# Official
# BASEBALL
# GUIDE

## 1986 EDITION

*Editor/Baseball Guide*
**DAVE SLOAN**

*Associate Editor/Baseball Guide*
**MIKE NAHRSTEDT**

*Contributing Editors/Baseball Guide*
**CRAIG CARTER**
**BARRY SIEGEL**
**LARRY WIGGE**

*President-Chief Executive Officer*
**RICHARD WATERS**

*Editor*
**TOM BARNIDGE**

*Director of Books and Periodicals*
**RON SMITH**

*Published by*

## The Sporting News

1212 North Lindbergh Boulevard
P.O. Box 56  —  St. Louis, MO 63166

Copyright © 1986
The Sporting News Publishing Company
A Times Mirror
Company

ISBN 0-89204-209-5                    ISSN 0078-3838

# TABLE OF CONTENTS

REVIEW OF 1985—The Positive Overshadows The Negative, Most Valuable Player Tables, Cy Young Tables..................................... **3**

AMERICAN LEAGUE—Team Reviews of '85 Season, Day-by-Day Scores, Official Batting, Fielding and Pitching Averages............. **29**

NATIONAL LEAGUE—Team Reviews of '85 Season, Day-by-Day Scores, Official Batting, Fielding and Pitching Averages............. **115**

AMERICAN LEAGUE CHAMPIONSHIP SERIES—Royals-Blue Jays Series Review, Box Scores, Composite Box Scores .................... **191**

NATIONAL LEAGUE CHAMPIONSHIP SERIES—Cardinals-Dodgers Series Review, Box Scores, Composite Box Scores .................... **199**

WORLD SERIES—Royals-Cardinals Series Review, Official Box Scores, Play-by-Play ................................................................. **209**

ALL-STAR GAME—1985 Game Review, Official Box Score, Play-by-Play, Results of Previous Games............................................. **227**

BATTING AND PITCHING FEATURES—Low-Hit Games, Top Strike-out Performances, Top Firemen, Pitchers Winning 1-0 Games, Multi-Homer Games, Grand Slam Hitters, One-Game Hitting Feats, Top Pinch-Hitters, Top Debut Performances, Homers by Parks, Award Winners, Hall of Fame Electees, List ................... **235**

1985 MAJOR LEAGUE TRANSACTIONS, MAJOR LEAGUE DRAFT, NECROLOGY ................................................................................. **279**

INFORMATION ON LEAGUES AND CLUBS—Major League and National Association Directories, American League Directory, American League Club Directories, National League Directory, National League Club Directories, Players Association Directory, Minor League Presidents, Major League Farm Systems............. **300**

OFFICIAL 1985 MINOR LEAGUE AVERAGES .................................... **334**

1986 AMERICAN LEAGUE SCHEDULE ............................................... **504**

1986 NATIONAL LEAGUE SCHEDULE ............................................... **506**

## For Index to Contents See Page 510

(Index to Minor League Cities on Page 511)

**ON THE COVER: Cardinals center fielder Willie McGee's league-leading .353 batting average and Gold Glove defense led St. Louis to the National League pennant and won him N.L. Most Valuable Player honors.**

**—Photo by Rich Pilling**

# '85 On-Field Accomplishments Overshadow Baseball's Woes

**By CLIFFORD KACHLINE**

Baseball's resilience and tremendous appeal were demonstrated as never before in 1985. It was a year that had almost everything—exciting performances, deep disappointments, shattered records, a players' strike, suspenseful pennant races, alarming drug disclosures and spectacular postseason series. In the end, the positive dramatically overshadowed the negative.

A lengthy labor dispute that culminated in the second player walkout in five years and a highly publicized drug trial in which seven players testified frequently dominated the baseball news. The strike, however, lasted only two days and exciting developments on the field captivated the public so completely that attendance soared to new heights and off-field problems were put in the background. Overall, the 1985 season was one to remember.

Milestone achievements by veterans Pete Rose, Tom Seaver, Rod Carew, Phil Niekro and Nolan Ryan, combined with remarkable statistics posted by Dwight Gooden, Don Mattingly, Willie McGee, Wade Boggs and Vince Coleman, among others, created a season-long air of excitement. The fact that three of the four division races remained undecided until the next-to-last day of the season added to the romance. But the best was yet to come. In the League Championship Series, newly expanded to seven games, the Los Angeles Dodgers and Toronto Blue Jays both jumped off to 2-0 leads, only to have the St. Louis Cardinals and Kansas City Royals rebound to capture their respective pennants. And then the Royals capped the season by staging an even more stunning comeback to win the World Series in seven games.

The closely contested races contributed to all-time attendance records. The American League's 14 teams attracted 24,532,225 paid admissions, while the 12-club National League drew 22,292,154. The combined total of 46,824,379 represented an average of 22,233 per date and exceeded by more than a million the previous mark of 45,540,338 set in 1983. Seven teams—the Chicago Cubs, New York Mets, St. Louis Cardinals, San Diego Padres, Baltimore Orioles, Minnesota Twins and Toronto Blue Jays—topped their former gate records.

One of the brightest lights of 1985 was New York Mets young pitching sensation Dwight Gooden, whose 24-4 record and 1.53 ERA earned him the National League's Cy Young Award.

Of the four division winners, Los Angeles had the easiest time. After struggling at a .500 clip in their first 56 games, the Dodgers took command in July and finished 5½ lengths in front of runnerup Cincinnati to give Manager Tommy Lasorda his fifth N.L. West title in nine years. In the N.L. East, St. Louis and the New York Mets battled down to the wire. The Mets moved within one game of first place by winning the first two games of a showdown series in St. Louis during the last week of the season, but Whitey Herzog's Cardinals, who had been picked by many observers to finish in the cellar, won the finale and clinched honors two days later.

Both American League races were decided in head-to-head clashes between the contenders. The California Angels entered the final week with a one-game lead, but dropped three of four contests at Kansas City and Dick Howser's Royals went on to capture the A.L. West. Toronto won its first A.L. East title ever when Bobby Cox's Blue Jays withstood a late surge by the New York Yankees. Going into their season-ending, three-game series at Toronto, the Yankees needed a sweep to tie for first place. But they fell victim to former teammate Doyle Alexander's five-hitter, 5-1, in the Saturday contest as the Blue Jays ended their nine-year championship quest.

The Royals continued their unbelievable come-from-behind heroics in both the league playoff and World Series. They opened the Championship Series by dropping the first two games on the road before rallying to win in seven games. The Cardinals, likewise, lost their first two Championship Series games in Los Angeles before winning four straight, the clinching sixth game being decided by Jack Clark's dramatic three-run, ninth-inning homer. In the All-Missouri, or so-called I-70, World Series, Howser's crew accomplished something that had never before been done in the fall classic. The Royals won the championship in seven games after losing the first two games at home.

Rose's run at the career hit record of Ty Cobb was a prime focus of attention through most of the season. Beginning his first full year as Cincinnati's player-manager, Rose entered the campaign needing 95 hits to top Cobb's career total of 4,191. Rose marked his 44th birthday on April 14, six days after the season opened, but quickly showed that age would not be a barrier in his quest for baseball immortality.

As the countdown to the record progressed, the pressures created by the media, merchandisers and others mounted steadily. Rose reveled in the attention and hype, orchestrating the chase into a months-long media event. Press boxes and clubhouses were jammed by ever-increasing numbers of media personnel as the countdown neared completion. By early September, hundreds of writers and photographers were on hand daily. Rose nevertheless maintained consistently that he felt no pressure. "I'm not on any timetable or schedule. There is no deadline," he said.

In a touch of irony, Rose equaled Cobb's record—and almost broke it—on a day when he hadn't expected to play. After launching a three-game series at Chicago's Wrigley Field by going 2 for 5 on September 6, Rose went hitless in four tries the next afternoon, leaving him two hits short of the record. With southpaw Steve Trout slated to pitch for the Cubs in the Sunday series finale, the Reds' skipper planned to sit out the game and use Tony Perez, his 43-year-old sidekick, at first base. Although a lifelong switch-hitter, Rose had decided early in the season to play only against righthanded pitching.

Trout, however, was a late scratch because of an elbow injury suffered in a bicycle accident and the Cubs named young righthander Reggie Patterson as his replacement. Rose inserted himself into the lineup and, using a black bat bearing the imprint "PR-4,192," he tagged the youngster for a single in the first inning. When he singled again in the fifth to catch Cobb, Wrigley Field fans gave him a five-minute standing ovation. Rose grounded out in his next at-bat and then, after a two-hour eighth-inning rain delay, struck out against reliever Lee Smith in the ninth with two teammates aboard. After the Cubs batted in the bottom of the ninth, the umpires called the game because of darkness with the score 5-5.

The Reds flew home that evening to await a Monday night contest against San Diego. With lefty Dave Dravecky starting for the Padres, Rose put his chase on hold, benching himself in favor of Perez. The following night a crowd of 51,045, including Commissioner Peter Ueberroth and league President Chub Feeney, packed Riverfront Stadium in hopes of witnessing the record-breaker. Unfortunately, Rose went hitless in four at-bats as LaMarr Hoyt and a trio of Padre relievers beat the Reds, 3-2.

The series windup on September 11 pitted San Diego righthander Eric Show

Cincinnati Player-Manager Pete Rose made baseball history in September when he collected career hit No. 4,192, passing Ty Cobb on the all-time list, and celebrated at first base by tearfully hugging son Petey.

California first baseman Rod Carew joined an exclusive club August 4 when he collected hit No. 3,000 against the Minnesota Twins, his former team.

against the Reds. With one away in the first inning and a 2-1 count, Rose slashed a line drive into left-center field for record-setting hit No. 4,192. The dramatic moment came at 8:01 EDT and, coincidentally, exactly 57 years to the day after Cobb played his last major league game. Following the historic hit, the standing-room crowd of 47,237 gave its hometown hero a monstrous ovation. Teammates dashed onto the field and mobbed Rose while Reds Owner Marge Schott came out of the stands and Rose's 15-year-old son, Petey, emerged from the dugout to congratulate him. Emotions caused Rose to break down at one point and weep on the shoulder of first-base coach Tommy Helms. To commemorate the achievement, Mrs. Schott presented Rose with a bright red Corvette

bearing a "PR 4192" license plate and, several days later, the Cincinnati city council passed a resolution changing the name of Second Street to Pete Rose Way.

Although the occasion of Rose's ascension to No. 1 on the game's all-time hit parade was rivaled in recent baseball history only by Hank Aaron's 715th homer in 1974, none of the television networks provided live coverage. Both NBC and ABC, however, showed taped replays within minutes after the event. Rose added to the memorable evening by smashing a triple in the seventh inning and by scoring both runs as the Reds won, 2-0, behind the five-hit pitching of Tom Browning and two relievers. To cap the night, Rose made a diving stop of Steve Garvey's grounder in the ninth inning and threw from a prone position to pitcher Ted Power covering first base for the final out.

Rose went on to collect 11 more hits over the remainder of the season and closed the year with 107 for a .264 average in 119 games. This boosted his career total to 4,204 hits and, equally important from Rose's viewpoint, the Reds climbed from fifth place in 1984 to second behind the Dodgers under his leadership.

The Cincinnati player-manager also profited financially. The sale of authorized ceramic plates and figurines, numbered color prints, gold and silver medallions, posters, books, etc., and the use of his picture on 12 million boxes of Wheaties produced sizeable royalties. In addition, he was rewarded with a hefty salary boost that made him the highest-paid manager ever. With the approval of the Players Association, he had taken a huge cut in salary—to $225,000 plus a $120,000 attendance bonus—on signing for 1985, but shortly after the season ended, Mrs. Schott rewarded him with a new three-year contract calling for $1 million each of the first two years.

The first of the other significant milestones was achieved by Ryan. The fireballing Houston righthander, playing in his 19th season in the majors at age 38, became the first major league pitcher to reach the 4,000-strikeout plateau. He did it by fanning Danny Heep of the New York Mets on three pitches to open the sixth inning of the Astros' 12-inning, 4-3 victory at the Astrodome on July 11. Ryan allowed only one earned run and struck out 11 in seven innings before bowing out for a pinch-hitter. He finished the season with 209 strikeouts in 232 innings and thus matched the major league record for most years with 200 or more strikeouts (10) that was held by Seaver.

Tom Seaver and his Chicago White Sox teammates had reason to celebrate August 4 after the veteran righthander had defeated the New York Yankees, 4-1, for career victory No. 300.

By an odd twist of fate, Seaver and Carew produced their milestone performances on the same day. Ironically, one did it in the city where he earned his greatest fame and the other against the team with which he spent most of his career.

Seaver, long-time New York Mets ace, joined the exclusive 300-victory club when he pitched the Chicago White Sox to a route-going 4-1 decision at Yankee Stadium on August 4. A near-capacity crowd of 54,032 turned out for the memorable occasion. The 40-year-old righthander, who had beaten the Boston Red Sox five nights earlier, responded by stopping the Yankees on six singles. He became the 17th pitcher to reach the cherished 300-win mark.

Carew gave 41,630 fans at Anaheim Stadium something to remember that same day. In the third inning he produced a single off Minnesota's Frank Viola for hit No. 3,000, becoming the 16th player to attain that magic figure. The 39-year-old Carew, who spent the first 12 years of his career with the Twins, was stopped in four other appearances that afternoon, but the Angels went on to win, 6-5.

Phil Niekro, the oldest player in the major leagues at 46, became the 18th player to enter the 300-victory ranks on October 6—the last day of the regular season. The knuckleball specialist had failed in four previous attempts before pitching the New York Yankees to a four-hit, 8-0 decision at Toronto. Having clinched the title the previous afternoon, the Blue Jays rested all except one of their regulars and Niekro in turn abandoned his trademark —the knuckler—completely until two were out in the ninth inning. That's when he fanned designated hitter Jeff Burroughs on three knuckleballs.

"A lot of people felt I couldn't get anybody out without a knuckler," the 22-year veteran said after the game. "I wanted to see what it would be like." Niekro also enjoyed the distinction of becoming the oldest man to pitch a shutout in the majors while marking his second straight season as a 16-game winner for the Yankees.

While activity on the playing fields was fascinating fans, much of management's attention was occupied by fiscal concerns, the bargaining table and the courts. Various clubs claimed to be experiencing serious financial problems, the Basic Agreement between the owners and players had expired and the drug situation was back in court. The glut of sticky issues served to put Peter Ueberroth to the test in his first full year as commissioner.

**Houston pitcher Nolan Ryan (above) made baseball history in July when he became the first pitcher to record 4,000 career strikeouts. Yankee veteran Phil Niekro recorded his 300th career win on the final day of the season.**

Negotiations on a new Basic Agreement, the union contract between the Players Association and the clubs, got underway six weeks prior to the expiration of the old one on December 31, 1984. However, it took almost nine months and another strike before settlement was reached. Unlike 1981 when a player walkout halted play for 50 days, this one ended after two days and caused little disruption in the schedule.

Two major issues emerged early in the bargaining. For the players the focal point was the lucrative new television package that took effect in 1984 and the big increase in revenue they expected from that source for their benefit plan. For management, the industry's economic problems and ways to slow the escalation of player salaries became the prime negotiating issue.

Under prior collective bargaining agreements, the players had received approximately one-third of the network television income for their industry's pension and benefit fund. In recent years the contribution had amounted to approximately $15.5 million annually. With the new television contract producing $1.1 billion over six years, the players sought to continue the arrangement giving them a one-third share, which would mean about $60 million annually.

Lee MacPhail, head of management's Player Relations Committee, introduced the subject of the club's financial dilemma into the negotiations at a meeting in New York on February 27. He asked the players' negotiators—Donald Fehr and Marvin Miller, acting executive director and consultant, respectively, of the Major League Players Association—to help management find a solution. One day earlier, also in New York, the club owners had gathered to discuss the situation and formulate policy. After that session, Commissioner Ueberroth issued a statement saying he would order the teams to open their financial books if the two sides "advise me this would be critical to the negotiations and will remove any lingering lack of trust between the parties."

In discussing the sport's fiscal problems, MacPhail said: "The owners agreed unanimously (at their February 26 meeting) that the situation was bad and was getting worse. If anything further happened that would be adverse to baseball's economics, it could be disastrous. The players have as much at stake as the clubs. . . ."

On March 12, MacPhail presented the Players Association negotiators with a letter detailing the clubs' areas of economic concern and a chart containing financial data for a 13-year period.

The chart indicated the 26 teams as a group made a profit only once in the last nine years—a mere $4,586 in 1978. According to the data, the clubs lost $613,189 in 1979, with losses escalating thereafter and reaching a high of $92,094,948 in 1982. The chart showed a loss for the 1981 strike season of $105,385,255, but strike insurance collected by the owners reduced the deficit by $46.8 million. In 1983, the last year for which complete records were available when the information was compiled, the owners claimed to have lost $66.6 million. They reported that 18 clubs finished in the red in 1983, with 10 teams dropping more than $3 million. Only one club reported a profit of more than $3 million that year. The chart did not identify any teams.

The financial data also revealed that only 11 clubs had submitted figures for 1984 up to that time, and they represented a combined loss of $27,447,307, or just shy of the $2.5 million average of 1983. The chart projected an overall loss of $58 million for 1985. While projecting that revenue would increase substantially through 1988, the owners foresaw expenses becoming so prohibitive that losses would total $155 million. Revenue was estimated at $826 million for 1988 with expenses projected at $981 million.

In his accompanying letter, MacPhail outlined management's concerns as follows:

• Enormous player payroll disparities among the clubs;

• The economic burden of a minor league system to develop talent;

• The growing risk to players of substantial amounts of unfunded deferred compensation, which MacPhail later said amounted to $250 million;

• A decline in TV network ratings and the failure of pay-TV to materially improve the clubs' financial position;

• The possibility of adverse government action, including proposals to curtail tax deductibility of business purchases of tickets, which he said account for nearly 50 percent of all tickets sold.

After studying the financial information provided by the clubs, Fehr said he had difficulty understanding the expense figures as they related to player costs and requested that additional data be supplied. He pointed out that while the clubs reported expenses of $588 million in 1983, Players Association figures pegged player salary costs at just over $200 million that year. Add the owners' contribution to the benefit plan to the total, Fehr said, and the figure would be around $220 million, which left $368 million unaccounted for. As for projections contained in the chart, he noted: "It appears that total costs are rising far faster than player costs figure to rise. In 1985 you're looking at non-major league player costs in excess of $400 million, which is an extreme amount. . . ."

Management subsequently furnished additional figures and also pared its projections of industry losses from (in millions) $58 to $29 for 1985, $94 to $59 for 1986, $113 to $64 for 1987 and from $155 to $86 for 1988. Still the Players Association representatives remained skeptical about the figures. Both sides hired experts to analyze the data, and the discussions soon deteriorated into a dispute over whose accountants were right and which accounting methods were proper. A basic difference between the battling accountants centered on depreciation, with the players' negotiators contending depreciation does not represent money spent and therefore should not be considered an expense. A further difficulty resulted from the fact that baseball ownership consisted of two disparate groups—those operating teams as separate entities as opposed to those who used their teams as advertising vehicles for other products or businesses.

To bolster their view of the financial information, the owners held a news conference at which they presented a New York University accounting professor, George Sorter. Having studied the baseball industry data, Sorter said he concluded the 26 clubs collectively lost $27 million in 1984. This was considerably less than the owners' revised total of $43 million. But it also was significantly different than the $9.3 million profit the Players Association concluded the clubs enjoyed in '84.

A few days after Sorter's presentation, the Players Association released the results of a 47-page report by Roger Noll, an economics professor at Stanford University. He had been commissioned by the players to analyze the figures provided by the clubs. Noll disagreed with the owners' contention that they have severe economic problems and wrote: "It takes either extravagant management or a poor team in a weak market to lose money." He acknowledged that problems exist in Seattle, Pittsburgh, Cleveland and the Bay Area (Oakland and San Francisco), but added that teams such as Baltimore, San Diego and Kansas City "show that solid operations are possible even in small markets."

In his report, Noll discussed some of the interesting and questionable items in the financial data of 11 clubs.

**Donald Fehr represented the players as executive director of the Major League Players Association.**

In the case of the New York Yankees, who reported losses of $9 million in 1984, he questioned the inclusion of $500,000 in charitable contributions as a cost of baseball operations as well as the inclusion of a club-owned hotel, the Bay Harbor Inn in Tampa Bay, Fla., in the team's financial data. He also concluded the Yankees' travel expenses were at least double the baseball-wide average.

Points raised by Noll in connection with other clubs included: The Oakland A's, who claimed the biggest losses ($15 million plus) in 1984, paid $4.1 million in general and administrative expenses ($1.3 million above the average), including $1.25 million in salaries to front-office personnel (more than $400,000 above the average), and spent $3.8 million on sales and promotion (more than $2 million

**Lee MacPhail represented the owners as head of management's Player Relations Committee.**

above the average); the St. Louis Cardinals received no revenue from concessions and parking, but the Civic Center Redevelopment Corp., which, like the Cardinals, is owned by Anheuser-Busch, reported a profit of about $2.5 million from that source; and the Atlanta Braves received only $1 million for local television rights from WTBS, the superstation that also is owned by Ted Turner, as compared to the average of $2,686,000.

It wasn't until May 20 that management presented its first proposal on major issues to the Players Association. The most significant element of the eight-point proposal was a club payroll plan. It provided that teams with payrolls above the 1985 average of the 26 teams would be barred from signing free agents unless the salary given the free agent didn't exceed

the average major league salary. In addition, trades for players who would put a team's payroll above the average would be prohibited, and playing bonuses and bonuses for signing contract extensions would count against the team involved. The plan also called for all clubs to be at or under the 1985 payroll level by 1988.

In a further bid to curb costs, the owners' negotiators later suggested that awards in salary arbitration be limited to no more than double the player's previous salary. Not surprisingly, the players rejected both the player payroll plan—or salary cap as the media termed it—and the idea of limiting arbitration awards. The owners meantime continued to withhold any offer on revenue from national television, contending they could make one only after other financial issues were resolved.

Despite the disagreements over the clubs' financial figures and the ploys employed by both sides, the discussions did not create the acrimony that marked the 1981 bargaining. At the same time, the negotiations were producing no notable progress in the stalemated talks. As a consequence, the team player representatives and the executive board of the Players Association met in Chicago on July 15, the day prior to the All-Star Game, and designated August 6 as the strike date if no settlement was reached.

MacPhail finally made the owners' long-awaited benefit-plan offer on July 30, but it only exacerbated the already-staggering state of negotiations. Under the proposal, the owners' contribution to the fund would be linked to player salaries. The plan called for the owners' contribution to remain at $15.5 million for both 1984 and 1985 and to increase to $25 million annually for the next four years, but with the proviso that the $25 million figure would be reduced by whatever amount that player payroll increases exceeded $13 million per year. The four-page proposal noted that one goal of the plan was to "eliminate the $86 million loss projected for 1988."

Two days later Ueberroth took his most visible step in the protracted labor dispute. He held a news conference to reveal several ideas he proposed to the negotiators in hopes they would lead to a settlement. Terming the owners' offers "frivolous" and declaring that they should "stop asking for the players to solve their financial problems," the commissioner urged management to drop its salary-cap plan and suggested the players agree to the owners' proposal of three years of service for salary arbitration eligibility instead of the current two years. He also recommended that the strike deadline be extended and that $44.5 million—the difference between the magnates' annual contribution to the benefit plan and the amount the players sought—be placed in escrow for 45 days while the two sides continued to negotiate. Under his plan, $1 million would be removed from the escrow account for each day the bargaining continued, with the money going to either amateur baseball or charity.

With the strike deadline rapidly approaching, the four owners on the Player Relations Committee's executive board—Bud Selig of Milwaukee, Edward Bennett Williams of Baltimore, John McMullen of Houston and Peter O'Malley of Los Angeles—gathered in New York on August 2 to discuss strategy. Following a two-day break in the talks, negotiators met again on August 4, and both sides offered compromise proposals. Management modified its benefit-plan contribution slightly but tied it to salary arbitration changes. The union, without citing any specific figure, offered to accept less than one-third of the national television revenue if the owners would agree to put the difference in a fund to help what Fehr called the "disadvantaged" clubs.

"What they (the owners) say, in essence, is that some clubs can't compete with other clubs because of poor markets and low revenues," Fehr commented afterward. "One way to change that is to redirect revenues. We're saying don't do it with your money; do it with the money the players believe is theirs." While acknowledging that management had "been thinking along similar lines" (presumably revenue sharing), MacPhail objected to the idea on the grounds that it was "something baseball should do rather than have the Players Association tell us how to do it."

When another meeting the following day (August 5) failed to break the stalemate, the player walkout officially began on August 6, and the day's games were cancelled. With everything in limbo, most of the players headed for their off-season homes. It appeared major league baseball might be in for another prolonged shutdown.

However, the negotiators held four separate meetings lasting a total of 9½ hours on the day the strike began. At 10 the next morning, August 7, members of the negotiating teams gathered at MacPhail's Manhattan apartment. Union chief Fehr and Barry Rona, the Player Relations

Committee's counsel, met privately in one room while MacPhail and Lou Hoynes, the National League's lawyer, waited in another room and the Players Association contingent—Marvin Miller, Mark Belanger, Fehr's assistant, and player representatives Kent Tekulve and Buck Martinez—remained in a third room.

With the owners agreeing to drop their demand for a salary cap in arbitration proceedings and the players consenting to a change in the eligibility requirement for salary arbitration, Fehr and Rona made quick progress and joined the other members of the negotiating teams to finalize the collective bargaining package. Ironically, the issue that led to the 1981 strike—compensation in the form of professional players for the signing of free agents—was eliminated altogether with the concurrence of both sides.

Commissioner Ueberroth arrived at MacPhail's apartment during the meeting and was informed that terms for the new Basic Agreement had been accepted by both parties. Shortly after noon he instructed his office to issue a statement saying a "tentative understanding" had been reached. A news conference was scheduled for 5 p.m. to make a formal announcement of the signing, but lawyers for the two groups needed additional time to put the agreement into contract language. Announcement of official ratification of the new agreement finally came at 10:45 p.m. The clubs and players already had been instructed to be ready to resume play the following day.

Provisions of the new Basic Agreement, a five-year document extending through 1989, included the following:

• Benefit plan: The owners agreed to add $9.5 million to the $15.5 million they already contributed in 1984 and to contribute $33 million annually from 1985 through 1988 and then $39 million in 1989. The $196 million total over six years (including 1984) represents about 18 percent of the $1.1 billion television package. Under the new plan, a player with 10 years of major league service will be eligible for an annual pension at age 62 of nearly $91,000 as contrasted to the former maximum of $57,000 for a 20-year major leaguer at age 65.

• Free agency: Professional compensation for free agents has been dropped. The re-entry draft, in existence since free agency began in 1976, was abolished, and any team can negotiate with any free agent. If a free agent's last team wants to retain negotiating rights to him, it must agree to go to salary arbitration if he so

**As the baseball strike date approached, fans everywhere expressed the same sentiments as the Chicago Cubs faithful.**

chooses.

• Salary arbitration: Beginning in 1987, players will need three years of major league service, instead of two years, to be eligible. There will be no cap on the increase a player can gain in arbitration. In addition, there will be no cap of any kind on salaries, and players released in the last 15 days of spring training will receive an increase in termination pay.

• Minimum salary: Effective immediately, it was raised from $40,000 to $60,000, with cost-of-living increases in ensuing years. The minimum pay for minor leaguers on option from the majors will be one-third of the major league minimum.

• Expansion: The National League was granted the right to expand by two clubs under a similar format to the one used in the past.

• World Series pool: The players' pool will receive 60 percent off the top of gate receipts from the first four games of the World Series. Previously, it was stipulated that the commissioner's office received 15 percent off the top and the players then received 60 percent of the remainder from the first four games. The change would have added approximately $500,000 to the 1984 players' pot.

• Playoffs: The League Championship Series will continue in the best-of-seven format approved earlier in the year.

• Grievances: The proviso allowing the commissioner to pull a grievance from standard procedure and decide the case himself, rather than having it go to an arbitrator, was left unchanged. If the commissioner takes that step, the players can demand to reopen the Basic Agreement or strike.

The announcement of the agreement and the end of the strike triggered the question: What role did Ueberroth have in the settlement? While some observers portrayed the commissioner as a hero, Murray Chass of the New York Times reported that sources close to both sides said Ueberroth had no influence on the outcome. The commissioner himself declared: "I want you to know very clearly that I had no role, that this was done by these two teams headed by Don Fehr and Lee

Lee MacPhail speaks to a press gathering about the settlement of the 1985 baseball strike.

MacPhail."

The two-day walkout caused cancellation of 25 games, 14 in the American League and 11 in the National. Five of the A.L. contests were made up in doubleheaders on August 8, the day that play resumed, and all of the others were immediately rescheduled for later in the season.

Earlier in the year, management had gained a significant victory over the Players Association. In a decision handed down in Chicago on May 23, U.S. District Judge Charles P. Kocoras ruled that the teams, not the players, own all broadcast rights to baseball games. The ruling came in a suit filed by the owners in 1982. The players had argued that their performances were not subject to copyright and that the teams did not have the right to negotiate TV contracts without their permission. However, Judge Kocoras held that baseball telecasts are "works made for hire" produced by employees within the scope of their employment and that the clubs own the copyright of the game telecasts.

Not long after the new Basic Agreement was accepted by both sides, the Players Association filed a grievance. It was precipitated by the action of major and minor league owners in revising the rules governing the eligibility of minor league players for the annual winter draft. The change provided that a player could be kept in the minors for four years (rather than three) before being eligible for selection.

Two months after the players' brief walkout, it appeared the umpires might stage a strike during the League Championship Series, as they had done a year earlier. Although Commissioner Ueberroth's arbitration ruling late in 1984 awarded them sizeable pay hikes, the umpires sought a $5,000 increase for working the LCS because of expansion of the playoffs to seven games. In addition, they asked for a $60,000 annual increase in the special-events pool that is split among all 60 major league umpires. The league presidents and the umpires' union agreed to submit the issue to binding arbitration and former President Richard M. Nixon was chosen as the arbitrator.

Nixon's verdict, announced on October 28, specified that because the LCS had "been expanded by a factor of 40 percent, the working umpires are entitled to a 40 percent increase in compensation" from $10,000 to $14,000 apiece for both 1985 and 1986. He further stipulated that no additional money should be put into the 1985 umpire pool of $240,000, but that the leagues should add $64,000 to the 1986 pot of $300,000.

Late in the year, figures released by the Players Association revealed that the average annual salary of major league players climbed to $371,157 in 1985. This compared with $329,408 a year earlier. A breakdown of the average salary by clubs in 1985 follows:

American League—Baltimore, $438,256; Boston, $386,597; California, $433,818; Chicago, $348,488; Cleveland, $219,879; Detroit, $406,755; Kansas City, $368,469; Milwaukee, $430,843; Minnesota, $258,039; New York, $546,364; Oakland, $352,004; Seattle, $169,694; Texas, $257,573; Toronto, $385,995.

National League—Atlanta, $540,988; Chicago, $413,765; Cincinnati, $336,786; Houston, $366,250; Los Angeles, $424,273; Montreal, $315,328; New York, $389,365; Philadelphia, $399,728; Pittsburgh, $392,271; St. Louis, $386,505; San Diego, $400,497; San Francisco, $320,370.

A study of documents filed with the Players Association and Player Relations Committee revealed that 43 players collected $1 million or more in salary and bonuses in '85. Mike Schmidt headed the pack at $2,130,300 followed by Gary Carter at $2,028,571. Several other players signed contract extensions that will reward them at even higher rates.

Shortly after the season began, the Cardinals' Ozzie Smith agreed to a four-year extension effective in 1986 that will yield him $8,700,000, including a $700,000 signing bonus, plus a $500,000 loan at 10 percent interest and primary consideration for a wholesale beer distributorship. In midseason, Baltimore's Eddie Murray received a five-year extension that starts in 1987 and will pay him a reported $13 million. To show his gratitude, Murray presented the city of Baltimore with a $500,000 gift toward development of an Outward Bound educational camp. And Kansas City co-owner Avron Fogelman, who signed George Brett to an innovative lifetime contract in 1984, also signed Dan Quisenberry and Willie Wilson to lifetime pacts. It was estimated the three Royals will collect nearly $93 million for 18 playing seasons, with less than $25 million being charged against the club's payroll and the remainder coming from investment of the trio's money, much of it in Fogelman's construction and real estate businesses.

Players salaries and benefits weren't the only things that rose sharply. So did concerns about baseball's drug situation. Several players experienced relapses, and revelations by others during a federal investigation and subsequent trial in Pittsburgh implicated far more players than had previously been identified. It all added up to what some in the media labeled the game's biggest black eye since the 1919 Black Sox scandal.

In an effort to cope with the drug problem, the owners and players' union had established a joint program in 1984. It established procedures to be followed in cases of player involvement with drugs and included a Joint Review Council, consisting of three doctors who are experts in chemical dependency, to make recommendations in cases of actual or suspected substance abuse.

Five players who previously underwent rehabilitation experienced more difficulties in 1985. They were Oakland pitcher Mike Norris, Atlanta outfielder Claudell Washington, San Diego second baseman Alan Wiggins, Pittsburgh pitcher Rod Scurry and Los Angeles pitcher Steve Howe. In addition, first baseman Daryl Sconiers of the California Angels missed much of the season after admitting to a substance abuse problem.

Norris, still recovering from shoulder surgery performed late in 1983, was arrested on February 13 in San Leandro, Calif., on cocaine possession charges. On April 7, Easter Sunday morning, he was arrested again in Albany, Calif., on suspicion of driving under the influence. Following treatment in a drug rehabilitation program, he was assigned in mid-June to Modesto (California). A few days later, a urine test administered to Norris showed traces of codeine and alcohol. He claimed he had been taking Tylenol 3 with a few aspirins before pitching to relieve stiffness and said he wasn't aware the codeine would show up. Norris, in the last year of a contract that could have earned him $500,000 for the season, subsequently was placed on the major league drug rehabilitation list and received only the major league minimum of $40,000 for the remainder of the season.

Washington was arrested in Walnut Creek, Calif., on February 18 after police allegedly found small amounts of marijuana in his car. A felony charge of cocaine possession later was dropped, but Washington's lawyer suggested he enter a drug diversion program again at the close of the season.

After missing the first 17 days of spring training, Sconiers reported to the Angels' camp on March 18 and disclosed his drug dependency. He immediately underwent medical evaluation and then spent a month in rehabilitation in Centinela Hospital's Life Start program in Inglewood, Calif.

Wiggins, who signed a four-year, $2.8 million contract during the winter, failed to show up for the Padres' games in Los Angeles on April 25 and 26. The following day he notified club officials that he had suffered a relapse and was entering a Minnesota drug center. On June 18, a week after the Joint Review Council had declared Wiggins ready to play, the Padres assigned him to Las Vegas (Pacific Coast) and then traded him to Baltimore on June 27. After spending six days with the Orioles' Rochester (International) affiliate to get in shape, Wiggins donned a Baltimore uniform for the first time on July 5.

Both Scurry and Howe found themselves in trouble on June 23. When Scurry did not appear for a game that day in Philadelphia, the Pirates suspended him. Following four weeks on the rehabilitation list, he returned to action with the Pirates and then was sold to the New York Yankees on September 13.

Howe, who sat out the entire 1984 season under suspension for cocaine abuse, saw his comeback bid endangered when he was a six-inning no-show at Dodger Stadium on June 23. The incident cost him a $300 fine. The following Saturday, Howe failed to appear at a Boy Scout dinner for which he was chairman. He also was a no-show again at Dodger Stadium the next day, June 30. Although his attorney said a drug test showed Howe was free of drugs, the Dodgers released the pitcher on July 3, despite his $325,000 contract.

The Minnesota Twins subsequently indicated an interest in Howe but held off signing him until August 11—after the players' strike ended. A month of good conduct with the Twins came to an end when he disappeared again. With the club's approval, he skipped the team flight from Chicago to Cleveland the night of September 12 so he could appear on ABC's "Nightline" and participate in a program on drug abuse in baseball. After missing the team's five-game series in Cleveland without explanation, Howe finally called Minnesota club officials and admitted to having a relapse. The Twins promptly released him.

Although the incidents involving the six aforementioned players left a bad taste, baseball's image was tarnished to an even greater extent during the September trials of alleged drug traffickers in Pittsburgh. The trials followed a 14-month investigation that led to the indictment of seven men by a Pittsburgh grand jury on

**Mets first baseman Keith Hernandez arrives at the courtroom before his testimony in the Pittsburgh drug trial.**

May 31 for alleged drug transactions with players. The seven, all but one from Pittsburgh, were said to have had access to the Pirates' clubhouse because of friendships with Pittsburgh players.

Several prominent performers were linked publicly to drug abuse for the first time during the proceedings. In fact, the focal point of the trial became the players, who were granted immunity from prosecution in exchange for cooperating with the federal government. The defendant was Curtis Strong, a 38-year-old Philadelphian who had served as a caterer in the Phillies' clubhouse briefly. He was charged with 16 counts of cocaine distribution to players.

The trial opened on September 5 in U.S. District Court in Pittsburgh before Judge Gustave Diamond. Lonnie Smith, Kansas City outfielder, was the first player called

by the prosecution and spent four hours on the witness stand. He said he met Strong through Dick Davis, a former Phillies' teammate, and named Davis, Gary Matthews, Dickie Noles, Keith Hernandez and Joaquin Andujar as players who used cocaine with him during his days with the Phillies and Cardinals.

Hernandez, New York Mets first baseman, and Dodgers infielder Enos Cabell testified next. Hernandez, who long had denied rumors that he used cocaine, admitted that he used the drug for three years while with the Cardinals and described it as "a demon in me" and "the devil on this earth." He said he gave up the drug for good "about June 1983," approximately the same time that Smith informed the Cardinals of his drug problem. The Cardinals traded the first baseman to the Mets shortly thereafter. In his testimony, Hernandez named Smith, Andujar, Bernie Carbo and Lary Sorensen as other drug users on the Cardinals at the time, while Cabell named Dave Parker, J. R. Richard, Al Holland, Jeff Leonard and Davis.

After a weekend recess, the trial resumed on September 9 with the government calling three more active players—Dale Berra of the New York Yankees, Parker of Cincinnati and Leonard of San Francisco—and former player John Milner to the witness stand. Among the additional players subsequently identified as alleged cocaine users, besides Howe and Scurry, were Dusty Baker, Derrel Thomas, Lee Lacy, Tim Raines, Rowland Office, Manny Sarmiento and Eddie Solomon.

In addition to the cocaine disclosures, both Berra and Parker said they obtained amphetamines or "greenies" (pills that are called "uppers") from Willie Stargell and Bill Madlock during their days with the Pirates. When contacted by the media, Stargell and Madlock both denied having dispensed the pills, which allegedly have been in widespread use in baseball for years and are not illegal. Milner injected the name of Willie Mays into the proceedings, declaring, "Willie had the red juice," a term for amphetamines dissolved in liquid, in his locker while both played with the Mets. Mays promptly denied any involvement with drugs and his longtime physician, Dr. John Jackson, later explained that the solution Milner saw was a prescription drug called Phenergin VC, a cough syrup which the doctor had prescribed.

The first witness to be called by the defense was Chuck Tanner, Pittsburgh manager. He was called after Berra testified that Tanner once warned him, "Don't talk to that gentleman (Strong)" while all three were in a hallway at Three Rivers Stadium before a game. Tanner rebutted Berra's statement and added that he did not know Strong.

The trial concluded on September 20 when the jury of nine women and three men found Strong guilty on 11 counts of cocaine distribution. On November 4, Judge Diamond sentenced the defendant to four to 12 years in prison. Strong was the sixth of the seven accused men to be sentenced.

Shortly before the Strong trial, the New York Times published a four-part series on the use of drugs in baseball. The articles listed the names of additional players who were identified by convicted drug dealers as cocaine users. In one account,

John McHale, president and chief executive officer of the Montreal Expos, was quoted as saying cocaine was the reason his team didn't win the National League East Division title in 1982. "I don't think there's any doubt in '82 that whole scenario (drugs) cost us a chance to win. . . . When we woke up to what was going on, we found there were at least eight players on our club who were into this thing. . . ." McHale said.

Whitey Herzog, Cardinals manager, supplied a similar observation late in the year. In an interview with Thomas Boswell of the Washington Post, Herzog said he was convinced cocaine "cost me a world title with the (Kansas City) Royals" in the late 1970s and claimed the 1980 Cardinals had 11 heavy cocaine users.

The testimony of the player-witnesses in the Strong trial indicated drug abuse peaked in the early 1980s and probably declined in recent years for one prime reason—fear of punishment, as demonstrated by the jail sentences imposed late in 1983 on four Kansas City Royals. Nevertheless, the fear that illegal drugs could lead to gambling-related scandals in baseball prompted Commissioner Ueberroth and the owners to continue to search for solutions.

In May, the commissioner announced a mandatory drug-testing program for all uniformed and non-uniformed personnel in professional baseball except for major league players and umpires. A few weeks later, the Major League Umpires Association agreed to go along with the testing plan. Management also intensified its efforts against drug abuse by having major league players do anti-drug announcements on national and local baseball telecasts. Officials of the Players Association, however, refused to accept the mandatory testing program, contending the joint program negotiated with the owners in 1984 was working.

A few days after the Strong trial ended, Ueberroth sent letters to all major league players, appealing for acceptance of voluntary drug testing in 1986. Many players voiced support for a testing program and asked that it be developed in negotiations with the Players Association. Ueberroth expressed optimism at the response and asked Player Relations Committee General Counsel Barry Rona to begin discussions immediately with the association. The negotiations did not produce an agreement. Thereafter, the owners voted on October 22 to terminate the 18-month-old joint drug agreement with the union.

Several clubs quickly announced that they'd seek to include a drug-testing clause in player contracts. The Dodgers had inserted such a clause in several contracts early in 1985, but later deleted them at the insistence of the Players Association.

The possibility that baseball might punish past drug offenders carried over into the new year. Published reports stated that 24 players were sent letters by the commissioner's office on November 27 inviting them to private, individual meetings with Ueberroth in January. The letters went to Wiggins, Sconiers, Washington and Norris, all of whom went through rehabilitation; former player John Milner; the seven who testified in the Strong trial, and all those mentioned during the proceedings who still were under a baseball contract.

Several retired former major leaguers also encountered drug-related difficulties in 1985. They included Denny McLain and Joe Pepitone. McLain, the former Detroit pitcher who won 30 games in 1968, was convicted of conspiracy and extortion, racketeering and attempting to deal cocaine following a 14-week trial in Tampa, Fla., and was sentenced on April 25 to 23 years in prison. Pepitone, former New York Yankee first baseman, was arrested in Brooklyn on March 18 and later indicted on drug and weapon possession charges.

On a brighter note, two former greats, Mickey Mantle of the New York Yankees and Willie Mays of the New York and San Francisco Giants, found themselves back in baseball's good graces. At a March 18 press conference, Ueberroth announced he was lifting the ban that his predecessor, Bowie Kuhn, had imposed on the pair because of their promotional roles with gambling casinos.

Besides the drug situation and player strike, two other subjects consumed much of Ueberroth's attention—the industry's economics and future expansion. With expenses rising and the annual income of the 26 clubs ranging from a low of $9 million to a high of $40 million, the need for fiscal responsibility and revenue equalization was becoming more pressing. Although declaring he was "convinced there will never be revenue sharing per se," the commissioner said steps were taken during the year to provide better balance. This involved sharing enhanced revenue from baseball superstation telecasts.

Shortly after taking over as commissioner, Ueberroth announced that one of his top priorities was to resolve the dilemma posed by the superstation telecasts. Before the '85 season opened he had reached agreement on five-year contracts with four of those clubs whose games were carried on a superstation—Atlanta (WTBS), New York Yankees (WPIX-TV), New York Mets (WOR-TV) and the Texas Rangers (KTVT). The fifth superstation club, the Chicago Cubs, owned by the Chicago Tribune, which also owns the broadcast station (WGN-TV), fell in line in June. While no financial terms were announced, it was reported that Turner, whose station boasted the largest audience (approximately 30 million households) outside its local viewing area, agreed to pay nearly $30 million over the five-year period and the other stations agreed to lesser fees.

In preparation for future expansion, Ueberroth invited representatives from various cities to make presentations at an informational meeting in New York on November 7-8. Criteria that franchise seekers were informed would be considered included (1) significant community identification of ownership, (2) long-term commitment to the club and community, (3) a net worth of $100 million or more for prospective owners, with a preference for individual rather than corporate ownership, (4) a commitment to 10,000 season tickets for the first five years of operation, and (5) a stadium with a capacity of 35,000 or 40,000 near public transportation and with parking facilities for at least 25 percent of capacity. Presentations were given by groups from Buffalo, Columbus, O., Denver, Indianapolis, Miami, Nashville, the Meadowlands Sports Complex in New Jersey, New Orleans, Phoenix, St. Petersburg, Tampa, Vancouver and Washington, D.C.

Six managers were fired during the season and five others were replaced after the close of the regular campaign. Two of the changes marked the return of controversial long-time favorites Billy Martin and Earl Weaver, although Martin's tenure was shortlived.

The first pilot to be fired was Yogi Berra. The Yankees lost 10 of their first 16 games and Berra was dismissed on April 28. Martin returned for his fourth hitch at the club's helm, marking the 12th managerial change in George Steinbrenner's 12-plus years as principal owner of the Yankees.

Doug Rader became the second manager to bow out. With the Texas Rangers owning a dismal 9-23 record, he was replaced on May 17 by Bobby Valentine, who had been serving as a coach with the

New York Mets.

Weaver, who retired after the 1982 season, resumed the Baltimore reins following the June 13 ouster of Joe Altobelli. The Orioles, 29-26 under Altobelli, won for coach Cal Ripken, Sr., on the night of Altobelli's dismissal and then played at a 53-52 clip under Weaver. It was the poorest showing of his 15-plus years as Orioles boss.

Billy Gardner was relieved as Minnesota manager on June 21 as the Twins languished in sixth place in the A.L. West with a 27-35 record. Ray Miller, long-time Baltimore pitching coach, replaced Gardner.

Eddie Haas' first season at the Atlanta helm came to an abrupt end on August 26 when he was replaced on an interim basis by coach Bobby Wine. The Braves had just lost 12 of 13 games to slip to 50-71.

In a wholesale change of leadership, both Manager Jim Davenport and General Manager Tom Haller were dismissed from their jobs with the San Francisco Giants on September 18. Roger Craig, who had quit as a Detroit coach after the Tigers' 1984 World Series victory, assumed the Giants' managerial reigns, while Al Rosen, deposed several days earlier as president-general manager of the Houston Astros, took over in a similar capacity with the Giants.

On October 7, one day after the season had ended, the Astros and Pittsburgh Pirates announced the release of managers Bob Lillis and Chuck Tanner, respectively. Tanner, who had two years remaining on his Pirates contract, was signed three days later by Atlanta to replace Wine.

After leading Toronto to its first division championship, Toronto Manager Bobby Cox resigned as the Blue Jays' skipper on October 22 to return to Atlanta, this time in the role of general manager. Cox had managed the Braves from 1978 through 1981 before moving to Toronto. The Blue Jays appointed coach Jimy Williams as their new manager.

Although the Yankees' 91-54 record under Martin was the best in the major leagues from the time of his arrival, Steinbrenner became disenchanted with his manager late in the season. As a result, coach Lou Piniella was elevated to the managerial post on October 27. Martin's involvement in two early-morning barroom brawls on successive days in Baltimore (September 21 and 22) and his griping over salary irked the Yankee owner. In the second of the two scuffles, Martin tangled with pitcher Ed Whitson and suffered a fractured right arm and two cracked ribs.

The two other managerial vacancies were filled when Hal Lanier, St. Louis Cardinals coach, was appointed to the Houston helm on November 5 and Pittsburgh named Jim Leyland, who had coached with the Chicago White Sox, as its skipper on December 15.

The episode that resulted in Martin's broken arm was only one of numerous bizarre events that highlighted the season. Late in July, the Yankee manager was hospitalized several days with a partially collapsed lung suffered while being administered a shot by Texas Rangers' team physician B. J. Mycoskie. A month later, Kansas City outfielder Willie Wilson was hospitalized after suffering an adverse reaction to a shot given by the same doctor.

Other unusual occurrences included:

• An infielder known as Jose Gonzalez during four seasons in the minors and a brief 1984 trial with St. Louis became Jose Uribe (his father's surname) as San Francisco's regular shortstop.

• The major leagues made it through a record 458 games without a postponement until a May 20 rainout at Cleveland ended the streak.

• Toronto catcher Buck Martinez completed a double play at Seattle on July 9 by tagging two runners at the plate, the second while lying flat on his back with a fractured leg.

• The Cardinals' Vince Coleman and Willie McGee were credited with four stolen bases (two each) on a single pitch in a game in Chicago on August 1.

• An apparent double by Yankee center fielder Rickey Henderson on August 2 was turned into a single and double play when two teammates, Bobby Meacham and Dale Berra, arrived at the plate just steps apart and were tagged in quick succession by catcher Carlton Fisk to help the White Sox to an 11-inning, 6-5 victory at Yankee Stadium.

• The fans and media in New York City were able to attend two battles for first place on the same day (September 12). The Cardinals and Mets played an afternoon game at Shea Stadium and the Blue Jays and Yankees met in a night contest at Yankee Stadium.

• Vince Coleman had to miss the World Series because of a freak accident in which the St. Louis stadium's automatic tarpaulin ran over his left leg prior to a playoff game.

Only one club underwent a change in primary ownership in 1985. Eleven months after placing the Pittsburgh Pi-

**Rookie speedster Vince Coleman ran into the baseball record books before a freak accident forced him to the sideline.**

of controlling interest in the Cincinnati Reds from brothers William and James Williams. Chiles' new partner was Gaylord Broadcasting of Oklahoma City, which acquired a one-third share as well as television rights to Ranger games for five years. In midseason, Frisch's Restaurants, Inc., of Cincinnati became the first new limited partner taken in by Mrs. Schott.

Like the Rangers, the Seattle, Oakland and San Francisco clubs encountered serious financial problems. In June, shortly before Owner George Argyros of the Mariners reportedly planned to begin bankruptcy proceedings, he and King County reached agreement on a new lease on the Kingdome. Besides netting the Mariners an estimated $1.3 million a year, the new deal contains an escape clause allowing the club to leave Seattle after 1987 if attendance or season-ticket sales over any two-year period fall short of 1.4 million and 10,000, respectively.

Rumors that the A's might move, possibly to Denver, were scotched when the Oakland club signed a new lease on Oakland-Alameda County Coliseum on September 17. The pact replaced one due to expire in 1987 and extends to the year 2000. According to President Roy Eisenhardt, the A's losses over the past five years totaled $28 million. In view of the situation, Coliseum officials approved inclusion of an escape clause allowing the club to terminate the lease in 1990 if the franchise continues to lose "significant amounts of money" and also agreed to make a $15 million loan to assist the A's in refinancing existing debts.

The Giants' dissatisfaction with Candlestick Park and the failure of plans for a new San Francisco stadium to materialize led Owner Bob Lurie to ponder a franchise move. The club reportedly lost $6 million in '85. Late in the season, Lurie disclosed that the Giants were hoping to play in Oakland-Alameda County Coliseum on an interim basis beginning in 1986 while San Francisco city officials continued to pursue efforts to build a new stadium. However, the Coliseum's board of directors turned down the Giants' bid. One reason supposedly was the fear that approval of such a proposal might adversely affect the city's legal efforts to bring the National Football League Raiders back from Los Angeles.

The 10th year of the salary arbitration process saw 98 players file. All but 13 reached agreement with their teams before the cases were to be heard in February. In three instances, players emerged

rates on the block, the John Galbreath family announced the sale of the team on October 2 to a coalition headed by Pittsburgh Mayor Richard Caliguiri. The price was said to be $22 million, far below the reported $35-40 million the Galbreaths originally sought. They owned 51 percent of the club stock and Warner Communications, Inc., held 48 percent. The new ownership consisted of local private and corporate investors, including Malcolm (Mac) Prine of Ryan Homes, who was named president; Carl Barger, managing partner of a law firm; Westinghouse Electric Co., and U.S. Steel.

Earlier in the year, Eddie Chiles sold a partial interest in the Texas Rangers to raise funds for his beleaguered franchise, while the National League approved the December 1984 purchase by Marge Schott

from the pre-hearing settlements with multi-year contracts worth more than $1 million a year. They were Bill Caudill, who signed a five-year, $7 million pact with Toronto; Joaquin Andujar of St. Louis, who signed for $3.45 million over three years, and Kent Hrbek of Minnesota, who agreed to a five-year, $5.9 million deal.

Of the 13 salary disputes that went to arbitration, two produced awards in the seven-figure range. Wade Boggs of Boston matched the old arbitration record of $1 million set by Fernando Valenzuela two years earlier, and then Tim Raines of Montreal established a record when he was awarded $1,200,000.

The six players who won their salary arbitration cases, with the club's offer in parentheses, were: Raines, $1,200,000 ($1,000,000); Boggs, $1,000,000 ($675,000); Mike Scioscia, Los Angeles, $435,000 ($350,000); Dave Palmer, Montreal, $375,000 ($235,000); Dave Schmidt, Texas, $344,000 ($230,000), and Bert Roberge, Montreal, $95,000 ($60,000).

The salaries of the seven who lost, with the player's rejected figure in parentheses, were: Leon Durham, Chicago Cubs, $800,000 ($1,100,000); Jesse Orosco, New York Mets, $650,000 ($850,000); Jerry Koosman, Philadelphia, $600,000 ($865,000); Tom Brunansky, Minnesota, $425,000 ($600,000); Doug Sisk, New York Mets, $275,000 ($470,000); Carlos Diaz, Los Angeles, $120,000 ($170,000), and Bobby Ramos, Montreal, $115,000 ($150,000).

Sixty-two players filed for free agency in November. It was the largest number since the process was initiated in 1976. Kirk Gibson, Detroit outfielder, was generally regarded as the top prize in the group with California reliever Donnie Moore running second. The list of those filing for free agency follows:

American League: Baltimore—Rich Dauer, Jim Dwyer, Lenn Sakata. Boston —Bruce Kison, Rick Miller. California— Juan Beniquez, Rod Carew, Bobby Grich, Al Holland, Donnie Moore, Don Sutton. Chicago—Carlton Fisk, Bart Johnson, Dan Spillner. Cleveland—Benny Ayala, Tony Bernazard, Jamie Easterly, Mike Hargrove, Vern Ruhle. Detroit—Tom Brookens, Doug Flynn, Kirk Gibson, Aurelio Lopez. Kansas City—Dane Iorg, Lynn Jones, Hal McRae, Jamie Quirk. Milwaukee—Danny Darwin. Minnesota— None. New York—Marty Bystrom, Joe Niekro, Phil Niekro, Butch Wynegar. Oakland—Bruce Bochte, Steve McCatty, Mike Norris, Rob Picciolo, Tommy John.

**First baseman Don Mattingly helped the Yankees stay in contention with an MVP season.**

Seattle—None. Texas—Alan Bannister, Bill Stein. Toronto—Jeff Burroughs, Steve Nicosia, Al Oliver.

National League: Atlanta—None. Chicago—Richie Hebner. Cincinnati—Tony Perez. Houston—Harry Spilman, Dickie Thon. Los Angeles—Steve Yeager. Montreal—Dave Palmer, U.L. Washington. New York—Larry Bowa, Rusty Staub. Philadelphia—Garry Maddox, Derrel Thomas. Pittsburgh—None. St. Louis— Doug Bair, Cesar Cedeno, Ivan DeJesus, Mike Jorgensen, Matt Keough. San Diego —Kurt Bevacqua, Al Bumbry, Miguel Dilone. San Francisco—Vida Blue.

Don Mattingly and Willie McGee were easy winners in the Most Valuable Player balloting conducted by the Baseball Writers' Association of America. The Yankee first baseman, who led the American League in RBIs with 145 while batting .324 and hitting 35 homers, received 23 of 28 first-place votes to beat George Brett of

Kansas City, 367 points to 274, in the A.L. poll. McGee, who hit .353 for the Cardinals to win the National League batting title, was the top choice of 14 of the 24 selectors and edged Dave Parker of Cincinnati, 280 to 220 points, in the N.L. voting. Results of the balloting, with each first-place vote worth 14 points, second place worth nine, third place eight and on down to one for 10th, follow:

## National League

| Player—Club | 1 | 2 | 3 | 4 | 5 | 6 | 7 | 8 | 9 | 10 | Pts. |
|---|---|---|---|---|---|---|---|---|---|---|---|
| Willie McGee | 14 | 6 | 3 | — | 1 | — | — | — | — | — | 280 |
| Dave Parker | 6 | 6 | 4 | 6 | — | 1 | — | 1 | — | — | 220 |
| Pedro Guerrero | 3 | 9 | 6 | 3 | 2 | — | 1 | — | — | — | 208 |
| Dwight Gooden | 1 | 2 | 6 | 6 | 3 | 3 | 1 | 1 | — | — | 162 |
| Tom Herr | — | 1 | — | 3 | 8 | 3 | 5 | 1 | 1 | 1 | 119 |
| Gary Carter | — | — | 5 | 2 | 3 | 5 | 3 | 1 | 2 | — | 116 |
| Dale Murphy | — | — | — | — | 3 | 3 | 2 | 3 | 5 | 3 | 63 |
| Keith Hernandez | — | — | — | 2 | 1 | 2 | 1 | 6 | 3 | 3 | 61 |
| John Tudor | — | — | — | — | 2 | 3 | 5 | 4 | — | 2 | 61 |
| Jack Clark | — | — | — | 2 | — | — | — | 1 | 1 | 1 | 20 |
| Vince Coleman | — | — | — | — | 1 | — | 2 | — | — | 2 | 16 |
| Tim Raines | — | — | — | — | — | 2 | 1 | — | — | 1 | 15 |
| Ryne Sandberg | — | — | — | — | — | — | 2 | 2 | — | — | 14 |
| Mike Marshall | — | — | — | — | — | 1 | — | 1 | 1 | 1 | 11 |
| Hubie Brooks | — | — | — | — | — | — | 1 | 1 | 1 | 2 | 11 |
| Orel Hershiser | — | — | — | — | — | 1 | — | — | 1 | 2 | 9 |
| Keith Moreland | — | — | — | — | — | — | — | 1 | 2 | 1 | 8 |
| Ozzie Smith | — | — | — | — | — | — | — | 1 | 1 | — | 5 |
| Mike Scioscia | — | — | — | — | — | — | — | — | 2 | 1 | 5 |
| Jeff Reardon | — | — | — | — | — | — | — | — | 2 | — | 4 |
| Jose Cruz | — | — | — | — | — | — | — | — | 1 | — | 2 |
| Bill Doran | — | — | — | — | — | — | — | — | 1 | — | 2 |
| Mariano Duncan | — | — | — | — | — | — | — | — | — | 1 | 1 |
| Tony Gwynn | — | — | — | — | — | — | — | — | — | 1 | 1 |
| Fernando Valenzuela | — | — | — | — | — | — | — | — | — | 1 | 1 |
| Glenn Wilson | — | — | — | — | — | — | — | — | — | 1 | 1 |

## American League

| Player—Club | 1 | 2 | 3 | 4 | 5 | 6 | 7 | 8 | 9 | 10 | Pts. |
|---|---|---|---|---|---|---|---|---|---|---|---|
| Don Mattingly | 23 | 5 | — | — | — | — | — | — | — | — | 367 |
| George Brett | 5 | 20 | 3 | — | — | — | — | — | — | — | 274 |
| Rickey Henderson | — | 1 | 8 | 10 | — | 3 | 3 | — | 2 | — | 174 |
| Wade Boggs | — | 2 | 5 | 3 | 8 | 3 | 1 | 3 | 2 | — | 159 |
| Eddie Murray | — | — | 1 | 5 | 4 | 6 | 5 | 2 | 3 | 1 | 130 |
| Donnie Moore | — | — | 5 | 2 | 2 | 4 | 1 | 1 | — | 3 | 96 |
| Jesse Barfield | — | — | 1 | 4 | 3 | 2 | 2 | 2 | 4 | 2 | 88 |
| George Bell | — | — | 3 | 2 | 3 | 2 | 3 | 1 | 1 | 1 | 84 |
| Harold Baines | — | — | — | — | 2 | 1 | 2 | 3 | 4 | 7 | 49 |
| Bret Saberhagen | — | — | 1 | 1 | 2 | 1 | 1 | 1 | 3 | — | 45 |
| Dan Quisenberry | — | — | — | — | 1 | 1 | 2 | 6 | — | 2 | 39 |
| Dave Winfield | — | — | — | 1 | 1 | 1 | 2 | 2 | 1 | 1 | 35 |
| Carlton Fisk | — | — | 1 | — | 1 | 1 | 2 | — | — | 2 | 29 |
| Darrell Evans | — | — | — | — | — | 2 | 2 | — | 3 | | 17 |
| Ron Guidry | — | — | — | — | — | 1 | 1 | 2 | — | — | 15 |
| Phil Bradley | — | — | — | — | — | — | — | 1 | 4 | 1 | 12 |
| Cal Ripken | — | — | — | — | — | — | 1 | — | 2 | 1 | 9 |
| Kirk Gibson | — | — | — | — | — | 1 | — | — | — | 2 | 7 |
| Steve Balboni | — | — | — | — | 1 | — | — | — | — | — | 6 |
| Tom Henke | — | — | — | — | — | 1 | — | — | — | — | 5 |
| Dennis Lamp | — | — | — | — | — | — | — | 1 | — | — | 3 |
| Kirby Puckett | — | — | — | — | — | — | — | 1 | — | — | 3 |
| Doyle Alexander | — | — | — | — | — | — | — | — | 1 | 1 | 3 |
| Damaso Garcia | — | — | — | — | — | — | — | — | 1 | — | 2 |
| Rich Gedman | — | — | — | — | — | — | — | — | — | 1 | 1 |

Dwight Gooden of the Mets, who at age 20 became the youngest 20-game winner in this century, and 21-year-old Bret Saberhagen of Kansas City were named Cy Young Award winners in the BBWAA voting. Gooden was a unanimous choice in the National League after leading both leagues in ERA (1.53), strikeouts (268) and victories (a 24-4 record). Saberhagen, who recorded a 20-6 mark, received 23 of 28 first-place votes to win handily over the Yankees' Ron Guidry in the A.L. poll. A breakdown of the Cy Young voting, with five points for a first-place vote, three points for a second and one for third, follows:

### American League

| Pitcher—Team | 1 | 2 | 3 | Pts. |
|---|---|---|---|---|
| Bret Saberhagen, K.C. | 23 | 4 | .. | 127 |
| Ron Guidry, New York | 4 | 22 | 2 | 88 |
| Bert Blyleven, Clev.-Minn. | 1 | .. | 4 | 9 |
| Dan Quisenberry, K.C. | .. | 2 | 3 | 9 |
| Charlie Leibrandt, K.C. | .. | .. | 7 | 7 |
| Doyle Alexander, Toronto.. | .. | .. | 5 | 5 |
| Britt Burns, Chicago | .. | .. | 2 | 2 |
| Donnie Moore, California... | .. | .. | 2 | 2 |
| Dave Stieb, Toronto | .. | .. | 2 | 2 |
| Mike Moore, Seattle | .. | .. | 1 | 1 |

### National League

| | 1 | 2 | 3 | Pts. |
|---|---|---|---|---|
| Dwight Gooden, New York | 24 | .. | .. | 120 |
| John Tudor, St. Louis | .. | 21 | 2 | 65 |
| Orel Hershiser, L.A. | .. | 1 | 14 | 17 |
| Joaquin Andujar, St. Louis | .. | 1 | 3 | 6 |
| Fernando Valenzuela, L.A. | .. | 1 | 1 | 4 |
| Tom Browning, Cincinnati | .. | .. | 3 | 3 |
| Jeff Reardon, Montreal | .. | .. | 1 | 1 |

Cardinals righthander Joaquin Andujar (above) and Yankee lefty Ron Guidry both won 20 games and received Cy Young Award votes.

Vince Coleman, who set a rookie record by stealing 110 bases for St. Louis, was a unanimous choice as National League Rookie of the Year by the Baseball Writers. Tom Browning, a 20-game winner with Cincinnati, was a unanimous pick for second place.

Shortstop Ozzie Guillen of the Chicago White Sox was named first on 16 of 28 ballots and edged Milwaukee pitcher Teddy Higuera, 101 points to 66, as the A.L. Rookie of the Year.

In the BBWAA's Manager of the Year poll, St. Louis' Whitey Herzog received 11 first-place votes to 10 for Cincinnati's Pete Rose and nosed him out, 86 points to 85, for National League honors. Toronto's Bobby Cox was the No. 1 choice on 16 of 28 American League ballots to beat Kansas City's Dick Howser, 104 to 66.

Rose, who enjoyed a spectacular season while chasing Ty Cobb's career hit record and guiding the Reds to their surprising

**George Brett's 30-homer, 112-RBI season helped Kansas City to its first-ever World Series victory.**

**Atlanta's Dale Murphy enjoyed another big offensive season while the Braves slid in the standings.**

second-place finish in the N.L. West, was named The Sporting News' Man of the Year for 1985.

A poll of the managers themselves resulted in Cox being named as The Sporting News' choice for Manager of the Year. Cox drew seven votes to six for Herzog and five for Tommy Lasorda. Other selections by The Sporting News included: Players of the Year—Mattingly in the A.L. and McGee in the N.L.; Pitchers of the Year—Saberhagen and Gooden, respectively; Firemen of the Year—Dan Quisenberry, Kansas City, and Jeff Reardon, Montreal; Comeback Players of the Year —Gorman Thomas, Seattle, and Rick Reuschel, Pittsburgh; Rookie Players of the Year—Guillen and Coleman; Rookie Pitchers of the Year—Higuera and Browning.

The annual All-Star Teams picked by The Sporting News consisted of the following:

American League: 1B—Mattingly, New York; 2B—Damaso Garcia, Toronto; SS— Cal Ripken, Baltimore; 3B—Wade Boggs, Boston; OF—Rickey Henderson, New York; Harold Baines, Chicago, and Phil Bradley, Seattle; C—Carlton Fisk, Chicago; DH—Don Baylor, New York; RHP— Saberhagen, Kansas City; LHP—Guidry, New York.

National League: 1B—Keith Hernandez, New York; 2B—Tommy Herr, St. Louis; SS—Ozzie Smith, St. Louis; 3B—Tim Wallach, Montreal; OF—Parker, Cincinnati; McGee, St. Louis, and Dale Murphy, Atlanta; C—Gary Carter, New York; RHP— Gooden, New York; LHP—John Tudor, St. Louis.

The Hillerich & Bradsby Silver Slugger Awards for the best offensive performers at each position, as chosen by the managers and coaches in a poll conducted by The Sporting News, went to the following: 1B —Mattingly in the American League and Jack Clark, St. Louis, in the National; 2B —Lou Whitaker, Detroit, and Ryne Sandberg, Chicago; SS—Ripken, Baltimore, and Hubie Brooks, Montreal; 3B—Brett, Kansas City, and Wallach, Montreal; OF —Henderson and Winfield of New York and George Bell, Toronto, in the American and McGee, Murphy and Parker in the National; C—Fisk, White Sox, and Carter, Mets; DH—Don Baylor, Yankees, and P— Rick Rhoden, Pittsburgh.

The Rawlings Gold Glove Award for fielding excellence, also selected by the managers and coaches, were 1B—Mattingly in the American and Hernandez in the National; 2B—Whitaker and Sandberg; SS—Alfredo Griffin, Oakland, and Smith, St. Louis; 3B—Brett and Wallach; OF—Winfield, Gary Pettis of California, Dwight Evans of Boston and Dwayne Murphy of Oakland in the American and McGee, Murphy and Andre Dawson of Montreal in the National; C—Lance Parrish, Detroit, Tony Pena, Pittsburgh; P— Guidry, New York, Reuschel, Pittsburgh.

In the minor leagues, The Sporting News named outfielder Jose Canseco, who hit 36 homers and drove in 127 runs in 118 games with Huntsville (Southern) and Tacoma (Pacific Coast) before joining Oakland late in the season, as Player of the Year. Jim Fregosi of Louisville (American Association) was designated as Manager of the Year, while choices for Executive of the Year were: Class AAA— Patty Cox Hampton of Oklahoma City (American Association), Class AA—Ben Bernard of Albany-Colonie (Eastern), and Class A—Pete Vonachen of Peoria (Midwest).

Kansas City Executive Vice President and General Manager John Schuerholz was honored as TSN's Major League Executive of the Year.

# AMERICAN LEAGUE

## Including

Team Reviews of 1985 Season

Team Day-by-Day Scores

1985 Standings, Home-Away Records

1985 Official A.L. Batting Averages

1985 Official A.L. Fielding Averages

1985 Official A.L. Pitching Averages

1985 Pitching Against Each Club

**Between strikeouts, first baseman Steve Balboni managed to hit a club-record 36 home runs while driving in 88.**

# Royals Fulfill Unlikely Dream

### By MIKE FISH

Winning a division title is tough; repeating is tougher. Just ask the Tigers or the Padres or the Cubs.

And while you're at it, ask the Kansas City Royals. They're becoming experts on the subject, having made seven postseason appearances in the last 10 years.

While the other defending champions were cleaning out their lockers when the 1985 regular season ended, the Royals were hung over from having celebrated another American League West title. That scenario hardly seemed likely after the Royals were swept by the Twins on the final weekend of September, leaving them one game behind California with seven games to go.

But the first four games were against the Angels, and Kansas City took command of the race by winning three of four to take a one-game lead. The Royals' pitching staff allowed the Angels just six runs in that series.

Offensively, the Angel wrecker was third baseman George Brett. Despite hitting just .226 in September, Brett hit three home runs and knocked in seven runs in the four games with California.

The Royals clinched the division title in dramatic style October 5. Having never rallied from more than a three-run deficit to win all year, they overcame a 4-0 Oakland lead to beat the A's, 5-4, in 10 innings.

That stunning comeback merely set the stage for the postseason. The Royals shrugged off 2-0 and 3-1 deficits in both the A.L. playoffs against Toronto and the World Series against St. Louis, rallying both times to win each seven-game series and emerging as unlikely world champions.

"If you ask me, we're a better club this year," Manager Dick Howser said. "We're not a dominant ball club, but we played about as well as you can the last six weeks of the season. We earned this thing.

"The biggest single factor was the strength of our starting pitching. No other club in the league runs out a better starting five than we do, plus we have Dan Quisenberry in relief. That's what did it early, and then we got better hitting as the season went on."

Kansas City's pitchers combined for a 3.49 earned-run average, which ranked second in the league. They also tied Detroit for the lead in shutouts with 11 and allowed only 103 homers, by far the best

**Lefthander Charlie Leibrandt's 2.69 ERA was the second-best in the A.L.**

mark in the league.

Heading the staff was Bret Saberhagen, who went 20-6 with a 2.87 ERA, 10 complete games and 158 strikeouts en route to the A.L. Cy Young Award. The 21-year-old righthander showed incredible confidence and poise for a pitcher in just his third professional season. After earning complete-game victories in both of his World Series starts, Saberhagen was named the fall classic's Most Valuable Player.

Posting an even better ERA (2.69) than Saberhagen was lefthander Charlie Leibrandt, who was dubbed "Rembrandt" by teammates who admired his pitching artistry. The former Cincinnati Reds journeyman won 17 games in 26 decisions.

Kansas City's 1984 ace, lefthander Bud Black, struggled most of the season and finished with a 10-15 record and a 4.33 ERA. But he came on strong when the Royals needed him most, posting a 4-0 shutout over California on October 2 to forge a first-place tie.

A pair of 23-year-olds, Danny Jackson (14-12) and Mark Gubicza (14-10), completed the five-man rotation, which did not miss a start. Doubleheaders necessi-

## SCORES OF KANSAS CITY ROYALS' 1985 GAMES

| APRIL | | | Winner | Loser |
|---|---|---|---|---|
| 8—Toronto | W | 2-1 | Black | Stieb |
| 10—Toronto | L | 0-1* | Caudill | Beckwith |
| 11—Toronto | L | 3-4* | Caudill | Quisenberry |
| 13—Detroit | L | 1-3 | Morris | Black |
| 14—Detroit | L | 1-5 | Petry | Saberhagen |
| 16—Boston | W | 2-0 | Jackson | Clemens |
| 17—Boston | W | 6-1 | Leibrandt | Nipper |
| 18—Boston | L | 3-4x | Ojeda | Jones |
| 19—At Detroit | W | 9-2 | Saberhagen | Petry |
| 20—At Detroit | L | 3-4 | Hernandez | Quisenberry |
| 21—At Detroit | W | 3-2§ | Quisenberry | Berenguer |
| 22—At Toronto | W | 2-0 | Leibrandt | Stieb |
| 23—At Toronto | W | 7-6 | Beckwith | Caudill |
| 24—At Toronto | L | 3-10 | Leal | Saberhagen |
| 26—At Boston | L | 2-5 | Clemens | Gubicza |
| 27—At Boston | W | 5-4 | Quisenberry | Stanley |
| 28—At Boston | W | 5-2 | Leibrandt | Boyd |
| 29—Cleveland | W | 3-2 | Black | Heaton |
| 30—Cleveland | W | 5-1 | Saberhagen | Roman |
| **Won 11, Lost 8** | | | | |

| MAY | | | | |
|---|---|---|---|---|
| 1—Cleveland | L | 5-6 | Schulze | Gubicza |
| 3—At N.Y. | L | 1-7 | Rasmussen | Jackson |
| 4—At N.Y. | L | 2-5 | Guidry | Leibrandt |
| 5—At N.Y. | L | 2-6 | Niekro | Black |
| 7—Baltimore | L | 2-4 | Dixon | Saberhagen |
| 8—Baltimore | W | 9-8 | LaCoss | McGregor |
| 10—New York | L | 4-6 | Guidry | Leibrandt |
| 11—New York | L | 3-11 | Rasmussen | Black |
| 12—New York | W | 6-5 | Quisenberry | Righetti |
| 13—At Balt. | W | 5-2 | Jackson | Davis |
| 14—At Balt. | W | 5-3 | Gubicza | McGregor |
| 15—At Cleve. | W | 5-1 | Leibrandt | Schulze |
| 16—At Cleve. | W | 7-1 | Black | Creel |
| 17—At Milw. | W | 3-0 | Saberhagen | Darwin |
| 18—At Milw. | L | 2-7 | Haas | Jackson |
| 19—At Milw. | L | 10-11 | Gibson | Quisenberry |
| 20—At Texas | L | 7-8 | Schmidt | Beckwith |
| 21—At Texas | W | 5-0 | Black | Tanana |
| 22—At Texas | W | 6-3 | Saberhagen | Noles |
| 24—Chicago | W | 8-4 | Jackson | Burns |
| 25—Chicago | W | 3-0 | Leibrandt | Seaver |
| 26—Chicago | W | 3-2 | Black | James |
| 27—Texas | W | 4-2 | Saberhagen | Noles |
| 28—Texas | L | 1-6 | Hooton | Gubicza |
| 29—Texas | W | 6-2 | Jackson | Hough |
| 30—At Chicago | L | 3-4 | Seaver | Leibrandt |
| 31—At Chicago | L | 3-8 | Bannister | Black |
| **Won 14, Lost 13** | | | | |

| JUNE | | | | |
|---|---|---|---|---|
| 1—At Chicago | L | 7-8 | James | Jones |
| 2—At Chicago | L | 1-4 | Dotson | Gubicza |
| 4—Milwaukee | W | 4-3 | Leibrandt | Vuckovich |
| 5—Milwaukee | L | 2-10 | Higuera | Black |
| 7—At Calif. | W | 6-0 | Saberhagen | Witt |
| 8—At Calif. | W | 4-1 | Gubicza | Slaton |
| 9—At Calif. | L | 0-1 | Romanick | Jackson |
| 10—At Oak. | L | 1-2* | Howell | Quisenberry |
| 11—At Oak. | L | 3-4 | Howell | Black |
| 12—At Oak. | W | 3-2x | Jones | McCatty |
| 13—At Seattle | W | 4-3 | Gubicza | Wilkinson |
| 14—At Seattle | L | 5-13 | Wills | Jackson |
| 15—At Seattle | L | 1-2 | Young | Leibrandt |
| 16—At Seattle | L | 1-2 | Best | Beckwith |
| 17—Minnesota | W | 10-3 | Saberhagen | Viola |
| 18—Minnesota | W | 10-1 | Gubicza | Smithson |
| 19—Minnesota | W | 3-2 | Jackson | Filson |
| 20—Minnesota | L | 8-11 | Eufemia | Beckwith |
| 22—Seattle | L | 1-2 | Swift | Saberhagen |
| 23—Seattle | L | 2-8 | Moore | Black |
| 24—At Minn. | W | 12-6 | Gubicza | Filson |
| 25—At Minn. | W | 3-0 | Jackson | Butcher |
| 26—At Minn. | L | 1-2 | Schrom | Leibrandt |
| 28—California | W | 5-4x | Quisenberry | Corbett |
| 29—California | L | 1-7 | Lugo | Black |
| 30—California | W | 3-1 | Gubicza | Romanick |
| **Won 12, Lost 14** | | | | |

| JULY | | | | |
|---|---|---|---|---|
| 1—Oakland | L | 3-4 | Atherton | Jackson |
| 2—Oakland | W | 10-1 | Leibrandt | Langford |
| 3—Oakland | W | 3-0 | Saberhagen | Codiroli |
| 4—Baltimore | L | 3-5 | D. Martinez | Black |
| 5—Baltimore | L | 3-6 | Boddicker | Gubicza |
| 6—Baltimore | L | 3-8 | McGregor | Jackson |
| 7—Baltimore | W | 8-4 | Leibrandt | Davis |
| 8—At N.Y. | W | 5-2 | Saberhagen | Niekro |
| 9—At N.Y. | L | 4-6 | Guidry | Black |
| 10—At N.Y. | L | 5-6 | Righetti | Quisenberry |

| JULY | | | Winner | Loser |
|---|---|---|---|---|
| 11—At Cleve. | W | 1-0 | Jackson | Ruhle |
| 12—At Cleve. | L | 4-5† | Waddell | Quisenberry |
| 13—At Cleve. | W | 5-1 | Saberhagen | Blyleven |
| 14—At Cleve. | W | 9-5 | Black | Heaton |
| 18—At Balt. | L | 3-8 | McGregor | Saberhagen |
| 19—At Balt. | W | 10-3 | Leibrandt | Boddicker |
| 20—At Balt. | W | 7-5 | Jackson | Flanagan |
| 21—At Balt. | L | 4-6 | T. Martinez | Black |
| 22—New York | W | 5-4 | Jones | Rasmussen |
| 23—New York | W | 5-2 | Saberhagen | Whitson |
| 24—New York | W | 5-3 | Leibrandt | Cowley |
| 26—Cleveland | W | 7-1 | Jackson | Romero |
| 27—Cleveland | W | 6-3 | Black | Reed |
| 28—Cleveland | W | 7-4 | Gubicza | Ruhle |
| 29—At Detroit | W | 4-2 | Saberhagen | Petry |
| 30—At Detroit | L | 7-11 | Morris | Leibrandt |
| 31—At Detroit | W | 5-2 | Jackson | Terrell |
| **Won 17, Lost 10** | | | | |

| AUGUST | | | | |
|---|---|---|---|---|
| 2—Boston | W | 4-3* | Quisenberry | Clear |
| 3—Boston | L | 4-5 | Clemens | Gubicza |
| 4—Boston | L | 5-6‡ | Stanley | LaCoss |
| 5—Detroit | L | 4-8 | Terrell | Jackson |
| 8—Detroit | W | 10-3 | Saberhagen | Tanana |
| 8—Detroit | W | 6-4 | Gubicza | Petry |
| 9—Toronto | W | 4-2 | Black | Stieb |
| 10—Toronto | W | 4-3* | Quisenberry | Caudill |
| 11—Toronto | L | 3-5* | Henke | Beckwith |
| 12—At Boston | W | 3-2 | Gubicza | Nipper |
| 13—At Boston | W | 6-3 | Saberhagen | Ojeda |
| 14—At Boston | L | 3-16 | Hurst | Black |
| 16—At Toronto | W | 4-2 | Leibrandt | Key |
| 17—At Toronto | W | 4-2 | Jackson | Alexander |
| 18—At Toronto | L | 6-10 | Filer | Gubicza |
| 19—Detroit | W | 2-1* | Saberhagen | Morris |
| 20—At Chicago | L | 1-2 | James | Quisenberry |
| 21—At Chicago | W | 2-1 | Leibrandt | Bannister |
| 22—At Chicago | W | 7-3 | Jackson | Davis |
| 23—Texas | L | 3-4 | Schmidt | Quisenberry |
| 24—Texas | W | 8-2 | Saberhagen | Hooton |
| 25—Texas | L | 3-7 | Hough | Black |
| 26—Texas | W | 9-2 | Leibrandt | Russell |
| 27—At Milw. | L | 5-8 | Cocanower | Jackson |
| 28—At Milw. | W | 8-2 | Gubicza | Vuckovich |
| 30—At Texas | L | 1-4 | Hough | Black |
| 31—At Texas | L | 4-6 | Harris | Leibrandt |
| **Won 15, Lost 12** | | | | |

| SEPTEMBER | | | | |
|---|---|---|---|---|
| 1—At Texas | L | 3-5 | Mason | Jackson |
| 2—Chicago | W | 3-2 | Gubicza | Nelson |
| 3—Chicago | W | 3-2 | Saberhagen | Seaver |
| 4—Chicago | W | 6-5* | Jones | James |
| 5—Milwaukee | W | 4-1 | Leibrandt | Haas |
| 6—Milwaukee | W | 4-3† | Quisenberry | Fingers |
| 6—Milwaukee | W | 7-1 | Farr | Burris |
| 7—Milwaukee | W | 7-4 | Gubicza | Cocanower |
| 8—Milwaukee | W | 13-11† | Farr | Fingers |
| 9—At Calif. | L | 1-7 | Candelaria | Saberhagen |
| 10—At Calif. | W | 6-0 | Leibrandt | McCaskill |
| 11—At Calif. | W | 2-1 | Jackson | Romanick |
| 13—At Oak. | W | 5-2 | Gubicza | Rijo |
| 14—At Oak. | W | 2-1 | Saberhagen | John |
| 15—At Oak. | L | 2-4 | Codiroli | Leibrandt |
| 15—At Oak. | W | 7-2 | Black | Young |
| 16—Seattle | L | 1-5 | Moore | Jackson |
| 17—Seattle | L | 0-7 | Young | Farr |
| 18—Seattle | L | 0-6 | Thomas | Gubicza |
| 19—Seattle | L | 4-6 | Nunez | Quisenberry |
| 20—Minnesota | W | 5-1 | Leibrandt | Blyleven |
| 21—Minnesota | W | 6-5* | Huismann | Davis |
| 22—Minnesota | L | 3-7 | Viola | Jackson |
| 24—At Seattle | L | 2-5 | Moore | Gubicza |
| 25—At Seattle | W | 5-4 | Saberhagen | Young |
| 26—At Seattle | W | 5-2 | Leibrandt | Swift |
| 27—At Minn. | L | 1-4 | Viola | Black |
| 28—At Minn. | L | 3-5 | Burtt | Jackson |
| 29—At Minn. | L | 3-6 | Butcher | Gubicza |
| 30—California | W | 3-1 | Saberhagen | Candelaria |
| **Won 18, Lost 12** | | | | |

| OCTOBER | | | | |
|---|---|---|---|---|
| 1—California | L | 2-4 | Witt | Leibrandt |
| 2—California | W | 4-0 | Black | Romanick |
| 3—California | W | 4-1 | Jackson | Sutton |
| 4—Oakland | W | 4-2 | Gubicza | Rijo |
| 5—Oakland | W | 5-4* | Quisenberry | Howell |
| 6—Oakland | L | 3-9 | Codiroli | Jones |
| **Won 4, Lost 2** | | | | |

*10 innings.   †11 innings.   ‡12 innings.   §13 innings.   x14 innings.

**Young lefthander Danny Jackson emerged as a vital member of the Royals' starting rotation.**

tated three starts by Steve Farr, and Mike Jones got the call on the last day of the season, but no other pitcher started a game for the Royals in 1985.

Middle relief was a source of some concern as Jones, Joe Beckwith and Mike La-Coss were inconsistent. So was Quisenberry, who still had a good year by any other stopper's standards. He led the league with 37 saves and was named the A.L. Fireman of the Year for the fifth time.

Despite the Royals' tremendous pitching, the All-Star break found the team floundering, two games above .500 and 7½ games behind the division-leading Angels. It was then that an anemic offense that had been batting just .241 through June 27 started to kick in. The Royals went 47-29 after the intermission and finished with a club-record 154 homers. Still, the team's .252 average and 687 runs both ranked 13th in the league.

The Royals' two most consistent offensive catalysts were Brett and center fielder Willie Wilson. Coming off a rigorous off-season conditioning program, Brett turned in his best performance since 1980, when he hit .390. While earning a Gold Glove at third, Brett led the league with a .585 slugging percentage and was among the leaders in hitting (.335), runs batted in (112), runs scored (108) and homers (30). He also managed to avoid serious injury for a change.

Wilson, who missed the first two weeks of September after suffering a reaction to a penicillin shot, batted .278 with 43 stolen bases and a league-high 21 triples. Right behind Wilson in steals was left fielder Lonnie Smith, who struggled after being acquired from St. Louis in a May trade but raised his average to .257 and stole 40 bases by season's end.

Second baseman Frank White sacrificed a few points from his average to hit for power and the results were impressive: 69 RBIs and a career-high 22 homers.

The key to the Royals' second-half surge, however, was the insertion of Hal McRae as the full-time designated hitter on July 22. Despite platooning with Jorge Orta before that point and then sitting out the final two weeks because of a strained muscle in his side, McRae finished with 14 homers and 70 RBIs.

"Once Hal started driving the ball again," Howser said, "there was no question he was the answer."

Catcher Jim Sundberg, who was sidelined for nearly a month in August and September with a torn cartilage in his rib cage, hit .245 with 10 homers. Surprisingly, the veteran struggled behind the plate, throwing out only 18 of 70 potential basestealers. But he did earn credit for his skillful handling of the young pitching staff, and so any offense he contributed was considered a bonus.

Similarly, first baseman Steve Balboni's 166 strikeouts were excusable because of the power he provided. He set a club record with 36 homers and knocked in 88 runs.

The weakest spots in the Kansas City lineup were right field and shortstop. Darryl Motley hit 17 homers as a platoon player in right, but he and Pat Sheridan combined for a meager .224 average.

Howser gave Onix Concepcion every opportunity to win the job at short, but he wound up on the bench after displaying little ability to field (21 errors) or hit (.204, 20 RBIs). Buddy Biancalana (.188) couldn't hit, either—late-night talk-show host David Letterman made light of that fact by starting a "Countdown to Rose" for the shortstop, who was more than 4,100 hits away—but he was a slick fielder, which earned him the starting job late in the season.

By that time, Howser had a lineup that could win, even if it didn't blow opponents away.

"We're not an overconfident club because we don't score a lot of runs," Howser said. "We get it done with our pitching. We couldn't be where we are without our five starters. That's the reason we won."

Veteran Donnie Moore was the key to California's 1985 success, coming out of the bullpen to record a team-record 31 saves and a 1.92 ERA.

# Angels Fall One Game Short

**By TOM SINGER**

With inventive and manipulative Gene Mauch back at the helm, the California Angels went much farther than anyone expected in 1985, but they came up one game short.

Consigned to the bottom of the American League West by the preseason prognosticators, the Angels foiled the experts by ruling the division for six months. Their unexpected success, however, was less surprising than their modus operandi. The club that for years pounded the ball and did little else suddenly did everything but.

The Angels hit 153 home runs—a total surpassed by eight A.L. clubs—and batted a league-low .251. The pitching staff, meanwhile, ranked fifth in the league with a 3.91 earned-run average. The pitchers were aided by a brilliant defense that turned a league-high 202 double plays and committed only 112 errors (No. 2 in the league).

And even though the offense sputtered, the Angels found ways to win. The result was a 90-72 record, the second best in the club's 25-year history.

Weaving it all together was Mauch, who conjured up 149 different lineups and signaled for a league-leading number of sacrifice bunts (99). The system worked well enough to keep the Angels atop the division for 142 of the season's 181 days.

But in the end, Mauch made one move too many.

On September 28, the Angels held a 5-0 lead at Cleveland and were within six outs of sole possession of first place. Don Sutton, who had been acquired as pennant insurance from Oakland 18 days earlier, was working on an effortless three-hitter.

Sutton never came out for the eighth inning. Mauch instead called on an unprepared Donnie Moore. The Indians tied it with five runs in that inning, and Jerry Willard's two-run homer stunned the Angels in the bottom of the ninth.

They never recovered. The Angels went to Kansas City, where they dropped three of four games, and then to Texas, where they were eliminated October 5.

Mauch was frustrated after failing in his 24th bid at his first pennant.

"I feel wrung out," he said. "I felt 92 to 93 wins alone would do it. A lot of people worked awful hard not to win. But I could never get used to this club not scoring."

Utilityman Juan Beniquez (.304) was the only player even close to a .300 batting average. Among the regulars, first baseman Rod Carew was next at .280. Right fielder-designated hitter Reggie Jackson led his teammates with 27 homers, and he and left fielder-DH Brian Downing (20 homers) shared the team lead with 85 runs batted in. The most paltry statistic is Downing's total of 137 hits. It topped the club.

Two of the weakest offensive performances were turned in by shortstop Dick Schofield, who batted just .219, and outfielder Ruppert Jones (.231). Jones, a streaky reserve who was leading the team with 18 homers and was second with 54 RBIs on August 10, added just three homers and 13 RBIs in the last two months of the season and finished in a 6-for-67 rut.

Second baseman Bobby Grich and backup Rob Wilfong combined for a .226 average, although they did contribute 17 homers and 66 RBIs. At third, Doug DeCinces hit 20 homers but saw his average drop to .244, his lowest mark since 1979.

Catcher Bob Boone hit only .248, although that was an improvement of 46 points over his 1984 performance.

Most of the year, though, it didn't seem to matter. The Angels always found a way to win. Fifteen different players had game-winning RBIs. Unearned runs accounted for the margin of victory in 15 of California's wins. The Angels thrived on pressure, going 30-13 in one-run games, by far the best in the league.

A sound and deep pitching staff, however, did the most to overcome the Angels' batting woes.

Mike Witt was the ace of the staff. The 25-year-old righthander went 15-9 with a 3.56 ERA and 180 strikeouts in 250 innings. Ron Romanick followed closely with a 14-9 record, although he had a 4.11 ERA and only one win after July 31.

Veteran Jim Slaton (6-10, 4.37 ERA) struggled all year, but the Angels were rescued by several rookies. Foremost on the list was starter Kirk McCaskill (12-12), along with swingman Rafael Lugo (3-4, 3.69) and relievers Stu Cliburn (9-3, 2.09, six saves) and Pat Clements (5-0 before being sacrificed in an August trade).

Perhaps the most important pitcher for the Angels, however, was Moore, whom the Angels had picked up from the free-agent compensation pool after the loss of Fred Lynn to Baltimore. Moore became

## SCORES OF CALIFORNIA ANGELS' 1985 GAMES

### APRIL

| Date | | Score | Winner | Loser |
|---|---|---|---|---|
| 9—Minnesota | L | 2-6 | Viola | Witt |
| 10—Minnesota | L | 3-6 | Smithson | Moore |
| 11—Minnesota | W | 4-3* | Moore | Lysander |
| 12—At Oak. | L | 6-15 | Sutton | John |
| 13—At Oak. | W | 6-1 | Romanick | Warren |
| 14—At Oak. | L | 1-8 | Codiroli | Witt |
| 15—At Minn. | W | 5-0 | Zahn | Smithson |
| 17—At Minn. | W | 4-3 | Slaton | Butcher |
| 18—At Minn. | W | 9-8 | Corbett | Schrom |
| 19—Seattle | W | 9-1 | Romanick | Moore |
| 20—Seattle | L | 2-3 | Langston | Witt |
| 21—Seattle | W | 9-2 | Zahn | Beattie |
| 22—Oakland | W | 6-1 | Slaton | Sutton |
| 23—Oakland | L | 9-14 | Atherton | Kipper |
| 24—Oakland | L | 4-6 | McCatty | Romanick |
| 25—At Seattle | W | 3-0 | Witt | Langston |
| 26—At Seattle | W | 11-3 | Corbett | Beattie |
| 27—At Seattle | W | 6-1 | Slaton | Young |
| 28—At Seattle | W | 2-1 | John | Barojas |
| 29—Boston | W | 7-6 | Clements | Crawford |
| 30—Boston | W | 3-2y | Cliburn | Ojeda |

Won 14, Lost 7

### MAY

| Date | | Score | Winner | Loser |
|---|---|---|---|---|
| 1—Toronto | L | 3-6 | Key | McCaskill |
| 2—Toronto | W | 3-2 | Clements | Stieb |
| 3—Milwaukee | L | 0-7 | Higuera | John |
| 4—Milwaukee | W | 4-3 | Romanick | Vuckovich |
| 5—Milwaukee | W | 5-1 | Witt | Darwin |
| 7—At Boston | L | 4-6 | Clemens | McCaskill |
| 8—At Boston | L | 1-6 | Boyd | Slaton |
| 10—At Milw. | W | 5-4 | Romanick | Vuckovich |
| 11—At Milw. | W | 6-5 | John | Kern |
| 12—At Milw. | L | 4-7 | Haas | McCaskill |
| 14—At Toronto | L | 3-6 | Alexander | Slaton |
| 15—At Toronto | W | 9-6 | Moore | Caudill |
| 17—New York | L | 0-6 | Niekro | Witt |
| 18—New York | L | 1-6 | Cowley | John |
| 19—New York | W | 4-1 | Slaton | Whitson |
| 20—Detroit | W | 7-2 | Romanick | Terrell |
| 21—Detroit | W | 2-1† | Moore | Hernandez |
| 22—Detroit | L | 2-3 | Petry | Witt |
| 24—Baltimore | L | 3-4 | Davis | Cliburn |
| 25—Baltimore | W | 5-3 | Romanick | D. Martinez |
| 26—Baltimore | W | 10-4 | Clements | Boddicker |
| 27—Baltimore | L | 4-6 | McGregor | John |
| 29—At N.Y. | L | 2-7 | Niekro | Slaton |
| 30—At N.Y. | L | 1-3 | Cowley | Romanick |
| 31—At Detroit | W | 6-3 | Clements | Morris |

Won 12, Lost 13

### JUNE

| Date | | Score | Winner | Loser |
|---|---|---|---|---|
| 1—At Detroit | W | 9-2 | Witt | Petry |
| 2—At Detroit | L | 3-4 | Hernandez | Moore |
| 3—At Balt. | L | 5-7 | Stewart | Moore |
| 4—At Balt. | W | 6-5y | Cliburn | Dixon |
| 5—At Balt. | L | 0-4 | D. Martinez | McCaskill |
| 7—Kan. City | L | 0-6 | Saberhagen | Witt |
| 8—Kan. City | L | 1-4 | Gubicza | Slaton |
| 9—Kan. City | W | 1-0 | Romanick | Jackson |
| 10—Texas | W | 8-1 | McCaskill | Mason |
| 11—Texas | L | 4-6 | Rozema | Lugo |
| 12—Texas | W | 3-2 | Witt | Hough |
| 13—Chicago | W | 2-1 | Moore | Nelson |
| 14—Chicago | L | 2-4 | Seaver | Romanick |
| 15—Chicago | L | 2-3 | Spillner | McCaskill |
| 16—Chicago | W | 3-1 | Lugo | Lollar |
| 18—At Cleve. | W | 7-3 | Witt | Heaton |
| 19—At Cleve. | L | 0-2 | Blyleven | Slaton |
| 20—At Cleve. | W | 4-0 | Romanick | Schulze |
| 21—At Chicago | W | 5-2 | McCaskill | Bannister |
| 22—At Chicago | W | 6-3 | Lugo | Lollar |
| 23—At Chicago | W | 11-1 | Witt | Tanner |
| 24—Cleveland | L | 1-2 | Blyleven | Slaton |
| 25—Cleveland | W | 7-3§ | Cliburn | Heaton |
| 26—Cleveland | W | 10-6 | Sanchez | Barkley |
| 28—At Kan. C. | L | 4-5x | Quisenberry | Corbett |
| 29—At Kan. C. | W | 7-1 | Lugo | Black |
| 30—At Kan. C. | L | 1-3 | Gubicza | Romanick |

Won 15, Lost 12

### JULY

| Date | | Score | Winner | Loser |
|---|---|---|---|---|
| 1—At Texas | L | 5-10 | Cook | Slaton |
| 2—At Texas | W | 7-2 | McCaskill | Sebra |
| 3—At Texas | W | 3-2† | Moore | Schmidt |
| 4—Boston | W | 5-4 | Clemens | Boyd |
| 5—Boston | W | 13-4 | Romanick | Ojeda |
| 6—Boston | L | 5-7 | Stanley | Cliburn |
| 7—Boston | W | 8-3 | McCaskill | Dorsey |
| 8—Milwaukee | W | 3-2† | Moore | Gibson |
| 9—Milwaukee | W | 5-4* | Moore | Fingers |
| 10—Milwaukee | W | 2-1 | Romanick | Burris |
| 11—Toronto | L | 3-5 | Alexander | Slaton |
| 12—Toronto | W | 5-3 | McCaskill | Key |
| 13—Toronto | W | 4-3 | Witt | Lavelle |
| 14—Toronto | W | 5-3 | Cliburn | Lavelle |
| 18—At Boston | L | 1-10 | Hurst | McCaskill |
| 19—At Boston | W | 3-2 | Romanick | Boyd |
| 20—At Boston | W | 5-3 | Witt | Ojeda |
| 21—At Boston | L | 4-8 | Nipper | Lugo |
| 22—At Milw. | L | 3-16 | Vuckovich | Slaton |
| 23—At Milw. | W | 2-0 | McCaskill | Darwin |
| 24—At Milw. | W | 8-4 | Romanick | Higuera |
| 25—At Toronto | L | 0-7 | Stieb | Witt |
| 26—At Toronto | L | 3-8 | Clancy | Lugo |
| 27—At Toronto | L | 3-8 | Filer | Mack |
| 28—At Toronto | L | 1-5 | Alexander | McCaskill |
| 30—At Oak. | L | 4-5* | Howell | Moore |
| 31—At Oak. | W | 8-5 | Romanick | Langford |

Won 16, Lost 11

### AUGUST

| Date | | Score | Winner | Loser |
|---|---|---|---|---|
| 1—At Oak. | L | 1-3 | Codiroli | Lugo |
| 2—Minnesota | W | 3-1 | McCaskill | Schrom |
| 3—Minnesota | W | 5-4 | Cliburn | Blyleven |
| 4—Minnesota | W | 6-5 | Cliburn | Eufemia |
| 5—Seattle | W | 3-1 | Witt | Swift |
| 8—At Minn. | L | 2-4 | Blyleven | Romanick |
| 9—At Minn. | L | 1-6 | Viola | Zahn |
| 10—At Minn. | W | 9-1 | McCaskill | Smithson |
| 11—At Minn. | W | 12-0 | Candelaria | Butcher |
| 12—At Seattle | L | 5-6 | Nunez | Moore |
| 13—At Seattle | W | 4-3 | Slaton | Lewis |
| 13—At Seattle | L | 4-11 | Langston | Romanick |
| 14—At Seattle | W | 3-1‡ | Cliburn | Nunez |
| 14—At Seattle | L | 1-6 | Beattie | Zahn |
| 16—Oakland | W | 5-2 | Candelaria | Birtsas |
| 17—Oakland | W | 9-5 | Witt | Codiroli |
| 18—Oakland | L | 3-4 | Rijo | Moore |
| 19—Oakland | W | 5-4 | McCaskill | Sutton |
| 20—New York | L | 5-8 | Bordi | Slaton |
| 21—New York | L | 10-13* | Righetti | Moore |
| 22—New York | W | 3-2 | Witt | Bordi |
| 23—Detroit | W | 7-6 | Sanchez | Hernandez |
| 24—Detroit | L | 2-13 | Morris | McCaskill |
| 25—Detroit | W | 7-1 | Cliburn | Terrell |
| 26—Baltimore | L | 3-17 | D. Martinez | Candelaria |
| 27—Baltimore | W | 7-3 | Witt | McGregor |
| 29—At N.Y. | L | 0-4 | Niekro | McCaskill |
| 30—At N.Y. | W | 4-1 | Candelaria | Bystrom |
| 31—At N.Y. | L | 4-10 | Righetti | Corbett |

Won 16, Lost 13

### SEPTEMBER

| Date | | Score | Winner | Loser |
|---|---|---|---|---|
| 1—At N.Y. | L | 3-5 | Shirley | Holland |
| 2—At Detroit | W | 11-1 | Slaton | Tanana |
| 3—At Detroit | L | 8-14 | Petry | McCaskill |
| 4—At Detroit | W | 5-2 | Candelaria | Morris |
| 6—At Balt. | L | 2-6 | D. Martinez | Romanick |
| 7—At Balt. | L | 3-4 | Aase | Moore |
| 8—At Balt. | W | 7-4† | Moore | T. Martinez |
| 9—Kan. City | W | 7-1 | Candelaria | Saberhagen |
| 10—Kan. City | L | 0-6 | Leibrandt | McCaskill |
| 11—Kan. City | L | 1-2 | Jackson | Romanick |
| 12—Texas | W | 5-3 | Witt | Henry |
| 13—Texas | W | 2-0 | Sutton | Hough |
| 14—Texas | L | 5-8 | Williams | Corbett |
| 15—Texas | W | 12-4 | McCaskill | Guzman |
| 17—At Chicago | L | 2-5 | Burns | Witt |
| 18—At Chicago | W | 9-3 | Sutton | Nelson |
| 19—At Chicago | W | 8-0 | Candelaria | Seaver |
| 20—Cleveland | W | 7-5 | Corbett | Von Ohlen |
| 21—Cleveland | W | 12-3 | McCaskill | Heaton |
| 22—Cleveland | W | 10-9‡ | Cliburn | Clark |
| 23—Chicago | L | 5-6 | Nelson | Sutton |
| 24—Chicago | L | 1-8 | Seaver | Candelaria |
| 25—Chicago | W | 7-4 | Romanick | Burns |
| 27—At Cleve. | L | 3-7 | Heaton | Witt |
| 28—At Cleve. | L | 5-7 | Reed | Cliburn |
| 29—At Cleve. | W | 9-3 | McCaskill | Wardle |
| 30—At Kan. C. | L | 1-3 | Saberhagen | Candelaria |

Won 14, Lost 13

### OCTOBER

| Date | | Score | Winner | Loser |
|---|---|---|---|---|
| 1—At Kan. C. | W | 4-2 | Witt | Leibrandt |
| 2—At Kan. C. | L | 0-4 | Black | Romanick |
| 3—At Kan. C. | L | 1-4 | Jackson | Sutton |
| 4—At Texas | L | 0-6 | Schmidt | McCaskill |
| 5—At Texas | W | 3-1 | Candelaria | Williams |
| 6—At Texas | W | 6-5 | Witt | Surhoff |

Won 3, Lost 3

*10 innings.   †11 innings.   ‡12 innings.   §13 innings.   x14 innings.   y15 innings.

**Gary Pettis struggled offensively but established himself as one of the top defensive center fielders in baseball.**

the bullpen stopper and registered a team-record 31 saves and a 1.92 ERA.

At the All-Star break, the link between California's league-leading 3.37 ERA and its six-game West lead was unmistakable, and even a battle-scarred veteran like Mauch was stunned by the club's first-half performance.

"No, I don't even see any room for improvement," Mauch said. "And no, I don't think I've ever before been in a position to say that."

But the three-day All-Star break was the first of two momentum-breaking lulls. The second—the two-day players strike—turned out to be fatal.

Climaxed by an emotional weekend sweep of Toronto, the Angels were on an 11-2 tear when first stopped by the schedule. An arduous 14-game trip that followed the All-Star break ended with a disastrous four-game sweep by the Blue Jays, whose ruthless treatment of three straight rookie starters prompted General Manager Mike Port to make a blockbuster trade with Pittsburgh.

The Angels received lefthander John Candelaria, who was invaluable during California's stretch drive as he won seven of 10 decisions. But the Angels also had to accept reliever Al Holland and outfielder George Hendrick, who did little more than eat up two roster spots. And Port broke up the youth-accented combination that had paved the team's rise as Clements and outfielder Mike Brown went to the Pirates.

Spurting again, the Angels had won four

straight and built their lead back to five games when play stopped so a new Basic Agreement could be pounded out.

Within 36 hours after play resumed, that lead was cut in half. Even worse, the strike robbed the Angels of two home dates—no small loss considering that they went 49-30 at home and lost the title by one game. The games were made up at Seattle in two doubleheaders, both of which the Angels split.

"If there's one thing that bothers me about the season, it's that we had two very important dates at home blown away," Mauch said.

The disappointing curtain obscured a number of individual highlights:

● Carew became the 16th member of the 3,000-hit circle with a single off Minnesota's Frank Viola on August 4.

● Jackson spent the season passing such immortals as Ernie Banks and Ted Williams on all-time charts, winding up in eighth place with 530 homers and in 15th with 1,601 RBIs.

● Grich's 13 homers left him with 145 as an Angel, supplanting Don Baylor as the team's all-time leader.

● Gold Glove winner Gary Pettis established himself as one of the best center fielders in baseball while stealing 56 bases.

All of the Angels' bright spots, though, could not soothe the pain over their one major drawback: a single game in the standings.

"Thanks to the efforts of a lot of people, we were a much better team," Port said. "But we couldn't finish the job."

Lefthander Britt Burns recovered from a bad 1984 season by recording an 18-11 record, four shutouts and a 3.96 ERA.

# White Sox Expected Better

### By JOE GODDARD

There was a time not too long ago when a first-division finish by the White Sox was a welcome accomplishment in Chicago.

Not anymore. The White Sox have come to know some degree of success in recent years—including 99 victories and an American League West crown in 1983—and so a third-place showing in 1985 just didn't cut it. Although the White Sox posted their fourth first-division finish in five years while going 85-77 (an 11-game improvement over their 1984 mark), co-Owners Jerry Reinsdorf and Eddie Einhorn still weren't satisfied.

"Expectations have been raised in this town," Reinsdorf said. "Third place may have been acceptable a few years ago, but not anymore."

The owners decided a change was in order, so with five days left in the season they promoted their local electric cowboy to the position of vice president of baseball operations. Ken (Hawk) Harrelson, the former slugger, pro golfer and television color commentator who is known for his loud outfits and cowboy hats, was made the club's top executive after submitting to the owners a plan on how to instill "aggressiveness" into the organization.

Roland Hemond, who as general manager was the Major League Executive of the Year in 1972 and 1983, was moved to the newly created position of special assistant to Reinsdorf and Einhorn. Harrelson was entrusted with the responsibility of naming a new general manager.

The Hawk also announced that he would expand the coaching staff in an effort to make the White Sox more than just competitive. One idea was to have two pitching coaches—one for starters and another (Moe Drabowsky) for relievers.

Feeling that help should have come in midseason from somewhere other than their rather barren Triple-A team at Buffalo, Manager Tony LaRussa's players weren't too surprised by the front-office change. Theirs was a frustrating season, making them anxious to watch Harrelson put his aggressive ideas to work in pursuit of a pennant-winning club.

Even with this emphasis on the future, White Sox fans could look back with pride on the championship-caliber performances of several players, from aging veterans to a green rookie.

Catcher Carlton Fisk came back from

**Slick-fielding shortstop Ozzie Guillen improved offensively and captured A.L. Rookie of the Year honors.**

an injury-plagued 1984 season to lead the league in home runs most of the campaign until yielding to Detroit's Darrell Evans down the stretch. Fisk, who also performed as the designated hitter, finished second with 37 homers, one for each year of his life, to tie a team record. He also was

## SCORES OF CHICAGO WHITE SOX' 1985 GAMES

### APRIL

| Date | W/L | Score | Winner | Loser |
|---|---|---|---|---|
| 9—At Milw. | W | 4-2 | Seaver | Haas |
| 11—At Milw. | L | 1-8 | Burris | Lollar |
| 13—At Boston | L | 2-7 | Boyd | Bannister |
| 14—At Boston | W | 11-6 | Burns | Crawford |
| 15—At Boston | W | 6-5§ | Jones | Stanley |
| 16—At N.Y. | L | 4-5 | Righetti | Spillner |
| 18—At N.Y. | L | 2-3 | Bordi | Bannister |
| 19—Boston | W | 8-1 | Burns | Trujillo |
| 20—Boston | L | 8-12 | Crawford | Nelson |
| 21—Boston | W | 7-2 | Lollar | Clemens |
| 22—Milwaukee | L | 2-4 | Darwin | Agosto |
| 23—Milwaukee | W | 6-5‡ | James | Fingers |
| 24—Milwaukee | L | 2-3 | Vuckovich | Burns |
| 26—New York | W | 4-2 | Seaver | Whitson |
| 27—New York | W | 5-4§ | Nelson | Shirley |
| 28—New York | W | 4-3 | Burns | Cowley |
| 30—At Balt. | L | 7-9 | Boddicker | Bannister |

**Won 9, Lost 8**

### MAY

| Date | W/L | Score | Winner | Loser |
|---|---|---|---|---|
| 1—At Balt. | L | 1-3 | Dixon | Burns |
| 3—At Detroit | W | 7-1 | Seaver | Petry |
| 4—At Detroit | L | 1-7 | Terrell | Lollar |
| 5—At Detroit | L | 3-4 | Berenguer | Dotson |
| 7—At Cleve. | W | 7-4 | Bannister | Blyleven |
| 8—At Cleve. | W | 4-0 | Burns | Heaton |
| 10—Detroit | L | 1-3 | Terrell | Seaver |
| 11—Detroit | W | 7-4 | Dotson | Berenguer |
| 12—Detroit | W | 4-0 | Bannister | Morris |
| 13—Cleveland | W | 8-0 | Burns | Heaton |
| 14—Cleveland | W | 2-1 | Nelson | Thompson |
| 15—Baltimore | W | 5-2 | Seaver | Aase |
| 16—Baltimore | L | 1-3* | Boddicker | Bannister |
| 17—Texas | W | 4-2 | Dotson | Noles |
| 18—Texas | L | 2-7 | Hooton | Burns |
| 19—Texas | W | 5-1 | Nelson | Hough |
| 20—At Toronto | L | 1-6 | Key | Seaver |
| 21—At Toronto | L | 3-4 | Lavelle | James |
| 22—At Toronto | L | 0-10 | Stieb | Dotson |
| 24—At Kan. C. | L | 4-8 | Jackson | Burns |
| 25—At Kan. C. | L | 0-3 | Leibrandt | Seaver |
| 26—At Kan. C. | L | 2-3 | Black | James |
| 28—Toronto | L | 1-6 | Stieb | Dotson |
| 29—Toronto | W | 8-5 | Burns | Clancy |
| 30—Kan. City | W | 4-3 | Seaver | Leibrandt |
| 31—Kan. City | W | 8-3 | Bannister | Black |

**Won 13, Lost 13**

### JUNE

| Date | W/L | Score | Winner | Loser |
|---|---|---|---|---|
| 1—Kan. City | W | 8-7 | James | Jones |
| 2—Kan. City | W | 4-1 | Dotson | Gubicza |
| 3—At Texas | L | 3-7 | Harris | Burns |
| 4—At Texas | L | 3-7 | Hough | Seaver |
| 6—At Texas | W | 4-3 | Bannister | Mason |
| 7—At Minn. | L | 3-6 | Filson | Dotson |
| 8—At Minn. | W | 3-1 | Burns | Butcher |
| 9—At Minn. | W | 5-1 | Seaver | Schrom |
| 10—At Seattle | W | 9-4 | Bannister | Young |
| 11—At Seattle | W | 7-1 | Lollar | Swift |
| 12—At Seattle | W | 6-3 | Tanner | Snyder |
| 13—At Calif. | L | 1-2 | Moore | Nelson |
| 14—At Calif. | W | 4-2 | Seaver | Romanick |
| 15—At Calif. | W | 3-2 | Spillner | McCaskill |
| 16—At Calif. | L | 1-3 | Lugo | Lollar |
| 18—Oakland | W | 4-3y | Nelson | Atherton |
| 19—Oakland | W | 8-7x | James | Langford |
| 20—Oakland | L | 1-12 | Birtsas | Seaver |
| 21—California | L | 2-5 | McCaskill | Bannister |
| 22—California | L | 3-6 | Lugo | Lollar |
| 23—California | L | 1-11 | Witt | Tanner |
| 24—At Oak. | W | 7-1 | Spillner | Birtsas |
| 25—At Oak. | L | 4-5y | Atherton | Nelson |
| 26—At Oak. | L | 0-10 | Sutton | Bannister |
| 28—Minnesota | L | 4-5 | Viola | Tanner |
| 29—Minnesota | L | 0-1 | Smithson | Burns |
| 30—Minnesota | L | 3-4 | Butcher | Seaver |

**Won 13, Lost 14**

### JULY

| Date | W/L | Score | Winner | Loser |
|---|---|---|---|---|
| 1—Seattle | L | 1-3 | Wills | Bannister |
| 2—Seattle | W | 12-4 | Lollar | Snyder |
| 3—Seattle | L | 1-5 | Swift | Spillner |
| 4—At Cleve. | W | 5-0 | Burns | Blyleven |
| 5—At Cleve. | W | 8-3 | Seaver | Reed |
| 6—At Cleve. | W | 6-4‡ | James | Thompson |
| 7—At Cleve. | L | 3-10 | Waddell | Lollar |
| 8—At Detroit | W | 9-4 | Nelson | Petry |
| 9—At Detroit | L | 5-6 | Hernandez | James |
| 10—At Detroit | L | 0-1 | Morris | Seaver |
| 11—At Balt. | L | 6-7 | Stewart | Stanton |
| 12—At Balt. | L | 3-10 | Dixon | Nelson |
| 13—At Balt. | W | 10-8 | Burns | D. Martinez |
| 14—At Balt. | W | 5-3 | Seaver | Boddicker |
| 18—Cleveland | W | 10-0 | Burns | Ruhle |
| 19—Cleveland | W | 1-0 | Seaver | Blyleven |
| 20—Cleveland | W | 8-6 | Agosto | Clark |
| 21—Cleveland | L | 3-4‡ | Thompson | Spillner |
| 22—Detroit | W | 9-4 | Nelson | O'Neal |
| 23—Detroit | W | 5-3 | Burns | Tanana |
| 24—Detroit | L | 4-5 | Petry | Seaver |
| 25—Baltimore | L | 1-5 | Flanagan | Bannister |
| 26—Baltimore | W | 9-8 | Agosto | Aase |
| 27—Baltimore | L | 1-9 | Davis | Nelson |
| 28—Baltimore | L | 1-6 | McGregor | Burns |
| 30—At Boston | W | 7-5‡ | Seaver | Boyd |
| 31—At Boston | T | 1-1† | ........ | ........ |

**Won 14, Lost 12**

### AUGUST

| Date | W/L | Score | Winner | Loser |
|---|---|---|---|---|
| 1—At Boston | W | 7-2 | Nelson | Nipper |
| 1—At Boston | L | 3-4 | Crawford | Agosto |
| 2—At N.Y. | W | 6-5§ | Agosto | Bordi |
| 3—At N.Y. | L | 4-8 | Whitson | Long |
| 4—At N.Y. | W | 4-1 | Seaver | Cowley |
| 5—At N.Y. | L | 3-7 | Guidry | Bannister |
| 8—Boston | W | 7-6 | Wehrmeister | Kison |
| 8—Boston | L | 1-6 | Lollar | Nelson |
| 9—Milwaukee | L | 7-8 | Waits | James |
| 10—Milwaukee | L | 2-5§ | Higuera | Agosto |
| 11—Milwaukee | W | 4-1 | Davis | Burris |
| 12—New York | L | 4-10 | Niekro | Nelson |
| 13—New York | W | 4-3 | Burns | Fisher |
| 14—New York | L | 7-10 | Fisher | James |
| 15—At Milw. | L | 5-7 | Higuera | Bannister |
| 16—At Milw. | L | 2-3 | Burris | Wehrmeister |
| 17—At Milw. | W | 12-7 | Spillner | Cocanower |
| 18—At Milw. | W | 8-4 | Burns | Vuckovich |
| 20—Kan. City | W | 2-1 | James | Quisenberry |
| 21—Kan. City | L | 1-2 | Leibrandt | Bannister |
| 22—Kan. City | L | 3-7 | Jackson | Davis |
| 23—Toronto | L | 3-6 | Filer | Burns |
| 23—Toronto | L | 3-10 | Acker | Nelson |
| 24—Toronto | L | 3-6 | Stieb | Seaver |
| 25—Toronto | W | 5-3 | Bannister | Key |
| 26—Boston | W | 7-6‡ | James | Stanley |
| 27—Texas | W | 7-4 | Burns | Noles |
| 28—Texas | W | 5-1 | Nelson | Stewart |
| 29—Texas | W | 6-5‡ | Spillner | Schmidt |
| 30—At Toronto | L | 3-5 | Key | Bannister |
| 31—At Toronto | L | 2-6 | Lavelle | Davis |

**Won 14, Lost 17**

### SEPTEMBER

| Date | W/L | Score | Winner | Loser |
|---|---|---|---|---|
| 1—At Toronto | W | 4-1 | Burns | Davis |
| 2—At Kan. C. | L | 2-3 | Gubicza | Nelson |
| 3—At Kan. C. | L | 2-3 | Saberhagen | Seaver |
| 4—At Kan. C. | L | 5-6‡ | Jones | James |
| 5—At Texas | W | 11-4 | Davis | Russell |
| 6—At Texas | W | 12-1 | Nelson | Mason |
| 7—At Texas | W | 3-2 | Agosto | Henry |
| 8—At Texas | W | 7-6 | Seaver | Hough |
| 9—Minnesota | L | 0-5 | Butcher | Bannister |
| 10—Minnesota | W | 7-2 | Davis | Blyleven |
| 11—Minnesota | W | 5-0 | Burns | Viola |
| 12—Minnesota | W | 4-2 | Nelson | Smithson |
| 13—At Seattle | W | 6-1 | Gleaton | Young |
| 14—At Seattle | L | 5-6 | Swift | Bannister |
| 15—At Seattle | W | 6-3 | Wehrmeister | Langston |
| 17—California | W | 5-2 | Burns | Witt |
| 18—California | L | 3-9 | Sutton | Nelson |
| 19—California | L | 0-8 | Candelaria | Seaver |
| 20—Oakland | W | 10-4 | Bannister | John |
| 21—Oakland | L | 3-8 | Codiroli | Burns |
| 22—Oakland | W | 7-5‡ | James | Howell |
| 23—At Calif. | W | 6-5 | Nelson | Sutton |
| 24—At Calif. | W | 8-1 | Seaver | Candelaria |
| 25—At Calif. | L | 4-7 | Romanick | Burns |
| 26—At Oak. | W | 11-7 | Bannister | Codiroli |
| 27—At Oak. | W | 4-3 | James | Ontiveros |
| 28—At Oak. | L | 4-7 | Rijo | Wehrmeister |
| 29—At Oak. | W | 3-0 | Seaver | Young |
| 30—At Minn. | L | 1-7 | Blyleven | Burns |

**Won 18, Lost 11**

### OCTOBER

| Date | W/L | Score | Winner | Loser |
|---|---|---|---|---|
| 1—At Minn. | W | 12-6 | Bannister | Smithson |
| 2—At Minn. | L | 1-3 | Viola | Davis |
| 3—Seattle | L | 4-5 | Swift | James |
| 4—Seattle | W | 7-5 | Seaver | Young |
| 5—Seattle | W | 10-4 | Bannister | Wills |
| 6—Seattle | W | 3-2 | Correa | Moore |

**Won 4, Lost 2**

*6 innings.  †7 innings.  ‡10 innings.  §11 innings.  x12 innings.  y13 innings.

eighth in runs batted in with 107, 13 of them the game-winning variety. His .488 slugging percentage compensated for his .238 batting average, and his 17 stolen bases tied his career high.

By getting off to his best spring start and having another fine finish, right fielder Harold Baines hit .309 with 22 home runs and 113 RBIs. Baines, who led the White Sox in runs scored with 86, was the club's most consistent performer.

Also turning in a good year was first baseman Greg Walker. Batting cleanup for a full season, Walker wound up with 24 homers, 38 doubles and 92 RBIs.

Rookie Ozzie Guillen not only broke Ron Hansen's 1963 club record for fewest errors by a shortstop with 12, but also led the major leagues. His .273 average and team-high nine triples also were respectable figures, although he contributed only 33 RBIs. He was a solid choice as A.L. Rookie of the Year, thus justifying the trade that brought Guillen to Chicago and sent 1983 Cy Young Award winner La-Marr Hoyt to San Diego.

There were some good pitching performances, too. Britt Burns had one of the league's most dramatic turnarounds, going from a 4-12 record and a 5.00 earned-run average in '84 to 18-11 and a 3.96 ERA, with four shutouts and 172 strikeouts. The lefthander had three chances to reach 20 victories, but the strain of pitching more than 100 more innings than the year before finally took its toll.

Durable Tom Seaver had a strong July to set up his 300th lifetime victory on August 4. The righthander finished 16-11 with a 3.17 ERA, bringing the future Hall of Famer to 31 White Sox wins in two years.

"Obviously, I've done what they brought me here for," Seaver said. "I think I did more than they thought I would."

Righthander Bob James, who was obtained from Montreal in one of Hemond's last deals, solved Chicago's bullpen woes. He broke Ed Farmer's 1980 club record for saves with 32 and fashioned a 2.13 ERA.

Although the White Sox shattered the club strikeout mark with 1,023, the pitching staff had its share of disappointments. Floyd Bannister was second in the league in strikeouts with 198 but was 10-14 with a 4.87 ERA. Richard Dotson missed most of the season following the removal of an overdeveloped muscle that was causing shoulder pain. LaRussa therefore was forced to bring righthander Gene Nelson (10-10, 4.26 ERA) out of his bullpen setup

role. Dan Spillner (4-3, 3.44) also made some spot starts.

When James went out for three weeks with a trick knee, LaRussa paraded relievers into the game like toy soldiers. Except for some late-season help from righthander Dave Wehrmeister, the relief was average at best.

In a season when the pitching overall was mediocre—the club's 4.07 ERA ranked seventh in the league—the White Sox had to take up the slack with a potent offense. They didn't. The team's collective batting average of .253 was tied for 10th in the league.

One of the biggest letdowns for the White Sox was the failure of Ron Kittle to match his 1983 Rookie of the Year performance. The left fielder struggled with an inflamed shoulder during the first half of the season and went to Buffalo for a brief rehabilitation period. Kittle hit 18 of his 26 homers after the All-Star break and wound up with a .230 average and 58 RBIs.

Center field was an equally unproductive spot for the White Sox. Rudy Law, who also played in left when Kittle was the DH or was injured, fell short of his goals for the second year in a row, batting .259 with 29 stolen bases. Law shared center with Luis Salazar, who hit .245 after coming to Chicago from San Diego in the Guillen trade, and Reid Nichols (.297 in Chicago), who was obtained in a July trade with Boston for pitcher Tim Lollar. Lollar, another part of the Guillen deal, did not pitch well in Chicago and was sent packing after going 3-5 with a 4.66 ERA.

Rookie Daryl Boston started the season in center field but spent much of his time in the minors trying to improve his hitting.

Led by Guillen, the White Sox sparkled defensively, committing a league-low 111 errors. The weakest spot was third base, where transplanted second baseman Tim Hulett made 23 errors (plus one more at second).

Hulett batted .268 and was one of several infielders who provided little run production. Bryan Little (.250) and Julio Cruz (.197) shared second base and combined for only 42 RBIs and two homers. Scott Fletcher, filling in at third and shortstop, hit .256 with 31 RBIs.

LaRussa, who used 103 different lineups in 1985, said his players did their best trying to win despite the injuries that afflicted key performers.

"I give all the players an 'A' for effort," the manager said. "They could have quit when we had those injuries, but didn't."

**Ace lefthander Frank Viola struggled early but returned to 1984 form with a September surge that lifted his final record to 18-14.**

# Early Collapse Dooms Twins

**By PATRICK REUSSE**

After finishing just three games behind American League West champion Kansas City in 1984, the Minnesota Twins entered the 1985 season expecting to contend. But poor pitching, mediocre defense and erratic hitting quickly put those expectations to rest as the Twins dropped out of the race early.

The Twins had both a nine-game losing streak and a 10-game winning streak in the first month, but they did themselves in with a 10-game losing streak from May 21 to June 1. When that streak started, the Twins were 21-16 and in second place, one game back. When it ended they were in fifth place, six games behind and fading.

The club settled into sixth place for most of the summer, but there remained some baseball excitement in the area because Minnesota hosted the All-Star Game on July 16. Buoyed by the interest in that game and the preseason optimism, the Twins set a franchise attendance record by surpassing 1.6 million for the first time. But the Twins' poor performance led to dwindling crowds in the second half, and the club's hopes of reaching 2 million fell short.

Manager Billy Gardner, who had been widely praised for putting the Twins in the race in 1984, did not make it to the All-Star break. He was fired by team President Howard Fox on June 21, when the Twins were 27-35 and 7½ games out of first.

"We tried to change things around by making a trade for Bert Blyleven," Fox said. "When we couldn't do that, we had to try something to get it turned around."

Ray Miller, Baltimore's longtime pitching coach, was brought in as Gardner's replacement. Miller signed a contract through the 1986 season.

After the change, the Twins faded farther from contention, but they rallied to finish with a .500 record (50-50) under Miller. For the season, the Twins went 77-85 and finished in a tie for fourth with Oakland, 14 games back.

One reason the Twins rallied was because they finally completed the Blyleven trade August 1. Blyleven, originally a member of the Twins before being traded to Texas in 1976, gave Minnesota its best starting pitching of the season once he arrived from Cleveland in exchange for pitcher Curt Wardle and two minor leaguers. The righthander was 8-5 with a 3.00

**Even the return of Bert Blyleven couldn't get the Twins back into the A.L. West Division race.**

ERA in 14 starts for Minnesota, and his combined Twins-Indians totals made him the league leader in strikeouts, shutouts, complete games and innings pitched.

The Twins' other attempt to improve their pitching didn't work out so well. On August 12, Minnesota signed reliever Steve Howe, who had been released by Los Angeles in July, just months after the Dodgers had given him another chance to resume his career after a long battle with drug dependency. But the lefthander was ineffective, going 2-3 with a 6.16 earned-run average and no saves in 13 appearances, and after admitting that he had suffered a relapse of cocaine use when he missed a weekend series in Cleveland, he was released September 17.

The Twins had not expected pitching—particularly starting pitching—to be a

## SCORES OF MINNESOTA TWINS' 1985 GAMES

### APRIL

| Date | | Score | Winner | Loser |
|---|---|---|---|---|
| 9—At Calif. | W | 6-2 | Viola | Witt |
| 10—At Calif. | W | 6-3 | Smithson | Moore |
| 11—At Calif. | L | 3-4* | Moore | Lysander |
| 12—At Seattle | L | 1-2 | Young | Schrom |
| 13—At Seattle | L | 7-8 | Stanton | Davis |
| 14—At Seattle | L | 1-5 | Moore | Viola |
| 15—California | L | 0-5 | Zahn | Smithson |
| 17—California | L | 3-4 | Slaton | Butcher |
| 18—California | L | 8-9 | Corbett | Schrom |
| 19—At Oak. | L | 2-4 | Codiroli | Viola |
| 20—At Oak. | L | 2-6 | Krueger | Smithson |
| 21—At Oak. | W | 2-0 | Butcher | Young |
| 22—Seattle | W | 9-5 | Schrom | Young |
| 23—Seattle | W | 4-2 | Viola | Barojas |
| 24—Seattle | W | 10-0 | Smithson | Moore |
| 25—Oakland | W | 5-4 | Butcher | Atherton |
| 26—Oakland | W | 8-7 | Davis | Atherton |
| 27—Oakland | W | 8-6 | Viola | Sutton |
| 28—Oakland | W | 10-1 | Smithson | Warren |
| 30—At Detroit | W | 11-2 | Butcher | Wilcox |
| **Won 11, Lost 9** | | | | |

### MAY

| Date | | Score | Winner | Loser |
|---|---|---|---|---|
| 1—At Detroit | W | 7-3 | Viola | Morris |
| 3—Baltimore | L | 7-8 | Aase | Wardle |
| 4—Baltimore | W | 8-6 | Schrom | D. Martinez |
| 5—Baltimore | L | 5-10 | Boddicker | Butcher |
| 7—New York | W | 8-6 | Viola | Whitson |
| 8—New York | W | 8-6 | Smithson | Cowley |
| 10—At Balt. | L | 5-6 | Aase | Davis |
| 11—At Balt. | L | 2-4 | Boddicker | Davis |
| 12—At Balt. | W | 7-3 | Viola | Dixon |
| 13—At N.Y. | L | 8-9 | Cowley | Davis |
| 14—At N.Y. | L | 7-10 | Fisher | Wardle |
| 15—Detroit | W | 5-4† | Wardle | Lopez |
| 16—Detroit | W | 7-5 | Schrom | Berenguer |
| 17—Toronto | W | 7-6† | Filson | Leal |
| 18—Toronto | L | 1-3 | Clancy | Smithson |
| 19—Toronto | W | 8-2 | Filson | Alexander |
| 20—Boston | W | 5-2 | Butcher | Nipper |
| 21—Boston | L | 1-9 | Kison | Schrom |
| 22—Boston | L | 3-4 | Clemens | Viola |
| 24—At Milw. | L | 2-5 | Burris | Smithson |
| 25—At Milw. | L | 7-9 | McClure | Filson |
| 26—At Milw. | L | 3-5 | Higuera | Butcher |
| 27—At Boston | L | 2-9 | Clemens | Schrom |
| 29—At Boston | L | 0-7 | Boyd | Viola |
| 30—At Boston | L | 7-8† | Stanley | Davis |
| 31—Milwaukee | L | 4-6 | Higuera | Filson |
| **Won 10, Lost 16** | | | | |

### JUNE

| Date | | Score | Winner | Loser |
|---|---|---|---|---|
| 1—Milwaukee | L | 2-7 | Darwin | Butcher |
| 2—Milwaukee | W | 5-4 | Schrom | Gibson |
| 4—At Toronto | L | 2-9 | Clancy | Viola |
| 5—At Toronto | L | 0-5 | Alexander | Smithson |
| 7—Chicago | W | 6-3 | Filson | Dotson |
| 8—Chicago | L | 1-3 | Burns | Butcher |
| 9—Chicago | L | 1-5 | Seaver | Schrom |
| 10—At Cleve. | W | 6-4 | Viola | Creel |
| 13—At Texas | W | 7-5 | Smithson | Tanana |
| 14—At Texas | L | 2-4 | Hooton | Filson |
| 15—At Texas | L | 2-11 | Mason | Butcher |
| 16—At Texas | W | 4-1 | Schrom | Hough |
| 17—At Kan. C. | L | 3-10 | Saberhagen | Viola |
| 18—At Kan. C. | L | 1-10 | Gubicza | Smithson |
| 19—At Kan. C. | L | 2-3 | Jackson | Filson |
| 20—At Kan. C. | W | 11-8 | Eufemia | Beckwith |
| 21—Texas | W | 3-2 | Schrom | Hough |
| 22—Texas | W | 3-2 | Viola | Mason |
| 23—Texas | L | 1-3 | Cook | Smithson |
| 24—Kan. City | L | 6-12 | Gubicza | Filson |
| 25—Kan. City | L | 0-3 | Jackson | Butcher |
| 26—Kan. City | W | 2-1 | Schrom | Leibrandt |
| 28—At Chicago | W | 5-4 | Viola | Tanner |
| 29—At Chicago | W | 1-0 | Smithson | Burns |
| 30—At Chicago | W | 4-3 | Butcher | Seaver |
| **Won 12, Lost 13** | | | | |

### JULY

| Date | | Score | Winner | Loser |
|---|---|---|---|---|
| 1—Cleveland | L | 2-5 | Ruhle | Schrom |
| 2—Cleveland | W | 8-7 | Eufemia | Waddell |
| 3—Cleveland | W | 7-0 | Smithson | Heaton |
| 4—At N.Y. | L | 2-3 | Guidry | Butcher |
| 5—At N.Y. | L | 3-6 | Rasmussen | Schrom |
| 7—At N.Y. | L | 2-3† | Righetti | Wardle |
| 7—At N.Y. | L | 2-14 | Bordi | Lysander |
| 8—At Balt. | W | 7-4* | Davis | Aase |
| 9—At Balt. | L | 6-11 | Snell | Schrom |
| 10—At Balt. | W | 2-1 | Viola | Boddicker |
| 11—At Detroit | W | 5-1 | Smithson | O'Neal |
| 12—At Detroit | W | 3-2 | Butcher | Tanana |
| 13—At Detroit | W | 6-4 | Schrom | Petry |
| 14—At Detroit | L | 0-8 | Terrell | Viola |
| 18—New York | W | 8-4 | Eufemia | Bordi |
| 19—New York | L | 4-6 | Cowley | Butcher |
| 20—New York | L | 3-8 | Guidry | Schrom |
| 21—New York | L | 2-5 | Niekro | Viola |
| 22—Baltimore | W | 5-4 | Smithson | Davis |
| 23—Baltimore | W | 5-2 | Butcher | McGregor |
| 24—Baltimore | L | 2-4 | Boddicker | Schrom |
| 25—Detroit | L | 2-7 | Morris | Viola |
| 26—Detroit | W | 6-5 | Smithson | Terrell |
| 27—Detroit | W | 11-4 | Butcher | Lopez |
| 28—Detroit | L | 2-3 | Tanana | Schrom |
| 29—At Seattle | L | 6-8 | Nunez | Eufemia |
| 30—At Seattle | W | 12-4 | Smithson | Swift |
| 31—At Seattle | L | 3-12 | Beattie | Butcher |
| **Won 13, Lost 15** | | | | |

### AUGUST

| Date | | Score | Winner | Loser |
|---|---|---|---|---|
| 2—At Calif. | L | 1-3 | McCaskill | Schrom |
| 3—At Calif. | L | 4-5 | Cliburn | Blyleven |
| 4—At Calif. | L | 5-6 | Cliburn | Eufemia |
| 5—At Oak. | L | 1-5 | Birtsas | Smithson |
| 8—California | W | 4-2 | Blyleven | Romanick |
| 9—California | W | 6-1 | Viola | Zahn |
| 10—California | L | 1-9 | McCaskill | Smithson |
| 11—California | L | 0-12 | Candelaria | Butcher |
| 12—Oakland | W | 4-3 | Blyleven | Rijo |
| 12—Oakland | W | 5-4 | Howe | Codiroli |
| 13—Oakland | W | 8-1 | Viola | John |
| 14—Oakland | L | 0-5 | Sutton | Smithson |
| 14—Oakland | L | 4-7 | Rijo | Portugal |
| 15—Seattle | W | 14-5 | Butcher | Young |
| 16—Seattle | L | 5-6 | Vande Berg | Howe |
| 17—Seattle | W | 2-0 | Blyleven | Wills |
| 18—Seattle | L | 2-7 | Langston | Viola |
| 19—At Milw. | L | 1-4 | Darwin | Smithson |
| 20—At Milw. | L | 2-3 | Higuera | Howe |
| 21—At Milw. | L | 2-3 | Burris | Howe |
| 23—At Boston | L | 5-2 | Viola | Lollar |
| 24—At Boston | W | 1-0 | Smithson | Hurst |
| 26—Toronto | L | 3-4 | Alexander | Blyleven |
| 27—Toronto | L | 0-8 | Davis | Viola |
| 28—Toronto | W | 6-5* | Filson | Henke |
| 30—Boston | L | 3-7 | Ojeda | Butcher |
| 31—Boston | W | 6-5 | Blyleven | Crawford |
| 31—Boston | W | 5-4 | Portugal | Nipper |
| **Won 12, Lost 16** | | | | |

### SEPTEMBER

| Date | | Score | Winner | Loser |
|---|---|---|---|---|
| 1—Boston | L | 3-10 | Trujillo | Viola |
| 2—Milwaukee | W | 6-1 | Smithson | Cocanower |
| 3—Milwaukee | W | 4-3 | Howe | Darwin |
| 4—Milwaukee | L | 10-11 | Waits | Burtt |
| 5—At Toronto | L | 0-7 | Alexander | Blyleven |
| 6—At Toronto | L | 3-8 | Davis | Viola |
| 7—At Toronto | W | 6-3 | Smithson | Stieb |
| 8—At Toronto | L | 9-10 | Lamp | Portugal |
| 9—At Chicago | W | 5-0 | Butcher | Bannister |
| 10—At Chicago | L | 2-7 | Davis | Blyleven |
| 11—At Chicago | L | 0-5 | Burns | Viola |
| 12—At Chicago | L | 2-4 | Nelson | Smithson |
| 13—At Cleve. | L | 2-3 | Wardle | Portugal |
| 13—At Cleve. | W | 3-1 | Viola | Schulze |
| 14—At Cleve. | L | 9-11 | Waddell | Butcher |
| 14—At Cleve. | W | 5-3 | Burtt | Thompson |
| 15—At Cleve. | W | 5-2 | Blyleven | Smith |
| 16—Texas | W | 7-6† | Eufemia | Harris |
| 17—Texas | W | 7-2 | Viola | Schmidt |
| 18—Texas | W | 4-3 | Schrom | Hough |
| 20—At Kan. C. | L | 1-5 | Leibrandt | Blyleven |
| 21—At Kan. C. | L | 5-6* | Huismann | Davis |
| 22—At Kan. C. | W | 7-3 | Viola | Jackson |
| 24—At Texas | L | 0-5 | Williams | Butcher |
| 25—At Texas | W | 5-1 | Blyleven | Russell |
| 26—At Texas | L | 0-2 | Guzman | Smithson |
| 27—Kan. City | W | 4-1 | Viola | Black |
| 28—Kan. City | W | 5-3 | Burtt | Jackson |
| 29—Kan. City | W | 6-3 | Butcher | Gubicza |
| 30—Chicago | W | 7-1 | Blyleven | Burns |
| **Won 16, Lost 14** | | | | |

### OCTOBER

| Date | | Score | Winner | Loser |
|---|---|---|---|---|
| 1—Chicago | L | 6-12 | Bannister | Smithson |
| 2—Chicago | W | 3-1 | Viola | Davis |
| 4—Cleveland | L | 6-8 | Reed | Burtt |
| 5—Cleveland | W | 8-2 | Blyleven | Easterly |
| 6—Cleveland | W | 4-2 | Smithson | Schulze |
| **Won 3, Lost 2** | | | | |

*10 innings.   †11 innings.

**Relief ace Ron Davis survived a slow start and recorded 25 saves.**

major problem when the season started. But the top three from 1984—lefthander Frank Viola and righthanders Mike Smithson and John Butcher—suffered a falloff.

Viola managed to equal his 1984 win total with a September surge that put him at 18-14, but his ERA rose from 3.21 in '84 to 4.09. Viola and Blyleven each threw nine complete games for the Twins.

Smithson (15-14, 4.34 ERA) also matched his previous year's victory total while watching his ERA jump. Butcher had the toughest time, going from 13-11 and a 3.44 ERA to 11-14 and 4.98 in '85. Ken Schrom (9-12, 4.99) completed the rotation, leaving Blyleven as the only regular starter with an ERA below 4.00.

The Twins' most valuable pitcher in 1985 was reliever Ron Davis. After a miserable start in which the righthander went 1-4 with a 6.92 ERA and four saves in seven opportunities through May 13, Davis did the best pitching of his four-year term with the Twins. After May 13, Davis was 1-2 with a 2.61 ERA and 21 saves in 22 opportunities.

The only other pitcher who saw considerable duty was middle reliever Pete Filson (4-5, 3.67).

As a team, the Twins' ERA soared from 3.85 in 1984 to 4.48. The pitchers also were hindered by a defense that turned over the second-fewest double plays (139) in the league.

The Twins made a move to improve that area when rookie Steve Lombardozzi took over for Tim Teufel at second base in September. Teufel's impressive performance at the plate (.260, 10 home runs, 50 runs batted in) did not make up for his defensive shortcomings, and when the slick-fielding Lombardozzi hit .370 in his brief trial, it appeared that Teufel had lost his job.

Overall, the Minnesota offense was fairly solid. The Twins batted .264, a point less than the year before, but clubbed 141 homers, up from 114 in '84.

Center fielder Kirby Puckett, in his second season, was the Twins' most consistent player. Puckett played spectacular defense, batted .288 and led the team with 199 hits, 13 triples, 80 runs scored and 21 stolen bases.

First baseman Kent Hrbek and right fielder Tom Brunansky both had cold spells but still wound up as the club's most productive batters. Hrbek hit .278 with 21 homers and 93 RBIs, while Brunansky, the host team's only representative at the All-Star Game, contributed 27 homers and 90 RBIs.

Third baseman Gary Gaetti rediscovered his power, hitting 20 homers, although his RBIs (63) and average (.246) both dropped.

Left fielder Mickey Hatcher batted .282, while catcher Mark Salas hit .300 with nine homers and 41 RBIs in 360 at-bats. The righthanded-hitting half of that catcher platoon—Tim Laudner and Dave Engle—combined for a .247 average and 14 homers.

Roy Smalley and Greg Gagne, who shared the shortstop position, combined for a .244 average.

Another platoon position was designated hitter, where Smalley, Engle, Mike Stenhouse, Randy Bush and others were used. Though the situation appeared chaotic, it was productive: Twins DHs hit .256 with 19 homers and 86 RBIs.

Miller said he hoped the disappointing 1985 season would serve as a lesson for his young players.

"This team had the elation of going right to the wire and almost winning in 1984," Miller said. "Even though they were a .500 club, that might have raised everyone's expectations too high for this season. I've learned the club well, and I think maybe the good future is still ahead of us. A lot of people thought we were, but we weren't quite ready to win in 1985."

**Former Yankee Jay Howell emerged as the big man in the A's bullpen, recording 29 saves and a 2.85 ERA.**

# Late-Season Swoon Kills A's

**By KIT STIER**

When the Oakland Athletics produce their 1985 highlight film, they can stop checking footage shot after August 10. Anything developed after that date would be too gruesome to include in a family-oriented movie.

On August 10 in Seattle, the day Dave Kingman hit his 400th career home run, the A's completed a stretch in which they won 11 of 14 games to climb to their high-water mark of the season at 10 games over .500. A day later they took a 6-0 lead against the Mariners, blew it and were never heard from again.

Turn out the lights. Pack up the camera. The A's won just 18 of their last 54 games to finish with a 77-85 record for the second year in a row. After occupying second or third place in the American League West much of the summer and always being within striking distance of the front-runners, the A's wound up tied with Minnesota for fourth place, 14 games out of first.

"At one time this year I thought we'd be better off, but it didn't happen," Manager Jackie Moore said. "We answered some questions. Some guys played their way onto the team and some played their way off. There are some things we need to do over the winter. If that happens, I think some exciting things will happen."

Some exciting things did happen to the A's before their big fall, which was caused by a combination of factors ranging from pitching and hitting to defense and even the players strike.

"It's a little bit of an enigma," said first baseman Bruce Bochte, who had one of his best seasons, batting .295 with 14 home runs and 60 runs batted in. "Usually there are one or two weaknesses that allow you to look up and pinpoint the causes."

The pluses included the team's strongest infield (offensively) since the world championship days of the mid-1970s. Bochte, third baseman Carney Lansford, shortstop Alfredo Griffin, second baseman Donnie Hill and versatile Tony Phillips all had fine seasons, although Lansford was sidelined after breaking his wrist July 23 and Hill missed the last month after breaking his hand. And Phillips was sidelined most of the year with a broken foot.

Griffin led his teammates in hits (166) and triples (seven) while stealing 24 bases, batting .270 and playing in all 162 games. Lansford hit .277 with 13 homers and 46 RBIs. Neither Hill nor Phillips provided much power, but they both had good batting averages (.285 and .280, respectively).

There also were two strong points in the bullpen, where Jay Howell saved 29 games and posted a 2.85 earned-run average. When Howell missed a few games with a shoulder ailment, righthanded rookie Steve Ontiveros proved himself an equally effective stopper. Ontiveros had eight saves and a 1.93 ERA after being called up from Tacoma (Pacific Coast) in June.

The negatives far outweighed the positives, however, on a team that many predicted would finish even lower than it finally did.

In its last 54 games, Oakland scored fewer than four runs 28 times while allowing the opposition to run up five or more runs 26 times. The A's hit 116 homers in their first 108 games and just 39 down the stretch, including four in one game and three in two others. An offense that struck out 497 times in 108 games whiffed 364 times in the final 54, while the team batted .254 after August 10, 15 points lower than before that date. Oakland went from scoring 4.9 runs per game to just 4.2.

The defense also rested, committing 59 of its 140 errors after the film should have stopped rolling. With that errors total and only 137 double plays, the A's had one of the worst defenses in the league. Still, two Oakland players—Griffin and center fielder Dwayne Murphy—won Gold Gloves.

The club traded its best pitcher, veteran Don Sutton with a 13-8 record, on September 10 when management finally decided the race was over. Sutton had been the team's only consistent starter.

Oakland's pitching staff compiled a 4.39 ERA, 10th in the league, while managing only 10 complete games. Seven individual A.L. pitchers had more than that.

One of the few bright spots was 20-year-old righthander Jose Rijo, who won six of the team's final 17 victories to finish with a 6-4 record and a 3.53 ERA. Righthander Chris Codiroli won four in that stretch to even his record at 14-14, although his 4.46 ERA was uninspiring.

Besides Howell, Ontiveros and Rijo, who pitched at Tacoma until being called up August 11, young pitchers whom the club had counted on to step forward failed to meet expectations. The only other youngster who came close was lefthander Tim

## SCORES OF OAKLAND ATHLETICS' 1985 GAMES

| APRIL | | | Winner | Loser |
|---|---|---|---|---|
| 9—At Seattle | L | 3-6 | Moore | Codiroli |
| 10—At Seattle | L | 4-5 | Langston | Krueger |
| 11—At Seattle | L | 6-14 | Morgan | Young |
| 12—California | W | 15-6 | Sutton | John |
| 13—California | L | 1-6 | Romanick | Warren |
| 14—California | W | 8-1 | Codiroli | Witt |
| 15—Seattle | W | 7-4 | Krueger | Langston |
| 16—Seattle | W | 9-7 | Warren | Morgan |
| 17—Seattle | W | 8-4 | Sutton | Young |
| 19—Minnesota | W | 4-2 | Codiroli | Viola |
| 20—Minnesota | W | 6-2 | Krueger | Smithson |
| 21—Minnesota | L | 0-2 | Butcher | Young |
| 22—At Calif. | L | 1-6 | Slaton | Sutton |
| 23—At Calif. | W | 14-9 | Atherton | Kipper |
| 24—At Calif. | W | 6-4 | McCatty | Romanick |
| 25—At Minn. | L | 4-5 | Butcher | Atherton |
| 26—At Minn. | L | 7-8 | Davis | Atherton |
| 27—At Minn. | L | 6-8 | Viola | Sutton |
| 28—At Minn. | L | 1-10 | Smithson | Warren |
| 29—Toronto | L | 1-2 | Leal | Krueger |
| 30—Toronto | L | 3-4 | Lamp | Howell |
| | | **Won 9, Lost 12** | | |

| MAY | | | | |
|---|---|---|---|---|
| 1—Milwaukee | L | 4-7 | Darwin | McCatty |
| 2—Milwaukee | W | 5-4 | Atherton | Searage |
| 3—Boston | L | 0-10 | Boyd | Warren |
| 4—Boston | L | 4-5 | Crawford | Krueger |
| 5—Boston | W | 6-3 | Codiroli | Hurst |
| 7—At Toronto | L | 1-10 | Stieb | Sutton |
| 8—At Toronto | W | 6-4 | McCatty | Alexander |
| 10—At Boston | L | 4-5* | Clear | Howell |
| 11—At Boston | W | 12-1 | Krueger | Hurst |
| 12—At Boston | W | 5-3 | Sutton | Clemens |
| 14—At Milw. | W | 6-3 | Codiroli | Fingers |
| 15—At Milw. | W | 19-3 | Krueger | Higuera |
| 17—Detroit | L | 2-10 | Morris | Sutton |
| 18—Detroit | L | 6-9 | Petry | McCatty |
| 19—Detroit | W | 9-7 | Codiroli | Wilcox |
| 21—Baltimore | W | 3-2* | Howell | Boddicker |
| 22—Baltimore | L | 0-3 | McGregor | Sutton |
| 23—Baltimore | W | 4-2 | Birtsas | Dixon |
| 24—New York | L | 3-10 | Cowley | Codiroli |
| 25—New York | W | 8-7 | Howell | Righetti |
| 26—New York | L | 1-13 | Guidry | Krueger |
| 27—New York | W | 2-1* | Howell | Righetti |
| 29—At Detroit | W | 4-2 | Codiroli | Wilcox |
| 30—At Detroit | L | 2-3 | Terrell | Birtsas |
| 31—At Balt. | L | 2-9 | D. Martinez | Krueger |
| | | **Won 13, Lost 12** | | |

| JUNE | | | | |
|---|---|---|---|---|
| 1—At Balt. | W | 3-1 | Sutton | Boddicker |
| 2—At Balt. | L | 1-10 | McGregor | Warren |
| 3—At N.Y. | L | 2-5 | Niekro | Codiroli |
| 4—At N.Y. | W | 2-0 | Birtsas | Cowley |
| 7—Texas | L | 2-4* | Schmidt | Howell |
| 8—Texas | W | 6-5 | Codiroli | Hough |
| 9—Texas | L | 4-8 | Noles | Krueger |
| 9—Texas | W | 6-5 | Howell | Welsh |
| 10—Kan. City | W | 2-1* | Howell | Quisenberry |
| 11—Kan. City | W | 4-3 | Howell | Black |
| 12—Kan. City | L | 2-3x | Jones | McCatty |
| 14—At Cleve. | L | 1-6 | Blyleven | Krueger |
| 15—At Cleve. | W | 8-6 | Birtsas | Heaton |
| 16—At Cleve. | W | 3-2 | Sutton | Waddell |
| 16—At Cleve. | W | 11-6 | McCatty | Ruhle |
| 18—At Chicago | L | 3-4§ | Nelson | Atherton |
| 19—At Chicago | L | 7-8‡ | James | Langford |
| 20—At Chicago | W | 12-1 | Birtsas | Seaver |
| 21—Cleveland | W | 9-1 | Sutton | Behenna |
| 22—Cleveland | W | 6-4† | Howell | Barkley |
| 23—Cleveland | W | 9-3 | Codiroli | Heaton |
| 24—Chicago | L | 1-7 | Spillner | Birtsas |
| 25—Chicago | W | 5-4§ | Atherton | Nelson |
| 26—Chicago | W | 10-0 | Sutton | Bannister |
| 28—At Texas | L | 5-7 | Harris | Atherton |
| 29—At Texas | W | 7-6 | Krueger | Rozema |
| 30—At Texas | W | 7-4 | McCatty | Hough |
| | | **Won 17, Lost 10** | | |

| JULY | | | | |
|---|---|---|---|---|
| 1—At Kan. C. | W | 4-3 | Atherton | Jackson |
| 2—At Kan. C. | L | 1-10 | Leibrandt | Langford |
| 3—At Kan. C. | L | 0-3 | Saberhagen | Codiroli |
| 4—Toronto | W | 3-2 | Howell | Caudill |
| 5—Toronto | L | 2-8 | Clancy | Krueger |
| 6—Toronto | W | 5-1 | Sutton | Alexander |
| 7—Toronto | L | 2-8 | Key | McCatty |
| 8—Boston | L | 1-2 | Hurst | Codiroli |
| 9—Boston | L | 3-6 | Boyd | Ontiveros |

| JULY | | | Winner | Loser |
|---|---|---|---|---|
| 10—Boston | W | 5-4 | Krueger | Ojeda |
| 11—Milwaukee | W | 9-3 | Sutton | Vuckovich |
| 12—Milwaukee | L | 3-5 | Higuera | Codiroli |
| 13—Milwaukee | W | 2-0 | Birtsas | Darwin |
| 14—Milwaukee | W | 11-2 | Krueger | Haas |
| 18—At Toronto | W | 6-4 | Ontiveros | Lavelle |
| 19—At Toronto | L | 1-5 | Key | Sutton |
| 20—At Toronto | W | 5-1 | Birtsas | Stieb |
| 21—At Toronto | L | 4-11 | Lamp | Krueger |
| 22—At Boston | L | 4-6 | Lollar | Codiroli |
| 23—At Boston | L | 2-3 | Hurst | Langford |
| 24—At Boston | L | 5-6 | Stanley | Howell |
| 25—At Milw. | W | 11-2 | Birtsas | Cocanower |
| 26—At Milw. | W | 7-3 | John | Burris |
| 27—At Milw. | L | 3-4 | Vuckovich | Codiroli |
| 28—At Milw. | W | 5-2 | Krueger | Darwin |
| 30—California | W | 5-4* | Howell | Moore |
| 31—California | L | 5-8 | Romanick | Langford |
| | | **Won 13, Lost 14** | | |

| AUGUST | | | | |
|---|---|---|---|---|
| 1—California | W | 3-1 | Codiroli | Lugo |
| 2—Seattle | W | 3-1 | Langford | Langston |
| 3—Seattle | L | 2-6 | Moore | Krueger |
| 4—Seattle | W | 5-3 | Sutton | Young |
| 5—Minnesota | W | 5-1 | Birtsas | Smithson |
| 8—At Seattle | W | 11-2 | Codiroli | Langston |
| 9—At Seattle | W | 6-4 | Sutton | Moore |
| 10—At Seattle | W | 11-5 | Birtsas | Young |
| 11—At Seattle | L | 6-9 | Swift | Langford |
| 12—At Minn. | L | 3-4 | Blyleven | Rijo |
| 12—At Minn. | L | 4-5 | Howe | Codiroli |
| 13—At Minn. | L | 1-8 | Viola | John |
| 14—At Minn. | W | 5-0 | Sutton | Smithson |
| 14—At Minn. | W | 7-4 | Rijo | Portugal |
| 16—At Calif. | L | 2-5 | Candelaria | Birtsas |
| 17—At Calif. | L | 5-9 | Witt | Codiroli |
| 18—At Calif. | W | 4-3 | Rijo | Moore |
| 19—At Calif. | L | 4-5 | McCaskill | Sutton |
| 20—Detroit | L | 1-4 | Terrell | Birtsas |
| 21—Detroit | W | 4-3 | Mura | Hernandez |
| 22—Detroit | L | 3-5§ | Scherrer | Atherton |
| 23—Baltimore | L | 2-7 | Boddicker | Howell |
| 24—Baltimore | L | 3-4† | Aase | Atherton |
| 25—Baltimore | W | 10-4 | Birtsas | Flanagan |
| 26—New York | W | 3-2y | Langford | Shirley |
| 27—New York | W | 3-0 | John | Guidry |
| 29—At Detroit | L | 2-3‡ | Scherrer | Mura |
| 30—At Detroit | W | 8-3 | Sutton | Morris |
| 31—At Detroit | L | 1-4 | Terrell | Birtsas |
| | | **Won 15, Lost 14** | | |

| SEPTEMBER | | | | |
|---|---|---|---|---|
| 1—At Detroit | L | 3-14 | Berenguer | Codiroli |
| 2—At Balt. | L | 4-12 | McGregor | John |
| 3—At Balt. | W | 3-2 | Rijo | Boddicker |
| 4—At Balt. | L | 1-6 | Davis | Sutton |
| 5—At N.Y. | L | 3-7 | Whitson | Atherton |
| 6—At N.Y. | L | 4-8 | Shirley | Codiroli |
| 7—At N.Y. | L | 2-3 | Guidry | John |
| 8—At N.Y. | L | 6-9 | P. Niekro | Rijo |
| 9—Texas | L | 1-3 | Russell | Ontiveros |
| 10—Texas | W | 10-3 | Codiroli | Guzman |
| 11—Texas | L | 3-6 | Mason | Conroy |
| 13—Kan. City | L | 2-5 | Gubicza | Rijo |
| 14—Kan. City | L | 1-2 | Saberhagen | John |
| 15—Kan. City | W | 4-2 | Codiroli | Leibrandt |
| 15—Kan. City | L | 5-7* | Black | Young |
| 17—At Cleve. | L | 8-15 | Wardle | Birtsas |
| 18—At Cleve. | W | 1-0 | Rijo | Schulze |
| 20—At Chicago | L | 4-10 | Bannister | John |
| 21—At Chicago | W | 8-3 | Codiroli | Burns |
| 22—At Chicago | L | 5-7* | James | Howell |
| 23—Cleveland | W | 8-7 | Rijo | Wardle |
| 24—Cleveland | W | 10-8 | Langford | Ruhle |
| 25—Cleveland | L | 2-7 | Creel | John |
| 26—Chicago | L | 7-11 | Bannister | Codiroli |
| 27—Chicago | L | 3-4 | James | Ontiveros |
| 28—Chicago | W | 7-4 | Rijo | Wehrmeister |
| 29—Chicago | L | 0-3 | Seaver | Young |
| 30—At Texas | L | 3-5 | Russell | Howell |
| | | **Won 8, Lost 20** | | |

| OCTOBER | | | | |
|---|---|---|---|---|
| 1—At Texas | L | 2-4 | Guzman | Codiroli |
| 2—At Texas | W | 14-3 | Krueger | Mason |
| 4—At Kan. C. | L | 2-4 | Gubicza | Rijo |
| 5—At Kan. C. | L | 4-5* | Quisenberry | Howell |
| 6—At Kan. C. | W | 9-3 | Codiroli | Jones |
| | | **Won 2, Lost 3** | | |

*10 innings. †11 innings. ‡12 innings. §13 innings. x14 innings. y15 innings.

**Right fielder Mike Davis enjoyed his best major league season, hitting 24 homers and driving in 82 runs.**

Birtsas, who went 10-6 with a 4.01 ERA.

Bill Krueger (9-10) had a 4.52 ERA and yielded 165 hits in 151⅓ innings, Tim Conroy (0-1, 4.26 ERA) issued 15 walks in 25⅓ innings. Middle reliever Keith Atherton (4-7, 4.30) coughed up 17 gopher balls in 104⅔ innings. Curt Young, who was injured part of the year, lost his only four decisions and had a 7.24 ERA. Jeff Kaiser had a whopping 14.58 ERA and surrendered six homers in 16⅔ innings.

Veterans Tommy John (2-6, 6.19), who was signed as a free agent in July, and Steve McCatty (4-4, 5.57) also did not perform as anticipated.

No one took the bull by the horns. Not a single member of the team could get hot when the club needed it most.

"It could have lessened the severity of our downfall," Bochte said. "If you look you will find that nearly every team has somebody who has been productive in the second half."

Designated hitter Kingman faltered in the second half, hitting just seven of his 30 homers and adding 27 of his 91 RBIs after August 10. Right fielder Mike Davis had a good season overall, batting .287 with 92 runs scored, 34 doubles, 82 RBIs and 24 stolen bases, but faded down the stretch, pounding just three of his 24 homers in the last 58 games. Murphy never got hot, finishing with a .233 average, 20 homers and just 59 RBIs. Dusty Baker, who platooned with Bochte at first and filled in as DH or in the outfield, drove in just five runs after August 10.

In left field, Steve Henderson hit .301 but saw less playing time than Dave Collins, who stole a team-high 29 bases but batted only .251.

Catcher also was a trouble spot for the A's. Mike Heath provided some power, knocking out 13 homers, but was replaced by Mickey Tettleton (.251) in late August.

Bochte said the A's collapse was partially due to the players strike on August 6 and 7. The strike forced the A's to play five games in three days at Minnesota after the series in Seattle. The Twins took the first three games.

"It piled up on us right when we were most vulnerable," Bochte said.

The A's then lost three of four games in Anaheim against then division-leading California, dropping them to six games out of first. The next road trip proved a killer as the club played a 2-9 tune in Detroit, Baltimore and New York to return home 10 games out and belly up.

"It was so impactful no one recovered," Bochte said. "The mental letdown to what happened to us on the Eastern road trip and then coming home and losing two of three to Texas and (three of four to) Kansas City was too much to recover from."

And that kept Oakland from making an Oscar-winning highlight film in 1985.

**Left fielder Phil Bradley surprised everyone by hitting 26 home runs while batting .300 and driving in 88.**

# Injury Bug Plagues Mariners

**By BILL PLASCHKE**

Mariners relief pitcher Ed Vande Berg described Seattle's 1985 season in one sentence.

"Our pitching staff doesn't need (coach) Phil Regan, it needs President Reagan," the lefthander said. "We need to be declared a national disaster area."

A summer in which city officials fought to keep the Mariners in Seattle by giving Owner George Argyros a new Kingdome lease ended with one disconcerting notion. Is something this sickly worth keeping?

Despite hefty improvement from outfielder Phil Bradley, designated hitter Gorman Thomas and pitcher Mike Moore, the season ended just as it had the year before. At 74-88. On the broken wings of four-fifths of the starting rotation and the top reliever, the club officially had gone nowhere. In fact, the Mariners dropped a notch in the American League West standings, from a fifth-place tie to sixth.

In the season's second week, No. 5 starter Mike Morgan went down with a torn groin muscle. He was finished for the season.

But the worst was yet to come. In a one-week period in June, starters Mike Moore, Mark Langston and Jim Beattie all went on the disabled list, as did long reliever Salome Barojas. A few days later, rookie Karl Best, who had won two games, saved four more and fashioned a 1.95 earned-run average in 15 relief appearances, was lost for the season.

These injuries resulted in starts by kids like Bill Wilkinson, who was promoted from Class A to Triple A just two weeks before his big-league debut, and Bill Swift, who had just seven starts at the Double-A level before coming up (the shortest minor league stint in Mariners history). Wilkinson was returned to Calgary (Pacific Coast) after two forgettable starts, but Swift, the club's No. 1 pick in the 1984 amateur draft, lasted the season. He went 6-10 with a 4.77 ERA.

"The biggest thing we need for next year is health," said lefthander Matt Young, Seattle's only healthy starter from opening day to the season finale. "It's no longer a joke. It's a nightmare."

It didn't help that Young had a 4.91 ERA and a club-record 19 losses against 12 wins. Nor did it help that lefty Mark Langston pitched poorly, winding up with a 7-14 record and a 5.47 ERA. After leading the league in strikeouts with 204 as a

**Third baseman Jim Presley surprised everybody by batting .275 with 28 homers and 84 RBIs.**

rookie in 1984, Langston had more walks (91) than strikeouts (72).

Beattie worked just 70⅓ innings for the Mariners, but it may have been just as well considering his 7.29 ERA. Frank Wills, a March acquisition from the Mets, started 18 games in 24 appearances and went 5-11 with a 6.00 ERA.

Overall, the Mariners had the league's second-worst ERA (4.68), and their totals in wild pitches (61) and hit batters (41) were exceeded by only one A.L. team.

## SCORES OF SEATTLE MARINERS' 1985 GAMES

### APRIL

| Date | W/L | Score | Winner | Loser |
|---|---|---|---|---|
| 9—Oakland | W | 6-3 | Moore | Codiroli |
| 10—Oakland | W | 5-4 | Langston | Krueger |
| 11—Oakland | W | 14-6 | Morgan | Young |
| 12—Minnesota | W | 2-1 | Young | Schrom |
| 13—Minnesota | W | 8-7 | Stanton | Davis |
| 14—Minnesota | W | 5-1 | Moore | Viola |
| 15—At Oak. | L | 4-7 | Krueger | Langston |
| 16—At Oak. | L | 7-9 | Warren | Morgan |
| 17—At Oak. | L | 4-8 | Sutton | Young |
| 19—At Calif. | L | 1-9 | Romanick | Moore |
| 20—At Calif. | W | 3-2 | Langston | Witt |
| 21—At Calif. | L | 2-9 | Zahn | Beattie |
| 22—At Minn. | L | 5-9 | Schrom | Young |
| 23—At Minn. | L | 2-4 | Viola | Barojas |
| 24—At Minn. | L | 0-10 | Smithson | Moore |
| 25—California | L | 0-3 | Witt | Langston |
| 26—California | L | 3-11 | Corbett | Beattie |
| 27—California | L | 1-6 | Slaton | Young |
| 28—California | L | 1-2 | John | Barojas |
| 29—Milwaukee | W | 9-7* | Nunez | Searage |
| 30—Milwaukee | W | 4-2 | Langston | Gibson |

**Won 9, Lost 12**

### MAY

| Date | W/L | Score | Winner | Loser |
|---|---|---|---|---|
| 1—Boston | W | 7-0 | Beattie | Clemens |
| 2—Boston | L | 1-2 | Nipper | Moore |
| 3—Toronto | L | 4-5 | Alexander | Barojas |
| 4—Toronto | W | 8-1 | Young | Leal |
| 5—Toronto | W | 4-1 | Langston | Clancy |
| 7—At Milw. | L | 2-5 | Haas | Beattie |
| 8—At Milw. | W | 4-2 | Moore | Burris |
| 10—At Toronto | L | 3-8 | Key | Langston |
| 11—At Toronto | L | 2-4 | Caudill | Young |
| 12—At Toronto | L | 5-9 | Stieb | Beattie |
| 14—At Boston | W | 5-0 | Moore | Boyd |
| 15—At Boston | W | 7-1 | Langston | Nipper |
| 17—Baltimore | L | 3-11 | Dixon | Young |
| 18—Baltimore | W | 8-7 | Nunez | T. Martinez |
| 19—Baltimore | L | 1-2 | D. Martinez | Moore |
| 21—New York | L | 1-11 | Guidry | Langston |
| 22—New York | W | 4-1 | Young | Rasmussen |
| 23—New York | W | 6-4 | Beattie | Niekro |
| 24—Detroit | L | 3-4† | Hernandez | Stanton |
| 25—Detroit | L | 2-3 | Terrell | Best |
| 26—Detroit | L | 0-6 | Morris | Barojas |
| 27—Detroit | W | 5-2 | Young | Petry |
| 29—At Balt. | W | 5-4† | Best | Aase |
| 30—At Balt. | L | 2-8 | Davis | Barojas |
| 31—At N.Y. | L | 3-8 | Fisher | Langston |

**Won 11, Lost 14**

### JUNE

| Date | W/L | Score | Winner | Loser |
|---|---|---|---|---|
| 1—At N.Y. | L | 2-8 | Guidry | Young |
| 2—At N.Y. | W | 7-6 | Nunez | Rasmussen |
| 3—At Detroit | W | 9-8 | Beattie | Lopez |
| 4—At Detroit | W | 7-6‡ | Thomas | Hernandez |
| 5—At Detroit | L | 2-5 | Morris | Langston |
| 6—At Cleve. | L | 1-9 | Blyleven | Young |
| 7—At Cleve. | W | 6-4 | Swift | Heaton |
| 8—At Cleve. | L | 8-12 | Waddell | Stanton |
| 9—At Cleve. | W | 10-6 | Wills | Schulze |
| 10—Chicago | L | 4-9 | Bannister | Young |
| 11—Chicago | L | 1-7 | Lollar | Swift |
| 12—Chicago | L | 3-6 | Tanner | Snyder |
| 13—Kan. City | L | 3-4 | Gubicza | Wilkinson |
| 14—Kan. City | W | 13-5 | Wills | Jackson |
| 15—Kan. City | W | 2-1 | Young | Leibrandt |
| 16—Kan. City | W | 2-1 | Best | Beckwith |
| 18—At Texas | L | 5-8 | Tanana | Wilkinson |
| 19—At Texas | L | 4-5 | Welsh | Wills |
| 20—At Texas | W | 11-3 | Young | Hooton |
| 22—At Kan. C. | W | 2-1 | Swift | Saberhagen |
| 23—At Kan. C. | W | 8-2 | Moore | Black |
| 24—Texas | W | 2-0 | Wills | Welsh |
| 25—Texas | W | 2-1 | Young | Hough |
| 26—Texas | W | 5-4* | Thomas | Stewart |
| 28—Cleveland | W | 8-6 | Thomas | Barkley |
| 29—Cleveland | W | 3-2 | Moore | Blyleven |
| 30—Cleveland | L | 3-7 | Thompson | Young |

**Won 16, Lost 11**

### JULY

| Date | W/L | Score | Winner | Loser |
|---|---|---|---|---|
| 1—At Chicago | W | 3-1 | Wills | Bannister |
| 2—At Chicago | L | 4-12 | Lollar | Snyder |
| 3—At Chicago | W | 5-1 | Swift | Spillner |
| 4—Milwaukee | W | 7-1 | Moore | Haas |
| 5—Milwaukee | W | 7-6† | Nunez | Waits |
| 6—Milwaukee | W | 5-3 | Thomas | Vuckovich |
| 7—Milwaukee | L | 1-2 | Higuera | Swift |
| 8—Toronto | L | 0-4 | Stieb | Moore |
| 9—Toronto | L | 4-9§ | Musselman | Vande Berg |
| 10—Toronto | L | 1-11 | Clancy | Wills |
| 11—Boston | L | 1-7 | Nipper | Swift |
| 12—Boston | L | 4-5 | Trujillo | Nunez |
| 13—Boston | W | 6-5 | Snyder | Stanley |
| 14—Boston | L | 2-6 | Boyd | Wills |
| 18—At Milw. | W | 5-2 | Moore | Darwin |
| 19—At Milw. | L | 7-9 | Higuera | Young |
| 20—At Milw. | W | 13-10 | Vande Berg | McClure |
| 21—At Milw. | L | 4-5 | Burris | Wills |
| 22—At Toronto | L | 1-3 | Filer | Langston |
| 23—At Toronto | L | 2-4 | Alexander | Moore |
| 24—At Toronto | L | 1-3 | Key | Young |
| 25—At Boston | L | 3-5 | Ojeda | Swift |
| 26—At Boston | L | 2-6 | Nipper | Beattie |
| 27—At Boston | W | 10-3 | Thomas | Lollar |
| 28—At Boston | W | 7-2 | Moore | Hurst |
| 29—Minnesota | W | 8-6 | Nunez | Eufemia |
| 30—Minnesota | L | 4-12 | Smithson | Swift |
| 31—Minnesota | W | 12-3 | Beattie | Butcher |

**Won 12, Lost 16**

### AUGUST

| Date | W/L | Score | Winner | Loser |
|---|---|---|---|---|
| 2—At Oak. | L | 1-3 | Langford | Langston |
| 3—At Oak. | W | 6-2 | Moore | Krueger |
| 4—At Oak. | L | 3-5 | Sutton | Young |
| 5—At Calif. | L | 1-3 | Witt | Swift |
| 8—Oakland | L | 2-11 | Codiroli | Langston |
| 9—Oakland | L | 4-6 | Sutton | Moore |
| 10—Oakland | L | 5-11 | Birtsas | Young |
| 11—Oakland | W | 9-6 | Swift | Langford |
| 12—California | W | 6-5 | Nunez | Moore |
| 12—California | L | 3-4 | Slaton | Lewis |
| 13—California | W | 11-4 | Langston | Romanick |
| 14—California | L | 1-3‡ | Cliburn | Nunez |
| 14—California | W | 6-1 | Beattie | Zahn |
| 15—At Minn. | L | 5-14 | Butcher | Young |
| 16—At Minn. | W | 6-5 | Vande Berg | Howe |
| 17—At Minn. | L | 0-2 | Blyleven | Wills |
| 18—At Minn. | W | 7-2 | Langston | Viola |
| 20—Baltimore | W | 4-3 | Moore | Snell |
| 21—Baltimore | L | 8-11 | D. Martinez | Beattie |
| 22—Baltimore | W | 4-0 | Young | McGregor |
| 23—New York | L | 1-3 | Niekro | Swift |
| 24—New York | L | 3-4 | Bystrom | Langston |
| 25—New York | L | 5-8 | Whitson | Moore |
| 26—Detroit | L | 3-6 | Berenguer | Wills |
| 27—Detroit | W | 3-1 | Young | Tanana |
| 29—At Balt. | L | 0-7 | Boddicker | Swift |
| 30—At Balt. | L | 0-6 | Davis | Langston |
| 31—At Balt. | W | 6-0 | Moore | Flanagan |

**Won 11, Lost 17**

### SEPTEMBER

| Date | W/L | Score | Winner | Loser |
|---|---|---|---|---|
| 1—At Balt. | W | 10-2 | Young | D. Martinez |
| 2—At N.Y. | L | 7-8 | Guidry | Wills |
| 3—At N.Y. | L | 3-6 | Niekro | Swift |
| 4—At N.Y. | L | 3-4 | Bordi | Langston |
| 6—At Detroit | W | 8-4 | Moore | Terrell |
| 7—At Detroit | W | 12-5 | Young | Berenguer |
| 8—At Detroit | W | 6-2 | Thomas | Tanana |
| 9—Cleveland | W | 8-7‡ | Tobik | Thompson |
| 10—Cleveland | L | 5-8 | Clark | Wills |
| 11—Cleveland | W | 9-5 | Moore | Smith |
| 13—Chicago | L | 1-6 | Gleaton | Young |
| 14—Chicago | W | 6-5 | Swift | Bannister |
| 15—Chicago | L | 3-6 | Wehrmeister | Langston |
| 16—At Kan. C. | W | 5-1 | Moore | Jackson |
| 17—At Kan. C. | W | 7-0 | Young | Farr |
| 18—At Kan. C. | W | 6-0 | Thomas | Gubicza |
| 19—At Kan. C. | W | 6-4 | Nunez | Quisenberry |
| 20—At Texas | L | 9-10 | Henry | Nunez |
| 21—At Texas | L | 2-7 | Guzman | Young |
| 22—At Texas | L | 0-6 | Mason | Wills |
| 23—At Texas | L | 4-11 | Schmidt | Langston |
| 24—Kan. City | W | 5-2 | Moore | Gubicza |
| 25—Kan. City | L | 4-5 | Saberhagen | Young |
| 26—Kan. City | L | 2-5 | Leibrandt | Swift |
| 27—Texas | W | 6-0 | Wills | Mason |
| 28—Texas | W | 3-2 | Moore | Schmidt |
| 29—Texas | L | 2-5 | Harris | Young |

**Won 14, Lost 13**

### OCTOBER

| Date | W/L | Score | Winner | Loser |
|---|---|---|---|---|
| 1—At Cleve. | L | 3-9 | Schulze | Wills |
| 2—At Cleve. | L | 2-12 | Creel | Moore |
| 3—At Chicago | W | 5-4 | Swift | James |
| 4—At Chicago | L | 5-7 | Seaver | Young |
| 5—At Chicago | L | 4-10 | Bannister | Wills |
| 6—At Chicago | L | 2-3 | Correa | Moore |

**Won 1, Lost 5**

*10 innings.   †11 innings.   ‡12 innings.   §13 innings.

**Righthander Mike Moore improved dramatically and recorded 17 victories.**

Seattle pitchers also allowed 637 walks and committed 18 balks, both tops in the league.

"It seemed like every time we went out on the field, we were down two or three runs," said right fielder Al Cowens, who batted .265 with 14 home runs. "You can't keep playing like that, you just can't."

How bad was the pitching? It overshadowed the top offensive year in club history. Under the direction of new hitting coach Deron Johnson, the Mariners set club marks for homers (171), runs scored (719), runs batted in (686), doubles (277), walks (564), total bases (2,276) and slugging percentage (.412).

How hard were they swinging? They also set a record for strikeouts with 942, the league high.

"I can't remember a more satisfying season," said Johnson, who came to Seattle immediately after leading Philadelphia to a National League batting crown. "There's so many young kids on this club who want to work. I never have to tell anybody to do anything."

One of the hardest workers was left fielder Bradley, who led the league in hitting for 11 days in June and finished seventh with a .300 average. He also had 88 RBIs, 22 stolen bases, 33 doubles, eight triples, 100 runs scored and a club-record 192 hits.

Bradley's most remarkable statistic, though, was his 26 homers (including three last-inning game-winners) in 641 at-bats. In his previous 389 big-league at-

bats, he hit no homers. In his previous 1,056 minor league at-bats, he hit three.

"I never dreamed I would hit with this kind of power," Bradley said. "I don't try for home runs. I knew I would have increased power, but nothing like this."

His bat almost blocked the public's view of Thomas, The Sporting News' A.L. Comeback Player of the Year. After missing most of the 1984 season because of rotator cuff surgery, Thomas contributed 32 homers and 87 RBIs.

Then there was Jim Presley, who won the third-base job from Darnell Coles in the spring and proceeded to hit .275 with 28 homers and 84 RBIs. After a slow start, the club's other rookie star of a year ago, first baseman Alvin Davis, hit .287 with 18 homers and 78 RBIs.

Center fielder Dave Henderson added 14 homers and 68 RBIs, while rookie outfielder Ivan Calderon batted .286 in a fill-in role.

"It makes you wonder what would have happened if our pitchers had stayed healthy and strong," Manager Chuck Cottier said. "There's just no telling."

The weakest spots in the Seattle lineup were second base, where Jack Perconte led the team with 31 stolen bases but knocked in only 23 runs; shortstop, where Spike Owen hit .259, and catcher, where Bob Kearney and Donnie Scott combined for a .235 average.

While Seattle batters were pounding in runs and Seattle pitchers were surrendering them even faster, one starter was consistently effective. Moore, who lost 17 games in 1984, came back to finish as high as third on more than one Cy Young Award ballot. He went 17-10 with a 3.46 ERA and 155 strikeouts and set club records for complete games (14) and innings pitched (247, tied with Floyd Bannister in 1982).

"He's no longer a thrower, he's a pitcher," Cottier said.

The relief corps managed to protect most of the leads it was given and had a 22-8 record, by far the best mark in the league. Bullpen ace Edwin Nunez went 7-3 with 16 saves and a 3.09 ERA, while Vande Berg, Best and Roy Thomas (7-0, 3.36) also were dependable.

As usual, a Mariner season cannot survive without a front-office shakeup. This time it was General Manager Hal Keller, who was fired a couple of days after sending Perconte to Calgary in a July move that caused the clubhouse to erupt in criticism. Keller was replaced in October by Dick Balderson, the Kansas City Royals' farm director.

Rookie center fielder Oddibe McDowell showed promise by hitting 18 home runs in 111 games while playing well defensively.

# Weak Pitching Hurts Rangers

**By JIM REEVES**

For the Texas Rangers, the best part of the 1985 season was the last few weeks—and not just because it was the end of another bad year.

More importantly for General Manager Tom Grieve and Manager Bobby Valentine, some of the Rangers' young starting pitchers began showing some signs of promise as the season mercifully wound down.

Having spent most of the season looking for such signs, the Ranger brain trust could only be relieved when they finally appeared, even if they were far too little and way too late. But from such pitchers as Jose Guzman, Mitch Williams and Jeff Russell, Valentine hopes to find capable starters to team with redoubtable warhorse Charlie Hough.

At season's end, Grieve looked carefully for something with which to salve the sting of a year in which the Rangers lost 99 games and settled into last place in the American League West in April, never to rise again. The club finished 28½ games behind Kansas City.

"It hasn't been a total failure," Grieve said. "As far as the won-loss record of the team, it was a very disappointing season, obviously. On the other hand, trying to find silver linings and be optimistic, the one thing the poor season did was allow Bobby the chance to pitch and play a lot of people. I think we'll go into spring training with a head start on evaluating the players we'll be playing next year."

The Rangers left Florida last spring with a lack of depth on the bench, questionable starting pitching and no proven stopper in the bullpen. They also left with a manager, Doug Rader, who wound up being fired in less than seven weeks, after the club had sputtered to a 9-23 start.

"I think everybody felt, coming out of spring training, that the depth of the team was a question mark, but that if we didn't have any injuries, we'd score runs," Grieve said. "The major breakdowns: Starting pitching and the offensive players, for one reason or another, didn't perform up to expectations."

The big if—injuries—was at least partially responsible for the Rangers finishing tied for 10th in the league in batting (.253) and last in runs scored (617).

Designated hitter Cliff Johnson, who was traded to Toronto in late August, and right fielder Larry Parrish both went down with knee injuries. Johnson, who was dispatched when the club decided to emphasize a youth movement, contributed 12 home runs and 56 runs batted in, but the loss of Parrish (17 homers, 51 RBIs) for 57 days particularly hurt.

Don Slaught batted .280 and nailed down Texas' shaky catcher position, but hamstring problems limited him to 102 games.

Rookie center fielder Oddibe McDowell pulled a hamstring September 15 and played only two more games defensively the rest of the season. Nevertheless, McDowell, who hit for the cycle July 23, finished with 18 homers and 25 stolen bases just one year after being selected in the amateur draft.

In all, nine different players spent time on the disabled list.

"I don't think any team has the kind of depth to survive the injuries we had," Valentine said.

Third baseman Buddy Bell slumped early and was batting .236 when the Rangers traded him to Cincinnati for Russell and outfielder Duane Walker in July. Rookie Steve Buechele performed admirably as Bell's replacement, although he hit only .219.

Outfielder George Wright, who hit .190 with 18 RBIs as his slump extended to two years, and infielder Curtis Wilkerson (.244) were additional drains on the Rangers' production.

The combination of injuries and weak performances was too much for the Texas offense to survive.

"We didn't prepare ourselves properly to win ball games," said left fielder Gary Ward, who turned in yet another solid season, hitting .287 with 15 homers, 70 RBIs and team-leading totals in steals (26) and runs scored (77). "We had a home run-hitting ball club, but when we lost a couple of key people, we had no alternate plans. We didn't know how to go out and win a one-run or two-run game. All our eggs were in the home run basket, and when that turned over, we went down."

That came as no surprise to shortstop Wayne Tolleson, who hit a career-high .313.

"Our start was just a carry-over from last year (1984)," Tolleson said. "We stunk the year before, and we came out doing the same thing this year.

"I'm not smart enough to know why it

## SCORES OF TEXAS RANGERS' 1985 GAMES

### APRIL

| Date | | Score | Winner | Loser |
|---|---|---|---|---|
| 8—At Balt. | L | 2-4 | Aase | Rozema |
| 10—At Balt. | L | 1-7 | Boddicker | Mason |
| 12—Milwaukee | L | 6-11 | Gibson | Tanana |
| 13—Milwaukee | L | 5-6 | Gibson | Noles |
| 14—Milwaukee | L | 1-8 | Haas | Rozema |
| 16—At Toronto | W | 9-4 | Mason | Leal |
| 17—At Toronto | L | 1-3* | Caudill | Stewart |
| 18—At Toronto | L | 2-4 | Stieb | Tanana |
| 19—At Milw. | W | 4-1 | Rozema | Searage |
| 20—At Milw. | W | 5-1 | Noles | Haas |
| 21—At Milw. | W | 5-2 | Mason | Burris |
| 22—Baltimore | W | 6-1 | Hough | McGregor |
| 23—Baltimore | L | 1-11 | Davis | Tanana |
| 24—Baltimore | L | 1-2 | Boddicker | Rozema |
| 26—Toronto | L | 5-6 | Lamp | Schmidt |
| 27—Toronto | L | 8-9* | Acker | Stewart |
| 28—Toronto | L | 3-6 | Alexander | Mason |
| 29—New York | W | 7-5 | Schmidt | Guidry |
| 30—New York | W | 8-4 | Noles | Niekro |

**Won 7, Lost 12**

### MAY

| Date | | Score | Winner | Loser |
|---|---|---|---|---|
| 1—New York | L | 1-5 | Whitson | Hough |
| 3—At Cleve. | L | 0-4 | Blyleven | Mason |
| 4—At Cleve. | L | 1-3 | Heaton | Tanana |
| 5—At Cleve. | W | 7-2 | Hough | Schulze |
| 7—Detroit | L | 1-10 | Morris | Noles |
| 8—Detroit | L | 1-4 | Petry | Mason |
| 10—Cleveland | W | 5-2 | Hough | Schulze |
| 11—Cleveland | L | 1-4 | Waddell | Harris |
| 12—Cleveland | L | 0-6 | Blyleven | Noles |
| 13—At Detroit | L | 4-7 | Petry | Hooton |
| 14—At Detroit | L | 1-4 | Wilcox | Hough |
| 15—At N.Y. | L | 5-6* | Righetti | Schmidt |
| 16—At N.Y. | L | 5-6 | Righetti | Stewart |
| 17—At Chicago | L | 2-4 | Dotson | Noles |
| 18—At Chicago | W | 7-2 | Hooton | Burns |
| 19—At Chicago | L | 1-5 | Nelson | Hough |
| 20—Kan. City | W | 8-7 | Schmidt | Beckwith |
| 21—Kan. City | L | 0-5 | Black | Tanana |
| 22—Kan. City | L | 3-6 | Saberhagen | Noles |
| 23—Boston | W | 7-6 | Rozema | Clear |
| 24—Boston | W | 1-0 | Hough | Boyd |
| 25—Boston | W | 10-3 | Mason | Nipper |
| 26—Boston | W | 5-3 | Tanana | Kison |
| 27—At Kan. C. | L | 2-4 | Saberhagen | Noles |
| 28—At Kan. C. | W | 6-1 | Hooton | Gubicza |
| 29—At Kan. C. | L | 2-6 | Jackson | Hough |
| 31—At Boston | W | 3-1 | Mason | Nipper |

**Won 10, Lost 17**

### JUNE

| Date | | Score | Winner | Loser |
|---|---|---|---|---|
| 1—At Boston | L | 0-6 | Kison | Tanana |
| 2—At Boston | L | 3-12 | Hurst | Rozema |
| 3—Chicago | W | 7-3 | Harris | Burns |
| 4—Chicago | W | 7-3 | Hough | Seaver |
| 6—Chicago | L | 3-4 | Bannister | Mason |
| 7—At Oak. | W | 4-2* | Schmidt | Howell |
| 8—At Oak. | L | 5-6 | Codiroli | Hough |
| 9—At Oak. | W | 8-4 | Noles | Krueger |
| 9—At Oak. | L | 5-6 | Howell | Welsh |
| 10—At Calif. | L | 1-8 | McCaskill | Mason |
| 11—At Calif. | W | 6-4 | Rozema | Lugo |
| 12—At Calif. | L | 2-3 | Witt | Hough |
| 13—Minnesota | L | 5-7 | Smithson | Tanana |
| 14—Minnesota | W | 4-2 | Hooton | Filson |
| 15—Minnesota | W | 11-2 | Mason | Butcher |
| 16—Minnesota | L | 1-4 | Schrom | Hough |
| 18—Seattle | W | 8-5 | Tanana | Wilkinson |
| 19—Seattle | W | 5-4 | Welsh | Wills |
| 20—Seattle | L | 3-11 | Young | Hooton |
| 21—At Minn. | L | 2-3 | Schrom | Hough |
| 22—At Minn. | L | 2-3 | Viola | Mason |
| 23—At Minn. | W | 3-1 | Cook | Smithson |
| 24—At Seattle | L | 0-2 | Wills | Welsh |
| 25—At Seattle | L | 1-2 | Young | Hough |
| 26—At Seattle | L | 4-5* | Thomas | Stewart |
| 28—Oakland | W | 7-5 | Harris | Atherton |
| 29—Oakland | L | 6-7 | Krueger | Rozema |
| 30—Oakland | L | 4-7 | McCatty | Hough |

**Won 11, Lost 17**

### JULY

| Date | | Score | Winner | Loser |
|---|---|---|---|---|
| 1—California | W | 10-5 | Cook | Slaton |
| 2—California | L | 2-7 | McCaskill | Sebra |
| 3—California | L | 2-3† | Moore | Schmidt |
| 4—Detroit | W | 4-1 | Hooton | Terrell |
| 5—Detroit | W | 3-1 | Hough | Morris |
| 6—Detroit | L | 3-4 | O'Neal | Rozema |
| 7—Detroit | L | 3-5 | Tanana | Harris |
| 8—At Cleve. | L | 0-4 | Heaton | Mason |

### JULY

| Date | | Score | Winner | Loser |
|---|---|---|---|---|
| 9—At Cleve. | L | 2-7 | Blyleven | Hooton |
| 10—At Cleve. | W | 4-1 | Hough | Reed |
| 11—At N.Y. | L | 7-11 | Shirley | Cook |
| 12—At N.Y. | L | 0-6 | Whitson | Sebra |
| 13—At N.Y. | L | 1-3 | Niekro | Mason |
| 14—At N.Y. | L | 1-7 | Guidry | Hooton |
| 18—At Detroit | W | 3-2 | Hough | Tanana |
| 19—At Detroit | W | 2-1 | Hooton | Petry |
| 20—At Detroit | L | 5-6‡ | Scherrer | Harris |
| 21—At Detroit | W | 7-5 | Schmidt | Lopez |
| 22—Cleveland | W | 2-1 | Harris | Ruhle |
| 23—Cleveland | W | 8-4 | Hough | Heaton |
| 24—Cleveland | L | 4-8 | Blyleven | Hooton |
| 26—New York | W | 9-8 | Noles | Righetti |
| 27—New York | L | 2-14 | Niekro | Cook |
| 28—New York | W | 8-2 | Welsh | Bystrom |
| 29—At Milw. | L | 2-3 | Higuera | Hough |
| 30—At Milw. | L | 3-6 | McClure | Rozema |
| 31—At Milw. | L | 2-5 | Cocanower | Mason |

**Won 11, Lost 16**

### AUGUST

| Date | | Score | Winner | Loser |
|---|---|---|---|---|
| 2—At Toronto | L | 3-5 | Alexander | Cook |
| 3—At Toronto | L | 1-4 | Lamp | Welsh |
| 4—At Toronto | W | 8-4 | Hough | Stieb |
| 8—Milwaukee | L | 4-7 | Waits | Russell |
| 8—Milwaukee | L | 1-3 | Vuckovich | Hooton |
| 9—Baltimore | W | 5-2 | Hough | Flanagan |
| 10—Baltimore | L | 8-9 | Davis | Welsh |
| 11—Baltimore | L | 4-9 | Stewart | Mason |
| 12—Toronto | W | 5-4 | Henry | Caudill |
| 13—Toronto | L | 3-5 | Filer | Russell |
| 14—Toronto | L | 1-4 | Stieb | Hough |
| 15—At Balt. | L | 1-9 | Davis | Welsh |
| 16—At Balt. | L | 2-4 | D. Martinez | Russell |
| 17—At Balt. | L | 2-9 | McGregor | Hooton |
| 19—At Balt. | L | 2-9 | Dixon | Mason |
| 20—At Boston | W | 3-1 | Hough | Ojeda |
| 21—At Boston | W | 5-3 | Russell | Boyd |
| 22—At Boston | L | 4-8 | Trujillo | Noles |
| 23—At Kan. C. | W | 4-3 | Schmidt | Quisenberry |
| 24—At Kan. C. | L | 2-8 | Saberhagen | Hooton |
| 25—At Kan. C. | W | 7-3 | Hough | Black |
| 26—At Kan. C. | L | 2-9 | Leibrandt | Russell |
| 27—At Chicago | L | 4-7 | Burns | Noles |
| 28—At Chicago | L | 1-5 | Nelson | Stewart |
| 29—At Chicago | L | 5-6* | Spillner | Schmidt |
| 30—Kan. City | W | 4-1 | Hough | Black |
| 31—Kan. City | W | 6-4 | Harris | Leibrandt |

**Won 9, Lost 18**

### SEPTEMBER

| Date | | Score | Winner | Loser |
|---|---|---|---|---|
| 1—Kan. City | W | 5-3 | Mason | Jackson |
| 2—Boston | L | 2-11 | Lollar | Stewart |
| 3—Boston | L | 4-6 | Hurst | Hough |
| 5—Chicago | L | 4-11 | Davis | Russell |
| 6—Chicago | L | 1-12 | Burns | Mason |
| 7—Chicago | L | 2-3 | Agosto | Henry |
| 8—Chicago | L | 6-7 | Seaver | Hough |
| 9—At Oak. | W | 3-1 | Russell | Ontiveros |
| 10—At Oak. | L | 3-10 | Codiroli | Guzman |
| 11—At Oak. | W | 6-3 | Mason | Conroy |
| 12—At Calif. | L | 3-5 | Witt | Henry |
| 13—At Calif. | L | 0-2 | Sutton | Hough |
| 14—At Calif. | W | 8-5 | Williams | Corbett |
| 15—At Calif. | L | 4-12 | McCaskill | Guzman |
| 16—At Minn. | L | 6-7† | Eufemia | Harris |
| 17—At Minn. | L | 2-7 | Viola | Schmidt |
| 18—At Minn. | L | 3-4 | Schrom | Hough |
| 20—Seattle | W | 10-9 | Henry | Nunez |
| 21—Seattle | W | 7-2 | Guzman | Young |
| 22—Seattle | W | 6-0 | Mason | Wills |
| 23—Seattle | W | 11-4 | Schmidt | Langston |
| 24—Minnesota | W | 5-0 | Williams | Butcher |
| 25—Minnesota | L | 1-5 | Blyleven | Russell |
| 26—Minnesota | W | 2-0 | Guzman | Smithson |
| 27—At Seattle | L | 0-6 | Wills | Mason |
| 28—At Seattle | L | 2-3 | Moore | Schmidt |
| 29—At Seattle | W | 5-2 | Harris | Young |
| 30—Oakland | W | 5-3 | Russell | Howell |

**Won 12, Lost 16**

### OCTOBER

| Date | | Score | Winner | Loser |
|---|---|---|---|---|
| 1—Oakland | W | 4-2 | Guzman | Codiroli |
| 2—Oakland | L | 3-14 | Krueger | Mason |
| 4—California | W | 6-0 | Schmidt | McCaskill |
| 5—California | L | 1-3 | Candelaria | Williams |
| 6—California | L | 5-6 | Witt | Surhoff |

**Won 2, Lost 3**

*10 innings.　†11 innings.　‡15 innings.

Pete O'Brien (above) emerged as the Rangers' most dangerous offensive threat and outfielder Gary Ward turned out another solid season.

happened, but I do know that even though we had some personnel changes, the atmosphere was the same. From a talent standpoint, we're definitely better than a last-place team."

One of those talented players was second baseman Toby Harrah, who batted .270, drew 113 walks and had a .432 on-base percentage. Another was first baseman Pete O'Brien, who rebounded from a slow start to hit .267 and post team and career highs in homers (22) and RBIs (92).

"We knew we weren't the deepest club in the world coming out of spring training," O'Brien said. "We have a good bench, but it's not all that versatile, so when Parrish went down, we just didn't have the people who could go out and play for a month and a half."

Valentine agreed. "It's true we need more depth," he said, "but some people you just can't replace."

On the other hand, the Rangers didn't hesitate to replace pitchers at any and every opportunity. Fourteen pitchers drew starting assignments in 1985 as only Hough and lefthander Mike Mason were part of both the season-opening and season-ending rotations.

The result was predictable: a team 4.56 earned-run average, which ranked 12th in the league.

Hough, who missed his last three starts because of arthroscopic knee surgery, was the only dependable starter. The knuckleballer led the staff with a 14-16 record, a 3.31 ERA, 14 complete games and 250⅓ innings pitched.

No other Ranger with more than five starts had an ERA below 4.00. Mason was 8-15 with a 4.83 ERA, while Burt Hooton (5-8, 5.23) and Dickie Noles (4-8, 5.06) fell in behind. Frank Tanana was 2-7 with a 5.91 ERA when he was traded to Detroit in June.

Greg Harris was the closest thing to a stopper the Rangers had. The righthander collected 11 saves and a 2.47 ERA.

By season's end, Guzman, Williams, Russell and Dave Schmidt all were starting, and in the last 15 games of the year, Ranger pitchers posted four shutouts and a 3.11 ERA. Texas won nine of those games.

"We're going to have to get more consistency out of our pitchers," Ward said, "but we've got some promising young pitchers who are going to be good pitchers in the major leagues. You've got to have pitching to win. When we get good pitching, we win. When we don't, we lose."

For the Rangers, there was a lot more of the latter than the former in 1985.

**Jesse Barfield's booming bat and strong defense helped Toronto hold off the Yankees' late pennant drive.**

# Jays Soar High in East

**By NEIL MacCARL**

With a team devoid of superstars but loaded with solid players, Manager Bobby Cox led the Toronto Blue Jays to the top of the American League East in the franchise's ninth year of existence.

Although the Blue Jays ruled the division for 152 (of 182) days in 1985, they still had to fight off a determined late challenge by the New York Yankees to establish their credentials.

Entering a four-game series that opened September 12 at Yankee Stadium, Toronto had won six of its previous seven games. But New York had won 11 of its previous 12 contests to narrow the Blue Jays' lead to 2½ games.

When 23-year-old shortstop Tony Fernandez made two damaging errors that helped the Yankees post a 7-5 victory in the opener, many people predicted the worst for the Blue Jays, saying they would fold before the more experienced Yankees.

But the Blue Jays outplayed the Yankees in the next three games, winning by scores of 3-2, 7-4 and 8-5. The Blue Jays had won three in a row in the Bronx for the first time in team history, and they left town with a 4½-game lead.

But they could not deliver the knockout punch—yet. They lost eight of their next 15 games, thus giving the Yankees, who finished the season with three games in Toronto, one last chance.

The Blue Jays' lead was down to three when the first- and second-place clubs met before a record crowd of 47,686 at Exhibition Stadium for the series opener. Toronto was one out from clinching the title when Butch Wynegar homered to tie the score, 3-3. Center fielder Lloyd Moseby then dropped a routine fly ball that allowed Bobby Meacham to score the winning run for the Yankees. It appeared once more that the Blue Jays might crumble.

After taking over sole possession of first place for good May 20, Toronto finally shut the door October 5 when righthander Doyle Alexander threw a masterful five-hitter. Moseby, catcher Ernie Whitt and first baseman Willie Upshaw hit home runs in a 5-1 victory that climaxed the club's nine-year climb from worst to first.

The Blue Jays—a team built on speed (144 stolen bases), defense (only 125 errors) and clutch hitting (a league-high 53 triples and a .269 batting average, No. 2 in the league)—were ideally suited to the artificial surface at Exhibition Stadium, where they won 54 of 80 games in 1985. They also piled up a huge margin (55-29) against the A.L. West en route to a 99-62 overall record.

But all of those statistics were rendered meaningless when the Kansas City Royals overcame a 3-1 deficit in the best-of-seven A.L. playoffs to win the pennant. The Royals won the last two games in Toronto, thereby preventing the Blue Jays from becoming the first team from Canada to play in the World Series.

Cox, who was named The Sporting News' Major League Manager of the Year, ended his four-year term when he accepted the general manager's job with the Atlanta Braves after the playoffs. Third base coach Jimy Williams was promoted to replace Cox.

Cox left behind what many consider the best all-around outfield in the league. Moseby, right fielder Jesse Barfield and left fielder George Bell—all just 25 years old at the end of the season—were the strongest part of Toronto's potent offense.

Bell batted .275, stole 21 bases and led the Blue Jays in home runs (28) and runs batted in (95), both career highs. Barfield, playing regularly for the first time, hit .289 with 27 homers, 84 RBIs, 94 runs scored, 22 steals and a .536 slugging percentage. He also led the league in outfield assists with 22. Moseby, who struggled the first half of the season, bounced back to lead the team in stolen bases with 37 while contributing 18 homers and 70 RBIs.

Their combined numbers represented 46 percent of Toronto's home runs, 36 percent of the runs scored, 35 percent of the RBIs and 56 percent of the stolen bases.

Several other players turned in good performances. Second baseman Damaso Garcia batted .282, stole 28 bases and had a career-high 65 RBIs from the leadoff spot. Fernandez, who succeeded Alfredo Griffin at shortstop and played in every game, showed tremendous potential in the field and knocked in 51 runs, a team record for both a shortstop and a switch-hitter, while batting .289. Whitt set personal peaks with 19 homers and 64 RBIs.

Veteran Buck Martinez, the other half of the catcher platoon, was sidelined for the season after breaking his leg July 9 in a home-plate collision in which he tagged out two runners on one play. As a result, Whitt had to catch every day—even when he was plagued by a sore shoulder—and

## SCORES OF TORONTO BLUE JAYS' 1985 GAMES

### APRIL

| Date | | | Winner | Loser |
|---|---|---|---|---|
| 8—At Kan. C. | L | 1-2 | Black | Stieb |
| 10—At Kan. C. | W | 1-0* | Caudill | Beckwith |
| 11—At Kan. C. | W | 4-3* | Caudill | Quisenberry |
| 12—At Balt. | L | 2-7 | McGregor | Key |
| 13—At Balt. | L | 7-8 | T. Martinez | Caudill |
| 14—At Balt. | W | 5-3 | Alexander | Boddicker |
| 16—Texas | L | 4-9 | Mason | Leal |
| 17—Texas | W | 3-1* | Caudill | Stewart |
| 18—Texas | W | 4-2 | Stieb | Tanana |
| 19—Baltimore | W | 6-5 | Alexander | Stewart |
| 20—Baltimore | W | 3-2 | Musselman | T. Martinez |
| 21—Baltimore | L | 2-3 | D. Martinez | Key |
| 22—Kan. City | L | 0-2 | Leibrandt | Stieb |
| 23—Kan. City | L | 6-7 | Beckwith | Caudill |
| 24—Kan. City | W | 10-3 | Leal | Saberhagen |
| 26—At Texas | W | 6-5 | Lamp | Schmidt |
| 27—At Texas | W | 9-8* | Acker | Stewart |
| 28—At Texas | W | 6-3 | Alexander | Mason |
| 29—At Oak. | W | 2-1 | Leal | Krueger |
| 30—At Oak. | W | 4-3 | Lamp | Howell |
| **Won 13, Lost 7** | | | | |

### MAY

| Date | | | Winner | Loser |
|---|---|---|---|---|
| 1—At Calif. | W | 6-3 | Key | McCaskill |
| 2—At Calif. | L | 2-3 | Clemente | Stieb |
| 3—At Seattle | W | 5-4 | Alexander | Barojas |
| 4—At Seattle | L | 1-8 | Young | Leal |
| 5—At Seattle | L | 1-4 | Langston | Clancy |
| 7—Oakland | W | 10-1 | Stieb | Sutton |
| 8—Oakland | L | 4-6 | McCatty | Alexander |
| 10—Seattle | W | 8-3 | Key | Langston |
| 11—Seattle | W | 4-2 | Caudill | Young |
| 12—Seattle | W | 9-5 | Stieb | Beattie |
| 14—California | W | 6-3 | Alexander | Slaton |
| 15—California | L | 6-9 | Moore | Caudill |
| 17—At Minn. | L | 6-7† | Filson | Leal |
| 18—At Minn. | W | 3-1 | Clancy | Smithson |
| 19—At Minn. | L | 2-8 | Filson | Alexander |
| 20—Chicago | W | 6-1 | Key | Seaver |
| 21—Chicago | W | 4-3 | Lavelle | James |
| 22—Chicago | W | 10-0 | Stieb | Dotson |
| 23—At Cleve. | W | 6-5 | Lamp | Waddell |
| 24—At Cleve. | W | 7-6 | Lamp | Creel |
| 25—At Cleve. | W | 10-7 | Musselman | Thompson |
| 26—At Cleve. | W | 6-5 | Lavelle | Creel |
| 28—At Chicago | W | 6-1 | Stieb | Dotson |
| 29—At Chicago | L | 5-8 | Burns | Clancy |
| 31—Cleveland | W | 7-2 | Alexander | Clark |
| **Won 17, Lost 8** | | | | |

### JUNE

| Date | | | Winner | Loser |
|---|---|---|---|---|
| 1—Cleveland | W | 8-3 | Key | Blyleven |
| 2—Cleveland | L | 4-5 | Heaton | Stieb |
| 2—Cleveland | W | 5-2 | Leal | Behenna |
| 4—Minnesota | W | 9-2 | Clancy | Viola |
| 5—Minnesota | W | 5-0 | Alexander | Smithson |
| 6—Detroit | W | 2-0‡ | Acker | Lopez |
| 7—Detroit | W | 9-2 | Stieb | Terrell |
| 8—Detroit | L | 1-10 | O'Neal | Leal |
| 9—Detroit | L | 3-8 | Bair | Clancy |
| 10—At N.Y. | L | 2-4 | Shirley | Alexander |
| 11—At N.Y. | W | 4-1† | Lamp | Fisher |
| 12—At N.Y. | W | 3-2* | Acker | Bordi |
| 13—At Boston | L | 7-8 | Trujillo | Lavelle |
| 14—At Boston | L | 1-4 | Boyd | Clancy |
| 15—At Boston | L | 5-7 | Stanley | Acker |
| 16—At Boston | L | 6-7 | Crawford | Lavelle |
| 17—At Milw. | L | 1-2 | Haas | Stieb |
| 18—At Milw. | L | 1-4 | Burris | Leal |
| 19—At Milw. | W | 5-1 | Clancy | Vuckovich |
| 20—Boston | W | 6-5 | Acker | Stanley |
| 21—Boston | W | 7-2 | Key | Hurst |
| 22—Boston | L | 3-5 | Stanley | Acker |
| 23—Boston | W | 8-1 | Stieb | Kison |
| 25—Milwaukee | W | 7-1 | Clancy | Burris |
| 26—Milwaukee | L | 4-5 | Gibson | Alexander |
| 27—Milwaukee | W | 7-3 | Key | Higuera |
| 28—At Detroit | W | 2-0 | Stieb | Petry |
| 29—At Detroit | L | 0-8 | Terrell | Leal |
| 30—At Detroit | W | 6-5 | Lavelle | Lopez |
| **Won 16, Lost 13** | | | | |

### JULY

| Date | | | Winner | Loser |
|---|---|---|---|---|
| 1—New York | L | 1-4 | Cowley | Alexander |
| 2—New York | L | 3-5 | Whitson | Key |
| 3—New York | W | 3-2* | Acker | Bordi |
| 4—At Oak. | L | 2-3 | Howell | Caudill |
| 5—At Oak. | W | 8-2 | Clancy | Krueger |
| 6—At Oak. | L | 1-5 | Sutton | Alexander |
| 7—At Oak. | W | 8-2 | Key | McCatty |
| 8—At Seattle | W | 4-0 | Stieb | Moore |
| 9—At Seattle | W | 9-4§ | Musselman | Vande Berg |
| 10—At Seattle | W | 11-1 | Clancy | Willis |
| 11—At Calif. | W | 5-3 | Alexander | Slaton |
| 12—At Calif. | L | 3-5 | McCaskill | Key |
| 13—At Calif. | L | 3-4 | Witt | Lavelle |
| 14—At Calif. | L | 3-5 | Cliburn | Lavelle |
| 18—Oakland | L | 4-6 | Ontiveros | Lavelle |
| 19—Oakland | W | 5-1 | Key | Sutton |
| 20—Oakland | L | 1-5 | Birtsas | Stieb |
| 21—Oakland | W | 11-4 | Lamp | Krueger |
| 22—Seattle | W | 3-1 | Filer | Langston |
| 23—Seattle | W | 4-2 | Alexander | Moore |
| 24—Seattle | W | 3-1 | Key | Young |
| 25—California | W | 7-0 | Stieb | Witt |
| 26—California | W | 8-3 | Clancy | Lugo |
| 27—California | W | 8-3 | Filer | Mack |
| 28—California | W | 5-1 | Alexander | McCaskill |
| 29—At Balt. | W | 4-3* | Henke | Boddicker |
| 30—At Balt. | L | 3-4* | Aase | Lavelle |
| 31—At Balt. | W | 5-3 | Henke | D. Martinez |
| **Won 18, Lost 10** | | | | |

### AUGUST

| Date | | | Winner | Loser |
|---|---|---|---|---|
| 1—At Balt. | W | 9-3 | Filer | Davis |
| 2—Texas | W | 5-3 | Alexander | Cook |
| 3—Texas | W | 4-1 | Lamp | Welsh |
| 4—Texas | L | 4-8 | Hough | Stieb |
| 8—Baltimore | W | 7-2 | Alexander | McGregor |
| 8—Baltimore | W | 7-4 | Filer | Boddicker |
| 9—At Kan. C. | L | 2-4 | Black | Stieb |
| 10—At Kan. C. | L | 3-4* | Quisenberry | Caudill |
| 11—At Kan. C. | W | 5-3* | Henke | Beckwith |
| 12—At Texas | L | 4-5 | Henry | Caudill |
| 13—At Texas | W | 5-3 | Filer | Russell |
| 14—At Texas | W | 4-1 | Stieb | Hough |
| 16—Kan. City | L | 2-4 | Leibrandt | Key |
| 17—Kan. City | L | 2-4 | Jackson | Alexander |
| 18—Kan. City | W | 10-6 | Filer | Gubicza |
| 19—At Cleve. | L | 3-5 | Waddell | Stieb |
| 20—At Cleve. | W | 3-2 | Key | Smith |
| 21—At Cleve. | L | 2-5 | Heaton | Alexander |
| 23—At Chicago | W | 6-3 | Filer | Burns |
| 23—At Chicago | W | 10-3 | Acker | Nelson |
| 24—At Chicago | W | 6-3 | Stieb | Seaver |
| 25—At Chicago | L | 3-5 | Bannister | Key |
| 26—At Minn. | W | 4-3 | Alexander | Blyleven |
| 27—At Minn. | W | 8-0 | Davis | Viola |
| 28—At Minn. | L | 5-6* | Filson | Henke |
| 30—Chicago | W | 5-3 | Key | Bannister |
| 31—Chicago | W | 6-2 | Lavelle | Davis |
| **Won 17, Lost 10** | | | | |

### SEPTEMBER

| Date | | | Winner | Loser |
|---|---|---|---|---|
| 1—Chicago | L | 1-4 | Burns | Davis |
| 2—Cleveland | W | 3-2 | Stieb | Wardle |
| 4—Cleveland | L | 4-5 | Clark | Henke |
| 5—Minnesota | W | 7-0 | Alexander | Blyleven |
| 6—Minnesota | W | 8-3 | Davis | Viola |
| 7—Minnesota | L | 3-6 | Smithson | Stieb |
| 8—Minnesota | W | 10-9 | Lamp | Portugal |
| 9—Detroit | W | 5-3 | Key | Mahler |
| 10—Detroit | W | 2-1 | Alexander | Morris |
| 11—Detroit | W | 3-2 | Lamp | Terrell |
| 12—At N.Y. | L | 5-7 | Guidry | Lavelle |
| 13—At N.Y. | W | 3-2 | Lavelle | P. Niekro |
| 14—At N.Y. | W | 7-4 | Key | Bordi |
| 15—At N.Y. | W | 8-5 | Alexander | Whitson |
| 17—At Boston | L | 5-6 | Boyd | Stieb |
| 18—At Boston | L | 1-13 | Nipper | Clancy |
| 20—Milwaukee | W | 7-5 | Key | Cocanower |
| 21—Milwaukee | W | 2-1x | Lamp | Darwin |
| 22—Milwaukee | L | 1-2 | Higuera | Stieb |
| 23—Milwaukee | W | 5-1 | Clancy | Leary |
| 24—Boston | W | 6-2 | Lamp | Nipper |
| 25—Boston | L | 2-4§ | Crawford | Cerutti |
| 26—Boston | L | 1-4 | Sellers | Alexander |
| 27—At Milw. | W | 5-1 | Stieb | Higuera |
| 28—At Milw. | W | 6-1 | Clancy | Leary |
| 29—At Milw. | W | 13-5 | Acker | Burris |
| **Won 17, Lost 9** | | | | |

### OCTOBER

| Date | | | Winner | Loser |
|---|---|---|---|---|
| 1—At Detroit | L | 1-6 | Tanana | Alexander |
| 2—At Detroit | L | 2-4 | Morris | Stieb |
| 3—At Detroit | L | 0-2 | Terrell | Clancy |
| 4—New York | L | 3-4 | Scurry | Henke |
| 5—New York | W | 5-1 | Alexander | Cowley |
| 6—New York | L | 0-8 | P. Niekro | Cerutti |
| **Won 1, Lost 5** | | | | |

*10 innings.    †11 innings.    ‡12 innings.    §13 innings.    x14 innings.

**Jimmy Key (left) emerged as the Blue Jays' top lefthanded starter while Tom Henke established himself as the team's bullpen ace.**

his average dipped to .245.

As usual, the third-base platoon of Rance Mulliniks (.295) and Garth Iorg (.313) had excellent production, totaling 17 homers and 94 RBIs.

Like Moseby, Upshaw had trouble in the first half of the season. But he hiked his average 42 points after the All-Star break to finish at .275 with 15 homers.

Strangely, the weakest spot in the Blue Jays' lineup was the designated hitter. Toronto started with Len Matuszek and Jeff Burroughs sharing the DH duties, but Matuszek was traded in July for veteran Al Oliver, and at the end of August, Toronto reacquired veteran Cliff Johnson. At .274 in 73 at-bats, Johnson had the best average of the bunch.

Many observers thought the Blue Jays could have won the division in 1984 if they had had a strong bullpen, so that was the club's top priority in the off-season. The Blue Jays seemed to have rectified their relief woes when they added righthander Bill Caudill, who had earned 36 saves with Oakland in 1984, and lefthander Gary Lavelle, who had saved 12 games for San Francisco. But neither lived up to expectations. They combined for only 22 saves, and they were responsible for 13 of the 20 bullpen losses.

The key acquisition turned out to be Tom Henke, who was picked up in the free-agent compensation pool from the Texas Rangers. The righthander started the season at Syracuse (International),

where he had fashioned an incredible 0.88 earned-run average by the time he was promoted in late July. Cox threw him right into the fray as his stopper, and he responded with a 3-3 record, a 2.03 ERA and 13 saves in 28 appearances.

Dennis Lamp, a major disappointment in '84, rebounded to post an amazing 11-0 record as a middle reliever. Jim Acker contributed seven wins and 10 saves, mostly in the first half. Put all these performances together and the bullpen produced 35 wins and a team-record 47 saves (second in the league).

Overall, Toronto pitchers led the league with a 3.29 ERA. The starting staff was paced by Alexander, who won 17 games for the second consecutive year, and righthander Dave Stieb, the A.L. ERA champion with a 2.48 mark. Stieb struggled in the second half, however, going 5-8 after the All-Star break to finish 14-13.

By adding Lavelle, Jimmy Key was freed from the bullpen, and he gave Toronto its first quality lefthanded starter in team history by going 14-6 with a 3.00 ERA. The Blue Jays had gone 614 games, dating to the 1980 season, without a win from a lefthanded starter.

Luis Leal (3-6, 5.75 ERA) was demoted in July, and Tom Filer, who replaced him in the rotation, ran up a 7-0 record before being sidelined with a tender elbow. Jim Clancy was on the disabled list twice, first because of an appendectomy and then tendinitis, but he still won nine games.

**Rickey Henderson ran up some impressive statistics in his first season as the Yankees center fielder.**

# Late Yankee Surge Falls Short

**By MOSS KLEIN**

The New York Yankees' season was filled with the usual controversies—firings and criticism by Owner George Steinbrenner and barroom scuffles involving Manager Billy Martin—as well as superb performances by several players. But more than anything else, the Yankees will remember the 1985 season for their abrupt collapse, the eight days in September that dimmed all the achievements of an otherwise outstanding campaign.

The Yankees had moved to within 1½ games of first place in the American League East on September 12 after winning the first game of a crucial four-game series against Toronto at Yankee Stadium. With that victory, New York had won 30 of its last 36 games and appeared ready to surge past the Blue Jays.

But then came the collapse. The Yankees lost the next three to Toronto, plus the next five to Cleveland, Detroit and Baltimore. After the eight-game losing streak, the Yankees regrouped, winning 10 of their next 12 to pull within two games of the Blue Jays. But they were eliminated in a loss at Toronto on the next-to-last day of the season, finishing with a 97-64 record, two games out of first.

The Yankees, who were confident they would catch Toronto, were baffled by that eight-game collapse.

"It's hard to figure out what happened," said first baseman Don Mattingly, who was named the league's Most Valuable Player. "Sometimes things just happen around here and nobody can figure out why."

Indeed, the only constant in the world of the Yankees during the past 10 years has been Steinbrenner, and once again the owner made his presence felt and his voice heard throughout the season.

Steinbrenner, who had promised Yogi Berra that he would be the manager "for the entire season, win or lose," fired Berra after 16 games, only six of which the Yankees had won. Steinbrenner summoned Martin, his on-again, off-again sparring partner, for a fourth term as Yankees manager.

For a while, the Yankees continued to struggle under Martin. They were in fifth place with a 28-29 record on June 15, but they fought back into contention by the All-Star break, when they were 2½ games back. They fell to 9½ games back as late

**Hard-throwing rookie Brian Fisher (above) joined Dave Righetti in the bullpen and recorded 14 saves.**

as August 4 before starting the surge that led to their key home series with Toronto in mid-September.

## SCORES OF NEW YORK YANKEES' 1985 GAMES

### APRIL

| Date | W/L | Score | Winner | Loser |
|---|---|---|---|---|
| 8—At Boston | L | 2-9 | Boyd | Niekro |
| 10—At Boston | L | 5-14 | Hurst | Whitson |
| 11—At Boston | L | 4-6 | Clemens | Rasmussen |
| 13—At Cleve. | W | 6-3 | Guidry | Blyleven |
| 14—At Cleve. | W | 2-1 | Niekro | Waddell |
| 16—Chicago | W | 5-4 | Righetti | Spillner |
| 18—Chicago | W | 3-2 | Bordi | Bannister |
| 19—Cleveland | L | 1-2 | Heaton | Guidry |
| 20—Cleveland | W | 5-2 | Niekro | Roman |
| 21—Cleveland | L | 0-3 | Von Ohlen | Whitson |
| 23—Boston | L | 4-5† | Ojeda | Righetti |
| 24—Boston | L | 6-7 | Crawford | Guidry |
| 25—Boston | W | 5-1 | Niekro | Hurst |
| 26—At Chicago | L | 2-4 | Seaver | Whitson |
| 27—At Chicago | L | 4-5† | Nelson | Shirley |
| 28—At Chicago | L | 3-4 | Burns | Cowley |
| 29—At Texas | L | 5-7 | Schmidt | Guidry |
| 30—At Texas | L | 4-8 | Noles | Niekro |

**Won 6, Lost 12**

### MAY

| Date | W/L | Score | Winner | Loser |
|---|---|---|---|---|
| 1—At Texas | W | 5-1 | Whitson | Hough |
| 3—Kan. City | W | 7-1 | Rasmussen | Jackson |
| 4—Kan. City | W | 5-2 | Guidry | Leibrandt |
| 5—Kan. City | W | 6-2 | Niekro | Black |
| 7—At Minn. | L | 6-8 | Viola | Whitson |
| 8—At Minn. | L | 6-8 | Smithson | Cowley |
| 10—At Kan. C. | W | 6-4 | Guidry | Leibrandt |
| 11—At Kan. C. | W | 11-3 | Rasmussen | Black |
| 12—At Kan. C. | L | 5-6 | Quisenberry | Righetti |
| 13—Minnesota | W | 9-8 | Cowley | Davis |
| 14—Minnesota | W | 10-7 | Fisher | Wardle |
| 15—Texas | W | 6-5* | Righetti | Schmidt |
| 16—Texas | W | 6-5 | Righetti | Stewart |
| 17—At Calif. | W | 6-0 | Niekro | Witt |
| 18—At Calif. | W | 6-1 | Cowley | John |
| 19—At Calif. | L | 1-4 | Slaton | Whitson |
| 21—At Seattle | W | 11-1 | Guidry | Langston |
| 22—At Seattle | L | 1-4 | Young | Rasmussen |
| 23—At Seattle | L | 4-6 | Beattie | Niekro |
| 24—At Oak. | W | 10-3 | Cowley | Codiroli |
| 25—At Oak. | L | 7-8 | Howell | Righetti |
| 26—At Oak. | W | 13-1 | Guidry | Krueger |
| 27—At Oak. | L | 1-2* | Howell | Righetti |
| 29—California | W | 7-2 | Niekro | Slaton |
| 30—California | W | 3-1 | Cowley | Romanick |
| 31—Seattle | W | 8-3 | Fisher | Langston |

**Won 18, Lost 8**

### JUNE

| Date | W/L | Score | Winner | Loser |
|---|---|---|---|---|
| 1—Seattle | W | 8-2 | Guidry | Young |
| 2—Seattle | L | 6-7 | Nunez | Rasmussen |
| 3—Oakland | W | 5-2 | Niekro | Codiroli |
| 4—Oakland | L | 0-2 | Birtsas | Cowley |
| 6—At Milw. | L | 1-5 | Darwin | Whitson |
| 7—At Milw. | L | 9-10* | Searage | Righetti |
| 8—At Milw. | W | 2-1‡ | Righetti | Gibson |
| 9—At Milw. | L | 4-9 | Vuckovich | Niekro |
| 10—Toronto | W | 4-2 | Shirley | Alexander |
| 11—Toronto | L | 1-4† | Lamp | Fisher |
| 12—Toronto | L | 2-3* | Acker | Bordi |
| 14—Detroit | L | 0-4 | Terrell | Rasmussen |
| 15—Detroit | L | 8-10 | Morris | Niekro |
| 16—Detroit | W | 2-1 | Shirley | O'Neal |
| 17—At Balt. | W | 10-0 | Guidry | McGregor |
| 18—At Balt. | W | 6-4 | Cowley | Davis |
| 19—At Balt. | W | 10-0 | Whitson | D. Martinez |
| 20—At Detroit | L | 9-10* | Bair | Righetti |
| 21—At Detroit | L | 4-6 | O'Neal | Niekro |
| 22—At Detroit | W | 4-0 | Guidry | Petry |
| 23—At Detroit | L | 1-3 | Tanana | Shirley |
| 24—Baltimore | W | 5-4 | Cowley | D. Martinez |
| 25—Baltimore | W | 7-4 | Whitson | Boddicker |
| 26—Baltimore | W | 4-3 | Righetti | Aase |
| 28—Milwaukee | W | 5-2 | Guidry | Darwin |
| 29—Milwaukee | L | 0-6 | Haas | Niekro |
| 30—Milwaukee | L | 5-7 | McClure | Fisher |

**Won 13, Lost 14**

### JULY

| Date | W/L | Score | Winner | Loser |
|---|---|---|---|---|
| 1—At Toronto | W | 4-1 | Cowley | Alexander |
| 2—At Toronto | W | 5-3 | Whitson | Key |
| 3—At Toronto | L | 2-3* | Acker | Bordi |
| 4—Minnesota | W | 3-2 | Guidry | Butcher |
| 5—Minnesota | W | 6-3 | Rasmussen | Schrom |
| 7—Minnesota | W | 3-2† | Righetti | Wardle |
| 7—Minnesota | W | 14-2 | Bordi | Lysander |
| 8—Kan. City | L | 2-5 | Saberhagen | Niekro |
| 9—Kan. City | W | 6-4 | Guidry | Black |
| 10—Kan. City | W | 6-5 | Righetti | Quisenberry |
| 11—Texas | W | 11-7 | Shirley | Cook |
| 12—Texas | W | 6-0 | Whitson | Sebra |
| 13—Texas | W | 3-1 | Niekro | Mason |
| 14—Texas | W | 7-1 | Guidry | Hooton |
| 18—At Minn. | L | 4-8 | Eufemia | Bordi |
| 19—At Minn. | W | 6-4 | Cowley | Butcher |
| 20—At Minn. | W | 8-3 | Guidry | Schrom |
| 21—At Minn. | W | 5-2 | Niekro | Viola |
| 22—At Kan. C. | L | 4-5 | Jones | Rasmussen |
| 23—At Kan. C. | L | 2-5 | Saberhagen | Whitson |
| 24—At Kan. C. | L | 3-5 | Leibrandt | Cowley |
| 26—At Texas | L | 8-9 | Noles | Righetti |
| 27—At Texas | W | 14-2 | Niekro | Cook |
| 28—At Texas | L | 2-8 | Welsh | Bystrom |
| 29—At Cleve. | W | 8-2 | Whitson | Blyleven |
| 30—At Cleve. | W | 8-5 | Cowley | Thompson |
| 30—At Cleve. | L | 2-3 | Romero | Shirley |
| 31—At Cleve. | L | 5-6 | Waddell | Guidry |

**Won 18, Lost 10**

### AUGUST

| Date | W/L | Score | Winner | Loser |
|---|---|---|---|---|
| 1—At Cleve. | L | 1-9 | Smith | Niekro |
| 2—Chicago | L | 5-6† | Agosto | Bordi |
| 3—Chicago | W | 8-4 | Whitson | Long |
| 4—Chicago | L | 1-4 | Seaver | Cowley |
| 5—Chicago | W | 7-3 | Guidry | Bannister |
| 8—Cleveland | W | 8-1 | Bystrom | Wardle |
| 8—Cleveland | W | 7-6 | Fisher | Reed |
| 9—At Boston | W | 10-6 | Bordi | Hurst |
| 10—At Boston | W | 7-3 | Cowley | Boyd |
| 11—At Boston | W | 5-3 | Guidry | Clemens |
| 12—At Chicago | W | 10-4 | Niekro | Nelson |
| 13—At Chicago | L | 3-4 | Burns | Fisher |
| 14—At Chicago | W | 10-7 | Fisher | James |
| 16—Boston | W | 5-4* | Righetti | Crawford |
| 17—Boston | W | 3-1 | Guidry | Nipper |
| 18—Boston | W | 4-2 | Righetti | Lollar |
| 19—Boston | W | 6-5 | Bystrom | Clear |
| 20—At Calif. | W | 8-5 | Bordi | Slaton |
| 21—At Calif. | W | 13-10* | Righetti | Moore |
| 22—At Calif. | L | 2-3 | Witt | Bordi |
| 23—At Seattle | W | 3-1 | Niekro | Swift |
| 24—At Seattle | W | 4-3 | Bystrom | Langston |
| 25—At Seattle | W | 8-5 | Whitson | Moore |
| 26—At Oak. | L | 2-3§ | Langford | Shirley |
| 27—At Oak. | L | 0-3 | John | Guidry |
| 29—California | W | 4-0 | Niekro | McCaskill |
| 30—California | L | 1-4 | Candelaria | Bystrom |
| 31—California | W | 10-4 | Righetti | Corbett |

**Won 20, Lost 8**

### SEPTEMBER

| Date | W/L | Score | Winner | Loser |
|---|---|---|---|---|
| 1—California | W | 5-3 | Shirley | Holland |
| 2—Seattle | W | 8-7 | Guidry | Wills |
| 3—Seattle | W | 6-3 | P. Niekro | Swift |
| 4—Seattle | W | 4-3 | Bordi | Langston |
| 5—Oakland | W | 7-3 | Whitson | Atherton |
| 6—Oakland | W | 8-4 | Shirley | Codiroli |
| 7—Oakland | W | 3-2 | Guidry | John |
| 8—Oakland | W | 9-6 | P. Niekro | Rijo |
| 9—At Milw. | W | 9-4* | Righetti | Searage |
| 10—At Milw. | W | 13-10 | Whitson | Burris |
| 11—At Milw. | L | 3-4 | Higuera | Bordi |
| 12—Toronto | W | 7-5 | Guidry | Lavelle |
| 13—Toronto | L | 2-3 | Lavelle | P. Niekro |
| 14—Toronto | L | 4-7 | Key | Bordi |
| 15—Toronto | L | 5-8 | Alexander | Whitson |
| 16—Cleveland | L | 5-9 | Reed | Fisher |
| 17—At Detroit | L | 1-9 | Petry | Guidry |
| 18—At Detroit | L | 2-5 | Mahler | P. Niekro |
| 19—At Detroit | L | 3-10 | Tanana | J. Niekro |
| 20—At Balt. | L | 2-4 | Flanagan | Bordi |
| 21—At Balt. | W | 5-2 | Cowley | Davis |
| 22—At Balt. | W | 5-4 | Guidry | Dixon |
| 24—Detroit | L | 1-4 | Tanana | P. Niekro |
| 25—Detroit | W | 10-2 | J. Niekro | Morris |
| 28—Baltimore | W | 6-5 | Guidry | Stewart |
| 29—Baltimore | W | 4-0 | Cowley | McGregor |
| 29—Baltimore | W | 9-2 | Bordi | Havens |
| 30—Baltimore | W | 5-4 | Allen | Aase |

**Won 18, Lost 10**

### OCTOBER

| Date | W/L | Score | Winner | Loser |
|---|---|---|---|---|
| 1—Milwaukee | W | 6-1 | J. Niekro | Cocanower |
| 2—Milwaukee | L | 0-1 | Higuera | Shirley |
| 3—Milwaukee | W | 3-0 | Guidry | Leary |
| 4—At Toronto | W | 4-3 | Scurry | Henke |
| 5—At Toronto | L | 1-5 | Alexander | Cowley |
| 6—At Toronto | W | 8-0 | P. Niekro | Cerutti |

**Won 4, Lost 2**

*10 innings.   †11 innings.   ‡13 innings.   §15 innings.

During the third game of that series, Steinbrenner strode into the press box and aired his disgust, singling out specific players and saying that Toronto "outplayed, out-managed, out-front officed and out-ownered us." He called Dave Winfield "Mr. May," a sarcastic reference to Reggie Jackson's "Mr. October" nickname. Although he later apologized for the remarks about Winfield and others, many players said the comments contributed to their losing streak.

Martin was under pressure throughout the skid, and in the five losses after the Toronto series he was criticized for staying too long with pitchers, for ordering lefthanded hitter Mike Pagliarulo to bat righthanded in a crucial situation and for inadvertently giving the pitchout sign (by rubbing his nose) in a key situation in a loss to Baltimore.

Martin's health, which had been affected after the Texas Rangers' team physician accidentally punctured his lung while administering an injection July 28, deteriorated further following his barroom scrapes on consecutive September nights in Baltimore. The first encounter was primarily a shouting and shoving match with an unidentified patron who thought Martin had insulted his wife. But the next night, Martin suffered a broken right arm in a three-round fight with pitcher Ed Whitson.

That last incident virtually sealed Martin's fate. Even though no manager bettered his .628 winning percentage in 1985, it came as no surprise when coach Lou Piniella was named as his replacement October 27.

Despite all the distractions, the Yankees played well. They were third in the league in both batting (.267) and pitching (3.69 earned-run average) as a team, and their 839 runs scored, 155 stolen bases and 49 saves all were A.L. highs.

Leading the way was Mattingly, who established himself as one of the game's top stars. The Gold Glove winner hit .324 with 35 home runs, 107 runs scored and 211 hits. He also led the league with an incredible 145 runs batted in, 21 game-winning RBIs and 48 doubles.

Though he slumped somewhat down the stretch, Winfield still batted .275 with 26 homers, 114 RBIs and 105 runs. The right fielder also won his fourth straight Gold Glove.

Center fielder Rickey Henderson, who had been acquired from Oakland in the off-season, was as good as the Yankees had hoped. He hit .314, led the league with a club-record 80 stolen bases and scored 146 runs, the most in the major leagues since Ted Williams scored 150 in 1949. Henderson also hit 24 homers, thus becoming the first player in A.L. history to hit 20 or more homers and steal 50 or more bases in a season.

Several other Yankees had fine offensive seasons, including designated hitter Don Baylor (23 homers, 91 RBIs), third baseman Pagliarulo (19 homers, 62 RBIs as a platoon player), left fielder Ken Griffey (.274, 69 RBIs), second baseman Willie Randolph (.276, 85 walks) and catcher-pinch-hitter Ron Hassey (.296, 13 homers). The only regular players who had weak years offensively were catcher Butch Wynegar (.223) and shortstop Bobby Meacham (.218).

The ace of the pitching staff was Ron Guidry, who bounced back from a 10-11 record in 1984 to post a 22-6 mark with a 3.27 ERA and 11 complete games, good enough for second place in the Cy Young Award voting. The 35-year-old lefthander revised his style, relying less on pure power and incorporating breaking pitches and changeups into his fastball-slider repertoire. Guidry also won a Gold Glove for his defensive play.

Phil Niekro, the 46-year-old knuckleballer, came through with a 16-12 record that included his 300th career victory. That 8-0 triumph over Toronto on the last day of the season made him the oldest major leaguer ever to pitch a shutout. And in his historic win, Niekro fulfilled a fantasy: He didn't throw any of his trademark knuckleballs until striking out Jeff Burroughs for the final out.

The bullpen was solid with lefthander Dave Righetti (12-7, 2.78 ERA, 29 saves) and hard-throwing rookie Brian Fisher (4-4, 2.38, 14 saves). Long relievers-starters Bob Shirley (5-5, 2.64) and Rich Bordi (6-8, 3.21) also performed capably. But a lack of quality starters behind Guidry was a big reason why the Yankees failed to win their division.

Though Niekro won 16 games, he had a 4.09 ERA. Also in that range were Joe Cowley, who went 12-6 with a 3.95 ERA, and Dennis Rasmussen (3-5, 3.98). But the weakest link in the rotation was Whitson, a free agent whom the Yankees had signed in the off-season. After an awful 1-6 start during which he was taunted mercilessly at Yankee Stadium, Whitson wound up with a 10-8 record and a 4.88 ERA.

"We don't need to make big changes," Righetti said after the season. "We need to improve our starting pitching. That's the main thing."

**Veteran first baseman Darrell Evans captured American League home run honors with 40 while driving in 94.**

# Defenseless Tigers Fall Hard

**By TOM GAGE**

They won their first six games, reviving memories of their 35-5 start in 1984. But after that, they were seldom heard from again.

Instead of leading wire to wire as they did in 1984, the Detroit Tigers led for 20 days before their season came unglued because of bad defense, an overdependence on power and the traditional malaise that afflicts defending champions in the American League East.

The Tigers went 84-77 to finish in third place, 15 games behind Toronto, but it was a struggle to get that far. They had to beat the Orioles on the final day in Baltimore to decide the difference between third and fourth. It was small consolation for a team that won its division by 15 games in 1984, swept Kansas City in the A.L. playoffs, beat San Diego in a five-game World Series and then considered itself improved in the off-season with the acquisition of pitcher Walt Terrell.

The Tigers, however, were not the next dynasty. Not even the next encore. Their one-year reign was doomed partly by a losing record at home against the A.L. West—including a combined 2-10 mark against Seattle and Minnesota—but mostly by a defensive collapse that surprised Manager Sparky Anderson.

"The only thing I'm disappointed in is our defense," Anderson said. "I'm not disappointed with our record, pitching, hitting or anything like that. Only the defense (which committed 143 errors). I don't believe you can play defense the way we did and win anything."

The Tigers peaked July 10 when they beat the White Sox to rise to 47-34, only 3½ games behind Toronto. The Tigers were never 13 games over .500 again, however, and they never considered themselves close to the Blue Jays again.

In some respects, mostly from the power standpoint, it was a good year for the Tigers. First baseman-designated hitter Darrell Evans hit 40 home runs and thus became, at 38, the oldest player ever to lead the American League in homers. Evans also contributed 94 runs batted in, 85 walks and a .519 slugging percentage.

Trailing Evans by one point in slugging percentage was Kirk Gibson, who followed up one good year with another. The right fielder batted .287 with 37 doubles and 97 RBIs and fell one home run short of becoming the first Tiger ever to steal 30

bases and hit 30 homers in the same season.

Catcher Lance Parrish had a productive year, leading the Tigers with 98 RBIs and smacking 28 homers. Lou Whitaker set a Detroit record for second basemen with 21 homers, and he and Parrish each won Gold Gloves for the third consecutive year. Center fielder Chet Lemon added 18 homers while batting .265.

The Tigers cleared the fences 202 times in 1985. It was their supreme skill, but all too often Anderson found runs difficult to come by with any other method.

"I've never had a team generate such a high percentage of its runs with home runs," he said. "Most of them meant nothing. All you need to know about home runs was in that final game we played against the Orioles. Here were two teams with more than 400 home runs between them . . . and we were playing to decide third and fourth place. Now if that doesn't tell you where home runs rank on the list of priorities, nothing will."

Anderson said the problem was fundamentals.

"We didn't do the little things right," he said. "Sure, it was a lot of bad defense, but it was also some little things that never show up in the box scores.

"We couldn't bunt, and we couldn't get a runner in from third with less than two out. I don't think I've ever seen it worse than our percentage this season. I think we failed to get the runner home from third 60 percent of the time. I can't imagine failing that often."

The unimaginable happened because of several undependable bats in the starting lineup. Shortstop Alan Trammell, who hit .314 in 1984 and was named the Most Valuable Player of the World Series, watched his average drop to .258. Left fielder Larry Herndon's average slipped 36 points to .244. And third baseman Tom Brookens hit just .237.

The averages for many of the part-time players were equally disturbing. Rookie DH Nelson Simmons batted .239, Barbaro Garbey .257, John Grubb .245 and Dave Bergman .179.

While the offense was floundering, the pitching was consistent. The Tigers ranked fourth in the league with a 3.78 earned-run average and tied for the lead in shutouts with 11. The strength of the staff was the starting rotation, which had only one regular (Juan Berenguer, who

## SCORES OF DETROIT TIGERS' 1985 GAMES

### APRIL

| Date—Opponent | W/L | Score | Winner | Loser |
|---|---|---|---|---|
| 8—Cleveland | W | 5-4 | Morris | Camacho |
| 10—Cleveland | W | 8-1 | Petry | Ruhle |
| 11—Cleveland | W | 11-10* | Hernandez | Von Ohlen |
| 13—At Kan. C. | W | 3-1 | Morris | Black |
| 14—At Kan. C. | W | 5-1 | Petry | Saberhagen |
| 16—Milwaukee | W | 2-1 | Terrell | Burris |
| 17—Milwaukee | L | 0-2 | Darwin | Morris |
| 19—Kan. City | L | 2-9 | Saberhagen | Petry |
| 20—Kan. City | W | 4-3 | Hernandez | Quisenberry |
| 21—Kan. City | L | 2-3§ | Quisenberry | Berenguer |
| 22—At Cleve. | L | 4-6 | Schulze | Morris |
| 23—At Cleve. | W | 4-3 | Petry | Blyleven |
| 24—At Cleve. | L | 6-7 | Easterly | Lopez |
| 25—At Milw. | L | 7-11 | Gibson | Scherrer |
| 26—At Milw. | W | 1-0 | Morris | Burris |
| 27—At Milw. | W | 3-2 | Petry | Darwin |
| 28—At Milw. | W | 5-0 | Terrell | Higuera |
| 30—Minnesota | L | 2-11 | Butcher | Wilcox |

Won 11, Lost 7

### MAY

| Date—Opponent | W/L | Score | Winner | Loser |
|---|---|---|---|---|
| 1—Minnesota | L | 3-7 | Viola | Morris |
| 3—Chicago | L | 1-7 | Seaver | Petry |
| 4—Chicago | W | 7-1 | Terrell | Lollar |
| 5—Chicago | W | 4-3 | Berenguer | Dotson |
| 7—At Texas | W | 10-1 | Morris | Noles |
| 8—At Texas | W | 4-1 | Petry | Mason |
| 10—At Chicago | W | 3-1 | Terrell | Seaver |
| 11—At Chicago | L | 4-7 | Dotson | Berenguer |
| 12—At Chicago | L | 0-4 | Bannister | Morris |
| 13—Texas | W | 7-4 | Petry | Hooton |
| 14—Texas | W | 4-1 | Wilcox | Hough |
| 15—At Minn. | L | 4-5† | Wardle | Lopez |
| 16—At Minn. | L | 5-7 | Schrom | Berenguer |
| 17—At Oak. | W | 10-2 | Morris | Sutton |
| 18—At Oak. | W | 9-6 | Petry | McCatty |
| 19—At Oak. | L | 7-9 | Codiroli | Wilcox |
| 20—At Calif. | L | 2-7 | Romanick | Terrell |
| 21—At Calif. | L | 1-2† | Moore | Hernandez |
| 22—At Calif. | W | 3-2 | Petry | Witt |
| 24—At Seattle | W | 4-3† | Hernandez | Stanton |
| 25—At Seattle | W | 3-2 | Terrell | Best |
| 26—At Seattle | W | 6-0 | Morris | Barojas |
| 27—Seattle | L | 2-5 | Young | Petry |
| 29—Oakland | L | 2-4 | Codiroli | Wilcox |
| 30—Oakland | W | 3-2 | Terrell | Birtsas |
| 31—California | L | 3-6 | Clements | Morris |

Won 14, Lost 12

### JUNE

| Date—Opponent | W/L | Score | Winner | Loser |
|---|---|---|---|---|
| 1—California | L | 2-9 | Witt | Petry |
| 2—California | W | 4-3 | Hernandez | Moore |
| 3—Seattle | L | 8-9 | Beattie | Lopez |
| 4—Seattle | L | 6-7‡ | Thomas | Hernandez |
| 5—Seattle | W | 5-2 | Morris | Langston |
| 6—At Toronto | L | 0-2‡ | Acker | Lopez |
| 7—At Toronto | L | 2-9 | Stieb | Terrell |
| 8—At Toronto | W | 10-1 | O'Neal | Leal |
| 9—At Toronto | W | 8-3 | Bair | Clancy |
| 10—Baltimore | W | 8-7† | Lopez | Stewart |
| 12—Baltimore | W | 6-2 | Petry | Boddicker |
| 14—At N.Y. | W | 4-0 | Terrell | Rasmussen |
| 15—At N.Y. | W | 10-8 | Morris | Niekro |
| 16—At N.Y. | L | 1-2 | Shirley | O'Neal |
| 17—Boston | L | 2-3 | Nipper | Hernandez |
| 18—Boston | W | 9-8 | Berenguer | Hurst |
| 19—Boston | W | 9-3 | Terrell | Boyd |
| 20—New York | W | 10-9* | Bair | Righetti |
| 21—New York | W | 6-4 | O'Neal | Niekro |
| 22—New York | L | 0-4 | Guidry | Petry |
| 23—New York | W | 3-1 | Tanana | Shirley |
| 24—At Boston | L | 2-9 | Boyd | Terrell |
| 25—At Boston | W | 3-0 | Morris | Ojeda |
| 26—At Boston | W | 3-0 | O'Neal | Nipper |
| 28—Toronto | L | 0-2 | Stieb | Petry |
| 29—Toronto | W | 8-0 | Terrell | Leal |
| 30—Toronto | L | 5-6 | Lavelle | Lopez |

Won 16, Lost 11

### JULY

| Date—Opponent | W/L | Score | Winner | Loser |
|---|---|---|---|---|
| 1—At Balt. | W | 7-1 | O'Neal | McGregor |
| 2—At Balt. | L | 4-5‡ | Aase | Hernandez |
| 3—At Balt. | W | 4-3* | Petry | Stewart |
| 4—At Texas | L | 1-4 | Hooton | Terrell |
| 5—At Texas | L | 1-3 | Hough | Morris |
| 6—At Texas | W | 4-3 | O'Neal | Rozema |
| 7—At Texas | W | 5-3 | Tanana | Harris |
| 8—Chicago | L | 4-9 | Nelson | Petry |
| 9—Chicago | W | 6-5 | Hernandez | James |
| 10—Chicago | W | 1-0 | Morris | Seaver |
| 11—Minnesota | L | 1-5 | Smithson | O'Neal |
| 12—Minnesota | L | 2-3 | Butcher | Tanana |
| 13—Minnesota | L | 4-6 | Schrom | Petry |
| 14—Minnesota | W | 8-0 | Terrell | Viola |
| 18—Texas | L | 2-3 | Hough | Tanana |
| 19—Texas | L | 1-2 | Hooton | Petry |
| 20—Texas | W | 6-5x | Scherrer | Harris |
| 21—Texas | L | 5-7 | Schmidt | Lopez |
| 22—At Chicago | L | 4-9 | Nelson | O'Neal |
| 23—At Chicago | L | 3-5 | Burns | Tanana |
| 24—At Chicago | W | 5-4 | Petry | Seaver |
| 25—At Minn. | W | 7-2 | Morris | Viola |
| 26—At Minn. | L | 5-6 | Smithson | Terrell |
| 27—At Minn. | L | 4-11 | Butcher | Lopez |
| 28—At Minn. | W | 3-2 | Tanana | Schrom |
| 29—Kan. City | L | 2-4 | Saberhagen | Petry |
| 30—Kan. City | W | 11-7 | Morris | Leibrandt |
| 31—Kan. City | L | 2-5 | Jackson | Terrell |

Won 12, Lost 16

### AUGUST

| Date—Opponent | W/L | Score | Winner | Loser |
|---|---|---|---|---|
| 2—Milwaukee | W | 4-1 | Tanana | Vuckovich |
| 3—Milwaukee | W | 9-3 | Petry | Darwin |
| 4—Milwaukee | W | 7-4 | Hernandez | Waits |
| 4—Milwaukee | L | 4-14 | Burris | O'Neal |
| 5—At Kan. C. | W | 8-4 | Terrell | Jackson |
| 8—At Kan. C. | L | 3-10 | Saberhagen | Tanana |
| 8—At Kan. C. | L | 4-6 | Gubicza | Petry |
| 9—At Cleve. | L | 2-4 | Easterly | Hernandez |
| 10—At Cleve. | W | 5-4† | Hernandez | Ruhle |
| 11—At Cleve. | L | 2-7 | Heaton | O'Neal |
| 12—At Milw. | L | 3-4 | Cocanower | Hernandez |
| 13—At Milw. | W | 5-4§ | Lopez | Gibson |
| 14—At Milw. | W | 4-3 | Morris | Darwin |
| 15—Cleveland | L | 6-7 | Wardle | Hernandez |
| 16—Cleveland | W | 3-2 | Lopez | Heaton |
| 17—Cleveland | W | 7-5 | Tanana | Wardle |
| 18—Cleveland | W | 4-0 | Petry | Romero |
| 19—At Kan. C. | L | 1-2* | Saberhagen | Morris |
| 20—At Oak. | W | 4-1 | Terrell | Birtsas |
| 21—At Oak. | L | 3-4 | Mura | Hernandez |
| 22—At Oak. | W | 5-3§ | Scherrer | Atherton |
| 23—At Calif. | L | 6-7 | Sanchez | Hernandez |
| 24—At Calif. | W | 13-2 | Morris | McCaskill |
| 25—At Calif. | L | 1-7 | Cliburn | Terrell |
| 26—At Seattle | W | 6-3 | Berenguer | Wills |
| 27—At Seattle | L | 1-3 | Young | Tanana |
| 29—Oakland | W | 3-2‡ | Scherrer | Mura |
| 30—Oakland | L | 3-8 | Sutton | Morris |
| 31—Oakland | W | 4-1 | Terrell | Birtsas |

Won 16, Lost 13

### SEPTEMBER

| Date—Opponent | W/L | Score | Winner | Loser |
|---|---|---|---|---|
| 1—Oakland | W | 14-3 | Berenguer | Codiroli |
| 2—California | L | 1-11 | Slaton | Tanana |
| 3—California | W | 14-8 | Petry | McCaskill |
| 4—California | L | 2-5 | Candelaria | Morris |
| 6—Seattle | L | 4-8 | Moore | Terrell |
| 7—Seattle | L | 5-12 | Young | Berenguer |
| 8—Seattle | L | 2-6 | Thomas | Tanana |
| 9—At Toronto | L | 3-5 | Key | Mahler |
| 10—At Toronto | L | 1-2 | Alexander | Morris |
| 11—At Toronto | L | 2-3 | Lamp | Terrell |
| 13—Baltimore | L | 4-6 | McGregor | Berenguer |
| 14—Baltimore | W | 10-3 | Tanana | Boddicker |
| 14—Baltimore | L | 4-5 | Flanagan | Mahler |
| 15—Baltimore | W | 4-1 | Hernandez | Stewart |
| 16—Baltimore | L | 7-14 | T. Martinez | Cary |
| 17—New York | W | 9-1 | Petry | Guidry |
| 18—New York | W | 5-2 | Mahler | P. Niekro |
| 19—New York | W | 10-3 | Tanana | J. Niekro |
| 20—At Boston | W | 6-2 | Morris | Hurst |
| 21—At Boston | L | 6-7 | Lollar | Terrell |
| 22—At Boston | L | 2-6 | Boyd | Petry |
| 23—At Boston | W | 2-1 | Berenguer | Ojeda |
| 24—At N.Y. | W | 9-1 | Tanana | P. Niekro |
| 25—At N.Y. | L | 2-10 | J. Niekro | Morris |
| 27—Boston | W | 5-1 | Terrell | Boyd |
| 28—Boston | L | 0-2* | Ojeda | Hernandez |
| 29—Boston | L | 4-8 | Woodward | Berenguer |

Won 11, Lost 16

### OCTOBER

| Date—Opponent | W/L | Score | Winner | Loser |
|---|---|---|---|---|
| 1—Toronto | W | 6-1 | Tanana | Alexander |
| 2—Toronto | W | 4-2 | Morris | Stieb |
| 3—Toronto | W | 2-0 | Terrell | Clancy |
| 4—At Balt. | L | 2-5 | McGregor | Petry |
| 5—At Balt. | L | 6-7 | Aase | Scherrer |
| 6—At Balt. | W | 11-3 | Tanana | D. Martinez |

Won 4, Lost 2

*10 innings.  †11 innings.  ‡12 innings.  §13 innings.  x15 innings.

**Catcher Lance Parrish (above) slugged 28 homers and drove in 98 runs while relief ace Willie Hernandez enjoyed his second straight successful season with 31 saves.**

was traded to San Francisco after the season) with an ERA over 3.85.

Jack Morris paced the staff with a 16-11 record and a 3.33 ERA. The righthander also tallied 13 complete games, four shutouts and 191 strikeouts in 257 innings.

Lefthander Frank Tanana, a Detroit native, came home in a trade with Texas and led the club with 10 victories from the day of the deal in mid-June. Righthander Dan Petry went 15-13 with a 3.36 ERA, while Terrell won 15 of 25 decisions.

Rookie Randy O'Neal (5-5, 3.24 ERA) showed promise for the future while working as both a starter and long reliever.

Willie Hernandez won't soon forget the 1985 season. Despite winning the Cy Young Award and Most Valuable Player honors the year before, when Hernandez was successful in 32 of 33 save situations, he often was booed at home.

"I got sick and tired" of the heckling, said Hernandez, who finished 8-10 with a 2.70 ERA and 31 saves.

Reliever Aurelio Lopez struggled even more, going 3-7 with five saves.

It was a frustrating year for all of the players, even the ones who weren't being booed. But no one wanted to dwell on it.

"Nobody likes to admit they didn't do the job," Brookens said, "but let's face it, we didn't. The best thing you can do with such a season is go home and forget about it."

**Shortstop Cal Ripken continued his assault on American League pitching, batting .282 with 26 homers and 110 RBIs.**

# Pitching Woes Doom Orioles

**By JIM HENNEMAN**

If somebody had suggested at the start of the 1985 season that Baltimore would set an Orioles record for runs scored, chances are that person also would have predicted the team's second World Series appearance in three years.

Alas, sound logic and baseball often don't mix. The team did score more runs than any Orioles club since the franchise was moved from St. Louis in 1954, but it ended up in a strange place—fourth in the American League East, 16 games out of first. It was, to put it mildly, the team's most disappointing finish in recent memory.

After a winter of heavy spending that saw them commit almost $12 million to sign free agents Fred Lynn, Lee Lacy and Don Aase, the Orioles expected a quick recovery from the slump that saw them go from world champions in 1983 to fifth in the division the next season. While they were shattering offensive records, however, some pitching marks also were established—but the wrong kind. For every significant batting record that was set, the Orioles duplicated it in reverse.

Baltimore baserunners scored 818 runs, but Baltimore pitchers allowed 764, just 10 shy of the Orioles' all-time high. The club hit 214 home runs, the A.L. high in 1985 as well as an Orioles record, but gave up 160 (also an Orioles record). And the team earned-run average of 4.38 was the highest in the franchise's 32-year Baltimore history.

"Slumps are part of the game," General Manager Hank Peters said after the season, "and you expect one or two individuals to have them every year. But never have I seen one that involved just about the entire pitching staff."

The pitching problems started the previous winter when lefthander Mike Flanagan suffered a ruptured Achilles tendon while playing in a charity basketball game. The injury sidelined him for more than half of the season, and when he did return, he went 4-5 with a 5.13 ERA.

More surprising was the breakdown of Mike Boddicker, the league's only 20-game winner in 1984. The righthander won six of his first seven decisions but then apparently victimized himself by picking up a habit that tipped off some of his pitches. He finished with a 12-17 record and a 4.07 ERA.

The most consistent of the starting

**Mike Boddicker, the O's 1984 ace, slumped to a 12-17 record and 4.07 earned-run average.**

pitchers was rookie Ken Dixon (8-4, 3.67 ERA), but he was in the rotation only half of the time. Scott McGregor (14-14), Dennis Martinez (13-11) and Storm Davis (10-8) all avoided losing records, but their ERAs (4.81, 5.15 and 4.53, respectively) were more indicative of their lack of effectiveness.

The bullpen wasn't much better. Aase (10-6) recovered from a horrible start to lead the club with just 14 saves. Rookie Nate Snell was brilliant as a long reliever through the first half of the schedule, but he missed a month after suffering a broken rib and finished 3-2 with a 2.69 ERA and five saves. And both Sammy Stewart (3.61 ERA, nine saves) and Tippy Martinez (5.40, four saves) were erratic.

Poor pitching undoubtedly cost Joe Altobelli his job as manager. By June 12, the Orioles were in fourth place with a 29-26

## SCORES OF BALTIMORE ORIOLES' 1985 GAMES

| APRIL | | | Winner | Loser |
|---|---|---|---|---|
| 8—Texas | W | 4-2 | Aase | Rozema |
| 10—Texas | W | 7-1 | Boddicker | Mason |
| 12—Toronto | W | 7-2 | McGregor | Key |
| 13—Toronto | W | 8-7 | T. Martinez | Caudill |
| 14—Toronto | L | 3-5 | Alexander | Boddicker |
| 16—At Cleve. | L | 3-6 | Ruhle | D. Martinez |
| 17—At Cleve. | W | 6-3 | Stewart | Roman |
| 18—At Cleve. | L | 5-11 | Von Ohlen | Snell |
| 19—At Toronto | L | 5-6 | Alexander | Stewart |
| 20—At Toronto | L | 2-3 | Musselman | T. Martinez |
| 21—At Toronto | W | 3-2 | D. Martinez | Key |
| 22—At Texas | L | 1-6 | Hough | McGregor |
| 23—At Texas | W | 11-1 | Davis | Tanana |
| 24—At Texas | W | 2-1 | Boddicker | Rozema |
| 25—Cleveland | W | 7-1 | Dixon | Roman |
| 26—Cleveland | W | 6-3 | D. Martinez | Ruhle |
| 27—Cleveland | L | 4-10 | Schulze | McGregor |
| 28—Cleveland | W | 8-7 | Aase | Waddell |
| 30—Chicago | W | 9-7 | Boddicker | Bannister |
| Won 12, Lost 7 | | | | |

| MAY | | | | |
|---|---|---|---|---|
| 1—Chicago | W | 3-1 | Dixon | Burns |
| 3—At Minn. | W | 8-7 | Aase | Wardle |
| 4—At Minn. | L | 6-8 | Schrom | D. Martinez |
| 5—At Minn. | W | 10-5 | Boddicker | Butcher |
| 7—At Kan. C. | W | 4-2 | Dixon | Saberhagen |
| 8—At Kan. C. | L | 8-9 | LaCoss | McGregor |
| 10—Minnesota | W | 6-5 | Aase | Davis |
| 11—Minnesota | W | 4-2 | Boddicker | Davis |
| 12—Minnesota | L | 3-7 | Viola | Dixon |
| 13—Kan. City | L | 2-5 | Jackson | Davis |
| 14—Kan. City | L | 3-5 | Gubicza | McGregor |
| 15—At Chicago | L | 2-5 | Seaver | Aase |
| 16—At Chicago | W | 3-1* | Boddicker | Bannister |
| 17—At Seattle | W | 11-3 | Dixon | Young |
| 18—At Seattle | L | 7-8 | Nunez | T. Martinez |
| 19—At Seattle | W | 2-1 | D. Martinez | Moore |
| 21—At Oak. | L | 2-3† | Howell | Boddicker |
| 22—At Oak. | W | 3-0 | McGregor | Sutton |
| 23—At Oak. | L | 2-4 | Birtsas | Dixon |
| 24—At Calif. | W | 4-3 | Davis | Cliburn |
| 25—At Calif. | L | 3-5 | Romanick | D. Martinez |
| 26—At Calif. | L | 4-10 | Clements | Boddicker |
| 27—At Calif. | W | 6-4 | McGregor | John |
| 29—Seattle | L | 4-5‡ | Best | Aase |
| 30—Seattle | W | 8-2 | Davis | Barojas |
| 31—Oakland | W | 9-2 | D. Martinez | Krueger |
| Won 14, Lost 12 | | | | |

| JUNE | | | | |
|---|---|---|---|---|
| 1—Oakland | L | 1-3 | Sutton | Boddicker |
| 2—Oakland | W | 10-1 | McGregor | Warren |
| 3—California | W | 7-5 | Stewart | Moore |
| 4—California | L | 5-6§ | Cliburn | Dixon |
| 5—California | W | 4-0 | D. Martinez | McCaskill |
| 7—Boston | L | 4-8 | Nipper | Boddicker |
| 8—Boston | L | 1-2 | Kison | McGregor |
| 9—Boston | L | 0-12 | Boyd | Davis |
| 10—At Detroit | L | 7-8‡ | Lopez | Stewart |
| 12—At Detroit | L | 2-6 | Petry | Boddicker |
| 13—Milwaukee | W | 8-3 | McGregor | Burris |
| 14—Milwaukee | W | 9-3 | Davis | Vuckovich |
| 15—Milwaukee | W | 7-5 | Snell | Gibson |
| 16—Milwaukee | W | 9-1 | Boddicker | Darwin |
| 17—New York | L | 0-10 | Guidry | McGregor |
| 18—New York | L | 4-6 | Cowley | Davis |
| 19—New York | L | 0-10 | Whitson | D. Martinez |
| 21—At Milw. | L | 10-13 | Cocanower | Stewart |
| 22—At Milw. | W | 3-2 | McGregor | Darwin |
| 23—At Milw. | W | 6-3 | Snell | Fingers |
| 24—At N.Y. | L | 4-5 | Cowley | D. Martinez |
| 25—At N.Y. | L | 4-7 | Whitson | Boddicker |
| 26—At N.Y. | L | 3-4 | Righetti | Aase |
| 28—At Boston | L | 1-6 | Hurst | Davis |
| 29—At Boston | W | 16-4 | D. Martinez | Boyd |
| 30—At Boston | W | 3-0 | Boddicker | Ojeda |
| Won 11, Lost 15 | | | | |

| JULY | | | | |
|---|---|---|---|---|
| 1—Detroit | L | 1-7 | O'Neal | McGregor |
| 2—Detroit | W | 5-4† | Aase | Hernandez |
| 3—Detroit | L | 3-4† | Petry | Stewart |
| 4—At Kan. C. | W | 5-3 | D. Martinez | Black |
| 5—At Kan. C. | W | 6-3 | Boddicker | Gubicza |
| 6—At Kan. C. | W | 8-3 | McGregor | Jackson |
| 7—At Kan. C. | L | 4-7† | Leibrandt | Davis |
| 8—Minnesota | L | 4-7† | Davis | Aase |
| 9—Minnesota | W | 11-6 | Snell | Schrom |
| 10—Minnesota | L | 1-2 | Viola | Boddicker |
| 11—Chicago | W | 7-6 | Stewart | Stanton |
| 12—Chicago | W | 10-3 | Dixon | Nelson |

| JULY | | | Winner | Loser |
|---|---|---|---|---|
| 13—Chicago | L | 8-10 | Burns | D. Martinez |
| 14—Chicago | L | 3-5 | Seaver | Boddicker |
| 18—Kan. City | W | 8-3 | McGregor | Saberhagen |
| 19—Kan. City | L | 3-10 | Leibrandt | Boddicker |
| 20—Kan. City | L | 5-7 | Jackson | Flanagan |
| 21—Kan. City | W | 6-4 | T. Martinez | Black |
| 22—At Minn. | L | 4-5 | Smithson | Davis |
| 23—At Minn. | L | 2-5 | Butcher | McGregor |
| 24—At Minn. | W | 4-2 | Boddicker | Schrom |
| 25—At Chicago | W | 5-1 | Flanagan | Bannister |
| 26—At Chicago | L | 8-9 | Agosto | Aase |
| 27—At Chicago | W | 9-1 | Davis | Nelson |
| 28—At Chicago | W | 6-1 | McGregor | Burns |
| 29—Toronto | L | 3-4† | Henke | Boddicker |
| 30—Toronto | W | 4-3† | Aase | Lavelle |
| 31—Toronto | L | 3-5 | Henke | D. Martinez |
| Won 14, Lost 14 | | | | |

| AUGUST | | | | |
|---|---|---|---|---|
| 1—Toronto | L | 3-9 | Filer | Davis |
| 2—At Cleve. | W | 8-6 | Stewart | Thompson |
| 3—At Cleve. | L | 4-10 | Wardle | Boddicker |
| 4—At Cleve. | W | 5-4 | D. Martinez | Thompson |
| 8—At Toronto | L | 2-7 | Alexander | McGregor |
| 8—At Toronto | L | 4-7 | Filer | Boddicker |
| 9—At Texas | L | 2-5 | Hough | Flanagan |
| 10—At Texas | W | 9-8 | Davis | Welsh |
| 11—At Texas | W | 9-4 | Stewart | Mason |
| 12—Cleveland | L | 5-8 | Wardle | McGregor |
| 13—Cleveland | W | 8-4 | Aase | Ruhle |
| 14—Cleveland | W | 8-4 | Flanagan | Clark |
| 15—Texas | W | 9-1 | Davis | Welsh |
| 16—Texas | W | 4-2 | D. Martinez | Russell |
| 17—Texas | W | 9-2 | McGregor | Hooton |
| 19—Texas | W | 9-2 | Dixon | Mason |
| 20—At Seattle | L | 3-4 | Moore | Snell |
| 21—At Seattle | W | 11-8 | D. Martinez | Beattle |
| 22—At Seattle | L | 0-4 | Young | McGregor |
| 23—At Oak. | W | 7-2 | Boddicker | Howell |
| 24—At Oak. | W | 4-3‡ | Aase | Atherton |
| 25—At Oak. | L | 4-10 | Birtsas | Flanagan |
| 26—At Calif. | W | 17-3 | D. Martinez | Candelaria |
| 27—At Calif. | L | 3-7 | Witt | McGregor |
| 29—Seattle | W | 7-0 | Boddicker | Swift |
| 30—Seattle | W | 6-0 | Davis | Langston |
| 31—Seattle | L | 0-6 | Moore | Flanagan |
| Won 16, Lost 11 | | | | |

| SEPTEMBER | | | | |
|---|---|---|---|---|
| 1—Seattle | L | 2-10 | Young | D. Martinez |
| 2—Oakland | W | 12-4 | McGregor | John |
| 3—Oakland | L | 2-3 | Rijo | Boddicker |
| 4—Oakland | W | 6-1 | Davis | Sutton |
| 6—California | W | 6-2 | D. Martinez | Romanick |
| 7—California | W | 4-3 | Aase | Moore |
| 8—California | L | 4-7‡ | Moore | T. Martinez |
| 10—At Boston | W | 7-5 | Davis | Hurst |
| 10—At Boston | L | 3-5 | Boyd | Boddicker |
| 11—At Boston | L | 1-4 | Ojeda | D. Martinez |
| 12—At Boston | W | 3-1 | Dixon | Nipper |
| 13—At Detroit | W | 6-4 | McGregor | Berenguer |
| 14—At Detroit | L | 3-10 | Tanana | Boddicker |
| 14—At Detroit | W | 5-4 | Flanagan | Mahler |
| 15—At Detroit | L | 1-4 | Hernandez | Stewart |
| 16—At Detroit | W | 14-7 | T. Martinez | Cary |
| 17—Milwaukee | W | 6-0 | Dixon | Higuera |
| 18—Milwaukee | W | 4-2 | McGregor | Leary |
| 19—Milwaukee | L | 2-5 | Wegman | Boddicker |
| 20—New York | W | 4-2 | Flanagan | Bordi |
| 21—New York | L | 2-5 | Cowley | Davis |
| 22—New York | L | 4-5 | Guidry | Dixon |
| 24—At Milw. | L | 6-10 | Wegman | McGregor |
| 25—At Milw. | L | 0-3 | Cocanower | Flanagan |
| 26—At Milw. | W | 9-1 | D. Martinez | Haas |
| 28—At N.Y. | L | 5-6 | Guidry | Stewart |
| 29—At N.Y. | L | 0-4 | Cowley | McGregor |
| 29—At N.Y. | L | 2-9 | Bordi | Havens |
| 30—At N.Y. | L | 4-5 | Allen | Aase |
| Won 13, Lost 16 | | | | |

| OCTOBER | | | | |
|---|---|---|---|---|
| 1—Boston | L | 3-10 | Hurst | D. Martinez |
| 3—Boston | L | 2-6 | Ojeda | Stewart |
| 3—Boston | W | 9-8 | Habyan | Crawford |
| 4—Detroit | W | 5-2 | McGregor | Petry |
| 5—Detroit | W | 7-6 | Aase | Scherrer |
| 6—Detroit | L | 3-11 | Tanana | D. Martinez |
| Won 3, Lost 3 | | | | |

*6 innings.　†10 innings.　‡11 innings.　§15 innings.

**Mike Young came on strong and produced 28 homers and 81 RBIs.**

record, and in 22 of those losses their opponents had scored four or more runs. In an effort to turn the season around, the Orioles rehired Earl Weaver, Altobelli's predecessor, but the change had no effect. The Orioles went 53-52 under Weaver, who was as mystified as anybody by the team's collapse.

"For a while it looked like we got it together, getting 12 games over .500 (79-67), but then everything just fell apart," said Weaver, who managed the Orioles to six division titles in a 14½-year tenure that ended with his retirement after the '82 season.

The Orioles finished with a .516 winning percentage, their lowest since 1967. The fact that their 83-78 record gave them their 18th straight winning season—the second-longest streak in major league history behind the Yankees' 39 successive winning campaigns from 1926-64—was of little consolation.

"I still feel this team, the way it is, is capable of winning it all," said Weaver, who agreed to return for another year.

The way the Orioles bruised the ball in 1985 had to encourage Weaver. Led by first baseman Eddie Murray and shortstop Cal Ripken, the Orioles had the most brutal offense in the league.

Murray paced the Orioles with a .297 average, 37 doubles, 31 homers and 124 runs batted in. The switch-hitter also scored 111 runs, just five fewer than Ripken, who batted .282 with 26 homers and 110 RBIs.

Even though nagging back and ankle injuries limited Lynn to 124 games, the center fielder still gave the Orioles the potent force they needed behind Murray in the lineup. Lynn batted .263 with 23 homers and 68 RBIs. And right fielder Lacy, who missed the first five weeks with a fractured thumb, gave Baltimore a strong No. 2 hitter, batting .293 with nine homers.

Second baseman Alan Wiggins, obtained in a June trade with San Diego, hit .285 and stole 30 bases as he provided some much-needed speed in the leadoff spot.

The biggest surprise of the year was Floyd Rayford, who entered the regular lineup at midseason, playing mostly at third base and also backing up catcher Rick Dempsey. Rayford hit .306 with 18 homers in only 359 at-bats to shed his label as a utilityman.

Dempsey, though slowed occasionally by a shoulder injury, had career highs in homers (12) and RBIs (52) while hitting a respectable .254. Baltimore's other big offensive contributors included left fielder-designated hitter Mike Young (.273, 28 homers, 81 RBIs), rookie DH Larry Sheets (.262, 17 homers, 50 RBIs in 328 at-bats) and backup outfielder John Shelby (.283).

The Orioles' only offensive slackers were such part-timers as Jim Dwyer (.249), Wayne Gross (.235), Fritz Connally (.232), Gary Roenicke (.218) and Rich Dauer (.202).

But the bottom line on the season was the fact that, for the first time in years, the Orioles' pitching didn't hold up.

"We have good people, some quality arms, although it is not reflected in the statistics," Peters said. "I can't explain what happened this year any more than anyone else can, except we didn't have anybody who escaped (the slump). It affected everybody on the staff, some worse than others. But we're not talking about physical problems or age, so . . . there's no reason we can't correct our problems."

**Third baseman Wade Boggs captured his second batting title and led the
American League with 240 hits and a .450 on-base percentage.**

# Red Sox Struggle to .500 Mark

**By JOE GIULIOTTI**

When you lose a potential 20-game winner (Roger Clemens) to shoulder surgery, have the major leagues' home run and RBI king (Tony Armas) all but crippled by an early-season injury and have a bullpen (collective effort) that's unable to provide consistent relief, winning probably will be difficult.

And it was for the Boston Red Sox, who thought they had a chance at contending for the American League East title in 1985 but struggled through a mediocre season. The Red Sox finished fifth with an 81-81 record, 18½ games behind Toronto.

There were several other factors that made John McNamara's first year as Red Sox manager one he'd like to forget. Left fielder Jim Rice played hurt most of the season and wound up having knee surgery. Bullpen stopper Bob Stanley wasn't his usual effective self because of a growth on the index finger of his pitching hand that required surgery. And right fielder Dwight Evans didn't start hitting until the Red Sox were far out of contention.

Despite the team's failure to reach its own lofty goals, there were some positive notes.

Third baseman Wade Boggs had another outstanding season, winning his second batting title in three years with his .368 average. He also led the league in hits (240) and on-base percentage (.450) while drawing 96 walks, slapping 42 doubles, scoring 107 runs and tallying 78 runs batted in.

Also reaching the 200-hit level was first baseman Bill Buckner, who batted .299 with 46 doubles, 16 homers and team-leading totals in RBIs (110) and stolen bases (18).

Steve Crawford wound up as the all-purpose man of the pitching staff, being used for both long and short relief as well as one start. The righthander went 6-5 with a 3.76 earned-run average and led the team with 12 saves.

After batting .189 and losing his starting shortstop job to Jackie Gutierrez in 1984, Glenn Hoffman made a comeback. He batted .276, made only 11 errors and put Gutierrez back on the bench. Gutierrez, meanwhile, hit .218 and had only 21 RBIs to go with his 23 errors.

Rich Gedman, who was as good defensively as any catcher in the league, also gave the fans something to cheer about. In addition to having more assists (78) than any other A.L. catcher, Gedman hit .295 with 18 homers and 80 RBIs.

But overall, 1985 was a nightmare. The injuries that haunted the team began cropping up in spring training when Al Nipper, one of the three young pitchers whom McNamara was counting on, was hospitalized with a blood disorder. That was just the first of several injuries for Nipper, who went 9-12 with a 4.06 ERA when he wasn't recuperating.

Nipper, Clemens and Dennis (Oil Can) Boyd all had shown in '84 that they were ready to be big winners. But only Boyd lasted the entire year, and his season nosedived after the All-Star break.

Boyd was 11-7 with a 3.15 ERA and 11 complete games by midseason but was not selected to the All-Star team. Oil Can became depressed, lost his confidence and went from July 14 to September 5 (nine starts) before winning another game. Still, he had the best numbers on the team —15-13, 3.70 ERA, 13 complete games, three shutouts and 272⅓ innings pitched.

Clemens was 6-4 at the end of May when he began having shoulder problems. He made only five more starts and eventually underwent season-ending arthroscopic surgery.

Armas, who led the major leagues with 43 homers and 123 RBIs in '84, was on a similar pace when he suffered a pulled leg muscle June 1. The center fielder returned June 16 and promptly reinjured the muscle, which just about ended his season. Even though he returned to full-time duty in mid-August, he never fully recovered and finished with 23 homers and 64 RBIs. Rookie Steve Lyons (.264, 30 RBIs) was an able replacement, but Armas' production was sorely missed.

Ironically, McNamara had pinpointed the reason for his team's eventual collapse long before it happened.

"It's all going to come down to pitching," he had said when the season began.

And so it did. While the offense was cranking out 800 runs (third in the league) and batting an A.L.-best .282, the pitchers were fashioning a 4.06 ERA. The injuries hurt, but the weakest link was the bullpen, which posted only 29 saves (13th in the league).

Not surprisingly, Boston's one brief moment of glory was sparked by pitching excellence. The Red Sox won 17 of 19 games from May 27 to June 17 to move from sixth place, 10 games out, to second, 2½

## SCORES OF BOSTON RED SOX' 1985 GAMES

### APRIL

| Date | | Score | Winner | Loser |
|---|---|---|---|---|
| 8—New York | W | 9-2 | Boyd | Niekro |
| 10—New York | W | 14-5 | Hurst | Whitson |
| 11—New York | W | 6-4 | Clemens | Rasmussen |
| 13—Chicago | W | 7-2 | Boyd | Bannister |
| 14—Chicago | L | 6-11 | Burns | Crawford |
| 15—Chicago | L | 5-6‡ | Jones | Stanley |
| 16—At Kan. C. | L | 0-2 | Jackson | Clemens |
| 17—At Kan. C. | L | 1-6 | Leibrandt | Nipper |
| 18—At Kan. C. | W | 4-3y | Ojeda | Jones |
| 19—At Chicago | L | 1-8 | Burns | Trujillo |
| 20—At Chicago | W | 12-8 | Crawford | Nelson |
| 21—At Chicago | L | 2-7 | Lollar | Clemens |
| 23—At N.Y. | W | 5-4‡ | Ojeda | Righetti |
| 24—At N.Y. | W | 7-6 | Crawford | Guidry |
| 25—At N.Y. | L | 1-5 | Niekro | Hurst |
| 26—Kan. City | W | 5-2 | Clemens | Gubicza |
| 27—Kan. City | L | 4-5 | Quisenberry | Stanley |
| 28—Kan. City | L | 2-5 | Leibrandt | Boyd |
| 29—At Calif. | L | 6-7 | Clemens | Crawford |
| 30—At Calif. | L | 2-3z | Cliburn | Ojeda |

**Won 9, Lost 11**

### MAY

| Date | | Score | Winner | Loser |
|---|---|---|---|---|
| 1—At Seattle | L | 0-7 | Beattie | Clemens |
| 2—At Seattle | W | 2-1 | Nipper | Moore |
| 3—At Oak. | W | 10-0 | Boyd | Warren |
| 4—At Oak. | W | 5-4 | Crawford | Krueger |
| 5—At Oak. | L | 3-6 | Codiroli | Hurst |
| 7—California | W | 6-4 | Clemens | McCaskill |
| 8—California | W | 6-1 | Boyd | Slaton |
| 10—Oakland | W | 5-4† | Clear | Howell |
| 11—Oakland | L | 1-12 | Krueger | Hurst |
| 12—Oakland | L | 3-5 | Sutton | Clemens |
| 14—Seattle | L | 0-5 | Moore | Boyd |
| 15—Seattle | L | 1-7 | Langston | Nipper |
| 17—At Cleve. | W | 5-0 | Clemens | Blyleven |
| 18—At Cleve. | L | 1-4 | Heaton | Hurst |
| 19—At Cleve. | L | 1-2 | Thompson | Boyd |
| 20—At Minn. | L | 2-5 | Butcher | Nipper |
| 21—At Minn. | W | 9-1 | Kison | Schrom |
| 22—At Minn. | W | 4-3 | Clemens | Viola |
| 23—At Texas | L | 6-7 | Rozema | Clear |
| 24—At Texas | L | 0-1 | Hough | Boyd |
| 25—At Texas | L | 3-10 | Mason | Nipper |
| 26—At Texas | L | 3-5 | Tanana | Kison |
| 27—Minnesota | W | 9-2 | Clemens | Schrom |
| 29—Minnesota | W | 7-0 | Boyd | Viola |
| 30—Minnesota | W | 8-7‡ | Stanley | Davis |
| 31—Texas | L | 1-3 | Mason | Nipper |

**Won 12, Lost 14**

### JUNE

| Date | | Score | Winner | Loser |
|---|---|---|---|---|
| 1—Texas | W | 6-0 | Kison | Tanana |
| 2—Texas | W | 12-3 | Hurst | Rozema |
| 3—Cleveland | W | 6-5 | Boyd | Schulze |
| 4—Cleveland | W | 5-0 | Ojeda | Creel |
| 7—At Balt. | W | 8-4 | Nipper | Boddicker |
| 8—At Balt. | W | 2-1 | Kison | McGregor |
| 9—At Balt. | W | 12-0 | Boyd | Davis |
| 10—Milwaukee | W | 4-2 | Ojeda | Higuera |
| 11—Milwaukee | L | 3-5 | Darwin | Hurst |
| 12—Milwaukee | W | 7-2 | Nipper | Haas |
| 13—Toronto | W | 8-7 | Trujillo | Lavelle |
| 14—Toronto | W | 4-1 | Boyd | Clancy |
| 15—Toronto | W | 7-5 | Stanley | Acker |
| 16—Toronto | W | 7-6 | Crawford | Lavelle |
| 17—At Detroit | W | 3-2 | Nipper | Hernandez |
| 18—At Detroit | L | 8-9 | Berenguer | Hurst |
| 19—At Detroit | L | 3-9 | Terrell | Boyd |
| 20—At Toronto | L | 5-6 | Acker | Stanley |
| 21—At Toronto | L | 2-7 | Key | Hurst |
| 22—At Toronto | W | 5-3 | Stanley | Acker |
| 23—At Toronto | L | 1-8 | Stieb | Kison |
| 24—Detroit | W | 9-2 | Boyd | Terrell |
| 25—Detroit | L | 0-3 | Morris | Ojeda |
| 26—Detroit | L | 0-3 | O'Neal | Nipper |
| 28—Baltimore | W | 6-1 | Hurst | Davis |
| 29—Baltimore | L | 4-16 | D. Martinez | Boyd |
| 30—Baltimore | L | 0-3 | Boddicker | Ojeda |

**Won 17, Lost 10**

### JULY

| Date | | Score | Winner | Loser |
|---|---|---|---|---|
| 1—At Milw. | L | 1-5 | Vuckovich | Trujillo |
| 2—At Milw. | L | 3-4† | Fingers | Stanley |
| 3—At Milw. | W | 9-0 | Hurst | Darwin |
| 4—At Calif. | L | 4-5 | Clemens | Boyd |
| 5—At Calif. | L | 4-13 | Romanick | Ojeda |
| 6—At Calif. | W | 7-5 | Stanley | Cliburn |
| 7—At Calif. | L | 3-8 | McCaskill | Dorsey |
| 8—At Oak. | W | 2-1 | Hurst | Codiroli |
| 9—At Oak. | W | 6-3 | Boyd | Ontiveros |
| 10—At Oak. | L | 4-5 | Krueger | Ojeda |
| 11—At Seattle | W | 7-1 | Nipper | Swift |
| 12—At Seattle | W | 5-4 | Trujillo | Nunez |
| 13—At Seattle | L | 5-6 | Snyder | Stanley |
| 14—At Seattle | W | 6-2 | Boyd | Wills |
| 18—California | W | 10-1 | Hurst | McCaskill |
| 19—California | L | 2-3 | Romanick | Boyd |
| 20—California | L | 3-5 | Witt | Ojeda |
| 21—California | W | 8-4 | Nipper | Lugo |
| 22—Oakland | W | 6-4 | Lollar | Codiroli |
| 23—Oakland | W | 3-2 | Hurst | Langford |
| 24—Oakland | W | 6-5 | Stanley | Howell |
| 25—Seattle | W | 5-3 | Ojeda | Swift |
| 26—Seattle | W | 6-2 | Nipper | Beattie |
| 27—Seattle | L | 3-10 | Thomas | Lollar |
| 28—Seattle | L | 2-7 | Moore | Hurst |
| 30—Chicago | L | 5-7† | Seaver | Boyd |
| 31—Chicago | T | 1-1* | ...... | ...... |

**Won 14, Lost 12**

### AUGUST

| Date | | Score | Winner | Loser |
|---|---|---|---|---|
| 1—Chicago | L | 2-7 | Nelson | Nipper |
| 1—Chicago | W | 4-3 | Crawford | Agosto |
| 2—At Kan. C. | L | 3-4† | Quisenberry | Clear |
| 3—At Kan. C. | W | 5-4 | Clemens | Gubicza |
| 4—At Kan. C. | W | 6-5§ | Stanley | LaCoss |
| 8—At Chicago | L | 6-7 | Wehrmeister | Kison |
| 8—At Chicago | W | 6-1 | Lollar | Nelson |
| 9—New York | L | 6-10 | Bordi | Hurst |
| 10—New York | L | 3-7 | Cowley | Boyd |
| 11—New York | L | 3-5 | Guidry | Clemens |
| 12—Kan. City | L | 2-3 | Gubicza | Nipper |
| 13—Kan. City | L | 3-6 | Saberhagen | Ojeda |
| 14—Kan. City | W | 16-3 | Hurst | Black |
| 16—At N.Y. | L | 4-5† | Righetti | Crawford |
| 17—At N.Y. | L | 1-3 | Guidry | Nipper |
| 18—At N.Y. | L | 2-4 | Righetti | Lollar |
| 19—At N.Y. | L | 5-6 | Bystrom | Clear |
| 20—Texas | L | 1-3 | Hough | Ojeda |
| 21—Texas | L | 3-5 | Russell | Boyd |
| 22—Texas | W | 8-4 | Trujillo | Noles |
| 23—Minnesota | L | 2-5 | Viola | Lollar |
| 24—Minnesota | L | 0-1 | Smithson | Hurst |
| 26—At Chicago | L | 6-7† | James | Stanley |
| 27—At Cleve. | L | 2-6 | Wardle | Trujillo |
| 28—At Cleve. | L | 4-7 | Easterly | Lollar |
| 29—At Cleve. | W | 17-2 | Hurst | Romero |
| 30—At Minn. | W | 7-3 | Ojeda | Butcher |
| 31—At Minn. | L | 5-6 | Blyleven | Crawford |
| 31—At Minn. | L | 4-5 | Portugal | Nipper |

**Won 8, Lost 21**

### SEPTEMBER

| Date | | Score | Winner | Loser |
|---|---|---|---|---|
| 1—At Minn. | W | 10-3 | Trujillo | Viola |
| 2—At Texas | W | 11-2 | Lollar | Stewart |
| 3—At Texas | W | 6-4 | Hurst | Hough |
| 5—Cleveland | W | 13-6 | Boyd | Heaton |
| 5—Cleveland | L | 5-9 | Easterly | Ojeda |
| 7—Cleveland | W | 11-9 | Kison | Reed |
| 7—Cleveland | W | 7-4 | Nipper | Wardle |
| 8—Cleveland | W | 8-1 | Lollar | Heaton |
| 10—Baltimore | L | 5-7 | Davis | Hurst |
| 10—Baltimore | W | 5-3 | Boyd | Boddicker |
| 11—Baltimore | W | 4-1 | Ojeda | D. Martinez |
| 12—Baltimore | L | 1-3 | Dixon | Nipper |
| 13—At Milw. | L | 3-6 | Leary | Lollar |
| 14—At Milw. | W | 10-8‡ | Kison | Darwin |
| 15—At Milw. | W | 4-2 | Sellers | Cocanower |
| 16—At Milw. | L | 3-5 | McClure | Ojeda |
| 17—Toronto | W | 6-5 | Boyd | Stieb |
| 18—Toronto | W | 13-1 | Nipper | Clancy |
| 20—Detroit | L | 2-6 | Morris | Hurst |
| 21—Detroit | W | 7-6 | Lollar | Terrell |
| 22—Detroit | W | 6-2 | Boyd | Petry |
| 23—Detroit | L | 1-2 | Berenguer | Ojeda |
| 24—At Toronto | L | 2-6 | Lamp | Nipper |
| 25—At Toronto | W | 4-2x | Crawford | Cerutti |
| 26—At Toronto | W | 4-1 | Sellers | Alexander |
| 27—At Detroit | L | 1-5 | Terrell | Boyd |
| 28—At Detroit | L | 2-0† | Ojeda | Hernandez |
| 29—At Detroit | W | 8-4 | Woodward | Berenguer |

**Won 19, Lost 9**

### OCTOBER

| Date | | Score | Winner | Loser |
|---|---|---|---|---|
| 1—At Balt. | W | 10-3 | Hurst | D. Martinez |
| 3—At Balt. | W | 6-2 | Ojeda | Stewart |
| 3—At Balt. | L | 8-9 | Habyan | Crawford |
| 4—Milwaukee | L | 7-8§ | Lesley | Trujillo |
| 5—Milwaukee | L | 3-5 | Cocanower | Boyd |
| 6—Milwaukee | L | 6-9 | Darwin | Hurst |

**Won 2, Lost 4**

*7 innings.  †10 innings.  ‡11 innings.  §12 innings.  x13 innings.  y14 innings.  z15 innings.

**Veteran first baseman Bill Buckner enjoyed one of his finest offensive seasons, hitting .299 with 110 RBIs.**

games behind Toronto. The pitching staff compiled a 2.55 ERA during that stretch.

But the next day a four-run lead was blown in Detroit, and two days after that another four-run lead went down the drain in Toronto. The skid proceeded from there.

Boston's two lefthanded starters, Bruce Hurst and Bob Ojeda, contributed little. Hurst broke the Red Sox mark for strikeouts by a lefthander (189), but he finished 11-13 with a 4.51 ERA. Ojeda (9-11, 4.00) was effective as neither a reliever nor a starter. He went 12 starts between June 10 and August 30 with only one victory. And injuries limited Bruce Kison to 92 innings.

The bullpen problems were exemplified by Stanley, who had a 2.87 ERA but saved only 10 games, his lowest total since 1981. But despite his injured finger, Stanley did not make excuses.

"I'm supposed to be the big man in the bullpen," he said, "and I didn't do the job."

Rice, whom McNamara had named team captain (Carl Yastrzemski was, for one year, the only other captain in Red Sox history), also blamed himself for the team's low finish.

"I had too many guys in scoring position all year and didn't capitalize," he said. "If I had, the team may have done better."

Rice's statistics—.291, 27 homers, 103 RBIs—show that a bad season for him still is outstanding by most other players' standards. Bearing in mind that Armas was injured, the only member of Boston's 300-RBI outfield from 1984 who really suffered a drop-off was Evans. The Gold Glove right fielder fell from .295, 32 homers and 104 RBIs in 1984 to .263, 29 homers and 78 RBIs. Evans did lead the league in walks (114), however, and scored 110 runs.

Designated hitter Mike Easler (.262, 16 homers, 74 RBIs) and second baseman Marty Barrett (.266) also saw their production plummet.

"Nothing can help make up for this year," Rice said. "It's been the worst of my professional career."

Paul Molitor made a triumphant return after surgery, hitting .297, scoring 93 runs and stealing 21 bases.

# Bamberger Can't Work Magic

By TOM FLAHERTY

Bambi was back, but the Brewers weren't.

The last time George Bamberger had been hired as Milwaukee's manager, he took over a team that had finished sixth in 1977 and promptly guided it to third place as the Brewers posted their first winning record ever. Two more first-division finishes followed, and even though Bamberger retired just before the end of the 1980 season, he had molded the Brewers into a strong club that would play in the 1982 World Series.

In 1985, there was no magic. Upon returning for his second stint as the Brewers' skipper, Bamberger took over a team that had finished last in the American League East in 1984 and moved it up one rung to sixth. The Brewers never rose above fifth place after May 1, and they settled into sixth for good on June 8.

Still, Bamberger figured, progress is progress.

"A lot of people picked us to finish last," he said, emphasizing the positive.

He had emphasized the positive in the spring, too.

Before the season opened, he predicted that the Brewers would hit 150 home runs. They hit 101, the lowest total in the league.

He said the bullpen would be one of the team's strengths. It turned out to be one of the biggest weaknesses. Although Rollie Fingers finished with 17 saves, he had a 5.04 earned-run average and struggled most of the year. The No. 2 reliever, Bob Gibson, had 11 saves but a 3.90 ERA.

He said the overall pitching would be strong. But the Brewers' staff compiled a 4.39 ERA, threw only five shutouts and allowed more homers (175) than any team in the league.

Danny Darwin, who was obtained from Texas during the winter, had 11 complete games and a 3.80 ERA but still lost a club-record 10 straight games and finished with an 8-18 record. Moose Haas (3.84 ERA) won only one game after June 29 and finished 8-8. Ray Burris (9-13, 4.81) and Jaime Cocanower (6-8, 4.33) fared even worse.

All in all, the Brewers looked a lot like the 1984 team that lost 94 games, tops in the league. The club's 71-90 record in 1985 was only a slight improvement, and it still left the Brewers 28 games out of first.

Although they hit a respectable .263 as a team, the lack of power again hurt them.

Shortstop Ernest Riles surprised the Brewers with his .286 average.

Catcher Bill Schroeder, who was supposed to be the Brewers' home run threat, hit five homers in the first three weeks but spent most of the season on the disabled list with elbow problems. He underwent surgery in September.

Bamberger may have found his power hitter in outfielder Paul Householder, but by the time he made the discovery it was too late. Householder, who warmed the bench for much of the season, hit 11 homers, including eight in the last month when he finally played on a regular basis.

Catcher Charlie Moore had his worst season since 1976 as he hit just .232 with 31 runs batted in. Other players who saw their production plummet were second

## SCORES OF MILWAUKEE BREWERS' 1985 GAMES

**APRIL**

| Date | | Score | Winner | Loser |
|---|---|---|---|---|
| 9—Chicago | L | 2-4 | Seaver | Haas |
| 11—Chicago | W | 8-1 | Burris | Lollar |
| 12—At Texas | W | 11-6 | Gibson | Tanana |
| 13—At Texas | W | 6-5 | Gibson | Noles |
| 14—At Texas | W | 8-1 | Haas | Rozema |
| 16—At Detroit | L | 1-2 | Terrell | Burris |
| 17—At Detroit | W | 2-0 | Darwin | Morris |
| 19—Texas | L | 1-4 | Rozema | Searage |
| 20—Texas | L | 1-5 | Noles | Haas |
| 21—Texas | L | 2-5 | Mason | Burris |
| 22—At Chicago | W | 4-2 | Darwin | Agosto |
| 23—At Chicago | L | 5-6* | James | Fingers |
| 24—At Chicago | W | 3-2 | Vuckovich | Burns |
| 25—Detroit | W | 11-7 | Gibson | Scherrer |
| 26—Detroit | L | 0-1 | Morris | Burris |
| 27—Detroit | L | 2-3 | Petry | Darwin |
| 28—Detroit | L | 0-5 | Terrell | Higuera |
| 29—At Seattle | L | 7-9* | Nunez | Searage |
| 30—At Seattle | L | 2-4 | Langston | Gibson |

Won 8, Lost 11

**MAY**

| Date | | Score | Winner | Loser |
|---|---|---|---|---|
| 1—At Oak. | W | 7-4 | Darwin | McCatty |
| 2—At Oak. | L | 4-5 | Atherton | Searage |
| 3—At Calif. | W | 7-0 | Higuera | John |
| 4—At Calif. | L | 3-4 | Romanick | Vuckovich |
| 5—At Calif. | L | 1-5 | Witt | Darwin |
| 7—Seattle | W | 5-2 | Haas | Beattie |
| 8—Seattle | L | 2-4 | Moore | Burris |
| 10—California | L | 4-5 | Romanick | Vuckovich |
| 11—California | L | 5-6 | John | Kern |
| 12—California | W | 7-4 | Haas | McCaskill |
| 14—Oakland | L | 3-6 | Codiroli | Fingers |
| 15—Oakland | L | 3-19 | Krueger | Higuera |
| 17—Kan. City | L | 0-3 | Saberhagen | Darwin |
| 18—Kan. City | W | 7-2 | Haas | Jackson |
| 19—Kan. City | W | 11-10 | Gibson | Quisenberry |
| 21—At Cleve. | L | 4-6 | Clark | Higuera |
| 22—At Cleve. | W | 6-5 | Gibson | Blyleven |
| 24—Minnesota | W | 5-2 | Burris | Smithson |
| 25—Minnesota | W | 9-7 | McClure | Filson |
| 26—Minnesota | W | 5-3 | Higuera | Butcher |
| 27—Cleveland | L | 0-8 | Blyleven | Darwin |
| 28—Cleveland | W | 3-2 | Haas | Heaton |
| 29—Cleveland | W | 7-2 | Burris | Schulze |
| 31—At Minn. | W | 6-4 | Higuera | Filson |

Won 13, Lost 11

**JUNE**

| Date | | Score | Winner | Loser |
|---|---|---|---|---|
| 1—At Minn. | W | 7-2 | Darwin | Butcher |
| 2—At Minn. | L | 4-5 | Schrom | Gibson |
| 4—At Kan. C. | L | 3-4 | Leibrandt | Vuckovich |
| 5—At Kan. C. | W | 10-2 | Higuera | Black |
| 6—New York | W | 5-1 | Darwin | Whitson |
| 7—New York | W | 10-9* | Searage | Righetti |
| 8—New York | L | 1-2§ | Righetti | Gibson |
| 9—New York | W | 9-4 | Vuckovich | Niekro |
| 10—At Boston | L | 2-4 | Ojeda | Higuera |
| 11—At Boston | W | 5-3 | Darwin | Hurst |
| 12—At Boston | L | 2-7 | Nipper | Haas |
| 13—At Balt. | L | 3-8 | McGregor | Burris |
| 14—At Balt. | L | 3-9 | Davis | Vuckovich |
| 15—At Balt. | L | 5-7 | Snell | Gibson |
| 16—At Balt. | L | 1-9 | Boddicker | Darwin |
| 17—Toronto | W | 2-1 | Haas | Stieb |
| 18—Toronto | W | 4-1 | Burris | Leal |
| 19—Toronto | L | 1-5 | Clancy | Vuckovich |
| 21—Baltimore | W | 13-10 | Cocanower | Stewart |
| 22—Baltimore | L | 2-3 | McGregor | Darwin |
| 23—Baltimore | L | 3-6 | Snell | Fingers |
| 25—At Toronto | L | 1-7 | Clancy | Burris |
| 26—At Toronto | W | 5-4 | Gibson | Alexander |
| 27—At Toronto | L | 3-7 | Key | Higuera |
| 28—At N.Y. | L | 2-5 | Guidry | Darwin |
| 29—At N.Y. | W | 6-0 | Haas | Niekro |
| 30—At N.Y. | W | 7-5 | McClure | Fisher |

Won 12, Lost 15

**JULY**

| Date | | Score | Winner | Loser |
|---|---|---|---|---|
| 1—Boston | W | 5-1 | Vuckovich | Trujillo |
| 2—Boston | W | 4-3* | Fingers | Stanley |
| 3—Boston | L | 0-9 | Hurst | Darwin |
| 4—At Seattle | L | 1-7 | Moore | Haas |
| 5—At Seattle | L | 6-7† | Nunez | Waits |
| 6—At Seattle | L | 3-5 | Thomas | Vuckovich |
| 7—At Seattle | W | 2-1 | Higuera | Swift |
| 8—At Calif. | L | 2-3† | Moore | Gibson |
| 9—At Calif. | L | 4-5* | Moore | Fingers |
| 10—At Calif. | L | 1-2 | Romanick | Burris |
| 11—At Oak. | L | 3-9 | Sutton | Vuckovich |
| 12—At Oak. | W | 5-3 | Higuera | Codiroli |
| 13—At Oak. | L | 0-2 | Birtsas | Darwin |
| 14—At Oak. | L | 2-11 | Krueger | Haas |
| 18—Seattle | L | 2-5 | Moore | Darwin |
| 19—Seattle | W | 9-7 | Higuera | Young |
| 20—Seattle | L | 10-13 | Vande Berg | McClure |
| 21—Seattle | W | 5-4 | Burris | Wills |
| 22—California | W | 16-3 | Vuckovich | Slaton |
| 23—California | L | 0-2 | McCaskill | Darwin |
| 24—California | L | 4-8 | Romanick | Higuera |
| 25—Oakland | L | 2-11 | Birtsas | Cocanower |
| 26—Oakland | L | 3-7 | John | Burris |
| 27—Oakland | W | 4-3 | Vuckovich | Codiroli |
| 28—Oakland | L | 2-5 | Krueger | Darwin |
| 29—Texas | W | 3-2 | Higuera | Hough |
| 30—Texas | W | 6-3 | McClure | Rozema |
| 31—Texas | W | 5-2 | Cocanower | Mason |

Won 11, Lost 17

**AUGUST**

| Date | | Score | Winner | Loser |
|---|---|---|---|---|
| 2—At Detroit | L | 1-4 | Tanana | Vuckovich |
| 3—At Detroit | L | 3-9 | Petry | Darwin |
| 4—At Detroit | L | 4-7 | Hernandez | Waits |
| 4—At Detroit | W | 14-4 | Burris | O'Neal |
| 8—At Texas | W | 7-4 | Waits | Russell |
| 8—At Texas | W | 3-1 | Vuckovich | Hooton |
| 9—At Chicago | W | 8-7 | Waits | James |
| 10—At Chicago | W | 5-2† | Higuera | Agosto |
| 11—At Chicago | L | 1-4 | Davis | Burris |
| 12—Detroit | W | 4-3 | Cocanower | Hernandez |
| 13—Detroit | L | 4-5§ | Lopez | Gibson |
| 14—Detroit | L | 3-4 | Morris | Darwin |
| 15—Chicago | W | 7-5 | Higuera | Bannister |
| 16—Chicago | W | 3-2 | Burris | Wehrmeister |
| 17—Chicago | L | 7-12 | Spillner | Cocanower |
| 18—Chicago | L | 4-8 | Burns | Vuckovich |
| 19—Minnesota | W | 4-1 | Darwin | Smithson |
| 20—Minnesota | W | 3-2 | Higuera | Howe |
| 21—Minnesota | W | 3-2 | Burris | Howe |
| 23—At Cleve. | L | 5-10 | Wardle | Cocanower |
| 25—At Cleve. | L | 2-6 | Waddell | Haas |
| 25—At Cleve. | L | 0-2 | Romero | Darwin |
| 26—At Cleve. | L | 3-4 | Heaton | Gibson |
| 26—At Cleve. | W | 8-3 | Burris | Smith |
| 27—Kan. City | W | 8-5 | Cocanower | Jackson |
| 28—Kan. City | L | 2-8 | Gubicza | Vuckovich |
| 30—Cleveland | W | 9-6 | Haas | Waddell |
| 31—Cleveland | W | 10-8 | Higuera | Heaton |

Won 15, Lost 13

**SEPTEMBER**

| Date | | Score | Winner | Loser |
|---|---|---|---|---|
| 1—Cleveland | L | 4-11 | Von Ohlen | Burris |
| 2—At Minn. | L | 1-6 | Smithson | Cocanower |
| 3—At Minn. | L | 3-4 | Howe | Darwin |
| 4—At Minn. | W | 11-10 | Waits | Burtt |
| 5—At Kan. C. | L | 1-4 | Leibrandt | Haas |
| 6—At Kan. C. | L | 3-4† | Quisenberry | Fingers |
| 6—At Kan. C. | L | 1-7 | Farr | Burris |
| 7—At Kan. C. | L | 4-7 | Gubicza | Cocanower |
| 8—At Kan. C. | L | 11-13† | Farr | Fingers |
| 9—New York | L | 4-9* | Righetti | Searage |
| 10—New York | L | 10-13 | Whitson | Burris |
| 11—New York | W | 4-3 | Higuera | Bordi |
| 13—Boston | W | 6-3 | Leary | Lollar |
| 14—Boston | L | 8-10† | Kison | Darwin |
| 15—Boston | L | 2-4 | Sellers | Cocanower |
| 16—Boston | W | 5-3 | McClure | Ojeda |
| 17—At Balt. | L | 0-6 | Dixon | Higuera |
| 18—At Balt. | L | 2-4 | McGregor | Leary |
| 19—At Balt. | W | 5-2 | Wegman | Boddicker |
| 20—At Toronto | L | 5-7 | Key | Cocanower |
| 21—At Toronto | L | 1-2x | Lamp | Darwin |
| 22—At Toronto | W | 2-1 | Higuera | Stieb |
| 23—At Toronto | L | 1-5 | Clancy | Leary |
| 24—Baltimore | W | 10-6 | Wegman | McGregor |
| 25—Baltimore | W | 3-0 | Cocanower | Flanagan |
| 26—Baltimore | L | 1-9 | D. Martinez | Haas |
| 27—Toronto | L | 1-5 | Stieb | Higuera |
| 28—Toronto | L | 1-6 | Clancy | Leary |
| 29—Toronto | L | 5-13 | Acker | Burris |

Won 8, Lost 21

**OCTOBER**

| Date | | Score | Winner | Loser |
|---|---|---|---|---|
| 1—At N.Y. | L | 1-6 | J. Niekro | Cocanower |
| 2—At N.Y. | W | 1-0 | Higuera | Shirley |
| 3—At N.Y. | L | 0-3 | Guidry | Leary |
| 4—At Boston | W | 8-7‡ | Lesley | Trujillo |
| 5—At Boston | W | 3-2 | Cocanower | Boyd |
| 6—At Boston | W | 9-6 | Darwin | Hurst |

Won 4, Lost 2

*10 innings.   †11 innings.   ‡12 innings.   §13 innings.   x14 innings.

**Lefthander Teddy Higuera won 10 of his last 13 decisions in a 15-8 rookie campaign.**

baseman Jim Gantner (.254, 44 RBIs) and part-time outfielder Rick Manning (.218 in 216 at-bats).

There were some bright spots, however, especially the play of a pair of rookies.

Teddy Higuera, a 26-year-old lefthander, opened the season with Milwaukee and got better as the season went on, winning 10 of his last 13 decisions to finish with a 15-8 record. Higuera also had a 3.90 ERA and was named The Sporting News' A.L. Rookie Pitcher of the Year.

Another rookie, Ernest Riles, was called up from Vancouver (Pacific Coast) in May and flirted with a .300 average for most of the season. Riles ended up hitting .286 while playing a steady, if not spectacular, shortstop.

Third baseman Paul Molitor, who had undergone surgery to rebuild his right elbow in 1984, made a triumphant return. His .297 average, 93 runs scored and 21 stolen bases paced the team.

Milwaukee's main offensive catalyst, however, was Cecil Cooper, who had slumped in 1984. The first baseman batted .293 with 16 homers and ranked among the league leaders in hits (185), doubles (39), triples (eight) and RBIs (99).

Designated hitter Ted Simmons (.273, 12 homers, 76 RBIs) and outfielder Ben Oglivie (.290, 10 homers, 61 RBIs) also made significant contributions.

Once again, the Brewers had more than their share of injuries. Robin Yount was hampered all season by shoulder problems and finally underwent surgery in early September. The former shortstop spent the entire season in the outfield and showed that he could roam far and wide in center, where he is expected to play in 1986. Despite his shoulder problems, Yount batted .277 and hit 15 homers, one short of Cooper's team-leading total.

There were other injuries, too. Outfielder Dion James, a .295 hitter in '84, dislocated his shoulder on his second day of spring training and returned to the lineup for only 18 games before suffering the same injury again and needing surgery. He was lost for the year.

Pete Vuckovich, who had pitched in only three games in two seasons because of shoulder problems, appeared to be well on the way to a comeback when his shoulder acted up again, requiring more surgery in September. The righthanded veteran went 6-10 with a 5.51 ERA in 112⅔ innings.

"With a bad arm throughout the season," General Manager Harry Dalton said, "he won about as many games as some of our other pitchers simply because he's that kind of competitor."

Brett Butler ranked among the American League leaders in five offensive categories while playing an impressive center field.

# Indians Sink to East Basement

**By SHELDON OCKER**

The 1985 Cleveland Indians carried an old maxim to extremes: Anything that possibly could go wrong, did.

The year began with designated hitter Andre Thornton's knee operation in spring training and ended with 102 defeats, tying the Tribe's all-time record for ineptness. Cleveland finished 39½ games behind American League East champion Toronto.

Thornton's arthroscopic surgery set him back in his preparedness more than two months, even though he missed less than three weeks of the season. But not having their perennial leader in home runs and runs batted in was not even the worst of the Indians' health problems.

Reliever Ernie Camacho, who had set a club record with 23 saves in 1984, underwent apparently routine surgery to remove bone chips from his elbow in mid-April. The righthander was expected to return in six weeks, but he was unable to throw a pitch in competition for the remainder of the year.

Camacho kept some calcium fragments in a jar in his locker as a joke, but as the months wore on, the humor of the situation evaporated. Camacho, still complaining of elbow pain as the season came to a close, made plans to visit famed orthopedic surgeon Frank Jobe in California.

Several other Indians pitchers missed significant portions of the season because of ill health. Two injuries caused starter/reliever Vern Ruhle, who went 2-10 with a 4.32 earned-run average, to spend five weeks on the disabled list. Starter Rick Behenna, still trying to come back from arthroscopic surgery to his right shoulder in May 1984, was inactive virtually the entire year. Reliever Dave Von Ohlen (3-2, 2.91 ERA) missed 3½ months with injuries. Starter Roy Smith (1-4, 5.34) was sidelined for a month after being hit in the ear with a line drive. And starter/reliever Tom Waddell underwent surgery to remove a calcium deposit from his elbow in September.

Thornton's knee operation was not the only blow to the offense, either. Starting left fielder Mel Hall received multiple injuries in a May car accident in Texas and spent the season recuperating from a broken pelvis and cracked collarbone. Hall was hitting .318 at the time. Joe Carter, another outfield regular, was slowed by a nagging wrist injury early in the season

**Shortstop Julio Franco drove in 90 runs but was inconsistent defensively.**

and did not regain his full capabilities until after the All-Star break. He wound up with a .262 average, 15 homers, 59 RBIs and 24 stolen bases.

But injuries do not fully explain Cleveland's biggest handicap, a lack of quality pitchers. The 1985 staff's league-high 4.91 ERA was the highest in club history.

"The biggest disappointment to me was the pitching," Manager Pat Corrales said. "I expected it to be half-decent. Even with all the injuries, we wouldn't have come close to losing 100 games if the pitching hadn't failed so badly."

The Indians had neither a 10-game winner nor a reliever with as many as 10 saves. Lefthander Neal Heaton was both the big winner and the big loser with a 9-17 record and a 4.90 ERA.

Heaton had been expected to be the No. 2 starter behind Bert Blyleven, who was traded to Minnesota in August after compiling a 9-11 record. But Corrales said Heaton was inconsistent because he was trying to overpower hitters rather than keep them off-stride by changing speeds.

"I guess I have to learn everything the hard way," Heaton said.

Waddell was second in wins with eight and first in saves with nine. Because of the

## SCORES OF CLEVELAND INDIANS' 1985 GAMES

### APRIL

| Date | W/L | Score | Winner | Loser |
|---|---|---|---|---|
| 8—At Detroit | L | 4-5 | Morris | Camacho |
| 10—At Detroit | L | 1-8 | Petry | Ruhle |
| 11—At Detroit | L | 10-11* | Hernandez | Von Ohlen |
| 13—New York | L | 3-6 | Guidry | Blyleven |
| 14—New York | L | 1-2 | Niekro | Waddell |
| 16—Baltimore | W | 6-3 | Ruhle | D. Martinez |
| 17—Baltimore | L | 3-6 | Stewart | Roman |
| 18—Baltimore | W | 11-5 | Von Ohlen | Snell |
| 19—At N.Y. | W | 2-1 | Heaton | Guidry |
| 20—At N.Y. | L | 2-5 | Niekro | Roman |
| 21—At N.Y. | W | 3-0 | Von Ohlen | Whitson |
| 22—Detroit | W | 6-4 | Schulze | Morris |
| 23—Detroit | L | 3-4 | Petry | Blyleven |
| 24—Detroit | W | 7-6 | Easterly | Lopez |
| 25—At Balt. | L | 1-7 | Dixon | Roman |
| 26—At Balt. | L | 3-6 | D. Martinez | Ruhle |
| 27—At Balt. | W | 10-4 | Schulze | McGregor |
| 28—At Balt. | L | 7-8 | Aase | Waddell |
| 29—At Kan. C. | L | 2-3 | Black | Heaton |
| 30—At Kan. C. | L | 1-5 | Saberhagen | Roman |

**Won 7, Lost 13**

### MAY

| Date | W/L | Score | Winner | Loser |
|---|---|---|---|---|
| 1—At Kan. C. | W | 6-5 | Schulze | Gubicza |
| 3—Texas | W | 4-0 | Blyleven | Mason |
| 4—Texas | W | 3-1 | Heaton | Tanana |
| 5—Texas | L | 2-7 | Hough | Schulze |
| 7—Chicago | L | 4-7 | Bannister | Blyleven |
| 8—Chicago | L | 0-4 | Burns | Heaton |
| 10—At Texas | L | 2-5 | Hough | Schulze |
| 11—At Texas | W | 4-1 | Waddell | Harris |
| 12—At Texas | W | 6-0 | Blyleven | Noles |
| 13—At Chicago | L | 0-8 | Burns | Heaton |
| 14—At Chicago | L | 1-2 | Nelson | Thompson |
| 15—Kan. City | L | 1-5 | Leibrandt | Schulze |
| 16—Kan. City | L | 1-7 | Black | Creel |
| 17—Boston | L | 0-5 | Clemens | Blyleven |
| 18—Boston | W | 4-1 | Heaton | Hurst |
| 19—Boston | W | 2-1 | Thompson | Boyd |
| 21—Milwaukee | W | 6-4 | Clark | Higuera |
| 22—Milwaukee | L | 5-6 | Gibson | Blyleven |
| 23—Toronto | L | 5-6 | Lamp | Waddell |
| 24—Toronto | L | 6-7 | Lamp | Creel |
| 25—Toronto | L | 7-10 | Musselman | Thompson |
| 26—Toronto | L | 5-6 | Lavelle | Creel |
| 27—At Milw. | W | 8-0 | Blyleven | Darwin |
| 28—At Milw. | L | 2-3 | Haas | Heaton |
| 29—At Milw. | L | 2-7 | Burris | Schulze |
| 31—At Toronto | L | 2-7 | Alexander | Clark |

**Won 9, Lost 17**

### JUNE

| Date | W/L | Score | Winner | Loser |
|---|---|---|---|---|
| 1—At Toronto | L | 3-8 | Key | Blyleven |
| 2—At Toronto | W | 5-4 | Heaton | Stieb |
| 2—At Toronto | L | 2-5 | Leal | Behenna |
| 3—At Boston | L | 5-6 | Boyd | Schulze |
| 4—At Boston | L | 0-5 | Ojeda | Creel |
| 6—Seattle | W | 9-1 | Blyleven | Young |
| 7—Seattle | L | 4-6 | Swift | Heaton |
| 8—Seattle | W | 12-8 | Waddell | Stanton |
| 9—Seattle | L | 6-10 | Wills | Schulze |
| 10—Minnesota | L | 4-6 | Viola | Creel |
| 14—Oakland | W | 6-1 | Blyleven | Krueger |
| 15—Oakland | L | 6-8 | Birtsas | Heaton |
| 16—Oakland | L | 2-3 | Sutton | Waddell |
| 16—Oakland | L | 6-11 | McCatty | Ruhle |
| 18—California | L | 3-7 | Witt | Heaton |
| 19—California | W | 2-0 | Blyleven | Slaton |
| 20—California | L | 0-4 | Romanick | Schulze |
| 21—At Oak. | L | 1-9 | Sutton | Behenna |
| 22—At Oak. | L | 4-6† | Howell | Barkley |
| 23—At Oak. | L | 3-9 | Codiroli | Heaton |
| 24—At Calif. | W | 2-1 | Blyleven | Slaton |
| 25—At Calif. | L | 3-7§ | Cliburn | Heaton |
| 26—At Calif. | L | 6-10 | Sanchez | Barkley |
| 28—At Seattle | L | 6-8 | Thomas | Barkley |
| 29—At Seattle | L | 2-3 | Moore | Blyleven |
| 30—At Seattle | W | 7-3 | Thompson | Young |

**Won 7, Lost 19**

### JULY

| Date | W/L | Score | Winner | Loser |
|---|---|---|---|---|
| 1—At Minn. | W | 5-2 | Ruhle | Schrom |
| 2—At Minn. | L | 7-8 | Eufemia | Waddell |
| 3—At Minn. | L | 0-7 | Smithson | Heaton |
| 4—Chicago | L | 0-5 | Burns | Blyleven |
| 5—Chicago | L | 3-8 | Seaver | Reed |
| 6—Chicago | L | 4-6* | James | Thompson |
| 7—Chicago | W | 10-3 | Waddell | Lollar |
| 8—Texas | W | 4-0 | Heaton | Mason |
| 9—Texas | W | 7-2 | Blyleven | Hooton |
| 10—Texas | L | 1-4 | Hough | Reed |
| 11—Kan. City | L | 0-1 | Jackson | Ruhle |
| 12—Kan. City | W | 5-4† | Waddell | Quisenberry |
| 13—Kan. City | L | 1-5 | Saberhagen | Blyleven |
| 14—Kan. City | L | 5-9 | Black | Heaton |
| 18—At Chicago | L | 0-10 | Burns | Ruhle |
| 19—At Chicago | L | 0-1 | Seaver | Blyleven |
| 20—At Chicago | L | 6-8 | Agosto | Clark |
| 21—At Chicago | W | 4-3* | Thompson | Spillner |
| 22—At Texas | L | 1-2 | Harris | Ruhle |
| 23—At Texas | L | 4-8 | Hough | Heaton |
| 24—At Texas | W | 8-4 | Blyleven | Hooton |
| 26—At Kan. C. | L | 1-7 | Jackson | Romero |
| 27—At Kan. C. | L | 3-6 | Black | Reed |
| 28—At Kan. C. | L | 4-7 | Gubicza | Ruhle |
| 29—New York | L | 2-8 | Whitson | Blyleven |
| 30—New York | L | 5-8 | Cowley | Thompson |
| 30—New York | W | 3-2 | Romero | Shirley |
| 31—New York | W | 6-5 | Waddell | Guidry |

**Won 9, Lost 19**

### AUGUST

| Date | W/L | Score | Winner | Loser |
|---|---|---|---|---|
| 1—New York | W | 9-1 | Smith | Niekro |
| 2—Baltimore | L | 6-8 | Stewart | Thompson |
| 3—Baltimore | W | 10-4 | Wardle | Boddicker |
| 4—Baltimore | L | 4-5 | D. Martinez | Thompson |
| 8—At N.Y. | L | 1-8 | Bystrom | Wardle |
| 8—At N.Y. | L | 6-7 | Fisher | Reed |
| 9—Detroit | W | 4-2 | Easterly | Hernandez |
| 10—Detroit | L | 4-5† | Hernandez | Ruhle |
| 11—Detroit | W | 7-2 | Heaton | O'Neal |
| 12—At Balt. | W | 8-5 | Wardle | McGregor |
| 13—At Balt. | L | 4-8 | Aase | Ruhle |
| 14—At Balt. | L | 4-8 | Flanagan | Clark |
| 15—At Detroit | W | 7-6 | Wardle | Hernandez |
| 16—At Detroit | L | 2-3 | Lopez | Heaton |
| 17—At Detroit | L | 5-7 | Tanana | Wardle |
| 18—At Detroit | L | 0-4 | Petry | Romero |
| 19—Toronto | W | 5-3 | Waddell | Stieb |
| 20—Toronto | L | 2-3 | Key | Smith |
| 21—Toronto | W | 5-2 | Heaton | Alexander |
| 23—Milwaukee | W | 10-5 | Wardle | Cocanower |
| 25—Milwaukee | W | 6-2 | Waddell | Haas |
| 25—Milwaukee | W | 2-0 | Romero | Darwin |
| 26—Milwaukee | W | 4-3 | Heaton | Gibson |
| 26—Milwaukee | L | 3-8 | Burris | Smith |
| 27—Boston | W | 6-2 | Wardle | Trujillo |
| 28—Boston | W | 7-4 | Easterly | Lollar |
| 29—Boston | L | 2-17 | Hurst | Romero |
| 30—At Milw. | L | 6-9 | Haas | Waddell |
| 31—At Milw. | L | 8-10 | Higuera | Heaton |

**Won 14, Lost 15**

### SEPTEMBER

| Date | W/L | Score | Winner | Loser |
|---|---|---|---|---|
| 1—At Milw. | W | 11-4 | Von Ohlen | Burris |
| 2—At Toronto | L | 2-3 | Stieb | Wardle |
| 4—At Toronto | W | 5-4 | Clark | Henke |
| 5—At Boston | L | 6-13 | Boyd | Heaton |
| 5—At Boston | W | 9-5 | Easterly | Ojeda |
| 7—At Boston | L | 9-11 | Kison | Reed |
| 7—At Boston | L | 4-7 | Nipper | Wardle |
| 8—At Boston | L | 1-8 | Lollar | Heaton |
| 9—At Seattle | L | 7-8‡ | Tobik | Thompson |
| 10—At Seattle | W | 8-5 | Clark | Willis |
| 11—At Seattle | L | 5-9 | Moore | Smith |
| 13—Minnesota | W | 3-2 | Wardle | Portugal |
| 13—Minnesota | L | 1-3 | Viola | Schulze |
| 14—Minnesota | W | 11-9 | Waddell | Butcher |
| 14—Minnesota | L | 3-5 | Burtt | Thompson |
| 15—Minnesota | L | 2-5 | Blyleven | Smith |
| 16—At N.Y. | W | 9-5 | Reed | Fisher |
| 17—Oakland | W | 15-8 | Wardle | Birtsas |
| 18—Oakland | L | 0-1 | Rijo | Schulze |
| 20—At Calif. | L | 5-7 | Corbett | Von Ohlen |
| 21—At Calif. | L | 3-12 | McCaskill | Heaton |
| 22—At Calif. | L | 9-10‡ | Cliburn | Clark |
| 23—At Oak. | L | 7-8 | Rijo | Wardle |
| 24—At Oak. | L | 8-10 | Langford | Ruhle |
| 25—At Oak. | W | 7-2 | Creel | John |
| 27—California | W | 7-3 | Heaton | Witt |
| 28—California | W | 7-5 | Reed | Cliburn |
| 29—California | L | 3-9 | McCaskill | Wardle |

**Won 11, Lost 17**

### OCTOBER

| Date | W/L | Score | Winner | Loser |
|---|---|---|---|---|
| 1—Seattle | W | 9-3 | Schulze | Wills |
| 2—Seattle | W | 12-2 | Creel | Moore |
| 4—At Minn. | W | 8-6 | Reed | Burtt |
| 5—At Minn. | L | 2-8 | Blyleven | Easterly |
| 6—At Minn. | L | 2-4 | Smithson | Schulze |

**Won 3, Lost 2**

*10 innings.　†11 innings.　‡12 innings.　§13 innings.

**Andre Thornton recovered from a slow start to hit 22 homers and drive in 88 runs.**

elbow injury, Waddell was unable to work regularly out of the bullpen after midseason and eventually was converted to a starter.

Lefthander Curt Wardle, one of the players obtained for Blyleven, was 7-6 with Cleveland and 8-9 overall. His 6.18 overall ERA was bettered only slightly by righthander Don Schulze, who went 4-10 with a 6.01 ERA and spent almost three months at Maine (International).

Two of the Tribe's more reliable pitchers were relievers Jerry Reed and Jamie Easterly. Reed, who was called up from Maine on July 1, came on strong late in the year to finish with eight saves and a 4.11 ERA. Easterly (4-1, 3.92) made several starts late in the season.

Despite the injuries to Thornton, Hall and Carter, offense was Cleveland's strength. The club batted .265 (fourth in the league), although its 116 homers ranked next to last.

The brightest performer at the plate was center fielder Brett Butler, who ranked among the league leaders in batting (.311), on-base percentage (.377), runs scored (106), steals (47) and triples (14). The leadoff man also was superb in the field, making countless circus catches

and committing only one error.

Thornton, who was batting just .146 with three homers and 14 RBIs through the end of June, hit at a .284 clip after that point to salvage his season. He finished with 22 homers, 88 RBIs and a .236 average.

The club RBI leadership was a three-way race among Thornton, third baseman Brook Jacoby and shortstop Julio Franco, who emerged as the winner with 90 despite hitting only six home runs. Jacoby was second in homers (20) and third in RBIs (87) in only his second year in the big leagues.

Franco's excellent season at the plate (.288, 183 hits, 33 doubles) was tempered by 36 errors (tops among A.L. shortstops), although only 13 of them came after the All-Star break. Because of his early difficulties in the field, Franco was the target of an abortive maneuver by the front office.

On May 7, the Indians acquired Johnnie LeMaster from San Francisco for pitcher Mike Jeffcoat and gave him Franco's job at short. In turn, Franco was moved to second (where he committed one of his errors), and Tony Bernazard, who was hitting .317 at the time, was shunted to the bench. After eight games of virtually no offense from LeMaster, Franco and Bernazard were restored to their normal positions and LeMaster was dealt to Pittsburgh.

Bernazard finished with a .274 average, 11 homers and 59 RBIs, while the first-base platoon of Pat Tabler and Mike Hargrove accounted for six homers, 86 RBIs and a .279 average.

The right-field platoon was slightly less productive. Carmen Castillo and George Vukovich combined for 19 homers and 70 RBIs but only a .244 average.

The weakest spot of the Cleveland offense, however, was catcher. The opening day starter, Chris Bando, had to struggle to bring his average up to .139. Bando found himself spending less time behind the plate than Jerry Willard, who raised his average to .270 by the end of the season.

While pitching was the most apparent reason for the Indians' poor season, they blew several games because of mental mistakes.

"We haven't played smart baseball day in and day out," Thornton said. "This is a young team, and it has to mature mentally.... We have to play good, sound fundamental baseball. I think not doing that hurt us as much as our pitching this season."

OFFICIAL BASEBALL GUIDE

# American League Averages for 1985
## CHAMPIONSHIP WINNERS IN PREVIOUS YEARS

| | | |
|---|---|---|
| 1900—Chicago* ....... .607 | 1929—Philadelphia ........ .693 | 1958—New York ......... .597 |
| 1901—Chicago ......... .610 | 1930—Philadelphia ........ .662 | 1959—Chicago ............ .610 |
| 1902—Philadelphia .... .610 | 1931—Philadelphia ........ .704 | 1960—New York ......... .630 |
| 1903—Boston .......... .659 | 1932—New York .......... .695 | 1961—New York ......... .673 |
| 1904—Boston .......... .617 | 1933—Washington ........ .651 | 1962—New York ......... .593 |
| 1905—Philadelphia .... .622 | 1934—Detroit ............ .656 | 1963—New York ......... .646 |
| 1906—Chicago ......... .616 | 1935—Detroit ............ .616 | 1964—New York ......... .611 |
| 1907—Detroit ......... .613 | 1936—New York .......... .667 | 1965—Minnesota ......... .630 |
| 1908—Detroit ......... .588 | 1937—New York .......... .662 | 1966—Baltimore ......... .606 |
| 1909—Detroit ......... .645 | 1938—New York .......... .651 | 1967—Boston ............ .568 |
| 1910—Philadelphia .... .680 | 1939—New York .......... .702 | 1968—Detroit ........... .636 |
| 1911—Philadelphia .... .669 | 1940—Detroit ............ .584 | 1969—Baltimore (East) .. .673 |
| 1912—Boston .......... .691 | 1941—New York .......... .656 | 1970—Baltimore (East) .. .667 |
| 1913—Philadelphia .... .627 | 1942—New York .......... .669 | 1971—Baltimore (East) .. .639 |
| 1914—Philadelphia .... .651 | 1943—New York .......... .636 | 1972—Oakland (West) ..... .600 |
| 1915—Boston .......... .669 | 1944—St. Louis .......... .578 | 1973—Oakland (West) ..... .580 |
| 1916—Boston .......... .591 | 1945—Detroit ............ .575 | 1974—Oakland (West) ..... .556 |
| 1917—Chicago ......... .649 | 1946—Boston ............ .675 | 1975—Boston (East) ...... .594 |
| 1918—Boston .......... .595 | 1947—New York .......... .630 | 1976—New York (East) .... .610 |
| 1919—Chicago ......... .629 | 1948—Cleveland† ......... .626 | 1977—New York (East) .... .617 |
| 1920—Cleveland ....... .636 | 1949—New York .......... .630 | 1978—New York (East) .... .613 |
| 1921—New York ....... .641 | 1950—New York .......... .636 | 1979—Baltimore (East) ... .642 |
| 1922—New York ....... .610 | 1951—New York .......... .636 | 1980—Kansas City (West) . .599 |
| 1923—New York ....... .645 | 1952—New York .......... .617 | 1981—New York (East) .... .551 |
| 1924—Washington ..... .597 | 1953—New York .......... .656 | 1982—Milwaukee (East) ... .586 |
| 1925—Washington ..... .636 | 1954—Cleveland .......... .721 | 1983—Baltimore (East) ... .605 |
| 1926—New York ....... .591 | 1955—New York .......... .623 | 1984—Detroit (East) ..... .642 |
| 1927—New York ....... .714 | 1956—New York .......... .630 | |
| 1928—New York ....... .656 | 1957—New York .......... .636 | |

*Not recognized as major league in 1900. †Defeated Boston in one-game playoff for pennant.

## STANDING OF CLUBS AT CLOSE OF SEASON
### EAST DIVISION

| Club | Tor. | N.Y. | Det. | Balt. | Bos. | Mil. | Cle. | K.C. | Cal. | Chi. | Min. | Oak. | Sea. | Tex. | W. | L. | Pct. | G.B. |
|---|---|---|---|---|---|---|---|---|---|---|---|---|---|---|---|---|---|---|
| Toronto | .. | 7 | 7 | 8 | 4 | 9 | 9 | 5 | 7 | 9 | 8 | 7 | 10 | 9 | 99 | 62 | .615 | ........ |
| New York | 6 | .. | 3 | 12 | 8 | 6 | 7 | 7 | 9 | 6 | 9 | 7 | 9 | 8 | 97 | 64 | .602 | 2 |
| Detroit | 6 | 9 | .. | 7 | 7 | 9 | 8 | 5 | 4 | 6 | 3 | 8 | 5 | 7 | 84 | 77 | .522 | 15 |
| Baltimore | 4 | 1 | 6 | .. | 5 | 9 | 8 | 6 | 7 | 8 | 6 | 7 | 6 | 10 | 83 | 78 | .516 | 16 |
| Boston | 9 | 5 | 6 | 8 | .. | 5 | 8 | 5 | 5 | 4 | 7 | 8 | 6 | 5 | 81 | 81 | .500 | 18½ |
| Milwaukee | 4 | 7 | 4 | 4 | 8 | .. | 6 | 4 | 3 | 7 | 9 | 3 | 4 | 8 | 71 | 90 | .441 | 28 |
| Cleveland | 4 | 6 | 5 | 5 | 5 | 7 | .. | 2 | 4 | 2 | 4 | 3 | 6 | 7 | 60 | 102 | .370 | 39½ |

### WEST DIVISION

| Club | K.C. | Cal. | Chi. | Min. | Oak. | Sea. | Tex. | Tor. | N.Y. | Det. | Balt. | Bos. | Mil. | Cle. | W. | L. | Pct. | G.B. |
|---|---|---|---|---|---|---|---|---|---|---|---|---|---|---|---|---|---|---|
| Kansas City | .. | 9 | 8 | 7 | 8 | 3 | 6 | 7 | 5 | 7 | 6 | 7 | 8 | 10 | 91 | 71 | .562 | ........ |
| California | 4 | .. | 8 | 9 | 6 | 9 | 9 | 5 | 3 | 8 | 5 | 7 | 9 | 8 | 90 | 72 | .556 | 1 |
| Chicago | 5 | 5 | .. | 6 | 8 | 9 | 10 | 3 | 6 | 6 | 4 | 8 | 5 | 10 | 85 | 77 | .525 | 6 |
| Minnesota | 6 | 4 | 7 | .. | 8 | 6 | 8 | 4 | 3 | 9 | 6 | 5 | 3 | 8 | 77 | 85 | .475 | 14 |
| Oakland | 5 | 7 | 5 | 5 | .. | 8 | 6 | 5 | 5 | 4 | 5 | 4 | 9 | 9 | 77 | 85 | .475 | 14 |
| Seattle | 10 | 4 | 4 | 7 | 5 | .. | 6 | 2 | 3 | 7 | 6 | 6 | 8 | 6 | 74 | 88 | .457 | 17 |
| Texas | 7 | 4 | 3 | 5 | 7 | 7 | .. | 3 | 4 | 5 | 2 | 7 | 3 | 5 | 62 | 99 | .385 | 28½ |

Tie Game—Chicago vs. Boston.
Championship Series—Kansas City defeated Toronto, four games to three.

## RECORD AT HOME
### EAST DIVISION

| Club | N.Y. | Tor. | Balt. | Det. | Bos. | Mil. | Cle. | Cal. | K.C. | Min. | Chi. | Oak. | Sea. | Tex. | W. | L. | Pct. |
|---|---|---|---|---|---|---|---|---|---|---|---|---|---|---|---|---|---|
| New York | .. | 2-5 | 7-0 | 2-3 | 5-2 | 3-3 | 3-3 | 5-1 | 6-0 | 4-2 | 5-1 | 5-1 | 6-0 | | 58 | 22 | .725 |
| Toronto | 2-4 | .. | 4-1 | 5-2 | 4-3 | 5-2 | 4-2 | 5-1 | 2-4 | 5-1 | 3-3 | 6-0 | 4-2 | | 54 | 26 | .675 |
| Baltimore | 1-5 | 3-4 | .... | 3-3 | 1-5 | 6-1 | 5-2 | 4-2 | 2-4 | 3-3 | 4-2 | 4-2 | 3-3 | 6-0 | 45 | 36 | .556 |
| Detroit | 6-1 | 4-2 | 4-3 | .... | 3-3 | 4-2 | 6-1 | 2-4 | 2-4 | 1-5 | 4-2 | 4-2 | 1-5 | 3-3 | 44 | 37 | .543 |
| Boston | 3-3 | 6-0 | 3-4 | 3-4 | .... | 2-4 | 6-1 | 4-2 | 4-2 | 3-2 | 2-4 | 4-2 | 2-4 | 3-3 | 43 | 37 | .538 |
| Milwaukee | 4-3 | 2-4 | 3-3 | 2-5 | 4-3 | .... | 4-2 | 2-4 | 3-2 | 6-0 | 3-3 | 1-5 | 3-3 | 3-3 | 40 | 40 | .500 |
| Cleveland | 3-4 | 2-5 | 3-3 | 4-2 | 4-2 | 5-2 | .... | 3-3 | 1-5 | 2-4 | 1-5 | 2-4 | 4-2 | 4-2 | 38 | 43 | .469 |

### WEST DIVISION

| Club | Cal. | K.C. | Min. | Chi. | Oak. | Sea. | Tex. | N.Y. | Tor. | Balt. | Det. | Bos. | Mil. | Cle. | W. | L. | Pct. |
|---|---|---|---|---|---|---|---|---|---|---|---|---|---|---|---|---|---|
| California | .... | 2-4 | 4-2 | 3-4 | 4-3 | 3-1 | 5-2 | 2-4 | 4-2 | 3-3 | 4-2 | 5-1 | 5-1 | 5-1 | 49 | 30 | .620 |
| Kansas City | 5-2 | .... | 5-2 | 6-0 | 4-2 | 0-6 | 4-3 | 4-2 | 3-3 | 2-4 | 3-3 | 3-3 | 6-1 | 5-1 | 50 | 32 | .610 |
| Minnesota | 2-5 | 4-2 | .... | 3-3 | 7-2 | 5-2 | 5-1 | 3-3 | 3-3 | 3-3 | 4-2 | 3-4 | 3-3 | 4-2 | 49 | 35 | .583 |
| Chicago | 1-5 | 5-2 | 3-4 | .... | 4-2 | 4-3 | 5-1 | 4-2 | 2-4 | 4-2 | 4-2 | 2-4 | 5-1 | 5-1 | 45 | 36 | .556 |
| Oakland | 4-2 | 3-4 | 3-1 | 3-4 | .... | 5-1 | 3-4 | 4-2 | 2-4 | 3-3 | 2-4 | 4-2 | 5-1 | 5-1 | 43 | 36 | .544 |
| Seattle | 3-6 | 4-3 | 5-1 | 1-5 | 4-3 | .... | 5-1 | 2-4 | 2-4 | 3-3 | 2-4 | 5-1 | 4-2 | 5-1 | 42 | 41 | .506 |
| Texas | 2-4 | 4-2 | 4-3 | 2-5 | 3-3 | 6-1 | .... | 4-2 | 1-5 | 2-4 | 2-4 | 4-2 | 0-5 | 3-3 | 37 | 43 | .463 |

## RECORD ABROAD

### EAST DIVISION

| Club | Tor. | Det. | N.Y. | Balt. | Bos. | Mil. | Cle. | K.C. | Cal. | Chi. | Oak. | Sea. | Min. | Tex. | W. | L. | Pct. |
|---|---|---|---|---|---|---|---|---|---|---|---|---|---|---|---|---|---|
| Toronto | .... | 2-4 | 5-2 | 4-3 | 0-6 | 4-2 | 5-2 | 3-3 | 2-4 | 4-2 | 4-2 | 4-2 | 3-3 | 5-1 | 45 | 36 | .556 |
| Detroit | 2-5 | .... | 3-2 | 3-3 | 4-3 | 5-2 | 2-4 | 3-3 | 2-4 | 2-4 | 4-2 | 4-2 | 2-4 | 4-2 | 40 | 40 | .500 |
| New York | 4-2 | 1-6 | .... | 5-1 | 3-3 | 3-4 | 4-3 | 2-4 | 4-2 | 2-4 | 2-4 | 4-2 | 3-3 | 2-4 | 39 | 42 | .481 |
| Baltimore | 1-4 | 3-4 | 0-7 | .... | 4-3 | 3-3 | 3-3 | 4-2 | 3-3 | 4-2 | 3-3 | 3-3 | 3-3 | 4-2 | 38 | 42 | .475 |
| Boston | 3-4 | 3-3 | 2-5 | 5-1 | .... | 3-4 | 2-4 | 3-3 | 1-5 | 2-4 | 4-2 | 4-2 | 4-3 | 2-4 | 38 | 44 | .463 |
| Milwaukee | 2-5 | 2-4 | 3-3 | 1-6 | 4-2 | .... | 2-5 | 1-6 | 1-5 | 4-2 | 2-4 | 1-5 | 3-3 | 5-0 | 31 | 50 | .383 |
| Cleveland | 2-4 | 1-6 | 3-3 | 2-5 | 1-6 | 2-4 | .... | 1-5 | 1-5 | 1-5 | 1-5 | 2-4 | 2-4 | 3-3 | 22 | 59 | .272 |

### WEST DIVISION

| Club | K.C. | Ca. | Chi. | Oak. | Sea. | Min. | Tex. | Tor. | Det. | N.Y. | Balt. | Bos. | Mil. | Cle. | W. | L. | Pct. |
|---|---|---|---|---|---|---|---|---|---|---|---|---|---|---|---|---|---|
| Kansas City | .... | 4-2 | 2-5 | 4-3 | 3-4 | 2-4 | 2-4 | 4-2 | 4-2 | 1-5 | 4-2 | 4-2 | 2-3 | 5-1 | 41 | 39 | .513 |
| California | 2-5 | .... | 5-1 | 2-4 | 6-3 | 5-2 | 4-2 | 1-5 | 4-2 | 1-5 | 2-4 | 2-4 | 4-2 | 3-3 | 41 | 42 | .494 |
| Chicago | 0-6 | 4-3 | .... | 4-3 | 5-1 | 3-3 | 5-2 | 1-5 | 2-4 | 2-4 | 4-2 | 3-3 | 5-1 | 4-0 | 41 | 42 | .494 |
| Oakland | 2-4 | 3-4 | 2-4 | .... | 3-4 | 2-7 | 3-3 | 3-3 | 2-4 | 1-5 | 2-4 | 2-4 | 5-1 | 4-2 | 34 | 49 | .410 |
| Seattle | 6-0 | 1-3 | 3-4 | 1-5 | .... | 2-5 | 1-6 | 0-6 | 5-1 | 1-5 | 3-3 | 4-2 | 3-2 | 2-4 | 32 | 47 | .405 |
| Minnesota | 2-5 | 2-4 | 4-3 | 1-3 | 1-5 | .... | 3-4 | 1-5 | 5-1 | 0-6 | 3-3 | 2-3 | 0-6 | 4-2 | 28 | 50 | .359 |
| Texas | 3-4 | 2-5 | 1-5 | 4-3 | 1-5 | 1-5 | .... | 2-4 | 3-3 | 0-6 | 0-6 | 3-3 | 3-3 | 2-4 | 25 | 56 | .309 |

## SHUTOUT GAMES

| Club | K.C. | Tor. | Det. | N.Y. | Oak. | Chi. | Bos. | Sea. | Balt. | Cal. | Clev. | Min. | Tex. | Mil. | W. | L. | Pct. |
|---|---|---|---|---|---|---|---|---|---|---|---|---|---|---|---|---|---|
| Kansas City | .. | 1 | 0 | 0 | 1 | 1 | 1 | 0 | 0 | 3 | 1 | 1 | 1 | 1 | 11 | 4 | .733 |
| Toronto | 1 | .. | 2 | 0 | 0 | 1 | 0 | 1 | 0 | 1 | 0 | 3 | 0 | 0 | 9 | 4 | .692 |
| Detroit | 0 | 2 | .. | 1 | 0 | 1 | 2 | 1 | 0 | 0 | 1 | 1 | 0 | 2 | 11 | 6 | .647 |
| New York | 0 | 1 | 1 | .. | 0 | 0 | 0 | 0 | 3 | 2 | 0 | 0 | 1 | 1 | 9 | 6 | .600 |
| Oakland | 0 | 0 | 0 | 2 | .. | 1 | 0 | 0 | 0 | 0 | 1 | 1 | 0 | 1 | 6 | 5 | .545 |
| Chicago | 0 | 0 | 1 | 0 | 1 | .. | 0 | 0 | 0 | 0 | 5 | 1 | 0 | 0 | 8 | 7 | .533 |
| Boston | 0 | 0 | 1 | 0 | 1 | 0 | .. | 0 | 1 | 0 | 2 | 1 | 1 | 1 | 8 | 8 | .500 |
| Seattle | 2 | 0 | 0 | 0 | 0 | 0 | 2 | .. | 2 | 0 | 0 | 2 | 0 | 0 | 8 | 8 | .500 |
| Baltimore | 0 | 0 | 0 | 0 | 1 | 0 | 1 | 2 | .. | 1 | 0 | 0 | 0 | 1 | 6 | 7 | .462 |
| California | 1 | 0 | 0 | 0 | 0 | 1 | 0 | 1 | 0 | .. | 1 | 2 | 1 | 1 | 8 | 10 | .444 |
| Cleveland | 0 | 0 | 0 | 1 | 0 | 0 | 0 | 0 | 0 | 1 | .. | 0 | 3 | 2 | 7 | 12 | .368 |
| Minnesota | 0 | 0 | 0 | 0 | 1 | 2 | 1 | 2 | 0 | 0 | 1 | .. | 0 | 0 | 7 | 12 | .368 |
| Texas | 0 | 0 | 0 | 0 | 0 | 1 | 1 | 1 | 0 | 1 | 0 | 2 | .. | 0 | 5 | 9 | .357 |
| Milwaukee | 0 | 0 | 1 | 2 | 1 | 0 | 0 | 0 | 1 | 1 | 0 | 0 | 0 | .. | 5 | 10 | .333 |

# OFFICIAL AMERICAN LEAGUE BATTING AVERAGES

Compiled by Sports Information Center

### CLUB BATTING

| Club | Pct. | G. | AB. | R. | OR. | H. | TB. | 2B. | 3B. | HR. | RBI. | SH. | SF. | SB. | CS. | LOB. |
|---|---|---|---|---|---|---|---|---|---|---|---|---|---|---|---|---|
| Boston | .282 | 163 | 5720 | 800 | 720 | 1615 | 2455 | 292 | 31 | 162 | 760 | 50 | 57 | 66 | 27 | 1241 |
| Toronto | .269 | 161 | 5508 | 759 | 588 | 1482 | 2343 | 281 | 53 | 158 | 714 | 21 | 44 | 144 | 77 | 1067 |
| New York | .267 | 161 | 5458 | 839 | 660 | 1458 | 2320 | 272 | 31 | 176 | 793 | 48 | 60 | 155 | 53 | 1125 |
| Cleveland | .265 | 162 | 5527 | 729 | 861 | 1465 | 2129 | 254 | 31 | 116 | 689 | 38 | 48 | 132 | 72 | 1068 |
| Oakland | .264 | 162 | 5581 | 757 | 787 | 1475 | 2238 | 230 | 34 | 155 | 690 | 63 | 47 | 117 | 58 | 1073 |
| Minnesota | .264 | 162 | 5509 | 705 | 782 | 1453 | 2240 | 282 | 41 | 141 | 678 | 39 | 47 | 68 | 44 | 1144 |
| Milwaukee | .263 | 161 | 5568 | 690 | 802 | 1467 | 2108 | 250 | 44 | 101 | 636 | 54 | 55 | 69 | 34 | 1130 |
| Baltimore | .263 | 161 | 5517 | 818 | 764 | 1451 | 2371 | 234 | 22 | 214 | 773 | 31 | 40 | 69 | 43 | 1124 |
| Seattle | .255 | 162 | 5521 | 719 | 818 | 1410 | 2276 | 277 | 38 | 171 | 686 | 28 | 41 | 94 | 35 | 1143 |
| Texas | .253 | 161 | 5361 | 617 | 785 | 1359 | 2041 | 213 | 41 | 129 | 578 | 34 | 45 | 130 | 76 | 1100 |
| Detroit | .253 | 161 | 5575 | 729 | 688 | 1413 | 2363 | 254 | 45 | 202 | 703 | 40 | 53 | 75 | 41 | 1142 |
| Chicago | .253 | 163 | 5470 | 736 | 720 | 1386 | 2145 | 247 | 37 | 146 | 695 | 59 | 45 | 108 | 56 | 1009 |
| Kansas City | .252 | 162 | 5500 | 687 | 639 | 1384 | 2205 | 261 | 49 | 154 | 657 | 44 | 41 | 128 | 48 | 1057 |
| California | .251 | 162 | 5442 | 732 | 703 | 1364 | 2100 | 215 | 31 | 153 | 685 | 99 | 35 | 106 | 51 | 1165 |
| Totals | .261 | 1132 | 77257 | 10317 | 10317 | 20182 | 31334 | 3562 | 528 | 2178 | 9737 | 648 | 658 | 1461 | 715 | 15588 |

### INDIVIDUAL BATTING

(Top Fifteen Qualifiers for Batting Championship—502 or More Plate Appearances)

*Bats lefthanded. †Switch-hitter.

| Player and Club | Pct. | G. | AB. | R. | H. | TB. | 2B. | 3B. | HR. | RBI. | GW. | SH. | SF. | SB. | CS. |
|---|---|---|---|---|---|---|---|---|---|---|---|---|---|---|---|
| Boggs, Wade, Boston* | .368 | 161 | 653 | 107 | 240 | 312 | 42 | 3 | 8 | 78 | 5 | 3 | 2 | 2 | 1 |
| Brett, George, Kansas City* | .335 | 155 | 550 | 108 | 184 | 322 | 38 | 5 | 30 | 112 | 16 | 0 | 9 | 9 | 1 |
| Mattingly, Donald, New York* | .324 | 159 | 652 | 107 | 211 | 370 | 48 | 3 | 35 | 145 | 21 | 2 | 15 | 2 | 2 |
| Henderson, Rickey, New York | .314 | 143 | 547 | 146 | 172 | 282 | 28 | 5 | 24 | 72 | 6 | 0 | 5 | 80 | 10 |
| Butler, Brett, Cleveland* | .311 | 152 | 591 | 106 | 184 | 255 | 28 | 14 | 5 | 50 | 6 | 8 | 3 | 47 | 20 |
| Baines, Harold, Chicago* | .309 | 160 | 640 | 86 | 198 | 299 | 29 | 3 | 22 | 113 | 13 | 0 | 10 | 1 | 1 |
| Bradley, Philip, Seattle | .300 | 159 | 641 | 100 | 192 | 319 | 33 | 8 | 26 | 88 | 12 | 4 | 2 | 22 | 9 |
| Buckner, William, Boston* | .299 | 162 | 673 | 89 | 201 | 301 | 46 | 3 | 16 | 110 | 11 | 2 | 11 | 18 | 4 |
| Molitor, Paul, Milwaukee | .297 | 140 | 576 | 93 | 171 | 235 | 28 | 3 | 10 | 48 | 2 | 7 | 4 | 21 | 7 |
| Murray, Eddie, Baltimore† | .297 | 156 | 583 | 111 | 173 | 305 | 37 | 1 | 31 | 124 | 15 | 0 | 8 | 5 | 2 |
| Gedman, Richard, Boston* | .295 | 144 | 498 | 66 | 147 | 241 | 30 | 5 | 18 | 80 | 10 | 3 | 2 | 2 | 0 |
| Cooper, Cecil, Milwaukee* | .293 | 154 | 631 | 82 | 185 | 288 | 39 | 8 | 16 | 99 | 10 | 1 | 10 | 10 | 3 |
| Lacy, Leondaus, Baltimore | .293 | 121 | 492 | 69 | 144 | 201 | 22 | 4 | 9 | 48 | 5 | 1 | 6 | 10 | 3 |
| Rice, James, Boston | .291 | 140 | 546 | 85 | 159 | 266 | 20 | 3 | 27 | 103 | 9 | 0 | 9 | 2 | 0 |
| Barfield, Jesse, Toronto | .289 | 155 | 539 | 94 | 156 | 289 | 34 | 9 | 27 | 84 | 12 | 0 | 3 | 22 | 8 |

DEPARTMENTAL LEADERS: G—Walker (Chi.), 163; AB—Puckett, 691; R—Henderson (N.Y.), 146; H—Boggs, 240; TB—Mattingly, 370; 2B—Mattingly, 48; 3B—Wilson, 21; HR—Evans (Det.), 40; RBI—Mattingly, 145; GW—Mattingly, 21; SH—Meacham, 23; SF—Mattingly, 15; SB—Henderson (N.Y.), 80; CS—Butler, 20.

(All Players—Listed Alphabetically)

| Player and Club | Pct. | G. | AB. | R. | H. | TB. | 2B. | 3B. | HR. | RBI. | GW. | SH. | SF. | SB. | CS. |
|---|---|---|---|---|---|---|---|---|---|---|---|---|---|---|---|
| Aikens, Willie, Toronto* | .200 | 12 | 20 | 2 | 4 | 8 | 1 | 0 | 1 | 5 | 1 | 0 | 1 | 0 | 0 |
| Allenson, Gary, Toronto | .118 | 14 | 34 | 2 | 4 | 5 | 1 | 0 | 0 | 3 | 0 | 0 | 0 | 0 | 0 |
| Armas, Antonio, Boston | .265 | 103 | 385 | 50 | 102 | 198 | 17 | 5 | 23 | 64 | 10 | 0 | 5 | 0 | 0 |
| Ayala, Benigno, Cleveland | .250 | 46 | 76 | 10 | 19 | 32 | 7 | 0 | 2 | 15 | 2 | 0 | 1 | 0 | 0 |
| Baines, Harold, Chicago* | .309 | 160 | 640 | 86 | 198 | 299 | 29 | 3 | 22 | 113 | 13 | 0 | 10 | 1 | 1 |
| Baker, Douglas, Detroit† | .185 | 15 | 27 | 4 | 5 | 6 | 1 | 0 | 0 | 1 | 0 | 0 | 0 | 0 | 0 |
| Baker, Johnnie, Oakland | .268 | 111 | 343 | 48 | 92 | 151 | 15 | 1 | 14 | 52 | 4 | 0 | 3 | 2 | 1 |
| Balboni, Stephen, Kansas City | .243 | 160 | 600 | 74 | 146 | 286 | 28 | 2 | 36 | 88 | 9 | 0 | 5 | 1 | 1 |
| Bando, Christopher, Cleveland† | .139 | 73 | 173 | 11 | 24 | 30 | 4 | 1 | 0 | 13 | 1 | 2 | 2 | 0 | 1 |
| Bannister, Alan, Texas | .262 | 57 | 122 | 17 | 32 | 41 | 4 | 1 | 1 | 6 | 0 | 1 | 0 | 8 | 2 |
| Barfield, Jesse, Toronto | .289 | 155 | 539 | 94 | 156 | 289 | 34 | 9 | 27 | 84 | 12 | 0 | 3 | 22 | 8 |
| Barrett, Martin, Boston | .266 | 156 | 534 | 59 | 142 | 183 | 26 | 0 | 5 | 56 | 3 | 12 | 4 | 7 | 5 |
| Baylor, Donald, New York | .231 | 142 | 477 | 70 | 110 | 205 | 24 | 1 | 23 | 91 | 10 | 1 | 10 | 0 | 4 |
| Bell, David, Texas | .236 | 84 | 313 | 33 | 74 | 105 | 13 | 3 | 4 | 32 | 3 | 0 | 4 | 3 | 2 |
| Bell, George, Toronto | .275 | 157 | 607 | 87 | 167 | 291 | 28 | 6 | 28 | 95 | 11 | 0 | 8 | 21 | 6 |
| Beniquez, Juan, California | .304 | 132 | 411 | 54 | 125 | 172 | 13 | 5 | 8 | 42 | 5 | 9 | 1 | 4 | 3 |
| Benton, Alfred, Cleveland | .179 | 31 | 67 | 5 | 12 | 16 | 4 | 0 | 0 | 7 | 0 | 1 | 2 | 0 | 0 |
| Bergman, David, Detroit* | .179 | 69 | 140 | 8 | 25 | 36 | 2 | 0 | 3 | 7 | 2 | 1 | 2 | 0 | 0 |
| Bernazard, Antonio, Cleveland† | .274 | 153 | 500 | 73 | 137 | 202 | 26 | 3 | 11 | 59 | 5 | 5 | 4 | 17 | 9 |
| Berra, Dale, New York | .229 | 48 | 109 | 8 | 25 | 35 | 5 | 1 | 1 | 8 | 1 | 0 | 1 | 1 | 1 |
| Biancalana, Roland, Kansas City† | .188 | 81 | 138 | 21 | 26 | 36 | 5 | 1 | 1 | 6 | 1 | 5 | 0 | 1 | 4 |
| Bochte, Bruce, Oakland* | .295 | 137 | 424 | 48 | 125 | 186 | 17 | 1 | 14 | 60 | 6 | 0 | 1 | 3 | 1 |
| Boddicker, Michael, Baltimore | .000 | 34 | 0 | 1 | 0 | 0 | 0 | 0 | 0 | 0 | 0 | 0 | 0 | 0 | 0 |
| Boggs, Wade, Boston* | .368 | 161 | 653 | 107 | 240 | 312 | 42 | 3 | 8 | 78 | 5 | 3 | 2 | 2 | 1 |
| Bonilla, Juan, New York | .125 | 8 | 16 | 0 | 2 | 3 | 1 | 0 | 0 | 2 | 0 | 0 | 0 | 0 | 0 |
| Bonnell, R. Barry, Seattle | .243 | 48 | 111 | 9 | 27 | 38 | 8 | 0 | 1 | 10 | 1 | 0 | 0 | 1 | 2 |
| Boone, Robert, California | .248 | 150 | 460 | 37 | 114 | 146 | 17 | 0 | 5 | 55 | 7 | 16 | 4 | 1 | 2 |
| Boston, Daryl, Chicago* | .228 | 95 | 232 | 20 | 53 | 77 | 13 | 1 | 3 | 15 | 2 | 1 | 1 | 8 | 6 |
| Bradley, Philip, Seattle | .300 | 159 | 641 | 100 | 192 | 319 | 33 | 8 | 26 | 88 | 12 | 4 | 2 | 22 | 9 |
| Bradley, Scott, New York* | .163 | 19 | 49 | 4 | 8 | 12 | 2 | 1 | 0 | 1 | 0 | 0 | 0 | 0 | 0 |
| Brett, George, Kansas City* | .335 | 155 | 550 | 108 | 184 | 322 | 38 | 5 | 30 | 112 | 16 | 0 | 9 | 9 | 1 |
| Brookens, Thomas, Detroit | .237 | 156 | 485 | 54 | 115 | 182 | 34 | 6 | 7 | 47 | 5 | 9 | 1 | 14 | 5 |
| Brouhard, Mark, Milwaukee | .259 | 37 | 108 | 11 | 28 | 42 | 7 | 2 | 1 | 13 | 1 | 1 | 0 | 0 | 0 |
| Brown, Michael C., California | .268 | 60 | 153 | 23 | 41 | 64 | 9 | 1 | 4 | 20 | 4 | 3 | 0 | 0 | 1 |
| Brummer, Glenn, Texas | .278 | 49 | 108 | 7 | 30 | 34 | 4 | 0 | 0 | 5 | 0 | 0 | 0 | 1 | 5 |
| Brunansky, Thomas, Minnesota | .242 | 157 | 567 | 71 | 137 | 254 | 28 | 4 | 27 | 90 | 10 | 0 | 13 | 5 | 3 |
| Buckner, William, Boston* | .299 | 162 | 673 | 89 | 201 | 301 | 46 | 3 | 16 | 110 | 11 | 2 | 11 | 18 | 4 |
| Buechele, Steven, Texas | .219 | 69 | 219 | 22 | 48 | 78 | 6 | 3 | 6 | 21 | 0 | 1 | 3 | 2 | 2 |
| Burroughs, Jeffrey, Toronto | .257 | 86 | 191 | 19 | 49 | 82 | 9 | 3 | 6 | 28 | 2 | 0 | 2 | 0 | 1 |
| Bush, R. Randall, Minnesota* | .239 | 97 | 234 | 26 | 56 | 105 | 13 | 3 | 10 | 35 | 4 | 0 | 2 | 3 | 0 |
| Butler, Brett, Cleveland* | .311 | 152 | 591 | 106 | 184 | 255 | 28 | 14 | 5 | 50 | 6 | 8 | 3 | 47 | 20 |
| Calderon, Ivan, Seattle | .286 | 67 | 210 | 37 | 60 | 108 | 16 | 4 | 8 | 28 | 2 | 1 | 1 | 4 | 2 |
| Cangelosi, John, Chicago† | .000 | 5 | 2 | 2 | 0 | 0 | 0 | 0 | 0 | 0 | 0 | 1 | 0 | 0 | 0 |
| Canseco, Jose, Oakland | .302 | 29 | 96 | 16 | 29 | 47 | 3 | 0 | 5 | 13 | 0 | 0 | 0 | 1 | 1 |
| Capra, Nick, Texas | .125 | 8 | 8 | 1 | 1 | 1 | 0 | 0 | 0 | 0 | 0 | 0 | 0 | 0 | 0 |
| Carew, Rodney, California* | .280 | 127 | 443 | 69 | 124 | 153 | 17 | 3 | 2 | 39 | 4 | 9 | 1 | 5 | 5 |
| Carter, Joseph, Cleveland | .262 | 143 | 489 | 64 | 128 | 200 | 27 | 0 | 15 | 59 | 7 | 3 | 4 | 24 | 6 |
| Castillo, Martin, Detroit | .119 | 57 | 84 | 4 | 10 | 18 | 2 | 0 | 2 | 5 | 0 | 0 | 1 | 0 | 2 |
| Castillo, M. Carmelo, Cleveland | .245 | 67 | 184 | 27 | 45 | 85 | 5 | 1 | 11 | 25 | 1 | 0 | 0 | 3 | 0 |
| Chambers, Albert, Seattle* | .000 | 4 | 4 | 0 | 0 | 0 | 0 | 0 | 0 | 0 | 0 | 0 | 0 | 0 | 0 |
| Clark, Robert, Milwaukee | .226 | 29 | 93 | 6 | 21 | 24 | 3 | 0 | 0 | 8 | 1 | 0 | 1 | 1 | 1 |
| Coles, Darnell, Seattle | .237 | 27 | 59 | 8 | 14 | 21 | 4 | 0 | 1 | 5 | 1 | 0 | 2 | 0 | 1 |
| Collins, David, Oakland† | .251 | 112 | 379 | 52 | 95 | 131 | 16 | 4 | 4 | 29 | 6 | 5 | 4 | 29 | 8 |
| Concepcion, Onix, Kansas City | .204 | 131 | 314 | 32 | 64 | 77 | 5 | 1 | 2 | 20 | 2 | 12 | 1 | 4 | 4 |
| Connally, Fritzie, Baltimore | .232 | 50 | 112 | 16 | 26 | 39 | 4 | 0 | 3 | 15 | 0 | 2 | 1 | 0 | 0 |
| Cooper, Cecil, Milwaukee* | .293 | 154 | 631 | 82 | 185 | 288 | 39 | 8 | 16 | 99 | 10 | 1 | 10 | 10 | 3 |
| Cotto, Henry, New York | .304 | 34 | 56 | 4 | 17 | 21 | 1 | 0 | 1 | 6 | 0 | 1 | 0 | 1 | 1 |
| Cowens, Alfred, Seattle | .265 | 122 | 452 | 59 | 120 | 204 | 32 | 5 | 14 | 69 | 5 | 0 | 4 | 0 | 0 |
| Cruz, Julio, Chicago† | .197 | 91 | 234 | 28 | 46 | 54 | 2 | 3 | 0 | 15 | 3 | 1 | 1 | 8 | 5 |
| Dauer, Richard, Baltimore | .202 | 85 | 208 | 25 | 42 | 55 | 7 | 0 | 2 | 14 | 2 | 5 | 0 | 0 | 1 |
| Davis, Alvin, Seattle* | .287 | 155 | 578 | 78 | 166 | 255 | 33 | 1 | 18 | 78 | 7 | 0 | 7 | 1 | 2 |
| Davis, Michael, Oakland* | .287 | 154 | 547 | 92 | 157 | 265 | 34 | 1 | 24 | 82 | 8 | 3 | 2 | 24 | 10 |
| DeCinces, Douglas, California | .244 | 120 | 427 | 50 | 104 | 188 | 22 | 1 | 20 | 78 | 9 | 5 | 7 | 1 | 4 |
| Dempsey, J. Rikard, Baltimore | .254 | 132 | 362 | 54 | 92 | 147 | 19 | 0 | 12 | 52 | 4 | 5 | 2 | 0 | 1 |
| DeSa, Joseph, Chicago* | .182 | 28 | 44 | 5 | 8 | 16 | 2 | 0 | 2 | 7 | 0 | 1 | 0 | 0 | 0 |
| Dixon, Kenneth, Baltimore | .000 | 37 | 0 | 0 | 0 | 0 | 0 | 0 | 0 | 0 | 0 | 0 | 0 | 0 | 0 |
| Downing, Brian, California | .263 | 150 | 520 | 80 | 137 | 222 | 23 | 1 | 20 | 85 | 12 | 5 | 4 | 5 | 3 |
| Dunbar, Thomas, Texas* | .202 | 45 | 104 | 7 | 21 | 28 | 4 | 0 | 1 | 5 | 0 | 0 | 0 | 0 | 3 |
| Dwyer, James, Baltimore* | .249 | 101 | 233 | 35 | 58 | 93 | 8 | 3 | 7 | 36 | 3 | 2 | 1 | 0 | 3 |
| Easler, Michael, Boston* | .262 | 155 | 568 | 71 | 149 | 234 | 29 | 4 | 16 | 74 | 7 | 0 | 7 | 0 | 1 |
| Engle, R. David, Minnesota | .256 | 70 | 172 | 28 | 44 | 77 | 8 | 2 | 7 | 25 | 3 | 0 | 2 | 2 | 2 |
| Espino, Juan, New York | .364 | 9 | 11 | 0 | 4 | 4 | 0 | 0 | 0 | 0 | 0 | 0 | 0 | 0 | 0 |
| Espinoza, Alvaro, Minnesota | .263 | 32 | 57 | 5 | 15 | 17 | 2 | 0 | 0 | 9 | 0 | 3 | 0 | 0 | 1 |
| Evans, Darrell, Detroit* | .248 | 151 | 505 | 81 | 125 | 262 | 17 | 0 | 40 | 94 | 10 | 1 | 2 | 0 | 4 |

| Player and Club | Pct. | G. | AB. | R. | H. | TB. | 2B. | 3B. | HR. | RBI. | GW. | SH. | SF. | SB. | CS. |
|---|---|---|---|---|---|---|---|---|---|---|---|---|---|---|---|
| Evans, Dwight, Boston | .263 | 159 | 617 | 110 | 162 | 280 | 29 | 1 | 29 | 78 | 13 | 1 | 7 | 7 | 2 |
| Felder, Mike, Milwaukee† | .196 | 15 | 56 | 8 | 11 | 12 | 1 | 0 | 0 | 0 | 0 | 1 | 0 | 4 | 1 |
| Fernandez, O. Antonio, Toronto† | .289 | 161 | 564 | 71 | 163 | 220 | 31 | 10 | 2 | 51 | 6 | 7 | 2 | 13 | 6 |
| Fielder, Cecil, Toronto | .311 | 30 | 74 | 6 | 23 | 39 | 4 | 0 | 4 | 16 | 4 | 0 | 1 | 0 | 0 |
| Fischlin, Michael, Cleveland | .200 | 73 | 60 | 12 | 12 | 18 | 4 | 1 | 0 | 2 | 0 | 4 | 0 | 0 | 1 |
| Fisk, Carlton, Chicago | .238 | 153 | 543 | 85 | 129 | 265 | 23 | 1 | 37 | 107 | 13 | 2 | 6 | 17 | 9 |
| Fletcher, Scott, Chicago | .256 | 119 | 301 | 38 | 77 | 93 | 8 | 1 | 2 | 31 | 1 | 11 | 1 | 5 | 5 |
| Flynn, R. Douglas, Detroit | .255 | 32 | 51 | 2 | 13 | 17 | 2 | 1 | 0 | 2 | 0 | 3 | 1 | 0 | 0 |
| Ford, Darnell, Baltimore | .187 | 28 | 75 | 4 | 14 | 19 | 2 | 0 | 1 | 1 | 0 | 0 | 0 | 0 | 1 |
| Franco, Julio, Cleveland | .288 | 160 | 636 | 97 | 183 | 242 | 33 | 4 | 6 | 90 | 9 | 0 | 9 | 13 | 9 |
| Funderburk, Mark, Minnesota | .314 | 23 | 70 | 7 | 22 | 37 | 7 | 1 | 2 | 13 | 1 | 0 | 2 | 0 | 1 |
| Gaetti, Gary, Minnesota | .246 | 160 | 560 | 71 | 138 | 229 | 31 | 0 | 20 | 63 | 8 | 3 | 1 | 13 | 5 |
| Gagne, Gregory, Minnesota | .225 | 114 | 293 | 37 | 66 | 93 | 15 | 3 | 2 | 23 | 4 | 3 | 3 | 10 | 4 |
| Gallego, Michael, Oakland | .208 | 76 | 77 | 13 | 16 | 26 | 5 | 1 | 1 | 9 | 1 | 2 | 1 | 1 | 1 |
| Gamble, Oscar, Chicago* | .203 | 70 | 148 | 20 | 30 | 47 | 5 | 0 | 4 | 20 | 1 | 0 | 1 | 0 | 0 |
| Gantner, James, Milwaukee* | .254 | 143 | 523 | 63 | 133 | 171 | 15 | 4 | 5 | 44 | 5 | 10 | 4 | 11 | 8 |
| Garbey, Barbaro, Detroit | .257 | 86 | 237 | 27 | 61 | 90 | 9 | 1 | 6 | 29 | 3 | 0 | 4 | 3 | 2 |
| Garcia, Damaso, Toronto | .282 | 146 | 600 | 70 | 169 | 226 | 25 | 4 | 8 | 65 | 10 | 5 | 3 | 28 | 15 |
| Gedman, Richard, Boston* | .295 | 144 | 498 | 66 | 147 | 241 | 30 | 5 | 18 | 80 | 10 | 3 | 2 | 2 | 0 |
| Gerber, Craig, California* | .264 | 65 | 91 | 8 | 24 | 29 | 1 | 2 | 0 | 6 | 0 | 3 | 1 | 0 | 3 |
| Gibson, Kirk, Detroit* | .287 | 154 | 581 | 96 | 167 | 301 | 37 | 5 | 29 | 97 | 8 | 3 | 10 | 30 | 4 |
| Gilbert, Mark, Chicago† | .273 | 7 | 22 | 3 | 6 | 7 | 1 | 0 | 0 | 3 | 0 | 0 | 0 | 0 | 0 |
| Giles, Brian, Milwaukee | .172 | 34 | 58 | 6 | 10 | 14 | 1 | 0 | 1 | 1 | 0 | 0 | 0 | 2 | 1 |
| Greenwell, Michael, Boston* | .323 | 17 | 31 | 7 | 10 | 23 | 1 | 0 | 4 | 8 | 2 | 0 | 0 | 1 | 0 |
| Grich, Robert, California | .242 | 144 | 479 | 74 | 116 | 178 | 17 | 3 | 13 | 53 | 5 | 8 | 0 | 3 | 5 |
| Griffey, G. Kenneth, New York* | .274 | 127 | 438 | 68 | 120 | 186 | 28 | 4 | 10 | 69 | 6 | 0 | 8 | 7 | 7 |
| Griffin, Alfredo, Oakland† | .270 | 162 | 614 | 75 | 166 | 204 | 18 | 7 | 2 | 64 | 8 | 5 | 7 | 24 | 9 |
| Gross, Wayne, Baltimore* | .235 | 103 | 217 | 31 | 51 | 92 | 8 | 0 | 11 | 18 | 1 | 1 | 0 | 1 | 1 |
| Grubb, John, Detroit* | .245 | 78 | 155 | 19 | 38 | 62 | 7 | 1 | 5 | 25 | 2 | 0 | 4 | 0 | 1 |
| Gruber, Kelly, Toronto | .231 | 5 | 13 | 0 | 3 | 3 | 0 | 0 | 0 | 1 | 1 | 0 | 0 | 0 | 0 |
| Guillen, Oswaldo, Chicago* | .273 | 150 | 491 | 71 | 134 | 176 | 21 | 9 | 1 | 33 | 3 | 8 | 1 | 7 | 4 |
| Gutierrez, Joaquin, Boston | .218 | 103 | 275 | 33 | 60 | 75 | 5 | 2 | 2 | 21 | 2 | 9 | 1 | 10 | 2 |
| Hairston, Jerry, Chicago† | .243 | 95 | 140 | 9 | 34 | 48 | 8 | 0 | 2 | 20 | 2 | 0 | 4 | 0 | 0 |
| Hall, Melvin, Cleveland* | .318 | 23 | 66 | 7 | 21 | 27 | 6 | 0 | 0 | 12 | 0 | 0 | 1 | 0 | 1 |
| Hargrove, D. Michael, Cleveland* | .285 | 107 | 284 | 31 | 81 | 100 | 14 | 1 | 1 | 27 | 0 | 2 | 1 | 1 | 0 |
| Harrah, Colbert, Texas | .270 | 126 | 396 | 65 | 107 | 154 | 18 | 1 | 9 | 44 | 6 | 2 | 6 | 11 | 4 |
| Hassey, Ronald, New York* | .296 | 92 | 267 | 31 | 79 | 136 | 16 | 1 | 13 | 42 | 6 | 0 | 0 | 0 | 0 |
| Hatcher, Michael, Minnesota | .282 | 116 | 444 | 46 | 125 | 162 | 28 | 0 | 3 | 49 | 5 | 3 | 2 | 0 | 0 |
| Hearron, Jeffrey, Toronto | .143 | 4 | 7 | 0 | 1 | 1 | 0 | 0 | 0 | 0 | 0 | 0 | 0 | 0 | 0 |
| Heath, Michael, Oakland | .250 | 138 | 436 | 71 | 109 | 178 | 18 | 6 | 13 | 55 | 5 | 10 | 4 | 7 | 7 |
| Hegman, Robert, Kansas City | .000 | 1 | 0 | 0 | 0 | 0 | 0 | 0 | 0 | 0 | 0 | 0 | 0 | 0 | 0 |
| Henderson, David, Seattle | .241 | 139 | 502 | 70 | 121 | 195 | 28 | 2 | 14 | 68 | 7 | 1 | 2 | 6 | 1 |
| Henderson, Rickey, New York | .314 | 143 | 547 | 146 | 172 | 282 | 28 | 5 | 24 | 72 | 6 | 0 | 5 | 80 | 10 |
| Henderson, Stephen, Oakland | .301 | 85 | 193 | 25 | 58 | 81 | 8 | 3 | 3 | 31 | 4 | 1 | 1 | 0 | 0 |
| Hendrick, George, California | .122 | 16 | 41 | 5 | 5 | 12 | 1 | 0 | 2 | 6 | 0 | 0 | 1 | 0 | 0 |
| Hernandez, Guillermo, Detroit* | .000 | 74 | 1 | 0 | 0 | 0 | 0 | 0 | 0 | 0 | 0 | 0 | 0 | 0 | 0 |
| Hernandez, Leonardo, Baltimore | .048 | 12 | 21 | 0 | 1 | 1 | 0 | 0 | 0 | 0 | 0 | 0 | 0 | 0 | 0 |
| Herndon, Larry, Detroit | .244 | 137 | 442 | 45 | 108 | 170 | 12 | 7 | 12 | 37 | 5 | 1 | 1 | 2 | 1 |
| Hill, Donald, Oakland† | .285 | 123 | 393 | 45 | 112 | 138 | 13 | 2 | 3 | 48 | 2 | 16 | 4 | 9 | 4 |
| Hill, Marc, Chicago | .133 | 40 | 75 | 5 | 10 | 12 | 2 | 0 | 0 | 4 | 1 | 8 | 0 | 0 | 0 |
| Hoffman, Glenn, Boston | .276 | 96 | 279 | 40 | 77 | 116 | 17 | 2 | 6 | 34 | 3 | 9 | 3 | 2 | 2 |
| Householder, Paul, Milwaukee† | .258 | 95 | 299 | 41 | 77 | 125 | 15 | 0 | 11 | 34 | 0 | 1 | 1 | 1 | 2 |
| Howell, Jack, California* | .197 | 43 | 137 | 19 | 27 | 46 | 4 | 0 | 5 | 18 | 2 | 4 | 1 | 1 | 1 |
| Hrbek, Kent, Minnesota* | .278 | 158 | 593 | 78 | 165 | 263 | 31 | 2 | 21 | 93 | 9 | 0 | 4 | 1 | 1 |
| Hudler, Rex, New York | .157 | 20 | 51 | 4 | 8 | 10 | 0 | 1 | 0 | 1 | 0 | 5 | 0 | 0 | 1 |
| Hulett, Timothy, Chicago | .268 | 141 | 395 | 52 | 106 | 148 | 19 | 4 | 5 | 37 | 2 | 4 | 3 | 6 | 4 |
| Huppert, David, Milwaukee | .048 | 15 | 21 | 1 | 1 | 1 | 0 | 0 | 0 | 0 | 0 | 2 | 0 | 0 | 0 |
| Iorg, Dane, Kansas City* | .223 | 64 | 130 | 7 | 29 | 43 | 9 | 1 | 1 | 21 | 4 | 0 | 0 | 0 | 1 |
| Iorg, Garth, Toronto | .313 | 131 | 288 | 33 | 90 | 135 | 22 | 1 | 7 | 37 | 0 | 2 | 1 | 3 | 6 |
| Jackson, Reginald, California* | .252 | 143 | 460 | 64 | 116 | 224 | 27 | 0 | 27 | 85 | 11 | 0 | 2 | 1 | 2 |
| Jacoby, Brook, Cleveland | .274 | 161 | 606 | 72 | 166 | 258 | 26 | 3 | 20 | 87 | 4 | 1 | 7 | 2 | 3 |
| James, Dion, Milwaukee* | .224 | 18 | 49 | 5 | 11 | 12 | 1 | 0 | 0 | 3 | 0 | 0 | 0 | 0 | 0 |
| Johnson, Clifford, Tex.-Tor. | .260 | 106 | 369 | 35 | 96 | 154 | 17 | 1 | 13 | 66 | 2 | 1 | 4 | 0 | 0 |
| Jones, Lynn, Kansas City | .211 | 110 | 152 | 12 | 32 | 39 | 7 | 0 | 0 | 9 | 1 | 4 | 2 | 0 | 1 |
| Jones, Robert, Texas* | .224 | 83 | 134 | 14 | 30 | 47 | 2 | 0 | 5 | 23 | 1 | 0 | 2 | 1 | 0 |
| Jones, Ruppert, California* | .231 | 125 | 389 | 66 | 90 | 174 | 17 | 2 | 21 | 67 | 9 | 8 | 2 | 7 | 4 |
| Jurak, Edward, Boston | .231 | 26 | 13 | 4 | 3 | 3 | 0 | 0 | 0 | 0 | 0 | 0 | 0 | 0 | 0 |
| Kearney, Robert, Seattle | .243 | 108 | 305 | 24 | 74 | 108 | 14 | 1 | 6 | 27 | 4 | 5 | 1 | 1 | 1 |
| Keedy, C. Patrick, California | .500 | 3 | 4 | 1 | 2 | 6 | 1 | 0 | 1 | 1 | 0 | 0 | 0 | 0 | 0 |
| Key, James, Toronto | .000 | 36 | 0 | 0 | 0 | 0 | 0 | 0 | 0 | 0 | 0 | 0 | 0 | 0 | 0 |
| Kiefer, Steven, Oakland | .197 | 40 | 66 | 8 | 13 | 19 | 1 | 1 | 1 | 10 | 1 | 2 | 2 | 0 | 0 |
| Kingman, David, Oakland | .238 | 158 | 592 | 66 | 141 | 247 | 16 | 0 | 30 | 91 | 9 | 2 | 8 | 3 | 2 |
| Kittle, Ronald, Chicago | .230 | 116 | 379 | 51 | 87 | 177 | 12 | 0 | 26 | 58 | 8 | 0 | 2 | 1 | 4 |
| Kunkel, Jeffrey, Texas | .250 | 2 | 4 | 1 | 1 | 1 | 0 | 0 | 0 | 0 | 0 | 0 | 0 | 0 | 0 |
| Kuntz, Russell, Detroit | .000 | 5 | 5 | 0 | 0 | 0 | 0 | 0 | 0 | 0 | 0 | 0 | 0 | 0 | 1 |
| Lacy, Leondaus, Baltimore | .293 | 121 | 492 | 69 | 144 | 201 | 22 | 4 | 9 | 48 | 5 | 1 | 6 | 10 | 3 |
| Laga, Michael, Detroit* | .167 | 9 | 36 | 3 | 6 | 13 | 1 | 0 | 2 | 6 | 0 | 0 | 0 | 0 | 0 |
| Lansford, Carney, Oakland | .277 | 98 | 401 | 51 | 111 | 172 | 18 | 2 | 13 | 46 | 7 | 4 | 5 | 2 | 3 |
| Laudner, Timothy, Minnesota | .238 | 72 | 164 | 16 | 39 | 65 | 5 | 0 | 7 | 19 | 2 | 4 | 1 | 0 | 1 |
| Law, Rudy, Chicago* | .259 | 125 | 390 | 62 | 101 | 146 | 21 | 6 | 4 | 36 | 3 | 6 | 1 | 29 | 6 |

| Player and Club | Pct. | G. | AB. | R. | H. | TB. | 2B. | 3B. | HR. | RBI. | GW. | SH. | SF. | SB. | CS. |
|---|---|---|---|---|---|---|---|---|---|---|---|---|---|---|---|
| Leach, Richard, Toronto* | .200 | 16 | 35 | 2 | 7 | 9 | 0 | 1 | 0 | 1 | 0 | 0 | 0 | 0 | 0 |
| Lee, Manuel, Toronto† | .200 | 64 | 40 | 9 | 8 | 8 | 0 | 0 | 0 | 0 | 0 | 1 | 0 | 1 | 4 |
| Leeper, David, Kansas City* | .088 | 15 | 34 | 1 | 3 | 3 | 0 | 0 | 0 | 4 | 2 | 0 | 0 | 0 | 0 |
| LeMaster, Johnnie, Cleveland | .150 | 11 | 20 | 0 | 3 | 3 | 0 | 0 | 0 | 2 | 0 | 1 | 0 | 0 | 1 |
| Lemon, Chester, Detroit | .265 | 145 | 517 | 69 | 137 | 227 | 28 | 4 | 18 | 68 | 9 | 0 | 3 | 0 | 2 |
| Linares, Rufino, California | .256 | 18 | 43 | 7 | 11 | 22 | 2 | 0 | 3 | 11 | 3 | 0 | 1 | 2 | 0 |
| Little, R. Bryan, Chicago† | .250 | 73 | 188 | 35 | 47 | 64 | 9 | 1 | 2 | 27 | 4 | 3 | 3 | 0 | 1 |
| Lollar, W. Timothy, Chi.-Bos.* | .000 | 35 | 1 | 0 | 0 | 0 | 0 | 0 | 0 | 0 | 0 | 0 | 0 | 0 | 0 |
| Loman, Douglas, Milwaukee* | .212 | 24 | 66 | 10 | 14 | 21 | 3 | 2 | 0 | 7 | 0 | 2 | 1 | 0 | 0 |
| Lombardozzi, Stephen, Minnesota | .370 | 28 | 54 | 10 | 20 | 26 | 4 | 1 | 0 | 6 | 0 | 4 | 1 | 3 | 2 |
| Lowenstein, John, Baltimore* | .077 | 12 | 26 | 0 | 2 | 2 | 0 | 0 | 0 | 2 | 1 | 0 | 1 | 0 | 0 |
| Lynn, Fredric, Baltimore* | .263 | 124 | 448 | 59 | 118 | 201 | 12 | 1 | 23 | 68 | 8 | 0 | 6 | 7 | 3 |
| Lyons, Stephen, Boston* | .264 | 133 | 371 | 52 | 98 | 133 | 14 | 3 | 5 | 30 | 3 | 2 | 3 | 12 | 9 |
| Madison, C. Scott, Detroit† | .000 | 6 | 11 | 0 | 0 | 0 | 0 | 0 | 0 | 1 | 0 | 0 | 1 | 0 | 0 |
| Manning, Richard, Milwaukee* | .218 | 79 | 216 | 19 | 47 | 64 | 9 | 1 | 2 | 18 | 3 | 1 | 0 | 1 | 0 |
| Martinez, John, Toronto | .162 | 42 | 99 | 11 | 16 | 31 | 3 | 0 | 4 | 14 | 3 | 0 | 3 | 0 | 0 |
| Mata, Victor, New York | .143 | 6 | 7 | 1 | 1 | 1 | 0 | 0 | 0 | 0 | 0 | 0 | 0 | 0 | 0 |
| Mattingly, Donald, New York* | .324 | 159 | 652 | 107 | 211 | 370 | 48 | 3 | 35 | 145 | 21 | 2 | 15 | 2 | 2 |
| Matuszek, Leonard, Toronto* | .212 | 62 | 151 | 23 | 32 | 48 | 6 | 2 | 2 | 15 | 0 | 0 | 4 | 2 | 1 |
| McDowell, Oddibe, Texas* | .239 | 111 | 406 | 63 | 97 | 175 | 14 | 5 | 18 | 42 | 7 | 5 | 2 | 25 | 7 |
| McRae, Harold, Kansas City | .259 | 112 | 320 | 41 | 83 | 144 | 19 | 0 | 14 | 70 | 9 | 2 | 2 | 0 | 1 |
| Meacham, Robert, New York† | .218 | 156 | 481 | 70 | 105 | 128 | 16 | 2 | 1 | 47 | 3 | 23 | 3 | 25 | 7 |
| Meier, David, Minnesota | .260 | 71 | 104 | 15 | 27 | 36 | 6 | 0 | 1 | 8 | 0 | 3 | 0 | 0 | 6 |
| Melvin, Robert, Detroit | .220 | 41 | 82 | 10 | 18 | 24 | 4 | 1 | 0 | 4 | 0 | 2 | 0 | 0 | 0 |
| Meyer, Daniel, Oakland* | .000 | 14 | 12 | 2 | 0 | 0 | 0 | 0 | 0 | 0 | 0 | 0 | 0 | 0 | 0 |
| Miller, Darrell, California | .375 | 51 | 48 | 8 | 18 | 28 | 2 | 1 | 2 | 7 | 0 | 0 | 0 | 0 | 1 |
| Miller, Richard, Boston* | .333 | 41 | 45 | 5 | 15 | 17 | 2 | 0 | 0 | 9 | 0 | 0 | 1 | 1 | 0 |
| Molitor, Paul, Milwaukee | .297 | 140 | 576 | 93 | 171 | 235 | 28 | 3 | 10 | 48 | 2 | 7 | 4 | 21 | 7 |
| Moore, Charles, Milwaukee | .232 | 105 | 349 | 35 | 81 | 102 | 13 | 4 | 0 | 31 | 8 | 8 | 1 | 4 | 0 |
| Moreno, Omar, N.Y.-K.C.* | .221 | 58 | 136 | 21 | 30 | 52 | 5 | 4 | 3 | 16 | 0 | 1 | 1 | 1 | 2 |
| Morris, John, Detroit | .000 | 36 | 0 | 0 | 0 | 0 | 0 | 0 | 0 | 0 | 0 | 0 | 0 | 0 | 0 |
| Moseby, Lloyd, Toronto* | .259 | 152 | 584 | 92 | 151 | 249 | 30 | 7 | 18 | 70 | 10 | 1 | 5 | 37 | 15 |
| Moses, John, Seattle† | .194 | 33 | 62 | 4 | 12 | 12 | 0 | 0 | 0 | 3 | 0 | 1 | 0 | 5 | 2 |
| Motley, Darryl, Kansas City | .222 | 123 | 383 | 45 | 85 | 158 | 20 | 1 | 17 | 49 | 4 | 0 | 5 | 6 | 4 |
| Mulliniks, S. Rance, Toronto* | .295 | 129 | 366 | 55 | 108 | 166 | 26 | 1 | 10 | 57 | 11 | 1 | 5 | 2 | 0 |
| Murphy, Dwayne, Oakland* | .233 | 152 | 523 | 77 | 122 | 209 | 21 | 3 | 20 | 59 | 7 | 5 | 4 | 4 | 5 |
| Murray, Eddie, Baltimore† | .297 | 156 | 583 | 111 | 173 | 305 | 37 | 1 | 31 | 124 | 15 | 0 | 8 | 5 | 2 |
| Narron, Jerry, California* | .220 | 67 | 132 | 12 | 29 | 48 | 4 | 0 | 5 | 14 | 2 | 0 | 0 | 0 | 0 |
| Nelson, Ricky, Seattle* | .000 | 6 | 2 | 2 | 0 | 0 | 0 | 0 | 0 | 0 | 0 | 0 | 0 | 0 | 0 |
| Nelson, W. Eugene, Chicago | .000 | 47 | 1 | 0 | 0 | 0 | 0 | 0 | 0 | 0 | 0 | 0 | 0 | 0 | 0 |
| Nichols, T. Reid, Bos.-Chi. | .273 | 72 | 150 | 23 | 41 | 57 | 8 | 1 | 2 | 18 | 4 | 3 | 2 | 6 | 5 |
| Nicosia, Steven, Toronto | .267 | 6 | 15 | 0 | 4 | 4 | 0 | 0 | 0 | 1 | 0 | 0 | 0 | 0 | 0 |
| Nixon, Otis, Cleveland† | .235 | 104 | 162 | 34 | 38 | 51 | 4 | 0 | 3 | 9 | 1 | 4 | 0 | 20 | 11 |
| Nolan, Joseph, Baltimore* | .132 | 31 | 38 | 1 | 5 | 7 | 2 | 0 | 0 | 6 | 0 | 0 | 1 | 0 | 0 |
| O'Brien, Charles, Oakland | .273 | 16 | 11 | 3 | 3 | 4 | 1 | 0 | 0 | 1 | 0 | 0 | 0 | 0 | 0 |
| O'Brien, Peter, Texas* | .267 | 159 | 573 | 69 | 153 | 259 | 34 | 3 | 22 | 92 | 10 | 3 | 9 | 5 | 10 |
| Oglivie, Benjamin, Milwaukee* | .290 | 101 | 341 | 40 | 99 | 150 | 17 | 2 | 10 | 61 | 7 | 4 | 10 | 0 | 2 |
| Oliver, Albert, Toronto* | .251 | 61 | 187 | 20 | 47 | 70 | 6 | 1 | 5 | 23 | 3 | 0 | 0 | 0 | 0 |
| O'Malley, Thomas, Baltimore* | .071 | 8 | 14 | 1 | 1 | 4 | 0 | 0 | 1 | 2 | 0 | 0 | 0 | 0 | 0 |
| Orta, Jorge, Kansas City* | .267 | 110 | 300 | 32 | 80 | 115 | 21 | 1 | 4 | 45 | 6 | 2 | 4 | 2 | 1 |
| Owen, Spike, Seattle† | .259 | 118 | 352 | 41 | 91 | 131 | 10 | 6 | 6 | 37 | 3 | 5 | 2 | 11 | 5 |
| Paciorek, Thomas, Chicago | .246 | 46 | 122 | 14 | 30 | 32 | 2 | 0 | 0 | 9 | 2 | 0 | 2 | 2 | 0 |
| Pagliarulo, Michael, New York* | .239 | 138 | 380 | 55 | 91 | 168 | 16 | 2 | 19 | 62 | 5 | 3 | 3 | 0 | 0 |
| Pardo, Alberto, Baltimore† | .133 | 34 | 75 | 3 | 10 | 11 | 1 | 0 | 0 | 1 | 0 | 0 | 0 | 0 | 0 |
| Paris, Kelly, Baltimore | .000 | 5 | 9 | 0 | 0 | 0 | 0 | 0 | 0 | 0 | 0 | 0 | 0 | 0 | 0 |
| Parrish, Lance, Detroit | .273 | 140 | 549 | 64 | 150 | 263 | 27 | 1 | 28 | 98 | 16 | 3 | 5 | 2 | 6 |
| Parrish, Larry, Texas | .249 | 94 | 346 | 44 | 86 | 150 | 11 | 1 | 17 | 51 | 4 | 0 | 2 | 0 | 2 |
| Pasqua, Daniel, New York* | .209 | 60 | 148 | 17 | 31 | 63 | 3 | 1 | 9 | 25 | 1 | 0 | 1 | 0 | 0 |
| Perconte, John, Seattle* | .264 | 125 | 485 | 60 | 128 | 165 | 17 | 7 | 2 | 23 | 2 | 2 | 2 | 31 | 2 |
| Petralli, Eugene, Texas† | .270 | 42 | 100 | 7 | 27 | 29 | 2 | 0 | 0 | 11 | 1 | 3 | 4 | 1 | 0 |
| Pettis, Gary, California† | .257 | 125 | 443 | 67 | 114 | 143 | 10 | 8 | 1 | 32 | 2 | 9 | 2 | 56 | 9 |
| Phelps, Kenneth, Seattle* | .207 | 61 | 116 | 18 | 24 | 54 | 3 | 0 | 9 | 24 | 3 | 0 | 0 | 2 | 0 |
| Phillips, K. Anthony, Oakland† | .280 | 42 | 161 | 23 | 45 | 73 | 12 | 2 | 4 | 17 | 2 | 3 | 1 | 3 | 2 |
| Picciolo, Robert, Oakland | .275 | 71 | 102 | 19 | 28 | 33 | 2 | 0 | 1 | 8 | 0 | 0 | 0 | 3 | 2 |
| Pittaro, Christopher, Detroit† | .242 | 28 | 62 | 10 | 15 | 20 | 3 | 1 | 0 | 7 | 1 | 1 | 0 | 1 | 1 |
| Polidor, Gustavo, California | 1.000 | 2 | 1 | 1 | 1 | 1 | 0 | 0 | 0 | 0 | 0 | 0 | 0 | 0 | 0 |
| Ponce, Carlos, Milwaukee | .161 | 21 | 60 | 4 | 10 | 15 | 2 | 0 | 1 | 5 | 0 | 1 | 2 | 0 | 0 |
| Presley, James, Seattle | .275 | 155 | 570 | 71 | 157 | 276 | 33 | 1 | 28 | 84 | 6 | 1 | 9 | 2 | 2 |
| Pryor, Gregory, Kansas City | .219 | 63 | 114 | 8 | 25 | 31 | 3 | 0 | 1 | 3 | 1 | 3 | 0 | 0 | 1 |
| Puckett, Kirby, Minnesota | .288 | 161 | 691 | 80 | 199 | 266 | 29 | 13 | 4 | 74 | 7 | 5 | 3 | 21 | 12 |
| Pujols, Luis, Texas | 1.000 | 1 | 1 | 0 | 1 | 1 | 0 | 0 | 0 | 0 | 0 | 0 | 0 | 0 | 0 |
| Quirk, James, Kansas City* | .281 | 19 | 57 | 3 | 16 | 21 | 3 | 1 | 0 | 4 | 2 | 0 | 0 | 0 | 0 |
| Ramos, Domingo, Seattle | .196 | 75 | 168 | 19 | 33 | 42 | 6 | 0 | 1 | 15 | 2 | 3 | 2 | 0 | 1 |
| Randolph, William, New York | .276 | 143 | 497 | 75 | 137 | 177 | 21 | 2 | 5 | 40 | 6 | 5 | 6 | 16 | 9 |
| Rayford, Floyd, Baltimore | .306 | 105 | 359 | 55 | 110 | 187 | 21 | 1 | 18 | 48 | 3 | 2 | 1 | 3 | 1 |
| Ready, Randy, Milwaukee | .265 | 48 | 181 | 29 | 48 | 70 | 9 | 5 | 1 | 21 | 3 | 2 | 2 | 0 | 0 |
| Reed, Jeffrey, Minnesota* | .200 | 7 | 10 | 2 | 2 | 2 | 0 | 0 | 0 | 0 | 0 | 0 | 0 | 0 | 0 |
| Reynolds, Harold, Seattle† | .144 | 67 | 104 | 15 | 15 | 20 | 3 | 1 | 0 | 6 | 0 | 1 | 0 | 3 | 2 |
| Rice, James, Boston | .291 | 140 | 546 | 85 | 159 | 266 | 20 | 3 | 27 | 103 | 9 | 0 | 9 | 2 | 0 |
| Riles, Ernest, Milwaukee* | .286 | 116 | 448 | 54 | 128 | 169 | 12 | 7 | 5 | 45 | 3 | 6 | 3 | 2 | 2 |

| Player and Club | Pct. | G. | AB. | R. | H. | TB. | 2B. | 3B. | HR. | RBI. | GW. | SH. | SF. | SB. | CS. |
|---|---|---|---|---|---|---|---|---|---|---|---|---|---|---|---|
| Ripken, Calvin, Baltimore | .282 | 161 | 642 | 116 | 181 | 301 | 32 | 5 | 26 | 110 | 15 | 0 | 8 | 2 | 3 |
| Robertson, Andre, New York | .328 | 50 | 125 | 16 | 41 | 52 | 5 | 0 | 2 | 17 | 0 | 2 | 2 | 1 | 2 |
| Robidoux, William, Milwaukee* | .176 | 18 | 51 | 5 | 9 | 20 | 2 | 0 | 3 | 8 | 3 | 0 | 0 | 0 | 0 |
| Roenicke, Gary, Baltimore | .218 | 114 | 225 | 36 | 49 | 103 | 9 | 0 | 15 | 43 | 5 | 2 | 3 | 2 | 2 |
| Romero, Edgardo, Milwaukee | 251 | 88 | 251 | 24 | 63 | 76 | 11 | 1 | 0 | 21 | 1 | 5 | 0 | 1 | 1 |
| Romine, Kevin, Boston | .214 | 24 | 28 | 3 | 6 | 8 | 2 | 0 | 0 | 1 | 0 | 2 | 0 | 1 | 0 |
| Ryal, Mark, Chicago* | .152 | 12 | 33 | 4 | 5 | 8 | 3 | 0 | 0 | 3 | 0 | 1 | 0 | 0 | 0 |
| Sakata, Lenn, Baltimore | .227 | 55 | 97 | 15 | 22 | 34 | 3 | 0 | 3 | 6 | 1 | 1 | 0 | 3 | 2 |
| Salas, Mark, Minnesota* | .300 | 120 | 360 | 51 | 108 | 165 | 20 | 5 | 9 | 41 | 7 | 0 | 3 | 0 | 1 |
| Salazar, Luis, Chicago | .245 | 122 | 327 | 39 | 80 | 132 | 18 | 2 | 10 | 45 | 5 | 9 | 5 | 14 | 4 |
| Sample, William, New York | .288 | 59 | 139 | 18 | 40 | 48 | 5 | 0 | 1 | 15 | 0 | 2 | 2 | 2 | 1 |
| Sanchez, Alejandro, Detroit | .248 | 71 | 133 | 19 | 33 | 61 | 6 | 2 | 6 | 12 | 2 | 0 | 0 | 2 | 2 |
| Sax, David, Boston | .306 | 22 | 36 | 2 | 11 | 14 | 3 | 0 | 0 | 6 | 0 | 3 | 1 | 0 | 1 |
| Schofield, Richard, California | .219 | 147 | 438 | 50 | 96 | 145 | 19 | 3 | 8 | 41 | 4 | 12 | 3 | 11 | 4 |
| Schroeder, A. William, Milwaukee | .242 | 53 | 194 | 18 | 47 | 79 | 8 | 0 | 8 | 25 | 1 | 0 | 2 | 0 | 1 |
| Sconiers, Daryl, California* | .286 | 44 | 98 | 14 | 28 | 42 | 6 | 1 | 2 | 12 | 1 | 0 | 3 | 2 | 1 |
| Scott, Donald, Seattle† | .222 | 80 | 185 | 18 | 41 | 66 | 13 | 0 | 4 | 23 | 4 | 1 | 4 | 1 | 1 |
| Scranton, James, Kansas City | .000 | 6 | 4 | 1 | 0 | 0 | 0 | 0 | 0 | 0 | 0 | 0 | 0 | 0 | 0 |
| Sheets, Larry, Baltimore* | .262 | 113 | 328 | 43 | 86 | 145 | 8 | 0 | 17 | 50 | 4 | 1 | 1 | 0 | 1 |
| Shelby, John, Baltimore† | .283 | 69 | 205 | 28 | 58 | 89 | 6 | 2 | 7 | 27 | 4 | 2 | 0 | 5 | 1 |
| Shepherd, Ronald, Toronto | .114 | 38 | 35 | 7 | 4 | 6 | 2 | 0 | 0 | 1 | 0 | 0 | 0 | 3 | 0 |
| Sheridan, Patrick, Kansas City* | .228 | 78 | 206 | 18 | 47 | 69 | 9 | 2 | 3 | 17 | 3 | 3 | 1 | 11 | 3 |
| Simmons, Nelson, Detroit† | .239 | 75 | 251 | 31 | 60 | 101 | 11 | 0 | 10 | 33 | 4 | 0 | 4 | 1 | 0 |
| Simmons, Ted, Milwaukee† | .273 | 143 | 528 | 60 | 144 | 212 | 28 | 2 | 12 | 76 | 13 | 1 | 5 | 1 | 1 |
| Skinner, Joel, Chicago | .341 | 22 | 44 | 9 | 15 | 24 | 4 | 1 | 1 | 5 | 0 | 1 | 0 | 0 | 0 |
| Slaught, Donald, Texas | .280 | 102 | 343 | 34 | 96 | 145 | 17 | 4 | 8 | 35 | 4 | 1 | 0 | 5 | 4 |
| Smalley, Roy, Minnesota† | .258 | 129 | 388 | 57 | 100 | 156 | 20 | 0 | 12 | 45 | 5 | 1 | 2 | 0 | 2 |
| Smith, Lonnie, Kansas City | .257 | 120 | 448 | 77 | 115 | 164 | 23 | 4 | 6 | 41 | 6 | 0 | 5 | 40 | 7 |
| Smith, P. Keith, New York† | .000 | 4 | 0 | 1 | 0 | 0 | 0 | 0 | 0 | 0 | 0 | 0 | 0 | 0 | 0 |
| Spillner, Daniel, Chicago | .000 | 53 | 0 | 0 | 0 | 0 | 0 | 0 | 0 | 0 | 0 | 0 | 0 | 0 | 0 |
| Squires, Michael, Chicago* | .000 | 2 | 0 | 1 | 0 | 0 | 0 | 0 | 0 | 0 | 0 | 0 | 0 | 0 | 0 |
| Stapleton, David, Boston | .227 | 30 | 66 | 4 | 15 | 21 | 6 | 0 | 0 | 2 | 0 | 1 | 0 | 0 | 0 |
| Stein, William, Texas | .253 | 44 | 79 | 5 | 20 | 28 | 3 | 1 | 1 | 12 | 1 | 0 | 0 | 0 | 0 |
| Stenhouse, Michael, Minnesota* | .223 | 81 | 179 | 23 | 40 | 60 | 5 | 0 | 5 | 21 | 3 | 0 | 1 | 1 | 0 |
| Sullivan, Marc, Boston | .174 | 32 | 69 | 10 | 12 | 20 | 2 | 0 | 2 | 3 | 0 | 2 | 0 | 0 | 0 |
| Sundberg, James, Kansas City | .245 | 115 | 367 | 38 | 90 | 140 | 12 | 4 | 10 | 35 | 4 | 4 | 2 | 0 | 2 |
| Tabler, Patrick, Cleveland | .275 | 117 | 404 | 47 | 111 | 150 | 18 | 3 | 5 | 59 | 5 | 2 | 3 | 0 | 6 |
| Tartabull, Danilo, Seattle | .328 | 19 | 61 | 8 | 20 | 32 | 7 | 1 | 1 | 7 | 0 | 0 | 0 | 1 | 0 |
| Tettleton, Mickey, Oakland† | .251 | 78 | 211 | 23 | 53 | 74 | 12 | 0 | 3 | 15 | 1 | 5 | 0 | 2 | 2 |
| Teufel, Timothy, Minnesota | .260 | 138 | 434 | 58 | 113 | 173 | 24 | 3 | 10 | 50 | 4 | 7 | 4 | 4 | 2 |
| Thomas, J. Gorman, Seattle | .215 | 135 | 484 | 76 | 104 | 218 | 16 | 1 | 32 | 87 | 10 | 2 | 3 | 3 | 2 |
| Thornton, Andre, Cleveland | .236 | 124 | 461 | 49 | 109 | 188 | 13 | 0 | 22 | 88 | 6 | 0 | 6 | 3 | 2 |
| Thornton, Louis, Toronto* | .236 | 56 | 72 | 18 | 17 | 23 | 1 | 1 | 1 | 8 | 1 | 0 | 0 | 1 | 0 |
| Tolleson, J. Wayne, Texas† | .313 | 123 | 323 | 45 | 101 | 123 | 9 | 5 | 1 | 18 | 6 | 9 | 2 | 21 | 12 |
| Trammell, Alan, Detroit | .258 | 149 | 605 | 79 | 156 | 230 | 21 | 7 | 13 | 57 | 5 | 11 | 9 | 14 | 5 |
| Upshaw, Willie, Toronto* | .275 | 148 | 501 | 79 | 138 | 224 | 31 | 5 | 15 | 65 | 7 | 1 | 3 | 8 | 8 |
| Valentine, Ellis, Texas | .211 | 11 | 38 | 5 | 8 | 15 | 1 | 0 | 2 | 4 | 2 | 0 | 0 | 0 | 1 |
| Valle, David, Seattle | .157 | 31 | 70 | 2 | 11 | 12 | 1 | 0 | 0 | 4 | 0 | 1 | 0 | 0 | 0 |
| Vukovich, George, Cleveland* | .244 | 149 | 434 | 43 | 106 | 152 | 22 | 0 | 8 | 45 | 4 | 1 | 4 | 2 | 2 |
| Waits, M. Richard, Milwaukee | .000 | 24 | 1 | 0 | 0 | 0 | 0 | 0 | 0 | 0 | 0 | 0 | 0 | 0 | 0 |
| Walker, Duane, Texas* | .174 | 53 | 132 | 14 | 23 | 40 | 2 | 0 | 5 | 11 | 0 | 0 | 0 | 2 | 1 |
| Walker, Gregory, Chicago* | .258 | 163 | 601 | 77 | 155 | 273 | 38 | 4 | 24 | 92 | 13 | 0 | 3 | 5 | 2 |
| Ward, Gary, Texas | .287 | 154 | 593 | 77 | 170 | 257 | 28 | 7 | 15 | 70 | 5 | 0 | 5 | 26 | 7 |
| Washington, Ronald, Minnesota | .274 | 70 | 135 | 24 | 37 | 54 | 6 | 4 | 1 | 14 | 2 | 3 | 3 | 5 | 1 |
| Wathan, John, Kansas City | .234 | 60 | 145 | 11 | 34 | 47 | 8 | 1 | 1 | 9 | 1 | 2 | 0 | 1 | 1 |
| Weaver, James, Detroit* | .143 | 12 | 7 | 2 | 1 | 2 | 1 | 0 | 0 | 0 | 0 | 0 | 0 | 0 | 1 |
| Webster, Mitchell, Toronto† | .000 | 4 | 1 | 0 | 0 | 0 | 0 | 0 | 0 | 0 | 0 | 0 | 0 | 0 | 0 |
| Whitaker, Louis, Detroit* | .279 | 152 | 609 | 102 | 170 | 278 | 29 | 8 | 21 | 73 | 9 | 5 | 5 | 6 | 4 |
| White, Devon, California† | .143 | 21 | 7 | 7 | 1 | 1 | 0 | 0 | 0 | 0 | 0 | 0 | 0 | 3 | 1 |
| White, Frank, Kansas City | .249 | 149 | 563 | 62 | 140 | 233 | 25 | 1 | 22 | 69 | 9 | 5 | 3 | 10 | 4 |
| Whitt, L. Ernest, Toronto* | .245 | 139 | 412 | 55 | 101 | 183 | 21 | 2 | 19 | 64 | 8 | 3 | 2 | 3 | 6 |
| Wiggins, Alan, Baltimore† | .285 | 76 | 298 | 43 | 85 | 104 | 11 | 4 | 0 | 21 | 0 | 6 | 0 | 30 | 13 |
| Wilfong, Robert, California* | .189 | 83 | 217 | 16 | 41 | 56 | 3 | 0 | 4 | 13 | 0 | 8 | 2 | 4 | 1 |
| Wilkerson, Curtis, Texas† | .244 | 129 | 360 | 35 | 88 | 111 | 11 | 6 | 0 | 22 | 3 | 6 | 3 | 14 | 7 |
| Willard, Gerald, Cleveland* | .270 | 104 | 300 | 39 | 81 | 115 | 13 | 0 | 7 | 36 | 6 | 4 | 1 | 0 | 0 |
| Wilson, James, Cleveland | .357 | 4 | 14 | 2 | 5 | 5 | 0 | 0 | 0 | 4 | 1 | 0 | 0 | 0 | 0 |
| Wilson, Willie, Kansas City† | .278 | 141 | 605 | 87 | 168 | 247 | 25 | 21 | 4 | 43 | 7 | 2 | 1 | 43 | 11 |
| Winfield, David, New York | .275 | 155 | 633 | 105 | 174 | 298 | 34 | 6 | 26 | 114 | 19 | 0 | 4 | 19 | 7 |
| Wright, George, Texas† | .190 | 109 | 363 | 21 | 69 | 88 | 13 | 0 | 2 | 18 | 1 | 3 | 2 | 4 | 7 |
| Wynegar, Harold, New York† | .223 | 102 | 309 | 27 | 69 | 99 | 15 | 0 | 5 | 32 | 3 | 1 | 1 | 0 | 0 |
| Young, Michael, Baltimore† | .273 | 139 | 450 | 72 | 123 | 231 | 22 | 1 | 28 | 81 | 9 | 1 | 1 | 5 | 5 |
| Yount, Robin, Milwaukee | .277 | 122 | 466 | 76 | 129 | 206 | 26 | 3 | 15 | 68 | 3 | 1 | 9 | 10 | 4 |

AWARDED FIRST BASE ON INTERFERENCE—G. Wright, Tex. 2 (Castillo, Bradley); Bell, Tor. (Sundberg); Bianca-lana, K.C. (Fisk); Buckner, Bos. (Parrish); Herndon, Det. (Wathan); Hulett, Chi. (Heath); Sheets, Balt. (Fisk); Tabler, Clev. (Hill); Trammell, Det. (Bando).

## PLAYERS WITH TWO OR MORE CLUBS
(Alphabetically Arranged With Player's First Club on Top)

| Player and Club | Pct. | G. | AB. | R. | H. | TB. | 2B. | 3B. | HR. | RBI. | GW. | SH. | SF. | Tot. BB. | Int. BB. | HP. | SO. | SB. | CS. | GI. DP. |
|---|---|---|---|---|---|---|---|---|---|---|---|---|---|---|---|---|---|---|---|---|
| Johnson, Texas | .257 | 82 | 296 | 31 | 76 | 131 | 17 | 1 | 12 | 56 | 2 | 1 | 3 | 31 | 2 | 3 | 44 | 0 | 0 | 3 |
| Johnson, Toronto | .274 | 24 | 73 | 4 | 20 | 23 | 0 | 0 | 1 | 10 | 0 | 0 | 1 | 9 | 0 | 0 | 15 | 0 | 0 | 1 |
| Lollar, Chicago | .000 | 18 | 0 | 0 | 0 | 0 | 0 | 0 | 0 | 0 | 0 | 0 | 0 | 0 | 0 | 0 | 0 | 0 | 0 | 0 |
| Lollar, Boston | .000 | 17 | 1 | 0 | 0 | 0 | 0 | 0 | 0 | 0 | 0 | 0 | 0 | 0 | 0 | 0 | 0 | 0 | 0 | 0 |
| Moreno, New York | .197 | 34 | 66 | 12 | 13 | 22 | 4 | 1 | 1 | 4 | 0 | 1 | 0 | 1 | 0 | 0 | 16 | 1 | 1 | 1 |
| Moreno, K.City | .243 | 24 | 70 | 9 | 17 | 30 | 1 | 3 | 2 | 12 | 0 | 0 | 1 | 3 | 0 | 1 | 8 | 0 | 1 | 1 |
| Nichols, Boston | .188 | 21 | 32 | 3 | 6 | 10 | 1 | 0 | 1 | 3 | 2 | 1 | 1 | 2 | 0 | 1 | 4 | 1 | 0 | 1 |
| Nichols, Chicago | .297 | 51 | 118 | 20 | 35 | 47 | 7 | 1 | 1 | 15 | 2 | 2 | 1 | 15 | 1 | 0 | 13 | 5 | 5 | 1 |

# OFFICIAL MISCELLANEOUS AMERICAN LEAGUE BATTING RECORDS

## CLUB MISCELLANEOUS BATTING RECORDS

| Club | Slg. Pct. | OB Pct. | Tot. BB. | Int. BB. | HP. | SO. | GIDP. | ShO. |
|---|---|---|---|---|---|---|---|---|
| Baltimore | .430 | .336 | 604 | 30 | 19 | 908 | 132 | 7 |
| Boston | .429 | .347 | 562 | 39 | 30 | 816 | 164 | 8 |
| Toronto | .425 | .331 | 503 | 44 | 30 | 807 | 121 | 5 |
| New York | .425 | .344 | 620 | 50 | 50 | 771 | 119 | 6 |
| Detroit | .424 | .318 | 526 | 56 | 27 | 926 | 81 | 6 |
| Seattle | .412 | .326 | 564 | 36 | 31 | 942 | 147 | 8 |
| Minnesota | .407 | .326 | 502 | 36 | 31 | 779 | 117 | 12 |
| Oakland | .401 | .325 | 508 | 29 | 16 | 861 | 129 | 5 |
| Kansas City | .401 | .313 | 473 | 57 | 36 | 840 | 125 | 4 |
| Chicago | .392 | .315 | 471 | 40 | 43 | 843 | 119 | 7 |
| California | .386 | .333 | 648 | 51 | 39 | 902 | 139 | 10 |
| Cleveland | .385 | .324 | 492 | 26 | 15 | 817 | 139 | 12 |
| Texas | .381 | .322 | 530 | 30 | 33 | 819 | 136 | 9 |
| Milwaukee | .379 | .319 | 462 | 33 | 19 | 746 | 145 | 10 |
| Totals | .406 | .327 | 7465 | 557 | 419 | 11777 | 1813 | 109 |

## INDIVIDUAL MISCELLANEOUS BATTING RECORDS
(Top Ten Qualifiers for Slugging Championship)

| Player—Club | Slg. Pct. | OB Pct. | Tot. BB. | Int. BB. | HP. | SO. | GI DP. |
|---|---|---|---|---|---|---|---|
| Brett, K.C. | .585 | .436 | 103 | 31 | 3 | 49 | 12 |
| Mattingly, N.Y. | .567 | .371 | 56 | 13 | 2 | 41 | 15 |
| Barfield, Tor. | .536 | .369 | 66 | 5 | 4 | 143 | 14 |
| Murray, Eddie, Balt. | .523 | .383 | 84 | 12 | 2 | 68 | 8 |
| Evans, Det. | .519 | .356 | 85 | 12 | 1 | 85 | 5 |
| Gibson, Det. | .518 | .364 | 71 | 16 | 5 | 137 | 5 |
| Henderson, N.Y. | .516 | .419 | 99 | 1 | 3 | 65 | 8 |
| Young, Balt. | .513 | .348 | 48 | 5 | 4 | 104 | 9 |
| Bradley, Sea. | .498 | .365 | 55 | 4 | 12 | 129 | 14 |
| Fisk, Chi. | .488 | .320 | 52 | 12 | 17 | 81 | 9 |

DEPARTMENTAL LEADERS: OBP—Boggs, .450; Tot. BB—Evans (Bos.), 114; Int. BB—Brett, 31; HP—Baylor, 24; SO—Balboni, 166; GIDP—Rice, 35.

| Player—Club | Slg. Pct. | OB Pct. | Tot. BB. | Int. BB. | HP. | SO. | GI DP. |
|---|---|---|---|---|---|---|---|
| Aikens, Tor. | .400 | .292 | 3 | 0 | 0 | 6 | 1 |
| Allenson, Tor. | .147 | .118 | 0 | 0 | 0 | 10 | 1 |
| Armas, Bos. | .514 | .298 | 18 | 4 | 2 | 90 | 14 |
| Ayala, Clev. | .421 | .284 | 4 | 1 | 0 | 17 | 2 |
| Baines, Chi. | .467 | .348 | 42 | 8 | 1 | 89 | 23 |
| Baker, Det. | .222 | .185 | 0 | 0 | 0 | 9 | 0 |
| Baker, Oak. | .440 | .359 | 50 | 0 | 0 | 47 | 12 |
| Balboni, K.C. | .477 | .307 | 52 | 4 | 5 | 166 | 14 |
| Bando, Clev. | .173 | .234 | 22 | 0 | 0 | 21 | 6 |
| Bannister, Tex. | .336 | .338 | 14 | 0 | 0 | 17 | 1 |
| Barfield, Tor. | .536 | .369 | 66 | 5 | 4 | 143 | 14 |
| Barrett, Bos. | .343 | .336 | 56 | 3 | 2 | 50 | 14 |
| Baylor, N.Y. | .430 | .330 | 52 | 6 | 24 | 90 | 10 |
| Bell, Tex. | .335 | .308 | 33 | 1 | 1 | 21 | 14 |
| Bell, Tor. | .479 | .327 | 43 | 6 | 8 | 90 | 8 |
| Beniquez, Cal. | .418 | .364 | 34 | 3 | 5 | 46 | 16 |
| Benton, Clev. | .239 | .208 | 3 | 2 | 0 | 9 | 1 |
| Bergman, Det. | .257 | .250 | 14 | 0 | 0 | 15 | 6 |
| Bernazard, Clev. | .404 | .361 | 69 | 2 | 1 | 72 | 11 |
| Berra, N.Y. | .321 | .276 | 7 | 0 | 0 | 20 | 2 |
| Biancalana, K.C. | .261 | .277 | 17 | 0 | 0 | 34 | 1 |
| Bochte, Oak. | .439 | .367 | 49 | 6 | 0 | 58 | 14 |

| Player—Club | Slg. Pct. | OB Pct. | Tot. BB. | Int. BB. | HP. | SO. | GI DP. |
|---|---|---|---|---|---|---|---|
| Boddicker, Balt. | .000 | .000 | 0 | 0 | 0 | 0 | 0 |
| Boggs, Bos. | .478 | .450 | 96 | 5 | 4 | 61 | 20 |
| Bonilla, N.Y. | .188 | .125 | 0 | 0 | 0 | 3 | 0 |
| Bonnell, Sea. | .342 | .282 | 6 | 1 | 0 | 19 | 1 |
| Boone, Cal. | .317 | .306 | 37 | 2 | 3 | 35 | 12 |
| Boston, Chi. | .332 | .271 | 14 | 1 | 0 | 44 | 3 |
| Bradley, Sea. | .498 | .365 | 55 | 4 | 12 | 129 | 14 |
| Bradley, N.Y. | .245 | .196 | 1 | 0 | 1 | 5 | 2 |
| Brett, K.C. | .585 | .436 | 103 | 31 | 3 | 49 | 12 |
| Brookens, Det. | .375 | .277 | 27 | 0 | 0 | 78 | 8 |
| Brouhard, Milw. | .389 | .298 | 5 | 1 | 1 | 26 | 2 |
| Brown, Cal. | .418 | .304 | 7 | 0 | 1 | 21 | 9 |
| Brummer, Tex. | .315 | .355 | 11 | 1 | 2 | 22 | 2 |
| Brunansky, Minn. | .448 | .320 | 71 | 7 | 0 | 86 | 12 |
| Buckner, Bos. | .447 | .325 | 30 | 5 | 2 | 36 | 16 |
| Buechele, Tex. | .356 | .271 | 14 | 2 | 2 | 38 | 11 |
| Burroughs, Tor. | .429 | .366 | 34 | 1 | 0 | 36 | 7 |
| Bush, Minn. | .449 | .321 | 24 | 1 | 5 | 30 | 3 |
| Butler, Clev. | .431 | .377 | 63 | 2 | 1 | 42 | 8 |
| Calderon, Sea. | .514 | .349 | 19 | 1 | 2 | 45 | 10 |
| Cangelosi, Chi. | .000 | .333 | 0 | 0 | 1 | 1 | 0 |
| Canseco, Oak. | .490 | .330 | 4 | 0 | 0 | 31 | 1 |
| Capra, Tex. | .125 | .125 | 0 | 0 | 0 | 0 | 0 |
| Carew, Cal. | .345 | .371 | 64 | 9 | 1 | 47 | 8 |
| Carter, Clev. | .409 | .298 | 25 | 2 | 2 | 74 | 9 |
| Castillo, Clev. | .462 | .298 | 11 | 0 | 3 | 40 | 6 |
| Castillo, Det. | .214 | .138 | 2 | 0 | 0 | 19 | 1 |
| Chambers, Sea. | .000 | .000 | 0 | 0 | 0 | 2 | 0 |
| Clark, Milw. | .258 | .277 | 7 | 0 | 0 | 19 | 3 |
| Coles, Sea. | .356 | .338 | 9 | 0 | 1 | 17 | 0 |
| Collins, Sea. | .346 | .303 | 29 | 2 | 1 | 37 | 6 |
| Concepcion, K.C. | .245 | .255 | 16 | 0 | 6 | 29 | 8 |
| Connally, Balt. | .348 | .346 | 19 | 0 | 1 | 21 | 1 |
| Cooper, Milw. | .456 | .322 | 30 | 3 | 2 | 77 | 24 |
| Cotto, N.Y. | .375 | .339 | 3 | 0 | 0 | 12 | 1 |
| Cowens, Sea. | .451 | .310 | 30 | 3 | 1 | 56 | 23 |
| Cruz, Chi. | .231 | .297 | 32 | 0 | 2 | 40 | 6 |
| Dauer, Balt. | .264 | .275 | 20 | 0 | 1 | 7 | 9 |

| Player—Club | Slg. Pct. | OB Pct. | Tot. BB. | Int. BB. | HP. | SO. | GI DP. |
|---|---|---|---|---|---|---|---|
| Davis, Sea. | .441 | .381 | 90 | 7 | 2 | 71 | 14 |
| Davis, Oak. | .484 | .348 | 50 | 8 | 2 | 99 | 10 |
| DeCinces, Cal. | .440 | .317 | 47 | 11 | 2 | 71 | 17 |
| Dempsey, Balt. | .406 | .345 | 50 | 0 | 1 | 87 | 2 |
| De Sa, Chi. | .364 | .234 | 3 | 1 | 0 | 6 | 0 |
| Dixon, Balt. | .000 | .000 | 0 | 0 | 0 | 0 | 0 |
| Downing, Cal. | .427 | .371 | 78 | 3 | 13 | 61 | 12 |
| Dunbar, Tex. | .269 | .291 | 12 | 3 | 1 | 9 | 5 |
| Dwyer, Balt. | .399 | .353 | 37 | 2 | 1 | 31 | 5 |
| Easler, Bos. | .412 | .325 | 53 | 1 | 3 | 129 | 15 |
| Engle, Minn. | .448 | .333 | 21 | 1 | 0 | 28 | 3 |
| Espino, N.Y. | .364 | .364 | 0 | 0 | 0 | 0 | 0 |
| Espinoza, Minn. | .298 | .288 | 1 | 0 | 1 | 9 | 2 |
| Evans, Det. | .519 | .356 | 85 | 12 | 1 | 85 | 5 |
| Evans, Bos. | .454 | .378 | 114 | 4 | 5 | 105 | 16 |
| Felder, Milw. | .214 | .262 | 5 | 0 | 0 | 6 | 2 |
| Fernandez, Tor. | .390 | .340 | 43 | 2 | 2 | 41 | 12 |
| Fielder, Tor. | .527 | .358 | 6 | 0 | 0 | 16 | 2 |
| Fischlin, Clev. | .300 | .262 | 5 | 0 | 0 | 7 | 0 |
| Fisk, Chi. | .488 | .320 | 52 | 12 | 17 | 81 | 9 |
| Fletcher, Chi. | .309 | .332 | 35 | 0 | 0 | 47 | 9 |
| Flynn, Det. | .333 | .250 | 0 | 0 | 0 | 3 | 1 |
| Ford, Balt. | .253 | .256 | 7 | 0 | 0 | 17 | 3 |
| Franco, Clev. | .381 | .343 | 54 | 2 | 4 | 74 | 26 |
| Funderburk, Minn. | .529 | .351 | 5 | 0 | 0 | 12 | 4 |
| Gaetti, Minn. | .409 | .301 | 37 | 3 | 7 | 89 | 15 |
| Gagne, Minn. | .317 | .279 | 20 | 0 | 3 | 57 | 5 |
| Gallego, Oak. | .338 | .319 | 12 | 0 | 1 | 14 | 2 |
| Gamble, Chi. | .318 | .353 | 34 | 3 | 1 | 22 | 1 |
| Gantner, Milw. | .327 | .300 | 33 | 7 | 3 | 42 | 13 |
| Garbey, Det. | .380 | .305 | 15 | 1 | 3 | 37 | 7 |
| Garcia, Tor. | .377 | .302 | 15 | 2 | 4 | 41 | 13 |
| Gedman, Bos. | .484 | .362 | 50 | 11 | 3 | 79 | 12 |
| Gerber, Cal. | .319 | .277 | 2 | 0 | 0 | 3 | 2 |
| Gibson, Det. | .518 | .364 | 71 | 16 | 5 | 137 | 5 |
| Gilbert, Chi. | .318 | .385 | 4 | 0 | 0 | 5 | 1 |
| Giles, Milw. | .241 | .262 | 7 | 0 | 0 | 16 | 1 |
| Greenwell, Bos. | .742 | .382 | 3 | 1 | 0 | 4 | 0 |
| Grich, Cal. | .372 | .355 | 81 | 3 | 3 | 77 | 18 |
| Griffey, N.Y. | .425 | .331 | 41 | 4 | 0 | 51 | 2 |
| Griffin, Oak. | .332 | .290 | 20 | 1 | 0 | 50 | 6 |
| Gross, Balt. | .424 | .369 | 46 | 0 | 0 | 48 | 3 |
| Grubb, Det. | .400 | .342 | 24 | 0 | 1 | 25 | 5 |
| Gruber, Tor. | .231 | .231 | 0 | 0 | 0 | 3 | 0 |
| Guillen, Chi. | .358 | .291 | 12 | 1 | 1 | 36 | 5 |
| Gutierrez, Bos. | .273 | .250 | 12 | 0 | 0 | 37 | 9 |
| Hairston, Chi. | .343 | .371 | 29 | 3 | 2 | 18 | 3 |
| Hall, Clev. | .409 | .387 | 8 | 0 | 0 | 12 | 2 |
| Hargrove, Clev. | .352 | .370 | 39 | 2 | 0 | 29 | 8 |
| Harrah, Tex. | .389 | .432 | 113 | 2 | 4 | 60 | 4 |
| Hassey, N.Y. | .509 | .369 | 28 | 4 | 3 | 21 | 7 |
| Hatcher, Minn. | .365 | .308 | 16 | 1 | 2 | 23 | 15 |
| Hearron, Tor. | .143 | .143 | 0 | 0 | 0 | 2 | 0 |
| Heath, Oak. | .408 | .313 | 41 | 0 | 1 | 63 | 13 |
| Hegman, K.C. | .000 | .000 | 0 | 0 | 0 | 0 | 0 |
| Henderson, Sea. | .388 | .310 | 48 | 2 | 3 | 104 | 11 |
| Henderson, N.Y. | .516 | .419 | 99 | 1 | 3 | 65 | 8 |
| Henderson, Oak. | .420 | .358 | 18 | 0 | 0 | 34 | 10 |
| Hendrick, Cal. | .293 | .196 | 4 | 1 | 0 | 8 | 4 |
| Hernandez, Balt. | .048 | .048 | 0 | 0 | 0 | 4 | 2 |
| Hernandez, Det. | .000 | .000 | 0 | 0 | 0 | 0 | 0 |
| Herndon, Det. | .385 | .298 | 33 | 1 | 1 | 79 | 9 |
| Hill, Oak. | .351 | .321 | 23 | 2 | 0 | 33 | 7 |
| Hill, Chi. | .160 | .253 | 12 | 0 | 0 | 9 | 2 |
| Hoffman, Bos. | .416 | .343 | 25 | 0 | 5 | 40 | 6 |
| Householder, Milw. | .418 | .320 | 27 | 0 | 1 | 60 | 5 |
| Howell, Cal. | .336 | .279 | 16 | 2 | 0 | 33 | 1 |
| Hrbek, Minn. | .444 | .351 | 67 | 12 | 2 | 87 | 12 |
| Hudler, N.Y. | .196 | .173 | 1 | 0 | 0 | 9 | 0 |
| Hulett, Chi. | .375 | .324 | 30 | 1 | 4 | 81 | 8 |
| Huppert, Milw. | .048 | .130 | 2 | 0 | 0 | 7 | 1 |
| Iorg, K.C. | .331 | .268 | 8 | 2 | 0 | 16 | 6 |
| Iorg, Tor. | .469 | .358 | 21 | 3 | 0 | 26 | 6 |
| Jackson, Cal. | .487 | .360 | 78 | 12 | 1 | 138 | 16 |
| Jacoby, Clev. | .426 | .324 | 48 | 3 | 0 | 120 | 17 |
| James, Milw. | .245 | .309 | 6 | 0 | 0 | 6 | 0 |
| Johnson, Tex.-Tor. | .417 | .334 | 40 | 2 | 3 | 59 | 4 |
| Jones, Tex. | .351 | .284 | 11 | 1 | 1 | 30 | 1 |
| Jones, K.C. | .257 | .261 | 8 | 0 | 3 | 15 | 6 |
| Jones, Cal. | .447 | .328 | 57 | 2 | 0 | 82 | 5 |
| Jurak, Bos. | .231 | .286 | 1 | 0 | 0 | 3 | 1 |
| Kearney, Sea. | .354 | .277 | 11 | 1 | 4 | 59 | 7 |
| Keedy, Cal. | 1.500 | .500 | 0 | 0 | 0 | 0 | 0 |
| Key, Tor. | .000 | .000 | 0 | 0 | 0 | 0 | 0 |
| Kiefer, Oak. | .288 | .203 | 1 | 0 | 0 | 18 | 1 |
| Kingman, Oak. | .417 | .309 | 62 | 6 | 2 | 114 | 17 |
| Kittle, Chi. | .467 | .295 | 31 | 1 | 5 | 92 | 12 |
| Kunkel, Tex. | .250 | .250 | 0 | 0 | 0 | 3 | 0 |
| Kuntz, Det. | .000 | .286 | 2 | 0 | 0 | 2 | 0 |
| Lacy, Balt. | .409 | .343 | 39 | 0 | 2 | 95 | 10 |
| Laga, Det. | .361 | .167 | 0 | 0 | 0 | 9 | 1 |
| Lansford, Oak. | .429 | .311 | 18 | 1 | 4 | 27 | 6 |
| Laudner, Minn. | .396 | .292 | 12 | 0 | 1 | 45 | 2 |
| Law, Chi. | .374 | .311 | 27 | 0 | 3 | 40 | 4 |
| Leach, Tor. | .257 | .263 | 3 | 1 | 0 | 9 | 0 |
| Lee, Tor. | .200 | .238 | 2 | 0 | 0 | 9 | 2 |
| Leeper, K.C. | .088 | .114 | 1 | 0 | 0 | 3 | 0 |
| LeMaster, Clev. | .150 | .150 | 0 | 0 | 0 | 6 | 0 |
| Lemon, Det. | .439 | .334 | 45 | 3 | 10 | 93 | 5 |
| Linares, Cal. | .512 | .283 | 2 | 0 | 0 | 5 | 1 |
| Little, Chi. | .340 | .345 | 26 | 0 | 3 | 21 | 4 |
| Lollar, Chi.-Bos. | .000 | .000 | 0 | 0 | 0 | 0 | 0 |
| Loman, Milw. | .318 | .221 | 1 | 0 | 0 | 12 | 0 |
| Lombardozzi, Minn. | .481 | .426 | 6 | 0 | 0 | 6 | 0 |
| Lowenstein, Balt. | .077 | .138 | 2 | 0 | 0 | 3 | 0 |
| Lynn, Balt. | .449 | .339 | 53 | 6 | 1 | 100 | 7 |
| Lyons, Bos. | .358 | .322 | 32 | 0 | 1 | 64 | 2 |
| Madison, Det. | .000 | .143 | 2 | 0 | 0 | 0 | 0 |
| Manning, Milw. | .296 | .265 | 14 | 0 | 0 | 19 | 2 |
| Martinez, Tor. | .313 | .239 | 10 | 0 | 1 | 12 | 3 |
| Mata, N.Y. | .143 | .143 | 0 | 0 | 0 | 0 | 0 |
| Mattingly, N.Y. | .567 | .371 | 56 | 13 | 2 | 41 | 15 |
| Matuszek, Tor. | .318 | .259 | 11 | 0 | 0 | 24 | 5 |
| McDowell, Tex. | .431 | .304 | 36 | 2 | 3 | 85 | 6 |
| McRae, K.C. | .450 | .349 | 44 | 3 | 1 | 45 | 12 |
| Meacham, N.Y. | .266 | .302 | 54 | 1 | 5 | 102 | 7 |
| Meier, Minn. | .346 | .374 | 18 | 0 | 1 | 12 | 0 |
| Melvin, Det. | .293 | .247 | 3 | 0 | 0 | 21 | 1 |
| Meyer, Oak. | .000 | .077 | 1 | 0 | 0 | 0 | 1 |
| Miller, Cal. | .583 | .400 | 1 | 0 | 1 | 10 | 0 |
| Miller, Bos. | .378 | .392 | 5 | 0 | 0 | 6 | 1 |
| Molitor, Milw. | .408 | .356 | 54 | 6 | 1 | 80 | 12 |
| Moore, Milw. | .292 | .288 | 27 | 0 | 1 | 53 | 12 |
| Moreno, N.Y.-K.C. | .382 | .246 | 4 | 0 | 1 | 24 | 2 |
| Morris, Det. | .000 | .000 | 0 | 0 | 0 | 0 | 0 |
| Moseby, Tor. | .426 | .345 | 76 | 4 | 4 | 91 | 12 |
| Moses, Sea. | .194 | .219 | 2 | 0 | 0 | 8 | 3 |
| Motley, K.C. | .413 | .257 | 18 | 2 | 2 | 57 | 17 |
| Mulliniks, Tor. | .454 | .383 | 55 | 2 | 0 | 54 | 10 |
| Murphy, Oak. | .400 | .340 | 84 | 3 | 3 | 123 | 14 |
| Murray, Balt. | .523 | .383 | 84 | 12 | 2 | 68 | 8 |
| Narron, Cal. | .364 | .280 | 11 | 2 | 0 | 17 | 2 |
| Nelson, Chi. | .000 | .000 | 0 | 0 | 0 | 0 | 0 |
| Nelson, Sea. | .000 | .000 | 0 | 0 | 0 | 1 | 0 |
| Nichols, Bos.-Chi. | .380 | .347 | 17 | 1 | 1 | 17 | 2 |
| Nicosia, Tor. | .267 | .267 | 0 | 0 | 0 | 3 | 0 |
| Nixon, Clev. | .315 | .271 | 8 | 0 | 0 | 27 | 2 |
| Nolan, Balt. | .184 | .227 | 5 | 1 | 0 | 5 | 1 |
| O'Brien, Sea. | .364 | .429 | 3 | 0 | 0 | 3 | 0 |
| O'Brien, Tex. | .452 | .342 | 69 | 4 | 1 | 53 | 18 |
| Oglivie, Milw. | .440 | .354 | 37 | 3 | 2 | 51 | 8 |
| Oliver, Tor. | .374 | .282 | 7 | 2 | 1 | 13 | 8 |
| O'Malley, Balt. | .286 | .071 | 0 | 0 | 0 | 2 | 1 |
| Orta, K.C. | .383 | .317 | 22 | 5 | 2 | 28 | 8 |
| Owen, Sea. | .372 | .322 | 34 | 0 | 0 | 27 | 5 |
| Paciorek, Chi. | .262 | .293 | 8 | 0 | 1 | 22 | 3 |
| Pagliarulo, N.Y. | .442 | .324 | 45 | 4 | 4 | 86 | 6 |
| Pardo, Balt. | .147 | .167 | 3 | 0 | 0 | 15 | 0 |
| Paris, Balt. | .000 | .000 | 0 | 0 | 0 | 1 | 0 |
| Parrish, Det. | .479 | .323 | 41 | 5 | 2 | 90 | 10 |
| Parrish, Tex. | .434 | .314 | 33 | 2 | 1 | 77 | 13 |
| Pasqua, N.Y. | .426 | .289 | 16 | 4 | 1 | 38 | 1 |
| Perconte, Sea. | .340 | .335 | 50 | 0 | 3 | 36 | 9 |
| Petralli, Tex. | .290 | .319 | 8 | 0 | 1 | 12 | 4 |
| Pettis, Cal. | .323 | .347 | 62 | 0 | 0 | 125 | 5 |
| Phelps, Sea. | .466 | .343 | 24 | 2 | 0 | 33 | 1 |
| Phillips, Oak. | .453 | .331 | 13 | 0 | 0 | 34 | 1 |
| Picciolo, Oak. | .324 | .288 | 2 | 0 | 0 | 17 | 1 |

| Player—Club | Slg. Pct. | OB Pct. | Tot. BB | Int. BB | HP | SO | GI DP | Player—Club | Slg. Pct. | OB Pct. | Tot. BB | Int. BB | HP | SO | GI DP |
|---|---|---|---|---|---|---|---|---|---|---|---|---|---|---|---|
| Pittaro, Det. | .323 | .299 | 5 | 0 | 0 | 13 | 0 | Smith, K.C. | .366 | .321 | 41 | 0 | 4 | 69 | 2 |
| Polidor, Cal. | 1.000 | 1.000 | 0 | 0 | 0 | 0 | 0 | Spillner, Chi. | .000 | 1.000 | 1 | 0 | 0 | 0 | 0 |
| Ponce, Milw. | .242 | .169 | 1 | 0 | 0 | 9 | 4 | Squires, Chi. | .000 | .000 | 0 | 0 | 0 | 0 | 0 |
| Presley, Sea. | .484 | .324 | 44 | 9 | 1 | 100 | 29 | Stapleton, Bos. | .318 | .271 | 4 | 0 | 0 | 11 | 1 |
| Pryor, K.C. | .272 | .270 | 8 | 0 | 0 | 12 | 6 | Stein, Tex. | .354 | .272 | 1 | 1 | 1 | 15 | 2 |
| Puckett, Minn. | .385 | .330 | 41 | 0 | 4 | 87 | 9 | Stenhouse, Minn. | .335 | .330 | 29 | 1 | 0 | 18 | 3 |
| Pujols, Tex. | 1.000 | 1.000 | 0 | 0 | 0 | 0 | 0 | Sullivan, Bos. | .290 | .240 | 6 | 0 | 0 | 15 | 0 |
| Quirk, K.C. | .368 | .305 | 2 | 0 | 0 | 9 | 1 | Sundberg, K.C. | .381 | .308 | 33 | 3 | 1 | 67 | 9 |
| Ramos, Sea. | .250 | .267 | 17 | 0 | 0 | 23 | 4 | Tabler, Clev. | .371 | .321 | 27 | 2 | 2 | 55 | 15 |
| Randolph, N.Y. | .356 | .382 | 85 | 3 | 4 | 39 | 24 | Tartabull, Sea. | .525 | .406 | 8 | 0 | 0 | 14 | 1 |
| Rayford, Balt. | .521 | .324 | 10 | 0 | 0 | 69 | 10 | Tettleton, Oak. | .351 | .344 | 28 | 0 | 2 | 59 | 6 |
| Ready, Milw. | .387 | .318 | 14 | 0 | 1 | 23 | 6 | Teufel, Minn. | .399 | .335 | 48 | 2 | 3 | 70 | 14 |
| Reed, Minn. | .200 | .200 | 0 | 0 | 0 | 3 | 0 | G. Thomas, Sea. | .450 | .330 | 84 | 6 | 1 | 126 | 11 |
| Reynolds, Sea. | .192 | .264 | 17 | 0 | 0 | 14 | 0 | Thornton, Clev. | .408 | .304 | 47 | 1 | 0 | 75 | 14 |
| Rice, Bos. | .487 | .349 | 51 | 5 | 2 | 75 | 35 | Thornton, Tor. | .319 | .267 | 2 | 0 | 1 | 24 | 2 |
| Riles, Bos. | .377 | .339 | 36 | 0 | 2 | 54 | 16 | Tolleson, Tex. | .381 | .353 | 21 | 0 | 0 | 46 | 6 |
| Ripken, Balt. | .469 | .347 | 67 | 1 | 1 | 68 | 32 | Trammell, Det. | .380 | .312 | 50 | 4 | 2 | 71 | 6 |
| Robertson, N.Y. | .416 | .358 | 6 | 0 | 1 | 24 | 3 | Upshaw, Tor. | .447 | .342 | 48 | 7 | 4 | 71 | 6 |
| Robidoux, Milw. | .392 | .333 | 12 | 0 | 0 | 16 | 1 | Valentine, Tex. | .395 | .250 | 2 | 0 | 0 | 8 | 1 |
| Roenicke, Balt. | .458 | .342 | 44 | 1 | 0 | 36 | 5 | Valle, Sea. | .171 | .181 | 1 | 0 | 1 | 17 | 1 |
| Romero, Milw. | .303 | .321 | 26 | 0 | 0 | 20 | 3 | Vukovich, Clev. | .350 | .292 | 30 | 6 | 1 | 75 | 9 |
| Romine, Bos. | .286 | .241 | 1 | 0 | 0 | 4 | 1 | Waits, Milw. | .000 | .000 | 0 | 0 | 0 | 1 | 0 |
| Ryal, Chi. | .242 | .222 | 3 | 0 | 0 | 3 | 2 | Walker, Tex. | .303 | .264 | 15 | 0 | 1 | 29 | 2 |
| Sakata, Balt. | .351 | .279 | 6 | 0 | 1 | 15 | 3 | Walker, Chi. | .454 | .309 | 44 | 6 | 2 | 100 | 16 |
| Salas, Minn. | .458 | .332 | 18 | 5 | 1 | 37 | 7 | Ward, Tex. | .433 | .329 | 39 | 3 | 1 | 97 | 19 |
| Salazar, Chi. | .404 | .267 | 12 | 2 | 0 | 60 | 5 | Washington, Minn. | .400 | .308 | 8 | 0 | 0 | 15 | 3 |
| Sample, N.Y. | .345 | .336 | 9 | 0 | 2 | 10 | 2 | Wathan, K.C. | .324 | .319 | 17 | 0 | 1 | 15 | 4 |
| Sanchez, Det. | .459 | .248 | 0 | 0 | 0 | 39 | 4 | Weaver, Det. | .286 | .250 | 1 | 0 | 0 | 4 | 0 |
| Sax, Bos. | .389 | .350 | 3 | 0 | 0 | 3 | 0 | Webster, Tor. | .000 | .000 | 0 | 0 | 0 | 0 | 0 |
| Schofield, Cal. | .331 | .287 | 35 | 0 | 8 | 70 | 8 | Whitaker, Det. | .456 | .362 | 80 | 9 | 2 | 56 | 3 |
| Schroeder, Milw. | .407 | .290 | 12 | 1 | 2 | 61 | 5 | White, Cal. | .143 | .333 | 1 | 0 | 1 | 3 | 0 |
| Sconiers, Cal. | .429 | .371 | 15 | 0 | 0 | 18 | 2 | White, K.C. | .414 | .284 | 28 | 2 | 1 | 86 | 8 |
| Scott, Sea. | .357 | .275 | 15 | 0 | 0 | 41 | 3 | Whitt, Tor. | .444 | .323 | 47 | 9 | 1 | 59 | 7 |
| Scranton, K.C. | .000 | .000 | 0 | 0 | 0 | 0 | 0 | Wiggins, Balt. | .349 | .353 | 29 | 0 | 2 | 16 | 2 |
| Sheets, Balt. | .442 | .323 | 28 | 2 | 2 | 52 | 15 | Wilfong, Cal. | .258 | .243 | 16 | 1 | 0 | 32 | 0 |
| Shelby, Balt. | .434 | .307 | 7 | 0 | 0 | 44 | 4 | Wilkerson, Tex. | .308 | .293 | 22 | 0 | 4 | 63 | 7 |
| Shepherd, Tor. | .171 | .162 | 2 | 0 | 0 | 12 | 1 | Willard, Clev. | .383 | .333 | 28 | 1 | 1 | 59 | 3 |
| Sheridan, K.C. | .335 | .307 | 23 | 2 | 1 | 38 | 4 | Wilson, Clev. | .357 | .400 | 1 | 0 | 0 | 3 | 0 |
| Simmons, Det. | .402 | .306 | 26 | 5 | 0 | 41 | 4 | Wilson, K.C. | .408 | .316 | 29 | 3 | 5 | 94 | 6 |
| Simmons, Milw. | .402 | .342 | 57 | 9 | 1 | 32 | 17 | Winfield, N.Y. | .471 | .328 | 52 | 8 | 0 | 96 | 17 |
| Skinner, Chi. | .545 | .408 | 5 | 0 | 0 | 13 | 2 | G. Wright, Tex. | .242 | .241 | 25 | 5 | 0 | 49 | 9 |
| Slaught, Tex. | .423 | .331 | 20 | 1 | 6 | 41 | 8 | Wynegar, N.Y. | .320 | .356 | 64 | 2 | 0 | 43 | 11 |
| Smalley, Minn. | .402 | .357 | 60 | 3 | 1 | 65 | 8 | Young, Balt. | .513 | .348 | 48 | 5 | 4 | 104 | 9 |
| Smith, N.Y. | .000 | .000 | 0 | 0 | 0 | 0 | 0 | Yount, Milw. | .442 | .342 | 49 | 3 | 2 | 56 | 8 |

# OFFICIAL AMERICAN LEAGUE DESIGNATED HITTING

## CLUB DESIGNATED HITTING

| Club | Pct. | AB | R | H | TB | 2B | 3B | HR | RBI | SH | SF | BB | HP | SO | SB | CS | GI DP |
|---|---|---|---|---|---|---|---|---|---|---|---|---|---|---|---|---|---|
| Boston | .263 | 640 | 87 | 168 | 276 | 36 | 3 | 22 | 94 | 3 | 9 | 56 | 3 | 141 | 0 | 1 | 14 |
| Kansas City | .256 | 620 | 75 | 159 | 257 | 39 | 1 | 19 | 114 | 4 | 7 | 66 | 3 | 76 | 2 | 2 | 19 |
| Minnesota | .256 | 609 | 82 | 156 | 258 | 39 | 3 | 19 | 86 | 0 | 6 | 70 | 3 | 80 | 3 | 1 | 8 |
| Detroit | .255 | 593 | 79 | 151 | 261 | 20 | 3 | 28 | 83 | 1 | 6 | 68 | 1 | 99 | 4 | 6 | 6 |
| Milwaukee | .252 | 627 | 73 | 158 | 237 | 27 | 2 | 16 | 83 | 0 | 10 | 57 | 2 | 68 | 3 | 1 | 18 |
| Toronto | .247 | 600 | 77 | 148 | 219 | 22 | 5 | 13 | 78 | 0 | 8 | 61 | 1 | 85 | 5 | 5 | 21 |
| Texas | .234 | 608 | 57 | 142 | 227 | 30 | 2 | 17 | 86 | 2 | 5 | 54 | 3 | 101 | 4 | 2 | 13 |
| New York | .232 | 596 | 88 | 138 | 254 | 28 | 2 | 28 | 111 | 1 | 10 | 59 | 26 | 110 | 0 | 4 | 12 |
| Baltimore | .231 | 614 | 72 | 142 | 239 | 17 | 1 | 26 | 82 | 1 | 5 | 56 | 5 | 112 | 1 | 7 | 21 |
| Chicago | .231 | 576 | 83 | 133 | 234 | 23 | 0 | 26 | 96 | 2 | 8 | 72 | 8 | 96 | 2 | 4 | 9 |
| Cleveland | .231 | 629 | 71 | 145 | 235 | 21 | 0 | 23 | 117 | 1 | 7 | 54 | 0 | 114 | 5 | 4 | 23 |
| Oakland | .229 | 619 | 74 | 142 | 252 | 14 | 0 | 32 | 100 | 2 | 9 | 70 | 2 | 117 | 3 | 3 | 22 |
| California | .225 | 605 | 88 | 136 | 244 | 27 | 3 | 25 | 97 | 2 | 7 | 84 | 5 | 143 | 6 | 5 | 16 |
| Seattle | .211 | 596 | 94 | 126 | 265 | 20 | 1 | 39 | 105 | 3 | 2 | 101 | 1 | 155 | 5 | 3 | 15 |
| Totals | .240 | 8532 | 1100 | 2044 | 3458 | 363 | 26 | 333 | 1332 | 21 | 100 | 928 | 63 | 1497 | 43 | 48 | 217 |

### INDIVIDUAL DESIGNATED HITTING
(Listed Alphabetically)

| Player and Club | Pct. | G. | AB. | R. | H. | TB. | 2B. | 3B. | HR. | RBI. | SH. | SF. | BB. | HP. | SO. | SB. | CS. | GI DP. |
|---|---|---|---|---|---|---|---|---|---|---|---|---|---|---|---|---|---|---|
| Aikens, Tor. | .158 | 11 | 19 | 1 | 3 | 4 | 1 | 0 | 0 | 3 | 0 | 1 | 3 | 0 | 6 | 0 | 0 | 1 |
| Armas, Bos. | .233 | 19 | 73 | 5 | 17 | 30 | 4 | 0 | 3 | 11 | 0 | 2 | 3 | 0 | 21 | 0 | 0 | 1 |
| Ayala, Clev. | .286 | 3 | 7 | 0 | 2 | 3 | 1 | 0 | 0 | 0 | 0 | 0 | 1 | 0 | 3 | 0 | 0 | 0 |
| Baines, Chi. | .000 | 1 | 3 | 0 | 0 | 0 | 0 | 0 | 0 | 0 | 0 | 0 | 0 | 0 | 0 | 0 | 0 | 0 |
| Baker, Oak. | .220 | 13 | 41 | 9 | 9 | 19 | 1 | 0 | 3 | 13 | 0 | 1 | 13 | 0 | 3 | 0 | 0 | 4 |
| Bannister, Tex. | .291 | 21 | 55 | 2 | 16 | 19 | 3 | 0 | 0 | 2 | 0 | 0 | 2 | 0 | 8 | 3 | 1 | 1 |
| Baylor, N.Y. | .232 | 140 | 475 | 70 | 110 | 205 | 24 | 1 | 23 | 91 | 1 | 10 | 52 | 24 | 89 | 0 | 4 | 10 |

| Player and Club | Pct. | G. | AB. | R. | H. | TB. | 2B. | 3B. | HR. | RBI. | SH. | SF. | BB. | HP. | SO. | SB. | CS. | GI DP. |
|---|---|---|---|---|---|---|---|---|---|---|---|---|---|---|---|---|---|---|
| Beniquez, Cal. | .281 | 14 | 32 | 4 | 9 | 16 | 1 | 0 | 2 | 6 | 0 | 0 | 2 | 1 | 7 | 0 | 0 | 1 |
| Bergman, Det. | .600 | 5 | 5 | 1 | 3 | 4 | 1 | 0 | 0 | 0 | 0 | 0 | 0 | 0 | 0 | 0 | 0 | 0 |
| Biancalana, K.C. | .000 | 2 | 0 | 2 | 0 | 0 | 0 | 0 | 0 | 0 | 0 | 0 | 0 | 0 | 0 | 0 | 0 | 0 |
| Boddicker, Balt. | .000 | 2 | 0 | 1 | 0 | 0 | 0 | 0 | 0 | 0 | 0 | 0 | 0 | 0 | 0 | 0 | 0 | 0 |
| Bonnell, Sea. | .375 | 2 | 8 | 1 | 3 | 4 | 1 | 0 | 0 | 0 | 0 | 0 | 0 | 0 | 0 | 1 | 0 | 0 |
| Boston, Chi. | .000 | 2 | 0 | 0 | 0 | 0 | 0 | 0 | 0 | 0 | 1 | 0 | 0 | 0 | 0 | 0 | 0 | 0 |
| Bradley, N.Y. | .226 | 9 | 31 | 3 | 7 | 9 | 2 | 0 | 0 | 1 | 0 | 0 | 1 | 1 | 2 | 0 | 0 | 2 |
| Brett, K.C. | .333 | 1 | 3 | 2 | 1 | 4 | 0 | 0 | 1 | 1 | 0 | 0 | .1 | 0 | 0 | 0 | 0 | 0 |
| Brookens, Det. | .000 | 1 | 0 | 1 | 0 | 0 | 0 | 0 | 0 | 1 | 0 | 0 | 1 | 0 | 0 | 1 | 0 | 0 |
| Brouhard, Milw. | .200 | 1 | 5 | 0 | 1 | 1 | 0 | 0 | 0 | 0 | 0 | 0 | 0 | 0 | 3 | 0 | 0 | 0 |
| Brown, Cal. | .100 | 7 | 10 | 1 | 1 | 1 | 0 | 0 | 0 | 0 | 0 | 0 | 1 | 1 | 3 | 0 | 0 | 0 |
| Brummer, Tex. | .000 | 1 | 0 | 0 | 0 | 0 | 0 | 0 | 0 | 0 | 0 | 0 | 0 | 0 | 0 | 0 | 0 | 0 |
| Burroughs, Tor. | .265 | 75 | 181 | 18 | 48 | 78 | 9 | 3 | 5 | 27 | 0 | 2 | 33 | 0 | 32 | 0 | 1 | 5 |
| Bush, Minn. | .233 | 28 | 90 | 14 | 21 | 44 | 4 | 2 | 5 | 15 | 0 | 1 | 8 | 2 | 12 | 0 | 0 | 1 |
| Butler, Clev. | .000 | 1 | 0 | 1 | 0 | 0 | 0 | 0 | 0 | 0 | 0 | 0 | 0 | 0 | 0 | 0 | 0 | 0 |
| Calderon, Sea. | .167 | 3 | 6 | 1 | 1 | 4 | 0 | 0 | 1 | 1 | 0 | 0 | 1 | 0 | 2 | 0 | 0 | 2 |
| Cangelosi, Chi. | .000 | 2 | 0 | 1 | 0 | 0 | 0 | 0 | 0 | 0 | 0 | 0 | 0 | 0 | 0 | 0 | 0 | 0 |
| Carter, Clev. | .231 | 7 | 26 | 7 | 6 | 11 | 2 | 0 | 1 | 4 | 0 | 0 | 1 | 0 | 12 | 0 | 0 | 1 |
| Castillo, Clev. | .138 | 9 | 29 | 2 | 4 | 4 | 0 | 0 | 0 | 0 | 0 | 0 | 1 | 0 | 9 | 0 | 0 | 2 |
| Coles, Sea. | .000 | 2 | 5 | 0 | 0 | 0 | 0 | 0 | 0 | 0 | 0 | 0 | 0 | 0 | 3 | 0 | 0 | 0 |
| Connally, Balt. | .000 | 1 | 3 | 0 | 0 | 0 | 0 | 0 | 0 | 0 | 0 | 0 | 1 | 0 | 1 | 0 | 0 | 0 |
| Cooper, Milw. | .244 | 30 | 127 | 10 | 31 | 43 | 6 | 0 | 2 | 13 | 0 | 1 | 5 | 1 | 25 | 1 | 0 | 4 |
| Cowens, Sea. | .111 | 5 | 18 | 1 | 2 | 3 | 1 | 0 | 0 | 1 | 0 | 0 | 1 | 0 | 4 | 0 | 0 | 2 |
| Cruz, Chi. | 1.000 | 2 | 1 | 1 | 1 | 1 | 0 | 0 | 0 | 1 | 0 | 0 | 0 | 0 | 0 | 0 | 0 | 0 |
| DeCinces, Cal. | .071 | 3 | 14 | 1 | 1 | 1 | 0 | 0 | 0 | 0 | 0 | 0 | 0 | 0 | 2 | 0 | 0 | 0 |
| De Sa, Chi. | .300 | 4 | 10 | 0 | 3 | 3 | 0 | 0 | 0 | 1 | 1 | 0 | 0 | 0 | 2 | 0 | 0 | 0 |
| Dixon, Balt. | .000 | 2 | 0 | 0 | 0 | 0 | 0 | 0 | 0 | 0 | 0 | 0 | 0 | 0 | 0 | 0 | 0 | 0 |
| Downing, Cal. | .217 | 25 | 83 | 12 | 18 | 30 | 3 | 0 | 3 | 15 | 0 | 1 | 13 | 2 | 9 | 1 | 0 | 4 |
| Dunbar, Tex. | .132 | 18 | 53 | 1 | 7 | 9 | 2 | 0 | 0 | 3 | 0 | 0 | 5 | 0 | 5 | 0 | 0 | 3 |
| Dwyer, Balt. | .400 | 3 | 5 | 0 | 2 | 2 | 0 | 0 | 0 | 1 | 0 | 1 | 2 | 0 | 1 | 0 | 0 | 0 |
| Easler, Bos. | .259 | 130 | 494 | 63 | 128 | 203 | 27 | 3 | 14 | 68 | 0 | 6 | 44 | 3 | 114 | 0 | 1 | 12 |
| Engle, Minn. | .250 | 38 | 116 | 18 | 29 | 47 | 6 | 0 | 4 | 15 | 0 | 2 | 14 | 0 | 21 | 1 | 0 | 1 |
| Evans, Bos. | .115 | 7 | 26 | 3 | 3 | 9 | 0 | 0 | 2 | 4 | 0 | 1 | 6 | 0 | 3 | 0 | 0 | 0 |
| Evans, Det. | .246 | 33 | 114 | 19 | 28 | 61 | 3 | 0 | 10 | 24 | 1 | 1 | 25 | 0 | 15 | 0 | 0 | 1 |
| Fischlin, Cleve. | .000 | 5 | 2 | 1 | 0 | 0 | 0 | 0 | 0 | 0 | 0 | 0 | 0 | 0 | 0 | 0 | 0 | 0 |
| Fisk, Chi. | .210 | 28 | 105 | 14 | 22 | 41 | 7 | 0 | 4 | 22 | 0 | 1 | 8 | 1 | 13 | 2 | 1 | 1 |
| Fletcher, Chi. | .000 | 2 | 0 | 0 | 0 | 0 | 0 | 0 | 0 | 0 | 0 | 0 | 0 | 0 | 0 | 0 | 0 | 0 |
| Ford, Balt. | .187 | 28 | 75 | 4 | 14 | 19 | 2 | 0 | 1 | 1 | 0 | 0 | 7 | 0 | 17 | 0 | 1 | 3 |
| Franco, Clev. | .200 | 1 | 5 | 1 | 1 | 1 | 0 | 0 | 0 | 1 | 0 | 0 | 0 | 0 | 0 | 0 | 0 | 0 |
| Funderburk, Minn. | .300 | 15 | 50 | 4 | 15 | 27 | 7 | 1 | 1 | 8 | 0 | 2 | 3 | 0 | 7 | 0 | 0 | 2 |
| Gaetti, Minn. | .000 | 1 | 0 | 0 | 0 | 0 | 0 | 0 | 0 | 0 | 0 | 0 | 0 | 0 | 0 | 0 | 0 | 0 |
| Gagne, Minn. | .333 | 5 | 6 | 0 | 2 | 2 | 0 | 0 | 0 | 0 | 0 | 0 | 0 | 0 | 0 | 0 | 0 | 0 |
| Gamble, Chi. | .211 | 48 | 128 | 20 | 27 | 44 | 5 | 0 | 4 | 18 | 0 | 1 | 32 | 1 | 20 | 0 | 0 | 0 |
| Garbey, Det. | .217 | 21 | 60 | 9 | 13 | 22 | 3 | 0 | 2 | 6 | 0 | 2 | 5 | 1 | 11 | 0 | 0 | 1 |
| Gerber, Cal. | .000 | 1 | 0 | 1 | 0 | 0 | 0 | 0 | 0 | 0 | 0 | 0 | 0 | 0 | 0 | 0 | 0 | 0 |
| Gibson, Det. | .367 | 8 | 30 | 3 | 11 | 19 | 2 | 0 | 2 | 6 | 0 | 0 | 4 | 0 | 3 | 2 | 0 | 0 |
| Giles, Milw. | .000 | 2 | 0 | 0 | 0 | 0 | 0 | 0 | 0 | 0 | 0 | 0 | 0 | 0 | 0 | 0 | 1 | 0 |
| Grich, Cal. | .238 | 6 | 21 | 0 | 5 | 7 | 2 | 0 | 0 | 1 | 0 | 0 | 1 | 0 | 3 | 1 | 0 | 2 |
| Griffey, N.Y. | .250 | 7 | 28 | 5 | 7 | 7 | 0 | 0 | 0 | 5 | 0 | 0 | 1 | 0 | 3 | 0 | 0 | 0 |
| Gross, Balt. | .158 | 10 | 19 | 3 | 3 | 6 | 0 | 0 | 1 | 1 | 0 | 0 | 3 | 0 | 3 | 0 | 0 | 0 |
| Grubb, Det. | .256 | 33 | 90 | 11 | 23 | 35 | 1 | 1 | 3 | 9 | 0 | 0 | 15 | 0 | 11 | 0 | 0 | 2 |
| Hairston, Chi. | .210 | 29 | 81 | 8 | 17 | 24 | 4 | 0 | 1 | 12 | 0 | 2 | 14 | 2 | 11 | 0 | 0 | 2 |
| Hall, Clev. | .231 | 5 | 13 | 1 | 3 | 5 | 2 | 0 | 0 | 4 | 0 | 0 | 2 | 0 | 2 | 0 | 0 | 0 |
| Hargrove, Clev. | .333 | 2 | 3 | 0 | 1 | 1 | 0 | 0 | 0 | 1 | 0 | 0 | 1 | 0 | 1 | 0 | 0 | 0 |
| Harrah, Tex. | .000 | 1 | 0 | 0 | 0 | 0 | 0 | 0 | 0 | 0 | 0 | 0 | 0 | 0 | 0 | 0 | 0 | 0 |
| Hassey, N.Y. | 1.000 | 2 | 6 | 1 | 6 | 7 | 1 | 0 | 0 | 4 | 0 | 0 | 0 | 0 | 0 | 0 | 0 | 0 |
| Hatcher, Minn. | .348 | 11 | 46 | 5 | 16 | 21 | 5 | 0 | 0 | 7 | 0 | 0 | 1 | 1 | 3 | 0 | 0 | 0 |
| Henderson, N.Y. | .000 | 1 | 4 | 0 | 0 | 0 | 0 | 0 | 0 | 0 | 0 | 0 | 0 | 0 | 2 | 0 | 0 | 0 |
| Henderson, Oak. | .000 | 1 | 4 | 0 | 0 | 0 | 0 | 0 | 0 | 0 | 0 | 0 | 0 | 0 | 1 | 0 | 0 | 1 |
| Hendrick, Cal. | .000 | 1 | 3 | 0 | 0 | 0 | 0 | 0 | 0 | 0 | 0 | 0 | 0 | 0 | 1 | 0 | 0 | 0 |
| Hernandez, Balt. | .059 | 8 | 17 | 0 | 1 | 1 | 0 | 0 | 0 | 0 | 0 | 0 | 0 | 0 | 4 | 0 | 0 | 1 |
| Householder, Milw. | .000 | 3 | 2 | 0 | 0 | 0 | 0 | 0 | 0 | 0 | 0 | 0 | 0 | 0 | 1 | 0 | 0 | 0 |
| Hrbek, Minn. | .250 | 2 | 8 | 1 | 2 | 5 | 0 | 0 | 1 | 4 | 0 | 0 | 0 | 0 | 2 | 0 | 0 | 0 |
| Iorg, K.C. | .000 | 2 | 2 | 0 | 0 | 0 | 0 | 0 | 0 | 0 | 0 | 0 | 0 | 0 | 2 | 0 | 0 | 0 |
| Jackson, Cal. | .196 | 52 | 168 | 25 | 33 | 65 | 8 | 0 | 8 | 26 | 0 | 2 | 35 | 1 | 65 | 0 | 2 | 6 |
| James, Milw. | .000 | 3 | 3 | 0 | 0 | 0 | 0 | 0 | 0 | 0 | 0 | 0 | 2 | 0 | 0 | 0 | 0 | 0 |
| Johnson, Tex-Tor. | .264 | 103 | 360 | 35 | 95 | 153 | 17 | 1 | 13 | 65 | 1 | 4 | 39 | 3 | 56 | 0 | 0 | 4 |
| Jones, K.C. | .000 | 2 | 2 | 0 | 0 | 0 | 0 | 0 | 0 | 0 | 0 | 0 | 0 | 0 | 1 | 0 | 0 | 0 |
| Jones, Tex. | .214 | 10 | 28 | 3 | 6 | 7 | 1 | 0 | 0 | 6 | 0 | 0 | 3 | 0 | 8 | 1 | 0 | 0 |
| Jones, Cal. | .262 | 43 | 130 | 27 | 34 | 64 | 8 | 2 | 6 | 30 | 1 | 1 | 19 | 0 | 30 | 1 | 1 | 0 |
| Jurak, Bos. | .000 | 2 | 1 | 1 | 0 | 0 | 0 | 0 | 0 | 0 | 0 | 0 | 0 | 0 | 0 | 0 | 0 | 0 |
| Key, Tor. | .000 | 1 | 0 | 0 | 0 | 0 | 0 | 0 | 0 | 0 | 0 | 0 | 0 | 0 | 0 | 0 | 0 | 0 |
| Kiefer, Oak. | 1.000 | 2 | 1 | 2 | 1 | 4 | 0 | 0 | 1 | 3 | 0 | 0 | 0 | 0 | 0 | 0 | 0 | 0 |
| Kingman, Oak. | .233 | 149 | 567 | 61 | 132 | 229 | 13 | 0 | 28 | 84 | 2 | 8 | 57 | 2 | 110 | 2 | 2 | 17 |
| Kittle, Chi. | .251 | 57 | 191 | 28 | 48 | 101 | 5 | 0 | 16 | 35 | 0 | 2 | 13 | 3 | 44 | 0 | 3 | 5 |
| Kuntz, Det. | .000 | 3 | 2 | 0 | 0 | 0 | 0 | 0 | 0 | 0 | 0 | 0 | 2 | 0 | 1 | 0 | 1 | 0 |
| Lacy, Balt. | .235 | 5 | 17 | 2 | 4 | 6 | 2 | 0 | 0 | 1 | 0 | 0 | 1 | 2 | 2 | 0 | 0 | 0 |
| Laga, Det. | .200 | 5 | 20 | 2 | 4 | 8 | 1 | 0 | 1 | 4 | 0 | 0 | 0 | 0 | 6 | 0 | 0 | 0 |
| Law, Chi. | .000 | 3 | 0 | 0 | 0 | 0 | 0 | 0 | 0 | 0 | 0 | 0 | 0 | 0 | 0 | 0 | 0 | 0 |

| Player and Club | Pct. | G. | AB. | R. | H. | TB. | 2B. | 3B. | HR. | RBI. | SH. | SF. | BB. | HP. | SO. | SB. | CS. | GI DP. |
|---|---|---|---|---|---|---|---|---|---|---|---|---|---|---|---|---|---|---|
| Lee, Tor. | .000 | 8 | 0 | 4 | 0 | 0 | 0 | 0 | 0 | 0 | 0 | 0 | 0 | 0 | 0 | 0 | 2 | 0 |
| Linares, Cal. | .250 | 14 | 40 | 6 | 10 | 21 | 2 | 0 | 3 | 10 | 0 | 1 | 1 | 0 | 4 | 1 | 0 | 1 |
| Lowenstein, Balt. | .071 | 6 | 14 | 0 | 1 | 1 | 0 | 0 | 0 | 2 | 0 | 1 | 2 | 0 | 1 | 0 | 0 | 0 |
| Lyons, Bos. | .500 | 5 | 2 | 3 | 1 | 1 | 0 | 0 | 0 | 0 | 0 | 0 | 0 | 0 | 0 | 0 | 0 | 0 |
| Madison, Det. | .000 | 3 | 9 | 0 | 0 | 0 | 0 | 0 | 0 | 1 | 0 | 1 | 1 | 0 | 0 | 0 | 0 | 0 |
| Manning, Milw. | .000 | 2 | 2 | 1 | 0 | 0 | 0 | 0 | 0 | 0 | 0 | 0 | 0 | 0 | 0 | 0 | 0 | 0 |
| Matuszek, Tor. | .216 | 54 | 139 | 21 | 30 | 44 | 6 | 1 | 2 | 15 | 0 | 4 | 10 | 0 | 20 | 2 | 1 | 5 |
| McDowell, Tex. | .143 | 4 | 14 | 1 | 2 | 5 | 0 | 0 | 1 | 2 | 0 | 0 | 0 | 0 | 3 | 0 | 0 | 1 |
| McRae, K.C. | .264 | 106 | 314 | 41 | 83 | 144 | 19 | 0 | 14 | 70 | 2 | 2 | 44 | 1 | 43 | 0 | 1 | 11 |
| Meier, Minn. | .000 | 3 | 2 | 0 | 0 | 0 | 0 | 0 | 0 | 0 | 0 | 0 | 0 | 0 | 0 | 0 | 0 | 0 |
| Meyer, Oak. | .000 | 1 | 1 | 0 | 0 | 0 | 0 | 0 | 0 | 0 | 0 | 0 | 0 | 0 | 0 | 0 | 0 | 0 |
| Miller, Bos. | .600 | 4 | 5 | 1 | 3 | 3 | 0 | 0 | 0 | 1 | 0 | 0 | 0 | 0 | 0 | 0 | 0 | 0 |
| Miller, Cal. | .400 | 4 | 10 | 0 | 4 | 4 | 0 | 0 | 0 | 0 | 0 | 0 | 0 | 0 | 2 | 0 | 1 | 0 |
| Molitor, Milw. | .167 | 4 | 18 | 4 | 3 | 6 | 0 | 0 | 1 | 1 | 0 | 0 | 2 | 0 | 2 | 1 | 0 | 1 |
| Moreno, N.Y. | .000 | 1 | 0 | 1 | 0 | 0 | 0 | 0 | 0 | 0 | 0 | 0 | 0 | 0 | 0 | 0 | 0 | 0 |
| Motley, K.C. | .059 | 7 | 17 | 0 | 1 | 1 | 0 | 0 | 0 | 3 | 0 | 1 | 2 | 0 | 5 | 0 | 0 | 0 |
| Murray, Balt. | .250 | 2 | 8 | 1 | 2 | 5 | 0 | 0 | 1 | 2 | 0 | 0 | 0 | 0 | 0 | 0 | 0 | 0 |
| Narron, Cal. | .182 | 7 | 22 | 1 | 4 | 8 | 1 | 0 | 1 | 1 | 0 | 0 | 1 | 0 | 2 | 0 | 0 | 0 |
| Nichols, Bos.-Chi. | .333 | 5 | 3 | 3 | 1 | 1 | 0 | 0 | 0 | 0 | 0 | 1 | 1 | 0 | 0 | 0 | 0 | 0 |
| Nixon, Clev. | .000 | 11 | 4 | 2 | 0 | 0 | 0 | 0 | 0 | 1 | 1 | 0 | 0 | 0 | 0 | 2 | 1 | 0 |
| Nolan, Balt. | .000 | 4 | 5 | 0 | 0 | 0 | 0 | 0 | 0 | 0 | 0 | 0 | 2 | 0 | 2 | 0 | 0 | 1 |
| Oglivie, Milw. | .250 | 4 | 12 | 4 | 3 | 7 | 1 | 0 | 1 | 2 | 0 | 0 | 3 | 0 | 2 | 0 | 0 | 0 |
| Oliver, Tor. | .253 | 59 | 186 | 20 | 47 | 70 | 6 | 1 | 5 | 23 | 0 | 0 | 5 | 1 | 13 | 0 | 0 | 8 |
| Orta, K.C. | .263 | 85 | 281 | 30 | 74 | 108 | 20 | 1 | 4 | 40 | 2 | 4 | 19 | 2 | 25 | 2 | 1 | 8 |
| Paciorek, Chi. | .308 | 12 | 26 | 6 | 8 | 8 | 0 | 0 | 0 | 1 | 0 | 1 | 2 | 0 | 2 | 0 | 0 | 1 |
| Paris, Balt. | .000 | 2 | 4 | 0 | 0 | 0 | 0 | 0 | 0 | 0 | 0 | 0 | 0 | 0 | 0 | 0 | 0 | 0 |
| Parrish, Det. | .298 | 22 | 84 | 7 | 25 | 38 | 4 | 0 | 3 | 12 | 0 | 0 | 6 | 0 | 19 | 1 | 3 | 0 |
| Parrish, Tex. | .277 | 22 | 83 | 11 | 23 | 39 | 4 | 0 | 4 | 13 | 0 | 1 | 9 | 0 | 18 | 0 | 0 | 3 |
| Pasqua, N.Y. | .114 | 14 | 44 | 6 | 5 | 16 | 0 | 1 | 3 | 7 | 0 | 0 | 4 | 1 | 12 | 0 | 0 | 0 |
| Phelps, Sea. | .211 | 25 | 76 | 15 | 16 | 36 | 2 | 0 | 6 | 16 | 0 | 0 | 16 | 0 | 20 | 2 | 0 | 1 |
| Picciolo, Oak. | .000 | 10 | 4 | 2 | 0 | 0 | 0 | 0 | 0 | 0 | 0 | 0 | 0 | 0 | 2 | 1 | 1 | 0 |
| Pittaro, Det. | .000 | 1 | 0 | 0 | 0 | 0 | 0 | 0 | 0 | 0 | 0 | 0 | 0 | 0 | 0 | 0 | 0 | 0 |
| Ponce, Milw. | .154 | 3 | 13 | 2 | 2 | 5 | 0 | 0 | 1 | 1 | 0 | 0 | 0 | 0 | 2 | 0 | 0 | 1 |
| Pryor, K.C. | .000 | 1 | 0 | 0 | 0 | 0 | 0 | 0 | 0 | 0 | 0 | 0 | 0 | 0 | 0 | 0 | 0 | 0 |
| Rayford, Balt. | .000 | 1 | 1 | 0 | 0 | 0 | 0 | 0 | 0 | 0 | 0 | 0 | 0 | 0 | 1 | 0 | 0 | 0 |
| Ready, Milw. | .000 | 2 | 3 | 1 | 0 | 0 | 0 | 0 | 0 | 0 | 0 | 0 | 1 | 0 | 1 | 0 | 0 | 0 |
| Rice, Bos. | .500 | 7 | 30 | 8 | 15 | 28 | 4 | 0 | 3 | 9 | 0 | 0 | 3 | 0 | 2 | 0 | 0 | 1 |
| Riles, Milw. | .000 | 1 | 6 | 1 | 0 | 0 | 0 | 0 | 0 | 0 | 0 | 0 | 0 | 0 | 0 | 0 | 0 | 0 |
| Robidoux, Milw. | .000 | 1 | 3 | 0 | 0 | 0 | 0 | 0 | 0 | 0 | 0 | 0 | 2 | 0 | 1 | 0 | 0 | 0 |
| Roenicke, Balt. | .240 | 17 | 25 | 4 | 6 | 10 | 0 | 1 | 1 | 5 | 0 | 1 | 2 | 0 | 4 | 0 | 1 | 0 |
| Romine, Bos. | .000 | 1 | 1 | 0 | 0 | 0 | 0 | 0 | 0 | 0 | 1 | 0 | 0 | 0 | 0 | 0 | 0 | 0 |
| Sakata, Balt. | .000 | 1 | 0 | 1 | 0 | 0 | 0 | 0 | 0 | 0 | 0 | 0 | 0 | 0 | 0 | 0 | 0 | 0 |
| Salas, Minn. | .286 | 3 | 7 | 1 | 2 | 3 | 1 | 0 | 0 | 1 | 0 | 0 | 1 | 0 | 1 | 0 | 0 | 0 |
| Salazar, Chi. | .143 | 8 | 7 | 2 | 1 | 1 | 0 | 0 | 0 | 1 | 0 | 0 | 1 | 0 | 2 | 0 | 0 | 0 |
| Sanchez, Det. | .306 | 28 | 62 | 11 | 19 | 34 | 2 | 2 | 3 | 6 | 0 | 0 | 0 | 0 | 13 | 0 | 1 | 0 |
| Schroeder, Milw. | .400 | 4 | 15 | 0 | 6 | 6 | 0 | 0 | 0 | 3 | 0 | 0 | 1 | 0 | 4 | 0 | 0 | 0 |
| Sconiers, Cal. | .250 | 20 | 68 | 10 | 17 | 27 | 2 | 1 | 2 | 8 | 0 | 2 | 11 | 0 | 15 | 2 | 1 | 2 |
| Sheets, Balt. | .262 | 93 | 294 | 37 | 77 | 123 | 7 | 0 | 13 | 43 | 1 | 1 | 25 | 2 | 46 | 0 | 1 | 13 |
| Shelby, Balt. | .286 | 3 | 7 | 1 | 2 | 5 | 0 | 0 | 1 | 2 | 0 | 0 | 0 | 0 | 2 | 0 | 0 | 0 |
| Shepherd, Tor. | .000 | 15 | 6 | 1 | 0 | 0 | 0 | 0 | 0 | 0 | 0 | 0 | 0 | 0 | 2 | 3 | 0 | 1 |
| Sheridan, K.C. | .000 | 1 | 1 | 0 | 0 | 0 | 0 | 0 | 0 | 0 | 0 | 0 | 0 | 0 | 0 | 0 | 0 | 0 |
| Simmons, Det. | .216 | 31 | 116 | 13 | 25 | 40 | 3 | 0 | 4 | 14 | 0 | 2 | 8 | 0 | 19 | 0 | 0 | 2 |
| Simmons, Milw. | .265 | 99 | 374 | 40 | 99 | 146 | 19 | 2 | 8 | 53 | 0 | 5 | 35 | 1 | 24 | 1 | 0 | 11 |
| Smalley, Minn. | .244 | 56 | 180 | 23 | 44 | 67 | 11 | 0 | 4 | 23 | 0 | 1 | 29 | 0 | 26 | 0 | 1 | 2 |
| Stapleton, Bos. | .167 | 5 | 6 | 1 | 1 | 2 | 1 | 0 | 0 | 1 | 1 | 0 | 0 | 0 | 1 | 0 | 0 | 0 |
| Stein, Tex. | .133 | 6 | 15 | 1 | 2 | 4 | 0 | 1 | 0 | 1 | 0 | 0 | 0 | 0 | 3 | 0 | 0 | 1 |
| Stenhouse, Minn. | .244 | 27 | 90 | 13 | 22 | 36 | 5 | 0 | 3 | 12 | 0 | 1 | 13 | 0 | 7 | 1 | 0 | 2 |
| Tabler, Clev. | .221 | 18 | 68 | 6 | 15 | 20 | 2 | 0 | 1 | 13 | 0 | 1 | 1 | 0 | 11 | 0 | 1 | 6 |
| Tettleton, Oak. | .000 | 1 | 1 | 0 | 0 | 0 | 0 | 0 | 0 | 0 | 0 | 0 | 0 | 0 | 1 | 0 | 0 | 0 |
| Teufel, Minn. | 1.000 | 1 | 1 | 1 | 1 | 4 | 0 | 0 | 1 | 1 | 0 | 0 | 0 | 0 | 0 | 0 | 0 | 0 |
| G. Thomas, Sea. | .215 | 133 | 483 | 76 | 104 | 218 | 16 | 1 | 32 | 87 | 2 | 3 | 83 | 1 | 126 | 3 | 2 | 10 |
| Thornton, Clev. | .235 | 122 | 460 | 48 | 108 | 184 | 13 | 0 | 21 | 87 | 0 | 6 | 46 | 0 | 75 | 3 | 2 | 14 |
| Thornton, Tex. | .000 | 16 | 1 | 7 | 0 | 0 | 0 | 0 | 0 | 0 | 0 | 0 | 0 | 0 | 0 | 0 | 0 | 0 |
| Tolleson, Tex. | .000 | 6 | 0 | 3 | 0 | 0 | 0 | 0 | 0 | 0 | 0 | 0 | 1 | 0 | 0 | 0 | 0 | 0 |
| Upshaw, Tor. | .333 | 1 | 3 | 1 | 1 | 1 | 0 | 0 | 0 | 1 | 0 | 0 | 2 | 0 | 0 | 0 | 0 | 0 |
| Valentine, Tex. | .125 | 4 | 16 | 0 | 2 | 2 | 0 | 0 | 0 | 0 | 0 | 0 | 0 | 0 | 4 | 0 | 1 | 1 |
| Walker, Chi. | .238 | 7 | 21 | 2 | 5 | 10 | 2 | 0 | 1 | 5 | 0 | 1 | 1 | 1 | 2 | 0 | 0 | 0 |
| Walker, Tex. | .067 | 10 | 30 | 1 | 2 | 2 | 0 | 0 | 0 | 1 | 0 | 0 | 2 | 0 | 7 | 0 | 0 | 0 |
| Ward, Tex. | .400 | 1 | 5 | 0 | 2 | 3 | 1 | 0 | 0 | 1 | 0 | 0 | 1 | 0 | 0 | 0 | 0 | 0 |
| Washington, Minn. | .154 | 7 | 13 | 2 | 2 | 2 | 0 | 0 | 0 | 0 | 0 | 0 | 1 | 0 | 1 | 1 | 0 | 0 |
| Wathan, K.C. | .000 | 2 | 0 | 0 | 0 | 0 | 0 | 0 | 0 | 0 | 0 | 0 | 0 | 0 | 0 | 0 | 0 | 0 |
| Weaver, Det. | .000 | 4 | 1 | 2 | 0 | 0 | 0 | 0 | 0 | 0 | 0 | 0 | 1 | 0 | 1 | 0 | 1 | 0 |
| Webster, Tor. | .000 | 2 | 1 | 0 | 0 | 0 | 0 | 0 | 0 | 0 | 0 | 0 | 0 | 0 | 1 | 0 | 1 | 0 |
| Wilfong, Cal. | .000 | 2 | 4 | 0 | 0 | 0 | 0 | 0 | 0 | 0 | 0 | 0 | 0 | 0 | 0 | 0 | 0 | 0 |
| Wilkerson, Tex. | .000 | 2 | 0 | 1 | 0 | 0 | 0 | 0 | 0 | 0 | 0 | 0 | 0 | 0 | 0 | 0 | 0 | 0 |
| Willard, Clev. | .500 | 1 | 4 | 0 | 2 | 3 | 1 | 0 | 0 | 3 | 0 | 0 | 0 | 0 | 0 | 0 | 0 | 0 |
| Wilson, Clev. | .375 | 2 | 8 | 2 | 3 | 3 | 0 | 0 | 0 | 0 | 0 | 0 | 1 | 0 | 1 | 0 | 0 | 0 |
| Winfield, N.Y. | .375 | 2 | 8 | 2 | 3 | 10 | 1 | 0 | 2 | 3 | 0 | 0 | 1 | 0 | 2 | 0 | 0 | 0 |
| G. Wright, Tex. | .308 | 4 | 13 | 2 | 4 | 6 | 2 | 0 | 0 | 1 | 1 | 1 | 0 | 0 | 0 | 0 | 0 | 0 |
| Young, Balt. | .250 | 37 | 120 | 18 | 30 | 61 | 5 | 1 | 8 | 24 | 0 | 1 | 11 | 1 | 28 | 1 | 4 | 3 |
| Yount, Milw. | .295 | 12 | 44 | 10 | 13 | 23 | 1 | 0 | 3 | 10 | 0 | 4 | 6 | 0 | 3 | 0 | 0 | 1 |

# OFFICIAL AMERICAN LEAGUE FIELDING AVERAGES

## CLUB FIELDING

| Club | Pct. | G. | PO. | A. | E. | TC. | DP. | TP. | PB. |
|---|---|---|---|---|---|---|---|---|---|
| California | .982 | 162 | 4372 | 1841 | 112 | 6325 | 202 | 0 | 8 |
| Chicago | .982 | 163 | 4355 | 1677 | 111 | 6143 | 152 | 0 | 11 |
| Seattle | .980 | 162 | 4296 | 1836 | 122 | 6254 | 156 | 0 | 22 |
| Minnesota | .980 | 162 | 4279 | 1732 | 120 | 6131 | 139 | 0 | 13 |
| Kansas City | .980 | 162 | 4383 | 1907 | 127 | 6417 | 160 | 1 | 10 |
| Texas | .980 | 161 | 4235 | 1703 | 120 | 6058 | 145 | 0 | 23 |
| Toronto | .980 | 161 | 4344 | 1729 | 125 | 6198 | 164 | 0 | 3 |
| New York | .979 | 161 | 4321 | 1563 | 126 | 6010 | 172 | 0 | 18 |
| Baltimore | .979 | 161 | 4282 | 1714 | 129 | 6125 | 168 | 0 | 4 |
| Boston | .977 | 163 | 4384 | 1846 | 145 | 6375 | 161 | 0 | 14 |
| Oakland | .977 | 162 | 4359 | 1566 | 140 | 6065 | 137 | 0 | 19 |
| Cleveland | .977 | 162 | 4263 | 1703 | 141 | 6107 | 161 | 0 | 13 |
| Milwaukee | .977 | 161 | 4311 | 1686 | 142 | 6139 | 153 | 0 | 12 |
| Detroit | .977 | 161 | 4368 | 1671 | 143 | 6182 | 152 | 0 | 10 |
| Totals | .979 | 1132 | 60552 | 24174 | 1803 | 86529 | 2222 | 1 | 180 |

## INDIVIDUAL FIELDING

*Throws lefthanded.

### FIRST BASEMEN

| LEADER—Club | Pct. | G. | PO. | A. | E. | DP. |
|---|---|---|---|---|---|---|
| MATTINGLY, N.Y.* | .995 | 159 | 1318 | 87 | 7 | 154 |

| PLAYER—Club | Pct. | G. | PO. | A. | E. | DP. |
|---|---|---|---|---|---|---|
| Baker, Oak. | .993 | 58 | 400 | 26 | 3 | 33 |
| Balboni, K.C. | .993 | 160 | 1573 | 101 | 12 | 138 |
| Beniquez, Cal. | .988 | 46 | 319 | 24 | 4 | 42 |
| Bergman, Det.* | .991 | 44 | 306 | 25 | 3 | 25 |
| Bochte, Oak.* | .990 | 128 | 942 | 60 | 10 | 83 |
| Buckner, Bos.* | .992 | 162 | 1384 | 184 | 12 | 140 |
| Carew, Cal. | .994 | 116 | 1055 | 65 | 7 | 121 |
| Carter, Clev. | .974 | 11 | 33 | 5 | 1 | 2 |
| Cooper, Milw.* | .986 | 123 | 1087 | 94 | 17 | 101 |
| Davis, Sea. | .992 | 154 | 1438 | 103 | 13 | 131 |
| Evans, Det. | .984 | 113 | 827 | 114 | 15 | 80 |
| Fielder, Tor. | .979 | 25 | 171 | 17 | 4 | 21 |
| Garbey, Det. | .991 | 37 | 190 | 20 | 2 | 24 |
| Grich, Cal. | 1.000 | 16 | 98 | 9 | 0 | 14 |
| Hargrove, Clev.* | .991 | 84 | 595 | 66 | 6 | 66 |
| Hrbek, Minn. | .9945 | 156 | 1339 | 114 | 8 | 114 |
| Leach, Tor.* | .987 | 10 | 72 | 6 | 1 | 8 |
| Mattingly, N.Y.* | .9950 | 159 | 1318 | 87 | 7 | 154 |
| Murray, Balt. | .987 | 154 | 1338 | 152 | 19 | 154 |
| O'Brien, Tex.* | .9948 | 159 | 1457 | 98 | 8 | 125 |
| Picciolo, Oak. | 1.000 | 13 | 19 | 4 | 0 | 2 |
| Ponce, Milw. | 1.000 | 10 | 54 | 3 | 0 | 7 |
| Ramos, Sea. | 1.000 | 14 | 15 | 0 | 0 | 1 |
| Simmons, Milw. | .992 | 28 | 226 | 17 | 2 | 22 |
| Tabler, Clev. | .983 | 92 | 739 | 72 | 14 | 77 |
| Upshaw, Tor.* | .992 | 147 | 1157 | 104 | 10 | 111 |
| Walker, Chi. | .994 | 151 | 1217 | 97 | 8 | 116 |

#### (Fewer Than Ten Games)

| PLAYER—Club | Pct. | G. | PO. | A. | E. | DP. |
|---|---|---|---|---|---|---|
| Bannister, Tex. | 1.000 | 4 | 11 | 1 | 0 | 2 |
| Bonnell, Sea. | 1.000 | 5 | 23 | 0 | 0 | 3 |
| Bush, Minn.* | 1.000 | 1 | 16 | 0 | 0 | 1 |
| Calderon, Sea. | 1.000 | 2 | 8 | 0 | 0 | 1 |
| Connally, Balt. | 1.000 | 2 | 16 | 0 | 0 | 1 |
| Dauer, Balt. | 1.000 | 1 | 2 | 0 | 0 | 0 |

| Player—Club | Pct. | G. | PO. | A. | E. | DP. |
|---|---|---|---|---|---|---|
| De Sa, Chi.* | 1.000 | 9 | 70 | 7 | 0 | 4 |
| Fischlin, Clev. | 1.000 | 6 | 8 | 0 | 0 | 0 |
| Funderburk, Minn. | 1.000 | 1 | 8 | 0 | 0 | 0 |
| Gaetti, Minn. | 1.000 | 1 | 6 | 0 | 0 | 0 |
| Griffey, N.Y.* | 1.000 | 1 | 5 | 0 | 0 | 0 |
| Gross, Balt. | 1.000 | 9 | 40 | 4 | 0 | 1 |
| Hassey, N.Y. | 1.000 | 2 | 18 | 0 | 0 | 2 |
| Hatcher, Minn. | .970 | 4 | 31 | 1 | 1 | 2 |
| Hernandez, Balt. | 1.000 | 1 | 2 | 0 | 0 | 0 |
| Hudler, N.Y. | 1.000 | 1 | 6 | 0 | 0 | 2 |
| Iorg, K.C. | 1.000 | 2 | 13 | 1 | 0 | 2 |
| Johnson, Tor. | .947 | 3 | 17 | 1 | 1 | 4 |
| Jones, Tex.* | 1.000 | 4 | 14 | 0 | 0 | 1 |
| Jurak, Bos. | .000 | 1 | 0 | 0 | 0 | 0 |
| Kingman, Oak. | 1.000 | 9 | 50 | 1 | 0 | 3 |
| Kuntz, Det. | .000 | 1 | 0 | 0 | 1 | 0 |
| Laga, Det.* | .974 | 4 | 33 | 5 | 1 | 4 |
| Laudner, Minn. | 1.000 | 1 | 3 | 0 | 0 | 0 |
| Matuszek, Tor.* | 1.000 | 5 | 19 | 2 | 0 | 1 |
| Narron, Cal. | 1.000 | 1 | 2 | 0 | 0 | 0 |
| Oliver, Tor.* | 1.000 | 1 | 3 | 0 | 0 | 0 |
| Paciorek, Chi. | 1.000 | 6 | 45 | 5 | 0 | 3 |
| Phelps, Sea.* | 1.000 | 8 | 31 | 2 | 0 | 5 |
| Pryor, K.C. | .000 | 1 | 0 | 0 | 0 | 0 |
| Quirk, K.C. | 1.000 | 1 | 2 | 0 | 0 | 0 |
| Robidoux, Milw. | 1.000 | 6 | 49 | 5 | 0 | 6 |
| Salazar, Chi. | 1.000 | 6 | 40 | 2 | 0 | 6 |
| Schroeder, Milw. | 1.000 | 1 | 5 | 0 | 0 | 1 |
| Sconiers, Cal.* | .973 | 6 | 35 | 1 | 1 | 2 |
| Sheets, Balt. | 1.000 | 1 | 5 | 1 | 0 | 1 |
| Smalley, Minn. | 1.000 | 1 | 4 | 1 | 0 | 0 |
| Stapleton, Bos. | .929 | 8 | 12 | 1 | 1 | 3 |
| Stein, Tex. | .977 | 8 | 40 | 3 | 1 | 2 |
| Stenhouse, Minn. | .985 | 8 | 59 | 8 | 1 | 4 |
| Washington, Minn. | 1.000 | 1 | 1 | 0 | 0 | 0 |
| Wathan, K.C. | 1.000 | 6 | 12 | 1 | 0 | 0 |
| Wilson, Clev. | 1.000 | 2 | 23 | 0 | 0 | 1 |
| Yount, Milw. | 1.000 | 2 | 9 | 1 | 0 | 0 |

Triple Play—Balboni.

### SECOND BASEMEN

| LEADER—Club | Pct. | G. | PO. | A. | E. | DP. |
|---|---|---|---|---|---|---|
| GRICH, Cal. | .997 | 116 | 224 | 380 | 2 | 99 |

| PLAYER—Club | Pct. | G. | PO. | A. | E. | DP. |
|---|---|---|---|---|---|---|
| Bannister, Tex. | .970 | 10 | 16 | 16 | 1 | 2 |
| Barrett, Bos. | .987 | 155 | 355 | 479 | 11 | 110 |
| Bernazard, Clev. | .978 | 147 | 311 | 399 | 16 | 86 |
| Cruz, Chi. | .982 | 87 | 158 | 220 | 7 | 59 |
| Dauer, Balt. | .990 | 73 | 117 | 181 | 3 | 44 |
| Fischlin, Clev. | .990 | 31 | 44 | 59 | 1 | 15 |
| Fletcher, Chi. | 1.000 | 37 | 38 | 55 | 0 | 11 |
| Flynn, Det. | .984 | 20 | 31 | 32 | 1 | 14 |
| Gallego, Oak. | .991 | 42 | 46 | 66 | 1 | 22 |

| Player—Club | Pct. | G. | PO. | A. | E. | DP. |
|---|---|---|---|---|---|---|
| Gantner, Milw. | .988 | 124 | 262 | 402 | 8 | 89 |
| Garcia, Tor. | .981 | 143 | 302 | 371 | 13 | 88 |
| Giles, Milw. | 1.000 | 13 | 27 | 27 | 0 | 5 |
| Grich, Cal. | .997 | 116 | 224 | 380 | 2 | 99 |
| Harrah, Tex. | .989 | 122 | 212 | 351 | 6 | 71 |
| Hill, Oak. | .973 | 122 | 228 | 320 | 15 | 56 |
| Hudler, N.Y. | .977 | 16 | 36 | 50 | 2 | 12 |
| Hulett, Chi. | .989 | 28 | 48 | 46 | 1 | 19 |
| Iorg, Tor. | 1.000 | 23 | 32 | 55 | 0 | 11 |
| Lee, Tor. | .971 | 38 | 27 | 40 | 2 | 8 |
| Little, Chi. | .989 | 68 | 100 | 164 | 3 | 33 |
| Lombardozzi, Minn. | .982 | 26 | 31 | 80 | 2 | 16 |

| Player—Club | Pct. | G. | PO. | A. | E. | DP. | Player—Club | Pct. | G. | PO. | A. | E. | DP. |
|---|---|---|---|---|---|---|---|---|---|---|---|---|---|
| Perconte, Sea. | .986 | 125 | 244 | 381 | 9 | 91 | Biancalana, K.C. | 1.000 | 4 | 3 | 1 | 0 | 1 |
| Phillips, Oak. | .984 | 24 | 18 | 43 | 1 | 7 | Bonilla, N.Y. | .955 | 7 | 7 | 14 | 1 | 3 |
| Picciolo, Oak. | .971 | 17 | 27 | 39 | 2 | 7 | Brookens, Det. | 1.000 | 3 | 2 | 6 | 0 | 1 |
| Pryor, K.C. | .988 | 20 | 35 | 46 | 1 | 11 | Buechele, Tex. | 1.000 | 1 | 0 | 1 | 0 | 0 |
| Ramos, Sea. | .953 | 20 | 25 | 36 | 3 | 9 | Carter, Clev. | 1.000 | 1 | 0 | 1 | 0 | 0 |
| Randolph, N.Y. | .985 | 143 | 303 | 425 | 11 | 104 | Concepcion, K.C. | 1.000 | 2 | 0 | 3 | 0 | 0 |
| Reynolds, Sea. | .960 | 61 | 69 | 123 | 8 | 22 | Franco, Clev. | .970 | 8 | 14 | 18 | 1 | 4 |
| Romero, Milw. | .979 | 31 | 80 | 104 | 4 | 26 | Gerber, Cal. | 1.000 | 1 | 1 | 0 | 0 | 0 |
| Sakata, Balt. | .960 | 50 | 58 | 87 | 6 | 18 | Gruber, Tor. | .000 | 1 | 0 | 0 | 0 | 0 |
| Stapleton, Bos. | 1.000 | 14 | 29 | 35 | 0 | 8 | Hegman, K.C. | .000 | 1 | 0 | 0 | 0 | 0 |
| Teufel, Minn. | .980 | 137 | 237 | 352 | 12 | 67 | Hoffman, Bos. | 1.000 | 3 | 2 | 0 | 0 | 0 |
| Tolleson, Tex. | .965 | 29 | 44 | 65 | 4 | 11 | Jacoby, Clev. | .000 | 1 | 0 | 0 | 0 | 0 |
| Washington, Minn. | .953 | 24 | 31 | 50 | 4 | 8 | Nichols, Bos. | 1.000 | 3 | 1 | 1 | 0 | 1 |
| Whitaker, Det. | .985 | 150 | 314 | 414 | 11 | 101 | Paris, Balt. | .857 | 2 | 3 | 3 | 1 | 0 |
| White, K.C. | .980 | 149 | 342 | 490 | 17 | 101 | Pittaro, Det. | .933 | 4 | 5 | 9 | 1 | 4 |
| Wiggins, Balt. | .960 | 76 | 148 | 186 | 14 | 58 | Ready, Milw. | 1.000 | 3 | 4 | 2 | 0 | 0 |
| Wilfong, Cal. | .986 | 69 | 124 | 216 | 5 | 45 | Robertson, N.Y. | 1.000 | 2 | 5 | 4 | 0 | 2 |
| Wilkerson, Tex. | .969 | 19 | 40 | 54 | 3 | 15 | Shelby, Balt. | 1.000 | 1 | 0 | 1 | 0 | 0 |
| | | | | | | | Stein, Tex. | 1.000 | 3 | 2 | 2 | 0 | 1 |
| | | | | | | | Tabler, Clev. | 1.000 | 1 | 1 | 2 | 0 | 1 |

(Fewer Than Ten Games)

| PLAYER—Club | Pct. | G. | PO. | A. | E. | DP. |
|---|---|---|---|---|---|---|
| Baker, Det. | .000 | 1 | 0 | 0 | 0 | 0 |

Triple Play—White.

## THIRD BASEMEN

| Leader—Club | Pct. | G. | PO. | A. | E. | DP. | Player—Club | Pct. | G. | PO. | A. | E. | DP. |
|---|---|---|---|---|---|---|---|---|---|---|---|---|---|
| MULLINIKS, Tor. | .971 | 119 | 75 | 162 | 7 | 16 | Smalley, Minn. | .980 | 14 | 9 | 41 | 1 | 2 |
| | | | | | | | Stein, Tex. | .952 | 11 | 5 | 15 | 1 | 1 |
| **Player—Club** | **Pct.** | **G.** | **PO.** | **A.** | **E.** | **DP.** | Tolleson, Tex. | .895 | 12 | 9 | 8 | 2 | 0 |
| Bell, Tex. | .942 | 83 | 70 | 192 | 16 | 22 | | | | | | | |
| Berra, N.Y. | .917 | 41 | 20 | 68 | 8 | 9 | | | | | | | |

| Player—Club | Pct. | G. | PO. | A. | E. | DP. |
|---|---|---|---|---|---|---|
| Boggs, Bos. | .965 | 161 | 134 | 335 | 17 | 30 |
| Brett, K.C. | .967 | 152 | 107 | 339 | 15 | 33 |
| Brookens, Det. | .943 | 151 | 123 | 261 | 23 | 26 |
| Buechele, Tex. | .969 | 69 | 52 | 137 | 6 | 17 |
| Castillo, Det. | .962 | 25 | 6 | 19 | 1 | 1 |
| Connally, Balt. | .976 | 46 | 23 | 57 | 2 | 3 |
| Dauer, Balt. | .966 | 17 | 7 | 21 | 1 | 0 |
| DeCinces, Calif. | .958 | 111 | 95 | 202 | 13 | 27 |
| Fletcher, Chi. | .934 | 55 | 29 | 70 | 7 | 7 |
| Gaetti, Minn. | .963 | 156 | 146 | 316 | 18 | 31 |
| Gallego, Oak. | 1.000 | 12 | 3 | 11 | 0 | 1 |
| Gantner, Milw. | .943 | 24 | 16 | 34 | 3 | 5 |
| Grich, Calif. | .966 | 15 | 9 | 19 | 1 | 2 |
| Gross, Balt. | .933 | 67 | 41 | 98 | 10 | 14 |
| Heath, Oak. | .962 | 13 | 7 | 18 | 1 | 1 |
| Howell, Calif. | .931 | 42 | 33 | 75 | 8 | 10 |
| Hulett, Chi. | .924 | 115 | 69 | 210 | 23 | 22 |
| Iorg, Tor. | .951 | 104 | 39 | 137 | 9 | 13 |
| Jacoby, Clev. | .958 | 161 | 114 | 319 | 19 | 26 |
| Kiefer, Oak. | .881 | 34 | 15 | 37 | 7 | 5 |
| Lansford, Oak. | .976 | 97 | 85 | 119 | 5 | 11 |
| Molitor, Milw. | .953 | 135 | 126 | 263 | 19 | 30 |
| Mulliniks, Tor. | .971 | 119 | 75 | 162 | 7 | 16 |
| Pagliarulo, N.Y. | .951 | 134 | 67 | 187 | 13 | 15 |
| Phillips, Oak. | .980 | 31 | 36 | 60 | 2 | 6 |
| Picciolo, Oak. | .889 | 19 | 6 | 18 | 3 | 2 |
| Pittaro, Det. | .881 | 22 | 10 | 27 | 5 | 1 |
| Presley, Sea. | .961 | 154 | 82 | 335 | 17 | 24 |
| Pryor, K.C. | .946 | 26 | 5 | 30 | 2 | 2 |
| Rayford, Balt. | .972 | 78 | 62 | 145 | 6 | 13 |
| Robertson, N.Y. | .867 | 33 | 11 | 41 | 8 | 6 |
| Salazar, Chi. | .925 | 39 | 22 | 52 | 6 | 5 |

(Fewer Than Ten Games)

| Player—Club | Pct. | G. | PO. | A. | E. | DP. |
|---|---|---|---|---|---|---|
| Bannister, Tex. | 1.000 | 5 | 0 | 1 | 0 | 0 |
| Bell, Tor. | 1.000 | 2 | 0 | 1 | 0 | 0 |
| Beniquez, Calif. | 1.000 | 1 | 1 | 0 | 0 | 0 |
| Carter, Clev. | .000 | 1 | 0 | 0 | 0 | 0 |
| Coles, Sea. | .900 | 7 | 2 | 7 | 1 | 0 |
| Evans, Det. | .750 | 7 | 4 | 11 | 5 | 1 |
| Fischlin, Clev. | 1.000 | 3 | 1 | 2 | 0 | 0 |
| Flynn, Det. | 1.000 | 4 | 0 | 1 | 0 | 0 |
| Garbey, Det. | .000 | 1 | 0 | 0 | 0 | 0 |
| Gerber, Calif. | 1.000 | 9 | 4 | 3 | 0 | 0 |
| Gruber, Tor. | 1.000 | 5 | 2 | 6 | 0 | 0 |
| Hill, Chi. | 1.000 | 1 | 0 | 2 | 0 | 0 |
| Hoffman, Bos. | .500 | 3 | 0 | 1 | 1 | 0 |
| Iorg, K.C. | 1.000 | 1 | 1 | 3 | 0 | 0 |
| Jurak, Bos. | .833 | 7 | 3 | 7 | 2 | 0 |
| Keedy, Calif. | .000 | 2 | 0 | 0 | 0 | 0 |
| Lee, Tor. | 1.000 | 5 | 0 | 3 | 0 | 0 |
| Little, Chi. | .000 | 2 | 0 | 2 | 0 | 0 |
| Lyons, Bos. | 1.000 | 1 | 0 | 2 | 0 | 0 |
| Meyer, Oak. | .000 | 1 | 0 | 0 | 0 | 0 |
| Miller, Calif. | 1.000 | 1 | 0 | 1 | 0 | 0 |
| O'Malley, Balt. | .833 | 3 | 2 | 3 | 1 | 0 |
| Parrish, Tex. | 1.000 | 2 | 0 | 3 | 0 | 0 |
| Ramos, Sea. | .929 | 7 | 3 | 10 | 1 | 1 |
| Ready, Milw. | 1.000 | 7 | 4 | 7 | 0 | 0 |
| Romero, Milw. | 1.000 | 1 | 1 | 0 | 0 | 0 |
| Simmons, Milw. | 1.000 | 2 | 0 | 5 | 0 | 0 |
| Tabler, Clev. | 1.000 | 4 | 4 | 3 | 0 | 0 |
| Tartabull, Sea. | 1.000 | 4 | 2 | 6 | 0 | 0 |
| Washington, Minn. | 1.000 | 7 | 3 | 12 | 0 | 1 |

## SHORTSTOPS

| Leader—Club | Pct. | G. | PO. | A. | E. | DP. | Player—Club | Pct. | G. | PO. | A. | E. | DP. |
|---|---|---|---|---|---|---|---|---|---|---|---|---|---|
| GUILLEN, Chi. | .980 | 150 | 220 | 382 | 12 | 80 | Gallego, Oak. | 1.000 | 21 | 8 | 17 | 0 | 2 |
| | | | | | | | Gerber, Calif. | .970 | 53 | 51 | 109 | 5 | 27 |
| **Player—Club** | **Pct.** | **G.** | **PO.** | **A.** | **E.** | **DP.** | Giles, Milw. | .963 | 20 | 21 | 31 | 2 | 5 |
| Baker, Det. | .960 | 12 | 12 | 12 | 1 | 2 | Griffin, Oak. | .960 | 162 | 278 | 440 | 30 | 87 |
| Biancalana, K.C. | .961 | 74 | 80 | 168 | 10 | 31 | Guillen, Chi. | .980 | 150 | 220 | 382 | 12 | 80 |
| Coles, Sea. | .918 | 15 | 19 | 37 | 5 | 10 | Gutierrez, Bos. | .943 | 99 | 143 | 238 | 23 | 47 |
| Concepcion, K.C. | .959 | 128 | 127 | 367 | 21 | 63 | Hoffman, Bos. | .975 | 93 | 155 | 231 | 10 | 61 |
| Espinoza, Minn. | .949 | 31 | 25 | 69 | 5 | 15 | LeMaster, Clev. | .949 | 10 | 19 | 18 | 2 | 7 |
| Fernandez, Tor. | .962 | 160 | 283 | 478 | 30 | 109 | Meacham, N.Y. | .963 | 155 | 236 | 390 | 24 | 103 |
| Fischlin, Clev. | .941 | 32 | 20 | 28 | 3 | 5 | Owen, Milw. | .975 | 117 | 196 | 361 | 14 | 76 |
| Fletcher, Chi. | .993 | 44 | 56 | 83 | 1 | 18 | Pryor, K.C. | .900 | 13 | 7 | 11 | 2 | 3 |
| Franco, Clev. | .949 | 151 | 238 | 419 | 35 | 95 | Ramos, Sea. | .951 | 36 | 44 | 73 | 6 | 15 |
| Gagne, Minn. | .968 | 106 | 149 | 269 | 14 | 48 | Riles, Milw. | .957 | 115 | 183 | 310 | 22 | 62 |

SHORTSTOPS—Continued

| Player—Club | Pct. | G. | PO. | A. | E. | DP. |
|---|---|---|---|---|---|---|
| Ripken, Balt. | .967 | 161 | 286 | 474 | 26 | 123 |
| Robertson, N.Y. | .950 | 14 | 16 | 22 | 2 | 8 |
| Romero, Milw. | .977 | 43 | 57 | 115 | 4 | 27 |
| Schofield, Calif. | .963 | 147 | 261 | 397 | 25 | 108 |
| Smalley, Minn. | .987 | 49 | 57 | 91 | 2 | 16 |
| Tartabull, Sea. | .940 | 16 | 26 | 37 | 4 | 11 |
| Tolleson, Tex. | .972 | 81 | 96 | 182 | 8 | 37 |
| Trammell, Det. | .977 | 149 | 225 | 400 | 15 | 89 |
| Washington, Minn. | .951 | 31 | 20 | 38 | 3 | 5 |
| Wilkerson, Tex. | .957 | 110 | 125 | 274 | 18 | 50 |

(Fewer Than Ten Games)

| Player—Club | Pct. | G. | PO. | A. | E. | DP. |
|---|---|---|---|---|---|---|
| Beniquez, Calif. | 1.000 | 1 | 0 | 1 | 0 | 0 |
| Bernazard, Clev. | 1.000 | 1 | 2 | 0 | 0 | 1 |
| Berra, N.Y. | .889 | 6 | 2 | 6 | 1 | 0 |
| Brookens, Det. | .923 | 8 | 3 | 9 | 1 | 1 |
| Flynn, Det. | 1.000 | 8 | 8 | 11 | 0 | 3 |
| Gantner, Milw. | .000 | 1 | 0 | 0 | 0 | 0 |
| Harrah, Tex. | .000 | 2 | 0 | 0 | 0 | 0 |
| Hudler, N.Y. | 1.000 | 1 | 0 | 1 | 0 | 0 |
| Jurak, Bos. | 1.000 | 3 | 2 | 3 | 0 | 0 |
| Kunkel, Tex. | 1.000 | 2 | 2 | 5 | 0 | 1 |
| Lee, Tor. | .952 | 8 | 7 | 13 | 1 | 3 |
| Little, Chi. | 1.000 | 1 | 1 | 1 | 0 | 1 |
| Lyons, Bos. | .000 | 1 | 0 | 0 | 0 | 0 |
| Picciolo, Oak. | 1.000 | 9 | 4 | 5 | 0 | 1 |
| Polidor, Calif. | 1.000 | 1 | 0 | 2 | 0 | 0 |
| Scranton, K.C. | 1.000 | 5 | 1 | 8 | 0 | 1 |
| Smith, N.Y. | 1.000 | 3 | 0 | 1 | 0 | 0 |

Triple Play—Concepcion.

## OUTFIELDERS

| Leader—Club | Pct. | G. | PO. | A. | E. | DP. |
|---|---|---|---|---|---|---|
| BUTLER, Clev.* | .998 | 150 | 437 | 19 | 1 | 5 |

| Player—Club | Pct. | G. | PO. | A. | E. | DP. |
|---|---|---|---|---|---|---|
| Armas, Bos. | .983 | 79 | 173 | 3 | 3 | 1 |
| Ayala, Clev. | .917 | 20 | 21 | 1 | 2 | 0 |
| Baines, Chi.* | .9939 | 159 | 318 | 8 | 2 | 2 |
| Baker, Oak. | .971 | 35 | 65 | 3 | 2 | 0 |
| Bannister, Tex. | 1.000 | 14 | 19 | 0 | 0 | 0 |
| Barfield, Tor. | .989 | 154 | 349 | 22 | 4 | 8 |
| Bell, Tor. | .968 | 157 | 320 | 13 | 11 | 3 |
| Beniquez, Calif. | 1.000 | 71 | 119 | 1 | 0 | 0 |
| Bonnell, Sea. | .976 | 22 | 38 | 2 | 1 | 0 |
| Boston, Chi.* | .989 | 93 | 179 | 7 | 2 | 1 |
| Bradley, Sea. | .986 | 159 | 336 | 10 | 5 | 3 |
| Brouhard, Milw. | .964 | 29 | 53 | 0 | 2 | 0 |
| Brown, Calif. | 1.000 | 48 | 78 | 3 | 0 | 1 |
| Brunansky, Minn. | .984 | 155 | 300 | 14 | 5 | 2 |
| Bush, Minn.* | .969 | 41 | 63 | 0 | 2 | 0 |
| Butler, Clev.* | .998 | 150 | 437 | 19 | 1 | 5 |
| Calderon, Sea. | .981 | 53 | 100 | 5 | 2 | 2 |
| Canseco, Oak. | .951 | 26 | 56 | 2 | 3 | 1 |
| Carter, Clev. | .983 | 135 | 278 | 11 | 5 | 2 |
| Castillo, Clev. | .953 | 51 | 101 | 0 | 5 | 0 |
| Clark, Milw. | 1.000 | 27 | 72 | 1 | 0 | 0 |
| Collins, Oak.* | .978 | 91 | 221 | 1 | 5 | 0 |
| Cotto, N.Y. | .977 | 30 | 41 | 2 | 1 | 0 |
| Cowens, Sea. | .967 | 110 | 198 | 10 | 7 | 2 |
| Davis, Oak.* | .979 | 151 | 370 | 6 | 8 | 1 |
| Downing, Calif. | .992 | 121 | 244 | 5 | 2 | 0 |
| Dunbar, Tex.* | .933 | 14 | 14 | 0 | 1 | 0 |
| Dwyer, Balt.* | .993 | 78 | 131 | 4 | 1 | 0 |
| Easler, Bos. | .914 | 20 | 32 | 0 | 3 | 0 |
| Evans, Bos. | .990 | 152 | 291 | 9 | 3 | 1 |
| Felder, Milw. | 1.000 | 14 | 32 | 1 | 0 | 0 |
| Garbey, Det. | .974 | 24 | 38 | 0 | 1 | 0 |
| Gibson, Det.* | .963 | 144 | 286 | 1 | 11 | 0 |
| Greenwell, Bos. | 1.000 | 17 | 14 | 0 | 0 | 0 |
| Griffey, N.Y.* | .970 | 110 | 222 | 8 | 7 | 3 |
| Grubb, Det. | 1.000 | 18 | 23 | 0 | 0 | 0 |
| Hall, Clev.* | 1.000 | 15 | 18 | 0 | 0 | 0 |
| Hatcher, Minn. | .991 | 97 | 215 | 6 | 2 | 2 |
| Heath, Oak. | .982 | 35 | 49 | 5 | 1 | 0 |
| Henderson, N.Y.* | .980 | 141 | 439 | 7 | 9 | 3 |
| Henderson, Oak* | .953 | 58 | 79 | 3 | 4 | 0 |
| Henderson, Sea. | .986 | 138 | 335 | 8 | 5 | 3 |
| Hendrick, Calif. | 1.000 | 12 | 18 | 1 | 0 | 0 |
| Herndon, Det. | .976 | 136 | 273 | 7 | 7 | 4 |
| Householder, Milw. | .986 | 91 | 202 | 5 | 3 | 0 |
| Iorg, K.C. | 1.000 | 32 | 41 | 0 | 0 | 0 |
| Jackson, Calif.* | .944 | 81 | 112 | 6 | 7 | 1 |
| James, Milw.* | 1.000 | 11 | 20 | 0 | 0 | 0 |
| L. Jones, K.C. | .983 | 100 | 115 | 2 | 2 | 1 |
| Jones, Tex.* | 1.000 | 30 | 30 | 0 | 0 | 0 |
| Jones, Calif.* | .995 | 73 | 179 | 12 | 1 | 5 |
| Kittle, Chi. | .989 | 57 | 88 | 2 | 1 | 1 |
| Lacy, Balt. | .984 | 115 | 231 | 9 | 4 | 0 |
| Law, Chi.* | .987 | 120 | 226 | 7 | 3 | 3 |
| Lemon, Det. | .990 | 144 | 411 | 6 | 4 | 3 |
| Loman, Milw.* | 1.000 | 20 | 41 | 4 | 0 | 2 |
| Lynn, Balt.* | .9938 | 123 | 314 | 6 | 2 | 2 |
| Lyons, Bos. | .973 | 114 | 253 | 4 | 7 | 0 |
| Manning, Milw. | .976 | 74 | 160 | 2 | 4 | 0 |
| McDowell, Tex.* | .993 | 103 | 282 | 9 | 2 | 2 |
| Meier, Minn. | .987 | 63 | 77 | 1 | 1 | 1 |
| Miller, Calif. | .952 | 45 | 38 | 2 | 2 | 0 |
| Moreno, N.Y.-K.C.* | 1.000 | 47 | 86 | 3 | 0 | 1 |
| Moseby, Tor. | .980 | 152 | 394 | 7 | 8 | 1 |
| Moses, Sea.* | 1.000 | 29 | 35 | 1 | 0 | 0 |
| Motley, K.C. | .967 | 114 | 198 | 4 | 7 | 1 |
| Murphy, Oak. | .989 | 150 | 432 | 6 | 5 | 1 |
| Nichols, Bos.-Chi. | .988 | 58 | 84 | 1 | 1 | 0 |
| Nixon, Clev. | .971 | 80 | 129 | 5 | 4 | 1 |
| Oglivie, Milw.* | .965 | 91 | 190 | 4 | 7 | 0 |
| Paciorek, Chi. | .970 | 23 | 31 | 1 | 1 | 0 |
| Parrish, Tex. | .991 | 69 | 111 | 4 | 1 | 0 |
| Pasqua, N.Y.* | 1.000 | 37 | 72 | 2 | 0 | 0 |
| Pettis, Calif. | .990 | 122 | 368 | 13 | 4 | 5 |
| Puckett, Minn. | .984 | 161 | 465 | 19 | 8 | 5 |
| Ready, Milw. | .989 | 37 | 85 | 5 | 1 | 1 |
| Rice, Bos. | .964 | 130 | 236 | 8 | 9 | 1 |
| Robidoux, Milw. | 1.000 | 11 | 15 | 1 | 0 | 0 |
| Roenicke, Balt. | .993 | 89 | 134 | 6 | 1 | 0 |
| Romero, Milw. | 1.000 | 14 | 19 | 0 | 0 | 0 |
| Romine, Bos. | 1.000 | 23 | 20 | 1 | 0 | 0 |
| Ryal, Chi.* | 1.000 | 12 | 21 | 0 | 0 | 0 |
| Salazar, Chi. | .968 | 84 | 118 | 3 | 4 | 2 |
| Sample, N.Y. | .989 | 55 | 89 | 1 | 1 | 0 |
| Sanchez, Det. | .923 | 31 | 35 | 1 | 3 | 0 |
| Shelby, Balt. | .981 | 59 | 148 | 3 | 3 | 0 |
| Shepherd, Tor. | 1.000 | 16 | 24 | 0 | 0 | 0 |
| Sheridan, K.C. | .983 | 69 | 116 | 3 | 2 | 0 |
| Simmons, Det. | .945 | 38 | 67 | 2 | 4 | 1 |
| Smith, K.C. | .958 | 119 | 195 | 10 | 9 | 3 |
| Stenhouse, Minn. | .929 | 16 | 24 | 2 | 2 | 0 |
| Thornton, Tor. | .957 | 35 | 44 | 0 | 2 | 0 |
| Vukovich, Clev. | .988 | 137 | 250 | 4 | 3 | 0 |
| Walker, Tex.* | 1.000 | 32 | 51 | 6 | 0 | 1 |
| Ward, Tex. | .969 | 153 | 304 | 11 | 10 | 2 |
| White, Calif. | 1.000 | 16 | 10 | 1 | 0 | 0 |
| Wilson, K.C. | .995 | 140 | 378 | 4 | 2 | 1 |
| Winfield, N.Y. | .991 | 152 | 316 | 13 | 3 | 3 |
| G. Wright, Tex. | .991 | 102 | 213 | 8 | 2 | 2 |
| Young, Balt. | .975 | 90 | 190 | 6 | 5 | 0 |
| Yount, Milw. | .970 | 108 | 258 | 4 | 8 | 2 |

(Fewer Than Ten Games)

| Player—Club | Pct. | G. | PO. | A. | E. | DP. |
|---|---|---|---|---|---|---|
| Bergman, Det.* | .000 | 1 | 0 | 0 | 0 | 0 |
| Brummer, Tex. | 1.000 | 1 | 1 | 0 | 0 | 0 |
| Cangelosi, Chi.* | 1.000 | 3 | 1 | 0 | 0 | 0 |
| Capra, Tex. | 1.000 | 8 | 11 | 0 | 0 | 0 |
| Coles, Sea. | 1.000 | 2 | 4 | 0 | 0 | 0 |
| De Sa, Chi.* | .000 | 1 | 0 | 0 | 0 | 0 |
| Engle, Minn. | 1.000 | 3 | 8 | 1 | 0 | 0 |
| Funderburk, Minn. | 1.000 | 5 | 7 | 0 | 0 | 0 |
| Gaetti, Minn. | 1.000 | 4 | 10 | 0 | 0 | 0 |
| Gilbert, Chi. | 1.000 | 7 | 14 | 0 | 0 | 0 |

## OUTFIELDERS—Continued

| Player—Club | Pct. | G. | PO. | A. | E. | DP. | Player—Club | Pct. | G. | PO. | A. | E. | DP. |
|---|---|---|---|---|---|---|---|---|---|---|---|---|---|
| Hairston, Chi. | 1.000 | 5 | 5 | 0 | 0 | 0 | Polidor, Calif. | .000 | 1 | 0 | 0 | 0 | 0 |
| Hargrove, Clev.* | 1.000 | 1 | 4 | 0 | 0 | 0 | Ponce, Milw. | 1.000 | 6 | 13 | 0 | 0 | 0 |
| Hernandez, Balt. | .000 | 1 | 0 | 0 | 0 | 0 | Sax, Bos. | .000 | 4 | 0 | 0 | 0 | 0 |
| Hulett, Chi. | .000 | 1 | 0 | 0 | 0 | 0 | Sheets, Balt. | .875 | 9 | 7 | 0 | 1 | 0 |
| Jurak, Bos. | .000 | 1 | 0 | 0 | 0 | 0 | Stein, Tex. | 1.000 | 3 | 5 | 0 | 0 | 0 |
| Keedy, Calif. | 1.000 | 1 | 1 | 0 | 0 | 0 | Valentine, Tex. | 1.000 | 7 | 7 | 0 | 0 | 0 |
| Leach, Tor.* | 1.000 | 4 | 6 | 0 | 0 | 0 | Weaver, Det.* | 1.000 | 4 | 1 | 0 | 0 | 0 |
| Leeper, K.C.* | .929 | 8 | 13 | 0 | 1 | 0 | Webster, Tor.* | .000 | 2 | 0 | 0 | 0 | 0 |
| Linares, Calif. | 1.000 | 2 | 1 | 0 | 0 | 0 | | | | | | | |
| Lowenstein, Balt. | 1.000 | 4 | 7 | 0 | 0 | 0 | | | | | | | |
| Mata, N.Y. | 1.000 | 3 | 1 | 0 | 0 | 0 | | | | | | | |
| Meyer, Oak. | 1.000 | 1 | 1 | 0 | 0 | 0 | | | | | | | |
| Miller, Bos.* | 1.000 | 8 | 9 | 0 | 0 | 0 | | | | | | | |
| Moore, Milw. | 1.000 | 3 | 7 | 0 | 0 | 0 | | | | | | | |
| Nelson, Sea. | 1.000 | 3 | 1 | 0 | 0 | 0 | | | | | | | |
| Picciolo, Oak. | .000 | 2 | 0 | 0 | 0 | 0 | | | | | | | |

### OUTFIELDERS WITH TWO OR MORE CLUBS

| Player—Club | Pct. | G. | PO. | A. | E. | DP. |
|---|---|---|---|---|---|---|
| Moreno, N.Y. | 1.000 | 26 | 56 | 2 | 0 | 0 |
| Moreno, K.C. | 1.000 | 21 | 30 | 1 | 0 | 1 |
| Nichols, Bos. | .933 | 10 | 14 | 0 | 1 | 0 |
| Nichols, Chi. | 1.000 | 48 | 70 | 1 | 0 | 0 |

## CATCHERS

| Leader—Club | Pct. | G. | PO. | A. | E. | DP. | PB. | Player—Club | Pct. | G. | PO. | A. | E. | DP. |
|---|---|---|---|---|---|---|---|---|---|---|---|---|---|---|
| KEARNEY, Sea. | .995 | 108 | 529 | 50 | 3 | 7 | 11 | Salas, Minn. | .991 | 115 | 529 | 39 | 5 | 10 | 11 |

| Player—Club | Pct. | G. | PO. | A. | E. | DP. | PB. |
|---|---|---|---|---|---|---|---|
| Allenson, Tor. | 1.000 | 14 | 39 | 2 | 0 | 0 | 0 |
| Bando, Clev. | .986 | 67 | 251 | 28 | 4 | 3 | 3 |
| Benton, Clev. | .957 | 26 | 75 | 13 | 4 | 1 | 5 |
| Boone, Calif. | .987 | 147 | 670 | 71 | 10 | 15 | 6 |
| Brummer, Tex. | .989 | 47 | 182 | 5 | 2 | 2 | 7 |
| Castillo, Det. | .977 | 32 | 117 | 12 | 3 | 1 | 1 |
| Dempsey, Balt. | .987 | 131 | 575 | 49 | 8 | 5 | 2 |
| Engle, Minn. | .984 | 17 | 58 | 3 | 1 | 1 | 0 |
| Fisk, Chi. | .989 | 130 | 801 | 60 | 10 | 13 | 10 |
| Gedman, Bos. | .983 | 139 | 768 | 78 | 15 | 13 | 11 |
| Hassey, N.Y. | .984 | 69 | 402 | 20 | 7 | 2 | 15 |
| Heath, Oak. | .981 | 112 | 483 | 44 | 10 | 9 | 9 |
| Hill, Chi. | .985 | 37 | 185 | 11 | 3 | 1 | 1 |
| Huppert, Milw. | .960 | 15 | 45 | 3 | 2 | 2 | 1 |
| Kearney, Sea. | .995 | 108 | 529 | 50 | 3 | 7 | 11 |
| Laudner, Minn. | .969 | 68 | 233 | 19 | 8 | 3 | 2 |
| Martinez, Tor. | .988 | 42 | 155 | 16 | 2 | 5 | 1 |
| Melvin, Det. | .989 | 41 | 175 | 13 | 2 | 1 | 1 |
| Moore, Milw. | .977 | 102 | 504 | 54 | 13 | 7 | 10 |
| Narron, Calif. | 1.000 | 45 | 144 | 14 | 0 | 4 | 2 |
| O'Brien, Oak. | .958 | 16 | 23 | 0 | 1 | 0 | 0 |
| Pardo, Balt. | .979 | 29 | 131 | 7 | 3 | 0 | 0 |
| Parrish, Det. | .993 | 120 | 695 | 53 | 5 | 9 | 8 |
| Petralli, Tex. | .990 | 41 | 179 | 16 | 2 | 6 | 3 |
| Quirk, K.C. | .986 | 17 | 64 | 8 | 1 | 1 | 2 |
| Rayford, Balt. | .992 | 29 | 114 | 7 | 1 | 0 | 2 |

| Player—Club | Pct. | G. | PO. | A. | E. | DP. |
|---|---|---|---|---|---|---|
| Sax, Bos. | .985 | 16 | 66 | 0 | 1 | 0 | 0 |
| Schroeder, Milw. | .987 | 48 | 211 | 23 | 3 | 4 | 0 |
| Scott, Sea. | .981 | 74 | 277 | 31 | 6 | 1 | 11 |
| Simmons, Milw. | .986 | 15 | 65 | 4 | 1 | 1 | 1 |
| Skinner, Chi. | .971 | 21 | 94 | 8 | 3 | 0 | 0 |
| Slaught, Tex. | .990 | 102 | 550 | 33 | 6 | 4 | 13 |
| Sullivan, Bos. | .993 | 32 | 129 | 8 | 1 | 1 | 3 |
| Sundberg, K.C. | .992 | 112 | 572 | 41 | 5 | 10 | 6 |
| Tettleton, Oak. | .989 | 76 | 344 | 24 | 4 | 9 | 10 |
| Valle, Sea. | .976 | 31 | 117 | 7 | 3 | 0 | 0 |
| Wathan, K.C. | .986 | 49 | 247 | 28 | 4 | 6 | 2 |
| Whitt, Tor. | .988 | 134 | 649 | 38 | 8 | 6 | 2 |
| Willard, Clev. | .990 | 96 | 427 | 52 | 5 | 11 | 5 |
| Wynegar, N.Y. | .990 | 96 | 547 | 34 | 6 | 7 | 3 |

### (Fewer Than Ten Games)

| Player—Club | Pct. | G. | PO. | A. | E. | DP. | PB. |
|---|---|---|---|---|---|---|---|
| Bradley, N.Y. | .923 | 3 | 12 | 0 | 1 | 0 | 0 |
| Brookens, Det. | 1.000 | 1 | 7 | 1 | 0 | 0 | 0 |
| Espino, N.Y. | 1.000 | 9 | 16 | 4 | 0 | 0 | 0 |
| Hearron, Tor. | 1.000 | 4 | 16 | 1 | 0 | 0 | 0 |
| Madison, Det. | 1.000 | 1 | 1 | 0 | 0 | 0 | 0 |
| Miller, Calif. | 1.000 | 1 | 1 | 0 | 0 | 0 | 0 |
| Nicosia, Tor. | 1.000 | 6 | 23 | 2 | 0 | 1 | 0 |
| Nolan, Balt. | 1.000 | 5 | 22 | 2 | 0 | 0 | 0 |
| Pujols, Tex. | 1.000 | 1 | 1 | 0 | 0 | 0 | 0 |
| Reed, Minn. | 1.000 | 7 | 9 | 3 | 0 | 0 | 0 |

## PITCHERS

| Leader—Club | Pct. | G. | PO. | A. | E. | DP. |
|---|---|---|---|---|---|---|
| PETRY, Det. | 1.000 | 34 | 36 | 26 | 0 | 3 |

| Player—Club | Pct. | G. | PO. | A. | E. | DP. |
|---|---|---|---|---|---|---|
| Aase, Balt. | 1.000 | 54 | 8 | 10 | 0 | 0 |
| Acker, Tor. | 1.000 | 61 | 10 | 16 | 0 | 1 |
| Agosto, Chi.* | .962 | 54 | 10 | 15 | 1 | 0 |
| Alexander, Tor. | .984 | 36 | 28 | 32 | 1 | 4 |
| Allen, N.Y. | 1.000 | 17 | 3 | 3 | 0 | 0 |
| Atherton, Oak. | .909 | 56 | 4 | 6 | 1 | 0 |
| Bair, Det. | 1.000 | 21 | 4 | 9 | 0 | 0 |
| Bannister, Chi.* | .963 | 34 | 4 | 22 | 1 | 0 |
| Barkley, Clev. | .900 | 21 | 4 | 5 | 1 | 0 |
| Barojas, Sea. | .923 | 17 | 5 | 7 | 1 | 0 |
| Beattie, Sea. | .909 | 18 | 4 | 6 | 1 | 0 |
| Beckwith, K.C. | .905 | 49 | 7 | 12 | 2 | 1 |
| Berenguer, Det. | .920 | 31 | 11 | 12 | 2 | 1 |
| Best, Sea. | .750 | 15 | 0 | 3 | 1 | 0 |
| Birtsas, Oak.* | .917 | 29 | 0 | 11 | 1 | 0 |
| Black, K.C.* | .900 | 33 | 6 | 30 | 4 | 0 |
| Blyleven, Clev.-Minn. | 1.000 | 37 | 17 | 32 | 0 | 2 |
| Boddicker, Balt. | .973 | 32 | 26 | 46 | 2 | 6 |
| Bordi, N.Y. | .933 | 51 | 2 | 12 | 1 | 1 |
| Boyd, Bos. | .988 | 35 | 42 | 41 | 1 | 2 |
| Burns, Chi.* | .943 | 36 | 6 | 27 | 2 | 0 |
| Burris, Milw. | .949 | 29 | 18 | 19 | 2 | 0 |
| Butcher, Minn. | .962 | 34 | 24 | 27 | 2 | 2 |

| Player—Club | Pct. | G. | PO. | A. | E. | DP. |
|---|---|---|---|---|---|---|
| Candelaria, Calif.* | .909 | 13 | 2 | 8 | 1 | 0 |
| Cary, Det.* | | 16 | 0 | 2 | 0 | 0 |
| Caudill, Tor. | 1.000 | 67 | 2 | 6 | 0 | 0 |
| Clancy, Tor. | .955 | 23 | 6 | 15 | 1 | 1 |
| Clark, Clev.* | .952 | 31 | 7 | 13 | 1 | 2 |
| Clear, Bos. | .889 | 41 | 4 | 12 | 2 | 0 |
| Clemens, Bos. | 1.000 | 15 | 12 | 9 | 0 | 1 |
| Clements, Calif.* | .944 | 41 | 2 | 15 | 1 | 2 |
| Cliburn, Calif. | 1.000 | 44 | 8 | 17 | 0 | 3 |
| Cocanower, Milw. | .871 | 24 | 7 | 20 | 4 | 1 |
| Codiroli, Oak. | .918 | 37 | 18 | 27 | 4 | 1 |
| Conroy, Oak.* | .750 | 16 | 0 | 3 | 1 | 0 |
| Corbett, Calif. | .909 | 30 | 1 | 9 | 1 | 0 |
| Cowley, N.Y. | .903 | 30 | 6 | 22 | 3 | 1 |
| Crawford, Bos. | .880 | 44 | 7 | 15 | 3 | 2 |
| Creel, Clev. | 1.000 | 15 | 4 | 2 | 0 | 1 |
| Darwin, Milw. | .939 | 39 | 15 | 16 | 2 | 1 |
| Davis, Balt. | 1.000 | 31 | 15 | 20 | 0 | 0 |
| Davis, Minn. | 1.000 | 57 | 3 | 5 | 0 | 1 |
| Davis, Chi. | .875 | 12 | 4 | 3 | 1 | 1 |
| Davis, Tor.* | 1.000 | 10 | 0 | 4 | 0 | 0 |
| Dixon, Balt. | .882 | 34 | 13 | 17 | 4 | 0 |
| Easterly, Clev.* | 1.000 | 50 | 11 | 10 | 0 | 1 |
| Eufemia, Minn. | 1.000 | 39 | 4 | 12 | 0 | 1 |
| Fallon, Chi.* | 1.000 | 10 | 2 | 3 | 0 | 1 |
| Farr, K.C. | 1.000 | 16 | 3 | 6 | 0 | 0 |

PITCHERS—Continued

| Player—Club | Pct. | G. | PO. | A. | E. | DP. |
|---|---|---|---|---|---|---|
| Filer, Tor. | 1.000 | 11 | 1 | 5 | 0 | 1 |
| Filson, Minn.* | .889 | 40 | 3 | 13 | 2 | 0 |
| Fingers, Milw. | 1.000 | 47 | 7 | 10 | 0 | 1 |
| Fisher, N.Y. | .944 | 55 | 4 | 13 | 1 | 1 |
| Flanagan, Balt.* | 1.000 | 15 | 4 | 11 | 0 | 0 |
| Geisel, Sea.* | 1.000 | 12 | 0 | 3 | 0 | 1 |
| Gibson, Milw. | 1.000 | 41 | 8 | 10 | 0 | 2 |
| Gleaton, Chi.* | 1.000 | 31 | 0 | 4 | 0 | 0 |
| Gubicza, K.C. | 1.000 | 29 | 23 | 26 | 0 | 4 |
| Guidry, N.Y.* | .976 | 34 | 6 | 34 | 1 | 3 |
| Haas, Milw. | .889 | 27 | 17 | 15 | 4 | 1 |
| Harris, Tex. | .960 | 58 | 8 | 16 | 1 | 4 |
| Heaton, Clev.* | .967 | 36 | 8 | 21 | 1 | 1 |
| Henke, Tor. | 1.000 | 28 | 3 | 3 | 0 | 0 |
| Henry, Tex. | .750 | 16 | 1 | 2 | 1 | 1 |
| Hernandez, Det.* | .933 | 74 | 7 | 7 | 1 | 0 |
| Higuera, Milw.* | .963 | 32 | 8 | 18 | 1 | 2 |
| Holland, Calif.* | 1.000 | 15 | 2 | 2 | 0 | 0 |
| Hooton, Tex. | .957 | 29 | 9 | 13 | 1 | 0 |
| Hough, Tex. | .964 | 34 | 18 | 35 | 2 | 5 |
| Howe, Minn.* | 1.000 | 13 | 3 | 1 | 0 | 0 |
| Howell, Oak. | 1.000 | 63 | 1 | 15 | 0 | 1 |
| Hurst, Bos.* | .935 | 35 | 11 | 32 | 3 | 0 |
| Jackson, K.C.* | .921 | 32 | 8 | 27 | 3 | 2 |
| James, Chi. | .952 | 69 | 12 | 8 | 1 | 0 |
| John, Calif.-Oak.* | 1.000 | 23 | 8 | 22 | 0 | 2 |
| M. Jones, K.C.* | 1.000 | 33 | 6 | 8 | 0 | 0 |
| Kaiser, Oak.* | 1.000 | 15 | 4 | 3 | 0 | 1 |
| Key, Tor.* | .957 | 35 | 15 | 52 | 3 | 3 |
| Kison, Bos. | 1.000 | 22 | 16 | 16 | 0 | 2 |
| Krueger, Oak.* | .929 | 32 | 3 | 23 | 2 | 0 |
| LaCoss, K.C. | 1.000 | 21 | 1 | 8 | 0 | 1 |
| Ladd, Milw. | .889 | 29 | 3 | 5 | 1 | 0 |
| Lamp, Tor. | 1.000 | 53 | 11 | 21 | 0 | 3 |
| Langford, Oak. | 1.000 | 23 | 2 | 9 | 0 | 1 |
| Langston, Sea.* | .946 | 24 | 9 | 26 | 2 | 4 |
| Lavelle, Tor.* | 1.000 | 69 | 2 | 9 | 0 | 1 |
| Lazorko, Sea. | 1.000 | 15 | 4 | 4 | 0 | 1 |
| Leal, Tor. | .938 | 15 | 5 | 10 | 1 | 1 |
| Leibrandt, K.C.* | .986 | 33 | 19 | 53 | 1 | 2 |
| Lollar, Chi.-Bos.* | 1.000 | 34 | 8 | 13 | 0 | 0 |
| Long, Sea. | 1.000 | 28 | 3 | 3 | 0 | 0 |
| Lopez, Det. | .938 | 51 | 5 | 10 | 1 | 1 |
| Lugo, Calif. | .895 | 20 | 4 | 13 | 2 | 2 |
| Lysander, Minn. | 1.000 | 35 | 7 | 5 | 0 | 1 |
| F. Martinez, Balt.* | .950 | 49 | 9 | 10 | 1 | 1 |
| J. Martinez, Balt. | .977 | 33 | 17 | 26 | 1 | 0 |
| Mason, Tex.* | .895 | 38 | 4 | 30 | 4 | 0 |
| McCaskill, Calif. | .927 | 30 | 11 | 27 | 3 | 1 |
| McCatty, Oak. | .944 | 30 | 4 | 13 | 1 | 4 |
| McClure, Milw.* | 1.000 | 38 | 3 | 11 | 0 | 2 |
| McGregor, Balt.* | .975 | 35 | 13 | 26 | 1 | 2 |
| Mirabella, Sea.* | 1.000 | 10 | 0 | 1 | 0 | 0 |
| Moore, Calif. | .889 | 65 | 4 | 12 | 2 | 1 |
| Moore, Sea. | .970 | 35 | 21 | 43 | 2 | 1 |
| Morris, Det. | .926 | 35 | 25 | 25 | 4 | 2 |
| Mura, Oak. | .889 | 23 | 2 | 6 | 1 | 0 |
| Musselman, Tor. | .857 | 25 | 2 | 4 | 1 | 0 |
| Nelson, Chi. | .967 | 46 | 10 | 19 | 1 | 0 |
| P. Niekro, N.Y. | 1.000 | 33 | 11 | 20 | 0 | 5 |
| Nipper, Bos. | .912 | 25 | 24 | 28 | 5 | 4 |
| Noles, Tex. | .906 | 28 | 13 | 16 | 3 | 2 |
| Nunez, Sea. | 1.000 | 70 | 5 | 12 | 0 | 1 |
| Ojeda, Bos.* | .923 | 39 | 13 | 23 | 3 | 0 |
| O'Neal, Det. | .929 | 28 | 9 | 17 | 2 | 1 |
| Ontiveros, Oak | .955 | 39 | 7 | 14 | 1 | 1 |
| Petry, Det. | 1.000 | 34 | 36 | 26 | 0 | 3 |
| Quisenberry, K.C. | .941 | 84 | 8 | 24 | 2 | 2 |
| Rasmussen, N.Y.* | 1.000 | 22 | 7 | 13 | 0 | 2 |
| Reed, Clev. | 1.000 | 33 | 13 | 8 | 0 | 1 |
| Righetti, N.Y.* | .929 | 74 | 1 | 12 | 1 | 2 |
| Rijo, Oak. | 1.000 | 12 | 2 | 5 | 0 | 0 |
| Romanick, Cal. | .966 | 31 | 10 | 18 | 1 | 0 |
| Romero, Clev.* | 1.000 | 19 | 0 | 6 | 0 | 0 |
| Rozema, Tex. | 1.000 | 34 | 2 | 18 | 0 | 0 |
| Ruhle, Clev. | 1.000 | 42 | 15 | 13 | 0 | 0 |
| Russell, Tex. | 1.000 | 13 | 6 | 10 | 0 | 1 |
| Saberhagen, K.C. | .968 | 32 | 22 | 38 | 2 | 4 |
| Sanchez, Cal. | .933 | 26 | 3 | 11 | 1 | 1 |
| Scherrer, Det.* | .900 | 48 | 7 | 11 | 2 | 2 |
| Schmidt, Tex. | .880 | 51 | 3 | 19 | 3 | 3 |
| Schrom, Minn. | .935 | 29 | 23 | 20 | 3 | 3 |
| Schulze, Clev. | .923 | 19 | 8 | 16 | 2 | 2 |
| Searage, Milw.* | .750 | 33 | 1 | 2 | 1 | 0 |
| Seaver, Chi. | .969 | 35 | 20 | 43 | 2 | 2 |
| Shirley, N.Y.* | .864 | 48 | 4 | 15 | 3 | 1 |
| Slaton, Cal. | .966 | 29 | 6 | 22 | 1 | 4 |
| Smith, Clev. | 1.000 | 12 | 6 | 3 | 0 | 0 |
| Smithson, Minn. | .957 | 37 | 16 | 28 | 2 | 4 |
| Snell, Balt. | .931 | 43 | 6 | 21 | 2 | 3 |
| Snyder, Sea.* | 1.000 | 15 | 4 | 7 | 0 | 0 |
| Spillner, Chi. | .857 | 52 | 4 | 2 | 1 | 0 |
| Stanley, Bos. | .952 | 48 | 8 | 12 | 1 | 1 |
| Stanton, Sea.-Chi. | .917 | 35 | 4 | 7 | 1 | 1 |
| Stewart, Balt. | 1.000 | 56 | 12 | 13 | 0 | 0 |
| Stewart, Tex. | .889 | 42 | 6 | 10 | 2 | 2 |
| Stieb, Tor. | .946 | 36 | 34 | 53 | 5 | 5 |
| Sutton, Oak.-Cal. | .909 | 34 | 8 | 32 | 4 | 1 |
| Swift, Sea. | .966 | 23 | 10 | 18 | 1 | 1 |
| Tanana, Tex.-Det.* | .978 | 33 | 14 | 31 | 1 | 2 |
| Tanner, Chi. | .909 | 10 | 3 | 7 | 1 | 1 |
| Tellmann, Oak. | 1.000 | 11 | 0 | 4 | 0 | 0 |
| Terrell, Det. | .970 | 34 | 21 | 43 | 2 | 8 |
| R. Thomas, Sea. | 1.000 | 40 | 7 | 7 | 0 | 1 |
| Thompson, Clev. | .750 | 57 | 2 | 7 | 3 | 1 |
| Trujillo, Bos. | .939 | 27 | 11 | 20 | 2 | 1 |
| Vande Berg, Sea.* | 1.000 | 76 | 8 | 11 | 0 | 1 |
| Viola, Minn.* | .886 | 36 | 6 | 33 | 5 | 0 |
| Von Ohlen, Clev.* | 1.000 | 26 | 2 | 9 | 0 | 1 |
| Vuckovich, Milw. | .950 | 22 | 5 | 14 | 1 | 1 |
| Waddell, Clev. | 1.000 | 49 | 10 | 15 | 0 | 0 |
| Waits, Milw.* | 1.000 | 24 | 8 | 4 | 0 | 0 |
| Wardle, Minn.-Clev.* | .952 | 50 | 5 | 15 | 1 | 1 |
| Warren, Oak. | .750 | 16 | 2 | 1 | 1 | 1 |
| Wehrmeister, Chi. | 1.000 | 23 | 3 | 2 | 0 | 2 |
| Welsh, Tex.* | 1.000 | 25 | 1 | 10 | 0 | 1 |
| Whitson, N.Y. | .889 | 30 | 8 | 16 | 3 | 3 |
| Wills, Sea. | 1.000 | 24 | 9 | 17 | 0 | 1 |
| Witt, Cal. | .961 | 35 | 16 | 33 | 2 | 2 |
| Young, Oak.* | 1.000 | 19 | 4 | 4 | 0 | 0 |
| Young, Sea.* | .968 | 37 | 6 | 24 | 1 | 1 |

(Fewer Than Ten Games)

| Player—Club | Pct. | G. | PO. | A. | E. | DP. |
|---|---|---|---|---|---|---|
| Armstrong, N.Y. | 1.000 | 9 | 1 | 1 | 0 | 0 |
| Behenna, Clev. | 1.000 | 4 | 0 | 1 | 0 | 0 |
| Bell, Balt.* | 1.000 | 4 | 2 | 1 | 0 | 0 |
| Boggs, Tex. | 1.000 | 4 | 0 | 2 | 0 | 0 |
| Brown, Bos. | .000 | 2 | 0 | 0 | 0 | 0 |
| Brown, Minn. | 1.000 | 6 | 1 | 1 | 0 | 0 |
| Burtt, Minn. | 1.000 | 5 | 1 | 5 | 0 | 1 |
| Bystrom, N.Y. | .909 | 8 | 1 | 9 | 1 | 0 |
| Camacho, Clev. | 1.000 | 2 | 0 | 1 | 0 | 0 |
| Cerutti, Tor.* | 1.000 | 4 | 0 | 1 | 0 | 0 |
| Clarke, Tor.* | 1.000 | 4 | 0 | 1 | 0 | 0 |
| Cook, Tex. | .833 | 9 | 3 | 2 | 1 | 1 |
| Cooper, N.Y. | .000 | 7 | 0 | 0 | 0 | 0 |
| Correa, Chi. | .000 | 5 | 0 | 0 | 0 | 0 |
| Dorsey, Bos. | .000 | 2 | 0 | 0 | 1 | 0 |
| Dotson, Chi. | 1.000 | 9 | 3 | 5 | 0 | 0 |
| Ferreira, K.C.* | 1.000 | 2 | 0 | 2 | 0 | 1 |
| Fireovid, Chi. | .000 | 4 | 0 | 0 | 0 | 0 |
| Fowlkes, Cal. | 1.000 | 2 | 1 | 1 | 0 | 0 |
| Gura, K.C.* | 1.000 | 3 | 2 | 0 | 0 | 0 |
| Guzman, Tex. | 1.000 | 5 | 0 | 5 | 0 | 0 |
| Habyan, Balt. | 1.000 | 2 | 1 | 0 | 0 | 0 |
| Havens, Balt.* | 1.000 | 8 | 0 | 1 | 0 | 0 |
| Huffman, Balt. | 1.000 | 2 | 2 | 0 | 0 | 0 |
| Huisman, K.C. | 1.000 | 9 | 1 | 3 | 0 | 0 |
| Jeffcoat, Clev.* | 1.000 | 9 | 1 | 5 | 0 | 0 |
| Jones, Chi. | 1.000 | 5 | 1 | 1 | 0 | 0 |
| Kern, Milw. | 1.000 | 5 | 2 | 3 | 0 | 1 |
| Kipper, Cal.* | 1.000 | 2 | 1 | 0 | 0 | 0 |
| Klawitter, Minn.* | 1.000 | 7 | 0 | 2 | 0 | 0 |
| Leary, Milw. | 1.000 | 5 | 1 | 7 | 0 | 0 |
| Leonard, K.C. | .000 | 2 | 0 | 0 | 0 | 0 |

PITCHERS—Continued

| Player—Club | Pct. | G. | PO. | A. | E. | DP. |
|---|---|---|---|---|---|---|
| Lesley, Milw. | 1.000 | 5 | 0 | 1 | 0 | 0 |
| Lewis, Sea. | .000 | 2 | 0 | 0 | 0 | 0 |
| Long, Chi. | 1.000 | 4 | 2 | 3 | 0 | 0 |
| Mack, Cal. | .000 | 1 | 0 | 0 | 0 | 0 |
| Mahler, Det.* | .750 | 3 | 1 | 2 | 1 | 0 |
| McCarthy, Bos. | 1.000 | 3 | 1 | 0 | 0 | 0 |
| Mitchell, Bos. | 1.000 | 2 | 1 | 1 | 0 | 0 |
| Montefusco, N.Y. | 1.000 | 3 | 1 | 1 | 0 | 0 |
| Morgan, Sea. | 1.000 | 2 | 0 | 1 | 0 | 0 |
| Murray, N.Y.-Tex. | 1.000 | 4 | 0 | 1 | 0 | 0 |
| J. Niekro, N.Y. | 1.000 | 3 | 3 | 2 | 0 | 0 |
| Porter, Milw. | .667 | 6 | 2 | 0 | 1 | 0 |
| Portugal, Minn. | .917 | 6 | 4 | 7 | 1 | 1 |
| Roman, Clev. | .800 | 5 | 3 | 1 | 1 | 0 |
| Scurry, N.Y.* | 1.000 | 5 | 0 | 1 | 0 | 0 |
| Sebra, Tex. | 1.000 | 7 | 1 | 1 | 0 | 1 |
| Sellers, Bos. | .750 | 4 | 2 | 4 | 2 | 0 |
| Smith, Cal. | 1.000 | 4 | 0 | 1 | 0 | 0 |
| Stoddard, Det. | 1.000 | 8 | 2 | 3 | 0 | 1 |
| Surhoff, Tex. | .000 | 7 | 0 | 0 | 0 | 0 |
| Swaggerty, Balt. | .000 | 1 | 0 | 0 | 0 | 0 |
| Tobik, Sea. | 1.000 | 8 | 1 | 0 | 0 | 0 |
| Wegman, Milw. | 1.000 | 3 | 3 | 0 | 0 | 0 |
| Whitehouse, Minn.* | 1.000 | 5 | 1 | 0 | 0 | 0 |
| Wilcox, Det. | .882 | 8 | 3 | 12 | 2 | 2 |
| Wilkinson, Sea.* | 1.000 | 2 | 0 | 2 | 0 | 0 |

| Player—Club | Pct. | G. | PO. | A. | E. | DP. |
|---|---|---|---|---|---|---|
| Williams, Tex. | .500 | 6 | 0 | 1 | 1 | 0 |
| Woodward, Bos. | .714 | 5 | 5 | 0 | 2 | 0 |
| R. Wright, Tex.* | 1.000 | 5 | 0 | 1 | 0 | 0 |
| Yett, Minn. | .000 | 1 | 0 | 0 | 0 | 0 |
| Zahn, Cal.* | 1.000 | 7 | 1 | 9 | 0 | 0 |

PITCHERS WITH TWO OR MORE CLUBS

| Player—Club | Pct. | G. | PO. | A. | E. | DP. |
|---|---|---|---|---|---|---|
| Blyleven, Clev. | 1.000 | 23 | 11 | 19 | 0 | 0 |
| Blyleven, Minn. | 1.000 | 14 | 6 | 13 | 0 | 2 |
| John, Cal. | 1.000 | 12 | 4 | 9 | 0 | 2 |
| John, Oak. | 1.000 | 11 | 4 | 13 | 0 | 0 |
| Lollar, Chi. | 1.000 | 18 | 6 | 8 | 0 | 0 |
| Lollar, Bos. | 1.000 | 16 | 2 | 5 | 0 | 0 |
| Murray, N.Y. | 1.000 | 3 | 0 | 0 | 0 | 0 |
| Murray, Tex. | 1.000 | 1 | 0 | 1 | 0 | 0 |
| Stanton, Sea. | 1.000 | 24 | 3 | 6 | 0 | 1 |
| Stanton, Chi. | .667 | 11 | 1 | 1 | 1 | 0 |
| Sutton, Oak. | .905 | 29 | 7 | 31 | 4 | 1 |
| Sutton, Cal. | 1.000 | 5 | 1 | 1 | 0 | 0 |
| Tanana, Tex. | .941 | 13 | 5 | 11 | 1 | 1 |
| Tanana, Det. | 1.000 | 20 | 9 | 20 | 0 | 1 |
| Wardle, Minn. | 1.000 | 35 | 4 | 11 | 0 | 1 |
| Wardle, Clev. | .833 | 15 | 1 | 4 | 1 | 0 |

# OFFICIAL AMERICAN LEAGUE PITCHING AVERAGES

## CLUB PITCHING

| Club | ERA. | G. | CG. | ShO. | Sv. | IP. | H. | BFP. | R. | ER. | HR. | SH. | SF. | HB. | Tot. BB. | Int. BB. | SO. | WP. | Bk. |
|---|---|---|---|---|---|---|---|---|---|---|---|---|---|---|---|---|---|---|---|
| Toronto | 3.29 | 161 | 18 | 9 | 47 | 1448.0 | 1312 | 6004 | 588 | 529 | 147 | 47 | 41 | 26 | 484 | 26 | 823 | 36 | 5 |
| Kansas City | 3.49 | 162 | 27 | 11 | 41 | 1461.0 | 1433 | 6165 | 639 | 566 | 103 | 48 | 42 | 28 | 463 | 37 | 846 | 43 | 9 |
| New York | 3.69 | 161 | 25 | 9 | 49 | 1440.1 | 1373 | 6065 | 660 | 590 | 157 | 32 | 42 | 13 | 518 | 20 | 907 | 34 | 5 |
| Detroit | 3.78 | 161 | 31 | 11 | 40 | 1456.0 | 1313 | 6135 | 688 | 612 | 141 | 43 | 49 | 23 | 556 | 67 | 943 | 62 | 6 |
| California | 3.91 | 162 | 22 | 8 | 41 | 1457.1 | 1453 | 6164 | 703 | 633 | 171 | 48 | 44 | 27 | 514 | 30 | 767 | 45 | 4 |
| Boston | 4.06 | 163 | 35 | 8 | 29 | 1461.1 | 1487 | 6281 | 720 | 659 | 130 | 49 | 38 | 35 | 540 | 54 | 913 | 34 | 13 |
| Chicago | 4.07 | 163 | 20 | 6 | 39 | 1451.2 | 1411 | 6221 | 720 | 656 | 161 | 57 | 47 | 36 | 569 | 35 | 1023 | 54 | 5 |
| Baltimore | 4.38 | 161 | 32 | 5 | 33 | 1427.1 | 1480 | 6182 | 764 | 694 | 160 | 59 | 41 | 23 | 568 | 57 | 793 | 32 | 7 |
| Milwaukee | 4.39 | 161 | 34 | 6 | 37 | 1437.0 | 1510 | 6212 | 802 | 701 | 175 | 52 | 51 | 33 | 499 | 31 | 777 | 51 | 4 |
| Oakland | 4.39 | 162 | 10 | 5 | 41 | 1453.0 | 1451 | 6327 | 787 | 709 | 172 | 39 | 46 | 25 | 607 | 32 | 785 | 48 | 6 |
| Minnesota | 4.48 | 162 | 41 | 7 | 34 | 1426.1 | 1468 | 6067 | 782 | 710 | 164 | 47 | 55 | 30 | 462 | 31 | 767 | 51 | 11 |
| Texas | 4.56 | 161 | 18 | 5 | 33 | 1411.2 | 1479 | 6112 | 785 | 715 | 173 | 28 | 44 | 36 | 501 | 38 | 863 | 43 | 7 |
| Seattle | 4.68 | 162 | 23 | 8 | 30 | 1432.0 | 1456 | 6260 | 818 | 744 | 154 | 38 | 48 | 41 | 637 | 54 | 868 | 61 | 18 |
| Cleveland | 4.91 | 162 | 24 | 7 | 28 | 1421.0 | 1556 | 6262 | 861 | 776 | 170 | 61 | 70 | 43 | 547 | 45 | 702 | 46 | 7 |
| Totals | 4.14 | 1132 | 360 | 108 | 522 | 20184.0 | 20182 | 86457 | 10317 | 9294 | 2178 | 648 | 658 | 419 | 7465 | 557 | 11777 | 640 | 107 |

NOTE—Totals for earned runs for several clubs do not agree with the composite totals for all pitchers of each respective club due to instances in which provisions of Section 10.18 (i) of the Scoring Rules were applied. The following difference are to be noted: Cleveland pitchers add to 777 earned runs, Detroit pitched add to 614, Milwaukee pitchers add to 703.

## PITCHERS' RECORDS

(Top Fifteen Qualifiers for Earned-Run Leadership—162 or More Innings)

*Throws lefthanded.

| Pitcher and Club | W. | L. | Pct. | ERA. | G. | GS. | CG. | ShO. | GF. | Sv. | IP. | H. | BFP. | R. | ER. | HR. | SH. | SF. | HB. | Tot. BB. | Int. BB. | SO. | WP. | Bk. |
|---|---|---|---|---|---|---|---|---|---|---|---|---|---|---|---|---|---|---|---|---|---|---|---|---|
| Stieb, David, Toronto | 14 | 13 | .519 | 2.48 | 36 | 36 | 8 | 2 | 0 | 0 | 265.0 | 206 | 1087 | 89 | 73 | 22 | 14 | 2 | 9 | 96 | 3 | 167 | 4 | 1 |
| Leibrandt, Charles, Kansas City* | 17 | 9 | .654 | 2.69 | 33 | 33 | 8 | 3 | 0 | 0 | 237.2 | 223 | 983 | 86 | 71 | 17 | 8 | 5 | 2 | 68 | 3 | 108 | 4 | 3 |
| Saberhagen, Bret, Kansas City | 20 | 6 | .769 | 2.87 | 32 | 32 | 10 | 1 | 0 | 0 | 235.1 | 211 | 931 | 79 | 75 | 19 | 9 | 1 | 1 | 38 | 1 | 158 | 1 | 3 |
| Key, James, Toronto* | 14 | 6 | .700 | 3.00 | 35 | 32 | 3 | 3 | 0 | 0 | 212.2 | 188 | 856 | 77 | 71 | 22 | 5 | 5 | 1 | 50 | 1 | 85 | 6 | 1 |
| Blyleven, Rikalbert, Clev.-Minn. | 17 | 16 | .515 | 3.16 | 37 | 37 | 24 | 5 | 0 | 0 | 293.2 | 264 | 1203 | 121 | 103 | 23 | 7 | 8 | 9 | 75 | 1 | 206 | 4 | 0 |
| Seaver, G. Thomas, Chicago | 16 | 11 | .593 | 3.17 | 35 | 33 | 6 | 1 | 0 | 0 | 238.2 | 223 | 993 | 103 | 84 | 22 | 8 | 8 | 0 | 69 | 6 | 134 | 10 | 1 |
| Guidry, Ronald, New York* | 22 | 6 | .786 | 3.27 | 33 | 33 | 11 | 2 | 0 | 0 | 259.0 | 243 | 1033 | 104 | 94 | 28 | 3 | 8 | 0 | 42 | 3 | 143 | 3 | 3 |
| Hough, Charles, Texas | 14 | 16 | .467 | 3.31 | 34 | 34 | 14 | 1 | 0 | 0 | 250.1 | 198 | 1018 | 102 | 92 | 23 | 1 | 7 | 7 | 83 | 7 | 141 | 11 | 0 |
| Morris, John, Detroit | 16 | 11 | .593 | 3.33 | 35 | 35 | 13 | 4 | 0 | 0 | 257.0 | 212 | 1077 | 102 | 95 | 21 | 11 | 5 | 5 | 110 | 7 | 191 | 15 | 3 |
| Petry, Daniel, Detroit | 15 | 13 | .536 | 3.36 | 34 | 34 | 8 | 0 | 0 | 0 | 238.2 | 190 | 962 | 98 | 89 | 24 | 5 | 2 | 6 | 81 | 9 | 109 | 6 | 0 |
| Jackson, Danny, Kansas City* | 14 | 12 | .538 | 3.42 | 32 | 32 | 4 | 3 | 0 | 0 | 208.0 | 203 | 893 | 94 | 79 | 7 | 5 | 4 | 3 | 76 | 0 | 114 | 4 | 2 |
| Alexander, Doyle, Toronto | 17 | 10 | .630 | 3.45 | 36 | 36 | 6 | 0 | 0 | 0 | 260.2 | 268 | 1090 | 105 | 100 | 28 | 6 | 3 | 6 | 67 | 2 | 142 | 9 | 0 |
| Moore, Michael, Seattle | 17 | 10 | .630 | 3.46 | 35 | 34 | 14 | 2 | 1 | 0 | 247.0 | 230 | 1016 | 100 | 95 | 18 | 7 | 7 | 4 | 70 | 0 | 155 | 10 | 3 |
| Witt, Michael, California | 15 | 9 | .625 | 3.56 | 35 | 35 | 9 | 2 | 0 | 0 | 250.0 | 228 | 1049 | 115 | 99 | 22 | 4 | 5 | 4 | 98 | 6 | 180 | 11 | 1 |
| Dixon, Kenneth, Baltimore | 8 | 4 | .667 | 3.67 | 34 | 18 | 3 | 1 | 1 | 1 | 162.0 | 144 | 683 | 68 | 66 | 20 | 8 | 2 | 2 | 64 | 7 | 108 | 5 | 2 |

DEPARTMENTAL LEADERS: W—Guidry, 22; L—Young (Sea.), 19; Pct.—Guidry, .786; G—Quisenberry, 84; GS—Smithson, Codiroli, Blyleven, 37; CG—Blyleven, 24; ShO—Blyleven, 5; GF—Quisenberry, 76; Sv.—Quisenberry, 37; IP—Blyleven, 293.2; H—Boyd, 273; BFP—Blyleven, 1,203; R—Viola, 136; HR—Darwin, McGregor, 34; SH—Stieb, 14; SF—Butcher, Higuera, 10; HB—Smithson, 15; Tot.BB—P. Niekro, 120; Int.BB—Scherrer, 13; SO—Blyleven, 206; WP—Morris, 15; Bk—Hurst, 4.

(All Pitchers—Listed Alphabetically)

| Pitcher and Club | W. | L. | Pct. | ERA. | G. | GS. | CG. | ShO. | GF. | Sv. | IP. | H. | BFP. | R. | ER. | HR. | SH. | SF. | HB. | Tot. BB. | Int. BB. | SO. | WP. | Bk. |
|---|---|---|---|---|---|---|---|---|---|---|---|---|---|---|---|---|---|---|---|---|---|---|---|---|
| Aase, Donald, Baltimore | 10 | 6 | .625 | 3.78 | 54 | 0 | 0 | 0 | 43 | 14 | 88.0 | 83 | 366 | 44 | 37 | 6 | 5 | 3 | 1 | 35 | 7 | 67 | 2 | 1 |
| Acker, James, Toronto | 7 | 2 | .778 | 3.23 | 61 | 0 | 0 | 0 | 26 | 10 | 86.1 | 86 | 370 | 35 | 31 | 7 | 1 | 2 | 3 | 43 | 1 | 42 | 0 | 0 |
| Agosto, Juan, Chicago* | 4 | 3 | .571 | 3.58 | 54 | 0 | 0 | 0 | 21 | 1 | 60.1 | 45 | 246 | 27 | 24 | 3 | 6 | 1 | 3 | 23 | 1 | 39 | 2 | 0 |
| Alexander, Doyle, Toronto | 17 | 10 | .630 | 3.45 | 36 | 36 | 6 | 1 | 0 | 0 | 260.2 | 268 | 1090 | 105 | 100 | 28 | 6 | 0 | 6 | 67 | 0 | 142 | 9 | 0 |
| Allen, Neil, New York | 1 | 0 | 1.000 | 2.76 | 17 | 0 | 0 | 0 | 10 | 1 | 29.1 | 26 | 124 | 9 | 9 | 1 | 0 | 0 | 0 | 13 | 0 | 16 | 1 | 1 |
| Armstrong, Michael, New York | 0 | 0 | .000 | 3.07 | 9 | 0 | 0 | 0 | 8 | 0 | 14.2 | 12 | 54 | 5 | 5 | 1 | 0 | 0 | 0 | 2 | 0 | 11 | 1 | 0 |
| Atherton, Keith, Oakland | 4 | 7 | .364 | 4.30 | 56 | 0 | 0 | 0 | 21 | 3 | 104.2 | 89 | 435 | 51 | 50 | 17 | 3 | 4 | 0 | 42 | 8 | 77 | 2 | 0 |
| Bair, C. Douglas, Detroit* | 0 | 3 | .000 | 6.24 | 21 | 0 | 0 | 0 | 4 | 0 | 49.0 | 54 | 224 | 38 | 34 | 3 | 4 | 4 | 1 | 25 | 5 | 30 | 6 | 1 |
| Bannister, Floyd, Chicago* | 10 | 14 | .417 | 4.87 | 34 | 34 | 4 | 1 | 0 | 0 | 210.2 | 211 | 928 | 121 | 114 | 30 | 5 | 8 | 6 | 100 | 3 | 198 | 11 | 0 |
| Barkley, Jeffrey, Cleveland | 0 | 3 | .000 | 5.27 | 21 | 0 | 0 | 0 | 6 | 0 | 41.0 | 37 | 174 | 26 | 24 | 5 | 3 | 2 | 0 | 15 | 5 | 30 | 6 | 1 |
| Barojas, Salome, Seattle | 0 | 1 | .000 | 5.98 | 17 | 0 | 0 | 0 | 3 | 0 | 52.2 | 65 | 250 | 40 | 35 | 6 | 5 | 5 | 3 | 33 | 3 | 27 | 2 | 0 |
| Beattie, James, Seattle | 5 | 6 | .455 | 7.29 | 18 | 15 | 1 | 1 | 1 | 0 | 70.1 | 93 | 335 | 61 | 57 | 9 | 5 | 2 | 3 | 61 | 5 | 45 | 5 | 0 |
| Beckwith, T. Joseph, Kansas City | 1 | 5 | .167 | 4.07 | 49 | 0 | 0 | 0 | 21 | 1 | 95.0 | 99 | 410 | 45 | 43 | 9 | 4 | 5 | 3 | 32 | 8 | 80 | 6 | 0 |
| Behenna, Richard, Cleveland | 0 | 2 | .000 | 7.78 | 4 | 4 | 0 | 0 | 0 | 0 | 19.2 | 29 | 91 | 17 | 17 | 3 | 0 | 3 | 0 | 8 | 0 | 4 | 2 | 0 |
| Bell, Eric, Baltimore* | 0 | 0 | .000 | 4.76 | 2 | 0 | 0 | 0 | 0 | 0 | 5.2 | 25 | 24 | 3 | 3 | 1 | 0 | 1 | 0 | 4 | 3 | 4 | 0 | 1 |
| Berenguer, Juan, Detroit | 5 | 6 | .455 | 5.59 | 31 | 13 | 0 | 0 | 9 | 0 | 95.0 | 96 | 424 | 67 | 59 | 12 | 6 | 4 | 3 | 48 | 0 | 82 | 6 | 0 |
| Best, Karl, Seattle | 0 | 1 | .000 | 1.95 | 15 | 0 | 0 | 0 | 7 | 0 | 32.1 | 25 | 128 | 7 | 7 | 1 | 9 | 0 | 0 | 6 | 0 | 32 | 2 | 0 |
| Birtsas, Timothy, Oakland* | 10 | 6 | .625 | 4.01 | 29 | 25 | 0 | 0 | 0 | 0 | 141.1 | 124 | 624 | 72 | 63 | 18 | 8 | 5 | 8 | 91 | 4 | 94 | 5 | 1 |
| Black, Harry, Kansas City* | 17 | 15 | .531 | 4.33 | 33 | 33 | 2 | 0 | 0 | 0 | 205.2 | 216 | 885 | 111 | 99 | 17 | 5 | 4 | 8 | 59 | 4 | 122 | 1 | 0 |
| Blyleven, Rikalbert, Clev.-Minn. | 17 | 16 | .515 | 3.16 | 37 | 37 | 24 | 5 | 0 | 0 | 293.2 | 264 | 1203 | 121 | 103 | 23 | 9 | 8 | 9 | 75 | 7 | 206 | 4 | 1 |
| Boddicker, Michael, Baltimore | 12 | 17 | .414 | 4.07 | 32 | 32 | 9 | 2 | 0 | 0 | 203.1 | 227 | 899 | 104 | 92 | 13 | 9 | 8 | 6 | 89 | 7 | 135 | 5 | 1 |
| Boggs, Thomas, Texas | 0 | 0 | .000 | 11.57 | 4 | 0 | 0 | 0 | 0 | 0 | 7.0 | 13 | 36 | 9 | 9 | 5 | 0 | 0 | 1 | 2 | 4 | 6 | 1 | 0 |
| Bordi, Richard, New York | 6 | 8 | .429 | 3.21 | 51 | 0 | 0 | 0 | 16 | 2 | 98.0 | 95 | 415 | 41 | 35 | 5 | 6 | 3 | 1 | 29 | 3 | 64 | 1 | 0 |
| Boyd, Dennis, Boston | 15 | 13 | .536 | 3.70 | 35 | 35 | 13 | 4 | 0 | 0 | 272.1 | 273 | 1132 | 117 | 112 | 26 | 9 | 7 | 4 | 67 | 0 | 154 | 0 | 0 |
| Brown, Mark, Minnesota | 0 | 0 | .000 | 6.89 | 6 | 0 | 0 | 0 | 4 | 0 | 15.2 | 21 | 73 | 13 | 12 | 8 | 3 | 0 | 0 | 7 | 0 | 5 | 0 | 0 |
| Brown, Michael G., Boston | 0 | 0 | .000 | 21.60 | 2 | 2 | 0 | 0 | 1 | 0 | 3.1 | 9 | 22 | 8 | 8 | 0 | 1 | 0 | 1 | 3 | 0 | 3 | 2 | 0 |
| Burns, R. Britt, Chicago* | 18 | 11 | .621 | 3.96 | 36 | 34 | 8 | 4 | 0 | 0 | 227.0 | 206 | 944 | 105 | 100 | 26 | 6 | 5 | 8 | 79 | 4 | 172 | 7 | 0 |
| Burris, B. Ray, Milwaukee | 13 | 13 | .500 | 4.81 | 29 | 28 | 6 | 0 | 0 | 0 | 170.1 | 182 | 738 | 95 | 91 | 25 | 2 | 2 | 1 | 53 | 0 | 81 | 1 | 2 |
| Burtt, Dennis, Minnesota | 2 | 3 | .400 | 3.81 | 5 | 5 | 0 | 0 | 1 | 0 | 28.1 | 20 | 109 | 13 | 12 | 2 | 6 | 0 | 0 | 7 | 0 | 9 | 5 | 0 |
| Butcher, John, Minnesota | 11 | 14 | .440 | 4.98 | 34 | 33 | 8 | 2 | 0 | 0 | 207.2 | 239 | 893 | 125 | 115 | 24 | 6 | 10 | 6 | 43 | 4 | 92 | 5 | 1 |
| Bystrom, Martin, New York | 3 | 2 | .600 | 5.71 | 8 | 8 | 0 | 0 | 0 | 0 | 41.0 | 44 | 180 | 29 | 26 | 8 | 2 | 2 | 0 | 19 | 0 | 16 | 2 | 0 |
| Camacho, Ernie, Cleveland | 0 | 1 | .000 | 8.10 | 2 | 0 | 0 | 0 | 1 | 0 | 3.1 | 4 | 15 | 3 | 3 | 0 | 0 | 0 | 1 | 1 | 0 | 1 | 1 | 0 |
| Candelaria, John, California* | 7 | 3 | .700 | 3.80 | 13 | 13 | 1 | 1 | 0 | 0 | 71.0 | 70 | 301 | 33 | 30 | 7 | 4 | 2 | 0 | 24 | 1 | 53 | 0 | 0 |
| Cary, Charles, Detroit* | 0 | 1 | .000 | 3.42 | 16 | 0 | 0 | 0 | 6 | 0 | 23.2 | 16 | 95 | 9 | 9 | 2 | 0 | 3 | 0 | 8 | 1 | 22 | 2 | 0 |
| Caudill, William, Toronto | 4 | 6 | .400 | 2.99 | 67 | 0 | 0 | 0 | 51 | 14 | 69.1 | 53 | 297 | 26 | 23 | 9 | 3 | 4 | 3 | 35 | 6 | 46 | 5 | 3 |
| Cerutti, John, Toronto* | 0 | 0 | .000 | 5.40 | 4 | 0 | 0 | 0 | 0 | 0 | 6.2 | 10 | 36 | 4 | 4 | 1 | 0 | 0 | 0 | 4 | 0 | 5 | 0 | 0 |
| Clancy, James, Toronto | 9 | 6 | .600 | 3.78 | 23 | 23 | 2 | 0 | 0 | 0 | 128.2 | 117 | 527 | 54 | 54 | 15 | 3 | 5 | 5 | 37 | 2 | 66 | 2 | 0 |
| Clark, Bryan, Cleveland* | 3 | 4 | .429 | 6.32 | 41 | 3 | 1 | 1 | 10 | 0 | 62.2 | 78 | 290 | 47 | 44 | 8 | 4 | 5 | 2 | 34 | 2 | 24 | 5 | 0 |
| Clarke, Stanley, Toronto* | 0 | 0 | .000 | 4.50 | 2 | 0 | 0 | 0 | 0 | 0 | 4.0 | 3 | 16 | 2 | 2 | 1 | 1 | 0 | 0 | 2 | 0 | 2 | 0 | 3 |
| Clear, Mark, Boston | 0 | 3 | .000 | 3.72 | 41 | 0 | 0 | 0 | 30 | 2 | 55.2 | 45 | 259 | 26 | 23 | 5 | 5 | 2 | 5 | 50 | 10 | 55 | 8 | 0 |
| Clemens, W. Roger, Boston | 7 | 5 | .583 | 3.29 | 15 | 15 | 3 | 1 | 0 | 0 | 98.1 | 83 | 407 | 38 | 36 | 5 | 4 | 2 | 5 | 37 | 2 | 74 | 11 | 0 |
| Clements, Patrick, California* | 5 | 0 | 1.000 | 3.34 | 41 | 0 | 0 | 0 | 12 | 0 | 62.0 | 47 | 247 | 23 | 23 | 5 | 5 | 2 | 1 | 25 | 6 | 19 | 4 | 0 |
| Cliburn, Stewart, California | 9 | 3 | .750 | 2.09 | 44 | 0 | 0 | 0 | 26 | 6 | 99.0 | 87 | 395 | 25 | 23 | 5 | 4 | 2 | 5 | 26 | 2 | 48 | 13 | 1 |
| Cocanower, James, Milwaukee | 6 | 8 | .429 | 4.33 | 24 | 15 | 0 | 0 | 0 | 0 | 116.1 | 122 | 534 | 72 | 56 | 6 | 4 | 8 | 8 | 73 | 2 | 44 | 8 | 0 |
| Codiroli, Christopher, Oakland | 14 | 14 | .500 | 4.46 | 37 | 37 | 4 | 0 | 1 | 0 | 226.0 | 228 | 975 | 125 | 112 | 23 | 5 | 4 | 1 | 78 | 1 | 111 | 4 | 0 |
| Conroy, Timothy, Oakland* | 0 | 4 | .000 | 4.26 | 16 | 4 | 0 | 0 | 2 | 0 | 25.1 | 22 | 110 | 15 | 12 | 3 | 0 | 8 | 3 | 15 | 1 | 18 | 1 | 0 |
| Cook, Glen, Texas | 2 | 3 | .400 | 9.45 | 9 | 7 | 0 | 0 | 0 | 0 | 40.0 | 53 | 187 | 42 | 42 | 12 | 2 | 1 | 1 | 18 | 1 | 19 | 1 | 0 |
| Cooper, Donald, New York | 0 | 3 | .000 | 5.40 | 7 | 0 | 0 | 0 | 7 | 0 | 10.0 | 12 | 44 | 6 | 6 | 2 | 0 | 1 | 0 | 3 | 0 | 4 | 1 | 0 |
| Corbett, Douglas, California | 3 | 3 | .500 | 4.89 | 30 | 0 | 0 | 0 | 11 | 0 | 46.0 | 49 | 203 | 33 | 25 | 7 | 2 | 2 | 1 | 20 | 3 | 24 | 0 | 0 |

| Pitcher and Club | W. | L. | Pct. | ERA. | G. | GS. | CG. | ShO. | GF. | Sv. | IP. | H. | BFP. | R. | ER. | HR. | SH. | SF. | HB. | Tot. BB. | Int. BB. | SO. | WP. | Bk. |
|---|---|---|---|---|---|---|---|---|---|---|---|---|---|---|---|---|---|---|---|---|---|---|---|---|
| Correa, Edwin, Chicago | 1 | 0 | 1.000 | 6.97 | 3 | 1 | 0 | 0 | 3 | 0 | 10.1 | 11 | 51 | 9 | 8 | 2 | 0 | 0 | 0 | 11 | 1 | 10 | 1 | 0 |
| Cowley, Joseph, New York | 12 | 6 | .667 | 3.95 | 30 | 26 | 1 | 0 | 2 | 0 | 159.2 | 132 | 684 | 75 | 70 | 29 | 1 | 4 | 6 | 85 | 8 | 97 | 5 | 1 |
| Crawford, Steven, Boston | 6 | 5 | .545 | 3.76 | 44 | 1 | 0 | 0 | 26 | 12 | 91.0 | 103 | 394 | 47 | 38 | 5 | 6 | 3 | 2 | 28 | 2 | 58 | 5 | 0 |
| Creel, S. Keith, Cleveland | 2 | 5 | .286 | 4.79 | 15 | 8 | 0 | 0 | 5 | 2 | 62.0 | 73 | 277 | 35 | 33 | 7 | 7 | 5 | 4 | 23 | 0 | 31 | 1 | 0 |
| Darwin, Danny, Milwaukee | 8 | 18 | .308 | 3.80 | 39 | 29 | 6 | 1 | 8 | 0 | 217.2 | 212 | 919 | 92 | 92 | 34 | 3 | 3 | 4 | 65 | 4 | 125 | 6 | 0 |
| Davis, George, Baltimore | 10 | 8 | .556 | 4.53 | 31 | 28 | 4 | 1 | 0 | 0 | 175.0 | 172 | 750 | 92 | 88 | 11 | 1 | 3 | 1 | 70 | 5 | 93 | 2 | 1 |
| Davis, Joel, Chicago | 3 | 3 | .500 | 4.16 | 11 | 11 | 1 | 0 | 0 | 0 | 71.1 | 71 | 307 | 34 | 33 | 6 | 0 | 2 | 1 | 26 | 0 | 37 | 1 | 0 |
| Davis, Ronald, Minnesota | 2 | 6 | .250 | 3.48 | 57 | 0 | 0 | 0 | 50 | 25 | 64.2 | 55 | 285 | 28 | 25 | 7 | 8 | 4 | 4 | 35 | 6 | 72 | 8 | 1 |
| Davis, Steven, Toronto* | 2 | 1 | .667 | 3.54 | 10 | 5 | 0 | 0 | 1 | 1 | 28.0 | 23 | 117 | 14 | 11 | 5 | 3 | 1 | 0 | 13 | 0 | 22 | 0 | 0 |
| Dixon, Kenneth, Baltimore | 8 | 4 | .667 | 3.67 | 34 | 18 | 3 | 1 | 7 | 0 | 162.0 | 144 | 683 | 68 | 66 | 20 | 8 | 2 | 4 | 64 | 7 | 108 | 5 | 2 |
| Dorsey, James, Boston | 0 | 1 | .000 | 20.25 | 2 | 1 | 0 | 0 | 0 | 0 | 5.1 | 12 | 37 | 12 | 12 | 2 | 0 | 2 | 0 | 10 | 1 | 2 | 0 | 0 |
| Dotson, Richard, Chicago | 3 | 4 | .429 | 4.47 | 9 | 9 | 1 | 0 | 0 | 0 | 52.1 | 53 | 226 | 30 | 26 | 5 | 5 | 2 | 4 | 17 | 4 | 33 | 0 | 0 |
| Easterly, James, Cleveland* | 4 | 1 | .800 | 3.92 | 50 | 0 | 0 | 0 | 18 | 2 | 98.2 | 96 | 435 | 52 | 43 | 9 | 5 | 3 | 0 | 53 | 7 | 58 | 7 | 0 |
| Eufemia, Frank, Minnesota | 4 | 2 | .667 | 3.79 | 39 | 0 | 0 | 0 | 21 | 2 | 61.2 | 56 | 250 | 27 | 26 | 7 | 2 | 3 | 4 | 21 | 2 | 30 | 2 | 2 |
| Fallon, Robert, Chicago* | 0 | 2 | .000 | 6.19 | 10 | 3 | 0 | 0 | 4 | 0 | 16.0 | 25 | 79 | 11 | 11 | 5 | 1 | 1 | 0 | 9 | 4 | 17 | 1 | 0 |
| Farr, Steven, Kansas City | 2 | 1 | .667 | 3.11 | 16 | 3 | 0 | 0 | 5 | 1 | 37.2 | 34 | 164 | 15 | 13 | 2 | 0 | 2 | 0 | 20 | 0 | 36 | 3 | 0 |
| Ferreira, Anthony, Kansas City* | 0 | 1 | .000 | 7.94 | 2 | 0 | 0 | 0 | 1 | 0 | 5.2 | 6 | 24 | 5 | 5 | 0 | 3 | 0 | 0 | 0 | 0 | 5 | 0 | 0 |
| Filer, Thomas, Toronto | 7 | 0 | 1.000 | 3.88 | 11 | 9 | 0 | 0 | 0 | 0 | 48.2 | 38 | 192 | 21 | 21 | 6 | 4 | 2 | 2 | 18 | 4 | 24 | 0 | 1 |
| Filson, W. Peter, Minnesota* | 4 | 5 | .444 | 3.67 | 40 | 6 | 0 | 0 | 12 | 2 | 95.2 | 93 | 406 | 42 | 39 | 13 | 0 | 2 | 2 | 30 | 5 | 42 | 1 | 1 |
| Fingers, Roland, Milwaukee | 1 | 6 | .143 | 5.04 | 47 | 0 | 0 | 0 | 37 | 17 | 55.1 | 59 | 241 | 33 | 31 | 14 | 3 | 0 | 1 | 19 | 0 | 24 | 4 | 0 |
| Fireovid, Stephen, Chicago | 0 | 1 | .000 | 5.14 | 4 | 0 | 0 | 0 | 2 | 0 | 7.0 | 17 | 38 | 4 | 4 | 0 | 0 | 2 | 0 | 2 | 3 | 2 | 3 | 0 |
| Fisher, Brian, New York | 4 | 4 | .500 | 2.38 | 55 | 0 | 0 | 0 | 23 | 14 | 98.1 | 77 | 391 | 32 | 26 | 4 | 5 | 2 | 2 | 29 | 3 | 85 | 3 | 0 |
| Flanagan, Michael, Baltimore* | 4 | 5 | .444 | 5.13 | 15 | 15 | 3 | 0 | 0 | 0 | 86.0 | 101 | 379 | 49 | 49 | 14 | 4 | 2 | 2 | 28 | 0 | 42 | 1 | 0 |
| Fowlkes, Alan, California | 0 | 0 | .000 | 9.00 | 2 | 0 | 0 | 0 | 0 | 0 | 7.0 | 8 | 33 | 7 | 7 | 3 | 1 | 0 | 0 | 4 | 3 | 5 | 0 | 1 |
| Geisel, J. David, Seattle* | 0 | 1 | .000 | 6.33 | 12 | 0 | 0 | 0 | 5 | 0 | 27.0 | 35 | 128 | 21 | 19 | 10 | 3 | 1 | 1 | 15 | 3 | 17 | 4 | 0 |
| Gibson, Robert, Milwaukee | 6 | 7 | .462 | 3.90 | 41 | 0 | 0 | 0 | 1 | 1 | 92.1 | 86 | 392 | 44 | 40 | 10 | 0 | 4 | 0 | 49 | 0 | 53 | 3 | 0 |
| Gleaton, Jerry, Chicago* | 4 | 5 | .444 | 5.76 | 31 | 0 | 0 | 0 | 25 | 11 | 29.2 | 37 | 135 | 19 | 19 | 1 | 4 | 1 | 5 | 13 | 2 | 22 | 12 | 0 |
| Gubicza, Mark, Kansas City | 14 | 10 | .583 | 4.06 | 29 | 28 | 2 | 0 | 0 | 0 | 177.1 | 160 | 760 | 88 | 80 | 14 | 1 | 6 | 1 | 77 | 0 | 99 | 3 | 0 |
| Guidry, Ronald, New York* | 22 | 6 | .786 | 3.27 | 34 | 33 | 11 | 2 | 0 | 0 | 259.0 | 243 | 1033 | 104 | 94 | 28 | 3 | 8 | 1 | 42 | 4 | 143 | 1 | 0 |
| Gura, Lawrence, Kansas City* | 0 | 2 | .000 | 12.46 | 3 | 1 | 0 | 0 | 2 | 0 | 4.1 | 7 | 23 | 6 | 6 | 2 | 0 | 0 | 0 | 14 | 0 | 1 | 2 | 1 |
| Guzman, Jose, Texas | 3 | 2 | .600 | 2.76 | 5 | 5 | 0 | 0 | 0 | 0 | 32.2 | 27 | 140 | 13 | 10 | 1 | 0 | 5 | 0 | 25 | 3 | 24 | 2 | 0 |
| Haas, Bryan, Milwaukee | 8 | 8 | .500 | 3.84 | 27 | 26 | 4 | 0 | 0 | 0 | 161.2 | 165 | 666 | 85 | 69 | 21 | 7 | 0 | 2 | 43 | 1 | 78 | 0 | 0 |
| Habyan, John, Baltimore | 1 | 0 | 1.000 | 0.00 | 3 | 0 | 0 | 0 | 1 | 0 | 2.2 | 4 | 12 | 0 | 0 | 0 | 0 | 2 | 0 | 10 | 3 | 1 | 1 | 1 |
| Harris, Greg, Texas | 5 | 4 | .556 | 2.47 | 58 | 0 | 0 | 0 | 35 | 11 | 113.0 | 74 | 450 | 35 | 31 | 7 | 3 | 0 | 0 | 43 | 0 | 111 | 2 | 0 |
| Havens, Bradley, Baltimore* | 0 | 2 | .000 | 8.79 | 8 | 1 | 0 | 0 | 3 | 0 | 14.1 | 20 | 70 | 14 | 14 | 4 | 0 | 7 | 0 | 10 | 2 | 19 | 0 | 0 |
| Heaton, Neal, Cleveland* | 9 | 17 | .346 | 4.90 | 36 | 33 | 5 | 0 | 0 | 0 | 207.2 | 244 | 921 | 119 | 113 | 19 | 7 | 8 | 4 | 80 | 2 | 82 | 1 | 0 |
| Henke, Thomas, Toronto | 3 | 3 | .500 | 2.03 | 28 | 0 | 0 | 0 | 22 | 13 | 40.0 | 29 | 153 | 12 | 9 | 4 | 0 | 2 | 1 | 14 | 1 | 42 | 2 | 3 |
| Henry, Dwayne, Texas | 2 | 0 | 1.000 | 2.57 | 16 | 0 | 0 | 0 | 10 | 0 | 21.0 | 16 | 86 | 6 | 6 | 0 | 2 | 1 | 0 | 8 | 2 | 20 | 4 | 0 |
| Hernandez, Guillermo, Detroit* | 8 | 10 | .444 | 2.70 | 74 | 0 | 0 | 0 | 64 | 31 | 106.2 | 82 | 415 | 38 | 32 | 13 | 4 | 5 | 0 | 37 | 0 | 76 | 1 | 0 |
| Higuera, Teodoro, Milwaukee* | 15 | 8 | .652 | 3.90 | 32 | 30 | 7 | 2 | 0 | 0 | 212.1 | 186 | 874 | 105 | 92 | 22 | 5 | 10 | 4 | 63 | 1 | 127 | 11 | 3 |
| Holland, Alfred, California* | 1 | 0 | 1.000 | 1.48 | 15 | 0 | 0 | 0 | 6 | 0 | 24.1 | 17 | 99 | 4 | 4 | 4 | 1 | 0 | 0 | 14 | 2 | 14 | 4 | 0 |
| Hooton, Burt, Texas | 5 | 8 | .385 | 5.23 | 29 | 20 | 2 | 0 | 0 | 0 | 124.0 | 149 | 546 | 78 | 72 | 18 | 5 | 5 | 0 | 40 | 3 | 62 | 0 | 1 |
| Hough, Charles, Texas | 14 | 16 | .467 | 3.31 | 34 | 34 | 14 | 1 | 2 | 0 | 250.1 | 198 | 1018 | 102 | 92 | 23 | 7 | 7 | 0 | 83 | 3 | 141 | 0 | 0 |
| Howe, Steven, Minnesota* | 2 | 3 | .400 | 6.16 | 13 | 0 | 0 | 0 | 5 | 0 | 19.0 | 28 | 94 | 16 | 13 | 5 | 3 | 3 | 0 | 7 | 0 | 10 | 3 | 0 |
| Howell, Jay, Oakland | 9 | 8 | .529 | 2.85 | 63 | 0 | 0 | 0 | 58 | 29 | 98.0 | 98 | 414 | 32 | 31 | 1 | 1 | 4 | 0 | 31 | 4 | 68 | 4 | 0 |
| Huffman, Phillip, Baltimore | 0 | 0 | .000 | 15.43 | 2 | 1 | 0 | 0 | 0 | 0 | 4.2 | 7 | 26 | 8 | 8 | 1 | 0 | 0 | 0 | 5 | 0 | 2 | 3 | 1 |
| Huismann, Mark, Kansas City | 1 | 0 | 1.000 | 1.93 | 9 | 0 | 0 | 0 | 6 | 0 | 18.2 | 14 | 70 | 4 | 4 | 1 | 3 | 2 | 2 | 7 | 2 | 9 | 0 | 0 |
| Hurst, Bruce, Boston* | 11 | 13 | .458 | 4.51 | 35 | 31 | 6 | 3 | 0 | 0 | 229.1 | 243 | 973 | 123 | 115 | 31 | 6 | 4 | 1 | 70 | 4 | 189 | 9 | 0 |
| Jackson, Danny, Kansas City* | 14 | 12 | .538 | 3.42 | 32 | 32 | 4 | 1 | 0 | 0 | 208.0 | 209 | 893 | 94 | 79 | 7 | 5 | 6 | 6 | 76 | 4 | 114 | 4 | 4 |
| James, Robert, Chicago | 8 | 7 | .533 | 2.13 | 69 | 0 | 0 | 0 | 60 | 32 | 110.0 | 90 | 436 | 31 | 26 | 5 | 7 | 5 | 2 | 23 | 2 | 88 | 3 | 2 |

| Pitcher and Club | W. | L. | Pct. | ERA. | G. | GS. | CG. | ShO. | GF. | Sv. | IP. | H. | BFP. | R. | ER. | HR. | SH. | SF. | HB. | Tot. BB. | Int. BB. | SO. | WP. | Bk. |
|---|---|---|---|---|---|---|---|---|---|---|---|---|---|---|---|---|---|---|---|---|---|---|---|---|
| Jeffcoat, J. Michael, Cleveland* | 0 | 0 | .000 | 2.79 | 9 | 0 | 0 | 0 | 3 | 0 | 9.2 | 8 | 44 | 5 | 3 | 1 | 2 | 2 | 0 | 6 | 1 | 4 | 0 | 0 |
| John, Thomas, Cal.-Oak.* | 4 | 10 | .286 | 5.53 | 23 | 17 | 2 | 0 | 2 | 0 | 86.1 | 117 | 397 | 59 | 53 | 9 | 9 | 4 | 2 | 28 | 1 | 25 | 7 | 0 |
| Jones, Alfornia, Chicago* | 1 | 0 | 1.000 | 1.50 | 5 | 1 | 0 | 0 | 2 | 0 | 6.0 | 3 | 21 | 2 | 1 | 0 | 1 | 0 | 0 | 3 | 0 | 2 | 0 | 0 |
| Jones, Michael, Kansas City* | 3 | 3 | .500 | 4.78 | 33 | 0 | 0 | 0 | 16 | 0 | 64.0 | 62 | 290 | 40 | 34 | 6 | 4 | 6 | 2 | 39 | 4 | 32 | 1 | 0 |
| Kaiser, Jeffrey, Oakland* | 0 | 1 | .000 | 14.58 | 15 | 0 | 0 | 0 | 4 | 0 | 16.2 | 25 | 97 | 32 | 27 | 6 | 1 | 0 | 1 | 20 | 2 | 10 | 2 | 0 |
| Kern, James, Milwaukee | 0 | 0 | .000 | 6.55 | 5 | 0 | 0 | 0 | 1 | 0 | 11.0 | 14 | 50 | 8 | 8 | 1 | 1 | 0 | 0 | 5 | 1 | 3 | 3 | 1 |
| Key, James, Toronto* | 14 | 6 | .700 | 3.00 | 35 | 32 | 3 | 0 | 0 | 0 | 212.2 | 188 | 856 | 77 | 71 | 22 | 5 | 5 | 2 | 50 | 1 | 85 | 6 | 0 |
| Kipper, Robert, California* | 0 | 1 | .000 | 21.60 | 2 | 1 | 0 | 0 | 0 | 0 | 3.1 | 7 | 20 | 8 | 8 | 1 | 0 | 2 | 0 | 5 | 0 | 0 | 0 | 0 |
| Kison, Bruce, Boston | 5 | 3 | .625 | 4.11 | 22 | 9 | 0 | 0 | 5 | 1 | 92.0 | 98 | 398 | 43 | 42 | 9 | 2 | 4 | 1 | 32 | 4 | 56 | 5 | 0 |
| Klawitter, Thomas, Minnesota* | 0 | 0 | .000 | 6.75 | 7 | 2 | 0 | 0 | 3 | 0 | 9.1 | 10 | 45 | 10 | 7 | 2 | 2 | 0 | 0 | 13 | 0 | 7 | 3 | 0 |
| Krueger, William, Oakland* | 9 | 10 | .474 | 4.52 | 32 | 26 | 0 | 0 | 4 | 0 | 151.1 | 165 | 674 | 95 | 76 | 13 | 5 | 5 | 2 | 69 | 6 | 56 | 6 | 3 |
| LaCoss, Michael, Kansas City | 1 | 1 | .500 | 5.09 | 21 | 3 | 0 | 0 | 7 | 1 | 40.2 | 49 | 193 | 25 | 23 | 5 | 2 | 0 | 0 | 29 | 3 | 26 | 2 | 1 |
| Ladd, Peter, Milwaukee | 0 | 1 | .000 | 4.53 | 29 | 0 | 0 | 0 | 13 | 2 | 45.2 | 58 | 202 | 26 | 23 | 7 | 3 | 6 | 2 | 10 | 6 | 22 | 1 | 0 |
| Lamp, Dennis, Toronto | 11 | 0 | 1.000 | 3.32 | 53 | 1 | 0 | 0 | 7 | 2 | 105.2 | 96 | 426 | 42 | 39 | 8 | 5 | 2 | 2 | 27 | 3 | 68 | 5 | 0 |
| Langford, J. Rick, Oakland | 3 | 5 | .375 | 3.51 | 24 | 10 | 1 | 0 | 0 | 0 | 59.0 | 60 | 247 | 24 | 23 | 5 | 2 | 3 | 0 | 15 | 2 | 21 | 2 | 0 |
| Langston, Mark, Seattle* | 7 | 14 | .333 | 5.47 | 24 | 24 | 4 | 0 | 0 | 0 | 126.2 | 122 | 577 | 85 | 77 | 22 | 3 | 2 | 8 | 91 | 5 | 72 | 5 | 3 |
| Lavelle, Gary, Toronto* | 5 | 7 | .417 | 3.10 | 69 | 0 | 0 | 0 | 19 | 8 | 72.2 | 54 | 298 | 30 | 25 | 5 | 2 | 2 | 2 | 36 | 7 | 50 | 2 | 0 |
| Lazorko, Jack, Seattle | 0 | 3 | .000 | 3.54 | 15 | 2 | 0 | 0 | 4 | 1 | 20.1 | 23 | 92 | 10 | 8 | 1 | 0 | 2 | 0 | 8 | 0 | 7 | 1 | 0 |
| Leal, Luis, Toronto | 3 | 6 | .333 | 5.75 | 15 | 14 | 0 | 0 | 0 | 0 | 67.1 | 82 | 303 | 46 | 43 | 13 | 2 | 0 | 3 | 24 | 3 | 33 | 3 | 0 |
| Leary, Timothy, Milwaukee | 1 | 4 | .200 | 4.05 | 15 | 5 | 0 | 0 | 4 | 0 | 33.1 | 40 | 146 | 18 | 15 | 5 | 1 | 0 | 0 | 8 | 0 | 29 | 4 | 0 |
| Leibrandt, Charles, Kansas City* | 17 | 9 | .654 | 2.69 | 33 | 33 | 8 | 3 | 0 | 0 | 237.2 | 223 | 983 | 86 | 71 | 17 | 8 | 5 | 5 | 68 | 3 | 108 | 4 | 3 |
| Leonard, Dennis, Kansas City | 0 | 0 | .000 | 0.00 | 1 | 0 | 0 | 0 | 1 | 0 | 2.0 | 1 | 7 | 0 | 0 | 0 | 0 | 0 | 0 | 2 | 0 | 1 | 0 | 0 |
| Lesley, Bradley, Milwaukee | 1 | 0 | 1.000 | 9.95 | 9 | 0 | 0 | 0 | 7 | 0 | 6.1 | 8 | 29 | 7 | 7 | 2 | 0 | 0 | 0 | 1 | 1 | 5 | 0 | 0 |
| Lewis, James, Seattle | 0 | 2 | .000 | 7.71 | 5 | 1 | 0 | 0 | 1 | 0 | 4.2 | 8 | 23 | 5 | 4 | 0 | 0 | 5 | 3 | 9 | 2 | 5 | 1 | 1 |
| Lollar, W. Timothy, Chi.-Bos.* | 8 | 10 | .444 | 4.62 | 34 | 23 | 0 | 0 | 7 | 0 | 150.0 | 140 | 669 | 85 | 77 | 19 | 4 | 5 | 1 | 98 | 1 | 105 | 10 | 0 |
| Long, Robert, Seattle | 0 | 1 | .000 | 3.76 | 28 | 0 | 0 | 0 | 13 | 1 | 38.1 | 30 | 162 | 17 | 16 | 4 | 1 | 1 | 2 | 17 | 2 | 29 | 2 | 0 |
| Long, William, Chicago | 3 | 7 | .300 | 10.29 | 4 | 3 | 0 | 0 | 0 | 0 | 14.0 | 25 | 71 | 17 | 16 | 4 | 1 | 6 | 0 | 5 | 9 | 13 | 1 | 0 |
| Lopez, Aurelio, Detroit | 3 | 4 | .429 | 4.80 | 51 | 0 | 1 | 0 | 22 | 3 | 86.1 | 82 | 379 | 50 | 46 | 15 | 0 | 3 | 1 | 41 | 2 | 53 | 5 | 2 |
| Lugo, Urbano, California | 3 | 3 | .500 | 3.69 | 20 | 10 | 1 | 0 | 5 | 0 | 83.0 | 86 | 351 | 36 | 34 | 10 | 3 | 2 | 0 | 29 | 2 | 42 | 4 | 0 |
| Lysander, Richard, Minnesota | 1 | 2 | .333 | 6.05 | 35 | 1 | 0 | 0 | 9 | 3 | 61.0 | 72 | 262 | 43 | 41 | 3 | 2 | 0 | 0 | 22 | 2 | 26 | 0 | 0 |
| Mack, Tony, California | 0 | 1 | .000 | 15.43 | 3 | 1 | 0 | 0 | 0 | 0 | 2.1 | 8 | 14 | 4 | 4 | 0 | 0 | 1 | 1 | 4 | 0 | 0 | 0 | 0 |
| Mahler, Michael, Detroit* | 1 | 2 | .333 | 1.74 | 16 | 2 | 0 | 0 | 9 | 0 | 20.2 | 19 | 84 | 8 | 4 | 2 | 1 | 1 | 0 | 4 | 3 | 14 | 4 | 0 |
| Martinez, J. Dennis, Baltimore | 13 | 11 | .542 | 5.15 | 31 | 30 | 3 | 1 | 0 | 0 | 180.0 | 203 | 789 | 110 | 103 | 29 | 4 | 2 | 9 | 63 | 3 | 68 | 5 | 0 |
| Martinez, Felix, Baltimore* | 4 | 9 | .308 | 5.40 | 50 | 0 | 0 | 0 | 20 | 4 | 70.0 | 70 | 312 | 48 | 42 | 8 | 3 | 4 | 0 | 37 | 8 | 47 | 4 | 1 |
| Mason, Michael, Texas* | 8 | 15 | .348 | 4.83 | 38 | 30 | 8 | 0 | 1 | 0 | 179.0 | 212 | 800 | 113 | 96 | 22 | 10 | 10 | 3 | 73 | 4 | 92 | 5 | 0 |
| McCarthy, Thomas, Boston | 0 | 0 | .000 | 10.80 | 10 | 0 | 0 | 0 | 2 | 0 | 5.0 | 7 | 25 | 6 | 6 | 0 | 1 | 5 | 1 | 4 | 0 | 2 | 1 | 0 |
| McCaskill, Kirk, California | 12 | 12 | .500 | 4.70 | 30 | 29 | 6 | 1 | 0 | 0 | 189.2 | 189 | 807 | 85 | 99 | 23 | 3 | 3 | 4 | 64 | 4 | 102 | 5 | 0 |
| McCatty, Steven, Oakland | 4 | 4 | .500 | 5.57 | 35 | 9 | 1 | 0 | 8 | 0 | 85.2 | 95 | 383 | 56 | 53 | 10 | 3 | 2 | 3 | 41 | 2 | 36 | 5 | 1 |
| McClure, Robert, Milwaukee* | 4 | 1 | .800 | 4.31 | 35 | 0 | 0 | 0 | 12 | 3 | 85.2 | 91 | 370 | 43 | 41 | 10 | 3 | 2 | 1 | 30 | 0 | 57 | 5 | 0 |
| McGregor, Scott, Baltimore* | 14 | 14 | .500 | 4.81 | 38 | 34 | 8 | 1 | 0 | 0 | 204.0 | 226 | 884 | 118 | 109 | 34 | 2 | 8 | 5 | 65 | 1 | 86 | 2 | 1 |
| Mirabella, Paul, Seattle* | 0 | 0 | .000 | 1.32 | 10 | 0 | 0 | 0 | 1 | 0 | 13.2 | 9 | 57 | 4 | 2 | 0 | 1 | 2 | 0 | 4 | 0 | 8 | 0 | 0 |
| Mitchell, Charles, Boston | 0 | 0 | .000 | 16.20 | 3 | 0 | 0 | 0 | 1 | 0 | 1.2 | 5 | 10 | 4 | 3 | 1 | 0 | 0 | 0 | 2 | 0 | 2 | 1 | 0 |
| Montefusco, John, New York | 0 | 0 | .000 | 10.29 | 2 | 1 | 0 | 0 | 0 | 0 | 7.0 | 12 | 34 | 8 | 8 | 2 | 1 | 2 | 2 | 2 | 0 | 8 | 5 | 0 |
| Moore, Donnie, California | 8 | 8 | .500 | 1.92 | 65 | 0 | 0 | 0 | 57 | 31 | 103.0 | 91 | 417 | 28 | 22 | 9 | 11 | 7 | 2 | 21 | 3 | 72 | 2 | 1 |
| Moore, Michael, Seattle | 17 | 10 | .630 | 3.46 | 35 | 34 | 14 | 2 | 0 | 0 | 247.0 | 230 | 1016 | 100 | 95 | 18 | 2 | 7 | 0 | 70 | 0 | 155 | 10 | 0 |
| Morgan, Michael, Seattle | 1 | 1 | .500 | 12.00 | 2 | 0 | 0 | 0 | 0 | 0 | 6.0 | 11 | 33 | 8 | 8 | 2 | 1 | 0 | 4 | 5 | 0 | 2 | 0 | 0 |
| Morris, John, Detroit | 16 | 11 | .593 | 3.33 | 35 | 35 | 13 | 4 | 0 | 0 | 257.0 | 212 | 1077 | 102 | 95 | 21 | 11 | 7 | 5 | 110 | 7 | 191 | 15 | 3 |
| Mura, Stephen, Oakland | 3 | 1 | .500 | 4.13 | 23 | 0 | 0 | 0 | 5 | 1 | 48.0 | 41 | 209 | 25 | 22 | 3 | 3 | 1 | 0 | 25 | 4 | 29 | 1 | 3 |
| Murray, Dale, N.Y.-Tex. | 0 | 0 | .000 | 15.00 | 4 | 0 | 0 | 0 | 2 | 0 | 3.0 | 7 | 15 | 5 | 5 | 0 | 1 | 0 | 0 | 0 | 0 | 0 | 0 | 0 |
| Musselman, R. Ronald, Toronto | 3 | 0 | 1.000 | 4.47 | 25 | 4 | 0 | 0 | 9 | 0 | 52.1 | 59 | 236 | 28 | 26 | 2 | 4 | 4 | 0 | 24 | 2 | 29 | 3 | 0 |

| Pitcher and Club | W. | L. | Pct. | ERA. | G. | GS. | CG. | ShO. | GF. | Sv. | IP. | H. | BFP. | R. | ER. | HR. | SH. | SF. | HB. | Tot. BB. | Int. BB. | SO. | WP. | Bk. |
|---|---|---|---|---|---|---|---|---|---|---|---|---|---|---|---|---|---|---|---|---|---|---|---|---|
| Nelson, W. Eugene, Chicago | 10 | 10 | .500 | 4.26 | 46 | 18 | 0 | 0 | 11 | 0 | 145.2 | 144 | 643 | 74 | 69 | 23 | 9 | 2 | 7 | 67 | 4 | 101 | 11 | 1 |
| Niekro, Joseph, New York | 2 | 1 | .667 | 5.84 | 3 | 3 | 0 | 0 | 0 | 0 | 12.1 | 14 | 58 | 8 | 8 | 3 | 1 | 0 | 0 | 8 | 0 | 4 | 2 | 0 |
| Niekro, Philip, New York | 16 | 12 | .571 | 4.09 | 33 | 33 | 7 | 1 | 0 | 0 | 220.0 | 203 | 955 | 110 | 100 | 29 | 4 | 3 | 2 | 120 | 1 | 149 | 5 | 2 |
| Nipper, Albert, Boston | 9 | 12 | .429 | 4.06 | 25 | 25 | 5 | 1 | 0 | 0 | 162.0 | 157 | 713 | 83 | 73 | 14 | 1 | 4 | 0 | 82 | 3 | 85 | 3 | 1 |
| Noles, Dickie, Texas | 4 | 8 | .333 | 5.06 | 28 | 13 | 0 | 0 | 3 | 1 | 110.1 | 129 | 488 | 67 | 62 | 11 | 4 | 0 | 6 | 33 | 1 | 59 | 1 | 0 |
| Nunez, Edwin, Seattle | 7 | 3 | .700 | 3.09 | 28 | 0 | 0 | 0 | 53 | 16 | 90.1 | 79 | 378 | 36 | 31 | 13 | 10 | 3 | 0 | 34 | 9 | 58 | 2 | 1 |
| Ojeda, Robert, Boston* | 9 | 11 | .450 | 4.00 | 39 | 22 | 5 | 0 | 10 | 1 | 157.2 | 166 | 671 | 74 | 70 | 8 | 1 | 3 | 2 | 48 | 9 | 102 | 5 | 3 |
| O'Neal, Randall, Detroit | 5 | 5 | .500 | 3.24 | 28 | 12 | 1 | 0 | 8 | 0 | 94.1 | 82 | 388 | 42 | 34 | 4 | 4 | 2 | 2 | 36 | 2 | 52 | 1 | 0 |
| Ontiveros, Steven, Oakland | 1 | 3 | .250 | 1.93 | 39 | 0 | 0 | 0 | 18 | 8 | 74.2 | 45 | 284 | 17 | 16 | 2 | 2 | 2 | 1 | 19 | 9 | 36 | 6 | 0 |
| Petry, Daniel, Detroit | 15 | 13 | .536 | 3.36 | 34 | 34 | 8 | 0 | 0 | 0 | 238.2 | 190 | 962 | 98 | 89 | 24 | 1 | 2 | 2 | 81 | 0 | 109 | 0 | 0 |
| Porter, Charles, Milwaukee | 1 | 3 | .250 | 1.98 | 6 | 4 | 0 | 1 | 1 | 0 | 13.2 | 15 | 58 | 16 | 8 | 1 | 0 | 0 | 1 | 4 | 0 | 8 | 1 | 1 |
| Portugal, Mark, Minnesota | 1 | 3 | .250 | 5.55 | 6 | 4 | 0 | 0 | 0 | 0 | 24.1 | 24 | 105 | 16 | 15 | 3 | 1 | 3 | 1 | 14 | 5 | 12 | 0 | 0 |
| Quisenberry, Daniel, Kansas City | 8 | 9 | .471 | 2.37 | 84 | 0 | 0 | 0 | 76 | 37 | 129.0 | 142 | 532 | 41 | 34 | 3 | 6 | 3 | 0 | 16 | 5 | 54 | 3 | 1 |
| Rasmussen, Dennis, New York* | 3 | 5 | .375 | 3.98 | 22 | 16 | 2 | 0 | 1 | 0 | 101.2 | 97 | 452 | 56 | 45 | 8 | 2 | 4 | 1 | 42 | 2 | 63 | 4 | 0 |
| Reed, Jerry, Cleveland | 3 | 5 | .375 | 4.11 | 33 | 5 | 0 | 0 | 19 | 0 | 72.1 | 67 | 301 | 41 | 33 | 10 | 2 | 3 | 3 | 19 | 3 | 37 | 7 | 0 |
| Righetti, David, New York* | 12 | 7 | .632 | 2.78 | 74 | 0 | 0 | 0 | 60 | 29 | 107.0 | 96 | 452 | 36 | 33 | 12 | 6 | 3 | 0 | 45 | 10 | 92 | 0 | 1 |
| Rijo, Jose, Oakland | 6 | 4 | .600 | 3.53 | 12 | 9 | 0 | 0 | 1 | 0 | 63.2 | 57 | 272 | 26 | 25 | 5 | 5 | 0 | 1 | 28 | 0 | 65 | 1 | 1 |
| Roman, Jose, Cleveland | 0 | 4 | .000 | 6.61 | 5 | 3 | 0 | 0 | 0 | 0 | 16.1 | 21 | 79 | 17 | 12 | 6 | 0 | 0 | 1 | 14 | 0 | 12 | 2 | 3 |
| Romanick, Ronald, California | 14 | 9 | .609 | 4.11 | 31 | 31 | 6 | 1 | 0 | 0 | 195.0 | 210 | 831 | 101 | 89 | 29 | 4 | 10 | 4 | 62 | 3 | 64 | 6 | 0 |
| Romero, Ramon, Clev.* | 2 | 3 | .400 | 6.58 | 10 | 10 | 0 | 0 | 5 | 0 | 64.1 | 69 | 295 | 48 | 47 | 13 | 0 | 1 | 5 | 38 | 0 | 38 | 1 | 0 |
| Rozema, David, Texas | 3 | 7 | .300 | 4.19 | 34 | 4 | 0 | 0 | 16 | 7 | 88.0 | 100 | 374 | 45 | 41 | 10 | 6 | 1 | 1 | 22 | 6 | 42 | 2 | 0 |
| Ruhle, Vernon, Cleveland | 2 | 10 | .167 | 4.32 | 42 | 16 | 7 | 0 | 7 | 3 | 125.0 | 139 | 532 | 65 | 60 | 16 | 0 | 4 | 2 | 30 | 1 | 54 | 2 | 0 |
| Russell, Jeffrey, Texas | 3 | 6 | .333 | 7.55 | 13 | 13 | 0 | 0 | 0 | 0 | 62.0 | 85 | 295 | 55 | 52 | 10 | 7 | 3 | 2 | 27 | 3 | 44 | 2 | 3 |
| Saberhagen, Bret, Kansas City | 20 | 6 | .769 | 2.87 | 32 | 32 | 10 | 1 | 0 | 0 | 235.1 | 211 | 931 | 79 | 75 | 19 | 1 | 7 | 1 | 38 | 3 | 158 | 5 | 0 |
| Sanchez, Luis, California | 3 | 2 | .600 | 5.72 | 26 | 0 | 0 | 0 | 16 | 2 | 61.1 | 67 | 268 | 41 | 39 | 9 | 3 | 3 | 2 | 27 | 13 | 34 | 2 | 3 |
| Scherrer, William, Detroit* | 3 | 2 | .600 | 4.36 | 48 | 0 | 0 | 0 | 14 | 0 | 66.0 | 62 | 299 | 35 | 32 | 3 | 0 | 2 | 2 | 22 | 8 | 46 | 3 | 0 |
| Schmidt, David, Texas | 7 | 6 | .538 | 3.15 | 51 | 0 | 0 | 0 | 35 | 5 | 85.2 | 81 | 356 | 36 | 30 | 10 | 5 | 8 | 5 | 59 | 2 | 46 | 2 | 1 |
| Schrom, Kenneth, Minnesota | 9 | 12 | .429 | 4.99 | 19 | 26 | 2 | 1 | 0 | 0 | 160.2 | 164 | 679 | 95 | 89 | 28 | 9 | 3 | 2 | 19 | 2 | 74 | 0 | 0 |
| Schulze, Donald, Cleveland | 4 | 0 | 1.000 | 6.01 | 5 | 18 | 1 | 0 | 0 | 0 | 94.1 | 128 | 429 | 75 | 63 | 10 | 6 | 0 | 0 | 10 | 1 | 37 | 0 | 0 |
| Scurry, Rodney, New York* | 2 | 5 | .286 | 2.84 | 33 | 0 | 0 | 0 | 18 | 1 | 12.2 | 5 | 51 | 4 | 4 | 2 | 4 | 1 | 2 | 24 | 4 | 17 | 10 | 0 |
| Searage, Raymond, Milwaukee* | 1 | 2 | .333 | 5.92 | 35 | 0 | 0 | 0 | 0 | 0 | 38.0 | 54 | 189 | 27 | 25 | 2 | 7 | 8 | 0 | 69 | 6 | 36 | 1 | 0 |
| Seaver, G. Thomas, Chicago | 16 | 11 | .593 | 3.17 | 7 | 33 | 6 | 0 | 0 | 0 | 238.2 | 223 | 993 | 103 | 84 | 22 | 0 | 8 | 1 | 14 | 2 | 134 | 1 | 0 |
| Sebra, Robert, Texas | 0 | 2 | .000 | 7.52 | 4 | 4 | 0 | 0 | 0 | 0 | 20.1 | 26 | 102 | 17 | 17 | 4 | 1 | 2 | 0 | 7 | 1 | 13 | 8 | 0 |
| Sellers, Jeffrey, Boston | 2 | 2 | .500 | 3.63 | 8 | 4 | 0 | 0 | 0 | 0 | 22.1 | 24 | 97 | 10 | 9 | 1 | 5 | 4 | 0 | 26 | 0 | 6 | 0 | 0 |
| Shirley, Robert, New York* | 5 | 0 | 1.000 | 2.64 | 48 | 8 | 0 | 0 | 9 | 2 | 109.0 | 103 | 446 | 34 | 32 | 5 | 5 | 4 | 0 | 63 | 0 | 55 | 1 | 0 |
| Slaton, James, California | 6 | 10 | .375 | 4.37 | 29 | 24 | 3 | 0 | 3 | 0 | 148.1 | 162 | 645 | 82 | 72 | 22 | 10 | 5 | 2 | 17 | 2 | 60 | 6 | 1 |
| Smith, David W., California | 0 | 4 | .000 | 7.20 | 4 | 0 | 0 | 0 | 0 | 0 | 5.0 | 5 | 20 | 5 | 4 | 1 | 4 | 0 | 0 | 5 | 0 | 3 | 1 | 0 |
| Smith, Leroy, Cleveland | 1 | 4 | .200 | 5.34 | 12 | 11 | 0 | 0 | 0 | 0 | 62.1 | 84 | 285 | 40 | 37 | 8 | 4 | 4 | 1 | 30 | 5 | 28 | 4 | 2 |
| Smithson, B. Mike, Minnesota | 15 | 14 | .517 | 4.34 | 37 | 37 | 8 | 3 | 0 | 0 | 257.0 | 264 | 1088 | 134 | 124 | 25 | 3 | 7 | 15 | 78 | 0 | 127 | 1 | 0 |
| Snell, Nathaniel, Baltimore | 3 | 2 | .600 | 2.69 | 15 | 0 | 0 | 0 | 15 | 5 | 100.1 | 44 | 421 | 44 | 30 | 2 | 1 | 1 | 1 | 19 | 5 | 41 | 5 | 0 |
| Snyder, Brian, Seattle* | 1 | 2 | .333 | 6.37 | 52 | 6 | 0 | 0 | 1 | 0 | 35.1 | 83 | 166 | 28 | 25 | 10 | 5 | 3 | 2 | 30 | 2 | 23 | 4 | 1 |
| Spillner, Daniel, Chicago | 4 | 3 | .571 | 3.44 | 48 | 0 | 0 | 0 | 15 | 1 | 91.2 | 76 | 378 | 39 | 35 | 7 | 0 | 4 | 2 | 29 | 3 | 41 | 5 | 1 |
| Stanley, Robert, Boston | 6 | 6 | .500 | 2.87 | 48 | 0 | 0 | 0 | 41 | 10 | 87.2 | 86 | 360 | 30 | 28 | 6 | 3 | 2 | 1 | 37 | 10 | 46 | 4 | 0 |
| Stanton, Michael, Seattle-Chicago | 3 | 9 | .250 | 6.42 | 42 | 0 | 0 | 0 | 16 | 4 | 40.2 | 47 | 200 | 34 | 29 | 13 | 5 | 5 | 9 | 30 | 3 | 29 | 2 | 0 |
| Stewart, David, Texas | 0 | 6 | .000 | 5.42 | 42 | 5 | 0 | 0 | 29 | 9 | 81.1 | 86 | 361 | 53 | 49 | 15 | 5 | 2 | 0 | 37 | 10 | 64 | 0 | 0 |
| Stewart, Samuel, Baltimore | 5 | 0 | 1.000 | 3.61 | 36 | 1 | 0 | 0 | 36 | 0 | 129.2 | 117 | 557 | 60 | 52 | 22 | 14 | 5 | 0 | 66 | 3 | 77 | 6 | 0 |
| Stieb, David, Toronto | 14 | 13 | .519 | 2.48 | 36 | 36 | 8 | 2 | 0 | 0 | 265.0 | 206 | 1087 | 89 | 73 | 12 | 2 | 4 | 0 | 96 | 3 | 167 | 0 | 0 |
| Stoddard, Robert, Detroit | 0 | 1 | .000 | 6.75 | 8 | 0 | 0 | 0 | 3 | 1 | 13.1 | 15 | 61 | 11 | 10 | 3 | 1 | 0 | 0 | 3 | 0 | 11 | 0 | 0 |
| Surhoff, Richard, Texas | 0 | 1 | .000 | 7.56 | 7 | 0 | 0 | 0 | 5 | 2 | 8.1 | 12 | 39 | 17 | 7 | 2 | 0 | 0 | 0 | 5 | 0 | 8 | 0 | 0 |
| Sutton, Donald, Oakland-California | 15 | 10 | .600 | 3.86 | 34 | 34 | 1 | 1 | 0 | 0 | 226.0 | 221 | 943 | 101 | 97 | 25 | 4 | 5 | 0 | 59 | 0 | 107 | 6 | 0 |

| Pitcher and Club | W. | L. | Pct. | ERA. | G. | GS. | CG. | ShO. | GF. | Sv. | IP. | H. | BFP. | R. | ER. | HR. | SH. | SF. | HB. | Tot. BB. | Int. BB. | SO. | WP. | Bk. |
|---|---|---|---|---|---|---|---|---|---|---|---|---|---|---|---|---|---|---|---|---|---|---|---|---|
| Swaggerty, William, Baltimore | 0 | 0 | .000 | 5.40 | 1 | 0 | 0 | 0 | 0 | 0 | 1.2 | 3 | 10 | 1 | 1 | 0 | 0 | 0 | 0 | 1 | 1 | 2 | 0 | 0 |
| Swift, William, Seattle | 6 | 10 | .375 | 4.77 | 23 | 21 | 0 | 0 | 0 | 0 | 120.2 | 131 | 532 | 71 | 64 | 8 | 6 | 3 | 5 | 48 | 5 | 55 | 5 | 3 |
| Tanana, Frank, Texas-Detroit* | 12 | 14 | .462 | 4.27 | 33 | 33 | 4 | 0 | 0 | 0 | 215.0 | 220 | 907 | 112 | 102 | 28 | 8 | 1 | 3 | 57 | 5 | 159 | 5 | 1 |
| Tanner, Bruce, Chicago | 1 | 2 | .333 | 5.33 | 10 | 4 | 0 | 0 | 3 | 0 | 27.0 | 34 | 128 | 17 | 16 | 3 | 5 | 1 | 1 | 13 | 3 | 9 | 0 | 0 |
| Tellmann, Thomas, Oakland | 0 | 0 | .000 | 5.06 | 11 | 0 | 0 | 0 | 3 | 0 | 21.1 | 33 | 106 | 12 | 12 | 3 | 2 | 1 | 4 | 9 | 1 | 9 | 0 | 0 |
| Terrell, C. Walter, Detroit | 15 | 10 | .600 | 3.85 | 34 | 34 | 5 | 3 | 0 | 0 | 229.0 | 221 | 983 | 107 | 98 | 9 | 11 | 7 | 2 | 95 | 1 | 130 | 5 | 0 |
| Thomas, Roy, Seattle | 7 | 8 | .467 | 3.36 | 40 | 0 | 0 | 0 | 9 | 1 | 93.1 | 66 | 385 | 37 | 35 | 8 | 5 | 2 | 6 | 48 | 5 | 70 | 4 | 2 |
| Thompson, Richard, Cleveland | 3 | 0 | 1.000 | 6.30 | 57 | 0 | 0 | 0 | 24 | 5 | 80.0 | 95 | 379 | 63 | 56 | 8 | 5 | 7 | 0 | 48 | 12 | 30 | 6 | 2 |
| Tobik, David, Seattle | 1 | 0 | 1.000 | 6.00 | 8 | 0 | 0 | 0 | 4 | 1 | 9.0 | 10 | 40 | 10 | 6 | 0 | 1 | 0 | 3 | 3 | 6 | 8 | 1 | 0 |
| Trujillo, Michael, Boston | 4 | 4 | .500 | 4.82 | 27 | 7 | 0 | 0 | 7 | 1 | 84.0 | 112 | 379 | 55 | 45 | 7 | 2 | 2 | 1 | 23 | 1 | 19 | 1 | 0 |
| Vande Berg, Edward, Seattle* | 2 | 1 | .667 | 3.72 | 76 | 0 | 0 | 0 | 22 | 8 | 67.2 | 71 | 296 | 30 | 28 | 4 | 1 | 3 | 0 | 31 | 3 | 34 | 4 | 2 |
| Viola, Frank, Minnesota* | 18 | 14 | .563 | 4.09 | 36 | 36 | 4 | 0 | 0 | 0 | 250.2 | 262 | 1059 | 136 | 114 | 26 | 5 | 5 | 7 | 68 | 1 | 135 | 6 | 0 |
| Von Ohlen, David, Cleveland* | 3 | 0 | 1.000 | 2.91 | 26 | 0 | 0 | 0 | 9 | 1 | 43.1 | 47 | 196 | 20 | 14 | 2 | 9 | 4 | 1 | 20 | 3 | 12 | 0 | 0 |
| Vuckovich, Peter, Milwaukee | 6 | 6 | .500 | 5.51 | 26 | 22 | 1 | 0 | 0 | 0 | 112.2 | 134 | 511 | 74 | 69 | 16 | 5 | 1 | 0 | 48 | 6 | 55 | 5 | 0 |
| Waddell, Thomas, Cleveland | 8 | 10 | .444 | 4.87 | 49 | 9 | 0 | 0 | 28 | 9 | 112.2 | 104 | 471 | 61 | 61 | 20 | 2 | 1 | 2 | 39 | 8 | 53 | 3 | 0 |
| Waits, M. Richard, Milwaukee* | 3 | 2 | .600 | 6.51 | 24 | 0 | 0 | 0 | 8 | 1 | 47.0 | 67 | 220 | 37 | 34 | 3 | 6 | 6 | 4 | 20 | 5 | 24 | 1 | 1 |
| Wardle, Curtis, Minnesota-Cleveland* | 8 | 9 | .471 | 6.18 | 50 | 12 | 0 | 0 | 13 | 0 | 115.0 | 127 | 523 | 83 | 79 | 20 | 6 | 6 | 0 | 62 | 0 | 84 | 3 | 1 |
| Warren, Michael, Oakland | 2 | 4 | .333 | 6.61 | 16 | 6 | 0 | 0 | 2 | 0 | 49.0 | 52 | 243 | 42 | 36 | 13 | 1 | 0 | 3 | 38 | 6 | 48 | 3 | 1 |
| Wegman, William, Milwaukee | 2 | 2 | .500 | 3.57 | 3 | 3 | 0 | 0 | 0 | 0 | 17.2 | 17 | 73 | 8 | 7 | 3 | 1 | 0 | 0 | 3 | 0 | 6 | 0 | 0 |
| Wehrmeister, David, Chicago | 2 | 5 | .286 | 3.43 | 23 | 6 | 0 | 0 | 4 | 2 | 39.1 | 35 | 159 | 15 | 15 | 3 | 4 | 7 | 4 | 10 | 0 | 32 | 5 | 0 |
| Welsh, Christopher, Texas* | 0 | 2 | .000 | 4.13 | 25 | 0 | 0 | 0 | 4 | 0 | 76.1 | 101 | 351 | 40 | 35 | 11 | 1 | 0 | 0 | 25 | 3 | 31 | 1 | 0 |
| Whitehouse, Leonard, Minnesota* | 0 | 5 | .000 | 11.05 | 5 | 0 | 0 | 0 | 0 | 1 | 7.1 | 12 | 36 | 9 | 9 | 4 | 0 | 0 | 0 | 2 | 0 | 4 | 2 | 0 |
| Whitson, Eddie, New York | 10 | 8 | .556 | 4.88 | 30 | 30 | 2 | 0 | 0 | 0 | 158.2 | 201 | 705 | 100 | 86 | 19 | 3 | 8 | 7 | 43 | 2 | 89 | 0 | 1 |
| Wilcox, Milton, Detroit | 1 | 3 | .250 | 4.85 | 8 | 8 | 0 | 0 | 0 | 0 | 39.0 | 51 | 177 | 24 | 21 | 6 | 1 | 5 | 2 | 14 | 0 | 20 | 2 | 1 |
| Wilkinson, William, Seattle* | 2 | 1 | .667 | 13.50 | 6 | 2 | 0 | 0 | 1 | 0 | 6.0 | 8 | 30 | 9 | 9 | 2 | 0 | 0 | 0 | 6 | 2 | 5 | 0 | 0 |
| Williams, Matthew, Texas | 2 | 1 | .667 | 2.42 | 24 | 2 | 0 | 0 | 2 | 0 | 26.0 | 20 | 106 | 7 | 7 | 3 | 4 | 8 | 0 | 10 | 0 | 22 | 2 | 0 |
| Wills, Frank, Seattle | 5 | 11 | .313 | 6.00 | 35 | 5 | 0 | 0 | 3 | 2 | 123.0 | 122 | 541 | 85 | 82 | 18 | 4 | 5 | 3 | 68 | 3 | 67 | 9 | 0 |
| Witt, Michael, California | 15 | 9 | .625 | 3.56 | 35 | 35 | 6 | 2 | 0 | 0 | 250.0 | 228 | 1049 | 115 | 99 | 22 | 4 | 4 | 4 | 98 | 6 | 180 | 11 | 0 |
| Woodward, Robert, Boston | 0 | 0 | .000 | 1.69 | 5 | 2 | 0 | 0 | 1 | 0 | 26.2 | 17 | 113 | 8 | 5 | 4 | 1 | 2 | 2 | 5 | 0 | 16 | 1 | 0 |
| Wright, J. Richard, Texas* | 0 | 1 | .000 | 4.70 | 5 | 1 | 0 | 0 | 0 | 0 | 7.2 | 5 | 32 | 4 | 4 | 0 | 0 | 0 | 0 | 2 | 1 | 7 | 0 | 0 |
| Yett, Richard, Minnesota | 0 | 0 | .000 | 27.00 | 1 | 0 | 0 | 0 | 0 | 0 | 0.1 | 3 | 5 | 1 | 1 | 0 | 0 | 1 | 0 | 1 | 0 | 0 | 0 | 0 |
| Young, Curtis, Oakland* | 0 | 4 | .000 | 7.24 | 19 | 7 | 0 | 0 | 5 | 0 | 46.0 | 57 | 214 | 38 | 37 | 15 | 7 | 3 | 1 | 22 | 0 | 19 | 1 | 0 |
| Young, Matthew, Seattle* | 12 | 19 | .387 | 4.91 | 37 | 34 | 5 | 2 | 0 | 0 | 218.1 | 242 | 951 | 135 | 119 | 23 | 5 | 7 | 7 | 76 | 3 | 136 | 6 | 2 |
| Zahn, Geoffrey, California* | 2 | 2 | .500 | 4.38 | 7 | 7 | 1 | 1 | 0 | 0 | 37.0 | 44 | 164 | 19 | 18 | 5 | 2 | 1 | 3 | 14 | 0 | 14 | 1 | 0 |

NOTE—Following pitchers combined to pitch shutout games: Boston (3)—Ojeda and Crawford 2; Kison and Crawford. California (3)—Romanick and Moore; Candelaria and Cliburn; Sutton, Cliburn and Moore. Chicago (2)—Burns, Nelson, Agosto and James; Seaver and James. Cleveland (2)—Ruhle, Von Ohlen and Waddell; Romero and Clark. Detroit (4)—Terrell and Hernandez 2; O'Neal and Hernandez; Petry and Hernandez. Kansas City (2)—Saberhagen and Quisenberry 2. Minnesota (1)—Smithson and Eufemia. New York (4)—P. Niekro, Guidry and Cooper; P. Niekro and Righetti; Cowley and Righetti; Guidry and Fisher. Oakland (5)—Birtsas, Atherton and Howell; Birtsas and Ontiveros; Sutton and Ontiveros; John and Ontiveros; Rijo and Howell. Seattle (3)—Wills and Nunez; Swift, R. Thomas and Nunez; Wills and Vande Berg. Texas (2)—Williams and Surhoff; Guzman and Henry. Toronto (6)—Alexander, Caudill and Lavelle; Stieb, Musselman and Caudill; Alexander and Lavelle; Key; Lavelle and Acker; Stieb and Acker; Filer, Davis, Lamp and Caudill.

## PITCHERS WITH TWO OR MORE CLUBS
(Alphabetically arranged with pitcher's first club on top)

| Pitcher and Club | W. | L. | Pct. | ERA. | G. | GS. | CG. | ShO. | GF. | Sv. | IP. | H. | BFP. | R. | ER. | HR. | SH. | SF. | HB. | Tot. BB. | Int. BB. | SO. | WP. | Bk. |
|---|---|---|---|---|---|---|---|---|---|---|---|---|---|---|---|---|---|---|---|---|---|---|---|---|
| Byleven, Rikalbert, Cleveland | 9 | 11 | .450 | 3.26 | 23 | 23 | 15 | 4 | 0 | 0 | 179.2 | 163 | 743 | 76 | 65 | 14 | 4 | 4 | 7 | 49 | 1 | 129 | 1 | 1 |
| Byleven, Rikalbert, Minnesota | 8 | 5 | .615 | 3.00 | 14 | 14 | 9 | 1 | 0 | 0 | 114.0 | 101 | 460 | 45 | 38 | 9 | 1 | 4 | 2 | 26 | 0 | 77 | 3 | 0 |
| John, Thomas, California | 2 | 4 | .333 | 4.70 | 12 | 6 | 0 | 0 | 2 | 0 | 38.1 | 51 | 176 | 22 | 20 | 3 | 3 | 2 | 1 | 15 | 1 | 17 | 5 | 0 |
| John, Thomas, Oakland | 2 | 6 | .250 | 6.19 | 11 | 11 | 0 | 0 | 0 | 0 | 48.0 | 66 | 221 | 37 | 33 | 6 | 6 | 1 | 1 | 13 | 0 | 8 | 2 | 0 |
| Lollar, W. Timothy, Chicago | 3 | 5 | .375 | 4.66 | 18 | 13 | 0 | 0 | 3 | 0 | 83.0 | 83 | 378 | 48 | 43 | 10 | 3 | 4 | 1 | 58 | 1 | 61 | 5 | 2 |
| Lollar, W. Timothy, Boston | 5 | 5 | .500 | 4.57 | 16 | 10 | 1 | 0 | 4 | 1 | 67.0 | 57 | 291 | 37 | 34 | 9 | 1 | 1 | 1 | 40 | 0 | 44 | 5 | 0 |
| Murray, Dale, New York | 0 | 0 | .000 | 13.50 | 3 | 0 | 0 | 0 | 2 | 0 | 2.0 | 4 | 10 | 3 | 3 | 0 | 0 | 0 | 0 | 0 | 0 | 0 | 1 | 0 |
| Murray, Dale, Texas | 0 | 0 | .000 | 18.00 | 1 | 0 | 0 | 0 | 0 | 0 | 1.0 | 3 | 5 | 2 | 2 | 0 | 1 | 0 | 0 | 0 | 0 | 0 | 0 | 0 |
| Stanton, Michael, Seattle | 1 | 2 | .333 | 5.28 | 24 | 0 | 0 | 0 | 11 | 1 | 29.0 | 32 | 140 | 20 | 17 | 4 | 1 | 0 | 3 | 21 | 3 | 17 | 2 | 0 |
| Stanton, Michael, Chicago | 0 | 1 | .000 | 9.26 | 11 | 0 | 0 | 0 | 5 | 0 | 11.2 | 15 | 60 | 14 | 12 | 2 | 0 | 1 | 0 | 8 | 3 | 12 | 1 | 0 |
| Sutton, Donald, Oakland | 13 | 8 | .619 | 3.89 | 29 | 29 | 1 | 1 | 0 | 0 | 194.1 | 194 | 819 | 88 | 84 | 19 | 4 | 5 | 3 | 51 | 0 | 91 | 6 | 0 |
| Sutton, Donald, California | 2 | 2 | .500 | 3.69 | 5 | 5 | 0 | 0 | 0 | 0 | 31.2 | 27 | 124 | 13 | 13 | 6 | 0 | 0 | 0 | 8 | 0 | 16 | 0 | 0 |
| Tanana, Frank, Texas | 2 | 7 | .222 | 5.91 | 13 | 13 | 0 | 0 | 0 | 0 | 77.2 | 89 | 340 | 53 | 51 | 15 | 2 | 4 | 4 | 23 | 2 | 52 | 3 | 1 |
| Tanana, Frank, Detroit | 10 | 7 | .588 | 3.34 | 20 | 20 | 4 | 0 | 0 | 0 | 137.1 | 131 | 567 | 59 | 51 | 13 | 3 | 4 | 2 | 34 | 6 | 107 | 2 | 1 |
| Wardle, Curtis, Minnesota | 1 | 3 | .250 | 5.51 | 35 | 0 | 0 | 0 | 13 | 1 | 49.0 | 49 | 218 | 32 | 30 | 9 | 4 | 1 | 1 | 28 | 0 | 47 | 1 | 1 |
| Wardle, Curtis, Cleveland | 7 | 6 | .538 | 6.68 | 15 | 12 | 0 | 0 | 0 | 0 | 66.0 | 78 | 305 | 51 | 49 | 11 | 2 | 5 | 1 | 34 | 0 | 37 | 2 | 0 |

# 1985 A.L. Pitching Against Each Club

## BALTIMORE—83-78

| Pitcher | Bos. W-L | Cal. W-L | Chi. W-L | Clev. W-L | Det. W-L | K.C. W-L | Mil. W-L | Min. W-L | N.Y. W-L | Oak. W-L | Sea. W-L | Tex. W-L | Tor. W-L | Totals W-L |
|---|---|---|---|---|---|---|---|---|---|---|---|---|---|---|
| Aase .......... | 0-0 | 1-0 | 0-2 | 2-0 | 2-0 | 0-0 | 0-0 | 2-1 | 0-2 | 1-0 | 0-1 | 1-0 | 1-0 | 10-6 |
| Boddicker... | 1-2 | 0-1 | 2-1 | 0-1 | 0-2 | 1-1 | 1-1 | 3-1 | 0-1 | 1-3 | 1-0 | 2-0 | 0-3 | 12-17 |
| Davis.......... | 1-2 | 1-0 | 1-0 | 0-0 | 0-0 | 0-2 | 1-0 | 0-1 | 0-2 | 1-0 | 2-0 | 3-0 | 0-1 | 10-8 |
| Dixon ......... | 1-0 | 0-1 | 2-0 | 1-0 | 0-0 | 1-0 | 1-0 | 0-1 | 0-1 | 0-1 | 1-0 | 1-0 | 0-0 | 8-4 |
| Flanagan .... | 0-0 | 0-0 | 1-0 | 1-0 | 1-0 | 0-1 | 0-1 | 0-0 | 1-0 | 0-1 | 0-1 | 0-1 | 0-0 | 4-5 |
| Habyan ...... | 1-0 | 0-0 | 0-0 | 0-0 | 0-0 | 0-0 | 0-0 | 0-0 | 0-0 | 0-0 | 0-0 | 0-0 | 0-0 | 1-0 |
| Havens....... | 0-0 | 0-0 | 0-0 | 0-0 | 0-0 | 0-0 | 0-0 | 0-0 | 0-1 | 0-0 | 0-0 | 0-0 | 0-0 | 0-1 |
| T. Martinez | 0-0 | 0-1 | 0-0 | 0-0 | 1-0 | 1-0 | 0-0 | 0-0 | 0-0 | 0-0 | 0-0 | 0-0 | 1-1 | 3-3 |
| D. Martinez | 1-2 | 3-1 | 0-1 | 2-1 | 0-1 | 1-0 | 1-0 | 0-1 | 0-2 | 1-0 | 2-1 | 1-0 | 1-1 | 13-11 |
| McGregor... | 0-1 | 1-1 | 1-0 | 0-2 | 2-1 | 2-2 | 3-1 | 0-1 | 0-2 | 3-0 | 0-1 | 1-1 | 1-1 | 14-14 |
| Snell .......... | 0-0 | 0-0 | 0-0 | 0-0 | 0-0 | 0-0 | 2-0 | 1-0 | 0-0 | 0-0 | 0-0 | 0-0 | 0-0 | 3-2 |
| Stewart ..... | 0-1 | 1-0 | 1-0 | 2-0 | 0-3 | 0-0 | 0-1 | 0-0 | 0-1 | 0-0 | 0-0 | 1-0 | 0-1 | 5-7 |
| Totals .... | 5-8 | 7-5 | 8-4 | 8-5 | 6-7 | 6-6 | 9-4 | 6-6 | 1-12 | 7-5 | 6-6 | 10-2 | 4-8 | 83-78 |

No Decisions—Bell, Huffman, Swaggerty.

## BOSTON—81-81

| Pitcher | Balt. W-L | Cal. W-L | Chi. W-L | Clev. W-L | Det. W-L | K.C. W-L | Mil. W-L | Min. W-L | N.Y. W-L | Oak. W-L | Sea. W-L | Tex. W-L | Tor. W-L | Totals W-L |
|---|---|---|---|---|---|---|---|---|---|---|---|---|---|---|
| Boyd .......... | 2-1 | 1-2 | 1-1 | 2-1 | 2-2 | 0-1 | 0-1 | 1-0 | 1-1 | 2-0 | 1-1 | 0-2 | 2-0 | 15-13 |
| Clear.......... | 0-0 | 0-0 | 0-0 | 0-0 | 0-0 | 0-1 | 0-0 | 0-0 | 0-1 | 1-0 | 0-0 | 0-1 | 0-0 | 1-3 |
| Clemens...... | 0-0 | 1-0 | 0-1 | 1-0 | 0-0 | 2-1 | 0-0 | 2-0 | 1-1 | 0-1 | 0-1 | 0-0 | 0-0 | 7-5 |
| Crawford.... | 0-1 | 0-1 | 2-1 | 0-0 | 0-0 | 0-0 | 0-0 | 0-1 | 1-1 | 1-0 | 0-0 | 0-0 | 2-0 | 6-5 |
| Dorsey....... | 0-0 | 0-1 | 0-0 | 0-0 | 0-0 | 0-0 | 0-0 | 0-0 | 0-0 | 0-0 | 0-0 | 0-0 | 0-0 | 0-1 |
| Hurst ......... | 2-1 | 1-0 | 0-0 | 1-1 | 0-2 | 1-0 | 1-2 | 0-1 | 1-2 | 2-2 | 0-1 | 2-0 | 0-1 | 11-13 |
| Kison ......... | 1-0 | 0-0 | 0-1 | 1-0 | 0-0 | 0-0 | 1-0 | 1-0 | 0-0 | 0-0 | 0-1 | 1-0 | 0-1 | 5-3 |
| Lollar ......... | 0-0 | 0-0 | 1-0 | 1-1 | 1-0 | 0-0 | 0-1 | 0-1 | 0-1 | 1-0 | 0-1 | 1-0 | 0-0 | 5-5 |
| Nipper........ | 1-1 | 1-0 | 0-1 | 1-0 | 1-1 | 0-2 | 1-0 | 0-2 | 0-1 | 0-0 | 3-1 | 0-2 | 1-1 | 9-12 |
| Ojeda ........ | 2-1 | 0-3 | 0-0 | 1-1 | 1-2 | 1-1 | 1-1 | 1-0 | 1-0 | 0-1 | 1-0 | 0-1 | 0-0 | 9-11 |
| Sellers ....... | 0-0 | 0-0 | 0-0 | 0-0 | 0-0 | 0-0 | 1-0 | 0-0 | 0-0 | 0-0 | 0-0 | 0-0 | 1-0 | 2-0 |
| Stanley ...... | 0-0 | 1-0 | 0-2 | 0-0 | 0-0 | 1-1 | 0-1 | 1-0 | 0-0 | 1-0 | 0-1 | 0-0 | 2-1 | 6-6 |
| Trujillo....... | 0-0 | 0-0 | 0-1 | 0-1 | 0-0 | 0-0 | 0-2 | 1-0 | 0-0 | 0-0 | 1-0 | 1-0 | 1-0 | 4-4 |
| Woodward . | 0-0 | 0-0 | 0-0 | 0-0 | 1-0 | 0-0 | 0-0 | 0-0 | 0-0 | 0-0 | 0-0 | 0-0 | 0-0 | 1-0 |
| Totals .... | 8-5 | 5-7 | 4-8 | 8-5 | 6-7 | 5-7 | 5-8 | 7-5 | 5-8 | 8-4 | 6-6 | 5-7 | 9-4 | 81-81 |

No Decisions—Brown, McCarthy, Mitchell.

## CALIFORNIA—90-72

| Pitcher | Balt. W-L | Bos. W-L | Chi. W-L | Clev. W-L | Det. W-L | K.C. W-L | Mil. W-L | Min. W-L | N.Y. W-L | Oak. W-L | Sea. W-L | Tex. W-L | Tor. W-L | otals W-L |
|---|---|---|---|---|---|---|---|---|---|---|---|---|---|---|
| Candelaria .. | 0-1 | 0-0 | 1-1 | 0-0 | 1-0 | 1-1 | 0-0 | 1-0 | 1-0 | 1-0 | 0-0 | 1-0 | 0-0 | 7-3 |
| Clements .... | 1-0 | 2-0 | 0-0 | 0-0 | 1-0 | 0-0 | 0-0 | 0-0 | 0-0 | 0-0 | 0-0 | 0-0 | 1-0 | 5-0 |
| Cliburn ....... | 1-1 | 1-1 | 0-0 | 2-1 | 1-0 | 0-0 | 0-0 | 2-0 | 0-0 | 0-0 | 1-0 | 0-0 | 1-0 | 9-3 |
| Corbett ...... | 0-0 | 0-0 | 0-0 | 1-0 | 0-0 | 0-1 | 0-0 | 1-0 | 0-1 | 0-0 | 1-0 | 0-1 | 0-0 | 3-3 |
| Holland ...... | 0-0 | 0-0 | 0-0 | 0-0 | 0-0 | 0-0 | 0-0 | 0-0 | 0-0 | 0-0 | 0-0 | 0-0 | 0-0 | 0-1 |
| John........... | 0-1 | 0-0 | 0-0 | 0-0 | 0-0 | 0-0 | 1-1 | 0-0 | 0-1 | 0-1 | 1-0 | 0-0 | 0-0 | 2-4 |
| Kipper ........ | 0-0 | 0-0 | 0-0 | 0-0 | 0-0 | 0-0 | 0-0 | 0-0 | 0-0 | 0-1 | 0-0 | 0-0 | 0-0 | 0-1 |
| Lugo .......... | 0-0 | 0-1 | 2-0 | 0-0 | 0-0 | 1-0 | 0-0 | 0-0 | 0-0 | 0-1 | 0-0 | 0-1 | 0-1 | 3-4 |
| Mack .......... | 0-0 | 0-0 | 0-0 | 0-0 | 0-0 | 0-0 | 0-0 | 0-0 | 0-0 | 0-0 | 0-0 | 0-0 | 0-1 | 0-1 |
| McCaskill.... | 0-1 | 1-2 | 1-1 | 2-0 | 0-2 | 0-1 | 1-1 | 2-0 | 0-1 | 1-0 | 0-0 | 3-1 | 1-2 | 12-12 |
| Moore......... | 1-2 | 0-0 | 1-0 | 0-0 | 1-1 | 0-0 | 2-0 | 1-1 | 0-1 | 0-2 | 0-1 | 1-0 | 1-0 | 8-8 |
| Romanick .... | 1-1 | 2-0 | 1-1 | 1-0 | 1-0 | 1-0 | 1-3 | 4-0 | 0-1 | 0-1 | 2-1 | 1-1 | 0-0 | 14-9 |
| Sanchez...... | 0-0 | 0-0 | 0-0 | 1-0 | 1-0 | 0-0 | 0-0 | 0-0 | 0-0 | 0-0 | 0-0 | 0-0 | 0-0 | 2-0 |
| Slaton........ | 0-0 | 0-1 | 0-0 | 0-2 | 1-0 | 0-1 | 0-1 | 1-0 | 1-2 | 1-0 | 2-0 | 0-1 | 0-2 | 6-10 |
| Sutton........ | 0-0 | 0-0 | 1-1 | 0-0 | 0-0 | 0-1 | 0-0 | 0-0 | 0-0 | 0-0 | 0-0 | 1-0 | 0-0 | 2-2 |
| Witt........... | 1-0 | 1-0 | 1-1 | 1-1 | 1-1 | 1-1 | 1-0 | 0-1 | 1-1 | 1-1 | 2-1 | 3-0 | 1-1 | 15-9 |
| Zahn .......... | 0-0 | 0-0 | 0-0 | 0-0 | 0-0 | 0-0 | 0-0 | 1-1 | 0-0 | 0-0 | 1-1 | 0-0 | 0-0 | 2-2 |
| Totals .... | 5-7 | 7-5 | 8-5 | 8-4 | 8-4 | 4-9 | 9-3 | 9-4 | 3-9 | 6-7 | 9-4 | 9-4 | 5-7 | 90-72 |

No Decisions—Fowlkes, Smith.

## CHICAGO—85-77

| Pitcher | Balt. W-L | Bos. W-L | Cal. W-L | Clev. W-L | Det. W-L | K.C. W-L | Mil. W-L | Min. W-L | N.Y. W-L | Oak. W-L | Sea. W-L | Tex. W-L | Tor. W-L | Totals W-L |
|---|---|---|---|---|---|---|---|---|---|---|---|---|---|---|
| Agosto........ | 1-0 | 0-1 | 0-0 | 1-0 | 0-0 | 0-0 | 0-2 | 0-0 | 1-0 | 0-0 | 0-0 | 1-0 | 0-0 | 4-3 |
| Bannister.... | 0-3 | 0-1 | 0-1 | 1-0 | 1-0 | 1-1 | 0-1 | 1-1 | 0-2 | 2-1 | 2-2 | 1-0 | 1-1 | 10-14 |
| Burns......... | 1-2 | 2-0 | 1-1 | 4-0 | 1-0 | 0-1 | 1-1 | 2-2 | 2-0 | 0-1 | 0-0 | 2-2 | 2-1 | 18-11 |
| Correa........ | 0-0 | 0-0 | 0-0 | 0-0 | 0-0 | 0-0 | 0-0 | 0-0 | 0-0 | 0-0 | 1-0 | 0-0 | 0-0 | 1-0 |
| Davis.......... | 0-0 | 0-0 | 0-0 | 0-0 | 0-0 | 0-1 | 1-0 | 1-1 | 0-0 | 0-0 | 0-0 | 1-0 | 0-1 | 3-3 |
| Dotson....... | 0-0 | 0-0 | 0-0 | 0-0 | 1-1 | 1-0 | 1-0 | 0-1 | 0-0 | 0-0 | 0-0 | 1-0 | 0-2 | 3-4 |
| Gleaton....... | 0-0 | 0-0 | 0-0 | 0-0 | 0-0 | 0-0 | 0-0 | 0-0 | 0-0 | 0-0 | 1-0 | 0-0 | 0-0 | 1-0 |
| James......... | 0-0 | 1-0 | 0-0 | 1-0 | 0-1 | 2-2 | 1-1 | 0-0 | 0-1 | 3-0 | 0-1 | 0-0 | 0-1 | 8-7 |
| Jones.......... | 0-0 | 1-0 | 0-0 | 0-0 | 0-0 | 0-0 | 0-0 | 0-0 | 0-0 | 0-0 | 0-0 | 0-0 | 0-0 | 1-0 |
| Lollar ......... | 0-0 | 1-0 | 0-2 | 0-1 | 0-1 | 0-0 | 0-1 | 0-0 | 0-0 | 0-0 | 2-0 | 0-0 | 0-0 | 3-5 |
| Long .......... | 0-0 | 0-0 | 0-0 | 0-0 | 0-0 | 0-0 | 0-0 | 0-0 | 0-0 | 0-1 | 0-0 | 0-0 | 0-0 | 0-1 |

| Pitcher | Balt. W-L | Bos. W-L | Cal. W-L | Clev. W-L | Det. W-L | K.C. W-L | Mil. W-L | Min. W-L | N.Y. W-L | Oak. W-L | Sea. W-L | Tex. W-L | Tor. W-L | Totals W-L |
|---|---|---|---|---|---|---|---|---|---|---|---|---|---|---|
| Nelson | 0-2 | 1-2 | 1-2 | 1-0 | 2-0 | 0-1 | 0-0 | 1-0 | 1-1 | 1-1 | 0-0 | 2-0 | 0-1 | 10-10 |
| Seaver | 2-0 | 1-0 | 2-1 | 2-0 | 1-3 | 1-2 | 1-0 | 1-1 | 2-0 | 1-1 | 1-0 | 1-1 | 0-2 | 16-11 |
| Spillner | 0-0 | 0-0 | 1-0 | 0-1 | 0-0 | 0-0 | 1-0 | 0-0 | 0-1 | 1-0 | 0-1 | 1-0 | 0-0 | 4-3 |
| Stanton | 0-1 | 0-0 | 0-0 | 0-0 | 0-0 | 0-0 | 0-0 | 0-0 | 0-0 | 0-0 | 0-0 | 0-0 | 0-0 | 0-1 |
| Tanner | 0-0 | 0-0 | 0-1 | 0-0 | 0-0 | 0-0 | 0-0 | 0-1 | 0-0 | 0-0 | 1-0 | 0-0 | 0-0 | 1-2 |
| Wehrm'st'r | 0-0 | 1-0 | 0-0 | 0-0 | 0-0 | 0-0 | 0-1 | 0-0 | 0-0 | 0-1 | 1-0 | 0-0 | 0-0 | 2-2 |
| Totals | 4-8 | 8-4 | 5-8 | 10-2 | 6-6 | 5-8 | 5-7 | 6-7 | 6-6 | 8-5 | 9-4 | 10-3 | 3-9 | 85-77 |

No Decisions—Fallon, Fireovid.

## CLEVELAND—60-102

| Pitcher | Balt. W-L | Bos. W-L | Cal. W-L | Chi. W-L | Det. W-L | K.C. W-L | Mil. W-L | Min. W-L | N.Y. W-L | Oak. W-L | Sea. W-L | Tex. W-L | Tor. W-L | Totals W-L |
|---|---|---|---|---|---|---|---|---|---|---|---|---|---|---|
| Barkley | 0-0 | 0-0 | 0-1 | 0-0 | 0-0 | 0-0 | 0-0 | 0-0 | 0-0 | 0-1 | 0-1 | 0-0 | 0-0 | 0-3 |
| Behenna | 0-0 | 0-0 | 0-0 | 0-0 | 0-0 | 0-0 | 0-0 | 0-0 | 0-0 | 0-1 | 0-0 | 0-0 | 0-1 | 0-2 |
| Blyleven | 0-0 | 0-1 | 2-0 | 0-3 | 0-1 | 0-1 | 1-1 | 0-0 | 0-2 | 1-0 | 1-1 | 4-0 | 0-1 | 9-11 |
| Camacho | 0-0 | 0-0 | 0-0 | 0-0 | 0-1 | 0-0 | 0-0 | 0-0 | 0-0 | 0-0 | 0-0 | 0-0 | 0-0 | 0-1 |
| Clark | 0-1 | 0-0 | 0-1 | 0-1 | 0-0 | 0-0 | 0-0 | 1-0 | 0-0 | 0-0 | 1-0 | 0-0 | 1-1 | 3-4 |
| Creel | 0-0 | 0-1 | 0-0 | 0-0 | 0-0 | 0-1 | 0-0 | 0-1 | 0-0 | 1-0 | 1-0 | 0-0 | 0-2 | 2-5 |
| Easterly | 0-0 | 2-0 | 0-0 | 0-0 | 2-0 | 0-0 | 0-0 | 0-1 | 0-0 | 0-0 | 0-0 | 0-0 | 0-0 | 4-1 |
| Heaton | 0-0 | 1-2 | 1-3 | 0-2 | 1-1 | 0-2 | 1-2 | 0-1 | 1-0 | 0-2 | 0-1 | 2-1 | 2-0 | 9-17 |
| Reed | 0-0 | 0-1 | 1-0 | 0-1 | 0-0 | 0-1 | 0-0 | 1-0 | 1-1 | 0-0 | 0-0 | 0-1 | 0-0 | 3-5 |
| Roman | 0-2 | 0-0 | 0-0 | 0-0 | 0-0 | 0-0 | 0-0 | 0-0 | 0-1 | 0-1 | 0-0 | 0-0 | 0-0 | 0-4 |
| Romero | 0-0 | 0-1 | 0-0 | 0-0 | 0-1 | 0-1 | 1-0 | 0-0 | 1-0 | 0-0 | 0-0 | 0-0 | 0-0 | 2-3 |
| Ruhle | 1-2 | 0-0 | 0-0 | 0-1 | 0-2 | 0-2 | 0-0 | 1-0 | 0-0 | 0-2 | 0-0 | 0-1 | 0-0 | 2-10 |
| Schulze | 1-0 | 0-1 | 0-1 | 0-0 | 1-0 | 1-1 | 0-1 | 0-2 | 0-0 | 0-1 | 1-1 | 0-2 | 0-0 | 4-10 |
| Smith | 0-0 | 0-0 | 0-0 | 0-0 | 0-0 | 0-0 | 0-1 | 0-1 | 1-0 | 0-0 | 0-1 | 0-0 | 0-1 | 1-4 |
| Thompson | 0-2 | 1-0 | 0-0 | 1-2 | 0-0 | 0-0 | 0-0 | 0-1 | 0-1 | 0-0 | 1-1 | 0-0 | 0-1 | 3-8 |
| Von Ohlen | 1-0 | 0-0 | 0-1 | 0-0 | 0-1 | 0-0 | 1-0 | 0-0 | 1-0 | 0-0 | 0-0 | 0-0 | 0-0 | 3-2 |
| Waddell | 0-1 | 0-0 | 0-0 | 1-0 | 0-0 | 1-0 | 1-1 | 1-1 | 1-1 | 0-1 | 1-0 | 1-0 | 1-1 | 8-6 |
| Wardle | 2-0 | 1-1 | 0-1 | 0-0 | 1-1 | 0-0 | 1-0 | 1-0 | 0-1 | 1-1 | 0-0 | 0-0 | 0-1 | 7-6 |
| Totals | 5-8 | 5-8 | 4-8 | 2-10 | 5-8 | 2-10 | 7-6 | 4-8 | 6-7 | 3-9 | 6-6 | 7-5 | 4-9 | 60-102 |

No Decisions—Jeffcoat.

## DETROIT—84-77

| Pitcher | Balt. W-L | Bos. W-L | Cal. W-L | Chi. W-L | Clev. W-L | K.C. W-L | Mil. W-L | Min. W-L | N.Y. W-L | Oak. W-L | Sea. W-L | Tex. W-L | Tor. W-L | Totals W-L |
|---|---|---|---|---|---|---|---|---|---|---|---|---|---|---|
| Bair | 0-0 | 0-0 | 0-0 | 0-0 | 0-0 | 0-0 | 0-0 | 0-0 | 1-0 | 0-0 | 0-0 | 0-0 | 1-0 | 2-0 |
| Berenguer | 0-1 | 2-1 | 0-0 | 1-1 | 0-0 | 0-1 | 0-0 | 0-1 | 0-0 | 1-0 | 1-1 | 0-0 | 0-0 | 5-6 |
| Cary | 0-1 | 0-0 | 0-0 | 0-0 | 0-0 | 0-0 | 0-0 | 0-0 | 0-0 | 0-0 | 0-0 | 0-0 | 0-0 | 0-1 |
| Hernandez | 1-1 | 0-2 | 1-2 | 1-0 | 2-2 | 1-0 | 1-1 | 0-0 | 0-1 | 1-1 | 0-0 | 0-0 | 0-1 | 8-10 |
| Lopez | 1-0 | 0-0 | 0-0 | 0-0 | 1-1 | 0-0 | 1-0 | 0-0 | 0-0 | 0-0 | 0-0 | 0-0 | 0-1 | 3-2 |
| Mahler | 0-1 | 0-0 | 0-0 | 0-0 | 0-0 | 0-0 | 0-0 | 0-0 | 1-0 | 0-0 | 0-0 | 0-0 | 0-1 | 1-2 |
| Morris | 0-0 | 2-0 | 1-2 | 1-1 | 1-1 | 2-1 | 2-1 | 1-1 | 1-1 | 2-0 | 1-1 | 1-1 | 1-1 | 16-11 |
| O'Neal | 1-0 | 1-0 | 0-0 | 0-1 | 0-1 | 0-0 | 0-1 | 0-1 | 1-1 | 1-0 | 0-1 | 2-1 | 0-1 | 5-5 |
| Petry | 2-1 | 0-1 | 2-1 | 1-2 | 3-0 | 1-3 | 2-0 | 0-1 | 1-1 | 1-0 | 0-1 | 2-1 | 0-1 | 15-13 |
| Scherrer | 0-1 | 0-0 | 0-0 | 0-0 | 0-0 | 0-0 | 0-1 | 0-0 | 0-0 | 2-0 | 0-0 | 1-0 | 0-0 | 3-2 |
| Tanana | 2-0 | 0-0 | 0-1 | 0-1 | 1-0 | 0-1 | 1-0 | 1-1 | 3-0 | 0-0 | 0-2 | 1-1 | 1-0 | 10-7 |
| Terrell | 0-0 | 2-2 | 0-2 | 2-0 | 0-0 | 1-1 | 2-0 | 1-1 | 1-0 | 3-0 | 1-1 | 0-1 | 2-2 | 15-10 |
| Wilcox | 0-0 | 0-0 | 0-0 | 0-0 | 0-0 | 0-0 | 0-0 | 0-1 | 0-0 | 0-2 | 0-0 | 1-0 | 0-0 | 1-3 |
| Totals | 7-6 | 7-6 | 4-8 | 6-6 | 8-5 | 5-7 | 9-4 | 3-9 | 9-3 | 8-4 | 5-7 | 7-5 | 6-7 | 84-77 |

No Decisions—Stoddard.

## KANSAS CITY—91-71

| Pitcher | Balt. W-L | Bos. W-L | Cal. W-L | Chi. W-L | Clev. W-L | Det. W-L | Mil. W-L | Min. W-L | N.Y. W-L | Oak. W-L | Sea. W-L | Tex. W-L | Tor. W-L | Totals W-L |
|---|---|---|---|---|---|---|---|---|---|---|---|---|---|---|
| Beckwith | 0-0 | 0-0 | 0-0 | 0-0 | 0-0 | 0-0 | 0-0 | 0-1 | 0-0 | 0-0 | 0-1 | 0-1 | 1-2 | 1-5 |
| Black | 0-2 | 0-1 | 1-1 | 1-1 | 4-0 | 0-1 | 0-1 | 0-3 | 1-1 | 0-1 | 0-1 | 1-2 | 2-0 | 10-15 |
| Farr | 0-0 | 0-0 | 0-0 | 0-0 | 0-0 | 0-0 | 2-0 | 0-0 | 0-0 | 0-0 | 0-1 | 0-0 | 0-0 | 2-1 |
| Gubicza | 1-1 | 1-2 | 2-0 | 1-1 | 1-1 | 1-0 | 2-0 | 2-1 | 0-0 | 2-0 | 1-2 | 0-1 | 0-1 | 14-10 |
| Huismann | 0-0 | 0-0 | 0-0 | 0-0 | 0-0 | 0-0 | 0-0 | 1-0 | 0-0 | 0-0 | 0-0 | 0-0 | 0-0 | 1-0 |
| Jackson | 2-1 | 1-0 | 2-1 | 2-0 | 2-0 | 1-1 | 0-2 | 2-2 | 0-1 | 0-1 | 0-2 | 1-1 | 1-0 | 14-12 |
| Jones | 0-0 | 0-1 | 0-0 | 1-1 | 0-0 | 0-0 | 0-0 | 0-0 | 1-0 | 1-1 | 0-0 | 0-0 | 0-0 | 3-3 |
| LaCoss | 1-0 | 0-1 | 0-0 | 0-0 | 0-0 | 0-0 | 0-0 | 0-0 | 0-0 | 0-0 | 0-0 | 0-0 | 0-0 | 1-1 |
| Leibrandt | 2-0 | 2-0 | 1-1 | 2-1 | 1-1 | 0-1 | 2-0 | 1-1 | 1-1 | 1-1 | 1-1 | 1-1 | 2-0 | 17-9 |
| Quisenberry | 0-0 | 2-0 | 1-0 | 0-1 | 0-1 | 1-1 | 1-1 | 0-0 | 1-1 | 1-1 | 0-1 | 0-1 | 1-1 | 8-9 |
| Saberhagen | 0-2 | 1-0 | 2-1 | 1-0 | 2-0 | 4-1 | 1-0 | 1-0 | 2-0 | 2-0 | 1-1 | 3-0 | 0-1 | 20-6 |
| Totals | 6-6 | 7-5 | 9-4 | 8-5 | 10-2 | 7-5 | 8-4 | 7-6 | 5-7 | 8-5 | 3-10 | 6-7 | 7-5 | 91-71 |

No Decisions—Ferreira, Gura, Leonard.

## MILWAUKEE—71-90

| Pitcher | Balt. W-L | Bos. W-L | Cal. W-L | Chi. W-L | Clev. W-L | Det. W-L | K.C. W-L | Min. W-L | N.Y. W-L | Oak. W-L | Sea. W-L | Tex. W-L | Tor. W-L | Totals W-L |
|---|---|---|---|---|---|---|---|---|---|---|---|---|---|---|
| Burris | 0-1 | 0-0 | 0-1 | 2-1 | 2-1 | 1-2 | 0-1 | 2-0 | 0-1 | 0-1 | 1-1 | 0-1 | 1-2 | 9-13 |
| Cocanower | 2-0 | 1-1 | 0-0 | 0-1 | 0-1 | 1-0 | 1-1 | 0-1 | 0-1 | 0-1 | 0-0 | 1-0 | 0-1 | 6-8 |
| Darwin | 0-2 | 2-2 | 0-2 | 1-0 | 0-2 | 1-3 | 0-1 | 2-1 | 1-1 | 1-2 | 0-1 | 0-0 | 0-1 | 8-18 |
| Fingers | 0-1 | 1-0 | 0-1 | 0-1 | 0-0 | 0-0 | 0-2 | 0-0 | 0-0 | 0-1 | 0-0 | 0-0 | 0-0 | 1-6 |

| Pitcher | Balt. W-L | Bos. W-L | Cal. W-L | Chi. W-L | Clev. W-L | Det. W-L | K.C. W-L | Min. W-L | N.Y. W-L | Oak. W-L | Sea. W-L | Tex. W-L | Tor. W-L | Totals W-L |
|---|---|---|---|---|---|---|---|---|---|---|---|---|---|---|
| Gibson | 0-1 | 0-0 | 0-1 | 0-0 | 1-1 | 1-1 | 1-0 | 0-0 | 0-1 | 0-0 | 0-1 | 2-0 | 1-0 | 6-7 |
| Haas | 0-1 | 0-1 | 1-0 | 0-1 | 2-1 | 0-0 | 1-1 | 0-0 | 1-0 | 0-1 | 1-1 | 1-1 | 1-0 | 8-8 |
| Higuera | 0-1 | 0-1 | 1-1 | 2-0 | 1-1 | 0-1 | 1-0 | 3-0 | 2-0 | 1-1 | 2-0 | 1-0 | 1-2 | 15-8 |
| Kern | 0-0 | 0-0 | 0-1 | 0-0 | 0-0 | 0-0 | 0-0 | 0-0 | 0-0 | 0-0 | 0-0 | 0-0 | 0-0 | 0-1 |
| Leary | 0-1 | 1-0 | 0-0 | 0-0 | 0-0 | 0-0 | 0-0 | 0-0 | 0-0 | 0-1 | 0-0 | 0-0 | 0-2 | 1-4 |
| Lesley | 0-0 | 1-0 | 0-0 | 0-0 | 0-0 | 0-0 | 0-0 | 0-0 | 0-0 | 0-0 | 0-0 | 0-0 | 0-0 | 1-0 |
| McClure | 0-0 | 1-0 | 0-0 | 0-0 | 0-0 | 0-0 | 0-0 | 1-0 | 1-0 | 0-0 | 0-1 | 1-0 | 0-0 | 4-1 |
| Searage | 0-0 | 0-0 | 0-0 | 0-0 | 0-0 | 0-0 | 0-0 | 0-0 | 1-1 | 0-1 | 0-1 | 0-1 | 0-0 | 1-4 |
| Vuckovich | 0-1 | 1-0 | 1-2 | 1-1 | 0-0 | 0-1 | 0-2 | 0-0 | 1-0 | 1-1 | 0-1 | 1-0 | 0-1 | 6-10 |
| Waits | 0-0 | 0-0 | 0-0 | 1-0 | 0-0 | 0-1 | 0-0 | 1-0 | 0-0 | 0-0 | 0-1 | 1-0 | 0-0 | 3-2 |
| Wegman | 2-0 | 0-0 | 0-0 | 0-0 | 0-0 | 0-0 | 0-0 | 0-0 | 0-0 | 0-0 | 0-0 | 0-0 | 0-0 | 2-0 |
| Totals | 4-9 | 8-5 | 3-9 | 7-5 | 6-7 | 4-9 | 4-8 | 9-3 | 7-6 | 3-9 | 4-8 | 8-3 | 4-9 | 71-90 |

No Decisions—Ladd, Porter.

## MINNESOTA—77-85

| Pitcher | Balt. W-L | Bos. W-L | Cal. W-L | Chi. W-L | Clev. W-L | Det. W-L | K.C. W-L | Mil. W-L | N.Y. W-L | Oak. W-L | Sea. W-L | Tex. W-L | Tor. W-L | Totals W-L |
|---|---|---|---|---|---|---|---|---|---|---|---|---|---|---|
| Blyleven | 0-0 | 1-0 | 1-1 | 1-1 | 2-0 | 0-0 | 0-1 | 0-0 | 0-0 | 1-0 | 1-0 | 1-0 | 0-2 | 8-5 |
| Burtt | 0-0 | 0-0 | 0-0 | 0-0 | 1-1 | 0-0 | 1-0 | 0-1 | 0-0 | 0-0 | 0-0 | 0-0 | 0-0 | 2-2 |
| Butcher | 1-1 | 1-1 | 0-2 | 2-1 | 0-1 | 3-0 | 1-1 | 0-2 | 0-2 | 2-0 | 1-1 | 0-2 | 0-0 | 11-14 |
| Davis | 1-2 | 0-1 | 0-0 | 0-0 | 0-0 | 0-0 | 0-1 | 0-0 | 0-1 | 1-0 | 0-1 | 0-0 | 0-0 | 2-6 |
| Eufemia | 0-0 | 0-0 | 0-1 | 0-0 | 1-0 | 0-0 | 1-0 | 0-0 | 1-0 | 0-0 | 0-1 | 1-0 | 0-0 | 4-2 |
| Filson | 0-0 | 0-0 | 0-0 | 1-0 | 0-0 | 0-0 | 0-2 | 0-2 | 0-0 | 0-0 | 0-0 | 0-1 | 3-0 | 4-5 |
| Howe | 0-0 | 0-0 | 0-0 | 0-0 | 0-0 | 0-0 | 0-0 | 1-2 | 0-0 | 1-0 | 0-1 | 0-0 | 0-0 | 2-3 |
| Lysander | 0-0 | 0-0 | 0-1 | 0-0 | 0-0 | 0-0 | 0-0 | 0-0 | 0-1 | 0-0 | 0-0 | 0-0 | 0-0 | 0-2 |
| Portugal | 0-0 | 1-0 | 0-0 | 0-0 | 0-1 | 0-0 | 0-0 | 0-0 | 0-0 | 0-1 | 0-0 | 0-0 | 0-1 | 1-3 |
| Schrom | 1-2 | 0-2 | 0-2 | 0-1 | 0-1 | 2-1 | 1-0 | 1-0 | 0-2 | 0-0 | 1-1 | 3-0 | 0-0 | 9-12 |
| Smithson | 1-0 | 1-0 | 1-2 | 1-2 | 2-0 | 2-0 | 0-1 | 1-2 | 1-0 | 1-3 | 2-0 | 1-2 | 1-2 | 15-14 |
| Viola | 2-0 | 1-3 | 2-0 | 2-1 | 2-0 | 1-2 | 2-1 | 0-0 | 1-1 | 2-1 | 1-2 | 2-0 | 0-3 | 18-14 |
| Wardle | 0-1 | 0-0 | 0-0 | 0-0 | 0-0 | 1-0 | 0-0 | 0-0 | 0-2 | 0-0 | 0-0 | 0-0 | 0-0 | 1-3 |
| Totals | 6-6 | 5-7 | 4-9 | 7-6 | 8-4 | 9-3 | 6-7 | 3-9 | 3-9 | 8-5 | 6-7 | 8-5 | 4-8 | 77-85 |

No Decisions—Brown, Klawitter, Whitehouse, Yett.

## NEW YORK—97-64

| Pitcher | Balt. W-L | Bos. W-L | Cal. W-L | Chi. W-L | Clev. W-L | Det. W-L | K.C. W-L | Mil. W-L | Min. W-L | Oak. W-L | Sea. W-L | Tex. W-L | Tor. W-L | Totals W-L |
|---|---|---|---|---|---|---|---|---|---|---|---|---|---|---|
| Allen | 1-0 | 0-0 | 0-0 | 0-0 | 0-0 | 0-0 | 0-0 | 0-0 | 0-0 | 0-0 | 0-0 | 0-0 | 0-0 | 1-0 |
| Bordi | 1-1 | 1-0 | 1-1 | 1-1 | 0-0 | 0-0 | 0-0 | 0-1 | 1-1 | 0-0 | 1-0 | 0-0 | 0-3 | 6-8 |
| Bystrom | 0-0 | 1-0 | 0-1 | 0-0 | 1-0 | 0-0 | 0-0 | 0-0 | 0-0 | 0-0 | 1-0 | 0-1 | 0-0 | 3-2 |
| Cowley | 4-0 | 1-0 | 2-0 | 0-2 | 1-0 | 0-0 | 0-1 | 0-0 | 2-1 | 1-1 | 0-0 | 0-0 | 1-1 | 12-6 |
| Fisher | 0-0 | 0-0 | 0-0 | 1-1 | 1-1 | 0-0 | 0-0 | 0-1 | 1-0 | 0-0 | 1-0 | 0-0 | 0-1 | 4-4 |
| Guidry | 3-0 | 2-1 | 0-0 | 1-0 | 1-2 | 1-1 | 3-0 | 2-0 | 2-0 | 2-1 | 3-0 | 1-1 | 1-0 | 22-6 |
| J. Niekro | 0-0 | 0-0 | 0-0 | 0-0 | 0-0 | 1-1 | 0-0 | 1-0 | 0-0 | 0-0 | 0-0 | 0-0 | 0-0 | 2-1 |
| P. Niekro | 0-0 | 1-1 | 3-0 | 1-0 | 2-1 | 0-4 | 1-1 | 0-2 | 1-0 | 2-0 | 2-1 | 2-1 | 1-1 | 16-12 |
| Rasmussen | 0-0 | 0-1 | 0-0 | 0-0 | 0-0 | 0-1 | 2-1 | 0-0 | 1-0 | 0-0 | 0-2 | 0-0 | 0-0 | 3-5 |
| Righetti | 1-0 | 2-1 | 2-0 | 1-0 | 0-0 | 0-1 | 1-1 | 2-1 | 1-0 | 0-2 | 0-0 | 2-1 | 0-0 | 12-7 |
| Scurry | 0-0 | 0-0 | 0-0 | 0-0 | 0-0 | 0-0 | 0-0 | 0-0 | 0-0 | 0-0 | 0-0 | 0-0 | 1-0 | 1-0 |
| Shirley | 0-0 | 0-0 | 1-0 | 0-1 | 0-1 | 1-1 | 0-0 | 0-1 | 0-0 | 0-0 | 1-0 | 1-0 | 1-0 | 5-5 |
| Whitson | 2-0 | 0-1 | 0-1 | 1-1 | 1-1 | 0-0 | 0-1 | 1-1 | 0-1 | 1-0 | 1-0 | 2-0 | 1-1 | 10-8 |
| Totals | 12-1 | 8-5 | 9-3 | 6-6 | 7-6 | 3-9 | 7-5 | 6-7 | 9-3 | 7-5 | 9-3 | 8-4 | 6-7 | 97-64 |

No Decisions—Armstrong, Cooper, Montefusco, Murray.

## OAKLAND—77-85

| Pitcher | Balt. W-L | Bos. W-L | Cal. W-L | Chi. W-L | Clev. W-L | Det. W-L | K.C. W-L | Mil. W-L | Min. W-L | N.Y. W-L | Sea. W-L | Tex. W-L | Tor. W-L | Totals W-L |
|---|---|---|---|---|---|---|---|---|---|---|---|---|---|---|
| Atherton | 0-1 | 0-0 | 1-0 | 1-1 | 0-0 | 0-1 | 1-0 | 1-0 | 0-2 | 0-1 | 0-0 | 0-1 | 0-0 | 4-7 |
| Birtsas | 2-0 | 0-0 | 0-1 | 1-1 | 1-1 | 0-3 | 0-0 | 2-0 | 1-0 | 1-0 | 1-0 | 0-0 | 1-0 | 10-6 |
| Codiroli | 0-0 | 1-2 | 2-1 | 1-1 | 1-0 | 2-1 | 2-1 | 1-2 | 1-1 | 0-3 | 1-1 | 2-1 | 0-0 | 14-14 |
| Conroy | 0-0 | 0-0 | 0-0 | 0-0 | 0-0 | 0-0 | 0-0 | 0-0 | 0-0 | 0-0 | 0-0 | 0-1 | 0-0 | 0-1 |
| Howell | 1-1 | 0-2 | 1-0 | 0-1 | 1-0 | 0-0 | 2-1 | 0-0 | 0-0 | 2-0 | 0-0 | 1-2 | 1-1 | 9-8 |
| John | 0-0 | 0-0 | 0-0 | 0-1 | 0-1 | 0-0 | 0-1 | 1-0 | 0-1 | 1-1 | 0-0 | 0-0 | 0-0 | 2-6 |
| Krueger | 0-1 | 2-1 | 0-0 | 0-0 | 0-1 | 0-0 | 0-0 | 3-0 | 1-0 | 0-1 | 1-2 | 2-1 | 0-3 | 9-10 |
| Langford | 0-0 | 0-1 | 0-1 | 0-1 | 1-0 | 0-0 | 0-1 | 0-0 | 0-0 | 1-0 | 1-1 | 0-0 | 0-0 | 3-5 |
| McCatty | 0-0 | 0-0 | 1-0 | 0-0 | 1-0 | 0-1 | 0-1 | 0-1 | 0-0 | 0-0 | 0-0 | 1-0 | 1-1 | 4-4 |
| Mura | 0-0 | 0-0 | 0-0 | 0-0 | 0-0 | 1-1 | 0-0 | 0-0 | 0-0 | 0-0 | 0-0 | 0-0 | 0-0 | 1-1 |
| Ontiveros | 0-0 | 0-1 | 0-0 | 0-1 | 0-0 | 0-0 | 0-0 | 0-0 | 0-0 | 0-0 | 0-1 | 1-0 | 0-0 | 1-3 |
| Rijo | 1-0 | 0-0 | 1-0 | 0-0 | 2-0 | 0-0 | 0-2 | 0-0 | 1-1 | 0-1 | 0-0 | 0-0 | 0-0 | 6-4 |
| Sutton | 1-2 | 1-0 | 1-2 | 1-0 | 2-0 | 1-1 | 0-0 | 1-0 | 1-1 | 0-0 | 3-0 | 0-0 | 1-2 | 13-8 |
| Warren | 0-1 | 0-1 | 0-1 | 0-0 | 0-0 | 0-0 | 0-0 | 0-0 | 0-1 | 0-0 | 1-0 | 0-0 | 0-0 | 1-4 |
| Young | 0-0 | 0-0 | 0-0 | 0-1 | 0-0 | 0-0 | 0-1 | 0-0 | 0-1 | 0-0 | 0-1 | 0-0 | 0-0 | 0-4 |
| Totals | 5-7 | 4-8 | 7-6 | 5-8 | 9-3 | 4-8 | 5-8 | 9-3 | 5-8 | 5-7 | 8-5 | 6-7 | 5-7 | 77-85 |

No Decisions—Kaiser, Tellmann.

**Righthander Joe Cowley, since traded by the Yankees to the White Sox, won all four of his decisions against Baltimore last season.**

## SEATTLE—74-88

| Pitcher | Balt. W-L | Bos. W-L | Cal. W-L | Chi. W-L | Clev. W-L | Det. W-L | K.C. W-L | Mil. W-L | Min. W-L | N.Y. W-L | Oak. W-L | Tex. W-L | Tor. W-L | Totals W-L |
|---|---|---|---|---|---|---|---|---|---|---|---|---|---|---|
| Barojas | 0-1 | 0-0 | 0-1 | 0-0 | 0-0 | 0-1 | 0-0 | 0-0 | 0-1 | 0-0 | 0-0 | 0-0 | 0-1 | 0-5 |
| Beattie | 0-1 | 1-1 | 1-2 | 0-0 | 0-0 | 1-0 | 0-0 | 0-1 | 1-0 | 1-0 | 0-0 | 0-0 | 0-1 | 5-6 |
| Best | 1-0 | 0-0 | 0-0 | 0-0 | 0-0 | 0-1 | 1-0 | 0-0 | 0-0 | 0-0 | 0-0 | 0-0 | 0-0 | 2-1 |
| Langston | 0-1 | 1-0 | 2-1 | 0-1 | 0-0 | 0-1 | 0-0 | 1-0 | 1-0 | 0-4 | 1-3 | 0-1 | 1-2 | 7-14 |
| Lewis | 0-0 | 0-0 | 0-1 | 0-0 | 0-0 | 0-0 | 0-0 | 0-0 | 0-0 | 0-0 | 0-0 | 0-0 | 0-0 | 0-1 |
| Moore | 2-1 | 2-1 | 0-1 | 0-1 | 2-1 | 1-0 | 3-0 | 3-0 | 1-1 | 0-1 | 2-1 | 1-0 | 0-2 | 17-10 |
| Morgan | 0-0 | 0-0 | 0-0 | 0-0 | 0-0 | 0-0 | 0-0 | 0-0 | 0-0 | 0-0 | 1-1 | 0-0 | 0-0 | 1-1 |
| Nunez | 1-0 | 0-1 | 1-1 | 0-0 | 0-0 | 0-0 | 1-0 | 2-0 | 1-0 | 1-0 | 0-0 | 0-1 | 0-0 | 7-3 |
| Snyder | 0-0 | 1-0 | 0-0 | 0-2 | 0-0 | 0-0 | 0-0 | 0-0 | 0-0 | 0-0 | 0-0 | 0-0 | 0-0 | 1-2 |
| Stanton | 0-0 | 0-0 | 0-0 | 0-0 | 0-1 | 0-1 | 0-0 | 0-0 | 1-0 | 0-0 | 0-0 | 0-0 | 0-0 | 1-2 |
| Swift | 0-1 | 0-2 | 0-1 | 3-1 | 1-0 | 0-0 | 1-1 | 0-1 | 0-1 | 0-2 | 1-0 | 0-0 | 0-0 | 6-10 |
| Thomas | 0-0 | 1-0 | 0-0 | 0-0 | 1-0 | 2-0 | 1-0 | 1-0 | 0-0 | 0-0 | 0-0 | 1-0 | 0-0 | 7-0 |
| Tobik | 0-0 | 0-0 | 0-0 | 0-0 | 1-0 | 0-0 | 0-0 | 0-0 | 0-0 | 0-0 | 0-0 | 0-0 | 0-0 | 1-0 |
| Vande Berg | 0-0 | 0-0 | 0-0 | 0-0 | 0-0 | 0-0 | 0-0 | 1-0 | 1-0 | 0-0 | 0-0 | 0-0 | 0-1 | 2-1 |
| Wilkinson | 0-0 | 0-0 | 0-0 | 0-0 | 0-0 | 0-0 | 0-1 | 0-0 | 0-0 | 0-0 | 0-0 | 0-1 | 0-0 | 0-2 |
| Wills | 0-0 | 0-1 | 0-0 | 1-1 | 1-2 | 0-1 | 1-0 | 0-1 | 0-1 | 0-1 | 0-0 | 2-2 | 0-1 | 5-11 |
| Young | 2-1 | 0-0 | 0-1 | 0-3 | 0-2 | 3-0 | 2-1 | 0-1 | 1-2 | 1-1 | 0-3 | 2-2 | 1-2 | 12-19 |
| Totals | 6-6 | 6-6 | 4-9 | 4-9 | 6-6 | 7-5 | 10-3 | 8-4 | 7-6 | 3-9 | 5-8 | 6-7 | 2-10 | 74-88 |

No Decisions—Geisel, Lazorko, Long, Mirabella.

## TEXAS—62-99

| Pitcher | Balt. W-L | Bos. W-L | Cal. W-L | Chi. W-L | Clev. W-L | Det. W-L | K.C. W-L | Mil. W-L | Min. W-L | N.Y. W-L | Oak. W-L | Sea. W-L | Tor. W-L | Totals W-L |
|---|---|---|---|---|---|---|---|---|---|---|---|---|---|---|
| Cook | 0-0 | 0-0 | 1-0 | 0-0 | 0-0 | 0-0 | 0-0 | 0-0 | 1-0 | 0-2 | 0-0 | 0-0 | 0-1 | 2-3 |
| Guzman | 0-0 | 0-0 | 0-1 | 0-0 | 0-0 | 0-0 | 0-0 | 0-0 | 1-0 | 0-0 | 1-1 | 1-0 | 0-0 | 3-2 |
| Harris | 0-0 | 0-0 | 0-0 | 1-0 | 1-1 | 0-2 | 1-0 | 0-0 | 0-1 | 0-0 | 1-0 | 1-0 | 0-0 | 5-4 |
| Henry | 0-0 | 0-0 | 0-1 | 0-1 | 0-0 | 0-0 | 0-0 | 0-0 | 0-0 | 0-0 | 0-0 | 1-0 | 1-0 | 2-2 |
| Hooton | 0-1 | 0-0 | 0-0 | 1-0 | 0-2 | 2-1 | 1-1 | 0-1 | 1-0 | 0-1 | 0-0 | 0-1 | 0-0 | 5-8 |
| Hough | 2-0 | 2-1 | 0-2 | 1-2 | 4-0 | 2-1 | 2-1 | 0-1 | 0-3 | 0-1 | 0-2 | 0-1 | 1-1 | 14-16 |
| Mason | 0-3 | 2-0 | 0-1 | 0-2 | 0-2 | 0-1 | 1-0 | 1-1 | 1-1 | 0-1 | 1-1 | 1-1 | 1-1 | 8-15 |
| Noles | 0-0 | 0-1 | 0-0 | 0-2 | 0-1 | 0-1 | 0-2 | 1-1 | 0-0 | 2-0 | 1-0 | 0-0 | 0-0 | 4-8 |
| Rozema | 0-2 | 1-1 | 1-0 | 0-0 | 0-0 | 0-1 | 0-0 | 1-2 | 0-0 | 0-0 | 0-1 | 0-0 | 0-0 | 3-7 |
| Russell | 0-1 | 1-0 | 0-0 | 0-1 | 0-0 | 0-0 | 0-1 | 0-1 | 0-1 | 0-0 | 2-0 | 0-0 | 0-1 | 3-6 |
| Schmidt | 0-0 | 0-0 | 1-1 | 0-1 | 0-0 | 1-0 | 2-0 | 0-0 | 1-1 | 1-0 | 1-1 | 0-1 | 0-0 | 7-6 |
| Sebra | 0-0 | 0-0 | 0-0 | 1-0 | 0-0 | 0-0 | 0-0 | 0-0 | 0-0 | 0-0 | 0-0 | 0-0 | 0-0 | 0-2 |
| Stewart | 0-0 | 0-1 | 0-0 | 0-1 | 0-0 | 0-0 | 0-0 | 0-0 | 0-0 | 0-1 | 0-0 | 0-1 | 0-2 | 0-6 |
| Surhoff | 0-0 | 0-0 | 0-1 | 0-0 | 0-0 | 0-0 | 0-0 | 0-0 | 0-0 | 0-0 | 0-0 | 0-0 | 0-0 | 0-1 |
| Tanana | 0-1 | 1-1 | 0-0 | 0-0 | 0-0 | 0-1 | 0-0 | 0-1 | 0-1 | 0-1 | 0-0 | 1-0 | 0-1 | 2-7 |
| Welsh | 0-2 | 0-0 | 0-0 | 0-0 | 0-0 | 0-0 | 0-0 | 0-0 | 0-0 | 1-0 | 0-1 | 1-1 | 0-1 | 2-5 |
| Williams | 0-0 | 0-0 | 1-1 | 0-0 | 0-0 | 0-0 | 0-0 | 0-0 | 1-0 | 0-0 | 0-0 | 0-0 | 0-0 | 2-1 |
| Totals | 2-10 | 7-5 | 4-9 | 3-10 | 5-7 | 5-7 | 7-6 | 3-8 | 5-8 | 4-8 | 7-6 | 7-6 | 3-9 | 62-99 |

No Decisions—Boggs, Murray, R. Wright.

## TORONTO—99-62

| Pitcher | Balt. W-L | Bos. W-L | Cal. W-L | Chi. W-L | Clev. W-L | Det. W-L | K.C. W-L | Mil. W-L | Min. W-L | N.Y. W-L | Oak. W-L | Sea. W-L | Tex. W-L | Totals W-L |
|---|---|---|---|---|---|---|---|---|---|---|---|---|---|---|
| Acker | 0-0 | 1-2 | 0-0 | 1-0 | 0-0 | 1-0 | 0-0 | 1-0 | 0-0 | 2-0 | 0-0 | 0-0 | 1-0 | 7-2 |
| Alexander | 3-0 | 0-1 | 3-0 | 0-0 | 1-1 | 1-1 | 0-1 | 0-1 | 3-1 | 2-2 | 0-2 | 2-0 | 2-0 | 17-10 |
| Caudill | 0-1 | 0-0 | 0-1 | 0-0 | 0-0 | 0-0 | 2-2 | 0-0 | 0-0 | 0-0 | 0-1 | 1-0 | 1-1 | 4-6 |
| Cerutti | 0-0 | 0-1 | 0-0 | 0-0 | 0-0 | 0-0 | 0-0 | 0-0 | 0-0 | 0-1 | 0-0 | 0-0 | 0-0 | 0-2 |
| Clancy | 0-0 | 0-2 | 1-0 | 0-1 | 0-0 | 0-2 | 0-0 | 4-0 | 2-0 | 0-0 | 1-0 | 1-1 | 0-0 | 9-6 |
| Davis | 0-0 | 0-0 | 0-0 | 0-1 | 0-0 | 0-0 | 0-0 | 0-0 | 2-0 | 0-0 | 0-0 | 0-0 | 0-0 | 2-1 |
| Filer | 2-0 | 0-0 | 1-0 | 1-0 | 0-0 | 0-0 | 1-0 | 0-0 | 0-0 | 0-0 | 0-0 | 1-0 | 1-0 | 7-0 |
| Henke | 2-0 | 0-0 | 0-0 | 0-0 | 0-1 | 0-0 | 1-0 | 0-0 | 0-1 | 0-1 | 0-0 | 0-0 | 0-0 | 3-3 |
| Key | 0-2 | 1-0 | 1-1 | 2-1 | 2-0 | 1-0 | 0-1 | 2-0 | 0-0 | 1-1 | 2-0 | 2-0 | 0-0 | 14-6 |
| Lamp | 0-0 | 1-0 | 0-0 | 2-0 | 1-0 | 1-0 | 0-0 | 1-0 | 1-0 | 1-0 | 2-0 | 0-0 | 2-0 | 11-0 |
| Lavelle | 0-1 | 0-2 | 0-2 | 2-0 | 1-0 | 1-0 | 0-0 | 0-0 | 0-0 | 1-1 | 0-1 | 0-0 | 0-0 | 5-7 |
| Leal | 0-0 | 0-0 | 0-0 | 0-0 | 1-0 | 0-0 | 2-1 | 0-1 | 0-1 | 0-0 | 1-0 | 0-1 | 0-1 | 3-6 |
| Musselman | 1-0 | 0-0 | 0-0 | 0-0 | 0-0 | 0-0 | 0-0 | 0-0 | 0-0 | 0-0 | 0-0 | 0-0 | 0-0 | 3-0 |
| Steib | 0-0 | 1-1 | 1-1 | 3-0 | 1-2 | 2-1 | 0-3 | 1-2 | 0-1 | 0-0 | 1-1 | 2-0 | 2-1 | 14-13 |
| Totals | 8-4 | 4-9 | 7-5 | 9-3 | 9-4 | 7-6 | 5-7 | 9-4 | 8-4 | 7-6 | 7-5 | 10-2 | 9-3 | 99-62 |

No Decisions—Clarke.

# NATIONAL LEAGUE

## Including

**Team Reviews of 1985 Season**

**Team Day-by-Day Scores**

**1985 Standings, Home-Away Records**

**1985 Official N.L. Batting Averages**

**1985 Official N.L. Fielding Averages**

**1985 Official N.L. Pitching Averages**

**1985 Pitching Against Each Club**

Lefthander John Tudor recovered from a 1-7 start to record 21 victories with an impressive 1.93 ERA.

# Underdog Cardinals Fly High

**By RICK HUMMEL**

Hitting, pitching, fielding—you name it, the St. Louis Cardinals did it well in 1985.

Ah, but running, that was the key. One must wonder whether the Cardinals could have won 101 games and edged out the New York Mets by three games in the National League East without their marvelous team speed.

The Cardinals became the fourth-best basestealing team in modern baseball history by totaling 314 stolen bases. Vince Coleman was the catalyst of this baserunning explosion with a rookie record 110 steals, and four other Cardinals had more than 30 steals each.

The result was a club that gave opposing pitchers fits. Pitchers became so preoccupied with trying to hold runners on base and give their catchers a reasonable chance of throwing out the jackrabbits that they were forced into making costly mistakes such as erratic pickoff throws and bad pitches. The Cardinals repeatedly capitalized on these blunders.

But the contribution of speed to the team's offensive production is only half of the story, as Manager Whitey Herzog pointed out.

"Speed probably is more important to us on defense," he said. "People overlook that."

Herzog cited his normal outfield of Coleman in left, Willie McGee in center and Andy Van Slyke in right.

"They might be the best defensive outfield in the history of the game," he said. "Andy and Willie both can run and have excellent arms. Vince can run and has a very good arm. You have to really hit it to get it between those guys."

The Cardinals, who also featured Ozzie Smith at shortstop, Tom Herr at second and a vastly improved Terry Pendleton at third, had the league's best defense. They committed a league-low 108 errors while turning 166 double plays (second among N.L. clubs).

The addition of Coleman to the roster is a perfect example of how championships often are a product of evolution, not design. In spring training, Coleman appeared to be a year away from the big leagues.

"We had no intention of bringing him up before July," Herzog said.

But when McGee and Tito Landrum got hurt early in the season, Coleman was called up from Louisville (American As-

Jack Clark came over from San Francisco and put some punch in the Cardinal lineup.

sociation) on April 17 as a temporary replacement.

Coleman stole two bases in his first game, then got four hits (including a game-winner) in his second, and suddenly he had galvanized a team and an entire city with his fearless running. He did not return to Louisville.

"When Vince came up," Herzog said, "the town got turned on. After that time, we played pretty steady baseball. I'm not saying he was our most valuable player, but he put the finishing touches on a good lineup."

Rookie of the Year Coleman, who hit

## SCORES OF ST. LOUIS CARDINALS' 1985 GAMES

### APRIL

| Date | W/L | Score | Winner | Loser |
|---|---|---|---|---|
| 9—At N.Y. | L | 5-6† | Gorman | Allen |
| 11—At N.Y. | L | 1-2‡ | McDowell | Hassler |
| 12—At Pitts. | L | 4-6 | Robinson | Kepshire |
| 13—At Pitts. | L | 3-4 | Candelaria | Campbell |
| 14—At Pitts. | W | 10-4 | Andujar | Rhoden |
| 15—Montreal | W | 6-1 | Forsch | Gullickson |
| 17—Montreal | L | 1-2 | Hesketh | Tudor |
| 18—Montreal | L | 1-7 | Rogers | Kepshire |
| 19—Pittsburgh | W | 5-4 | Andujar | Candelaria |
| 20—Pittsburgh | W | 4-3 | Cox | Tunnell |
| 21—Pittsburgh | W | 6-0 | Forsch | DeLeon |
| 22—New York | L | 6-7 | Schiraldi | Tudor |
| 23—New York | W | 8-3 | Kepshire | Gorman |
| 24—New York | W | 5-1 | Andujar | Gooden |
| 25—At Mon. | L | 2-4 | Gullickson | Cox |
| 26—At Mon. | L | 5-10 | Palmer | Forsch |
| 27—At Mon. | L | 3-8 | Hesketh | Tudor |
| 28—At Mon. | L | 3-5 | Rogers | Kepshire |
| 30—Los Ang. | W | 6-1 | Andujar | Reuss |

**Won 8, Lost 11**

### MAY

| Date | W/L | Score | Winner | Loser |
|---|---|---|---|---|
| 1—Los Ang. | L | 1-2§ | Howell | Allen |
| 3—San Fran. | W | 8-1 | Tudor | Krukow |
| 4—San Fran. | W | 6-4 | Kepshire | Hammaker |
| 5—San Fran. | L | 0-5 | LaPoint | Andujar |
| 6—San Diego | W | 5-2 | Cox | Show |
| 7—San Diego | L | 2-12 | Dravecky | Forsch |
| 8—At L.A. | L | 2-5 | Honeycutt | Tudor |
| 9—At L.A. | W | 5-4† | Allen | Howell |
| 10—At S. Fran. | W | 9-3 | Andujar | LaPoint |
| 11—At S. Fran. | W | 9-4 | Cox | Laskey |
| 12—At S. Fran. | L | 4-5† | Garrelts | Allen |
| 14—At S. Diego | L | 2-6 | Hawkins | Tudor |
| 15—At S. Diego | W | 14-4 | Andujar | Hoyt |
| 17—At Hous. | W | 8-6 | Campbell | Calhoun |
| 18—At Hous. | L | 5-6 | Ryan | Kepshire |
| 19—At Hous. | L | 3-7 | Mathis | Tudor |
| 20—Atlanta | W | 14-0 | Andujar | Smith |
| 21—Atlanta | W | 6-3 | Cox | Barker |
| 22—Atlanta | W | 5-3 | Forsch | Mahler |
| 24—At Cinn. | L | 6-7§ | Franco | Horton |
| 25—At Cinn. | W | 6-4 | Andujar | Tibbs |
| 26—At Cinn. | W | 7-2 | Cox | Stuper |
| 28—At Atlanta | W | 9-3 | Forsch | Smith |
| 29—At Atlanta | L | 3-5 | Bedrosian | Tudor |
| 30—At Atlanta | W | 6-0 | Andujar | Mahler |
| 31—Cincinnati | W | 5-0 | Cox | Stuper |

**Won 16, Lost 10**

### JUNE

| Date | W/L | Score | Winner | Loser |
|---|---|---|---|---|
| 1—Cincinnati | L | 3-9 | Browning | Kepshire |
| 2—Cincinnati | L | 3-8 | Tibbs | Forsch |
| 3—Houston | W | 9-5 | Tudor | Ryan |
| 4—Houston | W | 6-1 | Andujar | Niekro |
| 5—Houston | L | 3-8 | Knepper | Cox |
| 7—At N.Y. | W | 7-2x | Campbell | Sisk |
| 8—At N.Y. | W | 1-0 | Tudor | Gorman |
| 9—At N.Y. | L | 1-6 | Gooden | Forsch |
| 9—At N.Y. | W | 8-2 | Andujar | Schiraldi |
| 10—At Pitts. | W | 6-1 | Cox | Rhoden |
| 11—At Pitts. | L | 2-13 | Reuschel | Allen |
| 13—At Pitts. | W | 2-1 | Tudor | McWilliams |
| 14—At Chicago | W | 11-10 | Andujar | Ruthven |
| 15—At Chicago | W | 2-0 | Cox | Fontenot |
| 16—At Chicago | W | 5-2 | Kepshire | Eckersley |
| 18—Phila. | W | 6-2 | Tudor | Carlton |
| 19—Phila. | L | 0-1 | Koosman | Andujar |
| 20—Phila. | W | 5-0 | Cox | Gross |
| 21—Chicago | W | 7-5 | Kepshire | Eckersley |
| 22—Chicago | W | 2-1† | Dayley | Smith |
| 23—Chicago | W | 7-0 | Tudor | Ruthven |
| 25—At Phila. | L | 1-3 | Koosman | Andujar |
| 26—At Phila. | L | 4-6 | Denny | Cox |
| 27—At Phila. | W | 4-3 | Kepshire | Rawley |
| 28—New York | W | 3-2 | Tudor | Lynch |
| 29—New York | W | 6-0 | Andujar | Aguilera |
| 30—New York | W | 2-1‡ | Dayley | Orosco |

**Won 19, Lost 8**

### JULY

| Date | W/L | Score | Winner | Loser |
|---|---|---|---|---|
| 1—At Mon. | L | 2-3† | Lucas | Horton |
| 2—At Mon. | W | 4-0 | Tudor | Palmer |
| 4—Los Ang. | W | 3-2 | Andujar | Howell |
| 5—Los Ang. | L | 1-4 | Niedenfuer | Cox |
| 6—Los Ang. | L | 3-8 | Welch | Kepshire |
| 7—Los Ang. | W | 7-1 | Tudor | Hershiser |
| 8—San Fran. | W | 6-1 | Andujar | LaPoint |
| 9—San Fran. | W | 3-1 | Cox | Laskey |
| 10—San Fran. | W | 7-3 | Kepshire | Blue |
| 11—San Diego | W | 6-0 | Tudor | Thurmond |
| 12—San Diego | L | 0-2 | Hoyt | Andujar |
| 13—San Diego | W | 7-3 | Cox | Wojna |
| 14—San Diego | W | 2-1 | Kepshire | Dravecky |
| 18—At L.A. | L | 1-2 | Hershiser | Campbell |
| 19—At L.A. | L | 2-5 | Welch | Cox |
| 20—At L.A. | L | 0-3 | Valenzuela | Tudor |
| 21—At L.A. | W | 4-2 | Lahti | Niedenfuer |
| 22—At S. Fran. | W | 4-3 | Andujar | LaPoint |
| 23—At S. Fran. | W | 6-3 | Cox | Krukow |
| 24—At S. Fran. | W | 4-0 | Tudor | Gott |
| 25—At S. Diego | W | 9-6 | Dayley | Gossage |
| 26—At S. Diego | W | 2-1§ | Andujar | Stoddard |
| 27—At S. Diego | L | 0-2 | Hawkins | Cox |
| 28—At S. Diego | W | 4-2 | Tudor | Hoyt |
| 30—At Chicago | W | 11-3 | Kepshire | Engel |
| 31—At Chicago | L | 2-5 | Fontenot | Andujar |

**Won 17, Lost 9**

### AUGUST

| Date | W/L | Score | Winner | Loser |
|---|---|---|---|---|
| 1—At Chicago | L | 8-9y | Frazier | Dayley |
| 2—Phila. | W | 3-2 | Tudor | Hudson |
| 3—Phila. | L | 4-6† | Carman | Lahti |
| 4—Phila. | L | 0-6 | Gross | Andujar |
| 5—Phila. | L | 1-9 | Rawley | Cox |
| 8—Chicago | W | 8-0 | Tudor | Sanderson |
| 9—At Phila. | W | 5-4 | Andujar | Hudson |
| 10—At Phila. | W | 5-4 | Cox | Koosman |
| 10—At Phila. | W | 13-4 | Horton | Gross |
| 11—At Phila. | L | 1-4 | Rawley | Forsch |
| 12—Pittsburgh | W | 8-1 | Tudor | Winn |
| 13—Pittsburgh | W | 6-5 | Andujar | Robinson |
| 15—Pittsburgh | W | 3-1 | Kepshire | Reuschel |
| 15—Pittsburgh | W | 4-3§ | Campbell | Guante |
| 16—Montreal | W | 6-1 | Forsch | Laskey |
| 17—Montreal | L | 4-5 | Burke | Campbell |
| 18—Montreal | L | 5-6† | Lucas | Andujar |
| 20—At Hous. | L | 2-17 | Scott | Kepshire |
| 21—At Hous. | W | 7-4 | Lahti | Smith |
| 22—At Hous. | W | 2-1 | Horton | Calhoun |
| 23—At Atlanta | W | 6-2 | Andujar | McMurtry |
| 24—At Atlanta | W | 7-0* | Forsch | Barker |
| 25—At Atlanta | W | 5-2 | Kepshire | Mahler |
| 26—At Cinn. | W | 3-0 | Cox | Tibbs |
| 27—At Cinn. | W | 6-4 | Campbell | Power |
| 28—At Cinn. | L | 6-7§ | Power | Lahti |
| 30—Houston | L | 5-7 | Scott | Kepshire |
| 31—Houston | L | 1-3 | Knepper | Cox |

**Won 17, Lost 11**

### SEPTEMBER

| Date | W/L | Score | Winner | Loser |
|---|---|---|---|---|
| 1—Houston | W | 5-0 | Tudor | Niekro |
| 2—Cincinnati | L | 1-4 | Browning | Andujar |
| 3—Cincinnati | W | 6-4 | Lahti | Hume |
| 4—Cincinnati | W | 4-3 | Worrell | Robinson |
| 5—Chicago | W | 6-1 | Cox | Engel |
| 6—Atlanta | W | 8-0 | Tudor | Mahler |
| 7—Atlanta | L | 1-3 | Bedrosian | Andujar |
| 8—Atlanta | L | 3-7 | Johnson | Forsch |
| 9—Chicago | L | 1-3 | Fontenot | Kepshire |
| 10—At N.Y. | L | 4-5 | Darling | Cox |
| 11—At N.Y. | W | 1-0† | Tudor | Orosco |
| 12—At N.Y. | L | 6-7 | Orosco | Dayley |
| 13—At Chicago | W | 9-3 | Forsch | Trout |
| 14—At Chicago | W | 5-4 | Campbell | Sorensen |
| 15—At Chicago | L | 1-5 | Cox | Engel |
| 16—At Pitts. | W | 8-4 | Tudor | DeLeon |
| 16—At Pitts. | W | 3-1 | Perry | Clements |
| 17—At Pitts. | W | 10-4 | Andujar | Kipper |
| 18—At Phila. | W | 7-0 | Forsch | Denny |
| 19—At Phila. | L | 3-6 | Rucker | Keough |
| 20—Montreal | W | 5-3 | Worrell | St. Claire |
| 21—Montreal | W | 7-6 | Lahti | Roberge |
| 22—Montreal | W | 6-5 | Dayley | O'Connor |
| 23—Pittsburgh | W | 5-4 | Lahti | Guante |
| 24—Pittsburgh | W | 5-4 | Horton | Tunnell |
| 25—Phila. | W | 6-3 | Cox | Hudson |
| 26—Phila. | W | 5-0 | Tudor | Gross |
| 28—At Mon. | L | 0-2 | Gullickson | Andujar |
| 28—At Mon. | W | 4-2‡ | Worrell | Reardon |
| 29—At Mon. | L | 5-7 | Lucas | Dayley |

**Won 21, Lost 9**

### OCTOBER

| Date | W/L | Score | Winner | Loser |
|---|---|---|---|---|
| 1—New York | L | 0-1‡ | Orosco | Dayley |
| 2—New York | L | 2-5 | Gooden | Andujar |
| 3—New York | W | 4-3 | Cox | Aguilera |
| 4—Chicago | W | 4-2 | Forsch | Eckersley |
| 5—Chicago | W | 7-1 | Tudor | Trout |
| 6—Chicago | L | 2-8 | Patterson | Andujar |

**Won 3, Lost 3**

*5 innings.   †10 innings.   ‡11 innings.   §12 innings.   x13 innings.   y14 innings.

.267 with 10 triples and scored 107 runs, seemingly always was on base, and his presence sparked the rest of the lineup.

With Coleman on first, McGee saw fastballs. And McGee hit a league-high .353, the highest average for a switch-hitter in modern N.L. history. The Gold Glover also led the league in hits (216) and triples (18), hit 10 home runs, knocked in 82 runs and scored 114, stole 56 bases and was named the league's Most Valuable Player.

When Coleman and McGee both got on base, No. 3 hitter Herr was in an even better position. He batted a whopping 178 times with men in scoring position, which helps to explain how he was able to collect 110 runs batted in while hitting only eight homers. Herr batted .302 and stole 31 bases.

Then, after pitchers had fretted and fumed about this top three, there stood first baseman Jack Clark, imploring—almost daring—them to throw him their best fastballs. Though he missed most of the last six weeks because of an injured rib cage, Clark still bashed 22 homers and drove in 87 runs while batting .281.

Not surprisingly, St. Louis led the league in batting (.264), scoring (747 runs) and several other offensive categories.

Smith won his sixth consecutive Gold Glove while showing that the Cardinals were paying him $2 million a year for more than just his fielding prowess. He stole 31 bases and posted career highs in batting average (.276), homers (six) and RBIs (54).

Pendleton batted just .240 after a .324 rookie season, but many of his hits came in clutch situations, hence his 69 RBIs. Van Slyke contributed 13 homers and 34 steals. Landrum, who often platooned with Van Slyke, hit .280.

The weakest spot in the lineup was catcher, where Darrell Porter and Tom Nieto combined for a .223 average.

One late addition to the club was outfielder Cesar Cedeno, who homered on his first pitch as a Cardinal. He batted .434 after being acquired from Cincinnati on August 29.

"We would not have won without him," Herzog said.

The key off-season acquisitions had been Clark and pitcher John Tudor, who won 17 more games than the man for whom he was traded, George Hendrick, hit home runs (21 to four) in 1985.

Tudor got off to a horrible 1-7 start but then won 20 of his last 21 decisions. The lefthander led the league with 10 shutouts and was among the leaders in earned-run average (1.93), complete games (14), innings pitched (275) and strikeouts (169).

Joaquin Andujar's season was much like Tudor's, but in reverse. After winning his 20th game August 23, Andujar won only one more the rest of the way. Still, he finished with a 3.40 ERA, 10 complete games and his second consecutive 20-victory season.

Danny Cox came into his own in his third major league season, going 18-9 with a 2.88 ERA and 10 complete games. Kurt Kepshire won 10 games and Bob Forsch nine to complete the rotation.

The big surprise was the bullpen, of which little was expected after the loss of Bruce Sutter to free agency. But Herzog assembled a "bullpen by committee" that combined for 44 saves. The Cardinals did not lose a regular-season game in which they were winning after eight innings, and they were 83-1 and 78-3 in games they led after seven and six innings, respectively.

Jeff Lahti posted 19 saves and a 1.84 ERA as the righthanded stopper, while his lefthanded counterpart, Ken Dayley, had 11 saves. Ricky Horton (2.91 ERA) and Bill Campbell (five wins, four saves) provided strong middle relief, and rookie Todd Worrell collected five saves and three victories after being promoted from Louisville on August 27.

Overall, St. Louis pitchers allowed fewer homers (98) than any team in the league, and their 3.10 ERA was second only to the Dodgers' 2.96.

A July 21 game at Los Angeles offered a classic example of the Cardinals' come-from-behind heroics. St. Louis had been perched atop the division since June 29 but was in danger of slipping after losing the first three games after the All-Star break to the Dodgers. But in the 10th inning of a tie game, Pendleton pinch hit a double and Steve Braun pinch hit a homer to give the Cardinals a 4-2 victory that started a six-game winning streak.

The Cards and the Mets exchanged the lead several times after that, but a September stretch in which St. Louis won 14 of 15 games put the club four games up with nine games left. The Cardinals survived a scare by winning the last matchup of a three-game series against New York to prevent a tie October 3, and they clinched the division two days later.

The Cardinals then won the N.L. pennant by beating the Dodgers in six games but lost to Kansas City in a seven-game World Series.

"We had a great year," Herzog said. "It's just too bad we couldn't do it all. But we did a helluva lot more than people thought (we would)."

**Gary Carter solved the Mets' catching problems while contributing 32 home runs and 100 RBIs.**

# Mets Win Big, Still Fall Short

**By JACK LANG**

It was the second-best year in the New York Mets' history on the field and the greatest in New York baseball history at the turnstiles. But 1985 also was the most disappointing year the Mets have endured.

Picked by many to win the National League East title, the Mets were contenders all the way, and as late as September 13, after splitting a doubleheader in Montreal, they were in first place by half a game. But they fell to second the next day and remained there the balance of the season as the St. Louis Cardinals held on to win by three games. A 98-64 record is good enough to win in most years, but not in 1985.

The Mets' season had looked so promising after they had engineered one of the best deals in their history by obtaining veteran Gary Carter from Montreal. Carter was the one missing link in their 1984 quest for the title—a solid catcher who could hit home runs and drive in runs. When Carter's 10th-inning homer off Neil Allen on opening day beat the Cardinals, 6-5, the Mets were certain they had made the right moves.

And indeed, Carter had the kind of season the Mets expected of him, finishing with a .281 average, 32 homers and 100 runs batted in despite playing in pain most of the year because of a damaged ankle, rib and knee.

But, as is the case with all teams, injuries played a major role in the Mets' season. Without using them as an excuse, Manager Dave Johnson pointed out three injuries that kept the Mets at less than full strength.

The first came April 23 when Bruce Berenyi, the No. 3 starter, had to leave a game after just two innings with an aching right shoulder. He never pitched another inning and later underwent arthroscopic surgery. Berenyi, who had won 12 games the previous year, was the veteran of the staff, and his loss was a tremendous blow.

Less than three weeks later, on May 11, Darryl Strawberry dived for a fly ball in right field at Shea Stadium. In so doing he tore the ligaments in his right thumb and was sidelined for the next seven weeks.

"When I saw him dive and saw him come up holding his hand in pain, it was the darkest moment of the season for me," Johnson said.

**Darryl Strawberry only played 111 games, but he still hit 29 home runs.**

Considering that Strawberry, while playing in only 111 games, still hit 29 home runs, drove in 79, stole 26 bases and batted a respectable .277, the Mets winced when they realized what he might have accomplished in an entire season.

Danny Heep did a fine job filling in for Strawberry and finished the season with a .280 average. But Heep could not compensate for the loss of Strawberry's power, and the Mets had fallen to third place by the time Strawberry returned.

The third serious blow was the loss of center fielder Mookie Wilson for two months in July and August. Wilson came back to play in September and finished with a .276 average, but the Mets missed his bat, speed and defense during those long summer months. His replacement, 22-year-old rookie Len Dykstra, provided speed (15 steals) but little offense (.254) in the leadoff spot.

The Mets were able to overcome these key losses and stay close to the Cardinals because of the fine performances turned

## SCORES OF NEW YORK METS' 1985 GAMES

### APRIL

| Date | | Score | Winner | Loser |
|---|---|---|---|---|
| 9—St. Louis | W | 6-5* | Gorman | Allen |
| 11—St. Louis | W | 2-1† | McDowell | Hassler |
| 12—Cincinnati | W | 1-0 | Berenyi | Soto |
| 13—Cincinnati | W | 2-1 | McDowell | Franco |
| 14—Cincinnati | W | 4-0 | Gooden | Tibbs |
| 15—At Pitts. | L | 1-4 | Bielecki | Latham |
| 16—At Pitts. | W | 2-1 | Orosco | Candelaria |
| 17—At Pitts. | W | 10-6 | Sisk | McWilliams |
| 19—At Phila. | W | 1-0 | Gooden | Hudson |
| 20—At Phila. | L | 6-7 | Denny | Lynch |
| 21—At Phila. | L | 6-10 | Gross | Sisk |
| 22—At St. L. | W | 7-6 | Schiraldi | Tudor |
| 23—At St. L. | L | 3-8 | Kepshire | Gorman |
| 24—At St. L. | L | 1-5 | Andujar | Gooden |
| 26—Pittsburgh | W | 6-0 | Darling | DeLeon |
| 27—Pittsburgh | L | 2-3 | McWilliams | Orosco |
| 28—Pittsburgh | W | 5-4y | Gorman | Tunnell |
| 30—Houston | W | 4-1 | Gooden | Niekro |

**Won 12, Lost 6**

### MAY

| Date | | Score | Winner | Loser |
|---|---|---|---|---|
| 1—Houston | L | 3-10 | Knepper | Darling |
| 3—At Cinn. | W | 9-4 | Lynch | Soto |
| 4—At Cinn. | L | 2-14 | Tibbs | McDowell |
| 5—At Cinn. | W | 3-2 | Gooden | Browning |
| 7—Atlanta | W | 5-3 | Darling | Smith |
| 8—Atlanta | W | 4-0 | Lynch | Barker |
| 10—Phila. | W | 5-0 | Gooden | Carlton |
| 11—Phila. | W | 4-0 | Fernandez | Rawley |
| 12—Phila. | W | 3-2 | Darling | Gross |
| 13—At Atlanta | L | 0-1 | Barker | Lynch |
| 14—At Atlanta | W | 3-1 | McDowell | Mahler |
| 15—At Hous. | W | 5-3 | Gooden | Niekro |
| 16—At Hous. | L | 0-1 | Scott | Fernandez |
| 17—San Fran. | W | 3-2‡ | McDowell | Garrelts |
| 18—San Fran. | W | 2-8* | Davis | Gardner |
| 19—San Fran. | W | 3-2 | Gorman | Davis |
| 20—San Diego | L | 0-2 | Hoyt | Gooden |
| 22—San Diego | L | 4-5* | Thurmond | Orosco |
| 24—Los Ang. | L | 3-4 | Hershiser | Lynch |
| 25—Los Ang. | L | 2-6 | Valenzuela | Gooden |
| 26—Los Ang. | W | 2-1 | McDowell | Honeycutt |
| 27—Los Ang. | W | 8-1 | Darling | Reuss |
| 29—At S. Fran. | W | 4-3 | Lynch | Davis |
| 30—At S. Fran. | W | 2-1 | Gooden | Gott |
| 31—At S. Diego | L | 3-4 | Hoyt | Sisk |

**Won 15, Lost 10**

### JUNE

| Date | | Score | Winner | Loser |
|---|---|---|---|---|
| 1—At S. Diego | W | 5-3 | Darling | Thurmond |
| 2—At S. Diego | W | 7-3 | Schiraldi | Show |
| 3—At L. A. | W | 4-5‡ | Howe | Sisk |
| 4—At L. A. | W | 4-1 | Gooden | Valenzuela |
| 5—At L. A. | L | 1-2 | Welch | Fernandez |
| 7—St. Louis | L | 2-7§ | Campbell | Sisk |
| 8—St. Louis | L | 0-1 | Tudor | Gorman |
| 9—St. Louis | W | 6-1 | Gooden | Forsch |
| 9—St. Louis | L | 2-8 | Andujar | Schiraldi |
| 10—At Phila. | L | 4-6 | Denny | Fernandez |
| 11—At Phila. | L | 7-26 | Hudson | Gorman |
| 12—At Phila. | W | 7-3† | Aguilera | Rucker |
| 13—At Phila. | L | 4-5 | Rawley | Orosco |
| 14—At Mon. | L | 4-5 | Lucas | Sisk |
| 15—At Mon. | L | 2-3 | Burke | Fernandez |
| 16—At Mon. | L | 2-7 | Gullickson | Aguilera |
| 17—Chicago | W | 2-0 | Darling | Sutcliffe |
| 18—Chicago | W | 5-1 | Lynch | Trout |
| 19—Chicago | W | 1-0 | Gooden | Sanderson |
| 20—Chicago | W | 5-3 | Fernandez | Fontenot |
| 21—Montreal | W | 6-3 | Sisk | Mahler |
| 22—Montreal | L | 4-5* | St. Claire | McDowell |
| 23—Montreal | L | 1-5 | Smith | Lynch |
| 25—At Chicago | W | 3-2 | Gooden | Sanderson |
| 26—At Chicago | L | 3-7 | Fontenot | McDowell |
| 27—At Chicago | L | 2-4 | Sutcliffe | Darling |
| 28—At St. L. | L | 2-3 | Tudor | Lynch |
| 29—At St. L. | L | 0-6 | Andujar | Aguilera |
| 30—At St. L. | L | 1-2† | Dayley | Orosco |

**Won 11, Lost 18**

### JULY

| Date | | Score | Winner | Loser |
|---|---|---|---|---|
| 1—Pittsburgh | L | 0-1 | Reuschel | Fernandez |
| 2—Pittsburgh | W | 5-4 | Darling | McWilliams |
| 3—Pittsburgh | W | 6-2 | Lynch | DeLeon |
| 4—At Atlanta | W | 16-13z | Gorman | Camp |
| 5—At Atlanta | W | 6-1 | Aguilera | Perez |
| 7—At Atlanta | W | 4-0 | Fernandez | Smith |
| 7—At Atlanta | W | 8-5 | Darling | Dedmon |
| 8—At Cinn. | W | 7-5 | Lynch | Tibbs |
| 9—At Cinn. | W | 11-2 | Gooden | Soto |
| 10—At Cinn. | W | 2-1 | Aguilera | Browning |

### JULY

| Date | | Score | Winner | Loser |
|---|---|---|---|---|
| 11—At Hous. | L | 3-4‡ | Smith | Gorman |
| 12—At Hous. | W | 3-2* | Darling | Mathis |
| 13—At Hous. | W | 10-1 | Lynch | Knudson |
| 14—At Hous. | W | 1-0 | Gooden | Knepper |
| 18—Atlanta | W | 7-6 | Darling | Mahler |
| 19—Atlanta | L | 0-1 | Smith | Aguilera |
| 20—Atlanta | W | 16-4 | Gooden | Bedrosian |
| 21—Atlanta | W | 15-10 | Leach | Perez |
| 22—Cincinnati | L | 1-5 | Soto | Fernandez |
| 23—Cincinnati | L | 0-4 | Browning | Darling |
| 24—Cincinnati | L | 2-3 | Franco | McDowell |
| 25—Houston | W | 6-3 | Gooden | Scott |
| 27—Houston | W | 16-4 | Orosco | DePino |
| 27—Houston | W | 7-3 | Latham | Kerfeld |
| 28—Houston | L | 4-12 | Niekro | Darling |
| 29—Montreal | W | 3-2 | Aguilera | Smith |
| 30—Montreal | W | 2-0 | Gooden | Gullickson |
| 31—Montreal | W | 5-2 | Lynch | Schatzeder |

**Won 21, Lost 7**

### AUGUST

| Date | | Score | Winner | Loser |
|---|---|---|---|---|
| 2—At Chicago | L | 1-2 | Eckersley | Leach |
| 3—At Chicago | W | 5-4* | Orosco | Frazier |
| 4—At Chicago | W | 4-1 | Gooden | Fontenot |
| 5—At Chicago | W | 7-2 | Lynch | Botelho |
| 8—At Mon. | W | 14-7 | Aguilera | Hesketh |
| 9—Chicago | W | 6-4 | McDowell | Brusstar |
| 10—Chicago | W | 8-3 | Gooden | Fontenot |
| 11—Chicago | W | 6-2 | Lynch | Botelho |
| 12—Phila. | W | 4-3 | Fernandez | Denny |
| 13—Phila. | W | 4-2 | Aguilera | Hudson |
| 14—Phila. | L | 1-2 | Gross | Darling |
| 15—Phila. | W | 10-7 | Orosco | Carman |
| 16—At Pitts. | L | 1-7 | Rhoden | Lynch |
| 17—At Pitts. | W | 4-3 | Fernandez | Tunnell |
| 18—At Pitts. | L | 0-5 | Robinson | Aguilera |
| 19—At Mon. | W | 1-0 | Darling | Burke |
| 20—San Fran. | W | 3-0 | Gooden | Gott |
| 21—San Fran. | L | 2-3 | LaPoint | McDowell |
| 22—San Fran. | W | 7-0 | Leach | Blue |
| 23—San Diego | L | 1-6 | Thurmond | Aguilera |
| 23—San Diego | L | 0-3 | Jackson | Fernandez |
| 24—San Diego | W | 5-1 | Darling | Dravecky |
| 25—San Diego | W | 9-3 | Gooden | Show |
| 26—Los Ang. | L | 1-6 | Valenzuela | Lynch |
| 27—Los Ang. | L | 1-2 | Reuss | Fernandez |
| 29—At S. Fran. | L | 3-6* | Garrelts | Leach |
| 30—At S. Fran. | W | 2-1 | Darling | Krukow |
| 31—At S. Fran. | L | 2-3 | Gott | Gooden |

**Won 17, Lost 11**

### SEPTEMBER

| Date | | Score | Winner | Loser |
|---|---|---|---|---|
| 1—At S. Fran. | W | 4-3 | Sisk | Davis |
| 2—At S. Diego | W | 12-4 | Fernandez | Thurmond |
| 3—At S. Diego | W | 8-3 | Aguilera | Dravecky |
| 4—At S. Diego | W | 9-2 | Darling | Jackson |
| 6—At L. A. | W | 2-0§ | Orosco | Niedenfuer |
| 7—At L. A. | L | 6-7 | Niedenfuer | Leach |
| 8—At L. A. | W | 4-3x | Sisk | Diaz |
| 10—St. Louis | W | 5-4 | Darling | Cox |
| 11—St. Louis | L | 0-1* | Tudor | Orosco |
| 12—St. Louis | W | 7-6 | Orosco | Dayley |
| 13—At Mon. | L | 1-5 | Smith | Aguilera |
| 13—At Mon. | W | 7-2 | Leach | Schatzeder |
| 14—At Mon. | L | 1-5 | Palmer | Fernandez |
| 15—At Mon. | W | 6-2 | Darling | Dopson |
| 16—Phila. | W | 9-0 | Gooden | Gross |
| 17—Phila. | L | 1-5 | Rawley | Lynch |
| 18—Chicago | W | 4-2 | Aguilera | Trout |
| 19—Chicago | W | 5-1 | Fernandez | Fontenot |
| 20—Pittsburgh | L | 5-7† | Guante | Latham |
| 21—Pittsburgh | W | 12-1 | Gooden | Rhoden |
| 22—Pittsburgh | L | 3-5 | Kipper | Leach |
| 23—At Phila. | W | 4-1 | Aguilera | Toliver |
| 24—At Phila. | W | 7-1 | Fernandez | Rucker |
| 25—At Chicago | L | 4-5 | Smith | Orosco |
| 26—At Chicago | W | 3-0 | Gooden | Abrego |
| 27—At Pitts. | L | 7-8 | McWilliams | Gardner |
| 28—At Pitts. | W | 3-1 | Aguilera | Kipper |
| 29—At Pitts. | W | 9-7* | Orosco | McWilliams |

**Won 19, Lost 9**

### OCTOBER

| Date | | Score | Winner | Loser |
|---|---|---|---|---|
| 1—At St. L. | W | 1-0† | Orosco | Dayley |
| 2—At St. L. | W | 5-2 | Gooden | Andujar |
| 3—At St. L. | L | 3-4 | Cox | Aguilera |
| 4—Montreal | W | 9-4 | Fernandez | Gullickson |
| 5—Montreal | L | 3-8 | Youmans | Darling |
| 6—Montreal | L | 1-2 | Schatzeder | Latham |

**Won 3, Lost 3**

*10 innings.   †11 innings.   ‡12 innings.   §13 innings.   x14 innings.   y18 innings.   z19 innings.

**Ron Darling's 16-6 record was lost in the glare of Dwight Gooden's accomplishments.**

in by so many other players—especially N.L. Cy Young Award winner Dwight Gooden.

Gooden followed up his impressive 1984 rookie season with a campaign that included league-leading totals in earned-run average (1.53), victories (24) and strikeouts (268), making him the first pitcher since Steve Carlton in 1972 to win the "Triple Crown" of pitching. He lost only four games.

The 20-year-old righthander also led the league with 16 complete games and 276⅔ innings pitched while posting a club-record eight shutouts. He had a 14-game winning streak and a 31-inning scoreless streak.

Almost lost in the wake of Gooden's stunning season was Ron Darling, who could have been the ace of many a staff in the majors. The righthander went 16-6 with a 2.90 ERA and 167 strikeouts in 248 innings.

The Mets' most productive offensive player was first baseman Keith Hernandez, who won his eighth consecutive Gold Glove. His .309 average, 87 runs scored and 34 doubles were team highs, and of his 91 RBIs, 24 were game-winners, a new major league record.

The Mets got about as much offense as they could expect from the middle of their infield. Wally Backman batted .273, led the team with 30 stolen bases and played a slick second base, while shortstop Rafael Santana hit .257 (although he committed 25 errors).

The Mets also came up with three young pitchers who contributed mightily to their pennant pursuit.

Rookie Roger McDowell made the club in spring training and wound up the most dependable reliever on the staff with a 6-5 record and 17 saves. Sid Fernandez joined the team in mid-May and went 9-9 with a 2.80 ERA and a lot of tough luck. The lefthander finished fifth in the league in strikeouts with 180. The third big addition to the staff was rookie Rick Aguilera, who was promoted from Tidewater (International) in June and turned in a 10-7 record.

The highest ERA among regular Mets starters was recorded by Ed Lynch, whose 3.44 mark still was respectable. Overall, New York pitchers had the league's third-best ERA (3.11), which went nicely with the club's .257 batting average (No. 4 in the league).

But among all these pluses, the Mets also had a few minuses that contributed to their second-place finish.

One was the inability of lefthander Jesse Orosco to match his 1984 performance, when he had 31 saves. Orosco repeatedly denied he had elbow problems, but Johnson frequently would not even call on him, and disastrous results often followed when he did. Orosco wound up with only 17 saves and an 8-6 record.

Plagued by control problems, reliever Doug Sisk saved only two games, 13 fewer than in 1984. He underwent elbow surgery after the season.

Offensively, left fielder George Foster was inconsistent, and though he finished with 21 homers and 77 RBIs, it was not a typical season for the veteran slugger. And at third base, Howard Johnson and Ray Knight combined for 17 homers and 82 RBIs, but their combined batting average was only .232.

While the Mets beat up on teams like Atlanta (10-2) and Chicago (14-4), they had trouble with the last-place Pittsburgh Pirates, who won eight of the teams' 18 meetings. They also were only 8-10 against St. Louis, the team they had to beat.

"We put it all together this year," Hernandez said. "But the Cardinals put it together a little better."

**Jeff Reardon recorded a major league-leading 41 saves and was largely responsible for Montreal's 1985 revival.**

# Surprising Expos Earn Respect

### By IAN MacDONALD

Though they finished 16½ games behind the division-winning St. Louis Cardinals, the Montreal Expos made important strides in 1985.

After a 1984 season in which the Expos came in fifth in the National League East, five games below .500, the Expos jumped two notches in the standings, finishing a respectable seven games over .500 with an 84-77 record.

"When we started the season," first-year Manager Buck Rodgers said, "we knew we had to get over the .500 mark. We thought if we could get to 10 games over we would have a great season.

"At one point we were almost 20 games over, and at that point our aims were much higher than what we had originally thought about. But injuries finally broke our backs. We couldn't keep pace."

The Expos peaked August 18, after they had won successive one-run games in St. Louis. They were 17 games over .500 and just four games off the torrid pace being set by the Cardinals and the Mets. But injuries to pitchers David Palmer, Dan Schatzeder and Joe Hesketh quickly put the Expos in a bind.

The Expos didn't bemoan their fate because frankly, nobody really expected this team to contend. But the injuries were significant, as a brief comparison shows.

In 1979, when the Expos had their finest season with a 95-65 record, they had only one player on the disabled list all season. The club had six pitchers with wins in double figures and seven players with more than 480 at-bats. By comparison, Rodgers had to shuffle the lineup because of eight disablements in 1985, plus a handful of minor injuries. Only three pitchers earned 10 or more wins, and just five players had as many as 480 at-bats.

The Expos' pitching staff was hit hard by injuries. Charlie Lea, who went 15-10 in 1984, did not throw a pitch all season because of shoulder problems that required surgery. Other pitchers disabled during the season were Gary Lucas, Bert Roberge, Bill Gullickson, Schatzeder (twice), Palmer and Hesketh. Only Bryn Smith, Jeff Reardon and Tim Burke were on the active roster for the entire season, and both Smith and Reardon missed time because of injuries.

Despite all these medical setbacks, the Expos still managed to finish as high as third mainly because of their strong

**Righthander Bryn Smith emerged as the ace of the staff, recording an 18-5 record and 2.91 ERA.**

pitching. The Montreal staff posted a 3.55 earned-run average, which ranked fifth in the league, and the bullpen was responsible for an N.L.-high 53 saves.

The most successful Montreal pitcher was Smith, who filled the void created by the loss of Lea and the release of longtime ace Steve Rogers. The righthander went 18-5 with a 2.91 ERA and came through with the best winning percentage by any Expos pitcher ever with 20 or more decisions.

Gullickson (14-12, 3.52 ERA) and Hesketh (10-5, 2.49) were the only other Montreal pitchers who reached double figures in victories. Hesketh might have tallied even more wins had the rookie not broken his leg when he tripped over Dodgers catcher Mike Scioscia's leg August 23.

## SCORES OF MONTREAL EXPOS' 1985 GAMES

### APRIL

| Date | | Score | Winner | Loser |
|---|---|---|---|---|
| 8—At Cinn. | L | 1-4 | Soto | Rogers |
| 10—At Cinn. | W | 4-1 | Gullickson | Tibbs |
| 12—At Chicago | W | 5-1 | Smith | Eckersley |
| 13—At Chicago | L | 3-8 | Sanderson | Rogers |
| 14—At Chicago | W | 2-4 | Sutcliffe | Palmer |
| 15—At St. L. | L | 1-6 | Forsch | Gullickson |
| 17—At St. L. | W | 2-1 | Hesketh | Tudor |
| 18—At St. L. | W | 7-1 | Rogers | Kepshire |
| 19—Chicago | W | 5-3 | Smith | Sutcliffe |
| 20—Chicago | W | 4-0 | Gullickson | Trout |
| 21—Chicago | L | 0-4 | Eckersley | Palmer |
| 22—Phila. | L | 1-9 | Rawley | Hesketh |
| 23—Phila. | W | 5-4* | Reardon | Hudson |
| 24—Phila. | W | 7-6 | Smith | Denny |
| 25—St. Louis | W | 4-2 | Gullickson | Cox |
| 26—St. Louis | W | 10-5 | Palmer | Forsch |
| 27—St. Louis | W | 8-3 | Hesketh | Tudor |
| 28—St. Louis | W | 5-3 | Rogers | Kepshire |
| 29—At Phila. | L | 2-3* | Tekulve | Roberge |
| 30—At Phila. | L | 0-11 | Koosman | Gullickson |

**Won 12, Lost 8**

### MAY

| Date | | Score | Winner | Loser |
|---|---|---|---|---|
| 1—At Phila. | W | 3-2 | Palmer | Rawley |
| 3—At Atlanta | W | 9-2 | Hesketh | Barker |
| 4—At Atlanta | W | 9-3 | Smith | Perez |
| 5—At Atlanta | L | 1-6 | Mahler | Gullickson |
| 7—Houston | L | 1-3 | Knepper | Palmer |
| 8—Houston | W | 1-0 | Hesketh | Ryan |
| 10—Atlanta | W | 5-0 | Smith | Mahler |
| 11—Atlanta | W | 3-0 | Gullickson | Bedrosian |
| 12—Atlanta | W | 4-0 | Palmer | McMurtry |
| 13—At Hous. | L | 2-3* | Smith | Reardon |
| 14—At Hous. | L | 0-10 | Mathis | Rogers |
| 15—Cincinnati | L | 1-2 | Price | Smith |
| 16—Cincinnati | L | 2-4 | Tibbs | Gullickson |
| 17—San Diego | W | 2-1* | Reardon | Stoddard |
| 18—San Diego | L | 2-8 | Dravecky | Hesketh |
| 19—San Diego | L | 3-8 | Hawkins | Rogers |
| 20—Los Ang. | W | 9-1 | Schatzeder | Castillo |
| 21—Los Ang. | W | 6-1 | Gullickson | Honeycutt |
| 22—Los Ang. | L | 0-4 | Reuss | Palmer |
| 24—San Fran. | W | 2-0 | Hesketh | Laskey |
| 25—San Fran. | W | 3-1 | Schatzeder | Gott |
| 26—San Fran. | W | 3-1 | Gullickson | Krukow |
| 27—San Fran. | L | 1-6 | Hammaker | Palmer |
| 28—At S. Diego | W | 8-5 | Roberge | Gossage |
| 29—At S. Diego | W | 2-1 | Burke | Lefferts |
| 30—At S. Diego | L | 4-5 | Hawkins | Schatzeder |
| 31—At L.A. | L | 0-4 | Honeycutt | Gullickson |

**Won 15, Lost 12**

### JUNE

| Date | | Score | Winner | Loser |
|---|---|---|---|---|
| 1—At L.A. | W | 4-2† | Lucas | Howell |
| 2—At L.A. | L | 7-8 | Castillo | Smith |
| 3—At S. Fran. | W | 4-2§ | St. Claire | Williams |
| 4—At S. Fran. | L | 1-5 | Gott | Schatzeder |
| 5—At S. Fran. | W | 6-0 | Mahler | Krukow |
| 7—At Phila. | W | 3-1 | Palmer | Carlton |
| 8—At Phila. | W | 4-3 | Smith | Rawley |
| 9—At Phila. | L | 1-4 | Gross | Hesketh |
| 10—Chicago | L | 4-5 | Fontenot | Reardon |
| 11—Chicago | L | 3-5 | Frazier | St. Claire |
| 12—Chicago | W | 2-0 | Palmer | Sutcliffe |
| 13—Chicago | W | 9-7 | Smith | Trout |
| 14—New York | W | 5-4 | Lucas | Sisk |
| 15—New York | W | 3-2 | Burke | Fernandez |
| 16—New York | W | 7-2 | Gullickson | Aguilera |
| 17—Pittsburgh | L | 2-5 | Winn | Palmer |
| 18—Pittsburgh | L | 1-4 | McWilliams | Smith |
| 19—Pittsburgh | W | 4-3 | Burke | DeLeon |
| 20—Pittsburgh | L | 1-2 | Rhoden | Schatzeder |
| 21—At N.Y. | L | 3-6 | Sisk | Mahler |
| 22—At N.Y. | W | 5-4* | St. Claire | McDowell |
| 23—At N.Y. | W | 5-1 | Smith | Lynch |
| 25—At Pitts. | W | 3-2 | Burke | Holland |
| 26—At Pitts. | L | 2-11 | Reuschel | O'Connor |
| 27—At Pitts. | W | 4-2 | Palmer | McWilliams |
| 28—Phila. | W | 5-3 | Smith | Hudson |
| 29—Phila. | L | 2-6 | Gross | Mahler |
| 30—Phila. | L | 2-3 | Tekulve | Reardon |

**Won 16, Lost 12**

### JULY

| Date | | Score | Winner | Loser |
|---|---|---|---|---|
| 1—St. Louis | W | 3-2* | Lucas | Horton |
| 2—St. Louis | L | 0-4 | Tudor | Palmer |
| 4—At Hous. | W | 9-3‡ | St. Claire | DiPino |
| 5—At Hous. | L | 2-4 | Scott | Mahler |
| 6—At Hous. | L | 7-8 | Calhoun | Lucas |
| 7—At Hous. | W | 6-3x | Youmans | Mathis |
| 8—At Atlanta | L | 1-7 | Mahler | Gullickson |
| 9—At Atlanta | W | 5-1 | Smith | Perez |
| 10—At Atlanta | W | 6-5† | Burke | Sutter |
| 11—At Cinn. | L | 0-2 | Robinson | Hesketh |
| 12—At Cinn. | L | 4-5† | Franco | St. Claire |
| 13—At Cinn. | W | 6-3 | Gullickson | Soto |
| 14—At Cinn. | L | 4-5* | Power | Lucas |
| 18—Houston | W | 3-0 | Hesketh | Niekro |
| 19—Houston | W | 4-0 | Smith | Knepper |
| 20—Houston | W | 6-1 | Gullickson | Ryan |
| 21—Houston | L | 4-5 | Scott | Mahler |
| 22—Atlanta | L | 1-7 | Mahler | Palmer |
| 23—Atlanta | W | 4-2 | Hesketh | Smith |
| 24—Atlanta | W | 3-1 | Smith | Bedrosian |
| 25—Cincinnati | W | 1-0 | Gullickson | Hume |
| 26—Cincinnati | L | 6-7† | Buchanan | Reardon |
| 27—Cincinnati | L | 6-7 | Browning | Palmer |
| 28—Cincinnati | W | 6-0 | Hesketh | Robinson |
| 29—At N.Y. | L | 2-3 | Aguilera | Smith |
| 30—At N.Y. | L | 0-2 | Gooden | Gullickson |
| 31—At N.Y. | L | 2-5 | Lynch | Schatzeder |

**Won 13, Lost 14**

### AUGUST

| Date | | Score | Winner | Loser |
|---|---|---|---|---|
| 2—At Pitts. | W | 3-2 | Hesketh | Reuschel |
| 3—At Pitts. | W | 6-5 | Roberge | McWilliams |
| 4—At Pitts. | L | 3-4 | Rhoden | Gullickson |
| 5—At Pitts. | W | 5-2 | Burke | Winn |
| 8—New York | L | 7-14 | Aguilera | Hesketh |
| 9—Pittsburgh | W | 7-2 | Smith | Reuschel |
| 10—Pittsburgh | W | 7-5 | St. Claire | Rhoden |
| 11—Pittsburgh | W | 6-5 | Burke | Guante |
| 12—At Chi. | L | 7-8 | Gumpert | Reardon |
| 13—At Chi. | W | 4-1 | Hesketh | Sanderson |
| 14—At Chi. | W | 8-7 | Smith | Sorensen |
| 15—At Chi. | W | 7-3 | Gullickson | Engel |
| 16—At St. L. | L | 1-6 | Forsch | Laskey |
| 17—At St. L. | W | 5-4 | Burke | Campbell |
| 18—At St. L. | W | 6-5* | Lucas | Andujar |
| 19—New York | L | 0-1 | Darling | Burke |
| 20—San Diego | L | 0-1 | Dravecky | Gullickson |
| 21—San Diego | L | 2-6 | Show | Laskey |
| 22—San Diego | L | 0-3 | Hawkins | Youmans |
| 23—Los Ang. | L | 4-8 | Hershiser | Burke |
| 24—Los Ang. | W | 5-2 | Smith | Honeycutt |
| 25—Los Ang. | W | 6-1 | Gullickson | Welch |
| 26—San Fran. | L | 4-7 | LaPoint | Laskey |
| 27—San Fran. | L | 1-6 | Minton | Reardon |
| 29—At S. Diego | W | 8-5 | Roberge | Walter |
| 31—At S. Diego | W | 7-1 | Gullickson | Show |

**Won 15, Lost 11**

### SEPTEMBER

| Date | | Score | Winner | Loser |
|---|---|---|---|---|
| 1—At S. Diego | L | 1-5 | Hawkins | Youmans |
| 2—At L.A. | L | 4-5† | Diaz | Reardon |
| 3—At L.A. | L | 0-4 | Hershiser | Smith |
| 4—At L.A. | L | 2-4 | Welch | Dopson |
| 6—At S. Fran. | L | 3-8 | Gott | Gullickson |
| 7—At S. Fran. | W | 7-1 | Youmans | LaPoint |
| 8—At S. Fran. | W | 9-6* | Lucas | Garrelts |
| 10—At Phila. | L | 2-5† | Carman | Burke |
| 11—At Phila. | L | 1-4 | Gross | Gullickson |
| 12—At Phila. | W | 6-3 | Youmans | Rawley |
| 13—New York | W | 5-1 | Smith | Aguilera |
| 13—New York | L | 2-7 | Leach | Schatzeder |
| 14—New York | W | 5-1 | Palmer | Fernandez |
| 15—New York | L | 2-6 | Darling | Dopson |
| 16—Chicago | W | 8-5 | Burke | Frazier |
| 17—Chicago | L | 0-3 | Eckersley | Youmans |
| 18—Pittsburgh | L | 6-10† | Robinson | Roberge |
| 19—Pittsburgh | W | 6-8* | Winn | Burke |
| 20—At St. L. | L | 3-5 | Worrell | St. Claire |
| 21—At St. L. | L | 6-7 | Lahti | Roberge |
| 22—At St. L. | L | 5-6 | Dayley | O'Connor |
| 23—At Chicago | W | 10-7 | St. Claire | Frazier |
| 24—At Chicago | W | 17-15 | Smith | Fontenot |
| 25—At Pitts. | L | 2-8 | Reuschel | Laskey |
| 28—St. Louis | W | 2-0 | Gullickson | Andujar |
| 28—St. Louis | L | 2-4† | Worrell | Reardon |
| 29—St. Louis | W | 7-5 | Lucas | Dayley |

**Won 10, Lost 17**

### OCTOBER

| Date | | Score | Winner | Loser |
|---|---|---|---|---|
| 2—Phila. | W | 3-1 | Smith | Gross |
| 2—Phila. | L | 2-3 | Hudson | Palmer |
| 3—Phila. | L | 7-8 | Rawley | Laskey |
| 4—At N.Y. | L | 4-9 | Fernandez | Gullickson |
| 5—At N.Y. | W | 8-3 | Youmans | Darling |
| 6—At N.Y. | W | 2-1 | Schatzeder | Latham |

**Won 3, Lost 3**

*10 innings.   †11 innings.   ‡12 innings.   §15 innings.   x19 innings.

**Tim Raines was the picture of consistency, hitting .320 and stealing 70 bases.**

Palmer, Lucas, Schatzeder and Roberge combined for 19 victories between injuries.

Led by Reardon, the bullpen was brilliant. Despite being hampered by elbow problems in the second half of the season, the "Terminator" led the league with 41 saves and was named the N.L. Fireman of the Year.

"Jeff and Bryn Smith were our top pitchers, but because he finished the job so often and effectively, I pick Reardon as the (team's) Number 1 pitcher . . . (and) MVP," Rodgers said.

Burke blossomed dramatically, first as a setup man for Reardon and later as a closer. The righthander was 9-4 with eight saves and a 2.39 ERA, and he tied the major league record for rookie pitching appearances with 78.

The Montreal offense, however, batted only .247 and often provided little run support for the pitchers. In 57 of the club's 77 losses, the Expos scored three or fewer runs.

Left fielder Tim Raines was the team's

top offensive contributor. Raines ranked among the top three in the league in batting (.320), stolen bases (70), runs scored (115), triples (13) and on-base percentage (.405). He also hit 11 home runs.

While the Mets were patting themselves on the back for obtaining catcher Gary Carter from Montreal after the 1984 season, the Expos were enjoying the production of shortstop Hubie Brooks, one of the four players acquired for Carter. Brooks batted .269 with 34 doubles and 13 homers as well as a surprising 100 runs batted in, the most by an N.L. shortstop since 1960, when Chicago's Ernie Banks had 117. With 41 of his RBIs coming after two men were out, Brooks also became something of a clutch performer.

Less could be said of two of the other players obtained in the Carter deal, center fielder Herm Winningham and catcher Mike Fitzgerald. Winningham, a rookie, hit .237, and after a short stint on the disabled list he often shared his position with Mitch Webster, who hit .274 after being acquired from the Toronto organization in June. Fitzgerald saw more action than any other Expos catcher, but he batted just .207.

Another weak position was first base, where Dan Driessen contributed only 25 RBIs before being traded to San Francisco on August 1. His replacement, Terry Francona, hit .267.

Second baseman Vance Law, another off-season addition to the roster, was quietly effective. Law hit .266 and was second on the team in runs (75) and on-base percentage (.369).

Tim Wallach, gradually gaining recognition as the best third baseman in the league, produced handsomely with 22 homers and 81 RBIs. Though he ranked second in the league to the Giants' Chris Brown in fielding percentage (.967 to .971), Wallach led N.L. third basemen in putouts, assists, double plays and total chances and was awarded his first Gold Glove.

Right fielder Andre Dawson also won a Gold Glove (his sixth) while contributing 23 homers and 91 RBIs.

Even though the offense was not as productive as the Expos had hoped, they were pleased with their ability to stay in contention until their pitching staff was decimated by injuries.

"We proved this year that if we have reasonable health, we can compete in this division," Rodgers said. "We were right in the middle of things until we ran out of pitchers. Now we have to continue to improve."

After a slow start, second baseman Ryne Sandberg surged to a .305 average and 26 home runs while winning his second straight Gold Glove.

# Injury-Plagued Cubs Fall Hard

**By DAVE van DYCK**

If there is one word that can describe the Chicago Cubs' disappointing 1985 season, it would be "ouch."

The defending National League East champions had to spend the winter licking their wounded pride after injuries forced them into fourth place with a 77-84 record, 23½ games out of first.

Even though most Cubs fans probably would rather forget the 1985 season, it was memorable just because it was so unusual. In midseason, all five starting pitchers were on the disabled list at the same time.

The Cubs "would have won 100 games if our pitchers would have been healthy," Manager Jim Frey said. As it was, they were lucky to stay in contention for as long as they did.

How bad was it? On May 19, the day that 1984 Cy Young Award winner Rick Sutcliffe first hurt his leg and two days after Steve Trout first hurt his elbow, the Cubs were 2½ games out of first place and the pitching staff had an earned-run average of 2.56 with nine complete games. Over the next 75 games, the staff ERA was 4.12 with just seven complete games, and the Cubs tumbled to fourth, never to contend again.

With Sutcliffe and Trout hurt, the burden fell to Dennis Eckersley, Scott Sanderson and Dick Ruthven. All three also wound up disabled—Eckersley with shoulder tendinitis, Sanderson with a stretched knee ligament and Ruthven with a broken toe.

"I have never seen anything like it," said Jacob Suker, the team's longtime physician.

The injuries seemed to spread to almost every player and part of the body. Left fielder Gary Matthews underwent knee surgery and was on the disabled list twice. Center fielder Bob Dernier had foot surgery and played hobbled the last half of the season. Catcher Jody Davis spent time in the hospital with a stomach disorder. Young Brian Dayett hardly played at all because of ankle surgery.

Cubs fielders missed 242 games due to injuries. The five starting pitchers missed 60 starts. Eleven players spent 14 stretches on the disabled list, including Sutcliffe three times.

The result was that six pitchers won their first major league game and 18 different pitchers had at least one victory. The team ERA went from 3.75 in 1984 to

**Keith Moreland sparkled throughout the Cubs' dismal season, batting .307 with 106 RBIs.**

4.16, next to last in the league. Cubs pitchers surrendered a league-high 156 home runs.

Frey used 101 different lineups as the offense struggled. Despite the injuries, Frey thought the Cubs should have produced more runs.

"We had a lot of games where we had chances to do damage, but other than a couple of consistent guys, we had trouble finishing off the other team," Frey said. "Maybe three times during a game we get in a situation where one good pop would do it and we didn't get it done."

Matthews, third baseman Ron Cey and Davis batted a collective .233 in 1985.

## SCORES OF CHICAGO CUBS' 1985 GAMES

### APRIL

| Date | W/L | Score | Winner | Loser |
|---|---|---|---|---|
| 9—Pittsburgh | W | 2-1 | Sutcliffe | Rhoden |
| 11—Pittsburgh | W | 4-1 | Trout | DeLeon |
| 12—Montreal | L | 1-5 | Smith | Eckersley |
| 13—Montreal | W | 8-3 | Sanderson | Rogers |
| 14—Montreal | W | 4-2 | Sutcliffe | Palmer |
| 15—Phila. | W | 2-1 | Trout | Gross |
| 16—Phila. | W | 1-0* | Eckersley | Holland |
| 17—Phila. | W | 5-4 | Frazier | Gross |
| 19—At Mon. | L | 3-5 | Smith | Sutcliffe |
| 20—At Mon. | L | 0-4 | Gullickson | Trout |
| 21—At Mon. | W | 4-0 | Eckersley | Palmer |
| 22—At Pitts. | L | 3-5 | McWilliams | Ruthven |
| 23—At Pitts. | W | 5-0 | Sutcliffe | Bielecki |
| 24—At Pitts. | W | 5-2 | Trout | Rhoden |
| 26—At Phila. | W | 7-3 | Eckersley | Koosman |
| 27—At Phila. | L | 1-6 | Rawley | Sanderson |
| 28—At Phila. | L | 2-3 | Gross | Sutcliffe |
| 30—San Fran. | W | 3-1 | Trout | Laskey |

**Won 12, Lost 6**

### MAY

| Date | W/L | Score | Winner | Loser |
|---|---|---|---|---|
| 1—San Fran. | W | 4-3 | Eckersley | Garrelts |
| 3—San Diego | L | 5-6 | Hawkins | Sutcliffe |
| 4—San Diego | W | 12-8 | Sorensen | Booker |
| 5—San Diego | W | 6-3y | Frazier | DeLeon |
| 6—Los Ang. | L | 4-5* | Howell | Fontenot |
| 7—Los Ang. | W | 4-2 | Ruthven | Brennan |
| 8—At S. Fran. | W | 1-0 | Sutcliffe | Krukow |
| 9—At S. Fran. | L | 0-1‡ | Garrelts | Brusstar |
| 10—At S. Diego | W | 6-2 | Trout | Hoyt |
| 11—At S. Diego | L | 1-3 | Show | Eckersley |
| 12—At S. Diego | L | 3-5 | Dravecky | Ruthven |
| 14—At L.A. | W | 8-3 | Sutcliffe | Valenzuela |
| 15—At L.A. | W | 3-2 | Sanderson | Honeycutt |
| 17—At Atlanta | W | 7-5 | Smith | Sutter |
| 18—At Atlanta | L | 3-4 | Mahler | Eckersley |
| 19—At Atlanta | L | 0-3 | Bedrosian | Sutcliffe |
| 20—Cincinnati | W | 6-1 | Sanderson | Tibbs |
| 21—Cincinnati | L | 2-5 | Hume | Frazier |
| 22—Cincinnati | W | 7-4 | Eckersley | Browning |
| 24—Houston | L | 2-6 | Ryan | Ruthven |
| 25—Houston | W | 5-4 | Smith | Ross |
| 26—Houston | W | 10-8 | Frazier | Ross |
| 27—At Cinn. | W | 4-3 | Eckersley | Browning |
| 28—At Cinn. | L | 11-13 | Franco | Sorensen |
| 29—At Cinn. | L | 0-1 | Soto | Ruthven |
| 31—At Hous. | W | 6-2* | L. Smith | D. Smith |

**Won 15, Lost 11**

### JUNE

| Date | W/L | Score | Winner | Loser |
|---|---|---|---|---|
| 1—At Hous. | W | 4-1 | Eckersley | Knepper |
| 2—At Hous. | L | 3-4 | Scott | Gura |
| 4—Atlanta | W | 5-3 | Ruthven | Mahler |
| 5—Atlanta | L | 2-4† | Dedmon | Smith |
| 6—Pittsburgh | W | 3-2‡ | Brusstar | Holland |
| 7—Pittsburgh | W | 1-0 | Sutcliffe | DeLeon |
| 8—Pittsburgh | W | 7-3 | Trout | McWilliams |
| 9—Pittsburgh | W | 5-1 | Ruthven | Winn |
| 10—At Mon. | W | 5-4 | Fontenot | Reardon |
| 11—At Mon. | W | 5-3 | Frazier | St. Claire |
| 12—At Mon. | L | 0-2 | Palmer | Sutcliffe |
| 13—At Mon. | L | 7-9 | Smith | Trout |
| 14—St. Louis | L | 10-11 | Andujar | Ruthven |
| 15—St. Louis | L | 0-2 | Cox | Fontenot |
| 16—St. Louis | L | 2-5 | Kepshire | Eckersley |
| 17—At N.Y. | L | 0-2 | Darling | Sutcliffe |
| 18—At N.Y. | L | 1-5 | Lynch | Trout |
| 19—At N.Y. | L | 0-1 | Gooden | Sanderson |
| 20—At N.Y. | L | 3-5 | Fernandez | Fontenot |
| 21—At St. L. | L | 5-7 | Kepshire | Eckersley |
| 22—At St. L. | L | 1-2* | Dayley | Smith |
| 23—At St. L. | L | 0-7 | Tudor | Ruthven |
| 25—New York | L | 2-3 | Gooden | Sanderson |
| 26—New York | W | 7-3 | Fontenot | McDowell |
| 27—New York | W | 4-2 | Sutcliffe | Darling |
| 28—At Pitts. | W | 5-0 | Trout | DeLeon |
| 29—At Pitts. | L | 5-6x | Reuschel | Frazier |
| 30—At Pitts. | W | 9-2 | Sanderson | Robinson |

**Won 12, Lost 16**

### JULY

| Date | W/L | Score | Winner | Loser |
|---|---|---|---|---|
| 1—At Phila. | W | 3-1 | Fontenot | Denny |
| 2—At Phila. | L | 2-11 | Rawley | Sutcliffe |
| 3—At Phila. | W | 4-3 | Smith | Tekulve |
| 4—San Fran. | L | 4-6 | Garrelts | Trout |
| 5—San Fran. | L | 6-12 | Blue | Sanderson |
| 6—San Fran. | L | 4-6 | Garrelts | Smith |
| 7—San Fran. | W | 6-5 | Brusstar | Davis |
| 8—San Diego | L | 4-8 | Stoddard | Sorensen |
| 9—San Diego | W | 7-3 | Trout | Show |
| 10—San Diego | W | 4-3 | Sanderson | Dravecky |
| 11—Los Ang. | L | 1-3 | Welch | Fontenot |
| 12—Los Ang. | L | 4-7 | Niedenfuer | Smith |
| 13—Los Ang. | L | 1-9 | Valenzuela | Gura |
| 14—Los Ang. | W | 10-4 | Frazier | Honeycutt |
| 18—At S. Fran. | L | 0-1 | Krukow | Frazier |
| 19—At S. Fran. | W | 4-3 | Sorensen | Gott |
| 20—At S. Fran. | W | 2-1 | Ruthven | Hammaker |
| 21—At S. Fran. | L | 1-2 | Laskey | Gura |
| 22—At S. Diego | W | 5-3 | Meridith | Jackson |
| 23—At S. Diego | W | 8-1 | Sutcliffe | Hawkins |
| 24—At S. Diego | W | 4-3* | Smith | Stoddard |
| 25—At L.A. | L | 3-7 | Valenzuela | Fontenot |
| 26—At L.A. | L | 0-10 | Reuss | Ruthven |
| 27—At L.A. | L | 4-5 | Hershiser | Frazier |
| 28—At L.A. | W | 9-2 | Sorensen | Powell |
| 30—St. Louis | L | 3-11 | Kepshire | Engel |
| 31—St. Louis | W | 5-2 | Fontenot | Andujar |

**Won 13, Lost 14**

### AUGUST

| Date | W/L | Score | Winner | Loser |
|---|---|---|---|---|
| 1—St. Louis | W | 9-8§ | Frazier | Dayley |
| 2—New York | W | 2-1 | Eckersley | Leach |
| 3—New York | L | 4-5* | Orosco | Frazier |
| 4—New York | L | 1-4 | Gooden | Fontenot |
| 5—New York | L | 2-7 | Lynch | Botelho |
| 8—At St. L. | L | 0-8 | Tudor | Sanderson |
| 9—At N.Y. | L | 4-6 | McDowell | Brusstar |
| 10—At N.Y. | L | 3-8 | Gooden | Fontenot |
| 11—At N.Y. | L | 2-6 | Lynch | Botelho |
| 12—Montreal | W | 8-7 | Gumpert | Reardon |
| 13—Montreal | L | 1-4 | Hesketh | Sanderson |
| 14—Montreal | L | 7-8 | Smith | Sorensen |
| 15—Montreal | L | 3-7 | Gullickson | Engel |
| 16—Phila. | W | 6-5 | Smith | Tekulve |
| 17—Phila. | L | 4-10 | Denny | Sorensen |
| 18—Phila. | L | 5-9 | Hudson | Baller |
| 20—At Atlanta | W | 5-2 | Fontenot | Sutter |
| 21—At Atlanta | W | 9-5 | Brusstar | Garber |
| 22—At Atlanta | W | 3-2 | Meridith | Camp |
| 23—At Cinn. | L | 2-3 | Franco | Sorensen |
| 24—At Cinn. | W | 4-0 | Frazier | Soto |
| 25—At Cinn. | L | 3-5 | Browning | Brusstar |
| 26—At Hous. | W | 10-4 | Engel | Knepper |
| 27—At Hous. | L | 4-11 | Smith | Meridith |
| 28—At Hous. | L | 0-3 | Ryan | Baller |
| 29—Atlanta | L | 6-9 | Mahler | Sorensen |
| 30—Atlanta | L | 1-8 | Johnson | Fontenot |
| 31—Atlanta | W | 5-4† | Brusstar | Garber |

**Won 10, Lost 18**

### SEPTEMBER

| Date | W/L | Score | Winner | Loser |
|---|---|---|---|---|
| 1—Atlanta | W | 15-2 | Botelho | Barker |
| 2—Houston | L | 2-7 | Dawley | Baller |
| 3—Houston | L | 7-8* | Smith | Frazier |
| 4—Houston | L | 6-11 | Scott | Meridith |
| 5—At St. L. | L | 1-6 | Cox | Engel |
| 6—Cincinnati | L | 5-7 | Soto | Botelho |
| 7—Cincinnati | W | 9-7 | Baller | Franco |
| 8—Cincinnati | T | 5-5 | ....... | ....... |
| 9—At St. L. | W | 3-1 | Fontenot | Kepshire |
| 10—At Pitts. | L | 1-2 | Reuschel | Engel |
| 11—At Pitts. | W | 3-1 | Meridith | DeLeon |
| 12—At Pitts. | L | 2-10 | Rhoden | Eckersley |
| 13—St. Louis | L | 3-9 | Forsch | Trout |
| 14—St. Louis | L | 4-5 | Campbell | Sorensen |
| 15—St. Louis | L | 1-5 | Cox | Engel |
| 16—At Mon. | L | 5-8 | Burke | Frazier |
| 17—At Mon. | W | 3-0 | Eckersley | Youmans |
| 18—At N.Y. | L | 2-4 | Aguilera | Trout |
| 19—At N.Y. | L | 1-5 | Fernandez | Fontenot |
| 20—At Phila. | W | 3-1 | Patterson | Hudson |
| 21—At Phila. | W | 9-2 | Abrego | Gross |
| 22—At Phila. | W | 9-2 | Eckersley | Rawley |
| 23—Montreal | L | 7-10 | St. Claire | Frazier |
| 24—Montreal | L | 15-17 | Smith | Fontenot |
| 25—New York | W | 5-4 | Smith | Orosco |
| 26—New York | L | 0-3 | Gooden | Abrego |
| 27—Phila. | W | 9-7 | Baller | Tekulve |
| 28—Phila. | W | 11-10 | Eckersley | Denny |
| 29—Phila. | W | 6-2 | Trout | Toliver |

**Won 12, Lost 16**

### OCTOBER

| Date | W/L | Score | Winner | Loser |
|---|---|---|---|---|
| 1—Pittsburgh | W | 4-3 | Patterson | Reuschel |
| 2—Pittsburgh | L | 4-9 | Rhoden | Sutcliffe |
| 3—Pittsburgh | W | 13-5 | Perlman | Winn |
| 4—At St. L. | L | 2-4 | Forsch | Eckersley |
| 5—At St. L. | L | 1-7 | Tudor | Trout |
| 6—At St. L. | W | 8-2 | Patterson | Andujar |

**Won 3, Lost 3**

*10 innings.   †11 innings.   ‡12 innings.   §14 innings.   x15 innings.   ySuspended game, completed July 8.

**Fireballing Lee Smith continued his dominating ways and recorded 33 saves.**

Matthews' production slipped from 82 runs batted in to 40, Cey's from 97 to 63 RBIs, Davis' from 94 to 58 RBIs. That's not much run production from players who hit 13, 22 and 17 homers, respectively.

Dernier, who batted .278 with 45 stolen bases in 1984, slipped to .254 and 31 steals as he tried to overcome his foot injury.

Still, there were encouraging signs for the future. Right fielder Keith Moreland had his best season ever and second baseman Ryne Sandberg matched his 1984 Most Valuable Player performance.

Moreland had the most RBIs for a Cub (106) since Dave Kingman in 1979. He also led the team in hitting at .307, swatted 14 homers and stole a career-high 12 bases while leading the team with 161 games played.

Sandberg scored 113 runs, hit 26 homers, stole 54 bases (all team highs) and drove in 83 runs, most of those after being switched from No. 2 to No. 3 in the batting order for the last six weeks. He followed Joe Morgan and Cesar Cedeno to become

only the third player in major league history to have at least 25 homers and 50 stolen bases in one season. Sandberg also continued to sparkle in the field as he won his third consecutive Gold Glove.

First baseman Leon Durham turned in another solid performance, batting .282 with 21 homers and 75 RBIs.

While much of the offense sputtered, Davey Lopes motored right along. At 39, the reserve outfielder hit .284 with 11 homers and stole 47 bases, a remarkable number for a player his age.

Other players who produced when the Cubs were faltering late in the season were outfielder Thad Bosley, who hit .328 (including 20 pinch hits to set a team record and lead the National League), and shortstop Shawon Dunston.

Dunston was an early-season failure offensively and defensively, but he improved after a three-month stint at Iowa (American Association) that ended August 13, the day veteran Larry Bowa was released. He hit .287 in the final weeks to finish with a .260 average, and of his 65 hits, 20 were for extra bases.

The offense showed it had a good blend of power and speed when it was healthy, finishing first in the league in homers (150) and second in stolen bases (182). But the Cubs often failed to score runs when they were needed most, leaving too great a burden on an injury-depleted pitching staff.

Eckersley was the only Cubs pitcher to reach double figures in victories, going 11-7 with a team-leading 3.08 ERA. Sanderson, Sutcliffe and Trout also had ERAs below 3.40, an indication that they would have tallied more victories had they not been beset by injuries.

Ruthven (4.53 ERA) and Ray Fontenot (4.36), a converted middle reliever, were the only regular starters who struggled.

Middle relief was a disaster area for the Cubs. George Frazier, a righthander who went 7-8 with a 6.39 ERA, was the biggest disappointment, while Lary Sorensen (4.26) and Warren Brusstar (6.05) also had trouble holding leads.

One constant for the Cubs was Lee Smith, who had another exceptional year in the bullpen. The hard-throwing righthander saved 33 games despite being used sparingly during a September losing streak.

And although the Cubs went from a 51-29 record at Wrigley Field in 1984 to 41-39 in 1985, they set a Chicago attendance record.

The pocketbook was about the only area in which they weren't hurting.

Glenn Wilson swung a big bat, leading the Phillies with 102 RBIs while playing solid defense in right field.

# Young Phillies Look to Future

By PETER PASCARELLI

After a 1-8 start, the Philadelphia Phillies' 1985 season became a long, slow battle to gain respectability.

But just when first-year Manager John Felske's club appeared to have accomplished the task, the Phils collapsed. They reached the .500 mark for the first time all season on September 11 but then proceeded to lose 19 of their last 26 games to finish with a 75-87 record, 26 games behind the National League East champion Cardinals.

It was the Phillies' first losing season since 1974. Their fifth-place finish was their lowest since 1973.

The disappointing season came in what from the beginning obviously was a transitional year for Philadelphia, which had been the winningest N.L. club over the previous nine years.

The Phillies' opening day lineup included only three players with three or more years of major league experience. And as the season progressed, that lineup was constantly shuffled and reshuffled.

Heading the list of in-season changes was the May 29 switch of perennial All-Star third baseman Mike Schmidt to first base. And it turned out to be one of the Phils' few successful moves.

**Kevin Gross (above) and Shane Rawley formed a good right-left combination in the Phillies' rotation.**

Schmidt adapted well to defensive play at first, making only seven errors in 106 games at the position. And after a three-month slump that contributed mightily to the Phillies' slow start, Schmidt ended up with another solid statistical season that included a .277 average, 89 runs scored, 33 home runs and 93 runs batted in.

Rookie Rick Schu was brought up from Portland (Pacific Coast) to replace Schmidt at third. Although he was not as productive offensively as the Phillies had hoped (.252, 24 RBIs), Schu played solidly at third and offered promise for the future.

Some of the Phillies' other experiments weren't as successful. Rookie Steve Jeltz started the season at shortstop, but his weak hitting and costly defensive lapses eventually landed him back in the minors. The Phillies ended up acquiring infielder Tom Foley from Cincinnati in an August trade that sent catcher Bo Diaz to the Reds. And by season's end, the Phils were projecting Foley, who batted .266 after the trade, as their future shortstop.

Another rookie opening day starter was first baseman John Russell, perhaps the

## SCORES OF PHILADELPHIA PHILLIES' 1985 GAMES

### APRIL

| Date | | Score | Winner | Loser |
|---|---|---|---|---|
| 9—Atlanta | L | 0-6 | Mahler | Carlton |
| 11—Atlanta | L | 3-6 | Smith | Denny |
| 12—At Hous. | L | 3-8 | Smith | Andersen |
| 13—At Hous. | W | 4-2 | Rawley | Mathis |
| 14—At Hous. | L | 3-5 | Ryan | Carlton |
| 15—At Chicago | L | 1-2 | Trout | Gross |
| 16—At Chicago | L | 0-1* | Eckersley | Holland |
| 17—At Chicago | L | 4-5 | Frazier | Gross |
| 19—New York | L | 0-1 | Gooden | Hudson |
| 20—New York | W | 7-6 | Denny | Lynch |
| 21—New York | W | 10-6 | Gross | Sisk |
| 22—At Mon. | W | 9-1 | Rawley | Hesketh |
| 23—At Mon. | L | 4-5* | Reardon | Hudson |
| 24—At Mon. | L | 6-7 | Smith | Denny |
| 26—Chicago | L | 3-7 | Eckersley | Koosman |
| 27—Chicago | W | 6-1 | Rawley | Sanderson |
| 28—Chicago | W | 3-2 | Gross | Sutcliffe |
| 29—Montreal | W | 3-2* | Tekulve | Roberge |
| 30—Montreal | W | 11-0 | Koosman | Gullickson |

Won 8, Lost 11

### MAY

| Date | | Score | Winner | Loser |
|---|---|---|---|---|
| 1—Montreal | L | 2-3 | Palmer | Rawley |
| 3—Houston | W | 3-2 | Tekulve | DiPino |
| 4—Houston | W | 7-5‡ | Rucker | Dawley |
| 5—Houston | L | 3-4 | Niekro | Rawley |
| 7—Cincinnati | L | 0-2 | Soto | Gross |
| 8—Cincinnati | L | 2-8 | Tibbs | Denny |
| 10—At N.Y. | L | 0-5 | Gooden | Carlton |
| 11—At N.Y. | L | 0-4 | Fernandez | Rawley |
| 12—At N.Y. | L | 2-3 | Darling | Gross |
| 13—At Cinn. | L | 3-7 | Stuper | Denny |
| 14—At Cinn. | W | 7-1 | Hudson | Browning |
| 15—At Atlanta | L | 2-3* | Sutter | Tekulve |
| 16—At Atlanta | L | 3-6 | Dedmon | Andersen |
| 17—Los Ang. | W | 10-5 | Gross | Reuss |
| 18—Los Ang. | W | 7-5 | Andersen | Niedenfuer |
| 19—Los Ang. | L | 2-3 | Valenzuela | Hudson |
| 20—San Fran. | W | 2-1 | Carlton | Blue |
| 21—San Fran. | W | 6-5 | Rawley | Hammaker |
| 22—San Fran. | L | 2-6 | LaPoint | Gross |
| 24—San Diego | L | 0-1 | Dravecky | Denny |
| 25—San Diego | L | 1-4 | Hawkins | Hudson |
| 26—San Diego | L | 2-7 | Hoyt | Carlton |
| 27—San Diego | W | 10-9 | Tekulve | Lefferts |
| 29—At L.A. | L | 1-6 | Hershiser | Gross |
| 30—At L.A. | W | 6-1 | Denny | Valenzuela |
| 31—At S. Fran. | L | 3-4 | Krukow | Hudson |

Won 9, Lost 17

### JUNE

| Date | | Score | Winner | Loser |
|---|---|---|---|---|
| 1—At S. Fran. | L | 1-2 | Hammaker | Carlton |
| 2—At S. Fran. | L | 1-3 | Blue | Rawley |
| 3—At S. Diego | W | 3-2 | Gross | Dravecky |
| 4—At S. Diego | L | 5-6 | Lefferts | Tekulve |
| 5—At S. Diego | L | 1-3 | Hoyt | Hudson |
| 7—Montreal | L | 1-3 | Palmer | Carlton |
| 8—Montreal | L | 3-4 | Smith | Rawley |
| 9—Montreal | W | 4-1 | Gross | Hesketh |
| 10—New York | W | 6-4 | Denny | Fernandez |
| 11—New York | W | 26-7 | Hudson | Gorman |
| 12—New York | L | 3-7† | Aguilera | Rucker |
| 13—New York | W | 5-4 | Rawley | Orosco |
| 14—At Pitts. | L | 2-3 | DeLeon | Carman |
| 15—At Pitts. | W | 13-3 | Denny | Rhoden |
| 16—At Pitts. | W | 3-2 | Hudson | Reuschel |
| 18—At St. L. | L | 2-6 | Tudor | Carlton |
| 19—At St. L. | W | 1-0 | Koosman | Andujar |
| 20—At St. L. | L | 0-5 | Cox | Gross |
| 21—Pittsburgh | W | 4-3§ | Andersen | Winn |
| 22—Pittsburgh | W | 5-2 | Carman | Robinson |
| 23—Pittsburgh | W | 3-2 | Carman | Winn |
| 25—St. Louis | W | 3-1 | Koosman | Andujar |
| 26—St. Louis | W | 6-4 | Denny | Cox |
| 27—St. Louis | L | 3-4 | Kepshire | Rawley |
| 28—At Mon. | L | 3-5 | Smith | Hudson |
| 29—At Mon. | W | 6-2 | Gross | Mahler |
| 30—At Mon. | W | 3-2 | Tekulve | Reardon |

Won 15, Lost 12

### JULY

| Date | | Score | Winner | Loser |
|---|---|---|---|---|
| 1—Chicago | L | 1-3 | Fontenot | Denny |
| 2—Chicago | W | 11-2 | Rawley | Sutcliffe |
| 3—Chicago | L | 3-4 | Smith | Tekulve |
| 4—Cincinnati | W | 3-1 | Gross | Soto |
| 5—Cincinnati | W | 5-2 | Andersen | Browning |
| 6—Cincinnati | L | 2-4 | Robinson | Denny |
| 7—Cincinnati | W | 2-3* | Franco | Tekulve |
| 8—At Hous. | W | 7-4 | Hudson | Knudson |
| 9—At Hous. | W | 5-3 | Gross | Knepper |
| 10—At Hous. | L | 0-10 | Scott | Koosman |
| 11—At Atlanta | L | 2-3 | Sutter | Andersen |
| 12—At Atlanta | L | 4-7 | Forster | Carman |
| 13—At Atlanta | L | 5-13 | Mahler | Hudson |
| 14—At Atlanta | L | 3-12 | Perez | Gross |
| 18—At Cinn. | W | 6-3 | Koosman | Soto |
| 19—At Cinn. | L | 2-3 | Franco | Tekulve |
| 20—At Cinn. | W | 10-6 | Rawley | Robinson |
| 21—At Cinn. | L | 6-7 | Franco | Carman |
| 22—Houston | W | 7-6 | Carman | Heathcock |
| 23—Houston | W | 12-6 | Koosman | Knepper |
| 24—Houston | W | 3-1 | Gross | Ryan |
| 25—Atlanta | L | 2-3 | Sutter | Tekulve |
| 26—Atlanta | L | 4-6 | Mahler | Denny |
| 27—Atlanta | W | 5-4 | Hudson | Smith |
| 28—Atlanta | W | 7-3 | Koosman | Bedrosian |
| 30—At Pitts. | W | 2-0 | Gross | Rhoden |
| 31—At Pitts. | L | 3-4* | Guante | Tekulve |

Won 13, Lost 14

### AUGUST

| Date | | Score | Winner | Loser |
|---|---|---|---|---|
| 1—At Pitts. | W | 3-0 | Denny | Robinson |
| 2—At St. L. | L | 2-3 | Tudor | Hudson |
| 3—At St. L. | W | 6-4* | Carman | Lahti |
| 4—At St. L. | W | 6-0 | Gross | Andujar |
| 5—At St. L. | W | 9-1 | Rawley | Cox |
| 8—Pittsburgh | W | 7-3 | Denny | Robinson |
| 9—St. Louis | L | 4-5 | Andujar | Hudson |
| 10—St. Louis | L | 4-5 | Cox | Koosman |
| 10—St. Louis | L | 4-13 | Horton | Gross |
| 11—St. Louis | W | 4-1 | Rawley | Forsch |
| 12—At N.Y. | L | 3-4 | Fernandez | Denny |
| 13—At N.Y. | L | 2-4 | Aguilera | Hudson |
| 14—At N.Y. | W | 2-1 | Gross | Darling |
| 15—At N.Y. | L | 7-10 | Orosco | Carman |
| 16—At Chicago | L | 5-6 | Smith | Tekulve |
| 17—At Chicago | W | 10-4 | Denny | Sorensen |
| 18—At Chicago | W | 9-5 | Hudson | Baller |
| 20—Los Ang. | L | 4-5† | Niedenfuer | Tekulve |
| 21—Los Ang. | L | 6-15 | Valenzuela | Koosman |
| 22—Los Ang. | W | 2-0 | Rawley | Reuss |
| 23—San Fran. | L | 1-4 | Hammaker | Denny |
| 24—San Fran. | W | 9-2 | Hudson | Krukow |
| 25—San Fran. | W | 14-5 | Rucker | Gott |
| 26—San Diego | W | 4-3 | Carman | McCullers |
| 27—San Diego | L | 1-4 | Thurmond | Denny |
| 29—At L.A. | W | 3-2* | Carman | Honeycutt |
| 30—At L.A. | W | 5-2 | Gross | Welch |
| 31—At L.A. | W | 5-0 | Rawley | Valenzuela |

Won 16, Lost 12

### SEPTEMBER

| Date | | Score | Winner | Loser |
|---|---|---|---|---|
| 1—At L.A. | W | 4-1 | Denny | Reuss |
| 2—At S. Fran. | W | 4-3* | Carman | Jeffcoat |
| 3—At S. Fran. | W | 4-3‡ | Shipanoff | Minton |
| 4—At S. Fran. | L | 3-4 | Davis | Toliver |
| 6—At S. Diego | L | 2-3† | Gossage | Shipanoff |
| 7—At S. Diego | W | 2-0 | Denny | Hawkins |
| 8—At S. Diego | W | 9-7 | Surhoff | Wojna |
| 10—Montreal | W | 5-2† | Carman | Burke |
| 11—Montreal | W | 4-1 | Gross | Gullickson |
| 12—Montreal | L | 3-6 | Youmans | Rawley |
| 13—At Pitts. | W | 6-3 | Denny | Walk |
| 14—At Pitts. | L | 3-6 | Tunnell | Carlton |
| 15—At Pitts. | L | 4-5 | Reuschel | Shipanoff |
| 16—At N.Y. | L | 0-9 | Gooden | Gross |
| 17—At N.Y. | W | 5-1 | Rawley | Lynch |
| 18—St. Louis | L | 0-7 | Forsch | Denny |
| 19—St. Louis | W | 6-3 | Rucker | Keough |
| 20—Chicago | L | 1-3 | Patterson | Hudson |
| 21—Chicago | L | 2-9 | Abrego | Gross |
| 22—Chicago | L | 2-9 | Eckersley | Rawley |
| 23—New York | L | 1-4 | Aguilera | Toliver |
| 24—New York | L | 1-7 | Fernandez | Rucker |
| 25—At St. L. | L | 3-6 | Cox | Hudson |
| 26—At St. L. | L | 0-5 | Tudor | Gross |
| 27—At Chicago | L | 7-9 | Baller | Tekulve |
| 28—At Chicago | L | 10-11 | Eckersley | Denny |
| 29—At Chicago | L | 2-6 | Trout | Toliver |

Won 10, Lost 17

### OCTOBER

| Date | | Score | Winner | Loser |
|---|---|---|---|---|
| 2—At Mon. | L | 1-3 | Smith | Gross |
| 2—At Mon. | W | 3-2 | Hudson | Palmer |
| 3—At Mon. | W | 8-7 | Rawley | Laskey |
| 4—Pittsburgh | L | 2-7 | Walk | Denny |
| 4—Pittsburgh | W | 8-5 | Carman | DeLeon |
| 5—Pittsburgh | L | 2-4 | McWilliams | Toliver |
| 5—Pittsburgh | L | 0-5 | Bielecki | Childress |
| 6—Pittsburgh | W | 5-0 | Gross | Rhoden |

Won 4, Lost 4

*10 innings.   †11 innings.   ‡13 innings.   §16 innings.

**Though his numbers slipped slightly, Mike Schmidt still hit 33 homers and drove in 93 runs.**

best example of Philadelphia's frustrating season. Russell was quickly benched after striking out on 20 of his first 41 at-bats. He then was sent back to the minors to play the outfield and subsequently recalled, ending the season with a .218 average, nine homers and 23 RBIs.

Another youthful disappointment was outfielder Jeff Stone, whom the Phils had hoped would join with second baseman Juan Samuel and center fielder Von Hayes to form a dynamic basestealing trio.

Stone played inconsistently and tentatively for the season's first two months and was sent to Portland. He later was recalled for another trial but was sidelined for most of the final month with a chronic groin pull. Stone was the club's fourth-leading hitter with a .265 average, but he contributed only 11 RBIs and 15 stolen bases in 264 at-bats.

The Phils' disappointments weren't confined to youth. Pitchers Steve Carlton (age 40) and Jerry Koosman (41) ended the season with their careers in doubt. Carlton, who went 1-8 with a 3.33 earned-run average, was sidelined for nearly three months with a strained rotator cuff, while Koosman (6-4, 4.62 ERA) had his season curtailed by a knee injury that required surgery.

And the Phils were let down by their bullpen, which lost Al Holland but gained veteran Kent Tekulve in an April trade with Pittsburgh. But Tekulve ended up with a 4-10 record and only 14 saves (the team high).

Amid the disappointments were some highlights. Glenn Wilson, the first All-Star outfielder for the Phillies since Greg Luzinski in 1978, blossomed into one of the league's up-and-coming stars by driving in 102 runs and leading the league's outfielders with 18 assists. The right fielder also batted .275 with 39 doubles.

Samuel, who set a rookie record (since broken by St. Louis' Vince Coleman) for stolen bases with 72 in 1984, stole 53 in '85 and became the first Phillie ever to steal more than 50 bases in consecutive seasons. He also scored more than 100 runs for a second straight season. And Samuel was one of three N.L. players to reach double figures in doubles (31), triples (13), home runs (19) and stolen bases. His fielding improved, too, as his errors total dropped from 33 to 15.

In his first full major league season, Don Carman emerged as the Phils' top relief pitcher. With 71 appearances, he broke the club record for lefthanders. Carman finished with a 9-4 record, a 2.08 ERA and seven saves.

The Phils also got solid seasons from a pair of starting pitchers, Kevin Gross and Shane Rawley. Gross became the club's ace, compiling a 15-13 record and a 3.41 ERA and striking out 151 batters in 205⅔ innings. Rawley had a 3.31 ERA and a 13-8 record that included a six-game winning streak and Pitcher of the Month honors for August.

Righthander John Denny was the club's workhorse with 230⅔ innings pitched, but he won only 11 of 25 decisions. Charles Hudson, who started 26 of the 38 games in which he appeared, went 8-13.

A couple of players had solid if not outstanding seasons. Center fielder Von Hayes slipped somewhat after a strong 1984 campaign, batting .263 with 13 homers, 70 RBIs and 21 steals. Catcher Ozzie Virgil added 19 homers and 55 RBIs while batting .246.

Despite the Phillies' poor showing in 1985, Felske's contract was extended through the 1987 season.

"We all felt John did a good job under some trying circumstances," Phils President Bill Giles said. "We were trying a lot of young players and experimenting with many different lineups and combinations. And, despite our record, I was very satisfied with the job done by John."

**Veteran Rick Reuschel came out of nowhere to record a 14-8 record with an impressive 2.27 ERA.**

# Pirates Fall Deeper Into Cellar

## By CHARLEY FEENEY

The 1985 Pittsburgh Pirates opened the season with a cast of veterans and closed out with a youth movement that gave the club hope for the future, which was all they wanted to think about after posting a second straight last-place finish in the National League East.

The Pirates were pitiful in 1985. Before September, when they went 13-14, they never had a double-figure winning month. They had a 4-4 October to close out a 57-104 season, marking the first time since 1954 that a Pirates team had lost 100 or more games.

There were signs in spring training that the Pirates were in for a bad year. Left fielder Steve Kemp, acquired from the New York Yankees, reported with a sore left shoulder. He opened the season on the disabled list, then batted just .250 with two home runs and 21 runs batted in and was delegated to the bench.

When the club quickly plunged to the bottom of the standings, Manager Chuck Tanner did his best to keep team morale high. But it was difficult, especially when the younger players saw right fielder George Hendrick trotting to first base when he hit a grounder to the infield.

Hendrick, who came from St. Louis in a trade that enabled John Tudor to win 21 games for the Cardinals, made it clear from the start that he did not want to play in Pittsburgh. He sulked, didn't hustle and contributed only two home runs and 25 RBIs.

Pitcher John Candelaria, another disgruntled Pirate, was moved to the bullpen, where he earned a team-high nine saves in 37 relief appearances. He continued to demand a trade, however, and on August 2, Candelaria, Hendrick and relief pitcher Al Holland were traded to the California Angels for three youngsters—outfielder Mike Brown and pitchers Pat Clements and Bob Kipper.

It was the first major deal completed by General Manager Joe L. Brown, who replaced Harding (Pete) Peterson on May 23. Peterson was fired by club President Dan Galbreath, and Brown, who had retired as the club's general manager in 1976, agreed to return only until Galbreath sold the club.

The sale of the Pirates was announced during the last week of the season. Brown promised the new owners that he would remain as a consultant but said he was not interested in staying as general manager.

Brown made another big trade on August 31. He sent third baseman Bill Madlock to the Los Angeles Dodgers for outfielder R.J. Reynolds, first baseman Sid Bream and minor league infielder-outfielder Cecil Espy. Madlock, a four-time N.L. batting champion, was batting just .251 with 10 homers and 41 RBIs when he was traded. Brown said some negative remarks Madlock had made about the future of the Pirates had prompted the deal.

"His recent public and private statements indicate a lack of belief in the Pittsburgh Pirates, and it is doubtful that he can provide the kind of leadership that our fine young players need to reach their potential," the general manager said.

With the departure of Madlock, Candelaria, Hendrick and Holland—and their big contracts—the Pirates made a commitment to youth. The new faces were greeted with enthusiasm by the few fans who attended games at Three Rivers Stadium the last few weeks of the season, and some of the youngsters looked impressive.

Brown immediately took over in right field. He hit .332 with five homers and 33 RBIs in just 57 games with the Pirates. Reynolds also improved after arriving in Pittsburgh, batting .308 in 130 at-bats to finish at .282 overall.

Outfielder Joe Orsulak was another bright spot. The rookie hit .300 in 397 at-bats and stole a team-high 24 bases, although he showed no power. The leadoff man didn't hit a home run and had only 21 RBIs.

Rookie shortstop Sammy Khalifa, who appeared destined to spend the season at Hawaii (Pacific Coast), was called up in late June after Johnnie LeMaster (a May 30 acquisition from Cleveland) was injured. Khalifa, the sixth Pirate shortstop in 1985, was the first to hold onto the position. Even though he batted only .238 with little power, he played well defensively, which is all Tanner expected.

Tanner was disappointed, however, with the performances of some veterans. Catcher Tony Pena, considered the best player on the team, batted only .249 with 10 homers and 59 RBIs, although he won his third straight Gold Glove for his work behind the plate. Second baseman Johnny Ray needed a big surge to finish with a .274 average and club-leading totals in RBIs (70), runs scored (67), hits (163) and doubles (33).

## SCORES OF PITTSBURGH PIRATES' 1985 GAMES

### APRIL

| Date | W/L | Score | Winner | Loser |
|---|---|---|---|---|
| 9—At Chicago | L | 1-2 | Sutcliffe | Rhoden |
| 11—At Chicago | L | 1-4 | Trout | DeLeon |
| 12—St. Louis | W | 6-4 | Robinson | Kepshire |
| 13—St. Louis | W | 4-3 | Candelaria | Campbell |
| 14—St. Louis | L | 4-10 | Andujar | Rhoden |
| 15—New York | W | 4-1 | Bielecki | Latham |
| 16—New York | L | 1-2 | Orosco | Candelaria |
| 17—New York | L | 6-10 | Sisk | McWilliams |
| 19—At St. L. | L | 4-5 | Andujar | Candelaria |
| 20—At St. L. | L | 3-4 | Cox | Tunnell |
| 21—At St. L. | L | 0-6 | Forsch | DeLeon |
| 22—Chicago | W | 5-3 | McWilliams | Ruthven |
| 23—Chicago | L | 0-5 | Sutcliffe | Bielecki |
| 24—Chicago | L | 2-5 | Trout | Rhoden |
| 26—At N.Y. | L | 0-6 | Darling | DeLeon |
| 27—At N.Y. | W | 3-2 | McWilliams | Orosco |
| 28—At N.Y. | L | 4-5y | Gorman | Tunnell |
| 30—San Diego | W | 6-2 | Rhoden | Hoyt |

**Won 6, Lost 12**

### MAY

| Date | W/L | Score | Winner | Loser |
|---|---|---|---|---|
| 1—San Diego | L | 4-6 | Show | DeLeon |
| 3—Los Ang. | W | 16-2 | McWilliams | Honeycutt |
| 4—Los Ang. | L | 5-6* | Valenzuela | Candelaria |
| 5—Los Ang. | W | 3-2 | Rhoden | Niedenfuer |
| 6—San Fran. | L | 5-7 | Laskey | DeLeon |
| 7—San Fran. | L | 3-5 | Gott | Tunnell |
| 8—At S. Diego | L | 2-12 | Hawkins | McWilliams |
| 9—At S. Diego | L | 0-1 | Thurmond | Bielecki |
| 10—At L.A. | L | 0-1 | Reuss | Rhoden |
| 11—At L.A. | W | 5-2‡ | Holland | Brennan |
| 12—At L.A. | L | 0-2 | Castillo | Tunnell |
| 14—At S. Fran. | L | 1-3 | Krukow | McWilliams |
| 15—At S. Fran. | W | 3-2 | Robinson | Garrelts |
| 17—Cincinnati | L | 3-6 | Stuper | DeLeon |
| 18—Cincinnati | L | 0-8 | Browning | Bielecki |
| 19—Cincinnati | L | 1-7 | Soto | Tunnell |
| 20—Houston | W | 3-1 | Rhoden | Niekro |
| 21—Houston | W | 3-2 | Reuschel | Scott |
| 22—Houston | L | 3-5* | Dawley | Holland |
| 24—At Atlanta | W | 4-2 | Winn | Bedrosian |
| 25—At Atlanta | W | 8-2 | Rhoden | Perez |
| 26—At Atlanta | L | 4-5* | Dedmon | Krawczyk |
| 27—At Hous. | L | 2-4 | Knepper | DeLeon |
| 28—At Hous. | W | 4-3‡ | Guante | Solano |
| 29—At Hous. | L | 3-8 | Ryan | Krawczyk |
| 31—Atlanta | L | 2-8 | Camp | Rhoden |

**Won 9, Lost 17**

### JUNE

| Date | W/L | Score | Winner | Loser |
|---|---|---|---|---|
| 1—Atlanta | W | 6-3 | Reuschel | Garber |
| 2—Atlanta | W | 5-0 | DeLeon | Bedrosian |
| 4—At Cinn. | L | 3-9 | Soto | Guante |
| 5—At Cinn. | L | 9-11 | Pastore | Robinson |
| 6—At Chicago | L | 2-3‡ | Brusstar | Holland |
| 7—At Chicago | L | 0-1 | Sutcliffe | DeLeon |
| 8—At Chicago | L | 3-7 | Trout | McWilliams |
| 9—At Chicago | L | 1-5 | Ruthven | Winn |
| 10—St. Louis | L | 1-6 | Cox | Rhoden |
| 11—St. Louis | W | 13-2 | Reuschel | Allen |
| 13—St. Louis | L | 1-2 | Tudor | McWilliams |
| 14—Phila. | W | 3-2 | DeLeon | Carman |
| 15—Phila. | L | 3-13 | Denny | Rhoden |
| 16—Phila. | L | 2-3 | Hudson | Reuschel |
| 17—At Mon. | W | 5-2 | Winn | Palmer |
| 18—At Mon. | W | 4-1 | McWilliams | Smith |
| 19—At Mon. | L | 3-4 | Burke | DeLeon |
| 20—At Mon. | W | 2-1 | Rhoden | Schatzeder |
| 21—At Phila. | L | 3-4x | Andersen | Winn |
| 22—At Phila. | L | 2-5 | Carman | Robinson |
| 23—At Phila. | L | 2-3 | Carman | Winn |
| 25—Montreal | L | 2-3 | Burke | Holland |
| 26—Montreal | W | 11-2 | Reuschel | O'Connor |
| 27—Montreal | L | 2-4 | Palmer | McWilliams |
| 28—Chicago | L | 0-5 | Trout | DeLeon |
| 29—Chicago | W | 6-5§ | Reuschel | Frazier |
| 30—Chicago | L | 2-9 | Sanderson | Robinson |

**Won 9, Lost 18**

### JULY

| Date | W/L | Score | Winner | Loser |
|---|---|---|---|---|
| 1—At N.Y. | W | 1-0 | Reuschel | Fernandez |
| 2—At N.Y. | L | 4-5 | Darling | McWilliams |
| 3—At N.Y. | L | 2-6 | Lynch | DeLeon |
| 4—San Diego | L | 1-9 | Show | Rhoden |
| 5—San Diego | W | 5-4‡ | Reuschel | Lefferts |
| 6—San Diego | W | 8-7 | Candelaria | Lefferts |
| 7—San Diego | L | 0-3 | Hoyt | Reuschel |
| 8—Los Ang. | L | 3-4 | Valenzuela | DeLeon |
| 9—Los Ang. | L | 3-8 | Honeycutt | Rhoden |
| 10—Los Ang. | L | 4-5 | Reuss | Tunnell |
| 11—San Fran. | W | 6-4 | Guante | Krukow |
| 12—San Fran. | W | 3-1 | Reuschel | Gott |
| 13—San Fran. | L | 1-4 | LaPoint | DeLeon |
| 14—San Fran. | L | 3-7 | Laskey | Rhoden |
| 18—At S. Diego | L | 2-3 | Lefferts | Candelaria |
| 19—At S. Diego | L | 0-6 | Hawkins | DeLeon |
| 20—At S. Diego | L | 2-4 | Hoyt | Rhoden |
| 21—At S. Diego | W | 5-2 | Tunnell | Show |
| 22—At L.A. | W | 6-3 | McWilliams | Honeycutt |
| 23—At L.A. | L | 0-6 | Hershiser | Reuschel |
| 24—At L.A. | L | 1-9 | Welch | Robinson |
| 25—At S. Fran. | L | 3-4 | Minton | Guante |
| 26—At S. Fran. | L | 1-3 | Laskey | Tunnell |
| 27—At S. Fran. | L | 3-8 | LaPoint | Robinson |
| 28—At S. Fran. | L | 2-3* | Garrelts | Guante |
| 30—Phila. | L | 0-2 | Gross | Rhoden |
| 31—Phila. | W | 4-3* | Guante | Tekulve |

**Won 8, Lost 19**

### AUGUST

| Date | W/L | Score | Winner | Loser |
|---|---|---|---|---|
| 1—Phila. | L | 0-3 | Denny | Robinson |
| 2—Montreal | L | 2-3 | Hesketh | Reuschel |
| 3—Montreal | L | 5-6 | Roberge | McWilliams |
| 4—Montreal | W | 4-3 | Rhoden | Gullickson |
| 5—Montreal | L | 2-5 | Burke | Winn |
| 8—At Phila. | L | 3-7 | Denny | Robinson |
| 9—At Mon. | L | 2-7 | Smith | Reuschel |
| 10—At Mon. | L | 5-7 | St. Claire | Rhoden |
| 11—At Mon. | L | 5-6 | Burke | Guante |
| 12—At St. L. | L | 1-8 | Tudor | Winn |
| 13—At St. L. | L | 5-6 | Andujar | Robinson |
| 15—At St. L. | L | 1-3 | Kepshire | Reuschel |
| 15—At St. L. | L | 3-4‡ | Campbell | Guante |
| 16—New York | W | 7-1 | Rhoden | Lynch |
| 17—New York | L | 3-4 | Fernandez | Tunnell |
| 18—New York | W | 5-0 | Robinson | Aguilera |
| 20—Cincinnati | W | 3-2 | Reuschel | Soto |
| 21—Cincinnati | L | 5-8 | Browning | Walk |
| 22—Cincinnati | W | 5-1 | Rhoden | Tibbs |
| 23—Houston | L | 0-2* | Dawley | Clements |
| 25—Houston | W | 9-3 | Reuschel | Scott |
| 25—Houston | W | 10-9 | Robinson | Calhoun |
| 26—At Atlanta | L | 1-2 | Garber | Robinson |
| 27—At Atlanta | L | 6-7 | Garber | Robinson |
| 28—At Atlanta | L | 1-6 | Barker | Tunnell |
| 29—At Cinn. | L | 0-6 | Browning | DeLeon |
| 30—At Cinn. | L | 0-1 | Tibbs | Reuschel |
| 31—At Cinn. | W | 6-0 | Walk | McGaffigan |

**Won 8, Lost 20**

### SEPTEMBER

| Date | W/L | Score | Winner | Loser |
|---|---|---|---|---|
| 1—At Cinn. | L | 2-3 | Soto | Scurry |
| 2—Atlanta | W | 5-4 | Tunnell | Mahler |
| 3—Atlanta | L | 0-2 | Johnson | DeLeon |
| 4—Atlanta | W | 2-0 | Reuschel | Perez |
| 5—At Hous. | L | 3-4 | Knepper | Walk |
| 6—At Hous. | L | 3-4* | Dawley | Robinson |
| 7—At Hous. | W | 7-1 | Tunnell | Kerfeld |
| 10—Chicago | W | 2-1 | Reuschel | Engel |
| 11—Chicago | L | 1-3 | Meridith | DeLeon |
| 12—Chicago | W | 10-2 | Rhoden | Eckersley |
| 13—Phila. | L | 3-6 | Denny | Walk |
| 14—Phila. | W | 6-3 | Tunnell | Carlton |
| 15—Phila. | W | 5-4 | Reuschel | Shipanoff |
| 16—St. Louis | L | 4-8 | Tudor | DeLeon |
| 16—St. Louis | L | 1-3 | Perry | Clements |
| 17—St. Louis | L | 4-10 | Andujar | Kipper |
| 18—At Mon. | W | 10-6† | Robinson | Roberge |
| 19—At Mon. | W | 8-6* | Winn | Burke |
| 20—At N.Y. | W | 7-5† | Guante | Latham |
| 21—At N.Y. | L | 1-12 | Gooden | Rhoden |
| 22—At N.Y. | W | 5-3 | Kipper | Leach |
| 23—At St. L. | L | 4-5 | Lahti | Guante |
| 24—At St. L. | L | 4-5 | Horton | Tunnell |
| 25—Montreal | W | 8-2 | Reuschel | Laskey |
| 27—New York | W | 8-7 | McWilliams | Gardner |
| 28—New York | L | 1-3 | Aguilera | Kipper |
| 29—New York | L | 7-9* | Orosco | McWilliams |

**Won 13, Lost 14**

### OCTOBER

| Date | W/L | Score | Winner | Loser |
|---|---|---|---|---|
| 1—At Chicago | L | 3-4 | Patterson | Reuschel |
| 2—At Chicago | W | 9-4 | Rhoden | Sutcliffe |
| 3—At Chicago | L | 5-13 | Perlman | Winn |
| 4—At Phila. | W | 7-2 | Walk | Denny |
| 4—At Phila. | L | 5-8 | Carman | DeLeon |
| 5—At Phila. | W | 4-2 | McWilliams | Toliver |
| 5—At Phila. | W | 5-0 | Bielecki | Childress |
| 6—At Phila. | L | 0-5 | Gross | Rhoden |

**Won 4, Lost 4**

*10 innings.   †11 innings.   ‡12 innings.   §15 innings.   x16 innings.   y18 innings.

Catcher Tony Pena slumped to a .249 average, but still captured his third Gold Glove.

First baseman Jason Thompson, bothered by a sore knee most of the season, underwent arthroscopic surgery in September and finished with a .241 average, 12 homers (a team high) and 61 RBIs.

Center fielder Marvell Wynne never could find a groove between stints on the disabled list. He hit .205.

Jim Morrison (.254) was efficient as a backup infielder, utilityman Bill Almon hit .270 and Lee Mazzilli (.282) contributed at times as a pinch-hitter. But Sixto Lezcano (.207) was unproductive, and as a team, the Pirates were powerless. They hit a league-low 80 home runs.

Pittsburgh's pitching deteriorated in 1985, too. After leading the league with a 3.11 earned-run average in '84, the Pirates slumped to 3.97 (10th in the league).

The big surprise of 1985 was Rick Reuschel, who opened the season at Hawaii. Two days before he was fired, Peterson called up Reuschel, a 36-year-old whose career had seemed all but over. But the righthander went 14-8 with a 2.27 ERA and nine complete games to pace the Pirates' staff and was named The Sporting News' N.L. Comeback Player of the Year as well as a Gold Glove winner.

Leading the parade of losing pitchers was righthander Jose DeLeon, who finished with a 2-19 record and a 4.70 ERA and spent a month at Hawaii. Righthander Lee Tunnell, who also did time in the minors, was 4-10, making him 5-17 over the last two years. Lefthander Larry

McWilliams went 7-9 with a 4.70 ERA.

Righthander Rick Rhoden (10-15, 4.47 ERA), who led the 1984 staff with 14 victories, was the only Pittsburgh pitcher besides Reuschel to reach double figures in victories.

When the season opened, veteran Kent Tekulve was part of a bullpen that included Don Robinson, Rod Scurry and Cecilio Guante. On April 20, Peterson dealt Tekulve to the Phillies for Holland, and Brown sold Scurry to the New York Yankees in September. Guante performed admirably, notching five saves while fashioning a 2.72 ERA, and Robinson (5-11, 3.87 ERA) had three saves.

One day after the season ended, Tanner's nine-year reign as manager was over. The announcement of his firing came five days after a local coalition agreed to buy the team for $22 million and keep it in Pittsburgh.

Tanner, who had two years remaining on his contract, had said for months that if Galbreath sold the club, he was not interested in staying.

"They didn't want me and I didn't want them," he said.

Such was the Pirates' season. The team had players who didn't want to perform in Pittsburgh. The city had a federal drug investigation and later a name-dropping trial of accused drug dealers that it didn't want. And the fans sure didn't get what they wanted: a winning team.

"It was a season of turmoil," Galbreath said.

**Rookie shortstop Mariano Duncan solidified the Dodger defense while recording respectable offensive numbers.**

# Artful Dodgers Rise in West

**By GORDON VERRELL**

In searching out an explanation for the Los Angeles Dodgers' surprising conquest of the National League West in 1985, one begins with the quality pitching, includes Pedro Guerrero's incredible June boom and adds in career-best performances by catcher Mike Scioscia and right fielder Mike Marshall.

In addition, there was some slick boardroom work by Dodgers Vice President Al Campanis, who pulled off some timely trades. And the manager, Tom Lasorda, had an inordinate amount of patience when it appeared early on that 1985 might be a rerun of 1984, when Los Angeles finished fourth.

All that was true.

But the best thing to happen to the Dodgers in 1985 just might have been Bobby Grich of the California Angels falling atop second baseman Steve Sax in the final game of spring training. Sax injured his leg and could not play the first few games of the season, setting off a chain of events that resulted in Mariano Duncan performing acrobatics at shortstop rather than spending the summer in Albuquerque (Pacific Coast) learning the ropes at second base.

What Duncan, the most exciting infielder the Dodgers have brought along in years, did was solidify a defense that was all thumbs the first two months of the season, when the club was charged with 62 errors. The Dodgers still wound up leading the league in errors with 166, and 30 of those were committed by Duncan, but the rookie was able to make many outstanding plays on hits that would have gone through the Dodger infield of years past.

Duncan also was respectable at the plate, batting .244 with six triples and a team-high 38 stolen bases.

The other major move came June 1. That's when Guerrero was shifted to the outfield from third base, where he was playing because the Dodgers had failed to land a third baseman the previous winter.

The Dodgers pointed out that Guerrero had played third in 1983, when they won the N.L. West, and had hit 32 home runs and knocked in 103 runs. But he slumped in '84 and was switched to the outfield, but too late to salvage his season.

The Dodgers moved more swiftly in '85, and the results were astounding. After totaling only four homers and 16 runs batted in the first two months, Guerrero erupted

**Orel Hershiser enjoyed a phenomenal season, recording a 19-3 record and 2.03 ERA.**

to slug 15 homers in June (breaking the N.L. record for most home runs in that month), and he drove in 26 runs while batting .344. Guerrero wound up the season with 33 homers (although he hit only one after injuring his left wrist September 7), 87 RBIs and 99 runs scored. His .320 average was No. 2 in the league, and he led the loop in on-base percentage (.422) and slugging percentage (.577).

By itself, Guerrero's colossal month didn't spur the Dodgers—they were 5½ games behind the division-leading Padres

## SCORES OF LOS ANGELES DODGERS' 1985 GAMES

### APRIL

| | | | Winner | Loser |
|---|---|---|---|---|
| 9—At Hous. | L | 1-2 | Ryan | Valenzuela |
| 10—At Hous. | W | 5-4 | Reuss | Niekro |
| 11—At Hous. | W | 4-3 | Diaz | Dawley |
| 12—San Fran. | L | 1-4 | Krukow | Honeycutt |
| 13—San Fran. | W | 1-0 | Valenzuela | Davis |
| 14—San Fran. | L | 4-8 | Gott | Reuss |
| 15—Houston | W | 5-3 | Diaz | Niekro |
| 16—Houston | L | 3-7 | Smith | Howe |
| 17—Houston | W | 1-0† | Hershiser | DiPino |
| 18—At S. Diego | W | 5-0 | Valenzuela | Thurmond |
| 19—At S. Diego | L | 2-11 | Hoyt | Reuss |
| 20—At S. Diego | L | 3-4* | Gossage | Howell |
| 21—At S. Diego | W | 2-0 | Hershiser | Dravecky |
| 22—At S. Fran. | W | 3-2* | Niedenfuer | LaPoint |
| 23—At S. Fran. | L | 1-2 | Krukow | Valenzuela |
| 24—At S. Fran. | W | 4-2 | Brennan | Laskey |
| 25—San Diego | W | 6-3 | Honeycutt | Show |
| 26—San Diego | W | 2-0 | Hershiser | Dravecky |
| 27—San Diego | L | 3-4 | Hawkins | Brennan |
| 28—San Diego | L | 0-1 | Lefferts | Valenzuela |
| 30—At St. L. | L | 1-6 | Andujar | Reuss |

**Won 11, Lost 10**

### MAY

| | | | Winner | Loser |
|---|---|---|---|---|
| 1—At St. L. | W | 2-1‡ | Howell | Allen |
| 3—At Pitts. | L | 2-16 | McWilliams | Honeycutt |
| 4—At Pitts. | W | 6-5* | Valenzuela | Candelaria |
| 5—At Pitts. | L | 2-3 | Rhoden | Niedenfuer |
| 6—At Chicago | W | 5-4* | Howell | Fontenot |
| 7—At Chicago | L | 2-4 | Ruthven | Brennan |
| 8—St. Louis | W | 5-2 | Honeycutt | Tudor |
| 9—St. Louis | L | 4-5* | Allen | Howell |
| 10—Pittsburgh | W | 1-0 | Reuss | Rhoden |
| 11—Pittsburgh | L | 2-5‡ | Holland | Brennan |
| 12—Pittsburgh | W | 2-0 | Castillo | Tunnell |
| 14—Chicago | L | 3-8 | Sutcliffe | Valenzuela |
| 15—Chicago | L | 2-3 | Sanderson | Honeycutt |
| 17—At Phila. | L | 5-10 | Gross | Reuss |
| 18—At Phila. | L | 5-7 | Andersen | Niedenfuer |
| 19—At Phila. | W | 3-2 | Valenzuela | Hudson |
| 20—At Mon. | L | 1-9 | Schatzeder | Castillo |
| 21—At Mon. | L | 1-6 | Gullickson | Honeycutt |
| 22—At Mon. | W | 4-0 | Reuss | Palmer |
| 24—At N.Y. | W | 4-3 | Hershiser | Lynch |
| 25—At N.Y. | W | 6-2 | Valenzuela | Gooden |
| 26—At N.Y. | L | 1-2 | McDowell | Honeycutt |
| 27—At N.Y. | L | 1-8 | Darling | Reuss |
| 29—Phila. | W | 6-1 | Hershiser | Gross |
| 30—Phila. | L | 1-6 | Denny | Valenzuela |
| 31—Montreal | W | 4-0 | Honeycutt | Gullickson |

**Won 12, Lost 14**

### JUNE

| | | | Winner | Loser |
|---|---|---|---|---|
| 1—Montreal | L | 2-4† | Lucas | Howell |
| 2—Montreal | W | 8-7 | Castillo | Smith |
| 3—New York | W | 5-4‡ | Howe | Sisk |
| 4—New York | L | 1-4 | Gooden | Valenzuela |
| 5—New York | W | 2-1 | Welch | Fernandez |
| 7—At Atlanta | W | 7-2 | Niedenfuer | Bedrosian |
| 8—At Atlanta | L | 3-7 | Mahler | Hershiser |
| 9—At Atlanta | L | 3-10 | Shields | Valenzuela |
| 10—At Cinn. | W | 7-4 | Honeycutt | Stuper |
| 14—At Hous. | W | 10-2 | Reuss | Niekro |
| 15—At Hous. | W | 3-0 | Hershiser | Knepper |
| 16—At Hous. | W | 9-0 | Valenzuela | Scott |
| 17—San Diego | L | 2-3 | Show | Honeycutt |
| 18—San Diego | L | 0-4 | Dravecky | Welch |
| 19—San Diego | W | 5-1 | Reuss | Hawkins |
| 21—Houston | W | 7-2 | Hershiser | Scott |
| 22—Houston | W | 6-3 | Valenzuela | Ryan |
| 23—Houston | W | 6-2 | Honeycutt | Mathis |
| 24—Houston | L | 4-8 | Niekro | Reuss |
| 25—At S. Diego | W | 3-2 | Howell | Stoddard |
| 26—At S. Diego | L | 4-10 | Hoyt | Hershiser |
| 27—At S. Diego | L | 4-5 | Lefferts | Valenzuela |
| 28—Atlanta | L | 2-11 | Bedrosian | Honeycutt |
| 29—Atlanta | W | 3-2 | Reuss | Mahler |
| 30—Atlanta | W | 4-3 | Howell | Sutter |

**Won 15, Lost 10**

### JULY

| | | | Winner | Loser |
|---|---|---|---|---|
| 1—Cincinnati | W | 8-1 | Hershiser | Tibbs |
| 2—Cincinnati | W | 3-0 | Valenzuela | Price |
| 4—At St. L. | L | 2-3 | Andujar | Howell |
| 5—At St. L. | W | 4-1 | Niedenfuer | Cox |
| 6—At St. L. | W | 8-3 | Welch | Kepshire |
| 7—At St. L. | L | 1-7 | Tudor | Hershiser |
| 8—At Pitts. | W | 4-3 | Valenzuela | DeLeon |
| 9—At Pitts. | W | 8-3 | Honeycutt | Rhoden |
| 10—At Pitts. | W | 5-4 | Reuss | Tunnell |
| 11—At Chicago | W | 3-1 | Welch | Fontenot |

### JULY

| | | | Winner | Loser |
|---|---|---|---|---|
| 12—At Chicago | W | 7-4 | Niedenfuer | Smith |
| 13—At Chicago | W | 9-1 | Valenzuela | Gura |
| 14—At Chicago | L | 4-10 | Frazier | Honeycutt |
| 18—St. Louis | W | 2-1 | Hershiser | Campbell |
| 19—St. Louis | W | 5-2 | Welch | Cox |
| 20—St. Louis | W | 3-0 | Valenzuela | Tudor |
| 21—St. Louis | L | 2-4* | Lahti | Niedenfuer |
| 22—Pittsburgh | L | 3-6 | McWilliams | Honeycutt |
| 23—Pittsburgh | W | 6-0 | Hershiser | Reuschel |
| 24—Pittsburgh | W | 9-1 | Welch | Robinson |
| 25—Chicago | W | 7-3 | Valenzuela | Fontenot |
| 26—Chicago | W | 10-0 | Reuss | Ruthven |
| 27—Chicago | W | 5-4 | Hershiser | Frazier |
| 28—Chicago | L | 2-9 | Sorensen | Powell |
| 29—San Fran. | W | 10-5 | Welch | Blue |
| 30—San Fran. | W | 4-2 | Niedenfuer | Minton |
| 31—San Fran. | L | 5-7 | Laskey | Reuss |

**Won 20, Lost 7**

### AUGUST

| | | | Winner | Loser |
|---|---|---|---|---|
| 2—At Cinn. | W | 5-3 | Hershiser | Robinson |
| 2—At Cinn. | L | 2-5 | Tibbs | Honeycutt |
| 3—At Cinn. | W | 2-0 | Welch | Soto |
| 4—At Cinn. | L | 4-5 | Power | Howell |
| 5—At Atlanta | W | 6-1 | Reuss | Barker |
| 8—Cincinnati | L | 5-6§ | Power | Diaz |
| 9—Cincinnati | W | 3-1 | Welch | Browning |
| 10—Cincinnati | W | 2-1 | Valenzuela | Tibbs |
| 11—Cincinnati | W | 4-0 | Reuss | McGaffigan |
| 12—Atlanta | W | 3-0 | Honeycutt | Mahler |
| 13—Atlanta | W | 2-1 | Diaz | Forster |
| 14—Atlanta | W | 5-0 | Welch | McMurtry |
| 15—Atlanta | W | 5-4 | Valenzuela | Sutter |
| 16—At S. Fran. | W | 5-1 | Reuss | Blue |
| 17—At S. Fran. | L | 2-5 | Garrelts | Diaz |
| 18—At S. Fran. | L | 1-2* | Davis | Niedenfuer |
| 20—At Phila. | W | 5-4† | Niedenfuer | Tekulve |
| 21—At Phila. | W | 15-6 | Valenzuela | Koosman |
| 22—At Phila. | L | 0-2 | Rawley | Reuss |
| 23—At Mon. | W | 8-4 | Hershiser | Burke |
| 24—At Mon. | L | 2-5 | Smith | Honeycutt |
| 25—At Mon. | L | 1-6 | Gullickson | Welch |
| 26—At N.Y. | W | 6-1 | Valenzuela | Lynch |
| 27—At N.Y. | W | 2-1 | Reuss | Fernandez |
| 29—Phila. | L | 2-3* | Carman | Honeycutt |
| 30—Phila. | L | 2-5 | Gross | Welch |
| 31—Phila. | L | 0-5 | Rawley | Valenzuela |

**Won 16, Lost 11**

### SEPTEMBER

| | | | Winner | Loser |
|---|---|---|---|---|
| 1—Phila. | L | 1-4 | Denny | Reuss |
| 2—Montreal | W | 5-4† | Diaz | Reardon |
| 3—Montreal | W | 4-0 | Hershiser | Smith |
| 4—Montreal | W | 4-2 | Welch | Dopson |
| 6—New York | L | 0-2§ | Orosco | Niedenfuer |
| 7—New York | W | 7-6 | Niedenfuer | Leach |
| 8—New York | L | 3-4x | Sisk | Diaz |
| 9—At Atlanta | W | 9-7 | Holton | Sutter |
| 10—At Atlanta | W | 10-1 | Honeycutt | Perez |
| 10—At Atlanta | W | 10-4 | Powell | Smith |
| 11—At Atlanta | W | 12-3 | Valenzuela | Bedrosian |
| 12—At Atlanta | L | 6-11 | Smith | Castillo |
| 13—At Cinn. | W | 8-2 | Hershiser | McGaffigan |
| 13—At Cinn. | L | 5-6 | Power | Niedenfuer |
| 14—At Cinn. | W | 7-0 | Welch | Robinson |
| 15—At Cinn. | L | 6-10 | Browning | Valenzuela |
| 16—At S. Diego | L | 2-4 | Show | Reuss |
| 17—At S. Diego | W | 7-1 | Hershiser | Hawkins |
| 18—Houston | L | 2-7 | Scott | Howell |
| 19—Houston | L | 5-6 | Knepper | Welch |
| 20—At S. Fran. | L | 3-5 | Minton | Niedenfuer |
| 21—At S. Fran. | W | 11-2 | Reuss | Davis |
| 22—At S. Fran. | W | 5-3 | Hershiser | Blue |
| 23—At Hous. | W | 5-3 | Diaz | Calhoun |
| 24—At Hous. | W | 7-2 | Welch | Knepper |
| 25—At Hous. | L | 4-6* | Solano | Niedenfuer |
| 27—San Fran. | W | 6-2 | Hershiser | Blue |
| 28—San Fran. | W | 3-1 | Reuss | LaPoint |
| 29—San Fran. | W | 7-2 | Welch | Mason |
| 30—San Diego | L | 4-6 | Gossage | Howell |

**Won 18, Lost 12**

### OCTOBER

| | | | Winner | Loser |
|---|---|---|---|---|
| 1—San Diego | W | 10-3 | Diaz | Dravecky |
| 2—Atlanta | W | 9-3 | Hershiser | Johnson |
| 3—Atlanta | L | 0-5 | Smith | Holton |
| 4—Cincinnati | L | 2-4 | Stuper | Pena |
| 5—Cincinnati | W | 3-1 | Welch | Robinson |
| 6—Cincinnati | L | 5-6 | Power | Niedenfuer |

**Won 3, Lost 3**

*10 innings.   †11 innings.   ‡12 innings.   §13 innings.   x14 innings.

at the start of the month and still five back at the close of June—but it bought them time. They didn't get buried as they had the year before.

The big push began in earnest June 29. The Dodgers won 20 of 25 games, and they whipped past San Diego into first place July 13. The Dodgers never relinquished the top spot, opening a lead of as many as 9½ games on three occasions. They finished with a 95-67 record, 5½ games ahead of Cincinnati.

Guerrero was partly responsible for the surge with another big month—.460, four homers and 13 RBIs in July—but this time he wasn't alone. Some of his teammates finally got hot.

First baseman Greg Brock improved his average from .215 at the end of May to .277 on July 27. Brock finished with 21 homers and a .251 average.

Ken Landreaux jumped from .170 in mid-May to .279 by the end of August. The center fielder played in more games (147) than any other Dodger and hit .268 with 12 homers for the season.

Sax, dropped from the leadoff spot to No. 8 in the order, improved his average by 50 points to wind up at .279. He also stole 27 bases and kept his error total (22) down, indicating that his throwing problems may be behind him.

One of the biggest contributors for Los Angeles was Scioscia, the durable catcher who was hitting only .233 on May 30. He finished with the league's second-best on-base percentage (.407) and career highs of seven homers, 53 RBIs and a .296 average.

Marshall was absent during the Dodgers' big surge—he had an emergency appendectomy—but was a catalyst the final month, hitting .340 and driving in 37 runs in September-October. He finished at .293 with 28 homers and 95 RBIs.

The Dodgers didn't get much help from some of their role players, though, including infielder Dave Anderson (.199) and outfielders Candy Maldonado (.225) and R.J. Reynolds (.266).

To solve this problem, the Dodgers pulled off three player moves that added stability and experience to the club.

On July 9, Campanis traded outfielder Al Oliver to the American League, where he could be a designated hitter. In return, Toronto gave the Dodgers all-purpose player Len Matuszek, who hit .222 in Los Angeles.

The next day, Campanis came up with first baseman Enos Cabell from Houston in a deal for two minor leaguers. The timing was important because the Dodgers had a number of injuries then.

And on August 31, Campanis obtained his long-sought third baseman, Bill Madlock, in a deal with the Pirates. Reynolds and Sid Bream, the club's starting first baseman on opening day, were among three players sent to Pittsburgh.

Cabell, who hit .292 as a Dodger, and Madlock, who batted .360 with 15 RBIs and seven stolen bases in five weeks in Los Angeles, might have made their greatest contribution the morning of September 21, before a day game in San Francisco. The Dodgers had dropped a 5-3 decision to the Giants the night before, and suddenly the Reds had closed to within 4½ games.

Cabell, Madlock and some other Dodgers called a players-only meeting that apparently struck a chord. The Dodgers responded with an 11-2 trouncing of the Giants, opening a stretch in which they won nine of 11 games to clinch the title.

The one constant throughout the season was the pitching. Although the club did not have a 20-game winner, four Dodger starters posted earned-run averages below 3.00.

Lefthander Fernando Valenzuela had impressive numbers (17-10, 2.45 ERA, 208 strikeouts, five shutouts and 14 complete games) that would have been better with a little run support from his teammates, but the ace of the staff was mild-mannered Orel Hershiser. The righthander kept getting better after a strong rookie year and won his last 11 decisions. Hershiser went 19-3 with a 2.03 ERA, five shutouts and nine complete games.

Righthander Bob Welch, after making only one start in the first two months because of a tender elbow, posted a 14-4 record with a 2.31 ERA. Veteran Jerry Reuss had his best season since 1982, going 14-10 with a 2.92 ERA. Lefty Rick Honeycutt (8-12, 3.42) was the only thing close to a weak spot in the starting rotation.

The stopper in the bullpen was Tom Niedenfuer, who had 19 saves and a 2.71 ERA. Ken Howell added 12 saves.

It was Niedenfuer, however, who emerged as the goat in the N.L. Championship Series against St. Louis. The hard-throwing righthander gave up game-winning homers to Ozzie Smith (Game 5) and Jack Clark (Game 6) as the Cardinals came back from a 0-2 deficit to win the playoffs in six games.

Still, the Dodgers won the division in a year when they were not even expected to contend. And the club had another big year at the gate, surpassing the 3 million mark in attendance for the sixth time in eight years.

**Much of Cincinnati's 1985 success can be attributed to the booming bat of right fielder Dave Parker.**

# Reds Enjoy a Rosy Season

**By HAL McCOY**

Nobody doubted Pete Rose when he said he would break Ty Cobb's career hits record in 1985. The scrappy player-manager of the Cincinnati Reds entered the season with only 95 hits to go, so the only question was when and where he would get what he called "the big knock."

But when Rose told anybody who would listen during spring training that the Reds would contend for the National League West title, too, he had few believers outside the Cincinnati clubhouse.

"I'm going to be selling you guys this year until I'm blue in the face," he told his team. "You are going to get sick of reading how good I think you can be."

Rose was right on both counts. He chased and eventually passed the ghost of Ty Cobb, slapping the 4,192nd hit of his 23-year major league career on September 11 in Cincinnati, and used his pursuit of the record as a rallying point for his curious blend of young and old players. They responded with an 89-72 record to finish second in the division, only 5½ games behind Los Angeles. The Reds, whose 19½-game improvement over their 1984 record was the biggest jump in the major leagues, were not eliminated from the title race until October 2.

When it was all over, Rose was able to lean back in his office chair with an "I told you so" look on his face.

"If we had listened to people this spring, there would have been no sense playing the season," the 44-year-old hits champion said. "We would have finished fifth and that's it."

And if anybody had told Rose that the pitchers from whom he expected the most —righthanders Mario Soto and Jay Tibbs —would finish a combined 22-31, the manager wouldn't have been so optimistic.

Despite ranking among the league leaders in strikeouts (214), complete games (nine) and innings pitched (256⅔), Soto struggled all year, finishing with a 12-15 record and a 3.58 earned-run average. Tibbs (10-16, 3.92 ERA) spent time in Denver (American Association) trying to work out his problems.

After an 8-3 start, Soto lost eight straight decisions before beating the Mets on July 22.

"I got down during the losing streak," Soto said. "The guys told me not to worry, but I did worry. After I lost three or four in a row, I didn't even want to come to the

**Bullpen ace Ted Power saved 27 games and won eight more.**

stadium. I tried to not think about losing, but I got to where I didn't want to go out there."

One starter took up the slack. Lefthander Tom Browning became Cincinnati's first 20-game winner since 1970 and the first rookie to win 20 games since Bob Grim of the Yankees in 1954. Browning won his last 11 decisions to finish 20-9 with a 3.55 ERA and was named The Sporting News' N.L. Rookie Pitcher of the Year.

Rose started the season with a four-man rotation of Soto, Tibbs, Browning and righthander John Stuper (8-5, 4.55 ERA). That setup lasted until May 15, when Soto was scheduled to pitch against Montreal. Rose assembled his pitchers and told them that the four-man rotation was working so well, he wanted to use it all year.

Soto, saying that his elbow was sore and besides, he needed more than three days' rest to pitch effectively, balked at the idea. He missed his start against the Expos and Rose, trying to accommodate his ace, went with a five-man rotation.

But the staff was more effective with a four-man setup, and Rose reinstituted it just before the All-Star break. By the end

## SCORES OF CINCINNATI REDS' 1985 GAMES

### APRIL

| Date | W/L | Score | Winner | Loser |
|---|---|---|---|---|
| 8—Montreal | W | 4-1 | Soto | Rogers |
| 10—Montreal | L | 1-4 | Gullickson | Tibbs |
| 12—At N.Y. | L | 0-1 | Berenyi | Soto |
| 13—At N.Y. | L | 1-2 | McDowell | Franco |
| 14—At N.Y. | L | 0-4 | Gooden | Tibbs |
| 15—At Atlanta | W | 9-8 | Stuper | Perez |
| 16—At Atlanta | W | 2-1 | Soto | Camp |
| 17—At Atlanta | W | 6-1 | Browning | Bedrosian |
| 18—San Fran. | W | 4-3* | Willis | Minton |
| 19—San Fran. | W | 4-2 | Stuper | Laskey |
| 20—San Fran. | W | 2-1 | Soto | Williams |
| 21—San Fran. | W | 1-0 | Browning | Hammaker |
| 22—At Hous. | L | 1-4 | Scott | Tibbs |
| 23—At Hous. | L | 4-6 | Mathis | Stuper |
| 24—At Hous. | W | 8-3 | Soto | DiPino |
| 25—At S. Fran. | L | 3-7 | Davis | Hume |
| 26—At S. Fran. | L | 6-7 | Blue | Power |
| 27—At S. Fran. | W | 2-1 | Stuper | LaPoint |
| 28—At S. Fran. | L | 1-2† | Minton | Hume |
| 30—Atlanta | L | 4-8 | Garber | Tibbs |

**Won 10, Lost 10**

### MAY

| Date | W/L | Score | Winner | Loser |
|---|---|---|---|---|
| 1—Atlanta | L | 9-17 | Mahler | Stuper |
| 3—New York | L | 4-9 | Lynch | Soto |
| 4—New York | W | 14-2 | Tibbs | McDowell |
| 5—New York | L | 2-3 | Gooden | Browning |
| 7—At Phila. | W | 2-0 | Soto | Gross |
| 8—At Phila. | W | 8-2 | Tibbs | Denny |
| 10—Houston | W | 5-2 | Browning | DiPino |
| 11—Houston | L | 7-10 | Solano | Soto |
| 12—Houston | L | 5-10 | Knepper | Tibbs |
| 13—Phila. | W | 7-3 | Stuper | Denny |
| 14—Phila. | L | 1-7 | Hudson | Browning |
| 15—At Mon. | W | 2-1 | Price | Smith |
| 16—At Mon. | W | 4-2 | Tibbs | Gullickson |
| 17—At Pitts. | W | 6-3 | Stuper | DeLeon |
| 18—At Pitts. | W | 8-0 | Browning | Bielecki |
| 19—At Pitts. | W | 7-1 | Soto | Tunnell |
| 20—At Chicago | L | 1-6 | Sanderson | Tibbs |
| 21—At Chicago | W | 5-2 | Hume | Frazier |
| 22—At Chicago | L | 4-7 | Eckersley | Browning |
| 24—St. Louis | W | 7-6‡ | Franco | Horton |
| 25—St. Louis | L | 4-6 | Andujar | Tibbs |
| 26—St. Louis | L | 2-7 | Cox | Stuper |
| 27—Chicago | L | 3-4 | Eckersley | Browning |
| 28—Chicago | W | 13-11 | Franco | Sorensen |
| 29—Chicago | W | 1-0 | Soto | Ruthven |
| 31—At St. L. | L | 0-5 | Cox | Stuper |

**Won 14, Lost 12**

### JUNE

| Date | W/L | Score | Winner | Loser |
|---|---|---|---|---|
| 1—At St. L. | W | 9-3 | Browning | Kepshire |
| 2—At St. L. | W | 8-3 | Tibbs | Forsch |
| 4—Pittsburgh | W | 9-3 | Soto | Guante |
| 5—Pittsburgh | W | 11-9 | Pastore | Robinson |
| 7—San Diego | L | 3-9 | Thurmond | Browning |
| 7—San Diego | L | 2-3† | Lefferts | Power |
| 8—San Diego | W | 7-4 | Price | Dravecky |
| 9—San Diego | L | 3-5 | Hawkins | Soto |
| 10—Los Ang. | L | 4-7 | Honeycutt | Stuper |
| 13—At Atlanta | W | 9-2† | Franco | Garber |
| 14—At Atlanta | L | 4-6 | Sutter | Soto |
| 15—At Atlanta | L | 0-7 | Bedrosian | Price |
| 16—At Atlanta | W | 6-5* | Power | Sutter |
| 17—At S. Fran. | L | 0-4 | Hammaker | Tibbs |
| 18—At S. Fran. | W | 6-1 | Pastore | Laskey |
| 19—At S. Fran. | L | 2-5 | LaPoint | Soto |
| 21—Atlanta | W | 4-2 | Browning | Shields |
| 21—Atlanta | L | 4-5 | Camp | Tibbs |
| 22—Atlanta | W | 4-3 | Robinson | Forster |
| 23—Atlanta | L | 1-2 | Bedrosian | Pastore |
| 25—San Fran. | W | 7-6 | Stuper | Davis |
| 26—San Fran. | W | 6-4 | Browning | Krukow |
| 27—San Fran. | W | 7-6 | Robinson | Gott |
| 28—At S. Diego | W | 11-9 | Robinson | Show |
| 29—At S. Diego | W | 3-0 | Dravecky | Soto |
| 30—At S. Diego | W | 3-2 | Franco | Hawkins |

**Won 15, Lost 11**

### JULY

| Date | W/L | Score | Winner | Loser |
|---|---|---|---|---|
| 1—At L.A. | L | 1-8 | Hershiser | Tibbs |
| 2—At L.A. | L | 0-3 | Valenzuela | Price |
| 4—At Phila. | L | 1-3 | Gross | Soto |
| 5—At Phila. | L | 2-5 | Andersen | Browning |
| 6—At Phila. | W | 4-2 | Robinson | Denny |
| 7—At Phila. | W | 3-2* | Franco | Tekulve |
| 8—New York | L | 1-8 | Lynch | Tibbs |
| 9—New York | L | 2-11 | Gooden | Soto |
| 10—New York | L | 1-2 | Aguilera | Browning |
| 11—Montreal | W | 2-0 | Robinson | Hesketh |
| 12—Montreal | W | 5-4† | Franco | St. Claire |
| 13—Montreal | L | 3-6 | Gullickson | Soto |
| 14—Montreal | W | 5-4* | Power | Lucas |
| 18—Phila. | L | 3-6 | Koosman | Soto |
| 19—Phila. | W | 3-2 | Franco | Tekulve |
| 20—Phila. | L | 6-10 | Rawley | Robinson |
| 21—Phila. | W | 7-6 | Franco | Carman |
| 22—At N.Y. | W | 5-1 | Soto | Fernandez |
| 23—At N.Y. | W | 4-0 | Browning | Darling |
| 24—At N.Y. | W | 3-2 | Franco | McDowell |
| 25—At Mon. | L | 0-1 | Gullickson | Hume |
| 26—At Mon. | W | 7-6† | Buchanan | Reardon |
| 27—At Mon. | W | 7-6 | Browning | Palmer |
| 28—At Mon. | L | 0-6 | Hesketh | Robinson |
| 30—Houston | W | 4-1 | Soto | Ryan |
| 31—Houston | L | 2-9 | Scott | Browning |

**Won 13, Lost 13**

### AUGUST

| Date | W/L | Score | Winner | Loser |
|---|---|---|---|---|
| 1—Houston | W | 5-2 | McGaffigan | Knepper |
| 2—Los Ang. | L | 3-5 | Hershiser | Robinson |
| 2—Los Ang. | W | 5-2 | Tibbs | Honeycutt |
| 3—Los Ang. | L | 0-2 | Welch | Soto |
| 4—Los Ang. | W | 5-4 | Power | Howell |
| 5—San Diego | W | 8-7 | Hume | Jackson |
| 8—At L.A. | W | 6-5§ | Power | Diaz |
| 9—At L.A. | L | 1-3 | Welch | Browning |
| 10—At L.A. | L | 1-2 | Valenzuela | Tibbs |
| 11—At L.A. | L | 0-4 | Reuss | McGaffigan |
| 12—At S. Diego | L | 0-2 | Thurmond | Soto |
| 13—At S. Diego | W | 3-2 | Browning | Hoyt |
| 14—At S. Diego | L | 1-4 | Dravecky | Tibbs |
| 15—At S. Diego | W | 5-4* | Franco | Walter |
| 16—At Hous. | L | 4-5 | Smith | Power |
| 17—At Hous. | W | 8-0 | Browning | Niekro |
| 18—At Hous. | W | 8-3 | Tibbs | Ryan |
| 20—At Pitts. | L | 2-3 | Reuschel | Soto |
| 21—At Pitts. | W | 8-5 | Browning | Walk |
| 22—At Pitts. | L | 1-5 | Rhoden | Tibbs |
| 23—Chicago | W | 3-2 | Franco | Sorensen |
| 24—Chicago | L | 0-4 | Frazier | Soto |
| 25—Chicago | W | 5-3 | Browning | Brusstar |
| 26—St. Louis | L | 0-3 | Cox | Tibbs |
| 27—St. Louis | L | 4-6 | Campbell | Power |
| 28—St. Louis | L | 2-7§ | Power | Lahti |
| 29—Pittsburgh | W | 6-0 | Browning | DeLeon |
| 30—Pittsburgh | W | 1-0 | Tibbs | Reuschel |
| 31—Pittsburgh | L | 0-6 | Walk | McGaffigan |

**Won 15, Lost 14**

### SEPTEMBER

| Date | W/L | Score | Winner | Loser |
|---|---|---|---|---|
| 1—Pittsburgh | W | 3-2 | Soto | Scurry |
| 2—At St. L. | W | 4-1 | Browning | Andujar |
| 3—At St. L. | L | 4-6 | Lahti | Hume |
| 4—At St. L. | L | 3-4 | Worrell | Robinson |
| 6—At Chicago | W | 7-5 | Soto | Botelho |
| 7—At Chicago | L | 7-9 | Baller | Franco |
| 8—At Chicago | T | 5-5 | ....... | ....... |
| 9—San Diego | W | 2-1 | Franco | Gossage |
| 10—San Diego | L | 2-3 | Hoyt | Robinson |
| 11—San Diego | W | 2-0 | Browning | Show |
| 12—San Diego | W | 2-1 | Tibbs | Hawkins |
| 13—Los Ang. | L | 2-8 | Hershiser | McGaffigan |
| 13—Los Ang. | W | 6-5 | Power | Niedenfuer |
| 14—Los Ang. | L | 0-7 | Welch | Robinson |
| 15—Los Ang. | W | 10-6 | Browning | Valenzuela |
| 16—San Fran. | W | 7-6† | Stuper | Davis |
| 17—San Fran. | W | 6-1 | McGaffigan | LaPoint |
| 18—At Atlanta | W | 7-3 | Robinson | Barker |
| 19—At Atlanta | W | 15-5 | Browning | Perez |
| 20—At Hous. | W | 5-3 | Tibbs | Ryan |
| 21—At Hous. | L | 5-9 | Smith | Franco |
| 22—At Hous. | W | 6-5 | Power | Dawley |
| 24—Atlanta | W | 7-5 | Browning | Perez |
| 25—Atlanta | L | 2-4† | Garber | Power |
| 26—Atlanta | W | 6-1 | McGaffigan | Bedrosian |
| 27—Houston | W | 4-3 | Robinson | Calhoun |
| 28—Houston | W | 5-2 | Browning | Scott |
| 29—Houston | W | 5-0 | Tibbs | Knepper |
| 30—At S. Fran. | L | 3-4 | Garrelts | Power |

**Won 19, Lost 9**

### OCTOBER

| Date | W/L | Score | Winner | Loser |
|---|---|---|---|---|
| 1—At S. Fran. | W | 7-6 | Hume | Garrelts |
| 2—At S. Diego | L | 4-5 | Gossage | Hume |
| 3—At S. Diego | L | 4-9 | Hawkins | Tibbs |
| 4—At L.A. | W | 4-2 | Stuper | Pena |
| 5—At L.A. | L | 1-3 | Welch | Robinson |
| 6—At L.A. | W | 6-5 | Power | Niedenfuer |

**Won 3, Lost 3**

*10 innings.   †11 innings.   ‡12 innings.   §13 innings.

**Second baseman Ron Oester batted .295 and committed only nine errors.**

of the season, the Reds had lowered their staff ERA from 4.16 in 1984 to 3.71.

The other Cincinnati starters included Ron Robinson (7-7), Andy McGaffigan (3-3), Joe Price (2-2) and Frank Pastore (2-1).

The bullpen was the source of less controversy and more stability. Righthander Ted Power recorded 27 saves and eight victories with a 2.70 ERA, while John Franco had 12 saves, 12 victories and a 2.18 ERA in 67 games. After Franco's first loss, the lefty won 11 straight decisions. And Tom Hume lowered his monstrous 5.64 ERA of 1984 to 3.26.

Right fielder Dave Parker carried the club offensively with his most productive year ever. He paced the league in runs batted in (125) and doubles (42) and ranked among the leaders in home runs (34), hits (198), batting average (.312) and game-winning RBIs (18).

"My most satisfying season," Parker said. "To be a leader in all this magic taking place in Cincinnati—and I'd have to say it is magic because we've brought winning baseball back to the city—was most satisfying."

Said Rose: "He had some big years in Pittsburgh, but he never had a year as important to a team as he had this year."

Behind Parker, Cincinnati's steadiest performer was second baseman Ron Oester, who hit a career-high .295 and made only nine errors. "Without a doubt, the most underrated player in the National League," Rose said of Oester.

Rose shared first base with another aging veteran, Tony Perez, who hit .328 in 183 at-bats. Shortstop Dave Concepcion, their teammate from the days of the Big Red Machine in Cincinnati, batted .252.

The other positions in the Reds' lineup were less stable. There was little resemblance between Rose's opening day lineup and the late-season team that put pressure on the Dodgers.

On opening day, Dann Bilardello was the catcher, Nick Esasky was the third baseman, Cesar Cedeno was in left field and Eric Davis was in center. By midseason, Bilardello and Davis were in Denver and Cedeno was a pinch-hitter.

Rose knew he needed catching. Bilardello, Dave Van Gorder and Alan Knicely (despite his status as the Minor League Player of the Year in 1984) were not the answers. So, General Manager Bill Bergesch obtained veteran Bo Diaz from the Phillies, and, as a bonus, finagled a deal for third baseman Buddy Bell from Texas. To get them, Bergesch gave up such players as Knicely, seldom-used outfielder Duane Walker, infielder Tom Foley and minor league pitcher Jeff Russell, who lost 18 games for the Reds in '84.

These moves enabled Rose to install Bell at third base and to move Esasky to left field. Even though he never had played that position before, Esasky made no errors, and his hitting improved at that point, too. He wound up hitting .262 with a career-high 21 homers and 66 RBIs.

With Davis gone, Eddie Milner was a frequent starter in center field. He responded with a .254 average, 82 runs scored and 35 stolen bases. But the team leader in steals was outfielder Gary Redus, who had just 246 at-bats but still managed 48 steals.

Spot starters Wayne Krenchicki (.272) and Max Venable (.289) also provided some timely hitting for the Reds.

Bell (.219) and Diaz (.261 in Cincinnati) both started slowly in their new environs, and Rose took some heat for playing them. But both finished strong.

"It wouldn't surprise me if Bell was the All-Star third baseman next year," Rose said, "and I know Diaz is going to have a good season."

Bearing in mind Rose's accurate prognostications before the 1985 season, it might be wise to listen to him.

Second baseman Bill Doran was one of Houston's most consistent performers, hitting .287 with 84 runs scored and 23 stolen bases.

# Displeased Astros Clean House

**By NEIL HOHLFELD**

When the Houston Astros left their new spring training complex in Kissimmee, Fla., in April, Al Rosen was the general manager, Bob Lillis was the field manager and Joe Niekro was the senior pitcher on the team.

By the end of the 1985 season, none was a member of the Astros.

Despite an 83-79 record, a third-place tie with San Diego in the National League West and several outstanding individual efforts, the season was a major disappointment.

The Astros finished 12 games out of first for the third time in the last four years. Fans in Houston apparently sensed that the team would not be a contender because home attendance was the lowest since 1978. The final home game of the season drew a crowd of 2,600—the smallest in the 21-year history of the Astrodome.

With those numbers in mind, Astros Owner John J. McMullen decided changes were necessary. Ironically, the shuffle started in September, when the team was in the middle of its hottest month of the season.

Amid persistent rumblings that his job was in jeopardy, Rosen left in September to become the San Francisco Giants' general manager. He was replaced by Dick Wagner, a veteran baseball administrator.

Wagner's first move was to trade Niekro to the New York Yankees for two minor leaguers. The 40-year-old knuckleballer was eligible to become a free agent at the end of the season, and the Astros were not willing to give him a long-term contract.

Lillis, the club's manager since August 1982, was told by Wagner the day after the season ended that he would not be brought back for 1986. He was offered a job as vice president of player personnel, but he opted instead to become a coach with the Giants. Lillis had been associated with the Houston franchise as a player, scout, coach and manager since its inception in 1962.

The 1985 season had begun with the Astros intent on avoiding another slow start. In both 1983 and '84, they were 7½ games out of first at the end of April and never recovered.

The Astros broke even in April for a change, and despite injuries to Jose Cruz, Jerry Mumphrey and Terry Puhl—their

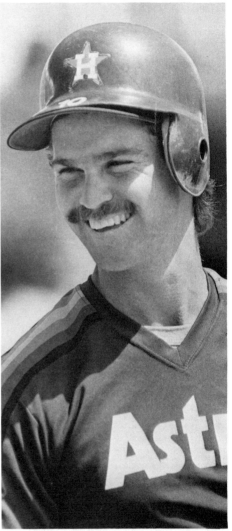

**The Astros were encouraged by the improvement of shortstop Dickie Thon, who still is on the comeback trail after a 1984 beaning.**

starting outfield—they entered June tied for second, four games out.

By June 12, they had crept to within 2½ games of first-place San Diego and appeared to be ready to stay in the race. But then the Dodger disaster struck.

Los Angeles, led by red-hot Pedro Guerrero, beat the Astros six out of seven games during an 11-day stretch. The

## SCORES OF HOUSTON ASTROS' 1985 GAMES

### APRIL

| Date | W/L | Score | Winner | Loser |
|---|---|---|---|---|
| 9—Los Ang. | W | 2-1 | Ryan | Valenzuela |
| 10—Los Ang. | L | 4-5 | Reuss | Niekro |
| 11—Los Ang. | L | 3-4 | Diaz | Dawley |
| 12—Phila. | W | 8-3 | Smith | Andersen |
| 13—Phila. | L | 2-4 | Rawley | Mathis |
| 14—Phila. | W | 5-3 | Ryan | Carlton |
| 15—At L.A. | L | 3-5 | Diaz | Niekro |
| 16—At L.A. | W | 7-3 | Smith | Howe |
| 17—At L.A. | L | 0-1† | Hershiser | DiPino |
| 19—At Atlanta | L | 5-9 | Mahler | Ryan |
| 20—At Atlanta | W | 8-1 | Niekro | Perez |
| 21—At Atlanta | W | 4-2 | Knepper | Barker |
| 22—Cincinnati | W | 4-1 | Scott | Tibbs |
| 23—Cincinnati | W | 6-4 | Mathis | Stuper |
| 24—Cincinnati | L | 3-8 | Soto | DiPino |
| 25—Atlanta | L | 2-3* | Z. Smith | D. Smith |
| 26—Atlanta | W | 3-2 | DiPino | Camp |
| 27—Atlanta | L | 2-8 | Mahler | Scott |
| 28—Atlanta | W | 2-1 | Smith | Forster |
| 30—At N.Y. | L | 1-4 | Gooden | Niekro |

**Won 10, Lost 10**

### MAY

| Date | W/L | Score | Winner | Loser |
|---|---|---|---|---|
| 1—At N.Y. | W | 10-3 | Knepper | Darling |
| 3—At Phila. | L | 2-3 | Tekulve | DiPino |
| 4—At Phila. | L | 5-7§ | Rucker | Dawley |
| 5—At Phila. | W | 4-3 | Niekro | Rawley |
| 7—At Mon. | W | 3-1 | Knepper | Palmer |
| 8—At Mon. | L | 0-1 | Hesketh | Ryan |
| 10—At Cinn. | L | 2-5 | Browning | DiPino |
| 11—At Cinn. | W | 10-7 | Solano | Soto |
| 12—At Cinn. | W | 10-5 | Knepper | Tibbs |
| 13—Montreal | W | 3-2* | Smith | Reardon |
| 14—Montreal | W | 10-0 | Mathis | Rogers |
| 15—New York | L | 3-5 | Gooden | Niekro |
| 16—New York | W | 1-0 | Scott | Fernandez |
| 17—St. Louis | L | 6-8 | Campbell | Calhoun |
| 18—St. Louis | W | 6-5 | Ryan | Kepshire |
| 19—St. Louis | W | 7-3 | Mathis | Tudor |
| 20—At Pitts. | L | 1-3 | Rhoden | Niekro |
| 21—At Pitts. | L | 2-3 | Reuschel | Scott |
| 22—At Pitts. | W | 5-3* | Dawley | Holland |
| 24—At Chicago | W | 6-2 | Ryan | Ruthven |
| 25—At Chicago | L | 4-5 | Smith | Ross |
| 26—At Chicago | L | 8-10 | Frazier | Ross |
| 27—Pittsburgh | W | 4-2 | Knepper | DeLeon |
| 28—Pittsburgh | L | 3-4‡ | Guante | Solano |
| 29—Pittsburgh | W | 8-3 | Ryan | Krawczyk |
| 31—Chicago | L | 2-6* | L. Smith | D. Smith |

**Won 14, Lost 12**

### JUNE

| Date | W/L | Score | Winner | Loser |
|---|---|---|---|---|
| 1—Chicago | L | 1-4 | Eckersley | Knepper |
| 2—Chicago | W | 4-3 | Scott | Gura |
| 3—At St. L. | L | 5-9 | Tudor | Ryan |
| 4—At St. L. | L | 1-6 | Andujar | Niekro |
| 5—At St. L. | W | 8-3 | Knepper | Cox |
| 7—San Fran. | W | 4-1 | Scott | Hammaker |
| 8—San Fran. | W | 4-1 | Ryan | Laskey |
| 9—San Fran. | W | 5-0 | Niekro | LaPoint |
| 10—San Diego | L | 1-9 | Hoyt | Knepper |
| 11—San Diego | W | 11-0 | Scott | Thurmond |
| 12—San Diego | W | 3-2 | Ryan | Show |
| 14—Los Ang. | L | 2-10 | Reuss | Niekro |
| 15—Los Ang. | L | 0-3 | Hershiser | Knepper |
| 16—Los Ang. | L | 0-9 | Valenzuela | Scott |
| 17—At Atlanta | W | 4-3 | Ryan | Shields |
| 18—At Atlanta | L | 2-3 | Sutter | Solano |
| 19—At Atlanta | W | 7-3 | Niekro | Bedrosian |
| 20—At Atlanta | W | 2-0 | Knepper | Mahler |
| 21—At L.A. | L | 2-7 | Hershiser | Scott |
| 22—At L.A. | L | 3-6 | Valenzuela | Ryan |
| 23—At L.A. | L | 2-6 | Honeycutt | Mathis |
| 24—At L.A. | W | 8-4 | Niekro | Reuss |
| 25—Atlanta | L | 4-6 | Mahler | Knepper |
| 26—Atlanta | L | 1-3† | Dedmon | Smith |
| 27—Atlanta | L | 1-4 | Smith | Ryan |
| 28—At S. Fran. | W | 3-1 | Niekro | Laskey |
| 29—At S. Fran. | W | 8-1 | Knepper | Hammaker |
| 30—At S. Fran. | W | 6-2 | Scott | LaPoint |
| 30—At S. Fran. | L | 4-7 | Blue | Mathis |

**Won 14, Lost 15**

### JULY

| Date | W/L | Score | Winner | Loser |
|---|---|---|---|---|
| 1—At S. Diego | L | 5-6* | Gossage | Ryan |
| 2—At S. Diego | W | 3-2 | Niekro | Wojna |
| 4—Montreal | L | 3-9‡ | St. Claire | DiPino |
| 5—Montreal | W | 4-2 | Scott | Mahler |
| 6—Montreal | W | 8-7 | Calhoun | Lucas |
| 7—Montreal | L | 3-6x | Youmans | Mathis |
| 8—Phila. | L | 4-7 | Hudson | Knudson |
| 9—Phila. | L | 3-5 | Gross | Knepper |
| 10—Phila. | W | 10-0 | Scott | Koosman |
| 11—New York | W | 4-3‡ | Smith | Gorman |
| 12—New York | L | 2-3* | Darling | Mathis |
| 13—New York | L | 1-10 | Lynch | Knudson |
| 14—New York | L | 0-1 | Gooden | Knepper |
| 18—At Mon. | L | 0-3 | Hesketh | Niekro |
| 19—At Mon. | L | 0-4 | Smith | Knepper |
| 20—At Mon. | L | 1-6 | Gullickson | Ryan |
| 21—At Mon. | W | 5-4 | Scott | Mahler |
| 22—At Phila. | L | 6-7 | Carman | Heathcock |
| 23—At Phila. | L | 6-12 | Koosman | Knepper |
| 24—At Phila. | L | 1-3 | Gross | Ryan |
| 25—At N.Y. | L | 3-6 | Gooden | Scott |
| 27—At N.Y. | L | 4-16 | Orosco | DiPino |
| 27—At N.Y. | L | 3-7 | Latham | Kerfeld |
| 28—At N.Y. | W | 12-4 | Niekro | Darling |
| 30—At Cinn. | L | 1-4 | Soto | Ryan |
| 31—At Cinn. | W | 9-2 | Scott | Browning |

**Won 8, Lost 18**

### AUGUST

| Date | W/L | Score | Winner | Loser |
|---|---|---|---|---|
| 1—At Cinn. | L | 2-5 | McGaffigan | Knepper |
| 2—San Diego | W | 12-9 | Niekro | Hoyt |
| 3—San Diego | W | 4-3 | Kerfeld | Lefferts |
| 4—San Diego | W | 2-1 | Scott | Dravecky |
| 5—San Fran. | W | 7-5 | Knepper | Hammaker |
| 8—At S. Diego | L | 5-6 | Lefferts | Smith |
| 9—At S. Diego | L | 4-6 | Dravecky | Ryan |
| 9—At S. Diego | L | 1-2 | Show | Scott |
| 11—At S. Diego | W | 7-2 | Knepper | Hawkins |
| 13—At S. Fran. | L | 2-4 | Krukow | Niekro |
| 14—At S. Fran. | W | 7-5 | Heathcock | Davis |
| 15—At S. Fran. | W | 4-1 | Scott | LaPoint |
| 16—Cincinnati | W | 5-4 | Smith | Power |
| 17—Cincinnati | L | 0-8 | Browning | Niekro |
| 18—Cincinnati | L | 3-8 | Tibbs | Ryan |
| 20—St. Louis | W | 17-2 | Scott | Kepshire |
| 21—St. Louis | L | 4-7 | Lahti | Smith |
| 22—St. Louis | L | 1-2 | Horton | Calhoun |
| 23—At Pitts. | W | 2-0* | Dawley | Clements |
| 25—At Pitts. | L | 3-9 | Reuschel | Scott |
| 25—At Pitts. | L | 9-10 | Robinson | Calhoun |
| 26—Chicago | L | 4-10 | Engel | Knepper |
| 27—Chicago | W | 11-4 | Smith | Meridith |
| 28—Chicago | W | 3-0 | Ryan | Baller |
| 30—At St. L. | W | 7-5 | Scott | Kepshire |
| 31—At St. L. | W | 3-1 | Knepper | Cox |

**Won 14, Lost 12**

### SEPTEMBER

| Date | W/L | Score | Winner | Loser |
|---|---|---|---|---|
| 1—At St. L. | L | 0-5 | Tudor | Niekro |
| 2—At Chicago | W | 7-2 | Dawley | Baller |
| 3—At Chicago | W | 8-7* | Smith | Frazier |
| 4—At Chicago | W | 11-6 | Scott | Meridith |
| 5—Pittsburgh | W | 4-3 | Knepper | Walk |
| 6—Pittsburgh | W | 4-3* | Dawley | Robinson |
| 7—Pittsburgh | L | 1-7 | Tunnell | Kerfeld |
| 9—San Fran. | W | 4-2 | Scott | Hammaker |
| 10—San Fran. | W | 4-1 | Knepper | Krukow |
| 11—San Fran. | L | 4-11 | Gott | Niekro |
| 11—San Fran. | W | 10-9 | DiPino | Davis |
| 12—San Fran. | W | 5-2 | Kerfeld | LaPoint |
| 13—San Diego | W | 3-2 | Scott | Thurmond |
| 14—San Diego | W | 4-3 | Knepper | Dravecky |
| 15—San Diego | W | 2-1 | Calhoun | Lefferts |
| 16—At Atlanta | W | 7-2 | Heathcock | Johnson |
| 17—At Atlanta | W | 10-6 | DiPino | Smith |
| 18—At L.A. | W | 7-2 | Scott | Howell |
| 19—At L.A. | W | 6-5 | Knepper | Welch |
| 20—Cincinnati | L | 3-5 | Tibbs | Ryan |
| 21—Cincinnati | W | 9-5 | Smith | Franco |
| 22—Cincinnati | L | 5-6 | Power | Dawley |
| 23—Los Ang. | L | 3-5 | Diaz | Calhoun |
| 24—Los Ang. | L | 2-7 | Welch | Knepper |
| 25—Los Ang. | W | 6-4* | Solano | Niedenfuer |
| 27—At Cinn. | L | 3-4 | Robinson | Calhoun |
| 28—At Cinn. | L | 2-5 | Browning | Scott |
| 29—At Cinn. | L | 0-5 | Tibbs | Knepper |
| 30—Atlanta | L | 3-6† | Camp | DiPino |

**Won 18, Lost 11**

### OCTOBER

| Date | W/L | Score | Winner | Loser |
|---|---|---|---|---|
| 1—Atlanta | W | 2-0 | Kerfeld | Bedrosian |
| 2—At S. Fran. | W | 7-2 | Dawley | Davis |
| 3—At S. Fran. | W | 7-2 | Heathcock | LaPoint |
| 4—At S. Diego | L | 3-4 | Thurmond | Knepper |
| 5—At S. Diego | W | 9-3 | Ryan | Wojna |
| 6—At S. Diego | W | 6-4 | Kerfeld | Show |

**Won 5, Lost 1**

*10 innings.   †11 innings.   ‡12 innings.   §13 innings.   x19 innings.

Astros were never in the race again, and the Dodgers began to pull away.

July was the killer for the Astros, though. They went 8-18 and fell deep into the second division. Included in the horrid month was a stretch during which they lost 12 of 13 games and were held scoreless for 42 consecutive innings (one short of the team record). They also went 32 straight innings without back-to-back hits.

"That was it, right there," Lillis said. "If you throw out that month, we played good baseball the rest of the season."

True, their record outside of July was 75-61. But their July record was only part of the reason why the Astros fell short.

In a year when the Astros' bats were hot —they led the league in hits, doubles and total bases and were second in scoring— their pitching went uncharacteristically sour. The club's earned-run average fell from 3.32 in 1984 to 3.66 (seventh in the league), marking the first time since 1978 that the Astros had ranked in the bottom half of the league in pitching.

The relief pitching was, on the whole, a big disappointment. Frank DiPino and Bill Dawley, who had combined for 53 saves and 24 wins in the two previous years, had a total of eight saves and eight wins. In all, the relievers lost 28 games.

The top loser among the starters was lefthander Bob Knepper, who went 15-13 despite a fairly respectable 3.55 ERA. Knepper also led the staff in innings pitched with 241.

Poor fielding plagued the Astros throughout the season. They committed 152 errors, the third-highest total in the league, and allowed 98 unearned runs, the second-highest N.L. total.

Injuries also slowed the Astros. Right fielder Puhl was on the disabled list four times, three of them for a recurring hamstring problem. He batted only 194 times. Left fielder Cruz had to sit out 22 games with a broken toe. Catcher Alan Ashby missed six weeks with a dislocated finger. And shortstop Dickie Thon was limited to 84 games as he attempted to come back from an eye injury that caused him to miss most of the 1984 season.

Despite being out of the race, the Astros didn't give up in September, winning nine straight games and 16 of 18 during one stretch. But with a chance to catch the Reds for second place, the Astros then went 2-7 against Los Angeles and Cincinnati in late September and fell to fourth. The Astros finished with a combined 13-23 record against the Dodgers and the Reds.

But the season did have its bright spots:

• Even though he endured a stretch of more than two months without a win and had his first sub-.500 season (10-12) since 1978, Nolan Ryan became the first pitcher ever to strike out 4,000 batters. Ryan finished with 209 to raise his career total to 4,083.

• Before he was traded, Niekro won his 138th game as an Astro, overtaking Larry Dierker as the club's all-time leading winner. He also won the 200th overall game of his career.

• Mike Scott, who had a 5-11 record in 1984, mastered a split-finger fastball and saw his record jump to 18-8. The righthander also fashioned a 3.29 ERA to pace the starters.

• Dave Smith, whose previous high for saves was 11, nailed down 27 games and won nine as the team's only consistent relief pitcher. He had a 2.27 ERA.

• First baseman Glenn Davis was called up from Tucson (Pacific Coast) in mid-June and then set a team record for home runs by a rookie with a club-leading 20. In 100 games he hit .271 with 64 runs batted in.

• Second baseman Bill Doran put together his most consistent season. Doran, always an excellent fielder, hit .287 and led the team in runs scored (84) and stolen bases (23). But most surprising was his 14 homers, which tied Joe Morgan's club record for a second baseman.

• In a heartening story, Thon made steady improvement from his career-threatening encounter with a Mike Torrez pitch in April 1984. While battling blurred vision, Thon struggled early in 1985 but managed to finish at .251.

• Despite the injury that forced him to miss more games in '85 than he had in the previous five years combined, Cruz homered in his next-to-last at-bat to finish the season with a .300 average, extending his string of .300-or-better seasons to three. Earlier in the season, Cruz, who also had 34 doubles and 79 RBIs, got the 2,000th hit of his career.

Several other players made substantial contributions. Center fielder Mumphrey hit .277. Third baseman Phil Garner batted .268 with 10 triples. Outfielder Kevin Bass took over when Puhl was injured and hit .269 with 16 homers and 68 RBIs. And catcher Mark Bailey (.265, 10 homers), shortstop Craig Reynolds (.272) and infielder Denny Walling (.270) performed capably when thrust into starting roles.

But it wasn't enough, and some personnel changes appeared to be in order.

"We've proven you can't stand pat and expect to win," Ryan said.

**Despite a late-season slump, righthander Andy Hawkins ranked among the National League's biggest winners with an 18-8 record.**

# Lack of Speed Slows Padres

**By PHIL COLLIER**

Alan Wiggins' role in bringing San Diego the 1984 National League championship wasn't put into proper perspective until the Padres tried to defend their title without him.

Their fall to third place in the N.L. West, a distant 12 games behind the division-winning Dodgers, was marked by offensive problems that occurred after Wiggins disappeared before an April 25 series opener in Los Angeles. The second baseman and leadoff batter suffered a drug relapse that led to his departure in a June trade with Baltimore.

"Losing Alan changed the entire character of our offense," said Manager Dick Williams, who was unable to replace Wiggins' 1984 contributions of 70 stolen bases and 106 runs scored. Both were club records.

Wiggins batted only .054 in the 10 games he played with the Padres in 1985, and for a while it appeared they could win without him. After all, they led second-place Los Angeles by five games on July 4. But San Diego went 37-48 the rest of the way and had to share third place with Houston, which matched its 83-79 record.

"Going into the season, I thought we were stronger than we were in 1984," General Manager Jack McKeon said. That estimation was based on the club's off-season acquisitions of former A.L. Cy Young Award winner LaMarr Hoyt, reliever Tim Stoddard and utilityman Jerry Royster as well as the presumption that key regulars such as Kevin McReynolds, Carmelo Martinez and Terry Kennedy would improve their performances.

The Padres did improve their pitching, lowering their staff earned-run average from 3.48 in 1984 to 3.40, the fourth-best figure in the league. Without Wiggins, however, their stolen-base output dropped from 152 to 60, the lowest total in the league. There was a corresponding decline in runs scored, from 686 to 650. In addition, the team's record in one-run games dropped from 34-24 to 31-30.

"Wiggins was the difference in the late innings of close games," Cubs Manager Jim Frey said. "He gave the Padres the ability to manufacture runs."

Wiggins' replacements, Royster and Tim Flannery, performed much better than expected. Each batted .281, and they combined to score 81 runs and drive in 71. But together they stole only eight bases in

**Off-season acquisition LaMarr Hoyt started off fast but could do no better than a 16-8 mark.**

18 attempts.

Wiggins' departure caused a domino effect on the San Diego lineup, particularly on 25-year-old right fielder Tony Gwynn, who bats second. Gwynn won the N.L. batting title in 1984, partly because he averaged .412 with Wiggins on base. With Wiggins gone, however, Gwynn had fewer fastballs to hit, and his average dropped from .351 to .317, the league's fourth-best figure in 1985.

At age 36, first baseman Steve Garvey batted .281 with 34 doubles, 17 home runs and 81 runs batted in. Those figures mask the fact, however, that he hit .239 in July, when the Padres lost 17 of 27 games and went from four games ahead of the Dodgers to five games behind.

Several other players contributed to the team's midsummer collapse with slumps. Kennedy, who batted .261 with 74 RBIs, reached a four-year low in home runs (10) and showed the effects of catching 140 games. He batted .296 in July but only .222 in June and .225 in August.

McReynolds suffered drop-offs in batting average (.278 to .234) and homers (20 to 15) after showing great potential in 1984, his first full season in the majors.

## SCORES OF SAN DIEGO PADRES' 1985 GAMES

### APRIL

| Date | | Score | Winner | Loser |
|---|---|---|---|---|
| 9—At S. Fran. | L | 3-4 | Blue | DeLeon |
| 10—At S. Fran. | W | 3-0 | Show | LaPoint |
| 12—At Atlanta | W | 7-3 | Hawkins | Camp |
| 13—At Atlanta | L | 5-7* | Sutter | Stoddard |
| 14—At Atlanta | L | 1-3 | Mahler | Hoyt |
| 15—San Fran. | W | 8-3 | Show | Hammaker |
| 16—San Fran. | W | 2-1 | Hawkins | LaPoint |
| 18—Los Ang. | L | 0-5 | Valenzuela | Thurmond |
| 19—Los Ang. | W | 11-2 | Hoyt | Reuss |
| 20—Los Ang. | W | 4-3* | Gossage | Howell |
| 21—Los Ang. | L | 0-2 | Hershiser | Dravecky |
| 22—Atlanta | W | 5-3 | Hawkins | Smith |
| 23—Atlanta | L | 2-4 | Mahler | Thurmond |
| 24—Atlanta | W | 3-1 | Hoyt | Perez |
| 25—At L.A. | L | 3-6 | Honeycutt | Show |
| 26—At L.A. | L | 0-2 | Hershiser | Dravecky |
| 27—At L.A. | W | 4-3 | Hawkins | Brennan |
| 28—At L.A. | W | 1-0 | Lefferts | Valenzuela |
| 30—At Pitts. | L | 2-6 | Rhoden | Hoyt |

**Won 10, Lost 9**

### MAY

| Date | | Score | Winner | Loser |
|---|---|---|---|---|
| 1—At Pitts. | W | 6-4 | Show | DeLeon |
| 3—At Chicago | W | 6-5 | Hawkins | Sutcliffe |
| 4—At Chicago | L | 8-12 | Sorensen | Booker |
| 5—At Chicago | L | 3-6x | Frazier | DeLeon |
| 6—At St. L. | L | 2-5 | Cox | Show |
| 7—At St. L. | W | 12-2 | Dravecky | Forsch |
| 8—Pittsburgh | W | 12-2 | Hawkins | McWilliams |
| 9—Pittsburgh | W | 1-0 | Thurmond | Bielecki |
| 10—Chicago | L | 2-6 | Trout | Hoyt |
| 11—Chicago | W | 3-1 | Show | Eckersley |
| 12—Chicago | W | 5-3 | Dravecky | Ruthven |
| 14—St. Louis | W | 6-2 | Hawkins | Tudor |
| 15—St. Louis | L | 4-14 | Andujar | Hoyt |
| 17—At Mon. | L | 1-2* | Reardon | Stoddard |
| 18—At Mon. | W | 8-2 | Dravecky | Hesketh |
| 19—At Mon. | W | 8-3 | Hawkins | Rogers |
| 20—At N.Y. | W | 2-0 | Hoyt | Gooden |
| 22—At N.Y. | W | 5-4* | Thurmond | Orosco |
| 24—At Phila. | W | 1-0 | Dravecky | Denny |
| 25—At Phila. | W | 4-1 | Hawkins | Hudson |
| 26—At Phila. | W | 7-2 | Hoyt | Carlton |
| 27—At Phila. | L | 9-10 | Tekulve | Lefferts |
| 28—Montreal | L | 5-8 | Roberge | Gossage |
| 29—Montreal | L | 1-2 | Burke | Lefferts |
| 30—Montreal | W | 5-4 | Hawkins | Schatzeder |
| 31—New York | W | 4-3 | Hoyt | Sisk |

**Won 17, Lost 9**

### JUNE

| Date | | Score | Winner | Loser |
|---|---|---|---|---|
| 1—New York | L | 3-5 | Darling | Thurmond |
| 2—New York | L | 3-7 | Schiraldi | Show |
| 3—Phila. | L | 2-3 | Gross | Dravecky |
| 4—Phila. | W | 6-5 | Lefferts | Tekulve |
| 5—Phila. | W | 3-1 | Hoyt | Hudson |
| 7—At Cinn. | W | 9-3 | Thurmond | Browning |
| 7—At Cinn. | W | 3-2† | Lefferts | Power |
| 8—At Cinn. | L | 4-7 | Price | Dravecky |
| 9—At Cinn. | W | 5-3 | Hawkins | Soto |
| 10—At Hous. | W | 9-1 | Hoyt | Knepper |
| 11—At Hous. | L | 0-11 | Scott | Thurmond |
| 12—At Hous. | L | 2-3 | Ryan | Show |
| 13—At S. Fran. | W | 3-0 | Dravecky | Laskey |
| 14—At S. Fran. | L | 4-5† | Davis | DeLeon |
| 15—At S. Fran. | W | 1-0 | Hoyt | Gott |
| 16—At S. Fran. | L | 3-7 | Krukow | Thurmond |
| 16—At S. Fran. | L | 4-5§ | Williams | Thurmond |
| 17—At L.A. | W | 3-2 | Show | Honeycutt |
| 18—At L.A. | W | 4-0 | Dravecky | Welch |
| 19—At L.A. | L | 1-5 | Reuss | Hawkins |
| 20—San Fran. | W | 6-5 | Hoyt | Davis |
| 21—San Fran. | W | 6-1 | Wojna | Blue |
| 22—San Fran. | W | 2-1 | Show | Laskey |
| 23—San Fran. | W | 6-1 | Dravecky | Hammaker |
| 25—Los Ang. | L | 2-3 | Howell | Stoddard |
| 26—Los Ang. | W | 10-4 | Hoyt | Hershiser |
| 27—Los Ang. | W | 5-4 | Lefferts | Valenzuela |
| 28—Cincinnati | L | 9-11 | Robinson | Show |
| 29—Cincinnati | W | 3-0 | Dravecky | Soto |
| 30—Cincinnati | L | 2-3 | Franco | Hawkins |

**Won 17, Lost 13**

### JULY

| Date | | Score | Winner | Loser |
|---|---|---|---|---|
| 1—Houston | W | 6-5* | Gossage | Ryan |
| 2—Houston | L | 2-3 | Niekro | Wojna |
| 4—At Pitts. | W | 9-1 | Show | Rhoden |
| 5—At Pitts. | L | 4-5‡ | Reuschel | Lefferts |
| 6—At Pitts. | L | 7-8 | Candelaria | Lefferts |
| 7—At Pitts. | W | 3-0 | Hoyt | Reuschel |
| 8—At Chicago | W | 8-4 | Stoddard | Sorensen |
| 9—At Chicago | L | 3-7 | Trout | Show |
| 10—At Chicago | L | 3-4 | Sanderson | Dravecky |
| 11—At St. L. | L | 0-6 | Tudor | Thurmond |
| 12—At St. L. | W | 2-0 | Hoyt | Andujar |
| 13—At St. L. | L | 3-7 | Cox | Wojna |
| 14—At St. L. | L | 1-2 | Kepshire | Dravecky |
| 18—Pittsburgh | W | 3-2 | Lefferts | Candelaria |
| 19—Pittsburgh | W | 6-0 | Hawkins | DeLeon |
| 20—Pittsburgh | W | 4-2 | Hoyt | Rhoden |
| 21—Pittsburgh | L | 2-5 | Tunnell | Show |
| 22—Chicago | L | 3-5 | Meredith | Jackson |
| 23—Chicago | L | 1-8 | Sutcliffe | Hawkins |
| 24—Chicago | L | 3-4* | Smith | Stoddard |
| 25—St. Louis | L | 6-9 | Dayley | Gossage |
| 26—St. Louis | L | 1-2‡ | Andujar | Stoddard |
| 27—St. Louis | W | 2-0 | Hawkins | Cox |
| 28—St. Louis | L | 2-4 | Tudor | Hoyt |
| 30—At Atlanta | W | 5-4‡ | Lefferts | Camp |
| 31—At Atlanta | L | 4-5* | Sutter | Stoddard |

**Won 10, Lost 16**

### AUGUST

| Date | | Score | Winner | Loser |
|---|---|---|---|---|
| 1—At Atlanta | W | 6-0 | Hawkins | Smith |
| 2—At Hous. | L | 9-12 | Niekro | Hoyt |
| 3—At Hous. | L | 3-4 | Kerfeld | Lefferts |
| 4—At Hous. | L | 1-2 | Scott | Dravecky |
| 5—At Cinn. | L | 7-8 | Hume | Jackson |
| 8—Houston | W | 6-5 | Lefferts | Smith |
| 9—Houston | W | 6-4 | Dravecky | Ryan |
| 9—Houston | W | 2-1 | Show | Scott |
| 11—Houston | L | 2-7 | Knepper | Hawkins |
| 12—Cincinnati | W | 2-0 | Thurmond | Soto |
| 13—Cincinnati | L | 2-3 | Browning | Hoyt |
| 14—Cincinnati | W | 4-1 | Dravecky | Tibbs |
| 15—Cincinnati | L | 4-5* | Franco | Walter |
| 16—Atlanta | W | 6-3 | Hawkins | Mahler |
| 18—Atlanta | W | 2-1 | Jackson | Bedrosian |
| 18—Atlanta | L | 3-6 | Forster | Hoyt |
| 20—At Mon. | W | 1-0 | Dravecky | Gullickson |
| 21—At Mon. | W | 6-2 | Show | Laskey |
| 22—At Mon. | W | 3-0 | Hawkins | Youmans |
| 23—At N.Y. | W | 6-1 | Thurmond | Aguilera |
| 23—At N.Y. | W | 3-0 | Jackson | Fernandez |
| 24—At N.Y. | L | 1-5 | Darling | Dravecky |
| 25—At N.Y. | L | 3-9 | Gooden | Show |
| 26—At Phila. | L | 3-4 | Carman | McCullers |
| 27—At Phila. | W | 4-1 | Thurmond | Denny |
| 29—Montreal | L | 5-8 | Roberge | Walter |
| 31—Montreal | L | 1-7 | Gullickson | Show |

**Won 14, Lost 13**

### SEPTEMBER

| Date | | Score | Winner | Loser |
|---|---|---|---|---|
| 1—Montreal | W | 5-1 | Hawkins | Youmans |
| 2—New York | L | 4-12 | Fernandez | Thurmond |
| 3—New York | L | 3-8 | Aguilera | Dravecky |
| 4—New York | L | 2-9 | Darling | Jackson |
| 6—Phila. | W | 3-2† | Gossage | Shipanoff |
| 7—Phila. | L | 0-2 | Denny | Hawkins |
| 8—Phila. | L | 7-9 | Surhoff | Wojna |
| 9—At Cinn. | L | 1-2 | Franco | Gossage |
| 10—At Cinn. | W | 3-2 | Hoyt | Robinson |
| 11—At Cinn. | L | 0-2 | Browning | Show |
| 12—At Cinn. | L | 1-2 | Tibbs | Hawkins |
| 13—At Hous. | L | 2-3 | Scott | Thurmond |
| 14—At Hous. | L | 3-4 | Knepper | Dravecky |
| 15—At Hous. | L | 1-2 | Calhoun | Lefferts |
| 16—Los Ang. | W | 4-2 | Show | Reuss |
| 17—Los Ang. | L | 1-7 | Hershiser | Hawkins |
| 18—At S. Fran. | L | 6-9 | Blue | Thurmond |
| 19—At S. Fran. | W | 11-3 | Dravecky | Hammaker |
| 20—Atlanta | W | 11-1 | Hoyt | Bedrosian |
| 21—Atlanta | W | 1-0 | Show | Johnson |
| 22—Atlanta | L | 5-7 | Smith | Hawkins |
| 23—San Fran. | L | 2-7 | Hammaker | Thurmond |
| 24—San Fran. | W | 4-3 | Dravecky | LaPoint |
| 25—San Fran. | W | 7-4 | Hoyt | Mason |
| 27—At Atlanta | W | 10-1 | Show | Johnson |
| 28—At Atlanta | W | 6-5§ | Wojna | Dedmon |
| 29—At Atlanta | L | 2-3 | Camp | McCullers |
| 30—At L.A. | W | 6-4 | Gossage | Howell |

**Won 12, Lost 16**

### OCTOBER

| Date | | Score | Winner | Loser |
|---|---|---|---|---|
| 1—At L.A. | L | 3-10 | Diaz | Dravecky |
| 2—Cincinnati | W | 5-4 | Gossage | Hume |
| 3—Cincinnati | W | 9-4 | Hawkins | Tibbs |
| 4—Houston | W | 4-3 | Thurmond | Knepper |
| 5—Houston | L | 3-9 | Ryan | Wojna |
| 6—Houston | L | 4-6 | Kerfeld | Show |

**Won 3, Lost 3**

*10 innings.   †11 innings.   ‡12 innings.   §13 innings.   xSuspended game, completed July 8.

**Tony Gwynn couldn't match his 1984 season, but still hit an impressive .317.**

The 25-year-old center fielder drove in 75 runs for the second year in a row, but he batted only .152 in July and .239 in August.

Martinez, who completed San Diego's trio of 25-year-old starting outfielders, improved on his 1984 totals in batting average (.250 to .253), homers (13 to 21) and RBIs (66 to 72). But like many of his teammates, the left fielder was cold in July, batting .205 with only nine RBIs.

Meanwhile, the Padres wasted fine years by Gwynn, Flannery, Royster, shortstop Garry Templeton (.282, six homers, 55 RBIs, 16 steals), 41-year-old third baseman Graig Nettles (.261, 15 homers, 61 RBIs) and reserve catcher Bruce Bochy (.268, six homers in 112 at-bats).

Williams was accused of not making proper use of his bench in 1985. Reserves Kurt Bevacqua, Al Bumbry and Bobby Brown played sparingly—Bevacqua had the most at-bats of the three with 138—and they all had subpar years.

Williams also had personality conflicts with several players, particularly McReynolds, and was accused of creating panic when the Padres reassembled after the All-Star break. Fearing a threatened players strike, Williams switched from a five-man to a four-man starting pitching rotation and instructed the team to play as if only 18 games were left in the season.

The idea was to be in first place by August 6, the announced strike date.

The Padres were half a game out of first after the intermission. They lost 12 of those next 18 games, however, and fell to third place, seven games back, by the start of the two-day strike.

The four-man rotation didn't seem to work as the starters went 4-5 with nine no-decisions after Mark Thurmond was dropped from the rotation. The lefthander rejoined the starters after the strike and the Padres promptly went on a 12-4 tear that still left them 6½ games behind Los Angeles.

Thurmond had a disappointing year, going 7-11 with a 3.97 ERA, but the rest of the rotation was fairly solid. Hoyt, who was 12-4 at midseason and was the starting and winning pitcher in the All-Star Game, encountered a midseason spell of arm problems but still wound up with a 16-8 record, a 3.47 ERA and three shutouts. Andy Hawkins, a 25-year-old righthander, won his first 11 decisions before finishing 18-8 with a 3.15 ERA. The other two starters, lefthander Dave Dravecky (13-11, 2.93 ERA) and righthander Eric Show (12-11, 3.09), pitched much better than their records indicated.

Stoddard, a free-agent signee, did not provide the relief support that the Padres had sought. Coming off a solid year with the Cubs, Stoddard went 1-6 with a 4.65 ERA and only one save. Lefthander Craig Lefferts pulled up much of the slack, going 7-6 with a 3.35 ERA and two saves.

The bullpen ace was, of course, Goose Gossage, who went 5-3 with 26 saves and a 1.82 ERA. Although the Padres lost Gossage for one month because of a mid-season knee injury, their prospects for 1986 were brightened by the performances of minor league prospects Lance McCullers (five saves, 2.31 ERA and 27 strikeouts in 35 innings) and Gene Walter (three saves, 2.05 ERA and 18 strikeouts in 22 innings).

Despite the Padres' failure to defend their division title, the club's management refused to blame Williams, who has led the club to four of its five .500-or-better seasons.

"We had a disappointing season," Padres President Ballard Smith said. "It's natural for people to gripe, but I'd like for someone to tell me who they would rather have manage the ball club."

Nevertheless, Williams was not offered a contract extension beyond the 1986 season.

"I have no problem with that," Williams said. "I won my first pennant (with Boston) on a one-year contract."

Center fielder Dale Murphy was his usual self, batting .300 with a league-leading 37 home runs, 111 RBIs and 118 runs scored.

# Braves' Collapse 'Depressing'

**By GERRY FRALEY**

When the Atlanta Braves' 1985 season opened, John Mullen was general manager, Eddie Haas was field manager and their players were confident that they could win the National League West after finishing first once and second twice in the previous three years.

How quickly things change. After the season, former manager Bobby Cox was back to be the Braves' general manager, Chuck Tanner was installed as the club's fourth field manager within 13 months and the players were sobered by the realization that they may need some major readjustments to be competitive. Losing 96 games and finishing fifth, 29 games behind the leader, can open some eyes.

"This was a very depressing year," Gold Glove center fielder Dale Murphy said.

"It'll take me a long time to forget this year," catcher Bruce Benedict added. "After this type of season, you not only reassess yourself, you do it as an organization. That's probably something that has to be done. There's a lot of food for thought for everybody."

In 1985, the Braves gave the world a pitcher (Pascual Perez) who operated on his own schedule and consulted a spiritualist, another pitcher (Terry Forster) who had as many saves as appearances on a nationally televised late-night talk show (one) and a manager (Haas) who said the leadoff hitter is overrated because "he only leads off once a game."

The effects showed in the standings. After a 4-1 start, the Braves fell below .500 on April 21, then again May 3, and never recovered. They dropped below fourth place for good (except for one day in July) on May 7, and their longest winning streak for the duration was five games. That streak started August 26, the day Haas was fired and coach Bobby Wine was named interim manager.

By the time Haas was released, the Braves had a 50-71 record and were on the verge of mutiny.

"He was a minor league guy," Claudell Washington said of Haas, a 20-year veteran of Atlanta's farm system, "and he managed us like we were a minor league team. He was overmatched. We sat back too much and waited for the two big guys. He never tried to get anything going."

The Braves' problems started with offense. They finished 10th in the league in batting with a .246 average and 10th in scoring with 632 runs while suffering more shutouts (18) than any team except Pittsburgh.

They reached these depths despite having Murphy and Bob Horner, who combined for 64 home runs and 126 extra-base hits. With just 62 homers and 241 extra-base hits by the rest of the team, it appeared that the Braves had lost the power base that carried them to a division title in 1982.

There were only three legitimate power spots in the lineup in 1985. Horner, who switched from third base to first June 10, hit .267 with 27 homers and 89 runs batted in. In center, Murphy batted .300, knocked in 111 runs and led the league in homers (37), runs scored (118) and walks (90). And in left field, Terry Harper broke a career pattern of mediocrity by producing 17 homers and 72 RBIs. But the rest of the offense was relatively weak.

Brad Komminsk and Gerald Perry, both Haas favorites, had been expected to correct that situation. They failed badly and put their futures with the Braves in jeopardy.

Komminsk began the year as the starting left fielder but lost the position after producing just two extra-base hits and eight RBIs in his first 103 at-bats. Komminsk later had a stretch of 102 at-bats without an RBI and wound up hitting .227 with four homers and 21 RBIs in 300 at-bats.

Perry was the starting first baseman (along with Chris Chambliss) until his .215 average forced Horner's switch. Batting .214 with only three homers and 13 RBIs for the season, Perry contributed even less offense than Komminsk.

The list of unproductive positions in Atlanta's lineup goes on. The worst spot was catcher, where Rick Cerone, Bruce Benedict and Larry Owen combined for a .214 average, five homers and 57 RBIs. Shortstop Rafael Ramirez (.248, 58 RBIs) and second baseman Glenn Hubbard (.232, 39 RBIs) fared little better.

Atlanta's overall lack of team speed was evidenced by Washington's team-high total of 14 stolen bases. The right fielder also hit .276 with 15 homers.

Ken Oberkfell, who assumed the regular third-base duties when Horner moved across the diamond, batted .272 but contributed only 35 RBIs.

The Braves did not take advantage of their small home park the way their oppo-

## SCORES OF ATLANTA BRAVES' 1985 GAMES

| APRIL | | | Winner | Loser |
|---|---|---|---|---|
| 9—At Phila. | W | 6-0 | Mahler | Carlton |
| 11—At Phila. | W | 6-3 | Smith | Denny |
| 12—San Diego | L | 3-7 | Hawkins | Camp |
| 13—San Diego | W | 7-5† | Sutter | Stoddard |
| 14—San Diego | W | 3-1 | Mahler | Hoyt |
| 15—Cincinnati | L | 8-9 | Stuper | Perez |
| 16—Cincinnati | L | 1-2 | Soto | Camp |
| 17—Cincinnati | L | 1-6 | Browning | Bedrosian |
| 19—Houston | W | 9-5 | Mahler | Ryan |
| 20—Houston | L | 1-8 | Niekro | Perez |
| 21—Houston | L | 2-4 | Knepper | Barker |
| 22—At S. Diego | L | 3-5 | Hawkins | Smith |
| 23—At S. Diego | W | 4-2 | Mahler | Thurmond |
| 24—At S. Diego | L | 1-3 | Hoyt | Perez |
| 25—At Hous. | W | 3-2† | Z. Smith | D. Smith |
| 26—At Hous. | L | 2-3 | DiPino | Camp |
| 27—At Hous. | W | 8-2 | Mahler | Scott |
| 28—At Hous. | L | 1-2 | Smith | Forster |
| 30—At Cinn. | W | 8-4 | Garber | Tibbs |
| **Won 9, Lost 10** | | | | |

| MAY | | | | |
|---|---|---|---|---|
| 1—At Cinn. | W | 17-9 | Mahler | Stuper |
| 3—Montreal | L | 2-9 | Hesketh | Barker |
| 4—Montreal | L | 3-9 | Smith | Perez |
| 5—Montreal | W | 6-1 | Mahler | Gullickson |
| 7—At N.Y. | L | 3-5 | Darling | Smith |
| 8—At N.Y. | L | 0-4 | Lynch | Barker |
| 10—At Mon. | L | 0-5 | Smith | Mahler |
| 11—At Mon. | L | 0-3 | Gullickson | Bedrosian |
| 12—At Mon. | L | 0-4 | Palmer | McMurtry |
| 13—New York | W | 1-0 | Barker | Lynch |
| 14—New York | L | 1-3 | McDowell | Mahler |
| 15—Phila. | W | 3-2† | Sutter | Tekulve |
| 16—Phila. | W | 6-3 | Dedmon | Andersen |
| 17—Chicago | L | 5-7 | Smith | Sutter |
| 18—Chicago | W | 4-3 | Mahler | Eckersley |
| 19—Chicago | W | 3-0 | Bedrosian | Sutcliffe |
| 20—At St. L. | L | 0-14 | Andujar | Smith |
| 21—At St. L. | L | 3-6 | Cox | Barker |
| 22—At St. L. | L | 3-5 | Forsch | Mahler |
| 24—Pittsburgh | L | 2-4 | Winn | Bedrosian |
| 25—Pittsburgh | L | 2-8 | Rhoden | Perez |
| 26—Pittsburgh | W | 5-4† | Dedmon | Krawczyk |
| 28—St. Louis | L | 3-9 | Forsch | Smith |
| 29—St. Louis | W | 5-3 | Bedrosian | Tudor |
| 30—St. Louis | L | 0-6 | Andujar | Mahler |
| 31—At Pitts. | W | 8-2 | Camp | Rhoden |
| **Won 10, Lost 16** | | | | |

| JUNE | | | | |
|---|---|---|---|---|
| 1—At Pitts. | L | 3-6 | Reuschel | Garber |
| 2—At Pitts. | L | 0-5 | DeLeon | Bedrosian |
| 4—At Chicago | L | 3-5 | Ruthven | Mahler |
| 5—At Chicago | W | 4-2‡ | Dedmon | Smith |
| 7—Los Ang. | L | 2-7 | Niedenfuer | Bedrosian |
| 8—Los Ang. | W | 7-3 | Mahler | Hershiser |
| 9—Los Ang. | W | 10-3 | Shields | Valenzuela |
| 10—San Fran. | W | 7-0 | Smith | Gott |
| 11—San Fran. | L | 4-5y | Williams | Garber |
| 12—San Fran. | W | 5-2 | Mahler | Hammaker |
| 13—Cincinnati | L | 2-9‡ | Franco | Garber |
| 14—Cincinnati | W | 6-4 | Sutter | Soto |
| 15—Cincinnati | W | 7-0 | Bedrosian | Price |
| 16—Cincinnati | L | 5-6† | Power | Sutter |
| 17—Houston | L | 3-4 | Ryan | Shields |
| 18—Houston | W | 3-2 | Sutter | Solano |
| 19—Houston | L | 3-5 | Niekro | Bedrosian |
| 20—Houston | L | 0-2 | Knepper | Mahler |
| 21—At Cinn. | L | 2-4 | Browning | Shields |
| 21—At Cinn. | W | 5-4 | Camp | Tibbs |
| 22—At Cinn. | L | 3-4 | Robinson | Forster |
| 23—At Cinn. | W | 2-1 | Bedrosian | Pastore |
| 25—At Hous. | W | 6-4 | Mahler | Knepper |
| 26—At Hous. | W | 3-1‡ | Dedmon | Smith |
| 27—At Hous. | W | 4-1 | Smith | Ryan |
| 28—At L.A. | W | 11-2 | Bedrosian | Honeycutt |
| 29—At L.A. | L | 2-3 | Reuss | Mahler |
| 30—At L.A. | L | 3-4 | Howell | Sutter |
| **Won 14, Lost 14** | | | | |

| JULY | | | | |
|---|---|---|---|---|
| 1—At S. Fran. | W | 4-1 | Smith | Krukow |
| 2—At S. Fran. | L | 3-8 | Gott | Bedrosian |
| 4—New York | L | 13-16z | Gorman | Camp |
| 5—New York | L | 1-6 | Aguilera | Perez |
| 7—New York | L | 0-4 | Fernandez | Smith |
| 7—New York | L | 5-8 | Darling | Dedmon |
| 8—Montreal | W | 7-1 | Mahler | Gullickson |
| 9—Montreal | L | 1-5 | Smith | Perez |
| 10—Montreal | L | 5-6‡ | Burke | Sutter |

| JULY | | | Winner | Loser |
|---|---|---|---|---|
| 11—Phila. | W | 3-2 | Sutter | Andersen |
| 12—Phila. | W | 7-4 | Forster | Carman |
| 13—Phila. | W | 13-5 | Mahler | Hudson |
| 14—Phila. | W | 12-3 | Perez | Gross |
| 18—At N.Y. | L | 6-7 | Darling | Mahler |
| 19—At N.Y. | W | 1-0 | Smith | Aguilera |
| 20—At N.Y. | L | 4-16 | Gooden | Bedrosian |
| 21—At N.Y. | L | 10-15 | Leach | Perez |
| 22—At Mon. | W | 7-1 | Mahler | Palmer |
| 23—At Mon. | L | 2-4 | Hesketh | Smith |
| 24—At Mon. | L | 1-3 | Smith | Bedrosian |
| 25—At Phila. | W | 3-2 | Sutter | Tekulve |
| 26—At Phila. | W | 6-4 | Mahler | Denny |
| 27—At Phila. | L | 4-5 | Hudson | Smith |
| 28—At Phila. | L | 3-7 | Koosman | Bedrosian |
| 30—San Diego | L | 4-5§ | Lefferts | Camp |
| 31—San Diego | W | 5-4† | Sutter | Stoddard |
| **Won 11, Lost 15** | | | | |

| AUGUST | | | | |
|---|---|---|---|---|
| 1—San Diego | L | 0-6 | Hawkins | Smith |
| 2—San Fran. | W | 12-7 | Garber | Williams |
| 3—San Fran. | L | 5-7 | Krukow | Mahler |
| 4—San Fran. | W | 5-4† | Garber | Jeffcoat |
| 5—Los Ang. | L | 1-6 | Reuss | Barker |
| 8—At S. Fran. | W | 2-0 | Mahler | Minton |
| 9—At S. Fran. | W | 6-5 | Dedmon | LaPoint |
| 10—At S. Fran. | L | 5-6 | Garrelts | Dedmon |
| 11—At S. Fran. | W | 7-4 | Johnson | Williams |
| 12—At L.A. | L | 0-3 | Honeycutt | Mahler |
| 13—At L.A. | L | 1-2 | Diaz | Forster |
| 14—At L.A. | L | 0-5 | Welch | McMurtry |
| 15—At L.A. | L | 4-5 | Valenzuela | Sutter |
| 16—At S. Diego | L | 3-6 | Hawkins | Mahler |
| 18—At S. Diego | L | 1-2 | Jackson | Bedrosian |
| 18—At S. Diego | W | 6-3 | Forster | Hoyt |
| 20—Chicago | L | 2-5 | Fontenot | Sutter |
| 21—Chicago | L | 5-9 | Brusstar | Garber |
| 22—Chicago | L | 2-3 | Meridith | Camp |
| 23—St. Louis | L | 2-6 | Andujar | McMurtry |
| 24—St. Louis | L | 0-7* | Forsch | Barker |
| 25—St. Louis | L | 2-5 | Kepshire | Mahler |
| 26—Pittsburgh | W | 2-1 | Garber | Robinson |
| 27—Pittsburgh | W | 7-6 | Garber | Robinson |
| 28—Pittsburgh | W | 6-1 | Barker | Tunnell |
| 29—At Chicago | W | 9-6 | Mahler | Sorensen |
| 30—At Chicago | W | 8-1 | Johnson | Fontenot |
| 31—At Chicago | W | 4-5‡ | Brusstar | Garber |
| **Won 11, Lost 17** | | | | |

| SEPTEMBER | | | | |
|---|---|---|---|---|
| 1—At Chicago | L | 2-15 | Botelho | Barker |
| 2—At Pitts. | L | 4-5 | Tunnell | Mahler |
| 3—At Pitts. | W | 2-0 | Johnson | DeLeon |
| 4—At Pitts. | L | 0-2 | Reuschel | Perez |
| 6—At St. L. | L | 0-8 | Tudor | Mahler |
| 7—At St. L. | W | 3-1 | Bedrosian | Andujar |
| 8—At St. L. | W | 7-3 | Johnson | Forsch |
| 9—Los Ang. | L | 7-9 | Holton | Sutter |
| 10—Los Ang. | L | 1-10 | Honeycutt | Perez |
| 10—Los Ang. | L | 4-10 | Powell | Smith |
| 11—Los Ang. | L | 3-12 | Valenzuela | Bedrosian |
| 12—Los Ang. | W | 11-6 | Smith | Castillo |
| 13—San Fran. | L | 3-9 | Blue | Barker |
| 14—San Fran. | L | 1-3 | Minton | Garber |
| 15—San Fran. | W | 4-1 | Bedrosian | Mason |
| 16—Houston | L | 2-7 | Heathcock | Johnson |
| 17—Houston | L | 6-10 | DiPino | Smith |
| 18—Cincinnati | L | 3-7 | Robinson | Barker |
| 19—Cincinnati | L | 5-15 | Browning | Perez |
| 20—At S. Diego | L | 1-11 | Hoyt | Bedrosian |
| 21—At S. Diego | L | 0-1 | Show | Johnson |
| 22—At S. Diego | W | 7-5 | Smith | Hawkins |
| 24—At Cinn. | L | 5-7 | Browning | Perez |
| 25—At Cinn. | W | 4-2‡ | Garber | Power |
| 26—At Cinn. | L | 1-6 | McGaffigan | Bedrosian |
| 27—San Diego | L | 1-10 | Show | Johnson |
| 28—San Diego | L | 5-6x | Wojna | Dedmon |
| 29—San Diego | W | 3-2 | Camp | McCullers |
| 30—At Hous. | W | 6-3‡ | Camp | DiPino |
| **Won 9, Lost 20** | | | | |

| OCTOBER | | | | |
|---|---|---|---|---|
| 1—At Hous. | L | 0-2 | Kerfeld | Bedrosian |
| 2—At L.A. | L | 3-9 | Hershiser | Johnson |
| 3—At L.A. | W | 5-0 | Smith | Holton |
| 4—At S. Fran. | L | 0-1 | Mason | Mahler |
| 5—At S. Fran. | L | 1-7 | Blue | Perez |
| 6—At S. Fran. | W | 8-7 | Dedmon | Garrelts |
| **Won 2, Lost 4** | | | | |

*5 innings.   †10 innings.   ‡11 innings.   §12 innings.   x13 innings.   y18 innings.   z19 innings.

**A big reason for the Braves' collapse was the disappointing performances of starter Pascual Perez (above) and relief ace Bruce Sutter.**

nents did. Atlanta was outhomered at home, 80-65, which at least partly explains the club's league-low home record of 32-49.

"We're not going to win games at home with pitching," said righthander Rick Mahler, who had 17 of the meager 39 wins recorded by the Braves' bedraggled starting pitching staff. "In our park, we're going to win with power. I'd rather go out there knowing I'm going to get four or five runs than knowing I have to win 2-1."

But the Braves' pitching was even worse than their hitting. The staff had the league's highest earned-run average (4.19), allowed the most runs (781), hits (1,512) and walks (642) and tallied the fewest complete games (nine). The only trustworthy starter was Mahler, who won his first seven decisions but still finished 17-15. He had a 3.48 ERA.

The Braves came to the All-Star break trailing by 9½ games but still harboring thoughts of a recovery. The starting rotation managed just 14 wins after the intermission, though.

Len Barker, Craig McMurtry and Pascual Perez, who combined for 30 wins in '84, compiled a 3-25 record. At 6.14, Perez had the best ERA of the trio.

By comparison, Steve Bedrosian's 7-15 record and 3.83 ERA looked pretty good. So did the performances of two rookies, Zane Smith and Joe Johnson. Smith, the only regular lefthander on the staff besides Forster, went 9-10 with a 3.80 ERA, while Johnson won four games in eight decisions after being called up from Richmond (International) in July.

Even the bullpen, which had gained Bruce Sutter from the free-agent market, collapsed. The Braves lost 19 games in which they led or were tied entering the seventh inning.

Sutter, who had 45 saves and a 1.54 ERA with St. Louis in '84, managed just 23 saves and a 4.48 ERA. He also allowed 13 homers in 88⅓ innings. He admitted he had a shoulder problem late in the year and did not pitch for the final 2½ weeks.

Relievers Gene Garber (3.61 ERA) and Rick Camp (3.95) had fewer saves but also allowed fewer runs per nine innings than Sutter.

The Braves' home attendance was surpassed by every N.L. club except for Houston, Pittsburgh and San Francisco, and only the Astros were less popular on the road. In addition, ratings for Braves games on Owner Ted Turner's cable superstation were down.

Apparently, "America's Team" loses its national appeal when it doesn't win.

**Scott Garrelts got a shot in San Francisco's bullpen and was one of the few bright spots in the Giants' dismal season.**

# Giants Drop Out of Sight

**By NICK PETERS**

According to Murphy's Law, anything that possibly can go wrong will go wrong.

In 1985, the San Francisco Giants proved that theory by exceeding everyone's expectations for futility.

It's hard to believe that a non-expansion team could go an entire season without a starting pitcher winning more than eight games, with no regular batting above .271 and with nobody notching more than 62 runs batted in. But it happened.

That's why the Giants lost 100 games for the first time in the franchise's long and tradition-steeped history. The previous club record of 98 losses was set in 1943—and that ragtag outfit from New York was ravaged by World War II.

The 1985 Giants had no excuses for their inept performance and last-place finish in the National League West. They simply didn't play well. The demise led to the firing of rookie Manager Jim Davenport and General Manager Tom Haller. They were replaced by Roger Craig and Al Rosen, respectively.

"I saw things I didn't want to see," Craig succinctly summed up following a three-week stint with his new club. But at least Craig only had to endure 18 games.

Those who observed the team for the entire season saw few encouraging signs, the exceptions being rookie third baseman Chris Brown and relief ace Scott Garrelts, the club's lone representative at the All-Star Game.

Two other non-disappointments were Vida Blue and rookie shortstop Jose Uribe. Blue, who had been inactive since 1983, capped his comeback by being a .500 pitcher (8-8) on a squad that finished 38 games below that level. Uribe played in a team-high 147 games and was effective defensively until a sore arm hampered his throwing down the stretch. But he batted only .237.

The Giants' pitching, on the whole, was better than their record suggests. The team earned-run average of 3.61 was in the middle of the pack, and the staff held up well in the early going—when hitting support was non-existent—and kept the club in most games. There were 36 one-run losses, second most in the league.

But the hitting was a disgrace. Despite being essentially the same club that ranked second in the league in hitting in 1984, the Giants suffered a collective team slump that produced the worst average in the majors (.233). The Giants scored three or fewer runs in 92 games, winning only 15 of them.

"There was the obvious lack of hitting, but there also was a lack of fundamentals," said left fielder Jeff Leonard, whose 62 RBIs represented a drop-off from his previous two seasons but still were good enough to lead the team.

"It's obvious what we had didn't work, so there have to be a lot of changes to alter the chemistry and the personality of the club," added Bob Brenly, whose 19 homers made him the first catcher in 100 years to lead the Giants in that department.

The dismal season was punctuated by doubt concerning where the club would play in 1986. Owner Bob Lurie insisted that the Giants would not return to Candlestick Park, but he had few options.

Plans for a new downtown stadium were more talk than substance as winter approached. A proposal for a stadium in nearby San Jose was discouraged when the City of San Francisco threatened legal action for tampering.

Lurie added to the club's humiliation by announcing a potential move to Oakland on an interim basis, only to have the cross-bay community overwhelmingly reject the Giants. There even was talk of a temporary move to Denver.

The Giants played almost exclusively in the daytime at home in an effort to attract spectators, but the club finished with its worst attendance (except for the 1981 strike season) since 1977. And the Giants were 38-43 in home games.

In other words, nothing worked in 1985. The poor hitting and a seven-game losing streak produced a 3-9 start from which the Giants never recovered. They were 7-12 in April, 10-16 in May and 10-20 in June en route to a 33-55 record at the All-Star break.

"We started off badly and Davenport lost control," said lefthander Dave La-Point, a victim of poor run support who won only seven of 24 decisions and was traded to Detroit after the season. "We were just two months into the schedule and already were at the point where we were just putting on the uniform and playing out the schedule."

Added righthander Mike Krukow, who went 8-11 with a 3.38 ERA and was the most consistent of the starting pitchers: "The uncertainty surrounding the club and the ball park made it tougher, but the

## SCORES OF SAN FRANCISCO GIANTS' 1985 GAMES

### APRIL

| Date | | Score | Winner | Loser |
|---|---|---|---|---|
| 9—San Diego | W | 4-3 | Blue | DeLeon |
| 10—San Diego | L | 0-3 | Show | LaPoint |
| 12—At L.A. | W | 4-1 | Krukow | Honeycutt |
| 13—At L.A. | L | 0-1 | Valenzuela | Davis |
| 14—At L.A. | W | 8-4 | Gott | Reuss |
| 15—At S. Diego | L | 3-8 | Show | Hammaker |
| 16—At S. Diego | L | 1-2 | Hawkins | LaPoint |
| 18—At Cinn. | L | 3-4* | Willis | Minton |
| 19—At Cinn. | L | 2-4 | Stuper | Laskey |
| 20—At Cinn. | L | 1-2 | Soto | Williams |
| 21—At Cinn. | L | 0-1 | Browning | Hammaker |
| 22—Los Ang. | L | 2-3* | Niedenfuer | LaPoint |
| 23—Los Ang. | W | 2-1 | Krukow | Valenzuela |
| 24—Los Ang. | L | 2-4 | Brennan | Laskey |
| 25—Cincinnati | W | 7-3 | Davis | Hume |
| 26—Cincinnati | W | 7-6 | Blue | Power |
| 27—Cincinnati | L | 1-2 | Stuper | LaPoint |
| 28—Cincinnati | W | 2-1† | Minton | Hume |
| 30—At Chicago | L | 1-3 | Trout | Laskey |

**Won 7, Lost 12**

### MAY

| Date | | Score | Winner | Loser |
|---|---|---|---|---|
| 1—At Chicago | L | 3-4 | Eckersley | Garrelts |
| 3—At St. L. | L | 1-8 | Tudor | Krukow |
| 4—At St. L. | L | 4-6 | Kepshire | Hammaker |
| 5—At St. L. | W | 5-0 | LaPoint | Andujar |
| 6—At Pitts. | W | 7-5 | Laskey | DeLeon |
| 7—At Pitts. | W | 5-3 | Gott | Tunnell |
| 8—Chicago | L | 0-1 | Sutcliffe | Krukow |
| 9—Chicago | W | 1-0‡ | Garrelts | Brusstar |
| 10—St. Louis | L | 3-9 | Andujar | LaPoint |
| 11—St. Louis | L | 4-9 | Cox | Laskey |
| 12—St. Louis | W | 5-4* | Garrelts | Allen |
| 14—Pittsburgh | W | 3-1 | Krukow | McWilliams |
| 15—Pittsburgh | L | 2-3 | Robinson | Garrelts |
| 17—At N.Y. | L | 2-3‡ | McDowell | Garrelts |
| 18—At N.Y. | W | 8-2* | Davis | Gardner |
| 19—At N.Y. | L | 2-3 | Gorman | Davis |
| 20—At Phila. | L | 1-2 | Carlton | Blue |
| 21—At Phila. | L | 5-6 | Rawley | Hammaker |
| 22—At Phila. | W | 6-2 | LaPoint | Gross |
| 24—At Mon. | L | 0-2 | Hesketh | Laskey |
| 25—At Mon. | L | 1-3 | Schatzeder | Gott |
| 26—At Mon. | L | 1-3 | Gullickson | Krukow |
| 27—At Mon. | W | 6-1 | Hammaker | Palmer |
| 29—New York | L | 3-4 | Lynch | Davis |
| 30—New York | L | 1-2 | Gooden | Gott |
| 31—Phila. | W | 4-3 | Krukow | Hudson |

**Won 10, Lost 16**

### JUNE

| Date | | Score | Winner | Loser |
|---|---|---|---|---|
| 1—Phila. | W | 2-1 | Hammaker | Carlton |
| 2—Phila. | W | 3-1 | Blue | Rawley |
| 3—Montreal | L | 2-4x | St. Claire | Williams |
| 4—Montreal | W | 5-1 | Gott | Schatzeder |
| 5—Montreal | L | 0-6 | Mahler | Krukow |
| 7—At Hous. | L | 1-4 | Scott | Hammaker |
| 8—At Hous. | L | 1-4 | Ryan | Laskey |
| 9—At Hous. | L | 0-5 | Niekro | LaPoint |
| 10—At Atlanta | L | 0-7 | Smith | Gott |
| 11—At Atlanta | W | 5-4y | Williams | Garber |
| 12—At Atlanta | L | 2-5 | Mahler | Hammaker |
| 13—San Diego | L | 0-3 | Dravecky | Laskey |
| 14—San Diego | W | 5-4† | Davis | DeLeon |
| 15—San Diego | L | 0-1 | Hoyt | Gott |
| 16—San Diego | W | 7-3 | Krukow | Thurmond |
| 16—San Diego | W | 5-4§ | Williams | Thurmond |
| 17—Cincinnati | W | 4-0 | Hammaker | Tibbs |
| 18—Cincinnati | L | 1-6 | Pastore | Laskey |
| 19—Cincinnati | W | 5-2 | LaPoint | Soto |
| 20—At S. Diego | L | 5-6 | Hoyt | Davis |
| 21—At S. Diego | L | 1-6 | Wojna | Blue |
| 22—At S. Diego | L | 1-2 | Show | Laskey |
| 23—At S. Diego | L | 1-6 | Dravecky | Hammaker |
| 25—At Cinn. | L | 6-7 | Stuper | Davis |
| 26—At Cinn. | L | 4-6 | Browning | Krukow |
| 27—At Cinn. | L | 6-7 | Robinson | Gott |
| 28—Houston | L | 1-3 | Niekro | Laskey |
| 29—Houston | L | 1-8 | Knepper | Hammaker |
| 30—Houston | L | 2-6 | Scott | LaPoint |
| 30—Houston | W | 7-4 | Blue | Mathis |

**Won 10, Lost 20**

### JULY

| Date | | Score | Winner | Loser |
|---|---|---|---|---|
| 1—Atlanta | L | 1-4 | Smith | Krukow |
| 2—Atlanta | W | 8-3 | Gott | Bedrosian |
| 4—At Chicago | W | 6-4 | Garrelts | Trout |
| 5—At Chicago | W | 12-6 | Blue | Sanderson |
| 6—At Chicago | W | 6-4 | Garrelts | Smith |
| 7—At Chicago | L | 5-6 | Brusstar | Davis |
| 8—At St. L. | L | 1-6 | Andujar | LaPoint |
| 9—At St. L. | L | 1-3 | Cox | Laskey |
| 10—At St. L. | L | 3-7 | Kepshire | Blue |
| 11—At Pitts. | L | 4-6 | Guante | Krukow |
| 12—At Pitts. | L | 1-3 | Reuschel | Gott |
| 13—At Pitts. | W | 4-1 | LaPoint | DeLeon |
| 14—At Pitts. | W | 7-3 | Laskey | Rhoden |
| 18—Chicago | W | 1-0 | Krukow | Frazier |
| 19—Chicago | L | 3-4 | Sorensen | Gott |
| 20—Chicago | L | 1-2 | Ruthven | Hammaker |
| 21—Chicago | W | 2-1 | Laskey | Gura |
| 22—St. Louis | L | 3-4 | Andujar | LaPoint |
| 23—St. Louis | L | 3-6 | Cox | Krukow |
| 24—St. Louis | L | 0-4 | Tudor | Gott |
| 25—Pittsburgh | W | 4-3 | Minton | Guante |
| 26—Pittsburgh | W | 3-1 | Laskey | Tunnell |
| 27—Pittsburgh | W | 8-3 | LaPoint | Robinson |
| 28—Pittsburgh | W | 3-2* | Garrelts | Guante |
| 29—At L.A. | L | 5-10 | Welch | Blue |
| 30—At L.A. | L | 2-4 | Niedenfuer | Minton |
| 31—At L.A. | W | 7-5 | Laskey | Reuss |

**Won 13, Lost 14**

### AUGUST

| Date | | Score | Winner | Loser |
|---|---|---|---|---|
| 2—At Atlanta | L | 7-12 | Garber | Williams |
| 3—At Atlanta | W | 7-5 | Krukow | Mahler |
| 4—At Atlanta | L | 4-5* | Garber | Jeffcoat |
| 5—At Hous. | L | 5-7 | Knepper | Hammaker |
| 8—Atlanta | L | 0-2 | Mahler | Minton |
| 9—Atlanta | L | 5-6 | Dedmon | LaPoint |
| 10—Atlanta | W | 6-5 | Garrelts | Dedmon |
| 11—Atlanta | L | 4-7 | Johnson | Williams |
| 13—Houston | W | 4-2 | Krukow | Niekro |
| 14—Houston | L | 5-7 | Heathcock | Davis |
| 15—Houston | L | 1-4 | Scott | LaPoint |
| 16—Los Ang. | L | 1-5 | Reuss | Blue |
| 17—Los Ang. | W | 5-2 | Garrelts | Diaz |
| 18—Los Ang. | W | 2-1* | Davis | Niedenfuer |
| 20—At N.Y. | L | 0-3 | Gooden | Gott |
| 21—At N.Y. | W | 3-2 | LaPoint | McDowell |
| 22—At N.Y. | L | 0-7 | Leach | Blue |
| 23—At Phila. | W | 4-1 | Hammaker | Denny |
| 24—At Phila. | L | 2-9 | Hudson | Krukow |
| 25—At Phila. | L | 5-14 | Rucker | Gott |
| 26—At Mon. | W | 7-4 | LaPoint | Laskey |
| 27—At Mon. | W | 6-1 | Minton | Reardon |
| 29—New York | W | 6-3* | Garrelts | Leach |
| 30—New York | L | 1-2 | Darling | Krukow |
| 31—New York | W | 3-2 | Gott | Gooden |

**Won 11, Lost 14**

### SEPTEMBER

| Date | | Score | Winner | Loser |
|---|---|---|---|---|
| 1—New York | L | 3-4 | Sisk | Davis |
| 2—Phila. | L | 3-4* | Carman | Jeffcoat |
| 3—Phila. | L | 3-4§ | Shipanoff | Minton |
| 4—Phila. | W | 4-3 | Davis | Toliver |
| 6—Montreal | W | 8-3 | Gott | Gullickson |
| 7—Montreal | L | 1-7 | Youmans | LaPoint |
| 8—Montreal | L | 6-9* | Lucas | Garrelts |
| 9—At Hous. | L | 2-4 | Scott | Hammaker |
| 10—At Hous. | L | 1-4 | Knepper | Krukow |
| 11—At Hous. | W | 11-4 | Gott | Niekro |
| 11—At Hous. | L | 9-10 | DiPino | Davis |
| 12—At Hous. | L | 2-5 | Kerfeld | LaPoint |
| 13—At Atlanta | W | 9-3 | Blue | Barker |
| 14—At Atlanta | W | 3-1 | Minton | Garber |
| 15—At Atlanta | L | 1-4 | Bedrosian | Mason |
| 16—At Cinn. | L | 6-7† | Stuper | Davis |
| 17—At Cinn. | L | 1-6 | McGaffigan | LaPoint |
| 18—San Diego | W | 9-6 | Blue | Thurmond |
| 19—San Diego | L | 3-11 | Dravecky | Hammaker |
| 20—Los Ang. | W | 5-3 | Minton | Niedenfuer |
| 21—Los Ang. | L | 2-11 | Reuss | Davis |
| 22—Los Ang. | L | 3-5 | Hershiser | Blue |
| 23—At S. Diego | W | 7-2 | Hammaker | Thurmond |
| 24—At S. Diego | L | 3-4 | Dravecky | LaPoint |
| 25—At S. Diego | L | 4-7 | Hoyt | Mason |
| 27—At L.A. | L | 2-6 | Hershiser | Blue |
| 28—At L.A. | L | 1-3 | Reuss | LaPoint |
| 29—At L.A. | L | 2-7 | Welch | Mason |
| 30—Cincinnati | W | 4-3 | Garrelts | Power |

**Won 9, Lost 20**

### OCTOBER

| Date | | Score | Winner | Loser |
|---|---|---|---|---|
| 1—Cincinnati | L | 6-7 | Hume | Garrelts |
| 2—Houston | L | 2-7 | Dawley | Davis |
| 3—Houston | L | 2-7 | Heathcock | LaPoint |
| 4—Atlanta | W | 1-0 | Mason | Mahler |
| 5—Atlanta | W | 7-1 | Blue | Perez |
| 6—Atlanta | L | 7-8 | Dedmon | Garrelts |

**Won 2, Lost 4**

*10 innings.   †11 innings.   ‡12 innings.   §13 innings.   x15 innings.   y18 innings.

**Rookie third baseman Chris Brown had a bad spring, but recovered to lead the Giants with a .271 average while hitting 16 homers and driving in 61.**

good teams don't make excuses."

Nothing clicked for the Giants except strong pitching in the first half and the steady play of Garrelts and Brown, each of whom was a question mark during spring training.

Garrelts had failed to make the grade as a starter in 1984, but he earned a chance to become the club's righthanded stopper in the bullpen when Greg Minton was ailing in the spring. He came through with a team-leading nine victories, a 2.30 ERA and 13 saves. Garrelts and lefty Mark Davis (seven saves) became the first relievers in San Francisco Giants history to strike out more than 100 batters. Minton, meanwhile, started slowly and finished with five wins and four saves.

Brown stumbled in the field and at the plate during a disappointing spring, but he regrouped to lead the club with a .271 average while belting 16 homers and 61 RBIs. He made only 10 errors.

But those highlights were overshadowed by the weak seasons turned in by such players as Leonard (.241), Brenly (.220), second baseman Manny Trillo (.224), first baseman David Green (.248) and center fielder Dan Gladden, who slipped from .351 in 1984 to .243. Gladden did lead the team, however, with 64 runs scored, eight triples and 32 stolen bases.

The San Francisco bench provided little help. Outfielder Joel Youngblood batted .270, but outfielders Ron Roenicke (.256) and Rob Deer (.185) and infielders Brad Wellman (.236) and Dan Driessen (.232 after being obtained from Montreal) were less productive.

Injuries played only a small part in the Giants' season. Right fielder Chili Davis batted a soft .270 and missed the last three weeks with a shoulder separation. Krukow and Jim Gott (7-10) also were on the shelf at season's end, but lefthander Atlee Hammaker (5-12) made it through 1985 without any serious arm trouble.

Small consolation.

# National League Averages for 1985

## CHAMPIONSHIP WINNERS IN PREVIOUS YEARS

| | | |
|---|---|---|
| 1876—Chicago .788 | 1913—New York .664 | 1949—Brooklyn .630 |
| 1877—Boston .646 | 1914—Boston .614 | 1950—Philadelphia .591 |
| 1878—Boston .683 | 1915—Philadelphia .592 | 1951—New York† .624 |
| 1879—Providence .705 | 1916—Brooklyn .610 | 1952—Brooklyn .627 |
| 1880—Chicago .798 | 1917—New York .636 | 1953—Brooklyn .682 |
| 1881—Chicago .667 | 1918—Chicago .651 | 1954—New York .630 |
| 1882—Chicago .655 | 1919—Cincinnati .686 | 1955—Brooklyn .641 |
| 1883—Boston .643 | 1920—Brooklyn .604 | 1956—Brooklyn .604 |
| 1884—Providence .750 | 1921—New York .614 | 1957—Milwaukee .617 |
| 1885—Chicago .777 | 1922—New York .604 | 1958—Milwaukee .597 |
| 1886—Chicago .726 | 1923—New York .621 | 1959—Los Angeles‡ .564 |
| 1887—Detroit .637 | 1924—New York .608 | 1960—Pittsburgh .617 |
| 1888—New York .641 | 1925—Pittsburgh .621 | 1961—Cincinnati .604 |
| 1889—New York .659 | 1926—St. Louis .578 | 1962—San Francisco§ .624 |
| 1890—Brooklyn .667 | 1927—Pittsburgh .610 | 1963—Los Angeles .611 |
| 1891—Boston .630 | 1928—St. Louis .617 | 1964—St. Louis .574 |
| 1892—Boston .680 | 1929—Chicago .645 | 1965—Los Angeles .599 |
| 1893—Boston .662 | 1930—St. Louis .597 | 1966—Los Angeles .586 |
| 1894—Baltimore .695 | 1931—St. Louis .656 | 1967—St. Louis .627 |
| 1895—Baltimore .669 | 1932—Chicago .584 | 1968—St. Louis .599 |
| 1896—Baltimore .698 | 1933—New York .599 | 1969—New York (East) .617 |
| 1897—Boston .705 | 1934—St. Louis .621 | 1970—Cincinnati (West) .630 |
| 1898—Boston .685 | 1935—Chicago .649 | 1971—Pittsburgh (East) .599 |
| 1899—Brooklyn .677 | 1936—New York .597 | 1972—Cincinnati (West) .617 |
| 1900—Brooklyn .603 | 1937—New York .625 | 1973—New York (East) .509 |
| 1901—Pittsburgh .647 | 1938—Chicago .586 | 1974—Los Angeles (West) .630 |
| 1902—Pittsburgh .741 | 1939—Cincinnati .630 | 1975—Cincinnati (West) .667 |
| 1903—Pittsburgh .650 | 1940—Cincinnati .654 | 1976—Cincinnati (West) .630 |
| 1904—New York .693 | 1941—Brooklyn .649 | 1977—Los Angeles (West) .605 |
| 1905—New York .686 | 1942—St. Louis .688 | 1978—Los Angeles (West) .586 |
| 1906—Chicago .763 | 1943—St. Louis .682 | 1979—Pittsburgh (East) .605 |
| 1907—Chicago .704 | 1944—St. Louis .682 | 1980—Philadelphia (East) .562 |
| 1908—Chicago .643 | 1945—Chicago .636 | 1981—Los Angeles (West) .573 |
| 1909—Pittsburgh .724 | 1946—St. Louis* .628 | 1982—St. Louis (East) .568 |
| 1910—Chicago .675 | 1947—Brooklyn .610 | 1983—Philadelphia (East) .556 |
| 1911—New York .647 | 1948—Boston .595 | 1984—San Diego (West) .568 |
| 1912—New York .682 | | |

*Defeated Brooklyn, two games to none, in playoff for pennant. †Defeated Brooklyn, two games to one, in playoff for pennant. ‡Defeated Milwaukee, two games to none, in playoff for pennant. §Defeated Los Angeles, two games to one, in playoff for pennant.

## STANDING OF CLUBS AT CLOSE OF SEASON

### EAST DIVISION

| Club | St.L. | N.Y. | Mon. | Chi. | Phil. | Pitt. | L.A. | Cin. | Hou. | S.D. | Atl. | S.F. | W. | L. | Pct. | G.B. |
|---|---|---|---|---|---|---|---|---|---|---|---|---|---|---|---|---|
| St. Louis | .. | 10 | 7 | 14 | 10 | 15 | 5 | 7 | 6 | 8 | 9 | 10 | 101 | 61 | .623 | ...... |
| New York | 8 | .. | 9 | 14 | 11 | 10 | 5 | 8 | 8 | 7 | 10 | 8 | 98 | 64 | .605 | 3 |
| Montreal | 11 | 9 | .. | 11 | 8 | 9 | 5 | 4 | 6 | 5 | 9 | 7 | 84 | 77 | .522 | 16½ |
| Chicago | 4 | 4 | 7 | .. | 13 | 13 | 5 | 5 | 5 | 8 | 7 | 6 | 77 | 84 | .478 | 23½ |
| Philadelphia | 8 | 7 | 10 | 5 | .. | 11 | 8 | 5 | 8 | 5 | 2 | 6 | 75 | 87 | .463 | 26 |
| Pittsburgh | 3 | 8 | 8 | 5 | 7 | .. | 4 | 3 | 6 | 4 | 6 | 3 | 57 | 104 | .354 | 43½ |

### WEST DIVISION

| Club | L.A. | Cin. | Hou. | S.D. | Atl. | S.F. | St.L. | N.Y. | Mon. | Chi. | Phil. | Pitt. | W. | L. | Pct. | G.B. |
|---|---|---|---|---|---|---|---|---|---|---|---|---|---|---|---|---|
| Los Angeles | .. | 11 | 12 | 8 | 13 | 11 | 7 | 7 | 7 | 7 | 4 | 8 | 95 | 67 | .586 | ...... |
| Cincinnati | 7 | .. | 11 | 9 | 11 | 12 | 5 | 4 | 8 | 6 | 7 | 9 | 89 | 72 | .553 | 5½ |
| Houston | 6 | 7 | .. | 12 | 10 | 15 | 6 | 4 | 6 | 7 | 4 | 6 | 83 | 79 | .512 | 12 |
| San Diego | 10 | 9 | 6 | .. | 11 | 12 | 4 | 5 | 7 | 4 | 7 | 8 | 83 | 79 | .512 | 12 |
| Atlanta | 5 | 7 | 8 | 7 | .. | 10 | 3 | 2 | 3 | 5 | 10 | 6 | 66 | 96 | .407 | 29 |
| San Francisco | 7 | 6 | 3 | 6 | 8 | .. | 2 | 4 | 5 | 6 | 6 | 9 | 62 | 100 | .383 | 33 |

Tie Game—Cincinnati vs. Chicago.
Championship Series—St. Louis defeated Los Angeles, four games to two.

## RECORD AT HOME

### EAST DIVISION

| Club | St.L. | N.Y. | Mon. | Chi. | Phil. | Pitt. | L.A. | Cin. | Hou. | S.D. | S.F. | Atl. | W. | L. | Pct. |
|---|---|---|---|---|---|---|---|---|---|---|---|---|---|---|---|
| St. Louis | .... | 6-3 | 5-4 | 7-2 | 5-4 | 9-0 | 3-3 | 3-3 | 3-3 | 4-2 | 5-1 | 4-2 | 54 | 27 | .667 |
| New York | 5-4 | .... | 5-4 | 9-0 | 7-2 | 5-4 | 2-4 | 3-3 | 4-2 | 4-2 | 5-1 | 5-1 | 51 | 30 | .630 |
| Montreal | 7-2 | 5-4 | .... | 5-4 | 4-5 | 4-5 | 4-2 | 2-4 | 4-2 | 1-5 | 3-3 | 5-1 | 44 | 37 | .543 |
| Chicago | 2-7 | 4-5 | 3-6 | .... | 7-2 | 8-1 | 2-4 | 3-2 | 2-4 | 4-2 | 3-3 | 3-3 | 41 | 39 | .513 |
| Philadelphia | 4-5 | 5-4 | 5-4 | 3-6 | .... | 6-3 | 3-3 | 2-4 | 5-1 | 2-4 | 4-2 | 2-4 | 41 | 40 | .506 |
| Pittsburgh | 3-6 | 4-5 | 3-5 | 4-5 | 4-5 | .... | 2-4 | 2-4 | 4-2 | 3-3 | 2-4 | 4-2 | 35 | 45 | .438 |

## WEST DIVISION

| Club | L.A. | Cin. | Hou. | S.D. | S.F. | Atl. | St.L. | N.Y. | Mon. | Chi. | Phil. | Pitt. | W. | L. | Pct. |
|---|---|---|---|---|---|---|---|---|---|---|---|---|---|---|---|
| Los Angeles | .... | 6-3 | 5-4 | 4-5 | 6-3 | 7-2 | 4-2 | 3-3 | 5-1 | 3-3 | 1-5 | 4-2 | 48 | 33 | .593 |
| Cincinnati | 4-5 | .... | 6-3 | 5-4 | 6-3 | 2-4 | 1-5 | 4-2 | 4-2 | 3-3 | 5-1 | 4-2 | 47 | 34 | .580 |
| Houston | 2-7 | 4-5 | .... | 8-1 | 8-1 | 3-6 | 3-3 | 2-4 | 4-2 | 3-3 | 3-3 | 4-2 | 44 | 37 | .543 |
| San Diego | 5-4 | 5-4 | 5-4 | .... | 8-1 | 6-3 | 2-4 | 1-5 | 2-4 | 2-4 | 3-3 | 5-1 | 44 | 37 | .543 |
| San Francisco | 4-5 | 6-3 | 2-7 | 5-4 | .... | 4-5 | 1-5 | 2-4 | 2-4 | 3-3 | 4-2 | 5-1 | 38 | 43 | .469 |
| Atlanta | 3-6 | 2-7 | 2-7 | 4-5 | 5-4 | .... | 1-5 | 1-5 | 2-4 | 2-4 | 6-0 | 4-2 | 32 | 49 | .395 |

## RECORD ABROAD

### EAST DIVISION

| Club | N.Y. | St.L. | Mon. | Chi. | Phil. | Pitt. | L.A. | Cin. | Hou. | S.D. | Atl. | S.F. | W. | L. | Pct. |
|---|---|---|---|---|---|---|---|---|---|---|---|---|---|---|---|
| New York | .... | 3-6 | 4-5 | 4-5 | 4-5 | 5-4 | 3-3 | 5-1 | 4-2 | 5-1 | 5-1 | 4-2 | 47 | 34 | .580 |
| St. Louis | 4-5 | .... | 2-7 | 7-2 | 5-4 | 6-3 | 2-4 | 4-2 | 3-3 | 4-2 | 5-1 | 5-1 | 47 | 34 | .580 |
| Montreal | 4-5 | 4-5 | .... | 6-3 | 4-5 | 5-3 | 1-5 | 2-4 | 2-4 | 4-2 | 4-2 | 4-2 | 40 | 40 | .500 |
| Chicago | 0-9 | 2-7 | 4-5 | .... | 6-3 | 3-6 | 3-3 | 2-4 | 3-3 | 4-2 | 3-3 | 4-2 | 36 | 45 | .444 |
| Philadelphia | 2-7 | 4-5 | 5-4 | 2-7 | .... | 5-4 | 5-1 | 3-3 | 3-3 | 3-3 | 0-6 | 2-4 | 34 | 47 | .420 |
| Pittsburgh | 4-5 | 0-9 | 5-4 | 1-8 | 3-6 | .... | 2-4 | 1-5 | 2-4 | 1-5 | 2-4 | 1-5 | 22 | 59 | .272 |

### WEST DIVISION

| Club | L.A. | Cin. | Hou. | S.D. | Atl. | S.F. | N.Y. | St.L. | Mon. | Chi. | Phil. | Pitt. | W. | L. | Pct. |
|---|---|---|---|---|---|---|---|---|---|---|---|---|---|---|---|
| Los Angeles | .... | 5-4 | 7-2 | 4-5 | 6-3 | 5-4 | 4-2 | 3-3 | 2-4 | 4-2 | 3-3 | 4-2 | 47 | 34 | .580 |
| Cincinnati | 3-6 | .... | 5-4 | 4-5 | 7-2 | 3-6 | 3-3 | 3-3 | 4-2 | 2-3 | 4-2 | 4-2 | 42 | 38 | .525 |
| Houston | 4-5 | 3-6 | .... | 4-5 | 7-2 | 7-2 | 2-4 | 3-3 | 2-4 | 4-2 | 1-5 | 2-4 | 39 | 42 | .481 |
| San Diego | 5-4 | 4-5 | 1-8 | .... | 5-4 | 4-5 | 4-2 | 2-4 | 5-1 | 2-4 | 2-4 | 3-3 | 39 | 42 | .481 |
| Atlanta | 2-7 | 5-4 | 6-3 | 3-6 | .... | 5-4 | 1-5 | 2-4 | 1-5 | 3-3 | 4-2 | 2-4 | 34 | 47 | .420 |
| San Francisco | 3-6 | 0-9 | 1-8 | 1-8 | 4-5 | .... | 2-4 | 1-5 | 3-3 | 3-3 | 2-4 | 4-2 | 24 | 57 | .296 |

## SHUTOUT GAMES

| Club | L.A. | S.D. | St.L. | N.Y. | Mon. | Hou. | Phil. | Cin. | Chi. | Atl. | S.F. | Pitt. | W. | L. | Pct. |
|---|---|---|---|---|---|---|---|---|---|---|---|---|---|---|---|
| Los Angeles | .. | 3 | 1 | 0 | 3 | 3 | 0 | 4 | 1 | 2 | 1 | 3 | 21 | 6 | .778 |
| San Diego | 2 | .. | 2 | 2 | 2 | 0 | 1 | 2 | 0 | 2 | 3 | 3 | 19 | 7 | .731 |
| St. Louis | 0 | 1 | .. | 3 | 1 | 1 | 3 | 2 | 3 | 4 | 1 | 1 | 20 | 8 | .714 |
| New York | 1 | 0 | 1 | .. | 2 | 1 | 4 | 2 | 3 | 2 | 2 | 1 | 19 | 11 | .633 |
| Montreal | 0 | 0 | 1 | 0 | .. | 3 | 0 | 2 | 2 | 3 | 2 | 0 | 13 | 13 | .500 |
| Houston | 0 | 1 | 0 | 1 | 1 | .. | 1 | 0 | 1 | 2 | 1 | 1 | 9 | 10 | .474 |
| Philadelphia | 2 | 1 | 2 | 0 | 1 | 0 | .. | 0 | 0 | 0 | 0 | 3 | 9 | 13 | .409 |
| Cincinnati | 0 | 1 | 0 | 1 | 1 | 2 | 1 | .. | 1 | 0 | 1 | 3 | 11 | 16 | .407 |
| Chicago | 0 | 0 | 0 | 0 | 2 | 0 | 1 | 1 | .. | 0 | 1 | 3 | 8 | 14 | .364 |
| Atlanta | 1 | 0 | 0 | 2 | 0 | 0 | 1 | 1 | 1 | .. | 2 | 1 | 9 | 18 | .333 |
| San Francisco | 0 | 0 | 1 | 0 | 0 | 0 | 0 | 1 | 2 | 1 | .. | 0 | 5 | 14 | .263 |
| Pittsburgh | 0 | 0 | 0 | 2 | 0 | 0 | 1 | 1 | 1 | 0 | 2 | .. | 6 | 19 | .240 |

# OFFICIAL NATIONAL LEAGUE BATTING AVERAGES

Compiled by Elias Sports Bureau

### CLUB BATTING

| Club | Pct. | G. | AB. | R. | OR. | H. | TB. | 2B. | 3B. | HR. | RBI. | SH. | SF. | SB. | CS. | LOB. |
|---|---|---|---|---|---|---|---|---|---|---|---|---|---|---|---|---|
| St. Louis | .264 | 162 | 5467 | 747 | 572 | 1446 | 2070 | 245 | 59 | 87 | 687 | 70 | 41 | 314 | 96 | 1105 |
| Houston | .261 | 162 | 5582 | 706 | 691 | 1457 | 2165 | 261 | 42 | 121 | 666 | 66 | 44 | 96 | 56 | 1117 |
| Los Angeles | .261 | 162 | 5502 | 682 | 579 | 1434 | 2103 | 226 | 28 | 129 | 632 | 104 | 46 | 136 | 58 | 1187 |
| New York | .257 | 162 | 5549 | 695 | 568 | 1425 | 2136 | 239 | 35 | 134 | 651 | 89 | 44 | 117 | 53 | 1149 |
| San Diego | .255 | 162 | 5507 | 650 | 622 | 1405 | 2029 | 241 | 28 | 109 | 611 | 75 | 32 | 60 | 39 | 1156 |
| Cincinnati | .255 | 162 | 5431 | 677 | 666 | 1385 | 2044 | 249 | 34 | 114 | 634 | 72 | 41 | 159 | 70 | 1134 |
| Chicago | .254 | 162 | 5492 | 686 | 729 | 1397 | 2142 | 239 | 28 | 150 | 640 | 66 | 39 | 182 | 49 | 1147 |
| Montreal | .247 | 162 | 5429 | 633 | 636 | 1342 | 2036 | 242 | 49 | 118 | 593 | 61 | 45 | 169 | 77 | 1061 |
| Pittsburgh | .247 | 161 | 5436 | 568 | 708 | 1340 | 1887 | 251 | 28 | 80 | 535 | 91 | 44 | 110 | 60 | 1132 |
| Atlanta | .246 | 162 | 5526 | 632 | 781 | 1359 | 2006 | 213 | 28 | 126 | 598 | 65 | 41 | 72 | 52 | 1163 |
| Philadelphia | .245 | 162 | 5477 | 667 | 673 | 1343 | 2098 | 238 | 47 | 141 | 628 | 49 | 44 | 122 | 51 | 1099 |
| San Fran. | .233 | 162 | 5420 | 556 | 674 | 1263 | 1887 | 217 | 31 | 115 | 517 | 93 | 25 | 99 | 55 | 1090 |
| Totals | .252 | 971 | 65818 | 7899 | 7899 | 16596 | 24603 | 2861 | 437 | 1424 | 7392 | 901 | 486 | 1636 | 716 | 13540 |

### INDIVIDUAL BATTING

(Top Fifteen Qualifiers for Batting Championship—502 or More Plate Appearances)

*Bats lefthanded. †Switch-hitter.

| Player and Club | Pct. | G. | AB. | R. | H. | TB. | 2B. | 3B. | HR. | RBI. | GW. | SH. | SF. | SB. | CS. |
|---|---|---|---|---|---|---|---|---|---|---|---|---|---|---|---|
| McGee, Willie, St. Louis† | .353 | 152 | 612 | 114 | 216 | 308 | 26 | 18 | 10 | 82 | 17 | 1 | 5 | 56 | 16 |
| Guerrero, Pedro, Los Angeles | .320 | 137 | 487 | 99 | 156 | 281 | 22 | 2 | 33 | 87 | 16 | 0 | 5 | 12 | 4 |
| Raines, Timothy, Montreal† | .320 | 150 | 575 | 115 | 184 | 273 | 30 | 13 | 11 | 41 | 4 | 3 | 3 | 70 | 9 |
| Gwynn, Anthony, San Diego* | .317 | 154 | 622 | 90 | 197 | 254 | 29 | 5 | 6 | 46 | 8 | 1 | 1 | 14 | 11 |
| Parker, David, Cincinnati* | .312 | 160 | 635 | 88 | 198 | 350 | 42 | 4 | 34 | 125 | 18 | 0 | 4 | 5 | 13 |
| Hernandez, Keith, New York* | .309 | 158 | 593 | 87 | 183 | 255 | 34 | 4 | 10 | 91 | 24 | 0 | 10 | 3 | 3 |
| Moreland, B. Keith, Chicago | .307 | 161 | 587 | 74 | 180 | 258 | 30 | 3 | 14 | 106 | 12 | 2 | 9 | 12 | 3 |
| Sandberg, Ryne, Chicago | .305 | 153 | 609 | 113 | 186 | 307 | 31 | 6 | 26 | 83 | 10 | 2 | 4 | 54 | 11 |
| Herr, Thomas, St. Louis† | .302 | 159 | 596 | 97 | 180 | 248 | 38 | 3 | 8 | 110 | 14 | 5 | 13 | 31 | 3 |
| Murphy, Dale, Atlanta | .300 | 162 | 616 | 118 | 185 | 332 | 32 | 2 | 37 | 111 | 14 | 0 | 5 | 10 | 3 |

| Player and Club | Pct. | G. | AB. | R. | H. | TB. | 2B. | 3B. | HR. | RBI. | GW. | SH. | SF. | SB. | CS. |
|---|---|---|---|---|---|---|---|---|---|---|---|---|---|---|---|
| Cruz, Jose, Houston* | .300 | 141 | 544 | 69 | 163 | 232 | 34 | 4 | 9 | 79 | 9 | 0 | 3 | 16 | 5 |
| Scioscia, Michael, Los Angeles* | .296 | 141 | 429 | 47 | 127 | 180 | 26 | 3 | 7 | 53 | 4 | 11 | 3 | 3 | 3 |
| Oester, Ronald, Cincinnati† | .295 | 152 | 526 | 59 | 155 | 190 | 26 | 3 | 1 | 34 | 4 | 2 | 5 | 5 | 0 |
| Marshall, Michael, Los Angeles | .293 | 135 | 518 | 72 | 152 | 267 | 27 | 2 | 28 | 95 | 12 | 2 | 4 | 3 | 10 |
| Doran, William, Houston† | .287 | 148 | 578 | 84 | 166 | 251 | 31 | 6 | 14 | 59 | 6 | 3 | 5 | 23 | 15 |

DEPARTMENTAL LEADERS: G—Garvey, Murphy, 162; AB—Samuel, 663; R—Murphy, 118; H—McGee, 216; TB—Parker, 350; 2B—Parker, 42; 3B—McGee, 18; HR—Murphy, 37; RBI—Parker, 125; GW—Hernandez, 24; SH—Backman, Ryan, 14; SF—Herr, 13; SB—Coleman, 110; CS—Coleman, 25.

(All Players—Listed Alphabetically)

| Player and Club | Pct. | G. | AB. | R. | H. | TB. | 2B. | 3B. | HR. | RBI. | GW. | SH. | SF. | SB. | CS. |
|---|---|---|---|---|---|---|---|---|---|---|---|---|---|---|---|
| Abrego, Johnny, Chicago | .000 | 6 | 9 | 0 | 0 | 0 | 0 | 0 | 0 | 1 | 0 | 0 | 0 | 0 | 0 |
| Adams, Ricky, San Francisco | .190 | 54 | 121 | 12 | 23 | 34 | 3 | 1 | 2 | 10 | 2 | 3 | 0 | 1 | 1 |
| Aguayo, Luis, Philadelphia | .279 | 91 | 165 | 27 | 46 | 77 | 7 | 3 | 6 | 21 | 4 | 4 | 3 | 1 | 0 |
| Aguilera, Richard, New York | .278 | 22 | 36 | 1 | 10 | 12 | 2 | 0 | 0 | 2 | 0 | 7 | 0 | 0 | 0 |
| Allen, Neil, St. Louis | .000 | 23 | 2 | 0 | 0 | 0 | 0 | 0 | 0 | 0 | 0 | 0 | 0 | 0 | 0 |
| Almon, William, Pittsburgh | .270 | 88 | 244 | 33 | 66 | 101 | 17 | 0 | 6 | 29 | 1 | 4 | 3 | 10 | 7 |
| Andersen, Larry, Philadelphia | .000 | 57 | 4 | 1 | 0 | 0 | 0 | 0 | 0 | 0 | 0 | 1 | 0 | 0 | 0 |
| Anderson, David, Los Angeles | .199 | 77 | 221 | 24 | 44 | 62 | 6 | 0 | 4 | 18 | 4 | 4 | 1 | 5 | 4 |
| Andujar, Joaquin, St. Louis† | .106 | 38 | 94 | 2 | 10 | 12 | 2 | 0 | 0 | 8 | 0 | 7 | 0 | 3 | 1 |
| Ashby, Alan, Houston† | .280 | 65 | 189 | 20 | 53 | 85 | 8 | 0 | 8 | 25 | 4 | 1 | 1 | 0 | 0 |
| Backman, Walter, New York† | .273 | 145 | 520 | 77 | 142 | 179 | 24 | 5 | 1 | 38 | 3 | 14 | 3 | 30 | 12 |
| Bailey, J. Mark, Houston† | .265 | 114 | 332 | 47 | 88 | 132 | 14 | 0 | 10 | 45 | 4 | 1 | 1 | 0 | 2 |
| Bailor, Robert, Los Angeles | .246 | 74 | 118 | 8 | 29 | 34 | 3 | 1 | 0 | 7 | 1 | 8 | 0 | 1 | 0 |
| Bair, C. Douglas, St. Louis | .000 | 2 | 0 | 0 | 0 | 0 | 0 | 0 | 0 | 0 | 0 | 0 | 0 | 0 | 0 |
| Baller, Jay, Chicago | .000 | 20 | 8 | 0 | 0 | 0 | 0 | 0 | 0 | 0 | 0 | 1 | 0 | 0 | 0 |
| Barker, Leonard, Atlanta | .000 | 20 | 17 | 0 | 0 | 0 | 0 | 0 | 0 | 0 | 0 | 4 | 0 | 0 | 1 |
| Barnes, William, Montreal | .154 | 19 | 26 | 0 | 4 | 5 | 1 | 0 | 0 | 0 | 0 | 0 | 0 | 0 | 1 |
| Bass, Kevin, Houston† | .269 | 150 | 539 | 72 | 145 | 230 | 27 | 5 | 16 | 68 | 6 | 4 | 2 | 19 | 8 |
| Beane, William, New York | .250 | 8 | 8 | 0 | 2 | 3 | 1 | 0 | 0 | 1 | 0 | 0 | 0 | 0 | 0 |
| Beard, David, Chicago* | .000 | 9 | 0 | 0 | 0 | 0 | 0 | 0 | 0 | 0 | 0 | 0 | 0 | 0 | 0 |
| Bedrosian, Stephen, Atlanta | .078 | 37 | 64 | 3 | 5 | 5 | 0 | 0 | 0 | 1 | 0 | 6 | 0 | 0 | 0 |
| Bell, David, Cincinnati | .219 | 67 | 247 | 28 | 54 | 91 | 15 | 2 | 6 | 36 | 4 | 1 | 2 | 0 | 1 |
| Belliard, Rafael, Pittsburgh | .200 | 17 | 20 | 1 | 4 | 4 | 0 | 0 | 0 | 1 | 0 | 0 | 0 | 0 | 0 |
| Benedict, Bruce, Atlanta | .202 | 70 | 208 | 12 | 42 | 48 | 6 | 0 | 0 | 20 | 1 | 4 | 2 | 0 | 1 |
| Berenyi, Bruce, New York | .250 | 3 | 4 | 1 | 1 | 2 | 1 | 0 | 0 | 1 | 0 | 2 | 0 | 0 | 0 |
| Bevacqua, Kurt, San Diego | .239 | 71 | 138 | 17 | 33 | 48 | 6 | 0 | 3 | 25 | 3 | 1 | 3 | 0 | 0 |
| Bielecki, Michael, Pittsburgh | .000 | 13 | 10 | 1 | 0 | 0 | 0 | 0 | 0 | 0 | 0 | 1 | 0 | 0 | 0 |
| Bilardello, Dann, Cincinnati | .167 | 42 | 102 | 6 | 17 | 20 | 0 | 0 | 1 | 9 | 2 | 1 | 0 | 0 | 0 |
| Blocker, Terry, New York* | .067 | 18 | 15 | 1 | 1 | 1 | 0 | 0 | 0 | 0 | 0 | 0 | 0 | 0 | 0 |
| Blue, Vida, San Francisco† | .133 | 33 | 30 | 0 | 4 | 5 | 1 | 0 | 0 | 0 | 0 | 8 | 0 | 0 | 0 |
| Bochy, Bruce, San Diego | .268 | 48 | 112 | 16 | 30 | 50 | 2 | 0 | 6 | 13 | 1 | 2 | 0 | 0 | 0 |
| Boever, Joseph, St. Louis | .000 | 13 | 0 | 0 | 0 | 0 | 0 | 0 | 0 | 0 | 0 | 0 | 0 | 0 | 0 |
| Booker, Gregory, San Diego | .000 | 17 | 1 | 0 | 0 | 0 | 0 | 0 | 0 | 0 | 0 | 0 | 0 | 0 | 0 |
| Bosley, Thaddis, Chicago* | .328 | 108 | 180 | 25 | 59 | 92 | 6 | 3 | 7 | 27 | 3 | 0 | 2 | 5 | 1 |
| Botelho, Derek, Chicago | .143 | 11 | 14 | 2 | 2 | 2 | 0 | 0 | 0 | 0 | 0 | 0 | 0 | 0 | 0 |
| Bowa, Lawrence, Chi.-N.Y.† | .234 | 86 | 214 | 15 | 50 | 65 | 7 | 4 | 0 | 15 | 4 | 6 | 1 | 5 | 1 |
| Braun, Stephen, St. Louis* | .239 | 64 | 67 | 7 | 16 | 23 | 4 | 0 | 1 | 6 | 2 | 0 | 1 | 0 | 0 |
| Bream, Sidney, L.A.-Pitt.* | .230 | 50 | 148 | 18 | 34 | 59 | 7 | 0 | 6 | 21 | 3 | 3 | 2 | 0 | 2 |
| Brenly, Robert, San Francisco | .220 | 133 | 440 | 41 | 97 | 172 | 16 | 1 | 19 | 56 | 5 | 4 | 2 | 1 | 4 |
| Brennan, Thomas, Los Angeles* | .125 | 12 | 8 | 0 | 1 | 1 | 0 | 0 | 0 | 0 | 0 | 1 | 0 | 0 | 0 |
| Brock, Gregory, Los Angeles* | .251 | 129 | 438 | 64 | 110 | 192 | 19 | 0 | 21 | 66 | 4 | 2 | 2 | 4 | 2 |
| Brooks, Hubert, Montreal | .269 | 156 | 605 | 67 | 163 | 250 | 34 | 7 | 13 | 100 | 13 | 0 | 8 | 6 | 9 |
| Brown, J. Christopher, San Fran. | .271 | 131 | 432 | 50 | 117 | 191 | 20 | 3 | 16 | 61 | 10 | 1 | 0 | 2 | 3 |
| Brown, Michael C., Pittsburgh | .332 | 57 | 205 | 29 | 68 | 105 | 18 | 2 | 5 | 33 | 2 | 3 | 3 | 2 | 2 |
| Brown, Rogers, San Diego† | .155 | 79 | 84 | 8 | 13 | 16 | 3 | 0 | 0 | 6 | 0 | 1 | 1 | 6 | 4 |
| Browning, Thomas, Cincinnati* | .193 | 39 | 88 | 4 | 17 | 21 | 2 | 1 | 0 | 2 | 0 | 9 | 0 | 0 | 0 |
| Brusstar, Warren, Chicago | .143 | 51 | 7 | 0 | 1 | 1 | 0 | 0 | 0 | 0 | 0 | 0 | 0 | 0 | 0 |
| Bryant, Ralph, Los Angeles* | .333 | 6 | 6 | 0 | 2 | 2 | 0 | 0 | 0 | 1 | 0 | 0 | 0 | 0 | 0 |
| Buchanan, Robert, Cincinnati* | .000 | 14 | 1 | 0 | 0 | 0 | 0 | 0 | 0 | 0 | 0 | 0 | 0 | 0 | 0 |
| Bullock, Eric, Houston* | .280 | 18 | 25 | 3 | 7 | 9 | 2 | 0 | 0 | 2 | 1 | 0 | 0 | 0 | 1 |
| Bumbry, Alonza, San Diego* | .200 | 68 | 95 | 6 | 19 | 25 | 3 | 0 | 1 | 10 | 1 | 1 | 0 | 2 | 0 |
| Burke, Timothy, Montreal | .100 | 78 | 10 | 0 | 1 | 1 | 0 | 0 | 0 | 0 | 0 | 0 | 0 | 0 | 0 |
| Butera, Salvatore, Montreal | .200 | 67 | 120 | 11 | 24 | 34 | 1 | 0 | 3 | 12 | 0 | 3 | 1 | 0 | 0 |
| Cabell, Enos, Houston-Los Angeles | .272 | 117 | 335 | 40 | 91 | 118 | 19 | 1 | 2 | 36 | 7 | 2 | 0 | 9 | 3 |
| Calhoun, Jeffrey, Houston* | .000 | 44 | 5 | 0 | 0 | 0 | 0 | 0 | 0 | 1 | 0 | 0 | 0 | 0 | 0 |
| Camp, Rick, Atlanta | .231 | 66 | 13 | 1 | 3 | 6 | 0 | 0 | 1 | 2 | 0 | 1 | 0 | 0 | 0 |
| Campbell, William, St. Louis | .333 | 50 | 6 | 2 | 2 | 2 | 0 | 0 | 0 | 1 | 0 | 0 | 0 | 0 | 1 |
| Candelaria, John, Pittsburgh† | .000 | 37 | 1 | 0 | 0 | 0 | 0 | 0 | 0 | 0 | 0 | 2 | 0 | 0 | 0 |
| Carlton, Steven, Philadelphia | .179 | 16 | 28 | 2 | 5 | 6 | 1 | 0 | 0 | 3 | 0 | 1 | 1 | 0 | 0 |
| Carman, Donald, Philadelphia* | .000 | 71 | 3 | 0 | 0 | 0 | 0 | 0 | 0 | 0 | 0 | 1 | 0 | 0 | 0 |
| Carter, Gary, New York | .281 | 149 | 555 | 83 | 156 | 271 | 17 | 1 | 32 | 100 | 18 | 0 | 3 | 1 | 1 |
| Castillo, Robert, Los Angeles | .100 | 36 | 10 | 0 | 1 | 1 | 0 | 0 | 0 | 0 | 0 | 2 | 0 | 0 | 0 |
| Cedeno, Cesar, Cin.-St. Louis | .291 | 111 | 296 | 38 | 86 | 131 | 16 | 1 | 9 | 49 | 8 | 1 | 3 | 14 | 6 |
| Cerone, Richard, Atlanta | .216 | 96 | 282 | 15 | 61 | 79 | 9 | 0 | 3 | 25 | 2 | 0 | 4 | 0 | 3 |
| Cey, Ronald, Chicago | .232 | 145 | 500 | 64 | 116 | 204 | 18 | 2 | 22 | 63 | 4 | 0 | 2 | 1 | 1 |
| Chambliss, C. Christopher, Atlanta* | .235 | 101 | 170 | 16 | 40 | 56 | 7 | 0 | 3 | 21 | 2 | 0 | 1 | 0 | 0 |
| Chapman, Kelvin, New York | .174 | 62 | 144 | 16 | 25 | 28 | 3 | 0 | 0 | 7 | 1 | 3 | 1 | 5 | 4 |
| Childress, Rodney, Philadelphia | .167 | 16 | 6 | 0 | 1 | 1 | 0 | 0 | 0 | 0 | 0 | 2 | 0 | 0 | 0 |

| Player and Club | Pct. | G. | AB. | R. | H. | TB. | 2B. | 3B. | HR. | RBI. | GW. | SH. | SF. | SB. | CS. |
|---|---|---|---|---|---|---|---|---|---|---|---|---|---|---|---|
| Christensen, John, New York | .186 | 51 | 113 | 10 | 21 | 36 | 4 | 1 | 3 | 13 | 0 | 1 | 0 | 1 | 2 |
| Clark, Jack, St. Louis | .281 | 126 | 442 | 71 | 124 | 222 | 26 | 3 | 22 | 87 | 7 | 0 | 5 | 1 | 4 |
| Clements, Patrick, Pittsburgh | .333 | 27 | 3 | 0 | 1 | 1 | 0 | 0 | 0 | 0 | 0 | 1 | 0 | 0 | 0 |
| Coleman, Vincent, St. Louis† | .267 | 151 | 636 | 107 | 170 | 213 | 20 | 10 | 1 | 40 | 3 | 5 | 1 | 110 | 25 |
| Concepcion, David, Cincinnati | .252 | 155 | 560 | 59 | 141 | 185 | 19 | 2 | 7 | 48 | 7 | 3 | 4 | 16 | 12 |
| Corcoran, Timothy, Philadelphia* | .214 | 103 | 182 | 11 | 39 | 47 | 6 | 1 | 0 | 22 | 2 | 1 | 7 | 0 | 0 |
| Cox, Danny, St. Louis | .152 | 35 | 79 | 3 | 12 | 13 | 1 | 0 | 0 | 6 | 0 | 8 | 1 | 0 | 0 |
| Cruz, Jose, Houston* | .300 | 141 | 544 | 69 | 163 | 232 | 34 | 4 | 9 | 79 | 9 | 0 | 3 | 16 | 5 |
| Darling, Ronald, New York | .171 | 42 | 76 | 9 | 13 | 17 | 4 | 0 | 0 | 0 | 0 | 13 | 0 | 1 | 0 |
| Daulton, Darren, Philadelphia* | .204 | 36 | 103 | 14 | 21 | 38 | 3 | 1 | 4 | 11 | 0 | 0 | 0 | 3 | 0 |
| Davis, Charles, San Francisco† | .270 | 136 | 481 | 53 | 130 | 198 | 25 | 2 | 13 | 56 | 3 | 1 | 7 | 15 | 7 |
| Davis, Eric, Cincinnati | .246 | 56 | 122 | 26 | 30 | 63 | 3 | 3 | 8 | 18 | 4 | 2 | 0 | 16 | 3 |
| Davis, Gerald, San Diego | .293 | 44 | 58 | 10 | 17 | 22 | 3 | 1 | 0 | 2 | 1 | 1 | 0 | 0 | 0 |
| Davis, Glenn, Houston | .271 | 100 | 350 | 51 | 95 | 166 | 11 | 0 | 20 | 64 | 7 | 2 | 4 | 0 | 1 |
| Davis, Jody, Chicago | .232 | 142 | 482 | 47 | 112 | 193 | 30 | 0 | 17 | 58 | 8 | 2 | 4 | 1 | 0 |
| Davis, Mark, San Francisco* | .250 | 77 | 12 | 0 | 3 | 5 | 0 | 1 | 0 | 0 | 0 | 4 | 0 | 0 | 1 |
| Davis, Trench, Pittsburgh* | .143 | 2 | 7 | 1 | 1 | 1 | 0 | 0 | 0 | 0 | 0 | 0 | 0 | 1 | 0 |
| Dawley, William, Houston | .200 | 49 | 10 | 1 | 2 | 2 | 0 | 0 | 0 | 0 | 0 | 0 | 0 | 0 | 0 |
| Dawson, Andre, Montreal | .255 | 139 | 529 | 65 | 135 | 235 | 27 | 2 | 23 | 91 | 12 | 1 | 7 | 13 | 4 |
| Dayett, Brian, Chicago | .231 | 22 | 26 | 1 | 6 | 9 | 0 | 0 | 1 | 4 | 1 | 0 | 0 | 0 | 0 |
| Dayley, Kenneth, St. Louis* | .400 | 57 | 5 | 0 | 2 | 2 | 0 | 0 | 0 | 0 | 0 | 0 | 0 | 0 | 0 |
| Dedmon, Jeffrey, Atlanta* | .111 | 60 | 9 | 0 | 1 | 1 | 0 | 0 | 0 | 1 | 0 | 1 | 0 | 0 | 0 |
| Deer, Robert, San Francisco | .185 | 78 | 162 | 22 | 30 | 61 | 5 | 1 | 8 | 20 | 2 | 0 | 2 | 0 | 1 |
| DeJesus, Ivan, St. Louis | .222 | 59 | 72 | 11 | 16 | 21 | 5 | 0 | 0 | 7 | 0 | 1 | 1 | 2 | 2 |
| DeLeon, Jose, Pittsburgh | .056 | 31 | 36 | 1 | 2 | 2 | 0 | 0 | 0 | 0 | 0 | 7 | 0 | 0 | 0 |
| DeLeon, Luis, San Diego | .200 | 29 | 5 | 1 | 1 | 1 | 0 | 0 | 0 | 0 | 0 | 0 | 0 | 0 | 0 |
| Denny, John, Philadelphia | .123 | 33 | 81 | 2 | 10 | 11 | 1 | 0 | 0 | 4 | 0 | 3 | 0 | 2 | 0 |
| Dernier, Robert, Chicago | .254 | 121 | 469 | 63 | 119 | 148 | 20 | 3 | 1 | 21 | 3 | 7 | 2 | 31 | 8 |
| Deshaies, James, Houston* | .000 | 2 | 0 | 0 | 0 | 0 | 0 | 0 | 0 | 0 | 0 | 0 | 0 | 0 | 0 |
| Diaz, Baudilio, Phil.-Cin. | .245 | 77 | 237 | 21 | 58 | 88 | 13 | 1 | 5 | 31 | 1 | 2 | 2 | 0 | 0 |
| Diaz, Carlos, Los Angeles | .000 | 46 | 4 | 0 | 0 | 0 | 0 | 0 | 0 | 0 | 0 | 0 | 0 | 0 | 0 |
| Dilone, Miguel, Mtl.-S.D.† | .200 | 78 | 130 | 18 | 26 | 32 | 0 | 3 | 0 | 7 | 2 | 0 | 1 | 17 | 6 |
| DiPino, Frank, Houston* | .167 | 54 | 12 | 1 | 2 | 2 | 0 | 0 | 0 | 1 | 0 | 0 | 0 | 0 | 0 |
| Dopson, John, Montreal* | .000 | 4 | 4 | 0 | 0 | 0 | 0 | 0 | 0 | 0 | 0 | 0 | 0 | 0 | 0 |
| Doran, William, Houston† | .287 | 148 | 578 | 84 | 166 | 251 | 31 | 6 | 14 | 59 | 6 | 3 | 5 | 23 | 15 |
| Dravecky, David, San Diego | .116 | 34 | 69 | 5 | 8 | 11 | 1 | 1 | 0 | 1 | 0 | 6 | 0 | 0 | 0 |
| Driessen, Daniel, Mtl.-S.F.* | .243 | 145 | 493 | 53 | 120 | 173 | 26 | 0 | 9 | 47 | 6 | 1 | 5 | 2 | 2 |
| Duncan, Mariano, Los Angeles† | .244 | 142 | 562 | 74 | 137 | 191 | 24 | 6 | 6 | 39 | 5 | 13 | 4 | 38 | 8 |
| Dunston, Shawon, Chicago | .260 | 74 | 250 | 40 | 65 | 97 | 12 | 4 | 4 | 18 | 2 | 1 | 2 | 11 | 3 |
| Durham, Leon, Chicago* | .282 | 153 | 542 | 58 | 153 | 252 | 32 | 2 | 21 | 75 | 6 | 0 | 1 | 7 | 6 |
| Dybzinski, Jerome, Pittsburgh | .000 | 5 | 4 | 0 | 0 | 0 | 0 | 0 | 0 | 0 | 0 | 0 | 0 | 0 | 0 |
| Dykstra, Leonard, New York* | .254 | 83 | 236 | 40 | 60 | 78 | 9 | 3 | 1 | 19 | 3 | 4 | 2 | 15 | 2 |
| Eckersley, Dennis, Chicago | .125 | 26 | 56 | 1 | 7 | 10 | 0 | 0 | 1 | 1 | 0 | 2 | 0 | 0 | 0 |
| Engel, Steven, Chicago | .188 | 11 | 16 | 1 | 3 | 6 | 0 | 0 | 1 | 4 | 0 | 0 | 0 | 0 | 0 |
| Esasky, Nicholas, Cincinnati | .262 | 125 | 413 | 61 | 108 | 192 | 21 | 0 | 21 | 66 | 9 | 3 | 3 | 3 | 4 |
| Fernandez, C. Sidney, New York*.. | .212 | 26 | 52 | 2 | 11 | 13 | 0 | 1 | 0 | 1 | 0 | 7 | 0 | 0 | 0 |
| Fitzgerald, Michael, Montreal | .207 | 108 | 295 | 25 | 61 | 85 | 7 | 1 | 5 | 34 | 6 | 1 | 5 | 5 | 3 |
| Flannery, Timothy, San Diego* | .281 | 126 | 384 | 50 | 108 | 131 | 14 | 3 | 1 | 40 | 6 | 3 | 2 | 2 | 5 |
| Flynn, R. Douglas, Montreal | .167 | 9 | 6 | 0 | 1 | 1 | 0 | 0 | 0 | 0 | 0 | 0 | 0 | 0 | 0 |
| Foley, Thomas, Cin.-Phil.* | .240 | 89 | 250 | 24 | 60 | 84 | 13 | 1 | 3 | 23 | 4 | 0 | 2 | 2 | 3 |
| Foli, Timothy, Pittsburgh | .189 | 19 | 37 | 1 | 7 | 7 | 0 | 0 | 0 | 2 | 0 | 0 | 0 | 0 | 0 |
| Fontenot, S. Ray, Chicago* | .049 | 38 | 41 | 2 | 2 | 2 | 0 | 0 | 0 | 0 | 0 | 4 | 0 | 0 | 0 |
| Ford, Curtis, St. Louis* | .500 | 11 | 12 | 2 | 6 | 8 | 2 | 0 | 0 | 3 | 1 | 0 | 0 | 1 | 0 |
| Forsch, Robert, St. Louis | .244 | 34 | 45 | 3 | 11 | 18 | 2 | 1 | 1 | 4 | 1 | 2 | 0 | 0 | 0 |
| Forster, Terry, Atlanta* | .000 | 46 | 4 | 0 | 0 | 0 | 0 | 0 | 0 | 0 | 0 | 1 | 0 | 0 | 0 |
| Foster, George, New York | .263 | 129 | 452 | 57 | 119 | 208 | 24 | 1 | 21 | 77 | 10 | 0 | 4 | 0 | 1 |
| Franco, John, Cincinnati* | .333 | 67 | 6 | 1 | 2 | 2 | 0 | 0 | 0 | 1 | 0 | 2 | 0 | 0 | 0 |
| Francona, Terry, Montreal* | .267 | 107 | 281 | 19 | 75 | 98 | 15 | 1 | 2 | 31 | 4 | 2 | 0 | 5 | 5 |
| Frazier, George, Chicago | .000 | 51 | 6 | 0 | 0 | 0 | 0 | 0 | 0 | 0 | 0 | 0 | 0 | 0 | 0 |
| Frobel, Douglas, Pitt.-Mtl.* | .189 | 65 | 132 | 17 | 25 | 34 | 6 | 0 | 1 | 11 | 2 | 3 | 0 | 4 | 3 |
| Gainey, Telmanch, Houston* | .162 | 13 | 37 | 5 | 6 | 6 | 0 | 0 | 0 | 0 | 0 | 1 | 0 | 0 | 0 |
| Galarraga, Andres, Montreal | .187 | 24 | 75 | 9 | 14 | 21 | 1 | 0 | 2 | 4 | 1 | 0 | 0 | 1 | 2 |
| Garber, H. Eugene, Atlanta | .200 | 59 | 5 | 1 | 1 | 1 | 0 | 0 | 0 | 1 | 0 | 1 | 0 | 0 | 0 |
| Garcia, Alfonso, Philadelphia | .000 | 4 | 3 | 0 | 0 | 0 | 0 | 0 | 0 | 0 | 0 | 0 | 0 | 0 | 0 |
| Gardenhire, Ronald, New York | .179 | 26 | 39 | 5 | 7 | 11 | 2 | 1 | 0 | 2 | 0 | 2 | 0 | 0 | 0 |
| Gardner, Wesley, New York | .000 | 9 | 0 | 0 | 0 | 0 | 0 | 0 | 0 | 0 | 0 | 0 | 0 | 0 | 0 |
| Garner, Philip, Houston | .268 | 135 | 463 | 65 | 124 | 185 | 23 | 10 | 6 | 51 | 9 | 1 | 5 | 4 | 4 |
| Garrelts, Scott, San Francisco | .222 | 74 | 9 | 1 | 2 | 3 | 1 | 0 | 0 | 2 | 0 | 0 | 0 | 0 | 0 |
| Garvey, Steven, San Diego | .281 | 162 | 654 | 80 | 184 | 281 | 34 | 6 | 17 | 81 | 11 | 1 | 6 | 0 | 0 |
| Gladden, C. Daniel, San Fran. | .243 | 142 | 502 | 64 | 122 | 174 | 15 | 8 | 7 | 41 | 6 | 10 | 2 | 32 | 15 |
| Glynn, Edward, Montreal | .000 | 3 | 0 | 0 | 0 | 0 | 0 | 0 | 0 | 0 | 0 | 0 | 0 | 0 | 0 |
| Gonzalez, Denio, Pittsburgh | .226 | 35 | 124 | 11 | 28 | 44 | 4 | 0 | 4 | 12 | 2 | 1 | 0 | 2 | 4 |
| Gonzalez, Jose, Los Angeles | .273 | 23 | 11 | 6 | 3 | 5 | 2 | 0 | 0 | 0 | 0 | 0 | 0 | 1 | 1 |
| Gooden, Dwight, New York | .226 | 35 | 93 | 11 | 21 | 26 | 2 | 0 | 1 | 9 | 0 | 9 | 0 | 0 | 0 |
| Gorman, Thomas, New York* | .000 | 34 | 5 | 0 | 0 | 0 | 0 | 0 | 0 | 0 | 0 | 2 | 0 | 0 | 0 |
| Gossage, Richard, San Diego | .000 | 50 | 11 | 1 | 0 | 0 | 0 | 0 | 0 | 0 | 0 | 0 | 0 | 0 | 0 |
| Gott, James, San Francisco | .196 | 26 | 51 | 6 | 10 | 21 | 2 | 0 | 3 | 3 | 0 | 4 | 0 | 0 | 1 |
| Grapenthin, Richard, Montreal | 1.000 | 5 | 1 | 0 | 1 | 1 | 0 | 0 | 0 | 0 | 0 | 0 | 0 | 0 | 0 |
| Green, David, San Francisco | .248 | 106 | 294 | 36 | 73 | 102 | 10 | 2 | 5 | 20 | 7 | 2 | 2 | 6 | 5 |

| Player and Club | Pct. | G. | AB. | R. | H. | TB. | 2B. | 3B. | HR. | RBI. | GW. | SH. | SF. | SB. | CS. |
|---|---|---|---|---|---|---|---|---|---|---|---|---|---|---|---|
| Gross, Gregory, Philadelphia* | .260 | 93 | 169 | 21 | 44 | 53 | 5 | 2 | 0 | 14 | 1 | 2 | 2 | 1 | 0 |
| Gross, Kevin, Philadelphia | .138 | 39 | 65 | 1 | 9 | 14 | 2 | 0 | 1 | 6 | 1 | 8 | 0 | 0 | 0 |
| Guante, Cecilio, Pittsburgh | .059 | 63 | 17 | 0 | 1 | 1 | 0 | 0 | 0 | 0 | 0 | 0 | 0 | 0 | 0 |
| Guerrero, Pedro, Los Angeles | .320 | 137 | 487 | 99 | 156 | 281 | 22 | 2 | 33 | 87 | 16 | 0 | 5 | 12 | 4 |
| Gullickson, William, Montreal | .188 | 29 | 64 | 2 | 12 | 16 | 4 | 0 | 0 | 6 | 0 | 4 | 0 | 0 | 0 |
| Gumpert, David, Chicago | .000 | 9 | 1 | 0 | 0 | 0 | 0 | 0 | 0 | 0 | 0 | 0 | 0 | 0 | 0 |
| Gura, Lawrence, Chicago* | .000 | 5 | 6 | 0 | 0 | 0 | 0 | 0 | 0 | 0 | 0 | 0 | 0 | 0 | 0 |
| Gwynn, Anthony, San Diego* | .317 | 154 | 622 | 90 | 197 | 254 | 29 | 5 | 6 | 46 | 8 | 1 | 1 | 14 | 11 |
| Hall, Albert, Atlanta† | .149 | 54 | 47 | 5 | 7 | 9 | 0 | 1 | 0 | 3 | 1 | 1 | 0 | 1 | 1 |
| Hammaker, C. Atlee, San Fran.† | .085 | 29 | 47 | 0 | 4 | 4 | 0 | 0 | 0 | 0 | 0 | 6 | 0 | 0 | 0 |
| Harper, Brian, St. Louis | .250 | 43 | 52 | 5 | 13 | 17 | 4 | 0 | 0 | 8 | 1 | 0 | 1 | 0 | 0 |
| Harper, Terry, Atlanta | .264 | 138 | 492 | 58 | 130 | 200 | 15 | 2 | 17 | 72 | 7 | 1 | 2 | 9 | 9 |
| Hassler, Andrew, St. Louis* | .000 | 10 | 0 | 0 | 0 | 0 | 0 | 0 | 0 | 0 | 0 | 0 | 0 | 0 | 0 |
| Hatcher, William, Chicago | .245 | 53 | 163 | 24 | 40 | 60 | 12 | 1 | 2 | 10 | 1 | 2 | 2 | 2 | 4 |
| Hawkins, M. Andrew, San Diego | .078 | 33 | 77 | 1 | 6 | 6 | 0 | 0 | 0 | 3 | 1 | 13 | 0 | 0 | 0 |
| Hayes, Von, Philadelphia* | .263 | 152 | 570 | 76 | 150 | 227 | 30 | 4 | 13 | 70 | 9 | 2 | 4 | 21 | 8 |
| Heathcock, R. Jeffery, Houston | .063 | 14 | 16 | 1 | 1 | 1 | 0 | 0 | 0 | 0 | 0 | 0 | 0 | 0 | 0 |
| Hebner, Richard, Chicago* | .217 | 83 | 120 | 10 | 26 | 37 | 2 | 0 | 3 | 22 | 3 | 0 | 0 | 0 | 1 |
| Heep, Daniel, New York* | .280 | 95 | 271 | 26 | 76 | 114 | 17 | 0 | 7 | 42 | 3 | 0 | 6 | 2 | 2 |
| Hendrick, George, Pittsburgh | .230 | 69 | 256 | 23 | 59 | 80 | 15 | 0 | 2 | 25 | 4 | 0 | 3 | 1 | 0 |
| Hernandez, Keith, New York* | .309 | 158 | 593 | 87 | 183 | 255 | 34 | 4 | 10 | 91 | 24 | 0 | 10 | 3 | 3 |
| Herr, Thomas, St. Louis† | .302 | 159 | 596 | 97 | 180 | 248 | 38 | 3 | 8 | 110 | 14 | 5 | 13 | 31 | 3 |
| Hershiser, Orel, Los Angeles | .197 | 37 | 76 | 5 | 15 | 16 | 1 | 0 | 0 | 4 | 0 | 10 | 0 | 1 | 0 |
| Hesketh, Joseph, Montreal* | .091 | 26 | 44 | 0 | 4 | 4 | 0 | 0 | 0 | 1 | 0 | 5 | 0 | 0 | 0 |
| Holland, Alfred, Phil.-Pitt. | .400 | 41 | 5 | 1 | 2 | 4 | 0 | 1 | 0 | 0 | 0 | 1 | 0 | 0 | 0 |
| Holton, Brian, Los Angeles | .000 | 3 | 0 | 0 | 0 | 0 | 0 | 0 | 0 | 0 | 0 | 0 | 0 | 0 | 0 |
| Honeycutt, Frederick, Los Angeles* | .132 | 32 | 38 | 5 | 5 | 6 | 1 | 0 | 0 | 1 | 1 | 8 | 0 | 0 | 0 |
| Horner, J. Robert, Atlanta | .267 | 130 | 483 | 61 | 129 | 241 | 25 | 3 | 27 | 89 | 6 | 0 | 6 | 1 | 1 |
| Horton, Ricky, St. Louis* | .063 | 49 | 16 | 1 | 1 | 1 | 0 | 0 | 0 | 0 | 0 | 2 | 0 | 0 | 0 |
| Howe, Arthur, St. Louis | .000 | 4 | 3 | 0 | 0 | 0 | 0 | 0 | 0 | 0 | 0 | 0 | 0 | 0 | 0 |
| Howe, Steven, Los Angeles* | .000 | 19 | 0 | 0 | 0 | 0 | 0 | 0 | 0 | 0 | 0 | 0 | 0 | 0 | 0 |
| Howell, Kenneth, Los Angeles | .000 | 56 | 4 | 0 | 0 | 0 | 0 | 0 | 0 | 0 | 0 | 0 | 0 | 0 | 0 |
| Hoyt, D. LaMarr, San Diego | .063 | 31 | 64 | 4 | 4 | 4 | 0 | 0 | 0 | 2 | 0 | 12 | 0 | 0 | 0 |
| Hubbard, Glenn, Atlanta | .232 | 142 | 439 | 51 | 102 | 138 | 21 | 0 | 5 | 39 | 5 | 7 | 6 | 4 | 3 |
| Hudson, Charles, Philadelphia† | .140 | 38 | 57 | 2 | 8 | 8 | 0 | 0 | 0 | 3 | 0 | 3 | 0 | 0 | 0 |
| Hume, Thomas, Cincinnati | .000 | 56 | 5 | 0 | 0 | 0 | 0 | 0 | 0 | 0 | 0 | 0 | 0 | 0 | 0 |
| Hunt, J. Randall, St. Louis | .158 | 14 | 19 | 1 | 3 | 3 | 0 | 0 | 0 | 1 | 0 | 1 | 0 | 0 | 1 |
| Hurdle, Clinton, New York* | .195 | 43 | 82 | 7 | 16 | 29 | 4 | 0 | 3 | 7 | 1 | 0 | 0 | 0 | 1 |
| Jackson, Darrin, Chicago | .091 | 5 | 11 | 0 | 1 | 1 | 0 | 0 | 0 | 0 | 0 | 0 | 0 | 0 | 0 |
| Jackson, Roy Lee, San Diego | .000 | 22 | 5 | 0 | 0 | 0 | 0 | 0 | 0 | 0 | 0 | 1 | 0 | 0 | 0 |
| Jeffcoat, J. Michael, San Fran.* | .000 | 19 | 1 | 0 | 0 | 0 | 0 | 0 | 0 | 0 | 0 | 0 | 0 | 0 | 0 |
| Jeltz, L. Steven, Philadelphia | .189 | 89 | 196 | 17 | 37 | 43 | 4 | 1 | 0 | 12 | 1 | 5 | 1 | 1 | 1 |
| Johnson, Howard, New York† | .242 | 126 | 389 | 38 | 94 | 153 | 18 | 4 | 11 | 46 | 8 | 1 | 4 | 6 | 4 |
| Johnson, Joseph, Atlanta | .043 | 15 | 23 | 0 | 1 | 2 | 1 | 0 | 0 | 2 | 0 | 3 | 0 | 0 | 0 |
| Johnson, Roy, Montreal* | .000 | 3 | 5 | 0 | 0 | 0 | 0 | 0 | 0 | 0 | 0 | 0 | 0 | 0 | 0 |
| Johnstone, John, Los Angeles* | .133 | 17 | 15 | 0 | 2 | 3 | 1 | 0 | 0 | 2 | 1 | 0 | 0 | 0 | 0 |
| Jones, Christopher, Houston* | .200 | 31 | 25 | 0 | 5 | 5 | 0 | 0 | 0 | 1 | 0 | 0 | 0 | 0 | 0 |
| Jorgensen, Michael, St. Louis* | .196 | 72 | 112 | 14 | 22 | 28 | 6 | 0 | 0 | 11 | 2 | 2 | 0 | 2 | 1 |
| Kemp, Steven, Pittsburgh* | .250 | 92 | 236 | 19 | 59 | 82 | 13 | 2 | 2 | 21 | 3 | 1 | 4 | 1 | 0 |
| Kennedy, Terrence, San Diego* | .261 | 143 | 532 | 54 | 139 | 198 | 27 | 1 | 10 | 74 | 9 | 0 | 2 | 0 | 0 |
| Keough, Matthew, St. Louis | .000 | 4 | 2 | 0 | 0 | 0 | 0 | 0 | 0 | 0 | 0 | 0 | 0 | 0 | 0 |
| Kepshire, Kurt, St. Louis* | .118 | 32 | 51 | 6 | 6 | 9 | 3 | 0 | 0 | 2 | 0 | 7 | 1 | 0 | 0 |
| Kerfeld, Charles, Houston | .000 | 11 | 14 | 0 | 0 | 0 | 0 | 0 | 0 | 0 | 0 | 2 | 0 | 0 | 0 |
| Khalifa, Sam, Pittsburgh | .238 | 95 | 320 | 30 | 76 | 102 | 14 | 3 | 2 | 31 | 3 | 9 | 4 | 5 | 2 |
| Kipper, Robert, Pittsburgh | .250 | 5 | 8 | 1 | 2 | 2 | 0 | 0 | 0 | 0 | 0 | 2 | 0 | 0 | 0 |
| Knepper, Robert, Houston* | .141 | 38 | 78 | 5 | 11 | 15 | 1 | 0 | 1 | 5 | 0 | 8 | 0 | 0 | 0 |
| Knicely, Alan, Cin.-Phil. | .242 | 55 | 165 | 17 | 40 | 64 | 9 | 0 | 5 | 26 | 2 | 1 | 2 | 0 | 0 |
| Knight, C. Ray, New York | .218 | 90 | 271 | 22 | 59 | 89 | 12 | 0 | 6 | 36 | 2 | 0 | 5 | 1 | 1 |
| Knudson, Mark, Houston | .000 | 2 | 2 | 0 | 0 | 0 | 0 | 0 | 0 | 0 | 0 | 0 | 0 | 0 | 0 |
| Komminsk, Brad, Atlanta | .227 | 106 | 300 | 52 | 68 | 98 | 12 | 3 | 4 | 21 | 2 | 2 | 2 | 10 | 8 |
| Koosman, Jerome, Philadelphia | .088 | 19 | 34 | 1 | 3 | 3 | 0 | 0 | 0 | 4 | 1 | 1 | 1 | 0 | 0 |
| Krawczyk, Raymond, Pittsburgh | .000 | 8 | 0 | 0 | 0 | 0 | 0 | 0 | 0 | 0 | 0 | 0 | 0 | 0 | 0 |
| Krenchicki, Wayne, Cincinnati* | .272 | 90 | 173 | 16 | 47 | 68 | 9 | 0 | 4 | 25 | 1 | 2 | 2 | 0 | 0 |
| Krukow, Michael, San Francisco | .218 | 28 | 55 | 2 | 12 | 19 | 4 | 0 | 1 | 3 | 0 | 8 | 0 | 1 | 1 |
| Kuiper, Duane, San Francisco* | .600 | 9 | 5 | 0 | 3 | 3 | 0 | 0 | 0 | 0 | 0 | 2 | 0 | 0 | 0 |
| Lahti, Jeffrey, St. Louis | .000 | 52 | 9 | 0 | 0 | 0 | 0 | 0 | 0 | 0 | 0 | 0 | 0 | 0 | 0 |
| LaPoint, David, San Francisco* | .167 | 31 | 60 | 4 | 10 | 11 | 1 | 0 | 0 | 6 | 1 | 5 | 0 | 0 | 0 |
| Lake, Steven, Chicago | .151 | 58 | 119 | 5 | 18 | 23 | 2 | 0 | 1 | 11 | 1 | 4 | 1 | 1 | 0 |
| Landreaux, Kenneth, Los Ang.* | .268 | 147 | 482 | 70 | 129 | 195 | 26 | 2 | 12 | 50 | 10 | 3 | 8 | 15 | 5 |
| Landrum, Terry, St. Louis | .280 | 85 | 161 | 21 | 45 | 69 | 8 | 2 | 4 | 21 | 3 | 1 | 0 | 1 | 4 |
| Laskey, William, S.F.-Mtl. | .135 | 30 | 37 | 2 | 5 | 5 | 0 | 0 | 0 | 2 | 0 | 8 | 0 | 0 | 0 |
| Latham, William, N.Y.* | .333 | 7 | 3 | 1 | 1 | 1 | 0 | 0 | 0 | 0 | 0 | 0 | 0 | 0 | 0 |
| Lavalliere, Michael, St. Louis* | .147 | 12 | 34 | 2 | 5 | 6 | 1 | 0 | 0 | 6 | 0 | 0 | 3 | 0 | 0 |
| Law, Vance, Montreal | .266 | 147 | 519 | 75 | 138 | 210 | 30 | 6 | 10 | 52 | 5 | 8 | 6 | 6 | 5 |
| Lawless, Thomas, St. Louis | .207 | 47 | 58 | 8 | 12 | 17 | 3 | 1 | 0 | 8 | 2 | 1 | 0 | 2 | 1 |
| Leach, Terry, New York | .167 | 22 | 12 | 1 | 2 | 3 | 1 | 0 | 0 | 0 | 0 | 1 | 0 | 0 | 0 |
| Lefferts, Craig, San Diego* | .250 | 60 | 4 | 0 | 1 | 1 | 0 | 0 | 0 | 0 | 0 | 0 | 0 | 0 | 0 |
| LeMaster, Johnnie, S.F.-Pitt. | .122 | 34 | 74 | 5 | 9 | 12 | 0 | 0 | 1 | 6 | 0 | 2 | 0 | 1 | 0 |
| Leonard, Jeffrey, San Francisco | .241 | 133 | 507 | 49 | 122 | 199 | 20 | 3 | 17 | 62 | 7 | 1 | 1 | 11 | 6 |
| Lezcano, Sixto, Pittsburgh | .207 | 72 | 116 | 16 | 24 | 35 | 2 | 0 | 3 | 9 | 0 | 0 | 1 | 0 | 0 |

| Player and Club | Pct. | G. | AB. | R. | H. | TB. | 2B. | 3B. | HR. | RBI. | GW. | SH. | SF. | SB. | CS. |
|---|---|---|---|---|---|---|---|---|---|---|---|---|---|---|---|
| Lopes, David, Chicago | .284 | 99 | 275 | 52 | 78 | 122 | 11 | 0 | 11 | 44 | 6 | 1 | 3 | 47 | 4 |
| Loucks, Scott, Pittsburgh | .286 | 4 | 7 | 1 | 2 | 4 | 2 | 0 | 0 | 1 | 0 | 0 | 0 | 0 | 0 |
| Lucas, Gary, Montreal* | .000 | 49 | 5 | 0 | 0 | 0 | 0 | 0 | 0 | 0 | 0 | 0 | 0 | 0 | 0 |
| Lynch, Edward, New York | .077 | 31 | 52 | 1 | 4 | 4 | 0 | 0 | 0 | 0 | 0 | 9 | 0 | 0 | 0 |
| Madden, Michael, Houston* | .000 | 13 | 0 | 0 | 0 | 0 | 0 | 0 | 0 | 0 | 0 | 0 | 0 | 0 | 0 |
| Maddox, Garry, Philadelphia | .239 | 105 | 218 | 22 | 52 | 74 | 8 | 1 | 4 | 23 | 3 | 1 | 3 | 4 | 2 |
| Madlock, Bill, Pitt.-L.A. | .275 | 144 | 513 | 69 | 141 | 206 | 27 | 1 | 12 | 56 | 6 | 3 | 4 | 10 | 4 |
| Mahler, Michael, Montreal† | .188 | 9 | 16 | 2 | 3 | 5 | 0 | 1 | 0 | 0 | 0 | 1 | 0 | 0 | 0 |
| Mahler, Richard, Atlanta | .156 | 39 | 90 | 9 | 14 | 15 | 1 | 0 | 0 | 8 | 3 | 11 | 1 | 0 | 0 |
| Maldonado, Candido, Los Angeles | .225 | 121 | 213 | 20 | 48 | 72 | 7 | 1 | 5 | 19 | 2 | 2 | 1 | 1 | 1 |
| Manrique, Fred, Montreal | .308 | 9 | 13 | 5 | 4 | 10 | 1 | 1 | 1 | 1 | 0 | 0 | 0 | 0 | 0 |
| Marshall, Michael, Los Angeles | .293 | 135 | 518 | 72 | 152 | 267 | 27 | 2 | 28 | 95 | 12 | 2 | 4 | 3 | 10 |
| Martinez, Carmelo, San Diego | .253 | 150 | 514 | 64 | 130 | 223 | 28 | 1 | 21 | 72 | 13 | 2 | 4 | 0 | 4 |
| Mason, Roger, San Francisco | .091 | 5 | 11 | 1 | 1 | 1 | 0 | 0 | 0 | 0 | 0 | 0 | 0 | 0 | 0 |
| Mathis, Ronald, Houston | .071 | 23 | 14 | 0 | 1 | 1 | 0 | 0 | 0 | 0 | 0 | 2 | 0 | 0 | 0 |
| Matthews, Gary, Chicago | .235 | 97 | 298 | 45 | 70 | 121 | 12 | 0 | 13 | 40 | 3 | 0 | 3 | 2 | 0 |
| Matuszek, Leonard, Los Angeles* | .222 | 43 | 63 | 10 | 14 | 27 | 2 | 1 | 3 | 13 | 2 | 1 | 3 | 0 | 1 |
| Mazzilli, Lee, Pittsburgh† | .282 | 92 | 117 | 20 | 33 | 44 | 8 | 0 | 1 | 9 | 1 | 1 | 0 | 4 | 1 |
| McCullers, Lance, San Diego† | .000 | 21 | 4 | 0 | 0 | 0 | 0 | 0 | 0 | 0 | 0 | 2 | 0 | 0 | 0 |
| McDowell, Roger, New York | .158 | 62 | 19 | 1 | 3 | 4 | 1 | 0 | 0 | 1 | 0 | 2 | 0 | 0 | 0 |
| McGaffigan, Andrew, Cincinnati | .034 | 15 | 29 | 0 | 1 | 2 | 1 | 0 | 0 | 1 | 1 | 1 | 0 | 0 | 0 |
| McGee, Willie, St. Louis† | .353 | 152 | 612 | 114 | 216 | 308 | 26 | 18 | 10 | 82 | 17 | 1 | 5 | 56 | 16 |
| McMurtry, J. Craig, Atlanta | .071 | 17 | 14 | 0 | 1 | 1 | 0 | 0 | 0 | 0 | 0 | 1 | 0 | 0 | 0 |
| McReynolds, W. Kevin, San Diego | .234 | 152 | 564 | 61 | 132 | 209 | 24 | 4 | 15 | 75 | 12 | 2 | 4 | 4 | 0 |
| McWilliams, Larry, Pittsburgh* | .125 | 32 | 40 | 2 | 5 | 6 | 1 | 0 | 0 | 2 | 0 | 4 | 0 | 0 | 0 |
| Meridith, Ronald, Chicago* | .250 | 32 | 4 | 0 | 1 | 1 | 0 | 0 | 0 | 0 | 0 | 0 | 0 | 0 | 0 |
| Milner, Eddie, Cincinnati* | .254 | 145 | 453 | 82 | 115 | 157 | 19 | 7 | 3 | 33 | 4 | 2 | 3 | 35 | 13 |
| Minton, Gregory, San Francisco† | .000 | 68 | 8 | 1 | 0 | 0 | 0 | 0 | 0 | 1 | 0 | 0 | 0 | 0 | 0 |
| Mizerock, John, Houston* | .237 | 15 | 38 | 6 | 9 | 13 | 4 | 0 | 0 | 6 | 2 | 0 | 0 | 0 | 0 |
| Moore, Robert, San Francisco | .000 | 11 | 2 | 0 | 0 | 0 | 0 | 0 | 0 | 0 | 0 | 0 | 0 | 0 | 0 |
| Moreland, B. Keith, Chicago | .307 | 161 | 587 | 74 | 180 | 258 | 30 | 3 | 14 | 106 | 12 | 2 | 9 | 12 | 3 |
| Morrison, James, Pittsburgh | .254 | 92 | 244 | 17 | 62 | 84 | 10 | 0 | 4 | 22 | 0 | 1 | 3 | 3 | 0 |
| Mumphrey, Jerry, Houston† | .277 | 130 | 444 | 52 | 123 | 176 | 25 | 2 | 8 | 61 | 3 | 1 | 6 | 6 | 7 |
| Murphy, Dale, Atlanta | .300 | 162 | 616 | 118 | 185 | 332 | 32 | 2 | 37 | 111 | 14 | 0 | 5 | 10 | 3 |
| Murphy, Robert, Cincinnati* | .000 | 2 | 0 | 0 | 0 | 0 | 0 | 0 | 0 | 0 | 0 | 0 | 0 | 0 | 0 |
| Myers, Randall, New York* | .000 | 1 | 0 | 0 | 0 | 0 | 0 | 0 | 0 | 0 | 0 | 0 | 0 | 0 | 0 |
| Nettles, Graig, San Diego* | .261 | 137 | 440 | 66 | 115 | 185 | 23 | 1 | 15 | 61 | 4 | 0 | 3 | 0 | 0 |
| Newman, Albert, Montreal† | .172 | 25 | 29 | 7 | 5 | 6 | 1 | 0 | 0 | 1 | 1 | 0 | 0 | 2 | 1 |
| Nicosia, Steven, Montreal | .169 | 42 | 71 | 4 | 12 | 14 | 2 | 0 | 0 | 1 | 0 | 1 | 0 | 1 | 0 |
| Niedenfuer, Thomas, Los Angeles | .111 | 64 | 9 | 0 | 1 | 1 | 0 | 0 | 0 | 0 | 0 | 1 | 0 | 0 | 0 |
| Niekro, Joseph, Houston | .250 | 32 | 68 | 6 | 17 | 18 | 1 | 0 | 0 | 6 | 1 | 10 | 1 | 0 | 0 |
| Niemann, Randy, New York* | .000 | 4 | 0 | 0 | 0 | 0 | 0 | 0 | 0 | 0 | 0 | 0 | 0 | 0 | 0 |
| Nieto, Thomas, St. Louis | .225 | 95 | 253 | 15 | 57 | 71 | 10 | 2 | 0 | 34 | 5 | 6 | 0 | 0 | 2 |
| Nokes, Matthew, San Francisco* | .208 | 19 | 53 | 3 | 11 | 19 | 2 | 0 | 2 | 5 | 0 | 0 | 0 | 0 | 0 |
| Oberkfell, Kenneth, Atlanta* | .272 | 134 | 412 | 30 | 112 | 148 | 19 | 4 | 3 | 35 | 2 | 1 | 2 | 1 | 2 |
| O'Berry, P. Michael, Montreal | .190 | 20 | 21 | 2 | 4 | 4 | 0 | 0 | 0 | 0 | 0 | 1 | 0 | 1 | 0 |
| O'Connor, Jack, Montreal* | .000 | 20 | 0 | 0 | 0 | 0 | 0 | 0 | 0 | 0 | 0 | 0 | 0 | 0 | 0 |
| Oester, Ronald, Cincinnati† | .295 | 152 | 526 | 59 | 155 | 190 | 26 | 3 | 1 | 34 | 4 | 2 | 5 | 5 | 0 |
| Oliver, Albert, Los Angeles* | .253 | 35 | 79 | 1 | 20 | 25 | 5 | 0 | 0 | 8 | 2 | 0 | 1 | 1 | 0 |
| O'Neill, Paul, Cincinnati* | .333 | 5 | 12 | 1 | 4 | 5 | 1 | 0 | 0 | 1 | 0 | 0 | 0 | 0 | 0 |
| Orosco, Jesse, New York* | .429 | 54 | 7 | 0 | 3 | 3 | 0 | 0 | 0 | 0 | 0 | 2 | 0 | 0 | 0 |
| Orsulak, Joseph, Pittsburgh* | .300 | 121 | 397 | 54 | 119 | 145 | 14 | 6 | 0 | 21 | 0 | 9 | 3 | 24 | 11 |
| Ortiz, Adalberto, Pittsburgh | .292 | 23 | 72 | 4 | 21 | 26 | 2 | 0 | 1 | 5 | 1 | 1 | 0 | 1 | 0 |
| Owen, Dave, Chicago† | .368 | 22 | 19 | 6 | 7 | 7 | 0 | 0 | 0 | 4 | 0 | 0 | 0 | 1 | 1 |
| Owen, Lawrence, Atlanta | .239 | 26 | 71 | 7 | 17 | 26 | 3 | 0 | 2 | 12 | 0 | 2 | 1 | 0 | 0 |
| Paciorek, Thomas, New York | .284 | 46 | 116 | 14 | 33 | 41 | 3 | 1 | 1 | 11 | 1 | 1 | 0 | 1 | 0 |
| Palmer, David, Montreal | .111 | 24 | 36 | 1 | 4 | 5 | 1 | 0 | 0 | 0 | 0 | 5 | 0 | 0 | 0 |
| Pankovits, James, Houston | .244 | 75 | 172 | 24 | 42 | 57 | 3 | 0 | 4 | 14 | 2 | 1 | 0 | 1 | 0 |
| Parker, David, Cincinnati* | .312 | 160 | 635 | 88 | 198 | 350 | 42 | 4 | 34 | 125 | 18 | 0 | 4 | 5 | 13 |
| Pastore, Frank, Cincinnati | .143 | 17 | 14 | 1 | 2 | 3 | 1 | 0 | 0 | 0 | 0 | 2 | 0 | 0 | 0 |
| Patterson, Reginald, Chicago* | .100 | 8 | 10 | 1 | 1 | 1 | 0 | 0 | 0 | 0 | 0 | 2 | 0 | 0 | 0 |
| Patterson, Robert, San Diego | .000 | 3 | 0 | 0 | 0 | 0 | 0 | 0 | 0 | 0 | 0 | 0 | 0 | 0 | 0 |
| Pederson, Stuart, Los Angeles* | .000 | 8 | 4 | 1 | 0 | 0 | 0 | 0 | 0 | 0 | 1 | 0 | 1 | 0 | 0 |
| Pena, Adalberto, Houston | .276 | 20 | 29 | 7 | 8 | 10 | 2 | 0 | 0 | 4 | 1 | 1 | 1 | 0 | 0 |
| Pena, Alejandro, Los Angeles | .000 | 2 | 1 | 0 | 0 | 0 | 0 | 0 | 0 | 0 | 0 | 0 | 0 | 0 | 0 |
| Pena, Antonio, Pittsburgh | .249 | 147 | 546 | 53 | 136 | 197 | 27 | 2 | 10 | 59 | 7 | 7 | 5 | 12 | 8 |
| Pendleton, Terry, St. Louis† | .240 | 149 | 559 | 56 | 134 | 171 | 16 | 3 | 5 | 69 | 12 | 3 | 3 | 17 | 12 |
| Perez, Atanasio, Cincinnati | .328 | 72 | 183 | 25 | 60 | 86 | 8 | 0 | 6 | 33 | 4 | 0 | 2 | 0 | 2 |
| Perez, Pascual, Atlanta | .120 | 22 | 25 | 0 | 3 | 3 | 0 | 0 | 0 | 1 | 1 | 4 | 0 | 0 | 0 |
| Perlman, Jonathan, Chicago* | .000 | 6 | 1 | 0 | 0 | 0 | 0 | 0 | 0 | 0 | 0 | 0 | 0 | 0 | 0 |
| Perry, Gerald, Atlanta* | .214 | 110 | 238 | 22 | 51 | 65 | 5 | 0 | 3 | 13 | 3 | 0 | 1 | 9 | 5 |
| Perry, W. Patrick, St. Louis* | .500 | 6 | 2 | 0 | 1 | 1 | 0 | 0 | 0 | 0 | 0 | 0 | 0 | 0 | 0 |
| Porter, Darrell, St. Louis* | .221 | 84 | 240 | 30 | 53 | 99 | 12 | 2 | 10 | 36 | 6 | 0 | 2 | 6 | 1 |
| Powell, Dennis, Los Angeles* | .000 | 16 | 3 | 0 | 0 | 0 | 0 | 0 | 0 | 0 | 0 | 2 | 0 | 0 | 0 |
| Power, Ted, Cincinnati | .000 | 64 | 0 | 0 | 0 | 0 | 0 | 0 | 0 | 0 | 0 | 0 | 0 | 0 | 0 |
| Price, Joseph, Cincinnati | .000 | 26 | 14 | 0 | 0 | 0 | 0 | 0 | 0 | 0 | 0 | 1 | 0 | 0 | 0 |
| Puhl, Terrance, Houston* | .284 | 57 | 194 | 34 | 55 | 81 | 14 | 3 | 2 | 23 | 1 | 4 | 3 | 6 | 2 |
| Rabb, John, Atlanta | .000 | 3 | 2 | 0 | 0 | 0 | 0 | 0 | 0 | 0 | 0 | 0 | 0 | 0 | 0 |
| Raines, Timothy, Montreal† | .320 | 150 | 575 | 115 | 184 | 273 | 30 | 13 | 11 | 41 | 4 | 3 | 3 | 70 | 9 |
| Rajsich, Gary, San Francisco* | .165 | 51 | 91 | 5 | 15 | 21 | 6 | 0 | 0 | 10 | 2 | 2 | 0 | 0 | 1 |

| Player and Club | Pct. | G. | AB. | R. | H. | TB. | 2B. | 3B. | HR. | RBI. | GW. | SH. | SF. | SB. | CS. |
|---|---|---|---|---|---|---|---|---|---|---|---|---|---|---|---|
| Ramirez, Mario, San Diego | .283 | 37 | 60 | 6 | 17 | 23 | 0 | 0 | 2 | 5 | 0 | 0 | 0 | 0 | 0 |
| Ramirez, Rafael, Atlanta | .248 | 138 | 568 | 54 | 141 | 189 | 25 | 4 | 5 | 58 | 5 | 2 | 5 | 2 | 6 |
| Ramsey, Michael, Los Angeles† | .133 | 9 | 15 | 1 | 2 | 3 | 1 | 0 | 0 | 0 | 0 | 0 | 0 | 0 | 0 |
| Rawley, Shane, Philadelphia | .138 | 36 | 58 | 3 | 8 | 9 | 1 | 0 | 0 | 6 | 0 | 7 | 2 | 0 | 0 |
| Ray, Johnny, Pittsburgh† | .274 | 154 | 594 | 67 | 163 | 223 | 33 | 3 | 7 | 70 | 5 | 5 | 6 | 13 | 9 |
| Reardon, Jeffrey, Montreal | .286 | 63 | 7 | 0 | 2 | 2 | 0 | 0 | 0 | 1 | 0 | 2 | 0 | 0 | 0 |
| Redus, Gary, Cincinnati | .252 | 101 | 246 | 51 | 62 | 102 | 14 | 4 | 6 | 28 | 4 | 2 | 1 | 48 | 12 |
| Reuschel, Ricky, Pittsburgh | .169 | 31 | 59 | 8 | 10 | 15 | 2 | 0 | 1 | 7 | 1 | 6 | 0 | 1 | 0 |
| Reuss, Jerry, Los Angeles* | .135 | 34 | 74 | 1 | 10 | 10 | 0 | 0 | 0 | 7 | 2 | 6 | 1 | 0 | 0 |
| Reyes, Gilberto, Los Angeles | .000 | 6 | 1 | 0 | 0 | 0 | 0 | 0 | 0 | 0 | 0 | 0 | 0 | 0 | 0 |
| Reynolds, G. Craig, Houston* | .272 | 107 | 379 | 43 | 103 | 149 | 18 | 8 | 4 | 32 | 7 | 3 | 2 | 4 | 4 |
| Reynolds, Robert, L.A.-Pitt.† | .282 | 104 | 337 | 44 | 95 | 133 | 15 | 7 | 3 | 42 | 8 | 7 | 3 | 18 | 5 |
| Reynolds, Ronn, New York | .209 | 28 | 43 | 4 | 9 | 11 | 2 | 0 | 0 | 1 | 0 | 2 | 0 | 0 | 0 |
| Rhoden, Richard, Pittsburgh | .189 | 37 | 74 | 2 | 14 | 17 | 3 | 0 | 0 | 6 | 3 | 2 | 0 | 0 | 0 |
| Rivera, German, Houston | .194 | 13 | 36 | 3 | 7 | 11 | 2 | 1 | 0 | 2 | 0 | 1 | 0 | 0 | 0 |
| Roberge, Bertrand, Montreal | .000 | 42 | 1 | 0 | 0 | 0 | 0 | 0 | 0 | 0 | 0 | 0 | 0 | 0 | 0 |
| Robinson, Don, Pittsburgh | .238 | 44 | 21 | 2 | 5 | 10 | 2 | 0 | 1 | 4 | 0 | 4 | 0 | 0 | 0 |
| Robinson, Jeffrey, San Francisco | .000 | 8 | 0 | 0 | 0 | 0 | 0 | 0 | 0 | 0 | 0 | 0 | 0 | 0 | 0 |
| Robinson, Ronald, Cincinnati | .091 | 33 | 22 | 0 | 2 | 2 | 0 | 0 | 0 | 1 | 0 | 5 | 0 | 0 | 0 |
| Rodriguez, Edwin, San Diego | .000 | 1 | 1 | 0 | 0 | 0 | 0 | 0 | 0 | 0 | 0 | 0 | 0 | 0 | 0 |
| Roenicke, Ronald, San Francisco† | .256 | 65 | 133 | 23 | 34 | 54 | 9 | 1 | 3 | 13 | 1 | 1 | 1 | 6 | 2 |
| Rogers, Stephen, Montreal | .143 | 8 | 14 | 1 | 2 | 3 | 1 | 0 | 0 | 1 | 0 | 0 | 0 | 0 | 0 |
| Rose, Peter, Cincinnati† | .264 | 119 | 405 | 60 | 107 | 129 | 12 | 2 | 2 | 46 | 6 | 1 | 4 | 8 | 1 |
| Ross, Mark, Houston | .000 | 8 | 1 | 0 | 0 | 0 | 0 | 0 | 0 | 1 | 0 | 0 | 0 | 0 | 0 |
| Rowdon, Wade, Cincinnati | .222 | 5 | 9 | 2 | 2 | 2 | 0 | 0 | 0 | 2 | 0 | 0 | 0 | 0 | 0 |
| Royster, Jeron, San Diego | .281 | 90 | 249 | 31 | 70 | 102 | 13 | 2 | 5 | 31 | 4 | 3 | 2 | 6 | 5 |
| Rucker, David, Philadelphia* | .333 | 41 | 12 | 2 | 4 | 5 | 1 | 0 | 0 | 0 | 0 | 1 | 0 | 0 | 0 |
| Runge, Paul, Atlanta | .218 | 50 | 87 | 15 | 19 | 25 | 3 | 0 | 1 | 5 | 0 | 4 | 1 | 0 | 1 |
| Runnells, Thomas, Cincinnati† | .200 | 28 | 35 | 3 | 7 | 8 | 1 | 0 | 0 | 0 | 0 | 4 | 0 | 0 | 0 |
| Russell, John, Philadelphia | .218 | 81 | 216 | 22 | 47 | 86 | 12 | 0 | 9 | 23 | 1 | 0 | 0 | 2 | 0 |
| Russell, William, Los Angeles | .260 | 76 | 169 | 19 | 44 | 52 | 6 | 1 | 0 | 13 | 2 | 3 | 1 | 4 | 0 |
| Ruthven, Richard, Chicago | .208 | 20 | 24 | 1 | 5 | 5 | 0 | 0 | 0 | 1 | 0 | 6 | 0 | 0 | 1 |
| Ryan, L. Nolan, Houston | .111 | 35 | 63 | 2 | 7 | 9 | 2 | 0 | 0 | 4 | 0 | 14 | 1 | 0 | 1 |
| St. Claire, Randy, Montreal | .200 | 42 | 5 | 1 | 1 | 1 | 0 | 0 | 0 | 0 | 0 | 1 | 0 | 0 | 0 |
| Sambito, Joseph, New York* | .000 | 8 | 0 | 0 | 0 | 0 | 0 | 0 | 0 | 0 | 0 | 0 | 0 | 0 | 0 |
| Samuel, Juan, Philadelphia | .264 | 161 | 663 | 101 | 175 | 289 | 31 | 13 | 19 | 74 | 13 | 2 | 5 | 53 | 19 |
| Sandberg, Ryne, Chicago | .305 | 153 | 609 | 113 | 186 | 307 | 31 | 6 | 26 | 83 | 10 | 2 | 4 | 51 | 11 |
| Sanderson, Scott, Chicago | .065 | 19 | 31 | 1 | 2 | 2 | 0 | 0 | 0 | 1 | 0 | 6 | 0 | 0 | 0 |
| Santana, Rafael, New York | .257 | 154 | 529 | 41 | 136 | 160 | 19 | 1 | 1 | 29 | 6 | 4 | 2 | 1 | 0 |
| Sax, Stephen, Los Angeles | .279 | 136 | 488 | 62 | 136 | 155 | 8 | 4 | 1 | 42 | 6 | 3 | 3 | 27 | 11 |
| Schatzeder, Daniel, Montreal* | .194 | 24 | 31 | 4 | 6 | 13 | 1 | 0 | 2 | 5 | 1 | 1 | 0 | 0 | 0 |
| Schiraldi, Calvin, New York | .125 | 10 | 8 | 0 | 1 | 1 | 0 | 0 | 0 | 0 | 0 | 0 | 0 | 0 | 0 |
| Schmidt, Michael, Philadelphia | .277 | 158 | 549 | 89 | 152 | 292 | 31 | 5 | 33 | 93 | 8 | 0 | 6 | 1 | 3 |
| Schu, Richard, Philadelphia | .252 | 112 | 416 | 54 | 105 | 155 | 21 | 4 | 7 | 24 | 2 | 1 | 0 | 8 | 6 |
| Schuler, David, Atlanta | .000 | 9 | 0 | 0 | 0 | 0 | 0 | 0 | 0 | 0 | 0 | 0 | 0 | 0 | 0 |
| Scioscia, Michael, Los Angeles* | .296 | 141 | 429 | 47 | 127 | 180 | 26 | 3 | 7 | 53 | 4 | 11 | 3 | 3 | 3 |
| Scott, Michael, Houston | .153 | 36 | 72 | 7 | 11 | 17 | 3 | 0 | 1 | 11 | 1 | 3 | 2 | 1 | 0 |
| Scurry, Rodney, Pittsburgh* | .000 | 30 | 4 | 0 | 0 | 0 | 0 | 0 | 0 | 0 | 0 | 0 | 0 | 0 | 0 |
| Shields, Stephen, Atlanta | .111 | 23 | 18 | 0 | 2 | 2 | 0 | 0 | 0 | 0 | 0 | 0 | 0 | 0 | 0 |
| Shines, A. Raymond, Montreal† | .120 | 47 | 50 | 6 | 6 | 6 | 0 | 0 | 0 | 3 | 1 | 0 | 0 | 0 | 1 |
| Shipanoff, David, Philadelphia | .000 | 26 | 3 | 0 | 0 | 0 | 0 | 0 | 0 | 0 | 0 | 0 | 0 | 0 | 0 |
| Show, Eric, San Diego | .127 | 35 | 79 | 3 | 10 | 13 | 0 | 0 | 1 | 6 | 0 | 7 | 0 | 0 | 0 |
| Sisk, Douglas, New York | .000 | 42 | 12 | 1 | 0 | 0 | 0 | 0 | 0 | 1 | 0 | 0 | 0 | 0 | 0 |
| Smith, Bryn, Montreal | .194 | 32 | 72 | 6 | 14 | 18 | 1 | 0 | 1 | 4 | 0 | 11 | 0 | 0 | 0 |
| Smith, David, Houston | .000 | 64 | 3 | 1 | 0 | 0 | 0 | 0 | 0 | 0 | 0 | 1 | 0 | 0 | 0 |
| Smith, Lee, Chicago | .000 | 65 | 6 | 0 | 0 | 0 | 0 | 0 | 0 | 0 | 0 | 0 | 0 | 0 | 0 |
| Smith, Lonnie, St. Louis | .260 | 28 | 96 | 15 | 25 | 31 | 2 | 2 | 0 | 7 | 1 | 1 | 0 | 12 | 6 |
| Smith, Michael, Cincinnati | .000 | 2 | 0 | 0 | 0 | 0 | 0 | 0 | 0 | 0 | 0 | 0 | 0 | 0 | 0 |
| Smith, Osborne, St. Louis† | .276 | 158 | 537 | 70 | 148 | 194 | 22 | 3 | 6 | 54 | 5 | 9 | 2 | 31 | 8 |
| Smith, Zane, Atlanta* | .162 | 43 | 37 | 1 | 6 | 6 | 0 | 0 | 0 | 3 | 1 | 6 | 0 | 0 | 0 |
| Solano, Julio, Houston | .000 | 20 | 2 | 0 | 0 | 0 | 0 | 0 | 0 | 0 | 0 | 0 | 0 | 0 | 0 |
| Sorensen, Lary, Chicago | .000 | 45 | 6 | 1 | 0 | 0 | 0 | 0 | 0 | 0 | 0 | 4 | 0 | 0 | 0 |
| Soto, Mario, Cincinnati | .133 | 37 | 83 | 3 | 11 | 13 | 0 | 1 | 0 | 4 | 1 | 6 | 0 | 0 | 0 |
| Speier, Chris, Chicago | .243 | 106 | 218 | 16 | 53 | 76 | 11 | 0 | 4 | 24 | 6 | 3 | 2 | 1 | 3 |
| Spilman, W. Harry, Houston* | .136 | 44 | 66 | 3 | 9 | 13 | 1 | 0 | 1 | 4 | 0 | 0 | 0 | 0 | 0 |
| Staub, Daniel, New York* | .267 | 54 | 45 | 2 | 12 | 18 | 3 | 0 | 1 | 8 | 0 | 0 | 0 | 0 | 0 |
| Stewart, David, Philadelphia | .000 | 4 | 0 | 0 | 0 | 0 | 0 | 0 | 0 | 0 | 0 | 0 | 0 | 0 | 0 |
| Stoddard, Timothy, San Diego | .000 | 44 | 5 | 0 | 0 | 0 | 0 | 0 | 0 | 0 | 0 | 1 | 0 | 0 | 0 |
| Stone, Jeffrey, Philadelphia* | .265 | 88 | 264 | 36 | 70 | 89 | 4 | 3 | 3 | 11 | 1 | 2 | 0 | 15 | 5 |
| Strawberry, Darryl, New York* | .277 | 111 | 393 | 78 | 109 | 219 | 15 | 4 | 29 | 79 | 8 | 0 | 3 | 26 | 11 |
| Stubbs, Franklin, Los Angeles* | .222 | 10 | 9 | 0 | 2 | 2 | 0 | 0 | 0 | 2 | 0 | 0 | 0 | 0 | 0 |
| Stuper, John, Cincinnati | .059 | 33 | 17 | 0 | 1 | 1 | 0 | 0 | 0 | 1 | 1 | 7 | 0 | 1 | 1 |
| Surhoff, Richard, Philadelphia | .000 | 2 | 0 | 0 | 0 | 0 | 0 | 0 | 0 | 0 | 0 | 0 | 0 | 0 | 0 |
| Sutcliffe, Richard, Chicago* | .233 | 20 | 43 | 4 | 10 | 13 | 0 | 0 | 1 | 3 | 0 | 2 | 1 | 0 | 0 |
| Sutter, H. Bruce, Atlanta | .000 | 58 | 4 | 0 | 0 | 0 | 0 | 0 | 0 | 0 | 0 | 0 | 0 | 0 | 0 |
| Tekulve, Kenton, Pitt.-Phil. | .000 | 61 | 3 | 0 | 0 | 0 | 0 | 0 | 0 | 0 | 0 | 0 | 0 | 0 | 0 |
| Templeton, Garry, San Diego† | .282 | 148 | 546 | 63 | 154 | 206 | 30 | 2 | 6 | 55 | 5 | 5 | 3 | 16 | 6 |
| Thomas, Andres, Atlanta | .278 | 15 | 18 | 6 | 5 | 5 | 0 | 0 | 0 | 2 | 0 | 1 | 0 | 0 | 0 |
| Thomas, Derrel, Philadelphia† | .207 | 63 | 92 | 16 | 19 | 33 | 2 | 0 | 4 | 12 | 2 | 0 | 0 | 2 | 0 |
| Thompson, Jason, Pittsburgh* | .241 | 123 | 402 | 42 | 97 | 152 | 17 | 1 | 12 | 61 | 6 | 0 | 4 | 0 | 0 |

| Player and Club | Pct. | G. | AB. | R. | H. | TB. | 2B. | 3B. | HR. | RBI. | GW. | SH. | SF. | SB. | CS. |
|---|---|---|---|---|---|---|---|---|---|---|---|---|---|---|---|
| Thompson, Milton, Atlanta* | .302 | 73 | 182 | 17 | 55 | 66 | 7 | 2 | 0 | 6 | 1 | 1 | 0 | 9 | 4 |
| Thompson, V. Scot, S.F.-Mtl.* | .224 | 98 | 143 | 10 | 32 | 38 | 6 | 0 | 0 | 10 | 3 | 1 | 1 | 0 | 0 |
| Thon, Richard, Houston | .251 | 84 | 251 | 26 | 63 | 89 | 6 | 1 | 6 | 29 | 5 | 1 | 2 | 8 | 3 |
| Thurmond, Mark, San Diego* | .088 | 36 | 34 | 2 | 3 | 3 | 0 | 0 | 0 | 2 | 1 | 9 | 1 | 0 | 0 |
| Tibbs, Jay, Cincinnati | .092 | 36 | 65 | 3 | 6 | 6 | 0 | 0 | 0 | 3 | 0 | 6 | 0 | 0 | 0 |
| Toliver, Freddie, Philadelphia | .500 | 11 | 4 | 0 | 2 | 2 | 0 | 0 | 0 | 0 | 0 | 0 | 0 | 0 | 0 |
| Tolman, Timothy, Houston | .140 | 31 | 43 | 4 | 6 | 13 | 1 | 0 | 2 | 8 | 2 | 1 | 0 | 0 | 1 |
| Tomlin, David, Pittsburgh* | .000 | 1 | 0 | 0 | 0 | 0 | 0 | 0 | 0 | 0 | 0 | 0 | 0 | 0 | 0 |
| Trevino, Alejandro, San Francisco... | .217 | 57 | 157 | 17 | 34 | 64 | 10 | 1 | 6 | 19 | 0 | 1 | 1 | 0 | 0 |
| Trillo, J. Manuel, San Francisco | .224 | 125 | 451 | 36 | 101 | 130 | 16 | 2 | 3 | 25 | 4 | 11 | 2 | 2 | 0 |
| Trout, Steven, Chicago* | .109 | 24 | 46 | 2 | 5 | 6 | 1 | 0 | 0 | 2 | 0 | 9 | 0 | 0 | 0 |
| Tudor, John, St. Louis* | .138 | 37 | 94 | 9 | 13 | 20 | 3 | 2 | 0 | 2 | 1 | 7 | 0 | 0 | 1 |
| Tunnell, B. Lee, Pittsburgh | .085 | 24 | 47 | 2 | 4 | 6 | 0 | 1 | 0 | 1 | 0 | 0 | 1 | 0 | 1 |
| Uribe, Jose, San Francisco† | .237 | 147 | 476 | 46 | 113 | 150 | 20 | 4 | 3 | 26 | 3 | 5 | 0 | 8 | 2 |
| Valenzuela, Fernando, Los Angeles* | .216 | 35 | 97 | 7 | 21 | 26 | 2 | 0 | 1 | 7 | 0 | 5 | 1 | 0 | 1 |
| Van Gorder, David, Cincinnati | .238 | 73 | 151 | 12 | 36 | 49 | 7 | 0 | 2 | 24 | 3 | 2 | 3 | 0 | 0 |
| Van Slyke, Andrew, St. Louis* | .259 | 146 | 424 | 61 | 110 | 186 | 25 | 6 | 13 | 55 | 7 | 1 | 1 | 34 | 6 |
| Venable, W. McKinley, Cincinnati*.. | .289 | 77 | 135 | 21 | 39 | 57 | 12 | 3 | 0 | 10 | 3 | 3 | 2 | 11 | 3 |
| Virgil, Osvaldo, Philadelphia | .246 | 131 | 426 | 47 | 105 | 184 | 16 | 3 | 19 | 55 | 7 | 1 | 2 | 0 | 0 |
| Walk, Robert, Pittsburgh | .000 | 9 | 17 | 0 | 0 | 0 | 0 | 0 | 0 | 0 | 0 | 4 | 0 | 0 | 0 |
| Walker, Cleotha, Chicago† | .083 | 21 | 12 | 3 | 1 | 1 | 0 | 0 | 0 | 0 | 0 | 0 | 0 | 1 | 0 |
| Walker, Duane, Cincinnati* | .167 | 37 | 48 | 5 | 8 | 18 | 2 | 1 | 2 | 6 | 0 | 0 | 0 | 1 | 0 |
| Wallach, Timothy, Montreal | .260 | 155 | 569 | 70 | 148 | 256 | 36 | 3 | 22 | 81 | 8 | 0 | 5 | 9 | 9 |
| Walling, Dennis, Houston* | .270 | 119 | 345 | 44 | 93 | 136 | 20 | 1 | 7 | 45 | 4 | 0 | 4 | 5 | 2 |
| Walter, Gene, San Diego* | .000 | 15 | 1 | 0 | 0 | 0 | 0 | 0 | 0 | 0 | 0 | 0 | 0 | 0 | 0 |
| Ward, Colin, San Francisco* | .000 | 6 | 2 | 0 | 0 | 0 | 0 | 0 | 0 | 0 | 0 | 0 | 0 | 0 | 0 |
| Washington, Claudell, Atlanta* | .276 | 122 | 398 | 62 | 110 | 181 | 14 | 6 | 15 | 43 | 2 | 0 | 2 | 14 | 4 |
| Washington, U.L., Montreal† | .249 | 68 | 193 | 24 | 48 | 68 | 9 | 4 | 1 | 17 | 1 | 0 | 1 | 6 | 3 |
| Webster, Mitchell, Montreal† | .274 | 74 | 212 | 32 | 58 | 103 | 8 | 2 | 11 | 30 | 2 | 1 | 1 | 15 | 9 |
| Welch, Robert, Los Angeles | .180 | 25 | 50 | 4 | 9 | 10 | 1 | 0 | 0 | 4 | 0 | 7 | 0 | 0 | 0 |
| Wellman, Brad, San Francisco | .236 | 71 | 174 | 16 | 41 | 54 | 11 | 1 | 0 | 16 | 2 | 5 | 1 | 5 | 2 |
| Whitfield, Terry, Los Angeles* | .260 | 79 | 104 | 8 | 27 | 43 | 7 | 0 | 3 | 16 | 2 | 0 | 0 | 0 | 0 |
| Wiggins, Alan, San Diego† | .054 | 10 | 37 | 3 | 2 | 3 | 1 | 0 | 0 | 0 | 0 | 1 | 0 | 0 | 1 |
| Williams, Frank, San Francisco | .000 | 49 | 3 | 0 | 0 | 0 | 0 | 0 | 0 | 0 | 0 | 1 | 0 | 0 | 0 |
| Williams, Reginald, Los Angeles | .333 | 22 | 9 | 4 | 3 | 3 | 0 | 0 | 0 | 0 | 0 | 0 | 0 | 1 | 0 |
| Willis, Carl, Cincinnati* | .000 | 11 | 1 | 0 | 0 | 0 | 0 | 0 | 0 | 0 | 0 | 1 | 0 | 0 | 0 |
| Wilson, Glenn, Philadelphia | .275 | 161 | 608 | 73 | 167 | 258 | 39 | 5 | 14 | 102 | 12 | 0 | 7 | 7 | 4 |
| Wilson, William, New York† | .276 | 93 | 337 | 56 | 93 | 143 | 16 | 8 | 6 | 26 | 1 | 1 | 1 | 24 | 9 |
| Winn, James, Pittsburgh | .111 | 30 | 18 | 2 | 2 | 3 | 1 | 0 | 0 | 0 | 0 | 2 | 0 | 0 | 0 |
| Winningham, Herman, Montreal* | .237 | 125 | 312 | 30 | 74 | 99 | 6 | 5 | 3 | 21 | 3 | 1 | 4 | 20 | 9 |
| Wockenfuss, Johnny, Philadelphia.... | .162 | 32 | 37 | 1 | 6 | 6 | 0 | 0 | 0 | 2 | 0 | 0 | 0 | 0 | 0 |
| Wohlford, James, Montreal | .192 | 70 | 125 | 7 | 24 | 34 | 5 | 1 | 1 | 15 | 6 | 1 | 0 | 0 | 2 |
| Wojna, Edward, San Diego | .167 | 15 | 12 | 0 | 2 | 2 | 0 | 0 | 0 | 0 | 0 | 0 | 0 | 0 | 0 |
| Woodard, Michael, San Francisco* . | .244 | 24 | 82 | 12 | 20 | 21 | 1 | 0 | 0 | 9 | 0 | 1 | 0 | 6 | 1 |
| Woods, Gary, Chicago | .244 | 81 | 82 | 11 | 20 | 23 | 3 | 0 | 0 | 4 | 0 | 1 | 0 | 0 | 1 |
| Worrell, Todd, St. Louis | .000 | 17 | 1 | 0 | 0 | 0 | 0 | 0 | 0 | 0 | 0 | 0 | 0 | 0 | 0 |
| Wynne, Marvell, Pittsburgh* | .205 | 103 | 337 | 21 | 69 | 87 | 6 | 3 | 2 | 18 | 2 | 7 | 0 | 10 | 5 |
| Yeager, Stephen, Los Angeles | .207 | 53 | 121 | 4 | 25 | 31 | 4 | 1 | 0 | 9 | 2 | 1 | 2 | 0 | 1 |
| Yost, Edgar, Montreal | .182 | 5 | 11 | 1 | 2 | 2 | 0 | 0 | 0 | 0 | 0 | 0 | 0 | 0 | 0 |
| Youmans, Floyd, Montreal | .053 | 14 | 19 | 1 | 1 | 1 | 0 | 0 | 0 | 0 | 0 | 3 | 0 | 0 | 0 |
| Youngblood, Joel, San Francisco | .270 | 95 | 230 | 24 | 62 | 80 | 6 | 0 | 4 | 24 | 1 | 1 | 1 | 3 | 2 |
| Zachry, Patrick, Philadelphia | .000 | 10 | 1 | 0 | 0 | 0 | 0 | 0 | 0 | 0 | 0 | 0 | 0 | 0 | 0 |
| Zuvella, Paul, Atlanta | .253 | 81 | 190 | 16 | 48 | 58 | 8 | 1 | 0 | 4 | 0 | 4 | 0 | 2 | 0 |

AWARDED FIRST BASE ON INTERFERENCE: Baker, Atl. (Fitzgerald); Redus, Cin. (Brenly); Reynolds, L.A. (Ashby); Rose, Cin. (Owen); Scioscia, L.A. (Cerone).

## PLAYERS WITH TWO OR MORE CLUBS
(Alphabetically Arranged With Player's First Club on Top)

| Player and Club | Pct. | G. | AB. | R. | H. | TB. | 2B. | 3B. | HR. | RBI. | GW. | SH. | SF. | Tot. BB. | Int. BB. | HP. | SO. | SB. | CS. | GI. DP. |
|---|---|---|---|---|---|---|---|---|---|---|---|---|---|---|---|---|---|---|---|---|
| Bowa, Chi. | .246 | 72 | 195 | 13 | 48 | 62 | 6 | 4 | 0 | 13 | 3 | 5 | 1 | 11 | 2 | 0 | 20 | 5 | 1 | 3 |
| Bowa, N.Y. | .105 | 14 | 19 | 2 | 2 | 3 | 1 | 0 | 0 | 2 | 1 | 1 | 0 | 2 | 0 | 0 | 2 | 0 | 0 | 0 |
| Bream, L.A. | .132 | 24 | 53 | 4 | 7 | 16 | 0 | 0 | 3 | 6 | 0 | 2 | 1 | 7 | 3 | 0 | 10 | 0 | 0 | 0 |
| Bream, Pitt. | .284 | 26 | 95 | 14 | 27 | 43 | 7 | 0 | 3 | 15 | 3 | 1 | 1 | 11 | 2 | 0 | 14 | 0 | 2 | 4 |
| Cabell, Hou. | .245 | 60 | 143 | 20 | 35 | 51 | 8 | 1 | 2 | 14 | 2 | 0 | 0 | 16 | 0 | 0 | 15 | 3 | 1 | 5 |
| Cabell, L.A. | .292 | 57 | 192 | 20 | 56 | 67 | 11 | 0 | 0 | 22 | 5 | 2 | 0 | 14 | 1 | 0 | 21 | 6 | 2 | 0 |
| Cedeno, Cin. | .241 | 83 | 220 | 24 | 53 | 74 | 12 | 0 | 3 | 30 | 4 | 1 | 2 | 19 | 1 | 3 | 35 | 9 | 5 | 5 |
| Cedeno, St.L. | .434 | 28 | 76 | 14 | 33 | 57 | 4 | 1 | 6 | 19 | 4 | 0 | 1 | 5 | 2 | 0 | 7 | 5 | 1 | 2 |
| Diaz, Phil. | .211 | 26 | 76 | 9 | 16 | 29 | 5 | 1 | 2 | 16 | 0 | 0 | 0 | 6 | 0 | 0 | 7 | 0 | 0 | 5 |
| Diaz, Cin. | .261 | 51 | 161 | 12 | 42 | 59 | 8 | 0 | 3 | 15 | 1 | 2 | 2 | 15 | 0 | 1 | 18 | 0 | 0 | 6 |
| Dilone, Mtl. | .190 | 51 | 84 | 10 | 16 | 20 | 0 | 2 | 0 | 6 | 1 | 0 | 1 | 6 | 0 | 0 | 11 | 7 | 3 | 4 |
| Dilone, S.D. | .217 | 27 | 46 | 8 | 10 | 12 | 0 | 1 | 0 | 1 | 1 | 0 | 0 | 4 | 0 | 0 | 8 | 10 | 3 | 0 |
| Driessen, Mtl. | .250 | 91 | 312 | 31 | 78 | 114 | 18 | 0 | 6 | 25 | 5 | 1 | 2 | 33 | 9 | 2 | 29 | 2 | 2 | 8 |
| Driessen, S.F. | .232 | 54 | 181 | 22 | 42 | 59 | 8 | 0 | 3 | 22 | 1 | 0 | 3 | 17 | 3 | 1 | 22 | 0 | 0 | 2 |
| Foley, Cin. | .196 | 43 | 92 | 7 | 18 | 25 | 5 | 1 | 0 | 6 | 1 | 0 | 0 | 6 | 1 | 0 | 16 | 1 | 0 | 0 |
| Foley, Phil. | .266 | 46 | 158 | 17 | 42 | 59 | 8 | 0 | 3 | 17 | 3 | 0 | 0 | 13 | 7 | 0 | 18 | 1 | 3 | 2 |

| Player and Club | Pct. | G. | AB. | R. | H. | TB. | 2B. | 3B. | HR. | RBI. | GW. | SH. | SF. | Tot. BB. | Int. BB. | HP. | SO. | SB. | CS. | GI. DP. |
|---|---|---|---|---|---|---|---|---|---|---|---|---|---|---|---|---|---|---|---|---|
| Frobel, Pitt. | .202 | 53 | 109 | 14 | 22 | 27 | 5 | 0 | 0 | 7 | 2 | 2 | 0 | 19 | 5 | 0 | 24 | 4 | 3 | 2 |
| Frobel, Mtl. | .130 | 12 | 23 | 3 | 3 | 7 | 1 | 0 | 1 | 4 | 0 | 1 | 0 | 2 | 0 | 0 | 6 | 0 | 0 | 2 |
| Holland, Phil. | .000 | 3 | 0 | 0 | 0 | 0 | 0 | 0 | 0 | 0 | 0 | 0 | 0 | 0 | 0 | 0 | 0 | 0 | 0 | 0 |
| Holland, Pitt. | .400 | 38 | 5 | 1 | 2 | 4 | 0 | 1 | 0 | 0 | 0 | 1 | 0 | 1 | 0 | 0 | 2 | 0 | 0 | 0 |
| Knicely, Cin. | .253 | 48 | 158 | 17 | 40 | 64 | 9 | 0 | 5 | 26 | 2 | 1 | 2 | 16 | 2 | 1 | 34 | 0 | 0 | 6 |
| Knicely, Phil. | .000 | 7 | 7 | 0 | 0 | 0 | 0 | 0 | 0 | 0 | 0 | 0 | 0 | 0 | 0 | 0 | 4 | 0 | 0 | 0 |
| Laskey, S.F. | .133 | 19 | 30 | 1 | 4 | 4 | 0 | 0 | 0 | 1 | 0 | 5 | 0 | 3 | 0 | 1 | 12 | 0 | 0 | 0 |
| Laskey, Mtl. | .143 | 11 | 7 | 1 | 1 | 1 | 0 | 0 | 0 | 1 | 0 | 3 | 0 | 0 | 0 | 0 | 4 | 0 | 0 | 0 |
| LeMaster, S.F. | .000 | 12 | 16 | 1 | 0 | 0 | 0 | 0 | 0 | 0 | 0 | 0 | 0 | 1 | 0 | 0 | 5 | 0 | 0 | 0 |
| LeMaster, Pitt. | .155 | 22 | 58 | 4 | 9 | 12 | 0 | 0 | 1 | 6 | 0 | 2 | 0 | 5 | 2 | 0 | 12 | 1 | 0 | 1 |
| Madlock, Pitt. | .251 | 110 | 399 | 49 | 100 | 155 | 23 | 1 | 10 | 41 | 4 | 3 | 3 | 39 | 2 | 5 | 42 | 3 | 3 | 12 |
| Madlock, L.A. | .360 | 34 | 114 | 20 | 41 | 51 | 4 | 0 | 2 | 15 | 2 | 0 | 1 | 10 | 0 | 3 | 11 | 7 | 1 | 3 |
| Reynolds, L.A. | .266 | 73 | 207 | 22 | 55 | 73 | 10 | 4 | 0 | 25 | 2 | 5 | 3 | 13 | 0 | 1 | 31 | 6 | 3 | 3 |
| Reynolds, Pitt. | .308 | 31 | 130 | 22 | 40 | 60 | 5 | 3 | 3 | 17 | 6 | 2 | 0 | 9 | 1 | 1 | 18 | 12 | 2 | 3 |
| Tekulve, Pitt. | .000 | 3 | 0 | 0 | 0 | 0 | 0 | 0 | 0 | 0 | 0 | 0 | 0 | 0 | 0 | 0 | 0 | 0 | 0 | 0 |
| Tekulve, Phil. | .000 | 58 | 3 | 0 | 0 | 0 | 0 | 0 | 0 | 0 | 0 | 0 | 0 | 0 | 0 | 0 | 1 | 0 | 0 | 0 |
| Thompson, S.F. | .207 | 64 | 111 | 8 | 23 | 28 | 5 | 0 | 0 | 6 | 1 | 1 | 0 | 2 | 0 | 0 | 10 | 0 | 0 | 5 |
| Thompson, Mtl. | .281 | 34 | 32 | 2 | 9 | 10 | 1 | 0 | 0 | 4 | 2 | 0 | 1 | 3 | 0 | 0 | 7 | 0 | 0 | 1 |

# OFFICIAL MISCELLANEOUS NATIONAL LEAGUE
## BATTING RECORDS
### CLUB MISCELLANEOUS BATTING RECORDS

| Club | Slg. Pct. | OB Pct. | Tot. BB. | Int. BB. | HP. | SO. | GIDP. | ShO. |
|---|---|---|---|---|---|---|---|---|
| Chicago | .390 | .324 | 562 | 62 | 18 | 937 | 119 | 14 |
| Houston | .388 | .319 | 477 | 63 | 23 | 873 | 127 | 10 |
| New York | .385 | .323 | 546 | 88 | 20 | 872 | 131 | 11 |
| Philadelphia | .383 | .312 | 527 | 51 | 25 | 1095 | 124 | 13 |
| Los Angeles | .382 | .328 | 539 | 69 | 31 | 846 | 108 | 6 |
| St. Louis | .379 | .335 | 586 | 61 | 18 | 853 | 91 | 8 |
| Cincinnati | .376 | .327 | 576 | 72 | 23 | 856 | 136 | 16 |
| Montreal | .375 | .310 | 492 | 73 | 26 | 880 | 112 | 13 |
| San Diego | .368 | .320 | 513 | 68 | 23 | 809 | 128 | 7 |
| Atlanta | .363 | .315 | 553 | 56 | 22 | 849 | 154 | 18 |
| San Francisco | .348 | .299 | 488 | 53 | 37 | 962 | 121 | 14 |
| Pittsburgh | .347 | .311 | 514 | 64 | 14 | 842 | 131 | 19 |
| Totals | .374 | .319 | 6373 | 780 | 280 | 10674 | 1482 | 149 |

### INDIVIDUAL MISCELLANEOUS BATTING RECORDS
(Top Ten Qualifiers for Slugging Championship)

| Player—Club | Slg. Pct. | OB Pct. | Tot. BB. | Int. BB. | HP. | SO. | GI DP. |
|---|---|---|---|---|---|---|---|
| Guerrero, L.A. | .577 | .422 | 83 | 14 | 6 | 68 | 13 |
| Parker, Cin. | .551 | .365 | 52 | 24 | 3 | 80 | 26 |
| Murphy, Atl. | .539 | .388 | 90 | 15 | 1 | 141 | 14 |
| Schmidt, Phila. | .532 | .375 | 87 | 8 | 3 | 117 | 10 |
| Marshall, L.A. | .515 | .342 | 37 | 6 | 3 | 137 | 8 |
| Sandberg, Chi. | .504 | .364 | 57 | 5 | 1 | 97 | 10 |
| McGee, St.L. | .503 | .384 | 34 | 2 | 0 | 86 | 3 |
| Clark, St.L. | .502 | .393 | 83 | 14 | 2 | 88 | 10 |
| Horner, Atl. | .499 | .333 | 50 | 4 | 1 | 57 | 18 |
| Carter, N.Y. | .488 | .365 | 69 | 16 | 6 | 46 | 18 |

DEPARTMENTAL LEADERS: OB Pct.—Guerrero, .422; TBB—Murphy, 90; IBB—Durham, Parker, Templeton, 24; HP—Brown (S.F.) 11; SO—Murphy, Samuel, 141; GIDP—Parker, 26.

| Player—Club | Slg. Pct. | OB Pct. | Tot. BB. | Int. BB. | HP. | SO. | GI DP. |
|---|---|---|---|---|---|---|---|
| Abrego, Chi. | .000 | .000 | 0 | 0 | 0 | 2 | 0 |
| Adams, S.F. | .281 | .228 | 5 | 3 | 1 | 23 | 2 |
| Aguayo, Phil. | .467 | .378 | 22 | 5 | 6 | 26 | 7 |
| Aguilera, N.Y. | .333 | .297 | 1 | 0 | 0 | 5 | 1 |
| Allen, St.L. | .000 | .000 | 0 | 0 | 0 | 2 | 0 |
| Almon, Pitt. | .414 | .330 | 22 | 0 | 1 | 61 | 6 |
| Andersen, Phil. | .000 | .000 | 0 | 0 | 0 | 0 | 0 |
| Anderson, L.A. | .281 | .310 | 35 | 3 | 1 | 42 | 4 |
| Andujar, St.L. | .128 | .152 | 5 | 0 | 0 | 50 | 2 |
| Ashby, Hou. | .450 | .363 | 24 | 2 | 1 | 27 | 9 |
| Backman, N.Y. | .344 | .320 | 36 | 1 | 1 | 72 | 3 |
| Bailey, Hou. | .398 | .389 | 67 | 13 | 1 | 70 | 16 |
| Bailor, L.A. | .288 | .270 | 3 | 0 | 1 | 5 | 3 |
| Bair, St.L. | .000 | .000 | 0 | 0 | 0 | 0 | 0 |
| Baller, Chi. | .000 | .000 | 0 | 0 | 0 | 6 | 0 |

| Player—Club | Slg. Pct. | OB Pct. | Tot. BB. | Int. BB. | HP. | SO. | GI DP. |
|---|---|---|---|---|---|---|---|
| Barker, Atl. | .000 | .000 | 0 | 0 | 0 | 7 | 0 |
| Barnes, Mtl. | .192 | .154 | 0 | 0 | 0 | 2 | 1 |
| Bass, Hou. | .427 | .315 | 31 | 1 | 6 | 63 | 10 |
| Beane, N.Y. | .375 | .250 | 0 | 0 | 0 | 3 | 0 |
| Beard, Chi. | .000 | .000 | 0 | 0 | 0 | 0 | 0 |
| Bedrosian, Atl. | .078 | .092 | 1 | 0 | 0 | 22 | 0 |
| Bell, Cin. | .368 | .311 | 34 | 2 | 0 | 27 | 10 |
| Belliard, Pitt. | .200 | .200 | 0 | 0 | 0 | 5 | 0 |
| Benedict, Atl. | .231 | .279 | 22 | 1 | 1 | 12 | 8 |
| Berenyi, N.Y. | .500 | .250 | 0 | 0 | 0 | 2 | 0 |
| Bevacqua, S.D. | .348 | .349 | 25 | 5 | 0 | 17 | 3 |
| Bielecki, Pitt. | .000 | .091 | 1 | 0 | 0 | 5 | 0 |
| Bilardello, Cin. | .196 | .206 | 4 | 1 | 1 | 15 | 5 |
| Blocker, N.Y. | .067 | .125 | 1 | 0 | 0 | 2 | 0 |
| Blue, S.F. | .167 | .212 | 3 | 0 | 0 | 12 | 0 |
| Bochy, S.D. | .446 | .305 | 6 | 1 | 0 | 30 | 1 |
| Boever, St.L. | .000 | .000 | 0 | 0 | 0 | 0 | 0 |
| Booker, S.D. | .000 | .000 | 0 | 0 | 0 | 0 | 0 |
| Bosley, Chi. | .511 | .391 | 20 | 1 | 0 | 29 | 3 |
| Botelho, Chi. | .143 | .200 | 1 | 0 | 0 | 5 | 0 |
| Bowa, Chi.-N.Y. | .304 | .276 | 13 | 2 | 0 | 22 | 3 |
| Braun, St.L. | .343 | .342 | 10 | 1 | 1 | 9 | 0 |
| Bream, L.A.-Pitt. | .399 | .310 | 18 | 5 | 0 | 24 | 4 |
| Brenly, S.F. | .391 | .311 | 57 | 5 | 2 | 62 | 6 |
| Brennan, L.A. | .125 | .125 | 0 | 0 | 0 | 1 | 0 |
| Brock, L.A. | .438 | .332 | 54 | 4 | 0 | 72 | 9 |
| Brooks, Mtl. | .413 | .310 | 34 | 6 | 5 | 79 | 20 |
| Brown, S.F. | .442 | .345 | 38 | 4 | 11 | 78 | 19 |
| Brown, Pitt. | .512 | .391 | 22 | 4 | 0 | 27 | 7 |
| Brown, S.D. | .190 | .200 | 5 | 0 | 0 | 20 | 2 |
| Browning, Cin. | .239 | .228 | 4 | 0 | 0 | 29 | 2 |
| Brusstar, Chi. | .143 | .250 | 1 | 0 | 0 | 5 | 0 |
| Bryant, L.A. | .333 | .333 | 0 | 0 | 0 | 2 | 0 |
| Buchanan, Cin. | .000 | .000 | 0 | 0 | 0 | 0 | 0 |

| Player—Club | Slg. Pct. | OB Pct. | Tot. BB. | Int. BB. | HP. | SO. | GI DP. |
|---|---|---|---|---|---|---|---|
| Bullock, Hou. | .360 | .308 | 1 | 0 | 0 | 3 | 0 |
| Bumbry, S.D. | .263 | .255 | 7 | 0 | 0 | 9 | 4 |
| Burke, Mtl. | .100 | .182 | 1 | 0 | 0 | 5 | 0 |
| Butera, Mtl. | .283 | .281 | 13 | 1 | 1 | 12 | 1 |
| Cabell, Hou.-L.A. | .352 | .332 | 30 | 1 | 0 | 36 | 5 |
| Calhoun, Hou. | .000 | .143 | 1 | 0 | 0 | 2 | 0 |
| Camp, Atl. | .462 | .286 | 1 | 0 | 0 | 5 | 0 |
| Campbell, St.L. | .333 | .556 | 3 | 0 | 0 | 2 | 0 |
| Candelaria, Pitt. | .000 | .000 | 0 | 0 | 0 | 1 | 0 |
| Carlton, Phil. | .214 | .200 | 1 | 0 | 0 | 8 | 1 |
| Carman, Phil. | .000 | .000 | 0 | 0 | 0 | 1 | 0 |
| Carter, N.Y. | .488 | .365 | 69 | 16 | 6 | 46 | 18 |
| Castillo, L.A. | .100 | .182 | 1 | 0 | 0 | 4 | 0 |
| Cedeno, Cin.-St.L. | .443 | .347 | 24 | 3 | 3 | 42 | 7 |
| Cerone, Atl. | .280 | .288 | 29 | 1 | 1 | 25 | 15 |
| Cey, Chi. | .408 | .316 | 58 | 9 | 4 | 106 | 10 |
| Chambliss, Atl. | .329 | .307 | 18 | 4 | 0 | 22 | 5 |
| Chapman, N.Y. | .194 | .231 | 9 | 0 | 2 | 15 | 2 |
| Childress, Phil. | .167 | .167 | 0 | 0 | 0 | 2 | 0 |
| Christensen, N.Y. | .319 | .303 | 19 | 1 | 0 | 23 | 3 |
| Clark, St.L. | .502 | .393 | 83 | 14 | 2 | 88 | 10 |
| Clements, Pitt. | .333 | .333 | 0 | 0 | 0 | 2 | 0 |
| Coleman, St.L. | .335 | .320 | 50 | 1 | 0 | 115 | 3 |
| Concepcion, Cin. | .330 | .314 | 50 | 3 | 3 | 67 | 23 |
| Corcoran, Phil. | .258 | .312 | 29 | 4 | 0 | 20 | 6 |
| Cox, St.L. | .165 | .200 | 4 | 0 | 1 | 24 | 1 |
| Cruz, Hou. | .426 | .349 | 43 | 10 | 0 | 74 | 11 |
| Darling, N.Y. | .224 | .213 | 4 | 0 | 0 | 25 | 0 |
| Daulton, Phil. | .369 | .311 | 16 | 0 | 0 | 37 | 1 |
| C. Davis, S.F. | .412 | .349 | 62 | 12 | 0 | 74 | 16 |
| Davis, Cin. | .516 | .287 | 7 | 0 | 0 | 39 | 1 |
| Davis, S.D. | .379 | .349 | 5 | 0 | 0 | 7 | 2 |
| Davis, Hou. | .474 | .332 | 27 | 6 | 7 | 68 | 12 |
| Davis, Chi. | .400 | .300 | 48 | 5 | 0 | 83 | 14 |
| M. Davis, S.F. | .417 | .250 | 0 | 0 | 0 | 5 | 0 |
| Davis, Pitt. | .143 | .143 | 0 | 0 | 0 | 0 | 1 |
| Dawley, Hou. | .200 | .273 | 1 | 0 | 0 | 3 | 0 |
| Dawson, Mtl. | .444 | .295 | 29 | 8 | 4 | 92 | 12 |
| Dayett, Chi. | .346 | .259 | 0 | 0 | 1 | 6 | 1 |
| Dayley, St.L. | .400 | .400 | 0 | 0 | 0 | 1 | 0 |
| Dedmon, Atl. | .111 | .200 | 1 | 0 | 0 | 3 | 0 |
| Deer, S.F. | .377 | .283 | 23 | 0 | 0 | 71 | 0 |
| DeJesus, St.L. | .292 | .260 | 4 | 0 | 0 | 16 | 0 |
| DeLeon, Pitt. | .056 | .128 | 3 | 0 | 0 | 19 | 0 |
| DeLeon, S.D. | .200 | .200 | 0 | 0 | 0 | 1 | 0 |
| Denny, Phil. | .136 | .165 | 4 | 0 | 0 | 19 | 0 |
| Dernier, Chi. | .316 | .315 | 40 | 1 | 3 | 44 | 7 |
| Deshaies, Hou. | .000 | .000 | 0 | 0 | 0 | 0 | 0 |
| Diaz, Phil.-Cin. | .371 | .307 | 21 | 0 | 1 | 25 | 11 |
| Diaz, L.A. | .000 | .000 | 0 | 0 | 0 | 1 | 0 |
| Dilone, Mtl.-S.D. | .246 | .255 | 10 | 0 | 0 | 19 | 4 |
| DiPino, Hou. | .167 | .167 | 0 | 0 | 0 | 7 | 0 |
| Dopson, Mtl. | .000 | .333 | 2 | 0 | 0 | 3 | 0 |
| Doran, Hou. | .434 | .362 | 71 | 6 | 0 | 69 | 10 |
| Dravecky, S.F. | .159 | .164 | 4 | 0 | 0 | 20 | 0 |
| Driessen, Mtl.-S.F. | .351 | .314 | 50 | 12 | 3 | 51 | 10 |
| Duncan, L.A. | .340 | .293 | 38 | 4 | 3 | 113 | 9 |
| Dunston, Chi. | .388 | .310 | 19 | 3 | 0 | 42 | 3 |
| Durham, Chi. | .465 | .357 | 64 | 24 | 0 | 99 | 5 |
| Dybzinski, Pitt. | .000 | .000 | 0 | 0 | 0 | 0 | 0 |
| Dykstra, N.Y. | .331 | .358 | 30 | 0 | 1 | 24 | 4 |
| Eckersley, Chi. | .179 | .222 | 7 | 0 | 0 | 25 | 0 |
| Engel, Chi. | .375 | .316 | 3 | 0 | 0 | 7 | 0 |
| Esasky, Cin. | .465 | .332 | 41 | 3 | 4 | 102 | 9 |
| Fernandez, N.Y. | .250 | .212 | 0 | 0 | 0 | 26 | 1 |
| Fitzgerald, Mtl. | .288 | .297 | 38 | 12 | 2 | 55 | 8 |
| Flannery, S.D. | .341 | .386 | 58 | 1 | 9 | 39 | 4 |
| Flynn, Mtl. | .167 | .167 | 0 | 0 | 0 | 0 | 0 |
| Foley, Cin.-Phil. | .336 | .294 | 19 | 8 | 0 | 34 | 2 |
| Foli, Pitt. | .189 | .268 | 4 | 1 | 0 | 2 | 4 |
| Fontenot, Chi. | .049 | .049 | 0 | 0 | 0 | 18 | 1 |
| Ford, St.L. | .667 | .625 | 4 | 0 | 0 | 1 | 0 |
| Forsch, St.L. | .400 | .244 | 0 | 0 | 0 | 10 | 0 |
| Forster, Atl. | .000 | .000 | 0 | 0 | 0 | 0 | 0 |
| Foster, N.Y. | .460 | .331 | 46 | 5 | 2 | 87 | 8 |
| Franco, Cin. | .333 | .333 | 0 | 0 | 0 | 0 | 0 |
| Francona, Mtl. | .349 | .299 | 12 | 4 | 1 | 12 | 1 |
| Frazier, Chi. | .000 | .000 | 0 | 0 | 0 | 4 | 0 |
| Frobel, Pitt.-Mtl. | .258 | .301 | 21 | 5 | 0 | 30 | 4 |
| Gainey, Hou. | .162 | .244 | 2 | 0 | 2 | 9 | 0 |
| Galarraga, Mtl. | .280 | .228 | 3 | 0 | 1 | 18 | 0 |
| Garber, Atl. | .200 | .200 | 0 | 0 | 0 | 1 | 0 |
| Garcia, Phil. | .000 | .000 | 0 | 0 | 0 | 1 | 0 |
| Gardenhire, N.Y. | .282 | .319 | 8 | 0 | 0 | 11 | 2 |
| Gardner, N.Y. | .000 | .000 | 0 | 0 | 0 | 0 | 0 |
| Garner, Hou. | .400 | .317 | 34 | 3 | 2 | 72 | 12 |
| Garrelts, S.F. | .333 | .300 | 1 | 0 | 0 | 4 | 0 |
| Garvey, S.D. | .430 | .318 | 35 | 7 | 3 | 67 | 25 |
| Gladden, S.F. | .347 | .307 | 40 | 1 | 7 | 78 | 10 |
| Glynn, Mtl. | .000 | .000 | 0 | 0 | 0 | 0 | 0 |
| Gonzalez, Pitt. | .355 | .299 | 13 | 2 | 0 | 27 | 1 |
| Gonzalez, L.A. | .455 | .333 | 1 | 0 | 0 | 3 | 1 |
| Gooden, N.Y. | .280 | .265 | 5 | 0 | 0 | 15 | 1 |
| Gorman, N.Y. | .000 | .000 | 0 | 0 | 0 | 3 | 0 |
| Gossage, S.D. | .000 | .154 | 2 | 0 | 0 | 5 | 0 |
| Gott, S.F. | .412 | .212 | 1 | 0 | 0 | 30 | 0 |
| Grapenthin, Mtl. | 1.000 | 1.000 | 0 | 0 | 0 | 0 | 0 |
| Green, S.F. | .347 | .301 | 22 | 3 | 1 | 58 | 12 |
| G. Gross, Phil. | .314 | .374 | 32 | 1 | 0 | 9 | 5 |
| K. Gross, Phil. | .215 | .164 | 2 | 0 | 0 | 23 | 1 |
| Guante, Pitt. | .059 | .059 | 0 | 0 | 0 | 12 | 0 |
| Guerrero, L.A. | .577 | .422 | 83 | 14 | 6 | 68 | 13 |
| Gullickson, Mtl. | .250 | .188 | 0 | 0 | 0 | 17 | 1 |
| Gumpert, Chi. | .000 | .000 | 0 | 0 | 0 | 1 | 0 |
| Gura, Chi. | .000 | .143 | 1 | 0 | 0 | 4 | 0 |
| Gwynn, S.D. | .408 | .364 | 45 | 4 | 2 | 33 | 17 |
| Hall, Atl. | .191 | .286 | 9 | 1 | 0 | 12 | 3 |
| Hammaker, S.F. | .085 | .085 | 0 | 0 | 0 | 17 | 0 |
| Harper, St.L. | .327 | .273 | 2 | 0 | 0 | 3 | 2 |
| Harper, Atl. | .407 | .327 | 44 | 4 | 3 | 76 | 13 |
| Hassler, St.L. | .000 | .000 | 0 | 0 | 0 | 0 | 0 |
| Hatcher, Chi. | .368 | .290 | 8 | 0 | 3 | 12 | 9 |
| Hawkins, S.D. | .078 | .113 | 3 | 0 | 0 | 16 | 1 |
| Hayes, Phil. | .398 | .332 | 61 | 6 | 0 | 99 | 6 |
| Heathcock, Hou. | .063 | .250 | 4 | 0 | 0 | 11 | 0 |
| Hebner, Chi. | .308 | .266 | 7 | 1 | 1 | 15 | 2 |
| Heep, N.Y. | .421 | .341 | 27 | 1 | 1 | 27 | 12 |
| Hendrick, Pitt. | .313 | .278 | 18 | 1 | 0 | 42 | 11 |
| Hernandez, N.Y. | .430 | .384 | 77 | 15 | 2 | 59 | 14 |
| Herr, St.L. | .416 | .379 | 80 | 5 | 2 | 55 | 6 |
| Hershiser, L.A. | .211 | .247 | 4 | 0 | 1 | 20 | 0 |
| Hesketh, Mtl. | .091 | .167 | 4 | 0 | 0 | 30 | 1 |
| Holland, Phil.-Pitt. | .800 | .500 | 1 | 0 | 0 | 2 | 0 |
| Holton, L.A. | .000 | .000 | 0 | 0 | 0 | 0 | 0 |
| Honeycutt, L.A. | .158 | .195 | 3 | 0 | 0 | 6 | 1 |
| Horner, Atl. | .499 | .333 | 50 | 4 | 1 | 57 | 18 |
| Horton, St.L. | .063 | .211 | 3 | 0 | 0 | 5 | 0 |
| Howe, St.L. | .000 | .000 | 0 | 0 | 0 | 0 | 0 |
| Howe, L.A. | .000 | .000 | 0 | 0 | 0 | 0 | 0 |
| Howell, L.A. | .000 | .000 | 0 | 0 | 0 | 2 | 0 |
| Hoyt, S.D. | .063 | .077 | 1 | 0 | 0 | 21 | 1 |
| Hubbard, Atl. | .314 | .321 | 56 | 2 | 4 | 54 | 11 |
| Hudson, Phil. | .140 | .169 | 1 | 0 | 1 | 18 | 1 |
| Hume, Cin. | .000 | .000 | 0 | 0 | 0 | 0 | 0 |
| Hunt, St.L. | .158 | .158 | 0 | 0 | 0 | 5 | 0 |
| Hurdle, N.Y. | .354 | .313 | 13 | 3 | 1 | 20 | 1 |
| Jackson, Chi. | .091 | .091 | 0 | 0 | 0 | 0 | 0 |
| Jackson, S.D. | .000 | .000 | 0 | 0 | 0 | 3 | 0 |
| Jeffcoat, S.F. | .000 | .500 | 1 | 0 | 0 | 0 | 0 |
| Jeltz, Phil. | .219 | .283 | 26 | 4 | 0 | 55 | 6 |
| Johnson, N.Y. | .393 | .300 | 34 | 10 | 0 | 78 | 6 |
| Johnson, Atl. | .087 | .154 | 3 | 0 | 0 | 8 | 0 |
| Johnson, St.L. | .000 | .000 | 0 | 0 | 0 | 0 | 0 |
| Johnstone, L.A. | .200 | .188 | 1 | 1 | 0 | 2 | 2 |
| Jones, Hou. | .200 | .286 | 3 | 0 | 0 | 7 | 0 |
| Jorgensen, St.L. | .250 | .375 | 31 | 0 | 1 | 27 | 3 |
| Kemp, Pitt. | .347 | .317 | 25 | 1 | 0 | 54 | 5 |
| Kennedy, S.D. | .372 | .301 | 31 | 10 | 0 | 102 | 19 |
| Keough, St.L. | .000 | .000 | 0 | 0 | 0 | 0 | 1 |
| Kepshire, St.L. | .176 | .132 | 1 | 0 | 0 | 18 | 0 |
| Kerfeld, Hou. | .000 | .000 | 0 | 0 | 0 | 9 | 0 |
| Khalifa, Pitt. | .319 | .307 | 34 | 8 | 0 | 56 | 9 |
| Kipper, Pitt. | .250 | .250 | 0 | 0 | 0 | 3 | 0 |
| Knepper, Hou. | .192 | .163 | 2 | 0 | 0 | 38 | 0 |
| Knicely, Cin.-Phil. | .388 | .310 | 16 | 2 | 1 | 38 | 6 |
| Knight, N.Y. | .328 | .252 | 13 | 1 | 1 | 32 | 17 |
| Knudson, Hou. | .000 | .333 | 1 | 0 | 0 | 2 | 0 |
| Komminsk, Atl. | .327 | .314 | 38 | 1 | 1 | 71 | 4 |

| Player—Club | Slg. Pct. | OB Pct. | Tot. BB. | Int. BB. | HP. | SO. | GI DP. |
|---|---|---|---|---|---|---|---|
| Koosman, Phil. | .088 | .111 | 1 | 0 | 0 | 9 | 2 |
| Krawczyk, Pitt. | .000 | .000 | 0 | 0 | 0 | 0 | 0 |
| Krenchicki, Cin. | .393 | .369 | 28 | 4 | 0 | 20 | 3 |
| Krukow, S.F. | .345 | .259 | 1 | 0 | 2 | 15 | 0 |
| Kuiper, S.F. | .600 | .667 | 1 | 0 | 0 | 0 | 0 |
| Lahti, St.L. | .000 | .000 | 0 | 0 | 0 | 5 | 0 |
| LaPoint, S.F. | .183 | .242 | 6 | 0 | 0 | 11 | 0 |
| Lake, Chi. | .193 | .177 | 3 | 1 | 1 | 21 | 3 |
| Landreaux, L.A. | .405 | .311 | 33 | 2 | 1 | 37 | 9 |
| Landrum, St.L. | .429 | .356 | 19 | 1 | 0 | 30 | 3 |
| Laskey, S.F.-Mtl. | .135 | .220 | 3 | 0 | 1 | 16 | 0 |
| Latham, N.Y. | .333 | .500 | 1 | 0 | 0 | 0 | 0 |
| Lavalliere, St.L. | .176 | .273 | 7 | 0 | 0 | 3 | 2 |
| Law, Mtl. | .405 | .369 | 86 | 0 | 2 | 96 | 11 |
| Lawless, St.L. | .293 | .270 | 5 | 0 | 0 | 4 | 0 |
| Leach, N.Y. | .250 | .231 | 1 | 0 | 0 | 8 | 0 |
| Lefferts, S.D. | .250 | .250 | 0 | 0 | 0 | 2 | 0 |
| LeMaster, SF-Pitt. | .162 | .188 | 6 | 2 | 0 | 17 | 1 |
| Leonard, S.F. | .393 | .272 | 21 | 5 | 1 | 107 | 19 |
| Lezcano, Pitt. | .302 | .392 | 35 | 3 | 1 | 17 | 3 |
| Lopes, Chi. | .444 | .383 | 46 | 1 | 0 | 37 | 14 |
| Loucks, Pitt. | .571 | .444 | 2 | 0 | 0 | 2 | 0 |
| Lucas, Mtl. | .000 | .000 | 0 | 0 | 0 | 4 | 0 |
| Lynch, N.Y. | .077 | .127 | 3 | 0 | 0 | 30 | 1 |
| Madden, Hou. | .000 | .000 | 0 | 0 | 0 | 0 | 0 |
| Maddox, Phil. | .339 | .281 | 13 | 2 | 1 | 26 | 4 |
| Madlock, Pitt.-L.A. | .402 | .345 | 49 | 2 | 8 | 53 | 15 |
| Mahler, Mtl. | .313 | .188 | 0 | 0 | 0 | 5 | 0 |
| Mahler, Atl. | .167 | .181 | 3 | 0 | 0 | 18 | 2 |
| Maldonado, L.A. | .338 | .288 | 19 | 4 | 0 | 40 | 3 |
| Manrique, Mtl. | .769 | .357 | 1 | 0 | 0 | 3 | 0 |
| Marshall, L.A. | .515 | .342 | 37 | 6 | 3 | 137 | 8 |
| Martinez, S.D. | .434 | .362 | 87 | 4 | 3 | 82 | 10 |
| Mason, S.F. | .091 | .167 | 0 | 0 | 1 | 5 | 1 |
| Mathis, Hou. | .071 | .133 | 1 | 0 | 0 | 6 | 0 |
| Matthews, Chi. | .406 | .362 | 59 | 2 | 2 | 64 | 8 |
| Matuszek, L.A. | .429 | .307 | 8 | 2 | 1 | 14 | 0 |
| Mazzilli, Pitt. | .376 | .425 | 29 | 1 | 0 | 17 | 3 |
| McCullers, S.D. | .000 | .000 | 0 | 0 | 0 | 4 | 0 |
| McDowell, N.Y. | .211 | .200 | 1 | 0 | 0 | 7 | 0 |
| McGaffigan, Cin. | .069 | .067 | 1 | 0 | 0 | 18 | 0 |
| McGee, St.L. | .503 | .384 | 34 | 2 | 0 | 86 | 3 |
| McMurtry, Atl. | .071 | .071 | 0 | 0 | 0 | 7 | 1 |
| McReynolds, S.D. | .371 | .290 | 43 | 6 | 3 | 81 | 17 |
| McWilliams, Pitt. | .150 | .146 | 1 | 0 | 0 | 19 | 1 |
| Meridith, Chi. | .250 | .400 | 1 | 0 | 0 | 1 | 0 |
| Milner, Cin. | .347 | .342 | 61 | 3 | 1 | 31 | 3 |
| Minton, S.F. | .000 | .111 | 1 | 0 | 0 | 6 | 0 |
| Mizerock, Hou. | .342 | .293 | 2 | 0 | 1 | 8 | 4 |
| Moore, S.F. | .000 | .000 | 0 | 0 | 0 | 0 | 0 |
| Moreland, Chi. | .440 | .374 | 68 | 7 | 1 | 58 | 14 |
| Morrison, Pitt. | .344 | .277 | 8 | 1 | 0 | 44 | 4 |
| Mumphrey, Hou. | .396 | .329 | 37 | 8 | 0 | 57 | 9 |
| Murphy, Atl. | .539 | .388 | 90 | 15 | 1 | 141 | 14 |
| Murphy, Cin. | .000 | .000 | 0 | 0 | 0 | 0 | 0 |
| Myers, N.Y. | .000 | .000 | 0 | 0 | 0 | 0 | 0 |
| Nettles, S.D. | .420 | .363 | 72 | 5 | 0 | 59 | 10 |
| Newman, Mtl. | .207 | .250 | 3 | 0 | 0 | 4 | 0 |
| Nicosia, Mtl. | .197 | .244 | 7 | 0 | 0 | 11 | 2 |
| Niedenfuer, L.A. | .111 | .111 | 0 | 0 | 0 | 3 | 0 |
| Niekro, Hou. | .265 | .257 | 1 | 0 | 0 | 16 | 4 |
| Niemann, N.Y. | .000 | .000 | 0 | 0 | 0 | 0 | 0 |
| Nieto, St.L. | .281 | .305 | 26 | 8 | 3 | 37 | 9 |
| Nokes, S.F. | .358 | .236 | 1 | 0 | 1 | 9 | 2 |
| Oberkfell, Atl. | .359 | .359 | 51 | 6 | 6 | 38 | 10 |
| O'Berry, Phil. | .190 | .320 | 4 | 0 | 0 | 3 | 0 |
| O'Connor, Mtl. | .000 | .000 | 0 | 0 | 0 | 0 | 0 |
| Oester, Cin. | .361 | .354 | 51 | 17 | 0 | 65 | 13 |
| Oliver, L.A. | .316 | .294 | 5 | 0 | 0 | 11 | 3 |
| O'Neill, Cin. | .417 | .333 | 0 | 0 | 0 | 2 | 0 |
| Orosco, N.Y. | .429 | .429 | 0 | 0 | 0 | 1 | 0 |
| Orsulak, Pitt. | .365 | .342 | 26 | 3 | 1 | 27 | 5 |
| Ortiz, Pitt. | .361 | .320 | 3 | 1 | 0 | 17 | 1 |
| Owen, Chi. | .368 | .400 | 1 | 0 | 0 | 5 | 0 |
| Owen, Atl. | .366 | .313 | 8 | 3 | 0 | 17 | 2 |
| Paciorek, N.Y. | .353 | .325 | 6 | 1 | 1 | 14 | 2 |
| Palmer, Mtl. | .139 | .111 | 0 | 0 | 0 | 10 | 2 |
| Pankovits, Hou. | .331 | .316 | 17 | 1 | 1 | 29 | 3 |
| Parker, Cin. | .551 | .365 | 52 | 24 | 3 | 80 | 26 |
| Pastore, Cin. | .214 | .143 | 0 | 0 | 0 | 6 | 0 |
| Patterson, Chi. | .100 | .182 | 1 | 0 | 0 | 4 | 0 |
| Patterson, S.D. | .000 | .000 | 0 | 0 | 0 | 0 | 0 |
| Pederson, L.A. | .000 | .000 | 0 | 0 | 0 | 2 | 0 |
| Pena, Hou. | .345 | .290 | 1 | 0 | 0 | 6 | 1 |
| Pena, L.A. | .000 | .000 | 0 | 0 | 0 | 0 | 0 |
| Pena, Pitt. | .361 | .284 | 29 | 4 | 0 | 67 | 19 |
| Pendleton, St.L. | .306 | .285 | 37 | 4 | 0 | 75 | 18 |
| Perez, Cin. | .470 | .396 | 22 | 1 | 0 | 22 | 2 |
| Perez, Atl. | .120 | .214 | 3 | 0 | 0 | 13 | 0 |
| Perlman, Chi. | .000 | .000 | 0 | 0 | 0 | 1 | 0 |
| Perry, Atl. | .273 | .282 | 23 | 1 | 0 | 28 | 7 |
| Perry, St.L. | .500 | .500 | 0 | 0 | 0 | 0 | 0 |
| Porter, St.L. | .413 | .335 | 41 | 6 | 1 | 48 | 3 |
| Powell, L.A. | .000 | .000 | 0 | 0 | 0 | 2 | 0 |
| Power, Cin. | .000 | 1.000 | 1 | 0 | 0 | 0 | 0 |
| Price, Cin. | .000 | .067 | 1 | 0 | 0 | 7 | 0 |
| Puhl, Hou. | .418 | .343 | 18 | 4 | 1 | 23 | 0 |
| Rabb, Atl. | .000 | .000 | 0 | 0 | 0 | 1 | 0 |
| Raines, Mtl. | .475 | .405 | 81 | 13 | 3 | 60 | 9 |
| Rajsich, S.F. | .231 | .296 | 17 | 4 | 0 | 22 | 0 |
| Ramirez, S.D. | .383 | .317 | 3 | 0 | 0 | 11 | 0 |
| Ramirez, Atl. | .333 | .272 | 20 | 1 | 0 | 63 | 21 |
| Ramsey, L.A. | .200 | .235 | 2 | 0 | 0 | 4 | 0 |
| Rawley, Phil. | .155 | .200 | 5 | 0 | 0 | 21 | 0 |
| Ray, Pitt. | .375 | .325 | 46 | 10 | 1 | 24 | 11 |
| Reardon, Mtl. | .286 | .286 | 0 | 0 | 0 | 4 | 0 |
| Redus, Cin. | .415 | .366 | 44 | 2 | 1 | 52 | 0 |
| Reuschel, Pitt. | .254 | .210 | 3 | 0 | 0 | 17 | 0 |
| Reuss, L.A. | .135 | .156 | 2 | 0 | 0 | 28 | 1 |
| Reyes, L.A. | .000 | .667 | 1 | 0 | 1 | 1 | 0 |
| Reynolds, Hou. | .393 | .293 | 12 | 2 | 0 | 30 | 4 |
| Reynolds, L.A.-Pitt. | .395 | .327 | 22 | 1 | 2 | 49 | 6 |
| Reynolds, N.Y. | .256 | .227 | 0 | 0 | 1 | 18 | 1 |
| Rhoden, Pitt. | .230 | .211 | 2 | 0 | 0 | 7 | 2 |
| Rivera, Hou. | .306 | .275 | 4 | 1 | 0 | 8 | 2 |
| Roberge, Mtl. | .000 | .000 | 0 | 0 | 0 | 1 | 0 |
| Robinson, Pitt. | .476 | .273 | 0 | 0 | 1 | 11 | 0 |
| Robinson, S.F. | .000 | .000 | 0 | 0 | 0 | 0 | 0 |
| Robinson, S.F. | .091 | .091 | 0 | 0 | 0 | 8 | 0 |
| Rodriguez, S.D. | .000 | .000 | 0 | 0 | 0 | 0 | 0 |
| Roenicke, S.F. | .406 | .408 | 35 | 3 | 0 | 27 | 1 |
| Rogers, Mtl. | .214 | .143 | 0 | 0 | 0 | 10 | 0 |
| Rose, Cin. | .319 | .395 | 86 | 5 | 4 | 35 | 10 |
| Ross, Hou. | .000 | .000 | 0 | 0 | 0 | 0 | 0 |
| Rowdon, Cin. | .222 | .364 | 2 | 0 | 0 | 1 | 0 |
| Royster, S.D. | .410 | .363 | 32 | 1 | 1 | 31 | 6 |
| Rucker, Phil. | .417 | .385 | 1 | 0 | 0 | 5 | 0 |
| Runge, Atl. | .287 | .349 | 18 | 0 | 0 | 18 | 3 |
| Runnells, Cin. | .229 | .263 | 3 | 0 | 0 | 4 | 1 |
| Russell, Phil. | .398 | .278 | 18 | 0 | 0 | 72 | 5 |
| Russell, L.A. | .308 | .333 | 18 | 1 | 1 | 9 | 2 |
| Ruthven, Chi. | .208 | .208 | 0 | 0 | 0 | 7 | 1 |
| Ryan, Hou. | .143 | .162 | 4 | 0 | 0 | 21 | 1 |
| St. Claire, Mtl. | .200 | .429 | 2 | 0 | 0 | 3 | 0 |
| Sambito, N.Y. | .000 | .000 | 0 | 0 | 0 | 0 | 0 |
| Samuel, Phil. | .436 | .303 | 33 | 2 | 6 | 141 | 8 |
| Sandberg, Chi. | .504 | .364 | 57 | 5 | 1 | 97 | 10 |
| Sanderson, Chi. | .065 | .121 | 1 | 0 | 0 | 17 | 0 |
| Santana, N.Y. | .302 | .295 | 29 | 12 | 0 | 54 | 14 |
| Sax, L.A. | .318 | .352 | 54 | 12 | 3 | 43 | 15 |
| Schatzeder, Mtl. | .419 | .219 | 1 | 0 | 0 | 10 | 1 |
| Schiraldi, N.Y. | .125 | .125 | 0 | 0 | 0 | 4 | 1 |
| Schmidt, Phil. | .532 | .375 | 87 | 8 | 3 | 117 | 10 |
| Schu, Phil. | .373 | .318 | 38 | 3 | 2 | 78 | 7 |
| Schuler, Atl. | .000 | .000 | 0 | 0 | 0 | 0 | 0 |
| Scioscia, L.A. | .420 | .407 | 77 | 9 | 5 | 21 | 10 |
| Scott, Hou. | .236 | .192 | 4 | 0 | 0 | 24 | 2 |
| Scurry, S.D. | .000 | .000 | 0 | 0 | 0 | 2 | 0 |
| Shields, Atl. | .111 | .158 | 1 | 0 | 0 | 6 | 0 |
| Shines, Mtl. | .120 | .185 | 4 | 0 | 0 | 9 | 2 |
| Shipanoff, Phil. | .000 | .000 | 0 | 0 | 0 | 3 | 0 |
| Show, S.D. | .165 | .138 | 0 | 0 | 1 | 30 | 0 |
| Sisk, N.Y. | .000 | .000 | 0 | 0 | 0 | 7 | 0 |
| Smith, Mtl. | .250 | .227 | 3 | 0 | 0 | 24 | 1 |
| Smith, Hou. | .000 | .250 | 1 | 0 | 0 | 2 | 0 |
| Smith, Chi. | .000 | .143 | 1 | 0 | 0 | 5 | 0 |
| L. Smith, St.L. | .323 | .377 | 15 | 0 | 3 | 20 | 2 |
| Smith, Cin. | .000 | .000 | 0 | 0 | 0 | 0 | 0 |

| Player—Club | Slg. Pct. | OB Pct. | Tot. BB. | Int. BB. | HP. | SO. | GI DP. |
|---|---|---|---|---|---|---|---|
| O. Smith, St.L. | .361 | .355 | 65 | 11 | 2 | 27 | 13 |
| Smith, Atl. | .162 | .184 | 1 | 0 | 0 | 5 | 1 |
| Solano, Hou. | .000 | .000 | 0 | 0 | 0 | 1 | 0 |
| Sorensen, Chi. | .000 | .143 | 1 | 0 | 0 | 4 | 1 |
| Soto, Cin. | .157 | .143 | 1 | 0 | 0 | 24 | 1 |
| Speier, Chi. | .349 | .295 | 17 | 0 | 0 | 34 | 7 |
| Spilman, Hou. | .197 | .174 | 3 | 0 | 0 | 7 | 2 |
| Staub, N.Y. | .400 | .400 | 10 | 3 | 0 | 4 | 1 |
| Stewart, Phil. | .000 | .000 | 0 | 0 | 0 | 0 | 0 |
| Stoddard, S.D. | .000 | .000 | 0 | 0 | 0 | 0 | 0 |
| Stone, Phil. | .337 | .307 | 15 | 0 | 1 | 50 | 3 |
| Strawberry, N.Y. | .557 | .389 | 73 | 13 | 1 | 96 | 9 |
| Stubbs, L.A. | .222 | .222 | 0 | 0 | 0 | 3 | 0 |
| Stuper, Cin. | .059 | .200 | 3 | 0 | 0 | 10 | 0 |
| Surhoff, Phil. | .000 | .000 | 0 | 0 | 0 | 0 | 0 |
| Sutcliffe, Chi. | .302 | .261 | 2 | 0 | 0 | 10 | 1 |
| Sutter, Atl. | .000 | .000 | 0 | 0 | 0 | 1 | 0 |
| Tekulve, Pitt.-Phil. | .000 | .000 | 0 | 0 | 0 | 1 | 0 |
| Templeton, S.D. | .377 | .332 | 41 | 24 | 1 | 88 | 5 |
| Thomas, Atl. | .278 | .278 | 0 | 0 | 0 | 2 | 1 |
| Thomas, Phil. | .359 | .291 | 11 | 1 | 0 | 14 | 3 |
| Thompson, Pitt. | .378 | .369 | 84 | 10 | 0 | 58 | 8 |
| Thompson, Atl. | .363 | .339 | 7 | 0 | 3 | 36 | 1 |
| Thompson, SF-Mt. | .266 | .248 | 5 | 0 | 0 | 17 | 6 |
| Thon, Hou. | .355 | .299 | 18 | 4 | 0 | 50 | 2 |
| Thurmond, S.D. | .088 | .111 | 1 | 0 | 0 | 10 | 0 |
| Tibbs, Cin. | .092 | .119 | 2 | 0 | 0 | 33 | 1 |
| Toliver, Phil. | .500 | .500 | 0 | 0 | 0 | 1 | 0 |
| Tolman, Hou. | .302 | .178 | 1 | 0 | 1 | 10 | 0 |
| Tomlin, Pitt. | .000 | .000 | 0 | 0 | 0 | 0 | 0 |
| Trevino, S.F. | .408 | .303 | 20 | 0 | 0 | 24 | 5 |
| Trillo, S.F. | .288 | .287 | 40 | 0 | 1 | 44 | 6 |
| Trout, Chi. | .130 | .146 | 2 | 0 | 0 | 13 | 0 |
| Tudor, St.L. | .213 | .182 | 5 | 0 | 0 | 25 | 1 |
| Tunnell, Pitt. | .128 | .102 | 1 | 0 | 0 | 20 | 0 |
| Uribe, S.F. | .315 | .285 | 30 | 8 | 2 | 57 | 5 |
| Valenzuela, L.A. | .268 | .214 | 0 | 0 | 0 | 9 | 3 |
| Van Gorder, Cin. | .325 | .280 | 9 | 2 | 1 | 19 | 6 |
| Van Slyke, St.L. | .439 | .335 | 47 | 6 | 2 | 54 | 7 |
| Venable, Cin. | .422 | .315 | 6 | 0 | 0 | 17 | 2 |
| Virgil, Phil. | .432 | .330 | 49 | 6 | 5 | 85 | 14 |
| Walk, Pitt. | .000 | .056 | 0 | 0 | 1 | 9 | 0 |
| Walker, Chi. | .083 | .083 | 0 | 0 | 0 | 5 | 0 |
| Walker, Cin. | .375 | .259 | 6 | 1 | 0 | 18 | 1 |
| Wallach, Mtl. | .450 | .310 | 38 | 8 | 5 | 79 | 17 |
| Walling, Hou. | .394 | .316 | 25 | 2 | 0 | 26 | 8 |
| Walter, S.D. | .000 | .500 | 1 | 0 | 0 | 0 | 0 |
| Ward, S.F. | .000 | .000 | 0 | 0 | 0 | 1 | 1 |
| Washington, Atl. | .455 | .342 | 40 | 11 | 1 | 66 | 11 |
| Washington, Mtl. | .352 | .301 | 15 | 1 | 0 | 33 | 2 |
| Webster, Mtl. | .486 | .335 | 20 | 3 | 0 | 33 | 3 |
| Welch, L.A. | .200 | .226 | 3 | 0 | 0 | 13 | 1 |
| Wellman, S.F. | .310 | .268 | 4 | 1 | 4 | 33 | 3 |
| Whitfield, L.A. | .413 | .300 | 6 | 1 | 0 | 27 | 2 |
| Wiggins, S.D. | .081 | .103 | 2 | 0 | 0 | 4 | 1 |
| Williams, S.F. | .000 | .000 | 0 | 0 | 0 | 0 | 0 |
| Williams, L.A. | .333 | .333 | 0 | 0 | 0 | 4 | 0 |
| Willis, Cin. | .000 | .500 | 1 | 0 | 0 | 0 | 0 |
| Wilson, Phil. | .424 | .311 | 35 | 1 | 0 | 117 | 24 |
| Wilson, N.Y. | .424 | .331 | 28 | 6 | 0 | 52 | 9 |
| Winn, Pitt. | .167 | .158 | 1 | 0 | 0 | 8 | 0 |
| Winningham, Mtl. | .317 | .297 | 28 | 3 | 0 | 72 | 1 |
| Wockenfuss, Phil. | .162 | .311 | 8 | 1 | 0 | 7 | 3 |
| Wohlford, Mtl. | .272 | .284 | 16 | 5 | 0 | 18 | 1 |
| Wojna, S.D. | .167 | .167 | 0 | 0 | 0 | 8 | 0 |
| Woodard, S.F. | .256 | .287 | 5 | 0 | 0 | 3 | 0 |
| Woods, Chi. | .280 | .354 | 14 | 0 | 0 | 18 | 2 |
| Worrell, St.L. | .000 | .000 | 0 | 0 | 0 | 1 | 0 |
| Wynne, Pitt. | .258 | .247 | 18 | 2 | 1 | 48 | 8 |
| Yeager, L.A. | .256 | .246 | 7 | 2 | 0 | 24 | 3 |
| Yost, Mtl. | .182 | .182 | 0 | 0 | 0 | 2 | 0 |
| Youmans, Mtl. | .053 | .182 | 3 | 0 | 0 | 10 | 0 |
| Youngblood, S.F. | .348 | .355 | 30 | 1 | 1 | 37 | 6 |
| Zachry, Phil. | .000 | .000 | 0 | 0 | 0 | 1 | 0 |
| Zuvella, Atl. | .305 | .311 | 16 | 1 | 0 | 14 | 3 |

# OFFICIAL NATIONAL LEAGUE FIELDING AVERAGES

## CLUB FIELDING

| Club | Pct. | G. | PO. | A. | E. | TC. | DP. | TP. | PB. |
|---|---|---|---|---|---|---|---|---|---|
| St. Louis | .983 | 162 | 4392 | 1859 | 108 | 6359 | 166 | 0 | 15 |
| New York | .982 | 162 | 4464 | 1696 | 115 | 6275 | 138 | 0 | 9 |
| Montreal | .981 | 161 | 4371 | 1856 | 121 | 6348 | 152 | 0 | 16 |
| Cincinnati | .980 | 162 | 4354 | 1679 | 122 | 6155 | 142 | 0 | 10 |
| San Diego | .980 | 162 | 4354 | 1730 | 124 | 6208 | 158 | 0 | 6 |
| Chicago | .979 | 162 | 4327 | 1934 | 134 | 6395 | 150 | 1 | 17 |
| Pittsburgh | .979 | 161 | 4336 | 1799 | 133 | 6268 | 127 | 0 | 6 |
| Philadelphia | .978 | 162 | 4341 | 1777 | 139 | 6257 | 142 | 0 | 15 |
| San Francisco | .976 | 162 | 4344 | 1773 | 148 | 6265 | 134 | 0 | 20 |
| Houston | .976 | 162 | 4374 | 1789 | 152 | 6315 | 159 | 0 | 36 |
| Atlanta | .976 | 162 | 4372 | 2028 | 159 | 6559 | 197 | 0 | 8 |
| Los Angeles | .974 | 162 | 4395 | 1903 | 166 | 6464 | 131 | 0 | 7 |
| Totals | .979 | 971 | 52424 | 21823 | 1621 | 75868 | 1796 | 1 | 165 |

## INDIVIDUAL FIELDING

*Throws lefthanded.

### FIRST BASEMEN

| Leader—Club | Pct. | G. | PO. | A. | E. | DP. |
|---|---|---|---|---|---|---|
| HERNANDEZ, N.Y.* | .997 | 157 | 1310 | 139 | 4 | 113 |

(Listed Alphabetically)

| Player—Club | Pct. | G. | PO. | A. | E. | DP. |
|---|---|---|---|---|---|---|
| Almon, Pitt. | .929 | 7 | 25 | 1 | 2 | 3 |
| Bailey, Hou. | 1.000 | 2 | 1 | 1 | 0 | 0 |
| Barnes, Mtl. | 1.000 | 1 | 4 | 0 | 0 | 0 |
| Bevacqua, S.D. | .909 | 9 | 16 | 4 | 2 | 1 |
| Bream, L.A.-Pitt.* | .993 | 41 | 367 | 35 | 3 | 29 |
| Brenly, S.F. | .978 | 10 | 42 | 3 | 1 | 4 |
| Brock, L.A. | .994 | 122 | 1113 | 84 | 7 | 86 |
| Cabell, Hou.-L.A. | .993 | 70 | 430 | 26 | 3 | 35 |
| Carter, N.Y. | 1.000 | 6 | 31 | 3 | 0 | 2 |
| Cedeno, Cin.-St.L. | .993 | 57 | 255 | 13 | 2 | 27 |
| Chambliss, Atl. | .997 | 39 | 299 | 25 | 1 | 31 |

| Leader—Club | Pct. | G. | PO. | A. | E. | DP. |
|---|---|---|---|---|---|---|
| Clark, St.L. | .988 | 121 | 1116 | 66 | 14 | 102 |
| Corcoran, Phil.* | .993 | 59 | 386 | 25 | 3 | 27 |
| Davis, Hou. | .985 | 89 | 749 | 57 | 12 | 76 |
| Deer, S.F. | .987 | 10 | 73 | 1 | 1 | 4 |
| Driessen, Mtl.-S.F.* | .997 | 137 | 1203 | 91 | 4 | 111 |
| Durham, Chi.* | .995 | 151 | 1421 | 107 | 7 | 121 |
| Esasky, Cin. | 1.000 | 12 | 37 | 3 | 0 | 3 |
| Francona, Mtl.* | .988 | 57 | 382 | 35 | 5 | 32 |
| Galarraga, Mtl. | .995 | 23 | 173 | 22 | 1 | 14 |
| Garvey, S.D. | .997 | 162 | 1442 | 92 | 5 | 138 |
| Green, Phil. | .987 | 78 | 628 | 42 | 9 | 54 |
| G. Gross, Phil.* | 1.000 | 8 | 18 | 4 | 0 | 1 |
| Guerrero, L.A. | 1.000 | 12 | 89 | 5 | 0 | 7 |
| Harper, St.L. | 1.000 | 1 | 2 | 0 | 0 | 0 |
| Hebner, Chi. | .991 | 12 | 108 | 6 | 1 | 15 |

## FIRST BASEMAN—Continued

| Leader—Club | Pct. | G. | PO. | A. | E. | DP. |
|---|---|---|---|---|---|---|
| Heep, N.Y.* | .970 | 4 | 28 | 4 | 1 | 3 |
| Hernandez, N.Y.* | .997 | 157 | 1310 | 139 | 4 | 113 |
| Horner, Atl. | 1.000 | 87 | 892 | 58 | 0 | 105 |
| Howe, St.L. | 1.000 | 1 | 4 | 0 | 0 | 1 |
| Jorgensen, St.L.* | .994 | 49 | 318 | 17 | 2 | 32 |
| Kennedy, S.D. | 1.000 | 5 | 8 | 1 | 0 | 0 |
| Knicely, Phil. | 1.000 | 1 | 4 | 0 | 0 | 1 |
| Knight, N.Y. | 1.000 | 1 | 2 | 1 | 0 | 0 |
| Law, Mtl. | .993 | 20 | 136 | 12 | 1 | 10 |
| Madlock, Pitt. | 1.000 | 12 | 81 | 5 | 0 | 3 |
| Marshall, L.A. | .969 | 7 | 59 | 3 | 2 | 7 |
| Martinez, S.D. | 1.000 | 3 | 4 | 1 | 0 | 2 |
| Matuszek, L.A. | 1.000 | 10 | 23 | 1 | 0 | 2 |
| Mazzilli, Pitt. | .986 | 19 | 139 | 6 | 2 | 15 |
| Moreland, Chi. | .962 | 12 | 70 | 6 | 3 | 4 |
| Nicosia, Mtl. | 1.000 | 2 | 6 | 0 | 0 | 0 |
| Paciorek, N.Y. | 1.000 | 8 | 41 | 3 | 0 | 3 |
| Pena, Pitt. | 1.000 | 1 | 3 | 2 | 0 | 0 |
| Perez, Cin. | .995 | 50 | 340 | 22 | 2 | 34 |
| Perry, Atl. | .985 | 55 | 541 | 37 | 9 | 48 |
| Rajsich, S.F. | .990 | 23 | 185 | 11 | 2 | 17 |
| Rose, Cin. | .995 | 110 | 870 | 73 | 5 | 80 |
| Russell, Phil. | .967 | 18 | 114 | 5 | 4 | 6 |
| Schmidt, Phil. | .993 | 106 | 880 | 83 | 7 | 89 |
| Shines, Mtl. | .950 | 5 | 34 | 4 | 2 | 1 |
| Spilman, Hou. | 1.000 | 19 | 131 | 4 | 0 | 15 |
| Stubbs, L.A.* | 1.000 | 4 | 11 | 0 | 0 | 1 |
| Thompson, Pitt.* | .992 | 114 | 995 | 82 | 9 | 69 |
| Thompson, S.F.-Mtl.* | .995 | 27 | 179 | 17 | 1 | 14 |
| Tolman, Hou. | 1.000 | 6 | 12 | 2 | 0 | 1 |
| Van Slyke, St.L. | 1.000 | 2 | 3 | 0 | 0 | 2 |
| Walling, Hou. | .993 | 46 | 283 | 20 | 2 | 22 |
| Wockenfuss, Phil. | 1.000 | 7 | 39 | 1 | 0 | 5 |

### FIRST BASEMEN WITH TWO OR MORE CLUBS

| Player—Club | Pct. | G. | PO. | A. | E. | DP. |
|---|---|---|---|---|---|---|
| Bream, L.A. | .994 | 16 | 148 | 14 | 1 | 8 |
| Bream, Pitt. | .992 | 25 | 219 | 21 | 2 | 21 |
| Cabell, Hou. | .994 | 49 | 311 | 22 | 2 | 30 |
| Cabell, L.A. | .992 | 21 | 119 | 4 | 1 | 5 |
| Cedeno, Cin. | .992 | 34 | 110 | 8 | 1 | 11 |
| Cedeno, St.L. | .993 | 23 | 145 | 5 | 1 | 16 |
| Driessen, Mtl. | .997 | 88 | 804 | 64 | 3 | 79 |
| Driessen, S.F. | .998 | 49 | 399 | 27 | 1 | 32 |
| Thompson, S.F. | .995 | 24 | 168 | 16 | 1 | 13 |
| Thompson, Mtl. | 1.000 | 3 | 11 | 1 | 0 | 1 |

Triple Play—Durham.

## SECOND BASEMEN

| Leader—Club | Pct. | G. | PO. | A. | E. | DP. |
|---|---|---|---|---|---|---|
| BACKMAN, N.Y. | .989 | 140 | 272 | 370 | 7 | 76 |

(Listed Alphabetically)

| Player—Club | Pct. | G. | PO. | A. | E. | DP. |
|---|---|---|---|---|---|---|
| Adams, S.F. | .957 | 6 | 9 | 13 | 1 | 1 |
| Aguayo, Phil. | .981 | 17 | 27 | 25 | 1 | 5 |
| Anderson, L.A. | 1.000 | 2 | 4 | 2 | 0 | 1 |
| Backman, N.Y. | .989 | 140 | 272 | 370 | 7 | 76 |
| Bailor, L.A. | 1.000 | 16 | 18 | 30 | 0 | 5 |
| Bowa, N.Y. | 1.000 | 4 | 9 | 7 | 0 | 2 |
| Chapman, N.Y. | .970 | 48 | 70 | 89 | 5 | 17 |
| Doran, Hou. | .980 | 147 | 345 | 440 | 16 | 108 |
| Duncan, L.A. | .969 | 19 | 50 | 44 | 3 | 7 |
| Flannery, S.D. | .977 | 121 | 261 | 287 | 13 | 72 |
| Flynn, Mtl. | 1.000 | 6 | 3 | 2 | 0 | 0 |
| Foley, Cin. | .983 | 18 | 23 | 36 | 1 | 10 |
| Gardenhire, N.Y. | 1.000 | 5 | 5 | 5 | 0 | 0 |
| Garner, Hou. | .983 | 15 | 26 | 32 | 1 | 10 |
| Gonzalez, Pitt. | 1.000 | 6 | 9 | 14 | 0 | 2 |
| Herr, St.L. | .985 | 158 | 337 | 448 | 12 | 120 |
| Hubbard, Atl. | .989 | 140 | 339 | 539 | 10 | 127 |
| Knight, N.Y. | 1.000 | 2 | 2 | 3 | 0 | 0 |
| Krenchicki, Cin. | 1.000 | 3 | 1 | 3 | 0 | 0 |
| Law, Mtl. | .985 | 126 | 276 | 367 | 10 | 86 |
| Lawless, St.L. | 1.000 | 11 | 10 | 20 | 0 | 2 |
| Lopes, Chi. | 1.000 | 1 | 1 | 2 | 0 | 1 |
| Manrique, Mtl. | 1.000 | 2 | 2 | 4 | 0 | 0 |
| Morrison, Pitt. | 1.000 | 15 | 34 | 37 | 0 | 5 |
| Newman, Mtl. | 1.000 | 15 | 18 | 33 | 0 | 6 |
| Oberkfell, Atl. | .982 | 16 | 18 | 37 | 1 | 7 |
| Oester, Cin. | .989 | 149 | 366 | 457 | 9 | 100 |
| Owen, Chi. | 1.000 | 4 | 1 | 1 | 0 | 0 |
| Pankovits, Hou. | 1.000 | 21 | 24 | 35 | 0 | 7 |
| Pena, Hou. | 1.000 | 2 | 1 | 0 | 0 | 0 |
| Ramirez, S.D. | 1.000 | 7 | 3 | 4 | 0 | 0 |
| Ramsey, L.A. | .800 | 2 | 1 | 3 | 1 | 0 |
| Ray, Pitt. | .976 | 151 | 305 | 423 | 18 | 89 |
| Reynolds, Hou. | 1.000 | 1 | 1 | 1 | 0 | 0 |
| Royster, S.D. | .975 | 58 | 112 | 165 | 7 | 33 |
| Runge, Atl. | .000 | 2 | 0 | 0 | 0 | 0 |
| Runnells, Cin. | 1.000 | 1 | 2 | 2 | 0 | 0 |
| Russell, L.A. | .964 | 8 | 10 | 17 | 1 | 0 |
| Samuel, Phil. | .983 | 159 | 389 | 463 | 15 | 88 |
| Sandberg, Chi. | .986 | 153 | 353 | 500 | 12 | 99 |
| Sax, L.A. | .969 | 135 | 330 | 357 | 22 | 84 |
| Speier, Chi. | .961 | 13 | 21 | 28 | 2 | 9 |
| Thomas, Phil. | .000 | 1 | 0 | 0 | 1 | 0 |
| Trillo, S.F. | .981 | 120 | 262 | 357 | 12 | 73 |
| Uribe, S.F. | .000 | 1 | 0 | 0 | 0 | 0 |
| Walker, Chi. | 1.000 | 2 | 1 | 0 | 0 | 0 |
| Washington, Mtl. | .978 | 43 | 70 | 104 | 4 | 22 |
| Wellman, S.F. | .983 | 36 | 55 | 60 | 2 | 11 |
| Wiggins, S.D. | 1.000 | 9 | 22 | 21 | 0 | 4 |
| Woodard, S.F. | .990 | 23 | 49 | 46 | 1 | 14 |
| Zuvella, Atl. | .986 | 42 | 55 | 88 | 2 | 15 |

Triple Play—Sandberg.

## THIRD BASEMEN

| Leader—Club | Pct. | G. | PO. | A. | E. | DP. |
|---|---|---|---|---|---|---|
| BROWN, S.F. | .971 | 120 | 94 | 243 | 10 | 15 |

(Listed Alphabetically)

| Player—Club | Pct. | G. | PO. | A. | E. | DP. |
|---|---|---|---|---|---|---|
| Adams, S.F. | .971 | 16 | 2 | 31 | 1 | 3 |
| Aguayo, Phil. | 1.000 | 7 | 4 | 16 | 0 | 1 |
| Almon, Pitt. | .857 | 7 | 2 | 4 | 1 | 0 |
| Anderson, L.A. | .957 | 51 | 28 | 107 | 6 | 10 |
| Bailor, L.A. | .963 | 45 | 14 | 63 | 3 | 6 |
| Barnes, Mtl. | 1.000 | 4 | 4 | 6 | 0 | 1 |
| Bell, Cin. | .946 | 67 | 54 | 105 | 9 | 13 |
| Bevacqua, S.D. | .946 | 33 | 32 | 56 | 5 | 7 |
| Brenly, S.F. | .897 | 17 | 15 | 20 | 4 | 4 |
| Brown, S.F. | .971 | 120 | 94 | 243 | 10 | 15 |
| Cabell, L.A. | .920 | 32 | 21 | 71 | 8 | 6 |
| Cey, Chi. | .943 | 140 | 75 | 273 | 21 | 21 |
| Chapman, N.Y. | .000 | 1 | 0 | 0 | 0 | 0 |
| Concepcion, Cin. | 1.000 | 5 | 2 | 1 | 0 | 0 |
| DeJesus, St.L. | 1.000 | 20 | 7 | 24 | 0 | 2 |
| Esasky, Cin. | .946 | 62 | 41 | 99 | 8 | 13 |
| Flannery, S.D. | .000 | 1 | 0 | 0 | 0 | 0 |
| Foley, Cin. | .000 | 1 | 0 | 0 | 0 | 0 |
| Francona, Mtl.* | 1.000 | 1 | 0 | 3 | 0 | 0 |
| Garcia, Phil. | .000 | 1 | 0 | 0 | 0 | 0 |
| Gardenhire, N.Y. | 1.000 | 2 | 1 | 1 | 0 | 0 |
| Garner, Hou. | .932 | 123 | 75 | 197 | 20 | 14 |
| Gonzalez, Pitt. | .894 | 21 | 14 | 28 | 5 | 3 |
| Guerrero, L.A. | .936 | 44 | 21 | 111 | 9 | 9 |
| Harper, St.L. | 1.000 | 6 | 5 | 5 | 0 | 0 |
| Hebner, Chi. | .870 | 7 | 2 | 18 | 3 | 0 |
| Horner, Atl. | .887 | 40 | 25 | 61 | 11 | 6 |
| Howe, St.L. | 1.000 | 1 | 1 | 1 | 0 | 0 |
| Johnson, N.Y. | .941 | 113 | 67 | 171 | 15 | 21 |
| Knight, N.Y. | .958 | 73 | 52 | 109 | 7 | 5 |
| Krenchicki, Cin. | .967 | 52 | 34 | 84 | 4 | 9 |
| Law, Mtl. | .969 | 11 | 8 | 23 | 1 | 2 |
| Lawless, St.L. | .971 | 13 | 9 | 24 | 1 | 2 |
| Lopes, Chi. | 1.000 | 4 | 1 | 2 | 0 | 0 |

## THIRD BASEMAN—Continued

| Player—Club | Pct. | G. | PO. | A. | E. | DP. | Player—Club | Pct. | G. | PO. | A. | E. | DP. |
|---|---|---|---|---|---|---|---|---|---|---|---|---|---|
| Madlock, Pitt.-L.A. | .943 | 130 | 74 | 238 | 19 | 17 | Schu, Phil. | .933 | 111 | 86 | 191 | 20 | 19 |
| Manrique, Mtl. | 1.000 | 1 | 1 | 3 | 0 | 1 | Speier, Chi. | .935 | 31 | 5 | 24 | 2 | 1 |
| Matuszek, L.A. | 1.000 | 1 | 0 | 1 | 0 | 0 | Thomas, Phil. | .000 | 1 | 0 | 0 | 0 | 0 |
| Moreland, Chi. | .840 | 11 | 8 | 13 | 4 | 1 | Trevino, S.F. | .000 | 1 | 0 | 0 | 0 | 0 |
| Morrison, Pitt. | .961 | 59 | 39 | 84 | 5 | 9 | Trillo, S.F. | .833 | 1 | 1 | 4 | 1 | 0 |
| Nettles, S.D. | .959 | 130 | 122 | 229 | 15 | 16 | Wallach, Mtl. | .967 | 154 | 148 | 383 | 18 | 34 |
| Oberkfell, Atl. | .963 | 117 | 70 | 220 | 11 | 19 | Walling, Hou. | .938 | 51 | 31 | 104 | 9 | 9 |
| Owen, Chi. | .875 | 7 | 2 | 5 | 1 | 0 | Washington, Mtl. | .500 | 3 | 1 | 1 | 2 | 0 |
| Pankovits, Hou. | .000 | 1 | 0 | 0 | 0 | 0 | Wellman, S.F. | .902 | 25 | 10 | 45 | 6 | 2 |
| Pena, Hou. | 1.000 | 7 | 3 | 7 | 0 | 0 | Youngblood, S.F. | .667 | 1 | 0 | 2 | 1 | 0 |
| Pendleton, St.L. | .965 | 149 | 129 | 361 | 18 | 26 | Zuvella, Atl. | 1.000 | 5 | 0 | 4 | 0 | 1 |
| Rivera, Hou. | .941 | 11 | 7 | 25 | 2 | 3 | | | | | | | |
| Rowdon, Chi. | .667 | 4 | 1 | 3 | 2 | 0 | | | | | | | |

### THIRD BASEMAN WITH TWO OR MORE CLUBS

| Player—Club | Pct. | G. | PO. | A. | E. | DP. |
|---|---|---|---|---|---|---|
| Royster, S.D. | .974 | 29 | 13 | 24 | 1 | 1 |
| Runge, Atl. | .929 | 28 | 10 | 55 | 5 | 3 |
| Russell, L.A. | 1.000 | 5 | 0 | 1 | 0 | 0 |
| Sax, L.A. | 1.000 | 1 | 0 | 1 | 0 | 0 |
| Schmidt, Phil. | .927 | 54 | 31 | 109 | 11 | 8 |

| Player—Club | Pct. | G. | PO. | A. | E. | DP. |
|---|---|---|---|---|---|---|
| Madlock, Pitt. | .940 | 98 | 46 | 175 | 14 | 10 |
| Madlock, L.A. | .948 | 32 | 28 | 63 | 5 | 7 |

Triple Play—Cey.

## SHORTSTOPS

| Leader—Club | Pct. | G. | PO. | A. | E. | DP. |
|---|---|---|---|---|---|---|
| O. SMITH, St.L. | .983 | 158 | 264 | 549 | 14 | 111 |

(Listed Alphabetically)

| Player—Club | Pct. | G. | PO. | A. | E. | DP. | Leader—Club | Pct. | G. | PO. | A. | E. | DP. |
|---|---|---|---|---|---|---|---|---|---|---|---|---|---|
| Adams, S.F. | .964 | 25 | 24 | 57 | 3 | 9 | Ramirez, S.D. | .918 | 27 | 22 | 34 | 5 | 9 |
| Aguayo, Phil. | .957 | 60 | 61 | 117 | 8 | 21 | Ramirez, Atl. | .954 | 133 | 214 | 451 | 32 | 115 |
| Almon, Pitt. | .987 | 43 | 50 | 101 | 2 | 19 | Ramsey, L.A. | .923 | 4 | 4 | 8 | 1 | 1 |
| Anderson, L.A. | .973 | 25 | 29 | 78 | 3 | 9 | Reynolds, Hou. | .977 | 102 | 158 | 318 | 11 | 65 |
| Backman, N.Y. | 1.000 | 1 | 1 | 0 | 0 | 0 | Royster, S.D. | 1.000 | 7 | 4 | 25 | 0 | 3 |
| Bailor, L.A. | 1.000 | 5 | 3 | 10 | 0 | 1 | Runge, Atl. | .889 | 5 | 5 | 11 | 2 | 2 |
| Belliard, Pitt. | .947 | 12 | 13 | 23 | 2 | 3 | Runnells, Cin. | 1.000 | 11 | 8 | 20 | 0 | 4 |
| Bowa, Chi.-N.Y. | .965 | 75 | 100 | 203 | 11 | 37 | Russell, L.A. | .919 | 23 | 27 | 64 | 8 | 11 |
| Brooks, Mtl. | .958 | 155 | 203 | 441 | 28 | 81 | Sandberg, Chi. | 1.000 | 1 | 0 | 1 | 0 | 0 |
| Concepcion, Cin. | .963 | 151 | 212 | 404 | 24 | 64 | Santana, N.Y. | .965 | 153 | 301 | 396 | 25 | 81 |
| DeJesus, St.L. | .923 | 13 | 8 | 16 | 2 | 1 | Schmidt, Phil. | 1.000 | 1 | 0 | 1 | 0 | 0 |
| Duncan, L.A. | .954 | 123 | 174 | 386 | 27 | 57 | O. Smith, St.L. | .983 | 158 | 264 | 549 | 14 | 111 |
| Dunston, Chi. | .958 | 73 | 144 | 248 | 17 | 39 | Speier, Chi. | .964 | 58 | 61 | 125 | 7 | 33 |
| Dybzinski, Pitt. | .900 | 5 | 4 | 5 | 1 | 0 | Templeton, S.D. | .968 | 148 | 245 | 460 | 23 | 96 |
| Flynn, Mtl. | .000 | 1 | 0 | 0 | 0 | 0 | Thomas, Atl. | .920 | 10 | 6 | 17 | 2 | 2 |
| Foley, Cin.-Phil. | .978 | 60 | 104 | 166 | 6 | 37 | Thomas, Phil. | .906 | 21 | 21 | 37 | 6 | 4 |
| Foli, Pitt. | .980 | 13 | 16 | 34 | 1 | 6 | Thon, Hou. | .967 | 79 | 106 | 218 | 11 | 48 |
| Garcia, Phil. | 1.000 | 3 | 0 | 2 | 0 | 0 | Uribe, S.F. | .961 | 145 | 209 | 438 | 26 | 77 |
| Gardenhire, N.Y. | .911 | 13 | 15 | 26 | 4 | 3 | Washington, Mtl. | .968 | 9 | 5 | 25 | 1 | 7 |
| Jeltz, Phil. | .958 | 86 | 106 | 215 | 14 | 38 | Wellman, S.F. | .750 | 3 | 1 | 2 | 1 | 2 |
| Johnson, N.Y. | .909 | 7 | 11 | 19 | 3 | 6 | Zuvella, Atl. | .958 | 33 | 57 | 81 | 6 | 23 |
| Khalifa, Pitt. | .967 | 95 | 156 | 316 | 16 | 45 | | | | | | | |
| LeMaster, S.F.-Pitt. | .978 | 31 | 55 | 80 | 3 | 13 | | | | | | | |

### SHORTSTOPS WITH TWO OR MORE CLUBS

| Player—Club | Pct. | G. | PO. | A. | E. | DP. |
|---|---|---|---|---|---|---|
| Manrique, Mtl. | 1.000 | 2 | 2 | 3 | 0 | 0 |
| Newman, Mtl. | 1.000 | 2 | 1 | 3 | 0 | 1 |
| Owen, Chi. | .917 | 7 | 3 | 8 | 1 | 2 |
| Pankovits, Hou. | .667 | 1 | 1 | 1 | 1 | 0 |
| Pena, Hou. | .929 | 6 | 5 | 8 | 1 | 2 |

| Player—Club | Pct. | G. | PO. | A. | E. | DP. |
|---|---|---|---|---|---|---|
| Bowa, Chi. | .970 | 66 | 91 | 197 | 9 | 34 |
| Bowa, N.Y. | .882 | 9 | 9 | 6 | 2 | 3 |
| Foley, Cin. | .971 | 15 | 29 | 38 | 2 | 11 |
| Foley, Phil. | .981 | 45 | 75 | 128 | 4 | 26 |
| LeMaster, S.F. | .955 | 10 | 12 | 9 | 1 | 1 |
| LeMaster, Pitt. | .983 | 21 | 43 | 71 | 2 | 12 |

Triple Play—Speier.

## OUTFIELDERS

| Leader—Club | Pct. | G. | PO. | A. | E. | DP. |
|---|---|---|---|---|---|---|
| BASS, HOU. | .997 | 141 | 328 | 10 | 1 | 1 |

(Listed Alphabetically)

| Player—Club | Pct. | G. | PO. | A. | E. | DP. | Leader—Club | Pct. | G. | PO. | A. | E. | DP. |
|---|---|---|---|---|---|---|---|---|---|---|---|---|---|
| | | | | | | | Christensen, N.Y. | .956 | 38 | 41 | 2 | 2 | 0 |
| | | | | | | | Clark, St.L. | 1.000 | 12 | 12 | 0 | 0 | 0 |
| | | | | | | | Coleman, St.L. | .979 | 150 | 305 | 16 | 7 | 1 |
| Almon, Pitt. | 1.000 | 32 | 27 | 2 | 0 | 0 | Corcoran, Phil.* | 1.000 | 3 | 3 | 0 | 0 | 0 |
| Bailor, L.A. | .000 | 1 | 0 | 0 | 0 | 0 | Cruz, Hou.* | .971 | 137 | 257 | 12 | 8 | 3 |
| Barnes, Mtl. | 1.000 | 3 | 5 | 0 | 0 | 0 | C. Davis, S.F. | .980 | 126 | 279 | 10 | 6 | 2 |
| Bass, Hou. | .997 | 141 | 328 | 10 | 1 | 1 | Davis, Cin. | .987 | 47 | 75 | 3 | 1 | 1 |
| Beane, N.Y. | 1.000 | 2 | 1 | 0 | 0 | 0 | Davis, S.D. | .952 | 23 | 18 | 2 | 1 | 0 |
| Bevacqua, S.D. | 1.000 | 1 | 1 | 0 | 0 | 0 | Davis, Hou. | 1.000 | 9 | 17 | 0 | 0 | 0 |
| Blocker, N.Y.* | 1.000 | 5 | 4 | 0 | 0 | 0 | Davis, Pitt.* | .667 | 2 | 2 | 0 | 1 | 0 |
| Bosley, Chi.* | .988 | 55 | 84 | 0 | 1 | 0 | Dawson, Mtl. | .973 | 131 | 248 | 9 | 7 | 1 |
| Braun, St.L. | 1.000 | 14 | 14 | 1 | 0 | 0 | Dayett, Chi. | 1.000 | 10 | 8 | 0 | 0 | 0 |
| Brown, Pitt. | .938 | 56 | 87 | 3 | 6 | 1 | Deer, S.F. | .982 | 37 | 54 | 1 | 1 | 0 |
| Brown, S.D. | 1.000 | 28 | 20 | 2 | 0 | 2 | Dernier, Chi. | .972 | 116 | 310 | 4 | 9 | 1 |
| Bryant, L.A. | .000 | 3 | 0 | 0 | 0 | 0 | Dilone, Mtl.-S.D. | .952 | 36 | 57 | 2 | 3 | 0 |
| Bullock, Hou.* | .750 | 7 | 6 | 0 | 2 | 0 | Dykstra, N.Y.* | .994 | 74 | 165 | 6 | 1 | 2 |
| Bumbry, S.D. | .939 | 17 | 31 | 0 | 2 | 0 | Esasky, Cin. | 1.000 | 54 | 91 | 4 | 0 | 0 |
| Cabell, L.A. | 1.000 | 4 | 5 | 0 | 0 | 0 | Ford, St.L. | .750 | 4 | 3 | 0 | 1 | 0 |
| Carter, N.Y. | .000 | 1 | 0 | 0 | 0 | 0 | Foster, N.Y. | .976 | 123 | 198 | 7 | 5 | 2 |
| Cedeno, Cin.-St.L. | .990 | 55 | 96 | 1 | 1 | 0 | Francona, Mtl.* | .981 | 28 | 49 | 2 | 1 | 0 |
| | | | | | | | Frobel, Pitt.-Mtl. | .938 | 42 | 58 | 2 | 4 | 1 |

## OUTFIELDERS—Continued

| Player—Club | Pct. | G. | PO. | A. | E. | DP. |
|---|---|---|---|---|---|---|
| Gainey, Hou.* | .913 | 9 | 21 | 0 | 2 | 0 |
| Gladden, S.F. | .975 | 124 | 273 | 3 | 7 | 0 |
| Gonzalez, Pitt. | .875 | 13 | 21 | 0 | 3 | 0 |
| Gonzalez, L.A. | 1.000 | 18 | 10 | 0 | 0 | 0 |
| Green, S.F.* | .944 | 12 | 17 | 0 | 1 | 0 |
| G. Gross, Phi.* | 1.000 | 52 | 48 | 4 | 0 | 0 |
| Guerrero, L.A. | .974 | 81 | 141 | 7 | 4 | 2 |
| Gwynn, S.D.* | .989 | 152 | 337 | 14 | 4 | 2 |
| Hall, Atl. | .900 | 13 | 7 | 2 | 1 | 0 |
| Harper, St.L. | 1.000 | 13 | 8 | 0 | 0 | 0 |
| Harper, Atl. | .978 | 131 | 215 | 10 | 5 | 0 |
| Hatcher, Chi. | .988 | 44 | 77 | 2 | 1 | 0 |
| Hayes, Phil. | .984 | 146 | 368 | 9 | 6 | 1 |
| Hebner, N.Y. | .000 | 1 | 0 | 0 | 0 | 0 |
| Heep, N.Y.* | .977 | 78 | 126 | 1 | 3 | 0 |
| Hendrick, Pitt. | .971 | 65 | 133 | 2 | 4 | 0 |
| Hurdle, N.Y. | .917 | 10 | 10 | 1 | 1 | 0 |
| Jackson, Chi. | 1.000 | 4 | 7 | 0 | 0 | 0 |
| Johnson, N.Y. | .000 | 1 | 0 | 0 | 0 | 0 |
| Johnson, Mtl.* | .000 | 3 | 0 | 0 | 0 | 0 |
| Jones, Hou.* | 1.000 | 15 | 15 | 0 | 0 | 0 |
| Jorgensen, St.L.* | .000 | 2 | 0 | 0 | 0 | 0 |
| Kemp, Pitt.* | 1.000 | 63 | 105 | 1 | 0 | 0 |
| Komminsk, Atl. | .959 | 92 | 161 | 2 | 7 | 0 |
| Landreaux, L.A. | .975 | 140 | 267 | 4 | 7 | 1 |
| Landrum, St.L. | 1.000 | 73 | 91 | 2 | 0 | 1 |
| Law, Mtl. | .000 | 1 | 0 | 0 | 0 | 0 |
| Leonard, S.F. | .977 | 126 | 203 | 10 | 5 | 0 |
| Lezcano, Pitt. | .967 | 40 | 57 | 2 | 2 | 0 |
| Lopes, Chi. | .991 | 79 | 113 | 2 | 1 | 0 |
| Loucks, Pitt. | 1.000 | 4 | 2 | 0 | 0 | 0 |
| Maddox, Phil. | .980 | 94 | 143 | 3 | 3 | 0 |
| Maldonado, L.A. | .984 | 113 | 121 | 6 | 2 | 0 |
| Marshall, L.A. | .991 | 125 | 206 | 9 | 2 | 0 |
| Martinez, S.D. | .978 | 150 | 298 | 13 | 7 | 3 |
| Matthews, Chi. | .977 | 85 | 119 | 7 | 3 | 2 |
| Matuszek, L.A. | 1.000 | 17 | 24 | 0 | 0 | 0 |
| Mazzilli, Pitt. | .929 | 5 | 13 | 0 | 1 | 0 |
| McGee, St.L. | .978 | 149 | 382 | 11 | 9 | 2 |
| McReynolds, S.D. | .993 | 150 | 430 | 12 | 3 | 3 |
| Milner, Cin.* | .983 | 135 | 340 | 12 | 6 | 3 |
| Moreland, Chi. | .976 | 148 | 233 | 10 | 6 | 2 |
| Morrison, Pitt. | .000 | 1 | 0 | 0 | 0 | 0 |
| Mumphrey, Hou. | .969 | 126 | 248 | 6 | 8 | 1 |
| Murphy, Atl. | .980 | 161 | 334 | 8 | 7 | 4 |
| Oliver, L.A.* | .882 | 17 | 13 | 2 | 2 | 0 |
| O'Neill, Cin.* | 1.000 | 2 | 3 | 1 | 0 | 0 |
| Orsulak, Pitt.* | .976 | 115 | 229 | 10 | 6 | 1 |
| Paciorek, N.Y. | 1.000 | 29 | 35 | 0 | 0 | 0 |
| Pankovits, Hou. | .983 | 33 | 56 | 2 | 1 | 1 |
| Parker, Cin. | .972 | 159 | 329 | 12 | 10 | 1 |
| Pederson, L.A.* | 1.000 | 5 | 2 | 0 | 0 | 0 |
| Perry, Atl. | .000 | 1 | 0 | 0 | 0 | 0 |
| Puhl, Hou. | 1.000 | 53 | 92 | 3 | 0 | 1 |
| Rabb, Atl. | .000 | 1 | 0 | 0 | 0 | 0 |
| Raines, Mtl. | .993 | 146 | 284 | 8 | 2 | 4 |
| Redus, Cin. | .986 | 85 | 140 | 3 | 2 | 0 |
| Reynolds, L.A.-Pitt. | .965 | 85 | 159 | 6 | 6 | 0 |
| Roenicke, S.F.* | .984 | 35 | 63 | 0 | 1 | 0 |
| Royster, S.D. | 1.000 | 2 | 1 | 0 | 0 | 0 |
| Russell, Phil. | 1.000 | 49 | 56 | 4 | 0 | 1 |
| Russell, L.A. | .958 | 21 | 23 | 0 | 1 | 0 |
| L. Smith, St.L. | 1.000 | 28 | 43 | 1 | 0 | 1 |
| Staub, N.Y. | 1.000 | 1 | 1 | 0 | 0 | 0 |
| Stone, Phil. | .966 | 69 | 82 | 4 | 3 | 0 |
| Strawberry, N.Y.* | .991 | 110 | 211 | 5 | 2 | 2 |
| Thomas, Phil. | 1.000 | 7 | 7 | 1 | 0 | 0 |
| Thompson, Atl. | .964 | 49 | 78 | 2 | 3 | 0 |
| Thompson, Mtl.* | 1.000 | 3 | 1 | 1 | 0 | 0 |
| Tolman, Hou. | 1.000 | 9 | 12 | 0 | 0 | 0 |
| Van Slyke, St.L. | .996 | 142 | 234 | 13 | 1 | 4 |
| Venable, Cin. | 1.000 | 39 | 60 | 3 | 0 | 0 |
| Walker, Chi. | 1.000 | 6 | 3 | 0 | 0 | 0 |
| Walker, Cin.* | .882 | 10 | 15 | 0 | 2 | 0 |
| Walling, Hou. | .923 | 13 | 12 | 0 | 1 | 0 |
| Washington, Atl.* | .962 | 99 | 122 | 3 | 5 | 1 |
| Webster, Mtl.* | .993 | 64 | 133 | 3 | 1 | 0 |
| Whitfield, L.A. | .926 | 28 | 23 | 2 | 2 | 0 |
| Williams, L.A. | .900 | 15 | 8 | 1 | 1 | 0 |
| Wilson, Phil. | .968 | 158 | 343 | 18 | 12 | 4 |
| Wilson, N.Y. | .964 | 83 | 216 | 0 | 8 | 0 |
| Winningham, Mtl. | .983 | 116 | 229 | 6 | 4 | 0 |
| Wohlford, Mtl. | 1.000 | 43 | 58 | 1 | 0 | 0 |
| Woods, Chi. | 1.000 | 56 | 42 | 1 | 0 | 0 |
| Wynne, Pitt.* | .987 | 99 | 229 | 7 | 3 | 1 |
| Youngblood, S.F. | .955 | 56 | 103 | 4 | 5 | 0 |

### OUTFIELDERS WITH TWO OR MORE CLUBS

| Player—Club | Pct. | G. | PO. | A. | E. | DP. |
|---|---|---|---|---|---|---|
| Cedeno, Cin. | .990 | 53 | 96 | 1 | 1 | 0 |
| Cedeno, St.L. | .000 | 2 | 0 | 0 | 0 | 0 |
| Dilone, Mtl. | .974 | 22 | 36 | 1 | 1 | 0 |
| Dilone, S.D. | .917 | 14 | 21 | 1 | 2 | 0 |
| Frobel, Pitt. | .941 | 36 | 46 | 2 | 3 | 1 |
| Frobel, Mtl. | 923 | 6 | 12 | 0 | 1 | 0 |
| Reynolds, L.A. | .970 | 54 | 94 | 3 | 3 | 0 |
| Reynolds, Pitt. | .958 | 31 | 65 | 3 | 3 | 0 |

Triple Play—Dernier.

# CATCHERS

| Leader—Club | Pct. | G. | PO. | A. | E. | DP. | PB. |
|---|---|---|---|---|---|---|---|
| VIRGIL, PHIL. | .994 | 120 | 667 | 52 | 4 | 11 | 12 |

(Listed Alphabetically)

| Player—Club | Pct. | G. | PO. | A. | E. | DP. | PB. |
|---|---|---|---|---|---|---|---|
| Ashby, Hou. | .978 | 60 | 312 | 37 | 8 | 1 | 14 |
| Bailey, Hou. | .979 | 110 | 565 | 51 | 13 | 6 | 19 |
| Benedict, Atl. | .989 | 70 | 314 | 35 | 4 | 1 | 1 |
| Bilardello, Cin. | .986 | 42 | 198 | 20 | 3 | 1 | 2 |
| Bochy, S.D. | .988 | 46 | 148 | 11 | 2 | 2 | 2 |
| Brenly, S.F. | .984 | 110 | 662 | 62 | 12 | 8 | 16 |
| Butera, Mtl. | .984 | 66 | 227 | 20 | 4 | 5 | 3 |
| Carter, N.Y. | .992 | 143 | 956 | 67 | 8 | 11 | 5 |
| Cerone, Atl. | .986 | 91 | 384 | 48 | 6 | 4 | 6 |
| Daulton, Phil. | .994 | 28 | 160 | 15 | 1 | 1 | 3 |
| Davis, Chi. | .990 | 138 | 694 | 84 | 8 | 7 | 14 |
| Diaz, Phil.-Cin. | .983 | 75 | 428 | 42 | 8 | 10 | 3 |
| Fitzgerald, Mtl. | .987 | 108 | 542 | 46 | 8 | 7 | 9 |
| Harper, St.L. | .000 | 2 | 0 | 0 | 0 | 0 | 0 |
| Hunt, St.L. | 1.000 | 13 | 33 | 1 | 0 | 0 | 0 |
| Hurdle, N.Y. | 1.000 | 17 | 79 | 6 | 0 | 0 | 3 |
| Kennedy, S.D. | .986 | 140 | 654 | 67 | 10 | 12 | 4 |
| Knicely, Cin. | .968 | 46 | 231 | 13 | 8 | 1 | 4 |
| Lake, Chi. | .995 | 55 | 182 | 25 | 1 | 1 | 3 |
| Lavalliere, St.L. | 1.000 | 12 | 48 | 5 | 0 | 3 | 0 |
| Mizerock, Hou. | .966 | 15 | 77 | 8 | 3 | 1 | 3 |
| Moreland, Chi. | 1.000 | 2 | 2 | 0 | 0 | 0 | 0 |
| Nicosia, Mtl. | .988 | 23 | 80 | 5 | 1 | 1 | 0 |
| Nieto, St.L. | .990 | 95 | 384 | 28 | 4 | 3 | 10 |
| Nokes, S.F. | .977 | 14 | 84 | 2 | 2 | 0 | 0 |
| O'Berry, Mtl. | 1.000 | 20 | 53 | 6 | 0 | 2 | 2 |
| Ortiz, Pitt. | .985 | 23 | 115 | 14 | 2 | 3 | 0 |
| Owen, Atl. | .966 | 25 | 129 | 11 | 5 | 1 | 1 |
| Pena, Pitt. | .988 | 146 | 922 | 100 | 12 | 9 | 6 |
| Porter, St.L. | .990 | 82 | 386 | 26 | 4 | 4 | 5 |
| Reyes, L.A. | 1.000 | 6 | 6 | 4 | 0 | 0 | 0 |
| Reynolds, N.Y. | .990 | 25 | 86 | 9 | 1 | 2 | 1 |
| Scioscia, L.A. | .986 | 139 | 818 | 66 | 13 | 8 | 5 |
| Spilman, Hou. | 1.000 | 2 | 3 | 0 | 0 | 0 | 0 |
| Thomas, Phil. | 1.000 | 1 | 3 | 0 | 0 | 0 | 0 |
| Trevino, S.F. | .978 | 55 | 299 | 19 | 7 | 1 | 4 |
| Van Gorder, Cin. | .989 | 70 | 255 | 11 | 3 | 2 | 1 |
| Virgil, Phil. | .994 | 120 | 667 | 52 | 4 | 11 | 12 |
| Wockenfuss, Phil. | 1.000 | 2 | 5 | 0 | 0 | 0 | 0 |
| Yeager, L.A. | .992 | 48 | 212 | 28 | 2 | 2 | 2 |
| Yost, Mtl. | .962 | 5 | 24 | 1 | 1 | 0 | 2 |

### CATCHER WITH TWO OR MORE CLUBS

| Player—Club | Pct. | G. | PO. | A. | E. | DP. | PB. |
|---|---|---|---|---|---|---|---|
| Diaz, Phil. | .972 | 24 | 127 | 10 | 4 | 2 | 0 |
| Diaz, Cin. | .988 | 51 | 301 | 32 | 4 | 8 | 3 |

## PITCHERS

| Leader—Club | Pct. | G. | PO. | A. | E. | DP. |
|---|---|---|---|---|---|---|
| REUSCHEL, PITT. | 1.000 | 31 | 24 | 40 | 0 | 2 |

(Listed Alphabetically)

| Player—Club | Pct. | G. | PO. | A. | E. | DP. |
|---|---|---|---|---|---|---|
| Abrego, Chi. | .875 | 6 | 1 | 6 | 1 | 0 |
| Aguilera, N.Y. | 1.000 | 21 | 8 | 16 | 0 | 1 |
| Allen, St.L. | 1.000 | 23 | 2 | 5 | 0 | 0 |
| Andersen, Phil. | .929 | 57 | 5 | 21 | 2 | 2 |
| Andujar, St.L. | .898 | 38 | 8 | 45 | 6 | 8 |
| Bair, St.L. | .000 | 2 | 0 | 0 | 0 | 0 |
| Baller, Chi. | 1.000 | 20 | 4 | 6 | 0 | 0 |
| Barker, Atl. | .917 | 20 | 2 | 9 | 1 | 0 |
| Beard, Chi. | 1.000 | 9 | 0 | 2 | 0 | 0 |
| Bedrosian, Atl. | .900 | 37 | 13 | 23 | 4 | 3 |
| Berenyi, N.Y. | 1.000 | 3 | 1 | 4 | 0 | 1 |
| Bielecki, Pitt. | 1.000 | 12 | 5 | 11 | 0 | 0 |
| Blue, S.F.* | .933 | 33 | 7 | 21 | 2 | 1 |
| Boever, St.L. | .000 | 13 | 0 | 0 | 0 | 0 |
| Booker, S.D. | .800 | 17 | 1 | 3 | 1 | 0 |
| Botelho, Chi. | 1.000 | 11 | 2 | 5 | 0 | 0 |
| Brennan, L.A. | 1.000 | 12 | 3 | 11 | 0 | 1 |
| Browning, Cin.* | .958 | 38 | 12 | 34 | 2 | 1 |
| Brusstar, Chi. | .818 | 51 | 6 | 3 | 2 | 0 |
| Buchanan, Cin.* | 1.000 | 14 | 1 | 3 | 0 | 0 |
| Burke, Mtl. | .963 | 78 | 5 | 21 | 1 | 2 |
| Butera, Mtl. | .000 | 1 | 0 | 0 | 0 | 0 |
| Calhoun, Hou.* | .882 | 44 | 5 | 10 | 2 | 2 |
| Camp, Atl. | .833 | 66 | 7 | 13 | 4 | 3 |
| Campbell, St.L. | .857 | 50 | 0 | 6 | 1 | 0 |
| Candelaria, Pitt.* | .900 | 37 | 1 | 8 | 1 | 0 |
| Carlton, Phil.* | 1.000 | 16 | 3 | 18 | 0 | 1 |
| Carman, Phil.* | .889 | 71 | 5 | 11 | 2 | 2 |
| Castillo, L.A. | .941 | 35 | 5 | 11 | 1 | 1 |
| Childress, Phil. | 1.000 | 16 | 1 | 4 | 0 | 0 |
| Clements, Pitt.* | 1.000 | 27 | 0 | 3 | 0 | 0 |
| Cox, St.L. | .964 | 35 | 22 | 31 | 2 | 1 |
| Darling, N.Y. | .973 | 36 | 24 | 47 | 2 | 5 |
| M. Davis, S.F.* | 1.000 | 77 | 2 | 12 | 0 | 0 |
| Dawley, Hou. | .950 | 49 | 6 | 13 | 1 | 2 |
| Dayley, St.L.* | 1.000 | 57 | 5 | 15 | 0 | 0 |
| Dedmon, Atl. | .947 | 60 | 9 | 27 | 2 | 4 |
| DeLeon, Pitt. | .962 | 31 | 9 | 16 | 1 | 1 |
| DeLeon, S.D. | 1.000 | 29 | 1 | 5 | 0 | 0 |
| Denny, Phil. | 1.000 | 33 | 15 | 39 | 0 | 4 |
| Deshaies, Hou.* | .000 | 2 | 0 | 0 | 0 | 0 |
| Diaz, L.A. | 1.000 | 46 | 1 | 8 | 0 | 0 |
| DiPino, Hou.* | .889 | 54 | 3 | 5 | 1 | 0 |
| Dopson, Mtl. | 1.000 | 4 | 0 | 2 | 0 | 0 |
| Dravecky, S.D.* | .935 | 34 | 13 | 30 | 3 | 2 |
| Eckersley, Chi. | .923 | 25 | 10 | 26 | 3 | 1 |
| Engel, Chi.* | 1.000 | 11 | 2 | 8 | 0 | 0 |
| Fernandez, N.Y.* | 1.000 | 26 | 1 | 23 | 0 | 0 |
| Fontenot, Chi.* | .976 | 38 | 6 | 35 | 1 | 3 |
| Forsch, St.L. | .970 | 34 | 12 | 20 | 1 | 0 |
| Forster, Atl.* | .900 | 46 | 2 | 7 | 1 | 0 |
| Franco, Cin.* | .968 | 67 | 9 | 21 | 1 | 1 |
| Frazier, Chi. | .933 | 51 | 5 | 9 | 1 | 2 |
| Garber, Atl. | 1.000 | 59 | 11 | 17 | 0 | 1 |
| Gardner, N.Y. | 1.000 | 9 | 0 | 4 | 0 | 0 |
| Garrelts, S.F. | .935 | 74 | 7 | 22 | 2 | 0 |
| Glynn, Mtl.* | .000 | 3 | 0 | 0 | 0 | 0 |
| Gooden, N.Y. | .969 | 35 | 25 | 38 | 2 | 6 |
| Gorman, N.Y.* | 1.000 | 34 | 3 | 14 | 0 | 1 |
| Gossage, S.D. | 1.000 | 50 | 0 | 7 | 0 | 1 |
| Gott, S.F. | 1.000 | 26 | 9 | 28 | 0 | 0 |
| Grapenthin, Mtl. | 1.000 | 5 | 0 | 1 | 0 | 0 |
| K. Gross, Phil. | .945 | 38 | 18 | 34 | 3 | 0 |
| Guante, Pitt. | .950 | 63 | 6 | 13 | 1 | 0 |
| Gullickson, Mtl. | .973 | 29 | 10 | 26 | 1 | 0 |
| Gumpert, Chi. | .000 | 9 | 0 | 0 | 0 | 0 |
| Gura, Chi.* | 1.000 | 5 | 4 | 4 | 0 | 0 |
| Hammaker, S.F.* | .974 | 29 | 6 | 32 | 1 | 1 |
| Hassler, St.L.* | .667 | 10 | 2 | 0 | 1 | 0 |
| Hawkins, S.D. | .981 | 33 | 21 | 30 | 1 | 3 |
| Heathcock, Hou. | 1.000 | 14 | 4 | 9 | 0 | 1 |
| Hershiser, L.A. | .903 | 36 | 20 | 45 | 7 | 4 |
| Hesketh, Mtl.* | 1.000 | 25 | 3 | 22 | 0 | 0 |
| Holland, Phil.-Pitt.* | 1.000 | 41 | 2 | 7 | 0 | 1 |

| Player—Club | Pct. | G. | PO. | A. | E. | DP. |
|---|---|---|---|---|---|---|
| Holton, L.A. | 1.000 | 3 | 0 | 1 | 0 | 0 |
| Honeycutt, L.A.* | .958 | 31 | 9 | 37 | 2 | 1 |
| Horton, St.L.* | .938 | 49 | 9 | 21 | 2 | 0 |
| Howe, L.A.* | .857 | 19 | 0 | 6 | 1 | 0 |
| Howell, L.A. | .947 | 56 | 7 | 11 | 1 | 0 |
| Hoyt, S.D. | .981 | 31 | 12 | 40 | 1 | 4 |
| Hudson, Phil. | 1.000 | 38 | 14 | 18 | 0 | 1 |
| Hume, Cin. | .941 | 56 | 4 | 12 | 1 | 1 |
| Jackson, S.D. | .909 | 22 | 5 | 5 | 1 | 0 |
| Jeffcoat, S.F.* | .889 | 19 | 1 | 7 | 1 | 0 |
| Johnson, Atl. | .917 | 15 | 4 | 7 | 1 | 0 |
| Keough, St.L. | 1.000 | 4 | 0 | 2 | 0 | 0 |
| Kepshire, St.L. | .960 | 32 | 5 | 19 | 1 | 1 |
| Kerfeld, Hou. | .875 | 11 | 5 | 2 | 1 | 1 |
| Kipper, Pitt.* | .833 | 5 | 0 | 5 | 1 | 0 |
| Knepper, Hou.* | .921 | 37 | 5 | 30 | 3 | 1 |
| Knudson, Hou. | 1.000 | 2 | 1 | 1 | 0 | 0 |
| Koosman, Phil.* | .947 | 19 | 4 | 14 | 1 | 1 |
| Krawczyk, Pitt. | .667 | 8 | 0 | 2 | 1 | 1 |
| Krukow, S.F. | .971 | 28 | 6 | 27 | 1 | 3 |
| Lahti, St.L. | .933 | 52 | 5 | 9 | 1 | 1 |
| LaPoint, S.F.* | .969 | 31 | 8 | 23 | 1 | 1 |
| Laskey, S.F.-Mtl. | .950 | 30 | 12 | 26 | 2 | 1 |
| Latham, N.Y.* | 1.000 | 7 | 0 | 7 | 0 | 0 |
| Leach, N.Y. | 1.000 | 22 | 5 | 14 | 0 | 0 |
| Lefferts, S.D.* | 1.000 | 60 | 4 | 11 | 0 | 1 |
| Lucas, Mtl.* | 1.000 | 49 | 2 | 11 | 0 | 1 |
| Lynch, N.Y. | .935 | 31 | 15 | 14 | 2 | 2 |
| Madden, Hou.* | 1.000 | 13 | 2 | 1 | 0 | 0 |
| Mahler, Mtl.* | .833 | 9 | 1 | 4 | 1 | 2 |
| Mahler, Atl. | .943 | 39 | 21 | 45 | 4 | 9 |
| Mason, S.F. | 1.000 | 5 | 4 | 2 | 0 | 0 |
| Mathis, Hou. | .938 | 23 | 5 | 10 | 1 | 0 |
| McCullers, S.D. | .800 | 21 | 2 | 6 | 2 | 0 |
| McDowell, N.Y. | .917 | 62 | 17 | 27 | 4 | 2 |
| McGaffigan, Cin. | .952 | 15 | 8 | 12 | 1 | 2 |
| McMurtry, Atl. | .875 | 17 | 2 | 12 | 2 | 0 |
| McWilliams, Pitt.* | 1.000 | 30 | 4 | 21 | 0 | 0 |
| Meridith, Chi. | 1.000 | 32 | 0 | 9 | 0 | 1 |
| Minton, S.F. | .971 | 68 | 7 | 27 | 1 | 1 |
| Moore, S.F. | .500 | 11 | 0 | 1 | 1 | 0 |
| Murphy, Cin.* | .000 | 2 | 0 | 0 | 0 | 0 |
| Myers, N.Y.* | 1.000 | 1 | 0 | 1 | 0 | 0 |
| Niedenfuer, L.A. | 1.000 | 64 | 8 | 7 | 0 | 0 |
| Niekro, Hou. | .980 | 32 | 14 | 34 | 1 | 1 |
| Niemann, N.Y.* | 1.000 | 4 | 0 | 2 | 0 | 0 |
| O'Connor, Mtl.* | 1.000 | 20 | 0 | 1 | 0 | 1 |
| Orosco, N.Y.* | .917 | 54 | 3 | 8 | 1 | 2 |
| Palmer, Mtl. | .974 | 24 | 17 | 21 | 1 | 3 |
| Pastore, Cin. | .923 | 17 | 3 | 9 | 1 | 1 |
| Patterson, Chi. | 1.000 | 8 | 4 | 4 | 0 | 0 |
| Patterson, S.D.* | .000 | 3 | 0 | 0 | 0 | 0 |
| Pena, L.A. | .500 | 2 | 0 | 1 | 1 | 0 |
| Perez, Atl. | .941 | 22 | 7 | 9 | 1 | 0 |
| Perlman, Chi. | 1.000 | 6 | 0 | 2 | 0 | 0 |
| Perry, St.L. | 1.000 | 6 | 0 | 1 | 0 | 0 |
| Powell, L.A.* | 1.000 | 16 | 0 | 6 | 0 | 2 |
| Power, Cin. | .875 | 64 | 3 | 4 | 1 | 0 |
| Price, Cin. | 1.000 | 26 | 1 | 4 | 0 | 1 |
| Rawley, Phil.* | .980 | 36 | 12 | 36 | 1 | 2 |
| Reardon, Mtl. | 1.000 | 63 | 9 | 8 | 0 | 0 |
| Reuschel, Pitt. | 1.000 | 31 | 24 | 40 | 0 | 2 |
| Reuss, L.A.* | .929 | 34 | 12 | 27 | 3 | 0 |
| Rhoden, Pitt. | 1.000 | 35 | 13 | 30 | 0 | 1 |
| Roberge, Mtl. | 1.000 | 42 | 5 | 12 | 0 | 0 |
| Robinson, Pitt. | 1.000 | 44 | 7 | 11 | 0 | 2 |
| Robinson, S.F. | .000 | 8 | 0 | 0 | 0 | 0 |
| Robinson, Cin. | .929 | 33 | 9 | 17 | 2 | 4 |
| Rogers, Mtl. | .941 | 8 | 5 | 11 | 1 | 0 |
| Ross, Hou. | 1.000 | 8 | 2 | 2 | 0 | 0 |
| Rucker, Phil.* | 1.000 | 39 | 5 | 14 | 0 | 1 |
| Ruthven, Chi. | .941 | 20 | 5 | 11 | 1 | 1 |
| Ryan, Hou. | .929 | 35 | 6 | 20 | 2 | 0 |
| St. Claire, Mtl. | 1.000 | 42 | 4 | 13 | 0 | 2 |
| Sambito, N.Y.* | 1.000 | 8 | 1 | 3 | 0 | 0 |
| Sanderson, Chi. | 1.000 | 19 | 11 | 21 | 0 | 2 |
| Schatzeder, Mtl.* | .852 | 24 | 3 | 20 | 4 | 1 |
| Schiraldi, N.Y. | 1.000 | 10 | 2 | 3 | 0 | 2 |

PITCHERS—Continued

| Player—Club | Pct. | G. | PO. | A. | E. | DP. | Player—Club | Pct. | G. | PO. | A. | E. | DP. |
|---|---|---|---|---|---|---|---|---|---|---|---|---|---|
| Schuler, Atl.* | 1.000 | 9 | 1 | 0 | 0 | 0 | Tomlin, Pitt.* | .000 | 1 | 0 | 0 | 0 | 0 |
| Scott, Hou. | .956 | 36 | 21 | 22 | 2 | 1 | Trout, Chi.* | .957 | 24 | 6 | 38 | 2 | 0 |
| Scurry, Pitt.* | 1.000 | 30 | 1 | 9 | 0 | 0 | Tudor, St.L.* | .955 | 36 | 18 | 45 | 3 | 4 |
| Shields, Atl. | .923 | 23 | 6 | 6 | 1 | 0 | Tunnell, Pitt. | 1.000 | 24 | 7 | 23 | 0 | 1 |
| Shines, Mtl. | .000 | 1 | 0 | 0 | 0 | 0 | Valenzuela, L.A.* | 1.000 | 35 | 18 | 45 | 0 | 0 |
| Shipanoff, Phil. | .800 | 26 | 2 | 2 | 1 | 0 | Walk, Pitt. | 1.000 | 9 | 7 | 2 | 0 | 0 |
| Show, S.D. | .905 | 35 | 14 | 24 | 4 | 2 | Walter, S.D.* | 1.000 | 15 | 1 | 4 | 0 | 0 |
| Sisk, N.Y. | 1.000 | 42 | 3 | 15 | 0 | 2 | Ward, S.F.* | 1.000 | 6 | 0 | 2 | 0 | 0 |
| Smith, Mtl. | .911 | 32 | 24 | 27 | 5 | 2 | Welch, L.A. | .933 | 23 | 15 | 27 | 3 | 1 |
| Smith, Hou. | .786 | 64 | 4 | 7 | 3 | 1 | Williams, S.F. | .800 | 49 | 4 | 12 | 4 | 2 |
| Smith, Chi. | 1.000 | 65 | 3 | 9 | 0 | 1 | Willis, Cin. | .500 | 11 | 0 | 1 | 1 | 0 |
| Smith, Cin. | 1.000 | 2 | 0 | 1 | 0 | 0 | Winn, Pitt. | 1.000 | 30 | 4 | 21 | 0 | 1 |
| Smith, Atl.* | .933 | 42 | 7 | 35 | 3 | 2 | Wojna, S.D. | .800 | 15 | 4 | 8 | 3 | 1 |
| Solano, Hou. | 1.000 | 20 | 0 | 2 | 0 | 0 | Worrell, St.L. | 1.000 | 17 | 3 | 0 | 0 | 0 |
| Sorensen, Chi. | .900 | 45 | 4 | 14 | 2 | 1 | Youmans, Mtl. | 1.000 | 14 | 6 | 1 | 0 | 0 |
| Soto, Cin. | .959 | 36 | 13 | 34 | 2 | 0 | Zachry, Phil. | 1.000 | 10 | 0 | 5 | 0 | 0 |
| Stewart, Phil. | .000 | 4 | 0 | 0 | 1 | 0 | | | | | | | |
| Stoddard, S.D. | 1.000 | 44 | 3 | 5 | 0 | 0 | PITCHERS WITH TWO OR MORE CLUBS | | | | | | |
| Stuper, Cin. | 1.000 | 33 | 12 | 14 | 0 | 0 | Player—Club | Pct. | G. | PO. | A. | E. | DP. |
| Surhoff, Phil. | .000 | 2 | 0 | 0 | 0 | 0 | Holland, Phil. | 1.000 | 3 | 0 | 2 | 0 | 0 |
| Sutcliffe, Chi. | .972 | 20 | 12 | 23 | 1 | 0 | Holland, Pitt. | 1.000 | 38 | 2 | 5 | 0 | 1 |
| Sutter, Atl. | 1.000 | 58 | 5 | 13 | 0 | 0 | Laskey, S.F. | .931 | 19 | 8 | 19 | 2 | 1 |
| Tekulve, Pitt.-Phil. | 1.000 | 61 | 4 | 14 | 0 | 0 | Laskey, Mtl. | 1.000 | 11 | 4 | 7 | 0 | 0 |
| Thurmond, S.D.* | .972 | 36 | 8 | 27 | 1 | 2 | Tekulve, Pitt. | 1.000 | 3 | 0 | 1 | 0 | 0 |
| Tibbs, Cin. | .948 | 35 | 15 | 40 | 3 | 4 | Tekulve, Phil. | 1.000 | 58 | 4 | 13 | 0 | 0 |
| Toliver, Phil. | .800 | 11 | 0 | 4 | 1 | 0 | | | | | | | |

# OFFICIAL NATIONAL LEAGUE PITCHING AVERAGES

## CLUB PITCHING

| Club | ERA. | G. | CG. | ShO. | Sv. | IP. | H. | BFP. | R. | ER. | HR. | SH. | SF. | HB. | Tot. BB. | Int. BB. | SO. | WP. | Bk. |
|---|---|---|---|---|---|---|---|---|---|---|---|---|---|---|---|---|---|---|---|
| Los Angeles | 2.96 | 162 | 37 | 21 | 36 | 1465.0 | 1280 | 6043 | 579 | 482 | 102 | 57 | 38 | 21 | 462 | 56 | 979 | 42 | 10 |
| St. Louis | 3.10 | 162 | 37 | 20 | 44 | 1464.0 | 1343 | 6048 | 572 | 505 | 98 | 60 | 39 | 28 | 453 | 80 | 798 | 33 | 6 |
| New York | 3.11 | 162 | 32 | 19 | 37 | 1488.0 | 1306 | 6146 | 568 | 514 | 111 | 66 | 27 | 18 | 515 | 36 | 1039 | 41 | 14 |
| San Diego | 3.40 | 162 | 26 | 19 | 44 | 1451.1 | 1399 | 6049 | 622 | 549 | 127 | 91 | 43 | 25 | 443 | 50 | 727 | 23 | 14 |
| Montreal | 3.55 | 161 | 13 | 13 | 53 | 1457.0 | 1346 | 6109 | 636 | 574 | 99 | 87 | 35 | 21 | 509 | 70 | 870 | 46 | 12 |
| San Francisco | 3.61 | 162 | 13 | 5 | 24 | 1448.0 | 1348 | 6168 | 674 | 581 | 125 | 88 | 40 | 19 | 572 | 76 | 985 | 57 | 16 |
| Houston | 3.66 | 162 | 17 | 9 | 42 | 1458.0 | 1393 | 6185 | 691 | 593 | 119 | 72 | 58 | 25 | 543 | 50 | 909 | 69 | 8 |
| Philadelphia | 3.68 | 162 | 24 | 9 | 30 | 1451.1 | 1424 | 6241 | 673 | 592 | 115 | 66 | 47 | 26 | 596 | 63 | 899 | 34 | 9 |
| Cincinnati | 3.71 | 162 | 15 | 11 | 45 | 1451.1 | 1347 | 6100 | 666 | 598 | 131 | 74 | 51 | 14 | 535 | 61 | 910 | 42 | 5 |
| Pittsburgh | 3.97 | 161 | 20 | 6 | 29 | 1445.1 | 1406 | 6205 | 708 | 638 | 107 | 57 | 28 | 32 | 584 | 72 | 962 | 48 | 11 |
| Chicago | 4.16 | 162 | 9 | 8 | 42 | 1442.1 | 1492 | 6195 | 729 | 666 | 156 | 95 | 45 | 23 | 519 | 83 | 820 | 31 | 11 |
| Atlanta | 4.19 | 162 | 24 | 9 | 29 | 1457.1 | 1512 | 6374 | 781 | 679 | 134 | 88 | 35 | 28 | 642 | 83 | 776 | 35 | 4 |
| Totals | 3.59 | 971 | 267 | 149 | 455 | 17474.2 | 16596 | 73863 | 7899 | 6971 | 1424 | 901 | 486 | 280 | 6373 | 780 | 10674 | 501 | 120 |

NOTE: Total earned runs for five clubs do not agree with composite total of respective club's pitchers due to provisions of Scoring Rule Section 10.18 (i). The following differences are to be noted: Atlanta pitching add to 682 earned runs, Chicago pitchers add to 668, Los Angeles pitchers add to 487, St. Louis pitchers add to 507, San Francisco pitchers add to 583.

## PITCHERS' RECORDS

(Top Fifteen Qualifiers for Earned-Run Leadership—162 or More Innings)

| Pitcher and Club | W. | L. | Pct. | ERA. | G. | GS. | CG. | ShO. | GF. | Sv. | IP. | H. | BFP. | R. | ER. | HR. | SH. | SF. | HB. | Tot. BB. | Int. BB. | SO. | WP. | Bk. |
|---|---|---|---|---|---|---|---|---|---|---|---|---|---|---|---|---|---|---|---|---|---|---|---|---|
| Gooden, Dwight, N.Y. | 24 | 4 | .857 | 1.53 | 35 | 35 | 16 | 8 | 0 | 0 | 276.2 | 198 | 1065 | 51 | 47 | 13 | 6 | 2 | 2 | 69 | 4 | 268 | 6 | 2 |
| Tudor, John, St.L.* | 21 | 8 | .724 | 1.93 | 36 | 36 | 14 | 10 | 0 | 0 | 275.0 | 209 | 1062 | 68 | 59 | 14 | 5 | 3 | 6 | 49 | 4 | 169 | 4 | 0 |
| Hershiser, Orel, L.A. | 19 | 3 | .864 | 2.03 | 36 | 34 | 9 | 5 | 1 | 1 | 239.2 | 179 | 953 | 72 | 54 | 8 | 5 | 6 | 4 | 68 | 5 | 157 | 5 | 0 |
| Reuschel, Ricky, Pitt. | 14 | 8 | .636 | 2.27 | 36 | 34 | 9 | 1 | 4 | 0 | 194.0 | 153 | 773 | 58 | 49 | 7 | 5 | 3 | 6 | 52 | 10 | 138 | 4 | 0 |
| Welch, Robert, L.A. | 14 | 4 | .778 | 2.31 | 23 | 23 | 8 | 3 | 0 | 0 | 167.1 | 141 | 675 | 49 | 43 | 16 | 13 | 8 | 0 | 35 | 5 | 96 | 7 | 4 |
| Valenzuela, Fernando, L.A.* | 17 | 10 | .630 | 2.45 | 35 | 35 | 14 | 5 | 0 | 0 | 272.1 | 211 | 1109 | 92 | 74 | 14 | 4 | 3 | 1 | 101 | 5 | 208 | 10 | 1 |
| Fernandez, C. Sidney, N.Y.* | 9 | 9 | .500 | 2.80 | 26 | 26 | 3 | 0 | 0 | 0 | 170.1 | 108 | 685 | 56 | 53 | 14 | 7 | 2 | 3 | 80 | 3 | 180 | 3 | 2 |
| Cox, Danny, St.L. | 18 | 9 | .667 | 2.88 | 35 | 35 | 10 | 4 | 0 | 0 | 241.0 | 226 | 989 | 91 | 77 | 21 | 13 | 8 | 3 | 64 | 1 | 131 | 3 | 1 |
| Darling, Ronald, N.Y. | 16 | 6 | .727 | 2.90 | 36 | 35 | 4 | 2 | 0 | 0 | 248.0 | 214 | 1043 | 93 | 80 | 13 | 13 | 4 | 3 | 114 | 7 | 167 | 7 | 1 |
| Smith, Bryn, Mtl. | 18 | 5 | .783 | 2.91 | 32 | 32 | 4 | 2 | 0 | 0 | 222.1 | 193 | 890 | 85 | 72 | 12 | 13 | 4 | 1 | 41 | 1 | 127 | 1 | 0 |
| Reuss, Jerry, L.A.* | 14 | 10 | .583 | 2.92 | 34 | 33 | 5 | 1 | 0 | 0 | 212.2 | 210 | 883 | 78 | 69 | 12 | 13 | 8 | 7 | 58 | 7 | 84 | 5 | 2 |
| Dravecky, David, S.D.* | 13 | 11 | .542 | 2.93 | 34 | 31 | 7 | 2 | 0 | 1 | 214.2 | 200 | 876 | 79 | 70 | 18 | 13 | 6 | 3 | 57 | 5 | 105 | 2 | 0 |
| Eckersley, Dennis, Chi. | 11 | 7 | .611 | 3.08 | 25 | 25 | 6 | 2 | 0 | 0 | 169.1 | 145 | 664 | 61 | 58 | 15 | 0 | 3 | 1 | 19 | 4 | 117 | 0 | 3 |
| Show, Eric, S.D. | 12 | 11 | .522 | 3.09 | 35 | 35 | 4 | 0 | 0 | 0 | 233.0 | 212 | 977 | 95 | 80 | 27 | 9 | 5 | 5 | 87 | 7 | 141 | 4 | 0 |
| Hawkins, M. Andrew, S.D. | 18 | 8 | .692 | 3.15 | 33 | 33 | 5 | 2 | 0 | 0 | 228.2 | 229 | 953 | 88 | 80 | 18 | 13 | 12 | 4 | 65 | 8 | 69 | 3 | 3 |

*Throws lefthanded

DEPARTMENTAL LEADERS: W—Gooden, 24; L—DeLeon (Pitt.), 19; Pct.—Hershiser, .864; G—Burke, 78; GS—Mahler (Atl.), 39; CG—Gooden, 16; ShO—Tudor, 10; GF—Smith (Chi.), 57; Sv.—Reardon, 41; IP—Gooden, 276.2; H—Mahler (Atl.), 272; BFP—Andujar, 1,127; R—Knepper, Rhoden, 119; ER—Rhoden, 106; HR—Soto, 30; SH—Smith (Atl.), 16; SF—Hawkins, Niekro, Ryan, 12; HB—Andujar, 11; Tot.BB—Darling, 114; Int.BB—Minton, 18; SO—Gooden, 268; WP—Niekro, 21; Bk—Roberge, 5.

(All Pitchers Listed Alphabetically)

| Pitcher and Club | W. | L. | Pct. | ERA. | G. | GS. | CG. | ShO. | GF. | Sv. | IP. | H. | BFP. | R. | ER. | HR. | SH. | SF. | HB. | Tot. BB. | Int. BB. | SO. | WP. | Bk. |
|---|---|---|---|---|---|---|---|---|---|---|---|---|---|---|---|---|---|---|---|---|---|---|---|---|
| Abrego, Johnny, Chi. | 1 | 1 | .500 | 6.38 | 6 | 5 | 0 | 0 | 0 | 0 | 24.0 | 32 | 109 | 18 | 17 | 3 | 5 | 1 | 0 | 12 | 1 | 13 | 2 | 0 |
| Aguilera, Richard, N.Y. | 10 | 7 | .588 | 3.24 | 21 | 19 | 2 | 0 | 1 | 0 | 122.1 | 118 | 507 | 49 | 44 | 8 | 7 | 4 | 2 | 37 | 2 | 74 | 5 | 2 |
| Allen, Neil, St.L. | 1 | 4 | .200 | 5.59 | 23 | 0 | 0 | 0 | 13 | 2 | 29.0 | 32 | 135 | 22 | 18 | 3 | 1 | 3 | 1 | 17 | 6 | 10 | 1 | 1 |
| Andersen, Larry, Phil. | 3 | 3 | .500 | 4.32 | 57 | 0 | 0 | 0 | 19 | 0 | 73.0 | 78 | 318 | 35 | 35 | 5 | 3 | 1 | 3 | 26 | 4 | 50 | 2 | 1 |
| Andujar, Joaquin, St.L. | 21 | 12 | .636 | 3.40 | 38 | 38 | 10 | 2 | 0 | 0 | 269.2 | 265 | 1127 | 113 | 102 | 15 | 11 | 4 | 11 | 82 | 12 | 112 | 3 | 0 |
| Bair, C. Douglas, St.L. | 2 | 0 | .000 | 0.00 | 2 | 0 | 0 | 0 | 1 | 0 | 2.0 | 1 | 8 | 0 | 0 | 0 | 0 | 0 | 0 | 2 | 0 | 1 | 0 | 0 |
| Baller, Jay, Chi. | 2 | 3 | .400 | 3.46 | 20 | 0 | 0 | 0 | 4 | 1 | 52.0 | 52 | 223 | 21 | 20 | 8 | 4 | 1 | 1 | 17 | 0 | 31 | 2 | 0 |
| Barker, Leonard, Atl. | 2 | 9 | .182 | 6.35 | 20 | 18 | 0 | 0 | 1 | 0 | 73.2 | 84 | 335 | 55 | 52 | 10 | 4 | 1 | 1 | 37 | 7 | 47 | 3 | 0 |
| Beard, David, Chi. | 0 | 3 | .000 | 6.39 | 9 | 0 | 0 | 0 | 5 | 0 | 12.2 | 16 | 59 | 9 | 9 | 2 | 4 | 1 | 0 | 7 | 1 | 4 | 6 | 0 |
| Bedrosian, Stephen, Atl. | 7 | 15 | .318 | 3.83 | 37 | 37 | 0 | 0 | 0 | 0 | 206.2 | 198 | 907 | 101 | 88 | 17 | 7 | 0 | 5 | 111 | 0 | 134 | 3 | 0 |
| Berenyi, Bruce, N.Y. | 0 | 1 | .000 | 2.63 | 3 | 3 | 0 | 0 | 0 | 0 | 13.2 | 8 | 58 | 6 | 4 | 0 | 0 | 3 | 0 | 10 | 1 | 10 | 1 | 0 |
| Blue, Vida, S.F.* | 8 | 8 | .500 | 4.47 | 33 | 20 | 1 | 0 | 5 | 0 | 131.0 | 115 | 574 | 70 | 65 | 17 | 11 | 3 | 3 | 80 | 1 | 103 | 5 | 1 |
| Boever, Joseph, St.L. | 0 | 0 | .000 | 4.41 | 13 | 0 | 0 | 0 | 5 | 0 | 16.1 | 17 | 69 | 9 | 8 | 3 | 0 | 1 | 0 | 4 | 1 | 20 | 1 | 0 |
| Booker, Gregory, S.D. | 0 | 1 | .000 | 6.85 | 17 | 0 | 0 | 0 | 9 | 0 | 22.1 | 20 | 102 | 17 | 17 | 3 | 4 | 0 | 2 | 17 | 1 | 7 | 5 | 1 |
| Botelho, Derek, Chi. | 1 | 3 | .250 | 5.32 | 11 | 7 | 0 | 0 | 2 | 0 | 44.0 | 52 | 203 | 27 | 26 | 8 | 4 | 0 | 3 | 23 | 2 | 23 | 2 | 0 |
| Brennan, Thomas, L.A. | 1 | 3 | .250 | 7.39 | 12 | 4 | 0 | 0 | 2 | 0 | 31.2 | 41 | 144 | 26 | 26 | 2 | 0 | 5 | 0 | 11 | 1 | 17 | 2 | 0 |
| Browning, Thomas, Cin.* | 20 | 9 | .690 | 3.55 | 38 | 38 | 6 | 4 | 0 | 0 | 261.1 | 242 | 1083 | 111 | 103 | 29 | 13 | 7 | 3 | 73 | 8 | 155 | 7 | 3 |
| Brusstar, Warren, Chi. | 4 | 3 | .571 | 6.05 | 51 | 0 | 0 | 0 | 20 | 4 | 74.1 | 87 | 346 | 55 | 50 | 8 | 8 | 5 | 3 | 36 | 11 | 34 | 3 | 0 |
| Buchanan, Robert, Cin.* | 1 | 0 | 1.000 | 8.44 | 14 | 0 | 0 | 0 | 3 | 0 | 16.0 | 25 | 77 | 15 | 15 | 4 | 0 | 0 | 0 | 9 | 1 | 3 | 7 | 0 |
| Burke, Timothy, Mtl. | 9 | 4 | .692 | 2.39 | 78 | 0 | 0 | 0 | 31 | 8 | 120.1 | 86 | 483 | 32 | 32 | 8 | 8 | 3 | 2 | 44 | 14 | 87 | 0 | 0 |
| Butera, Salvatore, Mtl. | 0 | 0 | .000 | 0.00 | 1 | 0 | 0 | 0 | 1 | 0 | 1.0 | 0 | 3 | 0 | 0 | 0 | 0 | 0 | 0 | 0 | 0 | 0 | 0 | 0 |
| Calhoun, Jeffrey, Hou.* | 2 | 5 | .286 | 2.54 | 44 | 0 | 0 | 0 | 21 | 4 | 63.2 | 56 | 259 | 21 | 18 | 2 | 5 | 2 | 0 | 24 | 11 | 47 | 4 | 1 |
| Camp, Rick, Atl. | 4 | 6 | .400 | 3.95 | 66 | 0 | 0 | 0 | 23 | 3 | 127.2 | 130 | 569 | 72 | 56 | 8 | 5 | 5 | 2 | 61 | 9 | 49 | 4 | 1 |
| Campbell, William, St.L. | 5 | 3 | .625 | 3.50 | 50 | 0 | 0 | 0 | 18 | 4 | 64.1 | 55 | 270 | 32 | 25 | 5 | 9 | 3 | 1 | 21 | 2 | 41 | 1 | 1 |
| Candelaria, John, Pitt.* | 2 | 4 | .333 | 3.64 | 37 | 0 | 0 | 0 | 26 | 0 | 54.1 | 57 | 229 | 34 | 22 | 7 | 0 | 1 | 0 | 14 | 3 | 41 | 2 | 0 |
| Carlton, Steven, Phil.* | 1 | 8 | .111 | 3.33 | 16 | 16 | 0 | 0 | 0 | 0 | 92.0 | 84 | 401 | 43 | 34 | 6 | 9 | 1 | 0 | 53 | 6 | 48 | 1 | 0 |
| Carman, Donald, Phil.* | 9 | 4 | .692 | 2.08 | 71 | 0 | 0 | 0 | 33 | 7 | 86.1 | 52 | 342 | 25 | 20 | 6 | 5 | 5 | 2 | 38 | 3 | 87 | 2 | 2 |
| Castillo, Robert, L.A. | 2 | 2 | .500 | 5.43 | 35 | 0 | 0 | 0 | 5 | 0 | 68.0 | 59 | 301 | 42 | 41 | 15 | 2 | 1 | 3 | 41 | 6 | 57 | 1 | 0 |
| Childress, Rodney, Phil. | 0 | 2 | .000 | 6.21 | 16 | 0 | 0 | 0 | 7 | 0 | 33.1 | 45 | 153 | 23 | 23 | 6 | 2 | 5 | 0 | 15 | 3 | 14 | 3 | 0 |
| Clements, Patrick, Pitt. | 0 | 2 | .000 | 3.67 | 27 | 0 | 0 | 0 | 7 | 2 | 34.1 | 39 | 151 | 14 | 14 | 3 | 2 | 2 | 0 | 18 | 5 | 17 | 7 | 0 |
| Cox, Danny, St.L. | 18 | 9 | .667 | 2.88 | 35 | 35 | 10 | 4 | 0 | 0 | 241.0 | 226 | 989 | 91 | 77 | 19 | 12 | 9 | 3 | 64 | 5 | 131 | 6 | 1 |
| Darling, Ronald, N.Y. | 16 | 6 | .727 | 2.90 | 36 | 35 | 4 | 2 | 1 | 0 | 248.0 | 214 | 1043 | 93 | 80 | 21 | 13 | 4 | 3 | 114 | 1 | 167 | 4 | 0 |
| Davis, Mark, S.F.* | 5 | 12 | .294 | 3.54 | 77 | 1 | 0 | 0 | 38 | 7 | 114.1 | 89 | 465 | 49 | 45 | 13 | 13 | 2 | 0 | 41 | 7 | 131 | 2 | 0 |
| Dayley, Kenneth, St.L.* | 4 | 4 | .500 | 2.76 | 36 | 0 | 0 | 0 | 19 | 11 | 65.1 | 65 | 271 | 24 | 20 | 4 | 2 | 4 | 0 | 37 | 9 | 62 | 7 | 0 |
| Dedmon, Jeffrey, Atl. | 4 | 3 | .571 | 4.08 | 57 | 0 | 0 | 0 | 27 | 3 | 86.0 | 84 | 377 | 52 | 39 | 7 | 8 | 2 | 1 | 49 | 14 | 41 | 1 | 0 |
| DeLeon, Jose, Pitt. | 2 | 19 | .095 | 4.70 | 31 | 25 | 0 | 0 | 1 | 0 | 162.2 | 138 | 700 | 89 | 85 | 15 | 7 | 8 | 3 | 89 | 5 | 149 | 8 | 1 |
| DeLeon, Luis, S.D. | 2 | 3 | .400 | 4.19 | 29 | 0 | 0 | 0 | 15 | 3 | 38.2 | 39 | 163 | 18 | 18 | 6 | 3 | 1 | 0 | 10 | 4 | 31 | 0 | 0 |
| Denny, John, Phil. | 11 | 14 | .440 | 3.82 | 33 | 33 | 6 | 2 | 0 | 0 | 230.2 | 252 | 998 | 112 | 98 | 15 | 11 | 8 | 0 | 83 | 5 | 123 | 4 | 0 |
| Deshaies, James, Hou.* | 0 | 0 | .000 | 0.00 | 2 | 0 | 0 | 0 | 0 | 0 | 3.0 | 1 | 10 | 0 | 0 | 0 | 1 | 0 | 0 | 3 | 0 | 6 | 2 | 0 |
| Diaz, Carlos, L.A.* | 6 | 3 | .667 | 2.61 | 46 | 0 | 0 | 0 | 21 | 6 | 79.1 | 70 | 326 | 28 | 23 | 4 | 3 | 1 | 0 | 18 | 6 | 73 | 2 | 1 |
| DiPino, Frank, Hou.* | 3 | 7 | .300 | 4.03 | 54 | 0 | 0 | 0 | 29 | 0 | 76.0 | 69 | 329 | 44 | 34 | 7 | 0 | 3 | 2 | 43 | 6 | 49 | 2 | 1 |
| Dopson, John, Mtl. | 0 | 2 | .000 | 11.08 | 4 | 3 | 0 | 0 | 1 | 0 | 13.0 | 25 | 70 | 17 | 16 | 4 | 0 | 0 | 1 | 13 | 0 | 4 | 0 | 1 |
| Dravecky, David, S.D.* | 13 | 11 | .542 | 2.93 | 34 | 31 | 7 | 2 | 0 | 0 | 214.2 | 200 | 876 | 79 | 70 | 18 | 13 | 3 | 0 | 57 | 5 | 105 | 3 | 0 |
| Eckersley, Dennis, Chi. | 11 | 7 | .611 | 3.08 | 25 | 25 | 6 | 2 | 0 | 0 | 169.1 | 145 | 664 | 61 | 58 | 15 | 6 | 2 | 1 | 19 | 4 | 117 | 3 | 1 |
| Engel, Steven, Chi.* | 1 | 5 | .167 | 5.57 | 11 | 8 | 0 | 0 | 1 | 0 | 51.2 | 61 | 237 | 36 | 32 | 6 | 5 | 2 | 0 | 26 | 3 | 29 | 2 | 0 |
| Fernandez, C. Sidney, N.Y.* | 9 | 9 | .500 | 2.80 | 26 | 26 | 3 | 1 | 0 | 0 | 170.1 | 108 | 685 | 61 | 53 | 15 | 6 | 3 | 2 | 80 | 3 | 180 | 3 | 2 |
| Fontenot, S. Ray, Chi.* | 6 | 10 | .375 | 4.36 | 38 | 23 | 0 | 0 | 5 | 0 | 154.2 | 177 | 661 | 86 | 75 | 23 | 12 | 3 | 2 | 45 | 4 | 70 | 2 | 0 |
| Forsch, Robert, St.L. | 9 | 6 | .600 | 3.90 | 34 | 19 | 1 | 1 | 4 | 2 | 136.0 | 132 | 567 | 63 | 59 | 11 | 5 | 1 | 2 | 47 | 4 | 48 | 3 | 0 |

| Pitcher and Club | W. | L. | Pct. | ERA. | G. | GS. | CG. | ShO. | GF. | Sv. | IP. | H. | BFP. | R. | ER. | HR. | SH. | SF. | HB. | Tot. BB. | Int. BB. | SO. | WP. | Bk. |
|---|---|---|---|---|---|---|---|---|---|---|---|---|---|---|---|---|---|---|---|---|---|---|---|---|
| Forster, Terry, Atl.* | 2 | 3 | .400 | 2.28 | 46 | 0 | 0 | 0 | 19 | 1 | 59.1 | 49 | 253 | 22 | 15 | 7 | 2 | 2 | 0 | 28 | 4 | 37 | 4 | 0 |
| Franco, John, Cin.* | 12 | 3 | .800 | 2.18 | 67 | 0 | 0 | 0 | 33 | 12 | 99.0 | 83 | 407 | 27 | 24 | 5 | 11 | 1 | 1 | 40 | 8 | 61 | 4 | 0 |
| Frazier, George, Chi.* | 7 | 8 | .467 | 6.39 | 51 | 0 | 0 | 0 | 17 | 1 | 76.0 | 88 | 357 | 57 | 54 | 11 | 7 | 1 | 3 | 52 | 9 | 46 | 6 | 2 |
| Garber, H. Eugene, Atl. | 6 | 6 | .500 | 3.61 | 59 | 0 | 0 | 0 | 31 | 24 | 97.1 | 98 | 409 | 41 | 39 | 8 | 9 | 1 | 2 | 25 | 8 | 66 | 1 | 0 |
| Gardner, Wesley, N.Y.* | 0 | 2 | .000 | 5.25 | 9 | 0 | 0 | 0 | 8 | 0 | 12.0 | 18 | 61 | 14 | 7 | 1 | 1 | 1 | 0 | 8 | 1 | 11 | 1 | 0 |
| Garrelts, Scott, S.F. | 9 | 6 | .600 | 2.30 | 74 | 0 | 0 | 0 | 44 | 13 | 105.2 | 76 | 454 | 37 | 27 | 2 | 6 | 3 | 2 | 58 | 12 | 106 | 7 | 1 |
| Glynn, Edward, Mtl.* | 0 | 0 | .000 | 19.29 | 3 | 0 | 0 | 0 | 0 | 0 | 2.1 | 5 | 16 | 5 | 5 | 0 | 0 | 0 | 0 | 4 | 0 | 2 | 0 | 0 |
| Gooden, Dwight, N.Y. | 24 | 4 | .857 | 1.53 | 35 | 35 | 16 | 8 | 0 | 0 | 276.2 | 198 | 1065 | 51 | 47 | 13 | 6 | 0 | 1 | 69 | 4 | 268 | 6 | 2 |
| Gorman, Thomas, N.Y.* | 4 | 4 | .500 | 5.13 | 34 | 0 | 0 | 0 | 12 | 0 | 52.2 | 56 | 227 | 32 | 30 | 8 | 6 | 2 | 0 | 18 | 2 | 32 | 2 | 0 |
| Gossage, Richard, S.D. | 5 | 3 | .625 | 1.82 | 50 | 0 | 0 | 0 | 38 | 26 | 79.0 | 64 | 308 | 21 | 16 | 1 | 3 | 4 | 1 | 17 | 1 | 52 | 3 | 0 |
| Gott, James, S.F. | 7 | 10 | .412 | 3.88 | 26 | 26 | 2 | 0 | 0 | 0 | 148.1 | 144 | 629 | 73 | 64 | 10 | 0 | 4 | 7 | 51 | 3 | 78 | 5 | 0 |
| Grapenthin, Richard, Mtl. | 0 | 0 | .000 | 14.14 | 5 | 0 | 0 | 0 | 1 | 0 | 7.0 | 13 | 43 | 11 | 11 | 1 | 0 | 1 | 1 | 7 | 2 | 4 | 1 | 1 |
| Gross, Kevin, Phil. | 15 | 13 | .536 | 3.41 | 38 | 31 | 6 | 2 | 1 | 0 | 205.2 | 194 | 873 | 86 | 78 | 11 | 5 | 3 | 1 | 81 | 3 | 151 | 2 | 1 |
| Guante, Cecilio, Pitt. | 4 | 6 | .400 | 2.72 | 63 | 0 | 0 | 0 | 31 | 5 | 109.0 | 84 | 445 | 34 | 33 | 8 | 12 | 2 | 5 | 40 | 9 | 92 | 5 | 2 |
| Gullickson, William, Mtl. | 14 | 12 | .538 | 3.52 | 29 | 29 | 4 | 1 | 0 | 0 | 181.1 | 187 | 759 | 78 | 71 | 15 | 8 | 2 | 8 | 47 | 9 | 68 | 5 | 0 |
| Gumpert, David, Chi. | 1 | 0 | 1.000 | 8.41 | 9 | 0 | 0 | 0 | 3 | 0 | 10.1 | 12 | 52 | 17 | 4 | 0 | 0 | 0 | 0 | 7 | 1 | 4 | 0 | 0 |
| Gura, Lawrence, Chi.* | 0 | 3 | .000 | 3.48 | 5 | 4 | 1 | 0 | 0 | 0 | 20.1 | 34 | 102 | 19 | 19 | 4 | 8 | 2 | 0 | 6 | 0 | 7 | 0 | 0 |
| Hammaker, C. Atlee, S.F.* | 5 | 12 | .294 | 3.74 | 29 | 29 | 5 | 0 | 0 | 0 | 170.2 | 161 | 713 | 81 | 71 | 17 | 8 | 6 | 0 | 47 | 5 | 100 | 4 | 4 |
| Hassler, Andrew, St.L.* | 3 | 1 | .750 | 1.80 | 10 | 0 | 1 | 0 | 4 | 1 | 10.0 | 9 | 45 | 5 | 2 | 0 | 1 | 0 | 1 | 4 | 0 | 5 | 0 | 0 |
| Hawkins, M. Andrew, S.D. | 18 | 8 | .692 | 3.15 | 33 | 33 | 9 | 2 | 0 | 0 | 228.2 | 229 | 953 | 88 | 80 | 18 | 13 | 12 | 6 | 65 | 8 | 69 | 3 | 3 |
| Heathcock, R. Jeffery, Hou. | 3 | 1 | .750 | 3.36 | 14 | 7 | 2 | 0 | 5 | 0 | 56.1 | 50 | 226 | 25 | 21 | 0 | 2 | 4 | 0 | 13 | 0 | 25 | 2 | 0 |
| Hershiser, Orel, L.A. | 19 | 3 | .864 | 2.03 | 36 | 34 | 9 | 5 | 0 | 0 | 239.2 | 179 | 953 | 72 | 54 | 8 | 8 | 6 | 2 | 68 | 5 | 157 | 5 | 3 |
| Hesketh, Joseph, Mtl.* | 10 | 5 | .667 | 2.49 | 25 | 25 | 2 | 1 | 0 | 0 | 155.1 | 125 | 618 | 52 | 43 | 10 | 5 | 2 | 4 | 45 | 1 | 113 | 5 | 3 |
| Holland, Alfred, Phil.-Pitt.* | 1 | 4 | .200 | 3.45 | 41 | 0 | 0 | 0 | 22 | 5 | 62.2 | 53 | 256 | 24 | 24 | 8 | 5 | 4 | 0 | 21 | 8 | 48 | 0 | 1 |
| Holton, Brian, L.A. | 1 | 1 | .500 | 9.00 | 1 | 0 | 0 | 0 | 0 | 0 | 4.0 | 9 | 21 | 4 | 4 | 0 | 0 | 0 | 0 | 1 | 0 | 1 | 2 | 0 |
| Honeycutt, Frederick, L.A.* | 8 | 12 | .400 | 3.42 | 31 | 25 | 5 | 0 | 2 | 1 | 142.0 | 141 | 600 | 71 | 54 | 9 | 5 | 3 | 3 | 49 | 9 | 67 | 3 | 2 |
| Horton, Rickey, St.L.* | 3 | 2 | .600 | 2.91 | 49 | 3 | 0 | 0 | 10 | 1 | 89.2 | 84 | 382 | 30 | 29 | 9 | 8 | 3 | 1 | 34 | 13 | 59 | 2 | 0 |
| Howe, Steven, L.A.* | 4 | 7 | .364 | 4.91 | 19 | 0 | 0 | 0 | 14 | 3 | 22.0 | 30 | 104 | 17 | 12 | 2 | 4 | 2 | 1 | 5 | 3 | 11 | 3 | 2 |
| Howell, Kenneth, L.A. | 4 | 2 | .667 | 3.77 | 56 | 0 | 0 | 0 | 31 | 12 | 86.0 | 66 | 356 | 41 | 36 | 8 | 9 | 3 | 1 | 35 | 5 | 85 | 4 | 4 |
| Hoyt, D. LaMarr, S.D. | 16 | 8 | .667 | 3.47 | 31 | 31 | 6 | 3 | 0 | 0 | 210.1 | 210 | 839 | 85 | 81 | 20 | 8 | 4 | 3 | 20 | 8 | 83 | 4 | 3 |
| Hudson, Charles, Phil. | 8 | 13 | .381 | 3.78 | 38 | 26 | 3 | 0 | 7 | 0 | 193.0 | 188 | 833 | 92 | 81 | 23 | 2 | 8 | 1 | 74 | 2 | 122 | 3 | 1 |
| Hume, Thomas, Cin. | 3 | 5 | .375 | 3.26 | 56 | 3 | 0 | 0 | 15 | 3 | 80.0 | 65 | 331 | 33 | 29 | 7 | 4 | 2 | 3 | 35 | 7 | 50 | 0 | 0 |
| Jackson, Roy Lee, S.D. | 2 | 3 | .400 | 2.70 | 22 | 2 | 0 | 0 | 6 | 2 | 40.0 | 32 | 163 | 13 | 12 | 4 | 2 | 2 | 3 | 13 | 5 | 28 | 1 | 0 |
| Jeffcoat, J. Michael, S.F.* | 0 | 0 |  | 5.32 | 19 | 1 | 0 | 0 | 7 | 0 | 22.0 | 27 | 99 | 13 | 13 | 4 | 4 | 1 | 1 | 6 | 3 | 10 | 2 | 0 |
| Johnson, Joseph, Atl. | 4 | 4 | .500 | 4.10 | 15 | 14 | 1 | 1 | 0 | 0 | 85.2 | 95 | 367 | 44 | 39 | 9 | 4 | 3 | 0 | 24 | 5 | 34 | 0 | 2 |
| Keough, Matthew, St.L. | 0 | 2 | .000 | 4.50 | 9 | 1 | 0 | 0 | 0 | 0 | 10.0 | 10 | 43 | 5 | 5 | 0 | 5 | 0 | 0 | 4 | 0 | 10 | 6 | 0 |
| Kepshire, Kurt, St.L. | 10 | 9 | .526 | 4.75 | 29 | 29 | 0 | 0 | 0 | 0 | 153.1 | 155 | 671 | 89 | 81 | 16 | 1 | 5 | 3 | 71 | 3 | 67 | 1 | 0 |
| Kerfeld, Charles, Hou.* | 0 | 2 | .000 | 4.06 | 37 | 6 | 0 | 0 | 0 | 0 | 44.1 | 44 | 193 | 22 | 20 | 2 | 15 | 3 | 1 | 25 | 2 | 30 | 0 | 2 |
| Kipper, Robert, Pitt.* | 2 | 1 | .667 | 5.11 | 6 | 4 | 0 | 0 | 2 | 0 | 24.0 | 21 | 104 | 16 | 14 | 4 | 1 | 9 | 0 | 7 | 1 | 13 | 4 | 0 |
| Knepper, Robert, Hou.* | 15 | 13 | .536 | 3.55 | 40 | 31 | 3 | 1 | 0 | 0 | 241.0 | 253 | 1016 | 119 | 95 | 21 | 10 | 0 | 0 | 54 | 3 | 131 | 2 | 3 |
| Knudson, Mark, Hou. | 0 | 2 | .000 | 9.00 | 5 | 2 | 0 | 0 | 3 | 0 | 11.0 | 21 | 53 | 11 | 11 | 0 | 0 | 4 | 0 | 3 | 3 | 4 | 1 | 0 |
| Koosman, Jerome, Phil.* | 6 | 4 | .600 | 4.62 | 28 | 28 | 6 | 1 | 0 | 0 | 99.1 | 107 | 433 | 56 | 51 | 14 | 7 | 3 | 0 | 34 | 3 | 60 | 4 | 3 |
| Krawczyk, Raymond, Pitt. | 0 | 2 | .000 | 14.04 | 7 | 0 | 0 | 0 | 3 | 0 | 8.1 | 20 | 51 | 13 | 13 | 1 | 0 | 0 | 0 | 6 | 0 | 9 | 0 | 0 |
| Krukow, Michael, S.F. | 8 | 11 | .421 | 3.38 | 34 | 31 | 2 | 2 | 1 | 0 | 194.2 | 176 | 804 | 80 | 73 | 19 | 10 | 3 | 3 | 49 | 10 | 150 | 3 | 2 |
| Lahti, Jeffrey, St.L. | 5 | 2 | .714 | 1.84 | 52 | 0 | 0 | 0 | 31 | 19 | 68.1 | 63 | 279 | 15 | 14 | 3 | 8 | 5 | 2 | 26 | 6 | 41 | 5 | 1 |
| LaPoint, David, S.F.* | 7 | 17 | .292 | 3.57 | 31 | 32 | 6 | 1 | 0 | 0 | 206.2 | 215 | 886 | 99 | 82 | 18 | 7 | 5 | 5 | 74 | 1 | 122 | 3 | 0 |
| Laskey, William, S.F.-Mtl.* | 5 | 16 | .238 | 4.91 | 30 | 26 | 0 | 0 | 1 | 1 | 148.1 | 165 | 656 | 91 | 81 | 19 | 13 | 5 | 2 | 53 | 1 | 60 | 3 | 1 |
| Latham, William, N.Y.* | 1 | 3 | .250 | 3.97 | 7 | 3 | 0 | 1 | 4 | 1 | 22.2 | 21 | 93 | 10 | 10 | 1 | 1 | 2 | 1 | 7 | 1 | 10 | 0 | 1 |
| Leach, Terry, N.Y. | 3 | 4 | .429 | 2.91 | 22 | 4 | 1 | 1 | 4 | 1 | 55.2 | 48 | 226 | 19 | 18 | 3 | 5 | 1 | 0 | 14 | 3 | 30 | 0 | 0 |
| Lefferts, Craig, S.D.* | 7 | 6 | .538 | 3.35 | 60 | 0 | 0 | 0 | 24 | 2 | 83.1 | 75 | 345 | 34 | 31 | 7 | 7 | 3 | 0 | 30 | 4 | 48 | 2 | 0 |

| Pitcher and Club | W. | L. | Pct. | ERA. | G. | GS. | CG. | ShO. | GF. | Sv. | IP. | H. | BFP. | R. | ER. | HR. | SH. | SF. | HB. | Tot. BB. | Int. BB. | SO. | WP. | Bk. |
|---|---|---|---|---|---|---|---|---|---|---|---|---|---|---|---|---|---|---|---|---|---|---|---|---|
| Lucas, Gary, Mtl.* | 6 | 2 | .750 | 3.19 | 49 | 0 | 0 | 0 | 18 | 1 | 67.2 | 63 | 284 | 29 | 24 | 6 | 7 | 2 | 0 | 24 | 8 | 31 | 5 | 0 |
| Lynch, Edward, N.Y.* | 10 | 8 | .556 | 3.44 | 31 | 29 | 6 | 1 | 4 | 0 | 191.0 | 188 | 777 | 76 | 73 | 19 | 9 | 5 | 1 | 27 | 1 | 65 | 0 | 0 |
| Madden, Michael, Hou.* | 0 | 0 | .000 | 4.26 | 13 | 0 | 0 | 1 | 8 | 0 | 19.0 | 20 | 92 | 15 | 9 | 1 | 0 | 1 | 0 | 11 | 0 | 16 | 1 | 0 |
| Mahler, Michael, Mtl.* | 1 | 4 | .000 | 3.54 | 9 | 7 | 1 | 0 | 2 | 0 | 48.1 | 40 | 203 | 22 | 19 | 3 | 2 | 1 | 1 | 24 | 1 | 32 | 3 | 1 |
| Mahler, Richard, Atl. | 17 | 15 | .531 | 3.48 | 39 | 39 | 6 | 1 | 0 | 0 | 266.2 | 272 | 1110 | 116 | 103 | 24 | 10 | 5 | 2 | 79 | 8 | 107 | 3 | 0 |
| Mason, Roger, S.F. | 1 | 3 | .250 | 2.12 | 5 | 5 | 1 | 1 | 0 | 0 | 29.2 | 28 | 128 | 13 | 7 | 1 | 2 | 1 | 1 | 11 | 1 | 26 | 0 | 1 |
| Mathis, Ronald, Hou. | 3 | 5 | .375 | 6.04 | 5 | 5 | 0 | 0 | 0 | 0 | 70.0 | 83 | 319 | 54 | 47 | 7 | 4 | 3 | 2 | 27 | 1 | 34 | 1 | 0 |
| McCullers, Lance, S.D. | 6 | 5 | .545 | 2.31 | 23 | 8 | 0 | 0 | 5 | 5 | 35.0 | 23 | 142 | 15 | 9 | 3 | 7 | 0 | 0 | 16 | 3 | 27 | 0 | 0 |
| McDowell, Roger, N.Y. | 6 | 5 | .545 | 2.83 | 62 | 2 | 0 | 0 | 11 | 17 | 127.1 | 108 | 516 | 43 | 40 | 9 | 6 | 2 | 2 | 37 | 8 | 70 | 6 | 2 |
| McGaffigan, Andrew, Cin. | 3 | 3 | .500 | 3.72 | 21 | 15 | 2 | 0 | 36 | 1 | 94.1 | 88 | 392 | 40 | 39 | 4 | 4 | 2 | 0 | 30 | 4 | 83 | 2 | 0 |
| McMurtry, J. Craig, Atl. | 7 | 9 | .438 | 6.60 | 62 | 17 | 2 | 0 | 3 | 0 | 45.0 | 56 | 220 | 36 | 33 | 6 | 4 | 2 | 1 | 27 | 11 | 28 | 3 | 0 |
| McWilliams, Larry, Pitt.* | 7 | 9 | .438 | 4.70 | 15 | 17 | 2 | 0 | 0 | 1 | 126.1 | 139 | 568 | 70 | 66 | 9 | 7 | 2 | 0 | 62 | 4 | 52 | 4 | 1 |
| Meridith, Ronald, Chi.* | 0 | 2 | .000 | 4.47 | 30 | 0 | 0 | 0 | 8 | 0 | 46.1 | 56 | 209 | 24 | 23 | 3 | 4 | 3 | 1 | 24 | 11 | 23 | 2 | 0 |
| Minton, Gregory, S.F. | 5 | 4 | .556 | 3.54 | 68 | 0 | 0 | 0 | 36 | 4 | 96.2 | 98 | 424 | 42 | 38 | 6 | 5 | 4 | 0 | 54 | 18 | 37 | 2 | 0 |
| Moore, Robert, S.F. | 0 | 0 | .000 | 3.24 | 11 | 0 | 0 | 0 | 4 | 0 | 16.2 | 18 | 78 | 6 | 6 | 1 | 6 | 3 | 0 | 10 | 2 | 10 | 0 | 0 |
| Murphy, Robert, Cin.* | 0 | 0 | .000 | 6.00 | 1 | 0 | 0 | 0 | 2 | 0 | 3.0 | 2 | 12 | 2 | 2 | 0 | 0 | 0 | 0 | 2 | 0 | 1 | 1 | 0 |
| Myers, Randall, N.Y.* | 0 | 0 | .000 | 0.00 | 1 | 0 | 0 | 0 | 0 | 0 | 2.0 | 0 | 7 | 0 | 0 | 0 | 1 | 0 | 0 | 1 | 0 | 2 | 0 | 0 |
| Niedenfuer, Thomas, L.A. | 9 | 9 | .438 | 2.71 | 64 | 0 | 0 | 0 | 43 | 19 | 106.1 | 86 | 415 | 32 | 32 | 6 | 0 | 3 | 1 | 24 | 5 | 102 | 2 | 0 |
| Niekro, Joseph, Hou. | 9 | 12 | .429 | 3.72 | 32 | 32 | 4 | 0 | 0 | 0 | 213.0 | 197 | 925 | 100 | 88 | 21 | 3 | 12 | 5 | 99 | 6 | 117 | 1 | 1 |
| Niemann, Randy, N.Y.* | 0 | 0 | .000 | 0.00 | 4 | 0 | 0 | 0 | 1 | 0 | 4.2 | 5 | 18 | 4 | 0 | 0 | 1 | 0 | 0 | 0 | 0 | 1 | 0 | 0 |
| O'Connor, Jack, Mtl.* | 8 | 2 | .000 | 4.94 | 20 | 0 | 0 | 0 | 7 | 0 | 23.2 | 21 | 106 | 14 | 13 | 0 | 3 | 2 | 0 | 13 | 7 | 16 | 2 | 0 |
| Orosco, Jesse, N.Y.* | 7 | 6 | .571 | 2.73 | 54 | 0 | 0 | 0 | 39 | 17 | 79.0 | 66 | 331 | 26 | 24 | 4 | 5 | 2 | 1 | 34 | 5 | 68 | 1 | 0 |
| Palmer, David, Mtl. | 2 | 1 | .412 | 3.71 | 24 | 23 | 1 | 0 | 0 | 0 | 135.2 | 128 | 588 | 60 | 56 | 6 | 5 | 2 | 1 | 67 | 1 | 106 | 0 | 0 |
| Pastore, Frank, Cin. | 3 | 2 | .667 | 3.83 | 17 | 5 | 1 | 0 | 3 | 0 | 54.0 | 60 | 232 | 23 | 23 | 5 | 5 | 3 | 2 | 16 | 5 | 29 | 4 | 0 |
| Patterson, Reginald, Chi. | 2 | 1 | 1.000 | 3.00 | 8 | 6 | 0 | 0 | 0 | 0 | 39.0 | 36 | 157 | 13 | 13 | 5 | 3 | 1 | 0 | 13 | 1 | 17 | 9 | 0 |
| Patterson, Robert, S.D.* | 0 | 0 | 1.000 | 8.31 | 3 | 1 | 1 | 0 | 2 | 0 | 4.0 | 13 | 26 | 11 | 11 | 2 | 1 | 0 | 0 | 10 | 0 | 1 | 2 | 0 |
| Pena, Alejandro, L.A. | 1 | 1 | .000 | 4.75 | 2 | 2 | 0 | 0 | 0 | 0 | 4.1 | 7 | 23 | 11 | 4 | 1 | 2 | 1 | 0 | 3 | 0 | 2 | 0 | 0 |
| Perez, Pascual, Atl. | 1 | 13 | .071 | 6.14 | 22 | 22 | 0 | 0 | 0 | 0 | 95.1 | 115 | 453 | 72 | 65 | 10 | 5 | 3 | 2 | 57 | 10 | 57 | 2 | 0 |
| Perlman, Jonathan, Chi. | 1 | 0 | 1.000 | 11.42 | 6 | 0 | 0 | 0 | 1 | 0 | 8.2 | 10 | 42 | 11 | 11 | 3 | 0 | 1 | 0 | 8 | 2 | 4 | 1 | 0 |
| Perry, W. Patrick, St.L.* | 1 | 0 | 1.000 | 0.00 | 6 | 0 | 0 | 0 | 1 | 0 | 12.1 | 3 | 42 | 1 | 0 | 0 | 5 | 1 | 0 | 3 | 1 | 6 | 1 | 0 |
| Powell, Dennis, L.A.* | 1 | 1 | .500 | 5.22 | 16 | 2 | 0 | 0 | 6 | 0 | 29.1 | 30 | 133 | 19 | 17 | 4 | 4 | 4 | 0 | 13 | 3 | 19 | 3 | 0 |
| Power, Ted, Cin. | 8 | 6 | .571 | 2.70 | 64 | 0 | 0 | 0 | 50 | 27 | 80.0 | 65 | 342 | 27 | 24 | 7 | 6 | 5 | 2 | 45 | 8 | 42 | 1 | 0 |
| Price, Joseph, Cin.* | 2 | 3 | .500 | 3.90 | 26 | 8 | 2 | 2 | 5 | 1 | 64.2 | 59 | 274 | 35 | 28 | 13 | 6 | 3 | 5 | 23 | 7 | 52 | 2 | 0 |
| Rawley, Shane, Phil.* | 13 | 8 | .619 | 3.31 | 36 | 31 | 6 | 1 | 4 | 0 | 198.2 | 188 | 849 | 82 | 73 | 18 | 8 | 3 | 2 | 81 | 6 | 106 | 7 | 3 |
| Reardon, Jeffrey, Mtl. | 14 | 8 | .636 | 3.18 | 63 | 0 | 0 | 0 | 50 | 41 | 87.2 | 68 | 356 | 31 | 31 | 10 | 6 | 6 | 1 | 26 | 4 | 67 | 4 | 0 |
| Reuschel, Ricky, Pitt. | 14 | 15 | .583 | 2.27 | 34 | 33 | 9 | 3 | 0 | 0 | 194.0 | 210 | 773 | 58 | 49 | 7 | 6 | 5 | 3 | 52 | 10 | 138 | 5 | 3 |
| Reuss, Jerry, L.A.* | 10 | 15 | .400 | 2.92 | 35 | 35 | 6 | 2 | 0 | 0 | 212.2 | 254 | 883 | 78 | 69 | 13 | 10 | 5 | 3 | 58 | 7 | 84 | 2 | 0 |
| Rhoden, Richard, Pitt. | 3 | 11 | .313 | 4.47 | 42 | 35 | 5 | 3 | 0 | 0 | 213.1 | 210 | 944 | 119 | 106 | 18 | 7 | 3 | 6 | 69 | 11 | 128 | 4 | 8 |
| Roberge, Bertrand, Mtl. | 5 | 0 | .500 | 3.44 | 44 | 6 | 0 | 0 | 15 | 0 | 68.0 | 58 | 280 | 28 | 26 | 5 | 2 | 0 | 2 | 22 | 3 | 34 | 8 | 3 |
| Robinson, Don, Pitt. | 0 | 3 | .313 | 3.87 | 8 | 0 | 0 | 0 | 22 | 0 | 95.1 | 95 | 418 | 49 | 41 | 6 | 6 | 0 | 2 | 42 | 11 | 65 | 5 | 0 |
| Robinson, Jeffrey, S.F. | 7 | 7 | .500 | 5.11 | 33 | 12 | 0 | 0 | 9 | 0 | 12.1 | 16 | 59 | 11 | 7 | 2 | 2 | 0 | 0 | 2 | 0 | 15 | 2 | 1 |
| Robinson, Ronald, Cin. | 2 | 4 | .333 | 3.99 | 8 | 7 | 0 | 0 | 4 | 1 | 108.1 | 107 | 453 | 53 | 48 | 11 | 3 | 4 | 1 | 32 | 3 | 76 | 2 | 2 |
| Rogers, Stephen, Mtl. | 3 | 2 | .600 | 5.68 | 8 | 8 | 1 | 0 | 11 | 0 | 38.0 | 51 | 179 | 25 | 24 | 2 | 2 | 2 | 0 | 20 | 1 | 18 | 2 | 0 |
| Ross, Mark, Hou. | 0 | 0 | .000 | 4.85 | 39 | 0 | 0 | 0 | 3 | 0 | 13.0 | 12 | 52 | 7 | 7 | 2 | 0 | 0 | 0 | 6 | 0 | 10 | 2 | 0 |
| Rucker, David, Phil.* | 3 | 2 | .600 | 4.31 | 20 | 3 | 0 | 0 | 4 | 0 | 79.1 | 83 | 350 | 42 | 38 | 6 | 4 | 6 | 0 | 40 | 10 | 41 | 2 | 0 |
| Ruthven, Richard, Chi. | 4 | 7 | .364 | 4.53 | 20 | 15 | 0 | 0 | 1 | 0 | 87.1 | 103 | 392 | 49 | 44 | 12 | 6 | 6 | 2 | 37 | 3 | 26 | 1 | 0 |
| Ryan, L. Nolan, Hou. | 10 | 12 | .455 | 3.80 | 35 | 35 | 4 | 0 | 0 | 0 | 232.0 | 205 | 983 | 108 | 98 | 14 | 11 | 6 | 9 | 95 | 8 | 209 | 14 | 2 |
| St. Claire, Randy, Mtl. | 5 | 3 | .625 | 3.93 | 42 | 0 | 0 | 0 | 14 | 0 | 68.2 | 69 | 294 | 32 | 30 | 3 | 12 | 1 | 1 | 26 | 7 | 25 | 1 | 0 |
| Sambito, Joseph, N.Y.* | 0 | 0 | .000 | 12.66 | 8 | 0 | 0 | 0 | 2 | 0 | 10.2 | 21 | 60 | 18 | 15 | 1 | 1 | 1 | 0 | 8 | 0 | 3 | 0 | 0 |

| Pitcher and Club | W. | L. | Pct. | ERA. | G. | GS. | CG. | ShO. | GF. | Sv. | IP. | H. | BFP. | R. | ER. | HR. | SH. | SF. | HB. | Tot. BB. | Int. BB. | SO. | WP. | Bk. |
|---|---|---|---|---|---|---|---|---|---|---|---|---|---|---|---|---|---|---|---|---|---|---|---|---|
| Sanderson, Scott, Chi. | 5 | 6 | .455 | 3.12 | 19 | 19 | 2 | 0 | 0 | 0 | 121.0 | 100 | 480 | 49 | 42 | 13 | 7 | 7 | 0 | 27 | 4 | 80 | 1 | 0 |
| Schatzeder, Daniel, N.Y.* | 3 | 5 | .375 | 3.80 | 24 | 15 | 1 | 0 | 2 | 0 | 104.1 | 101 | 431 | 52 | 44 | 13 | 7 | 3 | 3 | 31 | 4 | 64 | 4 | 0 |
| Schiraldi, Calvin, N.Y.* | 2 | 1 | .667 | 8.89 | 10 | 4 | 0 | 0 | 2 | 0 | 26.1 | 43 | 131 | 27 | 26 | 4 | 1 | 0 | 0 | 11 | 0 | 21 | 2 | 1 |
| Schuler, David, Atl.* | 0 | 0 | .000 | 6.75 | 9 | 0 | 0 | 0 | 5 | 0 | 10.2 | 19 | 50 | 8 | 8 | 4 | 0 | 0 | 0 | 3 | 0 | 10 | 0 | 0 |
| Scott, Michael, Hou. | 18 | 8 | .692 | 3.29 | 36 | 35 | 4 | 2 | 1 | 0 | 221.2 | 194 | 922 | 91 | 81 | 20 | 6 | 6 | 3 | 80 | 4 | 137 | 7 | 0 |
| Scurry, Rodney, Pitt.* | 1 | 2 | .333 | 3.21 | 30 | 0 | 0 | 0 | 13 | 3 | 47.2 | 42 | 210 | 22 | 17 | 4 | 2 | 2 | 0 | 28 | 3 | 43 | 1 | 0 |
| Shields, Stephen, Atl. | 1 | 2 | .333 | 5.16 | 23 | 6 | 0 | 0 | 3 | 0 | 68.0 | 86 | 311 | 46 | 39 | 9 | 6 | 1 | 1 | 32 | 6 | 29 | 3 | 2 |
| Shines, A. Raymond, Mtl. | 0 | 0 | .000 | 0.00 | 1 | 0 | 0 | 0 | 1 | 0 | 1.0 | 1 | 4 | 0 | 0 | 0 | 0 | 0 | 0 | 1 | 0 | 0 | 0 | 0 |
| Shipanoff, David, Phil. | 1 | 2 | .333 | 3.22 | 26 | 0 | 0 | 0 | 12 | 2 | 36.1 | 33 | 162 | 15 | 13 | 3 | 0 | 5 | 1 | 16 | 3 | 26 | 0 | 0 |
| Show, Eric, S.D. | 12 | 11 | .522 | 3.09 | 35 | 35 | 5 | 2 | 0 | 0 | 233.0 | 212 | 977 | 95 | 80 | 27 | 9 | 5 | 5 | 87 | 7 | 141 | 4 | 1 |
| Sisk, Douglas, N.Y. | 4 | 5 | .444 | 5.30 | 42 | 0 | 0 | 0 | 22 | 2 | 73.0 | 86 | 341 | 48 | 43 | 3 | 13 | 5 | 5 | 40 | 14 | 26 | 1 | 1 |
| Smith, Bryn, Mtl. | 18 | 5 | .783 | 2.91 | 32 | 32 | 5 | 2 | 0 | 0 | 222.1 | 193 | 890 | 85 | 72 | 12 | 13 | 4 | 1 | 41 | 4 | 127 | 1 | 1 |
| Smith, David, Hou. | 9 | 4 | .643 | 2.27 | 64 | 0 | 0 | 0 | 46 | 27 | 79.1 | 69 | 315 | 26 | 20 | 3 | 3 | 0 | 1 | 17 | 5 | 40 | 4 | 1 |
| Smith, Lee, Chi. | 7 | 4 | .636 | 3.04 | 65 | 0 | 0 | 0 | 57 | 33 | 97.2 | 87 | 397 | 35 | 33 | 9 | 0 | 1 | 1 | 32 | 6 | 112 | 4 | 0 |
| Smith, Michael, Cin. | 0 | 0 | .000 | 5.40 | 2 | 0 | 0 | 0 | 1 | 0 | 3.1 | 5 | 13 | 2 | 2 | 2 | 0 | 0 | 0 | 1 | 0 | 2 | 0 | 0 |
| Smith, Zane, Atl.* | 9 | 10 | .474 | 3.80 | 42 | 18 | 0 | 0 | 3 | 0 | 147.0 | 135 | 631 | 70 | 62 | 7 | 16 | 4 | 2 | 80 | 10 | 85 | 2 | 2 |
| Solano, Julio, Hou. | 2 | 2 | .500 | 3.48 | 20 | 0 | 0 | 0 | 9 | 0 | 33.2 | 34 | 144 | 13 | 13 | 2 | 1 | 1 | 2 | 13 | 5 | 17 | 0 | 0 |
| Sorensen, Lary, Chi. | 3 | 7 | .300 | 4.26 | 45 | 3 | 0 | 0 | 18 | 2 | 82.1 | 86 | 355 | 44 | 39 | 4 | 11 | 2 | 2 | 24 | 4 | 34 | 0 | 0 |
| Soto, Mario, Cin. | 12 | 15 | .444 | 3.58 | 36 | 36 | 9 | 1 | 0 | 0 | 256.2 | 196 | 1055 | 109 | 102 | 30 | 13 | 9 | 0 | 104 | 3 | 214 | 8 | 1 |
| Stewart, David, Phil.* | 0 | 0 | .000 | 6.23 | 4 | 0 | 0 | 0 | 3 | 0 | 4.1 | 5 | 22 | 3 | 3 | 1 | 0 | 2 | 0 | 4 | 2 | 2 | 1 | 0 |
| Stoddard, Timothy, S.D. | 1 | 6 | .143 | 4.65 | 44 | 0 | 0 | 0 | 20 | 1 | 60.0 | 63 | 279 | 35 | 31 | 3 | 6 | 0 | 4 | 37 | 7 | 42 | 5 | 0 |
| Stuper, John, Cin. | 8 | 5 | .615 | 4.55 | 33 | 13 | 0 | 0 | 11 | 0 | 99.0 | 116 | 432 | 60 | 50 | 8 | 5 | 7 | 1 | 37 | 3 | 38 | 1 | 0 |
| Surhoff, Richard, Phil. | 0 | 0 | 1.000 | 0.00 | 2 | 0 | 0 | 0 | 0 | 0 | 1.0 | 2 |  | 0 | 0 | 0 | 0 | 0 | 0 | 0 | 0 | 1 | 0 | 0 |
| Sutcliffe, Richard, Chi. | 8 | 8 | .500 | 3.18 | 20 | 20 | 6 | 3 | 0 | 0 | 130.0 | 119 | 549 | 51 | 46 | 12 | 3 | 4 | 3 | 44 | 3 | 102 | 6 | 0 |
| Sutter, H. Bruce, Atl. | 7 | 7 | .500 | 4.48 | 58 | 0 | 0 | 0 | 50 | 23 | 88.1 | 91 | 382 | 46 | 44 | 13 | 6 | 4 | 3 | 29 | 4 | 52 | 0 | 0 |
| Tekulve, Kenton, Pitt.-Phil. | 4 | 10 | .286 | 3.57 | 61 | 0 | 0 | 0 | 42 | 14 | 75.2 | 74 | 327 | 35 | 30 | 5 | 12 | 2 | 6 | 30 | 10 | 40 | 0 | 0 |
| Thurmond, Mark, S.D.* | 7 | 11 | .389 | 3.97 | 36 | 23 | 5 | 1 | 4 | 2 | 138.1 | 154 | 592 | 70 | 61 | 9 | 11 | 4 | 3 | 44 | 5 | 57 | 0 | 0 |
| Tibbs, Jay, Cin. | 10 | 16 | .385 | 3.92 | 35 | 34 | 5 | 2 | 0 | 0 | 218.0 | 216 | 928 | 111 | 95 | 14 | 0 | 8 | 1 | 83 | 10 | 98 | 12 | 0 |
| Toliver, Freddie, Phil. | 0 | 4 | .000 | 4.68 | 11 | 3 | 0 | 0 | 4 | 0 | 25.0 | 27 | 117 | 15 | 13 | 2 | 1 | 1 | 0 | 17 | 1 | 23 | 0 | 0 |
| Tomlin, David, Pitt.* | 0 | 0 | .000 | 0.00 | 1 | 0 | 0 | 0 | 0 | 0 | 1.0 | 2 | 4 | 0 | 0 | 0 | 0 | 0 | 0 | 1 | 0 | 0 | 1 | 0 |
| Trout, Steven, Chi.* | 9 | 7 | .563 | 3.39 | 24 | 24 | 3 | 1 | 0 | 0 | 140.2 | 142 | 601 | 57 | 53 | 14 | 8 | 5 | 1 | 63 | 7 | 44 | 4 | 0 |
| Tudor, John, St.L.* | 21 | 8 | .724 | 1.93 | 36 | 36 | 14 | 10 | 0 | 0 | 275.0 | 209 | 1062 | 68 | 59 | 11 | 7 | 5 | 5 | 57 | 4 | 169 | 4 | 0 |
| Tunnell, B. Lee, Pitt. | 4 | 10 | .286 | 4.01 | 24 | 23 | 0 | 0 | 0 | 0 | 132.1 | 126 | 565 | 70 | 59 | 14 | 3 | 2 | 1 | 57 | 4 | 74 | 3 | 0 |
| Valenzuela, Fernando, L.A.* | 17 | 10 | .630 | 2.45 | 35 | 35 | 14 | 5 | 0 | 1 | 272.1 | 211 | 1109 | 92 | 74 | 14 | 13 | 8 | 1 | 101 | 5 | 208 | 10 | 3 |
| Walk, Robert, Pitt. | 2 | 3 | .400 | 3.68 | 9 | 9 | 1 | 0 | 0 | 0 | 58.2 | 60 | 248 | 27 | 24 | 3 | 1 | 1 | 1 | 18 | 4 | 40 | 0 | 0 |
| Walter, Gene, S.D.* | 0 | 0 | .000 | 2.05 | 15 | 0 | 0 | 0 | 7 | 3 | 22.0 | 12 | 86 | 6 | 5 | 0 | 1 | 1 | 0 | 8 | 1 | 18 | 0 | 0 |
| Ward, Colin, S.F.* | 0 | 0 | .000 | 4.38 | 2 | 0 | 0 | 0 | 0 | 0 | 12.1 | 10 | 52 | 6 | 6 | 0 | 0 | 0 | 0 | 7 | 0 | 8 | 0 | 0 |
| Welch, Robert, L.A. | 14 | 4 | .778 | 2.31 | 23 | 23 | 8 | 3 | 0 | 0 | 167.1 | 141 | 675 | 49 | 43 | 16 | 6 | 2 | 6 | 35 | 2 | 96 | 7 | 1 |
| Williams, Frank, S.F.* | 2 | 4 | .333 | 4.19 | 49 | 0 | 0 | 0 | 15 | 0 | 73.0 | 65 | 318 | 39 | 34 | 5 | 4 | 4 | 6 | 35 | 7 | 54 | 3 | 2 |
| Willis, Carl, Cin. | 1 | 0 | 1.000 | 9.22 | 11 | 0 | 0 | 0 | 6 | 0 | 13.2 | 21 | 69 | 18 | 14 | 4 | 2 | 2 | 2 | 5 | 2 | 6 | 1 | 0 |
| Winn, James, Pitt. | 3 | 6 | .333 | 5.23 | 30 | 7 | 0 | 0 | 10 | 0 | 75.2 | 77 | 326 | 45 | 44 | 6 | 1 | 2 | 3 | 31 | 2 | 22 | 5 | 1 |
| Wojna, Edward, S.D. | 2 | 4 | .333 | 5.79 | 15 | 7 | 0 | 0 | 0 | 0 | 42.0 | 53 | 198 | 35 | 27 | 3 | 6 | 3 | 0 | 19 | 2 | 18 | 1 | 2 |
| Worrell, Todd, St.L. | 3 | 0 | 1.000 | 2.91 | 17 | 0 | 0 | 0 | 11 | 5 | 21.2 | 17 | 88 | 7 | 7 | 1 | 2 | 0 | 2 | 7 | 1 | 17 | 5 | 0 |
| Youmans, Floyd, Mtl. | 4 | 3 | .571 | 2.45 | 14 | 12 | 0 | 0 | 1 | 0 | 77.0 | 57 | 331 | 27 | 21 | 3 | 2 | 1 | 0 | 49 | 1 | 54 | 5 | 0 |
| Zachry, Patrick, Phil. | 0 | 3 | .000 | 4.26 | 10 | 0 | 0 | 0 | 1 | 1 | 12.2 | 14 | 61 | 7 | 7 | 0 | 0 | 0 | 1 | 11 | 1 | 8 | 0 | 0 |

NOTE—Following pitchers combined to pitch shutout games: Atlanta (6)—Barker and Sutter; Bedrosian and Dedmon; Bedrosian, Dedmon and Sutter; Johnson, Smith and Sutter; Mahler and Sutter; Smith and Sutter. Chicago (2)—Eckersley and Smith; Trout, Frazier and Smith. Cincinnati (4)—Browning, Franco and Power; Browning and Power; Robinson and Power; Soto, Franco and Power. Houston (6)—Kerfeld and Smith; Knepper and Smith; Mathis and Ross; Ryan, Dawley and DiPino; Ryan and Heathcock; Scott and Smith. Los Angeles (5)—Honeycutt and Niedenfuer 2; Castillo and Niedenfuer; Honeycutt and Hershiser; Reuss, Niedenfuer and Howe. Montreal (8)—Gullickson and Reardon 3; Hesketh and Reardon 3;

Palmer, Burke and Reardon; Palmer and Reardon. New York (7)—Fernandez and McDowell 2; Campbell; Forsch, Hassler and Campbell. San Diego (9)—Dravecky 2; Dravecky, Berenyi and Sisk; Darling and McDowell; Darling and Orosco; Gooden, McDowell, Leach and McCullers and Walter; Hawkins and Gossage; Hawkins and Stoddard; Hoyt and Gossage; Jack-Orosco; Gooden and Orosco. Philadelphia (2)—K. Gross, Carman and Tekulve; Koosman and son, Lefferts, Walter and McCullers; Thurmond, DeLeon, Lefferts and Gossage; Thurmond and Carman. Pittsburgh (4)—Bielecki, Clements, Reuschel and Kipper; DeLeon and Holland; Reus- McCullers. San Francisco (1)—Hammaker and Garrelts. chel and Candelaria; Robinson and Clements. St. Louis (3)—Andujar and Campbell; Forsch and

## PITCHERS WITH TWO OR MORE CLUBS
(Alphabetically Arranged With Pitcher's First Club on Top)

| Pitcher and Club | W. | L. | Pct. | ERA. | G. | GS. | CG. | ShO. | GF. | Sv. | IP. | H. | BFP. | R. | ER. | HR. | SH. | SF. | HB. | Tot. BB. | Int. BB. | SO. | WP. | Bk. |
|---|---|---|---|---|---|---|---|---|---|---|---|---|---|---|---|---|---|---|---|---|---|---|---|---|
| Holland, Phil. | 0 | 1 | .000 | 4.50 | 3 | 0 | 0 | 0 | 3 | 1 | 4.0 | 5 | 21 | 2 | 2 | 0 | 1 | 1 | 0 | 4 | 2 | 1 | 0 | 0 |
| Holland, Pitt. | 1 | 3 | .250 | 3.38 | 38 | 0 | 0 | 0 | 19 | 4 | 58.2 | 48 | 235 | 22 | 22 | 5 | 4 | 3 | 0 | 17 | 6 | 47 | 0 | 1 |
| Laskey, S.F. | 5 | 11 | .313 | 3.55 | 19 | 19 | 0 | 0 | 0 | 0 | 114.0 | 110 | 485 | 55 | 45 | 10 | 11 | 4 | 0 | 39 | 0 | 42 | 2 | 1 |
| Laskey, Mtl. | 0 | 5 | .000 | 9.44 | 11 | 7 | 0 | 0 | 3 | 0 | 34.1 | 55 | 171 | 36 | 36 | 9 | 2 | 1 | 2 | 14 | 1 | 18 | 1 | 0 |
| Tekulve, Pitt. | 0 | 0 | .000 | 16.20 | 3 | 0 | 0 | 0 | 1 | 0 | 3.1 | 7 | 21 | 7 | 6 | 1 | 1 | 0 | 0 | 5 | 1 | 4 | 0 | 0 |
| Tekulve, Phil. | 4 | 10 | .286 | 2.99 | 58 | 0 | 0 | 0 | 41 | 14 | 72.1 | 67 | 306 | 28 | 24 | 4 | 5 | 2 | 2 | 25 | 9 | 36 | 0 | 0 |

# 1985 N.L. Pitching Against Each Club

## ATLANTA—66-96

| Pitcher | Chi. W—L | Cin. W—L | Hou. W—L | L.A. W—L | Mtl. W—L | N.Y. W—L | Phil. W—L | Pitt. W—L | St.L. W—L | S.D. W—L | S.F. W—L | Totals W—L |
|---|---|---|---|---|---|---|---|---|---|---|---|---|
| Barker | 0—1 | 0—1 | 0—1 | 0—1 | 0—1 | 1—1 | 0—0 | 1—0 | 0—2 | 0—0 | 0—1 | 2—9 |
| Bedrosian | 1—0 | 2—2 | 0—2 | 1—2 | 0—2 | 0—1 | 0—1 | 0—2 | 2—0 | 0—2 | 1—1 | 7—15 |
| Camp | 0—1 | 1—1 | 1—1 | 0—0 | 0—0 | 0—1 | 0—0 | 1—0 | 0—0 | 1—2 | 0—0 | 4—6 |
| Dedmon | 1—0 | 0—0 | 1—0 | 0—0 | 0—0 | 0—1 | 1—0 | 1—0 | 0—0 | 0—1 | 2—1 | 6—3 |
| Forster | 0—0 | 0—1 | 0—1 | 0—1 | 0—0 | 0—0 | 1—0 | 0—0 | 1—0 | 0—0 | 0—0 | 2—3 |
| Garber | 0—2 | 2—1 | 0—0 | 0—0 | 0—0 | 0—0 | 0—0 | 2—1 | 0—0 | 0—0 | 2—2 | 6—6 |
| Johnson | 1—0 | 0—0 | 0—1 | 0—1 | 0—0 | 0—0 | 0—0 | 1—0 | 1—0 | 0—2 | 1—0 | 4—4 |
| Mahler | 2—1 | 1—0 | 3—1 | 1—2 | 3—1 | 0—2 | 3—0 | 0—1 | 0—4 | 2—1 | 2—2 | 17—15 |
| McMurtry | 0—0 | 0—0 | 0—0 | 0—1 | 0—1 | 0—0 | 0—0 | 0—0 | 0—1 | 0—0 | 0—0 | 0—3 |
| Perez | 0—0 | 0—3 | 0—1 | 0—1 | 0—2 | 0—2 | 1—0 | 0—2 | 0—0 | 0—1 | 0—1 | 1—13 |
| Shields | 0—0 | 0—0 | 0—1 | 1—0 | 0—0 | 0—0 | 0—0 | 0—0 | 0—0 | 0—0 | 0—0 | 1—2 |
| Smith | 0—0 | 0—0 | 2—1 | 2—1 | 0—1 | 1—2 | 1—1 | 0—0 | 0—2 | 1—2 | 2—0 | 9—10 |
| Sutter | 0—2 | 1—1 | 1—0 | 0—3 | 0—1 | 0—0 | 3—0 | 0—0 | 0—0 | 2—0 | 0—0 | 7—7 |
| Totals | 5—7 | 7—11 | 8—10 | 5—13 | 3—9 | 2—10 | 10—2 | 6—6 | 3—9 | 7—11 | 10—8 | 66—96 |

No Decision—Schuler.

## CHICAGO—77-84

| Pitcher | Atl. W—L | Cin. W—L | Hou. W—L | L.A. W—L | Mtl. W—L | N.Y. W—L | Phil. W—L | Pitt. W—L | St.L. W—L | S.D. W—L | S.F. W—L | Totals W—L |
|---|---|---|---|---|---|---|---|---|---|---|---|---|
| Abrego | 0—0 | 0—0 | 0—0 | 0—0 | 0—0 | 0—1 | 1—0 | 0—0 | 0—0 | 0—0 | 0—0 | 1—1 |
| Baller | 0—0 | 1—0 | 0—2 | 0—0 | 0—0 | 0—0 | 1—1 | 0—0 | 0—0 | 0—0 | 0—0 | 2—3 |
| Botelho | 1—0 | 0—1 | 0—0 | 0—0 | 0—0 | 0—2 | 0—0 | 0—0 | 0—0 | 0—0 | 0—0 | 1—3 |
| Brusstar | 2—0 | 0—1 | 0—0 | 0—0 | 0—0 | 0—1 | 0—0 | 1—0 | 0—0 | 0—0 | 1—1 | 4—3 |
| Eckersley | 0—1 | 2—0 | 1—0 | 0—0 | 2—1 | 1—0 | 4—0 | 0—1 | 0—3 | 0—1 | 0—0 | 11—7 |
| Engel | 0—0 | 0—0 | 1—0 | 0—0 | 0—1 | 0—0 | 0—0 | 0—1 | 0—3 | 0—0 | 0—0 | 1—5 |
| Fontenot | 1—1 | 0—0 | 0—0 | 0—3 | 1—1 | 1—4 | 1—0 | 0—0 | 2—1 | 0—0 | 0—0 | 6—10 |
| Frazier | 0—0 | 1—1 | 1—1 | 1—1 | 1—2 | 0—1 | 0—0 | 0—1 | 1—0 | 1—0 | 0—1 | 7—8 |
| Gumpert | 0—0 | 0—0 | 0—0 | 0—0 | 1—0 | 0—0 | 0—0 | 0—0 | 0—0 | 0—0 | 0—0 | 1—0 |
| Gura | 0—0 | 0—0 | 0—1 | 0—1 | 0—0 | 0—0 | 0—0 | 0—0 | 0—0 | 0—0 | 0—1 | 0—3 |
| Meridith | 1—0 | 0—0 | 0—2 | 0—0 | 0—0 | 0—0 | 0—0 | 1—0 | 0—0 | 1—0 | 0—0 | 3—2 |
| Patterson | 0—0 | 0—0 | 0—0 | 0—0 | 0—0 | 0—0 | 1—0 | 1—0 | 1—0 | 0—0 | 0—0 | 3—0 |
| Perlman | 0—0 | 0—0 | 0—0 | 0—0 | 0—0 | 0—0 | 0—0 | 1—0 | 0—0 | 0—0 | 0—0 | 1—0 |
| Ruthven | 1—0 | 0—1 | 0—1 | 1—1 | 0—0 | 0—0 | 0—0 | 1—1 | 0—2 | 0—1 | 1—0 | 4—7 |
| Sanderson | 0—0 | 1—0 | 0—0 | 1—0 | 1—1 | 0—2 | 0—1 | 1—0 | 0—1 | 1—0 | 0—1 | 5—6 |
| Smith | 1—1 | 0—0 | 2—0 | 0—1 | 0—0 | 1—0 | 2—0 | 0—0 | 0—1 | 1—0 | 0—1 | 7—4 |
| Sorensen | 0—1 | 0—2 | 0—0 | 1—0 | 0—1 | 0—0 | 0—1 | 0—0 | 0—1 | 1—1 | 0—0 | 3—7 |
| Sutcliffe | 0—1 | 0—0 | 0—0 | 1—0 | 1—2 | 1—1 | 0—2 | 3—1 | 0—0 | 1—1 | 1—0 | 8—8 |
| Trout | 0—0 | 0—0 | 0—0 | 0—0 | 0—2 | 0—2 | 2—0 | 4—0 | 0—2 | 2—0 | 1—1 | 9—7 |
| Totals | 7—5 | 5—6 | 5—7 | 5—7 | 7—11 | 4—14 | 13—5 | 13—5 | 4—14 | 8—4 | 6—6 | 77—84 |

No Decision—Beard.

## CINCINNATI—89-72

| Pitcher | Atl. W—L | Chi. W—L | Hou. W—L | L.A. W—L | Mtl. W—L | N.Y. W—L | Phil. W—L | Pitt. W—L | St.L. W—L | S.D. W—L | S.F. W—L | Totals W—L |
|---|---|---|---|---|---|---|---|---|---|---|---|---|
| Browning | 4—0 | 1—2 | 3—1 | 1—1 | 1—0 | 1—2 | 0—2 | 3—0 | 2—0 | 2—1 | 2—0 | 20—9 |
| Buchanan | 0—0 | 0—0 | 0—0 | 0—0 | 1—0 | 0—0 | 0—0 | 0—0 | 0—0 | 0—0 | 0—0 | 1—0 |
| Franco | 1—0 | 2—1 | 0—1 | 0—0 | 1—0 | 1—1 | 3—0 | 0—0 | 1—0 | 3—0 | 0—0 | 12—3 |
| Hume | 0—0 | 1—0 | 0—0 | 0—0 | 0—1 | 0—0 | 0—0 | 0—0 | 0—1 | 1—1 | 1—2 | 3—5 |
| McGaffigan | 1—0 | 0—0 | 1—0 | 0—2 | 0—0 | 0—0 | 0—0 | 0—1 | 0—0 | 0—0 | 1—0 | 3—3 |
| Pastore | 0—1 | 0—0 | 0—0 | 0—0 | 0—0 | 0—0 | 0—0 | 1—0 | 0—0 | 0—0 | 1—0 | 2—1 |
| Power | 1—1 | 0—0 | 1—1 | 4—0 | 1—0 | 0—0 | 0—0 | 0—0 | 1—1 | 0—1 | 0—2 | 8—6 |
| Price | 0—1 | 0—0 | 0—0 | 0—1 | 1—0 | 0—0 | 0—0 | 0—0 | 0—0 | 1—0 | 0—0 | 2—2 |
| Robinson | 2—0 | 0—0 | 1—0 | 0—3 | 1—1 | 0—0 | 1—1 | 0—0 | 0—1 | 1—1 | 1—0 | 7—7 |
| Soto | 1—1 | 2—1 | 2—1 | 0—1 | 1—1 | 1—3 | 1—2 | 3—1 | 0—0 | 0—3 | 1—1 | 12—15 |
| Stuper | 1—1 | 0—0 | 0—1 | 1—1 | 0—0 | 1—0 | 1—0 | 1—0 | 0—2 | 0—0 | 4—0 | 8—5 |
| Tibbs | 0—2 | 0—1 | 3—2 | 1—2 | 1—1 | 1—2 | 1—0 | 1—1 | 1—2 | 1—2 | 0—1 | 10—16 |
| Willis | 0—0 | 0—0 | 0—0 | 0—0 | 0—0 | 0—0 | 0—0 | 0—0 | 0—0 | 0—0 | 1—0 | 1—0 |
| Totals | 11—7 | 6—5 | 11—7 | 7—11 | 8—4 | 4—8 | 7—5 | 9—3 | 5—7 | 9—9 | 12—6 | 89—72 |

No Decisions—Murphy, Smith.

## HOUSTON—83-79

| Pitcher | Atl. W—L | Chi. W—L | Cin. W—L | L.A. W—L | Mtl. W—L | N.Y. W—L | Phil. W—L | Pitt. W—L | St.L. W—L | S.D. W—L | S.F. W—L | Totals W—L |
|---|---|---|---|---|---|---|---|---|---|---|---|---|
| Calhoun | 0—0 | 0—0 | 0—1 | 0—1 | 1—0 | 0—0 | 0—0 | 0—1 | 0—2 | 1—0 | 0—0 | 2—5 |
| Dawley | 0—0 | 1—0 | 0—1 | 0—1 | 0—0 | 0—0 | 0—1 | 3—0 | 0—0 | 0—0 | 1—0 | 5—3 |
| DiPino | 2—1 | 0—0 | 0—2 | 0—1 | 0—1 | 0—1 | 0—1 | 0—0 | 0—0 | 0—0 | 1—0 | 3—7 |
| Heathcock | 1—0 | 0—0 | 0—0 | 0—0 | 0—0 | 0—0 | 0—1 | 0—0 | 0—0 | 0—0 | 2—0 | 3—1 |
| Kerfeld | 1—0 | 0—0 | 0—0 | 0—0 | 0—0 | 0—1 | 1—0 | 0—0 | 0—0 | 2—0 | 1—0 | 4—2 |
| Knepper | 2—1 | 0—2 | 1—2 | 1—2 | 1—1 | 1—1 | 0—2 | 2—0 | 2—0 | 2—2 | 3—0 | 15—13 |
| Knudson | 0—0 | 0—0 | 0—0 | 0—0 | 0—0 | 0—1 | 0—0 | 0—0 | 0—0 | 0—0 | 0—0 | 0—2 |
| Mathis | 0—0 | 0—0 | 0—0 | 1—0 | 0—1 | 1—1 | 0—1 | 0—0 | 1—0 | 0—0 | 0—1 | 3—5 |
| Niekro | 2—0 | 0—0 | 0—1 | 1—3 | 0—1 | 1—2 | 1—0 | 0—1 | 0—2 | 2—0 | 2—2 | 9—12 |
| Ross | 0—0 | 0—2 | 0—0 | 0—0 | 0—0 | 0—0 | 0—0 | 0—0 | 0—0 | 0—0 | 0—0 | 0—2 |
| Ryan | 1—2 | 2—0 | 0—3 | 1—1 | 0—2 | 0—0 | 1—1 | 1—0 | 1—1 | 2—2 | 1—0 | 10—12 |

| Pitcher | Atl. W—L | Chi. W—L | Cin. W—L | L.A. W—L | Mtl. W—L | N.Y. W—L | Phil. W—L | Pitt. W—L | St.L. W—L | S.D. W—L | S.F. W—L | Totals W—L |
|---|---|---|---|---|---|---|---|---|---|---|---|---|
| Scott | 0—1 | 2—0 | 2—1 | 1—2 | 2—0 | 1—1 | 1—0 | 0—2 | 2—0 | 3—1 | 4—0 | 18—8 |
| Smith | 1—2 | 2—1 | 2—0 | 1—0 | 1—0 | 1—0 | 1—0 | 0—0 | 0—1 | 0—1 | 0—0 | 9—5 |
| Solano | 0—1 | 0—0 | 1—0 | 1—0 | 0—0 | 0—0 | 0—0 | 0—1 | 0—0 | 0—0 | 0—0 | 2—2 |
| Totals | 10—8 | 7—5 | 7—11 | 6—12 | 6—6 | 4—8 | 4—8 | 6—6 | 6—6 | 12—6 | 15—3 | 83—79 |

No Decisions—Deshaies, Madden.

## LOS ANGELES—95-67

| Pitcher | Atl. W—L | Chi. W—L | Cin. W—L | Hou. W—L | Mtl. W—L | N.Y. W—L | Phil. W—L | Pitt. W—L | St.L. W—L | S.D. W—L | S.F. W—L | Totals W—L |
|---|---|---|---|---|---|---|---|---|---|---|---|---|
| Brennan | 0—0 | 0—1 | 0—0 | 0—0 | 0—0 | 0—0 | 0—0 | 0—1 | 0—0 | 0—1 | 1—0 | 1—3 |
| Castillo | 0—1 | 0—0 | 0—0 | 0—0 | 1—1 | 0—0 | 0—0 | 1—0 | 0—0 | 0—0 | 0—0 | 2—2 |
| Diaz | 1—0 | 0—0 | 0—1 | 3—0 | 1—0 | 0—1 | 0—0 | 0—0 | 0—0 | 1—0 | 0—1 | 6—3 |
| Hershiser | 1—1 | 1—0 | 3—0 | 3—0 | 2—0 | 1—0 | 1—0 | 1—0 | 1—1 | 3—1 | 2—0 | 19—3 |
| Holton | 1—1 | 0—0 | 0—0 | 0—0 | 0—0 | 0—0 | 0—0 | 0—0 | 0—0 | 0—0 | 0—0 | 1—1 |
| Honeycutt | 2—1 | 0—2 | 1—1 | 1—0 | 1—2 | 0—1 | 0—1 | 1—2 | 1—0 | 1—1 | 0—1 | 8—12 |
| Howe | 0—0 | 0—0 | 0—0 | 0—1 | 0—0 | 1—0 | 0—0 | 0—0 | 0—0 | 0—0 | 0—0 | 1—1 |
| Howell | 1—0 | 1—0 | 0—1 | 0—1 | 0—1 | 0—0 | 0—0 | 0—0 | 1—2 | 1—2 | 0—0 | 4—7 |
| Niedenfuer | 1—0 | 1—0 | 0—2 | 0—1 | 0—0 | 1—1 | 1—1 | 0—1 | 1—1 | 0—0 | 2—2 | 7—9 |
| Pena | 0—0 | 0—0 | 0—1 | 0—0 | 0—0 | 0—0 | 0—0 | 0—0 | 0—0 | 0—0 | 0—0 | 0—1 |
| Powell | 1—0 | 0—1 | 0—0 | 0—0 | 0—0 | 0—0 | 0—0 | 0—0 | 0—0 | 0—0 | 0—0 | 1—1 |
| Reuss | 2—0 | 1—0 | 1—0 | 2—1 | 1—0 | 1—1 | 1—3 | 2—0 | 0—1 | 1—2 | 3—2 | 14—10 |
| Valenzuela | 2—1 | 2—1 | 2—1 | 2—1 | 0—0 | 2—1 | 2—2 | 2—0 | 1—0 | 1—2 | 1—1 | 17—10 |
| Welch | 1—0 | 1—0 | 4—0 | 1—1 | 1—1 | 1—0 | 0—1 | 1—0 | 2—0 | 0—1 | 2—0 | 14—4 |
| Totals | 13—5 | 7—5 | 11—7 | 12—6 | 7—5 | 7—5 | 4—8 | 8—4 | 7—5 | 8—10 | 11—7 | 95—67 |

## MONTREAL—84-77

| Pitcher | Atl. W—L | Chi. W—L | Cin. W—L | Hou. W—L | L.A. W—L | N.Y. W—L | Phil. W—L | Pitt. W—L | St.L. W—L | S.D. W—L | S.F. W—L | Totals W—L |
|---|---|---|---|---|---|---|---|---|---|---|---|---|
| Burke | 1—0 | 1—0 | 0—0 | 0—0 | 0—1 | 1—1 | 0—1 | 4—1 | 1—0 | 1—0 | 0—0 | 9—4 |
| Dopson | 0—0 | 0—0 | 0—0 | 0—0 | 0—1 | 0—1 | 0—0 | 0—0 | 0—0 | 0—0 | 0—0 | 0—2 |
| Gullickson | 1—2 | 2—0 | 3—1 | 1—0 | 2—1 | 1—2 | 0—2 | 0—1 | 2—1 | 1—1 | 1—1 | 14—12 |
| Hesketh | 2—0 | 1—0 | 1—1 | 2—0 | 0—0 | 0—1 | 0—2 | 1—0 | 2—0 | 0—1 | 1—0 | 10—5 |
| Laskey | 0—0 | 0—0 | 0—0 | 0—0 | 0—0 | 0—0 | 0—1 | 0—1 | 0—1 | 0—1 | 0—1 | 0—5 |
| Lucas | 0—0 | 0—0 | 0—1 | 0—1 | 1—0 | 1—0 | 0—0 | 0—0 | 3—0 | 0—0 | 1—0 | 6—2 |
| Mahler | 0—0 | 0—0 | 0—0 | 0—2 | 0—0 | 0—1 | 0—1 | 0—0 | 0—0 | 0—0 | 1—0 | 1—4 |
| O'Connor | 0—0 | 0—0 | 0—0 | 0—0 | 0—0 | 0—0 | 0—0 | 0—1 | 0—1 | 0—0 | 0—0 | 0—2 |
| Palmer | 1—1 | 1—2 | 0—1 | 0—1 | 0—1 | 1—0 | 2—1 | 1—1 | 1—1 | 0—0 | 0—1 | 7—10 |
| Reardon | 0—0 | 0—2 | 0—1 | 0—1 | 0—1 | 0—0 | 0—1 | 0—0 | 0—1 | 1—0 | 0—1 | 2—8 |
| Roberge | 0—0 | 0—0 | 0—0 | 0—0 | 0—0 | 0—0 | 0—1 | 1—1 | 0—1 | 2—0 | 0—0 | 3—3 |
| Rogers | 0—0 | 0—1 | 0—1 | 0—1 | 0—0 | 0—0 | 0—0 | 0—0 | 2—0 | 0—1 | 0—0 | 2—4 |
| St. Claire | 0—0 | 1—1 | 0—1 | 1—0 | 0—0 | 1—0 | 0—0 | 1—0 | 0—0 | 0—0 | 1—0 | 5—3 |
| Schatzeder | 0—0 | 0—0 | 0—0 | 0—0 | 1—0 | 1—2 | 0—0 | 0—1 | 0—0 | 0—1 | 1—1 | 3—5 |
| Smith | 4—0 | 5—0 | 0—1 | 1—0 | 1—2 | 2—1 | 4—0 | 1—1 | 0—0 | 0—0 | 0—0 | 18—5 |
| Youmans | 0—0 | 0—1 | 0—0 | 1—0 | 0—0 | 1—0 | 1—0 | 0—0 | 0—0 | 0—2 | 1—0 | 4—3 |
| Totals | 9—3 | 11—7 | 4—8 | 6—6 | 5—7 | 9—9 | 8—10 | 9—8 | 11—7 | 5—7 | 7—5 | 84—77 |

No Decisions—Butera, Glynn, Grapenthin, Shines.

## NEW YORK—98-64

| Pitcher | Atl. W—L | Chi. W—L | Cin. W—L | Hou. W—L | L.A. W—L | Mtl. W—L | Phil. W—L | Pitt. W—L | St.L. W—L | S.D. W—L | S.F. W—L | Totals W—L |
|---|---|---|---|---|---|---|---|---|---|---|---|---|
| Aguilera | 1—1 | 1—0 | 1—0 | 0—0 | 0—0 | 2—1 | 3—0 | 1—1 | 0—2 | 1—1 | 0—0 | 10—7 |
| Berenyi | 0—0 | 0—0 | 1—0 | 0—0 | 0—0 | 0—0 | 0—0 | 0—0 | 0—0 | 0—0 | 0—0 | 1—0 |
| Darling | 3—0 | 1—1 | 0—1 | 1—2 | 1—0 | 2—1 | 1—1 | 2—0 | 1—0 | 3—0 | 1—0 | 16—6 |
| Fernandez | 1—0 | 2—0 | 0—1 | 0—1 | 0—2 | 1—2 | 3—1 | 1—1 | 0—0 | 1—1 | 0—0 | 9—9 |
| Gardner | 0—0 | 0—0 | 0—0 | 0—0 | 0—0 | 0—0 | 0—0 | 0—1 | 0—0 | 0—0 | 0—1 | 0—2 |
| Gooden | 1—0 | 5—0 | 3—0 | 4—0 | 1—1 | 1—0 | 3—0 | 1—0 | 2—1 | 1—1 | 2—1 | 24—4 |
| Gorman | 1—0 | 0—0 | 0—0 | 0—1 | 0—0 | 0—0 | 0—1 | 1—0 | 1—2 | 0—0 | 1—0 | 4—4 |
| Latham | 0—0 | 0—0 | 0—0 | 1—0 | 0—0 | 0—1 | 0—0 | 0—2 | 0—0 | 0—0 | 0—0 | 1—3 |
| Leach | 1—0 | 0—1 | 0—0 | 0—0 | 0—1 | 1—0 | 0—0 | 0—1 | 0—0 | 0—0 | 1—1 | 3—4 |
| Lynch | 1—1 | 3—0 | 2—0 | 1—0 | 0—2 | 1—1 | 0—2 | 1—1 | 0—1 | 0—0 | 1—0 | 10—8 |
| McDowell | 1—0 | 1—1 | 1—2 | 0—0 | 1—0 | 0—1 | 0—0 | 0—0 | 1—0 | 0—0 | 1—1 | 6—5 |
| Orosco | 0—0 | 1—1 | 0—0 | 0—0 | 0—0 | 0—0 | 1—1 | 2—1 | 2—2 | 0—1 | 0—0 | 8—6 |
| Schiraldi | 0—0 | 0—0 | 0—0 | 0—0 | 0—0 | 0—0 | 0—0 | 0—0 | 1—1 | 1—0 | 0—0 | 2—1 |
| Sisk | 0—0 | 0—0 | 0—0 | 0—0 | 1—1 | 1—1 | 0—1 | 1—0 | 0—1 | 0—1 | 1—0 | 4—5 |
| Totals | 10—2 | 14—4 | 8—4 | 8—4 | 5—7 | 9—9 | 11—7 | 10—8 | 8—10 | 7—5 | 8—4 | 98—64 |

No Decisions—Myers, Niemann, Sambito.

## PHILADELPHIA—75-87

| Pitcher | Atl. W—L | Chi. W—L | Cin. W—L | Hou. W—L | L.A. W—L | Mtl. W—L | N.Y. W—L | Pitt. W—L | St.L. W—L | S.D. W—L | S.F. W—L | Totals W—L |
|---|---|---|---|---|---|---|---|---|---|---|---|---|
| Andersen | 0—2 | 0—0 | 1—0 | 0—1 | 1—0 | 0—0 | 0—0 | 1—0 | 0—0 | 0—0 | 0—0 | 3—3 |
| Carlton | 0—1 | 0—0 | 0—0 | 0—1 | 0—0 | 0—1 | 0—1 | 0—1 | 0—1 | 0—1 | 1—1 | 1—8 |
| Carman | 0—1 | 0—0 | 0—1 | 1—0 | 1—0 | 1—0 | 0—1 | 3—1 | 1—0 | 1—0 | 1—0 | 9—4 |
| Childress | 0—0 | 0—0 | 0—0 | 0—0 | 0—0 | 0—0 | 0—0 | 0—1 | 0—0 | 0—0 | 0—0 | 0—1 |
| Denny | 0—2 | 1—2 | 0—3 | 0—0 | 2—0 | 0—1 | 2—1 | 4—1 | 1—1 | 1—2 | 0—1 | 11—14 |
| K. Gross | 0—1 | 1—3 | 1—1 | 2—0 | 2—1 | 3—1 | 2—2 | 2—0 | 1—3 | 1—0 | 0—1 | 15—13 |
| Holland | 0—0 | 0—1 | 0—0 | 0—0 | 0—0 | 0—0 | 0—0 | 0—0 | 0—0 | 0—0 | 0—0 | 0—1 |

| Pitcher | Atl. W—L | Chi. W—L | Cin. W—L | Hou. W—L | L.A. W—L | Mtl. W—L | N.Y. W—L | Pitt. W—L | St.L. W—L | S.D. W—L | S.F. W—L | Totals W—L |
|---|---|---|---|---|---|---|---|---|---|---|---|---|
| Hudson | 1—1 | 1—1 | 1—0 | 1—0 | 0—1 | 1—2 | 1—2 | 1—0 | 0—3 | 0—2 | 1—1 | 8—13 |
| Koosman | 1—0 | 0—1 | 1—0 | 1—1 | 0—1 | 1—0 | 0—0 | 0—0 | 2—1 | 0—0 | 0—0 | 6—4 |
| Rawley | 0—0 | 2—1 | 1—0 | 1—1 | 2—0 | 2—3 | 2—1 | 0—0 | 2—1 | 0—0 | 1—1 | 13—8 |
| Rucker | 0—0 | 0—0 | 0—0 | 1—0 | 0—0 | 0—0 | 0—2 | 0—0 | 1—0 | 0—0 | 1—0 | 3—2 |
| Shipanoff | 0—0 | 0—0 | 0—0 | 0—0 | 0—0 | 0—0 | 0—0 | 0—1 | 0—0 | 0—1 | 1—0 | 1—2 |
| Surhoff | 0—0 | 0—0 | 0—0 | 0—0 | 0—0 | 0—0 | 0—0 | 0—0 | 0—0 | 1—0 | 0—0 | 1—0 |
| Tekulve | 0—2 | 0—3 | 0—2 | 1—0 | 0—1 | 2—0 | 0—0 | 0—1 | 0—0 | 1—1 | 0—0 | 4—10 |
| Toliver | 0—0 | 0—1 | 0—0 | 0—0 | 0—0 | 0—0 | 0—1 | 0—1 | 0—0 | 0—0 | 0—1 | 0—4 |
| Totals | 2—10 | 5—13 | 5—7 | 8—4 | 8—4 | 10—8 | 7—11 | 11—7 | 8—10 | 5—7 | 6—6 | 75—87 |

No Decisions—Stewart, Zachry.

### PITTSBURGH—57-104

| Pitcher | Atl. W—L | Chi. W—L | Cin. W—L | Hou. W—L | L.A. W—L | Mtl. W—L | N.Y. W—L | Phil. W—L | St.L. W—L | S.D. W—L | S.F. W—L | Totals W—L |
|---|---|---|---|---|---|---|---|---|---|---|---|---|
| Bielecki | 0—0 | 0—1 | 0—1 | 0—0 | 0—0 | 0—0 | 1—0 | 1—0 | 0—0 | 0—1 | 0—0 | 2—3 |
| Candelaria | 0—0 | 0—0 | 0—0 | 0—0 | 0—1 | 0—0 | 0—1 | 0—0 | 1—1 | 1—1 | 0—0 | 2—4 |
| Clements | 0—0 | 0—0 | 0—0 | 0—1 | 0—0 | 0—0 | 0—0 | 0—0 | 0—1 | 0—0 | 0—0 | 0—2 |
| DeLeon | 1—1 | 0—4 | 0—2 | 0—1 | 0—1 | 0—1 | 0—2 | 1—1 | 0—2 | 0—2 | 0—2 | 2—19 |
| Guante | 0—0 | 0—0 | 0—1 | 1—0 | 0—0 | 1—0 | 1—0 | 1—0 | 0—2 | 0—0 | 1—2 | 4—6 |
| Holland | 0—0 | 0—1 | 0—0 | 0—1 | 1—0 | 0—1 | 0—0 | 0—0 | 0—0 | 0—0 | 0—0 | 1—3 |
| Kipper | 0—0 | 0—0 | 0—0 | 0—0 | 0—0 | 0—0 | 1—1 | 0—0 | 0—1 | 0—0 | 0—0 | 1—2 |
| Krawczyk | 0—1 | 0—0 | 0—0 | 0—1 | 0—0 | 0—0 | 0—0 | 0—0 | 0—0 | 0—0 | 0—0 | 0—2 |
| McWilliams | 0—0 | 1—1 | 0—0 | 0—0 | 2—0 | 1—2 | 2—3 | 1—0 | 0—1 | 0—1 | 0—1 | 7—9 |
| Reuschel | 2—0 | 2—1 | 1—1 | 2—0 | 0—1 | 2—2 | 1—0 | 1—1 | 1—1 | 1—1 | 1—0 | 14—8 |
| Rhoden | 1—1 | 2—2 | 1—0 | 1—0 | 1—2 | 2—1 | 1—1 | 0—3 | 0—2 | 1—2 | 0—1 | 10—15 |
| Robinson | 0—2 | 0—1 | 0—1 | 1—1 | 0—1 | 1—0 | 1—0 | 0—3 | 1—1 | 0—0 | 1—1 | 5—11 |
| Scurry | 0—0 | 0—0 | 0—1 | 0—0 | 0—0 | 0—0 | 0—0 | 0—0 | 0—0 | 0—0 | 0—0 | 0—1 |
| Tunnell | 1—1 | 0—0 | 0—1 | 1—0 | 0—2 | 0—0 | 0—2 | 1—0 | 0—2 | 1—0 | 0—2 | 4—10 |
| Walk | 0—0 | 0—0 | 1—1 | 0—1 | 0—0 | 0—0 | 0—0 | 1—1 | 0—0 | 0—0 | 0—0 | 2—3 |
| Winn | 1—0 | 0—2 | 0—0 | 0—0 | 0—0 | 2—1 | 0—0 | 0—2 | 0—1 | 0—0 | 0—0 | 3—6 |
| Totals | 6—6 | 5—13 | 3—9 | 6—6 | 4—8 | 8—9 | 8—10 | 7—11 | 3—15 | 4—8 | 3—9 | 57—104 |

No Decisions—Tekulve, Tomlin.

### ST. LOUIS—101-61

| Pitcher | Atl. W—L | Chi. W—L | Cin. W—L | Hou. W—L | L.A. W—L | Mtl. W—L | N.Y. W—L | Phil. W—L | Pitt. W—L | S.D. W—L | S.F. W—L | Totals W—L |
|---|---|---|---|---|---|---|---|---|---|---|---|---|
| Allen | 0—0 | 0—0 | 0—0 | 0—0 | 1—1 | 0—0 | 0—1 | 0—0 | 0—1 | 0—0 | 0—1 | 1—4 |
| Andujar | 3—1 | 1—2 | 1—1 | 1—0 | 2—0 | 0—2 | 3—1 | 1—3 | 4—0 | 2—1 | 3—1 | 21—12 |
| Campbell | 0—0 | 1—0 | 1—0 | 1—0 | 0—1 | 0—1 | 1—0 | 0—0 | 1—1 | 0—0 | 0—0 | 5—3 |
| Cox | 1—0 | 3—0 | 3—0 | 0—2 | 0—2 | 0—1 | 1—1 | 3—2 | 2—0 | 2—1 | 3—0 | 18—9 |
| Dayley | 0—0 | 1—1 | 0—0 | 0—0 | 0—0 | 1—1 | 1—2 | 0—0 | 0—0 | 1—0 | 0—0 | 4—4 |
| Forsch | 3—1 | 2—0 | 0—1 | 0—0 | 0—0 | 2—1 | 0—1 | 1—1 | 1—0 | 0—1 | 0—0 | 9—6 |
| Hassler | 0—0 | 0—0 | 0—0 | 0—0 | 0—0 | 0—0 | 0—1 | 0—0 | 0—0 | 0—0 | 0—0 | 0—1 |
| Horton | 0—0 | 0—0 | 0—1 | 1—0 | 0—0 | 0—1 | 0—0 | 1—0 | 1—0 | 0—0 | 0—0 | 3—2 |
| Keough | 0—0 | 0—0 | 0—0 | 0—0 | 0—0 | 0—0 | 0—0 | 0—1 | 0—0 | 0—0 | 0—0 | 0—1 |
| Kepshire | 1—0 | 3—1 | 0—1 | 0—3 | 0—1 | 0—2 | 1—0 | 1—0 | 1—1 | 1—0 | 2—0 | 10—9 |
| Lahti | 0—0 | 0—0 | 1—1 | 0—0 | 0—0 | 1—0 | 0—0 | 0—1 | 1—0 | 0—0 | 0—0 | 5—2 |
| Perry | 0—0 | 0—0 | 0—0 | 0—0 | 0—0 | 0—0 | 0—0 | 0—0 | 1—0 | 0—0 | 0—0 | 1—0 |
| Tudor | 1—1 | 3—0 | 0—0 | 2—1 | 1—2 | 1—2 | 3—1 | 3—0 | 3—0 | 2—1 | 2—0 | 21—8 |
| Worrell | 0—0 | 0—0 | 1—0 | 0—0 | 0—0 | 2—0 | 0—0 | 0—0 | 0—0 | 0—0 | 0—0 | 3—0 |
| Totals | 9—3 | 14—4 | 7—5 | 6—6 | 5—7 | 7—11 | 10—8 | 10—8 | 15—3 | 8—4 | 10—2 | 101—61 |

No Decisions—Bair, Boever.

### SAN DIEGO—83-79

| Pitcher | Atl. W—L | Chi. W—L | Cin. W—L | Hou. W—L | L.A. W—L | Mtl. W—L | N.Y. W—L | Phil. W—L | Pitt. W—L | St.L. W—L | S.F. W—L | Totals W—L |
|---|---|---|---|---|---|---|---|---|---|---|---|---|
| Booker | 0—0 | 0—1 | 0—0 | 0—0 | 0—0 | 0—0 | 0—0 | 0—0 | 0—0 | 0—0 | 0—0 | 0—1 |
| DeLeon | 0—0 | 0—1 | 0—0 | 0—0 | 0—0 | 0—0 | 0—0 | 0—0 | 0—0 | 0—0 | 0—2 | 0—3 |
| Dravecky | 0—0 | 1—1 | 2—1 | 1—2 | 1—3 | 2—0 | 0—2 | 1—1 | 0—0 | 1—1 | 4—0 | 13—11 |
| Gossage | 0—0 | 0—0 | 1—1 | 1—0 | 2—0 | 0—1 | 0—0 | 1—0 | 0—0 | 0—1 | 0—0 | 5—3 |
| Hawkins | 4—1 | 1—1 | 2—2 | 0—1 | 1—2 | 4—0 | 0—0 | 1—1 | 2—0 | 2—0 | 1—0 | 18—8 |
| Hoyt | 2—2 | 0—1 | 1—1 | 1—1 | 2—0 | 0—0 | 2—0 | 2—0 | 2—1 | 1—2 | 3—0 | 16—8 |
| Jackson | 1—0 | 0—1 | 0—1 | 0—0 | 0—0 | 0—0 | 1—1 | 0—0 | 0—0 | 0—0 | 0—0 | 2—3 |
| Lefferts | 1—0 | 1—0 | 1—0 | 1—2 | 2—0 | 0—1 | 0—0 | 1—1 | 1—2 | 0—0 | 0—0 | 7—6 |
| McCullers | 0—1 | 0—0 | 0—0 | 0—0 | 0—0 | 0—0 | 0—0 | 0—1 | 0—0 | 0—0 | 0—0 | 0—2 |
| Show | 2—0 | 1—0 | 1—0 | 0—2 | 1—2 | 2—1 | 1—1 | 0—2 | 0—0 | 2—1 | 3—0 | 12—11 |
| Stoddard | 0—2 | 1—1 | 0—0 | 0—0 | 0—1 | 0—1 | 0—0 | 0—0 | 0—0 | 0—1 | 0—0 | 1—6 |
| Thurmond | 0—1 | 0—0 | 2—0 | 1—2 | 0—1 | 0—0 | 2—2 | 1—0 | 1—0 | 0—1 | 0—4 | 7—11 |
| Walter | 0—0 | 0—0 | 0—1 | 0—0 | 0—0 | 0—1 | 0—0 | 0—0 | 0—0 | 0—0 | 0—0 | 0—2 |
| Wojna | 1—0 | 0—0 | 0—0 | 0—2 | 0—0 | 0—0 | 0—0 | 0—1 | 0—0 | 0—1 | 1—0 | 2—4 |
| Totals | 11—7 | 4—8 | 9—9 | 6—12 | 10—8 | 7—5 | 5—7 | 7—5 | 8—4 | 4—8 | 12—6 | 83—79 |

No Decisions—Patterson.

### SAN FRANCISCO—62-100

| Pitcher | Atl. W—L | Chi. W—L | Cin. W—L | Hou. W—L | L.A. W—L | Mtl. W—L | N.Y. W—L | Phil. W—L | Pitt. W—L | St.L. W—L | S.D. W—L | Totals W—L |
|---|---|---|---|---|---|---|---|---|---|---|---|---|
| Blue | 2—0 | 1—0 | 1—0 | 1—0 | 0—4 | 0—0 | 0—1 | 1—1 | 0—0 | 0—1 | 2—1 | 8—8 |

**Lefthander Dave LaPoint, now with the Detroit Tigers, won't have to pitch against Houston in 1986. The Astros beat him five times last year.**

| Pitcher | Atl. W—L | Chi. W—L | Cin. W—L | Hou. W—L | L.A. W—L | Mtl. W—L | N.Y. W—L | Phil. W—L | Pitt. W—L | St.L. W—L | S.D. W—L | Totals W—L |
|---|---|---|---|---|---|---|---|---|---|---|---|---|
| M. Davis | 0—0 | 0—1 | 1—2 | 0—3 | 1—2 | 0—0 | 1—3 | 1—0 | 0—0 | 0—0 | 1—1 | 5—12 |
| Garrelts | 1—1 | 3—1 | 1—1 | 0—0 | 1—0 | 0—1 | 1—1 | 0—0 | 1—1 | 1—0 | 0—0 | 9—6 |
| Gott | 1—1 | 0—1 | 0—1 | 1—0 | 1—0 | 2—1 | 1—2 | 0—1 | 1—1 | 0—1 | 0—1 | 7—10 |
| Hammaker | 0—1 | 0—1 | 1—1 | 0—4 | 0—0 | 1—0 | 0—0 | 2—1 | 0—0 | 0—1 | 1—3 | 5—12 |
| Jeffcoat | 0—1 | 0—0 | 0—0 | 0—0 | 0—0 | 0—0 | 0—0 | 0—1 | 0—0 | 0—0 | 0—0 | 0—2 |
| Krukow | 1—1 | 1—1 | 0—1 | 1—1 | 2—0 | 0—2 | 0—1 | 1—1 | 1—1 | 0—2 | 1—0 | 8—11 |
| LaPoint | 0—1 | 0—0 | 1—2 | 0—5 | 0—2 | 1—1 | 1—0 | 1—0 | 2—0 | 1—3 | 0—3 | 7—17 |
| Laskey | 0—0 | 1—1 | 0—2 | 0—2 | 1—1 | 0—1 | 0—0 | 0—0 | 3—0 | 0—2 | 0—2 | 5—11 |
| Mason | 1—1 | 0—0 | 0—0 | 0—0 | 0—1 | 0—0 | 0—0 | 0—0 | 0—0 | 0—0 | 0—1 | 1—3 |
| Minton | 1—1 | 0—0 | 1—1 | 0—0 | 1—1 | 1—0 | 0—0 | 0—1 | 1—0 | 0—0 | 0—0 | 5—4 |
| Williams | 1—2 | 0—0 | 0—1 | 0—0 | 0—0 | 0—1 | 0—0 | 0—0 | 0—0 | 0—0 | 1—0 | 2—4 |
| Totals | 8—10 | 6—6 | 6—12 | 3—15 | 7—11 | 5—7 | 4—8 | 6—6 | 9—3 | 2—10 | 6—12 | 62—100 |

No Decisions—Moore, Robinson, Ward.

# 1985 CHAMPIONSHIP SERIES

## Including

**American League Review**

**American League Box Scores**

**American League Composite Box Score**

**National League Review**

**National League Box Scores**

**National League Composite Box Score**

**Pitcher Danny Jackson saved the Royals from elimination in Game 5 of the American League Championship Series with an eight-hit, 2-0 victory over Toronto.**

# Royals' Rally Jolts Jays in 7

**By LARRY WIGGE**

Some players go through an entire career without getting even a whiff of that sweet smell of success. They give it their all, day in and day out, but never get a chance to play in a League Championship Series or World Series. Give them their chance, however, and they produce.

Take Jim Sundberg, for example. For 10 years, the veteran catcher punched his time card for some pretty dreadful Texas Rangers clubs. Then he spent a season with a slumping Milwaukee Brewers club. Finally, he got the break of his life when he was traded to the Kansas City Royals prior to the 1985 season.

"I thought it was never going to happen," Sundberg said after driving in four runs to lead the Royals to a 6-2 victory over the Toronto Blue Jays in Game 7 of the American League Championship Series. "I always thought I had the ability and the confidence and the intense desire to win. I just wondered if I'd ever get the chance."

A six-time Gold Glove winner for his fielding excellence, Sundberg wasn't exactly tearing up the Blue Jays offensively through the first six playoff games. He had only two hits in 20 at-bats.

But Sundberg wasn't about to blow his opportunity. He drove in Kansas City's first run with a second-inning single. After right fielder Pat Sheridan added to the Royals' lead with a long solo home run in the fourth, Sundberg provided the game's biggest blow when he tripled off the top of the right-field fence with the bases loaded in the sixth, extending Kansas City's lead to 5-1. He then scored the Royals' sixth and final run on second baseman Frank White's single.

"No doubt about it, Sunny's hit was the knockout punch," said Hal McRae, Kansas City's veteran designated hitter.

Sundberg's blast, which knocked out starting and losing pitcher Dave Stieb, was lofted into a strong jet stream blowing out to right field and nearly carried over the fence for a grand slam.

"At first I didn't know if it had enough carry, but then I saw the wind grab it," Sundberg recalled. "When I saw (right fielder) Jesse Barfield just standing there looking at the ball, I wasn't sure what to think, so I ran as fast as I could."

Sundberg's big game allowed the Royals to take full advantage of the new best-of-seven format for the League Champion-

**Dave Stieb pitched eight scoreless innings as the Jays won the opener, 6-1.**

ship Series, previously a best-of-five affair. After dropping the first two games of the playoffs in Toronto, the Royals split the next two games with the Blue Jays in Kansas City. While that 3-1 edge in games would have given Toronto the pennant in previous years, it still gave Kansas City a chance in 1985. The Royals responded by winning the last three games—including the final two in Toronto—to earn their second ticket to the World Series in the 17-year history of the franchise.

"When we won the pennant in 1980, I thought there would be plenty more," said White, a longtime Royals veteran who has played on all six of Kansas City's A.L. West champion teams. "Then when no more came, I thought my time had gone. I got frustrated early in this series because it always seemed the last few years that we lacked the one hitter or the one pitcher we needed. Now, to see this, well, it's hard to express what it means. No one expected us to do it. I guess that makes it even sweeter."

Stieb was much sharper in Game 1 of the playoffs than in Game 7. The right-hander struck out eight batters and scattered three hits over eight innings in leading the Blue Jays to a 6-1 triumph in the opener.

Toronto tallied twice off lefthander Charlie Leibrandt in the second inning on run-scoring singles by catcher Ernie Whitt and shortstop Tony Fernandez. When Leibrandt surrendered a leadoff double to designated hitter Cliff Johnson, a walk to Barfield and a single to first baseman Willie Upshaw in the third, loading the bases with none out, he was replaced by righthander Steve Farr. All three baserunners eventually scored, however, on an RBI single by pinch-hitter Rance Mulliniks, a bases-loaded walk to Whitt and a sacrifice fly by Fernandez.

The Blue Jays' final run came in the fourth. Left fielder George Bell singled and then advanced to third on Johnson's groundout. Surprised to see Bell storming around second on the play, third baseman George Brett was late in covering the bag and first baseman Steve Balboni threw wildly, allowing Bell to score.

Knowing that Stieb would be pitching on three days' rest in Game 4, Toronto Manager Bobby Cox pulled his ace after eight scoreless innings. The Royals reached reliever Tom Henke for their only run in the ninth, following singles by center fielder Willie Wilson and Brett with a run-scoring forceout, but it wasn't enough. The setback stretched Kansas City's losing streak in postseason play (dating to the 1980 World Series) to nine games. And for Royals Manager Dick Howser, whose Yankees had been swept by Kansas City in the A.L. playoffs in '80, it was 10 straight postseason defeats.

Things didn't get any better for Howser or the Royals in Game 2 as Kansas City fell, 6-5, in a gut-wrenching, 10-inning loss.

The Royals built up a 3-0 lead in Game 2, scoring in the third inning on Wilson's two-run homer and in the fourth on Sundberg's RBI double. That was it for starter Jimmy Key, but Dennis Lamp came on to throw 3⅔ innings of scoreless relief. Meanwhile, the Blue Jays inched back with Johnson's run-scoring double (which followed an error by Brett) in their half of the fourth, and they tied it on a two-out, two-run single by Barfield in the sixth. A hit batter and a wild pitch by Kansas City

starter Bud Black contributed to that rally. Dan Quisenberry replaced Black in the eighth, when the Blue Jays took a 4-3 lead. This time, a throwing error by Sundberg on Lloyd Moseby's steal of second put the Toronto center fielder in position to score on Bell's sacrifice fly.

Then the game really got weird.

Sheridan, who had hit only three homers in 206 at-bats during the regular season, slugged a pinch homer off Henke in the ninth inning, tying the game, 4-4, and sending it into extra innings. In the top of the 10th, Wilson spanked a single to center and stole second base as Henke fanned McRae for the second out. White followed with a sinking liner to center, where Moseby galloped in and went down for the scoop. Second base umpire Ted Hendry was out of position and made no call. When right field umpire Dave Phillips ruled that Moseby had played the ball on one hop, allowing Wilson to cross the plate with the go-ahead run, bedlam arose in the friendly confines of Exhibition Stadium. Moseby vehemently argued that he fielded the ball cleanly, but to no avail.

"He made the right call if he's certain," Cox said. "Somebody had to make it."

At this point, Quisenberry was shaping up as the eventual winner and Henke as the goat. But in Toronto's half of the 10th, Fernandez legged out an infield hit as Royals shortstop Onix Concepcion had trouble getting the ball out of his glove. Fernandez went to second on a groundout by second baseman Damaso Garcia and scored on Moseby's single to right, tying the game. Moseby reached second when Balboni couldn't handle Quisenberry's pickoff attempt for an error. After Bell flied out, pinch-hitter Al Oliver singled to left to make Henke the winner and Quisenberry, a five-time A.L. Fireman of the Year, the loser.

"I can't remember a loss that hurt worse than this," a forlorn Brett said in the Kansas City clubhouse. "Every time we made a mistake, it cost us a run."

Brett could do no wrong in Game 3 as the scene shifted to Kansas City. The Royals' All-Star slugger and Gold Glove fielder took the Series into his own hands, leading the Royals to a 6-5 triumph with a 4-for-4 performance, including two homers.

Brett connected for a solo shot off right-hander Doyle Alexander in the first inning. The Royals' lead was extended to 2-0 in the fourth when Brett doubled off the top of the right-field fence and scored on a sacrifice fly by White. In between, Brett made a brilliant backhanded stab over the third-base bag of Moseby's hard grounder and threw out Garcia at the plate to prevent the Blue Jays from tying the score, 1-1, in the third.

Bret Saberhagen, Kansas City's 21-year-old righthander and a 20-game winner during the regular season, was sailing along smoothly until the fifth. Whitt led off the inning with a single and scored when Barfield followed with a home run that tied the score, 2-2. Saberhagen retired Fernandez on a fly to left, but Garcia then doubled. Next up was Moseby, who hit a sizzling line drive that ricocheted off Saberhagen's heel and into left field for a single, scoring Garcia. Saberhagen was in obvious pain, but he remained in the game to pitch to Mulliniks, who promptly clouted a two-run homer to extend Toronto's lead to 5-2. Howser then summoned Black from the bullpen, and the Royals escaped the inning without further damage.

Sundberg got one of those runs back for the Royals in their half of the fifth with a solo homer. But it was Brett who knotted the count, 5-5, with a two-run homer in the sixth. One batter later, Alexander was off to the showers.

Kansas City's Farr, who earned the victory, blanked the Blue Jays on two hits over the final 4⅓ innings while the Royals just waited for Brett to make his next appearance at the plate. That came as a leadoff hitter in the eighth.

Brett promptly singled to right off righthander Jim Clancy. After McRae sacrificed him to second, White grounded out and Sheridan was walked intentionally. Balboni then ended a 0-for-11 slump by blooping a single to center to score Brett with the winning run.

In Game 4, the Blue Jays stole another late-inning decision from Kansas City in a 3-1 game that bore a striking resemblance to Game 2. Just like before, Moseby and Oliver provided the game-tying and -winning hits, Henke was the winner for Toronto and Quisenberry was the victim for Kansas City.

But not the loser. That distinction went to Leibrandt, who pitched effectively for eight innings and took a 1-0 lead into the ninth. But he walked Garcia to open Toronto's half of the ninth, and Moseby followed with a run-scoring double to right-center, bringing Quisenberry to the mound with the game tied.

Bell greeted Quiz with a bloop single to center, Moseby stopping at third. That's when Cox sent Oliver in to bat for Johnson. Oliver laced a double to right field, scoring Moseby and Bell and clinching a 3-1 lead in the series for the Blue Jays.

Actually, the Royals would have been lucky to win Game 4. They scratched out only two hits, both by Wilson, and one was of the infield variety. Their only threat came in the sixth, when Toronto starter Stieb walked McRae with the bases loaded and none out to force in a run. But Stieb pitched out of that jam by getting Sheridan to pop out to the infield and White to hit into a double play. Henke allowed only two walks in 2⅓ innings of relief.

One more victory is all Toronto needed to make the trip to the World Series. But Kansas City lefthander Danny Jackson had other thoughts, limiting the Blue Jays to eight hits and shutting them out, 2-0, in Game 5.

Jackson was in several jams, but he repeatedly wriggled out of trouble. Meanwhile, his teammates gave him an early lead, scoring once in the first inning when left fielder Lonnie Smith greeted Key with a leadoff double, stole third and came home on Brett's grounder. The Royals added to their lead in the second when White beat out a bunt, went to third on a single by Balboni and scored on right fielder Darryl Motley's sacrifice fly.

When the series went back to Toronto for Game 6, the Royals once again dodged the executioner's blade, winning 5-3. The Royals jumped on top in the first when McRae singled home Wilson. After the Blue Jays tied it in their half of the first on Mulliniks' double-play grounder, Kansas City went in front again in the third on McRae's RBI double. Toronto quickly produced a 2-2 deadlock with one run in their half of the third on Moseby's run-scoring groundout. Enter Brett, the reigning Mr. October once again.

With one out in the fifth, Brett touched starter and loser Alexander for his third home run of the series, giving the Royals a 3-2 cushion. It was Brett's ninth career home run in League Championship Series play, breaking Steve Garvey's major league record of eight, and the series Most Valuable Player award was his—if the Royals could emerge as A.L. champs.

One inning later, the Royals padded their lead with run-scoring doubles by shortstop Buddy Biancalana and Smith. The Blue Jays' final tally came on Johnson's pinch single in the sixth. The victory went to righthanded starter Mark Gubicza, who went 5⅓ innings, with Black and Quisenberry combining for shutout relief for the final 3⅔ innings.

Kansas City's Saberhagen and Toronto's Stieb, the aces of their respective staffs, were matched in the decisive final game of the series, but with the home-field advantage, the odds appeared to be in the Blue Jays' favor entering Game 7. Those odds grew even larger when Upshaw smashed a first-inning line drive off Saberhagen's pitching hand, necessitating his removal after three scoreless innings. But Leibrandt, the hard-luck loser of Game 4 (as well as Game 1), made his first relief appearance of the season and rose to the occasion. A run-scoring double by Upshaw in the fifth and an RBI groundout by Garcia in the ninth were charged to the veteran lefty, but he earned the victory while allowing only five hits in 5⅓ innings.

Meanwhile, Sundberg was making the most of his opportunity at the plate with his 2-for-4, four-RBI performance. And Quisenberry atoned for his earlier breakdowns by recording the final out for the second night in a row.

Good fortune had smiled on the Royals in their dramatic comeback. But then, the club's co-owner, Avron Fogelman, had gotten a hint that this would be the Royals' day in the sun. Fogelman had dinner at a Chinese restaurant in Toronto several hours before the October 16 contest. The message in his fortune cookie couldn't have been more prophetic: "You will soon receive a gift of jewelry."

A World Series championship ring, perhaps?

### GAME OF TUESDAY, OCTOBER 8, AT TORONTO (N)

| Kansas City | AB. | R. | H. | RBI. | PO. | A. |
|---|---|---|---|---|---|---|
| Smith, lf | 4 | 0 | 0 | 0 | 0 | 1 |
| Wilson, cf | 4 | 1 | 1 | 0 | 2 | 0 |
| Brett, 3b | 4 | 0 | 3 | 0 | 3 | 0 |
| Orta, dh | 4 | 0 | 0 | 0 | 0 | 0 |
| Sheridan, rf | 3 | 0 | 0 | 1 | 6 | 0 |
| White, 2b | 4 | 0 | 0 | 0 | 0 | 1 |
| Balboni, 1b | 3 | 0 | 0 | 0 | 8 | 1 |
| Sundberg, c | 3 | 0 | 0 | 0 | 3 | 0 |
| Biancalana, ss | 2 | 0 | 0 | 0 | 1 | 7 |
| D. Iorg, ph | 1 | 0 | 1 | 0 | 0 | 0 |
| Concepcion, pr-ss | 0 | 0 | 0 | 0 | 0 | 0 |
| Leibrandt, p | 0 | 0 | 0 | 0 | 0 | 0 |
| Farr, p | 0 | 0 | 0 | 0 | 0 | 0 |
| Gubicza, p | 0 | 0 | 0 | 0 | 0 | 0 |
| Jackson, p | 0 | 0 | 0 | 0 | 1 | 0 |
| Totals | 32 | 1 | 5 | 1 | 24 | 10 |

| Toronto | AB. | R. | H. | RBI. | PO. | A. |
|---|---|---|---|---|---|---|
| Garcia, 2b | 5 | 0 | 2 | 0 | 0 | 2 |
| Lee, pr-2b | 0 | 0 | 0 | 0 | 0 | 0 |
| Moseby, cf | 5 | 0 | 0 | 0 | 4 | 0 |
| Bell, lf | 5 | 1 | 2 | 0 | 3 | 0 |
| Johnson, dh | 4 | 1 | 1 | 0 | 0 | 0 |
| Barfield, rf | 2 | 1 | 1 | 0 | 1 | 0 |
| Upshaw, 1b | 3 | 2 | 1 | 0 | 8 | 1 |
| G. Iorg, 3b | 1 | 1 | 0 | 1 | 1 | 1 |
| Mulliniks, ph-3b | 3 | 0 | 1 | 1 | 1 | 0 |
| Whitt, c | 3 | 0 | 1 | 2 | 8 | 0 |
| Fernandez, ss | 3 | 0 | 2 | 2 | 1 | 0 |
| Stieb, p | 0 | 0 | 0 | 0 | 0 | 1 |
| Henke, p | 0 | 0 | 0 | 0 | 0 | 0 |
| Totals | 34 | 6 | 11 | 5 | 27 | 5 |

Kansas City .......................... 0 0 0   0 0 0   0 0 1—1
Toronto ................................. 0 2 3   1 0 0   0 0 x—6

| Kansas City | IP. | H. | R. | ER. | BB. | SO. |
|---|---|---|---|---|---|---|
| Leibrandt (Loser) | 2* | 7 | 5 | 5 | 1 | 0 |
| Farr | 2 | 2 | 1 | 1 | 1 | 0 |
| Gubicza | 3 | 0 | 0 | 0 | 1 | 2 |
| Jackson | 1 | 2 | 0 | 0 | 0 | 1 |

| Toronto | IP. | H. | R. | ER. | BB. | SO. |
|---|---|---|---|---|---|---|
| Stieb (Winner) | 8 | 3 | 0 | 0 | 1 | 8 |
| Henke | 1 | 2 | 1 | 1 | 0 | 0 |

*Pitched to three batters in third.

Game-winning RBI—Whitt. Error—Balboni. Left on bases—Kansas City 5, Toronto 9. Two-base hits—Brett, Bell, Johnson, D. Iorg. Stolen base—Barfield. Sacrifice fly—Fernandez. Hit by pitcher—By Leibrandt (Upshaw). Umpires—Phillips, Ford, Evans, Hendry, Voltaggio and Cousins. Time—2:24. Attendance—39,115.

### GAME OF WEDNESDAY, OCTOBER 9, AT TORONTO

| Kansas City | AB. | R. | H. | RBI. | PO. | A. |
|---|---|---|---|---|---|---|
| Smith, lf | 5 | 0 | 0 | 0 | 0 | 1 |
| Wilson, cf | 5 | 2 | 3 | 2 | 3 | 0 |
| Brett, 3b | 4 | 0 | 0 | 1 | 2 | — |
| McRae, dh | 5 | 0 | 2 | 0 | 0 | 0 |
| White, 2b | 4 | 0 | 2 | 1 | 1 | 6 |
| Balboni, 1b | 5 | 0 | 0 | 0 | 8 | 1 |
| Motley, rf | 2 | 1 | 0 | 0 | 4 | 0 |
| Sheridan, ph-rf | 1 | 1 | 1 | 1 | 0 | 0 |
| Sundberg, c | 4 | 0 | 1 | 1 | 8 | 1 |
| Biancalana, ss | 2 | 1 | 1 | 0 | 1 | 1 |
| D. Iorg, ph | 0 | 0 | 0 | 0 | 0 | 0 |
| Concepcion, pr-ss | 0 | 0 | 0 | 0 | 0 | 0 |
| Black, p | 0 | 0 | 0 | 0 | 2 | 2 |
| Quisenberry, p | 0 | 0 | 0 | 0 | 1 | 0 |
| Totals | 37 | 5 | 10 | 5 | 29 | 14 |

| Toronto | AB. | R. | H. | RBI. | PO. | A. |
|---|---|---|---|---|---|---|
| Garcia, 2b | 5 | 0 | 0 | 0 | 1 | 2 |
| Moseby, cf | 5 | 2 | 2 | 1 | 1 | 0 |
| Bell, lf | 3 | 2 | 0 | 1 | 0 | 0 |
| Johnson, dh | 3 | 0 | 2 | 1 | 0 | 0 |
| Thornton, pr | 0 | 1 | 0 | 0 | 0 | 0 |
| Oliver, dh | 2 | 0 | 1 | 1 | 0 | 0 |
| Barfield, rf | 4 | 0 | 1 | 2 | 3 | 0 |
| Upshaw, 1b | 4 | 0 | 1 | 0 | 10 | 1 |
| G. Iorg, 3b | 3 | 0 | 1 | 0 | 2 | 3 |
| Mulliniks, ph-3b | 1 | 0 | 1 | 0 | 0 | 0 |
| Whitt, c | 4 | 0 | 0 | 0 | 9 | 2 |
| Fernandez, ss | 3 | 1 | 1 | 0 | 3 | 5 |
| Key, p | 0 | 0 | 0 | 0 | 0 | 0 |
| Lamp, p | 0 | 0 | 0 | 0 | 1 | 0 |
| Lavelle, p | 0 | 0 | 0 | 0 | 0 | 0 |
| Henke, p | 0 | 0 | 0 | 0 | 0 | 0 |
| Totals | 37 | 6 | 10 | 6 | 30 | 13 |

Kansas City ...................... 0 0 2   1 0 0   0 0 1   1—5
Toronto ............................. 0 0 0   1 0 2   0 1 0   2—6

Two out when winning run scored.

| Kansas City | IP. | H. | R. | ER. | BB. | SO. |
|---|---|---|---|---|---|---|
| Black | 7 | 5 | 3 | 2 | 1 | 5 |
| Quisenberry (Loser) | 2⅔ | 5 | 3 | 1 | 0 | 2 |

| Toronto | IP. | H. | R. | ER. | BB. | SO. |
|---|---|---|---|---|---|---|
| Key | 3⅓ | 7 | 3 | 3 | 1 | 2 |
| Lamp | 3⅔ | 0 | 0 | 0 | 0 | 3 |
| Lavelle | 0* | 0 | 0 | 0 | 1 | 0 |
| Henke (Winner) | 3 | 3 | 2 | 2 | 2 | 4 |

*Pitched to one batter in eighth.

Game-winning RBI—Oliver. Errors—Brett, Sundberg, Balboni. Double plays—Kansas City 1, Toronto 1. Left on bases—Kansas City 7, Toronto 5. Two-base hits—Sundberg, Johnson. Home runs—Wilson, Sheridan. Stolen bases—Moseby, Wilson. Sacrifice hit—Biancalana. Sacrifice fly—Bell. Hit by pitcher—By Black (Bell). Wild pitch—Black. Umpires—Ford, Evans, Voltaggio, Hendry, Cousins and Phillips. Time—3:39. Attendance—34,029.

## GAME OF FRIDAY, OCTOBER 11, AT KANSAS CITY (N)

| Toronto | AB. | R. | H. | RBI. | PO. | A. |
|---|---|---|---|---|---|---|
| Garcia, 2b | 5 | 1 | 2 | 0 | 1 | 1 |
| Moseby, cf | 4 | 1 | 1 | 1 | 1 | 0 |
| Mulliniks, 3b | 4 | 1 | 1 | 2 | 0 | 0 |
| Upshaw, 1b | 4 | 0 | 1 | 0 | 4 | 1 |
| Oliver, dh | 2 | 1 | 1 | 0 | 0 | 0 |
| Johnson, dh | 2 | 0 | 1 | 0 | 0 | 0 |
| Bell, lf | 4 | 0 | 3 | 0 | 2 | 0 |
| Whitt, c | 3 | 1 | 1 | 0 | 5 | 1 |
| Barfield, rf | 4 | 1 | 1 | 2 | 9 | 0 |
| Fernandez, ss | 4 | 0 | 1 | 0 | 1 | 2 |
| Alexander, p | 0 | 0 | 0 | 0 | 1 | 0 |
| Lamp, p | 0 | 0 | 0 | 0 | 0 | 1 |
| Clancy, p | 0 | 0 | 0 | 0 | 0 | 1 |
| Totals | 36 | 5 | 13 | 5 | 24 | 7 |

| Kansas City | AB. | R. | H. | RBI. | PO. | A. |
|---|---|---|---|---|---|---|
| Smith, lf | 4 | 0 | 1 | 0 | 3 | 0 |
| L. Jones, lf | 0 | 0 | 0 | 0 | 0 | 0 |
| Wilson, cf | 4 | 1 | 2 | 0 | 0 | 0 |
| Brett, 3b | 4 | 4 | 4 | 3 | 1 | 1 |
| McRae, dh | 3 | 0 | 1 | 0 | 0 | 0 |
| White, 2b | 3 | 0 | 0 | 1 | 2 | 4 |
| Sheridan, rf | 3 | 0 | 0 | 0 | 0 | 0 |
| Balboni, 1b | 4 | 0 | 1 | 1 | 10 | 0 |
| Sundberg, c | 4 | 1 | 1 | 1 | 8 | 1 |
| Biancalana, ss | 1 | 0 | 0 | 0 | 1 | 2 |
| D. Iorg, ph | 1 | 0 | 0 | 0 | 0 | 0 |
| Concepcion, ss | 1 | 0 | 0 | 0 | 2 | 4 |
| Saberhagen, p | 0 | 0 | 0 | 0 | 0 | 1 |
| Black, p | 0 | 0 | 0 | 0 | 0 | 1 |
| Farr, p | 0 | 0 | 0 | 0 | 0 | 1 |
| Totals | 32 | 6 | 10 | 6 | 27 | 14 |

Toronto .................................. 0 0 0    0 5 0    0 0 0—5
Kansas City ........................... 1 0 0    1 1 2    0 1 x—6

| Toronto | IP. | H. | R. | ER. | BB. | SO. |
|---|---|---|---|---|---|---|
| Alexander | 5* | 7 | 5 | 5 | 0 | 3 |
| Lamp | 2 | 1 | 0 | 0 | 0 | 2 |
| Clancy (Loser) | 1 | 2 | 1 | 1 | 1 | 0 |

| Kansas City | IP. | H. | R. | ER. | BB. | SO. |
|---|---|---|---|---|---|---|
| Saberhagen | 4⅓ | 9 | 5 | 5 | 1 | 4 |
| Black | ⅓ | 2 | 0 | 0 | 1 | 0 |
| Farr (Winner) | 4⅓ | 2 | 0 | 0 | 0 | 3 |

*Pitched to three batters in sixth.

Game-winning RBI—Balboni.
Errors—Upshaw, Smith. Double plays—Kansas City 3. Left on bases—Toronto 6, Kansas City 5. Two-base hits—Garcia 2, Upshaw, Brett, McRae. Home runs—Brett 2, Barfield, Mulliniks, Sundberg. Sacrifice hit—McRae. Sacrifice fly—White. Umpires—Evans, Hendry, Voltaggio, Cousins, Phillips and Ford. Time—2:51. Attendance—40,224.

## GAME OF SATURDAY, OCTOBER 12, AT KANSAS CITY (N)

| Toronto | AB. | R. | H. | RBI. | PO. | A. |
|---|---|---|---|---|---|---|
| Garcia, 2b | 3 | 1 | 1 | 0 | 2 | 2 |
| Moseby, cf | 4 | 1 | 1 | 1 | 4 | 0 |
| Bell, lf | 4 | 1 | 1 | 0 | 2 | 0 |
| Johnson, dh | 2 | 0 | 0 | 0 | 0 | 0 |
| Oliver, ph | 1 | 0 | 1 | 2 | 0 | 0 |
| Barfield, rf | 4 | 0 | 2 | 0 | 1 | 0 |
| Upshaw, 1b | 4 | 0 | 0 | 0 | 6 | 2 |
| G. Iorg, 3b | 4 | 0 | 0 | 0 | 1 | 2 |
| Whitt, c | 2 | 0 | 0 | 0 | 6 | 0 |
| Fielder, ph | 1 | 0 | 1 | 0 | 0 | 0 |
| Thornton, pr | 0 | 0 | 0 | 0 | 0 | 0 |
| Hearron, c | 0 | 0 | 0 | 0 | 0 | 0 |
| Fernandez, ss | 3 | 0 | 0 | 0 | 3 | 2 |
| Stieb, p | 0 | 0 | 0 | 0 | 1 | 1 |
| Henke, p | 0 | 0 | 0 | 0 | 1 | 0 |
| Totals | 32 | 3 | 7 | 3 | 27 | 9 |

| Kansas City | AB. | R. | H. | RBI. | PO. | A. |
|---|---|---|---|---|---|---|
| Smith, lf | 1 | 1 | 0 | 0 | 3 | 0 |
| L. Jones, lf | 0 | 0 | 0 | 0 | 2 | 0 |
| Quirk, ph | 1 | 0 | 0 | 0 | 0 | 0 |
| Wilson, cf | 3 | 0 | 2 | 0 | 2 | 0 |
| Brett, 3b | 2 | 0 | 0 | 0 | 0 | 1 |
| McRae, dh | 3 | 0 | 0 | 1 | 0 | 0 |
| Sheridan, rf | 4 | 0 | 0 | 0 | 1 | 0 |
| White, 2b | 4 | 0 | 0 | 0 | 0 | 3 |
| Balboni, 1b | 3 | 0 | 0 | 0 | 12 | 4 |
| Sundberg, c | 3 | 0 | 0 | 0 | 1 | 0 |
| Orta, ph | 1 | 0 | 0 | 0 | 0 | 0 |
| Biancalana, ss | 2 | 0 | 0 | 0 | 3 | 3 |
| D. Iorg, ph | 0 | 0 | 0 | 0 | 0 | 0 |
| Concepcion, pr-ss | 0 | 0 | 0 | 0 | 0 | 0 |
| Leibrandt, p | 0 | 0 | 0 | 0 | 3 | 5 |
| Quisenberry, p | 0 | 0 | 0 | 0 | 0 | 0 |
| Totals | 27 | 1 | 2 | 1 | 27 | 16 |

Toronto .......................... 0 0 0    0 0 0    0 0 3—3
Kansas City ..................... 0 0 0    0 0 1    0 0 0—1

| Toronto | IP. | H. | R. | ER. | BB. | SO. |
|---|---|---|---|---|---|---|
| Stieb | 6⅔ | 2 | 1 | 1 | 7 | 6 |
| Henke (Winner) | 2⅓ | 0 | 0 | 0 | 2 | 0 |

| Kansas City | IP. | H. | R. | ER. | BB. | SO. |
|---|---|---|---|---|---|---|
| Leibrandt (Loser) | 8* | 5 | 2 | 2 | 2 | 1 |
| Quisenberry | 1 | 2 | 1 | 1 | 0 | 0 |

*Pitched to two batters in ninth.

Game-winning RBI—Oliver.
Errors—None. Double plays—Toronto 1, Kansas City 1. Left on bases—Toronto 4, Kansas City 9. Two-base hits—Barfield, Garcia, Fielder, Moseby, Oliver. Sacrifice hit—Wilson. Umpires—Hendry, Voltaggio, Cousins, Phillips, Ford and Evans. Time—3:02. Attendance—41,112.

## GAME OF SUNDAY, OCTOBER 13, AT KANSAS CITY

| Toronto | AB. | R. | H. | RBI. | PO. | A. |
|---|---|---|---|---|---|---|
| Garcia, 2b | 4 | 0 | 0 | 0 | 3 | 2 |
| Moseby, cf | 4 | 0 | 0 | 0 | 1 | 0 |
| Bell, lf | 4 | 0 | 2 | 0 | 0 | 0 |
| Johnson, dh | 4 | 0 | 1 | 0 | 0 | 0 |
| Barfield, rf | 4 | 0 | 1 | 0 | 3 | 0 |
| Upshaw, 1b | 4 | 0 | 1 | 0 | 11 | 1 |
| G. Iorg, 3b | 3 | 0 | 1 | 0 | 0 | 2 |
| Whitt, c | 3 | 0 | 1 | 0 | 5 | 0 |
| Fielder, ph | 1 | 0 | 0 | 0 | 0 | 0 |
| Fernandez, ss | 3 | 0 | 1 | 0 | 1 | 2 |
| Key, p | 0 | 0 | 0 | 0 | 0 | 3 |
| Acker, p | 0 | 0 | 0 | 0 | 0 | 1 |
| Totals | 34 | 0 | 8 | 0 | 24 | 11 |

| Kansas City | AB. | R. | H. | RBI. | PO. | A. |
|---|---|---|---|---|---|---|
| Smith, lf | 4 | 1 | 3 | 0 | 0 | 1 |
| L. Jones, lf | 0 | 0 | 0 | 0 | 0 | 0 |
| Wilson, cf | 4 | 0 | 0 | 0 | 1 | 0 |
| Brett, 3b | 3 | 0 | 0 | 1 | 1 | 4 |
| McRae, dh | 4 | 0 | 0 | 0 | 0 | 0 |
| White, 2b | 3 | 1 | 2 | 0 | 3 | 3 |
| Balboni, 1b | 3 | 0 | 2 | 0 | 13 | 0 |
| Motley, rf | 1 | 0 | 1 | 1 | 0 | 0 |
| Sheridan, ph-rf | 1 | 0 | 0 | 0 | 3 | 0 |
| Sundberg, c | 3 | 0 | 0 | 0 | 6 | 0 |
| Biancalana, ss | 3 | 0 | 0 | 0 | 0 | 2 |
| Jackson, p | 0 | 0 | 0 | 0 | 0 | 1 |
| Totals | 29 | 2 | 8 | 2 | 27 | 11 |

Toronto .............................. 0 0 0    0 0 0    0 0 0—0
Kansas City ......................... 1 1 0    0 0 0    0 0 x—2

| Toronto | IP. | H. | R. | ER. | BB. | SO. |
|---|---|---|---|---|---|---|
| Key (Loser) | 5⅓ | 8 | 2 | 2 | 1 | 3 |
| Acker | 2⅔ | 0 | 0 | 0 | 0 | 2 |

| Kansas City | IP. | H. | R. | ER. | BB. | SO. |
|---|---|---|---|---|---|---|
| Jackson (Winner) ...... | 9 | 8 | 0 | 0 | 1 | 6 |

Game-winning RBI—Brett.
Errors—None. Double play—Toronto 1. Left on bases—Toronto 8, Kansas City 5. Two-base hits—Bell, Smith, Whitt. Stolen base—Smith. Sacrifice fly—Motley. Umpires—Voltaggio, Cousins, Phillips, Ford, Evans and Hendry. Time—2:21. Attendance—40,046.

### GAME OF TUESDAY, OCTOBER 15, AT TORONTO (N)

| Kansas City | AB. | R. | H. | RBI. | PO. | A. |
|---|---|---|---|---|---|---|
| Smith, lf | 5 | 0 | 1 | 1 | 0 | 0 |
| L. Jones, lf | 0 | 0 | 0 | 0 | 0 | 0 |
| Wilson, cf | 4 | 1 | 1 | 0 | 2 | 0 |
| Brett, 3b | 3 | 2 | 1 | 1 | 0 | 0 |
| McRae, dh | 5 | 0 | 3 | 2 | 0 | 0 |
| Sheridan, rf | 4 | 0 | 0 | 0 | 2 | 0 |
| Balboni, 1b | 4 | 0 | 0 | 0 | 11 | 0 |
| Sundberg, c | 3 | 1 | 0 | 0 | 8 | 0 |
| White, 2b | 3 | 0 | 0 | 0 | 1 | 6 |
| Biancalana, ss | 4 | 1 | 2 | 1 | 3 | 4 |
| Gubicza, p | 0 | 0 | 0 | 0 | 0 | 1 |
| Black, p | 0 | 0 | 0 | 0 | 0 | 1 |
| Quisenberry, p | 0 | 0 | 0 | 0 | 0 | 0 |
| Totals | 35 | 5 | 8 | 5 | 27 | 12 |

| Toronto | AB. | R. | H. | RBI. | PO. | A. |
|---|---|---|---|---|---|---|
| Garcia, 2b | 3 | 1 | 1 | 0 | 2 | 1 |
| Moseby, cf | 4 | 1 | 3 | 1 | 1 | 0 |
| Mulliniks, 3b | 2 | 0 | 0 | 0 | 0 | 2 |
| G. Iorg, ph-3b | 2 | 0 | 0 | 0 | 0 | 0 |
| Upshaw, 1b | 3 | 0 | 0 | 0 | 5 | 1 |
| Oliver, dh | 2 | 0 | 0 | 0 | 0 | 0 |
| Johnson, dh | 2 | 0 | 2 | 1 | 0 | 0 |
| Bell, lf | 4 | 0 | 0 | 0 | 3 | 0 |
| Whitt, c | 3 | 0 | 0 | 0 | 10 | 0 |
| Fielder, ph | 1 | 0 | 0 | 0 | 0 | 0 |
| Hearron, c | 0 | 0 | 0 | 0 | 2 | 0 |
| Barfield, rf | 4 | 0 | 0 | 0 | 3 | 0 |
| Fernandez, ss | 4 | 1 | 2 | 0 | 1 | 1 |
| Alexander, p | 0 | 0 | 0 | 0 | 0 | 0 |
| Lamp, p | 0 | 0 | 0 | 0 | 0 | 1 |
| Totals | 34 | 3 | 8 | 2 | 27 | 6 |

| Kansas City | | | 1 0 1 | 0 1 2 | 0 0 0—5 |
|---|---|---|---|---|---|
| Toronto | | | 1 0 1 | 0 0 1 | 0 0 0—3 |

| Kansas City | IP. | H. | R. | ER. | BB. | SO. |
|---|---|---|---|---|---|---|
| Gubicza (Winner) ...... | 5⅓ | 4 | 3 | 3 | 3 | 2 |
| Black | 3⅓ | 4 | 0 | 0 | 2 | 3 |
| Quisenberry (Save) .... | ⅓ | 0 | 0 | 0 | 0 | 1 |

| Toronto | IP. | H. | R. | ER. | BB. | SO. |
|---|---|---|---|---|---|---|
| Alexander (Loser) ...... | 5⅓ | 7 | 5 | 5 | 3 | 6 |
| Lamp | 3⅔ | 1 | 0 | 0 | 1 | 5 |

Game-winning RBI—Brett.
Errors—Fernandez, Barfield, Brett. Double plays—Kansas City 2. Left on bases—Kansas City 8, Toronto 9. Two-base hits—Garcia, McRae, Fernandez, Biancalana, Smith. Home run—Brett. Sacrifice hit—White. Wild pitches—Alexander, Gubicza, Black. Umpires—Cousins, Phillips, Ford, Evans, Hendry and Voltaggio. Time—3:12. Attendance—37,557.

### GAME OF WEDNESDAY, OCTOBER 16, AT TORONTO (N)

| Kansas City | AB. | R. | H. | RBI. | PO. | A. |
|---|---|---|---|---|---|---|
| Smith, lf | 5 | 0 | 2 | 0 | 2 | 0 |
| L. Jones, lf | 0 | 0 | 0 | 0 | 0 | 0 |
| Wilson, cf | 5 | 0 | 0 | 0 | 2 | 0 |
| Brett, 3b | 3 | 0 | 0 | 0 | 1 | 0 |
| McRae, dh | 3 | 1 | 0 | 0 | 0 | 0 |
| Sheridan, rf | 4 | 3 | 2 | 1 | 1 | 0 |
| Balboni, 1b | 3 | 1 | 0 | 0 | 10 | 1 |
| Sundberg, c | 4 | 1 | 2 | 4 | 7 | 0 |
| White, 2b | 4 | 0 | 1 | 1 | 2 | 5 |
| Biancalana, ss | 4 | 0 | 1 | 0 | 0 | 1 |
| Saberhagen, p | 0 | 0 | 0 | 0 | 2 | 0 |
| Leibrandt, p | 0 | 0 | 0 | 0 | 0 | 2 |
| Quisenberry, p | 0 | 0 | 0 | 0 | 0 | 1 |
| Totals | 35 | 6 | 8 | 6 | 27 | 10 |

| Toronto | AB. | R. | H. | RBI. | PO. | A. |
|---|---|---|---|---|---|---|
| Garcia, 2b | 5 | 1 | 1 | 1 | 1 | 2 |
| Moseby, cf | 5 | 0 | 0 | 0 | 4 | 0 |
| Mulliniks, 3b | 1 | 0 | 1 | 0 | 0 | 2 |
| G. Iorg, ph-3b | 2 | 0 | 0 | 0 | 1 | 2 |
| Upshaw, 1b | 4 | 0 | 2 | 1 | 9 | 0 |
| Oliver, dh | 1 | 0 | 0 | 0 | 0 | 0 |
| Johnson, dh | 2 | 0 | 0 | 0 | 0 | 0 |
| Bell, lf | 4 | 0 | 1 | 0 | 3 | 0 |
| Whitt, c | 3 | 0 | 1 | 0 | 7 | 0 |
| Burroughs, ph | 1 | 0 | 0 | 0 | 0 | 0 |
| Barfield, rf | 3 | 1 | 1 | 0 | 1 | 0 |
| Fernandez, ss | 4 | 0 | 1 | 0 | 1 | 3 |
| Stieb, p | 0 | 0 | 0 | 0 | 0 | 1 |
| Acker, p | 0 | 0 | 0 | 0 | 0 | 0 |
| Totals | 35 | 2 | 8 | 2 | 27 | 10 |

| Kansas City | | | 0 1 0 | 1 0 4 | 0 0 0—6 |
|---|---|---|---|---|---|
| Toronto | | | 0 0 0 | 0 1 0 | 0 0 1—2 |

| Kansas City | IP. | H. | R. | ER. | BB. | SO. |
|---|---|---|---|---|---|---|
| Saberhagen | 3 | 3 | 0 | 0 | 1 | 2 |
| Leibrandt (Winner) ... | 5⅓ | 5 | 2 | 2 | 1 | 5 |
| Quisenberry | ⅔ | 0 | 0 | 0 | 0 | 0 |

| Toronto | IP. | H. | R. | ER. | BB. | SO. |
|---|---|---|---|---|---|---|
| Stieb (Loser) | 5⅔ | 6 | 6 | 6 | 2 | 4 |
| Acker | 3⅓ | 2 | 0 | 0 | 0 | 3 |

Game-winning RBI—Sundberg.
Error—Fernandez. Double play—Toronto 1. Left on bases—Kansas City 5, Toronto 9. Two-base hits—Mulliniks, Bell, Upshaw, Fernandez. Three-base hit—Sundberg. Home run—Sheridan. Hit by pitcher—By Saberhagen (Oliver), by Stieb (McRae). Umpires—Phillips, Ford, Evans, Hendry, Voltaggio and Cousins. Time—2:49. Attendance—32,084.

### KANSAS CITY ROYALS' BATTING AND FIELDING AVERAGES

| Player—Position | G. | AB. | R. | H. | TB. | 2B. | 3B. | HR. | RBI. | B.A. | PO. | A. | E. | F.A. |
|---|---|---|---|---|---|---|---|---|---|---|---|---|---|---|
| D. Iorg, ph | 4 | 2 | 0 | 1 | 2 | 1 | 0 | 0 | 0 | .500 | 0 | 0 | 0 | .000 |
| Brett, 3b | 7 | 23 | 6 | 8 | 19 | 2 | 0 | 3 | 5 | .348 | 7 | 8 | 2 | .882 |
| Motley, rf | 2 | 3 | 1 | 1 | 1 | 0 | 0 | 0 | 1 | .333 | 4 | 0 | 0 | 1.000 |
| Wilson, cf | 7 | 29 | 5 | 9 | 12 | 0 | 0 | 1 | 2 | .310 | 12 | 0 | 0 | 1.000 |
| McRae, dh | 6 | 23 | 1 | 6 | 8 | 2 | 0 | 0 | 3 | .261 | 0 | 0 | 0 | .000 |
| Smith, lf | 7 | 28 | 2 | 7 | 9 | 2 | 0 | 0 | 1 | .250 | 8 | 3 | 1 | .917 |
| Biancalana, ss | 7 | 18 | 2 | 4 | 5 | 1 | 0 | 0 | 1 | .222 | 9 | 20 | 0 | 1.000 |
| White, 2b | 7 | 25 | 1 | 5 | 5 | 0 | 0 | 0 | 3 | .200 | 9 | 28 | 0 | 1.000 |
| Sundberg, c | 7 | 24 | 3 | 4 | 10 | 1 | 1 | 1 | 6 | .167 | 41 | 2 | 1 | .977 |
| Sheridan, rf-ph | 7 | 20 | 4 | 3 | 9 | 0 | 0 | 2 | 3 | .150 | 13 | 0 | 0 | 1.000 |
| Balboni, 1b | 7 | 25 | 1 | 3 | 3 | 0 | 0 | 0 | 1 | .120 | 72 | 7 | 2 | .975 |
| Jones, lf | 5 | 0 | 0 | 0 | 0 | 0 | 0 | 0 | 0 | .000 | 2 | 0 | 0 | 1.000 |

| Player—Position | G. | AB. | R. | H. | TB. | 2B. | 3B. | HR. | RBI. | B.A. | PO. | A. | E. | F.A. |
|---|---|---|---|---|---|---|---|---|---|---|---|---|---|---|
| Quisenberry, p | 4 | 0 | 0 | 0 | 0 | 0 | 0 | 0 | 0 | .000 | 1 | 1 | 0 | 1.000 |
| Black, p | 3 | 0 | 0 | 0 | 0 | 0 | 0 | 0 | 0 | .000 | 2 | 3 | 0 | 1.000 |
| Leibrandt, p | 3 | 0 | 0 | 0 | 0 | 0 | 0 | 0 | 0 | .000 | 3 | 7 | 0 | 1.000 |
| Farr, p | 2 | 0 | 0 | 0 | 0 | 0 | 0 | 0 | 0 | .000 | 0 | 1 | 0 | 1.000 |
| Gubicza, p | 2 | 0 | 0 | 0 | 0 | 0 | 0 | 0 | 0 | .000 | 0 | 1 | 0 | 1.000 |
| Jackson, p | 2 | 0 | 0 | 0 | 0 | 0 | 0 | 0 | 0 | .000 | 1 | 1 | 0 | 1.000 |
| Saberhagen, p | 2 | 0 | 0 | 0 | 0 | 0 | 0 | 0 | 0 | .000 | 2 | 1 | 0 | 1.000 |
| Quirk, ph | 1 | 1 | 0 | 0 | 0 | 0 | 0 | 0 | 0 | .000 | 0 | 0 | 0 | .000 |
| Concepcion, ss-pr | 4 | 1 | 0 | 0 | 0 | 0 | 0 | 0 | 0 | .000 | 2 | 4 | 0 | 1.000 |
| Orta, dh-ph | 2 | 5 | 0 | 0 | 0 | 0 | 0 | 0 | 0 | .000 | 0 | 0 | 0 | .000 |
| Totals | 7 | 227 | 26 | 51 | 83 | 9 | 1 | 7 | 26 | .225 | 188 | 87 | 6 | .979 |

## TORONTO BLUE JAYS' BATTING AND FIELDING AVERAGES

| Player—Position | G. | AB. | R. | H. | TB. | 2B. | 3B. | HR. | RBI. | B.A. | PO. | A. | E. | F.A. |
|---|---|---|---|---|---|---|---|---|---|---|---|---|---|---|
| Oliver, ph-dh | 5 | 8 | 0 | 3 | 4 | 1 | 0 | 0 | 3 | .375 | 0 | 0 | 0 | .000 |
| Johnson, dh-ph | 7 | 19 | 1 | 7 | 9 | 2 | 0 | 0 | 2 | .368 | 0 | 0 | 0 | .000 |
| Mulliniks, ph-3b | 5 | 11 | 1 | 4 | 8 | 1 | 0 | 1 | 3 | .364 | 1 | 4 | 0 | 1.000 |
| Fernandez, ss | 7 | 24 | 2 | 8 | 10 | 2 | 0 | 0 | 2 | .333 | 11 | 15 | 2 | .929 |
| Fielder, ph | 3 | 3 | 0 | 1 | 2 | 1 | 0 | 0 | 0 | .333 | 0 | 0 | 0 | .000 |
| Bell, lf | 7 | 28 | 4 | 9 | 12 | 3 | 0 | 0 | 1 | .321 | 13 | 0 | 0 | 1.000 |
| Barfield, rf | 7 | 25 | 3 | 7 | 11 | 1 | 0 | 1 | 4 | .280 | 21 | 0 | 1 | .955 |
| Garcia, 2b | 7 | 30 | 4 | 7 | 11 | 4 | 0 | 0 | 1 | .233 | 10 | 12 | 0 | 1.000 |
| Upshaw, 1b | 7 | 26 | 2 | 6 | 8 | 2 | 0 | 0 | 1 | .231 | 53 | 7 | 1 | .984 |
| Moseby, cf | 7 | 31 | 5 | 7 | 8 | 1 | 0 | 0 | 4 | .226 | 16 | 0 | 0 | 1.000 |
| Whitt, c | 7 | 21 | 1 | 4 | 5 | 1 | 0 | 0 | 2 | .190 | 50 | 3 | 0 | 1.000 |
| G. Iorg, 3b-ph | 6 | 15 | 1 | 2 | 2 | 0 | 0 | 0 | 0 | .133 | 5 | 10 | 0 | 1.000 |
| Henke, p | 3 | 0 | 0 | 0 | 0 | 0 | 0 | 0 | 0 | .000 | 1 | 0 | 0 | 1.000 |
| Lamp, p | 3 | 0 | 0 | 0 | 0 | 0 | 0 | 0 | 0 | .000 | 1 | 2 | 0 | 1.000 |
| Stieb, p | 3 | 0 | 0 | 0 | 0 | 0 | 0 | 0 | 0 | .000 | 1 | 3 | 0 | 1.000 |
| Thornton, pr | 2 | 0 | 1 | 0 | 0 | 0 | 0 | 0 | 0 | .000 | 0 | 0 | 0 | .000 |
| Acker, p | 2 | 0 | 0 | 0 | 0 | 0 | 0 | 0 | 0 | .000 | 0 | 1 | 0 | 1.000 |
| Alexander, p | 2 | 0 | 0 | 0 | 0 | 0 | 0 | 0 | 0 | .000 | 1 | 0 | 0 | 1.000 |
| Hearron, c | 2 | 0 | 0 | 0 | 0 | 0 | 0 | 0 | 0 | .000 | 2 | 0 | 0 | 1.000 |
| Key, p | 2 | 0 | 0 | 0 | 0 | 0 | 0 | 0 | 0 | .000 | 0 | 3 | 0 | 1.000 |
| Clancy, p | 1 | 0 | 0 | 0 | 0 | 0 | 0 | 0 | 0 | .000 | 0 | 1 | 0 | 1.000 |
| Lavelle, p | 1 | 0 | 0 | 0 | 0 | 0 | 0 | 0 | 0 | .000 | 0 | 0 | 0 | .000 |
| Lee, pr-2b | 1 | 0 | 0 | 0 | 0 | 0 | 0 | 0 | 0 | .000 | 0 | 0 | 0 | .000 |
| Burroughs, ph | 1 | 1 | 0 | 0 | 0 | 0 | 0 | 0 | 0 | .000 | 0 | 0 | 0 | .000 |
| Totals | 7 | 242 | 25 | 65 | 90 | 19 | 0 | 2 | 23 | .269 | 186 | 61 | 4 | .984 |

## KANSAS CITY ROYALS' PITCHING RECORDS

| Pitcher | G. | GS. | CG. | IP. | H. | R. | ER. | BB. | SO. | HB. | WP. | W. | L. | Pct. | ERA. |
|---|---|---|---|---|---|---|---|---|---|---|---|---|---|---|---|
| Jackson | 2 | 1 | 1 | 10 | 10 | 0 | 0 | 1 | 7 | 0 | 0 | 1 | 0 | 1.000 | 0.00 |
| Farr | 2 | 0 | 0 | 6⅓ | 4 | 1 | 1 | 1 | 3 | 0 | 0 | 1 | 0 | 1.000 | 1.42 |
| Black | 3 | 1 | 0 | 10⅔ | 11 | 3 | 2 | 4 | 8 | 1 | 2 | 0 | 0 | .000 | 1.69 |
| Gubicza | 2 | 1 | 0 | 8⅓ | 4 | 3 | 3 | 4 | 4 | 0 | 1 | 1 | 0 | 1.000 | 3.24 |
| Quisenberry | 4 | 0 | 0 | 4⅔ | 7 | 4 | 2 | 0 | 3 | 0 | 0 | 0 | 1 | .000 | 3.86 |
| Leibrandt | 3 | 2 | 0 | 15⅓ | 17 | 9 | 9 | 4 | 6 | 1 | 0 | 1 | 2 | .333 | 5.28 |
| Saberhagen | 2 | 2 | 0 | 7⅓ | 12 | 5 | 5 | 2 | 6 | 1 | 0 | 0 | 0 | .000 | 6.14 |
| Totals | 7 | 7 | 1 | 62⅔ | 65 | 25 | 22 | 16 | 37 | 3 | 3 | 4 | 3 | .571 | 3.16 |

Shutout—Jackson. Save—Quisenberry.

## TORONTO BLUE JAYS' PITCHING RECORDS

| Pitcher | G. | GS. | CG. | IP. | H. | R. | ER. | BB. | SO. | HB. | WP. | W. | L. | Pct. | ERA. |
|---|---|---|---|---|---|---|---|---|---|---|---|---|---|---|---|
| Lamp | 3 | 0 | 0 | 9⅓ | 2 | 0 | 0 | 1 | 10 | 0 | 0 | 0 | 0 | .000 | 0.00 |
| Acker | 2 | 0 | 0 | 6 | 2 | 0 | 0 | 5 | 0 | 0 | 0 | 0 | 0 | .000 | 0.00 |
| Lavelle | 1 | 0 | 0 | *0 | 0 | 0 | 0 | 1 | 0 | 0 | 0 | 0 | 0 | .000 | 0.00 |
| Stieb | 3 | 3 | 0 | 20⅓ | 11 | 7 | 7 | 10 | 18 | 1 | 0 | 1 | 1 | .500 | 3.10 |
| Henke | 3 | 0 | 0 | 6⅓ | 5 | 3 | 3 | 4 | 4 | 0 | 0 | 2 | 0 | 1.000 | 4.26 |
| Key | 2 | 2 | 0 | 8⅔ | 15 | 5 | 5 | 2 | 5 | 0 | 0 | 0 | 1 | .000 | 5.19 |
| Alexander | 2 | 2 | 0 | 10⅓ | 14 | 10 | 10 | 3 | 9 | 0 | 1 | 0 | 1 | .000 | 8.71 |
| Clancy | 1 | 0 | 0 | 1 | 2 | 1 | 1 | 1 | 0 | 0 | 0 | 0 | 1 | .000 | 9.00 |
| Totals | 7 | 7 | 0 | 62 | 51 | 26 | 26 | 22 | 51 | 1 | 1 | 3 | 4 | .429 | 3.77 |

*Pitched to one batter in eighth inning of Game 2.
No shutouts or saves.

## COMPOSITE SCORE BY INNINGS

| | | | | | | | | | | | | |
|---|---|---|---|---|---|---|---|---|---|---|---|---|
| Kansas City | 3 | 2 | 3 | 3 | 2 | 9 | 0 | 1 | 2 | 1 — 26 |
| Toronto | 1 | 2 | 4 | 2 | 6 | 3 | 0 | 1 | 4 | 2 — 25 |

Game-winning RBIs—Oliver 2, Brett 2, Whitt, Balboni, Sundberg.
Sacrifice hits—Biancalana, McRae, Wilson, White.
Sacrifice flies—Fernandez, Bell, White, Motley.
Stolen bases—Barfield, Moseby, Wilson, Smith.
Caught stealing—Brett, Concepcion, Wilson, Bell, Barfield, Smith.
Double plays—White, Biancalana and Balboni 2; Garcia and Upshaw 2; Black and Balboni; Whitt and Fernandez; Farr, Concepcion and Balboni; Sundberg and Concepcion; Biancalana (unassisted); Fernandez, Garcia and Upshaw; Gubicza, Biancalana and Balboni.
Left on bases—Kansas City 5, 7, 5, 9, 5, 8, 5—44; Toronto 9, 5, 6, 4, 8, 9, 9—50.
Official scorers—Del Black, Joe Sawchuk.

Cardinal slugger Jack Clark put St. Louis in the World Series with a dramatic, three-run homer in the ninth inning of Game 6 of the National League Championship Series.

# Clark's Clout Put Cards on Top

**By LARRY WIGGE**

Bobby Thomson's dramatic, ninth-inning home run won the 1951 National League pennant for the New York Giants and subsequently was dubbed the shot heard around the world. Bill Mazeroski dispatched the powerful New York Yankees and won the 1960 world championship for the Pittsburgh Pirates with another dramatic ninth-inning homer. Those two blasts rank near the top of all-time memorable occurrences in baseball history.

There are other homers that will remain forever implanted in the minds of baseball fans everywhere.

For pure suddenness, impact and staying power you might also include Boston catcher Carlton Fisk's game-winning blast in Game 6 of the 1975 World Series against Cincinnati. Or Yankee first baseman Chris Chambliss' American League pennant-winning homer in the 1976 Championship Series against Kansas City. There have been other dramatic homers, but none more vivid than the 1985 blows struck by Cardinals Ozzie Smith and Jack Clark.

Smith won Game 5 of the 1985 N.L. Championship Series with an unexpected one-out, ninth-inning homer off Tom Niedenfuer, giving St. Louis a 3-2 decision over Los Angeles and a sweep of the three games played in St. Louis after the Dodgers had won the first two games of the series in Los Angeles.

Clark shocked the Dodgers in Game 6 when he crushed a 450-foot homer into the left-field bleachers with two on and two out in the ninth inning and the Cardinals trailing, 5-4. The Redbirds' 7-5 triumph bought them a ticket to the World Series.

What made these two dramatic home runs even more special is that the Cardinals were not a power-hitting team. They won a major league-leading 101 games in 1985 with speed (a club-record 314 stolen bases), pitching (two 20-game winners in John Tudor and Joaquin Andujar) and timely hitting (a league-leading .264 average). Home runs? The Cardinals hit 87, the second lowest total in the major leagues.

"I guess you'd have to say I'm an unlikely hero," Smith said after his blast. Unlikely is an understatement. Entering the Championship Series, Smith was a .243 lifetime switch-hitter who had never hit a homer from the left side in more than 4,000 career at-bats.

"I don't fantasize much," Smith continued. "When you're young, sure, you dream of hitting the home run in the bottom of the ninth to help your team win. But I have to deal with reality. I'm 5-9, 155 pounds, not 6-3. I can't go into a bar and clean out the joint, just like I can't tell you that I'm going to go up to the plate and try to hit home runs. I was just trying to hit a line drive. I guess I made a mistake."

Some mistake!

"These are the ones that break another team's back," Clark said after Game 5. "They crush you much more than getting blown out of the stadium."

Clark's Game 6 homer didn't carry the element of surprise. The former Giant is a bona fide power hitter. But his blow was even more devastating. After the game, observers were second-guessing Dodgers Manager Tommy Lasorda for not walking Clark when he had a base open and Andy Van Slyke coming up next.

"I know it's an old rule of baseball that you never let a guy who can beat you with one swing of the bat do it," Clark said. "But I was really glad to see them not walk me."

Clark's hunger to hit in a clutch situation showed his character after having played for second-division clubs during his nine-year stay in San Francisco.

"The only way that shot would have stayed in the ballpark is if it hit the Goodyear blimp," said a disgusted Niedenfuer, a shocked loser for the second straight game.

When the series began, it looked like a Hollywood writer had produced a tidy little script for the Dodgers. Ace lefthander Fernando Valenzuela and Niedenfuer combined to limit the Cardinals to eight hits in a 4-1 Dodger triumph in Game 1.

The Dodgers opened the scoring in the fourth inning when Bill Madlock reached first base on an error by Cardinals third baseman Terry Pendleton, stole second and scored on a single by Pedro Guerrero. The Dodgers added to their lead with three more runs in the sixth on a double by Madlock, a two-out RBI single by Mike Scioscia, a run-scoring bunt single by Candy Maldonado and a run-producing double by Steve Sax.

The Cardinals' only run came on a seventh-inning RBI pinch-single by Tito Landrum.

The Dodgers routed Andujar for eight hits and six runs in 4⅓ innings and went

**Winning pitcher Orel Hershiser congratulates Greg Brock after the first baseman's two-run homer in the fourth inning of Game 2 helped the Dodgers to an 8-2 victory.**

on to an 8-2 triumph and a 2-0 series lead behind the eight-hit pitching of Orel Hershiser.

Dodgers catcher Scioscia served notice to the Cardinals that he wasn't going to be an easy mark for their base thiefs, throwing out both Vince Coleman and Willie McGee attempting to steal in the first inning. With one out in the third, however, the Cardinals opened the scoring when McGee singled and Tom Herr followed with a walk. McGee scored all the way from second on Hershiser's wild pitch.

The Dodgers came back to take the lead in their half of the third when Sax singled with one out and advanced to third on Andujar's errant pickoff attempt. Hershiser helped his own cause with a single to left, scoring Sax to tie the score. With two out, Ken Landreaux's double to left-center scored Hershiser with the go-ahead run. Madlock then singled to left to chase Landreaux home and give the Dodgers a 3-1 lead.

Scioscia led off the fourth with a bunt single and scored on Greg Brock's long home run into the right-field stands.

The Dodgers stretched their lead to 6-1 in the fifth when Landreaux doubled for the second time and scored on a single by Mike Marshall. Madlock collected his sec-

ond RBI single in the sixth and Guerrero accounted for the final Los Angeles run with a run-producing single.

Coleman's infield single accounted for the Cardinals' final run in the ninth.

Cardinals Manager Whitey Herzog told his players that Kansas City Star George Brett had the best advice for any team that starts a series down 0-2: "If we don't win this game, the hole is dug and you might as well put the dirt in."

The Cardinals took that advice to heart in Game 3, recording a 4-2 victory to cut the Dodgers' lead to 2-1.

Coleman singled to left and stole second to start the first inning. After McGee drew a walk, the Cardinals' speedsters went to work on Dodgers starter Bob Welch. Welch made a wild pickoff attempt to second base, Coleman scoring easily and McGee going to third. Herr walked and stole second. Then, after Clark struck out, Welch walked Van Slyke to load the bases before Pendleton's grounder plated McGee, giving the Cardinals a 2-0 lead.

The pesky Coleman walked with one out in the second. This time, he went to third on an errant pickoff attempt by Scioscia. After McGee singled to score Coleman, he was caught stealing. But Herr followed with a home run, increasing the Cardinals' lead to 4-0.

Danny Cox limited the Dodgers to only four hits in six-plus innings, yielding two runs. The first scored on back-to-back doubles by Guerrero and Marshall in the fourth and the second run crossed the plate in the seventh when Landreaux stroked an RBI single.

The Cardinals were aided by Pendleton's two dazzling defensive plays in the late innings. With two out and a runner on third in the eighth, Pendleton ranged far down the left-field line and made an over-the-shoulder catch of Brock's foul ball. Then, with a runner on second and nobody out in the ninth, the slick-fielding third baseman dived to make a backhanded stab of pinch-hitter Maldonado's smash near the bag and threw to first for the out.

Just when the Cardinals appeared to have their running game in gear, Coleman was lost in a freak accident prior to Game 4. The rookie sensation was disabled when an automatic tarp rolled over his left leg. But as so often happens when a team loses a key player, somebody comes off the bench and provides an Emmy-winning performance.

That role belonged to Tito Landrum, who went 4 for 5 with three RBIs in the Cardinals' 12-2 Game 4 rout of the Dodgers.

Landrum drove in the first run of the Cardinals' Championship Series-record nine-run second inning. That came after Clark and Cesar Cedeno led off the inning with singles. Pendleton plated the game's second run with a groundout. After Tom Nieto walked, John Tudor laid down a bunt, but all hands were safe when St. Louis native Jerry Reuss, the Dodgers starting pitcher, muffed the squeeze play as Landrum scored for a 3-0 cushion.

Smith, Herr and Clark followed with run-scoring singles to increase the margin to 6-0. After Cedeno walked to load the bases, Landrum picked up his second RBI of the inning with another single and Pendleton climaxed the big inning with a two-run single.

After Cedeno doubled to lead off the fourth, Landrum singled to score pinch-runner Van Slyke. The Cardinals rolled to an 11-0 lead in the fifth when Willie McGee opened the inning with a double and eventually scored on a sacrifice fly by Herr.

The Dodgers, who were held to only one hit over the first six innings by Tudor, finally broke the shutout when Bill Madlock homered to start the seventh. Pinch-hitter Len Matuszek opened the eighth with a single and later scored on a single

**Dodgers Manager Tommy Lasorda suffers through St. Louis' record-breaking nine-run, second inning in Game 4.**

by Guerrero, making the score 11-2.

The Dodgers sent Valenzuela to the mound in Game 5, while the Cardinals countered with Bob Forsch. But, in the end, it was the Smith-Niedenfuer confrontation that proved decisive and gave the Redbirds a 3-2 series edge as the teams headed back to Los Angeles.

Again the Cardinals struck first. McGee and Smith drew leadoff walks in the first. Both came home when Herr doubled to left. After that, however, Valenzuela found his good stuff and shut the Cardinals down.

The Dodgers scored the tying runs in the fourth when Landreaux led off with a single and scored ahead of Madlock's long home run to left.

The score remained knotted until Niedenfuer relieved Valenzuela in the ninth. The big reliever retired McGee on a foul pop to third base to start the inning and then got ahead in the count (1 and 2) to Smith. But the slick-fielding shortstop shocked the capacity Busch Stadium crowd by lashing a screamer down the right-field line for only the 14th homer of his major league career.

Smith leaped for joy when he rounded first and saw the ball hit off the cement pillar above the right-field wall and then literally danced around the bases.

"This series is like a tennis match," said

**Ozzie Smith celebrates his game-winning homer off Tom Niedenfuer in the ninth inning of Game 5.**

Dodgers pitcher Hershiser. "We won our service in the first two games and they won service in the three games in St. Louis. Now, we've got two serves left to win the series and they have a chance at break point."

Hershiser was asked to stop the Cardinals' momentum two days later against Andujar at Dodger Stadium. The Dodgers held the edge most of the way, until Clark found another one of those Niedenfuer fastballs to his liking in the ninth.

Madlock singled home Mariano Duncan, who had doubled to lead off the first, giving the Dodgers a 1-0 lead. They made it 2-0 in the second on Duncan's two-out RBI single.

The Cardinals got on the board in the third when Andujar hit a leadoff double and scored on Herr's two-out single. But the Dodgers rallied for two more runs in the fifth when Duncan, who had reached on an error by Andujar and stolen second, scored on a sacrifice fly by Guerrero and Madlock followed with his third home run of the series.

Hershiser scattered six hits and walked one, but he managed to hold the Dodgers' 4-1 lead until the seventh. Darrell Porter and Landrum opened that inning with

consecutive singles. They moved into scoring position when pinch-hitter Steve Braun grounded out. McGee followed with a single to center, scoring both Porter and Landrum and sending Hershiser to the showers.

It was Ozzie Smith against Niedenfuer once again. The little guy flexed his muscles one more time, rifling a triple into the right-field corner to score McGee and tie the score, 4-4. After walking Herr intentionally, Niedenfuer got out of the jam without further damage by striking out Clark and Van Slyke.

The Dodgers appeared to have weathered the storm when Marshall sent a Todd Worrell delivery over the right-center field fence in the bottom half of the eighth to put Los Angeles on top, 5-4.

But Niedenfuer couldn't stand prosperity, surrendering a one-out single to McGee. After McGee stole second and Smith drew a walk, Herr tapped easily to first baseman Brock, with the runners moving to second and third. That set the stage for the Clark-Niedenfuer matchup. Walk him or don't walk him?

Lasorda decided to face Clark and one pitch later the Cardinals led, 7-5, and were just three outs away from their second World Series visit in four years. St. Louis reliever Ken Dayley struck out Duncan and pinch-hitter Enos Cabell before finishing off the Dodgers by getting Guerrero on a fly ball to center.

Taped to the top of Niedenfuer's locker was a cartoon where the manager has visited the mound and is pleading with a bedraggled-looking reliever.

"I know this is your 150th relief appearance," the manager says, "but we really need this one."

No one will ever know whether that relief pitcher got the job done, but for Niedenfuer there was no comic relief—only the agony of defeat.

**GAME OF WEDNESDAY, OCTOBER 9,
AT LOS ANGELES (N)**

| St. Louis | AB. | R. | H. | RBI. | PO. | A. |
|---|---|---|---|---|---|---|
| Coleman, lf | 4 | 0 | 0 | 0 | 4 | 0 |
| McGee, cf | 4 | 0 | 0 | 0 | 2 | 0 |
| Herr, 2b | 3 | 0 | 1 | 0 | 1 | 2 |
| Clark, 1b | 3 | 0 | 1 | 0 | 10 | 0 |
| Cedeno, rf | 4 | 0 | 0 | 0 | 2 | 0 |
| Worrell, p | 0 | 0 | 0 | 0 | 0 | 0 |
| Pendleton, 3b | 4 | 1 | 2 | 0 | 0 | 4 |
| Porter, c | 4 | 0 | 1 | 0 | 3 | 1 |
| Smith, ss | 4 | 0 | 2 | 0 | 1 | 1 |
| Tudor, p | 2 | 0 | 0 | 0 | 0 | 1 |
| Dayley, p | 0 | 0 | 0 | 0 | 0 | 0 |
| Landrum, ph | 1 | 0 | 1 | 1 | 0 | 0 |
| Campbell, p | 0 | 0 | 0 | 0 | 0 | 0 |
| Van Slyke, rf | 0 | 0 | 0 | 0 | 1 | 0 |
| Totals | 33 | 1 | 8 | 1 | 24 | 9 |

| Los Angeles | AB. | R. | H. | RBI. | PO. | A. |
|---|---|---|---|---|---|---|
| Duncan, ss | 4 | 0 | 0 | 0 | 2 | 3 |
| Cabell, 1b | 4 | 0 | 0 | 0 | 9 | 1 |
| Madlock, 3b | 4 | 2 | 1 | 0 | 0 | 3 |
| Guerrero, lf | 3 | 1 | 2 | 1 | 1 | 0 |
| Marshall, rf | 4 | 0 | 0 | 0 | 0 | 0 |
| Scioscia, c | 4 | 1 | 1 | 1 | 8 | 0 |
| Maldonado, cf | 3 | 0 | 1 | 1 | 2 | 0 |
| Landreaux, ph-cf | 1 | 0 | 0 | 0 | 0 | 0 |
| Sax, 2b | 3 | 0 | 2 | 1 | 5 | 2 |
| Valenzuela, p | 2 | 0 | 1 | 0 | 0 | 1 |
| Niedenfuer, p | 0 | 0 | 0 | 0 | 0 | 0 |
| Totals | 32 | 4 | 8 | 4 | 27 | 10 |

St. Louis ............................. 0 0 0  0 0 0  1 0 0—1
Los Angeles ....................... 0 0 0  1 0 3  0 0 x—4

| St. Louis | IP. | H. | R. | ER. | BB. | SO. |
|---|---|---|---|---|---|---|
| Tudor (Loser) | 5⅔ | 7 | 4 | 3 | 1 | 3 |
| Dayley | ⅓ | 0 | 0 | 0 | 0 | 0 |
| Campbell | 1* | 1 | 0 | 0 | 0 | 0 |
| Worrell | 1 | 0 | 0 | 0 | 0 | 0 |

| Los Angeles | IP. | H. | R. | ER. | BB. | SO. |
|---|---|---|---|---|---|---|
| Valenzuela (Winner) | 6⅓ | 7 | 1 | 1 | 2 | 6 |
| Niedenfuer (Save) | 2⅔ | 1 | 0 | 0 | 0 | 2 |

*Pitched to one batter in eighth.

Game-winning RBI—Guerrero.
Error—Pendleton. Double play—Los Angeles 1. Left on bases—St. Louis 7, Los Angeles 6. Two-base hits—Herr, Madlock, Sax. Stolen bases—Smith, Madlock, Guerrero 2. Sacrifice hit—Valenzuela. Wild pitch—Worrell. Umpires—Stello, Froemming, McSherry, Tata, Runge and Crawford. Time—2:42. Attendance—55,270.

### GAME OF THURSDAY, OCTOBER 10, AT LOS ANGELES (N)

| St. Louis | AB. | R. | H. | RBI. | PO. | A. |
|---|---|---|---|---|---|---|
| Coleman, lf | 5 | 0 | 2 | 1 | 1 | 0 |
| McGee, cf | 5 | 1 | 1 | 0 | 5 | 0 |
| Herr, 2b | 3 | 0 | 1 | 0 | 1 | 1 |
| Clark, 1b | 3 | 0 | 1 | 0 | 6 | 0 |
| Van Slyke, rf | 3 | 0 | 0 | 0 | 1 | 0 |
| Pendleton, 3b | 4 | 1 | 1 | 0 | 1 | 2 |
| Porter, c | 2 | 0 | 0 | 0 | 8 | 0 |
| Smith, ss | 4 | 0 | 2 | 0 | 0 | 1 |
| Andujar, p | 2 | 0 | 0 | 0 | 0 | 0 |
| Horton, p | 0 | 0 | 0 | 0 | 1 | 2 |
| Campbell, p | 0 | 0 | 0 | 0 | 0 | 0 |
| Braun, ph | 1 | 0 | 0 | 0 | 0 | 0 |
| Dayley, p | 0 | 0 | 0 | 0 | 0 | 0 |
| Lahti, p | 0 | 0 | 0 | 0 | 0 | 0 |
| Jorgensen, ph | 1 | 0 | 0 | 0 | 0 | 0 |
| Totals | 33 | 2 | 8 | 1 | 24 | 6 |

| Los Angeles | AB. | R. | H. | RBI. | PO. | A. |
|---|---|---|---|---|---|---|
| Duncan, ss | 4 | 0 | 1 | 0 | 2 | 2 |
| Anderson, pr-ss | 1 | 1 | 0 | 0 | 1 | 0 |
| Landreaux, cf | 4 | 3 | 3 | 1 | 0 | 0 |
| Madlock, 3b | 5 | 0 | 3 | 2 | 0 | 3 |
| Bailor, pr-3b | 0 | 0 | 0 | 0 | 0 | 0 |
| Guerrero, lf | 3 | 0 | 1 | 1 | 1 | 0 |
| Maldonado, lf | 0 | 0 | 0 | 0 | 0 | 0 |
| Marshall, rf | 4 | 0 | 1 | 1 | 3 | 0 |
| Scioscia, c | 3 | 1 | 1 | 0 | 4 | 2 |
| Brock, 1b | 4 | 1 | 1 | 2 | 15 | 1 |
| Sax, 2b | 4 | 1 | 1 | 0 | 1 | 7 |
| Hershiser, p | 4 | 1 | 1 | 1 | 0 | 1 |
| Totals | 36 | 8 | 13 | 8 | 27 | 16 |

St. Louis ............................. 0 0 1  0 0 0  0 0 1—2
Los Angeles ....................... 0 0 3  2 1 2  0 0 x—8

| St. Louis | IP. | H. | R. | ER. | BB. | SO. |
|---|---|---|---|---|---|---|
| Andujar (Loser) | 4⅓ | 8 | 6 | 6 | 2 | 6 |
| Horton | 1⅓ | 1 | 2 | 2 | 2 | 0 |
| Campbell | ⅓ | 2 | 0 | 0 | 0 | 1 |
| Dayley | 1 | 0 | 0 | 0 | 0 | 0 |
| Lahti | 1 | 2 | 0 | 0 | 0 | 1 |

| Los Angeles | IP. | H. | R. | ER. | BB. | SO. |
|---|---|---|---|---|---|---|
| Hershiser (Winner) | 9 | 8 | 2 | 2 | 5 | 4 |

Game-winning RBI—Landreaux.
Errors—Duncan, Andujar. Double plays—St. Louis 1, Los Angeles 1. Left on bases—St. Louis 9, Los Angeles 8. Two-base hits—Herr, Landreaux 2, Duncan. Home run—Brock. Wild pitch—Hershiser. Passed ball—Porter. Umpires—Froemming, McSherry, Tata, Runge, Crawford and Stello. Time—3:04. Attendance—55,222.

### GAME OF SATURDAY, OCTOBER 12, AT ST. LOUIS

| Los Angeles | AB. | R. | H. | RBI. | PO. | A. |
|---|---|---|---|---|---|---|
| Anderson, ss | 3 | 0 | 0 | 0 | 1 | 2 |
| Landreaux, cf | 5 | 0 | 2 | 1 | 3 | 0 |
| Madlock, 3b | 4 | 0 | 0 | 0 | 1 | 0 |
| Guerrero, lf | 3 | 1 | 1 | 0 | 2 | 0 |
| Marshall, rf | 4 | 0 | 2 | 1 | 1 | 0 |
| Scioscia, c | 3 | 0 | 0 | 0 | 6 | 1 |
| Brock, 1b | 4 | 0 | 0 | 0 | 7 | 0 |
| Sax, 2b | 3 | 0 | 2 | 0 | 2 | 6 |
| Welch, p | 1 | 0 | 0 | 0 | 0 | 1 |
| Honeycutt, p | 0 | 0 | 0 | 0 | 0 | 1 |
| Johnstone, ph | 1 | 0 | 0 | 0 | 0 | 0 |
| Diaz, p | 0 | 0 | 0 | 0 | 1 | 0 |
| Matuszek, ph | 0 | 0 | 0 | 0 | 0 | 0 |
| Cabell, ph | 1 | 1 | 0 | 0 | 0 | 0 |
| Howell, p | 0 | 0 | 0 | 0 | 0 | 1 |
| Whitfield, ph | 0 | 0 | 0 | 0 | 0 | 0 |
| Maldonado, ph | 1 | 0 | 0 | 0 | 0 | 0 |
| Totals | 33 | 2 | 7 | 2 | 24 | 11 |

| St. Louis | AB. | R. | H. | RBI. | PO. | A. |
|---|---|---|---|---|---|---|
| Coleman, lf | 5 | 2 | 2 | 0 | 3 | 0 |
| McGee, cf | 4 | 1 | 2 | 1 | 2 | 0 |
| Herr, 2b | 4 | 1 | 2 | 1 | 3 | 4 |
| Clark, 1b | 2 | 0 | 0 | 0 | 10 | 0 |
| Van Slyke, rf | 1 | 0 | 0 | 0 | 1 | 0 |
| Cedeno, ph-rf | 2 | 0 | 0 | 0 | 0 | 0 |
| Worrell, p | 0 | 0 | 0 | 0 | 0 | 0 |
| Dayley, p | 0 | 0 | 0 | 0 | 0 | 0 |
| Pendleton, 3b | 4 | 0 | 0 | 1 | 2 | 3 |
| Porter, c | 3 | 0 | 1 | 0 | 4 | 1 |
| Smith, ss | 3 | 0 | 1 | 0 | 2 | 1 |
| Cox, p | 2 | 0 | 0 | 0 | 0 | 0 |
| Horton, p | 0 | 0 | 0 | 0 | 0 | 0 |
| Landrum, rf | 1 | 0 | 0 | 0 | 0 | 0 |
| Totals | 31 | 4 | 8 | 3 | 27 | 9 |

Los Angeles ....................... 0 0 0  1 0 0  1 0 0—2
St. Louis ............................. 2 2 0  0 0 0  0 0 x—4

| Los Angeles | IP. | H. | R. | ER. | BB. | SO. |
|---|---|---|---|---|---|---|
| Welch (Loser) | 2⅔ | 5 | 4 | 2 | 6 | 2 |
| Honeycutt | 1⅓ | 1 | 0 | 0 | 1 | 1 |
| Diaz | 2 | 2 | 0 | 0 | 1 | 1 |
| Howell | 2 | 0 | 0 | 0 | 0 | 2 |

| St. Louis | IP. | H. | R. | ER. | BB. | SO. |
|---|---|---|---|---|---|---|
| Cox (Winner) | 6* | 4 | 2 | 2 | 5 | 4 |
| Horton | ⅔ | 1 | 0 | 0 | 0 | 0 |
| Worrell | 1⅓† | 2 | 0 | 0 | 0 | 0 |
| Dayley (Save) | 1 | 0 | 0 | 0 | 0 | 0 |

*Pitched to one batter in seventh.
†Pitched to one batter in ninth.

Game-winning RBI—None.
Errors—Welch, Scioscia. Left on bases—Los Angeles 9, St. Louis 11. Two-base hits—Landreaux, Porter, Guerrero, Marshall 2, Smith, Herr, Sax. Home run—Herr. Stolen bases—Coleman, Herr, McGee. Wild pitch—Worrell. Umpires—McSherry, Tata, Runge, Crawford, Stello, Froemming. Time—3:21. Attendance—53,708.

## GAME OF SUNDAY, OCTOBER 13, AT ST. LOUIS (N)

| Los Angeles | AB. | R. | H. | RBI. | PO. | A. |
|---|---|---|---|---|---|---|
| Duncan, ss | 2 | 0 | 0 | 0 | 0 | 2 |
| Anderson, ss | 1 | 0 | 0 | 0 | 1 | 2 |
| Cabell, 1b | 4 | 0 | 0 | 0 | 8 | 1 |
| Guerrero, lf | 4 | 0 | 1 | 1 | 2 | 0 |
| Diaz, p | 0 | 0 | 0 | 0 | 0 | 0 |
| Madlock, 3b | 3 | 1 | 1 | 1 | 2 | 0 |
| Bailor, 3b | 1 | 0 | 0 | 0 | 0 | 1 |
| Marshall, rf | 4 | 0 | 1 | 0 | 3 | 0 |
| Scioscia, c | 1 | 0 | 0 | 0 | 1 | 0 |
| Yeager, ph-c | 2 | 0 | 0 | 0 | 4 | 0 |
| Maldonado, cf | 3 | 0 | 0 | 0 | 2 | 0 |
| Brock, ph | 1 | 0 | 0 | 0 | 0 | 0 |
| Sax, 2b | 3 | 0 | 1 | 0 | 0 | 1 |
| Reuss, p | 0 | 0 | 0 | 0 | 0 | 0 |
| Honeycutt, p | 0 | 0 | 0 | 0 | 0 | 0 |
| Castillo, p | 2 | 0 | 0 | 0 | 1 | 3 |
| Matuszek, ph-lf | 1 | 1 | 1 | 0 | 0 | 0 |
| Totals | 32 | 2 | 5 | 2 | 24 | 10 |

| St. Louis | AB. | R. | H. | RBI. | PO. | A. |
|---|---|---|---|---|---|---|
| McGee, cf | 5 | 1 | 1 | 0 | 2 | 0 |
| Smith, ss | 5 | 1 | 2 | 1 | 2 | 7 |
| Herr, 2b | 4 | 1 | 1 | 2 | 2 | 2 |
| Clark, 1b | 5 | 3 | 3 | 1 | 11 | 0 |
| Cedeno, rf | 2 | 2 | 2 | 0 | 1 | 0 |
| Van Slyke, pr-rf | 2 | 1 | 1 | 1 | 1 | 0 |
| Landrum, lf | 5 | 1 | 4 | 3 | 1 | 0 |
| Pendleton, 3b | 4 | 0 | 1 | 3 | 1 | 4 |
| Nieto, c | 3 | 1 | 0 | 0 | 7 | 0 |
| Tudor, p | 2 | 1 | 0 | 0 | 0 | 0 |
| Jorgensen, ph | 1 | 0 | 0 | 0 | 0 | 0 |
| Horton, p | 0 | 0 | 0 | 0 | 0 | 0 |
| Campbell, p | 0 | 0 | 0 | 0 | 0 | 0 |
| Totals | 38 | 12 | 15 | 11 | 27 | 13 |

Los Angeles .......................... 0 0 0  0 0 0  1 1 0—2
St. Louis ................................ 0 9 0  1 1 0  0 1 x—12

| Los Angeles | IP. | H. | R. | ER. | BB. | SO. |
|---|---|---|---|---|---|---|
| Reuss (Loser) | 1⅔ | 5 | 7 | 2 | 1 | 0 |
| Honeycutt | 0* | 3 | 2 | 2 | 1 | 0 |
| Castillo | 5⅓ | 4 | 2 | 2 | 2 | 4 |
| Diaz | 1 | 3 | 1 | 1 | 0 | 1 |

| St. Louis | IP. | H. | R. | ER. | BB. | SO. |
|---|---|---|---|---|---|---|
| Tudor (Winner) | 7 | 3 | 1 | 1 | 2 | 5 |
| Horton | 1 | 2 | 1 | 1 | 0 | 1 |
| Campbell | 1 | 0 | 0 | 0 | 0 | 1 |

*Pitched to four batters in second.

Game-winning RBI—Landrum.

Errors—Reuss, Maldonado. Double play—Los Angeles 1. Left on bases—Los Angeles 5, St. Louis 7. Two-base hits—Cedeno, McGee, Sax. Home run—Madlock. Sacrifice fly—Herr. Umpires—Tata, Runge, Crawford, Stello, Froemming and McSherry. Time—2:47. Attendance—53,708.

## GAME OF MONDAY, OCTOBER 14, AT ST. LOUIS

| Los Angeles | AB. | R. | H. | RBI. | PO. | A. |
|---|---|---|---|---|---|---|
| Duncan, ss | 3 | 0 | 0 | 0 | 1 | 3 |
| Landreaux, cf | 4 | 1 | 2 | 0 | 2 | 0 |
| Guerrero, lf | 4 | 0 | 0 | 0 | 4 | 0 |
| Madlock, 3b | 4 | 1 | 1 | 2 | 3 | 1 |
| Marshall, rf | 3 | 0 | 0 | 0 | 0 | 0 |
| xScioscia, c | 2 | 0 | 1 | 0 | 7 | 0 |
| Brock, 1b | 1 | 0 | 0 | 0 | 2 | 0 |
| Cabell, ph-1b | 3 | 0 | 1 | 0 | 3 | 1 |
| Niedenfuer, p | 0 | 0 | 0 | 0 | 0 | 0 |
| Sax, 2b | 3 | 0 | 0 | 0 | 2 | 0 |
| Valenzuela, p | 3 | 0 | 0 | 0 | 1 | 2 |
| Matuszek, 1b | 0 | 0 | 0 | 0 | 0 | 0 |
| Totals | 30 | 2 | 5 | 2 | 25 | 7 |

| St. Louis | AB. | R. | H. | RBI. | PO. | A. |
|---|---|---|---|---|---|---|
| McGee, cf | 3 | 1 | 0 | 0 | 3 | 0 |
| Smith, ss | 3 | 2 | 1 | 1 | 1 | 3 |
| Herr, 2b | 4 | 0 | 1 | 2 | 2 | 2 |
| Clark, 1b | 3 | 0 | 1 | 0 | 12 | 0 |
| Cedeno, rf | 3 | 0 | 0 | 0 | 3 | 0 |
| Landrum, lf | 3 | 0 | 0 | 0 | 2 | 0 |
| Pendleton, 3b | 4 | 0 | 1 | 0 | 1 | 3 |
| Porter, c | 2 | 0 | 0 | 0 | 3 | 0 |
| Forsch, p | 0 | 0 | 0 | 0 | 0 | 1 |
| Dayley, p | 2 | 0 | 1 | 0 | 0 | 1 |
| Worrell, p | 0 | 0 | 0 | 0 | 0 | 1 |
| Harper, ph | 1 | 0 | 0 | 0 | 0 | 0 |
| Lahti, p | 0 | 0 | 0 | 0 | 0 | 0 |
| Totals | 28 | 3 | 5 | 3 | 27 | 11 |

Los Angeles .......................... 0 0 0  2 0 0  0 0 0—2
St. Louis ................................ 2 0 0  0 0 0  0 0 1—3
One out when winning run scored.

| Los Angeles | IP. | H. | R. | ER. | BB. | SO. |
|---|---|---|---|---|---|---|
| Valenzuela | 8 | 4 | 2 | 2 | 8 | 7 |
| Niedenfuer (Loser) | ⅓ | 1 | 1 | 1 | 0 | 0 |

| St. Louis | IP. | H. | R. | ER. | BB. | SO. |
|---|---|---|---|---|---|---|
| Forsch | 3⅓ | 3 | 2 | 2 | 2 | 0 |
| Dayley | 2⅔* | 2 | 0 | 0 | 1 | 1 |
| Worrell | 2 | 0 | 0 | 0 | 0 | 1 |
| Lahti (Winner) | 1 | 0 | 0 | 0 | 0 | 0 |

*Pitched to two batters in seventh.

Game-winning RBI—Smith.

xAwarded first base on catcher's interference. Errors—Valenzuela, Porter. Double plays—St. Louis 2. Left on bases—Los Angeles 5, St. Louis 10. Two-base hits—Herr, Pendleton. Home runs—Madlock, Smith. Stolen base—Landrum. Sacrifice hits—Forsch, Smith. Wild pitch—Valenzuela. Umpires—Runge, Crawford, Stello, Froemming, McSherry and Tata. Time—2:56. Attendance—53,708.

## GAME OF WEDNESDAY, OCTOBER 16, AT LOS ANGELES

| St. Louis | AB. | R. | H. | RBI. | PO. | A. |
|---|---|---|---|---|---|---|
| McGee, cf | 5 | 2 | 3 | 2 | 4 | 0 |
| Smith, ss | 4 | 1 | 2 | 1 | 0 | 3 |
| Herr, 2b | 3 | 0 | 1 | 1 | 4 | 1 |
| Clark, 1b | 5 | 1 | 2 | 3 | 6 | 0 |
| Van Slyke, rf | 5 | 0 | 0 | 0 | 2 | 0 |
| Pendleton, 3b | 4 | 0 | 0 | 0 | 1 | 2 |
| Porter, c | 4 | 1 | 2 | 0 | 7 | 0 |
| Landrum, lf | 4 | 1 | 1 | 0 | 3 | 0 |
| Andujar, p | 2 | 1 | 1 | 0 | 0 | 0 |
| Braun, ph | 1 | 0 | 0 | 0 | 0 | 0 |
| Worrell, p | 0 | 0 | 0 | 0 | 0 | 0 |
| Cedeno, ph | 1 | 0 | 0 | 0 | 0 | 0 |
| Dayley, p | 0 | 0 | 0 | 0 | 0 | 0 |
| Totals | 38 | 7 | 12 | 7 | 27 | 6 |

| Los Angeles | AB. | R. | H. | RBI. | PO. | A. |
|---|---|---|---|---|---|---|
| Duncan, ss | 5 | 2 | 3 | 1 | 2 | 6 |
| Landreaux, cf | 4 | 0 | 0 | 0 | 2 | 0 |
| Cabell, ph | 1 | 0 | 0 | 0 | 0 | 0 |
| Guerrero, lf | 3 | 0 | 0 | 1 | 1 | 0 |
| Madlock, 3b | 4 | 1 | 2 | 2 | 0 | 2 |
| Anderson, 3b | 0 | 0 | 0 | 0 | 0 | 0 |
| Marshall, rf | 4 | 1 | 1 | 1 | 1 | 0 |
| Scioscia, c | 3 | 0 | 1 | 0 | 5 | 1 |
| Brock, 1b | 2 | 1 | 0 | 0 | 11 | 3 |
| Sax, 2b | 4 | 0 | 0 | 0 | 1 | 5 |
| Hershiser, p | 3 | 0 | 1 | 0 | 2 | 1 |
| Niedenfuer, p | 1 | 0 | 0 | 0 | 2 | 0 |
| Totals | 34 | 5 | 8 | 5 | 27 | 18 |

St. Louis .................................. 0 0 1  0 0 0  3 0 3—7
Los Angeles .......................... 1 1 0  0 2 0  0 1 0—5

| St. Louis | IP. | H. | R. | ER. | BB. | SO. |
|---|---|---|---|---|---|---|
| Andujar | 6 | 6 | 4 | 2 | 2 | 3 |
| Worrell (Winner) | 2 | 2 | 1 | 1 | 2 | 2 |
| Dayley (Save) | 1 | 0 | 0 | 0 | 0 | 2 |

| Los Angeles | IP. | H. | R. | ER. | BB. | SO. |
|---|---|---|---|---|---|---|
| Hershiser | 6⅓ | 9 | 4 | 4 | 1 | 1 |
| Niedenfuer (Loser) | 2⅔ | 3 | 3 | 3 | 2 | 3 |

Game-winning RBI—Clark.

Error—Andujar. Double play—St. Louis 1. Left on bases—St. Louis 7, Los Angeles 7. Two-base hits—Duncan, Andujar. Three-base hits—Smith, Duncan. Home runs—Madlock, Marshall, Clark. Stolen bases—Duncan, McGee. Sacrifice fly—Guerrero. Umpires—Crawford, Stello, Froemming, McSherry, Tata and Runge. Time—3:32. Attendance—55,208.

## ST. LOUIS CARDINALS' BATTING AND FIELDING AVERAGES

| Player—Position | G. | AB. | R. | H. | TB. | 2B. | 3B. | HR. | RBI. | B.A. | PO. | A. | E. | F.A. |
|---|---|---|---|---|---|---|---|---|---|---|---|---|---|---|
| Dayley, p | 5 | 2 | 0 | 1 | 1 | 0 | 0 | 0 | 0 | .500 | 0 | 1 | 0 | 1.000 |
| Smith, ss | 6 | 23 | 4 | 10 | 16 | 1 | 1 | 1 | 3 | .435 | 6 | 16 | 0 | 1.000 |
| Landrum, ph-rf-lf | 5 | 14 | 2 | 6 | 6 | 0 | 0 | 0 | 4 | .429 | 6 | 0 | 0 | 1.000 |
| Clark, 1b | 6 | 21 | 4 | 8 | 11 | 0 | 0 | 1 | 4 | .381 | 55 | 0 | 0 | 1.000 |
| Herr, 2b | 6 | 21 | 2 | 7 | 14 | 4 | 0 | 1 | 6 | .333 | 13 | 12 | 0 | 1.000 |
| Coleman, lf | 3 | 14 | 2 | 4 | 4 | 0 | 0 | 0 | 1 | .286 | 8 | 0 | 0 | 1.000 |
| McGee, cf | 6 | 26 | 6 | 7 | 8 | 1 | 0 | 0 | 3 | .269 | 18 | 0 | 0 | 1.000 |
| Porter, c | 5 | 15 | 1 | 4 | 5 | 1 | 0 | 0 | 0 | .267 | 25 | 2 | 1 | .964 |
| Andujar, p | 2 | 4 | 1 | 1 | 2 | 1 | 0 | 0 | 0 | .250 | 0 | 0 | 2 | .000 |
| Pendleton, 3b | 6 | 24 | 2 | 5 | 6 | 1 | 0 | 0 | 4 | .208 | 6 | 18 | 1 | .960 |
| Cedeno, rf-ph | 5 | 12 | 2 | 2 | 3 | 1 | 0 | 0 | 0 | .167 | 5 | 0 | 0 | 1.000 |
| Van Slyke, rf-pr | 5 | 11 | 1 | 1 | 1 | 0 | 0 | 0 | 1 | .091 | 6 | 0 | 0 | 1.000 |
| Worrell, p | 4 | 0 | 0 | 0 | 0 | 0 | 0 | 0 | 0 | .000 | 0 | 1 | 0 | 1.000 |
| Campbell, p | 3 | 0 | 0 | 0 | 0 | 0 | 0 | 0 | 0 | .000 | 0 | 0 | 0 | .000 |
| Horton, p | 3 | 0 | 0 | 0 | 0 | 0 | 0 | 0 | 0 | .000 | 1 | 2 | 0 | 1.000 |
| Lahti, p | 2 | 0 | 0 | 0 | 0 | 0 | 0 | 0 | 0 | .000 | 0 | 0 | 0 | .000 |
| Forsch, p | 1 | 0 | 0 | 0 | 0 | 0 | 0 | 0 | 0 | .000 | 0 | 1 | 0 | 1.000 |
| Harper, ph | 1 | 1 | 0 | 0 | 0 | 0 | 0 | 0 | 0 | .000 | 0 | 0 | 0 | .000 |
| Braun, ph | 2 | 2 | 0 | 0 | 0 | 0 | 0 | 0 | 0 | .000 | 0 | 0 | 0 | .000 |
| Jorgensen, ph | 2 | 2 | 0 | 0 | 0 | 0 | 0 | 0 | 0 | .000 | 0 | 0 | 0 | .000 |
| Cox, p | 1 | 2 | 0 | 0 | 0 | 0 | 0 | 0 | 0 | .000 | 0 | 0 | 0 | .000 |
| Nieto, c | 1 | 3 | 1 | 0 | 0 | 0 | 0 | 0 | 0 | .000 | 7 | 0 | 0 | 1.000 |
| Tudor, p | 2 | 4 | 1 | 0 | 0 | 0 | 0 | 0 | 0 | .000 | 0 | 1 | 0 | 1.000 |
| Totals | 6 | 201 | 29 | 56 | 77 | 10 | 1 | 3 | 26 | .279 | 156 | 54 | 4 | .981 |

## LOS ANGELES DODGERS' BATTING AND FIELDING AVERAGES

| Player—Position | G. | AB. | R. | H. | TB. | 2B. | 3B. | HR. | RBI. | B.A. | PO. | A. | E. | F.A. |
|---|---|---|---|---|---|---|---|---|---|---|---|---|---|---|
| Matuszek, ph-lf-1b | 3 | 1 | 1 | 1 | 1 | 0 | 0 | 0 | 0 | 1.000 | 0 | 0 | 0 | .000 |
| Landreaux, ph-cf | 5 | 18 | 4 | 7 | 10 | 3 | 0 | 0 | 2 | .389 | 7 | 0 | 0 | 1.000 |
| Madlock, 3b | 6 | 24 | 5 | 8 | 18 | 1 | 0 | 3 | 7 | .333 | 6 | 9 | 0 | 1.000 |
| Sax, 2b | 6 | 20 | 1 | 6 | 9 | 3 | 0 | 0 | 1 | .300 | 11 | 21 | 0 | 1.000 |
| Hershiser, p | 2 | 7 | 1 | 2 | 2 | 0 | 0 | 0 | 1 | .286 | 2 | 2 | 0 | 1.000 |
| Guerrero, lf | 6 | 20 | 2 | 5 | 6 | 1 | 0 | 0 | 4 | .250 | 11 | 0 | 0 | 1.000 |
| Scioscia, c | 6 | 16 | 2 | 4 | 4 | 0 | 0 | 0 | 1 | .250 | 31 | 4 | 1 | .972 |
| Duncan, ss | 5 | 18 | 2 | 4 | 8 | 2 | 1 | 0 | 1 | .222 | 7 | 16 | 1 | .958 |
| Marshall, rf | 6 | 23 | 1 | 5 | 10 | 2 | 0 | 1 | 3 | .217 | 8 | 0 | 0 | 1.000 |
| Valenzuela, p | 2 | 5 | 0 | 1 | 1 | 0 | 0 | 0 | 0 | .200 | 1 | 3 | 1 | .800 |
| Maldonado, cf-lf-ph | 4 | 7 | 0 | 1 | 1 | 0 | 0 | 0 | 0 | .143 | 4 | 0 | 1 | .800 |
| Brock, 1b-ph | 5 | 12 | 2 | 1 | 4 | 0 | 0 | 1 | 2 | .083 | 35 | 4 | 0 | 1.000 |
| Cabell, 1b-ph | 5 | 13 | 1 | 1 | 1 | 0 | 0 | 0 | 0 | .077 | 20 | 3 | 0 | 1.000 |
| Diaz, p | 2 | 0 | 0 | 0 | 0 | 0 | 0 | 0 | 0 | .000 | 1 | 0 | 0 | 1.000 |
| Honeycutt, p | 2 | 0 | 0 | 0 | 0 | 0 | 0 | 0 | 0 | .000 | 0 | 1 | 0 | 1.000 |
| Howell, p | 1 | 0 | 0 | 0 | 0 | 0 | 0 | 0 | 0 | .000 | 0 | 1 | 0 | 1.000 |
| Reuss, p | 1 | 0 | 0 | 0 | 0 | 0 | 0 | 0 | 0 | .000 | 0 | 0 | 1 | .000 |
| Whitfield, ph | 1 | 0 | 0 | 0 | 0 | 0 | 0 | 0 | 0 | .000 | 0 | 0 | 0 | .000 |
| Niedenfuer, p | 3 | 1 | 0 | 0 | 0 | 0 | 0 | 0 | 0 | .000 | 2 | 0 | 0 | 1.000 |
| Bailor, pr-3b | 2 | 1 | 0 | 0 | 0 | 0 | 0 | 0 | 0 | .000 | 0 | 1 | 0 | 1.000 |
| Johnstone, ph | 1 | 1 | 0 | 0 | 0 | 0 | 0 | 0 | 0 | .000 | 0 | 0 | 0 | .000 |
| Welch, p | 1 | 1 | 0 | 0 | 0 | 0 | 0 | 0 | 0 | .000 | 0 | 0 | 1 | .000 |
| Castillo, p | 1 | 2 | 0 | 0 | 0 | 0 | 0 | 0 | 0 | .000 | 1 | 3 | 0 | 1.000 |
| Yeager, ph-c | 1 | 2 | 0 | 0 | 0 | 0 | 0 | 0 | 0 | .000 | 4 | 0 | 0 | 1.000 |
| Anderson, pr-ss-3b | 4 | 5 | 1 | 0 | 0 | 0 | 0 | 0 | 0 | .000 | 3 | 4 | 0 | 1.000 |
| Totals | 6 | 197 | 23 | 46 | 75 | 12 | 1 | 5 | 23 | .234 | 154 | 72 | 6 | .974 |

## ST. LOUIS CARDINALS' PITCHING RECORDS

| Pitcher | G. | GS. | CG. | IP. | H. | R. | ER. | BB. | SO. | HB. | WP. | W. | L. | Pct. | ERA. |
|---|---|---|---|---|---|---|---|---|---|---|---|---|---|---|---|
| Dayley | 5 | 0 | 0 | 6 | 2 | 0 | 0 | 1 | 3 | 0 | 0 | 0 | 0 | .000 | 0.00 |
| Campbell | 3 | 0 | 0 | 2⅓ | 3 | 0 | 0 | 2 | 0 | 0 | 0 | 0 | 0 | .000 | 0.00 |
| Lahti | 2 | 0 | 0 | 2 | 2 | 0 | 0 | 1 | 0 | 0 | 0 | 1 | 0 | 1.000 | 0.00 |
| Worrell | 4 | 0 | 0 | 6⅓ | 4 | 1 | 1 | 2 | 3 | 0 | 2 | 1 | 0 | 1.000 | 1.42 |
| Cox | 1 | 1 | 0 | 6 | 4 | 1 | 1 | 5 | 4 | 0 | 0 | 1 | 0 | 1.000 | 1.50 |
| Tudor | 2 | 2 | 0 | 12⅔ | 10 | 5 | 4 | 3 | 8 | 0 | 0 | 1 | 1 | .500 | 2.84 |
| Forsch | 1 | 1 | 0 | 3⅓ | 3 | 2 | 2 | 2 | 0 | 0 | 0 | 0 | 0 | .000 | 5.40 |
| Andujar | 2 | 2 | 0 | 10⅓ | 14 | 10 | 8 | 4 | 9 | 0 | 0 | 0 | 1 | .000 | 6.97 |
| Horton | 3 | 0 | 0 | 3 | 4 | 4 | 4 | 2 | 1 | 0 | 0 | 0 | 0 | .000 | 12.00 |
| Totals | 6 | 6 | 0 | 52 | 46 | 23 | 20 | 19 | 31 | 0 | 2 | 4 | 2 | .667 | 3.46 |

No shutouts. Saves—Dayley 2.

## LOS ANGELES DODGERS' PITCHING RECORDS

| Pitcher | G. | GS. | CG. | IP. | H. | R. | ER. | BB. | SO. | HB. | WP. | W. | L. | Pct. | ERA. |
|---|---|---|---|---|---|---|---|---|---|---|---|---|---|---|---|
| Howell | 1 | 0 | 0 | 2 | 0 | 0 | 0 | 0 | 2 | 0 | 0 | 0 | 0 | .000 | 0.00 |
| Valenzuela | 2 | 2 | 0 | 14⅓ | 11 | 3 | 3 | 10 | 13 | 0 | 1 | 1 | 0 | 1.000 | 1.88 |
| Diaz | 2 | 0 | 0 | 3 | 5 | 1 | 1 | 1 | 2 | 0 | 0 | 0 | 0 | .000 | 3.00 |
| Castillo | 1 | 0 | 0 | 5⅓ | 4 | 2 | 2 | 2 | 4 | 0 | 0 | 0 | 0 | .000 | 3.38 |
| Hershiser | 2 | 2 | 1 | 15⅓ | 17 | 6 | 6 | 6 | 5 | 0 | 1 | 1 | 0 | 1.000 | 3.52 |
| Niedenfuer | 3 | 0 | 0 | 5⅔ | 5 | 4 | 4 | 2 | 5 | 0 | 0 | 0 | 2 | .000 | 6.35 |
| Welch | 1 | 1 | 0 | 2⅔ | 5 | 4 | 2 | 6 | 2 | 0 | 0 | 0 | 1 | .000 | 6.75 |
| Reuss | 1 | 1 | 0 | 1⅔ | 5 | 7 | 2 | 1 | 0 | 0 | 0 | 0 | 1 | .000 | 10.80 |
| Honeycutt | 2 | 0 | 0 | 1⅓ | 4 | 2 | 2 | 2 | 1 | 0 | 0 | 0 | 0 | .000 | 13.50 |
| Totals | 6 | 6 | 1 | 51⅓ | 56 | 29 | *20 | 30 | 34 | 0 | 2 | 2 | 4 | .333 | 3.51 |

*Individual earned runs do not add up to team total because of rule 10.18 (i) being applied in Game 4.

No shutouts. Save—Niedenfuer.

## COMPOSITE SCORE BY INNINGS

| | | | | | | | | | | |
|---|---|---|---|---|---|---|---|---|---|---|
| St. Louis | 4 | 11 | 2 | 1 | 1 | 0 | 4 | 1 | 5 — 29 |
| Los Angeles | 1 | 1 | 3 | 6 | 3 | 5 | 2 | 2 | 0 — 23 |

Game-winning RBIs—Guerrero, Landreaux, Landrum, Smith, Clark.
Catcher's interference—Scioscia awarded first base on interference by Porter.
Sacrifice hits—Valenzuela, Forsch, Smith.
Sacrifice flies—Herr, Guerrero.
Stolen bases—Guerrero 2, McGee 2, Smith, Madlock, Coleman, Herr, Landrum, Duncan.
Caught stealing—McGee 3, Coleman 2, Pendleton, Sax.
Double plays—Smith, Herr and Clark 2; Duncan and Cabell; Hershiser, Duncan and Sax; Horton and Pendleton; Castillo, Anderson and Cabell; Pendelton, Herr and Clark.
Left on bases—St. Louis 7, 9, 11, 7, 10, 7—51. Los Angeles 6, 8, 9, 5, 5, 7—40.
Hit by pitcher—None.
Passed ball—Porter.
Balks—None.
Time of games—First game, 2:42; second game, 3:04; third game, 3:21; fourth game, 2:47; fifth game, 2:56; sixth game, 3:32.
Attendance—First game, 55,270; second game, 55,222; third game, 53,708; fourth game, 53,708; fifth game, 53,708; sixth game, 55,208.
Umpires—Stello, Froemming, McSherry, Tata, Runge and Crawford.
Official scorers—Jack Herman, Wayne Monroe.

# 1985 WORLD SERIES

## Including

**Review of 1985 Series**

**Official Play-by-Play, Each Game**

**Official Composite Box Score**

Royals pitcher Bret Saberhagen and third baseman George Brett celebrate Kansas City's first-ever World Series championship following an 11-0 drubbing of St. Louis in Game 7.

# Royals' Pitching Cuffs Cards

## By LARRY WIGGE

The year 1985 will long be remembered for the base-hit countdown for Cincinnati's Pete Rose, who was trying to pass Ty Cobb's all-time hit mark of 4,191. Another countdown worth noting, however, was the baby watch for Kansas City pitcher Bret Saberhagen and his wife, Janeane, during the American League Championship Series and the World Series. While both seemed to last forever, they had Pulitzer Prize-winning endings.

Saberhagen's prize, son Drew William (born October 26), will be a one-of-a-kind reminder of just how good life was for his family and the Kansas City Royals in October of '85. It was cigars one day and champagne the next for Saberhagen and the Royals.

"There's nothing better than having a baby and winning the World Series," Saberhagen told President Ronald Reagan after limiting the St. Louis Cardinals to just five singles and showing impeccable control, walking nobody, in pitching the Royals to an 11-0 triumph in the seventh game of the World Series.

"I'm walking on sunshine," Saberhagen said later.

With the triumph, the 21-year-old Saberhagen recorded two victories (both complete games), finished with an earned-run average of 0.50 and was selected as the World Series Most Valuable Player.

While the score in the Series finale might make it appear as if the Royals waltzed to the title, they actually fought an uphill battle all the way. In fact, barely 24 hours before their victorious celebration, the Royals were within an inch of being eliminated. But that was before pinch-hitter Dane Iorg drove in two runs with a one-out single in the ninth inning for a 2-1 victory in Game 6. It was an incredible comeback, but beating the odds was natural for these Royals, who became the first team to lose the first two games of the World Series at home and still come back to win.

"It's been some kind of season," said Kansas City Manager Dick Howser, shaking his head. "I can't explain it. No club likes to have the odds against them during the regular season or in postseason series. But these players proved the ultimate. They proved you can get down and down and still beat the odds."

The Royals' comeback was no fluke. They rallied to edge the California Angels to win the A.L. West title. They also came from way back—one victory to Toronto's three after four games, to be precise—to defeat the Blue Jays in the A.L. playoffs. Timely hitting and an especially sharp pitching staff were the keys. Kansas City hurlers held the Cardinals, the National League's leading batters during the regular season, with a team average of .264, to 13 runs and a .185 average. That latter figure was 10 points lower than the previous nadir of any team that had engaged in a seven-game Series. Only once did the Redbirds score more than one run in an inning.

"I have to give them credit," St. Louis Manager Whitey Herzog said. "Their pitching was great. But our hitting had something to do with it, too. If their pitching was that good they would have won their division by 30 games."

The Royals' pitching was good in Game 1, but the Cardinals' was even better. Herzog's club won the Series opener, 3-1, behind the combined eight-hit pitching of 21-game winner John Tudor and rookie Todd Worrell and back-to-back doubles by Tito Landrum and Cesar Cedeno that broke a 1-1 tie in the fourth inning.

The Royals had taken a 1-0 lead in the second on a run-scoring single by first baseman Steve Balboni. With right fielder Darryl Motley advancing to third on the one-out play, the Royals threatened to score more, but shortstop Buddy Biancalana missed a suicide squeeze bunt attempt and left Motley hung out to dry between third and home. The Cardinals then tied the contest in the third on center fielder Willie McGee's run-scoring groundout.

Following Landrum's one-out double in the fourth, Cedeno broke his bat on a tight fastball by lefthander Danny Jackson, Kansas City's starting and losing pitcher. The right fielder got enough wood on the ball, however, to lift it safely down the left-field line.

The Royals threatened to tie the score in the bottom of the fourth, but Cardinals third baseman Terry Pendleton made a running over-the-shoulder grab of Balboni's foul pop near the stands and threw to catcher Darrell Porter to double up Jim Sundberg, who had doubled to open the inning. Then in the seventh, with the bases loaded and two out against a shaky Worrell, Royals center fielder Willie Wilson jumped on the first pitch, which he sliced high into foul territory. Landrum ran a

**Terry Pendleton's bases-loaded double was the big blow in St. Louis' four-run ninth inning in Game 2.**

long way from his post in left field to make the catch and squelch another threat. And Andy Van Slyke hauled in third baseman George Brett's bid for a game-tying home run near the right-field fence in the eighth.

First baseman Jack Clark doubled home an insurance run for the Cardinals in the ninth. The Royals wasted a leadoff double by pinch-hitter Pat Sheridan in their last chance as Worrell preserved Tudor's victory.

Game 2 was another game of ifs and buts for the Royals, who took a 2-0 lead against starter Danny Cox on a single by Wilson and back-to-back RBI doubles by Brett and second baseman Frank White in the fourth inning, only to fall to a four-run St. Louis uprising in the ninth inning and lose, 4-2. The rally made a winner of Ken Dayley, who relieved Cox after seven innings, and Jeff Lahti earned the save for pitching the ninth.

It was a heartbreaking loss for Kansas City lefthander Charlie Leibrandt, who had blanked the Cards on only two hits through eight innings and had set down 13 straight batters before McGee led off the ninth with a double.

Leibrandt still seemed destined to win after he retired shortstop Ozzie Smith on a groundout and second baseman Tom Herr on a fly ball. But then Clark grounded a single between short and third on a 3-and-0 count to drive in McGee and cut Kansas City's lead to 2-1. Landrum then reached across the plate and swatted a bloop double to right, sending Clark to third. After Leibrandt intentionally walked Cedeno to load the bases, Pendleton, a .240 hitter in the regular season and a .208 batsman in the N.L. playoffs, hit a soft liner to left to score three more runs and leave the experts to second-guess Howser for not bringing in his relief ace, Dan Quisenberry, earlier in the inning.

"He (Leibrandt) wasn't losing his stuff, his control was good, his stuff was great," Howser said in his own defense. "He was in complete command."

To others, Leibrandt appeared to be tiring.

"His pitches didn't have the pop (in the ninth) that they had in the earlier innings," Pendleton said.

The Cardinals' rally, which made them the first World Series team in 46 years to overcome a two-run deficit going into the top of the ninth inning and win, left the Royals wondering what they had to do to win.

"You can't play a better game than we played," Brett said. "We played fantastic. We played good enough to win both nights and we lost both. But this is the toughest way to lose a ball game."

It wasn't until the scene shifted to St. Louis that the Royals finally tasted victory. Saberhagen, who had injured his hand in the Royals' A.L. Championship Series clincher against Toronto, showed his 20-game-winning form in Game 3, allowing just one run on six hits and striking out eight. But it was a two-run double in the fourth inning by former Cardinal Lonnie Smith and White's three-RBI performance that really paced Kansas City to its first triumph.

Because Series rules dictated that no designated hitter would be used in 1985, thus taking Hal McRae out of the starting lineup, White became the first second baseman to bat in the cleanup position in the Series since Jackie Robinson did it for the Brooklyn Dodgers in 1952. The veteran responded by belting a two-run homer off starter and loser Joaquin Andujar in the fifth to give the Royals a 4-0 cushion. After the Cardinals scored on an RBI single by Clark in the sixth, White then doubled home yet another run in the seventh and scored on a single by Biancalana to clinch the 6-1 decision.

The Cardinals sent Tudor to the mound in Game 4 and the lefty scattered five hits and struck out eight in blanking the Royals, 3-0, to give the Series its first home-team victory and St. Louis a 3-1 Series lead. It was Tudor's second win in the Series, his 16th straight victory at Busch Stadium and his 23rd victory in 25 decisions since going 1-7 to start the '85 season.

St. Louis scored all three runs off starter Bud Black, a lefty who gave up only four hits, three of which were costly. Landrum slugged an opposite-field homer just inside the right-field foul pole in the second inning, while McGee clubbed another solo blast over the left-field wall in the third. In the fifth, catcher Tom Nieto laid down a perfect squeeze bunt to score Pendleton, who had tripled, for St. Louis' final run.

Kansas City's only threat came in the seventh when Brett led off with a single and went to second on a one-out single by Sundberg. With two out, Balboni walked to load the bases. But pinch-hitter McRae

grounded to Pendleton, who stepped on the bag at third for the third out.

Even though the Royals had to win three straight games to avoid elimination, they remained remarkably upbeat about their chances.

"This is nothing new," Saberhagen said after Game 4. "It's the same old stuff. They fell right into our trap, just like Toronto."

That lighthearted remark caused many a chuckle among confident Cardinals fans, but just when it looked as if St. Louis was ready to clinch its second world championship in four years, Jackson came to the Royals' rescue in Game 5—again. Jackson, who had shut out Toronto to keep the Royals alive after they fell behind, 3-1, in the A.L. playoffs, similarly stymied the Cardinals on five hits as he went the distance for a 6-1 victory.

The Royals jumped out to a 1-0 lead in the first inning on a run-scoring ground out by White. But the Cardinals rallied in their half of the first to tie the contest on a run-producing double by Clark. A three-run second, however, proved decisive for Kansas City.

Sundberg started the rally with a one-out hit that was ruled a double after left fielder Landrum, who initially started back on the ball, failed to make a diving catch. Biancalana followed with a single to right. Cedeno's throw home beat Sundberg by five feet, but home plate umpire John Shulock ruled that Sundberg's headlong, hooking dive for the plate beat Nieto's leg. After Cardinals starter Bob Forsch fanned Jackson and issued a walk to Lonnie Smith, Wilson tripled, scoring Biancalana and Smith to give the Royals a 4-1 lead.

The Royals added insurance with a run on a wild throw by Ozzie Smith in the eighth and another run on Pat Sheridan's RBI double in the ninth.

By this time, with the Series returning to Kansas City, the Cardinals were starting to get worried.

"We can't kid anybody," Herzog said. "We just ain't hitting."

Neither team was hitting much in Game 6. Leibrandt, Kansas City's hard-luck loser in Game 2, pitched perfect ball for five innings and was locked in a scoreless duel with Cox through seven. But the Cardinals broke through for one run in the eighth on pinch-hitter Brian Harper's bloop RBI single to center. All of that became academic, however, when Iorg came through with his aforementioned two-run pinch blow in the ninth to give the Royals a 2-1 victory and even the Se-

**Dane Iorg's two-run pinch single in the ninth inning gave the Royals a 2-1 victory in Game 6.**

ries at three games apiece. Quisenberry, who relieved Leibrandt with the bases loaded in the eighth, was the winner.

The scenario setting the stage for Iorg's safety had Herzog beside himself in rage.

Pinch-hitter Jorge Orta opened the ninth against Worrell, who was relieving Dayley, by hitting a chopper to the right side that was fielded by Clark. The first baseman tossed to Worrell to force Orta at first, but A.L. umpire Don Denkinger called Orta safe. Herzog argued vehemently—and television replays indicated that Denkinger blew the call—but Orta remained at first with an infield single. Herzog was further incensed when Balboni lifted a high pop near the first-base dugout that was playable but somehow fell untouched. Given a new life, Balboni promptly smacked a single to left. Sund-

berg, attempting to sacrifice, forced Orta at third when Worrell fielded his bunt and made a fine play. With McRae batting for Biancalana, Porter committed a passed ball that allowed pinch-runner Onix Concepcion and Sundberg to advance to third and second. The Cardinals then chose to walk McRae to load the bases with one out. Iorg followed with his winning hit to right, scoring Concepcion and Sundberg, who slid around Porter's tag—although Van Slyke's throw to the plate appeared to be there in plenty of time for Porter to make the play.

"I'm the luckiest guy in the world tonight," Howser said afterward, "and I'm the first to admit it."

Herzog, meanwhile, was more concerned about Denkinger's ruling at first than Clark's misplay of Balboni's foul pop or Porter's passed ball and missed tag.

"I ain't supposed to say anything about the umpiring," he said, "but if you want my opinion, it's been horse manure in this Series. It's been a real disgrace . . . As far as I'm concerned, we had the damned Series won tonight."

The Cardinals were still beefing about Denkinger's apparent blunder when Game 7 began. In fact, they had another ugly run-in with the A.L. umpire, who was stationed behind the plate in the finale. But the outcome of this game was decided long before that confrontation.

The Cardinals sent Tudor to the mound against Saberhagen, creating a matchup of pitchers who had been impeccable in their previous Series starts. But Motley reached Tudor for a two-run homer in the Kansas City half of the second, the blast coming immediately after Motley sent one just as far, but foul, down the left-field line. In the third, Tudor walked Lonnie Smith, allowed an infield single by Brett, then walked White and Sundberg to force in a run. Herzog could see that Tudor didn't have his usual stuff, and the left-hander was yanked after 2⅓ innings, his shortest stint of the season. Bill Campbell replaced Tudor and was greeted by Balboni's two-run single to put the Royals ahead, 5-0.

Kansas City added six runs in a fifth inning that will leave a black mark on baseball for a long time. It was an inning in which the Cardinals tied a Series record by using five pitchers and had their manager and one of their pitchers ejected from the game.

Lahti replaced Campbell after Sundberg produced a leadoff single. Balboni and Motley added singles to produce one run, and Biancalana and Saberhagen made outs (the latter reached base when Motley was forced on his sacrifice attempt) before Lonnie Smith knocked in two runners with a double. Wilson's RBI single made it 9-0. Brett then greeted reliever Ricky Horton with another single, moving Wilson to third, before Andujar took over on the mound.

White promptly made it 10-0 with a run-scoring single. Then, with a 2-and-2 count on Sundberg, Andujar fired a fastball over what he thought was the inside corner of the plate. Denkinger disagreed. Andujar charged off the mound and Herzog roared out of the dugout, resulting in the manager's dismissal from the game. After order was restored and Andujar fired another delivery to just about the same place, also ruled a ball, the St. Louis righthander again went bonkers and was quickly ejected from the game. For record's sake, Brett scored the final run of the inning, game and season when Forsch made a wild pitch on his first delivery. Saberhagen went on to record his five-hit shutout, pick up his MVP trophy and tell the President about becoming a father the day before.

The lopsided score and ugly arguments notwithstanding, the Royals proved themselves worthy champions. By coming back from a 3-1 deficit to win the seven-game A.L. playoffs, the Royals matched a feat previously performed by only four teams in World Series history. Then they did it again in the Series. Their pitching staff posted a composite 1.89 earned-run average (compared with the Cardinals' 3.96), and their lineup, even without their customary DH, batted .288 (103 points better than St. Louis).

"We had good pitching and good defense and just enough offense," said Biancalana, a .188 hitter in the regular season who batted .278 in the Series. "It took a lot of hard work. Maybe everyone was thinking we weren't the best, but we showed them differently."

# Game 1

**At Kansas City**
**October 19**

| St. Louis (N.L.) | AB. | R. | H. | PO. | A. | E. |
|---|---|---|---|---|---|---|
| McGee, cf | 4 | 0 | 1 | 1 | 0 | 0 |
| O. Smith, ss | 3 | 0 | 0 | 1 | 2 | 0 |
| Herr, 2b | 4 | 1 | 1 | 3 | 0 | 0 |
| Clark, 1b | 4 | 0 | 1 | 6 | 1 | 0 |
| Landrum, lf | 4 | 1 | 2 | 3 | 0 | 0 |
| Cedeno, rf | 3 | 0 | 1 | 3 | 0 | 0 |
| Worrell, p | 1 | 0 | 0 | 0 | 0 | 0 |
| Pendleton, 3b | 2 | 1 | 0 | 1 | 4 | 1 |
| Porter, c | 3 | 0 | 1 | 7 | 2 | 0 |
| Tudor, p | 1 | 0 | 0 | 0 | 2 | 0 |
| Van Slyke, rf | 2 | 0 | 0 | 2 | 0 | 0 |
| Totals | 31 | 3 | 7 | 27 | 11 | 1 |

| Kansas City (A.L.) | AB. | R. | H. | PO. | A. | E. |
|---|---|---|---|---|---|---|
| L. Smith, lf | 3 | 0 | 1 | 0 | 1 | 0 |
| Wilson, cf | 4 | 0 | 1 | 0 | 1 | 0 |
| Brett, 3b | 4 | 0 | 1 | 1 | 3 | 0 |
| White, 2b | 4 | 0 | 0 | 3 | 5 | 0 |
| Sundberg, c | 3 | 1 | 1 | 11 | 0 | 0 |
| Motley, rf | 3 | 0 | 1 | 1 | 0 | 0 |
| dSheridan | 1 | 0 | 1 | 0 | 0 | 0 |
| Balboni, 1b | 4 | 0 | 1 | 11 | 0 | 0 |
| Biancalana, ss | 1 | 0 | 0 | 0 | 1 | 0 |
| aL. Jones | 1 | 0 | 1 | 0 | 0 | 0 |
| Quisenberry, p | 0 | 0 | 0 | 0 | 0 | 0 |
| Black, p | 0 | 0 | 0 | 0 | 0 | 0 |
| eOrta | 1 | 0 | 0 | 0 | 0 | 0 |
| Jackson, p | 2 | 0 | 0 | 0 | 2 | 0 |
| bMcRae | 0 | 0 | 0 | 0 | 0 | 0 |
| cConcepcion, ss | 0 | 0 | 0 | 0 | 2 | 0 |
| fIorg | 1 | 0 | 0 | 0 | 0 | 0 |
| Totals | 32 | 1 | 8 | 27 | 15 | 0 |

St. Louis .................... 0 0 1   1 0 0   0 0 1—3
Kansas City ............. 0 1 0   0 0 0   0 0 0—1

| St. Louis | IP. | H. | R. | ER. | BB. | SO. |
|---|---|---|---|---|---|---|
| Tudor (W) | 6⅔ | 7 | 1 | 1 | 2 | 5 |
| Worrell (S) | 2⅓ | 1 | 0 | 0 | 1 | 0 |

| Kansas City | IP. | H. | R. | ER. | BB. | SO. |
|---|---|---|---|---|---|---|
| Jackson (L) | 7 | 4 | 2 | 2 | 2 | 7 |
| Quisenberry | 1⅔ | 3 | 1 | 1 | 0 | 2 |
| Black | ⅓ | 0 | 0 | 0 | 2 | 1 |

Bases on balls—Off Tudor 2 (Sundberg, Biancalana), off Worrell 1 (L. Smith), off Jackson 2 (Pendleton, O. Smith), off Black 2 (Pendleton, Porter).

Strikeouts—By Tudor 5 (L. Smith, Brett, Balboni, Jackson 2), by Jackson 7 (McGee, Clark, Cedeno, Pendleton, Porter 2, Tudor), by Quisenberry 2 (Van Slyke, Worrell), by Black 1 (Van Slyke).

Game-winning RBI—Cedeno.

aTripled for Biancalana in seventh. bHit by pitcher for Jackson in seventh. cRan for McRae in seventh. dDoubled for Motley in ninth. eFlied out for Black in ninth. fFlied out for Concepcion in ninth. Runs batted in—McGee, Clark, Cedeno, Balboni. Two-base hits—Landrum, Cedeno, Sundberg, McGee, Clark, Sheridan. Three-base hit—L. Jones. Stolen base—O. Smith. Caught stealing—Motley, L. Smith. Sacrifice hit—Tudor. Hit by pitcher—By Tudor (McRae). Passed ball—Sundberg. Double play—Pendleton and Porter. Left on bases—St. Louis 6, Kansas City 8. Umpires—Denkinger (A.L.) plate, B. Williams (N.L.) first, McKean (A.L.) second, Engel (N.L.) third, Shulock (A.L.) left, Quick (N.L.) right. Time—2:48. Attendance—41,650.

**FIRST INNING**

St. Louis—McGee struck out. Ozzie Smith grounded out to Biancalana. Herr bounced to Brett. No runs, no hits, no errors, none left.

Kansas City—Lonnie Smith flied to Cedeno. Wilson also flied to Cedeno. Brett struck out. No runs, no hits, no errors, none left.

**SECOND INNING**

St. Louis—Clark hit a soft liner to Balboni. Landrum lined to White. Cedeno struck out. No runs, no hits, no errors, none left.

Kansas City—White hit a nubber in front of home plate and was thrown out by Porter. Sundberg walked. Motley singled to left field, Sundberg stopping at second base. Balboni singled to left to score Sundberg for a 1-0 Royals lead, Motley moving to third when Pendleton mishandled Landrum's relay throw and Balboni staying at first. Biancalana missed the bunt on a suicide squeeze attempt and Motley was tagged out in a rundown, Porter to Pendleton to Tudor to Ozzie Smith. Balboni advanced to third on the play. Biancalana then walked. Jackson struck out. One run, two hits, one error, two left.

### THIRD INNING

St. Louis—Pendleton walked. Porter singled to right, Pendleton moving to third. Tudor sacrificed Porter to second, Jackson to White, with Pendleton holding third. McGee grounded out to White, Pendleton scoring to tie the game 1-1 and Porter moving to third. Ozzie Smith walked. Smith stole second. Jackson knocked down Herr's bouncer back to the mound and threw to Balboni for the out. One run, one hit, no errors, two left.

Kansas City—Lonnie Smith singled to left. Smith started running on the first pitch but was trapped by Tudor's pickoff throw, which then went from Clark to Ozzie Smith to Herr. Wilson popped to Herr. Brett reached first on an infield single when he beat Ozzie Smith's throw from deep short. White grounded out, Clark unassisted. No runs, two hits, no errors, one left.

### FOURTH INNING

St. Louis—Clark was called out on strikes. Landrum doubled down the right-field line. Cedeno hit a broken-bat double into the left-field corner, scoring Landrum to give the Cardinals a 2-1 lead. Pendleton grounded out to White, Cedeno advancing to third. Porter was called out on strikes. One run, two hits, no errors, one left.

Kansas City—Sundberg doubled down the left-field line. Motley flied to Cedeno, Sundberg moving to third after the catch. Balboni fouled out to Pendleton, who made an over-the-shoulder catch while running down the left-field line, then wheeled and threw to Porter to double up Sundberg who was trying to score after the catch. No runs, one hit, no errors, none left.

### FIFTH INNING

St. Louis—Tudor was called out on strikes. McGee doubled up the right-center alley but was out trying for a triple on a relay from Wilson to White to Brett. Ozzie Smith grounded out to White. No runs, one hit, no errors, none left.

Kansas City—Biancalana grounded to Ozzie Smith. Jackson struck out. Lonnie Smith also struck out. No runs, no hits, no errors, none left.

### SIXTH INNING

St. Louis—Herr was out at first when his bunt down the third-base line was fielded by Brett, who made a barehanded pickup and threw to Balboni for the out. Clark flied to Motley. Landrum fouled out to Sundberg. No runs, no hits, no errors, none left.

Kansas City—Wilson lined a single to left-center. Brett popped to Herr. Landrum made a fine running catch near the warning track in left-center on White's hard liner. Sundberg grounded to Pendleton. No runs, one hit, no errors, one left.

### SEVENTH INNING

St. Louis—Cedeno fouled out to Balboni, who made an over-the-shoulder catch while running toward the stands. Pendleton struck out. Porter also struck out. No runs, no hits, no errors, none left.

Kansas City—Motley flied to Landrum. Balboni struck out. Lynn Jones batted for Biancalana and tripled into the right-field corner. McRae, batting for Jackson, was hit by Tudor's 2-0 delivery. Worrell replaced Tudor on the mound for the Cardinals and Van Sylke went in to play right field. Concepcion ran for McRae. Lonnie Smith walked, loading the bases. Landrum

caught Wilson's foul ball after making a long run. No runs, one hit, no errors, three left.

### EIGHTH INNING

St. Louis—Concepcion stayed in the game at shortstop and Quisenberry came in to pitch for the Royals. Van Slyke was called out on strikes. White charged McGee's bouncer and made a fine play for the out. Ozzie Smith grounded to Concepcion. No runs, no hits, no errors, none left.

Kansas City—Van Slyke made a leaping catch against the wall of Brett's long drive to right-center. White fouled out to Porter. Sundberg grounded to Pendleton. No runs, no hits, no errors, none left.

### NINTH INNING

St. Louis—Herr bounced a single to center. Clark lined a double over Lonnie Smith's head, scoring Herr to give the Cardinals a 3-1 lead. Clark, however, rounded second too far and was thrown out, Lonnie Smith to Concepcion to Brett to White. Landrum blooped a single to right. Worrell struck out trying to sacrifice. Landrum went to second on Sundberg's passed ball. Black relieved Quisenberry with an 0-1 count on Pendleton but proceeded to walk him intentionally. Porter also walked, loading the bases. Van Slyke was called out on strikes. One run, three hits, no errors, three left.

Kansas City—Sheridan batted for Motley and doubled down the right-field line. Balboni bounced to Clark unassisted, Sheridan moving to third. Orta, batting for Black, flied to McGee in shallow center, Sheridan holding. Iorg batted for Concepcion and flied to Van Slyke. No runs, one hit, no errors, one left.

# Game 2

| St. Louis (N.L.) | AB. | R. | H. | PO. | A. | E. |
|---|---|---|---|---|---|---|
| McGee, cf | 4 | 1 | 1 | 2 | 0 | 0 |
| O. Smith, ss | 4 | 0 | 0 | 3 | 3 | 0 |
| Herr, 2b | 4 | 0 | 0 | 1 | 5 | 0 |
| Clark, 1b | 3 | 1 | 1 | 10 | 0 | 0 |
| Landrum, lf | 4 | 1 | 2 | 2 | 1 | 0 |
| Cedeno, rf | 3 | 1 | 0 | 0 | 0 | 0 |
| Lahti, p | 0 | 0 | 0 | 0 | 0 | 0 |
| Pendleton, 3b | 4 | 0 | 2 | 1 | 2 | 0 |
| Porter, c | 3 | 0 | 0 | 7 | 0 | 0 |
| Cox, p | 2 | 0 | 0 | 1 | 2 | 0 |
| aHarper | 1 | 0 | 0 | 0 | 0 | 0 |
| Dayley, p | 0 | 0 | 0 | 0 | 0 | 0 |
| bVan Slyke, rf | 1 | 0 | 0 | 0 | 0 | 0 |
| Totals | 33 | 4 | 6 | 27 | 13 | 0 |

| Kansas City (A.L.) | AB. | R. | H. | PO. | A. | E. |
|---|---|---|---|---|---|---|
| L. Smith, lf | 4 | 0 | 2 | 0 | 0 | 0 |
| L. Jones, lf | 0 | 0 | 0 | 2 | 0 | 0 |
| Wilson, cf | 4 | 1 | 2 | 3 | 0 | 0 |
| Brett, 3b | 4 | 1 | 1 | 1 | 5 | 0 |
| White, 2b | 3 | 0 | 3 | 0 | 0 | 0 |
| Sheridan, rf | 4 | 0 | 1 | 1 | 0 | 0 |
| Quisenberry, p | 0 | 0 | 0 | 0 | 0 | 0 |
| Sundberg, c | 4 | 0 | 0 | 7 | 0 | 0 |
| Balboni, 1b | 4 | 0 | 1 | 12 | 0 | 0 |
| Biancalana, ss | 1 | 0 | 0 | 1 | 4 | 0 |
| cOrta | 1 | 0 | 0 | 0 | 0 | 0 |
| Leibrandt, p | 2 | 0 | 0 | 0 | 2 | 0 |
| Motley, rf | 0 | 0 | 0 | 0 | 0 | 0 |
| Totals | 31 | 2 | 9 | 27 | 11 | 0 |

| | | | | | | |
|---|---|---|---|---|---|---|
| St. Louis | 000 | 000 | 004—4 | | | |
| Kansas City | 000 | 200 | 000—2 | | | |

| St. Louis | IP. | H. | R. | ER. | BB. | SO. |
|---|---|---|---|---|---|---|
| Cox | 7 | 7 | 2 | 2 | 3 | 5 |
| Dayley (W) | 1 | 1 | 0 | 0 | 0 | 1 |
| Lahti (S) | 1 | 1 | 0 | 0 | 0 | 0 |

| Kansas City | IP. | H. | R. | ER. | BB. | SO. |
|---|---|---|---|---|---|---|
| Leibrandt (L) | 8⅔ | 6 | 4 | 4 | 2 | 6 |
| Quisenberry | ⅓ | 0 | 0 | 0 | 1 | 0 |

Bases on balls—Off Cox 3 (White, Biancalana 2), off Leibrandt 2 (Clark, Cedeno), off Quisenberry 1 (Porter).

Strikeouts—By Cox 5 (Sheridan 2, Sundberg 2, Balboni), by Dayley 1 (Brett), by Leibrandt 6 (Clark, Landrum, Porter 2, Cox 2).

Game-winning RBI—Pendleton.

aFlied out for Cox in eighth. bFlied out for Dayley in ninth. cGrounded into double play for Biancalana in ninth. Runs batted in—Clark, Pendleton 3, Brett, White. Two-base hits—Brett, White 2, McGee, Landrum, Pendleton. Stolen bases—White, Wilson. Sacrifice hit—Leibrandt. Double plays—Herr, O. Smith and Clark 2; Cox, O. Smith and Herr. Left on bases—St. Louis 5, Kansas City 6. Umpires—B. Williams (N.L.) plate, McKean (A.L.) first, Engel (N.L.) second, Shulock (A.L.) third, Quick (N.L.) left, Denkinger (A.L.) right. Time—2:44. Attendance—41,656.

### FIRST INNING

St. Louis—McGee grounded to Biancalana. Ozzie Smith fouled out to Brett. Herr grounded to Brett, who charged the ball and made an off-balance throw to Balboni for the out. No runs, no hits, no errors, none left.

Kansas City—Lonnie Smith singled to left-center. Herr backhanded Wilson's grounder near second base and flipped to Ozzie Smith for one out, and Smith threw to Clark at first to complete the double play. Brett grounded out, Clark unassisted. No runs, one hit, no errors, none left.

### SECOND INNING

St. Louis—Clark struck out. Landrum was called out on strikes. Cedeno grounded to Biancalana. No runs, no hits, no errors, none left.

Kansas City—White laid down a perfect bunt and easily beat an off-balance throw to first by Cox for a single. With Sheridan at the plate, White stole second. Sheridan was called out on strikes. Sundberg struck out. Balboni also struck out. No runs, one hit, no errors, one left.

### THIRD INNING

St. Louis—Pendleton looped a single to right. Porter struck out. Cox, after failing to sacrifice twice, looked at the third strike. Wilson made a fine running catch of McGee's fly ball near the warning track in right-center. No runs, one hit, no errors, one left.

Kansas City—Biancalana walked. Leibrandt bunted back to Cox, who started a double play from Ozzie Smith to Herr covering first. Pendleton knocked down Lonnie Smith's hard smash with a backhanded stop near the third-base bag, scrambled to his feet and made a long throw to Clark to retire Smith. No runs, no hits, no errors, none left.

### FOURTH INNING

St. Louis—Ozzie Smith grounded back to the mound, Leibrandt to Balboni for the out. Herr grounded to Balboni. Clark walked. Landrum looped a single to right-center, Clark advancing to third. Cedeno hit a soft liner to Biancalana. No runs, one hit, no errors, two left.

Kansas City—Wilson grounded a single to right. With Wilson running on the pitch, Brett lined a double down the right-field line and Wilson came all the way around to score to give the Royals a 1-0 lead. White then doubled to left-center, Brett scoring to give Kansas City a 2-0 lead. Sheridan grounded out, Clark unassisted, White moving to third on the play. Sundberg struck out. Balboni flied to McGee, who ranged near the warning track in left-center to make the catch. Two runs, three hits, no errors, one left.

### FIFTH INNING

St. Louis—Brett backed up at third base to field Pendleton's high chopper and made the long throw to Balboni for the out. Porter was called out on strikes. Cox also was called out on strikes. No runs, no hits, no errors, none left.

Kansas City—Biancalana bounced to Herr. Leibrandt fouled out to Pendleton. Lonnie Smith flied to Landrum. No runs, no hits, no errors, none left.

### SIXTH INNING

St. Louis—Leibrandt stabbed McGee's high bouncer back to the mound and threw to Balboni for the out. Ozzie Smith flied to Wilson. Brett made a diving stop to his left on Herr's smash and threw to Balboni for the out. No runs, no hits, no errors, none left.

Kansas City—Herr fielded Wilson's high chop over the mound, but Wilson was ruled safe with an infield hit on a close play at first. Brett flied to Landrum. With White at the plate, Wilson stole second. White then walked. Sheridan struck out. Sundberg grounded back to Cox, who threw to Clark for the out. No runs, one hit, no errors, two left.

### SEVENTH INNING

St. Louis—Clark fouled out to Sundberg. Landrum bounced to Biancalana. Cedeno grounded to Brett. No runs, no hits, no errors, none left.

Kansas City—Balboni grounded to Pendleton. Biancalana walked. Leibrandt sacrificed Biancalana to second, Cox tagging Leibrandt for the out. Lonnie Smith singled sharply to left and Biancalana, trying to score from second, was called out at the plate on Landrum's throw to Porter. No runs, one hit, no errors, one left.

### EIGHTH INNING

St. Louis—Lynn Jones came in to play left field for the Royals. Pendleton grounded out, Balboni unassisted. Porter flied to Jones, Harper, batting for Cox, also flied to Jones. No runs, no hits, no errors, none left.

Kansas City—Dayley took over on the mound for the Cardinals. Wilson grounded to Herr. Brett stuck out. White doubled off the left-field wall. Sheridan grounded to Herr. No runs, one hit, no errors, one left.

### NINTH INNING

St. Louis—McGee's smash took a big bounce past a diving Brett and went into the left-field corner for a double. Ozzie Smith grounded out to Brett, McGee holding second. Herr flied to Sheridan, McGee again holding. Clark smacked a 3-0 delivery to left for a single, McGee scoring to cut the Royals' lead to 2-1. Landrum blooped a double down the right-field line, Clark advancing to third. Cedeno was walked intentionally to load the bases. Pendleton doubled down the left-field line, Clark, Landrum and Cedeno all scoring to give the Cardinals a 4-2 lead. Quisenberry replaced Leibrandt on the mound and Motley went in to play right field for the Royals. Porter was walked intentionally. Van Slyke batted for Dayley and flied to Wilson. Four runs, four hits, no errors, two left.

Kansas City—Van Slyke remained in the game and went to right field and Lahti went in to pitch for the Cardinals. Sundberg flied to McGee. Balboni was credited with a single when he squibbed one down the third-base line and Lahti had no play at first. Orta, batting for Biancalana, hit into the Royals' third double play of the game, Herr to Ozzie Smith to Clark. No runs, one hit, no errors, none left.

# Game 3

**At St. Louis**
**October 22**

| Kansas City (A.L.) | AB. | R. | H. | PO. | A. | E. |
|---|---|---|---|---|---|---|
| L. Smith, lf | 5 | 0 | 2 | 1 | 0 | 0 |
| L. Jones, lf | 0 | 0 | 0 | 1 | 0 | 0 |
| Wilson, cf | 5 | 0 | 2 | 3 | 0 | 0 |
| Brett, 3b | 2 | 2 | 2 | 2 | 3 | 0 |
| White, 2b | 4 | 2 | 2 | 1 | 3 | 0 |
| Sheridan, rf | 5 | 0 | 0 | 1 | 0 | 0 |
| Sundberg, c | 2 | 1 | 1 | 8 | 2 | 0 |
| Balboni, 1b | 4 | 0 | 0 | 9 | 0 | 0 |
| Biancalana, ss | 5 | 1 | 2 | 1 | 1 | 0 |
| Saberhagen, p | 3 | 0 | 0 | 0 | 0 | 0 |
| Totals | 35 | 6 | 11 | 27 | 9 | 0 |

| St. Louis (N.L.) | AB. | R. | H. | PO. | A. | E. |
|---|---|---|---|---|---|---|
| McGee, cf | 4 | 0 | 1 | 1 | 0 | 0 |
| O. Smith, ss | 4 | 1 | 1 | 1 | 5 | 0 |
| Herr, 2b | 3 | 0 | 1 | 2 | 1 | 0 |
| Clark, 1b | 4 | 0 | 1 | 9 | 0 | 0 |
| Van Slyke, rf | 4 | 0 | 0 | 1 | 0 | 0 |
| Pendleton, 3b | 4 | 0 | 1 | 0 | 0 | 0 |
| Porter, c | 3 | 0 | 0 | 8 | 1 | 0 |
| Landrum, lf | 3 | 0 | 1 | 4 | 0 | 0 |
| Andujar, p | 1 | 0 | 0 | 0 | 1 | 0 |
| Campbell, p | 0 | 0 | 0 | 0 | 0 | 0 |
| aJorgensen | 1 | 0 | 0 | 0 | 0 | 0 |
| Horton, p | 0 | 0 | 0 | 1 | 0 | 0 |
| bHarper | 1 | 0 | 0 | 0 | 0 | 0 |
| Dayley, p | 0 | 0 | 0 | 0 | 0 | 0 |
| Totals | 32 | 1 | 6 | 27 | 8 | 0 |

| | | | | |
|---|---|---|---|---|
| Kansas City | 000 | 220 | 200—6 |
| St. Louis | 000 | 001 | 000—1 |

| Kansas City | IP. | H. | R. | ER. | BB. | SO. |
|---|---|---|---|---|---|---|
| Saberhagen (W) | 9 | 6 | 1 | 1 | 1 | 8 |

| St. Louis | IP. | H. | R. | ER. | BB. | SO. |
|---|---|---|---|---|---|---|
| Andujar (L) | 4* | 9 | 4 | 4 | 3 | 3 |
| Campbell | 1 | 0 | 0 | 0 | 1 | 2 |
| Horton | 2 | 2 | 2 | 2 | 2 | 1 |
| Dayley | 2 | 0 | 0 | 0 | 2 | 2 |

*Pitched to two batters in fifth.

Bases on balls—Off Saberhagen 1 (Herr), off Andujar 3 (Brett, White, Sundberg), off Campbell 1 (Sundberg), off Horton 2 (Brett, Balboni), off Dayley 2 (Brett, Sundberg). Strikeouts—By Saberhagen 8 (McGee, Clark 3, Van Slyke 2, Landrum, Andujar), by Andujar 3 (L. Smith, Sheridan, Saberhagen), by Campbell 2 (Balboni, Biancalana), by Horton 1 (Wilson), by Dayley 2 (L. Smith, Wilson). Game-winning RBI—L. Smith. aGrounded out for Campbell in fifth. bGrounded out for Horton in seventh. Runs batted in—L. Smith 2, White 3, Biancalana, Clark. Two-base hits—L. Smith, White. Home run—White. Stolen bases—Wilson, McGee. Caught stealing—L. Smith. Sacrifice hit—Saberhagen. Balk—Horton. Double plays—Herr and Clark; Sundberg and Brett. Left on bases—Kansas City 11, St. Louis 5. Umpires—McKean (A.L.) plate, Engel (N.L.) first, Shulock (A.L.) second, Quick (N.L.) third, Denkinger (A.L.) left, B. Williams (N.L.) right. Time—2:59. Attendance—53,634.

## FIRST INNING

Kansas City—Lonnie Smith struck out. Wilson bounced a single to left. With Brett at the plate, Wilson stole second. Brett then was walked intentionally. With the runners moving on the pitch, Herr fielded White's grounder near second, stepped on the bag to retire Brett and then threw to Clark for the double play. No runs, one hit, no errors, one left.

St. Louis—McGee lined a single to left. Ozzie Smith fouled out to White. With Herr at the plate, McGee stole second. Herr walked. Clark was called out on strikes and McGee was caught trying to steal third, Sundberg to Brett, for a double play. No runs, one hit, no errors, one left.

## SECOND INNING

Kansas City—Sheridan flied to McGee. Sundberg lined a single to right-center. Balboni pinned Landrum up against the left-field wall to catch his long fly. Biancalana flied to Landrum. No runs, one hit, no errors, one left.

St. Louis—Brett went to his left to cut off Van Slyke's chopper and threw to Balboni for the out. White backhanded Pendleton's grounder near second but couldn't make a play, Pendleton getting an infield hit. Porter flied to Lonnie Smith. Landrum bounced out, Balboni unassisted. No runs, one hit, no errors, one left.

## THIRD INNING

Kansas City—Saberhagen struck out. Lonnie Smith lined a single to center. Smith was caught stealing, Porter to Ozzie Smith. Ozzie Smith backhanded Wilson's grounder to deep short, but Wilson beat Smith's throw to first for an infield hit. Brett grounded a single to right, Wilson advancing to third. White walked, loading the bases. Sheridan struck out. No runs, three hits, no errors, three left.

St. Louis—Andujar struck out. McGee also struck out. Ozzie Smith grounded to Brett. No runs, no hits, no errors, none left.

## FOURTH INNING

Kansas City—Sundberg walked. Balboni lined hard to Landrum. Andujar fielded Biancalana's high chop but had no play at first base as Biancalana was credited with an infield hit, Sundberg moving to second. Saberhagen sacrificed Sundberg to third and Biancalana to second, Andujar to Herr covering first. Lonnie Smith doubled off the glove of Van Slyke, who tried to make a diving catch in right-center, Sundberg and Biancalana both scoring to give the Royals a 2-0 lead. Wilson lined to Landrum. Two runs, two hits, no errors, one left.

St. Louis—Herr grounded to Biancalana. Clark was called out on strikes. Van Slyke also was called out on strikes. No runs, no hits, no errors, none left.

## FIFTH INNING

Kansas City—Brett lined a single to right. White belted Andujar's first pitch to him over the left-center field wall for a home run, boosting the Royals' lead to 4-0. Campbell replaced Andujar on the mound for the Cardinals. Sheridan bounced out, Clark unassisted. Sundberg walked. Balboni struck out. Biancalana also struck out. Two runs, two hits, no errors, one left.

St. Louis—Pendleton grounded to White. Porter flied to Wilson. Landrum singled to right. Jorgensen, batting for Campbell, hit a tap in front of the plate and was thrown out, Sundberg to Balboni. No runs, one hit, no errors, one left.

### SIXTH INNING

**Kansas City**—Horton came in to pitch for the Cardinals. Saberhagen grounded to Ozzie Smith, who made a fine play behind second base and threw to Clark for the out. Lonnie Smith grounded to Ozzie Smith. Wilson struck out. No runs, no hits, no errors, none left.

**St. Louis**—McGee popped to Brett. Ozzie Smith lined a single to center. Herr lined a single to right, Ozzie Smith stopping at second. Clark grounded a single up the middle, scoring Ozzie Smith and cutting Kansas City's lead to 4-1, with Herr stopping at second. Van Slyke flied to Wilson in short center. Pendleton line hard to Sheridan. One run, three hits, no errors, two left.

### SEVENTH INNING

**Kansas City**—Brett walked. Brett then advanced to second on a balk by Horton. White doubled into the left-field corner, scoring Brett to increase the Royals' lead to 5-1. Sheridan grounded to Ozzie Smith, White holding second. Horton snared Sundberg's liner back to the mound. Balboni was walked intentionally. Biancalana lined a single to right, White scoring to make the score 6-1, with Balboni going to third and Biancalana to second on Van Slyke's throw to the plate. Saberhagen grounded to Ozzie Smith. Two runs, two hits, no errors, two left.

**St. Louis**—Porter popped to Biancalana. Landrum struck out. Harper, batting for Horton, grounded to White. No runs, no hits, no errors, none left.

### EIGHTH INNING

**Kansas City**—Dayley came in to pitch for the Cardinals. Lonnie Smith struck out. Wilson was called out on strikes. Brett walked. White fouled to Clark. No runs, no hits, no errors, one left.

**St. Louis**—Lynn Jones replaced Lonnie Smith in left field for the Royals. McGee grounded to White. Ozzie Smith hit a smash to Brett, who ranged to his left to make a good play and threw to Balboni for the out. Herr lined hard to Wilson. No runs, no hits, no errors, none left.

### NINTH INNING

**Kansas City**—Sheridan grounded to Ozzie Smith. Sundberg walked. Balboni flied to Van Slyke. Biancalana popped to Clark. No runs, no hits, no errors, one left.

**St. Louis**—Clark struck out. Van Slyke also struck out. Pendleton lined to Lynn Jones. No runs, no hits, no errors, none left.

**John Tudor was splendid in the Cards' 3-0 victory in Game 4.**

# Game 4

**At St. Louis**
**October 23**

| Kansas City (A.L.) | AB. | R. | H. | PO. | A. | E. |
|---|---|---|---|---|---|---|
| L. Smith, lf | 4 | 0 | 0 | 1 | 1 | 0 |
| Wilson, cf | 4 | 0 | 1 | 1 | 0 | 0 |
| Brett, 3b | 4 | 0 | 1 | 0 | 3 | 0 |
| White, 2b | 4 | 0 | 0 | 2 | 3 | 0 |
| Sundberg, c | 4 | 0 | 1 | 7 | 1 | 0 |
| Motley, rf | 4 | 0 | 0 | 0 | 0 | 0 |
| Balboni, 1b | 2 | 0 | 1 | 11 | 1 | 0 |
| Biancalana, ss | 2 | 0 | 0 | 0 | 4 | 0 |
| bMcRae | 1 | 0 | 0 | 0 | 0 | 0 |
| Concepcion, ss | 0 | 0 | 0 | 0 | 0 | 0 |
| Black, p | 1 | 0 | 0 | 1 | 2 | 1 |
| aWathan | 1 | 0 | 0 | 0 | 0 | 0 |
| Beckwith, p | 0 | 0 | 0 | 0 | 0 | 0 |
| cL. Jones | 1 | 0 | 1 | 0 | 0 | 0 |
| Quisenberry, p | 0 | 0 | 0 | 1 | 1 | 0 |
| Totals | 32 | 0 | 5 | 24 | 16 | 1 |

| St. Louis (N.L.) | AB. | R. | H. | PO. | A. | E. |
|---|---|---|---|---|---|---|
| McGee, cf | 3 | 1 | 2 | 2 | 0 | 0 |
| O. Smith, ss | 2 | 0 | 0 | 0 | 0 | 0 |
| Herr, 2b | 3 | 0 | 1 | 0 | 2 | 0 |
| Clark, 1b | 3 | 0 | 1 | 10 | 0 | 0 |
| Landrum, lf | 4 | 1 | 1 | 1 | 0 | 0 |
| Cedeno, rf | 3 | 0 | 0 | 4 | 0 | 0 |
| Van Slyke, rf | 0 | 0 | 0 | 0 | 0 | 0 |
| Pendleton, 3b | 3 | 1 | 1 | 1 | 2 | 0 |
| Nieto, c | 1 | 0 | 0 | 9 | 0 | 0 |
| Tudor, p | 3 | 0 | 0 | 0 | 1 | 0 |
| Totals | 25 | 3 | 6 | 27 | 5 | 0 |

| | | | | | | |
|---|---|---|---|---|---|---|
| Kansas City | 0 0 0 | 0 0 0 | 0 0 0—0 |
| St. Louis | 0 1 1 | 0 1 0 | 0 0 x—3 |

| Kansas City | IP. | H. | R. | ER. | BB. | SO. |
|---|---|---|---|---|---|---|
| Black (L) | 5 | 4 | 3 | 3 | 3 | 3 |
| Beckwith | 2 | 1 | 0 | 0 | 0 | 3 |
| Quisenberry | 1 | 1 | 0 | 0 | 2 | 0 |

| St. Louis | IP. | H. | R. | ER. | BB. | SO. |
|---|---|---|---|---|---|---|
| Tudor (W) | 9 | 5 | 0 | 0 | 1 | 8 |

Bases on balls—Off Black 3 (McGee, O. Smith, Nieto), off Quisenberry 2 (Herr, Clark), off Tudor 1 (Balboni).

Strikeouts—By Black 3 (Herr, Clark, Tudor), by Beckwith 3 (Clark, Nieto, Tudor), by Tudor 8 (L. Smith 2, Brett 2, Motley, Biancalana, Black, Wathan).

Game-winning RBI—Landrum. aStruck out for Black in sixth. bGrounded into forceout for Biancalana in seventh. cDoubled for Beckwith in eighth. Runs batted in—McGee, Landrum, Nieto. Two-base hits—Herr, L. Jones. Three-base hit—Pendleton. Home runs—Landrum, McGee. Caught stealing—O. Smith. Sacrifice hits—Nieto, O. Smith. Wild pitch—Quisenberry. Double play—Black and White. Left on bases—Kansas City 6, St. Louis 5. Umpires—Engel (N.L.) plate, Shulock (A.L.) first, Quick (N.L.) second, Denkinger (A.L.) third, B. Williams (N.L.) left, McKean (A.L.) right. Time—2:19. Attendance—53,634.

## FIRST INNING

**Kansas City**—Lonnie Smith fouled out to Nieto on a two-strike bunt attempt. Wilson lined a single to center. Brett grounded out, Clark unassisted, with Wilson advancing to second. White flied to Cedeno. No runs, one hit, no errors, one left.

**St. Louis**—McGee smashed a one-hopper to Brett, who threw to Balboni for the out. Ozzie Smith walked on four pitches. Smith was picked off first and trapped in a rundown before being tagged out, Black to Balboni to Biancalana to Sundberg covering first. Herr struck out. No runs, no hits, no errors, none left.

## SECOND INNING

**Kansas City**—Sundberg lined to Cedeno. Motley struck out. Balboni grounded to Pendleton. No runs, no hits, no errors, none left.

**St. Louis**—Clark struck out. Landrum clouted Black's 3-2 delivery to the opposite field near the right-field foul pole for a home run, giving the Cardinals a 1-0 lead. Cedeno grounded to Biancalana. Pendleton grounded to White. One run, one hit, no errors, none left.

## THIRD INNING

**Kansas City**—Biancalana was called out on strikes. Black also struck out. Lonnie Smith became Tudor's third straight strikeout victim. No runs, no hits, no errors, none left.

**St. Louis**—Nieto walked. Tudor bunted into a double play, Black catching the pop-up for one out and then throwing to White covering first to retire Nieto. McGee hit a 1-2 pitch over the left-field wall for a home run to increase the Cardinals lead to 2-0. Ozzie Smith grounded to Biancalana, who went to his left, dived and then recovered to throw to Balboni for the out. One run, one hit, no errors, none left.

## FOURTH INNING

**Kansas City**—Wilson bounced out, Clark unassisted. Brett struck out. White grounded to Herr. No runs, no hits, no errors, none left.

**St. Louis**—Herr grounded to Brett. Clark singled to left but was thrown out at second when he tried for a double, Lonnie Smith to White. Landrum grounded to Biancalana. No runs, one hit, no errors, none left.

## FIFTH INNING

**Kansas City**—Sundberg hit a sinking liner to right-center, where Cedeno made a nice running catch. Motley grounded to Pendleton, with Clark leaving the base for the wide throw and tagging the runner for the out. Balboni lined a single to left. Biancalana flied to Cedeno, who made the catch near the right-field line. No runs, one hit, no errors, one left.

**St. Louis**—Cedeno popped to Balboni. Pendleton's smash to left-center eluded Wilson and went to the wall for a triple. With Pendleton breaking

for the plate on a 3-2 pitch, Nieto made a successful squeeze bunt, Black barehanding the ball and throwing it wildly past Sundberg to give the Cardinals a 3-0 lead. Nieto advanced to second on Black's error. Tudor then struck out. McGee was walked intentionally. Ozzie Smith flied to Lonnie Smith. One run, one hit, one error, two left.

## SIXTH INNING

**Kansas City**—Wathan batted for Black and struck out. Lonnie Smith popped to Clark. Wilson also popped to Clark. No runs, no hits, no errors, none left.

**St. Louis**—Beckwith came in to pitch for the Royals. Herr doubled off the right-field wall. Clark struck out. Brett went to his left to field Landrum's grounder and threw to Balboni for the out, Herr holding second. Cedeno flied to Wilson. No runs, one hit, no errors, one left.

## SEVENTH INNING

**Kansas City**—Van Slyke took over for Cedeno in right field for the Cardinals. Brett looped a single to left. White flied to McGee deep in center field, Brett holding first. Sundberg singled to right, Brett stopping at second. Motley flied to Landrum. Balboni walked, loading the bases. McRae batted for Biancalana and grounded to Pendleton, who stepped on third base to force Sundberg for the final out. No runs, two hits, no errors, three left.

**St. Louis**—Concepcion went in to play shortstop for the Royals. Pendleton grounded to White, who ranged to his left, whirled and threw to Balboni for the out. Nieto struck out. Tudor also struck out. No runs, no hits, no errors, none left.

## EIGHTH INNING

**Kansas City**—Lynn Jones, batting for Beckwith, lined a double to left-center. Lonnie Smith struck out. Wilson grounded to Herr, Jones advancing to third. Brett struck out. No runs, one hit, no errors, one left.

**St. Louis**—Quisenberry came in to pitch for the Royals. McGee looped a single to left. Ozzie Smith sacrificed McGee to second, Quisenberry to Balboni. Herr was walked intentionally. McGee tried to score from second base on a wild pitch by Quisenberry but was tagged out at the plate, Sundberg to Quisenberry, Herr advancing to third. Clark walked. Landrum bounced to White. No runs, one hit, no errors, two left.

## NINTH INNING

**Kansas City**—White bounced back to the mound, Tudor throwing to Clark for the out. Sundberg fouled to Clark. Motley flied to McGee. No runs, no hits, no errors, none left.

# Game 5

**At St. Louis**
**October 24**

| Kansas City (A.L.) | AB. | R. | H. | PO. | A. | E. |
|---|---|---|---|---|---|---|
| L. Smith, lf | 4 | 2 | 2 | 2 | 0 | 0 |
| L. Jones, lf | 0 | 0 | 0 | 0 | 0 | 0 |
| Wilson, cf | 5 | 0 | 2 | 2 | 0 | 0 |
| Brett, 3b | 4 | 0 | 1 | 1 | 1 | 1 |
| Pryor, 3b | 0 | 0 | 0 | 0 | 1 | 0 |
| White, 2b | 5 | 1 | 0 | 2 | 2 | 0 |
| Sheridan, rf | 5 | 0 | 2 | 2 | 0 | 0 |
| Balboni, 1b | 4 | 0 | 1 | 11 | 1 | 0 |
| Sundberg, c | 4 | 2 | 1 | 6 | 0 | 0 |
| Biancalana, ss | 3 | 1 | 2 | 1 | 5 | 0 |
| Jackson, p | 4 | 0 | 0 | 0 | 2 | 1 |
| Totals | 38 | 6 | 11 | 27 | 12 | 2 |

| St. Louis (N.L.) | AB. | R. | H. | PO. | A. | E. |
|---|---|---|---|---|---|---|
| McGee, cf | 4 | 0 | 2 | 0 | 0 | 0 |
| O. Smith, ss | 3 | 0 | 0 | 1 | 1 | 1 |
| Herr, 2b | 4 | 1 | 1 | 2 | 1 | 0 |
| Clark, 1b | 3 | 0 | 1 | 5 | 2 | 0 |
| Landrum, lf | 4 | 0 | 1 | 1 | 0 | 0 |
| Cedeno, rf | 4 | 0 | 0 | 1 | 0 | 0 |
| Pendleton, 3b | 3 | 0 | 0 | 1 | 4 | 0 |
| Nieto, c | 4 | 0 | 0 | 14 | 1 | 0 |
| Forsch, p | 0 | 0 | 0 | 0 | 0 | 0 |
| Horton, p | 1 | 0 | 0 | 1 | 0 | 0 |
| Campbell, p | 0 | 0 | 0 | 1 | 0 | 0 |
| aDeJesus | 1 | 0 | 0 | 0 | 0 | 0 |
| Worrell, p | 0 | 0 | 0 | 0 | 0 | 0 |
| bHarper | 1 | 0 | 0 | 0 | 0 | 0 |
| Lahti, p | 0 | 0 | 0 | 0 | 0 | 0 |
| Totals | 32 | 1 | 5 | 27 | 9 | 1 |

Kansas City .......................... 1 3 0  0 0 0  0 1 1—6
St. Louis.............................. 1 0 0  0 0 0  0 0 0—1

| Kansas City | IP. | H. | R. | ER. | BB. | SO. |
|---|---|---|---|---|---|---|
| Jackson (W) | 9 | 5 | 1 | 1 | 3 | 5 |

| St. Louis | IP. | H. | R. | ER. | BB. | SO. |
|---|---|---|---|---|---|---|
| Forsch (L) | 1⅔ | 5 | 4 | 4 | 1 | 2 |
| Horton | 2 | 1 | 0 | 0 | 3 | 4 |
| Campbell | 1⅓ | 0 | 0 | 0 | 0 | 2 |
| Worrell | 2 | 0 | 0 | 0 | 0 | 6 |
| Lahti | 2 | 5 | 2 | 1 | 0 | 1 |

Bases on balls—Off Jackson 3 (O. Smith, Clark, Pendleton), off Forsch 1 (L. Smith), off Horton 3 (Brett, Balboni, Biancalana).

Strikeouts—By Jackson 5 (McGee, Pendleton, Nieto, Horton, Harper), by Forsch 2 (Sheridan, Jackson) by Horton 4 (Wilson, White, Sheridan, Jackson), by Campbell 2 (White, Balboni), by Worrell 6 (L. Smith, Wilson, Brett, White, Biancalana, Jackson), by Lahti 1 (L. Smith).

Game-winning RBI—Biancalana.

aFlied out for Campbell in fifth. bStruck out for Worrell in seventh. Runs batted in—Wilson 2, White, Sheridan, Biancalana, Clark. Two-base hits—Herr, Clark, Sundberg, Sheridan. Three-base hit—Wilson. Stolen base—L. Smith. Caught stealing—McGee. Double play—Pendleton and Herr. Left on bases—Kansas City 9, St. Louis 7. Umpires—Shulock (A.L.) plate, Quick (N.L.) first, Denkinger (A.L.) second, B. Williams (N.L.) third, McKean (A.L.) left, Engel (N.L.) right. Time—2:52. Attendance—53,634.

### FIRST INNING

**Kansas City**—Lonnie Smith grounded a single to left. Wilson lined a single to left, Smith stopping at second. Brett flied to Landrum in fairly deep left-center, Smith and Wilson both tagging up and advancing one base after the catch. White grounded to Ozzie Smith, Lonnie Smith scoring to give the Royals a 1-0 lead and Wilson holding second. Sheridan struck out. One run, two hits, no errors, one left.

**St. Louis**—McGee bounced back to the mound, Jackson throwing to Balboni for the out. Ozzie Smith flied to Wilson. Herr hit a liner down the right-field line that bounced into the stands for a ground-rule double. Clark belted the first pitch from Jackson on one hop up against the right-field fence, Herr scoring to tie the game, 1-1. Landrum fouled to Balboni. One run, two hits, no errors, one left.

### SECOND INNING

**Kansas City**—Balboni flied to Cedeno, who made the catch at the right-field line. Sundberg blooped a ball to short left and Landrum, after misjudging the ball, just missed making a diving catch, Sundberg getting a double. Biancalana sin-

gled to right, Sundberg scoring on a close play at the plate as his headfirst slide just beat the tag by Nieto to give the Royals a 2-1 lead. Biancalana went to second on Cedeno's throw. Jackson then was called out on strikes. Lonnie Smith walked. Wilson tripled to right-center, scoring Biancalana and Lonnie Smith to extend the Royals' lead to 4-1. Horton replaced Forsch on the mound for the Cardinals. Brett grounded out, Clark to Horton covering first. Three runs, three hits, no errors, one left.

**St. Louis**—Cedeno popped to White. Pendleton grounded to White. Biancalana fielded Nieto's grounder behind second base and threw to Balboni for the out. No runs, no hits, no errors, none left.

### THIRD INNING

**Kansas City**—White struck out. Sheridan also struck out. Balboni walked. Sundberg grounded into a forceout at second, Herr to Ozzie Smith, No runs, no hits, no errors, one left.

**St. Louis**—Horton struck out. McGee singled to center. McGee went to second on Jackson's wild pickoff attempt. Ozzie Smith walked on four pitches. Herr popped to Balboni. Clark also walked on four pitches, loading the bases. Landrum fouled to Brett. No runs, one hit, one error, three left.

### FOURTH INNING

**Kansas City**—Biancalana walked. Jackson struck out when he bunted foul on the third strike. Lonnie Smith lined a single to right, Biancalana racing to third. With Wilson at the plate, Smith stole second. Wilson then struck out, Nieto throwing to Clark for the out after the catcher dropped the third strike. Brett was walked intentionally, loading the bases. Campbell came in to pitch for the Cardinals. White struck out. No runs, one hit, no errors, three left.

**St. Louis**—Cedeno grounded to Biancalana. Biancalana ranged to his left to field Pendleton's grounder and threw to Balboni for the out. Nieto flied to Lonnie Smith in left-center. No runs, no hits, no errors, none left.

### FIFTH INNING

**Kansas City**—Clark fielded Sheridan's tricky one-hopper and threw to Campbell covering first for the out. Balboni struck out. Sundberg grounded to Pendleton. No runs, no hits, no errors, none left.

**St. Louis**—DeJesus, batting for Campbell, flied to Sheridan. McGee hit a smash past a diving Brett into left field for a single. McGee was picked off and then thrown out attempting to steal, Jackson to Balboni to Biancalana. Ozzie Smith's smash went off Brett's glove and into short left-center for a two-base error. Herr flied to Lonnie Smith. No runs, one hit, one error, one left.

### SIXTH INNING

**Kansas City**—Worrell came in to pitch for the Cardinals. Biancalana struck out. Jackson also struck out. Lonnie Smith became Worrell's third straight strikeout victim. No runs, no hits, no errors, none left.

**St. Louis**—Clark fouled out to Sundberg. Landrum grounded to White. Cedeno grounded to Brett. No runs, no hits, no errors, none left.

### SEVENTH INNING

**Kansas City**—Wilson struck out. Brett also struck out. White struck out, becoming Worrell's sixth consecutive strikeout victim to tie a record set by Hod Eller of Cincinnati in 1919 and equaled by Moe Drabowsky of Baltimore in 1966. No runs, no hits, no errors, none left.

**St. Louis**—Pendleton struck out. Nieto was called out on strikes. Jackson also struck out the side when he fanned Harper, who was batting for Worrell. No runs, no hits, no errors, none left.

### EIGHTH INNING

**Kansas City**—Lahti came in to pitch for the Cardinals. Sheridan lined a single to center. Balboni smashed a single past a diving Pendleton and into left, Sheridan stopping at second. Pendleton fielded Sundberg's one-hopper to his left, tagged Sheridan and threw to Herr at second to double up Balboni. Biancalana lined a single to second, Sundberg stopping at second. Ozzie Smith went behind second to field Jackson's bouncer, but his off-balance throw to Clark was in the dirt for an error, Sundberg scoring to give the Royals a 5-1 lead and Biancalana advancing to third. Lonnie Smith was called out on strikes. One run, three hits, one error, two left.

**St. Louis**—Lynn Jones went in to play left field for the Royals. McGee struck out. Wilson raced to deep center field to make an over-the-shoulder grab of Ozzie Smith's long fly. Herr grounded to Biancalana. No runs, no hits, no errors, none left.

### NINTH INNING

**Kansas City**—Wilson grounded out, Clark unassisted. Brett grounded a single to right. Pendleton made a fine diving stop to his left on White's smash and recovered in time to throw to Herr at second to force Brett. Sheridan's liner went to the left-center field wall for a double, scoring White to boost the Royals' lead to 6-1. Balboni grounded to Pendleton. One run, two hits, no errors, one left.

**St. Louis**—Pryor replaced Brett at third base for the Royals. Clark grounded to Pryor. Landrum hit a high chop down the third-base line and was credited with a single when a charging Pryor could not make the play. Cedeno flied to Sheridan. Pendleton walked. Nieto grounded to Biancalana, who tossed to White covering second to force Pendleton for the final out. No runs, one hit, no errors, two left.

# Game 6

**At Kansas City**
**October 26**

| St. Louis (N.L.) | AB. | R. | H. | PO. | A. | E. |
|---|---|---|---|---|---|---|
| O. Smith, ss | 3 | 0 | 0 | 2 | 3 | 0 |
| McGee, cf | 4 | 0 | 0 | 4 | 0 | 0 |
| Herr, 2b | 4 | 0 | 0 | 1 | 2 | 0 |
| Clark, 1b | 4 | 0 | 0 | 5 | 0 | 0 |
| Landrum, lf | 4 | 0 | 1 | 1 | 0 | 0 |
| Pendleton, 3b | 4 | 1 | 1 | 1 | 1 | 0 |
| Cedeno, rf | 2 | 0 | 1 | 1 | 0 | 0 |
| bVan Slyke, rf | 0 | 0 | 0 | 0 | 0 | 0 |
| Porter, c | 3 | 0 | 1 | 10 | 1 | 0 |
| Cox, p | 2 | 0 | 0 | 0 | 0 | 0 |
| aHarper | 1 | 0 | 1 | 0 | 0 | 0 |
| cLawless | 0 | 0 | 0 | 0 | 0 | 0 |
| Dayley, p | 0 | 0 | 0 | 0 | 0 | 0 |
| Worrell, p | 0 | 0 | 0 | 0 | 1 | 0 |
| Totals | 31 | 1 | 5 | 25 | 8 | 0 |

| Kansas City (A.L.) | AB. | R. | H. | PO. | A. | E. |
|---|---|---|---|---|---|---|
| L. Smith, lf | 4 | 0 | 1 | 0 | 0 | 0 |
| Wilson, cf | 3 | 0 | 1 | 3 | 0 | 0 |
| Brett, 3b | 4 | 0 | 0 | 3 | 4 | 0 |
| White, 2b | 4 | 0 | 1 | 2 | 2 | 0 |
| Sheridan, rf | 3 | 0 | 1 | 2 | 0 | 0 |
| dMotley | 0 | 0 | 0 | 0 | 0 | 0 |
| eOrta | 1 | 0 | 1 | 0 | 0 | 0 |
| Balboni, 1b | 3 | 0 | 2 | 9 | 1 | 0 |
| fConcepcion | 0 | 1 | 0 | 0 | 0 | 0 |
| Sundberg, c | 4 | 1 | 1 | 6 | 0 | 0 |
| Biancalana, ss | 3 | 0 | 1 | 1 | 4 | 0 |

| Kansas City (A.L.) | AB. | R. | H. | PO. | A. | E. |
|---|---|---|---|---|---|---|
| gMcRae | 0 | 0 | 0 | 0 | 0 | 0 |
| hWathan | 0 | 0 | 0 | 0 | 0 | 0 |
| Leibrandt, p | 2 | 0 | 0 | 1 | 0 | 0 |
| Quisenberry, p | 0 | 0 | 0 | 0 | 0 | 0 |
| iIorg | 1 | 0 | 1 | 0 | 0 | 0 |
| Totals | 32 | 2 | 10 | 27 | 11 | 0 |

St. Louis .................................. 0 0 0  0 0 0  0 1 0—1
Kansas City ........................... 0 0 0  0 0 0  0 0 2—2
One out when winning run scored.

| St. Louis | IP. | H. | R. | ER. | BB. | SO. |
|---|---|---|---|---|---|---|
| Cox | 7 | 7 | 0 | 0 | 1 | 8 |
| Dayley | 1 | 0 | 0 | 0 | 1 | 2 |
| Worrell (L) | ⅓ | 3 | 2 | 2 | 1 | 0 |

| Kansas City | IP. | H. | R. | ER. | BB. | SO. |
|---|---|---|---|---|---|---|
| Leibrandt | 7⅔ | 4 | 1 | 1 | 2 | 4 |
| Quisenberry (W) | 1⅓ | 1 | 0 | 0 | 0 | 1 |

Bases on balls—Off Cox 1 (Balboni), off Dayley 1 (Wilson), off Worrell 1 (McRae), off Leibrandt 2 (Cedeno, O. Smith).

Strikeouts—By Cox 8 (Brett, White, Sheridan 2, Sundberg 2, Leibrandt 2), by Dayley 2 (L. Smith, Brett), by Leibrandt 4 (Herr, Clark, Cedeno, Porter), by Quisenberry 1 (Clark).

Game-winning RBI—Iorg.

aSingled in one run for Cox in eighth. bRan for Cedeno in eighth. cRan for Harper in eighth. dAnnounced as a pinch-hitter for Sheridan in ninth. eSingled for Motley in ninth. fRan for Balboni and scored in ninth. gWalked intentionally for Biancalana in ninth. hRan for McRae in ninth. iSingled in two runs for Quisenberry in ninth. Runs batted in—Harper, Iorg 2. Two-base hit—L. Smith. Caught stealing—White. Sacrifice hit—Leibrandt. Passed ball—Porter. Double plays—Biancalana, White and Balboni; Herr, O. Smith and Clark. Left on bases—St. Louis 5, Kansas City 9. Umpires—Quick (N.L.) plate, Denkinger (A.L.) first, B. Williams (N.L.) second, McKean (A.L.) third, Engel (N.L.) left, Shulock (A.L.) right. Time—2:47. Attendance—41,628.

### FIRST INNING

**St. Louis**—Brett temporarily fumbled Ozzie Smith's smash but recovered in time to throw him out at first. McGee flied to Wilson. Herr struck out. No runs, no hits, no errors, none left.

**Kansas City**—Lonnie Smith lined a double down the left-field line. Wilson grounded to Herr, Smith advancing to third. Brett was called out on strikes. White grounded to Ozzie Smith. No runs, one hit, no errors, one left.

### SECOND INNING

**St. Louis**—Clark popped to Brett. Landrum flied to Sheridan. Pendleton grounded to Brett, who charged in to field the one-hopper and make the throw to Balboni. No runs, no hits, no errors, none left.

**Kansas City**—Sheridan struck out. Balboni lined a single to center. Sundberg was called out on strikes. Ozzie Smith went behind second base to make a diving stop of Biancalana's grounder and then flipped to Herr to force Balboni at second. No runs, one hit, no errors, one left.

### THIRD INNING

**St. Louis**—Cedeno struck out. Porter fouled to Brett. Cox grounded to Balboni, who tossed to Leibrandt covering first for the out. No runs, no hits, no errors, none left.

**Kansas City**—Leibrandt struck out. Lonnie Smith flied to McGee near the warning track in center field. Wilson flied to Landrum. No runs, no hits, no errors, none left.

### FOURTH INNING

**St. Louis**—Ozzie Smith fouled out to Sundberg. Biancalana went behind second base to field McGee's grounder and threw to Balboni for the out. Herr bounced to Brett. No runs, no hits, no errors, none left.

**Kansas City**—Brett hit a towering drive to right field that Cedeno caught against the fence. White bunted down the third-base line and easily beat Pendleton's throw to first base for a single. White was caught stealing, Porter to Ozzie Smith. Sheridan singled past a diving Herr in the hole at second. Balboni lined to McGee. No runs, two hits, no errors, one left.

### FIFTH INNING

**St. Louis**—Clark popped to White, who made the catch in short center field. Landrum flied to Sheridan. Pendleton grounded to Brett. No runs, no hits, no errors, none left.

**Kansas City**—Sundberg lined a single to left. Biancalana flied to McGee in short center. Leibrandt sacrificed Sundberg to second, Clark tagging Leibrandt for the unassisted putout. Lonnie Smith grounded to Pendleton. No runs, one hit, no errors, one left.

### SIXTH INNING

**St. Louis**—Cedeno ended Leibrandt's hopes for a perfect game when he looped a single to left. Porter blooped a single to right, Cedeno advancing to second. Cox tried to sacrifice but popped the bunt in the air to Brett, both runners holding. Ozzie Smith grounded into a double play, Biancalana to White to Balboni. No runs, two hits, no errors, one left.

**Kansas City**—Wilson lined a single to right. Brett bounced into a double play, Herr to Ozzie Smith to Clark. White struck out. No runs, one hit, no errors, none left.

### SEVENTH INNING

**St. Louis**—Biancalana made a backhanded stab of McGee's grounder in the hole and beat McGee by an eyelash at first with his strong throw to Balboni. Biancalana then went behind second base to field Herr's grounder and threw to Balboni for another out. Clark struck out. No runs, no hits, no errors, none left.

**Kansas City**—Sheridan struck out. Balboni walked. Sundberg struck out. Biancalana singled to right, Balboni stopping at second. Leibrandt struck out on a check swing. No runs, one hit, no errors, two left.

### EIGHTH INNING

**St. Louis**—Landrum flied to Wilson. Pendleton grounded a single to right. Cedeno walked. Porter was called out on strikes. Harper, batting for Cox, looped a single to center, Pendleton scoring to give the Cardinals a 1-0 lead and Cedeno stopping at second. Van Slyke came in to run for Cedeno. Ozzie Smith walked to load the bases. Quisenberry replaced Leibrandt on the mound for the Royals. Lawless came in to run for Harper at second base. McGee grounded to White, who threw to Biancalana at second to force Ozzie Smith. One run, two hits, no errors, three left.

**Kansas City**—Van Slyke stayed in the game and played right field and Dayley came in to pitch for the Cardinals. Lonnie Smith struck out. Wilson walked. Brett struck out. White flied to McGee. No runs, no hits, no errors, one left.

### NINTH INNING

**St. Louis**—Herr grounded out, Balboni unassisted. Clark struck out. Landrum was credited with an infield hit when no play could be made on

his tapper in front of the plate. Pendleton flied to Wilson. No runs, one hit, no errors, one left.

**Kansas City**—After Motley was announced as a pinch-hitter for Sheridan, Cardinals Manager Herzog replaced Dayley on the mound with Worrell. Kansas City Manager Howser then switched batters from Motley to Orta. Orta was credited with a single when he was ruled safe on a disputed call after Clark fielded his grounder and threw to Worrell covering first. After getting another chance when his foul pop near the dugout was messed up by Clark, Balboni lined a single to left, Orta stopping at second. Concepcion ran for Balboni. Sundberg, attempting to sacrifice, bunted back to Worrell, who threw to Pendleton at third to force Orta. McRae batted for Biancalana and was given an intentional walk after both runners advanced on a passed ball by Porter. Wathan ran for McRae. Iorg, batting for Quisenberry, lined a single to right, scoring Concepcion and Sundberg to give the Royals a 2-1 victory. Two runs, three hits, no errors, two left.

## Game 7

**At Kansas City**
**October 27**

| St. Louis (N.L.) | AB. | R. | H. | PO. | A. | E. |
|---|---|---|---|---|---|---|
| O. Smith, ss | 4 | 0 | 1 | 2 | 2 | 0 |
| McGee, cf | 4 | 0 | 0 | 5 | 0 | 0 |
| Herr, 2b | 4 | 0 | 0 | 2 | 2 | 0 |
| Clark, 1b | 4 | 0 | 1 | 4 | 1 | 0 |
| Van Slyke, rf | 4 | 0 | 1 | 5 | 0 | 0 |
| Pendleton, 3b | 3 | 0 | 1 | 1 | 1 | 0 |
| Landrum, lf | 2 | 0 | 1 | 0 | 0 | 0 |
| Andujar, p | 0 | 0 | 0 | 0 | 0 | 0 |
| Forsch, p | 0 | 0 | 0 | 0 | 0 | 0 |
| aBraun | 1 | 0 | 0 | 0 | 0 | 0 |
| Dayley, p | 0 | 0 | 0 | 0 | 0 | 0 |
| Porter, c | 3 | 0 | 0 | 4 | 0 | 0 |
| Tudor, p | 1 | 0 | 0 | 0 | 0 | 0 |
| Campbell, p | 0 | 0 | 0 | 0 | 0 | 0 |
| Lahti, p | 0 | 0 | 0 | 0 | 0 | 0 |
| Horton, p | 0 | 0 | 0 | 0 | 0 | 0 |
| Jorgensen, lf | 2 | 0 | 0 | 1 | 0 | 0 |
| Totals | 32 | 0 | 5 | 24 | 6 | 0 |

| Kansas City (A.L.) | AB. | R. | H. | PO. | A. | E. |
|---|---|---|---|---|---|---|
| L. Smith, lf | 3 | 2 | 1 | 3 | 0 | 0 |
| L. Jones, lf | 1 | 0 | 0 | 1 | 0 | 0 |
| Wilson, cf | 5 | 1 | 2 | 7 | 0 | 0 |
| Brett, 3b | 5 | 2 | 4 | 2 | 0 | 0 |
| White, 2b | 4 | 1 | 1 | 0 | 5 | 0 |
| Sundberg, c | 3 | 1 | 1 | 2 | 0 | 0 |
| Balboni, 1b | 4 | 2 | 2 | 7 | 0 | 0 |
| Motley, rf | 4 | 1 | 3 | 3 | 0 | 0 |
| Biancalana, ss | 3 | 0 | 0 | 2 | 1 | 0 |
| Saberhagen, p | 4 | 1 | 0 | 0 | 0 | 0 |
| Totals | 36 | 11 | 14 | 27 | 6 | 0 |

| | | | | | | |
|---|---|---|---|---|---|---|
| St. Louis | 0 0 0 | 0 0 0 | 0 0 0— 0 |
| Kansas City | 0 2 3 | 0 6 0 | 0 0 x—11 |

| St. Louis | IP. | H. | R. | ER. | BB. | SO. |
|---|---|---|---|---|---|---|
| Tudor (L) | 2⅓ | 3 | 5 | 5 | 4 | 1 |
| Campbell | 1⅔* | 4 | 1 | 1 | 1 | 1 |
| Lahti | ⅔ | 4 | 4 | 4 | 0 | 1 |
| Horton | 0* | 1 | 1 | 1 | 0 | 0 |
| Andujar | 0† | 1 | 0 | 0 | 1 | 0 |
| Forsch | 1⅓ | 1 | 0 | 0 | 0 | 1 |
| Dayley | 2 | 0 | 0 | 0 | 0 | 0 |

| Kansas City | IP. | H. | R. | ER. | BB. | SO. |
|---|---|---|---|---|---|---|
| Saberhagen (W) | 9 | 5 | 0 | 0 | 0 | 2 |

*Pitched to one batter in fifth.
†Pitched to two batters in fifth.

Bases on balls—Off Tudor 4 (Balboni, L. Smith,

White, Sundberg), off Campbell 1 (Biancalana), off Andujar 1 (Sundberg).

Strikeouts—By Tudor 1 (Saberhagen), by Campbell 1 (Saberhagen), by Lahti 1 (Biancalana), by Forsch 1 (Saberhagen), by Saberhagen 2 (Van Slyke, Tudor).

Game-winning RBI—Motley.

aFlied out for Forsch in seventh. Runs batted in—L. Smith 2, Wilson, White, Sundberg, Balboni 2, Motley 3. Two-base hit—L. Smith. Home run—Motley. Stolen bases—L. Smith, Brett, Wilson. Wild pitch—Forsch. Double plays—Pendleton, Herr and Clark; Herr, O. Smith and Clark. Left on bases—St. Louis 5, Kansas City 7. Umpires—Denkinger (A.L.) plate, B. Williams (N.L.) first, McKean (A.L.) second, Engel (N.L.) third, Shulock (A.L.) left, Quick (N.L.) right. Time—2:46. Attendance—41,658.

### FIRST INNING

**St. Louis**—Ozzie Smith flied to Wilson. Wilson got a late jump but recovered in time to catch McGee's fly ball in short center. Herr flied to Biancalana, who ranged into short left to make the catch. No runs, no hits, no errors, none left.

**Kansas City**—Lonnie Smith flied to Van Slyke. Wilson grounded to Ozzie Smith. Brett lined a single to right. White flied to McGee, who made the catch in deep center field. No runs, one hit, no errors, one left.

### SECOND INNING

**St. Louis**—Clark lined a single to right. Van Slyke struck out. Pendleton flied to Wilson. Landrum popped to Brett. No runs, one hit, no errors, one left.

**Kansas City**—Sundberg flied to McGee. Balboni walked on a 3-2 delivery by Tudor. After breaking his bat on a long drive that hooked just foul, Motley sent another 3-2 pitch deep into the left-field bleachers for a home run to give the Royals a 2-0 lead. Biancalana lined hard to Pendleton. Saberhagen struck out. Two runs, one hit, no errors, none left.

### THIRD INNING

**St. Louis**—Porter popped to Lonnie Smith in short left. Tudor struck out trying to bunt. Ozzie Smith grounded to White. No runs, no hits, no errors, none left.

**Kansas City**—Lonnie Smith walked. Wilson flied to Van Slyke. Brett was credited with a hit on a check-swing tap down the third-base line, Smith advancing to second. With White at the plate, Smith and Brett executed a double steal. White walked on a 3-2 delivery to load the bases. Sundberg walked, forcing home Lonnie Smith to give the Royals a 3-0 lead. Campbell replaced Tudor on the mound for the Cardinals. Balboni bounced a single through the hole and into left field, scoring Brett and White to increase Kansas City's lead to 5-0. Motley grounded out, Clark unassisted, Sundberg going to third and Balboni to second on the play. Biancalana was walked intentionally to load the bases. Saberhagen struck out. Three runs, two hits, no errors, three left.

### FOURTH INNING

**St. Louis**—McGee grounded to White. Herr flied to Lonnie Smith. Clark grounded to Biancalana. No runs, no hits, no errors, none left.

**Kansas City**—Lonnie Smith flied to Van Slyke. Wilson lined a single to center. Brett lined a single to left, Wilson stopping at second. Wilson stole third base without a throw. White grounded into a double play, Pendleton to Herr to Clark. No runs, two hits, no errors, one left.

### FIFTH INNING

**St. Louis**—Van Slyke lined to Wilson. Pendleton flied to Lonnie Smith. Landrum grounded a single to left. Porter flied to Wilson. No runs, one hit, no errors, one left.

**Kansas City**—Sundberg lined a single to right. Lahti replaced Campbell on the mound for the Cardinals. Balboni grounded a single to left, Sundberg stopping at second. Motley singled to right-center, Sundberg scoring to give the Royals a 6-0 lead and Balboni stopping at second. Biancalana struck out. Saberhagen, attempting to sacrifice, forced Motley at second base, Clark to Ozzie Smith, Balboni advancing to third. Lonnie Smith doubled into the left-field corner, scoring Balboni and Saberhagen to give the Royals an 8-0 lead as Smith went to third on the throw to the plate. Wilson beat out a high hopper behind second base for a single, Lonnie Smith scoring to extend the Royals' lead to 9-0. Horton relieved Lahti for the Cardinals. Brett singled to center, Wilson going to third. With the count 2-0 on White, Andujar was brought in to pitch for the Cardinals and Jorgensen went in to play left field. White lined a single to left off the tip of Pendleton's glove, Wilson scoring to make it 10-0 and Brett stopping at second. With a 2-2 count on Sundberg, Andujar disputed an inside pitch. St. Louis Manager Herzog subsequently was ejected for arguing the call. When Andujar's next delivery also came inside and was ruled ball four by plate umpire Denkinger, loading the bases, the pitcher stormed off the mound, bumped into Denkinger and was ejected. Forsch became the Cardinals' fifth pitcher of the inning. Forsch's first delivery was a wild pitch, Brett scoring to boost the Royals' lead to 11-0. Balboni flied to McGee. Six runs, seven hits, no errors, two left.

### SIXTH INNING

**St. Louis**—Lynn Jones came in to play left field for the Royals. Jorgensen grounded to White, who made a nice backhanded stop. McGee singled to left-center. McGee flied to Motley. Herr popped to Biancalana. No runs, one hit, no errors, one left.

**Kansas City**—Motley lined a single to center. Biancalana grounded into a double play, Herr to Ozzie Smith to Clark. Saberhagen was called out on strikes. No runs, one hit, no errors, none left.

### SEVENTH INNING

**St. Louis**—Clark flied to Lynn Jones on the warning track in left field. Van Slyke singled to right. Pendleton singled to right, Van Slyke stopping at second. Braun batted for Forsch and flied to Wilson, Van Slyke advancing to third after the catch. Porter flied deep to Motley in right-center. No runs, two hits, no errors, two left.

**Kansas City**—Dayley came in to pitch for the Cardinals. Lynn Jones flied to Van Slyke. Wilson flied to McGee in deep center field. Brett also flied to McGee. No runs, no hits, no errors, none left.

### EIGHTH INNING

**St. Louis**—Jorgensen grounded out, Balboni unassisted. Ozzie Smith fouled to Brett. McGee grounded to White. No runs, no hits, no errors, none left.

**Kansas City**—White flied to Jorgensen. Sundberg popped to Herr. Balboni flied to Van Slyke. No runs, no hits, no errors, none left.

### NINTH INNING

**St. Louis**—Herr grounded to White. Clark flied to Wilson. Van Slyke flied to Motley on the warning track in right-center. No runs, no hits, no errors, none left.

## KANSAS CITY ROYALS' BATTING AND FIELDING AVERAGES

| Player—Position | G. | AB. | R. | H. | TB. | 2B. | 3B. | HR. | RBI. | BB. | IBB. | SO. | B.A. | PO. | A. | E. | F.A. |
|---|---|---|---|---|---|---|---|---|---|---|---|---|---|---|---|---|---|
| L. Jones, ph-lf | 6 | 3 | 0 | 2 | 5 | 1 | 1 | 0 | 0 | 0 | 0 | 0 | .667 | 4 | 0 | 0 | 1.000 |
| Iorg, ph | 2 | 2 | 0 | 1 | 1 | 0 | 0 | 0 | 2 | 0 | 0 | 0 | .500 | 0 | 0 | 0 | .000 |
| Brett, 3b | 7 | 27 | 5 | 10 | 11 | 1 | 0 | 0 | 1 | 4 | 2 | 7 | .370 | 10 | 19 | 1 | .967 |
| Wilson, cf | 7 | 30 | 2 | 11 | 13 | 0 | 1 | 0 | 3 | 1 | 0 | 4 | .367 | 19 | 1 | 0 | 1.000 |
| Motley, rf-ph | 5 | 11 | 1 | 4 | 7 | 0 | 0 | 1 | 3 | 0 | 0 | 1 | .364 | 4 | 0 | 0 | 1.000 |
| L. Smith, lf | 7 | 27 | 4 | 9 | 12 | 3 | 0 | 0 | 4 | 3 | 0 | 8 | .333 | 7 | 2 | 0 | 1.000 |
| Orta, ph | 3 | 3 | 0 | 1 | 1 | 0 | 0 | 0 | 0 | 0 | 0 | 0 | .333 | 0 | 0 | 0 | .000 |
| Balboni, 1b | 7 | 25 | 2 | 8 | 8 | 0 | 0 | 0 | 3 | 5 | 1 | 4 | .320 | 70 | 3 | 0 | 1.000 |
| Biancalana, ss | 7 | 18 | 2 | 5 | 5 | 0 | 0 | 0 | 2 | 5 | 1 | 4 | .278 | 6 | 20 | 0 | 1.000 |
| White, 2b | 7 | 28 | 4 | 7 | 13 | 3 | 0 | 1 | 6 | 3 | 0 | 4 | .250 | 10 | 20 | 0 | 1.000 |
| Sundberg, c | 7 | 24 | 6 | 6 | 8 | 2 | 0 | 0 | 1 | 6 | 0 | 4 | .250 | 47 | 3 | 0 | 1.000 |
| Sheridan, ph-rf | 5 | 18 | 0 | 4 | 6 | 2 | 0 | 0 | 1 | 0 | 0 | 7 | .222 | 6 | 0 | 0 | 1.000 |
| Beckwith, p | 1 | 0 | 0 | 0 | 0 | 0 | 0 | 0 | 0 | 0 | 0 | 0 | .000 | 0 | 0 | 0 | .000 |
| Concepcion, pr-ss | 3 | 0 | 1 | 0 | 0 | 0 | 0 | 0 | 0 | 0 | 0 | 0 | .000 | 0 | 2 | 0 | 1.000 |
| Pryor, 3b | 1 | 0 | 0 | 0 | 0 | 0 | 0 | 0 | 0 | 0 | 0 | 0 | .000 | 0 | 1 | 0 | 1.000 |
| Quisenberry, p | 4 | 0 | 0 | 0 | 0 | 0 | 0 | 0 | 0 | 0 | 0 | 0 | .000 | 1 | 1 | 0 | 1.000 |
| Black, p | 2 | 1 | 0 | 0 | 0 | 0 | 0 | 0 | 0 | 0 | 0 | 1 | .000 | 1 | 2 | 1 | .750 |
| McRae, ph | 3 | 1 | 0 | 0 | 0 | 0 | 0 | 0 | 0 | 1 | 1 | 0 | .000 | 0 | 0 | 0 | .000 |
| Wathan, ph-pr | 2 | 1 | 0 | 0 | 0 | 0 | 0 | 0 | 0 | 0 | 0 | 1 | .000 | 0 | 0 | 0 | .000 |
| Leibrandt, p | 2 | 4 | 0 | 0 | 0 | 0 | 0 | 0 | 0 | 0 | 0 | 2 | .000 | 1 | 2 | 0 | 1.000 |
| Jackson, p | 2 | 6 | 0 | 0 | 0 | 0 | 0 | 0 | 0 | 0 | 0 | 5 | .000 | 0 | 4 | 1 | .800 |
| Saberhagen, p | 2 | 7 | 1 | 0 | 0 | 0 | 0 | 0 | 0 | 0 | 0 | 4 | .000 | 0 | 0 | 0 | .000 |
| Totals | 7 | 236 | 28 | 68 | 90 | 12 | 2 | 2 | 26 | 28 | 5 | 56 | .288 | 186 | 80 | 3 | .989 |

Concepcion—Ran for McRae in seventh inning of first game; ran for Balboni in ninth inning of sixth game.

Iorg—Flied out for Concepcion in ninth inning of first game; singled for Quisenberry in ninth inning of sixth game.

L. Jones—Tripled for Biancalana in seventh inning of first game; doubled for Beckwith in eighth inning of fourth game.

McRae—Hit by pitcher for Jackson in seventh inning of first game; hit into forceout for Biancalana in seventh inning of fourth game; walked intentionally for Biancalana in ninth inning of sixth game.

Motley—Announced as pinch-hitter for Sheridan in ninth inning of sixth game.

Orta—Flied out for Black in ninth inning of first game; grounded into double play for Biancalana in ninth inning of second game; singled for Motley in ninth inning of sixth game.

Sheridan—Doubled for Motley in ninth inning of first game.

Wathan—Struck out for Black in sixth inning of fourth game; ran for McRae in ninth inning of sixth game.

## ST. LOUIS CARDINALS' BATTING AND FIELDING AVERAGES

| Player—Position | G. | AB. | R. | H. | TB. | 2B. | 3B. | HR. | RBI. | BB. | IBB. | SO. | B.A. | PO. | A. | E. | F.A. |
|---|---|---|---|---|---|---|---|---|---|---|---|---|---|---|---|---|---|
| Landrum, lf | 7 | 25 | 3 | 9 | 14 | 2 | 0 | 1 | 1 | 0 | 0 | 2 | .360 | 12 | 1 | 0 | 1.000 |
| Pendleton, 3b | 7 | 23 | 3 | 6 | 9 | 1 | 1 | 0 | 3 | 3 | 1 | 2 | .261 | 6 | 14 | 1 | .952 |
| McGee, cf | 7 | 27 | 2 | 7 | 12 | 2 | 0 | 1 | 2 | 1 | 1 | 3 | .259 | 15 | 0 | 0 | 1.000 |
| Harper, ph | 4 | 4 | 0 | 1 | 1 | 0 | 0 | 0 | 1 | 0 | 0 | 1 | .250 | 0 | 0 | 0 | .000 |
| Clark, 1b | 7 | 25 | 1 | 6 | 8 | 2 | 0 | 0 | 4 | 3 | 0 | 9 | .240 | 49 | 4 | 0 | 1.000 |
| Herr, 2b | 7 | 26 | 2 | 4 | 6 | 2 | 0 | 0 | 0 | 2 | 1 | 2 | .154 | 11 | 13 | 0 | 1.000 |
| Cedeno, rf | 5 | 15 | 1 | 2 | 3 | 1 | 0 | 0 | 1 | 2 | 1 | 2 | .133 | 9 | 0 | 0 | 1.000 |
| Porter, c | 5 | 15 | 0 | 2 | 2 | 0 | 0 | 0 | 0 | 2 | 1 | 5 | .133 | 36 | 4 | 0 | 1.000 |
| Van Slyke, rf-ph-pr | 6 | 11 | 0 | 1 | 1 | 0 | 0 | 0 | 0 | 0 | 0 | 5 | .091 | 8 | 0 | 0 | 1.000 |
| O. Smith, ss | 7 | 23 | 1 | 2 | 2 | 0 | 0 | 0 | 0 | 4 | 0 | 0 | .087 | 10 | 16 | 1 | .963 |
| Campbell, p | 3 | 0 | 0 | 0 | 0 | 0 | 0 | 0 | 0 | 0 | 0 | 0 | .000 | 1 | 0 | 0 | 1.000 |
| Dayley, p | 4 | 0 | 0 | 0 | 0 | 0 | 0 | 0 | 0 | 0 | 0 | 0 | .000 | 0 | 0 | 0 | .000 |
| Forsch, p | 2 | 0 | 0 | 0 | 0 | 0 | 0 | 0 | 0 | 0 | 0 | 0 | .000 | 0 | 0 | 0 | .000 |
| Lahti, p | 3 | 0 | 0 | 0 | 0 | 0 | 0 | 0 | 0 | 0 | 0 | 0 | .000 | 0 | 0 | 0 | .000 |
| Lawless, pr | 1 | 0 | 0 | 0 | 0 | 0 | 0 | 0 | 0 | 0 | 0 | 0 | .000 | 0 | 0 | 0 | .000 |
| Andujar, p | 2 | 1 | 0 | 0 | 0 | 0 | 0 | 0 | 0 | 0 | 0 | 1 | .000 | 0 | 1 | 0 | 1.000 |
| Braun, ph | 1 | 1 | 0 | 0 | 0 | 0 | 0 | 0 | 0 | 0 | 0 | 0 | .000 | 0 | 0 | 0 | .000 |
| DeJesus, ph | 1 | 1 | 0 | 0 | 0 | 0 | 0 | 0 | 0 | 0 | 0 | 0 | .000 | 0 | 0 | 0 | .000 |
| Horton, p | 3 | 1 | 0 | 0 | 0 | 0 | 0 | 0 | 0 | 0 | 0 | 1 | .000 | 2 | 0 | 0 | 1.000 |
| Worrell, p | 3 | 1 | 0 | 0 | 0 | 0 | 0 | 0 | 0 | 0 | 0 | 1 | .000 | 0 | 1 | 0 | 1.000 |
| Jorgensen, ph-lf | 2 | 3 | 0 | 0 | 0 | 0 | 0 | 0 | 0 | 0 | 0 | 0 | .000 | 1 | 0 | 0 | 1.000 |
| Cox, p | 2 | 4 | 0 | 0 | 0 | 0 | 0 | 0 | 0 | 0 | 0 | 2 | .000 | 1 | 2 | 0 | 1.000 |
| Nieto, c | 2 | 5 | 0 | 0 | 0 | 0 | 0 | 0 | 1 | 1 | 0 | 2 | .000 | 23 | 1 | 0 | 1.000 |
| Tudor, p | 3 | 5 | 0 | 0 | 0 | 0 | 0 | 0 | 0 | 0 | 0 | 4 | .000 | 0 | 3 | 0 | 1.000 |
| Totals | 7 | 216 | 13 | 40 | 58 | 10 | 1 | 2 | 13 | 18 | 5 | 42 | .185 | 184 | 60 | 2 | .992 |

Braun—Flied out for Forsch in seventh inning of seventh game.

DeJesus—Flied out for Campbell in fifth inning of fifth game.

Harper—Flied out for Cox in eighth inning of second game; grounded out for Horton in seventh inning of third game; struck out for Worrell in seventh inning of fifth game; singled for Cox in eighth inning of sixth game.

Jorgensen—Grounded out for Campbell in fifth inning of third game.

Lawless—Ran for Harper in eighth inning of sixth game.

Van Slyke—Flied out for Dayley in ninth inning of second game; ran for Cedeno in eighth inning of sixth game.

# OFFICIAL BASEBALL GUIDE

## KANSAS CITY ROYALS' PITCHING RECORDS

| Pitcher | G. | GS. | CG. | IP. | H. | R. | ER. | HR. | BB. | IBB. | SO. | HB. | WP. | W. | L. | Pct. | ERA. |
|---|---|---|---|---|---|---|---|---|---|---|---|---|---|---|---|---|---|
| Beckwith | 1 | 0 | 0 | 2 | 1 | 0 | 0 | 0 | 0 | 0 | 3 | 0 | 0 | 0 | 0 | .000 | 0.00 |
| Saberhagen | 2 | 2 | 2 | 18 | 11 | 1 | 1 | 0 | 1 | 0 | 10 | 0 | 0 | 2 | 0 | 1.000 | 0.50 |
| Jackson | 2 | 2 | 1 | 16 | 9 | 3 | 3 | 0 | 5 | 0 | 12 | 0 | 0 | 1 | 1 | .500 | 1.69 |
| Quisenberry | 4 | 0 | 0 | 4⅓ | 5 | 1 | 1 | 0 | 3 | 2 | 3 | 0 | 1 | 1 | 0 | 1.000 | 2.08 |
| Leibrandt | 2 | 2 | 0 | 16⅓ | 10 | 5 | 5 | 0 | 4 | 1 | 10 | 0 | 0 | 0 | 1 | .000 | 2.76 |
| Black | 2 | 1 | 0 | 5⅓ | 4 | 3 | 3 | 2 | 5 | 2 | 4 | 0 | 0 | 0 | 1 | .000 | 5.06 |
| Totals | 7 | 7 | 3 | 62 | 40 | 13 | 13 | 2 | 18 | 5 | 42 | 0 | 1 | 4 | 3 | .571 | 1.89 |

Shutout—Saberhagen. No saves.

## ST. LOUIS CARDINALS' PITCHING RECORDS

| Pitcher | G. | GS. | CG. | IP. | H. | R. | ER. | HR. | BB. | IBB. | SO. | HB. | WP. | W. | L. | Pct. | ERA. |
|---|---|---|---|---|---|---|---|---|---|---|---|---|---|---|---|---|---|
| Dayley | 4 | 0 | 0 | 6 | 1 | 0 | 0 | 0 | 3 | 0 | 5 | 0 | 0 | 1 | 0 | 1.000 | 0.00 |
| Cox | 2 | 2 | 0 | 14 | 14 | 2 | 2 | 0 | 4 | 0 | 13 | 0 | 0 | 0 | 0 | .000 | 1.29 |
| Campbell | 3 | 0 | 0 | 4 | 4 | 1 | 1 | 0 | 2 | 1 | 5 | 0 | 0 | 0 | 0 | .000 | 2.25 |
| Tudor | 3 | 3 | 1 | 18 | 15 | 6 | 6 | 1 | 7 | 0 | 14 | 1 | 0 | 2 | 1 | .667 | 3.00 |
| Worrell | 3 | 0 | 0 | 4⅔ | 4 | 2 | 2 | 0 | 2 | 1 | 6 | 0 | 0 | 0 | 1 | .000 | 3.86 |
| Horton | 3 | 0 | 0 | 4 | 4 | 3 | 3 | 0 | 5 | 2 | 5 | 0 | 0 | 0 | 0 | .000 | 6.75 |
| Andujar | 2 | 1 | 0 | 4 | 10 | 4 | 4 | 1 | 4 | 1 | 3 | 0 | 0 | 0 | 1 | .000 | 9.00 |
| Forsch | 2 | 1 | 0 | 3 | 6 | 4 | 4 | 0 | 1 | 0 | 3 | 0 | 1 | 0 | 1 | .000 | 12.00 |
| Lahti | 3 | 0 | 0 | 3⅔ | 10 | 6 | 5 | 0 | 0 | 0 | 2 | 0 | 0 | 0 | 0 | .000 | 12.27 |
| Totals | 7 | 7 | 1 | 61⅓ | 68 | 28 | 27 | 2 | 28 | 5 | 56 | 1 | 1 | 3 | 4 | .429 | 3.96 |

Shutout—Tudor. Saves—Worrell, Lahti.

## COMPOSITE SCORE BY INNINGS

| | | | | | | | | | | |
|---|---|---|---|---|---|---|---|---|---|---|
| Kansas City | 1 | 6 | 3 | 4 | 8 | 0 | 2 | 1 | 3 — 28 |
| St. Louis | 1 | 1 | 2 | 1 | 1 | 1 | 0 | 1 | 5 — 13 |

Game-winning RBI—Cedeno, Pendleton, L. Smith, Landrum, Biancalana, Iorg, Motley.

Sacrifice hits—Leibrandt 2, Tudor, Saberhagen, Nieto, O. Smith.

Sacrifice flies—None.

Stolen bases—Wilson 3, L. Smith 2, O. Smith, McGee, Brett.

Caught stealing—L. Smith 2, Motley, O. Smith, McGee, White.

Double plays—Herr, O. Smith and Clark 4; Pendleton and Porter; Cox, O. Smith and Herr; Herr and Clark; Sundberg and Brett; Black and White; Pendleton and Herr; Biancalana, White and Balboni; Pendleton, Herr and Clark.

Passed balls—Sundberg, Porter.

Hit by pitcher—By Tudor (McRae).

Balk—Horton.

Bases on balls—Off Black 5 (McGee, Nieto, Pendleton, Porter, O. Smith), off Jackson 5 (Pendleton 2, O. Smith 2, Clark), off Leibrandt 4 (Cedeno 2, Clark, O. Smith), off Quisenberry 3 (Clark, Herr, Porter), off Saberhagen 1 (Herr), off Tudor 7 (Balboni 2, Sundberg 2, Biancalana, L. Smith, White), off Horton 5 (Balboni 2, Brett 2, Biancalana), off Andujar 4 (Sundberg 2, Brett, White), off Cox 4 (Biancalana 2, Balboni, White), off Dayley 3 (Brett, Sundberg, Wilson), off Campbell 2 (Biancalana, Sundberg), off Worrell 2 (McRae, L. Smith), off Forsch 1 (L. Smith).

Strikeouts—By Jackson 12 (McGee 2, Pendleton 2, Porter 2, Cedeno, Clark, Harper, Horton, Nieto, Tudor), by Leibrandt 10 (Porter 3, Clark 2, Cox 2, Cedeno, Herr, Landrum), by Saberhagen 10 (Clark 3, Van Slyke 3, Andujar, Landrum, McGee, Tudor), by Black 4 (Clark, Herr, Tudor, Van Slyke), by Beckwith 3 (Clark, Nieto, Tudor), by Quisenberry 3 (Clark, Van Slyke, Worrell), by Tudor 14 (Brett 3, L. Smith 3, Jackson 2, Balboni, Biancalana, Black, Motley, Saberhagen, Wathan), by Cox 13 (Sheridan 4, Sundberg 4, Leibrandt 2, Balboni, Brett, White), by Worrell 6 (Biancalana, Brett, Jackson, L. Smith, White, Wilson), by Campbell 5 (Balboni 2, Biancalana, Saberhagen, White), by Dayley 5 (Brett 2, L. Smith 3, Wilson), by Horton 5 (Wilson 2, Jackson, Sheridan, White), by Andujar 3 (Saberhagen, Sheridan, L. Smith), by Forsch 3 (Jackson, Saberhagen, Sheridan), by Lahti 2 (Biancalana, L. Smith).

Left on bases—Kansas City 56—8, 6, 11, 6, 9, 9, 7; St. Louis 38—6, 5, 5, 5, 7, 5, 5.

Time of games—First game, 2:48; second game, 2:44; third game, 2:59; fourth game 2:19; fifth game, 2:52; sixth game, 2:47; seventh game, 2:46.

Attendance—First game, 41,650; second game, 41,656; third game, 53,634; fourth game, 53,634; fifth game, 53,634; sixth game, 41,628; seventh game, 41,658.

Umpires—Denkinger (A.L.), B. Williams (N.L.), McKean (A.L.), Engel (N.L.), Shulock (A.L.), Quick (N.L.).

Official scorers—Del Black, Kansas City Star/Times; Red Foley, New York Daily News; Jack Herman, St. Louis Globe Democrat-retired; Dave Nightingale, The Sporting News.

# 1985 ALL-STAR GAME

## Including

**Review of 1985 Game**

**Official Box Score**

**Official Play-by-Play**

**Results of Previous Games**

San Diego pitcher LaMarr Hoyt walks off with the Most Valuable Player trophy following the National League's 6-1 victory.

# Pitchers Extend A.L. Agony

**By DAVE SLOAN**

An old baseball adage says that good pitching always stops good hitting. The 1985 All-Star Game was a case in point.

Despite an American League roster loaded with power hitters, five National League pitchers kept those bats quiet in a 6-1 N.L. victory. It was the senior circuit's second straight win, its 13th in the previous 14 games and its 21st in the last 23.

A.L. batsmen came up with a paltry five hits—all singles—in the 56th All-Star Game, played July 16 at the Hubert H. Humphrey Metrodome in Minneapolis. So thorough was the N.L. pitchers' dominance that not even the ball park itself—referred to by many as the "Homerdome" because of its propensity for the long ball—was of help to the beleaguered American League on this night.

"The American League has a lot of big boppers, guys who can hit the ball out of the park," said San Diego righthander La-Marr Hoyt, the National League's starting and winning pitcher as well as the game's Most Valuable Player. "But you can pitch to free swingers. The National League has the great athletes, not just the big boppers. We have guys who can hit for average, hit the long ball, run and throw."

Hoyt should know; he spent five years with the Chicago White Sox and won the 1983 Cy Young Award before coming to the National League prior to the '85 season.

The American League took a 1-0 lead against Hoyt in the bottom of the first inning. Leadoff man Rickey Henderson of the Yankees singled to center and promptly stole second base, moving to third when catcher Terry Kennedy's throw sailed into center field. Kansas City's George Brett, the major leagues' leading hitter at the time, then lofted a sacrifice fly to left, scoring Henderson. It turned out to be the junior circuit's only run of the game, and an unearned one at that.

"When Henderson gets on, he's going to cause some problems," Hoyt said. "I felt like I gave the catcher a 50-50 chance to get the runner out, but I think Terry got the ball caught in his glove."

The National League tied the score in the second inning. Darryl Strawberry of the Mets singled off A.L. starter Jack Morris of Detroit with one out, then stole second and later scored on a single by San Diego's Kennedy.

**The Yankees' Rickey Henderson fields Dale Murphy's third-inning double.**

The Nationals took a 2-1 lead in the top of the third inning when St. Louis' Tom Herr doubled to left off Morris with two out and scored on a single to center by San Diego's Steve Garvey. Atlanta's Dale Murphy followed with a double to center, putting runners on second and third. Morris then walked Strawberry to load the bases, and A.L. Manager Sparky Anderson of Detroit yanked his own pitcher in favor of Toronto lefthander Jimmy Key. Key got San Diego's Graig Nettles, the National League's 40-year-old starting third baseman, to hit a foul pop to Brett at third.

"I thought I'd finish the inning, but I deserved to be taken out," said Morris, who

San Diego's Steve Garvey (above) laces a run-scoring single in the third inning. Montreal's Tim Wallach (below) scores the N.L.'s fourth run in the fifth inning after a single by Philadelphia's Ozzie Virgil.

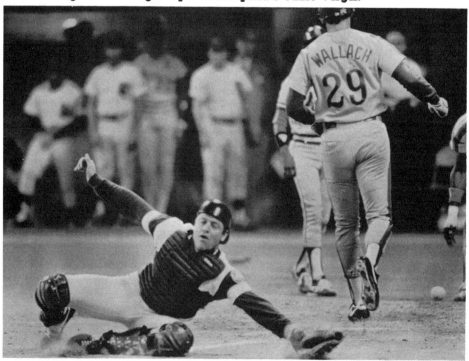

took the loss. "I didn't pitch as well as I would have liked. I had a lot of rest and I was probably rushing too much."

The National League increased its advantage to 4-1 in the fifth after Strawberry was hit by a pitch from Cleveland's Bert Blyleven and Montreal's Tim Wallach lined a ground-rule double to left, putting runners on second and third. Strawberry and Wallach both scored when Philadelphia's Ozzie Virgil lined a single to left.

"It was a breaking ball down and in," Virgil said, "and I got enough of the ball to hit it in the hole."

The National League closed out the scoring with two more runs in the ninth. Detroit's Dan Petry walked Chicago's Ryne Sandberg, Montreal's Tim Raines and St. Louis' Jack Clark to load the bases. The Cardinals' Willie McGee then tagged Detroit reliever Willie Hernandez for a ground-rule double to right-center, scoring Sandberg and Raines. Had the ball not taken a crazy bounce off the Metrodome's SuperTurf, McGee's hit easily would have been a triple and possibly an inside-the-park grand slam.

"We'll never know, will we?" McGee said afterward. "But it sure would have been fun to see what would have happened if I had been able to keep running."

Fun, that is, if you're an N.L. fan. But A.L. supporters have come to approach the midsummer classic like it's root-canal surgery.

"Maybe the National League players are a little more relaxed than we are because they've had so much success in this game," said Brett, who personally has tasted victory only once in nine All-Star Games. "Maybe there's more pressure on our side."

Anderson, who failed in his attempt to become the first manager to win an All-Star Game in each league (he won as the N.L. skipper in 1973, 1976 and 1977), rejected the notion that it's not important who wins baseball's annual showcase game for its best players.

"The guys really do want to win it," he said. "Everybody wants to walk away a winner."

"When I was playing for the American League (with the California Angels), I can remember we'd come into the locker room before a game and get a pep talk about how we had to beat the National League," said Houston pitcher Nolan Ryan, who relieved Hoyt and threw three scoreless innings. "There aren't any pep talks in the National League. Don't need 'em."

| NATIONALS | AB. | R. | H. | RBI. | PO. | A. |
|---|---|---|---|---|---|---|
| Gwynn, (Padres) lf | 1 | 0 | 0 | 0 | 1 | 0 |
| Cruz, (Astros) lf | 1 | 0 | 0 | 0 | 2 | 0 |
| fRaines, (Expos) lf | 0 | 1 | 0 | 0 | 0 | 0 |
| Herr, (Cardinals) 2b | 3 | 1 | 1 | 0 | 0 | 1 |
| Ryan, (Astros) p | 1 | 0 | 0 | 0 | 0 | 0 |
| Pena, (Pirates) c | 1 | 0 | 0 | 0 | 4 | 1 |
| Garvey, (Padres) 1b | 3 | 0 | 1 | 1 | 5 | 0 |
| Clark, (Cardinals) 1b | 1 | 0 | 0 | 0 | 4 | 0 |
| Murphy, (Braves) cf | 3 | 0 | 1 | 0 | 1 | 0 |
| McGee, (Cardinals) cf | 2 | 0 | 1 | 2 | 1 | 0 |
| Strawberry, (Mets) rf | 1 | 2 | 1 | 0 | 3 | 0 |
| Parker, (Reds) rf | 2 | 0 | 0 | 0 | 1 | 0 |
| Nettles, (Padres) 3b | 2 | 0 | 0 | 0 | 0 | 1 |
| Wallach, (Expos) 3b | 2 | 1 | 1 | 0 | 1 | 1 |
| Kennedy, (Padres) c | 2 | 0 | 1 | 1 | 0 | 0 |
| Virgil, (Phillies) c | 1 | 0 | 1 | 2 | 3 | 0 |
| Valenzuela, (Dodg.) p | 0 | 0 | 0 | 0 | 0 | 0 |
| eRose, (Reds) | 1 | 0 | 0 | 0 | 0 | 0 |
| Reardon, (Expos) p | 0 | 0 | 0 | 0 | 0 | 1 |
| gWilson, (Phillies) | 1 | 0 | 0 | 0 | 0 | 0 |
| Gossage, (Padres) p | 0 | 0 | 0 | 0 | 0 | 0 |
| Smith, (Cardinals) ss | 4 | 0 | 0 | 0 | 1 | 3 |
| Hoyt, (Padres) p | 1 | 0 | 0 | 0 | 0 | 0 |
| bTempleton, (Padres) | 1 | 0 | 1 | 0 | 0 | 0 |
| Sandberg, (Cubs) 2b | 1 | 1 | 0 | 0 | 0 | 3 |
| Totals | 35 | 6 | 9 | 6 | 27 | 11 |

| AMERICANS | AB. | R. | H. | RBI. | PO. | A. |
|---|---|---|---|---|---|---|
| Henderson, (Yanks) cf | 3 | 1 | 1 | 0 | 1 | 0 |
| Molitor, (Brew.) 3b-cf | 1 | 0 | 0 | 0 | 0 | 0 |
| Whitaker, (Tigers) 2b | 2 | 0 | 0 | 0 | 1 | 1 |
| Garcia, (Blue Jays) 2b | 2 | 0 | 1 | 0 | 0 | 3 |
| Brett, (Royals) 3b | 1 | 0 | 0 | 1 | 2 | 1 |
| Bradley, (Mariners) cf | 1 | 0 | 0 | 0 | 1 | 0 |
| Petry, (Tigers) p | 0 | 0 | 0 | 0 | 0 | 0 |
| Hernandez, (Tigers) p | 0 | 0 | 0 | 0 | 0 | 0 |
| Murray, (Orioles) 1b | 3 | 0 | 0 | 0 | 5 | 2 |
| Brunansky, (Twins) rf | 1 | 0 | 0 | 0 | 0 | 0 |
| Ripken, (Orioles) ss | 3 | 0 | 1 | 0 | 2 | 1 |
| Trammell, (Tigers) ss | 1 | 0 | 0 | 0 | 0 | 0 |
| Winfield, (Yankees) rf | 3 | 0 | 1 | 0 | 0 | 0 |
| Moore, (Angels) p | 0 | 0 | 0 | 0 | 0 | 1 |
| Boggs, (Red Sox) 3b | 0 | 0 | 0 | 0 | 0 | 0 |
| Rice, (Red Sox) lf | 3 | 0 | 0 | 0 | 1 | 0 |
| Fisk, (White Sox) c | 2 | 0 | 0 | 0 | 2 | 0 |
| Whitt, (Blue Jays) c | 0 | 0 | 0 | 0 | 2 | 0 |
| dWard, (Rangers) | 1 | 0 | 0 | 0 | 0 | 0 |
| Gedman, (Red Sox) c | 1 | 0 | 0 | 0 | 4 | 0 |
| Morris, (Tigers) p | 0 | 0 | 0 | 0 | 1 | 0 |
| Key, (Blue Jays) p | 0 | 0 | 0 | 0 | 0 | 0 |
| aBaines, (White Sox) | 1 | 0 | 1 | 0 | 0 | 0 |
| Blyleven, (Indians) p | 0 | 0 | 0 | 0 | 1 | 2 |
| cCooper, (Brewers) | 0 | 0 | 0 | 0 | 0 | 0 |
| Stieb, (Blue Jays) p | 0 | 0 | 0 | 0 | 0 | 0 |
| Mattingly, (Yanks) 1b | 1 | 0 | 0 | 0 | 4 | 0 |
| Totals | 30 | 1 | 5 | 1 | 27 | 11 |

Nationals .................................. 011 020 002—6
Americans ............................... 100 000 000—1

| NATIONALS | IP. | H. | R. | ER. | BB. | SO. |
|---|---|---|---|---|---|---|
| Hoyt (Padres) | 3 | 2 | 1 | 0 | 0 | 0 |
| Ryan (Astros) | 3 | 2 | 0 | 0 | 2 | 2 |
| Valenzuela (Dodgers) | 1 | 0 | 0 | 0 | 1 | 1 |
| Reardon (Expos) | 1 | 1 | 0 | 0 | 0 | 1 |
| Gossage (Padres) | 1 | 0 | 0 | 0 | 1 | 2 |

| AMERICANS | IP. | H. | R. | ER. | BB. | SO. |
|---|---|---|---|---|---|---|
| Morris (Tigers) | 2⅔ | 5 | 2 | 2 | 1 | 1 |
| Key (Blue Jays) | ⅓ | 0 | 0 | 0 | 0 | 0 |
| Blyleven (Indians) | 2 | 3 | 2 | 2 | 1 | 1 |
| Stieb (Blue Jays) | 1 | 0 | 0 | 0 | 1 | 2 |
| Moore (Angels) | 2 | 0 | 0 | 0 | 0 | 1 |
| Petry (Tigers) | ⅓ | 0 | 2 | 2 | 3 | 1 |
| Hernandez (Tigers) | ⅔ | 1 | 0 | 0 | 1 | 2 |

Winning pitcher—Hoyt. Losing pitcher—Morris.

Game-winning RBI—Garvey.

aSingled for Key in third. bSingled for Hoyt in fourth. cWalked for Blyleven in fifth. dLined out for Whitt in seventh. eGrounded out for Valenzuela in eighth. fWalked for Cruz in ninth. gStruck out for Reardon in ninth. Error—Kennedy. Double play—Pena, Sandberg, Reardon and Wallach. Left on bases—Nationals 10, Americans 7. Doubles—Herr, Murphy, Wallach, McGee. Stolen bases—Henderson, Strawberry, Winfield, Cruz, Garcia. Sacrifice fly—Brett. Hit by pitcher—By Blyleven (Strawberry). Wild pitch—Valenzuela. Bases on balls—Off Ryan 2 (Cooper, Brett), off Valenzuela 1 (Rice), off Gossage 1 (Boggs), off Morris 1 (Strawberry), off Blyleven 1 (Cruz), off Stieb 1 (Cruz), off Petry 3 (Sandberg, Raines, Clark), off Hernandez 1 (Wallach). Strikeouts—By Ryan 2 (Rice, Henderson), by Valenzuela 1 (Molitor), by Reardon 1 (Bradley), by Gossage 2 (Rice, Gedman), by Morris 1 (Hoyt), by Blyleven 1 (Murphy), by Stieb 2 (Sandberg, Ryan), by Moore 1 (Wallach), by Petry 1 (Pena), by Hernandez 2 (Parker, Wilson). Umpires—McCoy (A.L.) plate, Kibler (N.L.) first base, Bremigan (A.L.) second base, C. Williams (N.L.) third base, Coble (A.L.) left field, Marsh (N.L.) right field. Official scorers—Sheldon Ocker, Akron Beacon Journal, Bob Beebe (retired from the Minneapolis Star) and Red Foley, New York Daily News. Time—2:54. Attendance—54,960.

Players listed on roster but not used: N.L.—Darling, Garrelts, Gooden; A.L.—Howell.

### FIRST INNING

Nationals—Gwynn grounded to Whitaker. Herr popped to Ripken. Garvey was thrown out by Brett, who made a nice play on Garvey's one-hopper. No runs, no hits, no errors, none left.

Americans—Henderson smashed a single up the middle. Whitaker flied to Strawberry. With Brett batting, Henderson stole second base and moved to third when Kennedy's throw went into center field for an error. Brett lined hard to Gwynn in left field, Henderson scoring on the sacrifice fly. Murray popped to Smith in short center. One run, one hit, one error, none left.

### SECOND INNING

Nationals—Murphy popped to Ripken. Strawberry lined a single to left. With Nettles at the plate, Strawberry stole second. Nettles flied to Rice, Strawberry holding second on the play. Kennedy grounded a single to center, scoring Strawberry. Smith popped to Brett, who made an over-the-shoulder catch in short left field. One run, two hits, no errors, one left.

Americans—Cruz took over in left field for the Nationals. Ripken grounded to Smith. Winfield bounced to Herr. Rice flied to Strawberry, who made the catch near the right-field line. No runs, no hits, no errors, none left.

### THIRD INNING

Nationals—Hoyt struck out on three pitches. Cruz hit a high chop that Murray fielded and quickly relayed to Morris covering first base, beating Cruz on a close play. Herr sliced a double to left, beating Rice's strong throw to second base. Garvey lined a single to center, scoring Herr and giving the Nationals a 2-1 lead. Murphy was credited with a ground-rule double when his drive down the left-field line bounced into the stands, Garvey stopping at third. Strawberry walked, loading the bases. Key replaced Morris on the mound for the Americans. Nettles fouled out to Brett. One run, three hits, no errors, three left.

Americans—Fisk flied to Murphy, who made a fine running catch in left-center. Baines batted for Key and lined a single to right. Nettles threw out Henderson at first after fielding his chopper, Baines moving to second. Whitaker flied to Strawberry. No runs, one hit, no errors, one left.

### FOURTH INNING

Nationals—Blyleven became the third A.L. pitcher. Kennedy grounded to Murray, who made the play unassisted at first base. Blyleven made a barehanded play on Smith's high chopper and threw to Murray to beat Smith on a close play at first. Templeton batted for Hoyt and singled to center. Cruz walked. Herr grounded to Murray, who tossed to Blyleven covering first base for the out. No runs, one hit, no errors, two left.

Americans—Ryan took over on the mound for the Nationals, while Virgil became the new catcher, Sandberg went in to play second base and Wallach went to third. Brett grounded to Sandberg. Murray fouled out to Virgil. Ripken bounced to Smith. No runs, no hits, no errors, none left.

### FIFTH INNING

Nationals—Garvey grounded to Ripken, who made a backhanded stab before making the long throw to Murray for the out. Murphy struck out. Strawberry was hit on the leg by a Blyleven pitch. Wallach was credited with a ground-rule double when his liner bounced over the left-field fence, Strawberry stopping at third. Virgil bounced a single to left that scored Strawberry and Wallach, giving the Nationals a 4-1 lead. When Rice's throw to the plate got past Fisk, Virgil tried to advance to second but was thrown out, Blyleven to Whitaker. Two runs, two hits, no errors, none left.

Americans—Clark went in to play first base, McGee went to center and Parker took over in right for the Nationals. Winfield singled to center. Winfield stole second base while Ryan was striking out Rice. Cruz made a fine running catch in left-center to retire Fisk. Cooper batted for Blyleven and walked. Henderson struck out. No runs, one hit, no errors, two left.

### SIXTH INNING

Nationals—Stieb went in to pitch, Whitt to catch and Garcia to play second base for the Americans. Smith flied to Henderson in left-center field. Sandberg was called out on strikes. Cruz walked and stole second base. Ryan struck out. No runs, no hits, no errors, one left.

Americans—Garcia flied to Parker. Brett walked. Cruz made a backhanded stab on Murray's hard liner to left-center. Wallach made a diving stop on Ripken's hard smash down the third-base line but couldn't make a throw for a single, Brett stopping at second. Winfield grounded to Sandberg. No runs, one hit, no errors, two left.

### SEVENTH INNING

Nationals—Molitor went in to third, Bradley to center, Brunansky to right, Trammell to shortstop, Mattingly to first and Moore to pitch for the Americans. Clark grounded back to the mound, Moore to Mattingly for the out. McGee grounded to Garcia. Parker also grounded to Garcia. No runs, no hits, no errors, none left.

Americans—Valenzuela went in to pitch for the Nationals with Pena doing the catching. Rice walked. With Ward at the plate, batting for Whitt, Rice advanced to second base on Valenzuela's wild pitch. Clark made a leaping catch to snare Ward's liner, Rice getting back to second before Clark's attempt for a double play. McGee ran down Mattingly's long drive to right-center, Rice advancing to third safely when Smith's relay throw hit him in the back. Molitor struck out. No runs, no hits, no errors, one left.

## EIGHTH INNING

**Nationals**—Gedman went in to catch for the Americans. Wallach struck out. Rose batted for Valenzuela and grounded to Garcia. Smith flied to Bradley. No runs, no hits, no errors, none left.

**Americans**—Reardon took over as pitcher for the Nationals. Garcia grounded a single to left. Garcia stole second as Bradley struck out, and when Pena's low throw skipped away from Sandberg, Garcia attempted to take third but was thrown out when Reardon recovered the loose ball and threw to Wallach, who made the tag for a double play. Brunansky grounded to Smith. No runs, one hit, no errors, none left.

## NINTH INNING

**Nationals**—Molitor moved from third base to center field, Boggs came in to play third and Petry was the new A.L. pitcher. Sandberg walked. Raines, batting for Cruz, also walked. Pena struck out on three pitches. Clark drew the third walk of the inning from Petry, who was then replaced on the mound by Hernandez. McGee was credited with a ground-rule double when his smash bounced over the center-field wall, Sandberg and Raines scoring with Clark stopping at third. Parker struck out. Wallach was given an intentional walk, loading the bases. Wilson batted for Reardon and struck out. Two runs, one hit, no errors, three left.

**Americans**—Raines stayed in the game in left field and Gossage became the new pitcher for the Nationals. Trammell bounced to Wallach. Boggs walked. Rice struck out on a full-count pitch. Gedman also struck out. No runs, no hits, no errors, one left.

## RESULTS OF PREVIOUS GAMES

**1933**—At Comiskey Park, Chicago, July 6. Americans 4, Nationals 2. Managers—Connie Mack, John McGraw. Winning pitcher—Lefty Gomez. Losing pitcher—Bill Hallahan. Attendance —47,595.

**1934**—At Polo Grounds, New York, July 10. Americans 9, Nationals 7. Managers—Joe Cronin, Bill Terry. Winning pitcher—Mel Harder. Losing pitcher—Van Mungo. Attendance—48,363.

**1935**—At Municipal Stadium, Cleveland, July 8. Americans 4, Nationals 1. Managers—Mickey Cochrane, Frankie Frisch. Winning pitcher—Lefty Gomez. Losing pitcher—Bill Walker. Attendance—69,831.

**1936**—At Braves Field, Boston, July 7. Nationals 4, Americans 3. Managers—Charlie Grimm, Joe McCarthy. Winning pitcher—Dizzy Dean. Losing pitcher—Lefty Gomez. Attendance—25,556.

**1937**—At Griffith Stadium, Washington, July 7. Americans 8, Nationals 3. Managers—Joe McCarthy, Bill Terry. Winning pitcher—Lefty Gomez. Losing pitcher—Dizzy Dean. Attendance—31,391.

**1938**—At Crosley Field, Cincinnati, July 6. Nationals 4, Americans 1. Managers—Bill Terry, Joe McCarthy. Winning pitcher—Johnny Vander Meer. Losing pitcher—Lefty Gomez. Attendance—27,067.

**1939**—At Yankee Stadium, New York, July 11. Americans 3, Nationals 1. Managers—Joe McCarthy, Gabby Hartnett. Winning pitcher—Tommy Bridges. Losing pitcher—Bill Lee. Attendance—62,892.

**1940**—At Sportsman's Park, St. Louis, July 9. Nationals 4, Americans 0. Managers—Bill Mc-Kechnie, Joe Cronin. Winning pitcher—Paul Derringer. Losing pitcher—Red Ruffing. Attendance—32,373.

**1941**—At Briggs Stadium, Detroit, July 8. Americans 7, Nationals 5. Managers—Del Baker, Bill McKechnie. Winning pitcher—Ed Smith. Losing pitcher—Claude Passeau. Attendance—54,674.

**1942**—At Polo Grounds, New York, July 6. Americans 3, Nationals 1. Managers—Joe Cronin, Leo Durocher. Winning pitcher—Spud Chandler. Losing pitcher—Mort Cooper. Attendance—34,178.

**1943**—At Shibe Park, Philadelphia, July 13 (night). Americans 5, Nationals 3. Managers—Joe McCarthy, Billy Southworth. Winning pitcher—Dutch Leonard. Losing pitcher—Mort Cooper. Attendance—31,938.

**1944**—At Forbes Field, Pittsburgh, July 11 (night). Nationals 7, Americans 1. Managers—Billy Southworth, Joe McCarthy. Winning pitcher—Ken Raffensberger. Losing pitcher—Tex Hughson. Attendance—29,589.

**1945**—No game played.

**1946**—At Fenway Park, Boston, July 9. Americans 12, Nationals 0. Managers—Steve O'Neill, Charlie Grimm. Winning pitcher—Bob Feller. Losing pitcher—Claude Passeau. Attendance—34,906.

**1947**—At Wrigley Field, Chicago, July 8. Americans 2, Nationals 1. Managers—Joe Cronin, Eddie Dyer. Winning pitcher—Frank Shea. Losing pitcher—Johnny Sain. Attendance—41,123.

**1948**—At Sportsman's Park, St. Louis, July 13. Americans 5, Nationals 2. Managers—Bucky Harris, Leo Durocher. Winning pitcher—Vic Raschi. Losing pitcher—Johnny Schmitz. Attendance—34,009.

**1949**—At Ebbets Field, Brooklyn, July 12. Americans 11, Nationals 7. Managers—Lou Boudreau, Billy Southworth. Winning pitcher—Virgil Trucks. Losing pitcher—Don Newcombe. Attendance—32,577.

**1950**—At Comiskey Park, Chicago, July 11. Nationals 4, Americans 3 (14 innings). Managers—Burt Shotton, Casey Stengel. Winning pitcher—Ewell Blackwell. Losing pitcher—Ted Gray. Attendance—46,127.

**1951**—At Briggs Stadium, Detroit, July 10. Nationals 8, Americans 3. Managers—Eddie Sawyer, Casey Stengel. Winning pitcher—Sal Maglie. Losing pitcher—Ed Lopat. Attendance—52,075.

**1952**—At Shibe Park, Philadelphia, July 8. Nationals 3, Americans 2 (five innings—rain). Managers—Leo Durocher, Casey Stengel. Winning pitcher—Bob Rush. Losing pitcher—Bob Lemon. Attendance—32,785.

**1953**—At Crosley Field, Cincinnati, July 14. Nationals 5, Americans 1. Managers—Chuck Dressen, Casey Stengel. Winning pitcher—Warren Spahn. Losing pitcher—Allie Reynolds. Attendance—30,846.

**1954**—At Municipal Stadium, Cleveland, July 13. Americans 11, Nationals 9. Managers—Casey Stengel, Walter Alston. Winning pitcher—Dean Stone. Losing pitcher—Gene Conley. Attendance—68,751.

**1955**—At Milwaukee County Stadium, Milwaukee, July 12. Nationals 6, Americans 5 (12 innings). Managers—Leo Durocher, Al Lopez. Winning pitcher—Gene Conley. Losing pitcher—Frank Sullivan. Attendance—45,643.

**1956**—At Griffith Stadium, Washington, July 10. Nationals 7, Americans 3. Managers—Walter Alston, Casey Stengel. Winning pitcher—Bob Friend. Losing pitcher—Billy Pierce. Attendance—28,843.

**1957**—At Busch Stadium, St. Louis, July 9. Americans 6, Nationals 5. Managers—Casey Stengel, Walter Alston. Winning pitcher—Jim Bunning.

Losing pitcher—Curt Simmons. Attendance—30,693.

1958—At Memorial Stadium, Baltimore, July 8. Americans 4, Nationals 3. Managers—Casey Stengel, Fred Haney. Winning pitcher—Early Wynn. Losing pitcher—Bob Friend. Attendance—48,829.

1959 (first game)—At Forbes Field, Pittsburgh, July 7. Nationals 5, Americans 4. Managers—Fred Haney, Casey Stengel. Winning pitcher—Johnny Antonelli. Losing pitcher—Whitey Ford. Attendance—35,277.

1959 (second game)—At Memorial Coliseum, Los Angeles, August 3. Americans 5, Nationals 3. Managers—Casey Stengel, Fred Haney. Winning pitcher—Jerry Walker. Losing pitcher—Don Drysdale. Attendance—55,105.

1960 (first game)—At Municipal Stadium, Kansas City, July 11. Nationals 5, Americans 3. Managers—Walter Alston, Al Lopez. Winning pitcher—Bob Friend. Losing pitcher—Bill Monbouquette. Attendance—30,619.

1960 (second game)—At Yankee Stadium, New York, July 13. Nationals 6, Americans 0. Managers—Walter Alston, Al Lopez. Winning pitcher—Vernon Law. Losing pitcher—Whitey Ford. Attendance—38,362.

1961 (first game)—At Candlestick Park, San Francisco, July 11. Nationals 5, Americans 4 (10 innings). Managers—Danny Murtaugh, Paul Richards. Winning pitcher—Stu Miller. Losing pitcher—Hoyt Wilhelm. Attendance—44,115.

1961 (second game)—At Fenway Park, Boston, July 13. Americans 1, Nationals 1 (nine-inning tie, stopped by rain). Managers—Paul Richards, Danny Murtaugh. Attendance—31,851.

1962 (first game)—At District of Columbia Stadium, Washington, July 10. Nationals 3, Americans 1. Managers—Fred Hutchinson, Ralph Houk. Winning pitcher—Juan Marichal. Losing pitcher—Camilo Pascual. Attendance—45,480.

1962 (second game)—At Wrigley Field, Chicago, July 30. Americans 9, Nationals 4. Managers—Ralph Houk, Fred Hutchinson. Winning pitcher—Ray Herbert. Losing pitcher—Art Mahaffey. Attendance—38,359.

1963—At Municipal Stadium, Cleveland, July 9. Nationals 5, Americans 3. Managers—Alvin Dark, Ralph Houk. Winning pitcher—Larry Jackson. Losing pitcher—Jim Bunning. Attendance—44,160.

1964—At Shea Stadium, New York, July 7. Nationals 7, Americans 4. Managers—Walter Alston, Al Lopez. Winning pitcher—Juan Marichal. Losing pitcher—Dick Radatz. Attendance—50,850.

1965—At Metropolitan Stadium, Bloomington (Minnesota), July 13. Nationals 6, Americans 5. Managers—Gene Mauch, Al Lopez. Winning pitcher—Sandy Koufax. Losing pitcher—Sam McDowell. Attendance—46,706.

1966—At Busch Memorial Stadium, St Louis, July 12. Nationals 2, Americans 1 (10 innings). Managers—Walter Alston, Sam Mele. Winning pitcher—Gaylord Perry. Losing pitcher—Pete Richert. Attendance—49,936.

1967—At Anaheim Stadium, Anaheim (California), July 11. Nationals 2, Americans 1 (15 innings). Managers—Walter Alston, Hank Bauer. Winning pitcher—Don Drysdale. Losing pitcher—Jim Hunter. Attendance—46,309.

1968—At Astrodome, Houston, July 9 (night). Nationals 1, Americans 0. Managers—Red Schoendienst, Dick Williams. Winning pitcher—Don Drysdale. Losing pitcher—Luis Tiant. Attendance—48,321.

1969—At Robert F. Kennedy Memorial Stadium, Washington, July 23. Nationals 9, Americans 3. Managers—Red Schoendienst, Mayo Smith. Winning pitcher—Steve Carlton. Losing pitcher—Mel Stottlemyre. Attendance—45,259.

1970—At Riverfront Stadium, Cincinnati, July 14 (night). Nationals 5, Americans 4 (12 innings). Managers—Gil Hodges, Earl Weaver. Winning pitcher—Claude Osteen. Losing pitcher—Clyde Wright. Attendance—51,838.

1971—At Tiger Stadium, Detroit, July 13 (night). Americans 6, Nationals 4. Managers—Earl Weaver, George (Sparky) Anderson. Winning pitcher—Vida Blue. Losing pitcher—Dock Ellis. Attendance—53,559.

1972—At Atlanta Stadium, Atlanta, July 25 (night). Nationals 4, Americans 3 (10 innings). Managers—Danny Murtaugh, Earl Weaver. Winning pitcher—Tug McGraw. Losing pitcher—Dave McNally. Attendance—53,107.

1973—At Royals Stadium, Kansas City, July 24 (night). Nationals 7, Americans 1. Managers—George (Sparky) Anderson, Dick Williams. Winning pitcher—Rick Wise. Losing pitcher—Bert Blyleven. Attendance—40,849.

1974—At Three Rivers Stadium, Pittsburgh, July 23 (night). Nationals 7, Americans 2. Managers—Yogi Berra, Dick Williams. Winning pitcher—Ken Brett. Losing pitcher—Luis Tiant. Attendance—50,706.

1975—At Milwaukee County Stadium, Milwaukee, July 15 (night). Nationals 6, Americans 3. Managers—Walter Alston, Alvin Dark. Winning pitcher—Jon Matlack. Losing pitcher—Jim Hunter. Attendance—51,480.

1976—At Veterans Stadium, Philadelphia, July 13 (night). Nationals 7, Americans 1. Managers—George (Sparky) Anderson, Darrell Johnson. Winning pitcher—Randy Jones. Losing pitcher—Mark Fidrych. Attendance—63,974.

1977—At Yankee Stadium, New York, July 19 (night). Nationals 7, Americans 5. Managers—Alfred (Billy) Martin, George (Sparky) Anderson. Winning pitcher—Don Sutton. Losing pitcher—Jim Palmer. Attendance—56,683.

1978—At San Diego Stadium, San Diego, July 11 (night). Nationals 7, Americans 3. Managers—Alfred (Billy) Martin, Thomas Lasorda. Winning pitcher—Bruce Sutter. Losing pitcher—Rich Gossage. Attendance—51,549.

1979—At Kingdome, Seattle, July 17. Nationals 7, Americans 6. Managers—Chuck Tanner, Bob Lemon. Winning pitcher—Bruce Sutter. Losing pitcher—Jim Kern. Attendance—58,905.

1980—At Dodger Stadium, Los Angeles, July 8. Nationals 4, Americans 2. Managers—Chuck Tanner, Earl Weaver. Winning pitcher—Jerry Reuss. Losing pitcher—Tommy John. Attendance—56,088.

1981—At Municipal Stadium, Cleveland, August 9 (night). Nationals 5, Americans 4. Managers—Dallas Green, Jim Frey. Winning pitcher—Vida Blue. Losing pitcher—Rollie Fingers. Attendance—72,086.

1982—At Olympic Stadium, Montreal, July 13 (night). Nationals 4, Americans 1. Managers—Thomas Lasorda, Alfred (Billy) Martin. Winning pitcher—Steve Rogers. Losing pitcher—Dennis Eckersley. Attendance—59,057.

1983—At Comiskey Park, Chicago, July 6 (night). Americans 13, Nationals 3. Managers—Harvey Kuenn, Dorrel (Whitey) Herzog. Winning pitcher—Dave Stieb. Losing pitcher—Mario Soto. Attendance—43,801.

1984—At Candlestick Park, San Francisco, July 10 (night). Nationals 3, Americans 1. Managers—Paul Owens, Joseph Altobelli. Winning pitcher—Charlie Lea. Losing pitcher—Dave Stieb. Attendance—57,756.

# BATTING, PITCHING

# FEATURES

### Including

**Low-Hit Pitching Performances**

**Top Strikeout Performances**

**Baseball's Top Firemen**

**Pitchers Winning 1-0 Games**

**Multi-Home Run Performances**

**Batters Hitting Grand Slams**

**Top One-Game Hitting Performances**

**Baseball's Top Pinch-Hitters**

**Top Performances in Debuts**

**Homers by Parks**

**Award Winners**

**Hall of Fame Electees**

**Hall of Famers List, Years Selected**

**St. Louis' Danny Cox came within four outs of a perfect game May 31 before Cincinnati's Dave Concepcion broke it up.**

# Cox Close But No Cigar

**By DAVE SLOAN**

When Cincinnati veteran Dave Concepcion strolled to the plate in the eighth inning of the Reds' May 31 game at St. Louis, he was a man with a mission.

Cardinals righthander Danny Cox had set down in order the first 23 batters he faced and was within four outs of a perfect game. The Reds trailed, 5-0, and winning the game appeared unlikely. Concepcion just wanted to reach base.

"It's all over," Concepcion told home plate umpire Jerry Crawford and Cardinals catcher Darrell Porter, referring to Cox's perfect game. Crawford laughed, and Concepcion said, "Do you want to bet?"

Crawford declined, so Concepcion looked at Porter, who replied, "I can't bet against you; you're a dandy player."

After missing badly on Cox's first offering, Concepcion drilled the second pitch between third base and shortstop for a clean single. The perfect game was gone, and after Ron Oester followed with another single, Cox settled down to post a two-hit shutout victory.

No pitcher threw a perfect game or a no-hitter in 1985, but Cox's attempt came the closest. There were 49 low-hit games (one- and two-hitters), with 31 coming in the National League. The Los Angeles Dodgers led the major leagues with six low-hit performances, and no opposing pitcher threw one against L.A. batsmen. On the other hand, the Chicago Cubs fell victim to six low-hit games, but Cubs pitchers failed to throw even one.

Ironically, four of the Dodgers' low-hit gems came within an 11-day span in April, and all came against the N.L. West rival San Diego Padres. It also was ironic that 1984 N.L. batting champion Tony Gwynn had hits in each of the four games, including the Padres' first hit of the game three times.

On April 18 at San Diego, Fernando Valenzuela shut out the Padres, 5-0, on a two-hitter, with Gwynn's first-inning single and Kurt Bevacqua's eighth-inning single accounting for San Diego's only hits. Three days later, Dodgers righthander Orel Hershiser also pitched a two-hit shutout against the defending league champions, yielding only a double to Gwynn in the seventh inning and a single to Carmelo Martinez in the eighth.

When the two clubs resumed their rivalry one week later in Los Angeles, the two Dodger aces were at it again. On April 26,

Hershiser gave up only a fourth-inning single to Gwynn in a 2-0 L.A. victory. He faced the minimum 27 batters, however, because Gwynn was erased on a double play. Two nights later, Valenzuela threw another two-hitter at the Padres, but this time he ended up the losing pitcher after Gwynn's solo homer in the ninth gave the Padres a 1-0 triumph. Graig Nettles had singled in the second inning for San Diego's first hit.

Losing a low-hit game was not unique to Valenzuela and the Dodgers, however. Seven times in 1985 the club throwing the low-hit game ended up losing the contest. On April 14 at Chicago, Expos pitchers David Palmer and Bert Roberge held the Cubs to just two hits—but both were home runs. Jody Davis' second-inning blast and Gary Matthews' sixth-inning shot helped the Cubs to a 4-2 win.

Of the 14 one-hit games pitched during the '85 season, only two had home runs as the lone hit, and the Milwaukee Brewers were involved in both games. Coincidentally, both homers were hit in the fifth inning and both games ended with a 4-1 score. On August 2 at Detroit, Tigers lefthander Frank Tanana yielded a homer to Brewers outfielder Ben Oglivie, while on August 19 at Milwaukee, Brewers righthander Danny Darwin gave up only a home run to Minnesota's Roy Smalley.

Perhaps the season's most interesting one-hitter came June 5 at San Francisco, where Expos lefthander Mickey Mahler gave up only a third-inning single to Dan Gladden in a 6-0 Montreal victory. Mahler, a 32-year-old journeyman and brother of Braves pitcher Rick Mahler, was making his first major league start since 1979, when he played for Atlanta. Acquired by the Expos from St. Louis prior to the 1985 season, Mahler was released by Montreal on July 23 and was signed by Detroit late in the season.

For the second straight year, Hershiser led the National League with three low-hit games. Texas knuckleballer Charlie Hough also pitched three to lead the American League.

A complete list of one- and two-hit games for the 1985 season follows:

## NATIONAL LEAGUE
### One-Hit Games

April 16—Darling (seven innings) and Orosco (two innings), New York vs. Pittsburgh, 2-1—Ray, single in first.
April 26—Hershiser, Los Angeles vs. San Diego, 2-0—Gwynn, single in fourth.
May 11—Fernandez (six innings) and McDowell

(three innings), New York vs. Philadelphia, 4-0—Hayes, single in fourth.

June 2—Blue (five innings), Williams (1⅔ innings) and Davis (2⅓ innings), San Francisco vs. Philadelphia, 3-1—Schu, triple in fifth.

June 5—Mahler, Montreal vs. San Francisco, 6-0—Gladden, single in third.

July 23—Hershiser, Los Angeles vs. Pittsburgh, 6-0—Thompson, single in second.

Aug. 8—Tudor, St. Louis vs. Chicago, 8-0—Durham, single in fifth.

**Two-Hit Games**

April 14—Palmer (seven innings) and Roberge (one inning), Montreal vs. Chicago, 2-4—Davis, homer in second; Matthews, homer in sixth.

April 18—Valenzuela, Los Angeles vs. San Diego, 5-0—Gwynn, single in first; Bevacqua, single in eighth.

April 20—Gullickson (seven innings) and Reardon (two innings), Montreal vs. Chicago, 4-0—Lake, single in third; Cey, single in eighth.

April 20—Niekro (six innings) and DiPino (three innings), Houston vs. Atlanta, 8-1—Oberkfell, single in sixth; Cerone, single in seventh.

April 21—Hershiser, Los Angeles vs. San Diego, 2-0—Gwynn, double in seventh; Martinez, single in eighth.

April 27—Stuper, Cincinnati vs. San Francisco, 2-1—Davis, double in first; Thompson, single in eighth.

April 28—Valenzuela, Los Angeles vs. San Diego, 0-1—Nettles, single in second; Gwynn, homer in ninth.

May 8—Ryan (seven innings) and Smith (one inning), Houston vs. Montreal, 0-1—Driessen, single in third; Brooks, single in sixth.

May 16—Fernandez (seven innings) and Gorman (one inning), New York vs. Houston, 0-1—Cruz, double in first; Bass, single in seventh.

May 24—Hesketh (7⅓ innings) and Reardon (1⅔ innings), Montreal vs. San Francisco, 2-0—Laskey, single in third; Green, double in eighth.

May 29—Soto, Cincinnati vs. Chicago, 1-0—Sandberg, single in first; Moreland, single in fourth.

May 31—Cox, St. Louis vs. Cincinnati, 5-0—Concepcion, single in eighth; Oester, single in eighth.

June 2—DeLeon (five innings) and Holland (four innings), Pittsburgh vs. Atlanta, 5-0—Hubbard, double in third; Perry, single in ninth.

June 9—Niekro, Houston vs. San Francisco, 5-0—Uribe, single in fourth; Brenly, single in seventh.

June 13—McWilliams (seven innings) and Candelaria (two innings), Pittsburgh vs. St. Louis, 1-2—Clark, homer in second; Landrum, double in seventh.

June 22—Show (eight innings) and Stoddard (one inning), San Diego vs. San Francisco, 2-1—Brenly, single in second; Davis, homer in fifth.

June 23—Tudor, St. Louis vs. Chicago, 7-0—Lake, single in third; Sandberg, single in fourth.

Aug. 2—Hesketh (6⅓ innings) and Reardon (2⅔ innings), Montreal vs. Pittsburgh, 3-2—Ray, single in first; Almon, double in third.

Aug. 3—Welch, Los Angeles vs. Cincinnati, 2-0—Concepcion, single in fifth; Milner, double in sixth.

Aug. 23—Ryan (eight innings), Dawley (one inning) and DiPino (one inning), Houston vs. Pittsburgh, 2-0—Pena, double in second; Brown, single in seventh.

Aug. 27—Blue (six innings), Minton (two innings) and Davis (one inning), San Francisco vs. Montreal, 6-1—Butera, single in fifth; Raines, single in seventh.

Sept. 5—Cox, St. Louis vs. Chicago, 6-1—Dunston, double in first; Dernier, triple in sixth.

Sept. 16—Gooden, New York vs. Philadelphia, 9-0—Schmidt, double in fourth; Stone, single in ninth.

Sept. 24—Fernandez, New York vs. Philadelphia, 7-1—Schu, single in second; Aguayo, homer in eighth.

## AMERICAN LEAGUE

**One-Hit Games**

June 5—D. Martinez, Baltimore vs. California, 4-0—Narron, single in third.

June 26—Schrom, Minnesota vs. Kansas City, 2-1—Wilson, single in third.

June 29—Haas, Milwaukee vs. New York, 6-0—Mattingly, double in seventh.

July 11—Nipper (5⅓ innings) and Crawford (3⅔ innings), Boston vs. Seattle, 7-1—Calderon, single in sixth.

July 14—Terrell (7⅓ innings) and Hernandez (1⅔ innings), Detroit vs. Minnesota, 8-0—Brunansky, double in seventh.

Aug. 2—Tanana, Detroit vs. Milwaukee, 4-1—Oglivie, homer in fifth.

Aug. 19—Darwin, Milwaukee vs. Minnesota, 4-1—Smalley, homer in fifth.

**Two-Hit Games**

April 8—Hough (six innings) and Rozema (two innings), Texas vs. Baltimore, 2-4—Young, double in seventh; Murray, homer in eighth.

April 17—Darwin, Milwaukee vs. Detroit, 2-0—Whitaker, single in third; Parrish, single in fourth.

April 20—Noles (seven innings) and Schmidt (two innings), Texas vs. Milwaukee, 5-1—Giles, single in third; Simmons, double in eighth.

April 22—Hough, Texas vs. Baltimore, 6-1—Dwyer, double in first; Ripken, single in third.

May 17—Saberhagen, Kansas City vs. Milwaukee, 3-0—Yount, single in second; Gantner, single in sixth.

June 29—Terrell, Detroit vs. Toronto, 8-0—Moseby, double in first; Upshaw, single in seventh.

July 10—Hough, Texas vs. Cleveland, 4-1—Butler, singles in first and ninth.

Aug. 24—Langston (four innings) and Thomas (five innings), Seattle vs. New York, 3-4—Robertson, single in second; Mattingly, double in fourth.

Sept. 5—Alexander, Toronto vs. Minnesota, 7-0—Hrbek, double in fourth; Gagne, single in sixth.

Sept. 9—Candelaria (eight innings) and Corbett (one inning), California vs. Kansas City, 7-1—McRae, double in second; Motley, homer in eighth.

Sept. 27—Wills (eight innings) and Vande Berg (one inning), Seattle vs. Texas, 6-0—Slaught, double in fifth; Ward, single in ninth.

# Gooden Plenty Good in 10-K

**By DAVE SLOAN**

He first caught the attention of baseball men when he struck out 300 batters in 191 innings at Lynchburg of the Class A Carolina League in 1983. He followed that up by establishing a major league record for most strikeouts by a rookie pitcher with 276 whiffs in 1984. They salute him during his home games at Shea Stadium by holding aloft placards with a large letter 'K' on them every time he sets down a batter on strikes.

Dwight Gooden of the New York Mets receives plenty of acclaim for his remarkable pitching ability, and with good reason. In 1985, his 268 strikeouts led the major leagues for the second season in a row. The 1985 National League Cy Young Award winner struck out 10 or more batters in a game 11 times, and the next-best total was five, shared by three pitchers.

The ace righthander didn't play favorites in posting his 10-strikeout performances, either. Seven N.L. teams fell victim to Gooden at least once, with the Dodgers, Expos, Phillies and Giants falling twice. Gooden's 16 strikeouts against the Giants in a 3-0 victory August 20 was the best strikeout performance in the majors last year.

There were 88 10-or-more strikeout games in 1985, with N.L. pitchers hurling 48. Twenty-one clubs had a pitcher throw at least one such game, with the Orioles, Twins, A's, Braves and Cardinals being the exceptions. After Gooden, the three pitchers with five 10-strikeout performances were teammate Sid Fernandez, Bruce Hurst of the Red Sox and Britt Burns of the White Sox. Gooden was the only pitcher to surpass the 15-strikeout plateau.

Ironically, California's Mike Witt posted the American League high in strikeouts with 13 against Texas on October 6, the last day of the season. A year earlier, also against the Rangers in Arlington in the season finale, Witt threw a perfect game, becoming just the 13th pitcher in big-league history to accomplish the feat in a nine-inning game.

Houston fireballer Nolan Ryan had three games of 10 or more strikeouts to extend his major league record for such performances to 158. Ryan also became

**The Mets' Dwight Gooden.**

the first pitcher in baseball history to reach the 4,000 mark for career strikeouts when he fanned the Mets' Danny Heep in the sixth inning July 11 in the Astrodome.

Following is a list of all pitchers who achieved at least 10 strikeouts in a game in 1985, with the number of times the feat was accomplished:

AMERICAN LEAGUE: Baltimore—None. Boston (8)—Hurst 5, Boyd 2, Clemens. California (4)—Witt 3, McCaskill. Chicago (10)—Burns 5, Bannister 4, Seaver. Cleveland (4)—Blyleven 3, Heaton. Detroit (4)—Tanana 3, Morris. Kansas City (4)—Saberhagen 2, Black, Jackson. Milwaukee (1)—Higuera. Minnesota—None. New York (1)—Guidry. Oakland—None. Seattle (2)—Young, Moore. Texas (1)—Mason. Toronto (1)—Alexander.

NATIONAL LEAGUE: Atlanta—None. Chicago (4)—Eckersley 2, Sanderson, Sutcliffe. Cincinnati (5)—Soto 3, McGaffigan 2. Houston (3)—Ryan 3. Los Angeles (2)—Valenzuela 2. Montreal (3)—Hesketh, Schatzeder, Smith. New York (17)—Gooden 11, Fernandez 5, Darling. Philadelphia (3)—Denny, Gross, Hudson. Pittsburgh (5)—DeLeon 3, Reuschel, Tunnell. St. Louis—None. San Diego (1)—Show. San Francisco (5)—Blue 2, Krukow 2, Mason.

---

## 1985 Game With 15 or More Strikeouts

| Date | Pitcher—Club—Opp. | Place | IP. | H. | R. | ER. | BB. | SO. | Result |
|------|-------------------|-------|-----|-----|-----|-----|-----|-----|--------|
| Aug. 20—Gooden, Mets vs. Giants | | New York | 9 | 7 | 0 | 0 | 3 | 16 | W 3-0 |

# Quisenberry Is No. 1—Again

**By LARRY WIGGE**

Kansas City relief ace Dan Quisenberry put his name in the record books again in 1985, becoming the first player to win The Sporting News Fireman of the Year award five times.

Winning the award for the fifth time in the last six seasons, Quisenberry passed veterans Bruce Sutter and Rollie Fingers. Sutter was the National League's top relief pitcher in 1979 with Chicago and in 1981, '82 and '84 in St. Louis. Fingers was the N.L.'s top reliever with San Diego in 1977, '78 and '80 and the American League's top man in 1981 with Milwaukee.

Though Quisenberry couldn't match his 44-save, six-relief victory performance of 1984, his 37 saves and eight wins played a big part in helping the Royals win another A.L. West Division title en route to their World Series championship. New York's Dave Righetti, with 29 saves and 12 relief wins, was second, while Chicago's Bob

James was next with 32 saves and eight relief victories. Detroit's Willie Hernandez and California's Donnie Moore each compiled 39 points.

Montreal's Jeff Reardon led the major leagues with 41 saves and became a first-time winner of the Fireman Award. In supplanting Sutter as the top reliever in the N.L., Reardon became only the second Montreal pitcher to win the award. (Mike Marshall was Fireman of the Year in 1973).

Reardon's 41 saves and two relief wins gave him 43 points, three more than Chicago's Lee Smith, who had 33 saves and seven victories. Dave Smith of Houston was third with 36 points and Ted Power of Cincinnati was next with 35. Sutter, now with the Atlanta Braves, fell off his league-leading 50-point 1984 pace to 30 points with the Braves.

Following is a complete list of major league players who recorded saves or relief wins in 1985:

## AMERICAN LEAGUE

| Pitcher—Club | Saves | Relief Wins | Tot. Pts. |
|---|---|---|---|
| Quisenberry, Kansas City | 37 | 8 | 45 |
| Righetti, New York | 29 | 12 | 41 |
| James, Chicago | 32 | 8 | 40 |
| Hernandez, Detroit | 31 | 8 | 39 |
| Moore, California | 31 | 8 | 39 |
| Howell, Oakland | 29 | 9 | 38 |
| Davis, Minnesota | 25 | 2 | 27 |
| Aase, Baltimore | 14 | 10 | 24 |
| Nunez, Seattle | 16 | 7 | 23 |
| Caudill, Toronto | 14 | 4 | 18 |
| Fingers, Milwaukee | 17 | 1 | 18 |
| Fisher, New York | 14 | 4 | 18 |
| Acker, Toronto | 10 | 7 | 17 |
| Crawford, Boston | 12 | 5 | 17 |
| Gibson, Milwaukee | 11 | 6 | 17 |
| Harris, Texas | 11 | 5 | 16 |
| Henke, Toronto | 13 | 3 | 16 |
| Stanley, Boston | 10 | 6 | 16 |
| Cliburn, California | 6 | 9 | 15 |
| Stewart, Baltimore | 9 | 5 | 14 |
| Lamp, Toronto | 2 | 11 | 13 |
| Lavelle, Toronto | 8 | 5 | 13 |
| Waddell, Cleveland | 9 | 4 | 13 |
| Reed, Cleveland | 8 | 3 | 11 |
| Schmidt, Texas | 5 | 5 | 10 |
| Ontiveros, Oakland | 8 | 1 | 9 |
| Lopez, Detroit | 5 | 3 | 8 |
| Rozema, Texas | 7 | 1 | 8 |
| Snell, Baltimore | 5 | 3 | 8 |
| R. Thomas, Seattle | 1 | 7 | 8 |
| Thompson, Cleveland | 5 | 3 | 8 |
| Atherton, Oakland | 3 | 4 | 7 |
| T. Martinez, Baltimore | 4 | 3 | 7 |
| McClure, Milwaukee | 3 | 4 | 7 |
| Best, Seattle | 4 | 2 | 6 |
| Bordi, New York | 2 | 4 | 6 |
| Clements, California | 1 | 5 | 6 |
| Eufemia, Minnesota | 2 | 4 | 6 |
| Nelson, Chicago | 2 | 4 | 6 |
| Agosto, Chicago | 1 | 4 | 5 |
| Clark, Cleveland | 2 | 3 | 5 |
| Filson, Minnesota | 2 | 3 | 5 |

| Pitcher—Club | Saves | Relief Wins | Tot. Pts. |
|---|---|---|---|
| Henry, Texas | 3 | 2 | 5 |
| Shirley, New York | 2 | 3 | 5 |
| Spillner, Chicago | 1 | 4 | 5 |
| Vande Berg, Seattle | 3 | 2 | 5 |
| Clear, Boston | 3 | 1 | 4 |
| Sanchez, California | 2 | 2 | 4 |
| Stewart, Texas | 4 | 0 | 4 |
| Waits, Milwaukee | 1 | 3 | 4 |
| Wehrmeister, Chicago | 2 | 2 | 4 |
| Corbett, California | 0 | 3 | 3 |
| Darwin, Milwaukee | 2 | 1 | 3 |
| Kison, Boston | 1 | 2 | 3 |
| M. Jones, Kansas City | 0 | 3 | 3 |
| Langford, Oakland | 0 | 3 | 3 |
| Lysander, Minnesota | 3 | 0 | 3 |
| Musselman, Toronto | 0 | 3 | 3 |
| Ojeda, Boston | 1 | 2 | 3 |
| Ruhle, Cleveland | 3 | 0 | 3 |
| Scherrer, Detroit | 0 | 3 | 3 |
| Trujillo, Boston | 1 | 2 | 3 |
| Von Ohlen, Cleveland | 0 | 3 | 3 |
| Wardle, Minn.-Cleveland | 1 | 2 | 3 |
| Allen, New York | 1 | 1 | 2 |
| Beckwith, Kansas City | 1 | 1 | 2 |
| Cary, Detroit | 2 | 0 | 2 |
| Easterly, Cleveland | 0 | 2 | 2 |
| Farr, Kansas City | 1 | 1 | 2 |
| Gleaton, Chicago | 1 | 1 | 2 |
| Howe, Minnesota | 0 | 2 | 2 |
| LaCoss, Kansas City | 1 | 1 | 2 |
| Ladd, Milwaukee | 2 | 0 | 2 |
| Lollar, Chi.-Boston | 1 | 1 | 2 |
| Mura, Oakland | 1 | 1 | 2 |
| Noles, Texas | 1 | 1 | 2 |
| Rijo, Oakland | 0 | 2 | 2 |
| Scurry, New York | 1 | 1 | 2 |
| Searage, Milwaukee | 1 | 1 | 2 |
| Snyder, Seattle | 1 | 1 | 2 |
| Stanton, Seattle-Chicago | 1 | 1 | 2 |
| Surhoff, Texas | 2 | 0 | 2 |
| Tobik, Seattle | 1 | 1 | 2 |

**Kansas City's Dan Quisenberry won his fifth Fireman of the Year award in 1985.**

One save—Barkley, Cleveland; Dixon, Baltimore; Gura, Kansas City; Lazorko, Seattle; O'Neal, Detroit; Slaton, California; Stoddard, Detroit; Whitehouse, Minnesota; Wills, Seattle; Young, Seattle.

One relief win—Bair, Detroit; Berenguer, Detroit; Burns, Chicago; Cocanower, Milwaukee; Cowley, New York; Davis, Toronto; Gubicza, Kansas City; Habyan, Baltimore; Huismann, Kansas City; John, Calif.-Oakland; Jones, Chicago; Key, Toronto; Krueger, Oakland; Lesley, Milwaukee; Mahler, Detroit; D. Martinez, Baltimore; McCatty, Oakland; Swift, Seattle; Warren, Oakland; Welsh, Texas; Williams, Texas.

## NATIONAL LEAGUE

| Pitcher—Club | Saves | Relief Wins | Tot. Pts. | Pitcher—Club | Saves | Relief Wins | Tot. Pts. |
|---|---|---|---|---|---|---|---|
| Reardon, Montreal | 41 | 2 | 43 | Holland, Phil.-Pittsburgh | 5 | 1 | 6 |
| L. Smith, Chicago | 33 | 7 | 40 | Hume, Cincinnati | 3 | 3 | 6 |
| D. Smith, Houston | 27 | 9 | 36 | Sisk, New York | 2 | 4 | 6 |
| Power, Cincinnati | 27 | 8 | 35 | McCullers, San Diego | 5 | 0 | 5 |
| Gossage, San Diego | 26 | 5 | 31 | Roberge, Montreal | 2 | 3 | 5 |
| Sutter, Atlanta | 23 | 7 | 30 | St. Claire, Montreal | 0 | 5 | 5 |
| Niedenfuer, Los Angeles | 19 | 7 | 26 | Howe, Los Angeles | 3 | 1 | 4 |
| Orosco, New York | 17 | 8 | 25 | Meridith, Chicago | 1 | 3 | 4 |
| Franco, Cincinnati | 12 | 12 | 24 | R. Robinson, Cincinnati | 1 | 3 | 4 |
| Lahti, St. Louis | 19 | 5 | 24 | Shipanoff, Philadelphia | 3 | 1 | 4 |
| McDowell, New York | 17 | 6 | 23 | Allen, St. Louis | 2 | 1 | 3 |
| Garrelts, San Francisco | 13 | 9 | 22 | Baller, Chicago | 1 | 2 | 3 |
| Tekulve, Pitts.-Philadelphia | 14 | 4 | 18 | J. DeLeon, Pittsburgh | 3 | 0 | 3 |
| Burke, Montreal | 8 | 9 | 17 | L. DeLeon, San Diego | 3 | 0 | 3 |
| Carman, Philadelphia | 7 | 9 | 16 | Forsch, St. Louis | 2 | 1 | 3 |
| Howell, Los Angeles | 12 | 4 | 16 | Forster, Atlanta | 1 | 2 | 3 |
| Dayley, St. Louis | 11 | 4 | 15 | Gorman, New York | 0 | 3 | 3 |
| M. Davis, San Francisco | 7 | 5 | 12 | Horton, St. Louis | 1 | 2 | 3 |
| Candelaria, Pittsburgh | 9 | 2 | 11 | Jackson, San Diego | 2 | 1 | 3 |
| Campbell, St. Louis | 4 | 5 | 9 | Reuschel, Pittsburgh | 1 | 2 | 3 |
| DiPino, Houston | 6 | 3 | 9 | Rucker, Philadelphia | 1 | 2 | 3 |
| Frazier, Chicago | 2 | 7 | 9 | Z. Smith, Atlanta | 0 | 3 | 3 |
| Guante, Pittsburgh | 5 | 4 | 9 | Sorensen, Chicago | 0 | 3 | 3 |
| Lefferts, San Diego | 2 | 7 | 9 | Thurmond, San Diego | 2 | 1 | 3 |
| Minton, San Francisco | 4 | 5 | 9 | Walter, San Diego | 3 | 0 | 3 |
| Brusstar, Chicago | 4 | 4 | 8 | Blue, San Francisco | 0 | 2 | 2 |
| Worrell, St. Louis | 5 | 3 | 8 | Clements, Pittsburgh | 2 | 0 | 2 |
| Dawley, Houston | 2 | 5 | 7 | Heathcock, Houston | 1 | 1 | 2 |
| Garber, Atlanta | 1 | 6 | 7 | Kerfeld, Houston | 0 | 2 | 2 |
| Lucas, Montreal | 1 | 6 | 7 | Powell, Los Angeles | 1 | 1 | 2 |
| D. Robinson, Pittsburgh | 3 | 4 | 7 | Scurry, Pittsburgh | 2 | 0 | 2 |
| Andersen, Philadelphia | 3 | 3 | 6 | Solano, Houston | 0 | 2 | 2 |
| Calhoun, Houston | 4 | 2 | 6 | Stoddard, San Diego | 1 | 1 | 2 |
| Camp, Atlanta | 3 | 3 | 6 | Stuper, Cincinnati | 0 | 2 | 2 |
| Diaz, Los Angeles | 0 | 6 | 6 | Williams, San Francisco | 0 | 2 | 2 |
| Dedmon, Atlanta | 0 | 6 | 6 | Willis, Cincinnati | 1 | 1 | 2 |

One save—Engel, Chicago; Honeycutt, Los Angeles; Leach, New York; Mahler, Montreal; Mathis, Houston; McMurtry, Atlanta; Price, Cincinnati; Ross, Houston; Toliver, Philadelphia.

One relief win—Aguilera, New York; Brennan, Los Angeles; Buchanan, Cincinnati; K. Gross, Philadelphia; Gumpert, Chicago; Hershiser, Los Angeles; Holton, Los Angeles; McWilliams, Pittsburgh; Pastore, Cincinnati; Perlman, Chicago; Perry, St. Louis; Rawley, Philadelphia; Surhoff, Philadelphia; Winn, Pittsburgh; Wojna, San Diego; Youmans, Montreal.

# Mets Split Dozen 1-0 Games

**By DAVE SLOAN**

There were 44 games in the major leagues decided by a 1-0 score during the 1985 season, but the two most important and exciting 1-0 games were a pair of September matchups between the St. Louis Cardinals and the New York Mets with the National League East title on the line.

On September 11 at Shea Stadium, with the Mets holding a one-game lead in the division race, Mets ace Dwight Gooden and Cardinals standout John Tudor dueled through nine innings without either pitcher allowing a run. In the 10th, New York Manager Dave Johnson went with reliever Jesse Orosco after pinch hitting for Gooden in the bottom of the ninth. The move proved disastrous for the Mets. Cardinals pinch-hitter Cesar Cedeno led off the 10th by drilling a 0-2 slider from Orosco over the left-field wall for a St. Louis victory, knotting the race with 25 games to play.

On October 1 at Busch Stadium, with the Cardinals holding a three-game lead in the race, Tudor and Mets righthander Ron Darling hooked up in another nine-inning scoreless duel. Again, Johnson pulled his starter after nine innings in favor of Orosco. St. Louis Manager Whitey Herzog countered by pulling Tudor after 10 innings in favor of Ken Dayley, and the result this time was bad for the Cardinals. Mets right fielder Darryl Strawberry blasted a hanging curve off the scoreboard in right field, and New York moved to within two games of the Cards with five games left to play.

The Mets led all major league teams with 12 1-0 games, winning six and losing six. Gooden led all pitchers by winning three 1-0 decisions, while teammate Sid Fernandez was the only major leaguer to lose two 1-0 games. The Chicago Cubs and the San Francisco Giants followed the Mets with seven 1-0 games apiece, with each club winning three times and losing four.

Tudor, Jack Morris of Detroit, Mike Smithson of Minnesota, Dave Dravecky of San Diego and Rick Sutcliffe of the Cubs all won two 1-0 games. The Padres won all six of their 1-0 decisions.

There were 33 1-0 games in the National League last season, 11 in the American League. All clubs except for the Baltimore Orioles and the Seattle Mariners were involved in at least one 1-0 contest.

The season's longest 1-0 game was played May 9 at San Francisco, where the Giants ended a 24-inning scoreless drought by pushing across a run in the 12th inning to beat the Cubs.

The complete list of 1-0 games, including the winning and losing pitchers and the inning in which the run was scored, follows:

### AMERICAN LEAGUE (11)

**APRIL—**

| Date | Winner | Loser | Inning |
|---|---|---|---|
| 10 | *Caudill, Tor. | *Beckwith, K.C. | 10 |
| 26 | Morris, Det. | *Burris, Mil. | 1 |

**MAY—**

| Date | Winner | Loser | Inning |
|---|---|---|---|
| 24 | Hough, Tex. | Boyd, Bos. | 5 |

**JUNE—**

| Date | Winner | Loser | Inning |
|---|---|---|---|
| 9 | *Romanick, Cal. | Jackson, K.C. | 4 |
| 29 | *Smithson, Minn. | *Burns, Chi. | 4 |

**JULY—**

| Date | Winner | Loser | Inning |
|---|---|---|---|
| 10 | Morris, Det. | Seaver, Chi. | 8 |
| 11 | Jackson, K.C. | Ruhle, Clev. | 1 |
| 19 | Seaver, Chi. | Blyleven, Clev. | 2 |

**AUGUST—**

| Date | Winner | Loser | Inning |
|---|---|---|---|
| 24 | Smithson, Minn. | Hurst, Bos. | 5 |

**SEPTEMBER—**

| Date | Winner | Loser | Inning |
|---|---|---|---|
| 18 | *Rijo, Oak. | *Schulze, Clev. | 8 |

**OCTOBER—**

| Date | Winner | Loser | Inning |
|---|---|---|---|
| 2 | Higuera, Mil. | Shirley, N.Y. | 3 |

### NATIONAL LEAGUE (33)

**APRIL—**

| Date | Winner | Loser | Inning |
|---|---|---|---|
| 12 | *Berenyi, N.Y. | *Soto, Cin. | 4 |
| 13 | Valenzuela, L.A. | *Davis, S.F. | 8 |
| 16 | Eckersley, Chi. | *Holland, Phil. | 10 |
| 17 | *Hershiser, L.A. | *DiPino, Hou. | 11 |
| 19 | *Gooden, N.Y. | *Hudson, Phil. | 9 |
| 21 | *Browning, Cin. | *Hammaker, S.F. | 3 |
| 28 | *Lefferts, S.D. | Valenzuela, L.A. | 9 |

**MAY—**

| Date | Winner | Loser | Inning |
|---|---|---|---|
| 8 | Sutcliffe, Chi. | *Krukow, S.F. | 1 |
| 8 | *Hesketh, Mont. | *Ryan, Hou. | 2 |
| 9 | Thurmond, S.D. | *Bielecki, Pitt. | 7 |
| 9 | *Garrelts, S.F. | *Brusstar, Chi. | 12 |
| 10 | *Reuss, L.A. | *Rhoden, Pitt. | 6 |
| 13 | *Barker, Atl. | *Lynch, N.Y. | 2 |
| 16 | *Scott, Hou. | *Fernandez, N.Y. | 1 |
| 24 | *Dravecky, S.D. | Denny, Phil. | 8 |
| 29 | Soto, Cin. | *Ruthven, Chi. | 3 |

**JUNE—**

| Date | Winner | Loser | Inning |
|---|---|---|---|
| 7 | Sutcliffe, Chi. | *DeLeon, Pitt. | 2 |
| 8 | Tudor, St.L. | *Gorman, N.Y. | 9 |
| 15 | Hoyt, S.D. | *Gott, S.F. | 5 |
| 19 | *Koosman, Phil. | Andujar, St.L. | 2 |
| 19 | Gooden, N.Y. | *Sanderson, Chi. | 4 |

**JULY—**

| Date | Winner | Loser | Inning |
|---|---|---|---|
| 1 | *Reuschel, Pitt. | *Fernandez, N.Y. | 2 |
| 14 | Gooden, N.Y. | *Knepper, Hou. | 8 |
| 18 | Krukow, S.F. | *Frazier, Chi. | 9 |
| 19 | *Smith, Atl. | *Aguilera, N.Y. | 7 |
| 25 | *Gullickson, Mon. | *Hume, Cin. | 7 |

**AUGUST—**

| Date | Winner | Loser | Inning |
|---|---|---|---|
| 19 | *Darling, N.Y. | *Burke, Mon. | 8 |
| 20 | *Dravecky, S.D. | *Gullickson, Mon. | 5 |
| 30 | Tibbs, Cin. | Reuschel, Pitt. | 9 |

**SEPTEMBER—**

| Date | Winner | Loser | Inning |
|---|---|---|---|
| 11 | Tudor, St.L. | *Orosco, N.Y. | 10 |
| 21 | Show, S.D. | *Johnson, Atl. | 4 |

**OCTOBER—**

| Date | Winner | Loser | Inning |
|---|---|---|---|
| 1 | *Orosco, N.Y. | *Dayley, St.L. | 11 |
| 4 | Mason, S.F. | Mahler, Atl. | 9 |

*Did not pitch complete game.

# Parrish Ties 3-Homer Mark

**By DAVE SLOAN**

Normally, when a player belts three home runs and drives in eight runs in a single game, his club will coast to an easy victory. But normal games are seldom played at Chicago's Wrigley Field.

In a September 24 contest between the Montreal Expos and the Cubs, Expos outfielder Andre Dawson hammered three homers in the first five innings as Montreal grabbed a commanding 15-2 lead. The Expos scored 12 runs in the fifth inning—the most runs in a single inning in the major leagues in more than two years—as Dawson clubbed two homers and Tim Wallach one. But the Expos' pitching staff yielded three runs in the seventh inning, four in the eighth and five in the ninth before finally securing a 17-15 triumph. The Cubs had a runner on second base and the tying run at the plate when the game ended.

Dawson's three-homer performance was the sixth and final one in the majors in 1985. Seattle's Gorman Thomas, Texas' Larry Parrish, Baltimore's Eddie Murray and the New York Mets' Darryl Strawberry and Gary Carter earlier had accomplished the feat. Only Murray, who collected nine runs batted in during his three-homer game against California on August 26, had more RBIs than Dawson. The Orioles won that game, 17-3.

Parrish hit his three homers consecutively, making him only the third player in baseball history to perform the feat in both leagues. Parrish, who had three-homer games with Montreal in 1977, '78 and '80, joined Johnny Mize and Dave Kingman in that category.

Strawberry and Carter were the only teammates with three-homer games. Strawberry hit his against the Cubs on August 5 at Wrigley—the Cubs were the only club to be victimized twice—while Carter clubbed his three homers (they were consecutive) against the Padres on September 3. Carter came back the next day to wallop another two home runs against San Diego pitching.

Including the six three-homer performances, there were 171 multi-homer games in the big leagues last season. American League batters compiled 107 such games, with the New York Yankees leading all clubs with 16. Yankees first baseman Don Mattingly, the A.L. Most Valuable Player, collected five multi-homer games in 1985, tying with Seattle's

Thomas, Ron Kittle of the White Sox and Bob Horner of Atlanta for the most in baseball. The St. Louis Cardinals were the only club without at least one multi-homer performance.

Eleven times last season two players posted multi-homer performances in the same game, and three players did it in the same game once. In a September 28 game at Wrigley Field, the Cubs outlasted the Phillies, 11-10, with Ron Cey and Keith Moreland belting two homers each for Chicago and Mike Schmidt two for Philadelphia.

In an August 8 doubleheader at Yankee Stadium, Dave Winfield hit two homers in New York's 8-1 victory in the first game and Mattingly and Cleveland's Brett Butler hit two each in the Yankees' 7-6 triumph in the nightcap.

On four occasions last season, players hit homers from each side of the plate in the same game. Seattle's Donnie Scott (against Milwaukee) on April 29, Baltimore's Mike Young (vs. Cleveland) on August 13, Detroit's Nelson Simmons (vs. Baltimore) on September 16 and Baltimore's Murray each accomplished the feat. Murray's came in his three-homer game against the Angels, with two of the homers coming from the left side.

The season's most noteworthy multi-homer performance came from Philadelphia's Von Hayes, who had just 13 homers during 1985 and one multi-homer game. On June 11 at Veterans Stadium against the Mets, Hayes belted two home runs in the first inning as the Phillies scored nine times en route to a 26-7 blowout victory. Hayes became the first player in major league history to hit two homers in the first inning of a game as his team scored more runs in one game than any Phillies team in modern history. Ironically, Hayes' blasts were the only homers hit by the Phillies in a 27-hit attack.

Following is a list of players who had multi-homer games in '85 and the number of times they did it:

**AMERICAN LEAGUE:** Baltimore (12)—Gross 2, Lacy 2, Ripken 2, Young 2, Dempsey, Dwyer, Murray, Roenicke. Boston (6)—Armas, Easler, Evans, Gedman, Lyons, Rice. California (7)—Jackson 3, Jones 2, DeCinces, Howell. Chicago (8)—Kittle 5, Fisk 3. Cleveland (5)—Thornton 2, Butler, Carter, Castillo. Detroit (14)—Evans 4, Parrish 3, Lemon 2, Simmons 2, Gibson, Sanchez, Whitaker.

Don Mattingly's five multi-homer games tied for the major-league lead and helped the Yankees grab team honors with 16.

Kansas City (11)—Balboni 4, Brett 3, White 2, McRae, Sheridan. Milwaukee (4) —Robidoux, Schroeder, Simmons, Yount. Minnesota (2)—Brunansky, Gaetti. New York (16)—Mattingly 5, Hassey 2, Henderson 2, Winfield 2, Baylor, Griffey, Pagliarulo, Pasqua, Randolph. Oakland (7)— Davis 2, Lansford 2, Canseco, Kingman, Murphy. Seattle (8)—Thomas 5, Bradley, Presley, Scott. Texas (3)—Parrish 2, Jones. Toronto (4)—Barfield 2, Moseby, Upshaw.

**NATIONAL LEAGUE:** Atlanta (9)— Horner 5, Murphy 2, Harper, Owen. Chi- cago (10)—Sandberg 3, Cey 2, Durham 2, Bosley, Davis, Moreland. Cincinnati (2)— Parker 2. Houston (2)—Bass, Davis. Los Angeles (5)—Brock 2, Guerrero, Landreaux, Marshall. Montreal (7)—Dawson 2, Wallach 2, Fitzgerald, Raines, Webster. New York (6)—Carter 3, Strawberry 3. Philadelphia (11)—Virgil 3, Aguayo 2, Daulton, Diaz, Hayes, Schmidt, Stone, Wilson. Pittsburgh (2)—Madlock, Pena. St. Louis—None. San Diego (4)—Martinez 2, Garvey, Nettles. San Francisco (6)— Leonard 2, Brenly, Brown, Davis, Gott.

A recap of the three-homer games:

| Date | Player—Club—Opp. | Place | AB. | R. | H. | 2B. | 3B. | HR. | RBI. | Result |
|------|------------------|-------|-----|----|----|-----|-----|-----|------|--------|
| Apr. 11 | Thomas, Mariners vs. A's | H | 3 | 4 | 3 | 0 | 0 | 3 | 6 | W 14-6 |
| Apr. 29 | Parrish, Rangers vs. Yankees | H | 4 | 3 | 3 | 0 | 0 | 3 | 6 | W 7-5 |
| Aug. 5 | Strawberry, Mets vs. Cubs | A | 4 | 4 | 4 | 0 | 0 | 3 | 5 | W 7-2 |
| Aug. 26 | Murray, Orioles vs. Angels | A | 5 | 3 | 4 | 0 | 0 | 3 | 9 | W 17-3 |
| Sept. 3 | Carter, Mets vs. Padres | A | 4 | 3 | 3 | 0 | 0 | 3 | 6 | W 8-3 |
| Sept. 24 | Dawson, Expos vs. Cubs | A | 6 | 3 | 4 | 0 | 0 | 3 | 8 | W 17-15 |

# Murray, O's Set Pace in Slams

**By DAVE SLOAN**

Lou Gehrig's major league record of 23 grand slams is safe for now, but Orioles first baseman Eddie Murray last season continued to pound American League pitching for home runs when the bases were loaded.

Murray tied with the Twins' Kent Hrbek for the major league lead with three slams in 1985, giving him 12 in his nine-year career. Only Dave Kingman of the A's, who has hit 15 grand slams but is seven years older than Murray, has hit more among active major leaguers.

Murray's third slam of '85 came in Baltimore's 17-3 shellacking of the Angels on August 26 and was probably his most memorable. After clubbing a three-run homer off lefthander John Candelaria in the first inning and a solo homer off reliever Alan Fowlkes in the fourth, Murray nailed a grand slam off Fowlkes the following inning to give Baltimore a 14-3 lead. Murray finished the game with four hits in five at-bats and nine runs batted in. It was the third time in his career that he had hit three home runs in one game.

As a team, the Orioles hit seven grand slams to lead the major leagues for the fourth year in succession. Rookie third baseman Fritz Connally hit two slams for Baltimore—on April 19 and May 17—that also were the first two home runs of his major league career.

Besides Murray and Hrbek with three slams apiece, 16 other major leaguers, including Connally, hit two each. Cardinals third baseman Terry Pendleton's second slam of the season—off Mets reliever Joe Sambito on June 9—was the only inside-the-park grand slam of 1985.

All major league clubs except for the Atlanta Braves hit at least one slam, and all clubs yielded at least one. The Dodgers and the Brewers gave up just one each. The pitcher who led the majors in the dubious category of most grand slams allowed was White Sox lefthander Floyd Bannister, who gave up slams to the Indians' Brook Jacoby (on May 7), Murray (on July 25) and the Brewers' Cecil Cooper (on August 15).

On three occasions, final-inning grand slams provided the margin of victory. On April 13 at Seattle, the Mariners' Phil Bradley belted a slam off Twins reliever Ron Davis in the bottom of the ninth for an 8-7 Seattle victory. On April 25 at Milwaukee, the Brewers' Ted Simmons

**Baltimore's Eddie Murray blasted three more grand slams in '85.**

tagged the Tigers' Bill Scherrer for a grand slam to break a tie game and send Milwaukee to an 11-7 triumph. The Brewers scored five runs in both the eighth and ninth innings to erase a 7-1 Detroit lead.

On June 25 at Anaheim, after the Cleveland Indians had taken a 3-2 lead in the top of the 13th inning, the Angels' Ruppert Jones tagged Indians reliever Neal Heaton for a grand slam in the bottom of the inning to give California a 7-3 victory.

Darryl Strawberry of the Mets gave New York a quick 4-0 lead against Pittsburgh on April 28 when he connected off Mike Bielecki in the first inning. But the Mets failed to score in the next 16 innings before pushing across a run in the bottom of the 18th for a 5-4 triumph.

When the Mets traveled to Philadelphia on June 11, the Phils' Von Hayes led off the game with a home run off New York's Tom Gorman. Before the first inning was over, Hayes had hit a grand slam off Calvin Schiraldi and the Phillies were on their way to a resounding 26-7 victory, the most runs scored by a National League team in 41 years. Hayes' two first-inning home runs set a major league record.

Only once in 1985 did teammates hit

**Von Hayes' only slam came in a record-setting performance.**

grand slams in the same game. Pedro Guerrero and Mariano Duncan of the Dodgers turned the trick August 23 against Montreal. Guerrero's sixth-inning blast off Tim Burke and Duncan's seventh-inning shot off Gary Lucas accounted for all the Dodgers' runs in an 8-4 L.A. triumph. It marked the 34th time in major league history that one club had hit two slams in the same game.

There were a record 94 grand slams hit in the major leagues last season, with the American League hitting 51 for the second consecutive year. The 43 slams by N.L. batters was 17 more than the year before.

The complete list of grand slams, with the inning in which each was hit in parentheses, follows:

### AMERICAN LEAGUE (51)

**APRIL—**
| | |
|---|---|
| 11 —Thomas, Seattle vs. Kaiser, Oakland | (4) |
| 12 —Schofield, California vs. Atherton, Oakland | (9) |
| 12 —Schroeder, Milwaukee vs. Tanana, Texas | (3) |
| 13 —Bradley, Seattle vs. Davis, Minnesota | (9) |
| 19 —Connally, Baltimore vs. Alexander, Toronto | (5) |
| 20 —Barrett, Boston vs. James, Chicago | (9) |
| 25 —Simmons, Milwaukee vs. Scherrer, Detroit | (9) |
| 30 —Balboni, Kansas City vs. Roman, Cleveland | (3) |

**MAY—**
| | |
|---|---|
| 7 —Jacoby, Cleveland vs. Bannister, Chicago | (1) |
| 8 —Gaetti, Minnesota vs. Cowley, New York | (1) |
| 11 —Baylor, New York vs. Black, Kansas City | (4) |
| 12 —Bush, Minnesota vs. Dixon, Baltimore | (1) |
| 14 —Griffey, New York vs. Wardle, Minnesota | (7) |
| 15 —Narron, California vs. Caudill, Toronto | (9) |
| 17 —Connally, Baltimore vs. Young, Seattle | (1) |
| 23 —Phelps, Seattle vs. Niekro, New York | (3) |
| 23 —Ward, Texas vs. Hurst, Boston | (1) |

**JUNE—**
| | |
|---|---|
| 1 —Gedman, Boston vs. Tanana, Texas | (6) |
| 8 —Tabler, Cleveland vs. Beattie, Seattle | (1) |
| 18 —Parrish, Detroit vs. Hurst, Boston | (6) |
| 23 —Whitt, Toronto vs. Kison, Boston | (6) |
| 25 —Jones, California vs. Heaton, Cleveland | (13) |
| 26 —Jackson, California vs. Clark, Cleveland | (6) |

**JULY—**
| | |
|---|---|
| 2 —Evans, Detroit vs. Davis, Baltimore | (1) |
| 2 —Baines, Chicago vs. Barojas, Seattle | (8) |
| 6 —Lynn, Baltimore vs. Beckwith, Kansas City | (5) |
| 8 —Fisk, Chicago vs. Lopez, Detroit | (6) |
| 9 —Murray, Baltimore vs. Wardle, Minnesota | (6) |
| 9 —Bell, Toronto vs. Vande Berg, Seattle | (13) |
| 10 —White, Kansas City vs. Rasmussen, New York | (1) |
| 11 —Baylor, New York vs. Welsh, Texas | (4) |
| 13 —Roenicke, Baltimore vs. Burns, Chicago | (5) |
| 18 —Hrbek, Minnesota vs. Fisher, New York | (7) |
| 22 —Hrbek, Minnesota vs. Davis, Baltimore | (2) |
| 23 —Vukovich, Cleveland vs. Hough, Texas | (2) |
| 25 —Murray, Baltimore vs. Bannister, Chicago | (8) |

**AUGUST—**
| | |
|---|---|
| 2 —Bell, Toronto vs. Cook, Texas | (4) |
| 4 —Evans, Detroit vs. Gibson, Milwaukee | (7) |
| 14 —Buckner, Boston vs. Beckwith, Kansas City | (3) |
| 15 —Cooper, Milwaukee vs. Bannister, Chicago | (7) |
| 15 —Hrbek, Minnesota vs. Long, Seattle | (5) |
| 17 —Collins, Oakland vs. Witt, California | (4) |
| 26 —Murray, Baltimore vs. Fowlkes, California | (5) |
| 27 —Howell, California vs. McGregor, Baltimore | (2) |
| 28 —Franco, Cleveland vs. Clear, Boston | (7) |
| 31* —Easler, Boston vs. Blyleven, Minnesota | (6) |

**SEPTEMBER—**
| | |
|---|---|
| 2 —Easler, Boston vs. Welsh, Texas | (3) |
| 10 —Kingman, Oakland vs. Williams, Texas | (7) |
| 13 —De Sa, Chicago vs. Tobik, Seattle | (9) |
| 20 —Balboni, Kansas City vs. Blyleven, Minnesota | (1) |
| 22 —Grich, California vs. Easterly, Cleveland | (1) |

### NATIONAL LEAGUE (43)

**APRIL—**
| | |
|---|---|
| 15 —Martinez, San Diego vs. Minton, San Francisco | (7) |
| 21 —Pendleton, St. Louis vs. Scurry, Pittsburgh | (7) |
| 28 —Strawberry, New York vs. Bielecki, Pittsburgh | (1) |

**MAY—**
| | |
|---|---|
| 4 —Esasky, Cincinnati vs. Sisk, New York | (6) |
| 7 —Carter, New York vs. Sutter, Atlanta | (8) |
| 13 —Perez, Cincinnati vs. Rucker, Philadelphia | (6) |
| 22 —Dayett, Chicago vs. Browning, Cincinnati | (6) |
| 25 —Almon, Pittsburgh vs. Perez, Atlanta | (4) |
| 29 —Pankovits, Houston vs. Candelaria, Pittsburgh | (7) |

**JUNE—**
| | |
|---|---|
| 7* —Bevacqua, San Diego vs. Browning, Cincinnati | (5) |
| 9† —Pendleton, St. Louis vs. Sambito, New York | (5) |
| 11 —Hayes, Philadelphia vs. Schiraldi, New York | (1) |
| 11 —Durham, Chicago vs. Lucas, Montreal | (8) |
| 11 —Bailey, Houston vs. Lefferts, San Diego | (6) |
| 20 —Foster, New York vs. Fontenot, Chicago | (3) |
| 21 —Royster, San Diego vs. Minton, San Francisco | (8) |
| 23 —Bevacqua, San Diego vs. Hammaker, San Fran. | (5) |

**JULY—**
| | |
|---|---|
| 6 —Wallach, Montreal vs. Ryan, Houston | (5) |
| 20 —Strawberry, New York vs. Bedrosian, Atlanta | (1) |
| 22 —Russell, Philadelphia vs. Niekro, Houston | (1) |
| 24 —Brock, Los Angeles vs. Holland, Pittsburgh | (6) |
| 26 —Marshall, Los Angeles vs. Brusstar, Chicago | (6) |

**AUGUST—**
| | |
|---|---|
| 3 —Brown, San Francisco vs. Mahler, Atlanta | (3) |
| 14 —Cey, Chicago vs. Smith, Montreal | (3) |
| 17 —Concepcion, Cincinnati vs. Niekro, Houston | (1) |
| 20 —Bailey, Houston vs. Horton, St. Louis | (3) |
| 21 —Marshall, Los Angeles vs. Koosman, Phila. | (1) |
| 23 —Guerrero, Los Angeles vs. Burke, Montreal | (6) |
| 23 —Duncan, Los Angeles vs. Lucas, Montreal | (7) |

**SEPTEMBER—**
| | |
|---|---|
| 6 —Cedeno, St. Louis vs. Garber, Atlanta | (6) |
| 7 —Parker, Cincinnati vs. Smith, Chicago | (9) |
| 10 —Johnson, New York vs. Cox, St. Louis | (1) |
| 10† —Brock, Los Angeles vs. Shields, Atlanta | (7) |
| 12 —Robinson, Pittsburgh vs. Brusstar, Chicago | (8) |
| 12 —Brooks, Montreal vs. Rawley, Philadelphia | (5) |
| 16* —Almon, Pittsburgh vs. Tudor, St. Louis | (4) |
| 19 —Parker, Cincinnati vs. Sutter, Atlanta | (9) |
| 19 —Brooks, Montreal vs. Tunnell, Pittsburgh | (4) |
| 21 —Dawson, Montreal vs. Tudor, St. Louis | (3) |
| 25 —Carter, New York vs. Patterson, Chicago | (6) |
| 27 —Wilson, Philadelphia vs. Fontenot, Chicago | (3) |

**OCTOBER—**
| | |
|---|---|
| 4 —Krenchicki, Cincinnati vs. Pena, Los Angeles | (6) |
| 5 —Ashby, Houston vs. Wojna, San Diego | (2) |

*First game of doubleheader.
†Second game of doubleheader.

# Hernandez Tops Multi-Hit List

**By MIKE NAHRSTEDT**

When Atlanta Braves officials planned a fireworks display to top off an Independence Day game with the New York Mets, they had no way of knowing that the rockets' red glare and the bombs bursting in air would pale in comparison to the game preceding them.

Actually, the fireworks were pretty impressive—especially at four o'clock in the morning. The extravaganza didn't get under way before then because the game had just ended—six hours and 10 minutes after it began.

By that time, the Braves and the Mets had provided the 44,947 fans at Atlanta Stadium all the fireworks they could want —46 hits and 29 runs, to be exact. Only about 8,000 die-hards were around in the wee hours of July 5 when the 19-inning marathon came to an end.

Predictably, the game featured several impressive batting feats, not the least of which was Braves pitcher Rick Camp's first major league home run, which tied the game in the bottom of the 18th inning. The Mets then scored five runs in the top of the 19th and held off a Braves rally to win, 16-13. New York's Gary Carter and Atlanta's Terry Harper both had five hits in the game, while Wally Backman and Keith Hernandez of the Mets had four hits apiece. No other major league game in 1985 produced as many multi-hit (four or more) performances.

Hernandez's four hits comprised a single, double, triple and homer, making him the second of four players to hit for the cycle in 1985. San Francisco's Jeff Leonard did it against Cincinnati on June 27, while rookie outfielder Oddibe McDowell of the Texas Rangers completed the cycle with a home run—his fifth hit of the night —off Cleveland's Tom Waddell on July 23. Boston's Rich Gedman also hit for the cycle against Toronto on September 18.

McDowell, Carter and Harper turned in three of 22 five-hit performances in 1985. Hernandez was the only player, however, to do it more than once, and his three five-hit games all came in the last two months of the season. The first baseman collected five hits against the Expos on August 8, the Padres on September 2 and the Cardinals on October 3. His heroic effort in that last game was for naught, however, as the Mets lost, 4-3, and fell two games behind St. Louis with three games to play.

Hernandez also had four four-hit games, giving him seven multi-hit games for the

**The Mets' Keith Hernandez had seven multi-hit games.**

season. He was in good company. The National League batting champion, Willie McGee of the Cardinals, and the American League batting champion, Wade Boggs of the Red Sox, both had seven multi-hit performances, and no one bettered that number in 1985. One of the seven for McGee was a five-hit outing against Chicago on July 30.

The only other player in either league with more than a handful of multi-hit games was Pittsburgh rookie Joe Orsulak with six. Ryne Sandberg of the Cubs had five (including a five-hit showing against the Pirates on June 29), as did Detroit's Kirk Gibson.

Mickey Hatcher of the Twins helped Minnesota complete a four-game sweep of the A's by slapping a double and four singles on April 27 and two doubles and two singles April 28. His nine straight hits tied an A.L. record for consecutive hits over two nine-inning games.

Boston recorded the most multi-hit performances (22) of any team in the major leagues. The Mets were second with 20, followed by the Tigers (17), Orioles (16), Yankees (16) and Cardinals (14).

Boggs, whose .368 batting average led

both leagues, assembled the longest hitting streak of the season. When Boggs collected two hits in a June 24 game against Detroit, he started a string of 28 consecutive games in which he hit safely. That streak finally came to a close when Seattle shut him down July 26.

The second-longest streaks were turned in by Lee Lacy of the Orioles and Don Mattingly of the Yankees, both of whom hit safely in 20 straight games. Mattingly also had a 19-game streak, making him one of only two major league players with two separate hitting streaks of 15 or more games in '85. Milwaukee's Paul Molitor was the other, compiling streaks of 16 and 15 games.

In all, 25 major leaguers recorded hitting streaks of 15 or more games in '85. The others: 18 games—Keith Moreland, Cubs; Ryne Sandberg, Cubs; 17 games—Dave Concepcion, Reds; Donnie Hill, A's; Dave Parker, Reds; Cal Ripken, Orioles; 16 games—Jesse Barfield, Blue Jays; Julio Franco, Indians; Damaso Garcia, Blue Jays; Pedro Guerrero, Dodgers; 15 games—George Brett, Royals; Joe Carter, Indians; Brian Downing, Angels; Rich Gedman, Red Sox; Von Hayes, Phillies; Kevin McReynolds, Padres; Dale Murphy, Braves; Jack Perconte, Mariners; Steve Sax, Dodgers; Pat Tabler, Indians; Mike Young, Orioles.

The complete list of players with four or more hits in one game follows:

AMERICAN LEAGUE: Baltimore (16)—Lacy 4, Ripken 3, Murray 2, Buckner, Dempsey, Lynn, Rayford, Shelby, Wiggins, Young. Boston (22)—Boggs 7, Buckner 4, Gedman 4, Barrett 2, Easler 2, Rice 2, Evans. California (6)—Beniquez 4, DeCinces 2. Chicago (10)—Baines 2, Kittle 2, Fisk, Fletcher, Guillen, Law, Nichols, Salazar. Cleveland (7)—Butler, Carter, Franco, Hall, Hargrove, Jacoby, Thornton. Detroit (17)—Gibson 5, Evans 4, Parrish 3, Brookens, Herndon, Lemon, Simmons, Whitaker. Kansas City (8)—Wilson 3, Brett, Concepcion, Jones, Sundberg, White. Milwaukee (12)—Molitor 3, Riles 3, Householder 2, Manning, Ready, Schroeder, Simmons. Minnesota (9)—Puckett 4, Hrbek 3, Hatcher 2. New York (16)—Mattingly 4, Winfield 3, Hassey 2, Henderson 2, Meacham 2, Pagliarulo, Randolph, Sample. Oakland (8)—Baker, Canseco, Collins, Davis, Griffin, Heath, Hill, Murphy. Seattle (7)—Bradley 3, Presley 3, Perconte. Texas (3)—Dunbar, Harrah, McDowell. Toronto (10)—Garcia 4, Barfield, Bell, Fernandez, Matuszek, Mulliniks, Upshaw.

NATIONAL LEAGUE: Atlanta (10)—Chambliss 2, Benedict, Cerone, Harper, Horner, Hubbard, Murphy, Oberkfell, Ramirez. Chicago (12)—Sandberg 5, Moreland 2, Cey, Davis, Dernier, Dunston, Hatcher. Cincinnati (5)—Oester 2, Parker 2, Diaz. Houston (10)—Bass 2, Reynolds 2, Cabell, Cruz, Doran, Pankovits, Thon, Walling. Los Angeles (12)—Marshall 4, Duncan 2, Bailor, Cabell, Landreaux, Madlock, Maldonado, Scioscia. Montreal (11)—Dawson 3, Raines 2, Brooks, Driessen, Francona, Law, Wallach, Webster. New York (20)—Hernandez 7, Carter 4, Backman 3, Strawberry 2, Wilson 2, Foster, Knight. Philadelphia (10)—Samuel 4, Hayes 2, Aguayo, Daulton, Schu, Virgil. Pittsburgh (11)—Orsulak 6, Ray 2, Bream, Madlock, Pena. St. Louis (14)—McGee 7, Coleman 4, Cedeno, Clark, Herr. San Diego (10)—Garvey 3, Nettles 3, Templeton 2, Kennedy, McReynolds. San Francisco (6)—Brown 3, Leonard 2, Gladden.

The records of all players with five hits in a game follow:

| Date | Player—Club—Opp. | Place | AB. | R. | H. | 2B. | 3B. | HR. | RBI. | Result |
|---|---|---|---|---|---|---|---|---|---|---|
| April 26 | Backman, Mets vs. Pirates | H | 5 | 1 | 5 | 1 | 0 | 0 | 3 | W 6-0 |
| April 27 | Hatcher, Twins vs. A's | H | 5 | 1 | 5 | 1 | 0 | 0 | 2 | W 8-6 |
| May 5 | Ripken, Orioles vs. Twins | A | 6 | 0 | 5 | 2 | 0 | 0 | 4 | W 10-5 |
| June 8 | Bradley, Mariners vs. Indians | A | 5 | 0 | 5 | 0 | 1 | 0 | 3 | L 8-12 |
| June 11 | Samuel, Phillies vs. Mets | H | 7 | 3 | 5 | 1 | 0 | 0 | 2 | W 26-7 |
| June 15 | Evans, Tigers vs. Yankees | A | 5 | 3 | 5 | 1 | 0 | 1 | 3 | W 10-8 |
| June 17 | Henderson, Yankees vs. Orioles | A | 5 | 3 | 5 | 0 | 0 | 0 | 1 | W 10-0 |
| June 29 | Sandberg, Cubs vs. Pirates (15 innings) | A | 7 | 2 | 5 | 1 | 0 | 0 | 1 | L 5-6 |
| July 4 | Harper, Braves vs. Mets (19 innings) | H | 10 | 3 | 5 | 1 | 0 | 1 | 4 | L 13-16 |
| July 4 | Carter, Mets vs. Braves (19 innings) | A | 9 | 1 | 5 | 0 | 0 | 0 | 2 | W 16-13 |
| July 11 | Doran, Astros vs. Mets (12 innings) | H | 6 | 0 | 5 | 2 | 0 | 0 | 2 | W 4-3 |
| July 23 | McDowell, Rangers vs. Indians | H | 5 | 3 | 5 | 1 | 1 | 1 | 3 | W 8-4 |
| July 26 | Oester, Reds vs. Expos (11 innings) | A | 6 | 1 | 5 | 2 | 0 | 0 | 2 | W 7-6 |
| July 30 | McGee, Cardinals vs. Cubs | A | 6 | 3 | 5 | 1 | 0 | 1 | 2 | W 11-3 |
| Aug. 8 | Hernandez, Mets vs. Expos | A | 6 | 3 | 5 | 1 | 0 | 0 | 3 | W 14-7 |
| Aug. 17 | Baines, White Sox vs. Brewers | A | 6 | 2 | 5 | 2 | 0 | 0 | 3 | W 12-7 |
| Aug. 21 | Maldonado, Dodgers vs. Phillies | A | 6 | 1 | 5 | 1 | 0 | 1 | 2 | W 15-6 |
| Sept. 1 | Perconte, Mariners vs. Orioles | A | 6 | 2 | 5 | 0 | 0 | 0 | 1 | W 10-2 |
| Sept. 2 | Hernandez, Mets vs. Padres | A | 5 | 4 | 5 | 0 | 0 | 1 | 3 | W 12-4 |
| Sept. 10 | Ready, Brewers vs. Yankees | H | 5 | 3 | 5 | 0 | 0 | 0 | 0 | L 10-13 |
| Sept. 15 | Cedeno, Cardinals vs. Cubs | A | 5 | 1 | 5 | 2 | 0 | 1 | 4 | W 5-1 |
| Oct. 3 | Hernandez, Mets vs. Cardinals | A | 5 | 0 | 5 | 2 | 0 | 0 | 2 | L 3-4 |

# Mulliniks, Garner Led in Pinch

**The Cubs' Thad Bosley had 20 pinch hits in 60 at-bats, three home runs and 10 runs batted in.**

Houston infielder Phil Garner might have captured 1985 National League pinch-hitting honors with his .467 average (based on a minimum of 10 at-bats), but Chicago Cubs outfielder Thad Bosley should be remembered as the most prolific extra man.

Bosley, who has shuttled between the minor and major leagues in a professional career that began in 1974, compiled a .333 mark that included a major league-leading 20 pinch-hits, three home runs and 10 runs batted in. Garner collected seven hits in 15 pinch-hitting at-bats, edging Montreal rookie Herm Winningham (.462)

and Atlanta rookie Milt Thompson (13 hits, .433).

Toronto third baseman Rance Mulliniks captured American League pinch-hitting honors with a .474 average.

Ironically, team pinch-hitting honors went to a pair of last-place teams, Texas (a 62-99 record in 1985) in the A.L. with a .288 mark and Pittsburgh (57-104) in the N.L. at .286.

Major league teams produced 87 pinch-home runs in 1985, several of a dramatic variety.

On August 12, Wayne Gross and Larry Sheets connected for consecutive ninth-inning pinch-hit home runs against Cleveland, tying a major league record. Despite the two home runs, the Orioles still dropped an 8-5 decision to the Indians.

In consecutive pinch-hitting appearances on July 20 and 23, Detroit's Alejandro Sanchez tied an American League record by hitting home runs. And on June 10, Baltimore's Floyd Rayford and Detroit's Barbaro Garbey both hit pinch-homers in the Tigers' 8-7 victory.

One of the more interesting pinch-home runs in the N.L. occurred in the first week of the season when Dodger Candy Maldonado connected for the only run in Fernando Valenzuela's 1-0 victory over the San Francisco Giants.

Eight of the 87 pinch-homers were hit with the bases loaded, five of those by National Leaguers. Pinch-grand slam hitters were Cincinnati's Tony Perez and Wayne Krenchicki, Chicago Cubs outfielder Brian Dayett, St. Louis' Cesar Cedeno, Montreal's Hubie Brooks, California's Jerry Narron, Yankee slugger Don Baylor and Chicago White Sox first baseman Joe De Sa.

The only player besides Bosley to connect three times was San Francisco's Rob Deer, who collected only five pinch-hits for the season.

St. Louis pinch-hitting specialist Steve Braun completed another successful season, collecting 11 hits to move into sixth place on the all-time list with 113 pinch-hits. Mets veteran Rusty Staub also managed 11 pinch-hits, giving him 100 for his career and 10th place on the all-time list.

Following is a list of all pinch-hitters with at least 10 at-bats in 1985:

## AMERICAN LEAGUE PINCH-HITTING
(Compiled by Sports Information Center)
### Club Pinch-Hitting

| Club | AB. | H. | HR. | RBI. | Pct. | Club | AB. | H. | HR. | RBI. | Pct. |
|---|---|---|---|---|---|---|---|---|---|---|---|
| Texas | 146 | 42 | 3 | 31 | .288 | Seattle | 104 | 20 | 3 | 23 | .192 |
| Oakland | 116 | 31 | 0 | 17 | .267 | California | 149 | 28 | 2 | 22 | .188 |
| New York | 131 | 30 | 5 | 17 | .229 | Baltimore | 220 | 41 | 6 | 37 | .186 |
| Chicago | 214 | 49 | 3 | 35 | .229 | Minnesota | 172 | 31 | 5 | 20 | .180 |
| Boston | 83 | 19 | 1 | 6 | .229 | Kansas City | 147 | 23 | 1 | 17 | .156 |
| Cleveland | 128 | 29 | 1 | 21 | .227 | Milwaukee | 61 | 7 | 0 | 3 | .115 |
| Detroit | 133 | 30 | 5 | 26 | .226 | Totals | 1971 | 417 | 39 | 304 | .212 |
| Toronto | 167 | 37 | 4 | 29 | .222 | | | | | | |

### Individual Pinch-Hitting
(10 or More At-Bats)

| Player-Club | AB. | H. | HR. | RBI. | Pct. | Player-Club | AB. | H. | HR. | RBI. | Pct. |
|---|---|---|---|---|---|---|---|---|---|---|---|
| Mulliniks, Toronto | 19 | 9 | 1 | 6 | .474 | Evans, Detroit | 10 | 2 | 0 | 0 | .200 |
| Bannister, Texas | 14 | 6 | 0 | 0 | .429 | Phelps, Seattle | 25 | 5 | 1 | 6 | .200 |
| Stein, Texas | 24 | 10 | 0 | 11 | .417 | Willard, Cleveland | 10 | 2 | 0 | 0 | .200 |
| Baker, Oakland | 17 | 7 | 0 | 4 | .412 | Dwyer, Baltimore | 26 | 5 | 0 | 8 | .192 |
| Salazar, Chicago | 15 | 6 | 1 | 5 | .400 | Ayala, Cleveland | 22 | 4 | 0 | 4 | .182 |
| Baylor, New York | 13 | 5 | 2 | 6 | .385 | Oliver, Toronto | 11 | 2 | 0 | 1 | .182 |
| Law, Chicago | 17 | 6 | 0 | 4 | .353 | Wilfong, California | 11 | 2 | 0 | 1 | .182 |
| Sanchez, Detroit | 18 | 6 | 2 | 4 | .333 | Grubb, Detroit | 24 | 4 | 1 | 8 | .167 |
| Young, Baltimore | 18 | 6 | 0 | 4 | .333 | Jackson, California | 12 | 2 | 0 | 2 | .167 |
| Pagliarulo, N.Y. | 19 | 6 | 1 | 3 | .316 | McRae, Kansas City | 24 | 4 | 1 | 3 | .167 |
| Connally, Baltimore | 16 | 5 | 0 | 2 | .313 | Paciorek, Chicago | 12 | 2 | 0 | 0 | .167 |
| Calderon, Seattle | 10 | 3 | 1 | 4 | .300 | Washington, Minn. | 12 | 2 | 0 | 1 | .167 |
| Henderson, Oakland | 27 | 8 | 0 | 7 | .296 | Carew, California | 13 | 2 | 0 | 1 | .154 |
| Nichols, Bos.-Chi. | 17 | 5 | 0 | 3 | .294 | Lyons, Boston | 13 | 2 | 0 | 1 | .154 |
| Walker, Texas | 14 | 4 | 0 | 2 | .286 | Garbey, Detroit | 20 | 3 | 1 | 4 | .150 |
| Orta, Kansas City | 29 | 8 | 0 | 5 | .276 | Hargrove, Cleve. | 20 | 3 | 0 | 1 | .150 |
| Smalley, Minnesota | 26 | 7 | 0 | 3 | .269 | Iorg, Kansas City | 27 | 4 | 0 | 2 | .148 |
| Hairston, Chicago | 53 | 14 | 0 | 7 | .264 | De Sa, Chicago | 14 | 2 | 1 | 5 | .143 |
| Iorg, Toronto | 27 | 7 | 0 | 4 | .259 | Pasqua, New York | 15 | 2 | 0 | 1 | .133 |
| Bergman, Detroit | 24 | 6 | 0 | 1 | .250 | Bush, Minnesota | 32 | 4 | 1 | 4 | .125 |
| Fletcher, Chicago | 12 | 3 | 0 | 3 | .250 | Gamble, Chicago | 24 | 3 | 0 | 4 | .125 |
| Hassey, New York | 20 | 5 | 0 | 0 | .250 | Whitt, Toronto | 16 | 2 | 0 | 2 | .125 |
| Sheets, Baltimore | 16 | 4 | 2 | 5 | .250 | Griffey, New York | 18 | 2 | 1 | 2 | .111 |
| Shelby, Baltimore | 12 | 3 | 1 | 2 | .250 | Burroughs, Toronto | 29 | 3 | 2 | 6 | .103 |
| Vukovich, Cleve. | 20 | 5 | 0 | 2 | .250 | Roenicke, Baltimore | 29 | 3 | 0 | 3 | .103 |
| Gross, Baltimore | 29 | 7 | 1 | 1 | .241 | Scott, Seattle | 20 | 2 | 0 | 2 | .100 |
| Jones, Texas | 42 | 10 | 2 | 10 | .238 | Sheridan, Kan. City | 10 | 1 | 0 | 0 | .100 |
| Collins, Oakland | 17 | 4 | 0 | 1 | .235 | Nolan, Baltimore | 22 | 2 | 0 | 4 | .091 |
| Matuszek, Toronto | 13 | 3 | 0 | 2 | .231 | Salas, Minnesota | 12 | 1 | 1 | 2 | .083 |
| Narron, California | 22 | 5 | 1 | 5 | .227 | Guillen, Chicago | 13 | 1 | 0 | 0 | .077 |
| Miller, Boston | 31 | 7 | 0 | 3 | .226 | Dunbar, Texas | 14 | 1 | 0 | 0 | .071 |
| Bonnell, Seattle | 18 | 4 | 0 | 6 | .222 | Jones, Kansas City | 13 | 0 | 0 | 1 | .000 |
| Engle, Minnesota | 18 | 4 | 0 | 2 | .222 | Jones, California | 13 | 0 | 0 | 0 | .000 |
| Stenhouse, Minn. | 23 | 5 | 0 | 1 | .217 | Meier, Minnesota | 11 | 0 | 0 | 0 | .000 |
| Sconiers, California | 14 | 3 | 0 | 1 | .214 | Meyer, Oakland | 12 | 0 | 0 | 0 | .000 |
| Beniquez, California | 24 | 5 | 1 | 6 | .208 | Moreno, N.Y.-K.C. | 12 | 0 | 0 | 0 | .000 |

## NATIONAL LEAGUE PINCH-HITTING
(Compiled by Elias Sports Bureau)
### Club Pinch-Hitting

| Club | AB. | H. | HR. | RBI. | Pct. | Club | AB. | H. | HR. | RBI. | Pct. |
|---|---|---|---|---|---|---|---|---|---|---|---|
| Pittsburgh | 203 | 58 | 2 | 27 | .286 | Philadelphia | 244 | 50 | 4 | 29 | .205 |
| St. Louis | 199 | 52 | 4 | 34 | .261 | Montreal | 253 | 50 | 3 | 27 | .198 |
| Houston | 209 | 52 | 5 | 40 | .249 | New York | 213 | 41 | 4 | 24 | .192 |
| Cincinnati | 228 | 56 | 4 | 33 | .246 | San Francisco | 242 | 44 | 5 | 28 | .182 |
| Chicago | 259 | 62 | 8 | 45 | .239 | San Diego | 196 | 34 | 2 | 21 | .173 |
| Los Angeles | 277 | 63 | 3 | 37 | .227 | Totals | 2786 | 617 | 48 | 375 | .221 |
| Atlanta | 263 | 55 | 4 | 30 | .209 | | | | | | |

### Individual Pinch-Hitting
(10 or More At-Bats)

| Player-Club | AB. | H. | HR. | RBI. | Pct. | Player-Club | AB. | H. | HR. | RBI. | Pct. |
|---|---|---|---|---|---|---|---|---|---|---|---|
| Garner, Houston | 15 | 7 | 0 | 2 | .467 | Wockenfuss, Phila. | 24 | 5 | 0 | 2 | .208 |
| Winningham, Mon. | 13 | 6 | 0 | 1 | .462 | Chambliss, Atlanta | 54 | 11 | 1 | 10 | .204 |
| Thompson, Atlanta | 30 | 13 | 0 | 1 | .433 | Hebner, Chicago | 59 | 12 | 1 | 12 | .203 |
| Gladden, San Fran. | 19 | 8 | 0 | 2 | .421 | Bream, L.A.-Pitt. | 10 | 2 | 0 | 0 | .200 |
| Milner, Cincinnati | 12 | 5 | 0 | 1 | .417 | Oberkfell, Atl. | 10 | 2 | 0 | 0 | .200 |
| Speier, Chicago | 12 | 5 | 1 | 5 | .417 | Paciorek, New York | 15 | 3 | 0 | 2 | .200 |
| Backman, N.Y. | 15 | 6 | 0 | 0 | .400 | Perez, Cincinnati | 20 | 4 | 1 | 7 | .200 |
| Cedeno, Cin.-St.L. | 25 | 10 | 1 | 9 | .400 | Spilman, Houston | 20 | 4 | 1 | 3 | .200 |
| Esasky, Cincinnati | 10 | 4 | 0 | 2 | .400 | Thomas, Phila. | 35 | 7 | 0 | 4 | .200 |
| Mumphrey, Hous. | 10 | 4 | 0 | 5 | .400 | Francona, Montreal | 31 | 6 | 0 | 5 | .194 |
| Venable, Cincinnati | 35 | 13 | 0 | 4 | .371 | Bevacqua, S.D. | 26 | 5 | 0 | 4 | .192 |
| Almon, Pittsburgh | 14 | 5 | 1 | 2 | .357 | Brown, San Diego | 44 | 8 | 0 | 4 | .182 |
| Redus, Cincinnati | 17 | 6 | 0 | 2 | .353 | Davis, Chicago | 11 | 2 | 0 | 0 | .182 |
| Bass, Houston | 12 | 4 | 1 | 4 | .333 | Landreaux, L.A. | 22 | 4 | 0 | 1 | .182 |
| Bosley, Chicago | 60 | 20 | 3 | 10 | .333 | Lopes, Chicago | 22 | 4 | 1 | 5 | .182 |
| Johnson, New York | 12 | 4 | 1 | 1 | .333 | Matthews, Chicago | 11 | 2 | 1 | 5 | .182 |
| Kemp, Pittsburgh | 27 | 9 | 0 | 2 | .333 | Tolman, Houston | 17 | 3 | 1 | 5 | .176 |
| Landrum, St. Louis | 24 | 8 | 1 | 5 | .333 | Roenicke, S.F. | 23 | 4 | 1 | 2 | .174 |
| Virgil, Philadelphia | 12 | 4 | 0 | 2 | .333 | G. Gross, Phil. | 41 | 7 | 0 | 4 | .171 |
| Cabell, Hou.-L.A. | 31 | 10 | 0 | 9 | .323 | Deer, S. F. | 30 | 5 | 3 | 5 | .167 |
| Chapman, N.Y. | 20 | 6 | 0 | 3 | .300 | Runge, Atlanta | 12 | 2 | 0 | 0 | .167 |
| Frobel, Pitt.-Mon. | 20 | 6 | 1 | 5 | .300 | Maddox, Phil. | 25 | 4 | 0 | 2 | .160 |
| Reynolds, Houston | 10 | 3 | 0 | 1 | .300 | Reynolds, L.A. | 19 | 3 | 0 | 1 | .158 |
| Dayett, Chicago | 14 | 4 | 1 | 4 | .286 | Hall, Atlanta | 32 | 5 | 0 | 3 | .156 |
| Mazzilli, Pittsburgh | 56 | 16 | 0 | 7 | .286 | Krenchicki, Cin. | 32 | 5 | 1 | 6 | .156 |
| Youngblood, S.F. | 32 | 9 | 1 | 4 | .281 | Washington, Mon. | 20 | 3 | 0 | 0 | .150 |
| Whitfield, L.A. | 50 | 14 | 2 | 12 | .280 | Thompson, SF-Mon. | 62 | 9 | 0 | 7 | .145 |
| Stone, Philadelphia | 18 | 5 | 1 | 1 | .278 | Shines, Montreal | 36 | 5 | 0 | 3 | .139 |
| Harper, St. Louis | 26 | 7 | 0 | 5 | .269 | Dilone, Mon.-S.D. | 29 | 4 | 0 | 0 | .138 |
| Russell, Phila. | 15 | 4 | 1 | 3 | .267 | Jorgensen, St.L. | 22 | 3 | 0 | 5 | .136 |
| Staub, New York | 42 | 11 | 1 | 8 | .262 | Perry, Atlanta | 44 | 6 | 1 | 4 | .136 |
| Woods, Chicago | 27 | 7 | 0 | 0 | .259 | Johnstone, L.A. | 15 | 2 | 0 | 2 | .133 |
| Bullock, Houston | 12 | 3 | 0 | 2 | .250 | Corcoran, Phil. | 32 | 4 | 0 | 5 | .125 |
| DeJesus, St. Louis | 24 | 6 | 0 | 1 | .250 | Nicosia, Montreal | 17 | 2 | 0 | 0 | .118 |
| Harper, Atlanta | 12 | 3 | 1 | 3 | .250 | Walker, Cincinnati | 26 | 3 | 1 | 3 | .115 |
| Russell, Los Angeles | 20 | 5 | 0 | 4 | .250 | Bumbry, San Diego | 47 | 5 | 1 | 3 | .106 |
| Braun, St. Louis | 45 | 11 | 1 | 5 | .244 | Barnes, Montreal | 10 | 1 | 0 | 0 | .100 |
| Wohlford, Montreal | 21 | 5 | 1 | 6 | .238 | Royster, San Diego | 10 | 1 | 0 | 1 | .100 |
| Oliver, Los Angeles | 17 | 4 | 0 | 4 | .235 | Green, S.F. | 11 | 1 | 0 | 2 | .091 |
| Flannery, San Diego | 13 | 3 | 0 | 2 | .231 | Walling, Houston | 23 | 2 | 1 | 3 | .087 |
| Washington, Atl. | 26 | 6 | 1 | 3 | .231 | Foley, Cin.-Phil. | 12 | 1 | 0 | 0 | .083 |
| Maldonado, L.A. | 31 | 7 | 1 | 2 | .226 | Heep, New York | 13 | 1 | 0 | 2 | .077 |
| Lezcano, Pittsburgh | 27 | 6 | 0 | 1 | .222 | Christensen, N.Y. | 15 | 1 | 1 | 2 | .067 |
| Pankovits, Houston | 23 | 5 | 0 | 1 | .217 | Knight, New York | 16 | 1 | 0 | 1 | .063 |
| Jones, Houston | 14 | 3 | 0 | 0 | .214 | Matuszek, L.A. | 16 | 1 | 0 | 3 | .063 |
| Davis, San Diego | 19 | 4 | 0 | 0 | .211 | Rajsich, S.F. | 23 | 1 | 0 | 3 | .043 |
| Morrison, Pitt. | 19 | 4 | 1 | 4 | .211 | Hurdle, New York | 16 | 0 | 0 | 0 | .000 |
| Van Slyke, St.L. | 19 | 4 | 0 | 1 | .211 | Komminsk, Atlanta | 15 | 0 | 0 | 0 | .000 |

## PINCH-HOMERS FOR 1985

NATIONAL LEAGUE: Atlanta (4)—Chambliss, Harper, Perry, Washington. Chicago (8)—Bosley 3, Dayett, Hebner, Lopes, Matthews, Speier. Cincinnati (4)—Davis, Krenchicki, Perez, Walker. Houston (5)—Bass, Spilman, Thon, Tolman, Walling. Los Angeles (3)—Whitfield 2, Maldonado. Montreal (3)—Brooks, Frobel, Wohlford. New York (4)—Christensen, Hernandez, Johnson, Staub. Philadelphia (4)—Hayes, Russell, Stone, Wilson. Pittsburgh (4)—Almon, Morrison. St. Louis (4)—Braun, Cedeno, Landrum, Porter. San Diego (2)—Ramirez, Bumbry. San Francisco (5)—Deer 3, Roenicke, Youngblood.

AMERICAN LEAGUE: Baltimore (6)—Sheets 2, Dempsey, Gross, Rayford, Shelby. Boston (1)—Easler. California (2)—Beniquez, Narron. Chicago (3)—De Sa, Hulett, Salazar. Cleveland (1)—Thornton. Detroit (5)—Sanchez 2, Garbey, Grubb, Simmons. Kansas City (1)—McRae. Milwaukee (0). Minnesota (5)—Brunansky, Bush, Hrbek, Salas, Teufel. New York (5)—Baylor 2, Griffey, Pagliarulo, Wynegar. Oakland (0). Seattle (3)—Calderon, Cowens, Phelps. Texas (3)—Jones 2, McDowell. Toronto (4)—Burroughs 2, Aikens, Mulliniks.

# Coleman, Guillen Debut in '85

**By DAVE SLOAN**

Most young ball players break into their major league club's starting lineup by either 1), inheriting the position when the veteran incumbent suffers a disabling injury or is performing below expectations, or 2), being thrust into the lineup late in the season after the team's pennant hopes have been all but washed away. Seldom, however, is a youngster given a starting job with a World Series championship team.

But that luck, or fate, is what befell 23-year-old third baseman Chris Pittaro prior to the 1985 season. Pittaro, who batted .284 with 11 homers and 61 runs batted in with Detroit's Birmingham (Southern) club in 1984, so impressed the Tigers' brass that the '84 regular, Howard Johnson, was traded to the Mets. Even Manager Sparky Anderson, who had seen plenty of young players during his 15 years as a big-league skipper, called Pittaro "the best rookie I've ever seen."

Pittaro certainly lived up to Anderson's praise in his April 8 debut against the Indians. He had three singles in four at-bats with one RBI and a stolen base in a 5-4 Tigers victory. But Pittaro's good fortune didn't last. He struggled, spent time on the disabled list and even was sent back to the minors in midseason before rejoining the Tigers late in the year. Overall, Pittaro batted .242 in 28 major league games.

A total of 126 players made their big-league debuts in 1985, 71 in the American League and 55 in the National. Of the 126, 68 were pitchers and 58 were position players. Seven players, including Pittaro, debuted in their club's opening game.

Two St. Louis outfielders made impressive debuts in 1985. On June 22 against the Cubs, pinch-hitter Curt Ford singled home the winning run in the bottom of the 10th inning for a 2-1 St. Louis victory. Ford batted .500 (6 for 12) in 11 games for the Cardinals.

The more publicized Cardinals rookie, however, was the fleet-footed Vince Coleman, who gave a preview of things to come by stealing two bases and singling once in a 7-1 loss to Montreal on April 18. Coleman, whose insertion into the starting lineup was the spark to St. Louis' National League championship, stole a major league-leading 110 bases and captured N.L. Rookie of the Year honors.

The American League Rookie of the Year, Chicago shortstop Ozzie Guillen,

proved to be as good as advertised after the White Sox dealt former Cy Young Award winner LaMarr Hoyt to San Diego to acquire him. Guillen debuted on April 9 with a single in five at-bats in a 4-2 win over Milwaukee. Guillen went on to bat .273 in 150 games and led A.L. shortstops in fielding percentage with a .980 mark.

The season's best pitching debut was made by the Mariners' Bill Swift, who pitched five innings of one-hit, shutout relief to earn a 6-4 victory over Cleveland on June 7. Ironically, Swift was relieving Brian Snyder, who was pitching in just his third major league game, having debuted for Seattle on May 25 against Detroit.

The pitcher with the most forgettable debut was Oakland's Jeff Kaiser, who gave up a grand slam to Seattle's Gorman Thomas in his first inning as a reliever on April 11. Kaiser yielded five earned runs in 3⅓ innings but didn't take the loss in the A's 14-4 defeat.

Another fortunate pitcher was the Dodgers' Brian Holton, who won a 9-7 game against Atlanta on September 9 without retiring a batter. Holton entered the contest with two out in the Braves' seventh inning and Atlanta already holding a 6-3 lead. Holton yielded one hit but was on the mound when an Atlanta baserunner was caught stealing to end the inning. The Dodgers then scored six runs in the eighth for the victory.

The season's most unusual pitching debut, however, was achieved by the Astros' Ron Mathis. In an April 13 game against the Phillies, Mathis retired the side in the first inning without retiring a Philadelphia batter. Leadoff man Jeff Stone singled and took second base on a single by No. 2 hitter Juan Samuel. After running the count to 3-and-2 on third-place hitter Von Hayes, Mathis picked Stone off second base and Samuel off first. Hayes walked on the next pitch. On the second pitch to the cleanup hitter, Mike Schmidt, Hayes was caught stealing. Mathis' luck ran out, however, and he was tagged with a 4-2 defeat.

The oldest player to make his debut in 1985 was Reds second baseman Tom Runnells, who was 30 in his August 11 debut against the Dodgers. The youngest player was White Sox pitcher Ed Correa, who was 19 when he faced the Angels on September 18.

An alphabetical list of the players who made their debuts in '85 follows:

Chris Pittaro's rookie season fizzled after a good debut performance.

| Player | Pos. | Club | Date and Place of Birth | Debut |
|---|---|---|---|---|
| Abrego, Johnny Ray | P | Chicago N.L. | 7- 4-62—Corpus Christi, Tex. | 9- 4 |
| Aguilera, Richard Warren | P | New York N.L. | 12-31-61—San Gabriel, Calif. | 6-12 |
| Bell, Eric Alvin | P | Baltimore | 10-27-63—Modesto, Calif. | 9-24 |
| Birtsas, Timothy Dean | P | Oakland | 9- 5-60—Clarkston, Mich. | 5- 3 |
| Blocker, Terry Fennell | PR | New York N.L. | 8-18-59—Columbia, S.C. | 4-11 |
| Boever, Joseph Martin | P | St. Louis | 10- 4-60—St. Louis, Mo. | 7-19 |
| Bryant, Ralph Wendall | PH | Los Angeles | 5-20-61—Fort Gaines, Ga. | 9- 8 |
| Buchanan, Robert Gordon | P | Cincinnati | 5- 3-61—Ridley Park, Pa. | 7-13 |
| Buechele, Steven Bernard | 3B | Texas | 9-24-61—Lancaster, Calif. | 7-19 |
| Bullock, Eric Jerald | PH-OF | Houston | 2-16-60—Los Angeles, Calif. | 8-26 |
| Burke, Timothy Philip | P | Montreal | 2-19-59—Omaha, Neb. | 4- 8 |
| Burtt, Dennis Allen | P | Minnesota | 11-29-57—San Diego, Calif. | 9- 4 |
| Cangelosi, John Anthony | OF | Chicago A.L. | 3-10-63—Brooklyn, N.Y. | 6-30 |
| Canseco, Jose | OF | Oakland | 7- 2-64—Havana, Cuba | 9- 6 |
| Cary, Charles Douglas | P | Detroit | 3- 3-60—San Ramon, Calif. | 8-22 |
| Cerutti, John Joseph | P | Toronto | 4-28-60—Albany, N.Y. | 9- 1 |
| Childress, Rodney Osborne | P | Philadelphia | 2-18-62—Santa Rosa, Calif. | 5-22 |
| Clements, Patrick Brian | P | California | 2- 2-62—McCloud, Calif. | 4- 9 |
| Coleman, Vincent Maurice | OF | St. Louis | 9-22-60—Jacksonville, Fla. | 4-18 |
| Cook, Glen Patrick | P | Texas | 9- 8-59—Buffalo, N.Y. | 6-23 |
| Correa, Edwin Josue | P | Chicago A.L. | 4-29-66—Hato Rey, Puerto Rico | 9-18 |
| Davis, Joel Clark | P | Chicago A.L. | 1-30-65—Jacksonville, Fla. | 8-11 |
| Davis, Steven Kennon | P | Toronto | 8- 4-60—San Antonio, Tex. | 8-25 |
| Davis, Trench Neal | OF | Pittsburgh | 9-12-60—Baltimore, Md. | 6- 4 |
| Dopson, John Robert | P | Montreal | 7-14-63—Baltimore, Md. | 9- 4 |
| Duncan, Mariano | 2B | Los Angeles | 3-13-63—S.P. de Macoris, D.R. | 4- 9 |
| Dunston, Shawon Donnell | SS | Chicago N.L. | 3-21-63—Brooklyn, N.Y. | 4- 9 |
| Dykstra, Lenny Kyle | OF | New York N.L. | 2-10-63—Santa Ana, Calif. | 5- 3 |
| Engel, Steven Michael | P | Chicago N.L. | 12-31-61—Cincinnati, O. | 7-30 |
| Espinoza, Alvaro Alberto | SS | Minnesota | 2-19-62—Valencia, Venezuela | 8-11 |
| Eufemia, Frank Anthony | P | Minnesota | 12-23-59—Bronx, N.Y. | 5-21 |
| Felder, Michael Otis | PH | Milwaukee | 11-18-61—Vallejo, Calif. | 9-11 |
| Ferreira, Anthony Ross | P | Kansas City | 10- 4-62—Riverside, Calif. | 9-17 |
| Fielder, Cecil Grant | 1B | Toronto | 9-21-63—Los Angeles, Calif. | 7-20 |
| Fisher, Brian Kevin | P | New York A.L. | 3-18-62—Honolulu, Hawaii | 5- 7 |
| Ford, Curtis Glenn | PH | St. Louis | 10-11-60—Jackson, Miss. | 6-22 |
| Gainey, Telmanch | PH-OF | Houston | 12-25-60—Cheraw, S.C. | 4-24 |
| Galarraga, Andres Jose | 1B | Montreal | 6-18-61—Caracas, Venezuela | 8-23 |
| Gallego, Michael Anthony | SS | Oakland | 10-31-60—Whittier, Calif. | 4-11 |
| Gerber, Craig Stuart | PR | California | 1- 8-59—Chicago, Ill. | 4-11 |
| Gilbert, Mark David | PH-OF | Chicago A.L. | 8-22-56—Atlanta, Ga. | 7-21 |
| Gonzalez, Jose Rafael | PR | Los Angeles | 11-23-64—Puerto Plata, D.R. | 9- 2 |
| Greenwell, Michael Lewis | PR-OF | Boston | 7-18-63—Louisville, Ky. | 9- 5 |
| Guillen, Oswaldo Jose | SS | Chicago A.L. | 1-20-64—Miranda, Venezuela | 4- 9 |
| Guzman, Jose Alberto | P | Texas | 4- 9-63—Santa Isabel, P.R. | 9-10 |
| Habyan, John Gabriel | P | Baltimore | 1-29-64—Bayshore, N.Y. | 9-29 |

| Player | Pos. | Club | Date and Place of Birth | Debut |
|---|---|---|---|---|
| Hearron, Jeffrey Vernon | C | Toronto | 11-19-61—Long Beach, Calif. | 8-25 |
| Hegman, Robert Hilmer | 2B | Kansas City | 2-26-58—Springfield, Minn. | 8- 8 |
| Higuera, Teodoro Valenzuela | P | Milwaukee | 11- 9-58—Las Mochis, Mex. | 4-23 |
| Holton, Brian John | P | Los Angeles | 11-29-59—McKeesport, Pa. | 9- 9 |
| Howell, Jack Robert | 3B | California | 8-18-61—Tucson, Ariz. | 5-20 |
| Hunt, James Randall | C | St. Louis | 1- 3-60—Montgomery, Ala. | 6- 4 |
| Jackson, Darrin Jay | OF | Chicago N.L. | 8-22-63—Los Angeles, Calif. | 6-17 |
| Johnson, Joseph Richard | P | Atlanta | 10-30-61—Brookline, Mass. | 7-25 |
| Jones, Christopher Dale | OF | Houston | 7-13-57—Los Angeles, Calif. | 6- 8 |
| Kaiser, Jeffrey Patrick | P | Oakland | 7-24-60—Wyandotte, Mich. | 4-11 |
| Keedy, Charles Patrick | 3B | California | 1-10-59—Birmingham, Ala. | 9-10 |
| Kerfeld, Charles Patrick | P | Houston | 9-23-63—Carson City, Nev. | 7-27 |
| Khalifa, Sam | SS | Pittsburgh | 12- 5-63—Fontana, Calif. | 6-25 |
| Kipper, Robert Wayne | P | California | 7- 8-64—Aurora, Ill. | 4-12 |
| Klawitter, Thomas Carl | P | Minnesota | 6-24-58—LaCrosse, Wis. | 4-14 |
| Knudson, Mark Richard | P | Houston | 10-28-60—Denver, Colo. | 7- 8 |
| Latham, William Carol | P | New York N.L. | 8-29-60—Birmingham, Ala. | 4-15 |
| Lee, Manuel Lora | PR | Toronto | 6-17-65—S.P. de Macoris, D.R. | 4-10 |
| Lombardozzi, Stephen Paul | PH | Minnesota | 4-26-60—Malden, Mass. | 7-12 |
| Long, William Douglas | P | Chicago A.L. | 2-29-60—Cincinnati, O. | 7-21 |
| Lugo, Urbano Rafael | P | California | 8-12-62—Caracas, Venezuela | 4-28 |
| Lyons, Stephen John | PR | Boston | 6- 3-60—Tacoma, Wash. | 4-15 |
| Mack, Tony Lynn | P | California | 4-30-61—Lexington, Ky. | 7-27 |
| Madison, Charles Scott | DH | Detroit | 9-12-58—Lillian, Ala. | 7- 6 |
| Mathis, Ronald Vance | P | Houston | 9-15-58—Kansas City, Mo. | 4-13 |
| McCarthy, Thomas Michael | P | Boston | 6-18-61—Lundstahl, W. Germany | 7- 5 |
| McCaskill, Kirk Edward | P | California | 4- 9-61—Burlington, Vt. | 5- 1 |
| McCullers, Lance Graye | P | San Diego | 3- 8-64—Tampa, Fla. | 8-12 |
| McDowell, Oddibe | OF | Texas | 8-25-62—Hollywood, Fla. | 5-19 |
| McDowell, Roger Alan | P | New York N.L. | 12-21-60—Cincinnati, O. | 4-11 |
| Melvin, Robert Paul | C | Detroit | 10-28-61—Palo Alto, Calif. | 5-25 |
| Moore, Robert Devell | P | San Francisco | 11- 8-58—Jena, La. | 9-11 |
| Murphy, Robert Albert | P | Cincinnati | 5-26-60—Miami, Fla. | 9-13 |
| Myers, Randall Kirk | P | New York N.L. | 9-19-62—Vancouver, Wash. | 10- 6 |
| Newman, Albert Dwayne | PR | Montreal | 6-30-60—Kansas City, Mo. | 6-14 |
| Nokes, Matthew Dodge | C | San Francisco | 10-31-63—San Diego, Calif. | 9- 3 |
| O'Brien, Charles Hugh | C | Oakland | 5- 1-60—Tulsa, Okla. | 6- 2 |
| O'Neill, Paul Andrew | PH | Cincinnati | 2-25-63—Columbus, O. | 9- 3 |
| Ontiveros, Steven | P | Oakland | 3- 5-61—Tularosa, N.M. | 6-14 |
| Pardo, Alberto Judas | C | Baltimore | 9- 8-62—Oviedo, Spain | 7- 3 |
| Pasqua, Daniel Anthony | OF | New York A.L. | 10-17-61—Harrington Park, N.J. | 5-30 |
| Patterson, Robert Chandler | P | San Diego | 5-16-59—Jacksonville, Fla. | 9- 2 |
| Pederson, Stuart Russell | PH | Los Angeles | 1-28-60—Palo Alto, Calif. | 9- 8 |
| Perlman, Jonathan Samuel | P | Chicago N.L. | 12-13-56—Dallas, Tex. | 9- 6 |
| Perry, William Patrick | P | St. Louis | 2- 4-59—Taylorville, Ill. | 9-12 |
| Pittaro, Christopher Francis | 3B | Detroit | 9-16-61—Trenton, N.J. | 4- 8 |
| Polidor, Gustavo Adolfo | OF | California | 10-26-61—Caracas, Venezuela | 9- 7 |
| Ponce, Carlos Antonio | PH | Milwaukee | 2- 7-59—Rio Piedras, P.R. | 8-14 |
| Portugal, Mark Steven | P | Minnesota | 10-30-62—Los Angeles, Calif. | 8-14 |
| Powell, Dennis Clay | P | Los Angeles | 8-13-63—Moultrie, Ga. | 7- 7 |
| Riles, Ernest | SS | Milwaukee | 10- 2-60—Cairo, Ga. | 5-14 |
| Robidoux, William Joseph | PH | Milwaukee | 1-13-64—Ware, Mass. | 9-11 |
| Romine, Kevin Andrew | OF | Boston | 5-23-61—Exeter, N.H. | 9- 5 |
| Runnells, Thomas William | 2B | Cincinnati | 4-17-55—Greeley, Colo. | 8-11 |
| Sebra, Robert Bush | P | Texas | 12-11-61—Ridgewood, N.J. | 6-26 |
| Sellers, Jeffrey Doyle | P | Boston | 5-11-64—Compton, Calif. | 9-15 |
| Shields, Stephen Mack | P | Atlanta | 11-30-58—Etowah County, Ala. | 6- 1 |
| Shipanoff, David Noel | P | Philadelphia | 11-13-59—Edmonton, Alta. | 8-10 |
| Snyder, Brian Robert | P | Seattle | 2-20-58—Flemington, N.J. | 5-25 |
| Surhoff, Richard Clifford | P | Philadelphia | 10- 3-62—Bronx, N.Y. | 9- 8 |
| Swift, William Charles | P | Seattle | 12-27-61—Portland, Me. | 6- 7 |
| Tanner, Bruce Matthew | P | Chicago A.L. | 12- 9-61—New Castle, Pa. | 6-12 |
| Thomas, Andres Peres | PR | Atlanta | 11-10-63—Boca Chica, D.R. | 9- 3 |
| Thompson, Richard Neil | P | Cleveland | 11- 1-58—New York, N.Y. | 4-28 |
| Thornton, Louis | OF | Toronto | 4-26-63—Montgomery, Ala. | 4- 8 |
| Trujillo, Michael Andrew | P | Boston | 1-12-60—Denver, Colo. | 4-14 |
| Walter, Gene Winston | P | San Diego | 11-22-60—Chicago, Ill. | 8- 9 |
| Ward, Colin Norval | P | San Francisco | 11-22-60—Los Angeles, Calif. | 9-21 |
| Weaver, James Francis | OF | Detroit | 10-10-59—Kingston, N.Y. | 4-10 |
| Wegman, William Edward | P | Milwaukee | 12-19-62—Cincinnati, O. | 9-14 |
| White, Devon Markes | OF | California | 12-29-62—Kingston, Jamaica | 9- 2 |
| Wilkinson, William Carl | P | Seattle | 8-10-64—Greybull, Wyo. | 6-13 |
| Williams, Reginald Dewayne | OF | Los Angeles | 8-29-60—Memphis, Tenn. | 9- 2 |
| Wilson, James George | DH | Cleveland | 12-29-60—Corvallis, Ore. | 9-13 |
| Wojna, Edward David | P | San Diego | 8-20-60—Bridgeport, Conn. | 6-16 |
| Woodard, Michael Cary | 2B | San Francisco | 3- 2-60—Melrose Park, Ill. | 9-11 |
| Woodward, Robert John | P | Boston | 9-28-62—Hanover, N.H. | 9- 5 |
| Worrell, Todd Roland | P | St. Louis | 9-28-59—Arcadia, Calif. | 8-28 |
| Yett, Richard Martin | P | Minnesota | 10- 6-62—Pomona, Calif. | 4-13 |
| Youmans, Floyd Everett | P | Montreal | 5-11-64—Tampa, Fla. | 7- 1 |

# Homers by Parks for 1985

## National League

| | At Atl. | At Chi. | At Cin. | At Hou. | At L.A. | At Mont. | At N.Y. | At Phil. | At Pitt. | At St.L. | At S.D. | At S.F. | Totals 1985 | 1984 |
|---|---|---|---|---|---|---|---|---|---|---|---|---|---|---|
| Atlanta | 65 | 7 | 6 | 5 | 6 | 3 | 6 | 8 | 4 | 2 | 6 | 8 | 126 | 111 |
| Chicago | 8 | 98 | 3 | 3 | 6 | 6 | 4 | 6 | 7 | 3 | 5 | 1 | 150 | 136 |
| Cincinnati | 10 | 9 | 49 | 8 | 6 | 2 | 3 | 3 | 5 | 3 | 8 | 8 | 114 | 106 |
| Houston | 11 | 7 | 10 | 47 | 2 | 1 | 6 | 6 | 3 | 4 | 11 | 13 | 121 | 79 |
| Los Angeles | 16 | 5 | 13 | 8 | 47 | 4 | 4 | 5 | 5 | 4 | 10 | 8 | 129 | 102 |
| Montreal | 6 | 21 | 2 | 5 | 5 | 45 | 7 | 5 | 6 | 6 | 5 | 5 | 118 | 96 |
| New York | 3 | 10 | 9 | 2 | 6 | 8 | 58 | 8 | 8 | 6 | 11 | 5 | 134 | 107 |
| Philadelphia | 2 | 18 | 8 | 0 | 6 | 7 | 6 | 72 | 4 | 5 | 6 | 7 | 141 | 147 |
| Pittsburgh | 4 | 6 | 3 | 0 | 5 | 7 | 5 | 3 | 39 | 4 | 2 | 2 | 80 | 98 |
| St. Louis | 7 | 5 | 2 | 3 | 3 | 4 | 6 | 6 | 6 | 36 | 5 | 4 | 87 | 75 |
| San Diego | 8 | 9 | 4 | 4 | 1 | 2 | 6 | 3 | 0 | 2 | 64 | 6 | 109 | 109 |
| San Francisco | 5 | 7 | 5 | 9 | 8 | 1 | 5 | 4 | 5 | 0 | 8 | 58 | 115 | 112 |
| 1985 Totals | 145 | 202 | 114 | 94 | 101 | 90 | 116 | 129 | 92 | 75 | 141 | 125 | 1424 | .... |
| 1984 Totals | 125 | 156 | 131 | 47 | 89 | 101 | 103 | 124 | 92 | 71 | 121 | 118 | .... | 1278 |

**AT ATLANTA (145): Atlanta (65)**—Murphy 19, Horner 13, Harper 9, Ramirez 4, Washington 4, Cerone 3, Hubbard 3, Perry 3, Oberkfell 2, Owen 2, Camp, Chambliss, Komminsk. **Chicago (8)**—Sandberg 3, Bosley, Cey, Durham, Matthews, Speier. **Cincinnati (10)**—Esasky 4, Davis 2, Parker 2, Concepcion, Redus. **Houston (11)**—Cruz 2, Garner 2, Reynolds 2, Ashby, Davis, Doran, Mumphrey, Walling. **Los Angeles (16)**—Brock 3, Scioscia 3, Guerrero 2, Landreaux 2, Marshall 2, Anderson, Madlock, Matuszek, Valenzuela. **Montreal (6)**—Driessen 2, Fitzgerald 2, Brooks, Dawson. **New York (3)**—Backman, Hernandez, Johnson. **Philadelphia (2)**—Samuel, Schmidt. **Pittsburgh (4)**—Thompson 2, Almon, Madlock. **St. Louis (7)**—Van Slyke 3, Landrum 2, Clark, Herr. **San Diego (8)**—Garvey 2, McReynolds 2, Bochy, Kennedy, Nettles, Show. **San Francisco (5)**—Brenly, Brown, C. Davis, Roenicke, Youngblood.

**AT CHICAGO (202): Atlanta (7)**—Chambliss 2, Harper, Horner, Komminsk, Ramirez, Washington. **Chicago (98)**—Sandberg 17, Cey 15, Durham 15, Moreland 11, Davis 10, Matthews 8, Lopes 6, Bosley 4, Dunston 3, Hatcher 2, Hebner 2, Dayett, Dernier, Eckersley, Lake, Speier. **Cincinnati (9)**—Parker 2, Rose 2, Bell, Knicely, Milner, Oester, Perez. **Houston (7)**—Mumphrey 2, Bass, Davis, Garner, Puhl, Tolman. **Los Angeles (5)**—Brock 2, Anderson, Maldonado, Scioscia. **Montreal (21)**—Dawson 4, Wallach 4, Butera 2, Driessen 2, Law 2, Brooks, Frobel, Galarraga, Raines, Smith, Webster, Winningham. **New York (10)**—Carter 3, Strawberry 3, Johnson 2, Foster, Hurdle. **Philadelphia (18)**—Samuel 4, Schmidt 4, Daulton 3, Wilson 3, Virgil 2, Foley, Schu. **Pittsburgh (6)**—Brown 2, Almon, Bream, Ortiz, Ray. **St. Louis (5)**—Clark 2, Cedeno, McGee, Van Slyke. **San Diego (9)**—Nettles 3, Garvey 2, McReynolds 2, Templeton 2. **San Francisco (7)**—Brown 3, Trillo 2, Brenly, C. Davis.

**AT CINCINNATI (114): Atlanta (6)**—Horner 3, Murphy 2, Washington. **Chicago (3)**—Cey 2, Speier. **Cincinnati (49)**—Parker 16, Esasky 7, Bell 4, Perez 4, Redus 4, Knicely 3, Cedeno 2, Diaz 2, Krenchicki 2, Bilardello, Concepcion, Davis, Milner, Walker. **Houston (10)**—Bailey 2, Doran 2, Bass, Cruz, Davis, Scott, Thon, Walling. **Los Angeles (13)**—Guerrero 5, Marshall 4, Brock, Landreaux, Matuszek, Scioscia. **Montreal (2)**—Brooks, Winningham. **New York (9)**—Hernandez 3, Foster 2, Carter, Dykstra, Johnson, Strawberry. **Philadelphia (8)**—Samuel 3, Schmidt 3, Schu, Wilson. **Pittsburgh (3)**—Hendrick, LeMaster, Pena. **St. Louis (2)**—McGee, Van Slyke. **San Diego (4)**—Bevacqua, Gwynn, Martinez, Nettles. **San Francisco (5)**—Brown 3, Brenly, Leonard.

**AT HOUSTON (94): Atlanta (5)**—Murphy 2, Washington 2, Horner. **Chicago (3)**—Bosley, Engel, Moreland. **Cincinnati (8)**—Concepcion 2, Esasky 2, Bell, Milner, Parker, Walker. **Houston (47)**—Bass 9, Davis 8, Doran 5, Bailey 4, Mumphrey 4, Ashby 3, Thon 3, Garner 2, Pankovits 2, Walling 2, Cabell, Cruz, Puhl, Reynolds, Tolman. **Los Angeles (8)**—Guerrero 5, Brock, Landreaux, Marshall. **Montreal (5)**—Wallach 3, Webster 2. **New York (2)**—Heep, Strawberry. **Philadelphia—None. Pittsburgh—None. St. Louis (3)**—Clark, Porter, Van Slyke. **San Diego (4)**—Nettles 2, Bumbry, Royster. **San Francisco (9)**—Brown 2, Youngblood 2, Brenly, Gladden, Gott, Nokes, Trevino.

**AT LOS ANGELES (101): Atlanta (6)**—Murphy 2, Harper, Horner, Hubbard, Washington. **Chicago (6)**—Cey 2, Matthews 2, Davis, Lopes. **Cincinnati (6)**—Parker 2, Davis, Esasky, Krenchicki, Perez. **Houston (2)**—Bass, Davis. **Los Angeles (47)**—Marshall 15, Guerrero 13, Brock 7, Bream 2, Landreaux 2, Maldonado 2, Whitfield 2, Anderson, Duncan, Sax, Scioscia. **Montreal (5)**—Wallach 2, Brooks, Dawson, Law. **New York (6)**—Carter, Foster, Heep, Knight, Strawberry, Wilson. **Philadelphia (6)**—Samuel 2, Russell, Schmidt, Schu, Virgil. **Pittsburgh (5)**—Pena 2, Khalifa, Madlock, Thompson. **St. Louis (3)**—Clark 2, Braun. **San Diego (1)**—Gwynn. **San Francisco (8)**—Leonard 4, Deer, Green, Roenicke, Trevino.

**AT MONTREAL (90): Atlanta (3)**—Harper 2, Murphy. **Chicago (6)**—Davis 3, Cey 2, Durham. **Cincinnati (2)**—Esasky, Parker. **Houston (1)**—Davis. **Los Angeles (4)**—Guerrero 2, Brock, Duncan. **Montreal (45)**—Dawson 11, Wallach 9, Law 5, Brooks 4, Raines 4, Fitzgerald 3, Webster 3, Driessen 2, Manrique 2, Schatzeder 2, Washington 2, Wohlford. **New York (8)**—Carter 2, Foster 2, Heep, Johnson, Strawberry, Wilson. **Philadelphia (7)**—Schmidt 3, Virgil 2, Maddox, Wilson. **Pittsburgh (7)**—Pena 3, Almon, Bream, Reynolds, Wynne. **St. Louis (4)**—Clark, Herr, McGee, O. Smith. **San Diego (2)**—Kennedy, McReynolds. **San Francisco (1)**—C. Davis.

**AT NEW YORK (116): Atlanta (6)**—Washington 2, Harper, Horner, Hubbard, Murphy. **Chicago (4)**—Davis 2, Matthews, Moreland. **Cincinnati (3)**—Concepcion, Parker, Redus. **Houston (6)**—Davis 2, Bailey, Cruz, Doran, Walling. **Los Angeles (4)**—Brock 2, Scioscia. **Montreal (7)**—Raines 2, Brooks, Dawson, Francona, Law, Wallach. **New York (58)**—Strawberry 14, Carter 12, Foster 9, Johnson 5, Hernandez 4, Knight 4, Heep 2, Hurdle 2, Wilson 2, Christensen, Gooden, Paciorek, Staub. **Philadelphia (6)**—Wilson 2, Daulton, Schmidt, Schu, Virgil. **Pittsburgh (5)**—Pena 2, Hendrick, Madlock, Ray. **St. Louis (6)**—Herr 2, Cedeno, Clark, McGee, Pendleton. **San Diego (6)**—Garvey 2, Kennedy, Martinez, McReynolds, Nettles. **San Francisco (5)**—Brenly, Brown, C. Davis, Driessen, Leonard.

**AT PHILADELPHIA** (129): **Atlanta** (8)—Horner 4, Murphy 2, Harper, Runge. **Chicago** (6)—Sandberg 2, Davis, Dunston, Durham, Lopes. **Cincinnati** (3)—Cedeno, Esasky, Van Gorder. **Houston** (6)—Cruz 2, Davis 2, Spilman, Thon. **Los Angeles** (5)—Marshall 2, Brock, Guerrero, Maldonado. **Montreal** (5)—Brooks 2, Dawson, Wallach, Webster. **New York** (8)—Carter 3, Christensen 2, Foster, Heep, Strawberry. **Philadelphia** (72)—Schmidt 14, Hayes 12, Samuel 8, Virgil 7, Wilson 7, Russell 6, Aguayo 4, Thomas 3, Diaz 2, Foley 2, Maddox 2, Schu 2, Stone 2, K. Gross. **Pittsburgh** (3)—Ray 2, Reynolds. **St. Louis** (6)—Porter 2, McGee, Pendleton, O. Smith, Van Slyke. **San Diego** (3)—Bochy, Martinez, McReynolds. **San Francisco** (4)—Brown, Deer, Trevino, Uribe.

**AT PITTSBURGH** (92): **Atlanta** (4)—Washington 3, Harper. **Chicago** (7)—Durham 3, Lopes, Moreland, Sandberg, Sutcliffe. **Cincinnati** (5)—Parker 2, Concepcion, Davis, Esasky. **Houston** (3)—Bass, Doran, Reynolds. **Los Angeles** (5)—Guerrero 2, Marshall 2, Duncan. **Montreal** (6)—Brooks 2, Raines 2, Dawson, Wallach. **New York** (8)—Strawberry 4, Carter, Foster, Johnson, Santana. **Philadelphia** (4)—Hayes, Schmidt, Stone, Thomas. **Pittsburgh** (39)—Thompson 9, Madlock 6, Almon 3, Brown 3, Gonzalez 3, Ray 3, Lezcano 2, Morrison 2, Pena 2, Kemp, Khalifa, Reuschel, Reynolds, Robinson, Wynne. **St. Louis** (6)—Clark 3, Cedeno, McGee, O. Smith. **San Diego**—None. **San Francisco** (5)—Brenly 3, C. Davis, Green.

**AT ST. LOUIS** (75): **Atlanta** (2)—Horner 2. **Chicago** (3)—Bosley, Lopes, Speier. **Cincinnati** (3)—Parker 2, Knicely. **Houston** (4)—Davis 2, Bailey, Bass. **Los Angeles** (4)—Landreaux 2, Guerrero, Whitfield. **Montreal** (6)—Dawson 2, Butera, Galarraga, Schatzeder, Webster. **New York** (6)—Foster 3, Strawberry 2, Wilson. **Philadelphia** (5)—Schmidt 2, Virgil 2, Russell. **Pittsburgh** (4)—Morrison 2, Bream, Gonzalez. **St. Louis** (36)—Clark 8, Van Slyke 5, Herr 4, Porter 4, Cedeno 3, McGee 3, Pendleton 3, Landrum 2, O. Smith 2, Coleman, Forsch. **San Diego** (2)—Martinez, McReynolds. **San Francisco**—None.

**AT SAN DIEGO** (141): **Atlanta** (6)—Murphy 3, Horner, Oberkfell, Washington. **Chicago** (5)—Sandberg 2, Hebner, Lopes, Matthews. **Cincinnati** (8)—Parker 4, Diaz, Esasky, Krenchicki, Van Gorder. **Houston** (11)—Ashby 2, Cruz 2, Doran 2, Bailey, Bass, Garner, Mumphrey, Walling. **Los Angeles** (10)—Brock 2, Landreaux 2, Bream, Duncan, Guerrero, Maldonado, Marshall, Matuszek. **Montreal** (5)—Dawson, Francona, Law, Raines, Winningham. **New York** (11)—Carter 6, Heep, Hernandez, Knight, Strawberry, Wilson. **Philadelphia** (6)—Aguayo 2, Virgil 2, Russell, Schmidt. **Pittsburgh** (2)—Kemp, Lezcano. **St. Louis** (5)—Clark 2, Porter 2, Van Slyke. **San Diego** (64)—Martinez 15, Garvey 10, Kennedy 7, McReynolds 6, Nettles 6, Bochy 4, Royster 4, Templeton 4, Gwynn 3, Bevacqua 2, Ramirez 2, Flannery. **San Francisco** (8)—Leonard 3, Brenly 2, Adams, C. Davis, Deer.

**AT SAN FRANCISCO** (125): **Atlanta** (8)—Murphy 5, Komminsk 2, Harper. **Chicago** (1)—Sandberg. **Cincinnati** (8)—Davis 3, Esasky 3, Concepcion, Parker. **Houston** (13)—Ashby 2, Doran 2, Pankovits 2, Bailey, Bass, Cabell, Davis, Knepper, Thon, Walling. **Los Angeles** (8)—Duncan 2, Landreaux 2, Anderson, Guerrero, Madlock, Marshall. **Montreal** (5)—Webster 2, Raines, Wallach. **New York** (5)—Carter 3, Foster, Hernandez. **Philadelphia** (7)—Schmidt 2, Virgil 2, Maddox, Samuel, Schu. **Pittsburgh** (2)—Madlock, Mazzilli. **St. Louis** (4)—Clark, McGee, Porter, O. Smith. **San Diego** (6)—Martinez 2, Garvey, Gwynn, McReynolds, Nettles. **San Francisco** (58)—Brenly 9, Leonard 8, C. Davis 7, Gladden 6, Brown 5, Deer 5, Green 3, Trevino 3, Driessen 2, Gott 2, Uribe 2, Adams, Krukow, Nokes, Roenicke, Trillo, Youngblood.

## American League

| | At Balt. | At Bos. | At Cal. | At Chi. | At Clev. | At Det. | At K.C. | At Mil. | At Min. | At N.Y. | At Oak. | At Sea. | At Tex. | At Tor. | Totals 1985 | Totals 1984 |
|---|---|---|---|---|---|---|---|---|---|---|---|---|---|---|---|---|
| Baltimore | 103 | 9 | 12 | 9 | 11 | 16 | 5 | 7 | 9 | 6 | 5 | 6 | 8 | 8 | 214 | 160 |
| Boston | 7 | 71 | 6 | 10 | 5 | 6 | 3 | 6 | 9 | 8 | 8 | 10 | 7 | 6 | 162 | 181 |
| California | 2 | 4 | 75 | 12 | 5 | 10 | 4 | 8 | 3 | 4 | 5 | 9 | 7 | 5 | 153 | 150 |
| Chicago | 4 | 4 | 8 | 74 | 7 | 3 | 2 | 2 | 11 | 4 | 9 | 6 | 7 | 5 | 146 | 172 |
| Cleveland | 3 | 4 | 10 | 3 | 52 | 4 | 1 | 4 | 2 | 11 | 4 | 7 | 4 | 7 | 116 | 123 |
| Detroit | 11 | 5 | 9 | 3 | 3 | 108 | 6 | 7 | 8 | 9 | 10 | 5 | 12 | 6 | 202 | 187 |
| Kansas City | 9 | 5 | 6 | 4 | 6 | 11 | 67 | 7 | 8 | 7 | 4 | 4 | 9 | 7 | 154 | 117 |
| Milwaukee | 7 | 4 | 4 | 8 | 3 | 4 | 3 | 50 | 5 | 1 | 2 | 3 | 3 | 4 | 101 | 96 |
| Minnesota | 7 | 1 | 7 | 4 | 8 | 8 | 3 | 6 | 71 | 3 | 3 | 7 | 6 | 7 | 141 | 114 |
| New York | 7 | 1 | 7 | 7 | 6 | 7 | 5 | 11 | 6 | 92 | 5 | 8 | 7 | 7 | 176 | 130 |
| Oakland | 7 | 10 | 9 | 10 | 3 | 4 | 3 | 7 | 8 | 5 | 66 | 6 | 11 | 6 | 155 | 158 |
| Seattle | 4 | 8 | 3 | 5 | 6 | 9 | 4 | 10 | 4 | 5 | 8 | 92 | 7 | 6 | 171 | 129 |
| Texas | 4 | 5 | 9 | 2 | 3 | 6 | 1 | 5 | 7 | 1 | 4 | 2 | 76 | 4 | 129 | 120 |
| Toronto | 15 | 4 | 3 | 6 | 10 | 5 | 3 | 6 | 3 | 3 | 4 | 7 | 14 | 75 | 158 | 143 |
| 1985 Totals | 190 | 135 | 168 | 157 | 128 | 201 | 110 | 136 | 154 | 159 | 137 | 172 | 178 | 153 | 2178 | .... |
| 1984 Totals | 141 | 176 | 162 | 180 | 138 | 154 | 107 | 110 | 140 | 111 | 149 | 150 | 125 | 137 | .... | 1980 |

**AT BALTIMORE** (190): **Baltimore** (103)—Murray 15, Ripken 15, Young 15, Lynn 14, Gross 9, Roenicke 9, Rayford 6, Sheets 5, Dempsey 4, Shelby 4, Lacy 3, Sakata 2, Dauer, Dwyer. **Boston** (7)—Buckner 2, Evans 2, Armas, Greenwell, Rice. **California** (2)—Boone, DeCinces. **Chicago** (4)—Fisk 2, Baines, Salazar. **Cleveland** (3)—Bernazard, Jacoby, Thornton. **Detroit** (11)—Evans 2, Lemon 2, Parrish 2, Bergman, Brookens, Gibson, Herndon, Whitaker. **Kansas City** (9)—Brett 3, McRae 3, Balboni, Sundberg, White, Wilson. **Milwaukee** (7)—Cooper 2, Householder, Molitor, Riles, Robidoux, Schroeder. **Minnesota** (7)—Brunansky 3, Bush, Gaetti, Hrbek, Teufel. **New York** (7)—Hassey 3, Griffey 2, Henderson, Winfield. **Oakland** (7)—Murphy 3, Baker, Bochte, Davis, Henderson. **Seattle** (4)—Davis 2, Thomas 2. **Texas** (4)—Johnson, Parrish, Stein, Ward. **Toronto** (15)—Barfield 3, Bell 3, Upshaw 3, Mulliniks 2, Burroughs, Garcia, Oliver, Whitt.

**AT BOSTON** (135): **Baltimore** (9)—Murray 2, Rayford 2, Young 2, Roenicke, Sheets, Shelby. **Boston** (71)—Evans 14, Armas 10, Rice 10, Gedman 9, Boggs 6, Buckner 6, Easler 4, Lyons 4, Barrett 3, Hoffman 2, Sullivan 2, Greenwell. **California** (4)—Downing, Jackson, Linares, Schofield. **Chicago** (4)—Fisk 2, Salazar. **Cleveland** (4)—Thornton 2, Carter, Willard. **Detroit** (5)—Evans 2, Gibson, Lemon, Trammell. **Kansas City** (5)—White 3, McRae, Motley. **Milwaukee** (4)—Robidoux 2, Cooper, Householder. **Minnesota (1)** —Bush. **New York (1)** —Winfield. **Oakland (10)** —Kingman 3, Heath 2, Baker, Davis, Lansford, Murphy, Tettleton. **Seattle (8)** —Thomas 4, Calderon, Coles, Davis, Presley. **Texas (5)** —Parrish 2, Bell, Harrah, Ward. **Toronto (4)** —Barfield, Bell, Iorg, Matuszek.

**AT CALIFORNIA (168): Baltimore (12)** —Murray 4, Sheets 2, Connally, Dempsey, Lynn, Rayford, Roenicke, Shelby. **Boston (6)** —Easler 3, Armas, Gutierrez, Rice. **California (75)** —Jackson 15, DeCinces 12, Downing 10, Jones 10, Grich 7, Beniquez 6, Schofield 5, Narron 3, Howell 2, Wilfong 2, Brown, Carew, Sconiers. **Chicago (8)** —Fisk 3, Baines, Hulett, Kittle, Salazar, Walker. **Cleveland (10)** —Jacoby 3, Thornton 3, Bernazard, Carter, Castillo, Willard. **Detroit (9)** —Parrish 3, Gibson 2, Laga, Lemon, Trammell, Whitaker. **Kansas City (6)** —Balboni 2, White 2, Motley, Smith. **Milwaukee (4)** —Oglivie 2, Cooper, Householder. **Minnesota (7)** —Brunansky 2, Hatcher 2, Hrbek, Laudner, Smalley. **New York (7)** —Henderson 2, Mattingly 2, Pagliarulo 2, Winfield. **Oakland (9)** —Kingman 2, Baker, Bochte, Collins, Davis, Heath, Lansford, Murphy. **Seattle (3)** —Bradley, Phelps, Thomas. **Texas (9)** —Parrish 2, Bannister, Buechele, Johnson, McDowell, O'Brien, Walker, Ward. **Toronto (3)** —Barfield, Fernandez, Oliver.

**AT CHICAGO (157): Baltimore (9)** —Murray 3, Dauer, Dempsey, Dwyer, Ripken, Roenicke, Young. **Boston (10)** —Armas 3, Gedman 2, Barrett, Boggs, Buckner, Easler, Evans. **California (12)** —Boone 2, Brown 2, Downing 2, Jackson 2, Beniquez, DeCinces, Jones. Wilfong. **Chicago (74)** —Fisk 20, Baines 13, Kittle 12, Walker 11, Law 4, Salazar 4, Gamble 2, Hulett 2, Little 2, Boston, De Sa, Guillen, Skinner. **Cleveland (3)** —Bernazard, Castillo, Nixon. **Detroit (3)** —Evans, Gibson, Sanchez. **Kansas City (4)** —Balboni, Brett, Motley, Sundberg. **Milwaukee (8)** —Schroeder 3, Yount 2, Cooper, Householder, Ready. **Minnesota (4)** —Gaetti 2, Engle, Hrbek. **New York (7)** —Hassey 3, Mattingly 2, Henderson, Pagliarulo. **Oakland (10)** —Kingman 3, Baker, Bochte, Canseco, Gallego, Griffin, Lansford, Murphy. **Seattle (5)** —Bradley, Cowens, Owen, Presley, Scott. **Texas (2)** —Dunbar, O'Brien. **Toronto (6)** —Bell 3, Martinez, Upshaw, Whitt.

**AT CLEVELAND (128): Baltimore (11)** —Dempsey 2, Rayford 2, Sheets 2, Young 2, Lacy, Ripken, Roenicke. **Boston (5)** —Armas 2, Evans, Gedman, Gutierrez. **California (5)** —Jackson 2, DeCinces, Grich, Miller. **Chicago (7)** —Kittle 2, Walker 2, Fisk, Hairston, Hulett. **Cleveland (52)** —Thornton 12, Jacoby 9, Carter 5, Tabler 5, Bernazard 4, Castillo 4, Vukovich 4, Willard 4, Franco 3, Butler, Nixon. **Detroit (3)** —Parrish 2, Herndon. **Kansas City (6)** —Brett 2, White 2, Balboni, Wilson. **Milwaukee (3)** —Cooper, Gantner, Simmons. **Minnesota (8)** —Hrbek 2, Salas 2, Brunansky, Funderburk, Gaetti, Stenhouse. **New York (6)** —Baylor 2, Henderson 2, Winfield 2. **Oakland (3)** —Baker, Lansford, Murphy. **Seattle (6)** —Phelps 2, Presley 2, Bradley, Kearney. **Texas (3)** —McDowell, O'Brien, Slaught. **Toronto (10)** —Whitt 3, Barfield 2, Bell 2, Fielder, Moseby, Upshaw.

**AT DETROIT (201): Baltimore (16)** —Rayford 3, Lacy 2, Lynn 2, Murray 2, Ripken 2, Dempsey, Sakata, Sheets, Shelby, Young. **Boston (6)** —Evans 3, Buckner, Easler, Hoffman. **California (10)** —Grich 2, Jackson 2, Jones 2, Boone, Downing, Hendrick, Pettis. **Chicago (3)** —Fisk 3. **Cleveland (4)** —Butler, Carter, Franco, Thornton. **Detroit (108)** —Evans 21, Gibson 18, Parrish 11, Whitaker 11, Lemon 9, Herndon 7, Simmons 7, Trammell 7, Garbey 4, Grubb 4, Brookens 3, Bergman 2, Castillo 2, Sanchez 2. **Kansas City (11)** —Balboni 5, Brett 3, Motley, Sundberg, White. **Milwaukee (4)** —Oglivie 2, Cooper, Riles. **Minnesota (8)** —Hrbek 2, Smalley 2, Bush, Engle, Stenhouse, Teufel. **New York (7)** —Henderson 4, Baylor, Hassey, Mattingly. **Oakland (4)** —Lansford 2, Collins, Griffin. **Seattle (9)** —Bradley 3, Davis 2, Cowens, Kearney, Presley, Thomas. **Texas (6)** —Bell, Harrah, Johnson, O'Brien, Tolleson, Ward. **Toronto (5)** —Whitt 2, Bell, Garcia, Upshaw.

**AT KANSAS CITY (110): Baltimore (5)** —Lynn, Rayford, Ripken, Sheets, Young. **Boston (3)** —Buckner, Easler, Rice. **California (4)** —DeCinces, Grich, Jones, Sconiers. **Chicago (2)** —Baines, Walker. **Cleveland (1)** —Castillo. **Detroit (6)** —Evans 2, Parrish 2, Gibson, Whitaker. **Kansas City (67)** —Balboni 17, Brett 15, White 9, McRae 7, Motley 6, Moreno 2, Sheridan 2, Smith 2, Sundberg 2, Biancalana, Concepcion, Orta, Wathan, Wilson. **Milwaukee (3)** —Cooper, Householder, Molitor. **Minnesota (3)** —Funderburk, Hrbek, Laudner. **New York (5)** —Baylor 2, Mattingly, Pagliarulo, Wynegar. **Oakland (3)** —Baker, Bochte, Kingman. **Seattle (4)** —Bradley, Kearney, Owen, Tartabull. **Texas (1)** —McDowell. **Toronto (3)** —Bell, Iorg, Oliver.

**AT MILWAUKEE (136): Baltimore (7)** —Lynn 2, Dempsey, Rayford, Ripken, Sheets, Young. **Boston (6)** —Rice 2, Buckner, Easler, Evans, Gedman. **California (8)** —Jackson 2, Boone, Brown, DeCinces, Downing, Jones, Linares. **Chicago (2)** —Fletcher, Kittle. **Cleveland (4)** —Carter 2, Jacoby 2. **Detroit (7)** —Trammell 2, Lemon, Parrish, Sanchez, Simmons, Whitaker. **Kansas City (7)** —Balboni 2, Motley 2, Iorg, Smith, White. **Milwaukee (50)** —Yount 11, Simmons 8, Cooper 6, Molitor 6, Gantner 4, Oglivie 4, Householder 3, Riles 2, Schroeder 2, Brouhard, Giles, Manning, Ponce. **Minnesota (6)** —Gaetti 2, Brunansky, Bush, Smalley, Teufel. **New York (11)** —Winfield 3, Baylor 2, Griffey, Hassey, Henderson, Pagliarulo, Pasqua, Wynegar. **Oakland (7)** —Davis 3, Murphy 3, Bochte. **Seattle (10)** —Presley 3, Thomas 3, Davis 2, Henderson, Kearney. **Texas (5)** —O'Brien 2, Johnson, McDowell, Slaught. **Toronto (6)** —Moseby 2, Barfield, Fielder, Garcia, Whitt.

**AT MINNESOTA (154): Baltimore (9)** —Dwyer 2, Murray 2, Ripken 2, Gross, Lynn, Sheets. **Boston (9)** —Armas 3, Evans 3, Easler, Gedman, Rice. **California (3)** —DeCinces, Jones, Narron. **Chicago (11)** —Kittle 4, Salazar 2, Walker 2, Baines, Boston, Fisk. **Cleveland (2)** —Vukovich 2. **Detroit (8)** —Evans 5, Garbey, Gibson, Laga. **Kansas City (8)** —McRae 2, Sundberg 2, Motley, Orta, Smith, White. **Milwaukee (5)** —Cooper 2, Manning, Molitor, Riles. **Minnesota (71)** —Brunansky 12, Gaetti 10, Hrbek 10, Smalley 7, Salas 6, Teufel 6, Bush 5, Laudner 5, Engle 3, Puckett 2, Stenhouse 2 Hatcher, Meier, Washington. **New York (6)** —Baylor, Griffey, Henderson, Mattingly, Pagliarulo, Winfield. **Oakland (8)** —Davis 3, Bochte 2, Heath, Murphy, Picciolo. **Seattle (4)** —Bradley, Henderson, Phelps, Thomas. **Texas (7)** —O'Brien 3, Parrish 2, Slaught, Walker. **Toronto (3)** —Barfield, Bell, Burroughs.

**AT NEW YORK (159): Baltimore (6)** —Dwyer 2, Gross, Lynn, O'Malley, Roenicke. **Boston (8)** —Rice 3, Gedman 2, Armas, Easler, Evans. **California (4)** —Howell 3, Jones 2. **Chicago (2)** —Baines, Fisk, Gamble, Walker. **Cleveland (11)** —Bernazard 3, Thornton 3, Butler 2, Franco 2, Carter. **Detroit (9)** —Gibson 2, Brookens, Evans, Garbey, Grubb, Herndon, Parrish, Whitaker. **Kansas City (7)** —Balboni 2, Brett 2, Motley, Smith, White. **Milwaukee (1)** —Householder. **Minnesota (3)** —Brunansky 2, Bush. **New York (92)** —Mattingly 22, Winfield 15, Baylor 12, Henderson 8, Pagliarulo 8, Pasqua 7, Griffey 6, Hassey 3, Randolph 3, Robertson 2, Wynegar 2, Berra, Meacham, Moreno, Sample. **Oakland (5)** —Kingman 2, Phillips 2, Murphy. **Seattle (5)** —Henderson 2, Bradley, Cowens, Ramos. **Texas (1)** —McDowell. **Toronto (3)** —Barfield, Mulliniks, Whitt.

**AT OAKLAND** (137): **Baltimore** (5)—Lacy 2, Rayford, Ripken, Young. **Boston** (8)—Rice 3, Buckner 2, Easler 2, Nichols. **California** (5)—Downing 2, DeCinces, Jones, Schofield. **Chicago** (9)—Walker 4, Kittle 2, Baines, Fisk, Nichols. **Cleveland** (4)—Carter 2, Castillo, Jacoby. **Detroit** (10)—Evans 3, Parrish 2, Brookens, Gibson, Herndon, Trammell, Whitaker. **Kansas City** (4)—Balboni, Brett, McRae, White. **Milwaukee** (2)—Yount 2. **Minnesota** (3)—Brunansky, Engle, Gaetti. **New York** (5)—Hassey, Mattingly, Pagliarulo, Randolph, Winfield. **Oakland** (66)—Kingman 14, Davis 12, Heath 8, Lansford 7, Bochte 6, Baker 5, Murphy 5, Canseco 4, Phillips 2, Collins, Henderson, Tettleton. **Seattle** (8)—Presley 3, Cowens, 2, Thomas 2, Bradley. **Texas** (4)—Harrah, McDowell, Parrish, Slaught. **Toronto** (4)—Bell, Garcia, Mulliniks, Whitt.

**AT SEATTLE** (172): **Baltimore** (6)—Connally, Dempsey, Dwyer, Murray, Ripken, Sheets. **Boston** (10)—Gedman 2, Rice 2, Armas, Boggs, Buckner, Evans, Hoffman, Lyons. **California** (9)—Downing 3, Beniquez, Grich, Hendrick, Howell, Jackson, Schofield. **Chicago** (6)—Kittle 2, Baines, Boston, De Sa, Walker. **Cleveland** (7)—Castillo 3, Carter 2, Bernazard, Willard. **Detroit** (5)—Evans 2, Lemon 2, Trammell. **Kansas City** (4)—Balboni, Motley, Sheridan, Sundberg. **Milwaukee** (3)—Simmons 2, Schroeder. **Minnesota** (7)—Gaetti 2, Engle, Hrbek, Puckett, Smalley, Stenhouse. **New York** (8)—Baylor 2, Mattingly 2, Henderson, Pagliarulo, Pasqua, Winfield. **Oakland** (6)—Kingman 3, Baker, Hill, Murphy. **Seattle** (92)—Thomas 16, Bradley 15, Presley 12, Davis 11, Cowens 8, Henderson 8, Calderon 6, Phelps 5, Owen 3, Scott 3, Kearney 2, Perconte 2, Bonnell. **Texas** (2)—McDowell, Parrish. **Toronto** (7)—Bell 3, Barfield, Moseby, Mulliniks, Oliver.

**AT TEXAS** (178): **Baltimore** (8)—Young 3, Dempsey, Ford, Lacy, Murray, Rayford. **Boston** (7)—Rice 3, Hoffman 2, Armas, Easler. **California** (7)—DeCinces, Jackson, Jones, Keedy, Linares, Miller, Wilfong. **Chicago** (7)—Fisk 2, Baines, Hairston, Hulett, Kittle, Salazar. **Cleveland** (4)—Vukovich 2, Butler, Hargrove. **Detroit** (12)—Parrish 3, Whitaker 3, Sanchez 2, Brookens, Evans, Herndon, Simmons. **Kansas City** (9)—Brett 3, Sundberg 2, Balboni, Motley, Orta, Wilson. **Milwaukee** (3)—Householder, Oglivie, Schroeder. **Minnesota** (6)—Brunansky 2, Gagne 2, Gaetti, Puckett. **New York** (7)—Henderson 2, Pagliarulo 2, Hassey, Mattingly, Randolph. **Oakland** (11)—Kingman 2, Murphy 2, Baker, Bochte, Davis, Heath, Henderson, Kiefer, Tettleton. **Seattle** (7)—Presley 2, Bradley, Cowens, Henderson, Owen, Thomas. **Texas** (76)—O'Brien 12, McDowell 10, Ward 10, Johnson 8, Parrish 8, Buechele 5, Harrah 5, Jones 5, Slaught 4, Walker 3, Bell 2, Valentine 2, Wright 2. **Toronto** (14)—Moseby 3, Upshaw 3, Bell 2, Whitt 2, Aikens, Barfield, Martinez, Mulliniks.

**AT TORONTO** (153): **Baltimore** (8)—Sheets 2, Connally, Lynn, Murray, Ripken, Roenicke, Young. **Boston** (6)—Evans 2, Barrett, Buckner. **California** (5)—Carew, Grich, Jackson, Jones, Narron. **Chicago** (5)—Baines, Fletcher, Gamble, Kittle, Walker. **Cleveland** (7)—Jacoby 4, Ayala 2, Nixon. **Detroit** (6)—Lemon 2, Gibson, Parrish, Simmons, Whitaker. **Kansas City** (7)—Balboni 2, Concepcion, McRae, Motley, Orta, Pryor. **Milwaukee** (4)—Householder, Molitor, Oglivie, Simmons. **Minnesota** (7)—Brunansky 3, Hrbek 2, Salas, Teufel. **New York** (7)—Mattingly 2, Baylor, Cotto, Henderson, Pagliarulo, Wynegar. **Oakland** (6)—Davis 2, Hill 2, Baker, Collins. **Seattle** (6)—Presley 3, Calderon, Henderson, Thomas. **Texas** (4)—Harrah, McDowell, O'Brien, Ward. **Toronto** (75)—Barfield 15, Moseby 11, Bell 10, Whitt 7, Upshaw 6, Iorg 5, Burroughs 4, Garcia 4, Mulliniks 4, Fielder 2, Martinez 2, Fernandez, Johnson, Matuszek, Oliver, Thornton.

# The Sporting News AWARDS

## THE SPORTING NEWS MVP AWARDS

### AMERICAN LEAGUE

| Year | Player Club | Points |
|---|---|---|
| 1929—Al Simmons, Philadelphia, of | | 40 |
| 1930—Joseph Cronin, Washington, ss | | 52 |
| 1931—H. Louis Gehrig, New York, 1b | | 40 |
| 1932—James Foxx, Philadelphia, 1b | | 46 |
| 1933—James Foxx, Philadelphia, 1b | | 49 |
| 1934—H. Louis Gehrig, New York, 1b | | 51 |
| 1935—Henry Greenberg, Detroit, 1b | | 64 |
| 1936—H. Louis Gehrig, New York, 1b | | 55 |
| 1937—Charles Gehringer, Detroit, 2b | | 78 |
| 1938—James Foxx, Boston, 1b | | 304 |
| 1939—Joseph DiMaggio, New York, of | | 280 |
| 1940—Henry Greenberg, Detroit, of | | 292 |
| 1941—Joseph DiMaggio, New York, of | | 291 |
| 1942—Joseph Gordon, New York, 2b | | 270 |
| 1943—Spurgeon Chandler, New York, p | | 246 |
| 1944—Robert Doerr, Boston, 2b | | |
| 1945—Edward J. Mayo, Detroit, 2b | | |

### NATIONAL LEAGUE

| Player Club | Points |
|---|---|
| No selection | |
| William Terry, New York, 1b | 47 |
| Charles Klein, Philadelphia, of | 40 |
| Charles Klein, Philadelphia, of | 46 |
| Carl Hubbell, New York, p | 64 |
| Jerome Dean, St. Louis, p | 57 |
| J. Floyd Vaughan, Pittsburgh, ss | 42 |
| Carl Hubbell, New York, p | 61 |
| Joseph Medwick, St. Louis, of | 70 |
| Ernest Lombardi, Cincinnati, c | 229 |
| William Walters, Cincinnati, p | 303 |
| Frank McCormick, Cincinnati, 1b | 274 |
| Adolph Camilli, Brooklyn, 1b | 300 |
| Morton Cooper, St. Louis, p | 263 |
| Stanley Musial, St. Louis, of | 267 |
| Martin Marion, St. Louis, ss | |
| Thomas Holmes, Boston, of | |

## THE SPORTING NEWS PLAYER, PITCHER OF YEAR

### AMERICAN LEAGUE

1948—Louis Boudreau, Cleveland, ss
    Robert Lemon, Cleveland, p
1949—Theodore Williams, Boston, of
    Ellis Kinder, Boston, p
1950—Philip Rizzuto, New York, ss
    Robert Lemon, Cleveland, p
1951—Ferris Fain, Philadelphia, 1b
    Robert Feller, Cleveland, p
1952—Luscious Easter, Cleveland, 1b
    Robert Shantz, Philadelphia, p
1953—Albert Rosen, Cleveland, 3b
    Erv (Bob) Porterfield, Washington, p
1954—Roberto Avila, Cleveland, 2b
    Robert Lemon, Cleveland, p
1955—Albert Kaline, Detroit, of
    Edward Ford, New York, p
1956—Mickey Mantle, New York, of
    W. William Pierce, Chicago, p
1957—Theodore Williams, Boston, of
    W. William Pierce, Chicago, p
1958—Jack Jensen, Boston, of
    Robert Turley, New York, p
1959—J. Nelson Fox, Chicago, 2b
    Early Wynn, Chicago, p
1960—Roger Maris, New York, of
    Charles Estrada, Baltimore, p
1961—Roger Maris, New York, of
    Edward Ford, New York, p
1962—Mickey Mantle, New York, of
    Richard Donovan, Cleveland, p
1963—Albert Kaline, Detroit, of
    Edward Ford, New York, p
1964—Brooks Robinson, Baltimore, 3b
    Dean Chance, Los Angeles, p
1965—Pedro (Tony) Oliva, Minnesota, of
    James Grant, Minnesota, p
1966—Frank Robinson, Baltimore, of
    James Kaat, Minnesota, p
1967—Carl Yastrzemski, Boston, of
    Jim Lonborg, Boston, p
1968—Ken Harrelson, Boston, of
    Denny McLain, Detroit, p
1969—Harmon Killebrew, Minnesota, 1b-3b
    Denny McLain, Detroit, p
1970—Harmon Killebrew, Minnesota, 3b
    Sam McDowell, Cleveland, p
1971—Pedro (Tony) Oliva, Minnesota, of
    Vida Blue, Oakland, p
1972—Richie Allen, Chicago, 1b
    Wilbur Wood, Chicago, p

### NATIONAL LEAGUE

1948—Stanley Musial, St. Louis, of-1b
    John Sain, Boston, p
1949—Enos Slaughter, St. Louis, of
    Howard Pollet, St. Louis, p
1950—Ralph Kiner, Pittsburgh, of
    C. James Konstanty, Philadelphia, p
1951—Stanley Musial, St. Louis, of
    Elwin Roe, Brooklyn, p
1952—Henry Sauer, Chicago, of
    Robin Roberts, Philadelphia, p
1953—Roy Campanella, Brooklyn, c
    Warren Spahn, Milwaukee, p
1954—Willie Mays, New York, of
    John Antonelli, New York, p
1955—Edwin Snider, Brooklyn, of
    Robin Roberts, Philadelphia, p
1956—Henry Aaron, Milwaukee, of
    Donald Newcombe, Brooklyn, p
1957—Stanley Musial, St. Louis, 1b
    Warren Spahn, Milwaukee, p
1958—Ernest Banks, Chicago, ss
    Warren Spahn, Milwaukee, p
1959—Ernest Banks, Chicago, ss
    Samuel Jones, San Francisco, p
1960—Richard Groat, Pittsburgh, ss
    Vernon Law, Pittsburgh, p
1961—Frank Robinson, Cincinnati, of
    Warren Spahn, Milwaukee, p
1962—Maurice Wills, Los Angeles, ss
    Donald Drysdale, Los Angeles, p
1963—Henry Aaron, Milwaukee, of
    Sanford Koufax, Los Angeles, p
1964—Kenton Boyer, St. Louis, 3b
    Sanford Koufax, Los Angeles, p
1965—Willie Mays, San Francisco, of
    Sanford Koufax, Los Angeles, p
1966—Roberto Clemente, Pittsburgh, of
    Sanford Koufax, Los Angeles, p
1967—Orlando Cepeda, St. Louis, 1b
    Mike McCormick, San Francisco, p
1968—Pete Rose, Cincinnati, of
    Bob Gibson, St. Louis, p
1969—Willie McCovey, San Francisco, 1b
    Tom Seaver, New York, p
1970—Johnny Bench, Cincinnati, c
    Bob Gibson, St. Louis, p
1971—Joe Torre, St. Louis, 3b
    Ferguson Jenkins, Chicago, p
1972—Billy Williams, Chicago, of
    Steve Carlton, Philadelphia, p

## PLAYER, PITCHER OF YEAR—Continued

| AMERICAN LEAGUE | NATIONAL LEAGUE |
|---|---|
| 1973—Reggie Jackson, Oakland, of | 1973—Bobby Bonds, San Francisco, of |
| Jim Palmer, Baltimore, p | Ron Bryant, San Francisco, p |
| 1974—Jeff Burroughs, Texas, of | 1974—Lou Brock, St. Louis, of |
| Jim Hunter, Oakland, p | Mike Marshall, Los Angeles, p |
| 1975—Fred Lynn, Boston, of | 1975—Joe Morgan, Cincinnati, 2b |
| Jim Palmer, Baltimore, p | Tom Seaver, New York, p |
| 1976—Thurman Munson, New York, c | 1976—George Foster, Cincinnati, of |
| Jim Palmer, Baltimore, p | Randy Jones, San Diego, p |
| 1977—Rod Carew, Minnesota, 1b | 1977—George Foster, Cincinnati, of |
| Nolan Ryan, California, p | Steve Carlton, Philadelphia, p |
| 1978—Jim Rice, Boston, of | 1978—Dave Parker, Pittsburgh, of |
| Ron Guidry, New York, p | Vida Blue, San Francisco, p |
| 1979—Don Baylor, California, of | 1979—Keith Hernandez, St. Louis, 1b |
| Mike Flanagan, Baltimore, p | Joe Niekro, Houston, p |
| 1980—George Brett, Kansas City, 3b | 1980—Mike Schmidt, Philadelphia, 3b |
| Steve Stone, Baltimore, p | Steve Carlton, Philadelphia, p |
| 1981—Tony Armas, Oakland, of | 1981—Andre Dawson, Montreal, of |
| Jack Morris, Detroit, p | Fernando Valenzuela, Los Angeles, p |
| 1982—Robin Yount, Milwaukee, ss | 1982—Dale Murphy, Atlanta, of |
| Dave Stieb, Toronto, p | Steve Carlton, Philadelphia, p |
| 1983—Cal Ripken, Baltimore, ss | 1983—Dale Murphy, Atlanta, of |
| LaMarr Hoyt, Chicago, p | John Denny, Philadelphia, p |
| 1984—Don Mattingly, New York, 1b | 1984—Ryne Sandberg, Chicago, 2b |
| Willie Hernandez, Detroit, p | Rick Sutcliffe, Chicago, p |
| 1985—Don Mattingly, New York, 1b | 1985—Willie McGee, St. Louis, of |
| Bret Saberhagen, Kansas City, p | Dwight Gooden, New York, p |

## FIREMAN (Relief Pitcher) OF THE YEAR

| Year   Player   Club | Player   Club |
|---|---|
| 1960—Mike Fornieles, Boston | Lindy McDaniel, St. Louis |
| 1961—Luis Arroyo, New York | Stu Miller, San Francisco |
| 1962—Dick Radatz, Boston | Roy Face, Pittsburgh |
| 1963—Stu Miller, Baltimore | Lindy McDaniel, Chicago |
| 1964—Dick Radatz, Boston | Al McBean, Pittsburgh |
| 1965—Eddie Fisher, Chicago | Ted Abernathy, Chicago |
| 1966—Jack Aker, Kansas City | Phil Regan, Los Angeles |
| 1967—Minnie Rojas, California | Ted Abernathy, Cincinnati |
| 1968—Wilbur Wood, Chicago | Phil Regan, L.A.-Chicago |
| 1969—Ron Perranoski, Minnesota | Wayne Granger, Cincinnati |
| 1970—Ron Perranoski, Minnesota | Wayne Granger, Cincinnati |
| 1971—Ken Sanders, Milwaukee | Dave Giusti, Pittsburgh |
| 1972—Sparky Lyle, New York | Clay Carroll, Cincinnati |
| 1973—John Hiller, Detroit | Mike Marshall, Montreal |
| 1974—Terry Forster, Chicago | Mike Marshall, Los Angeles |
| 1975—Rich Gossage, Chicago | Al Hrabosky, St. Louis |
| 1976—Bill Campbell, Minnesota | Rawly Eastwick, Cincinnati |
| 1977—Bill Campbell, Boston | Rollie Fingers, San Diego |
| 1978—Rich Gossage, New York | Rollie Fingers, San Diego |
| 1979—Mike Marshall, Minnesota | Bruce Sutter, Chicago |
| Jim Kern, Texas | |
| 1980—Dan Quisenberry, Kansas City | Rollie Fingers, San Diego |
| | Tom Hume, Cincinnati |
| 1981—Rollie Fingers, Milwaukee | Bruce Sutter, St. Louis |
| 1982—Dan Quisenberry, Kansas City | Bruce Sutter, St. Louis |
| 1983—Dan Quisenberry, Kansas City | Al Holland, Philadelphia |
| | Lee Smith, Chicago |
| 1984—Dan Quisenberry, Kansas City | Bruce Sutter, St. Louis |
| 1985—Dan Quisenberry, Kansas City | Jeff Reardon, Montreal |

## THE SPORTING NEWS ROOKIE AWARDS

1946—Combined selection—Delmer Ennis, Philadelphia, N. L., of
1947—Combined selection—Jack Robinson, Brooklyn, 1b
1948—Combined selection—Richie Ashburn, Philadelphia, N. L., of

| AMERICAN LEAGUE | NATIONAL LEAGUE |
|---|---|
| Year   Player   Club | Player   Club |
| 1949—Roy Sievers, St. Louis, of | Donald Newcombe, Brooklyn, p |
| 1950—Combined selection—Edward Ford, New York, A. L., p | |
| 1951—Orestes Minoso, Chicago, of | Willie Mays, New York, of |
| 1952—Clinton Courtney, St. Louis, c | Joseph Black, Brooklyn, p |
| 1953—Harvey Kuenn, Detroit, ss | James Gilliam, Brooklyn, 2b |
| 1954—Robert Grim, New York, p | Wallace Moon, St. Louis, of |
| 1955—Herbert Score, Cleveland, p | William Virdon, St. Louis, of |
| 1956—Luis Aparicio, Chicago, ss | Frank Robinson, Cincinnati, of |

# THE SPORTING NEWS ROOKIE AWARDS—Continued

| AMERICAN LEAGUE | | | NATIONAL LEAGUE | |
|---|---|---|---|---|
| Year | Player | Club | Player | Club |
| 1957—Anthony Kubek, New York, inf-of (No pitcher named) | | | Edward Bouchee, Philadelphia, 1b Jack Sanford, Philadelphia, p | |
| 1958—Albert Pearson, Washington, of Ryne Duren, New York, p | | | Orlando Cepeda, San Francisco, 1b Carlton Willey, Milwaukee, p | |
| 1959—W. Robert Allison, Washington, of | | | Willie McCovey, San Francisco, 1b | |
| 1960—Ronald Hansen, Baltimore, ss | | | Frank Howard, Los Angeles, of | |
| 1961—Richard Howser, Kansas City, ss Donald Schwall, Boston, p | | | Billy Williams, Chicago, of Kenneth Hunt, Cincinnati, p | |
| 1962—Thomas Tresh, New York, of-ss | | | Kenneth Hubbs, Chicago, 2b | |
| 1963—Peter Ward, Chicago, 3b Gary Peters, Chicago, p | | | Peter Rose, Cincinnati, 2b Raymond Culp, Philadelphia, p | |
| 1964—Pedro (Tony) Oliva, Minnesota, of Wallace Bunker, Baltimore, p | | | Richard Allen, Philadelphia, 3b William McCool, Cincinnati, p | |
| 1965—Curtis Blefary, Baltimore, of Marcelino Lopez, California, p | | | Joseph Morgan, Houston, 2b Frank Linzy, San Francisco, p | |
| 1966—Tommie Agee, Chicago, of James Nash, Kansas City, p | | | Tommy Helms, Cincinnati, 3b Donald Sutton, Los Angeles, p | |
| 1967—Rod Carew, Minnesota, 2b Tom Phoebus, Baltimore, p | | | Lee May, Cincinnati, 1b Dick Hughes, St. Louis, p | |
| 1968—Del Unser, Washington, of Stan Bahnsen, New York, p | | | Johnny Bench, Cincinnati, c Jerry Koosman, New York, p | |
| 1969—Carlos May, Chicago, of Mike Nagy, Boston, p | | | Coco Laboy, Montreal, 3b Tom Griffin, Houston, p | |
| 1970—Roy Foster, Cleveland, of Bert Blyleven, Minnesota, p | | | Bernie Carbo, Cincinnati, of Carl Morton, Montreal, p | |
| 1971—Chris Chambliss, Cleveland, 1b Bill Parsons, Milwaukee, p | | | Earl Williams, Atlanta, c Reggie Cleveland, St. Louis, p | |
| 1972—Carlton Fisk, Boston, c Dick Tidrow, Cleveland, p | | | Dave Rader, San Francisco, c Jon Matlack, New York, p | |
| 1973—Al Bumbry, Baltimore, of Steve Busby, Kansas City, p | | | Gary Matthews, San Francisco, of Steve Rogers, Montreal, p  · | |
| 1974—Mike Hargrove, Texas, 1b Frank Tanana, California, p | | | Greg Gross, Houston, of John D'Acquisto, San Francisco, p | |
| 1975—Fred Lynn, Boston, of Dennis Eckersley, Cleveland, p | | | Gary Carter, Montreal, of-c John Montefusco, San Francisco, p | |
| 1976—Butch Wynegar, Minnesota, c Mark Fidrych, Detroit, p | | | Larry Herndon, San Francisco, of Butch Metzger, San Diego, p | |
| 1977—Mitchell Page, Oakland, of Dave Rozema, Detroit, p | | | Andre Dawson, Montreal, of Bob Owchinko, San Diego, p | |
| 1978—Paul Molitor, Milwaukee, 2b Rich Gale, Kansas City, p | | | Bob Horner, Atlanta, 3b Don Robinson, Pittsburgh, p | |
| 1979—Pat Putnam, Texas, 1b Mark Clear, California, p | | | Jeff Leonard, Houston, of Rick Sutcliffe, Los Angeles, p | |
| 1980—Joe Charboneau, Cleveland, of Britt Burns, Chicago, p | | | Lonnie Smith, Philadelphia, of Bill Gullickson, Montreal, p | |
| 1981—Rich Gedman, Boston, c Dave Righetti, New York, p | | | Tim Raines, Montreal, of Fernando Valenzuela, Los Angeles, p | |
| 1982—Cal Ripken, Baltimore, ss-3b Ed Vande Berg, Seattle, p | | | Johnny Ray, Pittsburgh, 2b Steve Bedrosian, Atlanta, p | |
| 1983—Ron Kittle, Chicago, of Mike Boddicker, Baltimore, p | | | Darryl Strawberry, New York, of Craig McMurtry, Atlanta, p | |
| 1984—Alvin Davis, Seattle, 1b Mark Langston, Seattle, p | | | Juan Samuel, Philadelphia, 2b Dwight Gooden, New York, p | |
| 1985—Ozzie Guillen, Chicago, ss Teddy Higuera, Milwaukee, p | | | Vince Coleman, St. Louis, of Tom Browning, Cincinnati, p | |

## MAJOR LEAGUE EXECUTIVE

| Year | Executive | Club | Year | Executive | Club |
|---|---|---|---|---|---|
| 1936—Branch Rickey, St. Louis NL | | | 1953—Louis Perini, Milwaukee NL | | |
| 1937—Edward Barrow, New York AL | | | 1954—Horace Stoneham, N. York NL | | |
| 1938—Warren Giles, Cincinnati NL | | | 1955—Walter O'Malley, Brooklyn NL | | |
| 1939—Larry MacPhail, Brooklyn NL | | | 1956—Gabe Paul, Cincinnati NL | | |
| 1940—W. O. Briggs, Sr., Detroit AL | | | 1957—Frank Lane, St. Louis NL | | |
| 1941—Edward Barrow, New York AL | | | 1958—Joe L. Brown, Pittsburgh NL | | |
| 1942—Branch Rickey, St. Louis NL | | | 1959—E. J. (Buzzie) Bavasi, L.A. NL | | |
| 1943—Clark Griffith, Washington AL | | | 1960—George Weiss, New York AL | | |
| 1944—Wm. O. DeWitt, St. Louis AL | | | 1961—Dan Topping, New York AL | | |
| 1945—Philip K. Wrigley, Chicago NL | | | 1962—Fred Haney, Los Angeles AL | | |
| 1946—Thomas A. Yawkey, Boston AL | | | 1963—Vaughan (Bing) Devine, St.L.NL | | |
| 1947—Branch Rickey, Brooklyn NL | | | 1964—Vaughan (Bing) Devine, St.L.NL | | |
| 1948—Bill Veeck, Cleveland AL | | | 1965—Calvin Griffith, Minnesota AL | | |
| 1949—Robt. Carpenter, Phila'phia NL | | | 1966—Lee MacPhail, Commissioner's Office | | |
| 1950—George Weiss, New York AL | | | 1967—Dick O'Connell, Boston AL | | |
| 1951—George Weiss, New York AL | | | 1968—James Campbell, Detroit AL | | |
| 1952—George Weiss, New York AL | | | | | |

## MAJOR LEAGUE EXECUTIVE — Continued

| Year | Executive | Club |
|------|-----------|------|
| 1969 | John Murphy, New York NL | |
| 1970 | Harry Dalton, Baltimore AL | |
| 1971 | Cedric Tallis, Kansas City AL | |
| 1972 | Roland Hemond, Chicago AL | |
| 1973 | Bob Howsam, Cincinnati NL | |
| 1974 | Gabe Paul, New York AL | |
| 1975 | Dick O'Connell, Boston AL | |
| 1976 | Joe Burke, Kansas City AL | |
| 1977 | Bill Veeck, Chicago AL | |

| Year | Executive | Club |
|------|-----------|------|
| 1978 | Spec Richardson, San Fran. NL | |
| 1979 | Hank Peters, Baltimore AL | |
| 1980 | Tal Smith, Houston NL | |
| 1981 | John McHale, Montreal NL | |
| 1982 | Harry Dalton, Milwaukee AL | |
| 1983 | Hank Peters, Baltimore AL | |
| 1984 | Dallas Green, Chicago NL | |
| 1985 | John Schuerholz, Kansas City AL | |

## MAJOR LEAGUE MANAGER

| Year | Manager | Club |
|------|---------|------|
| 1936 | Joe McCarthy, New York AL | |
| 1937 | Bill McKechnie, Boston NL | |
| 1938 | Joe McCarthy, New York AL | |
| 1939 | Leo Durocher, Brooklyn NL | |
| 1940 | Bill McKechnie, Cincinnati NL | |
| 1941 | Billy Southworth, St. Louis NL | |
| 1942 | Billy Southworth, St. Louis NL | |
| 1943 | Joe McCarthy, New York AL | |
| 1944 | Luke Sewell, St. Louis AL | |
| 1945 | Ossie Bluege, Washington AL | |
| 1946 | Eddie Dyer, St. Louis NL | |
| 1947 | Bucky Harris, New York AL | |
| 1948 | Bill Meyer, Pittsburgh NL | |
| 1949 | Casey Stengel, New York AL | |
| 1950 | Red Rolfe, Detroit AL | |
| 1951 | Leo Durocher, New York NL | |
| 1952 | Eddie Stanky, St. Louis NL | |
| 1953 | Casey Stengel, New York AL | |
| 1954 | Leo Durocher, New York NL | |
| 1955 | Walter Alston, Brooklyn NL | |
| 1956 | Birdie Tebbetts, Cincinnati NL | |
| 1957 | Fred Hutchinson, St. Louis NL | |
| 1958 | Casey Stengel, New York AL | |
| 1959 | Walter Alston, Los Angeles NL | |
| 1960 | Danny Murtaugh, Pitts. NL | |

| Year | Manager | Club |
|------|---------|------|
| 1961 | Ralph Houk, New York AL | |
| 1962 | Bill Rigney, Los Angeles AL | |
| 1963 | Walter Alston, Los Angeles NL | |
| 1964 | Johnny Keane, St. Louis NL | |
| 1965 | Sam Mele, Minnesota AL | |
| 1966 | Hank Bauer, Baltimore AL | |
| 1967 | Dick Williams, Boston AL | |
| 1968 | Mayo Smith, Detroit AL | |
| 1969 | Gil Hodges, New York NL | |
| 1970 | Danny Murtaugh, Pittsb'gh NL | |
| 1971 | Charlie Fox, San Francisco NL | |
| 1972 | Chuck Tanner, Chicago AL | |
| 1973 | Gene Mauch, Montreal NL | |
| 1974 | Bill Virdon, New York AL | |
| 1975 | Darrell Johnson, Boston AL | |
| 1976 | Danny Ozark, Philadelphia NL | |
| 1977 | Earl Weaver, Baltimore AL | |
| 1978 | George Bamberger, Milw'kee AL | |
| 1979 | Earl Weaver, Baltimore AL | |
| 1980 | Bill Virdon, Houston NL | |
| 1981 | Billy Martin, Oakland AL | |
| 1982 | Whitey Herzog, St. Louis NL | |
| 1983 | Tony LaRussa, Chicago AL | |
| 1984 | Jim Frey, Chicago NL | |
| 1985 | Bobby Cox, Toronto AL | |

## MAJOR LEAGUE PLAYER

| Year | Player | Club |
|------|--------|------|
| 1936 | Carl Hubbell, New York NL | |
| 1937 | Johnny Allen, Cleveland AL | |
| 1938 | Johnny Vander Meer, Cinn. NL | |
| 1939 | Joe DiMaggio, New York AL | |
| 1940 | Bob Feller, Cleveland AL | |
| 1941 | Ted Williams, Boston AL | |
| 1942 | Ted Williams, Boston AL | |
| 1943 | Spud Chandler, New York AL | |
| 1944 | Marty Marion, St. Louis NL | |
| 1945 | Hal Newhouser, Detroit AL | |
| 1946 | Stan Musial, St. Louis NL | |
| 1947 | Ted Williams, Boston AL | |
| 1948 | Lou Boudreau, Cleveland AL | |
| 1949 | Ted Williams, Boston AL | |
| 1950 | Phil Rizzuto, New York AL | |
| 1951 | Stan Musial, St. Louis NL | |
| 1952 | Robin Roberts, Philadelphia NL | |
| 1953 | Al Rosen, Cleveland AL | |
| 1954 | Willie Mays, New York NL | |
| 1955 | Duke Snider, Brooklyn NL | |
| 1956 | Mickey Mantle, New York AL | |
| 1957 | Ted Williams, Boston AL | |
| 1958 | Bob Turley, New York AL | |
| 1959 | Early Wynn, Chicago AL | |
| 1960 | Bill Mazeroski, Pittsburgh NL | |
| 1961 | Roger Maris, New York AL | |

| Year | Player | Club |
|------|--------|------|
| 1962 | Maury Wills, Los Angeles NL | |
| | Don Drysdale, Los Angeles NL | |
| 1963 | Sandy Koufax, Los Angeles NL | |
| 1964 | Ken Boyer, St. Louis NL | |
| 1965 | Sandy Koufax, Los Angeles NL | |
| 1966 | Frank Robinson, Baltimore AL | |
| 1967 | Carl Yastrzemski, Boston AL | |
| 1968 | Denny McLain, Detroit AL | |
| 1969 | Willie McCovey, San Fran. NL | |
| 1970 | Johnny Bench, Cin. NL | |
| 1971 | Joe Torre, St. Louis NL | |
| 1972 | Billy Williams, Chicago NL | |
| 1973 | Reggie Jackson, Oakland AL | |
| 1974 | Lou Brock, St. Louis NL | |
| 1975 | Joe Morgan, Cincinnati NL | |
| 1976 | Joe Morgan, Cincinnati NL | |
| 1977 | Rod Carew, Minnesota AL | |
| 1978 | Ron Guidry, New York AL | |
| 1979 | Willie Stargell, Pittsburgh NL | |
| 1980 | George Brett, Kansas City AL | |
| 1981 | Fernando Valenzuela, Los Angeles NL | |
| 1982 | Robin Yount, Milwaukee AL | |
| 1983 | Cal Ripken, Baltimore AL | |
| 1984 | Ryne Sandberg, Chicago NL | |
| 1985 | Don Mattingly, New York AL | |

## MINOR LEAGUE EXECUTIVE (HIGHER CLASSIFICATIONS)
### (Restricted to Class AAA Starting in 1963)

| Year | Executive | Club |
|------|-----------|------|
| 1936 | Earl Mann, Atlanta, Southern | |
| 1937 | Robt. LaMotte, Savannah, Sally | |
| 1938 | Louis McKenna, St. Paul, A.A. | |
| 1939 | Bruce Dudley, Louisville, A.A. | |

| Year | Executive | Club |
|------|-----------|------|
| 1940 | Roy Hamey, Kansas City, A.A. | |
| 1941 | Emil Sick, Seattle, PCL | |
| 1942 | Bill Veeck, Milwaukee, A.A. | |
| 1943 | Clar. Rowland, Los Angeles, PCL | |

## MINOR LEAGUE EXECUTIVE (HIGHER CLASSIFICATIONS)—Continued

| Year | Manager | Club |
|---|---|---|
| 1944 | William Mulligan, Seattle, PCL | |
| 1945 | Bruce Dudley, Louisville, A.A. | |
| 1946 | Earl Mann, Atlanta, Southern | |
| 1947 | Wm. Purnhage, Waterloo, I.I.I. | |
| 1948 | Ed. Glennon, Bir'ham, Southern | |
| 1949 | Ted Sullivan, Indianapolis, A.A. | |
| 1950 | Cl. (Brick) Laws, Oakland, PCL | |
| 1951 | Robert Howsam, Denver, West. | |
| 1952 | Jack Cooke, Toronto, Int. | |
| 1953 | Richard Burnett, Dallas, Texas | |
| 1954 | Edward Stumpf, Indpls., A.A. | |
| 1955 | Dewey Soriano, Seattle, PCL | |
| 1956 | Robert Howsam, Denver, A.A. | |
| 1957 | John Stiglmeier, Buffalo, Int. | |
| 1958 | Ed. Glennon, Bir'ham, Southern | |
| 1959 | Ed. Leishman, Salt Lake, PCL | |
| 1960 | Ray Winder, Little Rock, Sou. | |
| 1961 | Elten Schiller, Omaha, A.A. | |
| 1962 | Geo. Sisler, Jr., Rochester, Int. | |
| 1963 | Lewis Matlin, Hawaii, PCL | |
| 1964 | Ed. Leishman, San Diego, PCL | |

| Year | Manager | Club |
|---|---|---|
| 1965 | Harold Cooper, Columbus, Int. | |
| 1966 | John Quinn, Jr., Hawaii, PCL | |
| 1967 | Hillman Lyons, Richmond, Int. | |
| 1968 | Gabe Paul, Jr., Tulsa, PCL | |
| 1969 | Bill Gardner, Louisville, Int. | |
| 1970 | Dick King, Wichita, A.A. | |
| 1971 | Carl Steinfeldt, Jr., Roch'ter, Int. | |
| 1972 | Don Labbruzzo, Evansville, A.A. | |
| 1973 | Merle Miller, Tucson, PCL | |
| 1974 | John Carbray, Sacramento, PCL | |
| 1975 | Stan Naccarato, Tacoma, PCL | |
| 1976 | Art Teece, Salt Lake City, PCL | |
| 1977 | George Sisler, Jr., Col'bus, Int. | |
| 1978 | Willie Sanchez, Albu'que, PCL | |
| 1979 | George Sisler, Jr., Col'bus, Int. | |
| 1980 | Jim Burris, Denver, A.A. | |
| 1981 | Pat McKernan, Albuquerque, PCL | |
| 1982 | A. Ray Smith, Louisville, A.A. | |
| 1983 | A. Ray Smith, Louisville, A.A. | |
| 1984 | Mike Tamburro, Pawtucket, Int. | |
| 1985 | Patty Cox Hampton, Okla City, A.A. | |

## MINOR LEAGUE EXECUTIVE (LOWER CLASSIFICATIONS)
### (Separate Awards for Class AA and Class A Started in 1963)

| Year | Executive | Club |
|---|---|---|
| 1950 | H. Cooper, Hutch'son, West. A. | |
| 1951 | O. W. (Bill) Hayes, T'ple, B.S. | |
| 1952 | Hillman Lyons, Danville, MOV | |
| 1953 | Carl Roth, Peoria, III | |
| 1954 | James Meaghan, Cedar R., III | |
| 1955 | John Petrakis, Dubuque, MOV | |
| 1956 | Marvin Milkes, Fresno, Calif. | |
| 1957 | Richard Wagner, L'coln, West. | |
| 1958 | Gerald Waring, Macon, Sally | |
| 1959 | Clay Dennis, Des Moines, III | |
| 1960 | Hubert Kittle, Yakima, Northw. | |
| 1961 | David Steele, Fresno, California | |
| 1962 | John Quinn, Jr., S. Jose, Calif. | |
| 1963 | Hugh Finnerty, Tulsa, Texas | |
| | Ben Jewell, M. Valley, Pioneer | |
| 1964 | Glynn West, Birmingham, Sou. | |
| | Jas. Bayens, Rock Hill, W. Car. | |
| 1965 | Dick Butler, Dallas-Ft.W., Tex. | |
| | Ken. Blackman, Quad C., Midw. | |
| 1966 | Tom Fleming, Evansville, South. | |
| | Cappy Harada, Lodi, California | |
| 1967 | Robt. Quinn, Reading, East. | |
| | Pat Williams, Spar'burg, W. C. | |
| 1968 | Phil Howser, Charlotte, South. | |
| | Merle Miller, Burlington, Midw. | |
| 1969 | Charlie Blaney, Albuq., Texas | |
| | Bill Gorman, Visalia, Calif. | |
| 1970 | Carl Sawatski, Arkansas, Texas | |
| | Bob Williams, Bakersfield, Calif. | |

| Year | Executive | Club |
|---|---|---|
| 1971 | Miles Wolff, Savannah, Dixie A. | |
| | Ed Holtz, Appleton, Midwest | |
| 1972 | John Begzos, S. Antonio, Texas | |
| | Bob Piccinini, Modesto, Calif. | |
| 1973 | Dick Kravitz, Jacksonville, Sou. | |
| | Fritz Colschen, Clinton, Midw. | |
| 1974 | Jim Paul, El Paso, Texas | |
| | Bing Russell, Portland, N'west | |
| 1975 | Jim Paul, El Paso, Texas | |
| | Cordy Jensen, Eugene, N'west | |
| 1976 | Woodrow Reid, Chat'ooga, Sou. | |
| | Don Buchheister, Ced. Rap., Mid. | |
| 1977 | Jim Paul, El Paso, Texas | |
| | Harry Pells, Quad Cities, Midw. | |
| 1978 | Larry Schmittou, Nashville, Sou. | |
| | Dave Hersh, Appleton, Midwest | |
| 1979 | Bill Rigney Jr., Midland, Tex. | |
| | Tom Romenesko, G'sboro, W.C. | |
| 1980 | Frances Crockett, C'lotte, Sou. | |
| | Tom Romenesko, G'sboro, W.C. | |
| 1981 | Allie Prescott, Memphis, Southern | |
| | Dan Overstreet, Hagerstown, Caro. | |
| 1982 | Art Clarkson, Birmingham, Sou. | |
| | Bob Carruesco, Stockton, Calif. | |
| 1983 | Edward Kenney, New Britain, East. | |
| | Terry Reynolds, Vero Beach, Fla. St. | |
| 1984 | Bruce Baldwin, Greenville, Sou. | |
| | Dave Tarrolly, Beloit, Midwest | |
| 1985 | Ben Bernard, Albany-Colonie, Eastern | |
| | Pete Vonachen, Peoria, Midwest | |

## MINOR LEAGUE MANAGER

| Year | Manager | Club |
|---|---|---|
| 1936 | Al Sothoron, Milwaukee, A.A. | |
| 1937 | Jake Flowers, Salis'y, East. Sh. | |
| 1938 | Paul Richards, Atlanta, South. | |
| 1939 | Bill Meyer, Kansas City, A.A. | |
| 1940 | Larry Gilbert, Nashville, South. | |
| 1941 | Burt Shotton, Columbus, A.A. | |
| 1942 | Eddie Dyer, Columbus, A.A. | |
| 1943 | Nick Cullop, Columbus, A.A. | |
| 1944 | Al Thomas, Baltimore, Int. | |
| 1945 | Lefty O'Doul, San Fran., PCL | |
| 1946 | Clay Hopper, Montreal, Int. | |
| 1947 | Nick Cullop, Milwaukee, A.A. | |
| 1948 | Casey Stengel, Oakland, PCL | |
| 1949 | Fred Haney, Hollywood, PCL | |
| 1950 | Rollie Hemsley, Columbus, A.A. | |
| 1951 | Charlie Grimm, Milw., A.A. | |

| Year | Manager | Club |
|---|---|---|
| 1952 | Luke Appling, Memphis, South. | |
| 1953 | Bobby Bragan, Hollywood, PCL | |
| 1954 | Kerby Farrell, Indpls., A.A. | |
| 1955 | Bill Rigney, Minneapolis, A.A. | |
| 1956 | Kerby Farrell, Indpls., A.A. | |
| 1957 | Ben Geraghty, Wichita, A.A. | |
| 1958 | Cal Ermer, Birmingham, South. | |
| 1959 | Pete Reiser, Victoria, Texas | |
| 1960 | Mel McGaha, Toronto, Int. | |
| 1961 | Kerby Farrell, Buffalo, Int. | |
| 1962 | Ben Geraghty, Jackson'le, Int. | |
| 1963 | Rollie Hemsley, Indpls., Int. | |
| 1964 | Harry Walker, Jacks'vile, Int. | |
| 1965 | Grady Hatton, Okla. City, PCL | |
| 1966 | Bob Lemon, Seattle, PCL | |
| 1967 | Bob Skinner, San Diego, PCL | |

## MINOR LEAGUE MANAGER—Continued

Year  Manager          Club
1968—Jack Tighe, Toledo, Int.
1969—Clyde McCullough, Tide., Int.
1970—Tom Lasorda, Spokane, PCL
1971—Del Rice, Salt Lake City, PCL
1972—Hank Bauer, Tidewater, Int.
1973—Joe Morgan, Charleston, Int.
1974—Joe Altobelli, Rochester, Int.
1975—Joe Frazier, Tidewater, Int.
1976—Vern Rapp, Denver, A.A.

Year  Manager          Club
1977—Tommy Thompson, Arkan., Tex.
1978—Les Moss, Evansville, A.A.
1979—Vern Benson, Syracuse, Int.
1980—Hal Lanier, Springfield, A.A.
1981—Del Crandall, Albuquerque, PCL
1982—George Scherger, Indianapolis, A.A.
1983—Bill Dancy, Reading, East.
1984—Bob Rodgers, Indianapolis, A.A.
1985—Jim Fregosi, Louisville, A.A.

## MINOR LEAGUE PLAYER

Year  Player          Club
1936—Jn. Vander Meer, Durham, Pied.
1937—Charlie Keller, Newark, Int.
1938—Fred Hutchinson, Seattle, PCL
1939—Lou Novikoff, Tulsa-Los A'les.
1940—Phil Rizzuto, Kansas City, A.A.
1941—John Lindell, Newark, Int.
1942—Dick Barrett, Seattle, PCL
1943—Chet Covington, Scranton, East.
1944—Rip Collins, Albany, Eastern
1945—Gil Coan, Chattanooga, South.
1946—Sibby Sisti, Indianapolis, A.A.
1947—Hank Sauer, Syracuse, Int.
1948—Gene Woodling, S. F., PCL
1949—Orie Arntzen, Albany, Eastern
1950—Frank Saucier, San Ant'o, Tex.
1951—Gene Conley, Hartford, Eastern
1952—Bill Skowron, Kans. City, A.A.
1953—Gene Conley, Toledo, A.A.
1954—Herb Score, Indianapolis, A.A.
1955—John Murff, Dallas, Texas
1956—Steve Bilko, Los Angeles, PCL
1957—Norm Siebern, Denver, A.A.
1958—Jim O'Toole, Nashville, South.
1959—Frank Howard, Victoria-Spok.
1960—Willie Davis, Spokane, PCL

Year  Player          Club
1961—Howie Koplitz, Bir'ham, South.
1962—Bob Bailey, Columbus, Int.
1963—Don Buford, Indianapolis, Int.
1964—Mel Stottlemyre, Richm'd., Int.
1965—Joe Foy, Toronto, International
1966—Mike Epstein, Rochester, Int.
1967—Johnny Bench, Buffalo, Int.
1968—Merv Rettenmund, Roch'ter, Int.
1969—Danny Walton, Okla. City, A.A.
1970—Don Baylor, Rochester, Int.
1971—Bobby Grich, Rochester, Int.
1972—Tom Paciorek, Albuq'que, PCL
1973—Steve Ontiveros, Phoenix, PCL
1974—Jim Rice, Pawtucket, Int.
1975—Hector Cruz, Tulsa, A.A.
1976—Pat Putnam, Asheville, W. Car.
1977—Ken Landreaux, S.L.C., PCL-El Paso, Tex.
1978—Champ Summers, Indi'polis, A.A.
1979—Mark Bomback, Vancouver, PCL
1980—Tim Raines, Denver, A.A.
1981—Mike Marshall, Albuquerque, PCL
1982—Ron Kittle, Edmonton, PCL
1983—Kevin McReynolds, Las Vegas, PCL
1984—Alan Knicely, Wichita, A.A.
1985—Jose Canseco, Hunt., Sou.-Tac., PCL

# Major League All-Star Teams

### 1925
Bottomley, St. L. NL................ 1B
Hornsby, St. Louis NL.............. 2B
Wright, Pittsburgh NL............. SS
Traynor, Pittsb'gh NL ............. 3B
Cuyler, Pittsb'gh NL ................OF
Carey, Pittsb'gh NL..................OF
Goslin, Wash'ton AL.................OF
Cochrane, Phila. AL ................. C
Johnson, Wash'ton AL.............. P
Rommel, Phila. AL.................... P
Vance, Brooklyn NL.................. P

### 1926
G. Burns, Cleve. AL
Hornsby, St. Louis NL
J. Sewell, Cleve. AL
Traynor, Pittsb'gh NL
Goslin, Wash'ton AL
Mostil, Chicago AL
Ruth, New York AL
O'Farrell, St. Louis NL
Pennock, N. York AL
Uhle, Cleveland AL
Alexander, St. L. NL

### 1927
1B—Gehrig, N. York AL
2B—Hornsby, N. York NL
SS—Jackson, N. York NL
3B—Traynor, Pitts. NL
OF—Ruth, New York AL
OF—Simmons, Phila. AL
OF—P. Waner, Pitts. NL
C—Hartnett, Chicago NL
P—Root, Chicago, NL
P—Lyons, Chicago AL

### 1928
Gehrig, New York AL .............. 1B
Hornsby, Boston NL ................ 2B
Jackson, N. York NL................ SS
Lindstrom, N. Y. NL.................. 3B
Ruth, New York AL...................OF
Manush, St. Louis AL ...............OF
P. Waner, Pitts. NL ..................OF
Cochrane, Phila. AL ................. C
Grove, Phila'phia AL................ P
Hoyt, New York AL................... P

### 1929
Foxx, Phila'phia AL
Hornsby, Chicago NL
Jackson, N. York NL
Traynor, Pittsb'gh NL
Simmons, Phila. AL
L. Wilson, Chi. NL
Ruth, New York AL
Cochrane, Phila. AL
Grove, Phila'phia AL
Grimes, Pittsburgh NL

### 1930
1B—Terry, New York NL
2B—Frisch, St. Louis NL
SS—Cronin, Wash'ton, AL
3B—Lindstrom, N. Y. NL
OF—Simmons, Phila. AL
OF—L. Wilson, Chi. NL
OF—Ruth, New York AL
C—Cochrane, Phila. AL
P—Grove, Phila'phia AL
P—W. Ferrell, Cleve. AL

### 1931
Gehrig, New York AL .............. 1B
Frisch, St. Louis NL................. 2B
Cronin, Wash'ton AL................ SS
Traynor, Pittsb'gh NL ............. 3B
Simmons, Phila. AL..................OF
Averill, Cleve'd AL....................OF
Ruth, New York AL...................OF
Cochrane, Phila. AL ................. C
Grove, Phila'phia AL................ P
Earnshaw, Phila. AL................. P

### 1932
Foxx, Phila'phia AL
Lazzeri, N. York AL
Cronin, Wash'ton AL
Traynor, Pittsb'gh NL
O'Doul, Brooklyn NL
Averill, Cleveland AL
Klein, Phila'phia NL
Dickey, New York AL
Grove, Phila'phia AL
Warneke, Chicago NL

### 1933
1B—Foxx, Phila'phia AL
2B—Gehringer, Det. AL
SS—Cronin, Wash'ton AL
3B—Traynor, Pitts. NL
OF—Simmons, Chi. AL
OF—Berger, Boston NL
OF—Klein, Phila'phia NL
C—Dickey, N. York AL
P—Crowder, Wash. AL
P—Hubbell, N. York NL

### 1934

Gehrig, New York AL .............. 1B
Gehringer, Det. AL ................... 2B
Cronin, Wash'ton AL ................ SS
Higgins, Phil'phia AL ............... 3B
Simmons, Chicago AL ...............OF
Averill, Cleveland AL................OF
Ott, New York NL.....................OF
Cochrane, Detroit AL .............. C
Gomez, New York AL ............... P
Rowe, Detroit AL ...................... P
J. Dean, St. Louis NL................. P

### 1935

Greenberg, Det. AL
Gehringer, Det. AL
Vaughan, Pitts. NL
J. Martin, St. L. NL
Medwick, St. L. NL
Cramer, Phila. AL
Ott, New York NL
Cochrane, Detroit AL
Hubbell, N. York NL
J. Dean, St. Louis NL

### 1936

1B—Gehrig, New York AL
2B—Gehringer, Det. AL
SS—Appling, Chicago AL
3B—Higgins, Phila. AL
OF—Medwick, St. L. NL
OF—Averill, Cleve. AL
OF—Ott, New York NL
C—Dickey, N.Y. AL
P—Hubbell, N. York NL
P—J. Dean, St. Louis NL

### 1937

Gehrig, New York AL .............. 1B
Gehringer, Det. AL ................... 2B
Bartell, New York NL............... SS
Rolfe, New York AL .................. 3B
Medwick, St. L. NL ...................OF
J. DiMaggio, N.Y. AL................OF
P. Waner, Pitts. NL ..................OF
Hartnett, Chicago, NL.............. C
Hubbell, New York NL ............. P
Ruffing, New York AL.............. P

### 1938

Foxx, Boston AL
Gehringer, Detroit AL
Cronin, Boston AL
Rolfe, New York AL
Medwick, St. Louis NL
J. DiMaggio, N. Y. AL
Ott, New York NL
Dickey, New York AL
Ruffing, New York AL
Gomez, New York AL
Vander Meer, Cin. NL

### 1939

1B—Foxx, Boston, AL
2B—Gordon, N. York AL
SS—Cronin, Boston AL
3B—Rolfe, New York AL
OF—Medwick, St. L. NL
OF—J. DiMaggio, N.Y. AL
OF—Williams, Boston AL
C—Dickey, N. York AL
P—Ruffing, N. York AL
P—Feller, Cleveland AL
P—Walters, Cinn. NL

### 1940

F. McCormick, Cin. NL ............ 1B
Gordon, N. York AL.................. 2B
Appling, Chicago AL................. SS
Hack, Chicago NL...................... 3B
Greenberg, Det. AL...................OF
J. DiMaggio, N.Y. AL................OF
Williams, Boston AL.................OF
Danning, N. York NL ............. C
Feller, Cleveland AL ................. P
Walters, Cinn. NL ..................... P
Derringer, Cinn. NL ................. P

### 1941

Camilli, Brooklyn NL
Gordon, N. York AL
Travis, Wash'ton AL
Hack, Chicago NL
Williams, Boston AL
J. DiMaggio, N. Y. AL
Reiser, Brooklyn NL
Dickey, New York AL
Feller, Cleveland AL
Wyatt, Brooklyn NL
Lee, Chicago NL

### 1942

1B—Mize, New York NL
2B—Gordon, N. York AL
SS—Pesky, Boston AL
3B—Hack, Chicago NL
OF—Williams, Boston AL
OF—J. DiMaggio, N. Y. AL
OF—Slaughter, St. L. NL
C—Owen, Brooklyn NL
P—M. Cooper, St. L. NL
P—Bonham, N. York AL
P—Hughson, Boston AL

### 1943

York, Detroit AL....................... 1B
Herman, Brooklyn NL ............. 2B
Appling, Chicago AL................. SS
Johnson, N. York AL ................ 3B
Wakefield, Detroit AL..............OF
Musial, St. Louis NL.................OF
Nicholson, Chi. NL ...................OF
W. Cooper, St. L. NL ................ C
Chandler, N. Y. AL ................... P
M. Cooper, St. L. NL ................ P
Sewell, Pittsburgh NL.............. P

### 1944

Sanders, St. Louis NL
Doerr, Boston AL
Marion, St. Louis NL
Elliott, Pittsburgh NL
Musial, St. Louis NL
Wakefield, Detroit AL
F. Walker, Brkn. NL
W. Cooper, St. L. NL
Newhouser, Det. AL
M. Cooper, St. L. NL
Trout, Detroit AL

### 1945

1B—Cavarretta, Chi. NL
2B—Stirnweiss, N. Y. AL
SS—Marion, St. Louis NL
3B—Kurowski, St. L. NL
OF—Holmes, Boston NL
OF—Pafko, Chicago NL
OF—Rosen, Brooklyn, NL
C—Richards, Detroit AL
P—Newhouser, Det. AL
P—Ferriss, Boston AL
P—Borowy, Chicago NL

### 1946

Musial, St. Louis NL................. 1B
Doerr, Boston AL...................... 2B
Pesky, Boston AL ...................... SS
Kell, Detroit AL......................... 3B
Williams, Boston AL.................OF
D. DiMaggio, Bos. AL ..............OF
Slaughter, St. L. NL..................OF
Robinson, N. York AL .............. C
Newhouser, Detroit AL............. P
Feller, Cleveland AL ................. P
Ferriss, Boston AL .................... P

### 1947

Mize, New York NL
Gordon, Cleveland AL
Boudreau, Cleve. AL
Kell, Detroit AL
Williams, Boston AL
J. DiMaggio, N.Y. AL
Kiner, Pittsburgh NL
W. Cooper, N. Y. NL
Blackwell, Cinn. NL
Feller, Cleveland AL
Branca, Brooklyn NL

### 1948

1B—Mize, New York NL
2B—Gordon, Clevel'd AL
SS—Boudreau, Cleve. AL
3B—Elliott, Boston NL
OF—Williams, Boston AL
OF—J. DiMaggio, N.Y. AL
OF—Musial, St. Louis NL
C—Tebbetts, Boston AL
P—Sain, Boston NL
P—Lemon, Cleveland AL
P—Brecheen, St. L. NL

### 1949

Henrich, N. York AL ................ 1B
Robinson, Brkn. NL.................. 2B
Rizzuto, N. York AL ................. SS
Kell, Detroit AL......................... 3B
Williams, Boston AL.................OF
Musial, St. Louis NL.................OF
Kiner, Pittsburgh NL................OF
Campanella, Brkn. NL.............. C
Parnell, Boston AL.................... P
Kinder, Boston AL .................... P
Page, New York AL ................... P

### 1950

Dropo, Boston AL
Robinson, Brkn. NL
Rizzuto, New York AL
Kell, Detroit AL
Musial, St. Louis NL
Kiner, Pittsburgh NL
Doby, Cleveland AL
Berra, New York AL
Raschi, New York AL
Lemon, Cleveland AL
Konstanty, Phila. NL

### 1951

1B—Fain, Phila. AL
2B—Robinson, Brkn. NL
SS—Rizzuto, N. York AL
3B—Kell, Detroit AL
OF—Musial, St. Louis NL
OF—Williams, Boston AL
OF—Kiner, Pittsburgh NL
C—Campanella, Brk. NL
P—Maglie, N.Y. NL
P—Roe, Brooklyn NL
P—Reynolds, N. York AL

### 1952

Fain, Phila'phia AL ................... 1B
Robinson, Brkn. NL ..................... 2B
Rizzuto, New York AL .............. SS
Kell, Boston AL.......................... 3B
Musial, St. Louis NL .................OF
Sauer, Chicago NL ....................OF
Mantle, N. York AL ..................OF
Berra, New York AL ................ C
Roberts, Phila'phia NL ............. P
Shantz, Phila'phia AL .............. P
Reynolds, N. York AL .............. P

### 1953

Vernon, Wash'ton AL
Schoendi'st, St. L. NL
Reese, Brooklyn NL
Rosen, Cleveland AL
Musial, St. Louis NL
Snider, Brooklyn NL
Furillo, Brooklyn NL
Campanella, Brkn. NL
Roberts, Phila'phia NL
Spahn, Milwaukee NL
Porterfield, Wash. AL

### 1954

1B—Kluszewski, Cinn. NL
2B—Avila, Cleveland AL
SS—Dark, New York NL
3B—Rosen, Cleveland AL
OF—Mays, New York NL
OF—Musial, St. Louis NL
OF—Snider, Brooklyn NL
C—Berra, New York AL
P—Lemon, Cleveland AL
P—Antonelli, N.Y. NL
P—Roberts, Phila. NL

### 1955

Kluszewski, Cinn. NL ................ 1B
Fox, Chicago AL......................... 2B
Banks, Chicago NL .................... SS
Mathews, Milw. NL .................... 3B
Snider, Brooklyn NL..................OF
Williams, Boston AL..................OF
Kaline, Detroit AL ....................OF
Campanella, Brkn. NL.............. C
Roberts, Phila. NL..................... P
Newcombe, Brkn. NL................ P
Ford, New York AL................... P

### 1956

Kluszewski, Cinn. NL
Fox, Chicago AL
Kuenn, Detroit AL
Boyer, St. Louis NL
Mantle, New York AL
Aaron, Milwaukee NL
Williams, Boston AL
Berra, New York AL
Newcombe, Brkn. NL
Ford, New York AL
Pierce, Chicago AL

### 1957

1B—Musial, St. Louis NL
2B—Scho'st, N.Y-Mil. NL
SS—McDougald, N.Y. AL
3B—Mathews, Milw. NL
OF—Mantle, N. Y. AL
OF—Williams, Boston AL
OF—Mays, New York NL
C—Berra, New York AL
P—Spahn, Milw. NL
P—Pierce, Chicago AL
P—Bunning, Detroit AL

### 1958

Musial, St. Louis NL ................. 1B
Fox, Chicago AL......................... 2B
Banks, Chicago NL .................... SS
Thomas, Pitts. NL...................... 3B
Williams, Boston AL..................OF
Mays, San Fran. NL .................OF
Aaron, Milwaukee NL...............OF
Crandall, Milw. NL..................... C
Turley, New York AL .............. P
Spahn, Milwaukee NL................ P
Friend, Pittsburgh NL .............. P

### 1959

Cepeda, San Fran. NL
Fox, Chicago AL
Banks, Chicago NL
Mathews, Milw. NL
Minoso, Cleveland AL
Mays, San Fran. NL
Aaron, Milwaukee NL
Lollar, Chicago AL
Wynn, Chicago AL
S. Jones, S. Fran. NL
Antonelli, S. Fran. NL

### 1960

1B—Skowron, N. Y. AL
2B—Mazeroski, Pitts. NL
SS—Banks, Chicago NL
3B—Mathews, Milw. NL
OF—Minoso, Chicago AL
OF—Mays, San Fran. NL
OF—Maris, New York AL
C—Crandall, Milw. NL
P—Law, Pittsburgh NL
P—Spahn, Milw. NL
P—Broglio, St. Louis NL

### 1961—National

1B—Orlando Cepeda, S.F.
2B—Frank Bolling, Milw.
SS—Maury Wills, L.A.
3B—Ken Boyer, St. Louis
OF—Willie Mays, S.F.
OF—Frank Robinson, Cin.
OF—Roberto Clemente, Pitts.
C—Smoky Burgess, Pitts.
P—Joey Jay, Cin.
P—Warren Spahn, Milw.

### 1961—American

1B—Norm Cash, Detroit
2B—Bobby Richardson, N.Y.
SS—Tony Kubek, N.Y.
3B—Brooks Robinson, Balt.
OF—Mickey Mantle, N.Y.
OF—Roger Maris, N.Y.
OF—Rocky Colavito, Detroit
C—Elston Howard, N.Y.
P—Whitey Ford, N.Y.
P—Frank Lary, Detroit

### 1962—National

1B—Orlando Cepeda, S.F.
2B—Bill Mazeroski, Pitts.
SS—Maury Wills, L.A.
3B—Ken Boyer, St. Louis
OF—Tommy Davis, L.A.
OF—Willie Mays, S.F.
OF—Frank Robinson, Cin.
C—Del Crandall, Milw.
P—Don Drysdale, L.A.
P—Bob Purkey, Cin.

### 1962—American

1B—Norm Siebern, K.C.
2B—Bobby Richardson, N.Y.
SS—Tom Tresh, N.Y.
3B—Brooks Robinson, Balt.
OF—Leon Wagner, L.A.
OF—Mickey Mantle, N.Y.
OF—Al Kaline, Detroit
C—Earl Battey, Minnesota
P—Ralph Terry, N.Y.
P—Dick Donovan, Cleve.

### 1963—National

1B—Bill White, St. Louis
2B—Jim Gilliam, L.A.
SS—Dick Groat, St. Louis
3B—Ken Boyer, St. Louis
OF—Tommy Davis, L.A.
OF—Willie Mays, S.F.
OF—Hank Aaron, Milw.
C—John Edwards, Cin.
P—Sandy Koufax, L.A.
P—Juan Marichal, S.F.

### 1963—American

1B—Joe Pepitone, N.Y.
2B—Bobby Richardson, N.Y.
SS—Luis Aparicio, Balt.
3B—Frank Malzone, Boston
OF—Carl Yastrzemski, Boston
OF—Albie Pearson, L.A.
OF—Al Kaline, Detroit
C—Elston Howard, N.Y.
P—Whitey Ford, N.Y.
P—Gary Peters, Chicago

### 1964—American

1B—Dick Stuart, Boston
2B—Bobby Richardson, N.Y.
SS—Jim Fregosi, L.A.
3B—Brooks Robinson, Balt.
OF—Harmon Killebrew, Minn.
OF—Mickey Mantle, N.Y.
OF—Tony Oliva, Minn.
C—Elston Howard, N.Y.
P—Dean Chance, L.A.
P—Gary Peters, Chicago

### 1964—National

1B—Bill White, St. Louis
2B—Ron Hunt, New York
SS—Dick Groat, St. Louis
3B—Ken Boyer, St. Louis
OF—Billy Williams, Chicago
OF—Willie Mays, S.F.
OF—Roberto Clemente, Pitts.
C—Joe Torre, Milwaukee
P—Sandy Koufax, L.A.
P—Jim Bunning, Phila.

### 1965—American

1B—Fred Whitfield, Cleveland
2B—Bobby Richardson, N.Y.
SS—Zoilo Versalles, Minnesota
3B—Brooks Robinson, Balt.
LF—Carl Yastrzemski, Boston
CF—Jimmie Hall, Minnesota
RF—Tony Oliva, Minnesota
C—Earl Battey, Minnesota
P—Jim Grant, Minnesota
P—Mel Stottlemyre, N.Y.

**1965—National**
1B—Willie McCovey, S.F.
2B—Pete Rose, Cincinnati
SS—Maury Wills, Los Angeles
3B—Deron Johnson, Cincinnati
LF—Willie Stargell, Pittsburgh
CF—Willie Mays, San Francisco
RF—Hank Aaron, Milwaukee
C—Joe Torre, Milwaukee
P—Sandy Koufax, L.A.
P—Juan Marichal, S.F.

**1966—American**
1B—Boog Powell, Baltimore
2B—Bobby Richardson, N.Y.
SS—Luis Aparicio, Baltimore
3B—Brooks Robinson, Balt.
LF—Frank Robinson, Balt.
CF—Al Kaline, Detroit
RF—Tony Oliva, Minnesota
C—Paul Casanova, Wash.
P—Jim Kaat, Minnesota
P—Earl Wilson, Detroit

**1966—National**
1B—Felipe Alou, Atlanta
2B—Pete Rose, Cincinnati
SS—Gene Alley, Pittsburgh
3B—Ron Santo, Chicago
LF—Willie Stargell, Pittsburgh
CF—Willie Mays, San Francisco
RF—Roberto Clemente, Pitts.
C—Joe Torre, Atlanta
P—Sandy Koufax, L.A.
P—Juan Marichal, S.F.

**1967—American**
1B—Harmon Killebrew, Minn.
2B—Rod Carew, Minnesota
SS—Jim Fregosi, California
3B—Brooks Robinson, Balt.
LF—Carl Yastrzemski, Boston
CF—Al Kaline, Detroit
RF—Frank Robinson, Balt.
C—Bill Freehan, Detroit
P—Jim Lonborg, Boston
P—Earl Wilson, Detroit

**1967—National**
1B—Orlando Cepeda, St. Louis
2B—Bill Mazeroski, Pittsburgh
SS—Gene Alley, Pittsburgh
3B—Ron Santo, Chicago
LF—Hank Aaron, Atlanta
CF—Jim Wynn, Houston
RF—Roberto Clemente, Pitts.
C—Tim McCarver, St. Louis
P—Mike McCormick, S.F.
P—Ferguson Jenkins, Chi.

**1968—American**
1B—Boog Powell, Baltimore
2B—Rod Carew, Minnesota
SS—Luis Aparicio, Chicago
3B—Brooks Robinson, Balt.
OF—Ken Harrelson, Boston
OF—Willie Horton, Detroit
OF—Frank Howard, Wash.
C—Bill Freehan, Detroit
P—Dave McNally, Balt.
P—Denny McLain, Detroit

**1968—National**
1B—Willie McCovey, S.F.
2B—Tommy Helms, Cincinnati
SS—Don Kessinger, Chicago
3B—Ron Santo, Chicago
OF—Billy Williams, Chicago
OF—Curt Flood, St. Louis
OF—Pete Rose, Cincinnati
C—Johnny Bench, Cincinnati
P—Bob Gibson, St. Louis
P—Juan Marichal, S.F.

**1969—American**
1B—Boog Powell, Baltimore
2B—Rod Carew, Minnesota
SS—Rico Petrocelli, Boston
3B—Harmon Killebrew, Minn.
OF—Frank Howard, Wash.
OF—Paul Blair, Baltimore
OF—Reggie Jackson, Oak.
C—Bill Freehan, Detroit
RHP—Denny McLain, Detroit
LHP—Mike Cuellar, Baltimore

**1969—National**
1B—Willie McCovey, S.F.
2B—Glenn Beckert, Chicago
SS—Don Kessinger, Chicago
3B—Ron Santo, Chicago
OF—Cleon Jones, New York
OF—Matty Alou, Pittsburgh
OF—Hank Aaron, Atlanta
C—Johnny Bench, Cincinnati
RHP—Tom Seaver, New York
LHP—Steve Carlton, St. Louis

**1970—American**
1B—Boog Powell, Baltimore
2B—Dave Johnson, Baltimore
SS—Luis Aparicio, Chicago
3B—Harmon Killebrew, Minn.
OF—Frank Howard, Wash.
OF—Reggie Smith, Boston
OF—Tony Oliva, Minnesota
C—Ray Fosse, Cleveland
RHP—Jim Perry, Minnesota
LHP—Sam McDowell, Cleve.

**1970—National**
1B—Willie McCovey, S.F.
2B—Glenn Beckert, Chicago
SS—Don Kessinger, Chicago
3B—Tony Perez, Cincinnati
OF—Billy Williams, Chicago
OF—Bobby Tolan, Cincinnati
OF—Hank Aaron, Atlanta
C—Johnny Bench, Cincinnati
RHP—Bob Gibson, St. Louis
LHP—Jim Merritt, Cincinnati

**1971—American**
1B—Norm Cash, Detroit
2B—Cookie Rojas, K.C.
SS—Leo Cardenas, Minnesota
3B—Brooks Robinson, Balt.
LF—Merv Rettenmund, Balt.
CF—Bobby Murcer, N.Y.
RF—Tony Oliva, Minnesota
C—Bill Freehan, Detroit
RHP—Jim Palmer, Baltimore
LHP—Vida Blue, Oakland

**1971—National**
1B—Lee May, Cincinnati
2B—Glenn Beckert, Chicago
SS—Bud Harrelson, New York
3B—Joe Torre, St. Louis
LF—Willie Stargell, Pittsburgh
CF—Willie Davis, Los Angeles
RF—Hank Aaron, Atlanta
C—Manny Sanguillen, Pitts.
RHP—Ferguson Jenkins, Chi.
LHP—Steve Carlton, St. Louis

**1972—American**
1B—Dick Allen, Chicago
2B—Rod Carew, Minnesota
SS—Luis Aparicio, Boston
3B—Brooks Robinson, Balt.
LF—Joe Rudi, Oakland
CF—Bobby Murcer, N.Y.
RF—Richie Scheinblum, K.C.
C—Carlton Fisk, Boston
RHP—Gaylord Perry, Cleveland
LHP—Wilbur Wood, Chicago

**1972—National**
1B—Willie Stargell, Pittsburgh
2B—Joe Morgan, Cincinnati
SS—Chris Speier, S.F.
3B—Ron Santo, Chicago
LF—Billy Williams, Chicago
CF—Cesar Cedeno, Houston
RF—Roberto Clemente, Pitts.
C—Johnny Bench, Cincinnati
RHP—Ferguson Jenkins, Chi.
LHP—Steve Carlton, Phila.

**1973—American**
1B—John Mayberry, K.C.
2B—Rod Carew, Minnesota
SS—Bert Campaneris, Oak.
3B—Sal Bando, Oakland
LF—Reggie Jackson, Oak.
CF—Amos Otis, Kansas City
RF—Bobby Murcer, N.Y.
C—Thurman Munson, N.Y.
RHP—Jim Palmer, Baltimore
LHP—Ken Holtzman, Oakland

**1973—National**
1B—Tony Perez, Cincinnati
2B—Dave Johnson, Atlanta
SS—Bill Russell, Los Angeles
3B—Darrell Evans, Atlanta
LF—Bobby Bonds, S.F.
CF—Cesar Cedeno, Houston
RF—Pete Rose, Cincinnati
C—Johnny Bench, Cincinnati
RHP—Tom Seaver, New York
LHP—Ron Bryant, S.F.

**1974—American**
1B—Dick Allen, Chicago
2B—Rod Carew, Minnesota
SS—Bert Campaneris, Oak.
3B—Sal Bando, Oakland
LF—Joe Rudi, Oakland
CF—Paul Blair, Baltimore
RF—Jeff Burroughs, Texas
C—Thurman Munson, N.Y.
DH—Tommy Davis, Baltimore
RHP—Jim Hunter, Oakland
LHP—Mike Cuellar, Baltimore

### 1974—National
1B—Steve Garvey, Los Angeles
2B—Joe Morgan, Cincinnati
SS—Dave Concepcion, Cin.
3B—Mike Schmidt, Phila.
LF—Lou Brock, St. Louis
CF—Jim Wynn, Los Angeles
RF—Richie Zisk, Pittsburgh
C—Johnny Bench, Cincinnati
RHP—Andy Messersmith, L.A.
LHP—Don Gullett, Cincinnati

### 1975—American
1B—John Mayberry, K.C.
2B—Rod Carew, Minnesota
SS—Toby Harrah, Texas
3B—Graig Nettles, New York
LF—Jim Rice, Boston
CF—Fred Lynn, Boston
RF—Reggie Jackson, Oakland
C—Thurman Munson, N.Y.
DH—Willie Horton, Detroit
RHP—Jim Palmer, Baltimore
LHP—Jim Kaat, Chicago

### 1975—National
1B—Steve Garvey, Los Angeles
2B—Joe Morgan, Cincinnati
SS—Larry Bowa, Philadelphia
3B—Bill Madlock, Chicago
LF—Greg Luzinski, Phila.
CF—Al Oliver, Pittsburgh
RF—Dave Parker, Pittsburgh
C—Johnny Bench, Cincinnati
RHP—Tom Seaver, New York
LHP—Randy Jones, San Diego

### 1976—American
1B—Chris Chambliss, N.Y.
2B—Bobby Grich, Baltimore
3B—George Brett, K.C.
SS—Mark Belanger, Balt.
LF—Joe Rudi, Oakland
CF—Mickey Rivers, N.Y.
RF—Reggie Jackson, Balt.
C—Thurman Munson, N.Y.
DH—Hal McRae, Kansas City
RHP—Jim Palmer, Baltimore
LHP—Frank Tanana, Calif.

### 1976—National
1B—Willie Montanez, S.F.-Atl.
2B—Joe Morgan, Cincinnati
3B—Mike Schmidt, Phila.
SS—Dave Concepcion, Cin.
LF—George Foster, Cincinnati
CF—Cesar Cedeno, Houston
RF—Ken Griffey, Cincinnati
C—Bob Boone, Philadelphia
RHP—Don Sutton, Los Angeles
LHP—Randy Jones, San Diego

### 1977—American
1B—Rod Carew, Minn.
2B—Willie Randolph, N.Y.
3B—Graig Nettles, N.Y.
SS—Rick Burleson, Boston
OF—Jim Rice, Boston
OF—Larry Hisle, Minn.
OF—Bobby Bonds, Calif.
C—Carlton Fisk, Boston
DH—Hal McRae, K.C.
RHP—Nolan Ryan, Calif.
LHP—Frank Tanana, Calif.

### 1977—National
1B—Steve Garvey, L.A.
2B—Joe Morgan, Cincinnati
3B—Mike Schmidt, Phila.
SS—Garry Templeton, St. L.
OF—George Foster, Cin.
OF—Dave Parker, Pitts.
OF—Greg Luzinski, Phila.
C—Ted Simmons, St. Louis
RHP—Rick Reuschel, Chicago
LHP—Steve Carlton, Phila.

### 1978—American
1B—Rod Carew, Minnesota
2B—Frank White, K.C.
3B—Graig Nettles, N.Y.
SS—Robin Yount, Milw.
OF—Jim Rice, Boston
OF—Larry Hisle, Milw.
OF—Fred Lynn, Boston
C—Jim Sundberg, Texas
DH—Rusty Staub, Detroit
RHP—Jim Palmer, Balt.
LHP—Ron Guidry, N.Y.

### 1978—National
1B—Steve Garvey, L.A.
2B—Dave Lopes, Los Angeles
3B—Pete Rose, Cincinnati
SS—Larry Bowa, Phila.
OF—George Foster, Cin.
OF—Dave Parker, Pitts.
OF—Jack Clark, S.F.
C—Ted Simmons, St. Louis
RHP—Gaylord Perry, S.D.
LHP—Vida Blue, S.F.

### 1979—American
1B—Cecil Cooper, Milw.
2B—Bobby Grich, Calif.
3B—George Brett, K.C.
SS—Roy Smalley, Minn.
LF—Jim Rice, Boston
CF—Fred Lynn, Boston
RF—Ken Singleton, Balt.
C—Darrell Porter, K.C.
DH—Don Baylor, Calif.
RHP—Jim Kern, Texas
LHP—Mike Flanagan, Balt.

### 1979—National
1B—Keith Hernandez, St. L.
2B—Dave Lopes, Los Angeles
3B—Mike Schmidt, Phila.
SS—Garry Templeton, St. L.
LF—Dave Kingman, Chicago
CF—Omar Moreno, Pittsburgh
RF—Dave Winfield, San Diego
C—Ted Simmons, St. Louis
RHP—Joe Niekro, Houston
LHP—Steve Carlton, Phila.

### 1980—American
1B—Cecil Cooper, Milw.
2B—Willie Randolph, N.Y.
3B—George Brett, K.C.
SS—Robin Yount, Milw.
LF—Ben Oglivie, Milw.
CF—Al Bumbry, Baltimore
RF-DH—Reggie Jackson, N.Y.
C—Rick Cerone, N.Y.
RHP—Steve Stone, Balt.
LHP—Tommy John, N.Y.

### 1980—National
1B—Keith Hernandez, St. L.
2B—Manny Trillo, Phila.
3B—Mike Schmidt, Phila.
SS—Garry Templeton, St. L.
LF—Dusty Baker, L.A.
CF—Cesar Cedeno, Houston
RF—George Hendrick, St. L.
C—Gary Carter, Montreal
RHP—Jim Bibby, Pittsburgh
LHP—Steve Carlton, Phila.

### 1981—American
1B—Cecil Cooper, Milw.
2B—Bobby Grich, Calif.
3B—Buddy Bell, Texas
SS—Rick Burleson, Calif.
LF—Rickey Henderson, Oak.
CF—Dwayne Murphy, Oak.
RF—Tony Armas, Oak.
C—Jim Sundberg, Texas
DH—Richie Zisk, Seattle
RHP—Jack Morris, Detroit
LHP—Ron Guidry, N.Y.

### 1981—National
1B—Pete Rose, Phila.
2B—Manny Trillo, Phila.
3B—Mike Schmidt, Phila.
SS—Dave Concepcion, Cin.
LF—George Foster, Cin.
CF—Andre Dawson, Mon.
RF—Pedro Guerrero, L.A.
C—Gary Carter, Montreal
RHP—Tom Seaver, Cincinnati
LHP—Fernando Valenzuela, L.A.

### 1982—American
1B—Cecil Cooper, Milw.
2B—Damaso Garcia, Tor.
3B—Doug DeCinces, Calif.
SS—Robin Yount, Milw.
LF—Dave Winfield, N.Y.
CF—Gorman Thomas, Milw.
RF—Dwight Evans, Boston
C—Lance Parrish, Detroit
DH—Hal McRae, K.C.
RHP—Dave Stieb, Toronto
LHP—Geoff Zahn, Calif.

### 1982—National
1B—Al Oliver, Montreal
2B—Manny Trillo, Phila.
3B—Mike Schmidt, Phila.
SS—Ozzie Smith, St. Louis
LF—Lonnie Smith, St. Louis
CF—Dale Murphy, Atlanta
RF—Pedro Guerrero, L.A.
C—Gary Carter, Montreal
RHP—Steve Rogers, Montreal
LHP—Steve Carlton, Phila.

### 1983—American
1B—Eddie Murray, Balt.
2B—Lou Whitaker, Detroit
3B—Wade Boggs, Boston
SS—Cal Ripken, Balt.
OF—Jim Rice, Boston
OF—Dave Winfield, N.Y.
OF—Lloyd Moseby, Toronto
C—Carlton Fisk, Chicago
DH—Greg Luzinski, Chicago
RHP—LaMarr Hoyt, Chicago
LHP—Ron Guidry, New York

**1983—National**

1B—George Hendrick, St. L.
2B—Glenn Hubbard, Atlanta
3B—Mike Schmidt, Phila.
SS—Dickie Thon, Houston
OF—Dale Murphy, Atlanta
OF—Andre Dawson, Montreal
OF—Tim Raines, Montreal
C—Tony Pena, Pittsburgh
RHP—John Denny, Phila.
LHP—Larry McWilliams, Pitts.

**1984—American**

1B—Don Mattingly, N.Y.
2B—Lou Whitaker, Detroit
3B—Buddy Bell, Texas
SS—Cal Ripken, Baltimore
OF—Tony Armas, Boston
OF—Dwight Evans, Boston
OF—Dave Winfield, N.Y.
C—Lance Parrish, Detroit
DH—Dave Kingman, Oak.
RHP—Mike Boddicker, Balt.
LHP—Willie Hernandez, Det.

**1984—National**

1B—Keith Hernandez, N.Y.
2B—Ryne Sandberg, Chicago
3B—Mike Schmidt, Phila.
SS—Ozzie Smith, St. Louis
OF—Dale Murphy, Atlanta
OF—Jose Cruz, Houston
OF—Tony Gwynn, S.D.
C—Gary Carter, Montreal
RHP—Rick Sutcliffe, Chicago
LHP—Mark Thurmond, S.D.

**1985—American**

1B—Don Mattingly, N.Y.
2B—Damaso Garcia, Tor.
3B—Wade Boggs, Boston
SS—Cal Ripken, Balt.
OF—Rickey Henderson, N.Y.
OF—Harold Baines, Chicago
OF—Phil Bradley, Seattle
C—Carlton Fisk, Chicago
DH—Don Baylor, New York
RHP—Bret Saberhagen, K.C.
LHP—Ron Guidry, New York

**1985—National**

1B—Keith Hernandez, N.Y.
2B—Tom Herr, St. Louis
3B—Tim Wallach, Mon.
SS—Ozzie Smith, St. L.
OF—Dave Parker, Cin.
OF—Willie McGee, St. L.
OF—Dale Murphy, Atlanta
C—Gary Carter, N.Y.
RHP—Dwight Gooden, N.Y.
LHP—John Tudor, St. Louis

# Gold Glove Fielding Teams

**1957 Majors**

P—Shantz, N. Y. AL
C—Lollar, Chicago AL
1B—Hodges, Brooklyn
2B—Fox, Chicago AL
3B—Malzone, Boston
SS—McMillan, Cin.
LF—Minoso, Chicago AL
CF—Mays, N. Y. NL
RF—Kaline, Detroit

**1958 American**

P—Shantz, New York
C—Lollar, Chicago
1B—Power, Cleveland
2B—Bolling, Detroit
3B—Malzone, Boston
SS—Aparicio, Chicago
LF—Siebern, New York
CF—Piersall, Boston
RF—Kaline, Detroit

**1958 National**

P—Haddix, Cincinnati
C—Crandall, Milwaukee
1B—Hodges, Los Angeles
2B—Mazeroski, Pitt.
3B—Boyer, St. Louis
SS—McMillan, Cin.
LF—Robinson, Cin.
CF—Mays, S. Francisco
RF—Aaron, Milwaukee

**1959 American**

P—Shantz, New York
C—Lollar, Chicago
1B—Power, Cleveland
2B—Fox, Chicago
3B—Malzone, Boston
SS—Aparicio, Chicago
LF—Minoso, Cleveland
CF—Kaline, Detroit
RF—Jensen, Boston

**1959 National**

P—Haddix, Pittsburgh
C—Crandall, Milwaukee
1B—Hodges, Los Angeles
2B—Neal, Los Angeles
3B—Boyer, St. Louis
SS—McMillan, Cincinnati
LF—Brandt, S.F.
CF—Mays, San Francisco
RF—Aaron, Milwaukee

**1960 American**

P—Shantz, New York
C—Battey, Washington
1B—Power, Cleveland
2B—Fox, Chicago
3B—Robinson, Baltimore
SS—Aparicio, Chicago
LF—Minoso, Chicago
CF—Landis, Chicago
RF—Maris, New York

**1960 National**

P—Haddix, Pittsburgh
C—Crandall, Milwaukee
1B—White, St. Louis
2B—Mazeroski, Pittsburgh
3B—Boyer, St. Louis
SS—Banks, Chicago
LF—Moon, Los Angeles
CF—Mays, San Francisco
RF—Aaron, Milwaukee

**1961 American**

P—Lary, Detroit
C—Battey, Chicago
1B—Power, Cleveland
2B—Richardson, N.Y.
3B—Robinson, Baltimore
SS—Aparicio, Chicago
OF—Kaline, Detroit
OF—Piersall, Cleveland
OF—Landis, Chicago

**1961 National**

P—Shantz, Pittsburgh
C—Roseboro, Los Angeles
1B—White, St. Louis
2B—Mazeroski, Pittsburgh
3B—Boyer, St. Louis
SS—Wills, Los Angeles
OF—Mays, San Francisco
OF—Clemente, Pittsburgh
OF—Pinson, Cincinnati

**1962 American**

P—Kaat, Minnesota
C—Battey, Minnesota
1B—Power, Minnesota
2B—Richardson, N.Y.
3B—Robinson, Baltimore
SS—Aparicio, Chicago
OF—Landis, Chicago
OF—Mantle, New York
OF—Kaline, Detroit

**1962 National**

P—Shantz, St. Louis
C—Crandall, Milwaukee
1B—White, St. Louis
2B—Hubbs, Chicago
3B—Davenport, S.F.
SS—Wills, Los Angeles
OF—Mays, San Francisco
OF—Clemente, Pittsburgh
OF—Virdon, Pittsburgh

**1963 American**

P—Kaat, Minnesota
C—Howard, New York
1B—Power, Minnesota
2B—Richardson, N.Y.
3B—Robinson, Baltimore
SS—Versalles, Minnesota
OF—Kaline, Detroit
OF—Yastrzemski, Boston
OF—Landis, Chicago

### 1963 National
P—Shantz, St. Louis
C—Edwards, Cincinnati
1B—White, St. Louis
2B—Mazeroski, Pittsburgh
3B—Boyer, St. Louis
SS—Wine, Philadelphia
OF—Mays, San Francisco
OF—Clemente, Pittsburgh
OF—Flood, St. Louis

### 1964 American
P—Kaat, Minnesota
C—Howard, New York
1B—Power, Los Angeles
2B—Richardson, N.Y.
3B—Robinson, Baltimore
SS—Aparicio, Baltimore
OF—Kaline, Detroit
OF—Landis, Chicago
OF—Davalillo, Cleveland

### 1964 National
P—Shantz, Philadelphia
C—Edwards, Cincinnati
1B—White, St. Louis
2B—Mazeroski, Pittsburgh
3B—Santo, Chicago
SS—Amaro, Philadelphia
OF—Mays, San Francisco
OF—Clemente, Pittsburgh
OF—Flood, St. Louis

### 1965 American
P—Kaat, Minnesota
C—Freehan, Detroit
1B—Pepitone, New York
2B—Richardson, N.Y.
3B—Robinson, Baltimore
SS—Versalles, Minnesota
OF—Kaline, Detroit
OF—Tresh, New York
OF—Yastrzemski, Boston

### 1965 National
P—Gibson, St. Louis
C—Torre, Atlanta
1B—White, St. Louis
2B—Mazeroski, Pittsburgh
3B—Santo, Chicago
SS—Cardenas, Cincinnati
OF—Mays, San Francisco
OF—Clemente, Pittsburgh
OF—Flood, St. Louis

### 1966 American
P—Kaat, Minnesota
C—Freehan, Detroit
1B—Pepitone, New York
2B—Knoop, California
3B—B. Robinson, Balt.
SS—Aparicio, Baltimore
OF—Kaline, Detroit
OF—Agee, Chicago
OF—Oliva, Minnesota

### 1966 National
P—Gibson, St. Louis
C—Roseboro, Los Angeles
1B—White, Philadelphia
2B—Mazeroski, Pittsburgh
3B—Santo, Chicago
SS—Alley, Pittsburgh
OF—Mays, San Francisco
OF—Flood, St. Louis
OF—Clemente, Pittsburgh

### 1967 American
P—Kaat, Minnesota
C—Freehan, Detroit
1B—Scott, Boston
2B—Knoop, California
3B—B. Robinson, Balt.
SS—Fregosi, California
OF—Yastrzemski, Boston
OF—Blair, Baltimore
OF—Kaline, Detroit

### 1967 National
P—Gibson, St. Louis
C—Hundley, Chicago
1B—Parker, Los Angeles
2B—Mazeroski, Pittsburgh
3B—Santo, Chicago
SS—Alley, Pittsburgh
OF—Clemente, Pittsburgh
OF—Flood, St. Louis
OF—Mays, San Francisco

### 1968 American
P—Kaat, Minnesota
C—Freehan, Detroit
1B—Scott, Boston
2B—Knoop, California
3B—B. Robinson, Balt.
SS—Aparicio, Chicago
OF—Stanley, Detroit
OF—Yastrzemski, Boston
OF—Smith, Boston

### 1968 National
P—Gibson, St. Louis
C—Bench, Cincinnati
1B—Parker, Los Angeles
2B—Beckert, Chicago
3B—Santo, Chicago
SS—Maxvill, St. Louis
OF—Mays, San Francisco
OF—Clemente, Pittsburgh
OF—Flood, St. Louis

### 1969 American
P—Kaat, Minnesota
C—Freehan, Detroit
1B—Pepitone, New York
2B—Johnson, Baltimore
3B—B. Robinson, Balt.
SS—Belanger, Baltimore
OF—Blair, Baltimore
OF—Stanley, Detroit
OF—Yastrzemski, Boston

### 1969 National
P—Gibson, St. Louis
C—Bench, Cincinnati
1B—Parker, Los Angeles
2B—Millan, Atlanta
3B—Boyer, Atlanta
SS—Kessinger, Chicago
OF—Clemente, Pittsburgh
OF—Flood, St. Louis
OF—Rose, Cincinnati

### 1970 American
P—Kaat, Minnesota
C—Fosse, Cleveland
1B—Spencer, California
2B—Johnson, Baltimore
3B—B. Robinson, Balt.
SS—Aparicio, Chicago
OF—Stanley, Detroit
OF—Blair, Baltimore
OF—Berry, Chicago

### 1970 National
P—Gibson, St. Louis
C—Bench, Cincinnati
1B—Parker, Los Angeles
2B—Helms, Cincinnati
3B—Rader, Houston
SS—Kessinger, Chicago
OF—Clemente, Pittsburgh
OF—Agee, New York
OF—Rose, Cincinnati

### 1971 American
P—Kaat, Minnesota
C—Fosse, Cleveland
1B—Scott, Boston
2B—Johnson, Baltimore
3B—B. Robinson, Balt.
SS—Belanger, Baltimore
OF—Blair, Baltimore
OF—Otis, Kansas City
OF—Yastrzemski, Boston

### 1971 National
P—Gibson, St. Louis
C—Bench, Cincinnati
1B—Parker, Los Angeles
2B—Helms, Cincinnati
3B—Rader, Houston
SS—Harrelson, New York
OF—Clemente, Pittsburgh
OF—Bonds, San Francisco
OF—Davis, Los Angeles

### 1972 American
P—Kaat, Minnesota
C—Fisk, Boston
1B—Scott, Milwaukee
2B—Griffin, Boston
3B—Robinson, Baltimore
SS—Brinkman, Detroit
OF—Blair, Baltimore
OF—Murcer, New York
OF—Berry, California

### 1972 National
P—Gibson, St. Louis
C—Bench, Cincinnati
1B—Parker, Los Angeles
2B—Millan, Atlanta
3B—Rader, Houston
SS—Bowa, Philadelphia
OF—Clemente, Pittsburgh
OF—Cedeno, Houston
OF—Davis, Los Angeles

### 1973 American
P—Kaat, Chicago
C—Munson, New York
1B—Scott, Milwaukee
2B—Grich, Baltimore
3B—Robinson, Baltimore
SS—Belanger, Baltimore
OF—Blair, Baltimore
OF—Otis, Kansas City
OF—Stanley, Detroit

### 1973 National
P—Gibson, St. Louis
C—Bench, Cincinnati
1B—Jorgensen, Montreal
2B—Morgan, Cincinnati
3B—Rader, Houston
SS—Metzger, Houston
OF—Bonds, San Francisco
OF—Cedeno, Houston
OF—Davis, Los Angeles

### 1974 American
P—Kaat, Chicago
C—Munson, New York
1B—Scott, Milwaukee
2B—Grich, Baltimore
3B—Robinson, Baltimore
SS—Belanger, Baltimore
OF—Blair, Baltimore
OF—Otis, Kansas City
OF—Rudi, Oakland

### 1974 National
P—Messersmith, L.A.
C—Bench, Cincinnati
1B—Garvey, Los Angeles
2B—Morgan, Cincinnati
3B—Rader, Houston
SS—Concepcion, Cincinnati
OF—Cedeno, Houston
OF—Geronimo, Cincinnati
OF—Bonds, San Francisco

### 1975 American
P—Kaat, Chicago
C—Munson, New York
1B—Scott, Milwaukee
2B—Grich, Baltimore
3B—Robinson, Baltimore
SS—Belanger, Baltimore
OF—Blair, Baltimore
OF—Rudi, Oakland
OF—Lynn, Boston

### 1975 National
P—Messersmith, L.A.
C—Bench, Cincinnati
1B—Garvey, Los Angeles
2B—Morgan, Cincinnati
3B—Reitz, St. Louis
SS—Concepcion, Cincinnati
OF—Cedeno, Houston
OF—Geronimo, Cincinnati
OF—Maddox, Philadelphia

### 1976 American
P—Palmer, Baltimore
C—Sundberg, Texas
1B—Scott, Milwaukee
2B—Grich, Baltimore
3B—Rodriguez, Detroit
SS—Belanger, Baltimore
OF—Rudi, Oakland
OF—Evans, Boston
OF—Manning, Cleveland

### 1976 National
P—Kaat, Philadelphia
C—Bench, Cincinnati
1B—Garvey, Los Angeles
2B—Morgan, Cincinnati
3B—Schmidt, Philadelphia
SS—Concepcion, Cincinnati
OF—Cedeno, Houston
OF—Geronimo, Cincinnati
OF—Maddox, Philadelphia

### 1977 American
P—Palmer, Baltimore
C—Sundberg, Texas
1B—Spencer, Chicago
2B—White, Kansas City
13B—Nettles, New York
SS—Belanger, Baltimore
OF—Beniquez, Texas
OF—Yastrzemski, Boston
OF—Cowens, Kansas City

### 1977 National
P—Kaat, Philadelphia
C—Bench, Cincinnati
1B—Garvey, Los Angeles
2B—Morgan, Cincinnati
3B—Schmidt, Philadelphia
SS—Concepcion, Cincinnati
OF—Geronimo, Cincinnati
OF—Maddox, Philadelphia
OF—Parker, Pittsburgh

### 1978 American
P—Palmer, Baltimore
C—Sundberg, Texas
1B—Chambliss, New York
2B—White, Kansas City
3B—Nettles, New York
SS—Belanger, Baltimore
OF—Lynn, Boston
OF—Evans, Boston
OF—Miller, California

### 1978 National
P—Niekro, Atlanta
C—Boone, Philadelphia
1B—Hernandez, St. Louis
2B—Lopes, Los Angeles
3B—Schmidt, Philadelphia
SS—Bowa, Philadelphia
OF—Maddox, Philadelphia
OF—Parker, Pittsburgh
OF—Valentine, Montreal

### 1979 American
P—Palmer, Baltimore
C—Sundberg, Texas
1B—Cooper, Milwaukee
2B—White, Kansas City
3B—Bell, Texas
SS—Burleson, Boston
OF—Evans, Boston
OF—Lezcano, Milwaukee
OF—Lynn, Boston

### 1979 National
P—Niekro, Atlanta
C—Boone, Philadelphia
1B—Hernandez, St. Louis
2B—Trillo, Philadelphia
3B—Schmidt, Philadelphia
SS—Concepcion, Cincinnati
OF—Maddox, Philadelphia
OF—Parker, Pittsburgh
OF—Winfield, San Diego

### 1980 American
P—Norris, Oakland
C—Sundberg, Texas
1B—Cooper, Milwaukee
2B—White, Kansas City
3B—Bell, Texas
SS—Trammell, Detroit
OF—Lynn, Boston
OF—Murphy, Oakland
OF—Wilson, Kansas City

### 1980 National
P—Niekro, Atlanta
C—Carter, Montreal
1B—Hernandez, St. Louis
2B—Flynn, New York
3B—Schmidt, Philadelphia
SS—Smith, San Diego
OF—Dawson, Montreal
OF—Maddox, Philadelphia
OF—Winfield, San Diego

### 1981 American
P—Norris, Oakland
C—Sundberg, Texas
1B—Squires, Chicago
2B—White, Kansas City
3B—Bell, Texas
SS—Trammell, Detroit
OF—Murphy, Oakland
OF—Evans, Boston
OF—Henderson, Oakland

### 1981 National
P—Carlton, Philadelphia
C—Carter, Montreal
1B—Hernandez, St. Louis
2B—Trillo, Philadelphia
3B—Schmidt, Philadelphia
SS—Smith, San Diego
OF—Dawson, Montreal
OF—Maddox, Philadelphia
OF—Baker, Los Angeles

### 1982 American
P—Guidry, New York
C—Boone, California
1B—Murray, Baltimore
2B—White, Kansas City
3B—Bell, Texas
SS—Yount, Milwaukee
OF—Evans, Boston
OF—Winfield, New York
OF—Murphy, Oakland

### 1982 National
P—Niekro, Atlanta
C—Carter, Montreal
1B—Hernandez, St. Louis
2B—Trillo, Philadelphia
3B—Schmidt, Philadelphia
SS—O. Smith, St. Louis
OF—Dawson, Montreal
OF—Murphy, Atlanta
OF—Maddox, Philadelphia

### 1983 American
P—Guidry, New York
C—Parrish, Detroit
1B—Murray, Baltimore
2B—Whitaker, Detroit
3B—Bell, Texas
SS—Trammell, Detroit
OF—Evans, Boston
OF—Winfield, New York
OF—Murphy, Oakland

### 1983 National
P—Niekro, Atlanta
C—Pena, Pittsburgh
1B—Hernandez, St.L.-N.Y.
2B—Sandberg, Chicago
3B—Schmidt, Philadelphia
SS—O. Smith, St. Louis
OF—Dawson, Montreal
OF—Murphy, Atlanta
OF—McGee, St. Louis

### 1984 American
P—Guidry, New York
C—Parrish, Detroit
1B—Murray, Baltimore
2B—Whitaker, Detroit
3B—Bell, Texas
SS—Trammell, Detroit
OF—Evans, Boston
OF—Winfield, New York
OF—Murphy, Oakland

**1984 National**
P—Andujar, St. Louis
C—Pena, Pittsburgh
1B—Hernandez, New York
2B—Sandberg, Chicago
3B—Schmidt, Philadelphia
SS—O. Smith, St. Louis
OF—Murphy, Atlanta
OF—Dernier, Chicago
OF—Dawson, Montreal

**1985 American**
P—Guidry, New York
C—Parrish, Detroit
1B—Mattingly, New York
2B—Whitaker, Detroit
3B—Brett, Kansas City
SS—Griffin, Oakland
OF—Pettis, California
OF—Winfield, New York
OF—Evans, Boston (tie)
—Murphy, Oakland (tie)

**1985 National**
P—Reuschel, Pittsburgh
C—Pena, Pittsburgh
1B—Hernandez, New York
2B—Sandberg, Chicago
3B—Wallach, Montreal
SS—O. Smith, St. Louis
OF—McGee, St. Louis
OF—Murphy, Atlanta
OF—Dawson, Montreal
—

# Silver Slugger Teams

**1980 American**
1B—Cecil Cooper, Milw.
2B—Willie Randolph, N.Y.
3B—George Brett, K.C.
SS—Robin Yount, Milw.
OF—Ben Oglivie, Milw.
OF—Al Oliver, Texas
OF—Willie Wilson, K.C.
C—Lance Parrish, Detroit
DH—Reggie Jackson, N.Y.

**1980 National**
1B—Keith Hernandez, St.L.
2B—Manny Trillo, Phila.
3B—Mike Schmidt, Phila.
SS—Garry Templeton, St.L.
OF—Dusty Baker, Los Angeles
OF—Andre Dawson, Montreal
OF—George Hendrick, St. Louis
C—Ted Simmons, St. Louis
P—Bob Forsch, St. Louis

**1981 American**
1B—Cecil Cooper, Milw.
2B—Bobby Grich, Calif.
3B—Carney Lansford, Bos.
SS—Rick Burleson, Calif.
OF—Rickey Henderson, Oak.
OF—Dwight Evans, Boston
OF—Dave Winfield, N.Y.
C—Carlton Fisk, Chicago
DH—Al Oliver, Texas

**1981 National**
1B—Pete Rose, Philadelphia
2B—Manny Trillo, Phila.
3B—Mike Schmidt, Phila.
SS—Dave Concepcion, Cin.
OF—Andre Dawson, Montreal
OF—George Foster, Cincinnati
OF—Dusty Baker, Los Angeles
C—Gary Carter, Montreal
P—Fernando Valenzuela, L.A.

**1982 American**
1B—Cecil Cooper, Milw.
2B—Damaso Garcia, Tor.
3B—Doug DeCinces, Calif.
SS—Robin Yount, Milw.
OF—Dave Winfield, N.Y.
OF—Willie Wilson, K.C.
OF—Reggie Jackson, Calif.
C—Lance Parrish, Detroit
DH—Hal McRae, K.C.

**1982 National**
1B—Al Oliver, Montreal
2B—Joe Morgan, S.F.
3B—Mike Schmidt, Phila.
SS—Dave Concepcion, Cin.
OF—Dale Murphy, Atlanta
OF—Pedro Guerrero, L.A.
OF—Leon Durham, Chicago
C—Gary Carter, Montreal
P—Don Robinson, Pittsburgh

**1983 American**
1B—Eddie Murray, Balt.
2B—Lou Whitaker, Detroit
3B—Wade Boggs, Boston
SS—Cal Ripken, Baltimore
OF—Jim Rice, Boston
OF—Dave Winfield, N.Y.
OF—Lloyd Moseby, Toronto
C—Lance Parrish, Detroit
DH—Don Baylor, New York

**1983 National**
1B—George Hendrick, St.L.
2B—Johnny Ray, Pittsburgh
3B—Mike Schmidt, Phila.
SS—Dickie Thon, Houston
OF—Andre Dawson, Montreal
OF—Dale Murphy, Atlanta
OF—Jose Cruz, Houston
C—Terry Kennedy, San Diego
P—Fernando Valenzuela, L.A.

**1984 American**
1B—Eddie Murray, Balt.
2B—Lou Whitaker, Detroit
3B—Buddy Bell, Texas
SS  Cal Ripken, Baltimore
OF—Tony Armas, Boston
OF—Jim Rice, Boston
OF—Dave Winfield, N.Y.
C—Lance Parrish, Detroit
DH—Andre Thornton, Cleve.

**1984 National**
1B—Keith Hernandez, N.Y.
2B—Ryne Sandberg, Chicago
3B—Mike Schmidt, Phila.
SS—Garry Templeton, S.D.
OF—Dale Murphy, Atlanta
OF—Jose Cruz, Houston
OF—Tony Gwynn, San Diego
C—Gary Carter, Montreal
P—Rick Rhoden, Pittsburgh

**1985 American**
1B—Don Mattingly, N.Y.
2B—Lou Whitaker, Detroit
3B—George Brett, K.C.
SS—Cal Ripken, Baltimore
OF—Rickey Henderson, N.Y.
OF—Dave Winfield, N.Y.
OF—George Bell, Toronto
C—Carlton Fisk, Chicago
DH—Don Baylor, New York

**1985 National**
1B—Jack Clark, St. Louis
2B—Ryne Sandberg, Chi.
3B—Tim Wallach, Montreal
SS—Hubie Brooks, Montreal
OF—Willie McGee, St. Louis
OF—Dale Murphy, Atlanta
OF—Dave Parker, Cincinnati
C—Gary Carter, New York
P—Rick Rhoden, Pittsburgh

# Baseball Writers' Association Awards
## Most Valuable Player Citations

### CHALMERS AWARD

| AMERICAN LEAGUE | | | | NATIONAL LEAGUE | | |
|---|---|---|---|---|---|---|
| Year | Player | Club | Points | Player | Club | Points |
| 1911 | Tyrus Cobb, Detroit, of | | 64 | Frank Schulte, Chicago, of | | 29 |
| 1912 | Tristram Speaker, Boston, of | | 59 | Lawrence Doyle, New York, 2b | | 48 |
| 1913 | Walter Johnson, Washington, p | | 54 | Jacob Daubert, Brooklyn, 1b | | 50 |
| 1914 | Edward Collins, Philadelphia, 2b | | 63 | John Evers, Boston, 2b | | 50 |

### LEAGUE AWARDS

| AMERICAN LEAGUE | | | | NATIONAL LEAGUE | | |
|---|---|---|---|---|---|---|
| Year | Player | Club | Points | Player | Club | Points |
| 1922 | George Sisler, St. Louis, 1b | | 59 | No selection | | |
| 1923 | George Ruth, New York, of | | 64 | No selection | | |
| 1924 | Walter Johnson, Washington, p | | 55 | Arthur Vance, Brooklyn, p | | 74 |
| 1925 | Roger Peckinpaugh, Washington, ss | | 45 | Rogers Hornsby, St. Louis, 2b | | 73 |
| 1926 | George Burns, Cleveland, 1b | | 63 | Robert O'Farrell, St. Louis, c | | 79 |
| 1927 | H. Louis Gehrig, New York, 1b | | 56 | Paul Waner, Pittsburgh, of | | 72 |
| 1928 | Gordon Cochrane, Philadelphia, c | | 53 | James Bottomley, St. Louis, 1b | | 76 |
| 1929 | No selection | | | Rogers Hornsby, Chicago, 2b | | 60 |

### BASEBALL WRITERS' ASSOCIATION MVP AWARDS

| AMERICAN LEAGUE | | | | NATIONAL LEAGUE | | |
|---|---|---|---|---|---|---|
| Year | Player | Club | Points | Player | Club | Points |
| 1931 | Robert Grove, Philadelphia, p | | 78 | Frank Frisch, St. Louis, 2b | | 65 |
| 1932 | James Foxx, Philadelphia, 1b | | 75 | Charles Klein, Philadelphia, of | | 78 |
| 1933 | James Foxx, Philadelphia, 1b | | 74 | Carl Hubbell, New York, p | | 77 |
| 1934 | Gordon Cochrane, Detroit, c | | 67 | Jerome Dean, St. Louis, p | | 78 |
| 1935 | Henry Greenberg, Detroit, 1b | | *80 | Charles Hartnett, Chicago, c | | 75 |
| 1936 | H. Louis Gehrig, New York, 1b | | 73 | Carl Hubbell, New York, p | | 60 |
| 1937 | Charles Gehringer, Detroit, 2b | | 78 | Joseph Medwick, St. Louis, of | | 70 |
| 1938 | James Foxx, Boston, 1b | | 305 | Ernest Lombardi, Cincinnati, c | | 229 |
| 1939 | Joseph DiMaggio, New York, of | | 280 | William Walters, Cincinnati, p | | 303 |
| 1940 | Henry Greenberg, Detroit, of | | 292 | Frank McCormick, Cincinnati, 1b | | 274 |
| 1941 | Joseph DiMaggio, New York, of | | 291 | Adolph Camilli, Brooklyn, 1b | | 300 |
| 1942 | Joseph Gordon, New York, 2b | | 270 | Morton Cooper, St. Louis, p | | 263 |
| 1943 | Spurgeon Chandler, New York, p | | 246 | Stanley Musial, St. Louis, of | | 267 |
| 1944 | Harold Newhouser, Detroit, p | | 236 | Martin Marion, St. Louis, ss | | 190 |
| 1945 | Harold Newhouser, Detroit, p | | 236 | Philip Cavarretta, Chicago, 1b | | 279 |
| 1946 | Theodore Williams, Boston, of | | 224 | Stanley Musial, St. Louis, 1b | | 319 |
| 1947 | Joseph DiMaggio, New York, of | | 202 | Robert Elliott, Boston, 3b | | 205 |
| 1948 | Louis Boudreau, Cleveland, ss | | 324 | Stanley Musial, St. Louis, of | | 303 |
| 1949 | Theodore Williams, Boston, of | | 272 | Jack Robinson, Brooklyn, 2b | | 264 |
| 1950 | Philip Rizzuto, New York, ss | | 284 | C. James Konstanty, Philadelphia, p | | 286 |
| 1951 | Lawrence Berra, New York, c | | 184 | Roy Campanella, Brooklyn, c | | 243 |
| 1952 | Robert Shantz, Philadelphia, p | | 280 | Henry Sauer, Chicago, of | | 226 |
| 1953 | Albert Rosen, Cleveland, 3b | | *336 | Roy Campanella, Brooklyn, c | | 297 |
| 1954 | Lawrence Berra, New York, c | | 230 | Willie Mays, New York, of | | 283 |
| 1955 | Lawrence Berra, New York, c | | 218 | Roy Campanella, Brooklyn, c | | 226 |
| 1956 | Mickey Mantle, New York, of | | *336 | Donald Newcombe, Brooklyn, p | | 223 |
| 1957 | Mickey Mantle, New York, of | | 233 | Henry Aaron, Milwaukee, of | | 239 |
| 1958 | Jack Jensen, Boston, of | | 233 | Ernest Banks, Chicago, ss | | 283 |
| 1959 | J. Nelson Fox, Chicago, 2b | | 295 | Ernest Banks, Chicago, ss | | 232½ |
| 1960 | Roger Maris, New York, of | | 225 | Richard Groat, Pittsburgh, ss | | 276 |
| 1961 | Roger Maris, New York, of | | 202 | Frank Robinson, Cincinnati, of | | 219 |
| 1962 | Mickey Mantle, New York, of | | 234 | Maurice Wills, Los Angeles, ss | | 209 |
| 1963 | Elston Howard, New York, c | | 248 | Sanford Koufax, Los Angeles, p | | 237 |
| 1964 | Brooks Robinson, Baltimore, 3b | | 269 | Kenton Boyer, St. Louis, 3b | | 243 |
| 1965 | Zoilo Versalles, Minnesota, ss | | 275 | Willie Mays, San Francisco, of | | 224 |
| 1966 | Frank Robinson, Baltimore, of | | *280 | Roberto Clemente, Pittsburgh, of | | 218 |
| 1967 | Carl Yastrzemski, Boston, of | | 275 | Orlando Cepeda, St. Louis, 1b | | *280 |
| 1968 | Dennis McLain, Detroit, p | | *280 | Robert Gibson, St. Louis, p | | 242 |
| 1969 | Harmon Killebrew, Minnesota, 1-3b | | 294 | Willie McCovey, San Francisco, 1b | | 265 |
| 1970 | John (Boog) Powell, Baltimore, 1b | | 234 | Johnny Bench, Cincinnati, c | | 326 |
| 1971 | Vida Blue, Oakland, p | | 268 | Joseph Torre, St. Louis, 3b | | 318 |
| 1972 | Richie Allen, Chicago, 1b | | 321 | Johnny Bench, Cincinnati, c | | 263 |
| 1973 | Reggie Jackson, Oakland, of | | *336 | Pete Rose, Cincinnati, of | | 274 |
| 1974 | Jeff Burroughs, Texas, of | | 248 | Steve Garvey, Los Angeles, 1b | | 270 |
| 1975 | Fred Lynn, Boston, of | | 326 | Joe Morgan, Cincinnati, 2b | | 321½ |
| 1976 | Thurman Munson, New York, c | | 304 | Joe Morgan, Cincinnati, 2b | | 311 |
| 1977 | Rod Carew, Minnesota, 1b | | 273 | George Foster, Cincinnati, of | | 291 |
| 1978 | Jim Rice, Boston, of | | 352 | Dave Parker, Pittsburgh, of | | 320 |
| 1979 | Don Baylor, California, of | | 347 | Willie Stargell, Pittsburgh, 1b | | 216 |
| | | | | Keith Hernandez, St. Louis, 1b | | 216 |

## BASEBALL WRITERS' ASSOCIATION MVP AWARDS—Cont.

| AMERICAN LEAGUE | | | | NATIONAL LEAGUE | | |
|---|---|---|---|---|---|---|
| Year | Player | Club | Points | Player | Club | Points |
| 1980—George Brett, Kansas City, 3b | | | *335 | Mike Schmidt, Philadelphia, 3b | | *336 |
| 1981—Rollie Fingers, Milwaukee, p | | | 319 | Mike Schmidt, Philadelphia, 3b | | 321 |
| 1982—Robin Yount, Milwaukee, ss | | | 385 | Dale Murphy, Atlanta, of | | 283 |
| 1983—Cal Ripken, Baltimore, ss | | | 322 | Dale Murphy, Atlanta, of | | 318 |
| 1984—Willie Hernandez, Detroit, p | | | 306 | Ryne Sandberg, Chicago, 2b | | 326 |
| 1985—Don Mattingly, New York, 1b | | | 367 | Willie McGee, St. Louis, of | | 280 |

*Unanimous selection.

## BASEBALL WRITERS' ASSOCIATION ROOKIE AWARDS

1947—Combined selection—Jack Robinson, Brooklyn, 1b.
1948—Combined selection—Alvin Dark, Boston, N. L., ss.

| AMERICAN LEAGUE | | | NATIONAL LEAGUE | | |
|---|---|---|---|---|---|
| Year | Player Club | Votes | Player Club | | Votes |
| 1949—Roy Sievers, St. Louis, of | | 10 | Donald Newcombe, Brooklyn, p | | 21 |
| 1950—Walter Dropo, Boston, 1b | | 15 | Samuel Jethroe, Boston, of | | 11 |
| 1951—Gilbert McDougald, New York, 3b | | 13 | Willie Mays, New York, of | | 18 |
| 1952—Harry Byrd, Philadelphia, p | | 9 | Joseph Black, Brooklyn, p | | 19 |
| 1953—Harvey Kuenn, Detroit, ss | | 23 | James Gilliam, Brooklyn, 2b | | 11 |
| 1954—Robert Grim, New York, p | | 15 | Wallace Moon, St. Louis, of | | 17 |
| 1955—Herbert Score, Cleveland, p | | 18 | William Virdon, St. Louis, of | | 15 |
| 1956—Luis Aparicio, Chicago, ss | | 22 | Frank Robinson, Cincinnati, of | | *24 |
| 1957—Anthony Kubek, New York, inf-of | | 23 | John Sanford, Philadelphia, p | | 16 |
| 1958—Albert Pearson, Washington, of | | 14 | Orlando Cepeda, San Francisco, 1b | | *†21 |
| 1959—W. Robert Allison, Washington, of | | 18 | Willie McCovey, San Francisco, 1b | | *24 |
| 1960—Ronald Hansen, Baltimore, ss | | 22 | Frank Howard, Los Angeles, of | | 12 |
| 1961—Donald Schwall, Boston, p | | 7 | Billy Williams, Chicago, of | | 10 |
| 1962—Thomas Tresh, New York, of-ss | | 13 | Kenneth Hubbs, Chicago, 2b | | 19 |
| 1963—Gary Peters, Chicago, p | | 10 | Peter Rose, Cincinnati, 2b | | 17 |
| 1964—Pedro (Tony) Oliva, Minnesota, of | | 19 | Richard Allen, Philadelphia, 3b | | 18 |
| 1965—Curtis Blefary, Baltimore, of | | 19 | James Lefebvre, Los Angeles, 2b | | 13 |
| 1966—Tommie Agee, Chicago, of | | 16 | Tommy Helms, Cincinnati, 3b | | 12 |
| 1967—Rod Carew, Minnesota, 2b | | 19 | Tom Seaver, New York, p | | 11 |
| 1968—Stan Bahnsen, New York, p | | 17 | Johnny Bench, Cincinnati, c | | 10½ |
| 1969—Lou Piniella, Kansas City, of | | 9 | Ted Sizemore, Los Angeles, 2b | | 14 |
| 1970—Thurman Munson, New York, c | | 23 | Carl Morton, Montreal, p | | 11 |
| 1971—Chris Chambliss, Cleveland, 1b | | 11 | Earl Williams, Atlanta, c | | 18 |
| 1972—Carlton Fisk, Boston, c | | *24 | Jon Matlack, New York, p | | 19 |
| 1973—Al Bumbry, Baltimore, of | | 13½ | Gary Matthews, San Francisco, of | | 11 |
| 1974—Mike Hargrove, Texas, 1b | | 16½ | Bake McBride, St. Louis, of | | 16 |
| 1975—Fred Lynn, Boston, of | | 23 | John Montefusco, San Francisco, p | | 12 |
| 1976—Mark Fidrych, Detroit, p | | 22 | Butch Metzger, San Diego, p | | 11 |
| | | | Pat Zachry, Cincinnati, p | | 11 |
| 1977—Eddie Murray, Baltimore, dh-1b | | 12½ | Andre Dawson, Montreal, of | | 10 |
| 1978—Lou Whitaker, Detroit, 2b | | 21 | Bob Horner, Atlanta, 3b | | 12½ |
| 1979—John Castino, Minnesota, 3b | | 7 | Rick Sutcliffe, Los Angeles, p | | 20 |
| Alfredo Griffin, Toronto, ss | | 7 | | | |
| 1980—Joe Charboneau, Cleveland, of | | 103 | Steve Howe, Los Angeles, p | | 80 |
| 1981—Dave Righetti, New York, p | | 127 | Fernando Valenzuela, Los Angeles, p | | 107 |
| 1982—Cal Ripken, Baltimore, ss-3b | | 132 | Steve Sax, Los Angeles, 2b | | 63 |
| 1983—Ron Kittle, Chicago, of | | 104 | Darryl Strawberry, New York, of | | 109 |
| 1984—Alvin Davis, Seattle, 1b | | 134 | Dwight Gooden, New York, p | | 118 |
| 1985—Ozzie Guillen, Chicago, ss | | 101 | Vince Coleman, St. Louis, of | | *120 |

*Unanimous selection. †Three writers did not vote.

Kansas City's Bret Saberhagen capped his Cy Young Award-winning regular season with the World Series' Most Valuable Player honor as well.

## CY YOUNG MEMORIAL AWARD

| Year | Pitcher | Club | Votes |
|---|---|---|---|
| 1956—Donald Newcombe, Brooklyn | | | 10 |
| 1957—Warren Spahn, Milwaukee | | | 15 |
| 1958—Robert Turley, New York, A.L. | | | 5 |
| 1959—Early Wynn, Chicago, A.L. | | | 13 |
| 1960—Vernon Law, Pittsburgh | | | 8 |
| 1961—Edward Ford, New York, A.L. | | | 9 |
| 1962—Don Drysdale, Los Angeles, N.L. | | | 14 |
| 1963—Sanford Koufax, Los Angeles, N.L. | | | *20 |
| 1964—Dean Chance, Los Angeles, A.L. | | | 17 |
| 1965—Sanford Koufax, Los Angeles, N.L. | | | *20 |
| 1966—Sanford Koufax, Los Angeles, N.L. | | | *20 |
| **Year** | **Pitcher** | **Club** | **Votes** |
| 1967—A. L.—Jim Lonborg, Boston | | | 18 |
| N. L.—M. McCormick, San Francisco | | | 18 |
| 1968—A. L.—Dennis McLain, Detroit | | | *20 |
| N. L.—Bob Gibson, St. Louis | | | *20 |
| 1969—A. L.—Dennis McLain, Detroit | | | 10 |
| Mike Cuellar, Baltimore | | | 10 |
| N. L.—Tom Seaver, New York | | | 23 |
| **Year** | **Pitcher** | **Club** | **Votes** |
| 1970—A. L.—Jim Perry, Minnesota | | | †55 |
| N. L.—Bob Gibson, St. Louis | | | †118 |
| 1971—A. L.—Vida Blue, Oakland | | | †98 |
| N. L.—Fergy Jenkins, Chicago | | | †97 |
| 1972—A. L.—Gaylord Perry, Cleveland | | | †64 |
| N. L.—Steve Carlton, Philadelphia | | | *†120 |

| | |
|---|---|
| 1973—A. L.—Jim Palmer, Baltimore | †88 |
| N. L.—Tom Seaver, New York | †71 |
| 1974—A. L.—Jim Hunter, Oakland | †90 |
| N. L.—Mike Marshall, Los Angeles | †96 |
| 1975—A. L.—Jim Palmer, Baltimore | †98 |
| N. L.—Tom Seaver, New York | †98 |
| 1976—A. L.—Jim Palmer, Baltimore | †108 |
| N. L.—Randy Jones, San Diego | †96 |
| 1977—A. L.—Sparky Lyle, New York | †56½ |
| N. L.—Steve Carlton, Philadelphia | *†104 |
| 1978—A. L.—Ron Guidry, New York | *†140 |
| N. L.—Gaylord Perry, San Diego | ‡116 |
| 1979—A. L.—Mike Flanagan, Baltimore | †136 |
| N. L.—Bruce Sutter, Chicago | †72 |
| 1980—A. L.—Steve Stone, Baltimore | 100 |
| N. L.—Steve Carlton, Philadelphia | 118 |
| 1981—A. L.—Rollie Fingers, Milwaukee | 126 |
| N. L.—Fernando Valenzuela, Los Ang. | 70 |
| 1982—A. L.—Pete Vuckovich, Milwaukee | 87 |
| N. L.—Steve Carlton, Philadelphia | 112 |
| 1983—A. L.—LaMarr Hoyt, Chicago | 116 |
| N. L.—John Denny, Philadelphia | 103 |
| 1984—A. L.—Willie Hernandez, Detroit | 88 |
| N. L.—Rick Sutcliffe, Chicago | *120 |
| 1985—A. L.—Bret Saberhagen, Kansas City. | 127 |
| N. L.—Dwight Gooden, New York | *120 |

*Unanimous selection. †Point system used.

Former San Francisco Giants slugger Willie McCovey launches one of his 521 career home runs.

# McCovey Enters Hall of Fame

**By LARRY WIGGE**

A day rarely goes by that Willie McCovey isn't reminded about a line drive he hit on a 1962 October afternoon with two runners on base and two out in the ninth inning of the seventh game of the World Series.

One foot either way and New York Yankees second baseman Bobby Richardson probably wouldn't have been able to make the catch and the San Francisco Giants would have been World Series champions.

That was McCovey's last World Series at-bat, but not the last of his screaming line drives, many of which were not caught during his brilliant 22-year career with the Giants, San Diego and Oakland A's. McCovey slugged 521 career home runs and belted 18 grand slams while ranking as one of the most feared power hitters in National League history. His slugging feats were impressive enough to earn him election to baseball's Hall of Fame in January 1986—his first year of eligibility.

McCovey received 346 of 425 votes cast by 10-year members of the Baseball Writers Association of America to become the 194th member of the Hall of Fame and the 16th to be elected to enshrinement at Cooperstown, N.Y., in his first year on the ballot.

Former Cubs outfielder Billy Williams received 315 votes to finish second, but wound up four votes short of getting the required 75 percent necessary for election. Catfish Hunter was third with 289 votes, followed by Jim Bunning with 279 and the late Roger Maris with 177.

McCovey, whose major league career lasted from 1959 through July 1980, hit more homers than any other lefthanded hitter in National League history. His 18 grand slams were second on the all-time major league list behind Lou Gehrig's 23. His other records include hitting two home runs in an inning twice and leading the league in receiving intentional bases on balls four times. That's how much opposing teams feared the 6-foot-4, 200-pound slugger.

McCovey made his major league debut at old Seals Stadium in San Francisco in July 1959. After traveling all night to get from Phoenix (Pacific Coast League) to San Francisco, McCovey went 4 for 4 in his first big-league game, including two triples and two singles against Philadelphia's Hall of Fame righthander Robin Roberts. McCovey went on to hit .354 and win unanimous selection as N.L. Rookie of the Year.

McCovey's real potential, however, wasn't realized until 1963 when he tied Milwaukee's Hank Aaron for the N.L. home run title with 44. From 1965 through 1970, he never hit fewer than 31 homers in a season.

In 1968, McCovey led the league in home runs with 36 and runs batted in with 105. He accomplished the same feat in '69, belting 45 homers, driving in 126 runs and batting .320 en route to N.L. Most Valuable Player honors.

McCovey was traded by the Giants to San Diego after the 1973 season and was sold to Oakland in August 1976. He returned to the Giants in 1977 and, at age 39, was chosen The Sporting News Comeback Player of the Year after hitting 28 homers and driving in 86 runs.

McCovey's 521 homers place him in an eighth-place tie with Ted Williams on the all-time home run list—not bad for a guy who played with a bad knee and bad back for much of his career. He compiled a .270 career average, drove in 1,555 runs and led the National League in slugging percentage in 1968 (.545), 1969 (.656) and 1970 (.612). His two home runs in the 1969 All-Star Game at Washington represented yet another tribute to a prolific slugger.

The complete 1986 Hall of Fame voting totals follow:

McCovey, 346; Billy Williams, 315; Catfish Hunter, 289; Jim Bunning, 279; Roger Maris, 177; Tony Oliva, 154; Orlando Cepeda, 152; Harvey Kuenn, 144; Maury Wills, 124; Bill Mazeroski, 100; Lew Burdette, 96; Ken Boyer, 95; Mickey Lolich, 86; Roy Face, 74; Ron Santo, 64; Joe Torre, 60; Elston Howard, 51; Curt Flood, 45; Vada Pinson, 43; Richie Allen, 41; Thurman Munson, 35; Don Larsen, 33; Wilbur Wood, 23; Tim McCarver, 16; Dave McNally, 12; John Hiller, 11; Paul Blair, 8; J.R. Richard, 7; Ken Holtzman, 5; Willie Horton, 4; Jim Lonborg, 3; Andy Messersmith, 3; Dave Cash, 2; Manny Sanguillen, 2; Jack Billingham, 1; Jose Cardenal, 1; Bud Harrelson, 1; George Scott, 1. Failing to receive votes were Vic Davalillo and Darold Knowles.

Following is a complete list of those enshrined in the Hall of Fame prior to 1984 with the vote by which each enrollee was elected:

1936—Tyrus Cobb (222), John (Honus) Wagner (215), George (Babe) Ruth (215), Christy Mathewson (205), Walter Johnson (189), named by Baseball Writers' Association of America. Total ballots cast, 226.

1937—Napoleon Lajoie (168), Tristram Speaker (165), Denton (Cy) Young (153), named by the BBWAA. Total ballots cast, 201. George Wright, Morgan G. Bulkeley, Byron Bancroft Johnson, John J. McGraw, Cornelius McGillicuddy (Connie Mack), named by Centennial Commission.

1938—Grover C. Alexander (212), named by BBWAA. Total ballots, 262. Henry Chadwick, Alexander J. Cartwright, named by Centennial Commission.

1939—George Sisler (235), Edward Collins (213), William Keeler (207), Louis Gehrig, named by BBWAA (Gehrig by special election after retirement from game was announced). Total ballots cast, 274. Albert G. Spalding, Adrian C. Anson, Charles A. Comiskey, William (Buck) Ewing, Charles Radbourn, William A. (Candy) Cummings, named by committee of old-time players and writers.

1942—Rogers Hornsby (182), named by BBWAA. Total ballots cast, 233.

1944—Judge Kenesaw M. Landis, named by committee on old-timers.

1945—Hugh Duffy, Jimmy Collins, Hugh Jennings, Ed Delahanty, Fred Clarke, Mike Kelly, Wilbert Robinson, Jim O'Rourke, Dennis (Dan) Brouthers and Roger Bresnahan, named by committee on old-timers.

1946—Jesse Burkett, Frank Chance, Jack Chesbro, Johnny Evers, Clark Griffith, Tom McCarthy, Joe McGinnity, Eddie Plank, Joe Tinker, Rube Waddell and Ed Walsh, named by committee on old-timers.

1947—Carl Hubbell (140), Frank Frisch (136), Gordon (Mickey) Cochrane (128) and Robert (Lefty) Grove (123), named by BBWAA. Total ballots, 161.

1948—Herbert J. Pennock (94) and Harold (Pie) Traynor (93), named by BBWAA. Total ballots cast, 121.

1949—Charles Gehringer (159), named by BBWAA in runoff election. Total ballots cast, 187. Charles (Kid) Nichols and Mordecai (Three-Finger) Brown, named by committee on old timers.

1951—Mel Ott (197) and Jimmie Foxx (179), named by BBWAA. Total ballots cast, 226.

1952—Harry Heilmann (203) and Paul Waner (195), named by BBWAA. Total ballots cast, 234.

1953—Jerome (Dizzy) Dean (209) and Al Simmons (199), named by BBWAA. Total ballots cast, 264. Charles Albert (Chief) Bender, Roderick (Bobby) Wallace, William Klem, Tom Connolly, Edward G. Barrow and William Henry (Harry) Wright, named by the new Committee on Veterans.

1954—Walter (Rabbit) Maranville (209), William Dickey (202) and William Terry (195), named by BBWAA. Total ballots cast, 252.

1955—Joe DiMaggio (223), Ted Lyons

(217), Arthur (Dazzy) Vance (205) and Charles (Gabby) Hartnett (195), named by BBWAA. Total ballots cast, 251. J. Franklin (Home Run) Baker and Ray Schalk, named by Committee on Veterans.

1956—Hank Greenberg (164) and Joe Cronin (152), named by BBWAA. Total ballots cast, 193.

1957—Joseph V. McCarthy and Sam Crawford, named by Committee on Veterans.

1959—Zachariah (Zack) Wheat, named by Committee on Veterans.

1961—Max Carey and William Hamilton, named by Committee on Veterans.

1962—Bob Feller (150) and Jackie Robinson (124), named by BBWAA. Total ballots cast, 160. Bill McKechnie and Edd Roush, named by Committee on Veterans.

1963—Eppa Rixey, Edgar (Sam) Rice, Elmer Flick and John Clarkson, named by Committee on Veterans.

1964—Luke Appling (189), named by BBWAA in runoff election. Total ballots cast, 225. Urban (Red) Faber, Burleigh Grimes, Tim Keefe, Heinie Manush, Miller Huggins and John Montgomery Ward, named by Committee on Veterans.

1965—James (Pud) Galvin, named by Committee on Veterans.

1966—Ted Williams (282), named by BBWAA. Total ballots cast, 302. Casey Stengel, named by Committee on Veterans.

1967—Charles (Red) Ruffing (266), named by BBWAA in runoff election. Total ballots cast, 306. Branch Rickey and Lloyd Waner, named by Committee on Veterans.

1968—Joseph (Ducky) Medwick (240), named by BBWAA. Total ballots cast, 283. Leon (Goose) Goslin and Hazen (Kiki) Cuyler, named by Committee on Veterans.

1969—Stan (The Man) Musial (317) and Roy Campanella (270), named by BBWAA. Total ballots cast, 340. Stan Coveleski and Waite Hoyt, named by Committee on Veterans.

1970—Lou Boudreau (232), named by BBWAA. Total ballots cast, 300. Earle Combs, Jesse Haines and Ford Frick, named by Committee on Veterans.

1971—Chick Hafey, Rube Marquard, Joe Kelley, Dave Bancroft, Harry Hooper, Jake Beckley and George Weiss, named by Committee on Veterans. Satchel Paige, named by Special Committee on Negro Leagues.

1972—Sandy Koufax (344), Yogi Berra (339) and Early Wynn (301), named by BBWAA. Total ballots cast, 396. Lefty Gomez, Will Harridge and Ross Youngs, named by Committee on Veterans. Josh Gibson and Walter (Buck) Leonard, named by Special Committee on Negro Leagues.

1973—Warren Spahn (316), named by BBWAA. Total ballots cast, 380. Roberto Clemente (393), in special election by BBWAA in which 424 ballots were cast. Billy Evans, George Kelly and Mickey Welch, named by Committee on Veterans. Monte Irvin, named by Special Committee on Negro Leagues.

1974—Mickey Mantle (322) and Whitey Ford (284), named by BBWAA. Total ballots cast, 365. Jim Bottomley, Sam Thompson and Jocko Conlan, named by Committee on Veterans. James (Cool Papa) Bell, named by Special Committee on Negro Leagues.

1975—Ralph Kiner (273), named by BBWAA. Total ballots cast, 362. Earl Averill, Bucky Harris and Billy Herman, named by Committee on Veterans. William (Judy) Johnson, named by Special Committee on Negro Leagues.

1976—Robin Roberts (337) and Bob Lemon (305), named by BBWAA. Total ballots cast, 388. Roger Connor, Cal Hubbard and Fred Lindstrom, named by Committee on Veterans. Oscar Charleston, named by Special Committee on Negro Leagues.

1977—Ernie Banks (321), named by BBWAA. Total ballots cast, 383. Joe Sewell, Al Lopez and Amos Rusie, named by Committee on Veterans. Martin Dihigo and John Henry Lloyd, named by Special Committee on Negro Leagues.

1978—Eddie Mathews (301), named by BBWAA. Total ballots cast, 379. Larry MacPhail and Addie Joss, named by Committee on Veterans.

1979—Willie Mays (409), named by BBWAA. Total ballots cast, 432. Hack Wilson and Warren Giles, named by Committee on Veterans.

1980—Al Kaline (340) and Duke Snider (333), named by BBWAA. Total ballots cast, 385. Chuck Klein and Tom Yawkey, named by Committee on Veterans.

1981—Bob Gibson (337), named by BBWAA. Total ballots cast, 401. Johnny Mize and Rube Foster, named by Committee on Veterans.

1982—Henry Aaron (406) and Frank Robinson (370), named by BBWAA. Total ballots cast, 415. Albert B. (Happy) Chandler and Travis Jackson, named by Committee on Veterans.

1983—Brooks Robinson (344) and Juan Marichal (313), named by BBWAA. Total ballots cast, 374. George Kell and Walter Alston, named by Committee on Veterans.

1984—Luis Aparicio (341), Harmon Killebrew (335) and Don Drysdale (316), named by BBWAA. Total ballots cast, 403. Rick Ferrell and Pee Wee Reese, named by Committee on Veterans.

1985—Hoyt Wilhelm (331) and Lou Brock (315), named by BBWAA. Total ballots cast, 395. Enos Slaughter and Joseph (Arky) Vaughn, named by Committee on Veterans.

**MAJOR LEAGUE TRANSACTIONS**

**MINOR LEAGUE DRAFT**

**NECROLOGY**

Kansas City General Manager John Schuerholz' May 17 acquisition of left
fielder Lonnie Smith played a key part in the Royals' championship season.

# Herzog Dealt Cards a Winner

**By DAVE SLOAN**

Building a pennant winner can be difficult. With player contracts complicated by incentive bonuses, deferred payments and even weight clauses, dealing even a utility infielder for a journeyman outfielder can give a big-league general manager a headache. And even if the player you want comes with a price you can afford, re-signing that player after he becomes a free agent may be nearly impossible—especially if he is coming off a good year.

Trading in modern-day baseball is tough, but it can be done. And it can be done successfully if you know what you're doing. When Whitey Herzog took over a dilapidated St. Louis Cardinals franchise in 1980, he tore it apart after that season and rebuilt it into a world championship team two years later. Within a year of that World Series triumph, Herzog began dismantling his club again, beginning with a questionable trade of first baseman Keith Hernandez to the New York Mets. Two months into the 1985 season, four regulars from the '82 championship team were gone, but the St. Louis franchise was on its way to one of the best regular-season records in club history.

Two off-season deals transformed an 84-78 third-place club into a 101-61 National League pennant-winner last year. First, on December 12, Herzog dealt his only legitimate power threat, outfielder George Hendrick, and a minor leaguer to Pittsburgh for 12-game winner John Tudor and utility player Brian Harper. While Hendrick turned out to be an expensive mistake for the Pirates, Tudor became the ace of the Cardinals staff. He won 21 games and was nearly unbeatable down the stretch, winning 20 of his last 21 decisions. And Harper, who batted .250 as a righthanded pinch-hitter during the regular season, nearly came up with the World Series-winning hit when his eighth-inning single in Game 6 gave St. Louis a 1-0 lead before Kansas City rallied to win, 2-1.

In the Cardinals' second major off-season trade, pitcher Dave LaPoint, outfielder David Green, shortstop Jose Gonzalez (Uribe) and first baseman Gary Rajsich were sent to San Francisco for veteran outfielder Jack Clark. The deal was a steal. While LaPoint and Green struggled with the last-place Giants (and have since been traded again), Clark gave the Cards

a successor to Hendrick as the power man in the everyday lineup. Moved defensively to first base, Clark blasted 22 homers and drove in 87 runs and forced N.L. pitchers to throw strikes to third-place hitter Tom Herr, who proceeded to compile 61 more RBIs (110-49) than he had the year before. Herr's success, in turn, helped No. 2 hitter Willie McGee, the league's Most Valuable Player.

The cross-state Kansas City Royals, who defeated St. Louis in the seven-game World Series last fall, acquired veteran outfielder Lonnie Smith from the Cardinals on May 17. Smith, who became expendable because of the rapid development of rookie left fielder Vince Coleman, became the Royals' regular left fielder and a solid No. 2 hitter in the Kansas City lineup between Willie Wilson and George Brett. Smith, a liability on defense but a strong offensive player, hit .257 in 120 American League games and stole 40 bases.

Kansas City General Manager John Schuerholz, The Sporting News' Major League Executive of the Year in 1985, made another key trade before the Royals' championship season began. On January 18, Schuerholz acquired veteran catcher Jim Sundberg from Milwaukee in a six-player, four-team deal that also involved the New York Mets and Texas Rangers. A six-time Gold Glove recipient, Sundberg provided solid defense behind the plate—committing just five errors and six passed balls—and did an outstanding job handling Kansas City's young pitching staff.

Some of the biggest trades were made by teams still in contention late in the season and trying to gear up for the stretch drive. The California Angels picked up veteran lefthander John Candelaria, Hendrick and reliever Al Holland from Pittsburgh on August 2 in exchange for promising minor league pitchers Bob Kipper and Pat Clements and outfielder Mike Brown. Candelaria, who had requested a trade from the Pirates, responded by winning seven of 10 decisions, though the Angels still finished a game behind the Royals in the A.L. West.

The Dodgers picked up another disgruntled Pirate, third baseman Bill Madlock, on August 31 and went on to win the N.L. West by 5½ games over the surprising Cincinnati Reds. Los Angeles gave up three prospects—outfielders R.J. Reynolds and Cecil Espy and first baseman Sid

Bream—for the 34-year-old Madlock, a four-time N.L. batting champion. Madlock batted .360 in 34 games for the Dodgers.

The Yankees picked up veteran pitcher Joe Niekro from the Astros on September 15 for their stretch run against Toronto for the A.L. East Division title. The Yanks, who trailed by 4½ games at the time of the trade, nearly overtook the slumping Blue Jays before finishing two games behind. Niekro, whose 46-year-old brother, Phil, won 16 games for New York (including his 300th career victory on the season's final day), won two of three decisions for the Yankees.

In an unusual turn of events, Toronto, which lost free-agent designated hitter Cliff Johnson to Texas after the 1984 season, reacquired Johnson from the Rangers on August 28 for three minor-leaguers. Ironically, the player the Jays had received as compensation for losing Johnson to free agency—pitcher Tom Henke—played a bigger role than Johnson in the Jays' pennant drive, saving 13 games and winning three with a 2.03 ERA.

Henke wasn't the only player awarded as compensation for a free agent who enjoyed a productive season. The Angels received veteran pitcher Donnie Moore, a member of the Atlanta organization, as compensation for losing free-agent outfielder Fred Lynn to Baltimore. Moore, a 31-year-old journeyman with a 24-23 lifetime record prior to '85, proceeded to save 31 games and win eight more for California.

Veteran shortstop Johnnie LeMaster was the tough-luck tradee of 1985. He started the season with the last-place Giants of the N.L. West before being traded to the last-place Indians of the A.L. East on May 7. After hitting .150 in 11 games with Cleveland, LeMaster was traded to the last-place Pirates of the N.L. East on May 30. LeMaster hit a combined .122 for the Giants and Pirates.

The 1985 season proved to be the end of the line for a number of former stars who received unconditional releases from their teams. Pitchers Ron Reed, Joe Sambito, Larry Gura, Steve Rogers, Tommy John, Rollie Fingers and Jerry Koosman all were let go either during the season or shortly after. Sambito, Gura, Rogers and John all were picked up by other teams and given second chances. Other players released were outfielder John Lowenstein (by Baltimore), infielder Tim Foli (by Pittsburgh), outfielder Oscar Gamble (by the White Sox), infielder Larry Bowa (released by the Cubs but picked up by the

Mets) and catcher Darrell Porter (by St. Louis).

The saddest story of 1985 belongs to relief pitcher Steve Howe, whose recurring drug problems apparently have forced him from baseball at age 27. Howe, the National League Rookie of the Year in 1980 with the Dodgers, was suspended for part of the 1983 season and the entire '84 campaign because of involvement with cocaine. He had pitched 22 innings and compiled three saves for the Dodgers last season before asking for, and receiving, his release on July 3. Hoping a change of scenery might change his fortunes, Howe signed with the Minnesota Twins on August 12. But his problems with cocaine eventually returned and the Twins released him after only one month.

Although there were no blockbuster deals made at the winter meetings in San Diego, a few of the deals were more notable than others:

• The Cardinals traded temperamental righthander Joaquin Andujar to the A's for catcher Mike Heath and pitcher Tim Conroy. Andujar won 41 games the past two seasons in St. Louis but slumped badly during the final two months of the regular season and postseason. His outburst and ejection from Game 7 of the World Series probably sealed his fate as a Cardinal.

• The Braves traded reliever Steve Bedrosian and outfielder Milt Thompson to the Phillies for catcher Ozzie Virgil and pitcher Pete Smith.

• The Red Sox traded reliever Mark Clear to the Brewers for infielder Ed Romero. Boston followed up a week later by acquiring reliever Sammy Stewart from the Orioles for shortstop Jackie Gutierrez.

• The Dodgers acquired reliever Ed Vande Berg from the Mariners for veteran catcher Steve Yeager. Yeager became expendable when L.A. picked up catcher Alex Trevino from the Giants for outfielder Candy Maldonado the same day.

• The Reds acquired two pitchers who, if healthy, should be starters in 1986—Bill Gullickson (from Montreal) and John Denny (from Philadelphia). The Reds gave up outfielder Gary Redus and pitcher Tom Hume for Denny and four players, including three pitchers, for Gullickson.

Following is a list of all player transactions for the 1985 calendar year:

January 3—Padres signed infielder-outfielder Jerry Royster, a re-entry free agent formerly with the Braves.

January 3—Mets re-signed pinch-hitter Rusty Staub, a free agent.

January 7—Royals traded shortstop U.L. Washington to Expos for outfielder Ken Baker and pitcher Mike Kinnunen; Royals assigned Kinnunen and Baker to Omaha.

January 8—Yankees' Columbus affiliate purchased catcher Juan Espino from Indians.

January 8—Padres signed pitcher Tim Stoddard, a re-entry free agent formerly with the Cubs.

January 8—Brewers' Vancouver affiliate signed pitcher Jim Kern, a re-entry free agent.

January 9—Indians signed pitcher Dave Von Ohlen, a free agent, and assigned him to Maine.

January 9—Expos traded outfielder-first baseman Mike Stenhouse to Twins for pitcher Jack O'Connor; Expos assigned O'Connor to Indianapolis.

January 10—Angels re-signed infielder Rob Wilfong, a re-entry free agent.

January 11—Expos re-signed outfielder Jim Wohlford, a re-entry free agent.

January 11—Brewers released pitcher Mike Caldwell.

January 11—Angels released infielder Rob Picciolo.

January 12—White Sox' Buffalo affiliate signed pitcher Steve Fireovid, a free agent.

January 14—Tigers released pitcher John Martin.

January 14—Red Sox signed pitcher Bruce Kison, a re-entry free agent formerly with the Angels.

January 15—A's re-signed first baseman Dan Meyer, a re-entry free agent.

January 16—Mariners released outfielder Richie Zisk.

January 16—Brewers re-signed pitcher Rollie Fingers, a re-entry free agent.

January 18—In a six-player, four-team deal, Royals acquired catcher Jim Sundberg from Brewers, Rangers acquired catcher Don Slaught from Royals, Mets acquired pitcher Frank Wills from Royals, Brewers acquired pitcher Danny Darwin and a player to be named from Rangers and pitcher Tim Leary from Mets; Wills was assigned by Mets to Tidewater and Leary was assigned by Brewers to Vancouver. Catcher Bill Nance was acquired by Brewers from Rangers on January 30, and was assigned to El Paso.

January 22—Pirates signed outfielder Sixto Lezcano, a re-entry free agent formerly with the Phillies.

January 23—Phillies purchased pitcher Ralph Citarella from Cardinals, and assigned him to Portalnd.

January 23—Cardinals signed catcher Mike Lavalliere, a free agent, and assigned him to Louisville.

January 23—Red Sox signed catcher Dave Sax, a free agent, and assigned him to Pawtucket.

January 24—Angels selected pitcher Donnie Moore from Braves organization as compensation for the loss of Type A free-agent Fred Lynn, who signed with the Orioles.

January 24—Blue Jays selected pitcher Tom Henke from Rangers organization as compensation for the loss of Type A free-agent designated hitter Cliff Johnson, who signed with the Rangers; Henke was assigned to Syracuse.

January 24—Cardinals selected shortstop Argenis Salazar from Expos organization for the loss of Type A free-agent Bruce Sutter, who signed with the Braves; Salazar was assigned to Louisville.

January 26—Giants traded pitcher Gary Lavelle to Blue Jays for pitchers Jim Gott and Jack McKnight and infielder Augie Schmidt; Giants assigned McKnight to Phoenix.

January 29—Royals signed pitcher Renie Martin, a free agent, and assigned him to Omaha.

January 30—Angels signed outfielder Ruppert Jones, a re-entry free agent formerly with the Tigers.

February 1—Cardinals traded first baseman David Green and Gary Rajsich, pitcher Dave LaPoint and shortstop Jose Uribe (Jose Gonzalez) to Giants for outfielder-first baseman Jack Clark.

February 4—Phillies traded first baseman Al Oliver to Dodgers for pitcher Pat Zachry.

February 6—Cardinals traded pitcher Mickey Mahler to Expos for a player to be named; Cardinals' Louisville affiliate purchased infielder Tom Lawless on March 25.

February 7—Royals signed first baseman Pat Putnam, a re-entry free agent formerly with the Twins, and assigned him to Omaha.

February 7—Orioles traded second baseman Vic Rodriguez to Padres for third baseman Fritz Connally; Padres assigned Rodriguez to Las Vegas and Orioles assigned Connally to Rochester.

February 11—Dodgers signed pitcher Bobby Castillo, a re-entry free agent formerly with the Twins.

February 13—Rangers purchased pitcher Greg Harris from Padres.

February 15—Expos signed catcher Steve Nicosia, a re-entry free agent formerly with the Giants.

February 19—White Sox traded infielder Roy Smalley to Twins for first baseman Randy Johnson and outfielder Ron Scheer; White Sox assigned Johnson to Buffalo and Scheer was assigned to Glens Falls.

February 19—Royals signed pitcher Mike LaCoss, a re-entry free agent formerly with the Astros and assigned him to Omaha.

February 20—Dodgers signed outfielder Jay Johnstone, a free agent.

February 25—Royals signed catcher-infielder Jamie Quirk, a free agent, and assigned him to Memphis.

February 25—Blue Jays signed catcher Gary Allenson, a re-entry free agent, and assigned him to Syracuse.

February 27—Yankees traded third baseman Toby Harrah to Rangers for outfielder Billy Sample and a player to be named; Yankees acquired pitcher Eric Dersin on July 14 and assigned him to Fort Lauderdale.

February 28—Pirates signed pitcher Rick Reuschel, a re-entry free agent, and assigned him to Hawaii.

March 4—Expos re-signed outfielder Miguel Dilone, a re-entry free agent.

March 4—White Sox purchased infielder Nelson Barrera from Mexico City Reds in exchange for loan of infielder Manny Salinas and outfielder John Cangelosi; Barrera was assigned to Buffalo. Barrera was sold back to Mexico City on May 17, while Cangelosi was returned on June 1 to White Sox and Salinas was returned in August, 1985.

March 18—A's acquired outfielder Damon Farmar from Cubs, completing July 15, 1984 deal in which pitcher Chuck Rainey and a player to be named were traded to A's for a player to be named; Cubs acquired outfielder Davey Lopes as partial completion of deal, August 31, 1984.

March 19—Giants released infielder Roy Howell.

March 19—Royals traded pitcher Keith Creel to Indians for a player to be named; Indians acquired outfielder Dwight Taylor on October 3.

March 22—Indians released pitcher Jerry

Ujdur.

March 22—Cubs returned catcher Jamie Nelson to Brewers, who had sold him conditionally on December 2, 1984.

March 23—White Sox signed designated hitter-outfielder Oscar Gamble, a re-entry free agent formerly with the Yankees.

March 24—Cardinals released catcher Glenn Brummer.

March 24—Giants traded outfielder Dusty Baker to A's for pitcher Ed Puikunas and catcher Dan Winters, who were both assigned to Fresno.

March 25—Brewers acquired pitcher Ed Myers from A's completing December 7, 1984 deal in which Brewers traded pitcher Don Sutton to A's for pitcher Ray Burris and Eric Barry and a player to be named; Brewers assigned Myers to Vancouver.

March 26—White Sox released first baseman Mike Squires to become a scout.

March 27—Twins traded pitcher Brad Havens to Orioles for pitcher Mark Brown; Orioles assigned Havens to Rochester and Twins assigned Brown to Toledo.

March 28—Twins released outfielder Darrell Brown.

March 28—Expos released catcher Bobby Ramos.

March 28—Padres signed outfielder Al Bumbry, a re-entry free agent formerly with the Orioles.

March 28—Mets reclaimed pitcher Ed Olwine from Phillies, who had selected him from Tidewater in the 1984 major league draft; Olwine was assigned to Tidewater.

March 29—Mets traded pitcher Frank Wills to Mariners for pitcher Wray Bergendahl; Mariners assigned Wills to Calgary and Mets assigned Bergendahl to Lynchburg.

March 29—Orioles released third baseman Todd Cruz.

March 30—Padres released outfielder Ron Roenicke.

March 30—Tigers released pitcher Dave Gumpert.

March 30—Brewers released pitcher Tom Tellmann.

March 30—Mets traded pitcher Ken Reed and third baseman Gene Autry to White Sox for pitcher Randy Niemann; Mets assigned Niemann to Tidewater and White Sox assigned Reed and Autry to Appleton.

March 31—Mets traded outfielder Rusty Tillman to Padres for outfielder-first baseman Rick Lancellotti; Padres assigned Tillman to Las Vegas.

March 31—A's signed outfielder Steve Henderson, a re-entry free agent formerly with the Mariners.

March 31—Indians released pitcher Steve Farr.

March 31—A's released catcher Jim Essian.

April 1—Rangers released infielder Jim Anderson and catcher Ned Yost.

April 1—Blue Jays released pitcher Roy Lee Jackson and Bryan Clark.

April 1—Red Sox released pitcher John Henry Johnson.

April 1—White Sox released infielder Jerry Dybzinski and third baseman Tom O'Malley.

April 1—Indians traded pitcher Jay Baller to Cubs for infielder Dan Rohn; Indians assigned Rohn to Maine and Cubs assigned Baller to Iowa.

April 1—Phillies traded first baseman Len Matuszek to Blue Jays for infielder Jose Escobar, outfielder Ken Kinnard and pitcher Dave Shipanoff; Phillies assigned Escobar and Kinnard to Reading and assigned Shipanoff to Portland.

April 1—Mariners released pitcher Dave Beard.

April 1—Giants released pitcher Mark Calvert.

April 2—Cardinals traded shortstop Argenis Salazar and pitcher John Young to Mets for shortstop Jose Oquendo and pitcher Mark J. Davis; Cardinals assigned Oquendo to Louisville and Davis to St. Petersburg, and Met assigned Salazar to Tidewater and Young to Jackson.

April 3—Phillies released infielder Kiko Garcia.

April 4—Mariners' Calgary affiliate signed pitcher Dave Tobik, a free agent.

April 4—Rangers released outfielder Mickey Rivers.

April 4—Red Sox released catcher Jeff Newman.

April 4—Rangers traded catcher-outfielder Kevin Buckley to Indians for a player to be named and was assigned to Maine; Rangers acquired infielder Jeff Moronko on April 29. Moronko was assigned to Tulsa.

April 4—Rangers traded catcher Donnie Scott to Mariners for catcher Orlando Mercado; Mariners assigned Scott to Calgary and Rangers assigned Mercado to Oklahoma City.

April 4—Rangers signed catcher Glenn Brummer, a free agent, and assigned him to Oklahoma City.

April 4—Mariners traded pitcher Tom Burns to Mets for first baseman-designated hitter Paul Hollins; Mariners assigned Hollins to Chattanooga.

April 4—Twins released shortstop Lenny Faedo.

April 5—Royals traded outfielder Mike Brewer to Indians for a player to be named; Brewer was returned to Royals, September 17.

April 5—Phillies re-signed infielder Kiko Garcia, a free agent.

April 5—Cubs released infielder Tom Veryzer.

April 5—Giants traded outfielder Alejandro Sanchez to Tigers for pitcher Roger Mason; Tigers assigned Sanchez to Nashville and Giants assigned Mason to Phoenix.

April 6—Giants signed pitcher Vida Blue, a free agent.

April 6—White Sox released pitcher Ron Reed.

April 6—Cardinals traded pitcher Dave Rucker to Phillies for pitcher Bill Campbell and shortstop Ivan DeJesus; Phillies assigned Rucker to Portland.

April 6—Padres reclaimed pitcher Mitch Williams from Rangers, who had selected him from Las Vegas in the 1984 major league draft; Padres then traded Williams to Rangers for third baseman Randy Asadoor.

April 6—Expos released infielder Mike Ramsey.

April 7—Expos purchased infielder Fred Manrique from Blue Jays.

April 8—Pirates signed infielder Bill Almon, a re-entry free agent formerly with the A's.

April 8—Tigers' Nashville affiliate signed infielder Tom O'Malley a free agent.

April 8—Astros released pitcher Joe Sambito.

April 8—Cubs signed shortstop Chris Speier, a re-entry free agent formerly with the Twins.

April 10—Reds re-signed first baseman Tony Perez, a re-entry free agent.

April 11—Pirates signed pitcher John Henry Johnson and infielder Jerry Dybzinski, both free agents, and both assigned to Hawaii.

April 11—A's signed pitcher Tom Tellmann, a free agent, and assigned him to Tacoma.

April 13—Indians' Maine affiliate signed pitcher Dave Beard, a free agent.

April 15—Indians signed pitcher Bryan Clark, a free agent, and assigned him to Maine.

April 17—Braves traded catcher Alex Trevino to Giants for catcher-outfielder John Rabb; Braves assigned Rabb to Richmond.

April 18—Twins signed first baseman Mark Funderburk, a free agent, and assigned him to Orlando.

April 19—Indians signed outfielder Benny Ayala, a re-entry free agent formerly with the Orioles and assigned him to Maine.

April 20—Pirates traded pitcher Kent Tekulve to Phillies for pitchers Al Holland and Frankie Griffin; Pirates assigned Griffin to Nashua.

April 21—Cardinals signed pitcher Matt Keough, a free agent, and assigned him to Louisville.

April 22—Cardinals released infielder Art Howe.

April 23—Indians released catcher Geno Petralli and pitcher Jim Siwy.

April 26—Mets signed pitcher Joe Sambito, a free agent.

April 26—Expos traded outfielder Max Venable to Reds for infielder Skeeter Barnes; Expos assigned Barnes to Indianapolis and Reds assigned Venable to Denver.

April 27—Pirates traded catcher Steve Herz to Phillies for catcher Mike Diaz; Pirates assigned Diaz to Hawaii and Phillies assigned Herz to Portland.

April 28—Expos signed catcher Ned Yost, a free agent.

April 29—Yankees released pitcher Dale Murray.

April 30—Dodgers signed infielder Mike Ramsey, a free agent.

April 30—Giants released pitcher Jeff Cornell.

May 1—Red Sox traded pitcher Ed Glynn to Expos for a player to be named.

May 1—Orioles' Rochester affiliate signed pitcher Roy Lee Jackson, a free agent.

May 2—Angels signed pitcher Alan Fowlkes, a free agent, and assigned him to Edmonton.

May 3—Giants' Phoenix affiliate signed outfielder Ron Roenicke, a free agent.

May 7—Giants traded shortstop Johnnie Le-Master to Indians for pitcher Mike Jeffcoat and infielder Luis Quinones; Giants assigned Jeffcoat and Quinones to Phoenix.

May 7—Rangers signed pitcher Dale Murray, a free agent, and assigned him to Oklahoma City.

May 9—Blue Jays released first baseman Willie Aikens.

May 9—Royals signed pitcher Steve Farr and shortstop Lenny Faedo, both free agents; Farr was assigned to Omaha, and Faedo was assigned to Memphis.

May 15—Phillies purchased infielder Derrel Thomas from Miami (Independent).

May 15—Phillies signed pitcher Steve Comer, a free agent, and assigned him to Portland.

May 17—Rangers' Oklahoma City affiliate signed catcher Geno Petralli, a free agent.

May 17—Phillies released infielder Kiko Garcia.

May 17—Cardinals traded outfielder Lonnie Smith to Royals for outfielder John Morris; Cardinals assigned Morris to Louisville.

May 18—Royals released pitcher Larry Gura.

May 19—Blue Jays' Syracuse affiliate signed first baseman Willie Aikens, a free agent.

May 20—Angels' Edmonton affiliate signed outfielder Rufino Linares, a free agent.

May 21—Expos released pitcher Steve Rogers.

May 21—Orioles released outfielder John Lowenstein.

May 22—Twins reclaimed outfielder Jim Weaver from Tigers, who had selected him from Toledo in the 1984 major league draft; Weaver was assigned to Toledo.

May 25—Yankees' Columbus affiliate released catcher Mike O'Berry.

May 26—A's released first baseman Dan Meyer.

May 28—Cubs signed pitcher Larry Gura, a free agent.

May 30—Indians traded shortstop Johnnie Le-Master to Pirates for a player to be named; Indians acquired pitcher Scott Bailes on July 3 and assigned him to Waterbury.

June 2—Dodgers released infielder Mike Ramsey.

June 3—Angels signed pitcher Steve Rogers, a free agent, and assigned him to Edmonton.

June 6—Braves' Richmond affiliate purchased pitcher Charlie Puleo from Reds.

June 8—Phillies released pitcher Pat Zachry.

June 11—Expos released infielder Doug Flynn.

June 12—Astros' Tucson affiliate purchased catcher Brad Gulden from Reds.

June 17—Pirates released infielder Tim Foli.

June 19—Angels released pitcher Tommy John.

June 20—Rangers traded pitcher Frank Tanana to Tigers for pitcher Duane James; Tigers assigned James to Tulsa.

June 20—Tigers signed infielder Doug Flynn, a free agent.

June 20—Mariners released pitcher Mike Stanton.

June 21—Expos' Indianapolis affiliate signed catcher Mike O'Berry, a free agent.

June 22—Expos purchased outfielder Mitch Webster from Blue Jays.

June 25—Giants released pitcher Bob Lacey.

June 27—Padres traded second baseman Alan Wiggins to Orioles for pitcher Roy Lee Jackson and a player to be named; Orioles assigned Wiggins to Rochester and Padres assigned Jackson to Las Vegas. Padres acquired pitcher Rich Caldwell on September 16.

June 28—Giants released infielder Duane Kuiper.

June 28—Mariners' Calgary affiliate released pitcher Bob Stoddard.

July 1—Tigers' Nashville affiliate signed pitcher Bob Stoddard, a free agent.

July 2—Angels' Edmonton affiliate released pitcher Steve Rogers.

July 3—Dodgers released pitcher Steve Howe.

July 9—Dodgers traded first baseman-outfielder Al Oliver to Blue Jays for first baseman Len Matuszek.

July 10—Astros traded infielder Enos Cabell to Dodgers for pitcher Rafael Montalvo and a player to be named; Astros acquired third baseman German Rivera on July 15. Astros assigned both Montalvo and Rivera to Tucson.

July 10—Expos released outfielder Miguel Dilone.

July 11—White Sox traded pitcher Tim Lollar to Red Sox for outfielder Reid Nichols and a player to be named.

**Buddy Bell (left) became the Reds' regular third baseman following a July 19 trade with Texas. Bell's father, Gus, was a Cincinnati outfielder between 1953-61.**

July 12—A's Modesto affiliate signed pitcher Tommy John, a free agent.

July 16—White Sox traded outfielder Tom Paciorek to Mets for infielder Dave Cochrane; White Sox assigned Cochrane to Buffalo.

July 17—Cardinals traded pitcher Neil Allen to Yankees for a player to be named.

July 19—Rangers traded third baseman Buddy Bell to Reds for outfielder Duane Walker and a player to be named; Rangers acquired pitcher Jeff Russell on July 23 and assigned him to Oklahoma City.

July 22—Cardinals purchased first baseman Gary Rajsich from Giants.

July 23—Expos released pitcher Mickey Mahler.

July 26—Indians' Maine affiliate traded pitcher Dave Beard to Cubs' Iowa affiliate for outfielder Tom Grant.

July 27—Padres' Las Vegas affiliate signed outfielder Miguel Dilone, a free agent.

August 1—Expos traded first baseman Dan Driessen to Giants for pitcher Bill Laskey, first baseman Scot Thompson and a player to be named; deal settled when Laskey was traded back to Giants on October 24.

August 1—Indians traded pitcher Bert Blyleven to Twins for pitcher Curt Wardle, outfielder Jim Weaver and infielder Jay Bell; Indians assigned Weaver to Maine and Bell to Waterbury.

August 2—Mariners released infielder Larry Milbourne.

August 2—Pirates traded pitchers John Candelaria and Al Holland and outfielder George Hendrick to Angels for pitcher Pat Clements, outfielder Mike Brown and a player to be named; Pirates acquired pitcher Bob Kipper on August 16 and assigned him to Hawaii.

August 3—Tigers' Nashville affiliate signed pitcher Mickey Mahler, a free agent.

August 8—Phillies traded catcher Bo Diaz and pitcher Greg Simpson to Reds for shortstop Tom Foley, catcher Alan Knicely and a player to be named and cash; Reds assigned Simpson to Tampa. Phillies acquired pitcher Freddie Toliver on August 27.

August 8—White Sox' Buffalo affiliate signed pitcher Steve Rogers, a free agent.

August 12—Expos' Indianapolis affiliate purchased outfielder Doug Frobel from Pirates.

August 12—Twins signed pitcher Steve Howe, a free agent.

August 12—White Sox released outfielder Oscar Gamble and pitcher Mike Stanton.

August 13—Cubs released shortstop Larry Bowa.

August 14—Cubs released pitcher Larry Gura.

August 16—Yankees released outfielder Omar Moreno.

August 19—Phillies released catcher John Wockenfuss.

August 20—Mets signed shortstop Larry Bowa, a free agent.

August 22—Tigers released pitcher Doug Bair.

August 22—Expos released catcher Steve Nicosia.

August 23—Mets released pitcher Joe Sambito.

August 24—Blue Jays released catcher Gary Allenson.

August 28—Rangers traded designed hitter Cliff Johnson to Blue Jays for three players to be named; Rangers acquired pitchers Matt Williams and Jeff Mays on August 29 and pitcher Greg Ferlenda on November 14. Rangers assigned Williams to Oklahoma City and Mays to Daytona Beach.

August 29—Reds traded outfielder-first baseman Cesar Cedeno to Cardinals for outfielder Mark Jackson; Reds assigned Jackson to Tampa.

August 31—Pirates traded third baseman Bill Madlock to Dodgers for three players to be named; Pirates acquired outfielder R.J. Reynolds on September 3 and outfielder Cecil Espy and first baseman Sid Bream on September 9.

September 1—Blue Jays signed catcher Steve Nicosia, a free agent.

September 1—White Sox activated scout Mike Squires as a first baseman.

September 2—Cardinals signed pitcher Doug Bair, a free agent.

September 3—Royals signed outfielder Omar Moreno, a free agent.

September 10—A's traded pitcher Don Sutton to Angels for two players to be named; A's acquired pitcher Robert Sharpnack and outfielder Jerome Nelson on September 25.

September 13—Phillies traded pitcher Rick Surhoff to Rangers for pitcher Dave Stewart.

September 14—Yankees purchased pitcher Rod Scurry from Pirates.

September 15—Astros traded pitcher Joe Niekro to Yankees for pitcher Jim Deshaies and two players to be named; Astros acquired infielder Neder Horta on September 24 and pitcher Dody Rather on January 11, 1986. Astros assigned Horta to Sarasota.

September 17—Twins released pitcher Steve Howe.

September 17—Indians' Maine affiliate purchased pitcher Richard Yett from Twins' Toledo affiliate.

September 27—Brewers released outfielder Doug Loman.

October 4—Pirates released infielder Jerry Dybzinski, outfielder Mitchell Page and first baseman Hedi Vargas.

October 7—Giants traded pitchers Dave LaPoint and Eric King and catcher Matt Nokes to Tigers for pitcher Juan Berenguer, catcher Bob Melvin and a player to be named; Giants acquired pitcher Scott Medvin on December 11. Tigers assigned King to Birmingham.

October 9—Tigers released outfielder Rusty Kuntz and pitchers Mickey Mahler and Bob Stoddard.

October 9—Orioles released catcher Joe Nolan.

October 11—Twins released infielder John Castino.

October 15—Cardinals released pitcher Andy Hassler.

October 24—Expos traded pitcher Bill Laskey to Giants for pitcher George Riley and outfielder Alonzo Powell.

October 31—Dodgers released outfielder Jay Johnstone.

November 1—Mariners released pitchers Brian Snyder, Jim Lewis, Jack Lazorko, Bob Long and Dave Tobik.

November 2—Expos traded outfielder Pete Incaviglia to Rangers for pitcher Bob Sebra and infielder Jim Anderson.

November 9—Rangers released pitcher Chris Welsh.

November 11—Reds traded pitcher Bob Buchanan to Giants for pitcher Colin Ward; Reds assigned Ward to Denver.

November 12—Braves released pitcher Dave Schuler.

November 12—Indians released pitcher Bryan Clark.

November 12—Yankees released pitchers John Montefusco and Don Cooper and outfielder Matt Winters.

November 13—Braves released infielder Randy Johnson.

November 13—Rangers released catcher Glenn Brummer.

November 13—Mets released outfielder-first baseman Tom Paciorek, infielder Kelvin Chapman and pitcher Brent Gaff.

November 13—Red Sox traded pitchers Bob Ojeda, Tom McCarthy, John Mitchell and Chris Bayer to Mets for pitchers Calvin Schiraldi and Wes Gardner and outfielders John Christensen and LaSchelle Tarver.

November 13—Cubs released pitcher Dave Beard.

November 13—Tigers traded infielder Barbaro Garbey to A's for outfielder Dave Collins.

November 13—Astros released outfielder Chris Jones, first baseman-outfielder Tim Tolman and infielder Mike Richardt.

November 14—Brewers released pitchers Rollie Fingers and Rick Waits.

November 14—Cardinals released catcher Darrell Porter, pitcher Bill Campbell and infielder Willie Lozado.

November 14—Red Sox released pitcher Jim Dorsey.

November 15—Royals released outfielder Omar Moreno.

November 21—Brewers granted pitcher Pete Vuckovich free agency after refusing to report to minors.

November 22—Brewers released pitcher Brad Lesley and catcher Dave Huppert.

November 22—Brewers sold outfielder Mark Brouhard to Yakult Swallows of Japanese baseball.

November 25—Brewers released pitcher Pete Ladd.

November 25—Rangers traded infielder Wayne Tolleson and pitcher Dave Schmidt to White Sox for pitcher Ed Correa, infielder Scott Fletcher and a player to be named; Rangers acquired infielder Jose Mota on December 12.

December 4—Giants traded first baseman-outfielder David Green to Brewers for a player to be named; Giants acquired shortstop Hector Quinones on December 11.

December 4—Braves signed pitcher Dave Beard, a free agent.

December 5—A's signed pitchers Don Cooper and Ralph Citarella, both free agents.

December 6—Phillies released pitcher Jerry Koosman.

December 6—Cardinals sold first baseman Gary Rajsich to Chunichi Dragons of Japanese baseball.

December 6—Yankees traded outfielder Billy Sample to Brewers for infielder Miguel Sosa.

December 8—A's signed outfielder Rusty Kuntz, a free agent.

December 9—A's signed catcher Ray Smith, a free agent.

December 9—Astros traded pitcher Mark Ross to Cardinals for a player to be named.

December 10—Indians sold outfielder George Vukovich to Seibu Lions of Japanese baseball.

December 10—Red Sox released second baseman Jerry Remy.

December 10—Rangers signed outfielder Tom Paciorek, a free agent.

December 10—Cardinals traded pitcher Joaquin Andujar to A's for catcher Mike Heath and pitcher Tim Conroy.

December 10—Braves traded pitcher Steve Bedrosian and outfielder Milt Thompson to Phillies for catcher Ozzie Virgil and pitcher Pete Smith.

December 11—Red Sox traded pitcher Mark Clear to Brewers for infielder Ed Romero.

December 11—Dodgers traded outfielder Candy Maldonado to Giants for catcher Alex Trevino.

December 11—Dodgers traded catcher Steve Yeager to Mariners for pitcher Ed Vande Berg.

December 11—Indians traded infielder Mike Fischlin to Yankees for a player to be named.

December 11—Giants traded second baseman Manny Trillo to Cubs for infielder Dave Owen.

December 11—Yankees released second baseman Juan Bonilla.

December 11—Phillies traded pitchers John Denny and Jeff Gray to Reds for outfielder Gary Redus and pitcher Tom Hume.

December 12—Yankees traded pitcher Rich Bordi and infielder Rex Hudler to Orioles for outfielder Gary Roenicke and a player to be named; Yankees acquired outfielder Leo Hernandez on December 16.

December 12—Yankees traded catcher Ron Hassey and pitcher Joe Cowley to White Sox for pitcher Britt Burns, shortstop Mike Soper and outfielder Glen Braxton.

December 12—Mariners traded third baseman Darnell Coles to Tigers for pitcher Rich Monteleone.

December 12—Red Sox traded pitcher Charlie Mitchell to Twins for outfielder Mike Stenhouse.

December 12—Giants signed third baseman Randy Johnson and catcher Brad Gulden, both free agents.

December 12—Indians signed pitchers Ron Musselman and Tom Candiotti, both free agents.

December 12—Phillies released infielder Jose Escobar.

December 16—Astros traded outfielder Jerry Mumphrey to Cubs for outfielder Billy Hatcher and a player to be named.

December 16—Indians traded pitcher Rich Thompson to Brewers for pitcher Scott Roberts.

December 17—Red Sox traded shortstop Jackie Gutierrez to Orioles for pitcher Sammy Stewart.

December 18—Cardinals released outfielder Steve Braun.

December 18—Brewers traded pitchers Dean Freeland and Eric Pilkington to Giants for outfielder Rob Deer.

December 19—Expos released catcher Ned Yost.

December 19—Expos traded pitcher Bill Gullickson and catcher Sal Butera to Reds for pitchers Jay Tibbs, Andy McGaffigan and John Stuper and catcher Dann Bilardello.

December 20—Angels released pitchers Ken Forsch and Geoff Zahn and first baseman Daryl Sconiers.

December 20—Tigers released pitcher Milt Wilcox.

December 20—Twins released pitchers Ed Hodge and Rick Lysander and outfielder Dave Meier.

December 20—A's released designated hitter Dave Kingman and pitchers Steve Mura and Mike Warren.

December 20—Mariners released pitcher Salome Barojas and outfielder Al Cowens.

December 20—Rangers released pitcher Dickie Noles and outfielders Duane Walker and Ellis Valentine.

December 20—Cubs released pitchers Derek Botelho and Lary Sorensen.

December 20—Giants released infielder Joel Youngblood.

December 22—Phillies released first baseman Tim Corcoran.

December 22—White Sox signed outfielder Matt Winters, a free agent, and assigned him to Buffalo.

December 26—Braves signed second baseman Kelly Heath, a free agent.

December 27—Angels traded pitcher Luis Sanchez and catcher Tim Arnold to Expos for pitcher Gary Lucas.

The following is a list of players granted free agency on November 12, 1985 through the players' collective bargaining agreement:

November 13—Yankees re-signed pitcher Marty Bystrom.

November 21—Tigers re-signed infielder Doug Flynn.

November 26—Dodgers re-signed catcher Steve Yeager.

November 26—Angels re-signed second baseman Bobby Grich.

November 27—Royals re-signed catcher Jamie Quirk.

December 2—Royals re-signed outfielder Lynn Jones.

December 4—A's re-signed first baseman Bruce Bochte.

December 5—Angels re-signed pitcher Don Sutton.

December 6—Phillies re-signed outfielder Garry Maddox.

December 8—Royals re-signed designated hitter Hal McRae.

December 17—Giants re-signed pitcher Vida Blue.

December 22—Brewers re-signed pitcher Danny Darwin.

# Costs Keep Draft to Record Low

**By DAVE SLOAN**

With the cost per player having doubled from the previous year, only nine selections were made in the 1985 major league draft December 10 in San Diego. Whereas big-league general managers could have snatched unprotected, promising prospects from other clubs for just $25,000 at the 1984 winter meetings, the asking price of $50,000 last winter helped keep the number of selections down to a record low. Thirteen players had been chosen in '84.

With clubs drafting in inverse order of their '85 records and alternating by leagues, the Cleveland Indians opened the proceedings by taking 21-year-old third baseman Eddie Williams from the Reds' Denver (American Association) farm team. Williams, who had been selected fourth overall in the nation by the New York Mets in the June 1983 free-agent draft after a fabulous San Diego high school career, was traded by the Mets to the Reds a year later in a deal involving pitcher Bruce Berenyi. Williams spent the '85 season with the Reds' Cedar Rapids (Midwest) club, batting .261 in 119 games with 20 homers and 83 runs batted in.

The Texas Rangers, choosing second, opted for righthander Scott Patterson from the Yankees' organization. Patterson posted a 7-2 record with three saves and a 1.55 earned-run average in 27 games at Albany (Eastern) and a 5-2 record with three saves and a 3.35 ERA in 21 games at Columbus (International) in 1985. The San Diego Padres used the third pick on infielder Leon Roberts, a Pirates farmhand who batted .272 with one homer, 23 RBIs and 40 stolen bases in 105 games at Nashua (Eastern) in '85.

The most interesting pick of the draft was the Cardinals' selection of 28-year-old journeyman Clint Hurdle from the Mets' organization. Hurdle, who was projected by many observers as baseball's next superstar a decade ago when he started in the Kansas City Royals' farm system, never lived up to those lofty expectations during big-league stints with the Royals, Reds and Mets as an outfielder, third baseman and catcher. His selection by St. Louis would reunite him with Manager Whitey Herzog, who also managed the Royals during Hurdle's early years as a professional.

The Pirates, Brewers, Braves, Mariners, Phillies, Cubs, Red Sox, Reds, Dodgers, Mets and Yankees came in with full 40-man rosters and were not permitted to participate in the draft. However, three of those clubs—the Pirates, Reds and Mets—each lost two players.

Draft choices in order of selection:

**Indians** —Third baseman Eddie Williams from Denver (American Association) of the Reds' organization.

**Rangers** —Righthanded pitcher Scott Patterson from Columbus (International) of the Yankees' organization.

**Padres** —Infielder Leon Roberts from Hawaii (Pacific Coast) of the Pirates' organization.

**Expos** —Righthanded pitcher Jeff Parrett from Vancouver (Pacific Coast) of the Brewers' organization.

**White Sox** —First baseman-outfielder Bobby Bonilla from Hawaii (Pacific Coast) of the Pirates' organization.

**Angels** —Righthanded pitcher Carl Willis from Denver (American Association) of the Reds' organization.

**Cardinals** —Catcher Clint Hurdle from Tidewater (International) of the Mets' organization.

**Blue Jays** —Righthanded pitcher Jose DeJesus from Omaha (American Association) of the Royals' organization.

**Twins** —Righthanded pitcher Thomas Burns from Tidewater (International) of the Mets' organization.

## Major League Attendance for 1985

| NATIONAL LEAGUE | Home | Road |
|---|---|---|
| Atlanta | 1,350,137 | 1,655,362 |
| Chicago | 2,161,534 | 2,245,903 |
| Cincinnati | 1,834,619 | 1,821,193 |
| Houston | 1,184,314 | 1,645,925 |
| Los Angeles | 3,264,593 | 1,940,181 |
| Montreal | 1,502,494 | 1,849,541 |
| New York | 2,761,601 | 2,000,772 |
| Philadelphia | 1,830,350 | 1,704,226 |
| Pittsburgh | 735,900 | 1,693,499 |
| St. Louis | 2,637,563 | 1,886,919 |
| San Diego | 2,210,352 | 1,994,464 |
| San Francisco | 818,697 | 1,854,169 |
| Total | 22,292,154 | 22,292,154 |

| AMERICAN LEAGUE | Home | Road |
|---|---|---|
| Baltimore | 2,132,387 | 1,657,415 |
| Boston | 1,786,633 | 1,823,604 |
| California | 2,567,427 | 1,793,633 |
| Chicago | 1,669,888 | 1,856,675 |
| Cleveland | 655,181 | 1,567,866 |
| Detroit | 2,286,609 | 1,985,780 |
| Kansas City | 2,162,717 | 1,728,806 |
| Milwaukee | 1,360,265 | 1,568,577 |
| Minnesota | 1,651,814 | 1,604,574 |
| New York | 2,214,587 | 2,366,662 |
| Oakland | 1,334,599 | 1,666,480 |
| Seattle | 1,128,696 | 1,470,569 |
| Texas | 1,112,497 | 1,599,306 |
| Toronto | 2,468,925 | 1,842,278 |
| Total | 24,532,225 | 24,532,225 |

# Maris' Death Saddens Baseball

**Roger Maris stunned the baseball world on October 1, 1961, by hitting his 61st homer to break Babe Ruth's single-season record.**

**By RON SMITH**

Roger Maris, the man who broke one of baseball's most revered records, Burleigh Grimes, a member of the Hall of Fame, and Bill Wambsganss, the light-hitting second baseman who turned the only unassisted triple play in World Series history, were the most notable baseball personalities who died in 1985. All three died within a nine-day period in December.

Few could have foreseen the heights to which Maris would rise as the 1961 season opened for the New York Yankees. The lefthanded slugger, who was coming off a 39-homer, 112-RBI 1960 season in which he was named the American League's Most Valuable Player, hit one home run in April and looked as if he would have trouble duplicating his previous season's statistics.

But he caught fire and hit 11 home runs in May, added 15 in June and reached the 35 mark by the All-Star break in mid-July. He finished July with 40 and entered September with 51, locked in a battle with teammate Mickey Mantle for the A.L. home run championship. But Mantle suffered a September injury and fell out of the race as Maris continued his relentless march toward former Yankee great Babe Ruth's major league record of 60 (set in 1927).

On September 20, the Yankees' 154th game (the number of games Ruth played in '27), Maris connected for No. 59 off Baltimore's Milt Pappas. On September 26, in New York's 158th game, he hit No. 60 off the Orioles' Jack Fisher.

Then came the season finale on Sunday, October 1, at Yankee Stadium. The Yankees, who already had wrapped up the A.L. championship, drew a modest crowd of 23,154 to see Maris go for the record. With the count two balls and no strikes in the fourth inning, Maris connected on a fastball from Boston's Tracy Stallard, a rookie righthander, for the only run in a 1-0 Yankee victory.

The historic homer landed in the 15th row of the right-field stands and was retrieved by Sal Durante, a 19-year-old

Brooklyn truck driver. For his role in retrieving the ball, Durante received a $5,000 reward offered by a restaurant owner in Sacramento, Calif.

"My going after the record started off as such a dream," Maris said years later. "I was living a fairy tale for a while. I never thought I'd ever get a chance to break such a record. Too bad it ended so badly."

Maris was referring to the controversy created by his historic chase and the aggravation, frustration and asterisk that accompanied his journey into baseball's record book.

Because of Maris' stormy relationship with the media, the pressure mounted and the ghost of Babe Ruth began to haunt his would-be successor. Maris resented the fact that he was not accorded the respect or star status that other Yankee stars received and by the end of the summer began to lose his hair. There were rumors of friction between Maris and Mantle (later denied by both parties), and Maris said years later, "The Yankees played a part, too. Let's not kid anybody. They wanted Mantle, not me, to break the record. Some of them even tried to rig the lineup so he would get a better opportunity at it than me."

Mantle, who finished the '61 season with 54 homers, making the "M & M Boys" the most prolific one-season home run combination in baseball history, said in his autobiography, "The Mick," that the "single greatest feat I ever saw was Roger Maris hitting his 61 home runs to break Babe Ruth's record."

Mantle, however, was only a minor part of the controversy. The biggest problem was created by Commissioner Ford C. Frick, a former sportswriter who once had been a ghost writer for Ruth. Frick declared in July of '61 that should Maris need more than 154 games to break the record, an asterisk would be placed beside his name in the record book to show that it had been accomplished in a 162-game season. Frick's ruling reflected the view of traditionalists that the feats of Ruth needed to be protected against such evils as watered-down talent through expansion and the longer schedule.

Maris, vilified by fans as well as the media, eventually asked to be traded. After the 1966 season, the Yankees obliged and Maris spent his last two major league seasons in contentment with the St. Louis Cardinals. Though his highest home run total in St. Louis was nine, he enjoyed the distinction of helping the Cardinals to two World Series appearances and one championship.

After his astonishing 1961 season, an embittered Maris said, "Sometimes I think it wasn't worth the aggravation. Maybe I wouldn't do it over again if I had the chance. I had so many people on my tail. People hate me for breaking Ruth's record—the press especially."

Maris' career began in Cleveland when, in 1957, he hit a modest 14 homers and drove in 51 runs. The next season he split time between Cleveland and Kansas City, hitting 28 homers and driving in 80. A 16-homer season with the A's preceded his trade to New York and his 1960 MVP season.

After his trade to the Cardinals in 1966, Maris vowed that he would never return to Yankee Stadium. He kept his promise for almost 10 years before relenting to attend an Old-Timers Day event. At the 1985 season opener, both Mantle and Maris appeared at Yankee Stadium and Maris' old uniform No. 9 was retired. Recalling the moment, Yankee Owner George Steinbrenner recalled, "The fans stood and applauded for a good 15 minutes. That did a lot for him."

Maris, who operated a beer distributorship in Gainesville, Fla., after his 1968 retirement, was diagnosed as having cancer in November 1983 when he went to a doctor for treatment of what he believed to be a nagging sinus problem. Tests prompted by discovery of swollen lymph glands indicated that Maris had been suffering from lymphatic cancer for about five years.

In June 1984, Maris said that the cancer was in remission. But he began to feel ill in August 1984 and his condition grew steadily worse. After undergoing biological therapy—an experimental cancer treatment—in late 1985, he entered a Houston hospital November 20 and died December 14 at age 51.

Grimes, nicknamed "Old Stubblebeard" because he did not shave on the days he pitched, was a tenacious righthander who won 270 games in a 19-year major league career in which he pitched for six different National League teams.

Grimes was the last of the legal spitballers in major league baseball. When the pitch was outlawed in 1920, Grimes was one of 17 avowed throwers of the pitch who were allowed to continue. Not a hard thrower, Grimes' other major weapon was an intensity that bordered on meanness. Lee Allen, the late baseball historian, summed up his pitching personality when he said that Grimes' "idea of an intentional pass was four brushback pitches."

Utilizing a decent fastball and a screwball to complement his spitter, Grimes joined the Brooklyn Dodgers in 1918 and enjoyed four 20-victory seasons before being traded to the New York Giants in 1927. After winning 19 for the Giants that season, he was traded back to Pittsburgh, the team with which he began his career in 1916, and enjoyed his best major league season, recording a 25-14 record, a 2.99 ERA and leading N.L. pitchers in several major categories.

That was Old Stubblebeard's last big season. After one more year in Pittsburgh, Grimes made stops at Boston, St. Louis and Chicago before returning one more time to Pittsburgh (early 1934) and finishing out his major league career at age 40 in New York (late 1934).

Grimes pitched in four World Series. He was 1-2 with Brooklyn in 1920, 0-2 with St. Louis in 1930, 2-0 for the Cardinals in 1931 and had no record in two appearances for the Cubs in 1932. Grimes was a better hitter than pitcher in World Series play, batting .316 in nine games. He enjoyed a career batting average of .248.

Grimes' battles on the mound were almost legendary. Anybody who dared dig in at the plate paid a stiff penalty. Brushback pitches were standard operating procedure and he once knocked down a batter who was standing in the on-deck circle, explaining that the hitter appeared too anxious to get to the plate to face him. Longstanding feuds were not uncommon and one of his most memorable was with New York's Frankie Frisch.

Frisch handled Grimes' brushback offerings better than most and was particularly adept at taking the righthander to the opposite field. Once Frisch beat out a bunt against Grimes and the pitcher, covering first, was badly spiked. He sat out several months with a damaged Achilles tendon.

Frisch had apologized for the incident ("I didn't mean to hurt him that bad"), but the first time he stepped in against a recovered Grimes, he was hit squarely between the shoulder blades by Grimes' first pitch.

"Dammit, Burleigh," Frisch shouted as he trotted painfully to first base, "I said I was sorry."

"Yes," Grimes replied, "but you didn't smile."

The two later became teammates in St. Louis and good friends.

After his 1934 retirement, Grimes remained active in baseball, managing Brooklyn for two seasons and then managing in the minors, coaching in the major leagues and finally scouting for the Yan-

**Burleigh Grimes won 270 games in 19 big-league seasons.**

kees and Orioles.

With major league totals of 270 victories against 212 defeats, a 3.53 ERA, 4,180 innings and 35 shutouts, Grimes was inducted into baseball's Hall of Fame in 1964. He died at age 92 at his home in Clear Lake, Wis.,on December 6 after a long battle with cancer.

Wambsganss, better known as Wamby to intimidated typesetters and sportswriters, was an average player who made it to the record books with one memorable feat. That occurred in Game 5 of the 1920 World Series when Wambsganss and the Cleveland Indians were matched against the Brooklyn Dodgers and, ironically, ace righthander Burleigh Grimes.

The fifth inning of that game began with Brooklyn's Pete Kilduff and Otto Miller hitting singles. With the runners at first and second, Clarence Mitchell, a relief pitcher who had replaced Grimes, lined Indians pitcher Jim Bagby's offering to a leaping Wambsganss at second base. He stepped on second to double up Kilduff and then tagged a surprised Miller, who had broken for second.

**Bill Wambsganss pulled off the only unassisted triple play in World Series history.**

"I intended to throw to first to get Miller," Wambsganss said later, "but when I saw him so near I instinctively tagged him." The Indians won the game, 8-1, and the Series, five games to two. Grimes had entered the record book earlier in the game by surrendering the first grand slam in Series history (to Elmer Smith in the first inning) and the first home run to a pitcher (Bagby).

Wambsganss played in the major leagues from 1914 to 1926, all but three of those seasons as the regular second baseman for the Indians. He later played for the Boston Red Sox and Philadelphia A's while compiling a .259 average in 1,492 major league games.

He later managed in the minor leagues (at Springfield, Ill., and Fort Wayne, Ind.) before returning to the Cleveland suburb of Lakewood in 1934 to become a salesman for a hardware manufacturer.

Wambsganss, asked to retell the triple-play tale innumerable times, usually accommodated the request, contending that Miller, who was bearing down on second base, thought Mitchell's liner had gone through the infield for a hit.

"Of course, it was just luck," Wambsganss said. "Somebody, someday, who happens to be in just the right spot, will do it again. I remember (Miller) asked when I tagged him, 'where did you get the ball?' He thought Tris Speaker had thrown it in from center."

Wambsganss was 91 when he died at a Lakewood hospital while suffering from heart failure and complications.

Among the other baseball personalities who died in 1985 were Arthur C. Allyn, former owner of the Chicago White Sox; Bob Prince, the colorful play-by-play broadcaster who thrilled Pittsburgh fans for 28 years; Smoky Joe Wood, a right-hander who carved out a 34-5 record for the Boston Red Sox in 1912; Riggs Stephenson, a career .336 hitter and standout defensive outfielder for the Chicago Cubs in the 1920s and '30s; George Uhle, a 200-game winner in the 1920s and '30s who is credited with being the first pitcher to perfect a slider; Bob Scheffing, a former catcher, coach, manager, scout, broadcaster, farm director and general manager during his 50-year association with major league baseball; Bob Nieman, the only player in major league history to hit home runs in his first two big-league at-bats; Ray Jablonski, the National League's Rookie of the Year in 1953 for the St. Louis Cardinals; Bill Kunkel, a former major league pitcher and umpire; Dick Wakefield, a one-year sensation with the Detroit Tigers in 1941 after signing a hefty bonus contract; Sam West, a standout defensive outfielder who batted over .300 seven times in the 1920s and '30s; and Ralph (Lefty) Mellix, a pitcher for 43 years in the Old Negro leagues.

An alphabetical list of baseball deaths in 1985 follows:

**Arthur C. Allyn,** 71, a multimillionaire Chicago businessman who was owner and president of the Chicago White Sox from 1962-1969, at Sarasota, Fla., on March 22 after a long illness; Allyn was the son of the late Arthur C. Allyn Sr., who founded the family's investment firm and was a partner with Bill Veeck in the latter's association with the St. Louis, Cleveland and Chicago baseball operations; after Arthur Sr.'s death in 1959, Allyn and his late brother, John, became principal owners of the White Sox in 1961 and a year later, the Artnell Co., Allyn's widely diversified investment firm, acquired 100 percent of the ball club from Veeck; always outspoken and never a popular figure in Chicago, Allyn decided to sell his interest in the White Sox in 1969 so he could go into semi-retirement in Florida.

**Curt Barclay,** 53, a righthanded pitcher who appeared in 44 games for the New York and San Francisco Giants in the late 1950s, of cancer at Missoula, Mont., on March 25; after turning down an offer from the National Basketball Association's Boston Celtics to sign a contract with the Giants, Barclay spent two years in military service and 2½ years in the minors before joining the Giants in 1957, the team's final campaign in New York; posted his best numbers in '57, a 9-9 record and 3.44 earned-run average before the arm problems that eventually would end his career showed up; pitched in only six games with a 1-0 record in 1958, the Giants' first season in San Francisco, and ⅓ of an inning in 1959 before ending his baseball career at age 28.

**Lester Rowland (Les) Bell,** 84, a .325 hitter for the 1926 champion St. Louis Cardinals, of cancer, at Hershey, Pa., on December 26; a righthanded hitter who played parts of five seasons with the Cardinals and two each with the Boston Braves and Chicago Cubs; joined the Cardinals in 1924 as a shortstop and was converted to third by Manager Branch Rickey; enjoyed his best season for the '26 Cards, hitting .325 with 17 homers and 100 RBIs; after being traded to Boston, he finished his career in 1931 with the Cubs, sporting a lifetime .290 average with 66 homers and 509 RBIs; later managed at Harrisburg, Ottawa, Lincoln, Savannah and Springfield, Mass.; smashed three homers and a triple in a 1928 game for 15 total bases, a mark that still ranks fifth on the all-time list.

**John G. Bero,** 63, an infielder for the Detroit Tigers and St. Louis Browns during a two-year major league career, at Gardena, Calif., on May 11; Bero batted .201 in his 65-game big-league stay.

**Joseph A. Bird,** 82, a former minor league catcher and manager who scouted for the Philadelphia Phillies, Washington Senators and Houston Astros from 1952-62, at Allentown, Pa., on March 7; played eight minor league seasons in the 1920s and early 1930s, then managed several clubs, including Lexington, Trenton and Allentown.

**Roger Birtwell,** 84, a Boston Globe baseball writer for 30 years prior to his retirement in 1972, at Phoenix on October 16; the former New York sportswriter also was a longtime correspondent for The Sporting News.

**Ossie Bluege,** 84, a player, coach, manager, farm director and board member of the Washington Senators and their successors, the Minnesota Twins, for nearly half a century, at Edina, Minn., on October 15; an excellent defensive third baseman with quick hands and a strong arm, Bluege was purchased by the Senators in 1921 and spent 18 seasons in Washington's infield before retiring as a first baseman at age 39 in 1939; compiled a .272 career average in 1,867 games and was known as a rough-and-tumble player who helped the Senators win American League pennants in 1924, '25 and '33, the only titles in the franchise's Washington history; coached for three seasons under Manager Bucky Harris, then succeeded Harris in 1943 and compiled a 375-394 record and two second-place finishes in five seasons; became farm director in 1948 and was responsible for signing Hall of Famer Harmon Killebrew to the first bonus contract ($10,000) ever tendered by the Senators; when Twins Owner Clark Griffith died in 1955 and was succeeded by his son, Calvin, Bluege became the team's controller.

**John J. Broaca,** 75, a scholarly righthander signed off the Yale University campus in 1933 by the New York Yankees, at Lawrence, Mass., on May 18; compiled a 44-29 record over five seasons in a career clouded by unexplained disappearances from the Yankees; after spending less than a year in the minors, Broaca broke in spectacularly with the Yankees in 1934, pitching a three-hitter and a one-hitter in his first two starts; finished 15-7 in 1935 and was 12-7 in 1936 when he left the team for a period without explanation; followed the same pattern in 1937, compiling a 1-4 record and leaving the team before the Yankees' appearance in the World Series; remained on the suspended list in 1938 and pitched in 22 games for Cleveland in 1939, compiling a 4-2 record in a relief role.

**Edmund S. (Big Ed) Browalski,** 66, longtime writer for the Polish Daily News, official scorer at Tiger Stadium and former chairman of the Detroit chapter of the Baseball Writers' Association of America, of a heart attack at Detroit on January 3.

**Guy T. Bush,** 83, a righthanded pitcher who recorded a 176-136 record over 17 major league seasons, mostly with the Chicago Cubs, at Shannon, Miss., on July 2; dubbed the Mississippi Mudcat, Bush came off his father's cotton plantation in 1923 and joined the Cubs the same year; didn't blossom, however, until 1926 when he joined the Cubs rotation and won 13 games; reached the peak of his career in the early 1930s when he recorded consecutive 16, 19, 20 and 18-victory seasons; after being traded to Pittsburgh following the 1934 season, Bush did not enjoy another winning campaign; appeared in two World Series with the Cubs, winning one game in the 1929 Series against the Philadelphia A's and losing his only decision in the 1932 Series against the Yankees; known around trivia circles as the pitcher who, in 1935 while pitching in relief for the Pirates, surrendered Babe Ruth's final two career home runs.

**Harry G. Byrd,** 60, the Philadelphia A's 1952 Rookie of the Year who compiled a 46-54 record over seven major league seasons, at Darlington, S.C., on May 14; pitched all or parts of his seven seasons with the A's, New York Yankees, Baltimore Orioles, Chicago White Sox and Detroit Tigers between 1950 and 1957; Bush's best major league season was his rookie campaign when he compiled a 15-15 mark; was part of an 11-man trade in 1953 and a 17-player deal in 1954.

**Kendall F. Chase,** 71, an erratic lefthander who compiled a 53-84 record over eight major league seasons, most of them with perennial American League also-ran Washington, at Oneonta, N.Y., on January 16; his best seasons were 1939 and 1940, when he finished 10-19 and 15-17, respectively, with earned-run averages of 3.80 and 3.23; also led the A.L. by walking 143 batters in 1940; after slipping to 6-18 with a 5.08 ERA in 1941, Chase was traded to the Boston Red Sox; was traded the next season to the New York Giants, where he finished his career.

**Wilford C. (Lefty) Conway,** 69, a groundskeeper who spent nearly 50 years maintaining playing fields for five major league baseball teams, at Sarasota, Fla., on April 9; during his career, Conway worked for the Detroit Tigers, Houston Astros, St. Louis Cardinals, Atlanta Braves and Baltimore Orioles.

**John R. (Johnny Bob) Dixon,** 86, a pitcher with four Negro league teams from 1928-34 who barnstormed with the Cuban Red Sox in the 1930s, at Massillon, O., on February 3; the Chattanooga, Tenn., native pitched for the Cleveland Tigers, Detroit Stars, Cleveland Giants and Cleveland Red Sox; spent two seasons with the Ethiopian Clowns, a traveling comedy team, before retiring from baseball in 1940.

**Richard F. (Dick) Drott,** 49, a rookie pitching sensation for the Chicago Cubs in 1957, of stomach cancer at Glendale Heights, Ill., on August 16; recorded a 15-11 record in his rookie campaign but then won only 12 more games in the remaining six seasons of his major league career; after a 7-11 season in 1958 for a weak Cubs team, the righthander developed arm problems; after suffering through three more injury-plagued seasons in Chicago, Drott was selected by the Houston Colt 45s in the expansion draft that followed the 1961 season; his 3-12 mark in Houston left him with a career record of 27-46.

**Jake Early,** 70, a top-flight defensive catcher who excelled at handling knuckleball pitchers in the 1940s, at Melbourne, Fla., on May 31; the North Carolina native possessed the best throwing arm among catchers in the American League during his prime and was highly valued by the Washington Senators, with whom he spent eight of his nine major league seasons, because of his ability to handle knuckleballers Dutch Leonard, Johnny Niggeling, Roger Wolff and Mickey Haefner; known primarily for his incessant chattering, which constantly distracted batters and on more than one occasion caused them to double over with laughter; after two years of combat duty in World War II, he failed to regain his batting stroke and suffered through two off seasons with the Senators and St. Louis Browns before returning to Washington for the final two years of his career; finished with a career .241 average.

**Walter C. (Doc) Eberhardt,** 82, a widely known authority on physical fitness who conducted exercise programs in spring training for the St. Louis Cardinals and other teams, of a heart attack at St. Louis on January 23; the German-born Eberhardt was a professor of physical education at St. Louis University from 1927 until his retirement in 1971; hosted a radio exercise program from 1929 to 1971, making it the longest-running radio show in the country; began involvement with baseball in the winter of 1959-60 when, at the request of future Hall of Famer Stan Musial, began coordinating the physical conditioning program for the Cardinals; Eberhardt made annual spring-training trips to St. Petersburg, Fla., to oversee the Cardinals' conditioning from 1960 to 1980; also worked briefly with the Philadelphia Phillies and Cincinnati Reds.

**Clarence (Lefty) Fieber,** 71, a lefthanded pitcher who was 1-0 during his one-year stay with the 1932 Chicago White Sox, at Redwood City, Calif., on August 20; compiled a 1.69 earned-run average in his three-game career.

**Harold K. George,** 82, a bowling and baseball writer for more than 20 years before becoming assistant farm director for the Chicago Cubs during World War II and later vice president of the old Western League, at Juneau, Alaska, on March 15; began his sportswriting career in Omaha in 1921, joined the Chicago Times in 1931 and moved to the Chicago American three years later; took the Cubs job in 1944 and later served five years as vice president of the Cubs' Des Moines farm team before accepting his Western League position in 1952.

**Joe C. Glenn,** 76, the backup catcher for the New York Yankees in the 1930s who was behind the plate for the last game pitched by Babe Ruth, at Tunkhannock, Pa., on May 6; born Joseph Charles Guzensky, Glenn served as a caddy for Yankee catchers, primarily Hall of Famer Bill Dickey, between 1932 and 1938, finishing his 248-game major league career with a .252 average; caught for Ruth in the season-closing game of 1933, when the Yankees let the veteran return to the mound against his original team, the Boston Red Sox; Glenn closed his career with the St. Louis Browns in 1939 and the Red Sox in 1940.

**Harold E. (Hal) Goodnough,** 82, a scout and front-office executive for the old Boston and Milwaukee Braves, at Wellesley, Mass., on September 28; after briefly playing minor league baseball and teaching and coaching at a Wellesley high school, Goodnough began scouting for the Braves in New England in 1946; became head of the Braves' promotions department when the club moved to Milwaukee in 1953 and generally was regarded as one of baseball's best goodwill ambassadors and speechmakers.

**William F. Goodrich,** former publicity director for the New York Giants baseball team and prior to that a baseball writer for the old Brooklyn Eagle, at Brooklyn, N.Y.

**James M. (Jim) Gorey,** 65, former public address announcer for the New York Giants at the old Polo Grounds, on January 2.

**James R. Grant,** 91, a lefthander who appeared in the first night game in Organized Baseball history, of a respiratory ailment at Des Moines on November 30; appeared in two major league games for the Philadelphia Phillies in 1923;

pitched for the Des Moines Demons on May 2, 1930, in the precedent-setting night game.

**Burleigh A. (Old Stubblebeard) Grimes,** 92, the last of the legal spitballers, a 270-game major league winner and a member of baseball's Hall of Fame, of cancer at Clear Lake, Wis., on December 6; a righthander who spent 19 seasons in the major leagues and pitched for six National League teams, Grimes recorded four 20-plus victory seasons for the Brooklyn Dodgers between 1918 and 1926 and another in 1928 for the Pittsburgh Pirates; one of 17 avowed spitballers who were allowed to continue loading up the baseball after the pitch was outlawed in 1920; known for his competitive drive and penchant for moving opposing hitters off the plate; began his career with the Pirates, was traded to the Dodgers in 1918, to the New York Giants in 1927 and back to the Pirates in 1928; later pitched for the Boston Braves, the St. Louis Cardinals and the Chicago Cubs; compiled a career record of 270-212 for a .560 winning percentage, a 3.53 earned-run average and 35 shutouts; compiled a 3-4 record in four World Series with a .316 batting mark; compiled a .248 career batting average; after retiring in 1934, managed Brooklyn for two years and then managed another decade in the minor leagues; later coached for the Dodgers and scouted for the New York Yankees and Baltimore Orioles.

**Al Harper,** 71, a professional baseball scout for more than 35 years, at Bayside, N.Y., on September 16; spent the major portion of his career scouting for the Boston Red Sox but worked in later years for the New York Mets, Montreal Expos, St. Louis Cardinals and Atlanta Braves; responsible for signing such major leaguers as Ben Oglivie, Lee Mazzilli, Joe Hesketh and Mike Stenhouse.

**Fred A. Hawn,** 78, a manager and scout in the St. Louis Cardinals organization for more than 30 years, at Fayetteville, Ark., on August 23; a former minor league catcher, Hawn managed Fayetteville and New Iberia teams for St. Louis prior to World War II, then managed at Johnson City for one season before he began scouting Oklahoma, Texas and his native Arkansas on a full-time basis in 1945; signed Lindy and Von McDaniel, Wally Moon and Hal Smith to their first professional contracts.

**Robert W. Henderson,** 96, an English-born sports historian and New York City librarian who was primarily responsible for debunking the myth that baseball was an American game invented by Civil War Gen. Abner Doubleday, at Hartford, Conn., on August 18; a lifelong scholar and researcher who rose to chief of the main reading room at the New York City Public Library, Henderson began researching the origins of baseball when the game's officials prepared to observe baseball's 100th anniversary in conjunction with the opening of the Baseball Hall of Fame in Cooperstown, N.Y.; published a treatise that same year containing research that proved that Doubleday never in his life set foot in Cooperstown, much less invented the game there in 1839, as was the popular and officially recognized conception; that treatise and later documented evidence on the origins of the game eventually were accepted, reluctantly, by baseball officials and historians.

**Bruce F. Henry,** 81, traveling secretary for the New York Yankees during the 1960s and active as a baseball promoter and business manager from 1947 until his retirement, at Fort Lauderdale, Fla., on March 15; the New Jersey native began his front-office career as a publicist with the old Newark Bears in 1947 and later was associated with Yankees minor league operations as general manager of the Amsterdam (N.Y.) and Richmond clubs; served one year as stadium manager during his 11 seasons with the Yankees.

**Kirby Higbe,** 70, a high-living non-conformist who in 1941 helped lead the Brooklyn Dodgers to their first pennant in 21 years, at his native Columbia, S.C., on May 6; a high school dropout who signed with Pittsburgh at age 16, Higbe reached the major leagues with the Chicago Cubs in 1937 and went on to pitch for five National League teams, compiling a career record of 118-101 over 12 seasons; best record came in '41 when he and teammate Whitlow Wyatt tied for the N.L. lead with 22 victories for the league-champion Dodgers; inducted into the Army midway through World War II (1943) and rejoined the Dodgers during the 1946 campaign; was traded to Pittsburgh after that season, primarily because of his adamant opposition to the addition of Jackie Robinson to the team; never a big winner again, Higbe ended his major league career in 1950 with the New York Giants.

**Ray Jablonski,** 58, a third baseman who was the St. Louis Cardinals' Rookie of the Year in 1953, of kidney failure at Chicago on November 25; spent all or parts of eight seasons with five major league clubs after a rookie campaign in which he hit .268 with 21 home runs and 112 runs batted in; committed 27 errors in 1953, a problem that minimized his effectiveness and eventually led to the end of a promising career; started at third base for the 1954 National League All-Star team and finished that season batting .296 with 104 RBIs; traded to Cincinnati during the off-season and the Reds, disenchanted with his fielding, shipped him to the minors midway through the 1955 season; played in 130 games with the Reds in 1956 but was traded to the Chicago Cubs after the season; traded to the New York Giants before the 1957 season opened and batted only 535 times over the next two campaigns; traded back to the Cardinals in 1959, was sold to the Kansas City A's late that season and spent most of 1960 in the minors before being called up by the A's late in the season; served as player-coach for Atlanta Braves in 1964 before retiring.

**Frederic A. Johnson,** 90, the first attorney to challenge baseball's reserve clause on the grounds that it violated federal antitrust laws, at New York on February 7; represented former New York Giants outfielder Danny Gardella, one of a number of major leaguers who had been suspended for five years by Commissioner Happy Chandler for jumping to the Mexican League in 1946; case was dismissed by a lower court but the decision was reversed by a higher court and the matter eventually reached the Supreme Court docket; suit was dropped in 1949 when Organized Baseball made an out-of-court settlement and Chandler reinstated the suspended players the same year.

**Sylvester W. (Syl) Johnson,** 84, an injury-plagued righthander who appeared in 542 major league games for four teams over a 19-year period, at Portland, Ore., on February 20; purchased by the Detroit Tigers in 1921, Johnson's major league debut was delayed when he was struck on the hand by a line drive during spring training in 1922, fracturing three bones; in subsequent seasons in Detroit and St. Louis, he suffered a sinus infection and a torn muscle in his right elbow, was struck in the face by a line drive, fracturing his cheekbone in eight places, suffered a fractured big toe when hit by a line drive and suffered two fractured ribs when struck by another line drive; spent a year in the minor leagues before returning to St. Louis in 1928 to begin an injury-free stretch of six seasons in which he compiled a 52-47 record; traded to Cincinnati in 1934 and then sent to Philadelphia later that same year; ended his major league career with the Phillies in 1940 after compiling a 112-117 career record; pitched five more seasons in the Pacific Coast

League and later scouted for the New York Yankees, Brooklyn Dodgers and Los Angeles Dodgers.

**John E. Kimble,** 80, a righthander who pitched in the Brooklyn Dodgers, New York Yankees and Philadelphia Phillies organizations during a 15-year minor league career in the 1930s and '40s, at Drexel Hills, Pa., on April 7; twice was placed on the Brooklyn roster during the regular season but never appeared in a major league game.

**Theodore O. (Ted) Kleinhans,** 86, a lefthanded pitcher who compiled a 4-9 record in parts of four seasons with three major league clubs in the mid-1930s, at Redington Beach, Fla., on July 24; appeared in 56 games for the Philadelphia Phillies, Cincinnati Reds and New York Yankees, all but 12 in relief.

**Edward J. Kolo,** 58, a former minor league catcher and later a scout for the Cincinnati Reds, of cancer at Auburn, N.Y., on January 26.

**William G. (Bill) Kunkel,** 48, a former American League pitcher and umpire who fought a courageous five-year battle with cancer, at Leonardo, N.J., on May 3; a righthanded reliever, Kunkel played professional baseball for 11 years, rising briefly to the major leagues with the Kansas City A's in 1961-62 and the New York Yankees in 1963, compiling a 6-6 record in 89 appearances; turned to umpiring in 1966, breaking in with the Florida State League and joining the A.L. staff four years later; umpired in the 1974 and 1980 World Series, the 1972 and 1977 All-Star Games and the 1971, '75, '78 and '82 A.L. Championship Series; underwent surgery on two separate occasions to treat cancer and returned to umpiring both times; also served as a referee for the National Basketball Association and the now-defunct American Basketball Association; served for 20 years as a college basketball official, primarily for games in the Atlantic Coast Conference and Eastern College Athletic Conference.

**Paul D. Larson,** 46, an Iowa businessman who was vice president of the Midwest League's Central Division and past president of the Clinton Giants, at Clinton, Ia., on September 11; named Midwest League's executive of the year in 1982.

**Roy E. Lee,** 68, a lefthander who pitched in three games and compiled an 0-2 record with the New York Giants at the end of the 1945 season, at St. Louis on November 11; served as baseball coach at St. Louis University and Southern Illinois University-Edwardsville during the 1960s and '70s.

**Johnny Lindell,** 68, a 6-foot-5 pitcher-turned-outfielder who enjoyed several productive years with the New York Yankees during World War II, of lung cancer at Newport Beach, Calif., on August 27; broke in as a pitcher-outfielder at Joplin in 1936 and worked his way up through the Yankees chain, joining the club in 1942 after a 23-4 season with Newark; strapped for able outfielders because of the war, Yankee Manager Joe McCarthy made Lindell his regular right fielder and inserted him in the cleanup spot in the batting order; tied for the American League lead in triples in 1943 and '44, driving in 103 runs the latter season while batting .300 and leading the league in total bases; spent six months in military service in 1945 and his playing time was reduced when he returned to the Yankees in 1946; batted .317 in 1948, but appeared in only 88 games; acquired on waivers by the St. Louis Cardinals in 1950 and later was sent to the minors; at his request, Cardinals sold Lindell to Hollywood of the Pacific Coast League and he began a comeback as a knuckleball pitcher; named PCL's most valuable player in 1952 when he pitched 26 complete games and recorded a 24-9 record; was given a chance by the Pirates in 1953, but suffered through a 5-16 season and was sent to Philadelphia, where he ended his career; compiled a career batting average of .273 over 12 major league seasons and played in three World Series with the Yankees, hitting .324; finished his career with an 8-18 pitching mark.

**Ramon Lora,** 30, a former catcher in the Philadelphia and Toronto farm systems, in an automobile accident near Montecristi, Dominican Republic, on October 10; played last four seasons in the Mexican League.

**Ernest F. (Dutch) Lorbeer,** 84, a former minor league catcher, manager and executive for the Beaumont club of the Texas League in the 1930s, at Beaumont on October 29; later scouted for the Detroit Tigers, Cincinnati Reds and St. Louis Cardinals.

**Roy Luebbe,** 84, a well-traveled minor league catcher who played in eight 1925 games for the New York Yankees, at Omaha on August 21; made more than a dozen stops along the minor league trail; traded in 1924 with a teammate by the president of Omaha's Western League club for a private airplane; deal was voided and Luebbe was traded to the Yankees organization; spent the final weeks of the next season in New York going hitless in 15 at-bats.

**Dave Madison,** 64, a righthander who pitched for three major league clubs in the 1950s, of heart disease at Macon, Miss., on December 8; compiled an 8-7 major league record with the New York Yankees, St. Louis Browns and Detroit Tigers in 1950, '52 and '53; played and managed in the minors in 1954 and '55; scouted for the Yankees (1956-58), Baltimore (1965-67), Oakland (1968-74) and the New York Mets, for whom he had been a special-assignment scout since 1974.

**Roger Eugene Maris,** 51, the man who broke Babe Ruth's one-season home run record in 1961, of cancer at Houston on December 14; began his major league career in 1957 with the Cleveland Indians, hitting 14 homers and showing only a glimpse of the power-hitting form that later would vault him into baseball's record books; spent his next two seasons with Cleveland and Kansas City before a late 1959 trade to the New York Yankees; enjoyed his first big season with the Yankees in 1960, hitting 39 home runs, driving in 112 runs and winning the American League Most Valuable Player award; the Yankee right fielder began the 1961 season slowly, hitting only one home run in April, but had compiled 35 by the All-Star break in mid-July and 51 by the end of August; hit homer No. 59 in the Yankees' 154th game on September 20, No. 60 in the Yanks' 158th game on September 26 and then connected for his record-breaking 61st in the team's final regular-season game off Boston righthander Tracy Stallard; controversy plagued the lefthanded slugger as traditionalists, protective of the legendary Ruth's slugging accomplishments, downplayed Maris' feat because it had occurred over a 162-game schedule (Ruth hit his 60 in 154 games); Commissioner Ford Frick declared that because of the schedule differences, Maris' entry into the record book would have to be accompanied by an asterisk; after his second straight MVP season, an embittered Maris played five more years in New York and finally was granted his request to be traded; played two more seasons with St. Louis, helping the Cardinals to two World Series appearances (1967 and '68) and one championship; finished his career with a .260 lifetime average, 275 home runs and 851 RBIs; was only a .217 hitter in seven World Series with six homers and 18 RBIs.

**Cloy M. (Monk) Mattox,** 82, a catcher who appeared in three games for the 1929 World Series-champion Philadelphia Athletics, at Bassett, Va., on August 3; managed one hit in six at-bats for the A's and then played five seasons of minor league ball before calling it quits; one of five baseball-playing brothers, one of whom, Jim, also a catcher, appeared in 51 games for the Pittsburgh Pirates in the 1922 and '23 seasons.

**Archie (Hap) McKain,** 74, a lefthander who compiled a 26-21 record, mostly in relief, with three American League clubs between 1937 and 1943, at Salina, Kan., on May 21; compiled an 8-8 record with the Boston Red Sox in 1937 and a 5-0 mark in 1940 for the Detroit Tigers; finished his career in 1943 for the St. Louis Browns, choosing to retire rather than honor a trade to the Brooklyn Dodgers.

**Peter J. McNearney,** 82, who with his late brother, Jim, owned and operated the Schenectady, N.Y., franchise in the Canadian-American League in the 1940s and the Eastern League in the 1950s, at Schenectady on April 14; obtained a working agreement with the Philadelphia Phillies in 1946 and built McNearney Stadium; entered his franchise in the Eastern League in 1951.

**Ralph (Lefty) Mellix,** 88, a pitcher in the old Negro leagues for 43 years with at least 12 different clubs, at Pittsburgh on March 23; made his professional debut in 1915 at age 18 for the American Giants, throwing a one-hitter and striking out 17; played for the Homestead Grays, Pittsburgh Crawfords, Brooklyn Brown Dodgers, Atlantic City Bacharachs and Sell Hall's Cuban X Giants, among others; estimated that he appeared in 1,500 games as a pitcher, often playing first base when he was not on the mound; quit pitching competitively at age 55, laying claim to a reported nine league no-hitters.

**John L. Mokan,** 89, an outfielder with the Pittsburgh Pirates and Philadelphia Phillies between 1921 and 1927, at Buffalo on February 10; stood 5-foot-8 and weighed only 165 pounds; made his major league debut with the Pirates at the end of the 1921 season and was traded to the Phillies in 1922; batted .313 and hit 10 home runs in 113 games for the Phillies in 1923 and batted .303 in 127 games in 1926; traded to the St. Louis Cardinals in 1928 and was sent to the minors, resulting in his retirement in 1929; finished his 582-game major league career with a .291 average.

**Van Lingo Mungo,** 74, a hard-throwing, hard-living righthander noted for his off-the-field exploits and colorful name, at Pageland, S.C., on February 12; brought a blazing fastball and a high-kick delivery to Brooklyn in 1931 and proceeded to compile a 120-115 record over the next 14 seasons, 11 with the Dodgers and the final three with the New York Giants; never won 20 games in one season, though twice he came close with weak Brooklyn clubs; recorded a memorable victory in 1934 when he beat the cross-town rival Giants on the final weekend of the season, helping to knock them out of the pennant race; led the National League in bases on balls (118) and strikeouts (238) in 1936; injured his arm in the 1937 All-Star Game and suffered through 4-11 and 4-5 seasons before undergoing arm surgery in 1940; after an off-the-field incident in Cuba in the spring of 1941, Mungo was traded to the Giants; using guile and an assortment of breaking pitches to replace his once-vaunted fastball, he finished his major league career with a flourish, recording a 14-7 record in 1945; noted as the losing pitcher in the 1934 All-Star Game, in which N.L. teammate Carl Hubbell achieved fame by striking out Babe Ruth, Jimmy Foxx, Lou Gehrig, Al Simmons and Joe Cronin in succession.

**Robert C. (Bob) Nieman,** 58, the only player in history to hit home runs in his first two major league at-bats, of a heart attack at Corona, Calif., on March 10; broke in with the St. Louis Browns near the end of the 1951 season by hitting home runs at Fenway Park off Boston lefthander Mickey McDermott in his first two at-bats, a record that never has been equaled; became the Browns' regular left fielder in 1952 and responded by hitting .289 while driving in a career-high 74 runs; was traded to Detroit in 1953, to the Chicago White Sox in 1955 and then to Baltimore early in the 1956 season, in which he hit .322 in 114 games while winning the regular left-field job; later major league stops were with the St. Louis Cardinals, Cleveland Indians and San Francisco, where he ended his major league career in 1962 with a pennant winner; finished with a .295 career batting average; played one season in Japan before managing one season at Charleston, W. Va., in 1964; later scouted for the Indians, Los Angeles Dodgers, Oakland A's, the White Sox and the New York Yankees.

**Pat O'Connor,** 75, a longtime scout in the Northwest for the Pittsburgh Pirates, Chicago Cubs and Cincinnati Reds, at Caldwell, Idaho, on January 14.

**James Kenneth (Ken) O'Dea,** 72, a backup catcher and lefthanded pinch-hitting specialist for four National League teams between 1935 and 1946, at Lima, N.Y., on December 17; played backup roles to regular catchers Gabby Hartnett with the Chicago Cubs, Harry Danning with the New York Giants and Walker Cooper with the St. Louis Cardinals before finishing his 12-year career with the Boston Braves in 1946; compiled a .255 career batting average but hit a lofty .462 in 10 World Series Games with the Cubs and Cardinals.

**Hisel D. Patrick,** 59, a righthander who pitched 14 minor league seasons in the 1940s and '50s, most of them as a St. Louis Cardinals farmhand, at Paris, Ky., on February 23.

**Isaac O. (Ike) Pearson,** 67, a righthanded pitcher for the Philadelphia Phillies and Chicago White Sox in the 1940s after his graduation from the University of Mississippi, at Sarasota, Fla.; compiled a 13-50 major league record between 1939 and 1948, missing four years when he served for the Marine Corps in World War II.

**Grover D. Powell,** 44, whose only major league victory was a 1963 shutout over the Philadelphia Phillies, of Leukemia at Raleigh, N.C., on May 21; pitched 50 innings, mostly in relief, for the second-year New York Mets, compiling a 1-1 record and 2.72 earned-run average; suffered a serious arm injury the following winter while pitching in the Venezuelan League and never returned to the majors.

**Bob Prince,** 68, a colorful sports announcer who enjoyed a 28-year broadcasting career in Pittsburgh, of cancer at Pittsburgh on June 10; turned to broadcasting in 1941 and joined the Pirates' broadcasting team in 1947 as the No. 2 man behind Rosey Rowswell, Pittsburgh's play-by-play man for 19 seasons before his death in 1955; succeeded Rowswell and developed a colorful style and language that, combined with his 110 percent homerism for his beloved Pirates, made him one of the most popular figures in Pittsburgh; known for such phrases as "It's in the gap," "They're gonna run like bugs on a rug," and "You can kiss it goodbye" (a Pirates' home run); known for his outlandish wardrobe (he owned 60 colorful sports jackets), his non-conformist outlook on life (he often would strip to his skivvies while broadcasting a game on a hot day) and his crazy, devil-may-care attitude (he once jumped out of a third-floor St. Louis hotel window into a swimming pool to win a wager); also known for his benevolence in supporting charities; after differences with executives at Westinghouse Corp., owner of the Pirates flagship station KDKA, Prince made critical on-air comments that led to his dismissal after the 1975 season; Prince supporters staged a parade and protest, but the Pirates ownership supported the decision and the furor eventually died down; joined the Houston Astros broadcast team and became play-by-play man on ABC Monday Night baseball telecasts, but left those jobs after one year; returned to describing Pirates action in 1984 as chief announcer for Home Sports Entertainment, a now-defunct cable TV operation; was rehired in early 1985 by KDKA, but surgery to remove cancerous tumors from inside his mouth delayed his return; teamed with Joe Tucker to describe Steelers football for 14 years; also broadcast hockey and boxing during a career that spanned five decades.

**Robert B. (Bob) Scheffing,** 70, a former catcher, coach, manager, scout, broadcaster, farm director and general manager during his 50-year association with professional baseball, at Scottsdale, Ariz., on October 26; the St. Louis native broke in with the Cardinals organization in 1935 and played eight major league seasons, most with the Chicago Cubs, between 1941 and '51, with time out while serving with the Navy during World War II; finished his 517-game career with a .263 average; coached for the St. Louis Browns in 1952 and '53 and the Cubs in '54; managed the Cubs in 1957, '58 and '59 and the Detroit Tigers in 1961, '62 and '63; named Manager of the Year by both wire services after the 1961 Tigers won 101 games, though they still finished well behind the first-place Yankees; broadcast Tigers games in 1964 and scouted for the Tigers in 1965; became the New York Mets director of player development in 1966 and took over the team's general manager duties in 1970; served as Mets special consultant during his retirement years in Scottsdale.

**Wes Schulmerich,** 83, an outfielder for the Boston Braves, Philadelphia Phillies and Cincinnati Reds from 1931 through 1934, of cancer at Corvallis, Ore., on June 26; the righthanded batter compiled a .289 average in 429 major league games; hit .309 for Boston as a rookie in 1931 and had a .318 mark for the Braves and Phillies in 1933; played for Portland of the Pacific Coast League and managed at Lewiston, Idaho, after leaving the majors.

**Al Schuss,** 81, who did play-by-play broadcasts of San Diego Padres games from 1949-68 while the club was a member of the Pacific Coast League, at Santee, Calif., on May 13; early work included a stint as a baseball announcer for CBS radio in Chicago, five years as a play-by-play announcer in Milwaukee and two years teaming with Red Barber on Brooklyn Dodgers broadcasts.

**Hollis (Bud) Sheely,** 64, a catcher who appeared in 101 games for the Chicago White Sox from 1951 to 1953, at Sacramento, Calif., on October 17; spent most of his career in the minors, enjoying his greatest success in the Western International League where he hit .317 with 108 RBIs in 1948 for Spokane and .348 with 117 RBIs in 1949 for Vancouver; a beanball ended his career in 1955; son of former first baseman Earl (Whitey) Sheely, who played nine major league seasons (seven with the White Sox) between 1921 and 1931 and compiled a career .300 average.

**Clyde H. (Lefty) Smoll,** 71, a lefthanded pitcher who compiled a 2-8 record in 33 games for the 1940 Philadelphia Phillies, at Quakertown, Pa., on September 7; pitched and managed at Rome, Ga., and West Palm Beach, Fla., after World War II.

**Robert A. (Bob) Souza,** 22, a righthanded pitcher who was the Detroit Tigers' first choice in the June 1984 draft, in an automobile accident at Indiantown, Fla., on January 6; compiled a 2-2 record and 2.22 earned-run average for Lakeland of the Florida State League and an 0-2 mark and 4.82 ERA for Birmingham of the Southern League in his only season of professional baseball.

**Riggs (Old Hoss) Stephenson**, 87, a standout outfielder for the Chicago Cubs who compiled a career .336 batting average in 14 major league seasons, of heart failure at Tuscaloosa, Ala., on November 15; the four-sport letterman at the University of Alabama was signed by the Cleveland Indians in 1921 as a second baseman and experienced trouble making the double-play pivot; was converted to the outfield in 1925 while playing minor league ball and impressed Joe McCarthy, who took over as Cubs manager in 1926 and acquired the stocky righthanded-hitting Stephenson; became the regular left fielder and batted .319 or better in eight of the next nine seasons; batted fifth in the "North Side Murderers' Row" lineup that also featured Hall of Fame outfield teammates Hack Wilson and Kiki Cuyler plus Gabby Hartnett, Rogers Hornsby and Charlie Grimm; drove in 110 runs in the Cubs' pennant-winning 1929 season, joining with Wilson (159) and Cuyler (102) as the only National League outfield combination in history in which each member drove in 100 runs; batted a career-high .367 in 1930 and led the N.L. with 46 doubles in 1927; batted .316 in the 1929 World Series, a five-game loss to the Philadelphia A's, and .444 three years later, when the Cubs were swept by the New York Yankees; playing time was cut to 38 games in 1934 by arm and leg injuries, prompting Stephenson to retire; played and managed several more seasons in the minors at Birmingham, Helena, Ark., and Montgomery before leaving baseball in 1939.

**Joe Sullivan**, 74, a lefthanded pitcher who compiled a 30-37 record with the Detroit Tigers, Boston Braves and Pittsburgh Pirates between 1935 and 1941, of cancer at Sequin, Wash., on April 9; was 8-11 in two seasons with the Tigers as a reliever and spot starter before shuttling between the majors and minors as a member of the Braves and Pirates organizations until his retirement from baseball in 1945.

**Robert Sullivan**, 43, equipment manager for the Milwaukee Brewers, at Milwaukee on October 17; began his baseball association as a ball boy for the Boston Red Sox in 1958, became Boston's assistant equipment manager for six seasons and then joined the California Angels in 1968 as visiting clubhouse attendant; joined the Brewers staff in 1970.

**Alfred C. (Al) Todd**, 81, a catcher with four National League teams between 1932 and 1943, at Elmira, N.Y., on March 8; joined the Philadelphia Phillies in 1932, but never played in more than 100 games until 1935, the season in which he participated in major league baseball's first night game at Cincinnati's Crosley Field; sold to Pittsburgh, Todd became the Pirates starting catcher in 1937 and enjoyed his best major league season—.307 batting average with 86 runs batted in; set a major league record that season by catching 128 consecutive games without being charged with a passed ball; sold to the Brooklyn Dodgers in 1939 and traded to the Chicago Cubs in 1940; spent most of the 1941 and 1942 seasons in the minors, returning to Chicago to appear in 21 games before he was released in 1943; managed in the minor leagues for the next eight seasons at Mobile, Memphis and Des Moines; scouted for the Cubs, New York Mets and New York Yankees before retiring in 1963.

**George E. (The Bull) Uhle**, 86, a 200-game winner in the major leagues who is credited with being the first pitcher to throw an effective slider, at Lakewood, O., on February 19; joined the Cleveland Indians off the sandlots in 1919 and enjoyed his best seasons in 1923 and 1926 when he led the American League with 26 and 27 victories, respectively; the ironman pitcher started 44 games for the Indians in 1923, completing 29 of them and leading the A.L. in innings pitched with 358; discovered how to throw his slider later in his career while playing catch in the outfield with Tigers teammate Harry Heilmann; gave it its name because the pitch would "sort of slide across the plate."; the pitch, however, compounded Uhle's arm problems and by 1933 the Tigers figured he was finished; signed with the New York Yankees and hung around long enough to pick up his 200th victory, bringing his career mark to 200-166 in 17 seasons; compiled a .288 career batting average that remains a record for pitchers who compiled more than 1,000 plate appearances in the majors; once collected five hits in a 21-inning game; coached and scouted for the Indians, Chicago Cubs, Washington Senators and Brooklyn Dodgers after his retirement.

**Dick Wakefield**, 64, a one-year sensation with the Detroit Tigers after signing a then-record bonus contract off the University of Michigan campus in 1941, of cancer at Detroit on August 26; signed a $52,000 bonus and was touted as the game's next great star; started off with a bang in 1943 by leading the American League in hits (200) and doubles (38) while batting .316 in his first full season with the Tigers; after a short hitch in the Navy, returned to Detroit and batted .355 in 78 games at the end of the 1944 season; missed the 1945 season because of Navy duties and most of the 1946 season after suffering a broken arm; never returned to past form and was traded to the New York Yankees after the 1949 season; played in only three games with the Yankees because of a contract dispute and eventually was demoted and released; made one last brief appearance in the majors with the New York Giants in 1952.

**Dr. Leonard Wallenstein**, 68, the team physician for the Baltimore Orioles for 20 years, at Miami, Fla., on February 25; credited with drawing up major league baseball's original program for the prevention of drug abuse at the request of then-Commissioner Bowie Kuhn.

**Blaine Walsh**, 60, a play-by-play announcer for the Milwaukee Braves and Green Bay Packers in the 1950s and '60s, at Atlanta; teamed with Earl Gillespie to broadcast Braves games for 13 seasons and was the Packers' radio voice for four years.

**Bill (Wamby) Wambsganss**, 91, a slick-fielding, light-hitting infielder who was responsible for the only unassisted triple play in World Series history, at Lakewood, O., on December 8; played in the major leagues from 1914 to 1926, spending all but three of those seasons with the Cleveland Indians; was the Indians regular second baseman from 1915 through 1923; finished his career in 1926 with the Philadelphia A's with a career average of .259; greatest claim to fame came in Game 5 of the 1920 Series when he pulled off his unassisted triple play against the Brooklyn Dodgers; after his retirement, Wambsganss managed briefly in the minors at Springfield, Ill., and Fort Wayne, Ind.

**Sam West**, 81, an excellent defensive outfielder who batted .300 or better seven times during a 16-year major league career, at Lubbock, Tex., on November 23; began his major league career in 1927 with the Washington Senators and quickly established his reputation as one of baseball's top defensive outfielders; set an American League record in 1929 with a .996 fielding percentage; was traded to the St. Louis Browns in 1932 and enjoyed several good seasons before being traded back to the Senators in 1938; finished his career in 1942 with the Chicago White Sox; compiled a .299 career average in 1,753 major league games; served as Senators coach in 1948 and 1949.

**Vernon S. (Whitey) Wilshere**, 72, a lefthanded

Smoky Joe Wood
won 34 games,
including a
record-tying 16
straight, for Boston
in 1912.

pitcher who compiled a 10-12 record from 1934-36 with the Philadelphia Athletics, at Cooperstown, N.Y., on May 23; appeared in nine games for the A's as a rookie and lost his only decision; finished with a 9-9 mark in 1935 and suffered a serious arm injury that affected his 1936 season and resulted in his release.

**Joseph (Smoky Joe) Wood,** 95, a righthanded pitcher who posted a 34-5 record for the Boston Red Sox in 1912 at the age of 22, at West Haven, Conn., on July 27; the Kansas City native, who pitched for Boston from 1908-15, rocketed to fame when he pitched a no-hitter against the St. Louis Browns in 1911, a season in which he struck out 231 and finished with a 23-17 record; in his unbelievable 1912 season, Wood used his blazing fastball to strike out 258 batters in 344 innings, record a league-leading 10 shutouts, complete 35 of 38 starts and compile a record-tying streak of 16 consecutive victories; hampered by serious arm problems after that season, however, Wood's production dropped drastically, though he did lead the American League in earned-run average (1.49) and winning percentage (15-5, .750) in 1915, his last season as a full-time pitcher; sold to the Cleveland Indians in 1918 and began a second career as a sore-armed outfielder, filling in capably for one of the many teams depleted by military callups; hit .297 with 92 runs batted in for the Indians in 1922, his last season in the majors; pitched 1,434 innings in the majors with a 116-57 record and a 2.03 ERA; recorded a .283 career batting average; compiled a 3-1 record in the 1912 World Series and batted .200 in the 1920 Series for the Indians.

**Waldo W. (Rusty) Yarnall,** 82, a righthanded pitcher who was 0-1 in a brief stint with the 1926 Philadelphia Phillies, at Lowell, Mass., on October 9.

**Robert G. (Bobby) Young,** 60, the first player signed to a contract by the Baltimore Orioles franchise in 1954, of a heart attack at Baltimore on January 28; signed originally with the St. Louis Cardinals organization but was acquired in 1951 by the St. Louis Browns and appeared in 444 games, all at second base, over the next three seasons; became the first player to sign his contract in 1954 after the Browns left St. Louis for Baltimore following the 1953 season; later played for the Cleveland Indians and briefly for the Philadelphia Phillies; compiled a career average of .249 over all or parts of eight seasons.

**Carl Yowell,** 82, a lefthanded pitcher who recorded a 3-4 record in his two-year major league fling with the Cleveland Indians, at Jacksonville, Tex., on July 27.

**B.J. (Ben) Zientara,** 65, an infielder with the Cincinnati Reds for four seasons in the 1940s who later had a long career as a major league scout, at Lake Elsinore, Calif., on April 16; best season was 1947, when he played, mostly at second base, in 117 games, batting .258; managed and coached in the minors before becoming a Cleveland Indians scout in 1961; became a Chicago Cubs scout in 1971 and then became the Chicago-area representative for the Major League Scouting Bureau when it was formed in 1974.

**William (Billy) Zitzmann,** 87, an outfielder who appeared in 406 games over six seasons with the Pittsburgh Pirates and Cincinnati Reds, at Passaic, N.J., on May 29; his best season was 1928 when he batted .297 in 101 games.

# LEAGUE AND CLUB INFORMATION

## Including

**Major League Directory**

**American League Directory**

**American League Team Directories**

**National League Directory**

**National League Team Directories**

**Major League Players Association Directory**

**Major League Farm Systems**

**Minor League Presidents**

# Directory of Organized Baseball

## MAJOR LEAGUES

COMMISSIONER—Peter V. Ueberroth
SECRETARY-TREASURER & GENERAL COUNSEL—Edwin M. Durso
DEPUTY COMMISSIONER & SPECIAL PROJECTS—Alexander H. Hadden
HEADQUARTERS—350 Park Avenue
New York, N. Y. 10022
Telephone—371-7800 (area code 212)
Teletype—910-380-9482

EXECUTIVE COUNCIL—Peter V. Ueberroth, Commissioner; Robert W. Brown, President of American League; Charles S. Feeney, President of National League; Peter Bavasi, Roy Eisenhardt, Peter Hardy and Jerry Reinsdorf, representatives of American League, and Charles Bronfman, Nelson Doubleday, Bill Giles and Peter F. O'Malley, representatives of National League.

ADMINISTRATOR—William A. Murray
EXECUTIVE VICE-PRESIDENT OF BROADCASTING—Bryan L. Burns
NEWS DEPARTMENT—Richard Levin, Charles Adams & Richard Cerrone
DIRECTOR OF SECURITY—Horace J. Gibbs
CONTROLLER—Donald C. Marr, Jr.
ASSISTANTS TO ADMINISTRATIVE OFFICER—
George E. Pfister, Miguel A. Rodriguez
(Winter League Baseball Coordinators)
ASSISTANT COUNSEL—Thomas Ostertag
DIRECTOR OF BROADCAST ADMINISTRATION—David Alworth
MANAGER OF BROADCAST OPERATIONS—Leslie Lawrence
PERSONNEL ADMINISTRATION MANAGER—Barbara Ernst
OFFICE MANAGER—Mary Ann Burns
BOOKKEEPER—Rita Datz

NATIONAL ASSOCIATION REPRESENTATIVES—John H. Johnson, President of the National Association, and members of National Association Executive Committee.

## NATIONAL ASSOCIATION
## OF PROFESSIONAL BASEBALL LEAGUES

PRESIDENT-TREASURER—John H. Johnson
ADMINISTRATOR—Sal Artiaga
VICE-PRESIDENT—Bill Cutler
LEGAL COUNSEL—Charles J. Crist, Jr.
DIRECTOR OF PROMOTIONS—Bob Sparks
HEADQUARTERS—201 Bayshore Dr. S.E., P. O. Box A
St. Petersburg, Fla. 33731
Telephone—822-6937 (area code 813)
Teletype—810-863-0361

EXECUTIVE COMMITTEE—Bill Cutler, Chairman, President of the Pacific Coast League; Bill Walters, President of the Midwest League; and Charles Eshbach, President of the Eastern League.

# American League
**Organized 1900**

**ROBERT W. BROWN, M.D.**
President

**JOHN E. FETZER, GENE AUTRY, CALVIN R. GRIFFITH**
Vice-Presidents

**ROBERT O. FISHEL**
Executive Vice President

**DONALD C. MARR, Jr.**
Chief Financial Officer, Baseball

**MARTIN J. SPRINGSTEAD**
Chief Supervisor of Umpires

**RICHARD BUTLER**
Special Assistant

**PHYLLIS MERHIGE**
Director of Public Relations

**TESS BASTA, DAVID GLAZIER, CAROLYN COEN**
Administrators

**Headquarters—350 Park Avenue, New York, N. Y. 10022**

**Telephone—371-7600 (area code 212)**

ASSISTANT SUPERVISORS OF UMPIRES—Henry Soar, Larry Napp.

UMPIRES—Lawrence Barnett, Nicholas Bremigan, Joseph Brinkman, Alan Clark, Drew Coble, Terrance Cooney, Derryl Cousins, Donald Denkinger, James Evans, Dale Ford, Richard Garcia, Ted Hendry, John Hirschbeck, Mark Johnson, Kenneth Kaiser, Greg Kosc, Tim McClelland, Larry McCoy, James McKean, Durwood Merrill, Dan Morrison, Jerome Neudecker, Stephen Palermo, David Phillips, Rick Reed, Michael Reilly, John (Rocky) Roe, John Shulock, Vic Voltaggio, Tim Welke, Larry Young.

OFFICIAL STATISTICIANS—Sports Information Center, 1776 Heritage Drive, No. Quincy, Mass. 02171. Telephone—(617) 328-4674.

# BALTIMORE ORIOLES

Chairman of the Board and President—Edward Bennett Williams

Executive Vice-President, General Manager—Henry J. Peters
Vice-President, Secretary, General Counsel—Lawrence Lucchino
Vice-President, Stadium Operations—Jack Dunn, III
Vice-President, Finance—Joseph P. Hamper, Jr.
Treasurer—Robert J. Flanagan
Directors—Edward Bennett Williams, Joseph P. DiMaggio, Jack Dunn, III,
Jay Emmett, Robert J. Flanagan, Gerald T. Gabrys, Charles H. Hoffberger,
Jerold C. Hoffberger, Zanvyl Krieger, Lawrence Lucchino, Henry J. Peters,
Peter P. Weidenbruch, Jr.
Special Assistant to the General Manager—James J. Russo
Director of Business Affairs—Robert R. Aylward
Director of Public Relations—Robert W. Brown
Executive Director, Minor Leagues and Scouting—Thomas A. Giordano
Traveling Secretary—Philip E. Itzoe
Executive Director of Sales—Louis I. Michaelson
Promotions Manager—Martin Conway
Community Relations Manager—Julia A. Wagner
Director of Corporate Marketing—Daniel J. O'Dowd
Ticket Office Manager—Timothy Geraghty
Director, Scouting—Fred B. Uhlman
Administrator, Business Affairs, Minor Leagues & Scouting—John J. McCall
Assistant Public Relations Director—Richard L. Vaughn
Assistant Ticket Manager—Joseph B. Codd
Director of Broadcast Relations—Kenneth E. Nigro
Baltimore Sales Representative—Martin J. Smith
Manager—Earl S. Weaver
Club Physician—Dr. Sheldon Goldgeir
Executive Offices—Memorial Stadium, Baltimore, Md. 21218
Telephone—243-9800 (area code 301)

SCOUTS—(Major League)—Jim Russo, John Stokoe, Bill Werle. (Regular)—
Lefty Bagg, Jack Baker, Joe Bowman, Dan Cressman, Ray Crone, Ed Crosby, Joe
DeLucca, Jim Gilbert, Jesus Halabi, Len Johnston, Bill Lawlor, George Lauzerique,
Mike Ledna, Minnie Mendoza, Carl Moesche, Lamar North, Jim Pamlanye, Jack
Sanford, Jerry Zimmerman.

PARK LOCATION—Memorial Stadium, 33rd Street, Ellerslie Avenue, 36th
Street and Ednor Road.

Seating capacity—54,076.

FIELD DIMENSIONS—Home plate to left field at foul line, 309 feet; to center
field, 405 feet; to right field at foul line, 309 feet.

# BOSTON RED SOX

President—Jean R. Yawkey

Chief Executive Officer/Chief Operating Officer—Haywood C. Sullivan
General Partner—Edward G. LeRoux, Jr.
Vice-President, General Manager—James L. Gorman
Chief Financial Officer/Treasurer—Robert C. Furbush
V. P., Player Development Director—Edward F. Kenney
Minor League Administrative Assistant—Edward Kenney, Jr.
Scouting Director—Edward M. Kasko
Public Relations and Publicity Director—Richard L. Bresciani
Traveling Secretary—John J. Rogers
Broadcasting Director—James P. Healey
Executive Assistant—Joseph F. McDermott
Marketing Director—Lawrence C. Cancro
Controller—John J. Reilly
Ticket Director—Arthur J. Moscato
Assistant Publicity Director—Josh S. Spofford
Publicity Assistant—James A. Samia
Consultants—Theodore S. Williams, Carl M. Yastrzemski
Superintendent, Grounds & Maintenance—Joseph Mooney
Manager—John F. McNamara
Club Physician—Dr. Arthur M. Pappas
Executive Offices—24 Yawkey Way, Boston, Mass. 02215
Telephone—267-9440 (area code 617)

SCOUTS—Rafael Batista, Milton Bolling, Ray Boone, Wayne Britton, George Digby, Howard (Danny) Doyle, Bill Enos, Charles Koney, Wilfrid (Lefty) Lefebvre, Don Lenhardt, Howard McCullough, Tommy McDonald, Felix Maldonado, Frank Malzone, Sam Mele, Willie Paffen, Peter Randall, Philip Rossi, Edward Scott, Matt Sczesny, Joe Stephenson, Larry Thomas, Charlie Wagner.

PARK LOCATION—Fenway Park, Yawkey Way, Lansdowne Street and Ipswich Street.

Seating capacity—33,583.

FIELD DIMENSIONS—Home plate to left field at foul line, 315 feet; to center field, 420 feet; to right field at foul line, 302 feet; average right-field distance, 382 feet.

# CALIFORNIA ANGELS

President and Chairman of the Board—Gene Autry

Vice-President and General Manager—Mike Port
Vice-President—Jackie Autry
Vice-President/Secretary-Treasurer—Michael Schreter
Vice-President, Marketing—John Hays
Vice-President, Finance and Administration—James Wilson
Asst. to V.P., Public Relations & Promotions—Tom Seeberg
Assistant to General Manager—Preston Gomez
Director Publicity—Tim Mead
Director Publications—John Sevano
Controller—Jim Kaczmarek
Director Scouting & Player Development—Larry Himes
Director Minor League Operations—Bill Bavasi
Adm. Asst., Player Personnel & Development—Frank Marcos
Director Ticket Department—Carl Gordon
Assistant Ticket Director—Bob Terzes
Director Group Sales—Lynn Kirchmann Biggs
Group Sales Representative—Bob Wagner
Assistant Director Marketing—Jean (Corky) Lippert
Traveling Secretary—Frank Sims
Manager Stadium Operations—Kevin Uhlich
Medical Director—Dr. Robert Kerlan
General Medicine—Dr. Jules Rasinski
Orthopedist—Dr. Lewis Yocum
Trainers—Rick Smith, Ned Bergert
Physical Therapist—Roger Williams
Manager—Gene Mauch
Executive Offices—Anaheim Stadium, 2000 State College Blvd.,
Anaheim, Calif. 92806
Telephone—937-6700 (area code 714) or 625-1123 (area code 213)

SCOUTS—Mark Bernstein, Edmundo Borrome, Joe Carpenter, Alex Cosmidis, Pompeyo Davalillo, Preston Douglas, Jesse Flores, Ed Ford, Bob Gardner, Al Goldis, Steve Gruwell, Bruce Hines, Rick Ingalls, Nick Kamzic, Kevin Malone, Eusebio Perez, Vic Power, Philip Rizzo, Cookie Rojas, Rich Schlenker, Mark Snipp, Mark Weidemaier.

PARK LOCATION—Anaheim Stadium, 2000 State College Blvd.

Seating capacity—64,573.

FIELD DIMENSIONS—Home plate to left field at foul line, 333 feet; to center field, 404 feet; to right field at foul line, 333 feet.

# CHICAGO WHITE SOX

Chairman, Board of Directors—Jerry M. Reinsdorf

President—Eddie M. Einhorn
Special Assistant to the Chariman of the Board and President—Roland A. Hemond
Executive Vice-President/Baseball Operations—Ken Harrelson,
Executive Vice-President—Howard C. Pizer
Vice-President, Marketing—Michael D. McClure
Vice-President, Broadcasting and Special Projects—Laureen Ong
Vice-President, Baseball Administration—Jack Gould
Vice-President/Baseball Operations—David Dombrowski
Vice-President/Finance—Timothy L. Buzard
Assistant Vice-President, Marketing—Stephen M. Schanwald
Director of Player Development & Minor Leagues—Alvin Dark
Director of Public Relations—Paul H. Jensen
Sales Manager—Millie Johnson
Assistant to the Vice-President/Sales and Promotions—Jeff Overton
Director of Broadcast Sales—Edwin M. Doody
Controller—Terry Savarise
Director of Purchasing—Don Esposito
Traveling Secretary—Glen Rosenbaum
Ticket Manager—Robert K. Devoy
Coordinator of Promotions and Special Events—Christine O'Reilly
Assistant Director of Public Relations—Tim Clodjeaux
Assistant to the General Manager—Daniel Evans
Assistant Director of Player Development and Minor Leagues—Steve Noworyta
Administrative Assistant, Baseball Operations—Mitch Lukevics
General Counsel—Allan B. Muchin
Trainer—Herman Schneider
Team Physicians—Drs. Richard D. Corzatt, James B. Boscardin,
Hugo Cuadros
Manager—Tony LaRussa
Equipment/Club House Mgr., White Sox—Willie Thompson
Equipment/Club House Mgr., Visitors—John McNamara, Jr.
Director of Park Operations—David M. Schaffer
Groundskeepers—Gene and Roger Bossard
P.A. Announcer—Gene Honda
Organist—Nancy Faust
Executive Offices—Comiskey Park, Dan Ryan at 35th Street, Chicago, Ill. 60616
Telephone—924-1000 (area code 312)

SCOUTS—(Advance)—Ellis Clary, Bart Johnson, Joe Nossek, Mike Squires. (Special Assignment)—Walt Widmayer. (Director)—Terry Logan. (Regular)—Juan Bernhardt, George Bradley, Robert Fontaine Jr., Russ Gibson, Eric Gluck, Ben Hays, Joseph Ingalls, Leo Labossiere, Carlos Lareto, Dario Lodigiani, Larry Monroe, Victor Puig, Aurelio Rodriguez, Cucho Rodriguez, Duane Shaffer, Craig Wallenbrock, Stan Zielinski.

PARK LOCATION—Comiskey Park, Dan Ryan at 35th Street, Chicago, Ill. 60616.

Seating capacity—44,087.

FIELD DIMENSIONS—Home plate to left field at foul line, 347 feet; to center field, 409 feet; to right field at foul line, 347 feet.

# CLEVELAND INDIANS

Chairman of the Board—Patrick J. O'Neill
Directors—Walter Laich, Joseph O'Neill, Patrick J. O'Neill, Gabriel H. Paul
President/Chief Operating Officer/Treasurer—Peter Bavasi
Senior V.P., Baseball Administration & Player Relations—Dan O'Brien
Vice-President, Administration—Terry Barthelmas
Vice-President, Baseball Operations—Joe Klein
Director, Finance—Gregg Olson
Secretary and Club Legal Counsel—Edward C. Crouch
Senior Player Personnel Advisor—Phil Seghi
Manager—Pat Corrales
Director, Public Relations—Bob DiBiasio
Director, Ticket Services—Joan Eppich
Director, Sales/Promotions—Jeff Gregor
Director, Operations—Ben Jay
Director, Player Development & Scouting—Jeff Scott
Director, Team Travel—Mike Seghi
Controller—Ilona Kreischer
Trainer—Jim Warfield
Assistant Trainer—Paul Spicuzza
Medical Director—Dr. William Wilder
Orthopedic Specialist—Dr. John Bergfeld
Clubhouse and Equipment Manager—Cy Buynak
Executive Offices—Cleveland Stadium, Cleveland, Ohio 44114
Telephone—861-1200 (area code 216)

SCOUTS—Hector Acevedo, Eddie Bane, Dan Carnevale, Tom Chandler, Tom Couston, Red Gaskill, Orlando Gomez, Luis Issac, Bobby Malkmus, Bill Meyer, Jim Miller, Dave Roberts, Woody Smith, Dale Sutherland, Gary Sutherland, Birdie Tebbetts.

PARK LOCATION—Cleveland Stadium, Boudreau Blvd.

Seating capacity—74,208.

FIELD DIMENSIONS—Home plate to left field at foul line, 320 feet; to center field, 400 feet; to right field at foul line, 320 feet.

# DETROIT TIGERS

Board of Directors
John E. Fetzer, Thomas S. Monaghan, James A. Campbell

Chairman of the Board—John E. Fetzer
Vice-Chairman and Owner—Thomas S. Monaghan
President & Chief Executive Officer—James A. Campbell
Executive Vice-President & Chief Operating Officer—William E. Haase
Vice-President & General Manager—William R. Lajoie
Vice-President/Finance—Alexander C. Callam
Director of Public Relations—Dan Ewald
Director of Radio & TV—Neal Fenkell
Director of Stadium Operations—Ralph E. Snyder
Director of Ticket Sales—William H. Willis
Director of Player Development—Frank Franchi
Administrator of Player Development—Dave Miller
Data Processing Manager—Mary Lamthier
Executive Secretary/Baseball—Alice Sloane
Executive Secretary/Operations—Hazel McLane
Traveling Secretary—Bill Brown
Executive Consultant—Rick Ferrell
Special Assignment Scouts—Walter A. Evers, Jerry Walker
Eastern Scouting Coordinator—Jax Robertson
Midwest Scouting Coordinator—Bill Schudlich
Western Scouting Coordinator—Tom Gamboa
Assistant Director of Public Relations—Bob Miller
Assistant Director of Public Relations/Special Events/Scoreboard—Lew Matlin
Assistant Director of Public Relations/Community Relations—Vince Desmond
Group Sales Coordinator—Irwin Cohen
Assistant Director of Stadium Operations/Grounds Maintenance—Frank Feneck
Assistant Director of Stadium Operations/Grounds Maintenance—Ed Goward
Manager—Sparky Anderson
Club Physician—Clarence S. Livingood M.D.
Orthopedic Consultant—David Collon M.D.
Executive Offices—Tiger Stadium, Detroit, Mich. 48216
Telephone—962-4000 (area code 313)

SCOUTS—Rick Arnold, John Barkley, Ray Bellino, Wayne Blackburn, Phillip Favia, Joe Henderson, Joe Lewis, Kenneth Madeja, Joseph Nigro, Orlando Pena, Ramon Pena, Paul Robinson, Richard Wilson, Marti Wolever.

PARK LOCATION—Tiger Stadium, Michigan Avenue, Cochrane Avenue, Kaline Drive and Trumbull Avenue.

Seating capacity—52,806.

FIELD DIMENSIONS—Home plate to left field at foul line, 340 feet; to center field, 440 feet; to right field at foul line, 325 feet.

# KANSAS CITY ROYALS

Board of Directors
Joe Burke, William Deramus, III, Avron Fogelman, Charles Hughes,
Ewing Kauffman, Mrs. Ewing Kauffman, Earl Smith

Chairman of the Board (co-owner)—Ewing Kauffman
Vice Chairman of the Board (co-owner)—Avron Fogelman
President—Joe Burke
Executive Vice-President and General Manager—John Schuerholz
Executive Vice-President, Administration—Spencer (Herk) Robinson
Vice-President, Controller—Dale Rohr
Vice-President and Legal Counsel—Phil Koury
Vice-President, Public Relations—Dean Vogelaar
Director of Marketing and Broadcasting—Dennis Cryder
Traveling Secretary/Lancer Coordinator—Will Rudd
Assistant Director of Public Relations—Jeff Coy
Director of Scouting and Player Development—Art Stewart
Assistant to General Manager—Dean Taylor
Assistant Director of Player Development—Rick Mathews
Assistant Director of Marketing—Scott Pederson
Director of Ticket Operations—Stacy Sherrow
Director of Season Ticket Sales—Joe Grigoli
Director of Group Sales—Chris Muehlbach
Director of Event Personnel—Jay Hinrichs
Stadium Engineer—George Humphrey
Stadium Maintenance Coordinator—Bob Frank
Data Processing Manager—Loretta Kratzberg
Accountants—Tom Pfannenstiel, Ken Willeke
Manager—Dick Howser
Equipment Manager—Al Zych
Groundskeeper—George Toma
Team Physician—Dr. Paul Meyer
Trainers—Mickey Cobb, Paul McGannon
Executive Offices—Royals Stadium, Harry S Truman Sports Complex
Mailing Address—P. O. Box 1969, Kansas City, Mo. 64141
Telephone—921-2200 (area code 816)

SCOUTS—Carl Blando, Al Diez, Tom Ferrick, Rosey Gilhousen, Ken Gonzales, Ron Hopkins, Gary Johnson, Al Kubski, Tony Levato, Chuck McMichael, Jim Moran, Brian Murphy, George Noga, Herb Raybourn, Jerry Stephens, Roy Tanner, Jerry Terrell, Red Whitsett.

PARK LOCATION—Royals Stadium, Harry S Truman Sports Complex.

Seating capacity—40,625.

FIELD DIMENSIONS—Home plate to left field at foul line, 330 feet; to center field, 410 feet; to right field at foul line, 330 feet.

# MILWAUKEE BREWERS

President, Chief Executive Officer—Allan H. (Bud) Selig

Executive Vice-President, General Manager—Harry Dalton
Vice-President, Marketing—Richard Hackett
Vice-President, Broadcast Operations—William Haig
Vice-President, Finance—Richard Hoffmann
Vice-President, Stadium Operations—Gabe Paul, Jr.
Assistant General Manager—Walter Shannon
Special Assistants to the General Manager—Dee Fondy, Sal Bando
Traveling Secretary—Jimmy Bank
Special Assignments—Ray Poitevint
Farm Director—Bruce Manno
Coordinator of Player Development—Bob Humphreys
Scouting Coordinator—Dan Duquette
Director of Publicity—Tom Skibosh
Assistant Director of Stadium Operations and Advertising—Jack Hutchinson
Ticket Sales Director—Tim Trovato
Director of Community Relations—John Counsell
Director of Publications and Assistant Director of Publicity—Mario Ziino
Ticket Office Manager—John Barnes
Director of Ticket Office Computer Operations—Alice Boettcher
Manager—George Bamberger
Club Physician—Dr. Paul Jacobs
Trainers—John Adam, Freddie Frederico
Superintendent of Grounds and Maintenance—Harry Gill
Assistant Groundskeeper—Gary Vandenberg
Equipment Manager—Tony Migliaccio
P.A. Announcer—Bob Betts
Organist—Frank Charles
Executive Offices—Milwaukee Brewers Baseball Club
Milwaukee County Stadium, Milwaukee, Wis. 53214
Telephone—933-4114 (area code 414)

SCOUTS—Scouting supervisors: Julio Blanco-Herrera, Nelson Burbrink, Felix Delgado, Roland LeBlanc, Walter Youse. Regular scouts: Fred Beene, Tom Bourque, Ken Califano, Bill Castro, Lou Cohenour, Gerry Craft, Dick Foster, James Gabella, Dave Garcia, Hy Gomberg, Jack Hubbard, Gene Kerns, Phil Long, Cal McLish, Billy Moffitt, Johnny Neun, Frank Piet, Ken Richardson, Art Schuerman, Lee Sigman, Earl Silverthorn, Harry Smith, Milt Sobel, Sam Suplizio, Paul Tretiak.

PARK LOCATION—Milwaukee County Stadium, S. 46th St. off Bluemound Rd.

Seating capacity—53,192.

FIELD DIMENSIONS—Home plate to left field at foul line, 315 feet; to center field, 402 feet; to right field at foul line, 315 feet.

# MINNESOTA TWINS

Owner—Carl R. Pohlad

President—Howard T. Fox, Jr.
Consultant—Calvin R. Griffith
Directors—Donald E. Benson, Paul R. Christen, James O. Pohlad, Robert E. Woolley
Vice-President, Player Personnel—Andy MacPhail
Vice-President, Finance—Jim McHenry
Vice-President, Operations—Dave Moore
Vice-President, Marketing/Broadcasting—Don Schiel
Director of Minor Leagues—Jim Rantz
Director of Media Relations—Tom Mee
Traveling Secretary—Laurel Prieb
Manager—Ray Miller
Club Physicians—Dr. Leonard J. Michienzi, Dr. Harvey O'Phelan
Executive Offices—Hubert H. Humphrey Metrodome, 501 Chicago Ave. South,
Minneapolis, Minn. 55415
Telephone—375-1366 (area code 612)

SCOUTS—Floyd Baker, Joe Begani, Vern Borning, Ellsworth Brown, Edward Dunn, Jesse Flores, Jr., Jesse Flores, Sr., Billy Gardner, Angelo Giuliani, Bruce Haynes, Lee Irwin, Hank Izquierdo, Vern McKee, Bobby Morgan, Marvin Olson, Spencer (Red) Robbins, Herb Stein, Harry Warner, Fred Waters.

PARK LOCATION—Hubert H. Humphrey Metrodome, 501 Chicago Ave. South.

Seating capacity—55,244.

FIELD DIMENSIONS—Home plate to left field at foul line, 343 feet; to center field, 408 feet; to right field at foul line, 327 feet.

# NEW YORK YANKEES

Principal Owner—George M. Steinbrenner, III

Limited Partners—Harold M. Bowman, Lester Crown, Michael Friedman,
Marvin Goldklang, Barry Halper, Harvey Leighton, Daniel McCarthy,
Harry Nederlander, Robert Nederlander, William Rose Sr., Edward Rosenthal,
Jack Satter, Joan Z. Steinbrenner, Charlotte Witkind, Richard Witkind
President—Eugene J. McHale
Administrative Vice President and Treasurer—M. David Weidler
Vice President and General Manager—Clyde King
Manager—Lou Piniella
Vice President, Baseball Administration—Woody Woodward
Vice-President/Stadium Operations—Patrick Kelly
Vice-President/Customer Services—Jim Naples
Vice President—Ed Weaver
Director of Player Development—Bobby Hofman
Executive Director of Ticket Operations—Frank Swaine
Director of Marketing—Richard Kraft
Director of Publications, Publisher/Yankees Magazine—David Szen
Ticket Director—Mike Rendine
Traveling Secretary—Bill Kane
Assistant Ticket Director—Jim Hodge
Director of Group Sales—Debbie Tymon
Director of Accounting—Warren Atkinson
Assistant Player Development Director—Pete Jamison
Assistant Scouting Director—Roy Krasik
Assistant Media Relations Director—Lou D'Ermilio
Director, Television and Radio Relations—Kim Gallas
Message Board Operations Director—Betsy Leesman
Speakers Bureau—Bob Pelegrino
Public Relations Assistant—Keith Wiarda
Editor/Yankees Magazine—Tom Bannon
Video Coordination Director—Mike Barnett
Computer Statistics Director—Mark Batehko
Stadium Superintendent—Jimmy Esposito
Spring Training Coordinator—Marsh Samuel
Director, Alumni Association—Jim Ogle
Team Physician—Dr. John J. Bonamo
Public Address Announcer—Bob Sheppard
Organist—Eddie Layton
Executive Offices—Yankee Stadium, Bronx, N.Y. 10451
Telephone—293-4300 (area code 212)
Ticket Information—293-6000 (area code 212)

SCOUTS—Luis Arroyo, Hank Bauer, Al Cuccinello, Joe DiCarlo, Fred Ferreira,
Orrin Freeman, Jack Gillis, Ray Goodman, Dick Groch, Jim Gruzdis, Bob Lemon,
Don Lindeberg, Bill Livesey, Eddie Lopat, Russ Meyer, Jim Naples, Sr., Ramon
Naranjo, Dick Newberg, Greg Orr, Meade Palmer, Roberto Rivera, Brian Sabean,
Stan Saleski, Charlie Silvera, Tommy Thompson, Luis Tiant, Dick Tidrow, Mickey
Vernon, Stan Williams, Jeff Zimmerman.

PARK LOCATION—Yankee Stadium, E. 161st St. and River Ave., Bronx, N.Y.
10451.

Seating capacity—57,545.

FIELD DIMENSIONS—Home plate to left field at foul line, 312 feet; to center
field, 410 feet; to right field at foul line, 310 feet.

# OAKLAND A's

President—Roy Eisenhardt

Executive Vice-President—Walter J. Haas Jr.
Vice-President, Baseball Operations—Sandy Alderson
Vice-President, Business Operations—Andy Dolich
Vice-President, Finance—Kathleen McCracken
Director of Scouting—Dick Bogard
Special Asst. to V.P., Baseball Operations—Dick Wiencek
Director of Player Development—Karl Kuehl
Director of Baseball Administration—Walt Jocketty
Assistant to the President, Baseball Matters—Bill Rigney
Director of Latin American Scouting—Juan Marichal
Director of Team Travel—Mickey Morabito
Director of Sales & Telecommunications—David Rubinstein
Director of Public Relations—Ray Fosse
Director of Ticket Operations—Raymond B. Krise Jr.
Director of Stadium Operations—Jorge Costa
Director of Publications—Art Worthington
Director of Community Affairs—Dave Perron
Director of Ticket Sales—Steve Page
Director of Advertising Sales—Tom Cordova
Director of Season Sales—Doris Messina
Director of Group Sales—Bettina Flores
Assistant Director of Scouting—Jay Alves
Assistant Director of Public Relations—Kathy Jacobson
Business Oper. Coord/Dir. of Promotions—Sharon Kelly
Executive Assistant—Sharon Jones
Manager—Jackie Moore
Team Physician—Dr. Alan Pont
Team Orthopedist—Dr. Rick Bost
Trainers—Barry Weinberg, Larry Davis
Equipment Manager—Frank Ciensczyk
Visiting Clubhouse Manager—Steve Vucinich
Executive Offices—Oakland-Alameda County Coliseum, Oakland, Calif. 94621
Telephone—638-4900 (area code 415)

SCOUTS—Mark Conkin, Bruce Cudmore, Grady Fuson, Bill Gayton, Marty Miller, Mel Nelson, Camilo Pascual, John Ricciardi, Mike Sgobba, Ken Stauffer, Gary Wiencek.

PARK LOCATION—Oakland-Alameda County Coliseum, Nimitz Freeway and Hegenberger Road.

Seating capacity—50,219.

FIELD DIMENSIONS—Home plate to left field at foul line, 330 feet; to center field, 397 feet; to right field at foul line, 330 feet.

# SEATTLE MARINERS

Owner & Chairman of the Board—George L. Argyros

President—Charles G. Armstrong
Vice President, Baseball Operations—Dick Balderson
Asst. to V.P., Baseball Operations & Special Assignments—Bob Harrison
Vice President, Sales and Marketing—Bill Knudsen
Vice President, Administration & Finance—Brian Beggs
Director of Marketing & Community Relations—Randy Adamack
Director of Sales and Promotions—Roger King
Director of Player Development—Bill Haywood
Director of Scouting—Roger Jongewaard
Director of Public Relations—Bob Porter
Director of Ticket Services—Doug Hopkins
Director of Team Travel—Lee Pelekoudas
Director of Stadium Operations—Jeff Klein
Assistant Director of Player Development, Scouting—Gary Pellant
Assistant Director of Public Relations—Craig Detwiler
Assistant Director of Marketing—Ross Skinner
Assistant Director of Community Relations—Randy Stearnes
Assistant Director of Sales and Promotions—Larry Sindall
Assistant Director of Ticket Services—Mark Mitchell
Controller/Office Manager—Denise Podosek
Manager—Chuck Cottier
Club Physicians—Dr. Larry Pedegana, Dr. Mitchel Storey
Club Dentist—Dr. Richard Leshgold
Head Groundskeeper—Wilbur Loo
P.A. Announcer—Gary Spinnell
Executive Offices—P.O. Box 4100
100 South King Street, Suite 300, Seattle, Washington 98104
Telephone—628-3555 (area code 206)

SCOUTS—Bill Barkley, John Cole, Steve Hill, Bill Kearns, Coco Laboy, Jeff Malinoff, Tom Mooney, Whitey Piurek, Mike Roberts, Rick Sweet, Bill Tracy, Rip Tutor, Ray Vince, Steve Vrablik, Luke Wrenn, Bob Zuk.

PARK LOCATION—The Kingdome, 201 South King Street, Seattle, Washington.

Seating capacity—59,438.

FIELD DIMENSIONS—Home plate to left field at foul line, 316 feet; to center field, 410 feet; to right field at foul line, 316 feet.

# TEXAS RANGERS

Chairman of the Board, Chief Executive Officer—Eddie Chiles
Vice-Chairman—Dr. William S. Banowsky

President, Chief Operating Officer—Mike Stone
Vice President, General Manager—Tom Grieve
Vice President, Marketing and Administration—Larry Schmittou
Vice President, Finance and Secretary-Treasurer—Charles F. Wangner
General Counsel—Dee J. Kelly
Assistant G.M., Player Personnel and Scouting—Sandy Johnson
Assistant General Manager—Wayne Krivsky
Director of Player Development—Marty Scott
Director of Media Relations—John Blake
Director of Public Relations and Speakers' Bureau—Bobby Bragan
Director, Sales, Broadcasting and Producer, Diamond Vision—Chuck Morgan
Director of Promotions and Director, Diamond Vision—Dave Fendrick
Director of Ticket Sales and Management—Mary Ann Bosher
Stadium Manager—Mat Stolley
Traveling Secretary—Dan Schimek
Controller—John McMichael
Assistant Director of Season Ticket Sales—Jay Miller
Special Assistant, Baseball Operations—Paul Richards
Assistant Director of Media Relations—Jim Small
Manager—Bobby Valentine
Field Superintendent—Jim Anglea
Spring Training Director—John Welaj
Home Clubhouse and Equipment Manager—Joe Macko
Visiting Clubhouse Manager—Mike Wallace
Executive Offices—1200 Copeland Road, Suite 200, Arlington, Tex. 76011
Arlington Stadium—1500 Copeland Road, P.O. Box 1111, Arlington, Tex. 76010
Telephone—273-5222 (area code 817)

SCOUTS—Lee Anthony, Joseph Branzell, Jose Centeno, Paddy Cottrell, Amado Dinzey, Bill Earnhart, Dick Egan, Andy Hancock, Jack Hays, Sid Hudson, Dean Jongewaard, Bryan Lambe, Joseph Marchese, Jerry Marik, Jim McLaughlin, Omar Minaya, Cotton Nix, Luis Rosa, Eddie Santiago, Rick Schroeder, Danilo Troncoso, John Young.

PARK LOCATION—Arlington Stadium, 1500 Copeland Road, Arlington, Tex.

Seating capacity—43,508.

FIELD DIMENSIONS—Home plate to left field at foul line, 330 feet; to center field, 400 feet; to right field at foul line, 330 feet.

# TORONTO BLUE JAYS

Vice-Chairman, Chief Executive Officer—N. E. Hardy

Board of Directors—John Craig Eaton, L. G. Greenwood, N. E. Hardy,
R. Howard Webster, P. N. T. Widdrington
Chairman of the Board—R. Howard Webster
Executive Vice-President, Business—Paul Beeston
Executive Vice-President, Baseball—Pat Gillick
Vice-Presidents, Baseball—Bobby Mattick, Al LaMacchia
Vice-President, Finance—Bob Nicholson
Director, Public Relations—Howard Starkman
Director, Operations—Ken Erskine
Director, Ticket Operations—George Holm
Director of Marketing—Paul Markle
Director, Team Travel & Trainer—Ken Carson
Director, Group Sales—Maureen Haffey
Director, Canadian Scouting—Bob Prentice
Manager, Promotions—Colleen Burns
Assistant Director, Public Relations—Gary Oswald
Administrator, Player Personnel—Gord Ash
Assistant Director of Operations—Len Frejlich
Assistant Director, Ticket Operations—Randy Low
Director, Security—Fred Wootton
Equipment Manager—Jeff Ross
Coordinator, Promotions & Group Services—John MacLachlan
Supervisor, Grounds—Brad Bujold
Manager—Jimy Williams
Team Physician—Dr. Ron Taylor
Executive Offices—Exhibition Stadium, Exhibition Place,
Toronto, Ontario
Mailing Address—Box 7777, Adelaide St. P. O., Toronto, Ont. M5C 2K7
Telephone—595-0077 (area code 416)

SCOUTS—Dave Blume, Christopher Bourjos, Ellis Dungan, Robert Engle (Eastern Regional Scouting Director), Joe Ford, Moose Gordon, Epy Guerrero, Jim Hughes, Al LaMacchia, Duane Larson, Larry Maxie, Ben McLure, Steve Minor, Wayne Morgan (Western Regional Scouting Director), Bob Prentice, Don Welke, Bob Wilber, Tim Wilken, Dave Yoakum.

PARK LOCATION—Exhibition Stadium on the grounds of Exhibition Place. Entrances to Exhibition Place via Lakeshore Boulevard, Queen Elizabeth Way Highway and Dufferin and Bathurst Streets.

Seating capacity—43,737.

FIELD DIMENSIONS—Home plate to left field at foul line, 330 feet; to center field, 400 feet; to right field at foul line, 330 feet.

# National League

**Organized 1876**

**CHARLES S. FEENEY**
**President and Treasurer**

**JOHN J. McHALE**
**Vice-President**

**PHYLLIS B. COLLINS**
**Secretary**

**BLAKE CULLEN**
**Administrator and Public Relations Director**

**KATY FEENEY**
**Assistant Public Relations Director**

**LOUIS H. KREMS**
**Business Manager**

**JOSEPHINE TROY**
**Administrative Assistant**

**Headquarters—350 Park Avenue, New York, N. Y. 10022**

**Telephone—371-7300 (area code 212)**

UMPIRES—Fred Brocklander, Gerald Crawford, Robert Davidson, Gerry Davis, Dana DeMuth, Robert Engel, Bruce Froemming, Eric Gregg, H. Douglas Harvey, John Kibler, Randall Marsh, John McSherry, Edward Montague, David Pallone, Frank Pulli, James Quick, Lawrence (Dutch) Rennert, Steve Rippley, Paul Runge, Richard Stello, Terry Tata, Harry Wendelstedt, Joseph West, Lee Weyer, Charles Williams, William Williams.

OFFICIAL STATISTICIANS—Elias Sports Bureau, Inc., 500 5th Ave., Suite 2114, New York, N. Y. 10036. Telephone (212) 869-1530.

# ATLANTA BRAVES

Chairman of the Board—William C. Bartholomay

President—R.E. (Ted) Turner, III
Executive Vice-President—Allison Thornwell, Jr.
General Manager—Robert J. Cox
Assistant General Manager—John W. Mullen
Vice-President and Business Manager—Charles S. Sanders
Vice-President, Player Development—Henry L. Aaron
Assistant Vice-President, Scouting—Paul L. Snyder, Jr.
Assistant Scouting Director—Rod Gilbreath
Director of Broadcasting—Wayne Long
Ticket Distribution Manager—Ed Newman
Director of Public Relations, Promotions—Wayne Minshew
Publicity Director—Robin Monsky
Director of Stadium Operations and Security—Ken Little
Director of Matrix Operations—Bob Larson
Assistant Controller—Martin Mathews
Traveling Secretary and Equipment Manager—Bill Acree
Director of Ticket Sales—Andre DeLorenzo
Manager—Chuck Tanner
Club Physician—Dr. David T. Watson
Executive Offices—P.O. Box 4064, Atlanta, Ga. 30302
Telephone—522-7630 (area code 404)

SCOUTS—Mike Arbuckle, Sam Berry, Forrest (Smoky) Burgess, Jim Busby, Stu Cann, Joe Caputo, Harold Cronin, Tony DeMacio, Lou Fitzgerald, Pedro Gonzalez, Larry Grefer, John Groth, John Hageman, Gene Hassell, Herb Hippauf, Ray Holton, Jim Johnson, Bob Macius, Burney R. (Dickey) Martin, Bob Mavis, Tom Morgan, Rance Pless, Harry Postovc, Jose Salado, Bill Serena, Fred Shaffer, Charles Smith, Tony Stiel, Bob Turzilli, Bob Wadsworth, Wesley Westrum, William R. Wight, Don Williams, Bobby Wine, H.F. (Red) Wooten.

PARK LOCATION—Atlanta-Fulton County Stadium, on Capitol Avenue at the junction of Interstate Highways 20, 75 and 85.

Seating capacity—53,046.

FIELD DIMENSIONS—Home plate to left field at foul line, 330 feet; to center field, 402 feet; to right field at foul line, 330 feet.

# CHICAGO CUBS

Chairman of the Board—Andrew J. McKenna
President and General Manager—Dallas Green
Director of Minor Leagues and Scouting—Gordon Goldsberry
Vice President, Planning and Special Projects—Mark McGuire
Director of Marketing—Jeff Odenwald
Special Baseball Consultant to Exec. V. P. and G. M.—Charlie Fox
Executive Vice-President, Business Operations—Don Grenesko
Vice-President—E.R. Saltwell
General Counsel—Geoff Anderson
Assistant General Manager—John Cox
Director of Scouting—Scott Reid
Director of Player Development—Jim Snyder
Controller—Keith Bode
Secretary—Stanley J. Gradowski, Jr.
Director of Publications—Bob Ibach
Director of Media Relations—Ned Colletti
Traveling Secretary—Peter Durso
Director, Ticket Sales—Frank Maloney
Director, Stadium Operations—Tom Cooper
Director, Ticket Services—Lamar Vernon
Director, Promotions and Sales—John McDonough
Director of Minor League Operations—William Harford
Assistant Directors, Stadium Operations—Lubie Veal, Paul Rathje
Manager—Jim Frey
Executive Offices—Wrigley Field, N. Clark and Addison Streets, Chicago, Ill. 60613
Telephone—281-5050 (area code 312)

SCOUTS—(Major League)—Charlie Fox, Harley Anderson. (Supervisors)—
Brandon Davis, Frank DeMoss, Gene Handley, Gary Nickels. (Regular)—Dick Bank,
Billy Blitzer, William Capps, Billy Champion, Tom Davis, Warren Dewey, Edward
DiRamio, Walt Dixon, Cal Emery, Nino Espinosa, Morley Freitas, Louis Garcia,
Bobby Gardner, John Gracio, John Hennessy, Vedie Himsl, Ron Hollingsworth, Roy
Johnson, John "Spider" Jorgensen, Pat Kane, Don Kimura, Doug Laumann, Doug
Mapson, David Montfort, Julio Navarro, John "Buck" O'Neil, Lee Phillips, Andrew
Pienovi, Paul Provas, Joe Sayers, Joaquin Velilla, Harry Von Suskil, Wally Walker,
H.D. Wilson, Earl Winn, Harold Younghans, James Zerilla.

PARK LOCATION—Wrigley Field, Addison Street, N. Clark Street, Waveland
Avenue and Sheffield Avenue.

Seating capacity—38,040.

FIELD DIMENSIONS—Home plate to left field at foul line, 355 feet; to center
field, 400 feet; to right field at foul line, 353 feet.

# CINCINNATI REDS

General Partner—Marge Schott

President and Chief Executive Officer—Marge Schott
Executive Vice-President & General Manager—Bill Bergesch
Vice-President/Business Operations & Marketing—Roger Blaemire
Vice-President, Player Personnel—Sheldon Bender
Vice-President, Finance—D.L. Porco
Vice-President, Publicity—Jim Ferguson
Business Manager—Doug Bureman
Director, Scouting—Larry Doughty
Controller—Chris Krabbe
Director, Stadium Operations—Doug Duennes
Director, Promotions—Greg McCollam
Director, Ticket Department—Bill Stewart
Director, Season Tickets—Janet Wendel
Director, Group Sales—Tony Harris
Director of Speakers Bureau—Gordy Coleman
Traveling Secretary—Steve Cobb
Advance Scout—Jim Stewart
Assistant, Player Development and Scouting—Brian Granger
Assistant Publicity Director—Jon Braude
Assistant Ticket Director—John O'Brien
Chief Administrative Assistant—Joyce Pfarr
Manager—Pete Rose
Executive Offices—100 Riverfront Stadium, Cincinnati, O. 45202
Telephone—421-4510 (area code 513)

SCOUTS—Larry Barton, Jr., Gene Bennett, Cameron Bonifay, Dave Calaway, Bill Clark, Martin Daily, Roger Ferguson, Bill Fesh, Edwin Howsam, Chuck LaMar, Jeff McKay, Sam Mejias, Julian Mock, Chet Montgomery, Ed Roebuck, Tom Severtson, Neil Summers, Mickey White, George Zuraw.

PARK LOCATION—Riverfront Stadium, downtown Cincinnati, bounded by Second Street to Ohio River and from Walnut Street to Broadway.

Seating capacity—52,392.

FIELD DIMENSIONS—Home plate to left field at foul line, 330 feet; to center field, 404 feet; to right field at foul line, 330 feet.

# HOUSTON ASTROS

Board of Directors—Dr. John J. McMullen, Chairman. Owners—Dr. John J. McMullen, Mrs. R.E. (Bob) Smith, Mrs. Thomas E. (Mimi) Dompier, James A. Elkins, Jr., Alfred C. Glassell, Jr., Bob Marco, Don Sanders, Jack T. Trotter, H.L. Brown and Jacqueline, Peter, Catherine and John, Jr. McMullen.

President and General Manager—Dick Wagner
Vice-President, Baseball Operations—Fred Stanley
Assistant General Manager—William J. Wood
Director of Minor League Operations—Fred Nelson
Director of Scouting—Dan O'Brien, Jr.
Director of Public Relations—Rob Matwick
Traveling Secretary—John Davis
Director of Broadcasting—Art Elliott
Director of Promotions—Karen Williams
Special Assistant to the President—Donald Davidson
Assistant Director of Public Relations—Chuck Pool
Assistant to the Dirs., Minor Leagues/Scouting—Lew Temple
Scoreboard Operations—Paul Darst
Broadcast and Promotions Sales—Hugh Pickett, Art Bradshaw
Ticket Manager—Charles Wall
Manager, Season Ticket Sales—M.M. (Buddy) Hancken
Director, Group Ticket Sales—Evan Burian
Administrative Asst., Major League Operations—Allene Mutter
Secretary, Public Relations—Cinda Donovan
Club Physician—Dr. William Bryan
Public Address Announcer—J. Fred Duckett
Manager—Hal Lanier
Executive Offices—The Astrodome, P.O. Box 288
Houston, Tex. 77001
Telephone—799-9500 (area code 713)
HOUSTON SPORTS ASSOCIATION, INC.
President and Chief Operating Officer—Robert G. Harter
Executive Vice-President—Neal Gunn
Executive Vice-President, Astrodome-Astrohall Stadium Corporation—Jimmie Fore
Vice-President, Operations—W. Gary Keller
Vice-President, Marketing—Robert Carsia
Vice-President, Public Affairs—Jim Weidler
Treasurer—A. Eugene Stoffel
General Counsel—Frank Rynd
Controller—Adam C. Richards

SCOUTS—Clary Anderson, Stan Benjamin, Jack Bloomfield, Joe Campise, Walter Cress, Clark Crist, C.V. Davis, Doug Deutsch, Jim Fleming, Ben Galante, Carl Greene, Bill Hallauer, Bob Hartsfield, Red Hayworth, David Lakey, Julio Linares, Walter Matthews, Domingo Mercedes, Carlos Muro, Hal Newhouser, Tony Pacheco, Ramon Perez, Joe Pittman, Pico Prado, Adriano Rodriguez, Ross Sapp, Lynwood Stallings, Reggie Waller, Paul Weaver, Tom Wheeler, Harrison Wickel.

PARK LOCATION—The Astrodome, Kirby and Interstate Loop 610

Seating capacity—45,000.

FIELD DIMENSIONS—Home plate to left field at foul line, 330 feet; to center field, 400 feet; to right field at foul line, 330 feet.

# LOS ANGELES DODGERS

Board of Directors—Peter O'Malley, President; Harry M. Bardt;
Roland Seidler, Jr., Vice-President and Treasurer;
Mrs. Roland (Terry) Seidler, Secretary

President—Peter O'Malley
Executive Vice-President—Fred Claire
Vice-President, Player Personnel—Al Campanis
Vice-President, Minor League Operations—William P. Schweppe
Vice-President, Marketing—Merritt Willey
Controller and Assistant Treasurer—Ken Hasemann
Assistant Secretary—Irene Tanji
Assistant Secretary & General Counsel—Santiago Fernandez
Director, Advertising, Novelties and Souvenirs—Jim Campbell
Director, Dodgertown—Charles Blaney
Director, Financial Projects—Bob Graziano
Director, Stadium Operations—Bob Smith
Director, Ticket Department—Walter Nash
Director, Stadium Club and Transportation—Bob Schenz
Director, Dodger Network—David Van de Walker
Director, Scouting—Ben Wade
Director, Publicity—Steve Brener
Director, Publications—Toby Zwikel
Director, Community Relations—Don Newcombe
Community Relations—Roy Campanella, Lou Johnson
Director, Ticket Marketing and Promotions—Barry Stockhamer
Director, Community Services and Special Events—Bill Shumard
Assistant to the President—Ike Ikuhara
Traveling Secretary—Billy DeLury
Auditor—Michael Strange
Manager—Tom Lasorda
Club Physicians—Dr. Frank Jobe, Dr. Robert Woods
Executive Offices—Dodger Stadium, 1000 Elysian Park Avenue,
Los Angeles, Calif. 90012
Telephone—224-1500 (area code 213)

SCOUTS—Eleodoro Arias, Rafael Avila, Boyd Bartley, Bob Bishop, Gib Bodet,
Flores Boliavar, Mike Brito, Bob Darwin, Paul Duval, Eddie Fajardo, Sergio Ferrer,
Jim Garland, Rafael Gonzalez, Dick Hanlon, Dennis Haren, Gail Henley, Elvio Ji-
menez, Tony John, Tim Johnson, Hank Jones, John Keenan, Ron King, Steve Lembo,
Ed Liberatore, Carl Loewenstine, Frank Lucchesi, Don McMahon, Dale McReyn-
olds, Bob Miske, Tommy Mixon, Regie Otero, Bill Pleis, Glen Van Proyen, Jerry
Stephenson, Dick Teed, Corito Varona, Guy Wellman.

PARK LOCATION—Dodger Stadium, 1000 Elysian Park Avenue.

Seating capacity—56,000.

FIELD DIMENSIONS—Home plate to left field at foul line, 330 feet; to center
field, 395 feet; to right field at foul line, 330 feet.

# MONTREAL EXPOS

Board of Directors—Charles R. Bronfman, Lorne C. Webster, John J. McHale, Hugh Hallward, Sen. E. Leo Kolber, Arnold Ludwick

Honorary Directors—Louis R. Desmarais, Sydney Maislin

Chairman of the Board—Charles R. Bronfman
President and Chief Executive Officer—John J. McHale
Honorary Treasurer—Arnold Ludwick
Vice-President and General Manager—Murray Cook
Vice-President, Player Development—Jim Fanning
Vice-President, Baseball Administration—Bill Stoneman
Group Vice-President—Pierre Gauvreau
Vice-President, Business Operations—Gerry Trudeau
Vice-President, Marketing & Public Affairs—Rene Guimond
Director of Minor League Clubs—Bob Gebhard
Director of Scouting—Gary Hughes
Director, Team Travel—Dan Lunetta
Controller—Raymond St. Pierre
Executive Asst., Minor Leagues—Marilyn Elzer
Executive Asst., Scouting—Frank Wren
Publicists—Monique Giroux, Richard Griffin
Coordinator, Spring Training—Kevin McHale
Manager—Buck Rodgers
Club Physicians—Dr. Robert Brodrick, Dr. Mike Thomassin
Club Orthopedist—Dr. Larry Coughlin
Mailing Address—P. O. Box 500, Station M, Montreal, Quebec,
Canada H1V 3P2
Telephone—253-3434 (area code 514)

SCOUTS—(Special assignment)—Eddie Lyons, Carroll (Whitey) Lockman; (Supervisors)—Danny Menendez; (Regular)—Bill Adair, Jesus Alou, Kelvin Bowles, Lloyd Christopher, Ed Creech, Pat Daugherty, Richard Dehart, Cliff Ditto, Joe Frisina, Tom Hinkle, Bob Johnson, Dick Lemay, Roy McMillan, Felix Millan, Walter Millies, John (Red) Murff, Herb Newberry, Bob Oldis, Earl Rapp, Mark Servais.

PARK LOCATION—Olympic Stadium, 4545 Pierre de Coubertin, Montreal, Quebec, Canada H1V 3N7.

Seating capacity—59,149.

FIELD DIMENSIONS—Home plate to left field at foul line, 325 feet; to center field, 404 feet; to right field at foul line, 325 feet.

# NEW YORK METS

Chairman of the Board—Nelson Doubleday

Directors—Nelson Doubleday, Fred Wilpon, Walter E. Freese
John W. O'Donnell, John T. Sargent, Gerard Toner
President & Chief Executive Officer—Fred Wilpon
Exec. Vice-President, G.M. & Chief Operating Officer—J. Frank Cashen
Vice-President, Operations—Bob Mandt
Vice-President, Baseball Administration—Alan E. Harazin
Vice-President, Baseball Operations—Joseph McIlvaine
Vice-President, Finance and Administration—Harold W. O'Shaughnessy
Director of Amateur Baseball Relations—Tommy Holmes
Director of Broadcasting—Mike Ryan
Executive Asst. to General Manager—Joan Coen
Special Asst. to the G.M. & Team Travel Director—Arthur Richman
Director of Marketing—Drew Sheinman
Vice-President, Special Projects—John Doht
Ticket Manager—Bill Ianniciello
Controller—William Grundel
Director of Minor League Operations—Stephen Schryver
Director of Scouting—Roland Johnson
Director of Public Relations—Jay Horwitz
Stadium Manager—John McCarthy
Manager—Dave Johnson
Club Physician—Dr. James C. Parkes II
Team Trainer—Steve Garland
Executive Offices—William A. Shea Stadium, Roosevelt
Avenue and 126th Street, Flushing, N.Y. 11368
Telephone—507-6387 (area code 718)

SCOUTS—Carmen Fusco, Dick Gernert, Maury Harvat, Buddy Kerr, Joe Mason, Harry Minor, Robert Minor, Danny Monzon, Julian Morgan, Roy Partee, Carlos Pascual, Junior Roman, Marvin Scott, Eddy Toledo, Bob Wellman, Jim Woodward, Len Zanke, Jack Zduriencik.

PARK LOCATION—William A. Shea Stadium, Roosevelt Avenue and 126th Street, Flushing, N. Y. 11368.

Seating capacity—55,300.

FIELD DIMENSIONS—Home plate to left field at foul line, 338 feet; to center field, 410 feet; to right field at foul line, 338 feet.

# PHILADELPHIA PHILLIES

President—Bill Giles

Partners—The Taft Baseball Co., John Drew Betz Associates, Tri-Play Associates, Fitz Eugene Dixon Jr., Mrs. Rochelle Levy
Assistant to President—Paul Owens
Executive Vice-President—David Montgomery
Vice-President, Finance—Jerry Clothier
Vice-President, Baseball Administration—Tony Siegle
Vice-President, Public Relations—Larry Shenk
Secretary and Counsel—William Y. Webb
Financial Consultant—Robert D. Hedberg
Vice-President, Player Development and Scouting—Jim Baumer
Player Personnel Advisor—Hugh Alexander
Director of Promotions—Frank Sullivan
Director of Advertising—Tom Hudson
Traveling Secretary—Eddie Ferenz
Director of Sales and Ticket Operations—Richard Deats
Director of Scouting—Jack Pastore
Director of Community Relations and Broadcaster—Chris Wheeler
Director of Marketing—Dennis Lehman
Director of Stadium Operations—Mike DiMuzio
Director of Office Services—Pat Cassidy
Director of Management Information—Jeff Eisenberg
Director of Financial Analysis and Planning—Mike Kent
Director of Publicity—Vince Nauss
Director of Group Sales—Bettyanne Joyce
Director of Season Ticket Sales—Dennis Mannion
Assistant Director of Promotions—Chris Legault
Assistant Director of Marketing—Jo-Anne Levy
Executive Secretary to Minor Leagues—Bill Gargano
Club Physician—Dr. Phillip Marone
Club Trainer—Jeff Cooper
Strength and Flexibility Instructor—Gus Hoefling
Manager—John Felske
Executive Offices—Philadelphia Veterans Stadium
Mailing Address—P.O. Box 7575, Philadelphia, Pa. 19101
Telephone—463-6000 (area code 215)

SCOUTS—(Special assignment)—Hugh Alexander and Ray Shore. (Regular)—Oliver Bidwell, Edward Bockman, Carlos Cervo, George Farson, Tom Ferguson, Doug Gassaway, Bill Harper, Jerry Jordan, Dick Lawlor, Anthony Lucadello, Fred Mazuca, Joe McDonald, Bob Poole, Bob Reasonover, Larry Reasonover, Joe Reilly, Jay Robertson, Tony Roig, Rudy Terrasas, Randy Waddill, Don Williams.

PARK LOCATION—Philadelphia Veterans Stadium, Broad Street and Pattison Avenue.

Seating capacity—66,271.

FIELD DIMENSIONS—Home plate to left field at foul line, 330 feet; to center field, 408 feet; to right field at foul line, 330 feet.

# PITTSBURGH PIRATES

President & Chief Executive Officer—Malcolm Prine

Secretary & General Counsel—Carl F. Barger
Exec. V.P. & G.M./Baseball Operations—Syd Thrift
Vice-President—Harvey Walken
Administration—Joseph M. O'Toole
Treasurer—Douglas G. McCormick
Marketing—Steve Greenberg
Assistant Directors of Publicity—Greg Johnson, Sally O'Leary
Publicity Assistant—Jim Bowden
Director of Scouting—Elmer Gray
Minor League Director—Branch B. Rickey
Assistant Minor League Director—Tom Kayser
Assistant Director of Scouting—Jon Neiderer
Traveling Secretary—Charles Muse
Radio and TV Coordinator—Greg Brown
Community Relations Director—Patty Paytas
Assistant to the Treasurer—Kenneth C. Curcio
Ticket Manager—Norm DeLuca
Manager—Jim Leyland
Club Physician—Dr. Joseph Coroso
Team Orthopedist—Dr. Jack Failla
Team Trainer—Kent Biggerstaff
Equipment Manager—John Hallahan
Executive Offices—Three Rivers Stadium, 600 Stadium Circle, Pittsburgh, PA 15212
Telephone—323-5000 (area code 412)

SCOUTS—(Scouting Supervisors)—Gene Baker, Jack Bowen, Bart Braun, Joe L. Brown, Bill Bryk, Joe Consoli, Pablo Cruz, Larry D'Amato, George Detore, Angel Figueroa, Jerry Gardner, Pete Gebrian, Fred Goodman, Howie Haak, Buzzy Keller, Jim Maxwell, Lenny Yochim. (Associate Scouts)—Jose Luna, Boyd Odom, Steve Oleschuk, Mark Tanner, Bob Whalen.

PARK LOCATION—Three Rivers Stadium, 600 Stadium Circle.

Seating capacity—58,438.

FIELD DIMENSIONS—Home plate to left field at foul line, 335 feet; to center field, 400 feet; to right field at foul line, 335 feet.

# ST. LOUIS CARDINALS

Chairman of the Board, President and Chief Executive Officer—
August A. Busch, Jr.

Executive Vice-President, Chief Operating Officer—Fred L. Kuhlmann
Vice-Presidents—August A. Busch, III, Margaret S. Busch
Senior Vice-President—Stan Musial
Vice-President, Administration—Gary Blase
Secretary and Treasurer—John L. Hayward
Assistant Secretary—Richard Schwartz
Controller—John McMinn
Board of Directors—Adolphus A. Busch, IV, August A. Busch, Jr.,
August A. Busch, III, Margaret S. Busch, Frederic E. Giersch, Jr., Louis B. Hager,
John Hayward, Ben Kerner, Fred L. Kuhlmann, J.W. McAfee, Stanley F. Musial,
W.R. Persons, Walter C. Reisinger, Louis B. Susman
General Manager—Dal Maxvill
Manager—Whitey Herzog
Administrative Assistant to G.M.—Judy Lovelace
Director of Marketing—Marty Hendin
Administrative Asst. to Director of Marketing—Nancy McElroy
Director of Player Development—Lee Thomas
Director of Scouting—Fred McAlister
Director of Minor League Operations—Paul Fauks
Director of Public Relations—Jim Toomey
Assistant Director of Public Relations—Kip Ingle
Director of Promotions—Dan Farrell
Director of Sales—Joe Cunningham
Director of Season Ticket Sales—Sue Ann McClaren
Manager of Group Sales—Bridget Wynn
Director of Tickets and Stadium Operations—Mike Bertani
Assistant Director of Tickets—Josephine Arnold
Traveling Secretary—C.J. Cherre
Club Physician—Dr. Stan London
Executive Offices—Busch Stadium, 250 Stadium Plaza,
St. Louis, Mo. 63102
Telephone—421-3060 (area code 314)

SCOUTS—(Chief Scout)—Mo Mozzali. (Supervisors)—Jim Belz, Vern Benson, Steve Flores, Jim Johnston, Hank Kelly, Marty Keough, Marty Maier, Tom McCormack, Mike Roberts, Hal Smith, Charles (Tim) Thompson, Rube Walker (special assignment). (Part-time)—Jorge Aranzamendi, James Brown, Roberto Diaz, Cecil Espy, Manuel Guerra, Ray King, Juan Melo, Virgil Melvin, Bob Parks, Joe Popek, Kenneth Thomas.

PARK LOCATION—Busch Stadium, Broadway, Walnut Street, Stadium Plaza and Spruce Street.

Seating capacity—50,100.

FIELD DIMENSIONS—Home plate to left field at foul line, 330 feet; to center field, 414 feet; to right field at foul line, 330 feet.

# SAN DIEGO PADRES

Board of Directors—Joan Kroc, Ballard F. Smith, Jr., Anthony J. Zulfer, Jr.

President and Treasurer—Ballard F. Smith, Jr.
Senior Vice-President, Business Operations—Elten F. Schiller
Vice-President, Baseball Operations—Jack McKeon
Administrative Assistant—Rhoda Polley
Vice-President, Administration—Dick Freeman
Accounting Dept. Supervisor—Bob Wells
Major League Scout, Special Assignments—Dick Hager
Director, Minor Leagues and Scouting—Tom Romenesko
Director of Media Relations—Bill Beck
Assistant Director of Media Relations—Mike Swanson
Administrative Assistant—Mil Chipp
Media Relations Assistant—Be Barnes
Director of Community Development—Fred Whitacre
Asst. Dir. Community Relations/Publications—Jim Geschke
Director of Broadcasting—Jim Winters
Director of Group Sales—Tom Mulcahy
Director of Marketing—Andy Strasberg
Director of Ticket Sales—Dave Gilmore
Traveling Secretary—John Mattei
Manager—Dick Williams
Club Physician—Scripps Clinic
Executive Offices—P. O. Box 2000, San Diego, Calif. 92120
Telephone—283-7294 (area code 619)

SCOUTS—Santos Alomar, Dave Bartosch, Ken Bracey, Ray Coley, Jose Cora, Manny Crespo, David Freeland, Denny Galehouse, Jose Garcia, Jose Gonzales, Donald Hennelly, Ken Hennelly, Earl Jones, Pete Jones, Harvey Koepf, John Kosciak, Jim Marshall, Abe Martinez, Bill McKeon, Greg Riddoch, Tom Roberts, Ernie Sierra, Brad Sloan, Ed Stevens, Vince Valecce, Bob Warner, Henry Weaver, Hank Zacharias.

PARK LOCATION—San Diego Jack Murphy Stadium, 9949 Friars Road.

Seating capacity—58,402.

FIELD DIMENSIONS—Home plate to left field at foul line, 330 feet; to center field, 405 feet; to right field at foul line, 330 feet.

# SAN FRANCISCO GIANTS

Chairman—Robert A. Lurie

President & General Manager—Al Rosen
Executive Vice-President, Administration—Corey Busch
Vice-President, Baseball Operations—Bob Kennedy
Vice-President, Business Operations—Patrick J. Gallagher
Assistant General Manager—Ralph E. Nelson, Jr.
Director of Player Personnel and Scouting—Bob Fontaine
Minor League Administrator—Craig Bierach
Director of Travel—Dirk Smith
Director of Public Relations—Duffy Jennings
Director of Marketing—Mario Alioto
Director of Stadium Operations—Don Foreman
Ticket Manager—Arthur Schulze
Accounting Manager—Jeannie Adamo
Director of Sales—Bob Gaillard
Promotions Manager—Carlos Deza
Community Relations Manager—Dave Craig
Retail Sales Manager—Dave Alioto
Group Sales Manager—Pennie Lundberg
Stadium Club Manager—Ted Ince
Speakers Bureau—Joe Orengo
Community Representatives—Mike Sadek, Willie McCovey
Director of Graphics and Photography—Dennis Desprois
Manager—Roger Craig
Executive Offices—Candlestick Park, San Francisco, Calif. 94124
Telephone—468-3700 (area code 415)

SCOUTS—Harry Craft, Dutch Deutsch, Nino Escalera, Jim Fairey, Jack French, Robert Folkins, George M. Genovese, Milt Graff, Grady Hatton, Carl Hubbell, Herman Hannah, Al Heist, Richard Klaus, Andy Korenek, Jim Lyke, Alan Marr, T. McCarthy, D. McMillan, Frank Ontiveros, Jack Paepke, Bill Parese, Ken (Squeaky) Parker, A. Rodriguez, Hank Sauer, John Shafer, George Sobek, Marvin Stendel, Joe Strain, Bill Teed, Gene Thompson, Mike Toomey, Jack Uhey, John Van Ornum, Joe Winstead, Tom Zimmer.

PARK LOCATION—Candlestick Point, Bayshore Freeway.

Seating capacity—58,000.

FIELD DIMENSIONS—Home plate to left field at foul line, 335 feet; to center field, 400 feet; to right field at foul line, 330 feet.

**DON MATTINGLY**
● NEW YORK YANKEES ●
MAJOR LEAGUE
PLAYER OF THE YEAR

**JOHN SCHUERHOLZ**
● KANSAS CITY ROYALS ●
MAJOR LEAGUE EXECUTIVE

**BOBBY COX**
● TORONTO BLUE JAYS ●
MAJOR LEAGUE MANAGER

**JOSE CANSECO**
● HUNTSVILLE, TACOMA ●
MINOR LEAGUE PLAYER

𝕿𝖍𝖊 𝕾𝖕𝖔𝖗𝖙𝖎𝖓𝖌 𝕹𝖊𝖜𝖘

No. 1

# MEN

of

# 1985

**JIM FREGOSI**
● LOUISVILLE ●
MINOR LEAGUE MANAGER

**PATTY COX HAMPTON**
● OKLAHOMA CITY ●
MINOR LEAGUE EXECUTIVE
IN CLASS AAA

**BEN BERNARD**
● ALBANY-COLONIE ●
MINOR LEAGUE EXECUTIVE
IN CLASS AA

**PETE VONACHEN**
● PEORIA ●
MINOR LEAGUE EXECUTIVE
IN CLASS A

# Major League Players Association

805 Third Avenue
New York, N.Y. 10022
Telephone— (212) 826-0808

Executive Director & General Counsel—Donald Fehr
Special Assistant—Mark Belanger
Associate General Counsel—Eugene Orza
Assistant General Counsel—Lauren Rich
Counsel—Arthur Schack
Staff—Bonnie White and Tracy Freireich

### EXECUTIVE BOARD

Don Baylor—American League Representative
Buck Martinez—Alternate American League Representative
Keith Moreland—National League Representative
Vance Law—Alternate National League Representative
Ted Simmons—Pension Committee
Jim Beattie—Pension Committee Alternate
Rick Honeycutt—Pension Committee
Rick Horton—Pension Committee Alternate
Plus all remaining player representatives

### NATIONAL LEAGUE PLAYER REPRESENTATIVES

Bruce Benedict—Atlanta Braves
Keith Moreland—Chicago Cubs
Joe Price—Cincinnati Reds
Bob Knepper—Houston Astros
Mike Scioscia—Los Angeles Dodgers
Jim Wohlford—Montreal Expos
Keith Hernandez—New York Mets
Shane Rawley—Philadelphia Phillies
Jim Morrison—Pittsburgh Pirates
Tom Herr—St. Louis Cardinals
Terry Kennedy—San Diego Padres
Jim Gott—San Francisco Giants

### AMERICAN LEAGUE PLAYER REPRESENTATIVES

Scott McGregor—Baltimore Orioles
Rick Miller—Boston Red Sox
Ron Romanick—California Angels
Rich Dotson—Chicago White Sox
Brett Butler—Cleveland Indians
Alan Trammell—Detroit Tigers
Joe Beckwith—Kansas City Royals
Paul Molitor—Milwaukee Brewers
Ron Davis—Minnesota Twins
Dave Winfield—New York Yankees
Dwayne Murphy—Oakland A's
Jim Beattie—Seattle Mariners
Burt Hooton—Texas Rangers
Buck Martinez—Toronto Blue Jays

# Minor League Presidents for '86

### CLASS AAA

American Association—Joe Ryan, P. O. Box 382, Wichita, Kan. 67201

International League—Harold Cooper, P.O. Box 608, Grove City, Ohio 43123

Mexican League—Pedro Treto Cisneros, Av. Cuauhtemoc No. 451-101 Col. Narvarte C.P. 03020, Mexico, D.F.

Pacific Coast League—Bill Cutler, 2101 E. Broadway Rd., Tempe, Ariz. 85282

### CLASS AA

Eastern League—Charles Eshbach, P.O. Box 716, Plainville, Conn. 06062

Southern League—Jimmy Bragan, 235 Main St., Suite 200, Trussville, Ala. 35173

Texas League—Carl Sawatski, 10201 W. Markham St., Little Rock, Ark. 72205

### CLASS A

California League—Joe Gagliardi, P.O. Box 26400, San Jose, Calif. 95159

Carolina League—John Hopkins, 4241 United Street, Greensboro, N.C. 27407

Florida State League—George MacDonald, Jr., P.O. Box 414, Lakeland, Fla. 33802

Midwest League—Bill Walters, P.O. Box 444, Burlington, Ia. 52601

New York-Pennsylvania League—Leo A. Pinckney, 168 E. Genesee St., Auburn, N. Y. 13021

Northwest League—Jack Cain, P.O. Box 30025, Portland, Ore. 97230

South Atlantic League—John H. Moss, P.O. Box 49, Kings Mountain, N. C. 28086

### ROOKIE CLASSIFICATION

Appalachian League—Bill Halstead, 157 Carson Lane, Bristol, Va. 24201

Gulf Coast League—Thomas J. Saffell, 11 Sunset Drive, Suite 501, Sarasota, Fla. 33577

Pioneer League—Ralph C. Nelles, P. O. Box 1144, Billings, Mont. 59103

# Major League Farm Systems for '86

## AMERICAN LEAGUE

BALTIMORE (5): AAA—Rochester. AA—Charlotte. A—Hagerstown, Newark. Rookie—Bluefield.

BOSTON (5): AAA—Pawtucket. AA—New Britain, Conn. A—Elmira, Greensboro, Winter Haven.

CALIFORNIA (5): AAA—Edmonton. AA—Midland. A—Quad Cities, Palm Springs, Salem.

CHICAGO (5): AAA—Buffalo. AA—Birmingham. A—Appleton, Peninsula. Rookie—Sarasota.

CLEVELAND (5): AAA—Old Orchard Beach, Me. AA—Waterbury. A—Batavia, Waterloo. Rookie—Burlington, N.C.

DETROIT (5): AAA—Nashville. AA—Glens Falls. A—Lakeland, Gastonia. Rookie—Bristol, Va.

KANSAS CITY (5): AAA—Omaha. AA—Memphis. A—Eugene, Fort Myers. Rookie—Sarasota.

MILWAUKEE (5): AAA—Vancouver. AA—El Paso. A—Beloit, Stockton. Rookie—Helena.

MINNESOTA (5): AAA—Toledo. AA—Orlando. A—Kenosha, Visalia. Rookie—Elizabethton.

NEW YORK (5): AAA—Columbus, O. AA—Albany-Colonie, N.Y. A—Fort Lauderdale, Oneonta. Rookie—Sarasota.

OAKLAND (5): AAA—Tacoma. AA—Huntsville. A—Medford, Modesto, Madison.

SEATTLE (5): AAA—Calgary. AA—Chattanooga. A—Wausau, Salinas. Rookie—Bellingham.

TEXAS (5): AAA—Oklahoma City. AA—Tulsa. A—Salem, Daytona Beach. Rookie—Sarasota.

TORONTO (6): AAA—Syracuse. AA—Knoxville. A—Florence, St. Catherines, Ont., Ventura, Calif. Rookie—Medicine Hat.

## NATIONAL LEAGUE

ATLANTA (7): AAA—Richmond. AA—Greenville. A—Sumter, Durham. Rookie—Bradenton, Pulaski. Rookie—Pocatello.

CHICAGO (6): AAA—Iowa. AA—Pittsfield. A—Geneva, Peoria, Winston-Salem. Rookie—Wytheville.

CINCINNATI (6): AAA—Denver. AA—Burlington, Vt. A—Cedar Rapids, Tampa. Rookie—Billings, Sarasota.

HOUSTON (6): AAA—Tucson. AA—Columbus, Ga. A—Asheville, Auburn, Osceola, Fla. Rookie—Sarasota.

LOS ANGELES (6): AAA—Albuquerque. AA—San Antonio. A—Bakersfield, Vero Beach. Rookie—Great Falls, Sarasota.

MONTREAL (6): AAA—Indianapolis. AA—Jacksonville. A—Jamestown, West Palm Beach, Burlington, Ia. Rookie—Bradenton.

NEW YORK (6): AAA—Tidewater. AA—Jackson. A—Columbia, S.C., Little Falls, Lynchburg. Rookie—Kingsport.

PHILADELPHIA (6): AAA—Portland. AA—Reading. A—Clearwater, Bend, Spartanburg, Utica.

PITTSBURGH (6): AAA—Hawaii. AA—Nashua. A—Prince William, Macon, Watertown. Rookie—Bradenton.

ST. LOUIS (7): AAA—Louisville. AA—Arkansas. A—Erie, St. Petersburg, Savannah, Springfield. Rookie—Johnson City.

SAN DIEGO (5): AAA—Las Vegas. AA—Beaumont. A—Charleston, S.C., Reno, Spokane.

SAN FRANCISCO (5): AAA—Phoenix. AA—Shreveport. A—Clinton, Fresno, Everett.

# OFFICIAL MINOR LEAGUE AVERAGES

### Including

### Official Averages of All Class AAA, Class AA, Class A and Rookie Leagues

**National Association President John Johnson.**

# American Association

## CLASS AAA

**Leading Batter**
**SCOTTI MADISON**
Nashville

**League President**
**JOE RYAN**

**Leading Pitcher**
**STEVE FARR**
Omaha

### CHAMPIONSHIP WINNERS IN PREVIOUS YEARS

| | | |
|---|---|---|
| 1902—Indianapolis .683 | 1939—Kansas City .695 | 1961—Indianapolis .573 |
| 1903—St. Paul .657 |    Louisville (4th)‡ .490 |    Louisville (2nd)‡ .533 |
| 1904—St. Paul .646 | 1940—Kansas City .625 | 1962—Indianapolis .605 |
| 1905—Columbus .658 |    Louisville (4th)‡ .500 |    Louisville (4th)‡ .486 |
| 1906—Columbus .615 | 1941—Columbus† .621 | 1963-1968—Did not operate. |
| 1907—Columbus .584 | 1942—Kansas City .549 | 1969—Omaha .607 |
| 1908—Indianapolis .601 |    Columbus (3rd)‡ .532 | 1970—Omaha° .529 |
| 1909—Louisville .554 | 1943—Milwaukee .596 |    Denver .504 |
| 1910—Minneapolis .637 |    Columbus (3rd)‡ .532 | 1971—Indianapolis .604 |
| 1911—Minneapolis .600 | 1944—Milwaukee .667 |    Denver° .521 |
| 1912—Minneapolis .636 |    Louisville (3rd)‡ .574 | 1972—Wichita .621 |
| 1913—Milwaukee .599 | 1945—Milwaukee .604 |    Evansville° .593 |
| 1914—Milwaukee .590 |    Louisville (3rd)‡ .545 | 1973—Iowa .610 |
| 1915—Minneapolis .597 | 1946—Louisville† .601 |    Tulsa° .504 |
| 1916—Louisville .605 | 1947—Kansas City .608 | 1974—Indianapolis .578 |
| 1917—Indianapolis .588 |    Milwaukee (3rd)‡ .513 |    Tulsa° .567 |
| 1918—Kansas City .589 | 1948—Indianapolis .649 | 1975—Evansville° .566 |
| 1919—St. Paul .610 |    St. Paul (3rd)‡ .558 |    Denver .596 |
| 1920—St. Paul .701 | 1949—St. Paul .608 | 1976—Denver° .632 |
| 1921—Louisville .583 |    Indianapolis (2nd)‡ .604 |    Omaha .574 |
| 1922—St. Paul .641 | 1950—Minneapolis .584 | 1977—Omaha .563 |
| 1923—Kansas City .675 |    Columbus (3rd)‡ .549 |    Denver° .522 |
| 1924—St. Paul .578 | 1951—Milwaukee† .623 | 1978—Indianapolis .578 |
| 1925—Louisville .635 | 1952—Milwaukee .656 |    Omaha° .489 |
| 1926—Louisville .629 |    Kansas City (2nd)‡ .578 | 1979—Evansville° .574 |
| 1927—Toledo .601 | 1953—Toledo .584 |    Oklahoma City .533 |
| 1928—Indianapolis .593 |    Kansas City (2nd)‡ .571 | 1980—Denver .676 |
| 1929—Kansas City .665 | 1954—Indianapolis .625 |    Springfield° .551 |
| 1930—Louisville .608 |    Louisville (2nd)‡ .556 | 1981—Omaha .581 |
| 1931—St. Paul .623 | 1955—Minneapolis† .597 |    Denver° .559 |
| 1932—Minneapolis .595 | 1956—Indianapolis† .597 | 1982—Indianapolis° .551 |
| 1933—Columbus° .604 | 1957—Wichita .604 |    Omaha .518 |
|    Minneapolis .562 |    Denver (2nd)‡ .584 | 1983—Louisville .578 |
| 1934—Minneapolis .570 | 1958—Charleston .589 |    Denver‡ .545 |
|    Columbus° .556 |    Minneapolis (3rd)‡ .536 | 1984—Denver .513 |
| 1935—Minneapolis .591 | 1959—Louisville§ .599 |    Louisville‡ .510 |
| 1936—Milwaukee† .584 |    Omaha§ .516 | |
| 1937—Columbus† .584 |    Minneapolis (2nd)‡ .586 | |
| 1938—St. Paul .596 | 1960—Denver .571 | |
|    Kansas City (2nd)‡ .556 |    Louisville (2nd)‡ .556 | |

°Won playoff (East vs. West). †Won championship and four-team playoff. ‡Won four-team playoff. §Respective Eastern and Western division winners.

## STANDING OF CLUBS AT CLOSE OF SEASON, SEPTEMBER 2

### EASTERN DIVISION

| Club | W. | L. | T. | Pct. | G.B. |
|---|---|---|---|---|---|
| Louisville (Cardinals) | 74 | 68 | 2 | .521 | ....... |
| Nashville (Tigers) | 71 | 70 | 1 | .504 | 2½ |
| Buffalo (White Sox) | 66 | 76 | 0 | .465 | 8 |
| Indianapolis (Expos) | 61 | 81 | 0 | .430 | 13 |

### WESTERN DIVISION

| Club | W. | L. | T. | Pct. | G.B. |
|---|---|---|---|---|---|
| Oklahoma City (Rangers) | 79 | 63 | 1 | .556 | ....... |
| Denver (Reds) | 77 | 65 | 0 | .542 | 2 |
| Omaha (Royals) | 73 | 69 | 0 | .514 | 6 |
| Iowa (Cubs) | 66 | 75 | 0 | .468 | 12½ |

### COMPOSITE STANDING OF CLUBS AT CLOSE OF SEASON, SEPTEMBER 2

| Club | O.C. | Den. | Lou. | Oma. | Nash. | Iowa | Buf. | Ind. | W. | L. | T. | Pct. | G.B. |
|---|---|---|---|---|---|---|---|---|---|---|---|---|---|
| Oklahoma City (Rangers) | .... | 15 | 9 | 14 | 9 | 14 | 11 | 7 | 79 | 63 | 1 | .556 | ....... |
| Denver (Reds) | 11 | .... | 10 | 14 | 7 | 15 | 7 | 13 | 77 | 65 | 0 | .542 | 2 |
| Louisville (Cardinals) | 7 | 6 | .... | 7 | 14 | 9 | 14 | 17 | 74 | 68 | 2 | .521 | 5 |
| Omaha (Royals) | 12 | 12 | 9 | .... | 8 | 14 | 10 | 8 | 73 | 69 | 0 | .514 | 6 |
| Nashville (Tigers) | 7 | 9 | 12 | 8 | .... | 6 | 15 | 14 | 71 | 70 | 1 | .504 | 7½ |
| Iowa (Cubs) | 12 | 11 | 7 | 12 | 9 | .... | 8 | 7 | 66 | 75 | 0 | .468 | 12½ |
| Buffalo (White Sox) | 5 | 9 | 12 | 6 | 11 | 8 | .... | 15 | 66 | 76 | 0 | .465 | 13 |
| Indianapolis (Expos) | 9 | 3 | 9 | 8 | 12 | 9 | 11 | .... | 61 | 81 | 0 | .430 | 18 |

Iowa club represented Des Moines, Ia.

Major league affiliations in parentheses.

Playoffs—Louisville defeated Oklahoma City, four games to one, to win league championship.

Regular-Season Attendance—Buffalo, 362,762; Denver, 308,268; Indianapolis, 209,041; Iowa, 269,513; Louisville, 651,090; Nashville, 364,225; Oklahoma City, 364,247; Omaha, 175,329. Total, 2,704,475. Total Playoff Attendance, 20,202.

Managers—Buffalo, John Boles; Denver, Gene Dusan; Indianapolis, Felipe Alou; Iowa, Larry Cox; Louisville, Jim Fregosi; Nashville, Lee Walls (thru April 18), Leon Roberts (interim mgr. April 19 thru April 25), Gordy MacKenzie (April 26 thru end of season); Oklahoma City, Dave Oliver; Omaha, Gene Lamont.

All-Star Team—1B—Andres Galarraga, Indianapolis; 2B—Tom Runnells, Denver; 3B—Steve Buechele, Oklahoma City; SS—Wade Rowdon, Denver; OF—Darrell Brown, Nashville; Wally Johnson, Indianapolis; Paul O'Neill, Denver; C—Scotti Madison, Nashville and Joel Skinner, Buffalo; DH—Dave Hostetler, Iowa; RHP—Mark Huismann, Omaha; LHP—Tony Ferreira, Omaha; Most Valuable Player—Steve Buechele, Oklahoma City; Pitcher of the Year—Mark Huismann, Omaha; Co-Managers of the Year—Jim Fregosi, Louisville and Dave Oliver, Oklahoma City.

(Compiled by Howe News Bureau, Boston, Mass.)

### CLUB BATTING

| Club | Pct. | G. | AB. | R. | OR. | H. | TB. | 2B. | 3B. | HR. | RBI. | GW. | SH. | SF. | HP. | BB. | Int. BB. | SO. | SB. | CS. | LOB. |
|---|---|---|---|---|---|---|---|---|---|---|---|---|---|---|---|---|---|---|---|---|---|
| Denver | .272 | 142 | 4771 | 686 | 663 | 1300 | 2030 | 222 | 53 | 134 | 640 | 70 | 31 | 35 | 20 | 450 | 30 | 715 | 144 | 94 | 908 |
| Indianapolis | .266 | 142 | 4806 | 618 | 625 | 1277 | 1823 | 207 | 39 | 87 | 579 | 59 | 45 | 28 | 26 | 479 | 21 | 800 | 138 | 83 | 1010 |
| Buffalo | .257 | 142 | 4591 | 647 | 660 | 1181 | 1773 | 195 | 23 | 117 | 586 | 64 | 35 | 54 | 35 | 572 | 23 | 784 | 72 | 45 | 999 |
| Iowa | .253 | 141 | 4592 | 602 | 639 | 1161 | 1817 | 235 | 47 | 109 | 544 | 56 | 59 | 27 | 35 | 551 | 17 | 929 | 179 | 97 | 963 |
| Nashville | .252 | 142 | 4647 | 568 | 609 | 1171 | 1728 | 221 | 24 | 96 | 521 | 63 | 50 | 44 | 23 | 463 | 23 | 788 | 128 | 82 | 924 |
| Oklahoma City | .251 | 143 | 4601 | 630 | 542 | 1157 | 1788 | 207 | 59 | 102 | 579 | 71 | 30 | 43 | 46 | 585 | 24 | 813 | 109 | 60 | 1009 |
| Omaha | .249 | 142 | 4544 | 537 | 551 | 1131 | 1536 | 175 | 43 | 48 | 482 | 68 | 38 | 40 | 19 | 497 | 21 | 660 | 118 | 75 | 950 |
| Louisville | .239 | 144 | 4609 | 569 | 568 | 1103 | 1590 | 214 | 30 | 71 | 509 | 70 | 52 | 44 | 42 | 517 | 25 | 691 | 133 | 51 | 939 |

### INDIVIDUAL BATTING

(Leading Qualifiers for Batting Championship—383 or More Plate Appearances)

*Bats lefthanded.    †Switch-hitter.

| Player and Club | Pct. | G. | AB. | R. | H. | TB. | 2B. | 3B. | HR. | RBI. | GW. | SH. | SF. | HP. | BB. | Int. BB. | SO. | SB. | CS. |
|---|---|---|---|---|---|---|---|---|---|---|---|---|---|---|---|---|---|---|---|
| Madison, Scotti, Nashville† | .341 | 86 | 317 | 59 | 108 | 187 | 23 | 4 | 16 | 54 | 11 | 1 | 1 | 3 | 43 | 2 | 45 | 3 | 3 |
| Johnson, Wallace, Indianapolis† | .309 | 127 | 431 | 68 | 133 | 161 | 13 | 3 | 3 | 36 | 6 | 4 | 2 | 1 | 45 | 4 | 28 | 34 | 9 |
| O'Neill, Paul, Denver* | .305 | 137 | 509 | 63 | 155 | 214 | 32 | 3 | 7 | 74 | 13 | 1 | 6 | 1 | 28 | 4 | 73 | 5 | 7 |
| Christmas, Stephen, Denver* | .298 | 127 | 409 | 50 | 122 | 182 | 12 | 0 | 16 | 56 | 3 | 0 | 7 | 3 | 50 | 4 | 36 | 1 | 2 |
| Buechele, Steven, Oklahoma City | .297 | 89 | 350 | 56 | 104 | 165 | 20 | 7 | 9 | 64 | 7 | 0 | 2 | 4 | 33 | 2 | 62 | 6 | 3 |
| Brown, Darrell, Nashville† | .294 | 97 | 395 | 45 | 116 | 135 | 12 | 2 | 1 | 33 | 4 | 2 | 2 | 1 | 9 | 1 | 35 | 32 | 17 |
| Garcia, Leonardo, Denver* | .291 | 118 | 385 | 53 | 112 | 149 | 19 | 3 | 4 | 25 | 3 | 2 | 2 | 1 | 26 | 2 | 42 | 18 | 11 |
| Runnells, Thomas, Denver† | .290 | 114 | 466 | 55 | 135 | 188 | 22 | 8 | 5 | 51 | 4 | 4 | 4 | 1 | 34 | 3 | 41 | 5 | 11 |
| Rowdon, Wade, Denver | .289 | 128 | 457 | 61 | 132 | 230 | 31 | 5 | 19 | 78 | 7 | 3 | 3 | 4 | 48 | 5 | 81 | 7 | 10 |
| DeSa, Joseph, Buffalo* | .287 | 97 | 366 | 56 | 105 | 183 | 21 | 3 | 17 | 66 | 4 | 0 | 6 | 3 | 49 | 3 | 46 | 8 | 1 |

Departmental Leaders: G—O'Neill, 137; AB—O'Neill, 509; R—Galarraga, 75; H—O'Neill, 155; TB—Rowdon, 230; 2B—O'Neill, 32; 3B—Brower, 18; HR—Hostetler, 29; RBI—Hostetler, 89; GWRBI—Galarraga, O'Neill, 13; SH—Oquendo, 15; SF—J. Anderson, Castro, Christmas, Laga, Yobs, 7; HP—Lyons, 11; BB—Gillaspie, 77; IBB—Gillaspie, Roberts, 6; SO—Skinner, 115; SB—Ford, 45; CS—D. Brown, Cole, Ford, 17.

(All Players—Listed Alphabetically)

| Player and Club | Pct. | G. | AB. | R. | H. | TB. | 2B. | 3B. | HR. | RBI. | GW. | SH. | SF. | HP. | BB. | Int. BB. | SO. | SB. | CS. |
|---|---|---|---|---|---|---|---|---|---|---|---|---|---|---|---|---|---|---|---|
| Abrego, Johnny, Iowa | .000 | 5 | 5 | 0 | 0 | 0 | 0 | 0 | 0 | 0 | 0 | 0 | 0 | 0 | 0 | 0 | 2 | 0 | 0 |
| Anderson, James, Oklahoma City | .246 | 126 | 435 | 59 | 107 | 160 | 21 | 4 | 8 | 43 | 4 | 3 | 7 | 2 | 70 | 2 | 62 | 2 | 3 |
| Ayer, Jonathan, Louisville | .238 | 118 | 399 | 49 | 95 | 148 | 20 | 3 | 9 | 56 | 12 | 4 | 5 | 4 | 43 | 1 | 71 | 1 | 1 |
| Baker, Derrell, Indianapolis | .387 | 21 | 62 | 9 | 24 | 30 | 1 | 1 | 1 | 7 | 0 | 2 | 0 | 0 | 10 | 0 | 9 | 1 | 0 |
| Baker, Douglas, Nashville† | .218 | 107 | 325 | 42 | 71 | 94 | 9 | 4 | 2 | 30 | 4 | 10 | 4 | 3 | 41 | 0 | 50 | 6 | 2 |
| Baker, Kenneth, Omaha* | .253 | 73 | 194 | 26 | 49 | 63 | 7 | 2 | 1 | 23 | 6 | 3 | 2 | 1 | 27 | 0 | 19 | 2 | 3 |
| Baker, Steven, Indianapolis | .077 | 27 | 13 | 1 | 1 | 1 | 0 | 0 | 0 | 1 | 0 | 2 | 0 | 0 | 0 | 0 | 7 | 0 | 0 |
| Baller, Jay, Iowa | .000 | 24 | 5 | 0 | 0 | 0 | 0 | 0 | 0 | 0 | 0 | 0 | 0 | 0 | 0 | 0 | 4 | 0 | 0 |
| Bargar, Gregory, Indianapolis | .167 | 38 | 12 | 0 | 2 | 2 | 0 | 0 | 0 | 0 | 0 | 0 | 0 | 0 | 1 | 0 | 5 | 0 | 0 |
| Barnes, Richard, Iowa | .250 | 7 | 4 | 1 | 1 | 1 | 0 | 0 | 0 | 1 | 0 | 0 | 0 | 0 | 1 | 0 | 2 | 0 | 0 |
| Barnes, William, 12 Den-83 Ind | .279 | 95 | 340 | 51 | 95 | 135 | 16 | 0 | 8 | 63 | 7 | 3 | 3 | 5 | 38 | 3 | 45 | 20 | 8 |
| Barrera, Nelson, Buffalo | .176 | 25 | 74 | 9 | 13 | 22 | 3 | 0 | 2 | 4 | 0 | 0 | 1 | 10 | 3 | 15 | 2 | 1 |
| Bergman, David, Nashville* | .231 | 11 | 39 | 6 | 9 | 13 | 1 | 0 | 1 | 6 | 1 | 0 | 1 | 0 | 5 | 1 | 6 | 1 | 1 |
| Bernstine, Nehames, Iowa† | .318 | 83 | 302 | 52 | 96 | 121 | 11 | 4 | 2 | 18 | 1 | 2 | 1 | 3 | 28 | 1 | 55 | 33 | 11 |
| Bilardello, Dann, Denver | .242 | 67 | 236 | 41 | 57 | 98 | 5 | 3 | 10 | 37 | 6 | 0 | 2 | 2 | 25 | 0 | 37 | 4 | 5 |
| Bjorkman, George, Indianapolis | .226 | 11 | 31 | 3 | 7 | 10 | 3 | 0 | 0 | 0 | 0 | 0 | 0 | 0 | 2 | 0 | 7 | 2 | 0 |
| Boston, Daryl, Buffalo* | .274 | 63 | 241 | 45 | 66 | 110 | 12 | 1 | 10 | 36 | 4 | 2 | 1 | 4 | 33 | 0 | 48 | 15 | 5 |
| Botelho, Derek, Iowa | .353 | 22 | 17 | 0 | 6 | 6 | 0 | 0 | 0 | 0 | 0 | 1 | 0 | 0 | 0 | 0 | 3 | 0 | 1 |
| Brooks, Fred, Iowa | .242 | 106 | 327 | 39 | 79 | 126 | 18 | 1 | 9 | 35 | 6 | 5 | 1 | 1 | 52 | 0 | 52 | 8 | 3 |
| Brower, Robert, Oklahoma City | .249 | 133 | 445 | 56 | 111 | 175 | 13 | 18 | 5 | 50 | 4 | 4 | 2 | 2 | 54 | 0 | 86 | 33 | 12 |
| Brown, Darrell, Nashville† | .294 | 97 | 395 | 45 | 116 | 135 | 12 | 2 | 1 | 33 | 4 | 2 | 2 | 1 | 9 | 1 | 25 | 32 | 17 |
| Brown, Steven, Indianapolis | .000 | 45 | 5 | 0 | 0 | 0 | 0 | 0 | 0 | 0 | 0 | 0 | 0 | 0 | 0 | 0 | 3 | 0 | 0 |

| Player and Club | Pct. | G. | AB. | R. | H. | TB. | 2B. | 3B. | HR. | RBI. | GW. | SH. | SF. | HP. | BB. | Int. BB. | SO. | SB. | CS. |
|---|---|---|---|---|---|---|---|---|---|---|---|---|---|---|---|---|---|---|---|
| Brummer, Glenn, Oklahoma City | .000 | 1 | 4 | 0 | 0 | 0 | 0 | 0 | 0 | 0 | 0 | 0 | 0 | 0 | 0 | 0 | 0 | 0 | 0 |
| Brunenkant, Barry, Oklahoma City | .182 | 16 | 44 | 4 | 8 | 10 | 2 | 0 | 0 | 3 | 0 | 0 | 0 | 0 | 10 | 0 | 8 | 0 | 0 |
| Buechele, Steven, Oklahoma City | .297 | 89 | 350 | 56 | 104 | 165 | 20 | 7 | 9 | 64 | 7 | 0 | 2 | 4 | 33 | 2 | 62 | 6 | 3 |
| Burroughs, Darren, Denver | .125 | 15 | 8 | 0 | 1 | 1 | 0 | 0 | 0 | 0 | 0 | 2 | 0 | 0 | 0 | 0 | 1 | 0 | 0 |
| Butera, Salvatore, Indianapolis | .222 | 5 | 18 | 2 | 4 | 7 | 0 | 0 | 1 | 4 | 0 | 0 | 0 | 0 | 3 | 0 | 1 | 0 | 0 |
| Canady, Chuckie, Oklahoma City | .220 | 98 | 314 | 43 | 69 | 119 | 12 | 1 | 12 | 42 | 5 | 2 | 1 | 5 | 50 | 1 | 74 | 1 | 2 |
| Candaele, Casey, Indianapolis† | .259 | 127 | 390 | 55 | 101 | 124 | 13 | 5 | 0 | 35 | 2 | 11 | 1 | 0 | 44 | 2 | 33 | 13 | 10 |
| Cangelosi, John, Buffalo* | .238 | 78 | 244 | 34 | 58 | 79 | 8 | 5 | 1 | 21 | 3 | 3 | 2 | 1 | 46 | 1 | 32 | 14 | 7 |
| Capra, Nick, Oklahoma City | .272 | 97 | 353 | 53 | 96 | 115 | 17 | 1 | 0 | 27 | 4 | 2 | 1 | 4 | 68 | 1 | 45 | 25 | 16 |
| Castillo, Anthony, Iowa | .259 | 86 | 255 | 29 | 66 | 99 | 15 | 0 | 6 | 26 | 1 | 4 | 1 | 4 | 22 | 2 | 50 | 1 | 2 |
| Castro, Jose, Buffalo | .240 | 134 | 454 | 68 | 109 | 152 | 17 | 1 | 8 | 50 | 8 | 1 | 7 | 2 | 65 | 2 | 77 | 2 | 7 |
| Cates, Timothy, Indianapolis | .167 | 8 | 6 | 0 | 1 | 1 | 0 | 0 | 0 | 0 | 0 | 0 | 0 | 0 | 0 | 0 | 2 | 0 | 0 |
| Chavez, Pedro, Nashville | .227 | 51 | 154 | 14 | 35 | 46 | 3 | 1 | 2 | 14 | 0 | 3 | 1 | 0 | 12 | 0 | 17 | 6 | 6 |
| Christmas, Stephen, Buffalo* | .298 | 127 | 409 | 50 | 122 | 182 | 12 | 0 | 16 | 56 | 3 | 0 | 7 | 3 | 50 | 4 | 36 | 1 | 2 |
| Clements, David, Louisville | .105 | 31 | 57 | 3 | 6 | 8 | 2 | 0 | 0 | 7 | 0 | 0 | 0 | 0 | 4 | 0 | 13 | 0 | 0 |
| Cole, Michael, Omaha* | .339 | 69 | 227 | 41 | 77 | 94 | 7 | 5 | 0 | 19 | 2 | 1 | 1 | 2 | 56 | 0 | 14 | 28 | 17 |
| Coleman, Vincent, Louisville | .143 | 5 | 21 | 1 | 3 | 3 | 0 | 0 | 0 | 0 | 1 | 0 | 0 | 0 | 0 | 0 | 2 | 0 | 0 |
| Daniels, Kalvoski, Denver* | .302 | 76 | 285 | 59 | 86 | 161 | 12 | 9 | 15 | 43 | 5 | 1 | 1 | 2 | 37 | 1 | 34 | 10 | 11 |
| Darkis, William, Oklahoma City | .217 | 23 | 69 | 8 | 15 | 22 | 1 | 0 | 2 | 6 | 1 | 0 | 1 | 2 | 10 | 0 | 14 | 0 | 0 |
| Davis, Eric, Denver | .277 | 64 | 206 | 48 | 57 | 116 | 10 | 2 | 15 | 38 | 2 | 0 | 3 | 1 | 29 | 0 | 67 | 35 | 5 |
| Davis, Wallace, Omaha | .263 | 109 | 403 | 58 | 106 | 170 | 26 | 10 | 6 | 34 | 6 | 3 | 3 | 1 | 26 | 0 | 89 | 15 | 6 |
| Dayett, Brian, Iowa | .378 | 14 | 37 | 5 | 14 | 21 | 4 | 0 | 1 | 11 | 2 | 0 | 1 | 0 | 7 | 1 | 2 | 1 | 0 |
| DeSa, Joseph, Buffalo* | .287 | 97 | 366 | 56 | 105 | 183 | 21 | 3 | 17 | 66 | 4 | 0 | 6 | 3 | 39 | 3 | 46 | 8 | 1 |
| Dopson, John, Indianapolis* | .167 | 18 | 6 | 0 | 1 | 1 | 0 | 0 | 0 | 0 | 0 | 0 | 0 | 0 | 0 | 0 | 3 | 0 | 0 |
| Dunbar, Thomas, Oklahoma City* | .226 | 49 | 164 | 12 | 37 | 46 | 7 | 1 | 0 | 16 | 2 | 2 | 3 | 0 | 23 | 1 | 21 | 4 | 1 |
| Dunston, Shawon, Iowa | .268 | 73 | 272 | 24 | 73 | 100 | 9 | 6 | 2 | 28 | 1 | 5 | 1 | 1 | 5 | 0 | 49 | 17 | 12 |
| Earl, Scott, Nashville | .236 | 125 | 381 | 55 | 90 | 136 | 19 | 3 | 7 | 44 | 4 | 12 | 4 | 2 | 50 | 1 | 98 | 23 | 12 |
| Engel, Steven, Iowa | .200 | 11 | 5 | 0 | 1 | 1 | 0 | 0 | 0 | 2 | 1 | 2 | 0 | 0 | 1 | 0 | 2 | 0 | 0 |
| Foley, Marvis, Buffalo* | .218 | 40 | 78 | 15 | 17 | 33 | 2 | 1 | 4 | 17 | 1 | 0 | 2 | 1 | 22 | 1 | 15 | 0 | 0 |
| Ford, Curtis, Louisville* | .255 | 127 | 475 | 73 | 121 | 174 | 20 | 6 | 7 | 45 | 5 | 6 | 3 | 7 | 56 | 3 | 48 | 45 | 17 |
| Frobel, Douglas, Indianapolis* | .284 | 23 | 74 | 9 | 21 | 35 | 6 | 1 | 2 | 11 | 0 | 0 | 0 | 0 | 6 | 0 | 18 | 3 | 2 |
| Fuentes, Michael, Indianapolis | .256 | 121 | 391 | 58 | 100 | 147 | 11 | 0 | 12 | 58 | 4 | 0 | 1 | 3 | 70 | 0 | 114 | 4 | 6 |
| Galarraga, Andres, Indianapolis | .269 | 121 | 439 | 75 | 118 | 224 | 15 | 8 | 25 | 87 | 13 | 0 | 3 | 7 | 45 | 4 | 103 | 3 | 0 |
| Garcia, Leonardo, Denver* | .291 | 118 | 385 | 53 | 112 | 149 | 19 | 3 | 4 | 25 | 3 | 2 | 2 | 1 | 26 | 2 | 42 | 18 | 11 |
| Geren, Robert, Louisville | .357 | 5 | 14 | 2 | 5 | 10 | 2 | 0 | 1 | 3 | 1 | 0 | 0 | 0 | 0 | 0 | 1 | 0 | 0 |
| Gilbert, Mark, Buffalo† | .266 | 119 | 428 | 67 | 114 | 153 | 20 | 5 | 3 | 33 | 4 | 7 | 5 | 4 | 54 | 3 | 78 | 14 | 8 |
| Gillaspie, Mark, Iowa† | .257 | 117 | 377 | 54 | 97 | 169 | 30 | 3 | 12 | 63 | 4 | 1 | 4 | 2 | 77 | 6 | 102 | 3 | 4 |
| Glynn, Eugene, Indianapolis | .400 | 3 | 5 | 0 | 2 | 2 | 0 | 0 | 0 | 0 | 0 | 0 | 0 | 0 | 0 | 0 | 1 | 0 | 0 |
| Gonzales, Rene, Indianapolis | .226 | 130 | 340 | 21 | 77 | 90 | 11 | 1 | 0 | 25 | 3 | 4 | 1 | 0 | 22 | 0 | 49 | 3 | 5 |
| Gonzalez, Orlando, Denver | .253 | 75 | 265 | 25 | 67 | 105 | 10 | 2 | 8 | 34 | 3 | 2 | 3 | 0 | 18 | 0 | 27 | 2 | 7 |
| Grant, Thomas, Iowa* | .268 | 81 | 231 | 36 | 62 | 93 | 14 | 1 | 5 | 24 | 1 | 2 | 2 | 2 | 45 | 0 | 42 | 0 | 5 |
| Grapenthin, Richard, Indianapolis | .000 | 48 | 4 | 0 | 0 | 0 | 0 | 0 | 0 | 0 | 0 | 0 | 0 | 0 | 0 | 0 | 0 | 0 | 0 |
| Groves, Larry, Indianapolis | .000 | 13 | 2 | 1 | 0 | 0 | 0 | 0 | 0 | 0 | 0 | 0 | 0 | 1 | 2 | 0 | 0 | 0 | 0 |
| Gulden, Bradley, Denver* | .245 | 45 | 143 | 20 | 35 | 54 | 7 | 0 | 4 | 16 | 1 | 0 | 2 | 0 | 12 | 1 | 18 | 4 | 1 |
| Gumpert, David, Iowa | .000 | 42 | 4 | 0 | 0 | 0 | 0 | 0 | 0 | 0 | 0 | 1 | 0 | 0 | 0 | 0 | 2 | 0 | 0 |
| Gura, Lawrence, Iowa* | .300 | 10 | 10 | 0 | 3 | 3 | 0 | 0 | 0 | 2 | 0 | 1 | 0 | 0 | 0 | 0 | 4 | 0 | 0 |
| Hansen, Roger, Omaha | .276 | 11 | 29 | 2 | 8 | 10 | 2 | 0 | 0 | 5 | 1 | 0 | 0 | 0 | 2 | 1 | 7 | 0 | 0 |
| Harris, John, Nashville | .247 | 32 | 93 | 7 | 23 | 32 | 3 | 0 | 2 | 10 | 2 | 2 | 1 | 0 | 6 | 1 | 21 | 0 | 1 |
| Hatcher, William, Iowa | .280 | 67 | 279 | 39 | 78 | 117 | 14 | 5 | 5 | 19 | 4 | 2 | 2 | 2 | 24 | 0 | 40 | 17 | 11 |
| Hayes, William, Iowa | .188 | 86 | 260 | 33 | 49 | 80 | 8 | 1 | 7 | 31 | 0 | 8 | 2 | 2 | 26 | 1 | 57 | 3 | 2 |
| Hegman, Robert, Omaha | .232 | 89 | 207 | 16 | 48 | 55 | 5 | 1 | 0 | 19 | 1 | 2 | 3 | 0 | 24 | 0 | 37 | 2 | 2 |
| Hertzler, Paul, Indianapolis* | .241 | 70 | 203 | 28 | 49 | 75 | 11 | 3 | 3 | 27 | 4 | 1 | 1 | 4 | 19 | 1 | 53 | 4 | 5 |
| Hoeksema, David, Indianapolis | .301 | 66 | 146 | 14 | 44 | 60 | 8 | 1 | 2 | 23 | 1 | 4 | 3 | 0 | 13 | 0 | 35 | 1 | 1 |
| Hoffman, Guy, Iowa* | .000 | 9 | 3 | 0 | 0 | 0 | 0 | 0 | 0 | 0 | 0 | 0 | 0 | 0 | 0 | 0 | 2 | 0 | 0 |
| Holman, Scott, Iowa | .200 | 38 | 5 | 0 | 1 | 1 | 0 | 0 | 0 | 0 | 0 | 1 | 0 | 0 | 0 | 0 | 1 | 0 | 0 |
| Hostetler, David, 20 Ind-112 Iowa | .256 | 132 | 465 | 69 | 119 | 228 | 18 | 2 | 29 | 89 | 6 | 1 | 3 | 5 | 53 | 0 | 101 | 1 | 6 |
| Hunt, Randy, 34 Lou-29 OkC | .269 | 63 | 182 | 18 | 49 | 70 | 14 | 2 | 1 | 23 | 3 | 2 | 1 | 0 | 14 | 1 | 39 | 2 | 0 |
| Jackson, Darrin, Iowa | .175 | 10 | 40 | 0 | 7 | 11 | 2 | 1 | 0 | 1 | 0 | 0 | 0 | 0 | 3 | 0 | 10 | 1 | 0 |
| Jackson, Ronnie, Louisville | .238 | 62 | 181 | 23 | 43 | 65 | 8 | 1 | 4 | 34 | 5 | 0 | 3 | 2 | 14 | 2 | 30 | 3 | 0 |
| Jarrell, Joseph, Omaha | .128 | 11 | 39 | 4 | 5 | 13 | 0 | 1 | 2 | 3 | 1 | 0 | 0 | 0 | 1 | 0 | 14 | 1 | 0 |
| Jirschele, Michael, Oklahoma City | .217 | 52 | 143 | 20 | 31 | 44 | 4 | 3 | 1 | 18 | 4 | 1 | 2 | 1 | 19 | 0 | 36 | 5 | 2 |
| Johnson, Randall, Buffalo* | .224 | 58 | 170 | 30 | 38 | 67 | 6 | 1 | 7 | 27 | 5 | 0 | 3 | 1 | 20 | 2 | 34 | 2 | 2 |
| Johnson, Ronald, 20 Nash.-54 Buf. | .211 | 74 | 218 | 19 | 46 | 62 | 8 | 1 | 2 | 18 | 2 | 0 | 0 | 0 | 21 | 1 | 35 | 0 | 0 |
| Johnson, Rondin, Omaha† | .235 | 99 | 366 | 44 | 86 | 96 | 8 | 1 | 0 | 22 | 3 | 8 | 1 | 0 | 30 | 1 | 44 | 18 | 4 |
| Johnson, Roy, Indianapolis* | .278 | 26 | 90 | 15 | 25 | 40 | 6 | 0 | 3 | 12 | 0 | 0 | 1 | 0 | 6 | 0 | 16 | 4 | 3 |
| Johnson, Wallace, Indianapolis† | .309 | 127 | 431 | 68 | 133 | 161 | 13 | 3 | 3 | 36 | 6 | 4 | 2 | 1 | 45 | 4 | 28 | 34 | 9 |
| Jones, Tracy, Denver | .337 | 51 | 205 | 43 | 69 | 111 | 12 | 0 | 10 | 31 | 2 | 2 | 1 | 3 | 15 | 0 | 16 | 20 | 1 |
| Kable, David, Louisville* | .222 | 59 | 180 | 22 | 40 | 63 | 5 | 0 | 6 | 30 | 3 | 2 | 1 | 1 | 18 | 1 | 43 | 0 | 0 |
| Kemp, Hubert, Denver* | .000 | 7 | 4 | 0 | 0 | 0 | 0 | 0 | 0 | 0 | 0 | 0 | 0 | 0 | 0 | 0 | 3 | 0 | 0 |
| Kingery, Michael, Omaha* | .255 | 132 | 444 | 51 | 113 | 156 | 25 | 6 | 2 | 49 | 8 | 5 | 2 | 0 | 61 | 3 | 59 | 16 | 12 |
| Kittle, Ronald, Buffalo | .333 | 6 | 21 | 3 | 7 | 15 | 2 | 0 | 2 | 5 | 2 | 0 | 0 | 1 | 5 | 0 | 3 | 0 | 0 |
| Knicely, Alan, Denver | .413 | 29 | 109 | 20 | 45 | 76 | 10 | 0 | 7 | 29 | 5 | 0 | 1 | 0 | 13 | 2 | 13 | 0 | 0 |
| Knox, Michael, Denver | .000 | 2 | 1 | 0 | 0 | 0 | 0 | 0 | 0 | 0 | 0 | 0 | 0 | 0 | 0 | 0 | 0 | 0 | 0 |
| Koontz, James, 6 Lou-26 Ind | .000 | 32 | 6 | 0 | 0 | 0 | 0 | 0 | 0 | 0 | 0 | 0 | 0 | 0 | 0 | 0 | 3 | 0 | 0 |
| Kunkel, Jeffrey, Oklahoma City | .195 | 99 | 370 | 40 | 72 | 107 | 8 | 6 | 5 | 43 | 6 | 2 | 5 | 3 | 20 | 0 | 81 | 8 | 9 |
| Kuntz, Russell, Nashville | .222 | 74 | 167 | 24 | 37 | 63 | 5 | 0 | 7 | 29 | 5 | 3 | 3 | 2 | 33 | 0 | 39 | 7 | 6 |
| Laga, Michael, Nashville* | .263 | 117 | 430 | 58 | 113 | 207 | 30 | 2 | 20 | 79 | 8 | 1 | 7 | 1 | 39 | 4 | 95 | 2 | 3 |
| Landrum, William, Denver | .067 | 29 | 15 | 1 | 1 | 2 | 1 | 0 | 0 | 0 | 0 | 0 | 0 | 0 | 0 | 0 | 7 | 0 | 0 |
| Lavalliere, Michael, Louisville* | .203 | 83 | 231 | 19 | 47 | 73 | 12 | 1 | 4 | 26 | 2 | 3 | 6 | 1 | 48 | 2 | 20 | 0 | 1 |
| Lawless, Thomas, Louisville | .290 | 31 | 124 | 16 | 36 | 50 | 9 | 1 | 1 | 12 | 0 | 3 | 0 | 0 | 8 | 0 | 15 | 9 | 1 |
| Leeper, David, Omaha* | .279 | 98 | 380 | 52 | 106 | 161 | 21 | 4 | 10 | 52 | 11 | 2 | 3 | 2 | 26 | 1 | 33 | 6 | 5 |
| Little, Bryan, Buffalo† | .306 | 49 | 183 | 30 | 56 | 76 | 13 | 2 | 1 | 20 | 1 | 5 | 3 | 0 | 27 | 1 | 17 | 2 | 2 |
| Little, Ronald, Denver* | .212 | 72 | 184 | 20 | 39 | 55 | 6 | 2 | 2 | 12 | 0 | 1 | 0 | 0 | 13 | 1 | 53 | 4 | 3 |
| Lombarski, Thomas, Iowa* | .255 | 121 | 404 | 49 | 103 | 169 | 30 | 3 | 10 | 64 | 12 | 1 | 4 | 3 | 69 | 3 | 89 | 13 | 10 |
| Lowry, Dwight, Nashville* | .182 | 74 | 203 | 20 | 37 | 52 | 7 | 1 | 2 | 13 | 0 | 3 | 2 | 2 | 24 | 1 | 51 | 2 | 2 |
| Lozado, William, Louisville | .221 | 63 | 195 | 16 | 43 | 55 | 12 | 0 | 0 | 12 | 1 | 1 | 2 | 1 | 19 | 1 | 42 | 2 | 1 |
| Lyons, William, Louisville | .206 | 134 | 471 | 63 | 97 | 124 | 16 | 4 | 1 | 29 | 4 | 8 | 5 | 11 | 59 | 1 | 78 | 31 | 9 |
| Madison, Scotti, Nashville† | .341 | 86 | 317 | 59 | 108 | 187 | 23 | 4 | 16 | 54 | 11 | 1 | 1 | 3 | 43 | 2 | 45 | 3 | 3 |
| Mahler, Michael, 9 Ind-5 Nash.† | .125 | 14 | 8 | 2 | 1 | 2 | 1 | 0 | 0 | 0 | 0 | 0 | 0 | 0 | 1 | 0 | 4 | 0 | 0 |
| Maler, James, Oklahoma City | .257 | 105 | 369 | 42 | 95 | 157 | 18 | 1 | 14 | 48 | 7 | 2 | 3 | 7 | 18 | 1 | 58 | 0 | 0 |
| Manrique, Fred, Indianapolis | .240 | 123 | 409 | 46 | 98 | 153 | 21 | 5 | 8 | 37 | 4 | 5 | 4 | 2 | 20 | 1 | 71 | 2 | 8 |
| Martz, Randy, Iowa* | .000 | 4 | 1 | 0 | 0 | 0 | 0 | 0 | 0 | 0 | 0 | 0 | 0 | 0 | 0 | 0 | 1 | 0 | 0 |

| Player and Club | Pct. | G. | AB. | R. | H. | TB. | 2B. | 3B. | HR. | RBI. | GW. | SH. | SF. | HP. | BB. | Int. BB. | SO. | SB. | CS. |
|---|---|---|---|---|---|---|---|---|---|---|---|---|---|---|---|---|---|---|---|
| McClendon, Lloyd, Denver | .277 | 114 | 379 | 57 | 105 | 181 | 18 | 5 | 16 | 79 | 10 | 0 | 3 | 3 | 51 | 4 | 56 | 4 | 4 |
| McDowell, Oddibe, Oklahoma City* | .400 | 31 | 125 | 32 | 50 | 79 | 7 | 8 | 2 | 18 | 2 | 0 | 0 | 2 | 19 | 3 | 20 | 12 | 6 |
| McGaffigan, Andrew, Denver | .100 | 26 | 10 | 0 | 1 | 1 | 0 | 0 | 0 | 0 | 0 | 0 | 0 | 0 | 0 | 0 | 3 | 0 | 0 |
| McKeon, Joel, Buffalo* | 1.000 | 49 | 1 | 0 | 1 | 1 | 0 | 0 | 0 | 1 | 0 | 0 | 0 | 0 | 0 | 0 | 0 | 0 | 0 |
| Melvin, Robert, Nashville | .271 | 53 | 177 | 27 | 48 | 84 | 7 | 1 | 9 | 24 | 4 | 1 | 2 | 1 | 16 | 0 | 38 | 3 | 1 |
| Mercado, Orlando, Oklahoma City | .252 | 59 | 206 | 20 | 52 | 85 | 7 | 1 | 8 | 29 | 4 | 2 | 2 | 2 | 19 | 0 | 37 | 1 | 0 |
| Meridith, Ronald, Iowa* | .000 | 25 | 1 | 0 | 0 | 0 | 0 | 0 | 0 | 0 | 0 | 1 | 0 | 0 | 0 | 0 | 1 | 0 | 0 |
| Meyer, Daniel, Nashville* | .225 | 51 | 160 | 10 | 36 | 54 | 13 | 1 | 1 | 13 | 2 | 1 | 2 | 2 | 5 | 1 | 29 | 3 | 1 |
| Miley, David, Denver* | .180 | 63 | 167 | 9 | 30 | 36 | 6 | 0 | 0 | 19 | 0 | 2 | 1 | 0 | 14 | 0 | 15 | 1 | 2 |
| Mitchell, Robert, Nashville* | .246 | 111 | 325 | 47 | 80 | 111 | 16 | 3 | 3 | 29 | 3 | 2 | 1 | 1 | 45 | 0 | 50 | 5 | 9 |
| Moore, Kelvin, Buffalo | .222 | 13 | 27 | 3 | 6 | 6 | 0 | 0 | 0 | 0 | 0 | 0 | 0 | 0 | 4 | 0 | 5 | 0 | 0 |
| Morman, Russell, Buffalo | .297 | 21 | 64 | 16 | 19 | 45 | 3 | 1 | 7 | 14 | 0 | 0 | 2 | 0 | 10 | 0 | 16 | 2 | 0 |
| Moronko, Jeffrey, Oklahoma City | .247 | 54 | 166 | 23 | 41 | 64 | 8 | 0 | 5 | 17 | 0 | 4 | 2 | 4 | 17 | 0 | 38 | 2 | 2 |
| Morris, John, 23 Oma-107 Lou* | .251 | 130 | 466 | 64 | 117 | 169 | 25 | 6 | 5 | 50 | 9 | 3 | 1 | 3 | 72 | 5 | 57 | 21 | 8 |
| Mota, Jose, Buffalo† | .278 | 6 | 18 | 3 | 5 | 5 | 0 | 0 | 0 | 1 | 0 | 0 | 0 | 0 | 2 | 0 | 0 | 0 | 0 |
| Murphy, Robert, Denver* | .667 | 41 | 3 | 1 | 2 | 2 | 0 | 0 | 0 | 1 | 0 | 0 | 0 | 0 | 0 | 0 | 0 | 0 | 0 |
| Murray, Richard, Omaha | .250 | 79 | 208 | 25 | 52 | 79 | 7 | 1 | 6 | 27 | 3 | 1 | 1 | 2 | 18 | 4 | 32 | 4 | 2 |
| Newman, Albert, Indianapolis† | .282 | 87 | 301 | 42 | 85 | 105 | 16 | 2 | 0 | 23 | 2 | 3 | 1 | 2 | 46 | 1 | 27 | 31 | 11 |
| Noce, Paul, Iowa | .225 | 89 | 258 | 31 | 58 | 89 | 8 | 4 | 5 | 25 | 0 | 4 | 0 | 0 | 16 | 0 | 61 | 12 | 3 |
| O'Berry, Michael, Indianapolis | .174 | 44 | 121 | 8 | 21 | 28 | 4 | 0 | 1 | 10 | 2 | 2 | 1 | 0 | 11 | 0 | 22 | 2 | 0 |
| O'Connor, Jack, Indianapolis* | .000 | 42 | 2 | 0 | 0 | 0 | 0 | 0 | 0 | 0 | 0 | 0 | 0 | 0 | 0 | 0 | 1 | 0 | 0 |
| O'Malley, Thomas, Nashville* | .305 | 33 | 128 | 13 | 39 | 50 | 8 | 0 | 1 | 12 | 2 | 0 | 0 | 0 | 11 | 2 | 9 | 0 | 0 |
| O'Neill, Paul, Denver* | .305 | 137 | 509 | 63 | 155 | 214 | 32 | 3 | 7 | 74 | 13 | 1 | 6 | 1 | 28 | 4 | 73 | 5 | 7 |
| Oquendo, Jose, Louisville | .211 | 133 | 384 | 38 | 81 | 94 | 8 | 1 | 1 | 30 | 3 | 15 | 4 | 5 | 24 | 0 | 41 | 13 | 4 |
| Owen, Dave, Iowa† | .227 | 100 | 321 | 60 | 73 | 129 | 13 | 5 | 11 | 40 | 7 | 3 | 1 | 1 | 56 | 1 | 65 | 25 | 11 |
| Pagnozzi, Thomas, Louisville | .269 | 76 | 268 | 29 | 72 | 104 | 13 | 2 | 5 | 40 | 6 | 0 | 4 | 3 | 21 | 1 | 47 | 0 | 1 |
| Parrott, Michael, Oklahoma City | .333 | 21 | 3 | 0 | 1 | 1 | 0 | 0 | 0 | 0 | 0 | 0 | 0 | 0 | 0 | 0 | 0 | 0 | 0 |
| Parsons, Casey, Louisville* | .279 | 122 | 412 | 61 | 115 | 176 | 23 | 4 | 10 | 46 | 6 | 0 | 3 | 1 | 55 | 3 | 55 | 2 | 5 |
| Patterson, Reginald, Iowa | .357 | 22 | 14 | 4 | 5 | 6 | 1 | 0 | 0 | 2 | 0 | 2 | 0 | 0 | 0 | 0 | 3 | 0 | 0 |
| Pecota, William, Omaha | .240 | 130 | 409 | 47 | 98 | 124 | 17 | 3 | 1 | 34 | 4 | 2 | 5 | 5 | 57 | 0 | 55 | 21 | 10 |
| Perlman, Jonathan, Iowa* | .071 | 35 | 14 | 3 | 1 | 1 | 0 | 0 | 0 | 0 | 0 | 2 | 0 | 0 | 1 | 0 | 6 | 0 | 0 |
| Petralli, Eugene, Oklahoma City* | .263 | 27 | 80 | 11 | 21 | 32 | 8 | 0 | 1 | 5 | 1 | 1 | 0 | 0 | 10 | 1 | 9 | 0 | 0 |
| Pettini, Joseph, Louisville | .251 | 106 | 323 | 35 | 81 | 112 | 18 | 2 | 3 | 31 | 4 | 2 | 4 | 0 | 27 | 0 | 43 | 2 | 4 |
| Pittaro, Christopher, Nashville† | .194 | 60 | 175 | 22 | 34 | 49 | 4 | 1 | 3 | 19 | 3 | 4 | 0 | 2 | 22 | 0 | 32 | 4 | 2 |
| Pittman, Joseph, Nashville | .267 | 107 | 374 | 41 | 100 | 130 | 19 | 1 | 3 | 26 | 4 | 3 | 2 | 0 | 26 | 1 | 49 | 18 | 9 |
| Poldberg, Brian, Omaha | .140 | 42 | 107 | 9 | 15 | 16 | 1 | 0 | 0 | 7 | 1 | 0 | 2 | 1 | 22 | 0 | 11 | 2 | 0 |
| Porter, Darrell, Louisville* | .150 | 7 | 20 | 3 | 3 | 6 | 0 | 0 | 1 | 2 | 1 | 0 | 0 | 0 | 3 | 0 | 5 | 0 | 0 |
| Pryce, Kenneth, Iowa | .000 | 44 | 3 | 0 | 0 | 0 | 0 | 0 | 0 | 0 | 0 | 0 | 0 | 0 | 0 | 0 | 2 | 0 | 0 |
| Pryor, Buddy, Denver | .221 | 35 | 86 | 8 | 19 | 29 | 2 | 1 | 2 | 10 | 0 | 1 | 0 | 0 | 10 | 1 | 25 | 1 | 0 |
| Puleo, Charles, Denver | .250 | 11 | 4 | 0 | 1 | 1 | 0 | 0 | 0 | 1 | 0 | 0 | 0 | 0 | 0 | 0 | 3 | 0 | 0 |
| Putnam, Patrick, Omaha* | .257 | 123 | 416 | 50 | 107 | 154 | 16 | 2 | 9 | 67 | 10 | 1 | 5 | 2 | 48 | 4 | 72 | 0 | 2 |
| Quirk, James, Omaha* | .244 | 104 | 324 | 33 | 79 | 110 | 5 | 1 | 8 | 48 | 3 | 0 | 6 | 0 | 35 | 4 | 56 | 0 | 5 |
| Rajsich, Gary, Louisville* | .243 | 49 | 173 | 27 | 42 | 77 | 3 | 1 | 10 | 37 | 6 | 0 | 3 | 2 | 25 | 5 | 33 | 0 | 0 |
| Reynolds, Timothy, Denver† | .200 | 7 | 5 | 0 | 1 | 1 | 0 | 0 | 0 | 0 | 0 | 0 | 0 | 0 | 1 | 0 | 0 | 0 | 0 |
| Rizzo, Richard, Omaha | .255 | 16 | 51 | 4 | 13 | 21 | 4 | 2 | 0 | 7 | 1 | 1 | 0 | 1 | 6 | 0 | 7 | 0 | 0 |
| Roadcap, Steve, Iowa† | .333 | 2 | 3 | 1 | 1 | 1 | 0 | 0 | 0 | 1 | 0 | 0 | 0 | 0 | 0 | 0 | 0 | 0 | 0 |
| Roberts, Leon, Nashville | .267 | 97 | 311 | 31 | 83 | 114 | 19 | 0 | 4 | 39 | 5 | 1 | 6 | 1 | 39 | 6 | 47 | 6 | 6 |
| Robinson, Ronald, Denver | .500 | 6 | 2 | 0 | 1 | 1 | 0 | 0 | 0 | 0 | 0 | 1 | 0 | 0 | 0 | 0 | 0 | 0 | 0 |
| Romero, Ramon, Buffalo† | .200 | 28 | 65 | 7 | 13 | 17 | 1 | 0 | 1 | 7 | 1 | 3 | 2 | 0 | 11 | 0 | 15 | 0 | 1 |
| Roof, Eugene, Louisville† | .206 | 17 | 68 | 8 | 14 | 18 | 2 | 1 | 0 | 1 | 0 | 0 | 0 | 0 | 7 | 0 | 12 | 1 | 0 |
| Rosado, Luis, Nashville | .000 | 4 | 5 | 0 | 0 | 0 | 0 | 0 | 0 | 0 | 0 | 0 | 0 | 0 | 1 | 0 | 1 | 0 | 0 |
| Rothschild, Lawrence, Iowa* | .333 | 40 | 3 | 0 | 1 | 1 | 0 | 0 | 0 | 0 | 0 | 0 | 0 | 0 | 0 | 0 | 0 | 0 | 0 |
| Rowdon, Wade, Denver | .289 | 128 | 457 | 61 | 132 | 230 | 31 | 5 | 19 | 78 | 7 | 3 | 3 | 4 | 48 | 5 | 81 | 7 | 10 |
| Rubel, Michael, Oklahoma City | .240 | 63 | 208 | 38 | 50 | 84 | 10 | 0 | 8 | 34 | 5 | 1 | 3 | 2 | 47 | 2 | 55 | 0 | 5 |
| Runnells, Thomas, Denver† | .290 | 114 | 466 | 55 | 135 | 188 | 22 | 8 | 5 | 51 | 4 | 4 | 4 | 1 | 34 | 3 | 41 | 5 | 11 |
| Russell, Jeffrey, 19 Den-2 OkC | .167 | 21 | 12 | 3 | 2 | 5 | 0 | 0 | 1 | 2 | 1 | 0 | 0 | 0 | 2 | 0 | 8 | 0 | 0 |
| Ryal, Mark, Buffalo† | .265 | 106 | 392 | 50 | 104 | 166 | 21 | 1 | 13 | 66 | 10 | 0 | 5 | 2 | 18 | 1 | 50 | 1 | 1 |
| Sanchez, Alejandro, Nashville | .237 | 10 | 38 | 6 | 9 | 16 | 1 | 0 | 2 | 5 | 0 | 0 | 0 | 1 | 0 | 0 | 8 | 3 | 1 |
| Santovenia, Nelson, Indianapolis | .213 | 28 | 75 | 5 | 16 | 18 | 2 | 0 | 0 | 4 | 0 | 0 | 1 | 0 | 7 | 0 | 11 | 1 | 1 |
| Scott, Timothy, Denver | .000 | 12 | 3 | 0 | 0 | 0 | 0 | 0 | 0 | 0 | 0 | 0 | 0 | 0 | 0 | 0 | 1 | 0 | 0 |
| Scranton, James, Omaha† | .196 | 121 | 378 | 36 | 74 | 89 | 10 | 1 | 1 | 29 | 4 | 8 | 3 | 1 | 23 | 1 | 54 | 2 | 4 |
| Sheridan, Patrick, Omaha* | .357 | 8 | 28 | 1 | 10 | 11 | 1 | 0 | 0 | 1 | 0 | 0 | 0 | 1 | 5 | 0 | 7 | 0 | 0 |
| Shines, Raymond, Indianapolis† | .308 | 65 | 240 | 39 | 74 | 114 | 15 | 2 | 7 | 45 | 6 | 0 | 2 | 2 | 29 | 3 | 25 | 2 | 4 |
| Simmons, Nelson, Nashville† | .245 | 49 | 188 | 17 | 46 | 87 | 14 | 0 | 9 | 26 | 1 | 0 | 4 | 1 | 14 | 1 | 30 | 0 | 0 |
| Siwy, James, Buffalo | .000 | 16 | 1 | 0 | 0 | 0 | 0 | 0 | 0 | 0 | 0 | 0 | 0 | 0 | 0 | 0 | 1 | 0 | 0 |
| Skinner, Joel, Buffalo | .241 | 115 | 390 | 47 | 94 | 143 | 13 | 0 | 12 | 59 | 9 | 0 | 1 | 4 | 41 | 0 | 115 | 0 | 0 |
| Smith, Mark, Nashville | .213 | 26 | 80 | 5 | 17 | 24 | 4 | 0 | 1 | 8 | 0 | 0 | 1 | 1 | 4 | 0 | 9 | 0 | 0 |
| Smith, Michael, Denver | .000 | 47 | 3 | 0 | 0 | 0 | 0 | 0 | 0 | 0 | 0 | 0 | 0 | 0 | 0 | 0 | 2 | 0 | 0 |
| St. Claire, Randy, Indianapolis | 1.000 | 11 | 1 | 0 | 1 | 1 | 0 | 0 | 0 | 1 | 0 | 0 | 0 | 0 | 0 | 0 | 0 | 0 | 0 |
| Stearns, John, Denver | .264 | 72 | 235 | 46 | 62 | 85 | 8 | 3 | 3 | 19 | 1 | 2 | 3 | 1 | 39 | 2 | 34 | 9 | 8 |
| Stephans, Russell, Omaha | .286 | 10 | 28 | 6 | 8 | 12 | 2 | 1 | 0 | 5 | 2 | 0 | 0 | 0 | 4 | 0 | 7 | 0 | 0 |
| Stillwell, Kurt, Denver† | .264 | 59 | 182 | 28 | 48 | 66 | 7 | 4 | 1 | 22 | 3 | 3 | 0 | 0 | 21 | 2 | 23 | 5 | 3 |
| Stockstill, David, Oklahoma City* | .257 | 61 | 214 | 33 | 55 | 84 | 10 | 5 | 3 | 25 | 3 | 0 | 3 | 2 | 45 | 4 | 19 | 0 | 0 |
| Stoll, Richard, Indianapolis | .308 | 24 | 13 | 0 | 4 | 5 | 1 | 0 | 0 | 2 | 0 | 0 | 0 | 0 | 1 | 0 | 2 | 0 | 0 |
| Stryffeler, Daniel, Louisville* | .273 | 52 | 150 | 19 | 41 | 63 | 13 | 0 | 3 | 17 | 1 | 2 | 1 | 0 | 16 | 1 | 24 | 3 | 0 |
| Tabor, Gregory, Oklahoma City | .222 | 25 | 81 | 16 | 18 | 19 | 1 | 0 | 0 | 10 | 2 | 2 | 1 | 1 | 13 | 0 | 16 | 8 | 0 |
| Taveras, Alejandro, Buffalo | .218 | 109 | 266 | 36 | 58 | 87 | 14 | 0 | 5 | 30 | 2 | 8 | 3 | 0 | 40 | 0 | 50 | 2 | 4 |
| Terry, Scott, Denver | .158 | 29 | 19 | 1 | 3 | 3 | 0 | 0 | 0 | 0 | 0 | 0 | 0 | 0 | 1 | 0 | 3 | 0 | 0 |
| Toliver, Freddie, Denver | .111 | 21 | 18 | 1 | 2 | 3 | 1 | 0 | 0 | 0 | 0 | 2 | 0 | 0 | 0 | 0 | 4 | 0 | 1 |
| Valdez, Julio, Iowa† | .219 | 106 | 319 | 33 | 70 | 107 | 18 | 2 | 5 | 25 | 4 | 4 | 3 | 6 | 9 | 1 | 58 | 2 | 5 |
| Valentine, Ellis, Oklahoma City | .314 | 46 | 169 | 26 | 53 | 101 | 18 | 0 | 10 | 33 | 2 | 0 | 2 | 1 | 13 | 3 | 27 | 0 | 0 |
| Venable, William, 14 Ind-32 Den* | .244 | 46 | 172 | 27 | 42 | 71 | 7 | 5 | 4 | 19 | 4 | 1 | 0 | 0 | 12 | 2 | 19 | 10 | 3 |
| Wagner, Mark, Buffalo | .200 | 34 | 60 | 8 | 12 | 14 | 2 | 0 | 0 | 1 | 0 | 0 | 2 | 0 | 8 | 0 | 9 | 0 | 0 |
| Walker, Cleotha, Iowa† | .284 | 89 | 331 | 47 | 94 | 142 | 17 | 8 | 5 | 46 | 5 | 4 | 1 | 2 | 50 | 1 | 60 | 42 | 11 |
| Werner, Donald, 5 Nash.-15 OkC | .197 | 20 | 61 | 10 | 12 | 17 | 2 | 0 | 1 | 5 | 1 | 1 | 0 | 1 | 7 | 0 | 11 | 0 | 0 |
| Wherry, Clifton, Buffalo | .239 | 89 | 209 | 23 | 50 | 62 | 9 | 0 | 1 | 21 | 1 | 5 | 0 | 3 | 20 | 1 | 46 | 7 | 3 |
| Wilborn, Thaddeus, Nashville† | .200 | 37 | 100 | 11 | 20 | 21 | 1 | 0 | 0 | 4 | 0 | 1 | 0 | 0 | 10 | 0 | 26 | 4 | 0 |
| Wilkerson, Martin, Omaha* | .249 | 82 | 213 | 19 | 53 | 63 | 7 | 0 | 1 | 25 | 1 | 1 | 3 | 0 | 16 | 0 | 32 | 0 | 2 |
| Williams, Dallas, Indianapolis* | .287 | 77 | 244 | 34 | 70 | 106 | 14 | 5 | 4 | 27 | 2 | 4 | 3 | 0 | 24 | 0 | 32 | 5 | 10 |
| Williams, Matthew, Oklahoma City | .000 | 1 | 2 | 0 | 0 | 0 | 0 | 0 | 0 | 0 | 0 | 0 | 0 | 0 | 0 | 0 | 0 | 0 | 0 |
| Willis, Carl, Denver* | .000 | 37 | 5 | 0 | 0 | 0 | 0 | 0 | 0 | 2 | 1 | 0 | 0 | 0 | 0 | 0 | 2 | 0 | 0 |
| Winningham, Herman, Indianapolis* | .171 | 11 | 35 | 3 | 6 | 6 | 0 | 0 | 0 | 2 | 1 | 0 | 0 | 0 | 3 | 0 | 7 | 2 | 0 |

| Player and Club | Pct. | G. | AB. | R. | H. | TB. | 2B. | 3B. | HR. | RBI. | GW. | SH. | SF. | HP. | BB. | Int. BB. | SO. | SB. | CS. |
|---|---|---|---|---|---|---|---|---|---|---|---|---|---|---|---|---|---|---|---|
| Woods, Tony, Iowa | .230 | 22 | 74 | 11 | 17 | 27 | 5 | 1 | 1 | 4 | 0 | 1 | 0 | 1 | 8 | 0 | 17 | 0 | 0 |
| Wright, George, Oklahoma City† | .254 | 39 | 142 | 22 | 36 | 68 | 4 | 2 | 8 | 27 | 4 | 0 | 2 | 1 | 13 | 3 | 21 | 1 | 2 |
| Wright, Richard, Oklahoma City° | .500 | 19 | 6 | 1 | 3 | 5 | 2 | 0 | 0 | | 1 | 0 | 0 | 0 | 1 | 0 | 1 | 0 | 1 |
| Yobs, David, Buffalo° | .300 | 95 | 280 | 34 | 84 | 112 | 11· | 1 | 5 | 37 | 4 | 1 | 7 | 1 | 33 | 1 | 52 | 0 | 1 |
| Yost, Edgar, Indianapolis | .262 | 95 | 267 | 17 | 70 | 91 | 15 | 0 | 2 | 24 | 2 | 1 | 0 | 1 | 11 | 1 | 46 | 1 | 1 |
| Youmans, Floyd, Indianapolis | .286 | 6 | 7 | 0 | 2 | 2 | 0 | 0 | 0 | 0 | 0 | 0 | 0 | 0 | 0 | 0 | 3 | 0 | 0 |

The following pitchers, listed alphabetically by club, with games in parentheses, had no plate appearances, primarily through use of designated hitters:

BUFFALO—Agosto, Juan (6); Davis, Joel (10); Fallon, Robert (15); Fireovid, Stephen (24); Gleaton, Jerry Don (38); Hardy, John (3); Hickey, James (7); Jones, Alfornia (4); Long, William (26); Menendez, Antonio (1); Mullen, Thomas (21); Owchinko, Robert (10); Rogers, Stephen (4); Speck, Clifford (21); Stranski, Scott (48); Tanner, Bruce (20); Todd, Jackson (25); Wehrmeister, David (30).

DENVER—Buchanan, Robert (29); Nail, Charles (1); Tibbs, Jay (4).

INDIANAPOLIS—Barrett, Timothy (4); Breining, Fred (4); Cook, Kerry (6); Cutshall, William (7); Glynn, Edward (28); Lucas, Gary (1); Nicometi, Anthony (3); Roberge, Bertrand (1); Schatzeder, Daniel (1).

IOWA—Beard, David (11); Johnson, William (2).

LOUISVILLE—Anderson, Michael (18); Boever, Joseph (21); Epple, Thomas (5); Hagen, Kevin (28); Hassler, Andrew (26); Hayes, Ben (6); Keener, Jeffrey (43); Keough, Matthew (19); Koontz, James (16); Martin, John (2); Martinez, Alfredo (27); Mathews, Gregory (12); Ownbey, Richard (25); Perry, Patrick (45); Rajsich, David (24); Rasmussen, Eric (1); Rhodes, Michael (6); Shade, Michael (14); Worrell, Todd (34).

NASHVILLE—Breining, Fred (3); Cary, Charles (48); Conner, Jeffrey (33); Cruz, Victor (31); Denman, Brian (27); Heinkel, Donald (8); Kelly, Bryan (27); Mahler, Michael (5); Monge, Isidro (31); Monteleone, Richard (27); O'Neal, Randall (10); Pacella, John (37); Rasmussen, James (7); Shirley, Steven (21); Stoddard, Robert (22); Voigt, Paul (28).

OKLAHOMA CITY—Boggs, Thomas (13); Cook, Glen (18); Earley, William (41); Fossas, Anthony (30); Guzman, Jose (25); Hallgren, Tim (4); Mohorcic, Dale (40); Murray, Dale (26); Russell, Jeffrey (2); Sebra, Robert (22); Shimp, Tommy (24); Welsh, Christopher (8); Zwolensky, Mitchell (18).

OMAHA—Cone, David (28); Farr, Steven (17); Ferreira, Anthony (27); Griffin, Michael (24); Hargesheimer, Alan (32); Huismann, Mark (59); Keeton, Rickey (26); Kinnunen, Michael (53); LaCoss, Michael (4); Martin, Renie (39); Strode, Lester (21).

GRAND SLAM HOME RUNS—Gillaspie, 2; Canady, Castro, DeSa, Ford, Fuentes, Grant, W. Hayes, Hertzler, Hostetler, McClendon, Morris, Noce, O'Neill, Quirk, Skinner, Walker, Wilkerson, 1 each.

AWARDED FIRST BASE ON CATCHER'S INTERFERENCE—W. Barnes (Poldberg); Harris (Quirk); Miley (Lavalliere); Pecota (Yost); Walker (Quirk); G. Wright (Skinner).

## CLUB FIELDING

| Club | Pct. | G. | PO. | A. | E. | DP. | PB. | Club | Pct. | G. | PO. | A. | E. | DP. | PB. |
|---|---|---|---|---|---|---|---|---|---|---|---|---|---|---|---|
| Oklahoma City | .979 | 143 | 3692 | 1630 | 113 | 134 | 14 | Iowa | .974 | 141 | 3691 | 1528 | 138 | 103 | 5 |
| Louisville | .979 | 144 | 3758 | 1464 | 114 | 128 | 14 | Omaha | .973 | 142 | 3650 | 1463 | 144 | 122 | 33 |
| Buffalo | .976 | 142 | 3632 | 1478 | 128 | 154 | 11 | Nashville | .973 | 142 | 3729 | 1619 | 151 | 139 | 4 |
| Indianapolis | .975 | 142 | 3739 | 1566 | 138 | 147 | 5 | Denver | .971 | 142 | 3732 | 1577 | 160 | 148 | 7 |

Triple Play—Buffalo.

## INDIVIDUAL FIELDING

°Throws lefthanded.

### FIRST BASEMEN

| Player and Club | Pct. | G. | PO. | A. | E. | DP. | Player and Club | Pct. | G. | PO. | A. | E. | DP. |
|---|---|---|---|---|---|---|---|---|---|---|---|---|---|
| Anderson, Oklahoma City | .984 | 7 | 58 | 3 | 1 | 6 | Little, Denver° | .871 | 4 | 26 | 1 | 4 | 6 |
| Ayer, Louisville | .987 | 26 | 206 | 18 | 3 | 16 | Lombarski, Iowa | .986 | 30 | 257 | 30 | 4 | 18 |
| Barnes, 12 Den-19 Ind | .996 | 31 | 256 | 27 | 1 | 29 | Lozado, Louisville | 1.000 | 1 | 4 | 0 | 0 | 0 |
| Bergman, Nashville° | .990 | 9 | 87 | 8 | 1 | 11 | Madison, Nashville | .989 | 11 | 86 | 5 | 1 | 4 |
| Bilardello, Denver | .987 | 18 | 139 | 12 | 2 | 12 | Maler, Oklahoma City | .992 | 77 | 706 | 47 | 6 | 61 |
| Castillo, Iowa | 1.000 | 3 | 12 | 1 | 0 | 0 | McClendon, Denver | .989 | 53 | 402 | 39 | 5 | 40 |
| Christmas, Buffalo | .993 | 37 | 258 | 23 | 2 | 32 | Melvin, Nashville | 1.000 | 1 | 8 | 2 | 0 | 1 |
| Clements, Louisville | 1.000 | 1 | 4 | 0 | 0 | 1 | Meyer, Nashville | 1.000 | 2 | 4 | 0 | 0 | 1 |
| Davis, Omaha | 1.000 | 1 | 10 | 1 | 0 | 1 | Miley, Denver | 1.000 | 1 | 1 | 0 | 0 | 0 |
| DeSa, Buffalo° | .993 | 82 | 698 | 44 | 5 | 76 | Moore, Buffalo° | 1.000 | 7 | 39 | 2 | 0 | 3 |
| Galarraga, Indianapolis | .989 | 102 | 914 | 61 | 11 | 81 | Morman, Buffalo | .987 | 18 | 144 | 7 | 2 | 14 |
| Gillaspie, Iowa | .964 | 4 | 25 | 2 | 1 | 1 | Murray, Omaha | 1.000 | 44 | 305 | 21 | 0 | 30 |
| Gulden, Denver | .983 | 12 | 105 | 10 | 2 | 14 | O'Neill, Denver | 1.000 | 3 | 18 | 1 | 0 | 2 |
| Harris, Nashville° | .964 | 8 | 74 | 7 | 3 | 5 | PUTNAM, Omaha | .992 | 96 | 791 | 64 | 7 | 75 |
| Hegman, Omaha | 1.000 | 1 | 1 | 0 | 0 | 0 | Quirk, Omaha | 1.000 | 6 | 40 | 1 | 0 | 1 |
| Hostetler, 2 Ind-109 Iowa | .990 | 111 | 983 | 79 | 11 | 76 | G. Rajsich, Louisville | .989 | 49 | 401 | 43 | 5 | 35 |
| Jackson, Louisville | .990 | 33 | 267 | 20 | 3 | 24 | Roberts, Nashville | .966 | 3 | 27 | 1 | 1 | 1 |
| R. Johnson, Buffalo | .986 | 16 | 130 | 7 | 2 | 11 | Rubel, Oklahoma City | .982 | 63 | 596 | 41 | 12 | 55 |
| W. Johnson, Indianapolis | 1.000 | 12 | 110 | 2 | 0 | 15 | Shines, Indianapolis | 1.000 | 20 | 145 | 18 | 0 | 15 |
| Kable, Louisville° | .995 | 43 | 379 | 21 | 2 | 28 | Stearns, Omaha | .987 | 48 | 410 | 61 | 6 | 38 |
| Knicely, Denver | .971 | 5 | 32 | 1 | 1 | 6 | Stockstill, Oklahoma City | .958 | 2 | 21 | 2 | 1 | 1 |
| Kuntz, Denver | 1.000 | 1 | 0 | 1 | 0 | 0 | Werner, Oklahoma City | .929 | 1 | 13 | 0 | 1 | 1 |
| Laga, Nashville° | .990 | 114 | 1024 | 111 | 11 | 101 | Wilkerson, Omaha | .981 | 8 | 50 | 3 | 1 | 5 |
| Leeper, Omaha° | 1.000 | 1 | 0 | 1 | 0 | 0 | Yost, Indianapolis | 1.000 | 2 | 5 | 0 | 0 | 1 |

### SECOND BASEMEN

| Player and Club | Pct. | G. | PO. | A. | E. | DP. | Player and Club | Pct. | G. | PO. | A. | E. | DP. |
|---|---|---|---|---|---|---|---|---|---|---|---|---|---|
| Anderson, Oklahoma City | .989 | 62 | 82 | 177 | 3 | 33 | Lyons, Louisville | .989 | 30 | 39 | 50 | 1 | 11 |
| Brooks, Iowa | .981 | 95 | 167 | 294 | 9 | 41 | Manrique, Indianapolis | .968 | 40 | 49 | 101 | 5 | 21 |
| Buechele, Oklahoma City | 1.000 | 5 | 7 | 12 | 0 | 4 | Moronko, Oklahoma City | 1.000 | 1 | 1 | 9 | 0 | 1 |
| Candaele, Indianapolis | .991 | 48 | 74 | 142 | 2 | 36 | Mota, Buffalo | 1.000 | 6 | 10 | 12 | 0 | 2 |
| Capra, Oklahoma City | .992 | 26 | 65 | 64 | 1 | 13 | Newman, Indianapolis | .977 | 81 | 136 | 241 | 9 | 46 |
| Castro, Buffalo | .976 | 39 | 67 | 97 | 4 | 18 | Noce, Iowa | .980 | 13 | 19 | 31 | 1 | 7 |
| Chavez, Nashville | .958 | 15 | 30 | 38 | 3 | 10 | Owen, Iowa | .983 | 49 | 82 | 154 | 4 | 23 |
| Earl, Indianapolis | .982 | 118 | 263 | 325 | 11 | 78 | Pettini, Louisville | .984 | 91 | 161 | 216 | 6 | 42 |
| Foley, Buffalo | 1.000 | 1 | 2 | 5 | 0 | 2 | Pittaro, Indianapolis | .964 | 15 | 23 | 30 | 2 | 6 |
| Gonzalez, Denver | .965 | 19 | 27 | 56 | 3 | 12 | Pittman, Nashville | 1.000 | 5 | 4 | 9 | 0 | 3 |
| Hegman, Omaha | .960 | 40 | 69 | 74 | 6 | 16 | Romero, Buffalo | .961 | 16 | 24 | 49 | 3 | 11 |
| Jirschele, Oklahoma City | .984 | 36 | 70 | 119 | 3 | 25 | Rowdon, Denver | .968 | 11 | 15 | 15 | 1 | 2 |
| R. Johnson, Omaha | .978 | 96 | 181 | 257 | 10 | 46 | RUNNELLS, Denver | .989 | 114 | 256 | 391 | 7 | 83 |
| W. Johnson, Indianapolis | 1.000 | 3 | 0 | 3 | 0 | 1 | Tabor, Oklahoma City | .986 | 25 | 49 | 92 | 2 | 23 |
| Little, Buffalo | .988 | 49 | 98 | 145 | 3 | 34 | Wherry, Buffalo | .965 | 47 | 79 | 113 | 7 | 24 |
| Lozado, Louisville | .966 | 43 | 69 | 131 | 7 | 22 | Wilkerson, Omaha | .949 | 23 | 28 | 47 | 4 | 11 |

## THIRD BASEMEN

| Player and Club | Pct. | G. | PO. | A. | E. | DP. | Player and Club | Pct. | G. | PO. | A. | E. | DP. |
|---|---|---|---|---|---|---|---|---|---|---|---|---|---|
| Anderson, Oklahoma City | .958 | 17 | 12 | 34 | 2 | 4 | Madison, Nashville | .985 | 23 | 24 | 41 | 1 | 2 |
| Barnes, Indianapolis | .952 | 61 | 51 | 127 | 9 | 13 | Manrique, Indianapolis | .948 | 58 | 29 | 81 | 6 | 9 |
| Barrera, Buffalo | .951 | 23 | 13 | 45 | 3 | 4 | McClendon, Denver | .897 | 48 | 42 | 63 | 12 | 6 |
| Bilardello, Denver | .920 | 12 | 10 | 13 | 2 | 0 | Moronko, Oklahoma City | .932 | 46 | 26 | 84 | 8 | 7 |
| Buechele, Oklahoma City | .971 | 83 | 77 | 158 | 7 | 11 | Noce, Iowa | .922 | 18 | 13 | 34 | 4 | 2 |
| Candaele, Indianapolis | 1.000 | 2 | 0 | 4 | 0 | 0 | O'Malley, Nashville | .897 | 28 | 16 | 62 | 9 | 2 |
| Castro, Buffalo | .940 | 79 | 55 | 134 | 12 | 16 | Owen, Iowa | 1.000 | 4 | 1 | 1 | 0 | 0 |
| Chavez, Nashville | .867 | 9 | 7 | 19 | 4 | 2 | PECOTA, Omaha | .962 | 124 | 111 | 247 | 14 | 22 |
| Christmas, Buffalo | .937 | 55 | 43 | 91 | 9 | 11 | Pittaro, Nashville | .971 | 31 | 12 | 55 | 2 | 4 |
| Clements, Louisville | .950 | 28 | 21 | 36 | 3 | 2 | Pittman, Nashville | .897 | 63 | 35 | 113 | 17 | 7 |
| Dayett, Iowa | 1.000 | 1 | 1 | 1 | 0 | 0 | Pryor, Denver | .800 | 4 | 1 | 3 | 1 | 0 |
| Earl, Nashville | 1.000 | 5 | 2 | 13 | 0 | 2 | Quirk, Omaha | .889 | 4 | 5 | 3 | 1 | 0 |
| Foley, Buffalo | 1.000 | 3 | 0 | 1 | 0 | 0 | Romero, Buffalo | 1.000 | 1 | 0 | 1 | 0 | 0 |
| Ford, Louisville | .815 | 14 | 7 | 15 | 5 | 0 | Rowdon, Denver | .940 | 86 | 66 | 154 | 14 | 15 |
| Hegman, Omaha | 1.000 | 3 | 1 | 9 | 0 | 0 | Rubel, Oklahoma City | 1.000 | 1 | 0 | 1 | 0 | 0 |
| Hoeksema, Indianapolis | .891 | 38 | 18 | 31 | 6 | 3 | Shines, Indianapolis | .946 | 20 | 13 | 22 | 2 | 2 |
| Jarrell, Omaha | .889 | 3 | 4 | 4 | 1 | 1 | Stillwell, Denver | .889 | 3 | 3 | 5 | 1 | 0 |
| Jirschele, Oklahoma City | .875 | 2 | 1 | 6 | 1 | 0 | Valdez, Iowa | .942 | 62 | 45 | 85 | 8 | 8 |
| Lawless, Louisville | .963 | 30 | 20 | 58 | 3 | 9 | Wagner, Buffalo | 1.000 | 3 | 0 | 4 | 0 | 0 |
| Lombarski, Iowa | .945 | 48 | 38 | 83 | 7 | 7 | Walker, Iowa | 1.000 | 1 | 0 | 2 | 0 | 0 |
| Lozado, Louisville | 1.000 | 8 | 4 | 12 | 0 | 2 | Wilkerson, Omaha | .924 | 24 | 15 | 46 | 5 | 4 |
| Lyons, Louisville | .959 | 89 | 65 | 148 | 9 | 16 | Woods, Iowa | .923 | 22 | 18 | 30 | 4 | 3 |

## SHORTSTOPS

| Player and Club | Pct. | G. | PO. | A. | E. | DP. | Player and Club | Pct. | G. | PO. | A. | E. | DP. |
|---|---|---|---|---|---|---|---|---|---|---|---|---|---|
| Anderson, Oklahoma City | .988 | 34 | 50 | 108 | 2 | 26 | Moronko, Oklahoma City | 1.000 | 8 | 12 | 21 | 0 | 3 |
| Baker, Nashville | .958 | 107 | 179 | 318 | 22 | 74 | Newman, Indianapolis | .944 | 6 | 8 | 9 | 1 | 2 |
| Candaele, Indianapolis | 1.000 | 19 | 11 | 9 | 0 | 2 | Noce, Iowa | .875 | 2 | 1 | 6 | 1 | 0 |
| Castro, Buffalo | 1.000 | 6 | 7 | 11 | 0 | 4 | Oquendo, Louisville | .961 | 133 | 227 | 341 | 23 | 64 |
| Chavez, Nashville | .970 | 21 | 37 | 61 | 3 | 15 | Owen, Iowa | .985 | 42 | 74 | 125 | 3 | 19 |
| Dunston, Iowa | .963 | 68 | 138 | 176 | 12 | 33 | Pettini, Louisville | .977 | 23 | 19 | 24 | 1 | 8 |
| Gonzales, Indianapolis | .960 | 127 | 203 | 345 | 23 | 79 | Pittaro, Nashville | .972 | 16 | 28 | 41 | 2 | 8 |
| Gonzalez, Denver | .971 | 57 | 78 | 155 | 7 | 33 | Pittman, Nashville | 1.000 | 1 | 2 | 3 | 0 | 2 |
| Hegman, Omaha | .963 | 32 | 44 | 59 | 4 | 13 | Romero, Buffalo | .938 | 4 | 8 | 7 | 1 | 4 |
| Hoeksema, Indianapolis | 1.000 | 3 | 0 | 2 | 0 | 0 | Rowdon, Denver | .946 | 38 | 67 | 108 | 10 | 31 |
| Jarrell, Omaha | .889 | 1 | 1 | 7 | 1 | 0 | Scranton, Omaha | .950 | 119 | 216 | 297 | 27 | 70 |
| Jirschele, Oklahoma City | 1.000 | 12 | 10 | 26 | 0 | 2 | Stillwell, Denver | .906 | 57 | 100 | 130 | 24 | 36 |
| Kunkel, Oklahoma City | .947 | 99 | 152 | 308 | 26 | 62 | TAVERAS, Buffalo | .963 | 104 | 163 | 251 | 16 | 64 |
| Lozado, Louisville | 1.000 | 10 | 6 | 16 | 0 | 3 | Valdez, Iowa | .930 | 37 | 63 | 97 | 12 | 15 |
| Lyons, Louisville | .600 | 3 | 2 | 1 | 2 | 1 | Wagner, Buffalo | .957 | 26 | 43 | 45 | 4 | 17 |
| Manrique, Indianapolis | .935 | 42 | 48 | 67 | 8 | 14 | Wherry, Buffalo | .949 | 37 | 53 | 76 | 7 | 12 |

Triple Play—Taveras.

## OUTFIELDERS

| Player and Club | Pct. | G. | PO. | A. | E. | DP. | Player and Club | Pct. | G. | PO. | A. | E. | DP. |
|---|---|---|---|---|---|---|---|---|---|---|---|---|---|
| Anderson, Oklahoma City | .900 | 5 | 7 | 2 | 1 | 0 | Ro. Johnson, Indianapolis* | .931 | 25 | 51 | 3 | 4 | 1 |
| Ayer, Louisville | .991 | 67 | 112 | 3 | 1 | 1 | W. Johnson, Indianapolis | .965 | 76 | 130 | 9 | 5 | 3 |
| D. Baker, Indianapolis | 1.000 | 8 | 15 | 0 | 0 | 0 | Jones, Denver | 1.000 | 48 | 93 | 2 | 0 | 1 |
| K. Baker, Omaha* | .909 | 16 | 19 | 1 | 2 | 0 | Kingery, Omaha* | .981 | 129 | 247 | 17 | 5 | 3 |
| Barnes, Indianapolis | 1.000 | 3 | 1 | 0 | 0 | 0 | Kittle, Buffalo | 1.000 | 1 | 2 | 0 | 0 | 0 |
| Bernstine, Iowa | .994 | 82 | 168 | 6 | 1 | 0 | Kuntz, Nashville | 1.000 | 70 | 93 | 3 | 0 | 1 |
| Boston, Buffalo* | .981 | 61 | 151 | 3 | 3 | 2 | Leeper, Omaha* | .989 | 87 | 180 | 6 | 2 | 2 |
| Brooks, Iowa | 1.000 | 1 | 1 | 0 | 0 | 0 | Little, Denver* | .958 | 45 | 67 | 1 | 3 | 0 |
| Brower, Oklahoma City | .990 | 131 | 282 | 8 | 3 | 1 | Lyons, Louisville | 1.000 | 26 | 66 | 0 | 0 | 0 |
| Brown, Nashville | .978 | 97 | 213 | 9 | 5 | 1 | Madison, Nashville | 1.000 | 5 | 9 | 0 | 0 | 0 |
| Canady, Oklahoma City | .970 | 65 | 124 | 5 | 4 | 0 | McClendon, Denver | 1.000 | 3 | 5 | 0 | 0 | 0 |
| Candaele, Indianapolis | .979 | 82 | 181 | 5 | 4 | 1 | McDowell, Oklahoma City* | .987 | 31 | 72 | 4 | 1 | 1 |
| Cangelosi, Buffalo* | .987 | 77 | 148 | 9 | 2 | 0 | Melvin, Nashville | 1.000 | 3 | 2 | 0 | 0 | 0 |
| Capra, Oklahoma City | .993 | 74 | 136 | 6 | 1 | 0 | Meyer, Nashville | 1.000 | 5 | 2 | 0 | 0 | 0 |
| Castro, Buffalo | .955 | 29 | 40 | 2 | 2 | 1 | Mitchell, Nashville | .983 | 105 | 162 | 8 | 3 | 2 |
| Cole, Omaha | .989 | 54 | 93 | 1 | 1 | 0 | MORRIS, 23 Oma-107 Lou* | .994 | 130 | 330 | 11 | 2 | 3 |
| Coleman, Louisville | 1.000 | 5 | 8 | 0 | 0 | 0 | Noce, Iowa | .917 | 28 | 31 | 2 | 3 | 0 |
| Daniels, Denver | .957 | 61 | 83 | 5 | 4 | 1 | O'Neill, Denver | .973 | 115 | 230 | 19 | 7 | 8 |
| Darkis, Oklahoma City | .500 | 1 | 1 | 0 | 1 | 0 | Parsons, Louisville | .951 | 67 | 94 | 3 | 5 | 0 |
| E. Davis, Denver | .971 | 49 | 94 | 5 | 3 | 0 | Pittman, Nashville | .889 | 7 | 8 | 0 | 1 | 0 |
| W. Davis, Omaha | .957 | 96 | 199 | 2 | 9 | 0 | Rizzo, Omaha | .956 | 16 | 41 | 2 | 2 | 1 |
| Dayett, Iowa | .913 | 11 | 20 | 1 | 2 | 0 | Roberts, Nashville | .976 | 65 | 116 | 5 | 3 | 0 |
| DeSa, Buffalo* | .923 | 22 | 31 | 5 | 3 | 2 | Roof, Louisville | .964 | 16 | 25 | 2 | 1 | 1 |
| Dunbar, Oklahoma City* | .986 | 46 | 70 | 2 | 1 | 0 | Ryal, Buffalo* | .989 | 104 | 175 | 10 | 2 | 3 |
| Foley, Buffalo | 1.000 | 4 | 4 | 0 | 0 | 0 | Sanchez, Nashville | 1.000 | 10 | 17 | 0 | 0 | 0 |
| Ford, Louisville | .988 | 121 | 236 | 10 | 3 | 0 | Sheridan, Omaha | 1.000 | 7 | 8 | 1 | 0 | 0 |
| Frobel, Indianapolis | 1.000 | 22 | 29 | 1 | 0 | 0 | Simmons, Nashville | .990 | 49 | 93 | 7 | 1 | 4 |
| Fuentes, Indianapolis | .978 | 105 | 173 | 6 | 4 | 0 | Smith, Nashville | 1.000 | 26 | 46 | 1 | 0 | 0 |
| Galarraga, Indianapolis | .857 | 14 | 16 | 2 | 3 | 1 | Stockstill, Oklahoma City | 1.000 | 40 | 62 | 3 | 0 | 0 |
| Garcia, Denver* | .951 | 103 | 198 | 14 | 11 | 3 | Stryffeler, Louisville | 1.000 | 45 | 69 | 4 | 0 | 1 |
| Gilbert, Buffalo | .975 | 113 | 227 | 11 | 6 | 3 | Valentine, Oklahoma City | .947 | 9 | 15 | 3 | 1 | 1 |
| Gillaspie, Iowa | .965 | 100 | 186 | 6 | 7 | 0 | Venable, 14 Ind-30 Den | .990 | 44 | 93 | 2 | 1 | 1 |
| Glynn, Indianapolis | 1.000 | 1 | 1 | 0 | 0 | 0 | Walker, Iowa | .973 | 81 | 177 | 4 | 5 | 1 |
| Grant, Iowa | .954 | 64 | 100 | 3 | 5 | 1 | Werner, Oklahoma City | 1.000 | 5 | 7 | 1 | 0 | 0 |
| Harris, Iowa* | .867 | 10 | 13 | 0 | 2 | 0 | Wilborn, Nashville | .944 | 34 | 33 | 1 | 2 | 0 |
| Hatcher, Iowa | .976 | 67 | 157 | 4 | 4 | 1 | Williams, Indianapolis* | .987 | 72 | 145 | 4 | 2 | 1 |
| Hegman, Omaha | 1.000 | 9 | 6 | 0 | 0 | 0 | Winningham, Indianapolis | .957 | 11 | 22 | 0 | 1 | 0 |
| Hertzler, Indianapolis* | .948 | 66 | 101 | 8 | 6 | 0 | Wright, Oklahoma City | .991 | 38 | 108 | 2 | 1 | 0 |
| D. Jackson, Iowa | 1.000 | 10 | 19 | 0 | 0 | 0 | Yobs, Buffalo* | 1.000 | 4 | 2 | 0 | 0 | 0 |
| Ra. Johnson, Buffalo* | .939 | 44 | 59 | 3 | 4 | 1 | | | | | | | |

Triple Play—Cangelosi.

## CATCHERS

| Player and Club | Pct. | G. | PO. | A. | E. | DP. | PB. |
|---|---|---|---|---|---|---|---|
| Anderson, Oklahoma City | .978 | 20 | 76 | 12 | 2 | 0 | 7 |
| Bilardello, Denver | .992 | 34 | 216 | 25 | 2 | 3 | 3 |
| Bjorkman, Indianapolis | 1.000 | 8 | 39 | 1 | 0 | 0 | 1 |
| Brummer, Oklahoma City | 1.000 | 1 | 7 | 0 | 0 | 0 | 0 |
| Brunenkant, Oklahoma City | 1.000 | 16 | 68 | 8 | 0 | 2 | 0 |
| Butera, Indianapolis | 1.000 | 5 | 27 | 4 | 0 | 0 | 0 |
| Castillo, Iowa | .982 | 74 | 391 | 39 | 8 | 5 | 5 |
| Christmas, Buffalo | 1.000 | 13 | 59 | 5 | 0 | 0 | 1 |
| Foley, Buffalo | .979 | 19 | 81 | 13 | 2 | 1 | 1 |
| Geren, Louisville | 1.000 | 5 | 27 | 1 | 0 | 0 | 0 |
| Gulden, Denver | .983 | 25 | 158 | 14 | 3 | 2 | 1 |
| Hansen, Omaha | 1.000 | 10 | 47 | 2 | 0 | 0 | 0 |
| HAYES, Iowa | .989 | 84 | 407 | 51 | 5 | 6 | 0 |
| Hunt, 32 Lou-29 OkC | .987 | 61 | 333 | 38 | 5 | 6 | 8 |
| Knicely, Denver | .967 | 16 | 74 | 14 | 3 | 1 | 0 |
| Lavalliere, Louisville | .990 | 67 | 420 | 53 | 5 | 5 | 6 |
| Lowry, Nashville | .968 | 66 | 318 | 45 | 12 | 6 | 1 |
| Madison, Nashville | .967 | 38 | 233 | 28 | 9 | 3 | 1 |
| McClendon, Denver | 1.000 | 4 | 21 | 2 | 0 | 0 | 0 |
| Melvin, Nashville | .993 | 47 | 266 | 26 | 2 | 2 | 2 |
| Mercado, Oklahoma City | .987 | 57 | 268 | 26 | 4 | 3 | 3 |
| Miley, Denver | .994 | 53 | 278 | 35 | 2 | 6 | 0 |
| O'Berry, Indianapolis | .975 | 44 | 213 | 23 | 6 | 2 | 1 |
| Pagnozzi, Louisville | .986 | 48 | 266 | 25 | 4 | 3 | 4 |
| Petralli, Oklahoma City | .976 | 25 | 108 | 14 | 3 | 0 | 0 |
| Poldberg, Omaha | .976 | 42 | 255 | 30 | 7 | 3 | 8 |
| Porter, Louisville | 1.000 | 1 | 2 | 0 | 0 | 0 | 0 |
| Pryor, Denver | 1.000 | 30 | 143 | 14 | 0 | 0 | 3 |
| Quirk, Omaha | .977 | 92 | 480 | 63 | 13 | 6 | 23 |
| Roadcap, Iowa | 1.000 | 2 | 8 | 0 | 0 | 0 | 0 |
| Romero, Buffalo | 1.000 | 5 | 28 | 2 | 0 | 0 | 2 |
| Rosado, Nashville | 1.000 | 3 | 5 | 0 | 0 | 0 | 0 |
| Santovenia, Indianapolis | .994 | 25 | 135 | 20 | 1 | 2 | 0 |
| Skinner, Buffalo | .986 | 114 | 623 | 65 | 10 | 13 | 7 |
| Werner, 3 Nash.-9 OkC | .969 | 12 | 59 | 4 | 2 | 2 | 0 |
| Wilkerson, Omaha | .971 | 17 | 62 | 4 | 2 | 0 | 2 |
| Yost, Indianapolis | .972 | 84 | 370 | 48 | 12 | 4 | 3 |

## PITCHERS

| Player and Club | Pct. | G. | PO. | A. | E. | DP. |
|---|---|---|---|---|---|---|
| Abrego, Iowa | 1.000 | 5 | 1 | 3 | 0 | 0 |
| Agosto, Buffalo* | 1.000 | 6 | 0 | 3 | 0 | 0 |
| M. Anderson, Louisville* | .857 | 18 | 2 | 22 | 4 | 2 |
| S. Baker, Indianapolis | .973 | 27 | 16 | 20 | 1 | 0 |
| Baller, Iowa | .789 | 24 | 4 | 11 | 4 | 1 |
| Bargar, Indianapolis | .949 | 38 | 16 | 21 | 2 | 2 |
| Barnes, Iowa* | 1.000 | 6 | 2 | 7 | 0 | 0 |
| Beard, Iowa | .750 | 11 | 2 | 1 | 1 | 1 |
| Boever, Louisville | 1.000 | 21 | 0 | 3 | 0 | 0 |
| Boggs, Oklahoma City | 1.000 | 13 | 4 | 8 | 0 | 1 |
| BOTELHO, Iowa | 1.000 | 20 | 11 | 18 | 0 | 1 |
| Breining, 4 Ind-3 Nash | 1.000 | 7 | 2 | 4 | 0 | 0 |
| Brown, Indianapolis | .867 | 45 | 8 | 5 | 2 | 0 |
| Buchanan, Denver* | .875 | 29 | 0 | 7 | 1 | 0 |
| Burroughs, Denver* | .941 | 15 | 3 | 13 | 1 | 1 |
| Cary, Nashville | .947 | 48 | 6 | 12 | 1 | 2 |
| Cates, Indianapolis | 1.000 | 8 | 1 | 6 | 0 | 0 |
| Cone, Omaha | .742 | 28 | 12 | 11 | 8 | 1 |
| Conner, Nashville* | .862 | 33 | 7 | 18 | 4 | 1 |
| G. Cook, Oklahoma City | .905 | 18 | 11 | 8 | 2 | 0 |
| K. Cook, Indianapolis | 1.000 | 6 | 1 | 2 | 0 | 0 |
| Cruz, Nashville | 1.000 | 31 | 0 | 4 | 0 | 0 |
| Cutshall, Indianapolis | 1.000 | 7 | 1 | 6 | 0 | 0 |
| Davis, Buffalo | 1.000 | 10 | 0 | 7 | 0 | 0 |
| Denman, Nashville | .984 | 27 | 23 | 39 | 1 | 3 |
| Dopson, Indianapolis | .950 | 18 | 5 | 14 | 1 | 1 |
| Earley, Oklahoma City* | 1.000 | 41 | 6 | 18 | 0 | 1 |
| Engel, Iowa* | 1.000 | 10 | 1 | 7 | 0 | 0 |
| Epple, Louisville* | 1.000 | 5 | 2 | 3 | 0 | 0 |
| Fallon, Buffalo* | .824 | 15 | 3 | 11 | 3 | 0 |
| Farr, Omaha | .931 | 17 | 7 | 20 | 2 | 3 |
| Ferreira, Omaha* | .953 | 27 | 8 | 33 | 2 | 3 |
| Fireovid, Buffalo | .923 | 24 | 8 | 28 | 3 | 1 |
| Fossas, Oklahoma City* | .958 | 30 | 3 | 20 | 1 | 1 |
| Gleaton, Buffalo* | .900 | 38 | 2 | 7 | 1 | 0 |
| Glynn, Indianapolis* | 1.000 | 28 | 2 | 3 | 0 | 0 |
| Grapenthin, Indianapolis | .958 | 48 | 5 | 18 | 1 | 4 |
| Griffin, Omaha | .970 | 24 | 11 | 21 | 1 | 1 |
| Groves, Indianapolis | 1.000 | 12 | 1 | 0 | 0 | 0 |
| Gumpert, Iowa | 1.000 | 42 | 7 | 13 | 0 | 2 |
| Gura, Iowa* | .905 | 10 | 6 | 13 | 2 | 0 |
| Guzman, Oklahoma City | .976 | 25 | 12 | 29 | 1 | 1 |
| Hagen, Louisville | .964 | 28 | 21 | 32 | 2 | 2 |
| Hardy, Buffalo | 1.000 | 3 | 0 | 2 | 0 | 0 |
| Hargesheimer, Omaha | .973 | 32 | 12 | 24 | 1 | 3 |
| Hassler, Louisville* | 1.000 | 26 | 2 | 6 | 0 | 0 |
| Hayes, Louisville | 1.000 | 6 | 1 | 0 | 0 | 0 |
| Heinkel, Nashville | 1.000 | 8 | 2 | 9 | 0 | 0 |
| Hickey, Buffalo | 1.000 | 7 | 1 | 2 | 0 | 0 |
| Hoffman, Iowa* | 1.000 | 9 | 1 | 4 | 0 | 1 |
| Holman, Iowa | .935 | 38 | 11 | 18 | 2 | 2 |
| Huismann, Omaha | .950 | 59 | 11 | 8 | 1 | 0 |
| Johnson, Iowa | 1.000 | 2 | 0 | 1 | 0 | 0 |
| Jones, Buffalo | 1.000 | 4 | 0 | 2 | 0 | 0 |
| Keener, Louisville | 1.000 | 43 | 1 | 16 | 0 | 1 |
| Keeton, Omaha | .966 | 24 | 4 | 24 | 1 | 1 |
| Kelly, Nashville | .971 | 27 | 8 | 25 | 1 | 3 |
| Kemp, Denver | 1.000 | 7 | 4 | 8 | 0 | 0 |
| Keough, Louisville | 1.000 | 19 | 12 | 11 | 0 | 1 |
| Kinnunen, Omaha* | .929 | 53 | 3 | 10 | 1 | 0 |
| Knox, Denver | 1.000 | 2 | 1 | 3 | 0 | 0 |
| Koontz, 6 Lou-26 Ind | 1.000 | 32 | 8 | 10 | 0 | 1 |
| LaCoss, Omaha | 1.000 | 4 | 0 | 5 | 0 | 0 |
| Landrum, Iowa | .938 | 34 | 11 | 19 | 2 | 0 |
| Long, Buffalo | .935 | 25 | 13 | 16 | 2 | 3 |
| Mahler, 9 Ind-5 Nash* | 1.000 | 14 | 5 | 11 | 0 | 1 |
| J. Martin, Louisville | 1.000 | 2 | 0 | 1 | 0 | 0 |
| R. Martin, Omaha | .938 | 39 | 8 | 22 | 2 | 2 |
| Martinez, Louisville | .870 | 27 | 4 | 16 | 3 | 1 |
| Martz, Iowa | 1.000 | 4 | 0 | 3 | 0 | 0 |
| Mathews, Louisville* | .941 | 12 | 6 | 10 | 1 | 1 |
| McGaffigan, Denver | .893 | 26 | 13 | 12 | 3 | 1 |
| McKeon, Buffalo* | 1.000 | 49 | 6 | 11 | 0 | 0 |
| Meridith, Iowa* | .900 | 25 | 3 | 6 | 1 | 0 |
| Mohorcic, Oklahoma City | .964 | 40 | 10 | 17 | 1 | 2 |
| Monge, Nashville* | .909 | 31 | 2 | 8 | 1 | 1 |
| Monteleone, Nashville | .970 | 27 | 13 | 19 | 1 | 2 |
| Mullen, Buffalo | 1.000 | 19 | 0 | 3 | 0 | 0 |
| Murphy, Denver* | .875 | 41 | 5 | 9 | 2 | 0 |
| Murray, Oklahoma City | 1.000 | 26 | 0 | 2 | 0 | 0 |
| Nicometi, Indianapolis* | 1.000 | 3 | 0 | 2 | 0 | 0 |
| O'Connor, Indianapolis* | 1.000 | 42 | 2 | 8 | 0 | 1 |
| O'Neal, Nashville | 1.000 | 10 | 9 | 13 | 0 | 2 |
| Owchinko, Buffalo* | 1.000 | 10 | 1 | 7 | 0 | 0 |
| Ownbey, Louisville | .880 | 25 | 7 | 15 | 3 | 3 |
| Pacella, Nashville | .875 | 37 | 11 | 17 | 4 | 0 |
| Parrott, Oklahoma City | 1.000 | 21 | 4 | 15 | 0 | 3 |
| Patterson, Iowa | .905 | 22 | 14 | 24 | 4 | 1 |
| Perlman, Iowa | .979 | 32 | 17 | 29 | 1 | 1 |
| Perry, Louisville* | 1.000 | 45 | 4 | 23 | 0 | 2 |
| Pryce, Iowa | .963 | 44 | 10 | 16 | 1 | 2 |
| Puleo, Denver | .909 | 11 | 5 | 5 | 1 | 2 |
| D. Rajsich, Denver* | .929 | 24 | 6 | 7 | 1 | 0 |
| E. Rasmussen, Louisville | 1.000 | 1 | 1 | 1 | 0 | 0 |
| J. Rasmussen, Nashville | 1.000 | 7 | 3 | 1 | 0 | 0 |
| Reynolds, Denver | 1.000 | 7 | 4 | 4 | 0 | 1 |
| Robinson, Denver | .875 | 6 | 4 | 10 | 2 | 0 |
| Rogers, Buffalo | 1.000 | 4 | 2 | 4 | 0 | 1 |
| Rothschild, Iowa | .947 | 40 | 9 | 9 | 1 | 0 |
| Russell, 16 Den-2 OkC | .923 | 18 | 11 | 13 | 2 | 1 |
| Schatzeder, Indianapolis* | 1.000 | 1 | 0 | 0 | 0 | 0 |
| Scott, Denver | 1.000 | 12 | 4 | 4 | 0 | 1 |
| Sebra, Oklahoma City | .966 | 22 | 12 | 16 | 1 | 1 |
| Shade, Louisville | 1.000 | 14 | 2 | 0 | 0 | 1 |
| Shimp, Oklahoma City | .952 | 24 | 4 | 16 | 1 | 2 |
| Shirley, Nashville* | 1.000 | 21 | 0 | 4 | 0 | 0 |
| Siwy, Buffalo | .800 | 16 | 1 | 3 | 1 | 0 |
| Smith, Denver | 1.000 | 47 | 4 | 11 | 0 | 1 |
| Speck, Buffalo | 1.000 | 21 | 4 | 13 | 0 | 0 |
| St. Claire, Indianapolis | 1.000 | 11 | 0 | 1 | 0 | 0 |
| Stoddard, Nashville | .875 | 22 | 1 | 6 | 1 | 1 |
| Stoll, Oklahoma City | .967 | 23 | 6 | 23 | 1 | 2 |
| Stranski, Buffalo | .929 | 48 | 6 | 7 | 1 | 2 |
| Strode, Omaha* | .944 | 21 | 5 | 12 | 1 | 0 |
| Tanner, Buffalo | .974 | 20 | 7 | 30 | 1 | 4 |
| Terry, Denver | .966 | 28 | 21 | 36 | 2 | 3 |
| Tibbs, Denver | .941 | 4 | 8 | 8 | 1 | 0 |
| Todd, Buffalo | .889 | 25 | 2 | 6 | 1 | 0 |
| Toliver, Denver | 1.000 | 19 | 3 | 23 | 0 | 1 |
| Voigt, Nashville | .942 | 28 | 26 | 39 | 4 | 4 |
| Wehrmeister, Buffalo | .968 | 30 | 12 | 18 | 1 | 2 |
| Welsh, Oklahoma City* | 1.000 | 8 | 6 | 13 | 0 | 1 |
| Williams, Oklahoma City | 1.000 | 1 | 0 | 1 | 0 | 0 |
| Willis, Denver | .952 | 37 | 10 | 10 | 1 | 1 |
| Worrell, Louisville | .862 | 34 | 8 | 17 | 4 | 1 |
| Wright, Oklahoma City* | .950 | 17 | 2 | 17 | 1 | 0 |
| Youmans, Indianapolis | 1.000 | 6 | 3 | 3 | 0 | 0 |
| Zwolensky, Oklahoma City | .929 | 18 | 4 | 22 | 2 | 1 |

The following players do not have any recorded accepted chances at the positions indicated; therefore, are not listed in the fielding averages for those particular positions: J. Anderson, p; K. Baker, p; W. Barnes, 2b; Barrett, p; Hallgren, p; Hoeksema, 2b; R. Jackson, of; Ronald Johnson, 3b; Kunkel, of; Lawless, of; Lucas, p; Maler, of; Menendez, p; Moronko, of; Nail, p; Owen, of; Pecota, ss, of; Pittman, 1b; Rhodes, p; Roberge, p; Scranton, p; Shines, of; Stearns, c; Stockstill, 3b; Taveras, 3b.

## CLUB PITCHING

| Club | ERA. | G. | CG. | ShO. | Sv. | IP. | H. | R. | ER. | HR. | HB. | BB. | Int. BB. | SO. | WP. | Bk. |
|------|------|-----|-----|------|-----|--------|------|-----|-----|-----|-----|-----|----------|-----|-----|-----|
| Oklahoma City | 3.43 | 143 | 22 | 10 | 45 | 1230.2 | 1127 | 542 | 469 | 82 | 20 | 409 | 6 | 668 | 41 | 9 |
| Louisville | 3.51 | 144 | 22 | 7 | 39 | 1252.2 | 1124 | 568 | 488 | 95 | 37 | 553 | 20 | 856 | 58 | 15 |
| Omaha | 3.57 | 142 | 31 | 11 | 44 | 1216.2 | 1083 | 551 | 482 | 101 | 27 | 567 | 21 | 784 | 48 | 18 |
| Nashville | 3.84 | 142 | 28 | 10 | 29 | 1243.0 | 1144 | 609 | 531 | 95 | 40 | 559 | 23 | 783 | 67 | 17 |
| Indianapolis | 3.92 | 142 | 26 | 10 | 28 | 1246.1 | 1187 | 625 | 543 | 102 | 33 | 532 | 29 | 733 | 43 | 20 |
| Denver | 4.02 | 142 | 20 | 8 | 47 | 1244.0 | 1297 | 663 | 556 | 83 | 17 | 545 | 13 | 844 | 73 | 24 |
| Iowa | 4.10 | 141 | 22 | 13 | 27 | 1230.1 | 1213 | 639 | 560 | 93 | 36 | 458 | 46 | 764 | 46 | 18 |
| Buffalo | 4.30 | 142 | 24 | 8 | 29 | 1210.2 | 1306 | 660 | 579 | 113 | 36 | 491 | 26 | 748 | 44 | 10 |

## PITCHERS' RECORDS

(Leading Qualifiers for Earned-Run Average Leadership — 114 or More Innings)

*Throws lefthanded.

| Pitcher—Club | W. | L. | Pct. | ERA. | G. | GS. | CG. | GF. | ShO. | Sv. | IP. | H. | R. | ER. | HR. | HB. | BB. | Int. BB. | SO. | WP. |
|------|-----|-----|------|------|-----|-----|-----|-----|------|-----|-------|-----|-----|-----|-----|-----|-----|----------|-----|-----|
| Farr, Omaha | 10 | 4 | .714 | 2.02 | 17 | 16 | 7 | 0 | 3 | 0 | 133.2 | 105 | 36 | 30 | 6 | 3 | 41 | 0 | 98 | 1 |
| Hargesheimer, Omaha | 11 | 10 | .524 | 2.91 | 32 | 20 | 4 | 3 | 1 | 0 | 151.2 | 136 | 60 | 49 | 10 | 4 | 72 | 3 | 91 | 3 |
| Fireovid, Buffalo | 8 | 7 | .533 | 3.01 | 24 | 20 | 4 | 3 | 2 | 0 | 137.1 | 154 | 50 | 46 | 9 | 1 | 34 | 2 | 57 | 8 |
| Guzman, Oklahoma City | 10 | 5 | .667 | 3.13 | 25 | 23 | 4 | 2 | 1 | 1 | 149.2 | 131 | 60 | 52 | 11 | 2 | 40 | 0 | 76 | 2 |
| Voigt, Nashville | 11 | 9 | .550 | 3.17 | 28 | 27 | 7 | 1 | 1 | 0 | 176.0 | 155 | 75 | 62 | 10 | 10 | 85 | 2 | 95 | 8 |
| G. Cook, Oklahoma City | 9 | 5 | .643 | 3.21 | 18 | 18 | 2 | 0 | 0 | 0 | 120.2 | 92 | 50 | 43 | 8 | 3 | 32 | 0 | 80 | 4 |
| Ferreira, Omaha* | 11 | 10 | .524 | 3.21 | 27 | 26 | 6 | 0 | 0 | 0 | 173.2 | 142 | 73 | 62 | 15 | 3 | 89 | 6 | 105 | 7 |
| Pacella, Nashville | 7 | 7 | .500 | 3.23 | 37 | 12 | 2 | 12 | 1 | 3 | 122.2 | 90 | 47 | 44 | 4 | 0 | 54 | 2 | 79 | 10 |
| Toliver, Denver | 11 | 3 | .786 | 3.24 | 19 | 19 | 5 | 0 | 2 | 0 | 122.1 | 113 | 50 | 44 | 6 | 1 | 56 | 0 | 84 | 6 |
| Griffin, Omaha | 7 | 8 | .467 | 3.27 | 24 | 19 | 4 | 4 | 2 | 1 | 135.0 | 115 | 58 | 49 | 11 | 3 | 43 | 0 | 69 | 0 |
| Hagen, Louisville | 10 | 9 | .526 | 3.39 | 28 | 28 | 2 | 0 | 0 | 0 | 170.0 | 162 | 72 | 64 | 10 | 10 | 87 | 3 | 63 | 7 |

Departmental Leaders: G—Huismann, 59; W—Long, 13; L—Bargar, 17; Pct.—Gleaton, .800; GS—Hagen, Terry, 28; CG—S. Baker, Denman, Stoll, 8; GF—Huismann, 56; ShO—Denman, 4; Sv.—Huismann, 33; IP—S. Baker, Denman, 181.2; H—Terry, 203; R—Terry, 105; ER—Terry, 88; HR—Bargar, Keeton, Sebra, 17; HB—Hagen, Kelly, Voigt, 10; BB—Cone, 93; IBB—Grapenthin, Gumpert, 7; SO—Worrell, 126; WP—Kelly, Terry, 14.

| Pitcher—Club | W. | L. | Pct. | ERA. | G. | GS. | CG. | GF. | ShO. | Sv. | IP. | H. | R. | ER. | HR. | HB. | BB. | Int. BB. | SO. | WP. |
|------|-----|-----|------|------|-----|-----|-----|-----|------|-----|-------|-----|-----|-----|-----|-----|-----|----------|-----|-----|
| Abrego, Iowa | 0 | 5 | .000 | 7.92 | 5 | 5 | 0 | 0 | 0 | 0 | 25.0 | 29 | 24 | 22 | 2 | 2 | 15 | 3 | 12 | 4 |
| Agosto, Buffalo* | 0 | 0 | .000 | 2.13 | 6 | 0 | 0 | 5 | 0 | 2 | 12.2 | 13 | 3 | 3 | 0 | 0 | 2 | 0 | 11 | 0 |
| J. Anderson, Oklahoma City | 0 | 0 | .000 | 0.00 | 1 | 1 | 0 | 0 | 0 | 0 | 1.0 | 0 | 0 | 0 | 0 | 0 | 0 | 0 | 0 | 0 |
| M. Anderson, Louisville* | 3 | 4 | .429 | 4.16 | 18 | 8 | 5 | 4 | 1 | 1 | 84.1 | 81 | 43 | 39 | 5 | 0 | 50 | 0 | 61 | 6 |
| K. Baker, Omaha* | 0 | 0 | .000 | 0.00 | 1 | 0 | 0 | 0 | 0 | 0 | 2.0 | 3 | 0 | 0 | 0 | 1 | 1 | 0 | 0 | 0 |
| S. Baker, Indianapolis | 9 | 12 | .429 | 3.91 | 27 | 27 | 8 | 0 | 0 | 0 | 181.2 | 200 | 99 | 79 | 14 | 5 | 68 | 3 | 90 | 4 |
| Baller, Iowa | 8 | 9 | .471 | 4.65 | 38 | 22 | 5 | 9 | 1 | 2 | 162.2 | 150 | 97 | 84 | 17 | 6 | 85 | 3 | 119 | 8 |
| Bargar, Indianapolis | 5 | 17 | .227 | 4.65 | 24 | 24 | 7 | 0 | 3 | 0 | 149.0 | 140 | 77 | 70 | 12 | 5 | 63 | 6 | 119 | 7 |
| Barnes, Iowa* | 3 | 0 | 1.000 | 2.88 | 6 | 6 | 0 | 0 | 0 | 0 | 34.1 | 30 | 16 | 11 | 0 | 1 | 13 | 1 | 18 | 3 |
| Barrett, Indianapolis | 0 | 0 | .000 | 0.79 | 4 | 0 | 0 | 1 | 0 | 0 | 11.1 | 9 | 1 | 1 | 0 | 0 | 6 | 0 | 4 | 1 |
| Beard, Iowa | 2 | 0 | 1.000 | 0.56 | 11 | 0 | 0 | 10 | 0 | 3 | 16.0 | 10 | 1 | 1 | 0 | 0 | 9 | 3 | 9 | 0 |
| Boever, Louisville | 3 | 2 | .600 | 2.04 | 21 | 0 | 0 | 13 | 0 | 1 | 35.1 | 28 | 11 | 8 | 0 | 0 | 22 | 0 | 37 | 3 |
| Boggs, Oklahoma City | 5 | 7 | .417 | 3.43 | 13 | 13 | 4 | 0 | 0 | 0 | 78.2 | 79 | 39 | 30 | 5 | 3 | 23 | 0 | 31 | 2 |
| Botelho, Iowa | 11 | 7 | .611 | 4.30 | 20 | 20 | 4 | 0 | 0 | 0 | 125.2 | 117 | 64 | 60 | 12 | 3 | 53 | 2 | 94 | 5 |
| Breining, 4 Ind.-3 Nash. | 1 | 2 | .333 | 4.83 | 7 | 4 | 0 | 1 | 0 | 0 | 31.2 | 40 | 18 | 17 | 3 | 0 | 14 | 1 | 15 | 2 |
| Brown, Indianapolis | 4 | 3 | .571 | 3.82 | 45 | 2 | 0 | 12 | 0 | 1 | 92.0 | 84 | 44 | 39 | 9 | 3 | 30 | 4 | 53 | 1 |
| Buchanan, Denver* | 4 | 3 | .571 | 2.18 | 29 | 0 | 0 | 22 | 0 | 12 | 41.1 | 45 | 20 | 10 | 3 | 0 | 13 | 1 | 36 | 3 |
| Burroughs, Denver | 4 | 4 | .500 | 5.33 | 15 | 13 | 0 | 2 | 0 | 1 | 81.0 | 96 | 51 | 48 | 7 | 1 | 37 | 0 | 45 | 5 |
| Cary, Nashville | 2 | 1 | .667 | 3.00 | 48 | 0 | 0 | 16 | 0 | 8 | 66.0 | 55 | 27 | 22 | 6 | 3 | 27 | 1 | 54 | 4 |
| Cates, Indianapolis | 1 | 6 | .143 | 6.65 | 8 | 8 | 1 | 0 | 0 | 0 | 44.2 | 60 | 33 | 33 | 4 | 2 | 18 | 1 | 23 | 2 |
| Cone, Omaha | 9 | 15 | .375 | 4.65 | 28 | 27 | 5 | 0 | 1 | 0 | 158.2 | 157 | 90 | 82 | 13 | 2 | 93 | 3 | 115 | 7 |
| Conner, Nashville | 8 | 7 | .533 | 2.74 | 33 | 10 | 3 | 15 | 0 | 1 | 105.0 | 96 | 51 | 32 | 11 | 4 | 33 | 2 | 57 | 0 |
| G. Cook, Oklahoma City | 9 | 5 | .643 | 3.21 | 18 | 18 | 2 | 0 | 0 | 0 | 120.2 | 92 | 50 | 43 | 8 | 3 | 32 | 0 | 80 | 4 |
| K. Cook, Indianapolis | 1 | 1 | .500 | 0.69 | 6 | 1 | 0 | 4 | 0 | 0 | 13.0 | 10 | 1 | 1 | 0 | 0 | 2 | 1 | 2 | 0 |
| Cruz, Nashville | 1 | 2 | .333 | 7.23 | 31 | 0 | 0 | 14 | 0 | 2 | 37.1 | 43 | 32 | 30 | 4 | 0 | 23 | 6 | 24 | 2 |
| Cutshall, Indianapolis | 0 | 2 | .000 | 3.99 | 7 | 7 | 0 | 0 | 0 | 0 | 38.1 | 27 | 21 | 17 | 1 | 2 | 36 | 0 | 25 | 3 |
| Davis, Buffalo | 2 | 5 | .286 | 4.63 | 10 | 10 | 1 | 0 | 0 | 0 | 56.1 | 61 | 39 | 29 | 5 | 0 | 35 | 2 | 31 | 3 |
| Denman, Nashville | 10 | 8 | .556 | 4.06 | 27 | 26 | 8 | 0 | 4 | 0 | 181.2 | 198 | 93 | 82 | 12 | 5 | 51 | 0 | 65 | 1 |
| Dopson, Indianapolis | 4 | 7 | .364 | 3.78 | 18 | 18 | 3 | 0 | 2 | 0 | 95.1 | 88 | 44 | 40 | 7 | 3 | 44 | 1 | 48 | 3 |
| Earley, Oklahoma City* | 7 | 5 | .583 | 3.27 | 41 | 0 | 0 | 31 | 0 | 12 | 77.0 | 68 | 29 | 28 | 6 | 2 | 18 | 1 | 43 | 0 |
| Engel, Iowa* | 4 | 2 | .667 | 3.23 | 10 | 10 | 2 | 0 | 1 | 0 | 61.1 | 55 | 26 | 22 | 2 | 1 | 34 | 2 | 53 | 3 |
| Epple, Louisville* | 0 | 2 | .000 | 7.64 | 5 | 4 | 0 | 1 | 0 | 0 | 17.2 | 19 | 16 | 15 | 6 | 0 | 7 | 0 | 15 | 1 |
| Fallon, Buffalo* | 3 | 8 | .273 | 4.28 | 15 | 14 | 0 | 1 | 0 | 0 | 80.0 | 94 | 53 | 38 | 4 | 6 | 40 | 3 | 60 | 2 |
| Farr, Omaha | 10 | 4 | .714 | 2.02 | 17 | 16 | 7 | 0 | 3 | 0 | 133.2 | 105 | 36 | 30 | 6 | 3 | 41 | 0 | 98 | 1 |
| Ferreira, Omaha* | 11 | 10 | .524 | 3.21 | 27 | 26 | 6 | 0 | 0 | 0 | 173.2 | 142 | 73 | 62 | 15 | 3 | 89 | 6 | 105 | 7 |
| Fireovid, Buffalo | 8 | 7 | .533 | 3.01 | 24 | 20 | 4 | 3 | 2 | 0 | 137.1 | 154 | 50 | 46 | 9 | 1 | 34 | 2 | 57 | 8 |
| Fossas, Oklahoma City* | 7 | 6 | .538 | 4.75 | 30 | 13 | 2 | 8 | 0 | 2 | 110.0 | 121 | 65 | 58 | 6 | 1 | 36 | 1 | 49 | 3 |
| Gleaton, Buffalo* | 8 | 2 | .800 | 2.44 | 38 | 0 | 0 | 26 | 0 | 7 | 55.1 | 62 | 17 | 15 | 2 | 0 | 21 | 3 | 37 | 0 |
| Glynn, Indianapolis* | 4 | 2 | .667 | 1.71 | 28 | 0 | 0 | 19 | 0 | 4 | 42.0 | 25 | 11 | 8 | 1 | 0 | 17 | 1 | 48 | 4 |
| Grapenthin, Indianapolis | 5 | 7 | .417 | 3.74 | 48 | 0 | 0 | 33 | 0 | 11 | 84.1 | 77 | 38 | 35 | 7 | 2 | 31 | 7 | 24 | 2 |
| Griffin, Omaha | 7 | 8 | .467 | 3.27 | 24 | 19 | 4 | 4 | 2 | 1 | 135.0 | 115 | 58 | 49 | 11 | 3 | 43 | 0 | 69 | 0 |
| Groves, Indianapolis | 2 | 1 | .667 | 6.27 | 12 | 0 | 0 | 1 | 0 | 0 | 18.2 | 23 | 14 | 13 | 2 | 1 | 9 | 0 | 8 | 1 |
| Gumpert, Iowa | 3 | 4 | .429 | 4.19 | 42 | 0 | 0 | 30 | 0 | 10 | 66.2 | 74 | 36 | 31 | 6 | 2 | 23 | 7 | 33 | 2 |
| Gura, Iowa* | 7 | 3 | .700 | 2.54 | 10 | 10 | 0 | 0 | 0 | 0 | 71.0 | 69 | 24 | 20 | 4 | 1 | 8 | 0 | 45 | 1 |
| Guzman, Oklahoma City | 10 | 5 | .667 | 3.13 | 25 | 23 | 4 | 2 | 1 | 1 | 149.2 | 131 | 60 | 52 | 11 | 2 | 40 | 0 | 76 | 2 |
| Hagen, Louisville | 10 | 9 | .526 | 3.39 | 28 | 28 | 2 | 0 | 0 | 0 | 170.0 | 162 | 72 | 64 | 10 | 10 | 87 | 3 | 63 | 7 |
| Hallgren, Oklahoma City | 1 | 0 | 1.000 | 3.60 | 4 | 2 | 0 | 1 | 0 | 0 | 15.0 | 16 | 7 | 6 | 0 | 0 | 4 | 0 | 10 | 0 |
| Hardy, Buffalo | 0 | 1 | .000 | 6.52 | 3 | 2 | 0 | 1 | 0 | 0 | 9.2 | 13 | 7 | 7 | 3 | 0 | 4 | 0 | 6 | 2 |
| Hargesheimer, Omaha | 11 | 10 | .524 | 2.91 | 32 | 20 | 4 | 3 | 1 | 0 | 151.2 | 136 | 60 | 49 | 10 | 4 | 72 | 3 | 91 | 3 |
| Hassler, Louisville* | 4 | 5 | .444 | 3.29 | 26 | 0 | 0 | 14 | 0 | 2 | 41.0 | 39 | 17 | 15 | 7 | 0 | 19 | 1 | 32 | 3 |
| Hayes, Louisville | 0 | 1 | .000 | 1.35 | 6 | 0 | 0 | 2 | 0 | 0 | 6.2 | 7 | 1 | 1 | 0 | 0 | 3 | 0 | 2 | 2 |
| Heinkel, Nashville | 1 | 3 | .250 | 7.13 | 8 | 7 | 0 | 0 | 0 | 0 | 41.2 | 49 | 36 | 33 | 8 | 2 | 14 | 0 | 18 | 3 |
| Hickey, Buffalo | 1 | 0 | 1.000 | 7.71 | 7 | 1 | 0 | 0 | 0 | 0 | 16.1 | 25 | 14 | 14 | 3 | 1 | 5 | 0 | 12 | 1 |
| Hoffman, Iowa* | 4 | 0 | 1.000 | 1.50 | 9 | 6 | 0 | 1 | 0 | 0 | 36.0 | 23 | 9 | 6 | 2 | 0 | 17 | 0 | 37 | 2 |
| Holman, Iowa | 0 | 10 | .000 | 4.01 | 38 | 6 | 1 | 20 | 0 | 2 | 103.1 | 101 | 51 | 46 | 8 | 4 | 36 | 2 | 38 | 1 |
| Huismann, Omaha | 5 | 5 | .500 | 2.01 | 59 | 0 | 0 | 56 | 0 | 33 | 89.1 | 70 | 20 | 20 | 4 | 2 | 14 | 2 | 70 | 7 |
| Johnson, Iowa | 0 | 0 | .000 | 4.50 | 2 | 0 | 0 | 1 | 0 | 0 | 2.0 | 2 | 2 | 1 | 1 | 0 | 1 | 0 | 2 | 0 |
| Jones, Buffalo | 0 | 1 | .000 | 10.13 | 4 | 0 | 0 | 11 | 0 | 0 | 2.2 | 3 | 3 | 3 | 0 | 0 | 3 | 0 | 1 | 0 |

| Pitcher—Club | W. | L. | Pct. | ERA. | G. | GS. | CG. | GF. | ShO. | Sv. | IP. | H. | R. | ER. | HR. | HB. | BB. | Int. BB. | SO. | WP. |
|---|---|---|---|---|---|---|---|---|---|---|---|---|---|---|---|---|---|---|---|---|
| Keener, Louisville | 6 | 6 | .500 | 3.63 | 43 | 0 | 0 | 27 | 0 | 6 | 72.0 | 70 | 40 | 29 | 11 | 5 | 23 | 4 | 40 | 3 |
| Keeton, Omaha | 8 | 4 | .667 | 4.96 | 24 | 11 | 1 | 4 | 0 | 1 | 98.0 | 107 | 64 | 54 | 17 | 1 | 31 | 0 | 40 | 4 |
| Kelly, Nashville | 8 | 8 | .500 | 3.75 | 27 | 18 | 1 | 6 | 1 | 0 | 112.2 | 86 | 51 | 47 | 4 | 10 | 89 | 0 | 93 | 14 |
| Kemp, Denver | 2 | 3 | .400 | 3.12 | 7 | 7 | 0 | 0 | 0 | 0 | 40.1 | 41 | 20 | 14 | 4 | 0 | 20 | 0 | 33 | 0 |
| Keough, Louisville | 3 | 7 | .300 | 3.35 | 19 | 19 | 2 | 0 | 0 | 0 | 110.0 | 88 | 44 | 41 | 9 | 3 | 42 | 1 | 92 | 6 |
| Kinnunen, Omaha* | 2 | 0 | 1.000 | 3.46 | 53 | 0 | 0 | 25 | 0 | 6 | 52.0 | 41 | 24 | 20 | 3 | 1 | 41 | 1 | 30 | 4 |
| Knox, Denver | 0 | 1 | .000 | 7.27 | 2 | 1 | 0 | 1 | 0 | 0 | 8.2 | 11 | 9 | 7 | 1 | 0 | 3 | 0 | 3 | 0 |
| Koontz, 6 Lou.-26 Ind. | 5 | 3 | .625 | 4.02 | 32 | 12 | 0 | 6 | 0 | 0 | 103.0 | 93 | 49 | 46 | 10 | 1 | 40 | 1 | 57 | 1 |
| LaCoss, Omaha | 1 | 2 | .333 | 3.22 | 4 | 4 | 1 | 0 | 0 | 0 | 22.1 | 23 | 12 | 8 | 1 | 1 | 15 | 0 | 11 | 4 |
| Landrum, Denver | 6 | 6 | .500 | 3.98 | 29 | 19 | 3 | 6 | 1 | 2 | 138.0 | 148 | 72 | 61 | 9 | 3 | 49 | 1 | 88 | 4 |
| Long, Buffalo | 13 | 6 | .684 | 3.51 | 25 | 22 | 7 | 1 | 1 | 0 | 151.1 | 146 | 69 | 59 | 12 | 1 | 43 | 2 | 71 | 1 |
| Lucas, Indianapolis* | 0 | 0 | .000 | 0.00 | 1 | 1 | 0 | 0 | 0 | 0 | 2.0 | 1 | 0 | 0 | 0 | 0 | 2 | 0 | 2 | 0 |
| Mahler, 9 Ind.-5 Nash.* | 7 | 2 | .778 | 3.21 | 14 | 13 | 2 | 0 | 1 | 0 | 98.0 | 93 | 38 | 35 | 9 | 1 | 39 | 1 | 92 | 8 |
| J. Martin, Louisville | 2 | 0 | 1.000 | 1.42 | 2 | 1 | 0 | 1 | 0 | 0 | 6.1 | 4 | 1 | 1 | 1 | 0 | 2 | 0 | 4 | 2 |
| R. Martin, Omaha | 2 | 4 | .333 | 5.51 | 39 | 0 | 0 | 18 | 0 | 3 | 85.0 | 84 | 56 | 52 | 9 | 2 | 53 | 4 | 49 | 5 |
| Martinez, Louisville | 10 | 7 | .588 | 3.55 | 27 | 27 | 4 | 0 | 2 | 0 | 144.1 | 149 | 73 | 57 | 10 | 6 | 53 | 0 | 68 | 0 |
| Martz, Iowa | 0 | 1 | .000 | 4.91 | 4 | 0 | 0 | 0 | 0 | 0 | 7.1 | 10 | 4 | 4 | 0 | 0 | 4 | 1 | 0 | 0 |
| Mathews, Louisville* | 6 | 4 | .600 | 2.92 | 12 | 12 | 2 | 0 | 0 | 0 | 74.0 | 61 | 33 | 24 | 8 | 0 | 26 | 0 | 47 | 2 |
| McGaffigan, Denver | 11 | 5 | .688 | 2.95 | 26 | 13 | 4 | 8 | 2 | 2 | 106.2 | 105 | 43 | 35 | 3 | 2 | 37 | 1 | 91 | 4 |
| McKeon, Buffalo* | 6 | 4 | .600 | 3.72 | 49 | 5 | 0 | 26 | 0 | 12 | 82.1 | 85 | 40 | 34 | 10 | 1 | 36 | 0 | 62 | 1 |
| Menendez, Louisville | 0 | 1 | .000 | 19.29 | 1 | 1 | 0 | 0 | 0 | 0 | 2.1 | 9 | 5 | 5 | 0 | 0 | 1 | 1 | 2 | 0 |
| Meridith, Iowa* | 4 | 1 | .800 | 1.32 | 25 | 0 | 0 | 19 | 0 | 7 | 41.0 | 29 | 9 | 6 | 0 | 0 | 7 | 1 | 29 | 0 |
| Mohorcic, Oklahoma City | 3 | 7 | .300 | 2.87 | 40 | 0 | 0 | 32 | 0 | 15 | 84.2 | 72 | 32 | 27 | 8 | 1 | 21 | 0 | 47 | 3 |
| Monge, Nashville* | 4 | 4 | .500 | 3.64 | 31 | 0 | 0 | 24 | 0 | 8 | 47.0 | 50 | 21 | 19 | 4 | 1 | 16 | 5 | 26 | 2 |
| Monteleone, Nashville | 6 | 12 | .333 | 5.08 | 27 | 26 | 3 | 0 | 0 | 0 | 145.1 | 149 | 89 | 82 | 14 | 2 | 87 | 2 | 97 | 11 |
| Mullen, Buffalo | 0 | 3 | .000 | 9.53 | 19 | 0 | 0 | 10 | 0 | 4 | 28.1 | 40 | 33 | 30 | 6 | 1 | 12 | 0 | 15 | 2 |
| Murphy, Denver* | 5 | 5 | .500 | 4.61 | 41 | 0 | 0 | 18 | 0 | 5 | 84.0 | 94 | 55 | 43 | 8 | 2 | 57 | 4 | 66 | 8 |
| Murray, Oklahoma City | 1 | 4 | .200 | 2.83 | 26 | 0 | 0 | 22 | 0 | 8 | 35.0 | 29 | 17 | 11 | 3 | 0 | 7 | 0 | 20 | 2 |
| Nail, Denver | 0 | 0 | .000 | 1.93 | 1 | 0 | 0 | 0 | 0 | 0 | 4.2 | 5 | 1 | 1 | 0 | 0 | 0 | 0 | 3 | 0 |
| Nicometi, Indianapolis* | 1 | 1 | .500 | 2.79 | 3 | 2 | 0 | 0 | 0 | 0 | 9.2 | 7 | 3 | 3 | 0 | 0 | 6 | 0 | 5 | 0 |
| O'Connor, Indianapolis | 3 | 4 | .429 | 4.72 | 42 | 0 | 0 | 23 | 0 | 4 | 68.2 | 62 | 39 | 36 | 9 | 0 | 28 | 5 | 63 | 2 |
| O'Neal, Nashville | 5 | 4 | .556 | 3.59 | 10 | 10 | 3 | 0 | 1 | 0 | 67.2 | 57 | 29 | 27 | 9 | 0 | 19 | 0 | 44 | 0 |
| Owchinko, Buffalo* | 1 | 4 | .200 | 5.30 | 10 | 4 | 0 | 1 | 0 | 0 | 35.2 | 48 | 21 | 21 | 5 | 0 | 15 | 1 | 24 | 2 |
| Ownbey, Louisville | 10 | 9 | .526 | 3.42 | 25 | 25 | 5 | 0 | 0 | 0 | 166.0 | 154 | 68 | 63 | 10 | 3 | 74 | 1 | 122 | 6 |
| Pacella, Nashville | 7 | 7 | .500 | 3.23 | 37 | 12 | 2 | 12 | 1 | 3 | 122.2 | 90 | 47 | 44 | 4 | 0 | 54 | 2 | 79 | 10 |
| Parrott, Oklahoma City | 2 | 3 | .400 | 2.92 | 21 | 5 | 0 | 8 | 0 | 4 | 77.0 | 72 | 27 | 25 | 2 | 2 | 35 | 2 | 35 | 0 |
| Patterson, Iowa | 8 | 10 | .444 | 4.77 | 22 | 22 | 4 | 0 | 2 | 0 | 132.0 | 142 | 86 | 70 | 13 | 4 | 51 | 4 | 78 | 2 |
| Perlman, Iowa | 7 | 12 | .368 | 4.70 | 32 | 23 | 4 | 6 | 0 | 0 | 151.1 | 181 | 91 | 79 | 11 | 3 | 45 | 3 | 64 | 6 |
| Perry, Louisville | 4 | 3 | .571 | 2.37 | 45 | 2 | 0 | 24 | 0 | 14 | 91.0 | 56 | 33 | 24 | 2 | 3 | 39 | 3 | 63 | 3 |
| Pryce, Iowa | 4 | 6 | .400 | 4.40 | 44 | 6 | 0 | 19 | 0 | 5 | 118.2 | 100 | 61 | 58 | 10 | 6 | 45 | 6 | 75 | 3 |
| Puleo, Denver | 1 | 5 | .167 | 4.57 | 11 | 11 | 1 | 0 | 0 | 0 | 61.0 | 70 | 42 | 31 | 6 | 0 | 37 | 0 | 40 | 1 |
| D. Rajsich, Louisville | 4 | 1 | .800 | 3.42 | 24 | 1 | 0 | 11 | 0 | 3 | 50.0 | 41 | 20 | 19 | 1 | 1 | 24 | 5 | 37 | 6 |
| E. Rasmussen, Louisville | 0 | 0 | .000 | 0.00 | 1 | 0 | 0 | 0 | 0 | 0 | 4.2 | 3 | 0 | 0 | 0 | 0 | 0 | 0 | 4 | 1 |
| J. Rasmussen, Nashville | 0 | 1 | .000 | 6.75 | 7 | 1 | 0 | 2 | 0 | 0 | 14.2 | 20 | 14 | 11 | 2 | 2 | 10 | 1 | 12 | 2 |
| Reynolds, Denver | 2 | 2 | .500 | 7.14 | 7 | 4 | 0 | 1 | 0 | 0 | 29.0 | 39 | 24 | 23 | 4 | 0 | 8 | 0 | 20 | 1 |
| Rhodes, Oklahoma City | 1 | 0 | 1.000 | 8.00 | 6 | 0 | 0 | 2 | 0 | 0 | 9.0 | 12 | 8 | 8 | 1 | 0 | 3 | 1 | 5 | 0 |
| Roberge, Indianapolis | 0 | 0 | .000 | 4.50 | 1 | 0 | 0 | 0 | 0 | 0 | 2.0 | 2 | 1 | 1 | 0 | 1 | 1 | 0 | 2 | 0 |
| Robinson, Denver | 2 | 1 | .667 | 2.72 | 6 | 6 | 0 | 0 | 0 | 0 | 39.2 | 39 | 17 | 12 | 1 | 2 | 12 | 0 | 24 | 1 |
| Rogers, Buffalo | 1 | 2 | .333 | 4.35 | 4 | 4 | 0 | 0 | 0 | 0 | 20.2 | 21 | 12 | 10 | 1 | 0 | 9 | 0 | 13 | 1 |
| Rothschild, Iowa | 1 | 5 | .167 | 5.32 | 40 | 3 | 0 | 13 | 0 | 0 | 89.2 | 101 | 58 | 53 | 10 | 4 | 34 | 5 | 58 | 7 |
| Russell, 16 Den.-2 OkC | 7 | 4 | .636 | 4.06 | 18 | 18 | 1 | 0 | 1 | 0 | 115.1 | 105 | 55 | 52 | 6 | 1 | 51 | 1 | 94 | 6 |
| Schatzeder, Indianapolis* | 0 | 0 | .000 | 0.00 | 1 | 1 | 0 | 0 | 0 | 0 | 3.0 | 2 | 0 | 0 | 0 | 0 | 1 | 0 | 3 | 0 |
| Scott, Denver | 2 | 1 | .667 | 3.54 | 12 | 0 | 0 | 5 | 0 | 0 | 28.0 | 27 | 14 | 11 | 3 | 0 | 14 | 0 | 20 | 3 |
| Scranton, Omaha | 0 | 0 | .000 | 4.50 | 1 | 0 | 0 | 1 | 0 | 0 | 2.0 | 3 | 1 | 1 | 0 | 0 | 1 | 0 | 1 | 1 |
| Sebra, Oklahoma City | 10 | 6 | .625 | 3.83 | 22 | 22 | 2 | 0 | 0 | 0 | 138.2 | 121 | 62 | 59 | 17 | 2 | 57 | 0 | 84 | 7 |
| Shade, Louisville | 0 | 2 | .000 | 5.74 | 14 | 0 | 0 | 5 | 0 | 1 | 31.1 | 23 | 20 | 20 | 3 | 2 | 29 | 0 | 31 | 3 |
| Shimp, Oklahoma City | 5 | 5 | .500 | 2.67 | 24 | 9 | 2 | 9 | 1 | 1 | 104.2 | 101 | 41 | 31 | 4 | 0 | 35 | 2 | 49 | 3 |
| Shirley, Nashville* | 3 | 2 | .600 | 3.61 | 21 | 0 | 0 | 6 | 0 | 1 | 47.1 | 40 | 22 | 19 | 4 | 1 | 20 | 0 | 40 | 4 |
| Siwy, Buffalo | 3 | 5 | .375 | 4.93 | 16 | 3 | 0 | 3 | 0 | 0 | 38.1 | 54 | 25 | 21 | 4 | 1 | 19 | 0 | 28 | 0 |
| Smith, Denver | 5 | 4 | .556 | 4.85 | 47 | 0 | 0 | 35 | 0 | 17 | 68.2 | 65 | 40 | 37 | 5 | 1 | 38 | 1 | 67 | 9 |
| Speck, Buffalo | 6 | 7 | .462 | 4.86 | 21 | 20 | 5 | 1 | 2 | 0 | 122.1 | 113 | 66 | 66 | 13 | 1 | 67 | 1 | 88 | 5 |
| St. Claire, Indianapolis | 0 | 1 | .000 | 1.83 | 11 | 0 | 0 | 10 | 0 | 6 | 19.2 | 21 | 5 | 4 | 1 | 0 | 3 | 1 | 11 | 1 |
| Stoddard, Nashville | 2 | 1 | .667 | 0.59 | 22 | 0 | 0 | 17 | 0 | 6 | 30.2 | 15 | 3 | 2 | 0 | 0 | 14 | 1 | 31 | 2 |
| Stoll, Indianapolis | 9 | 9 | .500 | 4.08 | 23 | 23 | 8 | 0 | 1 | 0 | 145.2 | 148 | 83 | 66 | 13 | 4 | 46 | 0 | 57 | 1 |
| Stranski, Buffalo | 3 | 3 | .500 | 4.46 | 48 | 0 | 0 | 17 | 0 | 1 | 70.2 | 73 | 41 | 35 | 6 | 7 | 34 | 3 | 56 | 6 |
| Strode, Omaha* | 7 | 7 | .500 | 4.37 | 21 | 19 | 3 | 0 | 0 | 0 | 113.1 | 97 | 57 | 55 | 12 | 4 | 73 | 2 | 105 | 4 |
| Tanner, Buffalo | 5 | 7 | .417 | 3.46 | 20 | 17 | 4 | 3 | 0 | 0 | 109.1 | 99 | 49 | 42 | 9 | 4 | 44 | 4 | 49 | 3 |
| Terry, Denver | 11 | 12 | .478 | 4.43 | 28 | 28 | 4 | 0 | 1 | 0 | 178.2 | 203 | 105 | 88 | 11 | 3 | 76 | 2 | 101 | 14 |
| Tibbs, Denver | 1 | 2 | .333 | 2.27 | 4 | 4 | 2 | 0 | 0 | 0 | 31.2 | 20 | 10 | 8 | 0 | 0 | 12 | 0 | 15 | 1 |
| Todd, Buffalo | 2 | 2 | .333 | 3.76 | 25 | 1 | 0 | 9 | 0 | 0 | 52.2 | 59 | 25 | 22 | 5 | 1 | 12 | 1 | 38 | 2 |
| Toliver, Denver | 11 | 3 | .786 | 3.24 | 19 | 19 | 5 | 0 | 2 | 0 | 122.1 | 113 | 50 | 44 | 6 | 1 | 56 | 0 | 84 | 6 |
| Voigt, Nashville | 11 | 9 | .550 | 3.17 | 28 | 27 | 7 | 1 | 1 | 0 | 176.0 | 155 | 75 | 62 | 10 | 10 | 85 | 2 | 95 | 8 |
| Wehrmeister, Buffalo | 5 | 8 | .385 | 5.77 | 30 | 18 | 3 | 8 | 0 | 1 | 126.1 | 134 | 88 | 81 | 16 | 9 | 55 | 3 | 89 | 7 |
| Welsh, Oklahoma City* | 6 | 1 | .857 | 4.50 | 8 | 8 | 2 | 0 | 1 | 0 | 52.0 | 49 | 26 | 26 | 3 | 1 | 27 | 0 | 22 | 3 |
| Williams, Oklahoma City | 0 | 0 | .000 | 2.25 | 1 | 0 | 0 | 0 | 0 | 0 | 4.0 | 4 | 2 | 1 | 1 | 0 | 0 | 0 | 4 | 1 |
| Willis, Denver | 4 | 4 | .500 | 4.15 | 37 | 1 | 0 | 24 | 0 | 8 | 78.0 | 82 | 39 | 36 | 7 | 1 | 30 | 2 | 27 | 6 |
| Worrell, Louisville | 8 | 6 | .571 | 3.60 | 34 | 17 | 2 | 15 | 1 | 11 | 127.2 | 114 | 59 | 51 | 8 | 4 | 47 | 1 | 126 | 5 |
| Wright, Oklahoma City | 5 | 4 | .556 | 2.72 | 17 | 13 | 2 | 4 | 1 | 1 | 82.2 | 67 | 30 | 25 | 2 | 1 | 37 | 0 | 55 | 7 |
| Youmans, Indianapolis | 3 | 2 | .600 | 3.11 | 6 | 6 | 0 | 0 | 0 | 0 | 37.2 | 19 | 14 | 13 | 1 | 2 | 26 | 0 | 38 | 3 |
| Zwolensky, Oklahoma City | 7 | 5 | .583 | 4.45 | 18 | 14 | 2 | 4 | 0 | 1 | 87.0 | 94 | 51 | 43 | 5 | 2 | 32 | 0 | 50 | 3 |

BALKS—Stoll, 10; Landrum, 7; Pacella, 6; Cone, Keeton, McGaffigan, Ownbey, Perlman, Pryce, Strode, 4 each; Botelho, Brown, Kelly, Russell, Voigt, 3 each; Abrego, M. Anderson, Baller, Engel, Ferreira, Fossas, Guzman, Heinkel, Keener, Long, Mahler, Mathews, Mohorcic, Mullen, Robinson, Terry, 2 each; S. Baker, Boever, Buchanan, Burroughs, Cutshall, Denman, Epple, Farr, Groves, Hagen, Hardy, Hargesheimer, Hickey, Kinnunen, Koontz, Lucas, R. Martin, Martinez, Meridith, Murray, O'Neal, Puleo, Reynolds, Sebra, Shirley, Siwy, Tanner, Todd, Toliver, Wehrmeister, Willis, Worrell, Zwolensky, 1 each.

COMBINATION SHUTOUTS—Fireovid-Hickey-Mullen-Stranski, Long-Stranski, Rogers-McKeon, Buffalo; Robinson-Murphy, Denver; Bargar-Grapenthin, Stoll-O'Connor, Koontz-Grapenthin, Cook-Grapenthin, Youmans-Grapenthin, Indianapolis; Hoffman-Perlman, Gura-Gumpert, Botelho-Meridith, Baller-Gumpert, Hoffman-Pryce, Engel-Beard-Pryce, Barnes-Pryce, Iowa; Worrell-Boever, Keough-Worrell, Hagen-Worrell, Louisville; Heinkel-Cruz, Voigt-Pacella, Nashville; Cook-Wright, Cook-Shimp, Guzman-Fossas, Zwolensky-Earley, Guzman-Earley, Fossas-Earley, Oklahoma City; Cone-Martin, Griffin-Huismann, Hargesheimer-Kinnunen, Griffin-Martin-Kinnunen-Huismann, Omaha.

NO-HIT GAMES—Kelly, Nashville, defeated Oklahoma City, 6-0, July 17; Stoll, Indianapolis, defeated Buffalo, 3-0 (seven innings), August 27.

# International League

## CLASS AAA

**Leading Batter**
**JUAN BONILLA**
**Columbus**

**League President**
**HAROLD COOPER**

**Leading Pitcher**
**DON GORDON**
**Syracuse**

CHAMPIONSHIP WINNERS IN PREVIOUS YEARS

| | | |
|---|---|---|
| 1884—Trenton .520 | 1929—Rochester .613 | 1958—Montreal‡ .588 |
| 1885—Syracuse .584 | 1930—Rochester .629 | 1959—Buffalo .582 |
| 1886—Utica .646 | 1931—Rochester .601 | Havana (3rd)† .523 |
| 1887—Toronto .644 | 1932—Newark .649 | 1960—Toronto‡ .649 |
| 1888—Syracuse .723 | 1933—Newark .622 | 1961—Columbus .597 |
| 1889—Detroit .649 | Buffalo (4th)† .494 | Buffalo (3rd)† .559 |
| 1890—Detroit .617 | 1934—Newark .608 | 1962—Jacksonville .610 |
| 1891—Buffalo (reg. season) .727 | Toronto (3rd)† .559 | Atlanta (3rd)† .539 |
| Buffalo (supplem'l) .680 | 1935—Montreal .597 | 1963—Syracuse x .533 |
| 1892—Providence .615 | Syracuse (2nd)† .565 | Indianapolis‡ .562 |
| Binghamton* .667 | 1936—Buffalo‡ .610 | 1964—Jacksonville .589 |
| 1893—Erie .606 | 1937—Newark‡ .717 | Rochester (4th)† .532 |
| 1894—Providence .696 | 1938—Newark‡ .684 | 1965—Columbus .582 |
| 1895—Springfield .687 | 1939—Jersey City .582 | Toronto (3rd)† .556 |
| 1896—Providence .602 | Rochester (2nd)† .556 | 1966—Rochester .565 |
| 1897—Syracuse .632 | 1940—Rochester .611 | Toronto (2nd-tied)† .558 |
| 1898—Montreal .586 | Newark (2nd)† .594 | 1967—Richmond .574 |
| 1899—Rochester .624 | 1941—Newark .649 | Toledo (3rd)† .525 |
| 1900—Providence .616 | Montreal (2nd)† .584 | 1968—Toledo .565 |
| 1901—Rochester .642 | 1942—Newark .601 | Jacksonville (4th)† .514 |
| 1902—Toronto .669 | Syracuse (3rd)† .513 | 1969—Tidewater .563 |
| 1903—Jersey City .642 | 1943—Toronto .625 | Syracuse (3rd)† .536 |
| 1904—Buffalo .657 | Syracuse (3rd)† .536 | 1970—Syracuse‡ .600 |
| 1905—Providence .638 | 1944—Baltimore‡ .553 | 1971—Rochester‡ .614 |
| 1906—Buffalo .607 | 1945—Montreal .621 | 1972—Louisville .563 |
| 1907—Toronto .619 | Newark (2nd)† .582 | Tidewater (3rd)† .545 |
| 1908—Baltimore .593 | 1946—Montreal‡ .649 | 1973—Charleston .586 |
| 1909—Rochester .596 | 1947—Jersey City .610 | Pawtucket y† .534 |
| 1910—Rochester .601 | Syracuse (3rd)† .575 | 1974—Memphis .613 |
| 1911—Rochester .645 | 1948—Montreal‡ .614 | Rochester x‡ .611 |
| 1912—Toronto .595 | Buffalo .584 | 1975—Tidewater‡ .610 |
| 1913—Newark .625 | Montreal (3rd)† .545 | 1976—Rochester .638 |
| 1914—Providence .617 | 1950—Rochester .609 | Syracuse (2nd)† .590 |
| 1915—Buffalo .632 | Baltimore (3rd)† .556 | 1977—Pawtucket .571 |
| 1916—Buffalo .586 | 1951—Montreal‡ .617 | Charleston (2nd)‡ .557 |
| 1917—Toronto .604 | 1952—Montreal .629 | 1978—Charleston .607 |
| 1918—Toronto .693 | Rochester (3rd)† .619 | Richmond (4th)† .511 |
| 1919—Baltimore .671 | 1953—Rochester .630 | 1979—Columbus‡ .612 |
| 1920—Baltimore .719 | Montreal (2nd)† .586 | 1980—Columbus‡ .593 |
| 1921—Baltimore .717 | 1954—Toronto .630 | 1981—Columbus‡ .633 |
| 1922—Baltimore .689 | Syracuse (4th)§ .510 | 1982—Tidewater (3rd)† .540 |
| 1923—Baltimore .677 | 1955—Montreal .617 | Rochester .514 |
| 1924—Baltimore .709 | Rochester (4th)† .497 | 1983—Richmond .576 |
| 1925—Baltimore .633 | 1956—Toronto .566 | Tidewater† .511 |
| 1926—Toronto .657 | Rochester (2nd)† .553 | 1984—Maine .566 |
| 1927—Buffalo .667 | 1957—Toronto .575 | Pawtucket† .536 |
| 1928—Rochester .549 | Buffalo (2nd)† .571 | |

*Won split-season playoff. †Won four-team playoff. ‡Won championship and four-team playoff. §Defeated Havana in game to decide fourth place, then won four-team playoff. xLeague was divided into Northern, Southern divisions. yLeague divided into American, National divisions. (NOTE—Known as Eastern League in 1884, New York State League in 1885, International League in 1886-87, International Association in 1888, International League in 1889-90, Eastern Association in 1891, and Eastern League from 1892 until 1912.)

### STANDING OF CLUBS AT CLOSE OF SEASON, SEPTEMBER 2

| Club | Syr. | Me. | Tide. | Col. | Rich. | Tol. | Roch. | Paw. | W. | L. | T. | Pct. | G.B. |
|---|---|---|---|---|---|---|---|---|---|---|---|---|---|
| Syracuse (Blue Jays) | .... | 11 | 12 | 10 | 9 | 12 | 13 | 12 | 79 | 61 | 0 | .564 | ...... |
| Maine (Indians) | 9 | .... | 11 | 10 | 10 | 12 | 10 | 14 | 76 | 63 | 0 | .547 | 2½ |
| Tidewater (Mets) | 8 | 9 | .... | 11 | 12 | 8 | 11 | 16 | 75 | 64 | 0 | .540 | 3½ |
| Columbus (Yankees) | 10 | 10 | 9 | .... | 14 | 7 | 11 | 14 | 75 | 64 | 0 | .540 | 3½ |
| Richmond (Braves) | 11 | 10 | 8 | 6 | .... | 9 | 12 | 19 | 75 | 65 | 0 | .536 | 4 |
| Toledo (Twins) | 8 | 7 | 12 | 13 | 11 | .... | 12 | 8 | 71 | 68 | 0 | .511 | 7½ |
| Rochester (Orioles) | 7 | 10 | 8 | 9 | 8 | 8 | .... | 8 | 58 | 81 | 0 | .417 | 20½ |
| Pawtucket (Red Sox) | 8 | 6 | 4 | 5 | 1 | 12 | 12 | .... | 48 | 91 | 0 | .345 | 30½ |

Maine club represented Old Orchard Beach, Me.

Tidewater club represented Norfolk and Portsmouth, Va.

Major league affiliations in parentheses.

Playoffs—Columbus defeated Syracuse, three games to one; Tidewater defeated Maine, three games to two; Tidewater defeated Columbus, three games to one, to win Governor's Cup.

Regular-Season Attendance—Columbus, 568,735; Maine, 135,985; Pawtucket, 166,504; Richmond, 379,019; Rochester, 208,955; Syracuse, 222,813; Tidewater, 153,100; Toledo, 167,787. Total, 2,002,898. Playoffs, 31,679 (13 games).

Managers—Columbus, Doug Holmquist (thru May 6) and Carl "Stump" Merrill (May 7 thru end of season); Maine, Doc Edwards; Pawtucket, Rac Slider; Richmond, Roy Majtyka; Rochester, Frank Verdi (thru June 15) and Mark Wiley (June 17 thru end of season); Syracuse, Doug Ault; Tidewater, Bob Schaefer; Toledo, Cal Ermer.

All-Star Team—1B—Jim Wilson, Maine; 2B—Juan Bonilla, Columbus; 3B—Kelly Gruber, Syracuse; SS—Kelly Paris, Rochester; OF—Dan Pasqua, Columbus; Rick Leach, Syracuse; Billy Beane, Tidewater; C—Larry Owen, Richmond; DH—Willie Aikens, Syracuse; Starting Pitcher—Stan Clarke, Syracuse; Relief Pitcher—Tom Henke, Syracuse; Most Valuable Player—Dan Pasqua, Columbus; Most Valuable Pitcher—Tom Henke, Syracuse; Manager of the Year—Doug Ault, Syracuse.

(Compiled by Howe News Bureau, Boston, Mass.)

### CLUB BATTING

| Club | Pct. | G. | AB. | R. | OR. | H. | TB. | 2B. | 3B. | HR. | RBI. | GW. | SH. | SF. | HP. | BB. | Int. BB. | SO. | SB. | CS. | LOB. |
|---|---|---|---|---|---|---|---|---|---|---|---|---|---|---|---|---|---|---|---|---|---|
| Columbus | .270 | 139 | 4640 | 652 | 626 | 1254 | 1844 | 230 | 30 | 100 | 593 | 64 | 41 | 40 | 22 | 523 | 26 | 715 | 95 | 44 | 1017 |
| Syracuse | .269 | 140 | 4718 | 645 | 579 | 1271 | 1860 | 185 | 43 | 106 | 587 | 71 | 28 | 35 | 33 | 505 | 23 | 754 | 102 | 76 | 996 |
| Tidewater | .266 | 139 | 4669 | 558 | 512 | 1243 | 1749 | 216 | 31 | 76 | 510 | 68 | 47 | 34 | 37 | 415 | 26 | 777 | 129 | 51 | 978 |
| Toledo | .254 | 139 | 4666 | 630 | 611 | 1187 | 1808 | 170 | 32 | 129 | 575 | 63 | 67 | 38 | 35 | 545 | 26 | 686 | 57 | 45 | 1046 |
| Rochester | .248 | 139 | 4504 | 568 | 614 | 1119 | 1797 | 214 | 25 | 138 | 517 | 54 | 28 | 31 | 19 | 473 | 16 | 633 | 80 | 44 | 918 |
| Maine | .248 | 139 | 4466 | 602 | 564 | 1106 | 1635 | 162 | 20 | 109 | 555 | 72 | 56 | 56 | 23 | 514 | 18 | 710 | 135 | 58 | 914 |
| Richmond | .245 | 140 | 4522 | 559 | 547 | 1107 | 1557 | 162 | 30 | 76 | 499 | 67 | 70 | 53 | 25 | 534 | 27 | 619 | 135 | 60 | 985 |
| Pawtucket | .242 | 139 | 4587 | 512 | 673 | 1110 | 1618 | 177 | 20 | 97 | 471 | 45 | 46 | 30 | 29 | 486 | 22 | 758 | 74 | 52 | 971 |

### INDIVIDUAL BATTING
(Leading Qualifiers for Batting Championship—378 or More Plate Appearances)

°Bats lefthanded.     †Switch-hitter.

| Player and Club | Pct. | G. | AB. | R. | H. | TB. | 2B. | 3B. | HR. | RBI. | GW. | SH. | SF. | HP. | BB. | Int. BB. | SO. | SB. | CS. |
|---|---|---|---|---|---|---|---|---|---|---|---|---|---|---|---|---|---|---|---|
| Bonilla, Juan, Columbus | .330 | 102 | 388 | 60 | 128 | 153 | 22 | 0 | 1 | 52 | 11 | 3 | 7 | 1 | 36 | 3 | 26 | 9 | 4 |
| Aikens, Willie, Syracuse° | .311 | 105 | 373 | 65 | 116 | 185 | 19 | 1 | 16 | 61 | 7 | 0 | 1 | 1 | 67 | 5 | 81 | 0 | 0 |
| Tarver, LaSchelle, Tidewater° | .311 | 126 | 457 | 73 | 142 | 168 | 17 | 3 | 1 | 40 | 6 | 4 | 1 | 3 | 54 | 2 | 69 | 35 | 16 |
| Dalena, Peter, Columbus° | .305 | 114 | 357 | 34 | 109 | 165 | 21 | 4 | 9 | 65 | 7 | 1 | 1 | 1 | 25 | 1 | 32 | 1 | 0 |
| O'Malley, Thomas, Rochester° | .302 | 102 | 358 | 62 | 108 | 153 | 13 | 1 | 10 | 44 | 3 | 0 | 4 | 1 | 57 | 0 | 38 | 1 | 0 |
| Estes, Frank, Richmond° | .301 | 133 | 459 | 53 | 138 | 170 | 14 | 3 | 4 | 73 | 5 | 2 | 5 | 0 | 77 | 8 | 27 | 19 | 11 |
| Graham, Lee, Richmond° | .298 | 102 | 396 | 59 | 118 | 157 | 20 | 5 | 3 | 43 | 7 | 3 | 3 | 0 | 40 | 1 | 33 | 31 | 15 |
| Ullger, Scott, Toledo | .292 | 112 | 384 | 58 | 112 | 182 | 13 | 6 | 15 | 58 | 5 | 3 | 4 | 2 | 59 | 2 | 55 | 2 | 1 |
| Mitchell, Kevin, Tidewater | .290 | 95 | 348 | 44 | 101 | 156 | 24 | 2 | 9 | 43 | 7 | 0 | 3 | 2 | 32 | 1 | 60 | 3 | 1 |
| Sharperson, Michael, Syracuse | .289 | 134 | 536 | 86 | 155 | 191 | 19 | 7 | 1 | 59 | 4 | 3 | 4 | 2 | 71 | 1 | 75 | 14 | 15 |
| Noboa, Milciades, Maine | .288 | 122 | 403 | 62 | 116 | 146 | 11 | 2 | 5 | 32 | 4 | 10 | 3 | 3 | 34 | 0 | 28 | 14 | 15 |

Departmental Leaders: G—Wilson, 139; AB—Sharperson, 536; R—Sharperson, 86; H—Sharperson, 155; TB—Wilson, 251; 2B—Beane, 34; 3B—Sharperson, 7; HR—Wilson, 26; RBI—Wilson, 101; GWRBI—Wilson, 16; SH—Rios, 15; SF—Leach, 12; HP—Rabb, 10; BB—Rohn, 116; IBB—Estes, 8; SO—Beane, 130; SB—Taylor, 52; CS—McNealy, 19.

(All Players—Listed Alphabetically)

| Player and Club | Pct. | G. | AB. | R. | H. | TB. | 2B. | 3B. | HR. | RBI. | GW. | SH. | SF. | HP. | BB. | Int. BB. | SO. | SB. | CS. |
|---|---|---|---|---|---|---|---|---|---|---|---|---|---|---|---|---|---|---|---|
| Ackley, John, Pawtucket | .256 | 13 | 39 | 5 | 10 | 13 | 1 | 1 | 0 | 2 | 1 | 0 | 0 | 0 | 2 | 0 | 9 | 2 | 0 |
| Aguilera, Richard, Tidewater | .250 | 11 | 4 | 1 | 1 | 1 | 0 | 0 | 0 | 1 | 0 | 0 | 0 | 0 | 0 | 0 | 1 | 0 | 0 |
| Aikens, Willie, Syracuse° | .311 | 105 | 373 | 65 | 116 | 185 | 19 | 1 | 16 | 61 | 7 | 0 | 1 | 1 | 67 | 5 | 81 | 0 | 0 |
| Allen, Roderick, Rochester | .234 | 102 | 333 | 36 | 78 | 122 | 17 | 3 | 7 | 32 | 4 | 4 | 2 | 2 | 29 | 1 | 52 | 6 | 5 |
| Allenson, Gary, Syracuse | .249 | 62 | 205 | 21 | 51 | 79 | 10 | 0 | 6 | 22 | 4 | 0 | 1 | 3 | 21 | 0 | 23 | 0 | 1 |
| Anderson, Richard, Tidewater | .333 | 48 | 3 | 0 | 1 | 1 | 0 | 0 | 0 | 0 | 0 | 1 | 0 | 0 | 0 | 0 | 0 | 1 | 0 |
| Aragon, Steven, Toledo | .174 | 27 | 46 | 5 | 8 | 9 | 1 | 0 | 0 | 3 | 0 | 0 | 1 | 0 | 2 | 0 | 8 | 0 | 0 |
| Ayala, Benigno, Maine | .152 | 14 | 46 | 2 | 7 | 11 | 1 | 0 | 1 | 4 | 0 | 0 | 0 | 0 | 6 | 1 | 12 | 0 | 0 |
| Barrett, Thomas, Columbus† | .260 | 55 | 169 | 27 | 44 | 60 | 11 | 1 | 1 | 11 | 2 | 4 | 0 | 0 | 17 | 0 | 18 | 14 | 4 |
| Beane, William, Tidewater | .284 | 135 | 504 | 63 | 143 | 242 | 34 | 4 | 19 | 77 | 9 | 0 | 6 | 5 | 42 | 5 | 130 | 15 | 7 |
| Benton, Alfred, Maine | .283 | 48 | 187 | 16 | 53 | 71 | 10 | 1 | 2 | 30 | 5 | 1 | 2 | 3 | 7 | 2 | 15 | 2 | 1 |
| Benzinger, Todd, Pawtucket† | .250 | 70 | 256 | 31 | 64 | 112 | 13 | 1 | 11 | 47 | 6 | 2 | 3 | 0 | 12 | 1 | 49 | 0 | 0 |
| Bettendorf, Jeffrey, Tidewater | .500 | 28 | 2 | 0 | 1 | 1 | 0 | 0 | 0 | 0 | 0 | 0 | 0 | 0 | 0 | 0 | 0 | 0 | 0 |
| Bittiger, Jeffrey, Tidewater | .286 | 24 | 7 | 0 | 2 | 2 | 0 | 0 | 0 | 1 | 0 | 0 | 0 | 0 | 1 | 0 | 1 | 0 | 0 |
| Bjorkman, George, Rochester | .242 | 58 | 153 | 19 | 37 | 64 | 12 | 0 | 5 | 14 | 2 | 3 | 0 | 1 | 22 | 0 | 33 | 1 | 1 |
| Blocker, Terry, Tidewater° | .307 | 75 | 267 | 40 | 82 | 113 | 8 | 4 | 5 | 38 | 6 | 1 | 1 | 0 | 17 | 3 | 42 | 20 | 4 |
| Bonilla, Juan, Columbus | .330 | 102 | 388 | 60 | 128 | 153 | 22 | 0 | 1 | 52 | 11 | 3 | 7 | 1 | 36 | 3 | 26 | 9 | 4 |
| Bradley, Scott, Columbus° | .301 | 43 | 163 | 17 | 49 | 71 | 10 | 0 | 4 | 27 | 2 | 0 | 4 | 1 | 8 | 2 | 12 | 2 | 0 |
| Brewer, Michael, Maine | .235 | 119 | 413 | 58 | 97 | 169 | 17 | 2 | 17 | 53 | 8 | 3 | 3 | 2 | 46 | 2 | 103 | 12 | 7 |
| Briggs, Daniel, Columbus° | .268 | 132 | 403 | 51 | 108 | 164 | 27 | 4 | 7 | 60 | 6 | 0 | 5 | 2 | 42 | 6 | 64 | 1 | 2 |
| Brizzolara, Anthony, Richmond | .000 | 33 | 8 | 0 | 0 | 0 | 0 | 0 | 0 | 0 | 0 | 0 | 2 | 0 | 0 | 0 | 4 | 0 | 0 |
| Brown, Darrell, Rochester† | .180 | 17 | 61 | 4 | 11 | 14 | 1 | 1 | 0 | 3 | 0 | 0 | 0 | 5 | 3 | 0 | 7 | 3 | 0 |
| Buckley, Kevin, Maine | .221 | 86 | 294 | 39 | 65 | 120 | 10 | 0 | 15 | 45 | 4 | 0 | 3 | 5 | 35 | 0 | 83 | 0 | 0 |
| Burgess, Gus, Pawtucket° | .226 | 106 | 359 | 36 | 81 | 98 | 11 | 0 | 2 | 19 | 1 | 3 | 3 | 2 | 43 | 1 | 74 | 12 | 4 |
| Bustabad, Juan, Pawtucket° | .244 | 91 | 295 | 27 | 72 | 81 | 4 | 1 | 1 | 20 | 1 | 5 | 0 | 0 | 24 | 1 | 32 | 5 | 15 |
| Carreon, Mark, Tidewater° | .133 | 7 | 15 | 1 | 2 | 6 | 1 | 0 | 2 | 5 | 0 | 0 | 0 | 0 | 2 | 0 | 5 | 0 | 0 |
| Castillo, Carmelo, Maine | .240 | 26 | 96 | 12 | 23 | 35 | 2 | 2 | 2 | 18 | 2 | 0 | 2 | 0 | 9 | 0 | 13 | 2 | 1 |
| Chapman, Kelvin, Tidewater | .185 | 17 | 54 | 9 | 10 | 13 | 3 | 0 | 0 | 2 | 0 | 3 | 0 | 0 | 8 | 1 | 7 | 2 | 0 |
| Christensen, John, Tidewater | .212 | 43 | 156 | 14 | 33 | 42 | 4 | 1 | 1 | 13 | 1 | 2 | 2 | 5 | 11 | 2 | 25 | 0 | 0 |

| Player and Club | Pct. | G. | AB. | R. | H. | TB. | 2B. | 3B. | HR. | RBI. | GW. | SH. | SF. | HP. | BB. | Int. BB. | SO. | SB. | CS. |
|---|---|---|---|---|---|---|---|---|---|---|---|---|---|---|---|---|---|---|---|
| Clary, Martin, Richmond | .000 | 26 | 5 | 0 | 0 | 0 | 0 | 0 | 0 | 0 | 0 | 0 | 0 | 0 | 0 | 0 | 2 | 0 | 0 |
| Clay, David, Richmond | .000 | 47 | 3 | 0 | 0 | 0 | 0 | 0 | 0 | 0 | 1 | 0 | 0 | 0 | 0 | 0 | 2 | 0 | 0 |
| Connally, Fritzie, Rochester | .214 | 52 | 168 | 17 | 36 | 55 | 1 | 0 | 6 | 22 | 4 | 2 | 1 | 1 | 18 | 0 | 22 | 0 | 1 |
| Corbett, Raymond, Rochester | .222 | 5 | 9 | 1 | 2 | 3 | 1 | 0 | 0 | 1 | 0 | 0 | 0 | 0 | 0 | 0 | 2 | 0 | 1 |
| Cotto, Henry, Columbus | .257 | 75 | 272 | 38 | 70 | 111 | 16 | 2 | 7 | 36 | 3 | 1 | 3 | 2 | 19 | 0 | 61 | 10 | 4 |
| Craig, Rodney, Tidewater† | .261 | 9 | 23 | 1 | 6 | 7 | 1 | 0 | 0 | 2 | 1 | 0 | 0 | 0 | 2 | 0 | 6 | 0 | 0 |
| Cruz, Todd, Rochester | .091 | 5 | 11 | 0 | 1 | 1 | 0 | 0 | 0 | 1 | 0 | 0 | 0 | 0 | 2 | 0 | 5 | 0 | 0 |
| Curry, Stephen, Richmond | .222 | 104 | 311 | 50 | 69 | 100 | 13 | 0 | 6 | 31 | 4 | 7 | 1 | 1 | 50 | 0 | 65 | 3 | 1 |
| Dalena, Peter, Columbus° | .305 | 114 | 357 | 34 | 109 | 165 | 21 | 4 | 9 | 65 | 7 | 1 | 1 | 1 | 25 | 1 | 32 | 1 | 0 |
| David, Andre, Toledo° | .266 | 102 | 331 | 40 | 88 | 129 | 15 | 1 | 8 | 48 | 4 | 0 | 3 | 6 | 40 | 2 | 36 | 0 | 2 |
| Davis, Michael, Tidewater | .288 | 78 | 236 | 26 | 68 | 96 | 14 | 1 | 4 | 36 | 7 | 0 | 0 | 0 | 20 | 0 | 31 | 3 | 1 |
| Dempsey, Patrick, Maine | .244 | 57 | 164 | 13 | 40 | 48 | 2 | 0 | 2 | 18 | 1 | 2 | 1 | 0 | 5 | 0 | 25 | 3 | 2 |
| DeWillis, Jeffrey, Syracuse | .229 | 19 | 48 | 3 | 11 | 15 | 1 | 0 | 1 | 3 | 0 | 1 | 1 | 2 | 7 | 0 | 13 | 0 | 1 |
| Dodson, Patrick, Pawtucket° | .223 | 123 | 400 | 51 | 89 | 157 | 14 | 0 | 18 | 47 | 3 | 1 | 2 | 1 | 69 | 5 | 93 | 0 | 0 |
| Dugas, Shanie, Maine° | .218 | 104 | 326 | 40 | 71 | 109 | 14 | 0 | 8 | 40 | 2 | 2 | 4 | 1 | 35 | 2 | 67 | 5 | 4 |
| Dykstra, Leonard, Tidewater° | .310 | 58 | 229 | 44 | 71 | 94 | 8 | 6 | 1 | 25 | 2 | 1 | 2 | 1 | 31 | 0 | 20 | 26 | 6 |
| Eichelberger, Juan, Richmond | .000 | 17 | 1 | 0 | 0 | 0 | 0 | 0 | 0 | 0 | 0 | 0 | 0 | 0 | 0 | 0 | 1 | 0 | 0 |
| Espino, Juan, Columbus | .250 | 74 | 224 | 30 | 56 | 76 | 11 | 0 | 3 | 20 | 2 | 2 | 0 | 3 | 22 | 1 | 36 | 0 | 1 |
| Espinoza, Alvaro, Toledo | .229 | 82 | 266 | 24 | 61 | 75 | 11 | 0 | 1 | 33 | 4 | 8 | 2 | 3 | 14 | 0 | 30 | 1 | 3 |
| Estes, Frank, Richmond° | .301 | 133 | 459 | 53 | 138 | 170 | 14 | 3 | 4 | 73 | 5 | 2 | 5 | 0 | 77 | 8 | 27 | 19 | 11 |
| Evans, Barry, Maine | .269 | 70 | 242 | 34 | 65 | 92 | 5 | 2 | 6 | 30 | 6 | 4 | 7 | 2 | 29 | 0 | 30 | 0 | 1 |
| Falcone, David, Rochester° | .237 | 49 | 139 | 16 | 33 | 61 | 7 | 0 | 7 | 17 | 4 | 0 | 0 | 0 | 19 | 2 | 28 | 0 | 0 |
| Fernandez, Sidney, Tidewater° | .000 | 5 | 3 | 0 | 0 | 0 | 0 | 0 | 0 | 0 | 0 | 0 | 0 | 0 | 0 | 0 | 1 | 0 | 0 |
| Fultz, William, Tidewater | .167 | 19 | 6 | 0 | 1 | 1 | 0 | 0 | 0 | 0 | 0 | 0 | 0 | 2 | 0 | 0 | 2 | 0 | 0 |
| Gallagher, David, Maine | .242 | 132 | 488 | 71 | 118 | 173 | 22 | 3 | 9 | 55 | 5 | 11 | 8 | 3 | 65 | 0 | 38 | 16 | 8 |
| Gardenhire, Ronald, Tidewater | .211 | 22 | 71 | 3 | 15 | 20 | 2 | 0 | 1 | 10 | 2 | 0 | 0 | 0 | 6 | 0 | 13 | 0 | 2 |
| Gardner, Wesley, Tidewater | .000 | 53 | 1 | 0 | 0 | 0 | 0 | 0 | 0 | 0 | 0 | 0 | 0 | 0 | 0 | 0 | 0 | 0 | 0 |
| Gibbons, John, Tidewater | .259 | 108 | 370 | 35 | 96 | 137 | 10 | 2 | 9 | 30 | 2 | 3 | 2 | 7 | 35 | 3 | 78 | 3 | 2 |
| Graham, Lee, Richmond° | .298 | 102 | 396 | 59 | 118 | 157 | 20 | 5 | 3 | 43 | 7 | 3 | 3 | 0 | 40 | 1 | 33 | 31 | 15 |
| Granger, Lee, Rochester† | .245 | 77 | 277 | 32 | 68 | 103 | 10 | 5 | 5 | 18 | 0 | 2 | 1 | 3 | 15 | 0 | 51 | 19 | 10 |
| Grant, Thomas, Maine° | .172 | 19 | 64 | 8 | 11 | 18 | 2 | 1 | 1 | 7 | 0 | 0 | 1 | 0 | 4 | 0 | 10 | 0 | 0 |
| Gray, Lorenzo, Columbus | .259 | 71 | 147 | 16 | 38 | 43 | 2 | 0 | 1 | 19 | 1 | 1 | 0 | 0 | 11 | 2 | 23 | 0 | 2 |
| Greenwell, Michael, Pawtucket° | .256 | 117 | 418 | 47 | 107 | 169 | 21 | 1 | 13 | 52 | 5 | 1 | 4 | 6 | 38 | 2 | 45 | 3 | 4 |
| Gruber, Kelly, Syracuse | .249 | 121 | 473 | 71 | 118 | 207 | 16 | 5 | 21 | 69 | 8 | 1 | 5 | 7 | 28 | 2 | 92 | 20 | 8 |
| Guerrero, Inocencio, Richmond | .400 | 6 | 15 | 0 | 6 | 7 | 1 | 0 | 0 | 3 | 0 | 0 | 1 | 0 | 1 | 0 | 0 | 0 | 0 |
| Gulliver, Glenn, Richmond° | .189 | 44 | 95 | 16 | 18 | 21 | 3 | 0 | 0 | 7 | 0 | 0 | 3 | 2 | 32 | 0 | 8 | 1 | 0 |
| Hall, Albert, Richmond† | .224 | 38 | 98 | 12 | 22 | 28 | 0 | 3 | 0 | 5 | 1 | 3 | 1 | 0 | 15 | 0 | 14 | 6 | 2 |
| Hamric, Russell, Tidewater | .167 | 5 | 6 | 1 | 1 | 1 | 0 | 0 | 0 | 0 | 0 | 0 | 0 | 0 | 1 | 0 | 1 | 0 | 0 |
| Hart, Michael, Toledo° | .268 | 135 | 496 | 71 | 133 | 235 | 22 | 4 | 24 | 83 | 7 | 3 | 7 | 3 | 65 | 5 | 67 | 4 | 5 |
| Hawkins, Johnny, Columbus† | .250 | 22 | 28 | 3 | 7 | 7 | 0 | 0 | 0 | 5 | 2 | 2 | 0 | 0 | 0 | 0 | 5 | 0 | 0 |
| Hearn, Edward, Tidewater | .263 | 112 | 418 | 35 | 110 | 156 | 29 | 1 | 5 | 57 | 7 | 2 | 6 | 2 | 26 | 3 | 62 | 1 | 0 |
| Heath, Kelly, Columbus | .257 | 121 | 377 | 83 | 97 | 180 | 21 | 4 | 18 | 53 | 4 | 6 | 7 | 0 | 101 | 2 | 67 | 8 | 9 |
| Hernandez, Leonardo, Rochester | .269 | 124 | 475 | 59 | 128 | 214 | 31 | 2 | 17 | 69 | 10 | 0 | 3 | 4 | 22 | 3 | 52 | 1 | 5 |
| Hernandez, Tobias, Toledo | .203 | 28 | 74 | 8 | 15 | 16 | 1 | 0 | 0 | 5 | 1 | 4 | 0 | 1 | 6 | 0 | 10 | 0 | 0 |
| Hobson, Clell, Columbus | .236 | 107 | 347 | 44 | 82 | 129 | 9 | 1 | 12 | 56 | 5 | 0 | 4 | 3 | 47 | 1 | 64 | 0 | 2 |
| Holland, John, Syracuse | .000 | 2 | 4 | 0 | 0 | 0 | 0 | 0 | 0 | 0 | 0 | 0 | 0 | 0 | 0 | 0 | 1 | 0 | 0 |
| Holman, Dale, Syracuse° | .308 | 75 | 195 | 25 | 60 | 92 | 15 | 4 | 3 | 28 | 2 | 0 | 1 | 1 | 23 | 1 | 27 | 1 | 1 |
| Holmes, Stanley, Toledo | .228 | 93 | 307 | 32 | 70 | 108 | 9 | 1 | 9 | 38 | 3 | 5 | 4 | 0 | 15 | 0 | 73 | 0 | 0 |
| Howe, Gregory, Toledo | .257 | 86 | 292 | 49 | 75 | 107 | 10 | 5 | 4 | 31 | 6 | 6 | 1 | 7 | 35 | 2 | 66 | 15 | 9 |
| Hudler, Rex, Columbus° | .250 | 106 | 380 | 62 | 95 | 125 | 13 | 4 | 3 | 18 | 1 | 5 | 0 | 2 | 17 | 1 | 51 | 29 | 7 |
| Hughes, Keith, Columbus° | .296 | 18 | 54 | 7 | 16 | 29 | 4 | 0 | 3 | 8 | 0 | 0 | 0 | 2 | 11 | 0 | 11 | 0 | 2 |
| Hundhammer, Paul, Pawtucket | .241 | 110 | 378 | 48 | 91 | 142 | 15 | 3 | 10 | 40 | 6 | 5 | 2 | 3 | 50 | 3 | 64 | 9 | 6 |
| Infante, Alexis, Syracuse | .241 | 136 | 453 | 63 | 109 | 135 | 10 | 5 | 2 | 39 | 8 | 3 | 1 | 3 | 46 | 0 | 65 | 29 | 13 |
| Jimenez, Alfonso, Toledo | .223 | 113 | 390 | 47 | 87 | 112 | 14 | 1 | 3 | 25 | 0 | 12 | 2 | 0 | 35 | 1 | 53 | 12 | 4 |
| Johnson, Bobby, Columbus | .000 | 2 | 5 | 0 | 0 | 0 | 0 | 0 | 0 | 0 | 0 | 0 | 0 | 0 | 0 | 0 | 2 | 0 | 0 |
| Johnson, Joseph, Richmond | .000 | 9 | 2 | 0 | 0 | 0 | 0 | 0 | 0 | 0 | 0 | 1 | 0 | 0 | 0 | 0 | 1 | 0 | 0 |
| Johnson, Randall, Richmond | .193 | 122 | 337 | 30 | 65 | 89 | 13 | 1 | 3 | 22 | 2 | 8 | 4 | 3 | 41 | 1 | 38 | 3 | 3 |
| Jones, Ricky, Rochester | .173 | 14 | 52 | 3 | 9 | 10 | 1 | 0 | 0 | 4 | 0 | 0 | 0 | 0 | 1 | 0 | 11 | 0 | 0 |
| Jones, Ross, Tidewater | .232 | 50 | 82 | 14 | 19 | 24 | 2 | 0 | 1 | 3 | 0 | 2 | 0 | 1 | 19 | 0 | 22 | 0 | 0 |
| Jurak, Edward, Pawtucket | .259 | 72 | 263 | 33 | 68 | 101 | 11 | 2 | 6 | 38 | 4 | 7 | 2 | 3 | 37 | 2 | 34 | 4 | 3 |
| Keller, Charles, Syracuse | .208 | 69 | 221 | 18 | 46 | 72 | 5 | 0 | 7 | 24 | 4 | 1 | 1 | 0 | 26 | 3 | 49 | 0 | 0 |
| Kinnard, Kenneth, Syracuse | .000 | 2 | 1 | 0 | 0 | 0 | 0 | 0 | 0 | 0 | 0 | 0 | 0 | 0 | 0 | 0 | 0 | 0 | 0 |
| Knight, Timothy, Columbus° | .169 | 27 | 71 | 10 | 12 | 19 | 2 | 1 | 1 | 10 | 1 | 0 | 1 | 1 | 16 | 1 | 16 | 2 | 0 |
| Lancellotti, Richard, Tidewater° | .180 | 91 | 316 | 32 | 57 | 96 | 9 | 0 | 10 | 28 | 5 | 1 | 3 | 3 | 32 | 3 | 58 | 2 | 0 |
| Latham, William, Tidewater° | .167 | 24 | 6 | 0 | 1 | 1 | 0 | 0 | 0 | 1 | 0 | 1 | 0 | 0 | 0 | 0 | 2 | 0 | 0 |
| Leach, Richard, Syracuse° | .283 | 136 | 533 | 77 | 151 | 224 | 24 | 2 | 15 | 79 | 7 | 0 | 12 | 1 | 52 | 4 | 42 | 3 | 6 |
| Lickert, John, 63 Rich.-18 Paw. | .231 | 81 | 221 | 34 | 51 | 68 | 8 | 0 | 3 | 23 | 1 | 4 | 5 | 4 | 40 | 2 | 28 | 0 | 2 |
| Lindsey, John, Columbus | .211 | 27 | 71 | 10 | 15 | 23 | 5 | 0 | 1 | 9 | 2 | 2 | 0 | 2 | 14 | 0 | 12 | 0 | 0 |
| Lisi, Riccardo, Maine | .159 | 30 | 88 | 7 | 14 | 16 | 2 | 0 | 0 | 9 | 0 | 2 | 1 | 1 | 5 | 0 | 18 | 0 | 0 |
| Lomastro, Gerardo, Toledo | .243 | 117 | 400 | 54 | 97 | 159 | 11 | 0 | 17 | 58 | 11 | 2 | 5 | 7 | 35 | 1 | 65 | 1 | 1 |
| Lombardozzi, Stephen, Toledo | .264 | 118 | 451 | 55 | 119 | 188 | 21 | 3 | 14 | 48 | 7 | 7 | 0 | 0 | 48 | 2 | 51 | 10 | 8 |
| Malpeso, David, Pawtucket | .251 | 84 | 255 | 24 | 64 | 92 | 12 | 2 | 4 | 28 | 3 | 4 | 6 | 2 | 22 | 1 | 42 | 0 | 1 |
| Mata, Victor, Columbus | .261 | 104 | 375 | 39 | 98 | 125 | 14 | 2 | 3 | 27 | 1 | 1 | 3 | 1 | 27 | 2 | 58 | 2 | 2 |
| McGriff, Frederick, Syracuse° | .227 | 51 | 176 | 19 | 40 | 67 | 8 | 2 | 5 | 20 | 2 | 1 | 0 | 4 | 23 | 0 | 53 | 0 | 0 |
| McHenry, Vance, Syracuse | .209 | 68 | 134 | 16 | 28 | 43 | 1 | 1 | 4 | 12 | 1 | 3 | 0 | 0 | 14 | 1 | 29 | 6 | 3 |
| McMurtry, Craig, Richmond | .125 | 16 | 8 | 0 | 1 | 1 | 0 | 0 | 0 | 0 | 0 | 0 | 0 | 0 | 0 | 0 | 5 | 0 | 0 |
| McNealy, Derwin, Syracuse° | .265 | 135 | 472 | 49 | 125 | 153 | 13 | 6 | 1 | 42 | 5 | 7 | 1 | 5 | 36 | 1 | 74 | 22 | 19 |
| McPhail, Marlin, Tidewater | .304 | 10 | 23 | 1 | 7 | 8 | 1 | 0 | 0 | 1 | 0 | 0 | 0 | 1 | 0 | 0 | 4 | 0 | 0 |
| Mesh, Michael, Pawtucket | .215 | 97 | 298 | 35 | 64 | 82 | 8 | 2 | 2 | 23 | 2 | 7 | 1 | 5 | 43 | 0 | 57 | 18 | 9 |
| Miller, Lemmie, Rochester | .250 | 39 | 140 | 22 | 35 | 45 | 7 | 0 | 1 | 10 | 2 | 2 | 0 | 1 | 21 | 0 | 27 | 1 | 5 |
| Miller-Jones, Gary, Pawtucket† | .256 | 128 | 477 | 51 | 122 | 169 | 18 | 4 | 7 | 31 | 6 | 5 | 0 | 0 | 26 | 6 | 72 | 1 | 3 |
| Mitchell, Kevin, Tidewater | .290 | 95 | 348 | 44 | 101 | 156 | 24 | 2 | 9 | 43 | 7 | 0 | 3 | 2 | 32 | 1 | 60 | 3 | 1 |
| Molinaro, Robert, Rochester° | .250 | 111 | 328 | 41 | 82 | 138 | 18 | 1 | 12 | 35 | 5 | 0 | 1 | 1 | 38 | 2 | 22 | 13 | 1 |
| Morogiello, Daniel, Richmond° | 1.000 | 44 | 1 | 0 | 1 | 2 | 1 | 0 | 0 | 0 | 0 | 0 | 0 | 0 | 0 | 0 | 0 | 0 | 0 |
| Moronko, Jeffrey, Maine | .250 | 6 | 24 | 3 | 6 | 9 | 1 | 1 | 0 | 2 | 0 | 1 | 0 | 0 | 0 | 0 | 11 | 0 | 1 |
| Myers, Randall, Tidewater° | .000 | 8 | 2 | 0 | 0 | 0 | 0 | 0 | 0 | 0 | 0 | 0 | 0 | 0 | 0 | 0 | 0 | 0 | 0 |
| Nanni, Tito, Syracuse° | .200 | 18 | 60 | 9 | 12 | 20 | 3 | 1 | 1 | 7 | 2 | 0 | 0 | 0 | 4 | 0 | 17 | 0 | 1 |
| Nattile, Samuel, Pawtucket° | .230 | 85 | 261 | 26 | 60 | 93 | 10 | 1 | 7 | 34 | 1 | 0 | 3 | 0 | 18 | 0 | 38 | 1 | 1 |
| Niemann, Randy, Tidewater° | .333 | 30 | 3 | 0 | 1 | 1 | 0 | 0 | 0 | 0 | 0 | 1 | 0 | 0 | 0 | 0 | 0 | 0 | 0 |
| Noboa, Milciades, Maine | .288 | 122 | 403 | 62 | 116 | 146 | 11 | 2 | 5 | 32 | 4 | 10 | 3 | 3 | 34 | 0 | 28 | 14 | 15 |
| Norman, Nelson, Rochester | .186 | 84 | 204 | 19 | 38 | 52 | 4 | 2 | 2 | 11 | 1 | 6 | 3 | 0 | 35 | 0 | 17 | 3 | 2 |
| O'Berry, Michael, Columbus | .228 | 18 | 57 | 7 | 13 | 18 | 2 | 0 | 1 | 7 | 1 | 0 | 1 | 0 | 5 | 0 | 6 | 0 | 0 |

| Player and Club | Pct. | G. | AB. | R. | H. | TB. | 2B. | 3B. | HR. | RBI. | GW. | SH. | SF. | HP. | BB. | Int. BB. | SO. | SB. | CS. |
|---|---|---|---|---|---|---|---|---|---|---|---|---|---|---|---|---|---|---|---|
| O'Malley, Thomas, Rochester° | .302 | 102 | 358 | 62 | 108 | 153 | 13 | 1 | 10 | 44 | 3 | 0 | 4 | 1 | 57 | 0 | 38 | 1 | 0 |
| Owen, Lawrence, Richmond | .231 | 83 | 247 | 21 | 57 | 87 | 15 | 0 | 5 | 32 | 4 | 2 | 4 | 2 | 45 | 1 | 39 | 3 | 1 |
| Pardo, Alberto, Rochester† | .253 | 60 | 194 | 23 | 49 | 89 | 14 | 1 | 8 | 35 | 1 | 0 | 1 | 1 | 27 | 2 | 23 | 2 | 0 |
| Paris, Kelly, Rochester | .275 | 126 | 440 | 69 | 121 | 204 | 25 | 2 | 18 | 67 | 5 | 4 | 4 | 1 | 59 | 1 | 56 | 11 | 3 |
| Pasqua, Daniel, Columbus° | .321 | 78 | 287 | 52 | 92 | 172 | 16 | 5 | 18 | 69 | 9 | 0 | 2 | 2 | 48 | 2 | 62 | 5 | 0 |
| Pautt, Juan, Pawtucket | .237 | 40 | 118 | 18 | 28 | 41 | 5 | 1 | 2 | 15 | 1 | 0 | 0 | 0 | 16 | 0 | 19 | 0 | 2 |
| Payne, Michael, Richmond | .000 | 13 | 2 | 0 | 0 | 0 | 0 | 0 | 0 | 0 | 0 | 0 | 0 | 0 | 0 | 0 | 1 | 0 | 0 |
| Pedrique, Alfredo, Tidewater | .252 | 110 | 325 | 39 | 82 | 109 | 17 | 2 | 2 | 24 | 3 | 7 | 1 | 3 | 24 | 1 | 28 | 2 | 6 |
| Petralli, Eugene, Maine° | .143 | 2 | 7 | 0 | 1 | 1 | 0 | 0 | 0 | 1 | 0 | 1 | 0 | 0 | 0 | 0 | 0 | 0 | 0 |
| Poole, Mark, Syracuse | .295 | 75 | 237 | 29 | 70 | 103 | 9 | 0 | 8 | 37 | 4 | 2 | 2 | 2 | 15 | 2 | 23 | 0 | 0 |
| Puleo, Charles, Richmond | .000 | 16 | 2 | 0 | 0 | 0 | 0 | 0 | 0 | 0 | 0 | 1 | 0 | 0 | 0 | 0 | 1 | 0 | 0 |
| Quinones, Luis, Maine† | .178 | 14 | 45 | 4 | 8 | 15 | 2 | 1 | 1 | 2 | 0 | 0 | 0 | 0 | 6 | 0 | 5 | 0 | 0 |
| Rabb, John, Richmond | .252 | 111 | 369 | 55 | 93 | 178 | 12 | 5 | 21 | 62 | 9 | 3 | 3 | 10 | 39 | 1 | 74 | 16 | 1 |
| Reddish, Michael, Rochester | .271 | 74 | 229 | 39 | 62 | 109 | 8 | 0 | 13 | 37 | 4 | 0 | 3 | 0 | 33 | 2 | 42 | 0 | 0 |
| Redfield, Joseph, Tidewater | .300 | 4 | 10 | 0 | 3 | 4 | 1 | 0 | 0 | 0 | 0 | 0 | 0 | 0 | 1 | 0 | 1 | 0 | 0 |
| Reed, Jeffrey, Toledo° | .248 | 122 | 404 | 53 | 100 | 136 | 15 | 3 | 5 | 36 | 4 | 9 | 6 | 5 | 59 | 3 | 49 | 1 | 1 |
| Reynolds, Ronn, Tidewater | .300 | 3 | 10 | 0 | 3 | 4 | 1 | 0 | 0 | 2 | 0 | 0 | 0 | 0 | 0 | 0 | 2 | 0 | 0 |
| Rios, Carlos, Richmond | .242 | 128 | 396 | 44 | 96 | 112 | 10 | 3 | 0 | 30 | 1 | 15 | 4 | 2 | 23 | 1 | 26 | 3 | 2 |
| Robertson, Andre, Columbus | .393 | 9 | 28 | 3 | 11 | 12 | 1 | 0 | 0 | 1 | 0 | 1 | 0 | 0 | 1 | 0 | 3 | 0 | 0 |
| Rohn, Daniel, Maine° | .261 | 137 | 444 | 68 | 116 | 167 | 22 | 1 | 9 | 56 | 11 | 6 | 5 | 1 | 116 | 4 | 63 | 19 | 7 |
| Romine, Kevin, Pawtucket | .243 | 106 | 403 | 43 | 98 | 135 | 20 | 1 | 5 | 33 | 4 | 2 | 1 | 1 | 43 | 0 | 76 | 19 | 4 |
| Roof, Eugene, Richmond† | .221 | 86 | 263 | 28 | 58 | 70 | 3 | 0 | 3 | 28 | 11 | 4 | 7 | 1 | 31 | 4 | 39 | 3 | 4 |
| Rooney, Patrick, Syracuse | .250 | 6 | 12 | 2 | 3 | 3 | 0 | 0 | 0 | 1 | 1 | 0 | 0 | 0 | 0 | 0 | 3 | 0 | 0 |
| Rosado, Luis, Rochester | .200 | 20 | 55 | 2 | 11 | 17 | 4 | 1 | 0 | 4 | 1 | 0 | 0 | 0 | 5 | 0 | 8 | 0 | 0 |
| Sakata, Lenn, Rochester | .214 | 16 | 56 | 7 | 12 | 13 | 1 | 0 | 0 | 2 | 0 | 0 | 0 | 0 | 4 | 0 | 8 | 0 | 0 |
| Salazar, Argenis, Tidewater | .252 | 84 | 230 | 25 | 58 | 70 | 10 | 1 | 0 | 18 | 2 | 8 | 2 | 4 | 16 | 0 | 27 | 8 | 1 |
| Sambito, Joseph, Tidewater° | .000 | 19 | 0 | 0 | 0 | 0 | 0 | 0 | 0 | 0 | 0 | 1 | 0 | 0 | 0 | 0 | 0 | 0 | 0 |
| Sanchez, Orlando, Maine° | .237 | 12 | 38 | 1 | 9 | 10 | 1 | 0 | 0 | 4 | 0 | 1 | 1 | 0 | 5 | 1 | 9 | 1 | 0 |
| Sax, David, Pawtucket | .213 | 20 | 61 | 6 | 13 | 18 | 2 | 0 | 1 | 4 | 0 | 1 | 0 | 0 | 12 | 0 | 10 | 0 | 0 |
| Schaefer, Jeffrey, Rochester | .198 | 68 | 187 | 17 | 37 | 47 | 4 | 0 | 2 | 12 | 1 | 2 | 1 | 0 | 6 | 0 | 21 | 1 | 2 |
| Schiraldi, Calvin, Tidewater | .222 | 17 | 9 | 0 | 2 | 2 | 0 | 0 | 0 | 0 | 0 | 1 | 0 | 0 | 1 | 0 | 5 | 0 | 0 |
| Schuler, David, Richmond | .000 | 41 | 3 | 0 | 0 | 0 | 0 | 0 | 0 | 0 | 0 | 0 | 0 | 0 | 0 | 0 | 3 | 0 | 0 |
| Sharperson, Michael, Syracuse | .289 | 134 | 536 | 86 | 155 | 191 | 19 | 7 | 1 | 59 | 4 | 3 | 4 | 2 | 71 | 1 | 75 | 14 | 15 |
| Sheaffer, Danny, Pawtucket | .259 | 77 | 243 | 24 | 63 | 96 | 9 | 0 | 8 | 33 | 1 | 2 | 2 | 2 | 17 | 0 | 35 | 0 | 0 |
| Shelby, John, Rochester† | .286 | 52 | 206 | 31 | 59 | 107 | 16 | 4 | 8 | 21 | 0 | 1 | 3 | 0 | 19 | 2 | 35 | 14 | 4 |
| Shepherd, Ronald, Syracuse | .308 | 37 | 133 | 23 | 41 | 63 | 12 | 2 | 2 | 16 | 1 | 0 | 0 | 0 | 11 | 0 | 28 | 1 | 3 |
| Shields, Stephen, Richmond | .000 | 18 | 2 | 0 | 0 | 0 | 0 | 0 | 0 | 0 | 0 | 0 | 0 | 0 | 0 | 0 | 1 | 0 | 0 |
| Sinatro, Matthew, Richmond | .284 | 24 | 67 | 7 | 19 | 25 | 3 | 0 | 1 | 8 | 1 | 0 | 1 | 0 | 3 | 1 | 10 | 1 | 0 |
| Smith, Keith, Columbus | .241 | 123 | 307 | 40 | 74 | 97 | 9 | 1 | 4 | 21 | 2 | 9 | 1 | 0 | 39 | 0 | 66 | 10 | 5 |
| Smith, Kenneth, Richmond° | .167 | 22 | 36 | 8 | 6 | 9 | 0 | 0 | 1 | 7 | 0 | 0 | 1 | 0 | 11 | 0 | 12 | 1 | 0 |
| Sosa, Miguel, Richmond | .192 | 119 | 433 | 49 | 83 | 142 | 13 | 2 | 14 | 49 | 6 | 1 | 3 | 2 | 13 | 0 | 75 | 7 | 2 |
| Springer, Steven, Tidewater | .261 | 126 | 479 | 59 | 125 | 174 | 20 | 4 | 7 | 56 | 8 | 6 | 5 | 1 | 34 | 2 | 72 | 9 | 5 |
| Stapleton, David, Pawtucket | .214 | 5 | 14 | 1 | 3 | 4 | 1 | 0 | 0 | 0 | 0 | 0 | 0 | 0 | 2 | 0 | 1 | 0 | 0 |
| Stefero, John, Rochester° | .188 | 49 | 128 | 16 | 24 | 59 | 5 | 0 | 10 | 23 | 0 | 2 | 2 | 0 | 16 | 1 | 37 | 0 | 0 |
| Stegman, David, Syracuse | .319 | 89 | 257 | 36 | 82 | 135 | 15 | 4 | 10 | 45 | 5 | 2 | 4 | 1 | 40 | 2 | 35 | 1 | 1 |
| Sullivan, Marc, Pawtucket | .250 | 2 | 4 | 0 | 1 | 1 | 0 | 0 | 0 | 0 | 0 | 0 | 0 | 0 | 0 | 0 | 0 | 0 | 0 |
| Tarver, LaSchelle, Tidewater° | .311 | 126 | 457 | 73 | 142 | 168 | 17 | 3 | 1 | 40 | 6 | 4 | 1 | 3 | 54 | 2 | 69 | 35 | 16 |
| Taylor, Dwight, Maine° | .251 | 118 | 427 | 67 | 107 | 128 | 7 | 4 | 2 | 32 | 4 | 13 | 4 | 0 | 44 | 1 | 46 | 52 | 9 |
| Thomas, Andres, Richmond | .179 | 11 | 28 | 3 | 5 | 8 | 0 | 0 | 1 | 6 | 1 | 1 | 0 | 0 | 5 | 2 | 6 | 0 | 0 |
| Thompson, Milton, Richmond° | .314 | 82 | 312 | 52 | 98 | 116 | 10 | 1 | 2 | 22 | 2 | 5 | 3 | 1 | 32 | 3 | 30 | 34 | 11 |
| Thompson, Tommy, Richmond° | .167 | 3 | 6 | 1 | 1 | 2 | 1 | 0 | 0 | 3 | 0 | 0 | 0 | 0 | 1 | 0 | 1 | 0 | 0 |
| Tiburcio, Fredrick, Richmond° | .248 | 39 | 117 | 8 | 29 | 41 | 5 | 2 | 1 | 10 | 3 | 3 | 1 | 0 | 8 | 1 | 20 | 3 | 2 |
| Traber, James, Rochester° | .265 | 80 | 279 | 32 | 74 | 112 | 13 | 2 | 7 | 37 | 7 | 0 | 2 | 3 | 18 | 0 | 36 | 3 | 2 |
| Tumpane, Robert, Richmond° | .224 | 43 | 134 | 15 | 30 | 58 | 10 | 0 | 6 | 24 | 3 | 2 | 1 | 1 | 13 | 0 | 29 | 0 | 0 |
| Ullger, Scott, Toledo | .292 | 112 | 384 | 58 | 112 | 182 | 13 | 6 | 15 | 58 | 5 | 3 | 4 | 2 | 59 | 2 | 55 | 2 | 1 |
| Vargas, Leonel, Richmond | .091 | 4 | 11 | 0 | 1 | 1 | 0 | 0 | 0 | 1 | 0 | 0 | 1 | 0 | 1 | 0 | 0 | 0 | 0 |
| Weaver, James, 62 Tol-29 Maine° | .221 | 91 | 331 | 54 | 73 | 131 | 10 | 6 | 12 | 46 | 3 | 2 | 2 | 0 | 40 | 3 | 62 | 16 | 7 |
| Webster, Mitchell, Syracuse† | .275 | 47 | 189 | 32 | 52 | 72 | 5 | 3 | 3 | 23 | 6 | 4 | 1 | 1 | 20 | 1 | 24 | 5 | 4 |
| West, Matthew, Richmond† | .125 | 23 | 8 | 0 | 1 | 1 | 0 | 0 | 0 | 0 | 0 | 0 | 0 | 0 | 0 | 0 | 2 | 0 | 0 |
| Whisenton, Larry, Richmond° | .331 | 47 | 139 | 23 | 46 | 68 | 9 | 5 | 1 | 15 | 4 | 2 | 2 | 0 | 23 | 0 | 28 | 1 | 3 |
| Whittemore, Reginald, Toledo | .280 | 91 | 286 | 43 | 80 | 105 | 10 | 0 | 5 | 27 | 5 | 4 | 1 | 1 | 42 | 2 | 47 | 1 | 1 |
| Wiggins, Alan, Rochester† | .182 | 6 | 22 | 1 | 4 | 5 | 1 | 0 | 0 | 1 | 0 | 0 | 0 | 0 | 4 | 0 | 1 | 1 | 2 |
| Willard, Gerald, Maine° | .225 | 11 | 40 | 5 | 9 | 15 | 3 | 0 | 1 | 4 | 0 | 0 | 0 | 0 | 7 | 0 | 7 | 1 | 0 |
| Wilson, James, Maine | .287 | 139 | 523 | 75 | 150 | 251 | 23 | 1 | 26 | 101 | 16 | 0 | 9 | 1 | 50 | 5 | 104 | 0 | 1 |
| Winters, Matthew, Columbus° | .308 | 45 | 130 | 19 | 40 | 65 | 14 | 1 | 3 | 19 | 2 | 3 | 1 | 1 | 26 | 2 | 20 | 2 | 0 |
| Woods, Alvis, Toledo° | .283 | 94 | 315 | 54 | 89 | 147 | 12 | 2 | 14 | 48 | 3 | 2 | 1 | 0 | 56 | 3 | 37 | 2 | 4 |
| Zuvella, Paul, Richmond | .219 | 8 | 32 | 3 | 7 | 10 | 0 | 0 | 1 | 3 | 2 | 1 | 0 | 0 | 2 | 1 | 0 | 1 | 0 |

The following pitchers, listed alphabetically by club, with games in parentheses, had no plate appearances, primarily through use of designated hitters:

COLUMBUS—Armstrong, Michael (21); Bradley, Bert (11); Brown, Curtis (47); Bystrom, Martin (4); Christiansen, Clay (28); Cooper, Donald (33); Deshaies, James (21); Faulk, Kelly (18); Fisher, Brian (7); Patterson, Scott (21); Pulido, Alfonso (31); Rasmussen, Dennis (7); Scott, Kelly (21); Silva, Mark (43); Tewksbury, Robert (6); Underwood, Thomas (19); Williams, Alberto (26).

MAINE—Barkley, Jeffrey (24); Beard, David (16); Behenna, Richard (6); Calderon, Jose (42); Calvert, Mark (17); Clark, Bryan (4); Creel, Keith (19); Doyle, Richard (8); Elston, Guy (15); Fuson, Robin (21); Pippin, Craig (36); Reed, Jerry (14); Ritter, Reggie (10); Roman, Jose (11); Romero, Ramon (15); Rowe, Thomas (30); Schulze, Donald (15); Siwy, James (2); Smith, Leroy (15); Thompson, Richard (4); Von Ohlen, David (4).

PAWTUCKET—Brown, Michael (20); Dorsey, James (32); Fuson, Robin (10); Gering, Scott (6); Glynn, Edward (5); Gnacinski, Paul (34); Herron, Anthony (21); Johnson, Mitchell (30); Kane, Kevin (31); McCarthy, Thomas (26); Mecerod, George (29); Mitchell, Charles (64); Rochford, Michael (12); Woodward, Robert (15).

RICHMOND—Dedmon, Jeffrey (10); Leggatt, Richard (10); Reiter, Gary (4); Treadway, Andre (2); Ward, Duane (5).

ROCHESTER—Augustine, Gerald (43); Biercevicz, Gregory (27); Brito, Jose (8); Couchee, Michael (20); Havens, Bradley (34); Huffman, Phillip (23); Jackson, Roy Lee (15); Johnson, Jerry (28); Jones, Odell (41); Kucharski, Joseph (26); Rajsich, David (12); Snell, Nathaniel (2); Swaggerty, William (30); Welchel, Donald (26).

SYRACUSE—Alba, Gibson (17); Carlucci, Richard (39); Cerutti, John (28); Clarke, Stanley (43); Davis, Steven (6); Eichhorn, Mark (8); Filer, Thomas (12); Gillam, Keith (6); Gordon, Donald (51); Henke, Thomas (39); Howard, Dennis (25); Leal, Luis (12); McLaughlin, Colin (34); Musselman, Ronald (2); Rodgers, Timothy (13); Williams, Matthew (22).

TIDEWATER—Anderson, Karl (2); Berenyi, Bruce (1); Gaff, Brent (1); Leach, Terry (24); Olwine, Edward (55); Sisk, Douglas (4).

TOLEDO—Anderson, Allan (27); Broersma, Eric (47); Brown, Mark (26); Burtt, Dennis (27); Chiffer, Floyd (51); Eufemia, Frank (14);

Henderson, Craig (4); Hodge, Eddie (29); Lysander, Richard (7); Oelkers, Bryan (12); Portugal, Mark (19); Walters, Michael (11); Whitehouse, Leonard (37); Yett, Richard (25).

GRAND SLAM HOME RUNS—Dalena, Weaver, 2 each; Benzinger, Blocker, Brewer, Bustabad, David, Dugas, Gruber, Hart, Hobson, Holmes, Lickert, Miller-Jones, Pasqua, Reddish, Kei. Smith, Stefero, Stegman, Traber, Wilson, Woods, 1 each.

AWARDED FIRST BASE ON CATCHER'S INTERFERENCE—Hudler 3 (Owen, Poole, Jef. Reed); Dalena 2 (Poole 2); Dugas 2 (Owen, Rabb); Infante 2 (Espino, Owen); Miller-Jones 2 (Espino, Jef. Reed); Graham (Buckley); McGriff (Owen); McNealy (Gibbons); Paris (Owen); Schaefer (Malpeso); Sosa (Buckley).

## CLUB FIELDING

| Club | Pct. | G. | PO. | A. | E. | DP. | PB. | Club | Pct. | G. | PO. | A. | E. | DP. | PB. |
|---|---|---|---|---|---|---|---|---|---|---|---|---|---|---|---|
| Toledo | .975 | 139 | 3674 | 1539 | 134 | 163 | 12 | Maine | .973 | 139 | 3626 | 1444 | 143 | 124 | 22 |
| Syracuse | .974 | 140 | 3708 | 1522 | 142 | 134 | 12 | Rochester | .972 | 139 | 3539 | 1540 | 144 | 131 | 12 |
| Tidewater | .973 | 139 | 3689 | 1558 | 145 | 130 | 5 | Pawtucket | .971 | 139 | 3638 | 1503 | 151 | 128 | 17 |
| Richmond | .973 | 140 | 3673 | 1567 | 147 | 142 | 8 | Columbus | .967 | 139 | 3609 | 1491 | 175 | 127 | 25 |

Triple Play—Rochester.

## INDIVIDUAL FIELDING

*Throws lefthanded.

### FIRST BASEMEN

| Player and Club | Pct. | G. | PO. | A. | E. | DP. | Player and Club | Pct. | G. | PO. | A. | E. | DP. |
|---|---|---|---|---|---|---|---|---|---|---|---|---|---|
| Aikens, Syracuse | .986 | 23 | 200 | 16 | 3 | 22 | Leach, Syracuse* | .989 | 56 | 490 | 53 | 6 | 44 |
| Bjorkman, Rochester | .989 | 13 | 88 | 4 | 1 | 12 | Lickert, Richmond | 1.000 | 2 | 1 | 0 | 0 | 0 |
| Briggs, Columbus* | .984 | 98 | 730 | 46 | 13 | 60 | Lisi, Maine | .950 | 2 | 17 | 2 | 1 | 3 |
| Buckley, Maine | .964 | 3 | 26 | 1 | 1 | 7 | Malpeso, Pawtucket | 1.000 | 5 | 25 | 3 | 0 | 1 |
| Chapman, Tidewater | 1.000 | 3 | 33 | 2 | 0 | 3 | McGriff, Syracuse* | .989 | 51 | 433 | 37 | 5 | 43 |
| Connally, Rochester | 1.000 | 44 | 407 | 28 | 0 | 36 | McPhail, Tidewater | .938 | 3 | 14 | 1 | 1 | 1 |
| Curry, Richmond | .983 | 14 | 104 | 13 | 2 | 9 | Nanni, Syracuse* | .993 | 17 | 134 | 6 | 1 | 12 |
| Dalena, Columbus | .997 | 51 | 338 | 26 | 1 | 37 | Nattile, Pawtucket | .981 | 20 | 142 | 10 | 3 | 16 |
| David, Toledo* | .984 | 41 | 297 | 16 | 5 | 38 | O'Malley, Rochester | 1.000 | 1 | 2 | 1 | 0 | 0 |
| Davis, Tidewater | .981 | 37 | 235 | 19 | 5 | 18 | Pedrique, Tidewater | .981 | 14 | 46 | 5 | 1 | 6 |
| DODSON, Pawtucket* | .99226 | 110 | 942 | 83 | 8 | 78 | Rabb, Richmond | 1.000 | 1 | 8 | 0 | 0 | 0 |
| Estes, Richmond* | .990 | 76 | 641 | 55 | 7 | 72 | Reddish, Rochester | .981 | 31 | 296 | 10 | 6 | 33 |
| Evans, Maine | 1.000 | 1 | 1 | 0 | 0 | 0 | Roof, Rochester | 1.000 | 6 | 32 | 0 | 0 | 5 |
| Falcone, Rochester | .987 | 36 | 287 | 22 | 4 | 34 | Rosado, Rochester | .944 | 3 | 15 | 2 | 1 | 2 |
| Gray, Columbus | .993 | 22 | 120 | 18 | 1 | 12 | Sanchez, Maine | .969 | 11 | 87 | 6 | 3 | 11 |
| Guerrero, Richmond | 1.000 | 1 | 11 | 0 | 0 | 1 | Smith, Richmond | .972 | 16 | 98 | 5 | 3 | 12 |
| Hearn, Tidewater | .997 | 30 | 286 | 25 | 1 | 25 | Thompson, Richmond | 1.000 | 1 | 1 | 0 | 0 | 0 |
| Hernandez, Rochester | .976 | 4 | 36 | 4 | 1 | 3 | Traber, Rochester* | .994 | 20 | 155 | 17 | 1 | 12 |
| Hobson, Columbus | 1.000 | 8 | 49 | 3 | 0 | 5 | Tumpane, Richmond* | .989 | 39 | 338 | 22 | 4 | 36 |
| Johnson, Richmond | 1.000 | 8 | 73 | 1 | 0 | 3 | Ullger, Toledo | .997 | 38 | 306 | 24 | 1 | 31 |
| Jones, Tidewater | 1.000 | 3 | 6 | 0 | 0 | 2 | Whittemore, Toledo | .977 | 75 | 609 | 63 | 16 | 79 |
| Jurak, Pawtucket | .985 | 17 | 122 | 13 | 2 | 15 | Wilson, Maine | .99166 | 125 | 1104 | 85 | 10 | 96 |
| Keller, Syracuse | .667 | 2 | 2 | 0 | 1 | 0 | Woods, Toledo* | 1.000 | 1 | 1 | 0 | 0 | 0 |
| Lancellotti, Tidewater* | .987 | 79 | 701 | 38 | 10 | 69 | | | | | | | |

Triple Play—Falcone.

### SECOND BASEMEN

| Player and Club | Pct. | G. | PO. | A. | E. | DP. | Player and Club | Pct. | G. | PO. | A. | E. | DP. |
|---|---|---|---|---|---|---|---|---|---|---|---|---|---|
| Aragon, Toledo | .978 | 11 | 19 | 26 | 1 | 4 | MILLER-JONES, Pawtucket | .980 | 127 | 256 | 387 | 13 | 89 |
| Barrett, Columbus | 1.000 | 7 | 16 | 17 | 0 | 5 | Noboa, Maine | .979 | 122 | 270 | 379 | 14 | 85 |
| Bonilla, Columbus | .970 | 60 | 115 | 142 | 8 | 38 | Norman, Rochester | .970 | 67 | 121 | 174 | 9 | 41 |
| Chapman, Tidewater | .923 | 9 | 13 | 23 | 3 | 3 | Paris, Rochester | 1.000 | 7 | 3 | 13 | 0 | 1 |
| Curry, Richmond | .973 | 43 | 92 | 127 | 6 | 37 | Pedrique, Tidewater | 1.000 | 6 | 7 | 15 | 0 | 3 |
| Davis, Tidewater | 1.000 | 2 | 1 | 2 | 0 | 0 | Rios, Richmond | 1.000 | 7 | 11 | 14 | 0 | 6 |
| Dugas, Maine | .957 | 13 | 22 | 44 | 3 | 7 | Rohn, Maine | 1.000 | 5 | 18 | 16 | 0 | 6 |
| Evans, Maine | 1.000 | 1 | 3 | 5 | 0 | 3 | Sakata, Rochester | .962 | 15 | 28 | 48 | 3 | 8 |
| Gardenhire, Tidewater | .950 | 6 | 7 | 12 | 1 | 2 | Salazar, Tidewater | 1.000 | 1 | 2 | 3 | 0 | 1 |
| Gulliver, Richmond | 1.000 | 5 | 6 | 10 | 0 | 3 | Schaefer, Rochester | .990 | 60 | 126 | 179 | 3 | 38 |
| Heath, Columbus | .959 | 25 | 43 | 51 | 4 | 10 | Sharperson, Syracuse | .977 | 132 | 286 | 365 | 15 | 82 |
| Hudler, Columbus | .969 | 82 | 122 | 187 | 10 | 31 | Smith, Columbus | 1.000 | 3 | 1 | 1 | 0 | 0 |
| Hundhammer, Pawtucket | .985 | 14 | 31 | 36 | 1 | 2 | Sosa, Richmond | .951 | 100 | 179 | 283 | 24 | 58 |
| Jimenez, Toledo | .986 | 47 | 92 | 122 | 3 | 30 | Springer, Tidewater | .979 | 116 | 231 | 374 | 13 | 82 |
| Jones, Tidewater | 1.000 | 6 | 10 | 13 | 0 | 1 | Ullger, Toledo | 1.000 | 1 | 0 | 1 | 0 | 1 |
| Lombardozzi, Toledo | .981 | 92 | 246 | 261 | 10 | 85 | Wiggins, Rochester | .943 | 6 | 18 | 15 | 2 | 5 |
| McHenry, Syracuse | 1.000 | 14 | 26 | 34 | 0 | 8 | | | | | | | |

Triple Play—Norman.

### THIRD BASEMEN

| Player and Club | Pct. | G. | PO. | A. | E. | DP. | Player and Club | Pct. | G. | PO. | A. | E. | DP. |
|---|---|---|---|---|---|---|---|---|---|---|---|---|---|
| Aragon, Toledo | 1.000 | 13 | 4 | 15 | 0 | 3 | Lisi, Maine | .571 | 4 | 0 | 4 | 3 | 0 |
| Barrett, Columbus | .939 | 28 | 14 | 48 | 4 | 2 | Lombardozzi, Toledo | .920 | 29 | 24 | 56 | 7 | 5 |
| Bonilla, Columbus | .957 | 18 | 14 | 31 | 2 | 3 | Mata, Columbus | 1.000 | 1 | 0 | 1 | 0 | 0 |
| Bradley, Columbus | .941 | 17 | 8 | 40 | 3 | 2 | McHenry, Syracuse | .900 | 25 | 16 | 47 | 7 | 8 |
| Bustabad, Pawtucket | .944 | 8 | 5 | 12 | 1 | 0 | McPhail, Tidewater | .875 | 5 | 0 | 7 | 1 | 0 |
| Connally, Rochester | .963 | 6 | 6 | 20 | 1 | 2 | Mesh, Pawtucket | .941 | 7 | 3 | 13 | 1 | 1 |
| Curry, Richmond | .920 | 35 | 20 | 49 | 6 | 7 | Miller-Jones, Pawtucket | 1.000 | 1 | 1 | 3 | 0 | 0 |
| Davis, Tidewater | .921 | 18 | 11 | 24 | 3 | 1 | Mitchell, Tidewater | .923 | 93 | 55 | 209 | 22 | 17 |
| Dugas, Maine | .890 | 55 | 42 | 95 | 17 | 8 | Moronko, Maine | 1.000 | 1 | 1 | 5 | 0 | 1 |
| Evans, Maine | .953 | 67 | 51 | 133 | 9 | 11 | O'MALLEY, Rochester | .964 | 97 | 90 | 206 | 11 | 17 |
| Gardenhire, Tidewater | .941 | 8 | 6 | 10 | 1 | 1 | Paris, Rochester | .889 | 5 | 5 | 3 | 1 | 0 |
| Gray, Columbus | .889 | 15 | 5 | 19 | 3 | 1 | Pautt, Pawtucket | 1.000 | 3 | 3 | 2 | 0 | 1 |
| Gruber, Syracuse | .955 | 121 | 78 | 217 | 14 | 22 | Pedrique, Tidewater | .985 | 31 | 16 | 50 | 1 | 4 |
| Gulliver, Richmond | .974 | 19 | 11 | 27 | 1 | 4 | Rabb, Richmond | .750 | 2 | 2 | 1 | 1 | 0 |
| Hamric, Syracuse | 1.000 | 2 | 0 | 4 | 0 | 0 | Redfield, Tidewater | 1.000 | 1 | 0 | 2 | 0 | 0 |
| Hernandez, Rochester | .938 | 34 | 15 | 61 | 5 | 7 | Rios, Richmond | 1.000 | 1 | 2 | 1 | 0 | 0 |
| Hobson, Columbus | .929 | 82 | 74 | 135 | 16 | 13 | Rohn, Maine | .977 | 18 | 11 | 32 | 1 | 2 |
| Holmes, Toledo | .957 | 51 | 28 | 82 | 5 | 8 | Sax, Pawtucket | .833 | 3 | 0 | 5 | 1 | 1 |
| Hudler, Columbus | .667 | 1 | 1 | 1 | 1 | 1 | Springer, Tidewater | .800 | 2 | 3 | 5 | 2 | 1 |
| Hundhammer, Pawtucket | .922 | 92 | 69 | 169 | 20 | 19 | Stapleton, Pawtucket | 1.000 | 5 | 2 | 11 | 0 | 0 |
| Johnson, Richmond | .943 | 112 | 74 | 209 | 17 | 23 | Thompson, Richmond | 1.000 | 2 | 0 | 1 | 0 | 0 |
| Jones, Tidewater | .833 | 6 | 3 | 7 | 2 | 0 | Ullger, Toledo | .955 | 62 | 51 | 119 | 8 | 13 |
| Jurak, Pawtucket | .958 | 37 | 31 | 61 | 4 | 4 | | | | | | | |

## SHORTSTOPS

| Player and Club | Pct. | G. | PO. | A. | E. | DP. | Player and Club | Pct. | G. | PO. | A. | E. | DP. |
|---|---|---|---|---|---|---|---|---|---|---|---|---|---|
| Bonilla, Columbus | .932 | 23 | 26 | 43 | 5 | 9 | Mesh, Pawtucket | .944 | 73 | 121 | 214 | 20 | 50 |
| Bustabad, Pawtucket | .968 | 71 | 104 | 201 | 10 | 32 | Moronko, Maine | 1.000 | 5 | 7 | 16 | 0 | 5 |
| Cruz, Rochester | 1.000 | 3 | 1 | 6 | 0 | 0 | Norman, Rochester | .882 | 16 | 16 | 51 | 9 | 7 |
| Dugas, Maine | .904 | 20 | 33 | 33 | 7 | 7 | Paris, Rochester | .940 | 111 | 161 | 360 | 33 | 73 |
| Espinoza, Toledo | .959 | 80 | 132 | 245 | 16 | 64 | Pedrique, Tidewater | .967 | 74 | 101 | 191 | 10 | 41 |
| Gardenhire, Tidewater | .875 | 7 | 7 | 14 | 3 | 2 | Quinones, Maine | 1.000 | 6 | 13 | 12 | 0 | 4 |
| Gulliver, Richmond | .800 | 2 | 1 | 3 | 1 | 1 | RIOS, Richmond | .978 | 123 | 205 | 362 | 13 | 79 |
| Hudler, Columbus | .938 | 25 | 30 | 46 | 5 | 11 | Robertson, Columbus | .962 | 9 | 18 | 32 | 2 | 7 |
| Hundhammer, Pawtucket | .750 | 2 | 2 | 1 | 1 | 0 | Rohn, Maine | .963 | 111 | 171 | 325 | 19 | 66 |
| Infante, Syracuse | .940 | 136 | 225 | 432 | 42 | 84 | Salazar, Tidewater | .957 | 82 | 117 | 241 | 16 | 46 |
| Jimenez, Toledo | .953 | 69 | 109 | 218 | 16 | 53 | Schaefer, Rochester | .923 | 8 | 8 | 16 | 2 | 1 |
| Johnson, Richmond | .941 | 10 | 5 | 11 | 1 | 1 | Sharperson, Syracuse | .857 | 2 | 5 | 7 | 2 | 1 |
| Ri. Jones, Rochester | .953 | 14 | 24 | 37 | 3 | 7 | Smith, Columbus | .946 | 114 | 175 | 301 | 27 | 61 |
| Ro. Jones, Tidewater | .750 | 2 | 0 | 3 | 1 | 0 | Sosa, Richmond | .943 | 12 | 4 | 29 | 2 | 5 |
| Lombardozzi, Toledo | 1.000 | 3 | 2 | 7 | 0 | 1 | Thomas, Richmond | .938 | 11 | 15 | 30 | 3 | 9 |
| McHenry, Syracuse | .667 | 7 | 5 | 3 | 4 | 1 | Zuvella, Richmond | .930 | 8 | 10 | 30 | 3 | 3 |

## OUTFIELDERS

| Player and Club | Pct. | G. | PO. | A. | E. | DP. | Player and Club | Pct. | G. | PO. | A. | E. | DP. |
|---|---|---|---|---|---|---|---|---|---|---|---|---|---|
| Ackley, Pawtucket | .800 | 1 | 4 | 0 | 1 | 0 | Knight, Columbus* | .951 | 27 | 39 | 0 | 2 | 0 |
| Allen, Rochester | .961 | 88 | 145 | 3 | 6 | 0 | Leach, Syracuse* | .980 | 86 | 185 | 13 | 4 | 2 |
| Ayala, Maine | 1.000 | 1 | 2 | 0 | 0 | 0 | Lisi, Maine | .955 | 20 | 20 | 1 | 1 | 0 |
| Barrett, Columbus | .947 | 9 | 17 | 1 | 1 | 0 | Lomastro, Toledo | .974 | 82 | 145 | 2 | 4 | 0 |
| Beane, Tidewater | .978 | 134 | 255 | 10 | 6 | 2 | Malpeso, Pawtucket | 1.000 | 2 | 5 | 0 | 0 | 0 |
| Benzinger, Pawtucket | .973 | 52 | 106 | 3 | 3 | 0 | Mata, Columbus | .950 | 103 | 243 | 4 | 13 | 2 |
| Blocker, Tidewater* | .974 | 72 | 183 | 5 | 5 | 2 | McNealy, Syracuse* | .983 | 134 | 332 | 7 | 6 | 1 |
| Brewer, Maine | .975 | 117 | 264 | 11 | 7 | 1 | Mesh, Pawtucket | .938 | 13 | 13 | 2 | 1 | 0 |
| Briggs, Columbus* | .948 | 38 | 70 | 3 | 4 | 1 | Miller, Rochester | .968 | 38 | 86 | 5 | 3 | 0 |
| Brown, Rochester | 1.000 | 17 | 27 | 1 | 0 | 0 | Mitchell, Tidewater | 1.000 | 1 | 1 | 0 | 0 | 0 |
| Buckley, Maine | 1.000 | 3 | 4 | 1 | 0 | 1 | Molinaro, Rochester | .917 | 17 | 21 | 1 | 2 | 0 |
| Burgess, Pawtucket* | .964 | 104 | 227 | 13 | 9 | 3 | Nanni, Syracuse* | 1.000 | 1 | 2 | 0 | 0 | 0 |
| Carreon, Tidewater* | 1.000 | 2 | 2 | 0 | 0 | 0 | Pasqua, Columbus* | .974 | 76 | 141 | 9 | 4 | 2 |
| Castillo, Maine | 1.000 | 5 | 9 | 0 | 0 | 0 | Pautt, Pawtucket | .959 | 34 | 45 | 2 | 2 | 0 |
| Christensen, Tidewater | .947 | 43 | 65 | 7 | 4 | 1 | Quinones, Maine | 1.000 | 4 | 6 | 0 | 0 | 0 |
| Cotto, Columbus | .988 | 75 | 158 | 5 | 2 | 1 | Rabb, Richmond | .985 | 74 | 131 | 4 | 2 | 1 |
| Craig, Tidewater | 1.000 | 9 | 16 | 0 | 0 | 0 | Reddish, Rochester | .980 | 26 | 47 | 2 | 1 | 1 |
| David, Toledo* | 1.000 | 29 | 35 | 1 | 0 | 1 | Rohn, Maine | 1.000 | 3 | 12 | 0 | 0 | 0 |
| Davis, Tidewater | 1.000 | 14 | 18 | 2 | 0 | 0 | Romine, Pawtucket | .970 | 106 | 246 | 9 | 8 | 2 |
| Dykstra, Tidewater* | .974 | 58 | 184 | 4 | 5 | 1 | Roof, Richmond | .988 | 57 | 82 | 1 | 1 | 0 |
| Estes, Richmond* | .953 | 42 | 79 | 2 | 4 | 0 | Rooney, Syracuse | .857 | 4 | 6 | 0 | 1 | 0 |
| GALLAGHER, Maine | .992 | 132 | 357 | 9 | 3 | 0 | Sanchez, Maine | 1.000 | 1 | 1 | 0 | 0 | 0 |
| Graham, Rochester* | .979 | 101 | 221 | 9 | 5 | 4 | Sax, Pawtucket | .857 | 4 | 6 | 0 | 1 | 0 |
| Granger, Rochester | .980 | 75 | 192 | 5 | 4 | 0 | Shelby, Rochester | .992 | 52 | 124 | 4 | 1 | 2 |
| Grant, Maine | 1.000 | 4 | 4 | 0 | 0 | 0 | Shepherd, Syracuse | .952 | 37 | 60 | 0 | 3 | 0 |
| Gray, Columbus | .920 | 23 | 21 | 2 | 2 | 0 | Stegman, Syracuse | .992 | 81 | 123 | 8 | 1 | 0 |
| Greenwell, Pawtucket | .964 | 107 | 178 | 8 | 7 | 1 | Tarver, Tidewater* | .969 | 89 | 151 | 5 | 5 | 0 |
| Hall, Richmond | .963 | 34 | 77 | 2 | 3 | 1 | Taylor, Maine* | .961 | 116 | 266 | 4 | 11 | 0 |
| Hart, Toledo* | .986 | 133 | 345 | 11 | 5 | 0 | M. Thompson, Richmond | .981 | 81 | 209 | 3 | 4 | 0 |
| Heath, Columbus | .974 | 60 | 108 | 4 | 3 | 1 | Tiburcio, Richmond* | .973 | 31 | 72 | 1 | 2 | 0 |
| Hernandez, Rochester | .972 | 81 | 131 | 10 | 4 | 0 | Traber, Rochester* | .959 | 43 | 65 | 5 | 3 | 0 |
| Holman, Syracuse | .987 | 58 | 73 | 2 | 1 | 1 | Ullger, Toledo* | 1.000 | 13 | 21 | 0 | 0 | 0 |
| Holmes, Toledo | 1.000 | 6 | 7 | 0 | 0 | 0 | Vargas, Richmond | 1.000 | 3 | 6 | 0 | 0 | 0 |
| Howe, Toledo | 1.000 | 80 | 181 | 5 | 0 | 0 | Weaver, 54 Toledo-18 Maine* | .955 | 72 | 135 | 13 | 7 | 6 |
| Hudler, Columbus | .975 | 14 | 39 | 0 | 1 | 0 | Webster, Syracuse* | .989 | 46 | 83 | 10 | 1 | 1 |
| Hughes, Columbus* | .926 | 18 | 25 | 0 | 2 | 0 | Whisenton, Richmond* | .980 | 28 | 47 | 2 | 1 | 0 |
| Jones, Tidewater | .951 | 27 | 38 | 1 | 2 | 0 | Winters, Columbus | .979 | 28 | 45 | 1 | 1 | 0 |
| Jurak, Pawtucket | .939 | 18 | 30 | 1 | 2 | 0 | Woods, Toledo* | 1.000 | 41 | 72 | 1 | 0 | 0 |
| Kinnard, Syracuse | 1.000 | 2 | 2 | 0 | 0 | 0 | | | | | | | |

## CATCHERS

| Player and Club | Pct. | G. | PO. | A. | E. | DP. | PB. | Player and Club | Pct. | G. | PO. | A. | E. | DP. | PB. |
|---|---|---|---|---|---|---|---|---|---|---|---|---|---|---|---|
| Ackley, Pawtucket | 1.000 | 10 | 57 | 7 | 0 | 0 | 1 | Lindsey, Columbus | .972 | 25 | 121 | 18 | 4 | 0 | 5 |
| Allenson, Syracuse | .989 | 61 | 340 | 30 | 4 | 4 | 7 | Malpeso, Pawtucket | .968 | 65 | 365 | 34 | 13 | 10 | 7 |
| Benton, Maine | .965 | 28 | 116 | 20 | 5 | 0 | 4 | Nattile, Pawtucket | 1.000 | 7 | 10 | 1 | 0 | 1 | 0 |
| Bjorkman, Rochester | .980 | 41 | 172 | 23 | 4 | 4 | 3 | O'Berry, Columbus | .980 | 16 | 88 | 9 | 2 | 1 | 3 |
| Bradley, Columbus | .992 | 24 | 110 | 13 | 1 | 1 | 3 | Owen, Rochester | .977 | 81 | 436 | 65 | 12 | 6 | 4 |
| Buckley, Maine | .975 | 55 | 280 | 29 | 8 | 3 | 11 | Pardo, Rochester | .979 | 51 | 258 | 19 | 6 | 2 | 3 |
| Corbett, Rochester | 1.000 | 5 | 16 | 1 | 0 | 0 | 0 | Petralli, Maine | .929 | 2 | 12 | 1 | 1 | 0 | 0 |
| Dempsey, Maine | .984 | 52 | 219 | 20 | 4 | 3 | 6 | Poole, Syracuse | .985 | 73 | 370 | 24 | 6 | 5 | 5 |
| DeWillis, Syracuse | .975 | 19 | 106 | 9 | 3 | 1 | 0 | Rabb, Richmond | .833 | 2 | 10 | 0 | 2 | 0 | 0 |
| Espino, Columbus | .983 | 73 | 349 | 46 | 7 | 5 | 13 | Reed, Toledo | .983 | 120 | 627 | 81 | 12 | 8 | 6 |
| GIBBONS, Tidewater | .990 | 98 | 531 | 36 | 6 | 1 | 2 | Reynolds, Tidewater | 1.000 | 1 | 5 | 2 | 0 | 0 | 1 |
| Hawkins, Columbus | .981 | 20 | 44 | 7 | 1 | 0 | 1 | Rosado, Rochester | 1.000 | 14 | 81 | 8 | 0 | 0 | 3 |
| Hearn, Tidewater | .986 | 47 | 257 | 20 | 4 | 3 | 2 | Sax, Pawtucket | 1.000 | 9 | 36 | 4 | 0 | 0 | 1 |
| Hernandez, Toledo | .968 | 28 | 136 | 15 | 5 | 1 | 6 | Sheaffer, Pawtucket | .981 | 50 | 289 | 18 | 6 | 7 | 7 |
| Holland, Syracuse | .900 | 2 | 7 | 2 | 1 | 0 | 0 | Sinatro, Richmond | .970 | 22 | 89 | 8 | 3 | 1 | 0 |
| Johnson, Columbus | 1.000 | 2 | 9 | 0 | 0 | 0 | 0 | Stefero, Rochester | .982 | 47 | 192 | 24 | 4 | 0 | 3 |
| Keller, Syracuse | 1.000 | 6 | 23 | 0 | 0 | 0 | 0 | Sullivan, Pawtucket | 1.000 | 2 | 10 | 0 | 0 | 0 | 0 |
| Lickert, 45 Rich-15 Paw | .973 | 60 | 251 | 36 | 8 | 1 | 5 | Willard, Maine | .971 | 11 | 56 | 11 | 2 | 0 | 1 |

## PITCHERS

| Player and Club | Pct. | G. | PO. | A. | E. | DP. | Player and Club | Pct. | G. | PO. | A. | E. | DP. |
|---|---|---|---|---|---|---|---|---|---|---|---|---|---|
| Aguilera, Tidewater | 1.000 | 11 | 1 | 8 | 0 | 1 | Barkley, Maine | 1.000 | 24 | 2 | 2 | 0 | 0 |
| Alba, Syracuse* | 1.000 | 17 | 1 | 8 | 0 | 0 | Beard, Maine | 1.000 | 16 | 1 | 2 | 0 | 0 |
| A. Anderson, Toledo* | .914 | 27 | 4 | 28 | 3 | 2 | Behenna, Maine | 1.000 | 6 | 1 | 4 | 0 | 0 |
| K. Anderson, Tidewater | 1.000 | 2 | 0 | 1 | 0 | 0 | Bettendorf, Tidewater | .852 | 28 | 9 | 14 | 4 | 3 |
| R. Anderson, Tidewater | .917 | 48 | 5 | 6 | 1 | 1 | Biercevicz, Rochester | 1.000 | 27 | 3 | 8 | 0 | 1 |
| Armstrong, Columbus | 1.000 | 21 | 1 | 5 | 0 | 1 | Bittiger, Tidewater | .913 | 24 | 5 | 16 | 2 | 2 |
| Augustine, Rochester* | 1.000 | 43 | 6 | 10 | 0 | 1 | Bradley, Columbus | .947 | 11 | 8 | 10 | 1 | 2 |

PITCHERS—Continued

| Player and Club | Pct. | G. | PO. | A. | E. | DP. |
|---|---|---|---|---|---|---|
| Briggs, Columbus* | 1.000 | 2 | 1 | 0 | 0 | 0 |
| Brito, Rochester | 1.000 | 8 | 2 | 4 | 0 | 0 |
| Brizzolara, Richmond | 1.000 | 33 | 12 | 22 | 0 | 1 |
| Broersma, Toledo | .944 | 47 | 9 | 8 | 1 | 1 |
| C. Brown, Columbus | .917 | 47 | 5 | 17 | 2 | 2 |
| Ma. Brown, Toledo | .864 | 26 | 5 | 14 | 3 | 1 |
| Mi. Brown, Pawtucket | .875 | 20 | 1 | 6 | 1 | 0 |
| Burtt, Toledo | .938 | 27 | 8 | 22 | 2 | 2 |
| Bystrom, Columbus | .800 | 4 | 2 | 2 | 1 | 0 |
| Calderon, Maine* | .875 | 42 | 3 | 4 | 1 | 0 |
| Calvert, Maine | 1.000 | 17 | 5 | 5 | 0 | 0 |
| Carlucci, Syracuse | .909 | 39 | 6 | 14 | 2 | 1 |
| Cerutti, Syracuse* | .907 | 28 | 10 | 29 | 4 | 4 |
| Chiffer, Toledo | 1.000 | 51 | 3 | 12 | 0 | 0 |
| Christiansen, Columbus | .892 | 28 | 17 | 16 | 4 | 1 |
| Clark, Maine* | 1.000 | 4 | 2 | 6 | 0 | 1 |
| Clarke, Syracuse* | 1.000 | 43 | 6 | 9 | 0 | 1 |
| Clary, Richmond | .905 | 26 | 9 | 10 | 2 | 1 |
| Clay, Richmond | 1.000 | 47 | 3 | 18 | 0 | 2 |
| Cooper, Columbus | .857 | 33 | 3 | 9 | 2 | 0 |
| Couchee, Rochester | .900 | 20 | 3 | 6 | 1 | 1 |
| Creel, Maine | .958 | 19 | 8 | 15 | 1 | 0 |
| Dalena, Columbus | 1.000 | 2 | 2 | 0 | 0 | 0 |
| Davis, Syracuse* | 1.000 | 6 | 1 | 3 | 0 | 0 |
| Dedmon, Richmond | 1.000 | 10 | 0 | 3 | 0 | 0 |
| Deshaies, Columbus* | 1.000 | 21 | 3 | 11 | 0 | 1 |
| Dorsey, Pawtucket | .952 | 32 | 11 | 9 | 1 | 0 |
| Doyle, Maine | .889 | 8 | 3 | 5 | 1 | 1 |
| Eichelberger, Richmond | 1.000 | 17 | 1 | 0 | 0 | 0 |
| Eichhorn, Syracuse | 1.000 | 8 | 3 | 13 | 0 | 1 |
| Elston, Maine | 1.000 | 15 | 2 | 1 | 0 | 1 |
| Eufemia, Toledo | 1.000 | 14 | 4 | 1 | 0 | 0 |
| Faulk, Columbus | .882 | 18 | 7 | 23 | 4 | 2 |
| Fernandez, Tidewater* | 1.000 | 5 | 0 | 2 | 0 | 0 |
| Filer, Syracuse | .967 | 12 | 10 | 19 | 1 | 2 |
| Fisher, Columbus | 1.000 | 7 | 1 | 4 | 0 | 0 |
| Fultz, Tidewater | 1.000 | 18 | 9 | 9 | 0 | 1 |
| Fuson, 10 Paw-21 Maine | .938 | 31 | 20 | 25 | 3 | 3 |
| Gardner, Tidewater | .900 | 53 | 2 | 7 | 1 | 1 |
| Gering, Pawtucket | 1.000 | 6 | 1 | 3 | 0 | 1 |
| Gillam, Syracuse* | 1.000 | 6 | 0 | 4 | 0 | 1 |
| Gnacinski, Pawtucket | 1.000 | 34 | 10 | 11 | 0 | 2 |
| Gordon, Syracuse | .980 | 51 | 14 | 34 | 1 | 7 |
| Havens, Rochester* | .905 | 34 | 7 | 12 | 2 | 0 |
| Henderson, Toledo* | .833 | 4 | 2 | 3 | 1 | 0 |
| Henke, Syracuse | 1.000 | 39 | 2 | 4 | 0 | 0 |
| Herron, Pawtucket* | 1.000 | 21 | 1 | 6 | 0 | 0 |
| Hodge, Toledo* | .913 | 29 | 7 | 14 | 2 | 0 |
| Howard, Syracuse | 1.000 | 25 | 9 | 19 | 0 | 0 |
| Huffman, Rochester | .933 | 23 | 9 | 19 | 2 | 1 |
| Jackson, Rochester | .833 | 15 | 3 | 2 | 1 | 2 |
| Je. Johnson, Rochester | .933 | 28 | 3 | 11 | 1 | 0 |
| Jo. Johnson, Richmond | 1.000 | 9 | 4 | 6 | 0 | 3 |
| M. Johnson, Rochester | 1.000 | 30 | 11 | 16 | 0 | 1 |
| O. Jones, Rochester | 1.000 | 41 | 8 | 7 | 0 | 1 |
| Kane, Pawtucket | .967 | 31 | 6 | 23 | 1 | 0 |

| Player and Club | Pct. | G. | PO. | A. | E. | DP. |
|---|---|---|---|---|---|---|
| Kucharski, Rochester | .971 | 26 | 8 | 26 | 1 | 3 |
| Latham, Tidewater* | .980 | 24 | 15 | 33 | 1 | 3 |
| Leach, Tidewater | 1.000 | 24 | 2 | 9 | 0 | 1 |
| Leal, Syracuse | .929 | 12 | 6 | 7 | 1 | 0 |
| Leggatt, Richmond | 1.000 | 10 | 0 | 5 | 0 | 0 |
| Lysander, Toledo | 1.000 | 7 | 2 | 0 | 0 | 0 |
| McCarthy, Pawtucket | .957 | 26 | 10 | 12 | 1 | 1 |
| McLaughlin, Syracuse | 1.000 | 34 | 8 | 12 | 0 | 1 |
| McMurtry, Richmond | 1.000 | 16 | 9 | 33 | 0 | 1 |
| Mecerod, Pawtucket | .935 | 29 | 11 | 32 | 3 | 4 |
| Mitchell, Pawtucket | .971 | 64 | 13 | 21 | 1 | 3 |
| Morogiello, Richmond* | .833 | 44 | 6 | 9 | 3 | 2 |
| Musselman, Syracuse | .500 | 2 | 1 | 0 | 1 | 0 |
| Myers, Tidewater* | 1.000 | 8 | 1 | 4 | 0 | 0 |
| Niemann, Tidewater* | 1.000 | 30 | 14 | 27 | 0 | 0 |
| Oelkers, Toledo* | 1.000 | 12 | 3 | 5 | 0 | 0 |
| Olwine, Tidewater* | 1.000 | 55 | 3 | 13 | 0 | 1 |
| Patterson, Columbus | .917 | 21 | 3 | 8 | 1 | 0 |
| Payne, Richmond | 1.000 | 13 | 4 | 3 | 0 | 0 |
| Pippin, Maine | 1.000 | 36 | 6 | 9 | 0 | 2 |
| Portugal, Toledo | 1.000 | 19 | 15 | 20 | 0 | 3 |
| Puleo, Richmond | 1.000 | 16 | 5 | 9 | 0 | 1 |
| Pulido, Columbus* | 1.000 | 31 | 7 | 16 | 0 | 1 |
| Rajsich, Rochester* | .500 | 12 | 1 | 1 | 2 | 0 |
| Rasmussen, Columbus* | 1.000 | 7 | 2 | 8 | 0 | 0 |
| Reed, Maine | .960 | 14 | 12 | 12 | 1 | 1 |
| Ritter, Maine | 1.000 | 10 | 6 | 3 | 0 | 0 |
| Rochford, Pawtucket* | 1.000 | 12 | 7 | 6 | 0 | 1 |
| Rodgers, Syracuse | .857 | 13 | 2 | 4 | 1 | 1 |
| Roman, Maine | 1.000 | 11 | 4 | 3 | 0 | 0 |
| Romero, Maine* | .857 | 15 | 1 | 5 | 1 | 0 |
| Rowe, Maine | .875 | 30 | 6 | 22 | 4 | 1 |
| Sambito, Tidewater* | 1.000 | 19 | 0 | 6 | 0 | 1 |
| Schiraldi, Tidewater | .900 | 17 | 6 | 12 | 2 | 1 |
| Schuler, Richmond* | 1.000 | 41 | 2 | 11 | 0 | 0 |
| Schulze, Maine | 1.000 | 15 | 15 | 18 | 0 | 1 |
| Scott, Columbus | 1.000 | 21 | 6 | 16 | 0 | 1 |
| Shields, Richmond | .824 | 18 | 2 | 12 | 3 | 1 |
| Silva, Columbus | 1.000 | 43 | 2 | 9 | 0 | 1 |
| Sisk, Tidewater | 1.000 | 4 | 0 | 4 | 0 | 0 |
| Smith, Maine | .917 | 15 | 4 | 7 | 1 | 0 |
| SWAGGERTY, Rochester | 1.000 | 30 | 12 | 35 | 0 | 2 |
| Tewksbury, Columbus | .917 | 6 | 3 | 8 | 1 | 2 |
| Treadway, Richmond | 1.000 | 2 | 1 | 0 | 0 | 0 |
| Underwood, Columbus* | 1.000 | 19 | 0 | 4 | 0 | 0 |
| Von Ohlen, Maine* | 1.000 | 4 | 2 | 3 | 0 | 1 |
| Walters, Toledo | 1.000 | 11 | 2 | 6 | 0 | 2 |
| Ward, Richmond | 1.000 | 5 | 1 | 1 | 0 | 0 |
| Welchel, Rochester | 1.000 | 26 | 9 | 11 | 0 | 3 |
| West, Richmond | 1.000 | 23 | 14 | 19 | 0 | 1 |
| Whitehouse, Toledo* | .889 | 37 | 2 | 6 | 1 | 1 |
| A. Williams, Columbus | .889 | 26 | 10 | 14 | 3 | 1 |
| M. Williams, Syracuse | 1.000 | 22 | 17 | 17 | 0 | 1 |
| Woodward, Pawtucket | .900 | 15 | 7 | 11 | 2 | 1 |
| Yett, Toledo | .969 | 25 | 11 | 20 | 1 | 2 |

The following players do not have any recorded accepted chances at the positions indicated; therefore, are not listed in the fielding averages for those particular positions: Barrett, ss; Berenyi, p; Buckley, p; Burgess, p; Cruz, of; Curry, ss; Dalena, 3b; M. Davis, c; Dodson, of, p; Gaff, p; Glynn, p; Holman, p; Hudler, 1b; Ro. Jones, p; Lindsey, p; Molinaro, p; Paris, of; Reiter, p; Rosado, 3b; Siwy, p; Kei. Smith, 3b; Ken. Smith, of; Snell, p; Sosa, of; R. Thompson, p; T. Thompson, of.

## CLUB PITCHING

| Club | ERA. | G. | CG. | ShO. | Sv. | IP. | H. | R. | ER. | HR. | HB. | BB. | Int. BB. | SO. | WP. | Bk. |
|---|---|---|---|---|---|---|---|---|---|---|---|---|---|---|---|---|
| Tidewater | 3.10 | 139 | 18 | 11 | 36 | 1229.2 | 1127 | 512 | 423 | 74 | 26 | 468 | 29 | 726 | 37 | 8 |
| Richmond | 3.45 | 140 | 32 | 12 | 32 | 1224.1 | 1115 | 547 | 469 | 78 | 31 | 531 | 16 | 703 | 59 | 8 |
| Syracuse | 3.53 | 140 | 16 | 15 | 43 | 1236.0 | 1117 | 579 | 485 | 86 | 24 | 499 | 20 | 790 | 49 | 9 |
| Maine | 3.59 | 139 | 33 | 4 | 42 | 1208.2 | 1154 | 564 | 482 | 118 | 30 | 506 | 23 | 623 | 65 | 5 |
| Toledo | 3.88 | 139 | 26 | 6 | 36 | 1224.2 | 1257 | 611 | 528 | 121 | 26 | 526 | 11 | 710 | 62 | 16 |
| Columbus | 4.00 | 139 | 16 | 7 | 30 | 1203.0 | 1192 | 626 | 535 | 105 | 25 | 496 | 25 | 668 | 44 | 12 |
| Rochester | 4.14 | 139 | 29 | 12 | 20 | 1179.2 | 1213 | 614 | 542 | 104 | 24 | 436 | 30 | 664 | 46 | 6 |
| Pawtucket | 4.37 | 139 | 18 | 6 | 19 | 1212.2 | 1222 | 673 | 589 | 145 | 37 | 533 | 30 | 768 | 63 | 10 |

## PITCHERS' RECORDS
(Leading Qualifiers for Earned-Run Average Leadership — 112 or More Innings)

*Throws lefthanded.

| Pitcher — Club | W. | L. | Pct. | ERA. | G. | GS. | CG. | GF. | ShO. | Sv. | IP. | H. | R. | ER. | HR. | HB. | BB. | Int. BB. | SO. | WP. |
|---|---|---|---|---|---|---|---|---|---|---|---|---|---|---|---|---|---|---|---|---|
| Gordon, Syracuse | 8 | 5 | .615 | 2.07 | 51 | 0 | 0 | 30 | 0 | 12 | 113.0 | 93 | 39 | 26 | 4 | 5 | 21 | 2 | 43 | 1 |
| Shields, Richmond | 6 | 7 | .462 | 2.64 | 18 | 18 | 8 | 0 | 3 | 0 | 133.0 | 110 | 53 | 39 | 9 | 8 | 54 | 1 | 88 | 3 |
| Schulze, Maine | 6 | 4 | .600 | 2.65 | 15 | 15 | 5 | 0 | 1 | 0 | 115.1 | 105 | 41 | 34 | 7 | 2 | 29 | 0 | 45 | 2 |
| Latham, Tidewater* | 13 | 8 | .619 | 2.68 | 24 | 24 | 5 | 0 | 2 | 0 | 157.2 | 144 | 61 | 47 | 7 | 5 | 57 | 1 | 66 | 4 |
| Niemann, Tidewater* | 11 | 6 | .647 | 2.76 | 30 | 19 | 4 | 3 | 1 | 0 | 159.2 | 152 | 65 | 49 | 8 | 6 | 51 | 3 | 76 | 7 |
| Cerutti, Syracuse* | 11 | 9 | .550 | 2.97 | 28 | 27 | 7 | 1 | 2 | 0 | 182.0 | 165 | 84 | 60 | 10 | 2 | 60 | 2 | 110 | 6 |
| Swaggerty, Rochester | 11 | 13 | .458 | 3.24 | 30 | 26 | 10 | 1 | 2 | 0 | 189.0 | 187 | 73 | 68 | 11 | 2 | 52 | 4 | 58 | 9 |
| Brizzolara, Richmond | 10 | 12 | .455 | 3.27 | 33 | 22 | 8 | 6 | 2 | 2 | 165.0 | 146 | 72 | 60 | 12 | 2 | 63 | 2 | 76 | 9 |
| Clarke, Syracuse* | 14 | 4 | .778 | 3.37 | 43 | 14 | 1 | 17 | 0 | 2 | 117.2 | 106 | 52 | 44 | 13 | 0 | 66 | 2 | 98 | 5 |
| Pulido, Columbus* | 11 | 8 | .579 | 3.39 | 31 | 20 | 4 | 4 | 1 | 1 | 146.0 | 154 | 66 | 55 | 13 | 1 | 34 | 3 | 67 | 1 |

Departmental Leaders: G—Mitchell, 63; W—Burtt, Clarke, 14; L—Fuson, M. Johnson, Kucharski, Mecerod, Swaggerty, 13; Pct.—Clarke, .778; GS—Mecerod, 29; CG—Swaggerty, 10; GF—Mitchell, 56; ShO—Burtt, Shields, 3; Sv.—Gardner, Henke, 18; IP—Swaggerty, 189.0; H—Swaggerty, 187; R—Fuson, 102; ER—Fuson, 88; HR—Mecerod, 29; HB—Mi. Brown, Christiansen, Shields, 8; BB—Yett, 101; IBB—Je. Johnson, Mitchell, 8; SO—Havens, 129; WP—Yett, 16.

(All Pitchers—Listed Alphabetically)

| Pitcher—Club | W. | L. | Pct. | ERA. | G. | GS. | CG. | GF. | ShO. | Sv. | IP. | H. | R. | ER. | HR. | HB. | BB. | Int. BB. | SO. | WP. |
|---|---|---|---|---|---|---|---|---|---|---|---|---|---|---|---|---|---|---|---|---|
| Aguilera, Tidewater | 6 | 4 | .600 | 2.51 | 11 | 11 | 2 | 0 | 1 | 0 | 79.0 | 64 | 24 | 22 | 5 | 1 | 17 | 0 | 55 | 1 |
| Alba, Syracuse* | 2 | 3 | .400 | 5.66 | 17 | 7 | 0 | 6 | 0 | 1 | 55.2 | 48 | 41 | 35 | 2 | 1 | 51 | 0 | 33 | 3 |
| A. Anderson, Toledo* | 7 | 11 | .389 | 3.43 | 27 | 27 | 5 | 0 | 0 | 0 | 176.0 | 176 | 81 | 67 | 19 | 2 | 79 | 0 | 94 | 4 |
| K. Anderson, Tidewater | 1 | 0 | 1.000 | 0.00 | 2 | 0 | 0 | 0 | 0 | 0 | 6.2 | 3 | 0 | 0 | 0 | 0 | 2 | 1 | 2 | 0 |
| R. Anderson, Tidewater | 6 | 3 | .667 | 1.98 | 48 | 2 | 0 | 23 | 0 | 7 | 95.1 | 79 | 28 | 21 | 3 | 0 | 33 | 5 | 54 | 2 |
| Armstrong, Columbus | 2 | 2 | .500 | 6.64 | 21 | 3 | 0 | 5 | 0 | 2 | 40.2 | 49 | 31 | 30 | 7 | 0 | 26 | 0 | 40 | 7 |
| Augustine, Rochester* | 6 | 3 | .667 | 3.96 | 43 | 0 | 0 | 22 | 0 | 6 | 61.1 | 61 | 33 | 27 | 2 | 1 | 24 | 1 | 36 | 2 |
| Barkley, Maine | 1 | 4 | .200 | 1.62 | 24 | 0 | 0 | 21 | 0 | 13 | 39.0 | 32 | 12 | 7 | 0 | 1 | 21 | 3 | 34 | 2 |
| Beard, Maine | 1 | 0 | 1.000 | 2.49 | 16 | 0 | 0 | 10 | 0 | 1 | 21.2 | 21 | 7 | 6 | 2 | 0 | 11 | 1 | 15 | 2 |
| Behenna, Maine | 3 | 1 | .750 | 2.57 | 6 | 6 | 0 | 0 | 0 | 0 | 28.0 | 21 | 8 | 8 | 5 | 1 | 12 | 0 | 10 | 3 |
| Berenyi, Tidewater | 0 | 0 | .000 | 9.00 | 1 | 1 | 0 | 0 | 0 | 0 | 1.0 | 3 | 1 | 1 | 0 | 0 | 0 | 0 | 1 | 0 |
| Bettendorf, Tidewater | 0 | 7 | .000 | 5.47 | 28 | 9 | 0 | 9 | 0 | 2 | 82.1 | 89 | 54 | 50 | 7 | 2 | 39 | 1 | 43 | 1 |
| Biercevicz, Rochester | 0 | 3 | .000 | 3.72 | 27 | 2 | 1 | 11 | 0 | 3 | 67.2 | 68 | 31 | 28 | 5 | 3 | 28 | 1 | 33 | 2 |
| Bittiger, Tidewater | 11 | 7 | .611 | 3.69 | 24 | 24 | 2 | 0 | 0 | 0 | 131.2 | 131 | 62 | 54 | 14 | 1 | 52 | 2 | 66 | 2 |
| Bradley, Columbus | 1 | 7 | .125 | 4.83 | 11 | 8 | 0 | 2 | 0 | 0 | 54.0 | 68 | 35 | .29 | 6 | 0 | 15 | 0 | 11 | 0 |
| Briggs, Columbus* | 0 | 0 | .000 | 0.00 | 2 | 0 | 0 | 2 | 0 | 0 | 6.0 | 5 | 1 | 0 | 0 | 0 | 2 | 0 | 7 | 3 |
| Brito, Rochester | 0 | 1 | .000 | 7.30 | 8 | 0 | 0 | 2 | 0 | 0 | 12.1 | 15 | 11 | 10 | 0 | 0 | 11 | 3 | 9 | 0 |
| Brizzolara, Richmond | 10 | 12 | .455 | 3.27 | 33 | 22 | 8 | 6 | 2 | 2 | 165.0 | 146 | 72 | 60 | 12 | 2 | 63 | 2 | 76 | 9 |
| Broersma, Toledo | 4 | 5 | .444 | 3.74 | 46 | 0 | 0 | 26 | 0 | 8 | 79.1 | 73 | 38 | 33 | 8 | 4 | 31 | 1 | 63 | 4 |
| C. Brown, Columbus | 8 | 3 | .727 | 4.88 | 47 | 2 | 0 | 18 | 0 | 2 | 86.2 | 110 | 57 | 47 | 6 | 1 | 28 | 7 | 40 | 1 |
| Ma. Brown, Toledo | 2 | 2 | .500 | 2.94 | 26 | 2 | 0 | 10 | 0 | 5 | 67.1 | 71 | 30 | 22 | 3 | 2 | 22 | 1 | 26 | 4 |
| Mi. Brown, Pawtucket | 2 | 5 | .286 | 5.60 | 20 | 6 | 0 | 8 | 0 | 2 | 70.2 | 78 | 52 | 44 | 5 | 8 | 25 | 3 | 51 | 1 |
| Buckley, Toledo | 0 | 0 | .000 | 0.00 | 1 | 0 | 0 | 1 | 0 | 0 | 1.0 | 0 | 0 | 0 | 0 | 0 | 0 | 0 | 1 | 0 |
| Burgess, Pawtucket* | 0 | 0 | .000 | 18.00 | 1 | 0 | 0 | 1 | 0 | 0 | 1.0 | 1 | 2 | 2 | 0 | 0 | 4 | 0 | 1 | 0 |
| Burtt, Toledo | 14 | 8 | .636 | 4.13 | 27 | 27 | 6 | 0 | 3 | 0 | 172.1 | 182 | 96 | 79 | 15 | 3 | 67 | 1 | 95 | 9 |
| Bystrom, Columbus | 2 | 0 | 1.000 | 1.88 | 4 | 4 | 0 | 0 | 0 | 0 | 24.0 | 13 | 7 | 5 | 1 | 0 | 9 | 0 | 16 | 1 |
| Calderon, Maine* | 3 | 5 | .375 | 5.90 | 42 | 1 | 0 | 18 | 0 | 4 | 50.1 | 53 | 36 | 33 | 6 | 1 | 37 | 4 | 37 | 4 |
| Calvert, Maine | 2 | 4 | .333 | 4.82 | 17 | 6 | 0 | 3 | 0 | 1 | 61.2 | 68 | 42 | 33 | 5 | 2 | 32 | 2 | 23 | 4 |
| Carlucci, Syracuse | 4 | 3 | .571 | 2.35 | 39 | 0 | 0 | 18 | 0 | 8 | 72.2 | 77 | 30 | 19 | 1 | 4 | 26 | 4 | 50 | 3 |
| Cerutti, Syracuse* | 11 | 9 | .550 | 2.97 | 28 | 27 | 7 | 1 | 2 | 0 | 182.0 | 165 | 84 | 60 | 10 | 2 | 60 | 2 | 110 | 6 |
| Chiffer, Toledo | 9 | 7 | .563 | 2.49 | 51 | 0 | 0 | 40 | 0 | 13 | 79.2 | 83 | 26 | 22 | 9 | 3 | 19 | 1 | 49 | 7 |
| Christiansen, Columbus | 10 | 6 | .625 | 3.66 | 28 | 18 | 3 | 6 | 2 | 1 | 137.2 | 128 | 66 | 56 | 9 | 8 | 59 | 4 | 67 | 7 |
| Clark, Maine* | 1 | 0 | 1.000 | 0.96 | 4 | 2 | 0 | 1 | 0 | 0 | 18.2 | 15 | 2 | 2 | 0 | 0 | 8 | 0 | 9 | 4 |
| Clarke, Syracuse* | 14 | 4 | .778 | 3.37 | 43 | 14 | 1 | 17 | 0 | 2 | 117.2 | 106 | 52 | 44 | 13 | 0 | 66 | 2 | 98 | 5 |
| Clary, Richmond | 8 | 12 | .400 | 4.19 | 26 | 25 | 0 | 1 | 0 | 0 | 156.2 | 155 | 81 | 73 | 7 | 5 | 77 | 1 | 76 | 9 |
| Clay, Richmond | 4 | 5 | .444 | 3.57 | 47 | 2 | 1 | 18 | 0 | 5 | 98.1 | 112 | 46 | 39 | 9 | 6 | 34 | 2 | 48 | 5 |
| Cooper, Columbus | 7 | 3 | .700 | 2.37 | 33 | 4 | 0 | 25 | 0 | 10 | 68.1 | 61 | 23 | 18 | 7 | 0 | 21 | 1 | 59 | 1 |
| Couchee, Rochester | 1 | 4 | .200 | 6.49 | 20 | 2 | 1 | 11 | 0 | 0 | 52.2 | 59 | 39 | 38 | 3 | 3 | 23 | 4 | 20 | 4 |
| Creel, Maine | 7 | 7 | .500 | 3.70 | 19 | 19 | 6 | 0 | 1 | 0 | 124.0 | 121 | 59 | 51 | 13 | 4 | 38 | 1 | 58 | 3 |
| Dalena, Columbus | 0 | 0 | .000 | 12.00 | 2 | 0 | 0 | 1 | 0 | 0 | 3.0 | 5 | 5 | 4 | 1 | 0 | 3 | 0 | 1 | 0 |
| Davis, Syracuse* | 3 | 2 | .600 | 2.50 | 6 | 6 | 0 | 0 | 0 | 0 | 36.0 | 19 | 11 | 10 | 2 | 1 | 17 | 0 | 34 | 4 |
| Dedmon, Richmond | 1 | 1 | .500 | 1.50 | 10 | 0 | 0 | 10 | 0 | 5 | 12.0 | 12 | 2 | 2 | 0 | 0 | 3 | 0 | 7 | 1 |
| Deshaies, Columbus* | 8 | 6 | .571 | 4.31 | 21 | 21 | 3 | 0 | 0 | 0 | 131.2 | 124 | 67 | 63 | 16 | 1 | 59 | 1 | 106 | 3 |
| Dodson, Pawtucket* | 0 | 0 | .000 | 0.00 | 3 | 0 | 0 | 2 | 0 | 0 | 3.2 | 2 | 0 | 0 | 0 | 0 | 4 | 0 | 1 | 0 |
| Dorsey, Pawtucket | 8 | 8 | .500 | 4.31 | 32 | 18 | 3 | 7 | 1 | 1 | 146.1 | 136 | 73 | 70 | 16 | 6 | 53 | 2 | 110 | 7 |
| Doyle, Maine | 1 | 3 | .250 | 4.97 | 8 | 6 | 0 | 1 | 0 | 0 | 38.0 | 47 | 27 | 21 | 5 | 1 | 18 | 0 | 16 | 3 |
| Eichelberger, Richmond | 4 | 1 | .800 | 3.00 | 17 | 0 | 0 | 12 | 0 | 3 | 21.0 | 20 | 7 | 7 | 0 | 0 | 7 | 0 | 15 | 0 |
| Eichhorn, Syracuse | 2 | 5 | .286 | 4.82 | 8 | 7 | 0 | 1 | 0 | 0 | 37.1 | 38 | 24 | 20 | 5 | 0 | 7 | 0 | 27 | 1 |
| Elston, Maine | 2 | 1 | .667 | 6.06 | 15 | 1 | 0 | 7 | 0 | 2 | 32.2 | 37 | 23 | 22 | 5 | 2 | 28 | 1 | 28 | 1 |
| Eufemia, Toledo | 3 | 1 | .750 | 1.49 | 14 | 0 | 0 | 9 | 0 | 3 | 36.1 | 23 | 6 | 6 | 3 | 0 | 12 | 0 | 23 | 1 |
| Faulk, Columbus | 4 | 7 | .364 | 5.42 | 18 | 16 | 1 | 2 | 0 | 0 | 84.2 | 90 | 57 | 51 | 7 | 4 | 48 | 1 | 40 | 4 |
| Fernandez, Tidewater* | 4 | 1 | .800 | 2.04 | 5 | 5 | 1 | 0 | 0 | 0 | 35.1 | 17 | 8 | 8 | 2 | 0 | 21 | 0 | 42 | 1 |
| Filer, Syracuse | 7 | 2 | .778 | 2.53 | 12 | 12 | 1 | 0 | 0 | 0 | 78.1 | 67 | 24 | 22 | 6 | 1 | 22 | 0 | 31 | 4 |
| Fisher, Columbus | 0 | 0 | .000 | 2.38 | 7 | 0 | 0 | 4 | 0 | 0 | 11.1 | 8 | 4 | 3 | 0 | 1 | 7 | 0 | 12 | 2 |
| Fultz, Columbus | 5 | 4 | .556 | 3.88 | 18 | 17 | 3 | 0 | 1 | 0 | 109.0 | 110 | 51 | 47 | 12 | 1 | 27 | 3 | 52 | 0 |
| Fuson, 10 Paw-21 Maine | 5 | 13 | .278 | 4.94 | 31 | 25 | 5 | 1 | 0 | 1 | 160.1 | 183 | 102 | 88 | 15 | 6 | 88 | 7 | 84 | 14 |
| Gaff, Tidewater | 1 | 0 | 1.000 | 0.00 | 1 | 0 | 0 | 0 | 0 | 0 | 3.0 | 4 | 0 | 0 | 0 | 0 | 1 | 0 | 2 | 0 |
| Gardner, Tidewater | 7 | 6 | .538 | 2.82 | 53 | 0 | 0 | 42 | 0 | 18 | 76.2 | 57 | 31 | 24 | 6 | 1 | 34 | 3 | 75 | 5 |
| Gering, Pawtucket | 0 | 2 | .000 | 5.84 | 6 | 1 | 0 | 2 | 0 | 0 | 12.1 | 16 | 12 | 8 | 3 | 0 | 6 | 0 | 12 | 0 |
| Gillam, Syracuse* | 0 | 0 | .000 | 4.32 | 6 | 0 | 0 | 3 | 0 | 1 | 8.1 | 10 | 6 | 4 | 0 | 0 | 5 | 0 | 3 | 0 |
| Glynn, Pawtucket* | 0 | 0 | .000 | 5.40 | 5 | 0 | 0 | 1 | 0 | 1 | 5.0 | 7 | 3 | 3 | 0 | 0 | 2 | 0 | 8 | 0 |
| Gnacinski, Pawtucket | 2 | 7 | .222 | 4.39 | 34 | 3 | 0 | 18 | 0 | 1 | 82.0 | 73 | 44 | 40 | 9 | 1 | 48 | 2 | 44 | 5 |
| Gordon, Syracuse | 8 | 5 | .615 | 2.07 | 51 | 0 | 0 | 30 | 0 | 12 | 113.0 | 93 | 39 | 26 | 4 | 5 | 21 | 2 | 43 | 1 |
| Havens, Rochester* | 8 | 10 | .444 | 4.85 | 34 | 19 | 2 | 12 | 0 | 5 | 133.2 | 135 | 79 | 72 | 15 | 1 | 52 | 0 | 129 | 6 |
| Henderson, Toledo* | 1 | 2 | .333 | 4.91 | 4 | 4 | 0 | 0 | 0 | 0 | 18.1 | 23 | 10 | 10 | 0 | 0 | 15 | 0 | 8 | 2 |
| Henke, Syracuse | 2 | 1 | .667 | 0.88 | 39 | 0 | 0 | 32 | 0 | 18 | 51.1 | 13 | 5 | 5 | 2 | 1 | 18 | 2 | 60 | 1 |
| Herron, Pawtucket* | 0 | 0 | .000 | 0.00 | 4 | 0 | 0 | 8 | 0 | 0 | 33.0 | 39 | 29 | 25 | 8 | 0 | 22 | 2 | 31 | 6 |
| Hodge, Toledo* | 9 | 7 | .563 | 4.50 | 29 | 25 | 2 | 0 | 0 | 0 | 152.0 | 183 | 87 | 76 | 18 | 5 | 45 | 1 | 80 | 5 |
| Holman, Columbus | 0 | 0 | .000 | 13.50 | 1 | 0 | 0 | 1 | 0 | 0 | 2.0 | 4 | 3 | 3 | 0 | 0 | 2 | 0 | 0 | 1 |
| Howard, Syracuse | 7 | 9 | .438 | 5.05 | 25 | 19 | 1 | 3 | 0 | 0 | 130.0 | 141 | 79 | 73 | 12 | 2 | 53 | 2 | 63 | 5 |
| Huffman, Rochester | 10 | 10 | .500 | 3.49 | 23 | 23 | 6 | 0 | 2 | 0 | 152.0 | 140 | 73 | 59 | 15 | 3 | 48 | 2 | 78 | 4 |
| Jackson, Rochester | 1 | 1 | .500 | 3.00 | 15 | 0 | 0 | 11 | 0 | 2 | 27.0 | 26 | 12 | 9 | 4 | 2 | 8 | 2 | 25 | 2 |
| Je. Johnson, Rochester | 4 | 11 | .267 | 5.14 | 28 | 14 | 1 | 8 | 0 | 0 | 98.0 | 119 | 62 | 56 | 17 | 0 | 43 | 8 | 46 | 4 |
| Jo. Johnson, Richmond | 7 | 1 | .875 | 2.13 | 9 | 9 | 5 | 0 | 1 | 0 | 72.0 | 60 | 22 | 17 | 4 | 3 | 10 | 0 | 50 | 1 |
| M. Johnson, Pawtucket | 5 | 13 | .278 | 4.48 | 30 | 25 | 2 | 2 | 0 | 0 | 156.2 | 174 | 93 | 78 | 19 | 2 | 37 | 1 | 63 | 2 |
| O. Jones, Rochester | 4 | 6 | .400 | 4.20 | 41 | 7 | 1 | 21 | 0 | 3 | 105.0 | 97 | 52 | 49 | 13 | 4 | 45 | 0 | 104 | 4 |
| R. Jones, Tidewater | 0 | 0 | .000 | 18.00 | 1 | 0 | 0 | 1 | 0 | 0 | 1.0 | 4 | 2 | 2 | 0 | 0 | 0 | 0 | 0 | 0 |
| Kane, Pawtucket | 3 | 11 | .214 | 4.89 | 31 | 12 | 1 | 10 | 0 | 0 | 105.0 | 118 | 66 | 57 | 13 | 5 | 35 | 2 | 59 | 8 |
| Kucharski, Rochester | 6 | 13 | .316 | 4.36 | 26 | 25 | 1 | 0 | 0 | 0 | 144.1 | 159 | 79 | 70 | 12 | 4 | 45 | 3 | 54 | 4 |
| Latham, Tidewater* | 13 | 8 | .619 | 2.68 | 24 | 24 | 5 | 0 | 2 | 0 | 157.2 | 144 | 61 | 47 | 7 | 5 | 57 | 1 | 66 | 4 |
| Leach, Tidewater | 1 | 0 | 1.000 | 1.59 | 24 | 0 | 0 | 12 | 0 | 4 | 45.1 | 33 | 12 | 8 | 1 | 0 | 8 | 1 | 25 | 0 |
| Leal, Syracuse | 6 | 2 | .750 | 3.91 | 12 | 12 | 0 | 0 | 0 | 0 | 69.0 | 69 | 32 | 30 | 2 | 2 | 20 | 0 | 43 | 3 |
| Leggatt, Richmond | 0 | 0 | .000 | 2.79 | 10 | 1 | 0 | 4 | 0 | 0 | 19.1 | 17 | 9 | 6 | 2 | 0 | 9 | 0 | 11 | 3 |
| Lindsey, Columbus | 0 | 0 | .000 | 9.00 | 1 | 0 | 0 | 1 | 0 | 0 | 1.0 | 1 | 1 | 1 | 0 | 0 | 0 | 0 | 0 | 0 |
| Lysander, Toledo | 1 | 0 | 1.000 | 0.87 | 7 | 0 | 0 | 6 | 0 | 3 | 10.1 | 7 | 1 | 1 | 0 | 0 | 5 | 1 | 8 | 0 |
| McCarthy, Pawtucket | 5 | 6 | .455 | 3.59 | 26 | 10 | 3 | 6 | 1 | 0 | 85.1 | 72 | 48 | 34 | 6 | 2 | 62 | 1 | 65 | 11 |

| Pitcher—Club | W. | L. | Pct. | ERA. | G. | GS. | CG. | GF. | ShO. | Sv. | IP. | H. | R. | ER. | HR. | HB. | BB. | Int. BB. | SO. | WP. |
|---|---|---|---|---|---|---|---|---|---|---|---|---|---|---|---|---|---|---|---|---|
| McLaughlin, Syracuse | 4 | 3 | .571 | 4.35 | 34 | 10 | 1 | 4 | 0 | 1 | 101.1 | 91 | 56 | 49 | 9 | 0 | 66 | 2 | 73 | 7 |
| McMurtry, Richmond | 7 | 5 | .583 | 3.27 | 16 | 16 | 4 | 0 | 2 | 0 | 107.1 | 88 | 43 | 39 | 7 | 1 | 51 | 1 | 74 | 4 |
| Mecerod, Pawtucket | 9 | 13 | .409 | 3.93 | 29 | 29 | 3 | 0 | 1 | 0 | 185.1 | 167 | 90 | 81 | 29 | 6 | 85 | 3 | 105 | 6 |
| Mitchell, Pawtucket | 5 | 9 | .357 | 2.90 | 63 | 0 | 0 | 56 | 0 | 14 | 111.2 | 117 | 39 | 36 | 7 | 1 | 43 | 8 | 65 | 9 |
| Molinaro, Rochester | 0 | 0 | .000 | 0.00 | 1 | 0 | 0 | 1 | 0 | 0 | 1.0 | 1 | 0 | 0 | 0 | 0 | 1 | 0 | 0 | 0 |
| Morogiello, Richmond° | 6 | 0 | 1.000 | 4.57 | 44 | 1 | 0 | 22 | 0 | 4 | 86.2 | 91 | 47 | 44 | 9 | 0 | 22 | 2 | 31 | 2 |
| Musselman, Syracuse | 1 | 0 | 1.000 | 4.91 | 2 | 2 | 0 | 0 | 0 | 0 | 11.0 | 13 | 7 | 6 | 3 | 0 | 1 | 0 | 5 | 0 |
| Myers, Tidewater° | 1 | 1 | .500 | 1.84 | 8 | 7 | 0 | 0 | 0 | 0 | 44.0 | 40 | 13 | 9 | 1 | 1 | 20 | 1 | 25 | 4 |
| Niemann, Tidewater° | 11 | 6 | .647 | 2.76 | 30 | 19 | 4 | 3 | 1 | 0 | 159.2 | 152 | 65 | 49 | 8 | 6 | 51 | 3 | 76 | 7 |
| Oelkers, Toledo° | 0 | 4 | .000 | 6.75 | 12 | 8 | 0 | 2 | 0 | 0 | 48.0 | 58 | 39 | 36 | 12 | 0 | 26 | 0 | 30 | 3 |
| Olwine, Tidewater° | 4 | 7 | .364 | 2.86 | 55 | 0 | 0 | 21 | 0 | 5 | 66.0 | 60 | 23 | 21 | 2 | 5 | 26 | 5 | 50 | 6 |
| Patterson, Columbus | 5 | 2 | .714 | 3.35 | 21 | 0 | 0 | 9 | 0 | 3 | 37.2 | 30 | 16 | 14 | 3 | 1 | 12 | 3 | 26 | 0 |
| Payne, Richmond | 5 | 4 | .556 | 5.10 | 13 | 13 | 0 | 0 | 0 | 0 | 60.0 | 65 | 41 | 34 | 5 | 3 | 64 | 0 | 18 | 10 |
| Pippin, Maine | 7 | 3 | .700 | 2.70 | 36 | 0 | 0 | 29 | 0 | 15 | 60.0 | 41 | 20 | 18 | 5 | 2 | 35 | 1 | 52 | 7 |
| Portugal, Toledo | 8 | 5 | .615 | 3.78 | 19 | 19 | 5 | 0 | 1 | 0 | 128.2 | 129 | 60 | 54 | 10 | 0 | 60 | 0 | 89 | 4 |
| Puleo, Richmond | 5 | 4 | .556 | 2.79 | 16 | 9 | 2 | 5 | 1 | 2 | 71.0 | 50 | 23 | 22 | 2 | 1 | 37 | 0 | 63 | 6 |
| Pulido, Columbus° | 11 | 8 | .579 | 3.39 | 31 | 20 | 4 | 4 | 1 | 1 | 146.0 | 154 | 66 | 55 | 13 | 1 | 34 | 3 | 67 | 1 |
| Rajsich, Rochester° | 0 | 2 | .000 | 5.40 | 12 | 0 | 0 | 7 | 0 | 1 | 13.1 | 19 | 14 | 8 | 0 | 1 | 7 | 0 | 6 | 1 |
| Rasmussen, Columbus° | 0 | 3 | .000 | 3.80 | 7 | 7 | 1 | 0 | 0 | 0 | 45.0 | 41 | 24 | 19 | 1 | 1 | 25 | 0 | 43 | 3 |
| Reed, Maine | 8 | 5 | .615 | 3.40 | 14 | 14 | 5 | 0 | 0 | 0 | 95.1 | 88 | 41 | 36 | 10 | 2 | 37 | 0 | 47 | 4 |
| Reiter, Richmond° | 0 | 0 | .000 | 7.20 | 4 | 0 | 0 | 2 | 0 | 0 | 5.0 | 4 | 4 | 4 | 2 | 0 | 2 | 0 | 6 | 1 |
| Ritter, Maine | 4 | 3 | .571 | 4.25 | 10 | 9 | 3 | 0 | 1 | 0 | 53.0 | 51 | 26 | 25 | 8 | 0 | 17 | 0 | 24 | 1 |
| Rochford, Pawtucket° | 5 | 2 | .714 | 4.13 | 12 | 12 | 1 | 0 | 1 | 0 | 72.0 | 74 | 34 | 33 | 12 | 0 | 32 | 0 | 47 | 1 |
| Rodgers, Syracuse | 1 | 1 | .500 | 3.15 | 13 | 4 | 0 | 6 | 0 | 0 | 34.1 | 39 | 13 | 12 | 1 | 0 | 13 | 1 | 17 | 0 |
| Roman, Maine | 4 | 1 | .800 | 3.65 | 11 | 9 | 0 | 1 | 0 | 0 | 49.1 | 46 | 23 | 20 | 7 | 1 | 30 | 0 | 27 | 3 |
| Romero, Maine° | 0 | 2 | .000 | 3.00 | 15 | 1 | 1 | 6 | 0 | 4 | 42.0 | 35 | 17 | 14 | 4 | 2 | 23 | 4 | 23 | 5 |
| Rowe, Maine | 10 | 8 | .556 | 3.44 | 30 | 14 | 4 | 4 | 0 | 0 | 131.0 | 130 | 63 | 50 | 12 | 3 | 39 | 2 | 51 | 4 |
| Sambito, Tidewater° | 0 | 3 | .000 | 4.35 | 19 | 0 | 0 | 10 | 0 | 0 | 20.2 | 31 | 15 | 10 | 1 | 0 | 11 | 3 | 12 | 1 |
| Schiraldi, Tidewater | 4 | 5 | .444 | 3.50 | 17 | 17 | 1 | 0 | 0 | 0 | 100.1 | 91 | 50 | 39 | 5 | 3 | 56 | 0 | 76 | 1 |
| Schuler, Richmond° | 4 | 3 | .571 | 2.58 | 41 | 0 | 0 | 25 | 0 | 11 | 73.1 | 52 | 23 | 21 | 4 | 0 | 23 | 5 | 61 | 0 |
| Schulze, Maine | 6 | 4 | .600 | 2.65 | 15 | 15 | 5 | 0 | 1 | 0 | 115.1 | 105 | 41 | 34 | 7 | 2 | 29 | 0 | 45 | 2 |
| Scott, Columbus | 4 | 5 | .444 | 3.99 | 21 | 12 | 3 | 4 | 0 | 0 | 94.2 | 97 | 47 | 42 | 14 | 2 | 26 | 1 | 32 | 1 |
| Shields, Richmond | 6 | 7 | .462 | 2.64 | 18 | 18 | 8 | 0 | 3 | 0 | 133.0 | 110 | 53 | 39 | 9 | 8 | 54 | 1 | 88 | 3 |
| Silva, Columbus | 6 | 5 | .545 | 3.90 | 43 | 0 | 0 | 29 | 0 | 9 | 60.0 | 48 | 31 | 26 | 4 | 2 | 48 | 2 | 31 | 3 |
| Sisk, Tidewater | 0 | 2 | .000 | 7.20 | 4 | 3 | 0 | 0 | 0 | 0 | 15.0 | 15 | 12 | 12 | 0 | 0 | 13 | 0 | 4 | 2 |
| Siwy, Maine | 0 | 1 | .000 | 18.56 | 2 | 2 | 0 | 0 | 0 | 0 | 5.1 | 13 | 12 | 11 | 3 | 3 | 4 | 0 | 1 | 1 |
| Smith, Maine | 10 | 4 | .714 | 2.39 | 15 | 15 | 6 | 0 | 0 | 0 | 109.1 | 84 | 33 | 29 | 10 | 0 | 29 | 0 | 65 | 2 |
| Snell, Rochester | 0 | 0 | .000 | 0.00 | 2 | 2 | 0 | 0 | 0 | 0 | 4.2 | 4 | 0 | 0 | 0 | 0 | 0 | 0 | 3 | 0 |
| Swaggerty, Rochester | 11 | 13 | .458 | 3.24 | 30 | 26 | 10 | 1 | 2 | 0 | 189.0 | 187 | 73 | 68 | 11 | 2 | 52 | 4 | 58 | 9 |
| Tewksbury, Columbus | 3 | 0 | 1.000 | 1.02 | 6 | 6 | 1 | 0 | 1 | 0 | 44.0 | 27 | 5 | 5 | 2 | 0 | 5 | 0 | 21 | 0 |
| Thompson, Maine | 0 | 0 | .000 | 1.00 | 4 | 0 | 0 | 2 | 0 | 1 | 9.0 | 6 | 1 | 1 | 0 | 1 | 2 | 1 | 2 | 0 |
| Treadway, Richmond | 0 | 0 | .000 | 1.80 | 2 | 0 | 0 | 0 | 0 | 0 | 5.0 | 3 | 1 | 1 | 0 | 0 | 3 | 1 | 3 | 0 |
| Underwood, Columbus° | 1 | 2 | .333 | 6.64 | 19 | 2 | 0 | 9 | 0 | 2 | 20.1 | 18 | 21 | 15 | 2 | 1 | 16 | 0 | 11 | 1 |
| Von Ohlen, Maine° | 2 | 1 | .667 | 3.80 | 4 | 3 | 1 | 1 | 0 | 0 | 23.2 | 26 | 11 | 10 | 2 | 0 | 2 | 0 | 7 | 0 |
| Walters, Toledo | 2 | 1 | .667 | 1.98 | 11 | 1 | 0 | 3 | 0 | 0 | 27.1 | 18 | 7 | 6 | 3 | 0 | 10 | 1 | 16 | 1 |
| Ward, Richmond | 0 | 1 | .000 | 11.81 | 5 | 1 | 0 | 3 | 0 | 0 | 5.1 | 8 | 9 | 7 | 1 | 1 | 8 | 0 | 3 | 0 |
| Welchel, Rochester | 7 | 4 | .636 | 3.75 | 26 | 19 | 2 | 3 | 1 | 0 | 117.2 | 123 | 56 | 49 | 7 | 0 | 49 | 2 | 63 | 4 |
| West, Richmond | 8 | 9 | .471 | 3.71 | 23 | 23 | 4 | 0 | 0 | 0 | 133.1 | 122 | 64 | 55 | 5 | 1 | 64 | 1 | 73 | 5 |
| Whitehouse, Toledo° | 2 | 4 | .333 | 5.63 | 37 | 1 | 0 | 17 | 0 | 4 | 64.0 | 69 | 48 | 40 | 7 | 3 | 34 | 2 | 30 | 2 |
| A. Williams, Columbus | 3 | 5 | .375 | 4.40 | 26 | 16 | 0 | 2 | 0 | 0 | 106.1 | 115 | 62 | 52 | 6 | 2 | 52 | 2 | 38 | 6 |
| M. Williams, Syracuse | 7 | 12 | .368 | 4.43 | 22 | 20 | 5 | 2 | 2 | 0 | 136.0 | 124 | 73 | 67 | 14 | 5 | 51 | 3 | 100 | 5 |
| Woodward, Pawtucket | 3 | 8 | .273 | 4.46 | 15 | 14 | 2 | 0 | 0 | 0 | 82.2 | 79 | 46 | 41 | 9 | 2 | 41 | 2 | 70 | 3 |
| Yett, Toledo | 9 | 11 | .450 | 4.15 | 25 | 25 | 8 | 0 | 1 | 0 | 165.0 | 162 | 82 | 76 | 14 | 4 | 101 | 2 | 99 | 16 |

BALKS—Deshaies, 4; Alba, A. Anderson, Broersma, Dorsey, Portugal, West, 3 each; Aguilera, Brizzolara, Christiansen, Fuson, Havens, Je. Johnson, Leal, Niemann, Whitehouse, 2 each; Beard, Bittiger, Bradley, Ma. Brown, Calvert, Cerutti, Chiffer, Clary, Cooper, Faulk, Filer, Gillam, Gnacinski, Henderson, Herron, Hodge, M. Johnson, O. Jones, Kane, Kucharski, Latham, McLaughlin, McMurtry, Mecerod, Olwine, Pulido, Rasmussen, Reed, Romero, Schiraldi, Schulze, Shields, Tewksbury, Yett, 1 each.

COMBINATION SHUTOUTS—Williams-Pulido-Silva, Cooper-Brown, Armstrong-Cooper, Columbus; Smith-Pippin, Maine; McCarthy-Mitchell, Mecerod-Mitchell, Pawtucket; Clay-Schuler, McMurtry-Schuler, Brizzolara-Schuler-Morogiello, Richmond; Huffman-Augustine, Kucharski-Swaggerty-Welchel-Brito, Havens-Jackson, Welchel-Biercevicz, Johnson-O. Jones, Rochester; Howard-Henke, Williams-McLaughlin, Clarke-Carlucci, Clarke-Gordon, Leal-Gordon, Davis-Carlucci-Clarke, Leal-McLaughlin-Williams, Davis-Gordon, Leal-Clarke, Cerutti-Carlucci-Clarke-Gordon, Rodgers-Gordon, Syracuse; Fernandez-Anderson-Olwine-Gardner, Aguilera-Gardner, Bittiger-Leach, Fultz-Gardner, Myers-Gardner, Latham-Gardner, Tidewater; Hodge-Lysander, Toledo.

NO-HIT GAMES—None.

# Mexican League

## CLASS AAA

### CHAMPIONSHIP WINNERS IN PREVIOUS YEARS

| | | |
|---|---|---|
| 1955—Mexico City Tigers° ............. .539 | 1968—Mexico City Reds ................. .586 | 1977—Mexico City Reds ................. .623 |
| 1956—Mexico City Reds ................ .692 | 1969—Reynosa ................................ .591 | Nuevo Laredo x .................... .507 |
| 1957—Yucatan .............................. .567 | 1970—Aguila§ ................................ .580 | 1978—Aguascalientes x .................... .589 |
| Mex. C. Reds (2nd)† ........... .550 | Mexico City Reds ................. .607 | Union Laguna ........................ .523 |
| 1958—Nuevo Laredo ..................... .625 | 1971—Jalisco§ ................................ .558 | 1979—Saltillo .............................. .704 |
| 1959—Poza Rica ............................ .575 | Saltillo ................................ .593 | Puebla x ................................ .628 |
| Mex. C. Reds (3rd)† ........... .507 | 1972—Saltillo ................................ .636 | 1980—No champion y |
| 1960—Mexico City Tigers ............... .538 | Cordoba§ ............................ .541 | 1981—Mexico City Reds ................. .615 |
| 1961—Veracruz ............................ .575 | 1973—Saltillo ................................ .656 | Reynosa ................................ .492 |
| 1962—Monterrey .......................... .592 | Mexico City Reds x ............. .590 | 1982—Ciudad Juarez x ................... .570 |
| 1963—Puebla ............................... .606 | 1974—Jalisco ................................ .627 | Mexico City Tigers ............... .508 |
| 1964—Mexico City Reds ................ .586 | Mexico City Reds x ............. .551 | 1983—Campeche z ......................... .614 |
| 1965—Mexico City Tigers ............... .590 | 1975—Tampico x ............................ .541 | Ciudad Juarez ..................... .535 |
| 1966—Mexico City Tigers‡ ............. .614 | Cordoba ............................... .649 | 1984—Yucatan z ......................... .560 |
| Mexico City Reds ................ .571 | 1976—Mexico City Reds x ............. .543 | Ciudad Juarez ..................... .509 |
| 1967—Jalisco ................................ .607 | Union Laguna ....................... .547 | |

°Defeated Nuevo Laredo, two games to none, in playoff for pennant. †Won four-team playoff. ‡Won split-season playoff. §League divided into Northern, Southern divisions; won two-team playoff. xLeague divided into Northern, Southern zones; sub-divided into Eastern, Western divisions, won eight-team playoff. yA players strike on July 1 forced the cancellation of the regular season and playoff schedule. zLeague divided into Northern, Southern zones; four clubs from each zone qualified for postseason play. Won final series for league championship.

### STANDING OF CLUBS AT CLOSE OF SEASON
#### NORTHERN ZONE

| Club | Ags | N.L. | Mva | Tam | Sal | Leo | U.L. | Mon | M.R. | Yuc | M.T. | Cor | Pue | Cam | Tab | Ver | W. | L. | T. | Pct. | G.B. |
|---|---|---|---|---|---|---|---|---|---|---|---|---|---|---|---|---|---|---|---|---|---|
| Aguascalientes ............. | .... | 5 | 8 | 5 | 10 | 7 | 8 | 5 | 2 | 2 | 3 | 1 | 3 | 2 | 2 | 65 | 58 | 2 | .5284 | ...... |
| Nuevo Laredo ................ | 8 | .... | 6 | 9 | 8 | 12 | 6 | 5 | 2 | 0 | 2 | 2 | 1 | 1 | 2 | 3 | 67 | 60 | 1 | .5275 | ...... |
| Monclova ...................... | 5 | 8 | .... | 9 | 6 | 4 | 8 | 5 | 2 | 1 | 2 | 3 | 3 | 2 | 4 | 64 | 62 | 2 | .508 | 2½ |
| Tampico ....................... | 9 | 7 | 5 | .... | 10 | 7 | 5 | 10 | 2 | 1 | 0 | 1 | 2 | 2 | 1 | 4 | 66 | 64 | 0 | .508 | 2½ |
| Saltillo ........................ | 3 | 6 | 8 | 4 | .... | 9 | 9 | 11 | 2 | 2 | 1 | 0 | 3 | 1 | 2 | 3 | 64 | 65 | 2 | .496 | 4 |
| Leon ........................... | 9 | 1 | 7 | 6 | 5 | .... | 9 | 9 | 2 | 2 | 1 | 2 | 2 | 0 | 2 | 3 | 60 | 67 | 2 | .472 | 7 |
| Union Laguna ................ | 6 | 8 | 6 | 9 | 7 | 5 | .... | 6 | 2 | 0 | 0 | 2 | 1 | 3 | 3 | 3 | 61 | 70 | 1 | .466 | 8 |
| Monterrey ..................... | 7 | 9 | 10 | 4 | 3 | 5 | 8 | .... | 2 | 2 | 1 | 3 | 1 | 2 | 0 | 3 | 60 | 69 | 1 | .465 | 8 |

#### SOUTHERN ZONE

| Club | Ags | N.L. | Mva | Tam | Sal | Leo | U.L. | Mon | M.R. | Yuc | M.T. | Cor | Pue | Cam | Tab | Ver | W. | L. | T. | Pct. | G.B. |
|---|---|---|---|---|---|---|---|---|---|---|---|---|---|---|---|---|---|---|---|---|---|
| Mexico City Reds........... | 2 | 2 | 2 | 2 | 2 | 2 | 2 | 2 | .... | 8 | 8 | 8 | 8 | 11 | 12 | 9 | 80 | 52 | 0 | .606 | ...... |
| Yucatan ...................... | 0 | 4 | 2 | 2 | 2 | 2 | 4 | 2 | 6 | .... | 8 | 8 | 8 | 10 | 7 | 9 | 74 | 49 | 3 | .602 | 1½ |
| Mexico City Tigers ........ | 2 | 2 | 2 | 4 | 3 | 3 | 4 | 3 | 8 | 6 | .... | 3 | 10 | 3 | 8 | 11 | 72 | 54 | 1 | .571 | 5 |
| Cordoba ...................... | 1 | 2 | 2 | 3 | 4 | 2 | 1 | 1 | 6 | 5 | 10 | .... | 5 | 7 | 11 | 12 | 72 | 55 | 3 | .567 | 5½ |
| Puebla ......................... | 3 | 1 | 1 | 2 | 1 | 2 | 3 | 3 | 6 | 5 | 4 | 10 | .... | 6 | 12 | 11 | 70 | 54 | 2 | .565 | 6 |
| Campeche .................... | 0 | 2 | 1 | 2 | 2 | 4 | 1 | 2 | 3 | 4 | 7 | 6 | 5 | .... | 11 | 8 | 58 | 60 | 2 | .492 | 15 |
| Tabasco ...................... | 1 | 2 | 2 | 3 | 1 | 2 | 1 | 4 | 2 | 5 | 6 | 3 | 1 | 2 | .... | 8 | 43 | 83 | 4 | .341 | 34 |
| Veracruz ...................... | 2 | 1 | 0 | 0 | 1 | 1 | 1 | 1 | 5 | 5 | 3 | 12 | 3 | 6 | 8 | .... | 39 | 93 | 0 | .295 | 41 |

Playoffs—Nuevo Laredo defeated Aguascalientes, four games to two, in Northern Zone finals. Mexico City Reds defeated Mexico City Tigers, four games to one, in Southern Zone finals. Mexico City Reds defeated Nuevo Laredo, four games to one, in final series to capture league championship.

Regular-Season Attendance—Aguascalientes, 159,610; Campeche, 120,618; Cordoba, 138,652; Leon, 107,543; Mexico City Reds, 181,628; Mexico City Tigers, 181,508; Monclova, 259,724; Monterrey, 164,067; Nuevo Laredo, 123,553; Puebla, 71,389; Saltillo, 184,129; Tabasco, 82,624; Tampico, 197,210; Union Laguna, 132,802; Veracruz, 122,057; Yucatan, 364,326. Total, 2,591,440. Playoffs, 325,979.

Managers—Aguascalientes, David Garcia, Roberto Castellon; Campeche, Fransisco Estrada; Cordoba, Alberto Joachin, Eliseo Rodriguez, Alfredo Ortiz; Leon, Benjamin Valenzuela, Miguel Gaspar; Mexico City Reds, Benjamin Reyes, Roberto Castellon; Mexico City Tigers, Roberto Mendes; Monclova, Venicio Garcia; Monterrey, Jose Guerrero, Aurelio Rodriguez; Nuevo Laredo, Jorge Calvo; Puebla, Max Olivares; Saltillo, Roger Freed, Juan Navarrete; Tabasco, Javier Espinoza, Dolores Juarez; Tampico, Gregorio Lukuen; Union Laguna, Mario Pelaes, Rodolfo Sandoval, Gerardo Gutierrez, Hugo Rios; Veracruz, Federico Velazquez, Fransisco Rodriguez; Yucatan, Carlos Paz.

(Compiled by Ana Luisa Perea Talarico, League Statistician, Mexico, D.F.)

### CLUB BATTING

| Club | Pct. | G. | AB. | R. | OR. | H. | TB. | 2B. | 3B. | HR. | RBI. | GW. | SH. | SF. | HP. | BB. | Int. BB. | SO. | SB. | CS. | LOB. |
|---|---|---|---|---|---|---|---|---|---|---|---|---|---|---|---|---|---|---|---|---|---|
| Aguascalientes ......... | .311 | 125 | 4264 | 732 | 714 | 1324 | 1925 | 186 | 44 | 109 | 662 | 57 | 42 | 38 | 31 | 463 | 23 | 490 | 70 | 38 | 951 |
| Mexico City Tigers ... | .30/ | 127 | 4160 | 780 | 610 | 1279 | 1881 | 198 | 40 | 108 | 713 | 57 | 73 | 48 | 28 | 539 | 40 | 599 | 93 | 65 | 905 |
| Puebla ..................... | .305 | 126 | 3932 | 678 | 559 | 1200 | 1746 | 204 | 27 | 96 | 626 | 64 | 47 | 40 | 31 | 449 | 38 | 555 | 122 | 55 | 839 |
| Leon ....................... | .299 | 129 | 4177 | 713 | 752 | 1248 | 1957 | 178 | 24 | 161 | 666 | 53 | 36 | 38 | 39 | 448 | 25 | 558 | 66 | 45 | 883 |
| Monclova ................. | .298 | 128 | 4143 | 751 | 778 | 1236 | 1887 | 197 | 32 | 130 | 684 | 56 | 40 | 23 | 31 | 594 | 30 | 662 | 75 | 43 | 959 |
| Mexico City Reds...... | .296 | 132 | 4247 | 698 | 592 | 1259 | 1789 | 188 | 30 | 94 | 637 | 70 | 46 | 38 | 37 | 527 | 52 | 569 | 121 | 85 | 918 |
| Union Laguna ........... | .293 | 142 | 4375 | 672 | 722 | 1284 | 1879 | 206 | 34 | 107 | 619 | 52 | 63 | 37 | 31 | 458 | 42 | 602 | 92 | 59 | 953 |
| Saltillo .................... | .293 | 131 | 4260 | 721 | 706 | 1248 | 1867 | 213 | 35 | 112 | 677 | 54 | 64 | 35 | 50 | 530 | 48 | 646 | 42 | 58 | 962 |
| Nuevo Laredo .......... | .291 | 128 | 4167 | 702 | 579 | 1213 | 1919 | 178 | 24 | 160 | 621 | 52 | 50 | 29 | 57 | 419 | 39 | 597 | 75 | 51 | 853 |
| Campeche ................ | .288 | 120 | 3815 | 488 | 536 | 1097 | 1492 | 156 | 19 | 67 | 439 | 48 | 55 | 19 | 37 | 327 | 37 | 483 | 49 | 31 | 821 |
| Cordoba .................. | .285 | 130 | 4163 | 602 | 515 | 1188 | 1628 | 164 | 24 | 76 | 557 | 65 | 53 | 24 | 33 | 465 | 43 | 511 | 104 | 68 | 908 |
| Tampico .................. | .284 | 130 | 4245 | 692 | 688 | 1207 | 1879 | 196 | 28 | 140 | 624 | 58 | 53 | 31 | 50 | 487 | 29 | 725 | 55 | 49 | 923 |
| Yucatan .................. | .292 | 126 | 3997 | 576 | 476 | 1127 | 1594 | 178 | 23 | 81 | 522 | 63 | 50 | 28 | 40 | 470 | 39 | 482 | 85 | 54 | 884 |
| Monterrey ................ | .272 | 130 | 4111 | 586 | 667 | 1119 | 1622 | 191 | 27 | 86 | 522 | 48 | 57 | 33 | 37 | 417 | 31 | 676 | 63 | 50 | 848 |
| Tabasco ................... | .272 | 130 | 4113 | 486 | 650 | 1119 | 1479 | 170 | 14 | 54 | 420 | 39 | 73 | 22 | 32 | 409 | 34 | 487 | 77 | 61 | 907 |
| Veracruz .................. | .258 | 132 | 4174 | 463 | 796 | 1078 | 1443 | 169 | 17 | 54 | 403 | 34 | 49 | 27 | 34 | 395 | 26 | 605 | 54 | 40 | 999 |

## INDIVIDUAL BATTING

(Leading Qualifiers for Batting Championship—356 or More Plate Appearances)

*Bats lefthanded.    †Switch-hitter.

| Player and Club | Pct. | G. | AB. | R. | H. | TB. | 2B. | 3B. | HR. | RBI. | GW. | SH. | SF. | HP. | BB. | Int. BB. | SO. | SB. | CS. |
|---|---|---|---|---|---|---|---|---|---|---|---|---|---|---|---|---|---|---|---|
| Olivares, Oswaldo, Ags-Campeche* .... | .397 | 110 | 441 | 85 | 175 | 240 | 22 | 14 | 5 | 49 | 2 | 3 | 3 | 5 | 51 | 4 | 27 | 20 | 7 |
| Lora, Ramon, Puebla......................... | .380 | 109 | 376 | 84 | 143 | 231 | 24 | 5 | 18 | 81 | 15 | 0 | 4 | 4 | 43 | 4 | 39 | 20 | 8 |
| Bronson, Eddie, Union Laguna............ | .372 | 124 | 454 | 99 | 169 | 296 | 29 | 1 | 32 | 107 | 12 | 2 | 9 | 5 | 53 | 3 | 70 | 11 | 4 |
| Moore, Alvin, Leon........................... | .372 | 127 | 446 | 80 | 166 | 283 | 18 | 3 | 31 | 113 | 10 | 0 | 6 | 3 | 53 | 4 | 29 | 7 | 6 |
| Bryant, Derek, Tampico .................... | .367 | 122 | 446 | 92 | 164 | 318 | 38 | 1 | 38 | 121 | 11 | 0 | 8 | 3 | 68 | 4 | 65 | 8 | 6 |
| Perez, Julian, Tampico...................... | .366 | 125 | 448 | 120 | 164 | 267 | 25 | 0 | 26 | 89 | 11 | 1 | 3 | 2 | 92 | 4 | 39 | 13 | 11 |
| Bundy, Lorenzo, Mexico City Reds*.... | .366 | 105 | 350 | 78 | 128 | 213 | 15 | 5 | 20 | 77 | 12 | 1 | 2 | 5 | 66 | 14 | 54 | 7 | 2 |
| Mora, Andres, Nuevo Laredo ............. | .360 | 127 | 456 | 98 | 164 | 316 | 25 | 2 | 41 | 110 | 9 | 0 | 6 | 4 | 54 | 13 | 52 | 2 | 4 |
| Rodriguez, Rodolfo, Aguascalientes*.. | .353 | 104 | 388 | 76 | 137 | 178 | 24 | 4 | 3 | 42 | 6 | 6 | 3 | 2 | 53 | 0 | 29 | 1 | 2 |
| Carrillo, Matias, Mexico City Tigers*.. | .353 | 126 | 465 | 114 | 164 | 261 | 21 | 8 | 20 | 102 | 10 | 5 | 6 | 3 | 73 | 3 | 86 | 46 | 16 |
| Evans, John, Aguascalientes............. | .352 | 109 | 349 | 79 | 123 | 195 | 15 | 0 | 19 | 84 | 5 | 0 | 2 | 9 | 104 | 1 | 60 | 4 | 1 |
| Bellazetin, Jose, M.C. Tigers* ............ | .350 | 123 | 437 | 102 | 153 | 204 | 31 | 4 | 4 | 65 | 1 | 5 | 5 | 4 | 103 | 8 | 33 | 9 | 7 |

Departmental Leaders: G—Navarrete, 131; AB—L. Guerrero, 515; R—Ju. Perez, 120; H—Olivares, 175; TB—Bryant, 318; 2B—Bryant, 38; 3B—Olivares, 14; HR—Mora, 41; RBI—Renteria, 125; GWRBI—Lora, 15; SH—A. Gomez, 19; SF—Aguilar, M. Salinas, 10; HP—Machiria, 18; BB—Greene, 120; IBB—H. Cruz, 16; SO—A. Torres, 97; SB—Briones, 50; CS—Ju. Hernandez, 25.

(All Players—Listed Alphabetically)

| Player and Club | Pct. | G. | AB. | R. | H. | TB. | 2B. | 3B. | HR. | RBI. | GW. | SH. | SF. | HP. | BB. | Int. BB. | SO. | SB. | CS. |
|---|---|---|---|---|---|---|---|---|---|---|---|---|---|---|---|---|---|---|---|
| Abarca, David, Aguascalientes............ | .000 | 1 | 2 | 0 | 0 | 0 | 0 | 0 | 0 | 0 | 0 | 0 | 0 | 0 | 0 | 0 | 0 | 0 | 0 |
| Acosta, Marcos, Tabasco................... | .167 | 29 | 48 | 4 | 8 | 12 | 1 | 0 | 1 | 1 | 0 | 0 | 1 | 1 | 0 | 0 | 13 | 1 | 0 |
| Acosta, Martin, Campeche ................. | .143 | 7 | 7 | 0 | 1 | 1 | 0 | 0 | 0 | 0 | 0 | 0 | 0 | 0 | 0 | 0 | 1 | 0 | 0 |
| Adams, Calvin, 54 Tab-70 Veracruz.. | .322 | 124 | 435 | 61 | 140 | 178 | 23 | 3 | 3 | 45 | 5 | 3 | 1 | 4 | 59 | 4 | 50 | 19 | 13 |
| Aguilar, Enrique, Aguascalientes ....... | .323 | 120 | 474 | 106 | 153 | 255 | 23 | 2 | 25 | 107 | 6 | 2 | 10 | 2 | 44 | 3 | 48 | 12 | 5 |
| Aguilera, Antonio, Yucatan ............... | .138 | 54 | 58 | 14 | 8 | 10 | 0 | 1 | 0 | 3 | 0 | 0 | 0 | 2 | 10 | 0 | 18 | 2 | 0 |
| Almodobar, Ricardo, Tampico............. | .218 | 57 | 133 | 22 | 29 | 32 | 1 | 1 | 0 | 1 | 0 | 1 | 0 | 0 | 23 | 0 | 31 | 0 | 0 |
| Alonso, Hermilo, Puebla .................... | .313 | 38 | 99 | 11 | 31 | 37 | 6 | 0 | 0 | 5 | 0 | 2 | 0 | 0 | 5 | 0 | 10 | 0 | 0 |
| Alvarez, Juan Carlos, Union Laguna.... | .280 | 70 | 225 | 26 | 63 | 87 | 13 | 1 | 3 | 29 | 0 | 5 | 0 | 1 | 11 | 0 | 41 | 0 | 2 |
| Amador, Jose Luis, Veracruz ............. | .192 | 10 | 26 | 1 | 5 | 5 | 0 | 0 | 0 | 1 | 0 | 0 | 0 | 0 | 0 | 0 | 4 | 0 | 0 |
| Amaro, David, Mexico City Tigers ...... | .292 | 8 | 24 | 6 | 7 | 9 | 2 | 0 | 0 | 3 | 1 | 1 | 0 | 2 | 2 | 0 | 5 | 1 | 1 |
| Anderson, Karl, Nuevo Laredo ........... | .000 | 1 | 1 | 0 | 0 | 0 | 0 | 0 | 0 | 0 | 0 | 0 | 0 | 0 | 0 | 0 | 1 | 0 | 0 |
| Andrade, Reynaldo, 39 Tam-55 Mon. | .263 | 94 | 308 | 51 | 81 | 123 | 19 | 4 | 5 | 26 | 2 | 2 | 2 | 2 | 62 | 8 | 45 | 4 | 9 |
| Arce, Javier, Leon............................ | .297 | 80 | 202 | 35 | 60 | 83 | 8 | 0 | 5 | 25 | 4 | 2 | 1 | 2 | 29 | 2 | 33 | 3 | 2 |
| Arredondo, Heron, Veracruz ............. | .279 | 15 | 43 | 4 | 12 | 17 | 2 | 0 | 1 | 6 | 0 | 0 | 0 | 0 | 3 | 1 | 11 | 1 | 0 |
| Arzate, Martin, Aguascalientes .......... | .255 | 87 | 263 | 35 | 67 | 76 | 5 | 2 | 0 | 23 | 2 | 4 | 1 | 0 | 39 | 0 | 42 | 3 | 4 |
| Avila, Ruben, 5 Tam-19 UL ............... | .290 | 24 | 62 | 8 | 18 | 20 | 2 | 0 | 0 | 5 | 0 | 2 | 0 | 1 | 11 | 0 | 12 | 0 | 1 |
| Avina, Francisco Javier, Leon ........... | .177 | 15 | 17 | 2 | 3 | 4 | 1 | 0 | 0 | 2 | 1 | 1 | 0 | 0 | 4 | 0 | 3 | 0 | 1 |
| Baca, Manuel, Nuevo Laredo ............ | .278 | 96 | 273 | 44 | 76 | 106 | 10 | 1 | 6 | 37 | 3 | 10 | 3 | 4 | 19 | 1 | 42 | 5 | 3 |
| Barajas, Ismael, Tampico.................. | .162 | 13 | 37 | 8 | 6 | 9 | 1 | 1 | 0 | 2 | 0 | 2 | 0 | 0 | 6 | 0 | 13 | 1 | 0 |
| Barandica, Alberto, Union Laguna ...... | .161 | 31 | 31 | 6 | 5 | 6 | 1 | 0 | 0 | 1 | 0 | 1 | 1 | 0 | 0 | 0 | 8 | 1 | 0 |
| Barragan, Gerardo, M.C. Reds* ......... | .273 | 57 | 154 | 15 | 42 | 54 | 3 | 3 | 1 | 14 | 1 | 1 | 1 | 1 | 6 | 0 | 23 | 4 | 0 |
| Barrera, Jesus A., Nuevo Laredo ...... | .241 | 123 | 345 | 44 | 83 | 91 | 6 | 1 | 0 | 27 | 1 | 10 | 1 | 2 | 33 | 0 | 38 | 3 | 4 |
| Barrera, Nelson, Mexico City Reds ..... | .292 | 65 | 219 | 47 | 64 | 122 | 8 | 1 | 16 | 49 | 3 | 0 | 1 | 3 | 36 | 9 | 36 | 5 | 3 |
| Bautista, Antonio, Veracruz.............. | .305 | 57 | 190 | 29 | 58 | 87 | 6 | 1 | 7 | 26 | 1 | 0 | 1 | 3 | 32 | 3 | 32 | 4 | 4 |
| Bazan, Pedro, Yucatan* .................... | .290 | 75 | 221 | 36 | 64 | 92 | 16 | 0 | 4 | 38 | 2 | 5 | 2 | 2 | 43 | 13 | 21 | 1 | 1 |
| Bellazetin, Jose, M.C. Tigers* ............ | .350 | 123 | 437 | 102 | 153 | 204 | 31 | 4 | 4 | 65 | 1 | 5 | 5 | 4 | 103 | 8 | 33 | 9 | 7 |
| Benitez, Julio Cesar, Tampico............ | .207 | 103 | 329 | 34 | 68 | 96 | 9 | 2 | 5 | 29 | 3 | 4 | 3 | 5 | 32 | 0 | 68 | 1 | 3 |
| Blanks, Larvell, 50 Cam-22 Veracruz | .274 | 72 | 266 | 40 | 73 | 110 | 15 | 2 | 6 | 17 | 2 | 3 | 2 | 0 | 36 | 2 | 31 | 4 | 2 |
| Bobadilla, Manuel, Monclova ............. | .257 | 88 | 288 | 49 | 74 | 107 | 5 | 2 | 8 | 42 | 2 | 3 | 2 | 3 | 34 | 0 | 34 | 4 | 2 |
| Bocardo, Manuel, 18 MCR-11 Cor..... | .103 | 29 | 39 | 5 | 4 | 9 | 0 | 1 | 1 | 5 | 0 | 2 | 1 | 1 | 10 | 0 | 15 | 0 | 0 |
| Bojorquez, Jose, Campeche............... | .253 | 101 | 324 | 27 | 82 | 111 | 14 | 0 | 5 | 27 | 3 | 7 | 4 | 1 | 24 | 1 | 44 | 0 | 3 |
| Briones, Antonio, Union Laguna ......... | .239 | 120 | 410 | 70 | 98 | 111 | 5 | 1 | 2 | 30 | 2 | 16 | 3 | 3 | 59 | 0 | 54 | 50 | 20 |
| Bronson, Eddie, Union Laguna............ | .372 | 124 | 454 | 99 | 169 | 296 | 29 | 1 | 32 | 107 | 12 | 2 | 9 | 5 | 53 | 3 | 70 | 11 | 4 |
| Bruno, Joseph, Monterrey ................. | .271 | 22 | 70 | 10 | 19 | 27 | 0 | 1 | 2 | 13 | 1 | 0 | 1 | 1 | 12 | 0 | 9 | 4 | 3 |
| Bryant, Derek, Tampico .................... | .367 | 122 | 446 | 92 | 164 | 318 | 38 | 1 | 38 | 121 | 11 | 0 | 8 | 3 | 68 | 4 | 65 | 8 | 6 |
| Bundy, Lorenzo, Mexico City Reds*..... | .366 | 105 | 350 | 78 | 128 | 213 | 15 | 5 | 20 | 77 | 12 | 1 | 2 | 5 | 66 | 14 | 54 | 7 | 2 |
| Burke, Norberto, Saltillo ................... | .285 | 117 | 358 | 57 | 102 | 159 | 22 | 4 | 9 | 56 | 3 | 7 | 2 | 4 | 73 | 1 | 62 | 0 | 7 |
| Caballero, Juan, Monterrey ............... | .221 | 82 | 262 | 33 | 58 | 90 | 8 | 0 | 8 | 29 | 0 | 0 | 0 | 0 | 21 | 3 | 73 | 4 | 1 |
| Cabrales, Sergio, Campeche.............. | .208 | 86 | 216 | 29 | 45 | 53 | 6 | 1 | 0 | 13 | 0 | 3 | 2 | 3 | 31 | 0 | 52 | 0 | 3 |
| Cabrera, Jorge, Monclova ................. | .293 | 80 | 270 | 49 | 79 | 109 | 9 | 3 | 5 | 46 | 1 | 3 | 1 | 3 | 21 | 0 | 33 | 2 | 0 |
| Calderon, Francisco, Campeche ......... | .000 | 1 | 1 | 0 | 0 | 0 | 0 | 0 | 0 | 0 | 0 | 0 | 0 | 0 | 0 | 0 | 0 | 0 | 0 |
| Camacho, Adulfo, Mexico City Tigers. | .253 | 89 | 285 | 62 | 72 | 98 | 12 | 1 | 4 | 44 | 4 | 6 | 5 | 4 | 43 | 0 | 51 | 3 | 2 |
| Campos, Rosendo, Tabasco............... | .286 | 32 | 56 | 13 | 16 | 21 | 3 | 1 | 0 | 1 | 0 | 3 | 0 | 1 | 3 | 0 | 10 | 2 | 2 |
| Canedo, Alfredo, Monclova............... | .250 | 24 | 28 | 3 | 7 | 8 | 1 | 0 | 0 | 3 | 0 | 1 | 0 | 0 | 1 | 0 | 4 | 0 | 1 |
| Canedo, Donald, Monclova* .............. | .313 | 115 | 403 | 89 | 126 | 214 | 25 | 3 | 19 | 71 | 7 | 5 | 2 | 2 | 73 | 2 | 95 | 2 | 4 |
| Cangelosi, John, Mexico City Reds†.... | .353 | 61 | 201 | 46 | 71 | 91 | 9 | 4 | 1 | 30 | 3 | 4 | 0 | 4 | 50 | 3 | 19 | 17 | 16 |
| Cano, Javier, Saltillo ....................... | .270 | 84 | 230 | 36 | 62 | 78 | 5 | 1 | 3 | 28 | 2 | 8 | 2 | 2 | 24 | 2 | 31 | 4 | 4 |
| Carrillo, Francisco, Aguascalientes..... | .205 | 23 | 44 | 6 | 9 | 9 | 0 | 0 | 0 | 1 | 0 | 2 | 0 | 0 | 3 | 0 | 9 | 1 | 0 |
| Carrillo, Matias, Mexico City Tigers*.. | .353 | 126 | 465 | 114 | 164 | 261 | 21 | 8 | 20 | 102 | 10 | 5 | 6 | 3 | 73 | 3 | 86 | 46 | 16 |
| Castaneda, Antonio, Puebla............... | .157 | 62 | 108 | 15 | 17 | 23 | 0 | 0 | 2 | 12 | 1 | 5 | 3 | 2 | 19 | 0 | 38 | 1 | 1 |
| Castaneda, Aurelio, Cordoba............. | .000 | 1 | 1 | 0 | 0 | 0 | 0 | 0 | 0 | 0 | 0 | 0 | 0 | 0 | 1 | 0 | 0 | 0 | 0 |
| Castaneda, Nicholas, M.C. Tigers*...... | .318 | 53 | 176 | 43 | 56 | 109 | 6 | 1 | 15 | 53 | 6 | 0 | 3 | 2 | 42 | 2 | 47 | 0 | 1 |
| Castelan, Miguel Angel, Puebla* ........ | .276 | 116 | 348 | 61 | 96 | 123 | 10 | 4 | 3 | 39 | 3 | 6 | 5 | 3 | 49 | 6 | 64 | 14 | 10 |
| Castillo, Esteban, Cordoba* .............. | .294 | 106 | 395 | 55 | 116 | 168 | 20 | 1 | 10 | 59 | 5 | 2 | 4 | 0 | 51 | 8 | 23 | 1 | 8 |
| Castillo, Luis Trinidad, N. Laredo........ | .000 | 1 | 1 | 0 | 0 | 0 | 0 | 0 | 0 | 0 | 0 | 0 | 0 | 0 | 1 | 0 | 0 | 0 | 0 |
| Castillo, Raul, Cordoba..................... | .224 | 51 | 98 | 12 | 22 | 33 | 5 | 0 | 2 | 12 | 3 | 2 | 2 | 0 | 16 | 0 | 32 | 0 | 0 |
| Castro, Antonio, Mexico City Tigers*. | .317 | 124 | 439 | 89 | 139 | 228 | 17 | 3 | 22 | 86 | 5 | 1 | 4 | 0 | 58 | 11 | 45 | 5 | 5 |
| Castro, Jose Antonio, Tabasco.......... | .230 | 81 | 196 | 17 | 45 | 50 | 5 | 0 | 0 | 14 | 2 | 7 | 1 | 2 | 26 | 1 | 28 | 4 | 5 |
| Cazarin, Manuel, Veracruz................ | .283 | 32 | 99 | 11 | 28 | 34 | 6 | 0 | 0 | 6 | 1 | 3 | 1 | 1 | 12 | 0 | 14 | 2 | 2 |
| Chavarria, Miguel Angel, Saltillo......... | .108 | 28 | 37 | 6 | 4 | 5 | 1 | 0 | 0 | 1 | 0 | 0 | 1 | 0 | 4 | 0 | 14 | 0 | 1 |
| Chavez, Jose Angel, Veracruz........... | .199 | 46 | 151 | 14 | 30 | 34 | 4 | 0 | 0 | 6 | 0 | 5 | 0 | 0 | 2 | 0 | 10 | 0 | 4 |
| Chavez, Jose Santos, N. Laredo* ...... | .281 | 106 | 274 | 44 | 77 | 121 | 16 | 2 | 8 | 38 | 5 | 3 | 0 | 5 | 32 | 4 | 57 | 6 | 5 |
| Chavez, Luis, 3 MC Reds-12 Cam....... | .227 | 15 | 22 | 2 | 5 | 5 | 0 | 0 | 0 | 6 | 1 | 5 | 5 | 0 | 0 | 0 | 4 | 0 | 0 |
| Chavez, Ricardo, Campeche ............. | .255 | 97 | 318 | 26 | 81 | 87 | 6 | 0 | 0 | 19 | 5 | 7 | 1 | 3 | 10 | 0 | 45 | 4 | 3 |
| Clayton, Leonardo, Saltillo*.............. | .270 | 124 | 389 | 70 | 105 | 145 | 19 | 6 | 3 | 34 | 4 | 4 | 3 | 2 | 70 | 8 | 76 | 17 | 9 |
| Collins, James, 75 Cor-49 Vera.*........ | .317 | 124 | 445 | 72 | 141 | 193 | 30 | 2 | 6 | 56 | 4 | 0 | 2 | 2 | 66 | 9 | 57 | 14 | 6 |
| Cosey, Donald Ray, Campeche........... | .326 | 110 | 460 | 66 | 150 | 209 | 24 | 4 | 9 | 74 | 10 | 1 | 1 | 3 | 23 | 0 | 50 | 2 | 3 |
| Cota, Francisco, Mexico City Tigers... | .000 | 1 | 1 | 0 | 0 | 0 | 0 | 0 | 0 | 0 | 0 | 0 | 0 | 0 | 0 | 0 | 1 | 0 | 0 |

| Player and Club | Pct. | G. | AB. | R. | H. | TB. | 2B. | 3B. | HR. | RBI. | GW. | SH. | SF. | HP. | BB. | Int. BB. | SO. | SB. | CS. |
|---|---|---|---|---|---|---|---|---|---|---|---|---|---|---|---|---|---|---|---|
| Cotes, Eugenio, Cordoba | .316 | 87 | 291 | 61 | 92 | 126 | 8 | 4 | 6 | 48 | 3 | 1 | 1 | 4 | 48 | 4 | 41 | 22 | 4 |
| Craig, Rodney, Nuevo Laredo° | .331 | 117 | 408 | 80 | 135 | 239 | 15 | 4 | 27 | 76 | 2 | 2 | 3 | 9 | 61 | 6 | 62 | 13 | 10 |
| Cruz, Fernando, Nuevo Laredo | .205 | 26 | 44 | 7 | 9 | 10 | 1 | 0 | 0 | 4 | 0 | 1 | 0 | 1 | 4 | 0 | 7 | 0 | 0 |
| Cruz, Henry, Saltillo° | .305 | 127 | 466 | 96 | 142 | 260 | 33 | 2 | 27 | 108 | 12 | 1 | 1 | 6 | 73 | 16 | 48 | 0 | 2 |
| Cruz, Javier, Mexico City Tigers | .194 | 43 | 67 | 6 | 13 | 20 | 2 | 1 | 1 | 11 | 1 | 1 | 1 | 1 | 7 | 0 | 19 | 3 | 1 |
| Cruz, Luis Alfonso, Tampico | .263 | 116 | 403 | 55 | 106 | 181 | 23 | 2 | 16 | 60 | 4 | 2 | 3 | 8 | 30 | 1 | 81 | 1 | 5 |
| Daut, Manuel, Monterrey | .194 | 74 | 186 | 24 | 36 | 49 | 5 | 1 | 2 | 12 | 1 | 6 | 0 | 5 | 15 | 0 | 51 | 2 | 2 |
| DeFreites, Arturo, Yucatan | .299 | 124 | 455 | 67 | 136 | 217 | 22 | 1 | 19 | 74 | 8 | 2 | 5 | 0 | 45 | 7 | 73 | 8 | 4 |
| Delgado, Marcelo, Saltillo | .200 | 5 | 10 | 1 | 2 | 2 | 0 | 0 | 0 | 0 | 0 | 0 | 0 | 0 | 0 | 0 | 3 | 0 | 0 |
| Delgado, Tomas, Yucatan | .429 | 6 | 7 | 1 | 3 | 4 | 1 | 0 | 0 | 2 | 0 | 0 | 0 | 0 | 0 | 0 | 1 | 0 | 0 |
| De Los Santos, Carlos E., Cordoba | .222 | 113 | 342 | 46 | 76 | 81 | 5 | 0 | 0 | 20 | 2 | 12 | 0 | 5 | 37 | 0 | 27 | 1 | 3 |
| Diaz, Albino, Union Laguna | .266 | 105 | 327 | 53 | 87 | 125 | 9 | 4 | 7 | 42 | 4 | 4 | 2 | 4 | 52 | 3 | 47 | 3 | 3 |
| Diaz, Ernesto, Campeche | .276 | 41 | 105 | 14 | 29 | 36 | 4 | 0 | 1 | 16 | 1 | 5 | 1 | 1 | 6 | 0 | 20 | 4 | 0 |
| Diaz, Jesus, Leon | .318 | 26 | 66 | 15 | 21 | 29 | 2 | 0 | 2 | 12 | 0 | 0 | 3 | 1 | 7 | 0 | 11 | 0 | 2 |
| Diaz, Luis, Fernando, Nuevo Laredo | .103 | 18 | 29 | 2 | 3 | 6 | 0 | 0 | 1 | 1 | 0 | 0 | 0 | 0 | 0 | 0 | 6 | 0 | 0 |
| Dominguez, Herminio, Campeche° | 1.000 | 1 | 1 | 0 | 1 | 1 | 0 | 0 | 0 | 1 | 0 | 0 | 0 | 0 | 0 | 0 | 0 | 0 | 0 |
| Duran, Fierro Oscar Omar, MC Reds | .000 | 6 | 3 | 1 | 0 | 0 | 0 | 0 | 0 | 0 | 0 | 0 | 0 | 1 | 0 | 0 | 0 | 0 | 0 |
| Duran, Oscar, Saltillo | .398 | 40 | 113 | 17 | 45 | 59 | 11 | 0 | 1 | 24 | 2 | 1 | 0 | 4 | 14 | 3 | 16 | 1 | 2 |
| Duran, Ricardo, Monterrey | .300 | 126 | 424 | 78 | 127 | 191 | 26 | 1 | 12 | 77 | 9 | 1 | 5 | 5 | 86 | 3 | 52 | 2 | 2 |
| Elizondo, Fernando, Saltillo | .306 | 128 | 467 | 88 | 143 | 195 | 25 | 6 | 5 | 51 | 7 | 12 | 4 | 5 | 45 | 1 | 49 | 5 | 8 |
| Escalante, Isidro, Aguascalientes | .163 | 18 | 43 | 3 | 7 | 8 | 1 | 0 | 0 | 1 | 0 | 2 | 0 | 0 | 4 | 0 | 8 | 0 | 0 |
| Estrada, Francisco, Campeche | .230 | 77 | 213 | 24 | 49 | 64 | 9 | 0 | 2 | 20 | 3 | 4 | 2 | 2 | 36 | 3 | 8 | 2 | 2 |
| Evans, John, Aguascalientes | .352 | 109 | 349 | 79 | 123 | 195 | 15 | 0 | 19 | 84 | 5 | 0 | 2 | 9 | 104 | 1 | 60 | 4 | 1 |
| Ezquerra, Dennis, Mexico City Reds° | .265 | 63 | 155 | 17 | 41 | 59 | 9 | 0 | 3 | 27 | 1 | 0 | 1 | 0 | 9 | 2 | 33 | 1 | 3 |
| Fabela, Lorenzo, Veracruz | .210 | 106 | 329 | 35 | 69 | 90 | 16 | 1 | 1 | 20 | 1 | 4 | 2 | 2 | 19 | 0 | 53 | 2 | 7 |
| Felix, Alfredo, Veracruz | .248 | 56 | 145 | 16 | 36 | 50 | 7 | 2 | 1 | 10 | 0 | 2 | 1 | 1 | 7 | 0 | 32 | 0 | 0 |
| Felix, Victor Manuel, Yucatan | .241 | 35 | 83 | 8 | 20 | 25 | 2 | 0 | 1 | 9 | 1 | 0 | 0 | 0 | 16 | 1 | 18 | 1 | 2 |
| Fernandez, Daniel, Mexico City Reds° | .288 | 118 | 326 | 91 | 94 | 125 | 19 | 3 | 2 | 33 | 2 | 3 | 0 | 4 | 81 | 3 | 47 | 31 | 12 |
| Figueroa, Leobardo, Yucatan | .306 | 56 | 134 | 23 | 41 | 51 | 6 | 2 | 0 | 14 | 4 | 1 | 0 | 5 | 35 | 0 | 18 | 6 | 3 |
| Flores, Gilberto, 40 Pue-55 Yuc | .280 | 95 | 329 | 59 | 92 | 122 | 8 | 5 | 4 | 33 | 7 | 4 | 4 | 9 | 64 | 2 | 35 | 26 | 8 |
| Franco, Francisco, Veracruz | .667 | 1 | 3 | 1 | 2 | 2 | 0 | 0 | 0 | 0 | 0 | 0 | 0 | 0 | 0 | 0 | 1 | 0 | 0 |
| Franklin, Glenn, Cordoba | .335 | 68 | 218 | 41 | 73 | 102 | 10 | 2 | 5 | 37 | 4 | 4 | 0 | 2 | 43 | 4 | 36 | 33 | 8 |
| Gage, Ralph, Tabasco° | .285 | 126 | 400 | 58 | 114 | 161 | 24 | 1 | 7 | 42 | 2 | 0 | 3 | 3 | 90 | 12 | 48 | 10 | 4 |
| Galindo, Francisco Javier, N. Laredo | .299 | 81 | 268 | 40 | 80 | 113 | 18 | 0 | 5 | 25 | 1 | 3 | 0 | 3 | 16 | 0 | 28 | 1 | 0 |
| Gamundi, Timoteo, 2 Yuc-89 Vera | .280 | 91 | 261 | 26 | 73 | 84 | 11 | 0 | 0 | 26 | 4 | 2 | 2 | 2 | 29 | 0 | 41 | 3 | 0 |
| Garcia, Jesus, Monclova | .244 | 33 | 78 | 13 | 19 | 23 | 1 | 0 | 1 | 8 | 0 | 2 | 0 | 1 | 4 | 0 | 19 | 1 | 0 |
| Garcia, Jose Luis, Tampico | .238 | 20 | 21 | 4 | 5 | 5 | 0 | 0 | 0 | 0 | 0 | 0 | 1 | 0 | 0 | 0 | 10 | 1 | 0 |
| Garcia, Roberto, Nuevo Laredo | .167 | 5 | 6 | 0 | 1 | 1 | 0 | 0 | 0 | 0 | 0 | 0 | 0 | 0 | 0 | 0 | 3 | 0 | 0 |
| Garcia, Sabino, Campeche | .000 | 5 | 5 | 2 | 0 | 0 | 0 | 0 | 0 | 0 | 0 | 0 | 0 | 0 | 0 | 0 | 1 | 0 | 0 |
| Garibay, Guy, Nuevo Laredo | .167 | 31 | 42 | 10 | 7 | 9 | 1 | 0 | 0 | 3 | 1 | 1 | 0 | 1 | 3 | 0 | 12 | 1 | 1 |
| Garza, Adolfo, Tabasco° | .285 | 127 | 424 | 51 | 121 | 185 | 28 | 0 | 12 | 66 | 7 | 2 | 5 | 6 | 48 | 8 | 56 | 3 | 0 |
| Garza, Gerardo, Mexico City Reds | .250 | 7 | 8 | 0 | 2 | 3 | 1 | 0 | 0 | 3 | 0 | 0 | 0 | 0 | 0 | 0 | 0 | 0 | 0 |
| Garzon, Felix, Cordoba | .323 | 130 | 480 | 61 | 155 | 225 | 23 | 1 | 15 | 76 | 10 | 3 | 6 | 1 | 34 | 4 | 66 | 1 | 6 |
| Gomez, Alejandro, Tabasco | .244 | 124 | 459 | 46 | 112 | 127 | 11 | 2 | 0 | 24 | 4 | 19 | 4 | 2 | 23 | 1 | 39 | 14 | 13 |
| Gomez, Graciano, Leon | .315 | 120 | 419 | 57 | 132 | 204 | 16 | 4 | 16 | 58 | 2 | 2 | 2 | 6 | 21 | 2 | 56 | 7 | 4 |
| Gonzalez, Armando, Tampico | .000 | 8 | 9 | 2 | 0 | 0 | 0 | 0 | 0 | 0 | 0 | 0 | 0 | 0 | 0 | 0 | 5 | 0 | 0 |
| Gonzalez, Jesus, Puebla | .291 | 122 | 422 | 79 | 123 | 159 | 22 | 1 | 4 | 65 | 6 | 17 | 5 | 4 | 43 | 1 | 26 | 5 | 4 |
| Gonzalez, Mario, Monterrey | .269 | 13 | 26 | 3 | 7 | 9 | 0 | 1 | 0 | 4 | 0 | 0 | 0 | 0 | 0 | 0 | 11 | 0 | 1 |
| Gonzalez, Mario Angel, Monclova | .083 | 7 | 12 | 3 | 1 | 3 | 0 | 1 | 0 | 2 | 0 | 0 | 0 | 0 | 5 | 1 | 0 | 0 | 0 |
| Gonzalez, Noe, Monterrey | .264 | 95 | 284 | 45 | 75 | 123 | 17 | 5 | 7 | 34 | 2 | 2 | 4 | 3 | 21 | 1 | 55 | 3 | 3 |
| Gray, Gary, 72 Cam-48 Ags | .316 | 120 | 437 | 74 | 138 | 222 | 21 | 3 | 19 | 89 | 10 | 0 | 4 | 10 | 43 | 6 | 58 | 9 | 2 |
| Greene, Altar, Monclova° | .313 | 128 | 425 | 97 | 133 | 274 | 20 | 2 | 39 | 109 | 8 | 0 | 4 | 2 | 120 | 10 | 68 | 7 | 4 |
| Guerra, Ricardo, Union Laguna | .333 | 52 | 165 | 29 | 55 | 78 | 9 | 1 | 4 | 28 | 2 | 0 | 1 | 0 | 29 | 3 | 15 | 3 | 2 |
| Guerrero, Francisco, Union Laguna | .201 | 63 | 144 | 23 | 29 | 49 | 5 | 3 | 3 | 16 | 0 | 4 | 1 | 2 | 11 | 0 | 29 | 3 | 2 |
| Guerrero, Leobardo, Aguascalientes | .334 | 122 | 515 | 98 | 172 | 231 | 22 | 8 | 7 | 63 | 7 | 5 | 2 | 3 | 44 | 2 | 28 | 18 | 9 |
| Guzman, Andres, Tabasco | .298 | 111 | 336 | 29 | 100 | 128 | 12 | 2 | 4 | 41 | 6 | 4 | 1 | 2 | 13 | 2 | 53 | 1 | 1 |
| Guzman, Marco Antonio, Campeche | .306 | 116 | 385 | 50 | 118 | 182 | 22 | 0 | 14 | 63 | 7 | 4 | 1 | 4 | 55 | 4 | 46 | 4 | 4 |
| Hernandez, Gustavo, Cordoba | .230 | 25 | 61 | 10 | 14 | 22 | 5 | 0 | 1 | 7 | 1 | 2 | 0 | 0 | 2 | 0 | 12 | 0 | 0 |
| Hernandez, Javier, Leon° | .279 | 78 | 197 | 26 | 55 | 63 | 3 | 1 | 1 | 22 | 3 | 6 | 2 | 0 | 20 | 0 | 30 | 3 | 2 |
| Hernandez, Juan, Mexico City Reds | .283 | 125 | 438 | 67 | 124 | 154 | 19 | 4 | 1 | 39 | 2 | 5 | 3 | 2 | 53 | 3 | 76 | 25 | 19 |
| Hernandez, Miguel, Cordoba | .250 | 119 | 336 | 61 | 84 | 104 | 10 | 2 | 2 | 27 | 4 | 6 | 2 | 3 | 58 | 0 | 39 | 7 | 9 |
| Hernandez, Rodolfo, Yucatan | .238 | 95 | 298 | 31 | 71 | 104 | 12 | 0 | 7 | 43 | 11 | 5 | 2 | 6 | 37 | 2 | 50 | 0 | 2 |
| Herrera, Ricardo, Leon | .298 | 120 | 494 | 73 | 147 | 196 | 29 | 7 | 2 | 44 | 2 | 4 | 0 | 3 | 35 | 0 | 62 | 17 | 13 |
| Herring, Paul, Tampico | .297 | 122 | 444 | 67 | 132 | 218 | 20 | 6 | 18 | 85 | 10 | 2 | 3 | 3 | 53 | 11 | 43 | 5 | 2 |
| Isambert, Sergio, Yucatan | .304 | 36 | 138 | 21 | 42 | 59 | 4 | 2 | 3 | 15 | 2 | 0 | 1 | 1 | 12 | 3 | 24 | 0 | 3 |
| Jimenez, Leopoldo, Campeche | .280 | 72 | 189 | 21 | 53 | 65 | 6 | 0 | 2 | 14 | 2 | 1 | 1 | 8 | 21 | 2 | 22 | 2 | 2 |
| Johnes, Kenneth, Nuevo Laredo | .322 | 38 | 143 | 30 | 46 | 67 | 5 | 2 | 4 | 17 | 2 | 1 | 0 | 1 | 9 | 1 | 24 | 11 | 4 |
| Lara, Hugo, Cordoba | .000 | 3 | 4 | 0 | 0 | 0 | 0 | 0 | 0 | 0 | 0 | 0 | 0 | 0 | 0 | 0 | 0 | 0 | 0 |
| Leal, Guadalupe, Monclova° | .303 | 124 | 406 | 77 | 123 | 188 | 18 | 4 | 13 | 68 | 5 | 0 | 2 | 5 | 47 | 8 | 75 | 4 | 6 |
| Lee, Terry, Puebla° | .339 | 118 | 375 | 70 | 127 | 217 | 24 | 3 | 20 | 97 | 6 | 1 | 6 | 0 | 69 | 10 | 71 | 1 | 5 |
| Leon, Juan Carlos, Yucatan | .150 | 21 | 20 | 3 | 3 | 3 | 0 | 0 | 0 | 0 | 0 | 1 | 0 | 0 | 0 | 0 | 4 | 0 | 0 |
| Leon, Maximino, Mexico City Reds | .667 | 2 | 3 | 1 | 2 | 2 | 0 | 0 | 0 | 0 | 0 | 0 | 0 | 0 | 0 | 0 | 0 | 0 | 0 |
| Limon, Arturo, Tabasco | .289 | 44 | 83 | 8 | 24 | 27 | 3 | 0 | 0 | 10 | 0 | 2 | 2 | 0 | 6 | 0 | 6 | 2 | 1 |
| Limon, Salvador, Tabasco | .127 | 33 | 71 | 6 | 9 | 17 | 3 | 1 | 1 | 7 | 0 | 0 | 1 | 0 | 1 | 0 | 6 | 0 | 0 |
| Lizarraga, Alejandro, 70 UL-29 Yuc | .281 | 99 | 352 | 37 | 99 | 129 | 15 | 0 | 5 | 35 | 2 | 5 | 5 | 2 | 11 | 1 | 20 | 0 | 2 |
| Lopez, Alfonso, Mexico City Tigers | .327 | 103 | 346 | 46 | 113 | 129 | 12 | 2 | 0 | 38 | 3 | 7 | 5 | 0 | 23 | 1 | 22 | 2 | 11 |
| Lopez, Antonio, 43 Ags-70 Tab | .316 | 113 | 411 | 58 | 130 | 199 | 22 | 4 | 13 | 69 | 5 | 4 | 4 | 4 | 24 | 5 | 31 | 4 | 3 |
| Lopez, Carlos, 10 Mon-81 Tab | .301 | 91 | 299 | 53 | 90 | 127 | 15 | 2 | 6 | 34 | 4 | 2 | 0 | 5 | 35 | 0 | 28 | 5 | 6 |
| Lopez, Fernando, Saltillo | .248 | 79 | 218 | 50 | 54 | 71 | 9 | 4 | 0 | 16 | 1 | 4 | 3 | 2 | 43 | 0 | 55 | 5 | 5 |
| Lopez, Jamie, Union Laguna° | .349 | 96 | 315 | 52 | 110 | 143 | 21 | 0 | 4 | 47 | 7 | 2 | 4 | 0 | 25 | 12 | 8 | 0 | 2 |
| Lora, Ramon, Puebla | .380 | 109 | 376 | 84 | 143 | 231 | 24 | 5 | 18 | 81 | 15 | 0 | 4 | 4 | 43 | 4 | 39 | 20 | 8 |
| Lozano, Gustavo, Tampico | .000 | 2 | 1 | 0 | 0 | 0 | 0 | 0 | 0 | 0 | 0 | 0 | 0 | 0 | 0 | 0 | 1 | 0 | 0 |
| Luna, Jose Luis, Monterrey | .216 | 80 | 204 | 17 | 44 | 66 | 10 | 0 | 4 | 22 | 1 | 2 | 2 | 0 | 14 | 0 | 29 | 0 | 1 |
| Machaira, Pablo, Tampico | .274 | 118 | 416 | 69 | 114 | 178 | 17 | 4 | 13 | 60 | 5 | 15 | 2 | 18 | 39 | 0 | 88 | 5 | 5 |
| Marquez, Francisco, Saltillo | .246 | 72 | 175 | 28 | 43 | 71 | 11 | 1 | 5 | 30 | 2 | 2 | 2 | 3 | 23 | 0 | 37 | 0 | 1 |
| Martinez, Francisco, Cordoba | .255 | 88 | 247 | 25 | 63 | 77 | 8 | 0 | 2 | 28 | 2 | 4 | 3 | 3 | 17 | 0 | 31 | 2 | 4 |
| Martinez, Jose A., Mexico City Tigers | .000 | 1 | 1 | 0 | 0 | 0 | 0 | 0 | 0 | 0 | 0 | 0 | 0 | 0 | 0 | 0 | 0 | 0 | 0 |
| Martinez, Oscar, 29 Cor-38 Vera. | .194 | 67 | 196 | 17 | 38 | 44 | 3 | 0 | 1 | 14 | 2 | 3 | 2 | 3 | 11 | 0 | 34 | 2 | 2 |
| Martinez, Raul, Leon | .256 | 65 | 160 | 25 | 41 | 68 | 11 | 2 | 4 | 23 | 3 | 1 | 1 | 0 | 21 | 0 | 25 | 0 | 1 |
| Maza, Celerino, Union Laguna | .260 | 68 | 146 | 21 | 38 | 47 | 4 | 1 | 1 | 12 | 0 | 5 | 0 | 1 | 16 | 0 | 19 | 0 | 1 |
| Mendoza, Luis, Alonso, Monclova | .300 | 66 | 203 | 32 | 61 | 84 | 6 | 1 | 5 | 27 | 3 | 0 | 5 | 0 | 31 | 0 | 24 | 0 | 1 |
| Mendoza, Margarito, Union Laguna | .254 | 38 | 71 | 6 | 18 | 24 | 3 | 0 | 1 | 12 | 1 | 2 | 0 | 0 | 4 | 0 | 10 | 0 | 1 |

| Player and Club | Pct. | G. | AB. | R. | H. | TB. | 2B. | 3B. | HR. | RBI. | GW. | SH. | SF. | HP. | BB. | Int. BB. | SO. | SB. | CS. |
|---|---|---|---|---|---|---|---|---|---|---|---|---|---|---|---|---|---|---|---|
| Mendoza, Mario, Aguascalientes | .286 | 111 | 402 | 56 | 115 | 149 | 14 | 4 | 4 | 49 | 6 | 5 | 2 | 2 | 23 | 3 | 42 | 5 | 4 |
| Mendoza, Porfirio, Puebla | .286 | 102 | 311 | 43 | 89 | 137 | 25 | 1 | 7 | 52 | 2 | 5 | 3 | 2 | 38 | 1 | 45 | 13 | 4 |
| Mendoza, Saul, 25 Cam-26 Vera. | .237 | 51 | 118 | 15 | 28 | 33 | 5 | 0 | 0 | 9 | 0 | 3 | 1 | 1 | 24 | 0 | 17 | 0 | 0 |
| Meza, Leonel, Veracruz | .241 | 112 | 344 | 34 | 83 | 93 | 10 | 0 | 0 | 24 | 4 | 10 | 2 | 0 | 41 | 3 | 62 | 1 | 0 |
| Meza, Rigoberto, Leon | .000 | 2 | 0 | 1 | 0 | 0 | 0 | 0 | 0 | 0 | 0 | 0 | 0 | 0 | 0 | 0 | 0 | 0 | 0 |
| Monasterio, 51 MCR-31-Ve-21 Leo. | .271 | 113 | 414 | 52 | 112 | 155 | 18 | 2 | 7 | 37 | 6 | 1 | 1 | 3 | 29 | 3 | 42 | 7 | 8 |
| Monroy, Victor Hugo, Monclova | .283 | 84 | 269 | 35 | 76 | 118 | 10 | 4 | 8 | 39 | 5 | 2 | 0 | 2 | 13 | 0 | 40 | 3 | 3 |
| Montero, Danny, Union Laguna | .143 | 6 | 21 | 3 | 3 | 6 | 0 | 0 | 1 | 5 | 0 | 0 | 0 | 0 | 2 | 0 | 11 | 0 | 0 |
| Montiel, Julio Alfonso, Leon | .173 | 35 | 75 | 8 | 13 | 13 | 0 | 0 | 0 | 8 | 1 | 4 | 2 | 0 | 8 | 0 | 10 | 0 | 0 |
| Moore, Alvin, Leon | .372 | 127 | 446 | 80 | 166 | 283 | 18 | 3 | 31 | 113 | 10 | 0 | 6 | 3 | 53 | 4 | 29 | 7 | 6 |
| Mora, Andres, Nuevo Laredo | .360 | 127 | 456 | 98 | 164 | 316 | 25 | 2 | 41 | 110 | 9 | 0 | 6 | 4 | 54 | 13 | 52 | 2 | 4 |
| Morales, Carlos, Leon | .263 | 67 | 156 | 21 | 41 | 79 | 6 | 1 | 10 | 28 | 3 | 3 | 4 | 2 | 24 | 1 | 31 | 1 | 0 |
| Morales, Luis Arturo, Nuevo Laredo | .250 | 9 | 8 | 1 | 2 | 3 | 1 | 0 | 0 | 3 | 0 | 0 | 0 | 0 | 0 | 0 | 1 | 0 | 0 |
| Morales, Manuel, Mexico City Tigers | .240 | 104 | 342 | 54 | 82 | 98 | 11 | 1 | 1 | 31 | 2 | 16 | 3 | 3 | 44 | 0 | 32 | 5 | 8 |
| Moran, Jorge, Campeche | .242 | 19 | 33 | 3 | 8 | 8 | 0 | 0 | 0 | 1 | 1 | 0 | 0 | 0 | 2 | 1 | 13 | 0 | 0 |
| Moreno, Abel, Leon | .000 | 2 | 0 | 1 | 0 | 0 | 0 | 0 | 0 | 0 | 0 | 0 | 0 | 0 | 0 | 0 | 0 | 0 | 0 |
| Moreno, Jesus, Nuevo Laredo | .000 | 1 | 2 | 0 | 0 | 0 | 0 | 0 | 0 | 0 | 0 | 0 | 0 | 0 | 0 | 0 | 1 | 0 | 0 |
| Moreno, Jose, Aguascalientes | .287 | 49 | 171 | 24 | 49 | 69 | 2 | 0 | 6 | 28 | 6 | 0 | 1 | 1 | 25 | 4 | 24 | 6 | 4 |
| Mota, Benigno, Nuevo Laredo | .167 | 20 | 30 | 1 | 5 | 6 | 1 | 0 | 0 | 1 | 0 | 0 | 1 | 0 | 1 | 0 | 3 | 0 | 0 |
| Munoz, Jose Luis, Yucatan | .000 | 15 | 6 | 2 | 0 | 0 | 0 | 0 | 0 | 0 | 0 | 0 | 0 | 0 | 1 | 0 | 3 | 0 | 0 |
| Navarrete, Juan, Saltillo* | .305 | 131 | 511 | 85 | 156 | 192 | 20 | 2 | 4 | 85 | 9 | 9 | 7 | 2 | 49 | 4 | 16 | 5 | 9 |
| Navarro, Jose Angel, Saltillo | .500 | 6 | 4 | 2 | 2 | 5 | 0 | 0 | 1 | 3 | 0 | 0 | 0 | 0 | 1 | 0 | 2 | 0 | 0 |
| Navarro, Ruben, Monterrey | .182 | 23 | 66 | 9 | 12 | 17 | 2 | 0 | 1 | 5 | 1 | 2 | 0 | 0 | 11 | 1 | 25 | 0 | 0 |
| Negron, Miguel, 15 MCR-22 Tab* | .317 | 37 | 126 | 12 | 40 | 48 | 5 | 0 | 1 | 18 | 2 | 0 | 2 | 0 | 14 | 1 | 6 | 3 | 3 |
| Nunez, Arturo, Veracruz | .182 | 32 | 88 | 4 | 16 | 20 | 4 | 0 | 0 | 10 | 0 | 0 | 1 | 0 | 4 | 0 | 22 | 0 | 0 |
| Olivares, Oswaldo, 65 Ags-45 Cam* | .397 | 110 | 441 | 85 | 175 | 240 | 22 | 14 | 5 | 49 | 2 | 3 | 3 | 5 | 51 | 4 | 27 | 20 | 7 |
| Orejas, Enrique, Aguascalientes | .231 | 3 | 13 | 3 | 3 | 4 | 1 | 0 | 0 | 1 | 0 | 0 | 0 | 0 | 0 | 0 | 5 | 0 | 0 |
| Ortiz, Alejandro, Nuevo Laredo | .288 | 128 | 459 | 104 | 132 | 253 | 21 | 5 | 30 | 75 | 7 | 0 | 7 | 6 | 66 | 2 | 77 | 20 | 6 |
| Ortiz, Alfredo, 10 Vera.-10 Cor* | .389 | 20 | 18 | 5 | 7 | 7 | 0 | 0 | 0 | 5 | 3 | 0 | 0 | 0 | 6 | 2 | 0 | 0 | 0 |
| Ortiz, Jose Manuel, Monterrey | .239 | 33 | 71 | 5 | 17 | 21 | 1 | 0 | 1 | 8 | 1 | 0 | 0 | 0 | 2 | 0 | 13 | 0 | 0 |
| Ortiz, Rigoberto, Puebla | .500 | 2 | 2 | 0 | 1 | 1 | 0 | 0 | 0 | 0 | 0 | 0 | 0 | 1 | 0 | 0 | 0 | 0 | 0 |
| Pacho, Juan Jose, Yucatan | .259 | 117 | 386 | 40 | 100 | 124 | 18 | 3 | 0 | 44 | 4 | 5 | 4 | 1 | 31 | 0 | 35 | 2 | 4 |
| Paredes, Jesus, 33-Cor-3 Vera. | .233 | 36 | 103 | 11 | 24 | 27 | 3 | 0 | 0 | 6 | 0 | 2 | 1 | 0 | 9 | 0 | 21 | 3 | 1 |
| Paula, Julio Cesar, Union Laguna | .265 | 57 | 189 | 31 | 50 | 84 | 11 | 4 | 5 | 25 | 2 | 3 | 1 | 2 | 33 | 4 | 25 | 2 | 5 |
| Payton, Eric, Union Laguna | .331 | 103 | 381 | 75 | 126 | 231 | 27 | 6 | 22 | 77 | 7 | 3 | 3 | 2 | 48 | 10 | 51 | 10 | 4 |
| Peralta, Amado, Mexico City Tigers | .273 | 77 | 220 | 37 | 60 | 91 | 14 | 1 | 5 | 30 | 6 | 3 | 1 | 0 | 32 | 1 | 76 | 1 | 0 |
| Perez, Alfredo, Union Laguna | .000 | 2 | 2 | 0 | 0 | 0 | 0 | 0 | 0 | 0 | 0 | 0 | 0 | 0 | 0 | 0 | 1 | 0 | 0 |
| Perez, Jose Luis, Aguascalientes* | .264 | 93 | 322 | 44 | 85 | 145 | 23 | 2 | 11 | 50 | 4 | 2 | 3 | 1 | 24 | 2 | 44 | 1 | 2 |
| Perez, Julian, Tampico | .366 | 125 | 448 | 120 | 164 | 267 | 25 | 0 | 26 | 89 | 11 | 1 | 3 | 2 | 92 | 4 | 39 | 13 | 11 |
| Perez, Raul, Aguascalientes | .378 | 12 | 45 | 9 | 17 | 22 | 1 | 2 | 0 | 6 | 1 | 0 | 0 | 2 | 6 | 2 | 4 | 0 | 0 |
| Pierce, Jack, Leon* | .311 | 128 | 440 | 104 | 137 | 273 | 16 | 0 | 40 | 118 | 10 | 0 | 7 | 8 | 80 | 9 | 85 | 1 | 0 |
| Placencia, Juan, Puebla | .304 | 26 | 46 | 2 | 14 | 17 | 1 | 1 | 0 | 9 | 0 | 0 | 2 | 1 | 2 | 0 | 8 | 0 | 0 |
| Ponce, Hector, Puebla | .249 | 92 | 229 | 38 | 57 | 77 | 10 | 2 | 2 | 19 | 2 | 2 | 0 | 0 | 17 | 0 | 38 | 6 | 1 |
| Powell, Haskin, Saltillo | .289 | 40 | 128 | 22 | 37 | 58 | 5 | 2 | 4 | 16 | 0 | 1 | 0 | 2 | 8 | 3 | 12 | 1 | 1 |
| Quintero, Guadalupe, Veracruz | .246 | 101 | 301 | 25 | 74 | 102 | 12 | 2 | 4 | 33 | 2 | 9 | 2 | 2 | 38 | 0 | 45 | 1 | 3 |
| Quintero, Victor, Veracruz | .311 | 50 | 177 | 21 | 55 | 64 | 2 | 2 | 1 | 18 | 2 | 2 | 3 | 1 | 11 | 2 | 6 | 3 | 3 |
| Quiroz, Jose Julian, Nuevo Laredo* | .277 | 109 | 318 | 49 | 88 | 123 | 14 | 3 | 5 | 42 | 4 | 4 | 2 | 4 | 27 | 3 | 53 | 1 | 3 |
| Ramirez, Enrique, Nuevo Laredo | .429 | 7 | 7 | 0 | 3 | 3 | 0 | 0 | 0 | 1 | 1 | 0 | 0 | 0 | 0 | 0 | 2 | 0 | 0 |
| Ramirez, Manuel, Monclova | .330 | 128 | 482 | 83 | 159 | 211 | 23 | 4 | 7 | 75 | 8 | 4 | 3 | 5 | 47 | 2 | 33 | 6 | 5 |
| Ray, Larry, Mexico City Reds* | .274 | 76 | 241 | 43 | 66 | 109 | 14 | 1 | 9 | 41 | 8 | 0 | 3 | 3 | 50 | 4 | 36 | 5 | 6 |
| Raymundo, Oscar, Yucatan | .121 | 20 | 33 | 2 | 4 | 4 | 0 | 0 | 0 | 1 | 0 | 0 | 0 | 0 | 10 | 0 | 17 | 0 | 0 |
| Rendon, Jose, Saltillo | .324 | 128 | 469 | 76 | 152 | 273 | 21 | 2 | 32 | 114 | 8 | 2 | 7 | 3 | 45 | 7 | 77 | 0 | 5 |
| Renteria, Richard, Mexico City Tigers | .349 | 125 | 484 | 89 | 169 | 277 | 29 | 11 | 19 | 125 | 14 | 7 | 4 | 4 | 35 | 8 | 53 | 8 | 5 |
| Reyes, Enrique, Nuevo Laredo | .214 | 94 | 276 | 29 | 59 | 74 | 6 | 0 | 3 | 40 | 6 | 7 | 3 | 4 | 15 | 0 | 29 | 2 | 1 |
| Reyes, Gerardo, Mexico City Tigers | .200 | 12 | 25 | 4 | 5 | 5 | 0 | 0 | 0 | 3 | 0 | 0 | 0 | 0 | 1 | 0 | 4 | 0 | 0 |
| Reyes, Ignacio, Tabasco | .156 | 31 | 32 | 1 | 5 | 5 | 0 | 0 | 0 | 0 | 0 | 1 | 0 | 0 | 4 | 0 | 8 | 0 | 1 |
| Reyes, Juan, 40 Ags-39 Campeche* | .311 | 79 | 238 | 32 | 74 | 110 | 11 | 2 | 7 | 46 | 1 | 2 | 1 | 1 | 19 | 7 | 38 | 2 | 0 |
| Rios, Carlos, Monterrey | .265 | 128 | 457 | 50 | 121 | 170 | 20 | 1 | 9 | 53 | 5 | 4 | 2 | 3 | 25 | 2 | 62 | 14 | 4 |
| Rivera, Carlos, Campeche | .281 | 96 | 353 | 46 | 99 | 142 | 6 | 2 | 11 | 56 | 5 | 10 | 2 | 3 | 28 | 2 | 44 | 5 | 2 |
| Rivera, Eduardo, 48 Pue-40 Sal | .270 | 88 | 278 | 30 | 75 | 95 | 10 | 2 | 2 | 33 | 1 | 9 | 2 | 4 | 13 | 0 | 43 | 3 | 3 |
| Rivero, Genaro, Puebla | .500 | 5 | 2 | 1 | 1 | 1 | 0 | 0 | 0 | 0 | 0 | 0 | 0 | 0 | 0 | 0 | 0 | 0 | 0 |
| Rivero, Gener, Yucatan | .201 | 76 | 204 | 23 | 41 | 49 | 3 | 1 | 1 | 10 | 1 | 3 | 0 | 3 | 22 | 1 | 16 | 3 | 1 |
| Robles, Arturo, Saltillo | .000 | 1 | 1 | 1 | 0 | 0 | 0 | 0 | 0 | 0 | 0 | 0 | 0 | 0 | 0 | 0 | 1 | 0 | 0 |
| Robles, Eduardo, Tabasco | .222 | 8 | 9 | 2 | 2 | 2 | 0 | 0 | 0 | 1 | 0 | 1 | 0 | 0 | 0 | 0 | 3 | 0 | 0 |
| Robles, Humberto, Monterrey | .278 | 111 | 352 | 50 | 98 | 149 | 20 | 5 | 7 | 46 | 5 | 6 | 2 | 4 | 44 | 1 | 70 | 6 | 5 |
| Robles, Sergio, Mexico City Reds | .223 | 84 | 247 | 20 | 55 | 63 | 5 | 0 | 1 | 32 | 1 | 5 | 2 | 1 | 14 | 1 | 29 | 0 | 1 |
| Rodriguez, Aurelio, Monterrey | .304 | 107 | 378 | 57 | 115 | 181 | 25 | 1 | 13 | 69 | 5 | 8 | 7 | 0 | 35 | 3 | 47 | 1 | 2 |
| Rodriguez, I. Francisco, Veracruz | .200 | 2 | 5 | 0 | 1 | 1 | 0 | 0 | 0 | 1 | 0 | 0 | 0 | 0 | 2 | 0 | 1 | 0 | 0 |
| Rodriguez, Genaro, Union Laguna | .285 | 62 | 172 | 22 | 49 | 78 | 16 | 2 | 3 | 22 | 2 | 0 | 1 | 3 | 14 | 0 | 33 | 2 | 2 |
| Rodriguez, Guillermo, Puebla | .319 | 122 | 445 | 76 | 142 | 234 | 24 | 1 | 22 | 94 | 11 | 1 | 2 | 5 | 12 | 1 | 83 | 3 | 5 |
| Rodriguez, Jaime, Tabasco | .263 | 108 | 335 | 29 | 88 | 112 | 12 | 0 | 4 | 28 | 0 | 6 | 1 | 5 | 13 | 0 | 37 | 8 | 7 |
| Rodriguez, Jose de Jesus, M.C. Tigers | .322 | 78 | 292 | 54 | 94 | 119 | 9 | 2 | 4 | 38 | 2 | 9 | 2 | 1 | 22 | 0 | 27 | 7 | 4 |
| Rodriguez, Juan Francisco, Leon | .322 | 126 | 478 | 100 | 154 | 210 | 22 | 2 | 10 | 53 | 5 | 7 | 3 | 8 | 50 | 0 | 24 | 17 | 5 |
| Rodriguez, Roberto, Union Laguna* | .298 | 58 | 215 | 30 | 64 | 78 | 8 | 3 | 0 | 19 | 3 | 0 | 1 | 0 | 22 | 3 | 13 | 3 | 4 |
| Rodriguez, Rodolfo, Aguascalientes* | .353 | 104 | 388 | 76 | 137 | 178 | 24 | 4 | 3 | 42 | 6 | 6 | 3 | 2 | 53 | 0 | 29 | 1 | 2 |
| Rojas, Homar, Mexico City Tigers | .281 | 111 | 366 | 54 | 103 | 161 | 21 | 5 | 9 | 59 | 2 | 10 | 7 | 4 | 35 | 2 | 48 | 2 | 2 |
| Rojo, Diaz, Gonzalo, Saltillo | .254 | 48 | 130 | 9 | 33 | 40 | 2 | 1 | 1 | 14 | 0 | 2 | 0 | 1 | 7 | 0 | 27 | 0 | 0 |
| Roldan, Ricardo, Cordoba | .000 | 8 | 6 | 0 | 0 | 0 | 0 | 0 | 0 | 1 | 0 | 0 | 0 | 0 | 1 | 0 | 1 | 0 | 0 |
| Rosales, Arturo, 30 Cor-94 Mon | .299 | 124 | 431 | 62 | 129 | 206 | 19 | 8 | 14 | 61 | 8 | 6 | 4 | 5 | 22 | 5 | 67 | 13 | 9 |
| Rosario, Alfonso, 72 Vera.-47 Cor* | .305 | 126 | 466 | 57 | 142 | 227 | 36 | 2 | 15 | 66 | 6 | 3 | 1 | 6 | 34 | 9 | 56 | 9 | 3 |
| Rosas, Clemente, Aguascalientes | .289 | 61 | 211 | 25 | 61 | 84 | 11 | 0 | 4 | 33 | 3 | 1 | 4 | 0 | 12 | 0 | 33 | 0 | 0 |
| Royg, Luis, 48 Vera.-65 Cam | .301 | 113 | 413 | 64 | 128 | 213 | 16 | 3 | 21 | 72 | 5 | 1 | 4 | 11 | 19 | 1 | 58 | 9 | 1 |
| Rubio, Arturo, 15 Agu-10 Tab | .154 | 25 | 52 | 5 | 8 | 9 | 1 | 0 | 0 | 0 | 0 | 3 | 0 | 0 | 6 | 0 | 4 | 0 | 0 |
| Rubio, Mauricio, Saltillo | .259 | 14 | 27 | 5 | 7 | 10 | 1 | 1 | 0 | 3 | 0 | 0 | 0 | 0 | 3 | 0 | 7 | 0 | 1 |
| Ruiz, Demetrio, Tabasco | .321 | 43 | 84 | 15 | 27 | 27 | 0 | 0 | 0 | 10 | 3 | 5 | 0 | 0 | 13 | 0 | 3 | 4 | 2 |
| Ruiz, Porfirio, Leon | .208 | 72 | 207 | 20 | 43 | 53 | 7 | 0 | 1 | 12 | 1 | 1 | 1 | 1 | 12 | 0 | 24 | 1 | 0 |
| Saavedra, Edwin, 3 Vera.-3 MCR | .182 | 6 | 22 | 1 | 4 | 10 | 1 | 1 | 1 | 1 | 0 | 0 | 0 | 1 | 2 | 1 | 5 | 0 | 0 |
| Saenz, Ricardo, Puebla | .288 | 46 | 139 | 3 | 40 | 50 | 6 | 2 | 0 | 16 | 1 | 1 | 0 | 0 | 13 | 0 | 21 | 1 | 4 |
| Saiz, Herminio, Union Laguna | .315 | 103 | 333 | 49 | 105 | 139 | 15 | 5 | 3 | 44 | 1 | 7 | 4 | 4 | 19 | 1 | 42 | 4 | 4 |
| Salazar, Ronaldo, Tabasco | .245 | 94 | 282 | 41 | 69 | 106 | 13 | 3 | 6 | 33 | 4 | 1 | 2 | 1 | 32 | 5 | 29 | 3 | 4 |
| Salinas, Luis, Mexico City Reds | .252 | 53 | 119 | 15 | 30 | 50 | 8 | 0 | 4 | 13 | 2 | 2 | 1 | 1 | 13 | 2 | 38 | 0 | 1 |
| Salinas, Manuel, Mexico City Reds* | .331 | 112 | 408 | 60 | 135 | 163 | 15 | 2 | 3 | 80 | 7 | 4 | 10 | 0 | 24 | 1 | 19 | 1 | 4 |

| Player and Club | Pct. | G. | AB. | R. | H. | TB. | 2B. | 3B. | HR. | RBI. | GW. | SH. | SF. | HP. | BB. | Int. BB. | SO. | SB. | CS. |
|---|---|---|---|---|---|---|---|---|---|---|---|---|---|---|---|---|---|---|---|
| Samaniego, Manuel, Campeche | .217 | 33 | 46 | 7 | 10 | 13 | 1 | 1 | 0 | 3 | 0 | 1 | 0 | 0 | 2 | 0 | 4 | 0 | 0 |
| Sanchez, Armando, M.C. Reds° | .323 | 127 | 468 | 65 | 151 | 186 | 25 | 2 | 2 | 48 | 9 | 15 | 5 | 1 | 54 | 4 | 26 | 12 | 7 |
| Sanchez, Gerardo, Nuevo Laredo | .277 | 112 | 382 | 49 | 106 | 149 | 16 | 3 | 7 | 44 | 1 | 6 | 0 | 6 | 23 | 1 | 44 | 5 | 8 |
| Sanchez, Gustavo, Leon | .000 | 4 | 1 | 0 | 0 | 0 | 0 | 0 | 0 | 0 | 0 | 0 | 0 | 0 | 0 | 0 | 0 | 1 | 0 |
| Sanchez, Orlando, Puebla | .367 | 79 | 294 | 65 | 108 | 170 | 18 | 1 | 14 | 59 | 9 | 1 | 2 | 1 | 27 | 5 | 32 | 5 | 2 |
| Santana, Blas, Yucatan | .311 | 126 | 505 | 57 | 157 | 209 | 33 | 2 | 5 | 64 | 6 | 8 | 3 | 2 | 26 | 1 | 32 | 7 | 5 |
| Santos, Eduardo, Saltillo | .317 | 120 | 410 | 58 | 130 | 207 | 23 | 3 | 16 | 81 | 4 | 4 | 5 | 8 | 42 | 3 | 89 | 2 | 1 |
| Sarabia, Antonio, Monclova | .294 | 118 | 415 | 65 | 122 | 166 | 24 | 4 | 4 | 72 | 5 | 4 | 2 | 2 | 59 | 1 | 84 | 12 | 6 |
| Scott, Rodney, Puebla | .280 | 114 | 378 | 78 | 106 | 135 | 18 | 1 | 3 | 39 | 5 | 2 | 4 | 1 | 86 | 8 | 29 | 38 | 7 |
| Serna, Joel, Monclova | .265 | 119 | 419 | 72 | 111 | 165 | 29 | 2 | 7 | 60 | 9 | 8 | 3 | 3 | 76 | 6 | 76 | 6 | 3 |
| Serratos, Miguel, Mexico City Reds | .283 | 78 | 198 | 26 | 56 | 75 | 5 | 1 | 4 | 31 | 3 | 3 | 1 | 3 | 9 | 0 | 28 | 1 | 3 |
| Sharow, Dennis, Tabasco | .303 | 18 | 66 | 11 | 20 | 27 | 4 | 0 | 1 | 9 | 0 | 0 | 0 | 0 | 4 | 0 | 14 | 2 | 0 |
| Smith, Robert, Monclova° | .326 | 117 | 445 | 84 | 145 | 217 | 26 | 2 | 14 | 62 | 4 | 5 | 4 | 2 | 66 | 1 | 72 | 27 | 8 |
| Sommers, Jesus, Leon | .289 | 114 | 415 | 81 | 120 | 203 | 22 | 2 | 19 | 83 | 5 | 3 | 4 | 1 | 46 | 1 | 69 | 4 | 0 |
| Soriano, Hilario, Yucatan | .214 | 42 | 140 | 17 | 30 | 50 | 5 | 0 | 5 | 22 | 4 | 4 | 1 | 2 | 12 | 2 | 30 | 1 | 1 |
| Sosa, Arturo, Tampico | .194 | 40 | 72 | 8 | 14 | 16 | 2 | 0 | 0 | 10 | 1 | 0 | 0 | 2 | 4 | 0 | 14 | 1 | 1 |
| Sotelo, Emilio, Leon | .333 | 50 | 69 | 12 | 23 | 30 | 4 | 0 | 1 | 9 | 0 | 2 | 1 | 1 | 9 | 0 | 5 | 2 | 3 |
| Soto, Alvaro, Puebla | .000 | 1 | 1 | 0 | 0 | 0 | 0 | 0 | 0 | 0 | 0 | 0 | 0 | 0 | 0 | 0 | 1 | 0 | 0 |
| Soto, Carlos, Nuevo Laredo | .348 | 116 | 394 | 69 | 137 | 229 | 23 | 0 | 23 | 77 | 9 | 2 | 3 | 5 | 56 | 8 | 54 | 5 | 2 |
| Soto, Gregorio, Leon | .252 | 49 | 103 | 10 | 26 | 29 | 3 | 0 | 0 | 7 | 1 | 5 | 0 | 0 | 9 | 0 | 16 | 3 | 1 |
| Suarez, Miguel, 17 Vera.-97 Mon° | .259 | 114 | 383 | 49 | 99 | 120 | 12 | 0 | 3 | 49 | 7 | 10 | 4 | 7 | 45 | 7 | 30 | 4 | 10 |
| Sutton, John, Monclova | .000 | 1 | 1 | 0 | 0 | 0 | 0 | 0 | 0 | 0 | 0 | 0 | 0 | 0 | 0 | 0 | 1 | 0 | 0 |
| Tapia, Noe, Tabasco | .247 | 51 | 89 | 12 | 22 | 32 | 2 | 1 | 2 | 9 | 1 | 1 | 0 | 0 | 12 | 0 | 19 | 3 | 1 |
| Tellez, Alonso, Cordoba | .307 | 130 | 476 | 78 | 146 | 221 | 19 | 4 | 16 | 85 | 10 | 3 | 4 | 3 | 47 | 5 | 47 | 13 | 10 |
| Torres, Alf., 30 Tab-45 MCR-38 UL | .251 | 113 | 374 | 52 | 94 | 179 | 19 | 0 | 22 | 75 | 4 | 0 | 2 | 1 | 42 | 3 | 97 | 0 | 2 |
| Torres, Eduardo, Saltillo | .500 | 2 | 2 | 1 | 1 | 1 | 0 | 0 | 0 | 0 | 0 | 0 | 0 | 0 | 0 | 0 | 1 | 0 | 0 |
| Torres, Nemesio, 36 Vera.-58 Tab | .261 | 94 | 345 | 31 | 90 | 100 | 10 | 0 | 0 | 33 | 3 | 11 | 1 | 1 | 22 | 1 | 24 | 2 | 4 |
| Torres, Rafael, Aguascalientes | .156 | 25 | 45 | 8 | 7 | 9 | 2 | 0 | 0 | 1 | 0 | 1 | 0 | 0 | 5 | 0 | 6 | 0 | 0 |
| Torres, Raymundo, Yucatan | .341 | 110 | 355 | 73 | 121 | 216 | 18 | 4 | 23 | 79 | 8 | 3 | 6 | 7 | 54 | 2 | 48 | 9 | 7 |
| Trinidad, Ulin, Sergio, Cordoba | .262 | 64 | 145 | 8 | 38 | 42 | 2 | 1 | 0 | 19 | 1 | 2 | 1 | 2 | 7 | 0 | 27 | 0 | 0 |
| Uribe, Fernando, Tampico | .216 | 90 | 250 | 29 | 54 | 63 | 4 | 1 | 1 | 20 | 0 | 10 | 2 | 3 | 21 | 0 | 55 | 3 | 1 |
| Uzcanga, Ali, Monterrey | .306 | 124 | 481 | 78 | 147 | 182 | 23 | 3 | 2 | 40 | 5 | 11 | 2 | 1 | 36 | 0 | 68 | 7 | 8 |
| Valdez, Baltazar, Veracruz | .288 | 114 | 410 | 46 | 118 | 176 | 15 | 2 | 13 | 49 | 1 | 3 | 2 | 3 | 23 | 3 | 66 | 3 | 2 |
| Valdez, Rodolfo, Campeche | .000 | 1 | 1 | 0 | 0 | 0 | 0 | 0 | 0 | 0 | 0 | 0 | 0 | 0 | 0 | 0 | 0 | 0 | 0 |
| Valenzuela, Felipe, Saltillo | .000 | 1 | 1 | 0 | 0 | 0 | 0 | 0 | 0 | 0 | 0 | 0 | 0 | 0 | 0 | 0 | 0 | 0 | 0 |
| Valenzuela, Felipe, Tabasco | .000 | 20 | 24 | 5 | 4 | 5 | 1 | 0 | 0 | 1 | 0 | 2 | 0 | 0 | 6 | 0 | 4 | 0 | 0 |
| Valenzuela, Horacio, 71 Leo-40 Tig° | .285 | 111 | 347 | 55 | 99 | 175 | 18 | 2 | 18 | 68 | 4 | 0 | 2 | 2 | 37 | 9 | 71 | 2 | 3 |
| Valenzuela, Ricardo, M.C. Tigers | .188 | 20 | 48 | 1 | 9 | 12 | 3 | 0 | 0 | 2 | 0 | 0 | 1 | 1 | 4 | 0 | 15 | 0 | 1 |
| Valle, Guadalupe, Union Laguna | .285 | 106 | 341 | 43 | 97 | 126 | 13 | 2 | 4 | 46 | 4 | 0 | 0 | 1 | 38 | 1 | 64 | 0 | 2 |
| Vargas, Antonio, 8 MCT-57 Tam | .225 | 65 | 169 | 23 | 38 | 57 | 2 | 1 | 5 | 15 | 4 | 2 | 1 | 0 | 8 | 0 | 41 | 2 | 0 |
| Vega, Jesus, 31 MCR-75 Yuc | .275 | 106 | 363 | 66 | 100 | 149 | 17 | 1 | 10 | 45 | 3 | 3 | 6 | 5 | 44 | 4 | 40 | 17 | 4 |
| Vega, Jesus, Aguascalientes | .323 | 32 | 62 | 11 | 20 | 29 | 2 | 2 | 1 | 8 | 1 | 1 | 0 | 0 | 0 | 0 | 12 | 1 | 0 |
| Vega, Ramon, Aguascalientes | .293 | 63 | 188 | 18 | 55 | 70 | 4 | 4 | 1 | 22 | 0 | 8 | 1 | 1 | 6 | 0 | 19 | 0 | 4 |
| Veliz, Arballo, Francisco, Cordoba° | 1.000 | 1 | 1 | 1 | 1 | 1 | 0 | 0 | 0 | 0 | 0 | 0 | 0 | 0 | 0 | 0 | 0 | 0 | 0 |
| Vergara, Salvador, Veracruz | .172 | 31 | 93 | 12 | 16 | 19 | 3 | 0 | 0 | 2 | 0 | 0 | 2 | 0 | 8 | 0 | 13 | 5 | 1 |
| Villa, Victor, Veracruz | .455 | 4 | 11 | 2 | 5 | 5 | 0 | 0 | 0 | 1 | 0 | 0 | 0 | 0 | 0 | 0 | 2 | 0 | 0 |
| Villaescusa, Fernando, Yucatan° | .340 | 108 | 412 | 66 | 140 | 163 | 16 | 2 | 1 | 38 | 3 | 7 | 1 | 3 | 35 | 4 | 26 | 20 | 12 |
| Villagomez, David, Tampico | .296 | 126 | 449 | 64 | 133 | 193 | 27 | 3 | 9 | 63 | 4 | 4 | 2 | 3 | 43 | 6 | 68 | 1 | 4 |
| Villalobos, Juan E., 1 Leo-23 Pue | .291 | 24 | 55 | 6 | 16 | 22 | 2 | 2 | 0 | 7 | 0 | 4 | 0 | 0 | 0 | 0 | 13 | 0 | 0 |
| Villarreal, Ricardo, Puebla° | 1.000 | 2 | 1 | 0 | 1 | 2 | 1 | 0 | 0 | 2 | 0 | 0 | 0 | 0 | 0 | 0 | 0 | 0 | 0 |
| Villela, Carlos, Tampico | .303 | 125 | 478 | 76 | 145 | 198 | 17 | 6 | 8 | 58 | 4 | 10 | 3 | 2 | 41 | 2 | 88 | 12 | 4 |
| Walker, Michael, Mexico City Reds | .297 | 43 | 155 | 26 | 46 | 82 | 8 | 2 | 8 | 35 | 8 | 0 | 2 | 4 | 8 | 2 | 21 | 2 | 2 |
| Widales, Oscar, Nuevo Laredo | .000 | 1 | 1 | 0 | 0 | 0 | 0 | 0 | 0 | 0 | 0 | 0 | 0 | 0 | 0 | 0 | 1 | 0 | 0 |
| Zambrano, Rosario, Cordoba° | .280 | 96 | 322 | 34 | 90 | 111 | 7 | 1 | 4 | 43 | 10 | 6 | 1 | 0 | 21 | 5 | 24 | 6 | 6 |
| Zepeda, Alejandro, Tabasco | .053 | 9 | 19 | 0 | 1 | 1 | 0 | 0 | 0 | 0 | 0 | 0 | 0 | 0 | 0 | 0 | 1 | 0 | 0 |
| Zuniga, Armando, Mexico City Tigers | .143 | 8 | 7 | 1 | 1 | 1 | 0 | 0 | 0 | 0 | 0 | 0 | 0 | 0 | 0 | 0 | 3 | 0 | 0 |

The following pitchers, listed alphabetically by club, with games in parentheses, had no plate appearances, primarily through use of designated hitters:

AGUASCALIENTES—Byron, Quiroz, Ricardo (7); Chavez, Guadalupe (1); Delgadillo, Gustavo (20); Granillo, Carlos (27); Ibarra, Carlos (26); Lopez, Hector (15); Martinez, Gabriel (19); Matus, Nelson (26); Munoz, Miguel (3); Rodriguez, Arturo (15); Rodriguez, Mario A. (25); Sandate, Ricardo (25); Toribio, Manuel (5); Villanueva, Luis (34); Villegas, Mike (25).

CAMPECHE—Acosta, Cecilio (11); Baruch, Matias (18); Chavez, Luis (22); Divison, Julio Cesar (48); Flores, Jose Antonio (2); Hernandez, Angel (24); Madrigal, Jose (20); Menendez, Rolando (19); Moncada, Mario (3); Posadas, Rafael (2); Raygoza, Martin (7); Reyes, Hector (1); Rodriguez, Ramon (19), Valdez, Humberto (3).

CORDOBA—Aponte, Bonifacio (2); Beltran, Jorge (1); Colorado, Salvador (27); Cordova, Wilfrido (10); Gaxiola, Fernando (19); Leal, Bernabe (13); Morales, Mario (2); Morin, Paulino (8); Rivera, Oscar (6); Rodriguez, Jose (6); Romo, Vicente (14); Salinas, Guadalupe (3); Serafin, Hector (43); Silva, Eduardo (41); Tejeda, Gregorio (8); Torres, Martin (25); Urrea, Leonel (9); Vazquez, Marco A. (9).

LEON—Andujar, Ramon (4); Delgadillo, Gustavo (7); Enriquez, Martin (22); Jefferson, Jesse (7); Martinez, Jose Luis (17); Menendez, Rolando (7); Miranda, Francisco (20); Moncada, Mario (4); Ontiveros, Francisco (6); Osuna, Roberto (41); Peralta, Alvaro (4); Perez, Leonardo (20); Ramirez, Jose (22); Raygoza, Martin (41); Rios, Hector (23); Rodriguez, Arturo (25); Rodriguez, Mario A. (13); Valenzuela, Guillermo (19); Velazquez, Ildefonso (8).

MEXICO CITY REDS—Aponte, Luis (11); Chavez, Luis (6); Hernandez, Martin (28); Leal, Bernabe (10); Mendez, Luis Fernando (28); Morales, Isidro (22); Osuna, Ricardo (10); Palacios, Vicente (13); Pulido, Antonio (50); Pruneda, Armando (24); Sanchez, Daniel (18); Solis, Ricardo (31); Tejeda, Gregorio (8); Vizcarra, Matias (4).

MEXICO CITY TIGERS—Abad, Humberto (6); Aguilar, Jose Miguel (7); Alexander, Robert (3); Alvarado, Jose (26); Alvarez, Jose Refugio (1); Beltran, Jorge (7); Brunet, George (2); Buitimea, Martin (26); Cruz, Jesus (14); Cuevas, Rafael (3); Dimas, Rodolfo (7); Esquer, Mercedes (6); Fischer, Todd (8); Granillo, Ismael (1); Harper, Devallon (8); Marcheskie, Lee (29); Mejia, Octavio (5); Montano, Francisco (22); Palafox, Juan (15); Retes, Lorenzo (2); Rios, Jesus (26); Torres, Martin (9); Velazquez, Ildefonso (21); Villegas, Ramon (8).

MONCLOVA—Espinosa, Roberto (8); Feola, Larry (6); Garcia, Enrique (22); Garcia, Jose Luis (38); Guzman, Ramon (44); Ledon, Juan Carlos (35); Lugo, Manuel (9); Mariscal, Tomas (5); Martinez, Hector (4); Montes, Tim (26); Mundo, Jesus (14); Rivas, Lorenzo (14); Rodriguez, Ignacio (2); Rogers, Charles (27); Ruiz, Pablo (27); Sanchez, Daniel (9); Segui, Diego (13); Vazquez, Florentino (27).

MONTERREY—Antunez, Martin (8); Cota, Esteban (5); Dimas, Rodolfo (20); Duarte, Florentino (26); Feola, Larry (20); Ford, Dave (19); Gonzalez, Carlos (5); Guajardo, Arturo (6); Gutierrez, Porfirio (19); Lunar, Luis (26); Mariscal, Tomas (6); Morin, Paulino (1); Murillo, Felipe (22); Romero, Felipe DeJesus (8); Salinas, Guadalupe (6); Sanchez, Pablo (6); Vazquez, Jesse (5); Vila, Jesus (60).

NUEVO LAREDO—Buice, Dewayne (24); Carranza, Javier (7); Cordova, Wilfrido (8); Guajardo, Arturo (6); Huerta, Luis E. (26); Jackson, Reginald (28); Navarro, Adolfo (27); Ochoa, Porfirio (43); Sanchez, Felipe (7); Stone, Steve (15); Vaqueiro, Danny (20); Villegas, Ramon (13).

PUEBLA—Camarena, Martin (8); Jimenez, German (27); Jimenez, Issac (20); Lopez, Dave (1); Ochoa, Domingo (38); Orozco, Jaime (33); Orozco, Octavio (21); Perez, Cipriano (24); Quijano, Enrique (24); Taylor, John (1); Trevino, Noel (1); Urias, Reyes (5).

SALTILLO—Castaneda, Mario (33); Cecena, Jose Isabel (39); Contreras, Patricio (2); Cota, Esteban (17); Cutty, Francis (30); Franco, David (21); Montenegro, Francisco (1); Moya, Ramon (41); Padilla, Raymundo (43); Pimentel, Rafael (18); Solis, Miguel (22); Valenzuela, Adan (6); Valenzuela, Jairo (28); Vazquez, Rafael (2); Vidana, Alejandro (2); Viezca, Rodrigo (11).

TABASCO—Arano, Ramon (11); Breinning, Kevin (1); Diaz, Anibal (5); Garcia, Jorge Luis (29); Garcia, Victor (9); Gonzalez, Fernando (11); Inzunza, Sergio (49); Montes, Tim (1); Ochoa, Julio (5); Palacios, Raul (12); Pena, Manuel (4); Pollorena, Oscar (9); Rojo, Mendez, Gonzalo (51); Rondon, Gilberto (19); Salas, Ernesto (7); Sanchez, Felipe (17); Sanchez, Pablo (20); Torres, Nelson (16); Valdez, Humberto (11); Velazquez, Luis A. (18); Vidana, Alejandro (18); Yucupicio, J. Javier (38); Zamberino, Jesus (2).

TAMPICO—Aguilar, Ismael (27); Aguirre, Hector (14); Antunez, Martin (25); Armas, Isidro (5); Beltran, Eleazar (25); Buitimea, Martin (6); Chavez, Guadalupe (54); Gutierrez, Porfirio (10); Luna, Jose M. (8); Marquez, Isidro (13); Perez, Americo (31); Purata, Julio (29); Rivas, Martin (40); Sosa, Carlos (29); Tinajero, Juan (1); Torres, Martin (1); Villegas, Ramon (6).

UNION LAGUNA—Alicea, Miguel (24); Carranza, Javier (20); Castillo, Humberto (5); Contreras, Roberto (34); de los Santos, Ramon (13); Diaz, Octavio (9); Garcia, Lenny (3); Garcia, Rafael (12); Low, Gabriel (20); Montano, Nicolas (24); Pollorena, Antonio (23); Rivera, Abraham (20); Romo, Manuel (8); Romero, Emigdio (15); Ronquillo, Guillermo (8); Senteney, Steve (18); Serna, Ramon (30); Sombra, Francisco (17).

VERACRUZ—Arano, Ramon (7); Armas, Isidro (10); Castaneda, Aurelio (11); Cordova, Ernesto (13); Cuevas, Rafael (3); Delfin, Justino (12); Felix, Antonio (13); Figueroa, Miguel (41); Gonzalez, Fernando (3); Guzman, Gelacio (24); Luna, Jose M. (24); Morales, Mario (2); Ontiveros, Francisco (27); Pollorena, Oscar (23); Rincon, Juan (10); Rivera, Oscar (15); Urrea, Leonel (38); Vazquez, Marco A. (17); Zamudio, Aurelio (16).

YUCATAN—Arroyo, Freddie (7); Belman, Andres (22); Castillejos, Jose M. (22); Cordova, Ernesto (11); Diaz, Cesar (22); Escarrega, Ernesto (24); Espinosa, Javier (16); Navarrete, Jorge (4); Placencia, Jesse (9); Rincon, Juan (12); Rodriguez, Pilar (33); Ruiz, Cecilio (23); Sauceda, Ramiro (27); Uribe, Juan Carlos (1).

GRAND SLAM HOME RUNS—Rendon, A. Torres, 3 each; Bryant, Craig, Lee, Moore, Renteria, Gu. Rodriguez, 2 each; Aguilar, N. Barrera, Bronson, D. Canedo, M. Carrillo, E. Diaz, O. Duran, R. Duran, Ezquerra, A. Felix, L. Guerrero, M.A. Guzman, Leal, Lora, Machiria, Monasterio, Mora, C. Morales, Negron, Ju. Perez, Pierce, G. Quintero, Ray, J. Reyes, Rios, C. Rivera, E. Rivera, A. Rodriguez, Royg, A. Sanchez, Sarabia, Tellez, 1 each.

AWARDED FIRST BASE ON CATCHER'S INTERFERENCE—C. Lopez 4 (N. Barrera, M.A. Guzman, M. Hernandez, O. Sanchez); Bazan (S. Robles); An. Castaneda (S. Robles); Herring (Rosas); Navarrete (Rojas); A. Rodriguez (Rosas); Rojo (Monroy); Ge. Sanchez (L.A. Mendoza); Felipe Valenzuela, Tabasco (Soriano).

## CLUB FIELDING

| Club | Pct. | G. | PO. | A. | E. | DP. | PB. | Club | Pct. | G. | PO. | A. | E. | DP. | PB. |
|---|---|---|---|---|---|---|---|---|---|---|---|---|---|---|---|
| Cordoba | .977 | 130 | 3245 | 1325 | 109 | 127 | 12 | Saltillo | .969 | 131 | 3243 | 1486 | 139 | 137 | 15 |
| Puebla | .977 | 126 | 3001 | 1357 | 104 | 131 | 19 | Tabasco | .969 | 130 | 3201 | 1357 | 145 | 112 | 26 |
| Mexico City Tigers | .976 | 127 | 3192 | 1439 | 113 | 130 | 14 | Tampico | .968 | 130 | 3272 | 1350 | 152 | 125 | 18 |
| Yucatan | .975 | 126 | 3142 | 1403 | 116 | 128 | 10 | Leon | .968 | 129 | 3131 | 1416 | 150 | 160 | 16 |
| Mexico City Reds | .973 | 132 | 3300 | 1514 | 134 | 138 | 10 | Veracruz | .967 | 132 | 3290 | 1624 | 167 | 141 | 16 |
| Nuevo Laredo | .971 | 128 | 3172 | 1239 | 130 | 111 | 14 | Union Laguna | .966 | 132 | 3317 | 1364 | 166 | 108 | 36 |
| Campeche | .971 | 120 | 2978 | 1326 | 127 | 112 | 23 | Aguascalientes | .964 | 125 | 3127 | 1370 | 167 | 113 | 12 |
| Monterrey | .971 | 130 | 3182 | 1398 | 138 | 146 | 32 | Monclova | .963 | 128 | 3165 | 1344 | 175 | 127 | 22 |

Triple Plays—Monterrey, Tabasco, Yucatan.

## INDIVIDUAL FIELDING

*Throws lefthanded.

### FIRST BASEMEN

| Player and Club | Pct. | G. | PO. | A. | E. | DP. | Player and Club | Pct. | G. | PO. | A. | E. | DP. |
|---|---|---|---|---|---|---|---|---|---|---|---|---|---|
| Evans, Aguascalientes | 1.000 | 20 | 169 | 11 | 0 | 14 | An. Lopez, 40 Ags-65 Tab | .991 | 105 | 899 | 54 | 9 | 63 |
| L. Salinas, Mexico City Reds* | 1.000 | 19 | 115 | 6 | 0 | 8 | Villaescusa, Yucatan | .991 | 42 | 392 | 29 | 4 | 34 |
| R. Hernandez, Yucatan | 1.000 | 13 | 113 | 6 | 0 | 17 | Quiroz, Nuevo Laredo | .989 | 19 | 83 | 3 | 1 | 4 |
| GU. RODRIGUEZ, Puebla | .999 | 90 | 751 | 48 | 1 | 90 | Ge. Rodriguez, Union Laguna | .988 | 42 | 319 | 12 | 4 | 29 |
| Garzon, Cordoba | .998 | 129 | 1162 | 61 | 3 | 119 | Pierce, Leon | .988 | 126 | 1146 | 65 | 15 | 143 |
| Lee, Puebla | .995 | 23 | 195 | 6 | 1 | 20 | B. Valdez, Veracruz | .987 | 107 | 1016 | 66 | 14 | 108 |
| Sosa, Tampico | .995 | 27 | 189 | 8 | 1 | 15 | A. Felix, Veracruz | .987 | 18 | 146 | 5 | 2 | 9 |
| Mora, Nuevo Laredo | .994 | 110 | 846 | 38 | 5 | 82 | J. Lopez, Union Laguna* | .986 | 68 | 543 | 33 | 8 | 59 |
| Gray, 60 Cam-33 Ags | .994 | 93 | 849 | 33 | 5 | 74 | A. Torres, 2 Tab-4 MCR-4 UL | .986 | 10 | 66 | 3 | 1 | 6 |
| A. Peralta, Mexico City Tigers | .994 | 59 | 491 | 38 | 3 | 61 | A. Garza, Tabasco* | .985 | 57 | 496 | 21 | 8 | 47 |
| Al. Lopez, Mexico City Tigers | .993 | 70 | 541 | 41 | 4 | 58 | Cabrera, Monclova | .985 | 26 | 184 | 9 | 3 | 19 |
| J.L. Perez, Aguascalientes* | .992 | 14 | 123 | 8 | 1 | 10 | Villagomez, Tampico | .985 | 112 | 989 | 30 | 16 | 83 |
| H. Cruz, Saltillo* | .992 | 15 | 120 | 6 | 1 | 10 | R. Guerra, Union Laguna | .982 | 15 | 106 | 5 | 2 | 6 |
| Bundy, Mexico City Reds* | .992 | 99 | 920 | 53 | 8 | 96 | C. Soto, Nuevo Laredo | .981 | 13 | 95 | 9 | 2 | 5 |
| Clayton, Saltillo | .992 | 93 | 780 | 62 | 7 | 95 | Lora, Puebla | .981 | 19 | 145 | 6 | 3 | 16 |
| Bojorquez, Campeche | .991 | 38 | 331 | 18 | 3 | 36 | Greene, Monclova* | .979 | 100 | 812 | 31 | 18 | 83 |
| R. Duran, Monterrey* | .991 | 122 | 1092 | 52 | 10 | 135 | Payton, Union Laguna | .977 | 21 | 123 | 7 | 3 | 6 |
| J. Vega, 19 MCR-63 Yuc* | .991 | 82 | 744 | 51 | 7 | 78 | Santos, Saltillo | .977 | 36 | 250 | 9 | 6 | 27 |
| DeFreites, Yucatan | .991 | 11 | 106 | 4 | 1 | 3 | J. Reyes, 19 Ags-24 Cam* | .977 | 43 | 359 | 19 | 9 | 31 |

### (Fewer Than Ten Games)

| Player and Club | Pct. | G. | PO. | A. | E. | DP. | Player and Club | Pct. | G. | PO. | A. | E. | DP. |
|---|---|---|---|---|---|---|---|---|---|---|---|---|---|
| C. Lopez, Tabasco | 1.000 | 8 | 53 | 1 | 0 | 5 | Salazar, Tabasco | 1.000 | 1 | 6 | 1 | 0 | 1 |
| A. Castro, Mexico City Tigers* | 1.000 | 6 | 37 | 2 | 0 | 2 | Rendon, Saltillo | 1.000 | 1 | 6 | 0 | 0 | 1 |
| Bobadilla, Monclova | 1.000 | 8 | 36 | 1 | 0 | 4 | A. Guzman, Tabasco | 1.000 | 1 | 6 | 0 | 0 | 1 |
| H. Robles, Monterrey | 1.000 | 7 | 31 | 3 | 0 | 2 | L.A. Morales, Nuevo Laredo | 1.000 | 4 | 5 | 0 | 0 | 2 |
| Avila, Tampico | 1.000 | 4 | 31 | 2 | 0 | 6 | Roldan, Cordoba | 1.000 | 2 | 4 | 0 | 0 | 0 |
| Ezquerra, Mexico City Reds* | 1.000 | 6 | 27 | 1 | 0 | 3 | Placencia, Puebla | 1.000 | 1 | 4 | 0 | 0 | 0 |
| N. Castaneda, M.C. Tigers* | 1.000 | 2 | 21 | 3 | 0 | 3 | Marg. Morales, Union Laguna | 1.000 | 1 | 2 | 1 | 0 | 0 |
| C. Morales, Leon | 1.000 | 3 | 20 | 0 | 0 | 1 | Rojas, Mexico City Tigers | 1.000 | 1 | 3 | 0 | 0 | 0 |
| Arredondo, Veracruz | 1.000 | 4 | 18 | 2 | 0 | 3 | Bautista, Veracruz* | .985 | 7 | 62 | 4 | 1 | 8 |
| Cosey, Campeche | 1.000 | 4 | 15 | 0 | 0 | 0 | H. Valenzuela, 3 Leo-5 MCT* | .983 | 8 | 55 | 2 | 1 | 3 |
| Gage, Tabasco* | 1.000 | 3 | 11 | 0 | 0 | 3 | Vergara, Veracruz | .967 | 3 | 28 | 1 | 1 | 1 |
| Bronson, Union Laguna | 1.000 | 3 | 9 | 1 | 0 | 1 | Sarabia, Monclova | .937 | 7 | 57 | 2 | 4 | 1 |
| Alf. Ortiz, 1 Vera.-2 Cor* | 1.000 | 3 | 10 | 0 | 0 | 2 | L. Meza, Veracruz | .929 | 3 | 24 | 2 | 2 | 1 |
| J.M. Ortiz, Monterrey | 1.000 | 1 | 8 | 0 | 0 | 0 | Marc. Acosta, Tabasco | .929 | 3 | 12 | 1 | 1 | 0 |
| R. Valenzuela, M.C. Tigers | 1.000 | 1 | 8 | 0 | 0 | 0 | Rosales, Cordoba | .889 | 1 | 7 | 1 | 1 | 0 |
| V.M. Felix, Yucatan | 1.000 | 1 | 7 | 1 | 0 | 2 | Scott, Puebla | .500 | 1 | 1 | 0 | 1 | 0 |
| N. Gonzalez, Monterrey | 1.000 | 1 | 7 | 0 | 0 | 1 | Negron, Tabasco* | .000 | 1 | 0 | 1 | 0 | 0 |

Triple Plays—R. Duran, An. Lopez, J. Vega.

## SECOND BASEMEN

| Player and Club | Pct. | G. | PO. | A. | E. | DP. |
|---|---|---|---|---|---|---|
| Trinidad, Ulin, Cordoba | 1.000 | 22 | 34 | 34 | 0 | 8 |
| J.M. Ortiz, Monterrey | 1.000 | 10 | 25 | 25 | 0 | 8 |
| A. SANCHEZ, Mexico City Reds | .991 | 127 | 307 | 356 | 6 | 92 |
| Navarrete, Saltillo | .990 | 131 | 312 | 377 | 7 | 107 |
| N. Torres, 35 Vera.-57 Tab | .990 | 92 | 236 | 243 | 5 | 50 |
| Campos, Tabasco | .984 | 21 | 23 | 40 | 1 | 7 |
| I. Reyes, Tabasco | .983 | 23 | 32 | 26 | 1 | 10 |
| Galindo, Nuevo Laredo | .982 | 53 | 94 | 124 | 4 | 34 |
| Blanks, Campeche | .982 | 22 | 43 | 65 | 2 | 11 |
| Scott, Puebla | .980 | 59 | 145 | 152 | 6 | 36 |
| A. Camacho, Mexico City Tigers | .979 | 51 | 140 | 138 | 6 | 35 |
| J. Gonzalez, Puebla | .978 | 85 | 173 | 226 | 7 | 69 |
| Briones, Union Laguna | .980 | 120 | 263 | 314 | 12 | 65 |
| J.A. Castro, Tabasco | .977 | 29 | 51 | 74 | 3 | 10 |
| Ju. Rodriguez, Leon | .976 | 122 | 302 | 389 | 17 | 107 |
| Jo. Rodriguez, M.C. Tigers | .976 | 78 | 211 | 232 | 11 | 61 |
| Serna, Monclova | .975 | 90 | 228 | 248 | 12 | 59 |
| Villela, Tampico | .975 | 123 | 305 | 396 | 18 | 82 |
| Pacho, Yucatan | .974 | 61 | 142 | 195 | 9 | 39 |
| R. Chavez, Campeche | .973 | 97 | 242 | 305 | 15 | 76 |
| Villaescusa, Yucatan | .973 | 65 | 145 | 183 | 9 | 53 |
| C. Rios, Monterrey | .972 | 128 | 312 | 342 | 19 | 97 |
| F. Martinez, Cordoba | .971 | 69 | 126 | 174 | 9 | 48 |
| Franklin, Cordoba | .966 | 59 | 125 | 132 | 9 | 32 |
| Ge. Sanchez, Nuevo Laredo | .963 | 81 | 160 | 205 | 14 | 45 |
| O. Martinez, 3 Cor-27 Vera | .962 | 30 | 60 | 66 | 5 | 13 |
| Fabela, Veracruz | .958 | 65 | 167 | 197 | 16 | 53 |
| L. Guerrero, Aguascalientes | .951 | 120 | 294 | 342 | 33 | 69 |
| Cabrera, Monclova | .950 | 52 | 112 | 115 | 12 | 35 |
| A. Limon, Tabasco | .948 | 42 | 81 | 82 | 9 | 22 |
| Almodobar, Tampico | .944 | 10 | 16 | 18 | 2 | 3 |
| J.C. Leon, Yucatan | .941 | 12 | 8 | 8 | 1 | 1 |
| Paula, Union Laguna | .870 | 10 | 18 | 22 | 6 | 6 |

### (Fewer Than Ten Games)

| Player and Club | Pct. | G. | PO. | A. | E. | DP. |
|---|---|---|---|---|---|---|
| Raf. Torres, Aguascalientes | 1.000 | 5 | 19 | 8 | 0 | 2 |
| J.A. Barrera, Nuevo Laredo | 1.000 | 9 | 7 | 17 | 0 | 2 |
| Alonso, Puebla | 1.000 | 3 | 5 | 5 | 0 | 2 |
| J.A. Chavez, Veracruz | 1.000 | 3 | 4 | 3 | 0 | 0 |
| N. Gonzalez, Monclova | 1.000 | 1 | 2 | 2 | 0 | 0 |
| Uribe, Tampico | 1.000 | 3 | 1 | 3 | 0 | 0 |
| Maza, Union Laguna | 1.000 | 2 | 1 | 2 | 0 | 0 |
| S. Limon, Tabasco | 1.000 | 1 | 0 | 2 | 0 | 0 |
| A. Canedo, Monclova | 1.000 | 3 | 1 | 1 | 0 | 0 |
| Gu. Sanchez, Leon | 1.000 | 2 | 0 | 1 | 0 | 0 |
| Zuniga, Mexico City Tigers | 1.000 | 3 | 1 | 0 | 0 | 0 |
| Cabrales, Campeche | .974 | 9 | 17 | 20 | 1 | 1 |
| Gamundi, Veracruz | .969 | 5 | 13 | 18 | 1 | 4 |
| Barragan, Mexico City Reds | .950 | 9 | 25 | 13 | 2 | 2 |
| Avina, Leon | .939 | 9 | 11 | 20 | 2 | 5 |
| Renteria, Mexico City Tigers | .923 | 7 | 10 | 14 | 2 | 3 |
| Barandica, Union Laguna | .909 | 9 | 14 | 16 | 3 | 3 |
| F. Guerrero, Union Laguna | .900 | 8 | 10 | 17 | 3 | 6 |
| Montiel, Leon | .900 | 7 | 8 | 10 | 2 | 6 |
| Munoz, Yucatan | .857 | 5 | 1 | 5 | 1 | 0 |

Triple Plays—Rios, Villaescusa.

## THIRD BASEMEN

| Player and Club | Pct. | G. | PO. | A. | E. | DP. |
|---|---|---|---|---|---|---|
| Je. Garcia, Monclova | .980 | 19 | 12 | 36 | 1 | 4 |
| S. Limon, Tabasco | .976 | 23 | 12 | 28 | 1 | 1 |
| N. Barrera, Mexico City Reds | .970 | 30 | 31 | 65 | 3 | 7 |
| E. CASTILLO, Cordoba | .968 | 106 | 91 | 242 | 11 | 27 |
| Alonso, Puebla | .966 | 29 | 17 | 67 | 3 | 8 |
| Cazarin, Veracruz | .964 | 16 | 23 | 31 | 2 | 3 |
| R. Guerra, Union Laguna | .964 | 16 | 10 | 17 | 1 | 0 |
| B. Santana, Yucatan | .963 | 126 | 100 | 285 | 15 | 30 |
| J. Gonzalez, Puebla | .962 | 46 | 61 | 66 | 5 | 8 |
| A. Rodriguez, Monterrey | .961 | 79 | 83 | 161 | 10 | 24 |
| Saiz, Union Laguna | .960 | 98 | 74 | 235 | 13 | 15 |
| C. Rivera, Campeche | .954 | 79 | 72 | 135 | 10 | 13 |
| Renteria, Mexico City Tigers | .952 | 117 | 111 | 227 | 17 | 22 |
| M. Salinas, Mexico City Reds | .950 | 88 | 74 | 194 | 14 | 15 |
| Serratos, Mexico City Reds | .948 | 22 | 21 | 52 | 4 | 4 |
| Bobadilla, Monclova | .946 | 77 | 73 | 155 | 13 | 18 |
| Ju. Perez, Tampico | .946 | 122 | 102 | 231 | 19 | 24 |
| L. Meza, Veracruz | .944 | 96 | 68 | 200 | 16 | 20 |
| Scott, Puebla | .941 | 18 | 13 | 35 | 3 | 6 |
| E. Aguilar, Aguascalientes | .941 | 119 | 103 | 279 | 24 | 23 |
| J.A. Castro, Tabasco | .939 | 47 | 31 | 77 | 7 | 2 |
| Ale. Ortiz, Nuevo Laredo | .937 | 128 | 123 | 247 | 25 | 18 |
| L. Jimenez, Campeche | .937 | 32 | 29 | 45 | 5 | 1 |
| N. Gonzalez, Monterrey | .935 | 58 | 44 | 101 | 10 | 8 |
| Sommers, Leon | .935 | 62 | 39 | 106 | 10 | 14 |
| O. Martinez, 23 Cor-11 Vera | .935 | 34 | 20 | 67 | 6 | 8 |
| M. Rubio, Saltillo | .933 | 13 | 12 | 30 | 3 | 4 |
| R. Salazar, Tabasco | .933 | 78 | 69 | 125 | 14 | 12 |
| An. Castaneda, Puebla | .929 | 30 | 9 | 43 | 4 | 3 |
| Bautista, Veracruz | .924 | 24 | 27 | 58 | 7 | 4 |
| Montiel, Leon | .920 | 11 | 6 | 17 | 2 | 5 |
| Arce, Leon | .919 | 74 | 54 | 138 | 17 | 18 |
| Rendon, Saltillo | .917 | 12 | 12 | 32 | 4 | 2 |
| Burke, Saltillo | .915 | 115 | 97 | 248 | 32 | 32 |
| Serna, Monclova | .913 | 38 | 31 | 64 | 9 | 4 |
| Saenz, Puebla | .897 | 21 | 14 | 38 | 6 | 1 |
| Paula, Union Laguna | .860 | 26 | 22 | 52 | 12 | 1 |

### (Fewer Than Ten Games)

| Player and Club | Pct. | G. | PO. | A. | E. | DP. |
|---|---|---|---|---|---|---|
| A. Camacho, Mexico City Tigers | 1.000 | 7 | 7 | 12 | 0 | 3 |
| S. Mendoza, Campeche | 1.000 | 8 | 2 | 13 | 0 | 0 |
| J.M. Ortiz, Monterrey | 1.000 | 3 | 4 | 6 | 0 | 0 |
| Trinidad, Ulin, Cordoba | 1.000 | 3 | 3 | 6 | 0 | 1 |
| N. Torres, Tabasco | 1.000 | 3 | 1 | 7 | 0 | 1 |
| Blanks, Campeche | 1.000 | 3 | 1 | 6 | 0 | 2 |
| Chavarria, Saltillo | 1.000 | 1 | 4 | 1 | 0 | 1 |
| R. Valenzuela, M. C. Tigers | 1.000 | 2 | 1 | 3 | 0 | 1 |
| Zepeda, Tabasco | 1.000 | 2 | 1 | 2 | 0 | 1 |
| J.A. Barrera, Union Laredo | 1.000 | 1 | 0 | 2 | 0 | 0 |
| I. Reyes, Tabasco | 1.000 | 1 | 0 | 2 | 0 | 0 |
| B. Valdez, Veracruz | 1.000 | 1 | 1 | 0 | 0 | 0 |
| L.A. Cruz, Tampico | .944 | 9 | 6 | 11 | 1 | 4 |
| Cabrera, Monclova | .909 | 7 | 7 | 3 | 1 | 1 |
| D. Canedo, Monclova | .867 | 2 | 4 | 9 | 2 | 2 |
| Bojorquez, Campeche | .857 | 3 | 2 | 4 | 1 | 1 |
| M.A. Guzman, Campeche | .824 | 5 | 6 | 8 | 3 | 1 |
| A. Peralta, Mexico City Tigers | .813 | 6 | 4 | 9 | 3 | 2 |
| Raf. Torres, Aguascalientes | .769 | 7 | 4 | 6 | 3 | 1 |
| Garzon, Cordoba | .667 | 2 | 1 | 1 | 1 | 0 |
| A. Torres, Tabasco | .000 | 1 | 0 | 0 | 1 | 0 |

Triple Play—Santana.

## SHORTSTOPS

| Player and Club | Pct. | G. | PO. | A. | E. | DP. |
|---|---|---|---|---|---|---|
| Gene. Rivero, Yucatan | .991 | 74 | 120 | 204 | 3 | 35 |
| Scott, Puebla | .987 | 30 | 49 | 105 | 2 | 21 |
| A. Camacho, Mexico City Tigers | .979 | 37 | 59 | 125 | 4 | 17 |
| Trinidad, Ulin, Cordoba | .977 | 32 | 22 | 63 | 2 | 12 |
| DE LOS SANTOS, Cordoba | .967 | 115 | 186 | 312 | 17 | 64 |
| Montiel, Leon | .965 | 15 | 19 | 36 | 2 | 7 |
| P. Mendoza, Puebla | .964 | 102 | 129 | 295 | 16 | 51 |
| Blanks, 24 Cam.-22 Vera | .961 | 46 | 69 | 150 | 9 | 22 |
| M. Morales, Mexico City Tigers | .960 | 101 | 154 | 297 | 19 | 66 |
| A. Gomez, Tabasco | .960 | 124 | 199 | 394 | 25 | 65 |
| Uzcanga, Monterrey | .959 | 124 | 223 | 382 | 26 | 94 |
| C. Rivera, Campeche | .956 | 25 | 36 | 72 | 5 | 11 |
| Elizondo, Saltillo | .955 | 126 | 236 | 408 | 30 | 81 |
| Fabela, Veracruz | .954 | 36 | 59 | 128 | 9 | 22 |
| Barragan, Mexico City Reds | .953 | 37 | 58 | 126 | 9 | 23 |
| Ju. Hernandez, MC Reds | .952 | 106 | 180 | 319 | 25 | 66 |
| J.A. Barrera, Nuevo Laredo | .950 | 110 | 174 | 264 | 23 | 56 |
| Cabrales, Campeche | .948 | 65 | 151 | 194 | 19 | 45 |
| J.A. Chavez, Veracruz | .945 | 45 | 79 | 128 | 12 | 29 |
| Pacho, Yucatan | .945 | 63 | 99 | 176 | 16 | 45 |
| Uribe, Tampico | .945 | 75 | 123 | 184 | 18 | 35 |
| Mario Mendoza, Aguascalientes | .944 | 109 | 197 | 344 | 32 | 56 |
| V. Quintero, Veracruz | .943 | 34 | 53 | 113 | 10 | 23 |
| Herrera, Leon | .940 | 119 | 215 | 366 | 37 | 94 |
| F. Guerrero, Union Laguna | .936 | 53 | 84 | 105 | 13 | 23 |
| Galindo, Nuevo Laredo | .934 | 21 | 22 | 35 | 4 | 6 |
| Escalante, Aguascalientes | .929 | 18 | 33 | 46 | 6 | 7 |
| D. Canedo, Monclova | .929 | 116 | 192 | 354 | 42 | 62 |
| Almodobar, Tampico | .908 | 41 | 63 | 105 | 17 | 15 |
| Valle, Union Laguna | .903 | 99 | 137 | 215 | 38 | 40 |
| L. Jimenez, Campeche | .879 | 17 | 22 | 36 | 8 | 5 |
| Barajas, Tampico | .857 | 11 | 13 | 35 | 8 | 5 |
| L.A. Cruz, Tampico | .814 | 10 | 12 | 23 | 8 | 1 |

(Fewer Than Ten Games)

| Player and Club | Pct. | G. | PO. | A. | E. | DP. | Player and Club | Pct. | G. | PO. | A. | E. | DP. |
|---|---|---|---|---|---|---|---|---|---|---|---|---|---|
| R. Campos, Tabasco | 1.000 | 6 | 3 | 15 | 0 | 1 | Bobadilla, Monclova | .955 | 8 | 3 | 18 | 1 | 1 |
| Zepeda, Tabasco | 1.000 | 3 | 4 | 10 | 0 | 3 | C. Rios, Monterrey | .938 | 6 | 4 | 11 | 1 | 4 |
| S. Limon, Tabasco | 1.000 | 6 | 5 | 5 | 0 | 3 | Bautista, Veracruz | .897 | 7 | 9 | 26 | 4 | 7 |
| An. Castaneda, Puebla | 1.000 | 2 | 1 | 4 | 0 | 2 | Je. Garcia, Monclova | .880 | 9 | 7 | 15 | 3 | 2 |
| Villaescusa, Yucatan | 1.000 | 3 | 3 | 2 | 0 | 0 | M. Delgado, Saltillo | .857 | 5 | 3 | 9 | 2 | 2 |
| E. Ramirez, Nuevo Laredo | 1.000 | 3 | 1 | 3 | 0 | 0 | A. Canedo, Monclova | .833 | 9 | 8 | 12 | 4 | 5 |
| F. Rodriguez, Veracruz | 1.000 | 1 | 0 | 4 | 0 | 1 | Baca, Nuevo Laredo | .800 | 1 | 0 | 4 | 1 | 0 |
| Ju. Perez, Tampico | 1.000 | 4 | 2 | 2 | 0 | 0 | Raf. Torres, Aguascalientes | .571 | 6 | 1 | 3 | 3 | 0 |
| Ju. Rodriguez, Leon | 1.000 | 3 | 1 | 1 | 0 | 0 | S. Mendoza, Campeche | .500 | 1 | 0 | 2 | 2 | 0 |

Triple Plays—A. Gomez, Uzcanga.

## OUTFIELDERS

| Player and Club | Pct. | G. | PO. | A. | E. | DP. | Player and Club | Pct. | G. | PO. | A. | E. | DP. |
|---|---|---|---|---|---|---|---|---|---|---|---|---|---|
| Vargas, 2 MC Tig.-34 Tampico | 1.000 | 36 | 52 | 6 | 0 | 2 | Gage, Tabasco* | .969 | 123 | 243 | 10 | 8 | 3 |
| Clayton, Saltillo | 1.000 | 23 | 52 | 2 | 0 | 1 | Rod. Rodriguez, Aguascalientes* | .969 | 98 | 148 | 10 | 5 | 1 |
| Tapia, Tabasco | 1.000 | 36 | 50 | 3 | 0 | 1 | Ray, Mexico City Reds* | .969 | 74 | 118 | 8 | 4 | 1 |
| Figueroa, Yucatan | 1.000 | 29 | 53 | 0 | 0 | 0 | N. Gonzalez, Monterrey | .969 | 21 | 31 | 0 | 1 | 0 |
| Negron, 12 M.C. Reds-18 Tab.* | 1.000 | 30 | 48 | 2 | 0 | 0 | Villagomez, Tampico | .969 | 14 | 29 | 2 | 1 | 1 |
| A. Felix, Veracruz | 1.000 | 21 | 38 | 2 | 0 | 0 | Maza, Union Laguna | .968 | 35 | 60 | 1 | 2 | 0 |
| Moran, Campeche | 1.000 | 18 | 25 | 0 | 0 | 0 | Bronson, Union Laguna | .967 | 107 | 195 | 8 | 7 | 1 |
| Paredes, Cordoba | 1.000 | 19 | 23 | 1 | 0 | 0 | G. Gomez, Leon | .966 | 120 | 221 | 9 | 8 | 2 |
| F. Carrillo, Aguascalientes | 1.000 | 14 | 21 | 0 | 0 | 0 | Baca, Nuevo Laredo | .966 | 87 | 133 | 9 | 5 | 1 |
| Garibay, Nuevo Laredo | 1.000 | 18 | 15 | 0 | 0 | 0 | Sarabia, Monclova | .965 | 109 | 182 | 12 | 7 | 1 |
| Jo. Garcia, Tampico | 1.000 | 13 | 12 | 1 | 0 | 0 | Cotes, Cordoba | .964 | 56 | 79 | 2 | 3 | 0 |
| Monroy, Monclova | 1.000 | 12 | 10 | 0 | 0 | 0 | C. Lopez, Tabasco | .964 | 59 | 126 | 6 | 5 | 2 |
| G. Reyes, Mexico City Tigers | 1.000 | 11 | 7 | 3 | 0 | 1 | Leal, Monclova* | .963 | 122 | 222 | 13 | 9 | 1 |
| A. CASTRO, M.C. Tigers* | .996 | 119 | 225 | 15 | 1 | 3 | Walker, Mexico City Reds | .963 | 43 | 69 | 9 | 3 | 0 |
| Cano, Saltillo | .993 | 77 | 144 | 8 | 1 | 0 | Payton, Union Laguna | .962 | 88 | 165 | 14 | 7 | 1 |
| Ponce, Puebla | .992 | 89 | 123 | 9 | 1 | 2 | O. Duran, Saltillo | .962 | 34 | 50 | 1 | 2 | 0 |
| Bryant, Tampico | .991 | 63 | 108 | 4 | 1 | 0 | Craig, Nuevo Laredo | .962 | 108 | 192 | 9 | 8 | 2 |
| Cosey, Campeche | .991 | 118 | 205 | 15 | 2 | 2 | Ray. Torres, Yucatan | .960 | 107 | 258 | 6 | 11 | 3 |
| Caballero, Monterrey | .988 | 57 | 79 | 2 | 1 | 1 | Royg, 46 Vera.-62 Campeche | .959 | 108 | 237 | 20 | 11 | 2 |
| Collins, 42 Cordoba-44 Vera.* | .986 | 86 | 128 | 8 | 2 | 2 | Quiroz, Nuevo Laredo | .958 | 68 | 87 | 4 | 4 | 1 |
| L.A. Cruz, Tampico | .984 | 86 | 173 | 11 | 3 | 3 | Monasterio, 51 MR-31 V-31 L. | .957 | 113 | 216 | 9 | 10 | 1 |
| Greene, Monclova* | .984 | 39 | 54 | 6 | 1 | 1 | Sherow, Tabasco | .957 | 16 | 43 | 2 | 2 | 1 |
| Ja. Hernandez, Leon | .981 | 45 | 49 | 4 | 1 | 1 | Cangelosi, Mexico City Reds | .957 | 60 | 127 | 7 | 6 | 1 |
| Gu. Rodriguez, Puebla | .981 | 38 | 49 | 3 | 1 | 1 | E. Diaz, Campeche | .955 | 40 | 62 | 1 | 3 | 1 |
| DeFreites, Yucatan | .981 | 99 | 198 | 4 | 4 | 0 | Ja. Rodriguez, Tabasco | .954 | 104 | 195 | 11 | 10 | 2 |
| Rosales, 27 Cor.-94 Mon. | .980 | 121 | 238 | 8 | 5 | 0 | Scott, Puebla | .952 | 14 | 19 | 1 | 1 | 0 |
| Ge. Sanchez, Nuevo Laredo | .980 | 25 | 40 | 8 | 1 | 1 | Santos, Saltillo | .952 | 76 | 110 | 9 | 6 | 1 |
| Tellez, Cordoba | .980 | 130 | 333 | 6 | 7 | 2 | Zambrano, Cordoba* | .952 | 72 | 131 | 7 | 7 | 1 |
| Rendon, Saltillo | .979 | 104 | 174 | 16 | 4 | 4 | Sotelo, Leon | .951 | 37 | 38 | 1 | 2 | 0 |
| Moore, Leon | .979 | 116 | 177 | 8 | 4 | 2 | Arzate, Aguascalientes | .950 | 83 | 184 | 8 | 10 | 2 |
| A. Diaz, Union Laguna | .979 | 96 | 181 | 4 | 4 | 0 | Rubio, 10 Vera.-4 Tabasco | .950 | 14 | 19 | 0 | 1 | 0 |
| Powell, Saltillo | .979 | 39 | 88 | 4 | 2 | 1 | R. Guerra, Union Laguna | .950 | 13 | 17 | 2 | 1 | 1 |
| Vergara, Aguascalientes | .978 | 25 | 45 | 0 | 1 | 0 | Isambert, Yucatan | .949 | 31 | 53 | 3 | 3 | 1 |
| Serratos, Mexico City Reds | .976 | 25 | 38 | 2 | 1 | 0 | Adams, 50 Tabasco-69 Vera. | .948 | 119 | 212 | 9 | 12 | 2 |
| J.S. Chavez, Nuevo Laredo* | .975 | 94 | 149 | 10 | 4 | 1 | Suarez, 12 Vera.-30 Mon.* | .948 | 42 | 53 | 2 | 3 | 2 |
| R. Navarro, Monterrey | .975 | 23 | 35 | 4 | 1 | 2 | O. Sanchez, Puebla | .944 | 21 | 32 | 2 | 2 | 0 |
| D. Fernandez, M.C. Reds* | .974 | 112 | 212 | 11 | 6 | 2 | Andrade, 30 Tam.-50 Mon.* | .944 | 80 | 130 | 5 | 8 | 1 |
| Herring, Tampico | .973 | 75 | 138 | 8 | 4 | 3 | An. Castaneda, Puebla | .941 | 21 | 16 | 0 | 1 | 0 |
| Machiria, Tampico | .973 | 105 | 172 | 8 | 5 | 1 | V.M. Felix, Yucatan | .938 | 18 | 28 | 2 | 2 | 0 |
| Castelan, Puebla* | .973 | 113 | 205 | 9 | 6 | 0 | Mario Gonzalez, Monterrey | .938 | 11 | 15 | 0 | 1 | 0 |
| Olivares 64 Agua.-39 Cam.* | .972 | 93 | 190 | 20 | 6 | 2 | H. Valenzuela, Leon* | .935 | 56 | 72 | 0 | 5 | 0 |
| F. Lopez, Saltillo | .972 | 74 | 131 | 9 | 4 | 1 | Gamundi, 1 Laguna-53 Agua. | .935 | 54 | 87 | 13 | 7 | 1 |
| Flores, 36 Puebla-52 Yucatan | .972 | 88 | 166 | 7 | 5 | 1 | Tovar, Aguascalientes | .929 | 11 | 24 | 2 | 2 | 0 |
| Bellazetin, Mexico City Tigers* | .972 | 122 | 159 | 12 | 5 | 3 | Jo. Perez, Aguascalientes* | .927 | 62 | 110 | 5 | 9 | 1 |
| M.A. Guzman, Campeche | .972 | 55 | 99 | 4 | 3 | 0 | Johnes, Nuevo Laredo | .926 | 37 | 61 | 2 | 5 | 1 |
| Smith, Monclova* | .971 | 117 | 236 | 2 | 7 | 1 | Ju. Hernandez, MC Reds | .923 | 21 | 32 | 4 | 3 | 1 |
| Lizarraga, 63 UL.-28 Yuc. | .971 | 91 | 162 | 6 | 5 | 0 | Lora, Puebla | .917 | 65 | 90 | 9 | 9 | 0 |
| M. Carrillo, Mexico City Tigers* | .971 | 126 | 320 | 13 | 10 | 4 | Aguilera, Yucatan | .912 | 25 | 29 | 2 | 3 | 0 |
| G. Soto, Campeche | .971 | 40 | 59 | 7 | 2 | 0 | G. Hernandez, Cordoba | .909 | 13 | 28 | 2 | 3 | 0 |
| Saenz, Puebla | .971 | 20 | 32 | 1 | 1 | 0 | Bruno, Monterrey | .907 | 22 | 45 | 4 | 5 | 1 |
| Rosario, 71 Vera.-46 Cordoba | .970 | 117 | 215 | 15 | 7 | 4 | J. Cruz, Mexico City Tigers | .897 | 24 | 23 | 3 | 3 | 0 |
| H. Robles, Monterrey | .969 | 98 | 122 | 5 | 4 | 0 | Bautista, Aguascalientes | .875 | 13 | 17 | 4 | 3 | 0 |
| Jo. Moreno, Aguascalientes | .969 | 45 | 87 | 8 | 3 | 1 | C. Morales, Leon | .818 | 13 | 9 | 0 | 2 | 0 |

(Fewer Than Ten Games)

| Player and Club | Pct. | G. | PO. | A. | E. | DP. | Player and Club | Pct. | G. | PO. | A. | E. | DP. |
|---|---|---|---|---|---|---|---|---|---|---|---|---|---|
| Saavedra, 3 Vera.-4 MC Reds | 1.000 | 7 | 17 | 0 | 0 | 0 | Mart. Acosta, Campeche | 1.000 | 4 | 3 | 1 | 0 | 0 |
| F. Valenzuela, Tabasco | 1.000 | 5 | 6 | 1 | 0 | 0 | Bundy, Mexico City Reds* | 1.000 | 3 | 3 | 0 | 0 | 0 |
| Montero, Union Laguna | 1.000 | 5 | 7 | 0 | 0 | 0 | Chavarria, Saltillo | 1.000 | 9 | 2 | 0 | 0 | 0 |
| L. Jimenez, Campeche | 1.000 | 5 | 6 | 0 | 0 | 0 | Bojorquez, Campeche | 1.000 | 3 | 2 | 0 | 0 | 0 |
| N. Barrera, Mexico City Reds | 1.000 | 9 | 5 | 1 | 0 | 0 | S. Limon, Tabasco | 1.000 | 1 | 1 | 1 | 0 | 0 |
| Rob. Rodriguez, Union Laguna | 1.000 | 8 | 6 | 0 | 0 | 0 | O. Duran, Mexico City Reds | 1.000 | 2 | 1 | 0 | 0 | 0 |
| Ju. Rodriguez, Leon | 1.000 | 5 | 6 | 0 | 0 | 0 | M. Ramirez, Monclova | 1.000 | 2 | 1 | 0 | 0 | 0 |
| R. Valenzuela, MC Tigers | 1.000 | 2 | 5 | 0 | 0 | 0 | L. Diaz, Nuevo Laredo | .938 | 9 | 13 | 2 | 1 | 1 |
| T. Delgado, Yucatan | 1.000 | 2 | 5 | 0 | 0 | 0 | An. Lopez, Tabasco | .875 | 3 | 7 | 0 | 1 | 0 |
| J. Vega, Yucatan | 1.000 | 4 | 5 | 0 | 0 | 0 | Oreja, Aguascalientes | .833 | 2 | 5 | 0 | 1 | 0 |
| Marc. Acosta, Tabasco | 1.000 | 3 | 4 | 1 | 0 | 0 | M.A. Gonzalez, Monclova | .800 | 4 | 4 | 0 | 1 | 0 |
| Cazarin, Veracruz | 1.000 | 1 | 4 | 0 | 0 | 0 | Salazar, Tabasco | .000 | 2 | 0 | 0 | 1 | 0 |

## CATCHERS

| Player and Club | Pct. | G. | PO. | A. | E. | DP. | PB. | Player and Club | Pct. | G. | PO. | A. | E. | DP. | PB. |
|---|---|---|---|---|---|---|---|---|---|---|---|---|---|---|---|
| J. Diaz, Leon | 1.000 | 15 | 69 | 13 | 0 | 1 | 2 | E. Rivera, 33 Pue.-49 Sal. | .989 | 82 | 334 | 26 | 4 | 3 | 5 |
| Samaniego, Campeche | 1.000 | 16 | 21 | 1 | 0 | 0 | 0 | Villalobos, 1 Leon-20 Puebla | .987 | 21 | 68 | 7 | 1 | 1 | 3 |
| C. Soto, Nuevo Laredo | .996 | 45 | 224 | 18 | 1 | 3 | 5 | Marg. Mendoza, UL | .986 | 36 | 125 | 21 | 2 | 2 | 3 |
| R. Vega, Aguascalientes | .994 | 64 | 308 | 42 | 2 | 5 | 8 | P. Ruiz, Leon | .986 | 74 | 322 | 41 | 5 | 3 | 6 |
| Lora, Puebla | .992 | 21 | 111 | 6 | 1 | 3 | 4 | Luna, Monterrey | .985 | 78 | 330 | 63 | 6 | 4 | 15 |
| E. REYES, Nuevo Laredo | .991 | 87 | 498 | 51 | 5 | 3 | 5 | Nunez, Veracruz | .984 | 30 | 102 | 23 | 2 | 1 | 8 |

### CATCHERS

| Player and Club | Pct. | G. | PO. | A. | E. | DP. | PB. |
|---|---|---|---|---|---|---|---|
| Alvarez, Union Laguna | .984 | 70 | 386 | 50 | 7 | 2 | 15 |
| Raymundo, Yucatan | .984 | 18 | 56 | 6 | 1 | 0 | 2 |
| M.A. Guzman, Campeche | .984 | 50 | 198 | 43 | 4 | 2 | 8 |
| F. Cruz, Nuevo Laredo | .981 | 20 | 100 | 6 | 2 | 2 | 4 |
| L. Mendoza, Monclova | .981 | 64 | 336 | 26 | 7 | 4 | 16 |
| Torres, 17 Tb-33 MR-30 U.. | .980 | 80 | 360 | 42 | 8 | 4 | 14 |
| Rosas, Aguascalientes | .980 | 57 | 270 | 29 | 6 | 2 | 3 |
| M. Hernandez, Cordoba | .979 | 120 | 562 | 57 | 13 | 5 | 9 |
| Benitez, Tampico | .979 | 100 | 507 | 64 | 12 | 12 | 11 |
| D. Ruiz, Tabasco | .978 | 39 | 111 | 24 | 3 | 2 | 6 |
| Marquez, Saltillo | .977 | 69 | 265 | 31 | 7 | 2 | 9 |
| Estrada, Campeche | .977 | 71 | 320 | 59 | 9 | 5 | 15 |
| S. Robles, Mexico City Reds.. | .976 | 83 | 327 | 41 | 9 | 3 | 7 |
| L.A. Cruz, Tampico | .976 | 18 | 70 | 10 | 2 | 1 | 3 |
| Bazan, Yucatan | .975 | 75 | 273 | 43 | 8 | 5 | 3 |
| R. Martinez, Leon | .975 | 56 | 207 | 23 | 6 | 0 | 8 |
| A. Guzman, Tabasco | .974 | 95 | 390 | 60 | 12 | 8 | 12 |
| Daut, Monterrey | .974 | 73 | 318 | 52 | 10 | 8 | 17 |
| Al. Lopez, Mexico City Tigers | .973 | 27 | 97 | 12 | 3 | 5 | 2 |
| Rojas, Mexico City Tigers | .972 | 108 | 491 | 65 | 16 | 7 | 12 |
| Monroy, Monclova | .971 | 71 | 303 | 35 | 10 | 6 | 6 |
| J. Vega, Aguascalientes | .969 | 17 | 57 | 5 | 2 | 0 | 1 |
| Rojo, Saltillo | .968 | 51 | 180 | 33 | 7 | 4 | 5 |
| Vargas, Tampico | .968 | 23 | 84 | 7 | 3 | 1 | 4 |
| O. Sanchez, Puebla | .966 | 63 | 277 | 32 | 11 | 0 | 8 |
| Soriano, Yucatan | .963 | 41 | 177 | 31 | 8 | 2 | 5 |
| N. Barrera, Mexico City Reds | .963 | 14 | 46 | 8 | 2 | 1 | 0 |
| R. Castillo, Cordoba | .957 | 25 | 59 | 7 | 3 | 2 | 3 |
| G. Quintero, Veracruz | .956 | 95 | 373 | 79 | 11 | 7 | 7 |
| Bocardo, 18 MC Reds-7 Cor. | .942 | 25 | 70 | 11 | 5 | 2 | 1 |
| Avila, Union Laguna | .923 | 18 | 90 | 6 | 6 | 0 | 4 |

#### (Fewer Than Ten Games)

| Player and Club | Pct. | G. | PO. | A. | E. | DP. | PB. |
|---|---|---|---|---|---|---|---|
| Amador, Veracruz | 1.000 | 4 | 22 | 2 | 0 | 1 | 0 |
| G. Garza, Mexico City Reds.. | 1.000 | 5 | 5 | 1 | 0 | 0 | 0 |
| Vila, Veracruz | 1.000 | 3 | 6 | 0 | 0 | 0 | 0 |
| Sarabia, Monclova | 1.000 | 1 | 4 | 1 | 0 | 0 | 0 |
| E. Robles, Tabasco | 1.000 | 3 | 4 | 0 | 0 | 0 | 4 |
| B. Valdez, Veracruz | 1.000 | 1 | 3 | 0 | 0 | 0 | 1 |
| An. Lopez, Aguascalientes | 1.000 | 1 | 3 | 0 | 0 | 0 | 0 |
| J.A. Navarro, Saltillo | 1.000 | 1 | 1 | 0 | 0 | 0 | 0 |
| A. Gonzalez, Tampico | 1.000 | 1 | 1 | 0 | 0 | 0 | 0 |
| Cazarin, Veracruz | .949 | 9 | 32 | 5 | 2 | 0 | 0 |
| Ezquerra, Mexico City Reds | .909 | 4 | 6 | 4 | 1 | 1 | 0 |
| M. Ramirez, Monclova | .600 | 2 | 3 | 0 | 2 | 1 | 0 |

Triple Play—D. Ruiz.

### PITCHERS

| Player and Club | Pct. | G. | PO. | A. | E. | DP. |
|---|---|---|---|---|---|---|
| M. VILLEGAS, Aguascalientes .. | 1.000 | 25 | 8 | 36 | 0 | 3 |
| Rogers, Monclova | 1.000 | 27 | 13 | 29 | 0 | 2 |
| Colorado, Cordoba | 1.000 | 27 | 8 | 33 | 0 | 4 |
| G. Jimenez, Puebla* | 1.000 | 27 | 1 | 37 | 0 | 4 |
| F. Vazquez, Monclova | 1.000 | 27 | 6 | 30 | 0 | 1 |
| Jackson, Nuevo Laredo | 1.000 | 28 | 12 | 21 | 0 | 3 |
| O. Pollorena, 9 Tab-29 Vera. .... | 1.000 | 32 | 7 | 24 | 0 | 1 |
| G. Valenzuela, Leon | 1.000 | 19 | 9 | 19 | 0 | 1 |
| Contreras, Union Laguna | 1.000 | 34 | 3 | 23 | 0 | 2 |
| Marcheskie, Mexico City Tigers. | 1.000 | 29 | 5 | 21 | 0 | 3 |
| E. Cordova, 11 Yuc-13 Vera. | 1.000 | 24 | 1 | 25 | 0 | 2 |
| C. Diaz, Yucatan | 1.000 | 22 | 4 | 21 | 0 | 2 |
| Inzunza, Tabasco | 1.000 | 49 | 6 | 17 | 0 | 1 |
| Moya, Saltillo | 1.000 | 41 | 7 | 16 | 0 | 1 |
| Menendez, 19 Cam-7 Leon | 1.000 | 26 | 3 | 20 | 0 | 1 |
| Vila, Monterrey | 1.000 | 60 | 6 | 16 | 0 | 2 |
| Ford, Monterrey | 1.000 | 19 | 7 | 15 | 0 | 0 |
| A. Perez, Tampico | 1.000 | 31 | 3 | 18 | 0 | 0 |
| Pulido, Mexico City Reds | 1.000 | 50 | 4 | 16 | 0 | 0 |
| J.L. Martinez, Leon | 1.000 | 17 | 6 | 14 | 0 | 2 |
| Jo. Garcia, Monclova* | 1.000 | 38 | 3 | 15 | 0 | 0 |
| Alvarado, Mexico City Tigers.. | 1.000 | 26 | 1 | 17 | 0 | 1 |
| F. Sanchez, 7 NL-17 Tab | 1.000 | 24 | 6 | 12 | 0 | 2 |
| A. Rivera, Union Laguna | 1.000 | 20 | 2 | 16 | 0 | 3 |
| M. Rivas, Tampico | 1.000 | 40 | 1 | 16 | 0 | 1 |
| Alicea, Union Laguna | 1.000 | 24 | 4 | 12 | 0 | 0 |
| I. Jimenez, Puebla* | 1.000 | 20 | 0 | 16 | 0 | 1 |
| G. Martinez, Aguascalientes | 1.000 | 19 | 8 | 8 | 0 | 0 |
| Divison, Campeche | 1.000 | 48 | 3 | 12 | 0 | 0 |
| P. Ruiz, Monclova* | 1.000 | 27 | 5 | 10 | 0 | 0 |
| E. Cota, 5 Mon-17 Sal | 1.000 | 22 | 1 | 14 | 0 | 2 |
| Dimas, 7 MCT-20 Mon | 1.000 | 27 | 2 | 11 | 0 | 0 |
| D. Franco, Saltillo | 1.000 | 21 | 3 | 10 | 0 | 1 |
| Figueroa, Veracruz | 1.000 | 41 | 2 | 10 | 0 | 1 |
| Huerta, Nuevo Laredo | 1.000 | 26 | 4 | 8 | 0 | 1 |
| Silva, Cordoba | 1.000 | 41 | 3 | 8 | 0 | 0 |
| V. Romo, Cordoba | 1.000 | 14 | 1 | 10 | 0 | 2 |
| Montes, Monclova | 1.000 | 26 | 1 | 9 | 0 | 0 |
| Quijano, Puebla | 1.000 | 24 | 2 | 8 | 0 | 1 |
| J. Ramirez, Leon | 1.000 | 22 | 1 | 9 | 0 | 1 |
| Stone, Nuevo Laredo | 1.000 | 15 | 2 | 8 | 0 | 0 |
| C. Acosta, Campeche | 1.000 | 11 | 0 | 10 | 0 | 1 |
| D. Sanchez, 18 MCR-9 Mva.. | 1.000 | 27 | 1 | 8 | 0 | 0 |
| Sauceda, Yucatan | 1.000 | 27 | 4 | 5 | 0 | 0 |
| G. Guzman, Veracruz | 1.000 | 24 | 1 | 8 | 0 | 1 |
| A. Hernandez, Campeche | 1.000 | 24 | 1 | 8 | 0 | 0 |
| Buice, Nuevo Laredo | 1.000 | 24 | 2 | 7 | 0 | 1 |
| J. Espinosa, Yucatan | 1.000 | 16 | 1 | 8 | 0 | 2 |
| Zamudio, Veracruz | 1.000 | 16 | 2 | 7 | 0 | 1 |
| Armas, 10 Vera.-5 Tam | 1.000 | 15 | 1 | 8 | 0 | 1 |
| D. Ochoa, Puebla | 1.000 | 38 | 0 | 8 | 0 | 1 |
| Ra. Rodriguez, Campeche | 1.000 | 19 | 1 | 7 | 0 | 0 |
| Romero, Union Laguna | 1.000 | 15 | 0 | 8 | 0 | 0 |
| Palafox, Mexico City Reds | 1.000 | 15 | 0 | 8 | 0 | 1 |
| Ri. Osuna, Mexico City Reds.. | 1.000 | 10 | 0 | 8 | 0 | 0 |
| M. Torres, 9 MCT-25 Cor.... | 1.000 | 34 | 0 | 7 | 0 | 1 |
| N. Montano, Union Laguna | 1.000 | 24 | 0 | 7 | 0 | 0 |
| Vaqueiro, Nuevo Laredo | 1.000 | 20 | 1 | 6 | 0 | 0 |
| F. Cota, Mexico City Tigers .... | 1.000 | 34 | 0 | 6 | 0 | 1 |
| E. Garcia, Monclova | 1.000 | 22 | 1 | 5 | 0 | 0 |
| Murillo, Monterrey | 1.000 | 22 | 2 | 4 | 0 | 1 |
| Vidana, Tabasco | 1.000 | 18 | 4 | 2 | 0 | 0 |
| R. Meza, Leon | 1.000 | 16 | 2 | 4 | 0 | 0 |
| Sombra, Union Laguna | 1.000 | 17 | 2 | 4 | 0 | 0 |
| Rivas, Monclova | 1.000 | 14 | 1 | 5 | 0 | 0 |
| L. Aponte, Mexico City Reds | 1.000 | 11 | 0 | 6 | 0 | 0 |
| Au. Castaneda, Veracruz | 1.000 | 11 | 1 | 5 | 0 | 0 |
| Villarreal, Puebla* | 1.000 | 21 | 1 | 4 | 0 | 0 |
| Deladillo, Aguascalientes | 1.000 | 20 | 2 | 3 | 0 | 1 |
| Baruch, Campeche | 1.000 | 18 | 1 | 3 | 0 | 0 |
| Senteney, Union Laguna | 1.000 | 18 | 1 | 3 | 0 | 1 |
| J. Cruz, Mexico City Tigers | 1.000 | 14 | 1 | 3 | 0 | 0 |
| I. Aguilar, Tampico | 1.000 | 27 | 0 | 3 | 0 | 0 |
| H. Valdez, 3 Cam-11 Tab | 1.000 | 14 | 1 | 2 | 0 | 0 |
| A. Felix, Veracruz | 1.000 | 13 | 1 | 2 | 0 | 0 |
| R. Palacios, Tabasco | 1.000 | 12 | 0 | 3 | 0 | 0 |
| Viesca, Saltillo | 1.000 | 11 | 0 | 3 | 0 | 0 |
| Marquez, Saltillo | 1.000 | 13 | 1 | 1 | 0 | 0 |
| A. Robles, Saltillo | 1.000 | 13 | 0 | 2 | 0 | 0 |
| A. Moreno, Leon | 1.000 | 11 | 0 | 1 | 0 | 0 |
| Serna, Union Laguna | .981 | 30 | 15 | 36 | 1 | 1 |
| J. Valenzuela, Saltillo | .979 | 28 | 11 | 36 | 1 | 1 |
| Escarrega, Yucatan | .979 | 24 | 11 | 35 | 1 | 2 |
| Ontiveros, 27 Vera.-6 Leon | .970 | 33 | 4 | 28 | 1 | 6 |
| P. Sanchez, 20 Tab-6 Mon | .970 | 26 | 8 | 24 | 1 | 1 |
| G. Chavez, Tampico | .969 | 54 | 2 | 29 | 1 | 2 |
| M.A. Rodriguez, 25 Ag-13 Le.. | .967 | 38 | 5 | 24 | 1 | 1 |
| Mendez, Mexico City Reds | .967 | 28 | 5 | 24 | 1 | 2 |
| C. Ruiz, Yucatan* | .966 | 23 | 4 | 24 | 1 | 1 |
| F. Montano, Mexico City Tigers. | .966 | 22 | 7 | 21 | 1 | 2 |
| M. Leon, Mexico City Reds | .960 | 27 | 9 | 39 | 2 | 3 |
| Luna, 8 Tam-24 Vera. | .960 | 32 | 8 | 16 | 1 | 1 |
| Serafin, Cordoba | .960 | 43 | 5 | 19 | 1 | 1 |
| O. Orozco, Puebla | .960 | 21 | 4 | 20 | 1 | 1 |
| R. Solis, Mexico City Reds* | .958 | 31 | 10 | 36 | 2 | 6 |
| A. Soto, Puebla | .958 | 34 | 4 | 19 | 1 | 2 |
| Enriquez, Leon | .958 | 22 | 5 | 18 | 1 | 2 |
| P. Ochoa, Nuevo Laredo | .958 | 43 | 3 | 20 | 1 | 4 |
| Gutierrez, 10 Tam-19 Mon.... | .957 | 29 | 4 | 18 | 1 | 1 |
| I. Velazquez, 21 MCT-8 Leon | .957 | 29 | 3 | 19 | 1 | 1 |
| Buitimea 26 MCT-6 Tam | .957 | 32 | 3 | 19 | 1 | 3 |
| Madrigal, Campeche | .957 | 20 | 5 | 17 | 1 | 1 |
| M. Solis, Saltillo | .956 | 22 | 16 | 27 | 2 | 5 |
| Ledon, Monclova | .955 | 35 | 4 | 17 | 1 | 0 |
| H. Rios, Leon | .952 | 23 | 6 | 34 | 2 | 1 |
| Raygoza, 41 Leon-7 Cam | .952 | 48 | 4 | 16 | 1 | 0 |
| Carranza, Union Laguna* | .952 | 20 | 3 | 17 | 1 | 5 |
| Arballo, Cordoba* | .952 | 27 | 2 | 18 | 1 | 0 |
| M. Hernandez, Mexico City Reds | .952 | 28 | 2 | 18 | 1 | 1 |
| Antunez, 8 Mon-25 Tam*.... | .950 | 33 | 3 | 16 | 1 | 0 |
| Sandate, Aguascalientes | .947 | 25 | 7 | 29 | 2 | 3 |
| J. Rios, Mexico City Tigers | .947 | 26 | 7 | 29 | 2 | 0 |
| A. Pollorena, Union Laguna | .947 | 23 | 4 | 14 | 1 | 0 |
| R. Garcia, Union Laguna | .947 | 12 | 6 | 12 | 1 | 1 |
| O. Rivera, 6 Cor-15 Vera. | .944 | 21 | 4 | 13 | 1 | 2 |
| A. Rodriguez, 25 Leon-15 Ags.. | .944 | 40 | 5 | 12 | 1 | 0 |
| Mundo, Monclova | .944 | 14 | 3 | 14 | 1 | 2 |
| Dominguez, Campeche* | .943 | 28 | 3 | 30 | 2 | 1 |

## PITCHERS—Continued

| Player and Club | Pct. | G. | PO. | A. | E. | DP. | Player and Club | Pct. | G. | PO. | A. | E. | DP. |
|---|---|---|---|---|---|---|---|---|---|---|---|---|---|
| Purta, Tampico* | .941 | 29 | 5 | 27 | 2 | 1 | Rojo, Tabasco | .900 | 51 | 2 | 16 | 2 | 0 |
| Miranda, Leon | .941 | 20 | 4 | 12 | 1 | 0 | Gaxiola, Cordoba | .900 | 19 | 3 | 15 | 2 | 0 |
| R. Valdez, Campeche | .939 | 28 | 6 | 25 | 2 | 1 | Widales, Nuevo Laredo | .900 | 12 | 1 | 8 | 1 | 1 |
| J. Orozco, Puebla | .938 | 33 | 8 | 37 | 3 | 2 | W. Cordova, Cordoba | .900 | 10 | 1 | 8 | 1 | 0 |
| Yucupicio, Tabasco | .938 | 38 | 2 | 13 | 1 | 0 | M.A. Castaneda, Saltillo* | .889 | 33 | 0 | 8 | 1 | 0 |
| Rondon, Tabasco | .938 | 19 | 6 | 9 | 2 | 2 | M.A. Vazquez, 17 Vera.-9 Cor.. | .885 | 26 | 4 | 19 | 3 | 2 |
| Lara, Cordoba | .938 | 18 | 4 | 11 | 1 | 1 | A. Navarro, Nuevo Laredo | .882 | 27 | 3 | 12 | 2 | 2 |
| Ibarra, Aguascalientes | .933 | 26 | 9 | 19 | 2 | 0 | Feola, 6 Mva-20 Mon | .875 | 26 | 4 | 17 | 3 | 0 |
| Matus, Aguascalientes | .933 | 26 | 11 | 17 | 2 | 1 | Anderson, Nuevo Laredo | .875 | 21 | 0 | 7 | 1 | 0 |
| de los Santos, Union Laguna* | .933 | 13 | 2 | 12 | 1 | 0 | Low, Union Laguna | .875 | 20 | 1 | 6 | 1 | 0 |
| Cutty, Saltillo | .932 | 30 | 7 | 34 | 3 | 3 | Delfin, Veracruz | .875 | 12 | 3 | 4 | 1 | 0 |
| Villanueva, Aguascalientes* | .929 | 34 | 2 | 24 | 2 | 1 | L.T. Castillo, Nuevo Laredo | .867 | 27 | 5 | 34 | 6 | 1 |
| Belman, Yucatan | .929 | 22 | 7 | 19 | 2 | 2 | R. Guzman, Monclova | .867 | 44 | 1 | 12 | 2 | 1 |
| F. Franco, 11 Vera.-22 MCR | .928 | 33 | 3 | 10 | 1 | 1 | Urrea, 38 Vera.-9 Cor | .867 | 47 | 5 | 8 | 2 | 1 |
| Je. Moreno, Nuevo Laredo | .925 | 27 | 15 | 34 | 4 | 0 | Rincon, 10 Vera.-12 Yuc | .857 | 22 | 5 | 19 | 4 | 2 |
| Castillejos, Yucatan | .923 | 22 | 3 | 9 | 1 | 1 | V. Palacios, Mexico City Reds | .857 | 13 | 4 | 8 | 2 | 1 |
| Pruneda, Mexico City Reds | .923 | 24 | 3 | 9 | 1 | 0 | N. Torres, Tabasco | .857 | 16 | 0 | 6 | 1 | 0 |
| Duarte, Monterrey | .919 | 26 | 10 | 24 | 3 | 4 | Sosa, Tampico | .846 | 29 | 3 | 19 | 4 | 3 |
| E. Beltran, Tampico | .917 | 25 | 5 | 28 | 3 | 2 | L.A. Velazquez, Tabasco | .846 | 18 | 0 | 11 | 2 | 2 |
| Arano, 7 Vera.-11 Tab | .917 | 18 | 3 | 19 | 2 | 2 | Lunar, Monterrey | .840 | 26 | 11 | 31 | 8 | 3 |
| Segui, Monclova | .917 | 13 | 1 | 10 | 1 | 0 | Ro. Osuna, Leon | .833 | 41 | 1 | 4 | 1 | 2 |
| P. Rodriguez, Yucatan | .917 | 33 | 1 | 10 | 1 | 1 | Pimentel, Saltillo | .833 | 18 | 2 | 3 | 1 | 0 |
| R. Villegas, 8 Tig-13 NL-6 Tam | .917 | 27 | 2 | 9 | 1 | 1 | F. Gonzalez, 13 Vera.-11 Tab.. | .800 | 24 | 1 | 7 | 2 | 1 |
| L. Chavez, 6 MCR-22 Cam* | .914 | 28 | 5 | 27 | 3 | 0 | Granillo, Aguascalientes | .800 | 27 | 0 | 8 | 2 | 0 |
| Sutton, Monterrey | .913 | 24 | 4 | 38 | 4 | 2 | L. Perez, Leon | .800 | 20 | 2 | 6 | 2 | 0 |
| Alf. Ortiz, Veracruz* | .913 | 16 | 2 | 19 | 2 | 2 | Tejeda, 8 Cor-8 MCR | .800 | 16 | 2 | 2 | 1 | 0 |
| Cecena, Saltillo | .909 | 24 | 2 | 17 | 2 | 0 | I. Morales, Mexico City Reds* | .800 | 22 | 1 | 3 | 1 | 0 |
| Leal, 10 MCR-13 Cor | .909 | 39 | 5 | 15 | 2 | 1 | Padilla, Saltillo | .750 | 43 | 1 | 5 | 2 | 0 |
| C. Perez, Puebla* | .905 | 24 | 2 | 17 | 2 | 0 | H. Lopez, Aguascalientes | .667 | 15 | 1 | 3 | 2 | 0 |
| Jo. Garcia, Tabasco | .903 | 29 | 9 | 19 | 3 | 0 | | | | | | | |

### (Fewer Than Ten Games)

| Player and Club | Pct. | G. | PO. | A. | E. | DP. | Player and Club | Pct. | G. | PO. | A. | E. | DP. |
|---|---|---|---|---|---|---|---|---|---|---|---|---|---|
| Arroyo, Yucatan | 1.000 | 7 | 4 | 13 | 0 | 1 | Fischer, Mexico City Tigers | 1.000 | 8 | 0 | 2 | 0 | 1 |
| G. Salinas, 6 Mon-3 Cor | 1.000 | 9 | 1 | 10 | 0 | 1 | Jo. Rodriguez, Cordoba | 1.000 | 6 | 1 | 1 | 0 | 0 |
| R. Espinosa, Monclova | 1.000 | 8 | 1 | 9 | 0 | 0 | Navarrete, Yucatan | 1.000 | 4 | 1 | 1 | 0 | 0 |
| Salas, Tabasco | 1.000 | 7 | 1 | 6 | 0 | 0 | Alexander, Mexico City Tigers | 1.000 | 3 | 1 | 1 | 0 | 0 |
| Abad, Mexico City Tigers* | 1.000 | 6 | 2 | 5 | 0 | 2 | Peralta, Leon | 1.000 | 1 | 1 | 1 | 0 | 0 |
| A. Valenzuela, Saltillo | 1.000 | 6 | 1 | 6 | 0 | 0 | Breinning, Tabasco | 1.000 | 1 | 0 | 2 | 0 | 1 |
| Harper, Mexico City Tigers | 1.000 | 9 | 2 | 4 | 0 | 0 | Byron, Quiroz, Aguascalientes | 1.000 | 7 | 0 | 1 | 0 | 0 |
| Mejia, Mexico City Tigers* | 1.000 | 5 | 1 | 5 | 0 | 0 | M. Aguilar, Mexico City Tigers | 1.000 | 7 | 0 | 1 | 0 | 0 |
| Placencia, Yucatan* | 1.000 | 9 | 2 | 3 | 0 | 0 | Guajardo, Nuevo Laredo | 1.000 | 6 | 0 | 1 | 0 | 0 |
| Ronquillo, Union Laguna | 1.000 | 8 | 1 | 4 | 0 | 1 | Moncada, Leon | 1.000 | 4 | 1 | 0 | 0 | 0 |
| Jefferson, Leon | 1.000 | 7 | 2 | 3 | 0 | 0 | H. Martinez, Monclova | 1.000 | 4 | 0 | 1 | 0 | 0 |
| Esquer, Mexico City Tigers* | 1.000 | 6 | 1 | 4 | 0 | 1 | Vargas, Mexico City Tigers | 1.000 | 2 | 0 | 1 | 0 | 1 |
| Vizcarra, Mexico City Reds | 1.000 | 4 | 1 | 4 | 0 | 0 | Retes, Mexico City Tigers | 1.000 | 2 | 0 | 1 | 0 | 0 |
| V. Garcia, Tabasco | 1.000 | 9 | 0 | 3 | 0 | 0 | H. Reyes, Campeche | 1.000 | 1 | 0 | 1 | 0 | 1 |
| J. Beltran, Mexico City Tigers | 1.000 | 7 | 0 | 3 | 0 | 0 | M. Romo, Union Laguna | .889 | 8 | 0 | 8 | 1 | 0 |
| J. Vazquez, Monterrey | 1.000 | 5 | 3 | 0 | 0 | 0 | Lugo, Monclova | .800 | 9 | 1 | 3 | 1 | 0 |
| Urias, Puebla | 1.000 | 5 | 1 | 2 | 0 | 1 | Munoz, Aguascalientes | .000 | 3 | 0 | 0 | 1 | 0 |
| F. Romero, Monterrey | 1.000 | 8 | 1 | 1 | 0 | 0 | | | | | | | |

## CLUB PITCHING

| Club | ERA. | G. | CG. | ShO. | Sv. | IP. | H. | R. | ER. | HR. | HB. | BB. | Int. BB. | SO. | WP. | Bk. |
|---|---|---|---|---|---|---|---|---|---|---|---|---|---|---|---|---|
| Yucatan | 3.63 | 126 | 50 | 12 | 15 | 1047.1 | 1106 | 476 | 422 | 74 | 34 | 322 | 21 | 469 | 40 | 6 |
| Cordoba | 3.79 | 130 | 33 | 13 | 10 | 1081.2 | 1097 | 515 | 455 | 79 | 38 | 439 | 66 | 594 | 55 | 3 |
| Mexico City Reds | 4.21 | 132 | 35 | 14 | 30 | 1100.0 | 1151 | 592 | 515 | 79 | 29 | 480 | 26 | 531 | 53 | 3 |
| Nuevo Laredo | 4.26 | 128 | 38 | 14 | 21 | 1057.1 | 1053 | 599 | 501 | 106 | 27 | 510 | 49 | 813 | 50 | 8 |
| Campeche | 4.28 | 120 | 36 | 5 | 17 | 992.2 | 1090 | 536 | 472 | 94 | 17 | 462 | 18 | 516 | 33 | 1 |
| Mexico City Tigers | 4.39 | 127 | 45 | 8 | 14 | 1064.0 | 1196 | 610 | 519 | 83 | 31 | 464 | 26 | 533 | 43 | 5 |
| Tampico | 4.56 | 130 | 14 | 8 | 20 | 1090.2 | 1138 | 688 | 552 | 132 | 40 | 545 | 41 | 594 | 45 | 2 |
| Tabasco | 4.60 | 130 | 27 | 8 | 9 | 1067.0 | 1228 | 650 | 545 | 76 | 30 | 430 | 45 | 524 | 52 | 5 |
| Puebla | 4.61 | 126 | 44 | 10 | 15 | 1000.1 | 1140 | 559 | 512 | 63 | 42 | 404 | 51 | 567 | 62 | 0 |
| Saltillo | 4.91 | 131 | 28 | 2 | 22 | 1081.0 | 1301 | 706 | 590 | 156 | 48 | 409 | 32 | 543 | 48 | 1 |
| Monterrey | 4.96 | 130 | 18 | 8 | 22 | 1060.2 | 1228 | 667 | 585 | 99 | 61 | 520 | 23 | 592 | 45 | 2 |
| Union Laguna | 4.98 | 132 | 36 | 6 | 18 | 1105.2 | 1274 | 722 | 612 | 123 | 40 | 478 | 26 | 724 | 65 | 2 |
| Aguascalientes | 5.27 | 125 | 47 | 5 | 10 | 1042.1 | 1299 | 714 | 610 | 118 | 37 | 376 | 24 | 603 | 39 | 1 |
| Leon | 5.52 | 129 | 32 | 0 | 12 | 1043.2 | 1234 | 757 | 640 | 147 | 25 | 498 | 33 | 587 | 70 | 0 |
| Veracruz | 5.55 | 132 | 13 | 2 | 15 | 1096.2 | 1387 | 796 | 676 | 86 | 35 | 561 | 57 | 461 | 82 | 4 |
| Monclova | 5.60 | 128 | 26 | 6 | 23 | 1055.0 | 1304 | 778 | 657 | 120 | 64 | 499 | 38 | 596 | 53 | 3 |

## PITCHERS' RECORDS
(Leading Qualifiers for Earned-Run Average Leadership — 94 or More Innings)

*Throws lefthanded.

| Pitcher—Club | W. | L. | Pct. | ERA. | G. | GS. | CG. | GF. | ShO. | Sv. | IP. | H. | R. | ER. | HR. | HB. | BB. | Int. BB. | SO. | WP. |
|---|---|---|---|---|---|---|---|---|---|---|---|---|---|---|---|---|---|---|---|---|
| J. Rios, Mexico City Tigers | 21 | 4 | .840 | 2.52 | 26 | 26 | 26 | 0 | 5 | 0 | 225.0 | 183 | 76 | 63 | 15 | 10 | 66 | 1 | 152 | 3 |
| Serafin, Cordoba | 10 | 5 | .667 | 2.81 | 43 | 5 | 1 | 38 | 0 | 14 | 134.1 | 106 | 47 | 42 | 6 | 5 | 54 | 8 | 79 | 10 |
| Vila, Monterrey | 10 | 6 | .625 | 3.00 | 60 | 1 | 0 | 59 | 0 | 19 | 120.0 | 97 | 46 | 40 | 11 | 6 | 46 | 5 | 101 | 2 |
| G. Jimenez, Puebla* | 18 | 9 | .667 | 3.13 | 27 | 27 | 16 | 0 | 4 | 0 | 195.1 | 186 | 75 | 68 | 8 | 3 | 54 | 1 | 130 | 7 |
| Serna, Union Laguna | 16 | 12 | .571 | 3.16 | 30 | 29 | 22 | 1 | 3 | 0 | 236.1 | 222 | 103 | 83 | 15 | 11 | 61 | 4 | 200 | 5 |
| C. Ruiz, Yucatan* | 9 | 7 | .563 | 3.25 | 23 | 23 | 10 | 0 | 3 | 0 | 163.1 | 166 | 66 | 59 | 7 | 4 | 66 | 4 | 84 | 5 |
| Navarro, Nuevo Laredo | 10 | 8 | .556 | 3.28 | 27 | 27 | 19 | 0 | 3 | 0 | 164.2 | 138 | 68 | 60 | 11 | 1 | 96 | 3 | 145 | 11 |
| Dominguez, Campeche* | 11 | 9 | .550 | 3.31 | 28 | 28 | 11 | 0 | 1 | 0 | 187.1 | 181 | 73 | 69 | 15 | 1 | 85 | 1 | 118 | 2 |
| M. Villegas, Aguascalientes | 12 | 9 | .571 | 3.32 | 25 | 23 | 13 | 2 | 1 | 0 | 176.0 | 180 | 76 | 65 | 18 | 6 | 49 | 6 | 130 | 3 |
| Escarrega, Yucatan | 14 | 9 | .609 | 3.35 | 24 | 24 | 14 | 0 | 3 | 0 | 166.2 | 182 | 67 | 62 | 8 | 5 | 27 | 4 | 75 | 7 |
| L. Castillo, Nuevo Laredo | 16 | 10 | .615 | 3.38 | 27 | 26 | 16 | 1 | 5 | 1 | 181.0 | 156 | 77 | 68 | 14 | 4 | 73 | 3 | 165 | 3 |
| Mendez, Mexico City Reds | 14 | 6 | .700 | 3.38 | 28 | 26 | 7 | 2 | 1 | 1 | 181.1 | 171 | 76 | 68 | 18 | 6 | 54 | 2 | 73 | 3 |
| E. Beltran, Tampico | 18 | 3 | .857 | 3.60 | 25 | 25 | 4 | 0 | 1 | 0 | 162.1 | 147 | 75 | 65 | 15 | 6 | 65 | 2 | 79 | 2 |
| Belman, Yucatan | 7 | 8 | .467 | 3.62 | 22 | 22 | 7 | 0 | 3 | 0 | 139.1 | 151 | 67 | 56 | 9 | 5 | 49 | 1 | 62 | 2 |

Departmental Leaders: G—Vila, 60; W—J. Rios, 21; L—O. Pollorena, 19; Pct.—E. Beltran, .857; GS—Cutty, J. Orozco, Serna, R. Solis, 29; CG—J. Rios, 26; GF—Vila, 59; ShO—L. Castillo, J. Rios, 5; Sv.—Pulido, 20; IP—Serna, 236.1; H—Rogers, 249; R—Rogers, 121; ER—Rogers, 107; HR—J. Valenzuela, 37; HB—Lunar, 15; BB—Lunar, 118; IBB—J. Orozco, 17; SO—Serna, 200; WP—Jackson, I. Jimenez, Lunar, M.A. Vazquez, 14.

(All Pitchers—Listed Alphabetically)

| Pitcher—Club | W. | L. | Pct. | ERA. | G. | GS. | CG. | GF. | ShO. | Sv. | IP. | H. | R. | ER. | HR. | HB. | BB. | Int. BB. | SO. | WP. |
|---|---|---|---|---|---|---|---|---|---|---|---|---|---|---|---|---|---|---|---|---|
| Abad, Mexico City Tigers | 1 | 2 | .333 | 4.60 | 6 | 4 | 1 | 2 | 0 | 0 | 29.1 | 29 | 15 | 15 | 0 | 1 | 15 | 1 | 12 | 1 |
| Acosta, Campeche | 2 | 5 | .286 | 4.92 | 11 | 10 | 1 | 1 | 0 | 0 | 53.0 | 71 | 32 | 29 | 5 | 5 | 16 | 2 | 19 | 0 |
| I. Aguilar, Tampico | 2 | 1 | .667 | 6.53 | 27 | 2 | 0 | 25 | 0 | 0 | 51.0 | 64 | 48 | 37 | 12 | 4 | 34 | 1 | 21 | 4 |
| J.M. Aguilar, M.C. Tigers | 0 | 0 | .000 | 6.08 | 7 | 1 | 0 | 6 | 0 | 0 | 13.1 | 15 | 10 | 9 | 4 | 0 | 7 | 0 | 4 | 1 |
| Aguirre, Tampico | 0 | 1 | .000 | 7.07 | 14 | 0 | 0 | 14 | 0 | 0 | 14.0 | 18 | 12 | 11 | 4 | 0 | 3 | 0 | 6 | 3 |
| Alexander, M.C. Tigers | 1 | 0 | 1.000 | 4.32 | 3 | 3 | 0 | 0 | 0 | 0 | 16.2 | 20 | 9 | 8 | 2 | 0 | 4 | 1 | 4 | 0 |
| Alicea, Union Laguna | 7 | 1 | .875 | 1.74 | 24 | 0 | 0 | 24 | 0 | 7 | 51.2 | 48 | 10 | 2 | 0 | 0 | 8 | 2 | 33 | 2 |
| Alvarado, M.C. Tigers | 11 | 5 | .688 | 3.87 | 26 | 23 | 3 | 3 | 0 | 0 | 149.0 | 177 | 80 | 64 | 7 | 4 | 58 | 5 | 77 | 8 |
| Alvarez, M.C. Tigers | 0 | 0 | .000 | 0.00 | 1 | 0 | 0 | 1 | 0 | 0 | 0.0 | 1 | 0 | 0 | 0 | 0 | 1 | 0 | 0 | 0 |
| Anderson, Nuevo Laredo | 3 | 4 | .429 | 4.42 | 21 | 5 | 0 | 16 | 0 | 7 | 55.0 | 63 | 30 | 27 | 3 | 0 | 21 | 3 | 45 | 5 |
| Andujar, Leon | 0 | 1 | .000 | 7.71 | 4 | 0 | 0 | 4 | 0 | 0 | 4.2 | 7 | 7 | 4 | 0 | 0 | 4 | 0 | 3 | 1 |
| Antunez, 8 Mon.-25 Tam.° | 4 | 14 | .222 | 5.20 | 33 | 23 | 1 | 10 | 0 | 1 | 173.0 | 179 | 108 | 100 | 24 | 4 | 69 | 3 | 74 | 10 |
| B. Aponte, Cordoba | 0 | 2 | .000 | 11.17 | 2 | 2 | 0 | 0 | 0 | 0 | 9.2 | 16 | 13 | 12 | 2 | 0 | 3 | 1 | 6 | 1 |
| L. Aponte, Mexico City Reds | 1 | 1 | .500 | 2.77 | 11 | 0 | 0 | 11 | 0 | 7 | 13.0 | 14 | 6 | 4 | 0 | 1 | 7 | 2 | 5 | 1 |
| Arano, 7 Vera.-11 Tab. | 4 | 9 | .308 | 4.45 | 18 | 18 | 0 | 0 | 0 | 0 | 95.0 | 131 | 59 | 47 | 4 | 0 | 18 | 2 | 24 | 1 |
| Armas, 10 Vera.-5 Tam. | 0 | 3 | .000 | 7.53 | 15 | 5 | 1 | 10 | 0 | 1 | 34.2 | 46 | 37 | 29 | 7 | 6 | 26 | 1 | 9 | 4 |
| Arroyo, Yucatan | 2 | 3 | .400 | 4.26 | 7 | 7 | 1 | 0 | 0 | 0 | 38.0 | 42 | 18 | 18 | 3 | 1 | 8 | 0 | 10 | 1 |
| Baruch, Campeche | 1 | 0 | 1.000 | 4.46 | 18 | 1 | 0 | 17 | 0 | 0 | 42.1 | 54 | 24 | 21 | 6 | 2 | 16 | 1 | 18 | 3 |
| Belman, Yucatan | 7 | 8 | .467 | 3.62 | 22 | 22 | 7 | 0 | 3 | 0 | 139.1 | 151 | 67 | 56 | 9 | 5 | 49 | 1 | 62 | 2 |
| E. Beltran, Tampico | 18 | 3 | .857 | 3.60 | 25 | 25 | 4 | 0 | 1 | 0 | 162.1 | 147 | 75 | 65 | 15 | 6 | 65 | 2 | 79 | 2 |
| J. Beltran, 1 Cor.-7 MCT | 0 | 1 | .000 | 6.00 | 8 | 0 | 0 | 8 | 0 | 0 | 12.0 | 14 | 14 | 8 | 3 | 0 | 11 | 1 | 2 | 1 |
| Breinning, Tabasco | 0 | 1 | .000 | 13.50 | 1 | 1 | 0 | 0 | 0 | 0 | 2.0 | 3 | 3 | 3 | 0 | 1 | 3 | 0 | 2 | 0 |
| Brunet, Mexico City Tigers° | 0 | 0 | .000 | 0.00 | 2 | 0 | 0 | 2 | 0 | 0 | 0.1 | 0 | 0 | 0 | 0 | 0 | 0 | 0 | 0 | 0 |
| Buice, Nuevo Laredo | 0 | 1 | .000 | 3.21 | 24 | 0 | 0 | 24 | 0 | 3 | 33.2 | 33 | 13 | 12 | 3 | 3 | 15 | 5 | 37 | 2 |
| Buitimea, 26 MCT-6 Sal. | 6 | 7 | .462 | 4.53 | 32 | 12 | 2 | 20 | 0 | 1 | 113.1 | 138 | 69 | 57 | 8 | 2 | 47 | 5 | 74 | 4 |
| Byron, Quiroz, Aguascalientes | 1 | 0 | 1.000 | 4.50 | 7 | 0 | 0 | 7 | 0 | 0 | 10.0 | 12 | 7 | 5 | 1 | 0 | 7 | 0 | 6 | 1 |
| Camarena, Puebla | 0 | 0 | 1.000 | 7.30 | 8 | 0 | 0 | 8 | 0 | 0 | 12.1 | 11 | 11 | 10 | 1 | 0 | 11 | 0 | 5 | 1 |
| Carranza, 20 UL-7 NL° | 6 | 8 | .429 | 4.98 | 27 | 18 | 3 | 9 | 1 | 0 | 106.2 | 134 | 81 | 59 | 18 | 2 | 57 | 3 | 68 | 6 |
| An. Castaneda, Puebla | 0 | 0 | .000 | 13.50 | 2 | 0 | 0 | 2 | 0 | 0 | 1.1 | 2 | 2 | 2 | 0 | 0 | 0 | 0 | 1 | 0 |
| Au. Castaneda, 1 Cor.-11 Vera. | 0 | 5 | .000 | 6.31 | 12 | 7 | 2 | 5 | 0 | 0 | 51.1 | 65 | 42 | 36 | 4 | 3 | 28 | 2 | 12 | 8 |
| M.A. Castaneda, Saltillo | 1 | 2 | .333 | 7.00 | 33 | 5 | 0 | 28 | 0 | 1 | 45.0 | 66 | 37 | 35 | 7 | 2 | 25 | 1 | 31 | 4 |
| Castillejos, Yucatan | 4 | 1 | .800 | 6.21 | 22 | 4 | 0 | 18 | 0 | 0 | 62.1 | 83 | 47 | 43 | 10 | 2 | 8 | 0 | 30 | 1 |
| H. Castillo, Union Laguna | 0 | 0 | .000 | 6.91 | 5 | 0 | 0 | 5 | 0 | 0 | 14.1 | 21 | 13 | 11 | 1 | 1 | 4 | 0 | 2 | 0 |
| L. Castillo, Nuevo Laredo | 16 | 10 | .615 | 3.38 | 27 | 26 | 16 | 1 | 5 | 1 | 181.0 | 156 | 77 | 68 | 14 | 4 | 73 | 3 | 165 | 3 |
| Cecena, Saltillo | 7 | 13 | .350 | 5.14 | 39 | 16 | 3 | 23 | 0 | 6 | 108.2 | 125 | 73 | 62 | 13 | 3 | 53 | 3 | 100 | 8 |
| G. Chavez, 1 Agua.-54 Tam | 7 | 10 | .412 | 5.21 | 55 | 5 | 0 | 50 | 0 | 7 | 114.1 | 123 | 81 | 66 | 13 | 3 | 62 | 13 | 83 | 9 |
| L. Chavez, 6 MCR-22 Cam. | 8 | 11 | .421 | 5.32 | 28 | 24 | 3 | 4 | 0 | 0 | 132.0 | 156 | 89 | 78 | 14 | 2 | 67 | 1 | 72 | 5 |
| Colorado, Cordoba | 15 | 9 | .625 | 3.68 | 27 | 27 | 19 | 0 | 3 | 0 | 212.2 | 242 | 92 | 87 | 19 | 2 | 46 | 15 | 119 | 1 |
| P. Contreras, Saltillo | 0 | 0 | .000 | 11.81 | 2 | 0 | 0 | 2 | 0 | 0 | 5.1 | 9 | 8 | 7 | 6 | 0 | 2 | 0 | 2 | 2 |
| R. Contreras, Union Laguna | 9 | 6 | .600 | 5.45 | 34 | 17 | 1 | 17 | 0 | 0 | 107.1 | 112 | 66 | 65 | 10 | 6 | 79 | 0 | 79 | 10 |
| E. Cordova, 4 Tam.-13 Vera. | 4 | 11 | .267 | 5.02 | 24 | 22 | 5 | 2 | 1 | 0 | 127.1 | 170 | 79 | 71 | 10 | 2 | 41 | 4 | 51 | 3 |
| W. Cordova, 10 Cor.-8 NL | 4 | 4 | .500 | 6.05 | 18 | 2 | 0 | 16 | 0 | 0 | 38.2 | 44 | 29 | 26 | 5 | 1 | 27 | 11 | 37 | 2 |
| E. Cota, 5 Mon.-17 Sal. | 1 | 3 | .250 | 5.37 | 22 | 6 | 0 | 16 | 0 | 1 | 53.2 | 69 | 36 | 32 | 7 | 1 | 17 | 2 | 26 | 2 |
| F. Cota, Mexico City Tigers | 10 | 1 | .909 | 5.42 | 34 | 0 | 0 | 34 | 0 | 1 | 78.0 | 90 | 56 | 47 | 5 | 0 | 43 | 2 | 39 | 1 |
| Cruz, Mexico City Tigers | 1 | 2 | .333 | 6.98 | 14 | 2 | 1 | 12 | 0 | 0 | 20.2 | 22 | 19 | 16 | 3 | 0 | 15 | 1 | 7 | 0 |
| Cuevas, 3 Vera.-3 MCT | 0 | 2 | .000 | 5.40 | 6 | 1 | 0 | 5 | 0 | 0 | 10.0 | 12 | 8 | 6 | 0 | 0 | 12 | 3 | 6 | 3 |
| Cutty, Saltillo | 13 | 10 | .565 | 4.44 | 30 | 29 | 10 | 1 | 0 | 0 | 182.1 | 216 | 120 | 90 | 16 | 8 | 86 | 4 | 105 | 6 |
| Delfin, Veracruz | 0 | 1 | .000 | 5.57 | 12 | 1 | 0 | 11 | 0 | 1 | 21.0 | 31 | 15 | 13 | 1 | 2 | 9 | 3 | 3 | 2 |
| Delgadillo, 20 Agua.-7 Leon | 0 | 0 | .000 | 5.79 | 27 | 0 | 0 | 27 | 0 | 1 | 42.0 | 60 | 32 | 27 | 8 | 0 | 12 | 1 | 18 | 1 |
| de los Santos, Union Laguna° | 2 | 3 | .400 | 5.96 | 13 | 2 | 0 | 11 | 0 | 0 | 25.2 | 32 | 20 | 17 | 5 | 1 | 19 | 1 | 21 | 4 |
| A. Diaz, Tabasco | 2 | 0 | .000 | 6.48 | 5 | 2 | 0 | 3 | 0 | 0 | 8.1 | 12 | 11 | 6 | 2 | 0 | 9 | 0 | 1 | 1 |
| C. Diaz, Yucatan | 8 | 7 | .533 | 4.07 | 22 | 22 | 7 | 0 | 0 | 0 | 115.0 | 131 | 69 | 52 | 8 | 8 | 47 | 1 | 57 | 5 |
| O. Diaz, Union Laguna | 2 | 0 | .000 | 13.79 | 9 | 2 | 0 | 7 | 0 | 0 | 15.2 | 26 | 27 | 24 | 4 | 0 | 20 | 0 | 12 | 3 |
| Dimas, 7 MCT-20 Mon. | 1 | 6 | .143 | 6.53 | 27 | 0 | 0 | 27 | 0 | 2 | 41.1 | 57 | 32 | 30 | 4 | 0 | 23 | 4 | 20 | 0 |
| Divison, Campeche | 14 | 4 | .778 | 0.94 | 48 | 0 | 0 | 48 | 0 | 14 | 76.1 | 62 | 15 | 8 | 1 | 0 | 24 | 4 | 50 | 0 |
| Dominguez, Campeche° | 11 | 9 | .550 | 3.31 | 28 | 28 | 11 | 0 | 1 | 0 | 187.1 | 181 | 73 | 69 | 15 | 1 | 85 | 1 | 118 | 2 |
| Duarte, Monterrey | 7 | 8 | .467 | 5.40 | 26 | 26 | 3 | 0 | 1 | 0 | 141.2 | 191 | 99 | 85 | 12 | 11 | 59 | 5 | 60 | 2 |
| Duran, Saltillo | 0 | 0 | .000 | 0.00 | 1 | 0 | 0 | 1 | 0 | 0 | 0.1 | 0 | 0 | 0 | 0 | 0 | 0 | 0 | 0 | 0 |
| Enriquez, Leon | 5 | 6 | .455 | 5.60 | 22 | 16 | 1 | 6 | 0 | 0 | 82.0 | 98 | 72 | 51 | 15 | 1 | 38 | 1 | 31 | 12 |
| Escarrega, Yucatan | 14 | 9 | .609 | 3.35 | 24 | 24 | 14 | 0 | 3 | 0 | 166.2 | 182 | 67 | 62 | 8 | 5 | 74 | 4 | 75 | 7 |
| J. Espinosa, Yucatan | 2 | 0 | 1.000 | 5.25 | 16 | 0 | 0 | 16 | 0 | 1 | 48.0 | 58 | 28 | 28 | 7 | 2 | 27 | 2 | 17 | 1 |
| R. Espinosa, Monclova | 2 | 3 | .400 | 5.10 | 8 | 7 | 1 | 1 | 0 | 0 | 30.0 | 39 | 24 | 17 | 3 | 1 | 22 | 0 | 14 | 2 |
| Esquer, Mexico City Tigers° | 3 | 1 | .750 | 4.00 | 6 | 6 | 1 | 0 | 0 | 0 | 36.0 | 41 | 17 | 16 | 2 | 1 | 18 | 0 | 18 | 2 |
| Al. Felix, Veracruz | 0 | 0 | .000 | 0.00 | 1 | 0 | 1 | 0 | 0 | 0 | 0.0 | 0 | 0 | 0 | 0 | 0 | 2 | 0 | 0 | 0 |
| An. Felix, Veracruz | 0 | 2 | .000 | 14.29 | 13 | 2 | 0 | 11 | 0 | 0 | 17.0 | 19 | 35 | 27 | 1 | 3 | 36 | 0 | 13 | 10 |
| Feola, 6 Mva.-20 Mon.° | 6 | 10 | .375 | 7.87 | 26 | 19 | 2 | 7 | 0 | 0 | 100.2 | 137 | 99 | 88 | 16 | 5 | 75 | 0 | 66 | 9 |
| Figueroa, Veracruz | 1 | 4 | .200 | 6.82 | 41 | 1 | 0 | 40 | 0 | 2 | 95.0 | 122 | 80 | 72 | 17 | 5 | 56 | 5 | 30 | 7 |
| Fischer, Mexico City Tigers | 0 | 2 | .000 | 5.06 | 8 | 0 | 0 | 8 | 0 | 3 | 10.2 | 15 | 9 | 9 | 1 | 1 | 4 | 2 | 4 | 0 |
| Flores, Campeche | 0 | 0 | .000 | 0.00 | 2 | 0 | 0 | 2 | 0 | 0 | 2.0 | 2 | 0 | 0 | 0 | 0 | 1 | 0 | 2 | 0 |
| Ford, Monterrey | 9 | 8 | .529 | 4.24 | 19 | 19 | 5 | 0 | 2 | 0 | 116.2 | 130 | 58 | 55 | 16 | 2 | 40 | 2 | 56 | 4 |
| D. Franco, Saltillo | 6 | 2 | .750 | 4.29 | 21 | 9 | 0 | 12 | 0 | 0 | 92.1 | 112 | 46 | 44 | 19 | 9 | 20 | 1 | 23 | 2 |
| F. Franco, 11 Vera.-22 MCR | 6 | 2 | .750 | 4.28 | 33 | 1 | 0 | 32 | 0 | 2 | 82.0 | 79 | 43 | 39 | 5 | 0 | 41 | 5 | 27 | 1 |
| Gage, Tabasco | 0 | 0 | .000 | 0.00 | 1 | 0 | 0 | 1 | 0 | 0 | 3.1 | 1 | 0 | 0 | 0 | 0 | 2 | 0 | 2 | 0 |
| Gamundi, Veracruz | 0 | 0 | .000 | 13.50 | 5 | 0 | 0 | 5 | 0 | 0 | 5.1 | 9 | 8 | 8 | 0 | 1 | 1 | 0 | 2 | 0 |
| E. Garcia, Monclova | 0 | 4 | .000 | 7.11 | 22 | 7 | 0 | 15 | 0 | 1 | 57.0 | 83 | 56 | 45 | 7 | 2 | 28 | 0 | 25 | 1 |
| Jor. Garcia, Tabasco° | 9 | 7 | .563 | 3.85 | 29 | 22 | 9 | 7 | 1 | 0 | 149.2 | 163 | 70 | 64 | 11 | 5 | 44 | 2 | 81 | 6 |
| Jos. Garcia, Monclova° | 3 | 7 | .300 | 7.15 | 38 | 10 | 1 | 28 | 0 | 1 | 61.2 | 89 | 62 | 49 | 5 | 3 | 33 | 5 | 40 | 11 |
| L. Garcia, Union Laguna | 1 | 1 | .500 | 5.40 | 3 | 3 | 0 | 0 | 0 | 0 | 11.2 | 16 | 9 | 7 | 1 | 1 | 10 | 0 | 3 | 0 |
| R. Garcia, Union Laguna | 4 | 4 | .500 | 5.38 | 12 | 12 | 4 | 0 | 1 | 0 | 80.0 | 98 | 62 | 51 | 14 | 2 | 42 | 0 | 63 | 5 |
| V. Garcia, Tabasco | 2 | 3 | .400 | 5.87 | 9 | 9 | 1 | 0 | 1 | 0 | 46.0 | 57 | 38 | 30 | 4 | 2 | 24 | 1 | 24 | 4 |
| Gaxiola, Cordoba | 6 | 9 | .400 | 4.28 | 19 | 19 | 3 | 0 | 0 | 0 | 113.2 | 124 | 61 | 54 | 12 | 10 | 47 | 2 | 60 | 8 |
| C. Gonzalez, Monterrey | 0 | 0 | .000 | 6.43 | 5 | 0 | 0 | 5 | 0 | 0 | 7.0 | 8 | 6 | 5 | 2 | 0 | 4 | 0 | 3 | 0 |
| F. Gonzalez, 3 Yuc.-1 Tab | 0 | 5 | .000 | 4.17 | 14 | 4 | 0 | 10 | 0 | 2 | 41.0 | 37 | 24 | 19 | 2 | 1 | 24 | 2 | 28 | 0 |
| C. Granillo, Aguascalientes | 4 | 4 | .500 | 5.65 | 27 | 6 | 2 | 21 | 0 | 4 | 71.2 | 90 | 55 | 45 | 11 | 1 | 32 | 2 | 64 | 2 |
| I. Granillo, Mexico City Tigers | 0 | 0 | .000 | 0.00 | 1 | 0 | 0 | 1 | 0 | 0 | 1.2 | 1 | 0 | 0 | 0 | 0 | 0 | 0 | 1 | 0 |
| Guajardo, 6 NL-6 Mon. | 0 | 0 | .000 | 7.04 | 12 | 0 | 0 | 12 | 0 | 0 | 15.1 | 23 | 14 | 12 | 2 | 1 | 5 | 0 | 5 | 1 |

| Pitcher — Club | W. | L. | Pct. | ERA. | G. | GS. | CG. | GF. | ShO. | Sv. | IP. | H. | R. | ER. | HR. | HB. | BB. | Int. BB. | SO. | WP. |
|---|---|---|---|---|---|---|---|---|---|---|---|---|---|---|---|---|---|---|---|---|
| Gutierrez, 10 Tam.-19 Mon | 0 | 9 | .000 | 3.63 | 29 | 9 | 0 | 20 | 0 | 2 | 96.2 | 97 | 61 | 39 | 10 | 7 | 59 | 2 | 71 | 7 |
| G. Guzman, Veracruz | 3 | 3 | .500 | 6.53 | 24 | 4 | 0 | 20 | 0 | 1 | 40.0 | 60 | 39 | 29 | 2 | 3 | 30 | 3 | 21 | 1 |
| R. Guzman, Monclova | 5 | 4 | .556 | 3.47 | 44 | 0 | 0 | 44 | 0 | 19 | 72.2 | 77 | 33 | 28 | 7 | 1 | 28 | 3 | 45 | 3 |
| Harper, Mexico City Tigers | 4 | 3 | .571 | 3.83 | 9 | 8 | 3 | 1 | 0 | 1 | 51.2 | 56 | 23 | 22 | 2 | 0 | 38 | 0 | 32 | 7 |
| A. Hernandez, Campeche | 2 | 1 | .667 | 6.67 | 24 | 0 | 0 | 24 | 0 | 1 | 58.0 | 76 | 52 | 43 | 8 | 0 | 16 | 1 | 29 | 1 |
| M. Hernandez, Mexico City Reds | 6 | 7 | .462 | 4.08 | 28 | 16 | 2 | 12 | 0 | 1 | 108.0 | 94 | 67 | 49 | 6 | 2 | 68 | 3 | 38 | 11 |
| Huerta, Nuevo Laredo | 2 | 6 | .250 | 7.11 | 26 | 4 | 0 | 22 | 0 | 1 | 50.2 | 67 | 51 | 40 | 11 | 3 | 28 | 6 | 28 | 1 |
| Ibarra, Aguascalientes | 7 | 9 | .438 | 6.33 | 26 | 23 | 4 | 3 | 0 | 0 | 135.0 | 188 | 115 | 95 | 16 | 5 | 48 | 0 | 61 | 7 |
| Inzunza, Tabasco | 0 | 6 | .000 | 3.44 | 49 | 0 | 0 | 49 | 0 | 1 | 65.1 | 71 | 34 | 25 | 4 | 0 | 25 | 2 | 24 | 2 |
| Jackson, Nuevo Laredo | 9 | 9 | .500 | 4.38 | 28 | 24 | 6 | 4 | 1 | 1 | 168.2 | 166 | 93 | 82 | 17 | 4 | 85 | 7 | 148 | 14 |
| Jefferson, Leon | 2 | 2 | .500 | 6.04 | 7 | 7 | 0 | 0 | 0 | 0 | 28.1 | 33 | 20 | 19 | 4 | 1 | 15 | 0 | 17 | 1 |
| G. Jimenez, Puebla | 18 | 9 | .667 | 3.13 | 27 | 27 | 16 | 0 | 4 | 0 | 195.1 | 186 | 75 | 68 | 8 | 3 | 54 | 1 | 130 | 7 |
| I. Jimenez, Puebla | 5 | 6 | .455 | 6.63 | 20 | 19 | 1 | 1 | 1 | 0 | 74.2 | 87 | 58 | 55 | 1 | 13 | 67 | 1 | 58 | 14 |
| Lara, Cordoba | 3 | 3 | .500 | 3.48 | 18 | 12 | 2 | 6 | 2 | 0 | 85.1 | 65 | 37 | 33 | 6 | 4 | 22 | 2 | 41 | 0 |
| Leal, 10 M.C. Reds-13 Cor. | 5 | 3 | .625 | 5.05 | 23 | 9 | 1 | 14 | 0 | 0 | 57.0 | 51 | 35 | 32 | 4 | 1 | 43 | 1 | 34 | 5 |
| Ledon, Monclova | 4 | 5 | .444 | 6.48 | 35 | 3 | 0 | 32 | 0 | 0 | 91.2 | 106 | 75 | 66 | 12 | 9 | 44 | 2 | 50 | 6 |
| Leon, Mexico City Reds | 13 | 9 | .591 | 3.88 | 27 | 27 | 10 | 0 | 2 | 0 | 164.2 | 167 | 76 | 71 | 9 | 5 | 44 | 1 | 68 | 12 |
| D. Lopez, Puebla | 0 | 0 | .000 | 54.00 | 1 | 0 | 0 | 1 | 0 | 0 | 0.1 | 2 | 2 | 2 | 0 | 0 | 1 | 0 | 0 | 1 |
| H. Lopez, Aguascalientes | 1 | 1 | .500 | 8.23 | 15 | 0 | 0 | 15 | 0 | 0 | 35.0 | 59 | 37 | 32 | 4 | 0 | 11 | 2 | 19 | 2 |
| Lora, Puebla | 0 | 0 | .000 | 9.00 | 1 | 0 | 0 | 1 | 0 | 0 | 1.0 | 2 | 1 | 1 | 0 | 0 | 0 | 0 | 0 | 0 |
| Low, Union Laguna | 1 | 4 | .200 | 2.86 | 20 | 2 | 0 | 18 | 0 | 7 | 34.2 | 29 | 12 | 11 | 5 | 1 | 12 | 5 | 25 | 1 |
| Lugo, Monclova | 0 | 1 | .000 | 4.82 | 9 | 0 | 0 | 9 | 0 | 1 | 9.1 | 13 | 10 | 5 | 1 | 2 | 6 | 0 | 5 | 0 |
| Luna, 8 Tam.-24 Vera | 3 | 10 | .231 | 6.15 | 32 | 16 | 1 | 16 | 0 | 0 | 112.2 | 142 | 94 | 77 | 12 | 0 | 64 | 7 | 48 | 12 |
| Lunar, Monterrey | 12 | 10 | .546 | 4.19 | 26 | 26 | 5 | 0 | 2 | 0 | 152.2 | 147 | 79 | 71 | 7 | 15 | 118 | 2 | 109 | 14 |
| Madrigal, Campeche | 7 | 6 | .538 | 4.32 | 20 | 17 | 6 | 3 | 2 | 0 | 127.0 | 143 | 65 | 61 | 8 | 1 | 53 | 1 | 64 | 3 |
| Marcheskie, Mexico City Tigers | 3 | 6 | .333 | 4.42 | 29 | 2 | 1 | 27 | 0 | 10 | 53.0 | 63 | 29 | 26 | 6 | 3 | 18 | 2 | 26 | 0 |
| Mariscal, 6 Mon.-5 Mva. | 0 | 1 | .000 | 10.34 | 11 | 0 | 0 | 11 | 0 | 0 | 15.2 | 31 | 23 | 18 | 4 | 1 | 13 | 0 | 8 | 5 |
| Marquez, Tampico | 0 | 0 | .000 | 3.90 | 13 | 0 | 0 | 13 | 0 | 0 | 27.2 | 28 | 13 | 12 | 4 | 1 | 14 | 1 | 17 | 5 |
| G. Martinez, Aguascalientes | 4 | 8 | .333 | 6.50 | 19 | 14 | 3 | 5 | 0 | 0 | 80.1 | 108 | 66 | 58 | 13 | 5 | 33 | 3 | 37 | 2 |
| H. Martinez, Monclova | 0 | 0 | .000 | 10.50 | 4 | 0 | 0 | 4 | 0 | 0 | 6.0 | 11 | 12 | 7 | 3 | 1 | 2 | 0 | 3 | 1 |
| J. Martinez, Leon | 6 | 5 | .545 | 6.20 | 17 | 17 | 2 | 0 | 0 | 0 | 90.0 | 98 | 65 | 62 | 15 | 2 | 51 | 1 | 35 | 4 |
| Matus, Aguascalientes | 9 | 6 | .600 | 4.78 | 26 | 17 | 6 | 9 | 1 | 0 | 113.0 | 142 | 77 | 60 | 11 | 3 | 53 | 6 | 39 | 2 |
| Mejia, Mexico City Tigers* | 1 | 1 | .500 | 3.13 | 5 | 3 | 2 | 2 | 0 | 0 | 23.0 | 23 | 9 | 8 | 2 | 0 | 14 | 0 | 5 | 1 |
| Mendez, Mexico City Reds | 14 | 6 | .700 | 3.38 | 28 | 26 | 7 | 2 | 1 | 1 | 181.1 | 171 | 76 | 68 | 18 | 6 | 54 | 2 | 73 | 3 |
| Menendez, 19 Cam-7 Leon | 5 | 14 | .263 | 4.74 | 26 | 21 | 6 | 5 | 0 | 0 | 136.2 | 151 | 77 | 72 | 19 | 1 | 52 | 4 | 64 | 1 |
| Meza, Leon | 1 | 0 | 1.000 | 5.55 | 16 | 1 | 0 | 15 | 0 | 0 | 37.1 | 41 | 23 | 23 | 6 | 0 | 23 | 0 | 21 | 7 |
| Miranda, Leon | 3 | 1 | .750 | 3.55 | 20 | 0 | 0 | 20 | 0 | 2 | 45.2 | 40 | 24 | 18 | 2 | 2 | 25 | 3 | 33 | 7 |
| Moncada, 4 Leon-3 Cam. | 0 | 0 | .000 | 6.75 | 7 | 0 | 0 | 7 | 0 | 0 | 5.1 | 10 | 4 | 4 | 1 | 0 | 3 | 0 | 3 | 0 |
| F. Montano, Mex. City Tigers | 11 | 5 | .688 | 3.74 | 22 | 21 | 4 | 1 | 1 | 0 | 120.1 | 137 | 57 | 50 | 7 | 1 | 40 | 0 | 45 | 6 |
| N. Montano, Union Laguna | 0 | 2 | .000 | 7.97 | 24 | 3 | 0 | 21 | 0 | 2 | 55.1 | 71 | 55 | 49 | 8 | 1 | 29 | 0 | 35 | 3 |
| Montenegro, Saltillo | 0 | 0 | .000 | 9.00 | 1 | 0 | 0 | 1 | 0 | 0 | 1.0 | 3 | 1 | 1 | 1 | 0 | 0 | 0 | 0 | 0 |
| Montes, 1 Tab-26 Monclova | 4 | 4 | .500 | 7.19 | 27 | 4 | 0 | 23 | 0 | 1 | 56.1 | 79 | 49 | 45 | 4 | 3 | 25 | 2 | 20 | 1 |
| I. Morales, Mex. City Reds* | 4 | 2 | .667 | 6.35 | 22 | 0 | 0 | 22 | 0 | 0 | 22.2 | 38 | 19 | 16 | 1 | 1 | 15 | 1 | 7 | 3 |
| M. Morales, 2 Vera.-2 Cor. | 0 | 1 | .000 | 12.00 | 4 | 1 | 0 | 3 | 0 | 0 | 3.0 | 13 | 5 | 4 | 1 | 0 | 0 | 0 | 1 | 0 |
| A. Moreno, Leon | 0 | 1 | .000 | 9.31 | 11 | 1 | 0 | 10 | 0 | 1 | 9.2 | 8 | 10 | 10 | 3 | 0 | 8 | 0 | 4 | 1 |
| J. Moreno, Nuevo Laredo | 12 | 7 | .632 | 4.15 | 27 | 26 | 6 | 1 | 2 | 0 | 160.2 | 166 | 89 | 74 | 19 | 5 | 67 | 9 | 111 | 3 |
| Morin, 8 Cor.-1 Mon. | 1 | 0 | 1.000 | 6.60 | 9 | 1 | 0 | 8 | 0 | 0 | 15.0 | 15 | 11 | 11 | 1 | 2 | 15 | 0 | 9 | 1 |
| Moya, Saltillo | 5 | 6 | .455 | 4.35 | 41 | 5 | 1 | 36 | 0 | 6 | 99.1 | 125 | 57 | 48 | 16 | 2 | 29 | 3 | 52 | 2 |
| Mundo, Monclova | 6 | 4 | .600 | 4.77 | 14 | 11 | 3 | 3 | 0 | 0 | 66.0 | 76 | 43 | 35 | 7 | 3 | 30 | 2 | 19 | 0 |
| Munoz, Aguascalientes | 1 | 0 | 1.000 | 0.79 | 3 | 1 | 1 | 2 | 1 | 0 | 11.1 | 11 | 2 | 1 | 0 | 0 | 1 | 0 | 7 | 0 |
| Murillo, Monterrey | 0 | 2 | .000 | 6.02 | 22 | 1 | 0 | 21 | 0 | 0 | 49.1 | 66 | 41 | 33 | 7 | 3 | 25 | 1 | 26 | 5 |
| Navarrete, Yucatan | 0 | 0 | .000 | 2.84 | 4 | 0 | 0 | 4 | 0 | 0 | 12.2 | 15 | 5 | 4 | 2 | 1 | 7 | 0 | 5 | 1 |
| Navarro, Nuevo Laredo | 10 | 8 | .556 | 3.28 | 27 | 27 | 9 | 0 | 3 | 0 | 164.2 | 138 | 68 | 60 | 11 | 1 | 96 | 3 | 145 | 11 |
| D. Ochoa, Puebla | 4 | 3 | .571 | 4.29 | 38 | 0 | 0 | 38 | 0 | 3 | 56.2 | 69 | 30 | 27 | 3 | 1 | 22 | 5 | 31 | 6 |
| J. Ochoa, Tabasco | 0 | 0 | .000 | 27.00 | 5 | 0 | 0 | 5 | 0 | 0 | 2.0 | 9 | 7 | 6 | 0 | 1 | 2 | 1 | 0 | 3 |
| P. Ochoa, Nuevo Laredo | 5 | 4 | .556 | 4.15 | 43 | 1 | 0 | 42 | 0 | 4 | 80.1 | 78 | 44 | 37 | 7 | 0 | 31 | 4 | 34 | 1 |
| Ontiveros, 27 Vera.-6 Leon | 5 | 4 | .556 | 4.32 | 33 | 4 | 0 | 29 | 0 | 0 | 77.0 | 89 | 42 | 37 | 9 | 3 | 23 | 2 | 33 | 2 |
| J. Orozco, Puebla | 14 | 7 | .667 | 4.22 | 33 | 29 | 17 | 4 | 4 | 2 | 194.0 | 232 | 92 | 91 | 13 | 8 | 48 | 17 | 113 | 7 |
| O. Orozco, Puebla | 6 | 5 | .545 | 4.45 | 21 | 13 | 3 | 8 | 1 | 1 | 91.0 | 101 | 47 | 45 | 10 | 5 | 35 | 5 | 27 | 10 |
| Ortiz, 16 Vera.-1 Cor.* | 2 | 7 | .222 | 5.35 | 17 | 14 | 0 | 3 | 0 | 0 | 77.1 | 117 | 57 | 46 | 1 | 0 | 26 | 3 | 32 | 4 |
| Ri. Osuna, Mexico City Reds | 1 | 1 | .500 | 7.52 | 10 | 1 | 0 | 9 | 0 | 0 | 20.1 | 24 | 17 | 17 | 3 | 1 | 13 | 0 | 8 | 0 |
| Ro. Osuna, Leon | 6 | 3 | .667 | 6.13 | 41 | 1 | 0 | 40 | 0 | 2 | 101.1 | 117 | 83 | 69 | 15 | 2 | 62 | 3 | 84 | 7 |
| Padilla, Saltillo | 4 | 7 | .364 | 4.86 | 43 | 0 | 0 | 43 | 0 | 6 | 53.2 | 55 | 39 | 29 | 7 | 5 | 32 | 5 | 19 | 4 |
| R. Palacios, Tabasco | 0 | 0 | .000 | 4.50 | 12 | 0 | 0 | 12 | 0 | 0 | 22.0 | 23 | 22 | 11 | 2 | 1 | 10 | 1 | 14 | 5 |
| V. Palacios, Mexico City Reds | 7 | 2 | .778 | 3.87 | 13 | 13 | 4 | 0 | 1 | 0 | 74.1 | 86 | 44 | 32 | 3 | 3 | 44 | 0 | 49 | 4 |
| Palafox, Mexico City Tigers | 0 | 4 | .000 | 8.85 | 15 | 2 | 0 | 13 | 0 | 0 | 20.1 | 26 | 22 | 20 | 2 | 3 | 19 | 3 | 13 | 1 |
| Pena, Tabasco* | 0 | 1 | .000 | 8.59 | 4 | 1 | 0 | 3 | 0 | 0 | 7.1 | 13 | 9 | 7 | 2 | 0 | 6 | 1 | 3 | 0 |
| Peralta, Leon | 0 | 1 | .000 | 4.91 | 4 | 1 | 0 | 3 | 0 | 0 | 3.2 | 2 | 2 | 2 | 0 | 1 | 6 | 1 | 3 | 0 |
| A. Perez, Tampico | 5 | 7 | .417 | 4.14 | 31 | 14 | 3 | 17 | 0 | 1 | 117.1 | 125 | 67 | 53 | 17 | 5 | 65 | 7 | 64 | 2 |
| C. Perez, Puebla* | 10 | 8 | .556 | 4.45 | 24 | 24 | 6 | 0 | 0 | 0 | 147.2 | 162 | 80 | 73 | 12 | 5 | 61 | 7 | 89 | 6 |
| L. Perez, Leon | 3 | 4 | .429 | 7.71 | 20 | 12 | 0 | 8 | 0 | 0 | 51.1 | 65 | 51 | 44 | 11 | 2 | 42 | 3 | 23 | 7 |
| Pimentel, Saltillo | 2 | 4 | .333 | 4.24 | 18 | 5 | 2 | 13 | 1 | 2 | 46.2 | 48 | 23 | 22 | 4 | 2 | 17 | 1 | 32 | 3 |
| Placencia, Yucatan* | 3 | 2 | .600 | 3.86 | 9 | 2 | 1 | 7 | 0 | 0 | 35.0 | 39 | 16 | 15 | 4 | 0 | 16 | 0 | 7 | 1 |
| A. Pollorena, Union Laguna | 6 | 9 | .400 | 4.20 | 23 | 23 | 3 | 0 | 2 | 0 | 139.1 | 184 | 79 | 65 | 14 | 3 | 27 | 4 | 65 | 3 |
| O. Pollorena, 9 Tab-23 Vera. | 7 | 19 | .269 | 5.08 | 32 | 27 | 6 | 5 | 0 | 0 | 170.0 | 207 | 112 | 96 | 13 | 4 | 80 | 4 | 60 | 7 |
| Posadas, Campeche | 0 | 0 | .000 | 9.00 | 2 | 0 | 0 | 2 | 0 | 0 | 3.0 | 6 | 6 | 3 | 1 | 0 | 2 | 1 | 3 | 2 |
| Pulido, Mexico City Reds | 4 | 6 | .400 | 3.88 | 50 | 0 | 0 | 50 | 0 | 20 | 69.2 | 77 | 34 | 30 | 3 | 0 | 32 | 8 | 51 | 2 |
| Purata, Tampico | 6 | 7 | .462 | 5.28 | 29 | 25 | 3 | 4 | 1 | 0 | 121.0 | 145 | 89 | 71 | 15 | 2 | 68 | 2 | 73 | 1 |
| Pruneda, Mexico City Reds | 4 | 8 | .333 | 5.95 | 24 | 15 | 3 | 9 | 1 | 1 | 87.2 | 87 | 62 | 58 | 15 | 0 | 59 | 1 | 62 | 8 |
| Quijano, Puebla | 5 | 4 | .556 | 7.56 | 24 | 10 | 1 | 14 | 0 | 0 | 72.2 | 100 | 69 | 61 | 7 | 2 | 31 | 4 | 22 | 4 |
| Quiroz, Nuevo Laredo* | 0 | 2 | .000 | 6.14 | 13 | 0 | 0 | 13 | 0 | 3 | 7.1 | 11 | 5 | 5 | 0 | 1 | 3 | 0 | 7 | 0 |
| Ramirez, Leon | 1 | 2 | .333 | 8.49 | 22 | 8 | 0 | 14 | 0 | 0 | 46.2 | 68 | 49 | 44 | 9 | 3 | 33 | 0 | 21 | 3 |
| Raygoza, 41 Leon-7 Cam | 9 | 6 | .600 | 6.10 | 48 | 3 | 1 | 45 | 0 | 1 | 97.1 | 125 | 75 | 66 | 9 | 1 | 54 | 3 | 54 | 7 |
| Retes, Mexico City Tigers | 0 | 0 | .000 | 10.80 | 2 | 0 | 0 | 2 | 0 | 0 | 3.1 | 5 | 6 | 4 | 1 | 0 | 3 | 0 | 2 | 0 |
| Reyes, Campeche | 0 | 1 | .000 | 8.10 | 1 | 1 | 0 | 0 | 0 | 0 | 3.1 | 5 | 4 | 3 | 0 | 2 | 2 | 0 | 1 | 0 |
| Rincon, 10 Vera-12 Yuc | 10 | 12 | .455 | 3.84 | 22 | 22 | 9 | 0 | 2 | 0 | 138.1 | 129 | 63 | 59 | 11 | 2 | 41 | 6 | 67 | 4 |
| H. Rios, Leon | 11 | 11 | .500 | 4.36 | 23 | 23 | 11 | 0 | 0 | 0 | 154.2 | 181 | 91 | 75 | 19 | 3 | 33 | 3 | 71 | 2 |
| J. Rios, Mexico City Tigers | 21 | 4 | .840 | 2.52 | 26 | 26 | 26 | 0 | 5 | 0 | 225.0 | 183 | 76 | 63 | 15 | 10 | 66 | 1 | 152 | 3 |
| L. Rivas, Monclova | 2 | 1 | .667 | 4.73 | 14 | 0 | 0 | 14 | 0 | 0 | 26.2 | 31 | 16 | 14 | 5 | 2 | 15 | 1 | 13 | 1 |
| M. Rivas, Tampico | 11 | 5 | .688 | 2.81 | 40 | 0 | 0 | 40 | 0 | 11 | 83.1 | 75 | 38 | 26 | 1 | 6 | 34 | 5 | 40 | 1 |
| A. Rivera, Union Laguna | 3 | 11 | .214 | 7.43 | 20 | 17 | 3 | 3 | 0 | 0 | 95.2 | 121 | 84 | 79 | 12 | 8 | 58 | 2 | 67 | 9 |
| O. Rivera, 6 Cor-15 Vera | 2 | 7 | .222 | 5.63 | 21 | 14 | 1 | 7 | 1 | 0 | 84.2 | 95 | 62 | 53 | 8 | 4 | 58 | 4 | 46 | 9 |
| Robles, Saltillo | 1 | 1 | .500 | 4.67 | 13 | 0 | 0 | 13 | 0 | 0 | 17.1 | 16 | 9 | 9 | 1 | 1 | 10 | 3 | 8 | 1 |

| Pitcher—Club | W. | L. | Pct. | ERA. | G. | GS. | CG. | GF. | ShO. | Sv. | IP. | H. | R. | ER. | HR. | HB. | BB. | Int. BB. | SO. | WP. |
|---|---|---|---|---|---|---|---|---|---|---|---|---|---|---|---|---|---|---|---|---|
| A. Rodriguez, 25 Leon-15 Agua. | 7 | 5 | .583 | 4.96 | 40 | 2 | 0 | 38 | 0 | 7 | 78.0 | 85 | 51 | 43 | 6 | 1 | 40 | 4 | 63 | 9 |
| I. Rodriguez, Monclova | 0 | 0 | .000 | 0.00 | 2 | 0 | 0 | 2 | 0 | 0 | 1.0 | 1 | 0 | 0 | 0 | 0 | 1 | 1 | 1 | 0 |
| J. Rodriguez, Cordoba | 0 | 0 | .000 | 5.40 | 6 | 0 | 0 | 6 | 0 | 0 | 6.2 | 7 | 5 | 4 | 1 | 1 | 12 | 2 | 4 | 1 |
| M.A. Rod'guez, 25 Ag-13 Le | 4 | 12 | .250 | 5.68 | 38 | 11 | 5 | 27 | 0 | 1 | 126.2 | 155 | 85 | 80 | 11 | 9 | 65 | 5 | 83 | 7 |
| P. Rodriguez, Yucatan | 7 | 4 | .636 | 2.64 | 33 | 0 | 0 | 33 | 0 | 13 | 47.2 | 48 | 16 | 14 | 1 | 1 | 11 | 2 | 18 | 4 |
| R. Rodriguez, Campeche | 1 | 2 | .333 | 4.14 | 19 | 0 | 0 | 19 | 0 | 2 | 41.1 | 47 | 21 | 19 | 3 | 1 | 17 | 1 | 23 | 3 |
| Rogers, Monclova | 13 | 11 | .542 | 5.10 | 27 | 27 | 10 | 0 | 1 | 0 | 189.0 | 249 | 121 | 107 | 18 | 13 | 50 | 6 | 93 | 9 |
| Rojo, Mendez, Tabasco | 5 | 5 | .500 | 3.52 | 51 | 1 | 0 | 50 | 0 | 8 | 87.0 | 98 | 38 | 34 | 6 | 9 | 26 | 9 | 39 | 2 |
| E. Romero, Union Laguna | 5 | 1 | .833 | 5.40 | 15 | 0 | 0 | 15 | 0 | 0 | 31.2 | 43 | 22 | 19 | 3 | 0 | 12 | 1 | 15 | 2 |
| F. Romero, Monterrey | 0 | 0 | .000 | 6.08 | 8 | 0 | 0 | 8 | 0 | 0 | 13.1 | 16 | 9 | 9 | 3 | 0 | 11 | 0 | 9 | 2 |
| M. Romo, Union Laguna | 2 | 1 | .667 | 4.22 | 8 | 5 | 2 | 3 | 0 | 0 | 42.2 | 53 | 23 | 20 | 4 | 2 | 13 | 0 | 15 | 8 |
| V. Romo, Cordoba | 4 | 2 | .667 | 2.11 | 14 | 14 | 1 | 0 | 1 | 0 | 59.2 | 42 | 18 | 14 | 4 | 1 | 13 | 0 | 44 | 3 |
| Rondon, Tabasco | 5 | 10 | .333 | 4.86 | 19 | 18 | 5 | 1 | 3 | 0 | 102.0 | 130 | 61 | 55 | 9 | 1 | 24 | 2 | 62 | 4 |
| Ronquillo, Union Laguna | 0 | 1 | .000 | 4.42 | 8 | 1 | 0 | 7 | 0 | 0 | 18.1 | 18 | 15 | 9 | 3 | 1 | 13 | 0 | 5 | 4 |
| C. Ruiz, Yucatan | 9 | 7 | .563 | 3.25 | 23 | 23 | 10 | 0 | 3 | 0 | 163.1 | 166 | 66 | 59 | 7 | 4 | 66 | 4 | 84 | 5 |
| P. Ruiz, Monclova* | 10 | 7 | .588 | 5.21 | 27 | 27 | 7 | 0 | 3 | 0 | 157.1 | 183 | 107 | 91 | 11 | 10 | 98 | 7 | 156 | 8 |
| Salas, Tabasco | 1 | 3 | .250 | 5.25 | 7 | 4 | 1 | 3 | 0 | 0 | 24.0 | 27 | 19 | 14 | 2 | 1 | 15 | 3 | 12 | 3 |
| Salinas, 6 Mon-3 Cor | 2 | 5 | .286 | 6.10 | 9 | 8 | 2 | 1 | 1 | 0 | 41.1 | 58 | 32 | 28 | 3 | 1 | 10 | 1 | 17 | 3 |
| D. Sanchez, 18 MCR-9 Mva | 0 | 1 | .000 | 5.61 | 27 | 0 | 0 | 27 | 0 | 1 | 43.1 | 60 | 33 | 27 | 3 | 5 | 29 | 5 | 16 | 0 |
| F. Sanchez, 7 NL-17 Tab | 3 | 5 | .375 | 5.58 | 24 | 10 | 2 | 14 | 0 | 0 | 79.0 | 92 | 52 | 49 | 5 | 3 | 44 | 5 | 27 | 5 |
| P. Sanchez, 20 Tab-6 Mon | 7 | 11 | .389 | 4.83 | 26 | 26 | 9 | 0 | 1 | 0 | 149.0 | 156 | 90 | 80 | 11 | 7 | 66 | 5 | 77 | 5 |
| Sandate, Aguascalientes* | 10 | 7 | .588 | 5.21 | 25 | 25 | 10 | 0 | 0 | 0 | 162.1 | 209 | 111 | 94 | 18 | 4 | 43 | 0 | 103 | 4 |
| Sauceda, Yucatan | 7 | 0 | 1.000 | 2.13 | 27 | 0 | 0 | 27 | 0 | 1 | 67.2 | 53 | 16 | 16 | 5 | 3 | 23 | 4 | 41 | 6 |
| Segui, Monclova | 5 | 4 | .556 | 4.26 | 13 | 12 | 1 | 1 | 1 | 0 | 63.1 | 57 | 31 | 30 | 9 | 3 | 24 | 1 | 31 | 1 |
| Senteney, Union Laguna | 1 | 1 | .500 | 3.13 | 18 | 0 | 0 | 18 | 0 | 2 | 31.2 | 26 | 15 | 11 | 1 | 0 | 13 | 5 | 25 | 2 |
| Serafin, Cordoba | 10 | 5 | .667 | 2.81 | 43 | 5 | 1 | 38 | 0 | 4 | 134.1 | 106 | 47 | 42 | 6 | 5 | 54 | 8 | 79 | 10 |
| Serna, Union Laguna | 16 | 12 | .571 | 3.16 | 30 | 29 | 22 | 1 | 3 | 0 | 236.1 | 222 | 103 | 83 | 15 | 11 | 61 | 4 | 200 | 5 |
| Silva, Cordoba | 7 | 7 | .500 | 2.98 | 41 | 2 | 2 | 39 | 0 | 5 | 81.2 | 81 | 32 | 27 | 2 | 2 | 21 | 3 | 51 | 5 |
| M. Solis, Saltillo | 12 | 6 | .667 | 4.07 | 22 | 22 | 5 | 0 | 0 | 0 | 154.2 | 166 | 82 | 70 | 14 | 12 | 43 | 5 | 47 | 5 |
| R. Solis, Mexico City Reds* | 19 | 4 | .826 | 3.67 | 31 | 29 | 9 | 2 | 4 | 0 | 203.1 | 212 | 97 | 83 | 10 | 5 | 57 | 1 | 104 | 3 |
| Sombra, Union Laguna | 1 | 3 | .250 | 6.88 | 17 | 3 | 0 | 14 | 0 | 0 | 35.1 | 43 | 28 | 27 | 5 | 0 | 15 | 1 | 11 | 0 |
| Sosa, Tampico | 11 | 10 | .524 | 4.16 | 29 | 25 | 3 | 4 | 2 | 0 | 151.1 | 162 | 91 | 70 | 12 | 6 | 83 | 6 | 85 | 3 |
| Soto, Puebla | 7 | 10 | .412 | 4.17 | 34 | 4 | 0 | 30 | 0 | 7 | 99.1 | 125 | 54 | 46 | 3 | 4 | 38 | 10 | 51 | 2 |
| Stone, Nuevo Laredo | 2 | 3 | .400 | 4.66 | 15 | 2 | 0 | 13 | 0 | 1 | 29.0 | 25 | 16 | 15 | 2 | 1 | 18 | 3 | 14 | 1 |
| Sutton, Monterrey | 13 | 9 | .591 | 4.86 | 24 | 24 | 11 | 0 | 1 | 0 | 159.1 | 195 | 101 | 86 | 14 | 10 | 52 | 0 | 58 | 3 |
| Taylor, Puebla | 0 | 0 | .000 | 27.00 | 1 | 0 | 0 | 1 | 0 | 0 | 1.0 | 4 | 4 | 3 | 0 | 0 | 1 | 0 | 1 | 1 |
| Tejeda, 8 Cor-8 MCR | 0 | 1 | .000 | 4.64 | 16 | 1 | 0 | 15 | 0 | 0 | 42.2 | 51 | 23 | 22 | 4 | 1 | 11 | 0 | 24 | 3 |
| Tinajero, Tampico | 0 | 0 | .000 | 27.00 | 1 | 0 | 0 | 1 | 0 | 0 | 1.0 | 2 | 4 | 3 | 0 | 0 | 0 | 0 | 0 | 2 |
| Toribio, Aguascalientes | 0 | 2 | .000 | 34.36 | 5 | 2 | 0 | 3 | 0 | 0 | 3.2 | 12 | 15 | 14 | 2 | 1 | 10 | 0 | 4 | 2 |
| Torres, 9 MT-1 Tam-25 Co | 3 | 1 | .750 | 7.14 | 35 | 0 | 0 | 35 | 0 | 2 | 40.1 | 54 | 36 | 32 | 4 | 2 | 22 | 6 | 21 | 9 |
| N. Torres, Tabasco | 0 | 3 | .000 | 2.51 | 16 | 2 | 0 | 14 | 0 | 4 | 32.1 | 30 | 12 | 9 | 0 | 0 | 13 | 2 | 17 | 2 |
| Trevino, Puebla | 0 | 0 | .000 | 0.00 | 1 | 0 | 0 | 1 | 0 | 0 | 1.2 | 2 | 0 | 0 | 0 | 0 | 1 | 0 | 3 | 0 |
| Urias, Puebla | 0 | 0 | .000 | 5.40 | 5 | 0 | 0 | 5 | 0 | 1 | 13.1 | 16 | 11 | 8 | 3 | 0 | 8 | 0 | 4 | 0 |
| Uribe, Yucatan | 0 | 0 | .000 | 20.25 | 1 | 0 | 0 | 1 | 0 | 0 | 1.1 | 4 | 3 | 3 | 1 | 0 | 0 | 0 | 1 | 0 |
| Urrea, 38 Vera-9 Cor | 7 | 8 | .467 | 2.51 | 47 | 0 | 0 | 47 | 0 | 11 | 68.0 | 87 | 35 | 29 | 6 | 0 | 19 | 10 | 36 | 1 |
| H. Valdez, 3 Cam-11 Tab | 0 | 1 | .000 | 3.99 | 14 | 0 | 0 | 14 | 0 | 0 | 38.1 | 46 | 23 | 17 | 2 | 2 | 12 | 1 | 16 | 2 |
| R. Valdez, Campeche | 11 | 9 | .550 | 4.00 | 28 | 27 | 6 | 1 | 0 | 0 | 171.0 | 175 | 80 | 76 | 19 | 1 | 108 | 3 | 76 | 12 |
| A. Valenzuela, Saltillo | 2 | 1 | .667 | 6.35 | 6 | 6 | 1 | 0 | 0 | 0 | 28.1 | 48 | 25 | 20 | 1 | 0 | 13 | 2 | 14 | 1 |
| G. Valenzuela, Leon | 7 | 8 | .467 | 4.24 | 19 | 17 | 11 | 2 | 0 | 1 | 116.2 | 137 | 67 | 55 | 15 | 3 | 38 | 6 | 68 | 6 |
| J. Valenzuela, Saltillo | 9 | 8 | .529 | 5.10 | 28 | 27 | 6 | 1 | 1 | 0 | 166.0 | 193 | 112 | 94 | 37 | 2 | 42 | 1 | 67 | 1 |
| Vaqueiro, Nuevo Laredo* | 2 | 1 | .667 | 2.30 | 20 | 0 | 0 | 20 | 0 | 1 | 15.2 | 9 | 5 | 4 | 1 | 1 | 7 | 1 | 16 | 1 |
| Vargas, Mexico City Tigers | 0 | 0 | .000 | 0.00 | 2 | 0 | 0 | 2 | 0 | 0 | 4.0 | 4 | 0 | 0 | 0 | 0 | 4 | 0 | 0 | 1 |
| F. Vazquez, Monclova | 9 | 5 | .643 | 5.28 | 27 | 16 | 3 | 11 | 0 | 0 | 129.2 | 144 | 86 | 76 | 16 | 7 | 69 | 8 | 56 | 1 |
| J. Vazquez, Monterrey | 0 | 0 | .000 | 8.16 | 5 | 0 | 0 | 5 | 0 | 0 | 14.1 | 21 | 15 | 13 | 1 | 1 | 5 | 0 | 6 | 1 |
| M. Vazquez, 17 Vera-9 Cor | 9 | 7 | .563 | 3.85 | 26 | 26 | 1 | 0 | 0 | 0 | 149.2 | 183 | 77 | 64 | 5 | 4 | 67 | 11 | 84 | 14 |
| R. Vazquez, Saltillo | 0 | 0 | .000 | 10.80 | 2 | 2 | 0 | 0 | 0 | 0 | 6.2 | 13 | 10 | 8 | 3 | 0 | 1 | 0 | 3 | 1 |
| I. Velazquez, 21 MCT-8 Leon | 1 | 6 | .143 | 7.55 | 29 | 13 | 1 | 16 | 0 | 0 | 76.1 | 116 | 75 | 64 | 13 | 4 | 40 | 3 | 26 | 3 |
| L. Velazquez, Tabasco | 5 | 11 | .313 | 5.38 | 18 | 18 | 2 | 0 | 1 | 0 | 95.1 | 102 | 60 | 57 | 8 | 1 | 62 | 1 | 65 | 7 |
| Veliz, Cordoba* | 8 | 7 | .533 | 3.72 | 27 | 23 | 3 | 4 | 1 | 0 | 130.2 | 135 | 62 | 54 | 7 | 5 | 88 | 6 | 59 | 6 |
| Vergara, Veracruz | 0 | 0 | .000 | 135.00 | 1 | 0 | 0 | 1 | 0 | 0 | 0.1 | 3 | 5 | 5 | 0 | 0 | 3 | 0 | 1 | 1 |
| Vidana, 2 Sal-18 Tab | 1 | 1 | .500 | 6.15 | 20 | 1 | 0 | 19 | 0 | 0 | 41.0 | 49 | 28 | 28 | 6 | 1 | 10 | 0 | 16 | 1 |
| Viezca, Saltillo | 1 | 0 | 1.000 | 6.75 | 11 | 0 | 0 | 11 | 0 | 0 | 22.2 | 30 | 19 | 17 | 4 | 1 | 19 | 1 | 8 | 6 |
| Vila, Monterrey | 10 | 6 | .625 | 3.00 | 60 | 1 | 0 | 59 | 0 | 19 | 120.0 | 97 | 46 | 40 | 11 | 6 | 46 | 5 | 101 | 2 |
| Villaescusa, Yucatan | 0 | 0 | .000 | 2.25 | 1 | 0 | 0 | 1 | 0 | 0 | 4.0 | 2 | 1 | 1 | 0 | 0 | 1 | 0 | 2 | 1 |
| Villanueva, Aguascalientes* | 10 | 6 | .625 | 4.41 | 34 | 14 | 8 | 20 | 2 | 2 | 128.2 | 152 | 67 | 63 | 12 | 5 | 33 | 2 | 63 | 4 |
| Villarreal, Puebla* | 0 | 2 | .000 | 4.74 | 21 | 0 | 0 | 21 | 0 | 1 | 38.0 | 39 | 23 | 20 | 2 | 1 | 26 | 1 | 33 | 2 |
| M. Villegas, Aguascalientes | 12 | 9 | .571 | 3.32 | 25 | 23 | 13 | 2 | 1 | 0 | 176.0 | 180 | 76 | 65 | 18 | 6 | 49 | 6 | 130 | 3 |
| R. Villegas, 8 MT-13 N-6 Tam | 0 | 6 | .000 | 7.67 | 27 | 9 | 0 | 18 | 0 | 0 | 58.2 | 83 | 61 | 50 | 11 | 1 | 32 | 2 | 35 | 1 |
| Vizcarra, Mexico City Reds | 0 | 0 | .000 | 3.55 | 4 | 0 | 0 | 4 | 0 | 0 | 12.2 | 13 | 5 | 5 | 2 | 0 | 2 | 0 | 2 | 0 |
| Widales, Nuevo Laredo | 2 | 2 | .500 | 6.48 | 12 | 5 | 0 | 7 | 0 | 0 | 33.1 | 41 | 28 | 24 | 6 | 1 | 12 | 1 | 12 | 1 |
| Yucupicio, Tabasco | 1 | 6 | .143 | 5.92 | 38 | 1 | 0 | 37 | 0 | 0 | 48.2 | 62 | 46 | 32 | 5 | 1 | 36 | 4 | 23 | 2 |
| Zamberino, Tabasco | 0 | 0 | .000 | 6.75 | 2 | 0 | 0 | 2 | 0 | 0 | 1.1 | 2 | 1 | 1 | 0 | 0 | 0 | 0 | 0 | 0 |
| Zamudio, Veracruz | 3 | 1 | .750 | 4.66 | 16 | 3 | 0 | 13 | 0 | 0 | 36.2 | 39 | 25 | 19 | 2 | 3 | 16 | 2 | 13 | 4 |

BALKS—P. Ochoa, 3; L. Chavez, C. Diaz, Duarte, R. Espinosa, Jor. Garcia, J. Moreno, 2 each; Au. Casteneda, Castillejos, E. Cordova, F. Cota, Cutty, O. Diaz, M. Hernandez, Huerta, Jackson, Lara, Leal, Marquez, Mundo, Navarro, Ortiz, R. Palacios, Palafox, Retes, J. Rios, O. Rivera, P. Rodriguez, C. Ruiz, Serna, R. Solis, Sosa, N. Torres, Toribio, M.A. Vazquez, I. Velazquez, L. Velazquez, Veliz, 1 each.

COMBINATION SHUTOUTS—R. Valdez-Divison, Madrigal-Divison, Campeche; V. Romo-Serafin-Silva, Leal-Serafin, Gaxiola-Urrea-M. Torres-Silva, V. Romo-Urrea, M.A. Vazquez-M. Torres, Lara-Serafin, Cordoba; L. Chavez-Pulido, Mendez-Pulido, V. Palacios-L. Aponte, Mexico City Reds; F. Montano-Fischer, F. Montano-Harper, Mexico City Tigers; Segui-Jos. Garcia-R. Guzman, Monclova; Duarte-Vila, Monterrey; J. Moreno-Anderson, J. Moreno-P. Ochoa, Nuevo Laredo; O. Pollorena-Inzunza-Rojo, Mendez, Tabasco; E. Beltran-I. Aguilar-Antunez, E. Beltran-G. Chavez, E. Beltran-M. Rivas, Purata-G. Chavez, Tampico; R. Contreras-Alicea, Union Laguna; M.A. Vazquez-Urrea, Veracruz.

PERFECT GAME—Dominguez, Campeche, defeated Cordoba, 1-0 (seven innings), April 14.

NO-HIT GAMES—Sosa, Tampico, defeated Puebla, 4-0, June 8; Colorado, Cordoba, defeated Monterrey, 4-0 (six innings), June 14.

# Pacific Coast League

## CLASS AAA

**Leading Batter
JOHN KRUK
Las Vegas**

**League President
BILL CUTLER**

**Leading Pitcher
BOB WALK
Hawaii**

CHAMPIONSHIP WINNERS IN PREVIOUS YEARS

| | | | | | |
|---|---|---|---|---|---|
| 1903—Los Angeles | .630 | 1935—Los Angeles | .648 | 1966—Seattle a | .561 |
| 1904—Tacoma | .589 | San Francisco° | .608 | Tulsa | .578 |
| Tacoma§ | .571 | 1936—Portland‡ | .549 | 1967—San Diego a | .574 |
| Los Angeles§ | .571 | 1937—Sacramento | .573 | Spokane | .541 |
| 1905—Tacoma | .583 | San Diego (3rd)† | .545 | 1968—Tulsa a | .642 |
| Los Angeles° | .604 | 1938—Los Angeles | .590 | Spokane | .586 |
| 1906—Portland | .657 | Sacramento (3rd)† | .537 | 1969—Tacoma a | .589 |
| 1907—Los Angeles | .608 | 1939—Seattle | .589 | Eugene | .603 |
| 1908—Los Angeles | .585 | Sacramento (4th)† | .500 | 1970—Spokane a | .644 |
| 1909—San Francisco | .623 | 1940—Seattle‡ | .629 | Hawaii | .671 |
| 1910—Portland | .567 | 1941—Seattle‡ | .598 | 1971—Salt Lake City | .534 |
| 1911—Portland | .589 | 1942—Sacramento | .590 | Tacoma | .545 |
| 1912—Oakland | .591 | Seattle (3rd)† | .539 | 1972—Albuquerque | .622 |
| 1913—Portland | .559 | 1943—Los Angeles | .710 | Eugene | .534 |
| 1914—Portland | .574 | S. Francisco (2nd)† | .574 | 1973—Tucson | .583 |
| 1915—San Francisco | .570 | 1944—Los Angeles | .586 | Spokane a | .563 |
| 1916—Los Angeles | .601 | S. Francisco (3rd)† | .509 | 1974—Spokane a | .549 |
| 1917—San Francisco | .561 | 1945—Portland | .622 | Albuqerque | .535 |
| 1918—Vernon | .569 | S. Francisco (4th)† | .525 | 1975—Salt Lake City | .556 |
| Los Angeles (2nd) x | .548 | 1946—San Francisco‡ | .628 | Hawaii a | .611 |
| 1919—Vernon | .613 | 1947—Los Angeles†† | .567 | 1976—Salt Lake City | .625 |
| 1920—Vernon | .556 | 1948—Oakland‡ | .606 | Hawaii a | .531 |
| 1921—Los Angeles | .574 | 1949—Hollywood‡ | .583 | 1977—Phoenix a | .579 |
| 1922—San Francisco | .638 | 1950—Oakland | .590 | Hawaii | .541 |
| 1923—San Francisco | .617 | 1951—Seattle‡ | .593 | 1978—Tacoma b | .584 |
| 1924—Seattle | .545 | 1952—Hollywood | .606 | Albuquerque b | .557 |
| 1925—San Francisco | .643 | 1953—Hollywood | .589 | 1979—Albuquerque | .581 |
| 1926—Los Angeles | .599 | 1954—San Diego y | .604 | Salt Lake City c | .541 |
| 1927—Oakland | .615 | 1955—Seattle | .552 | 1980—Albuquerque° | .578 |
| 1928—San Francisco° | .630 | 1956—Los Angeles | .637 | Hawaii | .539 |
| Sacramento§§ | .626 | 1957—San Francisco | .601 | 1981—Albuquerque° | .712 |
| San Francisco§§ | .626 | 1958—Phoenix | .578 | Tacoma | .561 |
| 1929—Mission | .643 | 1959—Salt Lake City | .552 | 1982—Albuquerque° | .594 |
| Hollywood° | .592 | 1960—Spokane | .601 | Spokane | .545 |
| 1930—Los Angeles | .576 | 1961—Tacoma | .630 | 1983—Albuquerque | .594 |
| Hollywood° | .650 | 1962—San Diego | .604 | Portland° | .528 |
| 1931—Hollywood | .626 | 1963—Spokane | .620 | 1984—Hawaii | .621 |
| San Francisco° | .608 | Oklahoma City a | .632 | Edmonton° | .486 |
| 1932—Portland | .587 | 1964—Arkansas | .609 | | |
| 1933—Los Angeles | .610 | San Diego a | .576 | | |
| 1934—Los Angeles z | .786 | 1965—Oklahoma City a | .628 | | |
| Portland | .689 | Portland | .547 | | |

°Won split-season playoff. †Won four-team playoff. ‡Won pennant and four-team playoff. §Tied for second-half title with Tacoma winning playoff. §§Tied for second-half title, with Sacramento winning playoff. ††Ended regular season in tie with San Francisco and won one-game playoff for pennant, then won four-club playoff. xWon playoff from first-place Vernon and awarded championship. yDefeated Hollywood in one-game playoff for pennant. zWon both halves, no playoff. aLeague was divided into Northern, Southern divisions in 1963, 1969-70-71, and Eastern, Western divisions in 1964 through 1968 and 1972 through 1977, won two-team playoff. bLeague divided into Eastern and Western divisions, Tacoma and Albuquerque declared co-champions following cancellation of four-team playoff due to continuing rain and wet grounds. cWon second-half title and defeated Hawaii in four-team playoff.

## STANDING OF CLUBS AT CLOSE OF FIRST HALF, JUNE 21

### NORTHERN DIVISION

| Club | W. | L. | T. | Pct. | G.B. |
|---|---|---|---|---|---|
| Calgary (Mariners) | 37 | 32 | 0 | .536 | ....... |
| Vancouver (Brewers) | 38 | 34 | 0 | .528 | ½ |
| Portland (Phillies) | 36 | 34 | 0 | .514 | 1½ |
| Tacoma (A's) | 30 | 40 | 1 | .429 | 7½ |
| Edmonton (Angels) | 28 | 42 | 0 | .400 | 9½ |

### SOUTHERN DIVISION

| Club | W. | L. | T. | Pct. | G.B. |
|---|---|---|---|---|---|
| Hawaii (Pirates) | 42 | 29 | 0 | .592 | ....... |
| Phoenix (Giants) | 37 | 33 | 0 | .529 | 4½ |
| Tucson (Astros) | 35 | 34 | 0 | .507 | 6 |
| Albuquerque (Dodgers) | 36 | 35 | 1 | .507 | 6 |
| Las Vegas (Padres) | 33 | 39 | 0 | .458 | 9½ |

## STANDING OF CLUBS AT CLOSE OF SECOND HALF, SEPTEMBER 1

### NORTHERN DIVISION

| Club | W. | L. | T. | Pct. | G.B. |
|---|---|---|---|---|---|
| Vancouver (Brewers) | 41 | 30 | 0 | .577 | ....... |
| Edmonton (Angels) | 38 | 34 | 0 | .528 | 3½ |
| Tacoma (A's) | 36 | 36 | 0 | .500 | 5½ |
| Calgary (Mariners) | 34 | 38 | 0 | .472 | 7½ |
| Portland (Phillies) | 32 | 40 | 0 | .444 | 9½ |

### SOUTHERN DIVISION

| Club | W. | L. | T. | Pct. | G.B. |
|---|---|---|---|---|---|
| Phoenix (Giants) | 43 | 29 | 0 | .597 | ....... |
| Hawaii (Pirates) | 42 | 30 | 0 | .583 | 1 |
| Las Vegas (Padres) | 32 | 40 | 0 | .444 | 11 |
| Albuquerque (Dodgers) | 31 | 41 | 0 | .431 | 12 |
| Tucson (Astros) | 30 | 41 | 0 | .423 | 12½ |

## COMPOSITE STANDING OF CLUBS AT CLOSE OF SEASON, SEPTEMBER 1

### NORTHERN DIVISION

| Club | Van. | Cal. | Port. | Edm. | Tac. | Haw. | Phx. | Alb. | Tuc. | LV | W. | L. | T. | Pct. | G.B. |
|---|---|---|---|---|---|---|---|---|---|---|---|---|---|---|---|
| Vancouver (Brewers) | .... | 9 | 8 | 8 | 6 | 6 | 9 | 10 | 12 | 11 | 79 | 64 | 0 | .552 | ....... |
| Calgary (Mariners) | 7 | .... | 8 | 9 | 10 | 4 | 6 | 6 | 10 | 11 | 71 | 70 | 0 | .504 | 7 |
| Portland (Phillies) | 8 | 8 | .... | 11 | 7 | 4 | 8 | 6 | 8 | 8 | 68 | 74 | 0 | .479 | 10½ |
| Edmonton (Angels) | 8 | 7 | 5 | .... | 7 | 7 | 7 | 12 | 7 | 6 | 66 | 76 | 0 | .465 | 12½ |
| Tacoma (A's) | 10 | 6 | 8 | 9 | .... | 8 | 5 | 4 | 9 | 7 | 66 | 76 | 1 | .465 | 12½ |

### SOUTHERN DIVISION

| Club | Van. | Cal. | Port. | Edm. | Tac. | Haw. | Phx. | Alb. | Tuc. | LV | W. | L. | T. | Pct. | G.B. |
|---|---|---|---|---|---|---|---|---|---|---|---|---|---|---|---|
| Hawaii (Pirates) | 10 | 12 | 11 | 9 | 8 | .... | 7 | 10 | 7 | 10 | 84 | 59 | 0 | .587 | ....... |
| Phoenix (Giants) | 7 | 10 | 8 | 7 | 11 | 9 | .... | 12 | 6 | 10 | 80 | 62 | 0 | .563 | 3½ |
| Albuquerque (Dodgers) | 6 | 10 | 10 | 4 | 11 | 6 | 4 | .... | 8 | 8 | 67 | 76 | 1 | .469 | 17 |
| Tucson (Astros) | 3 | 3 | 8 | 9 | 7 | 9 | 10 | 8 | .... | 8 | 65 | 75 | 0 | .464 | 17½ |
| Las Vegas (Padres) | 5 | 5 | 8 | 10 | 9 | 6 | 6 | 8 | 8 | .... | 65 | 79 | 0 | .451 | 19½ |

Hawaii club represented Honolulu, Haw.

Major league affiliations in parentheses.

Playoffs—Vancouver defeated Calgary, three games to none; Phoenix defeated Hawaii, three games to none; Vancouver defeated Phoenix, three games to none, to win league championship.

Regular-Season Attendance—Albuquerque, 252,453; Calgary, 272,322; Edmonton, 229,112; Hawaii, 134,864; Las Vegas, 313,783; Phoenix, 168,620; Portland, 188,042; Tacoma, 208,534; Tucson, 128,540; Vancouver, 199,781. Total, 2,096,051.

Managers—Albuquerque, Terry Collins; Calgary, Bobby Floyd; Edmonton, Winston Llenas; Hawaii, Tommy Sandt; Las Vegas, Bob Cluck; Phoenix, Jim Lefebvre; Portland, Bill Dancy; Tacoma, Keith Lieppman; Tucson, Jimmy Johnson; Vancouver, Tom Trebelhorn.

All-Star Team: 1B—Franklin Stubbs, Albuquerque; 2B—Mike Woodard, Phoenix; 3B—Jack Howell, Edmonton; SS—Danny Tartabull, Calgary; OF—John Moses, Calgary; John Kruk, Las Vegas; Mike Felder, Vancouver; C—Mike Diaz, Hawaii; DH—Carlos Ponce, Vancouver; RHP—Bob Walk, Hawaii; LHP—Tim Conroy, Tacoma; Rel. P—Ray Krawczyk, Hawaii; Manager of the Year—Jim Lefebvre, Phoenix; Most Valuable Player—Danny Tartabull, Calgary.

(Compiled by William J. Weiss, League Statistician, San Mateo, Calif.)

## CLUB BATTING

| Club | Pct. | G. | AB. | R. | OR. | H. | TB. | 2B. | 3B. | HR. | RBI. | GW. | SH. | SF. | HP. | BB. | Int. BB. | SO. | SB. | CS. | LOB. |
|---|---|---|---|---|---|---|---|---|---|---|---|---|---|---|---|---|---|---|---|---|---|
| Calgary | .2840 | 141 | 4824 | 789 | 787 | 1370 | 2200 | 281 | 36 | 159 | 734 | 62 | 40 | 41 | 22 | 566 | 36 | 859 | 125 | 49 | 1031 |
| Las Vegas | .2838 | 144 | 4979 | 636 | 736 | 1413 | 2073 | 295 | 46 | 91 | 600 | 62 | 60 | 33 | 16 | 387 | 37 | 816 | 101 | 50 | 1027 |
| Edmonton | .277 | 142 | 4795 | 679 | 688 | 1328 | 1962 | 237 | 59 | 93 | 621 | 62 | 32 | 47 | 23 | 542 | 24 | 805 | 79 | 73 | 1028 |
| Vancouver | .274 | 143 | 4762 | 657 | 578 | 1307 | 1880 | 239 | 47 | 80 | 608 | 68 | 25 | 48 | 33 | 572 | 46 | 796 | 175 | 76 | 1066 |
| Albuquerque | .273 | 144 | 4775 | 690 | 712 | 1305 | 1991 | 250 | 38 | 120 | 533 | 61 | 41 | 42 | 26 | 434 | 40 | 812 | 105 | 45 | 968 |
| Phoenix | .271 | 142 | 4690 | 701 | 624 | 1273 | 1807 | 206 | 44 | 80 | 621 | 72 | 54 | 53 | 28 | 572 | 43 | 753 | 129 | 56 | 1062 |
| Portland | .267 | 142 | 4688 | 596 | 619 | 1253 | 1831 | 208 | 65 | 80 | 546 | 62 | 64 | 48 | 34 | 429 | 41 | 765 | 124 | 78 | 958 |
| Tucson | .264 | 140 | 4696 | 611 | 709 | 1239 | 1745 | 232 | 47 | 60 | 550 | 56 | 51 | 43 | 23 | 536 | 48 | 835 | 147 | 48 | 1060 |
| Tacoma | .263 | 143 | 4839 | 668 | 673 | 1275 | 1892 | 271 | 26 | 98 | 625 | 61 | 51 | 54 | 27 | 611 | 32 | 882 | 115 | 62 | 1120 |
| Hawaii | .255 | 143 | 4581 | 627 | 528 | 1170 | 1814 | 228 | 58 | 100 | 560 | 72 | 37 | 29 | 29 | 499 | 37 | 809 | 162 | 73 | 938 |

## INDIVIDUAL BATTING

(Leading Qualifiers for Batting Championship—389 or More Plate Appearances)

*Bats lefthanded.  †Switch-hitter.

| Player and Club | Pct. | G. | AB. | R. | H. | TB. | 2B. | 3B. | HR. | RBI. | GW. | SH. | SF. | HP. | BB. | Int. BB. | SO. | SB. | CS. |
|---|---|---|---|---|---|---|---|---|---|---|---|---|---|---|---|---|---|---|---|
| Kruk, John, Las Vegas* | .351 | 123 | 422 | 61 | 148 | 206 | 29 | 4 | 7 | 59 | 8 | 0 | 3 | 1 | 67 | 12 | 48 | 2 | 4 |
| Tillman, Kerry, Las Vegas | .337 | 115 | 412 | 66 | 139 | 216 | 27 | 7 | 12 | 75 | 4 | 3 | 3 | 1 | 23 | 2 | 73 | 18 | 3 |
| Smith, Raymond, Las Vegas | .325 | 104 | 397 | 48 | 129 | 188 | 32 | 3 | 7 | 42 | 6 | 3 | 4 | 16 | 1 | 37 | 1 | 2 |
| Moses, John, Calgary† | .321 | 113 | 473 | 75 | 152 | 206 | 37 | 1 | 5 | 47 | 3 | 5 | 0 | 46 | 4 | 56 | 35 | 11 |
| Ponce, Carlos, Vancouver | .320 | 109 | 394 | 53 | 126 | 197 | 25 | 5 | 12 | 78 | 11 | 0 | 5 | 6 | 34 | 5 | 54 | 21 | 8 |
| Bullock, Eric, Tucson* | .319 | 124 | 467 | 81 | 149 | 203 | 26 | 8 | 4 | 57 | 11 | 1 | 3 | 7 | 45 | 7 | 50 | 48 | 14 |
| Wilson, Michael, Phoenix | .319 | 140 | 518 | 109 | 165 | 206 | 20 | 6 | 3 | 45 | 6 | 9 | 4 | 2 | 93 | 2 | 38 | 56 | 22 |
| Woodard, Michael, Phoenix* | .316 | 140 | 573 | 85 | 181 | 224 | 16 | 9 | 3 | 63 | 6 | 5 | 7 | 0 | 51 | 3 | 42 | 33 | 14 |
| James, Christopher, Phoenix† | .316 | 135 | 507 | 78 | 160 | 244 | 35 | 8 | 11 | 73 | 9 | 5 | 3 | 7 | 33 | 1 | 72 | 23 | 10 |
| Felder, Michael, Vancouver† | .314 | 137 | 563 | 91 | 177 | 221 | 16 | 11 | 2 | 43 | 3 | 3 | 5 | 2 | 55 | 1 | 70 | 61 | 12 |

Departmental Leaders: G—Wilson, Woodard, 140; AB—Woodard, 573; R—Wilson, 109; H—Woodard, 181; TB—Tartabull, 291; 2B—J. Moses, 37; 3B—T. Davis, 12; HR—Tartabull, 43; RBI—Tartabull, 109; GWRBI—V. Rodriguez, 16; SH—Followell, 12; SF—Loman, Reyes, 8; HP—Bullock, Diaz, C. James, Miscik, Schultz, 7; BB—C. Clark, 108; IBB—Kruk, 12; SO—King, 126; SB—Felder, 61; CS—Wilson, 22.

| Player and Club | Pct. | G. | AB. | R. | H. | TB. | 2B. | 3B. | HR. | RBI. | GW. | SH. | SF. | HP. | BB. | Int. BB. | SO. | SB. | CS. |
|---|---|---|---|---|---|---|---|---|---|---|---|---|---|---|---|---|---|---|---|
| Acker, Larry, Tucson* | .083 | 36 | 24 | 2 | 2 | 2 | 0 | 0 | 0 | 2 | 0 | 2 | 0 | 0 | 2 | 0 | 12 | 0 | 0 |
| Adams, Patrick, Phoenix | .262 | 116 | 401 | 47 | 105 | 159 | 19 | 1 | 11 | 63 | 14 | 1 | 5 | 2 | 63 | 4 | 119 | 0 | 1 |
| Adams, Ricky, Phoenix | .305 | 42 | 154 | 22 | 47 | 73 | 8 | 3 | 4 | 31 | 3 | 2 | 2 | 1 | 6 | 0 | 22 | 7 | 0 |
| Adduci, James, Vancouver* | .277 | 112 | 393 | 63 | 109 | 201 | 28 | 2 | 20 | 77 | 9 | 0 | 6 | 1 | 49 | 7 | 93 | 8 | 3 |
| Alderete, Michael, Phoenix* | .125 | 3 | 8 | 0 | 1 | 2 | 1 | 0 | 0 | 1 | 0 | 0 | 0 | 0 | 0 | 0 | 3 | 0 | 0 |
| Allen, James, Calgary | .244 | 90 | 315 | 41 | 77 | 129 | 19 | 0 | 11 | 50 | 3 | 5 | 1 | 5 | 38 | 1 | 58 | 2 | 2 |

| Player and Club | Pct. | G. | AB. | R. | H. | TB. | 2B. | 3B. | HR. | RBI. | GW. | SH. | SF. | HP. | BB. | Int. BB. | SO. | SB. | CS. |
|---|---|---|---|---|---|---|---|---|---|---|---|---|---|---|---|---|---|---|---|
| Allen, Robert, Albuquerque | .264 | 38 | 91 | 12 | 24 | 31 | 7 | 0 | 0 | 10 | 0 | 0 | 0 | 1 | 1 | 0 | 10 | 0 | 0 |
| Amelung, Edward, Albuquerque* | .291 | 137 | 561 | 70 | 163 | 222 | 29 | 3 | 8 | 61 | 6 | 1 | 6 | 0 | 27 | 6 | 66 | 12 | 10 |
| Anderson, David, Albuquerque | .289 | 28 | 97 | 23 | 28 | 44 | 7 | 0 | 3 | 16 | 0 | 0 | 1 | 1 | 22 | 0 | 17 | 10 | 4 |
| Asadoor, Randall, Las Vegas | .254 | 126 | 413 | 57 | 105 | 183 | 27 | 0 | 17 | 58 | 4 | 6 | 4 | 2 | 50 | 1 | 110 | 8 | 1 |
| Ashford, Thomas, Portland | .100 | 16 | 30 | 0 | 3 | 3 | 0 | 0 | 0 | 2 | 0 | 1 | 0 | 3 | 0 | 1 | 0 | 0 |
| Ashman, Michael, Tacoma* | .278 | 47 | 133 | 19 | 37 | 43 | 6 | 0 | 0 | 13 | 0 | 0 | 1 | 1 | 16 | 1 | 19 | 2 | 0 |
| Barnes, Richard, Tucson | .000 | 25 | 4 | 0 | 0 | 0 | 0 | 0 | 0 | 0 | 0 | 1 | 0 | 0 | 0 | 0 | 3 | 0 | 0 |
| Bathe, Robert, Tacoma | .235 | 104 | 327 | 46 | 77 | 136 | 20 | 3 | 11 | 42 | 7 | 3 | 2 | 0 | 70 | 2 | 59 | 4 | 5 |
| Bathe, William, Tacoma | .279 | 108 | 359 | 43 | 100 | 144 | 26 | 0 | 6 | 45 | 3 | 3 | 4 | 3 | 48 | 0 | 60 | 0 | 2 |
| Belliard, Rafael, Hawaii | .246 | 100 | 341 | 35 | 84 | 107 | 12 | 4 | 1 | 18 | 2 | 3 | 1 | 1 | 4 | 0 | 49 | 9 | 7 |
| Bielecki, Michael, Hawaii | .000 | 20 | 27 | 2 | 0 | 0 | 0 | 0 | 0 | 1 | 0 | 0 | 0 | 2 | 0 | 13 | 0 | 0 |
| Blobaum, Jeffrey, Phoenix | .000 | 39 | 2 | 0 | 0 | 0 | 0 | 0 | 0 | 0 | 0 | 0 | 0 | 0 | 0 | 1 | 0 | 0 |
| Bonine, Eddie, Tucson | .429 | 47 | 7 | 0 | 3 | 4 | 1 | 0 | 0 | 1 | 0 | 0 | 0 | 2 | 0 | 2 | 0 | 0 |
| Booker, Gregory, Las Vegas | .167 | 10 | 6 | 0 | 1 | 1 | 0 | 0 | 0 | 0 | 0 | 0 | 0 | 1 | 0 | 2 | 0 | 0 |
| Brantley, Michael, Calgary | .244 | 74 | 279 | 52 | 68 | 126 | 13 | 6 | 11 | 45 | 5 | 2 | 3 | 0 | 28 | 2 | 27 | 11 | 1 |
| Bream, Sidney, Albuquerque* | .370 | 85 | 297 | 51 | 110 | 192 | 25 | 3 | 17 | 57 | 4 | 1 | 0 | 0 | 35 | 1 | 38 | 1 | 1 |
| Brennan, Thomas, Albuquerque | .125 | 20 | 16 | 0 | 2 | 3 | 1 | 0 | 0 | 2 | 0 | 5 | 0 | 4 | 0 | 7 | 0 | 0 |
| Brewer, Anthony, Albuquerque | .265 | 117 | 344 | 49 | 91 | 154 | 23 | 5 | 10 | 44 | 8 | 3 | 3 | 3 | 31 | 1 | 60 | 12 | 1 |
| Brouhard, Mark, Vancouver | .219 | 15 | 64 | 7 | 14 | 17 | 3 | 0 | 0 | 7 | 0 | 0 | 2 | 1 | 0 | 0 | 11 | 3 | 1 |
| Bryant, Ralph, Albuquerque* | .268 | 120 | 400 | 62 | 107 | 185 | 27 | 3 | 15 | 64 | 6 | 0 | 2 | 5 | 28 | 7 | 103 | 7 | 5 |
| Bullock, Eric, Tucson* | .319 | 124 | 467 | 81 | 149 | 203 | 26 | 8 | 4 | 57 | 11 | 1 | 3 | 7 | 45 | 7 | 50 | 48 | 14 |
| Cabrera, Antonio, Tacoma | .000 | 1 | 1 | 0 | 0 | 0 | 0 | 0 | 0 | 0 | 0 | 0 | 0 | 0 | 0 | 0 | 0 | 0 | 0 |
| Calise, Michael, Tucson | .278 | 116 | 363 | 53 | 101 | 170 | 17 | 5 | 14 | 60 | 5 | 0 | 1 | 0 | 47 | 2 | 94 | 1 | 0 |
| Callahan, Benjamin, Las Vegas | .000 | 4 | 2 | 1 | 0 | 0 | 0 | 0 | 0 | 0 | 0 | 0 | 0 | 0 | 0 | 0 | 0 | 0 | 0 |
| Canseco, Jose, Tacoma | .348 | 60 | 233 | 41 | 81 | 132 | 16 | 1 | 11 | 47 | 1 | 0 | 3 | 1 | 40 | 5 | 66 | 5 | 0 |
| Carrasco, Norman, Edmonton | .236 | 114 | 402 | 41 | 95 | 123 | 13 | 3 | 3 | 47 | 1 | 1 | 5 | 0 | 15 | 1 | 41 | 6 | 6 |
| Carter, Don, Hawaii* | .275 | 18 | 51 | 7 | 14 | 14 | 0 | 0 | 0 | 0 | 0 | 0 | 0 | 0 | 5 | 1 | 9 | 6 | 2 |
| Casey, Patrick, Calgary | .265 | 109 | 392 | 71 | 104 | 184 | 29 | 3 | 15 | 57 | 5 | 0 | 4 | 3 | 68 | 3 | 70 | 3 | 1 |
| Castillo, Juan, Vancouver† | .270 | 118 | 440 | 71 | 119 | 145 | 17 | 3 | 1 | 32 | 2 | 11 | 2 | 4 | 55 | 0 | 66 | 37 | 16 |
| Cato, Keefe, Las Vegas | .105 | 45 | 19 | 1 | 2 | 2 | 0 | 0 | 0 | 3 | 0 | 0 | 0 | 1 | 0 | 9 | 0 | 0 |
| Chambers, Albert, Calgary* | .308 | 100 | 354 | 64 | 109 | 173 | 31 | 3 | 9 | 64 | 7 | 2 | 6 | 1 | 59 | 7 | 75 | 10 | 3 |
| Childress, Rodney, Portland | .000 | 34 | 2 | 0 | 0 | 0 | 0 | 0 | 0 | 0 | 0 | 0 | 0 | 0 | 0 | 0 | 1 | 0 | 0 |
| Citarella, Ralph, Portland | .000 | 30 | 28 | 0 | 0 | 0 | 0 | 0 | 0 | 0 | 0 | 4 | 0 | 1 | 0 | 14 | 0 | 0 |
| Clark, Christopher, Edmonton† | .279 | 134 | 462 | 75 | 129 | 204 | 33 | 6 | 10 | 57 | 8 | 0 | 6 | 1 | 108 | 5 | 70 | 3 | 3 |
| Clark, Robert, Vancouver | .282 | 29 | 110 | 17 | 31 | 48 | 7 | 2 | 2 | 20 | 4 | 0 | 2 | 2 | 12 | 2 | 21 | 1 | 0 |
| Clements, Wesley, Vancouver | .269 | 70 | 238 | 34 | 64 | 115 | 12 | 3 | 11 | 42 | 4 | 0 | 2 | 0 | 29 | 0 | 73 | 0 | 1 |
| Cliburn, Stanley, Hawaii | .252 | 54 | 123 | 8 | 31 | 51 | 6 | 1 | 4 | 22 | 2 | 0 | 2 | 0 | 14 | 0 | 20 | 0 | 0 |
| Colbert, Richard, Tucson | .143 | 29 | 63 | 4 | 9 | 12 | 0 | 0 | 1 | 7 | 1 | 1 | 1 | 0 | 3 | 0 | 21 | 1 | 0 |
| Cole, Rodgers, Portland | .250 | 40 | 8 | 1 | 2 | 2 | 0 | 0 | 0 | 0 | 0 | 0 | 0 | 0 | 0 | 2 | 0 | 0 |
| Coles, Darnell, Calgary | .320 | 31 | 97 | 16 | 31 | 51 | 8 | 0 | 4 | 24 | 4 | 1 | 1 | 2 | 17 | 0 | 15 | 2 | 1 |
| Comer, Steven, Portland† | .000 | 19 | 8 | 0 | 0 | 0 | 0 | 0 | 0 | 0 | 0 | 3 | 0 | 2 | 0 | 5 | 0 | 0 |
| Crone, William, Calgary | .255 | 84 | 294 | 35 | 75 | 94 | 16 | 0 | 1 | 29 | 3 | 8 | 1 | 1 | 29 | 0 | 37 | 5 | 1 |
| Cummings, Robert, Phoenix | .000 | 2 | 6 | 0 | 0 | 0 | 0 | 0 | 0 | 0 | 0 | 0 | 0 | 0 | 0 | 1 | 0 | 0 |
| Daulton, Darren, Portland* | .297 | 23 | 64 | 13 | 19 | 36 | 5 | 3 | 2 | 10 | 3 | 0 | 1 | 1 | 16 | 0 | 13 | 6 | 1 |
| David, Brian, Calgary | .280 | 6 | 25 | 6 | 7 | 11 | 1 | 0 | 1 | 3 | 0 | 0 | 0 | 4 | 0 | 2 | 0 | 0 |
| Davidsmeier, Daniel, Vancouver | .281 | 107 | 356 | 38 | 100 | 129 | 21 | 1 | 2 | 40 | 4 | 3 | 1 | 5 | 28 | 2 | 53 | 2 | 3 |
| Davis, Gerald, Las Vegas | .286 | 17 | 63 | 7 | 18 | 19 | 1 | 0 | 0 | 9 | 0 | 1 | 2 | 0 | 8 | 2 | 5 | 4 | 2 |
| Davis, Glenn, Tucson | .305 | 60 | 220 | 22 | 67 | 110 | 24 | 2 | 5 | 35 | 3 | 0 | 3 | 3 | 13 | 3 | 23 | 1 | 0 |
| Davis, Trench, Hawaii* | .270 | 132 | 534 | 59 | 144 | 190 | 16 | 12 | 2 | 56 | 5 | 2 | 5 | 2 | 28 | 0 | 58 | 33 | 18 |
| Davisson, Jay, Portland | .000 | 9 | 10 | 0 | 0 | 0 | 0 | 0 | 0 | 0 | 0 | 0 | 0 | 1 | 0 | 7 | 0 | 0 |
| Decker, Martin, Las Vegas | .000 | 5 | 2 | 1 | 0 | 0 | 0 | 0 | 0 | 0 | 0 | 0 | 0 | 0 | 0 | 0 | 0 | 0 |
| DeLeon, Jose, Hawaii | .071 | 5 | 14 | 1 | 1 | 1 | 0 | 0 | 0 | 1 | 0 | 0 | 0 | 1 | 0 | 4 | 0 | 0 |
| DeLeon, Luis, Las Vegas | .000 | 9 | 4 | 0 | 0 | 0 | 0 | 0 | 0 | 0 | 0 | 0 | 0 | 0 | 0 | 2 | 0 | 0 |
| Diaz, Michael, 10 Port.-118 Haw. | .312 | 128 | 445 | 65 | 139 | 242 | 29 | 4 | 22 | 85 | 8 | 4 | 2 | 7 | 46 | 6 | 70 | 3 | 3 |
| Dilone, Miguel, Las Vegas† | .326 | 11 | 43 | 6 | 14 | 22 | 5 | 0 | 1 | 4 | 0 | 1 | 0 | 0 | 3 | 0 | 3 | 2 | 1 |
| Distefano, Benito, Hawaii* | .238 | 136 | 480 | 74 | 114 | 199 | 27 | 8 | 14 | 67 | 10 | 1 | 1 | 1 | 69 | 11 | 53 | 5 | 2 |
| Dowell, Kenneth, Portland | .211 | 114 | 303 | 32 | 64 | 79 | 6 | 3 | 1 | 23 | 1 | 3 | 5 | 1 | 34 | 1 | 42 | 5 | 5 |
| Downs, Kelly, Phoenix | .192 | 37 | 26 | 1 | 5 | 5 | 0 | 0 | 0 | 3 | 0 | 2 | 1 | 0 | 2 | 0 | 9 | 0 | 0 |
| Dybzinski, Jerome, Hawaii | .199 | 55 | 176 | 19 | 35 | 48 | 6 | 2 | 1 | 13 | 1 | 5 | 1 | 4 | 16 | 1 | 24 | 0 | 1 |
| Escobar, Jose, Calgary | .321 | 46 | 109 | 21 | 35 | 46 | 4 | 2 | 1 | 8 | 0 | 2 | 1 | 0 | 8 | 0 | 16 | 4 | 0 |
| Felder, Michael, Vancouver† | .314 | 137 | 563 | 91 | 177 | 221 | 16 | 11 | 2 | 43 | 3 | 3 | 5 | 2 | 55 | 1 | 70 | 61 | 12 |
| Fimple, John, Albuquerque | .229 | 95 | 231 | 25 | 53 | 79 | 11 | 0 | 5 | 29 | 2 | 4 | 4 | 2 | 29 | 0 | 64 | 0 | 1 |
| Followell, Vernon, Tucson† | .248 | 114 | 355 | 42 | 88 | 103 | 10 | 1 | 1 | 40 | 1 | 12 | 6 | 1 | 45 | 2 | 33 | 4 | 2 |
| Gainey, Telmanch (Ty), Tucson | .336 | 68 | 232 | 42 | 78 | 111 | 14 | 2 | 5 | 46 | 7 | 0 | 3 | 0 | 37 | 4 | 48 | 10 | 5 |
| Garcia, Steven, Las Vegas* | .281 | 92 | 278 | 31 | 78 | 108 | 18 | 3 | 2 | 23 | 3 | 4 | 1 | 0 | 14 | 0 | 25 | 12 | 5 |
| Gaynor, Richard, Portland | .000 | 8 | 0 | 0 | 0 | 0 | 0 | 0 | 0 | 0 | 0 | 1 | 0 | 0 | 0 | 0 | 0 | 0 | 0 |
| Ghelfi, Anthony, Portland | .067 | 24 | 15 | 0 | 1 | 1 | 0 | 0 | 0 | 2 | 0 | 1 | 0 | 0 | 0 | 5 | 0 | 0 |
| Giddings, Wayne, Tacoma | 1.000 | 3 | 1 | 0 | 1 | 1 | 0 | 0 | 0 | 0 | 0 | 0 | 0 | 0 | 0 | 0 | 0 | 0 |
| Giles, Brian, Vancouver | .234 | 40 | 128 | 21 | 30 | 45 | 7 | 1 | 2 | 15 | 4 | 1 | 4 | 0 | 22 | 0 | 25 | 3 | 2 |
| Gomez, Randall, Phoenix | .265 | 79 | 279 | 25 | 74 | 95 | 14 | 2 | 1 | 34 | 6 | 3 | 3 | 1 | 16 | 1 | 29 | 0 | 0 |
| Gonzalez, Arturo, Portland | .200 | 30 | 35 | 4 | 7 | 14 | 1 | 0 | 2 | 7 | 0 | 4 | 0 | 0 | 0 | 4 | 0 | 0 |
| Gonzalez, Denio, Hawaii | .288 | 106 | 365 | 68 | 105 | 174 | 21 | 6 | 12 | 57 | 11 | 0 | 3 | 3 | 51 | 6 | 79 | 39 | 13 |
| Goodwin, Danny, Tacoma* | .291 | 87 | 316 | 44 | 92 | 146 | 18 | 0 | 12 | 65 | 6 | 0 | 7 | 3 | 45 | 3 | 52 | 1 | 1 |
| Grant, Mark, Phoenix | .167 | 30 | 36 | 0 | 6 | 6 | 0 | 0 | 0 | 2 | 0 | 0 | 0 | 1 | 0 | 11 | 0 | 0 |
| Green, Christopher, Hawaii* | .143 | 35 | 14 | 1 | 2 | 4 | 0 | 1 | 0 | 0 | 0 | 0 | 0 | 1 | 0 | 5 | 0 | 0 |
| Groh, Donald, Edmonton* | .000 | 34 | 1 | 0 | 0 | 0 | 0 | 0 | 0 | 0 | 0 | 0 | 0 | 0 | 0 | 0 | 0 | 0 |
| Gulden, Bradley, Tucson* | .268 | 47 | 153 | 20 | 41 | 64 | 10 | 2 | 3 | 21 | 0 | 4 | 0 | 15 | 1 | 20 | 0 | 1 |
| Gwosdz, Douglas, Phoenix | .252 | 52 | 143 | 25 | 36 | 68 | 12 | 1 | 6 | 25 | 4 | 2 | 1 | 27 | 2 | 35 | 1 | 0 |
| Harper, Devallon, Las Vegas | .000 | 10 | 6 | 0 | 0 | 0 | 0 | 0 | 0 | 0 | 0 | 0 | 0 | 0 | 0 | 0 | 0 | 0 |
| Harrison, Ronald, Tacoma* | .251 | 119 | 387 | 55 | 97 | 135 | 13 | 2 | 7 | 42 | 5 | 11 | 3 | 1 | 20 | 1 | 53 | 10 | 8 |
| Hayward, Raymond, Las Vegas* | .279 | 31 | 43 | 1 | 12 | 15 | 3 | 0 | 0 | 3 | 0 | 1 | 0 | 0 | 2 | 0 | 4 | 0 | 0 |
| Heathcock, Jeffrey, Tucson | .067 | 23 | 30 | 1 | 2 | 3 | 1 | 0 | 0 | 1 | 0 | 2 | 0 | 0 | 12 | 0 | 0 |
| Hengel, David, Calgary | .087 | 6 | 23 | 1 | 2 | 3 | 1 | 0 | 0 | 3 | 0 | 0 | 0 | 4 | 0 | 6 | 0 | 0 |
| Hensley, Charles, Phoenix* | .000 | 35 | 7 | 0 | 0 | 0 | 0 | 0 | 0 | 0 | 0 | 0 | 0 | 0 | 0 | 7 | 0 | 0 |
| Hernandez, Manuel, Tucson | .000 | 11 | 6 | 0 | 0 | 0 | 0 | 0 | 0 | 0 | 0 | 0 | 0 | 2 | 0 | 4 | 0 | 0 |
| Hernandez, Pedro, Tucson | .235 | 34 | 68 | 10 | 16 | 26 | 3 | 2 | 1 | 6 | 2 | 0 | 0 | 0 | 2 | 0 | 15 | 1 | 0 |
| Herz, Steven, 4 Haw.-85 Port. | .259 | 89 | 266 | 28 | 69 | 96 | 12 | 0 | 5 | 28 | 2 | 4 | 4 | 2 | 15 | 1 | 30 | 0 | 1 |
| Hill, Clay, Phoenix | .302 | 86 | 288 | 40 | 87 | 122 | 17 | 3 | 4 | 34 | 0 | 4 | 3 | 2 | 26 | 2 | 39 | 0 | 0 |
| Hill, Roger, Calgary* | .270 | 15 | 63 | 10 | 17 | 21 | 4 | 0 | 0 | 6 | 1 | 1 | 0 | 4 | 0 | 7 | 0 | 1 |
| Hinshaw, George, Las Vegas | .279 | 101 | 337 | 41 | 94 | 128 | 13 | 6 | 3 | 49 | 5 | 0 | 4 | 1 | 27 | 1 | 60 | 9 | 7 |
| Holton, Brian, Albuquerque | .103 | 28 | 29 | 2 | 3 | 3 | 0 | 0 | 0 | 1 | 0 | 0 | 0 | 0 | 0 | 10 | 0 | 0 |
| Hough, Stanley, Tucson | .154 | 6 | 13 | 0 | 2 | 2 | 0 | 0 | 0 | 0 | 0 | 0 | 0 | 0 | 0 | 4 | 0 | 0 |

| Player and Club | Pct. | G. | AB. | R. | H. | TB. | 2B. | 3B. | HR. | RBI. | GW. | SH. | SF. | HP. | BB. | Int. BB. | SO. | SB. | CS. |
|---|---|---|---|---|---|---|---|---|---|---|---|---|---|---|---|---|---|---|---|
| Howell, Jack, Edmonton* | .373 | 79 | 284 | 55 | 106 | 173 | 22 | 3 | 13 | 48 | 3 | 0 | 0 | 0 | 52 | 3 | 57 | 3 | 2 |
| Howell, Roy, Portland* | .262 | 68 | 244 | 38 | 64 | 104 | 9 | 2 | 9 | 37 | 5 | 1 | 2 | 5 | 17 | 4 | 39 | 0 | 1 |
| Huppert, David, Vancouver | .308 | 9 | 26 | 3 | 8 | 8 | 0 | 0 | 0 | 1 | 0 | 0 | 0 | 0 | 9 | 0 | 7 | 0 | 0 |
| Ireland, Timothy, Vancouver† | .200 | 2 | 5 | 2 | 1 | 1 | 0 | 0 | 0 | 0 | 0 | 0 | 0 | 0 | 2 | 0 | 0 | 0 | 0 |
| Jackson, Charles, Tucson | .180 | 19 | 61 | 7 | 11 | 18 | 2 | 1 | 1 | 4 | 1 | 1 | 0 | 0 | 11 | 0 | 18 | 7 | 0 |
| Jackson, Roy Lee, Las Vegas | .000 | 3 | 1 | 0 | 0 | 0 | 0 | 0 | 0 | 0 | 0 | 0 | 0 | 0 | 0 | 0 | 0 | 0 | 0 |
| James, Christopher, Portland | .316 | 135 | 507 | 78 | 160 | 244 | 35 | 8 | 11 | 73 | 9 | 5 | 3 | 7 | 33 | 1 | 72 | 23 | 10 |
| James, Dion, Vancouver* | .108 | 10 | 37 | 2 | 4 | 6 | 2 | 0 | 0 | 5 | 0 | 0 | 0 | 0 | 4 | 0 | 6 | 0 | 0 |
| Jeffcoat, Michael, Phoenix* | .357 | 10 | 14 | 3 | 5 | 5 | 0 | 0 | 0 | 2 | 0 | 2 | 0 | 0 | 2 | 0 | 4 | 0 | 0 |
| Jeltz, Steven, Portland† | .296 | 21 | 71 | 6 | 21 | 30 | 4 | 1 | 1 | 9 | 0 | 1 | 0 | 0 | 8 | 1 | 15 | 2 | 1 |
| Johnson, John H., 20 Haw.-3 Van.* | .000 | 23 | 12 | 0 | 0 | 0 | 0 | 0 | 0 | 0 | 0 | 0 | 0 | 0 | 2 | 0 | 3 | 0 | 0 |
| Jones, Christopher, Tucson* | .338 | 76 | 281 | 44 | 95 | 138 | 21 | 8 | 2 | 33 | 3 | 0 | 2 | 0 | 48 | 5 | 29 | 24 | 6 |
| Jones, James, Tacoma | .500 | 2 | 2 | 0 | 1 | 1 | 0 | 0 | 0 | 0 | 0 | 0 | 0 | 1 | 1 | 0 | 0 | 0 | 0 |
| Joyner, Wallace, Edmonton* | .283 | 126 | 477 | 68 | 135 | 210 | 29 | 5 | 12 | 73 | 5 | 3 | 3 | 2 | 60 | 2 | 64 | 2 | 2 |
| Keedy, Patrick, Edmonton | .277 | 107 | 365 | 59 | 101 | 184 | 24 | 4 | 17 | 61 | 11 | 4 | 5 | 4 | 38 | 2 | 115 | 11 | 9 |
| Kerfeld, Charles, Tucson | .081 | 26 | 37 | 1 | 3 | 3 | 0 | 0 | 0 | 2 | 0 | 0 | 0 | 2 | 0 | 0 | 20 | 0 | 0 |
| Khalifa, Sam, Hawaii | .281 | 67 | 217 | 36 | 61 | 88 | 14 | 5 | 1 | 22 | 4 | 2 | 1 | 1 | 25 | 0 | 27 | 5 | 2 |
| Kibbe, Jay, Albuquerque* | .286 | 31 | 14 | 1 | 4 | 5 | 1 | 0 | 0 | 1 | 0 | 3 | 0 | 0 | 1 | 0 | 6 | 0 | 0 |
| Kiefer, Steven, Tacoma | .263 | 85 | 331 | 41 | 87 | 152 | 25 | 2 | 12 | 53 | 4 | 1 | 3 | 1 | 17 | 0 | 80 | 2 | 2 |
| King, Kevin, Calgary† | .272 | 96 | 335 | 64 | 91 | 164 | 17 | 4 | 16 | 46 | 3 | 1 | 2 | 3 | 37 | 1 | 126 | 2 | 1 |
| Kipper, Robert, 1 Edm.-6 Haw. | .000 | 7 | 8 | 0 | 0 | 0 | 0 | 0 | 0 | 0 | 0 | 0 | 0 | 0 | 0 | 0 | 4 | 0 | 0 |
| Klipstein, David, Vancouver | .189 | 12 | 37 | 3 | 7 | 7 | 0 | 0 | 0 | 1 | 0 | 0 | 0 | 0 | 3 | 1 | 5 | 0 | 1 |
| Knicely, Alan, Portland | .286 | 21 | 77 | 11 | 22 | 33 | 2 | 0 | 3 | 11 | 2 | 0 | 1 | 0 | 8 | 0 | 8 | 1 | 0 |
| Knight, Timothy, Portland* | .300 | 48 | 130 | 22 | 39 | 60 | 9 | 3 | 2 | 15 | 4 | 2 | 4 | 2 | 17 | 2 | 26 | 2 | 1 |
| Knudson, Mark, Tucson | .115 | 24 | 26 | 1 | 3 | 3 | 0 | 0 | 0 | 2 | 0 | 3 | 0 | 0 | 4 | 0 | 14 | 0 | 0 |
| Koenigsfeld, Ronald, Tucson | .217 | 64 | 203 | 26 | 44 | 63 | 3 | 2 | 4 | 17 | 1 | 3 | 2 | 0 | 35 | 2 | 38 | 2 | 2 |
| Krauss, Timothy, Edmonton* | .244 | 93 | 308 | 38 | 75 | 101 | 15 | 1 | 3 | 36 | 6 | 1 | 4 | 1 | 29 | 2 | 49 | 2 | 1 |
| Krawczyk, Raymond, Hawaii | .000 | 38 | 2 | 0 | 0 | 0 | 0 | 0 | 0 | 0 | 0 | 0 | 0 | 0 | 0 | 0 | 1 | 0 | 0 |
| Kruk, John, Las Vegas* | .351 | 123 | 422 | 61 | 148 | 206 | 29 | 4 | 7 | 59 | 8 | 0 | 3 | 1 | 67 | 12 | 48 | 2 | 4 |
| Kutcher, Randy, Phoenix | .237 | 97 | 228 | 36 | 54 | 76 | 15 | 2 | 1 | 20 | 2 | 3 | 2 | 1 | 20 | 1 | 45 | 10 | 3 |
| Lacey, Robert, Phoenix† | .000 | 21 | 0 | 0 | 0 | 0 | 0 | 0 | 0 | 0 | 0 | 1 | 0 | 0 | 0 | 0 | 0 | 0 | 0 |
| Lancellotti, Richard, Phoenix* | .210 | 33 | 119 | 17 | 25 | 51 | 4 | 2 | 6 | 29 | 7 | 0 | 5 | 1 | 14 | 2 | 18 | 0 | 0 |
| Landestoy, Rafael, Tucson† | .067 | 6 | 15 | 0 | 1 | 1 | 0 | 0 | 0 | 2 | 0 | 0 | 0 | 2 | 0 | 1 | 0 | 0 | 0 |
| Lansford, Joseph, Las Vegas | .214 | 104 | 318 | 44 | 68 | 133 | 26 | 3 | 11 | 45 | 3 | 1 | 3 | 1 | 41 | 4 | 113 | 2 | 3 |
| Lazorko, Jack, 22 Phx.-23 Cal. | .000 | 45 | 2 | 0 | 0 | 0 | 0 | 0 | 0 | 0 | 0 | 0 | 0 | 0 | 0 | 0 | 1 | 0 | 0 |
| LeBoeuf, Alan, Portland* | .205 | 20 | 44 | 3 | 9 | 15 | 2 | 2 | 0 | 5 | 0 | 1 | 1 | 0 | 2 | 1 | 2 | 1 | 1 |
| Legg, Gregory, Portland | .283 | 115 | 420 | 48 | 119 | 165 | 11 | 7 | 7 | 50 | 5 | 5 | 4 | 2 | 39 | 2 | 46 | 9 | 5 |
| Leopold, James, Las Vegas | .385 | 24 | 13 | 0 | 5 | 5 | 0 | 0 | 0 | 1 | 0 | 1 | 0 | 0 | 0 | 0 | 1 | 0 | 0 |
| Lerch, Randy, Portland* | .188 | 22 | 16 | 2 | 3 | 5 | 2 | 0 | 0 | 1 | 0 | 2 | 0 | 0 | 1 | 0 | 4 | 0 | 0 |
| Lewis, James, Calgary | .250 | 20 | 4 | 0 | 1 | 1 | 0 | 0 | 0 | 1 | 0 | 0 | 0 | 0 | 0 | 0 | 2 | 0 | 0 |
| Liddle, Steven, Edmonton | .307 | 25 | 75 | 12 | 23 | 36 | 7 | 0 | 2 | 13 | 0 | 0 | 2 | 0 | 12 | 1 | 12 | 0 | 1 |
| Linares, Rufino, Edmonton | .311 | 98 | 383 | 64 | 119 | 196 | 13 | 8 | 16 | 65 | 4 | 2 | 3 | 1 | 34 | 2 | 51 | 3 | 7 |
| Loman, Douglas, Vancouver* | .294 | 104 | 385 | 61 | 113 | 178 | 23 | 6 | 10 | 66 | 9 | 3 | 8 | 3 | 47 | 10 | 48 | 9 | 3 |
| Loucks, Scott, Hawaii | .282 | 91 | 330 | 61 | 93 | 133 | 21 | 2 | 5 | 27 | 2 | 4 | 1 | 1 | 54 | 1 | 61 | 34 | 10 |
| Lubratich, Steven, Las Vegas | .231 | 64 | 229 | 22 | 53 | 70 | 11 | 0 | 2 | 27 | 2 | 0 | 0 | 1 | 17 | 0 | 27 | 0 | 2 |
| Madden, Michael, Tucson* | .000 | 6 | 6 | 0 | 0 | 0 | 0 | 0 | 0 | 0 | 0 | 0 | 0 | 0 | 0 | 0 | 5 | 0 | 0 |
| Maddux, Michael, Portland | .048 | 27 | 21 | 2 | 1 | 1 | 0 | 0 | 0 | 0 | 0 | 5 | 0 | 0 | 5 | 0 | 6 | 0 | 0 |
| Madril, Michael, Edmonton† | .216 | 17 | 51 | 4 | 11 | 12 | 1 | 0 | 0 | 4 | 1 | 1 | 0 | 0 | 2 | 0 | 7 | 1 | 1 |
| Malkin, John, Hawaii | .186 | 96 | 307 | 36 | 57 | 110 | 18 | 1 | 11 | 40 | 7 | 0 | 4 | 2 | 32 | 0 | 97 | 0 | 0 |
| Martin, Michael, Vancouver* | .230 | 77 | 248 | 24 | 57 | 75 | 9 | 3 | 1 | 25 | 2 | 2 | 1 | 1 | 34 | 2 | 44 | 0 | 3 |
| Martin, Steven, Albuquerque | .077 | 42 | 13 | 1 | 1 | 1 | 0 | 0 | 0 | 1 | 0 | 0 | 0 | 0 | 0 | 0 | 4 | 0 | 0 |
| Martinez, Edgar, Calgary | .353 | 20 | 68 | 8 | 24 | 33 | 7 | 1 | 0 | 14 | 0 | 0 | 0 | 0 | 12 | 1 | 7 | 1 | 0 |
| Martz, Randy, Tucson* | .250 | 24 | 20 | 2 | 4 | 6 | 2 | 0 | 0 | 1 | 0 | 1 | 0 | 0 | 1 | 0 | 11 | 0 | 0 |
| Mason, Roger, Phoenix | .000 | 24 | 39 | 0 | 0 | 0 | 0 | 0 | 0 | 0 | 1 | 0 | 0 | 0 | 1 | 0 | 26 | 0 | 0 |
| Mathis, Ronald, Tucson | .545 | 7 | 11 | 0 | 6 | 6 | 0 | 0 | 0 | 1 | 0 | 1 | 0 | 0 | 0 | 0 | 1 | 0 | 0 |
| McCullers, Lance, Las Vegas† | .143 | 25 | 35 | 1 | 5 | 6 | 1 | 0 | 0 | 0 | 0 | 2 | 0 | 0 | 1 | 0 | 17 | 0 | 0 |
| McKnight, Jonathan, Phoenix | .111 | 17 | 18 | 1 | 2 | 3 | 1 | 0 | 0 | 0 | 0 | 3 | 0 | 0 | 1 | 0 | 4 | 0 | 0 |
| Meeks, Timothy, Albuquerque | .111 | 32 | 27 | 0 | 3 | 5 | 0 | 1 | 0 | 0 | 0 | 0 | 0 | 0 | 2 | 0 | 9 | 0 | 0 |
| Melendez, Francisco, Portland* | .280 | 130 | 397 | 41 | 111 | 146 | 25 | 2 | 2 | 54 | 4 | 3 | 3 | 3 | 42 | 5 | 42 | 4 | 6 |
| Milbourne, Lawrence, Calgary† | .278 | 9 | 36 | 5 | 10 | 10 | 0 | 0 | 0 | 0 | 0 | 1 | 0 | 0 | 2 | 0 | 4 | 0 | 0 |
| Miller, Darrell, Edmonton | .282 | 17 | 71 | 10 | 20 | 28 | 3 | 1 | 1 | 6 | 1 | 0 | 0 | 0 | 7 | 0 | 15 | 2 | 1 |
| Miller, Lemmie, Albuquerque | .283 | 61 | 159 | 25 | 45 | 61 | 7 | 3 | 1 | 14 | 2 | 1 | 1 | 0 | 14 | 1 | 29 | 3 | 5 |
| Mills, Bradley, Tucson* | .237 | 104 | 308 | 18 | 73 | 90 | 10 | 2 | 1 | 35 | 8 | 3 | 4 | 0 | 44 | 7 | 30 | 0 | 0 |
| Miner, James, Tucson* | .333 | 39 | 9 | 3 | 3 | 4 | 1 | 0 | 0 | 2 | 0 | 2 | 1 | 0 | 2 | 0 | 2 | 0 | 0 |
| Mirabella, Paul, Calgary* | .000 | 53 | 1 | 0 | 0 | 0 | 0 | 0 | 0 | 0 | 0 | 0 | 0 | 0 | 0 | 0 | 1 | 0 | 0 |
| Miscik, Robert, Hawaii | .274 | 127 | 419 | 66 | 115 | 175 | 18 | 6 | 10 | 48 | 9 | 2 | 0 | 7 | 75 | 8 | 50 | 13 | 9 |
| Mizerock, John, Tucson* | .211 | 75 | 223 | 24 | 47 | 63 | 11 | 1 | 1 | 19 | 2 | 3 | 0 | 1 | 32 | 6 | 28 | 0 | 1 |
| Montalvo, Rafael, 30 Alb.-22 Tuc. | .333 | 52 | 3 | 0 | 1 | 1 | 0 | 0 | 0 | 0 | 0 | 0 | 0 | 0 | 0 | 0 | 1 | 0 | 0 |
| Moore, Robert, Phoenix | .375 | 50 | 8 | 1 | 3 | 4 | 1 | 0 | 0 | 0 | 0 | 1 | 0 | 0 | 0 | 0 | 2 | 0 | 0 |
| Moses, John, Calgary† | .321 | 113 | 473 | 75 | 152 | 206 | 37 | 1 | 5 | 47 | 3 | 3 | 5 | 0 | 46 | 4 | 56 | 35 | 11 |
| Moses, Stephen, Portland* | .264 | 99 | 231 | 25 | 61 | 80 | 7 | 3 | 2 | 17 | 0 | 8 | 1 | 0 | 17 | 2 | 16 | 7 | 9 |
| Mullins, Francis, Phoenix | .267 | 77 | 232 | 33 | 62 | 96 | 13 | 0 | 7 | 30 | 2 | 5 | 2 | 3 | 30 | 1 | 54 | 0 | 0 |
| Murphy, Daniel, Edmonton* | .234 | 45 | 154 | 11 | 36 | 43 | 5 | 1 | 0 | 17 | 3 | 1 | 2 | 1 | 7 | 1 | 34 | 0 | 3 |
| Nago, Garrett, Vancouver† | .282 | 58 | 142 | 15 | 40 | 51 | 8 | 0 | 1 | 14 | 3 | 1 | 1 | 1 | 33 | 4 | 19 | 0 | 3 |
| Nahorodny, William, Portland | .275 | 102 | 316 | 34 | 87 | 130 | 10 | 3 | 9 | 42 | 6 | 1 | 6 | 1 | 14 | 2 | 52 | 0 | 2 |
| Nelson, James, Vancouver | .167 | 7 | 12 | 3 | 2 | 2 | 0 | 0 | 0 | 1 | 0 | 0 | 0 | 0 | 2 | 0 | 0 | 0 | 0 |
| Nelson, Ricky, Calgary* | .268 | 120 | 489 | 75 | 131 | 217 | 30 | 4 | 16 | 70 | 8 | 4 | 5 | 0 | 26 | 6 | 71 | 25 | 4 |
| O'Brien, Charles, Tacoma | .158 | 18 | 57 | 5 | 9 | 13 | 4 | 0 | 0 | 7 | 1 | 0 | 1 | 1 | 6 | 0 | 17 | 0 | 0 |
| Olander, James, Portland | .222 | 44 | 72 | 6 | 16 | 18 | 2 | 0 | 0 | 6 | 1 | 0 | 2 | 0 | 2 | 0 | 17 | 3 | 0 |
| Opie, James, Hawaii | .216 | 50 | 139 | 18 | 30 | 44 | 6 | 1 | 2 | 11 | 1 | 1 | 3 | 1 | 13 | 0 | 36 | 6 | 4 |
| Ouellette, Philip, Phoenix† | .177 | 27 | 79 | 7 | 14 | 19 | 0 | 0 | 1 | 11 | 1 | 1 | 1 | 1 | 12 | 3 | 15 | 0 | 0 |
| Paciorek, James, Vancouver | .220 | 53 | 177 | 20 | 39 | 47 | 8 | 0 | 0 | 13 | 1 | 0 | 0 | 2 | 14 | 0 | 29 | 1 | 2 |
| Page, Mitchell, Hawaii* | .258 | 74 | 151 | 25 | 39 | 83 | 10 | 2 | 10 | 32 | 4 | 0 | 0 | 4 | 20 | 4 | 40 | 5 | 2 |
| Parent, Mark, Las Vegas | .241 | 105 | 361 | 36 | 87 | 137 | 23 | 3 | 7 | 45 | 4 | 1 | 1 | 0 | 29 | 2 | 58 | 1 | 3 |
| Patterson, Robert, Las Vegas* | .074 | 27 | 27 | 3 | 2 | 2 | 0 | 0 | 0 | 1 | 0 | 6 | 0 | 0 | 1 | 0 | 7 | 0 | 0 |
| Pederson, Stuart, Albuquerque* | .328 | 111 | 287 | 54 | 94 | 144 | 20 | 3 | 8 | 55 | 7 | 1 | 2 | 4 | 48 | 4 | 39 | 6 | 5 |
| Pena, Adalberto, Tucson | .260 | 59 | 204 | 24 | 53 | 66 | 10 | 0 | 1 | 19 | 0 | 2 | 1 | 3 | 15 | 0 | 31 | 1 | 0 |
| Perconte, James, Calgary* | .288 | 14 | 52 | 17 | 15 | 21 | 2 | 2 | 0 | 5 | 0 | 0 | 1 | 1 | 14 | 2 | 5 | 0 | 0 |
| Peters, Richard, Tacoma† | .296 | 126 | 423 | 73 | 125 | 160 | 17 | 6 | 2 | 43 | 6 | 9 | 4 | 4 | 91 | 2 | 62 | 28 | 18 |
| Phillips, Anthony, Tacoma† | .130 | 20 | 69 | 9 | 9 | 10 | 1 | 0 | 0 | 5 | 0 | 0 | 0 | 0 | 6 | 0 | 28 | 3 | 0 |
| Plunk, Eric, Tacoma | .000 | 10 | 1 | 0 | 0 | 0 | 0 | 0 | 0 | 0 | 0 | 0 | 0 | 0 | 0 | 0 | 1 | 0 | 0 |
| Polidor, Gustavo, Edmonton | .285 | 132 | 460 | 56 | 131 | 169 | 18 | 7 | 2 | 51 | 7 | 10 | 3 | 1 | 37 | 0 | 53 | 5 | 6 |
| Ponce, Carlos, Vancouver | .320 | 109 | 394 | 53 | 126 | 197 | 25 | 5 | 12 | 78 | 11 | 0 | 5 | 6 | 34 | 5 | 54 | 21 | 8 |

| Player and Club | Pct. | G. | AB. | R. | H. | TB. | 2B. | 3B. | HR. | RBI. | GW. | SH. | SF. | HP. | BB. | Int. BB. | SO. | SB. | CS. |
|---|---|---|---|---|---|---|---|---|---|---|---|---|---|---|---|---|---|---|---|
| Powell, Dennis, Albuquerque | .176 | 20 | 17 | 2 | 3 | 3 | 0 | 0 | 0 | 2 | 0 | 1 | 0 | 0 | 0 | 0 | 5 | 0 | 0 |
| Pyznarski, Timothy, Las Vegas | .284 | 115 | 359 | 51 | 102 | 153 | 22 | 4 | 7 | 37 | 4 | 2 | 3 | 0 | 38 | 3 | 86 | 13 | 4 |
| Quinones, Luis, Phoenix† | .257 | 85 | 304 | 46 | 78 | 129 | 13 | 7 | 8 | 47 | 3 | 4 | 5 | 1 | 28 | 5 | 41 | 4 | 1 |
| Rabb, John, Phoenix | .318 | 6 | 22 | 3 | 7 | 8 | 1 | 0 | 0 | 0 | 0 | 0 | 0 | 0 | 4 | 0 | 9 | 0 | 0 |
| Rajsich, Gary, Phoenix° | .375 | 10 | 40 | 8 | 15 | 29 | 3 | 1 | 3 | 12 | 1 | 0 | 1 | 0 | 2 | 0 | 3 | 0 | 0 |
| Ramirez, Mario, Las Vegas | .277 | 13 | 47 | 6 | 13 | 21 | 4 | 2 | 0 | 6 | 0 | 1 | 0 | 0 | 6 | 1 | 8 | 0 | 0 |
| Ramos, Roberto, Edmonton | .269 | 96 | 320 | 39 | 86 | 113 | 12 | 3 | 3 | 35 | 2 | 4 | 1 | 3 | 56 | 1 | 53 | 3 | 2 |
| Randall, James, Edmonton† | .282 | 35 | 103 | 12 | 29 | 36 | 5 | 1 | 0 | 16 | 1 | 1 | 1 | 0 | 17 | 2 | 18 | 1 | 2 |
| Ready, Randy, Vancouver | .326 | 52 | 190 | 33 | 62 | 92 | 12 | 3 | 4 | 29 | 2 | 0 | 2 | 0 | 30 | 2 | 14 | 14 | 3 |
| Reece, Thad, Tacoma° | .262 | 130 | 474 | 51 | 124 | 154 | 20 | 2 | 2 | 50 | 10 | 8 | 6 | 3 | 46 | 2 | 65 | 6 | 4 |
| Reid, Jessie, Phoenix° | .263 | 54 | 179 | 26 | 47 | 80 | 6 | 3 | 7 | 32 | 3 | 0 | 2 | 1 | 18 | 1 | 32 | 3 | 3 |
| Renteria, Richard, Hawaii | .194 | 7 | 31 | 2 | 6 | 8 | 2 | 0 | 0 | 2 | 0 | 0 | 0 | 0 | 0 | 0 | 4 | 0 | 0 |
| Reuschel, Ricky, Hawaii | .222 | 8 | 9 | 1 | 2 | 2 | 0 | 0 | 0 | 1 | 0 | 3 | 0 | 0 | 1 | 0 | 4 | 0 | 0 |
| Reyes, Gilberto, Albuquerque | .265 | 111 | 366 | 35 | 97 | 135 | 20 | 0 | 6 | 54 | 6 | 2 | 8 | 3 | 15 | 1 | 74 | 0 | 0 |
| Reynolds, Harold, Calgary† | .363 | 52 | 212 | 36 | 77 | 109 | 11 | 3 | 5 | 30 | 2 | 3 | 4 | 1 | 28 | 1 | 18 | 9 | 13 |
| Rhomberg, Kevin, Phoenix | .279 | 116 | 383 | 76 | 107 | 140 | 12 | 6 | 3 | 45 | 5 | 3 | 5 | 4 | 49 | 2 | 54 | 8 | 5 |
| Richardt, Michael, Tucson | .250 | 13 | 16 | 4 | 4 | 6 | 2 | 0 | 0 | 3 | 0 | 0 | 1 | 0 | 5 | 0 | 5 | 0 | 0 |
| Riles, Ernest, Vancouver° | .347 | 30 | 118 | 19 | 41 | 56 | 7 | 1 | 2 | 20 | 3 | 0 | 2 | 1 | 17 | 4 | 13 | 2 | 2 |
| Riley, George, Phoenix° | .000 | 46 | 1 | 0 | 0 | 0 | 0 | 0 | 0 | 0 | 0 | 1 | 0 | 0 | 1 | 0 | 1 | 0 | 0 |
| Rincones, Hector, Albuquerque | .238 | 117 | 366 | 53 | 87 | 109 | 9 | 5 | 1 | 31 | 4 | 3 | 3 | 1 | 25 | 1 | 28 | 2 | 2 |
| Rivera, German, 85 Alb.-23 Tuc. | .281 | 108 | 384 | 45 | 108 | 158 | 22 | 2 | 8 | 44 | 4 | 2 | 3 | 1 | 25 | 4 | 61 | 5 | 2 |
| Robinson, Jeffrey, Phoenix | .167 | 30 | 36 | 3 | 6 | 9 | 3 | 0 | 0 | 4 | 1 | 3 | 0 | 0 | 0 | 0 | 13 | 0 | 0 |
| Rodriguez, Angel, Vancouver | .111 | 2 | 9 | 1 | 1 | 4 | 0 | 0 | 1 | 1 | 0 | 0 | 0 | 0 | 0 | 0 | 1 | 0 | 0 |
| Rodriguez, Edwin, Las Vegas | .289 | 115 | 436 | 78 | 126 | 177 | 21 | 6 | 6 | 35 | 2 | 3 | 1 | 2 | 32 | 1 | 76 | 19 | 7 |
| Rodriguez, Ruben, Hawaii | .250 | 1 | 4 | 0 | 1 | 1 | 0 | 0 | 0 | 0 | 0 | 0 | 0 | 0 | 0 | 0 | 0 | 0 | 0 |
| Rodriguez, Victor, Las Vegas | .312 | 127 | 462 | 56 | 144 | 214 | 31 | 3 | 11 | 58 | 16 | 9 | 4 | 1 | 20 | 4 | 41 | 0 | 2 |
| Roenicke, Ronald, Phoenix† | .308 | 60 | 214 | 36 | 66 | 97 | 16 | 0 | 5 | 48 | 2 | 1 | 4 | 0 | 54 | 11 | 41 | 8 | 4 |
| Romano, Thomas, Tacoma | .263 | 118 | 415 | 66 | 109 | 177 | 28 | 5 | 10 | 54 | 6 | 3 | 6 | 1 | 40 | 2 | 61 | 11 | 7 |
| Romero, Albert, Edmonton | .260 | 82 | 246 | 38 | 64 | 97 | 9 | 3 | 6 | 26 | 1 | 0 | 4 | 2 | 18 | 1 | 48 | 5 | 3 |
| Rood, Nelson, Tucson | .245 | 69 | 269 | 46 | 66 | 76 | 6 | 2 | 0 | 16 | 4 | 4 | 1 | 3 | 26 | 2 | 41 | 19 | 4 |
| Ross, Mark, Tucson | .000 | 46 | 3 | 0 | 0 | 0 | 0 | 0 | 0 | 0 | 0 | 0 | 0 | 0 | 0 | 0 | 3 | 0 | 0 |
| Rucker, David, Portland° | .000 | 10 | 2 | 0 | 0 | 0 | 0 | 0 | 0 | 0 | 0 | 0 | 0 | 0 | 0 | 0 | 1 | 0 | 0 |
| Russell, John, Portland | .306 | 16 | 49 | 8 | 15 | 33 | 2 | 2 | 4 | 11 | 0 | 0 | 0 | 1 | 13 | 3 | 15 | 0 | 0 |
| Salava, Randy, Portland° | .224 | 115 | 362 | 43 | 81 | 120 | 17 | 2 | 6 | 46 | 7 | 2 | 5 | 0 | 34 | 8 | 77 | 8 | 5 |
| Sarmiento, Manuel, Hawaii | .190 | 18 | 21 | 0 | 4 | 4 | 0 | 0 | 0 | 2 | 0 | 3 | 0 | 0 | 1 | 0 | 3 | 0 | 0 |
| Schefsky, Steven, Las Vegas | .000 | 13 | 4 | 0 | 0 | 0 | 0 | 0 | 0 | 0 | 0 | 0 | 0 | 0 | 0 | 0 | 3 | 0 | 0 |
| Schmidt, August, Phoenix | .269 | 59 | 167 | 22 | 45 | 53 | 6 | 1 | 0 | 12 | 3 | 0 | 0 | 1 | 30 | 0 | 29 | 1 | 1 |
| Schu, Richard, Portland | .280 | 42 | 150 | 19 | 42 | 68 | 8 | 3 | 4 | 22 | 2 | 0 | 0 | 2 | 14 | 0 | 20 | 1 | 6 |
| Schultz, Greg, Portland | .283 | 109 | 364 | 56 | 103 | 156 | 20 | 0 | 11 | 54 | 1 | 1 | 1 | 7 | 30 | 1 | 35 | 0 | 1 |
| Schuster, Mark, Phoenix° | .159 | 30 | 88 | 12 | 14 | 19 | 2 | 0 | 1 | 10 | 2 | 0 | 1 | 1 | 17 | 4 | 8 | 0 | 1 |
| Sconiers, Daryl, Edmonton° | .350 | 6 | 20 | 3 | 7 | 9 | 2 | 0 | 0 | 4 | 1 | 0 | 1 | 0 | 5 | 0 | 2 | 0 | 0 |
| Scott, Donald, Calgary† | .462 | 7 | 26 | 6 | 12 | 17 | 3 | 1 | 0 | 9 | 0 | 0 | 1 | 0 | 4 | 0 | 0 | 0 | 0 |
| See, Laurence, Albuquerque | .260 | 23 | 77 | 7 | 20 | 34 | 3 | 1 | 3 | 9 | 0 | 0 | 2 | 0 | 3 | 0 | 18 | 0 | 1 |
| Seibert, Gibson, Portland | .268 | 119 | 410 | 48 | 110 | 164 | 17 | 11 | 5 | 34 | 7 | 2 | 4 | 2 | 45 | 2 | 98 | 15 | 10 |
| Semall, Paul, Hawaii | .200 | 24 | 10 | 0 | 2 | 3 | 1 | 0 | 0 | 0 | 0 | 1 | 0 | 0 | 1 | 0 | 5 | 0 | 0 |
| Senteney, Steven, Calgary | .000 | 28 | 2 | 0 | 0 | 0 | 0 | 0 | 0 | 0 | 0 | 0 | 0 | 0 | 0 | 0 | 1 | 0 | 0 |
| Serna, Paul, Calgary | .198 | 38 | 111 | 10 | 22 | 26 | 1 | 0 | 1 | 9 | 0 | 3 | 0 | 0 | 2 | 0 | 15 | 0 | 3 |
| Shipanoff, David, Portland | .000 | 51 | 5 | 0 | 0 | 0 | 0 | 0 | 0 | 0 | 0 | 0 | 0 | 0 | 0 | 0 | 3 | 0 | 0 |
| Shipley, Craig, Albuquerque† | .242 | 124 | 414 | 50 | 100 | 113 | 9 | 2 | 0 | 30 | 3 | 3 | 3 | 1 | 22 | 3 | 43 | 24 | 6 |
| Shirley, Steven, Hawaii° | .091 | 16 | 11 | 0 | 1 | 1 | 0 | 0 | 0 | 1 | 0 | 1 | 0 | 0 | 0 | 0 | 5 | 0 | 0 |
| Skube, Robert, Vancouver° | .232 | 89 | 276 | 34 | 64 | 97 | 18 | 3 | 3 | 30 | 2 | 0 | 3 | 2 | 43 | 1 | 62 | 11 | 7 |
| Smith, Don, Albuquerque | .125 | 55 | 8 | 2 | 1 | 4 | 0 | 0 | 1 | 1 | 0 | 0 | 0 | 0 | 0 | 0 | 4 | 0 | 0 |
| Smith, Raymond, Las Vegas | .325 | 104 | 397 | 48 | 129 | 188 | 32 | 3 | 7 | 42 | 6 | 6 | 3 | 4 | 16 | 1 | 37 | 1 | 2 |
| Solano, Julio, Tucson | .000 | 23 | 1 | 0 | 0 | 0 | 0 | 0 | 0 | 0 | 0 | 0 | 0 | 0 | 0 | 0 | 0 | 0 | 0 |
| Sonberg, Eric, Albuquerque | .000 | 26 | 6 | 0 | 0 | 0 | 0 | 0 | 0 | 1 | 0 | 1 | 1 | 0 | 0 | 0 | 6 | 0 | 0 |
| Steels, James, Las Vegas° | .261 | 111 | 394 | 39 | 103 | 145 | 19 | 4 | 5 | 46 | 3 | 1 | 3 | 3 | 23 | 5 | 59 | 13 | 6 |
| Stephenson, Phillip, Tacoma° | .211 | 56 | 171 | 30 | 36 | 62 | 11 | 0 | 5 | 24 | 2 | 1 | 2 | 0 | 46 | 1 | 32 | 5 | 1 |
| Stone, Jeffrey, Portland | .329 | 67 | 252 | 58 | 83 | 121 | 16 | 8 | 2 | 28 | 4 | 2 | 3 | 3 | 37 | 5 | 45 | 34 | 14 |
| Stubbs, Franklin, Albuquerque° | .280 | 132 | 421 | 86 | 118 | 247 | 23 | 5 | 32 | 93 | 9 | 1 | 3 | 1 | 83 | 10 | 105 | 23 | 3 |
| Strucher, Mark, Tucson | .256 | 82 | 285 | 34 | 73 | 119 | 17 | 4 | 7 | 44 | 2 | 3 | 4 | 1 | 21 | 1 | 55 | 0 | 1 |
| Surhoff, Richard, Portland | .333 | 70 | 6 | 0 | 2 | 3 | 1 | 0 | 0 | 0 | 0 | 0 | 0 | 0 | 0 | 0 | 2 | 0 | 0 |
| Sveum, Dale, Vancouver† | .236 | 122 | 415 | 42 | 98 | 139 | 17 | 3 | 6 | 48 | 5 | 1 | 2 | 2 | 48 | 6 | 79 | 4 | 5 |
| Tartabull, Danilo, Calgary | .300 | 125 | 473 | 102 | 142 | 291 | 14 | 3 | 43 | 109 | 12 | 1 | 4 | 1 | 67 | 4 | 123 | 17 | 4 |
| Thoma, Raymond, Tacoma | .118 | 7 | 17 | 0 | 2 | 3 | 1 | 0 | 0 | 0 | 0 | 0 | 0 | 0 | 0 | 0 | 5 | 0 | 0 |
| Thomas, James, Las Vegas† | .234 | 41 | 107 | 14 | 25 | 42 | 6 | 1 | 3 | 14 | 1 | 2 | 0 | 0 | 14 | 1 | 37 | 0 | 1 |
| Thrower, Keith, Tacoma† | .287 | 131 | 464 | 61 | 133 | 159 | 15 | 1 | 3 | 48 | 2 | 8 | 4 | 3 | 40 | 2 | 52 | 40 | 8 |
| Tillman, Kerry, Las Vegas | .337 | 115 | 412 | 66 | 139 | 216 | 27 | 7 | 12 | 75 | 4 | 3 | 3 | 1 | 23 | 2 | 73 | 18 | 3 |
| Tingley, Ronald, Calgary | .253 | 83 | 277 | 36 | 70 | 120 | 11 | 3 | 11 | 47 | 6 | 2 | 0 | 2 | 30 | 1 | 74 | 3 | 3 |
| Tobik, David, Calgary | .000 | 57 | 0 | 0 | 0 | 0 | 0 | 0 | 0 | 0 | 0 | 1 | 0 | 0 | 0 | 0 | 0 | 0 | 0 |
| Tolentino, Jose, Tacoma° | .257 | 106 | 339 | 38 | 87 | 131 | 24 | 1 | 6 | 41 | 5 | 1 | 4 | 3 | 38 | 5 | 53 | 1 | 3 |
| Tolman, Timothy, Tucson | .302 | 40 | 149 | 30 | 45 | 69 | 10 | 1 | 4 | 27 | 2 | 0 | 3 | 1 | 24 | 1 | 26 | 0 | 2 |
| Tomlin, David, Hawaii° | .182 | 33 | 11 | 2 | 2 | 3 | 1 | 0 | 0 | 3 | 0 | 1 | 0 | 0 | 0 | 0 | 3 | 0 | 0 |
| Tunnell, Lee, Hawaii | .000 | 7 | 3 | 0 | 0 | 0 | 0 | 0 | 0 | 0 | 1 | 0 | 1 | 0 | 0 | 0 | 1 | 0 | 0 |
| Valle, David, Calgary | .344 | 42 | 131 | 17 | 45 | 71 | 8 | 0 | 6 | 26 | 0 | 0 | 0 | 0 | 20 | 1 | 19 | 0 | 0 |
| Vanderbush, Walter, Las Vegas° | .200 | 42 | 5 | 0 | 1 | 1 | 0 | 0 | 0 | 0 | 0 | 0 | 0 | 0 | 0 | 0 | 2 | 0 | 0 |
| Vargas, Hediberto, Hawaii° | .270 | 102 | 304 | 40 | 82 | 126 | 17 | 3 | 7 | 48 | 6 | 0 | 4 | 0 | 38 | 0 | 70 | 1 | 1 |
| Vavra, Joseph, Albuquerque° | .272 | 61 | 202 | 31 | 55 | 69 | 9 | 1 | 1 | 15 | 0 | 1 | 3 | 3 | 21 | 1 | 13 | 2 | 0 |
| Vila, Jesus, Albuquerque | .667 | 11 | 3 | 2 | 2 | 2 | 0 | 0 | 0 | 1 | 0 | 0 | 0 | 0 | 0 | 0 | 0 | 0 | 0 |
| Walk, Robert, Hawaii | .325 | 24 | 40 | 6 | 13 | 16 | 3 | 0 | 0 | 6 | 0 | 3 | 0 | 0 | 0 | 0 | 11 | 3 | 1 |
| Waller, Tyrone, Tucson | .277 | 125 | 458 | 62 | 127 | 175 | 25 | 4 | 5 | 46 | 2 | 3 | 3 | 2 | 49 | 5 | 120 | 22 | 5 |
| Walter, Gene, Las Vegas° | .000 | 46 | 7 | 1 | 0 | 0 | 0 | 0 | 0 | 0 | 0 | 0 | 0 | 0 | 0 | 0 | 2 | 0 | 0 |
| Ward, Colin, Phoenix° | .000 | 22 | 3 | 0 | 0 | 0 | 0 | 0 | 0 | 0 | 0 | 0 | 0 | 0 | 0 | 0 | 0 | 0 | 0 |
| West, Reginald, Edmonton° | .273 | 95 | 326 | 40 | 89 | 118 | 10 | 8 | 1 | 30 | 3 | 2 | 4 | 3 | 24 | 1 | 36 | 10 | 15 |
| White, Devon, Edmonton† | .253 | 66 | 277 | 53 | 70 | 108 | 16 | 5 | 4 | 39 | 3 | 1 | 3 | 4 | 24 | 0 | 77 | 21 | 9 |
| White, Larry, Albuquerque | .308 | 36 | 26 | 7 | 8 | 15 | 2 | 1 | 1 | 3 | 1 | 4 | 1 | 0 | 1 | 0 | 2 | 0 | 0 |
| Wiggins, Alan, Las Vegas† | .250 | 2 | 8 | 2 | 2 | 2 | 0 | 0 | 0 | 1 | 0 | 0 | 0 | 0 | 1 | 0 | 0 | 0 | 0 |
| Wiggins, Kevin, Las Vegas° | .211 | 12 | 19 | 4 | 4 | 6 | 2 | 0 | 0 | 1 | 0 | 1 | 0 | 0 | 4 | 0 | 4 | 0 | 0 |
| Wilkinson, William, Calgary | .500 | 9 | 2 | 0 | 1 | 1 | 0 | 0 | 0 | 1 | 0 | 0 | 0 | 0 | 0 | 0 | 0 | 0 | 0 |
| Wilson, Michael, Phoenix | .319 | 140 | 518 | 109 | 165 | 206 | 20 | 6 | 3 | 45 | 6 | 9 | 4 | 2 | 93 | 2 | 38 | 56 | 22 |
| Winn, James, Hawaii | .000 | 7 | 6 | 0 | 0 | 0 | 0 | 0 | 0 | 0 | 0 | 0 | 0 | 0 | 0 | 0 | 0 | 0 | 0 |
| Wojna, Edward, Las Vegas | .056 | 18 | 18 | 1 | 1 | 4 | 0 | 0 | 1 | 2 | 0 | 3 | 0 | 0 | 0 | 0 | 8 | 0 | 0 |
| Woodard, Michael, Phoenix° | .316 | 140 | 573 | 85 | 181 | 224 | 16 | 9 | 3 | 63 | 6 | 5 | 7 | 0 | 51 | 3 | 42 | 33 | 14 |
| Zaske, Jeffrey, Hawaii | .000 | 46 | 3 | 0 | 0 | 0 | 0 | 0 | 0 | 0 | 0 | 0 | 0 | 0 | 0 | 0 | 3 | 0 | 0 |

The following pitchers, listed alphabetically by club, with games in parentheses, had no plate appearances, primarily through use of designated hitters:

ALBUQUERQUE—Hausman, Thomas (19); Rennicke, Dean (2); Rodas, Richard (2); Scudder, William (11); Tejeda, Felix (9).

CALGARY—Bartley, Gregory (17); Best, Karl (4); Cuellar, Robert (1); Geisel, David (20); Guetterman, Lee (20); Long, Robert (19); Luecken, Richard (18); Martin, Victor (6); Morgan, Michael (1); Murray, Jed (3); Snyder, Brian (20); Stoddard, Robert (7); Thomas, Roy (15); Whitmer, Joseph (29); Wills, Frank (9).

EDMONTON—Bastian, Robert (27); Bryden, Thomas (36); Chadwick, Ray (2); Cliburn, Stewart (2); Corbett, Douglas (1); Finch, Steven (25); Fowlkes, Alan (23); Kain, Martin (29); Kaufman, Curt (22); Lugo, Rafael (4); Mack, Tony (25); McCaskill, Kirk (3); Oliver, Scott (32); Rogers, Stephen (5); Sanchez, Luis (4); Smith, David (42).

HAWAII—Fansler, Stanley (3); Jones, Barry (1); Monge, Isidro (14).

LAS VEGAS—Couchee, Michael (1); Hausman, Thomas (15); Kristan, Kevin (11); Simmons, Todd (6).

PHOENIX—Cornell, Jeffrey (5); Crews, Lawrence (1); Williams, Frank (9).

PORTLAND—Arnold, Jerry (14); Money, Kyle (6).

TACOMA—Bauer, Mark (4); Birtsas, Timothy (4); Chris, Michael (32); Conroy, Timothy (22); Dozier, Thomas (6); Kaiser, Jeffrey (27); Krueger, William (2); Kyles, Stanley (43); Lambert, Timothy (28); Leiper, David (15); McLaughlin, Joey (38); McLaughlin, Michael (38); Mooneyham, William (21); Mura, Stephen (16); Ontiveros, Steven (15); Owchinko, Robert (16); Rijo, Jose (24); Rodriguez, Ricardo (7); Scherer, Douglas (8); Tellmann, Thomas (8); Warren, Michael (12); Young, Curtis (3).

TUCSON—Montgomery, Larry (12).

VANCOUVER—Candiotti, Thomas (24); Clutterbuck, Bryan (29); Cocanower, James (9); Crim, Charles (49); Duquette, Bryan (41); Kern, James (5); Ladd, Peter (5); Leary, Timothy (27); Lesley, Bradley (48); Myers, Edward (14); Nieves, Juan (13); Roberts, Scott (12); Searage, Raymond (23); Waits, Richard (16); Wegman, William (28).

GRAND SLAM HOME RUNS—Kiefer, Loman, 2 each; Diaz, Joyner, Legg, S. Moses, Pederson, Reid, Rhomberg, Schultz, Steels, Tartabull, Tolman, Valle, 1 each.

AWARDED FIRST BASE ON CATCHER'S INTERFERENCE—Amelung 4 (Ashman, Clements, Nago, Ramos); Krauss 2 (Ashman, Malkin); Sveum 2 (Gomez, Knicely); R. Allen (Gulden); Bullock (Smith); Casey (Knicely); C. Clark (Reyes); Diaz (Clements); C. Jones (Smith); Ready (Reyes); Woodard (Bathe).

## CLUB FIELDING

| Club | Pct. | G. | PO. | A. | E. | DP. | PB. | Club | Pct. | G. | PO. | A. | E. | DP. | PB. |
|------|------|----|-----|----|----|----|----|------|------|----|-----|----|----|----|----|
| Hawaii | .976 | 143 | 3659 | 1439 | 126 | 120 | 13 | Edmonton | .971 | 142 | 3699 | 1580 | 158 | 152 | 14 |
| Tacoma | .974 | 143 | 3779 | 1595 | 143 | 143 | 22 | Portland | .971 | 142 | 3704 | 1579 | 159 | 133 | 10 |
| Phoenix | .974 | 142 | 3672 | 1529 | 141 | 136 | 8 | Albuquerque | .970 | 144 | 3652 | 1708 | 167 | 151 | 31 |
| Vancouver | .974 | 143 | 3742 | 1590 | 145 | 142 | 22 | Las Vegas | .970 | 144 | 3792 | 1533 | 167 | 117 | 20 |
| Tucson | .972 | 140 | 3668 | 1627 | 150 | 124 | 20 | Calgary | .967 | 141 | 3667 | 1542 | 179 | 135 | 15 |

## INDIVIDUAL FIELDING
### FIRST BASEMEN

*Throws lefthanded.

| Player and Club | Pct. | G. | PO. | A. | E. | DP. | Player and Club | Pct. | G. | PO. | A. | E. | DP. |
|------|------|----|-----|----|----|----|------|------|----|-----|----|----|----|
| P. Adams, Phoenix | .987 | 108 | 866 | 90 | 13 | 84 | Lubratich, Las Vegas | .965 | 8 | 54 | 1 | 2 | 7 |
| Adduci, Vancouver* | .983 | 91 | 782 | 63 | 15 | 71 | Malkin, Hawaii | 1.000 | 23 | 169 | 8 | 0 | 16 |
| J. Allen, Calgary | .992 | 27 | 215 | 22 | 2 | 25 | Melendez, Portland* | .986 | 115 | 971 | 69 | 15 | 91 |
| Asadoor, Las Vegas | 1.000 | 4 | 17 | 4 | 0 | 2 | J. Moses, Calgary* | 1.000 | 10 | 93 | 3 | 0 | 7 |
| Ashford, Portland | 1.000 | 1 | 2 | 0 | 0 | 0 | Murphy, Edmonton* | .976 | 5 | 36 | 5 | 1 | 4 |
| Bream, Albuquerque* | .995 | 41 | 338 | 50 | 2 | 41 | Nahorodny, Portland | .995 | 26 | 189 | 11 | 1 | 19 |
| Calise, Tucson | .987 | 76 | 672 | 29 | 9 | 61 | Parent, Las Vegas | 1.000 | 8 | 48 | 3 | 0 | 3 |
| CASEY, Calgary | .991 | 104 | 925 | 58 | 9 | 87 | Ponce, Vancouver | .992 | 41 | 351 | 33 | 3 | 33 |
| Clements, Vancouver | .993 | 16 | 136 | 7 | 1 | 14 | Pyznarski, Las Vegas | .990 | 104 | 788 | 76 | 9 | 67 |
| Davidsmeier, Vancouver | 1.000 | 2 | 5 | 0 | 0 | 1 | Rajsich, Phoenix* | 1.000 | 4 | 29 | 4 | 0 | 2 |
| Gl. Davis, Tucson | .988 | 43 | 378 | 26 | 5 | 30 | Randall, Edmonton* | 1.000 | 4 | 32 | 0 | 0 | 5 |
| Diaz, Hawaii | .992 | 27 | 229 | 14 | 2 | 17 | Reyes, Albuquerque | 1.000 | 4 | 20 | 1 | 0 | 0 |
| Distefano, Hawaii* | 1.000 | 22 | 187 | 8 | 0 | 18 | Roenicke, Phoenix* | 1.000 | 1 | 1 | 0 | 0 | 1 |
| Goodwin, Tacoma | .990 | 12 | 89 | 7 | 1 | 10 | Russell, Portland | 1.000 | 1 | 1 | 0 | 0 | 0 |
| Gulden, Tucson | 1.000 | 2 | 3 | 0 | 0 | 0 | Schultz, Phoenix | .991 | 13 | 100 | 8 | 1 | 11 |
| P. Hernandez, Tucson | 1.000 | 1 | 0 | 0 | 0 | 0 | Schuster, Phoenix* | .980 | 13 | 88 | 10 | 2 | 13 |
| Herz, Portland | 1.000 | 1 | 2 | 0 | 0 | 0 | R. Smith, Las Vegas | 1.000 | 8 | 61 | 3 | 0 | 5 |
| C. Hill, Calgary | .983 | 8 | 57 | 2 | 1 | 6 | Stephenson, Tacoma* | 1.000 | 10 | 45 | 2 | 0 | 4 |
| R. Howell, Portland | .985 | 8 | 63 | 3 | 1 | 4 | Stubbs, Albuquerque* | .986 | 105 | 919 | 85 | 14 | 92 |
| Joyner, Edmonton* | .988 | 126 | 1107 | 107 | 15 | 121 | Strucher, Tucson | .988 | 26 | 216 | 24 | 3 | 16 |
| Keedy, Edmonton | 1.000 | 13 | 100 | 8 | 0 | 6 | Thomas, Las Vegas | 1.000 | 7 | 42 | 3 | 0 | 2 |
| Knicely, Portland | .986 | 7 | 65 | 4 | 1 | 7 | Tillman, Las Vegas | .947 | 3 | 18 | 0 | 1 | 1 |
| Kruk, Las Vegas | .986 | 28 | 202 | 12 | 3 | 17 | Tolentino, Tacoma* | .988 | 100 | 801 | 77 | 11 | 79 |
| Lancellotti, Phoenix* | .992 | 13 | 117 | 3 | 1 | 13 | Tolman, Tucson | .962 | 7 | 72 | 4 | 3 | 5 |
| Lansford, Tacoma | .984 | 43 | 348 | 24 | 6 | 34 | Vargas, Hawaii | .989 | 83 | 662 | 46 | 8 | 51 |
| LeBoeuf, Portland | 1.000 | 1 | 2 | 0 | 0 | 0 | Vavra, Albuquerque | 1.000 | 1 | 8 | 1 | 0 | 2 |
| Liddle, Edmonton | 1.000 | 1 | 1 | 0 | 0 | 0 | | | | | | | |

### SECOND BASEMEN

| Player and Club | Pct. | G. | PO. | A. | E. | DP. | Player and Club | Pct. | G. | PO. | A. | E. | DP. |
|------|------|----|-----|----|----|----|------|------|----|-----|----|----|----|
| J. Allen, Calgary | 1.000 | 2 | 4 | 4 | 0 | 1 | Koenigsfeld, Tucson | .977 | 32 | 75 | 98 | 4 | 15 |
| R. Allen, Albuquerque | .985 | 18 | 23 | 42 | 1 | 4 | Krauss, Edmonton | .960 | 41 | 77 | 113 | 8 | 30 |
| Anderson, Albuquerque | 1.000 | 6 | 10 | 11 | 0 | 3 | Kutcher, Phoenix | 1.000 | 1 | 0 | 1 | 0 | 0 |
| Belliard, Hawaii | .992 | 25 | 45 | 74 | 1 | 15 | Landestoy, Tucson | .943 | 6 | 13 | 20 | 2 | 3 |
| Carrasco, Edmonton | .978 | 112 | 245 | 326 | 13 | 69 | Legg, Portland | .977 | 112 | 203 | 339 | 13 | 60 |
| Castillo, Vancouver | .972 | 52 | 102 | 173 | 8 | 29 | Lubratich, Las Vegas | 1.000 | 13 | 26 | 42 | 0 | 5 |
| Crone, Calgary | .966 | 50 | 107 | 152 | 9 | 34 | Martinez, Calgary | 1.000 | 2 | 3 | 3 | 0 | 1 |
| David, Calgary | .958 | 4 | 11 | 12 | 1 | 3 | Milbourne, Calgary | .600 | 1 | 2 | 1 | 2 | 1 |
| Davidsmeier, Vancouver | .980 | 91 | 184 | 251 | 9 | 52 | Miscik, Hawaii | .959 | 98 | 170 | 273 | 19 | 42 |
| Dowell, Portland | .995 | 40 | 71 | 131 | 1 | 30 | Mullins, Phoenix | 1.000 | 1 | 1 | 2 | 0 | 1 |
| Dybzinski, Hawaii | .964 | 7 | 12 | 15 | 1 | 3 | Pena, Tucson | .900 | 5 | 11 | 16 | 3 | 3 |
| Escobar, Portland | 1.000 | 2 | 1 | 1 | 0 | 0 | Perconte, Calgary | .975 | 14 | 31 | 47 | 2 | 12 |
| Felder, Vancouver | 1.000 | 2 | 1 | 0 | 0 | 0 | Peters, Tacoma | 1.000 | 2 | 0 | 2 | 0 | 0 |
| Followell, Tucson | .976 | 81 | 181 | 259 | 11 | 46 | Phillips, Tacoma | .921 | 10 | 12 | 23 | 3 | 2 |
| Garcia, Las Vegas | 1.000 | 9 | 13 | 19 | 0 | 2 | Quinones, Tacoma | 1.000 | 2 | 6 | 0 | 0 | 5 |
| D. Gonzalez, Hawaii | 1.000 | 5 | 11 | 19 | 0 | 5 | Ready, Vancouver | .870 | 8 | 14 | 6 | 3 | 2 |
| P. Hernandez, Tucson | .970 | 7 | 14 | 18 | 1 | 6 | REECE, Tacoma | .9788 | 127 | 242 | 357 | 13 | 86 |
| Ireland, Vancouver | 1.000 | 1 | 0 | 3 | 0 | 0 | Renteria, Hawaii | 1.000 | 6 | 5 | 15 | 0 | 2 |
| Khalifa, Hawaii | 1.000 | 4 | 5 | 12 | 0 | 3 | Reynolds, Calgary | .957 | 52 | 119 | 171 | 13 | 37 |

## SECOND BASEMEN—Continued

| Player and Club | Pct. | G. | PO. | A. | E. | DP. |
|---|---|---|---|---|---|---|
| Rincones, Albuquerque | .982 | 81 | 184 | 254 | 8 | 53 |
| E. Rodriguez, Las Vegas | .964 | 84 | 164 | 206 | 14 | 42 |
| V. Rodriguez, Las Vegas | .969 | 54 | 105 | 147 | 8 | 28 |
| Rood, Tucson | .972 | 23 | 43 | 60 | 3 | 16 |
| Schultz, Phoenix | 1.000 | 2 | 2 | 5 | 0 | 1 |
| Serna, Calgary | .967 | 21 | 41 | 47 | 3 | 10 |
| Thoma, Tacoma | .900 | 3 | 6 | 3 | 1 | 1 |
| Thrower, Tacoma | 1.000 | 13 | 32 | 38 | 0 | 7 |
| Vavra, Albuquerque | .959 | 56 | 122 | 184 | 13 | 43 |
| A. Wiggins, Las Vegas | 1.000 | 1 | 2 | 6 | 0 | 2 |
| Wilson, Phoenix | 1.000 | 2 | 3 | 2 | 0 | 0 |
| Woodard, Phoenix | .9786 | 139 | 283 | 404 | 15 | 89 |

## THIRD BASEMEN

| Player and Club | Pct. | G. | PO. | A. | E. | DP. |
|---|---|---|---|---|---|---|
| J. Allen, Calgary | .894 | 60 | 41 | 136 | 21 | 13 |
| R. Allen, Albuquerque | .818 | 14 | 4 | 23 | 6 | 1 |
| Anderson, Albuquerque | .714 | 7 | 0 | 10 | 4 | 1 |
| Asadoor, Las Vegas | .925 | 111 | 90 | 195 | 23 | 15 |
| Ashford, Portland | .778 | 4 | 2 | 5 | 2 | 1 |
| Ashman, Tacoma | .875 | 2 | 2 | 5 | 1 | 0 |
| R. Bathe, Tacoma | .943 | 86 | 62 | 154 | 13 | 7 |
| Coles, Calgary | .914 | 24 | 14 | 39 | 5 | 3 |
| Crone, Calgary | .948 | 30 | 16 | 39 | 3 | 3 |
| Davidsmeier, Vancouver | .885 | 11 | 10 | 13 | 3 | 1 |
| Diaz, Port-Haw | 1.000 | 4 | 0 | 4 | 0 | 0 |
| Dowell, Portland | 1.000 | 4 | 1 | 9 | 0 | 1 |
| Dybzinski, Hawaii | .947 | 34 | 21 | 51 | 4 | 5 |
| Fimple, Albuquerque | 1.000 | 15 | 7 | 25 | 0 | 2 |
| D. Gonzalez, Hawaii | .936 | 83 | 57 | 162 | 15 | 12 |
| C. Hill, Calgary | .952 | 10 | 5 | 15 | 1 | 1 |
| J. Howell, Edmonton | .942 | 73 | 67 | 128 | 12 | 13 |
| R. Howell, Portland | .916 | 30 | 28 | 48 | 7 | 4 |
| Ireland, Vancouver | 1.000 | 1 | 1 | 0 | 0 | 0 |
| Keedy, Edmonton | .930 | 39 | 24 | 82 | 8 | 5 |
| Kiefer, Tacoma | .962 | 56 | 38 | 89 | 5 | 12 |
| Koenigsfeld, Tucson | .667 | 1 | 2 | 0 | 1 | 0 |
| Krauss, Edmonton | .925 | 34 | 27 | 59 | 7 | 9 |
| LeBoeuf, Portland | .900 | 10 | 4 | 14 | 2 | 1 |
| Lubratich, Las Vegas | .929 | 5 | 3 | 10 | 1 | 1 |
| Martinez, Calgary | .930 | 19 | 12 | 41 | 4 | 3 |
| L. Miller, Albuquerque | 1.000 | 4 | 1 | 1 | 0 | 0 |
| Mills, Tucson | .959 | 84 | 49 | 162 | 9 | 12 |
| Miscik, Hawaii | .963 | 21 | 13 | 39 | 2 | 6 |
| Mullins, Phoenix | .988 | 32 | 16 | 65 | 1 | 6 |
| Nahorodny, Portland | .900 | 12 | 2 | 7 | 1 | 0 |
| Opie, Hawaii | .880 | 7 | 7 | 15 | 3 | 2 |
| Phillips, Tacoma | .941 | 11 | 3 | 13 | 1 | 0 |
| Ponce, Vancouver | .867 | 31 | 24 | 48 | 11 | 2 |
| Quinones, Phoenix | 1.000 | 1 | 0 | 2 | 0 | 0 |
| Ready, Vancouver | .929 | 15 | 10 | 29 | 3 | 3 |
| Rincones, Albuquerque | .978 | 17 | 11 | 34 | 1 | 1 |
| RIVERA, Alb-Tuc | .937 | 99 | 76 | 191 | 18 | 21 |
| V. Rodriguez, Las Vegas | .975 | 41 | 20 | 58 | 2 | 3 |
| Schmidt, Phoenix | .921 | 46 | 31 | 109 | 12 | 9 |
| Schu, Portland | .933 | 20 | 11 | 31 | 3 | 1 |
| Schultz, Phoenix | .918 | 75 | 61 | 119 | 16 | 9 |
| See, Albuquerque | .900 | 23 | 25 | 29 | 6 | 4 |
| Seibert, Portland | .903 | 87 | 80 | 143 | 24 | 14 |
| Serna, Calgary | .923 | 5 | 3 | 9 | 1 | 0 |
| R. Smith, Las Vegas | 1.000 | 1 | 1 | 1 | 0 | 0 |
| Strucher, Tucson | .895 | 21 | 12 | 39 | 6 | 1 |
| Sveum, Vancouver | .920 | 92 | 72 | 168 | 21 | 11 |
| Tartabull, Calgary | .833 | 1 | 0 | 5 | 1 | 0 |
| Thoma, Tacoma | 1.000 | 2 | 0 | 6 | 0 | 1 |
| Thomas, Las Vegas | .842 | 9 | 6 | 10 | 3 | 2 |
| Tillman, Las Vegas | 1.000 | 1 | 0 | 1 | 0 | 1 |
| Waller, Tucson | .938 | 28 | 19 | 42 | 4 | 5 |

## SHORTSTOPS

| Player and Club | Pct. | G. | PO. | A. | E. | DP. |
|---|---|---|---|---|---|---|
| R. Adams, Phoenix | .953 | 36 | 58 | 103 | 8 | 25 |
| J. Allen, Calgary | .957 | 5 | 6 | 16 | 1 | 3 |
| Anderson, Alburquerque | .896 | 16 | 19 | 41 | 7 | 7 |
| Belliard, Hawaii | .988 | 76 | 127 | 215 | 4 | 40 |
| Castillo, Vancouver | .946 | 66 | 120 | 194 | 18 | 51 |
| Coles, Calgary | 1.000 | 4 | 2 | 10 | 0 | 1 |
| David, Calgary | .909 | 2 | 1 | 9 | 1 | 1 |
| Dowell, Portland | .961 | 73 | 111 | 211 | 13 | 46 |
| Dybzinski, Hawaii | .975 | 10 | 15 | 24 | 1 | 4 |
| Escobar, Portland | .959 | 41 | 49 | 113 | 7 | 20 |
| Followell, Tucson | .972 | 28 | 45 | 96 | 4 | 14 |
| Garcia, Las Vegas | .934 | 61 | 78 | 163 | 17 | 29 |
| Giles, Vancouver | .950 | 40 | 47 | 125 | 9 | 28 |
| D. Gonzalez, Hawaii | 1.000 | 1 | 1 | 0 | 0 | 0 |
| J. Howell, Edmonton | 1.000 | 1 | 0 | 2 | 0 | 0 |
| Jeltz, Portland | .959 | 21 | 28 | 66 | 4 | 10 |
| Keedy, Edmonton | .913 | 11 | 16 | 26 | 4 | 5 |
| Khalifa, Hawaii | .960 | 63 | 84 | 181 | 11 | 33 |
| Kiefer, Tacoma | .939 | 28 | 42 | 82 | 8 | 22 |
| Koenigsfeld, Tucson | .933 | 27 | 39 | 101 | 10 | 13 |
| Krauss, Edmonton | 1.000 | 5 | 8 | 11 | 0 | 4 |
| Lubratich, Las Vegas | .948 | 12 | 19 | 36 | 3 | 4 |
| Mullins, Phoenix | .971 | 34 | 38 | 94 | 4 | 22 |
| Pena, Tucson | .942 | 53 | 76 | 153 | 14 | 27 |
| Polidor, Edmonton | .966 | 132 | 250 | 396 | 23 | 93 |
| Quinones, Phoenix | .962 | 76 | 104 | 228 | 13 | 49 |
| Ramirez, Las Vegas | .947 | 12 | 16 | 20 | 2 | 4 |
| Reece, Tacoma | 1.000 | 3 | 4 | 4 | 0 | 0 |
| Riles, Vancouver | .965 | 30 | 47 | 120 | 6 | 18 |
| Rincones, Albuquerque | .946 | 19 | 25 | 45 | 4 | 11 |
| E. Rodriguez, Las Vegas | .911 | 34 | 43 | 80 | 12 | 17 |
| V. Rodriguez, Las Vegas | .965 | 39 | 58 | 106 | 6 | 20 |
| Rood, Tucson | .956 | 38 | 59 | 113 | 8 | 18 |
| Schmidt, Phoenix | .828 | 2 | 2 | 6 | 3 | 1 |
| Schu, Portland | .914 | 23 | 25 | 60 | 8 | 8 |
| Serna, Calgary | .972 | 10 | 9 | 26 | 1 | 2 |
| Shipley, Albuquerque | .964 | 122 | 202 | 367 | 21 | 82 |
| Sveum, Vancouver | .891 | 10 | 9 | 32 | 5 | 4 |
| Tartabull, Calgary | .943 | 124 | 181 | 394 | 35 | 92 |
| Thoma, Tacoma | 1.000 | 1 | 2 | 2 | 0 | 0 |
| THROWER, Tacoma | .967 | 123 | 188 | 368 | 19 | 77 |

## OUTFIELDERS

| Player and Club | Pct. | G. | PO. | A. | E. | DP. |
|---|---|---|---|---|---|---|
| R. Adams, Phoenix | 1.000 | 1 | 1 | 0 | 0 | 0 |
| Adduci, Vancouver* | .889 | 5 | 6 | 2 | 1 | 0 |
| Aldrete, Phoenix* | 1.000 | 3 | 3 | 0 | 0 | 0 |
| Amelung, Albuquerque* | .984 | 137 | 288 | 17 | 5 | 3 |
| Ashford, Portland | 1.000 | 1 | 4 | 0 | 0 | 0 |
| Brantley, Calgary | .982 | 63 | 165 | 1 | 3 | 0 |
| Bream, Albuquerque* | 1.000 | 28 | 43 | 1 | 0 | 1 |
| BREWER, Albuquerque | .994 | 97 | 165 | 5 | 1 | 0 |
| Brouhard, Vancouver | 1.000 | 13 | 28 | 0 | 0 | 0 |
| Bryant, Albuquerque | .933 | 109 | 171 | 11 | 13 | 3 |
| Bullock, Tucson* | .967 | 119 | 199 | 5 | 7 | 0 |
| Canseco, Tacoma | .978 | 58 | 81 | 7 | 2 | 1 |
| Carter, Hawaii | .846 | 14 | 22 | 0 | 4 | 0 |
| Casey, Calgary | 1.000 | 3 | 7 | 0 | 0 | 0 |
| Chambers, Calgary* | .955 | 60 | 124 | 2 | 6 | 1 |
| C. Clark, Edmonton* | .972 | 109 | 194 | 14 | 6 | 2 |
| R. Clark, Vancouver | .985 | 29 | 63 | 2 | 1 | 0 |
| Ge. Davis, Las Vegas | 1.000 | 17 | 50 | 3 | 0 | 0 |
| Gl. Davis, Hawaii | 1.000 | 22 | 42 | 3 | 0 | 0 |
| T. Davis, Hawaii* | .974 | 132 | 293 | 10 | 8 | 2 |
| Diaz, Hawaii | .984 | 31 | 59 | 3 | 1 | 1 |
| Dilone, Las Vegas | .900 | 8 | 9 | 0 | 1 | 0 |
| Distefano, Hawaii* | .961 | 117 | 188 | 10 | 8 | 2 |
| Felder, Vancouver | .987 | 134 | 294 | 13 | 4 | 1 |
| Gainey, Tucson* | .969 | 51 | 119 | 4 | 4 | 1 |
| Harrison, Tacoma | .980 | 112 | 184 | 12 | 4 | 2 |
| Hengel, Calgary | 1.000 | 6 | 13 | 0 | 0 | 0 |
| P. Hernandez, Tucson | 1.000 | 4 | 2 | 0 | 0 | 0 |
| C. Hill, Calgary | .933 | 34 | 40 | 2 | 3 | 0 |
| R. Hill, Calgary | .971 | 15 | 33 | 0 | 1 | 0 |
| Hinshaw, Las Vegas | .952 | 94 | 207 | 9 | 11 | 1 |
| C. Jackson, Tucson | .979 | 19 | 43 | 3 | 1 | 1 |
| C. James, Portland | .980 | 133 | 328 | 16 | 7 | 3 |
| D. James, Vancouver* | 1.000 | 8 | 17 | 0 | 0 | 0 |
| C. Jones, Tucson* | .993 | 70 | 142 | 7 | 1 | 3 |
| Keedy, Edmonton | 1.000 | 12 | 60 | 0 | 0 | 0 |
| King, Calgary* | .875 | 37 | 48 | 1 | 7 | 0 |
| Klipstein, Vancouver | 1.000 | 12 | 12 | 0 | 0 | 0 |
| Knight, Portland* | .988 | 35 | 71 | 9 | 1 | 2 |
| Kruk, Las Vegas* | .976 | 94 | 154 | 6 | 4 | 0 |
| Kutcher, Phoenix | .974 | 82 | 143 | 8 | 4 | 1 |
| Lancellotti, Phoenix* | 1.000 | 17 | 19 | 0 | 0 | 0 |
| Lansford, Tacoma | 1.000 | 25 | 28 | 1 | 0 | 0 |
| Linares, Edmonton | .964 | 31 | 52 | 1 | 2 | 0 |
| Loman, Vancouver* | .977 | 102 | 204 | 9 | 5 | 2 |
| Loucks, Hawaii | .985 | 89 | 127 | 3 | 2 | 0 |
| Lubratich, Las Vegas | .875 | 12 | 14 | 0 | 2 | 0 |
| Madrid, Edmonton | .972 | 17 | 34 | 1 | 1 | 0 |
| D. Miller, Edmonton | .964 | 12 | 25 | 2 | 1 | 0 |
| L. Miller, Albuquerque | .977 | 28 | 42 | 1 | 1 | 0 |

## OUTFIELDERS—Continued

| Player and Club | Pct. | G. | PO. | A. | E. | DP. |
|---|---|---|---|---|---|---|
| Miscik, Hawaii | 1.000 | 7 | 12 | 0 | 0 | 0 |
| J. Moses, Calgary° | .983 | 103 | 223 | 9 | 4 | 2 |
| S. Moses, Portland | .980 | 66 | 97 | 1 | 2 | 1 |
| Murphy, Edmonton° | 1.000 | 34 | 76 | 0 | 0 | 0 |
| R. Nelson, Calgary | .973 | 106 | 210 | 5 | 6 | 1 |
| Olander, Portland | .960 | 27 | 23 | 1 | 1 | 0 |
| Opie, Hawaii | .971 | 40 | 63 | 3 | 2 | 0 |
| Paciorek, Vancouver | .977 | 51 | 81 | 3 | 2 | 2 |
| Page, Hawaii | 1.000 | 1 | 1 | 0 | 0 | 0 |
| Pederson, Albuquerque° | .934 | 65 | 109 | 5 | 8 | 0 |
| Peters, Tacoma | .968 | 120 | 260 | 8 | 9 | 1 |
| Pyznarski, Las Vegas | 1.000 | 2 | 3 | 0 | 0 | 0 |
| Quinones, Phoenix | .833 | 3 | 5 | 0 | 1 | 0 |
| Rabb, Phoenix | .929 | 5 | 13 | 0 | 1 | 0 |
| Rajsich, Phoenix° | 1.000 | 3 | 6 | 0 | 0 | 0 |
| Randall, Edmonton° | .952 | 16 | 18 | 2 | 1 | 1 |
| Ready, Vancouver | .973 | 32 | 36 | 0 | 1 | 0 |
| Reece, Tacoma | 1.000 | 1 | 1 | 0 | 0 | 0 |
| Reid, Phoenix° | .972 | 52 | 101 | 3 | 3 | 0 |
| Rhomberg, Phoenix | .969 | 98 | 182 | 5 | 6 | 0 |
| Roenicke, Phoenix° | .993 | 59 | 129 | 6 | 1 | 1 |
| Romano, Tacoma | .971 | 101 | 161 | 8 | 5 | 1 |
| Romero, Edmonton | .953 | 49 | 76 | 5 | 4 | 0 |
| Rood, Tucson | .955 | 11 | 18 | 3 | 1 | 0 |
| Russell, Portland | .957 | 16 | 21 | 1 | 1 | 0 |
| Salava, Portland | .975 | 100 | 178 | 14 | 5 | 5 |
| Seibert, Portland | .897 | 25 | 34 | 1 | 4 | 0 |
| Skube, Vancouver° | 1.000 | 62 | 111 | 4 | 0 | 3 |
| R. Smith, Las Vegas | 1.000 | 32 | 44 | 5 | 0 | 0 |
| Steels, Las Vegas° | .983 | 105 | 163 | 12 | 3 | 4 |
| Stephenson, Tacoma° | .938 | 46 | 72 | 4 | 5 | 1 |
| Stone, Portland | .948 | 65 | 103 | 6 | 6 | 0 |
| Strucher, Tucson | .842 | 10 | 15 | 1 | 3 | 0 |
| Stubbs, Albuquerque° | 1.000 | 12 | 26 | 2 | 0 | 1 |
| Thomas, Las Vegas | 1.000 | 8 | 9 | 0 | 0 | 0 |
| Tillman, Las Vegas | .973 | 90 | 175 | 6 | 5 | 0 |
| Tingley, Calgary | .895 | 9 | 17 | 0 | 2 | 0 |
| Tolman, Portland | .984 | 31 | 61 | 1 | 1 | 0 |
| Waller, Tucson | .991 | 99 | 220 | 13 | 2 | 3 |
| Walter, Las Vegas° | 1.000 | 1 | 1 | 0 | 0 | 0 |
| West, Edmonton | .983 | 89 | 166 | 10 | 3 | 0 |
| D. White, Edmonton | .991 | 66 | 205 | 6 | 2 | 1 |
| K. Wiggins, Las Vegas° | 1.000 | 8 | 12 | 0 | 0 | 0 |
| Wilson, Phoenix | .976 | 135 | 307 | 14 | 8 | 1 |

## CATCHERS

| Player and Club | Pct. | G. | PO. | A. | E. | DP. | PB. |
|---|---|---|---|---|---|---|---|
| Ashman, Tacoma | .973 | 41 | 260 | 25 | 8 | 3 | 9 |
| W. Bathe, Tacoma | .990 | 97 | 613 | 64 | 7 | 9 | 12 |
| Clements, Vancouver | .972 | 18 | 93 | 10 | 3 | 0 | 5 |
| Cliburn, Hawaii | .970 | 29 | 186 | 9 | 6 | 2 | 1 |
| Colbert, Tucson | .980 | 27 | 79 | 18 | 2 | 2 | 0 |
| Daulton, Portland | 1.000 | 18 | 110 | 9 | 0 | 1 | 2 |
| Diaz, Portland-Hawaii | .991 | 65 | 410 | 16 | 4 | 0 | 2 |
| Fimple, Albuquerque | .988 | 72 | 297 | 38 | 4 | 2 | 7 |
| Gomez, Phoenix | .980 | 79 | 502 | 47 | 11 | 11 | 2 |
| Gulden, Tucson | .978 | 38 | 200 | 25 | 5 | 3 | 2 |
| Gwosdz, Phoenix | .996 | 49 | 243 | 22 | 1 | 2 | 4 |
| Herz, Hawaii-Portland | .989 | 79 | 395 | 39 | 5 | 3 | 6 |
| C. Hill, Calgary | .975 | 35 | 182 | 16 | 5 | 0 | 3 |
| Hough, Tucson | .960 | 6 | 22 | 2 | 1 | 1 | 1 |
| Huppert, Vancouver | .986 | 9 | 63 | 8 | 1 | 2 | 1 |
| J. Jones, Tacoma | 1.000 | 2 | 8 | 2 | 0 | 0 | 0 |
| Knicely, Portland | .957 | 12 | 62 | 4 | 3 | 1 | 1 |
| Liddle, Edmonton | .977 | 24 | 109 | 21 | 3 | 0 | 1 |
| Malkin, Hawaii | .988 | 63 | 395 | 31 | 5 | 5 | 9 |
| M. MARTIN, Vancouver | .993 | 76 | 400 | 40 | 3 | 9 | 9 |
| D. Miller, Edmonton | 1.000 | 5 | 18 | 3 | 0 | 0 | 2 |
| Mizerock, Tucson | .987 | 71 | 333 | 43 | 5 | 3 | 7 |
| Nago, Vancouver | .997 | 56 | 289 | 47 | 1 | 5 | 6 |
| Nahorodny, Portland | .980 | 52 | 269 | 26 | 6 | 0 | 2 |
| J. Nelson, Vancouver | 1.000 | 3 | 10 | 0 | 0 | 0 | 1 |
| O'Brien, Tacoma | .975 | 17 | 110 | 9 | 3 | 0 | 1 |
| Ouellette, Phoenix | .992 | 20 | 114 | 10 | 1 | 0 | 2 |
| Parent, Las Vegas | .990 | 84 | 538 | 51 | 6 | 5 | 10 |
| Ramos, Edmonton | .974 | 92 | 462 | 57 | 14 | 7 | 8 |
| Reyes, Albuquerque | .958 | 96 | 419 | 65 | 21 | 10 | 24 |
| A. Rodriguez, Vancouver | 1.000 | 2 | 14 | 0 | 0 | 0 | 0 |
| R. Rodriguez, Hawaii | 1.000 | 1 | 9 | 0 | 0 | 0 | 0 |
| Romero, Edmonton | .932 | 25 | 95 | 15 | 8 | 3 | 3 |
| Russell, Portland | 1.000 | 1 | 2 | 0 | 0 | 0 | 0 |
| Scott, Calgary | .936 | 7 | 39 | 5 | 3 | 0 | 2 |
| R. Smith, Las Vegas | .978 | 64 | 454 | 43 | 11 | 4 | 10 |
| Strucher, Tucson | .989 | 17 | 80 | 11 | 1 | 0 | 0 |
| Thomas, Las Vegas | 1.000 | 4 | 10 | 1 | 0 | 0 | 0 |
| Tingley, Calgary | .982 | 73 | 382 | 51 | 8 | 7 | 6 |
| Valle, Calgary | .995 | 39 | 202 | 11 | 1 | 1 | 4 |

## PITCHERS

| Player and Club | Pct. | G. | PO. | A. | E. | DP. |
|---|---|---|---|---|---|---|
| Acker, Tucson° | .970 | 36 | 12 | 20 | 1 | 4 |
| R. Allen, Albuquerque | 1.000 | 3 | 0 | 1 | 0 | 0 |
| Arnold, Portland° | 1.000 | 14 | 3 | 2 | 0 | 0 |
| Barnes, Tucson° | .857 | 25 | 4 | 8 | 2 | 1 |
| Bartley, Calgary | 1.000 | 17 | 3 | 6 | 0 | 1 |
| Bastian, Edmonton | .889 | 27 | 9 | 15 | 3 | 1 |
| Bauer, Tacoma | .667 | 4 | 0 | 2 | 1 | 0 |
| Best, Calgary | 1.000 | 4 | 0 | 1 | 0 | 0 |
| Bielecki, Hawaii | .969 | 20 | 8 | 23 | 1 | 1 |
| Birtsas, Tacoma° | 1.000 | 4 | 1 | 5 | 0 | 0 |
| Blobaum, Phoenix | .800 | 39 | 3 | 5 | 2 | 2 |
| Bonine, Tucson | .929 | 46 | 5 | 21 | 2 | 3 |
| Booker, Las Vegas | .727 | 10 | 2 | 6 | 3 | 2 |
| Brennan, Albuquerque | 1.000 | 20 | 13 | 17 | 0 | 2 |
| Bryden, Edmonton | 1.000 | 36 | 8 | 7 | 0 | 0 |
| Callahan, Las Vegas | 1.000 | 4 | 1 | 1 | 0 | 0 |
| Candiotti, Vancouver | .981 | 24 | 18 | 33 | 1 | 4 |
| Cato, Las Vegas | 1.000 | 44 | 12 | 25 | 0 | 1 |
| Childress, Portland | 1.000 | 34 | 3 | 5 | 0 | 1 |
| Chris, Tacoma° | .950 | 32 | 5 | 14 | 1 | 0 |
| Citarelli, Portland | .935 | 30 | 9 | 20 | 2 | 3 |
| Cliburn, Edmonton | 1.000 | 2 | 0 | 1 | 0 | 0 |
| Clutterbuck, Vancouver | 1.000 | 29 | 13 | 15 | 0 | 3 |
| Cocanower, Vancouver | .813 | 9 | 5 | 8 | 3 | 1 |
| Cole, Portland | .815 | 40 | 8 | 14 | 5 | 1 |
| Comer, Portland | 1.000 | 19 | 6 | 16 | 0 | 1 |
| Conroy, Tacoma° | .905 | 22 | 7 | 12 | 2 | 0 |
| Corbett, Edmonton | 1.000 | 1 | 0 | 2 | 0 | 1 |
| Cornell, Portland | .667 | 5 | 0 | 2 | 1 | 0 |
| Crim, Vancouver | 1.000 | 48 | 10 | 23 | 0 | 5 |
| Davisson, Portland | 1.000 | 9 | 0 | 13 | 0 | 0 |
| Decker, Las Vegas | 1.000 | 5 | 1 | 1 | 0 | 0 |
| J. DeLeon, Hawaii | 1.000 | 5 | 0 | 8 | 0 | 0 |
| L. DeLeon, Las Vegas | 1.000 | 9 | 1 | 7 | 0 | 1 |
| Downs, Phoenix | .950 | 37 | 6 | 13 | 1 | 2 |
| Dozier, Tacoma° | 1.000 | 6 | 1 | 4 | 0 | 0 |
| Duquette, Vancouver° | 1.000 | 41 | 2 | 9 | 0 | 1 |
| Fansler, Hawaii | 1.000 | 3 | 0 | 1 | 0 | 0 |
| Finch, Edmonton | .913 | 25 | 19 | 23 | 4 | 2 |
| Fowlkes, Edmonton | .878 | 23 | 19 | 24 | 6 | 1 |
| Gaynor, Portland | 1.000 | 8 | 1 | 4 | 0 | 0 |
| Geisel, Calgary° | .957 | 20 | 4 | 18 | 1 | 0 |
| Ghelfi, Portland | .947 | 20 | 3 | 15 | 1 | 2 |
| Giddings, Tacoma | 1.000 | 3 | 0 | 1 | 0 | 0 |
| A. Gonzalez, Portland | .974 | 28 | 9 | 29 | 1 | 2 |
| Grant, Phoenix | .917 | 29 | 13 | 9 | 2 | 1 |
| Green, Hawaii° | .950 | 35 | 0 | 19 | 1 | 1 |
| Groh, Edmonton° | .889 | 33 | 1 | 7 | 1 | 1 |
| Guetterman, Calgary° | .920 | 20 | 8 | 15 | 2 | 1 |
| Harper, Las Vegas | .867 | 10 | 5 | 8 | 2 | 0 |
| Hausman, L.V.-Alb | .941 | 34 | 4 | 12 | 1 | 2 |
| Hayward, Las Vegas° | .932 | 28 | 10 | 31 | 3 | 4 |
| Heathcock, Tucson | .972 | 23 | 11 | 24 | 1 | 5 |
| Hensley, Phoenix° | 1.000 | 35 | 6 | 9 | 0 | 1 |
| M. Hernandez, Tucson | 1.000 | 11 | 2 | 4 | 0 | 2 |
| Holton, Albuquerque | .980 | 27 | 19 | 30 | 1 | 4 |
| R.L. Jackson, Las Vegas | 1.000 | 3 | 0 | 1 | 0 | 0 |
| Jeffcoat, Phoenix | 1.000 | 10 | 5 | 6 | 0 | 0 |
| Johnson, Haw-Van° | .857 | 23 | 8 | 16 | 4 | 1 |
| B. Jones, Hawaii | 1.000 | 1 | 0 | 2 | 0 | 0 |
| Kain, Edmonton | .957 | 29 | 11 | 33 | 2 | 0 |
| Kaiser, Tacoma° | .833 | 27 | 3 | 7 | 2 | 3 |
| Kaufman, Edmonton | 1.000 | 22 | 4 | 2 | 0 | 0 |
| Keedy, Edmonton | 1.000 | 2 | 1 | 0 | 0 | 0 |
| Kerfeld, Tucson | .947 | 26 | 9 | 27 | 2 | 0 |
| Kern, Vancouver | 1.000 | 5 | 1 | 3 | 0 | 0 |
| Kibbe, Albuquerque | .913 | 31 | 6 | 15 | 2 | 2 |
| Kipper, Edm-Haw° | .833 | 7 | 1 | 4 | 1 | 0 |
| Knudson, Tucson | 1.000 | 24 | 10 | 16 | 0 | 0 |
| Krawczyk, Hawaii | 1.000 | 38 | 1 | 6 | 0 | 2 |
| Kristan, Las Vegas | 1.000 | 11 | 0 | 2 | 0 | 0 |
| Krueger, Tacoma° | .500 | 2 | 0 | 1 | 1 | 0 |
| Kyles, Tacoma | 1.000 | 43 | 4 | 23 | 0 | 2 |
| Lacey, Phoenix° | 1.000 | 21 | 2 | 6 | 0 | 1 |
| Ladd, Vancouver | 1.000 | 5 | 3 | 1 | 0 | 0 |
| LAMBERT, Tacoma | 1.000 | 28 | 15 | 23 | 0 | 1 |
| Lazorko, Phx-Cal | 1.000 | 44 | 5 | 19 | 0 | 1 |
| Leary, Vancouver | .974 | 27 | 11 | 27 | 1 | 2 |
| Leiper, Tacoma° | 1.000 | 15 | 1 | 4 | 0 | 0 |
| Leopold, Las Vegas | .889 | 22 | 5 | 11 | 2 | 0 |
| Lerch, Portland° | 1.000 | 20 | 9 | 18 | 0 | 0 |
| Lesley, Vancouver | 1.000 | 48 | 5 | 10 | 0 | 1 |
| Lewis, Calgary | .880 | 20 | 6 | 16 | 3 | 1 |
| Long, Calgary | 1.000 | 19 | 2 | 6 | 0 | 0 |

## PITCHERS—Continued

| Player and Club | Pct. | G. | PO. | A. | E. | DP. |
|---|---|---|---|---|---|---|
| Luecken, Calgary | 1.000 | 18 | 6 | 12 | 0 | 0 |
| Lugo, Edmonton | 1.000 | 4 | 5 | 4 | 0 | 0 |
| Mack, Edmonton | .962 | 25 | 9 | 16 | 1 | 0 |
| Madden, Tucson* | .667 | 6 | 0 | 2 | 1 | 1 |
| Maddux, Portland | .969 | 27 | 12 | 19 | 1 | 3 |
| S. Martin, Albuquerque | 1.000 | 42 | 14 | 22 | 0 | 4 |
| V. Martin, Calgary | 1.000 | 6 | 5 | 2 | 0 | 0 |
| Martz, Tucson | 1.000 | 24 | 4 | 9 | 0 | 0 |
| Mason, Phoenix | .953 | 24 | 16 | 25 | 2 | 1 |
| Mathis, Tucson | .923 | 7 | 6 | 6 | 1 | 0 |
| McCaskill, Edmonton | 1.000 | 3 | 0 | 1 | 0 | 0 |
| McCullers, Las Vegas | .917 | 24 | 14 | 19 | 3 | 1 |
| McKnight, Phoenix | .909 | 17 | 9 | 11 | 2 | 1 |
| J. McLaughlin, Tacoma | 1.000 | 38 | 4 | 12 | 0 | 2 |
| M. McLaughlin, Tacoma | .875 | 38 | 4 | 10 | 2 | 1 |
| Meeks, Albuquerque | .950 | 32 | 13 | 25 | 2 | 2 |
| Miner, Tucson | .688 | 39 | 5 | 6 | 5 | 1 |
| Mirabella, Calgary* | 1.000 | 53 | 3 | 13 | 0 | 1 |
| Money, Portland | 1.000 | 6 | 1 | 2 | 0 | 0 |
| Monge, Hawaii* | 1.000 | 14 | 2 | 1 | 0 | 1 |
| Montalvo, Alb-Tuc | 1.000 | 52 | 5 | 16 | 0 | 1 |
| Mooneyham, Tacoma | .947 | 21 | 9 | 9 | 1 | 1 |
| Moore, Phoenix | .909 | 50 | 5 | 5 | 1 | 2 |
| Morgan, Calgary | 1.000 | 1 | 0 | 1 | 0 | 0 |
| S. Moses, Portland* | 1.000 | 1 | 1 | 0 | 0 | 0 |
| Mura, Tacoma | .875 | 16 | 6 | 15 | 3 | 0 |
| Myers, Vancouver | 1.000 | 14 | 2 | 2 | 0 | 0 |
| Nieves, Vancouver* | 1.000 | 12 | 8 | 4 | 0 | 1 |
| Oliver, Edmonton | .929 | 32 | 12 | 14 | 2 | 3 |
| Ontiveros, Tacoma | .714 | 15 | 3 | 7 | 4 | 1 |
| Owchinko, Tacoma* | 1.000 | 16 | 1 | 5 | 0 | 0 |
| PATTERSON, Las Vegas* | 1.000 | 42 | 9 | 29 | 0 | 1 |
| Pederson, Albuquerque* | 1.000 | 1 | 1 | 0 | 0 | 0 |
| Plunk, Tacoma | .750 | 10 | 4 | 5 | 3 | 0 |
| Powell, Albuquerque* | 1.000 | 18 | 2 | 24 | 0 | 2 |
| Reece, Tacoma | 1.000 | 2 | 0 | 1 | 0 | 0 |
| Reuschel, Hawaii | 1.000 | 8 | 0 | 6 | 0 | 0 |
| Rijo, Tacoma | 1.000 | 24 | 7 | 16 | 0 | 1 |
| Riley, Phoenix* | .842 | 46 | 1 | 15 | 3 | 2 |
| Roberts, Vancouver | 1.000 | 12 | 1 | 3 | 0 | 0 |
| Robinson, Phoenix | .980 | 29 | 21 | 27 | 1 | 1 |
| Rogers, Edmonton | 1.000 | 5 | 3 | 6 | 0 | 0 |
| R. Rodriguez, Tacoma | 1.000 | 7 | 3 | 3 | 0 | 0 |
| Ross, Tucson | 1.000 | 46 | 4 | 19 | 0 | 2 |
| Sanchez, Edmonton | 1.000 | 4 | 1 | 0 | 0 | 0 |
| Sarmiento, Hawaii | .941 | 18 | 3 | 13 | 1 | 2 |
| Schefsky, Las Vegas | 1.000 | 13 | 0 | 2 | 0 | 1 |
| Scherer, Tacoma | 1.000 | 8 | 1 | 8 | 0 | 1 |
| Scudder, Albuquerque | 1.000 | 11 | 2 | 2 | 0 | 0 |
| Searage, Vancouver* | 1.000 | 23 | 2 | 1 | 0 | 1 |
| Semall, Hawaii | .929 | 24 | 2 | 11 | 1 | 0 |
| Senteney, Calgary | .800 | 28 | 3 | 5 | 2 | 0 |
| Shipanoff, Portland | .800 | 51 | 2 | 2 | 1 | 0 |
| Shirley, Hawaii* | .750 | 15 | 1 | 8 | 3 | 0 |
| Simmons, Las Vegas | 1.000 | 6 | 0 | 1 | 0 | 0 |
| Da. Smith, Edmonton | .962 | 42 | 7 | 18 | 1 | 0 |
| Do. Smith, Albuquerque | 1.000 | 55 | 11 | 23 | 0 | 2 |
| Snyder, Calgary* | 1.000 | 20 | 5 | 13 | 0 | 1 |
| Solano, Tucson | 1.000 | 23 | 1 | 2 | 0 | 0 |
| Sonberg, Albuquerque | .769 | 26 | 2 | 8 | 3 | 1 |
| Stoddard, Calgary | .875 | 7 | 2 | 5 | 1 | 0 |
| Surhoff, Portland | .958 | 70 | 7 | 16 | 1 | 0 |
| Tellmann, Tacoma | 1.000 | 8 | 1 | 5 | 0 | 0 |
| Thomas, Calgary | 1.000 | 15 | 0 | 5 | 0 | 0 |
| Tobik, Calgary | .882 | 56 | 6 | 9 | 2 | 0 |
| Tomlin, Hawaii* | 1.000 | 33 | 3 | 16 | 0 | 1 |
| Tunnell, Hawaii | .933 | 7 | 6 | 8 | 1 | 0 |
| Vanderbush, Las Vegas | .923 | 42 | 4 | 8 | 1 | 2 |
| Vila, Albuquerque | 1.000 | 11 | 1 | 2 | 0 | 1 |
| Waits, Vancouver* | .962 | 16 | 7 | 18 | 1 | 0 |
| Walk, Hawaii | .971 | 24 | 10 | 24 | 1 | 2 |
| Walter, Las Vegas* | 1.000 | 45 | 9 | 17 | 0 | 1 |
| Ward, Phoenix* | 1.000 | 22 | 0 | 9 | 0 | 0 |
| Warren, Tacoma | 1.000 | 12 | 1 | 1 | 0 | 0 |
| Wegman, Vancouver | .957 | 28 | 17 | 27 | 2 | 3 |
| L. White, Albuquerque | .940 | 31 | 17 | 30 | 3 | 3 |
| Whitmer, Calgary | .978 | 29 | 19 | 25 | 1 | 2 |
| Wilkinson, Calgary* | 1.000 | 9 | 1 | 9 | 0 | 0 |
| Williams, Phoenix | 1.000 | 9 | 2 | 3 | 0 | 0 |
| Wills, Calgary | .947 | 9 | 6 | 12 | 1 | 1 |
| Winn, Hawaii | .900 | 7 | 0 | 9 | 1 | 0 |
| Wojna, Las Vegas | .889 | 18 | 8 | 16 | 3 | 0 |
| Young, Tacoma* | 1.000 | 3 | 0 | 3 | 0 | 1 |
| Zaske, Hawaii | 1.000 | 46 | 1 | 4 | 0 | 0 |

The following players do not have any recorded accepted chances at the positions indicated; therefore, are not listed in the fielding averages for those particular positions: R. Allen, ss; Ashman, p; Chadwick, p; Coles, of; Couchee, p; Crews, p; Cuellar, p; Davidsmeier, ss; Dybzinski, of; Escobar, 3b; Followell, p; Garcia, of; Keedy, 2b, c; Krauss, p; Krawczyk, 1b; Lazorko, 3b, of; Mills, 2b, of; Miscik, 1b; Montgomery, p; Murray, p; Nago, p; Nahorodny, 2b; Opie, 2b; Page, p; Rennicke, p; Rodas, p; Romero, p; Rucker, p; Serna, p; Skube, 1b; Smith, p; Tejeda, p; Thomas, p; Tillman, p; Tolentino, of; Vavra, of.

## CLUB PITCHING

| Club | ERA. | G. | CG. | ShO. | Sv. | IP. | H. | R. | ER. | HR. | HB. | BB. | Int. BB. | SO. | WP. | Bk. |
|---|---|---|---|---|---|---|---|---|---|---|---|---|---|---|---|---|
| Hawaii | 3.39 | 143 | 30 | 13 | 35 | 1219.2 | 1074 | 528 | 460 | 89 | 23 | 484 | 21 | 963 | 70 | 10 |
| Vancouver | 3.68 | 143 | 26 | 9 | 35 | 1247.1 | 1230 | 578 | 510 | 92 | 33 | 421 | 29 | 832 | 35 | 13 |
| Portland | 3.94 | 142 | 16 | 7 | 41 | 1234.2 | 1258 | 619 | 541 | 86 | 22 | 537 | 40 | 788 | 48 | 13 |
| Phoenix | 4.05 | 142 | 20 | 10 | 41 | 1224.0 | 1240 | 624 | 551 | 102 | 25 | 555 | 59 | 811 | 64 | 10 |
| Edmonton | 4.12 | 142 | 28 | 7 | 27 | 1233.0 | 1413 | 688 | 565 | 98 | 32 | 429 | 18 | 654 | 59 | 13 |
| Tacoma | 4.19 | 143 | 14 | 12 | 31 | 1259.2 | 1197 | 673 | 587 | 86 | 22 | 703 | 55 | 963 | 61 | 32 |
| Albuquerque | 4.37 | 144 | 25 | 10 | 25 | 1217.1 | 1384 | 712 | 591 | 104 | 17 | 494 | 49 | 683 | 60 | 13 |
| Las Vegas | 4.49 | 144 | 26 | 6 | 35 | 1264.0 | 1291 | 736 | 630 | 115 | 40 | 580 | 46 | 974 | 61 | 13 |
| Tucson | 4.53 | 140 | 17 | 5 | 28 | 1222.2 | 1428 | 709 | 616 | 80 | 18 | 452 | 39 | 674 | 40 | 13 |
| Calgary | 4.95 | 141 | 19 | 3 | 25 | 1222.1 | 1418 | 787 | 672 | 109 | 29 | 493 | 28 | 790 | 63 | 7 |

## PITCHERS' RECORDS

(Leading Qualifiers for Earned-Run Average Leadership — 115 or More Innings)

*Throws lefthanded.

| Pitcher—Club | W. | L. | Pct. | ERA. | G. | GS. | CG. | GF. | ShO. | Sv. | IP. | H. | R. | ER. | HR. | HB. | BB. | Int. BB. | SO. | WP. |
|---|---|---|---|---|---|---|---|---|---|---|---|---|---|---|---|---|---|---|---|---|
| Walk, Hawaii | 16 | 5 | .762 | 2.65 | 24 | 24 | 12 | 0 | 1 | 0 | 173.0 | 143 | 57 | 51 | 10 | 4 | 61 | 1 | 124 | 12 |
| Waits, Vancouver* | 10 | 5 | .667 | 2.87 | 16 | 16 | 5 | 0 | 1 | 0 | 116.0 | 108 | 43 | 37 | 6 | 0 | 22 | 3 | 64 | 4 |
| Rijo, Tacoma | 7 | 10 | .412 | 2.90 | 24 | 24 | 3 | 0 | 1 | 0 | 149.0 | 116 | 64 | 48 | 6 | 0 | 108 | 3 | 179 | 4 |
| Patterson, Las Vegas* | 10 | 11 | .476 | 3.14 | 42 | 20 | 7 | 16 | 1 | 6 | 186.1 | 187 | 80 | 65 | 19 | 1 | 52 | 5 | 146 | 5 |
| Gonzalez, Portland | 10 | 10 | .500 | 3.22 | 28 | 26 | 6 | 0 | 3 | 0 | 164.2 | 168 | 63 | 59 | 11 | 0 | 40 | 4 | 85 | 3 |
| Conroy, Tacoma* | 11 | 3 | .786 | 3.27 | 22 | 22 | 2 | 0 | 1 | 0 | 129.1 | 106 | 52 | 47 | 8 | 1 | 71 | 1 | 166 | 4 |
| Mason, Phoenix | 12 | 1 | .923 | 3.33 | 24 | 24 | 5 | 0 | 2 | 0 | 167.1 | 145 | 67 | 62 | 12 | 4 | 72 | 6 | 120 | 6 |
| Citarella, Portland | 7 | 9 | .438 | 3.44 | 30 | 18 | 1 | 1 | 0 | 0 | 136.0 | 128 | 67 | 52 | 9 | 2 | 58 | 4 | 62 | 4 |
| Clutterbuck, Vancouver | 11 | 7 | .611 | 3.53 | 29 | 19 | 3 | 5 | 0 | 0 | 147.2 | 156 | 68 | 58 | 9 | 2 | 41 | 2 | 101 | 7 |
| Holton, Albuquerque* | 9 | 10 | .474 | 3.61 | 27 | 27 | 7 | 0 | 1 | 0 | 179.2 | 183 | 83 | 72 | 15 | 0 | 40 | 1 | 86 | 4 |

Departmental Leaders: G—Surhoff, 70; W—Walk, 16; L—Grant, Meeks, 15; Pct.—Mason, .923; GS—Grant, Meeks, Robinson, 29; CG—Walk, 12; GF—Surhoff, 41; ShO—Gonzalez, Grant, Mack, 3; Sv.—Krawczyk, 20; IP—Hayward, 191.1; H—Acker, 221; R—Whitmer, 115; ER—Acker, 103; HR—Wegman, 21; HB—Comer, Hayward, Lazorko, McCullers, Whitmer, 6; BB—Rijo, 108; IBB—Do. Smith, 17; SO—Rijo, 179; WP—Grant, 18.

### (All Pitchers—Listed Alphabetically)

| Pitcher—Club | W. | L. | Pct. | ERA. | G. | GS. | CG. | GF. | ShO. | Sv. | IP. | H. | R. | ER. | HR. | HB. | BB. | Int. BB. | SO. | WP. |
|---|---|---|---|---|---|---|---|---|---|---|---|---|---|---|---|---|---|---|---|---|
| Acker, Tucson* | 10 | 12 | .455 | 5.45 | 36 | 25 | 2 | 0 | 0 | 0 | 170.0 | 221 | 110 | 103 | 14 | 3 | 68 | 4 | 80 | 2 |
| Allen, Albuquerque | 0 | 0 | .000 | 0.00 | 3 | 0 | 0 | 3 | 0 | 0 | 3.0 | 3 | 0 | 0 | 0 | 0 | 1 | 0 | 1 | 0 |
| Arnold, Portland* | 0 | 0 | .000 | 2.41 | 14 | 0 | 0 | 2 | 0 | 1 | 18.2 | 19 | 7 | 5 | 2 | 1 | 6 | 1 | 7 | 0 |
| Ashman, Tacoma | 0 | 0 | .000 | 4.50 | 1 | 0 | 0 | 1 | 0 | 0 | 2.0 | 1 | 1 | 1 | 0 | 0 | 2 | 0 | 0 | 0 |

| Pitcher—Club | W. | L. | Pct. | ERA. | G. | GS. | CG. | GF. | ShO. | Sv. | IP. | H. | R. | ER. | HR. | HB. | BB. | Int. BB. | SO. | WP. |
|---|---|---|---|---|---|---|---|---|---|---|---|---|---|---|---|---|---|---|---|---|
| Barnes, Tucson* | 3 | 2 | .600 | 3.35 | 25 | 4 | 0 | 8 | 0 | 1 | 48.1 | 45 | 21 | 18 | 4 | 1 | 17 | 0 | 30 | 2 |
| Bartley, Calgary | 1 | 2 | .333 | 4.91 | 17 | 2 | 0 | 9 | 0 | 3 | 36.2 | 43 | 25 | 20 | 6 | 0 | 17 | 3 | 17 | 0 |
| Bastian, Edmonton | 11 | 12 | .478 | 4.36 | 27 | 27 | 5 | 0 | 0 | 0 | 173.1 | 199 | 102 | 84 | 18 | 3 | 56 | 1 | 91 | 6 |
| Bauer, Tacoma | 0 | 1 | .000 | 13.03 | 4 | 1 | 0 | 2 | 0 | 1 | 9.2 | 20 | 14 | 14 | 3 | 2 | 4 | 0 | 5 | 1 |
| Best, Calgary | 0 | 0 | .000 | 0.00 | 4 | 0 | 0 | 2 | 0 | 0 | 5.1 | 2 | 1 | 0 | 0 | 0 | 4 | 0 | 8 | 0 |
| Bielecki, Hawaii | 8 | 6 | .571 | 3.83 | 20 | 20 | 2 | 0 | 0 | 0 | 129.1 | 117 | 58 | 55 | 13 | 1 | 56 | 1 | 111 | 6 |
| Birtsas, Tacoma* | 2 | 2 | .500 | 3.04 | 4 | 4 | 1 | 0 | 0 | 0 | 26.2 | 21 | 10 | 9 | 3 | 0 | 14 | 0 | 25 | 0 |
| Blobaum, Phoenix | 4 | 1 | .800 | 3.88 | 39 | 0 | 0 | 14 | 0 | 5 | 58.0 | 76 | 29 | 25 | 4 | 0 | 20 | 3 | 29 | 3 |
| Bonine, Tucson | 3 | 9 | .250 | 5.44 | 46 | 3 | 0 | 18 | 0 | 3 | 92.2 | 113 | 65 | 56 | 3 | 1 | 35 | 8 | 75 | 2 |
| Booker, Las Vegas | 1 | 1 | .500 | 5.40 | 10 | 7 | 0 | 2 | 0 | 1 | 45.0 | 46 | 34 | 27 | 5 | 0 | 34 | 4 | 16 | 6 |
| Brennan, Albuquerque | 6 | 5 | .545 | 3.75 | 20 | 14 | 3 | 1 | 1 | 0 | 100.2 | 105 | 44 | 42 | 5 | 4 | 29 | 3 | 72 | 4 |
| Bryden, Edmonton | 5 | 6 | .455 | 4.76 | 36 | 1 | 0 | 22 | 0 | 7 | 73.2 | 73 | 45 | 39 | 3 | 5 | 36 | 1 | 52 | 12 |
| Callahan, Las Vegas | 0 | 1 | .000 | 4.70 | 4 | 0 | 0 | 0 | 0 | 0 | 7.2 | 5 | 4 | 4 | 0 | 0 | 8 | 0 | 6 | 1 |
| Candiotti, Vancouver | 9 | 13 | .409 | 3.94 | 24 | 24 | 5 | 0 | 1 | 0 | 150.2 | 178 | 83 | 66 | 14 | 4 | 36 | 2 | 97 | 5 |
| Cato, Las Vegas | 7 | 10 | .412 | 5.28 | 44 | 10 | 3 | 19 | 0 | 3 | 134.2 | 166 | 91 | 79 | 12 | 4 | 39 | 4 | 104 | 2 |
| Chadwick, Edmonton | 1 | 1 | .500 | 3.09 | 2 | 2 | 0 | 0 | 0 | 0 | 11.2 | 9 | 7 | 4 | 2 | 1 | 6 | 0 | 9 | 1 |
| Childress, Portland | 5 | 2 | .714 | 1.27 | 34 | 0 | 0 | 18 | 0 | 6 | 56.2 | 48 | 12 | 8 | 1 | 2 | 23 | 2 | 30 | 0 |
| Chris, Tacoma* | 4 | 2 | .667 | 5.95 | 32 | 0 | 0 | 8 | 0 | 0 | 56.0 | 65 | 41 | 37 | 2 | 1 | 50 | 8 | 38 | 8 |
| Citarella, Portland | 7 | 9 | .438 | 3.44 | 30 | 18 | 1 | 1 | 0 | 0 | 136.0 | 128 | 67 | 52 | 9 | 2 | 58 | 4 | 86 | 2 |
| Cliburn, Edmonton | 0 | 0 | .000 | 0.00 | 2 | 0 | 0 | 1 | 0 | 0 | 3.2 | 3 | 0 | 0 | 0 | 0 | 0 | 0 | 2 | 0 |
| Clutterbuck, Vancouver | 11 | 7 | .611 | 3.53 | 29 | 19 | 3 | 5 | 0 | 0 | 147.2 | 156 | 68 | 58 | 9 | 2 | 41 | 2 | 101 | 7 |
| Cocanower, Vancouver | 5 | 2 | .714 | 3.16 | 9 | 9 | 2 | 0 | 1 | 0 | 62.2 | 59 | 27 | 22 | 2 | 3 | 23 | 0 | 19 | 2 |
| Cole, Portland | 3 | 6 | .333 | 4.69 | 40 | 6 | 2 | 13 | 0 | 3 | 86.1 | 101 | 57 | 45 | 8 | 1 | 50 | 3 | 47 | 6 |
| Comer, Portland | 4 | 3 | .571 | 5.79 | 19 | 17 | 0 | 1 | 0 | 0 | 98.0 | 125 | 65 | 63 | 7 | 6 | 32 | 6 | 49 | 0 |
| Conroy, Tacoma* | 11 | 3 | .786 | 3.27 | 22 | 22 | 2 | 0 | 1 | 0 | 129.1 | 106 | 52 | 47 | 8 | 1 | 71 | 1 | 166 | 4 |
| Corbett, Edmonton | 0 | 1 | .000 | 3.00 | 1 | 0 | 0 | 1 | 0 | 0 | 3.0 | 3 | 1 | 1 | 0 | 0 | 0 | 0 | 1 | 0 |
| Cornell, Phoenix | 0 | 2 | .000 | 9.82 | 5 | 0 | 0 | 2 | 0 | 0 | 3.2 | 6 | 4 | 4 | 0 | 1 | 5 | 1 | 3 | 1 |
| Couchee, Las Vegas | 0 | 0 | .000 | 0.00 | 1 | 0 | 0 | 1 | 0 | 0 | 2.1 | 1 | 0 | 0 | 0 | 0 | 0 | 0 | 3 | 0 |
| Crews, Phoenix | 0 | 0 | .000 | 3.38 | 1 | 0 | 0 | 0 | 0 | 0 | 2.2 | 3 | 2 | 1 | 0 | 0 | 3 | 1 | 2 | 0 |
| Crim, Vancouver | 3 | 6 | .333 | 4.56 | 48 | 5 | 0 | 23 | 0 | 6 | 106.2 | 110 | 58 | 54 | 8 | 4 | 38 | 3 | 68 | 3 |
| Cuellar, Calgary | 0 | 0 | .000 | 0.00 | 1 | 0 | 0 | 1 | 0 | 0 | 1.0 | 1 | 1 | 0 | 0 | 0 | 1 | 0 | 1 | 1 |
| Davisson, Portland | 2 | 4 | .333 | 3.99 | 9 | 9 | 0 | 0 | 0 | 0 | 49.2 | 55 | 26 | 22 | 1 | 1 | 22 | 1 | 15 | 2 |
| Decker, Las Vegas | 1 | 3 | .250 | 7.98 | 5 | 5 | 0 | 0 | 0 | 0 | 14.2 | 16 | 14 | 13 | 2 | 2 | 17 | 1 | 12 | 1 |
| J. de Leon, Hawaii | 4 | 0 | 1.000 | 0.88 | 5 | 5 | 4 | 0 | 2 | 0 | 41.0 | 15 | 4 | 4 | 3 | 1 | 10 | 0 | 45 | 1 |
| L. de Leon, Las Vegas | 2 | 1 | .667 | 5.40 | 9 | 3 | 0 | 3 | 0 | 0 | 23.1 | 27 | 14 | 14 | 3 | 2 | 8 | 1 | 19 | 0 |
| Downs, Phoenix | 9 | 10 | .474 | 4.01 | 37 | 19 | 2 | 6 | 1 | 1 | 137.0 | 138 | 69 | 61 | 9 | 1 | 56 | 4 | 109 | 7 |
| Dozier, Tacoma | 0 | 0 | .000 | 4.24 | 6 | 4 | 0 | 0 | 0 | 0 | 34.0 | 27 | 18 | 16 | 1 | 1 | 14 | 2 | 22 | 0 |
| Duquette, Vancouver* | 5 | 3 | .625 | 3.25 | 41 | 0 | 0 | 14 | 0 | 4 | 63.2 | 61 | 25 | 23 | 1 | 1 | 29 | 8 | 48 | 1 |
| Fansler, Hawaii | 1 | 0 | 1.000 | 2.31 | 3 | 2 | 0 | 0 | 0 | 0 | 11.2 | 9 | 5 | 3 | 0 | 1 | 9 | 1 | 8 | 0 |
| Finch, Edmonton | 8 | 7 | .533 | 4.11 | 25 | 21 | 5 | 2 | 2 | 0 | 142.1 | 170 | 74 | 65 | 2 | 3 | 38 | 1 | 52 | 4 |
| Followell, Tucson | 0 | 0 | .000 | 18.00 | 1 | 0 | 0 | 1 | 0 | 0 | 1.0 | 3 | 2 | 2 | 0 | 0 | 0 | 0 | 0 | 0 |
| Fowlkes, Edmonton | 9 | 8 | .529 | 3.79 | 23 | 21 | 3 | 2 | 0 | 0 | 142.1 | 171 | 75 | 60 | 20 | 5 | 39 | 0 | 69 | 2 |
| Gaynor, Portland | 1 | 1 | .500 | 5.61 | 8 | 3 | 0 | 0 | 0 | 0 | 25.2 | 33 | 18 | 16 | 1 | 1 | 12 | 1 | 12 | 1 |
| Geisel, Calgary* | 5 | 7 | .417 | 5.75 | 20 | 19 | 2 | 1 | 0 | 0 | 114.1 | 153 | 92 | 73 | 12 | 1 | 45 | 0 | 69 | 3 |
| Ghelfi, Portland | 8 | 5 | .615 | 5.01 | 20 | 17 | 0 | 3 | 0 | 0 | 91.2 | 84 | 58 | 51 | 7 | 2 | 91 | 2 | 62 | 12 |
| Giddings, Tacoma | 0 | 0 | .000 | 9.53 | 3 | 0 | 0 | 1 | 0 | 0 | 5.2 | 9 | 7 | 6 | 1 | 0 | 3 | 0 | 4 | 1 |
| Gonzalez, Portland | 10 | 10 | .500 | 3.22 | 28 | 26 | 6 | 0 | 3 | 0 | 164.2 | 168 | 63 | 59 | 11 | 0 | 40 | 4 | 85 | 3 |
| Grant, Phoenix | 8 | 15 | .348 | 4.52 | 29 | 29 | 4 | 0 | 3 | 0 | 183.0 | 182 | 101 | 92 | 17 | 3 | 90 | 5 | 133 | 18 |
| Green, Hawaii* | 3 | 6 | .333 | 4.24 | 35 | 11 | 0 | 19 | 0 | 6 | 97.2 | 108 | 50 | 46 | 12 | 2 | 28 | 1 | 91 | 4 |
| Groh, Edmonton | 1 | 4 | .200 | 4.26 | 33 | 4 | 0 | 17 | 0 | 1 | 61.1 | 82 | 34 | 29 | 5 | 1 | 29 | 2 | 25 | 5 |
| Guetterman, Calgary* | 5 | 8 | .385 | 5.79 | 20 | 18 | 2 | 1 | 0 | 0 | 110.1 | 138 | 86 | 71 | 7 | 1 | 44 | 0 | 48 | 6 |
| Harper, Las Vegas | 2 | 4 | .333 | 4.58 | 10 | 8 | 1 | 1 | 0 | 0 | 57.0 | 47 | 30 | 29 | 4 | 0 | 32 | 1 | 44 | 4 |
| Hausman, 15 LV-19 Alb. | 3 | 4 | .429 | 5.25 | 34 | 3 | 0 | 14 | 0 | 0 | 61.2 | 77 | 45 | 36 | 9 | 3 | 28 | 6 | 20 | 2 |
| Hayward, Las Vegas* | 11 | 10 | .524 | 4.00 | 28 | 28 | 6 | 0 | 1 | 0 | 191.1 | 198 | 104 | 85 | 14 | 6 | 79 | 4 | 150 | 15 |
| Heathcock, Tucson | 7 | 10 | .412 | 5.08 | 23 | 22 | 3 | 0 | 0 | 0 | 141.2 | 180 | 91 | 80 | 9 | 1 | 27 | 3 | 59 | 3 |
| Hensley, Phoenix* | 3 | 1 | .750 | 3.15 | 35 | 5 | 0 | 10 | 0 | 2 | 74.1 | 75 | 30 | 26 | 5 | 3 | 27 | 4 | 52 | 2 |
| Hernandez, Tucson | 1 | 1 | .500 | 3.58 | 11 | 6 | 0 | 4 | 0 | 0 | 37.2 | 35 | 19 | 15 | 0 | 1 | 10 | 0 | 25 | 1 |
| Holton, Albuquerque | 9 | 10 | .474 | 3.61 | 27 | 27 | 7 | 0 | 1 | 0 | 179.2 | 183 | 83 | 72 | 15 | 0 | 40 | 1 | 86 | 4 |
| Jackson, Las Vegas | 1 | 0 | 1.000 | 1.59 | 3 | 0 | 0 | 3 | 0 | 0 | 5.2 | 3 | 1 | 1 | 0 | 0 | 0 | 0 | 3 | 0 |
| Jeffcoat, Phoenix* | 4 | 5 | .444 | 3.62 | 10 | 10 | 2 | 0 | 0 | 0 | 59.2 | 64 | 26 | 24 | 11 | 2 | 9 | 2 | 28 | 2 |
| Johnson, 20 Haw-3 Van* | 4 | 7 | .364 | 4.95 | 23 | 17 | 3 | 3 | 1 | 0 | 109.0 | 116 | 64 | 60 | 13 | 2 | 44 | 0 | 70 | 3 |
| Jones, Hawaii | 0 | 0 | .000 | 9.00 | 1 | 0 | 0 | 1 | 0 | 0 | 3.0 | 5 | 5 | 3 | 0 | 0 | 1 | 0 | 2 | 0 |
| Kain, Edmonton | 9 | 11 | .450 | 4.03 | 29 | 23 | 6 | 3 | 1 | 1 | 160.2 | 185 | 95 | 72 | 14 | 1 | 36 | 1 | 75 | 5 |
| Kaiser, Tacoma* | 4 | 2 | .667 | 1.75 | 27 | 4 | 0 | 11 | 0 | 5 | 46.1 | 33 | 10 | 9 | 3 | 0 | 18 | 4 | 36 | 2 |
| Kaufman, Edmonton | 1 | 2 | .333 | 2.33 | 22 | 1 | 0 | 15 | 0 | 3 | 46.1 | 40 | 14 | 12 | 2 | 2 | 15 | 2 | 40 | 1 |
| Keedy, Edmonton | 0 | 0 | .000 | 3.00 | 2 | 0 | 0 | 1 | 0 | 0 | 3.0 | 1 | 1 | 1 | 0 | 0 | 2 | 0 | 0 | 1 |
| Kerfeld, Tucson | 10 | 11 | .476 | 4.41 | 26 | 25 | 5 | 0 | 2 | 0 | 163.1 | 176 | 95 | 80 | 8 | 3 | 74 | 2 | 123 | 11 |
| Kern, Vancouver | 0 | 0 | .000 | 2.89 | 5 | 0 | 0 | 4 | 0 | 0 | 9.1 | 3 | 3 | 3 | 1 | 0 | 8 | 0 | 4 | 0 |
| Kibbe, Albuquerque | 5 | 8 | .385 | 5.88 | 31 | 16 | 0 | 3 | 0 | 0 | 104.0 | 144 | 86 | 68 | 11 | 1 | 48 | 2 | 51 | 12 |
| Kipper, 1 Edm-6 Haw* | 3 | 0 | 1.000 | 1.99 | 7 | 6 | 1 | 1 | 1 | 0 | 49.2 | 36 | 15 | 11 | 4 | 1 | 12 | 0 | 42 | 1 |
| Knudson, Tucson | 8 | 5 | .615 | 4.01 | 24 | 22 | 4 | 0 | 2 | 0 | 146.0 | 171 | 69 | 65 | 10 | 1 | 37 | 1 | 68 | 6 |
| Krauss, Edmonton | 1 | 0 | 1.000 | 0.00 | 2 | 0 | 0 | 2 | 0 | 0 | 3.0 | 1 | 1 | 0 | 0 | 0 | 2 | 0 | 1 | 2 |
| Krawczyk, Hawaii | 5 | 3 | .625 | 2.26 | 38 | 0 | 0 | 31 | 0 | 20 | 55.2 | 35 | 15 | 14 | 4 | 0 | 22 | 2 | 54 | 3 |
| Kristan, Las Vegas | 1 | 0 | 1.000 | 5.00 | 11 | 0 | 0 | 4 | 0 | 1 | 18.0 | 24 | 11 | 10 | 0 | 1 | 2 | 0 | 13 | 0 |
| Krueger, Tacoma* | 0 | 1 | .000 | 9.31 | 2 | 2 | 0 | 0 | 0 | 0 | 9.2 | 12 | 10 | 10 | 2 | 0 | 6 | 0 | 10 | 0 |
| Kyles, Tacoma | 1 | 7 | .125 | 5.13 | 43 | 2 | 0 | 28 | 0 | 11 | 72.0 | 92 | 47 | 41 | 2 | 1 | 39 | 9 | 31 | 10 |
| Lacey, Tacoma* | 3 | 2 | .600 | 3.09 | 21 | 0 | 0 | 13 | 0 | 2 | 23.1 | 24 | 15 | 8 | 2 | 1 | 11 | 3 | 11 | 0 |
| Ladd, Vancouver | 0 | 0 | .000 | 2.00 | 5 | 0 | 0 | 3 | 0 | 1 | 9.0 | 6 | 2 | 2 | 0 | 1 | 1 | 0 | 5 | 0 |
| Lambert, Tacoma | 10 | 10 | .500 | 4.27 | 28 | 28 | 3 | 0 | 2 | 0 | 173.0 | 165 | 93 | 82 | 20 | 2 | 80 | 0 | 66 | 9 |
| Lazorko, 22 Phx-22 Cal | 5 | 5 | .500 | 2.06 | 44 | 0 | 0 | 30 | 0 | 8 | 74.1 | 56 | 20 | 17 | 5 | 6 | 21 | 7 | 52 | 3 |
| Leary, Vancouver | 10 | 7 | .588 | 4.00 | 27 | 27 | 3 | 0 | 1 | 0 | 177.2 | 174 | 85 | 79 | 9 | 5 | 57 | 1 | 136 | 6 |
| Leiper, Tacoma* | 0 | 1 | .000 | 5.40 | 15 | 0 | 0 | 5 | 0 | 2 | 23.1 | 29 | 16 | 14 | 1 | 1 | 12 | 2 | 7 | 0 |
| Leopold, Las Vegas | 3 | 4 | .429 | 5.66 | 22 | 11 | 0 | 3 | 0 | 0 | 68.1 | 73 | 48 | 43 | 8 | 4 | 50 | 1 | 33 | 1 |
| Lerch, Portland* | 6 | 6 | .500 | 2.75 | 20 | 17 | 1 | 1 | 0 | 0 | 108.0 | 84 | 44 | 33 | 8 | 2 | 56 | 1 | 68 | 7 |
| Lesley, Vancouver | 3 | 5 | .375 | 2.24 | 48 | 0 | 0 | 42 | 0 | 17 | 56.1 | 41 | 15 | 14 | 3 | 1 | 26 | 2 | 50 | 2 |
| Lewis, Calgary | 7 | 7 | .500 | 6.47 | 20 | 16 | 1 | 0 | 0 | 0 | 103.0 | 130 | 83 | 74 | 8 | 1 | 37 | 2 | 52 | 3 |
| Long, Calgary | 3 | 1 | .750 | 2.10 | 19 | 0 | 0 | 9 | 0 | 5 | 34.1 | 24 | 9 | 8 | 1 | 4 | 15 | 2 | 32 | 2 |
| Luecken, Calgary | 4 | 8 | .333 | 6.93 | 18 | 14 | 2 | 4 | 0 | 0 | 85.2 | 111 | 70 | 66 | 12 | 1 | 39 | 1 | 44 | 5 |
| Lugo, Edmonton | 1 | 0 | 1.000 | 4.56 | 4 | 4 | 1 | 0 | 0 | 0 | 25.2 | 20 | 14 | 13 | 3 | 1 | 14 | 0 | 19 | 2 |
| Mack, Edmonton | 8 | 14 | .364 | 4.74 | 25 | 25 | 6 | 0 | 3 | 0 | 153.2 | 179 | 103 | 81 | 13 | 2 | 81 | 2 | 100 | 4 |
| Madden, Tucson* | 2 | 0 | 1.000 | 3.52 | 6 | 3 | 0 | 1 | 0 | 0 | 23.0 | 24 | 11 | 9 | 1 | 0 | 11 | 0 | 14 | 1 |
| Maddux, Portland | 9 | 12 | .429 | 5.31 | 27 | 26 | 6 | 1 | 1 | 0 | 166.0 | 195 | 106 | 98 | 15 | 4 | 51 | 4 | 96 | 13 |

| Pitcher—Club | W. | L. | Pct. | ERA. | G. | GS. | CG. | GF. | ShO. | Sv. | IP. | H. | R. | ER. | HR. | HB. | BB. | Int. BB. | SO. | WP. |
|---|---|---|---|---|---|---|---|---|---|---|---|---|---|---|---|---|---|---|---|---|
| S. Martin, Albuquerque | 3 | 5 | .375 | 5.08 | 42 | 5 | 0 | 10 | 0 | 1 | 102.2 | 122 | 72 | 58 | 11 | 1 | 62 | 2 | 53 | 9 |
| V. Martin, Calgary | 2 | 2 | .500 | 4.44 | 6 | 5 | 0 | 0 | 0 | 0 | 26.1 | 29 | 13 | 13 | 2 | 0 | 14 | 0 | 22 | 0 |
| Martz, Tucson | 2 | 5 | .286 | 5.33 | 24 | 15 | 0 | 5 | 0 | 1 | 101.1 | 121 | 70 | 60 | 8 | 2 | 41 | 3 | 33 | 3 |
| Mason, Phoenix | 12 | 1 | .923 | 3.33 | 24 | 24 | 5 | 0 | 2 | 0 | 167.1 | 145 | 67 | 62 | 12 | 4 | 72 | 6 | 120 | 6 |
| Mathis, Tucson | 4 | 2 | .667 | 4.50 | 7 | 6 | 1 | 0 | 0 | 0 | 44.0 | 45 | 24 | 22 | 6 | 0 | 19 | 0 | 29 | 0 |
| McCaskill, Edmonton | 1 | 1 | .500 | 2.04 | 3 | 3 | 0 | 0 | 0 | 0 | 17.2 | 17 | 7 | 4 | 1 | 0 | 6 | 0 | 18 | 0 |
| McCullers, Las Vegas | 11 | 8 | .579 | 3.98 | 24 | 24 | 3 | 0 | 1 | 0 | 149.1 | 135 | 75 | 66 | 11 | 6 | 83 | 2 | 148 | 2 |
| McKnight, Phoenix | 8 | 4 | .667 | 3.44 | 17 | 17 | 0 | 0 | 0 | 0 | 99.1 | 89 | 47 | 38 | 4 | 1 | 65 | 4 | 55 | 5 |
| J. McLaughlin, Tacoma | 2 | 4 | .333 | 4.13 | 38 | 0 | 0 | 17 | 0 | 1 | 56.2 | 50 | 29 | 26 | 3 | 0 | 24 | 4 | 39 | 1 |
| M. McLaughlin, Tacoma | 7 | 6 | .538 | 3.57 | 38 | 4 | 0 | 15 | 0 | 0 | 80.2 | 80 | 35 | 32 | 6 | 3 | 31 | 4 | 51 | 4 |
| Meeks, Albuquerque | 12 | 15 | .444 | 3.93 | 32 | 29 | 6 | 3 | 1 | 0 | 183.0 | 187 | 93 | 80 | 14 | 0 | 62 | 3 | 120 | 1 |
| Miner, Tucson | 4 | 6 | .400 | 3.72 | 39 | 9 | 2 | 12 | 0 | 2 | 92.0 | 88 | 46 | 38 | 4 | 3 | 42 | 2 | 51 | 1 |
| Mirabella, Calgary* | 5 | 4 | .556 | 4.08 | 53 | 0 | 0 | 28 | 0 | 5 | 68.1 | 84 | 34 | 31 | 8 | 1 | 29 | 1 | 42 | 1 |
| Money, Portland | 0 | 0 | .000 | 8.10 | 6 | 1 | 0 | 4 | 0 | 0 | 10.0 | 15 | 9 | 9 | 0 | 0 | 6 | 0 | 6 | 0 |
| Monge, Hawaii* | 1 | 0 | 1.000 | 4.66 | 14 | 0 | 0 | 6 | 0 | 0 | 19.1 | 21 | 10 | 10 | 3 | 1 | 8 | 1 | 6 | 3 |
| Montalvo, 30 Alb-22 Tuc | 2 | 7 | .222 | 4.20 | 52 | 0 | 0 | 30 | 0 | 13 | 75.0 | 97 | 39 | 35 | 6 | 1 | 53 | 13 | 42 | 5 |
| Montgomery, Tucson | 0 | 2 | .000 | 4.60 | 12 | 0 | 0 | 9 | 0 | 0 | 15.2 | 17 | 9 | 8 | 0 | 1 | 4 | 1 | 8 | 0 |
| Mooneyham, Tacoma | 2 | 6 | .250 | 4.18 | 21 | 7 | 0 | 12 | 0 | 6 | 60.1 | 56 | 28 | 28 | 4 | 1 | 38 | 4 | 49 | 0 |
| Moore, Phoenix | 6 | 2 | .750 | 3.50 | 50 | 0 | 0 | 31 | 0 | 14 | 79.2 | 69 | 31 | 31 | 7 | 0 | 41 | 6 | 60 | 3 |
| Morgan, Calgary | 0 | 0 | .000 | 4.50 | 1 | 1 | 0 | 0 | 0 | 0 | 2.0 | 3 | 1 | 1 | 0 | 0 | 0 | 0 | 0 | 0 |
| Moses, Portland* | 0 | 0 | .000 | 0.00 | 1 | 0 | 0 | 1 | 0 | 0 | 1.0 | 1 | 0 | 0 | 0 | 0 | 0 | 0 | 0 | 0 |
| Mura, Tacoma | 7 | 5 | .583 | 3.65 | 16 | 16 | 4 | 0 | 1 | 0 | 111.0 | 103 | 55 | 45 | 5 | 2 | 35 | 1 | 89 | 3 |
| Murray, Calgary | 1 | 1 | .500 | 6.17 | 3 | 2 | 0 | 0 | 0 | 0 | 11.2 | 19 | 14 | 8 | 0 | 1 | 6 | 0 | 12 | 1 |
| Myers, Vancouver | 2 | 0 | 1.000 | 3.48 | 14 | 0 | 0 | 4 | 0 | 0 | 33.2 | 33 | 14 | 13 | 2 | 3 | 19 | 1 | 23 | 2 |
| Nago, Vancouver | 0 | 0 | .000 | 0.00 | 1 | 0 | 0 | 0 | 0 | 0 | 1.1 | 2 | 0 | 0 | 0 | 0 | 0 | 0 | 1 | 0 |
| Nahorodny, Portland | 0 | 0 | .000 | 9.00 | 4 | 0 | 0 | 4 | 0 | 0 | 4.0 | 7 | 4 | 4 | 0 | 0 | 2 | 0 | 2 | 2 |
| Nieves, Vancouver* | 8 | 3 | .727 | 3.80 | 12 | 12 | 0 | 0 | 0 | 0 | 68.2 | 56 | 30 | 29 | 9 | 2 | 44 | 0 | 54 | 0 |
| Oliver, Edmonton | 2 | 0 | 1.000 | 4.25 | 32 | 4 | 0 | 13 | 0 | 2 | 91.0 | 124 | 54 | 43 | 8 | 4 | 32 | 1 | 39 | 7 |
| Ontiveros, Tacoma | 3 | 0 | 1.000 | 2.94 | 15 | 0 | 0 | 7 | 0 | 2 | 33.2 | 26 | 13 | 11 | 1 | 2 | 21 | 2 | 30 | 1 |
| Owchinko, Tacoma* | 3 | 5 | .375 | 5.73 | 16 | 7 | 1 | 5 | 0 | 1 | 37.2 | 52 | 30 | 24 | 3 | 1 | 18 | 4 | 20 | 1 |
| Page, Hawaii | 0 | 0 | .000 | 27.00 | 1 | 0 | 0 | 1 | 0 | 0 | 1.0 | 3 | 3 | 3 | 1 | 0 | 2 | 0 | 1 | 0 |
| Patterson, Las Vegas* | 10 | 11 | .476 | 3.14 | 42 | 20 | 7 | 16 | 1 | 6 | 186.1 | 187 | 80 | 65 | 19 | 1 | 52 | 5 | 146 | 5 |
| Pederson, Albuquerque* | 0 | 0 | .000 | 0.00 | 1 | 0 | 0 | 1 | 0 | 0 | 1.0 | 1 | 0 | 0 | 0 | 0 | 1 | 0 | 0 | 0 |
| Plunk, Tacoma | 0 | 5 | .000 | 5.77 | 11 | 10 | 0 | 0 | 0 | 0 | 53.0 | 51 | 41 | 34 | 3 | 2 | 50 | 3 | 43 | 4 |
| Powell, Albuquerque* | 9 | 0 | 1.000 | 2.74 | 18 | 17 | 3 | 1 | 0 | 0 | 111.2 | 106 | 40 | 34 | 5 | 1 | 48 | 0 | 55 | 6 |
| Reece, Tacoma | 0 | 0 | .000 | 0.00 | 2 | 0 | 0 | 2 | 0 | 0 | 1.2 | 0 | 0 | 0 | 0 | 0 | 1 | 0 | 0 | 0 |
| Rennicke, Albuquerque | 0 | 0 | .000 | 10.13 | 2 | 0 | 0 | 1 | 0 | 0 | 2.2 | 7 | 6 | 3 | 0 | 0 | 2 | 0 | 1 | 1 |
| Reuschel, Hawaii | 6 | 2 | .750 | 2.50 | 8 | 8 | 2 | 0 | 0 | 0 | 54.0 | 52 | 18 | 15 | 2 | 1 | 12 | 1 | 46 | 5 |
| Rijo, Tacoma | 7 | 10 | .412 | 2.90 | 24 | 24 | 3 | 0 | 1 | 0 | 149.0 | 116 | 64 | 48 | 6 | 0 | 108 | 3 | 179 | 4 |
| Riley, Phoenix* | 6 | 7 | .462 | 4.84 | 46 | 7 | 1 | 24 | 0 | 11 | 89.1 | 97 | 52 | 48 | 8 | 0 | 43 | 6 | 64 | 3 |
| Roberts, Vancouver | 1 | 2 | .333 | 6.26 | 12 | 3 | 0 | 6 | 0 | 0 | 27.1 | 33 | 21 | 19 | 2 | 0 | 13 | 0 | 17 | 1 |
| Robinson, Phoenix | 9 | 9 | .500 | 5.14 | 29 | 29 | 5 | 0 | 1 | 0 | 161.0 | 192 | 107 | 92 | 14 | 4 | 60 | 7 | 80 | 11 |
| Rodas, Albuquerque* | 0 | 0 | .000 | 4.50 | 2 | 0 | 0 | 2 | 0 | 0 | 2.0 | 4 | 1 | 1 | 0 | 0 | 0 | 0 | 0 | 0 |
| Rodriguez, Tacoma | 0 | 1 | .000 | 4.05 | 7 | 1 | 0 | 4 | 0 | 0 | 13.1 | 18 | 9 | 6 | 2 | 0 | 7 | 2 | 5 | 1 |
| Rogers, Edmonton | 1 | 2 | .333 | 4.08 | 5 | 5 | 2 | 0 | 0 | 0 | 35.1 | 42 | 19 | 16 | 2 | 2 | 13 | 0 | 20 | 1 |
| Romero, Edmonton | 0 | 0 | .000 | 9.00 | 1 | 0 | 0 | 1 | 0 | 0 | 1.0 | 2 | 1 | 1 | 0 | 1 | 0 | 0 | 0 | 1 |
| Ross, Tucson | 8 | 5 | .615 | 3.62 | 46 | 0 | 0 | 38 | 0 | 11 | 77.0 | 109 | 38 | 31 | 3 | 0 | 21 | 6 | 31 | 2 |
| Rucker, Portland* | 1 | 0 | 1.000 | 4.50 | 10 | 0 | 0 | 5 | 0 | 1 | 16.0 | 15 | 9 | 8 | 2 | 0 | 4 | 0 | 17 | 0 |
| Sanchez, Edmonton | 0 | 0 | .000 | 10.13 | 4 | 0 | 0 | 4 | 0 | 0 | 5.1 | 7 | 6 | 6 | 1 | 0 | 2 | 1 | 4 | 1 |
| Sarmiento, Hawaii | 5 | 8 | .385 | 3.18 | 18 | 16 | 3 | 0 | 1 | 0 | 107.2 | 102 | 48 | 38 | 6 | 3 | 31 | 3 | 81 | 1 |
| Schefsky, Las Vegas | 0 | 4 | .000 | 5.20 | 13 | 2 | 0 | 6 | 0 | 1 | 27.2 | 26 | 22 | 16 | 6 | 2 | 10 | 1 | 17 | 0 |
| Scherer, Tacoma | 0 | 1 | .000 | 7.89 | 8 | 3 | 0 | 2 | 0 | 0 | 21.2 | 26 | 20 | 19 | 2 | 0 | 23 | 0 | 10 | 2 |
| Scudder, Albuquerque | 0 | 2 | .000 | 11.85 | 11 | 1 | 0 | 5 | 0 | 0 | 13.2 | 25 | 20 | 18 | 1 | 2 | 21 | 2 | 10 | 0 |
| Searage, Vancouver* | 2 | 0 | 1.000 | 2.42 | 23 | 0 | 0 | 15 | 0 | 7 | 26.0 | 22 | 10 | 7 | 5 | 2 | 12 | 2 | 31 | 0 |
| Semall, Hawaii | 6 | 5 | .545 | 5.17 | 24 | 10 | 0 | 3 | 0 | 0 | 85.1 | 93 | 65 | 49 | 8 | 3 | 35 | 0 | 49 | 4 |
| Senteney, Calgary | 2 | 2 | .500 | 4.76 | 28 | 1 | 0 | 5 | 0 | 0 | 62.1 | 86 | 41 | 33 | 11 | 2 | 16 | 0 | 39 | 2 |
| Serna, Calgary | 0 | 0 | .000 | 3.00 | 3 | 0 | 0 | 3 | 0 | 0 | 6.0 | 6 | 2 | 2 | 0 | 1 | 4 | 0 | 3 | 0 |
| Shipanoff, Portland | 8 | 5 | .615 | 2.65 | 51 | 2 | 0 | 32 | 0 | 13 | 91.2 | 73 | 30 | 27 | 8 | 0 | 40 | 6 | 115 | 0 |
| Shirley, Hawaii* | 3 | 5 | .375 | 4.56 | 15 | 7 | 1 | 0 | 0 | 0 | 53.1 | 51 | 34 | 27 | 2 | 0 | 19 | 1 | 40 | 4 |
| Simmons, Las Vegas | 0 | 1 | .000 | 11.12 | 6 | 1 | 0 | 2 | 0 | 0 | 5.2 | 8 | 11 | 7 | 1 | 1 | 9 | 1 | 5 | 1 |
| Da. Smith, Edmonton | 6 | 7 | .462 | 3.75 | 42 | 0 | 0 | 30 | 0 | 12 | 72.0 | 78 | 32 | 30 | 3 | 1 | 20 | 6 | 29 | 4 |
| Do. Smith, Albuquerque | 7 | 6 | .538 | 4.15 | 55 | 0 | 0 | 35 | 0 | 12 | 95.1 | 120 | 55 | 44 | 12 | 2 | 33 | 17 | 39 | 3 |
| R. Smith, Las Vegas | 0 | 0 | .000 | 0.00 | 1 | 0 | 0 | 1 | 0 | 0 | 1.0 | 1 | 0 | 0 | 0 | 0 | 0 | 0 | 0 | 0 |
| Snyder, Calgary* | 4 | 2 | .667 | 4.00 | 20 | 9 | 2 | 3 | 0 | 1 | 69.2 | 76 | 36 | 31 | 7 | 2 | 26 | 0 | 46 | 5 |
| Solano, Tucson | 2 | 3 | .400 | 3.98 | 23 | 0 | 0 | 19 | 0 | 6 | 31.2 | 25 | 16 | 14 | 4 | 1 | 21 | 3 | 23 | 4 |
| Sonberg, Albuquerque* | 2 | 6 | .250 | 7.45 | 26 | 9 | 0 | 6 | 0 | 2 | 54.1 | 65 | 54 | 45 | 7 | 2 | 33 | 5 | 30 | 6 |
| Stoddard, Calgary | 1 | 3 | .250 | 5.90 | 7 | 7 | 0 | 0 | 0 | 0 | 39.2 | 55 | 31 | 26 | 3 | 2 | 13 | 3 | 33 | 1 |
| Surhoff, Calgary | 7 | 8 | .467 | 3.17 | 70 | 0 | 0 | 41 | 0 | 16 | 110.2 | 107 | 44 | 39 | 6 | 0 | 44 | 5 | 91 | 0 |
| Tejeda, Albuquerque* | 2 | 0 | 1.000 | 7.71 | 9 | 0 | 0 | 5 | 0 | 0 | 16.1 | 24 | 16 | 14 | 1 | 0 | 8 | 0 | 14 | 1 |
| Tellmann, Tacoma | 0 | 2 | .000 | 5.84 | 8 | 0 | 0 | 5 | 0 | 1 | 12.1 | 12 | 8 | 8 | 2 | 1 | 3 | 1 | 6 | 0 |
| J. Thomas, Las Vegas | 0 | 0 | .000 | 9.00 | 1 | 0 | 0 | 1 | 0 | 0 | 1.0 | 1 | 1 | 1 | 0 | 0 | 0 | 0 | 0 | 0 |
| R. Thomas, Calgary | 2 | 2 | .500 | 4.55 | 15 | 0 | 0 | 9 | 0 | 1 | 29.2 | 29 | 15 | 15 | 2 | 0 | 13 | 1 | 40 | 1 |
| Tillman, Las Vegas | 0 | 0 | .000 | 27.00 | 1 | 0 | 0 | 0 | 0 | 0 | 1.0 | 5 | 6 | 3 | 0 | 1 | 1 | 0 | 1 | 1 |
| Tobik, Calgary | 12 | 6 | .667 | 5.18 | 56 | 1 | 0 | 30 | 0 | 5 | 88.2 | 98 | 59 | 51 | 8 | 2 | 58 | 9 | 97 | 9 |
| Tomlin, Hawaii* | 8 | 2 | .800 | 2.09 | 33 | 4 | 0 | 19 | 0 | 4 | 82.0 | 62 | 22 | 19 | 3 | 0 | 35 | 3 | 65 | 3 |
| Tunnell, Hawaii | 4 | 1 | .800 | 2.31 | 7 | 7 | 2 | 0 | 2 | 0 | 46.2 | 32 | 12 | 12 | 2 | 1 | 24 | 0 | 29 | 3 |
| Vanderbush, Las Vegas | 2 | 4 | .333 | 6.44 | 42 | 3 | 0 | 23 | 0 | 5 | 88.0 | 94 | 69 | 63 | 13 | 3 | 66 | 11 | 73 | 7 |
| Vila, Albuquerque | 1 | 2 | .333 | 4.11 | 11 | 0 | 0 | 9 | 0 | 1 | 15.1 | 15 | 8 | 7 | 1 | 0 | 7 | 0 | 8 | 2 |
| Waits, Vancouver* | 10 | 5 | .667 | 2.87 | 16 | 16 | 5 | 0 | 1 | 0 | 116.0 | 108 | 43 | 37 | 6 | 0 | 22 | 3 | 64 | 4 |
| Walk, Hawaii | 16 | 5 | .762 | 2.65 | 24 | 24 | 12 | 0 | 1 | 0 | 173.0 | 143 | 57 | 51 | 10 | 4 | 61 | 1 | 124 | 0 |
| Walter, Las Vegas* | 7 | 5 | .583 | 2.75 | 45 | 2 | 0 | 27 | 0 | 12 | 95.0 | 75 | 34 | 29 | 3 | 5 | 35 | 5 | 107 | 6 |
| Ward, Phoenix* | 3 | 0 | 1.000 | 5.88 | 22 | 2 | 0 | 2 | 0 | 1 | 41.1 | 45 | 27 | 27 | 3 | 2 | 30 | 2 | 31 | 1 |
| Warren, Tacoma | 1 | 2 | .333 | 5.09 | 12 | 1 | 0 | 4 | 0 | 1 | 23.0 | 17 | 15 | 13 | 2 | 2 | 24 | 1 | 24 | 5 |
| Wegman, Vancouver | 10 | 11 | .476 | 4.02 | 28 | 28 | 8 | 0 | 2 | 0 | 188.0 | 187 | 93 | 84 | 21 | 5 | 52 | 5 | 113 | 2 |
| White, Albuquerque | 8 | 12 | .400 | 4.34 | 31 | 25 | 6 | 4 | 2 | 0 | 159.2 | 186 | 96 | 77 | 15 | 1 | 54 | 2 | 114 | 7 |
| Whitmer, Calgary | 7 | 8 | .467 | 4.90 | 29 | 28 | 4 | 0 | 0 | 0 | 180.0 | 208 | 115 | 98 | 15 | 6 | 50 | 3 | 84 | 14 |
| Wilkinson, Calgary* | 5 | 1 | .833 | 2.67 | 9 | 9 | 3 | 0 | 0 | 0 | 57.1 | 44 | 21 | 17 | 0 | 1 | 25 | 0 | 42 | 5 |
| Williams, Phoenix | 1 | 1 | .500 | 3.95 | 9 | 0 | 0 | 3 | 0 | 0 | 13.2 | 10 | 8 | 6 | 3 | 0 | 14 | 1 | 10 | 0 |
| Wills, Calgary | 4 | 3 | .571 | 4.86 | 9 | 9 | 3 | 0 | 2 | 0 | 46.1 | 44 | 27 | 25 | 5 | 0 | 25 | 0 | 31 | 3 |
| Winn, Hawaii | 5 | 2 | .714 | 3.38 | 7 | 7 | 0 | 0 | 0 | 0 | 42.2 | 31 | 19 | 16 | 1 | 0 | 20 | 0 | 33 | 4 |
| Wojna, Las Vegas | 5 | 8 | .385 | 4.45 | 18 | 18 | 6 | 0 | 0 | 0 | 111.1 | 121 | 63 | 55 | 9 | 1 | 43 | 3 | 66 | 10 |
| Young, Tacoma* | 2 | 0 | 1.000 | 3.60 | 3 | 3 | 0 | 0 | 0 | 0 | 15.0 | 10 | 7 | 6 | 1 | 0 | 7 | 0 | 8 | 0 |
| Zaske, Hawaii | 2 | 7 | .222 | 3.41 | 46 | 0 | 0 | 30 | 0 | 5 | 68.2 | 51 | 28 | 26 | 3 | 1 | 57 | 6 | 75 | 15 |

BALKS—Rijo, 11; Candiotti, Chris, 5 each; Crim, Downs, Ghelfi, S. Martin, Walk, 4 each; Dozier, Fowlkes, Heathcock, Holton, Plunk, 3 each; Bastian, Gonzalez, Groh, Hayward, Kerfeld, Kyles, Lambert, Maddux, Mathis, McCullers, Meeks, Miner, Murray, Oliver, Patterson, Powell, Riley, Roberts, Scherer, Shirley, Snyder, Walter, Whitmer, Wojna, 2 each; Acker, Barnes, Bielecki, Callahan, Citarella, Clutterbuck, Comer, Finch, Gaynor, Giddings, Hausman, Hensley, Jeffcoat, Kain, Kaiser, Kibbe, Kipper, Leary, Mack, Madden, McKnight, Montalvo, Mooneyham, Mura, Page, Reuschel, Rodriguez, Scudder, Shipanoff, Simmons, Stoddard, Surhoff, Ward, Winn, 1 each.

COMBINATION SHUTOUTS—Brennan-Sonberg, Kibbe-Montalvo, Kibbe-Smith, Holton-Tejeda-Martin, Powell-Montalvo, Albuquerque; Wilkinson-Long, Calgary; McCaskill-Kaufman, Edmonton; Fansler-Tomlin-Krawczyk, Sarmiento-Shirley-Krawczyk, Sarmiento-Tomlin, Walk-Krawczyk, Walk-Zaske, Hawaii; McCullers-Walter, Patterson-Leopold, Patterson-Walter, Las Vegas; Jeffcoat-Moore, Mason-Riley, McKnight-Hensley, Phoenix; Citarella-Childress, Comer-Surhoff, Davisson-Childress, Portland; Conroy-Kaiser, Conroy-Kyles, Kaiser-Kyles-Mooneyham, Lambert-Kaiser, Owchinko-Ontiveros, Rijo-Owchinko-Tellmann, Rijo-Warren, Tacoma; Acker-Martz, Tucson; Wegman-Lesley 2, Candiotti-Crim, Vancouver.

NO-HIT GAMES—Sonberg-Martin, Albuquerque, defeated Hawaii, 7-1, April 25; Johnson, Hawaii, defeated Calgary, 5-0, May 2; Conroy, Tacoma, defeated Tucson, 1-0 (seven innings, first game), May 14; Wills, Calgary, defeated Tacoma, 1-0 (seven innings, first game), May 31; Waits, Vancouver, defeated Portland, 7-0, June 20.

# Eastern League

## CLASS AA

**Leading Batter**
**ANDY ALLANSON**
**Waterbury**

**League President**
**CHARLES ESHBACH**

**Leading Pitcher**
**BRAD ARNSBERG**
**Albany**

### CHAMPIONSHIP WINNERS IN PREVIOUS YEARS

| | | |
|---|---|---|
| 1923—Williamsport .661 | 1946—Scranton† .691 | Reading (2nd)‡ .579 |
| 1924—Williamsport .654 | 1947—Utica† .652 | 1969—York .640 |
| 1925—York§ .583 | 1948—Scranton† .636 | 1970—Waterbury a .560 |
| Williamsport§ .583 | 1949—Albany .664 | Reading a .553 |
| 1926—Scranton .627 | Binghamton (4th)‡ .500 | 1971—Three Rivers .569 |
| 1927—Harrisburg .630 | 1950—Wilkes-Barre‡ .652 | Elmira b .561 |
| 1928—Harrisburg .603 | 1951—Wilkes-Barre .612 | 1972—West Haven b .600 |
| 1929—Binghamton .597 | Scranton (2nd)† .562 | Three Rivers .559 |
| 1930—Wilkes-Barre .572 | 1952—Albany .603 | 1973—Reading b .551 |
| 1931—Harrisburg .597 | Binghamton (2nd)‡ .562 | Pittsfield .551 |
| 1932—Wilkes-Barre .561 | 1953—Reading .682 | 1974—Thetford Mines (2nd)c .536 |
| 1933—Binghamton .690 | Binghamton (2nd)‡ .636 | Pittsfield (2nd) .496 |
| 1934—Binghamton .694 | 1954—Wilkes-Barre .576 | 1975—Reading .613 |
| Williamsport* .603 | Albany (3rd)‡ .540 | Bristol* .587 |
| 1935—Scranton .657 | 1955—Reading .613 | 1976—Three Rivers .601 |
| Binghamton* .580 | Allentown (2nd)‡ .565 | West Haven d .576 |
| 1936—Scranton* .609 | 1956—Schenectady† .609 | 1977—West Haven e .623 |
| Elmira .629 | 1957—Binghamton .607 | Three Rivers .551 |
| 1937—Elmira† .622 | Reading (3rd)‡ .529 | 1978—Reading .642 |
| 1938—Binghamton .622 | 1958—Lancaster x .568 | Bristol* .580 |
| Elmira (3rd)‡ .522 | Binghamton (6th)‡ .493 | 1979—West Haven f .597 |
| 1939—Scranton† .571 | 1959—Springfield† .607 | 1980—Holyoke* .561 |
| 1940—Scranton .568 | 1960—Williamsport y .551 | Waterbury .540 |
| Binghamton (2nd)‡ .554 | Springfield (3rd)y .496 | 1981—Glens Falls .615 |
| 1941—Wilkes-Barre .630 | 1961—Springfield .612 | Bristol* .577 |
| Elmira (3rd)‡ .514 | 1962—Williamsport .593 | 1982—West Haven* .614 |
| 1942—Albany .600 | Elmira (2nd)‡ .514 | Lynn .590 |
| Scranton (2nd)‡ .593 | 1963—Charleston .593 | 1983—Lynn .554 |
| 1943—Scranton .630 | 1964—Elmira .586 | New Britain‡ .518 |
| Elmira (2nd)‡ .568 | 1965—Pittsfield .607 | 1984—Waterbury .543 |
| 1944—Hartford .723 | 1966—Elmira .633 | Vermont‡ .536 |
| Binghamton (4th)‡ .474 | 1967—Binghamton z .586 | |
| 1945—Utica .615 | Elmira .532 | |
| Albany (3rd)‡ .564 | 1968—Pittsfield .604 | |

*Won split-season playoff. †Won championship and four-team playoff. ‡Won four-team playoff. §Tied for pennant, York winning playoff. xLeague was divided into Northern, Southern divisions and played a split season; Lancaster over-all season leader. yPlayoff finals canceled after one game because of rain with Williamsport and Springfield declared playoff co-champions. zLeague was divided into Eastern, Western divisions; Binghamton won playoff. aTied for pennant, Waterbury winning playoff. bLeague was divided into American, National divisions; won playoff. cLeague was divided into American and National divisions; won four-team playoff. dLeague was divided into Northern, Southern divisions, won playoff. eLeague was divided into New England and Canadian-American divisions; won playoff. fWon both halves of split season (no playoffs). (NOTE—Known as New York-Pennsylvania League prior to 1938.)

## STANDING OF CLUBS AT CLOSE OF SEASON, AUGUST 31

| Club | Alb. | Wat. | N.B. | Vrt. | G.F. | Nash. | Pitt. | Read. | W. | L. | T. | Pct. | G.B. |
|---|---|---|---|---|---|---|---|---|---|---|---|---|---|
| Albany (Yankees) | .... | 13 | 11 | 10 | 12 | 12 | 13 | 11 | 82 | 57 | 0 | .590 | ........ |
| Waterbury (Indians) | 7 | .... | 6 | 12 | 8 | 10 | 17 | 15 | 75 | 64 | 0 | .540 | 7 |
| New Britain (Red Sox) | 9 | 14 | .... | 11 | 10 | 9 | 11 | 11 | 75 | 64 | 0 | .540 | 7 |
| Vermont (Reds) | 10 | 8 | 9 | .... | 10 | 9 | 11 | 14 | 71 | 67 | 0 | .514 | 10½ |
| Glens Falls (White Sox) | 8 | 11 | 10 | 10 | .... | 12 | 8 | 9 | 68 | 71 | 0 | .489 | 14 |
| Nashua (Pirates) | 7 | 10 | 11 | 11 | 8 | .... | 7 | 12 | 66 | 73 | 0 | .475 | 16 |
| Pittsfield (Cubs) | 7 | 3 | 8 | 9 | 12 | 13 | .... | 7 | 59 | 79 | 0 | .428 | 22½ |
| Reading (Phillies) | 9 | 5 | 9 | 4 | 11 | 8 | 12 | .... | 58 | 79 | 0 | .423 | 23 |

Vermont club represented Burlington, Vt.

Major league affiliations in parentheses.

Playoffs—Vermont defeated Albany, three games to one; New Britain defeated Waterbury, three games to one; Vermont defeated New Britain, three games to one, to win league championship.

Regular-Season Attendance—Albany, 324,003; Glens Falls, 69,260; Nashua, 73,867; New Britain, 90,802; Pittsfield, 60,585; Reading, 76,819; Vermont, 90,478; Waterbury, 37,318. Total, 823,132; Playoffs, 16,380 (12 games); All-Star Game at Nashua, N.H. 1,385.

Managers—Albany, Barry Foote; Glens Falls, Steve Dillard; Nashua, Johnny Lipon; New Britain, Ed Nottle; Pittsfield, Tom Spencer; Reading, Tony Taylor; Vermont, Jack Lind; Waterbury, Jack Aker.

All-Star Team—1B—Russ Morman, Glens Falls; 2B—Jeff Treadway, Vermont; 3B—Cory Snyder, Waterbury; SS—Mike Brumley, Pittsfield; OF—Randy Washington, Waterbury; Dave Clark, Waterbury; Dana Williams, New Britain; C—Andy Allanson, Waterbury; DH—Orestes Destrade, Albany; RHP—Brad Arnsberg, Albany; LHP—Scott Bailes, Nashua/Waterbury; Relief Pitcher—Barry Jones, Nashua; Most Valuable Player—Cory Snyder, Waterbury; Manager of the Year—Barry Foote, Albany.

(Compiled by Howe News Bureau, Boston, Mass.)

## CLUB BATTING

| Club | Pct. | G. | AB. | R. | OR. | H. | TB. | 2B. | 3B. | HR. | RBI. | GW. | SH. | SF. | HP. | BB. | Int. BB. | SO. | SB. | CS. | LOB. |
|---|---|---|---|---|---|---|---|---|---|---|---|---|---|---|---|---|---|---|---|---|---|
| Vermont | .269 | 138 | 4546 | 617 | 549 | 1221 | 1708 | 163 | 39 | 82 | 539 | 61 | 50 | 38 | 34 | 523 | 32 | 666 | 129 | 47 | 1058 |
| New Britain | .261 | 139 | 4364 | 613 | 515 | 1138 | 1649 | 198 | 50 | 71 | 545 | 64 | 64 | 42 | 45 | 579 | 28 | 648 | 113 | 83 | 1001 |
| Reading | .257 | 137 | 4338 | 546 | 635 | 1115 | 1550 | 173 | 38 | 62 | 494 | 52 | 43 | 36 | 39 | 450 | 31 | 759 | 101 | 76 | 945 |
| Waterbury | .255 | 139 | 4465 | 640 | 628 | 1137 | 1604 | 176 | 27 | 79 | 565 | 71 | 35 | 63 | 36 | 575 | 20 | 809 | 140 | 76 | 979 |
| Glens Falls | .254 | 139 | 4408 | 603 | 651 | 1118 | 1613 | 177 | 30 | 86 | 546 | 61 | 39 | 46 | 30 | 544 | 19 | 710 | 97 | 68 | 967 |
| Pittsfield | .248 | 138 | 4334 | 547 | 587 | 1076 | 1440 | 168 | 44 | 36 | 485 | 54 | 56 | 42 | 27 | 579 | 27 | 711 | 134 | 60 | 993 |
| Albany | .240 | 139 | 4437 | 624 | 553 | 1065 | 1613 | 189 | 52 | 85 | 532 | 67 | 62 | 35 | 28 | 581 | 28 | 788 | 123 | 65 | 935 |
| Nashua | .235 | 139 | 4337 | 495 | 567 | 1021 | 1370 | 154 | 27 | 47 | 420 | 58 | 61 | 39 | 44 | 415 | 25 | 703 | 173 | 92 | 839 |

## INDIVIDUAL BATTING

(Leading Qualifiers for Batting Championship—378 or More Plate Appearances)

*Bats lefthanded.     †Switch-hitter.

| Player and Club | Pct. | G. | AB. | R. | H. | TB. | 2B. | 3B. | HR. | RBI. | GW. | SH. | SF. | HP. | BB. | Int. BB. | SO. | SB. | CS. |
|---|---|---|---|---|---|---|---|---|---|---|---|---|---|---|---|---|---|---|---|
| Allanson, Andrew, Waterbury | .312 | 120 | 420 | 69 | 131 | 150 | 17 | 1 | 0 | 47 | 4 | 8 | 4 | 3 | 52 | 1 | 25 | 22 | 9 |
| Morman, Russell, Glens Falls | .310 | 119 | 422 | 64 | 131 | 216 | 24 | 5 | 17 | 81 | 9 | 1 | 3 | 5 | 65 | 3 | 51 | 11 | 10 |
| Williams, Dana, New Britain | .309 | 115 | 450 | 56 | 139 | 172 | 16 | 7 | 1 | 39 | 5 | 3 | 4 | 5 | 34 | 3 | 24 | 20 | 16 |
| Washington, Randy, Waterbury | .307 | 125 | 449 | 75 | 138 | 204 | 14 | 5 | 14 | 84 | 10 | 0 | 8 | 3 | 78 | 1 | 94 | 12 | 7 |
| Clark, David, Waterbury* | .302 | 132 | 463 | 75 | 140 | 214 | 24 | 7 | 12 | 64 | 7 | 1 | 4 | 1 | 86 | 0 | 79 | 27 | 12 |
| Treadway, Jeffrey, Vermont* | .302 | 129 | 431 | 63 | 130 | 155 | 17 | 1 | 2 | 49 | 3 | 5 | 5 | 2 | 71 | 2 | 40 | 6 | 5 |
| Hammond, Steven, Pittsfield* | .299 | 130 | 455 | 51 | 136 | 186 | 23 | 3 | 7 | 84 | 9 | 1 | 5 | 2 | 61 | 5 | 37 | 4 | 4 |
| Soper, Michael, Glens Falls | .296 | 132 | 480 | 50 | 142 | 170 | 16 | 0 | 4 | 49 | 7 | 2 | 6 | 3 | 26 | 0 | 51 | 5 | 6 |
| Miller, Keith, Reading† | .295 | 134 | 499 | 77 | 147 | .203 | 24 | 7 | 6 | 59 | 5 | 3 | 2 | 1 | 65 | 4 | 61 | 20 | 10 |
| Lee, Terry, Vermont | .289 | 121 | 409 | 56 | 118 | 178 | 20 | 2 | 12 | 62 | 9 | 4 | 4 | 3 | 48 | 2 | 51 | 4 | 0 |
| McLaughlin, David, Reading* | .286 | 109 | 388 | 52 | 111 | 133 | 16 | 3 | 0 | 32 | 3 | 7 | 3 | 0 | 38 | 2 | 26 | 4 | 3 |

Departmental Leaders: G—Snyder, 139; AB—K. Williams, 520; R—K. Williams, 87; H—Miller, 147; TB—Snyder, 255; 2B—Horn, 32; 3B—Brumley, 14; HR—Snyder, 28; RBI—Snyder, 94; GWRBI—Snyder, 14; SH—Russell, 22; SF—Snyder, 12; HP—Quinonez, 9; BB—Cannizzaro, 98; IBB—Horn, 14; SO—Destrade, 129; SB—R. Guzman, Roberts, Varsho, 40; CS—D. Williams, 16.

(All Players—Listed Alphabetically)

| Player and Club | Pct. | G. | AB. | R. | H. | TB. | 2B. | 3B. | HR. | RBI. | GW. | SH. | SF. | HP. | BB. | Int. BB. | SO. | SB. | CS. |
|---|---|---|---|---|---|---|---|---|---|---|---|---|---|---|---|---|---|---|---|
| Abrego, Johnny, Pittsfield | .207 | 24 | 29 | 2 | 6 | 6 | 0 | 0 | 0 | 2 | 0 | 4 | 0 | 0 | 2 | 0 | 7 | 0 | 0 |
| Ackley, John, New Britain | .267 | 41 | 120 | 18 | 32 | 50 | 6 | 0 | 4 | 20 | 1 | 5 | 0 | 0 | 17 | 0 | 26 | 4 | 0 |
| Alcazar, George, Glens Falls | .333 | 1 | 3 | 1 | 1 | 1 | 0 | 0 | 0 | 0 | 0 | 0 | 0 | 0 | 0 | 0 | 1 | 0 | 0 |
| Allanson, Andrew, Waterbury | .312 | 120 | 420 | 69 | 131 | 150 | 17 | 1 | 0 | 47 | 4 | 8 | 4 | 3 | 52 | 1 | 25 | 22 | 9 |
| Arnold, Jerry, Reading* | .077 | 27 | 13 | 1 | 1 | 1 | 0 | 0 | 0 | 0 | 0 | 2 | 0 | 0 | 0 | 0 | 5 | 0 | 0 |
| Arnsberg, Bradley, Albany | .000 | 21 | 1 | 0 | 0 | 0 | 0 | 0 | 0 | 0 | 0 | 0 | 0 | 0 | 0 | 0 | 0 | 0 | 0 |
| Bailes, Scott, 29 Nash-13 Water* | .000 | 42 | 4 | 0 | 0 | 0 | 0 | 0 | 0 | 1 | 0 | 0 | 0 | 0 | 0 | 0 | 2 | 0 | 0 |
| Baker, Kerry, Nashua | .174 | 47 | 121 | 10 | 21 | 34 | 5 | 1 | 2 | 6 | 0 | 2 | 1 | 0 | 11 | 0 | 36 | 0 | 3 |
| Barranca, German, Waterbury | .244 | 64 | 197 | 27 | 48 | 56 | 6 | 1 | 0 | 13 | 0 | 1 | 1 | 1 | 22 | 1 | 19 | 7 | 9 |
| Barrett, Thomas, Albany† | .262 | 57 | 233 | 40 | 61 | 78 | 8 | 3 | 1 | 18 | 1 | 1 | 1 | 2 | 25 | 1 | 19 | 23 | 9 |
| Beal, Anthony, New Britain | .226 | 108 | 301 | 53 | 68 | 105 | 8 | 7 | 5 | 26 | 2 | 2 | 1 | 7 | 65 | 1 | 71 | 14 | 9 |
| Bell, Jay, Waterbury | .298 | 29 | 114 | 13 | 34 | 52 | 11 | 2 | 1 | 14 | 1 | 1 | 0 | 0 | 9 | 1 | 16 | 3 | 3 |
| Bennett, James, New Britain* | .257 | 106 | 343 | 57 | 88 | 157 | 21 | 3 | 14 | 59 | 9 | 1 | 1 | 3 | 54 | 3 | 75 | 4 | 3 |
| Berge, Jordan, Vermont* | .417 | 4 | 12 | 3 | 5 | 5 | 0 | 0 | 0 | 2 | 0 | 0 | 0 | 0 | 0 | 0 | 0 | 0 | 0 |
| Berger, Michael, Nashua | .247 | 129 | 430 | 53 | 106 | 157 | 20 | 2 | 9 | 57 | 10 | 4 | 2 | 4 | 42 | 4 | 84 | 15 | 9 |
| Bernstine, Nehames, Pittsfield† | .312 | 50 | 202 | 33 | 63 | 82 | 6 | 5 | 1 | 17 | 1 | 1 | 0 | 3 | 20 | 0 | 26 | 17 | 2 |
| Blaser, Mark, Albany | .190 | 57 | 184 | 15 | 35 | 48 | 5 | 1 | 2 | 21 | 0 | 1 | 4 | 1 | 20 | 2 | 29 | 3 | 1 |
| Blevins, Bradley, Pittsfield | .000 | 38 | 3 | 1 | 0 | 0 | 0 | 0 | 0 | 0 | 0 | 1 | 0 | 0 | 0 | 0 | 2 | 0 | 0 |
| Bolton, Thomas, New Britain* | .000 | 34 | 0 | 0 | 0 | 0 | 0 | 0 | 0 | 0 | 0 | 1 | 0 | 0 | 0 | 0 | 0 | 0 | 0 |
| Bowden, Mark, Reading* | .167 | 15 | 6 | 2 | 1 | 1 | 0 | 0 | 0 | 0 | 0 | 0 | 0 | 0 | 0 | 0 | 0 | 0 | 0 |
| Bradley, Scott, Albany* | .125 | 6 | 24 | 2 | 3 | 4 | 1 | 0 | 2 | 1 | 0 | 0 | 0 | 2 | 0 | 1 | 0 | 0 | |
| Brown, Anthony, Reading* | .254 | 127 | 448 | 36 | 114 | 156 | 18 | 6 | 4 | 48 | 10 | 2 | 1 | 2 | 18 | 4 | 79 | 14 | 11 |
| Brown, Craig, Nashua | .214 | 121 | 379 | 45 | 81 | 139 | 18 | 2 | 12 | 50 | 7 | 6 | 5 | 4 | 39 | 0 | 79 | 6 | 7 |
| Brumley, Michael, Pittsfield† | .276 | 131 | 460 | 66 | 127 | 187 | 23 | 14 | 3 | 58 | 4 | 2 | 9 | 0 | 74 | 5 | 95 | 29 | 7 |
| Bulls, David, Reading | .000 | 16 | 7 | 0 | 0 | 0 | 0 | 0 | 0 | 0 | 0 | 2 | 0 | 0 | 0 | 0 | 1 | 0 | 0 |
| Burks, Ellis, New Britain | .254 | 133 | 476 | 66 | 121 | 190 | 25 | 7 | 10 | 61 | 7 | 2 | 4 | 3 | 42 | 0 | 85 | 17 | 14 |
| Burroughs, Darren, Vermont | .000 | 24 | 1 | 0 | 0 | 0 | 0 | 0 | 0 | 0 | 0 | 0 | 0 | 0 | 1 | 0 | 1 | 0 | 0 |
| Byron, Timothy, Albany | .000 | 27 | 1 | 0 | 0 | 0 | 0 | 0 | 0 | 0 | 0 | 0 | 1 | 0 | 0 | 0 | 0 | 0 | 0 |
| Cannizzaro, Chris, New Britain† | .262 | 134 | 466 | 77 | 122 | 153 | 16 | 6 | 1 | 38 | 6 | 16 | 1 | 1 | 98 | 2 | 26 | 16 | 13 |
| Capel, Michael, Pittsfield | .176 | 38 | 17 | 1 | 3 | 3 | 0 | 0 | 0 | 0 | 1 | 0 | 0 | 0 | 0 | 0 | 4 | 0 | 0 |
| Carpenter, Douglas, Albany | .305 | 71 | 203 | 27 | 62 | 88 | 11 | 6 | 1 | 26 | 4 | 2 | 2 | 2 | 18 | 0 | 38 | 10 | 4 |

| Player and Club | Pct. | G. | AB. | R. | H. | TB. | 2B. | 3B. | HR. | RBI. | GW. | SH. | SF. | HP. | BB. | Int. BB. | SO. | SB. | CS. |
|---|---|---|---|---|---|---|---|---|---|---|---|---|---|---|---|---|---|---|---|
| Carroll, Carson, Albany | .273 | 12 | 44 | 5 | 12 | 17 | 1 | 2 | 0 | 1 | 0 | 3 | 0 | 0 | 1 | 0 | 5 | 0 | 1 |
| Carter, Don, Waterbury° | .184 | 24 | 76 | 13 | 14 | 14 | 0 | 0 | 0 | 5 | 2 | 0 | 1 | 1 | 6 | 0 | 14 | 6 | 3 |
| Cathcart, Gary, Albany° | .244 | 20 | 45 | 4 | 11 | 13 | 2 | 0 | 0 | 5 | 0 | 1 | 0 | 0 | 6 | 1 | 10 | 1 | 0 |
| Cecchetti, George, Waterbury° | .242 | 115 | 389 | 59 | 94 | 137 | 23 | 1 | 6 | 52 | 8 | 0 | 5 | 4 | 56 | 2 | 71 | 6 | 4 |
| Chapman, Ronald, Albany† | .237 | 107 | 363 | 74 | 86 | 120 | 10 | 6 | 4 | 29 | 5 | 11 | 1 | 5 | 78 | 4 | 32 | 21 | 11 |
| Chestnut, Troy, Pittsfield | .053 | 31 | 19 | 0 | 1 | 1 | 0 | 0 | 0 | 1 | 0 | 0 | 1 | 0 | 1 | 0 | 9 | 0 | 0 |
| Christensen, Kim, Nashua | .170 | 38 | 100 | 11 | 17 | 20 | 1 | 1 | 0 | 13 | 1 | 1 | 2 | 2 | 10 | 0 | 23 | 0 | 0 |
| Cipolloni, Joseph, Reading | .244 | 87 | 287 | 21 | 70 | 95 | 11 | 1 | 4 | 34 | 1 | 1 | 4 | 4 | 13 | 3 | 43 | 1 | 7 |
| Clark, David, Waterbury° | .302 | 132 | 463 | 75 | 140 | 214 | 24 | 7 | 12 | 64 | 7 | 1 | 4 | 1 | 86 | 8 | 79 | 27 | 12 |
| Cordova, Antonio, Pittsfield | .227 | 30 | 97 | 8 | 22 | 30 | 6 | 1 | 0 | 11 | 2 | 0 | 1 | 1 | 10 | 0 | 20 | 3 | 0 |
| Cornell, Jeffrey, Pittsfield° | .000 | 30 | 12 | 0 | 0 | 0 | 0 | 0 | 0 | 0 | 0 | 2 | 0 | 0 | 3 | 0 | 10 | 0 | 0 |
| Cox, Jeffrey, Vermont | .250 | 4 | 4 | 1 | 1 | 1 | 0 | 0 | 0 | 0 | 0 | 0 | 0 | 0 | 1 | 0 | 0 | 0 | 0 |
| Dale, Charles, New Britain | .000 | 46 | 2 | 0 | 0 | 0 | 0 | 0 | 0 | 0 | 0 | 0 | 0 | 0 | 0 | 0 | 1 | 0 | 0 |
| Day, Randall, Reading | .228 | 73 | 232 | 25 | 53 | 88 | 8 | 0 | 9 | 34 | 1 | 1 | 6 | 2 | 26 | 1 | 45 | 1 | 1 |
| DeLaRosa, Nelson, Nashua° | .180 | 69 | 194 | 19 | 35 | 51 | 1 | 0 | 5 | 9 | 1 | 2 | 0 | 2 | 23 | 0 | 47 | 4 | 4 |
| Destrade, Orestes, Albany† | .253 | 136 | 471 | 82 | 119 | 222 | 24 | 5 | 23 | 72 | 9 | 0 | 6 | 1 | 86 | 8 | 129 | 9 | 4 |
| Dodd, Timothy, Vermont | .250 | 7 | 4 | 1 | 1 | 1 | 0 | 0 | 0 | 0 | 2 | 2 | 0 | 1 | 0 | 0 | 0 | 0 | 0 |
| Edwards, Glenn, Waterbury | .206 | 86 | 248 | 28 | 51 | 73 | 7 | 0 | 5 | 27 | 3 | 4 | 4 | 4 | 17 | 0 | 55 | 9 | 5 |
| Engel, Steven, Pittsfield | .167 | 12 | 12 | 1 | 2 | 3 | 1 | 0 | 0 | 2 | 1 | 2 | 0 | 0 | 0 | 0 | 3 | 0 | 0 |
| Escobar, Jose, Reading | .254 | 40 | 122 | 17 | 31 | 38 | 4 | 0 | 1 | 8 | 0 | 1 | 1 | 0 | 11 | 1 | 17 | 3 | 2 |
| Evetts, Anthony, Reading | .000 | 39 | 9 | 1 | 0 | 0 | 0 | 0 | 0 | 0 | 0 | 0 | 0 | 0 | 1 | 0 | 8 | 0 | 0 |
| Fansler, Stanley, Nashua | .300 | 24 | 20 | 1 | 6 | 6 | 0 | 0 | 0 | 0 | 0 | 0 | 2 | 0 | 2 | 0 | 2 | 0 | 0 |
| Fennell, Michael, Albany° | .175 | 16 | 40 | 5 | 7 | 17 | 2 | 1 | 2 | 5 | 0 | 0 | 0 | 0 | 5 | 0 | 13 | 0 | 0 |
| Fermin, Felix, Nashua | .226 | 137 | 443 | 32 | 100 | 114 | 10 | 2 | 0 | 27 | 1 | 10 | 2 | 3 | 37 | 0 | 30 | 29 | 15 |
| Ficklin, Winston, Waterbury† | .230 | 119 | 382 | 49 | 88 | 112 | 16 | 1 | 2 | 43 | 7 | 1 | 7 | 3 | 45 | 0 | 61 | 25 | 7 |
| Foley, Marvis, Glens Falls° | .248 | 49 | 145 | 18 | 36 | 55 | 7 | 0 | 4 | 31 | 1 | 0 | 2 | 1 | 36 | 1 | 20 | 1 | 1 |
| Ford, Kenneth, Nashua | .282 | 116 | 380 | 51 | 107 | 145 | 13 | 2 | 7 | 53 | 9 | 0 | 4 | 3 | 26 | 5 | 42 | 15 | 5 |
| Freeman, Marvin, Reading | .000 | 11 | 4 | 0 | 0 | 0 | 0 | 0 | 0 | 0 | 0 | 2 | 0 | 0 | 1 | 0 | 3 | 0 | 0 |
| Fryer, Paul, Nashua | .185 | 50 | 162 | 12 | 30 | 33 | 3 | 0 | 0 | 13 | 3 | 4 | 3 | 0 | 4 | 0 | 29 | 3 | 0 |
| Gallegos, Matthew, Albany† | .231 | 9 | 26 | 5 | 6 | 6 | 0 | 0 | 0 | 1 | 0 | 0 | 0 | 0 | 6 | 0 | 5 | 4 | 0 |
| Gaynor, Richard, Reading | .120 | 19 | 25 | 2 | 3 | 8 | 0 | 1 | 1 | 3 | 0 | 3 | 0 | 0 | 0 | 0 | 13 | 0 | 0 |
| Gillaspie, Mark, Pittsfield† | .263 | 17 | 57 | 7 | 15 | 23 | 5 | 0 | 1 | 12 | 2 | 0 | 2 | 0 | 11 | 0 | 15 | 2 | 1 |
| Glass, Timothy, Waterbury | .190 | 92 | 263 | 26 | 50 | 87 | 8 | 1 | 9 | 34 | 6 | 2 | 3 | 3 | 38 | 1 | 71 | 0 | 0 |
| Goldthorn, Burk, Nashua° | .154 | 4 | 13 | 1 | 2 | 2 | 0 | 0 | 0 | 0 | 0 | 0 | 0 | 0 | 1 | 0 | 3 | 0 | 1 |
| Gomez, Jorge, Pittsfield | .259 | 100 | 293 | 38 | 76 | 111 | 11 | 3 | 6 | 31 | 4 | 5 | 2 | 5 | 53 | 0 | 42 | 1 | 5 |
| Gonzalez, Orlando, Vermont | .279 | 60 | 226 | 26 | 63 | 89 | 7 | 2 | 5 | 32 | 3 | 4 | 2 | 1 | 11 | 0 | 24 | 0 | 0 |
| Griffin, Frankie, 15 Read-3 Nash° | .000 | 18 | 3 | 0 | 0 | 0 | 0 | 0 | 0 | 0 | 0 | 0 | 0 | 0 | 0 | 0 | 3 | 0 | 0 |
| Grimm, Peter, Vermont | .167 | 12 | 6 | 0 | 1 | 1 | 0 | 0 | 0 | 0 | 0 | 1 | 0 | 0 | 0 | 0 | 1 | 0 | 0 |
| Guzman, Ruben, Vermont | .285 | 115 | 417 | 60 | 119 | 146 | 10 | 4 | 3 | 38 | 6 | 4 | 0 | 5 | 31 | 1 | 82 | 40 | 13 |
| Hale, Demarlo, New Britain | .260 | 133 | 430 | 65 | 112 | 159 | 19 | 5 | 6 | 57 | 4 | 8 | 3 | 7 | 41 | 3 | 49 | 17 | 5 |
| Hammond, Steven, Pittsfield° | .299 | 130 | 455 | 51 | 136 | 186 | 23 | 3 | 7 | 84 | 9 | 1 | 5 | 2 | 61 | 5 | 37 | 4 | 4 |
| Haro, Samuel, Nashua | .267 | 120 | 386 | 58 | 103 | 122 | 8 | 4 | 1 | 21 | 1 | 8 | 2 | 4 | 40 | 1 | 59 | 37 | 16 |
| Harper, Milton, Waterbury | .234 | 15 | 47 | 5 | 11 | 12 | 1 | 0 | 0 | 5 | 0 | 0 | 2 | 0 | 10 | 1 | 9 | 0 | 0 |
| Hawkins, Johnny, Albany† | .138 | 13 | 29 | 4 | 4 | 4 | 0 | 0 | 0 | 2 | 1 | 1 | 0 | 0 | 3 | 0 | 6 | 1 | 0 |
| Hawley, William, Vermont° | .250 | 18 | 8 | 2 | 2 | 5 | 0 | 0 | 1 | 2 | 0 | 1 | 0 | 0 | 0 | 0 | 2 | 0 | 0 |
| Heidenreich, Curtis, Vermont | .059 | 23 | 17 | 0 | 1 | 1 | 0 | 0 | 0 | 0 | 0 | 2 | 0 | 0 | 1 | 0 | 6 | 0 | 0 |
| Henderson, Joseph, Pittsfield° | .231 | 100 | 294 | 33 | 68 | 86 | 9 | 0 | 3 | 29 | 3 | 2 | 3 | 1 | 41 | 4 | 59 | 1 | 3 |
| Henderson, Ramon, Reading | .244 | 17 | 45 | 3 | 11 | 13 | 2 | 0 | 0 | 4 | 0 | 0 | 0 | 3 | 0 | 5 | 1 | 0 |
| Henika, Ronald, Vermont° | .278 | 121 | 389 | 57 | 108 | 157 | 16 | 6 | 7 | 58 | 9 | 1 | 6 | 2 | 49 | 4 | 36 | 5 | 2 |
| Henry, Timothy, Pittsfield° | .000 | 10 | 7 | 1 | 0 | 0 | 0 | 0 | 0 | 0 | 0 | 0 | 0 | 0 | 1 | 0 | 3 | 0 | 0 |
| Hickey, Kevin, 11 Alb.-33 Read.° | .000 | 44 | 3 | 0 | 0 | 0 | 0 | 0 | 0 | 0 | 0 | 0 | 0 | 0 | 0 | 0 | 2 | 0 | 0 |
| Hicks, Robert, Reading | .000 | 41 | 3 | 0 | 0 | 0 | 0 | 0 | 0 | 0 | 0 | 0 | 0 | 0 | 1 | 0 | 2 | 0 | 0 |
| Hill, Orsino, Vermont° | .251 | 121 | 414 | 49 | 104 | 162 | 18 | 2 | 12 | 50 | 3 | 2 | 3 | 2 | 48 | 10 | 88 | 9 | 5 |
| Hoppie, Bryan, Reading† | .228 | 79 | 171 | 11 | 39 | 42 | 3 | 0 | 0 | 14 | 1 | 1 | 0 | 0 | 16 | 3 | 25 | 4 | 2 |
| Horn, Samuel, New Britain° | .282 | 134 | 457 | 64 | 129 | 194 | 32 | 0 | 11 | 82 | 11 | 1 | 9 | 4 | 64 | 14 | 107 | 4 | 6 |
| Housey, Joseph, Pittsfield | .400 | 32 | 5 | 1 | 2 | 2 | 0 | 0 | 0 | 0 | 0 | 1 | 0 | 0 | 0 | 0 | 2 | 0 | 0 |
| Hughes, Darrell, Albany | .286 | 9 | 14 | 3 | 4 | 4 | 0 | 0 | 0 | 1 | 0 | 0 | 0 | 0 | 4 | 0 | 3 | 0 | 0 |
| Hughes, Keith, Albany° | .269 | 104 | 361 | 53 | 97 | 159 | 22 | 5 | 10 | 54 | 9 | 0 | 1 | 3 | 51 | 1 | 73 | 4 | 4 |
| Jackson, Darrin, Pittsfield | .252 | 91 | 325 | 38 | 82 | 103 | 10 | 1 | 3 | 60 | 6 | 5 | 3 | 0 | 34 | 3 | 64 | 8 | 7 |
| Jackson, Kenneth, Reading | .234 | 121 | 423 | 66 | 99 | 127 | 15 | 2 | 3 | 34 | 3 | 2 | 2 | 3 | 69 | 1 | 83 | 16 | 6 |
| Jefferson, James, Vermont | .231 | 25 | 26 | 3 | 6 | 6 | 0 | 0 | 0 | 1 | 0 | 5 | 0 | 0 | 5 | 0 | 9 | 0 | 0 |
| Jelks, Gregory, Reading | .266 | 127 | 447 | 63 | 119 | 162 | 15 | 2 | 8 | 55 | 9 | 1 | 2 | 6 | 44 | 0 | 68 | 10 | 12 |
| Jensen, Roger, Glens Falls | .227 | 50 | 181 | 22 | 41 | 58 | 6 | 1 | 3 | 29 | 1 | 1 | 4 | 0 | 8 | 1 | 28 | 1 | 2 |
| Johnson, David, Nashua | .105 | 34 | 19 | 1 | 2 | 2 | 0 | 0 | 0 | 0 | 0 | 3 | 0 | 0 | 1 | 0 | 10 | 0 | 0 |
| Jones, Barry, Nashua | .000 | 23 | 1 | 0 | 0 | 0 | 0 | 0 | 0 | 0 | 0 | 0 | 0 | 0 | 1 | 0 | 0 | 0 | 0 |
| Jones, Gary, Pittsfield | .252 | 111 | 325 | 56 | 82 | 99 | 7 | 5 | 0 | 30 | 3 | 6 | 3 | 1 | 72 | 2 | 51 | 17 | 9 |
| Jones, Jeffry, Pittsfield | .196 | 31 | 92 | 11 | 18 | 25 | 4 | 0 | 1 | 12 | 1 | 1 | 0 | 2 | 22 | 3 | 25 | 0 | 2 |
| Jones, Tracy, Vermont | .317 | 75 | 284 | 40 | 90 | 120 | 12 | 3 | 4 | 31 | 5 | 0 | 3 | 2 | 26 | 3 | 23 | 26 | 3 |
| Jordan, Scott, Waterbury | .074 | 8 | 27 | 2 | 2 | 3 | 1 | 0 | 0 | 2 | 1 | 0 | 1 | 0 | 2 | 0 | 6 | 0 | 0 |
| Karkovice, Ronald, Glens Falls | .216 | 99 | 324 | 37 | 70 | 118 | 9 | 3 | 11 | 37 | 5 | 0 | 0 | 2 | 49 | 1 | 105 | 6 | 2 |
| Kelly, Patrick, Glens Falls | .315 | 30 | 92 | 14 | 29 | 40 | 3 | 1 | 2 | 9 | 0 | 0 | 1 | 2 | 16 | 1 | 16 | 2 | 1 |
| Kemp, Hubert, Vermont° | .429 | 12 | 7 | 1 | 3 | 3 | 0 | 0 | 0 | 0 | 0 | 0 | 0 | 0 | 0 | 0 | 2 | 0 | 0 |
| Kinnard, Kenneth, Reading | .184 | 79 | 277 | 40 | 51 | 80 | 11 | 3 | 4 | 23 | 2 | 3 | 1 | 1 | 16 | 0 | 68 | 9 | 6 |
| Knight, Timothy, Albany° | .225 | 26 | 80 | 13 | 18 | 23 | 5 | 0 | 0 | 9 | 2 | 0 | 2 | 0 | 16 | 0 | 11 | 1 | 1 |
| Knox, Michael, Vermont | .000 | 7 | 5 | 0 | 0 | 0 | 0 | 0 | 0 | 0 | 0 | 0 | 0 | 0 | 1 | 0 | 2 | 0 | 0 |
| Konderla, Michael, Vermont | .111 | 44 | 9 | 1 | 1 | 1 | 0 | 0 | 0 | 0 | 0 | 0 | 0 | 0 | 2 | 0 | 4 | 0 | 0 |
| Labay, Stephen, Reading | .333 | 9 | 6 | 0 | 2 | 2 | 0 | 0 | 0 | 0 | 0 | 0 | 0 | 0 | 1 | 0 | 1 | 0 | 0 |
| Laird, Anthony, Nashua° | .258 | 125 | 395 | 53 | 102 | 140 | 22 | 2 | 4 | 43 | 3 | 3 | 3 | 4 | 63 | 8 | 60 | 7 | 3 |
| Lamonde, Lawrence, Nashua | .000 | 24 | 12 | 0 | 0 | 0 | 0 | 0 | 0 | 0 | 0 | 3 | 0 | 0 | 1 | 0 | 5 | 0 | 0 |
| Landestoy, Rafael, Albany† | .232 | 55 | 181 | 18 | 42 | 54 | 3 | 3 | 1 | 13 | 2 | 3 | 0 | 2 | 10 | 0 | 14 | 4 | 5 |
| Larkin, Barry, Vermont | .267 | 72 | 255 | 42 | 68 | 88 | 13 | 2 | 1 | 31 | 5 | 4 | 3 | 3 | 23 | 1 | 21 | 12 | 1 |
| Layton, Thomas, 7 GF-23 Pitts° | .000 | 30 | 5 | 0 | 0 | 0 | 0 | 0 | 0 | 0 | 0 | 0 | 0 | 0 | 0 | 0 | 4 | 0 | 0 |
| Lee, Terry, Vermont | .289 | 121 | 409 | 56 | 118 | 178 | 20 | 2 | 12 | 62 | 9 | 0 | 4 | 3 | 48 | 2 | 51 | 4 | 0 |
| Lindsey, William, Albany | .282 | 69 | 227 | 30 | 64 | 98 | 16 | 0 | 6 | 41 | 7 | 1 | 2 | 2 | 31 | 1 | 23 | 2 | 3 |
| Lombardi, Phillip, Albany | .256 | 76 | 250 | 44 | 64 | 96 | 13 | 2 | 5 | 32 | 1 | 3 | 3 | 2 | 39 | 0 | 29 | 5 | 2 |
| Long, Bruce, Reading | .100 | 14 | 10 | 0 | 1 | 1 | 0 | 0 | 0 | 0 | 0 | 2 | 0 | 0 | 1 | 0 | 7 | 0 | 0 |
| MacKay, Joey, Albany | .207 | 22 | 58 | 3 | 12 | 22 | 3 | 2 | 1 | 9 | 0 | 0 | 0 | 4 | 1 | 0 | 15 | 0 | 0 |
| Madden, Morris, Vermont° | .000 | 6 | 1 | 0 | 0 | 0 | 0 | 0 | 0 | 0 | 0 | 0 | 0 | 0 | 0 | 0 | 0 | 0 | 0 |
| Manfre, Michael, Vermont | .253 | 47 | 146 | 20 | 37 | 43 | 4 | 1 | 0 | 12 | 3 | 0 | 0 | 0 | 20 | 1 | 24 | 3 | 0 |
| Manzanillo, Ravelo, Nashua° | .167 | 37 | 24 | 4 | 4 | 5 | 1 | 0 | 0 | 2 | 0 | 1 | 0 | 1 | 0 | 0 | 5 | 1 | 1 |
| Marzano, John, New Britain | .246 | 103 | 350 | 36 | 86 | 124 | 14 | 6 | 4 | 51 | 4 | 7 | 9 | 3 | 19 | 0 | 43 | 4 | 3 |
| McAllister, Steven, Nashua† | .231 | 36 | 91 | 5 | 21 | 23 | 2 | 0 | 0 | 7 | 1 | 2 | 0 | 1 | 3 | 0 | 9 | 0 | 1 |

| Player and Club | Pct. | G. | AB. | R. | H. | TB. | 2B. | 3B. | HR. | RBI. | GW. | SH. | SF. | HP. | BB. | Int. BB. | SO. | SB. | CS. |
|---|---|---|---|---|---|---|---|---|---|---|---|---|---|---|---|---|---|---|---|
| McGriff, Terence, Vermont | .253 | 110 | 363 | 52 | 92 | 149 | 10 | 4 | 13 | 60 | 4 | 0 | 1 | 3 | 54 | 2 | 81 | 1 | 0 |
| McKelvey, Mitch, Nashua | .400 | 19 | 5 | 0 | 2 | 2 | 0 | 0 | 0 | 0 | 0 | 0 | 0 | 0 | 0 | 0 | 2 | 0 | 0 |
| McLaughlin, David, 33 GF.-76 Read° | .286 | 109 | 388 | 52 | 111 | 133 | 16 | 3 | 0 | 32 | 3 | 7 | 3 | 0 | 38 | 2 | 26 | 4 | 3 |
| Meleski, Mark, New Britain° | .230 | 42 | 87 | 7 | 20 | 22 | 2 | 0 | 0 | 9 | 0 | 2 | 1 | 0 | 12 | 0 | 19 | 0 | 0 |
| Menard, Darryl, Reading | .136 | 30 | 22 | 1 | 3 | 3 | 0 | 0 | 0 | 2 | 0 | 2 | 1 | 0 | 0 | 0 | 9 | 0 | 0 |
| Miller, Keith, Reading† | .295 | 134 | 499 | 77 | 147 | 203 | 24 | 7 | 6 | 59 | 5 | 3 | 2 | 1 | 65 | 4 | 61 | 20 | 10 |
| Montgomery, Jeff, Vermont | .000 | 53 | 5 | 0 | 0 | 0 | 0 | 0 | 0 | 0 | 0 | 0 | 0 | 0 | 1 | 0 | 2 | 0 | 0 |
| Moritz, Thomas, Glens Falls | .262 | 126 | 447 | 61 | 117 | 169 | 25 | 3 | 7 | 68 | 8 | 2 | 3 | 3 | 62 | 0 | 72 | 0 | 4 |
| Morman, Russell, Glens Falls | .310 | 119 | 422 | 64 | 131 | 216 | 24 | 5 | 17 | 81 | 9 | 1 | 3 | 5 | 65 | 3 | 51 | 11 | 10 |
| Moyer, Jamie, Pittsfield° | .000 | 15 | 10 | 3 | 0 | 0 | 0 | 0 | 0 | 1 | 0 | 1 | 0 | 0 | 2 | 0 | 5 | 0 | 0 |
| Neal, Scott, Nashua° | .000 | 26 | 4 | 0 | 0 | 0 | 0 | 0 | 0 | 0 | 0 | 0 | 0 | 0 | 0 | 0 | 3 | 0 | 0 |
| Olander, James, Reading | .322 | 64 | 208 | 30 | 67 | 98 | 15 | 2 | 4 | 39 | 3 | 2 | 1 | 3 | 29 | 1 | 45 | 2 | 2 |
| Oliva, David, New Britain | .297 | 44 | 118 | 15 | 35 | 44 | 4 | 1 | 1 | 12 | 2 | 2 | 0 | 1 | 4 | 1 | 13 | 2 | 3 |
| Oliverio, Stephen, Vermont | .250 | 8 | 4 | 1 | 1 | 1 | 0 | 0 | 0 | 0 | 0 | 1 | 0 | 0 | 1 | 0 | 0 | 0 | 0 |
| Olson, James, Reading | .263 | 30 | 19 | 2 | 5 | 6 | 1 | 0 | 0 | 2 | 0 | 5 | 0 | 0 | 4 | 0 | 2 | 0 | 0 |
| Opie, James, Nashua | .282 | 74 | 241 | 31 | 68 | 95 | 18 | 0 | 3 | 37 | 6 | 0 | 6 | 2 | 39 | 1 | 44 | 8 | 8 |
| Pacillo, Patrick, Vermont | .000 | 22 | 1 | 0 | 0 | 0 | 0 | 0 | 0 | 0 | 0 | 0 | 0 | 0 | 0 | 0 | 0 | 0 | 0 |
| Parmenter, Gary, Pittsfield | .056 | 17 | 18 | 1 | 1 | 1 | 0 | 0 | 0 | 1 | 1 | 3 | 0 | 0 | 0 | 0 | 6 | 0 | 0 |
| Pastornicky, Clifford, Glens Falls | .221 | 75 | 263 | 30 | 58 | 87 | 12 | 1 | 5 | 24 | 4 | 1 | 1 | 2 | 16 | 0 | 33 | 3 | 0 |
| Pedraza, Nelson, Waterbury | .183 | 106 | 290 | 37 | 53 | 58 | 5 | 0 | 0 | 20 | 2 | 5 | 5 | 4 | 43 | 0 | 54 | 0 | 2 |
| Peruso, Steven, Albany | .135 | 14 | 37 | 4 | 5 | 9 | 1 | 0 | 1 | 4 | 1 | 1 | 1 | 0 | 5 | 0 | 12 | 1 | 0 |
| Pino, Rolando, Glens Falls | .214 | 127 | 370 | 56 | 79 | 107 | 18 | 2 | 2 | 27 | 4 | 7 | 3 | 1 | 83 | 0 | 84 | 14 | 5 |
| Potestio, Douglas, Pittsfield | .083 | 26 | 12 | 1 | 1 | 1 | 0 | 0 | 0 | 1 | 0 | 1 | 0 | 0 | 1 | 0 | 3 | 0 | 0 |
| Pryor, Buddy, Vermont | .183 | 33 | 82 | 4 | 15 | 23 | 0 | 1 | 2 | 10 | 0 | 0 | 1 | 1 | 17 | 2 | 23 | 1 | 0 |
| Quinonez, Rey, New Britain | .257 | 134 | 439 | 67 | 113 | 169 | 19 | 5 | 9 | 50 | 6 | 7 | 5 | 9 | 73 | 1 | 50 | 6 | 6 |
| Rembielak, Richard, Pittsfield | .241 | 21 | 58 | 9 | 14 | 19 | 3 | 1 | 0 | 6 | 1 | 1 | 1 | 0 | 8 | 0 | 2 | 0 | 1 |
| Reynolds, Timothy, Vermont† | .118 | 19 | 17 | 1 | 2 | 3 | 1 | 0 | 0 | 0 | 0 | 3 | 0 | 0 | 1 | 0 | 6 | 0 | 0 |
| Rice, Cepedia, Nashua | .400 | 12 | 10 | 1 | 4 | 5 | 1 | 0 | 0 | 1 | 0 | 1 | 0 | 0 | 0 | 0 | 5 | 0 | 0 |
| Riggs, James, Albany° | .234 | 121 | 415 | 51 | 97 | 141 | 19 | 2 | 7 | 60 | 8 | 1 | 2 | 0 | 57 | 2 | 50 | 2 | 4 |
| Riley, Thomas, Vermont | .193 | 49 | 114 | 14 | 22 | 29 | 2 | 1 | 1 | 9 | 1 | 1 | 0 | 1 | 16 | 0 | 17 | 0 | 1 |
| Roadcap, Steve, Pittsfield† | .164 | 32 | 73 | 6 | 12 | 13 | 1 | 0 | 0 | 4 | 0 | 1 | 1 | 0 | 23 | 1 | 22 | 1 | 1 |
| Roberts, Leon, Nashua† | .272 | 105 | 401 | 64 | 109 | 141 | 19 | 5 | 1 | 23 | 4 | 4 | 2 | 6 | 29 | 2 | 43 | 40 | 12 |
| Robinson, Brian, Vermont | .222 | 3 | 9 | 3 | 2 | 3 | 1 | 0 | 0 | 0 | 0 | 0 | 0 | 0 | 0 | 0 | 0 | 0 | 0 |
| Rodriguez, Ruben, Nashua | .214 | 104 | 341 | 28 | 73 | 99 | 9 | 4 | 3 | 40 | 8 | 3 | 2 | 6 | 16 | 3 | 56 | 5 | 6 |
| Romero, Ramon, Glens Falls† | .118 | 16 | 34 | 3 | 4 | 4 | 0 | 0 | 0 | 4 | 1 | 1 | 0 | 0 | 9 | 0 | 13 | 0 | 0 |
| Ronk, Jeffrey, Pittsfield | .234 | 103 | 346 | 34 | 81 | 99 | 14 | 2 | 0 | 30 | 4 | 2 | 3 | 1 | 18 | 0 | 28 | 4 | 5 |
| Russell, Anthony, Albany | .246 | 123 | 415 | 64 | 102 | 152 | 16 | 8 | 6 | 36 | 2 | 22 | 5 | 3 | 42 | 4 | 96 | 15 | 6 |
| Rutledge, Jeffrey, Pittsfield | .236 | 103 | 318 | 41 | 75 | 106 | 12 | 2 | 5 | 39 | 3 | 5 | 3 | 2 | 43 | 1 | 52 | 3 | 3 |
| Sabo, Christopher, Vermont | .278 | 124 | 428 | 66 | 119 | 171 | 19 | 0 | 11 | 46 | 5 | 6 | 4 | 7 | 50 | 1 | 39 | 7 | 5 |
| Sanchez, Leopoldo, Nashua° | .200 | 26 | 5 | 1 | 1 | 1 | 0 | 0 | 0 | 0 | 0 | 0 | 0 | 0 | 0 | 0 | 1 | 0 | 0 |
| Santarelli, Calvin, Waterbury | .000 | 31 | 0 | 0 | 0 | 0 | 0 | 0 | 0 | 0 | 0 | 0 | 0 | 0 | 2 | 0 | 0 | 0 | 0 |
| Sauveur, Richard, Nashua° | .167 | 27 | 24 | 4 | 4 | 4 | 0 | 0 | 0 | 1 | 0 | 1 | 1 | 0 | 5 | 0 | 4 | 1 | 0 |
| Schaum, Brian, Nashua | .211 | 8 | 19 | 1 | 4 | 4 | 0 | 0 | 0 | 1 | 0 | 0 | 0 | 0 | 1 | 0 | 4 | 1 | 0 |
| Scheer, Ronald, Glens Falls | .232 | 101 | 354 | 42 | 82 | 123 | 9 | 1 | 10 | 42 | 2 | 1 | 7 | 0 | 34 | 4 | 64 | 6 | 6 |
| Schmidt, Eric, Glens Falls† | .000 | 27 | 1 | 0 | 0 | 0 | 0 | 0 | 0 | 0 | 0 | 0 | 0 | 0 | 0 | 0 | 0 | 0 | 0 |
| Scott, Richard, Albany | .214 | 97 | 299 | 30 | 64 | 99 | 15 | 4 | 4 | 34 | 10 | 6 | 2 | 3 | 27 | 0 | 73 | 6 | 7 |
| Scott, Timothy, Vermont | .500 | 36 | 2 | 0 | 1 | 1 | 0 | 0 | 0 | 1 | 0 | 0 | 0 | 0 | 1 | 0 | 0 | 0 | 0 |
| Sedar, Edward, Glens Falls | .193 | 72 | 207 | 32 | 40 | 54 | 4 | 2 | 2 | 18 | 2 | 5 | 2 | 3 | 40 | 1 | 31 | 4 | 8 |
| Seoane, Mitchell, Albany° | .196 | 32 | 102 | 9 | 20 | 22 | 2 | 0 | 0 | 7 | 0 | 3 | 0 | 0 | 9 | 0 | 10 | 3 | 0 |
| Smajstrla, Craig, 71 GF.-53 Water†. | .277 | 124 | 470 | 84 | 130 | 160 | 20 | 5 | 0 | 43 | 7 | 5 | 3 | 2 | 36 | 2 | 32 | 25 | 12 |
| Smith, Philander, Albany | .211 | 10 | 38 | 5 | 8 | 9 | 1 | 0 | 0 | 3 | 0 | 1 | 0 | 0 | 2 | 0 | 1 | 1 | 1 |
| Snyder, Cory, Waterbury | .281 | 139 | 512 | 77 | 144 | 255 | 25 | 1 | 28 | 94 | 14 | 3 | 12 | 4 | 44 | 2 | 123 | 5 | 9 |
| Soares, Todd, Reading° | .284 | 125 | 423 | 60 | 120 | 195 | 23 | 5 | 14 | 70 | 10 | 0 | 9 | 8 | 63 | 8 | 74 | 9 | 8 |
| Soper, Michael, Glens Falls | .296 | 132 | 480 | 50 | 142 | 170 | 16 | 0 | 4 | 49 | 7 | 2 | 6 | 3 | 26 | 0 | 51 | 5 | 6 |
| Squires, Michael, Glens Falls° | .067 | 4 | 15 | 0 | 1 | 1 | 0 | 0 | 0 | 0 | 0 | 0 | 0 | 0 | 2 | 0 | 1 | 0 | 0 |
| Stalp, Joseph, Vermont | .667 | 6 | 3 | 1 | 2 | 2 | 0 | 0 | 0 | 1 | 0 | 0 | 0 | 0 | 1 | 0 | 1 | 0 | 0 |
| Syverson, Dain, Waterbury | .235 | 71 | 204 | 29 | 48 | 64 | 8 | 1 | 2 | 31 | 3 | 1 | 3 | 3 | 34 | 2 | 43 | 6 | 0 |
| Taylor, Donald, Nashua | .000 | 26 | 11 | 0 | 0 | 0 | 0 | 0 | 0 | 0 | 0 | 1 | 0 | 0 | 1 | 0 | 3 | 0 | 0 |
| Tejada, Wilfredo, Reading | .271 | 69 | 210 | 24 | 57 | 73 | 7 | 0 | 3 | 25 | 2 | 3 | 3 | 3 | 17 | 3 | 52 | 1 | 1 |
| Thompson, Timothy, Pittsfield° | .215 | 44 | 130 | 15 | 28 | 41 | 8 | 1 | 1 | 18 | 1 | 2 | 2 | 2 | 14 | 0 | 23 | 2 | 0 |
| Torve, Kenton, Glens Falls° | .291 | 52 | 175 | 27 | 51 | 69 | 5 | 2 | 3 | 19 | 2 | 5 | 4 | 1 | 22 | 3 | 25 | 2 | 2 |
| Treadway, Jeffrey, Vermont† | .302 | 129 | 431 | 63 | 130 | 155 | 17 | 1 | 2 | 49 | 3 | 5 | 5 | 2 | 71 | 2 | 40 | 6 | 5 |
| Tremblay, Gary, New Britain | .213 | 22 | 61 | 3 | 13 | 22 | 3 | 0 | 2 | 13 | 2 | 0 | 0 | 0 | 4 | 0 | 20 | 0 | 0 |
| Valera, Alcadio, Waterbury† | .200 | 83 | 180 | 20 | 36 | 48 | 4 | 4 | 0 | 16 | 0 | 6 | 3 | 1 | 15 | 0 | 60 | 1 | 1 |
| Varsho, Gary, Pittsfield° | .242 | 115 | 418 | 62 | 101 | 136 | 14 | 6 | 3 | 37 | 4 | 5 | 1 | 5 | 40 | 1 | 53 | 40 | 8 |
| Vincent, Michael, Vermont | .244 | 19 | 45 | 2 | 11 | 17 | 0 | 0 | 2 | 9 | 1 | 0 | 1 | 1 | 8 | 1 | 9 | 1 | 1 |
| Walck, Craig, New Britain | .227 | 99 | 264 | 29 | 60 | 88 | 13 | 3 | 3 | 28 | 5 | 7 | 4 | 2 | 52 | 0 | 39 | 5 | 5 |
| Walker, Kurt, Glens Falls | .000 | 46 | 1 | 0 | 0 | 0 | 0 | 0 | 0 | 0 | 0 | 0 | 0 | 0 | 0 | 0 | 1 | 0 | 0 |
| Ward, Kevin, Reading | .303 | 42 | 132 | 23 | 40 | 64 | 9 | 6 | 1 | 21 | 2 | 0 | 2 | 5 | 23 | 1 | 19 | 7 | 5 |
| Washington, Randy, Waterbury | .307 | 125 | 449 | 75 | 138 | 204 | 14 | 5 | 14 | 84 | 10 | 0 | 8 | 3 | 78 | 1 | 94 | 12 | 7 |
| Watts, Leonard, Reading° | .000 | 6 | 3 | 0 | 0 | 0 | 0 | 0 | 0 | 0 | 0 | 0 | 0 | 1 | 0 | 0 | 0 | 0 | 0 |
| Williams, Dana, New Britain | .309 | 115 | 450 | 56 | 139 | 172 | 16 | 7 | 1 | 39 | 5 | 3 | 4 | 5 | 34 | 3 | 24 | 20 | 16 |
| Williams, Kenneth, Glens Falls | .250 | 133 | 520 | 87 | 130 | 206 | 16 | 6 | 16 | 66 | 10 | 7 | 5 | 6 | 47 | 1 | 83 | 27 | 14 |
| Winkler, Bradley, Albany° | .197 | 73 | 249 | 27 | 49 | 87 | 7 | 2 | 9 | 41 | 3 | 1 | 3 | 2 | 26 | 2 | 81 | 7 | 1 |
| Winters, Matthew, Albany° | .277 | 14 | 47 | 7 | 13 | 21 | 2 | 0 | 2 | 6 | 1 | 0 | 0 | 0 | 8 | 1 | 10 | 0 | 1 |
| Woods, Tony, Pittsfield | .248 | 78 | 242 | 27 | 60 | 77 | 11 | 0 | 2 | 29 | 4 | 2 | 2 | 2 | 34 | 2 | 40 | 2 | 2 |
| Wotus, Ronald, Nashua | .186 | 37 | 102 | 9 | 19 | 26 | 3 | 2 | 0 | 14 | 3 | 1 | 4 | 1 | 20 | 1 | 13 | 1 | 1 |
| Wright, Scott, 19 Read.-20 Nas. | .000 | 39 | 1 | 0 | 0 | 0 | 0 | 0 | 0 | 0 | 0 | 0 | 0 | 0 | 0 | 0 | 1 | 0 | 0 |
| Young, Delwyn, Vermont† | .241 | 115 | 399 | 47 | 96 | 147 | 13 | 10 | 6 | 35 | 4 | 4 | 5 | 1 | 30 | 2 | 73 | 14 | 7 |

The following pitchers, listed alphabetically by club, with games in parentheses, had no plate appearances, primarily through use of designated hitters:

ALBANY—Bradley, Bert (25); Cloninger, Darin (13); Drabek, Douglas (26); Easley, Logan (29); Faulk, Kelly (6); Ferguson, Mark (17); Frey, Steven (40); Graham, Randle (46); Nielsen, Scott (11); Patterson, Scott (27); Scott, Kelly (8); Tewksbury, Robert (17); Torres, Ricardo (1); Underwood, Thomas (4); Wever, Stefan (5); Wex, Gary (9).

GLENS FALLS—Brecht, Michael (25); Correa, Edwin (8); Davis, Joel (4); DeVincenzo, Richard (21); Filippi, James (2); Guzman, Pedro (20); Hardy, John (37); Hickey, James (25); Imig, Paul (8); Johnson, John (28); Mullen, Thomas (18); Oswald, Steven (2); Palacios, Vicente (8); Renz, Kevin (9); Williams, Mark (35).

NASHUA—Holman, Shawn (2); Marcheskie, Lee (7).

NEW BRITAIN—Cappadona, Anthony (12); Davis, Charles (23); Ellsworth, Steven (20); Gering, Scott (34); Leister, John (27); Mitchell, John (29); Rochford, Michael (14); Sellers, Jeffrey (25); Woodward, Robert (12).

PITTSFIELD—Fruge, Jeffrey (5); Moreno, Angel (5).

READING—Caraballo, Ramon (4); Culver, George (3).

VERMONT—Lono, Joel (1); Reburn, Scott (5).

WATERBURY—Arney, Jeffrey (28); Beasley, Christopher (9); Belleman, Michael (2); Doyle, Richard (15); Elston, Guy (8); Farrell, John (25); Johnson, Wayne (8); Jones, Douglas (39); Leach, Martin (13); Miglio, John (46); Murphy, Kent (4); Pippin, Craig (18); Ritter, Reggie (15); Smith, Daryl (16); Street, Michael (16).

GRAND SLAM HOME RUNS—Moritz, 3; Bennett, Clark, Ford, Glass, Gomez, K. Hughes, Laird, Lindsey, Miller, Morman, R. Scott, Snyder, Soares, Torve, Tremblay, Vincent, 1 each.

AWARDED FIRST BASE ON CATCHER'S INTERFERENCE—Pastornicky 2 (Hammond, Lombardi); Treadway 2 (Baker, Hammond); Cannizzaro (McGriff); Fryer (McGriff); Oliva (Foley).

## CLUB FIELDING

| Club | Pct. | G. | PO. | A. | E. | DP. | PB. | Club | Pct. | G. | PO. | A. | E. | DP. | PB. |
|---|---|---|---|---|---|---|---|---|---|---|---|---|---|---|---|
| Vermont | .972 | 138 | 3530 | 1373 | 139 | 117 | 15 | Nashua | .967 | 139 | 3552 | 1474 | 173 | 121 | 23 |
| Waterbury | .970 | 139 | 3562 | 1326 | 152 | 119 | 20 | Glens Falls | .966 | 139 | 3495 | 1407 | 174 | 112 | 18 |
| New Britain | .968 | 139 | 3507 | 1514 | 165 | 125 | 14 | Albany | .965 | 139 | 3621 | 1482 | 186 | 114 | 20 |
| Pittsfield | .967 | 138 | 3482 | 1512 | 168 | 97 | 23 | Reading | .962 | 137 | 3365 | 1391 | 188 | 127 | 9 |

Triple Play—Pittsfield.

## INDIVIDUAL FIELDING

*Throw lefthanded.

### FIRST BASEMEN

| Player and Club | Pct. | G. | PO. | A. | E. | DP. | Player and Club | Pct. | G. | PO. | A. | E. | DP. |
|---|---|---|---|---|---|---|---|---|---|---|---|---|---|
| Berger, Nashua | .994 | 40 | 308 | 22 | 2 | 27 | Lee, Vermont | .986 | 79 | 589 | 53 | 9 | 45 |
| Blaser, Albany | 1.000 | 1 | 2 | 1 | 0 | 0 | Lindsey, Albany | .941 | 5 | 46 | 2 | 3 | 1 |
| Cecchetti, Waterbury* | .982 | 112 | 885 | 58 | 17 | 77 | Manfre, Vermont | 1.000 | 2 | 12 | 3 | 0 | 1 |
| Day, Reading | .992 | 61 | 536 | 53 | 5 | 45 | McAllister, Nashua | 1.000 | 1 | 3 | 0 | 0 | 0 |
| Destrade, Albany | .985 | 134 | 1103 | 73 | 18 | 99 | McLaughlin, 4 GF-51 Read* | .986 | 55 | 402 | 25 | 6 | 35 |
| Fennell, Albany | .933 | 2 | 13 | 1 | 1 | 1 | Moritz, Glens Falls | 1.000 | 1 | 2 | 0 | 0 | 0 |
| Foley, Glens Falls | 1.000 | 2 | 5 | 1 | 0 | 0 | MORMAN, Glens Falls | .9879 | 118 | 903 | 79 | 12 | 81 |
| Gillaspie, Pittsfield | .944 | 3 | 17 | 0 | 1 | 1 | Rembielak, Pittsfield | 1.000 | 1 | 3 | 0 | 0 | 0 |
| Glass, Waterbury | .985 | 10 | 62 | 5 | 1 | 5 | Roadcap, Pittsfield | 1.000 | 1 | 3 | 0 | 0 | 0 |
| Hale, New Britain | .988 | 62 | 472 | 35 | 6 | 49 | Romero, Glens Falls | 1.000 | 1 | 0 | 1 | 0 | 0 |
| Hammond, Pittsfield | .993 | 34 | 256 | 18 | 2 | 22 | Scott, Albany | 1.000 | 2 | 1 | 0 | 0 | 0 |
| Harper, Waterbury | .988 | 15 | 144 | 14 | 2 | 15 | Sedar, Glens Falls | 1.000 | 12 | 95 | 9 | 0 | 9 |
| Henderson, Pittsfield | .958 | 10 | 61 | 7 | 3 | 3 | Squires, Glens Falls* | 1.000 | 4 | 31 | 3 | 0 | 0 |
| Henika, Vermont | .987 | 71 | 548 | 39 | 8 | 56 | Syverson, Waterbury | .988 | 9 | 74 | 5 | 1 | 6 |
| Horn, New Britain* | .973 | 89 | 751 | 63 | 23 | 68 | Tejada, Reading | 1.000 | 1 | 4 | 1 | 0 | 0 |
| Jelks, Reading | .980 | 31 | 238 | 12 | 5 | 31 | Thompson, Pittsfield* | .983 | 26 | 215 | 14 | 4 | 13 |
| Jones, Pittsfield | 1.000 | 15 | 106 | 3 | 0 | 5 | Torve, Glens Falls | .971 | 3 | 30 | 3 | 1 | 2 |
| Laird, Nashua* | .9875 | 113 | 882 | 72 | 12 | 81 | Varsho, Pittsfield | .991 | 67 | 579 | 50 | 6 | 39 |

Triple Play—Varsho.

### SECOND BASEMEN

| Player and Club | Pct. | G. | PO. | A. | E. | DP. | Player and Club | Pct. | G. | PO. | A. | E. | DP. |
|---|---|---|---|---|---|---|---|---|---|---|---|---|---|
| Barranca, Waterbury | .986 | 25 | 29 | 43 | 1 | 10 | Pastornicky, Glens Falls | .976 | 8 | 18 | 22 | 1 | 2 |
| Barrett, Albany | .953 | 18 | 49 | 52 | 5 | 10 | PEDRAZA, Waterbury | .980 | 101 | 178 | 217 | 8 | 51 |
| Blaser, Albany | .929 | 6 | 6 | 7 | 1 | 0 | Pino, Glens Falls | .966 | 127 | 313 | 313 | 22 | 64 |
| Cannizzaro, New Britain | .975 | 131 | 273 | 355 | 16 | 90 | Rembielak, Pittsfield | .976 | 8 | 17 | 23 | 1 | 5 |
| Carroll, Albany | .957 | 7 | 8 | 14 | 1 | 4 | Riley, Vermont | .925 | 17 | 25 | 37 | 5 | 5 |
| Chapman, Albany | .965 | 99 | 236 | 283 | 19 | 59 | Roberts, Nashua | .941 | 95 | 217 | 249 | 29 | 41 |
| Christensen, Nashua | .972 | 20 | 35 | 34 | 2 | 10 | Robinson, Vermont | 1.000 | 3 | 10 | 8 | 0 | 3 |
| Escobar, Reading | 1.000 | 3 | 4 | 4 | 0 | 1 | Romero, Glens Falls | 1.000 | 6 | 17 | 7 | 0 | 4 |
| Fermin, Nashua | 1.000 | 1 | 0 | 1 | 0 | 1 | Ronk, Pittsfield | 1.000 | 1 | 6 | 2 | 0 | 1 |
| Fryer, Nashua | .971 | 8 | 18 | 15 | 1 | 5 | Rutledge, Pittsfield | .963 | 51 | 97 | 136 | 9 | 22 |
| Hoppie, Reading | .952 | 7 | 10 | 10 | 1 | 3 | Schaum, Nashua | .833 | 7 | 9 | 11 | 4 | 1 |
| Hughes, Albany | 1.000 | 1 | 0 | 1 | 0 | 0 | Seoane, Albany | 1.000 | 1 | 1 | 2 | 0 | 1 |
| Jones, Pittsfield | .965 | 91 | 191 | 246 | 16 | 42 | Smajstrla, 2 GF-38 Water | .977 | 40 | 80 | 93 | 4 | 27 |
| Landestoy, Albany | .952 | 17 | 27 | 33 | 3 | 9 | Smith, Albany | .970 | 6 | 9 | 23 | 1 | 2 |
| McAllister, Nashua | .962 | 23 | 33 | 42 | 3 | 8 | Torve, Glens Falls | 1.000 | 1 | 0 | 1 | 0 | 0 |
| Meleski, New Britain | 1.000 | 12 | 13 | 28 | 0 | 5 | Treadway, Vermont | .976 | 127 | 271 | 332 | 15 | 66 |
| Miller, Reading | .956 | 132 | 273 | 355 | 29 | 81 | Valera, Waterbury | 1.000 | 2 | 1 | 3 | 0 | 0 |

Triple Play—Jones.

### THIRD BASEMEN

| Player and Club | Pct. | G. | PO. | A. | E. | DP. | Player and Club | Pct. | G. | PO. | A. | E. | DP. |
|---|---|---|---|---|---|---|---|---|---|---|---|---|---|
| Barrett, Albany | .863 | 18 | 17 | 27 | 7 | 2 | McAllister, Nashua | .968 | 12 | 15 | 15 | 1 | 2 |
| Berger, Nashua | .857 | 14 | 8 | 16 | 4 | 0 | Meleski, New Britain | 1.000 | 5 | 2 | 10 | 0 | 1 |
| Blaser, Albany | .881 | 36 | 18 | 78 | 13 | 5 | Morman, Glens Falls | 1.000 | 3 | 1 | 2 | 0 | 0 |
| Bradley, Albany | .846 | 6 | 8 | 14 | 4 | 2 | Opie, Nashua | .941 | 71 | 46 | 146 | 12 | 20 |
| Carroll, Albany | 1.000 | 3 | 3 | 11 | 0 | 0 | Pastornicky, Glens Falls | .929 | 62 | 53 | 90 | 11 | 9 |
| Christensen, Nashua | .926 | 9 | 7 | 18 | 2 | 3 | Rembielak, Pittsfield | .960 | 7 | 7 | 17 | 1 | 4 |
| Day, Reading | 1.000 | 1 | 1 | 2 | 0 | 0 | Riggs, Albany | .952 | 71 | 56 | 143 | 10 | 15 |
| Escobar, Reading | .900 | 14 | 10 | 26 | 4 | 0 | Riley, Vermont | 1.000 | 14 | 6 | 14 | 0 | 1 |
| Fryer, Nashua | .912 | 41 | 34 | 70 | 10 | 5 | Ronk, Pittsfield | .943 | 22 | 16 | 50 | 4 | 2 |
| Gomez, Pittsfield | 1.000 | 3 | 2 | 1 | 0 | 0 | Rutledge, Pittsfield | .948 | 40 | 26 | 101 | 7 | 4 |
| Hale, New Britain | .871 | 52 | 33 | 109 | 21 | 8 | Sabo, Vermont | .951 | 120 | 97 | 236 | 17 | 19 |
| J. Henderson, Pittsfield | .943 | 13 | 14 | 19 | 2 | 3 | Seoane, Albany | 1.000 | 1 | 1 | 1 | 0 | 0 |
| R. Henderson, Reading | .939 | 15 | 12 | 19 | 2 | 0 | Smajstrla, 57 GF-3 Water | .890 | 60 | 46 | 100 | 18 | 10 |
| Hoppie, Reading | .896 | 21 | 12 | 31 | 5 | 3 | Snyder, Waterbury | .921 | 136 | 132 | 228 | 31 | 26 |
| Jelks, Reading | .872 | 99 | 83 | 176 | 38 | 17 | Syverson, Waterbury | .870 | 14 | 9 | 11 | 3 | 2 |
| Landestoy, Albany | .828 | 9 | 9 | 15 | 5 | 3 | Torve, Glens Falls | .943 | 22 | 14 | 52 | 4 | 5 |
| Lee, Vermont | .909 | 4 | 4 | 6 | 1 | 2 | Valera, Waterbury | 1.000 | 3 | 1 | 4 | 0 | 0 |
| Lombardi, Albany | 1.000 | 3 | 0 | 1 | 0 | 0 | WALCK, New Britain | .967 | 93 | 70 | 197 | 9 | 15 |
| Manfre, Vermont | .900 | 10 | 3 | 15 | 2 | 1 | Woods, Pittsfield | .890 | 69 | 56 | 105 | 20 | 12 |

## SHORTSTOPS

| Player and Club | Pct. | G. | PO. | A. | E. | DP. | Player and Club | Pct. | G. | PO. | A. | E. | DP. |
|---|---|---|---|---|---|---|---|---|---|---|---|---|---|
| Barranca, Waterbury | .961 | 48 | 58 | 88 | 6 | 18 | Meleski, New Britain | .914 | 18 | 9 | 23 | 3 | 8 |
| Bell, Waterbury | .952 | 29 | 41 | 79 | 6 | 16 | Opie, Nashua | 1.000 | 2 | 0 | 4 | 0 | 0 |
| Brumley, Pittsfield | .940 | 126 | 182 | 333 | 33 | 54 | Pastornicky, Glens Falls | 1.000 | 2 | 6 | 5 | 0 | 2 |
| Chapman, Albany | .000 | 2 | 0 | 0 | 1 | 0 | Quinonez, New Britain | .947 | 133 | 207 | 402 | 34 | 75 |
| Christensen, Nashua | .857 | 5 | 5 | 7 | 2 | 1 | Rembielak, Pittsfield | 1.000 | 1 | 1 | 3 | 0 | 0 |
| Escobar, Reading | .930 | 22 | 25 | 55 | 6 | 11 | Riley, Vermont | .840 | 9 | 10 | 11 | 4 | 5 |
| FERMIN, Nashua | .964 | 136 | 251 | 386 | 24 | 64 | Romero, Glens Falls | .870 | 4 | 7 | 13 | 3 | 4 |
| Fryer, Nashua | 1.000 | 2 | 3 | 5 | 0 | 2 | Rutledge, Pittsfield | .905 | 15 | 17 | 40 | 6 | 4 |
| Gallegos, Albany | .870 | 6 | 12 | 8 | 3 | 0 | Sabo, Vermont | .000 | 1 | 0 | 0 | 1 | 0 |
| Gonzalez, Vermont | .932 | 59 | 85 | 136 | 16 | 33 | Scott, Albany | .941 | 92 | 149 | 231 | 24 | 49 |
| Hoppie, Reading | 1.000 | 4 | 3 | 4 | 0 | 1 | Seoane, Albany | .963 | 30 | 51 | 80 | 5 | 15 |
| Jackson, Reading | .935 | 120 | 169 | 305 | 33 | 57 | Smajstrla, 4 GF-16 Water | .955 | 20 | 21 | 43 | 3 | 6 |
| Landestoy, Albany | .968 | 21 | 14 | 47 | 2 | 3 | Snyder, Waterbury | .714 | 10 | 2 | 3 | 2 | 1 |
| Larkin, Vermont | .942 | 71 | 110 | 166 | 17 | 31 | Soper, Glens Falls | .945 | 131 | 208 | 325 | 31 | 56 |
| Manfre, Vermont | .958 | 6 | 9 | 14 | 1 | 3 | Valera, Waterbury | .954 | 71 | 84 | 145 | 11 | 29 |
| McAllister, Nashua | 1.000 | 1 | 1 | 4 | 0 | 1 | | | | | | | |

Triple Play—Brumley.

## OUTFIELDERS

| Player and Club | Pct. | G. | PO. | A. | E. | DP. | Player and Club | Pct. | G. | PO. | A. | E. | DP. |
|---|---|---|---|---|---|---|---|---|---|---|---|---|---|
| Ackley, New Britain | 1.000 | 14 | 32 | 2 | 0 | 1 | Jackson, Pittsfield | 1.000 | 89 | 221 | 5 | 0 | 1 |
| Baker, Nashua | 1.000 | 1 | 1 | 0 | 0 | 0 | Jensen, Glens Falls | .984 | 50 | 116 | 10 | 2 | 0 |
| Barrett, Albany | 1.000 | 2 | 3 | 0 | 0 | 0 | J. Jones, Pittsfield | 1.000 | 16 | 27 | 0 | 0 | 0 |
| Beal, New Britain | .959 | 96 | 200 | 11 | 9 | 2 | T. Jones, Vermont | .992 | 73 | 117 | 4 | 1 | 1 |
| Bennett, New Britain* | .987 | 46 | 71 | 5 | 1 | 1 | Jordan, Waterbury | 1.000 | 8 | 20 | 1 | 0 | 0 |
| Berge, Vermont | .889 | 4 | 8 | 0 | 1 | 0 | Kinnard, Reading | .972 | 75 | 172 | 4 | 5 | 0 |
| Berger, Nashua | .958 | 84 | 152 | 6 | 7 | 0 | Knight, Albany* | 1.000 | 22 | 32 | 3 | 0 | 0 |
| Bernstine, Pittsfield | .954 | 50 | 120 | 5 | 6 | 3 | Lee, Vermont | 1.000 | 7 | 6 | 0 | 0 | 0 |
| A. Brown, Reading | .963 | 107 | 176 | 8 | 7 | 0 | Lombardi, Albany | 1.000 | 10 | 14 | 0 | 0 | 0 |
| C. Brown, Nashua | .975 | 119 | 220 | 12 | 6 | 4 | MacKay, Albany | .976 | 19 | 39 | 2 | 1 | 0 |
| Burks, New Britain | .975 | 130 | 306 | 9 | 8 | 4 | Manfre, Vermont | .950 | 31 | 54 | 3 | 3 | 1 |
| Cannizzaro, New Britain | 1.000 | 2 | 1 | 0 | 0 | 0 | McLaughlin, 18 GF-19 Read* | .986 | 37 | 69 | 4 | 1 | 0 |
| Carpenter, Albany | .973 | 66 | 105 | 4 | 3 | 1 | Moritz, Glens Falls | .933 | 88 | 141 | 11 | 11 | 1 |
| Carroll, Albany | .500 | 1 | 1 | 0 | 1 | 0 | Morman, Glens Falls | 1.000 | 1 | 1 | 0 | 0 | 0 |
| Carter, Waterbury | .976 | 19 | 37 | 3 | 1 | 1 | Olander, Reading | .985 | 61 | 125 | 6 | 2 | 3 |
| Cathcart, Albany* | .976 | 19 | 38 | 2 | 1 | 1 | Oliva, New Britain | .956 | 33 | 64 | 1 | 3 | 1 |
| Cecchetti, Waterbury* | 1.000 | 4 | 7 | 0 | 0 | 0 | Opie, Nashua | 1.000 | 1 | 2 | 0 | 0 | 0 |
| Clark, Waterbury | .951 | 125 | 204 | 11 | 11 | 2 | Peruso, Albany | 1.000 | 1 | 2 | 0 | 0 | 0 |
| Cordova, Pittsfield | .980 | 25 | 46 | 3 | 1 | 1 | Ronk, Pittsfield | .992 | 81 | 122 | 7 | 1 | 2 |
| DeLaRosa, Nashua* | .972 | 56 | 102 | 2 | 3 | 1 | Russell, Albany | .982 | 122 | 332 | 4 | 6 | 2 |
| Edwards, Waterbury | .983 | 81 | 166 | 8 | 3 | 3 | Scheer, Glens Falls | .969 | 100 | 197 | 19 | 7 | 6 |
| Ficklin, Waterbury | .982 | 107 | 254 | 14 | 5 | 1 | Scott, Albany | 1.000 | 2 | 4 | 0 | 0 | 0 |
| Ford, Nashua | .965 | 73 | 129 | 7 | 5 | 2 | Sedar, Glens Falls | .958 | 42 | 63 | 6 | 3 | 1 |
| Gallegos, Albany | .875 | 3 | 6 | 1 | 1 | 0 | Smajstrla, 7 GF-3 Water | 1.000 | 10 | 15 | 1 | 0 | 0 |
| Gillaspie, Pittsfield | 1.000 | 13 | 20 | 1 | 0 | 1 | Soares, Reading | .966 | 122 | 216 | 9 | 8 | 4 |
| Gomez, Pittsfield | .944 | 69 | 96 | 5 | 6 | 1 | Varsho, Pittsfield | 1.000 | 46 | 91 | 1 | 0 | 0 |
| Guzman, Vermont | .967 | 104 | 174 | 4 | 6 | 0 | Ward, Reading | 1.000 | 37 | 84 | 1 | 0 | 0 |
| Hale, New Britain | .750 | 4 | 2 | 1 | 1 | 0 | Washington, Waterbury | .980 | 92 | 179 | 16 | 4 | 3 |
| Hammond, Pittsfield | .975 | 55 | 115 | 4 | 3 | 1 | D. Williams, New Britain | .986 | 109 | 198 | 6 | 3 | 0 |
| Haro, Nashua | .982 | 112 | 274 | 6 | 5 | 2 | K. Williams, Glens Falls | .958 | 123 | 296 | 20 | 14 | 3 |
| Hill, Vermont | .971 | 119 | 194 | 9 | 6 | 3 | Winkler, Albany | .957 | 65 | 109 | 2 | 5 | 0 |
| Hoppie, Reading | 1.000 | 14 | 8 | 0 | 0 | 0 | Winters, Albany | 1.000 | 14 | 19 | 0 | 0 | 0 |
| D. Hughes, Albany | .667 | 5 | 2 | 0 | 1 | 0 | YOUNG, Vermont | .988 | 109 | 243 | 12 | 3 | 4 |
| K. Hughes, Albany* | .987 | 104 | 218 | 7 | 3 | 4 | | | | | | | |

## CATCHERS

| Player and Club | Pct. | G. | PO. | A. | E. | DP. | PB. | Player and Club | Pct. | G. | PO. | A. | E. | DP. | PB. |
|---|---|---|---|---|---|---|---|---|---|---|---|---|---|---|---|
| Ackley, New Britain | .983 | 23 | 102 | 15 | 2 | 0 | 2 | Karkovice, Glens Falls | .980 | 97 | 573 | 103 | 14 | 13 | 11 |
| Alcazar, Glens Falls | 1.000 | 1 | 7 | 1 | 0 | 1 | 0 | Kelly, Glens Falls | .971 | 25 | 114 | 18 | 4 | 3 | 5 |
| Allanson, Waterbury | .985 | 98 | 578 | 64 | 10 | 5 | 12 | Lindsey, Albany | .985 | 54 | 272 | 49 | 5 | 4 | 8 |
| Baker, Nashua | .974 | 45 | 197 | 30 | 6 | 4 | 6 | Lombardi, Albany | .975 | 65 | 376 | 47 | 11 | 5 | 7 |
| Blaser, Albany | 1.000 | 10 | 44 | 3 | 0 | 1 | 2 | Marzano, New Britain | .980 | 101 | 530 | 70 | 12 | 4 | 8 |
| Cipolloni, Reading | .986 | 84 | 437 | 67 | 7 | 11 | 5 | McGRIFF, Vermont | .992 | 101 | 636 | 89 | 6 | 9 | 10 |
| Fennell, Albany | .973 | 14 | 66 | 5 | 2 | 0 | 1 | Pryor, Vermont | .983 | 27 | 158 | 18 | 3 | 0 | 4 |
| Foley, Glens Falls | .989 | 15 | 75 | 11 | 1 | 1 | 1 | Roadcap, Pittsfield | .958 | 28 | 111 | 25 | 6 | 1 | 1 |
| Glass, Waterbury | .986 | 13 | 63 | 5 | 1 | 0 | 2 | Rodriguez, Nashua | .982 | 100 | 498 | 96 | 11 | 6 | 17 |
| Goldthorn, Nashua | 1.000 | 4 | 19 | 1 | 0 | 0 | 0 | Romero, Glens Falls | .941 | 5 | 16 | 0 | 1 | 1 | 1 |
| Hammond, Pittsfield | .960 | 47 | 218 | 21 | 10 | 0 | 14 | Syverson, Waterbury | .977 | 38 | 187 | 24 | 5 | 3 | 6 |
| Hawkins, Albany | 1.000 | 12 | 35 | 3 | 0 | 0 | 2 | Tejada, Reading | .988 | 58 | 291 | 29 | 4 | 5 | 4 |
| Henderson, Pittsfield | .978 | 74 | 356 | 51 | 9 | 3 | 8 | Tremblay, New Britain | .967 | 21 | 76 | 13 | 3 | 2 | 4 |
| Hoppie, Reading | 1.000 | 4 | 4 | 0 | 0 | 0 | 0 | Vincent, Vermont | 1.000 | 17 | 84 | 4 | 0 | 2 | 1 |

Triple Play—Hammond.

## PITCHERS

| Player and Club | Pct. | G. | PO. | A. | E. | DP. | Player and Club | Pct. | G. | PO. | A. | E. | DP. |
|---|---|---|---|---|---|---|---|---|---|---|---|---|---|
| Abrego, Pittsfield | .909 | 22 | 11 | 29 | 4 | 2 | Capel, Pittsfield | .917 | 33 | 5 | 17 | 2 | 0 |
| Arney, Waterbury | 1.000 | 28 | 1 | 9 | 0 | 0 | Cappadona, New Britain* | 1.000 | 12 | 4 | 5 | 0 | 0 |
| Arnold, Reading* | .966 | 27 | 3 | 25 | 1 | 0 | Caraballo, Reading | .500 | 4 | 0 | 1 | 1 | 0 |
| Arnsberg, Albany | .927 | 20 | 9 | 29 | 3 | 0 | Chestnut, Pittsfield | .976 | 28 | 8 | 33 | 1 | 1 |
| Bailes, 29 Nas-13 Water.* | .917 | 42 | 4 | 18 | 2 | 2 | Cloninger, Albany | .900 | 13 | 3 | 6 | 1 | 0 |
| Beasley, Waterbury | .938 | 9 | 2 | 13 | 1 | 0 | Cornell, Pittsfield | 1.000 | 29 | 9 | 11 | 0 | 1 |
| Belleman, Waterbury | 1.000 | 2 | 4 | 2 | 0 | 0 | Correa, Glens Falls | .938 | 8 | 0 | 15 | 1 | 0 |
| Blevins, Pittsfield | .917 | 38 | 3 | 8 | 1 | 0 | Culver, Reading | 1.000 | 3 | 0 | 2 | 0 | 0 |
| Bolton, New Britain* | .967 | 34 | 8 | 21 | 1 | 3 | Dale, New Britain | .933 | 46 | 4 | 10 | 1 | 0 |
| Bowden, Reading* | 1.000 | 15 | 2 | 1 | 0 | 0 | C. Davis, New Britain | 1.000 | 23 | 8 | 10 | 0 | 1 |
| Bradley, Albany | .917 | 25 | 3 | 8 | 1 | 1 | J. Davis, Glens Falls | 1.000 | 4 | 1 | 4 | 0 | 0 |
| Brecht, Glens Falls* | 1.000 | 25 | 2 | 2 | 0 | 0 | DeLaRosa, Nashua* | 1.000 | 2 | 0 | 1 | 0 | 0 |
| Bulls, Reading | .870 | 16 | 6 | 14 | 3 | 0 | DeVincenzo, Glens Falls* | 1.000 | 21 | 1 | 19 | 0 | 0 |
| Burroughs, Vermont* | 1.000 | 24 | 0 | 10 | 0 | 0 | Dodd, Vermont | 1.000 | 7 | 0 | 3 | 0 | 0 |
| Byron, Albany | .909 | 27 | 10 | 30 | 4 | 6 | Doyle, Waterbury | .875 | 15 | 7 | 7 | 2 | 1 |

## PITCHERS—Continued

| Player and Club | Pct. | G. | PO. | A. | E. | DP. |
|---|---|---|---|---|---|---|
| Drabek, Albany | .921 | 26 | 10 | 25 | 3 | 1 |
| Easley, Albany | .905 | 29 | 3 | 16 | 2 | 0 |
| Ellsworth, New Britain | 1.000 | 20 | 6 | 20 | 0 | 2 |
| Elston, Waterbury | 1.000 | 8 | 1 | 1 | 0 | 0 |
| Engle, Pittsfield° | 1.000 | 12 | 1 | 12 | 0 | 0 |
| Evetts, Reading | .966 | 39 | 6 | 22 | 1 | 0 |
| Fansler, Nashua | .885 | 24 | 19 | 27 | 6 | 0 |
| Farrell, Waterbury | .952 | 25 | 7 | 13 | 1 | 1 |
| Faulk, Albany | 1.000 | 6 | 1 | 9 | 0 | 0 |
| Ferguson, Albany | .929 | 17 | 2 | 11 | 1 | 3 |
| Filippi, Glens Falls | 1.000 | 2 | 0 | 1 | 0 | 0 |
| Freeman, Reading | .923 | 11 | 4 | 8 | 1 | 0 |
| Frey, Albany° | .938 | 40 | 1 | 14 | 1 | 0 |
| Fruge, Pittsfield | 1.000 | 5 | 1 | 0 | 0 | 0 |
| GAYNOR, Reading | 1.000 | 18 | 10 | 27 | 0 | 2 |
| Gering, New Britain | 1.000 | 34 | 8 | 6 | 0 | 1 |
| Gomez, Pittsfield | 1.000 | 1 | 0 | 1 | 0 | 0 |
| Graham, Albany | .800 | 46 | 7 | 1 | 2 | 1 |
| Griffin, 15 Read-3 Nashua° | .917 | 18 | 1 | 10 | 1 | 1 |
| Grimm, Vermont | 1.000 | 12 | 1 | 5 | 0 | 0 |
| Guzman, Glens Falls | .857 | 19 | 7 | 11 | 3 | 1 |
| Hardy, Glens Falls | 1.000 | 37 | 6 | 10 | 0 | 2 |
| Hawley, Vermont | .875 | 17 | 5 | 9 | 2 | 0 |
| Heidenreich, Vermont | .861 | 23 | 12 | 19 | 5 | 3 |
| Henika, Vermont | 1.000 | 2 | 1 | 0 | 0 | 0 |
| Henry, Pittsfield° | .875 | 10 | 0 | 7 | 1 | 0 |
| J. Hickey, Glens Falls | 1.000 | 25 | 7 | 11 | 0 | 2 |
| K. Hickey, 11 Alb-33 Read.° | 1.000 | 44 | 4 | 12 | 0 | 0 |
| Hicks, Reading | .833 | 41 | 1 | 9 | 2 | 2 |
| Holman, Nashua | 1.000 | 2 | 1 | 1 | 0 | 0 |
| Housey, Pittsfield | 1.000 | 32 | 4 | 11 | 0 | 0 |
| Imig, Glens Falls | 1.000 | 8 | 1 | 0 | 0 | 1 |
| Jefferson, Vermont | .923 | 25 | 8 | 16 | 2 | 0 |
| D. Johnson, Nashua | .952 | 34 | 10 | 30 | 2 | 0 |
| J. Johnson, Glens Falls | .969 | 28 | 12 | 19 | 1 | 2 |
| W. Johnson, Waterbury° | 1.000 | 8 | 1 | 1 | 0 | 0 |
| B. Jones, Nashua | 1.000 | 23 | 3 | 3 | 0 | 0 |
| D. Jones, Waterbury | .897 | 39 | 6 | 20 | 3 | 0 |
| Kelly, Glens Falls | 1.000 | 1 | 0 | 1 | 0 | 1 |
| Kemp, Vermont | .800 | 12 | 6 | 6 | 3 | 0 |
| Knox, Vermont | 1.000 | 7 | 5 | 13 | 0 | 3 |
| Konderla, Vermont | .900 | 44 | 3 | 15 | 2 | 0 |
| Labay, Reading° | 1.000 | 6 | 2 | 5 | 0 | 1 |
| Lamonde, Nashua | .933 | 24 | 13 | 15 | 2 | 2 |
| Layton, 7 GF-23 Pittsfield° | .963 | 30 | 5 | 21 | 1 | 1 |
| Leach, Waterbury | 1.000 | 13 | 5 | 7 | 0 | 0 |
| Leister, New Britain | .938 | 27 | 4 | 11 | 1 | 1 |
| Long, Reading | .895 | 14 | 6 | 11 | 2 | 1 |
| Lono, Vermont° | 1.000 | 1 | 0 | 1 | 0 | 0 |
| Madden, Vermont° | | 6 | 1 | 7 | 0 | 0 |
| Manzanillo, Nashua° | .889 | 33 | 6 | 18 | 3 | 2 |
| Marcheskie, Nashua | 1.000 | 7 | 3 | 4 | 0 | 1 |
| McKelvey, Nashua | 1.000 | 19 | 0 | 5 | 0 | 0 |
| Menard, Reading | .857 | 30 | 6 | 12 | 3 | 1 |
| Miglio, Waterbury° | 1.000 | 46 | 4 | 6 | 0 | 1 |
| Mitchell, New Britain | .984 | 26 | 23 | 38 | 1 | 1 |
| Montgomery, Vermont | 1.000 | 53 | 6 | 18 | 0 | 0 |
| Moyer, Pittsfield° | 1.000 | 15 | 3 | 25 | 0 | 3 |
| Mullen, Glens Falls | 1.000 | 18 | 6 | 16 | 0 | 0 |
| Murphy, Waterbury° | 1.000 | 4 | 1 | 2 | 0 | 0 |
| Neal, Nashua° | 1.000 | 26 | 2 | 9 | 0 | 0 |
| Nielsen, Albany | .929 | 11 | 3 | 10 | 1 | 0 |
| Oliverio, Vermont | 1.000 | 8 | 4 | 8 | 0 | 0 |
| Olson, Reading | .875 | 28 | 4 | 24 | 4 | 1 |
| Oswald, Glens Falls° | 1.000 | 2 | 3 | 1 | 0 | 0 |
| Pacillo, Vermont | 1.000 | 22 | 4 | 3 | 0 | 0 |
| Palacios, Glens Falls | 1.000 | 8 | 2 | 2 | 0 | 0 |
| Parmenter, Pittsfield | .941 | 17 | 8 | 24 | 2 | 1 |
| Patterson, Albany | 1.000 | 27 | 1 | 10 | 0 | 0 |
| Pippin, Waterbury | 1.000 | 18 | 0 | 3 | 0 | 0 |
| Potestio, Pittsfield | 1.000 | 26 | 9 | 19 | 0 | 2 |
| Reburn, Vermont | 1.000 | 5 | 1 | 1 | 0 | 0 |
| Renz, Glens Falls | .625 | 9 | 1 | 4 | 3 | 0 |
| Reynolds, Vermont | 1.000 | 19 | 13 | 16 | 0 | 0 |
| Rice, Nashua | 1.000 | 11 | 3 | 4 | 0 | 1 |
| Ritter, Waterbury | .885 | 15 | 10 | 13 | 3 | 0 |
| Rochford, New Britain° | 1.000 | 14 | 7 | 11 | 0 | 0 |
| Sanchez, Nashua° | .867 | 26 | 1 | 12 | 2 | 0 |
| Santarelli, Waterbury | .941 | 31 | 12 | 20 | 2 | 2 |
| Sauveur, Nashua° | .927 | 25 | 10 | 41 | 4 | 3 |
| Schmidt, Glens Falls | .927 | 27 | 11 | 27 | 3 | 0 |
| K. Scott, Albany | 1.000 | 8 | 3 | 3 | 0 | 0 |
| T. Scott, Vermont | 1.000 | 36 | 5 | 6 | 0 | 0 |
| Sedar, Glens Falls | 1.000 | 5 | 2 | 1 | 0 | 0 |
| Sellers, New Britain | .892 | 25 | 15 | 18 | 4 | 2 |
| Smith, Waterbury | .900 | 16 | 1 | 8 | 1 | 1 |
| Stalp, Vermont | 1.000 | 6 | 2 | 4 | 0 | 0 |
| Street, Waterbury | .800 | 16 | 1 | 7 | 2 | 1 |
| Taylor, Nashua | .947 | 26 | 5 | 13 | 1 | 1 |
| Tewksbury, Albany | 1.000 | 17 | 4 | 24 | 0 | 3 |
| Torres, Albany | 1.000 | 1 | 2 | 1 | 0 | 0 |
| Underwood, Albany° | .000 | 4 | 0 | 0 | 1 | 0 |
| Walker, Glens Falls | .955 | 46 | 4 | 17 | 1 | 1 |
| Watts, Reading° | .800 | 6 | 3 | 1 | 1 | 0 |
| Wever, Albany | 1.000 | 5 | 2 | 2 | 0 | 0 |
| Wex, Albany | 1.000 | 9 | 0 | 2 | 0 | 0 |
| Williams, Glens Falls | 1.000 | 35 | 11 | 17 | 0 | 0 |
| Woodward, New Britain | .850 | 12 | 8 | 9 | 3 | 0 |
| Wright, 19 Rea-20 Nashua° | .882 | 39 | 6 | 9 | 2 | 1 |

The following players do not have any recorded accepted chances at the positions indicated; therefore, are not listed in the fielding averages for those particular positions: Baker, p; Berger, p; Brumley, of; Carroll, ss; Cordova, c; Cox, p; Ford, 1b; Hill, p; D. Hughes, 3b, p; Landestoy, of; Lindsey, of; Lombardi, ss; Moreno, p; Schaum, 3b; P. Smith, of; Torve, of.

## CLUB PITCHING

| Club | ERA | G. | CG. | ShO. | Sv. | IP. | H. | R. | ER. | HR. | HB. | BB. | Int. BB. | SO. | WP. | Bk. |
|---|---|---|---|---|---|---|---|---|---|---|---|---|---|---|---|---|
| New Britain | 3.36 | 139 | 48 | 16 | 19 | 1169.0 | 1063 | 515 | 436 | 52 | 29 | 452 | 30 | 664 | 44 | 9 |
| Albany | 3.37 | 139 | 33 | 12 | 29 | 1207.0 | 1129 | 553 | 452 | 68 | 44 | 440 | 38 | 767 | 32 | 4 |
| Nashua | 3.52 | 139 | 17 | 15 | 36 | 1184.0 | 1027 | 567 | 463 | 59 | 21 | 621 | 20 | 677 | 59 | 13 |
| Vermont | 3.66 | 138 | 18 | 8 | 27 | 1176.2 | 1037 | 549 | 478 | 77 | 20 | 600 | 23 | 835 | 58 | 16 |
| Pittsfield | 3.81 | 138 | 35 | 8 | 16 | 1160.2 | 1083 | 587 | 491 | 55 | 44 | 511 | 27 | 647 | 63 | 10 |
| Waterbury | 3.99 | 139 | 33 | 11 | 35 | 1187.1 | 1179 | 628 | 527 | 79 | 44 | 553 | 26 | 782 | 62 | 8 |
| Reading | 4.12 | 137 | 21 | 8 | 26 | 1121.2 | 1137 | 635 | 513 | 70 | 35 | 506 | 28 | 691 | 55 | 17 |
| Glens Falls | 4.16 | 139 | 25 | 9 | 26 | 1165.0 | 1236 | 651 | 538 | 88 | 44 | 563 | 18 | 731 | 46 | 13 |

## PITCHERS' RECORDS
(Leading Qualifiers for Earned-Run Average Leadership — 112 or More Innings)

°Throws lefthanded.

| Pitcher—Club | W. | L. | Pct. | ERA | G. | GS. | CG. | GF. | ShO. | Sv. | IP. | H. | R. | ER. | HR. | HB. | BB. | Int. BB. | SO. | WP. |
|---|---|---|---|---|---|---|---|---|---|---|---|---|---|---|---|---|---|---|---|---|
| Arnsberg, Albany | 14 | 2 | .875 | 1.59 | 20 | 20 | 9 | 0 | 2 | 0 | 141.1 | 105 | 34 | 25 | 0 | 8 | 35 | 0 | 82 | 3 |
| Parmenter, Pittsfield | 6 | 5 | .545 | 2.44 | 17 | 17 | 6 | 0 | 1 | 0 | 121.2 | 81 | 40 | 33 | 5 | 5 | 49 | 0 | 62 | 8 |
| Gaynor, Reading | 9 | 4 | .692 | 2.57 | 18 | 18 | 7 | 0 | 1 | 0 | 126.0 | 117 | 47 | 36 | 3 | 3 | 35 | 0 | 84 | 3 |
| Mitchell, New Britain | 12 | 8 | .600 | 2.70 | 26 | 26 | 10 | 0 | 1 | 0 | 190.1 | 143 | 71 | 57 | 4 | 2 | 61 | 4 | 108 | 11 |
| Bailes, Waterbury° | 9 | 6 | .600 | 2.71 | 42 | 11 | 3 | 22 | 1 | 9 | 126.1 | 123 | 58 | 38 | 7 | 4 | 43 | 2 | 93 | 8 |
| Abrego, Pittsfield | 6 | 6 | .500 | 2.76 | 22 | 22 | 6 | 0 | 2 | 0 | 156.1 | 119 | 60 | 48 | 8 | 9 | 72 | 2 | 92 | 7 |
| Sellers, New Britain | 14 | 7 | .667 | 2.78 | 25 | 25 | 15 | 0 | 5 | 0 | 184.2 | 165 | 67 | 57 | 2 | 4 | 67 | 1 | 115 | 9 |
| Lamonde, Nashua | 9 | 8 | .529 | 2.93 | 24 | 21 | 1 | 0 | 0 | 0 | 132.0 | 119 | 61 | 43 | 10 | 4 | 69 | 0 | 47 | 4 |
| Reynolds, Vermont | 5 | 8 | .385 | 2.98 | 19 | 18 | 4 | 0 | 0 | 0 | 121.0 | 105 | 50 | 40 | 6 | 4 | 49 | 2 | 85 | 7 |
| Drabek, Albany | 13 | 7 | .650 | 2.99 | 26 | 26 | 9 | 0 | 2 | 0 | 192.2 | 153 | 71 | 64 | 12 | 6 | 55 | 2 | 153 | 2 |

Departmental Leaders: G—Montgomery, 53; W—Arnsberg, Sellers, 14; L—Chestnut, 15; Pct.—Arnsberg, .875; GS—Chestnut, J. Johnson, 28; CG—Sellers, 15; GF—Dale, 40; ShO—Sellers, 5; Sv.—Graham, 17; IP—Drabek, 192.2; H—Chestnut, 191; R—Farrell, 106; ER—Chestnut, 88; HR—J. Johnson, 15; HB—Abrego, Santarelli, 9; BB—Manzanillo, 96; IBB—Dale, D. Jones, 8; SO—Drabek, 153; WP—Santarelli, 12.

(All Pitchers—Listed Alphabetically)

| Pitcher—Club | W. | L. | Pct. | ERA. | G. | GS. | CG. | GF. | ShO. | Sv. | IP. | H. | R. | ER. | HR. | HB. | BB. | Int. BB. | SO. | WP. |
|---|---|---|---|---|---|---|---|---|---|---|---|---|---|---|---|---|---|---|---|---|
| Abrego, Pittsfield | 6 | 6 | .500 | 2.76 | 22 | 22 | 6 | 0 | 2 | 0 | 156.1 | 119 | 60 | 48 | 8 | 9 | 72 | 2 | 92 | 7 |
| Arney, Waterbury | 6 | 2 | .750 | 2.18 | 28 | 2 | 0 | 18 | 0 | 8 | 70.1 | 62 | 19 | 17 | 4 | 0 | 22 | 1 | 47 | 1 |
| Arnold, Reading° | 3 | 8 | .273 | 2.79 | 27 | 13 | 4 | 9 | 2 | 3 | 106.1 | 103 | 54 | 33 | 4 | 2 | 41 | 5 | 65 | 3 |
| Arnsberg, Albany | 14 | 2 | .875 | 1.59 | 20 | 20 | 9 | 0 | 2 | 0 | 141.1 | 105 | 34 | 25 | 0 | 8 | 35 | 0 | 82 | 3 |
| Bailes, Waterbury° | 9 | 6 | .600 | 2.71 | 42 | 11 | 3 | 22 | 1 | 9 | 126.1 | 123 | 58 | 38 | 7 | 4 | 43 | 2 | 93 | 8 |
| Baker, Nashua | 0 | 0 | .000 | 0.00 | 1 | 0 | 0 | 1 | 0 | 0 | 1.0 | 0 | 0 | 0 | 0 | 0 | 1 | 0 | 1 | 0 |
| Beasley, Waterbury | 2 | 6 | .250 | 4.18 | 9 | 9 | 4 | 0 | 0 | 0 | 56.0 | 44 | 28 | 26 | 4 | 3 | 35 | 1 | 27 | 1 |
| Belleman, Waterbury | 2 | 0 | 1.000 | 1.13 | 2 | 2 | 1 | 0 | 1 | 0 | 16.0 | 9 | 3 | 2 | 0 | 0 | 3 | 0 | 12 | 1 |
| Berger, Nashua | 0 | 0 | .000 | 18.00 | 1 | 0 | 0 | 1 | 0 | 0 | 1.0 | 2 | 2 | 2 | 1 | 0 | 1 | 0 | 0 | 0 |
| Blevins, Pittsfield | 5 | 6 | .455 | 3.40 | 38 | 0 | 0 | 31 | 0 | 8 | 50.1 | 50 | 24 | 19 | 1 | 0 | 26 | 4 | 33 | 2 |
| Bolton, New Britain° | 5 | 6 | .455 | 4.28 | 34 | 10 | 1 | 14 | 0 | 1 | 101.0 | 106 | 53 | 48 | 3 | 2 | 40 | 1 | 74 | 3 |
| Bowden, Reading° | 1 | 0 | 1.000 | 4.96 | 15 | 4 | 0 | 3 | 0 | 1 | 32.2 | 27 | 18 | 18 | 3 | 1 | 20 | 0 | 25 | 2 |
| Bradley, Albany | 1 | 6 | .143 | 5.30 | 25 | 5 | 1 | 13 | 0 | 3 | 56.0 | 69 | 42 | 33 | 6 | 2 | 26 | 3 | 24 | 1 |
| Brecht, Glens Falls° | 1 | 3 | .250 | 6.21 | 25 | 2 | 0 | 10 | 0 | 2 | 33.1 | 43 | 29 | 23 | 3 | 1 | 20 | 0 | 30 | 1 |
| Bulls, Reading | 4 | 8 | .333 | 4.25 | 16 | 15 | 0 | 0 | 0 | 0 | 89.0 | 96 | 51 | 42 | 4 | 7 | 40 | 0 | 53 | 6 |
| Burroughs, Vermont° | 2 | 4 | .333 | 2.32 | 24 | 2 | 0 | 11 | 0 | 0 | 50.1 | 34 | 14 | 13 | 5 | 0 | 21 | 2 | 49 | 6 |
| Byron, Albany | 10 | 7 | .588 | 3.33 | 27 | 25 | 5 | 2 | 0 | 0 | 165.0 | 158 | 83 | 61 | 6 | 5 | 79 | 6 | 89 | 9 |
| Capel, Pittsfield | 3 | 6 | .333 | 4.91 | 33 | 4 | 0 | 16 | 0 | 0 | 73.1 | 74 | 44 | 40 | 4 | 1 | 47 | 2 | 53 | 6 |
| Cappadona, New Britain | 0 | 2 | .000 | 4.36 | 12 | 2 | 1 | 5 | 0 | 1 | 33.0 | 31 | 16 | 16 | 0 | 2 | 17 | 1 | 18 | 1 |
| Caraballo, Reading | 0 | 0 | .000 | 6.23 | 4 | 0 | 0 | 1 | 0 | 0 | 4.1 | 7 | 4 | 3 | 0 | 0 | 4 | 0 | 3 | 0 |
| Chestnut, Pittsfield | 8 | 15 | .348 | 4.29 | 28 | 28 | 10 | 0 | 2 | 0 | 184.2 | 191 | 103 | 88 | 6 | 4 | 66 | 5 | 89 | 8 |
| Cloninger, Albany | 1 | 3 | .250 | 5.35 | 13 | 6 | 0 | 3 | 0 | 0 | 38.2 | 48 | 26 | 23 | 3 | 3 | 23 | 1 | 16 | 0 |
| Cornell, Pittsfield | 8 | 7 | .533 | 3.46 | 29 | 10 | 0 | 15 | 0 | 5 | 91.0 | 91 | 42 | 35 | 3 | 3 | 35 | 4 | 64 | 5 |
| Correa, Glens Falls | 1 | 5 | .167 | 6.75 | 8 | 8 | 0 | 0 | 0 | 0 | 40.0 | 37 | 41 | 30 | 6 | 4 | 35 | 0 | 34 | 4 |
| Cox, Vermont | 0 | 0 | .000 | 0.00 | 2 | 0 | 0 | 2 | 0 | 0 | 3.0 | 5 | 1 | 0 | 0 | 0 | 0 | 0 | 1 | 0 |
| Culver, Reading | 0 | 0 | .000 | 16.62 | 3 | 0 | 0 | 1 | 0 | 0 | 4.1 | 11 | 8 | 8 | 0 | 1 | 1 | 0 | 0 | 1 |
| Dale, New Britain | 4 | 3 | .571 | 3.15 | 46 | 0 | 0 | 40 | 0 | 12 | 68.2 | 73 | 28 | 24 | 8 | 0 | 29 | 8 | 34 | 2 |
| C. Davis, New Britain | 7 | 8 | .467 | 3.82 | 23 | 15 | 3 | 6 | 1 | 1 | 110.2 | 99 | 48 | 47 | 6 | 7 | 47 | 6 | 41 | 1 |
| J. Davis, Glens Falls | 1 | 1 | .500 | 2.84 | 4 | 4 | 0 | 0 | 0 | 0 | 25.1 | 21 | 8 | 8 | 4 | 2 | 16 | 2 | 20 | 0 |
| DeLaRosa, Nashua° | 0 | 0 | .000 | 4.50 | 2 | 0 | 0 | 2 | 0 | 0 | 2.0 | 2 | 3 | 1 | 0 | 0 | 3 | 0 | 1 | 0 |
| DeVincenzo, Glens Falls° | 5 | 7 | .417 | 3.87 | 21 | 19 | 4 | 1 | 1 | 0 | 109.1 | 127 | 56 | 47 | 11 | 1 | 64 | 1 | 64 | 4 |
| Dodd, Vermont | 0 | 1 | .000 | 11.25 | 7 | 5 | 0 | 1 | 0 | 0 | 24.0 | 35 | 34 | 30 | 2 | 0 | 28 | 0 | 21 | 4 |
| Doyle, Waterbury | 8 | 4 | .667 | 4.38 | 15 | 15 | 4 | 0 | 1 | 0 | 86.1 | 95 | 47 | 42 | 5 | 6 | 26 | 0 | 50 | 3 |
| Drabek, Albany | 13 | 7 | .650 | 2.99 | 26 | 26 | 9 | 0 | 2 | 0 | 192.2 | 153 | 71 | 64 | 12 | 6 | 55 | 2 | 153 | 2 |
| Easley, Albany | 5 | 3 | .625 | 3.18 | 29 | 5 | 0 | 9 | 0 | 0 | 85.0 | 85 | 40 | 30 | 6 | 4 | 38 | 1 | 58 | 1 |
| Ellsworth, New Britain | 7 | 8 | .467 | 4.26 | 20 | 20 | 2 | 0 | 0 | 0 | 120.1 | 136 | 66 | 57 | 8 | 1 | 31 | 1 | 63 | 7 |
| Elston, Waterbury | 0 | 0 | .000 | 4.20 | 8 | 1 | 0 | 4 | 0 | 0 | 15.0 | 13 | 8 | 7 | 2 | 1 | 12 | 0 | 14 | 4 |
| Engel, Pittsfield° | 3 | 6 | .333 | 3.89 | 12 | 12 | 4 | 0 | 2 | 0 | 76.1 | 67 | 36 | 33 | 1 | 6 | 44 | 0 | 52 | 3 |
| Evetts, Reading | 6 | 6 | .500 | 4.09 | 39 | 5 | 1 | 16 | 1 | 3 | 94.2 | 93 | 48 | 43 | 3 | 2 | 38 | 2 | 51 | 4 |
| Fansler, Nashua | 9 | 7 | .563 | 3.01 | 24 | 24 | 5 | 0 | 2 | 0 | 158.2 | 137 | 67 | 53 | 4 | 4 | 75 | 1 | 74 | 4 |
| Farrell, Waterbury | 7 | 13 | .350 | 5.19 | 25 | 25 | 5 | 0 | 1 | 0 | 149.0 | 161 | 106 | 86 | 8 | 5 | 76 | 1 | 75 | 7 |
| Faulk, Albany | 3 | 0 | 1.000 | 3.09 | 6 | 5 | 0 | 0 | 0 | 0 | 35.0 | 32 | 12 | 12 | 3 | 0 | 14 | 1 | 24 | 0 |
| Ferguson, Albany | 5 | 3 | .625 | 3.19 | 17 | 9 | 0 | 2 | 0 | 0 | 62.0 | 63 | 30 | 22 | 2 | 0 | 29 | 5 | 36 | 4 |
| Filippi, Glens Falls | 0 | 0 | .000 | 3.00 | 2 | 2 | 0 | 0 | 0 | 0 | 9.0 | 7 | 3 | 3 | 0 | 0 | 6 | 0 | 8 | 1 |
| Freeman, Reading | 1 | 7 | .125 | 5.37 | 11 | 11 | 2 | 0 | 0 | 0 | 65.1 | 51 | 41 | 39 | 11 | 1 | 52 | 1 | 35 | 3 |
| Frey, Albany° | 4 | 7 | .364 | 3.82 | 40 | 0 | 0 | 14 | 0 | 3 | 61.1 | 53 | 30 | 26 | 4 | 3 | 25 | 5 | 54 | 0 |
| Fruge, Pittsburgh | 0 | 0 | .000 | 12.38 | 5 | 0 | 0 | 0 | 0 | 0 | 8.0 | 14 | 12 | 11 | 2 | 0 | 6 | 0 | 4 | 0 |
| Gaynor, Reading | 9 | 4 | .692 | 2.57 | 18 | 18 | 7 | 0 | 1 | 0 | 126.0 | 117 | 47 | 36 | 3 | 3 | 35 | 0 | 84 | 3 |
| Gering, New Britain | 3 | 6 | .333 | 3.33 | 34 | 2 | 0 | 17 | 0 | 3 | 75.2 | 64 | 37 | 28 | 4 | 1 | 34 | 3 | 47 | 1 |
| Gomez, Pittsfield | 0 | 0 | .000 | 0.00 | 1 | 0 | 0 | 1 | 0 | 0 | 2.1 | 0 | 0 | 0 | 0 | 0 | 2 | 0 | 0 | 0 |
| Graham, Albany | 4 | 4 | .500 | 3.54 | 46 | 0 | 0 | 36 | 0 | 17 | 56.0 | 60 | 26 | 22 | 2 | 0 | 7 | 1 | 46 | 1 |
| Griffin, 15 Read-3 Nash° | 2 | 2 | .500 | 3.76 | 18 | 6 | 0 | 7 | 0 | 0 | 55.0 | 48 | 30 | 23 | 3 | 0 | 30 | 0 | 33 | 1 |
| Grimm, Vermont | 5 | 5 | .500 | 3.91 | 12 | 12 | 1 | 0 | 0 | 0 | 69.0 | 72 | 32 | 30 | 11 | 0 | 25 | 0 | 37 | 1 |
| Guzman, Glens Falls | 2 | 2 | .500 | 5.21 | 19 | 9 | 1 | 1 | 1 | 0 | 74.1 | 60 | 48 | 43 | 9 | 3 | 59 | 0 | 39 | 4 |
| Hardy, Glens Falls | 7 | 3 | .700 | 2.90 | 37 | 0 | 0 | 30 | 0 | 15 | 59.0 | 50 | 23 | 19 | 2 | 0 | 26 | 3 | 48 | 2 |
| Hawley, Vermont | 7 | 8 | .467 | 4.63 | 17 | 17 | 2 | 0 | 0 | 0 | 101.0 | 102 | 60 | 52 | 9 | 2 | 30 | 3 | 52 | 1 |
| Heidenreich, Vermont | 8 | 7 | .533 | 4.98 | 23 | 22 | 2 | 0 | 1 | 0 | 119.1 | 122 | 73 | 66 | 9 | 3 | 81 | 0 | 49 | 6 |
| Henka, Vermont | 0 | 0 | .000 | 15.00 | 2 | 0 | 0 | 1 | 0 | 0 | 3.0 | 3 | 5 | 5 | 1 | 1 | 5 | 0 | 2 | 0 |
| Henry, Pittsfield° | 0 | 3 | .000 | 8.33 | 10 | 6 | 0 | 0 | 0 | 0 | 31.1 | 44 | 31 | 29 | 3 | 0 | 23 | 0 | 17 | 2 |
| J. Hickey, Nashua | 7 | 6 | .538 | 3.86 | 25 | 10 | 4 | 11 | 1 | 2 | 93.1 | 90 | 46 | 40 | 6 | 3 | 42 | 1 | 39 | 3 |
| K. Hickey, 11 Alb-33 Read° | 5 | 5 | .500 | 2.69 | 44 | 0 | 0 | 31 | 0 | 11 | 60.1 | 53 | 22 | 18 | 3 | 3 | 22 | 3 | 44 | 1 |
| Hicks, Reading | 6 | 6 | .500 | 3.62 | 41 | 0 | 0 | 35 | 0 | 8 | 59.2 | 53 | 30 | 24 | 4 | 0 | 28 | 5 | 50 | 3 |
| Hill, Vermont | 0 | 0 | .000 | 9.00 | 1 | 0 | 0 | 1 | 0 | 0 | 1.0 | 1 | 1 | 1 | 0 | 0 | 1 | 0 | 0 | 0 |
| Holman, Nashua | 0 | 1 | .000 | 4.50 | 2 | 2 | 0 | 0 | 0 | 0 | 8.0 | 10 | 6 | 4 | 0 | 0 | 7 | 0 | 2 | 0 |
| Housey, Pittsfield | 1 | 3 | .250 | 3.34 | 32 | 1 | 0 | 22 | 0 | 1 | 64.2 | 49 | 31 | 24 | 5 | 5 | 33 | 4 | 36 | 5 |
| Hughes, Albany | 0 | 0 | .000 | 22.50 | 1 | 0 | 0 | 0 | 0 | 0 | 2.0 | 4 | 5 | 5 | 0 | 0 | 5 | 1 | 1 | 1 |
| Imig, Glens Falls | 0 | 0 | .000 | 8.49 | 8 | 0 | 0 | 4 | 0 | 0 | 11.2 | 20 | 15 | 11 | 1 | 2 | 10 | 0 | 4 | 0 |
| Jefferson, Vermont | 9 | 7 | .563 | 4.32 | 25 | 25 | 1 | 0 | 0 | 0 | 148.0 | 154 | 78 | 71 | 9 | 2 | 85 | 3 | 93 | 9 |
| D. Johnson, Nashua | 6 | 9 | .400 | 3.12 | 34 | 18 | 4 | 9 | 1 | 2 | 153.0 | 129 | 66 | 53 | 9 | 2 | 45 | 1 | 84 | 6 |
| J. Johnson, Glens Falls | 8 | 9 | .417 | 4.76 | 28 | 28 | 4 | 0 | 2 | 0 | 164.2 | 188 | 97 | 87 | 15 | 8 | 71 | 0 | 110 | 6 |
| W. Johnson, Waterbury° | 0 | 1 | .000 | 3.98 | 8 | 1 | 0 | 1 | 0 | 0 | 20.1 | 30 | 17 | 9 | 0 | 2 | 16 | 2 | 8 | 1 |
| B. Jones, Nashua | 3 | 2 | .600 | 1.55 | 23 | 0 | 0 | 20 | 0 | 12 | 29.0 | 19 | 6 | 5 | 1 | 0 | 10 | 0 | 24 | 4 |
| D. Jones, Waterbury | 9 | 4 | .692 | 3.65 | 39 | 1 | 0 | 25 | 0 | 7 | 116.0 | 123 | 59 | 47 | 11 | 3 | 36 | 8 | 113 | 8 |
| Kelly, Glens Falls | 0 | 0 | .000 | 18.00 | 1 | 0 | 0 | 1 | 0 | 0 | 1.0 | 3 | 2 | 2 | 1 | 0 | 0 | 0 | 0 | 0 |
| Kemp, Vermont | 5 | 3 | .625 | 3.33 | 12 | 12 | 3 | 0 | 1 | 0 | 78.1 | 63 | 33 | 29 | 9 | 1 | 28 | 1 | 67 | 2 |
| Knox, Vermont | 3 | 2 | .600 | 3.02 | 7 | 7 | 1 | 0 | 1 | 0 | 50.2 | 41 | 20 | 17 | 0 | 0 | 15 | 2 | 25 | 2 |
| Konderla, Vermont | 10 | 5 | .667 | 2.55 | 44 | 1 | 0 | 27 | 0 | 4 | 91.2 | 56 | 32 | 26 | 2 | 1 | 58 | 1 | 96 | 5 |
| Labay, Reading° | 1 | 3 | .250 | 4.50 | 6 | 4 | 0 | 1 | 0 | 0 | 20.0 | 26 | 13 | 10 | 2 | 1 | 7 | 0 | 9 | 0 |
| Lamonde, Nashua | 9 | 8 | .529 | 2.93 | 24 | 21 | 1 | 0 | 0 | 0 | 132.0 | 119 | 61 | 43 | 10 | 4 | 69 | 0 | 47 | 4 |
| Layton, 7 GF-23 Pitts. | 7 | 6 | .538 | 3.10 | 30 | 8 | 2 | 7 | 0 | 0 | 95.2 | 81 | 45 | 33 | 6 | 4 | 46 | 2 | 46 | 3 |
| Leach, Waterbury | 4 | 2 | .667 | 4.60 | 13 | 8 | 0 | 2 | 0 | 0 | 58.2 | 62 | 32 | 30 | 4 | 2 | 33 | 1 | 25 | 2 |
| Leister, New Britain | 8 | 6 | .571 | 3.17 | 27 | 13 | 4 | 9 | 2 | 1 | 105.0 | 91 | 48 | 37 | 4 | 2 | 49 | 0 | 68 | 4 |
| Long, Reading | 4 | 8 | .333 | 5.02 | 14 | 14 | 2 | 0 | 0 | 0 | 75.1 | 69 | 50 | 42 | 3 | 3 | 50 | 2 | 31 | 10 |
| Lono, Vermont° | 0 | 0 | .000 | 0.00 | 1 | 0 | 0 | 1 | 0 | 0 | 3.1 | 2 | 0 | 0 | 0 | 0 | 3 | 0 | 3 | 0 |
| Madden, Vermont° | 1 | 3 | .250 | 3.06 | 6 | 4 | 2 | 1 | 1 | 0 | 32.1 | 25 | 11 | 11 | 2 | 0 | 19 | 0 | 31 | 2 |
| Manzanillo, Nashua° | 6 | 10 | .375 | 4.67 | 33 | 17 | 2 | 10 | 0 | 5 | 123.1 | 99 | 70 | 64 | 4 | 3 | 96 | 3 | 62 | 11 |
| Marcheskie, Nashua | 1 | 1 | .500 | 2.92 | 7 | 0 | 0 | 2 | 0 | 0 | 12.1 | 11 | 5 | 4 | 1 | 0 | 5 | 1 | 6 | 0 |
| McKelvey, Nashua | 2 | 5 | .286 | 4.47 | 19 | 3 | 0 | 10 | 0 | 2 | 44.1 | 39 | 25 | 22 | 0 | 2 | 33 | 2 | 48 | 3 |
| Menard, Reading | 8 | 9 | .471 | 4.75 | 30 | 17 | 2 | 6 | 0 | 0 | 132.2 | 183 | 87 | 70 | 9 | 3 | 28 | 7 | 80 | 4 |
| Miglio, Waterbury° | 5 | 1 | .833 | 4.59 | 46 | 0 | 0 | 28 | 0 | 8 | 64.2 | 63 | 38 | 33 | 5 | 3 | 52 | 2 | 54 | 2 |
| Mitchell, New Britain | 12 | 8 | .600 | 2.70 | 26 | 26 | 10 | 0 | 1 | 0 | 190.1 | 143 | 71 | 57 | 4 | 2 | 61 | 4 | 108 | 11 |

| Pitcher—Club | W. | L. | Pct. | ERA. | G. | GS. | CG. | GF. | ShO. | Sv. | IP. | H. | R. | ER. | HR. | HB. | BB. | Int. BB. | SO. | WP. |
|---|---|---|---|---|---|---|---|---|---|---|---|---|---|---|---|---|---|---|---|---|
| Montgomery, Vermont | 5 | 3 | .625 | 2.05 | 53 | 1 | 0 | 33 | 0 | 9 | 101.0 | 63 | 25 | 23 | 6 | 1 | 48 | 4 | 89 | 2 |
| Moreno, Pittsfield* | 0 | 2 | .000 | 9.00 | 5 | 0 | 0 | 2 | 0 | 0 | 7.0 | 9 | 7 | 7 | 0 | 0 | 3 | 0 | 4 | 2 |
| Moyer, Pittsfield* | 7 | 6 | .538 | 3.72 | 15 | 15 | 3 | 0 | 0 | 0 | 96.2 | 99 | 49 | 40 | 4 | 5 | 32 | 1 | 51 | 4 |
| Mullen, Glens Falls | 8 | 3 | .727 | 2.52 | 18 | 9 | 5 | 4 | 1 | 0 | 85.2 | 96 | 33 | 24 | 4 | 3 | 16 | 0 | 56 | 3 |
| Murphy, Waterbury* | 1 | 1 | .500 | 3.32 | 4 | 4 | 0 | 0 | 0 | 0 | 21.2 | 22 | 10 | 8 | 1 | 0 | 12 | 0 | 8 | 1 |
| Neal, Nashua* | 5 | 3 | .625 | 3.32 | 26 | 0 | 0 | 8 | 0 | 3 | 62.1 | 43 | 27 | 23 | 4 | 0 | 37 | 1 | 60 | 0 |
| Nielsen, Albany | 6 | 1 | .857 | 2.95 | 11 | 11 | 4 | 0 | 1 | 0 | 73.1 | 60 | 26 | 24 | 9 | 5 | 14 | 0 | 31 | 2 |
| Oliverio, Vermont | 3 | 1 | .750 | 3.94 | 8 | 7 | 2 | 1 | 0 | 0 | 45.2 | 49 | 24 | 20 | 2 | 0 | 25 | 0 | 21 | 4 |
| Olson, Reading | 8 | 9 | .471 | 4.20 | 28 | 23 | 3 | 2 | 1 | 0 | 143.2 | 130 | 85 | 67 | 11 | 5 | 86 | 3 | 89 | 11 |
| Oswald, Glens Falls* | 0 | 1 | .000 | 5.84 | 2 | 2 | 0 | 0 | 0 | 0 | 12.1 | 14 | 10 | 8 | 0 | 1 | 6 | 0 | 2 | 1 |
| Pacillo, Vermont | 0 | 4 | .000 | 2.45 | 22 | 0 | 0 | 12 | 0 | 3 | 36.2 | 27 | 11 | 10 | 1 | 0 | 24 | 1 | 39 | 2 |
| Palacios, Glens Falls | 1 | 1 | .500 | 4.76 | 8 | 4 | 0 | 1 | 0 | 1 | 39.2 | 44 | 25 | 21 | 1 | 2 | 29 | 1 | 20 | 5 |
| Parmenter, Pittsfield | 6 | 5 | .545 | 2.44 | 17 | 17 | 6 | 0 | 1 | 0 | 121.2 | 81 | 40 | 33 | 5 | 5 | 49 | 0 | 62 | 8 |
| Patterson, Albany | 7 | 2 | .778 | 1.55 | 27 | 0 | 0 | 19 | 0 | 3 | 46.1 | 32 | 12 | 8 | 0 | 1 | 17 | 5 | 35 | 2 |
| Pippin, Waterbury | 3 | 3 | .500 | 2.97 | 18 | 0 | 0 | 14 | 0 | 6 | 39.1 | 32 | 13 | 13 | 1 | 1 | 17 | 3 | 47 | 1 |
| Potestio, Pittsfield | 5 | 9 | .357 | 4.08 | 26 | 16 | 4 | 9 | 0 | 2 | 121.1 | 127 | 70 | 55 | 8 | 4 | 40 | 3 | 54 | 10 |
| Reburn, Vermont | 1 | 0 | 1.000 | 6.94 | 5 | 0 | 0 | 2 | 0 | 0 | 11.2 | 16 | 10 | 9 | 3 | 0 | 8 | 0 | 3 | 1 |
| Renz, Glens Falls | 0 | 3 | .000 | 4.34 | 9 | 4 | 0 | 4 | 0 | 0 | 29.0 | 31 | 18 | 14 | 1 | 1 | 10 | 1 | 15 | 2 |
| Reynolds, Vermont | 5 | 8 | .385 | 2.98 | 19 | 18 | 4 | 0 | 0 | 0 | 121.0 | 105 | 50 | 40 | 6 | 4 | 49 | 2 | 85 | 7 |
| Rice, Nashua | 2 | 2 | .500 | 3.71 | 11 | 11 | 0 | 0 | 0 | 0 | 43.2 | 36 | 26 | 18 | 0 | 0 | 34 | 2 | 36 | 5 |
| Ritter, Waterbury | 7 | 6 | .538 | 3.21 | 15 | 15 | 7 | 0 | 2 | 0 | 101.0 | 91 | 40 | 36 | 6 | 0 | 33 | 1 | 31 | 2 |
| Rochford, New Britain* | 8 | 5 | .615 | 2.99 | 14 | 14 | 9 | 0 | 3 | 0 | 93.1 | 84 | 39 | 31 | 11 | 1 | 41 | 0 | 42 | 1 |
| Sanchez, Nashua* | 2 | 2 | .500 | 3.56 | 26 | 1 | 0 | 16 | 0 | 2 | 55.2 | 47 | 25 | 22 | 7 | 1 | 29 | 1 | 29 | 3 |
| Santarelli, Waterbury | 9 | 11 | .450 | 4.73 | 31 | 25 | 7 | 4 | 2 | 1 | 160.0 | 158 | 93 | 84 | 9 | 9 | 78 | 5 | 128 | 12 |
| Sauveur, Nashua* | 9 | 10 | .474 | 3.55 | 25 | 25 | 4 | 0 | 2 | 0 | 157.1 | 146 | 73 | 62 | 7 | 3 | 78 | 2 | 85 | 7 |
| Schmidt, Glens Falls | 11 | 12 | .478 | 3.38 | 27 | 27 | 4 | 0 | 1 | 0 | 173.1 | 187 | 80 | 65 | 12 | 5 | 74 | 2 | 97 | 2 |
| K. Scott, Albany | 1 | 3 | .250 | 4.81 | 8 | 8 | 1 | 0 | 0 | 0 | 33.2 | 39 | 20 | 18 | 0 | 2 | 12 | 0 | 19 | 2 |
| T. Scott, Vermont | 6 | 3 | .667 | 2.24 | 36 | 0 | 0 | 26 | 0 | 11 | 60.1 | 40 | 22 | 15 | 0 | 4 | 32 | 4 | 65 | 3 |
| Sedar, Glens Falls | 0 | 0 | .000 | 1.59 | 5 | 0 | 0 | 4 | 0 | 0 | 5.2 | 4 | 3 | 1 | 1 | 0 | 1 | 0 | 4 | 0 |
| Sellers, New Britain | 14 | 7 | .667 | 2.78 | 25 | 25 | 15 | 0 | 5 | 0 | 184.2 | 165 | 67 | 57 | 2 | 4 | 67 | 1 | 115 | 9 |
| Smith, Waterbury | 2 | 2 | .500 | 3.52 | 16 | 6 | 1 | 8 | 0 | 4 | 53.2 | 42 | 25 | 21 | 5 | 1 | 37 | 1 | 38 | 5 |
| Stalp, Vermont | 1 | 3 | .250 | 3.55 | 6 | 5 | 0 | 1 | 0 | 0 | 25.1 | 22 | 13 | 10 | 2 | 1 | 18 | 0 | 6 | 1 |
| Street, Waterbury | 4 | 5 | .444 | 4.82 | 16 | 14 | 1 | 0 | 0 | 0 | 80.1 | 94 | 54 | 43 | 9 | 4 | 42 | 0 | 52 | 7 |
| Taylor, Nashua | 6 | 9 | .400 | 4.31 | 16 | 17 | 1 | 5 | 1 | 0 | 112.2 | 101 | 63 | 54 | 7 | 1 | 57 | 2 | 64 | 8 |
| Tewksbury, Albany | 6 | 5 | .545 | 3.54 | 17 | 17 | 4 | 0 | 2 | 0 | 106.2 | 101 | 48 | 42 | 9 | 2 | 19 | 0 | 63 | 2 |
| Torres, Albany | 0 | 1 | .000 | 9.00 | 1 | 1 | 0 | 0 | 0 | 0 | 4.0 | 5 | 5 | 4 | 0 | 0 | 2 | 0 | 4 | 0 |
| Underwood, Albany* | 0 | 0 | .000 | 9.64 | 4 | 0 | 0 | 0 | 0 | 0 | 4.2 | 13 | 8 | 5 | 0 | 1 | 4 | 1 | 3 | 0 |
| Walker, Glens Falls | 10 | 6 | .625 | 4.26 | 46 | 4 | 1 | 30 | 0 | 5 | 80.1 | 93 | 48 | 38 | 3 | 3 | 40 | 5 | 69 | 2 |
| Watts, Reading* | 1 | 3 | .250 | 6.03 | 6 | 6 | 0 | 0 | 0 | 0 | 31.1 | 39 | 24 | 21 | 3 | 0 | 20 | 1 | 27 | 3 |
| Wever, Albany | 0 | 0 | .000 | 4.91 | 5 | 0 | 0 | 1 | 0 | 1 | 11.0 | 12 | 6 | 6 | 0 | 0 | 10 | 2 | 5 | 1 |
| Wex, Albany | 1 | 3 | .250 | 8.10 | 9 | 1 | 0 | 2 | 0 | 1 | 20.0 | 26 | 24 | 18 | 6 | 1 | 19 | 3 | 13 | 1 |
| Williams, Glens Falls | 6 | 8 | .429 | 4.68 | 35 | 6 | 2 | 13 | 0 | 1 | 98.0 | 108 | 59 | 51 | 7 | 5 | 25 | 2 | 62 | 4 |
| Woodward, New Britain | 7 | 5 | .583 | 3.54 | 12 | 12 | 3 | 0 | 1 | 0 | 86.1 | 71 | 42 | 34 | 2 | 7 | 36 | 5 | 54 | 4 |
| Wright, 19 Read-20 Nash. | 3 | 2 | .600 | 4.64 | 39 | 1 | 0 | 23 | 0 | 1 | 73.2 | 84 | 48 | 38 | 6 | 5 | 32 | 3 | 37 | 0 |

BALKS—Palacios, Sauveur, 4 each; Brecht, Kemp, Rice, Rochford, Sanchez, 3 each; Bailes, Bolton, Bowden, Bulls, Engel, Evetts, Gaynor, Hawley, Hicks, Konderla, Long, Olson, Reynolds, Ritter, 2 each; Abrego, Arney, Arnold, Arnsberg, Blevins, Capel, Chestnut, DeVincenzo, Dodd, Doyle, Fansler, Farrell, Gering, Guzman, Heidenreich, Henry, J. Hickey, Jefferson, J. Johnson, Knox, Labay, Lamonde, Madden, McKelvey, Mitchell, Moyer, Oliverio, Oswald, Parmenter, Pippin, Potestio, Schmidt, K. Scott, T. Scott, Sellers, Tewksbury, Wex, Woodward, Wright, 1 each.

COMBINATION SHUTOUTS—Ferguson-Patterson, Drabek-Graham, Tewksbury-Graham, K. Scott-Ferguson-Easley, Scott-Ferguson-Graham-Frey, Albany; Brecht-Hardy, Johnson-Hardy, Glens Falls; Rice-Bailes, Fansler-Bailes, Sauveur-Bailes, Fansler-Bailes-Johnson, Rice-Neal-Johnson, Fansler-Jones, Johnson-Neal-DeLaRosa, Johnson-Jones, Lamonde-Jones, Nashua; Mitchell-Davis-Leister, Ellsworth-Davis, Leister-Cappadona-Dale, New Britain; Abrego-Capel-Potestio, Pittsfield; Menard-Bowden-Hicks, Labay-Hicks, Evetts-Hickey, Reading; Hawley-Burroughs, Jefferson-Burroughs, Hawley-Scott, Kemp-Montgomery, Vermont; Ritter-Miglio-Jones, Ritter-Pippin, Doyle-Arney, Waterbury.

NO-HIT GAMES—Parmenter, Pittsfield, defeated Nashua, 6-0, June 8; Heidenreich, Vermont, defeated Pittsfield, 2-0 (five innings), June 20; Abrego, Pittsfield, defeated Nashua, 1-0, August 1.

# Southern League

## CLASS AA

Leading Batter
**BRUCE FIELDS**
Birmingham

League President
**JIMMY BRAGAN**

Leading Pitcher
**STEVE DAVIS**
Knoxville

### CHAMPIONSHIP WINNERS IN PREVIOUS YEARS

| | | |
|---|---|---|
| 1904—Macon | .598 | |
| 1905—Macon | .625 | |
| 1906—Savannah | .637 | |
| 1907—Charleston | .620 | |
| 1908—Jacksonville | .694 | |
| 1909—Chattanooga° | .738 | |
| Augusta | .702 | |
| 1910—Columbus | .588 | |
| 1911—Columbus° | .681 | |
| Columbia | .710 | |
| 1912—Jacksonville° | .679 | |
| Columbus | .632 | |
| 1913—Savannah | .754 | |
| Savannah | .593 | |
| 1914—Savannah° | .667 | |
| Albany | .650 | |
| 1915—Macon | .588 | |
| Columbus° | .686 | |
| 1916—Augusta° | .617 | |
| Columbia | .631 | |
| 1917—Charleston | .741 | |
| Columbia° | .667 | |
| 1918—Did not operate. | | |
| 1919—Columbia | .585 | |
| 1920—Columbia | .633 | |
| 1921—Columbia | .642 | |
| 1922—Charleston | .625 | |
| 1923—Charlotte° | .653 | |
| Macon | .580 | |
| 1924—Augusta | .612 | |
| 1925—Spartanburg | .620 | |
| 1926—Greenville | .662 | |
| 1927—Greenville | .622 | |
| 1928—Asheville | .664 | |
| 1929—Asheville | .605 | |
| Knoxville° | .634 | |
| 1930—Greenville° | .620 | |
| Macon | .643 | |
| 1931-35—Did not operate. | | |
| 1936—Jacksonville | .652 | |
| Columbus° | .650 | |
| 1937—Columbus | .572 | |
| Savannah (3rd)† | .565 | |

| | | |
|---|---|---|
| 1938—Savannah | .574 | |
| Macon (2nd)† | .570 | |
| 1939—Columbus | .601 | |
| Augusta (2nd)† | .597 | |
| 1940—Savannah | .627 | |
| Columbus (2nd)† | .583 | |
| 1941—Macon | .643 | |
| Columbia (2nd)† | .636 | |
| 1942—Charleston | .620 | |
| Macon (2nd)† | .585 | |
| 1943-45—Did not operate. | | |
| 1946—Columbus | .568 | |
| Augusta (4th)† | .547 | |
| 1947—Columbus | .575 | |
| Savannah (2nd)† | .563 | |
| 1948—Charleston | .572 | |
| Greenville (3rd)† | .549 | |
| 1949—Macon‡ | .623 | |
| 1950—Macon‡ | .588 | |
| 1951—Montgomery | .607 | |
| 1952—Columbia | .649 | |
| Montgomery (3rd)† | .558 | |
| 1953—Jacksonville | .679 | |
| Savannah (2nd)† | .571 | |
| 1954—Jacksonville | .593 | |
| Savannah (2nd)† | .571 | |
| 1955—Columbia | .636 | |
| Augusta (3rd)† | .543 | |
| 1956—Jacksonville‡ | .621 | |
| 1957—Augusta | .636 | |
| Charlotte (2nd)† | .562 | |
| 1958—Augusta | .550 | |
| Macon (3rd)† | .500 | |
| 1959—Knoxville | .557 | |
| Gastonia (4th)† | .504 | |
| 1960—Columbia | .597 | |
| Savannah (3rd)† | .561 | |
| 1961—Asheville | .635 | |
| 1962—Savannah | .662 | |
| Macon (3rd)† | .576 | |
| 1963—Augusta† | .661 | |
| Lynchburg | .662 | |
| 1964—Lynchburg | .579 | |

| | | |
|---|---|---|
| 1965—Columbus | .572 | |
| 1966—Mobile | .629 | |
| 1967—Birmingham | .604 | |
| 1968—Asheville | .614 | |
| 1969—Charlotte | .579 | |
| 1970—Columbus | .569 | |
| 1971—Did not operate as league—clubs were members of Dixie Association. | | |
| 1972—Asheville | .583 | |
| Montgomery§ | .561 | |
| 1973—Montgomery§ | .580 | |
| Jacksonville | .559 | |
| 1974—Jacksonville | .565 | |
| Knoxville§ | .533 | |
| 1975—Orlando | .587 | |
| Montgomery§ | .545 | |
| 1976—Montgomery x | .591 | |
| Orlando | .540 | |
| 1977—Montgomery x | .628 | |
| Jacksonville | .522 | |
| 1978—Knoxville x | .611 | |
| Savannah | .500 | |
| 1979—Columbus | .587 | |
| Nashville x | .576 | |
| 1980—Memphis | .576 | |
| Charlotte x | .500 | |
| 1981—Nashville | .566 | |
| Orlando x | .556 | |
| 1982—Jacksonville | .576 | |
| Nashville x | .535 | |
| 1983—Birmingham x | .628 | |
| Jacksonville | .531 | |
| 1984—Charlotte x | .510 | |
| Knoxville | .483 | |

°Won split-season playoff. †Won four-club playoff. ‡Won championship and four-club playoff. §League was divided into Eastern and Western divisions; won playoff. xLeague was divided into Eastern and Western divisions and played split season; won playoff.

## STANDING OF CLUBS AT CLOSE OF FIRST HALF, JUNE 22

### EASTERN DIVISION

| Club | W. | L. | T. | Pct. | G.B. |
|---|---|---|---|---|---|
| Columbus (Astros) | 41 | 28 | 0 | .594 | ....... |
| Jacksonville (Expos) | 36 | 31 | 0 | .537 | 4 |
| Greenville (Braves) | 37 | 35 | 0 | .514 | 5½ |
| Charlotte (Orioles) | 35 | 34 | 0 | .507 | 6 |
| Orlando (Twins) | 29 | 35 | 0 | .453 | 9½ |

### WESTERN DIVISION

| Club | W. | L. | T. | Pct. | G.B. |
|---|---|---|---|---|---|
| Huntsville (A's) | 39 | 32 | 0 | .549 | ....... |
| Knoxville (Blue Jays) | 37 | 34 | 0 | .521 | 2 |
| Chattanooga (Mariners) | 36 | 35 | 0 | .507 | 3 |
| Memphis (Royals) | 33 | 36 | 0 | .478 | 5 |
| Birmingham (Tigers) | 24 | 47 | 0 | .338 | 15 |

## STANDING OF CLUBS AT CLOSE OF SECOND HALF, SEPTEMBER 2

### EASTERN DIVISION

| Club | W. | L. | T. | Pct. | G.B. |
|---|---|---|---|---|---|
| Charlotte (Orioles) | 43 | 31 | 0 | .581 | ....... |
| Orlando (Twins) | 43 | 36 | 0 | .544 | 2½ |
| Columbus (Astros) | 38 | 37 | 0 | .507 | 5½ |
| Jacksonville (Expos) | 37 | 39 | 0 | .487 | 7 |
| Greenville (Braves) | 33 | 39 | 0 | .458 | 9 |

### WESTERN DIVISION

| Club | W. | L. | T. | Pct. | G.B. |
|---|---|---|---|---|---|
| Knoxville (Blue Jays) | 42 | 30 | 0 | .583 | ....... |
| Huntsville (A's) | 39 | 34 | 0 | .534 | 3½ |
| Birmingham (Tigers) | 33 | 39 | 0 | .458 | 9 |
| Memphis (Royals) | 32 | 43 | 0 | .427 | 11½ |
| Chattanooga (Mariners) | 30 | 42 | 0 | .417 | 12 |

## COMPOSITE STANDING OF CLUBS AT CLOSE OF SEASON, SEPTEMBER 2

| Club | Knox. | Col. | Char. | Hunt. | Jax. | Orl. | Grn. | Chat. | Mem. | Birm. | W. | L. | T. | Pct. | G.B. |
|---|---|---|---|---|---|---|---|---|---|---|---|---|---|---|---|
| Knoxville (Blue Jays) | ... | 9 | 6 | 12 | 8 | 9 | 9 | 10 | 8 | 8 | 79 | 64 | 0 | .552 | ....... |
| Columbus (Astros) | 7 | ... | 7 | 6 | 7 | 11 | 9 | 11 | 11 | 10 | 79 | 65 | 0 | .549 | ½ |
| Charlotte (Orioles) | 9 | 9 | ... | 7 | 9 | 6 | 8 | 10 | 9 | 11 | 78 | 65 | 0 | .545 | 1 |
| Huntsville (A's) | 4 | 10 | 9 | ... | 9 | 9 | 6 | 11 | 9 | 11 | 78 | 66 | 0 | .542 | 1½ |
| Jacksonville (Expos) | 8 | 9 | 7 | 7 | ... | 8 | 8 | 7 | 9 | 10 | 73 | 70 | 0 | .510 | 6 |
| Orlando (Twins) | 7 | 5 | 10 | 7 | 7 | ... | 10 | 5 | 9 | 12 | 72 | 71 | 0 | .503 | 7 |
| Greenville (Braves) | 7 | 7 | 8 | 10 | 8 | 6 | ... | 9 | 7 | 8 | 70 | 74 | 0 | .486 | 9½ |
| Chattanooga (Mariners) | 6 | 5 | 6 | 5 | 9 | 11 | 7 | ... | 9 | 8 | 66 | 77 | 0 | .462 | 13 |
| Memphis (Royals) | 8 | 5 | 7 | 7 | 7 | 7 | 9 | 7 | ... | 8 | 65 | 79 | 0 | .451 | 14½ |
| Birmingham (Tigers) | 8 | 6 | 5 | 5 | 6 | 4 | 8 | 7 | 8 | ... | 57 | 86 | 0 | .399 | 22 |

Major league affiliations in parentheses.

Playoffs—Charlotte defeated Columbus, three games to one; Huntsville defeated Knoxville, three games to one, and Huntsville defeated Charlotte, three games to two, to win league championship.

Regular-Season Attendance—Birmingham, 140,671; Charlotte, 104,085; Chattanooga, 112,700; Columbus, 109,603; Greenville, 214,471; Huntsville, 300,810; Jacksonville, 82,907; Knoxville, 108,952; Memphis, 200,682; Orlando, 62,122. Total, 1,437,003. Total Playoff Attendance 23,886. All-Star Attendance, 2,709.

Managers—Birmingham, Gordy MacKenzie (thru April 24), Mark DeJohn (April 25 thru May 18), Frank Franchi (May 19 thru May 26) and Jerry Grote (May 27 thru end of season); Charlotte, John Hart; Chattanooga, Bill Plummer; Columbus, Carlos Alfonso; Greenville, Jim Beauchamp; Huntsville, Brad Fischer; Jacksonville, Tommy Thompson; Knoxville, John McLaren; Memphis, Tommy Jones; Orlando, Charlie Manuel.

All-Star Team—1B—Rob Nelson, Huntsville; 2B—Brian David, Chattanooga; 3B—Jim Sherman, Columbus; SS—Luis Rivera, Jacksonville; OF—Randy Braun, Chattanooga; Bill Moore, Jacksonville; Mark Davidson, Orlando; Jose Canseco, Huntsville; Alexis Marte, Orlando; C—Robbie Wine, Columbus; DH—Mark Funderburk, Orlando; RHP—John Habyan, Charlotte; LHP—Steve Davis, Knoxville; Most Valuable Player—Jose Canseco, Huntsville; Pitcher of the Year—Steve Davis, Knoxville; Co-Managers of the Year—John McLaren, Knoxville and Carlos Alfonso, Columbus.

(Compiled by Howe News Bureau, Boston, Mass.)

## CLUB BATTING

| Club | Pct. | G. | AB. | R. | OR. | H. | TB. | 2B. | 3B. | HR. | RBI. | GW. | SH. | SF. | HP. | BB. | Int. BB. | SO. | SB. | CS. | LOB. |
|---|---|---|---|---|---|---|---|---|---|---|---|---|---|---|---|---|---|---|---|---|---|
| Orlando | .276 | 143 | 4655 | 708 | 719 | 1287 | 1938 | 203 | 32 | 128 | 654 | 66 | 28 | 53 | 49 | 560 | 22 | 601 | 102 | 55 | 1056 |
| Huntsville | .268 | 144 | 4751 | 729 | 667 | 1275 | 1988 | 214 | 41 | 139 | 652 | 69 | 47 | 45 | 37 | 631 | 30 | 761 | 148 | 55 | 1088 |
| Charlotte | .266 | 143 | 4735 | 761 | 619 | 1261 | 1988 | 230 | 25 | 149 | 698 | 68 | 51 | 44 | 49 | 681 | 37 | 673 | 87 | 52 | 1106 |
| Chattanooga | .263 | 143 | 4680 | 640 | 707 | 1232 | 1750 | 193 | 50 | 75 | 581 | 58 | 79 | 58 | 31 | 552 | 39 | 538 | 81 | 54 | 1071 |
| Columbus | .262 | 144 | 4591 | 664 | 616 | 1202 | 1833 | 206 | 46 | 111 | 598 | 71 | 42 | 54 | 47 | 583 | 22 | 749 | 170 | 87 | 998 |
| Greenville | .260 | 144 | 4783 | 679 | 677 | 1243 | 1896 | 222 | 28 | 125 | 614 | 58 | 44 | 50 | 17 | 571 | 24 | 738 | 61 | 33 | 1079 |
| Birmingham | .258 | 143 | 4637 | 636 | 784 | 1198 | 1720 | 195 | 27 | 91 | 570 | 49 | 37 | 40 | 31 | 539 | 18 | 675 | 49 | 49 | 998 |
| Knoxville | .258 | 143 | 4726 | 629 | 615 | 1220 | 1808 | 199 | 46 | 99 | 580 | 71 | 40 | 46 | 44 | 564 | 27 | 865 | 95 | 62 | 1065 |
| Memphis | .258 | 144 | 4703 | 630 | 698 | 1213 | 1734 | 178 | 35 | 91 | 559 | 59 | 44 | 39 | 42 | 549 | 26 | 752 | 134 | 69 | 1034 |
| Jacksonville | .257 | 143 | 4653 | 662 | 636 | 1196 | 1882 | 225 | 25 | 137 | 597 | 67 | 34 | 38 | 50 | 554 | 25 | 708 | 84 | 74 | 997 |

## INDIVIDUAL BATTING

(Leading Qualifiers for Batting Championship—389 or More Plate Appearances)

*Bats lefthanded.    †Switch-hitter.

| Player and Club | Pct. | G. | AB. | R. | H. | TB. | 2B. | 3B. | HR. | RBI. | GW. | SH. | SF. | HP. | BB. | Int. BB. | SO. | SB. | CS. |
|---|---|---|---|---|---|---|---|---|---|---|---|---|---|---|---|---|---|---|---|
| Fields, Bruce, Birmingham* | .323 | 114 | 421 | 59 | 136 | 174 | 24 | 4 | 2 | 41 | 3 | 0 | 4 | 3 | 54 | 1 | 50 | 9 | 6 |
| Marte, Alexis, Orlando* | .320 | 141 | 534 | 117 | 171 | 204 | 15 | 9 | 0 | 33 | 3 | 6 | 4 | 1 | 63 | 1 | 43 | 64 | 21 |
| Braun, Randall, Chattanooga* | .314 | 132 | 493 | 78 | 155 | 266 | 33 | 6 | 22 | 100 | 11 | 0 | 7 | 4 | 53 | 10 | 58 | 8 | 6 |
| Jackson, Charles, Columbus | .310 | 108 | 361 | 62 | 112 | 162 | 10 | 8 | 8 | 46 | 5 | 3 | 3 | 3 | 77 | 2 | 51 | 32 | 14 |
| Schulz, Jeffrey, Memphis* | .305 | 136 | 488 | 73 | 149 | 186 | 15 | 5 | 4 | 53 | 7 | 4 | 8 | 0 | 59 | 5 | 42 | 8 | 4 |
| Davidson, Mark, Orlando | .302 | 134 | 453 | 93 | 137 | 233 | 17 | 2 | 25 | 106 | 16 | 2 | 6 | 10 | 92 | 13 | 92 | 13 | 5 |
| Carpenter, Glenn, Columbus | .302 | 127 | 420 | 54 | 127 | 169 | 24 | 0 | 6 | 47 | 4 | 5 | 2 | 4 | 58 | 1 | 70 | 2 | 6 |
| David, Brian, Chattanooga | .301 | 117 | 418 | 71 | 126 | 165 | 23 | 8 | 0 | 51 | 7 | 8 | 6 | 3 | 76 | 3 | 30 | 5 | 2 |
| Ralston, Robert, Orlando | .301 | 126 | 419 | 66 | 126 | 139 | 11 | 1 | 0 | 28 | 2 | 10 | 4 | 2 | 38 | 0 | 25 | 16 | 15 |
| Walker, Anthony, Columbus† | .294 | 135 | 530 | 88 | 156 | 225 | 23 | 5 | 12 | 65 | 6 | 4 | 2 | 2 | 59 | 2 | 63 | 42 | 8 |
| Fielder, Cecil, Knoxville | .294 | 96 | 361 | 52 | 106 | 190 | 26 | 2 | 18 | 81 | 4 | 0 | 5 | 3 | 45 | 3 | 83 | 0 | 0 |
| Baker, Derrell, Jacksonville | .291 | 102 | 340 | 57 | 99 | 135 | 19 | 4 | 3 | 48 | 7 | 3 | 2 | 3 | 50 | 0 | 19 | 2 | 5 |
| Torve, Kelvin, Charlotte* | .290 | 134 | 482 | 85 | 140 | 221 | 34 | 1 | 15 | 77 | 8 | 4 | 7 | 2 | 75 | 9 | 53 | 5 | 2 |
| Green, Otis, Knoxville* | .290 | 115 | 442 | 68 | 128 | 190 | 19 | 5 | 11 | 68 | 14 | 1 | 3 | 2 | 44 | 5 | 71 | 9 | 8 |

Departmental Leaders: G—Rollin, 142; AB—Rivera, 538; R—Marte, 117; H—Marte, 171; TB—Funderburk, 272; 2B—Sherman, Torve, 34; 3B—Polonia, 18; HR—Funderburk, 34; RBI—Funderburk, 116; GWRBI—Davidson, 16; SH—M. Diaz, 14; SF—E. Martinez, 12; HP—Johnston, 13; BB—Javier, 112; IBB—Braun, Hollins, 10; SO—Rollin, 143; SB—Marte, 64; CS—Marte, 21.

(All Players—Listed Alphabetically)

| Player and Club | Pct. | G. | AB. | R. | H. | TB. | 2B. | 3B. | HR. | RBI. | GW. | SH. | SF. | HP. | BB. | Int. BB. | SO. | SB. | CS. |
|---|---|---|---|---|---|---|---|---|---|---|---|---|---|---|---|---|---|---|---|
| Allen, Edward, Memphis | .203 | 46 | 143 | 12 | 29 | 41 | 4 | 1 | 2 | 15 | 0 | 1 | 1 | 0 | 14 | 0 | 37 | 9 | 3 |
| Alvarez, Jose, 13 Mem-10 Jack | .143 | 23 | 7 | 1 | 1 | 1 | 0 | 0 | 0 | 0 | 0 | 0 | 0 | 0 | 0 | 0 | 2 | 0 | 0 |
| Aragon, Steven, Orlando | .217 | 42 | 120 | 12 | 26 | 35 | 3 | 0 | 2 | 20 | 0 | 2 | 2 | 1 | 7 | 0 | 8 | 1 | 0 |
| Ashman, Michael, Huntsville* | .279 | 40 | 129 | 9 | 36 | 48 | 4 | 1 | 2 | 13 | 1 | 1 | 1 | 1 | 14 | 0 | 8 | 0 | 0 |
| Ashmore, Mitchell, Memphis | .200 | 18 | 25 | 4 | 5 | 5 | 0 | 0 | 0 | 1 | 0 | 0 | 0 | 0 | 6 | 0 | 6 | 0 | 0 |
| Assenmacher, Paul, Greenville* | .000 | 29 | 1 | 0 | 0 | 0 | 0 | 0 | 0 | 0 | 0 | 0 | 0 | 0 | 0 | 0 | 0 | 0 | 0 |
| August, Donald, Columbus | .077 | 27 | 13 | 0 | 1 | 1 | 0 | 0 | 0 | 0 | 0 | 1 | 0 | 0 | 1 | 0 | 5 | 0 | 0 |
| Aviles, Brian, Greenville | .200 | 14 | 5 | 0 | 1 | 1 | 0 | 0 | 0 | 0 | 0 | 0 | 0 | 0 | 0 | 0 | 2 | 0 | 0 |
| Baker, Derrell, Jacksonville | .291 | 102 | 340 | 57 | 99 | 135 | 19 | 4 | 3 | 48 | 7 | 3 | 2 | 3 | 50 | 0 | 19 | 2 | 5 |
| Barrett, Timothy, Jacksonville* | .200 | 37 | 5 | 0 | 1 | 1 | 0 | 0 | 0 | 0 | 0 | 1 | 0 | 0 | 2 | 0 | 1 | 0 | 0 |
| Beauchamp, Kash, Knoxville | .276 | 137 | 496 | 68 | 137 | 173 | 14 | 5 | 4 | 35 | 7 | 6 | 8 | 6 | 60 | 3 | 62 | 25 | 16 |
| Bishop, James, Knoxville | .176 | 57 | 182 | 17 | 32 | 50 | 7 | 1 | 3 | 14 | 3 | 3 | 1 | 0 | 19 | 0 | 46 | 2 | 1 |
| Blackwell, Orlando, Knoxville† | .233 | 130 | 485 | 62 | 113 | 132 | 9 | 5 | 0 | 45 | 5 | 5 | 4 | 2 | 52 | 1 | 43 | 8 | 6 |
| Bockhorn, Glen, Greenville | .271 | 122 | 395 | 63 | 107 | 191 | 25 | 1 | 19 | 69 | 6 | 3 | 5 | 5 | 55 | 3 | 81 | 0 | 1 |
| Bodie, Keith, Columbus | .000 | 2 | 3 | 0 | 0 | 0 | 0 | 0 | 0 | 0 | 0 | 0 | 0 | 0 | 0 | 0 | 1 | 0 | 0 |
| Bogener, Terry, Charlotte* | .300 | 86 | 323 | 59 | 97 | 142 | 19 | 4 | 6 | 38 | 4 | 7 | 0 | 4 | 54 | 2 | 46 | 2 | 5 |
| Bombard, Richard, Columbus | .000 | 52 | 2 | 0 | 0 | 0 | 0 | 0 | 0 | 0 | 0 | 0 | 0 | 0 | 0 | 0 | 1 | 0 | 0 |
| Borowsky, Erez, Orlando | .200 | 14 | 30 | 2 | 6 | 7 | 1 | 0 | 0 | 5 | 0 | 3 | 1 | 0 | 2 | 0 | 2 | 0 | 0 |
| Botkin, Michael, Columbus* | .262 | 108 | 317 | 44 | 83 | 115 | 18 | 4 | 2 | 23 | 3 | 1 | 2 | 0 | 54 | 4 | 27 | 9 | 10 |
| Bradford, Larry, Greenville | .333 | 46 | 3 | 1 | 1 | 1 | 0 | 0 | 0 | 0 | 0 | 0 | 0 | 0 | 0 | 0 | 1 | 0 | 0 |
| Brahs, Gary, Jacksonville* | .091 | 33 | 11 | 1 | 1 | 1 | 0 | 0 | 0 | 0 | 0 | 0 | 0 | 0 | 0 | 0 | 3 | 0 | 0 |
| Braun, Randall, Chattanooga* | .314 | 132 | 493 | 78 | 155 | 266 | 33 | 6 | 22 | 100 | 11 | 0 | 7 | 4 | 53 | 10 | 58 | 8 | 6 |
| Brown, Renard, Chattanooga | .236 | 109 | 348 | 51 | 82 | 99 | 9 | 4 | 0 | 27 | 4 | 7 | 2 | 3 | 49 | 2 | 39 | 6 | 8 |
| Burke, Curtis, Columbus | .179 | 22 | 78 | 10 | 14 | 29 | 3 | 3 | 2 | 11 | 1 | 1 | 1 | 1 | 7 | 0 | 24 | 0 | 2 |
| Callahan, Benjamin, Greenville | .500 | 13 | 2 | 0 | 1 | 1 | 0 | 0 | 0 | 0 | 0 | 0 | 0 | 0 | 0 | 0 | 1 | 0 | 0 |
| Campusano, Silvestre, Knoxville | .303 | 45 | 178 | 30 | 54 | 81 | 9 | 0 | 6 | 29 | 4 | 3 | 1 | 0 | 14 | 0 | 32 | 10 | 4 |
| Canseco, Jose, Huntsville | .318 | 58 | 211 | 47 | 67 | 156 | 10 | 2 | 25 | 80 | 8 | 0 | 5 | 5 | 30 | 6 | 55 | 6 | 0 |
| Carl, Jeffrey, Jacksonville | .204 | 105 | 318 | 32 | 65 | 116 | 14 | 2 | 11 | 38 | 5 | 2 | 2 | 1 | 40 | 0 | 55 | 1 | 5 |
| Carpenter, Glenn, Columbus | .302 | 127 | 420 | 54 | 127 | 169 | 24 | 0 | 6 | 47 | 4 | 5 | 2 | 4 | 58 | 1 | 70 | 2 | 6 |
| Castro, Edgar, Charlotte* | .100 | 6 | 10 | 0 | 1 | 1 | 0 | 0 | 0 | 0 | 0 | 0 | 0 | 0 | 5 | 2 | 3 | 0 | 0 |
| Cates, Timothy, Jacksonville | .222 | 15 | 9 | 0 | 2 | 3 | 1 | 0 | 0 | 0 | 0 | 0 | 0 | 0 | 0 | 0 | 3 | 0 | 0 |
| Chavez, Pedro, Birmingham | .222 | 55 | 189 | 20 | 42 | 46 | 2 | 1 | 0 | 18 | 2 | 2 | 1 | 1 | 15 | 0 | 21 | 7 | 2 |
| Childress, Willie, Greenville* | .289 | 13 | 45 | 7 | 13 | 20 | 2 | 1 | 1 | 9 | 3 | 0 | 0 | 0 | 5 | 1 | 3 | 0 | 0 |
| Chmil, Stephen, Greenville | .000 | 1 | 3 | 0 | 0 | 0 | 0 | 0 | 0 | 0 | 0 | 0 | 0 | 0 | 0 | 0 | 0 | 0 | 0 |
| Citari, Joseph, Memphis | .253 | 141 | 490 | 79 | 124 | 226 | 21 | 6 | 23 | 84 | 12 | 2 | 3 | 5 | 97 | 6 | 87 | 4 | 4 |
| Colbert, Cary, Birmingham | .211 | 6 | 19 | 1 | 4 | 4 | 0 | 0 | 0 | 0 | 0 | 0 | 0 | 0 | 4 | 1 | 2 | 0 | 1 |
| Colbert, Richard, Greenville | .261 | 60 | 161 | 25 | 42 | 77 | 10 | 2 | 7 | 18 | 2 | 0 | 1 | 3 | 24 | 0 | 24 | 2 | 1 |
| Cole, Michael, 11 Green-29 Mem° | .280 | 40 | 150 | 27 | 42 | 56 | 5 | 3 | 1 | 13 | 4 | 1 | 0 | 0 | 25 | 0 | 9 | 22 | 9 |
| Conklin, Graham, Huntsville | .237 | 95 | 279 | 45 | 66 | 110 | 9 | 1 | 11 | 37 | 4 | 7 | 4 | 1 | 29 | 2 | 42 | 1 | 0 |
| Cornwell, Curtis, Birmingham* | .248 | 38 | 121 | 13 | 30 | 42 | 5 | 2 | 1 | 9 | 1 | 3 | 1 | 0 | 11 | 0 | 16 | 0 | 0 |
| Coyle, Rock, Huntsville | .282 | 96 | 294 | 46 | 83 | 114 | 16 | 0 | 5 | 25 | 4 | 7 | 1 | 3 | 32 | 1 | 21 | 8 | 3 |
| Cummings, Robert, Chattanooga | .292 | 35 | 113 | 14 | 33 | 42 | 6 | 0 | 1 | 11 | 2 | 0 | 1 | 0 | 17 | 0 | 12 | 1 | 2 |
| Cutshall, William, Jacksonville* | .143 | 10 | 7 | 1 | 1 | 1 | 0 | 0 | 0 | 0 | 0 | 0 | 0 | 0 | 0 | 0 | 2 | 0 | 0 |
| Datz, Jeffrey, Columbus | .193 | 53 | 150 | 16 | 29 | 43 | 5 | 0 | 3 | 13 | 0 | 1 | 3 | 6 | 7 | 0 | 20 | 1 | 1 |
| David, Brian, Chattanooga | .301 | 117 | 418 | 71 | 126 | 165 | 23 | 8 | 0 | 51 | 7 | 8 | 6 | 3 | 76 | 3 | 30 | 5 | 2 |
| Davidson, Mark, Orlando | .302 | 134 | 453 | 93 | 137 | 233 | 17 | 2 | 25 | 106 | 16 | 2 | 6 | 10 | 92 | 1 | 92 | 13 | 5 |
| Davis, Robert, Memphis | .185 | 33 | 65 | 4 | 12 | 16 | 2 | 1 | 0 | 4 | 0 | 1 | 0 | 0 | 6 | 0 | 8 | 0 | 1 |
| Delgado, Juan, Columbus | .254 | 68 | 201 | 27 | 51 | 89 | 7 | 5 | 7 | 36 | 3 | 3 | 2 | 4 | 14 | 1 | 41 | 1 | 4 |
| Dennis, Eduardo, Knoxville | .000 | 5 | 4 | 1 | 0 | 0 | 0 | 0 | 0 | 0 | 0 | 0 | 0 | 0 | 0 | 0 | 1 | 0 | 0 |
| DeWillis, Jeffrey, Knoxville | .219 | 68 | 196 | 22 | 43 | 58 | 7 | 1 | 2 | 22 | 5 | 4 | 0 | 4 | 39 | 0 | 45 | 0 | 2 |
| Diaz, Jose, Knoxville | .214 | 100 | 266 | 30 | 57 | 85 | 14 | 1 | 4 | 32 | 4 | 5 | 2 | 1 | 34 | 0 | 66 | 2 | 0 |
| Diaz, Mario, Chattanooga | .253 | 115 | 400 | 39 | 101 | 121 | 6 | 7 | 0 | 38 | 4 | 14 | 7 | 0 | 21 | 2 | 20 | 3 | 4 |
| Dodd, Thomas, Charlotte | .307 | 85 | 287 | 51 | 88 | 161 | 18 | 2 | 17 | 52 | 7 | 0 | 3 | 5 | 39 | 2 | 54 | 1 | 0 |
| Dorsett, Brian, Huntsville | .268 | 88 | 313 | 38 | 84 | 141 | 18 | 3 | 11 | 43 | 4 | 3 | 0 | 0 | 38 | 1 | 61 | 2 | 0 |
| Eagar, Stephen, Birmingham | .196 | 94 | 285 | 29 | 56 | 75 | 10 | 0 | 3 | 18 | 2 | 9 | 2 | 2 | 37 | 0 | 47 | 0 | 0 |
| Faedo, Leonardo, Memphis | .284 | 98 | 388 | 46 | 110 | 144 | 12 | 2 | 6 | 57 | 2 | 5 | 4 | 1 | 20 | 1 | 22 | 4 | 4 |
| Falls, Robert, Columbus† | .285 | 95 | 263 | 23 | 75 | 105 | 12 | 0 | 6 | 37 | 5 | 2 | 4 | 3 | 13 | 0 | 63 | 12 | 3 |
| Felix, Paul, Orlando† | .245 | 101 | 278 | 36 | 68 | 116 | 15 | 3 | 9 | 37 | 0 | 0 | 3 | 7 | 36 | 2 | 66 | 0 | 0 |
| Fielder, Cecil, Knoxville | .294 | 96 | 361 | 52 | 106 | 190 | 26 | 2 | 18 | 81 | 4 | 0 | 5 | 3 | 45 | 3 | 83 | 0 | 0 |
| Fields, Bruce, Birmingham* | .323 | 114 | 421 | 59 | 136 | 174 | 24 | 4 | 2 | 41 | 3 | 0 | 4 | 3 | 54 | 1 | 50 | 9 | 6 |
| Firova, Daniel, Chattanooga | .240 | 110 | 346 | 28 | 83 | 110 | 14 | 2 | 3 | 22 | 0 | 8 | 1 | 6 | 12 | 1 | 32 | 0 | 2 |
| Foussianes, George, Memphis | .208 | 29 | 77 | 8 | 16 | 21 | 3 | 1 | 0 | 10 | 0 | 1 | 0 | 2 | 18 | 1 | 14 | 0 | 0 |
| Funderburk, Mark, Orlando | .283 | 140 | 523 | 70 | 148 | 272 | 20 | 1 | 34 | 116 | 13 | 0 | 6 | 11 | 40 | 3 | 63 | 0 | 3 |
| Gerhart, Kenneth, Charlotte | .275 | 68 | 222 | 55 | 61 | 130 | 16 | 1 | 17 | 52 | 7 | 3 | 2 | 3 | 48 | 2 | 46 | 20 | 4 |
| Gould, Robert, Huntsville | .333 | 3 | 3 | 1 | 1 | 1 | 0 | 0 | 0 | 0 | 0 | 1 | 0 | 0 | 0 | 0 | 1 | 0 | 0 |
| Graham, Brian, Huntsville | .289 | 95 | 298 | 37 | 86 | 110 | 13 | 1 | 3 | 28 | 0 | 1 | 2 | 2 | 24 | 0 | 44 | 8 | 8 |
| Granger, Lee, Charlotte† | .265 | 44 | 166 | 31 | 44 | 62 | 6 | 3 | 2 | 21 | 0 | 1 | 1 | 4 | 26 | 1 | 35 | 17 | 10 |
| Graybill, David, Jacksonville | .000 | 10 | 1 | 0 | 0 | 0 | 0 | 0 | 0 | 0 | 0 | 0 | 0 | 0 | 0 | 0 | 1 | 0 | 0 |
| Green, Otis, Knoxville* | .290 | 115 | 442 | 68 | 128 | 190 | 19 | 5 | 11 | 68 | 14 | 1 | 3 | 2 | 44 | 5 | 71 | 9 | 8 |
| Griffin, David, Greenville | .364 | 7 | 22 | 5 | 8 | 13 | 2 | 0 | 1 | 5 | 1 | 0 | 0 | 0 | 3 | 0 | 4 | 0 | 0 |
| Grote, Gerald, Birmingham | .000 | 1 | 1 | 0 | 0 | 0 | 0 | 0 | 0 | 0 | 0 | 0 | 0 | 0 | 0 | 0 | 0 | 0 | 0 |
| Groves, Larry, Jacksonville | .333 | 36 | 3 | 1 | 1 | 1 | 0 | 0 | 0 | 0 | 0 | 0 | 0 | 0 | 1 | 0 | 0 | 0 | 0 |
| Guerrero, Inocencio, Greenville | .279 | 118 | 419 | 72 | 117 | 202 | 27 | 5 | 16 | 68 | 9 | 1 | 7 | 1 | 63 | 1 | 87 | 1 | 2 |
| Guinn, Brian, Huntsville* | .209 | 30 | 86 | 9 | 18 | 25 | 1 | 0 | 2 | 9 | 2 | 1 | 0 | 1 | 14 | 0 | 16 | 4 | 1 |
| Hamric, Russell, Knoxville | .216 | 71 | 213 | 29 | 46 | 61 | 7 | 4 | 0 | 13 | 1 | 4 | 2 | 1 | 38 | 3 | 21 | 6 | 2 |
| Hanggie, Daniel, Orlando† | .269 | 134 | 409 | 63 | 110 | 174 | 21 | 2 | 13 | 53 | 9 | 0 | 3 | 4 | 73 | 4 | 83 | 4 | 3 |
| Hansen, Roger, Memphis | .331 | 55 | 181 | 15 | 60 | 74 | 8 | 0 | 2 | 28 | 5 | 1 | 2 | 2 | 18 | 1 | 26 | 0 | 1 |
| Harvey, Randall, Huntsville* | 1.000 | 22 | 2 | 0 | 2 | 2 | 0 | 0 | 0 | 0 | 0 | 0 | 0 | 0 | 0 | 0 | 0 | 0 | 0 |
| Hatcher, Harold, Memphis | .230 | 59 | 183 | 18 | 42 | 66 | 9 | 0 | 5 | 24 | 2 | 0 | 2 | 3 | 7 | 0 | 44 | 0 | 0 |
| Hatcher, Johnny, Greenville | .255 | 25 | 98 | 11 | 25 | 31 | 3 | 0 | 1 | 8 | 0 | 0 | 1 | 0 | 9 | 0 | 15 | 4 | 2 |
| Hayes, Thomas, Greenville | .211 | 89 | 280 | 27 | 59 | 75 | 12 | 2 | 0 | 23 | 2 | 0 | 1 | 3 | 32 | 0 | 38 | 2 | 1 |
| Hearron, Jeffrey, Knoxville | .223 | 45 | 130 | 17 | 29 | 52 | 6 | 1 | 5 | 15 | 0 | 1 | 1 | 1 | 24 | 2 | 20 | 0 | 2 |
| Hengel, Daniel, Chattanooga | .287 | 122 | 460 | 71 | 132 | 223 | 30 | 5 | 17 | 89 | 5 | 2 | 8 | 4 | 38 | 3 | 66 | 7 | 2 |
| Hernandez, Pedro, Columbus | .196 | 13 | 46 | 3 | 9 | 13 | 2 | 1 | 0 | 3 | 0 | 0 | 1 | 1 | 0 | 1 | 4 | 0 | 2 |
| Hertzler, Paul, Greenville* | .319 | 50 | 185 | 31 | 59 | 85 | 11 | 3 | 3 | 15 | 2 | 0 | 1 | 0 | 18 | 3 | 18 | 6 | 4 |
| Hill, Roger, Chattanooga* | .172 | 37 | 122 | 17 | 21 | 32 | 2 | 3 | 1 | 10 | 0 | 1 | 1 | 0 | 11 | 0 | 12 | 5 | 1 |
| Hobbs, Rodney, Birmingham | .284 | 135 | 496 | 88 | 141 | 199 | 23 | 7 | 7 | 66 | 9 | 2 | 7 | 4 | 73 | 0 | 77 | 7 | 13 |
| Hocutt, Michael, Chattanooga | .259 | 139 | 495 | 85 | 128 | 250 | 22 | 8 | 28 | 92 | 11 | 4 | 7 | 6 | 79 | 3 | 100 | 9 | 7 |
| Hoeksema, David, Jacksonville | .284 | 22 | 81 | 13 | 23 | 38 | 6 | 0 | 3 | 12 | 0 | 1 | 0 | 1 | 7 | 0 | 14 | 0 | 0 |
| Hogan, Michael, Columbus | .200 | 27 | 10 | 1 | 2 | 4 | 2 | 0 | 0 | 1 | 0 | 0 | 0 | 0 | 2 | 0 | 2 | 0 | 0 |
| Holland, John, Knoxville | .450 | 5 | 20 | 4 | 9 | 12 | 0 | 0 | 1 | 5 | 0 | 0 | 0 | 0 | 0 | 0 | 0 | 0 | 0 |

| Player and Club | Pct. | G. | AB. | R. | H. | TB. | 2B. | 3B. | HR. | RBI. | GW. | SH. | SF. | HP. | BB. | Int. BB. | SO. | SB. | CS. |
|---|---|---|---|---|---|---|---|---|---|---|---|---|---|---|---|---|---|---|---|
| Hollins, Paul, Chattanooga° | .257 | 131 | 474 | 64 | 122 | 204 | 26 | 4 | 16 | 78 | 9 | 0 | 4 | 1 | 60 | 10 | 110 | 4 | 1 |
| Holmes, Stanley, Orlando | .303 | 9 | 33 | 4 | 10 | 21 | 3 | 1 | 2 | 8 | 0 | 0 | 1 | 0 | 7 | 0 | 12 | 0 | 0 |
| Hoover, John, Charlotte | .000 | 29 | 0 | 0 | 0 | 0 | 0 | 0 | 0 | 0 | 0 | 0 | 0 | 0 | 1 | 0 | 0 | 0 | 0 |
| Hotchkiss, John, Birmingham | .198 | 73 | 232 | 23 | 46 | 72 | 9 | 1 | 5 | 29 | 1 | 1 | 3 | 1 | 23 | 3 | 39 | 1 | 2 |
| Ingle, Randy, Greenville | .256 | 102 | 340 | 38 | 87 | 134 | 18 | 1 | 9 | 46 | 6 | 4 | 5 | 1 | 22 | 3 | 44 | 0 | 0 |
| Jackson, Charles, Columbus | .310 | 108 | 361 | 62 | 112 | 162 | 10 | 8 | 8 | 46 | 5 | 3 | 3 | 3 | 77 | 2 | 51 | 32 | 14 |
| Jacobson, Jeffrey, Charlotte | .238 | 131 | 411 | 60 | 98 | 123 | 10 | 3 | 3 | 45 | 2 | 3 | 3 | 3 | 46 | 1 | 44 | 0 | 4 |
| Jarrell, Joseph, Memphis | .232 | 85 | 289 | 27 | 67 | 112 | 15 | 0 | 10 | 32 | 2 | 4 | 2 | 2 | 23 | 1 | 84 | 4 | 2 |
| Javier, Stanley, Huntsville† | .284 | 140 | 486 | 105 | 138 | 203 | 22 | 8 | 9 | 64 | 7 | 4 | 6 | 5 | 112 | 6 | 92 | 61 | 15 |
| Johnson, Joseph, Greenville | .000 | 12 | 5 | 1 | 0 | 0 | 0 | 0 | 0 | 0 | 0 | 1 | 0 | 0 | 2 | 0 | 0 | 0 | 0 |
| Johnson, Roy, Jacksonville° | .252 | 78 | 274 | 39 | 69 | 117 | 13 | 1 | 11 | 37 | 4 | 2 | 1 | 5 | 32 | 5 | 31 | 9 | 1 |
| Johnston, Christopher, Knoxville | .260 | 135 | 496 | 56 | 129 | 219 | 32 | 2 | 18 | 81 | 9 | 1 | 8 | 13 | 44 | 1 | 138 | 1 | 3 |
| Jones, Ricky, Charlotte | .280 | 108 | 386 | 64 | 108 | 196 | 20 | 1 | 22 | 64 | 4 | 5 | 5 | 3 | 45 | 2 | 59 | 3 | 5 |
| Kasprzak, Michael, Columbus | .000 | 38 | 2 | 0 | 0 | 0 | 0 | 0 | 0 | 0 | 0 | 1 | 0 | 0 | 1 | 0 | 0 | 0 | 0 |
| Kelley, Anthony, Columbus | .000 | 22 | 8 | 0 | 0 | 0 | 0 | 0 | 0 | 1 | 0 | 1 | 0 | 0 | 4 | 0 | 4 | 0 | 0 |
| Kenaga, Jeffrey, Charlotte° | .265 | 73 | 260 | 24 | 69 | 110 | 21 | 1 | 6 | 40 | 6 | 1 | 0 | 2 | 16 | 1 | 37 | 1 | 0 |
| Kinnard, Kenneth, Knoxville | .231 | 17 | 13 | 7 | 3 | 4 | 1 | 0 | 0 | 1 | 0 | 0 | 0 | 0 | 4 | 0 | 3 | 0 | 1 |
| Kinns, Glenn, Jacksonville | .200 | 37 | 5 | 0 | 1 | 1 | 0 | 0 | 0 | 0 | 0 | 0 | 0 | 0 | 0 | 0 | 2 | 0 | 0 |
| Knox, Michael, Greenville | .210 | 137 | 485 | 49 | 102 | 134 | 16 | 2 | 4 | 40 | 5 | 10 | 9 | 1 | 50 | 1 | 65 | 6 | 3 |
| Koenigsfeld, Ronald, Columbus | .269 | 26 | 93 | 15 | 25 | 41 | 1 | 0 | 5 | 15 | 1 | 0 | 1 | 1 | 12 | 0 | 13 | 2 | 1 |
| Lamb, Todd, Greenville | .333 | 40 | 18 | 1 | 6 | 7 | 1 | 0 | 0 | 0 | 1 | 0 | 0 | 1 | 0 | 6 | 0 | 0 |
| Lawrence, Theodore, Birmingham | .125 | 3 | 8 | 0 | 1 | 1 | 0 | 0 | 0 | 1 | 0 | 0 | 0 | 1 | 3 | 0 | 2 | 0 | 0 |
| Leggatt, Richard, Greenville° | .250 | 46 | 4 | 0 | 1 | 1 | 0 | 0 | 0 | 0 | 0 | 0 | 0 | 0 | 0 | 0 | 1 | 0 | 0 |
| Lockwood, Richard, Charlotte† | .223 | 129 | 404 | 55 | 90 | 155 | 14 | 3 | 15 | 67 | 6 | 6 | 6 | 3 | 57 | 5 | 58 | 7 | 1 |
| Longenecker, Jere, Memphis | .247 | 95 | 292 | 46 | 72 | 108 | 13 | 1 | 7 | 32 | 4 | 3 | 2 | 5 | 40 | 0 | 43 | 16 | 4 |
| Lucas, Arbrey, Columbus | 1.000 | 7 | 1 | 0 | 1 | 1 | 0 | 0 | 0 | 0 | 0 | 0 | 0 | 0 | 0 | 0 | 0 | 0 | 0 |
| Lusader, Scott, Birmingham° | .338 | 21 | 77 | 13 | 26 | 43 | 3 | 4 | 2 | 14 | 3 | 0 | 1 | 0 | 5 | 0 | 12 | 0 | 0 |
| Luzon, Robert, Greenville | .201 | 75 | 149 | 21 | 30 | 39 | 6 | 0 | 1 | 10 | 1 | 1 | 0 | 0 | 20 | 0 | 34 | 0 | 5 |
| MacFarlane, Michael, Memphis | .269 | 65 | 223 | 29 | 60 | 107 | 15 | 4 | 8 | 39 | 2 | 2 | 2 | 5 | 11 | 0 | 30 | 0 | 0 |
| Madison, Scotti, Birmingham† | .322 | 37 | 121 | 28 | 39 | 64 | 8 | 1 | 5 | 25 | 1 | 0 | 0 | 1 | 35 | 5 | 12 | 2 | 1 |
| Marquardt, John, Huntsville | .266 | 109 | 353 | 43 | 94 | 115 | 10 | 1 | 3 | 40 | 6 | 7 | 4 | 0 | 37 | 1 | 39 | 7 | 3 |
| Marquardt, Roger, Knoxville | .000 | 3 | 3 | 0 | 0 | 0 | 0 | 0 | 0 | 0 | 0 | 0 | 0 | 0 | 1 | 0 | 2 | 0 | 0 |
| Marte, Alexis, Orlando° | .320 | 141 | 534 | 117 | 171 | 204 | 15 | 9 | 0 | 33 | 3 | 6 | 4 | 1 | 63 | 1 | 43 | 64 | 21 |
| Martinez, Edgar, Chattanooga | .258 | 111 | 357 | 43 | 92 | 126 | 15 | 5 | 3 | 47 | 5 | 10 | 12 | 5 | 71 | 2 | 30 | 1 | 3 |
| McKay, Troy, Jacksonville | .333 | 14 | 3 | 1 | 1 | 1 | 0 | 0 | 0 | 0 | 0 | 0 | 0 | 0 | 1 | 0 | 1 | 0 | 0 |
| McNealy, Robert, Chattanooga° | .254 | 115 | 426 | 80 | 108 | 131 | 15 | 4 | 0 | 32 | 0 | 8 | 0 | 0 | 71 | 3 | 39 | 35 | 19 |
| Meadows, Michael, Columbus° | .233 | 140 | 476 | 76 | 111 | 185 | 16 | 8 | 14 | 67 | 13 | 2 | 7 | 6 | 70 | 5 | 85 | 23 | 7 |
| Miller, Michael, Memphis | .264 | 98 | 371 | 56 | 98 | 127 | 13 | 2 | 4 | 36 | 2 | 4 | 2 | 2 | 41 | 0 | 83 | 25 | 9 |
| Mills, Craig, Birmingham | .256 | 113 | 371 | 42 | 95 | 112 | 9 | 1 | 2 | 29 | 2 | 3 | 3 | 5 | 34 | 0 | 55 | 4 | 4 |
| Moore, William, Jacksonville | .259 | 140 | 509 | 83 | 132 | 265 | 30 | 2 | 33 | 104 | 7 | 0 | 5 | 11 | 73 | 3 | 97 | 4 | 5 |
| Moreno, Armando, Jacksonville | .286 | 105 | 371 | 67 | 106 | 155 | 25 | 0 | 8 | 32 | 5 | 8 | 4 | 4 | 60 | 3 | 46 | 4 | 9 |
| Moreno, Michael, 36 Orl-23 Mem | .209 | 59 | 177 | 15 | 37 | 46 | 4 | 1 | 1 | 13 | 1 | 4 | 1 | 0 | 19 | 0 | 29 | 2 | 3 |
| Morhardt, Gregory, Orlando° | .263 | 121 | 411 | 55 | 108 | 174 | 17 | 5 | 13 | 63 | 6 | 1 | 6 | 7 | 21 | 1 | 38 | 0 | 1 |
| Myers, David, Chattanooga | .241 | 82 | 261 | 26 | 63 | 70 | 3 | 2 | 0 | 17 | 1 | 12 | 2 | 1 | 24 | 0 | 22 | 1 | 1 |
| Nelson, Robert, Huntsville° | .232 | 140 | 499 | 68 | 116 | 237 | 25 | 0 | 32 | 98 | 9 | 1 | 5 | 2 | 86 | 8 | 137 | 2 | 0 |
| Neuzil, Jeffrey, Memphis | .238 | 118 | 341 | 54 | 81 | 94 | 6 | 2 | 1 | 22 | 3 | 5 | 0 | 1 | 34 | 1 | 53 | 18 | 3 |
| Nichols, Carl, Charlotte | .236 | 115 | 331 | 45 | 78 | 99 | 11 | 2 | 2 | 37 | 2 | 4 | 7 | 9 | 48 | 2 | 51 | 7 | 4 |
| Nicometi, Anthony, Jacksonville° | .000 | 41 | 1 | 0 | 0 | 0 | 0 | 0 | 0 | 0 | 0 | 0 | 0 | 0 | 0 | 0 | 1 | 0 | 0 |
| Noble, Rayner, Columbus† | .200 | 38 | 5 | 0 | 1 | 1 | 0 | 0 | 0 | 0 | 0 | 0 | 0 | 0 | 0 | 0 | 2 | 0 | 0 |
| Norman, Daniel, 86 Birm-32 Char | .264 | 118 | 439 | 67 | 116 | 194 | 19 | 1 | 19 | 80 | 11 | 0 | 2 | 3 | 38 | 1 | 76 | 2 | 3 |
| O'Brien, Charles, Huntsville | .209 | 33 | 115 | 20 | 24 | 50 | 5 | 0 | 7 | 16 | 0 | 1 | 1 | 2 | 16 | 0 | 20 | 0 | 1 |
| Padia, Steven, Charlotte° | .246 | 19 | 57 | 10 | 14 | 30 | 4 | 0 | 4 | 11 | 1 | 0 | 0 | 7 | 0 | 8 | 1 | 0 |
| Palacios, Rey, Birmingham | .264 | 35 | 110 | 14 | 29 | 39 | 4 | 0 | 2 | 16 | 0 | 2 | 1 | 2 | 11 | 0 | 13 | 2 | 2 |
| Paredes, Johnny, Jacksonville | .315 | 21 | 73 | 11 | 23 | 25 | 2 | 0 | 0 | 5 | 0 | 2 | 0 | 2 | 6 | 0 | 7 | 3 | 4 |
| Perez, Edgar, Chattanooga | .231 | 10 | 26 | 4 | 6 | 6 | 0 | 0 | 0 | 4 | 2 | 1 | 0 | 0 | 2 | 0 | 6 | 1 | 1 |
| Perez, Oriol, Chattanooga | .212 | 10 | 33 | 2 | 7 | 12 | 2 | 0 | 1 | 5 | 1 | 2 | 1 | 1 | 0 | 0 | 6 | 1 | 0 |
| Polonia, Luis, Huntsville† | .289 | 130 | 515 | 82 | 149 | 206 | 15 | 18 | 2 | 36 | 5 | 6 | 4 | 0 | 59 | 3 | 54 | 39 | 20 |
| Price, Kevin, Jacksonville | .125 | 21 | 8 | 1 | 1 | 1 | 0 | 0 | 0 | 0 | 0 | 0 | 0 | 0 | 0 | 0 | 6 | 0 | 0 |
| Ralston, Robert, Orlando | .301 | 126 | 419 | 66 | 126 | 139 | 11 | 1 | 0 | 28 | 2 | 10 | 4 | 2 | 38 | 0 | 25 | 16 | 15 |
| Ramsey, Michael, Charlotte† | .143 | 6 | 14 | 2 | 2 | 3 | 1 | 0 | 0 | 1 | 0 | 0 | 0 | 2 | 0 | 3 | 2 | 1 |
| Ransom, Jeffrey, Greenville† | .219 | 53 | 169 | 14 | 37 | 58 | 4 | 1 | 5 | 19 | 1 | 1 | 2 | 1 | 18 | 0 | 32 | 0 | 0 |
| Reddish, Michael, Charlotte | .307 | 51 | 166 | 34 | 51 | 92 | 5 | 0 | 12 | 38 | 5 | 2 | 1 | 4 | 40 | 1 | 23 | 4 | 2 |
| Reilly, Edward, Columbus | .333 | 18 | 3 | 0 | 1 | 1 | 0 | 0 | 0 | 0 | 0 | 0 | 0 | 0 | 0 | 0 | 0 | 0 | 0 |
| Reynolds, Jeffrey, Jacksonville | .259 | 137 | 499 | 53 | 129 | 203 | 30 | 1 | 14 | 69 | 7 | 1 | 4 | 2 | 45 | 2 | 118 | 3 | 6 |
| Ripken, William, Charlotte | .137 | 18 | 51 | 2 | 7 | 8 | 1 | 0 | 0 | 3 | 0 | 1 | 0 | 0 | 6 | 0 | 4 | 0 | 0 |
| Rivera, Luis, Jacksonville | .240 | 138 | 538 | 74 | 129 | 201 | 20 | 2 | 16 | 72 | 7 | 3 | 6 | 7 | 44 | 1 | 69 | 18 | 15 |
| Rizzo, Richard, Memphis | .236 | 109 | 322 | 42 | 76 | 90 | 9 | 1 | 1 | 18 | 1 | 7 | 3 | 5 | 43 | 2 | 40 | 15 | 12 |
| Rodriguez, Ricardo, Huntsville | .000 | 8 | 1 | 0 | 0 | 0 | 0 | 0 | 0 | 0 | 0 | 0 | 0 | 0 | 1 | 0 | 0 | 0 | 0 |
| Rollin, Rondal, Birmingham | .259 | 142 | 518 | 80 | 134 | 254 | 28 | 1 | 30 | 108 | 6 | 1 | 6 | 4 | 40 | 4 | 143 | 1 | 1 |
| Rood, Nelson, Columbus | .262 | 64 | 225 | 31 | 59 | 76 | 8 | 3 | 1 | 17 | 3 | 4 | 2 | 3 | 48 | 1 | 24 | 19 | 6 |
| Rosado, Luis, Birmingham | .344 | 37 | 122 | 12 | 42 | 55 | 7 | 0 | 2 | 19 | 2 | 0 | 2 | 0 | 9 | 0 | 11 | 0 | 1 |
| Rosario, Maximo, Greenville° | .000 | 22 | 8 | 0 | 0 | 0 | 0 | 0 | 0 | 0 | 0 | 0 | 0 | 0 | 0 | 0 | 6 | 0 | 0 |
| Ruiz, Benny, Birmingham | .233 | 112 | 352 | 33 | 82 | 94 | 10 | 1 | 0 | 28 | 1 | 7 | 4 | 0 | 25 | 1 | 32 | 4 | 3 |
| Salcedo, Ronnie, Charlotte° | .265 | 92 | 321 | 54 | 85 | 129 | 17 | 0 | 9 | 51 | 5 | 1 | 2 | 2 | 75 | 4 | 19 | 4 | 4 |
| Samuels, Roger, Columbus° | .000 | 33 | 10 | 0 | 0 | 0 | 0 | 0 | 0 | 0 | 0 | 1 | 0 | 0 | 1 | 0 | 6 | 0 | 0 |
| Santovenia, Nelson, Jacksonville | .217 | 57 | 184 | 15 | 40 | 52 | 6 | 0 | 2 | 15 | 3 | 4 | 1 | 1 | 14 | 1 | 18 | 2 | 0 |
| Schaefer, Jeffrey, Charlotte | .260 | 49 | 181 | 19 | 47 | 62 | 7 | 1 | 2 | 19 | 1 | 3 | 1 | 0 | 12 | 0 | 14 | 6 | 5 |
| Schulz, Jeffrey, Memphis° | .305 | 136 | 488 | 73 | 149 | 186 | 15 | 5 | 4 | 53 | 7 | 4 | 8 | 0 | 59 | 5 | 42 | 8 | 4 |
| Seitzer, Kevin, Memphis | .348 | 52 | 187 | 26 | 65 | 78 | 6 | 2 | 1 | 20 | 2 | 1 | 0 | 5 | 25 | 1 | 21 | 9 | 3 |
| Shaddy, Christopher, Knoxville | .240 | 106 | 341 | 35 | 82 | 118 | 12 | 6 | 4 | 36 | 3 | 4 | 2 | 3 | 30 | 2 | 83 | 2 | 3 |
| Sherman, James, Columbus | .279 | 118 | 423 | 68 | 118 | 216 | 34 | 2 | 20 | 90 | 11 | 0 | 8 | 5 | 32 | 3 | 66 | 4 | 8 |
| Silva, Jose, Jacksonville† | .185 | 42 | 108 | 8 | 20 | 23 | 3 | 0 | 0 | 7 | 1 | 0 | 0 | 1 | 9 | 0 | 17 | 3 | 1 |
| Sinatro, Matthew, Greenville | .279 | 49 | 172 | 25 | 48 | 72 | 4 | 1 | 6 | 28 | 3 | 5 | 2 | 0 | 13 | 0 | 13 | 4 | 0 |
| Sliwinski, Kevin, Knoxville | .289 | 139 | 502 | 77 | 145 | 243 | 26 | 9 | 18 | 68 | 10 | 0 | 8 | 5 | 61 | 2 | 92 | 3 | 4 |
| Smith, Brick, Chattanooga | .262 | 80 | 275 | 38 | 72 | 103 | 7 | 0 | 8 | 37 | 6 | 3 | 4 | 1 | 39 | 2 | 34 | 2 | 1 |
| Smith, Kenneth, Greenville° | .301 | 66 | 183 | 38 | 55 | 98 | 11 | 1 | 10 | 43 | 2 | 0 | 2 | 1 | 40 | 2 | 37 | 9 | 3 |
| Smith, Lawrence, Huntsville° | .000 | 48 | 1 | 0 | 0 | 0 | 0 | 0 | 0 | 0 | 0 | 0 | 0 | 0 | 0 | 0 | 1 | 0 | 0 |
| Smith, Mark, Birmingham | .246 | 88 | 338 | 37 | 83 | 117 | 17 | 1 | 5 | 34 | 3 | 0 | 3 | 3 | 12 | 1 | 30 | 0 | 1 |
| Snider, Van, Memphis° | .236 | 85 | 292 | 43 | 69 | 116 | 15 | 4 | 8 | 39 | 3 | 1 | 4 | 1 | 43 | 6 | 63 | 4 | 8 |
| Sorce, Samuel, Orlando | .278 | 122 | 421 | 45 | 117 | 163 | 26 | 1 | 6 | 59 | 7 | 0 | 10 | 1 | 32 | 3 | 31 | 1 | 1 |
| Springer, Gary, Birmingham° | .252 | 120 | 408 | 78 | 103 | 148 | 19 | 1 | 8 | 41 | 6 | 5 | 0 | 2 | 105 | 1 | 39 | 9 | 8 |
| Stark, Matthew, Knoxville† | .245 | 18 | 53 | 3 | 13 | 17 | 1 | 0 | 1 | 3 | 0 | 0 | 0 | 5 | 1 | 8 | 0 | 0 |

| Player and Club | Pct. | G. | AB. | R. | H. | TB. | 2B. | 3B. | HR. | RBI. | GW. | SH. | SF. | HP. | BB. | Int. BB. | SO. | SB. | CS. |
|---|---|---|---|---|---|---|---|---|---|---|---|---|---|---|---|---|---|---|---|
| Stefero, John, Charlotte° | .219 | 57 | 169 | 31 | 37 | 66 | 8 | 0 | 7 | 19 | 2 | 1 | 2 | 0 | 33 | 2 | 41 | 0 | 0 |
| Steinbach, Terry, Huntsville | .272 | 128 | 456 | 64 | 124 | 188 | 31 | 3 | 9 | 72 | 9 | 4 | 7 | 3 | 45 | 2 | 36 | 4 | 1 |
| Stenhouse, David, Knoxville | .228 | 26 | 79 | 8 | 18 | 20 | 2 | 0 | 0 | 11 | 0 | 1 | 1 | 0 | 16 | 2 | 11 | 2 | 0 |
| Strasser, Richard, Columbus | .111 | 30 | 9 | 2 | 1 | 1 | 0 | 0 | 0 | 0 | 0 | 1 | 0 | 0 | 1 | 0 | 6 | 0 | 0 |
| Stromer, Richard, Huntsville | .298 | 64 | 178 | 28 | 53 | 77 | 9 | 0 | 5 | 27 | 2 | 0 | 4 | 4 | 37 | 0 | 23 | 1 | 1 |
| Strucher, Mark, Columbus | .267 | 40 | 131 | 26 | 35 | 55 | 9 | 1 | 3 | 26 | 2 | 0 | 4 | 2 | 21 | 0 | 13 | 1 | 1 |
| Szajko, Daniel, Jacksonville | .249 | 73 | 185 | 33 | 46 | 57 | 3 | 1 | 2 | 13 | 2 | 1 | 0 | 2 | 35 | 1 | 23 | 11 | 3 |
| Tatis, Bernardo, Knoxville† | .286 | 105 | 266 | 43 | 76 | 103 | 7 | 4 | 4 | 21 | 2 | 3 | 0 | 3 | 34 | 2 | 37 | 25 | 10 |
| Taylor, Jeffrey, 22 Green-10 Orl° | .000 | 32 | 3 | 0 | 0 | 0 | 0 | 0 | 0 | 0 | 0 | 0 | 0 | 0 | 0 | 0 | 2 | 0 | 0 |
| Thielker, David, Charlotte° | .303 | 27 | 89 | 16 | 27 | 37 | 4 | 0 | 2 | 14 | 0 | 1 | 1 | 3 | 12 | 0 | 12 | 0 | 0 |
| Thiessen, Timothy, Jacksonville | .222 | 40 | 135 | 15 | 30 | 39 | 6 | 0 | 1 | 13 | 2 | 1 | 0 | 2 | 11 | 1 | 18 | 1 | 3 |
| Thoma, Raymond, Huntsville | .265 | 123 | 464 | 75 | 123 | 183 | 21 | 3 | 11 | 55 | 8 | 4 | 1 | 6 | 38 | 0 | 93 | 5 | 1 |
| Thomas, Andres, Greenville | .249 | 114 | 458 | 53 | 114 | 167 | 18 | 4 | 9 | 59 | 6 | 3 | 2 | 1 | 23 | 2 | 63 | 3 | 3 |
| Thomas, James, Columbus† | .279 | 129 | 423 | 65 | 118 | 148 | 19 | 4 | 1 | 43 | 5 | 9 | 9 | 5 | 74 | 1 | 34 | 20 | 10 |
| Thomas, Reginald, Birmingham° | .220 | 19 | 50 | 6 | 11 | 15 | 1 | 0 | 1 | 5 | 1 | 0 | 1 | 0 | 4 | 0 | 12 | 1 | 0 |
| Thompson, Tommy, Greenville° | .321 | 95 | 324 | 61 | 104 | 162 | 18 | 2 | 12 | 38 | 0 | 4 | 4 | 0 | 50 | 1 | 26 | 0 | 0 |
| Tiburcio, Fredrick, Greenville | .250 | 86 | 340 | 55 | 85 | 125 | 10 | 3 | 8 | 41 | 1 | 2 | 2 | 1 | 24 | 3 | 49 | 9 | 7 |
| Torres, Miguel, 11 Jack-24 Col | .000 | 35 | 4 | 0 | 0 | 0 | 0 | 0 | 0 | 0 | 0 | 0 | 0 | 0 | 0 | 0 | 3 | 0 | 0 |
| Torve, Kelvin, Charlotte° | .290 | 134 | 482 | 85 | 140 | 221 | 34 | 1 | 15 | 77 | 8 | 4 | 7 | 2 | 75 | 9 | 53 | 5 | 2 |
| Treadway, Andre, Greenville | .000 | 31 | 10 | 0 | 0 | 0 | 0 | 0 | 0 | 0 | 0 | 0 | 3 | 0 | 0 | 0 | 4 | 0 | 0 |
| Trout, Jeffrey, Orlando° | .279 | 95 | 294 | 44 | 82 | 117 | 20 | 3 | 3 | 40 | 3 | 0 | 2 | 1 | 51 | 4 | 22 | 0 | 3 |
| Tumpane, Robert, Greenville° | .300 | 68 | 207 | 43 | 62 | 114 | 14 | 1 | 12 | 41 | 4 | 0 | 3 |  | 53 | 2 | 36 | 0 | 0 |
| Tutt, Johnny, Charlotte | .150 | 6 | 20 | 4 | 3 | 5 | 0 | 1 | 0 | 2 | 0 | 0 | 0 |  | 2 | 0 | 5 | 0 | 0 |
| Vargas, Leonel, Greenville | .270 | 105 | 352 | 39 | 95 | 140 | 22 | 1 | 7 | 32 | 3 | 3 | 3 | 1 | 26 | 2 | 41 | 9 | 3 |
| Verkuilen, Michael, Orlando° | .261 | 107 | 284 | 47 | 74 | 131 | 19 | 1 | 12 | 41 | 5 | 1 | 1 | 1 | 48 | 3 | 44 | 0 | 0 |
| Vetsch, David, Orlando° | .195 | 19 | 41 | 6 | 8 | 12 | 1 | 0 | 1 | 5 | 0 | 0 | 0 |  | 4 | 0 | 10 | 0 | 0 |
| Walewander, James, Birmingham† | .289 | 14 | 45 | 3 | 13 | 15 | 0 | 1 | 0 | 2 | 1 | 1 | 0 |  | 2 | 0 | 3 | 0 | 1 |
| Walker, Anthony, Columbus† | .294 | 135 | 530 | 88 | 156 | 225 | 23 | 5 | 12 | 65 | 6 | 4 | 2 | 2 | 59 | 2 | 63 | 42 | 8 |
| Walker, Glen, Memphis | .206 | 50 | 180 | 22 | 37 | 68 | 7 | 0 | 8 | 31 | 7 | 0 | 4 | 3 | 15 | 1 | 28 | 1 | 1 |
| Wallace, Timothy, Jacksonville | .296 | 55 | 189 | 26 | 56 | 66 | 7 | 0 | 1 | 18 | 3 | 0 | 2 | 1 | 16 | 1 | 26 | 4 | 4 |
| Ward, Duane, Greenville | .125 | 28 | 8 | 1 | 1 | 4 | 0 | 0 | 1 | 1 | 0 | 0 | 0 | 0 | 0 | 0 | 2 | 0 | 0 |
| Wayne, Gary, Jacksonville° | .500 | 21 | 6 | 1 | 3 | 3 | 0 | 0 | 0 | 0 | 0 | 0 | 0 | 0 | 2 | 0 | 1 | 0 | 0 |
| Werner, Donald, Birmingham | .188 | 10 | 32 | 6 | 6 | 12 | 1 | 1 | 1 | 4 | 0 | 0 | 1 |  | 2 | 0 | 2 | 0 | 0 |
| Whisenton, Larry, Greenville° | .323 | 70 | 226 | 44 | 73 | 92 | 8 | 1 | 3 | 32 | 3 | 0 | 0 |  | 54 | 3 | 46 | 4 | 2 |
| Wilborn, Thaddeus, Charlotte† | .288 | 69 | 267 | 44 | 77 | 101 | 10 | 1 | 4 | 29 | 2 | 8 | 2 | 0 | 28 | 1 | 39 | 7 | 5 |
| Wilder, David, Huntsville | .162 | 29 | 68 | 11 | 11 | 22 | 5 | 0 | 2 | 8 | 0 | 0 | 2 | 0 | 19 | 0 | 18 | 0 | 1 |
| Williams, Dallas, Jacksonville° | .281 | 39 | 96 | 12 | 27 | 36 | 7 | 1 | 0 | 5 | 1 | 0 | 2 | 0 | 9 | 1 | 9 | 4 | 2 |
| Williams, David, Orlando | .210 | 65 | 124 | 13 | 26 | 29 | 1 | 1 | 0 | 12 | 0 | 1 | 2 | 0 | 11 | 0 | 23 | 0 | 1 |
| Wilson, Ricky, Chattanooga | .194 | 27 | 67 | 6 | 13 | 13 | 0 | 0 | 0 | 6 | 1 | 2 | 2 | 1 | 6 | 0 | 14 | 1 | 0 |
| Wine, Robert, Columbus | .190 | 109 | 384 | 53 | 73 | 153 | 13 | 2 | 21 | 55 | 8 | 1 | 3 | 1 | 28 | 2 | 121 | 2 | 4 |
| Worden, William, Chattanooga | .262 | 17 | 61 | 7 | 16 | 27 | 2 | 0 | 3 | 7 | 0 | 1 | 0 | 1 | 2 | 1 | 6 | 0 | 1 |
| Youmans, Floyd, Jacksonville | .286 | 14 | 7 | 1 | 2 | 5 | 0 | 1 | 0 | 1 | 0 | 0 | 0 | 0 | 0 | 0 | 0 | 0 | 0 |
| Ziem, Stephen, Greenville | .125 | 48 | 8 | 4 | 1 | 1 | 0 | 0 | 0 | 0 | 1 | 0 | 0 |  | 2 | 0 | 1 | 0 | 0 |

The following pitchers, listed alphabetically by club, with games in parentheses, had no plate appearances, primarily through use of designated hitters:

BIRMINGHAM—Barlow, Ricky (18); Breining, Fred (12); Conner, Jeffrey (3); Cook, Kerry (3); Dotson, Wayne (8); Furman, Jon (19); Gibson, Paul (36); Gorman, Michael (9); Heinkel, Donald (10); Henneman, Michael (46); Hinz, William (7); James, Duane (18); Labozzetta, Albert (10); Medvin, Scott (13); Pena, Ramon (47); Perrotte, Joseph (2); Phillion, Gerald (1); Rasmussen, James (3); Robinson, Jeffrey (22); Searcy, Stephen (7); Shiflett, Mark (19); Siwy, James (5); St. Clair, Daniel (5); Zmudosky, Thomas (27).

CHARLOTTE—Arnold, Tony (31); Bernard, Robert (22); Biercevicz, Gregory (4); Boudreau, James (28); Brito, Jose (9); Caldwell, Richard (45); Couchee, Michael (22); Dooner, Glenn (27); Flinn, John (13); Gilbert, Jeffrey (23); Habyan, John (28); Johnson, Jerry (3); Konopa, Robert (3); Lavelle, William (2); Leiter, Mark (5); Mariano, Robert (4); Oliveras, Francisco (12); Ramirez, Allan (2); Skinner, Michael (16); Steirer, Ricky (5); Summers, Jeffrey (8); Todd, Jackson (3).

CHATTANOOGA—Adair, Richard (37); Bargerhuff, Brian (30); Bartley, Gregory (42); Bryant, James (24); Evans, Michael (47); Grimsley, Ross (1); Gunnarsson, Robert (3); Johnson, Michael (6); Jones, Kenneth (32); Martin, Victor (22); McDonald, Jeffrey (35); Mendek, William (4); Murray, Jed (27); Newman, Randall (28); Swift, William (7); Taylor, Terry (28).

COLUMBUS—Cook, Mitchell (5); Montgomery, Larry (16); Shouppe, Jamey (11).

GREENVILLE—Barker, Leonard (1); Cole, Timothy (4); Morris, David (4); Payne, Michael (2); Santiago, Michael (3).

HUNTSVILLE—Akerfelds, Darrel (17); Bauer, Mark (22); Belcher, Timothy (29); Burns, Todd (4); Cadaret, Gregory (17); Dozier, Thomas (13); Giddings, Wayne (49); Gorman, Michael (14); Hallas, Robert (20); Kendrick, Peter (13); Law, Joseph (37); Mooneyham, William (10); Plunk, Eric (13); Whaley, Scott (40); Zmudosky, Thomas (15).

JACKSONVILLE—Cook, Kerry (9); Dopson, John (5); Fedor, Francis (13); Flores, David (11); Moran, Steven (1); Torres, Miguel (11).

KNOXVILLE—Alba, Gibson (11); Aquino, Luis (50); Bencomo, Omar (9); Carlucci, Richard (12); Clancy, James (2); Clemons, Mark (2); Cullen, Michael (1); Davis, Steven (27); Dickman, Mark (28); Eichhorn, Mark (26); Elam, Scot (33); Esquer, Mercedes (3); Gillam, Keith (42); Harper, Devallon (6); Moore, Gregory (7); Peraza, Oswald (9); Rodgers, Timothy (1); Shanks, William (31); Valenzuela, Guillermo (4); Walsh, David (38); Yearout, Michael (31).

MEMPHIS—Bankhead, Scott (24); Benedict, James (43); Dacko, Mark (4); Daniel, Jimmy (7); Davis, Bradley (3); Davis, John (27); Leonard, Dennis (1); Martinez, Arthur (11); Mohr, Thomas (15); Morgan, Eugene (14); Radtke, John (29); Reiter, Gary (16); Reyes, Jose (39); Tabor, Scott (38); Walberg, Mark (29); Wilder, William (45).

ORLANDO—Alfonzo, Osvaldo (38); Cardwood, Alfredo (11); Clay, Danny (31); Felt, Richard (3); Heimueller, Gorman (41); Henderson, Craig (19); Innis, Brian (1); Klump, Kenneth (14); Mancuso, Paul (37); Martin, John (12); Oelkers, Bryan (6); Smith, Robert (13); Straker, Lester (27); Taylor, Jeffrey (10); Walters, Michael (3); Wiseman, Timothy (10).

GRAND SLAM HOME RUNS—Rivera, 3; Canseco, Davidson, B. Moore, Tumpane, 2 each; Bockhorn, Burke, Citari, J. Diaz, Funderburk, H. Hatcher, R. Johnson, R. Jones, Lockwood, Lusader, Madison, Nichols, Reddish, Rollin, Sherman, Tatis, A. Thomas, Tiburico, T. Walker, Wilborn, Wine, 1 each.

AWARDED FIRST BASE ON CATCHER'S INTERFERENCE—Hengel 5 (R. Colbert 2, Dorsett, Eager, Nichols); Rizzo 3 (Colbert, Eager, Silva); Baker 2 (R. Colbert, Eager); Botkin 2 (Firova, Hansen); Allen (Dorsett); Felix (Steinbach); Firova (Sorce); Funderburk (Hearron); Hotchkiss (Wine).

## CLUB FIELDING

| Club | Pct. | G. | PO. | A. | E. | DP. | PB. | Club | Pct. | G. | PO. | A. | E. | DP. | PB. |
|---|---|---|---|---|---|---|---|---|---|---|---|---|---|---|---|
| Charlotte | .974 | 143 | 3724 | 1516 | 141 | 150 | 23 | Columbus | .967 | 144 | 3675 | 1628 | 183 | 125 | 24 |
| Jacksonville | .973 | 143 | 3672 | 1482 | 144 | 148 | 15 | Memphis | .967 | 144 | 3694 | 1487 | 179 | 110 | 14 |
| Knoxville | .969 | 143 | 3746 | 1557 | 171 | 134 | 22 | Birmingham | .966 | 143 | 3616 | 1402 | 174 | 146 | 21 |
| Greenville | .968 | 144 | 3690 | 1400 | 166 | 139 | 9 | Orlando | .965 | 143 | 3582 | 1518 | 184 | 129 | 23 |
| Chattanooga | .968 | 143 | 3677 | 1550 | 174 | 139 | 19 | Huntsville | .964 | 144 | 3719 | 1438 | 192 | 130 | 17 |

## INDIVIDUAL FIELDING

*Throws lefthanded.

### FIRST BASEMEN

| Player and Club | Pct. | G. | PO. | A. | E. | DP. | Player and Club | Pct. | G. | PO. | A. | E. | DP. |
|---|---|---|---|---|---|---|---|---|---|---|---|---|---|
| Ashman, Huntsville | 1.000 | 4 | 13 | 2 | 0 | 1 | Mills, Birmingham | 1.000 | 5 | 27 | 4 | 0 | 3 |
| Bockhorn, Greenville | 1.000 | 4 | 8 | 2 | 0 | 0 | Moore, Jacksonville* | .982 | 6 | 50 | 5 | 1 | 8 |
| Braun, Chattanooga | .985 | 72 | 585 | 51 | 10 | 61 | Morhardt, Orlando* | .992 | 46 | 353 | 21 | 3 | 34 |
| Carpenter, Columbus* | .992 | 105 | 956 | 56 | 8 | 89 | Myers, Chattanooga | .955 | 4 | 41 | 1 | 2 | 2 |
| Castro, Charlotte* | .974 | 6 | 33 | 5 | 1 | 3 | Nelson, Huntsville* | .981 | 137 | 1101 | 86 | 23 | 109 |
| CITARI, Memphis | .993 | 135 | 1147 | 111 | 9 | 90 | Neuzil, Memphis | 1.000 | 1 | 5 | 0 | 0 | 2 |
| Colbert, Birmingham | .947 | 5 | 34 | 2 | 2 | 6 | Norman, 13 Bir-2 Char. | .966 | 15 | 82 | 2 | 3 | 12 |
| Cummings, Chattanooga | 1.000 | 2 | 11 | 1 | 0 | 3 | Palacios, Birmingham | .989 | 10 | 79 | 8 | 1 | 8 |
| Datz, Columbus | 1.000 | 5 | 30 | 5 | 0 | 1 | Ransom, Greenville | 1.000 | 1 | 6 | 1 | 0 | 1 |
| Eagar, Birmingham | 1.000 | 1 | 8 | 2 | 0 | 1 | Reddish, Charlotte | .992 | 15 | 122 | 6 | 1 | 10 |
| Felix, Orlando | .990 | 27 | 198 | 6 | 2 | 17 | Rosado, Birmingham | .995 | 24 | 182 | 16 | 1 | 19 |
| Fielder, Knoxville | .987 | 53 | 444 | 26 | 6 | 38 | Seitzer, Memphis | .983 | 7 | 50 | 7 | 1 | 4 |
| Funderburk, Orlando | .995 | 52 | 414 | 25 | 2 | 41 | Sherman, Columbus | 1.000 | 1 | 5 | 1 | 0 | 0 |
| Griffin, Greenville | 1.000 | 5 | 36 | 2 | 0 | 6 | Sliwinski, Knoxville | .975 | 29 | 222 | 10 | 6 | 22 |
| Guerrero, Greenville | .985 | 103 | 825 | 41 | 13 | 92 | B. Smith, Chattanooga | .987 | 72 | 563 | 45 | 8 | 57 |
| Hamric, Knoxville | 1.000 | 1 | 1 | 0 | 0 | 0 | K. Smith, Greenville | 1.000 | 12 | 106 | 7 | 0 | 10 |
| Hanggie, Orlando | .957 | 5 | 22 | 0 | 1 | 2 | M. Smith, Birmingham | .994 | 59 | 439 | 26 | 3 | 43 |
| Hatcher, Memphis | 1.000 | 1 | 2 | 0 | 0 | 0 | Steinbach, Huntsville | .975 | 8 | 35 | 4 | 1 | 3 |
| Hayes, Greenville | 1.000 | 1 | 4 | 0 | 0 | 0 | Stromer, Huntsville | .833 | 3 | 4 | 1 | 1 | 0 |
| Hocutt, Jacksonville | .992 | 137 | 1144 | 104 | 10 | 125 | Strucher, Columbus | 1.000 | 4 | 36 | 1 | 0 | 3 |
| Hotchkiss, Birmingham | .992 | 30 | 223 | 11 | 2 | 30 | Thielker, Charlotte | 1.000 | 6 | 42 | 1 | 0 | 5 |
| Johnston, Knoxville | .988 | 66 | 609 | 49 | 8 | 69 | Torve, Charlotte | .992 | 119 | 1074 | 68 | 9 | 114 |
| Kenaga, Charlotte | 1.000 | 3 | 15 | 1 | 0 | 2 | Tumpane, Greenville* | 1.000 | 25 | 198 | 8 | 0 | 14 |
| Longenecker, Memphis | 1.000 | 2 | 20 | 0 | 0 | 4 | Vargas, Greenville | 1.000 | 1 | 1 | 0 | 0 | 0 |
| Madison, Birmingham | .992 | 15 | 116 | 9 | 1 | 8 | Verkuilen, Orlando* | 1.000 | 36 | 252 | 18 | 0 | 23 |
| Meadows, Columbus* | .979 | 40 | 349 | 27 | 8 | 23 | | | | | | | |

### SECOND BASEMEN

| Player and Club | Pct. | G. | PO. | A. | E. | DP. | Player and Club | Pct. | G. | PO. | A. | E. | DP. |
|---|---|---|---|---|---|---|---|---|---|---|---|---|---|
| Aragon, Orlando | .979 | 29 | 68 | 73 | 3 | 11 | Marquardt, Huntsville | .975 | 54 | 124 | 106 | 6 | 23 |
| Baker, Jacksonville | 1.000 | 1 | 3 | 1 | 0 | 0 | Miller, Memphis | .976 | 65 | 146 | 178 | 8 | 43 |
| Blackwell, Knoxville | .981 | 122 | 268 | 303 | 11 | 78 | A. Moreno, Jacksonville | .974 | 105 | 262 | 258 | 14 | 68 |
| Bockhorn, Greenville | 1.000 | 3 | 7 | 8 | 0 | 3 | M. Moreno, Memphis | .974 | 18 | 39 | 35 | 2 | 3 |
| Botkin, Columbus | .500 | 1 | 0 | 1 | 1 | 1 | Myers, Chattanooga | .978 | 24 | 77 | 57 | 3 | 19 |
| Chavez, Birmingham | .959 | 14 | 37 | 34 | 3 | 12 | Neuzil, Memphis | .972 | 72 | 133 | 176 | 9 | 24 |
| David, Chattanooga | .977 | 113 | 274 | 284 | 13 | 75 | Paredes, Jacksonville | .980 | 20 | 47 | 51 | 2 | 14 |
| Diaz, Knoxville | .947 | 4 | 11 | 7 | 1 | 1 | Perez, Chattanooga | .980 | 10 | 23 | 27 | 1 | 2 |
| Dodd, Charlotte | 1.000 | 2 | 0 | 1 | 0 | 0 | Ralston, Orlando | .977 | 55 | 102 | 106 | 5 | 26 |
| Falls, Columbus | .964 | 33 | 71 | 88 | 6 | 21 | Ramsey, Charlotte | 1.000 | 4 | 3 | 2 | 0 | 1 |
| Graham, Huntsville | .945 | 51 | 111 | 113 | 13 | 27 | Ruiz, Birmingham | 1.000 | 17 | 29 | 25 | 0 | 6 |
| Hamric, Knoxville | .981 | 26 | 51 | 55 | 2 | 14 | Schaefer, Charlotte | .972 | 14 | 30 | 40 | 2 | 11 |
| Hanggie, Orlando | .979 | 67 | 172 | 158 | 7 | 52 | Springer, Birmingham | .973 | 106 | 233 | 272 | 14 | 76 |
| Hernandez, Columbus | .976 | 9 | 22 | 19 | 1 | 6 | Szajko, Jacksonville | 1.000 | 21 | 36 | 42 | 0 | 11 |
| Ingle, Greenville | .953 | 15 | 22 | 19 | 2 | 2 | Tatis, Knoxville | 1.000 | 1 | 4 | 1 | 0 | 1 |
| JACOBSON, Charlotte | .985 | 130 | 291 | 319 | 9 | 89 | Thiessen, Jacksonville | 1.000 | 3 | 5 | 10 | 0 | 3 |
| Knox, Greenville | .982 | 134 | 297 | 307 | 11 | 88 | Thoma, Huntsville | .971 | 47 | 101 | 99 | 6 | 33 |
| Lockwood, Charlotte | .982 | 15 | 28 | 26 | 1 | 6 | Thomas, Columbus | .961 | 107 | 238 | 304 | 22 | 64 |
| Longenecker, Memphis | 1.000 | 2 | 1 | 0 | 0 | 0 | Trout, Orlando | .894 | 23 | 46 | 38 | 10 | 10 |
| Mariano, Charlotte | 1.000 | 2 | 1 | 0 | 0 | 0 | Walewander, Birmingham | .982 | 14 | 22 | 33 | 1 | 8 |

### THIRD BASEMEN

| Player and Club | Pct. | G. | PO. | A. | E. | DP. | Player and Club | Pct. | G. | PO. | A. | E. | DP. |
|---|---|---|---|---|---|---|---|---|---|---|---|---|---|
| Aragon, Orlando | .933 | 7 | 3 | 11 | 1 | 0 | Madison, Birmingham | .857 | 3 | 1 | 5 | 1 | 0 |
| Ashman, Huntsville | .909 | 15 | 9 | 21 | 3 | 1 | MARTINEZ, Chattanooga | .947 | 110 | 94 | 247 | 19 | 34 |
| Bishop, Knoxville | .920 | 57 | 45 | 116 | 14 | 11 | Mills, Birmingham | .907 | 89 | 75 | 159 | 24 | 16 |
| Blackwell, Knoxville | .929 | 7 | 3 | 10 | 1 | 1 | Myers, Chattanooga | .918 | 24 | 22 | 45 | 6 | 5 |
| Bockhorn, Greenville | .842 | 8 | 8 | 8 | 3 | 0 | Neuzil, Memphis | 1.000 | 9 | 2 | 13 | 0 | 1 |
| Botkin, Columbus | .500 | 1 | 0 | 1 | 1 | 0 | Palacios, Birmingham | .897 | 13 | 8 | 27 | 4 | 3 |
| Chavez, Birmingham | .929 | 7 | 2 | 11 | 1 | 0 | Ralston, Orlando | 1.000 | 2 | 1 | 1 | 0 | 0 |
| Chmil, Greenville | 1.000 | 1 | 0 | 5 | 0 | 0 | Ramsey, Charlotte | 1.000 | 2 | 0 | 3 | 0 | 0 |
| Colbert, Orlando | 1.000 | 3 | 1 | 2 | 0 | 0 | Reynolds, Jacksonville | .921 | 85 | 79 | 155 | 20 | 13 |
| Conklin, Huntsville | .875 | 36 | 16 | 40 | 8 | 2 | Ruiz, Birmingham | .940 | 18 | 11 | 52 | 4 | 7 |
| Davidson, Orlando | .667 | 1 | 0 | 2 | 1 | 0 | Schaefer, Charlotte | .973 | 14 | 7 | 29 | 1 | 3 |
| Dennis, Orlando | .667 | 2 | 1 | 1 | 1 | 0 | Seitzer, Memphis | .880 | 24 | 22 | 44 | 9 | 6 |
| Dodd, Charlotte | .853 | 45 | 23 | 87 | 19 | 13 | Shaddy, Knoxville | .873 | 44 | 22 | 88 | 16 | 8 |
| Falls, Columbus | .966 | 16 | 5 | 23 | 1 | 3 | Sherman, Columbus | .877 | 24 | 15 | 42 | 8 | 6 |
| Foussianes, Memphis | .906 | 29 | 19 | 39 | 6 | 5 | Smith, Chattanooga | 1.000 | 1 | 0 | 1 | 0 | 0 |
| Hamric, Knoxville | .938 | 39 | 23 | 98 | 8 | 13 | Sorce, Orlando | .880 | 27 | 18 | 48 | 9 | 4 |
| Hanggie, Orlando | .947 | 74 | 51 | 146 | 11 | 11 | Springer, Birmingham | 1.000 | 2 | 0 | 5 | 0 | 0 |
| Hayes, Greenville | .914 | 59 | 43 | 106 | 14 | 12 | Steinbach, Huntsville | .913 | 13 | 6 | 15 | 2 | 3 |
| Hocutt, Jacksonville | .600 | 1 | 0 | 3 | 2 | 0 | Stromer, Huntsville | .918 | 50 | 41 | 104 | 13 | 10 |
| Hoeksema, Jacksonville | .946 | 20 | 14 | 39 | 3 | 2 | Strucher, Columbus | .873 | 23 | 14 | 55 | 10 | 4 |
| Holmes, Orlando | .778 | 3 | 2 | 5 | 2 | 1 | Szajko, Jacksonville | 1.000 | 4 | 2 | 11 | 0 | 1 |
| Hotchkiss, Birmingham | .889 | 20 | 19 | 29 | 6 | 5 | Tatis, Knoxville | .893 | 10 | 6 | 19 | 3 | 1 |
| Ingle, Greenville | .917 | 72 | 43 | 145 | 17 | 15 | Thielker, Charlotte | 1.000 | 3 | 5 | 1 | 0 | 0 |
| Jackson, Columbus | .907 | 93 | 68 | 226 | 30 | 18 | Thiessen, Jacksonville | .950 | 38 | 36 | 77 | 6 | 5 |
| Jacobson, Charlotte | 1.000 | 1 | 0 | 1 | 0 | 0 | Thoma, Huntsville | .954 | 54 | 43 | 101 | 7 | 12 |
| Jarrell, Memphis | .914 | 59 | 49 | 120 | 16 | 8 | Thompson, Greenville | .911 | 16 | 11 | 30 | 4 | 4 |
| Lockwood, Charlotte | .925 | 107 | 52 | 194 | 20 | 16 | Trout, Orlando | .943 | 54 | 36 | 113 | 9 | 10 |
| Longenecker, Memphis | .915 | 37 | 31 | 66 | 9 | 5 | Worden, Chattanooga | .830 | 15 | 13 | 31 | 9 | 3 |

## SHORTSTOPS

| Player and Club | Pct. | G. | PO. | A. | E. | DP. |
|---|---|---|---|---|---|---|
| Aragon, Orlando | 1.000 | 1 | 2 | 2 | 0 | 1 |
| Ashman, Huntsville | 1.000 | 6 | 5 | 11 | 0 | 2 |
| Blackwell, Knoxville | 1.000 | 1 | 0 | 2 | 0 | 0 |
| Bockhorn, Greenville | .857 | 2 | 3 | 3 | 1 | 1 |
| Chavez, Birmingham | .951 | 35 | 50 | 86 | 7 | 16 |
| Childress, Greenville | .982 | 13 | 24 | 31 | 1 | 13 |
| Conklin, Huntsville | .902 | 12 | 13 | 24 | 4 | 5 |
| J. Diaz, Knoxville | .951 | 92 | 125 | 266 | 20 | 37 |
| M. Diaz, Chattanooga | .942 | 115 | 186 | 314 | 31 | 53 |
| Faedo, Memphis | .943 | 98 | 159 | 254 | 25 | 52 |
| Falls, Columbus | .950 | 38 | 63 | 107 | 9 | 19 |
| Graham, Huntsville | .926 | 28 | 52 | 61 | 9 | 20 |
| Guinn, Huntsville | .973 | 29 | 42 | 101 | 4 | 15 |
| Hamric, Knoxville | .917 | 3 | 5 | 6 | 1 | 0 |
| Hayes, Greenville | .909 | 2 | 3 | 7 | 1 | 2 |
| Hoeksema, Jacksonville | 1.000 | 1 | 0 | 4 | 0 | 1 |
| Hotchkiss, Birmingham | .927 | 28 | 31 | 58 | 7 | 11 |
| Ingle, Columbus | .966 | 15 | 20 | 36 | 2 | 7 |
| Jarrell, Memphis | .900 | 28 | 48 | 69 | 13 | 10 |
| JONES, Charlotte | .966 | 102 | 161 | 316 | 17 | 72 |
| Knox, Greenville | .909 | 3 | 7 | 3 | 1 | 2 |
| Koenigsfeld, Columbus | .942 | 26 | 42 | 87 | 8 | 18 |
| Lockwood, Charlotte | .905 | 10 | 15 | 23 | 4 | 6 |
| Longenecker, Memphis | 1.000 | 2 | 1 | 4 | 0 | 0 |
| Marquardt, Huntsville | .927 | 54 | 79 | 136 | 17 | 21 |
| Mills, Birmingham | 1.000 | 1 | 3 | 3 | 0 | 0 |
| Moreno, 31 Orl-3 Mem | .931 | 34 | 60 | 88 | 11 | 18 |
| Myers, Chattanooga | .942 | 32 | 49 | 82 | 8 | 16 |
| Neuzil, Memphis | .929 | 23 | 24 | 41 | 5 | 8 |
| Ralston, Orlando | .910 | 86 | 103 | 250 | 35 | 42 |
| Ramsey, Charlotte | 1.000 | 1 | 1 | 2 | 0 | 0 |
| Ripken, Charlotte | .946 | 18 | 18 | 52 | 4 | 10 |
| Rivera, Jacksonville | .949 | 138 | 198 | 412 | 33 | 107 |
| Rood, Columbus | .964 | 64 | 119 | 204 | 12 | 29 |
| Ruiz, Birmingham | .956 | 81 | 122 | 223 | 16 | 55 |
| Schaefer, Charlotte | .952 | 20 | 37 | 43 | 4 | 7 |
| Shaddy, Knoxville | .935 | 64 | 93 | 193 | 20 | 42 |
| Springer, Birmingham | .933 | 13 | 13 | 29 | 3 | 9 |
| Szajko, Jacksonville | .920 | 7 | 9 | 14 | 2 | 5 |
| Thoma, Huntsville | .949 | 30 | 46 | 85 | 7 | 17 |
| A. Thomas, Greenville | .941 | 112 | 155 | 339 | 31 | 64 |
| J. Thomas, Columbus | .933 | 22 | 20 | 63 | 6 | 17 |
| Williams, Orlando | .892 | 61 | 45 | 112 | 19 | 14 |

## OUTFIELDERS

| Player and Club | Pct. | G. | PO. | A. | E. | DP. |
|---|---|---|---|---|---|---|
| Allen, Memphis | .956 | 44 | 83 | 4 | 4 | 1 |
| Ashmore, Memphis | 1.000 | 1 | 3 | 0 | 0 | 0 |
| Baker, Jacksonville | .992 | 60 | 127 | 5 | 1 | 0 |
| Beauchamp, Knoxville | .988 | 135 | 310 | 9 | 4 | 1 |
| Bockhorn, Greenville | .965 | 93 | 158 | 8 | 6 | 0 |
| Bogener, Charlotte* | .974 | 80 | 144 | 5 | 4 | 0 |
| Botkin, Columbus | .985 | 74 | 130 | 3 | 2 | 0 |
| Braun, Chattanooga | .978 | 55 | 83 | 4 | 2 | 0 |
| Brown, Chattanooga | .977 | 103 | 210 | 6 | 5 | 0 |
| Burke, Columbus | .973 | 20 | 35 | 1 | 1 | 0 |
| Campusano, Knoxville | .972 | 45 | 135 | 3 | 4 | 0 |
| Canseco, Huntsville | .947 | 56 | 117 | 9 | 7 | 2 |
| Carl, Jacksonville | .981 | 82 | 152 | 6 | 3 | 2 |
| Carpenter, Columbus* | .968 | 22 | 29 | 1 | 1 | 0 |
| Colbert, Orlando | 1.000 | 4 | 13 | 0 | 0 | 0 |
| Cole, 11 Green.-28 Mem* | .951 | 39 | 72 | 5 | 4 | 1 |
| Conklin, Huntsville | .981 | 41 | 49 | 3 | 1 | 0 |
| Cornwell, Birmingham* | .930 | 33 | 63 | 3 | 5 | 0 |
| Coyle, Huntsville | .990 | 89 | 187 | 7 | 2 | 1 |
| Davidson, Orlando | .984 | 134 | 305 | 12 | 5 | 1 |
| Delgado, Columbus | .947 | 38 | 54 | 0 | 3 | 0 |
| Dodd, Charlotte | .934 | 31 | 55 | 2 | 4 | 0 |
| Falls, Columbus | 1.000 | 4 | 4 | 0 | 0 | 0 |
| Fields, Birmingham | .979 | 93 | 228 | 10 | 5 | 3 |
| Funderburk, Orlando | .977 | 55 | 82 | 3 | 2 | 1 |
| Gerhart, Charlotte | .995 | 62 | 177 | 4 | 1 | 2 |
| Gould, Huntsville | 1.000 | 1 | 1 | 0 | 0 | 0 |
| Graham, Huntsville | 1.000 | 4 | 8 | 0 | 0 | 0 |
| Granger, Charlotte | .953 | 40 | 78 | 3 | 4 | 2 |
| Green, Knoxville* | .987 | 114 | 221 | 4 | 3 | 1 |
| Harvey, Huntsville* | 1.000 | 1 | 1 | 0 | 0 | 0 |
| Hatcher, Greenville | .934 | 25 | 57 | 0 | 4 | 0 |
| Hayes, Greenville | 1.000 | 1 | 2 | 0 | 0 | 0 |
| Hengel, Chattanooga | .980 | 121 | 277 | 14 | 6 | 3 |
| Hernandez, Columbus | 1.000 | 4 | 9 | 1 | 0 | 1 |
| Hertzler, Jacksonville* | .979 | 22 | 45 | 1 | 1 | 0 |
| Hill, Chattanooga | .922 | 33 | 57 | 2 | 5 | 1 |
| Hobbs, Birmingham | .979 | 135 | 370 | 4 | 8 | 2 |
| Hollins, Chattanooga | .929 | 14 | 12 | 1 | 1 | 0 |
| Holmes, Orlando | 1.000 | 2 | 3 | 1 | 0 | 0 |
| Jackson, Columbus | .947 | 16 | 30 | 6 | 2 | 0 |
| Javier, Huntsville | .981 | 121 | 363 | 6 | 7 | 3 |
| Johnson, Jacksonville* | .987 | 54 | 144 | 3 | 2 | 1 |
| Johnston, Knoxville | 1.000 | 1 | 3 | 0 | 0 | 0 |
| Kenaga, Charlotte | 1.000 | 43 | 73 | 5 | 0 | 2 |
| Kinnard, Knoxville | 1.000 | 9 | 6 | 0 | 0 | 0 |
| Longenecker, Memphis | .978 | 24 | 41 | 3 | 1 | 0 |
| Lusader, Birmingham* | 1.000 | 21 | 49 | 1 | 0 | 0 |
| Luzon, Greenville | .986 | 68 | 142 | 4 | 2 | 3 |
| Marte, Orlando* | .966 | 137 | 320 | 18 | 12 | 3 |
| McNealy, Chattanooga* | .972 | 114 | 300 | 11 | 9 | 5 |
| Meadows, Columbus* | .977 | 93 | 165 | 5 | 4 | 3 |
| Moore, Jacksonville* | .972 | 130 | 261 | 16 | 8 | 3 |
| Moreno, Orlando* | 1.000 | 5 | 9 | 0 | 0 | 0 |
| Morhardt, Orlando* | .965 | 73 | 130 | 9 | 5 | 2 |
| Nichols, Charlotte | .972 | 12 | 31 | 4 | 1 | 1 |
| Noble, Columbus* | 1.000 | 3 | 1 | 0 | 0 | 0 |
| Norman, 35 Bir-23 Char | .949 | 58 | 104 | 7 | 6 | 5 |
| Perez, Chattanooga | 1.000 | 10 | 18 | 3 | 0 | 2 |
| Polonia, Huntsville* | .954 | 122 | 236 | 13 | 12 | 1 |
| Ransom, Greenville | 1.000 | 2 | 3 | 1 | 0 | 0 |
| Reddish, Charlotte | .981 | 31 | 51 | 0 | 1 | 0 |
| Reynolds, Jacksonville | .984 | 42 | 61 | 1 | 1 | 0 |
| RIZZO, Memphis | .992 | 104 | 233 | 5 | 2 | 0 |
| Rollin, Birmingham | .977 | 82 | 164 | 5 | 4 | 0 |
| Salcedo, Charlotte | .988 | 52 | 76 | 5 | 1 | 1 |
| Schaefer, Charlotte | 1.000 | 7 | 10 | 0 | 0 | 0 |
| Schulz, Memphis | .962 | 134 | 263 | 12 | 11 | 4 |
| Seitzer, Memphis | 1.000 | 6 | 7 | 0 | 0 | 0 |
| Sherman, Columbus | .966 | 52 | 82 | 2 | 3 | 1 |
| Sliwinski, Knoxville | .985 | 87 | 127 | 3 | 2 | 0 |
| K. Smith, Greenville | .986 | 40 | 68 | 2 | 1 | 0 |
| M. Smith, Birmingham | .984 | 31 | 58 | 3 | 1 | 1 |
| Snider, Memphis | .931 | 83 | 166 | 9 | 13 | 3 |
| Sorce, Orlando | 1.000 | 17 | 24 | 4 | 0 | 1 |
| Stefero, Charlotte | 1.000 | 2 | 3 | 0 | 0 | 0 |
| Strucher, Columbus | .667 | 3 | 2 | 0 | 1 | 0 |
| Szajko, Jacksonville | 1.000 | 34 | 70 | 2 | 0 | 1 |
| Tatis, Knoxville | .983 | 82 | 113 | 2 | 2 | 0 |
| Thielker, Charlotte | 1.000 | 4 | 7 | 0 | 0 | 0 |
| Thoma, Huntsville | 1.000 | 3 | 7 | 0 | 0 | 0 |
| R. Thomas, Birmingham* | .875 | 12 | 13 | 1 | 2 | 1 |
| Thompson, Greenville | .947 | 10 | 16 | 2 | 1 | 1 |
| Tiburcio, Greenville | .959 | 83 | 207 | 5 | 9 | 2 |
| Torve, Charlotte* | 1.000 | 2 | 3 | 0 | 0 | 0 |
| Tumpane, Greenville* | .941 | 7 | 16 | 0 | 1 | 0 |
| Tutt, Charlotte | .900 | 5 | 9 | 0 | 1 | 0 |
| Vargas, Greenville | .933 | 80 | 119 | 6 | 9 | 2 |
| Verkuilen, Orlando* | 1.000 | 16 | 21 | 0 | 0 | 0 |
| Vetsch, Orlando | 1.000 | 18 | 25 | 1 | 0 | 0 |
| A. Walker, Columbus | .980 | 133 | 335 | 16 | 7 | 1 |
| G. Walker, Memphis | 1.000 | 30 | 47 | 4 | 0 | 1 |
| Whisenton, Greenville* | .986 | 61 | 133 | 3 | 2 | 1 |
| Wilborn, Charlotte | 1.000 | 69 | 158 | 0 | 0 | 0 |
| Wilder, Huntsville | .909 | 19 | 39 | 1 | 4 | 1 |
| Williams, Jacksonville* | .984 | 31 | 61 | 1 | 1 | 0 |
| Wine, Columbus | 1.000 | 2 | 1 | 0 | 0 | 0 |

## CATCHERS

| Player and Club | Pct. | G. | PO. | A. | E. | DP. | PB. |
|---|---|---|---|---|---|---|---|
| Ashman, Huntsville | 1.000 | 5 | 23 | 2 | 0 | 0 | 0 |
| Ashmore, Memphis | 1.000 | 14 | 46 | 1 | 0 | 0 | 1 |
| Bockhorn, Greenville | .929 | 2 | 10 | 3 | 1 | 0 | 0 |
| Borowsky, Orlando | .980 | 13 | 42 | 8 | 1 | 1 | 2 |
| Colbert, Orlando | .969 | 54 | 219 | 28 | 8 | 2 | 4 |
| Cummings, Chattanooga | .966 | 21 | 105 | 10 | 4 | 1 | 1 |
| Datz, Columbus | .972 | 47 | 184 | 22 | 6 | 4 | 6 |
| Davis, Memphis | .965 | 32 | 96 | 15 | 4 | 1 | 0 |
| DeWillis, Knoxville | .993 | 68 | 377 | 45 | 3 | 4 | 5 |
| Dodd, Charlotte | 1.000 | 1 | 1 | 0 | 0 | 0 | 0 |
| Dorsett, Birmingham | .980 | 79 | 437 | 51 | 10 | 7 | 6 |
| Eagar, Birmingham | .970 | 93 | 444 | 43 | 15 | 5 | 17 |
| Felix, Orlando | .857 | 7 | 10 | 2 | 2 | 0 | 2 |
| Firova, Chattanooga | .976 | 110 | 483 | 89 | 14 | 12 | 15 |
| Grote, Birmingham | 1.000 | 1 | 5 | 0 | 0 | 0 | 0 |
| Hansen, Memphis | .984 | 32 | 170 | 9 | 3 | 1 | 3 |
| Hatcher, Memphis | .981 | 33 | 183 | 20 | 4 | 2 | 5 |
| Hearron, Knoxville | .986 | 34 | 190 | 20 | 3 | 1 | 6 |
| Holland, Knoxville | 1.000 | 5 | 33 | 1 | 0 | 0 | 1 |
| Hollins, Chattanooga | 1.000 | 2 | 3 | 0 | 0 | 0 | 1 |
| Lawrence, Birmingham | .810 | 3 | 16 | 1 | 4 | 0 | 1 |
| MacFarlane, Memphis | .973 | 61 | 295 | 24 | 9 | 1 | 5 |
| Madison, Birmingham | 1.000 | 19 | 88 | 13 | 0 | 1 | 2 |
| Marquardt, Knoxville | .875 | 3 | 7 | 0 | 1 | 0 | 0 |
| Nichols, Charlotte | .974 | 98 | 465 | 67 | 14 | 9 | 16 |
| O'Brien, Huntsville | .977 | 33 | 182 | 29 | 5 | 1 | 4 |

## CATCHERS—Continued

| Player and Club | Pct. | G. | PO. | A. | E. | DP. | PB. | Player and Club | Pct. | G. | PO. | A. | E. | DP. | PB. |
|---|---|---|---|---|---|---|---|---|---|---|---|---|---|---|---|
| Padia, Charlotte | 1.000 | 19 | 109 | 15 | 0 | 1 | 3 | Stefero, Charlotte | 1.000 | 41 | 200 | 30 | 0 | 3 | 4 |
| Palacios, Birmingham | .961 | 15 | 66 | 8 | 3 | 3 | 1 | Steinbach, Huntsville | .983 | 35 | 146 | 24 | 3 | 2 | 7 |
| Ransom, Greenville | .980 | 51 | 310 | 25 | 7 | 1 | 3 | Stenhouse, Knoxville | .988 | 25 | 146 | 13 | 2 | 1 | 6 |
| Rosado, Birmingham | 1.000 | 9 | 42 | 4 | 0 | 1 | 0 | Strucher, Columbus | 1.000 | 1 | 3 | 0 | 0 | 0 | 0 |
| Santovenia, Jacksonville | .971 | 57 | 281 | 20 | 9 | 3 | 5 | Thompson, Greenville | .987 | 48 | 270 | 31 | 4 | 2 | 4 |
| Silva, Jacksonville | .961 | 42 | 172 | 24 | 8 | 2 | 7 | Wallace, Jacksonville | .994 | 55 | 328 | 28 | 2 | 3 | 3 |
| Sinatro, Greenville | .978 | 48 | 265 | 49 | 7 | 8 | 2 | Werner, Birmingham | .966 | 9 | 52 | 4 | 2 | 0 | 0 |
| Smith, Greenville | 1.000 | 1 | 3 | 0 | 0 | 0 | 0 | Wilson, Chattanooga | .972 | 26 | 97 | 7 | 3 | 0 | 3 |
| SORCE, Orlando | .988 | 87 | 381 | 41 | 5 | 6 | 15 | Wine, Columbus | .986 | 105 | 502 | 63 | 8 | 4 | 18 |
| Stark, Knoxville | .959 | 18 | 85 | 8 | 4 | 1 | 4 | Worden, Chattanooga | 1.000 | 1 | 5 | 1 | 0 | 0 | 0 |

## PITCHERS

| Player and Club | Pct. | G. | PO. | A. | E. | DP. | Player and Club | Pct. | G. | PO. | A. | E. | DP. |
|---|---|---|---|---|---|---|---|---|---|---|---|---|---|
| Adair, Chattanooga° | .957 | 37 | 3 | 19 | 1 | 1 | Hinz, Birmingham | 1.000 | 7 | 1 | 2 | 0 | 0 |
| Akerfelds, Huntsville | 1.000 | 17 | 5 | 10 | 0 | 1 | Hogan, Columbus | .921 | 27 | 5 | 30 | 3 | 2 |
| Alba, Knoxville | .778 | 11 | 1 | 6 | 2 | 0 | Hoover, Charlotte | .972 | 29 | 11 | 24 | 1 | 3 |
| Alfonzo, Orlando | .960 | 38 | 9 | 15 | 1 | 1 | James, Birmingham | .625 | 18 | 3 | 2 | 3 | 0 |
| Alvarez, 13 Mem-10 Jack | .875 | 23 | 5 | 16 | 3 | 2 | Je. Johnson, Charlotte | 1.000 | 3 | 0 | 1 | 0 | 0 |
| Aquino, Knoxville | .813 | 50 | 0 | 13 | 3 | 0 | Jo. Johnson, Greenville | .857 | 12 | 2 | 10 | 2 | 1 |
| Arnold, Charlotte | .976 | 31 | 16 | 25 | 1 | 5 | M. Johnson, Chattanooga | 1.000 | 6 | 1 | 0 | 0 | 0 |
| Assenmacher, Greenville° | 1.000 | 29 | 4 | 3 | 0 | 0 | Jones, Chattanooga | 1.000 | 30 | 8 | 16 | 0 | 1 |
| August, Columbus | 1.000 | 27 | 10 | 33 | 0 | 2 | Kasprzak, Columbus | 1.000 | 38 | 4 | 10 | 0 | 0 |
| Aviles, Greenville | .947 | 14 | 6 | 12 | 1 | 0 | Kelley, Columbus | .871 | 22 | 7 | 20 | 4 | 0 |
| Bankhead, Memphis | 1.000 | 24 | 10 | 21 | 0 | 0 | Kendrick, Huntsville° | .946 | 13 | 8 | 27 | 2 | 1 |
| Bargerhuff, Chattanooga | .941 | 30 | 5 | 11 | 1 | 0 | Kinns, Jacksonville | 1.000 | 37 | 7 | 9 | 0 | 2 |
| Barker, Greenville | 1.000 | 1 | 1 | 0 | 0 | 0 | Klump, Orlando | 1.000 | 14 | 2 | 11 | 0 | 0 |
| Barlow, Birmingham | .818 | 18 | 3 | 6 | 2 | 1 | Labozzetta, Birmingham° | 1.000 | 10 | 4 | 3 | 0 | 1 |
| Barrett, Jacksonville | .917 | 37 | 15 | 18 | 3 | 2 | Lamb, Greenville | .880 | 40 | 4 | 18 | 3 | 0 |
| Bartley, Chattanooga | .974 | 42 | 10 | 27 | 1 | 3 | Law, Huntsville | .947 | 37 | 6 | 12 | 1 | 1 |
| Bauer, Huntsville | 1.000 | 22 | 12 | 17 | 0 | 2 | Leggatt, Greenville | 1.000 | 46 | 5 | 12 | 0 | 0 |
| Belcher, Huntsville | .957 | 29 | 9 | 13 | 1 | 1 | Leiter, Charlotte | 1.000 | 5 | 0 | 1 | 0 | 0 |
| Bencomo, Knoxville | 1.000 | 9 | 1 | 9 | 0 | 1 | Leonard, Memphis | 1.000 | 1 | 0 | 1 | 0 | 0 |
| Benedict, Memphis | 1.000 | 43 | 3 | 14 | 0 | 0 | Lucas, Columbus | .750 | 7 | 2 | 1 | 1 | 0 |
| Bernard, Charlotte | 1.000 | 22 | 2 | 3 | 0 | 1 | Mancuso, Orlando° | .962 | 37 | 10 | 15 | 1 | 0 |
| Biercevicz, Charlotte | 1.000 | 4 | 0 | 1 | 0 | 0 | J. Martin, Orlando° | .900 | 12 | 0 | 9 | 1 | 1 |
| Bombard, Columbus | 1.000 | 52 | 1 | 11 | 0 | 2 | V. Martin, Chattanooga | 1.000 | 22 | 12 | 26 | 0 | 1 |
| Boudreau, Charlotte° | .900 | 28 | 2 | 7 | 1 | 1 | Martinez, Memphis | 1.000 | 11 | 4 | 1 | 0 | 1 |
| Bradford, Greenville° | .933 | 46 | 2 | 12 | 1 | 3 | McDonald, Chattanooga | .935 | 35 | 13 | 16 | 2 | 0 |
| Brahs, Jacksonville° | .958 | 33 | 5 | 18 | 1 | 3 | McKay, Jacksonville | .905 | 14 | 7 | 12 | 2 | 1 |
| Breining, Birmingham | 1.000 | 12 | 4 | 6 | 0 | 1 | Medvin, Birmingham | 1.000 | 13 | 1 | 2 | 0 | 0 |
| Brito, Charlotte | 1.000 | 9 | 3 | 3 | 0 | 1 | Mohr, Memphis° | .800 | 15 | 2 | 2 | 1 | 1 |
| Bryant, Chattanooga | 1.000 | 24 | 2 | 5 | 0 | 0 | Montgomery, Columbus | 1.000 | 16 | 2 | 1 | 0 | 0 |
| Burns, Huntsville | .667 | 4 | 0 | 2 | 1 | 0 | Mooneyham, Huntsville | .667 | 10 | 1 | 3 | 2 | 0 |
| Cadaret, Huntsville | .917 | 17 | 2 | 20 | 2 | 1 | Moore, Knoxville | 1.000 | 7 | 1 | 2 | 0 | 0 |
| Caldwell, Charlotte | .941 | 45 | 3 | 13 | 1 | 1 | Morgan, Memphis | .900 | 14 | 1 | 8 | 1 | 0 |
| Callahan, Greenville | 1.000 | 13 | 2 | 2 | 0 | 1 | Morris, Greenville | 1.000 | 4 | 1 | 0 | 0 | 0 |
| Cardwood, Orlando | .941 | 11 | 5 | 11 | 1 | 1 | Murray, Chattanooga° | 1.000 | 27 | 9 | 15 | 0 | 1 |
| Carlucci, Knoxville | 1.000 | 12 | 2 | 2 | 0 | 0 | Newman, Columbus° | .864 | 28 | 5 | 33 | 6 | 1 |
| Cates, Jacksonville | 1.000 | 15 | 5 | 7 | 0 | 1 | Nicometi, Jacksonville | .926 | 41 | 4 | 21 | 2 | 0 |
| Clancy, Knoxville | 1.000 | 2 | 1 | 3 | 0 | 0 | Noble, Columbus° | .952 | 35 | 4 | 16 | 1 | 1 |
| Clay, Orlando | .895 | 31 | 9 | 25 | 4 | 3 | Oelkers, Orlando° | 1.000 | 6 | 1 | 2 | 0 | 0 |
| Conner, Birmingham° | 1.000 | 3 | 3 | 5 | 0 | 0 | Oliveras, Charlotte | .625 | 12 | 1 | 4 | 3 | 0 |
| K. Cook, 3 Birm-9 Jack | .667 | 12 | 3 | 1 | 2 | 0 | Payne, Greenville | 1.000 | 2 | 1 | 2 | 0 | 0 |
| M. Cook, Columbus | 1.000 | 5 | 0 | 4 | 0 | 0 | Pena, Birmingham | .947 | 47 | 4 | 14 | 1 | 0 |
| Couchee, Charlotte | 1.000 | 22 | 4 | 8 | 0 | 0 | Peraza, Knoxville | 1.000 | 9 | 4 | 5 | 0 | 1 |
| Cutshall, Jacksonville | .867 | 10 | 4 | 9 | 2 | 1 | Plunk, Huntsville | .944 | 13 | 6 | 11 | 1 | 0 |
| Dacko, Memphis | 1.000 | 4 | 4 | 4 | 0 | 0 | Price, Jacksonville | 1.000 | 21 | 4 | 10 | 0 | 2 |
| Daniel, Memphis | .889 | 7 | 4 | 4 | 1 | 0 | Radtke, Memphis | .976 | 29 | 17 | 23 | 1 | 1 |
| B. Davis, Memphis | 1.000 | 3 | 0 | 2 | 0 | 0 | Ramirez, Charlotte | 1.000 | 2 | 0 | 2 | 0 | 0 |
| J. Davis, Memphis | .913 | 27 | 15 | 27 | 4 | 1 | Reilly, Columbus | .909 | 18 | 3 | 7 | 1 | 2 |
| S. Davis, Knoxville° | .933 | 27 | 5 | 23 | 2 | 1 | Reiter, Memphis° | 1.000 | 16 | 1 | 3 | 0 | 1 |
| Dickman, Knoxville | .938 | 28 | 8 | 7 | 1 | 1 | REYES, Birmingham | 1.000 | 39 | 24 | 28 | 0 | 1 |
| Dooner, Charlotte | .857 | 27 | 2 | 4 | 1 | 1 | Robinson, Birmingham | .964 | 22 | 4 | 23 | 1 | 4 |
| Dopson, Jacksonville | 1.000 | 5 | 4 | 9 | 0 | 1 | Rodriguez, Huntsville | .955 | 8 | 9 | 12 | 1 | 0 |
| Dotson, Birmingham | .933 | 8 | 6 | 8 | 1 | 1 | Rosario, Greenville° | 1.000 | 21 | 3 | 11 | 0 | 2 |
| Dozier, Huntsville | .929 | 12 | 4 | 9 | 1 | 1 | Samuels, Columbus° | .951 | 33 | 4 | 35 | 2 | 2 |
| Eichhorn, Knoxville | .966 | 26 | 4 | 24 | 1 | 1 | Santiago, Greenville° | 1.000 | 3 | 1 | 0 | 0 | 0 |
| Elam, Knoxville | .867 | 33 | 5 | 21 | 4 | 2 | Searcy, Birmingham | .833 | 7 | 1 | 4 | 1 | 0 |
| Esquer, Knoxville° | 1.000 | 3 | 0 | 2 | 0 | 0 | Shanks, Knoxville | .778 | 31 | 4 | 10 | 4 | 0 |
| Evans, Chattanooga° | .952 | 47 | 7 | 13 | 1 | 2 | Shiflett, Birmingham° | .880 | 19 | 2 | 20 | 3 | 0 |
| Fedor, Jacksonville | 1.000 | 13 | 0 | 3 | 0 | 0 | Shouppe, Columbus° | 1.000 | 11 | 1 | 0 | 0 | 0 |
| Felt, Orlando° | 1.000 | 3 | 0 | 1 | 0 | 0 | Siwy, Birmingham | .667 | 5 | 1 | 1 | 1 | 0 |
| Flinn, Columbus | 1.000 | 13 | 6 | 3 | 0 | 0 | Skinner, Charlotte | .842 | 16 | 4 | 12 | 3 | 0 |
| Flores, Jacksonville | 1.000 | 11 | 1 | 3 | 0 | 0 | L. Smith, Huntsville° | 1.000 | 48 | 4 | 14 | 0 | 1 |
| Furman, Birmingham | .900 | 19 | 3 | 6 | 1 | 0 | R. Smith, Orlando | .933 | 13 | 2 | 12 | 1 | 0 |
| Gibson, Birmingham° | .938 | 36 | 2 | 13 | 1 | 1 | Sorce, Greenville | 1.000 | 4 | 0 | 2 | 0 | 0 |
| Giddings, Huntsville | .846 | 49 | 3 | 8 | 2 | 1 | St. Clair, Birmingham | 1.000 | 5 | 0 | 1 | 0 | 0 |
| Gilbert, Charlotte° | .941 | 23 | 5 | 11 | 1 | 3 | Steirer, Charlotte | 1.000 | 5 | 0 | 2 | 0 | 0 |
| Gillam, Knoxville | .920 | 42 | 3 | 20 | 2 | 2 | Straker, Orlando | .929 | 27 | 4 | 35 | 3 | 1 |
| Gorman, 14 Hunt-9 Birm | 1.000 | 23 | 3 | 3 | 0 | 0 | Strasser, Columbus | .966 | 28 | 10 | 18 | 1 | 1 |
| Graybill, Jacksonville | 1.000 | 10 | 8 | 11 | 0 | 0 | Summers, Charlotte | .667 | 8 | 1 | 5 | 3 | 0 |
| Groves, Jacksonville | 1.000 | 36 | 6 | 15 | 0 | 0 | Swift, Chattanooga | 1.000 | 7 | 4 | 14 | 0 | 3 |
| Gunnarsson, Chattanooga° | .667 | 3 | 0 | 2 | 1 | 0 | Tabor, Memphis | 1.000 | 38 | 10 | 29 | 0 | 2 |
| Habyan, Charlotte | 1.000 | 28 | 8 | 26 | 0 | 1 | J. Taylor, 22 Green-10 Orl° | 1.000 | 32 | 1 | 4 | 0 | 0 |
| Hallas, Huntsville | 1.000 | 20 | 1 | 7 | 0 | 0 | T. Taylor, Chattanooga | .935 | 28 | 10 | 19 | 2 | 3 |
| Harper, Knoxville | 1.000 | 6 | 1 | 2 | 0 | 0 | Todd, Charlotte | 1.000 | 3 | 0 | 1 | 0 | 0 |
| Harvey, Huntsville | 1.000 | 21 | 2 | 6 | 0 | 1 | Torres, 11 Jack-24 Col | .958 | 35 | 5 | 18 | 1 | 0 |
| Heimueller, Orlando° | .923 | 41 | 9 | 15 | 2 | 2 | Treadway, Greenville | 1.000 | 31 | 10 | 14 | 0 | 0 |
| Heinkel, Birmingham | 1.000 | 10 | 4 | 7 | 0 | 0 | Valenzuela, Knoxville | 1.000 | 4 | 0 | 2 | 0 | 0 |
| Henderson, Orlando° | 1.000 | 19 | 2 | 9 | 0 | 0 | Walberg, Memphis | .927 | 29 | 9 | 29 | 3 | 4 |
| Henneman, Birmingham | 1.000 | 46 | 1 | 16 | 0 | 0 | Walsh, Knoxville° | .930 | 38 | 10 | 30 | 3 | 4 |

## PITCHERS—Continued

| Player and Club | Pct. | G. | PO. | A. | E. | DP. | Player and Club | Pct. | G. | PO. | A. | E. | DP. |
|---|---|---|---|---|---|---|---|---|---|---|---|---|---|
| Walters, Orlando | 1.000 | 3 | 0 | 6 | 0 | 1 | Wiseman, Orlando | 1.000 | 10 | 0 | 4 | 0 | 0 |
| Ward, Greenville | .969 | 28 | 9 | 22 | 1 | 2 | Yearout, Knoxville° | .903 | 31 | 10 | 18 | 3 | 3 |
| Wayne, Jacksonville° | .909 | 21 | 3 | 17 | 2 | 1 | Youmans, Jacksonville | .923 | 14 | 4 | 8 | 1 | 0 |
| Whaley, Huntsville | .909 | 40 | 5 | 5 | 1 | 0 | Ziem, Greenville | .976 | 48 | 11 | 29 | 1 | 4 |
| Wilder, Memphis | 1.000 | 45 | 2 | 15 | 0 | 1 | Zmudosky, 15 Hunts-27 Birm | .905 | 42 | 11 | 27 | 4 | 3 |

The following players do not have any recorded accepted chances at the positions indicated; therefore, are not listed in the fielding averages for those particular positions: Ashman, p; Citari, of; Clemons, p; T. Cole, p; Cullen, p; R. Davis, 3b; Dennis, p; Grimsley, p; Hamric, p; H. Hatcher, p; Hotchkiss, p; Innis, p; Konopa, p; Lavelle, p; Mariano, 3b, ss; J. Marquardt, 3b; McNealy, p; Mendek, p; Moran, p; Myers, of; Neuzil, of; Nichols, 1b; Perrotte, p; Phillion, p; Rasmussen, p; Rodgers, p; Springer, p; Steinbach, of, p; Strucher, p; Szajko, p; Tatis, ss; A. Thomas, of.

## CLUB PITCHING

| Club | ERA. | G. | CG. | ShO. | Sv. | IP. | H. | R. | ER. | HR. | HB. | BB. | Int. BB. | SO. | WP. | Bk. |
|---|---|---|---|---|---|---|---|---|---|---|---|---|---|---|---|---|
| Columbus | 3.56 | 144 | 22 | 10 | 29 | 1225.0 | 1193 | 616 | 484 | 121 | 37 | 480 | 34 | 643 | 52 | 11 |
| Knoxville | 3.73 | 143 | 17 | 10 | 38 | 1248.2 | 1121 | 615 | 517 | 93 | 27 | 626 | 22 | 790 | 79 | 15 |
| Charlotte | 3.92 | 143 | 30 | 8 | 30 | 1241.1 | 1220 | 619 | 541 | 115 | 27 | 482 | 25 | 736 | 43 | 8 |
| Huntsville | 3.92 | 144 | 20 | 11 | 30 | 1239.2 | 1216 | 667 | 540 | 109 | 31 | 619 | 16 | 740 | 67 | 14 |
| Jacksonville | 4.15 | 143 | 17 | 11 | 33 | 1224.0 | 1210 | 636 | 565 | 87 | 45 | 615 | 29 | 711 | 86 | 4 |
| Greenville | 4.19 | 144 | 13 | 4 | 34 | 1230.0 | 1221 | 677 | 573 | 111 | 34 | 636 | 22 | 799 | 78 | 5 |
| Memphis | 4.31 | 144 | 18 | 4 | 25 | 1231.1 | 1264 | 698 | 590 | 134 | 50 | 521 | 38 | 737 | 68 | 7 |
| Chattanooga | 4.39 | 143 | 18 | 7 | 24 | 1225.2 | 1327 | 707 | 598 | 102 | 54 | 535 | 37 | 663 | 63 | 11 |
| Orlando | 4.51 | 143 | 40 | 5 | 23 | 1194.0 | 1238 | 719 | 598 | 134 | 32 | 626 | 30 | 588 | 57 | 10 |
| Birmingham | 5.05 | 143 | 23 | 8 | 18 | 1205.1 | 1317 | 784 | 676 | 139 | 60 | 644 | 17 | 653 | 86 | 21 |

## PITCHERS' RECORDS
### (Leading Qualifiers for Earned-Run Average Leadership — 115 or More Innings)

°Throws lefthanded.

| Pitcher—Club | W. | L. | Pct. | ERA. | G. | GS. | CG. | GF. | ShO. | Sv. | IP. | H. | R. | ER. | HR. | HB. | BB. | Int. BB. | SO. | WP. |
|---|---|---|---|---|---|---|---|---|---|---|---|---|---|---|---|---|---|---|---|---|
| S. Davis, Knoxville° | 17 | 6 | .739 | 2.45 | 27 | 24 | 5 | 2 | 3 | 1 | 154.0 | 114 | 49 | 42 | 8 | 4 | 72 | 1 | 107 | 7 |
| August, Columbus | 14 | 8 | .636 | 2.96 | 27 | 27 | 4 | 0 | 2 | 0 | 176.1 | 183 | 77 | 58 | 11 | 3 | 49 | 4 | 78 | 9 |
| Eichhorn, Knoxville | 5 | 1 | .833 | 3.02 | 26 | 10 | 2 | 2 | 1 | 0 | 116.1 | 101 | 49 | 39 | 11 | 4 | 34 | 2 | 76 | 2 |
| Straker, Orlando | 16 | 6 | .727 | 3.08 | 27 | 26 | 12 | 1 | 3 | 0 | 193.0 | 164 | 75 | 66 | 14 | 2 | 79 | 2 | 106 | 3 |
| Habyan, Charlotte | 13 | 5 | .722 | 3.27 | 28 | 28 | 8 | 0 | 2 | 0 | 189.2 | 157 | 73 | 69 | 11 | 2 | 90 | 0 | 123 | 13 |
| Reyes, Memphis | 11 | 8 | .579 | 3.45 | 39 | 19 | 4 | 5 | 0 | 0 | 151.1 | 147 | 72 | 58 | 10 | 16 | 70 | 5 | 81 | 28 |
| Murray, Chattanooga | 8 | 7 | .533 | 3.53 | 27 | 17 | 3 | 5 | 1 | 1 | 135.0 | 135 | 67 | 53 | 10 | 3 | 40 | 1 | 75 | 3 |
| Bankhead, Memphis | 8 | 6 | .571 | 3.59 | 24 | 24 | 2 | 0 | 1 | 0 | 140.1 | 117 | 63 | 56 | 16 | 3 | 56 | 0 | 128 | 3 |
| Hogan, Columbus | 7 | 14 | .333 | 3.71 | 27 | 27 | 3 | 0 | 0 | 0 | 160.0 | 163 | 89 | 66 | 24 | 4 | 64 | 2 | 69 | 10 |
| Newman, Chattanooga° | 13 | 6 | .684 | 3.82 | 28 | 28 | 4 | 0 | 1 | 0 | 174.1 | 193 | 88 | 74 | 13 | 2 | 61 | 0 | 91 | 6 |

Departmental Leaders: G—Bombard, 52; W—S. Davis, 17; L—Hoover, 16; Pct.—Skinner, .917; GS—Hoover, 29; CG—Straker, 12; GF—Aquino, Bombard, 42; ShO—S. Davis, Straker, 3; Sv.—Aquino, 20; IP—Straker, 193.0; H—Clay, 195; R—T. Taylor, 114; ER—T. Taylor, 97; HR—Hogan, Walberg, 24; HB—Reyes, T. Taylor, 16; BB—Ward, 105; IBB—Bartley, 10; SO—Bankhead, Hoover, 128; WP—Reyes, 28.

### (All Pitchers—Listed Alphabetically)

| Pitcher—Club | W. | L. | Pct. | ERA. | G. | GS. | CG. | GF. | ShO. | Sv. | IP. | H. | R. | ER. | HR. | HB. | BB. | Int. BB. | SO. | WP. |
|---|---|---|---|---|---|---|---|---|---|---|---|---|---|---|---|---|---|---|---|---|
| Adair, Chattanooga° | 5 | 10 | .333 | 4.42 | 37 | 10 | 2 | 16 | 0 | 2 | 91.2 | 101 | 53 | 45 | 12 | 5 | 47 | 2 | 55 | 4 |
| Akerfelds, Huntsville | 9 | 6 | .600 | 3.46 | 17 | 17 | 1 | 0 | 1 | 0 | 96.1 | 75 | 42 | 37 | 12 | 1 | 64 | 0 | 56 | 4 |
| Alba, Knoxville° | 0 | 3 | .000 | 8.24 | 11 | 6 | 0 | 2 | 0 | 0 | 31.2 | 25 | 29 | 29 | 6 | 0 | 38 | 0 | 24 | 3 |
| Alfonzo, Orlando | 7 | 9 | .438 | 2.56 | 38 | 1 | 0 | 27 | 0 | 6 | 95.0 | 99 | 47 | 27 | 10 | 1 | 48 | 5 | 62 | 3 |
| Alvarez, 13 Mem-10 Jack | 3 | 7 | .300 | 4.54 | 23 | 13 | 1 | 5 | 0 | 2 | 101.0 | 90 | 59 | 51 | 16 | 8 | 63 | 1 | 78 | 4 |
| Aquino, Knoxville | 5 | 7 | .417 | 2.60 | 50 | 0 | 0 | 42 | 0 | 20 | 83.0 | 58 | 29 | 24 | 4 | 0 | 32 | 0 | 82 | 1 |
| Arnold, Charlotte | 11 | 7 | .611 | 3.87 | 31 | 18 | 6 | 7 | 2 | 1 | 160.2 | 163 | 74 | 69 | 12 | 2 | 21 | 1 | 85 | 3 |
| Ashman, Huntsville | 0 | 0 | .000 | 0.00 | 1 | 0 | 0 | 1 | 0 | 0 | 1.0 | 0 | 0 | 0 | 0 | 0 | 1 | 0 | 0 | 0 |
| Assenmacher, Greenville° | 6 | 0 | 1.000 | 2.56 | 29 | 0 | 0 | 21 | 0 | 4 | 52.2 | 47 | 16 | 15 | 0 | 1 | 11 | 3 | 59 | 1 |
| August, Columbus | 14 | 8 | .636 | 2.96 | 27 | 27 | 4 | 0 | 2 | 0 | 176.1 | 183 | 77 | 58 | 11 | 3 | 49 | 4 | 78 | 9 |
| Aviles, Greenville | 5 | 6 | .455 | 4.76 | 14 | 14 | 2 | 0 | 0 | 0 | 81.1 | 95 | 54 | 43 | 12 | 2 | 28 | 0 | 44 | 5 |
| Bankhead, Memphis | 8 | 6 | .571 | 3.59 | 24 | 24 | 2 | 0 | 1 | 0 | 140.1 | 117 | 63 | 56 | 16 | 3 | 56 | 0 | 128 | 3 |
| Bargerhuff, Chattanooga | 5 | 2 | .714 | 4.02 | 30 | 0 | 0 | 10 | 0 | 0 | 56.0 | 55 | 28 | 25 | 6 | 4 | 26 | 3 | 21 | 1 |
| Barker, Greenville | 1 | 0 | 1.000 | 1.80 | 1 | 1 | 0 | 0 | 0 | 0 | 5.0 | 1 | 1 | 1 | 0 | 0 | 1 | 0 | 7 | 1 |
| Barlow, Birmingham | 1 | 5 | .167 | 8.38 | 18 | 11 | 0 | 3 | 0 | 0 | 63.1 | 88 | 74 | 59 | 13 | 2 | 55 | 1 | 39 | 6 |
| Barrett, Jacksonville | 13 | 8 | .619 | 4.03 | 37 | 17 | 1 | 15 | 1 | 4 | 145.1 | 145 | 70 | 65 | 12 | 4 | 63 | 5 | 111 | 4 |
| Bartley, Chattanooga | 8 | 6 | .571 | 2.10 | 42 | 0 | 0 | 35 | 0 | 12 | 64.1 | 61 | 20 | 15 | 2 | 3 | 23 | 10 | 24 | 2 |
| Bauer, Huntsville | 5 | 8 | .385 | 4.74 | 22 | 20 | 2 | 1 | 0 | 0 | 123.1 | 156 | 79 | 65 | 14 | 2 | 37 | 1 | 63 | 5 |
| Belcher, Huntsville | 11 | 10 | .524 | 4.69 | 29 | 26 | 3 | 1 | 1 | 0 | 149.2 | 145 | 99 | 78 | 12 | 7 | 99 | 0 | 90 | 11 |
| Bencomo, Huntsville | 3 | 2 | .600 | 2.93 | 9 | 8 | 0 | 0 | 0 | 0 | 58.1 | 57 | 23 | 19 | 1 | 2 | 22 | 2 | 25 | 2 |
| Benedict, Memphis | 6 | 8 | .429 | 3.26 | 43 | 0 | 0 | 40 | 0 | 15 | 66.1 | 56 | 28 | 24 | 6 | 4 | 37 | 9 | 50 | 4 |
| Bernard, Charlotte | 2 | 3 | .400 | 2.79 | 22 | 0 | 0 | 15 | 0 | 4 | 29.0 | 28 | 13 | 9 | 1 | 1 | 18 | 5 | 18 | 1 |
| Biercevicz, Charlotte | 2 | 1 | .667 | 3.75 | 4 | 4 | 0 | 0 | 0 | 0 | 24.0 | 26 | 11 | 10 | 4 | 0 | 8 | 0 | 12 | 0 |
| Bombard, Columbus | 7 | 3 | .700 | 3.31 | 52 | 1 | 0 | 42 | 0 | 15 | 73.1 | 76 | 32 | 27 | 2 | 0 | 39 | 3 | 34 | 1 |
| Boudreau, Charlotte | 3 | 2 | .600 | 2.10 | 28 | 4 | 1 | 10 | 1 | 4 | 68.2 | 47 | 17 | 16 | 4 | 1 | 20 | 4 | 59 | 2 |
| Bradford, Greenville° | 8 | 3 | .727 | 3.34 | 46 | 0 | 0 | 23 | 0 | 9 | 72.2 | 64 | 33 | 27 | 6 | 3 | 43 | 2 | 65 | 6 |
| Brahs, Jacksonville° | 5 | 7 | .417 | 5.27 | 33 | 15 | 2 | 8 | 1 | 1 | 124.2 | 136 | 80 | 73 | 15 | 5 | 56 | 2 | 86 | 4 |
| Breining, Birmingham | 8 | 4 | .667 | 2.88 | 12 | 12 | 8 | 0 | 1 | 0 | 97.0 | 93 | 36 | 31 | 6 | 2 | 20 | 0 | 45 | 3 |
| Brito, Charlotte | 1 | 1 | .500 | 9.00 | 9 | 2 | 0 | 3 | 0 | 1 | 18.0 | 20 | 18 | 18 | 4 | 0 | 11 | 0 | 6 | 1 |
| Bryant, Chattanooga | 3 | 2 | .600 | 3.41 | 24 | 0 | 0 | 22 | 0 | 5 | 29.0 | 24 | 12 | 11 | 3 | 2 | 11 | 1 | 19 | 2 |
| Burns, Huntsville | 3 | 1 | .750 | 1.19 | 4 | 4 | 1 | 0 | 1 | 0 | 22.2 | 16 | 6 | 3 | 0 | 0 | 13 | 0 | 8 | 0 |
| Cadaret, Huntsville° | 3 | 7 | .300 | 6.12 | 17 | 17 | 0 | 0 | 0 | 0 | 82.1 | 96 | 61 | 56 | 9 | 3 | 57 | 0 | 60 | 9 |
| Caldwell, Charlotte | 7 | 4 | .636 | 2.98 | 45 | 8 | 2 | 26 | 0 | 6 | 105.2 | 100 | 43 | 35 | 15 | 6 | 27 | 3 | 56 | 0 |
| Callahan, Charlotte | 0 | 1 | .000 | 6.07 | 13 | 1 | 0 | 5 | 0 | 0 | 29.2 | 32 | 22 | 20 | 2 | 3 | 14 | 0 | 15 | 5 |
| Cardwood, Orlando | 2 | 4 | .333 | 4.73 | 11 | 9 | 1 | 1 | 0 | 0 | 72.1 | 54 | 46 | 38 | 10 | 4 | 46 | 1 | 34 | 9 |
| Carlucci, Knoxville | 1 | 1 | .500 | 1.17 | 12 | 0 | 0 | 10 | 0 | 5 | 23.0 | 17 | 6 | 3 | 0 | 1 | 4 | 0 | 16 | 0 |
| Cates, Jacksonville | 4 | 7 | .364 | 5.42 | 15 | 14 | 2 | 0 | 2 | 0 | 74.2 | 85 | 52 | 45 | 8 | 5 | 29 | 0 | 36 | 4 |
| Clancy, Knoxville | 1 | 0 | 1.000 | 3.38 | 2 | 2 | 0 | 0 | 0 | 0 | 8.0 | 7 | 3 | 3 | 0 | 0 | 2 | 0 | 0 | 0 |
| Clay, Orlando | 13 | 9 | .591 | 4.48 | 31 | 28 | 11 | 2 | 1 | 1 | 190.2 | 195 | 112 | 95 | 15 | 5 | 89 | 2 | 79 | 10 |
| Clemons, Knoxville | 0 | 1 | .000 | 23.14 | 1 | 0 | 0 | 0 | 0 | 0 | 2.1 | 5 | 6 | 6 | 1 | 0 | 3 | 0 | 1 | 2 |
| Cole, Greenville° | 0 | 0 | .000 | 20.25 | 4 | 0 | 0 | 0 | 0 | 0 | 4.0 | 5 | 9 | 9 | 1 | 0 | 11 | 0 | 3 | 2 |

| Pitcher—Club | W. | L. | Pct. | ERA. | G. | GS. | CG. | GF. | ShO. | Sv. | IP. | H. | R. | ER. | HR. | HB. | BB. | Int. BB. | SO. | WP. |
|---|---|---|---|---|---|---|---|---|---|---|---|---|---|---|---|---|---|---|---|---|
| Conner, Birmingham* | 1 | 0 | 1.000 | 2.29 | 3 | 3 | 0 | 0 | 0 | 0 | 19.2 | 17 | 5 | 5 | 0 | 0 | 9 | 0 | 12 | 3 |
| K. Cook, 3 Birm.-9 Jack | 1 | 4 | .200 | 9.64 | 12 | 4 | 0 | 7 | 0 | 0 | 23.1 | 34 | 27 | 25 | 3 | 4 | 12 | 2 | 7 | 2 |
| M. Cook, Columbus | 2 | 1 | .667 | 5.20 | 5 | 5 | 0 | 0 | 0 | 0 | 27.2 | 26 | 22 | 16 | 5 | 1 | 8 | 0 | 24 | 2 |
| Couchee, Charlotte | 4 | 4 | .500 | 3.69 | 22 | 0 | 0 | 21 | 0 | 6 | 31.2 | 30 | 13 | 13 | 3 | 1 | 12 | 5 | 14 | 1 |
| Cullen, Knoxville | 0 | 0 | .000 | 5.40 | 1 | 0 | 0 | 0 | 0 | 0 | 1.2 | 0 | 1 | 1 | 0 | 0 | 6 | 0 | 2 | 2 |
| Cutshall, Jacksonville | 6 | 2 | .750 | 3.12 | 10 | 10 | 0 | 0 | 0 | 0 | 57.2 | 55 | 25 | 20 | 5 | 2 | 23 | 0 | 43 | 1 |
| Dacko, Memphis | 0 | 3 | .000 | 10.00 | 4 | 4 | 0 | 0 | 0 | 0 | 18.0 | 23 | 20 | 20 | 6 | 0 | 6 | 0 | 13 | 1 |
| Daniel, Memphis | 2 | 4 | .333 | 3.77 | 7 | 7 | 1 | 0 | 0 | 0 | 43.0 | 48 | 22 | 18 | 2 | 1 | 12 | 0 | 21 | 1 |
| B. Davis, Memphis | 0 | 0 | .000 | 5.14 | 3 | 0 | 1 | 0 | 0 | 0 | 7.0 | 8 | 4 | 4 | 1 | 0 | 1 | 0 | 7 | 0 |
| J. Davis, Memphis | 6 | 15 | .286 | 5.39 | 27 | 27 | 4 | 0 | 0 | 0 | 160.1 | 186 | 113 | 96 | 13 | 11 | 75 | 4 | 103 | 7 |
| S. Davis, Knoxville* | 17 | 6 | .739 | 2.45 | 27 | 24 | 5 | 2 | 3 | 1 | 154.0 | 114 | 49 | 42 | 8 | 4 | 72 | 1 | 107 | 7 |
| Dennis, Knoxville | 0 | 0 | .000 | 0.00 | 1 | 0 | 0 | 1 | 0 | 0 | 1.0 | 1 | 0 | 0 | 0 | 0 | 1 | 0 | 0 | 0 |
| Dickman, Knoxville | 5 | 6 | .455 | 4.92 | 28 | 9 | 0 | 7 | 0 | 0 | 71.1 | 67 | 41 | 39 | 8 | 1 | 61 | 1 | 45 | 10 |
| Dooner, Charlotte | 2 | 3 | .400 | 3.77 | 27 | 0 | 0 | 15 | 0 | 6 | 43.0 | 47 | 23 | 18 | 3 | 2 | 9 | 1 | 19 | 1 |
| Dopson, Jacksonville | 3 | 0 | 1.000 | 1.11 | 5 | 5 | 1 | 0 | 0 | 0 | 32.1 | 27 | 5 | 4 | 2 | 1 | 10 | 0 | 20 | 1 |
| Dotson, Birmingham | 1 | 5 | .167 | 4.85 | 8 | 8 | 1 | 0 | 0 | 0 | 42.2 | 42 | 26 | 23 | 6 | 2 | 30 | 0 | 22 | 8 |
| Dozier, Huntsville | 5 | 2 | .714 | 3.17 | 12 | 8 | 3 | 1 | 1 | 0 | 59.2 | 42 | 28 | 21 | 5 | 0 | 26 | 1 | 54 | 4 |
| Eichhorn, Knoxville | 5 | 1 | .833 | 3.02 | 26 | 10 | 2 | 2 | 1 | 0 | 116.1 | 101 | 49 | 39 | 11 | 4 | 34 | 2 | 76 | 2 |
| Elam, Knoxville | 4 | 4 | .500 | 3.44 | 33 | 11 | 1 | 10 | 1 | 2 | 107.1 | 103 | 55 | 41 | 3 | 1 | 56 | 3 | 50 | 11 |
| Esquer, Knoxville* | 1 | 0 | 1.000 | 0.00 | 3 | 0 | 0 | 1 | 0 | 0 | 5.2 | 4 | 0 | 0 | 0 | 1 | 4 | 0 | 9 | 0 |
| Evans, Chattanooga* | 3 | 5 | .375 | 3.44 | 47 | 2 | 0 | 16 | 0 | 3 | 70.2 | 86 | 35 | 27 | 5 | 3 | 14 | 3 | 51 | 1 |
| Fedor, Jacksonville | 2 | 1 | .667 | 4.22 | 13 | 0 | 0 | 4 | 0 | 0 | 21.1 | 18 | 10 | 10 | 2 | 3 | 18 | 2 | 15 | 5 |
| Felt, Orlando* | 0 | 1 | .000 | 20.25 | 3 | 1 | 0 | 1 | 0 | 0 | 4.0 | 6 | 14 | 9 | 3 | 0 | 10 | 1 | 2 | 1 |
| Flinn, Charlotte | 1 | 5 | .167 | 4.45 | 13 | 0 | 0 | 4 | 0 | 0 | 32.1 | 39 | 18 | 16 | 3 | 1 | 7 | 0 | 26 | 0 |
| Flores, Jacksonville | 1 | 2 | .333 | 5.19 | 11 | 0 | 0 | 7 | 0 | 0 | 17.1 | 22 | 17 | 10 | 1 | 1 | 12 | 1 | 12 | 4 |
| Furman, Birmingham | 1 | 2 | .333 | 5.01 | 19 | 4 | 0 | 7 | 0 | 1 | 41.1 | 46 | 37 | 23 | 5 | 2 | 26 | 0 | 17 | 4 |
| Gibson, Birmingham* | 8 | 8 | .500 | 4.12 | 36 | 14 | 2 | 5 | 2 | 1 | 144.1 | 135 | 73 | 66 | 13 | 0 | 63 | 1 | 79 | 4 |
| Giddings, Huntsville | 6 | 6 | .500 | 2.89 | 49 | 0 | 0 | 40 | 0 | 12 | 71.2 | 70 | 29 | 23 | 4 | 1 | 26 | 1 | 40 | 5 |
| Gilbert, Charlotte* | 5 | 3 | .625 | 4.65 | 23 | 12 | 1 | 4 | 1 | 0 | 91.0 | 101 | 56 | 47 | 7 | 1 | 38 | 1 | 32 | 2 |
| Gillam, Knoxville* | 6 | 5 | .545 | 2.68 | 42 | 0 | 0 | 31 | 0 | 7 | 77.1 | 70 | 29 | 23 | 3 | 0 | 31 | 5 | 41 | 2 |
| Gorman, 14 Hunts-9 Birm | 6 | 0 | 1.000 | 3.35 | 23 | 2 | 1 | 8 | 0 | 2 | 40.1 | 32 | 21 | 15 | 3 | 1 | 25 | 1 | 29 | 4 |
| Graybill, Jacksonville | 4 | 2 | .667 | 3.65 | 10 | 9 | 1 | 0 | 0 | 0 | 56.2 | 62 | 25 | 23 | 2 | 3 | 23 | 0 | 26 | 4 |
| Grimsley, Chattanooga* | 0 | 0 | .000 | 27.00 | 1 | 0 | 0 | 1 | 0 | 0 | 1.0 | 2 | 3 | 3 | 1 | 0 | 2 | 0 | 2 | 1 |
| Groves, Jacksonville | 6 | 4 | .600 | 1.34 | 36 | 0 | 0 | 33 | 0 | 19 | 67.1 | 42 | 13 | 10 | 1 | 0 | 20 | 2 | 33 | 4 |
| Gunnarsson, Chattanooga* | 1 | 1 | .500 | 7.62 | 3 | 2 | 0 | 0 | 0 | 0 | 13.0 | 23 | 12 | 11 | 3 | 1 | 4 | 0 | 5 | 1 |
| Habyan, Charlotte | 13 | 5 | .722 | 3.27 | 28 | 28 | 8 | 0 | 2 | 0 | 189.2 | 157 | 73 | 69 | 11 | 2 | 90 | 0 | 123 | 13 |
| Hallas, Huntsville | 1 | 3 | .250 | 4.43 | 20 | 1 | 0 | 3 | 0 | 0 | 44.2 | 49 | 23 | 22 | 9 | 0 | 11 | 1 | 19 | 1 |
| Hamric, Knoxville | 0 | 0 | .000 | 0.00 | 1 | 0 | 0 | 1 | 0 | 0 | 1.0 | 0 | 0 | 0 | 0 | 0 | 0 | 0 | 0 | 0 |
| Harper, Knoxville | 1 | 2 | .333 | 4.97 | 6 | 4 | 0 | 1 | 0 | 0 | 25.1 | 27 | 18 | 14 | 1 | 0 | 19 | 0 | 22 | 1 |
| Harvey, Huntsville* | 1 | 2 | .333 | 3.77 | 21 | 1 | 0 | 11 | 0 | 2 | 28.2 | 28 | 15 | 12 | 1 | 0 | 10 | 2 | 17 | 5 |
| Hatcher, Memphis | 0 | 0 | .000 | 0.00 | 1 | 0 | 0 | 0 | 0 | 0 | 1.0 | 0 | 0 | 0 | 0 | 0 | 3 | 0 | 1 | 0 |
| Heimueller, Orlando* | 7 | 3 | .700 | 2.88 | 41 | 2 | 1 | 36 | 1 | 14 | 75.0 | 70 | 31 | 24 | 3 | 0 | 33 | 7 | 38 | 4 |
| Heinkel, Birmingham | 2 | 5 | .286 | 4.89 | 10 | 10 | 2 | 0 | 0 | 0 | 57.0 | 77 | 31 | 31 | 9 | 3 | 18 | 0 | 33 | 4 |
| Henderson, Birmingham | 3 | 7 | .300 | 6.11 | 19 | 16 | 0 | 2 | 0 | 0 | 101.2 | 128 | 89 | 69 | 14 | 1 | 58 | 3 | 51 | 5 |
| Henneman, Birmingham | 3 | 5 | .375 | 5.76 | 46 | 0 | 0 | 38 | 0 | 9 | 70.1 | 88 | 50 | 45 | 6 | 7 | 28 | 4 | 40 | 3 |
| Hinz, Birmingham | 1 | 3 | .250 | 5.88 | 7 | 5 | 0 | 0 | 0 | 0 | 26.0 | 19 | 18 | 17 | 4 | 2 | 35 | 0 | 9 | 0 |
| Hogan, Columbus | 7 | 14 | .333 | 3.71 | 27 | 27 | 3 | 0 | 0 | 0 | 160.0 | 163 | 89 | 66 | 24 | 5 | 64 | 2 | 69 | 10 |
| Hoover, Charlotte | 8 | 16 | .333 | 4.72 | 29 | 29 | 7 | 0 | 0 | 0 | 183.0 | 186 | 108 | 96 | 20 | 4 | 81 | 1 | 128 | 5 |
| Hotchkiss, Birmingham | 0 | 0 | .000 | 0.00 | 2 | 0 | 0 | 2 | 0 | 0 | 2.2 | 2 | 0 | 0 | 0 | 0 | 0 | 0 | 1 | 0 |
| Innis, Orlando | 0 | 0 | .000 | 36.00 | 1 | 1 | 0 | 0 | 0 | 0 | 1.0 | 2 | 5 | 4 | 0 | 1 | 6 | 0 | 1 | 0 |
| James, Birmingham | 4 | 7 | .364 | 5.38 | 18 | 12 | 3 | 2 | 0 | 1 | 77.0 | 72 | 52 | 46 | 6 | 7 | 58 | 2 | 59 | 11 |
| Je. Johnson, Charlotte | 2 | 1 | .667 | 1.54 | 3 | 3 | 2 | 0 | 0 | 0 | 23.1 | 18 | 7 | 4 | 1 | 0 | 10 | 0 | 20 | 0 |
| Jo. Johnson, Greenville | 6 | 3 | .667 | 4.07 | 12 | 11 | 1 | 0 | 0 | 0 | 59.2 | 78 | 30 | 27 | 3 | 1 | 12 | 0 | 29 | 1 |
| M. Johnson, Chattanooga | 0 | 1 | .000 | 9.45 | 6 | 0 | 0 | 1 | 0 | 0 | 6.2 | 12 | 11 | 7 | 2 | 1 | 6 | 1 | 4 | 0 |
| Jones, Chattanooga | 5 | 6 | .455 | 6.11 | 30 | 14 | 2 | 7 | 1 | 1 | 109.0 | 120 | 88 | 74 | 12 | 4 | 61 | 2 | 41 | 6 |
| Kasprzak, Columbus | 2 | 8 | .200 | 3.03 | 38 | 1 | 0 | 16 | 0 | 1 | 86.0 | 73 | 37 | 29 | 5 | 2 | 45 | 5 | 59 | 2 |
| Kelley, Columbus | 10 | 8 | .556 | 3.86 | 22 | 20 | 4 | 1 | 1 | 0 | 133.0 | 119 | 75 | 57 | 19 | 2 | 39 | 3 | 60 | 4 |
| Kendrick, Huntsville* | 6 | 4 | .600 | 2.45 | 13 | 12 | 5 | 1 | 1 | 0 | 88.0 | 83 | 28 | 24 | 5 | 3 | 26 | 1 | 39 | 3 |
| Kinns, Jacksonville | 4 | 7 | .364 | 4.53 | 37 | 6 | 2 | 16 | 0 | 3 | 101.1 | 108 | 55 | 51 | 6 | 5 | 56 | 2 | 46 | 8 |
| Klump, Orlando | 5 | 7 | .417 | 4.96 | 14 | 14 | 4 | 0 | 0 | 0 | 90.2 | 101 | 57 | 50 | 8 | 5 | 51 | 1 | 25 | 4 |
| Konopa, Charlotte* | 0 | 1 | 1.000 | 6.00 | 3 | 0 | 0 | 1 | 0 | 0 | 6.0 | 8 | 5 | 4 | 1 | 0 | 7 | 1 | 3 | 0 |
| Labozzetta, Birmingham* | 2 | 3 | .400 | 6.49 | 10 | 10 | 0 | 0 | 0 | 0 | 52.2 | 74 | 43 | 38 | 11 | 1 | 27 | 0 | 23 | 0 |
| Lamb, Greenville | 6 | 9 | .400 | 4.68 | 40 | 20 | 3 | 7 | 1 | 0 | 150.0 | 164 | 95 | 78 | 16 | 1 | 67 | 3 | 83 | 9 |
| Lavelle, Charlotte | 1 | 0 | 1.000 | 1.93 | 2 | 0 | 0 | 2 | 0 | 0 | 4.2 | 1 | 1 | 1 | 0 | 0 | 4 | 1 | 4 | 0 |
| Law, Huntsville | 8 | 8 | .500 | 6.11 | 37 | 15 | 2 | 7 | 1 | 1 | 106.0 | 115 | 86 | 72 | 12 | 6 | 78 | 1 | 53 | 6 |
| Leggatt, Greenville | 5 | 2 | .714 | 2.64 | 46 | 2 | 0 | 36 | 0 | 17 | 92.0 | 70 | 31 | 27 | 7 | 4 | 47 | 5 | 75 | 4 |
| Leiter, Charlotte | 0 | 1 | .000 | 1.42 | 5 | 0 | 0 | 2 | 0 | 1 | 6.1 | 3 | 1 | 1 | 0 | 2 | 0 | 0 | 8 | 0 |
| Leonard, Memphis | 0 | 0 | .000 | 7.20 | 1 | 0 | 0 | 0 | 0 | 0 | 5.0 | 9 | 4 | 4 | 1 | 0 | 1 | 0 | 1 | 0 |
| Lucas, Columbus | 1 | 1 | .500 | 3.78 | 4 | 0 | 0 | 6 | 0 | 2 | 16.2 | 12 | 7 | 7 | 1 | 0 | 16 | 3 | 9 | 0 |
| Mancuso, Birmingham* | 9 | 8 | .529 | 4.08 | 37 | 14 | 6 | 17 | 0 | 2 | 132.1 | 137 | 65 | 60 | 17 | 4 | 66 | 3 | 79 | 1 |
| J. Martin, Orlando* | 4 | 5 | .444 | 6.20 | 12 | 10 | 3 | 1 | 0 | 0 | 69.2 | 86 | 50 | 48 | 13 | 3 | 27 | 0 | 16 | 0 |
| V. Martin, Chattanooga | 7 | 9 | .438 | 4.21 | 22 | 22 | 3 | 0 | 1 | 0 | 149.2 | 165 | 75 | 70 | 10 | 4 | 58 | 6 | 82 | 5 |
| Martinez, Memphis | 3 | 1 | .750 | 2.33 | 11 | 6 | 2 | 3 | 1 | 1 | 46.1 | 34 | 16 | 12 | 5 | 0 | 16 | 0 | 37 | 4 |
| McDonald, Chattanooga | 2 | 6 | .250 | 5.03 | 35 | 13 | 2 | 7 | 0 | 0 | 116.1 | 137 | 79 | 65 | 7 | 4 | 62 | 5 | 63 | 15 |
| McKay, Jacksonville | 3 | 6 | .333 | 5.57 | 14 | 14 | 1 | 0 | 0 | 0 | 76.0 | 86 | 53 | 47 | 2 | 1 | 36 | 1 | 27 | 12 |
| McNealy, Chattanooga* | 0 | 0 | .000 | 18.00 | 1 | 0 | 0 | 1 | 0 | 0 | 1.0 | 2 | 2 | 2 | 0 | 0 | 1 | 0 | 1 | 1 |
| Medvin, Birmingham | 3 | 3 | .500 | 3.13 | 13 | 0 | 0 | 12 | 0 | 1 | 23.0 | 14 | 10 | 8 | 1 | 3 | 12 | 0 | 17 | 6 |
| Mendek, Chattanooga* | 0 | 0 | .000 | 7.36 | 4 | 0 | 0 | 4 | 0 | 0 | 3.2 | 6 | 4 | 3 | 0 | 0 | 2 | 1 | 1 | 0 |
| Mohr, Memphis* | 2 | 1 | .667 | 4.11 | 15 | 0 | 0 | 5 | 0 | 0 | 30.2 | 29 | 14 | 14 | 5 | 0 | 16 | 3 | 25 | 0 |
| Montgomery, Columbus | 2 | 1 | .667 | 3.91 | 16 | 0 | 0 | 13 | 0 | 3 | 23.0 | 29 | 10 | 10 | 1 | 0 | 8 | 2 | 19 | 1 |
| Mooneyham, Huntsville | 2 | 1 | .667 | 1.98 | 10 | 4 | 0 | 4 | 0 | 2 | 36.1 | 27 | 13 | 8 | 2 | 1 | 15 | 0 | 28 | 3 |
| Moore, Knoxville | 0 | 2 | .000 | 6.55 | 7 | 3 | 0 | 1 | 0 | 0 | 22.0 | 28 | 17 | 16 | 1 | 1 | 12 | 1 | 12 | 6 |
| Moran, Jacksonville* | 0 | 0 | .000 | 0.00 | 1 | 0 | 0 | 1 | 0 | 0 | 1.0 | 1 | 0 | 0 | 0 | 0 | 1 | 0 | 0 | 0 |
| Morgan, Memphis | 2 | 0 | 1.000 | 3.15 | 14 | 0 | 0 | 13 | 0 | 2 | 20.0 | 19 | 7 | 7 | 2 | 2 | 9 | 0 | 14 | 1 |
| Morris, Greenville | 2 | 2 | .500 | 4.12 | 4 | 4 | 1 | 0 | 1 | 0 | 19.2 | 16 | 9 | 9 | 2 | 1 | 10 | 0 | 8 | 0 |
| Murray, Chattanooga | 8 | 7 | .533 | 3.53 | 27 | 17 | 3 | 5 | 1 | 1 | 135.0 | 135 | 67 | 53 | 10 | 3 | 40 | 1 | 75 | 3 |
| Newman, Chattanooga* | 13 | 6 | .684 | 3.82 | 28 | 28 | 4 | 0 | 0 | 0 | 174.1 | 193 | 88 | 74 | 13 | 2 | 61 | 0 | 91 | 6 |
| Nicometi, Jacksonville* | 4 | 4 | .500 | 3.80 | 41 | 0 | 0 | 23 | 0 | 4 | 73.1 | 84 | 37 | 31 | 3 | 5 | 40 | 6 | 23 | 7 |
| Noble, Columbus* | 6 | 0 | 1.000 | 2.52 | 35 | 1 | 0 | 11 | 0 | 2 | 75.0 | 70 | 28 | 21 | 6 | 1 | 28 | 3 | 47 | 2 |
| Oelkers, Orlando* | 2 | 3 | .400 | 6.00 | 6 | 6 | 0 | 0 | 0 | 0 | 33.0 | 46 | 27 | 22 | 5 | 0 | 18 | 0 | 15 | 5 |
| Oliveras, Charlotte | 2 | 1 | .667 | 6.64 | 12 | 7 | 0 | 2 | 0 | 0 | 40.2 | 57 | 40 | 30 | 3 | 1 | 25 | 0 | 20 | 5 |
| Payne, Greenville | 0 | 1 | .000 | 5.87 | 2 | 2 | 0 | 0 | 0 | 0 | 7.2 | 8 | 5 | 5 | 0 | 1 | 4 | 0 | 4 | 0 |

| Pitcher—Club | W. | L. | Pct. | ERA. | G. | GS. | CG. | GF. | ShO. | Sv. | IP. | H. | R. | ER. | HR. | HB. | BB. | Int. BB. | SO. | WP. |
|---|---|---|---|---|---|---|---|---|---|---|---|---|---|---|---|---|---|---|---|---|
| Pena, Birmingham | 6 | 7 | .462 | 4.34 | 47 | 1 | 0 | 31 | 0 | 3 | 95.1 | 95 | 53 | 46 | 12 | 8 | 44 | 4 | 70 | 5 |
| Peraza, Knoxville | 5 | 2 | .714 | 4.06 | 9 | 8 | 1 | 0 | 0 | 0 | 51.0 | 53 | 31 | 23 | 6 | 0 | 30 | 2 | 28 | 6 |
| Perrotte, Birmingham* | 0 | 1 | .000 | 27.00 | 2 | 2 | 0 | 0 | 0 | 0 | 5.2 | 15 | 17 | 17 | 1 | 1 | 10 | 0 | 3 | 1 |
| Phillion, Birmingham* | 0 | 0 | .000 | 14.73 | 1 | 0 | 0 | 0 | 0 | 0 | 3.2 | 4 | 6 | 6 | 1 | 0 | 4 | 0 | 1 | 0 |
| Plunk, Huntsville | 8 | 2 | .800 | 3.40 | 13 | 13 | 2 | 0 | 1 | 0 | 79.1 | 61 | 36 | 30 | 9 | 2 | 56 | 0 | 68 | 4 |
| Price, Jacksonville | 4 | 2 | .667 | 3.49 | 21 | 8 | 3 | 6 | 1 | 0 | 87.2 | 83 | 38 | 34 | 11 | 2 | 36 | 2 | 27 | 2 |
| Radtke, Memphis | 7 | 12 | .368 | 4.24 | 29 | 24 | 3 | 3 | 0 | 0 | 152.2 | 180 | 98 | 72 | 15 | 2 | 56 | 4 | 55 | 7 |
| Ramirez, Charlotte | 0 | 1 | .000 | 7.94 | 2 | 2 | 0 | 0 | 0 | 0 | 11.1 | 13 | 10 | 10 | 1 | 0 | 6 | 0 | 5 | 3 |
| Rasmussen, Birmingham | 0 | 0 | .000 | 6.14 | 3 | 0 | 0 | 1 | 0 | 0 | 7.1 | 7 | 5 | 5 | 1 | 0 | 3 | 0 | 3 | 0 |
| Reilly, Columbus | 2 | 0 | 1.000 | 4.20 | 18 | 1 | 1 | 8 | 0 | 0 | 40.2 | 47 | 28 | 19 | 7 | 2 | 16 | 0 | 22 | 2 |
| Reiter, Memphis* | 1 | 2 | .333 | 4.01 | 16 | 0 | 0 | 6 | 0 | 1 | 24.2 | 25 | 13 | 11 | 3 | 1 | 12 | 2 | 19 | 1 |
| Reyes, Memphis | 11 | 8 | .579 | 3.45 | 39 | 19 | 4 | 5 | 0 | 0 | 151.1 | 147 | 72 | 58 | 10 | 16 | 70 | 5 | 81 | 28 |
| Robinson, Birmingham | 4 | 8 | .333 | 5.09 | 22 | 22 | 2 | 0 | 1 | 0 | 115.0 | 142 | 79 | 65 | 14 | 6 | 59 | 0 | 67 | 14 |
| Rodgers, Knoxville | 0 | 0 | .000 | 0.00 | 1 | 0 | 0 | 1 | 0 | 0 | 1.0 | 0 | 0 | 0 | 0 | 0 | 0 | 0 | 1 | 0 |
| Rodriguez, Huntsville | 2 | 1 | .667 | 2.34 | 8 | 6 | 1 | 1 | 1 | 1 | 50.0 | 40 | 18 | 13 | 5 | 1 | 13 | 0 | 25 | 0 |
| Rosario, Greenville* | 6 | 11 | .353 | 4.16 | 21 | 19 | 0 | 0 | 0 | 0 | 106.0 | 87 | 62 | 49 | 14 | 2 | 81 | 3 | 67 | 5 |
| Samuels, Columbus* | 10 | 9 | .526 | 3.96 | 33 | 25 | 1 | 4 | 0 | 2 | 147.2 | 132 | 73 | 65 | 18 | 4 | 82 | 2 | 85 | 8 |
| Santiago, Greenville* | 0 | 1 | .000 | 3.86 | 3 | 1 | 0 | 2 | 0 | 0 | 9.1 | 12 | 5 | 4 | 1 | 0 | 4 | 0 | 6 | 0 |
| Searcy, Birmingham* | 2 | 2 | .500 | 3.19 | 7 | 7 | 0 | 0 | 0 | 0 | 36.2 | 39 | 17 | 13 | 1 | 2 | 23 | 1 | 19 | 2 |
| Shanks, Knoxville | 3 | 2 | .600 | 4.73 | 31 | 1 | 0 | 8 | 0 | 3 | 64.2 | 56 | 41 | 34 | 5 | 1 | 28 | 4 | 36 | 2 |
| Shiflett, Birmingham* | 4 | 8 | .333 | 5.28 | 19 | 14 | 2 | 4 | 1 | 0 | 90.1 | 106 | 61 | 53 | 14 | 1 | 40 | 0 | 48 | 3 |
| Shouppe, Columbus* | 1 | 0 | 1.000 | 1.38 | 11 | 0 | 0 | 11 | 0 | 3 | 13.0 | 4 | 2 | 2 | 1 | 1 | 6 | 0 | 7 | 0 |
| Siwy, Birmingham | 0 | 1 | .000 | 6.75 | 5 | 0 | 0 | 2 | 0 | 0 | 8.0 | 8 | 9 | 6 | 0 | 0 | 7 | 0 | 2 | 1 |
| Skinner, Charlotte | 11 | 1 | .917 | 2.59 | 16 | 15 | 3 | 1 | 0 | 0 | 111.1 | 97 | 37 | 32 | 12 | 3 | 43 | 1 | 70 | 3 |
| L. Smith, Huntsville* | 4 | 1 | .800 | 3.36 | 48 | 0 | 0 | 26 | 0 | 3 | 72.1 | 79 | 38 | 27 | 3 | 2 | 38 | 5 | 31 | 3 |
| R. Smith, Orlando | 4 | 4 | .500 | 4.87 | 13 | 10 | 1 | 0 | 0 | 0 | 61.0 | 69 | 42 | 33 | 8 | 3 | 33 | 4 | 27 | 4 |
| Sorce, Orlando | 0 | 0 | .000 | 4.09 | 4 | 0 | 0 | 3 | 0 | 0 | 11.0 | 15 | 8 | 5 | 2 | 0 | 2 | 0 | 8 | 2 |
| Springer, Birmingham | 0 | 0 | .000 | 4.50 | 3 | 0 | 0 | 3 | 0 | 0 | 4.0 | 2 | 2 | 2 | 1 | 0 | 2 | 0 | 3 | 0 |
| St. Clair, Birmingham | 0 | 0 | .000 | 10.24 | 5 | 0 | 0 | 2 | 0 | 1 | 9.2 | 15 | 12 | 11 | 2 | 3 | 9 | 1 | 3 | 0 |
| Steinbach, Huntsville | 0 | 0 | .000 | 0.00 | 1 | 0 | 0 | 0 | 0 | 0 | 1.0 | 0 | 0 | 0 | 0 | 0 | 0 | 0 | 0 | 0 |
| Steirer, Charlotte | 3 | 1 | .750 | 4.50 | 5 | 4 | 0 | 0 | 0 | 0 | 22.0 | 30 | 17 | 11 | 3 | 2 | 9 | 0 | 5 | 2 |
| Straker, Orlando | 16 | 6 | .727 | 3.08 | 27 | 26 | 12 | 1 | 3 | 0 | 193.0 | 164 | 75 | 66 | 14 | 2 | 79 | 2 | 106 | 3 |
| Strasser, Columbus | 12 | 9 | .571 | 3.87 | 28 | 28 | 6 | 0 | 2 | 0 | 176.2 | 188 | 100 | 76 | 17 | 14 | 49 | 6 | 99 | 8 |
| Strucher, Columbus | 0 | 0 | .000 | 0.00 | 1 | 0 | 0 | 0 | 0 | 0 | 2.0 | 1 | 1 | 0 | 0 | 0 | 1 | 0 | 1 | 0 |
| Summers, Charlotte | 0 | 4 | .000 | 6.69 | 8 | 7 | 0 | 0 | 0 | 0 | 35.0 | 40 | 28 | 26 | 5 | 0 | 32 | 1 | 21 | 1 |
| Swift, Chattanooga | 2 | 1 | .667 | 3.69 | 7 | 7 | 0 | 0 | 0 | 0 | 39.0 | 34 | 16 | 16 | 2 | 2 | 21 | 0 | 21 | 3 |
| Szajko, Jacksonville | 0 | 0 | .000 | 0.00 | 1 | 0 | 0 | 1 | 0 | 0 | 2.0 | 4 | 0 | 0 | 0 | 0 | 0 | 0 | 0 | 0 |
| Tabor, Memphis | 6 | 3 | .667 | 2.89 | 38 | 2 | 0 | 14 | 0 | 4 | 87.1 | 80 | 33 | 28 | 5 | 1 | 31 | 5 | 48 | 2 |
| J. Taylor, 22 Green-10 Orl* | 3 | 8 | .273 | 6.01 | 32 | 10 | 1 | 16 | 0 | 0 | 91.1 | 88 | 67 | 61 | 10 | 6 | 100 | 0 | 72 | 9 |
| T. Taylor, Chattanooga | 4 | 15 | .211 | 5.28 | 28 | 28 | 2 | 0 | 0 | 0 | 165.1 | 171 | 114 | 97 | 14 | 16 | 96 | 2 | 107 | 12 |
| Todd, Charlotte | 0 | 0 | .000 | 13.50 | 3 | 0 | 0 | 0 | 0 | 0 | 4.0 | 9 | 6 | 6 | 1 | 0 | 2 | 0 | 2 | 0 |
| Torres, 11 Jack-24 Col | 4 | 3 | .571 | 3.53 | 35 | 8 | 3 | 15 | 1 | 1 | 99.1 | 82 | 43 | 39 | 5 | 3 | 52 | 2 | 41 | 4 |
| Treadway, Greenville | 6 | 7 | .462 | 4.33 | 31 | 24 | 1 | 1 | 0 | 0 | 166.1 | 179 | 92 | 80 | 21 | 2 | 58 | 0 | 101 | 10 |
| Valenzuela, Knoxville | 0 | 0 | .000 | 3.79 | 4 | 4 | 0 | 0 | 0 | 0 | 19.0 | 18 | 9 | 8 | 1 | 0 | 10 | 0 | 14 | 0 |
| Walberg, Memphis | 9 | 11 | .450 | 5.17 | 29 | 25 | 2 | 3 | 0 | 0 | 158.1 | 168 | 99 | 91 | 24 | 2 | 63 | 1 | 74 | 6 |
| Walsh, Knoxville* | 11 | 8 | .579 | 4.50 | 38 | 25 | 3 | 6 | 1 | 0 | 154.0 | 147 | 89 | 77 | 11 | 5 | 89 | 0 | 103 | 14 |
| Walters, Orlando | 0 | 0 | .000 | 2.57 | 3 | 1 | 0 | 2 | 0 | 0 | 7.0 | 8 | 2 | 2 | 1 | 0 | 3 | 0 | 3 | 0 |
| Ward, Greenville | 11 | 10 | .524 | 4.20 | 28 | 24 | 3 | 1 | 0 | 0 | 150.0 | 141 | 83 | 70 | 4 | 4 | 105 | 1 | 100 | 9 |
| Wayne, Jacksonville* | 3 | 12 | .200 | 5.29 | 21 | 20 | 2 | 0 | 0 | 0 | 102.0 | 108 | 67 | 60 | 3 | 1 | 70 | 3 | 62 | 11 |
| Whaley, Huntsville | 3 | 2 | .600 | 2.95 | 40 | 0 | 0 | 16 | 0 | 6 | 85.1 | 79 | 36 | 28 | 4 | 1 | 28 | 2 | 65 | 3 |
| Wilder, Memphis | 1 | 0 | 1.000 | 5.81 | 45 | 0 | 0 | 29 | 0 | 1 | 74.1 | 85 | 61 | 48 | 10 | 2 | 31 | 5 | 24 | 2 |
| Wiseman, Orlando | 0 | 1 | .000 | 6.75 | 10 | 1 | 0 | 4 | 0 | 0 | 32.0 | 34 | 25 | 24 | 7 | 1 | 24 | 1 | 17 | 4 |
| Yearout, Knoxville* | 11 | 12 | .478 | 4.03 | 31 | 28 | 5 | 0 | 2 | 0 | 169.2 | 163 | 90 | 76 | 23 | 6 | 72 | 1 | 96 | 8 |
| Youmans, Jacksonville | 7 | 3 | .700 | 3.36 | 14 | 14 | 1 | 0 | 1 | 0 | 85.2 | 65 | 35 | 32 | 5 | 2 | 57 | 0 | 86 | 5 |
| Ziem, Greenville | 5 | 14 | .263 | 4.18 | 48 | 14 | 2 | 25 | 0 | 13 | 157.1 | 158 | 87 | 73 | 16 | 6 | 73 | 5 | 86 | 13 |
| Zmudosky, 15 Hunts-27 Bir | 1 | 8 | .111 | 4.99 | 42 | 5 | 2 | 10 | 1 | 2 | 106.1 | 133 | 68 | 59 | 11 | 5 | 48 | 2 | 31 | 5 |

BALKS—Shiflett, 10; Newman, 7; Kendrick, Walsh, 6 each; James, Samuels, 5 each; Hoover, 4; Heimueller, Law, Tabor, 3 each; Barrett, Belcher, Cardwood, J. Davis, Harper, Labozzetta, Rosario, Straker, T. Taylor, 2 each; Alba, Alfonzo, Alvarez, Arnold, August, Bargerhuff, Barlow, Bartley, Bencomo, Clay, S. Davis, Dickman, Dotson, Dozier, Eichhorn, Furman, Giddings, Groves, Je. Johnson, Kasprzak, Kelley, Lamb, Lucas, Noble, Peraza, Plunk, Skinner, R. Smith, Strasser, Todd, Treadway, Walberg, Wayne, Yearout, Ziem, Zmudosky, 1 each.

COMBINATION SHUTOUTS—Robinson-Siwy-Zmudosky-Henneman, Searcy-Zmudosky-Henneman, Birmingham; Newman-Bartley, Martin-Adair, Swift-Murray, Evans-Bargerhuff, Chattanooga; Hogan-Kasprzak-Shouppe, Samuels-Kasprzak, Noble-Kasprzak, Samuels-Bombard, Columbus; Lamb-Ziem, Rosario-Leggatt, Greenville; Belcher-Giddings, Plunk-Smith, Cadaret-Belcher, Huntsville; Graybill-Groves, Wayne-Brahs, Cutshall-Cook, Alvarez-Groves, Jacksonville; Yearout-Dickman, Knoxville; Bankhead-Tabor, Daniel-Wilder, Memphis.

NO-HIT GAMES—Elam, Knoxville, defeated Memphis, 2-0, May 10; Habyan, Charlotte, defeated Columbus, 6-0, May 13.

# Texas League

## CLASS AA

**Leading Batter**
**BILLY JOE ROBIDOUX**
**El Paso**

**League President**
**CARL SAWATSKI**

**Leading Pitcher**
**RANDY BOCKUS**
**Shreveport**

CHAMPIONSHIP WINNERS IN PREVIOUS YEARS

| | | |
|---|---|---|
| 1888—Dallas | .671 | |
| 1889—Houston | .551 | |
| 1890—Galveston | .705 | |
| 1892—Houston | .741 | |
| Houston | .613 | |
| 1895—Dallas | .754 | |
| Fort Worth° | .750 | |
| 1896—Fort Worth | .757 | |
| Houston° | .679 | |
| Galveston | .548 | |
| 1897—San Antonio† | .657 | |
| Galveston† | .717 | |
| 1898—League disbanded. | | |
| 1899—Galveston | .632 | |
| Galveston | .762 | |
| 1900-01—Did not operate. | | |
| 1902—Corsicana | .866 | |
| Corsicana | .682 | |
| 1903—Paris-Waco | .615 | |
| Dallas° | .648 | |
| 1904—Corsicana° | .615 | |
| Fort Worth | .800 | |
| 1905—Fort Worth | .545 | |
| 1906—Fort Worth | .677 | |
| Cleburne x | .609 | |
| 1907—Austin | .629 | |
| 1908—San Antonio | .664 | |
| 1909—Houston | .601 | |
| 1910—Dallas† | .586 | |
| Houston† | .586 | |
| 1911—Austin | .575 | |
| 1912—Houston | .626 | |
| 1913—Houston | .620 | |
| 1914—Houston† | .671 | |
| Waco† | .671 | |
| 1915—Waco | .592 | |
| 1916—Waco | .587 | |
| 1917—Dallas | .600 | |
| 1918—Dallas | .584 | |
| 1919—Shreveport° | .677 | |
| Fort Worth | .651 | |
| 1920—Fort Worth | .703 | |
| Fort Worth | .750 | |
| 1921—Fort Worth | .691 | |
| Fort Worth | .662 | |
| 1922—Fort Worth | .694 | |
| Fort Worth | .711 | |
| 1923—Fort Worth | .632 | |
| 1924—Fort Worth | .689 | |
| Fort Worth | .763 | |
| 1925—Fort Worth | .711 | |
| Fort Worth y | .653 | |

| | | |
|---|---|---|
| 1926—Dallas | .574 | |
| 1927—Wichita Falls | .654 | |
| 1928—Houston° | .679 | |
| Wichita Falls | .731 | |
| 1929—Dallas° | .588 | |
| Wichita Falls | .620 | |
| 1930—Wichita Falls | .697 | |
| Fort Worth° | .632 | |
| 1931—Houston a | .625 | |
| Houston | .734 | |
| 1932—Beaumont° | .640 | |
| Dallas | .727 | |
| 1933—Houston | .623 | |
| San Antonio (4th)§ | .523 | |
| 1934—Galveston‡ | .579 | |
| 1935—Oklahoma City‡ | .590 | |
| 1936—Dallas | .604 | |
| Tulsa (3rd)§ | .519 | |
| 1937—Oklahoma City | .635 | |
| Fort Worth (3rd)§ | .535 | |
| 1938—Beaumont | .635 | |
| 1939—Houston | .606 | |
| Fort Worth (4th)§ | .540 | |
| 1940—Houston‡ | .652 | |
| 1941—Houston | .673 | |
| Dallas (4th)§ | .519 | |
| 1942—Beaumont | .605 | |
| Shreveport (2nd)§ | .576 | |
| 1943-44-45—Did not operate. | | |
| 1946—Fort Worth | .656 | |
| Dallas (2nd)§ | .591 | |
| 1947—Houston‡ | .623 | |
| 1948—Fort Worth‡ | .601 | |
| 1949—Fort Worth | .649 | |
| Tulsa (2nd)§ | .584 | |
| 1950—Beaumont | .595 | |
| San Antonio (4th)§ | .513 | |
| 1951—Houston‡ | .619 | |
| 1952—Dallas | .571 | |
| Shreveport (3rd)§ | .522 | |
| 1953—Dallas‡ | .571 | |
| 1954—Shreveport | .559 | |
| Houston (2nd)§ | .553 | |
| 1955—Dallas | .581 | |
| Shreveport (3rd)§ | .540 | |
| 1956—Houston‡ | .623 | |
| 1957—Dallas | .662 | |
| Houston (2nd)§ | .630 | |
| 1958—Fort Worth | .582 | |
| Cor. Christi (3rd)§ | .507 | |
| 1959—Victoria | .589 | |
| Austin (2nd)§ | .548 | |

| | | |
|---|---|---|
| 1960—Rio Grande Valley | .590 | |
| Tulsa (3rd) | .528 | |
| 1961—Amarillo | .643 | |
| San Antonio (3rd)§ | .532 | |
| 1962—El Paso | .571 | |
| Tulsa (2nd)§ | .550 | |
| 1963—San Antonio | .564 | |
| Tulsa (3rd)§ | .529 | |
| 1964—San Antonio‡ | .607 | |
| 1965—Tulsa | .574 | |
| Albuquerque b | .550 | |
| 1966—Arkansas | .579 | |
| 1967—Albuquerque | .557 | |
| 1968—Arkansas | .586 | |
| El Paso b | .562 | |
| 1969—Amarillo | .593 | |
| Memphis b | .504 | |
| 1970—Albuquerque a | .615 | |
| Memphis | .507 | |
| 1971—Did not operate as league—clubs were members of Dixie Association. | | |
| 1972—Alexandria | .600 | |
| El Paso b | .557 | |
| 1973—San Antonio | .590 | |
| Memphis b | .558 | |
| 1974—Victoria b | .581 | |
| El Paso | .555 | |
| 1975—Lafayette c | .558 | |
| Midland c | .604 | |
| 1976—Amarillo b | .600 | |
| Shreveport | .515 | |
| 1977—El Paso | .600 | |
| Arkansas d | .485 | |
| 1978—El Paso d | .593 | |
| Jackson | .567 | |
| 1979—Arkansas d | .571 | |
| Midland | .563 | |
| 1980—Arkansas d | .596 | |
| San Antonio | .544 | |
| 1981—San Antonio | .571 | |
| Jackson d | .507 | |
| 1982—El Paso | .559 | |
| Tulsa d | .515 | |
| 1983—Jackson | .507 | |
| Beaumont d | .500 | |
| 1984—Beaumont | .654 | |
| Jackson d | .610 | |

°Won split-season playoff. †No playoff for title. ‡Finished first and won four-club playoff. §Won four-club playoff. xTitle to Cleburne by default. yTied with Dallas in second half and won playoff for championship. zFort Worth disbanded. aTied with Beaumont at end of first half and won title in best-of-five series played as part of second half schedule. bLeague divided into Eastern, Western divisions; won two-team playoff. cLeague divided into Eastern, Western divisions; declared co-champions when playoffs were not completed. dLeague divided into Eastern and Western divisions and played split-season; won playoffs. NOTE—Championship awarded to winner of four-team playoff, 1933-51; first-place team and playoff winner co-champions, 1952-64.

## STANDING OF CLUBS AT CLOSE OF FIRST HALF, JUNE 18

### EASTERN DIVISION

| Club | W. | L. | T. | Pct. | G.B. |
|---|---|---|---|---|---|
| Arkansas (Cardinals) | 33 | 30 | 1 | .524 | ...... |
| Shreveport (Giants) | 33 | 33 | 0 | .500 | 1½ |
| Jackson (Mets) | 31 | 35 | 1 | .470 | 3½ |
| Tulsa (Rangers) | 28 | 39 | 0 | .418 | 7 |

### WESTERN DIVISION

| Club | W. | L. | T. | Pct. | G.B. |
|---|---|---|---|---|---|
| El Paso (Brewers) | 39 | 29 | 0 | .574 | ...... |
| Beaumont (Padres) | 36 | 30 | 0 | .545 | 2 |
| San Antonio (Dodgers) | 33 | 29 | 0 | .532 | 3 |
| Midland (Angels) | 29 | 37 | 0 | .439 | 9 |

## STANDING OF CLUBS AT CLOSE OF SECOND HALF, AUGUST 31

### EASTERN DIVISION

| Club | W. | L. | T. | Pct. | G.B. |
|---|---|---|---|---|---|
| Jackson (Mets) | 42 | 28 | 1 | .600 | ...... |
| Shreveport (Giants) | 39 | 31 | 0 | .557 | 3 |
| Tulsa (Rangers) | 32 | 37 | 1 | .464 | 9½ |
| Arkansas (Cardinals) | 31 | 40 | 0 | .437 | 11½ |

### WESTERN DIVISION

| Club | W. | L. | T. | Pct. | G.B. |
|---|---|---|---|---|---|
| El Paso (Brewers) | 47 | 21 | 0 | .691 | ...... |
| Beaumont (Padres) | 33 | 37 | 0 | .471 | 15 |
| Midland (Angels) | 30 | 40 | 0 | .429 | 18 |
| San Antonio (Dodgers) | 26 | 46 | 0 | .361 | 23 |

## COMPOSITE STANDING OF CLUBS AT CLOSE OF SEASON, AUGUST 31

| Club | ElP. | Jax. | Shrv. | Beau. | Ark. | Tul. | S.A. | Mid. | W. | L. | T. | Pct. | G.B. |
|---|---|---|---|---|---|---|---|---|---|---|---|---|---|
| El Paso (Brewers) | .... | 6 | 7 | 18 | 6 | 7 | 19 | 23 | 86 | 50 | 0 | .632 | ...... |
| Jackson (Mets) | 4 | .... | 17 | 7 | 17 | 18 | 4 | 6 | 73 | 63 | 2 | .537 | 13 |
| Shreveport (Giants) | 3 | 15 | .... | 4 | 21 | 15 | 7 | 7 | 72 | 64 | 0 | .529 | 14 |
| Beaumont (Padres) | 14 | 3 | 6 | .... | 2 | 8 | 18 | 18 | 69 | 67 | 0 | .507 | 17 |
| Arkansas (Cardinals) | 4 | 15 | 11 | 8 | .... | 17 | 4 | 5 | 64 | 70 | 1 | .478 | 21 |
| Tulsa (Rangers) | 3 | 14 | 17 | 2 | 15 | .... | 5 | 4 | 60 | 76 | 1 | .441 | 26 |
| San Antonio (Dodgers) | 13 | 6 | 3 | 14 | 4 | 5 | .... | 14 | 59 | 75 | 0 | .440 | 26 |
| Midland (Angels) | 9 | 4 | 3 | 14 | 5 | 6 | 18 | .... | 59 | 77 | 0 | .434 | 27 |

Arkansas club represented Little Rock, Ark.

Major league affiliations in parentheses.

Playoffs—Jackson defeated Arkansas, two games to none; Jackson defeated El Paso, four games to none to win league championship.

Regular-Season Attendance—Arkansas, 207,985; Beaumont, 108,729; El Paso, 245,744; Jackson, 132,021; Midland, 127,836; San Antonio, 106,183; Shreveport, 56,025; Tulsa, 154,514. Total, 1,139,037. Total Playoff Attendance, 12,026. All-Star Game Attendance, 4,341.

Managers—Arkansas, Jim Riggleman; Beaumont, Bobby Tolan; El Paso, Terry Bevington; Jackson, Sam Perlozzo; Midland, Joe Maddon; San Antonio, Gary Larocque; Shreveport, Duane Espy; Tulsa, Orlando Gomez.

All-Star Team—1B-Billy Joe Robidoux, El Paso; 2B-Mark McLemore, Midland; 3B-Jeff Hamilton, San Antonio; SS-Rod Booker, Arkansas; OF-Glenn Braggs, El Paso; Johnny Tutt, Beaumont; Jose Gonzalez, San Antonio; C-Barry Lyons, Jackson and Benito Santiago, Beaumont; DH-Joey Meyer, El Paso; Pitchers-Chris Bosio, El Paso; Juan Nieves, El Paso; Dan Plesac, El Paso; Terry Mulholland, Shreveport; Scott May, San Antonio; Most Valuable Player-Billy Joe Robidoux, El Paso; Most Valuable Pitcher-Juan Nieves, El Paso; Manager of the Year-Terry Bevington, El Paso.

(Compiled by Howe News Bureau, Boston, Mass.)

## CLUB BATTING

| Club | Pct. | G. | AB. | R. | OR. | H. | TB. | 2B. | 3B. | HR. | RBI. | GW. | SH. | SF. | HP. | BB. | Int. BB. | SO. | SB. | CS. | LOB. |
|---|---|---|---|---|---|---|---|---|---|---|---|---|---|---|---|---|---|---|---|---|---|
| El Paso | .294 | 136 | 4674 | 882 | 662 | 1373 | 2035 | 244 | 26 | 122 | 803 | 82 | 34 | 47 | 41 | 674 | 24 | 701 | 115 | 79 | 1063 |
| Midland | .275 | 136 | 4638 | 725 | 820 | 1274 | 1909 | 237 | 22 | 118 | 669 | 52 | 39 | 48 | 24 | 524 | 28 | 768 | 131 | 77 | 974 |
| Beaumont | .274 | 136 | 4543 | 631 | 639 | 1244 | 1674 | 195 | 26 | 61 | 547 | 58 | 77 | 35 | 30 | 421 | 31 | 727 | 121 | 54 | 930 |
| Jackson | .263 | 138 | 4546 | 657 | 541 | 1197 | 1668 | 207 | 30 | 68 | 596 | 64 | 48 | 35 | 30 | 571 | 30 | 808 | 99 | 52 | 1036 |
| San Antonio | .262 | 134 | 4435 | 606 | 728 | 1162 | 1631 | 173 | 25 | 82 | 531 | 53 | 58 | 30 | 23 | 508 | 27 | 783 | 138 | 88 | 931 |
| Arkansas | .257 | 135 | 4330 | 552 | 594 | 1113 | 1553 | 194 | 33 | 60 | 490 | 59 | 79 | 41 | 33 | 437 | 35 | 740 | 90 | 59 | 909 |
| Shreveport | .254 | 136 | 4363 | 582 | 538 | 1107 | 1613 | 189 | 28 | 87 | 503 | 60 | 57 | 38 | 31 | 522 | 30 | 872 | 124 | 58 | 942 |
| Tulsa | .249 | 137 | 4483 | 549 | 662 | 1115 | 1703 | 208 | 34 | 104 | 508 | 50 | 45 | 31 | 34 | 479 | 33 | 893 | 98 | 68 | 934 |

## INDIVIDUAL BATTING

(Leading Qualifiers for Batting Championship—367 or More Plate Appearances)

*Bats lefthanded.      †Switch-hitter.

| Player and Club | Pct. | G. | AB. | R. | H. | TB. | 2B. | 3B. | HR. | RBI. | GW. | SH. | SF. | HP. | BB. | Int. BB. | SO. | SB. | CS. |
|---|---|---|---|---|---|---|---|---|---|---|---|---|---|---|---|---|---|---|---|
| Robidoux, William, El Paso* | .342 | 133 | 515 | 111 | 176 | 297 | 46 | 3 | 23 | 132 | 13 | 0 | 4 | 0 | 97 | 7 | 62 | 9 | 4 |
| Aldrete, Michael, Shreveport* | .333 | 127 | 441 | 80 | 147 | 226 | 32 | 1 | 15 | 77 | 12 | 2 | 4 | 0 | 94 | 9 | 57 | 16 | 7 |
| Klipstein, David, El Paso | .333 | 94 | 396 | 92 | 132 | 159 | 19 | 1 | 2 | 40 | 3 | 3 | 4 | 5 | 42 | 0 | 44 | 14 | 13 |
| Hamilton, Jeffrey, San Antonio | .332 | 101 | 377 | 48 | 125 | 184 | 14 | 3 | 13 | 59 | 8 | 1 | 2 | 0 | 28 | 6 | 52 | 1 | 2 |
| Smith, Gregory, Beaumont* | .317 | 114 | 394 | 75 | 125 | 199 | 30 | 1 | 14 | 69 | 9 | 4 | 2 | 4 | 45 | 11 | 59 | 12 | 2 |
| Tutt, Johnny, Beaumont | .315 | 120 | 454 | 59 | 143 | 181 | 19 | 2 | 5 | 67 | 10 | 1 | 3 | 2 | 39 | 1 | 61 | 12 | 8 |
| Cartwright, Alan, El Paso* | .314 | 125 | 475 | 82 | 149 | 225 | 35 | 4 | 11 | 74 | 7 | 1 | 5 | 3 | 48 | 4 | 58 | 12 | 15 |
| Carreon, Mark, Jackson | .313 | 123 | 447 | 96 | 140 | 191 | 23 | 5 | 6 | 51 | 4 | 3 | 4 | 6 | 87 | 3 | 32 | 23 | 6 |
| Braggs, Glenn, El Paso | .310 | 117 | 448 | 105 | 139 | 233 | 26 | 4 | 20 | 103 | 12 | 0 | 4 | 10 | 68 | 4 | 77 | 20 | 7 |
| Milligan, Randy, Jackson | .309 | 119 | 391 | 60 | 121 | 186 | 22 | 2 | 13 | 77 | 8 | 1 | 4 | 4 | 53 | 5 | 78 | 11 | 6 |
| Heath, David, Midland | .309 | 98 | 362 | 49 | 112 | 171 | 21 | 1 | 12 | 54 | 7 | 1 | 1 | 1 | 21 | 0 | 62 | 1 | 1 |
| Magadan, David, Jackson* | .309 | 134 | 466 | 84 | 144 | 166 | 22 | 0 | 0 | 76 | 9 | 4 | 1 | 5 | 106 | 2 | 57 | 0 | 3 |
| Lyons, Barry, Jackson | .307 | 126 | 486 | 69 | 149 | 228 | 34 | 6 | 11 | 108 | 16 | 0 | 3 | 5 | 25 | 2 | 67 | 3 | 0 |

Departmental Leaders: G—R. Sierra, 137; AB—R. Sierra, 545; R—Robidoux, 111; H—Robidoux, 176; TB—Robidoux, 297; 2B—Robidoux, 46; 3B—R. Sierra, 8; HR—Meyer, 37; RBI—Robidoux, 132; GWRBI—Alfaro, Lyons, 16; SH—Green, 15; SF—Merrifield, 12; HP—Braggs, 10; BB—Magadan, 106; IBB—Smith, 11; SO—Cockrell, 137; SB—Jefferson, 39; CS—Espy, J. Gonzalez, Ramsey, 17.

(All Players—Listed Alphabetically)

| Player and Club | Pct. | G. | AB. | R. | H. | TB. | 2B. | 3B. | HR. | RBI. | GW. | SH. | SF. | HP. | BB. | Int. BB. | SO. | SB. | CS. |
|---|---|---|---|---|---|---|---|---|---|---|---|---|---|---|---|---|---|---|---|
| Adamczak, James, Jackson | 1.000 | 57 | 2 | 1 | 2 | 4 | 0 | 1 | 0 | 2 | 0 | 2 | 0 | 0 | 0 | 0 | 0 | 0 | 0 |
| Adams, John, Arkansas | .067 | 33 | 15 | 1 | 1 | 1 | 0 | 0 | 0 | 0 | 0 | 0 | 0 | 0 | 1 | 0 | 6 | 1 | 0 |
| Aldrete, Michael, Shreveport* | .333 | 127 | 441 | 80 | 147 | 226 | 32 | 1 | 15 | 77 | 12 | 2 | 4 | 0 | 94 | 9 | 57 | 16 | 7 |
| Alfaro, Jesus, El Paso | .299 | 131 | 508 | 70 | 152 | 231 | 25 | 3 | 16 | 112 | 16 | 2 | 6 | 3 | 56 | 0 | 77 | 3 | 6 |
| Allen, Robert, San Antonio | .204 | 35 | 98 | 7 | 20 | 26 | 0 | 0 | 2 | 13 | 2 | 2 | 3 | 0 | 12 | 0 | 14 | 0 | 2 |
| Amante, Thomas, Arkansas | .200 | 21 | 40 | 3 | 8 | 12 | 1 | 0 | 1 | 2 | 0 | 1 | 0 | 2 | 4 | 0 | 8 | 1 | 0 |
| Banning, Douglas, Midland | .000 | 10 | 2 | 0 | 0 | 0 | 0 | 0 | 0 | 0 | 0 | 0 | 0 | 0 | 0 | 0 | 2 | 0 | 0 |
| Bass, Barry, Tulsa | .000 | 43 | 4 | 4 | 0 | 0 | 0 | 0 | 0 | 0 | 0 | 0 | 0 | 0 | 0 | 0 | 1 | 1 | 0 |
| Beuerlein, John, El Paso | .250 | 41 | 124 | 22 | 31 | 39 | 5 | 0 | 1 | 8 | 1 | 1 | 0 | 1 | 26 | 0 | 33 | 2 | 1 |
| Bitker, Joseph, Beaumont | .235 | 16 | 17 | 2 | 4 | 6 | 2 | 0 | 0 | 1 | 1 | 4 | 0 | 0 | 1 | 0 | 4 | 0 | 0 |

| Player and Club | Pct. | G. | AB. | R. | H. | TB. | 2B. | 3B. | HR. | RBI. | GW. | SH. | SF. | HP. | BB. | Int. BB. | SO. | SB. | CS. |
|---|---|---|---|---|---|---|---|---|---|---|---|---|---|---|---|---|---|---|---|
| Bockus, Randy, Shreveport° | .325 | 28 | 40 | 4 | 13 | 14 | 1 | 0 | 0 | 9 | 0 | 3 | 1 | 0 | 2 | 0 | 7 | 0 | 0 |
| Boever, Joseph, Arkansas | .000 | 27 | 2 | 0 | 0 | 0 | 0 | 0 | 0 | 0 | 0 | 0 | 0 | 0 | 0 | 0 | 1 | 0 | 0 |
| Bonner, Mark, Midland | .222 | 32 | 99 | 14 | 22 | 37 | 3 | 0 | 4 | 13 | 1 | 0 | 0 | 1 | 19 | 0 | 29 | 3 | 1 |
| Booker, Roderick, Arkansas | .264 | 129 | 466 | 59 | 123 | 150 | 18 | 3 | 1 | 47 | 4 | 8 | 4 | 1 | 55 | 4 | 43 | 13 | 7 |
| Braggs, Glenn, El Paso | .310 | 117 | 448 | 105 | 139 | 233 | 26 | 4 | 20 | 103 | 12 | 0 | 4 | 10 | 68 | 4 | 77 | 20 | 7 |
| Brassil, Thomas, Beaumont | .281 | 106 | 377 | 48 | 106 | 144 | 12 | 1 | 8 | 45 | 5 | 3 | 3 | 2 | 22 | 1 | 53 | 2 | 1 |
| Brown, Kevin, Jackson° | .250 | 12 | 8 | 2 | 2 | 2 | 0 | 0 | 0 | 0 | 0 | 2 | 0 | 0 | 0 | 0 | 2 | 0 | 0 |
| Brunenkant, Barry, Tulsa | .299 | 102 | 348 | 35 | 104 | 147 | 11 | 4 | 8 | 41 | 5 | 4 | 2 | 0 | 53 | 4 | 51 | 3 | 4 |
| Bryant, John, El Paso | .000 | 14 | 1 | 0 | 0 | 0 | 0 | 0 | 0 | 0 | 0 | 0 | 0 | 0 | 0 | 0 | 1 | 0 | 0 |
| Buonantony, Richard, Arkansas | .143 | 27 | 35 | 2 | 5 | 6 | 1 | 0 | 0 | 4 | 1 | 2 | 1 | 0 | 1 | 0 | 16 | 0 | 0 |
| Burns, Daniel, El Paso | .000 | 15 | 1 | 0 | 0 | 0 | 0 | 0 | 0 | 0 | 0 | 0 | 0 | 0 | 0 | 0 | 1 | 0 | 0 |
| Burns, Thomas, Jackson | .000 | 31 | 3 | 0 | 0 | 0 | 0 | 0 | 0 | 0 | 0 | 0 | 0 | 0 | 0 | 0 | 1 | 0 | 0 |
| Carlucci, Anthony, Tulsa | .233 | 11 | 30 | 1 | 7 | 11 | 1 | 0 | 1 | 2 | 0 | 0 | 0 | 0 | 3 | 0 | 10 | 0 | 1 |
| Carreon, Mark, Jackson | .313 | 123 | 447 | 96 | 140 | 191 | 23 | 5 | 6 | 51 | 4 | 3 | 4 | 6 | 87 | 3 | 32 | 23 | 6 |
| Cartwright, Alan, El Paso° | .314 | 125 | 475 | 82 | 149 | 225 | 35 | 4 | 11 | 74 | 7 | 1 | 5 | 3 | 48 | 4 | 58 | 12 | 15 |
| Castro, Edgar, Tulsa° | .193 | 33 | 83 | 7 | 16 | 27 | 2 | 0 | 3 | 6 | 1 | 1 | 1 | 0 | 13 | 1 | 34 | 0 | 1 |
| Castro, Frank, Beaumont | .195 | 71 | 220 | 21 | 43 | 72 | 12 | 1 | 5 | 19 | 3 | 3 | 0 | 0 | 17 | 2 | 43 | 1 | 1 |
| Cataline, Daniel, San Antonio | .216 | 99 | 301 | 34 | 65 | 102 | 10 | 0 | 9 | 34 | 1 | 1 | 0 | 1 | 39 | 4 | 90 | 2 | 2 |
| Chapman, Christopher, San Antonio° | .200 | 22 | 70 | 12 | 14 | 23 | 3 | 0 | 2 | 6 | 1 | 0 | 2 | 1 | 11 | 2 | 11 | 0 | 1 |
| Cherry, Michael, San Antonio | .000 | 20 | 9 | 1 | 0 | 0 | 0 | 0 | 0 | 0 | 0 | 0 | 0 | 0 | 0 | 0 | 2 | 0 | 0 |
| Childers, Jeffrey, Beaumont | .000 | 24 | 4 | 0 | 0 | 0 | 0 | 0 | 0 | 0 | 0 | 1 | 0 | 0 | 0 | 0 | 2 | 0 | 0 |
| Chmil, Stephen, San Antonio | .197 | 26 | 66 | 10 | 13 | 14 | 1 | 0 | 0 | 4 | 0 | 0 | 0 | 0 | 10 | 0 | 13 | 3 | 0 |
| Clark, Robert, Tulsa° | .000 | 27 | 2 | 0 | 0 | 0 | 0 | 0 | 0 | 0 | 0 | 0 | 0 | 0 | 1 | 0 | 0 | 0 | 0 |
| Clark, Terry, Arkansas | .077 | 42 | 13 | 0 | 1 | 1 | 0 | 0 | 0 | 0 | 0 | 1 | 0 | 0 | 1 | 0 | 4 | 0 | 0 |
| Clements, David, Arkansas | .205 | 26 | 88 | 10 | 18 | 27 | 6 | 0 | 1 | 9 | 0 | 1 | 2 | 0 | 4 | 0 | 24 | 1 | 0 |
| Coatney, Rickey, Tulsa | .000 | 8 | 1 | 0 | 0 | 0 | 0 | 0 | 0 | 0 | 0 | 0 | 0 | 0 | 0 | 0 | 1 | 0 | 0 |
| Cochrane, David, Jackson | .223 | 33 | 103 | 14 | 23 | 36 | 1 | 0 | 4 | 20 | 0 | 1 | 3 | 0 | 20 | 3 | 45 | 0 | 2 |
| Cockrell, Alan, Shreveport | .253 | 126 | 455 | 53 | 115 | 179 | 25 | 3 | 11 | 68 | 6 | 3 | 2 | 3 | 54 | 2 | 137 | 12 | 3 |
| Coleman, Rickey, Beaumont | .281 | 111 | 449 | 75 | 126 | 145 | 11 | 4 | 0 | 29 | 5 | 6 | 2 | 2 | 32 | 2 | 51 | 22 | 7 |
| Corman, David, Beaumont | .281 | 125 | 399 | 49 | 112 | 147 | 18 | 4 | 3 | 50 | 4 | 5 | 5 | 2 | 62 | 0 | 65 | 14 | 9 |
| Crews, Lawrence, Shreveport | .080 | 21 | 25 | 1 | 2 | 4 | 0 | 1 | 0 | 0 | 0 | 6 | 0 | 0 | 3 | 0 | 9 | 0 | 0 |
| Crum, George, Tulsa | .235 | 59 | 213 | 35 | 50 | 67 | 6 | 1 | 3 | 12 | 1 | 2 | 0 | 0 | 30 | 0 | 42 | 12 | 8 |
| Cruz, Juan, Midland | .267 | 37 | 105 | 19 | 28 | 36 | 8 | 0 | 0 | 17 | 3 | 2 | 2 | 0 | 24 | 0 | 14 | 4 | 3 |
| Darkis, William, Tulsa | .285 | 86 | 330 | 36 | 94 | 168 | 20 | 3 | 16 | 54 | 5 | 0 | 3 | 3 | 21 | 0 | 74 | 2 | 4 |
| Davis, Douglas, Tulsa | .153 | 42 | 118 | 10 | 18 | 32 | 2 | 0 | 4 | 11 | 3 | 3 | 1 | 0 | 10 | 0 | 31 | 1 | 2 |
| Davis, Douglas, Midland | .258 | 79 | 252 | 26 | 65 | 94 | 11 | 0 | 6 | 29 | 3 | 7 | 1 | 2 | 20 | 2 | 48 | 2 | 1 |
| Davis, Kevin, Midland | .263 | 100 | 354 | 47 | 93 | 138 | 19 | 1 | 8 | 42 | 3 | 4 | 3 | 2 | 28 | 0 | 64 | 7 | 10 |
| Debus, Jon, San Antonio | .287 | 110 | 390 | 49 | 112 | 160 | 23 | 2 | 7 | 64 | 6 | 3 | 3 | 2 | 43 | 0 | 60 | 2 | 2 |
| Denby, Darryl, Jackson | .197 | 84 | 229 | 25 | 45 | 75 | 15 | 0 | 5 | 20 | 2 | 1 | 3 | 2 | 13 | 0 | 52 | 2 | 2 |
| Diaz, Edgar, El Paso | .267 | 132 | 501 | 90 | 134 | 156 | 14 | 4 | 0 | 55 | 3 | 4 | 5 | 2 | 62 | 0 | 47 | 21 | 7 |
| Dougherty, Mark, Arkansas | .264 | 126 | 421 | 51 | 111 | 142 | 14 | 1 | 5 | 43 | 2 | 13 | 5 | 1 | 41 | 2 | 71 | 22 | 7 |
| Doughty, Jamie, Tulsa | .192 | 45 | 125 | 14 | 24 | 34 | 4 | 0 | 2 | 9 | 0 | 5 | 2 | 1 | 14 | 0 | 33 | 4 | 4 |
| Dunne, Michael, Arkansas | .125 | 23 | 24 | 2 | 3 | 4 | 1 | 0 | 0 | 0 | 0 | 0 | 0 | 0 | 4 | 0 | 11 | 0 | 1 |
| Eichhorn, David, San Antonio | .333 | 54 | 3 | 0 | 1 | 1 | 0 | 0 | 0 | 0 | 0 | 0 | 0 | 0 | 0 | 0 | 1 | 0 | 0 |
| Elster, Kevin, Jackson | .257 | 59 | 214 | 30 | 55 | 74 | 13 | 0 | 2 | 22 | 4 | 0 | 0 | 2 | 19 | 1 | 27 | 2 | 3 |
| Embser, Richard, Arkansas | .000 | 6 | 1 | 0 | 0 | 0 | 0 | 0 | 0 | 0 | 0 | 0 | 0 | 0 | 0 | 0 | 0 | 0 | 0 |
| Epple, Thomas, Arkansas† | .143 | 10 | 7 | 0 | 1 | 1 | 0 | 0 | 0 | 1 | 0 | 2 | 0 | 0 | 1 | 0 | 2 | 0 | 0 |
| Espy, Cecil, San Antonio† | .280 | 124 | 461 | 64 | 129 | 174 | 24 | 3 | 5 | 49 | 5 | 4 | 3 | 2 | 47 | 1 | 59 | 20 | 17 |
| Felice, Jason, Jackson | .260 | 127 | 416 | 51 | 108 | 161 | 15 | 4 | 10 | 67 | 5 | 1 | 10 | 2 | 39 | 5 | 90 | 7 | 5 |
| Ferran, George, Shreveport | .222 | 6 | 9 | 1 | 2 | 2 | 0 | 0 | 0 | 1 | 0 | 1 | 0 | 0 | 2 | 0 | 3 | 0 | 0 |
| Foussianes, George, Tulsa | .266 | 56 | 188 | 35 | 50 | 91 | 12 | 1 | 9 | 30 | 4 | 1 | 0 | 3 | 26 | 1 | 49 | 2 | 3 |
| Francis, Thomas, Shreveport° | .265 | 92 | 257 | 30 | 68 | 93 | 10 | 3 | 3 | 33 | 4 | 0 | 3 | 2 | 11 | 1 | 26 | 3 | 4 |
| Fryer, Paul, Shreveport | .241 | 39 | 133 | 14 | 32 | 45 | 8 | 1 | 1 | 4 | 1 | 1 | 0 | 1 | 10 | 1 | 29 | 5 | 0 |
| Fultz, William, Jackson | .125 | 8 | 8 | 0 | 1 | 1 | 0 | 0 | 0 | 0 | 1 | 0 | 3 | 0 | 0 | 1 | 0 | 3 | 0 |
| Galvez, Balvino, San Antonio | .259 | 27 | 27 | 2 | 7 | 7 | 0 | 0 | 0 | 4 | 1 | 4 | 0 | 0 | 1 | 0 | 7 | 0 | 0 |
| Gauntlett, Todd, San Antonio | .224 | 64 | 192 | 21 | 43 | 58 | 7 | 1 | 2 | 23 | 5 | 3 | 1 | 1 | 19 | 1 | 23 | 1 | 0 |
| Geren, Robert, Arkansas | .225 | 103 | 315 | 38 | 71 | 106 | 18 | 1 | 5 | 40 | 10 | 7 | 5 | 5 | 31 | 2 | 74 | 3 | 1 |
| Gergen, Robert, Tulsa | .271 | 89 | 295 | 34 | 80 | 132 | 30 | 2 | 6 | 29 | 3 | 5 | 1 | 3 | 26 | 8 | 61 | 5 | 5 |
| Gibbons, Jim Montgomery, El Paso° | .302 | 63 | 169 | 31 | 51 | 66 | 8 | 2 | 1 | 19 | 1 | 5 | 1 | 1 | 41 | 2 | 17 | 10 | 7 |
| Gile, Mark, Tulsa° | .199 | 127 | 433 | 47 | 86 | 104 | 12 | 3 | 0 | 38 | 1 | 6 | 1 | 1 | 51 | 3 | 71 | 11 | 8 |
| Gill, Gary, Arkansas | .164 | 29 | 61 | 4 | 10 | 15 | 3 | 1 | 0 | 6 | 0 | 0 | 0 | 0 | 8 | 2 | 17 | 0 | 0 |
| Glynn, Dennis, Jackson | .201 | 70 | 169 | 13 | 34 | 39 | 3 | 1 | 0 | 12 | 1 | 4 | 1 | 1 | 15 | 1 | 42 | 0 | 0 |
| Gonzalez, Jose, San Antonio | .306 | 128 | 448 | 82 | 137 | 210 | 22 | 6 | 13 | 62 | 2 | 1 | 3 | 4 | 60 | 4 | 80 | 34 | 17 |
| Gonzalez, Otto, Tulsa | .226 | 28 | 84 | 8 | 19 | 23 | 1 | 0 | 1 | 14 | 2 | 1 | 0 | 0 | 11 | 0 | 14 | 0 | 4 |
| Graham, Everett, Shreveport° | .266 | 130 | 451 | 74 | 120 | 186 | 17 | 5 | 13 | 64 | 10 | 4 | 3 | 3 | 54 | 4 | 61 | 15 | 7 |
| Graves, Joseph, Jackson | .167 | 50 | 6 | 0 | 1 | 1 | 0 | 0 | 0 | 0 | 0 | 2 | 0 | 0 | 0 | 0 | 4 | 0 | 0 |
| Green, Gary, Beaumont | .257 | 119 | 409 | 44 | 105 | 127 | 17 | 1 | 1 | 51 | 7 | 15 | 4 | 1 | 27 | 2 | 54 | 8 | 7 |
| Hamilton, Jeffrey, San Antonio | .332 | 101 | 347 | 48 | 125 | 184 | 14 | 3 | 13 | 59 | 8 | 1 | 2 | 0 | 28 | 6 | 52 | 1 | 2 |
| Hardgrave, Eric, Beaumont | .258 | 46 | 155 | 23 | 40 | 66 | 9 | 1 | 5 | 26 | 2 | 1 | 1 | 5 | 15 | 4 | 31 | 2 | 0 |
| Hartshorn, Kyle, Jackson° | .000 | 3 | 4 | 0 | 0 | 0 | 0 | 0 | 0 | 0 | 0 | 0 | 0 | 0 | 0 | 0 | 2 | 0 | 0 |
| Hartsock, Brian, Midland° | .318 | 50 | 179 | 43 | 57 | 115 | 15 | 2 | 13 | 32 | 2 | 3 | 0 | 0 | 29 | 2 | 36 | 1 | 2 |
| Harvey, Kenneth, San Antonio | .225 | 85 | 249 | 35 | 56 | 66 | 8 | 1 | 0 | 21 | 3 | 7 | 3 | 5 | 37 | 0 | 42 | 11 | 6 |
| Hayes, Ben, Arkansas | .333 | 23 | 6 | 1 | 2 | 2 | 0 | 0 | 0 | 1 | 0 | 2 | 0 | 0 | 0 | 0 | 3 | 0 | 0 |
| Heath, David, Midland | .309 | 98 | 362 | 49 | 112 | 171 | 21 | 1 | 12 | 54 | 7 | 1 | 1 | 1 | 21 | 0 | 62 | 1 | 1 |
| Hensley, Charles, Shreveport° | .000 | 13 | 1 | 0 | 0 | 0 | 0 | 0 | 0 | 0 | 0 | 0 | 0 | 0 | 1 | 0 | 1 | 0 | 0 |
| Heuer, Mark, San Antonio | .053 | 25 | 19 | 2 | 1 | 1 | 0 | 0 | 0 | 0 | 0 | 6 | 0 | 0 | 3 | 0 | 9 | 0 | 0 |
| Hillegas, Shawn, San Antonio | .100 | 23 | 10 | 1 | 1 | 1 | 0 | 0 | 0 | 0 | 0 | 0 | 0 | 0 | 3 | 0 | 4 | 0 | 0 |
| Hummel, Dean, Shreveport° | .250 | 11 | 8 | 1 | 2 | 5 | 0 | 0 | 1 | 1 | 0 | 0 | 0 | 0 | 2 | 0 | 2 | 0 | 0 |
| Huppert, David, El Paso | .227 | 96 | 309 | 46 | 70 | 101 | 14 | 1 | 5 | 34 | 3 | 10 | 3 | 2 | 63 | 0 | 89 | 3 | 9 |
| Jefferson, Stanley, Jackson† | .277 | 133 | 524 | 97 | 145 | 202 | 21 | 6 | 8 | 30 | 8 | 5 | 0 | 1 | 72 | 2 | 79 | 39 | 16 |
| Jirschele, Michael, Tulsa | .261 | 23 | 88 | 15 | 23 | 32 | 4 | 1 | 1 | 6 | 1 | 1 | 0 | 5 | 12 | 1 | 15 | 4 | 1 |
| Johnston, Jody, San Antonio | .250 | 26 | 4 | 0 | 1 | 1 | 0 | 0 | 0 | 0 | 0 | 0 | 0 | 0 | 1 | 0 | 3 | 0 | 0 |
| Jones, James, Beaumont | .200 | 16 | 10 | 2 | 2 | 2 | 0 | 0 | 0 | 0 | 0 | 0 | 1 | 0 | 0 | 0 | 5 | 0 | 0 |
| Jones, Ross, Jackson | .143 | 19 | 63 | 4 | 9 | 10 | 1 | 0 | 0 | 6 | 0 | 0 | 0 | 0 | 12 | 1 | 18 | 0 | 2 |
| Kable, David, Arkansas° | .251 | 56 | 187 | 34 | 47 | 90 | 8 | 1 | 11 | 34 | 4 | 0 | 1 | 4 | 34 | 4 | 48 | 0 | 2 |
| Kaull, Kurtis, Arkansas | .232 | 29 | 56 | 3 | 13 | 16 | 3 | 0 | 0 | 3 | 1 | 1 | 1 | 3 | 0 | 10 | 0 | 1 | |
| Key, Gregory, Midland | .215 | 94 | 261 | 39 | 56 | 76 | 12 | 1 | 2 | 25 | 2 | 6 | 4 | 2 | 30 | 1 | 66 | 9 | 9 |
| King, Eric, Shreveport | .100 | 15 | 20 | 1 | 2 | 2 | 0 | 0 | 0 | 0 | 0 | 4 | 0 | 0 | 1 | 0 | 10 | 0 | 0 |
| Klein, Larry, Tulsa | .273 | 44 | 161 | 15 | 44 | 61 | 6 | 1 | 3 | 20 | 3 | 4 | 2 | 5 | 9 | 0 | 32 | 2 | 1 |
| Klipstein, David, El Paso | .333 | 94 | 396 | 92 | 132 | 159 | 19 | 1 | 2 | 40 | 3 | 3 | 4 | 5 | 42 | 0 | 44 | 14 | 13 |
| Kockenmeister, Ted, Beaumont° | .000 | 7 | 1 | 0 | 0 | 0 | 0 | 0 | 0 | 0 | 0 | 0 | 0 | 0 | 0 | 0 | 0 | 0 | 0 |
| Kutsukos, Peter, Beaumont | .333 | 47 | 6 | 0 | 2 | 2 | 0 | 0 | 0 | 0 | 0 | 0 | 0 | 0 | 0 | 0 | 0 | 0 | 0 |

| Player and Club | Pct. | G. | AB. | R. | H. | TB. | 2B. | 3B. | HR. | RBI. | GW. | SH. | SF. | HP. | BB. | Int. BB. | SO. | SB. | CS. |
|---|---|---|---|---|---|---|---|---|---|---|---|---|---|---|---|---|---|---|---|
| Lane, Eric, Shreveport | .202 | 66 | 198 | 12 | 40 | 52 | 6 | 0 | 2 | 14 | 2 | 1 | 2 | 2 | 12 | 1 | 40 | 2 | 2 |
| Ledbetter, Jeffrey, Arkansas° | .255 | 79 | 231 | 34 | 59 | 98 | 9 | 3 | 8 | 37 | 8 | 0 | 5 | 1 | 41 | 4 | 54 | 4 | 4 |
| Lindeman, James, Arkansas | .282 | 128 | 450 | 54 | 127 | 199 | 30 | 6 | 10 | 63 | 5 | 2 | 3 | 6 | 41 | 1 | 82 | 11 | 13 |
| Long, Donald, Shreveport† | .190 | 27 | 84 | 7 | 16 | 25 | 3 | 0 | 2 | 6 | 0 | 1 | 1 | 2 | 15 | 1 | 25 | 1 | 2 |
| Lovelace, Vance, San Antonio° | .333 | 7 | 3 | 0 | 1 | 1 | 0 | 0 | 0 | 0 | 0 | 0 | 0 | 0 | 0 | 0 | 1 | 0 | 0 |
| Lozado, William, Arkansas | .276 | 44 | 116 | 15 | 32 | 39 | 5 | 1 | 0 | 16 | 3 | 2 | 2 | 0 | 20 | 1 | 25 | 0 | 0 |
| Lundgren, Kurt, Jackson | .000 | 22 | 22 | 0 | 0 | 0 | 0 | 0 | 0 | 0 | 0 | 4 | 0 | 0 | 2 | 0 | 7 | 0 | 0 |
| Lusted, Charles, Shreveport | .067 | 19 | 15 | 0 | 1 | 1 | 0 | 0 | 0 | 0 | 0 | 2 | 0 | 0 | 2 | 0 | 8 | 0 | 1 |
| Lyons, Barry, Jackson | .307 | 126 | 486 | 69 | 149 | 228 | 34 | 6 | 11 | 108 | 16 | 0 | 3 | 5 | 25 | 2 | 67 | 3 | 0 |
| Mace, Jeffrey, Tulsa | .231 | 125 | 433 | 50 | 100 | 157 | 18 | 3 | 11 | 51 | 2 | 6 | 6 | 5 | 28 | 3 | 68 | 6 | 5 |
| Mack, Shane, Beaumont | .260 | 125 | 430 | 59 | 112 | 159 | 23 | 3 | 6 | 55 | 3 | 7 | 1 | 3 | 38 | 2 | 89 | 12 | 5 |
| Madril, Michael, Midland† | .271 | 81 | 292 | 46 | 79 | 95 | 9 | 2 | 1 | 21 | 1 | 2 | 1 | 4 | 35 | 0 | 37 | 10 | 10 |
| Magadan, David, Jackson° | .309 | 134 | 466 | 84 | 144 | 166 | 22 | 0 | 0 | 76 | 9 | 4 | 1 | 5 | 106 | 2 | 57 | 0 | 3 |
| Martin, John, Arkansas | .056 | 26 | 18 | 4 | 1 | 1 | 0 | 0 | 0 | 0 | 0 | 2 | 0 | 0 | 1 | 0 | 7 | 0 | 0 |
| Mason, Martin, Arkansas | 1.000 | 13 | 1 | 0 | 1 | 1 | 0 | 0 | 0 | 0 | 0 | 1 | 0 | 0 | 0 | 0 | 0 | 0 | 0 |
| Mattson, Kurt, Shreveport | .000 | 53 | 5 | 0 | 0 | 0 | 0 | 0 | 0 | 0 | 0 | 1 | 0 | 0 | 0 | 0 | 3 | 0 | 0 |
| May, Scott, San Antonio | .087 | 26 | 23 | 2 | 2 | 2 | 0 | 0 | 0 | 2 | 0 | 7 | 0 | 0 | 3 | 0 | 9 | 0 | 1 |
| Mayberry, Gregory, San Antonio° | .000 | 8 | 6 | 0 | 0 | 0 | 0 | 0 | 0 | 0 | 0 | 0 | 0 | 0 | 0 | 0 | 4 | 0 | 0 |
| McClain, Michael, Beaumont | .250 | 27 | 24 | 1 | 6 | 6 | 0 | 0 | 0 | 0 | 0 | 1 | 0 | 1 | 0 | 0 | 7 | 0 | 0 |
| McCulla, Henry, Arkansas | .214 | 7 | 14 | 3 | 3 | 5 | 0 | 1 | 0 | 0 | 0 | 0 | 0 | 0 | 1 | 0 | 2 | 0 | 0 |
| McKnight, Jonathan, Shreveport | .000 | 5 | 7 | 1 | 0 | 0 | 0 | 0 | 0 | 0 | 0 | 2 | 0 | 0 | 0 | 0 | 5 | 0 | 0 |
| McLemore, Mark, Midland† | .271 | 117 | 458 | 80 | 124 | 159 | 17 | 6 | 2 | 46 | 3 | 6 | 3 | 1 | 66 | 4 | 59 | 31 | 16 |
| McPhail, Marlin, Jackson | .229 | 66 | 166 | 17 | 38 | 48 | 4 | 3 | 0 | 10 | 1 | 2 | 0 | 0 | 20 | 0 | 36 | 0 | 2 |
| Meagher, Adrian, San Antonio | .000 | 45 | 7 | 0 | 0 | 0 | 0 | 0 | 0 | 0 | 0 | 1 | 0 | 0 | 0 | 0 | 4 | 0 | 0 |
| Mejia, Oscar, Tulsa | .347 | 31 | 98 | 19 | 34 | 41 | 5 | 1 | 0 | 6 | 0 | 1 | 0 | 1 | 12 | 1 | 2 | 1 | 1 |
| Merrifield, Billie, Midland | .280 | 133 | 507 | 77 | 142 | 221 | 28 | 3 | 15 | 83 | 4 | 4 | 12 | 0 | 49 | 1 | 49 | 5 | 4 |
| Meyer, Joe, El Paso | .304 | 131 | 506 | 79 | 154 | 286 | 17 | 2 | 37 | 123 | 12 | 1 | 5 | 5 | 41 | 6 | 92 | 1 | 2 |
| Miller, Edward, Beaumont† | .222 | 52 | 158 | 20 | 35 | 46 | 7 | 2 | 0 | 11 | 0 | 1 | 2 | 3 | 14 | 0 | 32 | 10 | 2 |
| Miller, Keith, Jackson | .224 | 46 | 165 | 17 | 37 | 56 | 8 | 1 | 3 | 22 | 2 | 1 | 1 | 1 | 12 | 0 | 38 | 8 | 1 |
| Miller, Stephen, Shreveport° | .204 | 113 | 362 | 29 | 74 | 88 | 7 | 2 | 1 | 32 | 2 | 3 | 5 | 3 | 40 | 7 | 47 | 5 | 4 |
| Milligan, Randy, Jackson | .309 | 119 | 391 | 60 | 121 | 186 | 22 | 2 | 13 | 77 | 8 | 1 | 4 | 4 | 53 | 5 | 78 | 11 | 6 |
| Mills, Gotay, Arkansas | .258 | 89 | 236 | 39 | 61 | 89 | 7 | 3 | 5 | 21 | 2 | 4 | 0 | 0 | 31 | 1 | 39 | 14 | 5 |
| Mills, Michael, Beaumont | .150 | 26 | 20 | 1 | 3 | 3 | 0 | 0 | 0 | 1 | 0 | 2 | 0 | 0 | 5 | 0 | 10 | 0 | 0 |
| Montgomery, Reginald, Midland | .289 | 112 | 450 | 57 | 130 | 221 | 23 | 1 | 22 | 101 | 10 | 0 | 9 | 2 | 25 | 6 | 65 | 1 | 1 |
| Morales, Joseph, El Paso† | .133 | 6 | 15 | 3 | 2 | 2 | 0 | 0 | 0 | 1 | 0 | 0 | 0 | 0 | 4 | 0 | 1 | 0 | 0 |
| Moreno, Jaime, Beaumont | .180 | 20 | 50 | 7 | 9 | 9 | 0 | 0 | 0 | 3 | 0 | 0 | 1 | 2 | 8 | 1 | 0 | 0 | 0 |
| Morlock, Allen, Arkansas | .120 | 27 | 25 | 2 | 3 | 4 | 1 | 0 | 0 | 0 | 0 | 5 | 0 | 0 | 2 | 0 | 11 | 0 | 0 |
| Moronko, Jeffrey, Tulsa | .262 | 63 | 233 | 31 | 61 | 102 | 10 | 2 | 9 | 36 | 3 | 2 | 3 | 0 | 27 | 2 | 56 | 4 | 3 |
| Mulholland, Terence, Shreveport | .065 | 26 | 31 | 1 | 2 | 2 | 0 | 0 | 0 | 2 | 1 | 4 | 0 | 0 | 1 | 0 | 22 | 0 | 0 |
| Murphy, Daniel, Midland° | .300 | 36 | 120 | 26 | 36 | 47 | 5 | 0 | 2 | 19 | 4 | 0 | 1 | 0 | 29 | 1 | 19 | 1 | 0 |
| Murray, Scott, Jackson | .143 | 30 | 7 | 1 | 1 | 1 | 0 | 0 | 0 | 0 | 0 | 2 | 0 | 0 | 0 | 0 | 4 | 0 | 0 |
| Myers, Randall, Jackson° | .250 | 19 | 28 | 4 | 7 | 8 | 1 | 0 | 0 | 1 | 0 | 1 | 0 | 0 | 1 | 0 | 9 | 0 | 0 |
| Nandin, Robert, El Paso† | .250 | 20 | 48 | 12 | 12 | 15 | 3 | 0 | 0 | 8 | 2 | 0 | 2 | 1 | 12 | 0 | 2 | 2 | 1 |
| Nanni, Tito, Midland° | .263 | 53 | 167 | 23 | 44 | 62 | 6 | 0 | 4 | 21 | 0 | 0 | 1 | 0 | 15 | 1 | 37 | 5 | 4 |
| Newsom, Gary, San Antonio | .249 | 68 | 249 | 36 | 62 | 75 | 7 | 0 | 2 | 24 | 1 | 6 | 0 | 0 | 27 | 0 | 27 | 10 | 2 |
| Nix, David, Jackson° | .224 | 77 | 246 | 33 | 55 | 80 | 11 | 1 | 4 | 30 | 2 | 1 | 3 | 0 | 30 | 4 | 34 | 3 | 1 |
| Nokes, Matthew, Shreveport° | .294 | 105 | 344 | 52 | 101 | 169 | 24 | 1 | 14 | 56 | 7 | 2 | 7 | 2 | 41 | 2 | 47 | 2 | 0 |
| Norman, Scott, Shreveport | .105 | 22 | 19 | 2 | 2 | 3 | 1 | 0 | 0 | 3 | 0 | 0 | 0 | 0 | 1 | 0 | 4 | 0 | 0 |
| North, Jay, Arkansas | .000 | 2 | 3 | 0 | 0 | 0 | 0 | 0 | 0 | 0 | 0 | 1 | 0 | 0 | 0 | 0 | 1 | 0 | 0 |
| Norton, Douglas, El Paso | .000 | 36 | 1 | 0 | 0 | 0 | 0 | 0 | 0 | 0 | 0 | 0 | 0 | 0 | 0 | 0 | 1 | 0 | 0 |
| Oliveras, Francisco, Beaumont | .333 | 7 | 3 | 0 | 1 | 1 | 0 | 0 | 0 | 0 | 0 | 0 | 0 | 0 | 1 | 0 | 1 | 0 | 0 |
| Olson, Gregory, Jackson | .270 | 69 | 211 | 21 | 57 | 67 | 7 | 0 | 1 | 32 | 2 | 3 | 2 | 1 | 23 | 1 | 20 | 1 | 3 |
| Ortiz, Javier, Tulsa | .247 | 86 | 304 | 47 | 75 | 108 | 12 | 3 | 5 | 31 | 3 | 0 | 1 | 4 | 52 | 2 | 75 | 11 | 3 |
| Owen, Timothy, Tulsa | .167 | 3 | 6 | 0 | 1 | 2 | 1 | 0 | 0 | 0 | 0 | 0 | 0 | 0 | 1 | 0 | 1 | 0 | 0 |
| Paciorek, James, El Paso | .290 | 36 | 138 | 37 | 40 | 58 | 7 | 1 | 3 | 22 | 4 | 1 | 2 | 3 | 19 | 0 | 20 | 6 | 1 |
| Pagnozzi, Thomas, Arkansas | .309 | 41 | 139 | 15 | 43 | 67 | 7 | 1 | 5 | 29 | 3 | 1 | 0 | 0 | 13 | 1 | 21 | 0 | 0 |
| Penigar, Charles Lee, Shreveport† | .224 | 103 | 357 | 39 | 80 | 94 | 8 | 0 | 2 | 21 | 2 | 6 | 1 | 1 | 33 | 1 | 107 | 20 | 10 |
| Pickett, Richard, Jackson° | .000 | 3 | 1 | 0 | 0 | 0 | 0 | 0 | 0 | 0 | 0 | 0 | 0 | 0 | 0 | 0 | 0 | 0 | 0 |
| Piper, Brian, San Antonio | .000 | 22 | 7 | 0 | 0 | 0 | 0 | 0 | 0 | 0 | 0 | 1 | 0 | 0 | 0 | 0 | 3 | 0 | 0 |
| Poston, Mark, Beaumont | .000 | 38 | 6 | 1 | 0 | 0 | 0 | 0 | 0 | 0 | 0 | 0 | 0 | 0 | 1 | 0 | 3 | 0 | 0 |
| Pott, Lawrence, Tulsa | .171 | 25 | 70 | 6 | 12 | 17 | 3 | 1 | 0 | 4 | 0 | 0 | 0 | 0 | 10 | 0 | 14 | 0 | 0 |
| Pruitt, Edwin, Jackson° | .000 | 52 | 4 | 0 | 0 | 0 | 0 | 0 | 0 | 0 | 0 | 0 | 0 | 0 | 0 | 0 | 0 | 0 | 0 |
| Psaltis, Spiro, Midland° | .000 | 45 | 4 | 1 | 0 | 0 | 0 | 0 | 0 | 0 | 0 | 0 | 0 | 0 | 1 | 0 | 3 | 0 | 0 |
| Purpura, Daniel, El Paso | .269 | 115 | 409 | 81 | 110 | 138 | 20 | 1 | 2 | 57 | 4 | 4 | 6 | 5 | 77 | 0 | 62 | 4 | 5 |
| Ramsey, Michael James, San Antonio | .238 | 106 | 365 | 47 | 87 | 105 | 7 | 4 | 1 | 23 | 3 | 2 | 1 | 0 | 41 | 4 | 73 | 17 | 17 |
| Randall, James, Midland† | .311 | 81 | 302 | 54 | 94 | 164 | 23 | 1 | 15 | 61 | 4 | 0 | 1 | 1 | 38 | 5 | 51 | 3 | 5 |
| Redfield, Joseph, Jackson | .137 | 39 | 73 | 12 | 10 | 17 | 4 | 0 | 1 | 5 | 0 | 2 | 0 | 0 | 15 | 0 | 23 | 0 | 0 |
| Reibel, Douglas, Midland° | .286 | 8 | 14 | 6 | 4 | 4 | 0 | 0 | 0 | 1 | 0 | 0 | 0 | 0 | 6 | 0 | 2 | 1 | 0 |
| Reitz, Kenneth, Tulsa | .222 | 45 | 126 | 13 | 28 | 50 | 4 | 0 | 6 | 17 | 1 | 1 | 2 | 0 | 11 | 1 | 29 | 1 | 1 |
| Rhodes, Michael, Arkansas° | .000 | 23 | 3 | 0 | 0 | 0 | 0 | 0 | 0 | 0 | 0 | 0 | 0 | 0 | 0 | 0 | 1 | 0 | 0 |
| Roberts, Scott, El Paso | .500 | 13 | 2 | 0 | 1 | 1 | 0 | 0 | 0 | 0 | 0 | 0 | 0 | 0 | 0 | 0 | 1 | 0 | 0 |
| Robidoux, William, El Paso° | .342 | 133 | 515 | 111 | 176 | 297 | 46 | 3 | 23 | 132 | 13 | 0 | 4 | 0 | 97 | 7 | 62 | 9 | 4 |
| Robinson, Michael, Arkansas | .000 | 1 | 2 | 0 | 0 | 0 | 0 | 0 | 0 | 0 | 0 | 0 | 0 | 0 | 0 | 0 | 1 | 0 | 0 |
| Robles, Ruben, Arkansas | .269 | 27 | 78 | 13 | 21 | 30 | 4 | 1 | 1 | 7 | 2 | 0 | 0 | 1 | 9 | 0 | 21 | 5 | 3 |
| Rodriguez, Angel, El Paso | .208 | 10 | 24 | 4 | 5 | 9 | 1 | 0 | 1 | 6 | 0 | 0 | 0 | 0 | 1 | 0 | 4 | 0 | 0 |
| Rodriguez, Jose, Arkansas† | .251 | 128 | 386 | 48 | 97 | 117 | 13 | 2 | 1 | 30 | 3 | 13 | 2 | 9 | 19 | 6 | 44 | 6 | 8 |
| Rodriguez, Rigo, Beaumont | .188 | 30 | 64 | 8 | 12 | 13 | 1 | 0 | 0 | 3 | 0 | 2 | 0 | 0 | 9 | 0 | 10 | 0 | 1 |
| Roman, Luis, Arkansas° | .100 | 52 | 10 | 4 | 1 | 1 | 0 | 0 | 0 | 1 | 0 | 0 | 0 | 0 | 0 | 0 | 1 | 0 | 1 |
| Ronan, Kernan, Shreveport | .167 | 29 | 6 | 0 | 1 | 1 | 0 | 0 | 0 | 0 | 0 | 1 | 0 | 0 | 0 | 0 | 0 | 0 | 0 |
| Ross, Carey, El Paso | .167 | 5 | 6 | 0 | 1 | 2 | 1 | 0 | 0 | 0 | 0 | 0 | 0 | 0 | 0 | 0 | 1 | 0 | 0 |
| Santiago, Benito, Beaumont | .298 | 101 | 372 | 55 | 111 | 154 | 16 | 6 | 5 | 52 | 4 | 8 | 3 | 2 | 16 | 1 | 59 | 12 | 2 |
| Schefsky, Steven, Beaumont | .000 | 21 | 2 | 0 | 0 | 0 | 0 | 0 | 0 | 0 | 0 | 1 | 0 | 0 | 0 | 0 | 1 | 0 | 0 |
| Schmidt, August, Shreveport | .290 | 12 | 31 | 3 | 9 | 11 | 2 | 0 | 0 | 2 | 1 | 1 | 0 | 0 | 11 | 0 | 5 | 1 | 0 |
| Schulte, Mark, Arkansas° | .278 | 46 | 151 | 16 | 42 | 53 | 7 | 2 | 0 | 20 | 1 | 1 | 3 | 1 | 8 | 1 | 13 | 1 | 0 |
| Sconiers, Daryl, Midland° | .224 | 15 | 58 | 7 | 13 | 22 | 6 | 0 | 1 | 10 | 0 | 0 | 0 | 0 | 7 | 0 | 13 | 0 | 0 |
| Scudder, William, San Antonio° | .400 | 27 | 5 | 0 | 2 | 3 | 1 | 0 | 0 | 0 | 0 | 0 | 0 | 0 | 0 | 0 | 3 | 0 | 0 |
| See, Laurence, San Antonio | .268 | 99 | 373 | 55 | 100 | 164 | 17 | 1 | 15 | 58 | 5 | 1 | 5 | 3 | 51 | 2 | 70 | 1 | 3 |
| Sferrazza, Matthew, El Paso | .179 | 24 | 78 | 14 | 14 | 17 | 3 | 0 | 0 | 9 | 1 | 2 | 0 | 0 | 17 | 1 | 11 | 8 | 1 |
| Sierra, Ruben, Tulsa† | .253 | 137 | 545 | 63 | 138 | 227 | 34 | 8 | 13 | 74 | 11 | 1 | 5 | 1 | 35 | 6 | 111 | 22 | 7 |
| Sierra, Ulises, Beaumont | .182 | 23 | 11 | 1 | 2 | 2 | 0 | 0 | 0 | 1 | 0 | 1 | 0 | 0 | 1 | 0 | 4 | 0 | 0 |
| Smith, Gregory, Beaumont° | .317 | 114 | 394 | 75 | 125 | 199 | 30 | 1 | 14 | 69 | 9 | 4 | 2 | 4 | 45 | 11 | 59 | 12 | 2 |
| Soff, Raymond, Arkansas | .000 | 19 | 1 | 0 | 0 | 0 | 0 | 0 | 0 | 0 | 0 | 0 | 0 | 0 | 0 | 0 | 0 | 0 | 0 |

| Player and Club | Pct. | G. | AB. | R. | H. | TB. | 2B. | 3B. | HR. | RBI. | GW. | SH. | SF. | HP. | BB. | Int. BB. | SO. | SB. | CS. |
|---|---|---|---|---|---|---|---|---|---|---|---|---|---|---|---|---|---|---|---|
| Stanicek, Stephen, Shreveport | .282 | 119 | 401 | 57 | 113 | 173 | 17 | 2 | 13 | 54 | 10 | 2 | 6 | 2 | 37 | 1 | 74 | 4 | 3 |
| Stanley, Michael, Tulsa | .309 | 46 | 165 | 24 | 51 | 70 | 10 | 0 | 3 | 17 | 1 | 1 | 1 | 2 | 24 | 0 | 18 | 6 | 2 |
| Steen, Gregory, Midland | .215 | 51 | 177 | 16 | 38 | 43 | 5 | 0 | 0 | 14 | 0 | 0 | 2 | 1 | 11 | 0 | 33 | 4 | 0 |
| Stephenson, Phillip, Midland° | .295 | 50 | 176 | 39 | 52 | 87 | 14 | 0 | 7 | 41 | 3 | 0 | 0 | 1 | 35 | 3 | 27 | 5 | 2 |
| Stryffeler, Daniel, Arkansas° | .301 | 58 | 183 | 35 | 55 | 83 | 13 | 3 | 3 | 27 | 3 | 1 | 1 | 1 | 15 | 2 | 26 | 4 | 3 |
| Szekely, Joseph, San Antonio° | .264 | 30 | 106 | 9 | 28 | 40 | 9 | 0 | 1 | 18 | 2 | 0 | 0 | 1 | 6 | 0 | 26 | 0 | 0 |
| Tanner, Edwin, Arkansas° | .280 | 123 | 414 | 52 | 116 | 149 | 18 | 3 | 3 | 38 | 6 | 4 | 4 | 2 | 29 | 4 | 26 | 4 | 2 |
| Thomas, Christopher, San Antonio° | .500 | 17 | 4 | 0 | 2 | 2 | 0 | 0 | 0 | 1 | 0 | 0 | 0 | 0 | 0 | 0 | 1 | 0 | 0 |
| Thomas, Jimmy, Beaumont | .200 | 16 | 50 | 4 | 10 | 14 | 4 | 0 | 0 | 4 | 0 | 1 | 0 | 0 | 8 | 0 | 16 | 1 | 0 |
| Thomas, Todd, Shreveport° | .227 | 79 | 211 | 35 | 48 | 60 | 8 | 2 | 0 | 16 | 2 | 3 | 0 | 5 | 32 | 0 | 37 | 10 | 8 |
| Thompson, Robert, Shreveport | .261 | 121 | 449 | 85 | 117 | 178 | 20 | 7 | 9 | 40 | 0 | 5 | 3 | 5 | 65 | 0 | 101 | 28 | 7 |
| Towers, Kevin, Beaumont | .000 | 7 | 1 | 0 | 0 | 0 | 0 | 0 | 0 | 0 | 0 | 0 | 0 | 0 | 1 | 0 | 0 | 0 | 0 |
| Tutt, Johnny, Beaumont | .315 | 120 | 454 | 59 | 143 | 181 | 19 | 2 | 5 | 67 | 10 | 1 | 3 | 2 | 39 | 1 | 61 | 12 | 8 |
| Vaughn, DeWayne, Jackson | .048 | 24 | 21 | 2 | 1 | 1 | 0 | 0 | 0 | 1 | 0 | 1 | 0 | 0 | 2 | 0 | 10 | 0 | 0 |
| Villaescusa, Fernando, Midland° | .205 | 14 | 39 | 4 | 8 | 10 | 2 | 0 | 0 | 4 | 0 | 1 | 0 | 1 | 0 | 0 | 6 | 0 | 0 |
| Vosberg, Edward, Beaumont° | .225 | 33 | 40 | 5 | 9 | 12 | 0 | 0 | 1 | 6 | 0 | 2 | 0 | 0 | 0 | 0 | 14 | 0 | 0 |
| Wallace, Timothy, Arkansas | .282 | 46 | 131 | 10 | 37 | 44 | 7 | 0 | 0 | 11 | 1 | 3 | 2 | 2 | 17 | 0 | 26 | 0 | 1 |
| Wasinger, Mark, Beaumont | .302 | 114 | 411 | 71 | 124 | 161 | 13 | 0 | 8 | 52 | 5 | 8 | 9 | 2 | 65 | 5 | 46 | 12 | 10 |
| Weissman, Craig, Jackson | .095 | 28 | 21 | 1 | 2 | 2 | 0 | 0 | 0 | 2 | 0 | 2 | 0 | 0 | 2 | 0 | 6 | 0 | 0 |
| White, Devon, Midland° | .296 | 70 | 260 | 52 | 77 | 107 | 10 | 4 | 4 | 35 | 2 | 3 | 6 | 6 | 35 | 2 | 46 | 38 | 8 |
| White, William, San Antonio | .205 | 54 | 127 | 16 | 26 | 29 | 3 | 0 | 0 | 11 | 3 | 1 | 1 | 0 | 20 | 1 | 29 | 3 | 1 |
| Williams, Reginald, San Antonio | .291 | 120 | 436 | 73 | 127 | 182 | 17 | 4 | 10 | 53 | 5 | 4 | 3 | 3 | 47 | 2 | 63 | 33 | 15 |
| Williamson, Mark, Beaumont | .333 | 42 | 6 | 0 | 2 | 3 | 1 | 0 | 0 | 2 | 0 | 0 | 0 | 0 | 0 | 0 | 0 | 0 | 0 |
| Wilmet, Paul, Arkansas | .000 | 9 | 1 | 0 | 0 | 0 | 0 | 0 | 0 | 0 | 0 | 0 | 0 | 0 | 0 | 0 | 1 | 0 | 0 |
| Wyatt, David, Jackson | .125 | 10 | 16 | 1 | 2 | 2 | 0 | 0 | 0 | 1 | 0 | 0 | 0 | 0 | 2 | 0 | 7 | 0 | 0 |
| Yokubaitis, Dan, Shreveport° | .000 | 35 | 3 | 0 | 0 | 0 | 0 | 0 | 0 | 0 | 0 | 0 | 0 | 0 | 0 | 0 | 3 | 0 | 0 |
| Young, John, Jackson° | .308 | 24 | 26 | 2 | 8 | 10 | 2 | 0 | 0 | 0 | 0 | 0 | 0 | 0 | 0 | 0 | 14 | 0 | 0 |

The following pitchers, listed alphabetically by club, with games in parentheses, had no plate appearances, primarily through use of designated hitters:

ARKANSAS—Shade, Michael (32); Thurberg, Thomas (6).

EL PASO—Aldrich, Jay (42); Barry, Eric (31); Beene, Andrew (2); Birkbeck, Michael (24); Bosio, Christopher (28); Candiotti Thomas (4); Ciardi, Mark (10); Fingers, Robert (16); Ford, David (3); Myers, Edward (32); Nieves, Juan (17); Plesac Daniel (25); Schroeck, Robert (27).

JACKSON—Lockenmeyer, Mark (3).

MIDLAND—Angulo, Kenneth (21); Bryden, Thomas (7); Cannon, Scott (8); Chadwick, Ray (10); Delzer, Edwin (29); Finch, Steven (3); Fischer, Todd (43); Gonzales, Julian (53); Kemmerling, Byron (26); Kipper, Robert (9); McKenzie, Douglas (26); Orozco, Jaime (6); Price, Bryan (12); Suehr, Scott (35); Timberlake, Donald (23); Wilburn, Fred (10).

SAN ANTONIO—Hamilton, Robert (1); Heredia, Hector (3).

SHREVEPORT—Alexander, Tommy (1); Bargerhuff, Brian (7); Murtha, Brian (2).

TULSA—Anderson, Scott (28); Hallgren, Tim (3); Harman, David (9); Henry, Dwayne (34); Hudson, Anthony (51); James, Duane (15); Johnson, Terrance (26); Killingsworth, Kirk (39); Kordish, Steve (7); Lachowicz, Allen (1); Reichard, Clyde (38); Taylor, William (20); Williams, Mitchell (6); Witt, Robert (11).

GRAND SLAM HOME RUNS—Alfaro, Braggs, Lyons, 2 each; Aldrete, Bonner, Booker, Brassil, Darkis, Espy, Gergen, O. Gonzalez, Hamilton, Heath, Key, Lindeman, Meyer, Montgomery, Nix, Robidoux, See, R. Sierra, Smith, Stephenson, Stryffeler, D. White, 1 each.

AWARDED FIRST BASE ON CATCHER'S INTERFERENCE—Mulholland (Lyons); Robidoux (Santiago).

## CLUB FIELDING

| Club | Pct. | G. | PO. | A. | E. | DP. | PB. | Club | Pct. | G. | PO. | A. | E. | DP. | PB. |
|---|---|---|---|---|---|---|---|---|---|---|---|---|---|---|---|
| Arkansas | .976 | 135 | 3444 | 1442 | 121 | 121 | 15 | Shreveport | .963 | 136 | 3502 | 1550 | 193 | 135 | 10 |
| El Paso | .970 | 136 | 3582 | 1626 | 162 | 143 | 24 | Beaumont | .963 | 136 | 3554 | 1651 | 199 | 128 | 21 |
| Jackson | .967 | 138 | 3555 | 1549 | 176 | 112 | 10 | San Antonio | .962 | 134 | 3488 | 1444 | 196 | 116 | 26 |
| Midland | .965 | 136 | 3547 | 1665 | 188 | 133 | 13 | Tulsa | .961 | 137 | 3563 | 1577 | 208 | 124 | 15 |

Triple Play—El Paso.

## INDIVIDUAL FIELDING

°Throws lefthanded

### FIRST BASEMEN

| Player and Club | Pct. | G. | PO. | A. | E. | DP. | Player and Club | Pct. | G. | PO. | A. | E. | DP. |
|---|---|---|---|---|---|---|---|---|---|---|---|---|---|
| Aldrete, Shreveport° | .992 | 88 | 795 | 35 | 7 | 74 | Meyer, El Paso | .978 | 30 | 252 | 15 | 6 | 28 |
| Bonner, Midland | .984 | 27 | 231 | 13 | 4 | 21 | Miller, Beaumont | .900 | 2 | 8 | 1 | 1 | 0 |
| Brassil, Beaumont | .988 | 30 | 238 | 14 | 3 | 18 | Milligan, Jackson | .986 | 85 | 726 | 49 | 11 | 60 |
| Brunenkant, Tulsa | .986 | 24 | 196 | 12 | 3 | 19 | Murphy, Midland° | .993 | 13 | 128 | 9 | 1 | 9 |
| Castro, Tulsa° | .985 | 31 | 228 | 27 | 4 | 25 | Ortiz, Tulsa | .981 | 17 | 149 | 8 | 3 | 11 |
| Cataline, San Antonio | .944 | 2 | 17 | 0 | 1 | 2 | Pagnozzi, Arkansas | 1.000 | 3 | 12 | 0 | 0 | 0 |
| Chapman, San Antonio | .990 | 22 | 182 | 13 | 2 | 17 | Pott, Tulsa | .983 | 7 | 53 | 5 | 1 | 4 |
| Clements, Arkansas | .990 | 26 | 192 | 9 | 2 | 25 | Randall, Midland° | .969 | 42 | 410 | 22 | 14 | 39 |
| Darkis, Tulsa | .990 | 10 | 97 | 2 | 1 | 7 | Redfield, Jackson | 1.000 | 15 | 82 | 4 | 0 | 8 |
| D. Davis, Tulsa | .973 | 20 | 137 | 7 | 4 | 10 | Reibel, Midland° | 1.000 | 3 | 25 | 3 | 0 | 1 |
| Debus, San Antonio | .991 | 13 | 109 | 5 | 1 | 7 | Reitz, Tulsa | 1.000 | 12 | 83 | 3 | 0 | 8 |
| Foussianes, Tulsa | 1.000 | 7 | 60 | 6 | 0 | 5 | ROBIDOUX, El Paso | .988 | 109 | 1025 | 68 | 13 | 102 |
| Geren, Arkansas | .986 | 21 | 124 | 12 | 2 | 8 | Rodriguez, Beaumont | 1.000 | 1 | 2 | 0 | 0 | 0 |
| Gergen, Tulsa | .991 | 26 | 208 | 18 | 2 | 14 | Santiago, Beaumont | 1.000 | 2 | 10 | 0 | 0 | 2 |
| Gibbons, El Paso° | 1.000 | 1 | 1 | 0 | 0 | 0 | Schulte, Arkansas° | .992 | 38 | 327 | 28 | 3 | 34 |
| Gonzalez, Tulsa | .750 | 1 | 2 | 1 | 1 | 0 | Sconiers, Midland° | .989 | 8 | 84 | 3 | 1 | 6 |
| Hardgrave, Beaumont | .979 | 40 | 354 | 20 | 8 | 35 | See, San Antonio | .985 | 99 | 879 | 57 | 14 | 80 |
| Kable, Arkansas° | .993 | 48 | 418 | 24 | 3 | 36 | Smith, Beaumont | .991 | 70 | 583 | 58 | 6 | 53 |
| Kaull, Arkansas | .974 | 13 | 68 | 7 | 2 | 5 | Stanicek, Shreveport | .976 | 53 | 495 | 29 | 13 | 46 |
| Ledbetter, Arkansas° | 1.000 | 5 | 19 | 4 | 0 | 1 | Stanley, Tulsa | .964 | 8 | 80 | 1 | 3 | 6 |
| Lyons, Jackson | .989 | 36 | 334 | 19 | 4 | 27 | Stephenson, Midland° | .991 | 36 | 316 | 25 | 3 | 29 |
| Magadan, Jackson | 1.000 | 2 | 19 | 1 | 0 | 2 | Tanner, Arkansas | 1.000 | 1 | 2 | 0 | 0 | 0 |
| McCulla, Arkansas | 1.000 | 2 | 13 | 0 | 0 | 3 | Thomas, Beaumont | .950 | 11 | 90 | 6 | 5 | 3 |
| McPhail, Jackson | 1.000 | 8 | 60 | 3 | 0 | 6 | Villaescusa, Midland | 1.000 | 1 | 8 | 0 | 0 | 0 |
| Merrifield, Midland | .992 | 12 | 119 | 3 | 1 | 10 | White, San Antonio | .944 | 4 | 15 | 2 | 1 | 1 |

Triple Play—Robidoux.

## SECOND BASEMEN

| Player and Club | Pct. | G. | PO. | A. | E. | DP. | Player and Club | Pct. | G. | PO. | A. | E. | DP. |
|---|---|---|---|---|---|---|---|---|---|---|---|---|---|
| Alfaro, El Paso | 1.000 | 2 | 2 | 2 | 0 | 0 | McPhail, Jackson | .963 | 22 | 52 | 51 | 4 | 10 |
| Allen, San Antonio | .936 | 21 | 34 | 54 | 6 | 9 | Mejia, Tulsa | 1.000 | 4 | 6 | 10 | 0 | 4 |
| Brassil, Beaumont | .895 | 9 | 13 | 21 | 4 | 3 | Miller, Jackson | .968 | 43 | 108 | 131 | 8 | 21 |
| Chmil, San Antonio | 1.000 | 12 | 13 | 24 | 0 | 3 | Morales, El Paso | .833 | 3 | 5 | 5 | 2 | 2 |
| Corman, Beaumont | .969 | 113 | 261 | 333 | 19 | 76 | Moronko, Tulsa | .923 | 3 | 3 | 9 | 1 | 1 |
| Cruz, Midland | .950 | 19 | 40 | 56 | 5 | 15 | Nandin, El Paso | .938 | 15 | 27 | 34 | 4 | 9 |
| Dougherty, Arkansas | .981 | 119 | 251 | 321 | 11 | 70 | Newsom, San Antonio | .971 | 37 | 77 | 88 | 5 | 26 |
| Doughty, Tulsa | 1.000 | 2 | 1 | 13 | 0 | 0 | Nix, Jackson | .953 | 65 | 142 | 183 | 16 | 42 |
| Foussianes, Tulsa | .778 | 1 | 3 | 4 | 2 | 0 | Purpura, El Paso | .971 | 105 | 228 | 313 | 16 | 76 |
| Gauntlett, San Antonio | 1.000 | 1 | 1 | 2 | 0 | 0 | Reitz, Tulsa | .920 | 9 | 10 | 13 | 2 | 1 |
| Gile, Tulsa | .964 | 126 | 234 | 386 | 23 | 79 | Rodriguez, Beaumont | 1.000 | 1 | 0 | 3 | 0 | 0 |
| Glynn, Jackson | .959 | 17 | 34 | 36 | 3 | 6 | Sferrazza, El Paso | .952 | 16 | 37 | 43 | 4 | 9 |
| Harvey, San Antonio | .966 | 74 | 158 | 207 | 13 | 36 | Steen, Midland | .986 | 16 | 24 | 47 | 1 | 14 |
| Jirschele, Tulsa | 1.000 | 1 | 1 | 3 | 0 | 1 | Tanner, Arkansas | .956 | 11 | 20 | 23 | 2 | 7 |
| Klein, Tulsa | 1.000 | 5 | 6 | 13 | 0 | 3 | Thomas, Shreveport | .943 | 19 | 39 | 61 | 6 | 12 |
| Lozado, Arkansas | .940 | 11 | 18 | 29 | 3 | 5 | THOMPSON, Shreveport | .982 | 120 | 291 | 361 | 12 | 91 |
| Madril, Midland | 1.000 | 2 | 5 | 4 | 0 | 1 | Villaescusa, Midland | 1.000 | 4 | 3 | 6 | 0 | 0 |
| McLemore, Midland | .977 | 104 | 276 | 310 | 14 | 80 | Wasinger, Beaumont | .978 | 20 | 30 | 59 | 2 | 11 |

Triple Play—Purpura.

## THIRD BASEMEN

| Player and Club | Pct. | G. | PO. | A. | E. | DP. | Player and Club | Pct. | G. | PO. | A. | E. | DP. |
|---|---|---|---|---|---|---|---|---|---|---|---|---|---|
| ALFARO, El Paso | .944 | 127 | 60 | 274 | 20 | 25 | Madril, Midland | .889 | 3 | 0 | 8 | 1 | 0 |
| Allen, San Antonio | 1.000 | 3 | 0 | 1 | 0 | 1 | Magadan, Jackson | .921 | 127 | 87 | 275 | 31 | 27 |
| Brassil, Beaumont | .936 | 28 | 15 | 58 | 5 | 3 | McPhail, Jackson | 1.000 | 4 | 2 | 9 | 0 | 1 |
| Brunenkant, Tulsa | .667 | 1 | 1 | 1 | 1 | 1 | Mejia, Tulsa | .889 | 2 | 2 | 6 | 1 | 1 |
| Corman, Beaumont | .913 | 8 | 7 | 14 | 2 | 1 | Merrifield, Midland | .932 | 119 | 76 | 266 | 25 | 34 |
| Cruz, Midland | .750 | 3 | 2 | 4 | 2 | 0 | Moreno, Beaumont | .667 | 4 | 0 | 2 | 1 | 0 |
| D. Davis, Midland | 1.000 | 2 | 2 | 8 | 0 | 0 | Moronko, Tulsa | .955 | 30 | 22 | 63 | 4 | 8 |
| Debus, San Antonio | .905 | 8 | 7 | 12 | 2 | 0 | Newsom, San Antonio | 1.000 | 2 | 0 | 1 | 0 | 0 |
| Doughty, Tulsa | .750 | 1 | 3 | 0 | 1 | 0 | Purpura, El Paso | .903 | 9 | 6 | 22 | 3 | 0 |
| Foussianes, Tulsa | .935 | 47 | 22 | 93 | 8 | 11 | Redfield, Jackson | .813 | 7 | 3 | 10 | 3 | 1 |
| Fryer, Shreveport | .874 | 39 | 26 | 92 | 17 | 11 | Reitz, Tulsa | .896 | 18 | 9 | 34 | 5 | 4 |
| Gauntlett, San Antonio | 1.000 | 5 | 2 | 8 | 0 | 1 | Robidoux, El Paso | .500 | 2 | 0 | 1 | 1 | 0 |
| Gergen, Tulsa | .931 | 49 | 32 | 90 | 9 | 3 | Rodriguez, Beaumont | .727 | 8 | 6 | 10 | 6 | 0 |
| Glynn, Jackson | 1.000 | 3 | 1 | 4 | 0 | 0 | Ross, El Paso | 1.000 | 2 | 0 | 2 | 0 | 0 |
| Hamilton, San Antonio | .941 | 96 | 69 | 186 | 16 | 11 | Schmidt, Shreveport | .929 | 10 | 6 | 20 | 2 | 0 |
| Hardgrave, Beaumont | 1.000 | 1 | 2 | 1 | 0 | 0 | Smith, Beaumont | 1.000 | 11 | 6 | 17 | 0 | 3 |
| Jirschele, Tulsa | 1.000 | 2 | 0 | 2 | 0 | 0 | Stanicek, Shreveport | .857 | 47 | 21 | 111 | 22 | 8 |
| Jones, Jackson | .750 | 1 | 0 | 3 | 1 | 0 | Steen, Midland | .933 | 13 | 10 | 32 | 3 | 3 |
| Kaull, Arkansas | 1.000 | 3 | 4 | 3 | 0 | 0 | Tanner, Arkansas | 1.000 | 10 | 1 | 11 | 0 | 1 |
| Klein, Tulsa | .667 | 3 | 0 | 2 | 1 | 0 | Thomas, Shreveport | .948 | 19 | 9 | 46 | 3 | 6 |
| Lindeman, Arkansas | .929 | 121 | 74 | 238 | 24 | 24 | Villaescusa, Midland | 1.000 | 2 | 1 | 1 | 0 | 0 |
| Long, Shreveport | .825 | 27 | 16 | 50 | 14 | 4 | Wasinger, Beaumont | .930 | 89 | 62 | 176 | 18 | 16 |
| Lozado, Arkansas | .933 | 14 | 14 | 28 | 3 | 2 | White, San Antonio | .972 | 28 | 24 | 46 | 2 | 2 |

## SHORTSTOPS

| Player and Club | Pct. | G. | PO. | A. | E. | DP. | Player and Club | Pct. | G. | PO. | A. | E. | DP. |
|---|---|---|---|---|---|---|---|---|---|---|---|---|---|
| Allen, San Antonio | 1.000 | 6 | 6 | 14 | 0 | 2 | McPhail, Jackson | 1.000 | 2 | 1 | 1 | 0 | 1 |
| BOOKER, Arkansas | .956 | 126 | 198 | 362 | 26 | 71 | Mejia, Tulsa | .911 | 8 | 8 | 33 | 4 | 4 |
| Brassil, Beaumont | .899 | 20 | 20 | 51 | 8 | 9 | Merrifield, Midland | .750 | 2 | 1 | 5 | 2 | 0 |
| Chmil, San Antonio | .879 | 10 | 14 | 15 | 4 | 5 | K. Miller, Jackson | 1.000 | 1 | 0 | 1 | 0 | 0 |
| Cochrane, Jackson | .900 | 30 | 39 | 87 | 14 | 13 | S. Miller, Shreveport | .941 | 113 | 140 | 356 | 31 | 71 |
| Cruz, Midland | .935 | 5 | 10 | 19 | 2 | 2 | Morales, El Paso | .889 | 2 | 2 | 6 | 1 | 2 |
| K. Davis, Midland | .943 | 98 | 160 | 366 | 32 | 62 | Moronko, Tulsa | .941 | 32 | 47 | 112 | 10 | 14 |
| Diaz, El Paso | .950 | 132 | 217 | 489 | 37 | 101 | Newsom, San Antonio | .958 | 19 | 23 | 45 | 3 | 5 |
| Doughty, Tulsa | .909 | 42 | 58 | 112 | 17 | 20 | Purpura, El Paso | .900 | 3 | 3 | 6 | 1 | 2 |
| Elster, Jackson | .970 | 59 | 107 | 220 | 10 | 36 | Redfield, Jackson | .833 | 2 | 3 | 7 | 2 | 2 |
| Espy, San Antonio | .911 | 109 | 164 | 345 | 50 | 59 | Rodriguez, Beaumont | .800 | 1 | 2 | 2 | 1 | 0 |
| Glynn, Jackson | .935 | 41 | 45 | 113 | 11 | 13 | Schmidt, Shreveport | 1.000 | 1 | 1 | 1 | 0 | 0 |
| Green, Beaumont | .949 | 118 | 157 | 405 | 30 | 71 | Steen, Midland | .929 | 23 | 23 | 56 | 6 | 11 |
| Jirschele, Tulsa | .970 | 21 | 48 | 80 | 4 | 25 | Tanner, Arkansas | .833 | 1 | 4 | 6 | 2 | 2 |
| Jones, Jackson | .957 | 16 | 25 | 41 | 3 | 5 | Thomas, Shreveport | .942 | 30 | 35 | 62 | 6 | 13 |
| Kaull, Arkansas | 1.000 | 1 | 0 | 1 | 0 | 0 | Thompson, Midland | 1.000 | 1 | 1 | 5 | 0 | 0 |
| Klein, Tulsa | .921 | 40 | 57 | 130 | 16 | 23 | Villaescusa, Midland | 1.000 | 2 | 3 | 7 | 0 | 1 |
| Lozado, Arkansas | .926 | 15 | 21 | 29 | 4 | 5 | Wasinger, Beaumont | .750 | 3 | 1 | 5 | 2 | 2 |
| McLemore, Midland | .915 | 11 | 25 | 29 | 5 | 5 | | | | | | | |

Triple Play—Diaz.

## OUTFIELDERS

| Player and Club | Pct. | G. | PO. | A. | E. | DP. | Player and Club | Pct. | G. | PO. | A. | E. | DP. |
|---|---|---|---|---|---|---|---|---|---|---|---|---|---|
| Aldrete, Shreveport° | .970 | 42 | 59 | 6 | 2 | 2 | Denby, Jackson | .960 | 66 | 91 | 5 | 4 | 2 |
| Amante, Arkansas | 1.000 | 9 | 8 | 0 | 0 | 0 | Espy, San Antonio | .952 | 9 | 19 | 1 | 1 | 1 |
| Braggs, El Paso | .958 | 116 | 239 | 10 | 11 | 1 | Felice, Jackson | .976 | 110 | 193 | 8 | 5 | 2 |
| Brassil, Beaumont | 1.000 | 10 | 12 | 0 | 0 | 0 | Francis, Shreveport | .986 | 46 | 70 | 1 | 1 | 1 |
| Brunenkant, Tulsa | 1.000 | 4 | 2 | 0 | 0 | 0 | Gauntlett, San Antonio | .667 | 1 | 2 | 0 | 1 | 0 |
| Carreon, Jackson° | .995 | 120 | 201 | 8 | 1 | 0 | Geren, Arkansas | 1.000 | 7 | 8 | 1 | 0 | 1 |
| Cartwright, El Paso° | .967 | 116 | 192 | 13 | 7 | 0 | Gergen, Tulsa | 1.000 | 12 | 13 | 0 | 0 | 0 |
| Cataline, San Antonio | .992 | 72 | 116 | 9 | 1 | 2 | Gibbons, El Paso° | .977 | 44 | 82 | 2 | 2 | 0 |
| Clark, Arkansas | 1.000 | 1 | 1 | 0 | 0 | 0 | Gill, Arkansas | .941 | 12 | 15 | 1 | 1 | 0 |
| Cockrell, Shreveport | .949 | 124 | 177 | 10 | 10 | 2 | Gonzalez, San Antonio | .966 | 123 | 294 | 15 | 11 | 2 |
| Coleman, Beaumont | .946 | 107 | 156 | 19 | 10 | 1 | Graham, Shreveport° | .981 | 123 | 293 | 18 | 6 | 4 |
| Crum, Tulsa | .915 | 40 | 54 | 0 | 5 | 0 | Hartsock, Midland | 1.000 | 25 | 47 | 5 | 0 | 0 |
| Darkis, Tulsa | 1.000 | 48 | 74 | 2 | 0 | 0 | Jefferson, Jackson | .976 | 132 | 276 | 9 | 7 | 0 |
| D. A. Davis, Tulsa | .750 | 3 | 3 | 0 | 1 | 0 | Jones, Arkansas | 1.000 | 1 | 1 | 0 | 0 | 0 |
| D. R. Davis, Midland | .889 | 4 | 7 | 1 | 1 | 0 | Kaull, Arkansas | 1.000 | 2 | 4 | 0 | 0 | 0 |
| Debus, San Antonio | .938 | 10 | 15 | 0 | 1 | 0 | Key, Midland | .952 | 81 | 153 | 6 | 8 | 1 |

## OUTFIELDERS—Continued

| Player and Club | Pct. | G. | PO. | A. | E. | DP. |
|---|---|---|---|---|---|---|
| Klipstein, El Paso | .975 | 89 | 184 | 14 | 5 | 3 |
| Ledbetter, Arkansas° | .974 | 46 | 69 | 5 | 2 | 2 |
| MACE, Tulsa | .996 | 123 | 219 | 12 | 1 | 2 |
| Mack, Beaumont | .974 | 124 | 252 | 12 | 7 | 2 |
| Madril, Midland | .985 | 78 | 192 | 10 | 3 | 0 |
| McCulla, Arkansas | 1.000 | 4 | 5 | 0 | 0 | 0 |
| McPhail, Jackson | 1.000 | 7 | 11 | 0 | 0 | 0 |
| Miller, Beaumont | .980 | 36 | 46 | 4 | 1 | 0 |
| Mills, Arkansas | .986 | 74 | 139 | 3 | 2 | 0 |
| Montgomery, Midland | .964 | 78 | 119 | 15 | 5 | 3 |
| Murphy, Midland° | 1.000 | 13 | 18 | 1 | 0 | 0 |
| Nanni, Midland° | .909 | 39 | 78 | 2 | 8 | 0 |
| Ortiz, Tulsa | .953 | 65 | 115 | 7 | 6 | 0 |
| Paciorek, El Paso | .971 | 34 | 65 | 1 | 2 | 0 |
| Penigar, Shreveport | .969 | 88 | 119 | 8 | 4 | 1 |
| Ramsey, San Antonio° | .984 | 102 | 231 | 9 | 4 | 1 |
| Randall, Midland° | 1.000 | 34 | 42 | 3 | 0 | 1 |
| Reibel, Midland° | 1.000 | 2 | 1 | 0 | 0 | 0 |
| Robidoux, El Paso | .833 | 9 | 5 | 0 | 1 | 0 |
| Robinson, Arkansas | .500 | 1 | 1 | 0 | 1 | 0 |
| Robles, Arkansas | .971 | 26 | 32 | 1 | 1 | 0 |
| J. Rodriguez, Arkansas | .982 | 121 | 259 | 10 | 5 | 3 |
| R. Rodriguez, Beaumont | .950 | 11 | 15 | 4 | 1 | 0 |
| Roman, Arkansas° | 1.000 | 2 | 1 | 0 | 0 | 0 |
| Schulte, Arkansas° | 1.000 | 4 | 2 | 1 | 0 | 1 |
| Sferrazza, El Paso | 1.000 | 4 | 3 | 1 | 0 | 0 |
| Sierra, Tulsa | .943 | 129 | 234 | 12 | 15 | 2 |
| Smith, Beaumont | .957 | 34 | 63 | 4 | 3 | 1 |
| Stanley, Tulsa | .000 | 1 | 0 | 0 | 1 | 0 |
| Stephenson, Midland° | 1.000 | 15 | 24 | 2 | 0 | 0 |
| Stryffeler, Arkansas | .972 | 57 | 69 | 1 | 2 | 1 |
| Tanner, Arkansas | .984 | 84 | 114 | 11 | 2 | 0 |
| Tutt, Beaumont | .961 | 114 | 241 | 7 | 10 | 2 |
| Wallace, Arkansas | 1.000 | 7 | 9 | 0 | 0 | 0 |
| D. White, Midland | .979 | 70 | 176 | 10 | 4 | 1 |
| W. White, San Antonio | 1.000 | 2 | 4 | 0 | 0 | 0 |
| Williams, San Antonio | .953 | 101 | 209 | 14 | 11 | 2 |

## CATCHERS

| Player and Club | Pct. | G. | PO. | A. | E. | DP. | PB. |
|---|---|---|---|---|---|---|---|
| Amante, Arkansas | 1.000 | 2 | 16 | 0 | 0 | 0 | 0 |
| Beuerlein, El Paso | .983 | 39 | 216 | 21 | 4 | 4 | 6 |
| Brunenkant, Tulsa | .973 | 72 | 430 | 42 | 13 | 4 | 7 |
| Carlucci, Tulsa | .964 | 11 | 71 | 9 | 3 | 1 | 2 |
| Castro, Beaumont | .960 | 45 | 237 | 28 | 11 | 3 | 3 |
| D. A. Davis, Tulsa | .973 | 18 | 66 | 7 | 2 | 0 | 3 |
| D. R. Davis, Midland | .974 | 63 | 284 | 50 | 9 | 3 | 4 |
| Debus, San Antonio | .966 | 67 | 351 | 42 | 14 | 1 | 13 |
| Gauntlett, San Antonio | .983 | 45 | 253 | 29 | 5 | 2 | 8 |
| GEREN, Arkansas | .996 | 77 | 430 | 47 | 2 | 3 | 7 |
| Hartsock, Midland | 1.000 | 1 | 1 | 0 | 0 | 0 | 1 |
| Heath, Midland | .977 | 82 | 360 | 70 | 10 | 3 | 8 |
| Huppert, El Paso | .987 | 96 | 612 | 70 | 9 | 5 | 14 |
| Lane, Shreveport | .989 | 58 | 331 | 30 | 4 | 3 | 1 |
| Lyons, Jackson | .966 | 79 | 500 | 46 | 19 | 4 | 5 |
| McCulla, Arkansas | 1.000 | 1 | 7 | 1 | 0 | 0 | 0 |
| Moreno, Arkansas | .963 | 15 | 67 | 12 | 3 | 1 | 2 |
| Nokes, Shreveport | .979 | 88 | 520 | 40 | 12 | 6 | 9 |
| Olson, Jackson | .986 | 64 | 353 | 56 | 6 | 5 | 5 |
| Owen, Tulsa | 1.000 | 3 | 17 | 2 | 0 | 0 | 0 |
| Pagnozzi, Arkansas | .996 | 41 | 231 | 27 | 1 | 1 | 3 |
| Pott, Tulsa | .982 | 16 | 95 | 13 | 2 | 1 | 0 |
| Reitz, Tulsa | 1.000 | 1 | 1 | 0 | 0 | 0 | 0 |
| Rodriguez, El Paso | 1.000 | 7 | 44 | 5 | 0 | 1 | 4 |
| Santiago, Beaumont | .975 | 89 | 515 | 78 | 15 | 5 | 16 |
| Stanley, Tulsa | .991 | 31 | 209 | 17 | 2 | 3 | 3 |
| Szekely, San Antonio | .993 | 29 | 136 | 12 | 1 | 2 | 4 |
| Thomas, Beaumont | 1.000 | 2 | 11 | 0 | 0 | 0 | 0 |
| Wallace, Arkansas | .991 | 35 | 187 | 28 | 2 | 3 | 5 |
| White, San Antonio | 1.000 | 3 | 1 | 0 | 0 | 0 | 1 |

## PITCHERS

| Player and Club | Pct. | G. | PO. | A. | E. | DP. |
|---|---|---|---|---|---|---|
| Adamczak, Jackson | .875 | 57 | 2 | 12 | 2 | 0 |
| Adams, Arkansas | .938 | 33 | 4 | 11 | 1 | 2 |
| Aldrich, El Paso | .941 | 42 | 1 | 15 | 1 | 3 |
| Anderson, Tulsa | 1.000 | 28 | 19 | 23 | 0 | 1 |
| Angulo, Midland° | .913 | 21 | 4 | 17 | 2 | 0 |
| Banning, Midland | .933 | 10 | 2 | 12 | 1 | 0 |
| Bargerhuff, Shreveport | 1.000 | 7 | 0 | 2 | 0 | 0 |
| Barry, El Paso° | .900 | 31 | 2 | 16 | 2 | 4 |
| BASS, Tulsa | 1.000 | 34 | 12 | 36 | 0 | 2 |
| Beene, Beaumont | 1.000 | 2 | 1 | 2 | 0 | 0 |
| Birkbeck, El Paso | .977 | 24 | 17 | 25 | 1 | 1 |
| Bitker, Beaumont | .889 | 15 | 2 | 6 | 1 | 0 |
| Bockus, Shreveport | .852 | 28 | 8 | 38 | 8 | 1 |
| Boever, Arkansas | .875 | 27 | 3 | 4 | 1 | 1 |
| Bosio, El Paso | .955 | 28 | 14 | 28 | 2 | 1 |
| Brown, Jackson° | 1.000 | 12 | 0 | 7 | 0 | 1 |
| Bryant, El Paso | 1.000 | 14 | 1 | 1 | 0 | 0 |
| Bryden, Midland | 1.000 | 7 | 0 | 4 | 0 | 0 |
| Buonantony, Arkansas | .938 | 27 | 11 | 19 | 2 | 1 |
| D. Burns, El Paso | 1.000 | 15 | 2 | 2 | 0 | 0 |
| T. Burns, Jackson | .905 | 31 | 2 | 17 | 2 | 1 |
| Candiotti, Tulsa | 1.000 | 4 | 1 | 7 | 0 | 1 |
| Chadwick, Midland | .938 | 10 | 5 | 10 | 1 | 0 |
| Cherry, San Antonio | 1.000 | 20 | 7 | 6 | 0 | 0 |
| Childers, Beaumont | 1.000 | 24 | 4 | 9 | 0 | 0 |
| Ciardi, El Paso | 1.000 | 10 | 4 | 9 | 0 | 1 |
| R. Clark, Tulsa° | .939 | 26 | 12 | 19 | 2 | 0 |
| T. Clark, Arkansas | 1.000 | 42 | 2 | 19 | 0 | 3 |
| Coatney, Tulsa | 1.000 | 8 | 0 | 1 | 0 | 0 |
| Crews, Shreveport | .972 | 21 | 6 | 29 | 1 | 1 |
| Delzer, Midland° | .875 | 29 | 3 | 11 | 2 | 1 |
| Dunne, Arkansas | .932 | 23 | 11 | 30 | 3 | 6 |
| Eichhorn, San Antonio | .935 | 54 | 6 | 23 | 2 | 3 |
| Embser, Arkansas° | .667 | 6 | 0 | 2 | 1 | 0 |
| Epple, Arkansas° | 1.000 | 10 | 1 | 1 | 0 | 0 |
| Ferran, Shreveport | 1.000 | 6 | 4 | 5 | 0 | 1 |
| Finch, Midland | 1.000 | 3 | 0 | 4 | 0 | 0 |
| Fingers, El Paso | 1.000 | 16 | 1 | 4 | 0 | 0 |
| Fischer, Midland | .905 | 43 | 9 | 10 | 2 | 3 |
| Ford, El Paso | 1.000 | 3 | 0 | 1 | 0 | 0 |
| Fultz, Jackson | 1.000 | 8 | 1 | 3 | 0 | 0 |
| Galvez, San Antonio | .804 | 26 | 6 | 31 | 9 | 2 |
| Gergen, Tulsa | 1.000 | 1 | 0 | 0 | 0 | 0 |
| Gonzales, Midland | .960 | 53 | 6 | 18 | 1 | 0 |
| Graves, Jackson | .952 | 50 | 9 | 11 | 1 | 0 |
| Harman, Tulsa | 1.000 | 6 | 2 | 2 | 0 | 0 |
| Hartshorn, Jackson | .750 | 3 | 2 | 1 | 1 | 0 |
| Hayes, Arkansas | 1.000 | 23 | 0 | 8 | 0 | 1 |
| Henry, Tulsa | .900 | 34 | 6 | 3 | 1 | 1 |
| Hensley, Shreveport° | 1.000 | 13 | 2 | 7 | 0 | 0 |
| Heredia, San Antonio | 1.000 | 3 | 1 | 0 | 0 | 0 |
| Heuer, San Antonio | .893 | 25 | 2 | 23 | 3 | 1 |
| Hillegas, San Antonio | .944 | 23 | 12 | 22 | 2 | 1 |
| Hudson, Tulsa | .913 | 51 | 7 | 14 | 2 | 1 |
| Hummel, Shreveport° | 1.000 | 9 | 1 | 2 | 0 | 0 |
| James, Tulsa | .900 | 15 | 4 | 5 | 1 | 2 |
| Johnson, Tulsa° | .806 | 26 | 5 | 20 | 6 | 1 |
| Johnston, San Antonio | 1.000 | 26 | 0 | 8 | 0 | 1 |
| Jones, Beaumont | .880 | 16 | 6 | 16 | 3 | 0 |
| Kemmerling, Midland | 1.000 | 26 | 2 | 4 | 0 | 0 |
| Key, Midland | 1.000 | 7 | 0 | 2 | 0 | 0 |
| Killingsworth, Tulsa | .944 | 39 | 8 | 9 | 1 | 2 |
| King, Shreveport | .893 | 15 | 3 | 22 | 3 | 0 |
| Kipper, Midland° | 1.000 | 9 | 1 | 6 | 0 | 1 |
| Kockenmeister, Beaumont° | 1.000 | 7 | 1 | 3 | 0 | 0 |
| Kordish, Tulsa | .900 | 7 | 6 | 3 | 1 | 1 |
| Kutsukos, Beaumont | .947 | 47 | 5 | 13 | 1 | 0 |
| Lockenmeyer, Jackson | 1.000 | 3 | 0 | 2 | 0 | 0 |
| Lovelace, San Antonio° | .667 | 7 | 0 | 4 | 2 | 0 |
| Lundgren, Jackson | .944 | 22 | 3 | 14 | 1 | 0 |
| Lusted, Shreveport | .920 | 19 | 7 | 16 | 2 | 1 |
| Martin, Arkansas | .968 | 26 | 7 | 23 | 1 | 0 |
| Mason, Arkansas | 1.000 | 13 | 1 | 3 | 0 | 0 |
| Mattson, Shreveport | 1.000 | 53 | 6 | 15 | 0 | 0 |
| May, San Antonio | .911 | 26 | 14 | 27 | 4 | 2 |
| Mayberry, San Antonio | 1.000 | 8 | 1 | 6 | 0 | 0 |
| McClain, Beaumont | .900 | 27 | 13 | 50 | 7 | 3 |
| McKenzie, Midland | .938 | 26 | 8 | 22 | 2 | 0 |
| McKnight, Shreveport | .800 | 5 | 1 | 3 | 1 | 0 |
| Meagher, San Antonio | 1.000 | 45 | 6 | 13 | 0 | 2 |
| Mills, Beaumont | .975 | 26 | 18 | 21 | 1 | 1 |
| Morlock, Arkansas | .938 | 27 | 6 | 24 | 2 | 1 |
| Mulholland, Shreveport° | .935 | 26 | 9 | 34 | 3 | 4 |
| Murray, Jackson | 1.000 | 30 | 4 | 7 | 0 | 0 |
| Murtha, Shreveport° | 1.000 | 2 | 0 | 1 | 0 | 0 |
| E. Myers, El Paso | .923 | 32 | 3 | 9 | 1 | 2 |
| R. Myers, Jackson° | .967 | 19 | 7 | 22 | 1 | 1 |
| Nieves, El Paso° | 1.000 | 17 | 4 | 23 | 0 | 0 |
| Norman, Shreveport | .867 | 22 | 2 | 11 | 2 | 0 |
| North, Arkansas | 1.000 | 2 | 0 | 1 | 0 | 0 |
| Norton, El Paso | .956 | 36 | 14 | 29 | 2 | 2 |
| Oliveras, Beaumont | 1.000 | 7 | 2 | 3 | 0 | 0 |
| Orozco, Midland | 1.000 | 6 | 2 | 5 | 0 | 0 |
| Piper, San Antonio | .929 | 22 | 4 | 9 | 1 | 0 |
| Plesac, El Paso° | .920 | 25 | 4 | 19 | 2 | 0 |
| Poston, Beaumont | .889 | 38 | 2 | 14 | 2 | 2 |
| Price, Midland° | .923 | 12 | 0 | 12 | 1 | 0 |
| Pruitt, Jackson° | .938 | 52 | 5 | 10 | 1 | 1 |
| Psaltis, Midland° | .882 | 43 | 4 | 11 | 2 | 1 |
| Reichard, Tulsa | .818 | 38 | 5 | 4 | 2 | 0 |

PITCHERS—Continued

| Player and Club | Pct. | G. | PO. | A. | E. | DP. | Player and Club | Pct. | G. | PO. | A. | E. | DP. |
|---|---|---|---|---|---|---|---|---|---|---|---|---|---|
| Rhodes, Arkansas* | 1.000 | 23 | 0 | 4 | 0 | 0 | Thurberg, Arkansas | 1.000 | 6 | 0 | 1 | 0 | 0 |
| Roberts, El Paso | .913 | 12 | 5 | 16 | 2 | 2 | Timberlake, Midland | .906 | 23 | 13 | 16 | 3 | 0 |
| Rodriguez, Beaumont | 1.000 | 7 | 0 | 1 | 0 | 0 | Towers, Beaumont | 1.000 | 6 | 2 | 1 | 0 | 0 |
| Roman, Arkansas* | .947 | 43 | 8 | 10 | 1 | 1 | Vaughn, Jackson | 1.000 | 24 | 7 | 14 | 0 | 1 |
| Ronan, Shreveport | 1.000 | 29 | 7 | 11 | 0 | 1 | Vosberg, Beaumont* | .985 | 27 | 9 | 56 | 1 | 1 |
| Schefsky, Beaumont | 1.000 | 20 | 1 | 4 | 0 | 0 | Weissman, Jackson | .923 | 28 | 8 | 16 | 2 | 0 |
| Schroeck, El Paso* | 1.000 | 27 | 1 | 3 | 0 | 0 | Wilburn, Midland | 1.000 | 10 | 1 | 7 | 0 | 0 |
| Scudder, San Antonio | .882 | 27 | 3 | 12 | 2 | 1 | Williams, Tulsa* | .455 | 6 | 1 | 4 | 6 | 1 |
| Shade, Arkansas | .889 | 32 | 1 | 7 | 1 | 0 | Williamson, Beaumont | 1.000 | 42 | 6 | 15 | 0 | 1 |
| Sierra, Beaumont | .941 | 23 | 1 | 15 | 1 | 0 | Wilmet, Arkansas | 1.000 | 9 | 0 | 2 | 0 | 0 |
| Soff, Arkansas | 1.000 | 19 | 2 | 1 | 0 | 0 | Witt, Tulsa | .750 | 11 | 1 | 2 | 1 | 0 |
| Suehr, Midland | .952 | 35 | 3 | 17 | 1 | 2 | Wyatt, Jackson* | .917 | 10 | 5 | 17 | 2 | 0 |
| Taylor, Tulsa | .833 | 20 | 5 | 10 | 3 | 0 | Yokubaitis, Shreveport* | .923 | 35 | 2 | 10 | 1 | 0 |
| Thomas, San Antonio | .833 | 17 | 1 | 4 | 1 | 1 | Young, Jackson* | 1.000 | 21 | 4 | 16 | 0 | 0 |

The following players do not have any recorded accepted chances at the position indicated, therefore, are not listed in the fielding averages for those particular positions: Alexander, p; Bass, of; Cannon, p; Gibbons, p; Gile, 3b; Hallgren, p; J. Hamilton, of; R. Hamilton, p; Hardgrave, ss; Lachowicz, p; Mack, 3b; G. Mills, ss; Moreno, p; Newsom, p; Pickett, p; Reitz, ss, of, p; Santiago, 3b; Smith, ss; Stanley, 2b; Tanner, p.

CLUB PITCHING

| Club | ERA. | G. | CG. | ShO. | Sv. | IP. | H. | R. | ER. | HR. | HB. | BB. | Int. BB. | SO. | WP. | Bk. |
|---|---|---|---|---|---|---|---|---|---|---|---|---|---|---|---|---|
| Shreveport | 3.22 | 136 | 42 | 10 | 17 | 1167.2 | 1107 | 538 | 418 | 74 | 44 | 396 | 16 | 805 | 56 | 14 |
| Jackson | 3.36 | 138 | 9 | 12 | 27 | 1185.0 | 1121 | 541 | 443 | 62 | 31 | 468 | 28 | 822 | 59 | 12 |
| Arkansas | 3.93 | 135 | 14 | 9 | 30 | 1148.0 | 1114 | 594 | 501 | 87 | 34 | 513 | 42 | 851 | 60 | 11 |
| Tulsa | 4.01 | 137 | 11 | 7 | 27 | 1187.2 | 1117 | 662 | 529 | 77 | 31 | 620 | 39 | 857 | 68 | 27 |
| Beaumont | 4.06 | 136 | 13 | 5 | 31 | 1184.2 | 1222 | 639 | 534 | 54 | 30 | 573 | 36 | 804 | 59 | 26 |
| El Paso | 4.18 | 136 | 25 | 10 | 35 | 1194.0 | 1283 | 662 | 555 | 106 | 13 | 422 | 26 | 843 | 60 | 13 |
| San Antonio | 4.43 | 134 | 22 | 5 | 21 | 1162.2 | 1234 | 728 | 572 | 101 | 23 | 576 | 29 | 693 | 78 | 16 |
| Midland | 5.42 | 136 | 18 | 2 | 25 | 1162.1 | 1387 | 820 | 712 | 141 | 40 | 568 | 22 | 617 | 92 | 19 |

PITCHERS' RECORDS

(Leading Qualifiers for Earned-Run Average Leadership — 109 or More Innings)

*Throws lefthanded.

| Pitcher—Club | W. | L. | Pct. | ERA. | G. | GS. | CG. | GF. | ShO. | Sv. | IP. | H. | R. | ER. | HR. | HB. | BB. | Int. BB. | SO. | WP. |
|---|---|---|---|---|---|---|---|---|---|---|---|---|---|---|---|---|---|---|---|---|
| Bockus, Shreveport | 14 | 11 | .560 | 2.73 | 28 | 27 | 15 | 1 | 2 | 0 | 201.0 | 196 | 85 | 61 | 13 | 3 | 44 | 0 | 126 | 11 |
| Mulholland, Shreveport* | 9 | 8 | .529 | 2.90 | 26 | 26 | 8 | 0 | 3 | 0 | 176.2 | 166 | 79 | 57 | 9 | 2 | 87 | 2 | 122 | 6 |
| Weissman, Jackson | 8 | 8 | .500 | 2.93 | 28 | 19 | 1 | 5 | 1 | 0 | 132.0 | 122 | 57 | 43 | 4 | 4 | 53 | 2 | 72 | 7 |
| Dunne, Arkansas | 4 | 9 | .308 | 3.08 | 23 | 23 | 3 | 0 | 1 | 0 | 146.0 | 133 | 72 | 50 | 9 | 5 | 57 | 5 | 91 | 7 |
| Crews, Shreveport | 9 | 8 | .529 | 3.15 | 21 | 21 | 7 | 0 | 0 | 0 | 142.2 | 133 | 71 | 50 | 7 | 6 | 28 | 0 | 69 | 2 |
| Hillegas, San Antonio | 4 | 10 | .286 | 3.17 | 23 | 23 | 3 | 0 | 0 | 0 | 139.1 | 134 | 72 | 49 | 6 | 3 | 67 | 1 | 56 | 5 |
| Lundgren, Jackson | 8 | 4 | .667 | 3.29 | 22 | 21 | 1 | 1 | 1 | 0 | 128.2 | 113 | 54 | 47 | 8 | 2 | 34 | 1 | 74 | 7 |
| Martin, Arkansas | 8 | 8 | .500 | 3.30 | 26 | 23 | 4 | 1 | 1 | 0 | 142.0 | 136 | 60 | 52 | 6 | 5 | 43 | 2 | 94 | 5 |
| Birkbeck, El Paso | 9 | 9 | .500 | 3.43 | 24 | 24 | 4 | 0 | 0 | 0 | 155.0 | 154 | 67 | 59 | 9 | 1 | 64 | 4 | 103 | 11 |
| Vaughn, Jackson | 9 | 7 | .563 | 3.47 | 24 | 18 | 2 | 3 | 0 | 1 | 124.2 | 133 | 59 | 48 | 8 | 3 | 35 | 1 | 58 | 3 |
| May, San Antonio | 10 | 6 | .625 | 3.47 | 26 | 26 | 9 | 0 | 2 | 0 | 191.2 | 181 | 85 | 74 | 15 | 1 | 99 | 3 | 125 | 10 |

Departmental Leaders: G—Adamczak, 57; W—Bockus, 14; L—McKenzie, 14; Pct.—Nieves, .800; GS—Anderson, Bockus, McClain, Vosberg, 27; CG—Bockus, 15; GF—Eichhorn, Mattson, 36; ShO—Mulholland, 3; Sv.—Fischer, 15; IP—Bockus, 201.0; H—McKenzie, 203; R—Timberlake, 110; ER—McKenzie, 92; HR—McKenzie, 19; HB—Buonantony, McClain, 8; BB—May, 99; IBB—Graves, 10; SO—Bosio, 155; WP—Angulo, 17.

(All Pitchers—Listed Alphabetically)

| Pitcher—Club | W. | L. | Pct. | ERA. | G. | GS. | CG. | GF. | ShO. | Sv. | IP. | H. | R. | ER. | HR. | HB. | BB. | Int. BB. | SO. | WP. |
|---|---|---|---|---|---|---|---|---|---|---|---|---|---|---|---|---|---|---|---|---|
| Adamczak, Jackson | 7 | 6 | .538 | 2.25 | 57 | 0 | 0 | 34 | 0 | 10 | 84.0 | 75 | 25 | 21 | 0 | 3 | 24 | 4 | 66 | 5 |
| Adams, Tulsa | 3 | 6 | .333 | 4.49 | 33 | 11 | 1 | 8 | 1 | 2 | 104.1 | 119 | 55 | 52 | 10 | 1 | 39 | 3 | 71 | 16 |
| Aldrich, El Paso | 4 | 1 | .800 | 3.55 | 42 | 0 | 0 | 29 | 0 | 12 | 63.1 | 61 | 28 | 25 | 7 | 1 | 13 | 1 | 35 | 3 |
| Alexander, Shreveport | 0 | 0 | .000 | 94.50 | 1 | 0 | 0 | 0 | 0 | 0 | 0.2 | 4 | 7 | 7 | 0 | 0 | 3 | 0 | 0 | 0 |
| Anderson, Tulsa | 9 | 6 | .600 | 3.67 | 28 | 27 | 2 | 0 | 1 | 0 | 174.1 | 177 | 87 | 71 | 15 | 4 | 51 | 1 | 123 | 3 |
| Angulo, Midland* | 10 | 5 | .667 | 4.62 | 21 | 21 | 3 | 0 | 1 | 0 | 126.2 | 140 | 77 | 65 | 8 | 6 | 65 | 0 | 74 | 17 |
| Banning, Midland | 2 | 5 | .286 | 5.51 | 10 | 9 | 3 | 0 | 0 | 0 | 63.2 | 64 | 41 | 39 | 9 | 0 | 27 | 1 | 27 | 2 |
| Bargerhuff, Shreveport | 0 | 1 | .000 | 6.52 | 7 | 0 | 0 | 2 | 0 | 0 | 9.2 | 16 | 7 | 7 | 0 | 2 | 5 | 1 | 10 | 2 |
| Barry, El Paso* | 6 | 3 | .667 | 4.81 | 31 | 2 | 0 | 13 | 0 | 4 | 58.0 | 76 | 32 | 31 | 10 | 0 | 23 | 1 | 31 | 3 |
| Bass, Tulsa | 3 | 11 | .214 | 3.74 | 34 | 14 | 4 | 11 | 0 | 0 | 132.1 | 125 | 72 | 55 | 4 | 2 | 49 | 6 | 68 | 5 |
| Beene, El Paso | 2 | 0 | 1.000 | 4.05 | 2 | 2 | 0 | 0 | 0 | 0 | 13.1 | 18 | 6 | 6 | 1 | 0 | 3 | 0 | 13 | 1 |
| Birkbeck, El Paso | 9 | 9 | .500 | 3.43 | 24 | 24 | 4 | 0 | 0 | 0 | 155.0 | 154 | 67 | 59 | 9 | 1 | 64 | 4 | 103 | 11 |
| Bitker, Beaumont | 8 | 1 | .889 | 3.12 | 15 | 14 | 4 | 0 | 1 | 0 | 98.0 | 91 | 43 | 34 | 3 | 2 | 41 | 2 | 64 | 3 |
| Bockus, Shreveport | 14 | 11 | .560 | 2.73 | 28 | 27 | 15 | 1 | 2 | 0 | 201.0 | 196 | 85 | 61 | 13 | 3 | 44 | 0 | 126 | 11 |
| Boever, Arkansas | 3 | 1 | .750 | 1.19 | 27 | 0 | 0 | 20 | 0 | 9 | 37.2 | 21 | 5 | 5 | 1 | 0 | 23 | 4 | 45 | 2 |
| Bosio, Tulsa | 11 | 6 | .647 | 3.82 | 28 | 25 | 6 | 3 | 1 | 2 | 181.1 | 186 | 108 | 77 | 14 | 4 | 49 | 4 | 155 | 4 |
| Brown, Jackson* | 3 | 4 | .429 | 5.08 | 12 | 12 | 1 | 0 | 1 | 0 | 51.1 | 62 | 38 | 29 | 4 | 1 | 27 | 0 | 44 | 4 |
| Bryant, El Paso | 2 | 1 | .667 | 4.13 | 14 | 0 | 0 | 6 | 0 | 1 | 24.0 | 23 | 12 | 11 | 1 | 0 | 12 | 1 | 23 | 2 |
| Bryden, Midland | 1 | 2 | .333 | 6.97 | 7 | 0 | 0 | 5 | 0 | 0 | 10.1 | 13 | 11 | 8 | 1 | 1 | 4 | 1 | 4 | 0 |
| Buonantony, Arkansas | 10 | 11 | .476 | 4.64 | 27 | 25 | 4 | 1 | 1 | 0 | 147.1 | 141 | 90 | 76 | 11 | 8 | 92 | 4 | 121 | 8 |
| D. Burns, El Paso | 1 | 2 | .333 | 6.38 | 15 | 0 | 0 | 10 | 0 | 4 | 18.1 | 24 | 16 | 13 | 3 | 0 | 10 | 1 | 15 | 1 |
| T. Burns, Jackson | 7 | 1 | .875 | 1.41 | 31 | 0 | 0 | 24 | 0 | 6 | 51.0 | 47 | 8 | 8 | 3 | 0 | 15 | 4 | 35 | 6 |
| Candiotti, El Paso | 1 | 0 | 1.000 | 2.76 | 4 | 4 | 1 | 0 | 0 | 0 | 29.1 | 29 | 11 | 9 | 2 | 0 | 7 | 1 | 16 | 0 |
| Cannon, Midland | 1 | 2 | .333 | 15.63 | 8 | 1 | 0 | 0 | 0 | 0 | 12.2 | 17 | 22 | 22 | 3 | 4 | 19 | 0 | 7 | 2 |
| Chadwick, Midland | 5 | 2 | .714 | 5.25 | 10 | 10 | 3 | 0 | 0 | 0 | 60.0 | 53 | 36 | 35 | 4 | 2 | 47 | 0 | 44 | 9 |
| Cherry, San Antonio | 2 | 8 | .200 | 5.35 | 20 | 13 | 1 | 4 | 0 | 0 | 74.0 | 95 | 61 | 44 | 9 | 3 | 45 | 1 | 44 | 5 |
| Childers, Beaumont | 1 | 3 | .250 | 5.21 | 24 | 5 | 0 | 9 | 0 | 2 | 57.0 | 68 | 36 | 33 | 5 | 0 | 42 | 1 | 38 | 5 |
| Ciardi, El Paso | 8 | 1 | .889 | 2.66 | 10 | 9 | 3 | 1 | 2 | 1 | 67.2 | 55 | 27 | 20 | 9 | 1 | 13 | 0 | 50 | 4 |
| R. Clark, Tulsa* | 9 | 6 | .600 | 3.48 | 26 | 26 | 3 | 0 | 2 | 0 | 175.2 | 178 | 84 | 68 | 14 | 4 | 47 | 0 | 100 | 2 |
| T. Clark, Arkansas | 6 | 5 | .545 | 4.93 | 42 | 7 | 0 | 8 | 0 | 2 | 96.2 | 102 | 64 | 53 | 9 | 4 | 38 | 2 | 67 | 0 |
| Coatney, Tulsa | 0 | 2 | .000 | 7.58 | 4 | 0 | 0 | 0 | 0 | 0 | 19.0 | 28 | 17 | 16 | 2 | 1 | 20 | 0 | 13 | 2 |
| Crews, Shreveport | 9 | 8 | .529 | 3.15 | 21 | 21 | 7 | 0 | 0 | 0 | 142.2 | 133 | 71 | 50 | 7 | 6 | 28 | 0 | 69 | 2 |
| Delzer, Midland* | 2 | 6 | .250 | 4.25 | 29 | 0 | 0 | 18 | 0 | 4 | 53.0 | 55 | 33 | 25 | 6 | 1 | 31 | 4 | 37 | 6 |

| Pitcher—Club | W. | L. | Pct. | ERA. | G. | GS. | CG. | GF. | ShO. | Sv. | IP. | H. | R. | ER. | HR. | HB. | BB. | Int. BB. | SO. | WP. |
|---|---|---|---|---|---|---|---|---|---|---|---|---|---|---|---|---|---|---|---|---|
| Dunne, Arkansas | 4 | 9 | .308 | 3.08 | 23 | 23 | 3 | 0 | 1 | 0 | 146.0 | 133 | 72 | 50 | 9 | 5 | 57 | 5 | 91 | 7 |
| Eichhorn, San Antonio | 6 | 9 | .400 | 2.82 | 54 | 0 | 0 | 36 | 0 | 10 | 73.1 | 77 | 41 | 23 | 4 | 0 | 35 | 8 | 21 | 4 |
| Embser, Arkansas* | 0 | 1 | .000 | 5.63 | 6 | 1 | 0 | 1 | 0 | 0 | 8.0 | 7 | 5 | 5 | 0 | 0 | 9 | 0 | 4 | 0 |
| Epple, Arkansas* | 3 | 2 | .600 | 4.26 | 10 | 7 | 0 | 0 | 0 | 0 | 38.0 | 35 | 24 | 18 | 3 | 0 | 13 | 0 | 34 | 2 |
| Ferran, Shreveport | 4 | 1 | .800 | 3.21 | 6 | 6 | 1 | 0 | 0 | 0 | 42.0 | 38 | 18 | 15 | 1 | 4 | 14 | 0 | 44 | 1 |
| Finch, Midland | 0 | 1 | .000 | 5.74 | 3 | 3 | 0 | 0 | 0 | 0 | 15.2 | 25 | 16 | 10 | 1 | 1 | 3 | 0 | 13 | 0 |
| Fingers, El Paso | 0 | 3 | .000 | 5.40 | 16 | 0 | 0 | 7 | 0 | 0 | 23.1 | 34 | 19 | 14 | 2 | 0 | 2 | 1 | 17 | 0 |
| Fischer, Midland | 6 | 3 | .667 | 3.43 | 43 | 0 | 0 | 35 | 0 | 15 | 76.0 | 69 | 32 | 29 | 10 | 0 | 29 | 7 | 43 | 5 |
| Ford, El Paso | 0 | 2 | .000 | 7.90 | 3 | 3 | 0 | 0 | 0 | 0 | 13.2 | 22 | 12 | 12 | 4 | 1 | 5 | 1 | 4 | 0 |
| Fultz, Jackson | 3 | 4 | .429 | 3.23 | 8 | 8 | 1 | 0 | 0 | 0 | 53.0 | 53 | 22 | 19 | 3 | 1 | 5 | 0 | 37 | 1 |
| Galvez, San Antonio | 10 | 9 | .526 | 4.54 | 26 | 26 | 4 | 0 | 1 | 0 | 170.2 | 181 | 99 | 86 | 15 | 0 | 79 | 2 | 111 | 12 |
| Gergen, Tulsa | 0 | 0 | .000 | 0.00 | 1 | 0 | 0 | 1 | 0 | 0 | 2.0 | 1 | 1 | 0 | 0 | 1 | 1 | 0 | 3 | 0 |
| Gibbons, El Paso* | 1 | 0 | 1.000 | 0.00 | 3 | 1 | 0 | 1 | 0 | 0 | 8.0 | 3 | 1 | 0 | 0 | 0 | 2 | 0 | 0 | 1 |
| Gonzales, Midland | 8 | 5 | .615 | 3.82 | 53 | 0 | 0 | 29 | 0 | 4 | 77.2 | 84 | 38 | 33 | 3 | 4 | 50 | 3 | 45 | 11 |
| Graves, El Paso | 5 | 8 | .385 | 3.82 | 50 | 1 | 0 | 32 | 0 | 7 | 96.2 | 93 | 56 | 41 | 6 | 7 | 62 | 10 | 61 | 7 |
| Hallgren, Tulsa | 0 | 0 | .000 | 5.40 | 3 | 1 | 0 | 1 | 0 | 0 | 3.1 | 6 | 2 | 2 | 0 | 0 | 2 | 0 | 3 | 0 |
| Hamilton, San Antonio | 1 | 0 | 1.000 | 0.00 | 1 | 1 | 0 | 0 | 0 | 0 | 8.0 | 5 | 1 | 0 | 0 | 0 | 4 | 0 | 3 | 1 |
| Harman, Tulsa | 1 | 0 | 1.000 | 2.08 | 6 | 0 | 0 | 5 | 0 | 1 | 8.2 | 6 | 2 | 2 | 0 | 0 | 6 | 1 | 3 | 1 |
| Hartshorn, Jackson | 0 | 2 | .000 | 6.89 | 3 | 3 | 0 | 0 | 0 | 0 | 15.2 | 22 | 12 | 12 | 0 | 1 | 5 | 1 | 6 | 0 |
| Hayes, Arkansas | 3 | 1 | .750 | 2.90 | 23 | 7 | 0 | 11 | 0 | 6 | 59.0 | 55 | 19 | 19 | 3 | 2 | 26 | 0 | 49 | 3 |
| Henry, Tulsa | 7 | 6 | .538 | 2.66 | 34 | 11 | 0 | 19 | 0 | 9 | 81.1 | 51 | 32 | 24 | 1 | 1 | 44 | 3 | 97 | 8 |
| Hensley, Shreveport* | 4 | 3 | .571 | 2.81 | 13 | 0 | 0 | 11 | 0 | 0 | 25.2 | 20 | 9 | 8 | 3 | 0 | 5 | 0 | 20 | 0 |
| Heredia, San Antonio | 1 | 0 | 1.000 | 1.93 | 3 | 0 | 0 | 1 | 0 | 0 | 4.2 | 4 | 1 | 1 | 1 | 0 | 0 | 0 | 2 | 1 |
| Heuer, San Antonio | 8 | 8 | .500 | 4.39 | 25 | 24 | 3 | 0 | 1 | 0 | 158.0 | 174 | 107 | 77 | 13 | 3 | 55 | 0 | 93 | 10 |
| Hillegas, San Antonio | 4 | 10 | .286 | 3.17 | 23 | 23 | 3 | 0 | 0 | 0 | 139.1 | 134 | 72 | 49 | 6 | 3 | 67 | 1 | 56 | 5 |
| Hudson, Tulsa | 8 | 4 | .667 | 2.17 | 51 | 0 | 0 | 35 | 0 | 10 | 78.2 | 69 | 29 | 19 | 4 | 1 | 34 | 6 | 39 | 5 |
| Hummel, Shreveport* | 2 | 2 | .500 | 4.73 | 9 | 3 | 0 | 1 | 0 | 0 | 26.2 | 25 | 14 | 14 | 1 | 1 | 12 | 1 | 17 | 2 |
| James, Tulsa | 3 | 9 | .250 | 6.85 | 15 | 13 | 0 | 2 | 0 | 0 | 71.0 | 78 | 60 | 54 | 7 | 3 | 66 | 1 | 44 | 10 |
| Johnson, Tulsa* | 1 | 3 | .250 | 4.35 | 26 | 5 | 0 | 9 | 0 | 1 | 78.2 | 89 | 50 | 38 | 4 | 3 | 48 | 6 | 34 | 3 |
| Johnston, San Antonio | 3 | 3 | .500 | 8.26 | 26 | 0 | 0 | 13 | 0 | 0 | 40.1 | 63 | 44 | 37 | 5 | 2 | 27 | 2 | 24 | 3 |
| Jones, Beaumont | 7 | 5 | .583 | 4.66 | 16 | 16 | 1 | 0 | 0 | 0 | 85.0 | 84 | 51 | 44 | 3 | 0 | 66 | 3 | 57 | 5 |
| Kemmerling, Midland | 1 | 1 | .500 | 6.86 | 26 | 0 | 0 | 8 | 0 | 0 | 39.1 | 64 | 38 | 30 | 2 | 0 | 13 | 0 | 11 | 3 |
| Key, Midland | 0 | 0 | .000 | 7.71 | 7 | 0 | 0 | 7 | 0 | 0 | 7.0 | 6 | 6 | 6 | 2 | 0 | 3 | 0 | 5 | 1 |
| Killingsworth, Tulsa | 3 | 3 | .500 | 5.17 | 39 | 1 | 0 | 13 | 0 | 0 | 94.0 | 103 | 66 | 54 | 8 | 2 | 45 | 8 | 79 | 10 |
| King, Shreveport | 5 | 3 | .625 | 2.32 | 15 | 15 | 2 | 0 | 1 | 0 | 104.2 | 74 | 34 | 27 | 8 | 4 | 30 | 0 | 80 | 1 |
| Kipper, Midland* | 3 | 3 | .500 | 3.08 | 9 | 9 | 1 | 0 | 1 | 0 | 49.2 | 52 | 22 | 17 | 5 | 0 | 10 | 0 | 31 | 1 |
| Kochenmeister, Beaumont* | 0 | 0 | .000 | 7.11 | 7 | 0 | 0 | 4 | 0 | 0 | 12.2 | 21 | 14 | 10 | 3 | 0 | 10 | 0 | 3 | 1 |
| Kordish, Tulsa | 2 | 2 | .500 | 4.70 | 7 | 5 | 0 | 2 | 0 | 0 | 30.2 | 33 | 21 | 16 | 5 | 2 | 11 | 2 | 21 | 1 |
| Kutsukos, Beaumont | 1 | 4 | .200 | 4.93 | 47 | 0 | 0 | 29 | 0 | 6 | 80.1 | 101 | 55 | 44 | 3 | 1 | 33 | 2 | 39 | 0 |
| Lachowicz, Tulsa | 0 | 0 | .000 | 1.80 | 1 | 1 | 0 | 0 | 0 | 0 | 5.0 | 4 | 1 | 1 | 0 | 0 | 4 | 0 | 2 | 1 |
| Lockenmeyer, Jackson | 0 | 0 | .000 | 7.20 | 3 | 1 | 0 | 2 | 0 | 0 | 5.0 | 6 | 4 | 4 | 1 | 0 | 1 | 0 | 6 | 0 |
| Lovelace, San Antonio* | 0 | 4 | .000 | 7.61 | 7 | 5 | 0 | 1 | 0 | 0 | 23.2 | 22 | 27 | 20 | 0 | 1 | 30 | 0 | 12 | 5 |
| Lundgren, Jackson | 8 | 4 | .667 | 3.29 | 22 | 21 | 1 | 1 | 1 | 0 | 128.2 | 113 | 54 | 47 | 8 | 2 | 34 | 1 | 74 | 7 |
| Lusted, Shreveport | 4 | 8 | .333 | 3.69 | 19 | 15 | 3 | 2 | 0 | 0 | 105.0 | 101 | 51 | 43 | 6 | 4 | 33 | 0 | 73 | 9 |
| Martin, Arkansas | 8 | 8 | .500 | 3.30 | 26 | 23 | 4 | 1 | 1 | 0 | 142.0 | 136 | 60 | 52 | 6 | 5 | 43 | 2 | 94 | 5 |
| Mason, Arkansas | 1 | 1 | .500 | 4.37 | 13 | 0 | 0 | 9 | 0 | 1 | 22.2 | 26 | 12 | 11 | 5 | 0 | 9 | 3 | 12 | 2 |
| Mattson, Shreveport | 8 | 8 | .500 | 2.79 | 53 | 0 | 0 | 36 | 0 | 12 | 80.2 | 78 | 34 | 25 | 7 | 4 | 40 | 8 | 94 | 6 |
| May, San Antonio | 10 | 6 | .625 | 3.47 | 26 | 26 | 9 | 0 | 2 | 0 | 191.2 | 181 | 85 | 74 | 15 | 1 | 99 | 3 | 125 | 10 |
| Mayberry, San Antonio | 2 | 4 | .333 | 4.39 | 8 | 8 | 1 | 0 | 0 | 0 | 41.0 | 35 | 28 | 20 | 3 | 3 | 18 | 0 | 31 | 4 |
| McClain, Beaumont | 4 | 11 | .267 | 4.61 | 27 | 27 | 2 | 0 | 0 | 0 | 171.2 | 176 | 100 | 88 | 11 | 8 | 90 | 4 | 129 | 12 |
| McKenzie, Midland | 4 | 14 | .222 | 5.01 | 26 | 26 | 3 | 0 | 0 | 0 | 165.1 | 203 | 108 | 92 | 19 | 7 | 57 | 1 | 65 | 9 |
| McKnight, Shreveport | 2 | 1 | .667 | 1.66 | 5 | 5 | 3 | 0 | 1 | 0 | 38.0 | 28 | 10 | 7 | 2 | 2 | 10 | 0 | 40 | 2 |
| Meagher, San Antonio | 8 | 5 | .615 | 3.70 | 45 | 3 | 1 | 28 | 0 | 9 | 87.2 | 72 | 38 | 36 | 9 | 0 | 44 | 7 | 76 | 5 |
| Mills, Beaumont | 10 | 9 | .526 | 3.73 | 26 | 26 | 4 | 0 | 0 | 0 | 166.2 | 164 | 84 | 69 | 4 | 6 | 71 | 3 | 94 | 8 |
| Moreno, Beaumont | 0 | 0 | .000 | 0.00 | 1 | 0 | 0 | 1 | 0 | 0 | 1.0 | 0 | 0 | 0 | 0 | 0 | 0 | 0 | 0 | 0 |
| Morlock, Arkansas | 10 | 6 | .625 | 3.51 | 27 | 25 | 2 | 2 | 1 | 1 | 156.1 | 139 | 70 | 61 | 17 | 5 | 64 | 1 | 110 | 7 |
| Mulholland, Shreveport* | 9 | 8 | .529 | 2.90 | 26 | 26 | 8 | 0 | 3 | 0 | 176.2 | 166 | 79 | 57 | 9 | 2 | 87 | 2 | 122 | 6 |
| Murray, Jackson | 3 | 3 | .500 | 3.30 | 30 | 6 | 0 | 8 | 0 | 0 | 79.0 | 68 | 34 | 29 | 6 | 5 | 17 | 2 | 57 | 0 |
| Murtha, Shreveport* | 0 | 0 | .000 | 7.71 | 2 | 0 | 0 | 0 | 0 | 0 | 2.1 | 2 | 3 | 2 | 1 | 0 | 1 | 0 | 1 | 1 |
| E. Myers, El Paso | 5 | 5 | .500 | 3.38 | 32 | 0 | 0 | 22 | 0 | 6 | 50.2 | 52 | 24 | 19 | 2 | 1 | 18 | 3 | 41 | 2 |
| R. Myers, Jackson* | 4 | 8 | .333 | 3.96 | 19 | 19 | 2 | 0 | 1 | 0 | 120.1 | 99 | 61 | 53 | 4 | 1 | 69 | 1 | 116 | 8 |
| Newsom, San Antonio | 0 | 0 | .000 | 6.00 | 5 | 0 | 0 | 5 | 0 | 0 | 6.0 | 6 | 4 | 4 | 1 | 0 | 3 | 0 | 0 | 0 |
| Nieves, El Paso* | 8 | 2 | .800 | 3.53 | 17 | 17 | 5 | 0 | 2 | 0 | 120.0 | 106 | 53 | 47 | 10 | 0 | 44 | 2 | 91 | 2 |
| Norman, Shreveport | 6 | 5 | .545 | 4.40 | 22 | 17 | 3 | 4 | 1 | 0 | 100.1 | 115 | 60 | 49 | 4 | 7 | 43 | 0 | 51 | 6 |
| North, Arkansas | 0 | 2 | .000 | 7.59 | 2 | 2 | 0 | 0 | 0 | 0 | 10.2 | 13 | 9 | 9 | 0 | 1 | 7 | 0 | 5 | 1 |
| Norton, El Paso | 5 | 8 | .385 | 5.38 | 36 | 13 | 2 | 9 | 0 | 0 | 110.1 | 142 | 85 | 66 | 9 | 2 | 47 | 4 | 53 | 7 |
| Oliveras, Beaumont | 3 | 1 | .750 | 5.00 | 7 | 4 | 0 | 0 | 0 | 0 | 27.0 | 23 | 17 | 15 | 2 | 1 | 9 | 0 | 24 | 2 |
| Orozco, Beaumont | 2 | 3 | .400 | 5.49 | 6 | 6 | 0 | 0 | 0 | 0 | 39.1 | 42 | 25 | 24 | 10 | 0 | 11 | 0 | 25 | 0 |
| Pickett, Jackson* | 0 | 0 | .000 | 0.00 | 3 | 0 | 0 | 0 | 0 | 0 | 4.0 | 2 | 0 | 0 | 0 | 0 | 4 | 0 | 1 | 0 |
| Piper, Jackson | 2 | 4 | .333 | 3.66 | 22 | 5 | 0 | 9 | 0 | 2 | 59.0 | 57 | 29 | 24 | 6 | 2 | 24 | 1 | 43 | 8 |
| Plesac, El Paso* | 12 | 5 | .706 | 4.97 | 25 | 24 | 2 | 0 | 0 | 0 | 150.1 | 171 | 91 | 83 | 12 | 0 | 68 | 1 | 128 | 13 |
| Poston, Beaumont | 8 | 4 | .667 | 2.82 | 38 | 1 | 0 | 24 | 0 | 6 | 67.0 | 71 | 28 | 21 | 0 | 2 | 33 | 8 | 41 | 2 |
| Price, Midland* | 2 | 4 | .333 | 6.05 | 12 | 12 | 1 | 0 | 0 | 0 | 58.0 | 73 | 44 | 39 | 14 | 4 | 38 | 1 | 37 | 4 |
| Pruitt, Jackson* | 4 | 4 | .500 | 2.12 | 52 | 0 | 0 | 20 | 0 | 3 | 68.0 | 66 | 25 | 16 | 4 | 1 | 17 | 0 | 58 | 1 |
| Psaltis, Midland* | 3 | 2 | .600 | 5.99 | 43 | 4 | 0 | 15 | 0 | 2 | 79.2 | 97 | 60 | 53 | 6 | 2 | 54 | 3 | 50 | 6 |
| Reichard, Tulsa | 9 | 7 | .563 | 4.26 | 38 | 1 | 0 | 24 | 0 | 6 | 61.1 | 41 | 33 | 29 | 4 | 2 | 52 | 4 | 65 | 3 |
| Reitz, Tulsa | 0 | 0 | .000 | 0.00 | 1 | 0 | 0 | 0 | 0 | 0 | 1.0 | 0 | 0 | 0 | 0 | 0 | 0 | 0 | 0 | 0 |
| Rhodes, Arkansas* | 2 | 3 | .400 | 4.19 | 23 | 3 | 0 | 11 | 0 | 0 | 43.0 | 48 | 26 | 20 | 4 | 1 | 21 | 1 | 39 | 2 |
| Roberts, El Paso | 7 | 2 | .778 | 5.68 | 12 | 11 | 2 | 1 | 0 | 0 | 76.0 | 93 | 53 | 48 | 10 | 2 | 26 | 0 | 47 | 6 |
| Rodriguez, Beaumont | 0 | 0 | .000 | 3.29 | 7 | 0 | 0 | 5 | 0 | 0 | 13.2 | 15 | 10 | 5 | 0 | 0 | 5 | 0 | 5 | 0 |
| Roman, Arkansas* | 5 | 3 | .625 | 5.17 | 43 | 1 | 0 | 11 | 0 | 0 | 54.0 | 58 | 35 | 31 | 3 | 0 | 26 | 5 | 37 | 0 |
| Ronan, Arkansas | 5 | 1 | .833 | 3.09 | 29 | 1 | 0 | 11 | 0 | 2 | 64.0 | 54 | 23 | 22 | 3 | 4 | 18 | 2 | 30 | 2 |
| Schefsky, Beaumont | 5 | 2 | .714 | 1.97 | 20 | 0 | 0 | 16 | 0 | 7 | 32.0 | 30 | 8 | 7 | 1 | 2 | 14 | 2 | 24 | 2 |
| Schroeck, El Paso* | 4 | 0 | 1.000 | 4.31 | 21 | 1 | 0 | 9 | 0 | 2 | 31.1 | 34 | 17 | 15 | 1 | 0 | 16 | 1 | 21 | 0 |
| Scudder, San Antonio | 1 | 3 | .250 | 9.38 | 27 | 0 | 0 | 9 | 0 | 0 | 54.2 | 85 | 66 | 57 | 12 | 5 | 33 | 2 | 28 | 2 |
| Shade, Arkansas | 7 | 7 | .000 | 4.39 | 32 | 0 | 0 | 21 | 0 | 3 | 41.0 | 44 | 27 | 20 | 4 | 1 | 20 | 4 | 36 | 2 |
| Sierra, Beaumont | 3 | 6 | .333 | 4.74 | 23 | 16 | 0 | 2 | 0 | 1 | 104.1 | 109 | 65 | 55 | 10 | 3 | 60 | 1 | 93 | 7 |
| Soff, Arkansas | 5 | 3 | .625 | 1.38 | 19 | 0 | 0 | 15 | 0 | 6 | 26.0 | 16 | 5 | 4 | 0 | 0 | 9 | 4 | 26 | 2 |
| Suehr, Midland | 3 | 2 | .600 | 6.42 | 35 | 5 | 0 | 5 | 0 | 0 | 88.1 | 112 | 69 | 63 | 13 | 6 | 30 | 1 | 33 | 8 |
| Tanner, Arkansas | 0 | 0 | .000 | 0.00 | 1 | 0 | 0 | 1 | 0 | 0 | 1.0 | 1 | 0 | 0 | 0 | 0 | 0 | 0 | 1 | 0 |
| Taylor, Tulsa | 3 | 9 | .250 | 3.47 | 20 | 17 | 2 | 0 | 0 | 0 | 103.2 | 84 | 55 | 40 | 7 | 2 | 48 | 1 | 87 | 4 |
| Thomas, San Antonio | 1 | 2 | .333 | 5.87 | 17 | 0 | 0 | 6 | 0 | 0 | 30.2 | 43 | 25 | 20 | 2 | 0 | 13 | 2 | 24 | 3 |

| Pitcher—Club | W. | L. | Pct. | ERA. | G. | GS. | CG. | GF. | ShO. | Sv. | IP. | H. | R. | ER. | HR. | HB. | BB. | Int. BB. | SO. | WP. |
|---|---|---|---|---|---|---|---|---|---|---|---|---|---|---|---|---|---|---|---|---|
| Thurberg, Arkansas | 1 | 1 | .500 | 7.50 | 6 | 0 | 0 | 0 | 0 | 0 | 6.0 | 4 | 5 | 5 | 0 | 0 | 12 | 3 | 7 | 1 |
| Timberlake, Midland | 5 | 12 | .294 | 6.71 | 23 | 23 | 2 | 0 | 0 | 0 | 120.2 | 168 | 110 | 90 | 17 | 1 | 65 | 0 | 45 | 7 |
| Towers, Beaumont | 0 | 1 | .000 | 4.91 | 6 | 0 | 0 | 1 | 0 | 1 | 14.2 | 19 | 9 | 8 | 2 | 0 | 5 | 0 | 5 | 0 |
| Vaughn, Jackson | 9 | 7 | .563 | 3.47 | 24 | 18 | 2 | 3 | 0 | 1 | 124.2 | 133 | 59 | 48 | 8 | 3 | 35 | 1 | 58 | 3 |
| Vosberg, Beaumont° | 9 | 11 | .450 | 3.91 | 27 | 27 | 2 | 0 | 1 | 0 | 175.0 | 178 | 92 | 76 | 6 | 3 | 69 | 3 | 124 | 9 |
| Weissman, Jackson | 8 | 8 | .500 | 2.93 | 28 | 19 | 1 | 5 | 1 | 0 | 132.0 | 122 | 57 | 43 | 4 | 4 | 53 | 2 | 72 | 7 |
| Wilburn, Midland | 1 | 5 | .167 | 7.32 | 10 | 7 | 0 | 0 | 0 | 0 | 39.1 | 50 | 32 | 32 | 8 | 1 | 12 | 0 | 21 | 1 |
| Williams, Tulsa° | 2 | 2 | .500 | 4.64 | 6 | 6 | 0 | 0 | 0 | 0 | 33.0 | 17 | 24 | 17 | 1 | 2 | 48 | 0 | 37 | 3 |
| Williamson, Beaumont | 10 | 9 | .526 | 2.86 | 42 | 0 | 0 | 32 | 0 | 8 | 78.2 | 72 | 27 | 25 | 1 | 2 | 23 | 7 | 64 | 3 |
| Wilmet, Arkansas | 0 | 0 | .000 | 10.80 | 9 | 0 | 0 | 1 | 0 | 0 | 8.1 | 16 | 11 | 10 | 2 | 1 | 5 | 1 | 2 | 0 |
| Witt, Tulsa | 0 | 6 | .000 | 6.43 | 11 | 8 | 0 | 1 | 0 | 0 | 35.0 | 26 | 26 | 25 | 1 | 1 | 44 | 0 | 39 | 7 |
| Wyatt, Jackson° | 6 | 1 | .857 | 3.92 | 10 | 10 | 1 | 0 | 0 | 0 | 59.2 | 64 | 32 | 26 | 3 | 2 | 24 | 1 | 40 | 1 |
| Yokubaitis, Shreveport° | 0 | 4 | .000 | 4.56 | 35 | 0 | 0 | 26 | 0 | 3 | 47.1 | 57 | 33 | 24 | 9 | 1 | 23 | 2 | 28 | 5 |
| Young, Jackson° | 6 | 3 | .667 | 3.78 | 21 | 20 | 0 | 0 | 0 | 0 | 112.0 | 96 | 54 | 47 | 8 | 0 | 76 | 1 | 91 | 9 |

BALKS—Bass, 9; James, McClain, Vosberg, 6 each; Bosio, Jones, 5 each; Bockus, May, McKenzie, Taylor, Yokubaitis, 4 each; Adams, Buonantony, Chadwick, Galvez, Hillegas, Johnson, Lundgren, Meagher, Rogerts, Wyatt, 3 each; Banning, Childers, Dunne, Ferran, Fultz, Gonzales, Mills, Norman, Timberlake, Wilburn, 2 each; Anderson, Angulo Birkbeck, Bitker, Brown, T. Clark, Crews, Delzer, Eichhorn, Henry, Kipper, Kordish, Kutsukos, Lovelace, Morlock, E. Myers, R. Myers, Norton, Orozco, Plesac, Rodriguez, Ronan, Schefsky, Schroeck, Scudder, Soff, Towers, Vaughn, Weissman, Williams, Witt, 1 each.

COMBINATION SHUTOUTS—Martin-Boever, Morlock-Hayes, Clark-Roman-Shade, Hayes-Soff, Arkansas; Mills-Williamson, Mills-Poston, Vosberg-Poston, Beaumont; Birkbeck-Barry 2, Gibbons-Bosio, Ciardi-Plesac-Bryant-Barry-Aldrich, El Paso; Fultz-Graves, Brown-Adamczak, Young-Pruitt, Lundgren-Vaughn-Burns, Young-Adamczak, Young-Graves, Murray-Burns, Hartshorn-Pruitt, Jackson; Heuer-Eichhorn, San Antonio; Hummel-Yokubaitis, King-Hummel-Mattson, Shreveport; Anderson-Reichard, Bass-Reichard, Henry-Hudson, Taylor-Johnson-Hudson, Tulsa.

NO-HIT GAMES—None.

# California League

## CLASS A

### CHAMPIONSHIP WINNERS IN PREVIOUS YEARS

| | | | | | |
|---|---|---|---|---|---|
| 1914—Fresno | .571 | 1959—Bakersfield | .592 | 1972—Modesto§ | .547 |
| 1915—Modesto | .857 | Modesto§ | .643 | Bakersfield | .629 |
| 1916-40—Did not operate. | | 1960—Reno | .614 | 1973—Lodi§ | .657 |
| 1941—Fresno | .643 | Reno | .657 | Bakersfield | .571 |
| S. Barbara (2nd)° | .597 | 1961—Reno | .743 | 1974—Fresno§ | .607 |
| 1942—Santa Barbara† | .642 | Reno | .643 | San Jose | .579 |
| 1943-44-45—Did not operate. | | 1962—San Jose§ | .686 | 1975—Reno | .614 |
| 1946—Stockton‡ | .600 | Reno | .587 | Reno | .614 |
| 1947—Stockton‡ | .679 | 1963—Modesto | .589 | 1976—Salinas | .650 |
| 1948—Fresno | .607 | Stockton§ | .687 | Reno§ | .547 |
| S. Barbara (3rd)° | .529 | 1964—Fresno | .638 | 1977—Salinas | .564 |
| 1949—Bakersfield | .612 | Fresno | .600 | Lodi§ | .579 |
| San Jose (4th)° | .543 | 1965—San Jose | .586 | 1978—Visalia§ | .698 |
| 1950—Ventura | .607 | Stockton§ | .614 | Lodi | .607 |
| Modesto (2nd)° | .586 | 1966—Modesto | .577 | 1979—San Jose§ | .636 |
| 1951—Santa Barbara‡ | .599 | Modesto | .671 | Reno | .525 |
| 1952—Fresno‡ | .629 | 1967—San Jose§ | .676 | 1980—Stockton§ | .638 |
| 1953—San Jose‡ | .664 | Modesto | .586 | Visalia | .507 |
| 1954—Modesto‡ | .623 | 1968—San Jose | .629 | 1981—Visalia | .621 |
| 1955—Stockton | .733 | Fresno§ | .623 | Lodi§ | .521 |
| Fresno§ | .718 | 1969—Stockton§ | .600 | 1982—Modesto§ | .671 |
| 1956—Fresno‡ | .650 | Visalia | .614 | Visalia | .586 |
| 1957—Visalia x | .622 | 1970—Bakersfield | .667 | 1983—Visalia | .621 |
| Salinas (4th)° | .504 | Bakersfield | .671 | Redwood§ | .529 |
| 1958—Fresno° | .639 | 1971—Visalia§ | .583 | 1984—Modesto§ | .597 |
| Bakersfield | .672 | Fresno | .500 | Bakersfield | .486 |

°Won four-club playoff. †League disbanded June 28. ‡Won championship and four-club playoff. §Won split-season playoff. xWon both halves of split-season.

### STANDING OF CLUBS AT CLOSE OF FIRST HALF, JUNE 19

#### NORTHERN DIVISION

| Club | W. | L. | T. | Pct. | G.B. |
|---|---|---|---|---|---|
| Modesto (A's) | 43 | 29 | 0 | .597 | ........ |
| Stockton (Brewers) | 41 | 32 | 0 | .562 | 2½ |
| San Jose (Independent) | 32 | 40 | 0 | .444 | 11 |
| Redwood (Angels) | 32 | 42 | 0 | .432 | 12 |
| Reno (Padres) | 28 | 45 | 0 | .384 | 15½ |

#### SOUTHERN DIVISION

| Club | W. | L. | T. | Pct. | G.B. |
|---|---|---|---|---|---|
| Salinas (Mariners) | 50 | 22 | 0 | .694 | ........ |
| Fresno (Giants) | 35 | 37 | 0 | .486 | 15 |
| Visalia (Twins) | 33 | 38 | 0 | .465 | 16½ |
| Bakersfield (Dodgers) | 32 | 41 | 0 | .438 | 18½ |

### STANDING OF CLUBS AT CLOSE OF SECOND HALF, SEPTEMBER 1

#### NORTHERN DIVISION

| Club | W. | L. | T. | Pct. | G.B. |
|---|---|---|---|---|---|
| Stockton (Brewers) | 41 | 31 | 0 | .569 | ........ |
| Redwood (Angels) | 38 | 34 | 0 | .528 | 3 |
| Reno (Padres) | 36 | 36 | 0 | .500 | 5 |
| Modesto (A's) | 33 | 39 | 0 | .458 | 8 |
| San Jose (Independent) | 23 | 48 | 0 | .324 | 17½ |

#### SOUTHERN DIVISION

| Club | W. | L. | T. | Pct. | G.B. |
|---|---|---|---|---|---|
| Fresno (Giants) | 49 | 25 | 0 | .662 | ........ |
| Salinas (Mariners) | 39 | 33 | 0 | .542 | 9 |
| Bakersfield (Dodgers) | 33 | 39 | 0 | .458 | 15 |
| Visalia (Twins) | 33 | 40 | 0 | .452 | 15½ |

### COMPOSITE STANDING OF CLUBS AT CLOSE OF SEASON, SEPTEMBER 1

#### NORTHERN DIVISION

| Club | Sto. | Mod. | Red. | Reno | S.J. | Sal. | Fr. | Vis. | Bak. | W. | L. | T. | Pct. | G.B. |
|---|---|---|---|---|---|---|---|---|---|---|---|---|---|---|
| Stockton (Brewers) | .... | 12 | 14 | 12 | 11 | 6 | 9 | 10 | 8 | 82 | 63 | 0 | .566 | ........ |
| Modesto (A's) | 14 | .... | 10 | 14 | 13 | 7 | 3 | 7 | 8 | 76 | 68 | 0 | .528 | 5½ |
| Redwood (Angels) | 11 | 14 | .... | 16 | 14 | 5 | 5 | 2 | 3 | 70 | 76 | 0 | .479 | 12½ |
| Reno (Padres) | 12 | 10 | 9 | .... | 15 | 2 | 3 | 5 | 8 | 64 | 81 | 0 | .441 | 18 |
| San Jose (Independent) | 11 | 9 | 10 | 9 | .... | 6 | 2 | 6 | 2 | 55 | 88 | 0 | .385 | 26 |

#### SOUTHERN DIVISION

| Club | Sto. | Mod. | Red. | Reno | S.J. | Sal. | Fr. | Vis. | Bak. | W. | L. | T. | Pct. | G.B. |
|---|---|---|---|---|---|---|---|---|---|---|---|---|---|---|
| Salinas (Mariners) | 6 | 5 | 7 | 10 | 10 | .... | 17 | 16 | 18 | 89 | 55 | 0 | .618 | ........ |
| Frenso (Giants) | 3 | 9 | 7 | 9 | 10 | 10 | .... | 14 | 22 | 84 | 62 | 0 | .575 | 6 |
| Visalia (Twins) | 2 | 5 | 10 | 7 | 5 | 10 | 16 | .... | 11 | 66 | 78 | 0 | .458 | 23 |
| Bakersfield (Dodgers) | 4 | 4 | 9 | 4 | 10 | 9 | 7 | 18 | .... | 65 | 80 | 0 | .448 | 24½ |

Major league affiliations in parentheses.

Playoffs—Stockton defeated Modesto, three games to one; Fresno defeated Salinas, three games to one; and Fresno defeated Stockton, three games to two, to win league championship.

Regular Season Attendance—Bakersfield, 74,054; Fresno, 83,351; Modesto, 73,661; Redwood, 25,836; Reno, 77,693; Salinas, 39,720; San Jose, 53,423; Stockton, 69,334; Visalia, 74,407. Total, 571,479. Playoffs, 17,747.

Managers—Bakersfield, Melvin Queen; Fresno, Wendell Kim; Modesto, George Mitterwald; Redwood, John Kotchman; Reno, Steve Smith; Salinas, Bob Harrison; San Jose; Jethro McIntyre; Stockton, Tom Gamboa; Visalia; Dan Schmitz.

All-Star Team: 1B—Jim Eppard, Modesto; 2B—Phil Smith, San Jose; 3B—Mark McGwire, Modesto; SS—Brian Guinn, Modesto; OF—Mike Jones, Fresno; Bob Loscalzo, Modesto; Mack Sasser, Fresno; C—Jeff Brown, Bakersfield; DH—(tie) Chris Chapman, Bakersfield; Tim Hill, San Jose; P—Charlie Corbell, Fresno; Jeff Parrett, Stockton; Ed Puikunas, Fresno; Rick Moore, Salinas; Most Valuable Player—Eric Hardgrave, Reno; Pitcher of the Year—Charlie Corbell, Fresno; Manager of the Year—Wendell Kim, Fresno.

(Compiled by William J. Weiss, League Statistician, San Mateo, Calif.)

## CLUB BATTING

| Club | Pct. | G. | AB. | R. | OR. | H. | TB. | 2B. | 3B. | HR. | RBI. | GW. | SH. | SF. | HP. | BB. | Int. BB. | SO. | SB. | CS. | LOB. |
|---|---|---|---|---|---|---|---|---|---|---|---|---|---|---|---|---|---|---|---|---|---|
| Fresno | .284 | 146 | 4859 | 816 | 667 | 1381 | 1902 | 222 | 34 | 77 | 737 | 76 | 64 | 61 | 39 | 703 | 17 | 837 | 145 | 78 | 1214 |
| Reno | .276 | 145 | 4880 | 815 | 915 | 1348 | 1897 | 221 | 44 | 80 | 714 | 55 | 32 | 35 | 43 | 622 | 13 | 819 | 158 | 77 | 1108 |
| Visalia | .267 | 144 | 4737 | 678 | 754 | 1267 | 1672 | 162 | 27 | 63 | 616 | 57 | 58 | 59 | 43 | 624 | 21 | 724 | 133 | 72 | 1176 |
| Bakersfield | .265 | 145 | 4749 | 675 | 766 | 1257 | 1686 | 184 | 16 | 71 | 590 | 57 | 43 | 37 | 47 | 581 | 18 | 860 | 209 | 90 | 1085 |
| Modesto | .264 | 144 | 4710 | 779 | 699 | 1245 | 1809 | 214 | 37 | 92 | 697 | 67 | 33 | 46 | 43 | 734 | 21 | 1042 | 166 | 83 | 1139 |
| San Jose | .263 | 143 | 4519 | 594 | 728 | 1188 | 1594 | 194 | 28 | 52 | 513 | 48 | 76 | 40 | 33 | 575 | 12 | 883 | 123 | 75 | 1068 |
| Redwood | .261 | 146 | 4748 | 641 | 700 | 1240 | 1735 | 238 | 40 | 59 | 571 | 61 | 71 | 37 | 48 | 595 | 21 | 997 | 147 | 74 | 1143 |
| Salinas | .261 | 144 | 4498 | 706 | 603 | 1172 | 1600 | 181 | 35 | 59 | 596 | 76 | 36 | 50 | 48 | 663 | 8 | 756 | 162 | 99 | 1059 |
| Stockton | .256 | 145 | 4734 | 775 | 647 | 1212 | 1647 | 181 | 31 | 64 | 679 | 71 | 45 | 56 | 62 | 813 | 21 | 844 | 252 | 88 | 1190 |

## INDIVIDUAL BATTING

(Leading Qualifiers for Batting Championship—391 or More Plate Appearances)

*Bats lefthanded.      †Switch-hitter.

| Player and Club | Pct. | G. | AB. | R. | H. | TB. | 2B. | 3B. | HR. | RBI. | GW. | SH. | SF. | HP. | BB. | Int. BB. | SO. | SB. | CS. |
|---|---|---|---|---|---|---|---|---|---|---|---|---|---|---|---|---|---|---|---|
| Eppard, James, Modesto* | .345 | 141 | 531 | 97 | 183 | 223 | 23 | 4 | 3 | 88 | 14 | 5 | 11 | 2 | 69 | 6 | 49 | 14 | 6 |
| Chapman, Christopher, Bakersfield* | .341 | 102 | 364 | 69 | 124 | 221 | 29 | 1 | 22 | 82 | 9 | 2 | 5 | 2 | 70 | 8 | 36 | 9 | 5 |
| Williams, Brian, Bakersfield* | .340 | 109 | 441 | 65 | 150 | 184 | 29 | 1 | 1 | 65 | 5 | 2 | 4 | 1 | 23 | 2 | 47 | 19 | 9 |
| Sasser, Mack, Fresno* | .338 | 133 | 497 | 79 | 168 | 245 | 27 | 4 | 14 | 102 | 16 | 3 | 9 | 3 | 36 | 4 | 35 | 3 | 3 |
| Jones, Michael, Fresno* | .332 | 124 | 398 | 92 | 132 | 179 | 21 | 4 | 6 | 47 | 4 | 4 | 5 | 4 | 101 | 2 | 68 | 36 | 17 |
| Smith, Philander, San Jose | .318 | 121 | 444 | 76 | 141 | 163 | 12 | 2 | 2 | 44 | 3 | 4 | 5 | 3 | 60 | 1 | 48 | 30 | 20 |
| McCue, Deron, Fresno* | .316 | 110 | 367 | 69 | 116 | 153 | 17 | 4 | 4 | 54 | 4 | 9 | 4 | 5 | 38 | 0 | 58 | 10 | 5 |
| Freeman, Lavel, Stockton* | .314 | 137 | 544 | 89 | 171 | 221 | 25 | 2 | 7 | 92 | 12 | 1 | 5 | 3 | 53 | 3 | 74 | 38 | 6 |
| Loscalzo, Robert, Modesto* | .308 | 120 | 413 | 72 | 127 | 187 | 20 | 5 | 10 | 63 | 7 | 1 | 1 | 1 | 65 | 5 | 88 | 22 | 14 |
| Larkin, Eugene, Visalia† | .305 | 142 | 528 | 90 | 161 | 231 | 25 | 3 | 13 | 106 | 12 | 0 | 14 | 2 | 81 | 5 | 61 | 0 | 1 |

Departmental Leaders: G—Farmar, Larkin, 142; AB—Litton, 564; R—Wrona, 107; H—Eppard, 183; TB—Sasser, 245; 2B—Litton, 33; 3B—Varoz, 10; HR—Hardgrave, McGwire, 24; RBI—Larkin, McGwire, 106; GWRBI—Sasser, Wishnevski, 16; SH—Tomashino, 20; SF—Larkin, 14; HP—Finley, 15; BB—Thornton, 113; IBB—Chapman, 8; SO—Pettis, 143; SB—Sferrazza, 57; CS—Finley, 23.

(All Players—Listed Alphabetically)

| Player and Club | Pct. | G. | AB. | R. | H. | TB. | 2B. | 3B. | HR. | RBI. | GW. | SH. | SF. | HP. | BB. | Int. BB. | SO. | SB. | CS. |
|---|---|---|---|---|---|---|---|---|---|---|---|---|---|---|---|---|---|---|---|
| Alarid, David, Bakersfield* | .238 | 28 | 84 | 8 | 20 | 24 | 4 | 0 | 0 | 10 | 1 | 0 | 1 | 0 | 8 | 0 | 12 | 5 | 2 |
| Alexander, Tommy, 20 Fr.-34 Reno | .000 | 54 | 2 | 1 | 0 | 0 | 0 | 0 | 0 | 0 | 0 | 0 | 0 | 0 | 1 | 0 | 2 | 0 | 0 |
| Alfonso, Antonio, Redwood | .246 | 43 | 122 | 14 | 30 | 38 | 6 | 1 | 0 | 10 | 2 | 5 | 3 | 1 | 24 | 0 | 23 | 3 | 1 |
| Allen, James, 107 SJ-33 Sto† | .274 | 140 | 482 | 72 | 132 | 173 | 18 | 1 | 7 | 65 | 8 | 8 | 6 | 3 | 92 | 2 | 70 | 5 | 7 |
| Allen, David, Fresno | .243 | 81 | 218 | 33 | 53 | 71 | 11 | 2 | 1 | 26 | 2 | 2 | 3 | 4 | 19 | 0 | 39 | 6 | 3 |
| Alvarez, Carmelo, Bakersfield† | .209 | 52 | 153 | 19 | 32 | 33 | 1 | 0 | 0 | 7 | 1 | 5 | 0 | 0 | 20 | 1 | 28 | 10 | 3 |
| Amaya, Benjamin, Salinas | .253 | 74 | 194 | 33 | 49 | 64 | 7 | 1 | 2 | 24 | 2 | 3 | 0 | 8 | 36 | 0 | 34 | 4 | 4 |
| Anderson, Kent, Redwood | .250 | 117 | 420 | 53 | 105 | 127 | 17 | 1 | 1 | 47 | 8 | 10 | 2 | 2 | 40 | 1 | 66 | 4 | 7 |
| Antonelli, John, Stockton | .282 | 85 | 252 | 38 | 71 | 91 | 10 | 2 | 2 | 40 | 4 | 1 | 5 | 5 | 26 | 1 | 38 | 8 | 6 |
| Arnold, Timothy, Redwood | .299 | 43 | 137 | 12 | 41 | 53 | 7 | 1 | 1 | 16 | 4 | 1 | 1 | 0 | 21 | 1 | 15 | 0 | 0 |
| Austin, Terry, Reno | .252 | 106 | 298 | 42 | 75 | 94 | 11 | 4 | 0 | 33 | 3 | 0 | 3 | 3 | 36 | 1 | 54 | 11 | 6 |
| Barnhouse, Scott, Reno | .333 | 41 | 6 | 0 | 2 | 2 | 0 | 0 | 0 | 0 | 0 | 0 | 0 | 0 | 0 | 0 | 2 | 0 | 0 |
| Barton, Gregory, San Jose | .148 | 23 | 54 | 4 | 8 | 9 | 1 | 0 | 0 | 5 | 0 | 0 | 0 | 0 | 4 | 0 | 9 | 0 | 0 |
| Barton, Shawn, San Jose | .253 | 75 | 261 | 35 | 66 | 86 | 12 | 1 | 2 | 23 | 2 | 6 | 1 | 0 | 25 | 0 | 28 | 1 | 2 |
| Bates, William, Stockton* | .298 | 59 | 218 | 36 | 65 | 84 | 8 | 1 | 3 | 31 | 3 | 2 | 1 | 1 | 35 | 0 | 27 | 18 | 5 |
| Beall, Peter, Redwood | .242 | 133 | 405 | 48 | 98 | 142 | 18 | 1 | 8 | 55 | 4 | 9 | 3 | 7 | 58 | 1 | 85 | 8 | 2 |
| Bell, Jay, Visalia | .282 | 106 | 376 | 56 | 106 | 161 | 16 | 6 | 9 | 59 | 6 | 4 | 7 | 4 | 41 | 0 | 73 | 10 | 6 |
| Bell, Terence, Salinas | .236 | 92 | 263 | 40 | 62 | 82 | 15 | 1 | 1 | 40 | 4 | 0 | 6 | 3 | 54 | 0 | 49 | 4 | 3 |
| Benitez, Manuel, Bakersfield | .100 | 10 | 30 | 1 | 3 | 4 | 1 | 0 | 0 | 1 | 0 | 0 | 1 | 0 | 0 | 0 | 8 | 1 | 1 |
| Beringhele, Vincent, Bakersfield | .237 | 47 | 156 | 18 | 37 | 43 | 3 | 0 | 1 | 13 | 1 | 0 | 0 | 0 | 26 | 0 | 29 | 8 | 2 |
| Bernardo, Robert, Salinas | .244 | 27 | 82 | 13 | 20 | 33 | 7 | 0 | 2 | 7 | 1 | 1 | 0 | 1 | 18 | 0 | 22 | 4 | 1 |
| Bierley, Bradley, Visalia* | .287 | 74 | 282 | 45 | 81 | 126 | 17 | 2 | 8 | 41 | 4 | 4 | 1 | 0 | 33 | 1 | 59 | 3 | 6 |
| Boyd, Mark, Bakersfield | .229 | 66 | 192 | 20 | 44 | 58 | 5 | 0 | 3 | 25 | 1 | 1 | 3 | 0 | 25 | 0 | 36 | 1 | 1 |
| Bradley, Paul, Modesto | .216 | 72 | 213 | 27 | 46 | 65 | 6 | 2 | 3 | 26 | 3 | 3 | 1 | 5 | 40 | 0 | 53 | 1 | 0 |
| Brady, Brian, Redwood* | .290 | 123 | 441 | 65 | 128 | 195 | 28 | 6 | 9 | 56 | 5 | 10 | 1 | 7 | 43 | 4 | 74 | 16 | 9 |
| Brantley, Jeffrey, Fresno | .000 | 14 | 6 | 0 | 0 | 0 | 0 | 0 | 0 | 0 | 0 | 0 | 0 | 0 | 0 | 0 | 1 | 0 | 0 |
| Brown, Jeffrey, Bakersfield | .303 | 138 | 495 | 93 | 150 | 221 | 30 | 1 | 13 | 85 | 6 | 3 | 5 | 12 | 71 | 0 | 91 | 20 | 12 |
| Brown, Waymon, San Jose† | .125 | 23 | 48 | 6 | 6 | 9 | 3 | 0 | 0 | 1 | 0 | 0 | 1 | 2 | 6 | 0 | 12 | 2 | 1 |
| Bruno, Joseph, Stockton | .238 | 36 | 84 | 11 | 20 | 22 | 2 | 0 | 0 | 10 | 0 | 1 | 0 | 1 | 19 | 0 | 9 | 4 | 1 |
| Bruzik, Robert, Salinas | .291 | 94 | 306 | 42 | 89 | 103 | 7 | 2 | 1 | 32 | 5 | 4 | 3 | 6 | 25 | 0 | 37 | 14 | 5 |
| Buchanon, Bobby, Redwood* | .222 | 13 | 45 | 9 | 10 | 12 | 0 | 1 | 0 | 3 | 1 | 0 | 0 | 0 | 7 | 0 | 10 | 1 | 2 |
| Burkett, John, Fresno | .071 | 20 | 14 | 2 | 1 | 1 | 0 | 0 | 0 | 0 | 0 | 1 | 0 | 0 | 1 | 0 | 11 | 0 | 0 |
| Buss, Scott, Salinas | .278 | 110 | 352 | 62 | 98 | 128 | 4 | 1 | 8 | 34 | 5 | 1 | 3 | 1 | 63 | 1 | 58 | 17 | 11 |
| Cabrera, Antonio, Modesto | .229 | 72 | 218 | 23 | 50 | 57 | 7 | 0 | 0 | 16 | 1 | 6 | 1 | 1 | 14 | 0 | 22 | 1 | 2 |
| Calley, Robert, Visalia | .285 | 122 | 439 | 48 | 125 | 149 | 15 | 0 | 3 | 55 | 6 | 3 | 6 | 1 | 45 | 2 | 46 | 1 | 2 |
| Calvert, Christopher, Visalia | .255 | 68 | 200 | 32 | 51 | 72 | 4 | 1 | 5 | 31 | 5 | 3 | 4 | 3 | 36 | 1 | 34 | 3 | 0 |
| Campbell, Michael, Redwood* | .258 | 28 | 66 | 14 | 17 | 24 | 5 | 1 | 0 | 10 | 2 | 1 | 2 | 0 | 11 | 0 | 16 | 2 | 0 |
| Candelaria, Albert, Fresno* | .000 | 34 | 6 | 0 | 0 | 0 | 0 | 0 | 0 | 0 | 0 | 0 | 0 | 0 | 0 | 0 | 6 | 0 | 0 |
| Carlson, John, Reno | .205 | 59 | 156 | 18 | 32 | 36 | 4 | 0 | 0 | 16 | 0 | 1 | 0 | 2 | 13 | 0 | 35 | 1 | 2 |
| Carlucci, David, Bakersfield | .227 | 77 | 229 | 22 | 52 | 60 | 5 | 0 | 1 | 21 | 1 | 4 | 4 | 1 | 26 | 0 | 47 | 3 | 4 |
| Casey, Timothy, Stockton* | .204 | 105 | 348 | 67 | 71 | 132 | 11 | 4 | 14 | 70 | 11 | 1 | 8 | 6 | 75 | 1 | 93 | 23 | 11 |
| Chapman, Christopher, Bakersfield* | .341 | 102 | 364 | 69 | 124 | 221 | 29 | 1 | 22 | 82 | 9 | 2 | 5 | 2 | 70 | 8 | 36 | 9 | 5 |
| Childers, Jeffrey, Reno | .250 | 12 | 4 | 1 | 1 | 2 | 1 | 0 | 0 | 0 | 0 | 0 | 0 | 0 | 1 | 0 | 0 | 0 | 0 |
| Clark, Daniel, Salinas | .256 | 134 | 450 | 87 | 115 | 175 | 19 | 7 | 9 | 68 | 4 | 6 | 3 | 3 | 72 | 0 | 95 | 14 | 6 |
| Clark, William, Fresno* | .309 | 65 | 217 | 41 | 67 | 111 | 14 | 0 | 10 | 48 | 5 | 3 | 5 | 2 | 62 | 2 | 46 | 11 | 2 |
| Cobbs, Todd, Bakersfield | .000 | 34 | 10 | 0 | 0 | 0 | 0 | 0 | 0 | 0 | 0 | 0 | 0 | 0 | 2 | 0 | 6 | 0 | 0 |
| Colton, Bradford, Salinas | .224 | 64 | 214 | 33 | 48 | 71 | 6 | 1 | 5 | 23 | 4 | 0 | 2 | 6 | 29 | 0 | 52 | 2 | 7 |
| Copeland, Thomas, Visalia* | .303 | 62 | 208 | 35 | 63 | 92 | 8 | 3 | 5 | 31 | 6 | 1 | 2 | 0 | 43 | 4 | 11 | 7 | 6 |
| Corbell, Charles, Fresno | .167 | 26 | 12 | 3 | 2 | 2 | 0 | 0 | 0 | 0 | 0 | 1 | 0 | 0 | 0 | 0 | 6 | 0 | 1 |
| Crabtree, Gary, Salinas† | .238 | 127 | 378 | 61 | 90 | 130 | 18 | 5 | 4 | 44 | 6 | 3 | 1 | 0 | 73 | 0 | 66 | 14 | 6 |
| Cucjen, Romulo, Fresno | .266 | 108 | 342 | 41 | 91 | 144 | 14 | 3 | 11 | 54 | 6 | 0 | 2 | 3 | 43 | 1 | 90 | 0 | 4 |
| Culberson, Charles, Fresno | .237 | 101 | 266 | 36 | 63 | 81 | 7 | 4 | 1 | 40 | 2 | 2 | 7 | 1 | 33 | 0 | 55 | 18 | 3 |
| DeButch, Michael, Reno | .270 | 120 | 460 | 88 | 124 | 159 | 19 | 5 | 2 | 46 | 5 | 7 | 3 | 3 | 80 | 1 | 55 | 49 | 14 |
| de Chavez, Oscar, Modesto | 1.000 | 31 | 1 | 0 | 1 | 1 | 0 | 0 | 0 | 0 | 0 | 0 | 0 | 0 | 0 | 0 | 0 | 0 | 0 |
| DiCeglio, Thomas, Visalia | .226 | 74 | 226 | 26 | 51 | 66 | 7 | 1 | 2 | 22 | 3 | 4 | 0 | 1 | 10 | 0 | 36 | 0 | 1 |
| Dillard, David, Reno* | .306 | 52 | 183 | 37 | 56 | 85 | 11 | 3 | 4 | 28 | 2 | 0 | 2 | 1 | 17 | 1 | 37 | 6 | 5 |
| Doran, Mark, Redwood | .279 | 104 | 330 | 49 | 92 | 139 | 18 | 4 | 7 | 41 | 5 | 0 | 2 | 6 | 47 | 0 | 89 | 14 | 8 |
| Duggan, Thomas, Salinas | .176 | 14 | 34 | 2 | 6 | 11 | 2 | 0 | 1 | 6 | 1 | 1 | 0 | 0 | 7 | 0 | 10 | 0 | 0 |
| Duncan, John, Salinas | .301 | 88 | 296 | 42 | 89 | 109 | 14 | 0 | 2 | 37 | 5 | 1 | 1 | 2 | 28 | 1 | 37 | 9 | 6 |

| Player and Club | Pct. | G. | AB. | R. | H. | TB. | 2B. | 3B. | HR. | RBI. | GW. | SH. | SF. | HP. | BB. | Int. BB. | SO. | SB. | CS. |
|---|---|---|---|---|---|---|---|---|---|---|---|---|---|---|---|---|---|---|---|
| Dunlop, David, Reno | .000 | 30 | 0 | 0 | 0 | 0 | 0 | 0 | 0 | 0 | 0 | 0 | 0 | 0 | 0 | 0 | 0 | 1 | 0 |
| Dunton, Kevin, San Jose | .276 | 74 | 254 | 29 | 70 | 99 | 9 | 1 | 6 | 34 | 3 | 0 | 4 | 1 | 33 | 0 | 50 | 0 | 3 |
| Edwards, Jeffrey, Bakersfield° | .000 | 16 | 5 | 0 | 0 | 0 | 0 | 0 | 0 | 0 | 0 | 3 | 0 | 0 | 0 | 0 | 1 | 0 | 0 |
| Eppard, James, Modesto° | .345 | 141 | 531 | 97 | 183 | 223 | 23 | 4 | 3 | 88 | 14 | 5 | 11 | 2 | 69 | 6 | 49 | 14 | 6 |
| Escobar, Angel, Fresno† | .251 | 109 | 386 | 62 | 97 | 117 | 13 | 2 | 1 | 34 | 3 | 15 | 4 | 1 | 59 | 1 | 57 | 18 | 7 |
| Eurton, James, San Jose | .274 | 21 | 62 | 5 | 17 | 22 | 2 | 0 | 1 | 8 | 2 | 1 | 0 | 1 | 7 | 1 | 16 | 0 | 0 |
| Falkner, Belgee, San Jose | .241 | 121 | 402 | 57 | 97 | 156 | 16 | 8 | 9 | 48 | 2 | 10 | 5 | 4 | 49 | 1 | 119 | 31 | 11 |
| Farmar, Damon, Modesto | .225 | 142 | 519 | 63 | 117 | 170 | 15 | 4 | 10 | 86 | 10 | 2 | 12 | 2 | 52 | 1 | 123 | 32 | 9 |
| Finley, Brian, Stockton° | .243 | 141 | 530 | 100 | 129 | 150 | 10 | 4 | 1 | 45 | 2 | 5 | 6 | 15 | 112 | 2 | 42 | 54 | 23 |
| Flores, Richard, Bakersfield° | .231 | 103 | 295 | 38 | 68 | 98 | 9 | 3 | 5 | 26 | 1 | 3 | 1 | 2 | 30 | 1 | 65 | 10 | 6 |
| Forgione, Christopher, Visalia° | .230 | 116 | 382 | 41 | 88 | 110 | 12 | 2 | 2 | 40 | 3 | 5 | 3 | 1 | 38 | 2 | 68 | 6 | 3 |
| Freeman, Lavel, Stockton° | .314 | 137 | 544 | 89 | 171 | 221 | 25 | 2 | 7 | 92 | 12 | 1 | 5 | 3 | 53 | 3 | 74 | 38 | 6 |
| Gallego, Michael, Modesto | .200 | 6 | 25 | 1 | 5 | 6 | 1 | 0 | 0 | 2 | 1 | 0 | 0 | 0 | 2 | 0 | 8 | 1 | 1 |
| Garner, Michael, Bakersfield† | .268 | 84 | 313 | 80 | 84 | 91 | 3 | 2 | 0 | 18 | 0 | 3 | 1 | 10 | 61 | 1 | 63 | 56 | 12 |
| Garrett, Eric, Modesto | .176 | 55 | 165 | 15 | 29 | 34 | 5 | 0 | 0 | 16 | 1 | 1 | 1 | 0 | 19 | 0 | 37 | 4 | 4 |
| Gatewood, Henry, Bakersfield | .333 | 5 | 12 | 1 | 4 | 4 | 0 | 0 | 0 | 0 | 0 | 0 | 0 | 0 | 3 | 0 | 1 | 0 | 0 |
| Gentle, Michael, Bakersfield° | .192 | 24 | 26 | 3 | 5 | 8 | 1 | 1 | 0 | 4 | 0 | 0 | 0 | 0 | 0 | 0 | 3 | 2 | 0 |
| Gibree, Robert, Salinas | .200 | 2 | 5 | 0 | 1 | 1 | 0 | 0 | 0 | 0 | 0 | 0 | 0 | 0 | 1 | 0 | 2 | 0 | 0 |
| Gilbert, Gregory, Fresno | .000 | 21 | 1 | 0 | 0 | 0 | 0 | 0 | 0 | 0 | 0 | 0 | 0 | 0 | 0 | 0 | 0 | 0 | 0 |
| Gildehaus, Michael, Reno° | .000 | 21 | 1 | 0 | 0 | 0 | 0 | 0 | 0 | 0 | 0 | 0 | 0 | 0 | 0 | 0 | 1 | 0 | 0 |
| Grandstaff, Robert, Reno | .283 | 124 | 431 | 75 | 122 | 182 | 16 | 4 | 12 | 70 | 2 | 1 | 0 | 4 | 75 | 2 | 77 | 14 | 3 |
| Grimes, John, Fresno | .298 | 87 | 262 | 48 | 78 | 106 | 16 | 0 | 4 | 45 | 6 | 1 | 2 | 1 | 63 | 2 | 61 | 0 | 2 |
| Guinn, Brian, Modesto† | .291 | 109 | 444 | 103 | 129 | 189 | 29 | 5 | 7 | 54 | 3 | 2 | 2 | | 62 | 5 | 100 | 42 | 14 |
| Hall, Matthew, Salinas° | .273 | 135 | 517 | 80 | 141 | 191 | 27 | 7 | 3 | 73 | 8 | 3 | 4 | 6 | 70 | 0 | 81 | 41 | 16 |
| Hamrick, Randy, Bakersfield | .000 | 16 | 7 | 0 | 0 | 0 | 0 | 0 | 0 | 0 | 0 | 0 | 0 | 0 | 0 | 0 | 3 | 0 | 0 |
| Hance, William, Stockton° | .306 | 102 | 291 | 42 | 89 | 135 | 21 | 2 | 7 | 63 | 5 | 3 | 4 | 2 | 70 | 7 | 36 | 1 | 4 |
| Hancock, Boris, San Jose | .000 | 3 | 5 | 0 | 0 | 0 | 0 | 0 | 0 | 0 | 0 | 0 | 0 | 0 | 0 | 0 | 1 | 0 | 0 |
| Hanyuda, Tadayuki, San Jose† | .220 | 71 | 177 | 27 | 39 | 44 | 3 | 1 | 0 | 11 | 0 | 5 | 1 | 1 | 24 | 0 | 36 | 4 | 3 |
| Hardgrave, Eric, Reno | .375 | 77 | 291 | 58 | 109 | 207 | 24 | 1 | 24 | 85 | 12 | 0 | 3 | 8 | 18 | 4 | 42 | 2 | 1 |
| Hartsock, Brian, Redwood° | .320 | 86 | 309 | 45 | 99 | 138 | 22 | 4 | 3 | 48 | 8 | 2 | 2 | 1 | 39 | 1 | 55 | 6 | 5 |
| Harvey, Randall, Modesto° | 1.000 | 24 | 1 | 0 | 1 | 2 | 1 | 0 | 0 | 0 | 0 | 0 | 0 | 0 | 0 | 0 | 0 | 0 | 0 |
| Hayes, Charles, Fresno | .283 | 131 | 467 | 73 | 132 | 165 | 17 | 2 | 4 | 68 | 6 | 1 | 4 | 6 | 56 | 0 | 95 | 7 | 8 |
| Henning, Richard, Fresno | .182 | 15 | 11 | 2 | 2 | 2 | 0 | 0 | 0 | 2 | 0 | 2 | 0 | 0 | 1 | 0 | 4 | 0 | 1 |
| Hill, Timothy, San Jose | .269 | 126 | 439 | 47 | 118 | 179 | 30 | 2 | 9 | 68 | 8 | 2 | 2 | 5 | 18 | 2 | 89 | 2 | 0 |
| Hillman, Thomas, Visalia | .229 | 15 | 48 | 4 | 11 | 14 | 3 | 0 | 0 | 4 | 0 | 0 | 2 | 0 | 11 | 0 | 14 | 1 | 1 |
| Holcomb, Ted, Bakersfield° | .283 | 132 | 456 | 54 | 129 | 142 | 11 | 1 | 0 | 57 | 6 | 4 | 6 | 2 | 41 | 1 | 45 | 19 | 9 |
| Hornacek, Jay, Bakersfield | .205 | 72 | 239 | 26 | 49 | 70 | 9 | 0 | 4 | 27 | 3 | 3 | 2 | 5 | 14 | 0 | 62 | 4 | 3 |
| Howard, Steven, Modesto | .221 | 110 | 349 | 59 | 77 | 140 | 15 | 3 | 14 | 64 | 2 | 1 | 2 | 8 | 67 | 0 | 138 | 10 | 9 |
| Hubbard, Henry, Reno | .233 | 120 | 339 | 47 | 79 | 92 | 6 | 2 | 1 | 36 | 1 | 1 | 4 | 2 | 32 | 1 | 59 | 5 | 9 |
| Humphrey, Sylester, San Jose° | .250 | 35 | 84 | 9 | 21 | 23 | 2 | 0 | 0 | 6 | 0 | 1 | 2 | 0 | 15 | 0 | 21 | 1 | 0 |
| Husband, Perry, Visalia° | .217 | 97 | 295 | 41 | 64 | 71 | 7 | 0 | 0 | 27 | 3 | 13 | 5 | 0 | 40 | 0 | 41 | 9 | 5 |
| Jacas, Andre, Modesto | .215 | 37 | 107 | 24 | 23 | 29 | 1 | 1 | 1 | 10 | 0 | 2 | 1 | 2 | 33 | 0 | 25 | 8 | 5 |
| Jackson, Larry, Stockton° | .305 | 66 | 187 | 31 | 57 | 70 | 7 | 3 | 0 | 32 | 3 | 0 | 4 | 0 | 30 | 2 | 20 | 15 | 2 |
| Jaremko, Thomas, Visalia | .176 | 27 | 74 | 3 | 13 | 14 | 1 | 0 | 0 | 4 | 0 | 1 | 0 | 1 | 4 | 0 | 17 | 0 | 1 |
| Jones, Gary, San Jose | .263 | 121 | 376 | 42 | 99 | 122 | 15 | 1 | 2 | 30 | 1 | 4 | 2 | 1 | 37 | 3 | 75 | 0 | 2 |
| Jones, James, Modesto | .252 | 98 | 330 | 40 | 83 | 108 | 14 | 1 | 3 | 48 | 2 | 5 | 3 | 2 | 59 | 1 | 61 | 2 | 4 |
| Jones, Michael, Fresno° | .332 | 124 | 398 | 92 | 132 | 179 | 21 | 4 | 6 | 47 | 4 | 4 | 5 | 4 | 101 | 2 | 68 | 36 | 17 |
| Jones, Terrance, Redwood° | .206 | 33 | 101 | 12 | 21 | 27 | 2 | 2 | 0 | 15 | 2 | 0 | 1 | 0 | 13 | 2 | 20 | 3 | 0 |
| Kline, Kris, Redwood | .286 | 117 | 402 | 48 | 115 | 146 | 22 | 3 | 1 | 41 | 5 | 5 | 6 | 3 | 27 | 0 | 63 | 12 | 5 |
| Kockenmeister, Ted, Reno | .000 | 13 | 1 | 0 | 0 | 0 | 0 | 0 | 0 | 0 | 0 | 0 | 0 | 0 | 0 | 0 | 0 | 0 | 0 |
| Kopetsky, Brian, Bakersfield | .145 | 46 | 124 | 14 | 18 | 20 | 0 | 1 | 0 | 14 | 2 | 3 | 1 | 0 | 14 | 1 | 37 | 2 | 0 |
| Krause, Thomas, Salinas° | .307 | 88 | 254 | 50 | 78 | 90 | 8 | 2 | 0 | 29 | 3 | 2 | 1 | 0 | 31 | 0 | 15 | 17 | 10 |
| Kubala, Brian, San Jose | .217 | 30 | 60 | 3 | 13 | 17 | 2 | 1 | 0 | 8 | 2 | 2 | 0 | 1 | 5 | 0 | 20 | 0 | 0 |
| Kuhn, Todd, Fresno | .111 | 21 | 9 | 0 | 1 | 1 | 0 | 0 | 0 | 0 | 0 | 0 | 0 | 0 | 0 | 0 | 5 | 0 | 0 |
| Larkin, Eugene, Visalia† | .305 | 142 | 528 | 90 | 161 | 231 | 25 | 3 | 13 | 106 | 12 | 0 | 14 | 2 | 81 | 5 | 61 | 0 | 0 |
| Leake, Jon, 32 Sto-33 SJ | .217 | 65 | 212 | 17 | 46 | 52 | 6 | 0 | 0 | 17 | 1 | 1 | 2 | 2 | 23 | 0 | 39 | 0 | 2 |
| Litton, Gregory, Fresno | .266 | 141 | 564 | 88 | 150 | 233 | 33 | 7 | 12 | 103 | 13 | 2 | 7 | 3 | 50 | 0 | 86 | 8 | 4 |
| Livingston, Dennis, Bakersfield | .077 | 27 | 13 | 0 | 1 | 1 | 0 | 0 | 0 | 0 | 0 | 0 | 0 | 0 | 1 | 0 | 6 | 0 | 0 |
| Loscalzo, Robert, Modesto° | .308 | 120 | 413 | 72 | 127 | 187 | 20 | 5 | 10 | 63 | 7 | 1 | 1 | 1 | 65 | 5 | 88 | 22 | 14 |
| Marsh, Scott, Reno | .500 | 12 | 2 | 0 | 1 | 1 | 0 | 0 | 0 | 0 | 0 | 0 | 0 | 0 | 0 | 0 | 1 | 0 | 0 |
| McCue, Deron, Fresno | .316 | 110 | 367 | 69 | 116 | 153 | 17 | 4 | 4 | 54 | 4 | 9 | 4 | 5 | 38 | 0 | 58 | 10 | 5 |
| McGwire, Mark, Modesto | .274 | 138 | 489 | 95 | 134 | 235 | 23 | 3 | 24 | 106 | 10 | 0 | 7 | 4 | 96 | 2 | 108 | 1 | 2 |
| McLoughlin, Timothy, Reno | .000 | 38 | 3 | 0 | 0 | 0 | 0 | 0 | 0 | 0 | 0 | 1 | 0 | 0 | 0 | 0 | 2 | 0 | 0 |
| Mena, Andres, Bakersfield | .278 | 30 | 18 | 1 | 5 | 9 | 1 | 0 | 1 | 1 | 0 | 0 | 0 | 0 | 0 | 0 | 7 | 0 | 0 |
| Mooneyham, William, Modesto | .000 | 8 | 1 | 0 | 0 | 0 | 0 | 0 | 0 | 0 | 0 | 0 | 0 | 1 | 0 | 0 | 0 | 0 | 0 |
| Moran, Mitchell, Bakersfield | .259 | 130 | 455 | 53 | 118 | 155 | 19 | 3 | 4 | 53 | 8 | 2 | 2 | 5 | 47 | 0 | 98 | 22 | 11 |
| Moriarty, Todd, Fresno | .000 | 12 | 1 | 0 | 0 | 0 | 0 | 0 | 0 | 0 | 0 | 0 | 0 | 0 | 0 | 0 | 0 | 0 | 0 |
| Murray, Stephen, Salinas | .204 | 127 | 456 | 55 | 93 | 104 | 11 | 0 | 0 | 40 | 2 | 13 | 3 | 4 | 53 | 0 | 76 | 8 | 9 |
| Nicolosi, Salvatore, Visalia | .213 | 42 | 150 | 18 | 32 | 47 | 5 | 2 | 2 | 20 | 1 | 1 | 4 | 2 | 15 | 0 | 25 | 0 | 1 |
| Oakes, Todd, Fresno | .000 | 51 | 3 | 1 | 0 | 0 | 0 | 0 | 0 | 0 | 0 | 2 | 0 | 0 | 1 | 0 | 2 | 0 | 0 |
| O'Brien, Charles, Modesto | .296 | 9 | 27 | 5 | 8 | 17 | 4 | 1 | 1 | 2 | 0 | 0 | 0 | | 2 | 1 | 5 | 0 | 0 |
| O'Connor, William, Visalia | .234 | 36 | 94 | 9 | 22 | 25 | 3 | 0 | 0 | 5 | 0 | 2 | 1 | 1 | 8 | 1 | 22 | 1 | 1 |
| Ohnoutka, Brian, Fresno | .125 | 12 | 8 | 1 | 1 | 1 | 0 | 0 | 0 | 2 | 0 | 0 | 0 | 0 | 1 | 0 | 4 | 0 | 0 |
| Palmer, Douglas, Visalia | .292 | 120 | 411 | 68 | 120 | 128 | 8 | 0 | 0 | 40 | 2 | 7 | 2 | 10 | 87 | 1 | 36 | 35 | 16 |
| Parks, Jeffrey, Reno | .200 | 23 | 5 | 0 | 1 | 1 | 0 | 0 | 0 | 0 | 0 | 0 | 0 | 0 | 0 | 0 | 2 | 0 | 0 |
| Pequignot, Jonathan, Bakersfield° | .272 | 110 | 364 | 67 | 99 | 168 | 19 | 1 | 16 | 66 | 11 | 0 | 1 | 3 | 71 | 3 | 70 | 7 | 4 |
| Pettis, Stacey, Redwood° | .229 | 99 | 376 | 60 | 86 | 123 | 15 | 5 | 4 | 28 | 0 | 3 | 1 | 2 | 47 | 1 | 143 | 44 | 16 |
| Porter, Jason, Reno | .262 | 112 | 355 | 50 | 93 | 126 | 23 | 2 | 2 | 58 | 5 | 0 | 2 | 2 | 39 | 0 | 57 | 4 | 3 |
| Powell, Alonzo, San Jose | .258 | 136 | 473 | 79 | 122 | 188 | 27 | 6 | 9 | 62 | 4 | 3 | 6 | 3 | 71 | 0 | 118 | 34 | 11 |
| Puig, Edward, Reno° | .000 | 28 | 5 | 2 | 0 | 0 | 0 | 0 | 0 | 0 | 0 | 0 | 1 | 0 | 1 | 0 | 0 | 0 | 0 |
| Puikunas, Edmund, Fresno | .000 | 60 | 2 | 0 | 0 | 0 | 0 | 0 | 0 | 0 | 0 | 0 | 0 | 1 | 1 | 0 | 2 | 0 | 0 |
| Quinones, Hector, Stockton | .241 | 132 | 449 | 70 | 108 | 145 | 23 | 7 | 0 | 62 | 7 | 5 | 3 | 4 | 43 | 0 | 103 | 6 | 2 |
| Rainey, Scott, Reno | .242 | 77 | 248 | 29 | 60 | 75 | 10 | 1 | 1 | 32 | 6 | 1 | 2 | 2 | 21 | 0 | 37 | 2 | 2 |
| Raymer, Gregory, Reno | .000 | 29 | 6 | 1 | 0 | 0 | 0 | 0 | 0 | 0 | 0 | 1 | 0 | 0 | 1 | 0 | 3 | 0 | 0 |
| Reibel, Douglas, Redwood° | .268 | 119 | 381 | 57 | 102 | 170 | 26 | 3 | 12 | 69 | 5 | 0 | 4 | 3 | 101 | 1 | 74 | 10 | 8 |
| Reid, Jessie, Fresno° | .323 | 72 | 254 | 45 | 82 | 124 | 14 | 2 | 8 | 55 | 4 | 1 | 6 | 2 | 55 | 4 | 33 | 15 | 4 |
| Robertson, Randy, Reno | .000 | 14 | 2 | 0 | 0 | 0 | 0 | 0 | 0 | 0 | 0 | 0 | 0 | 0 | 0 | 0 | 0 | 0 | 0 |
| Robles, Gregory, San Jose° | .286 | 109 | 332 | 44 | 95 | 128 | 22 | 0 | 3 | 49 | 7 | 0 | 2 | 3 | 64 | 3 | 46 | 0 | 1 |
| Rodriguez, Angel, Stockton° | .268 | 40 | 127 | 19 | 34 | 47 | 4 | 0 | 3 | 18 | 2 | 1 | 1 | 5 | 10 | 0 | 16 | 2 | 1 |
| Rodriguez, Rigo, Reno | .667 | 10 | 3 | 0 | 2 | 3 | 1 | 0 | 0 | 0 | 0 | 0 | 0 | 0 | 1 | 0 | 0 | 0 | 0 |
| Ross, Carey, Stockton | .214 | 10 | 28 | 2 | 6 | 7 | 1 | 0 | 0 | 1 | 0 | 1 | 1 | 0 | 3 | 0 | 7 | 0 | 0 |
| Rowen, Robert, Bakersfield° | .000 | 13 | 8 | 0 | 0 | 0 | 0 | 0 | 0 | 0 | 0 | 0 | 1 | 0 | 0 | 0 | 3 | 0 | 0 |

| Player and Club | Pct. | G. | AB. | R. | H. | TB. | 2B. | 3B. | HR. | RBI. | GW. | SH. | SF. | HP. | BB. | Int. BB. | SO. | SB. | CS. |
|---|---|---|---|---|---|---|---|---|---|---|---|---|---|---|---|---|---|---|---|
| Sasser, Mack, Fresno° | .338 | 133 | 497 | 79 | 168 | 245 | 27 | 4 | 14 | 102 | 16 | 3 | 9 | 3 | 36 | 4 | 35 | 3 | 3 |
| Satnat, David, Bakersfield° | .000 | 47 | 7 | 1 | 0 | 0 | 0 | 0 | 0 | 0 | 0 | 0 | 0 | 0 | 1 | 0 | 3 | 0 | 0 |
| Schugel, Jeffrey, Visalia | .224 | 73 | 219 | 34 | 49 | 63 | 4 | 2 | 2 | 22 | 0 | 4 | 0 | 2 | 27 | 1 | 35 | 8 | 5 |
| Sciacca, Steven, Redwood | .226 | 43 | 106 | 15 | 24 | 25 | 1 | 0 | 0 | 6 | 0 | 4 | 0 | 1 | 4 | 0 | 18 | 2 | 1 |
| Scott, Timothy, Bakersfield | .214 | 16 | 14 | 0 | 3 | 4 | 1 | 0 | 0 | 2 | 0 | 0 | 0 | 0 | 2 | 0 | 5 | 1 | 0 |
| Segura, Americo, Redwood | .276 | 80 | 228 | 24 | 63 | 72 | 7 | 1 | 0 | 24 | 3 | 4 | 2 | 3 | 23 | 1 | 43 | 2 | 3 |
| Serritella, John, Bakersfield° | .000 | 17 | 3 | 1 | 0 | 0 | 0 | 0 | 0 | 0 | 0 | 1 | 0 | 0 | 0 | 0 | 0 | 0 | 0 |
| Sexton, Matthew, Redwood | .177 | 60 | 147 | 12 | 26 | 34 | 3 | 1 | 1 | 9 | 0 | 6 | 1 | 0 | 9 | 1 | 30 | 1 | 2 |
| Sferrazza, Matthew, Stockton | .298 | 97 | 359 | 75 | 107 | 130 | 19 | 2 | 0 | 45 | 4 | 8 | 3 | 4 | 78 | 2 | 54 | 57 | 13 |
| Simmons, Todd, Reno | .067 | 24 | 15 | 2 | 1 | 1 | 0 | 0 | 0 | 0 | 0 | 0 | 0 | 0 | 0 | 0 | 7 | 0 | 0 |
| Smith, David, Salinas° | .224 | 65 | 201 | 27 | 45 | 74 | 9 | 1 | 6 | 31 | 4 | 0 | 4 | 2 | 39 | 4 | 36 | 7 | 5 |
| Smith, Philander, San Jose | .318 | 121 | 444 | 76 | 141 | 163 | 12 | 2 | 2 | 44 | 3 | 4 | 5 | 3 | 60 | 1 | 48 | 30 | 20 |
| Smith, Richard, Redwood | .205 | 29 | 78 | 8 | 16 | 18 | 2 | 0 | 0 | 2 | 0 | 2 | 0 | 0 | 3 | 0 | 22 | 1 | 0 |
| Smith, Stephen, Fresno† | .000 | 27 | 9 | 3 | 0 | 0 | 0 | 0 | 0 | 1 | 0 | 2 | 0 | 0 | 5 | 0 | 4 | 0 | 0 |
| Sohma, Katsuya, San Jose | .219 | 77 | 192 | 14 | 42 | 47 | 5 | 0 | 0 | 15 | 3 | 7 | 2 | 0 | 26 | 0 | 47 | 0 | 1 |
| Spalt, Steven, Stockton | .212 | 86 | 217 | 36 | 46 | 50 | 2 | 1 | 0 | 15 | 2 | 7 | 1 | 2 | 23 | 0 | 34 | 2 | 2 |
| Sparks, Gregory, Reno° | .282 | 123 | 436 | 57 | 123 | 169 | 23 | 1 | 7 | 73 | 5 | 2 | 3 | 1 | 36 | 0 | 89 | 4 | 4 |
| Stanek, Michael, Stockton | .137 | 54 | 168 | 14 | 23 | 32 | 3 | 0 | 2 | 20 | 1 | 0 | 4 | 3 | 22 | 1 | 46 | 5 | 0 |
| Steen, Gregory, Redwood | .233 | 75 | 292 | 44 | 68 | 92 | 18 | 0 | 2 | 39 | 2 | 7 | 2 | 6 | 25 | 2 | 52 | 10 | 1 |
| Stephens, Darryl, San Jose | .248 | 42 | 145 | 22 | 36 | 45 | 3 | 0 | 2 | 8 | 2 | 4 | 1 | 1 | 26 | 0 | 37 | 3 | 9 |
| Stock, Kevin, Modesto | .284 | 131 | 483 | 86 | 137 | 197 | 26 | 5 | 8 | 65 | 7 | 4 | 2 | 9 | 89 | 0 | 133 | 2 | 4 |
| Stone, Shawn, San Jose° | .000 | 43 | 2 | 0 | 0 | 0 | 0 | 0 | 0 | 0 | 0 | 0 | 0 | 0 | 0 | 0 | 2 | 0 | 0 |
| Strong, Joseph, Modesto† | .000 | 42 | 1 | 0 | 0 | 0 | 0 | 0 | 0 | 0 | 0 | 0 | 0 | 0 | 0 | 0 | 1 | 0 | 0 |
| Tate, Stuart, Fresno | .125 | 34 | 8 | 2 | 1 | 1 | 0 | 0 | 0 | 2 | 0 | 1 | 0 | 0 | 4 | 0 | 3 | 0 | 0 |
| Tejeda, Felix, Bakersfield† | .000 | 7 | 2 | 0 | 0 | 0 | 0 | 0 | 0 | 0 | 0 | 0 | 0 | 0 | 0 | 0 | 0 | 0 | 0 |
| Tettleton, Mickey, Modesto† | .214 | 4 | 14 | 1 | 3 | 6 | 3 | 0 | 0 | 2 | 0 | 0 | 0 | 0 | 0 | 0 | 4 | 0 | 0 |
| Thornton, John, Stockton | .245 | 117 | 363 | 72 | 89 | 175 | 18 | 1 | 22 | 74 | 7 | 4 | 3 | 2 | 113 | 1 | 125 | 9 | 6 |
| Tomashino, Seiji, San Jose | .296 | 73 | 230 | 28 | 68 | 91 | 11 | 3 | 2 | 30 | 2 | 20 | 0 | 3 | 25 | 0 | 44 | 10 | 4 |
| Torres, Philip, Bakersfield | .250 | 58 | 4 | 0 | 1 | 1 | 0 | 0 | 0 | 0 | 0 | 1 | 0 | 0 | 0 | 0 | 0 | 0 | 0 |
| Utecht, Timothy, Stockton | .275 | 72 | 189 | 27 | 52 | 69 | 12 | 1 | 1 | 28 | 4 | 0 | 4 | 3 | 30 | 0 | 38 | 1 | 2 |
| Van Burkleo, Tyler, Redwood° | .276 | 118 | 366 | 53 | 101 | 161 | 20 | 5 | 10 | 52 | 5 | 2 | 5 | 5 | 52 | 4 | 99 | 8 | 4 |
| Varoz, Eric, Reno° | .296 | 137 | 497 | 105 | 147 | 233 | 27 | 10 | 13 | 84 | 5 | 2 | 3 | 10 | 99 | 2 | 97 | 30 | 7 |
| Vetsch, David, Visalia° | .268 | 87 | 313 | 36 | 84 | 129 | 15 | 0 | 10 | 63 | 4 | 1 | 2 | 4 | 36 | 2 | 74 | 0 | 2 |
| Walker, Steven, Bakersfield | .000 | 8 | 2 | 0 | 0 | 0 | 0 | 0 | 0 | 0 | 0 | 0 | 0 | 0 | 0 | 0 | 1 | 0 | 0 |
| Ward, James, Bakersfield | .296 | 32 | 98 | 10 | 29 | 30 | 1 | 0 | 0 | 3 | 0 | 1 | 0 | 2 | 16 | 0 | 14 | 5 | 4 |
| Wasem, James, Fresno | .269 | 84 | 264 | 56 | 71 | 83 | 12 | 0 | 0 | 31 | 0 | 8 | 1 | 3 | 50 | 1 | 31 | 12 | 13 |
| Weiss, Walter, Modesto† | .197 | 30 | 122 | 17 | 24 | 30 | 4 | 1 | 0 | 7 | 1 | 1 | 0 | 0 | 12 | 0 | 20 | 3 | 3 |
| White, Marvin, San Jose | .125 | 3 | 8 | 0 | 1 | 1 | 0 | 0 | 0 | 0 | 0 | 0 | 0 | 1 | 0 | 0 | 1 | 0 | 0 |
| White, Michael, Bakersfield | .222 | 32 | 108 | 10 | 24 | 26 | 2 | 0 | 0 | 7 | 1 | 0 | 0 | 1 | 7 | 0 | 27 | 3 | 0 |
| Wiggins, Kevin, Reno° | .279 | 102 | 326 | 50 | 91 | 127 | 18 | 3 | 4 | 37 | 3 | 6 | 2 | 0 | 41 | 1 | 59 | 12 | 9 |
| Wilder, David, Modesto | .259 | 70 | 239 | 48 | 62 | 102 | 15 | 2 | 7 | 37 | 5 | 0 | 1 | 4 | 45 | 0 | 62 | 23 | 5 |
| Williams, Brian, Bakersfield° | .340 | 109 | 441 | 65 | 150 | 184 | 29 | 1 | 1 | 65 | 5 | 2 | 4 | 1 | 23 | 2 | 47 | 19 | 9 |
| Williams, Fred, Stockton† | .158 | 59 | 158 | 23 | 25 | 27 | 0 | 1 | 0 | 14 | 1 | 2 | 1 | 4 | 37 | 0 | 37 | 9 | 2 |
| Wilson, Phillip, Visalia | .297 | 127 | 492 | 92 | 146 | 174 | 12 | 5 | 2 | 46 | 3 | 4 | 2 | 9 | 67 | 1 | 72 | 49 | 16 |
| Wilson, Ricky, Salinas | .280 | 28 | 82 | 9 | 23 | 32 | 1 | 1 | 2 | 17 | 2 | 0 | 3 | 0 | 7 | 0 | 12 | 0 | 3 |
| Winters, Daniel, Fresno | .286 | 81 | 255 | 38 | 73 | 82 | 6 | 0 | 1 | 24 | 5 | 2 | 2 | 0 | 19 | 0 | 37 | 1 | 0 |
| Wishnevski, Michael, Salinas° | .302 | 119 | 414 | 70 | 125 | 202 | 26 | 6 | 13 | 91 | 16 | 0 | 12 | 5 | 60 | 2 | 73 | 7 | 7 |
| Wolff, Steven, Reno | .276 | 94 | 272 | 46 | 75 | 85 | 6 | 2 | 0 | 34 | 0 | 4 | 2 | 0 | 48 | 0 | 37 | 4 | 2 |
| Wrona, William, Reno | .288 | 139 | 535 | 107 | 154 | 217 | 21 | 6 | 10 | 78 | 6 | 3 | 6 | 5 | 64 | 0 | 61 | 13 | 10 |
| Xavier, Joseph, Modesto° | .333 | 6 | 18 | 3 | 6 | 11 | 2 | 0 | 1 | 5 | 0 | 0 | 1 | 1 | 7 | 0 | 5 | 0 | 1 |
| Young, Raymond, Bakersfield | .364 | 23 | 22 | 1 | 8 | 11 | 1 | 1 | 0 | 3 | 0 | 1 | 0 | 0 | 0 | 0 | 7 | 1 | 2 |

The following pitchers, listed alphabetically by club, with games in parentheses, had no plate appearances, primarily through use of designated hitters:

BAKERSFIELD—Anderson, David (1).

FRESNO—Lee, Kurt (4); Wilhelmi, David (3).

MODESTO—Balsley, Darren (3); Bauer, Mark (4); Cadaret, Gregory (12); Coughlon, Kevin (37); Figueroa, Victor (11); Fulmer, Michael (45); Harris, Twayne (2); Heath, Allan (40); Hilton, Stan (9); John, Thomas (2); Kendrick, Peter (15); Langford, Rick (1); Leiper, David (21); Norris, Michael (2); Odom, Joe (16); Rodriguez, Ricardo (16); Scherer, Douglas (20); Whitehurst, Walter (2); Young, Curtis (2).

REDWOOD—Cannon, Scott (17); Carter, Richard (8); Cedeno, Vinicio (38); Chadwick, Ray (4); Cipres, Mark (26); Corbett, Sherman (28); Cozzolino, Paul (8); Delzer, Edwin (18); Gallo, Bernard (38); Kemmerling, Byron (24); Marrett, Scott (15); Migliore, Brian (29); Price, Bryan (12); Reed, Marty (34); Rentschler, Thomas (27); Tinkey, James (36).

RENO—Ferraro, Carl (17); Forbes, Terence (25); Morales, Edwin (6).

SALINAS—Bryant, James (21); Campbell, Michael (10); Christ, Michael (22); Gunnarsson, Robert (31); Hinson, Robert (2); Johnson, Michael (22); Malave, Benito (8); McCormick, Ronald (16); Moore, Richard (51); Poloni, John (5); Ramirez, Randolph (28); Schneider, Paul (44); Swearingen, Douglas (44); Walker, James (8); Wilkinson, William (9).

SAN JOSE—Bryant, John (18); Ferran, George (23); Foley, Rickey (9); Gladden, Jeffrey (18); Gotoh, Akemi (22); Hardwick, Willie (4); Kobernus, Jeffrey (24); Kushihara, Yasuo (22); Murai, Kazuo (27); Price, Kevin (5); Ueda, Sadahito (21); Watkins, Troy (8); Zamba, Michael (15).

STOCKTON—Barry, Eric (16); Bryant, John (4); Ciardi, Mark (18); Crews, Timothy (16); Evans, Gary (19); Fingers, Robert (19); Madrid, Alexander (8); Morris, James (19); Murphy, Daniel (24); Parrett, Jeffrey (45); Pimentel, Rafael (20); Reece, Jeffrey (24); Rice, Woolsey (27); Stapleton, David (52); Walker, Cameron (27); Williams, Bruce (13).

VISALIA—Budke, Todd (21); Dominguez, Jose (56); Galloway, Troy (23); Guerrero, Tony (27); Klingbeil, Scott (25); Landmark, Neil (26); Lee, Robert (27); Pierorazio, Wesley (51); Rojas, Jeffrey (26); Velasquez, Raymond (53).

GRAND SLAM HOME RUNS—Hardgrave, Litton, McGwire, 2 each; Brady, J. Brown, Chapman, Cucjen, Culberson, DeButch, Hartsock, Hill, Hornacek, M. Jones, Pettis, Powell, Reid, Schugel, D. Smith, Sparks, Stock, Varoz, 1 each.

AWARDED FIRST BASE ON CATCHER'S INTERFERENCE—Hill 3 (Calvert 2, Segura); Anronelli 2 (Arnold, Segura); T. Bell (Ward); Carlson (Segura); Jacas (Segura); Litton (Bell); Ward (Bell); P. Wilson (Arnold).

## CLUB FIELDING

| Club | Pct. | G. | PO. | A. | E. | DP. | PB. | Club | Pct. | G. | PO. | A. | E. | DP. | PB. |
|---|---|---|---|---|---|---|---|---|---|---|---|---|---|---|---|
| Fresno | .965 | 146 | 3721 | 1606 | 192 | 130 | 36 | San Jose | .959 | 143 | 3544 | 1392 | 213 | 101 | 31 |
| Modesto | .964 | 144 | 3662 | 1635 | 200 | 108 | 26 | Visalia | .958 | 144 | 3662 | 1608 | 229 | 170 | 37 |
| Redwood | .963 | 146 | 3711 | 1505 | 200 | 118 | 27 | Bakersfield | .958 | 145 | 3672 | 1533 | 228 | 112 | 29 |
| Stockton | .962 | 145 | 3779 | 1516 | 207 | 113 | 28 | Salinas | .957 | 144 | 3575 | 1489 | 228 | 125 | 21 |
| Reno | .962 | 145 | 3668 | 1579 | 207 | 149 | 30 | | | | | | | | |

Triple Play—Visalia.

## INDIVIDUAL FIELDING

*Throws lefthanded.

### FIRST BASEMEN

| Player and Club | Pct. | G. | PO. | A. | E. | DP. | | Player and Club | Pct. | G. | PO. | A. | E. | DP. |
|---|---|---|---|---|---|---|---|---|---|---|---|---|---|---|
| Allen, Stockton | 1.000 | 1 | 6 | 0 | 0 | 2 | | Hance, Stockton | .977 | 12 | 78 | 8 | 2 | 3 |
| Amaya, Salinas | 1.000 | 1 | 2 | 0 | 0 | 0 | | Hardgrave, Reno | .992 | 66 | 553 | 36 | 5 | 59 |
| G. Barton, San Jose | 1.000 | 2 | 13 | 0 | 0 | 2 | | Humphrey, San Jose* | 1.000 | 9 | 69 | 3 | 0 | 5 |
| Beall, Redwood | .954 | 9 | 60 | 2 | 3 | 8 | | G. Jones, San Jose | 1.000 | 1 | 10 | 2 | 0 | 0 |
| Boyd, Bakersfield | .981 | 36 | 240 | 23 | 5 | 17 | | T. Jones, Redwood* | .996 | 27 | 219 | 14 | 1 | 14 |
| Brown, Bakersfield | .958 | 17 | 126 | 12 | 6 | 10 | | Kubala, San Jose | .979 | 17 | 132 | 7 | 3 | 4 |
| Bruno, Stockton* | .979 | 14 | 89 | 5 | 2 | 9 | | Larkin, Visalia | .991 | 137 | 1227 | 62 | 12 | 140 |
| Bruzik, Salinas | 1.000 | 1 | 4 | 1 | 0 | 0 | | Loscalzo, Modesto* | 1.000 | 1 | 6 | 1 | 0 | 1 |
| Calley, Visalia | 1.000 | 1 | 4 | 0 | 0 | 0 | | McGwire, Modesto | 1.000 | 2 | 23 | 1 | 0 | 1 |
| Carlson, Reno | 1.000 | 1 | 5 | 1 | 0 | 1 | | Powell, San Jose | 1.000 | 3 | 16 | 0 | 0 | 2 |
| Chapman, Bakersfield | .985 | 98 | 796 | 61 | 13 | 61 | | Reibel, Redwood* | .990 | 58 | 468 | 28 | 5 | 53 |
| D. Clark, Salinas | .967 | 5 | 26 | 3 | 1 | 3 | | Reid, Fresno* | 1.000 | 3 | 20 | 3 | 0 | 0 |
| W. Clark, Fresno* | .990 | 60 | 520 | 51 | 6 | 48 | | Robles, San Jose* | .985 | 64 | 502 | 34 | 8 | 30 |
| Colton, Salinas | .972 | 22 | 172 | 4 | 5 | 15 | | Sasser, Fresno | .985 | 15 | 129 | 6 | 2 | 12 |
| Cucjen, Fresno | .988 | 76 | 646 | 38 | 8 | 63 | | Schugel, Visalia | 1.000 | 10 | 63 | 0 | 0 | 7 |
| Dillard, Reno* | 1.000 | 2 | 1 | 0 | 0 | 1 | | Smith, Salinas* | .982 | 53 | 409 | 27 | 8 | 36 |
| Duggan, Salinas | 1.000 | 4 | 25 | 1 | 0 | 3 | | Sparks, Reno* | .985 | 80 | 672 | 35 | 11 | 71 |
| Duncan, Salinas | .985 | 67 | 580 | 25 | 9 | 55 | | THORNTON, Stockton | .992 | 100 | 810 | 51 | 7 | 65 |
| Dunton, San Jose | .987 | 57 | 418 | 27 | 6 | 46 | | Utecht, Stockton | .996 | 33 | 255 | 20 | 1 | 20 |
| Eppard, Modesto* | .991 | 140 | 1204 | 125 | 12 | 91 | | Van Burkleo, Redwood* | .987 | 60 | 484 | 35 | 7 | 31 |
| Garrett, Modesto | .947 | 5 | 17 | 1 | 1 | 1 | | Williams, Bakersfield* | 1.000 | 1 | 6 | 2 | 0 | 1 |
| Grandstaff, Reno | .963 | 4 | 24 | 2 | 1 | 4 | | Wilson, Salinas | 1.000 | 3 | 9 | 0 | 0 | 0 |

Triple Play—Larkin.

### SECOND BASEMEN

| Player and Club | Pct. | G. | PO. | A. | E. | DP. | | Player and Club | Pct. | G. | PO. | A. | E. | DP. |
|---|---|---|---|---|---|---|---|---|---|---|---|---|---|---|
| Alfonso, Redwood | .949 | 39 | 84 | 85 | 9 | 20 | | Palmer, Visalia | .968 | 46 | 116 | 127 | 8 | 28 |
| Bates, Stockton | .973 | 58 | 115 | 175 | 8 | 23 | | Pequignot, Bakersfield | 1.000 | 5 | 10 | 12 | 0 | 0 |
| Brown, San Jose | .909 | 5 | 6 | 14 | 2 | 1 | | Sexton, Redwood | 1.000 | 2 | 2 | 3 | 0 | 1 |
| Cabrera, Modesto | .965 | 61 | 111 | 195 | 11 | 26 | | Sferrazza, Stockton | .850 | 6 | 4 | 13 | 3 | 2 |
| Crabtree, Salinas | .944 | 4 | 5 | 12 | 1 | 4 | | Smith, San Jose | .953 | 113 | 240 | 310 | 27 | 39 |
| DiCeglio, Visalia | 1.000 | 2 | 3 | 4 | 0 | 0 | | Spalt, Stockton | .982 | 45 | 53 | 109 | 3 | 18 |
| Escobar, Fresno | .667 | 2 | 1 | 1 | 1 | 0 | | Stanek, Stockton | 1.000 | 1 | 0 | 3 | 0 | 1 |
| Gallego, Modesto | .952 | 5 | 11 | 9 | 1 | 2 | | Steen, Redwood | .963 | 74 | 171 | 215 | 15 | 45 |
| Garner, Bakersfield | .889 | 4 | 5 | 11 | 2 | 3 | | Stock, Modesto | .966 | 86 | 204 | 227 | 15 | 42 |
| Garrett, Modesto | .917 | 2 | 5 | 6 | 1 | 1 | | Tomashino, San Jose | .934 | 14 | 39 | 32 | 5 | 10 |
| Hanyuda, San Jose | .906 | 10 | 22 | 26 | 5 | 3 | | Varoz, Reno | .925 | 9 | 21 | 28 | 4 | 7 |
| Hillman, Visalia | .962 | 13 | 25 | 25 | 2 | 5 | | Ward, Bakersfield | .981 | 25 | 41 | 65 | 2 | 11 |
| Holcomb, Bakersfield | .967 | 117 | 270 | 338 | 21 | 55 | | Wasem, Fresno | .880 | 9 | 21 | 23 | 6 | 7 |
| Husband, Salinas | .954 | 95 | 219 | 322 | 26 | 93 | | White, San Jose | .929 | 3 | 6 | 7 | 1 | 1 |
| Jones, San Jose | .765 | 6 | 5 | 8 | 4 | 2 | | F. Williams, Stockton | .973 | 55 | 93 | 159 | 7 | 29 |
| Kline, Redwood | .957 | 38 | 78 | 98 | 8 | 18 | | Wolff, Reno | .971 | 16 | 31 | 36 | 2 | 10 |
| Krause, Salinas | .966 | 21 | 38 | 47 | 3 | 14 | | WRONA, Reno | .972 | 123 | 260 | 409 | 19 | 91 |
| Litton, Fresno | .963 | 139 | 268 | 453 | 28 | 86 | | Xavier, Modesto | .846 | 2 | 3 | 8 | 2 | 1 |
| Murray, Salinas | .955 | 126 | 272 | 343 | 29 | 71 | | | | | | | | |

Triple Play—Husband.

### THIRD BASEMEN

| Player and Club | Pct. | G. | PO. | A. | E. | DP. | | Player and Club | Pct. | G. | PO. | A. | E. | DP. |
|---|---|---|---|---|---|---|---|---|---|---|---|---|---|---|
| Allen, San Jose-Stockton | .916 | 139 | 96 | 208 | 28 | 15 | | Kline, Redwood | .874 | 34 | 17 | 66 | 12 | 7 |
| Amaya, Salinas | .931 | 10 | 10 | 17 | 2 | 0 | | Leake, Stockton-San Jose | .912 | 65 | 34 | 91 | 12 | 10 |
| Beall, Redwood | .915 | 119 | 82 | 207 | 27 | 16 | | McGwire, Modesto | .907 | 130 | 82 | 239 | 33 | 23 |
| Beringhele, Bakersfield | .889 | 7 | 5 | 11 | 2 | 0 | | Palmer, Visalia | .952 | 60 | 54 | 104 | 8 | 10 |
| Brown, San Jose | 1.000 | 1 | 0 | 2 | 0 | 0 | | Pequignot, Bakersfield | .950 | 75 | 43 | 127 | 9 | 8 |
| Calley, Visalia | .882 | 75 | 52 | 143 | 26 | 17 | | Ross, Stockton | .818 | 10 | 3 | 15 | 4 | 1 |
| Carlson, Reno | .600 | 3 | 0 | 3 | 2 | 0 | | Sasser, Fresno | 1.000 | 1 | 1 | 0 | 0 | 0 |
| Clark, Salinas | .893 | 127 | 88 | 220 | 37 | 16 | | Schugel, Visalia | .500 | 1 | 1 | 1 | 2 | 1 |
| Crabtree, Salinas | 1.000 | 7 | 6 | 17 | 0 | 2 | | Sexton, Redwood | 1.000 | 3 | 1 | 4 | 0 | 0 |
| Cucjen, Fresno | .864 | 10 | 9 | 10 | 3 | 1 | | Sferrazza, Stockton | 1.000 | 1 | 1 | 0 | 0 | 0 |
| DiCeglio, Visalia | .902 | 20 | 13 | 42 | 6 | 4 | | Spalt, Stockton | .914 | 20 | 8 | 24 | 3 | 3 |
| Duggan, Salinas | 1.000 | 7 | 7 | 9 | 0 | 1 | | Stanek, Stockton | .935 | 53 | 25 | 105 | 9 | 8 |
| Duncan, Salinas | 1.000 | 2 | 1 | 1 | 0 | 0 | | Steen, Redwood | 1.000 | 1 | 1 | 0 | 0 | 0 |
| Flores, Bakersfield | .789 | 5 | 5 | 10 | 4 | 0 | | Stock, Modesto | .917 | 13 | 6 | 16 | 2 | 1 |
| Garrett, Modesto | .875 | 3 | 3 | 4 | 1 | 0 | | Tomashino, San Jose | 1.000 | 3 | 2 | 3 | 0 | 1 |
| Grandstaff, Reno | .913 | 114 | 96 | 208 | 29 | 26 | | Utecht, Stockton | .778 | 15 | 3 | 11 | 4 | 1 |
| HAYES, Fresno | .949 | 128 | 100 | 233 | 18 | 21 | | Wasem, Fresno | .914 | 15 | 12 | 20 | 3 | 1 |
| Hillman, Visalia | .857 | 3 | 2 | 4 | 1 | 0 | | B. Williams, Bakersfield | .571 | 4 | 1 | 3 | 3 | 0 |
| Hornacek, Bakersfield | .895 | 68 | 42 | 120 | 19 | 8 | | F. Williams, Stockton | 1.000 | 2 | 2 | 6 | 0 | 1 |
| G. Jones, San Jose | .400 | 2 | 0 | 2 | 3 | 0 | | Wolff, Reno | .912 | 30 | 8 | 54 | 6 | 7 |
| J. Jones, Modesto | .636 | 3 | 0 | 7 | 4 | 0 | | | | | | | | |

Triple Play—Calley.

### SHORTSTOPS

| Player and Club | Pct. | G. | PO. | A. | E. | DP. | | Player and Club | Pct. | G. | PO. | A. | E. | DP. |
|---|---|---|---|---|---|---|---|---|---|---|---|---|---|---|
| Alvarez, Bakersfield | .902 | 48 | 84 | 109 | 21 | 25 | | Holcomb, Bakersfield | 1.000 | 1 | 3 | 3 | 0 | 1 |
| ANDERSON, Redwood | .945 | 115 | 182 | 316 | 29 | 58 | | Hornacek, Bakersfield | .750 | 2 | 0 | 3 | 1 | 0 |
| S. Barton, San Jose | .950 | 75 | 138 | 201 | 18 | 40 | | Kline, Redwood | 1.000 | 1 | 0 | 1 | 0 | 0 |
| Bell, Visalia | .905 | 102 | 176 | 330 | 53 | 84 | | Kopetsky, Bakersfield | .882 | 20 | 33 | 38 | 9 | 6 |
| Brown, San Jose | .952 | 6 | 7 | 13 | 1 | 0 | | Krause, Salinas | .920 | 45 | 82 | 114 | 17 | 25 |
| Cabrera, Modesto | .945 | 12 | 14 | 38 | 3 | 6 | | Quinones, Stockton | .908 | 132 | 195 | 355 | 56 | 50 |
| Crabtree, Salinas | .923 | 103 | 171 | 296 | 39 | 61 | | Sexton, Redwood | .976 | 43 | 56 | 104 | 4 | 19 |
| Cucjen, Fresno | .889 | 4 | 6 | 10 | 2 | 0 | | Smith, San Jose | .957 | 9 | 10 | 12 | 1 | 1 |
| DeButch, Reno | .941 | 115 | 199 | 331 | 33 | 78 | | Spalt, Stockton | .918 | 23 | 34 | 56 | 8 | 11 |
| DiCeglio, Visalia | .948 | 45 | 61 | 121 | 10 | 29 | | Tomashino, San Jose | .927 | 57 | 79 | 148 | 18 | 21 |
| Escobar, Fresno | .930 | 102 | 173 | 289 | 35 | 63 | | Ward, Bakersfield | 1.000 | 3 | 4 | 8 | 0 | 0 |
| Flores, Bakersfield | .917 | 79 | 152 | 225 | 34 | 38 | | Wasem, Fresno | .920 | 44 | 68 | 116 | 16 | 22 |
| Gallego, Modesto | 1.000 | 1 | 1 | 2 | 0 | 0 | | Weiss, Modesto | .950 | 30 | 36 | 97 | 7 | 19 |
| Guinn, Modesto | .921 | 104 | 181 | 299 | 41 | 44 | | Wolff, Reno | .946 | 23 | 29 | 58 | 5 | 9 |
| Hancock, San Jose | 1.000 | 2 | 3 | 1 | 0 | 0 | | Wrona, Reno | .966 | 10 | 21 | 36 | 2 | 6 |
| Hillman, Visalia | .833 | 1 | 2 | 3 | 1 | 2 | | | | | | | | |

## OUTFIELDERS

| Player and Club | Pct. | G. | PO. | A. | E. | DP. | Player and Club | Pct. | G. | PO. | A. | E. | DP. |
|---|---|---|---|---|---|---|---|---|---|---|---|---|---|
| Alarid, Bakersfield* | .967 | 27 | 27 | 2 | 1 | 0 | Howard, Modesto | .903 | 64 | 101 | 1 | 11 | 0 |
| Allen, Fresno | .980 | 66 | 98 | 2 | 2 | 0 | Hubbard, Reno | .944 | 113 | 198 | 6 | 12 | 0 |
| Austin, Reno | .966 | 95 | 137 | 5 | 5 | 1 | Humphrey, San Jose* | .895 | 13 | 15 | 2 | 2 | 0 |
| Bates, Stockton | 1.000 | 1 | 2 | 0 | 0 | 0 | Jacas, Modesto | .937 | 36 | 56 | 3 | 4 | 1 |
| Benitez, Bakersfield | .947 | 9 | 17 | 1 | 1 | 0 | Jackson, Stockton* | 1.000 | 10 | 15 | 0 | 0 | 0 |
| Beringhele, Bakersfield | .988 | 41 | 79 | 3 | 1 | 0 | Jaremko, Visalia | 1.000 | 22 | 24 | 0 | 0 | 0 |
| Bernardo, Salinas | 1.000 | 19 | 20 | 2 | 0 | 0 | M. Jones, Fresno* | .981 | 111 | 145 | 7 | 3 | 1 |
| Bierley, Visalia | .957 | 62 | 106 | 4 | 5 | 0 | Kopetsky, Bakersfield | .950 | 17 | 17 | 2 | 1 | 0 |
| Brady, Redwood* | .957 | 123 | 192 | 10 | 9 | 1 | Litton, Fresno | 1.000 | 1 | 1 | 0 | 0 | 0 |
| J. Brown, Bakersfield | .889 | 23 | 32 | 0 | 4 | 0 | Loscalzo, Modesto* | .976 | 113 | 226 | 14 | 6 | 4 |
| W. Brown, San Jose | .900 | 7 | 7 | 2 | 1 | 1 | McCue, Fresno | .973 | 99 | 177 | 4 | 5 | 0 |
| Bruno, Stockton* | 1.000 | 6 | 3 | 0 | 0 | 0 | Moran, Bakersfield | .965 | 98 | 160 | 7 | 6 | 2 |
| Bruzik, Salinas | .942 | 65 | 93 | 4 | 6 | 0 | O'Connor, Visalia | .939 | 32 | 45 | 1 | 3 | 0 |
| Buchanon, Redwood | .889 | 6 | 7 | 1 | 1 | 0 | Pequignot, Bakersfield | 1.000 | 27 | 26 | 3 | 0 | 1 |
| Buss, Salinas | .980 | 89 | 141 | 6 | 3 | 2 | PETTIS, Redwood | .988 | 97 | 230 | 7 | 3 | 1 |
| Campbell, Redwood | .967 | 21 | 26 | 3 | 1 | 0 | Porter, Reno | .889 | 20 | 22 | 2 | 3 | 0 |
| Carlson, Reno | 1.000 | 3 | 1 | 1 | 0 | 0 | Powell, San Jose | .967 | 128 | 276 | 21 | 10 | 3 |
| Carlucci, Bakersfield | 1.000 | 3 | 1 | 0 | 0 | 0 | Reid, Fresno* | .968 | 68 | 119 | 3 | 4 | 0 |
| Casey, Stockton* | .959 | 90 | 158 | 7 | 7 | 2 | Sasser, Fresno | .970 | 58 | 89 | 7 | 3 | 1 |
| Clark, Fresno* | 1.000 | 3 | 3 | 0 | 0 | 0 | Sexton, Redwood | 1.000 | 1 | 1 | 0 | 0 | 0 |
| Colton, Salinas | .936 | 27 | 43 | 1 | 3 | 1 | Sferrazza, Stockton | .975 | 84 | 150 | 5 | 4 | 1 |
| Copeland, Visalia* | .986 | 41 | 60 | 8 | 1 | 2 | Sparks, Reno* | 1.000 | 9 | 15 | 0 | 0 | 0 |
| Culberson, Fresno | .936 | 74 | 115 | 2 | 8 | 0 | Stephens, San Jose | .965 | 42 | 81 | 1 | 3 | 0 |
| Dillard, Reno* | .951 | 51 | 71 | 6 | 4 | 0 | Utecht, Stockton | 1.000 | 1 | 1 | 0 | 0 | 0 |
| Doran, Redwood | .975 | 101 | 195 | 4 | 5 | 1 | Van Burkleo, Redwood* | .933 | 21 | 39 | 3 | 3 | 0 |
| Duncan, Salinas | 1.000 | 4 | 5 | 2 | 0 | 0 | Varoz, Reno | .960 | 128 | 206 | 8 | 9 | 1 |
| Falkner, San Jose | .940 | 114 | 196 | 9 | 13 | 0 | Vetsch, Visalia | .975 | 65 | 110 | 6 | 3 | 0 |
| Farmar, Modesto | .980 | 141 | 279 | 8 | 6 | 3 | Wasem, Fresno | 1.000 | 4 | 1 | 1 | 0 | 0 |
| Finley, Stockton | .956 | 138 | 303 | 4 | 14 | 2 | White, Bakersfield | .921 | 25 | 33 | 2 | 3 | 0 |
| Forgione, Visalia* | .962 | 111 | 197 | 8 | 8 | 1 | Wiggins, Reno* | .924 | 59 | 77 | 8 | 7 | 0 |
| Freeman, Stockton* | .957 | 119 | 189 | 11 | 9 | 1 | Wilder, Modesto | .942 | 66 | 120 | 9 | 8 | 0 |
| Garner, Bakersfield | .959 | 76 | 157 | 5 | 7 | 1 | B. Williams, Bakersfield* | .978 | 107 | 215 | 11 | 5 | 3 |
| Garrett, Modesto | 1.000 | 22 | 22 | 2 | 0 | 0 | F. Williams, Stockton | 1.000 | 1 | 2 | 0 | 0 | 0 |
| Gentle, Bakersfield* | 1.000 | 7 | 9 | 0 | 0 | 0 | Wilson, Visalia | .984 | 125 | 298 | 11 | 5 | 3 |
| Hall, Salinas* | .966 | 135 | 275 | 5 | 10 | 2 | Winters, Fresno | .500 | 2 | 1 | 0 | 1 | 0 |
| Hanyuda, San Jose | .941 | 49 | 60 | 4 | 4 | 0 | Wishnevski, Salinas* | .970 | 109 | 189 | 8 | 6 | 0 |
| Hartsock, Redwood | .966 | 52 | 76 | 8 | 3 | 1 | Wrona, Reno | .800 | 1 | 4 | 0 | 1 | 0 |
| Hill, San Jose | .922 | 99 | 160 | 6 | 14 | 0 | | | | | | | |

## CATCHERS

| Player and Club | Pct. | G. | PO. | A. | E. | DP. | PB. | Player and Club | Pct. | G. | PO. | A. | E. | DP. | PB. |
|---|---|---|---|---|---|---|---|---|---|---|---|---|---|---|---|
| Amaya, Salinas | .974 | 54 | 331 | 44 | 10 | 4 | 7 | G. Jones, San Jose | .978 | 64 | 309 | 40 | 8 | 4 | 16 |
| Antonelli, Stockton | .983 | 53 | 317 | 27 | 6 | 8 | 5 | J. Jones, Modesto | .982 | 78 | 449 | 56 | 9 | 6 | 12 |
| Arnold, Redwood | .987 | 39 | 264 | 35 | 4 | 2 | 4 | Nicolosi, Visalia | .970 | 42 | 224 | 35 | 8 | 5 | 8 |
| G. Barton, San Jose | .966 | 15 | 80 | 5 | 3 | 1 | 5 | O'Brien, Modesto | .976 | 6 | 33 | 8 | 1 | 0 | 2 |
| Bell, Reno | .972 | 90 | 495 | 67 | 16 | 7 | 14 | Porter, Reno | .970 | 50 | 306 | 45 | 11 | 4 | 9 |
| Bradley, Modesto | .997 | 62 | 342 | 27 | 1 | 3 | 10 | Rainey, Reno | .979 | 73 | 456 | 58 | 11 | 6 | 15 |
| BROWN, Bakersfield | .994 | 87 | 556 | 73 | 4 | 9 | 15 | Rodriguez, Stockton | .978 | 35 | 200 | 21 | 5 | 0 | 11 |
| Calvert, Visalia | .964 | 67 | 357 | 42 | 15 | 8 | 11 | Sasser, Fresno | .959 | 36 | 183 | 29 | 9 | 3 | 19 |
| Carlson, Reno | .977 | 35 | 192 | 19 | 5 | 4 | 6 | Schugel, Visalia | .968 | 41 | 171 | 38 | 7 | 1 | 18 |
| Carlucci, Bakersfield | .986 | 60 | 364 | 49 | 6 | 2 | 13 | Sciacca, Redwood | .961 | 38 | 176 | 19 | 8 | 0 | 7 |
| Eurton, San Jose | 1.000 | 6 | 32 | 3 | 0 | 0 | 0 | Segura, Redwood | .960 | 64 | 368 | 42 | 17 | 1 | 12 |
| Garrett, Modesto | 1.000 | 2 | 4 | 2 | 0 | 0 | 0 | Smith, Redwood | .983 | 22 | 108 | 10 | 2 | 0 | 4 |
| Gatewood, Bakersfield | .970 | 4 | 27 | 5 | 1 | 0 | 1 | Sohma, San Jose | .986 | 77 | 447 | 63 | 7 | 3 | 10 |
| Gibree, Salinas | 1.000 | 2 | 9 | 4 | 0 | 0 | 0 | Tettleton, Modesto | 1.000 | 4 | 20 | 1 | 0 | 0 | 2 |
| Grimes, Fresno | .992 | 61 | 299 | 53 | 3 | 3 | 8 | Wilson, Salinas | .909 | 8 | 16 | 4 | 2 | 0 | 0 |
| Hance, Stockton | .990 | 75 | 548 | 36 | 6 | 3 | 12 | Winters, Fresno | .987 | 72 | 410 | 55 | 6 | 5 | 9 |

## PITCHERS

| Player and Club | Pct. | G. | PO. | A. | E. | DP. | Player and Club | Pct. | G. | PO. | A. | E. | DP. |
|---|---|---|---|---|---|---|---|---|---|---|---|---|---|
| Alexander, Fresno-Reno | 1.000 | 54 | 2 | 7 | 0 | 2 | Dunlop, Reno | .800 | 29 | 1 | 3 | 1 | 0 |
| Balsley, Modesto | 1.000 | 3 | 1 | 2 | 0 | 1 | Edwards, Bakersfield* | .962 | 16 | 4 | 21 | 1 | 0 |
| Barnhouse, Reno | .909 | 41 | 2 | 18 | 2 | 2 | Evans, Stockton | 1.000 | 19 | 5 | 12 | 0 | 0 |
| Barry, Stockton* | .917 | 16 | 3 | 8 | 1 | 0 | Ferran, San Jose | .857 | 23 | 10 | 20 | 5 | 3 |
| Bauer, Modesto | .818 | 4 | 5 | 4 | 2 | 0 | Ferraro, Reno* | 1.000 | 17 | 0 | 5 | 0 | 0 |
| Brantley, Fresno | .941 | 14 | 8 | 8 | 1 | 0 | Figueroa, Modesto | 1.000 | 11 | 3 | 10 | 0 | 0 |
| Ja. Bryant, Salinas | 1.000 | 21 | 2 | 3 | 0 | 0 | Fingers, Stockton | 1.000 | 19 | 4 | 4 | 0 | 1 |
| Jo. Bryant, San Jose-Stockton | .871 | 22 | 6 | 21 | 4 | 0 | Flores, Bakersfield | .900 | 14 | 2 | 7 | 1 | 1 |
| Budke, Visalia | 1.000 | 21 | 6 | 16 | 0 | 0 | Foley, San Jose | 1.000 | 8 | 2 | 2 | 0 | 0 |
| Burkett, Fresno | .867 | 20 | 5 | 8 | 2 | 0 | Forbes, Reno | .938 | 25 | 5 | 10 | 1 | 1 |
| Cadaret, Modesto* | .929 | 12 | 2 | 11 | 1 | 0 | Fulmer, Modesto* | .929 | 45 | 5 | 21 | 2 | 1 |
| Campbell, Salinas | 1.000 | 10 | 1 | 6 | 0 | 0 | Gallo, Redwood* | 1.000 | 38 | 2 | 12 | 0 | 0 |
| Candelaria, Fresno* | 1.000 | 34 | 3 | 7 | 0 | 2 | Galloway, Visalia* | .889 | 23 | 2 | 14 | 2 | 3 |
| Cannon, Redwood | .846 | 17 | 3 | 8 | 2 | 0 | Garrett, Modesto | 1.000 | 1 | 1 | 0 | 0 | 0 |
| Carter, Redwood | 1.000 | 8 | 0 | 1 | 0 | 0 | Gentle, Bakersfield* | 1.000 | 16 | 4 | 7 | 0 | 0 |
| Cedeno, Redwood | .600 | 38 | 0 | 3 | 2 | 0 | Gilbert, Fresno | 1.000 | 21 | 9 | 6 | 0 | 1 |
| Chadwick, Redwood | 1.000 | 4 | 1 | 3 | 0 | 0 | Gildehaus, Reno | .895 | 21 | 4 | 13 | 2 | 0 |
| Childers, Reno | 1.000 | 12 | 2 | 3 | 0 | 0 | Gladden, San Jose | .783 | 18 | 5 | 13 | 5 | 0 |
| Christ, Salinas | .933 | 22 | 6 | 22 | 2 | 1 | Gotoh, San Jose | .885 | 22 | 5 | 18 | 3 | 0 |
| Ciardi, Stockton | .931 | 18 | 5 | 22 | 2 | 3 | Guerrero, Visalia* | .906 | 27 | 4 | 25 | 3 | 3 |
| Cipres, Redwood | 1.000 | 26 | 2 | 2 | 0 | 0 | Gunnarsson, Salinas* | .929 | 31 | 9 | 17 | 2 | 2 |
| Cobbs, Bakersfield | .892 | 34 | 15 | 18 | 4 | 0 | Hamrick, Bakersfield* | .917 | 16 | 1 | 10 | 1 | 1 |
| Corbell, Fresno | .934 | 26 | 16 | 41 | 4 | 3 | Hardwick, San Jose | 1.000 | 4 | 1 | 1 | 0 | 0 |
| Corbett, Redwood* | .958 | 28 | 8 | 38 | 2 | 1 | Harris, Modesto | 1.000 | 2 | 0 | 1 | 0 | 0 |
| Coughlon, Modesto | 1.000 | 37 | 12 | 19 | 0 | 3 | Harvey, Modesto* | 1.000 | 24 | 7 | 12 | 0 | 0 |
| Cozzolino, Redwood | 1.000 | 8 | 1 | 2 | 0 | 0 | Heath, Modesto* | 1.000 | 40 | 4 | 8 | 0 | 2 |
| Crews, Stockton | .933 | 16 | 4 | 10 | 1 | 2 | Henning, Fresno | .852 | 15 | 8 | 15 | 4 | 1 |
| de Chavez, Modesto | 1.000 | 30 | 6 | 20 | 0 | 1 | Hilton, Modesto | .944 | 9 | 3 | 14 | 1 | 0 |
| Delzer, Redwood* | 1.000 | 18 | 0 | 5 | 0 | 0 | John, Modesto* | 1.000 | 2 | 0 | 1 | 0 | 0 |
| Dominguez, Visalia | .941 | 56 | 2 | 14 | 1 | 0 | Johnson, Salinas | .846 | 22 | 3 | 8 | 2 | 0 |

## PITCHERS—Continued

| Player and Club | Pct. | G. | PO. | A. | E. | DP. | Player and Club | Pct. | G. | PO. | A. | E. | DP. |
|---|---|---|---|---|---|---|---|---|---|---|---|---|---|
| Kemmerling, Redwood | 1.000 | 24 | 4 | 4 | 0 | 1 | Puikunas, Fresno* | .944 | 60 | 4 | 13 | 1 | 1 |
| Kendrick, Modesto* | .950 | 15 | 5 | 33 | 2 | 0 | Ramirez, Salinas | .897 | 28 | 8 | 27 | 4 | 1 |
| Klingbeil, Visalia | .762 | 25 | 4 | 12 | 5 | 2 | Raymer, Reno | .878 | 29 | 12 | 24 | 5 | 2 |
| Kobernus, San Jose* | .818 | 24 | 6 | 3 | 2 | 0 | Reece, Stockton* | .943 | 24 | 9 | 24 | 2 | 2 |
| Kockenmeister, Reno* | 1.000 | 13 | 1 | 4 | 0 | 0 | Reed, Redwood* | .929 | 34 | 5 | 21 | 2 | 0 |
| Kubala, San Jose | .857 | 10 | 4 | 8 | 2 | 1 | Rentschler, Redwood* | .905 | 27 | 12 | 26 | 4 | 0 |
| Kuhn, Fresno | .857 | 21 | 5 | 13 | 3 | 2 | Rice, Stockton | .875 | 27 | 3 | 4 | 1 | 0 |
| Kushihara, San Jose | .943 | 22 | 6 | 27 | 2 | 1 | Robertson, Reno | .941 | 14 | 7 | 9 | 1 | 1 |
| Landmark, Visalia | .926 | 26 | 8 | 17 | 2 | 2 | Ric. Rodriguez, Modesto | .976 | 16 | 17 | 24 | 1 | 5 |
| Langford, Modesto | 1.000 | 1 | 0 | 1 | 0 | 0 | Rig. Rodriguez, Reno | .923 | 9 | 2 | 10 | 1 | 1 |
| K. Lee, Fresno* | 1.000 | 4 | 0 | 5 | 0 | 0 | Rojas, Visalia | .927 | 26 | 11 | 27 | 3 | 0 |
| R. Lee, Visalia* | 1.000 | 27 | 1 | 12 | 0 | 0 | Rowen, Bakersfield* | .810 | 13 | 2 | 15 | 4 | 0 |
| Leiper, Modesto* | 1.000 | 21 | 3 | 9 | 0 | 0 | Satnat, Bakersfield* | .923 | 47 | 7 | 17 | 2 | 0 |
| Livingston, Bakersfield* | .868 | 27 | 5 | 28 | 5 | 0 | Scherer, Modesto | .886 | 20 | 11 | 20 | 4 | 2 |
| Madrid, Stockton | .867 | 8 | 4 | 9 | 2 | 0 | Schneider, Salinas | 1.000 | 44 | 6 | 13 | 0 | 1 |
| Malave, Salinas | .833 | 8 | 0 | 5 | 1 | 0 | Scott, Bakersfield | .786 | 12 | 6 | 5 | 3 | 0 |
| Marrett, Redwood | .944 | 15 | 3 | 14 | 1 | 0 | Serritella, Bakersfield | 1.000 | 17 | 4 | 15 | 0 | 0 |
| Marsh, Reno* | 1.000 | 12 | 1 | 6 | 0 | 1 | Simmons, Reno | .920 | 24 | 7 | 16 | 2 | 1 |
| McCormack, Salinas | 1.000 | 16 | 0 | 7 | 0 | 0 | R. Smith, Redwood | 1.000 | 2 | 1 | 0 | 0 | 0 |
| McLoughlin, Reno | .909 | 38 | 5 | 15 | 2 | 2 | S. Smith, Fresno | 1.000 | 27 | 5 | 13 | 0 | 1 |
| Mena, Bakersfield | .824 | 30 | 15 | 13 | 6 | 3 | Stapleton, Stockton* | .889 | 52 | 4 | 12 | 2 | 2 |
| Migliore, Redwood | .963 | 29 | 8 | 18 | 1 | 1 | Stone, San Jose | 1.000 | 43 | 4 | 14 | 0 | 0 |
| Mooneyham, Modesto | 1.000 | 8 | 1 | 4 | 0 | 1 | Strong, Modesto | .821 | 42 | 8 | 15 | 5 | 3 |
| Moore, Salinas | .964 | 51 | 4 | 23 | 1 | 3 | Swearingen, Salinas* | .821 | 44 | 5 | 18 | 5 | 1 |
| Moran, Bakersfield | 1.000 | 5 | 1 | 1 | 0 | 0 | Tate, Fresno | .939 | 34 | 11 | 20 | 2 | 1 |
| Moriarty, Fresno* | 1.000 | 12 | 3 | 6 | 0 | 1 | Tejeda, Bakersfield* | 1.000 | 7 | 0 | 3 | 0 | 0 |
| Morris, Stockton* | 1.000 | 19 | 1 | 10 | 0 | 2 | Tinkey, Redwood | .913 | 36 | 5 | 16 | 2 | 1 |
| Murai, San Jose | .889 | 27 | 3 | 5 | 1 | 0 | Torres, Bakersfield | .867 | 58 | 2 | 11 | 2 | 0 |
| Murphy, Stockton | .929 | 24 | 12 | 14 | 2 | 1 | Ueda, San Jose | .931 | 21 | 5 | 22 | 2 | 3 |
| Norris, Modesto | .750 | 2 | 1 | 2 | 1 | 0 | Velasquez, Visalia | 1.000 | 53 | 5 | 12 | 0 | 1 |
| Oakes, Fresno | .966 | 51 | 7 | 21 | 1 | 1 | C. Walker, Stockton | .907 | 27 | 17 | 32 | 5 | 1 |
| Odom, Modesto | .800 | 16 | 0 | 3 | 1 | 1 | J. Walker, Salinas | .962 | 28 | 7 | 43 | 2 | 1 |
| Ohnoutka, Fresno | .913 | 12 | 11 | 10 | 2 | 2 | S. Walker, Bakersfield | .750 | 8 | 2 | 1 | 1 | 0 |
| Parks, Reno | .889 | 23 | 5 | 11 | 2 | 1 | Watkins, San Jose | 1.000 | 8 | 1 | 5 | 0 | 0 |
| Parrett, Stockton | .946 | 45 | 15 | 20 | 2 | 1 | Whitehurst, Modesto | 1.000 | 2 | 1 | 2 | 0 | 0 |
| Pierorazio, Visalia* | .864 | 51 | 2 | 17 | 3 | 0 | Wilhelmi, Fresno | 1.000 | 3 | 1 | 0 | 0 | 0 |
| Pimentel, Stockton | 1.000 | 20 | 0 | 4 | 0 | 2 | Wilkinson, Salinas* | .929 | 9 | 2 | 11 | 1 | 1 |
| Poloni, Salinas* | .750 | 5 | 0 | 3 | 1 | 0 | B. Williams, Stockton | 1.000 | 13 | 0 | 1 | 0 | 0 |
| B. Price, Redwood* | .913 | 12 | 5 | 16 | 2 | 0 | R. Young, Bakersfield | .750 | 19 | 6 | 12 | 6 | 1 |
| K. Price, San Jose | 1.000 | 5 | 0 | 4 | 0 | 0 | Zamba, San Jose | 1.000 | 15 | 5 | 13 | 0 | 0 |
| PUIG, Reno | 1.000 | 28 | 8 | 32 | 0 | 2 | | | | | | | |

The following players do not have any recorded accepted chances at the positions indicated; therefore, are not listed in the fielding averages for those particular positions: Alfonso, 3b; Amaya, p; Anderson, of, p; Austin, 1b; Carlson, 2b; Chapman, of; D. Clark, 2b; Copeland, p; Flores, of; Freeman, p; Gallego, 3b; Grimes, 3b; Hinson, p; Husband, p; Jackson, 1b; G. Jones, of; Morales, p; Murray, 3b; Porter, p; Schugel, of, p; Spalt, p; Wolff, of, p; C. Young, p.

### CLUB PITCHING

| Club | ERA. | G. | CG. | ShO. | Sv. | IP. | H. | R. | ER. | HR. | HB. | BB. | Int. BB. | SO. | WP. | Bk. |
|---|---|---|---|---|---|---|---|---|---|---|---|---|---|---|---|---|
| Salinas | 3.73 | 144 | 30 | 18 | 37 | 1191.2 | 1191 | 603 | 494 | 75 | 37 | 505 | 15 | 808 | 54 | 6 |
| Stockton | 3.74 | 145 | 18 | 7 | 31 | 1259.2 | 1213 | 647 | 523 | 39 | 26 | 597 | 15 | 1048 | 66 | 6 |
| Fresno | 3.85 | 146 | 20 | 10 | 35 | 1240.1 | 1163 | 667 | 530 | 63 | 47 | 686 | 3 | 880 | 125 | 13 |
| Redwood | 4.09 | 146 | 26 | 8 | 29 | 1237.0 | 1232 | 700 | 562 | 55 | 41 | 673 | 17 | 891 | 87 | 3 |
| Modesto | 4.25 | 144 | 21 | 9 | 29 | 1220.2 | 1246 | 699 | 577 | 85 | 36 | 607 | 10 | 810 | 55 | 8 |
| San Jose | 4.42 | 143 | 45 | 6 | 20 | 1181.1 | 1254 | 728 | 580 | 63 | 69 | 603 | 26 | 807 | 77 | 20 |
| Visalia | 4.49 | 144 | 22 | 5 | 25 | 1220.2 | 1355 | 754 | 609 | 72 | 39 | 653 | 20 | 720 | 138 | 12 |
| Bakersfield | 4.54 | 145 | 20 | 9 | 31 | 1224.0 | 1249 | 766 | 618 | 59 | 53 | 769 | 8 | 900 | 90 | 11 |
| Reno | 5.61 | 145 | 20 | 7 | 26 | 1222.2 | 1407 | 915 | 762 | 106 | 58 | 817 | 38 | 903 | 90 | 10 |

### PITCHERS' RECORDS

(Leading Qualifiers for Earned-Run Average Leadership — 116 or More Innings)

*Throws lefthanded.

| Pitcher—Club | W. | L. | Pct. | ERA. | G. | GS. | CG. | GF. | ShO. | Sv. | IP. | H. | R. | ER. | HR. | HB. | BB. | Int. BB. | SO. | WP. |
|---|---|---|---|---|---|---|---|---|---|---|---|---|---|---|---|---|---|---|---|---|
| Parrett, Stockton | 7 | 4 | .636 | 2.75 | 45 | 2 | 0 | 21 | 0 | 11 | 127.2 | 97 | 50 | 39 | 5 | 1 | 75 | 2 | 120 | 7 |
| Gunnarsson, Salinas* | 10 | 8 | .556 | 3.12 | 31 | 18 | 6 | 6 | 2 | 0 | 130.0 | 125 | 54 | 45 | 5 | 6 | 44 | 4 | 91 | 0 |
| Reece, Stockton* | 8 | 8 | .500 | 3.20 | 24 | 22 | 2 | 2 | 0 | 1 | 126.2 | 112 | 63 | 45 | 4 | 2 | 77 | 0 | 129 | 10 |
| Corbell, Fresno | 17 | 4 | .810 | 3.23 | 26 | 26 | 9 | 0 | 3 | 0 | 181.1 | 174 | 77 | 65 | 7 | 6 | 61 | 0 | 89 | 14 |
| Kushihara, San Jose | 8 | 13 | .381 | 3.33 | 22 | 22 | 13 | 0 | 0 | 0 | 165.0 | 147 | 82 | 61 | 12 | 7 | 63 | 1 | 131 | 4 |
| Rentschler, Redwood* | 10 | 10 | .500 | 3.40 | 27 | 27 | 7 | 0 | 1 | 0 | 193.1 | 191 | 84 | 73 | 11 | 2 | 63 | 1 | 137 | 6 |
| Simmons, Reno | 8 | 10 | .444 | 3.42 | 24 | 18 | 7 | 4 | 1 | 1 | 142.0 | 133 | 70 | 54 | 7 | 4 | 73 | 6 | 117 | 5 |
| Ferran, San Jose | 8 | 9 | .471 | 3.43 | 23 | 16 | 10 | 7 | 1 | 1 | 126.0 | 112 | 57 | 48 | 3 | 7 | 74 | 4 | 98 | 11 |
| Mena, Bakersfield | 10 | 13 | .435 | 3.46 | 30 | 21 | 7 | 5 | 1 | 0 | 176.2 | 181 | 92 | 68 | 4 | 7 | 86 | 0 | 105 | 7 |
| Walker, Salinas | 13 | 10 | .565 | 3.49 | 28 | 27 | 11 | 1 | 2 | 0 | 180.1 | 186 | 89 | 70 | 14 | 5 | 39 | 1 | 79 | 7 |

Departmental Leaders: G—Puikunas, 60; W—Corbell, 17; L—Guerrero, 15; Pct.—Corbell, .810; GS—Corbett, Raymer, 28; CG—Kushihara, 13; GF—Puikunas, 54; ShO—Corbell, Corbett, Ramirez, 3; Sv.—Puikunas, 21; IP—Rentschler, 193.1; H—Raymer, 207; R—Raymer, 123; ER—Livingston, 98; HR—Ramirez, 18; HB—Ueda, 12; BB—Raymer, 125; IBB—Barnhouse, 8; SO—Livingston, 166; WP—Guerrero, 29.

(All Pitchers—Listed Alphabetically)

| Pitcher—Club | W. | L. | Pct. | ERA. | G. | GS. | CG. | GF. | ShO. | Sv. | IP. | H. | R. | ER. | HR. | HB. | BB. | Int. BB. | SO. | WP. |
|---|---|---|---|---|---|---|---|---|---|---|---|---|---|---|---|---|---|---|---|---|
| Alexander, 20 Fresno-34 Reno | 4 | 7 | .364 | 2.70 | 54 | 1 | 0 | 39 | 0 | 12 | 76.2 | 63 | 33 | 23 | 1 | 0 | 58 | 6 | 63 | 3 |
| Amaya, Salinas | 0 | 0 | .000 | 2.25 | 1 | 0 | 0 | 1 | 0 | 0 | 4.0 | 3 | 1 | 1 | 1 | 0 | 2 | 0 | 3 | 0 |
| Anderson, Bakersfield | 0 | 0 | .000 | 4.50 | 1 | 0 | 0 | 1 | 0 | 0 | 2.0 | 4 | 1 | 1 | 0 | 0 | 1 | 0 | 2 | 0 |
| Balsley, Modesto | 0 | 0 | .000 | 1.26 | 3 | 2 | 0 | 0 | 0 | 0 | 14.1 | 12 | 5 | 2 | 0 | 0 | 9 | 0 | 8 | 0 |
| Barnhouse, Reno | 6 | 9 | .400 | 5.24 | 41 | 4 | 0 | 19 | 0 | 4 | 87.2 | 105 | 69 | 51 | 8 | 2 | 56 | 8 | 55 | 5 |
| Barry, Stockton* | 5 | 4 | .556 | 1.66 | 16 | 3 | 1 | 9 | 0 | 2 | 48.2 | 38 | 11 | 9 | 0 | 2 | 8 | 0 | 42 | 2 |
| Bauer, Modesto | 2 | 1 | .667 | 3.49 | 4 | 4 | 0 | 0 | 0 | 0 | 28.1 | 26 | 11 | 11 | 1 | 0 | 10 | 0 | 14 | 1 |

| Pitcher—Club | W. | L. | Pct. | ERA. | G. | GS. | CG. | GF. | ShO. | Sv. | IP. | H. | R. | ER. | HR. | HB. | BB. | Int. BB. | SO. | WP. |
|---|---|---|---|---|---|---|---|---|---|---|---|---|---|---|---|---|---|---|---|---|
| Brantley, Fresno | 8 | 2 | .800 | 3.33 | 14 | 13 | 3 | 0 | 0 | 0 | 94.2 | 83 | 39 | 35 | 4 | 1 | 37 | 0 | 85 | 7 |
| Ja. Bryant, Salinas | 4 | 0 | 1.000 | 0.34 | 21 | 0 | 0 | 21 | 0 | 12 | 26.2 | 17 | 2 | 1 | 0 | 1 | 11 | 4 | 36 | 4 |
| Jo. Bryant, 18 SJ-4 Sto | 5 | 5 | .500 | 2.55 | 22 | 9 | 1 | 12 | 0 | 8 | 81.1 | 56 | 31 | 23 | 2 | 2 | 44 | 3 | 65 | 8 |
| Budke, Visalia | 10 | 4 | .714 | 4.18 | 21 | 21 | 8 | 0 | 1 | 0 | 137.2 | 124 | 73 | 64 | 11 | 2 | 71 | 0 | 82 | 15 |
| Burkett, Fresno | 7 | 4 | .636 | 2.87 | 20 | 20 | 1 | 0 | 1 | 0 | 109.2 | 98 | 43 | 35 | 3 | 6 | 46 | 0 | 72 | 6 |
| Cadaret, Modesto* | 3 | 9 | .250 | 5.87 | 12 | 12 | 1 | 0 | 1 | 0 | 61.1 | 59 | 50 | 40 | 4 | 1 | 54 | 0 | 43 | 10 |
| Campbell, Salinas | 4 | 4 | .500 | 3.24 | 10 | 10 | 0 | 0 | 0 | 0 | 50.0 | 41 | 22 | 18 | 3 | 1 | 22 | 0 | 50 | 3 |
| Candelaria, Fresno* | 4 | 4 | .500 | 3.95 | 34 | 6 | 0 | 14 | 0 | 1 | 79.2 | 68 | 49 | 35 | 6 | 3 | 84 | 0 | 61 | 8 |
| Cannon, Redwood | 2 | 4 | .333 | 4.30 | 17 | 10 | 0 | 0 | 0 | 0 | 69.0 | 72 | 47 | 33 | 2 | 4 | 41 | 0 | 36 | 8 |
| Carter, Redwood | 1 | 1 | .500 | 1.00 | 8 | 0 | 0 | 8 | 0 | 2 | 9.0 | 6 | 2 | 1 | 0 | 0 | 3 | 1 | 8 | 1 |
| Cedeno, Redwood | 4 | 7 | .364 | 3.26 | 38 | 0 | 0 | 28 | 0 | 8 | 47.0 | 43 | 26 | 17 | 1 | 1 | 42 | 4 | 48 | 13 |
| Chadwick, Redwood | 0 | 1 | .000 | 6.43 | 4 | 2 | 0 | 0 | 0 | 0 | 14.0 | 13 | 14 | 10 | 0 | 0 | 11 | 0 | 10 | 2 |
| Childers, Reno | 2 | 1 | .667 | 4.38 | 12 | 6 | 0 | 5 | 0 | 0 | 37.0 | 37 | 20 | 18 | 2 | 2 | 29 | 2 | 26 | 3 |
| Christ, Salinas | 8 | 7 | .533 | 4.97 | 22 | 22 | 3 | 0 | 1 | 0 | 114.0 | 130 | 80 | 63 | 3 | 4 | 82 | 0 | 70 | 8 |
| Ciardi, Stockton | 10 | 6 | .625 | 3.69 | 18 | 18 | 4 | 0 | 1 | 0 | 129.1 | 116 | 59 | 53 | 5 | 3 | 39 | 0 | 119 | 4 |
| Cipres, Redwood | 1 | 2 | .333 | 4.10 | 26 | 0 | 0 | 12 | 0 | 1 | 41.2 | 39 | 20 | 19 | 2 | 1 | 33 | 0 | 34 | 6 |
| Cobbs, Bakersfield | 8 | 7 | .533 | 4.18 | 34 | 14 | 1 | 11 | 0 | 6 | 114.0 | 119 | 68 | 53 | 9 | 5 | 55 | 1 | 67 | 6 |
| Copeland, Visalia* | 0 | 0 | .000 | 0.00 | 1 | 0 | 0 | 1 | 0 | 0 | 2.0 | 2 | 0 | 0 | 0 | 0 | 0 | 0 | 0 | 0 |
| Corbell, Fresno | 17 | 4 | .810 | 3.23 | 26 | 26 | 9 | 0 | 3 | 0 | 181.1 | 174 | 77 | 65 | 7 | 6 | 61 | 0 | 89 | 14 |
| Corbett, Redwood* | 11 | 12 | .478 | 4.03 | 28 | 28 | 7 | 0 | 3 | 0 | 174.0 | 165 | 108 | 78 | 7 | 5 | 101 | 0 | 122 | 12 |
| Coughlon, Modesto | 6 | 12 | .333 | 5.48 | 37 | 13 | 1 | 15 | 0 | 3 | 111.2 | 132 | 78 | 68 | 7 | 2 | 51 | 1 | 60 | 5 |
| Cozzolino, Redwood | 1 | 0 | 1.000 | 7.31 | 8 | 0 | 0 | 4 | 0 | 0 | 16.0 | 17 | 17 | 13 | 0 | 1 | 15 | 0 | 18 | 3 |
| Crews, Stockton | 8 | 1 | .889 | 3.30 | 16 | 14 | 0 | 1 | 0 | 0 | 90.0 | 101 | 46 | 33 | 4 | 2 | 17 | 0 | 56 | 1 |
| de Chavez, Modesto | 10 | 5 | .667 | 4.93 | 30 | 16 | 1 | 6 | 0 | 0 | 115.0 | 121 | 73 | 63 | 7 | 6 | 82 | 1 | 60 | 1 |
| Delzer, Redwood* | 0 | 2 | .000 | 1.93 | 18 | 0 | 0 | 15 | 0 | 7 | 18.2 | 9 | 4 | 4 | 2 | 1 | 11 | 0 | 24 | 3 |
| Dominguez, Visalia | 8 | 6 | .571 | 2.95 | 56 | 0 | 0 | 45 | 0 | 11 | 106.2 | 104 | 42 | 35 | 1 | 3 | 61 | 6 | 90 | 13 |
| Dunlop, Reno | 1 | 2 | .333 | 7.91 | 29 | 2 | 0 | 6 | 0 | 0 | 60.1 | 75 | 61 | 53 | 5 | 6 | 59 | 0 | 58 | 11 |
| Edwards, Bakersfield* | 3 | 3 | .500 | 3.87 | 16 | 14 | 1 | 0 | 1 | 0 | 88.1 | 80 | 44 | 38 | 3 | 2 | 49 | 0 | 73 | 3 |
| Evans, Stockton | 2 | 4 | .333 | 5.44 | 19 | 13 | 0 | 2 | 0 | 0 | 81.0 | 91 | 60 | 49 | 4 | 0 | 45 | 0 | 54 | 3 |
| Ferran, San Jose | 8 | 9 | .471 | 3.43 | 23 | 16 | 10 | 7 | 1 | 1 | 126.0 | 112 | 57 | 48 | 3 | 7 | 74 | 4 | 98 | 11 |
| Ferraro, Reno* | 1 | 2 | .333 | 7.20 | 17 | 1 | 0 | 7 | 0 | 3 | 30.0 | 37 | 26 | 24 | 6 | 0 | 19 | 0 | 20 | 0 |
| Figueroa, Modesto | 2 | 5 | .286 | 5.83 | 11 | 10 | 1 | 1 | 0 | 0 | 54.0 | 63 | 43 | 35 | 7 | 3 | 22 | 0 | 29 | 0 |
| Fingers, Stockton | 1 | 0 | 1.000 | 3.47 | 19 | 0 | 0 | 14 | 0 | 0 | 23.1 | 33 | 9 | 9 | 0 | 0 | 7 | 2 | 22 | 0 |
| Flores, Bakersfield | 0 | 0 | .000 | 3.30 | 14 | 0 | 0 | 12 | 0 | 2 | 30.0 | 26 | 11 | 11 | 2 | 1 | 15 | 0 | 25 | 3 |
| Foley, San Jose | 1 | 2 | .333 | 8.86 | 8 | 3 | 1 | 4 | 0 | 0 | 21.1 | 32 | 25 | 21 | 1 | 3 | 12 | 0 | 15 | 3 |
| Forbes, Reno | 2 | 2 | .500 | 7.17 | 25 | 4 | 0 | 6 | 0 | 1 | 69.0 | 82 | 64 | 55 | 3 | 11 | 59 | 2 | 40 | 9 |
| Freeman, Stockton* | 0 | 0 | .000 | 9.00 | 1 | 0 | 0 | 0 | 0 | 0 | 2.0 | 4 | 2 | 2 | 0 | 0 | 0 | 0 | 2 | 0 |
| Fulmer, Modesto* | 6 | 5 | .545 | 3.15 | 45 | 1 | 0 | 20 | 0 | 5 | 105.2 | 108 | 47 | 37 | 5 | 4 | 40 | 2 | 87 | 3 |
| Gallo, Redwood* | 5 | 2 | .714 | 3.43 | 38 | 4 | 0 | 13 | 0 | 2 | 65.2 | 56 | 30 | 25 | 3 | 0 | 45 | 2 | 65 | 4 |
| Galloway, Visalia* | 11 | 6 | .647 | 4.39 | 23 | 22 | 2 | 0 | 0 | 0 | 125.0 | 142 | 78 | 61 | 7 | 3 | 71 | 0 | 61 | 22 |
| Garrett, Modesto | 0 | 0 | .000 | 9.00 | 1 | 0 | 0 | 1 | 0 | 0 | 1.0 | 2 | 1 | 1 | 1 | 0 | 0 | 0 | 1 | 0 |
| Gentle, Bakersfield* | 1 | 4 | .200 | 7.09 | 16 | 4 | 0 | 5 | 0 | 0 | 45.2 | 61 | 44 | 36 | 2 | 6 | 41 | 1 | 35 | 4 |
| Gilbert, Fresno | 3 | 5 | .375 | 5.28 | 21 | 9 | 0 | 1 | 0 | 1 | 73.1 | 82 | 54 | 43 | 6 | 1 | 61 | 1 | 50 | 6 |
| Gildehaus, Reno | 3 | 8 | .273 | 8.95 | 21 | 11 | 1 | 5 | 1 | 0 | 64.1 | 102 | 80 | 64 | 10 | 2 | 32 | 0 | 36 | 6 |
| Gladden, San Jose | 4 | 8 | .333 | 4.80 | 18 | 11 | 3 | 6 | 1 | 0 | 86.1 | 96 | 61 | 46 | 7 | 3 | 44 | 0 | 62 | 3 |
| Gotoh, San Jose | 5 | 12 | .294 | 4.75 | 22 | 22 | 7 | 0 | 2 | 0 | 140.1 | 161 | 85 | 74 | 6 | 5 | 62 | 5 | 61 | 10 |
| Guerrero, Visalia* | 7 | 15 | .318 | 4.49 | 27 | 27 | 1 | 0 | 0 | 0 | 152.1 | 176 | 95 | 76 | 5 | 3 | 99 | 1 | 87 | 29 |
| Gunnarsson, Salinas* | 10 | 8 | .556 | 3.12 | 31 | 18 | 6 | 6 | 2 | 0 | 130.0 | 125 | 54 | 45 | 5 | 6 | 44 | 4 | 91 | 0 |
| Hamrick, Bakersfield* | 2 | 7 | .222 | 4.05 | 16 | 12 | 3 | 3 | 0 | 0 | 80.0 | 69 | 45 | 36 | 2 | 2 | 61 | 0 | 43 | 9 |
| Hardwick, San Jose | 0 | 1 | .000 | 6.00 | 4 | 4 | 0 | 0 | 0 | 0 | 15.0 | 19 | 14 | 10 | 1 | 0 | 10 | 0 | 10 | 1 |
| Harris, Modesto | 0 | 2 | .000 | 8.22 | 2 | 2 | 0 | 0 | 0 | 0 | 7.2 | 13 | 7 | 7 | 1 | 1 | 2 | 0 | 2 | 0 |
| Harvey, Modesto* | 4 | 2 | .667 | 2.20 | 24 | 4 | 3 | 17 | 0 | 6 | 57.1 | 29 | 14 | 14 | 6 | 0 | 22 | 1 | 43 | 0 |
| Heath, Modesto* | 4 | 5 | .444 | 5.71 | 44 | 4 | 0 | 19 | 0 | 2 | 75.2 | 94 | 57 | 48 | 4 | 0 | 52 | 1 | 70 | 7 |
| Henning, Fresno | 6 | 6 | .500 | 4.46 | 15 | 13 | 1 | 0 | 0 | 0 | 70.2 | 51 | 52 | 35 | 2 | 6 | 62 | 0 | 47 | 10 |
| Hilton, Modesto | 3 | 3 | .500 | 4.06 | 9 | 8 | 2 | 1 | 1 | 0 | 44.1 | 49 | 21 | 20 | 3 | 1 | 21 | 0 | 16 | 1 |
| Hinson, Salinas | 0 | 0 | .000 | 2.00 | 2 | 1 | 0 | 0 | 0 | 0 | 9.0 | 7 | 2 | 2 | 0 | 1 | 3 | 0 | 5 | 0 |
| Husband, Visalia | 0 | 0 | .000 | 9.00 | 1 | 0 | 0 | 1 | 0 | 0 | 1.0 | 0 | 1 | 1 | 0 | 0 | 4 | 0 | 1 | 2 |
| John, Modesto* | 0 | 0 | .000 | 5.73 | 2 | 2 | 0 | 0 | 0 | 0 | 11.0 | 12 | 8 | 7 | 0 | 1 | 6 | 0 | 11 | 0 |
| Johnson, Salinas | 8 | 5 | .615 | 5.47 | 22 | 10 | 0 | 1 | 0 | 0 | 79.0 | 96 | 63 | 48 | 9 | 3 | 58 | 1 | 54 | 7 |
| Kemmerling, Redwood | 2 | 2 | .500 | 1.80 | 24 | 0 | 0 | 13 | 0 | 4 | 40.0 | 36 | 11 | 8 | 4 | 0 | 11 | 2 | 23 | 5 |
| Kendrick, Modesto* | 9 | 4 | .692 | 2.78 | 15 | 14 | 3 | 0 | 1 | 0 | 97.0 | 96 | 43 | 30 | 6 | 3 | 27 | 1 | 70 | 3 |
| Klingbeil, Visalia | 5 | 11 | .313 | 5.23 | 25 | 22 | 4 | 3 | 1 | 0 | 144.2 | 171 | 106 | 84 | 12 | 7 | 72 | 3 | 71 | 11 |
| Kobernus, San Jose* | 4 | 7 | .364 | 5.44 | 24 | 4 | 0 | 12 | 0 | 1 | 56.2 | 69 | 41 | 34 | 3 | 2 | 30 | 1 | 32 | 3 |
| Kockenmeister, Reno* | 0 | 1 | .000 | 13.50 | 13 | 0 | 0 | 4 | 0 | 0 | 18.2 | 39 | 30 | 28 | 7 | 0 | 15 | 0 | 8 | 1 |
| Kubala, San Jose | 3 | 5 | .375 | 5.98 | 10 | 10 | 1 | 0 | 0 | 0 | 55.2 | 68 | 43 | 37 | 2 | 5 | 46 | 1 | 31 | 5 |
| Kuhn, Fresno | 4 | 2 | .667 | 5.43 | 21 | 11 | 0 | 2 | 0 | 0 | 68.0 | 66 | 49 | 41 | 7 | 0 | 37 | 0 | 49 | 4 |
| Kushihara, San Jose | 8 | 13 | .381 | 3.33 | 22 | 22 | 13 | 0 | 0 | 0 | 165.0 | 147 | 82 | 61 | 12 | 7 | 63 | 1 | 131 | 4 |
| Landmark, Visalia | 4 | 10 | .286 | 6.49 | 26 | 21 | 1 | 0 | 0 | 0 | 131.2 | 181 | 119 | 95 | 13 | 7 | 58 | 3 | 67 | 7 |
| Langford, Modesto | 0 | 0 | .000 | 6.00 | 1 | 1 | 0 | 0 | 0 | 0 | 6.0 | 10 | 5 | 4 | 1 | 0 | 2 | 0 | 3 | 1 |
| K. Lee, Fresno* | 0 | 2 | .000 | 6.75 | 4 | 3 | 0 | 0 | 0 | 0 | 14.2 | 14 | 12 | 11 | 1 | 0 | 14 | 0 | 12 | 4 |
| R. Lee, Visalia | 2 | 5 | .286 | 5.10 | 27 | 8 | 2 | 6 | 0 | 2 | 102.1 | 111 | 67 | 58 | 5 | 7 | 58 | 2 | 46 | 13 |
| Leiper, Modesto* | 1 | 0 | 1.000 | 7.80 | 21 | 0 | 0 | 11 | 0 | 1 | 30.0 | 53 | 31 | 26 | 2 | 1 | 19 | 1 | 24 | 5 |
| Livingston, Bakersfield* | 10 | 11 | .476 | 5.23 | 27 | 27 | 5 | 0 | 1 | 0 | 168.2 | 173 | 111 | 98 | 6 | 5 | 117 | 0 | 166 | 17 |
| Madrid, Stockton | 7 | 0 | 1.000 | 1.97 | 8 | 8 | 2 | 0 | 1 | 0 | 59.1 | 53 | 16 | 13 | 1 | 1 | 15 | 0 | 52 | 1 |
| Malave, Salinas | 4 | 2 | .667 | 4.40 | 8 | 8 | 0 | 0 | 0 | 0 | 43.0 | 43 | 23 | 21 | 5 | 1 | 18 | 0 | 27 | 1 |
| Marrett, Redwood | 5 | 5 | .500 | 4.74 | 15 | 15 | 1 | 0 | 0 | 0 | 81.2 | 98 | 60 | 43 | 4 | 7 | 45 | 0 | 49 | 3 |
| Marsh, Reno* | 3 | 2 | .600 | 5.40 | 12 | 8 | 1 | 1 | 0 | 0 | 45.0 | 49 | 31 | 27 | 3 | 1 | 34 | 1 | 31 | 4 |
| McCormack, Salinas | 2 | 1 | .667 | 8.40 | 16 | 1 | 0 | 6 | 0 | 0 | 45.0 | 71 | 44 | 42 | 4 | 0 | 25 | 1 | 18 | 2 |
| McLoughlin, Reno | 5 | 4 | .538 | 4.18 | 38 | 1 | 0 | 21 | 0 | 6 | 92.2 | 87 | 53 | 43 | 3 | 8 | 71 | 7 | 85 | 2 |
| Mena, Bakersfield | 10 | 13 | .435 | 3.46 | 30 | 21 | 7 | 5 | 1 | 0 | 176.2 | 181 | 92 | 68 | 4 | 7 | 86 | 0 | 105 | 7 |
| Migliore, Visalia | 9 | 9 | .500 | 4.73 | 29 | 19 | 4 | 4 | 0 | 0 | 131.1 | 131 | 81 | 69 | 5 | 6 | 75 | 1 | 84 | 6 |
| Mooneyham, Modesto | 2 | 0 | 1.000 | 1.26 | 8 | 0 | 0 | 6 | 0 | 4 | 14.1 | 9 | 3 | 2 | 0 | 0 | 8 | 0 | 13 | 0 |
| Moore, Salinas | 10 | 1 | .909 | 2.10 | 51 | 0 | 0 | 36 | 0 | 14 | 85.2 | 68 | 25 | 20 | 2 | 3 | 23 | 1 | 61 | 4 |
| Morales, Reno | 0 | 2 | .000 | 28.29 | 6 | 3 | 0 | 2 | 0 | 1 | 7.0 | 21 | 24 | 22 | 6 | 0 | 13 | 0 | 6 | 0 |
| Moran, Bakersfield | 0 | 0 | .000 | 0.00 | 5 | 0 | 0 | 4 | 0 | 0 | 9.1 | 5 | 1 | 0 | 0 | 2 | 3 | 0 | 3 | 0 |
| Moriarty, Modesto | 0 | 4 | .000 | 6.94 | 12 | 1 | 0 | 5 | 0 | 1 | 23.1 | 27 | 20 | 18 | 3 | 0 | 18 | 0 | 18 | 4 |
| Morris, Stockton* | 5 | 6 | .455 | 6.04 | 19 | 13 | 0 | 2 | 0 | 0 | 73.0 | 85 | 63 | 49 | 3 | 2 | 57 | 2 | 43 | 7 |
| Murai, San Jose | 2 | 5 | .286 | 6.48 | 24 | 4 | 0 | 16 | 0 | 2 | 62.0 | 80 | 55 | 43 | 3 | 11 | 44 | 1 | 48 | 5 |
| Murphy, Stockton | 9 | 7 | .563 | 3.95 | 24 | 21 | 3 | 2 | 1 | 0 | 132.0 | 114 | 65 | 58 | 1 | 4 | 84 | 2 | 157 | 10 |
| Norris, Modesto | 1 | 0 | 1.000 | 0.00 | 2 | 2 | 0 | 0 | 0 | 0 | 13.0 | 4 | 1 | 0 | 0 | 1 | 0 | 0 | 6 | 0 |
| Oakes, Fresno | 4 | 4 | .500 | 3.77 | 51 | 0 | 0 | 29 | 0 | 6 | 88.1 | 89 | 46 | 37 | 5 | 3 | 27 | 1 | 51 | 10 |
| Odom, Modesto | 1 | 0 | 1.000 | 2.48 | 16 | 1 | 0 | 7 | 0 | 1 | 29.0 | 23 | 14 | 8 | 3 | 1 | 17 | 0 | 26 | 0 |

| Pitcher—Club | W. | L. | Pct. | ERA | G. | GS. | CG. | GF. | ShO. | Sv. | IP. | H. | R. | ER. | HR. | HB. | BB. | Int. BB. | SO. | WP. |
|---|---|---|---|---|---|---|---|---|---|---|---|---|---|---|---|---|---|---|---|---|
| Ohnoutka, Fresno | 7 | 2 | .778 | 2.52 | 12 | 12 | 2 | 0 | 1 | 0 | 75.0 | 53 | 27 | 21 | 1 | 8 | 42 | 0 | 73 | 6 |
| Parks, Reno | 2 | 5 | .286 | 6.68 | 23 | 7 | 0 | 9 | 0 | 1 | 62.0 | 83 | 55 | 46 | 8 | 3 | 57 | 1 | 35 | 7 |
| Parrett, Stockton | 7 | 4 | .636 | 2.75 | 45 | 2 | 0 | 21 | 0 | 11 | 127.2 | 97 | 50 | 39 | 5 | 1 | 75 | 2 | 120 | 7 |
| Pierorazio, Visalia° | 6 | 2 | .750 | 3.74 | 51 | 0 | 0 | 28 | 0 | 2 | 67.1 | 73 | 37 | 28 | 2 | 4 | 42 | 2 | 43 | 10 |
| Pimentel, Stockton | 4 | 2 | .667 | 2.54 | 20 | 0 | 0 | 8 | 0 | 1 | 46.0 | 37 | 17 | 13 | 0 | 1 | 19 | 2 | 44 | 2 |
| Poloni, Salinas° | 0 | 1 | .000 | 1.93 | 5 | 1 | 1 | 1 | 0 | 0 | 14.0 | 14 | 4 | 3 | 1 | 0 | 2 | 0 | 3 | 0 |
| Porter, Reno | 0 | 0 | .000 | 0.00 | 1 | 0 | 0 | 1 | 0 | 0 | 2.0 | 2 | 0 | 0 | 0 | 0 | 0 | 0 | 1 | 0 |
| B. Price, Redwood° | 8 | 1 | .889 | 2.20 | 12 | 12 | 4 | 0 | 1 | 0 | 86.0 | 67 | 26 | 21 | 2 | 3 | 53 | 0 | 109 | 3 |
| K. Price, San Jose | 1 | 1 | .500 | 3.06 | 5 | 5 | 1 | 0 | 0 | 0 | 35.1 | 36 | 16 | 12 | 4 | 4 | 13 | 2 | 20 | 0 |
| Puig, Reno° | 9 | 7 | .563 | 4.86 | 28 | 25 | 4 | 0 | 2 | 0 | 153.2 | 164 | 101 | 83 | 14 | 6 | 78 | 1 | 121 | 8 |
| Puikunas, Fresno° | 7 | 5 | .583 | 1.93 | 60 | 0 | 0 | 54 | 0 | 21 | 84.0 | 64 | 24 | 18 | 3 | 1 | 36 | 0 | 67 | 12 |
| Ramirez, Salinas | 9 | 9 | .500 | 3.61 | 28 | 28 | 5 | 0 | 3 | 0 | 177.0 | 172 | 89 | 71 | 18 | 8 | 51 | 1 | 108 | 4 |
| Raymer, Reno | 10 | 11 | .476 | 4.44 | 29 | 28 | 6 | 1 | 0 | 0 | 188.2 | 207 | 123 | 93 | 13 | 3 | 125 | 3 | 165 | 24 |
| Reece, Stockton° | 8 | 8 | .500 | 3.20 | 24 | 22 | 2 | 2 | 0 | 1 | 126.2 | 112 | 63 | 45 | 4 | 2 | 77 | 0 | 129 | 10 |
| Reed, Redwood° | 3 | 11 | .214 | 5.93 | 34 | 16 | 1 | 8 | 0 | 1 | 123.0 | 142 | 91 | 81 | 7 | 6 | 73 | 2 | 50 | 9 |
| Rentschler, Redwood° | 10 | 10 | .500 | 3.40 | 27 | 27 | 7 | 0 | 1 | 0 | 193.1 | 191 | 84 | 73 | 11 | 2 | 63 | 1 | 137 | 6 |
| Rice, Stockton | 1 | 1 | .500 | 3.46 | 27 | 1 | 0 | 15 | 0 | 1 | 41.2 | 44 | 25 | 16 | 1 | 3 | 30 | 2 | 26 | 4 |
| Robertson, Reno | 5 | 7 | .417 | 7.77 | 14 | 12 | 1 | 1 | 1 | 0 | 63.2 | 99 | 60 | 55 | 4 | 3 | 30 | 1 | 26 | 0 |
| Ric. Rodriguez, Modesto | 8 | 1 | .889 | 3.30 | 16 | 16 | 3 | 0 | 1 | 0 | 103.2 | 103 | 42 | 38 | 6 | 5 | 41 | 1 | 50 | 3 |
| Rig. Rodriguez, Reno | 3 | 2 | .600 | 5.44 | 9 | 8 | 0 | 0 | 0 | 0 | 43.0 | 44 | 29 | 26 | 4 | 4 | 25 | 1 | 16 | 3 |
| Rojas, Visalia | 6 | 12 | .333 | 4.40 | 26 | 22 | 4 | 1 | 0 | 0 | 159.2 | 193 | 106 | 78 | 10 | 0 | 66 | 1 | 84 | 8 |
| Rowen, Bakersfield° | 3 | 5 | .375 | 5.97 | 13 | 10 | 0 | 1 | 0 | 0 | 60.1 | 73 | 49 | 40 | 1 | 4 | 45 | 0 | 43 | 12 |
| Satnat, Bakersfield° | 5 | 7 | .417 | 4.48 | 47 | 3 | 1 | 25 | 0 | 2 | 82.1 | 106 | 52 | 41 | 3 | 2 | 41 | 3 | 43 | 2 |
| Scherer, Modesto | 6 | 7 | .462 | 3.89 | 20 | 17 | 3 | 1 | 2 | 1 | 113.1 | 108 | 59 | 49 | 10 | 2 | 50 | 1 | 84 | 5 |
| Schneider, Salinas | 3 | 3 | .500 | 3.46 | 44 | 3 | 0 | 22 | 0 | 9 | 88.1 | 84 | 40 | 34 | 3 | 2 | 62 | 2 | 65 | 6 |
| Schugel, Visalia | 0 | 0 | .000 | 18.00 | 1 | 0 | 0 | 1 | 0 | 0 | 1.0 | 3 | 2 | 2 | 0 | 0 | 1 | 0 | 0 | 0 |
| Scott, Bakersfield | 3 | 4 | .429 | 5.80 | 12 | 10 | 2 | 1 | 0 | 0 | 63.2 | 84 | 46 | 41 | 4 | 1 | 28 | 0 | 31 | 2 |
| Serritella, Bakersfield | 5 | 4 | .556 | 5.22 | 17 | 9 | 0 | 1 | 0 | 0 | 69.0 | 85 | 50 | 40 | 6 | 3 | 41 | 0 | 38 | 2 |
| Simmons, Reno | 8 | 10 | .444 | 3.42 | 24 | 18 | 7 | 4 | 1 | 1 | 142.0 | 133 | 70 | 54 | 7 | 4 | 73 | 6 | 117 | 5 |
| R. Smith, Redwood | 0 | 0 | .000 | 2.25 | 2 | 0 | 0 | 2 | 0 | 0 | 4.0 | 2 | 1 | 1 | 0 | 0 | 2 | 0 | 1 | 1 |
| S. Smith, Fresno | 6 | 6 | .500 | 4.14 | 27 | 16 | 2 | 3 | 2 | 2 | 115.1 | 134 | 61 | 53 | 5 | 3 | 48 | 0 | 70 | 9 |
| Spalt, Stockton | 0 | 0 | .000 | 3.00 | 3 | 0 | 0 | 2 | 0 | 0 | 3.0 | 2 | 1 | 1 | 0 | 0 | 4 | 0 | 2 | 0 |
| Stapleton, Stockton° | 2 | 9 | .182 | 2.54 | 52 | 0 | 0 | 41 | 0 | 15 | 71.0 | 68 | 32 | 20 | 0 | 0 | 26 | 2 | 58 | 3 |
| Stone, San Jose | 7 | 4 | .636 | 4.41 | 43 | 1 | 0 | 34 | 0 | 8 | 112.1 | 121 | 75 | 55 | 4 | 6 | 72 | 4 | 91 | 13 |
| Strong, Modesto | 7 | 7 | .500 | 5.06 | 42 | 11 | 2 | 18 | 0 | 6 | 110.1 | 103 | 79 | 62 | 10 | 3 | 60 | 0 | 82 | 10 |
| Swearingen, Salinas° | 8 | 3 | .727 | 3.72 | 44 | 6 | 1 | 19 | 1 | 2 | 87.0 | 83 | 46 | 36 | 5 | 1 | 39 | 0 | 63 | 6 |
| Tate, Fresno | 9 | 6 | .600 | 4.32 | 34 | 12 | 2 | 7 | 0 | 0 | 123.0 | 112 | 73 | 59 | 8 | 3 | 86 | 0 | 118 | 24 |
| Tejeda, Bakersfield° | 1 | 0 | 1.000 | 2.70 | 7 | 2 | 0 | 2 | 0 | 1 | 23.1 | 16 | 11 | 7 | 2 | 0 | 4 | 0 | 18 | 0 |
| Tinkey, Redwood | 8 | 7 | .533 | 4.71 | 36 | 13 | 3 | 12 | 1 | 4 | 122.1 | 145 | 78 | 64 | 5 | 4 | 49 | 4 | 73 | 2 |
| Torres, Bakersfield | 12 | 4 | .750 | 3.74 | 58 | 0 | 0 | 49 | 0 | 19 | 101.0 | 84 | 50 | 42 | 8 | 3 | 54 | 3 | 112 | 8 |
| Ueda, Stockton | 3 | 10 | .231 | 4.79 | 21 | 21 | 6 | 0 | 0 | 0 | 133.1 | 139 | 80 | 71 | 5 | 12 | 63 | 4 | 80 | 6 |
| Velasquez, Visalia | 7 | 7 | .500 | 2.39 | 53 | 1 | 0 | 36 | 0 | 10 | 90.1 | 75 | 28 | 24 | 6 | 3 | 50 | 2 | 88 | 9 |
| C. Walker, Stockton | 9 | 10 | .474 | 4.03 | 27 | 27 | 6 | 0 | 2 | 0 | 172.0 | 185 | 90 | 77 | 9 | 2 | 60 | 1 | 106 | 5 |
| J. Walker, Salinas | 13 | 10 | .565 | 3.49 | 28 | 27 | 11 | 1 | 2 | 0 | 180.1 | 186 | 89 | 70 | 14 | 5 | 39 | 1 | 79 | 7 |
| S. Walker, Bakersfield | 1 | 2 | .333 | 5.92 | 8 | 2 | 0 | 4 | 0 | 1 | 24.1 | 22 | 18 | 16 | 0 | 1 | 18 | 0 | 15 | 4 |
| Watkins, San Jose | 0 | 3 | .000 | 8.27 | 8 | 0 | 0 | 7 | 0 | 0 | 16.1 | 21 | 15 | 15 | 3 | 2 | 11 | 0 | 12 | 3 |
| Whitehurst, Modesto | 1 | 0 | 1.000 | 1.80 | 2 | 2 | 0 | 0 | 0 | 0 | 10.0 | 10 | 3 | 2 | 1 | 1 | 5 | 0 | 5 | 0 |
| Wilhelmi, Fresno | 0 | 3 | .000 | 8.25 | 3 | 3 | 0 | 0 | 0 | 0 | 12.0 | 21 | 19 | 11 | 1 | 3 | 9 | 0 | 5 | 0 |
| Wilkinson, Salinas° | 6 | 1 | .857 | 2.72 | 9 | 9 | 3 | 0 | 2 | 0 | 59.2 | 47 | 19 | 18 | 2 | 1 | 23 | 0 | 75 | 2 |
| Williams, Stockton | 1 | 0 | 1.000 | 13.91 | 13 | 0 | 0 | 7 | 0 | 0 | 11.0 | 15 | 25 | 17 | 0 | 2 | 23 | 0 | 6 | 5 |
| Wolff, Reno | 0 | 0 | .000 | 7.94 | 5 | 0 | 0 | 4 | 0 | 0 | 5.2 | 5 | 5 | 5 | 2 | 0 | 4 | 0 | 7 | 0 |
| C. Young, Modesto° | 0 | 0 | .000 | 4.76 | 2 | 2 | 0 | 0 | 0 | 0 | 5.2 | 7 | 4 | 3 | 0 | 1 | 6 | 0 | 3 | 0 |
| R. Young, Bakersfield | 1 | 9 | .100 | 5.70 | 19 | 17 | 0 | 1 | 0 | 0 | 85.1 | 61 | 73 | 54 | 7 | 8 | 111 | 0 | 81 | 12 |
| Zamba, San Jose | 7 | 4 | .636 | 3.84 | 15 | 14 | 3 | 0 | 0 | 0 | 96.0 | 115 | 61 | 41 | 9 | 1 | 26 | 0 | 65 | 4 |

BALKS—Kushihara, 8; Guerrero, Landmark, Scott, 4 each; Ciardi, Corbell, R. Lee, Puikunas, Ueda, 3 each; deChavez, Fulmer, Gotoh, Kubala, Livingston, McLoughlin, Murai, Oakes, Parks, Parrett, Puig, J. Walker, 2 each; Campbell, Candelaria, Chadwick, Coughlon, Ferran, Figueroa, Gentle, Gilbert, Hamrick, Johnson, Klingbeil, Kobernus, Kockenmeister, Kuhn, Leiper, Malave, Marsh, Moriarty, K. Price, Reed, Rentschler, Robertson, Satnat, Scherer, Serritella, Simmons, Tate, Torres, C. Walker, Wilkinson, R. Young, Zamba, 1 each.

COMBINATION SHUTOUTS—Rowen-Torres 2, Cobbs-Tejeda-Satnat, Cobbs-Edwards-Flores, Mena-Cobbs, Serritella-Torres, Bakersfield; Ohnoutka-Candelaria, Smith-Moriarty, Tate-Moriarty, Fresno; deChavez-Fulmer, Norris-Fulmer, Heath-Odom, Modesto; Corbett-Tinkey, Gallo-Cipres, Redwood; Raymer-Barnhouse, Rodriguez-Alexander, Reno; Walker-Moore 2, Campbell-Swearingen-Moore, Campbell-Moore, Johnson-Moore, Johnson-Schneider, Malave-Moore, Salinas; Kushihara-Kobernus, Murai-Ferran, San Jose; Crews-Stapleton, Walker-Rice-Stapleton, Stockton; Galloway-Lee, Guerrero-Velasquez, Rojas-Pierorazio, Visalia.

NO-HIT GAME—Henning-Puikunas, Fresno, defeated Bakersfield, 5-2, April 18.

# Carolina League

## CLASS A

### CHAMPIONSHIP WINNERS IN PREVIOUS YEARS

| | | |
|---|---|---|
| 1945—Danville ...................................681 | 1960—Greensboro‡ ..........................636 | 1971—Peninsula‡ ..............................647 |
| 1946—Greensboro...........................599 | Burlington.............................586 | Kinston .................................623 |
| Raleigh (2nd)† ...............563 | 1961—Wilson....................................594 | 1972—Salem‡ ...................................657 |
| 1947—Burlington..............................613 | 1962—Durham..................................636 | Burlington.............................632 |
| Raleigh (3rd)† ...............574 | Wilson....................................600 | 1973—Lynchburg..............................588 |
| 1948—Raleigh....................................592 | Kinston (2nd)† ....................593 | Winston-Salem‡..................557 |
| Martinsville (2nd)† ........570 | 1963—Kinston§.................................538 | 1974—Salem.....................................671 |
| 1949—Danville ..................................601 | Greensboro§.........................590 | Salem....................................582 |
| Burlington (4th)† ...........500 | Wilson (2nd)† .......................535 | 1975—Rocky Mount..........................667 |
| 1950—Winston-Salem° .......................693 | 1964—Kinston§.................................572 | Rocky Mount........................614 |
| 1951—Durham...................................600 | Winston-Salem§† ................590 | 1976—Winston-Salem ........................618 |
| Wins-Salem (2nd)† ........583 | 1965—Peninsula§...............................597 | Winston-Salem ....................551 |
| 1952—Raleigh....................................581 | Durham§...............................580 | 1977—Lynchburg..............................591 |
| Reidsville (4th)† .............536 | Tidewater† ...........................528 | Peninsula‡ ...........................556 |
| 1953—Raleigh....................................593 | 1966—Kinston§.................................547 | 1978—Peninsula................................696 |
| Danville (2nd)† ..............572 | Winston-Salem§ ..................586 | Lynchburg‡ ..........................614 |
| 1954—Fayetteville° ............................628 | Rocky Mount† ......................533 | 1979—Winston-Salem a ......................607 |
| 1955—HP-Thomasville .........................580 | 1967—Durham x (West.).....................536 | 1980—Peninsula‡ ..............................714 |
| Danville (2nd)† ..............533 | Raleigh (East.).....................542 | Durham ................................600 |
| 1956—HP-Thomasville .........................591 | 1968—Salem (West.) ..........................607 | 1981—Peninsula................................522 |
| Fayetteville (4th)† .........523 | Ral-Dur (East.).....................597 | Hagerstown‡.........................507 |
| 1957—Durham...................................632 | HP-Thom. y (W.)..................493 | 1982—Alexandria‡..............................597 |
| HP-Thomasville.............622 | 1969—Rocky M (East.)........................569 | Durham ................................588 |
| 1958—Danville ..................................576 | Salem (West.) ......................542 | 1983—Lynchburg‡..............................691 |
| Burlington (4th)† ...........511 | Ral-Dur z (East.)..................560 | Winston-Salem ....................529 |
| 1959—Raleigh....................................600 | 1970—Winston-Salem‡........................586 | 1984—Lynchburg‡..............................645 |
| Wilson (2nd)† .................550 | Burlington.............................597 | Durham ................................486 |

°Won championship and four-club playoff. †Won four-club playoff. ‡Won split-season playoff. §League was divided into Eastern, Western divisions. xWon eight-club, two-division playoff. yWon eight-club, two-division playoff against Raleigh-Durham. zWon eight-club, two-division playoff against Burlington. aWon both halves of split-season (no playoffs).

### STANDING OF CLUBS AT CLOSE OF FIRST HALF, JUNE 19

#### NORTHERN DIVISION

| Club | W. | L. | T. | Pct. | G.B. |
|---|---|---|---|---|---|
| Lynchburg (Mets) ..................................... | 48 | 22 | 0 | .686 | ........ |
| Hagerstown (Orioles)............................. | 41 | 28 | 0 | .594 | 6½ |
| Salem (Rangers) ..................................... | 40 | 30 | 1 | .571 | 8 |
| Prince William (Pirates) ......................... | 32 | 37 | 0 | .464 | 15½ |

#### SOUTHERN DIVISION

| Club | W. | L. | T. | Pct. | G.B. |
|---|---|---|---|---|---|
| Winston-Salem (Cubs)............................ | 35 | 35 | 0 | .500 | ........ |
| Durham (Braves)..................................... | 32 | 38 | 0 | .457 | 3 |
| Peninsula (Phillies)................................. | 28 | 42 | 0 | .400 | 7 |
| Kinston (Blue Jays)................................. | 23 | 47 | 1 | .329 | 12 |

### STANDING OF CLUBS AT CLOSE OF SECOND HALF, AUGUST 31

#### NORTHERN DIVISION

| Club | W. | L. | T. | Pct. | G.B. |
|---|---|---|---|---|---|
| Lynchburg (Mets) ..................................... | 47 | 23 | 0 | .671 | ........ |
| Salem (Rangers) ..................................... | 32 | 35 | 0 | .478 | 13½ |
| Prince William (Pirates) ......................... | 33 | 37 | 0 | .471 | 14 |
| Hagerstown (Orioles)............................. | 24 | 44 | 0 | .353 | 22 |

#### SOUTHERN DIVISION

| Club | W. | L. | T. | Pct. | G.B. |
|---|---|---|---|---|---|
| Kinston (Blue Jays)................................. | 41 | 26 | 0 | .612 | ........ |
| Peninsula (Phillies)................................. | 39 | 26 | 0 | .600 | 1 |
| Durham (Braves)..................................... | 34 | 36 | 0 | .486 | 8½ |
| Winston-Salem (Cubs)............................ | 23 | 46 | 0 | .333 | 19 |

### COMPOSITE STANDING OF CLUBS AT CLOSE OF SEASON, AUGUST 31

| Club | Lyn. | Sal. | Pen. | Hag. | Dur. | P.W. | Kin. | W-S | W. | L. | T. | Pct. | G.B. |
|---|---|---|---|---|---|---|---|---|---|---|---|---|---|
| Lynchburg (Mets) ......................... | .... | 16 | 10 | 14 | 15 | 13 | 13 | 14 | 95 | 45 | 0 | .679 | ........ |
| Salem (Rangers) ........................... | 4 | .... | 11 | 10 | 13 | 16 | 10 | 8 | 72 | 65 | 1 | .526 | 21½ |
| Peninsula (Phillies)........................ | 10 | 7 | .... | 8 | 8 | 12 | 12 | 10 | 67 | 68 | 0 | .496 | 25½ |
| Hagerstown (Orioles)..................... | 6 | 10 | 9 | .... | 10 | 8 | 9 | 13 | 65 | 72 | 0 | .474 | 28½ |
| Durham (Braves)........................... | 5 | 7 | 12 | 10 | .... | 9 | 12 | 11 | 66 | 74 | 0 | .471 | 29 |
| Prince William (Pirates) ................ | 7 | 4 | 8 | 12 | 11 | .... | 11 | 12 | 65 | 74 | 0 | .468 | 29½ |
| Kinston (Blue Jays)....................... | 7 | 9 | 8 | 11 | 8 | 8 | .... | 13 | 64 | 73 | 1 | .467 | 29½ |
| Winston-Salem (Cubs).................... | 6 | 12 | 10 | 7 | 9 | 8 | 6 | .... | 58 | 81 | 0 | .417 | 36½ |

Major league affiliations in parentheses.

Playoffs—Winston-Salem defeated Kinston, two games to none; Winston-Salem defeated Lynchburg, three games to one, to win league championship.

Regular-Season Attendance—Durham, 182,720; Hagerstown, 112,978; Kinston, 74,722; Lynchburg, 95,657; Peninsula, 59,151; Prince William, 127,356; Salem, 71,788; Winston-Salem, 98,434. Total—822,806. Total Playoff Attendance, 4,260. All-Star Game attendance at Winston-Salem, 7,358.

Managers—Durham, Jim Beauchamp; Hagerstown, Greg Biagini; Kinston, Grady Little; Lynchburg, Mike Cubbage; Peninsula, Ron Clark; Prince William, Ed Ott; Salem, Bill Stearns; Winston-Salem, Cal Emery.

All-Star Team—1B—Chris Padget, Hagerstown; 2B—Jerry Browne, Salem; 3B—Dimas Gutierrez, Prince William; SS—Kevin Elster, Lynchburg and D.L. Smith, Hagerstown; OF—Shawn Abner, Lynchburg; Dave Martinez, Winston-Salem; Eric Yelding, Kinston; C—Burk Goldthorn, Prince William; LHP—Shawn Barton, Peninsula; RHP—Kyle Hartshorn, Lynchburg; Most Valuable Player—Shawn Abner, Lynchburg; Pitcher of the Year—Kyle Hartshorn, Lynchburg; Manager of the Year—Grady Little, Kinston.

(Compiled by Howe News Bureau, Boston, Mass.)

## CLUB BATTING

| Club | Pct. | G. | AB. | R. | OR. | H. | TB. | 2B. | 3B. | HR. | RBI. | GW. | SH. | SF. | HP. | BB. | Int. BB. | SO. | SB. | CS. | LOB. |
|---|---|---|---|---|---|---|---|---|---|---|---|---|---|---|---|---|---|---|---|---|---|
| Lynchburg | .255 | 140 | 4567 | 624 | 411 | 1164 | 1688 | 197 | 42 | 81 | 545 | 78 | 50 | 38 | 41 | 524 | 23 | 969 | 148 | 47 | 1027 |
| Salem | .247 | 138 | 4588 | 670 | 642 | 1135 | 1668 | 188 | 39 | 89 | 606 | 64 | 36 | 29 | 56 | 611 | 15 | 1069 | 165 | 70 | 1053 |
| Kinston | .247 | 138 | 4505 | 546 | 589 | 1113 | 1529 | 161 | 18 | 73 | 461 | 57 | 19 | 43 | 29 | 477 | 8 | 951 | 221 | 98 | 927 |
| Winston-Salem | .242 | 139 | 4413 | 510 | 587 | 1069 | 1504 | 170 | 26 | 71 | 457 | 54 | 46 | 44 | 30 | 452 | 18 | 940 | 144 | 71 | 916 |
| Prince William | .240 | 139 | 4401 | 529 | 533 | 1058 | 1460 | 163 | 34 | 57 | 461 | 57 | 41 | 44 | 41 | 498 | 25 | 825 | 137 | 76 | 946 |
| Durham | .239 | 140 | 4494 | 626 | 674 | 1072 | 1570 | 162 | 24 | 96 | 558 | 60 | 50 | 37 | 46 | 647 | 24 | 902 | 132 | 62 | 1035 |
| Peninsula | .237 | 135 | 4293 | 518 | 552 | 1017 | 1439 | 181 | 29 | 61 | 459 | 60 | 56 | 34 | 32 | 471 | 17 | 914 | 145 | 41 | 935 |
| Hagerstown | .234 | 137 | 4341 | 535 | 570 | 1017 | 1412 | 185 | 33 | 48 | 446 | 55 | 33 | 42 | 23 | 625 | 31 | 773 | 113 | 53 | 1059 |

## INDIVIDUAL BATTING

(Leading Qualifiers for Batting Championship—378 or More Plate Appearances)

°Bats lefthanded.　　†Switch-hitter.

| Player and Club | Pct. | G. | AB. | R. | H. | TB. | 2B. | 3B. | HR. | RBI. | GW. | SH. | SF. | HP. | BB. | Int. BB. | SO. | SB. | CS. |
|---|---|---|---|---|---|---|---|---|---|---|---|---|---|---|---|---|---|---|---|
| Martinez, David, Winston-Salem° | .342 | 115 | 386 | 52 | 132 | 169 | 14 | 4 | 5 | 54 | 7 | 1 | 2 | 3 | 62 | 5 | 35 | 38 | 14 |
| Wilson, John, Lynchburg° | .302 | 121 | 377 | 70 | 114 | 143 | 11 | 3 | 4 | 31 | 7 | 3 | 2 | 4 | 49 | 3 | 105 | 50 | 7 |
| Abner, Shawn, Lynchburg | .301 | 139 | 542 | 71 | 163 | 263 | 30 | 11 | 16 | 89 | 18 | 0 | 7 | 9 | 28 | 1 | 77 | 8 | 7 |
| Farmer, Albert, Salem | .300 | 127 | 506 | 68 | 152 | 191 | 11 | 5 | 6 | 70 | 10 | 1 | 10 | 2 | 34 | 1 | 52 | 9 | 5 |
| Liriano, Nelson, Kinston† | .288 | 139 | 451 | 68 | 130 | 173 | 23 | 1 | 6 | 36 | 3 | 4 | 0 | 2 | 39 | 1 | 55 | 25 | 11 |
| Malave, Omar, Kinston | .288 | 105 | 354 | 42 | 102 | 150 | 16 | 1 | 10 | 55 | 10 | 3 | 5 | 1 | 32 | 0 | 57 | 9 | 3 |
| Lawrence, Andy, Lynchburg° | .281 | 113 | 356 | 44 | 100 | 134 | 23 | 1 | 3 | 50 | 7 | 0 | 9 | 2 | 34 | 3 | 75 | 7 | 4 |
| Padget, Chris, Hagerstown° | .277 | 136 | 483 | 56 | 134 | 183 | 20 | 4 | 7 | 70 | 6 | 3 | 10 | 3 | 74 | 6 | 73 | 11 | 8 |
| Lind, Jose, Prince William | .276 | 105 | 377 | 42 | 104 | 121 | 9 | 4 | 0 | 28 | 9 | 0 | 0 | 0 | 32 | 1 | 42 | 11 | 7 |
| Roberts, Drexel, Kinston° | .276 | 105 | 312 | 56 | 86 | 119 | 19 | 1 | 4 | 30 | 5 | 0 | 2 | 3 | 64 | 5 | 64 | 16 | 8 |
| Amaral, Richard, Winston-Salem | .271 | 124 | 428 | 62 | 116 | 150 | 15 | 5 | 3 | 36 | 3 | 5 | 1 | 2 | 59 | 1 | 68 | 26 | 7 |
| Engram, Graylin, Peninsula | .270 | 108 | 359 | 49 | 97 | 124 | 11 | 2 | 4 | 32 | 3 | 1 | 0 | 4 | 46 | 1 | 52 | 10 | 6 |
| Yastrzemski, Michael, Durham† | .270 | 132 | 493 | 64 | 133 | 196 | 20 | 5 | 11 | 63 | 3 | 6 | 3 | 3 | 53 | 2 | 76 | 3 | 5 |

Departmental Leaders: G—Little, 140; AB—Abner, 542; R—Bootay, Leiva, 73; H—Abner, 163; TB—Abner, 263; 2B—Abner, 30; 3B—Abner, 11; HR—Dickerson, 28; RBI—Abner, 89; GWRBI—Abner, 18; SH—Kennard, 10; SF—Farmer, Guttierez, Padget, 10; HP—Ro. Martinez, 13; BB—Baird, 94; IBB—Goldthorn, 10; SO—Hill, 211; SB—Yelding, 62; CS—Yelding, 26.

(All Players—Listed Alphabetically)

| Player and Club | Pct. | G. | AB. | R. | H. | TB. | 2B. | 3B. | HR. | RBI. | GW. | SH. | SF. | HP. | BB. | Int. BB. | SO. | SB. | CS. |
|---|---|---|---|---|---|---|---|---|---|---|---|---|---|---|---|---|---|---|---|
| Abner, Shawn, Lynchburg | .301 | 139 | 542 | 71 | 163 | 263 | 30 | 11 | 16 | 89 | 18 | 0 | 7 | 9 | 28 | 1 | 77 | 8 | 7 |
| Adkins, Terry, Prince William | .000 | 6 | 1 | 0 | 0 | 0 | 0 | 0 | 0 | 0 | 0 | 0 | 0 | 0 | 0 | 0 | 0 | 0 | 0 |
| Alfaro, Flavio, Durham | .193 | 110 | 378 | 60 | 73 | 103 | 13 | 4 | 3 | 34 | 4 | 7 | 0 | 5 | 82 | 1 | 78 | 29 | 8 |
| Amaral, Richard, Winston-Salem | .271 | 124 | 428 | 62 | 116 | 150 | 15 | 5 | 3 | 36 | 3 | 5 | 1 | 2 | 59 | 1 | 68 | 26 | 7 |
| Assenmacher, Paul, Durham° | .200 | 14 | 5 | 0 | 1 | 1 | 0 | 0 | 0 | 0 | 0 | 0 | 0 | 0 | 0 | 0 | 1 | 0 | 0 |
| Bailey, Gregory, Salem | .256 | 117 | 426 | 65 | 109 | 171 | 17 | 3 | 13 | 73 | 8 | 2 | 2 | 5 | 41 | 1 | 150 | 18 | 3 |
| Baird, Christopher, Durham° | .264 | 118 | 382 | 61 | 101 | 146 | 12 | 3 | 9 | 50 | 7 | 2 | 5 | 6 | 94 | 7 | 83 | 17 | 9 |
| Barger, Vincent, Durham° | .238 | 18 | 21 | 7 | 5 | 7 | 2 | 0 | 0 | 0 | 0 | 1 | 0 | 0 | 5 | 0 | 7 | 0 | 0 |
| Barnard, Steve, Prince William† | .199 | 53 | 151 | 16 | 30 | 43 | 7 | 0 | 2 | 18 | 3 | 2 | 3 | 0 | 29 | 5 | 24 | 1 | 2 |
| Barringer, Reginald, Prince William | .220 | 117 | 395 | 48 | 87 | 103 | 7 | 3 | 1 | 32 | 2 | 5 | 0 | 8 | 73 | 0 | 55 | 14 | 18 |
| Barton, Shawn, Peninsula | .240 | 23 | 25 | 1 | 6 | 7 | 1 | 0 | 0 | 2 | 1 | 5 | 0 | 0 | 1 | 0 | 7 | 0 | 0 |
| Bates, Kirk, Salem° | .217 | 51 | 175 | 12 | 38 | 48 | 7 | 0 | 1 | 18 | 1 | 0 | 1 | 3 | 13 | 1 | 50 | 1 | 0 |
| Bautista, Jose, Lynchburg | .111 | 29 | 27 | 2 | 3 | 3 | 0 | 0 | 0 | 2 | 0 | 5 | 1 | 0 | 0 | 0 | 8 | 0 | 0 |
| Beamesderfer, Kurt, Hagerstown | .205 | 29 | 88 | 7 | 18 | 22 | 4 | 0 | 0 | 5 | 1 | 0 | 0 | 0 | 4 | 0 | 18 | 1 | 0 |
| Belen, Lance, Prince William | .268 | 124 | 421 | 40 | 113 | 163 | 20 | 0 | 10 | 65 | 7 | 1 | 5 | 1 | 27 | 1 | 84 | 2 | 3 |
| Bell, Eric, Hagerstown° | 1.000 | 28 | 1 | 0 | 1 | 1 | 0 | 0 | 0 | 0 | 0 | 0 | 0 | 0 | 0 | 0 | 0 | 0 | 0 |
| Bell, Gregory, Winston-Salem° | .000 | 22 | 6 | 0 | 0 | 0 | 0 | 0 | 0 | 0 | 0 | 1 | 0 | 0 | 0 | 0 | 1 | 0 | 0 |
| Bellini, Robert, Hagerstown | .234 | 15 | 47 | 6 | 11 | 11 | 0 | 0 | 0 | 1 | 1 | 1 | 0 | 0 | 6 | 0 | 9 | 2 | 3 |
| Ben, Elijah, Salem | .198 | 101 | 323 | 62 | 64 | 119 | 15 | 2 | 12 | 39 | 3 | 1 | 0 | 4 | 71 | 0 | 142 | 23 | 9 |
| Benkert, Robert, Prince William | .000 | 3 | 8 | 0 | 0 | 0 | 0 | 0 | 0 | 0 | 0 | 0 | 0 | 1 | 1 | 0 | 3 | 0 | 0 |
| Bennett, Eric, Peninsula | .182 | 27 | 55 | 8 | 10 | 15 | 0 | 1 | 1 | 4 | 2 | 1 | 0 | 0 | 15 | 1 | 23 | 2 | 2 |
| Bergendahl, Wray, Lynchburg | .154 | 18 | 26 | 6 | 4 | 8 | 0 | 2 | 0 | 3 | 0 | 0 | 0 | 1 | 0 | 3 | 0 | 0 | |
| Berroa, Geronimo, Kinston | .186 | 19 | 43 | 4 | 8 | 11 | 0 | 0 | 1 | 4 | 0 | 0 | 1 | 0 | 4 | 0 | 10 | 0 | 1 |
| Berryhill, Damon, Winston-Salem† | .233 | 117 | 386 | 31 | 90 | 144 | 25 | 1 | 9 | 50 | 7 | 4 | 7 | 1 | 32 | 3 | 90 | 4 | 4 |
| Bethel, Donald, Winston-Salem | .087 | 25 | 23 | 1 | 2 | 2 | 0 | 0 | 0 | 1 | 0 | 2 | 0 | 0 | 0 | 0 | 9 | 0 | 0 |
| Blair, Martin, Salem† | .264 | 75 | 201 | 37 | 53 | 74 | 9 | 3 | 2 | 28 | 2 | 3 | 4 | 3 | 37 | 0 | 36 | 9 | 6 |
| Blankenship, Kevin, Durham | .167 | 30 | 18 | 1 | 3 | 3 | 0 | 0 | 0 | 1 | 0 | 4 | 0 | 0 | 0 | 0 | 7 | 0 | 0 |
| Blasucci, Anthony, Prince William° | .000 | 1 | 1 | 0 | 0 | 0 | 0 | 0 | 0 | 0 | 0 | 1 | 0 | 0 | 0 | 0 | 1 | 0 | 0 |
| Bonds, Barry, Prince William° | .299 | 71 | 254 | 49 | 76 | 139 | 16 | 4 | 13 | 37 | 3 | 1 | 4 | 0 | 37 | 0 | 52 | 15 | 3 |
| Bonilla, Roberto, Prince William† | .262 | 39 | 130 | 15 | 34 | 49 | 4 | 1 | 3 | 11 | 0 | 0 | 1 | 0 | 16 | 2 | 29 | 1 | 1 |
| Bootay, Kevin, Salem | .253 | 130 | 501 | 73 | 127 | 168 | 20 | 6 | 3 | 46 | 7 | 8 | 0 | 8 | 47 | 1 | 75 | 40 | 20 |
| Borders, Patrick, Kinston | .261 | 127 | 460 | 43 | 120 | 168 | 16 | 1 | 10 | 60 | 9 | 0 | 2 | 1 | 45 | 1 | 116 | 6 | 5 |
| Bormann, Michael, Durham | .500 | 11 | 2 | 0 | 1 | 1 | 0 | 0 | 0 | 0 | 0 | 1 | 0 | 0 | 0 | 0 | 1 | 0 | 0 |
| Boudreau, James, Winston-Salem° | .500 | 12 | 2 | 0 | 1 | 1 | 0 | 0 | 0 | 0 | 0 | 0 | 0 | 0 | 0 | 0 | 1 | 0 | 0 |
| Bowden, Mark, Peninsula° | .400 | 20 | 5 | 0 | 2 | 3 | 1 | 0 | 0 | 0 | 0 | 0 | 0 | 0 | 0 | 0 | 3 | 0 | 0 |
| Brewer, Jeffrey, Winston-Salem | .000 | 10 | 3 | 0 | 0 | 0 | 0 | 0 | 0 | 0 | 0 | 0 | 0 | 0 | 0 | 0 | 1 | 0 | 0 |
| Brown, Kevin, Lynchburg | .000 | 11 | 9 | 0 | 0 | 0 | 0 | 0 | 0 | 0 | 0 | 1 | 0 | 0 | 1 | 0 | 3 | 0 | 0 |
| Browne, Jerome, Salem† | .267 | 122 | 460 | 69 | 123 | 158 | 18 | 4 | 3 | 58 | 7 | 1 | 1 | 1 | 82 | 2 | 62 | 24 | 16 |
| Burns, Thomas, Lynchburg | .000 | 24 | 2 | 0 | 0 | 0 | 0 | 0 | 0 | 0 | 0 | 0 | 0 | 0 | 0 | 0 | 1 | 0 | 0 |
| Burrell, Kevin, Lynchburg | .237 | 110 | 392 | 44 | 93 | 149 | 16 | 5 | 10 | 54 | 7 | 1 | 4 | 6 | 24 | 2 | 99 | 2 | 1 |
| Butters, David, Prince William | .167 | 15 | 36 | 4 | 6 | 6 | 0 | 0 | 0 | 0 | 0 | 1 | 0 | 0 | 4 | 0 | 16 | 0 | 0 |
| Cadahia, Benito, Salem | .205 | 68 | 185 | 21 | 38 | 63 | 7 | 0 | 6 | 25 | 2 | 7 | 0 | 2 | 26 | 0 | 45 | 1 | 0 |
| Caraballo, Wilmer, Lynchburg | .231 | 94 | 333 | 39 | 77 | 141 | 13 | 0 | 17 | 49 | 1 | 0 | 0 | 0 | 17 | 3 | 74 | 4 | 0 |
| Carlucci, Anthony, Salem | .212 | 51 | 137 | 13 | 29 | 42 | 7 | 0 | 2 | 13 | 2 | 2 | 0 | 2 | 16 | 0 | 43 | 0 | 0 |
| Carmichael, Alan, Lynchburg | .287 | 52 | 115 | 16 | 33 | 41 | 8 | 0 | 0 | 5 | 1 | 3 | 1 | 2 | 22 | 2 | 24 | 0 | 1 |
| Carter, Don, Prince William° | .210 | 47 | 176 | 28 | 37 | 43 | 0 | 3 | 0 | 9 | 1 | 1 | 1 | 2 | 19 | 0 | 34 | 30 | 8 |
| Cash, Johnny, Durham° | .200 | 8 | 10 | 0 | 2 | 2 | 0 | 0 | 0 | 0 | 0 | 0 | 1 | 0 | 0 | 0 | 4 | 0 | 0 |
| Castro, Edgar, 38 Hag-12 PW° | .264 | 50 | 110 | 17 | 29 | 46 | 5 | 0 | 4 | 13 | 3 | 2 | 1 | 1 | 45 | 3 | 25 | 1 | 1 |
| Chambers, Travis, Peninsula° | .100 | 9 | 10 | 1 | 1 | 2 | 1 | 0 | 0 | 0 | 0 | 0 | 0 | 0 | 0 | 0 | 3 | 0 | 0 |
| Childress, Willie, Durham° | .246 | 121 | 406 | 55 | 100 | 139 | 16 | 1 | 7 | 49 | 1 | 4 | 8 | 4 | 59 | 4 | 69 | 19 | 12 |
| Cimo, Matthew, Hagerstown | .283 | 88 | 314 | 50 | 89 | 135 | 26 | 1 | 6 | 29 | 2 | 2 | 5 | 4 | 38 | 4 | 45 | 18 | 9 |
| Cooper, Mark, Kinston | .259 | 98 | 301 | 27 | 78 | 92 | 9 | 1 | 1 | 36 | 4 | 1 | 4 | 0 | 20 | 0 | 32 | 5 | 1 |
| Cordner, Steven, Winston-Salem | .217 | 49 | 143 | 16 | 31 | 36 | 5 | 0 | 0 | 6 | 0 | 1 | 0 | 1 | 15 | 1 | 38 | 2 | 2 |
| Cordova, Antonio, Winston-Salem | .210 | 76 | 257 | 33 | 54 | 87 | 10 | 1 | 7 | 29 | 2 | 3 | 4 | 5 | 4 | 0 | 59 | 5 | 1 |
| Cormack, Terry, Durham° | .211 | 29 | 57 | 3 | 12 | 13 | 1 | 0 | 0 | 5 | 0 | 1 | 0 | 0 | 9 | 0 | 10 | 0 | 0 |
| Coveney, Patrick, Peninsula° | .243 | 88 | 251 | 21 | 61 | 86 | 13 | 3 | 2 | 28 | 3 | 0 | 4 | 1 | 16 | 0 | 61 | 9 | 2 |
| Cox, John, Winston-Salem° | .400 | 31 | 10 | 0 | 4 | 4 | 0 | 0 | 0 | 2 | 0 | 0 | 0 | 0 | 1 | 0 | 4 | 0 | 0 |

| Player and Club | Pct. | G. | AB. | R. | H. | TB. | 2B. | 3B. | HR. | RBI. | GW. | SH. | SF. | HP. | BB. | Int. BB. | SO. | SB. | CS. |
|---|---|---|---|---|---|---|---|---|---|---|---|---|---|---|---|---|---|---|---|
| Cruz, Luis, Winston-Salem | .258 | 121 | 415 | 55 | 107 | 133 | 15 | 4 | 1 | 29 | 3 | 3 | 5 | 0 | 37 | 0 | 81 | 16 | 13 |
| Cunningham, Charles, Prince William | .500 | 32 | 8 | 1 | 4 | 4 | 0 | 0 | 0 | 0 | 0 | 0 | 0 | 0 | 2 | 0 | 0 | 0 | 0 |
| D'Alessandro, Salvatore, Durham | .256 | 108 | 324 | 52 | 83 | 130 | 15 | 1 | 10 | 60 | 3 | 3 | 3 | 6 | 61 | 1 | 58 | 3 | 1 |
| Dahse, David, Hagerstown | .158 | 14 | 38 | 7 | 6 | 6 | 0 | 0 | 0 | 3 | 0 | 0 | 0 | 0 | 5 | 0 | 5 | 1 | 1 |
| Dannenberg, Wayne, Peninsula* | .216 | 121 | 430 | 39 | 93 | 137 | 17 | 3 | 7 | 61 | 10 | 0 | 5 | 0 | 22 | 0 | 96 | 3 | 1 |
| Davis, Lee, Peninsula* | .196 | 20 | 46 | 2 | 9 | 11 | 2 | 0 | 0 | 5 | 1 | 0 | 0 | 0 | 0 | 0 | 15 | 0 | 0 |
| DelRosario, Maximo, Durham | .000 | 39 | 5 | 0 | 0 | 0 | 0 | 0 | 0 | 0 | 0 | 0 | 0 | 0 | 1 | 0 | 5 | 0 | 0 |
| Delucchi, Ronald, Prince William | .224 | 40 | 107 | 5 | 24 | 27 | 3 | 0 | 0 | 10 | 1 | 0 | 0 | 1 | 3 | 0 | 22 | 0 | 2 |
| Dennis, Eduardo, Kinston | .200 | 2 | 5 | 0 | 1 | 1 | 0 | 0 | 0 | 1 | 0 | 0 | 0 | 0 | 0 | 0 | 0 | 0 | 0 |
| DeWillis, Jeffrey, Kinston | .184 | 27 | 87 | 12 | 16 | 24 | 3 | 1 | 1 | 8 | 1 | 0 | 0 | 5 | 19 | 0 | 22 | 1 | 1 |
| Dickerson, James, Winston-Salem | .235 | 128 | 439 | 65 | 103 | 203 | 14 | 1 | 28 | 82 | 11 | 0 | 9 | 8 | 55 | 2 | 125 | 10 | 6 |
| Dobie, Reginald, Lynchburg | .067 | 28 | 30 | 2 | 2 | 2 | 0 | 0 | 0 | 0 | 0 | 5 | 0 | 0 | 2 | 0 | 14 | 0 | 0 |
| Dodd, Thomas, Hagerstown | .267 | 10 | 30 | 3 | 8 | 15 | 2 | 1 | 1 | 3 | 0 | 0 | 0 | 1 | 4 | 0 | 7 | 0 | 0 |
| Doerr, Jeffrey, Hagerstown | .218 | 101 | 339 | 46 | 74 | 118 | 18 | 4 | 6 | 43 | 7 | 3 | 3 | 0 | 42 | 1 | 97 | 5 | 1 |
| Doggett, Geoffrey, Lynchburg† | .176 | 34 | 68 | 10 | 12 | 15 | 3 | 0 | 0 | 7 | 1 | 1 | 0 | 0 | 11 | 0 | 16 | 0 | 2 |
| Dombek, Damon, Peninsula† | .250 | 24 | 12 | 1 | 3 | 3 | 0 | 0 | 0 | 1 | 0 | 4 | 0 | 0 | 1 | 0 | 5 | 0 | 0 |
| Doughty, Jamie, Salem | .232 | 30 | 95 | 12 | 22 | 34 | 3 | 3 | 1 | 11 | 0 | 0 | 1 | 0 | 7 | 0 | 26 | 0 | 1 |
| Edens, Thomas, Lynchburg | .364 | 16 | 11 | 2 | 4 | 4 | 0 | 0 | 0 | 1 | 0 | 1 | 0 | 0 | 2 | 0 | 1 | 0 | 0 |
| Elster, Kevin, Lynchburg | .295 | 59 | 224 | 41 | 66 | 96 | 9 | 0 | 7 | 26 | 4 | 0 | 1 | 2 | 33 | 2 | 21 | 8 | 2 |
| Engram, Graylyn, Peninsula | .270 | 108 | 359 | 49 | 97 | 124 | 11 | 2 | 4 | 32 | 3 | 1 | 0 | 4 | 46 | 1 | 52 | 10 | 6 |
| Epps, Riley, Salem† | .283 | 77 | 226 | 29 | 64 | 103 | 7 | 1 | 10 | 28 | 4 | 0 | 0 | 6 | 35 | 3 | 69 | 5 | 3 |
| Evans, Evan, Prince William | .228 | 40 | 123 | 14 | 28 | 38 | 5 | 1 | 1 | 12 | 3 | 2 | 2 | 2 | 19 | 0 | 42 | 2 | 2 |
| Farmer, Albert, Salem | .300 | 127 | 506 | 68 | 152 | 191 | 11 | 5 | 6 | 70 | 10 | 1 | 10 | 2 | 34 | 1 | 52 | 9 | 5 |
| Ferreiras, Salvador, Prince William | .000 | 5 | 6 | 1 | 0 | 0 | 0 | 0 | 0 | 0 | 0 | 0 | 0 | 0 | 1 | 0 | 2 | 0 | 0 |
| Fiepke, Scott, Prince William* | .000 | 13 | 1 | 0 | 0 | 0 | 0 | 0 | 0 | 0 | 0 | 2 | 0 | 0 | 0 | 0 | 1 | 0 | 0 |
| Fredymond, Juan, Durham | .195 | 52 | 169 | 12 | 33 | 37 | 2 | 1 | 0 | 8 | 3 | 2 | 1 | 0 | 16 | 1 | 40 | 7 | 2 |
| Freeman, Donald, Salem† | .184 | 54 | 158 | 23 | 29 | 41 | 5 | 2 | 1 | 17 | 1 | 0 | 1 | 1 | 20 | 0 | 55 | 5 | 2 |
| Freytes, Hector, Winston-Salem | .237 | 118 | 384 | 33 | 91 | 127 | 21 | 3 | 3 | 35 | 4 | 1 | 3 | 0 | 20 | 1 | 54 | 4 | 2 |
| Frohwirth, Todd, Peninsula | .000 | 54 | 6 | 0 | 0 | 0 | 0 | 0 | 0 | 0 | 0 | 0 | 0 | 1 | 0 | 0 | 5 | 0 | 0 |
| Garcia, Agustin, Lynchburg | 1.000 | 4 | 1 | 0 | 1 | 1 | 0 | 0 | 0 | 0 | 0 | 0 | 0 | 0 | 0 | 0 | 0 | 0 | 0 |
| Garrison, Webster, Kinston | .203 | 129 | 449 | 40 | 91 | 110 | 14 | 1 | 1 | 30 | 4 | 2 | 5 | 3 | 42 | 0 | 76 | 22 | 5 |
| Gay, Steven, Lynchburg | .154 | 21 | 13 | 1 | 2 | 3 | 1 | 0 | 0 | 0 | 0 | 1 | 0 | 0 | 0 | 0 | 3 | 0 | 0 |
| Giansiracusa, Roberto, Peninsula* | .260 | 20 | 50 | 8 | 13 | 16 | 0 | 0 | 1 | 5 | 1 | 1 | 1 | 0 | 6 | 0 | 5 | 2 | 0 |
| Gideon, Ronnie, Peninsula* | .244 | 112 | 360 | 49 | 88 | 151 | 25 | 1 | 12 | 58 | 3 | 2 | 2 | 3 | 44 | 2 | 119 | 3 | 3 |
| Goldthorn, Burk, Prince William* | .254 | 117 | 362 | 46 | 92 | 145 | 20 | 0 | 11 | 59 | 6 | 1 | 4 | 6 | 77 | 10 | 61 | 3 | 5 |
| Gordon, Kevin, Prince William | .182 | 22 | 22 | 2 | 4 | 4 | 0 | 0 | 0 | 2 | 0 | 1 | 0 | 0 | 2 | 0 | 1 | 0 | 0 |
| Griffin, David, Durham | .274 | 82 | 226 | 35 | 62 | 90 | 11 | 1 | 5 | 32 | 7 | 0 | 2 | 2 | 38 | 2 | 55 | 0 | 1 |
| Groves, Jeffrey, Durham | .250 | 20 | 24 | 2 | 6 | 6 | 0 | 0 | 0 | 3 | 1 | 1 | 0 | 0 | 0 | 0 | 6 | 0 | 0 |
| Grudzinski, Gary, Prince William | .333 | 15 | 3 | 0 | 1 | 1 | 0 | 0 | 0 | 1 | 0 | 0 | 0 | 0 | 0 | 0 | 1 | 0 | 0 |
| Gutierrez, Dimas, Prince William | .265 | 121 | 419 | 62 | 111 | 152 | 24 | 4 | 3 | 49 | 6 | 0 | 10 | 3 | 26 | 1 | 51 | 15 | 5 |
| Hall, Andrew, Winston-Salem* | .182 | 24 | 22 | 2 | 4 | 5 | 1 | 0 | 0 | 1 | 0 | 1 | 1 | 0 | 2 | 0 | 12 | 0 | 0 |
| Hamilton, Carlton, Winston-Salem* | .250 | 25 | 24 | 2 | 6 | 6 | 0 | 0 | 0 | 3 | 0 | 3 | 0 | 0 | 2 | 0 | 6 | 0 | 0 |
| Hammonds, Reginald, Prince William | .287 | 68 | 223 | 36 | 64 | 100 | 7 | 4 | 7 | 26 | 1 | 1 | 1 | 10 | 22 | 0 | 32 | 9 | 4 |
| Harrison, Wayne, Durham | .222 | 94 | 279 | 46 | 62 | 103 | 12 | 1 | 9 | 35 | 4 | 1 | 3 | 9 | 44 | 0 | 65 | 0 | 1 |
| Hartshorn, Kyle, Lynchburg | .243 | 25 | 37 | 7 | 9 | 13 | 2 | 1 | 0 | 4 | 0 | 5 | 0 | 0 | 1 | 0 | 16 | 0 | 0 |
| Hatcher, Johnny, Durham | .263 | 89 | 312 | 46 | 82 | 110 | 10 | 0 | 6 | 47 | 8 | 1 | 2 | 1 | 26 | 1 | 47 | 17 | 3 |
| Henderson, Ramon, Peninsula | .188 | 72 | 218 | 21 | 41 | 54 | 8 | 1 | 1 | 18 | 2 | 1 | 1 | 1 | 17 | 0 | 57 | 2 | 1 |
| Hill, Glenallen, Kinston | .210 | 131 | 466 | 57 | 98 | 171 | 13 | 0 | 20 | 56 | 8 | 2 | 4 | 1 | 57 | 0 | 211 | 42 | 15 |
| Holland, John, Kinston | .000 | 2 | 1 | 0 | 0 | 0 | 0 | 0 | 0 | 0 | 0 | 0 | 0 | 0 | 0 | 0 | 0 | 0 | 0 |
| Holman, Shawn, Prince William | .050 | 26 | 20 | 2 | 1 | 1 | 0 | 0 | 0 | 0 | 0 | 0 | 0 | 0 | 2 | 0 | 7 | 0 | 0 |
| Holtz, Gerald, Hagerstown* | .223 | 108 | 391 | 56 | 87 | 127 | 19 | 3 | 5 | 46 | 4 | 1 | 5 | 2 | 74 | 0 | 67 | 17 | 5 |
| Hopkins, Richard, Winston-Salem* | .183 | 85 | 169 | 16 | 31 | 39 | 8 | 0 | 0 | 10 | 0 | 4 | 2 | 3 | 34 | 2 | 41 | 2 | 4 |
| Householder, Brian, Peninsula | .077 | 39 | 13 | 3 | 1 | 4 | 0 | 0 | 1 | 3 | 0 | 3 | 0 | 0 | 1 | 0 | 4 | 0 | 0 |
| Howard, James, Kinston | .000 | 1 | 1 | 0 | 0 | 0 | 0 | 0 | 0 | 0 | 0 | 0 | 0 | 0 | 0 | 0 | 0 | 0 | 0 |
| Innis, Jeffrey, Lynchburg | .200 | 53 | 5 | 0 | 1 | 1 | 0 | 0 | 0 | 0 | 0 | 0 | 0 | 0 | 0 | 0 | 1 | 0 | 0 |
| Jackson, Michael, Peninsula | .238 | 32 | 21 | 2 | 5 | 8 | 1 | 1 | 0 | 1 | 0 | 1 | 1 | 0 | 0 | 0 | 3 | 0 | 0 |
| Jensen, David, Lynchburg* | .333 | 14 | 3 | 2 | 1 | 1 | 0 | 0 | 0 | 0 | 0 | 0 | 0 | 0 | 5 | 0 | 0 | 0 | 0 |
| Johnson, Steven, Kinston | .265 | 44 | 117 | 20 | 31 | 43 | 5 | 2 | 1 | 12 | 1 | 0 | 2 | 1 | 29 | 0 | 31 | 9 | 4 |
| Johnson, Todd, Peninsula | .214 | 15 | 42 | 3 | 9 | 10 | 1 | 0 | 0 | 3 | 0 | 0 | 0 | 1 | 4 | 0 | 17 | 1 | 0 |
| Jones, Barry, Prince William | .000 | 28 | 4 | 0 | 0 | 0 | 0 | 0 | 0 | 0 | 0 | 0 | 0 | 0 | 0 | 0 | 0 | 0 | 0 |
| Jones, Brian, Prince William | .233 | 100 | 331 | 39 | 77 | 98 | 13 | 4 | 0 | 29 | 2 | 5 | 3 | 0 | 38 | 1 | 77 | 10 | 6 |
| Jones, David, Durham | .188 | 32 | 16 | 4 | 3 | 3 | 0 | 0 | 0 | 0 | 0 | 0 | 0 | 0 | 0 | 0 | 5 | 0 | 0 |
| Kaiser, Bart, Peninsula* | .306 | 10 | 36 | 1 | 11 | 13 | 2 | 0 | 0 | 3 | 1 | 0 | 0 | 0 | 2 | 0 | 10 | 3 | 2 |
| Karr, Jeffrey, Lynchburg | .000 | 2 | 0 | 1 | 0 | 0 | 0 | 0 | 0 | 0 | 0 | 0 | 0 | 0 | 1 | 0 | 0 | 0 | 0 |
| Kenaga, Jeffrey, Hagerstown* | .313 | 20 | 80 | 10 | 25 | 35 | 4 | 0 | 2 | 10 | 2 | 0 | 0 | 0 | 4 | 1 | 8 | 0 | 0 |
| Kennard, David, Peninsula | .223 | 131 | 422 | 50 | 94 | 137 | 16 | 3 | 7 | 44 | 7 | 10 | 2 | 3 | 47 | 2 | 59 | 13 | 5 |
| King, Ronald, Salem* | .258 | 102 | 326 | 66 | 84 | 126 | 13 | 1 | 9 | 48 | 6 | 4 | 4 | 2 | 76 | 1 | 67 | 26 | 4 |
| Klink, Joseph, Lynchburg* | .000 | 44 | 2 | 0 | 0 | 0 | 0 | 0 | 0 | 0 | 0 | 0 | 0 | 0 | 0 | 0 | 1 | 0 | 0 |
| Klopp, Francis, 81 PW-23 Hag | .221 | 104 | 340 | 30 | 75 | 108 | 15 | 3 | 4 | 32 | 7 | 2 | 2 | 5 | 24 | 2 | 53 | 4 | 2 |
| Knox, Jeffrey, Peninsula | .000 | 3 | 4 | 0 | 0 | 0 | 0 | 0 | 0 | 0 | 0 | 0 | 0 | 0 | 0 | 0 | 3 | 0 | 0 |
| Knox, Scott, Prince William | .163 | 80 | 209 | 18 | 34 | 44 | 5 | 1 | 1 | 15 | 3 | 2 | 3 | 1 | 10 | 0 | 46 | 8 | 3 |
| Kopf, David, Winston-Salem | .091 | 24 | 11 | 0 | 1 | 1 | 0 | 0 | 0 | 1 | 0 | 0 | 0 | 0 | 1 | 0 | 1 | 0 | 0 |
| Kraft, Kenneth, Peninsula | .240 | 71 | 246 | 31 | 59 | 72 | 13 | 0 | 0 | 27 | 1 | 2 | 4 | 0 | 30 | 0 | 30 | 4 | 2 |
| Latmore, Robert, Hagerstown | .167 | 6 | 18 | 0 | 3 | 3 | 0 | 0 | 0 | 0 | 0 | 0 | 0 | 1 | 0 | 0 | 6 | 0 | 0 |
| Lawrence, Andy, Lynchburg | .281 | 113 | 356 | 44 | 100 | 134 | 23 | 1 | 3 | 50 | 7 | 0 | 9 | 2 | 34 | 3 | 75 | 7 | 4 |
| Leiva, Jose, Peninsula | .258 | 95 | 306 | 73 | 79 | 98 | 7 | 3 | 2 | 20 | 1 | 3 | 0 | 4 | 69 | 1 | 60 | 58 | 4 |
| Lenderman, David, Winston-Salem* | .250 | 41 | 8 | 1 | 2 | 5 | 0 | 0 | 1 | 3 | 0 | 0 | 0 | 0 | 1 | 0 | 4 | 0 | 0 |
| Lewis, John, Winston-Salem* | .500 | 1 | 2 | 0 | 1 | 1 | 0 | 0 | 0 | 0 | 0 | 0 | 0 | 0 | 0 | 0 | 0 | 1 | 0 |
| Lind, Jose, Prince William | .276 | 105 | 377 | 42 | 104 | 121 | 9 | 4 | 0 | 28 | 9 | 0 | 0 | 0 | 32 | 1 | 42 | 11 | 7 |
| Lind, Orlando, Prince William | .091 | 36 | 22 | 1 | 2 | 2 | 0 | 0 | 0 | 1 | 0 | 2 | 0 | 0 | 1 | 0 | 7 | 0 | 0 |
| Liriano, Nelson, Kinston† | .288 | 134 | 451 | 68 | 130 | 173 | 23 | 1 | 6 | 36 | 3 | 4 | 0 | 2 | 39 | 1 | 55 | 25 | 11 |
| Little, Scott, Lynchburg | .236 | 140 | 470 | 70 | 111 | 147 | 16 | 7 | 2 | 44 | 6 | 9 | 3 | 2 | 79 | 2 | 94 | 29 | 10 |
| Lloyd, Raymond, Peninsula | .200 | 12 | 5 | 0 | 1 | 2 | 1 | 0 | 0 | 0 | 0 | 1 | 0 | 0 | 0 | 0 | 0 | 0 | 0 |
| Long, Bruce, Peninsula | .000 | 11 | 10 | 0 | 0 | 0 | 0 | 0 | 0 | 0 | 0 | 0 | 0 | 0 | 1 | 0 | 8 | 0 | 0 |
| Lopez, Michael, Hagerstown* | .212 | 92 | 293 | 42 | 62 | 90 | 8 | 4 | 4 | 38 | 6 | 2 | 2 | 1 | 29 | 5 | 59 | 2 | 4 |
| Magrann, Thomas, Peninsula | .157 | 31 | 51 | 2 | 8 | 10 | 2 | 0 | 0 | 0 | 0 | 0 | 0 | 0 | 10 | 0 | 12 | 0 | 0 |
| Malave, Omar, Kinston | .288 | 105 | 354 | 42 | 102 | 150 | 16 | 1 | 10 | 55 | 10 | 3 | 5 | 1 | 32 | 0 | 57 | 9 | 3 |
| Maloney, Christopher, Lynchburg† | .201 | 72 | 159 | 12 | 32 | 44 | 7 | 1 | 1 | 21 | 5 | 0 | 2 | 1 | 22 | 1 | 38 | 0 | 0 |
| Mancini, Peter, Hagerstown | .177 | 22 | 62 | 2 | 11 | 13 | 0 | 1 | 0 | 4 | 0 | 1 | 0 | 0 | 6 | 1 | 10 | 0 | 0 |
| Martinez, David, Winston-Salem* | .342 | 115 | 386 | 52 | 132 | 169 | 14 | 4 | 5 | 54 | 7 | 1 | 2 | 3 | 62 | 5 | 35 | 38 | 14 |
| Martinez, Rey, Lynchburg* | .273 | 31 | 88 | 9 | 24 | 32 | 2 | 0 | 2 | 10 | 1 | 0 | 0 | 0 | 15 | 4 | 19 | 0 | 0 |
| Martinez, Robert, Salem | .227 | 113 | 406 | 50 | 92 | 156 | 26 | 1 | 12 | 64 | 3 | 1 | 3 | 13 | 35 | 1 | 103 | 0 | 0 |

| Player and Club | Pct. | G. | AB. | R. | H. | TB. | 2B. | 3B. | HR. | RBI. | GW. | SH. | SF. | HP. | BB. | Int. BB. | SO. | SB. | CS. |
|---|---|---|---|---|---|---|---|---|---|---|---|---|---|---|---|---|---|---|---|
| Masters, David, Winston-Salem | .000 | 14 | 14 | 0 | 0 | 0 | 0 | 0 | 0 | 0 | 0 | 5 | 0 | 0 | 0 | 0 | 8 | 0 | 0 |
| Maye, Stephen, Winston-Salem | .095 | 17 | 21 | 1 | 2 | 2 | 0 | 0 | 0 | 0 | 0 | 0 | 0 | 1 | 0 | 0 | 9 | 0 | 0 |
| McClanahan, Scott, Peninsula | .000 | 16 | 2 | 0 | 0 | 0 | 0 | 0 | 0 | 0 | 0 | 0 | 0 | 0 | 0 | 0 | 2 | 0 | 0 |
| McDevitt, Stephen, Peninsula | .200 | 6 | 5 | 0 | 1 | 1 | 0 | 0 | 0 | 0 | 0 | 0 | 0 | 0 | 0 | 0 | 1 | 0 | 0 |
| McKelvey, Mitch, Prince William | .067 | 11 | 15 | 1 | 1 | 1 | 0 | 0 | 0 | 0 | 0 | 0 | 0 | 0 | 1 | 0 | 8 | 0 | 0 |
| McKnight, Jefferson, Lynchburg° | .220 | 49 | 150 | 19 | 33 | 41 | 6 | 1 | 0 | 21 | 4 | 4 | 3 | 0 | 29 | 0 | 19 | 0 | 0 |
| McLarnan, John, Peninsula | .000 | 48 | 9 | 0 | 0 | 0 | 0 | 0 | 0 | 0 | 0 | 1 | 0 | 1 | 0 | 0 | 5 | 0 | 0 |
| McMorris, Mark, Winston-Salem° | .250 | 1 | 4 | 0 | 1 | 1 | 0 | 0 | 0 | 0 | 0 | 0 | 0 | 0 | 0 | 0 | 0 | 0 | 0 |
| Mejia, Simon, Winston-Salem† | .196 | 64 | 112 | 11 | 22 | 24 | 2 | 0 | 0 | 11 | 0 | 2 | 4 | 3 | 9 | 0 | 28 | 12 | 2 |
| Melendez, Jose, Prince William | .444 | 9 | 9 | 1 | 4 | 4 | 0 | 0 | 0 | 0 | 1 | 0 | 0 | 1 | 0 | 0 | 4 | 0 | 0 |
| Melillo, Gerry, Hagerstown | .211 | 89 | 299 | 28 | 63 | 82 | 13 | 0 | 2 | 28 | 1 | 1 | 2 | 2 | 36 | 1 | 36 | 6 | 0 |
| Miller, Keith, Lynchburg | .302 | 89 | 325 | 51 | 98 | 145 | 16 | 5 | 7 | 54 | 9 | 1 | 0 | 4 | 39 | 0 | 52 | 14 | 2 |
| Miller, Michael, Winston-Salem | .500 | 2 | 2 | 0 | 1 | 1 | 0 | 0 | 0 | 0 | 0 | 0 | 0 | 0 | 0 | 0 | 1 | 0 | 0 |
| Moore, Bryant, Prince William | .273 | 41 | 143 | 21 | 39 | 51 | 8 | 2 | 0 | 13 | 1 | 0 | 0 | 1 | 24 | 3 | 22 | 11 | 4 |
| Morales, Joseph, Salem† | .234 | 101 | 333 | 54 | 78 | 120 | 17 | 2 | 7 | 49 | 6 | 6 | 2 | 2 | 57 | 3 | 49 | 2 | 0 |
| Morelock, Charles, Durham | .000 | 28 | 2 | 0 | 0 | 0 | 0 | 0 | 0 | 0 | 0 | 0 | 0 | 0 | 0 | 0 | 1 | 0 | 0 |
| Morris, David, Durham | .074 | 27 | 27 | 1 | 2 | 5 | 0 | 0 | 1 | 2 | 0 | 4 | 0 | 0 | 2 | 0 | 12 | 0 | 0 |
| Morrow, Benjamin, Prince William | .167 | 34 | 6 | 0 | 1 | 1 | 0 | 0 | 0 | 1 | 0 | 2 | 0 | 0 | 0 | 0 | 3 | 0 | 0 |
| Morton, William, Peninsula | .133 | 32 | 15 | 1 | 2 | 2 | 0 | 0 | 0 | 3 | 0 | 2 | 1 | 0 | 3 | 0 | 1 | 0 | 0 |
| Moscat, Fernando, Lynchburg | .239 | 68 | 218 | 22 | 52 | 65 | 10 | 0 | 1 | 12 | 1 | 3 | 1 | 0 | 14 | 0 | 48 | 3 | 3 |
| Moyer, Jamie, Winston-Salem° | .200 | 12 | 15 | 1 | 3 | 3 | 0 | 0 | 0 | 0 | 0 | 2 | 0 | 0 | 4 | 0 | 4 | 0 | 0 |
| Mucha, Keith, Hagerstown | .225 | 64 | 187 | 22 | 42 | 64 | 14 | 1 | 2 | 31 | 3 | 0 | 4 | 3 | 32 | 1 | 36 | 1 | 0 |
| Neal, Scott, Prince William° | .333 | 18 | 6 | 0 | 2 | 3 | 1 | 0 | 0 | 0 | 0 | 0 | 0 | 0 | 1 | 0 | 1 | 0 | 0 |
| Neidlinger, James, Prince William† | .160 | 26 | 25 | 1 | 4 | 5 | 1 | 0 | 0 | 1 | 1 | 5 | 1 | 0 | 1 | 0 | 12 | 0 | 0 |
| Nichols, Howard, Peninsula | .287 | 41 | 150 | 19 | 43 | 59 | 9 | 2 | 1 | 20 | 3 | 0 | 3 | 3 | 23 | 0 | 25 | 6 | 2 |
| Nipper, Michael, Durham | .255 | 111 | 365 | 45 | 93 | 140 | 15 | 1 | 10 | 55 | 5 | 1 | 3 | 4 | 36 | 3 | 67 | 0 | 3 |
| Nowakowski, Joseph, Kinston | .118 | 6 | 17 | 1 | 2 | 2 | 0 | 0 | 0 | 3 | 0 | 1 | 1 | 0 | 0 | 0 | 5 | 0 | 0 |
| Odgers, Daniel, Peninsula | .248 | 92 | 322 | 34 | 80 | 120 | 15 | 5 | 5 | 37 | 8 | 1 | 3 | 5 | 23 | 3 | 47 | 17 | 4 |
| Padget, Chris, Hagerstown° | .277 | 136 | 483 | 56 | 134 | 183 | 20 | 4 | 7 | 70 | 6 | 3 | 10 | 3 | 74 | 6 | 73 | 11 | 8 |
| Padia, Steven, Hagerstown° | .208 | 44 | 120 | 15 | 25 | 40 | 6 | 0 | 3 | 17 | 1 | 0 | 0 | 0 | 23 | 0 | 23 | 1 | 2 |
| Pena, Hipolito, Prince William° | .000 | 20 | 3 | 0 | 0 | 0 | 0 | 0 | 0 | 0 | 0 | 1 | 0 | 0 | 2 | 0 | 2 | 0 | 0 |
| Perez, Sergio, Peninsula | .269 | 53 | 186 | 25 | 50 | 73 | 11 | 0 | 4 | 26 | 4 | 6 | 2 | 0 | 16 | 2 | 28 | 6 | 3 |
| Phillips, James, Winston-Salem | .188 | 3 | 16 | 0 | 3 | 4 | 1 | 0 | 0 | 0 | 0 | 0 | 0 | 0 | 0 | 0 | 5 | 0 | 1 |
| Phillips, Stephen, Lynchburg° | .216 | 121 | 348 | 48 | 75 | 109 | 13 | 3 | 5 | 37 | 3 | 4 | 3 | 2 | 53 | 0 | 96 | 12 | 4 |
| Posey, Robert, Durham° | .263 | 48 | 179 | 32 | 47 | 74 | 6 | 0 | 7 | 22 | 2 | 0 | 1 | 2 | 25 | 0 | 32 | 2 | 1 |
| Powers, Scott, Durham | .170 | 34 | 100 | 13 | 17 | 29 | 0 | 0 | 4 | 11 | 2 | 2 | 0 | 0 | 12 | 0 | 23 | 1 | 0 |
| Ransom, Jeffrey, Durham† | .227 | 24 | 75 | 7 | 17 | 22 | 2 | 0 | 1 | 6 | 2 | 0 | 1 | 0 | 10 | 1 | 14 | 0 | 0 |
| Ray, Louis, Peninsula | .178 | 26 | 45 | 3 | 8 | 9 | 1 | 0 | 0 | 2 | 1 | 0 | 2 | 0 | 9 | 0 | 10 | 0 | 0 |
| Redfield, Joseph, Lynchburg | .242 | 41 | 132 | 22 | 32 | 49 | 8 | 0 | 3 | 18 | 1 | 0 | 0 | 4 | 33 | 0 | 29 | 10 | 3 |
| Rembielak, Richard, Winston-Salem | .261 | 105 | 371 | 39 | 97 | 109 | 7 | 1 | 1 | 31 | 4 | 4 | 2 | 2 | 41 | 1 | 45 | 6 | 4 |
| Reyes, Joselito, Kinston | .229 | 13 | 35 | 4 | 8 | 9 | 1 | 0 | 0 | 4 | 0 | 0 | 2 | 0 | 2 | 0 | 7 | 0 | 0 |
| Reynolds, Michael, Durham° | .173 | 50 | 133 | 18 | 23 | 30 | 4 | 0 | 1 | 18 | 2 | 1 | 2 | 1 | 22 | 0 | 27 | 1 | 3 |
| Riley, Randall, Hagerstown° | .208 | 10 | 24 | 2 | 5 | 8 | 0 | 0 | 1 | 4 | 1 | 0 | 1 | 0 | 2 | 0 | 12 | 0 | 0 |
| Ripken, William, Hagerstown | .255 | 14 | 47 | 9 | 12 | 14 | 0 | 1 | 0 | 0 | 0 | 0 | 0 | 2 | 1 | 0 | 2 | 0 | 2 |
| Roadcap, Steve, Winston-Salem† | .159 | 40 | 82 | 13 | 13 | 16 | 3 | 0 | 0 | 3 | 1 | 1 | 0 | 0 | 24 | 0 | 18 | 0 | 0 |
| Roberts, Drexel, Kinston° | .276 | 105 | 312 | 56 | 86 | 119 | 19 | 1 | 4 | 30 | 5 | 0 | 2 | 3 | 64 | 5 | 64 | 16 | 8 |
| Rogers, MacArthur, Durham | .158 | 36 | 19 | 1 | 3 | 3 | 0 | 0 | 0 | 0 | 0 | 3 | 0 | 0 | 1 | 0 | 4 | 0 | 1 |
| Romagna, Randolph, Kinston | .237 | 110 | 329 | 48 | 78 | 96 | 10 | 1 | 2 | 32 | 2 | 1 | 7 | 5 | 52 | 0 | 44 | 12 | 12 |
| Roman, Ray, Peninsula | .247 | 87 | 296 | 39 | 73 | 120 | 15 | 1 | 10 | 34 | 5 | 3 | 1 | 6 | 29 | 3 | 63 | 2 | 0 |
| Rooker, David, Prince William | .000 | 17 | 7 | 0 | 0 | 0 | 0 | 0 | 0 | 0 | 1 | 0 | 1 | 0 | 1 | 0 | 1 | 0 | 0 |
| Roomes, Rolando, Winston-Salem | .242 | 131 | 433 | 57 | 105 | 175 | 19 | 6 | 13 | 51 | 8 | 2 | 1 | 2 | 29 | 1 | 147 | 17 | 9 |
| Rosario, Maximo, Durham° | .100 | 17 | 10 | 3 | 1 | 1 | 0 | 0 | 0 | 0 | 0 | 1 | 0 | 0 | 0 | 0 | 6 | 1 | 0 |
| Rosario, Simon, Durham | .188 | 36 | 96 | 7 | 18 | 30 | 3 | 0 | 3 | 16 | 1 | 0 | 1 | 0 | 6 | 1 | 17 | 1 | 0 |
| Russell, Robert, Prince William° | .063 | 35 | 16 | 1 | 1 | 1 | 0 | 0 | 0 | 0 | 0 | 1 | 0 | 1 | 0 | 0 | 8 | 0 | 0 |
| Rypien, Timothy, Kinston | .228 | 40 | 92 | 6 | 21 | 31 | 1 | 0 | 3 | 13 | 1 | 0 | 1 | 0 | 0 | 0 | 22 | 0 | 0 |
| Santiago, Michael, Durham° | .000 | 44 | 2 | 0 | 0 | 0 | 0 | 0 | 0 | 0 | 0 | 0 | 0 | 0 | 0 | 0 | 2 | 0 | 0 |
| Schreiber, Martin, Durham° | .333 | 12 | 3 | 0 | 1 | 1 | 0 | 0 | 0 | 2 | 0 | 1 | 0 | 0 | 1 | 0 | 0 | 0 | 0 |
| Sciacca, Christopher, Win-Sal† | .188 | 13 | 32 | 2 | 6 | 7 | 1 | 0 | 0 | 3 | 1 | 0 | 1 | 0 | 0 | 0 | 13 | 0 | 0 |
| Scott, Michael, Lynchburg | .000 | 4 | 5 | 0 | 0 | 0 | 0 | 0 | 0 | 0 | 0 | 0 | 0 | 0 | 0 | 0 | 1 | 0 | 0 |
| Simpson, Danny, Salem | .231 | 35 | 121 | 14 | 28 | 49 | 6 | 6 | 1 | 16 | 2 | 0 | 0 | 2 | 13 | 1 | 44 | 2 | 1 |
| Slowik, Thaddeus, Winston-Salem | .000 | 10 | 1 | 0 | 0 | 0 | 0 | 0 | 0 | 0 | 0 | 0 | 0 | 0 | 0 | 0 | 1 | 0 | 0 |
| Smiley, John, Prince William° | .000 | 10 | 8 | 1 | 0 | 0 | 0 | 0 | 0 | 0 | 0 | 2 | 0 | 0 | 1 | 0 | 1 | 0 | 0 |
| Smith, Dana, Hagerstown | .216 | 85 | 245 | 24 | 53 | 60 | 2 | 1 | 1 | 16 | 3 | 6 | 3 | 1 | 32 | 0 | 54 | 2 | 4 |
| Smith, David, Hagerstown | .234 | 122 | 393 | 48 | 92 | 110 | 16 | 1 | 0 | 29 | 3 | 3 | 2 | 0 | 55 | 1 | 52 | 4 | 4 |
| Smith, Timothy, Hagerstown | .150 | 16 | 40 | 3 | 6 | 8 | 2 | 0 | 0 | 7 | 1 | 1 | 0 | 0 | 4 | 1 | 7 | 0 | 0 |
| Soto, Jose, Peninsula° | .262 | 56 | 149 | 16 | 39 | 41 | 2 | 0 | 0 | 8 | 1 | 4 | 1 | 0 | 17 | 0 | 43 | 4 | 4 |
| Stanley, Michael, Salem | .556 | 4 | 9 | 2 | 5 | 5 | 0 | 0 | 0 | 3 | 0 | 0 | 0 | 0 | 1 | 0 | 1 | 0 | 0 |
| Stevens, Michael, Prince William | .171 | 25 | 70 | 4 | 12 | 14 | 2 | 0 | 0 | 5 | 1 | 0 | 2 | 1 | 2 | 0 | 22 | 2 | 1 |
| Sullivan, James, Hagerstown° | .217 | 6 | 23 | 0 | 5 | 6 | 1 | 0 | 0 | 3 | 1 | 0 | 1 | 0 | 0 | 0 | 4 | 1 | 0 |
| Thielker, David, Hagerstown° | .179 | 28 | 84 | 5 | 15 | 21 | 3 | 0 | 1 | 6 | 1 | 1 | 0 | 1 | 20 | 1 | 12 | 0 | 3 |
| Thompson, Scott, Lynchburg | .235 | 34 | 85 | 13 | 20 | 36 | 3 | 2 | 3 | 7 | 2 | 0 | 1 | 3 | 8 | 0 | 25 | 0 | 0 |
| Tomsick, Troy, Durham | .100 | 17 | 10 | 1 | 1 | 1 | 0 | 0 | 0 | 0 | 0 | 0 | 0 | 0 | 0 | 0 | 6 | 0 | 0 |
| Traylor, Keith, Lynchburg | .250 | 3 | 4 | 0 | 1 | 1 | 0 | 0 | 0 | 0 | 0 | 0 | 0 | 0 | 0 | 0 | 2 | 1 | 1 |
| True, Steven, Peninsula° | .000 | 9 | 2 | 1 | 0 | 0 | 0 | 0 | 0 | 0 | 0 | 2 | 0 | 0 | 0 | 0 | 1 | 0 | 0 |
| Tubbs, Gregory, Durham | .282 | 70 | 266 | 44 | 75 | 126 | 15 | 6 | 8 | 32 | 4 | 2 | 1 | 3 | 36 | 0 | 52 | 29 | 12 |
| Tullier, Michael, Winston-Salem° | .203 | 51 | 143 | 13 | 29 | 34 | 5 | 0 | 0 | 14 | 3 | 0 | 1 | 1 | 16 | 1 | 17 | 1 | 1 |
| Velleggia, Frank, Hagerstown | .212 | 58 | 189 | 19 | 40 | 53 | 8 | 1 | 1 | 15 | 2 | 2 | 0 | 0 | 19 | 1 | 40 | 4 | 0 |
| Wagner, Jeffrey, Durham† | .170 | 22 | 53 | 5 | 9 | 15 | 3 | 0 | 1 | 7 | 1 | 0 | 1 | 0 | 5 | 0 | 15 | 2 | 0 |
| Weatherford, Brant, Peninsula | .250 | 14 | 8 | 0 | 2 | 4 | 0 | 1 | 0 | 0 | 0 | 0 | 0 | 0 | 0 | 0 | 4 | 0 | 0 |
| Weston, Michael, Lynchburg | .000 | 49 | 8 | 0 | 0 | 0 | 0 | 0 | 0 | 0 | 0 | 0 | 0 | 0 | 0 | 0 | 5 | 0 | 0 |
| Wetherby, Jeffrey, Durham° | .136 | 6 | 22 | 1 | 3 | 3 | 0 | 0 | 0 | 2 | 0 | 0 | 0 | 2 | 0 | 0 | 4 | 0 | 0 |
| Whitfield, Kenneth, Kinston | .231 | 127 | 459 | 59 | 106 | 164 | 17 | 4 | 11 | 50 | 6 | 0 | 4 | 2 | 39 | 1 | 129 | 12 | 6 |
| Williams, Jeffrey, Hagerstown° | .268 | 95 | 339 | 57 | 91 | 130 | 10 | 10 | 3 | 41 | 6 | 2 | 3 | 0 | 68 | 3 | 64 | 35 | 6 |
| Wilson, John, Lynchburg° | .302 | 121 | 377 | 70 | 114 | 143 | 11 | 3 | 4 | 31 | 7 | 3 | 2 | 4 | 49 | 3 | 105 | 50 | 7 |
| Wrona, Richard, Winston-Salem† | .224 | 20 | 49 | 4 | 11 | 15 | 4 | 0 | 0 | 2 | 0 | 0 | 0 | 3 | 0 | 0 | 15 | 0 | 1 |
| Wyatt, David, Lynchburg | .143 | 9 | 7 | 0 | 1 | 1 | 0 | 0 | 0 | 0 | 0 | 1 | 0 | 0 | 0 | 0 | 0 | 0 | 0 |
| Yastrzemski, Michael, Durham† | .270 | 132 | 493 | 64 | 133 | 196 | 20 | 5 | 11 | 63 | 3 | 6 | 3 | 3 | 53 | 2 | 76 | 3 | 5 |
| Yelding, Eric, Kinston | .260 | 135 | 526 | 59 | 137 | 165 | 14 | 4 | 2 | 31 | 3 | 5 | 3 | 4 | 33 | 0 | 70 | 62 | 26 |
| Zayas, Carlos, Peninsula | .231 | 43 | 121 | 15 | 28 | 47 | 6 | 2 | 3 | 13 | 2 | 0 | 1 | 0 | 18 | 2 | 27 | 0 | 0 |

The following pitchers, listed alphabetically by club, with games in parentheses, had no plate appearances, primarily through use of designated hitters:

DURHAM—Coffman, Kevin (3); LaFrancois, Roger (1); Mathews, Edward (2).

**HAGERSTOWN**—Bianchi, Ben (17); Dooner, Glenn (19); Egelston, Christopher (24); Flanagan, Michael (1); Flinn, John (11); Gannon, Justin (3); Gilbert, Jeffrey (1); Heise, Larry (12); Hixon, Alan (21); Lavelle, William (38); Leiter, Mark (34); Milacki, Robert (7); Raczka, Michael (35); Reiter, Gary (11); Skinner, Michael (11); Stanhope, Chester (2); Steirer, Ricky (13); Summers, Jeffrey (8); Talamantez, Gregory (10); Wilson, Roger (23).

**KINSTON**—Anthony, Dane (2); Bencomo, Omar (25); Burgos, Enrique (7); Castillo, Antonio (35); Castro, Eddy (24); Clemons, Mark (32); Cullen, Michael (8); Dickman, Mark (10); Lychak, Perry (48); McKay, Alan (39); Mesa, Jose (30); Moore, Gregory (4); Palo, David (1); Peraza, Oswald (2); Reyes, Pablo (36); Segura, Jose (34); Shanks, William (9); Stephenson, Joseph (4).

**LYNCHBURG**—Barba, Michael (2).

**PENINSULA**—Hicks, Robert (7).

**PRINCE WILLIAM**—Lein, Christopher (2).

**SALEM**—Bass, Regan (27); Coatney, Rickey (10); Hallgren, Tim (15); Harman, David (42); Harrington, John (10); Hartman, Albert (46); Hester, Ricky (18); Kilgus, Paul (38); Knapp, Richard (29); Kordish, Steve (10); Kramer, Randall (25); Mortimer, Robert (4); Thomas, Mitchell (5); Williams, Mitchell (22); Winbush, Michael (25).

**WINSTON-SALEM**—Hallas, Robert (1); Kranitz, Richard (1).

**GRAND SLAM HOME RUNS**—Abner, Alfaro, Amaral, Baird, Caraballo, Childress, Coveney, D'Alessandro, Dickerson, Gideon, Goldthorn, King, Ro. Martinez, Melillo, K. Miller, Nipper, Roomes, Tubbs, 1 each.

**AWARDED FIRST BASE ON CATCHER'S INTERFERENCE**—Lopez 3 (Carmichael, Cooper, Roadcap); Ben 2 (D'Alessandro, Melillo); Edens 2 (Berryhill, Roman); Bailey (D'Alessandro); Bellini (Burrell); Berryhill (Cadahia); Evans (Cooper); Roadcap (Cooper).

## CLUB FIELDING

| Club | Pct. | G. | PO. | A. | E. | DP. | PB. |
|---|---|---|---|---|---|---|---|
| Prince William | .970 | 139 | 3550 | 1331 | 151 | 96 | 18 |
| Hagerstown | .967 | 137 | 3469 | 1497 | 171 | 107 | 18 |
| Lynchburg | .966 | 140 | 3646 | 1496 | 182 | 135 | 17 |
| Durham | .963 | 140 | 3597 | 1541 | 200 | 134 | 9 |
| Winston-Salem | .962 | 139 | 3523 | 1548 | 202 | 108 | 21 |
| Kinston | .961 | 138 | 3592 | 1375 | 203 | 125 | 14 |
| Salem | .958 | 138 | 3604 | 1603 | 226 | 137 | 29 |
| Peninsula | .951 | 135 | 3422 | 1438 | 250 | 125 | 20 |

Triple Play—Winston-Salem.

## INDIVIDUAL FIELDING

*Throws lefthanded.

### FIRST BASEMEN

| Player and Club | Pct. | G. | PO. | A. | E. | DP. |
|---|---|---|---|---|---|---|
| Barnard, Prince William | .994 | 20 | 157 | 11 | 1 | 14 |
| Bates, Salem | .992 | 39 | 355 | 26 | 3 | 37 |
| Beamesderfer, Hagerstown | 1.000 | 1 | 6 | 3 | 0 | 1 |
| Belen, Prince William | .990 | 91 | 646 | 62 | 7 | 54 |
| Bennett, Peninsula | 1.000 | 10 | 72 | 5 | 0 | 8 |
| Berryhill, Winston-Salem | 1.000 | 1 | 0 | 1 | 0 | 0 |
| Bonilla, Prince William | .990 | 29 | 180 | 9 | 2 | 10 |
| Borders, Kinston | .978 | 110 | 854 | 42 | 20 | 80 |
| Burrell, Lynchburg | 1.000 | 1 | 2 | 0 | 0 | 0 |
| Cadahia, Salem | .966 | 5 | 26 | 2 | 1 | 2 |
| Caraballo, Lynchburg | .989 | 34 | 253 | 19 | 3 | 19 |
| Carter, Prince William | 1.000 | 1 | 2 | 0 | 0 | 1 |
| Castro, 33 Hag-4 PR* | .980 | 37 | 273 | 26 | 6 | 31 |
| Childress, Durham | 1.000 | 2 | 17 | 1 | 0 | 1 |
| Cordner, Winston-Salem | .987 | 44 | 338 | 28 | 5 | 28 |
| Cordova, Winston-Salem | .995 | 22 | 177 | 10 | 1 | 15 |
| Delucchi, Prince William | 1.000 | 1 | 6 | 2 | 0 | 1 |
| Doerr, Hagerstown | .971 | 15 | 124 | 10 | 4 | 8 |
| Freeman, Salem | .968 | 9 | 56 | 5 | 2 | 8 |
| Freytes, Winston-Salem | .990 | 75 | 625 | 42 | 7 | 47 |
| Gideon, Peninsula* | .980 | 110 | 856 | 48 | 18 | 82 |
| Griffin, Durham | .992 | 43 | 333 | 21 | 3 | 34 |
| Harrison, Durham | .989 | 82 | 687 | 44 | 8 | 64 |
| Hatcher, Durham | .956 | 10 | 81 | 6 | 4 | 3 |
| Jones, Prince William | 1.000 | 2 | 11 | 1 | 0 | 0 |
| Kaiser, Peninsula | 1.000 | 10 | 89 | 6 | 0 | 9 |
| Kenaga, Hagerstown | 1.000 | 8 | 76 | 13 | 0 | 2 |
| King, Salem* | 1.000 | 1 | 2 | 0 | 0 | 0 |
| LAWRENCE, Lynchburg | .992 | 97 | 779 | 45 | 7 | 75 |
| Magrann, Peninsula | 1.000 | 1 | 8 | 0 | 0 | 0 |
| Malave, Kinston | .993 | 41 | 267 | 17 | 2 | 24 |
| Maloney, Lynchburg | .959 | 12 | 65 | 5 | 3 | 8 |
| Re. Martinez, Lynchburg* | .975 | 19 | 150 | 8 | 4 | 21 |
| Ro. Martinez, Salem | .984 | 91 | 820 | 61 | 14 | 71 |
| McMorris, Winston-Salem* | 1.000 | 1 | 8 | 0 | 0 | 1 |
| Melillo, Hagerstown | 1.000 | 1 | 1 | 0 | 0 | 0 |
| Mucha, Hagerstown | 1.000 | 5 | 34 | 0 | 0 | 4 |
| Nichols, Peninsula | 1.000 | 8 | 44 | 3 | 0 | 3 |
| Nipper, Durham | .967 | 3 | 25 | 4 | 1 | 1 |
| Padget, Hagerstown | .992 | 70 | 558 | 51 | 5 | 40 |
| Padia, Hagerstown | 1.000 | 4 | 26 | 2 | 0 | 2 |
| Reynolds, Durham | 1.000 | 1 | 1 | 0 | 0 | 0 |
| Roman, Peninsula | 1.000 | 6 | 40 | 2 | 0 | 4 |
| Rosario, Durham | .959 | 9 | 66 | 4 | 3 | 7 |
| Simpson, Salem | 1.000 | 1 | 5 | 1 | 0 | 0 |
| Smith, Winston-Salem* | .923 | 3 | 8 | 4 | 1 | 0 |
| Stanley, Salem | .947 | 2 | 18 | 0 | 1 | 2 |
| Stevens, Prince William | 1.000 | 3 | 17 | 1 | 0 | 1 |
| Thielker, Winston-Salem | 1.000 | 9 | 83 | 7 | 0 | 6 |
| Tullier, Winston-Salem* | .989 | 10 | 90 | 2 | 1 | 3 |
| Zayas, Peninsula | 1.000 | 5 | 32 | 1 | 0 | 3 |

Triple Play—Cordner.

### SECOND BASEMEN

| Player and Club | Pct. | G. | PO. | A. | E. | DP. |
|---|---|---|---|---|---|---|
| Alfaro, Durham | .987 | 70 | 177 | 210 | 5 | 51 |
| Amaral, Winston-Salem | .953 | 107 | 217 | 294 | 25 | 51 |
| Blair, Salem | .958 | 14 | 34 | 34 | 3 | 6 |
| BROWNE, Salem | .9703 | 118 | 265 | 390 | 20 | 77 |
| Caraballo, Lynchburg | 1.000 | 1 | 1 | 3 | 0 | 0 |
| Childress, Durham | .976 | 47 | 120 | 123 | 6 | 38 |
| Cruz, Winston-Salem | .953 | 32 | 61 | 81 | 7 | 21 |
| Doggett, Lynchburg | 1.000 | 1 | 1 | 0 | 0 | 1 |
| Engram, Peninsula | .920 | 5 | 14 | 9 | 2 | 2 |
| Freeman, Salem | 1.000 | 5 | 18 | 19 | 0 | 4 |
| Henderson, Peninsula | .920 | 17 | 31 | 38 | 6 | 10 |
| Holtz, Hagerstown | .9696 | 106 | 226 | 254 | 15 | 53 |
| Hopkins, Winston-Salem | .935 | 12 | 13 | 16 | 2 | 2 |
| Jones, Prince William | .966 | 92 | 164 | 209 | 13 | 46 |
| Kennard, Peninsula | .962 | 109 | 247 | 317 | 22 | 70 |
| Kraft, Peninsula | 1.000 | 9 | 18 | 13 | 0 | 5 |
| LaFrancois, Durham | 1.000 | 1 | 1 | 0 | 0 | 0 |
| Lind, Prince William | .987 | 54 | 104 | 131 | 3 | 24 |
| Liriano, Kinston | .959 | 131 | 261 | 328 | 25 | 79 |
| Malave, Kinston | 1.000 | 6 | 11 | 15 | 0 | 4 |
| Mancini, Hagerstown | .949 | 17 | 35 | 39 | 4 | 9 |
| McKnight, Lynchburg | 1.000 | 5 | 8 | 7 | 0 | 2 |
| Miller, Lynchburg | .961 | 30 | 61 | 87 | 6 | 17 |
| Morales, Lynchburg | .889 | 2 | 5 | 3 | 1 | 0 |
| Moscat, Lynchburg | .947 | 15 | 25 | 29 | 3 | 8 |
| Odgers, Peninsula | .909 | 2 | 7 | 3 | 1 | 0 |
| Phillips, Lynchburg | .966 | 109 | 192 | 287 | 17 | 66 |
| Redfield, Lynchburg | .969 | 6 | 14 | 17 | 1 | 6 |
| Reyes, Kinston | .900 | 4 | 4 | 14 | 2 | 0 |
| Reynolds, Durham | .945 | 34 | 63 | 74 | 8 | 19 |
| Ripken, Hagerstown | 1.000 | 1 | 3 | 2 | 0 | 0 |
| Smith, Hagerstown | .983 | 19 | 24 | 33 | 1 | 4 |

Triple Play—Amaral.

### THIRD BASEMEN

| Player and Club | Pct. | G. | PO. | A. | E. | DP. |
|---|---|---|---|---|---|---|
| Amaral, Winston-Salem | .946 | 11 | 11 | 24 | 2 | 0 |
| Barnard, Prince William | .810 | 8 | 4 | 13 | 4 | 0 |
| Beamesderfer, Hagerstown | .857 | 6 | 2 | 4 | 1 | 0 |
| Bennett, Peninsula | 1.000 | 2 | 2 | 0 | 0 | 0 |
| Blair, Salem | .692 | 11 | 6 | 12 | 8 | 0 |
| Caraballo, Lynchburg | .920 | 49 | 26 | 78 | 9 | 9 |
| Childress, Durham | .904 | 48 | 32 | 91 | 13 | 10 |
| Cordner, Winston-Salem | 1.000 | 1 | 6 | 0 | 0 | 0 |
| Cruz, Winston-Salem | .880 | 82 | 51 | 140 | 26 | 11 |
| Dennis, Kinston | 1.000 | 1 | 0 | 2 | 0 | 0 |
| Doerr, Hagerstown | .884 | 41 | 26 | 81 | 14 | 7 |
| Doughty, Salem | .941 | 19 | 8 | 24 | 2 | 5 |

## THIRD BASEMEN—Continued

| Player and Club | Pct. | G. | PO. | A. | E. | DP. | Player and Club | Pct. | G. | PO. | A. | E. | DP. |
|---|---|---|---|---|---|---|---|---|---|---|---|---|---|
| Engram, Peninsula | .833 | 3 | 1 | 4 | 1 | 0 | Miller, Lynchburg | .893 | 63 | 42 | 116 | 19 | 16 |
| Farmer, Salem | .856 | 89 | 45 | 145 | 32 | 15 | Morales, Salem | .846 | 7 | 5 | 17 | 4 | 3 |
| Freeman, Salem | .853 | 12 | 8 | 21 | 5 | 2 | Moscat, Lynchburg | 1.000 | 3 | 0 | 1 | 0 | 0 |
| Freytes, Winston-Salem | .879 | 38 | 14 | 66 | 11 | 2 | Mucha, Hagerstown | .878 | 20 | 6 | 30 | 5 | 3 |
| Gutierrez, Prince William | .946 | 117 | 73 | 208 | 16 | 13 | Nichols, Peninsula | .792 | 30 | 18 | 43 | 16 | 5 |
| Henderson, Peninsula | .816 | 19 | 17 | 23 | 9 | 1 | Nipper, Durham | .902 | 103 | 50 | 227 | 30 | 12 |
| Hopkins, Winston-Salem | .929 | 21 | 15 | 24 | 3 | 2 | Odgers, Peninsula | .889 | 89 | 64 | 169 | 29 | 15 |
| Lind, Prince William | .846 | 22 | 13 | 31 | 8 | 3 | Padia, Hagerstown | .750 | 4 | 4 | 5 | 3 | 0 |
| Malave, Kinston | .911 | 37 | 21 | 71 | 9 | 4 | Redfield, Lynchburg | .932 | 36 | 23 | 59 | 6 | 9 |
| Maloney, Lynchburg | .667 | 1 | 0 | 2 | 1 | 0 | Reyes, Kinston | .900 | 4 | 1 | 8 | 1 | 1 |
| Mancini, Hagerstown | .733 | 4 | 2 | 9 | 4 | 0 | Reynolds, Durham | 1.000 | 1 | 1 | 1 | 0 | 1 |
| Martinez, Salem | .886 | 14 | 7 | 24 | 4 | 1 | Ripken, Hagerstown | .958 | 11 | 11 | 35 | 2 | 2 |
| McKnight, Lynchburg | .900 | 8 | 2 | 16 | 2 | 1 | ROMAGNA, Kinston | .954 | 109 | 82 | 209 | 14 | 21 |
| Mejia, Winston-Salem | 1.000 | 3 | 0 | 3 | 0 | 0 | Smith, Hagerstown | .860 | 50 | 24 | 93 | 19 | 11 |
| Melillo, Hagerstown | .966 | 12 | 6 | 22 | 1 | 0 | | | | | | | |

## SHORTSTOPS

| Player and Club | Pct. | G. | PO. | A. | E. | DP. | Player and Club | Pct. | G. | PO. | A. | E. | DP. |
|---|---|---|---|---|---|---|---|---|---|---|---|---|---|
| Alfaro, Durham | .961 | 37 | 70 | 127 | 8 | 31 | Latmore, Hagerstown | .917 | 6 | 6 | 16 | 2 | 4 |
| Barringer, Prince William | .935 | 116 | 166 | 280 | 31 | 53 | Lind, Prince William | .972 | 25 | 45 | 59 | 3 | 8 |
| Blair, Salem | .827 | 18 | 16 | 51 | 14 | 13 | Malave, Kinston | .881 | 16 | 21 | 31 | 7 | 5 |
| Childress, Durham | .919 | 30 | 39 | 63 | 9 | 10 | McKnight, Lynchburg | .922 | 31 | 35 | 83 | 10 | 16 |
| Cruz, Winston-Salem | .600 | 5 | 1 | 2 | 2 | 0 | Mejia, Winston-Salem | .778 | 3 | 3 | 4 | 2 | 2 |
| Doughty, Salem | .918 | 11 | 19 | 37 | 5 | 10 | Morales, Salem | .938 | 90 | 138 | 318 | 30 | 54 |
| Elster, Lynchburg | .945 | 59 | 82 | 195 | 16 | 37 | Moscat, Lynchburg | .945 | 47 | 49 | 141 | 11 | 20 |
| Fredymond, Durham | .874 | 51 | 66 | 143 | 30 | 25 | Perez, Peninsula | .945 | 53 | 82 | 177 | 15 | 34 |
| Freeman, Salem | .907 | 26 | 36 | 62 | 10 | 10 | Phillips, Lynchburg | .900 | 9 | 17 | 19 | 4 | 3 |
| Garrison, Kinston | .916 | 129 | 205 | 353 | 51 | 74 | Powers, Durham | .930 | 33 | 43 | 104 | 11 | 15 |
| Gutierrez, Prince William | .900 | 4 | 7 | 2 | 1 | 0 | Rembielak, Winston-Salem | .956 | 105 | 126 | 347 | 22 | 45 |
| Henderson, Peninsula | 1.000 | 3 | 4 | 8 | 0 | 2 | Reynolds, Durham | .800 | 2 | 3 | 1 | 1 | 0 |
| Hopkins, Winston-Salem | .912 | 31 | 45 | 79 | 12 | 14 | Sciacca, Winston-Salem | .875 | 11 | 13 | 29 | 6 | 5 |
| Kennard, Peninsula | .915 | 21 | 33 | 53 | 8 | 14 | Dan. Smith, Hagerstown | .957 | 16 | 8 | 37 | 2 | 1 |
| Kraft, Peninsula | .894 | 63 | 82 | 188 | 32 | 30 | DAV. SMITH, Hagerstown | .963 | 120 | 186 | 394 | 22 | 61 |

Triple Play—Hopkins.

## OUTFIELDERS

| Player and Club | Pct. | G. | PO. | A. | E. | DP. | Player and Club | Pct. | G. | PO. | A. | E. | DP. |
|---|---|---|---|---|---|---|---|---|---|---|---|---|---|
| Abner, Lynchburg | .966 | 139 | 332 | 8 | 12 | 4 | Lewis, Winston-Salem | 1.000 | 1 | 1 | 0 | 0 | 0 |
| Bailey, Salem | .979 | 100 | 174 | 10 | 4 | 4 | Lind, Prince William | 1.000 | 2 | 2 | 0 | 0 | 0 |
| Baird, Durham | .982 | 105 | 219 | 5 | 4 | 0 | Little, Lynchburg | .978 | 140 | 252 | 12 | 6 | 2 |
| Bates, Salem | 1.000 | 1 | 2 | 0 | 0 | 0 | Lopez, Hagerstown* | .967 | 87 | 141 | 7 | 5 | 1 |
| Beamesderfer, Hagerstown | 1.000 | 6 | 4 | 0 | 0 | 0 | Malave, Kinston | .833 | 10 | 14 | 1 | 3 | 0 |
| Belen, Prince William | .957 | 19 | 20 | 2 | 1 | 1 | Maloney, Lynchburg | 1.000 | 12 | 15 | 0 | 0 | 0 |
| Bellini, Hagerstown* | 1.000 | 15 | 21 | 1 | 0 | 1 | D. Martinez, Winston-Salem* | .969 | 110 | 206 | 11 | 7 | 3 |
| Ben, Salem | .975 | 89 | 113 | 4 | 3 | 0 | Re. Martinez, Lynchburg* | 1.000 | 4 | 6 | 0 | 0 | 0 |
| Berroa, Kinston | .933 | 11 | 13 | 1 | 1 | 0 | McKnight, Lynchburg | 1.000 | 4 | 2 | 0 | 0 | 0 |
| Bonds, Prince William* | .976 | 70 | 202 | 4 | 5 | 1 | Mejia, Winston-Salem | 1.000 | 45 | 49 | 3 | 0 | 0 |
| Bootay, Salem | .945 | 129 | 229 | 12 | 14 | 5 | Melillo, Hagerstown | 1.000 | 4 | 2 | 0 | 0 | 0 |
| Carter, Prince William | .989 | 47 | 90 | 4 | 1 | 0 | Moore, Prince William | .950 | 41 | 92 | 3 | 5 | 1 |
| Childress, Durham | 1.000 | 6 | 8 | 2 | 0 | 0 | Mucha, Hagerstown | 1.000 | 8 | 11 | 0 | 0 | 0 |
| Cimo, Hagerstown | 1.000 | 79 | 115 | 6 | 0 | 1 | Nichols, Peninsula | 1.000 | 7 | 9 | 0 | 0 | 0 |
| Cordova, Winston-Salem | .957 | 37 | 42 | 2 | 2 | 0 | Nowakowski, Kinston | 1.000 | 2 | 4 | 0 | 0 | 0 |
| Coveney, Peninsula* | .960 | 67 | 114 | 7 | 5 | 0 | Padget, Hagerstown | .959 | 69 | 89 | 5 | 4 | 1 |
| Dahse, Hagerstown | .947 | 11 | 18 | 0 | 1 | 0 | Padia, Hagerstown | 1.000 | 4 | 4 | 0 | 0 | 0 |
| Dannenberg, Peninsula* | .966 | 117 | 215 | 15 | 8 | 6 | Posey, Durham | .969 | 46 | 62 | 1 | 2 | 0 |
| Davis, Peninsula* | .880 | 13 | 21 | 1 | 3 | 0 | Ray, Peninsula | .778 | 12 | 7 | 0 | 2 | 0 |
| Delucchi, Prince William | 1.000 | 4 | 8 | 0 | 0 | 0 | Riley, Hagerstown | .875 | 9 | 13 | 1 | 2 | 1 |
| Dickerson, Winston-Salem | .935 | 103 | 107 | 8 | 8 | 2 | Roomes, Winston-Salem | .978 | 125 | 254 | 14 | 6 | 2 |
| Dodd, Hagerstown | 1.000 | 8 | 12 | 1 | 0 | 0 | Rosario, Durham | 1.000 | 8 | 7 | 0 | 0 | 0 |
| Doerr, Hagerstown | 1.000 | 7 | 12 | 0 | 0 | 0 | Simpson, Salem | .949 | 27 | 34 | 3 | 2 | 1 |
| Doggett, Lynchburg | .974 | 28 | 37 | 0 | 1 | 0 | D. Smith, Hagerstown | 1.000 | 1 | 1 | 0 | 0 | 0 |
| Engram, Peninsula | .955 | 93 | 123 | 4 | 6 | 0 | T. Smith, Hagerstown* | 1.000 | 7 | 9 | 0 | 0 | 0 |
| Evans, Prince William | .979 | 32 | 44 | 3 | 1 | 0 | Soto, Peninsula* | .948 | 41 | 69 | 4 | 4 | 2 |
| Giansiracusa, Peninsula | .950 | 13 | 18 | 1 | 1 | 0 | Stevens, Prince William | .903 | 18 | 25 | 3 | 3 | 1 |
| Hammonds, Prince William | .962 | 67 | 94 | 7 | 4 | 1 | Sullivan, Hagerstown* | 1.000 | 6 | 17 | 0 | 0 | 0 |
| Hatcher, Durham | .989 | 49 | 82 | 4 | 1 | 3 | Thompson, Lynchburg | 1.000 | 26 | 34 | 0 | 0 | 0 |
| Hill, Kinston | .950 | 127 | 234 | 12 | 13 | 2 | Traylor, Lynchburg | 1.000 | 2 | 3 | 0 | 0 | 0 |
| Holtz, Hagerstown | 1.000 | 2 | 3 | 0 | 0 | 0 | Tubbs, Durham | .990 | 70 | 188 | 3 | 2 | 1 |
| S. Johnson, Kinston | 1.000 | 25 | 42 | 1 | 0 | 0 | Tullier, Winston-Salem* | .984 | 40 | 59 | 2 | 1 | 1 |
| T. Johnson, Peninsula | .900 | 15 | 17 | 1 | 2 | 0 | Wagner, Durham | 1.000 | 10 | 26 | 0 | 0 | 0 |
| Kenaga, Hagerstown | 1.000 | 2 | 5 | 0 | 0 | 0 | Wetherby, Durham* | 1.000 | 5 | 7 | 0 | 0 | 0 |
| Kennard, Peninsula | .857 | 6 | 12 | 0 | 2 | 0 | Whitfield, Kinston | .959 | 124 | 199 | 13 | 9 | 3 |
| King, Salem* | .983 | 82 | 113 | 5 | 2 | 1 | Williams, Hagerstown* | .985 | 93 | 185 | 7 | 3 | 0 |
| Klopp, 76 PW-21 Hagers. | .953 | 97 | 170 | 14 | 9 | 2 | WILSON, Lynchburg | .986 | 115 | 131 | 8 | 2 | 0 |
| Knox, Prince William | .981 | 64 | 102 | 4 | 2 | 1 | Yastrzemski, Durham | .952 | 129 | 202 | 17 | 11 | 6 |
| Leiva, Peninsula | .941 | 68 | 142 | 1 | 9 | 0 | Yelding, Kinston | .973 | 133 | 310 | 10 | 9 | 3 |

## CATCHERS

| Player and Club | Pct. | G. | PO. | A. | E. | DP. | PB. | Player and Club | Pct. | G. | PO. | A. | E. | DP. | PB. |
|---|---|---|---|---|---|---|---|---|---|---|---|---|---|---|---|
| Barnard, Prince William | .993 | 17 | 131 | 7 | 1 | 0 | 2 | Carmichael, Lynchburg | .985 | 41 | 233 | 24 | 4 | 3 | 3 |
| Beamesderfer, Hagerstown | .980 | 15 | 88 | 10 | 2 | 1 | 6 | Cooper, Kinston | .983 | 94 | 589 | 51 | 11 | 7 | 5 |
| Benkert, Prince William | 1.000 | 3 | 25 | 3 | 0 | 0 | 2 | Cordova, Winston-Salem | 1.000 | 4 | 16 | 2 | 0 | 0 | 0 |
| Bennett, Peninsula | 1.000 | 11 | 61 | 1 | 0 | 1 | 1 | Cormack, Durham | .989 | 15 | 85 | 5 | 1 | 0 | 0 |
| Berryhill, Winston-Salem | .984 | 99 | 625 | 70 | 11 | 6 | 18 | D'Alessandro, Durham | .975 | 106 | 594 | 77 | 17 | 12 | 8 |
| BURRELL, Lynchburg | .988 | 104 | 705 | 45 | 9 | 9 | 13 | DeWillis, Kinston | .987 | 25 | 206 | 26 | 3 | 4 | 6 |
| Butters, Prince William | .961 | 13 | 69 | 4 | 3 | 0 | 4 | Epps, Salem | .981 | 52 | 317 | 41 | 7 | 4 | 9 |
| Cadahia, Salem | .982 | 63 | 386 | 49 | 8 | 4 | 15 | Goldthorn, Prince William | .986 | 113 | 804 | 96 | 13 | 9 | 10 |
| Carlucci, Salem | .983 | 48 | 263 | 26 | 5 | 1 | 5 | Henderson, Peninsula | .991 | 15 | 96 | 10 | 1 | 1 | 7 |

## CATCHERS —Continued

| Player and Club | Pct. | G. | PO. | A. | E. | DP. | PB. | Player and Club | Pct. | G. | PO. | A. | E. | DP. | PB. |
|---|---|---|---|---|---|---|---|---|---|---|---|---|---|---|---|
| Holland, Kinston | 1.000 | 1 | 1 | 0 | 0 | 0 | 0 | Ransom, Durham | .987 | 22 | 148 | 9 | 2 | 4 | 0 |
| Karr, Lynchburg | 1.000 | 2 | 2 | 0 | 0 | 0 | 0 | Reynolds, Durham | 1.000 | 5 | 31 | 1 | 0 | 0 | 1 |
| Magrann, Peninsula | 1.000 | 19 | 102 | 12 | 0 | 1 | 0 | Roadcap, Winston-Salem | .982 | 34 | 197 | 19 | 4 | 2 | 3 |
| Maloney, Lynchburg | 1.000 | 2 | 6 | 0 | 0 | 0 | 1 | Roman, Peninsula | .967 | 82 | 469 | 53 | 18 | 7 | 7 |
| Melillo, Hagerstown | .982 | 71 | 502 | 40 | 10 | 3 | 6 | Rypien, Kinston | .984 | 37 | 170 | 15 | 3 | 4 | 3 |
| Miller, Winston-Salem | 1.000 | 1 | 1 | 0 | 0 | 0 | 0 | Stanley, Salem | 1.000 | 1 | 1 | 1 | 0 | 1 | 0 |
| Nipper, Durham | 1.000 | 1 | 1 | 0 | 0 | 0 | 0 | Velleggia, Hagerstown | .981 | 48 | 333 | 33 | 7 | 6 | 5 |
| Nowakowski, Kinston | .969 | 4 | 28 | 3 | 1 | 0 | 0 | Wrona, Winston-Salem | .971 | 16 | 90 | 10 | 3 | 1 | 0 |
| Padia, Hagerstown | 1.000 | 13 | 62 | 6 | 0 | 3 | 1 | Zayas, Peninsula | .970 | 21 | 143 | 19 | 5 | 4 | 5 |

## PITCHERS

| Player and Club | Pct. | G. | PO. | A. | E. | DP. | Player and Club | Pct. | G. | PO. | A. | E. | DP. |
|---|---|---|---|---|---|---|---|---|---|---|---|---|---|
| Adkins, Prince William | 1.000 | 6 | 1 | 3 | 0 | 0 | B. Jones, Prince William | 1.000 | 28 | 3 | 10 | 0 | 1 |
| Anthony, Kinston | 1.000 | 2 | 0 | 2 | 0 | 0 | D. Jones, Durham | .950 | 26 | 4 | 15 | 1 | 0 |
| Assenmacher, Durham° | 1.000 | 14 | 0 | 5 | 0 | 0 | Kilgus, Salem° | 1.000 | 38 | 6 | 15 | 0 | 1 |
| Barba, Lynchburg | 1.000 | 2 | 1 | 0 | 0 | 0 | Klink, Lynchburg° | 1.000 | 44 | 1 | 7 | 0 | 0 |
| Barger, Durham° | .895 | 18 | 5 | 12 | 2 | 0 | Knapp, Salem | .974 | 29 | 11 | 26 | 1 | 2 |
| Barton, Peninsula° | .872 | 22 | 3 | 31 | 5 | 0 | J. Knox, Peninsula | 1.000 | 3 | 0 | 3 | 0 | 0 |
| Bass, Salem | .889 | 27 | 6 | 10 | 2 | 0 | Kopf, Winston-Salem | .833 | 24 | 6 | 9 | 3 | 3 |
| Bautista, Lynchburg | .909 | 27 | 9 | 21 | 3 | 1 | Kordish, Salem | 1.000 | 10 | 5 | 14 | 0 | 0 |
| E. Bell, Hagerstown | 1.000 | 26 | 4 | 27 | 0 | 2 | Kramer, Salem | .931 | 25 | 6 | 21 | 2 | 3 |
| G. Bell, Winston-Salem° | 1.000 | 22 | 5 | 13 | 0 | 1 | Lavelle, Hagerstown | 1.000 | 38 | 6 | 18 | 0 | 4 |
| Bencomo, Kinston | .962 | 25 | 7 | 18 | 1 | 1 | Lein, Prince William | 1.000 | 2 | 0 | 2 | 0 | 0 |
| Bergendahl, Lynchburg | .774 | 18 | 5 | 19 | 7 | 2 | Leiter, Hagerstown | .920 | 34 | 5 | 18 | 2 | 6 |
| BETHEL, Winston-Salem | 1.000 | 25 | 12 | 35 | 0 | 1 | Lenderman, Winston-Salem | .905 | 41 | 7 | 12 | 2 | 0 |
| Bianchi, Hagerstown | .667 | 17 | 1 | 5 | 3 | 2 | Lind, Prince William | 1.000 | 36 | 13 | 19 | 0 | 1 |
| Blankenship, Durham | .969 | 29 | 7 | 24 | 1 | 0 | Lloyd, Peninsula | 1.000 | 12 | 0 | 8 | 0 | 1 |
| Blasucci, Prince William° | 1.000 | 1 | 1 | 0 | 0 | 0 | Long, Peninsula | .941 | 11 | 2 | 14 | 1 | 3 |
| Bormann, Durham | .750 | 11 | 2 | 4 | 2 | 0 | Lychak, Kinston° | .917 | 48 | 1 | 10 | 1 | 0 |
| Bowden, Peninsula° | 1.000 | 20 | 0 | 14 | 0 | 4 | Magrann, Peninsula | .833 | 10 | 1 | 4 | 1 | 0 |
| Brewer, Winston-Salem | 1.000 | 10 | 1 | 5 | 0 | 1 | Masters, Winston-Salem | .667 | 14 | 1 | 9 | 5 | 0 |
| Brown, Lynchburg° | .938 | 11 | 2 | 13 | 1 | 0 | Maye, Winston-Salem | .667 | 17 | 1 | 7 | 4 | 1 |
| Burgos, Kinston° | 1.000 | 7 | 0 | 1 | 0 | 0 | McClanahan, Peninsula | .818 | 16 | 2 | 7 | 2 | 0 |
| Burns, Lynchburg | .900 | 24 | 1 | 8 | 1 | 0 | McDevitt, Peninsula | 1.000 | 6 | 0 | 3 | 0 | 0 |
| Butters, Prince William | 1.000 | 1 | 0 | 1 | 0 | 0 | McKay, Kinston° | .882 | 39 | 3 | 12 | 2 | 0 |
| Carter, Prince William | 1.000 | 1 | 1 | 0 | 0 | 0 | McKelvey, Prince William | .917 | 11 | 3 | 8 | 1 | 0 |
| Cash, Durham° | 1.000 | 8 | 1 | 6 | 0 | 1 | McLarnan, Peninsula | 1.000 | 48 | 6 | 11 | 0 | 1 |
| Castillo, Kinston | .957 | 35 | 6 | 16 | 1 | 3 | Melendez, Prince William | .750 | 9 | 2 | 1 | 1 | 0 |
| Castro, Kinston | .600 | 24 | 1 | 2 | 2 | 0 | Mesa, Kinston | .800 | 30 | 2 | 10 | 3 | 0 |
| Chambers, Peninsula | .833 | 9 | 4 | 6 | 2 | 0 | Milacki, Hagerstown | 1.000 | 7 | 4 | 7 | 0 | 0 |
| Clemons, Kinston | .943 | 32 | 9 | 24 | 2 | 1 | Moore, Kinston | 1.000 | 4 | 0 | 1 | 0 | 0 |
| Coatney, Salem | 1.000 | 10 | 1 | 3 | 0 | 0 | Morelock, Durham | .900 | 28 | 2 | 7 | 1 | 1 |
| Coffman, Durham | .500 | 3 | 0 | 1 | 1 | 0 | Morris, Durham | .892 | 26 | 14 | 19 | 4 | 0 |
| Cox, Winston-Salem° | .943 | 31 | 7 | 26 | 2 | 2 | Morrow, Prince William | 1.000 | 34 | 6 | 8 | 0 | 1 |
| Cullen, Kinston | .600 | 8 | 1 | 2 | 2 | 1 | Mortimer, Salem° | 1.000 | 4 | 0 | 2 | 0 | 1 |
| Cunningham, Prince William | .917 | 32 | 9 | 13 | 2 | 1 | Morton, Peninsula° | .833 | 32 | 2 | 8 | 2 | 0 |
| DelRosario, Durham | .952 | 39 | 6 | 14 | 1 | 1 | Moyer, Winston-Salem° | 1.000 | 12 | 4 | 17 | 0 | 2 |
| Dickman, Kinston | 1.000 | 10 | 0 | 1 | 0 | 0 | Neal, Prince William° | .900 | 18 | 1 | 8 | 1 | 0 |
| Dobie, Lynchburg | .867 | 26 | 2 | 24 | 4 | 0 | Neidlinger, Prince William | .792 | 26 | 9 | 10 | 5 | 0 |
| Dombek, Peninsula° | 1.000 | 24 | 3 | 22 | 0 | 3 | Pena, Prince William° | 1.000 | 20 | 0 | 4 | 0 | 0 |
| Dooner, Hagerstown | .545 | 19 | 2 | 4 | 5 | 0 | Peraza, Kinston | .889 | 25 | 10 | 14 | 3 | 1 |
| Edens, Lynchburg | .957 | 16 | 10 | 12 | 1 | 2 | Phillips, Winston-Salem | .862 | 33 | 7 | 18 | 4 | 0 |
| Egelston, Hagerstown | .923 | 24 | 2 | 10 | 1 | 0 | Raczka, Prince William | 1.000 | 35 | 5 | 12 | 0 | 1 |
| Fiepke, Prince William° | 1.000 | 13 | 0 | 3 | 0 | 0 | Reiter, Hagerstown° | .857 | 11 | 1 | 5 | 1 | 0 |
| Flanagan, Hagerstown° | 1.000 | 1 | 0 | 2 | 0 | 0 | Reyes, Kinston° | 1.000 | 36 | 8 | 11 | 0 | 1 |
| Flinn, Hagerstown | 1.000 | 11 | 2 | 2 | 0 | 0 | Rogers, Durham | .933 | 36 | 3 | 11 | 1 | 0 |
| Frohwirth, Peninsula | .852 | 54 | 7 | 16 | 4 | 1 | Romagna, Kinston | 1.000 | 1 | 0 | 1 | 0 | 1 |
| Gannon, Hagerstown° | 1.000 | 3 | 0 | 3 | 0 | 0 | Rooker, Prince William | 1.000 | 17 | 4 | 10 | 0 | 1 |
| Garcia, Lynchburg | 1.000 | 4 | 2 | 0 | 0 | 0 | Rosario, Durham° | .909 | 13 | 2 | 8 | 1 | 1 |
| Gay, Lynchburg | .944 | 21 | 7 | 10 | 1 | 3 | Russell, Prince William° | 1.000 | 15 | 2 | 12 | 0 | 0 |
| Gilbert, Hagerstown° | 1.000 | 1 | 0 | 1 | 0 | 0 | Santiago, Durham° | 1.000 | 44 | 3 | 11 | 0 | 1 |
| Gordon, Prince William | .926 | 22 | 8 | 17 | 2 | 0 | Schreiber, Durham° | .944 | 12 | 3 | 14 | 1 | 1 |
| Groves, Durham | .833 | 20 | 5 | 10 | 3 | 1 | Scott, Durham | .875 | 4 | 2 | 5 | 1 | 0 |
| Grudzinski, Prince William | 1.000 | 15 | 1 | 1 | 0 | 0 | Segura, Kinston | .929 | 34 | 6 | 20 | 2 | 2 |
| Hall, Winston-Salem° | .931 | 24 | 1 | 26 | 2 | 0 | Shanks, Kinston | 1.000 | 9 | 0 | 5 | 0 | 0 |
| Hallgren, Salem | 1.000 | 15 | 5 | 11 | 0 | 1 | Skinner, Hagerstown | .905 | 11 | 4 | 15 | 2 | 0 |
| Hamilton, Winston-Salem° | .925 | 25 | 9 | 28 | 3 | 0 | Slowik, Winston-Salem | .900 | 10 | 1 | 8 | 1 | 2 |
| Harman, Salem | .938 | 42 | 5 | 10 | 1 | 0 | Smiley, Prince William° | 1.000 | 10 | 4 | 6 | 0 | 0 |
| Harrington, Salem | .875 | 10 | 4 | 3 | 1 | 0 | Steirer, Hagerstown | 1.000 | 13 | 5 | 19 | 0 | 1 |
| Hartman, Salem | .850 | 46 | 11 | 23 | 6 | 2 | Stephenson, Kinston | 1.000 | 4 | 1 | 2 | 0 | 0 |
| Hartshorn, Lynchburg | .886 | 25 | 8 | 23 | 4 | 1 | Summers, Hagerstown | .818 | 8 | 2 | 7 | 2 | 0 |
| Heise, Hagerstown° | .667 | 12 | 0 | 2 | 1 | 0 | Talamantez, Hagerstown | .800 | 10 | 2 | 6 | 2 | 0 |
| Hester, Salem | .875 | 18 | 3 | 11 | 2 | 2 | Thomas, Salem | 1.000 | 5 | 4 | 8 | 0 | 2 |
| Hicks, Peninsula | 1.000 | 7 | 0 | 1 | 0 | 0 | Tomsick, Salem | .875 | 17 | 3 | 7 | 0 | 1 |
| Hixon, Hagerstown | .931 | 21 | 8 | 19 | 2 | 0 | True, Peninsula° | .857 | 7 | 0 | 6 | 1 | 0 |
| Holman, Prince William | .944 | 24 | 10 | 24 | 2 | 1 | Weatherford, Peninsula | .800 | 14 | 1 | 3 | 1 | 0 |
| Hopkins, Winston-Salem° | 1.000 | 2 | 0 | 2 | 0 | 0 | Weston, Lynchburg | .929 | 49 | 9 | 17 | 2 | 1 |
| Householder, Peninsula° | 1.000 | 33 | 4 | 20 | 0 | 2 | Williams, Salem° | .909 | 22 | 4 | 16 | 2 | 1 |
| Innis, Lynchburg | .923 | 53 | 11 | 11 | 2 | 2 | Wilson, Hagerstown° | .833 | 21 | 0 | 25 | 5 | 2 |
| Jackson, Peninsula | .833 | 31 | 8 | 22 | 6 | 3 | Winbush, Salem | .878 | 25 | 9 | 27 | 5 | 1 |
| Jensen, Lynchburg° | .667 | 14 | 0 | 2 | 1 | 0 | Wyatt, Lynchburg° | 1.000 | 9 | 3 | 15 | 0 | 1 |

The following players had no recorded accepted chances at the positions indicated; therefore, are not listed in the fielding averages for those particular positions: Barringer, of; Bonilla, 3b; Boudreau, p; Carter, 2b, 3b, ss, c; Cordner, of; Cordova, 3b; Freytes, 2b, ss; Gutierrez, 2b, of; Hallas, p; Hopkins, 1b; Br. Jones, 3b; S. Knox, 2b, p; Kranitz, p; Latmore, 2b; Lein, of; Little, 2b; Mathews, p; McKelvey, of; McKnight, 1b; Melillo, 2b, ss, p; K. Miller, of; Moyer, 1b; Palo, p; Powers, p; Reynolds, of, p; Roadcap, 1b; Romagna, ss; Sciacca, 2b; Stanhope, p.

## CLUB PITCHING

| Club | ERA | G | CG | ShO | Sv | IP | H | R | ER | HR | HB | BB | Int. BB | SO | WP | Bk |
|---|---|---|---|---|---|---|---|---|---|---|---|---|---|---|---|---|
| Lynchburg | 2.42 | 140 | 27 | 18 | 41 | 1215.1 | 979 | 411 | 327 | 61 | 20 | 425 | 10 | 903 | 59 | 11 |
| Peninsula | 3.33 | 135 | 14 | 13 | 34 | 1140.2 | 1013 | 552 | 422 | 66 | 32 | 552 | 18 | 836 | 63 | 16 |
| Prince William | 3.35 | 139 | 20 | 10 | 34 | 1183.1 | 995 | 533 | 441 | 64 | 52 | 606 | 21 | 1021 | 87 | 17 |
| Kinston | 3.50 | 138 | 13 | 14 | 30 | 1197.1 | 1088 | 589 | 465 | 74 | 39 | 530 | 34 | 964 | 58 | 11 |
| Winston-Salem | 3.56 | 139 | 34 | 12 | 19 | 1174.1 | 1069 | 587 | 464 | 63 | 40 | 549 | 34 | 905 | 80 | 25 |
| Hagerstown | 3.63 | 137 | 22 | 9 | 27 | 1156.1 | 1143 | 570 | 466 | 56 | 41 | 479 | 5 | 941 | 64 | 11 |
| Salem | 3.80 | 138 | 15 | 5 | 39 | 1201.1 | 1118 | 642 | 507 | 83 | 41 | 636 | 21 | 961 | 96 | 13 |
| Durham | 4.13 | 140 | 24 | 6 | 30 | 1199.0 | 1240 | 674 | 550 | 109 | 33 | 528 | 18 | 812 | 61 | 17 |

## PITCHERS' RECORDS
### (Leading Qualifiers for Earned-Run Average Leadership — 112 or More Innings)

*Throws lefthanded.

| Pitcher—Club | W | L | Pct. | ERA | G | GS | CG | GF | ShO | Sv | IP | H | R | ER | HR | HB | BB | Int. BB | SO | WP |
|---|---|---|---|---|---|---|---|---|---|---|---|---|---|---|---|---|---|---|---|---|
| Hartshorn, Lynchburg | 17 | 4 | .810 | 1.69 | 25 | 25 | 8 | 0 | 2 | 0 | 170.2 | 125 | 45 | 32 | 5 | 9 | 53 | 0 | 98 | 4 |
| O. Lind, Prince William | 11 | 7 | .611 | 1.82 | 36 | 14 | 6 | 12 | 4 | 3 | 148.0 | 93 | 38 | 30 | 5 | 3 | 64 | 3 | 149 | 5 |
| Castillo, Kinston* | 11 | 7 | .611 | 1.90 | 36 | 12 | 0 | 8 | 0 | 3 | 127.2 | 111 | 44 | 27 | 5 | 3 | 48 | 3 | 136 | 2 |
| Clemons, Kinston | 12 | 3 | .800 | 2.04 | 32 | 18 | 7 | 7 | 2 | 1 | 159.0 | 138 | 49 | 36 | 4 | 1 | 33 | 3 | 117 | 7 |
| Barton, Peninsula* | 12 | 4 | .750 | 2.30 | 22 | 22 | 7 | 0 | 5 | 0 | 140.2 | 108 | 45 | 36 | 5 | 1 | 43 | 1 | 82 | 4 |
| Bautista, Lynchburg | 15 | 8 | .652 | 2.34 | 27 | 25 | 7 | 1 | 3 | 1 | 169.0 | 145 | 49 | 44 | 8 | 3 | 33 | 0 | 109 | 3 |
| Dobie, Lynchburg | 12 | 5 | .706 | 2.63 | 26 | 26 | 5 | 0 | 3 | 0 | 167.2 | 118 | 61 | 49 | 11 | 0 | 77 | 1 | 144 | 11 |
| Hamilton, Winston-Salem* | 11 | 10 | .524 | 2.72 | 25 | 24 | 11 | 1 | 4 | 0 | 155.2 | 110 | 61 | 47 | 3 | 1 | 108 | 5 | 152 | 10 |
| Dombek, Peninsula* | 7 | 8 | .467 | 2.86 | 24 | 17 | 4 | 2 | 0 | 0 | 113.1 | 71 | 48 | 36 | 9 | 4 | 76 | 0 | 75 | 9 |
| Bencomo, Kinston | 10 | 8 | .556 | 3.09 | 25 | 24 | 3 | 0 | 1 | 0 | 160.1 | 141 | 69 | 55 | 8 | 3 | 39 | 3 | 109 | 3 |

Departmental Leaders: G—Frohwirth, 54; W—Hartshorn, 17; L—Neidlinger, Segura, 13; Pct.—Hartshorn, .810; GS—E. Bell, Dobie, Neidlinger, 26; CG—Hamilton, 11; GF—Frohwirth, 48; ShO—Barton, 5; Sv.—Frohwirth, 18; IP—Knapp, 180.0; H—Knapp, 187; R—Kramer, 99; ER—Kramer, 86; HR—D. Jones, 24; HB—Hartshorn, Mesa, 9; BB—Williams, 117; IBB—Bethel, Hartman, 6; SO—E. Bell, 162; WP—Winbush, 25.

### (All Pitchers—Listed Alphabetically)

| Pitcher—Club | W | L | Pct. | ERA | G | GS | CG | GF | ShO | Sv | IP | H | R | ER | HR | HB | BB | Int. BB | SO | WP |
|---|---|---|---|---|---|---|---|---|---|---|---|---|---|---|---|---|---|---|---|---|
| Adkins, Prince William | 0 | 1 | .000 | 1.59 | 6 | 0 | 0 | 5 | 0 | 2 | 11.1 | 8 | 3 | 2 | 1 | 1 | 9 | 0 | 7 | 1 |
| Anthony, Kinston | 0 | 0 | .000 | 3.68 | 2 | 0 | 0 | 0 | 0 | 0 | 7.1 | 10 | 3 | 3 | 0 | 0 | 0 | 0 | 7 | 0 |
| Assenmacher, Durham* | 3 | 2 | .600 | 3.29 | 14 | 0 | 0 | 11 | 0 | 1 | 38.1 | 38 | 16 | 14 | 1 | 2 | 13 | 4 | 36 | 0 |
| Barba, Lynchburg | 0 | 1 | .000 | 10.80 | 2 | 0 | 0 | 1 | 0 | 0 | 1.2 | 3 | 2 | 2 | 0 | 1 | 3 | 1 | 2 | 1 |
| Barger, Durham* | 8 | 8 | .500 | 5.20 | 18 | 18 | 5 | 0 | 0 | 0 | 105.2 | 137 | 70 | 61 | 16 | 3 | 41 | 1 | 64 | 4 |
| Barton, Peninsula* | 12 | 4 | .750 | 2.30 | 22 | 22 | 7 | 0 | 5 | 0 | 140.2 | 108 | 45 | 36 | 5 | 1 | 43 | 1 | 82 | 4 |
| Bass, Salem | 1 | 4 | .200 | 5.27 | 27 | 4 | 1 | 11 | 0 | 3 | 85.1 | 96 | 59 | 50 | 7 | 3 | 32 | 3 | 88 | 7 |
| Bautista, Lynchburg | 15 | 8 | .652 | 2.34 | 27 | 25 | 7 | 1 | 3 | 1 | 169.0 | 145 | 49 | 44 | 8 | 3 | 33 | 0 | 109 | 3 |
| E. Bell, Hagerstown* | 11 | 6 | .647 | 3.13 | 26 | 26 | 5 | 0 | 2 | 0 | 158.1 | 141 | 73 | 55 | 7 | 1 | 63 | 0 | 162 | 4 |
| G. Bell, Winston-Salem* | 3 | 4 | .429 | 2.97 | 22 | 4 | 1 | 11 | 0 | 0 | 63.2 | 44 | 22 | 21 | 2 | 2 | 28 | 3 | 52 | 4 |
| Bencomo, Kinston | 10 | 8 | .556 | 3.09 | 25 | 24 | 3 | 0 | 1 | 0 | 160.1 | 141 | 69 | 55 | 8 | 3 | 39 | 3 | 109 | 3 |
| Bergendahl, Lynchburg | 10 | 3 | .769 | 3.62 | 18 | 16 | 2 | 0 | 1 | 0 | 104.1 | 94 | 51 | 42 | 8 | 1 | 41 | 1 | 71 | 14 |
| Bethel, Winston-Salem | 7 | 8 | .467 | 3.10 | 25 | 21 | 5 | 3 | 1 | 0 | 154.0 | 153 | 65 | 53 | 8 | 6 | 60 | 6 | 73 | 6 |
| Bianchi, Hagerstown | 2 | 7 | .222 | 2.70 | 17 | 6 | 1 | 3 | 0 | 0 | 63.1 | 58 | 24 | 19 | 3 | 7 | 35 | 0 | 53 | 8 |
| Blankenship, Durham | 8 | 8 | .500 | 3.78 | 29 | 16 | 3 | 4 | 0 | 0 | 116.2 | 124 | 63 | 49 | 8 | 2 | 53 | 0 | 89 | 7 |
| Blasucci, Prince William* | 0 | 0 | .000 | 7.71 | 1 | 1 | 0 | 0 | 0 | 0 | 4.2 | 4 | 4 | 4 | 0 | 0 | 3 | 0 | 6 | 0 |
| Bormann, Durham* | 0 | 2 | .000 | 3.33 | 11 | 1 | 0 | 5 | 0 | 1 | 24.1 | 29 | 15 | 9 | 1 | 0 | 3 | 0 | 13 | 0 |
| Boudreau, Winston-Salem* | 0 | 2 | .000 | 7.07 | 12 | 0 | 0 | 2 | 0 | 0 | 14.0 | 18 | 12 | 11 | 1 | 0 | 9 | 1 | 16 | 2 |
| Bowden, Peninsula* | 3 | 1 | .750 | 3.57 | 20 | 0 | 0 | 6 | 0 | 1 | 35.1 | 30 | 18 | 14 | 2 | 3 | 21 | 1 | 21 | 5 |
| Brewer, Winston-Salem | 1 | 5 | .167 | 3.24 | 10 | 1 | 0 | 7 | 0 | 0 | 25.0 | 24 | 12 | 9 | 1 | 3 | 10 | 1 | 15 | 1 |
| Brown, Lynchburg* | 3 | 5 | .375 | 3.00 | 11 | 9 | 0 | 0 | 0 | 0 | 54.0 | 35 | 23 | 18 | 4 | 0 | 41 | 0 | 54 | 5 |
| Burgos, Kinston* | 0 | 2 | .000 | 11.88 | 7 | 1 | 0 | 1 | 0 | 0 | 8.1 | 12 | 11 | 11 | 1 | 0 | 10 | 0 | 5 | 1 |
| Burns, Lynchburg | 2 | 0 | 1.000 | 1.04 | 24 | 0 | 0 | 19 | 0 | 10 | 52.0 | 41 | 11 | 6 | 2 | 0 | 10 | 1 | 48 | 2 |
| Butters, Prince William | 0 | 0 | .000 | .000 | 1 | 0 | 0 | 1 | 0 | 0 | 1.0 | 0 | 0 | 0 | 0 | 0 | 2 | 0 | 0 | 0 |
| Carter, Prince William | 0 | 0 | .000 | 0.00 | 1 | 0 | 0 | 1 | 0 | 0 | 0.2 | 2 | 0 | 0 | 0 | 0 | 0 | 0 | 1 | 0 |
| Cash, Durham* | 3 | 3 | .500 | 3.75 | 8 | 8 | 2 | 0 | 1 | 0 | 48.0 | 45 | 22 | 20 | 2 | 1 | 13 | 0 | 48 | 4 |
| Castillo, Kinston* | 11 | 7 | .611 | 1.90 | 36 | 12 | 0 | 8 | 0 | 3 | 127.2 | 111 | 44 | 27 | 5 | 3 | 48 | 3 | 136 | 2 |
| Castro, Kinston | 3 | 0 | 1.000 | 4.68 | 23 | 1 | 0 | 14 | 0 | 2 | 32.2 | 30 | 23 | 17 | 2 | 1 | 18 | 3 | 21 | 0 |
| Chambers, Peninsula | 2 | 3 | .400 | 3.52 | 9 | 9 | 0 | 0 | 0 | 0 | 46.0 | 37 | 19 | 18 | 1 | 3 | 21 | 0 | 23 | 1 |
| Clemons, Kinston | 12 | 3 | .800 | 2.04 | 32 | 18 | 7 | 7 | 2 | 1 | 159.0 | 138 | 49 | 36 | 4 | 1 | 33 | 3 | 117 | 7 |
| Coatney, Salem | 4 | 0 | 1.000 | 3.77 | 10 | 0 | 0 | 5 | 0 | 2 | 28.2 | 29 | 12 | 12 | 3 | 0 | 15 | 1 | 26 | 3 |
| Coffman, Durham | 0 | 1 | .000 | 10.38 | 3 | 0 | 0 | 2 | 0 | 0 | 4.1 | 4 | 5 | 5 | 0 | 1 | 11 | 2 | 1 | 2 |
| Cox, Winston-Salem* | 2 | 5 | .286 | 4.08 | 31 | 8 | 1 | 10 | 0 | 0 | 81.2 | 74 | 49 | 37 | 5 | 1 | 42 | 0 | 53 | 8 |
| Cullen, Kinston | 0 | 3 | .000 | 5.92 | 8 | 7 | 0 | 0 | 0 | 0 | 24.1 | 20 | 23 | 16 | 1 | 0 | 22 | 0 | 39 | 6 |
| Cunningham, Prince William | 4 | 4 | .500 | 3.96 | 32 | 1 | 0 | 16 | 0 | 1 | 63.2 | 69 | 35 | 28 | 3 | 6 | 35 | 3 | 25 | 5 |
| DelRosario, Durham | 4 | 1 | .800 | 4.06 | 39 | 1 | 0 | 12 | 0 | 2 | 82.0 | 92 | 51 | 37 | 5 | 6 | 37 | 2 | 28 | 1 |
| Dickman, Kinston | 0 | 3 | .000 | 2.66 | 10 | 0 | 0 | 8 | 0 | 3 | 20.1 | 15 | 7 | 6 | 0 | 0 | 11 | 2 | 26 | 3 |
| Dobie, Lynchburg | 12 | 5 | .706 | 2.63 | 26 | 26 | 5 | 0 | 3 | 0 | 167.2 | 118 | 61 | 49 | 11 | 0 | 77 | 1 | 144 | 11 |
| Dombek, Peninsula* | 7 | 8 | .467 | 2.86 | 24 | 17 | 4 | 2 | 0 | 0 | 113.1 | 71 | 48 | 36 | 9 | 4 | 76 | 0 | 75 | 9 |
| Dooner, Hagerstown | 1 | 1 | .500 | 3.09 | 19 | 2 | 0 | 13 | 0 | 2 | 43.2 | 53 | 17 | 15 | 3 | 1 | 3 | 0 | 25 | 1 |
| Edens, Lynchburg | 6 | 4 | .600 | 3.84 | 16 | 16 | 0 | 0 | 0 | 0 | 82.0 | 86 | 40 | 35 | 4 | 2 | 34 | 0 | 48 | 3 |
| Egelston, Hagerstown | 4 | 3 | .571 | 5.69 | 24 | 11 | 0 | 5 | 0 | 1 | 74.1 | 96 | 56 | 47 | 8 | 2 | 40 | 0 | 69 | 5 |
| Fiepke, Prince William* | 1 | 2 | .333 | 4.29 | 13 | 2 | 0 | 7 | 0 | 0 | 21.0 | 16 | 10 | 10 | 2 | 0 | 24 | 0 | 24 | 6 |
| Flanagan, Hagerstown* | 0 | 0 | .000 | 0.00 | 1 | 1 | 0 | 0 | 0 | 0 | 6.0 | 1 | 0 | 0 | 0 | 0 | 0 | 0 | 5 | 0 |
| Flinn, Hagerstown | 2 | 1 | .667 | 2.04 | 11 | 0 | 0 | 10 | 0 | 2 | 17.2 | 16 | 4 | 4 | 1 | 0 | 3 | 0 | 18 | 1 |
| Frohwirth, Peninsula | 7 | 5 | .583 | 2.20 | 54 | 0 | 0 | 48 | 0 | 18 | 82.0 | 70 | 33 | 20 | 2 | 4 | 48 | 3 | 74 | 6 |
| Gannon, Hagerstown* | 0 | 1 | .000 | 9.00 | 3 | 0 | 0 | 2 | 0 | 0 | 7.0 | 12 | 7 | 7 | 1 | 0 | 2 | 0 | 4 | 1 |
| Garcia, Lynchburg | 0 | 0 | .000 | 9.64 | 4 | 0 | 0 | 1 | 0 | 0 | 4.2 | 6 | 5 | 5 | 1 | 0 | 5 | 1 | 2 | 0 |
| Gay, Lynchburg | 4 | 1 | .800 | 2.08 | 21 | 6 | 0 | 6 | 0 | 0 | 73.2 | 77 | 26 | 17 | 6 | 2 | 18 | 0 | 43 | 1 |
| Gilbert, Lynchburg* | 0 | 1 | .000 | 3.60 | 1 | 1 | 0 | 0 | 0 | 0 | 5.0 | 5 | 2 | 2 | 0 | 0 | 2 | 0 | 6 | 0 |
| Gordon, Prince William | 10 | 8 | .556 | 3.54 | 22 | 21 | 3 | 0 | 1 | 0 | 129.2 | 122 | 59 | 51 | 4 | 5 | 60 | 0 | 129 | 1 |
| Groves, Durham | 9 | 5 | .643 | 4.19 | 20 | 13 | 4 | 3 | 2 | 0 | 101.0 | 95 | 54 | 47 | 6 | 5 | 43 | 1 | 53 | 7 |
| Grudzinski, Prince William | 0 | 1 | .000 | 6.84 | 15 | 2 | 0 | 5 | 0 | 0 | 26.1 | 30 | 23 | 20 | 1 | 4 | 23 | 0 | 13 | 3 |
| Hall, Winston-Salem* | 10 | 7 | .588 | 4.67 | 24 | 23 | 6 | 0 | 3 | 0 | 140.2 | 131 | 92 | 73 | 12 | 8 | 83 | 1 | 135 | 19 |
| Hallas, Winston-Salem | 0 | 0 | .000 | 0.00 | 1 | 1 | 0 | 0 | 0 | 0 | 2.0 | 1 | 0 | 0 | 0 | 0 | 0 | 0 | 0 | 0 |
| Hallgren, Salem | 5 | 5 | .500 | 3.04 | 15 | 15 | 1 | 0 | 1 | 0 | 91.2 | 88 | 37 | 31 | 4 | 3 | 27 | 0 | 75 | 3 |
| Hamilton, Winston-Salem* | 11 | 10 | .524 | 2.72 | 25 | 24 | 11 | 1 | 4 | 0 | 155.2 | 110 | 61 | 47 | 3 | 1 | 108 | 5 | 152 | 10 |
| Harman, Salem | 5 | 3 | .625 | 1.75 | 42 | 0 | 0 | 39 | 0 | 14 | 77.1 | 65 | 21 | 15 | 6 | 2 | 14 | 4 | 40 | 0 |

| Pitcher—Club | W. | L. | Pct. | ERA. | G. | GS. | CG. | GF. | ShO. | Sv. | IP. | H. | R. | ER. | HR. | HB. | BB. | Int. BB. | SO. | WP. |
|---|---|---|---|---|---|---|---|---|---|---|---|---|---|---|---|---|---|---|---|---|
| Harrington, Salem | 3 | 2 | .600 | 4.89 | 10 | 10 | 0 | 0 | 0 | 0 | 49.2 | 47 | 34 | 27 | 6 | 1 | 36 | 0 | 44 | 2 |
| Hartman, Salem | 6 | 9 | .400 | 2.24 | 46 | 0 | 0 | 36 | 0 | 9 | 100.1 | 88 | 41 | 25 | 3 | 2 | 56 | 6 | 68 | 7 |
| Hartshorn, Lynchburg | 17 | 4 | .810 | 1.69 | 25 | 25 | 8 | 0 | 2 | 0 | 170.2 | 125 | 45 | 32 | 5 | 9 | 53 | 0 | 98 | 4 |
| Heise, Hagerstown* | 1 | 0 | 1.000 | 3.18 | 12 | 0 | 0 | 6 | 0 | 2 | 22.2 | 17 | 11 | 8 | 0 | 3 | 11 | 0 | 10 | 1 |
| Hester, Salem | 4 | 1 | .800 | 4.75 | 18 | 3 | 1 | 6 | 0 | 0 | 53.0 | 63 | 35 | 28 | 7 | 2 | 24 | 1 | 24 | 4 |
| Hicks, Peninsula | 0 | 2 | .000 | 0.84 | 7 | 0 | 0 | 5 | 0 | 2 | 10.2 | 6 | 5 | 1 | 0 | 1 | 3 | 0 | 7 | 0 |
| Hixon, Hagerstown | 6 | 10 | .375 | 3.47 | 21 | 19 | 5 | 2 | 1 | 0 | 122.0 | 118 | 55 | 47 | 3 | 2 | 42 | 0 | 67 | 5 |
| Holman, Prince William | 10 | 11 | .476 | 3.54 | 24 | 23 | 4 | 0 | 2 | 0 | 142.1 | 123 | 69 | 56 | 11 | 6 | 53 | 2 | 65 | 11 |
| Hopkins, Winston-Salem | 0 | 0 | .000 | 0.00 | 2 | 0 | 0 | 2 | 0 | 0 | 1.1 | 1 | 0 | 0 | 0 | 0 | 3 | 0 | 1 | 1 |
| Householder, Peninsula* | 4 | 5 | .444 | 3.39 | 33 | 14 | 2 | 8 | 0 | 1 | 109.0 | 76 | 55 | 41 | 6 | 2 | 82 | 2 | 114 | 10 |
| Innis, Lynchburg | 6 | 3 | .667 | 2.34 | 53 | 0 | 0 | 39 | 0 | 14 | 77.0 | 46 | 26 | 20 | 2 | 1 | 40 | 1 | 91 | 3 |
| Jackson, Peninsula | 7 | 9 | .438 | 4.60 | 31 | 18 | 0 | 2 | 0 | 1 | 125.1 | 127 | 71 | 64 | 11 | 5 | 53 | 1 | 96 | 6 |
| Jensen, Lynchburg* | 3 | 2 | .600 | 2.75 | 14 | 5 | 0 | 5 | 0 | 1 | 39.1 | 32 | 14 | 12 | 4 | 0 | 9 | 0 | 21 | 1 |
| B. Jones, Prince William | 3 | 2 | .600 | 1.21 | 28 | 0 | 0 | 23 | 0 | 10 | 37.1 | 26 | 7 | 5 | 0 | 0 | 19 | 3 | 42 | 9 |
| D. Jones, Durham | 6 | 11 | .353 | 6.75 | 26 | 22 | 2 | 3 | 0 | 0 | 110.2 | 129 | 93 | 83 | 24 | 1 | 73 | 2 | 74 | 4 |
| Kilgus, Salem* | 3 | 1 | .750 | 2.03 | 38 | 0 | 0 | 19 | 0 | 10 | 84.1 | 69 | 28 | 19 | 5 | 6 | 26 | 2 | 67 | 4 |
| Klink, Lynchburg* | 3 | 3 | .500 | 2.26 | 44 | 0 | 0 | 17 | 0 | 5 | 51.2 | 41 | 16 | 13 | 1 | 0 | 26 | 2 | 59 | 5 |
| Knapp, Salem | 13 | 7 | .650 | 3.40 | 29 | 25 | 6 | 1 | 1 | 0 | 180.0 | 187 | 89 | 68 | 15 | 3 | 55 | 1 | 127 | 5 |
| J. Knox, Peninsula | 2 | 1 | .667 | 2.25 | 3 | 3 | 1 | 0 | 0 | 0 | 20.0 | 23 | 5 | 5 | 1 | 0 | 2 | 0 | 19 | 0 |
| S. Knox, Prince William | 0 | 0 | .000 | 0.00 | 2 | 0 | 0 | 2 | 0 | 0 | 2.1 | 1 | 0 | 0 | 0 | 0 | 4 | 0 | 1 | 0 |
| Kopf, Winston-Salem | 3 | 5 | .375 | 3.83 | 24 | 8 | 2 | 12 | 1 | 0 | 82.1 | 79 | 46 | 35 | 5 | 1 | 48 | 1 | 51 | 7 |
| Kordish, Salem | 3 | 6 | .333 | 4.09 | 9 | 9 | 2 | 0 | 0 | 0 | 55.0 | 56 | 38 | 25 | 5 | 1 | 20 | 0 | 32 | 1 |
| Kramer, Salem | 7 | 11 | .389 | 6.71 | 25 | 24 | 1 | 0 | 0 | 0 | 115.1 | 143 | 99 | 86 | 11 | 3 | 77 | 0 | 86 | 20 |
| Kranitz, Winston-Salem | 0 | 1 | .000 | 9.00 | 1 | 0 | 0 | 1 | 0 | 0 | 1.0 | 2 | 1 | 1 | 0 | 0 | 2 | 0 | 2 | 1 |
| Lavelle, Hagerstown | 9 | 7 | .563 | 3.33 | 38 | 0 | 0 | 30 | 0 | 7 | 73.0 | 65 | 28 | 27 | 2 | 0 | 22 | 2 | 44 | 2 |
| Lein, Prince William | 0 | 0 | .000 | 0.00 | 2 | 1 | 0 | 1 | 0 | 0 | 2.0 | 1 | 1 | 0 | 0 | 0 | 0 | 0 | 1 | 1 |
| Leiter, Hagerstown | 2 | 8 | .200 | 3.46 | 34 | 6 | 1 | 22 | 0 | 8 | 83.1 | 77 | 44 | 32 | 2 | 7 | 29 | 3 | 82 | 3 |
| Lenderman, Winston-Salem | 3 | 4 | .429 | 2.44 | 41 | 0 | 0 | 32 | 0 | 15 | 70.0 | 64 | 22 | 19 | 0 | 5 | 25 | 2 | 59 | 8 |
| O. Lind, Prince William | 11 | 7 | .611 | 1.82 | 36 | 14 | 6 | 12 | 4 | 3 | 148.0 | 93 | 38 | 30 | 5 | 3 | 64 | 3 | 149 | 5 |
| Lloyd, Peninsula | 1 | 2 | .333 | 4.13 | 12 | 5 | 0 | 3 | 0 | 0 | 32.2 | 37 | 20 | 15 | 3 | 1 | 17 | 0 | 19 | 0 |
| Long, Peninsula | 4 | 6 | .400 | 3.72 | 11 | 10 | 0 | 1 | 0 | 0 | 58.0 | 63 | 27 | 24 | 3 | 3 | 20 | 1 | 38 | 3 |
| Lychak, Kinston* | 4 | 2 | .667 | 1.75 | 48 | 0 | 0 | 39 | 0 | 14 | 56.2 | 42 | 20 | 11 | 2 | 1 | 28 | 4 | 45 | 1 |
| Magrann, Peninsula | 0 | 1 | .000 | 5.63 | 10 | 0 | 0 | 5 | 0 | 0 | 24.0 | 35 | 16 | 15 | 1 | 0 | 11 | 0 | 18 | 3 |
| Masters, Winston-Salem | 1 | 11 | .083 | 5.59 | 14 | 13 | 0 | 1 | 0 | 0 | 67.2 | 59 | 53 | 42 | 7 | 6 | 42 | 2 | 49 | 5 |
| Mathews, Durham | 0 | 0 | .000 | 1.42 | 2 | 0 | 0 | 2 | 0 | 1 | 6.1 | 5 | 1 | 1 | 0 | 0 | 2 | 0 | 5 | 0 |
| Maye, Winston-Salem | 4 | 6 | .400 | 4.25 | 17 | 13 | 1 | 3 | 0 | 0 | 91.0 | 94 | 51 | 43 | 12 | 1 | 35 | 1 | 51 | 2 |
| McClanahan, Peninsula | 1 | 2 | .333 | 2.90 | 16 | 3 | 0 | 4 | 0 | 0 | 40.1 | 44 | 20 | 13 | 2 | 1 | 19 | 3 | 17 | 2 |
| McDevitt, Peninsula | 2 | 3 | .400 | 6.53 | 6 | 6 | 0 | 0 | 0 | 0 | 20.2 | 24 | 21 | 15 | 1 | 1 | 21 | 0 | 14 | 1 |
| McKay, Kinston* | 6 | 4 | .600 | 2.83 | 39 | 9 | 0 | 12 | 0 | 4 | 108.0 | 85 | 38 | 34 | 6 | 1 | 51 | 5 | 96 | 5 |
| McKelvey, Prince William | 3 | 3 | .500 | 3.05 | 11 | 9 | 1 | 1 | 0 | 0 | 62.0 | 48 | 29 | 21 | 3 | 5 | 32 | 1 | 72 | 6 |
| McLarnan, Peninsula | 3 | 3 | .500 | 1.43 | 48 | 0 | 0 | 30 | 0 | 11 | 94.1 | 60 | 24 | 15 | 4 | 0 | 25 | 3 | 90 | 2 |
| Melendez, Prince William | 3 | 2 | .600 | 2.44 | 9 | 8 | 1 | 1 | 0 | 1 | 44.1 | 25 | 17 | 12 | 2 | 0 | 26 | 0 | 41 | 2 |
| Melillo, Hagerstown | 0 | 0 | .000 | 0.00 | 1 | 0 | 0 | 1 | 0 | 0 | 1.0 | 2 | 0 | 0 | 0 | 0 | 0 | 0 | 1 | 1 |
| Mesa, Kinston | 5 | 10 | .333 | 6.16 | 30 | 20 | 0 | 5 | 0 | 1 | 106.2 | 110 | 89 | 73 | 11 | 9 | 79 | 2 | 71 | 12 |
| Milacki, Hagerstown | 3 | 2 | .600 | 2.66 | 7 | 7 | 1 | 0 | 0 | 0 | 40.2 | 32 | 16 | 12 | 1 | 2 | 22 | 0 | 37 | 0 |
| Moore, Kinston | 0 | 2 | .000 | 11.57 | 4 | 0 | 0 | 1 | 0 | 0 | 4.2 | 8 | 7 | 6 | 3 | 0 | 3 | 0 | 5 | 0 |
| Morelock, Durham | 4 | 4 | .500 | 3.40 | 28 | 0 | 0 | 16 | 0 | 4 | 42.1 | 40 | 22 | 16 | 1 | 2 | 26 | 2 | 36 | 5 |
| Morris, Durham | 6 | 10 | .375 | 3.65 | 26 | 22 | 5 | 3 | 1 | 0 | 150.1 | 152 | 83 | 61 | 17 | 1 | 51 | 2 | 77 | 8 |
| Morrow, Prince William | 3 | 5 | .375 | 1.33 | 34 | 0 | 0 | 28 | 0 | 11 | 54.0 | 33 | 12 | 8 | 1 | 3 | 15 | 2 | 67 | 3 |
| Mortimer, Salem* | 1 | 0 | 1.000 | 3.38 | 4 | 0 | 0 | 3 | 0 | 0 | 13.1 | 13 | 11 | 5 | 1 | 0 | 10 | 1 | 8 | 1 |
| Morton, Peninsula* | 9 | 5 | .643 | 4.31 | 32 | 14 | 0 | 5 | 0 | 0 | 102.1 | 115 | 71 | 49 | 11 | 2 | 50 | 2 | 58 | 3 |
| Moyer, Winston-Salem* | 8 | 2 | .800 | 2.30 | 12 | 12 | 6 | 1 | 2 | 0 | 94.0 | 82 | 36 | 24 | 1 | 5 | 22 | 3 | 94 | 0 |
| Neal, Prince William | 1 | 3 | .250 | 3.27 | 18 | 3 | 0 | 6 | 0 | 2 | 41.1 | 31 | 15 | 15 | 3 | 3 | 25 | 2 | 47 | 4 |
| Neidlinger, Prince William | 8 | 13 | .381 | 4.30 | 26 | 26 | 4 | 0 | 0 | 0 | 165.1 | 141 | 86 | 79 | 14 | 7 | 83 | 0 | 143 | 8 |
| Palo, Kinston | 0 | 0 | .000 | 0.00 | 1 | 0 | 0 | 1 | 0 | 0 | 1.0 | 0 | 0 | 0 | 0 | 0 | 2 | 0 | 1 | 0 |
| Pena, Prince William* | 2 | 1 | .667 | 2.86 | 20 | 1 | 0 | 6 | 0 | 3 | 44.0 | 31 | 14 | 14 | 2 | 2 | 21 | 1 | 63 | 4 |
| Peraza, Kinston | 6 | 10 | .375 | 3.20 | 25 | 25 | 2 | 0 | 1 | 0 | 154.2 | 132 | 69 | 55 | 9 | 6 | 72 | 2 | 134 | 5 |
| Phillips, Winston-Salem | 4 | 9 | .308 | 3.74 | 33 | 12 | 1 | 14 | 0 | 3 | 113.0 | 118 | 63 | 47 | 6 | 3 | 25 | 5 | 91 | 2 |
| Powers, Durham | 0 | 0 | .000 | 0.00 | 1 | 0 | 0 | 0 | 0 | 0 | 1.0 | 1 | 0 | 0 | 0 | 0 | 1 | 0 | 1 | 0 |
| Raczka, Hagerstown | 3 | 2 | .600 | 3.32 | 35 | 6 | 1 | 10 | 0 | 3 | 97.2 | 101 | 55 | 36 | 4 | 6 | 48 | 0 | 93 | 12 |
| Reiter, Hagerstown* | 0 | 3 | .000 | 4.18 | 11 | 4 | 1 | 4 | 0 | 1 | 32.1 | 32 | 17 | 15 | 2 | 0 | 11 | 0 | 21 | 2 |
| Reyes, Kinston* | 3 | 5 | .375 | 5.66 | 36 | 6 | 0 | 12 | 0 | 1 | 89.0 | 102 | 62 | 56 | 9 | 5 | 35 | 3 | 57 | 2 |
| Reynolds, Durham | 0 | 0 | .000 | 4.15 | 3 | 0 | 0 | 3 | 0 | 0 | 4.1 | 7 | 2 | 2 | 0 | 0 | 1 | 0 | 0 | 0 |
| Rogers, Durham | 5 | 7 | .417 | 4.63 | 36 | 14 | 1 | 10 | 0 | 4 | 118.2 | 127 | 71 | 61 | 19 | 1 | 33 | 0 | 114 | 2 |
| Romagna, Kinston | 0 | 0 | .000 | 0.00 | 1 | 0 | 0 | 1 | 0 | 0 | 1.0 | 0 | 0 | 0 | 0 | 0 | 1 | 0 | 1 | 1 |
| Rooker, Prince William | 1 | 5 | .167 | 4.23 | 17 | 4 | 0 | 4 | 0 | 1 | 44.2 | 47 | 37 | 21 | 2 | 2 | 42 | 3 | 29 | 12 |
| Rosario, Durham* | 5 | 3 | .625 | 3.19 | 13 | 11 | 2 | 0 | 1 | 0 | 73.1 | 62 | 30 | 26 | 2 | 1 | 34 | 0 | 54 | 5 |
| Russell, Prince William* | 3 | 4 | .429 | 3.65 | 15 | 13 | 1 | 0 | 0 | 0 | 81.1 | 80 | 38 | 33 | 7 | 1 | 39 | 1 | 51 | 3 |
| Santiago, Kinston | 1 | 2 | .333 | 2.17 | 44 | 0 | 0 | 38 | 0 | 16 | 58.0 | 53 | 17 | 14 | 2 | 0 | 23 | 1 | 51 | 1 |
| Schreiber, Durham* | 0 | 2 | .000 | 4.25 | 12 | 1 | 0 | 3 | 0 | 1 | 29.2 | 26 | 18 | 14 | 0 | 1 | 24 | 1 | 25 | 2 |
| Scott, Durham | 0 | 0 | .000 | 2.21 | 4 | 3 | 0 | 0 | 0 | 0 | 20.1 | 17 | 7 | 5 | 0 | 2 | 15 | 0 | 11 | 3 |
| Segura, Kinston | 4 | 13 | .235 | 4.16 | 34 | 15 | 1 | 10 | 1 | 1 | 110.1 | 109 | 62 | 51 | 9 | 7 | 69 | 4 | 73 | 7 |
| Shanks, Kinston | 0 | 0 | .000 | 2.95 | 9 | 0 | 0 | 4 | 0 | 0 | 18.1 | 14 | 8 | 6 | 3 | 1 | 8 | 0 | 14 | 2 |
| Skinner, Hagerstown | 5 | 4 | .556 | 4.50 | 11 | 10 | 2 | 0 | 0 | 0 | 74.0 | 69 | 40 | 37 | 8 | 2 | 16 | 0 | 70 | 4 |
| Slowik, Winston-Salem | 1 | 1 | .500 | 1.04 | 10 | 0 | 0 | 5 | 0 | 1 | 17.1 | 15 | 2 | 2 | 0 | 1 | 7 | 3 | 11 | 4 |
| Smiley, Prince William* | 2 | 2 | .500 | 5.14 | 10 | 10 | 0 | 0 | 0 | 0 | 56.0 | 64 | 36 | 32 | 3 | 4 | 27 | 0 | 45 | 3 |
| Stanhope, Hagerstown | 0 | 0 | .000 | 3.86 | 2 | 0 | 0 | 1 | 0 | 0 | 4.2 | 5 | 2 | 2 | 0 | 0 | 0 | 0 | 4 | 0 |
| Steirer, Hagerstown | 8 | 3 | .727 | 2.23 | 13 | 13 | 3 | 0 | 0 | 0 | 88.2 | 84 | 24 | 22 | 4 | 5 | 20 | 0 | 69 | 1 |
| Stephenson, Kinston | 1 | 0 | 1.000 | 3.86 | 4 | 0 | 0 | 2 | 0 | 0 | 7.0 | 9 | 5 | 3 | 1 | 0 | 1 | 0 | 7 | 1 |
| Summers, Hagerstown | 0 | 6 | .000 | 7.67 | 8 | 6 | 1 | 0 | 0 | 0 | 29.1 | 35 | 26 | 25 | 2 | 0 | 25 | 0 | 19 | 2 |
| Talamantez, Hagerstown | 3 | 1 | .500 | 4.75 | 10 | 10 | 1 | 0 | 0 | 0 | 47.1 | 46 | 30 | 25 | 2 | 1 | 46 | 0 | 38 | 8 |
| Thomas, Salem | 3 | 1 | .750 | 1.82 | 5 | 5 | 1 | 0 | 0 | 0 | 34.2 | 27 | 8 | 7 | 4 | 1 | 18 | 0 | 19 | 2 |
| Tomsick, Durham | 4 | 3 | .571 | 3.82 | 17 | 10 | 1 | 0 | 0 | 0 | 63.2 | 57 | 34 | 27 | 5 | 4 | 31 | 0 | 32 | 6 |
| True, Peninsula* | 1 | 4 | .200 | 4.09 | 7 | 6 | 0 | 0 | 0 | 0 | 33.0 | 33 | 20 | 15 | 2 | 0 | 18 | 1 | 27 | 4 |
| Weatherford, Peninsula | 2 | 4 | .333 | 4.42 | 14 | 8 | 0 | 2 | 0 | 0 | 53.0 | 54 | 34 | 26 | 2 | 1 | 22 | 0 | 44 | 4 |
| Weston, Lynchburg | 6 | 5 | .545 | 2.15 | 49 | 3 | 1 | 24 | 1 | 10 | 100.1 | 81 | 29 | 24 | 4 | 0 | 22 | 2 | 62 | 4 |
| Williams, Salem* | 6 | 9 | .400 | 5.45 | 22 | 21 | 1 | 1 | 0 | 0 | 99.0 | 57 | 64 | 60 | 6 | 6 | 117 | 0 | 138 | 12 |
| Wilson, Hagerstown | 5 | 4 | .556 | 4.06 | 21 | 9 | 6 | 0 | 1 | 0 | 64.1 | 78 | 39 | 29 | 3 | 2 | 35 | 0 | 44 | 4 |
| Winbush, Salem | 8 | 6 | .571 | 3.30 | 25 | 22 | 1 | 2 | 0 | 1 | 133.2 | 90 | 66 | 49 | 0 | 8 | 109 | 2 | 119 | 25 |
| Wyatt, Lynchburg | 8 | 1 | .889 | 1.47 | 9 | 9 | 4 | 0 | 2 | 0 | 67.1 | 51 | 12 | 11 | 1 | 1 | 13 | 0 | 51 | 2 |

BALKS—Jackson, 7; Cox, D. Jones, 5 each; G. Bell, Maye, Morris, 4 each; Bencomo, Blankenship, Cunningham, Frohwirth, Kopf, Moyer, Winbush, 3 each; Barton, Bianchi, Clemons, Dickman, Edens, Gordon, Groves, Hamilton, Harrington, Holman, Klink, Knapp, Lenderman, Lind,

Pena, Skinner, Smiley, Tomsick, Wyatt, 2 each; Barger, Bass, Bautista, Bergendahl, Brewer, Chambers, Dobie, Dombek, Egelston, Grudzinski, Hartman, Hartshorn, Heise, Hester, Hixon, Householder, Kilgus, McClanahan, McKelvey, Mesa, Morrow, Peraza, Phillips, Raczka, Reiter, Reyes, Rooker, Segura, Steirer, Talamantez, Thomas, Weston, Williams, 1 each.

COMBINATION SHUTOUTS—Tomsick-Rogers-Santiago, Durham; Wilson-Egelston, Skinner-Dooner, Wilson-Dooner, Steirer-Raczka, Steirer-Leiter, Hagerstown; Bencomo-Lychak 2, Segura-Lychak 2, Castillo-Dickman, Bencomo-McKay, Peraza-Lychak, Castro-McKay, Castillo-Reyes, Kinston; Jensen-Burns, Edens-Innis, Hartshorn-Gay-Klink-Innis, Bergendahl-Klink, Brown-Klink, Jensen-Innis, Lynchburg; Dombek-McLarnon, Morton-McLarnon, Jackson-McLarnon, Weatherford-McLarnon, Chambers-McLarnon, Morton-Frohwirth, Knox-Frohwirth, Jackson-Morton-McClanahan-Householder, Peninsula; Neidlinger-Ba. Jones, O. Lind-Morrow, Gordon-Pena, Prince William; Hallgren-Coatney, Williams-Harman, Williams-Hartman, Salem; Kopf-Lenderman, Winston-Salem.

NO-HIT GAME—Bautista, Lynchburg, defeated Prince William, 6-0 (first game), May 26.

# Florida State League

## CLASS A

### CHAMPIONSHIP WINNERS IN PREVIOUS YEARS

| Year | Club | Pct. |
|---|---|---|
| 1919 | Sanford* | .605 |
| | Orlando* | .703 |
| 1920 | Tampa | .654 |
| | Tampa | .722 |
| 1921 | Orlando | .635 |
| 1922 | St. Petersburg | .503 |
| | St. Petersburg | .618 |
| 1923 | Orlando | .667 |
| | Orlando | .678 |
| 1924 | Lakeland | .695 |
| | Lakeland | .683 |
| 1925 | St. Petersburg | .667 |
| | Tampa† | .696 |
| 1926 | Sanford | .647 |
| | Sanford | .623 |
| 1927 | Orlando† | .600 |
| | Miami | .661 |
| 1928-35 | Did not operate. | |
| 1936 | Gainesville | .542 |
| | St. Augustine (4th)† | .492 |
| 1937 | Gainesville§ | .616 |
| 1938 | Leesburg | .626 |
| | Gainesville (2nd)‡ | .615 |
| 1939 | Sanford§ | .787 |
| 1940 | Daytona Beach | .619 |
| | Orlando (4th)‡ | .507 |
| 1941 | St. Augustine | .659 |
| | Leesburg (4th)‡ | .488 |
| 1942-45 | Did not operate. | |
| 1946 | Orlando§ | .681 |
| 1947 | St. Augustine | .625 |
| | Gainesville (2nd)‡ | .584 |
| 1948 | Orlando | .643 |
| | Daytona Beach (2nd)‡ | .616 |
| 1949 | Gainesville | .635 |
| | St. Augustine (3rd)‡ | .556 |
| 1950 | Orlando | .629 |
| | DeLand (3rd)‡ | .590 |
| 1951 | DeLand§ | .643 |
| 1952 | DeLand x | .704 |
| | Palatka (3rd)‡ | .569 |
| 1953 | Daytona Beach† | .657 |
| | DeLand | .703 |
| 1954 | Jacksonville Beach | .629 |
| | Lakeland† | .594 |
| 1955 | Orlando | .671 |
| | Orlando | .643 |
| 1956 | Cocoa | .614 |
| | Cocoa | .671 |
| 1957 | Palatka | .629 |
| | Tampa† | .681 |
| 1958 | St. Petersburg | .732 |
| | St. Petersburg | .681 |
| 1959 | Tampa | .591 |
| | St. Petersburg† | .612 |
| 1960 | Lakeland | .731 |
| | Palatka† | .614 |
| 1961 | Tampa† | .710 |
| | Sarasota | .696 |
| 1962 | Sarasota | .689 |
| | Fort Lauderdale† | .623 |
| 1963 | Sarasota | .645 |
| | Sarasota | .667 |
| 1964 | Fort Lauderdale† | .629 |
| | St. Petersburg | .594 |
| 1965 | Fort Lauderdale | .627 |
| | Fort Lauderdale | .634 |
| 1966 | Leesburg† | .781 |
| | St. Petersburg | .700 |
| 1967 | St. Petersburg y | .691 |
| | Orlando | .638 |
| 1968 | Miami | .613 |
| | Orlando z | .579 |
| 1969 | Miami a | .606 |
| | Orlando | .606 |
| 1970 | Miami b | .662 |
| | St. Petersburg | .600 |
| 1971 | Miami b | .667 |
| | Daytona Beach | .586 |
| 1972 | Miami c | .562 |
| | Daytona Beach | .606 |
| 1973 | St. Petersburg d | .575 |
| | West Palm Beach | .580 |
| 1974 | West Palm Beach d | .598 |
| | Fort Lauderdale | .626 |
| 1975 | St. Petersburg d | .652 |
| | Miami | .581 |
| 1976 | Tampa | .559 |
| | Lakeland d | .536 |
| 1977 | Lakeland d | .616 |
| | West Palm Beach | .583 |
| 1978 | Lakeland | .565 |
| | Miami§ | .539 |
| 1979 | Fort Lauderdale | .643 |
| | Winter Haven e | .577 |
| 1980 | Daytona Beach | .628 |
| | Fort Lauderdale d | .606 |
| 1981 | Fort Myers | .554 |
| | Daytona Beach f | .504 |
| 1982 | Fort Lauderdale f | .621 |
| | Tampa | .546 |
| 1983 | Daytona Beach | .634 |
| | Vero Beach f | .515 |
| 1984 | Tampa | .532 |
| | Fort Lauderdale f | .521 |

*Split-season playoff abandoned after each team won three games. †Won split-season playoff. ‡Won four-club playoff. §Won championship and four-club playoff. xWon both halves of split season. yLeague divided into Eastern and Western divisions with split season. St. Petersburg and Orlando won both halves of split season; St. Petersburg won playoff. zLeague divided into Eastern and Western divisions. Miami won regular-season pennant on basis of highest won-lost percentage. Orlando won four-club playoff involving first two teams in each division. aLeague divided into Southern and Central divisions. Miami won playoff between division leaders. (NOTE—Pennant awarded to playoff winner in 1936.) bLeague divided into Eastern and Western divisions. Miami won regular-season pennant on basis of highest won-loss percentage, and also won four-club playoff involving first two teams in each division. cLeague divided into Eastern and Western divisions. Won four-club playoff involving first two teams in each division. dLeague divided into Northern and Southern divisions. Won four-club playoff involving first two teams in each division. eLeague divided into Northern and Southern divisions. Same two clubs won both halves; won playoffs. fWon split-season playoff.

### STANDING OF CLUBS AT CLOSE OF SEASON, AUGUST 29

#### WESTERN DIVISION

| Club | W. | L. | T. | Pct. | G.B. |
|---|---|---|---|---|---|
| Fort Myers (Royals) | 82 | 57 | 0 | .590 | ........ |
| St. Petersburg (Cardinals) | 78 | 62 | 0 | .557 | 4½ |
| Tampa (Reds) | 73 | 62 | 0 | .541 | 7 |
| Clearwater (Phillies) | 69 | 72 | 0 | .489 | 14 |

#### SOUTHERN DIVISION

| Club | W. | L. | T. | Pct. | G.B. |
|---|---|---|---|---|---|
| Fort Lauderdale (Yankees) | 77 | 63 | 0 | .550 | ........ |
| West Palm Beach (Expos) | 74 | 66 | 0 | .529 | 3 |
| Vero Beach (Dodgers) | 67 | 73 | 0 | .479 | 10 |
| Miami (Independent) | 58 | 83 | 0 | .411 | 19½ |

#### CENTRAL DIVISION

| Club | W. | L. | T. | Pct. | G.B. |
|---|---|---|---|---|---|
| Osceola (Astros) | 77 | 58 | 0 | .570 | ........ |
| Winter Haven (Red Sox) | 71 | 68 | 0 | .511 | 8 |
| Lakeland (Tigers) | 56 | 84 | 0 | .400 | 23½ |
| Daytona Beach (Co-op) | 53 | 87 | 0 | .379 | 26½ |

### COMPOSITE STANDING OF CLUBS AT CLOSE OF SEASON, AUGUST 29

| Club | Ft.M. | Osc. | St.P. | Ft.L. | Tam. | WPB | WH | Clw. | V.B. | Mia. | Lak. | Day. | W. | L. | T. | Pct. | G.B. |
|---|---|---|---|---|---|---|---|---|---|---|---|---|---|---|---|---|---|
| Fort Myers (Royals) | .... | 3 | 13 | 4 | 13 | 4 | 4 | 18 | 4 | 5 | 7 | 7 | 82 | 57 | 0 | .590 | ........ |
| Osceola (Astros) | 5 | .... | 0 | 4 | 4 | 4 | 12 | 3 | 6 | 4 | 17 | 18 | 77 | 58 | 0 | .570 | 3 |
| St. Petersburg (Cardinals) | 13 | 8 | .... | 5 | 12 | 1 | 2 | 15 | 4 | 6 | 7 | 5 | 78 | 62 | 0 | .557 | 4½ |
| Fort Lauderdale (Yankees) | 4 | 3 | 2 | .... | 4 | 13 | 6 | 4 | 16 | 18 | 3 | 4 | 77 | 63 | 0 | .550 | 5½ |
| Tampa (Reds) | 13 | 1 | 14 | 4 | .... | 4 | 5 | 17 | 4 | 3 | 4 | 4 | 73 | 62 | 0 | .541 | 7 |
| West Palm Beach (Expos) | 4 | 3 | 7 | 13 | 3 | .... | 4 | 2 | 11 | 16 | 5 | 6 | 74 | 66 | 0 | .529 | 8½ |
| Winter Haven (Red Sox) | 3 | 13 | 5 | 2 | 3 | 4 | .... | 3 | 4 | 3 | 15 | 16 | 71 | 68 | 0 | .511 | 11 |
| Clearwater (Phillies) | 8 | 4 | 11 | 4 | 9 | 6 | 5 | .... | 6 | 5 | 8 | 3 | 69 | 72 | 0 | .489 | 14 |
| Vero Beach (Dodgers) | 2 | 2 | 4 | 10 | 4 | 15 | 4 | 2 | .... | 18 | 3 | 3 | 67 | 73 | 0 | .479 | 15½ |
| Miami (Independent) | 3 | 4 | 2 | 8 | 5 | 10 | 5 | 3 | 8 | .... | 5 | 5 | 58 | 83 | 0 | .411 | 25 |
| Lakeland (Tigers) | 1 | 9 | 1 | 5 | 3 | 3 | 11 | 0 | 5 | 2 | .... | 16 | 56 | 84 | 0 | .400 | 26½ |
| Daytona Beach (Co-op) | 1 | 8 | 3 | 4 | 2 | 2 | 10 | 5 | 5 | 3 | 10 | .... | 53 | 87 | 0 | .379 | 29½ |

Major league affiliations in parentheses.

Playoffs—Fort Lauderdale defeated Osceola, two games to one; Fort Myers defeated St. Petersburg, two games to one; Fort Myers defeated Fort Lauderdale, three games to one, to win league championship.

Regular-Season Attendance—Clearwater, 44,081; Daytona Beach, 30,736; Fort Lauderdale, 52,115; Fort Myers, 46,163; Lakeland, 50,229; Miami, 32,321; Osceola, 38,082; St. Petersburg, 136,689; Tampa, 60,764; Vero Beach, 81,800; West Palm Beach, 114,659; Winter Haven, 18,788. Total—706,827. Total Playoff Attendance—5,589. All-Star Game Attendance at Fort Myers—991.

Managers—Clearwater, Ramon Aviles; Daytona Beach, Jim Hutto; Fort Lauderdale, Bucky Dent; Fort Myers, Duane Gustavson; Lakeland, Jerry Grote (thru May 19) and Moby Benedict (May 20 thru end of season); Miami, Tommy Burgess (thru May 24) and Jim Essian (May 25 thru end of season); Osceola, Dave Cripe; St. Petersburg, Dave Bialas; Tampa, Marc Bombard; Vero Beach, Stan Wasiak; West Palm Beach, Junior Minor; Winter Haven, Dave Holt.

All-Star Team—1B—Jack Daugherty, West Palm Beach; 2B—Carson Carroll, Miami; 3B—Ken Caminiti, Osceola; SS—Jody Reed, Winter Haven; C—Marty Pevey, St. Petersburg and Joe Oliver, Tampa; LF—Pete Camelo, West Palm Beach; CF—Jay Buhner, Fort Lauderdale; RF—Darren Reed, Fort Lauderdale; DH—Steve DeAngelis, Clearwater; RHP—Scott Young, St. Petersburg and Andy Araujo, Winter Haven; LHP—Cliff Young, West Palm Beach and Rob Mallicoat, Osceola; Relief Pitcher—Jeff Gray, Clearwater and Mark Baker, Osceola; Most Valuable Player—Jack Daugherty, West Palm Beach; Manager of the Year—Dave Bialas, St. Petersburg.

(Compiled by Howe News Bureau, Boston, Mass.)

## CLUB BATTING

| Club | Pct. | G. | AB. | R. | OR. | H. | TB. | 2B. | 3B. | HR. | RBI. | GW. | SH. | SF. | HP. | BB. | Int. BB. | SO. | SB. | CS. | LOB. |
|---|---|---|---|---|---|---|---|---|---|---|---|---|---|---|---|---|---|---|---|---|---|
| Fort Lauderdale | .259 | 140 | 4452 | 652 | 533 | 1151 | 1636 | 187 | 56 | 62 | 565 | 68 | 28 | 44 | 30 | 572 | 20 | 844 | 172 | 70 | 983 |
| Fort Myers | .258 | 139 | 4473 | 607 | 465 | 1156 | 1447 | 158 | 35 | 21 | 497 | 68 | 18 | 49 | 22 | 626 | 19 | 817 | 276 | 102 | 1034 |
| St. Petersburg | .258 | 140 | 4519 | 536 | 431 | 1165 | 1471 | 162 | 45 | 18 | 467 | 66 | 60 | 42 | 17 | 534 | 39 | 613 | 85 | 63 | 1067 |
| Vero Beach | .254 | 140 | 4491 | 538 | 513 | 1139 | 1468 | 161 | 51 | 22 | 454 | 55 | 61 | 46 | 67 | 440 | 31 | 679 | 112 | 66 | 1015 |
| West Palm Beach | .251 | 140 | 4410 | 591 | 588 | 1105 | 1481 | 164 | 22 | 56 | 530 | 65 | 57 | 50 | 32 | 629 | 40 | 744 | 153 | 68 | 1056 |
| Tampa | .247 | 135 | 4254 | 513 | 485 | 1050 | 1391 | 143 | 39 | 40 | 463 | 63 | 56 | 52 | 30 | 546 | 32 | 776 | 122 | 47 | 1006 |
| Winter Haven | .245 | 139 | 4495 | 536 | 502 | 1103 | 1465 | 173 | 30 | 43 | 475 | 64 | 29 | 42 | 21 | 520 | 33 | 739 | 116 | 71 | 978 |
| Osceola | .244 | 135 | 4282 | 625 | 536 | 1044 | 1408 | 163 | 57 | 29 | 532 | 66 | 33 | 57 | 27 | 583 | 21 | 684 | 147 | 66 | 922 |
| Lakeland | .242 | 140 | 4517 | 523 | 701 | 1095 | 1418 | 153 | 40 | 30 | 459 | 52 | 29 | 32 | 21 | 486 | 21 | 852 | 80 | 43 | 1003 |
| Daytona Beach | .239 | 140 | 4336 | 474 | 649 | 1036 | 1281 | 127 | 38 | 14 | 397 | 44 | 60 | 29 | 32 | 560 | 18 | 766 | 163 | 76 | 995 |
| Clearwater | .239 | 141 | 4545 | 517 | 555 | 1085 | 1448 | 172 | 37 | 39 | 443 | 58 | 43 | 37 | 35 | 391 | 35 | 810 | 189 | 99 | 894 |
| Miami | .229 | 141 | 4393 | 477 | 631 | 1005 | 1301 | 153 | 37 | 23 | 403 | 45 | 92 | 31 | 20 | 475 | 17 | 742 | 196 | 79 | 905 |

## INDIVIDUAL BATTING
(Leading Qualifiers for Batting Championship—378 or More Plate Appearances)

*Bats lefthanded.     †Switch-hitter.

| Player and Club | Pct. | G. | AB. | R. | H. | TB. | 2B. | 3B. | HR. | RBI. | GW. | SH. | SF. | HP. | BB. | Int. BB. | SO. | SB. | CS. |
|---|---|---|---|---|---|---|---|---|---|---|---|---|---|---|---|---|---|---|---|
| Reed, Jody, Winter Haven | .321 | 134 | 489 | 95 | 157 | 184 | 25 | 1 | 0 | 45 | 6 | 4 | 4 | 1 | 94 | 2 | 26 | 16 | 11 |
| Reed, Darren, Fort Lauderdale | .317 | 100 | 369 | 63 | 117 | 176 | 21 | 4 | 10 | 61 | 10 | 0 | 7 | 7 | 36 | 3 | 56 | 13 | 3 |
| Daugherty, John, West Palm Beach† | .316 | 133 | 481 | 76 | 152 | 213 | 25 | 3 | 10 | 87 | 13 | 0 | 5 | 0 | 75 | 11 | 58 | 33 | 6 |
| Seitzer, Kevin, Fort Myers | .314 | 90 | 290 | 61 | 91 | 120 | 10 | 5 | 3 | 46 | 5 | 0 | 5 | 2 | 85 | 4 | 30 | 28 | 7 |
| Thurman, Gary, Fort Myers | .302 | 134 | 453 | 68 | 137 | 164 | 9 | 9 | 0 | 45 | 5 | 3 | 4 | 4 | 68 | 1 | 93 | 70 | 18 |
| Buhner, Jay, Fort Lauderdale | .296 | 117 | 409 | 65 | 121 | 192 | 18 | 10 | 11 | 76 | 15 | 1 | 4 | 2 | 65 | 4 | 76 | 6 | 4 |
| Pevey, Marty, St. Petersburg* | .290 | 104 | 393 | 48 | 114 | 143 | 12 | 4 | 3 | 41 | 8 | 2 | 2 | 1 | 28 | 6 | 56 | 5 | 2 |
| Nunez, Mauricio, St. Petersburg | .290 | 128 | 438 | 50 | 127 | 163 | 22 | 4 | 2 | 46 | 6 | 10 | 1 | 2 | 38 | 1 | 66 | 5 | 7 |
| Berge, Jordan, Tampa* | .289 | 132 | 477 | 57 | 138 | 185 | 20 | 3 | 7 | 86 | 7 | 1 | 10 | 2 | 66 | 5 | 29 | 8 | 3 |
| Jacobo, Edward, Vero Beach | .287 | 112 | 376 | 42 | 108 | 147 | 19 | 4 | 4 | 58 | 10 | 2 | 6 | 2 | 39 | 5 | 68 | 2 | 5 |
| Weinberger, Gary, West Palm Beach* | .285 | 138 | 554 | 81 | 158 | 193 | 19 | 2 | 4 | 55 | 6 | 5 | 8 | 5 | 51 | 3 | 55 | 23 | 15 |

Departmental Leaders: G—Jordan, 139; AB—Weinberger, 554; R—J. Reed, 95; H—Weinberger, 158; TB—Daugherty, 213; 2B—DeAngelis, 32; 3B—Kelly, 13; HR—DeAngelis, 16; RBI—Daugherty, 87; GWRBI—Buhner, 15; SH—Carroll, 15; SF—Berge, O'Dell, 10; HP—Francois, 17; BB—J. Reed, 94; IBB—M. Harris, 12; SO—Shumate, 112; SB—Thurman, 70; CS—Mabe, 20.

(All Players—Listed Alphabetically)

| Player and Club | Pct. | G. | AB. | R. | H. | TB. | 2B. | 3B. | HR. | RBI. | GW. | SH. | SF. | HP. | BB. | Int. BB. | SO. | SB. | CS. |
|---|---|---|---|---|---|---|---|---|---|---|---|---|---|---|---|---|---|---|---|
| Abner, Benjamin, West Palm Beach | .190 | 86 | 231 | 19 | 44 | 60 | 9 | 2 | 1 | 25 | 2 | 2 | 4 | 1 | 14 | 2 | 33 | 0 | 4 |
| Afenir, Troy, Osceola | .248 | 99 | 323 | 38 | 80 | 119 | 19 | 1 | 6 | 41 | 6 | 2 | 2 | 0 | 20 | 1 | 86 | 3 | 1 |
| Agostinelli, Salvatore, St. Pete | .270 | 98 | 326 | 34 | 88 | 99 | 11 | 0 | 0 | 43 | 4 | 2 | 4 | 1 | 28 | 1 | 23 | 5 | 2 |
| Allaire, Karl, Osceola* | .211 | 107 | 289 | 41 | 61 | 79 | 8 | 5 | 0 | 16 | 3 | 7 | 3 | 0 | 39 | 0 | 46 | 8 | 5 |
| Allen, Edward, Fort Myers | .305 | 72 | 256 | 40 | 78 | 102 | 11 | 5 | 1 | 35 | 6 | 1 | 4 | 2 | 37 | 3 | 54 | 25 | 11 |
| Altobelli, John, Miami* | .114 | 15 | 35 | 5 | 4 | 4 | 0 | 0 | 0 | 0 | 0 | 1 | 0 | 0 | 6 | 0 | 5 | 2 | 1 |
| Amante, Thomas, St. Petersburg | .272 | 20 | 81 | 9 | 22 | 35 | 5 | 1 | 2 | 5 | 1 | 0 | 0 | 0 | 5 | 0 | 13 | 0 | 0 |
| Amble, Robyn, Daytona Beach† | .269 | 126 | 432 | 37 | 116 | 138 | 19 | 0 | 1 | 46 | 6 | 3 | 4 | 6 | 41 | 3 | 71 | 7 | 5 |
| Amity, Christopher, Miami | .308 | 4 | 13 | 2 | 4 | 4 | 0 | 0 | 0 | 2 | 0 | 0 | 0 | 0 | 1 | 0 | 0 | 0 | 0 |
| Antone, Ralph, West Palm Beach | .221 | 98 | 271 | 32 | 60 | 82 | 11 | 1 | 3 | 41 | 4 | 2 | 4 | 0 | 52 | 3 | 48 | 0 | 2 |
| Antonio, Ramon, Vero Beach† | .200 | 2 | 5 | 1 | 1 | 2 | 1 | 0 | 0 | 0 | 0 | 0 | 0 | 0 | 0 | 0 | 1 | 0 | 0 |
| Aquino, Fausto, Daytona Beach* | .364 | 17 | 33 | 5 | 12 | 14 | 2 | 0 | 0 | 0 | 0 | 0 | 0 | 0 | 0 | 0 | 7 | 4 | 1 |
| Arzola, Ricardo, St. Petersburg* | .291 | 103 | 306 | 48 | 89 | 115 | 16 | 5 | 0 | 28 | 3 | 5 | 0 | 4 | 57 | 2 | 51 | 7 | 12 |
| Bachman, Kent, West Palm Beach | .227 | 116 | 366 | 49 | 83 | 107 | 11 | 5 | 1 | 27 | 5 | 4 | 4 | 2 | 45 | 0 | 85 | 10 | 1 |
| Bacon, Ernest, Tampa | .125 | 36 | 8 | 1 | 1 | 1 | 0 | 0 | 0 | 1 | 1 | 0 | 0 | 1 | 0 | 0 | 5 | 0 | 0 |
| Baker, Mark, Osceola | .333 | 46 | 3 | 0 | 1 | 1 | 0 | 0 | 0 | 1 | 1 | 0 | 0 | 0 | 0 | 0 | 1 | 0 | 0 |
| Balcomb, Alan, St. Petersburg† | .202 | 52 | 104 | 8 | 21 | 23 | 2 | 0 | 0 | 10 | 0 | 4 | 0 | 0 | 26 | 4 | 10 | 2 | 1 |
| Barker, Timothy, West Palm Beach | .221 | 32 | 113 | 17 | 25 | 28 | 1 | 1 | 0 | 2 | 0 | 1 | 0 | 1 | 15 | 0 | 11 | 17 | 3 |
| Batista, Juan, West Palm Beach | .208 | 13 | 24 | 1 | 5 | 7 | 2 | 0 | 0 | 1 | 0 | 0 | 0 | 0 | 2 | 0 | 6 | 1 | 0 |
| Bautista, Bienvenido, Daytona B.* | .267 | 24 | 75 | 10 | 20 | 21 | 1 | 0 | 0 | 5 | 1 | 0 | 1 | 1 | 6 | 0 | 18 | 5 | 4 |
| Beamesderfer, Kurt, Daytona B. | .224 | 89 | 272 | 36 | 61 | 78 | 9 | 1 | 2 | 31 | 2 | 4 | 3 | 3 | 40 | 1 | 56 | 5 | 8 |
| Behrend, Michael, St. Petersburg | .000 | 9 | 1 | 0 | 0 | 0 | 0 | 0 | 0 | 0 | 0 | 0 | 0 | 0 | 1 | 0 | 0 | 0 | 0 |
| Bellver, Juan, Miami | .257 | 41 | 70 | 10 | 18 | 22 | 4 | 0 | 0 | 5 | 0 | 5 | 0 | 1 | 5 | 0 | 5 | 1 | 2 |
| Berge, Jordan, Tampa* | .289 | 132 | 477 | 57 | 138 | 185 | 20 | 3 | 7 | 86 | 7 | 1 | 10 | 2 | 66 | 5 | 29 | 8 | 3 |
| Beringhele, Vincent, Vero Beach | .235 | 42 | 98 | 12 | 23 | 27 | 4 | 0 | 0 | 8 | 1 | 0 | 1 | 1 | 18 | 1 | 20 | 2 | 2 |
| Bernaldo, Richard, Fort Lauderdale | .200 | 16 | 25 | 4 | 5 | 6 | 1 | 0 | 0 | 2 | 1 | 0 | 0 | 0 | 6 | 0 | 2 | 0 | 0 |
| Birriel, Jose, Winter Haven* | .242 | 123 | 454 | 41 | 110 | 158 | 22 | 1 | 8 | 76 | 13 | 1 | 9 | 2 | 47 | 7 | 67 | 0 | 2 |
| Blaser, Mark, Fort Lauderdale | .291 | 53 | 175 | 24 | 51 | 73 | 13 | 0 | 3 | 30 | 0 | 0 | 0 | 0 | 26 | 0 | 28 | 0 | 2 |
| Blunt, Bradley, St. Petersburg | .000 | 4 | 4 | 0 | 0 | 0 | 0 | 0 | 0 | 0 | 0 | 1 | 0 | 0 | 0 | 0 | 1 | 0 | 0 |
| Bochesa, Gregory, Winter Haven | .243 | 42 | 111 | 11 | 27 | 39 | 6 | 0 | 2 | 11 | 1 | 1 | 2 | 1 | 26 | 1 | 23 | 2 | 2 |
| Bogener, Terry, Miami* | .311 | 48 | 161 | 28 | 50 | 71 | 10 | 4 | 1 | 19 | 2 | 0 | 3 | 1 | 27 | 2 | 19 | 10 | 0 |
| Boling, John, Lakeland* | .000 | 14 | 1 | 0 | 0 | 0 | 0 | 0 | 0 | 0 | 0 | 0 | 0 | 0 | 0 | 0 | 0 | 0 | 0 |
| Boudreaux, Eric, Clearwater | .000 | 14 | 6 | 1 | 0 | 0 | 0 | 0 | 0 | 0 | 0 | 3 | 0 | 0 | 1 | 0 | 1 | 0 | 0 |
| Braukmiller, Kurt, West Palm Beach. | .000 | 20 | 2 | 0 | 0 | 0 | 0 | 0 | 0 | 0 | 0 | 0 | 0 | 0 | 1 | 0 | 1 | 0 | 0 |
| Breedlove, Larry, St. Petersburg | .266 | 97 | 316 | 46 | 84 | 96 | 8 | 2 | 0 | 27 | 5 | 3 | 0 | 1 | 48 | 1 | 36 | 6 | 3 |
| Brennan, William, Vero Beach | .071 | 22 | 14 | 1 | 1 | 1 | 0 | 0 | 0 | 2 | 0 | 2 | 0 | 0 | 2 | 0 | 3 | 0 | 0 |

| Player and Club | Pct. | G. | AB. | R. | H. | TB. | 2B. | 3B. | HR. | RBI. | GW. | SH. | SF. | HP. | BB. | Int. BB. | SO. | SB. | CS. |
|---|---|---|---|---|---|---|---|---|---|---|---|---|---|---|---|---|---|---|---|
| Brisco, Jamie, St. Petersburg | .083 | 29 | 12 | 1 | 1 | 1 | 0 | 0 | 0 | 0 | 0 | 0 | 0 | 2 | 0 | 7 | 0 | 0 |
| Brown, Jeffrey, Fort Myers | .206 | 61 | 180 | 16 | 37 | 50 | 6 | 2 | 1 | 29 | 6 | 0 | 5 | 1 | 18 | 0 | 34 | 1 | 1 |
| Bryant, John, Tampa | .252 | 121 | 404 | 73 | 102 | 121 | 14 | 1 | 1 | 30 | 9 | 4 | 4 | 10 | 91 | 5 | 62 | 27 | 6 |
| Buhner, Jay, Fort Lauderdale | .296 | 117 | 409 | 65 | 121 | 192 | 18 | 10 | 11 | 76 | 15 | 1 | 4 | 2 | 65 | 4 | 76 | 6 | 4 |
| Burke, Curtis, Osceola | .241 | 86 | 274 | 43 | 66 | 95 | 14 | 3 | 3 | 40 | 6 | 1 | 4 | 4 | 39 | 2 | 51 | 3 | 2 |
| Caffrey, Robert, West Palm Beach | .244 | 110 | 315 | 37 | 77 | 118 | 14 | 0 | 9 | 58 | 5 | 2 | 4 | 3 | 57 | 3 | 88 | 4 | 2 |
| Camelo, Peter, West Palm Beach° | .271 | 131 | 432 | 59 | 117 | 187 | 21 | 2 | 15 | 68 | 7 | 3 | 3 | 2 | 85 | 4 | 89 | 13 | 11 |
| Camilli, Kevin, Winter Haven° | .152 | 35 | 66 | 4 | 10 | 11 | 1 | 0 | 0 | 6 | 0 | 1 | 2 | 0 | 6 | 1 | 21 | 0 | 0 |
| Caminiti, Kenneth, Osceola† | .284 | 126 | 468 | 83 | 133 | 189 | 26 | 9 | 4 | 73 | 11 | 1 | 6 | 1 | 51 | 5 | 54 | 14 | 4 |
| Campbell, Michael, Tampa | .167 | 23 | 12 | 2 | 2 | 2 | 0 | 0 | 0 | 3 | 1 | 2 | 1 | 0 | 2 | 0 | 3 | 0 | 0 |
| Carpenter, Douglas, Fort Lauderdale. | .232 | 40 | 99 | 18 | 23 | 31 | 5 | 0 | 1 | 14 | 1 | 0 | 5 | 2 | 24 | 0 | 20 | 4 | 1 |
| Carrasco, Ernest, St. Petersburg | .071 | 33 | 14 | 2 | 1 | 2 | 1 | 0 | 0 | 0 | 0 | 1 | 0 | 0 | 2 | 0 | 4 | 0 | 0 |
| Carroll, Carson, Miami | .273 | 126 | 454 | 63 | 124 | 149 | 12 | 5 | 1 | 56 | 10 | 15 | 4 | 3 | 54 | 2 | 65 | 45 | 9 |
| Carson, Henry, St. Petersburg | .154 | 27 | 13 | 0 | 2 | 2 | 0 | 0 | 0 | 1 | 0 | 0 | 0 | 0 | 2 | 0 | 3 | 0 | 0 |
| Cash, Timothy, Osceola | .400 | 37 | 5 | 1 | 2 | 3 | 1 | 0 | 0 | 0 | 0 | 0 | 0 | 0 | 0 | 0 | 1 | 0 | 0 |
| Cathcart, Gary, Fort Lauderdale° | .250 | 76 | 256 | 35 | 64 | 78 | 8 | 3 | 0 | 24 | 2 | 0 | 1 | 2 | 31 | 4 | 44 | 7 | 4 |
| Cecchini, James, West Palm Beach | .182 | 11 | 11 | 0 | 2 | 2 | 0 | 0 | 0 | 1 | 0 | 0 | 0 | 0 | 0 | 0 | 4 | 0 | 0 |
| Cerefin, Michael, Osceola° | .000 | 26 | 4 | 0 | 0 | 0 | 0 | 0 | 0 | 0 | 0 | 1 | 0 | 0 | 2 | 0 | 2 | 0 | 0 |
| Charlton, Norman, W. P. Beach† | .000 | 24 | 15 | 1 | 0 | 0 | 0 | 0 | 0 | 1 | 0 | 1 | 0 | 0 | 1 | 0 | 12 | 0 | 0 |
| Cherry, Michael, Vero Beach | .000 | 6 | 6 | 0 | 0 | 0 | 0 | 0 | 0 | 0 | 0 | 1 | 0 | 0 | 0 | 0 | 1 | 0 | 0 |
| Cherry, Paul, St. Petersburg° | .231 | 32 | 13 | 1 | 3 | 3 | 0 | 0 | 0 | 1 | 0 | 1 | 0 | 0 | 1 | 0 | 3 | 0 | 0 |
| Ching, Mauricio, Fort Lauderdale° | .300 | 90 | 293 | 38 | 88 | 134 | 28 | 3 | 4 | 54 | 9 | 1 | 4 | 0 | 47 | 3 | 66 | 9 | 6 |
| Christy, Alexander, Lakeland | .173 | 37 | 139 | 14 | 24 | 40 | 5 | 1 | 3 | 17 | 3 | 1 | 2 | 0 | 10 | 0 | 50 | 1 | 0 |
| Cobb, Robert, West Palm Beach° | .231 | 67 | 182 | 25 | 42 | 49 | 7 | 0 | 0 | 13 | 0 | 7 | 2 | 2 | 24 | 2 | 23 | 3 | 4 |
| Colbert, Cary, Lakeland | .190 | 6 | 21 | 0 | 4 | 4 | 0 | 0 | 0 | 2 | 0 | 1 | 0 | 1 | 4 | 0 | 4 | 0 | 0 |
| Colpitt, Michael, Clearwater | .133 | 11 | 30 | 3 | 4 | 4 | 0 | 0 | 0 | 2 | 0 | 2 | 0 | 0 | 3 | 0 | 6 | 0 | 0 |
| Corbett, Raymond, Daytona Beach | .215 | 36 | 93 | 6 | 20 | 26 | 3 | 0 | 1 | 5 | 1 | 2 | 0 | 0 | 14 | 0 | 22 | 0 | 0 |
| Cornwell, Curtis, Lakeland° | .215 | 69 | 251 | 27 | 54 | 79 | 10 | 6 | 1 | 25 | 6 | 1 | 0 | 2 | 24 | 4 | 54 | 1 | 2 |
| Crone, Raymond, Daytona Beach° | .130 | 30 | 69 | 9 | 9 | 10 | 1 | 0 | 0 | 4 | 0 | 2 | 0 | 0 | 17 | 0 | 19 | 3 | 3 |
| Cruz, Todd, Miami | .222 | 42 | 144 | 12 | 32 | 55 | 6 | 1 | 5 | 21 | 4 | 0 | 2 | 2 | 12 | 2 | 26 | 1 | 2 |
| Cunningham, Joseph, St. Petersburg | .259 | 77 | 224 | 22 | 58 | 71 | 5 | 1 | 2 | 25 | 7 | 1 | 2 | 2 | 34 | 1 | 30 | 0 | 1 |
| Cutshall, William, West Palm Beach° | .000 | 10 | 8 | 0 | 0 | 0 | 0 | 0 | 0 | 0 | 0 | 0 | 0 | 0 | 0 | 0 | 1 | 0 | 0 |
| Daily, Richard, Lakeland† | .177 | 25 | 79 | 6 | 14 | 15 | 1 | 0 | 0 | 4 | 0 | 0 | 1 | 1 | 14 | 0 | 16 | 0 | 1 |
| Dale, Phil, Tampa | .000 | 10 | 2 | 0 | 0 | 0 | 0 | 0 | 0 | 0 | 0 | 0 | 0 | 0 | 0 | 0 | 2 | 0 | 0 |
| Daniel, Clay, Tampa† | .000 | 3 | 3 | 0 | 0 | 0 | 0 | 0 | 0 | 0 | 0 | 0 | 0 | 0 | 0 | 0 | 0 | 0 | 0 |
| Daugherty, John, West Palm Beach† | .316 | 133 | 481 | 76 | 152 | 213 | 25 | 3 | 10 | 87 | 13 | 0 | 5 | 0 | 75 | 11 | 58 | 33 | 6 |
| Davis, Lee, Clearwater° | .167 | 11 | 36 | 2 | 6 | 7 | 1 | 0 | 0 | 0 | 0 | 0 | 0 | 0 | 1 | 0 | 8 | 1 | 1 |
| Davis, Robert, Miami | .222 | 45 | 144 | 20 | 32 | 40 | 2 | 0 | 2 | 12 | 0 | 4 | 0 | 1 | 13 | 0 | 30 | 3 | 4 |
| Day, Michael, West Palm Beach° | .261 | 51 | 142 | 29 | 37 | 53 | 7 | 0 | 3 | 17 | 2 | 2 | 4 | 1 | 51 | 2 | 24 | 1 | 1 |
| DeAngelis, Steven, Clearwater° | .271 | 128 | 450 | 64 | 122 | 212 | 32 | 5 | 16 | 86 | 13 | 0 | 6 | 3 | 57 | 4 | 85 | 8 | 6 |
| DeFrancesco, Anthony, Winter Haven | .240 | 38 | 104 | 7 | 25 | 31 | 3 | 0 | 1 | 5 | 1 | 1 | 0 | 0 | 14 | 1 | 18 | 0 | 0 |
| Delgado, Juan, Osceola | .323 | 29 | 93 | 20 | 30 | 49 | 9 | 5 | 0 | 17 | 3 | 0 | 0 | 1 | 13 | 0 | 9 | 1 | 3 |
| DeLosSantos, Luis, Fort Myers | .264 | 123 | 454 | 44 | 120 | 142 | 18 | 2 | 0 | 48 | 2 | 0 | 6 | 0 | 37 | 2 | 53 | 2 | 2 |
| Dempsay, Adam, Lakeland | .250 | 21 | 64 | 6 | 16 | 19 | 1 | 1 | 0 | 7 | 0 | 0 | 0 | 0 | 3 | 0 | 15 | 0 | 0 |
| Denis, Orlando, Vero Beach | .125 | 5 | 16 | 3 | 2 | 3 | 1 | 0 | 0 | 0 | 0 | 0 | 0 | 0 | 1 | 0 | 3 | 0 | 0 |
| Denny, David, Clearwater | .255 | 55 | 157 | 12 | 40 | 48 | 8 | 0 | 0 | 12 | 1 | 3 | 1 | 0 | 10 | 1 | 34 | 0 | 4 |
| Dixon, William, West Palm Beach | .143 | 9 | 7 | 0 | 1 | 2 | 1 | 0 | 0 | 0 | 0 | 1 | 0 | 0 | 0 | 0 | 5 | 0 | 0 |
| Dodd, Timothy, Tampa | .357 | 19 | 14 | 3 | 5 | 9 | 1 | 0 | 1 | 2 | 0 | 1 | 0 | 0 | 0 | 0 | 3 | 0 | 0 |
| Dube, Gregory, Osceola | .429 | 23 | 7 | 0 | 3 | 3 | 0 | 0 | 0 | 1 | 0 | 0 | 0 | 0 | 2 | 0 | 0 | 0 | 0 |
| Dyrek, David, Osceola° | .163 | 19 | 49 | 7 | 8 | 11 | 1 | 1 | 0 | 7 | 1 | 0 | 1 | 0 | 14 | 0 | 10 | 0 | 0 |
| Edmiston, Craig, Lakeland | .151 | 53 | 159 | 13 | 24 | 33 | 1 | 1 | 2 | 16 | 2 | 3 | 1 | 0 | 17 | 1 | 42 | 0 | 1 |
| Englehart, William, Fort Lauderdale°. | .272 | 38 | 114 | 14 | 31 | 44 | 8 | 1 | 1 | 19 | 1 | 0 | 2 | 0 | 25 | 2 | 23 | 0 | 1 |
| Essian, James, Miami | .200 | 28 | 75 | 8 | 15 | 15 | 0 | 0 | 0 | 6 | 0 | 2 | 0 | 0 | 16 | 0 | 10 | 2 | 1 |
| Estes, Mark, St. Petersburg° | .000 | 13 | 1 | 0 | 0 | 0 | 0 | 0 | 0 | 1 | 0 | 1 | 0 | 0 | 0 | 0 | 1 | 0 | 0 |
| Estrada, Eduardo, Winter Haven | .274 | 114 | 423 | 43 | 116 | 144 | 11 | 7 | 1 | 62 | 11 | 0 | 4 | 1 | 22 | 3 | 67 | 6 | 1 |
| Figueroa, Noel, Miami | .140 | 25 | 43 | 3 | 6 | 7 | 1 | 0 | 0 | 1 | 0 | 2 | 0 | 0 | 4 | 0 | 9 | 0 | 0 |
| Fischer, Jeffrey, West Palm Beach | .250 | 13 | 8 | 1 | 2 | 5 | 0 | 0 | 1 | 2 | 0 | 0 | 1 | 0 | 3 | 0 | 3 | 0 | 0 |
| Flores, Norberto, Vero Beach° | .228 | 135 | 430 | 61 | 98 | 141 | 9 | 11 | 4 | 45 | 2 | 3 | 5 | 2 | 71 | 5 | 68 | 14 | 4 |
| Foli, Timothy, Miami | .250 | 1 | 4 | 0 | 1 | 1 | 0 | 0 | 0 | 0 | 0 | 1 | 0 | 0 | 0 | 0 | 0 | 0 | 0 |
| Fortenberry, Jimmy, Clearwater° | .178 | 27 | 101 | 14 | 18 | 27 | 6 | 0 | 1 | 14 | 1 | 0 | 1 | 1 | 7 | 2 | 18 | 4 | 1 |
| Francois, Manuel, Vero Beach | .277 | 115 | 390 | 70 | 108 | 142 | 13 | 9 | 1 | 38 | 2 | 7 | 1 | 17 | 45 | 1 | 84 | 20 | 18 |
| Freeman, Martin, Lakeland | .271 | 134 | 499 | 55 | 135 | 187 | 28 | 3 | 6 | 61 | 8 | 0 | 4 | 2 | 33 | 1 | 106 | 3 | 6 |
| Freeman, Marvin, Clearwater | .133 | 14 | 15 | 1 | 2 | 2 | 0 | 0 | 0 | 1 | 0 | 0 | 0 | 0 | 0 | 0 | 6 | 0 | 1 |
| Friedrich, Michael, Osceola† | .083 | 24 | 12 | 0 | 1 | 1 | 0 | 0 | 0 | 0 | 0 | 1 | 0 | 0 | 0 | 0 | 5 | 0 | 0 |
| Gaeta, Christopher, Daytona Beach | .185 | 12 | 27 | 5 | 5 | 9 | 0 | 2 | 0 | 5 | 0 | 0 | 0 | 0 | 4 | 0 | 2 | 2 | 0 |
| Gardner, Mark, West Palm Beach | .167 | 10 | 12 | 1 | 2 | 3 | 1 | 0 | 0 | 1 | 0 | 0 | 0 | 0 | 1 | 0 | 3 | 0 | 0 |
| Gatewood, Henry, Vero Beach | .225 | 66 | 178 | 12 | 40 | 47 | 3 | 2 | 0 | 15 | 1 | 4 | 1 | 1 | 11 | 1 | 11 | 3 | 1 |
| Gentile, Gene, Miami° | .232 | 92 | 293 | 33 | 68 | 104 | 16 | 4 | 4 | 30 | 2 | 2 | 4 | 1 | 43 | 0 | 66 | 16 | 8 |
| Gentile, Michael, Vero Beach° | .000 | 13 | 3 | 0 | 0 | 0 | 0 | 0 | 0 | 0 | 0 | 0 | 0 | 0 | 0 | 0 | 1 | 0 | 0 |
| Germann, Mark, Tampa | .266 | 128 | 379 | 49 | 101 | 120 | 7 | 6 | 0 | 24 | 1 | 8 | 3 | 1 | 49 | 0 | 42 | 13 | 3 |
| Giddens, Ronnie, Tampa | .257 | 108 | 335 | 37 | 86 | 98 | 5 | 2 | 1 | 26 | 4 | 6 | 4 | 3 | 30 | 4 | 62 | 10 | 5 |
| Gilcrease, Douglas, Fort Myers | .276 | 130 | 482 | 70 | 133 | 164 | 25 | 3 | 0 | 42 | 9 | 3 | 2 | 2 | 54 | 0 | 59 | 24 | 11 |
| Gill, Gary, St. Petersburg | .103 | 40 | 87 | 3 | 9 | 12 | 3 | 0 | 0 | 4 | 0 | 1 | 0 | 0 | 14 | 0 | 17 | 0 | 1 |
| Gilles, Thomas, Fort Lauderdale | .200 | 2 | 5 | 1 | 1 | 1 | 0 | 0 | 0 | 2 | 0 | 0 | 0 | 0 | 2 | 0 | 0 | 0 | 0 |
| Goff, Michael, Winter Haven | .202 | 89 | 262 | 36 | 53 | 73 | 11 | 0 | 3 | 22 | 4 | 4 | 1 | 4 | 44 | 1 | 28 | 2 | 6 |
| Gonzalez, Angel, Winter Haven† | .252 | 107 | 317 | 49 | 80 | 108 | 11 | 7 | 1 | 26 | 2 | 3 | 1 | 1 | 38 | 1 | 40 | 24 | 5 |
| Gonzalez, Fredi, Fort Lauderdale | .204 | 48 | 137 | 13 | 28 | 40 | 1 | 1 | 3 | 13 | 1 | 3 | 0 | 1 | 20 | 0 | 34 | 0 | 4 |
| Gray, Jeffrey, Clearwater | .000 | 55 | 6 | 0 | 0 | 0 | 0 | 0 | 0 | 0 | 0 | 0 | 0 | 0 | 0 | 0 | 1 | 0 | 0 |
| Grimm, Peter, Tampa | .091 | 14 | 11 | 1 | 1 | 1 | 0 | 0 | 0 | 0 | 0 | 0 | 0 | 0 | 0 | 0 | 4 | 0 | 0 |
| Groth, Jonathan, Tampa° | .199 | 100 | 196 | 26 | 39 | 50 | 4 | 2 | 1 | 22 | 5 | 3 | 3 | 4 | 49 | 0 | 83 | 5 | 1 |
| Gsellman, Bob, Clearwater | .143 | 12 | 28 | 0 | 4 | 4 | 0 | 0 | 0 | 3 | 1 | 0 | 1 | 0 | 1 | 0 | 13 | 0 | 0 |
| Gutierrez, Felipe, Vero Beach | .256 | 119 | 403 | 34 | 103 | 121 | 16 | 1 | 0 | 28 | 4 | 6 | 3 | 11 | 18 | 1 | 25 | 5 | 1 |
| Gutierrez, Roberto, Daytona Beach | .264 | 50 | 174 | 22 | 46 | 54 | 5 | 0 | 1 | 14 | 1 | 3 | 1 | 0 | 23 | 0 | 16 | 6 | 3 |
| Gwynn, Christopher, Vero Beach° | .257 | 52 | 179 | 19 | 46 | 66 | 8 | 6 | 0 | 17 | 1 | 1 | 1 | 2 | 16 | 0 | 34 | 2 | 2 |
| Halasz, Michael, Daytona Beach | .236 | 30 | 72 | 6 | 17 | 17 | 0 | 0 | 0 | 5 | 0 | 4 | 0 | 0 | 12 | 0 | 11 | 3 | 1 |
| Haller, Timothy, Daytona Beach | .245 | 42 | 94 | 12 | 23 | 27 | 2 | 1 | 0 | 9 | 1 | 0 | 2 | 0 | 7 | 0 | 26 | 7 | 2 |
| Hamb, Andre, Lakeland° | .200 | 5 | 15 | 0 | 3 | 3 | 0 | 0 | 0 | 0 | 0 | 0 | 0 | 0 | 3 | 0 | 6 | 0 | 0 |
| Hamilton, Alvin, Winter Haven | .191 | 86 | 209 | 28 | 40 | 63 | 7 | 2 | 4 | 19 | 2 | 1 | 1 | 1 | 33 | 1 | 67 | 12 | 6 |
| Hamilton, Robert, Vero Beach | .067 | 27 | 15 | 0 | 1 | 1 | 0 | 0 | 0 | 0 | 0 | 1 | 0 | 0 | 0 | 0 | 7 | 0 | 0 |
| Hampton, Anthony, Osceola° | .203 | 47 | 133 | 16 | 27 | 33 | 2 | 2 | 0 | 14 | 3 | 0 | 1 | 1 | 13 | 2 | 28 | 9 | 3 |
| Hansen, Raymond, Winter Haven° | .231 | 108 | 351 | 31 | 81 | 107 | 15 | 1 | 3 | 31 | 4 | 1 | 4 | 0 | 33 | 3 | 67 | 2 | 4 |
| Harris, Leonard, Tampa° | .259 | 132 | 499 | 66 | 129 | 165 | 11 | 8 | 3 | 51 | 7 | 5 | 7 | 1 | 37 | 2 | 57 | 15 | 8 |

| Player and Club | Pct. | G. | AB. | R. | H. | TB. | 2B. | 3B. | HR. | RBI. | GW. | SH. | SF. | HP. | BB. | Int. BB. | SO. | SB. | CS. |
|---|---|---|---|---|---|---|---|---|---|---|---|---|---|---|---|---|---|---|---|
| Harris, Michael, St Petersburg† | .227 | 135 | 458 | 45 | 104 | 127 | 9 | 7 | 0 | 44 | 5 | 5 | 6 | 1 | 41 | 12 | 72 | 11 | 11 |
| Harrison, Brett, St. Petersburg | .264 | 115 | 382 | 50 | 101 | 127 | 20 | 3 | 0 | 36 | 4 | 11 | 5 | 1 | 69 | 1 | 72 | 4 | 2 |
| Heeney, Joseph, Fort Lauderdale | .094 | 14 | 32 | 4 | 3 | 3 | 0 | 0 | 0 | 2 | 0 | 1 | 0 | 0 | 9 | 0 | 4 | 1 | 1 |
| Heidenreich, Curtis, Tampa | .000 | 7 | 2 | 0 | 0 | 0 | 0 | 0 | 0 | 0 | 0 | 1 | 0 | 0 | 0 | 0 | 1 | 0 | 0 |
| Held, Thomas, Lakeland | .000 | 26 | 1 | 0 | 0 | 0 | 0 | 0 | 0 | 0 | 0 | 0 | 0 | 0 | 0 | 0 | 0 | 0 | 0 |
| Henderson, Rickey, Fort Lauderdale | .167 | 3 | 6 | 5 | 1 | 3 | 0 | 1 | 0 | 3 | 0 | 0 | 0 | 0 | 5 | 0 | 2 | 1 | 1 |
| Hermann, Jeffrey, Lakeland* | .259 | 101 | 340 | 37 | 88 | 127 | 20 | 2 | 5 | 49 | 4 | 1 | 2 | 1 | 58 | 3 | 75 | 4 | 2 |
| Herzog, Hans, St. Petersburg* | .000 | 43 | 3 | 0 | 0 | 0 | 0 | 0 | 0 | 0 | 0 | 0 | 0 | 0 | 0 | 0 | 1 | 0 | 0 |
| Hester, Ricky, Daytona Beach* | .000 | 14 | 0 | 0 | 0 | 0 | 0 | 0 | 0 | 0 | 0 | 0 | 0 | 0 | 1 | 0 | 0 | 0 | 0 |
| Hilgenberg, Scott, Tampa* | .214 | 110 | 345 | 29 | 74 | 108 | 14 | 1 | 6 | 39 | 6 | 2 | 3 | 1 | 40 | 3 | 49 | 4 | 2 |
| Holman, Brian, West Palm Beach | .227 | 25 | 22 | 1 | 5 | 6 | 1 | 0 | 0 | 2 | 0 | 0 | 0 | 0 | 8 | 0 | 8 | 0 | 0 |
| Holmes, Darren, Vero Beach | .667 | 33 | 3 | 0 | 2 | 2 | 0 | 0 | 0 | 0 | 1 | 0 | 0 | 0 | 0 | 0 | 1 | 0 | 0 |
| Houp, Scott, Osceola | .169 | 42 | 65 | 8 | 11 | 16 | 0 | 1 | 1 | 6 | 0 | 0 | 1 | 0 | 14 | 0 | 17 | 1 | 0 |
| Hoyt, David, St. Petersburg | .000 | 24 | 5 | 0 | 0 | 0 | 0 | 0 | 0 | 0 | 0 | 0 | 0 | 0 | 1 | 0 | 1 | 0 | 0 |
| Hubbard, Jeffrey, Daytona Beach | .290 | 90 | 317 | 39 | 92 | 115 | 6 | 7 | 1 | 42 | 5 | 5 | 1 | 0 | 43 | 2 | 38 | 4 | 7 |
| Hudson, Lance, Miami† | .229 | 119 | 436 | 49 | 100 | 133 | 19 | 7 | 0 | 27 | 1 | 11 | 2 | 2 | 29 | 1 | 85 | 34 | 12 |
| Hutson, Lee, West Palm Beach | .224 | 29 | 67 | 5 | 15 | 19 | 1 | 0 | 1 | 11 | 3 | 0 | 2 | 0 | 14 | 0 | 13 | 2 | 2 |
| Infante, Kennedy, St. Petersburg | .116 | 13 | 43 | 4 | 5 | 6 | 1 | 0 | 0 | 2 | 0 | 0 | 0 | 1 | 3 | 0 | 4 | 0 | 0 |
| Ireland, Timothy, Miami | .221 | 49 | 172 | 16 | 38 | 47 | 9 | 0 | 0 | 17 | 2 | 2 | 1 | 1 | 14 | 0 | 15 | 5 | 4 |
| Jacobo, Edward, Vero Beach | .287 | 112 | 376 | 42 | 108 | 147 | 19 | 4 | 4 | 58 | 10 | 2 | 6 | 2 | 39 | 5 | 68 | 2 | 5 |
| Jacobsen, Robert, Vero Beach | .167 | 43 | 6 | 0 | 1 | 1 | 0 | 0 | 0 | 0 | 0 | 1 | 0 | 0 | 1 | 0 | 1 | 0 | 0 |
| Jacoby, Donald, Miami* | .213 | 95 | 300 | 20 | 64 | 91 | 13 | 1 | 4 | 30 | 4 | 4 | 2 | 2 | 26 | 2 | 58 | 2 | 3 |
| Jarrell, Joseph, Fort Myers | .270 | 28 | 111 | 19 | 30 | 58 | 2 | 1 | 8 | 21 | 3 | 0 | 0 | 0 | 8 | 0 | 35 | 3 | 0 |
| Jester, William, Clearwater* | .222 | 25 | 18 | 3 | 4 | 4 | 0 | 0 | 0 | 1 | 0 | 2 | 0 | 0 | 1 | 0 | 6 | 0 | 0 |
| Jimenez, Raul, St. Petersburg | .065 | 12 | 31 | 1 | 2 | 2 | 0 | 0 | 0 | 1 | 1 | 0 | 0 | 0 | 2 | 0 | 8 | 0 | 0 |
| Job, Ryan, Osceola | .246 | 104 | 349 | 42 | 86 | 98 | 6 | 3 | 0 | 51 | 4 | 4 | 4 | 0 | 20 | 0 | 39 | 8 | 6 |
| Johns, Ronald, St. Petersburg | .266 | 135 | 489 | 53 | 130 | 170 | 22 | 6 | 2 | 59 | 14 | 2 | 9 | 3 | 40 | 5 | 51 | 1 | 1 |
| Johnson, Bobby, Fort Lauderdale | .222 | 13 | 45 | 7 | 10 | 12 | 2 | 0 | 0 | 0 | 0 | 0 | 0 | 1 | 9 | 0 | 10 | 0 | 0 |
| Johnson, Lance, St. Petersburg* | .270 | 129 | 497 | 68 | 134 | 177 | 17 | 10 | 2 | 55 | 6 | 2 | 9 | 0 | 58 | 5 | 39 | 33 | 19 |
| Johnson, Roger, Clearwater | .276 | 34 | 105 | 8 | 29 | 36 | 4 | 0 | 1 | 10 | 0 | 0 | 1 | 0 | 4 | 2 | 12 | 2 | 3 |
| Johnson, Ronald, Daytona Beach | .000 | 15 | 1 | 0 | 0 | 0 | 0 | 0 | 0 | 0 | 0 | 0 | 0 | 0 | 0 | 0 | 1 | 0 | 0 |
| Johnson, Thomas, Fort Myers* | .160 | 12 | 25 | 4 | 4 | 5 | 1 | 0 | 0 | 0 | 0 | 0 | 0 | 1 | 5 | 0 | 8 | 2 | 1 |
| Johnson, Todd, Clearwater | .189 | 32 | 106 | 13 | 20 | 34 | 7 | 2 | 1 | 10 | 2 | 0 | 1 | 2 | 10 | 0 | 35 | 12 | 4 |
| Jordan, Paul, Clearwater | .277 | 139 | 528 | 60 | 146 | 205 | 22 | 8 | 7 | 62 | 9 | 2 | 4 | 1 | 25 | 3 | 59 | 26 | 8 |
| Juenke, Daniel, Miami* | .301 | 58 | 176 | 10 | 53 | 69 | 14 | 1 | 0 | 13 | 2 | 0 | 2 | 1 | 19 | 1 | 28 | 1 | 1 |
| Karmeris, Joseph, Vero Beach | .143 | 11 | 14 | 0 | 2 | 3 | 1 | 0 | 0 | 1 | 0 | 0 | 0 | 0 | 2 | 0 | 6 | 0 | 0 |
| Kaye, Jeffrey, Clearwater | .138 | 40 | 94 | 10 | 13 | 19 | 6 | 0 | 0 | 4 | 0 | 3 | 0 | 3 | 16 | 0 | 36 | 1 | 1 |
| Kelley, Anthony, Osceola | .000 | 6 | 6 | 1 | 0 | 0 | 0 | 0 | 0 | 0 | 0 | 0 | 0 | 0 | 1 | 0 | 4 | 0 | 0 |
| Kelly, Roberto, Fort Lauderdale† | .247 | 114 | 417 | 86 | 103 | 142 | 4 | 13 | 3 | 38 | 6 | 3 | 6 | 3 | 58 | 1 | 70 | 49 | 14 |
| Kemp, Hubert, Tampa* | .231 | 10 | 13 | 3 | 3 | 4 | 1 | 0 | 0 | 2 | 0 | 0 | 0 | 0 | 3 | 0 | 4 | 0 | 0 |
| Kinns, Glenn, West Palm Beach | .000 | 4 | 2 | 0 | 0 | 0 | 0 | 0 | 0 | 0 | 0 | 0 | 0 | 0 | 0 | 0 | 0 | 0 | 0 |
| Kirby, Wayne, Vero Beach* | .281 | 122 | 437 | 70 | 123 | 138 | 9 | 3 | 0 | 28 | 5 | 4 | 3 | 3 | 41 | 1 | 41 | 31 | 14 |
| Kopetsky, Brian, Vero Beach | .185 | 14 | 27 | 3 | 5 | 5 | 0 | 0 | 0 | 4 | 0 | 0 | 0 | 0 | 1 | 0 | 7 | 0 | 0 |
| Kraft, Kenneth, Clearwater | .267 | 54 | 206 | 23 | 55 | 61 | 4 | 1 | 0 | 15 | 1 | 4 | 0 | 2 | 17 | 0 | 18 | 8 | 2 |
| Krynitsky, Mark, Fort Myers | .080 | 11 | 25 | 2 | 2 | 2 | 0 | 0 | 0 | 1 | 1 | 0 | 0 | 0 | 5 | 0 | 7 | 0 | 1 |
| Lane, Phillip, 11 Ft.L-28 Miami | .179 | 39 | 112 | 8 | 20 | 23 | 3 | 0 | 0 | 11 | 1 | 1 | 0 | 1 | 15 | 0 | 27 | 2 | 1 |
| Langdon, Ted, Tampa | .143 | 29 | 7 | 1 | 1 | 1 | 0 | 0 | 0 | 0 | 0 | 1 | 0 | 0 | 2 | 0 | 2 | 0 | 0 |
| Lange, Clarke, Osceola | .217 | 73 | 175 | 29 | 38 | 57 | 8 | 1 | 3 | 24 | 1 | 0 | 2 | 3 | 38 | 1 | 47 | 5 | 0 |
| Latmore, Robert, Daytona Beach | .267 | 7 | 15 | 3 | 4 | 4 | 0 | 0 | 0 | 1 | 0 | 0 | 0 | 1 | 0 | 0 | 3 | 1 | 0 |
| Lawhon, Duane, Fort Lauderdale | .000 | 6 | 4 | 0 | 0 | 0 | 0 | 0 | 0 | 0 | 0 | 0 | 0 | 0 | 0 | 0 | 1 | 0 | 0 |
| Ledbetter, Jeffrey, St. Petersburg* | .295 | 33 | 122 | 19 | 36 | 57 | 4 | 1 | 5 | 26 | 1 | 0 | 2 | 0 | 12 | 0 | 15 | 1 | 1 |
| Legumina, Gary, Vero Beach | .333 | 42 | 3 | 0 | 1 | 1 | 0 | 0 | 0 | 1 | 0 | 1 | 0 | 0 | 0 | 0 | 0 | 0 | 0 |
| Leiper, Timothy, Lakeland† | .221 | 25 | 77 | 13 | 17 | 21 | 2 | 1 | 0 | 5 | 1 | 0 | 1 | 0 | 10 | 0 | 11 | 1 | 0 |
| Lemon, Ricky, St. Petersburg* | .267 | 8 | 15 | 4 | 4 | 4 | 0 | 0 | 0 | 2 | 0 | 0 | 0 | 0 | 1 | 0 | 3 | 1 | 0 |
| Lemons, Timothy, Fort Myers | .165 | 38 | 115 | 12 | 19 | 22 | 3 | 0 | 0 | 13 | 2 | 0 | 0 | 2 | 8 | 0 | 26 | 1 | 0 |
| Lewis, Jay, Miami | .183 | 92 | 289 | 29 | 53 | 83 | 15 | 3 | 3 | 35 | 2 | 3 | 2 | 0 | 37 | 0 | 64 | 4 | 4 |
| Lloyd, Raymond, Clearwater* | .000 | 11 | 2 | 0 | 0 | 0 | 0 | 0 | 0 | 0 | 0 | 0 | 0 | 0 | 0 | 0 | 1 | 0 | 0 |
| Long, Anthony, Lakeland | .284 | 98 | 334 | 37 | 95 | 112 | 10 | 2 | 1 | 25 | 3 | 2 | 3 | 0 | 43 | 0 | 40 | 13 | 5 |
| Longenecker, Jere, Fort Myers | .214 | 15 | 56 | 8 | 12 | 18 | 1 | 1 | 1 | 10 | 0 | 0 | 1 | 2 | 2 | 0 | 11 | 5 | 0 |
| Lono, Joel, Tampa* | .136 | 42 | 22 | 1 | 3 | 3 | 0 | 0 | 0 | 1 | 0 | 0 | 0 | 0 | 0 | 0 | 7 | 0 | 0 |
| Lopez, Luis, Vero Beach | .277 | 120 | 382 | 47 | 106 | 131 | 18 | 2 | 1 | 43 | 12 | 3 | 3 | 6 | 25 | 3 | 41 | 2 | 2 |
| Lovelace, Vance, Vero Beach* | 1.000 | 13 | 1 | 1 | 1 | 1 | 0 | 0 | 0 | 0 | 0 | 0 | 0 | 0 | 1 | 0 | 0 | 0 | 0 |
| Lowe, Dion, Clearwater* | .231 | 96 | 333 | 26 | 77 | 88 | 9 | 1 | 0 | 21 | 2 | 3 | 1 | 2 | 39 | 1 | 63 | 11 | 11 |
| Loy, Darren, Clearwater | .261 | 100 | 310 | 23 | 81 | 102 | 18 | 0 | 1 | 36 | 3 | 1 | 4 | 0 | 17 | 4 | 38 | 5 | 2 |
| Lucas, Arbrey, Osceola | .000 | 34 | 2 | 0 | 0 | 0 | 0 | 0 | 0 | 0 | 0 | 0 | 0 | 0 | 0 | 0 | 1 | 0 | 0 |
| Lusader, Scott, Lakeland* | .289 | 27 | 97 | 16 | 28 | 41 | 5 | 1 | 2 | 22 | 5 | 0 | 1 | 0 | 12 | 1 | 22 | 0 | 1 |
| Lyden, Mitchell, Fort Lauderdale | .255 | 116 | 400 | 43 | 102 | 155 | 21 | 1 | 10 | 58 | 5 | 1 | 5 | 5 | 27 | 0 | 93 | 1 | 2 |
| Mabe, Todd, Fort Myers† | .268 | 129 | 492 | 73 | 132 | 152 | 20 | 0 | 0 | 31 | 2 | 3 | 4 | 2 | 80 | 3 | 79 | 41 | 20 |
| Machado, Ruben, Tampa | .167 | 49 | 96 | 8 | 16 | 18 | 2 | 0 | 0 | 6 | 0 | 1 | 0 | 0 | 13 | 0 | 29 | 0 | 1 |
| MacKay, Joey, Fort Lauderdale | .239 | 48 | 138 | 23 | 33 | 50 | 4 | 2 | 3 | 17 | 1 | 0 | 2 | 0 | 19 | 0 | 31 | 1 | 2 |
| Madden, Morris, Tampa* | .111 | 28 | 9 | 1 | 1 | 1 | 0 | 0 | 0 | 0 | 0 | 0 | 0 | 0 | 0 | 0 | 5 | 0 | 0 |
| Madden, Scott, Clearwater | .000 | 27 | 14 | 0 | 0 | 0 | 0 | 0 | 0 | 0 | 0 | 2 | 0 | 0 | 2 | 0 | 10 | 0 | 0 |
| Magrane, Joseph, St. Petersburg | .154 | 5 | 13 | 1 | 2 | 2 | 0 | 0 | 0 | 0 | 0 | 1 | 0 | 0 | 1 | 0 | 6 | 0 | 0 |
| Mallicoat, Robbin, Osceola* | .222 | 26 | 18 | 0 | 4 | 4 | 0 | 0 | 0 | 1 | 0 | 2 | 0 | 0 | 0 | 0 | 5 | 0 | 0 |
| Manfre, Michael, Tampa | .262 | 84 | 301 | 43 | 79 | 113 | 17 | 4 | 3 | 34 | 4 | 0 | 4 | 1 | 35 | 5 | 62 | 15 | 5 |
| Mann, Scott, West Palm Beach* | .272 | 93 | 257 | 25 | 70 | 91 | 10 | 1 | 3 | 31 | 4 | 0 | 2 | 1 | 27 | 6 | 25 | 4 | 0 |
| Manning, Otis, Lakeland* | .235 | 7 | 17 | 5 | 4 | 5 | 1 | 0 | 0 | 1 | 0 | 0 | 0 | 0 | 7 | 0 | 2 | 1 | 0 |
| Martinez, Carlos, Fort Lauderdale | .248 | 93 | 311 | 39 | 77 | 124 | 15 | 7 | 6 | 44 | 3 | 4 | 2 | 2 | 14 | 1 | 65 | 8 | 4 |
| Martinez, Christian, St. Petersburg | .000 | 4 | 3 | 0 | 0 | 0 | 0 | 0 | 0 | 0 | 0 | 0 | 0 | 0 | 0 | 0 | 3 | 0 | 0 |
| Martinez, Porfirio, Lakeland† | .236 | 41 | 148 | 11 | 35 | 56 | 5 | 5 | 2 | 14 | 3 | 0 | 0 | 0 | 6 | 2 | 33 | 3 | 3 |
| Martinez, Reynaldo, Fort Myers* | .262 | 76 | 248 | 35 | 65 | 84 | 9 | 5 | 0 | 29 | 6 | 1 | 3 | 1 | 31 | 3 | 42 | 11 | 5 |
| Mason, Martin, St. Petersburg | .000 | 41 | 1 | 0 | 0 | 0 | 0 | 0 | 0 | 0 | 0 | 1 | 0 | 0 | 1 | 0 | 0 | 0 | 0 |
| Masters, Frank, Lakeland | .175 | 31 | 97 | 4 | 17 | 18 | 1 | 0 | 0 | 4 | 0 | 2 | 1 | 0 | 13 | 0 | 29 | 0 | 0 |
| Mathews, Charles, Osceola | .182 | 29 | 11 | 1 | 2 | 2 | 0 | 0 | 0 | 0 | 1 | 0 | 0 | 0 | 0 | 0 | 5 | 0 | 0 |
| Mathews, Gregory, St. Petersburg† | .222 | 16 | 9 | 4 | 2 | 4 | 0 | 1 | 0 | 2 | 0 | 3 | 0 | 0 | 2 | 0 | 3 | 0 | 0 |
| Mattocks, Richard, 66 FtL-44 M. | .267 | 110 | 344 | 68 | 92 | 106 | 4 | 5 | 0 | 26 | 3 | 6 | 0 | 2 | 67 | 0 | 50 | 61 | 15 |
| Mauch, Thomas, St. Petersburg* | .200 | 12 | 25 | 4 | 5 | 6 | 1 | 0 | 0 | 1 | 0 | 0 | 0 | 0 | 3 | 0 | 8 | 0 | 0 |
| Mayberry, Gregory, Vero Beach* | .174 | 17 | 23 | 1 | 4 | 4 | 0 | 0 | 0 | 1 | 1 | 0 | 0 | 0 | 2 | 0 | 16 | 0 | 0 |
| Maynard, Chris, Fort Lauderdale | .286 | 22 | 70 | 13 | 20 | 24 | 4 | 0 | 0 | 8 | 2 | 2 | 0 | 0 | 9 | 0 | 9 | 2 | 3 |
| McDevitt, Stephen, Clearwater | .000 | 17 | 3 | 0 | 0 | 0 | 0 | 0 | 0 | 0 | 1 | 0 | 0 | 1 | 0 | 0 | 1 | 0 | 0 |
| McHugh, Charles, Lakeland | .000 | 38 | 1 | 0 | 0 | 0 | 0 | 0 | 0 | 0 | 0 | 0 | 0 | 0 | 0 | 0 | 0 | 0 | 0 |
| McInnis, William, Winter Haven* | .266 | 54 | 177 | 19 | 47 | 55 | 6 | 1 | 0 | 17 | 2 | 2 | 2 | 0 | 15 | 1 | 27 | 7 | 5 |

| Player and Club | Pct. | G. | AB. | R. | H. | TB. | 2B. | 3B. | HR. | RBI. | GW. | SH. | SF. | HP. | BB. | Int. BB. | SO. | SB. | CS. |
|---|---|---|---|---|---|---|---|---|---|---|---|---|---|---|---|---|---|---|---|
| McKnight, James, Miami | .125 | 15 | 32 | 2 | 4 | 5 | 1 | 0 | 0 | 0 | 0 | 2 | 0 | 0 | 1 | 0 | 4 | 0 | 0 |
| Meadows, Geoffrey, Vero Beach | .000 | 6 | 2 | 0 | 0 | 0 | 0 | 0 | 0 | 0 | 0 | 0 | 0 | 0 | 0 | 0 | 0 | 0 | 0 |
| Melrose, Jeffrey, Daytona Beach* | .253 | 119 | 396 | 32 | 100 | 123 | 6 | 4 | 3 | 43 | 6 | 5 | 3 | 2 | 21 | 1 | 49 | 13 | 4 |
| Millis, Joseph, Lakeland | .242 | 43 | 120 | 15 | 29 | 31 | 2 | 0 | 0 | 7 | 0 | 3 | 0 | 2 | 10 | 0 | 29 | 5 | 0 |
| Mills, Gotay, St. Petersburg | .230 | 25 | 61 | 9 | 14 | 17 | 3 | 0 | 0 | 4 | 1 | 0 | 0 | 0 | 10 | 0 | 8 | 3 | 0 |
| Minick, Jeffrey, Lakeland* | .083 | 4 | 12 | 0 | 1 | 2 | 1 | 0 | 0 | 0 | 0 | 0 | 0 | 0 | 1 | 0 | 5 | 0 | 0 |
| Mirabito, Timothy, Tampa | .111 | 15 | 9 | 0 | 1 | 1 | 0 | 0 | 0 | 1 | 0 | 1 | 0 | 0 | 1 | 0 | 3 | 0 | 0 |
| Mitchell, Reginald, Tampa* | .176 | 35 | 91 | 7 | 16 | 26 | 1 | 3 | 1 | 11 | 1 | 1 | 0 | 0 | 10 | 1 | 23 | 6 | 1 |
| Mitchell, Thomas, Osceola | .277 | 55 | 191 | 18 | 53 | 72 | 8 | 4 | 1 | 22 | 2 | 0 | 1 | 0 | 16 | 0 | 47 | 4 | 10 |
| Moreno, Michael, Fort Myers | .293 | 38 | 123 | 21 | 36 | 50 | 11 | 0 | 1 | 23 | 3 | 0 | 3 | 0 | 18 | 1 | 35 | 7 | 3 |
| Morris, Angel, Fort Myers | .254 | 91 | 256 | 34 | 65 | 78 | 5 | 1 | 2 | 25 | 2 | 1 | 3 | 0 | 44 | 0 | 47 | 2 | 1 |
| Murcer, Bobby, Fort Lauderdale* | .083 | 4 | 12 | 3 | 1 | 1 | 0 | 0 | 0 | 1 | 0 | 1 | 0 | 3 | 0 | 3 | 0 | 0 |
| Murray, David, Daytona Beach | .253 | 121 | 387 | 63 | 98 | 120 | 14 | 4 | 0 | 33 | 1 | 4 | 0 | 4 | 92 | 2 | 41 | 20 | 2 |
| Newark, Douglas, Miami | .175 | 93 | 212 | 25 | 37 | 41 | 4 | 0 | 0 | 17 | 3 | 12 | 1 | 1 | 30 | 0 | 34 | 4 | 0 |
| Newsom, Gary, Vero Beach | .228 | 57 | 158 | 24 | 36 | 42 | 3 | 0 | 1 | 26 | 1 | 3 | 2 | 1 | 30 | 1 | 16 | 1 | 4 |
| Newsome, Timothy, Lakeland | .267 | 123 | 445 | 63 | 119 | 162 | 18 | 5 | 5 | 56 | 6 | 3 | 2 | 5 | 61 | 2 | 49 | 1 | 2 |
| Nichols, Howard, Clearwater | .250 | 101 | 376 | 51 | 94 | 145 | 21 | 3 | 8 | 45 | 8 | 0 | 3 | 4 | 25 | 0 | 44 | 7 | 3 |
| Nichols, Ty, Daytona Beach | .174 | 53 | 155 | 11 | 27 | 35 | 4 | 2 | 0 | 11 | 1 | 4 | 2 | 2 | 9 | 0 | 42 | 3 | 1 |
| Niemann, Thomas, Fort Myers | .192 | 60 | 156 | 12 | 30 | 36 | 6 | 0 | 0 | 13 | 0 | 2 | 1 | 3 | 18 | 0 | 29 | 2 | 0 |
| Nunez, Mauricio, St. Petersburg | .290 | 128 | 438 | 50 | 127 | 163 | 22 | 4 | 2 | 46 | 6 | 10 | 1 | 2 | 38 | 1 | 66 | 5 | 7 |
| O'Dell, James, Osceola* | .263 | 129 | 449 | 62 | 118 | 150 | 22 | 5 | 0 | 67 | 10 | 3 | 10 | 5 | 60 | 3 | 41 | 16 | 3 |
| Odekirk, Richard, Tampa* | .188 | 31 | 16 | 2 | 3 | 6 | 1 | 1 | 0 | 1 | 0 | 1 | 0 | 0 | 3 | 0 | 0 |
| Odgers, Daniel, Clearwater | .255 | 29 | 94 | 13 | 24 | 35 | 5 | 3 | 0 | 12 | 0 | 0 | 2 | 0 | 12 | 0 | 22 | 8 | 5 |
| Oliva, David, Winter Haven | .268 | 62 | 224 | 27 | 60 | 82 | 12 | 2 | 2 | 20 | 4 | 1 | 2 | 0 | 15 | 2 | 31 | 11 | 5 |
| Oliver, Joseph, Tampa | .269 | 112 | 386 | 38 | 104 | 152 | 23 | 2 | 7 | 62 | 9 | 4 | 5 | 1 | 32 | 3 | 75 | 1 | 5 |
| Oquendo, Jorge, Lakeland* | .176 | 24 | 74 | 10 | 13 | 18 | 3 | 1 | 0 | 10 | 1 | 1 | 1 | 0 | 8 | 0 | 21 | 0 | 2 |
| Pacillo, Patrick, Tampa | .000 | 25 | 5 | 0 | 0 | 0 | 0 | 0 | 0 | 0 | 0 | 0 | 1 | 0 | 1 | 0 | 2 | 0 | 0 |
| Palacios, Rey, Lakeland | .232 | 85 | 280 | 35 | 65 | 84 | 11 | 1 | 2 | 27 | 2 | 1 | 2 | 1 | 42 | 2 | 47 | 3 | 1 |
| Paredes, Johnny, West Palm Beach | .261 | 101 | 322 | 65 | 84 | 105 | 7 | 4 | 2 | 34 | 4 | 9 | 2 | 9 | 49 | 2 | 49 | 31 | 11 |
| Parker, Robert, Osceola* | .254 | 122 | 389 | 65 | 99 | 104 | 5 | 0 | 0 | 41 | 2 | 2 | 6 | 3 | 69 | 0 | 39 | 35 | 10 |
| Peppio, Richard, Miami† | .000 | 3 | 2 | 0 | 0 | 0 | 0 | 0 | 0 | 0 | 0 | 1 | 0 | 0 | 0 | 0 | 0 | 0 |
| Perdomo, Felix, Fort Lauderdale | .245 | 90 | 273 | 37 | 67 | 87 | 10 | 2 | 2 | 25 | 1 | 3 | 4 | 0 | 23 | 0 | 53 | 16 | 5 |
| Pereira, Ramon, Miami | .165 | 55 | 127 | 7 | 21 | 28 | 4 | 0 | 1 | 7 | 0 | 4 | 0 | 2 | 7 | 1 | 27 | 3 | 1 |
| Perez, Sergio, Clearwater | .273 | 77 | 271 | 26 | 74 | 83 | 5 | 2 | 0 | 21 | 4 | 4 | 0 | 2 | 28 | 4 | 39 | 19 | 8 |
| Perkins, Broderick, Miami* | .253 | 22 | 79 | 10 | 20 | 26 | 4 | 1 | 0 | 10 | 1 | 0 | 0 | 1 | 5 | 0 | 4 | 0 | 1 |
| Peruso, Steven, Fort Lauderdale | .175 | 15 | 40 | 3 | 7 | 8 | 1 | 0 | 0 | 1 | 0 | 1 | 0 | 0 | 6 | 0 | 5 | 1 | 0 |
| Pesavento, Michael, Vero Beach* | .000 | 24 | 7 | 1 | 0 | 0 | 0 | 0 | 0 | 1 | 0 | 1 | 0 | 0 | 3 | 0 | 4 | 0 | 0 |
| Peters, Steven, St. Petersburg* | .294 | 10 | 17 | 2 | 5 | 5 | 0 | 0 | 0 | 0 | 0 | 0 | 2 | 0 | 0 | 0 | 3 | 0 | 0 |
| Pevey, Marty, St. Petersburg* | .290 | 104 | 393 | 48 | 114 | 143 | 12 | 4 | 3 | 41 | 8 | 2 | 2 | 1 | 28 | 6 | 56 | 5 | 2 |
| Posillico, James, Miami† | .000 | 5 | 10 | 0 | 0 | 0 | 0 | 0 | 0 | 0 | 0 | 0 | 0 | 0 | 0 | 0 | 3 | 0 | 0 |
| Pottinger, Mark, Clearwater† | .221 | 97 | 303 | 32 | 67 | 77 | 8 | 1 | 0 | 25 | 6 | 5 | 2 | 3 | 28 | 7 | 49 | 23 | 6 |
| Poznanski, Richard, Daytona Beach | .231 | 102 | 308 | 34 | 71 | 91 | 9 | 4 | 1 | 25 | 4 | 5 | 0 | 1 | 32 | 0 | 63 | 3 | 1 |
| Ratliff, Daniel, West Palm Beach | .000 | 27 | 3 | 0 | 0 | 0 | 0 | 0 | 0 | 0 | 0 | 1 | 0 | 0 | 0 | 0 | 2 | 0 | 0 |
| Raziano, Scott, West Palm Beach | .200 | 82 | 185 | 30 | 37 | 43 | 3 | 0 | 1 | 17 | 4 | 9 | 1 | 1 | 38 | 1 | 26 | 9 | 2 |
| Reburn, Scott, Tampa | .083 | 23 | 12 | 0 | 1 | 1 | 0 | 0 | 0 | 1 | 0 | 2 | 0 | 0 | 2 | 0 | 3 | 0 | 0 |
| Reed, Darren, Fort Lauderdale | .317 | 100 | 369 | 63 | 117 | 176 | 21 | 4 | 10 | 61 | 10 | 0 | 7 | 7 | 36 | 3 | 56 | 13 | 3 |
| Reed, Jody, Winter Haven | .321 | 134 | 489 | 95 | 157 | 184 | 25 | 1 | 0 | 45 | 6 | 4 | 4 | 1 | 94 | 2 | 26 | 16 | 11 |
| Reid, Patrick, Miami | .263 | 7 | 19 | 1 | 5 | 5 | 0 | 0 | 0 | 2 | 0 | 0 | 0 | 2 | 0 | 4 | 0 | 1 |
| Reynolds, Mark, Osceola* | .238 | 79 | 193 | 24 | 46 | 78 | 6 | 1 | 8 | 29 | 4 | 0 | 2 | 1 | 37 | 2 | 23 | 3 | 1 |
| Richardson, Billy, Winter Haven | .244 | 74 | 234 | 22 | 57 | 91 | 9 | 2 | 7 | 38 | 5 | 2 | 1 | 2 | 15 | 2 | 60 | 0 | 2 |
| Richardson, Tim, 101 Mia-21 FtM | .278 | 122 | 407 | 49 | 113 | 127 | 4 | 5 | 0 | 38 | 5 | 9 | 4 | 0 | 36 | 1 | 25 | 17 | 10 |
| Riley, Randall, Daytona Beach* | .220 | 57 | 159 | 11 | 35 | 46 | 6 | 1 | 1 | 12 | 2 | 1 | 2 | 0 | 29 | 4 | 44 | 1 | 1 |
| Ripken, William, Daytona Beach | .230 | 67 | 222 | 23 | 51 | 62 | 11 | 0 | 0 | 18 | 5 | 5 | 1 | 0 | 22 | 1 | 24 | 7 | 4 |
| Ritch, Harris, Vero Beach | .217 | 76 | 143 | 16 | 31 | 34 | 1 | 1 | 0 | 12 | 0 | 2 | 2 | 1 | 13 | 1 | 22 | 2 | 1 |
| Ritchie, Wallace, Clearwater* | .111 | 14 | 9 | 1 | 1 | 1 | 0 | 0 | 0 | 1 | 0 | 1 | 0 | 1 | 0 | 2 | 0 | 0 |
| Rivera, Jose, 35 FtL-7 Mia | .241 | 42 | 133 | 13 | 32 | 46 | 6 | 4 | 0 | 15 | 0 | 0 | 0 | 1 | 17 | 1 | 33 | 0 | 1 |
| Roberts, John, Winter Haven | .271 | 117 | 340 | 45 | 92 | 106 | 8 | 3 | 0 | 20 | 3 | 5 | 1 | 1 | 22 | 1 | 27 | 22 | 11 |
| Rodiles, Jose, Fort Myers | .000 | 40 | 2 | 0 | 0 | 0 | 0 | 0 | 0 | 0 | 0 | 0 | 0 | 0 | 0 | 0 | 2 | 0 | 0 |
| Rodriguez, Ignacio, West Palm Beach | .200 | 35 | 55 | 7 | 11 | 14 | 3 | 0 | 0 | 4 | 2 | 1 | 2 | 3 | 19 | 0 | 1 |
| Roman, Ray, Clearwater | .114 | 15 | 44 | 3 | 5 | 5 | 0 | 0 | 0 | 5 | 0 | 0 | 0 | 5 | 1 | 15 | 1 | 0 |
| Ross, Cordell, Lakeland† | .263 | 31 | 95 | 7 | 25 | 27 | 2 | 0 | 0 | 13 | 0 | 1 | 2 | 1 | 9 | 0 | 18 | 0 | 1 |
| Rosthenhausler, Ramon, Lakeland | .169 | 40 | 136 | 12 | 23 | 29 | 4 | 1 | 0 | 11 | 2 | 0 | 1 | 1 | 14 | 0 | 45 | 2 | 2 |
| Rowen, Robert, Vero Beach* | .000 | 9 | 4 | 0 | 0 | 0 | 0 | 0 | 0 | 0 | 0 | 1 | 0 | 0 | 0 | 4 | 0 | 0 |
| Ruffin, Bruce, Clearwater* | .063 | 14 | 16 | 1 | 1 | 1 | 0 | 0 | 0 | 1 | 0 | 0 | 0 | 2 | 0 | 10 | 0 | 0 |
| Sambo, Ramon, Clearwater† | .262 | 110 | 397 | 63 | 104 | 116 | 2 | 5 | 0 | 21 | 3 | 5 | 3 | 2 | 37 | 5 | 57 | 28 | 17 |
| Santiago, Norman, Fort Lauderdale | .200 | 32 | 90 | 10 | 18 | 22 | 1 | 0 | 1 | 6 | 0 | 1 | 0 | 0 | 8 | 0 | 9 | 0 | 0 |
| Schlichting, John, Vero Beach* | .275 | 125 | 415 | 39 | 114 | 145 | 17 | 4 | 2 | 38 | 6 | 9 | 5 | 6 | 20 | 2 | 52 | 15 | 5 |
| Schwartz, Lawrence, Tampa* | .333 | 13 | 6 | 0 | 2 | 2 | 0 | 0 | 0 | 0 | 0 | 1 | 0 | 0 | 3 | 0 | 0 |
| Schweighoffer, Michael, Vero Beach | .059 | 25 | 17 | 2 | 1 | 1 | 0 | 0 | 0 | 1 | 0 | 0 | 0 | 6 | 0 | 10 | 0 | 0 |
| Sciacca, Christopher, Miami† | .194 | 29 | 62 | 3 | 12 | 13 | 1 | 0 | 0 | 3 | 0 | 1 | 0 | 0 | 15 | 2 | 3 |
| Seitzer, Kevin, Fort Myers | .314 | 90 | 290 | 61 | 91 | 120 | 10 | 5 | 3 | 46 | 5 | 0 | 5 | 2 | 85 | 4 | 30 | 28 | 7 |
| Seoane, Mitchell, Fort Lauderdale* | .275 | 63 | 182 | 22 | 50 | 56 | 2 | 2 | 0 | 6 | 1 | 2 | 0 | 2 | 11 | 0 | 21 | 10 | 3 |
| Shaab, Douglas, Osceola* | .000 | 35 | 1 | 0 | 0 | 0 | 0 | 0 | 0 | 0 | 0 | 0 | 0 | 0 | 0 | 0 | 0 | 0 |
| Shaw, Theodore, Fort Myers | .204 | 80 | 240 | 24 | 49 | 70 | 12 | 0 | 3 | 37 | 3 | 0 | 2 | 0 | 17 | 0 | 89 | 13 | 9 |
| Sherlock, Glenn, Osceola* | .198 | 40 | 81 | 8 | 16 | 20 | 2 | 1 | 0 | 8 | 0 | 3 | 1 | 1 | 8 | 0 | 16 | 2 | 1 |
| Shumake, Brooks, Tampa | .252 | 126 | 405 | 53 | 102 | 156 | 15 | 6 | 9 | 44 | 6 | 5 | 4 | 4 | 62 | 3 | 112 | 17 | 5 |
| Simpson, Gregory, 25 Clw-7 Tam* | .333 | 32 | 3 | 1 | 1 | 1 | 0 | 0 | 0 | 0 | 0 | 0 | 0 | 0 | 1 | 0 | 0 |
| Smiciklas, Michael, Miami | .000 | 2 | 5 | 0 | 0 | 0 | 0 | 0 | 0 | 0 | 0 | 0 | 0 | 0 | 0 | 4 | 0 | 0 |
| Smith, Peter, Clearwater | .067 | 26 | 15 | 2 | 1 | 2 | 1 | 0 | 0 | 0 | 0 | 0 | 0 | 0 | 2 | 0 | 7 | 0 | 0 |
| Smith, Timothy, Daytona Beach | .257 | 54 | 179 | 15 | 46 | 64 | 8 | 2 | 2 | 18 | 0 | 0 | 3 | 1 | 22 | 1 | 32 | 2 | 0 |
| Snyder, Doug, Osceola* | .196 | 52 | 158 | 27 | 31 | 47 | 4 | 6 | 0 | 21 | 3 | 1 | 7 | 0 | 36 | 0 | 40 | 2 | 4 |
| Solis, Julio, Miami | .171 | 44 | 82 | 8 | 14 | 16 | 2 | 0 | 0 | 6 | 1 | 3 | 0 | 0 | 12 | 0 | 23 | 0 | 2 |
| Soto, Jose, Clearwater* | .159 | 25 | 69 | 8 | 11 | 16 | 2 | 0 | 1 | 3 | 1 | 2 | 0 | 0 | 7 | 0 | 16 | 3 | 2 |
| Soto, Maximilliano, Lakeland | .256 | 115 | 383 | 45 | 98 | 110 | 5 | 2 | 1 | 37 | 0 | 7 | 1 | 1 | 21 | 1 | 67 | 12 | 3 |
| Spagnola, Glenn, Tampa* | .000 | 21 | 8 | 0 | 0 | 0 | 0 | 0 | 0 | 0 | 0 | 0 | 0 | 0 | 3 | 0 | 6 | 0 | 0 |
| Stearns, Donald, Miami† | .189 | 82 | 259 | 33 | 49 | 64 | 7 | 1 | 2 | 23 | 3 | 3 | 3 | 0 | 26 | 4 | 65 | 18 | 2 |
| Stellern, Michael, Osceola | .117 | 27 | 60 | 3 | 7 | 9 | 2 | 0 | 0 | 2 | 0 | 0 | 0 | 5 | 0 | 17 | 2 | 0 |
| Stewart, Charles, Miami† | .211 | 14 | 38 | 3 | 8 | 8 | 0 | 0 | 0 | 2 | 0 | 1 | 0 | 0 | 3 | 0 | 8 | 0 | 0 |
| Stone, Jerome, Miami* | .169 | 51 | 59 | 6 | 10 | 14 | 2 | 1 | 0 | 4 | 0 | 0 | 0 | 0 | 3 | 0 | 24 | 5 | 4 |
| Stuart, Jervis, Daytona Beach* | .143 | 18 | 49 | 6 | 7 | 7 | 0 | 0 | 0 | 1 | 0 | 1 | 0 | 0 | 12 | 0 | 17 | 1 | 1 |
| Sullivan, Daniel, Winter Haven† | .167 | 22 | 54 | 4 | 9 | 10 | 1 | 0 | 0 | 4 | 0 | 1 | 0 | 1 | 14 | 0 | 12 | 0 | 0 |
| Szekely, Joseph, Vero Beach* | .246 | 68 | 211 | 24 | 52 | 68 | 8 | 4 | 0 | 25 | 0 | 2 | 4 | 4 | 20 | 2 | 48 | 3 | 2 |

| Player and Club | Pct. | G. | AB. | R. | H. | TB. | 2B. | 3B. | HR. | RBI. | GW. | SH. | SF. | HP. | Int. BB. | BB. | SO. | SB. | CS. |
|---|---|---|---|---|---|---|---|---|---|---|---|---|---|---|---|---|---|---|---|
| Tackett, Jeffrey, Daytona Beach....... | .194 | 40 | 103 | 8 | 20 | 29 | 5 | 2 | 0 | 10 | 1 | 0 | 1 | 1 | 13 | 0 | 16 | 1 | 3 |
| Tenacen, Francisco, Clearwater........ | .214 | 105 | 327 | 46 | 70 | 98 | 9 | 5 | 3 | 27 | 2 | 0 | 6 | 9 | 30 | 1 | 68 | 17 | 10 |
| Thiessen, Timothy, West Palm Beach | .243 | 76 | 276 | 24 | 67 | 82 | 9 | 0 | 2 | 27 | 3 | 4 | 2 | 3 | 18 | 1 | 36 | 2 | 4 |
| Thomas, Derrel, Miami† .................... | .292 | 27 | 89 | 6 | 26 | 28 | 2 | 0 | 0 | 9 | 2 | 1 | 1 | 0 | 16 | 1 | 6 | 8 | 2 |
| Thoutsis, Paul, Winter Haven* .......... | .230 | 75 | 209 | 18 | 48 | 57 | 6 | 0 | 1 | 18 | 1 | 1 | 0 | 3 | 18 | 1 | 44 | 0 | 3 |
| Thurman, Gary, Fort Myers.............. | .302 | 134 | 453 | 68 | 137 | 164 | 9 | 9 | 0 | 45 | 5 | 3 | 4 | 4 | 68 | 1 | 93 | 70 | 18 |
| Traen, Thomas, West Palm Beach†.... | .267 | 31 | 15 | 1 | 4 | 6 | 0 | 1 | 0 | 1 | 0 | 0 | 0 | 0 | 0 | 0 | 5 | 0 | 0 |
| Trautwein, John, West Palm Beach ... | .000 | 35 | 4 | 0 | 0 | 0 | 0 | 0 | 0 | 0 | 0 | 0 | 0 | 0 | 1 | 0 | 4 | 0 | 0 |
| Tremblay, Gary, Winter Haven ........ | .159 | 53 | 151 | 14 | 24 | 39 | 6 | 0 | 3 | 18 | 0 | 0 | 2 | 0 | 15 | 0 | 34 | 0 | 0 |
| Triplett, Antonio, Daytona Beach...... | .234 | 123 | 393 | 42 | 92 | 113 | 10 | 4 | 1 | 38 | 4 | 7 | 5 | 2 | 60 | 2 | 82 | 42 | 17 |
| True, Steven, Clearwater* ................ | .000 | 3 | 1 | 0 | 0 | 0 | 0 | 0 | 0 | 0 | 0 | 0 | 0 | 0 | 0 | 0 | 0 | 0 | 0 |
| Tuck, Kevin, Miami ........................... | .000 | 18 | 1 | 1 | 0 | 0 | 0 | 0 | 0 | 0 | 0 | 0 | 0 | 0 | 0 | 0 | 1 | 0 | 0 |
| Tucker, Robert, Vero Beach.............. | .400 | 4 | 5 | 0 | 2 | 2 | 0 | 0 | 0 | 0 | 0 | 0 | 0 | 0 | 1 | 0 | 1 | 0 | 0 |
| Valliant, Robert, West Palm Beach .... | .000 | 6 | 2 | 0 | 0 | 0 | 0 | 0 | 0 | 0 | 0 | 0 | 0 | 0 | 0 | 0 | 2 | 0 | 0 |
| Vanacore, Derek, Fort Myers............ | .235 | 89 | 255 | 33 | 60 | 65 | 3 | 1 | 0 | 19 | 3 | 4 | 1 | 0 | 48 | 0 | 38 | 25 | 8 |
| Van Blaricom, Mark, Fort Myers ....... | .172 | 68 | 174 | 22 | 30 | 38 | 5 | 0 | 1 | 22 | 8 | 0 | 5 | 0 | 36 | 2 | 40 | 8 | 2 |
| Van Cleve, Dandridge, Day. Beach* .. | .215 | 75 | 284 | 37 | 61 | 75 | 6 | 4 | 0 | 25 | 3 | 3 | 2 | 1 | 28 | 1 | 58 | 22 | 8 |
| Van Heyningen, Patrick, Day. Beach* | .111 | 12 | 27 | 1 | 3 | 3 | 0 | 0 | 0 | 1 | 0 | 0 | 0 | 0 | 8 | 0 | 8 | 0 | 0 |
| Vargas, Miguel, Clearwater* ............ | .000 | 44 | 1 | 0 | 0 | 0 | 0 | 0 | 0 | 0 | 0 | 0 | 1 | 0 | 1 | 0 | 0 | 0 | 0 |
| Wade, Scott, Winter Haven .............. | .209 | 104 | 320 | 42 | 67 | 107 | 13 | 3 | 7 | 37 | 5 | 1 | 3 | 4 | 49 | 5 | 80 | 12 | 8 |
| Walewander, James, Lakeland† ........ | .283 | 129 | 499 | 80 | 141 | 168 | 13 | 7 | 0 | 36 | 5 | 1 | 6 | 2 | 48 | 4 | 28 | 30 | 10 |
| Watts, Leonard, Clearwater* ............ | .083 | 22 | 12 | 1 | 1 | 1 | 0 | 0 | 0 | 0 | 0 | 0 | 0 | 0 | 0 | 0 | 5 | 0 | 0 |
| Waylock, Edmund, Lakeland ............ | .173 | 43 | 133 | 12 | 23 | 27 | 4 | 0 | 0 | 10 | 1 | 1 | 0 | 2 | 18 | 0 | 38 | 0 | 1 |
| Wayne, Gary, West Palm Beach* ...... | .600 | 8 | 5 | 2 | 3 | 4 | 1 | 0 | 0 | 3 | 1 | 0 | 0 | 1 | 0 | 2 | 0 | 0 |
| Weinberger, Gary, West Palm Beach* | .285 | 138 | 554 | 81 | 158 | 193 | 19 | 2 | 4 | 55 | 6 | 5 | 8 | 5 | 51 | 3 | 55 | 23 | 15 |
| Welch, Robert, Vero Beach.............. | .000 | 3 | 2 | 0 | 0 | 0 | 0 | 0 | 0 | 0 | 0 | 0 | 0 | 0 | 0 | 0 | 1 | 0 | 0 |
| Winkler, Bradley, Fort Lauderdale* ... | .264 | 40 | 121 | 20 | 32 | 53 | 7 | 1 | 4 | 23 | 7 | 0 | 1 | 0 | 18 | 1 | 35 | 3 | 0 |
| Wohler, Barry, Vero Beach* .............. | .071 | 29 | 14 | 0 | 1 | 1 | 0 | 0 | 0 | 0 | 0 | 1 | 0 | 0 | 3 | 0 | 4 | 0 | 0 |
| Woleslagel, Thomas, Fort Lauderdale | .173 | 25 | 81 | 3 | 14 | 18 | 4 | 0 | 0 | 4 | 0 | 1 | 0 | 0 | 3 | 0 | 14 | 1 | 1 |
| Woodson, Tracy, Vero Beach ............ | .250 | 138 | 504 | 55 | 126 | 191 | 30 | 4 | 9 | 62 | 9 | 5 | 8 | 9 | 50 | 6 | 78 | 10 | 5 |
| Young, Clifford, West Palm Beach* ... | .095 | 25 | 21 | 2 | 2 | 2 | 0 | 0 | 0 | 1 | 0 | 3 | 0 | 0 | 3 | 0 | 4 | 0 | 0 |
| Young, Gerald, Osceola .................... | .255 | 133 | 474 | 88 | 121 | 168 | 20 | 9 | 3 | 48 | 6 | 2 | 9 | 5 | 86 | 5 | 48 | 31 | 13 |
| Young, Scott, St. Petersburg ............ | .167 | 27 | 12 | 0 | 2 | 2 | 0 | 0 | 0 | 2 | 0 | 2 | 0 | 0 | 7 | 0 | 2 | 0 | 0 |
| Zeratsky, Rodney, Tampa ................ | .221 | 69 | 181 | 12 | 40 | 47 | 7 | 0 | 0 | 15 | 2 | 4 | 4 | 1 | 17 | 1 | 35 | 1 | 2 |

The following pitchers, listed alphabetically by club, with games in parentheses, had no plate appearances, primarily through use of designated hitters:

CLEARWATER—Garces, Robinson (11); Ledbetter, David (24).

DAYTONA BEACH—Bianchi, Ben (7); Biercevicz, Gregory (3); Dersin, Eric (17); Fay, Michael (4); Gannon, Justin (27); Gonzalez, Julian (5); Heise, Larry (28); Holm, Michael (12); King, Randy (5); Kipper, Bruce (12); Lackie, Jeffrey (9); Ledbetter, David (4); LoSauro, Carmelo (27); Milacki, Robert (8); Oliveras, Francisco (3); Ramirez, Allan (4); Reynolds, Jay (5); Rice, Richard (13); Rogers, Kenneth (6); Rohan, Edward (17); Sanchez, Geraldo (19); Summers, Jeffrey (30); Thorpe, Paul (24); Willsher, Christopher (21); Wilson, Roger (11); Wilson, Wayne (11).

FORT LAUDERDALE—Beahan, Scot (3); Blum, Brent (4); Canseco, Oswaldo (11); Chastain, Dennis (22); Cloninger, Darin (19); Dersin, Eric (3); Devlin, Robert (32); Dougherty, Patrick (4); Easley, Logan (17); Frey, Steven (19); Fulton, William (15); George, Stephen (24); Guercio, Maurice (22); Harrison, Matthew (22); Leiter, Alois (18); Pries, Jeffrey (22); Raftice, Robert (11); Rather, Dody (6); Rodriguez, Yonis (30); Torres, Ricardo (17); Trudeau, Kevin (1); Underwood, Thomas (5); Yeager, Charles (20).

FORT MYERS—Bass, Edward (36); Berrios, Hector (9); Crew, Kenneth (10); Daniel, Jimmy (13); Davis, Bradley (36); DeJesus, Jose (27); George, Phillip (30); Hull, Jeffrey (27); Leonard, Dennis (3); Mohr, Thomas (29); Nunez, Jose (11); Sanchez, Israel (28); Sparling, Donald (27); Walter, Craig (28); Wyatt, Reginald (4).

LAKELAND—Agar, Jeffrey (4); Barlow, Ricky (9); Cook, Kerry (5); Cooper, William (27); Diez, Scott (4); Dotson, Wayne (17); Duffy, John (45); Gorman, Michael (15); Labozzetta, Albert (12); Medvin, Scott (31); Melchert, Gregory (3); Minnema, David (26); Perrotte, Joseph (13); Phillion, Gerald (11); Poissant, Rodney (22); Raubolt, Arthur (12).

MIAMI—Bear, David (31); Devine, Kevin (15); Eichelberger, Juan (7); Erickson, Paul (14); Farmer, Edward (48); Harris, Randy (1); Kohler, Adam (14); Lacey, Robert (11); McEnaney, William (39); Pena, Hipolito (25); Perkins, Ray (59); Pettaway, Felix (6); Pratt, Louis (3); Rasmussen, Eric (27); Russo, Francis (18); Taft, Dennie (32); Torrez, Michael (19).

OSCEOLA—Cole, Timothy (19); Hartman, Robert (2); Mangham, Mark (23).

TAMPA—Simpson, Gregory (7).

VERO BEACH—Devine, Kevin (1); Torres, Philip (2).

WEST PALM BEACH—Fedor, Francis (31); Impagliazzo, Joseph (37); Johnson, Wayne (5); Lucas, Gary (3); McKay, Troy (2); Moran, Steven (25).

WINTER HAVEN—Araujo, Anazario (32); Cappadona, Anthony (21); Clarkin, Michael (10); Curry, Stephen (27); Dalton, Michael (49); Fenn, Michael (37); Hale, Daniel (38); Kiecker, Dana (29); Parkins, Robert (26); Slifko, Paul (34); Stewart, Hector (37).

GRAND SLAM HOME RUNS—Afenir, Berge, 2 each; Ching, DeAngelis, Jordan, J. Ledbetter, Longenecker, Winkler, 1 each.

AWARDED FIRST BASE ON CATCHER'S INTERFERENCE—Roberts 6 (Afenir, Day, Essian, Jiminez, Niemann, Palacios); Oliva 3 (Beamesderfer, Gatewood, Loy); Abner (Lyden); Essian (Palacios); Francois (F. Gonzalez); Gilcrease (Jiminez); Kelly (Szekely); Sherlock (Oliver); Tenacen (Morris); Tremblay (Gatewood); Triplett (Edmiston).

## CLUB FIELDING

| Club | Pct. | G. | PO. | A. | E. | DP. | PB. | Club | Pct. | G. | PO. | A. | E. | DP. | PB. |
|---|---|---|---|---|---|---|---|---|---|---|---|---|---|---|---|
| St. Petersburg............ | .970 | 140 | 3599 | 1628 | 161 | 140 | 11 | West Palm Beach......... | .964 | 140 | 3540 | 1448 | 185 | 128 | 22 |
| Tampa........................ | .967 | 135 | 3409 | 1526 | 166 | 132 | 46 | Lakeland .................... | .964 | 140 | 3529 | 1472 | 186 | 103 | 29 |
| Osceola...................... | .966 | 135 | 3462 | 1529 | 174 | 121 | 39 | Fort Myers.................. | .964 | 139 | 3589 | 1321 | 186 | 107 | 13 |
| Clearwater.................. | .966 | 141 | 3645 | 1536 | 181 | 129 | 14 | Vero Beach................. | .960 | 140 | 3543 | 1496 | 208 | 119 | 19 |
| Winter Haven.............. | .966 | 139 | 3616 | 1736 | 190 | 165 | 25 | Miami ........................ | .960 | 141 | 3592 | 1614 | 216 | 155 | 26 |
| Fort Lauderdale .......... | .965 | 140 | 3515 | 1449 | 180 | 108 | 18 | Daytona Beach............ | .960 | 140 | 3492 | 1497 | 208 | 123 | 36 |

Triple Plays—Fort Lauderdale, Miami, Winter Haven.

## INDIVIDUAL FIELDING

*Throws lefthanded.

### FIRST BASEMEN

| Player and Club | Pct. | G. | PO. | A. | E. | DP. | Player and Club | Pct. | G. | PO. | A. | E. | DP. |
|---|---|---|---|---|---|---|---|---|---|---|---|---|---|
| Antone, West Palm Beach.......... | .986 | 25 | 191 | 19 | 3 | 18 | Breedlove, St. Petersburg.......... | .667 | 1 | 2 | 0 | 1 | 0 |
| Beamesderfer, Daytona Beach.. | 1.000 | 3 | 12 | 1 | 0 | 1 | Brown, Fort Myers.................... | .970 | 25 | 146 | 13 | 5 | 14 |
| Berge, Tampa.......................... | 1.000 | 1 | 1 | 0 | 0 | 0 | Cathcart, Fort Lauderdale*......... | .986 | 32 | 270 | 10 | 4 | 24 |
| Birriel, Winter Haven* .............. | .986 | 108 | 996 | 76 | 15 | 102 | Ching, Fort Lauderdale*............ | .993 | 66 | 525 | 36 | 4 | 35 |
| Blaser, Fort Lauderdale ............ | .993 | 21 | 127 | 13 | 1 | 15 | Colbert, Lakeland..................... | .974 | 3 | 35 | 3 | 1 | 2 |

| Player and Club | Pct. | G. | PO. | A. | E. | DP. |
|---|---|---|---|---|---|---|
| Corbett, Daytona Beach | 1.000 | 1 | 3 | 0 | 0 | 0 |
| Cunningham, St. Petersburg | 1.000 | 2 | 10 | 0 | 0 | 0 |
| Daily, Lakeland | .988 | 16 | 148 | 11 | 2 | 9 |
| Daugherty, West Palm Beach* | .987 | 119 | 1041 | 50 | 14 | 95 |
| Davis, Miami | 1.000 | 5 | 11 | 2 | 0 | 5 |
| Day, West Palm Beach | 1.000 | 1 | 7 | 0 | 0 | 0 |
| Edmiston, Lakeland | 1.000 | 3 | 18 | 4 | 0 | 2 |
| Englehart, Fort Lauderdale* | .983 | 28 | 215 | 23 | 4 | 23 |
| Gentile, Miami* | 1.000 | 1 | 4 | 2 | 0 | 0 |
| Gill, St. Petersburg | .971 | 5 | 27 | 6 | 1 | 2 |
| Gilles, Fort Lauderdale | 1.000 | 1 | 3 | 1 | 0 | 1 |
| Gonzalez, Fort Lauderdale | 1.000 | 6 | 50 | 7 | 0 | 1 |
| Hamilton, Winter Haven | 1.000 | 15 | 109 | 5 | 0 | 14 |
| Hermann, Lakeland | .984 | 85 | 674 | 49 | 12 | 54 |
| Hilgenberg, Tampa* | .991 | 104 | 846 | 55 | 8 | 86 |
| Ireland, Miami | 1.000 | 1 | 8 | 0 | 0 | 1 |
| Jacobo, Vero Beach | .981 | 78 | 628 | 47 | 13 | 49 |
| JOHNS, St. Petersburg | .993 | 134 | 1286 | 78 | 9 | 123 |
| Johnson, Fort Lauderdale | .889 | 1 | 7 | 1 | 1 | 0 |
| Jordan, Clearwater | .985 | 139 | 1252 | 86 | 20 | 117 |
| Juenke, Miami* | .981 | 33 | 247 | 16 | 5 | 38 |
| Lange, Osceola | .985 | 11 | 57 | 8 | 1 | 8 |
| Ledbetter, St. Petersburg* | .956 | 6 | 41 | 2 | 2 | 4 |
| Leiper, Lakeland | .984 | 7 | 53 | 7 | 1 | 5 |
| Lemons, Fort Myers | .976 | 37 | 229 | 16 | 6 | 16 |
| Lopez, Vero Beach | .983 | 69 | 542 | 33 | 10 | 53 |
| Loy, Clearwater | 1.000 | 2 | 6 | 1 | 0 | 1 |
| Manfre, Tampa | .986 | 26 | 196 | 17 | 3 | 15 |
| Mann, West Palm Beach | 1.000 | 1 | 1 | 0 | 0 | 0 |
| Masters, Lakeland | .990 | 12 | 90 | 9 | 1 | 6 |
| Melrose, Daytona Beach* | .986 | 114 | 920 | 58 | 14 | 89 |
| Newark, Miami | .963 | 3 | 23 | 3 | 1 | 0 |
| Newsome, Lakeland | .977 | 15 | 108 | 18 | 3 | 8 |
| Nichols, Clearwater | 1.000 | 1 | 12 | 0 | 0 | 1 |
| O'Dell, Osceola* | .989 | 127 | 1111 | 96 | 14 | 93 |
| Odgers, Clearwater | 1.000 | 2 | 14 | 0 | 0 | 1 |
| Oliver, Tampa | .976 | 17 | 112 | 10 | 3 | 15 |
| Palacios, Lakeland | 1.000 | 7 | 38 | 1 | 0 | 4 |
| Perkins, Miami* | .989 | 21 | 171 | 12 | 2 | 20 |
| Pevey, St. Petersburg | 1.000 | 1 | 4 | 0 | 0 | 1 |
| Poznanski, Daytona Beach | .984 | 41 | 277 | 22 | 5 | 22 |
| Reynolds, Osceola | 1.000 | 8 | 30 | 3 | 0 | 3 |
| B. Richardson, Winter Haven | .993 | 15 | 140 | 11 | 1 | 18 |
| T. Richardson, 94 Mia-18 FtM | .991 | 112 | 912 | 82 | 9 | 85 |
| Riley, Daytona Beach | 1.000 | 1 | 3 | 0 | 0 | 0 |
| Seitzer, Fort Myers | .989 | 74 | 561 | 73 | 7 | 51 |
| Sullivan, Winter Haven | 1.000 | 15 | 144 | 7 | 0 | 14 |
| Tackett, Daytona Beach | 1.000 | 2 | 1 | 0 | 0 | 0 |
| Woodson, Vero Beach | 1.000 | 7 | 20 | 3 | 0 | 1 |

Triple Plays—Birriel, T. Richardson.

## SECOND BASEMEN

| Player and Club | Pct. | G. | PO. | A. | E. | DP. |
|---|---|---|---|---|---|---|
| Balcomb, St. Petersburg | .950 | 30 | 54 | 79 | 7 | 21 |
| Barker, West Palm Beach | .961 | 23 | 41 | 57 | 4 | 8 |
| Batista, West Palm Beach | 1.000 | 3 | 4 | 3 | 0 | 1 |
| Bautista, Daytona Beach | .909 | 21 | 37 | 53 | 9 | 14 |
| Beamesderfer, Daytona Beach | .957 | 6 | 15 | 7 | 1 | 3 |
| Bernaldo, Fort Lauderdale | .923 | 10 | 10 | 14 | 2 | 1 |
| Breedlove, St. Petersburg | 1.000 | 2 | 0 | 5 | 0 | 2 |
| Carroll, Miami | .973 | 120 | 292 | 363 | 18 | 85 |
| Cobb, West Palm Beach | .925 | 20 | 28 | 58 | 7 | 10 |
| Crone, Daytona Beach | .921 | 26 | 50 | 55 | 9 | 10 |
| Denny, Clearwater | 1.000 | 1 | 2 | 1 | 0 | 1 |
| Germann, Tampa | 1.000 | 28 | 63 | 81 | 0 | 11 |
| Giddens, Tampa | .966 | 102 | 209 | 280 | 17 | 69 |
| Gilcrease, Fort Myers | .988 | 18 | 37 | 47 | 1 | 7 |
| Goff, Winter Haven | .969 | 81 | 174 | 288 | 15 | 62 |
| Gonzalez, Winter Haven | .968 | 64 | 135 | 203 | 11 | 52 |
| Gutierrez, Vero Beach | .971 | 101 | 211 | 300 | 15 | 60 |
| Haller, Daytona Beach | .907 | 15 | 25 | 24 | 5 | 3 |
| Harrison, St. Petersburg | .968 | 114 | 243 | 341 | 19 | 74 |
| Heeney, Fort Lauderdale | .889 | 4 | 7 | 9 | 2 | 1 |
| Hubbard, Daytona Beach | 1.000 | 4 | 10 | 6 | 0 | 1 |
| Ireland, Miami | 1.000 | 1 | 2 | 4 | 0 | 1 |
| Jacoby, Miami | .667 | 2 | 1 | 3 | 2 | 0 |
| Job, Osceola | .972 | 62 | 115 | 166 | 8 | 27 |
| Kopetsky, Vero Beach | 1.000 | 1 | 0 | 1 | 0 | 0 |
| Mabe, Fort Myers | .932 | 123 | 256 | 292 | 40 | 58 |
| Machado, Tampa | .980 | 15 | 19 | 31 | 1 | 4 |
| Manning, Lakeland | 1.000 | 2 | 4 | 4 | 0 | 0 |
| Mattocks, 58 FtL-20 Mia | .955 | 78 | 169 | 216 | 18 | 41 |
| Maynard, Fort Lauderdale | 1.000 | 1 | 1 | 1 | 0 | 0 |
| Moreno, Fort Myers | 1.000 | 4 | 7 | 11 | 0 | 2 |
| Murray, Daytona Beach | .967 | 77 | 159 | 193 | 12 | 45 |
| Newark, Miami | 1.000 | 2 | 1 | 2 | 0 | 1 |
| Newsom, Vero Beach | 1.000 | 20 | 27 | 50 | 0 | 3 |
| Newsome, Lakeland | 1.000 | 13 | 29 | 21 | 0 | 5 |
| Odgers, Clearwater | 1.000 | 1 | 1 | 2 | 0 | 2 |
| PAREDES, West Palm Beach | .981 | 93 | 184 | 281 | 9 | 66 |
| Parker, Osceola | .962 | 86 | 183 | 247 | 17 | 50 |
| Perdomo, Fort Lauderdale | .972 | 44 | 85 | 120 | 6 | 29 |
| Pottinger, Clearwater | .968 | 52 | 96 | 143 | 8 | 26 |
| Riley, Daytona Beach | 1.000 | 2 | 1 | 0 | 0 | 0 |
| Ripken, Daytona Beach | 1.000 | 8 | 9 | 27 | 0 | 6 |
| Ritch, Vero Beach | .949 | 38 | 49 | 81 | 7 | 15 |
| Sambo, Clearwater | .941 | 95 | 205 | 256 | 29 | 52 |
| Seoane, Fort Lauderdale | 1.000 | 40 | 55 | 72 | 0 | 14 |
| Soto, Lakeland | .958 | 5 | 7 | 16 | 1 | 2 |
| Stearns, Miami | 1.000 | 3 | 5 | 3 | 0 | 3 |
| Thiessen, West Palm Beach | .976 | 13 | 14 | 27 | 1 | 3 |
| Walewander, Lakeland | .980 | 125 | 267 | 417 | 14 | 69 |
| Woleslagel, Fort Lauderdale | 1.000 | 2 | 8 | 6 | 0 | 5 |

Triple Play—Carroll.

## THIRD BASEMEN

| Player and Club | Pct. | G. | PO. | A. | E. | DP. |
|---|---|---|---|---|---|---|
| Amity, Miami | .667 | 4 | 3 | 7 | 5 | 1 |
| Balcomb, St. Petersburg | 1.000 | 2 | 0 | 1 | 0 | 0 |
| Barker, West Palm Beach | .857 | 9 | 5 | 19 | 4 | 1 |
| Beamesderfer, Daytona Beach | .870 | 9 | 7 | 13 | 3 | 1 |
| Blaser, Fort Lauderdale | .924 | 35 | 17 | 68 | 7 | 3 |
| Bochesa, Winter Haven | 1.000 | 2 | 4 | 1 | 0 | 0 |
| Breedlove, St. Petersburg | .924 | 77 | 51 | 169 | 18 | 23 |
| Caminiti, Osceola | .925 | 81 | 53 | 193 | 20 | 21 |
| Carroll, Miami | 1.000 | 1 | 0 | 2 | 0 | 0 |
| Cobb, West Palm Beach | .898 | 42 | 25 | 72 | 11 | 8 |
| Colpitt, Clearwater | .880 | 11 | 5 | 17 | 3 | 2 |
| Crone, Daytona Beach | .857 | 2 | 1 | 5 | 1 | 0 |
| Cruz, Miami | .977 | 27 | 22 | 63 | 2 | 13 |
| Cunningham, St. Petersburg | .944 | 55 | 39 | 95 | 8 | 4 |
| DeLosSantos, Fort Myers | .877 | 104 | 87 | 141 | 32 | 13 |
| Denny, Clearwater | .750 | 1 | 0 | 3 | 1 | 1 |
| Essian, Miami | 1.000 | 1 | 2 | 0 | 0 | 0 |
| Estrada, Winter Haven | .915 | 86 | 55 | 183 | 22 | 22 |
| Figueroa, St. Petersburg | .750 | 2 | 2 | 10 | 4 | 1 |
| Germann, Tampa | 1.000 | 5 | 4 | 7 | 0 | 1 |
| Gilcrease, Fort Myers | 1.000 | 12 | 7 | 12 | 0 | 0 |
| Gilles, Fort Lauderdale | .500 | 2 | 1 | 0 | 1 | 0 |
| Gonzalez, Winter Haven | .969 | 13 | 6 | 25 | 1 | 2 |
| Gutierrez, Vero Beach | 1.000 | 8 | 4 | 13 | 0 | 0 |
| Halasz, Daytona Beach | .913 | 9 | 5 | 16 | 2 | 1 |
| Haller, Daytona Beach | .879 | 24 | 18 | 40 | 8 | 3 |
| Hamilton, Winter Haven | .908 | 55 | 27 | 111 | 14 | 9 |
| Harris, Tampa | .913 | 128 | 89 | 277 | 35 | 34 |
| Heeney, Fort Lauderdale | .765 | 8 | 5 | 8 | 4 | 0 |
| Hubbard, Daytona Beach | .920 | 86 | 45 | 162 | 18 | 8 |
| Hudson, Miami | .750 | 1 | 0 | 3 | 1 | 0 |
| Infante, St. Petersburg | .853 | 12 | 6 | 23 | 5 | 0 |
| Jacoby, Miami | .921 | 48 | 20 | 73 | 8 | 6 |
| Jarrell, Fort Myers | .900 | 15 | 7 | 20 | 3 | 2 |
| Job, Osceola | .909 | 24 | 20 | 40 | 6 | 3 |
| Lane, Fort Lauderdale | 1.000 | 3 | 3 | 5 | 0 | 2 |
| Lange, Osceola | .963 | 40 | 17 | 61 | 3 | 4 |
| Leiper, Lakeland | .903 | 15 | 7 | 21 | 3 | 4 |
| Longenecker, Fort Myers | 1.000 | 2 | 0 | 2 | 0 | 0 |
| Machado, Tampa | .913 | 12 | 5 | 16 | 2 | 2 |
| Manning, Lakeland | .909 | 4 | 3 | 7 | 1 | 1 |
| Mattocks, Miami | 1.000 | 1 | 2 | 1 | 0 | 0 |
| Maynard, Fort Lauderdale | .833 | 1 | 0 | 5 | 1 | 1 |
| McKnight, Miami | .889 | 6 | 2 | 6 | 1 | 3 |
| Murray, Daytona Beach | .926 | 11 | 5 | 20 | 2 | 2 |
| Newark, Miami | .924 | 24 | 14 | 59 | 6 | 5 |
| Newsome, Lakeland | .918 | 56 | 47 | 88 | 12 | 5 |
| Nichols, Clearwater | .931 | 84 | 65 | 137 | 15 | 13 |
| Odgers, Clearwater | .947 | 25 | 13 | 41 | 3 | 1 |
| Perdomo, Fort Lauderdale | .909 | 11 | 6 | 14 | 2 | 0 |
| Pereira, Miami | .911 | 30 | 21 | 30 | 5 | 3 |
| Pottinger, Clearwater | .934 | 29 | 17 | 68 | 6 | 4 |
| Raziano, West Palm Beach | .911 | 69 | 40 | 103 | 14 | 10 |
| Reid, Miami | .842 | 6 | 2 | 14 | 3 | 0 |
| Ripken, Daytona Beach | .952 | 9 | 12 | 8 | 1 | 2 |
| Rivera, 28 FtL-3 Mia | .910 | 31 | 21 | 60 | 8 | 4 |
| Ross, Lakeland | .943 | 18 | 14 | 36 | 3 | 3 |
| Rosthenhausler, Lakeland | .912 | 16 | 11 | 20 | 3 | 2 |
| Santiago, Fort Lauderdale | .932 | 24 | 16 | 39 | 4 | 5 |
| Seitzer, Fort Myers | .920 | 12 | 8 | 15 | 2 | 1 |
| Seoane, Fort Lauderdale | .872 | 20 | 9 | 32 | 6 | 1 |
| Soto, Lakeland | .667 | 1 | 0 | 2 | 1 | 1 |
| Stearns, Miami | .850 | 5 | 7 | 10 | 3 | 0 |
| Thiessen, West Palm Beach | .883 | 39 | 26 | 65 | 12 | 9 |
| Triplett, Daytona Beach | .923 | 6 | 4 | 8 | 1 | 2 |
| Van Blaricom, Fort Myers | 1.000 | 4 | 2 | 2 | 0 | 0 |
| Waylock, Lakeland | .934 | 35 | 26 | 59 | 6 | 6 |
| Woleslagel, Fort Lauderdale | .934 | 19 | 9 | 48 | 4 | 2 |
| WOODSON, Vero Beach | .926 | 136 | 111 | 267 | 30 | 26 |

Triple Plays—Jacoby, Woleslagel.

## SHORTSTOPS

| Player and Club | Pct. | G. | PO. | A. | E. | DP. |
|---|---|---|---|---|---|---|
| Allaire, Osceola | .936 | 105 | 140 | 296 | 30 | 59 |
| Antonio, Vero Beach | 1.000 | 2 | 1 | 4 | 0 | 1 |
| Bachman, West Palm Beach | .914 | 112 | 150 | 327 | 45 | 66 |
| Balcomb, St. Petersburg | .892 | 15 | 10 | 23 | 4 | 8 |
| Batista, West Palm Beach | .913 | 7 | 7 | 14 | 2 | 4 |
| Carroll, Miami | 1.000 | 2 | 3 | 4 | 0 | 1 |
| Cruz, Miami | .885 | 15 | 27 | 42 | 9 | 12 |
| Denny, Clearwater | 1.000 | 1 | 0 | 3 | 0 | 0 |
| Estrada, Winter Haven | .900 | 17 | 19 | 17 | 4 | 2 |
| Foli, Miami | 1.000 | 1 | 1 | 5 | 0 | 2 |
| Francois, Vero Beach | .889 | 111 | 151 | 283 | 54 | 50 |
| Germann, Tampa | .967 | 79 | 122 | 202 | 11 | 39 |
| Gilcrease, Fort Myers | .956 | 72 | 116 | 187 | 14 | 36 |
| Gutierrez, Vero Beach | .902 | 15 | 22 | 33 | 6 | 5 |
| Halasz, Daytona Beach | .978 | 19 | 32 | 58 | 2 | 16 |
| Hamilton, Winter Haven | 1.000 | 1 | 0 | 1 | 0 | 0 |
| Harris, St. Petersburg | .942 | 135 | 205 | 466 | 41 | 89 |
| Heeney, Fort Lauderdale | .667 | 1 | 0 | 4 | 2 | 0 |
| Hudson, Miami | .853 | 35 | 50 | 72 | 21 | 21 |
| Ireland, Miami | .967 | 46 | 72 | 132 | 7 | 28 |
| Job, Osceola | .871 | 8 | 13 | 14 | 4 | 5 |
| Kopetsky, Vero Beach | .852 | 8 | 8 | 15 | 4 | 4 |
| Kraft, Clearwater | .971 | 53 | 83 | 183 | 8 | 33 |
| Latmore, Daytona Beach | 1.000 | 5 | 6 | 6 | 0 | 2 |
| Martinez, Fort Lauderdale | .938 | 91 | 123 | 254 | 25 | 45 |
| Maynard, Fort Lauderdale | .916 | 19 | 29 | 58 | 8 | 11 |
| McKnight, Miami | .950 | 6 | 6 | 13 | 1 | 1 |
| Moreno, Fort Myers | .952 | 28 | 40 | 60 | 5 | 9 |
| Murray, Daytona Beach | .922 | 29 | 48 | 71 | 10 | 10 |
| Newsom, Vero Beach | .911 | 16 | 16 | 35 | 5 | 4 |
| Nichols, Daytona Beach | .903 | 46 | 91 | 141 | 25 | 33 |
| Parker, Osceola | .942 | 41 | 48 | 82 | 8 | 16 |
| Peppio, Miami | .625 | 2 | 2 | 3 | 3 | 2 |
| Perdomo, Fort Lauderdale | .892 | 34 | 32 | 84 | 14 | 14 |
| Pereira, Miami | .878 | 25 | 37 | 71 | 15 | 10 |
| Perez, Clearwater | .956 | 74 | 115 | 236 | 16 | 47 |
| Pottinger, Clearwater | .982 | 15 | 20 | 35 | 1 | 6 |
| REED, Winter Haven | .952 | 133 | 256 | 478 | 37 | 101 |
| Reid, Miami | 1.000 | 1 | 1 | 4 | 0 | 2 |
| Reynolds, Osceola | 1.000 | 1 | 1 | 0 | 0 | 0 |
| Ripken, Daytona Beach | .971 | 50 | 69 | 163 | 7 | 24 |
| Rivera, Miami | 1.000 | 1 | 3 | 3 | 0 | 0 |
| Ross, Lakeland | .917 | 4 | 1 | 10 | 1 | 3 |
| Rosthenhausler, Lakeland | .912 | 24 | 55 | 70 | 12 | 14 |
| Sciacca, Miami | .914 | 21 | 20 | 54 | 7 | 11 |
| Seoane, Fort Lauderdale | 1.000 | 2 | 0 | 5 | 0 | 0 |
| Shumake, Tampa | .924 | 59 | 110 | 183 | 24 | 36 |
| Soto, Lakeland | .935 | 104 | 158 | 290 | 31 | 38 |
| Thiessen, West Palm Beach | .940 | 30 | 29 | 81 | 7 | 16 |
| Thomas, Miami | .875 | 4 | 5 | 9 | 2 | 1 |
| Van Blaricom, Fort Myers | .931 | 50 | 73 | 130 | 15 | 20 |
| Waylock, Lakeland | .929 | 8 | 15 | 24 | 3 | 5 |
| Woleslagel, Fort Lauderdale | 1.000 | 3 | 2 | 7 | 0 | 2 |

Triple Plays—Maynard, Reed.

## OUTFIELDERS

| Player and Club | Pct. | G. | PO. | A. | E. | DP. |
|---|---|---|---|---|---|---|
| Abner, West Palm Beach | .986 | 82 | 138 | 7 | 2 | 3 |
| Agostinelli, St. Petersburg | 1.000 | 4 | 4 | 0 | 0 | 0 |
| Allen, Fort Myers | .984 | 71 | 171 | 9 | 3 | 6 |
| Altobelli, Miami | 1.000 | 12 | 13 | 0 | 0 | 0 |
| Amante, St. Petersburg | .970 | 20 | 29 | 3 | 1 | 0 |
| Amble, Daytona Beach | .962 | 95 | 145 | 7 | 6 | 1 |
| Antone, West Palm Beach | 1.000 | 1 | 1 | 0 | 0 | 0 |
| Aquino, Daytona Beach° | .941 | 15 | 16 | 0 | 1 | 0 |
| Arzola, St. Petersburg | .978 | 84 | 125 | 6 | 3 | 2 |
| Balcomb, St. Petersburg | 1.000 | 1 | 1 | 0 | 0 | 0 |
| Barker, West Palm Beach | 1.000 | 1 | 2 | 0 | 0 | 0 |
| Bautista, Daytona Beach | 1.000 | 1 | 2 | 0 | 0 | 0 |
| Beamesderfer, Daytona Beach.. | .945 | 27 | 48 | 4 | 3 | 1 |
| Bellver, Miami | .939 | 29 | 45 | 1 | 3 | 0 |
| Berge, Tampa | .978 | 114 | 164 | 10 | 4 | 1 |
| Beringhele, Vero Beach | .945 | 37 | 47 | 5 | 3 | 2 |
| Birriel, Winter Haven° | 1.000 | 4 | 6 | 1 | 0 | 0 |
| Bogener, Miami° | 1.000 | 45 | 83 | 6 | 0 | 1 |
| Bryant, Tampa | .975 | 98 | 181 | 12 | 5 | 3 |
| Buhner, Fort Lauderdale | .972 | 113 | 235 | 12 | 7 | 4 |
| Burke, Osceola | .972 | 73 | 99 | 7 | 3 | 2 |
| Camelo, West Palm Beach° | .990 | 128 | 189 | 8 | 2 | 2 |
| Carpenter, Fort Lauderdale | .944 | 38 | 50 | 1 | 3 | 1 |
| Carroll, Miami | 1.000 | 2 | 1 | 0 | 0 | 0 |
| Cathcart, Fort Lauderdale° | 1.000 | 33 | 57 | 1 | 0 | 1 |
| Christy, Lakeland | 1.000 | 30 | 51 | 2 | 0 | 1 |
| Cornwell, Lakeland° | .976 | 63 | 117 | 5 | 3 | 0 |
| Cruz, Miami | 1.000 | 1 | 1 | 0 | 0 | 0 |
| Cunningham, St. Petersburg | .957 | 10 | 21 | 1 | 1 | 0 |
| Davis, Clearwater° | .957 | 10 | 21 | 1 | 1 | 0 |
| DeAngelis, Clearwater° | .964 | 109 | 195 | 19 | 8 | 1 |
| Delgado, Osceola | .939 | 21 | 31 | 0 | 2 | 0 |
| Denny, Clearwater | 1.000 | 42 | 47 | 3 | 0 | 2 |
| Dyrek, Osceola° | 1.000 | 16 | 18 | 0 | 0 | 0 |
| Flores, Vero Beach° | .982 | 133 | 270 | 7 | 5 | 2 |
| Fortenberry, Clearwater | .985 | 26 | 64 | 3 | 1 | 2 |
| FREEMAN, Lakeland | .997 | 127 | 288 | 10 | 1 | 1 |
| Gaeta, Daytona Beach | 1.000 | 10 | 16 | 0 | 0 | 0 |
| Gentile, Miami° | .960 | 90 | 114 | 6 | 5 | 1 |
| Gilcrease, Fort Myers | .985 | 34 | 63 | 1 | 1 | 0 |
| Gill, St. Petersburg | .880 | 20 | 22 | 0 | 3 | 0 |
| Groth, Tampa | .970 | 84 | 125 | 4 | 4 | 1 |
| Gutierrez, Daytona Beach° | .955 | 41 | 60 | 3 | 3 | 0 |
| Gwynn, Vero Beach° | 1.000 | 38 | 43 | 2 | 0 | 1 |
| Hamb, Lakeland | .889 | 5 | 8 | 0 | 1 | 0 |
| Hampton, Osceola° | .936 | 45 | 71 | 2 | 5 | 0 |
| Hansen, Winter Haven° | .915 | 67 | 124 | 6 | 12 | 0 |
| Henderson, Fort Lauderdale° | 1.000 | 3 | 6 | 0 | 0 | 0 |
| Hermann, Lakeland | .962 | 12 | 23 | 2 | 1 | 0 |
| Houp, Osceola | .971 | 31 | 30 | 3 | 1 | 1 |
| Hudson, Miami | .976 | 81 | 196 | 8 | 5 | 1 |
| Hutson, West Palm Beach | .944 | 20 | 17 | 0 | 1 | 0 |
| L. Johnson, St. Petersburg° | .986 | 128 | 338 | 16 | 5 | 4 |
| Th. Johnson, Fort Myers° | 1.000 | 10 | 11 | 0 | 0 | 0 |
| To. Johnson, Clearwater | .989 | 30 | 90 | 1 | 1 | 0 |
| Juenke, Miami° | 1.000 | 2 | 4 | 0 | 0 | 0 |
| Karmeris, Vero Beach | .875 | 5 | 6 | 1 | 1 | 0 |
| Kelly, Fort Lauderdale | .995 | 113 | 187 | 1 | 1 | 0 |
| Kirby, Vero Beach | .984 | 110 | 231 | 10 | 4 | 2 |
| Kopetsky, Vero Beach | 1.000 | 2 | 3 | 0 | 0 | 0 |
| Lane, 6 FtL-13 Miami | .962 | 19 | 21 | 4 | 1 | 1 |
| Lange, Osceola | 1.000 | 6 | 4 | 0 | 0 | 0 |
| Latmore, Daytona Beach | 1.000 | 2 | 0 | 1 | 0 | 0 |
| Ledbetter, St. Petersburg° | 1.000 | 20 | 35 | 3 | 0 | 1 |
| Lemon, St. Petersburg° | 1.000 | 4 | 3 | 0 | 0 | 0 |
| Lewis, Miami | .956 | 89 | 184 | 11 | 9 | 2 |
| Long, Lakeland | .957 | 74 | 126 | 6 | 6 | 1 |
| Longenecker, Fort Myers | 1.000 | 5 | 9 | 0 | 0 | 0 |
| Lowe, Clearwater | .985 | 96 | 193 | 10 | 3 | 3 |
| Lusader, Lakeland° | .943 | 25 | 47 | 3 | 3 | 1 |
| MacKay, Fort Lauderdale | 1.000 | 25 | 32 | 0 | 0 | 0 |
| Manfre, Tampa | .957 | 63 | 103 | 7 | 5 | 0 |
| Mann, West Palm Beach | .991 | 75 | 111 | 5 | 1 | 0 |
| P. Martinez, Lakeland | .963 | 36 | 101 | 2 | 4 | 2 |
| R. Martinez, Fort Myers° | .977 | 71 | 161 | 7 | 4 | 0 |
| Mattocks, Miami | .960 | 21 | 22 | 2 | 1 | 0 |
| Mauch, St. Petersburg | .889 | 7 | 7 | 1 | 1 | 0 |
| McInnis, Winter Haven° | .992 | 52 | 115 | 7 | 1 | 2 |
| Millis, Lakeland | .979 | 38 | 89 | 3 | 2 | 0 |
| Mills, St. Petersburg | .976 | 23 | 39 | 1 | 1 | 0 |
| Minick, Lakeland° | 1.000 | 4 | 8 | 1 | 0 | 0 |
| R. Mitchell, Tampa | .917 | 20 | 31 | 2 | 3 | 0 |
| T. Mitchell, Osceola | .941 | 52 | 78 | 2 | 5 | 1 |
| Newsome, Lakeland | .955 | 12 | 20 | 1 | 1 | 0 |
| Nichols, Clearwater | 1.000 | 5 | 3 | 0 | 0 | 0 |
| Nunez, St. Petersburg | .971 | 125 | 229 | 9 | 7 | 1 |
| Oliva, Winter Haven | .987 | 59 | 141 | 7 | 2 | 2 |
| Oquendo, Lakeland° | .909 | 7 | 10 | 0 | 1 | 0 |
| Peruso, Fort Lauderdale | .900 | 13 | 17 | 1 | 2 | 0 |
| Posillico, Miami° | 1.000 | 3 | 3 | 1 | 0 | 0 |
| Reed, Fort Lauderdale | .966 | 96 | 191 | 8 | 7 | 3 |
| Reynolds, Osceola | 1.000 | 10 | 9 | 1 | 0 | 0 |
| Richardson, Miami | 1.000 | 1 | 2 | 0 | 0 | 0 |
| Riley, Daytona Beach | .944 | 9 | 16 | 1 | 1 | 0 |
| Rivera, Miami | 1.000 | 1 | 1 | 0 | 0 | 0 |
| Roberts, Winter Haven | .977 | 110 | 201 | 10 | 5 | 3 |
| Rodriguez, West Palm Beach | .955 | 24 | 21 | 0 | 1 | 0 |
| Schlichting, Vero Beach | .970 | 120 | 253 | 6 | 8 | 1 |
| Sciacca, Miami | 1.000 | 1 | 3 | 0 | 0 | 0 |
| Seoane, Fort Lauderdale | 1.000 | 1 | 1 | 0 | 0 | 0 |
| Shaw, Fort Myers | .946 | 35 | 51 | 2 | 3 | 1 |
| Shumake, Tampa | .973 | 54 | 141 | 5 | 4 | 1 |
| Smith, Daytona Beach° | .923 | 38 | 44 | 4 | 4 | 1 |
| Snyder, Osceola | .976 | 48 | 77 | 3 | 2 | 1 |
| Soto, Clearwater° | 1.000 | 18 | 30 | 1 | 0 | 0 |
| Stearns, Miami | .976 | 64 | 114 | 6 | 3 | 1 |
| Stellern, Osceola | 1.000 | 18 | 26 | 0 | 0 | 0 |
| Stone, Clearwater | .960 | 12 | 22 | 2 | 1 | 1 |
| Stuart, Daytona Beach° | .971 | 17 | 34 | 0 | 1 | 0 |
| Tenacen, Clearwater | .928 | 95 | 212 | 7 | 17 | 2 |
| Thomas, Miami | 1.000 | 5 | 6 | 0 | 0 | 0 |
| Thoutsis, Winter Haven | .991 | 61 | 103 | 3 | 1 | 1 |
| Thurman, Fort Myers | .975 | 132 | 368 | 18 | 10 | 3 |
| Triplett, Daytona Beach | .979 | 113 | 226 | 10 | 5 | 5 |
| Vanacore, Fort Myers° | .983 | 87 | 160 | 13 | 3 | 3 |
| Van Cleve, Daytona Beach | .988 | 74 | 165 | 4 | 2 | 2 |
| Van Heyningen, Daytona Beach° | .667 | 5 | 2 | 0 | 1 | 0 |
| Wade, Winter Haven | .947 | 99 | 171 | 8 | 10 | 1 |
| Weinberger, West Palm Beach° | .991 | 138 | 326 | 5 | 3 | 1 |
| Winkler, Fort Lauderdale | 1.000 | 7 | 14 | 1 | 0 | 0 |
| Young, Osceola | .981 | 131 | 251 | 11 | 5 | 5 |

Triple Plays—Buhner, Thoutsis.

## CATCHERS

| Player and Club | Pct. | G. | PO. | A. | E. | DP. | PB. |
|---|---|---|---|---|---|---|---|
| Afenir, Osceola | .975 | 89 | 557 | 72 | 16 | 5 | 28 |
| Agostinelli, St. Petersburg | .985 | 51 | 226 | 29 | 4 | 5 | 4 |
| Antone, West Palm Beach | .995 | 65 | 366 | 30 | 2 | 7 | 12 |
| Balcomb, St. Petersburg | 1.000 | 1 | 10 | 1 | 0 | 0 | 0 |
| Beamesderfer, Day. Beach | .983 | 46 | 251 | 39 | 5 | 2 | 9 |
| Bochesa, Winter Haven | .978 | 27 | 115 | 21 | 3 | 2 | 4 |
| Caffrey, West Palm Beach | .984 | 36 | 220 | 29 | 4 | 2 | 5 |
| Camilli, Winter Haven | .971 | 33 | 93 | 7 | 3 | 2 | 5 |
| Corbett, Daytona Beach | .985 | 25 | 112 | 19 | 2 | 0 | 4 |
| Daily, Lakeland | 1.000 | 4 | 11 | 1 | 0 | 0 | 1 |
| Davis, Miami | .973 | 41 | 211 | 43 | 7 | 7 | 6 |
| Day, West Palm Beach | .963 | 49 | 305 | 29 | 13 | 3 | 5 |
| DeFrancesco, Winter Haven | .979 | 36 | 162 | 23 | 4 | 5 | 1 |
| Dempsay, Lakeland | .929 | 13 | 57 | 8 | 5 | 0 | 2 |
| Denis, Vero Beach | .966 | 4 | 27 | 1 | 1 | 0 | 2 |
| Edmiston, Lakeland | .988 | 44 | 217 | 37 | 3 | 3 | 15 |
| Essian, Miami | .967 | 14 | 83 | 5 | 3 | 4 | 2 |
| Gatewood, Vero Beach | .974 | 61 | 335 | 38 | 10 | 8 | 9 |
| Gonzalez, Fort Lauderdale | .983 | 37 | 218 | 18 | 4 | 2 | 2 |
| Gsellman, Clearwater | 1.000 | 7 | 23 | 0 | 0 | 0 | 0 |
| Jimenez, St. Petersburg | .966 | 11 | 54 | 3 | 2 | 0 | 1 |
| B. Johnson, Fort Lauderdale | 1.000 | 8 | 42 | 1 | 0 | 0 | 1 |
| R. Johnson, Clearwater | .969 | 33 | 172 | 16 | 6 | 0 | 3 |
| Kaye, Clearwater | .969 | 30 | 109 | 15 | 4 | 0 | 5 |
| Krynitsky, Fort Myers | 1.000 | 11 | 57 | 4 | 0 | 0 | 2 |
| Lawhon, Fort Lauderdale | 1.000 | 4 | 5 | 0 | 0 | 0 | 1 |
| Lopez, Vero Beach | .969 | 28 | 113 | 13 | 4 | 1 | 6 |
| Loy, Clearwater | .985 | 75 | 419 | 46 | 7 | 3 | 5 |
| LYDEN, Fort Lauderdale | .988 | 101 | 607 | 63 | 8 | 5 | 14 |
| Masters, Lakeland | .981 | 19 | 93 | 9 | 2 | 0 | 3 |
| Morris, Fort Myers | .980 | 91 | 493 | 57 | 11 | 7 | 10 |
| Newark, Miami | .994 | 64 | 263 | 56 | 2 | 5 | 8 |
| Niemann, Fort Myers | .968 | 56 | 245 | 28 | 9 | 3 | 1 |
| Oliver, Tampa | .978 | 86 | 503 | 84 | 13 | 6 | 33 |
| Palacios, Lakeland | .970 | 67 | 372 | 44 | 13 | 4 | 8 |
| Pevey, St. Petersburg | .981 | 83 | 419 | 57 | 9 | 0 | 6 |
| Poznanski, Daytona Beach | .980 | 50 | 257 | 39 | 6 | 1 | 14 |
| Reynolds, Osceola | .980 | 33 | 172 | 26 | 4 | 3 | 5 |
| Richardson, Winter Haven | .986 | 17 | 62 | 9 | 1 | 1 | 2 |
| Roman, Clearwater | .967 | 12 | 77 | 10 | 3 | 1 | 1 |
| Sherlock, Osceola | .995 | 36 | 163 | 23 | 1 | 0 | 6 |
| Solis, Miami | .970 | 44 | 163 | 32 | 6 | 4 | 8 |
| Stewart, Miami | .977 | 14 | 71 | 13 | 2 | 3 | 2 |
| Szekely, Vero Beach | .982 | 63 | 337 | 46 | 7 | 7 | 2 |
| Tackett, Daytona Beach | .975 | 36 | 172 | 21 | 5 | 1 | 9 |
| Tremblay, Winter Haven | .965 | 52 | 181 | 41 | 8 | 3 | 13 |
| Tucker, Vero Beach | 1.000 | 2 | 4 | 0 | 0 | 0 | 0 |
| Zeratsky, Tampa | .971 | 66 | 320 | 52 | 11 | 12 | 13 |

## PITCHERS

| Player and Club | Pct. | G. | PO. | A. | E. | DP. |
|---|---|---|---|---|---|---|
| Agar, Lakeland | 1.000 | 4 | 1 | 1 | 0 | 0 |
| Antone, West Palm Beach | 1.000 | 1 | 0 | 1 | 0 | 0 |
| Araujo, Winter Haven | .979 | 32 | 16 | 30 | 1 | 0 |
| Bacon, Tampa | .964 | 36 | 8 | 19 | 1 | 2 |
| Baker, Osceola | .952 | 46 | 8 | 12 | 1 | 1 |
| Barlow, Lakeland | .917 | 9 | 3 | 8 | 1 | 0 |
| Bass, Fort Myers | .923 | 36 | 12 | 12 | 2 | 1 |
| Beahan, Fort Lauderdale | 1.000 | 3 | 1 | 0 | 0 | 0 |
| Bear, Miami | .865 | 31 | 14 | 18 | 5 | 2 |
| Behrend, St. Petersburg | 1.000 | 9 | 1 | 2 | 0 | 0 |
| Berrios, Fort Myers* | 1.000 | 9 | 3 | 1 | 0 | 0 |
| Bianchi, Daytona Beach | .778 | 7 | 2 | 5 | 2 | 0 |
| Biercevicz, Daytona Beach | 1.000 | 3 | 0 | 1 | 0 | 0 |
| Blum, Fort Lauderdale* | 1.000 | 4 | 1 | 4 | 0 | 2 |
| Blunt, St. Petersburg | 1.000 | 4 | 2 | 0 | 0 | 0 |
| Boling, Lakeland* | 1.000 | 14 | 3 | 8 | 0 | 0 |
| Boudreaux, Clearwater | .864 | 14 | 6 | 13 | 3 | 0 |
| Braukmiller, West Palm Beach | .833 | 20 | 2 | 3 | 1 | 0 |
| Brennan, Vero Beach | .838 | 22 | 13 | 18 | 6 | 0 |
| Brisco, St. Petersburg | .939 | 29 | 6 | 25 | 2 | 1 |
| Campbell, Tampa | .933 | 23 | 9 | 19 | 2 | 1 |
| Canseco, Fort Lauderdale | .667 | 11 | 0 | 6 | 3 | 0 |
| Cappadona, Winter Haven* | 1.000 | 21 | 4 | 6 | 0 | 1 |
| Carrasco, St. Petersburg | 1.000 | 33 | 8 | 35 | 0 | 1 |
| Carson, St. Petersburg | .962 | 27 | 10 | 15 | 1 | 0 |
| Cash, Osceola | .955 | 37 | 6 | 15 | 1 | 2 |
| Cerefin, Osceola | .846 | 26 | 6 | 16 | 4 | 0 |
| Charlton, West Palm Beach* | .829 | 24 | 3 | 26 | 6 | 0 |
| Chastain, Fort Lauderdale | 1.000 | 22 | 4 | 5 | 0 | 1 |
| M. Cherry, Vero Beach | .750 | 6 | 1 | 2 | 1 | 0 |
| P. Cherry, St. Petersburg* | .958 | 32 | 5 | 18 | 1 | 4 |
| Clarkin, Winter Haven | 1.000 | 10 | 5 | 1 | 0 | 0 |
| Cloninger, Fort Lauderdale | 1.000 | 19 | 5 | 6 | 0 | 0 |
| Cole, Osceola* | .889 | 19 | 7 | 9 | 2 | 3 |
| Cook, Lakeland | 1.000 | 5 | 1 | 0 | 0 | 0 |
| Cooper, Lakeland | .867 | 27 | 10 | 16 | 4 | 1 |
| Crew, Fort Myers | .929 | 10 | 2 | 11 | 1 | 1 |
| Curry, Winter Haven | .941 | 27 | 12 | 20 | 2 | 2 |
| Cutshall, West Palm Beach | .846 | 10 | 1 | 10 | 2 | 0 |
| Dale, Tampa | .750 | 10 | 0 | 3 | 1 | 1 |
| Dalton, Winter Haven* | .895 | 49 | 4 | 13 | 2 | 0 |
| C. Daniel, Tampa* | 1.000 | 3 | 4 | 0 | 0 | 0 |
| J. Daniel, Fort Myers | 1.000 | 13 | 3 | 8 | 0 | 1 |
| Davis, Fort Myers | 1.000 | 36 | 4 | 9 | 0 | 1 |
| DeJesus, Fort Myers | .786 | 27 | 4 | 7 | 3 | 1 |
| Dersin, 17 Day-8 FtL | .913 | 25 | 5 | 16 | 2 | 0 |
| Devine, 4 Mia-1 Vero B. | .913 | 15 | 9 | 12 | 2 | 1 |
| Devlin, Fort Lauderdale | 1.000 | 32 | 1 | 9 | 0 | 0 |
| Diez, Lakeland* | .000 | 4 | 0 | 0 | 1 | 0 |
| Dixon, West Palm Beach | .833 | 9 | 1 | 9 | 2 | 0 |
| Dodd, Tampa | .938 | 13 | 4 | 11 | 1 | 0 |
| Dotson, Lakeland | .739 | 17 | 7 | 10 | 6 | 1 |
| Dougherty, Fort Lauderdale | 1.000 | 4 | 0 | 2 | 0 | 0 |
| Dube, Osceola | .867 | 23 | 3 | 10 | 2 | 0 |
| Duffy, Lakeland* | .900 | 45 | 3 | 15 | 2 | 2 |
| Easley, Fort Lauderdale | 1.000 | 17 | 2 | 1 | 0 | 1 |
| Eichelberger, Miami | .636 | 7 | 2 | 5 | 4 | 0 |
| Erickson, Miami* | .909 | 14 | 3 | 7 | 1 | 0 |
| Estes, St. Petersburg* | .909 | 13 | 0 | 10 | 1 | 0 |
| Farmer, Miami | 1.000 | 48 | 3 | 9 | 0 | 0 |
| Fay, Daytona Beach | 1.000 | 4 | 1 | 0 | 0 | 0 |
| Fedor, West Palm Beach | .929 | 31 | 5 | 8 | 1 | 0 |
| Fenn, Winter Haven | .833 | 37 | 4 | 6 | 2 | 1 |
| Fischer, West Palm Beach | .944 | 13 | 8 | 9 | 1 | 1 |
| Freeman, Clearwater | .950 | 14 | 7 | 12 | 1 | 1 |
| Frey, Fort Lauderdale* | 1.000 | 19 | 1 | 3 | 0 | 0 |
| Friedrich, Osceola | .966 | 24 | 11 | 17 | 1 | 2 |
| Fulton, Fort Lauderdale | .917 | 15 | 7 | 15 | 2 | 0 |
| Gannon, Daytona Beach* | 1.000 | 27 | 6 | 12 | 0 | 0 |
| Garces, Clearwater* | 1.000 | 11 | 0 | 2 | 0 | 0 |
| Gardner, West Palm Beach | .846 | 10 | 7 | 4 | 2 | 0 |
| Gentle, Vero Beach* | 1.000 | 13 | 1 | 1 | 0 | 1 |
| P. George, Fort Myers* | .939 | 30 | 5 | 26 | 2 | 2 |
| S. George, Fort Lauderdale* | .788 | 24 | 7 | 19 | 7 | 2 |
| Gonzalez, Daytona Beach* | 1.000 | 5 | 0 | 5 | 0 | 0 |
| Gorman, Clearwater | .900 | 15 | 3 | 6 | 1 | 1 |
| Gray, Clearwater | 1.000 | 55 | 6 | 20 | 0 | 2 |
| Grimm, Tampa | 1.000 | 14 | 3 | 1 | 0 | 0 |
| Guercio, Fort Lauderdale | 1.000 | 22 | 4 | 9 | 0 | 0 |
| Hale, Winter Haven | .960 | 38 | 7 | 17 | 1 | 4 |
| A. Hamilton, Winter Haven | 1.000 | 2 | 0 | 1 | 0 | 0 |
| R. Hamilton, Vero Beach | .900 | 26 | 8 | 19 | 3 | 3 |
| Harrison, Fort Lauderdale* | 1.000 | 22 | 4 | 7 | 0 | 0 |
| Hartman, Osceola | .667 | 2 | 1 | 1 | 1 | 0 |
| Heidenreich, Tampa | 1.000 | 6 | 2 | 6 | 0 | 1 |
| Heise, Daytona Beach* | .818 | 28 | 2 | 7 | 2 | 0 |
| Held, Lakeland | .906 | 26 | 10 | 19 | 3 | 0 |
| Herzog, St. Petersburg* | 1.000 | 43 | 2 | 22 | 0 | 1 |
| Hester, Daytona Beach | 1.000 | 13 | 0 | 3 | 0 | 0 |
| Holm, Daytona Beach* | .875 | 12 | 1 | 13 | 2 | 1 |
| Holman, West Palm Beach | .913 | 25 | 4 | 17 | 2 | 0 |
| Holmes, Vero Beach | .941 | 33 | 5 | 11 | 1 | 2 |
| Hoyt, St. Petersburg | 1.000 | 20 | 9 | 5 | 0 | 1 |
| Hull, Fort Myers | 1.000 | 27 | 11 | 23 | 0 | 0 |
| Impagliazzo, West Palm Beach | .909 | 37 | 3 | 7 | 1 | 0 |
| Jacobsen, Vero Beach | .870 | 43 | 8 | 12 | 3 | 1 |
| Jester, Clearwater* | .958 | 25 | 9 | 37 | 2 | 2 |
| R. Johnson, Daytona Beach | 1.000 | 14 | 4 | 15 | 0 | 1 |
| Kelley, Osceola | .923 | 6 | 4 | 8 | 1 | 0 |
| Kemp, Tampa | 1.000 | 9 | 3 | 12 | 0 | 0 |
| Kiecker, Winter Haven | .882 | 29 | 13 | 32 | 6 | 2 |
| King, Daytona Beach | .500 | 5 | 1 | 0 | 1 | 0 |
| Kipper, Daytona Beach* | .906 | 22 | 7 | 22 | 3 | 3 |
| Kohler, Miami | 1.000 | 14 | 0 | 8 | 0 | 1 |
| Labozzetta, Lakeland* | 1.000 | 12 | 2 | 9 | 0 | 0 |
| Lacey, Miami* | 1.000 | 11 | 3 | 8 | 0 | 0 |
| Lackie, Daytona Beach* | .667 | 9 | 1 | 1 | 1 | 0 |
| Langdon, Tampa | .800 | 29 | 3 | 9 | 3 | 1 |
| Ledbetter, 4 Day-24 Clw | .867 | 28 | 8 | 5 | 2 | 0 |
| Legumina, Vero Beach | .875 | 42 | 3 | 11 | 2 | 0 |
| Leiter, Fort Lauderdale | .921 | 18 | 10 | 25 | 3 | 0 |
| Leonard, Fort Myers | 1.000 | 3 | 1 | 2 | 0 | 0 |
| Lloyd, Clearwater* | 1.000 | 11 | 0 | 1 | 0 | 0 |
| Lono, Tampa* | .971 | 41 | 7 | 26 | 1 | 4 |
| LoSauro, Daytona Beach | .897 | 27 | 9 | 17 | 3 | 0 |
| Lovelace, Vero Beach* | 1.000 | 12 | 2 | 5 | 0 | 1 |
| A. Lucas, Osceola | 1.000 | 34 | 10 | 16 | 0 | 1 |
| G. Lucas, West Palm Beach* | 1.000 | 3 | 0 | 1 | 0 | 0 |
| M. Madden, Tampa* | .952 | 23 | 4 | 16 | 1 | 0 |
| S. Madden, Clearwater* | .750 | 27 | 1 | 20 | 7 | 2 |
| Magrane, St. Petersburg* | .917 | 5 | 6 | 5 | 1 | 0 |
| Mallicoat, Osceola* | .974 | 26 | 7 | 30 | 1 | 2 |
| Mangham, Osceola | 1.000 | 23 | 8 | 6 | 0 | 0 |
| Martinez, St. Petersburg | 1.000 | 4 | 4 | 8 | 0 | 0 |
| Mason, St. Petersburg | 1.000 | 41 | 2 | 11 | 0 | 0 |
| C. Mathews, Osceola | .925 | 29 | 13 | 24 | 3 | 2 |
| G. Mathews, St. Petersburg* | .958 | 16 | 2 | 21 | 1 | 2 |
| Mayberry, Vero Beach | .935 | 17 | 9 | 20 | 2 | 0 |

PITCHERS—Continued

| Player and Club | Pct. | G. | PO. | A. | E. | DP. | Player and Club | Pct. | G. | PO. | A. | E. | DP. |
|---|---|---|---|---|---|---|---|---|---|---|---|---|---|
| McDevitt, Clearwater | .917 | 17 | 4 | 7 | 1 | 0 | Rogers, Daytona Beach* | 1.000 | 6 | 0 | 2 | 0 | 0 |
| McEnaney, Miami* | .923 | 39 | 5 | 7 | 1 | 2 | Rohan, Daytna Beach | 1.000 | 17 | 2 | 13 | 0 | 0 |
| McHugh, Lakeland | .722 | 38 | 4 | 9 | 5 | 0 | Rowen, Vero Beach* | .800 | 9 | 2 | 6 | 2 | 0 |
| McKay, West Palm Beach | 1.000 | 2 | 1 | 0 | 0 | 0 | Ruffin, Clearwater* | 1.000 | 14 | 3 | 10 | 0 | 1 |
| Meadows, Vero Beach | 1.000 | 6 | 4 | 4 | 0 | 0 | Russo, Miami* | .957 | 15 | 8 | 14 | 1 | 0 |
| Medvin, Lakeland | .750 | 31 | 1 | 5 | 2 | 0 | G. Sanchez, Daytona Beach | 1.000 | 19 | 1 | 8 | 0 | 0 |
| Melchert, Lakeland* | 1.000 | 3 | 0 | 1 | 0 | 0 | I. Sanchez, Fort Myers* | 1.000 | 28 | 10 | 8 | 0 | 2 |
| Melrose, Daytona Beach* | 1.000 | 4 | 0 | 1 | 0 | 0 | Schwartz, Tampa* | 1.000 | 13 | 0 | 4 | 0 | 0 |
| Milacki, Daytona Beach | 1.000 | 8 | 1 | 8 | 0 | 0 | SCHWEIGHOFFER, Vero Beach | 1.000 | 25 | 14 | 34 | 0 | 6 |
| Minnema, Lakeland | .944 | 26 | 18 | 16 | 2 | 0 | Shaab, Osceola* | .867 | 35 | 4 | 9 | 2 | 0 |
| Mirabito, Tampa | 1.000 | 15 | 5 | 9 | 0 | 2 | Simpson, 25 Clw-7 Tam* | .900 | 32 | 0 | 9 | 1 | 0 |
| Mohr, Fort Myers* | .875 | 29 | 2 | 5 | 1 | 0 | Slifko, Winter Haven | .952 | 34 | 2 | 18 | 1 | 0 |
| Moran, West Palm Beach* | .700 | 22 | 1 | 6 | 3 | 1 | Smith, Clearwater | .962 | 26 | 11 | 14 | 1 | 0 |
| Nunez, Fort Myers | 1.000 | 11 | 4 | 9 | 0 | 0 | Spagnola, Tampa | .938 | 21 | 4 | 11 | 1 | 0 |
| Odekirk, Tampa* | .958 | 31 | 5 | 18 | 1 | 4 | Sparling, Fort Myers | 1.000 | 27 | 7 | 16 | 0 | 0 |
| Oliveras, Daytona Beach | 1.000 | 3 | 1 | 1 | 0 | 0 | Stewart, Winter Haven* | .926 | 37 | 2 | 23 | 2 | 2 |
| Pacillo, Tampa | .833 | 25 | 1 | 4 | 1 | 0 | Summers, Daytona Beach | .833 | 3 | 3 | 2 | 1 | 1 |
| Parkins, Winter Haven | .903 | 26 | 8 | 20 | 3 | 1 | Taft, Miami* | .833 | 32 | 6 | 14 | 4 | 0 |
| Pena, Miami* | .923 | 25 | 3 | 9 | 1 | 0 | Thorpe, Daytona Beach | .833 | 24 | 1 | 4 | 1 | 1 |
| Perkins, Miami | .889 | 59 | 3 | 29 | 4 | 3 | R. Torres, Fort Lauderdale | .870 | 17 | 8 | 12 | 3 | 0 |
| Perrotte, Lakeland* | .917 | 13 | 3 | 8 | 1 | 0 | Torrez, Miami | .955 | 19 | 7 | 14 | 1 | 0 |
| Pesavento, Vero Beach* | 1.000 | 24 | 4 | 23 | 0 | 1 | Traen, West Palm Beach | 1.000 | 30 | 4 | 13 | 0 | 1 |
| Peters, St. Petersburg | 1.000 | 10 | 6 | 12 | 0 | 0 | Trautwein, West Palm Beach | 1.000 | 35 | 3 | 6 | 0 | 0 |
| Pettaway, Miami | .667 | 6 | 0 | 2 | 1 | 0 | True, Clearwater* | 1.000 | 3 | 0 | 2 | 0 | 0 |
| Phillion, Lakeland* | 1.000 | 11 | 3 | 12 | 0 | 0 | Tuck, Miami | 1.000 | 15 | 1 | 5 | 0 | 0 |
| Poissant, Lakeland | .933 | 22 | 10 | 4 | 1 | 0 | Underwood, Fort Lauderdale* | 1.000 | 5 | 0 | 1 | 0 | 0 |
| Pratt, Miami* | 1.000 | 3 | 1 | 0 | 0 | 0 | Valliant, West Palm Beach* | 1.000 | 6 | 0 | 2 | 0 | 0 |
| Pries, Fort Lauderdale | .938 | 22 | 20 | 25 | 3 | 1 | Vargas, Clearwater* | .944 | 44 | 4 | 13 | 1 | 0 |
| Raftice, Fort Lauderdale* | .800 | 11 | 1 | 3 | 1 | 0 | Walter, Fort Myers | 1.000 | 28 | 7 | 3 | 0 | 1 |
| Ramirez, Daytona Beach | 1.000 | 4 | 0 | 3 | 0 | 0 | Watts, Clearwater* | 1.000 | 22 | 3 | 16 | 0 | 2 |
| Rasmussen, Miami | .976 | 27 | 15 | 25 | 1 | 3 | Wayne, West Palm Beach* | .875 | 8 | 1 | 6 | 1 | 0 |
| Rather, Fort Lauderdale | 1.000 | 6 | 3 | 4 | 0 | 1 | Welch, Vero Beach | 1.000 | 3 | 3 | 2 | 0 | 1 |
| Ratliff, West Palm Beach | 1.000 | 27 | 5 | 12 | 0 | 0 | Willsher, Daytona Beach | .828 | 21 | 10 | 14 | 5 | 1 |
| Raubolt, Lakeland | 1.000 | 12 | 1 | 4 | 0 | 0 | R. Wilson, Daytona Beach* | .857 | 10 | 2 | 10 | 2 | 1 |
| Reburn, Tampa | 1.000 | 23 | 7 | 19 | 0 | 2 | W. Wilson, Daytona Beach | 1.000 | 11 | 1 | 3 | 0 | 0 |
| Reynolds, Daytona Beach | .750 | 5 | 2 | 1 | 1 | 0 | Wohler, Vero Beach* | .976 | 28 | 7 | 34 | 1 | 6 |
| Rice, Daytona Beach | .667 | 13 | 0 | 4 | 2 | 0 | Yeager, Fort Lauderdale* | 1.000 | 20 | 1 | 10 | 0 | 0 |
| Ritchie, Clearwater* | 1.000 | 14 | 1 | 8 | 0 | 0 | C. Young, West Palm Beach* | .955 | 25 | 2 | 19 | 1 | 1 |
| Rodiles, Fort Myers | .931 | 40 | 14 | 13 | 2 | 0 | S. Young, St. Petersburg | .912 | 27 | 10 | 21 | 3 | 2 |
| Rodriguez, Fort Lauderdale | .889 | 30 | 5 | 11 | 2 | 1 | | | | | | | |

The following players do not have any recorded accepted chances at the positions indicated; therefore, are not listed in the fielding averages for those particular positions: Afenir, ss; Bachman, 3b; Beringhele, 3b; Cecchini, c; Cruz, p; DeFrancesco, of; Germann, of; Giddens, p; A. Gonzalez, ss; R. Harris, c; Hoyt, of; W. Johnson, p; Kinns, p; Lewis, 3b; McKnight, p; Odgers, of; Pereira, 2b, of; Poznanski, of; Raziano, c; Ritch, of; Sciacca, 3b; Stone, c; Tackett, 3b, of; P. Torres, p; Trudeau, p; Wyatt, p.

## CLUB PITCHING

| Club | ERA. | G. | CG. | ShO. | Sv. | IP. | H. | R. | ER. | HR. | HB. | BB. | Int. BB. | SO. | WP. | Bk. |
|---|---|---|---|---|---|---|---|---|---|---|---|---|---|---|---|---|
| St. Petersburg | 2.53 | 140 | 40 | 24 | 22 | 1199.2 | 1010 | 431 | 337 | 30 | 38 | 470 | 28 | 667 | 57 | 14 |
| Fort Myers | 2.79 | 139 | 12 | 12 | 37 | 1196.1 | 1049 | 465 | 371 | 34 | 35 | 432 | 20 | 756 | 40 | 12 |
| Winter Haven | 2.99 | 139 | 20 | 10 | 30 | 1205.1 | 1084 | 502 | 401 | 35 | 16 | 446 | 21 | 557 | 58 | 17 |
| Tampa | 3.09 | 135 | 27 | 16 | 23 | 1136.1 | 1034 | 485 | 390 | 23 | 20 | 546 | 46 | 766 | 85 | 20 |
| Vero Beach | 3.12 | 140 | 29 | 12 | 24 | 1181.0 | 1018 | 513 | 409 | 19 | 24 | 543 | 26 | 773 | 72 | 27 |
| Clearwater | 3.21 | 141 | 23 | 12 | 43 | 1215.0 | 1164 | 555 | 434 | 37 | 17 | 506 | 35 | 767 | 49 | 18 |
| Fort Lauderdale | 3.23 | 140 | 32 | 18 | 31 | 1171.2 | 1037 | 533 | 421 | 38 | 30 | 527 | 9 | 830 | 78 | 14 |
| Osceola | 3.32 | 135 | 17 | 12 | 35 | 1154.0 | 1013 | 536 | 426 | 28 | 25 | 602 | 31 | 859 | 74 | 17 |
| West Palm Beach | 3.51 | 140 | 33 | 10 | 28 | 1180.0 | 1097 | 588 | 460 | 57 | 28 | 570 | 18 | 872 | 82 | 25 |
| Miami | 3.59 | 141 | 24 | 10 | 21 | 1197.1 | 1246 | 631 | 477 | 27 | 38 | 503 | 27 | 751 | 86 | 24 |
| Daytona Beach | 3.89 | 140 | 30 | 4 | 19 | 1164.0 | 1137 | 649 | 503 | 29 | 35 | 655 | 54 | 754 | 114 | 23 |
| Lakeland | 4.34 | 140 | 19 | 8 | 26 | 1176.1 | 1245 | 701 | 567 | 40 | 48 | 562 | 11 | 714 | 81 | 17 |

## PITCHERS' RECORDS

(Leading Qualifiers for Earned-Run Average Leadership—112 or More Innings)

*Throws lefthanded.

| Pitcher—Club | W. | L. | Pct. | ERA. | G. | GS. | CG. | GF. | ShO. | Sv. | IP. | H. | R. | ER. | HR. | HB. | BB. | Int. BB. | SO. | WP. |
|---|---|---|---|---|---|---|---|---|---|---|---|---|---|---|---|---|---|---|---|---|
| G. Mathews, St. Petersburg* | 13 | 1 | .929 | 1.11 | 16 | 16 | 8 | 0 | 4 | 0 | 122.0 | 76 | 17 | 15 | 3 | 2 | 47 | 0 | 96 | 3 |
| Mallicoat, Osceola* | 16 | 6 | .727 | 1.36 | 26 | 25 | 5 | 0 | 2 | 0 | 178.2 | 119 | 41 | 27 | 2 | 3 | 74 | 3 | 158 | 14 |
| Fulton, Fort Lauderdale | 11 | 2 | .846 | 1.61 | 15 | 15 | 9 | 0 | 1 | 0 | 112.0 | 91 | 31 | 20 | 2 | 2 | 30 | 0 | 71 | 6 |
| S. George, Fort Lauderdale* | 13 | 7 | .650 | 1.75 | 24 | 24 | 12 | 0 | 5 | 0 | 164.2 | 120 | 48 | 32 | 2 | 1 | 76 | 0 | 141 | 14 |
| P. Cherry, St. Petersburg* | 10 | 4 | .714 | 1.88 | 32 | 19 | 7 | 7 | 3 | 4 | 148.2 | 130 | 43 | 31 | 1 | 2 | 46 | 2 | 88 | 3 |
| Sparling, Fort Myers | 8 | 6 | .571 | 2.31 | 27 | 22 | 1 | 1 | 0 | 0 | 140.1 | 135 | 48 | 36 | 2 | 5 | 44 | 0 | 69 | 1 |
| Mayberry, Vero Beach | 11 | 4 | .733 | 2.35 | 17 | 17 | 5 | 0 | 1 | 0 | 118.2 | 101 | 40 | 31 | 1 | 3 | 37 | 2 | 97 | 2 |
| Traen, West Palm Beach | 8 | 4 | .667 | 2.49 | 30 | 10 | 2 | 11 | 0 | 3 | 112.0 | 97 | 39 | 31 | 5 | 0 | 41 | 1 | 98 | 4 |
| Araujo, Winter Haven | 12 | 10 | .545 | 2.55 | 32 | 25 | 1 | 5 | 1 | 0 | 176.1 | 169 | 67 | 50 | 5 | 2 | 33 | 3 | 96 | 9 |
| Kiecker, Winter Haven | 12 | 12 | .500 | 2.60 | 29 | 29 | 9 | 0 | 2 | 0 | 193.2 | 176 | 72 | 56 | 4 | 2 | 59 | 2 | 60 | 7 |

Departmental Leaders: G—Perkins, 59; W—Mallicoat, 16; L—Kiecker, Minnema, Schweighoffer, 12; Pct.—G. Mathews, .929; GS—Kiecker, 29; CG—S. George, 12; GF—Gray, 47; ShO—S. George, 5; Sv.—Baker, 24; IP—Kiecker, 193.2; H—Rasmussen, 177; R—Dube, 88; ER—Dube, 76; HR—C. Young, 13; HB—S. Young, 11; BB—Cerefin, 134; IBB—Thorpe, Vargas, 10; SO—Mallicoat, 158; WP—Reburn, 20.

(All Pitchers—Listed Alphabetically)

| Pitcher—Club | W. | L. | Pct. | ERA. | G. | GS. | CG. | GF. | ShO. | Sv. | IP. | H. | R. | ER. | HR. | HB. | BB. | Int. BB. | SO. | WP. |
|---|---|---|---|---|---|---|---|---|---|---|---|---|---|---|---|---|---|---|---|---|
| Agar, Lakeland | 0 | 0 | .000 | 7.50 | 4 | 0 | 0 | 2 | 0 | 1 | 12.0 | 12 | 10 | 10 | 0 | 1 | 10 | 0 | 13 | 1 |
| Antone, West Palm Beach | 0 | 0 | .000 | 0.00 | 1 | 0 | 0 | 1 | 0 | 0 | 2.0 | 4 | 0 | 0 | 0 | 0 | 0 | 0 | 1 | 0 |
| Araujo, Winter Haven | 12 | 10 | .545 | 2.55 | 32 | 25 | 1 | 5 | 1 | 0 | 176.1 | 169 | 67 | 50 | 5 | 2 | 33 | 3 | 96 | 9 |
| Bacon, Tampa | 5 | 4 | .556 | 3.90 | 36 | 5 | 1 | 14 | 1 | 2 | 64.2 | 69 | 34 | 28 | 0 | 3 | 34 | 5 | 21 | 4 |
| Baker, Osceola | 4 | 5 | .444 | 3.09 | 46 | 0 | 0 | 41 | 0 | 24 | 64.0 | 59 | 24 | 22 | 1 | 0 | 25 | 6 | 60 | 4 |
| Barlow, Lakeland | 1 | 7 | .125 | 5.54 | 9 | 9 | 2 | 0 | 0 | 0 | 50.1 | 51 | 34 | 31 | 4 | 5 | 27 | 0 | 35 | 4 |

| Pitcher—Club | W. | L. | Pct. | ERA. | G. | GS. | CG. | GF. | ShO. | Sv. | IP. | H. | R. | ER. | HR. | HB. | BB. | Int. BB. | SO. | WP. |
|---|---|---|---|---|---|---|---|---|---|---|---|---|---|---|---|---|---|---|---|---|
| Bass, Fort Myers | 5 | 4 | .556 | 2.50 | 36 | 2 | 1 | 20 | 0 | 5 | 90.0 | 83 | 39 | 25 | 1 | 0 | 29 | 4 | 55 | 5 |
| Beahan, Fort Lauderdale | 0 | 0 | .000 | 0.00 | 3 | 0 | 0 | 1 | 0 | 0 | 6.1 | 5 | 0 | 0 | 1 | 0 | 5 | 0 | 4 | 1 |
| Bear, Miami | 6 | 11 | .353 | 3.92 | 31 | 18 | 2 | 6 | 0 | 0 | 128.2 | 146 | 76 | 56 | 3 | 2 | 49 | 4 | 59 | 4 |
| Behrend, St. Petersburg | 1 | 1 | .500 | 3.27 | 9 | 2 | 0 | 5 | 0 | 0 | 22.0 | 26 | 9 | 8 | 0 | 1 | 11 | 0 | 13 | 4 |
| Berrios, Fort Myers* | 1 | 1 | .500 | 6.23 | 9 | 0 | 0 | 6 | 0 | 0 | 17.1 | 23 | 13 | 12 | 2 | 2 | 8 | 1 | 9 | 0 |
| Bianchi, Daytona Beach | 0 | 4 | .000 | 6.81 | 7 | 7 | 1 | 0 | 0 | 0 | 38.1 | 30 | 30 | 29 | 5 | 1 | 31 | 2 | 32 | 5 |
| Biercevicz, Daytona Beach | 2 | 0 | 1.000 | 0.57 | 3 | 3 | 0 | 0 | 0 | 0 | 15.2 | 7 | 5 | 1 | 0 | 0 | 3 | 0 | 16 | 0 |
| Blum, Fort Lauderdale* | 2 | 1 | .667 | 5.50 | 4 | 3 | 1 | 1 | 0 | 0 | 18.0 | 22 | 13 | 11 | 1 | 1 | 5 | 0 | 7 | 2 |
| Blunt, St. Petersburg | 0 | 2 | .000 | 3.86 | 4 | 4 | 0 | 0 | 0 | 0 | 18.2 | 16 | 12 | 8 | 1 | 0 | 14 | 0 | 8 | 4 |
| Boling, Lakeland* | 3 | 5 | .375 | 4.15 | 14 | 9 | 3 | 1 | 1 | 0 | 65.0 | 68 | 35 | 30 | 1 | 0 | 28 | 0 | 26 | 2 |
| Boudreaux, Clearwater | 6 | 4 | .600 | 3.26 | 14 | 14 | 0 | 0 | 0 | 0 | 85.2 | 90 | 44 | 31 | 2 | 2 | 30 | 2 | 47 | 2 |
| Braukmiller, West Palm Beach | 0 | 1 | .000 | 3.26 | 20 | 0 | 0 | 6 | 0 | 0 | 38.2 | 27 | 15 | 14 | 0 | 0 | 40 | 2 | 26 | 8 |
| Brennan, Vero Beach | 10 | 9 | .526 | 2.85 | 22 | 21 | 5 | 0 | 1 | 0 | 142.0 | 121 | 64 | 45 | 1 | 5 | 59 | 1 | 74 | 11 |
| Brisco, St. Petersburg | 6 | 7 | .462 | 3.34 | 29 | 17 | 4 | 3 | 1 | 2 | 126.2 | 129 | 64 | 47 | 4 | 3 | 43 | 1 | 45 | 4 |
| Campbell, Tampa | 5 | 5 | .500 | 2.90 | 23 | 16 | 1 | 2 | 1 | 0 | 99.1 | 101 | 41 | 32 | 2 | 1 | 31 | 3 | 52 | 2 |
| Canseco, Fort Lauderdale | 5 | 4 | .556 | 3.61 | 11 | 11 | 1 | 0 | 0 | 0 | 57.1 | 42 | 33 | 23 | 1 | 2 | 42 | 1 | 37 | 10 |
| Cappadona, Winter Haven | 0 | 2 | .000 | 2.45 | 21 | 0 | 0 | 13 | 0 | 5 | 36.2 | 24 | 13 | 10 | 0 | 1 | 19 | 1 | 25 | 2 |
| Carrasco, St. Petersburg | 7 | 9 | .438 | 2.90 | 33 | 13 | 3 | 8 | 2 | 2 | 118.0 | 113 | 48 | 38 | 2 | 7 | 40 | 4 | 49 | 5 |
| Carson, St. Petersburg | 7 | 9 | .438 | 3.75 | 27 | 18 | 5 | 4 | 2 | 0 | 129.2 | 111 | 64 | 54 | 5 | 5 | 57 | 2 | 59 | 3 |
| Cash, Osceola | 6 | 4 | .600 | 3.50 | 37 | 6 | 0 | 20 | 0 | 3 | 92.2 | 80 | 44 | 36 | 2 | 3 | 54 | 6 | 63 | 3 |
| Cerefin, Osceola | 6 | 10 | .375 | 4.95 | 26 | 20 | 1 | 2 | 0 | 0 | 120.0 | 86 | 83 | 66 | 1 | 9 | 134 | 0 | 104 | 12 |
| Charlton, West Palm Beach* | 7 | 10 | .412 | 4.57 | 24 | 23 | 5 | 0 | 2 | 0 | 128.0 | 135 | 79 | 65 | 7 | 4 | 79 | 1 | 71 | 9 |
| Chastain, Fort Lauderdale* | 3 | 2 | .600 | 2.12 | 22 | 0 | 0 | 6 | 0 | 3 | 34.0 | 20 | 11 | 8 | 3 | 1 | 12 | 0 | 35 | 2 |
| M. Cherry, Vero Beach | 2 | 3 | .400 | 3.76 | 6 | 6 | 0 | 0 | 0 | 0 | 38.1 | 35 | 17 | 16 | 1 | 0 | 17 | 2 | 50 | 0 |
| P. Cherry, St. Petersburg* | 10 | 4 | .714 | 1.88 | 32 | 19 | 7 | 7 | 3 | 4 | 148.2 | 130 | 43 | 31 | 2 | 2 | 46 | 2 | 88 | 3 |
| Clarkin, Winter Haven | 2 | 0 | 1.000 | 2.25 | 10 | 3 | 0 | 1 | 0 | 0 | 24.0 | 19 | 8 | 6 | 0 | 0 | 8 | 0 | 8 | 2 |
| Cloninger, Fort Lauderdale | 4 | 4 | .500 | 3.70 | 19 | 6 | 1 | 3 | 1 | 0 | 58.1 | 62 | 28 | 24 | 1 | 1 | 21 | 0 | 18 | 2 |
| Cole, Osceola* | 1 | 2 | .333 | 5.10 | 19 | 5 | 0 | 6 | 0 | 0 | 47.2 | 41 | 29 | 27 | 1 | 2 | 45 | 1 | 25 | 0 |
| Cook, Lakeland | 0 | 2 | .000 | 12.38 | 5 | 0 | 0 | 1 | 0 | 0 | 8.0 | 14 | 11 | 11 | 0 | 2 | 5 | 0 | 4 | 1 |
| Cooper, Lakeland | 6 | 8 | .429 | 4.56 | 27 | 20 | 3 | 1 | 0 | 0 | 134.1 | 144 | 86 | 68 | 6 | 5 | 52 | 1 | 65 | 4 |
| Crew, Fort Myers | 7 | 0 | 1.000 | 1.91 | 10 | 10 | 0 | 0 | 0 | 0 | 56.2 | 46 | 13 | 12 | 0 | 1 | 24 | 0 | 34 | 3 |
| Cruz, Miami | 0 | 0 | .000 | 0.00 | 1 | 0 | 0 | 1 | 0 | 0 | 1.0 | 0 | 0 | 0 | 0 | 1 | 0 | 0 | 3 | 0 |
| Curry, Winter Haven | 9 | 10 | .474 | 3.69 | 27 | 25 | 4 | 0 | 0 | 0 | 161.0 | 157 | 75 | 66 | 9 | 5 | 63 | 1 | 81 | 14 |
| Cutshall, West Palm Beach | 3 | 5 | .375 | 3.00 | 10 | 10 | 4 | 0 | 0 | 0 | 63.0 | 53 | 24 | 21 | 3 | 2 | 21 | 1 | 60 | 2 |
| Dale, Tampa | 2 | 1 | .667 | 2.20 | 10 | 0 | 0 | 5 | 0 | 0 | 16.1 | 13 | 4 | 4 | 0 | 1 | 8 | 1 | 10 | 2 |
| Dalton, Winter Haven* | 2 | 3 | .400 | 1.13 | 49 | 0 | 0 | 42 | 0 | 18 | 72.0 | 45 | 14 | 9 | 0 | 0 | 27 | 3 | 41 | 1 |
| C. Daniel, Tampa* | 0 | 1 | .000 | 3.86 | 3 | 3 | 0 | 0 | 0 | 0 | 16.1 | 12 | 8 | 7 | 0 | 0 | 8 | 0 | 15 | 1 |
| J. Daniel, Fort Myers | 6 | 2 | .750 | 2.67 | 13 | 10 | 0 | 0 | 0 | 0 | 70.2 | 66 | 28 | 21 | 1 | 2 | 15 | 0 | 32 | 3 |
| Davis, Fort Myers | 0 | 3 | .000 | 1.89 | 36 | 0 | 0 | 24 | 0 | 7 | 52.1 | 46 | 12 | 11 | 1 | 1 | 13 | 2 | 37 | 0 |
| DeJesus, Fort Myers | 8 | 10 | .444 | 4.30 | 27 | 26 | 3 | 0 | 1 | 0 | 129.2 | 119 | 70 | 62 | 9 | 7 | 59 | 0 | 94 | 4 |
| Dersin, 17 Day-8 Fort Laud. | 9 | 8 | .529 | 2.97 | 25 | 25 | 5 | 0 | 0 | 0 | 154.2 | 153 | 65 | 51 | 1 | 5 | 69 | 5 | 109 | 11 |
| Devine, 14 Mia-1 Vero Beach | 4 | 5 | .444 | 2.59 | 15 | 13 | 3 | 0 | 2 | 0 | 87.0 | 64 | 25 | 25 | 2 | 1 | 42 | 3 | 64 | 5 |
| Devlin, Fort Lauderdale | 3 | 5 | .375 | 4.19 | 32 | 0 | 0 | 22 | 0 | 4 | 38.2 | 34 | 21 | 18 | 2 | 2 | 23 | 1 | 45 | 0 |
| Diez, Lakeland* | 0 | 0 | .000 | 4.22 | 4 | 0 | 0 | 2 | 0 | 0 | 10.2 | 10 | 6 | 5 | 3 | 1 | 5 | 1 | 6 | 1 |
| Dixon, West Palm Beach | 3 | 2 | .600 | 3.15 | 9 | 9 | 1 | 0 | 1 | 0 | 54.1 | 49 | 25 | 19 | 0 | 2 | 19 | 0 | 38 | 1 |
| Dodd, Tampa | 4 | 2 | .667 | 3.41 | 13 | 4 | 1 | 3 | 0 | 0 | 58.0 | 63 | 27 | 22 | 1 | 0 | 36 | 2 | 46 | 4 |
| Dotson, Lakeland | 6 | 8 | .429 | 5.44 | 17 | 17 | 1 | 0 | 0 | 0 | 101.0 | 107 | 78 | 61 | 1 | 4 | 61 | 0 | 71 | 10 |
| Dougherty, Fort Lauderdale | 0 | 0 | .000 | 9.00 | 4 | 0 | 0 | 1 | 0 | 0 | 8.0 | 14 | 8 | 8 | 0 | 0 | 3 | 0 | 8 | 0 |
| Dube, Osceola | 8 | 10 | .444 | 6.11 | 23 | 23 | 1 | 0 | 0 | 0 | 112.0 | 127 | 88 | 76 | 2 | 2 | 75 | 2 | 89 | 11 |
| Duffy, Lakeland* | 3 | 4 | .429 | 2.15 | 45 | 0 | 0 | 37 | 0 | 6 | 79.2 | 66 | 27 | 19 | 2 | 4 | 32 | 2 | 73 | 7 |
| Easley, Fort Lauderdale | 1 | 1 | .500 | 0.95 | 17 | 0 | 0 | 14 | 0 | 4 | 19.0 | 19 | 6 | 2 | 0 | 1 | 6 | 0 | 16 | 0 |
| Eichelberger, Miami | 2 | 3 | .400 | 4.07 | 7 | 7 | 1 | 0 | 0 | 0 | 42.0 | 50 | 31 | 19 | 1 | 1 | 23 | 0 | 40 | 1 |
| Erickson, Miami | 0 | 8 | .000 | 5.67 | 14 | 11 | 2 | 1 | 0 | 0 | 60.1 | 77 | 47 | 38 | 2 | 2 | 37 | 1 | 33 | 7 |
| Estes, St. Petersburg* | 0 | 3 | .000 | 3.19 | 13 | 4 | 0 | 6 | 0 | 0 | 42.1 | 40 | 19 | 15 | 1 | 0 | 27 | 2 | 17 | 5 |
| Farmer, Miami | 7 | 5 | .583 | 2.73 | 48 | 0 | 0 | 32 | 0 | 4 | 66.0 | 73 | 30 | 20 | 0 | 3 | 35 | 5 | 54 | 8 |
| Fay, Daytona Beach | 0 | 0 | .000 | 9.82 | 4 | 0 | 0 | 2 | 0 | 0 | 7.1 | 14 | 9 | 8 | 0 | 0 | 5 | 0 | 5 | 2 |
| Fedor, West Palm Beach | 2 | 1 | .667 | 1.69 | 31 | 0 | 0 | 20 | 0 | 8 | 48.0 | 32 | 18 | 9 | 1 | 2 | 27 | 5 | 49 | 4 |
| Fenn, Winter Haven | 3 | 3 | .500 | 3.72 | 37 | 1 | 0 | 17 | 0 | 2 | 67.2 | 68 | 32 | 28 | 4 | 0 | 31 | 3 | 41 | 3 |
| Fischer, West Palm Beach | 6 | 5 | .545 | 3.51 | 13 | 13 | 4 | 0 | 2 | 0 | 84.2 | 92 | 40 | 33 | 4 | 1 | 18 | 0 | 40 | 5 |
| Freeman, Clearwater | 6 | 5 | .545 | 3.06 | 14 | 13 | 3 | 1 | 3 | 0 | 88.1 | 72 | 32 | 30 | 0 | 1 | 36 | 1 | 55 | 7 |
| Frey, Fort Lauderdale | 1 | 1 | .500 | 1.21 | 19 | 0 | 0 | 13 | 0 | 7 | 22.1 | 11 | 4 | 3 | 0 | 1 | 12 | 0 | 15 | 0 |
| Friedrich, Osceola | 8 | 9 | .471 | 3.29 | 24 | 24 | 3 | 0 | 2 | 0 | 142.1 | 130 | 74 | 52 | 6 | 2 | 62 | 1 | 125 | 9 |
| Fulton, Fort Lauderdale | 11 | 2 | .846 | 1.61 | 15 | 15 | 9 | 0 | 1 | 0 | 112.0 | 91 | 31 | 20 | 2 | 2 | 30 | 0 | 71 | 6 |
| Gannon, Daytona Beach* | 4 | 3 | .571 | 3.36 | 27 | 3 | 1 | 11 | 0 | 0 | 61.2 | 63 | 29 | 23 | 0 | 2 | 27 | 1 | 32 | 4 |
| Garces, Clearwater* | 0 | 2 | .000 | 6.08 | 11 | 0 | 0 | 7 | 0 | 1 | 23.2 | 30 | 20 | 16 | 0 | 3 | 15 | 0 | 17 | 0 |
| Gardner, West Palm Beach | 5 | 4 | .556 | 2.37 | 10 | 9 | 4 | 1 | 0 | 0 | 60.2 | 54 | 24 | 16 | 4 | 2 | 18 | 1 | 44 | 6 |
| Gentle, Vero Beach* | 1 | 0 | 1.000 | 2.84 | 13 | 2 | 0 | 4 | 0 | 0 | 38.0 | 30 | 14 | 12 | 0 | 0 | 25 | 0 | 33 | 3 |
| P. George, Fort Myers* | 10 | 6 | .625 | 3.23 | 30 | 16 | 2 | 4 | 0 | 0 | 128.1 | 128 | 53 | 46 | 2 | 4 | 19 | 0 | 76 | 3 |
| S. George, Fort Lauderdale | 13 | 7 | .650 | 1.75 | 24 | 24 | 12 | 0 | 5 | 0 | 164.2 | 120 | 48 | 32 | 2 | 1 | 76 | 0 | 141 | 14 |
| Giddens, Tampa | 0 | 0 | .000 | 0.00 | 1 | 0 | 0 | 1 | 0 | 0 | 1.0 | 1 | 0 | 0 | 0 | 0 | 2 | 0 | 0 | 0 |
| Gonzalez, Daytona Beach* | 0 | 1 | .000 | 7.56 | 5 | 3 | 0 | 0 | 0 | 0 | 16.2 | 24 | 16 | 14 | 3 | 2 | 7 | 0 | 12 | 3 |
| Gorman, Lakeland | 1 | 0 | 1.000 | 1.40 | 15 | 0 | 0 | 11 | 0 | 4 | 25.2 | 26 | 7 | 4 | 1 | 0 | 1 | 1 | 15 | 0 |
| Gray, Clearwater | 5 | 9 | .357 | 3.18 | 55 | 0 | 0 | 47 | 0 | 23 | 87.2 | 80 | 38 | 31 | 4 | 1 | 33 | 9 | 80 | 6 |
| Grimm, Tampa | 3 | 6 | .333 | 4.13 | 14 | 12 | 1 | 0 | 0 | 0 | 69.2 | 76 | 45 | 32 | 5 | 3 | 36 | 2 | 36 | 2 |
| Guercio, Fort Lauderdale | 2 | 2 | .500 | 3.09 | 22 | 0 | 0 | 10 | 0 | 4 | 43.2 | 26 | 19 | 15 | 5 | 0 | 27 | 0 | 41 | 4 |
| Hale, Winter Haven | 4 | 6 | .400 | 3.11 | 38 | 3 | 1 | 20 | 0 | 4 | 72.1 | 51 | 35 | 25 | 1 | 1 | 41 | 3 | 37 | 5 |
| A. Hamilton, Winter Haven | 1 | 0 | 1.000 | 0.00 | 2 | 0 | 0 | 2 | 0 | 0 | 2.0 | 1 | 0 | 0 | 0 | 1 | 1 | 1 | 0 | 0 |
| R. Hamilton, Vero Beach | 5 | 8 | .385 | 4.05 | 26 | 17 | 3 | 3 | 1 | 0 | 117.2 | 104 | 62 | 53 | 3 | 1 | 74 | 2 | 84 | 12 |
| Harrison, Fort Lauderdale* | 1 | 0 | 1.000 | 2.15 | 22 | 0 | 0 | 10 | 0 | 6 | 37.2 | 27 | 11 | 9 | 1 | 1 | 14 | 0 | 23 | 6 |
| Hartman, Osceola | 1 | 0 | 1.000 | 0.00 | 2 | 0 | 0 | 1 | 0 | 0 | 3.2 | 2 | 1 | 0 | 0 | 0 | 3 | 0 | 3 | 0 |
| Heidenreich, Tampa | 1 | 0 | .667 | 1.95 | 6 | 3 | 2 | 1 | 0 | 0 | 27.2 | 19 | 6 | 6 | 0 | 0 | 12 | 1 | 21 | 4 |
| Heise, Daytona Beach* | 5 | 1 | .833 | 1.99 | 28 | 0 | 0 | 26 | 0 | 18 | 40.2 | 23 | 12 | 9 | 0 | 0 | 21 | 5 | 36 | 2 |
| Held, Lakeland | 4 | 10 | .286 | 4.20 | 26 | 16 | 2 | 7 | 1 | 1 | 111.1 | 116 | 63 | 52 | 0 | 2 | 50 | 5 | 52 | 9 |
| Herzog, St. Petersburg | 3 | 4 | .571 | 1.97 | 43 | 0 | 0 | 26 | 0 | 4 | 59.1 | 49 | 17 | 13 | 2 | 1 | 17 | 5 | 25 | 3 |
| Hester, Daytona Beach* | 0 | 2 | .000 | 11.72 | 13 | 0 | 0 | 4 | 0 | 0 | 17.2 | 35 | 24 | 23 | 1 | 1 | 12 | 1 | 6 | 3 |
| Holm, Daytona Beach* | 3 | 4 | .429 | 3.34 | 12 | 8 | 2 | 1 | 0 | 0 | 62.0 | 57 | 29 | 23 | 2 | 2 | 26 | 2 | 46 | 1 |
| Holman, West Palm Beach | 9 | 9 | .500 | 3.96 | 25 | 24 | 6 | 0 | 2 | 0 | 143.1 | 124 | 79 | 63 | 6 | 2 | 90 | 1 | 103 | 10 |
| Holmes, St. Petersburg | 4 | 3 | .571 | 3.11 | 33 | 0 | 0 | 20 | 0 | 2 | 63.2 | 57 | 31 | 22 | 0 | 0 | 35 | 2 | 46 | 6 |
| Hoyt, St. Petersburg | 2 | 3 | .400 | 3.40 | 20 | 2 | 0 | 9 | 0 | 1 | 45.0 | 30 | 21 | 17 | 2 | 5 | 36 | 4 | 27 | 5 |
| Hull, Fort Myers | 9 | 8 | .529 | 3.12 | 27 | 27 | 2 | 0 | 0 | 0 | 147.1 | 120 | 58 | 51 | 6 | 7 | 76 | 0 | 91 | 5 |
| Impagliazzo, West Palm Beach | 3 | 3 | .500 | 2.56 | 37 | 0 | 0 | 21 | 0 | 3 | 59.2 | 57 | 27 | 17 | 2 | 1 | 30 | 2 | 45 | 9 |

| Pitcher—Club | W. | L. | Pct. | ERA. | G. | GS. | CG. | GF. | ShO. | Sv. | IP. | H. | R. | ER. | HR. | HB. | BB. | Int. BB. | SO. | WP. |
|---|---|---|---|---|---|---|---|---|---|---|---|---|---|---|---|---|---|---|---|---|
| Jacobsen, Vero Beach | 4 | 5 | .444 | 1.74 | 43 | 0 | 0 | 32 | 0 | 11 | 82.2 | 52 | 18 | 16 | 1 | 3 | 43 | 5 | 64 | 5 |
| Jester, Clearwater° | 9 | 7 | .563 | 2.88 | 25 | 25 | 5 | 0 | 0 | 0 | 159.1 | 162 | 70 | 51 | 5 | 1 | 49 | 2 | 84 | 2 |
| R. Johnson, Daytona Beach | 1 | 5 | .167 | 5.64 | 14 | 7 | 2 | 4 | 0 | 0 | 60.2 | 73 | 44 | 38 | 4 | 2 | 29 | 4 | 39 | 14 |
| W. Johnson, W. Palm Beach° | 0 | 0 | .000 | 15.63 | 5 | 0 | 0 | 2 | 0 | 0 | 6.1 | 15 | 11 | 11 | 2 | 0 | 3 | 0 | 2 | 1 |
| Kelley, Osceola | 5 | 1 | .833 | 1.06 | 6 | 6 | 4 | 0 | 1 | 0 | 51.0 | 45 | 11 | 6 | 1 | 0 | 6 | 0 | 29 | 1 |
| Kemp, Tampa | 5 | 1 | .833 | 1.56 | 9 | 9 | 5 | 0 | 4 | 0 | 69.1 | 47 | 14 | 12 | 1 | 0 | 22 | 1 | 54 | 4 |
| Kiecker, Winter Haven | 12 | 12 | .500 | 2.60 | 29 | 29 | 9 | 0 | 2 | 0 | 193.2 | 176 | 72 | 56 | 4 | 2 | 59 | 2 | 60 | 7 |
| King, Daytona Beach | 0 | 1 | .000 | 1.93 | 5 | 0 | 0 | 2 | 0 | 1 | 4.2 | 4 | 7 | 1 | 0 | 0 | 6 | 2 | 4 | 1 |
| Kinns, West Palm Beach | 1 | 1 | .500 | 6.48 | 4 | 1 | 0 | 0 | 0 | 0 | 8.1 | 11 | 12 | 6 | 0 | 0 | 11 | 0 | 11 | 3 |
| Kipper, Daytona Beach° | 6 | 10 | .375 | 2.85 | 22 | 21 | 3 | 0 | 1 | 0 | 129.2 | 109 | 56 | 41 | 1 | 5 | 74 | 1 | 65 | 5 |
| Kohler, Miami | 0 | 0 | .000 | 5.87 | 14 | 0 | 0 | 6 | 0 | 0 | 23.0 | 25 | 17 | 15 | 1 | 2 | 21 | 1 | 8 | 4 |
| Labozzetta, Lakeland° | 4 | 4 | .500 | 4.30 | 12 | 12 | 1 | 0 | 1 | 0 | 69.0 | 78 | 40 | 33 | 3 | 3 | 24 | 0 | 30 | 7 |
| Lacey, Miami° | 4 | 5 | .444 | 3.77 | 11 | 10 | 4 | 0 | 1 | 0 | 59.2 | 74 | 32 | 25 | 4 | 0 | 11 | 0 | 38 | 3 |
| Lackie, Daytona Beach° | 0 | 3 | .000 | 2.25 | 9 | 0 | 0 | 4 | 0 | 0 | 16.0 | 16 | 8 | 4 | 0 | 1 | 11 | 1 | 9 | 3 |
| Langdon, Tampa | 6 | 2 | .750 | 2.19 | 29 | 6 | 0 | 15 | 0 | 5 | 65.2 | 37 | 20 | 16 | 0 | 1 | 51 | 7 | 53 | 5 |
| Ledbetter, 4 Day-24 Clw | 2 | 6 | .250 | 4.86 | 28 | 7 | 0 | 8 | 0 | 2 | 70.1 | 84 | 47 | 38 | 4 | 2 | 29 | 4 | 35 | 6 |
| Legumina, Vero Beach° | 3 | 3 | .500 | 1.63 | 42 | 0 | 0 | 35 | 0 | 10 | 66.1 | 49 | 19 | 12 | 0 | 0 | 22 | 3 | 56 | 1 |
| Leiter, Fort Lauderdale | 1 | 6 | .143 | 6.48 | 17 | 17 | 1 | 0 | 0 | 0 | 82.0 | 87 | 70 | 59 | 3 | 2 | 57 | 1 | 44 | 3 |
| Leonard, Fort Myers | 2 | 0 | 1.000 | 1.10 | 3 | 3 | 0 | 0 | 0 | 0 | 16.1 | 5 | 3 | 2 | 0 | 0 | 2 | 0 | 10 | 1 |
| Lloyd, Clearwater | 2 | 0 | 1.000 | 1.23 | 11 | 0 | 0 | 4 | 0 | 0 | 14.2 | 8 | 3 | 2 | 0 | 1 | 9 | 0 | 9 | 0 |
| Lono, Tampa° | 8 | 11 | .421 | 2.74 | 41 | 12 | 5 | 18 | 0 | 4 | 125.0 | 125 | 46 | 38 | 0 | 0 | 43 | 9 | 82 | 4 |
| LoSauro, Daytona Beach | 7 | 11 | .389 | 4.84 | 27 | 19 | 3 | 2 | 0 | 1 | 111.2 | 126 | 80 | 60 | 4 | 3 | 70 | 3 | 41 | 17 |
| Lovelace, Vero Beach° | 1 | 2 | .333 | 6.14 | 11 | 3 | 0 | 4 | 0 | 0 | 29.1 | 31 | 22 | 20 | 0 | 1 | 23 | 1 | 26 | 4 |
| A. Lucas, Osceola | 4 | 2 | .667 | 1.76 | 34 | 3 | 0 | 18 | 0 | 5 | 92.0 | 64 | 24 | 18 | 2 | 1 | 37 | 1 | 63 | 4 |
| G. Lucas, W. Palm Beach° | 0 | 0 | .000 | 7.20 | 3 | 3 | 0 | 0 | 0 | 0 | 5.0 | 4 | 5 | 4 | 1 | 0 | 1 | 0 | 3 | 1 |
| M. Madden, Tampa° | 6 | 8 | .429 | 3.39 | 23 | 12 | 3 | 8 | 0 | 1 | 82.1 | 76 | 48 | 31 | 2 | 3 | 64 | 1 | 78 | 9 |
| S. Madden, Clearwater° | 8 | 11 | .421 | 3.03 | 27 | 25 | 5 | 0 | 1 | 0 | 157.1 | 139 | 65 | 53 | 5 | 0 | 95 | 0 | 87 | 6 |
| Magrane, St. Petersburg° | 3 | 1 | .750 | 1.04 | 5 | 5 | 1 | 0 | 1 | 0 | 34.2 | 21 | 8 | 4 | 0 | 1 | 14 | 0 | 17 | 2 |
| Mallicoat, Osceola° | 16 | 6 | .727 | 1.36 | 26 | 25 | 5 | 0 | 2 | 0 | 178.2 | 119 | 41 | 27 | 2 | 3 | 74 | 3 | 158 | 14 |
| Mangham, Osceola | 3 | 1 | .750 | 3.91 | 23 | 1 | 1 | 11 | 0 | 0 | 50.2 | 51 | 24 | 22 | 2 | 1 | 21 | 5 | 26 | 6 |
| Martinez, St. Petersburg | 2 | 0 | 1.000 | 1.85 | 4 | 3 | 1 | 0 | 1 | 0 | 24.1 | 16 | 5 | 5 | 0 | 0 | 6 | 0 | 21 | 0 |
| Mason, St. Petersburg | 6 | 7 | .462 | 1.40 | 41 | 0 | 0 | 32 | 0 | 9 | 64.1 | 44 | 17 | 10 | 0 | 0 | 20 | 7 | 33 | 4 |
| C. Mathews, Osceola | 12 | 6 | .667 | 3.18 | 29 | 22 | 2 | 2 | 1 | 0 | 152.2 | 159 | 66 | 54 | 6 | 2 | 47 | 1 | 74 | 7 |
| G. Mathews, St. Petersburg° | 13 | 1 | .929 | 1.11 | 16 | 16 | 8 | 0 | 4 | 0 | 122.0 | 76 | 17 | 15 | 3 | 2 | 47 | 0 | 96 | 3 |
| Mayberry, Vero Beach | 11 | 4 | .733 | 2.35 | 17 | 17 | 5 | 0 | 1 | 0 | 118.2 | 101 | 40 | 31 | 1 | 3 | 37 | 2 | 97 | 2 |
| McDevitt, Clearwater | 2 | 2 | .500 | 2.87 | 17 | 2 | 0 | 5 | 0 | 1 | 31.1 | 34 | 15 | 10 | 0 | 0 | 16 | 2 | 33 | 2 |
| McEnaney, Miami° | 1 | 4 | .200 | 3.82 | 39 | 0 | 0 | 22 | 0 | 3 | 37.2 | 45 | 24 | 16 | 4 | 3 | 13 | 3 | 30 | 4 |
| McHugh, Lakeland | 9 | 5 | .643 | 3.72 | 38 | 2 | 0 | 19 | 0 | 4 | 84.2 | 91 | 45 | 35 | 2 | 3 | 41 | 2 | 77 | 2 |
| McKay, West Palm Beach | 0 | 0 | .000 | 11.12 | 2 | 2 | 0 | 0 | 0 | 0 | 5.2 | 9 | 7 | 7 | 2 | 0 | 5 | 0 | 4 | 0 |
| McKnight, Miami | 0 | 0 | .000 | .000 | 1 | 0 | 0 | 0 | 0 | 0 | 1.0 | 1 | 0 | 0 | 0 | 0 | 0 | 0 | 0 | 0 |
| Meadows, Vero Beach | 1 | 2 | .333 | 3.95 | 6 | 5 | 0 | 0 | 0 | 0 | 27.1 | 21 | 16 | 12 | 2 | 0 | 22 | 0 | 16 | 2 |
| Medvin, Lakeland | 5 | 4 | .556 | 2.79 | 31 | 0 | 0 | 28 | 0 | 5 | 51.2 | 48 | 20 | 16 | 1 | 0 | 20 | 1 | 47 | 1 |
| Melchert, Lakeland° | 0 | 0 | .000 | 4.50 | 3 | 0 | 0 | 1 | 0 | 0 | 6.0 | 10 | 3 | 3 | 0 | 1 | 3 | 0 | 1 | 2 |
| Melrose, Daytona Beach° | 0 | 0 | .000 | .000 | 4 | 0 | 0 | 4 | 0 | 0 | 3.1 | 2 | 0 | 0 | 0 | 1 | 3 | 0 | 4 | 0 |
| Milacki, Daytona Beach | 1 | 4 | .200 | 3.99 | 8 | 6 | 2 | 1 | 0 | 0 | 38.1 | 32 | 23 | 17 | 0 | 0 | 26 | 1 | 24 | 7 |
| Minnema, Lakeland | 8 | 12 | .400 | 3.46 | 26 | 24 | 6 | 2 | 2 | 0 | 153.1 | 152 | 81 | 59 | 7 | 3 | 66 | 1 | 89 | 8 |
| Mirabito, Tampa | 5 | 5 | .500 | 2.76 | 15 | 11 | 3 | 2 | 1 | 0 | 78.1 | 64 | 29 | 24 | 0 | 0 | 25 | 1 | 37 | 3 |
| Mohr, Fort Myers° | 4 | 4 | .500 | 1.13 | 29 | 0 | 0 | 27 | 0 | 12 | 48.0 | 32 | 9 | 6 | 0 | 0 | 16 | 3 | 43 | 1 |
| Moran, West Palm Beach° | 2 | 4 | .333 | 4.96 | 22 | 7 | 0 | 4 | 0 | 0 | 45.1 | 47 | 36 | 25 | 2 | 5 | 33 | 0 | 46 | 3 |
| Nunez, Fort Myers | 3 | 2 | .600 | 2.44 | 11 | 8 | 0 | 0 | 0 | 0 | 44.1 | 32 | 14 | 12 | 1 | 4 | 12 | 0 | 23 | 2 |
| Odekirk, Tampa° | 5 | 3 | .625 | 3.36 | 31 | 2 | 1 | 11 | 0 | 1 | 80.1 | 71 | 31 | 30 | 3 | 6 | 30 | 2 | 48 | 9 |
| Oliveras, Daytona Beach | 3 | 0 | 1.000 | 1.90 | .3 | 3 | 1 | 0 | 0 | 0 | 23.2 | 13 | 6 | 5 | 0 | 1 | 9 | 0 | 25 | 1 |
| Pacillo, Tampa | 8 | 1 | .889 | 3.03 | 25 | 0 | 0 | 21 | 0 | 7 | 38.2 | 28 | 17 | 13 | 1 | 1 | 28 | 5 | 39 | 3 |
| Parkins, Winter Haven | 6 | 11 | .353 | 4.04 | 26 | 21 | 2 | 2 | 1 | 0 | 133.2 | 119 | 66 | 60 | 4 | 2 | 72 | 0 | 69 | 6 |
| Pena, Miami° | 2 | 4 | .333 | 4.79 | 25 | 6 | 0 | 6 | 0 | 2 | 71.1 | 69 | 54 | 38 | 0 | 3 | 41 | 3 | 73 | 12 |
| Perkins, Miami | 4 | 3 | .571 | 2.69 | 59 | 1 | 0 | 25 | 0 | 5 | 97.0 | 100 | 37 | 29 | 1 | 7 | 36 | 2 | 44 | 4 |
| Perrotte, Lakeland° | 1 | 4 | .200 | 4.75 | 13 | 11 | 0 | 0 | 0 | 0 | 55.0 | 51 | 34 | 29 | 5 | 3 | 47 | 0 | 27 | 0 |
| Pesavento, Vero Beach° | 6 | 7 | .462 | 3.62 | 24 | 15 | 4 | 5 | 2 | 0 | 109.1 | 102 | 47 | 44 | 5 | 6 | 38 | 0 | 59 | 4 |
| Peters, St. Petersburg | 4 | 3 | .571 | 2.51 | 10 | 10 | 2 | 0 | 1 | 0 | 64.2 | 52 | 21 | 18 | 2 | 0 | 29 | 1 | 60 | 2 |
| Pettaway, Miami | 1 | 2 | .333 | 4.09 | 6 | 1 | 0 | 4 | 0 | 2 | 11.0 | 11 | 9 | 5 | 0 | 0 | 5 | 0 | 8 | 3 |
| Phillion, Lakeland | 1 | 5 | .167 | 5.87 | 11 | 10 | 0 | 0 | 0 | 0 | 53.2 | 64 | 40 | 35 | 1 | 3 | 28 | 0 | 33 | 8 |
| Poissant, Lakeland | 5 | 4 | .556 | 6.10 | 22 | 10 | 1 | 4 | 0 | 1 | 79.2 | 108 | 63 | 54 | 3 | 3 | 39 | 0 | 37 | 10 |
| Pratt, Miami | 1 | 0 | 1.000 | 3.00 | 3 | 0 | 0 | 0 | 0 | 0 | 6.0 | 9 | 7 | 2 | 0 | 0 | 4 | 0 | 2 | 2 |
| Pries, Fort Lauderdale | 11 | 7 | .611 | 3.83 | 22 | 22 | 4 | 0 | 0 | 0 | 131.2 | 117 | 66 | 56 | 7 | 6 | 49 | 1 | 50 | 7 |
| Raftice, Fort Lauderdale° | 0 | 2 | .000 | 4.58 | 11 | 0 | 0 | 5 | 0 | 0 | 17.2 | 18 | 11 | 9 | 0 | 0 | 11 | 1 | 11 | 1 |
| Ramirez, Daytona Beach | 0 | 2 | .000 | 3.43 | 4 | 4 | 0 | 0 | 0 | 0 | 21.0 | 22 | 12 | 8 | 0 | 0 | 10 | 1 | 14 | 0 |
| Rasmussen, Miami | 15 | 6 | .714 | 2.75 | 27 | 27 | 8 | 0 | 3 | 0 | 186.2 | 177 | 64 | 57 | 3 | 4 | 35 | 1 | 118 | 3 |
| Rather, Fort Lauderdale | 2 | 3 | .400 | 3.47 | 6 | 6 | 1 | 0 | 0 | 0 | 36.1 | 31 | 17 | 14 | 0 | 2 | 20 | 0 | 35 | 5 |
| Ratliff, West Palm Beach | 5 | 5 | .500 | 2.30 | 27 | 0 | 0 | 16 | 0 | 6 | 54.2 | 45 | 21 | 14 | 1 | 0 | 23 | 0 | 39 | 3 |
| Raubolt, Lakeland | 0 | 1 | .000 | 5.68 | 12 | 0 | 0 | 5 | 0 | 2 | 25.1 | 29 | 18 | 16 | 0 | 5 | 23 | 0 | 13 | 4 |
| Reburn, Tampa | 5 | 6 | .455 | 3.60 | 23 | 18 | 3 | 1 | 0 | 0 | 110.0 | 118 | 58 | 44 | 1 | 0 | 56 | 3 | 82 | 20 |
| Reynolds, Daytona Beach | 1 | 3 | .250 | 5.47 | 5 | 5 | 1 | 0 | 0 | 0 | 26.1 | 29 | 19 | 16 | 1 | 0 | 20 | 2 | 12 | 1 |
| Rice, Daytona Beach | 0 | 1 | .000 | 6.65 | 13 | 1 | 0 | 9 | 0 | 0 | 23.0 | 31 | 17 | 17 | 0 | 2 | 13 | 0 | 16 | 1 |
| Ritchie, Clearwater° | 3 | 1 | .750 | 3.47 | 14 | 6 | 0 | 3 | 0 | 1 | 46.2 | 49 | 30 | 18 | 5 | 0 | 12 | 0 | 24 | 0 |
| Rodiles, Fort Myers | 10 | 3 | .769 | 1.72 | 40 | 3 | 1 | 19 | 0 | 4 | 99.1 | 74 | 29 | 19 | 3 | 1 | 56 | 5 | 67 | 3 |
| Rodriguez, Fort Lauderdale | 6 | 5 | .545 | 3.09 | 30 | 9 | 1 | 9 | 0 | 0 | 96.0 | 100 | 41 | 33 | 3 | 1 | 35 | 1 | 48 | 2 |
| Rogers, Daytona Beach° | 0 | 1 | .000 | 7.20 | 6 | 0 | 0 | 1 | 0 | 0 | 10.0 | 12 | 9 | 8 | 0 | 1 | 11 | 1 | 9 | 3 |
| Rohan, Daytona Beach | 3 | 1 | .750 | 4.08 | 17 | 1 | 0 | 4 | 0 | 2 | 46.1 | 44 | 26 | 21 | 0 | 2 | 27 | 3 | 27 | 7 |
| Rowen, Fort Myers° | 2 | 4 | .333 | 6.75 | 9 | 9 | 0 | 0 | 0 | 0 | 32.0 | 37 | 27 | 24 | 1 | 0 | 25 | 0 | 21 | 7 |
| Ruffin, Clearwater° | 5 | 5 | .500 | 2.88 | 14 | 14 | 3 | 0 | 1 | 0 | 97.0 | 87 | 33 | 31 | 2 | 2 | 34 | 1 | 74 | 3 |
| Russo, Miami | 0 | 7 | .000 | 4.34 | 15 | 11 | 1 | 4 | 0 | 0 | 66.1 | 77 | 40 | 32 | 1 | 4 | 27 | 1 | 42 | 4 |
| G. Sanchez, Daytona Beach | 2 | 1 | .667 | 3.17 | 19 | 2 | 0 | 8 | 0 | 2 | 48.1 | 50 | 20 | 17 | 2 | 0 | 22 | 4 | 28 | 2 |
| I. Sanchez, Fort Myers° | 8 | 6 | .571 | 2.11 | 28 | 12 | 2 | 8 | 2 | 3 | 98.1 | 72 | 32 | 23 | 4 | 0 | 27 | 1 | 86 | 3 |
| Schwartz, Tampa° | 2 | 3 | .400 | 3.35 | 13 | 4 | 0 | 2 | 0 | 0 | 43.0 | 37 | 17 | 16 | 1 | 0 | 21 | 0 | 28 | 4 |
| Schweighoffer, Vero Beach | 10 | 12 | .455 | 3.11 | 25 | 25 | 5 | 0 | 1 | 0 | 153.1 | 146 | 68 | 53 | 3 | 2 | 60 | 6 | 59 | 5 |
| Shaab, Osceola° | 3 | 2 | .600 | 4.24 | 35 | 0 | 0 | 17 | 0 | 3 | 46.2 | 50 | 27 | 22 | 2 | 0 | 22 | 5 | 40 | 3 |
| Simpson, 25 Clw-7 Tampa° | 1 | 4 | .200 | 3.81 | 32 | 0 | 0 | 19 | 0 | 6 | 49.2 | 55 | 26 | 21 | 0 | 1 | 17 | 0 | 30 | 1 |
| Slifko, Winter Haven | 10 | 4 | .714 | 3.40 | 34 | 15 | 0 | 7 | 0 | 1 | 119.0 | 106 | 64 | 45 | 2 | 2 | 55 | 1 | 46 | 5 |
| Smith, Clearwater | 12 | 10 | .545 | 3.29 | 26 | 25 | 4 | 0 | 1 | 0 | 153.0 | 135 | 68 | 56 | 2 | 2 | 80 | 1 | 86 | 3 |
| Spagnola, Tampa | 2 | 2 | .500 | 3.70 | 21 | 18 | 1 | 1 | 0 | 0 | 80.1 | 69 | 37 | 33 | 6 | 1 | 35 | 3 | 58 | 5 |
| Sparling, Fort Myers | 8 | 6 | .571 | 2.31 | 27 | 22 | 1 | 1 | 0 | 0 | 140.1 | 135 | 48 | 36 | 2 | 5 | 44 | 0 | 69 | 1 |
| Stewart, Winter Haven° | 10 | 7 | .588 | 2.82 | 37 | 17 | 3 | 10 | 0 | 0 | 147.0 | 149 | 56 | 46 | 6 | 0 | 37 | 3 | 52 | 4 |

| Pitcher—Club | W. | L. | Pct. | ERA. | G. | GS. | CG. | GF. | ShO. | Sv. | IP. | H. | R. | ER. | HR. | HB. | BB. | Int. BB. | SO. | WP. |
|---|---|---|---|---|---|---|---|---|---|---|---|---|---|---|---|---|---|---|---|---|
| Summers, Daytona Beach ........... | 1 | 1 | .500 | 2.05 | 3 | 3 | 1 | 0 | 0 | 0 | 22.0 | 11 | 7 | 5 | 0 | 0 | 11 | 0 | 19 | 4 |
| Taft, Miami* ................................ | 3 | 9 | .250 | 3.59 | 32 | 14 | 0 | 7 | 0 | 0 | 87.2 | 89 | 52 | 35 | 2 | 1 | 41 | 0 | 39 | 6 |
| Thorpe, Daytona Beach ............... | 1 | 5 | .167 | 2.51 | 24 | 0 | 0 | 20 | 0 | 4 | 28.2 | 33 | 12 | 8 | 1 | 1 | 16 | 10 | 9 | 1 |
| P. Torres, Vero Beach ................ | 0 | 0 | .000 | 0.00 | 2 | 0 | 0 | 2 | 0 | 1 | 6.0 | 1 | 1 | 0 | 0 | 0 | 3 | 0 | 10 | 0 |
| R. Torres, Fort Lauderdale ........ | 6 | 6 | .500 | 4.68 | 17 | 17 | 1 | 0 | 1 | 0 | 92.1 | 103 | 56 | 48 | 7 | 1 | 36 | 0 | 107 | 7 |
| Torrez, Miami ............................. | 7 | 8 | .467 | 2.80 | 19 | 19 | 3 | 0 | 2 | 0 | 132.0 | 115 | 56 | 41 | 0 | 1 | 55 | 3 | 66 | 9 |
| Traen, West Palm Beach ............. | 8 | 4 | .667 | 2.49 | 30 | 10 | 2 | 11 | 0 | 3 | 112.0 | 97 | 39 | 31 | 5 | 0 | 41 | 1 | 98 | 4 |
| Trautwein, West Palm Beach ..... | 3 | 5 | .375 | 2.16 | 35 | 0 | 0 | 23 | 0 | 8 | 66.2 | 52 | 20 | 16 | 2 | 1 | 22 | 4 | 54 | 2 |
| Trudeau, Fort Lauderdale .......... | 0 | 0 | .000 | 0.00 | 1 | 0 | 0 | 1 | 0 | 0 | 2.0 | 0 | 0 | 0 | 0 | 1 | 0 | 1 | 1 | 0 |
| True, Clearwater* ...................... | 0 | 1 | .000 | 4.82 | 3 | 2 | 0 | 0 | 0 | 0 | 9.1 | 10 | 5 | 5 | 0 | 0 | 5 | 0 | 9 | 0 |
| Tuck, Miami ............................... | 1 | 3 | .250 | 6.03 | 15 | 3 | 0 | 2 | 0 | 0 | 37.1 | 46 | 31 | 25 | 3 | 4 | 32 | 1 | 32 | 7 |
| Underwood, Fort Lauderdale* .... | 0 | 1 | .000 | 1.35 | 5 | 2 | 0 | 1 | 0 | 0 | 13.1 | 14 | 5 | 2 | 0 | 1 | 4 | 0 | 12 | 1 |
| Valliant, West Palm Beach ......... | 0 | 0 | .000 | 3.86 | 6 | 0 | 0 | 1 | 0 | 0 | 9.1 | 4 | 6 | 4 | 1 | 0 | 10 | 0 | 8 | 0 |
| Vargas, Clearwater* .................. | 3 | 3 | .500 | 3.27 | 44 | 1 | 0 | 21 | 0 | 11 | 85.1 | 85 | 41 | 31 | 5 | 1 | 23 | 10 | 50 | 6 |
| Walter, Fort Myers ..................... | 0 | 2 | .000 | 5.66 | 28 | 0 | 0 | 18 | 0 | 3 | 47.2 | 54 | 37 | 30 | 2 | 1 | 25 | 2 | 21 | 4 |
| Watts, Clearwater* .................... | 5 | 3 | .625 | 2.13 | 22 | 7 | 3 | 7 | 1 | 1 | 71.2 | 56 | 25 | 17 | 3 | 0 | 30 | 3 | 57 | 5 |
| Wayne, West Palm Beach* ........ | 2 | 2 | .500 | 5.58 | 8 | 4 | 0 | 1 | 0 | 0 | 30.2 | 37 | 23 | 19 | 1 | 0 | 22 | 0 | 18 | 5 |
| Welch, Vero Beach ..................... | 0 | 0 | .000 | 2.12 | 3 | 3 | 0 | 0 | 0 | 0 | 17.0 | 15 | 4 | 4 | 0 | 0 | 1 | 0 | 9 | 0 |
| Willsher, Daytona Beach ............ | 6 | 11 | .353 | 3.27 | 21 | 17 | 6 | 0 | 1 | 0 | 107.1 | 104 | 60 | 39 | 4 | 3 | 65 | 2 | 86 | 11 |
| R. Wilson, Daytona Beach* ........ | 2 | 3 | .400 | 2.53 | 10 | 5 | 1 | 2 | 0 | 0 | 42.2 | 40 | 20 | 12 | 0 | 0 | 25 | 1 | 42 | 5 |
| W. Wilson, Daytona Beach* ....... | 0 | 3 | .000 | 8.10 | 11 | 5 | 0 | 4 | 0 | 0 | 26.2 | 28 | 28 | 24 | 0 | 1 | 27 | 2 | 12 | 2 |
| Wohler, Vero Beach* .................. | 7 | 11 | .389 | 2.93 | 28 | 18 | 7 | 5 | 2 | 0 | 135.0 | 114 | 62 | 44 | 1 | 3 | 55 | 1 | 67 | 10 |
| Wyatt, Fort Myers ..................... | 1 | 0 | 1.000 | 2.79 | 4 | 0 | 0 | 0 | 0 | 0 | 9.2 | 14 | 7 | 3 | 0 | 0 | 7 | 2 | 9 | 2 |
| Yeager, Fort Lauderdale* ........... | 1 | 1 | .500 | 1.60 | 20 | 0 | 0 | 11 | 0 | 3 | 33.2 | 22 | 6 | 6 | 0 | 2 | 14 | 3 | 32 | 3 |
| C. Young, West Palm Beach* ...... | 15 | 5 | .750 | 3.98 | 25 | 25 | 7 | 0 | 0 | 0 | 153.2 | 149 | 77 | 68 | 13 | 6 | 57 | 0 | 112 | 6 |
| S. Young, St. Petersburg ........... | 13 | 9 | .591 | 2.71 | 27 | 27 | 9 | 0 | 3 | 0 | 179.1 | 157 | 66 | 54 | 7 | 11 | 63 | 0 | 109 | 10 |

BALKS—Curry, 11; Bear, Smith, 6 each; Fischer, Held, Pena, Pesavento, 5 each; Carson, Cerefin, Devine, Dube, Mayberry, Perrotte, Russo, Schweighoffer, C. Young, 4 each; Canseco, DeJesus, Dodd, Friedrich, S. George, Hale, R. Hamilton, Holm, Lono, Minnema, Mirabito, Moran, Ratliff, Reynolds, Rodriguez, Rohan, G. Sanchez, Trautwein, 3 each; Araujo, Brennan, Campbell, Cash, P. Cherry, Cutshall, Estes, Hull, Jacobsen, Jester, Lovelace, S. Madden, Mallicoat, G. Mathews, Odekirk, Rasmussen, Rodiles, Willsher, R. Wilson, 2 each; Agar, Barlow, Bass, Berrios, Bianchi, Boudreaux, Cooper, Crew, Dale, C. Daniel, J. Daniel, Dixon, Dougherty, Freeman, Gannon, Gardner, Gonzalez, Gray, Harrison, Holman, Holmes, Hoyt, R. Johnson, Kohler, Lacey, Langdon, Leiter, A. Lucas, Magrane, McDevitt, McHugh, Meadows, Medvin, Milacki, Pacillo, Perkins, Peters, Pries, Rather, Reburn, Rowen, Ruffin, Schwartz, Shaab, Simpson, Slifko, Spagnola, Summers, Taft, Thorpe, P. Torres, Traen, Valliant, Vargas, Walter, Watts, S. Young, 1 each.

COMBINATION SHUTOUTS—Smith-True-Simpson, Madden-Gray, Smith-Vargas, Madden-Vargas, Freeman-McDevitt-Gray, Clearwater; Kipper-Sanchez-Heise, Holm-Heise, Daytona Beach; Pries-Frey 2, Canseco-Frey, George-Easley-Frey, George-Cloninger-Devlin, Dersin-Guercio, Cloninger-Guercio, Rodriguez-Harrison, Dersin-Rodriguez, Pries-Blum, Fort Lauderdale; DeJesus-Rodiles, Nunez-Walter, Sparling-Sanchez-Rodiles, Daniel-Mohr, Hull-Rodiles, Sparling-Davis, Crew-Rodiles-Mohr, DeJesus-George-Rodiles, Leonard-George, Fort Myers; McHugh-Duffy, Perrotte-Minnema, Perrotte-McHugh, Lakeland; Torrez-Perkins-Farmer, Taft-Farmer-McEnaney, Miami; Friedrich-Baker, Mathews-Baker, Lucas-Shaab, Cerefin-Cash-Baker, Cash-Lucas-Baker, Mallicoat-Baker, Mallicoat-Baker, Osceola; Mathews-Carrasco, Young-Cherry, Mathews-Herzog-Hoyt, Cherry-Herzog-Mason, Peters-Brisco, Hoyt-Carrasco-Mason, St. Petersburg; Daniel-Heidenreich-Pacillo, Reburn-Heidenreich, Reburn-Lono, Campbell-Lono-Pacillo, Kemp-Campbell, Grimm-Campbell, Mirabito-Langdon-Madden, Spagnola-Schwartz-Langdon, Mirabito-Langdon, Tampa; Cherry-Jacobsen, Rowen-Jacobsen, Mayberry-Jacobsen, Brennan-Legumina, Vero Beach; Holman-Fedor, Young-Traen, Charlton-Trautwein, West Palm Beach; Curry-Cappadona, Araujo-Slifko-Fenn-Cappadona, Araujo-Cappadona-Dalton, Slifko-Hale-Stewart-Fenn, Araujo-Dalton, Clarkin-Stewart, Winter Haven.

NO-HIT GAMES—Fulton, Fort Lauderdale, defeated Lakeland, 5-0 (first game), July 2; Bacon, Tampa, defeated Miami, 1-0 (second game), July 3; Wohler, Vero Beach, defeated St. Petersburg, 1-0, July 17; Friedrich, Osceola, defeated Lakeland, 2-0 (first game), August 4; George, Fort Lauderdale, defeated Miami, 6-0 (five innings), August 14.

# Midwest League

## CLASS A

### CHAMPIONSHIP WINNERS IN PREVIOUS YEARS

| | | |
|---|---|---|
| 1947—Belleville .667 | 1961—Waterloo .613 | 1973—Wisconsin Rapids a .562 |
| Belleville .672 | Quincy z .594 | Danville .537 |
| 1948—West Frankfort* .708 | 1962—Dubuque z .667 | 1974—Appleton .593 |
| 1949—Centralia .627 | Waterloo .625 | Danville a .517 |
| Paducah (4th)† .454 | 1963—Clinton .710 | 1975—Waterloo a .727 |
| 1950—Centralia‡ .675 | Clinton .629 | Quad Cities .624 |
| 1951—Paris§ .700 | 1964—Clinton .667 | 1976—Waterloo a .600 |
| Danville (4th)† .432 | Fox Cities z .667 | Cedar Rapids .595 |
| 1952—Danville x .685 | 1965—Burlington .667 | 1977—Waterloo .580 |
| Decatur (3rd)† .584 | Burlington .677 | Burlington a .511 |
| 1953—Decatur* .576 | 1966—Fox Cities z .689 | 1978—Appleton a .708 |
| 1954—Decatur .587 | Cedar Rapids .762 | Burlington .500 |
| Danville (2nd)‡ .528 | 1967—Wisconsin Rapids .685 | 1979—Waterloo .600 |
| 1955—Dubuque* .587 | Appleton z .587 | Quad Cities a .579 |
| 1956—Paris y .656 | 1968—Decatur .656 | 1980—Waterloo a .610 |
| Dubuque .603 | Quad Cities z .648 | Quad Cities .532 |
| 1957—Decatur y .683 | 1969—Appleton .648 | 1981—Wausau a .636 |
| Clinton .623 | Appleton .690 | Quad Cities .570 |
| 1958—Michigan City .623 | 1970—Quincy z .691 | 1982—Madison .626 |
| Waterloo z .613 | Quad Cities .581 | Appleton b .579 |
| 1959—Waterloo .613 | 1971—Appleton .642 | 1983—Appleton c .635 |
| Waterloo .613 | Quad Cities a .548 | Springfield .576 |
| 1960—Waterloo .629 | 1972—Appleton a .598 | 1984—Appleton c .640 |
| Waterloo .677 | Danville a .584 | Springfield .504 |

*Won championship and four-club playoff. †Won four-club playoff. ‡Playoff finals canceled because of bad weather. §Won both halves of split-season. xWon first half of split-season and tied Paris for second-half title. yWon first-half title and four-team playoff. zWon split-season playoff. aLeague divided into Northern and Southern divisions and played split-season. Playoff winner. bLeague divided into Northern, Central and Southern. Playoff winner. cLeague divided into Northern, Central and Southern divisions; regular-season and playoff winner. (NOTE—Known as Illinois State League in 1947-48 and Mississippi-Ohio Valley League from 1949 through 1955.)

### STANDING OF CLUBS AT CLOSE OF SEASON, SEPTEMBER 2

#### NORTHERN DIVISION

| Club | W. | L. | T. | Pct. | G.B. |
|---|---|---|---|---|---|
| Appleton (White Sox) | 85 | 54 | 0 | .662 | ....... |
| Kenosha (Twins) | 79 | 60 | 0 | .568 | 6 |
| Madison (A's) | 65 | 73 | 0 | .464 | 19½ |
| Wausau (Mariners) | 52 | 85 | 0 | .387 | 32 |

#### CENTRAL DIVISION

| Club | W. | L. | T. | Pct. | G.B. |
|---|---|---|---|---|---|
| Beloit (Brewers) | 79 | 57 | 0 | .581 | ....... |
| Cedar Rapids (Reds) | 78 | 61 | 0 | .561 | 2½ |
| Clinton (Giants) | 71 | 69 | 0 | .507 | 10 |
| Waterloo (Indians) | 67 | 73 | 0 | .479 | 14 |

#### SOUTHERN DIVISION

| Club | W. | L. | T. | Pct. | G.B. |
|---|---|---|---|---|---|
| Peoria (Cubs) | 75 | 65 | 0 | .536 | ....... |
| Springfield (Cardinals) | 66 | 74 | 0 | .471 | 9 |
| Quad Cities (Angels) | 66 | 74 | 0 | .471 | 9 |
| Burlington (Rangers) | 50 | 88 | 0 | .362 | 24 |

### COMPOSITE STANDING OF CLUBS AT CLOSE OF SEASON, SEPTEMBER 2

| Club | Apl. | Bel. | Ken. | C.R. | Pea. | Cln. | Wat. | Spr. | Q.C. | Mad. | Wau. | Bur. | W. | L. | T. | Pct. | G.B. |
|---|---|---|---|---|---|---|---|---|---|---|---|---|---|---|---|---|---|
| Appleton (White Sox) | ... | 5 | 13 | 5 | 6 | 5 | 5 | 6 | 6 | 12 | 15 | 7 | 85 | 54 | 0 | .612 | ....... |
| Beloit (Brewers) | 5 | ... | 5 | 10 | 4 | 12 | 12 | 5 | 6 | 6 | 7 | 7 | 79 | 57 | 0 | .581 | 4½ |
| Kenosha (Twins) | 7 | 4 | ... | 6 | 3 | 7 | 6 | 6 | 9 | 15 | 10 | 79 | 60 | 0 | .568 | 6 |
| Cedar Rapids (Reds) | 5 | 9 | 4 | ... | 8 | 11 | 13 | 4 | 4 | 5 | 7 | 8 | 78 | 61 | 0 | .561 | 7 |
| Peoria (Cubs) | 4 | 6 | 7 | 2 | ... | 4 | 5 | 14 | 9 | 6 | 4 | 14 | 75 | 65 | 0 | .536 | 10½ |
| Clinton (Giants) | 5 | 8 | 3 | 9 | 6 | ... | 11 | 3 | 7 | 6 | 7 | 6 | 71 | 69 | 0 | .507 | 14½ |
| Waterloo (Indians) | 5 | 8 | 4 | 7 | 5 | 9 | ... | 6 | 6 | 4 | 7 | 6 | 67 | 73 | 0 | .479 | 18½ |
| Springfield (Cardinals) | 4 | 5 | 4 | 6 | 6 | 7 | 4 | ... | 9 | 6 | 5 | 10 | 66 | 74 | 0 | .471 | 19½ |
| Quad Cities (Angels) | 4 | 4 | 4 | 6 | 11 | 3 | 4 | 11 | ... | 3 | 6 | 10 | 66 | 74 | 0 | .471 | 19½ |
| Madison (Athletics) | 8 | 4 | 11 | 5 | 4 | 4 | 6 | 4 | 7 | ... | 6 | 6 | 65 | 73 | 0 | .464 | 19½ |
| Wausau (Mariners) | 4 | 3 | 5 | 3 | 6 | 3 | 3 | 5 | 4 | 12 | ... | 4 | 52 | 85 | 0 | .387 | 32 |
| Burlington (Rangers) | 3 | 1 | 0 | 2 | 6 | 4 | 4 | 10 | 10 | 4 | 6 | ... | 50 | 88 | 0 | 362 | 34½ |

Quad Cities' home games played in Davenport, Ia.
Major league affiliations in parentheses.

Playoffs—Peoria defeated Beloit, two games to one; Kenosha defeated Appleton, two games to one; Kenosha defeated Peoria, three games to one, to win league championship.

Regular-Season Attendance—Appleton, 76,860; Beloit, 93,638; Burlington, 64,763; Cedar Rapids, 155,034; Clinton, 101,499; Kenosha, 60,977; Madison, 110,949; Peoria, 165,053; Quad Cities, 153,414; Springfield, 149,069; Waterloo, 78,125; Wausau, 50,352. Total—1,259,733. Total Playoff Attendance, 14,093. All-Star Game Attendance, 1,259.

Managers—Appleton, Sal Rende; Beloit, Dave Machemer; Burlington, Mike Bucci; Cedar Rapids, Jay Ward; Clinton, Tim Blackwell; Kenosha, Duffy Dyer; Madison, Jim Nettles; Peoria, Pete Mackanin; Quad Cities, Bill Lachemann; Springfield, Lloyd Merritt; Waterloo, Steve Swisher; Wausau, Greg Mahlberg.

All-Star Team—1B—Greg Monda, Cedar Rapids; 2B—Pete Coachman, Quad Cities and Bryan House, Peoria; 3B—Eddie Williams, Cedar Rapids; SS—Julius McDougal, Peoria; OF—Darryel Walters, Beloit; Tom Thomas, Kenosha; Dante Bichette, Quad Cities; Troy Thomas, Appleton; Miguel Roman, Waterloo; and Oriol Perez, Wausau; C—B.J. Surhoff, Beloit; DH—Tom Amante, Springfield; LHP—Dan Scarpetta, Beloit; RHP—Alan Sontag, Kenosha; RH Reliever—Greg Dunn, Springfield; LH Reliever—Bill Mendek, Wausau; Most Valuable Player—Eddie Williams, Cedar Rapids; Manager of the Year—Duffy Dyer, Kenosha.

(Compiled by Howe News Bureau, Boston, Mass.)

OFFICIAL BASEBALL GUIDE

## CLUB BATTING

| Club | Pct. | G. | AB. | R. | OR. | H. | TB. | 2B. | 3B. | HR. | RBI. | GW. | SH. | SF. | HP. | BB. | Int. BB. | SO. | SB. | CS. | LOB. |
|---|---|---|---|---|---|---|---|---|---|---|---|---|---|---|---|---|---|---|---|---|---|
| Beloit | .263 | 136 | 4459 | 624 | 536 | 1172 | 1624 | 168 | 25 | 78 | 532 | 68 | 55 | 32 | 37 | 515 | 20 | 878 | 200 | 95 | 999 |
| Springfield | .261 | 140 | 4780 | 691 | 686 | 1247 | 1815 | 168 | 41 | 106 | 612 | 61 | 34 | 32 | 44 | 550 | 8 | 976 | 166 | 73 | 1032 |
| Appleton | .261 | 139 | 4716 | 782 | 614 | 1229 | 1790 | 221 | 50 | 80 | 674 | 73 | 37 | 49 | 27 | 636 | 25 | 938 | 194 | 68 | 1045 |
| Peoria | .258 | 140 | 4654 | 653 | 571 | 1203 | 1691 | 221 | 27 | 71 | 563 | 64 | 41 | 31 | 52 | 545 | 20 | 785 | 171 | 77 | 1022 |
| Cedar Rapids | .248 | 139 | 4536 | 645 | 551 | 1127 | 1648 | 189 | 25 | 94 | 564 | 68 | 26 | 40 | 44 | 482 | 15 | 928 | 100 | 47 | 948 |
| Waterloo | .246 | 140 | 4613 | 619 | 685 | 1136 | 1722 | 195 | 23 | 115 | 547 | 57 | 28 | 30 | 38 | 523 | 16 | 923 | 95 | 56 | 997 |
| Quad Cities | .244 | 140 | 4534 | 642 | 673 | 1107 | 1569 | 192 | 36 | 66 | 559 | 59 | 37 | 39 | 52 | 599 | 16 | 911 | 198 | 91 | 989 |
| Kenosha | .243 | 139 | 4582 | 670 | 631 | 1114 | 1558 | 183 | 30 | 67 | 580 | 67 | 44 | 45 | 44 | 660 | 25 | 823 | 83 | 63 | 1052 |
| Wausau | .242 | 137 | 4472 | 523 | 644 | 1081 | 1536 | 171 | 13 | 86 | 467 | 49 | 48 | 27 | 28 | 500 | 13 | 877 | 120 | 75 | 996 |
| Burlington | .236 | 138 | 4487 | 550 | 756 | 1058 | 1481 | 165 | 18 | 74 | 478 | 44 | 63 | 26 | 47 | 487 | 7 | 944 | 129 | 98 | 952 |
| Clinton | .236 | 140 | 4475 | 513 | 541 | 1055 | 1436 | 188 | 35 | 41 | 448 | 60 | 49 | 29 | 42 | 439 | 16 | 940 | 139 | 92 | 895 |
| Madison | .235 | 138 | 4575 | 573 | 597 | 1075 | 1512 | 198 | 25 | 63 | 488 | 58 | 32 | 41 | 56 | 516 | 18 | 962 | 137 | 77 | 959 |

## INDIVIDUAL BATTING

(Leading Qualifiers for Batting Championship—378 or More Plate Appearances)

°Bats lefthanded.     †Switch-hitter.

| Player and Club | Pct. | G. | AB. | R. | H. | TB. | 2B. | 3B. | HR. | RBI. | GW. | SH. | SF. | HP. | BB. | Int. BB. | SO. | SB. | CS. |
|---|---|---|---|---|---|---|---|---|---|---|---|---|---|---|---|---|---|---|---|
| McCulla, Henry, Springfield | .317 | 112 | 382 | 61 | 121 | 184 | 21 | 3 | 12 | 70 | 7 | 1 | 2 | 5 | 57 | 1 | 77 | 2 | 1 |
| Crabbe, Bruce, Peoria | .313 | 125 | 470 | 53 | 147 | 205 | 31 | 3 | 7 | 68 | 6 | 7 | 3 | 6 | 47 | 2 | 53 | 8 | 6 |
| Harper, Milton, Waterloo | .302 | 112 | 374 | 61 | 113 | 183 | 27 | 5 | 11 | 61 | 6 | 0 | 4 | 0 | 64 | 4 | 53 | 7 | 2 |
| Hill, Bradley, Burlington° | .301 | 103 | 375 | 57 | 113 | 175 | 22 | 2 | 12 | 59 | 4 | 0 | 3 | 2 | 36 | 0 | 61 | 13 | 4 |
| Thomas, Troy, Appleton° | .290 | 131 | 462 | 94 | 134 | 171 | 19 | 6 | 2 | 72 | 12 | 0 | 2 | 3 | 105 | 5 | 76 | 43 | 9 |
| Bertolani, Jerry, Appleton | .289 | 135 | 495 | 94 | 143 | 208 | 23 | 6 | 10 | 74 | 7 | 2 | 7 | 8 | 76 | 2 | 85 | 20 | 5 |
| Kent, Bernard, Beloit° | .285 | 126 | 477 | 50 | 136 | 188 | 20 | 7 | 6 | 57 | 11 | 1 | 3 | 3 | 38 | 4 | 77 | 10 | 6 |
| Thomas, Thomas, Kenosha° | .284 | 130 | 482 | 97 | 137 | 168 | 18 | 5 | 1 | 51 | 5 | 2 | 8 | 5 | 102 | 6 | 55 | 39 | 14 |
| Boever, Daniel, Cedar Rapids | .283 | 134 | 481 | 61 | 136 | 209 | 30 | 5 | 11 | 70 | 12 | 0 | 7 | 2 | 32 | 1 | 66 | 6 | 4 |
| St. Laurent, James, Burlington° | .282 | 130 | 471 | 66 | 133 | 184 | 25 | 1 | 8 | 63 | 6 | 4 | 3 | 2 | 46 | 0 | 64 | 11 | 11 |
| Mattox, Frank, Beloit† | .282 | 126 | 476 | 92 | 134 | 159 | 16 | 3 | 1 | 34 | 6 | 6 | 1 | 2 | 63 | 1 | 58 | 59 | 17 |

Departmental Leaders: G—Monda, 138; AB—Roman, 548; R—Taylor, 107; H—Crabbe, 147; TB—Brito, 244; 2B—Monda, 32; 3B—House, Perezchica, Venturini, Winters, 8; HR—Brito, 29; RBI—Winters, 91; GWRBI—Bichette, 13; SH—DeWolf, 9; SF—Th. Thomas, 8; HP—E. Williams, 15; BB—Taylor, 106; IBB—Forrester, 8; SO—Walters, 141; SB—Coachman, 69; CS—Grant, 22.

(All Players—Listed Alphabetically)

| Player and Club | Pct. | G. | AB. | R. | H. | TB. | 2B. | 3B. | HR. | RBI. | GW. | SH. | SF. | HP. | BB. | Int. BB. | SO. | SB. | CS. |
|---|---|---|---|---|---|---|---|---|---|---|---|---|---|---|---|---|---|---|---|
| Ackerman, John, Clinton | .000 | 45 | 2 | 0 | 0 | 0 | 0 | 0 | 0 | 0 | 0 | 0 | 0 | 0 | 0 | 0 | 0 | 0 | 0 |
| Alfonzo, Edgar, Quad Cities | .286 | 8 | 21 | 3 | 6 | 6 | 0 | 0 | 0 | 0 | 0 | 0 | 1 | 2 | 0 | 2 | 0 | 2 | |
| Alfredson, Thomas, Quad Cities | .213 | 120 | 418 | 54 | 89 | 135 | 16 | 0 | 10 | 46 | 7 | 3 | 4 | 5 | 44 | 1 | 123 | 6 | 7 |
| Alvis, David, Waterloo° | .220 | 39 | 118 | 8 | 26 | 31 | 5 | 0 | 0 | 7 | 0 | 0 | 1 | 0 | 10 | 2 | 15 | 0 | 0 |
| Amante, Thomas, Springfield | .313 | 82 | 323 | 42 | 101 | 187 | 14 | 6 | 20 | 73 | 6 | 0 | 2 | 2 | 24 | 0 | 67 | 1 | 1 |
| Anderson, John, Wausau° | .251 | 111 | 386 | 42 | 97 | 126 | 14 | 3 | 3 | 22 | 3 | 5 | 1 | 2 | 38 | 0 | 85 | 28 | 9 |
| Anderson, Roy, Madison | .213 | 88 | 296 | 27 | 63 | 86 | 8 | 0 | 5 | 27 | 3 | 2 | 0 | 2 | 32 | 0 | 85 | 2 | 0 |
| Aragon, Joey, Kenosha | .228 | 121 | 460 | 59 | 105 | 122 | 13 | 2 | 0 | 47 | 6 | 6 | 4 | 1 | 53 | 0 | 46 | 7 | 9 |
| Arias, Antonio, Madison | .208 | 133 | 457 | 61 | 95 | 158 | 25 | 1 | 12 | 60 | 8 | 4 | 3 | 4 | 49 | 3 | 137 | 2 | 3 |
| Autry, Gene, Appleton | .186 | 94 | 312 | 32 | 58 | 79 | 13 | 1 | 2 | 27 | 4 | 3 | 2 | 1 | 26 | 0 | 71 | 1 | 3 |
| Balelo, Onesimo, Wausau | .240 | 68 | 225 | 29 | 54 | 84 | 16 | 1 | 4 | 18 | 1 | 0 | | 4 | 23 | 0 | 49 | 6 | 3 |
| Barton, Shawn, Wausau° | .185 | 21 | 65 | 5 | 12 | 12 | 0 | 0 | 0 | 4 | 0 | 1 | 0 | | 5 | 0 | 5 | 0 | 1 |
| Bates, Kirk, Burlington° | .288 | 33 | 125 | 10 | 36 | 49 | 7 | 0 | 2 | 17 | 1 | 1 | 1 | 1 | 9 | 1 | 23 | 5 | 1 |
| Bayron, Angel, Kenosha° | .269 | 46 | 145 | 28 | 39 | 50 | 9 | 1 | 0 | 17 | 2 | 0 | 0 | 1 | 21 | 1 | 28 | 0 | 1 |
| Beardman, Lawrence, Madison | .202 | 26 | 94 | 8 | 19 | 24 | 3 | 1 | 0 | 8 | 0 | 0 | 1 | 0 | 14 | 0 | 25 | 2 | 0 |
| Belinskas, Dan, Cedar Rapids | .000 | 11 | 0 | 0 | 0 | 0 | 0 | 0 | 0 | 0 | 0 | 0 | 0 | 0 | 0 | 1 | 0 | 0 | 0 |
| Bell, Gregory, Peoria° | .000 | 9 | 5 | 0 | 0 | 0 | 0 | 0 | 0 | 0 | 0 | 0 | 0 | 0 | 0 | 0 | 2 | 0 | 0 |
| Bennett, Keith, Waterloo | .168 | 39 | 107 | 13 | 18 | 19 | 1 | 0 | 0 | 5 | 0 | 0 | | 2 | 13 | 0 | 17 | 14 | 2 |
| Berry, Mark, Cedar Rapids | .266 | 93 | 319 | 35 | 85 | 126 | 16 | 2 | 7 | 38 | 7 | 0 | 1 | 1 | 37 | 0 | 55 | 2 | 2 |
| Bertolani, Jerry, Appleton | .289 | 135 | 495 | 94 | 143 | 208 | 23 | 6 | 10 | 74 | 7 | 2 | 7 | 8 | 76 | 2 | 85 | 20 | 5 |
| Bichette, Dante, Quad Cities | .265 | 137 | 547 | 58 | 145 | 214 | 28 | 4 | 11 | 78 | 13 | 0 | 7 | 3 | 25 | 1 | 89 | 25 | 11 |
| Blair, Paul, Clinton | .248 | 110 | 399 | 51 | 99 | 111 | 6 | 3 | 0 | 19 | 3 | 4 | 0 | 7 | 36 | 2 | 43 | 13 | 17 |
| Boderick, Stanley, Peoria | .196 | 20 | 46 | 2 | 9 | 15 | 3 | 0 | 1 | 2 | 0 | 0 | 0 | 1 | 6 | 2 | 10 | 4 | 0 |
| Boever, Daniel, Cedar Rapids | .283 | 134 | 481 | 61 | 136 | 209 | 30 | 5 | 11 | 70 | 12 | 0 | 7 | 2 | 32 | 1 | 66 | 6 | 4 |
| Borg, Gary, Kenosha° | .281 | 78 | 278 | 48 | 78 | 132 | 14 | 2 | 12 | 61 | 8 | 0 | 5 | 5 | 43 | 2 | 50 | 5 | 3 |
| Boyles, John, Cedar Rapids | .067 | 27 | 15 | 0 | 1 | 2 | 1 | 0 | 0 | 1 | 0 | 3 | 0 | 0 | 2 | 0 | 6 | 0 | 0 |
| Bresnahan, David, Wausau† | .177 | 31 | 96 | 7 | 17 | 25 | 2 | 0 | 2 | 10 | 3 | 1 | 0 | 0 | 15 | 1 | 21 | 0 | 1 |
| Brilinski, Tyler, Madison° | .212 | 65 | 231 | 27 | 49 | 82 | 10 | 1 | 7 | 38 | 6 | 0 | 4 | 1 | 29 | 3 | 64 | 2 | 0 |
| Brinkman, Gregory, Wausau | .000 | 27 | 2 | 0 | 0 | 0 | 0 | 0 | 0 | 0 | 0 | 0 | 0 | 0 | 0 | 0 | 1 | 0 | 0 |
| Brito, Bernardo, Waterloo | .257 | 135 | 498 | 66 | 128 | 244 | 27 | 1 | 29 | 78 | 5 | 0 | 3 | 4 | 24 | 1 | 133 | 1 | 4 |
| Brown, Todd, Beloit | .185 | 17 | 54 | 3 | 10 | 10 | 0 | 0 | 0 | 4 | 0 | 0 | 0 | | 6 | 0 | 7 | 1 | 1 |
| Bruno, Joseph, Beloit° | .275 | 43 | 142 | 31 | 39 | 50 | 5 | 0 | 2 | 20 | 1 | 3 | 0 | 0 | 26 | 0 | 21 | 7 | 4 |
| Bucci, Michael, Burlington | .000 | 3 | 2 | 1 | 0 | 0 | 0 | 0 | 0 | 0 | 0 | 0 | 0 | 0 | 2 | 0 | 1 | 1 | 0 |
| Byrd, James, Appleton† | .213 | 60 | 174 | 18 | 37 | 48 | 4 | 2 | 1 | 16 | 0 | 2 | 1 | 0 | 23 | 0 | 33 | 6 | 3 |
| Caianiello, John, Appleton° | .191 | 60 | 178 | 17 | 34 | 41 | 7 | 0 | 0 | 14 | 1 | 4 | 0 | 1 | 26 | 1 | 35 | 1 | 2 |
| Campbell, Michael, Quad Cities° | .208 | 56 | 168 | 34 | 35 | 55 | 12 | 1 | 2 | 20 | 1 | 4 | 3 | 1 | 47 | 0 | 39 | 9 | 3 |
| Cantrell, Gregory, Quad Cities | .274 | 87 | 288 | 43 | 79 | 129 | 14 | 3 | 10 | 44 | 4 | 1 | 0 | 0 | 43 | 1 | 91 | 14 | 5 |
| Carganilla, Peter, Waterloo | .185 | 110 | 351 | 29 | 65 | 75 | 10 | 0 | 0 | 24 | 3 | 6 | 2 | 2 | 29 | 1 | 71 | 0 | 4 |
| Carrasco, Claudio, Waterloo† | .233 | 103 | 322 | 41 | 75 | 100 | 10 | 3 | 3 | 25 | 1 | 5 | 2 | 3 | 36 | 0 | 60 | 8 | 11 |
| Casey, Mark, Kenosha | .159 | 23 | 63 | 6 | 10 | 14 | 0 | 2 | 0 | 2 | 1 | 0 | 0 | 1 | 5 | 0 | 21 | 0 | 1 |
| Cieslak, Mark, Cedar Rapids† | .500 | 9 | 2 | 0 | 1 | 1 | 0 | 0 | 0 | 0 | 0 | 0 | 0 | 0 | 0 | 0 | 0 | 2 | 0 |
| Clements, Wesley, Beloit | .297 | 30 | 111 | 23 | 33 | 67 | 4 | 0 | 10 | 35 | 4 | 1 | 2 | 0 | 18 | 5 | 27 | 2 | 0 |
| Coachman, Bobby, Quad Cities | .264 | 135 | 530 | 93 | 140 | 172 | 21 | 4 | 1 | 38 | 2 | 4 | 2 | 12 | 74 | 1 | 77 | 69 | 16 |
| Coffey, Michael, Cedar Rapids | .000 | 9 | 2 | 2 | 0 | 0 | 0 | 0 | 0 | 0 | 0 | 0 | 2 | 0 | 0 | 2 | 0 | 0 | |
| Coin, Michael, Beloit | .193 | 47 | 135 | 7 | 26 | 33 | 5 | 1 | 0 | 11 | 0 | 3 | 0 | 2 | 17 | 1 | 18 | 4 | 3 |
| Conley, Virgil, Cedar Rapids° | .000 | 33 | 5 | 0 | 0 | 0 | 0 | 0 | 0 | 0 | 0 | 0 | 0 | 0 | 0 | 0 | 0 | 0 | 0 |
| Cook, Dennis, Clinton° | .000 | 15 | 5 | 1 | 0 | 0 | 0 | 0 | 0 | 0 | 0 | 0 | 0 | 0 | 6 | 0 | 3 | 1 | 2 |
| Cooper, Kent, Clinton | .180 | 75 | 222 | 20 | 40 | 53 | 5 | 1 | 2 | 15 | 0 | 1 | 0 | 1 | 28 | 1 | 71 | 0 | 1 |
| Cosby, Robert, Clinton | .196 | 55 | 163 | 20 | 32 | 46 | 9 | 1 | 1 | 13 | 2 | 0 | 1 | 3 | 10 | 0 | 41 | 3 | 3 |
| Costello, John, Springfield | .056 | 28 | 18 | 1 | 1 | 1 | 0 | 0 | 0 | 0 | 0 | 1 | 0 | 0 | 1 | 0 | 4 | 0 | 0 |
| Coyle, Rock, Madison | .333 | 24 | 90 | 11 | 30 | 39 | 9 | 0 | 0 | 8 | 1 | 0 | 0 | 2 | 16 | 0 | 8 | 7 | 1 |
| Crabbe, Bruce, Peoria | .313 | 125 | 470 | 53 | 147 | 205 | 31 | 3 | 7 | 68 | 6 | 7 | 3 | 6 | 47 | 2 | 53 | 8 | 6 |
| Crosby, Patrick, Kenosha° | .241 | 47 | 158 | 16 | 38 | 50 | 9 | 0 | 1 | 17 | 0 | 1 | 1 | 2 | 23 | 1 | 23 | 0 | 0 |
| Cullers, Steven, Burlington | .227 | 18 | 44 | 3 | 10 | 13 | 1 | 1 | 0 | 9 | 0 | 2 | 0 | 0 | 8 | 0 | 6 | 1 | 1 |

| Player and Club | Pct. | G. | AB. | R. | H. | TB. | 2B. | 3B. | HR. | RBI. | GW. | SH. | SF. | HP. | BB. | Int. BB. | SO. | SB. | CS. |
|---|---|---|---|---|---|---|---|---|---|---|---|---|---|---|---|---|---|---|---|
| Cupples, Michael, Madison | .228 | 98 | 311 | 30 | 71 | 96 | 11 | 1 | 4 | 25 | 2 | 2 | 1 | 1 | 43 | 2 | 43 | 1 | 1 |
| Dacus, Barry, Quad Cities | .000 | 51 | 1 | 0 | 0 | 0 | 0 | 0 | 0 | 0 | 0 | 0 | 0 | 0 | 0 | 0 | 0 | 0 | 0 |
| Daddario, Paul, Waterloo | .257 | 116 | 362 | 59 | 93 | 127 | 17 | 4 | 3 | 33 | 4 | 3 | 2 | 6 | 92 | 1 | 68 | 9 | 3 |
| Danek, William, Peoria | .000 | 16 | 1 | 0 | 0 | 0 | 0 | 0 | 0 | 0 | 0 | 0 | 0 | 0 | 0 | 0 | 1 | 0 | 0 |
| Daniel, Clay, Cedar Rapids† | .118 | 25 | 17 | 3 | 2 | 3 | 1 | 0 | 0 | 0 | 0 | 2 | 0 | 0 | 2 | 0 | 7 | 0 | 0 |
| Darretta, David, Burlington | .198 | 101 | 323 | 46 | 64 | 89 | 10 | 3 | 3 | 19 | 1 | 9 | 0 | 3 | 30 | 1 | 97 | 13 | 12 |
| Davidson, Jackie, Peoria† | .286 | 30 | 14 | 3 | 4 | 4 | 0 | 0 | 0 | 2 | 0 | 1 | 0 | 1 | 0 | 2 | 0 | 0 |
| Davis, Harry, Clinton | .205 | 84 | 302 | 39 | 62 | 95 | 11 | 2 | 6 | 39 | 7 | 4 | 1 | 7 | 23 | 0 | 66 | 12 | 10 |
| Demeter, Todd, Springfield | .260 | 132 | 462 | 66 | 120 | 179 | 19 | 2 | 12 | 55 | 6 | 3 | 0 | 8 | 65 | 0 | 127 | 2 | 3 |
| Denbo, Gary, Cedar Rapids | .210 | 85 | 233 | 25 | 49 | 51 | 2 | 0 | 0 | 18 | 3 | 2 | 1 | 2 | 33 | 0 | 41 | 7 | 2 |
| DeWolf, Robert, Beloit° | .252 | 107 | 330 | 47 | 83 | 105 | 11 | 1 | 3 | 35 | 7 | 9 | 2 | 2 | 49 | 1 | 84 | 21 | 9 |
| Dibble, Robert, Cedar Rapids | .000 | 45 | 1 | 0 | 0 | 0 | 0 | 0 | 0 | 0 | 0 | 0 | 0 | 0 | 1 | 0 | 1 | 0 | 0 |
| Dietrick, Patrick, Madison | .250 | 51 | 176 | 33 | 44 | 61 | 9 | 1 | 2 | 24 | 4 | 1 | 4 | 4 | 24 | 0 | 54 | 12 | 5 |
| Digioia, John, Springfield | .196 | 97 | 265 | 37 | 52 | 99 | 7 | 2 | 12 | 36 | 2 | 0 | 1 | 3 | 53 | 1 | 93 | 1 | 3 |
| Dorsett, Brian, Madison | .267 | 40 | 161 | 15 | 43 | 60 | 11 | 0 | 2 | 30 | 4 | 1 | 2 | 2 | 12 | 1 | 23 | 0 | 2 |
| Dressler, Kenneth, Clinton | .091 | 38 | 11 | 1 | 1 | 1 | 0 | 0 | 0 | 0 | 0 | 0 | 0 | 0 | 0 | 0 | 2 | 0 | 0 |
| Dunlap, Joe, Cedar Rapids | .272 | 81 | 301 | 50 | 82 | 116 | 12 | 2 | 6 | 33 | 7 | 3 | 3 | 7 | 33 | 0 | 57 | 2 | 7 |
| Dunn, Gregory, Springfield | .000 | 55 | 3 | 1 | 0 | 0 | 0 | 0 | 0 | 1 | 0 | 1 | 0 | 0 | 0 | 0 | 1 | 0 | 0 |
| Eichorst, Timothy, Madison° | .258 | 29 | 93 | 10 | 24 | 29 | 2 | 0 | 1 | 6 | 0 | 1 | 0 | 2 | 7 | 0 | 13 | 0 | 1 |
| Embser, Richard, Springfield | .217 | 23 | 23 | 2 | 5 | 5 | 0 | 0 | 0 | 2 | 1 | 1 | 0 | 0 | 1 | 0 | 7 | 0 | 0 |
| Erickson, Donald, Clinton° | 1.000 | 39 | 3 | 1 | 3 | 5 | 2 | 0 | 0 | 2 | 0 | 0 | 0 | 0 | 0 | 0 | 0 | 0 | 0 |
| Fassero, Jeffrey, Springfield° | .000 | 29 | 4 | 0 | 0 | 0 | 0 | 0 | 0 | 0 | 0 | 0 | 0 | 0 | 0 | 0 | 4 | 0 | 0 |
| Fazzini, Frank, Beloit | .234 | 44 | 145 | 17 | 34 | 48 | 6 | 1 | 2 | 16 | 3 | 0 | 0 | 0 | 15 | 0 | 49 | 1 | 2 |
| Felt, Richard, Kenosha | .500 | 12 | 2 | 0 | 1 | 1 | 0 | 0 | 0 | 0 | 0 | 0 | 0 | 0 | 0 | 0 | 1 | 0 | 0 |
| Fick, Barry, Cedar Rapids | .250 | 31 | 4 | 1 | 1 | 1 | 0 | 0 | 0 | 0 | 0 | 0 | 0 | 0 | 0 | 0 | 2 | 0 | 0 |
| Fitzgerald, Michael, Springfield | .254 | 113 | 413 | 58 | 105 | 174 | 21 | 0 | 16 | 62 | 5 | 1 | 4 | 4 | 32 | 0 | 64 | 1 | 2 |
| Forrester, Thomas, Appleton° | .264 | 96 | 352 | 58 | 93 | 160 | 18 | 2 | 15 | 81 | 9 | 2 | 7 | 2 | 46 | 8 | 61 | 3 | 0 |
| Fregosi, James, Springfield | .302 | 54 | 192 | 20 | 58 | 70 | 7 | 1 | 1 | 31 | 4 | 0 | 0 | 1 | 42 | 1 | 37 | 1 | 3 |
| Fulgencio, Elvin, Cedar Rapids | .236 | 94 | 301 | 41 | 71 | 95 | 7 | 1 | 5 | 32 | 2 | 0 | 2 | 3 | 24 | 2 | 76 | 3 | 3 |
| Garcia, Victor, Waterloo | .259 | 113 | 421 | 66 | 109 | 200 | 19 | 6 | 20 | 76 | 9 | 0 | 4 | 8 | 39 | 2 | 87 | 2 | 2 |
| Garner, Darrin, Burlington | .171 | 47 | 158 | 11 | 27 | 30 | 1 | 1 | 0 | 5 | 2 | 3 | 0 | 3 | 25 | 0 | 33 | 10 | 8 |
| Gass, Jeffrey, Springfield | .000 | 8 | 1 | 1 | 0 | 0 | 0 | 0 | 0 | 0 | 0 | 0 | 0 | 0 | 1 | 0 | 1 | 0 | 0 |
| Glendening, Robert, Peoria | .235 | 95 | 307 | 31 | 72 | 113 | 17 | 0 | 8 | 35 | 4 | 0 | 1 | 1 | 37 | 0 | 56 | 2 | 2 |
| Glidewell, John, Springfield | .000 | 7 | 3 | 0 | 0 | 0 | 0 | 0 | 0 | 0 | 0 | 0 | 0 | 0 | 0 | 0 | 1 | 0 | 0 |
| Gobbo, Michael, Beloit | .252 | 78 | 206 | 22 | 52 | 60 | 5 | 0 | 1 | 14 | 1 | 2 | 1 | 0 | 32 | 0 | 23 | 2 | 2 |
| Goedde, Michael, Cedar Rapids | .000 | 28 | 1 | 0 | 0 | 0 | 0 | 0 | 0 | 0 | 0 | 0 | 0 | 0 | 0 | 0 | 1 | 0 | 0 |
| Gonzalez, Felipe, Clinton | .272 | 70 | 217 | 26 | 59 | 73 | 8 | 0 | 2 | 28 | 3 | 2 | 2 | 0 | 5 | 0 | 29 | 7 | 1 |
| Gould, Robert, Madison | .248 | 98 | 314 | 45 | 78 | 114 | 20 | 2 | 4 | 24 | 2 | 7 | 4 | 9 | 26 | 1 | 85 | 19 | 6 |
| Grant, Kenneth, Quad Cities | .235 | 137 | 481 | 73 | 113 | 153 | 18 | 5 | 4 | 62 | 6 | 6 | 4 | 5 | 76 | 3 | 101 | 26 | 22 |
| Grayston, Joseph, Burlington | .199 | 110 | 287 | 32 | 57 | 83 | 6 | 1 | 6 | 23 | 6 | 8 | 1 | 7 | 32 | 1 | 90 | 12 | 10 |
| Haley, Samuel, Wausau | .229 | 100 | 358 | 46 | 82 | 126 | 17 | 0 | 9 | 31 | 3 | 6 | 3 | 2 | 24 | 1 | 72 | 23 | 4 |
| Hamstra, Daniel, Clinton | .143 | 33 | 7 | 0 | 1 | 1 | 0 | 0 | 0 | 1 | 0 | 1 | 0 | 0 | 0 | 0 | 4 | 0 | 0 |
| Hardamon, Derrick, Peoria | .231 | 42 | 130 | 14 | 30 | 36 | 4 | 1 | 0 | 11 | 1 | 1 | 0 | 3 | 16 | 0 | 20 | 14 | 7 |
| Harper, Milton, Waterloo | .302 | 112 | 374 | 61 | 113 | 183 | 27 | 5 | 11 | 61 | 6 | 0 | 4 | 0 | 64 | 4 | 53 | 7 | 2 |
| Hartley, Michael, Springfield | .250 | 34 | 8 | 1 | 2 | 2 | 0 | 0 | 0 | 0 | 0 | 0 | 0 | 0 | 2 | 0 | 2 | 0 | 0 |
| Harvey, Steven, Peoria | .294 | 19 | 51 | 8 | 15 | 25 | 2 | 1 | 2 | 11 | 1 | 1 | 2 | 0 | 0 | 0 | 11 | 3 | 0 |
| Higgins, Mark, Waterloo | .254 | 108 | 355 | 47 | 90 | 159 | 17 | 2 | 16 | 55 | 6 | 0 | 3 | 4 | 38 | 1 | 71 | 1 | 4 |
| Hill, Bradley, Burlington° | .301 | 103 | 375 | 57 | 113 | 175 | 22 | 2 | 12 | 59 | 4 | 0 | 3 | 2 | 36 | 0 | 61 | 13 | 4 |
| Hill, Gregory, Kenosha | .260 | 113 | 389 | 57 | 101 | 156 | 15 | 2 | 12 | 65 | 10 | 3 | 4 | 5 | 50 | 1 | 58 | 0 | 4 |
| Hill, Roger, Wausau° | .340 | 60 | 212 | 29 | 72 | 86 | 9 | 1 | 1 | 21 | 3 | 3 | 1 | 0 | 26 | 2 | 18 | 17 | 10 |
| Hinnrichs, David, Clinton | .200 | 31 | 5 | 0 | 1 | 1 | 0 | 0 | 0 | 0 | 0 | 0 | 0 | 0 | 0 | 0 | 2 | 0 | 0 |
| Hopkins, Mark, Waterloo | .313 | 22 | 48 | 12 | 15 | 21 | 3 | 0 | 1 | 8 | 1 | 0 | 2 | 1 | 18 | 0 | 14 | 1 | 0 |
| House, Bryan, Peoria† | .260 | 129 | 477 | 80 | 124 | 187 | 23 | 8 | 8 | 76 | 5 | 3 | 3 | 5 | 78 | 4 | 74 | 45 | 16 |
| Howie, Mark, Madison | .265 | 130 | 486 | 72 | 129 | 158 | 13 | 5 | 2 | 46 | 6 | 0 | 4 | 4 | 62 | 3 | 57 | 26 | 14 |
| Jagnow, James, Burlington | .159 | 35 | 88 | 8 | 14 | 16 | 2 | 0 | 0 | 7 | 0 | 4 | 1 | 1 | 10 | 0 | 19 | 3 | 2 |
| Jenkins, David, Waterloo | .247 | 31 | 81 | 12 | 20 | 23 | 3 | 0 | 0 | 6 | 0 | 1 | 0 | 0 | 4 | 0 | 24 | 3 | 0 |
| Jennings, Douglas, Quad Cities° | .254 | 95 | 319 | 50 | 81 | 127 | 17 | 7 | 5 | 54 | 5 | 2 | 6 | 5 | 62 | 1 | 76 | 10 | 8 |
| Jimenez, Genaro, Quad Cities | .200 | 9 | 25 | 4 | 5 | 6 | 1 | 0 | 0 | 0 | 0 | 0 | 0 | 0 | 3 | 0 | 10 | 0 | 1 |
| Johnigan, Stephen, Waterloo | .246 | 26 | 65 | 5 | 16 | 18 | 2 | 0 | 0 | 8 | 4 | 0 | 1 | 0 | 7 | 0 | 9 | 0 | 0 |
| Johnson, John, Peoria | .250 | 2 | 4 | 0 | 1 | 1 | 0 | 0 | 0 | 0 | 0 | 0 | 0 | 0 | 1 | 0 | 1 | 1 | 0 |
| Jones, Terence, Quad Cities° | .262 | 76 | 275 | 33 | 72 | 96 | 21 | 0 | 1 | 31 | 3 | 3 | 1 | 4 | 14 | 0 | 30 | 7 | 1 |
| Jordan, Robert, Waterloo | .255 | 118 | 463 | 70 | 118 | 168 | 23 | 0 | 9 | 46 | 7 | 1 | 2 | 2 | 46 | 2 | 88 | 25 | 13 |
| Jose, Felix, Madison† | .218 | 117 | 409 | 46 | 89 | 117 | 13 | 3 | 3 | 33 | 2 | 1 | 2 | 5 | 33 | 2 | 82 | 6 | 6 |
| Kampsen, Douglas, Cedar Rapids° | .000 | 29 | 3 | 0 | 0 | 0 | 0 | 0 | 0 | 0 | 0 | 1 | 0 | 0 | 0 | 0 | 2 | 0 | 0 |
| Kanter, John, Madison° | .232 | 121 | 413 | 50 | 96 | 143 | 25 | 2 | 6 | 45 | 4 | 3 | 2 | 6 | 32 | 0 | 92 | 18 | 13 |
| Kavanaugh, Timothy, Springfield | .333 | 13 | 6 | 1 | 2 | 3 | 1 | 0 | 0 | 1 | 0 | 0 | 0 | 0 | 0 | 0 | 0 | 0 | 0 |
| Kelley, Thomas, Burlington° | .220 | 13 | 41 | 6 | 9 | 10 | 1 | 0 | 0 | 3 | 0 | 1 | 0 | 1 | 4 | 1 | 16 | 0 | 1 |
| Kent, Bernard, Beloit° | .285 | 126 | 477 | 50 | 136 | 188 | 20 | 7 | 6 | 57 | 11 | 1 | 3 | 3 | 38 | 4 | 77 | 10 | 6 |
| Kent, Wesley, Appleton | .232 | 82 | 276 | 37 | 64 | 126 | 14 | 3 | 14 | 54 | 3 | 1 | 4 | 1 | 30 | 0 | 110 | 2 | 0 |
| Kindred, Curtis, Kenosha | .000 | 10 | 1 | 0 | 0 | 0 | 0 | 0 | 0 | 1 | 0 | 0 | 0 | 0 | 1 | 0 | 0 | 0 | 0 |
| Kinzer, Matthew, Springfield | .000 | 11 | 5 | 0 | 0 | 0 | 0 | 0 | 0 | 1 | 1 | 0 | 0 | 0 | 0 | 0 | 3 | 0 | 0 |
| Klein, Larry, Burlington | .268 | 74 | 280 | 41 | 75 | 93 | 8 | 2 | 2 | 25 | 2 | 8 | 1 | 3 | 29 | 1 | 44 | 16 | 6 |
| Komeiji, Keith, Wausau | .192 | 72 | 213. | 23 | 41 | 61 | 9 | 1 | 3 | 25 | 1 | 4 | 2 | 1 | 43 | 0 | 61 | 3 | 3 |
| Kramer, Joseph, Madison | .290 | 84 | 293 | 55 | 85 | 126 | 14 | 3 | 7 | 38 | 5 | 2 | 6 | 10 | 53 | 2 | 61 | 29 | 10 |
| Kramer, Mark, Burlington° | .233 | 96 | 287 | 36 | 67 | 103 | 11 | 2 | 7 | 38 | 3 | 4 | 2 | 3 | 31 | 0 | 48 | 9 | 6 |
| Krause, Andrew, Madison° | .228 | 121 | 390 | 49 | 89 | 125 | 18 | 3 | 4 | 43 | 7 | 2 | 7 | 1 | 55 | 1 | 57 | 10 | 10 |
| Kreuter, Chad, Burlington | .266 | 69 | 199 | 25 | 53 | 74 | 9 | 0 | 4 | 26 | 7 | 5 | 3 | 1 | 38 | 0 | 48 | 3 | 2 |
| Lanik, Dale, Burlington° | .175 | 49 | 154 | 17 | 27 | 39 | 6 | 0 | 2 | 17 | 0 | 0 | 0 | 0 | 19 | 2 | 42 | 2 | 1 |
| Larson, Daniel, Wausau | .244 | 94 | 308 | 41 | 75 | 96 | 12 | 0 | 3 | 32 | 3 | 1 | 1 | 1 | 52 | 0 | 43 | 6 | 5 |
| Leon, Ronald, Springfield° | .292 | 100 | 322 | 43 | 94 | 128 | 10 | 6 | 4 | 43 | 2 | 3 | 0 | 2 | 33 | 1 | 37 | 9 | 3 |
| Lezcano, Manuel, Peoria | .238 | 62 | 193 | 27 | 46 | 67 | 9 | 0 | 4 | 18 | 4 | 0 | 0 | 5 | 21 | 0 | 33 | 5 | 4 |
| Lopez, Anthony, Kenosha | .243 | 35 | 107 | 14 | 26 | 40 | 5 | 0 | 3 | 15 | 2 | 0 | 1 | 0 | 22 | 0 | 35 | 0 | 2 |
| Lopez, Juan, Waterloo | .156 | 39 | 96 | 4 | 15 | 17 | 2 | 0 | 0 | 8 | 0 | 3 | 2 | 1 | 3 | 0 | 27 | 0 | 0 |
| Luther, Bradley, Springfield | .230 | 112 | 374 | 45 | 86 | 107 | 8 | 2 | 3 | 32 | 2 | 4 | 2 | 2 | 35 | 1 | 61 | 7 | 4 |
| Machalec, Mark, Wausau | .256 | 119 | 410 | 47 | 105 | 125 | 11 | 0 | 3 | 36 | 6 | 7 | 2 | 0 | 31 | 1 | 37 | 3 | 9 |
| Maddux, Gregory, Peoria | .238 | 27 | 21 | 1 | 5 | 6 | 1 | 0 | 0 | 1 | 0 | 0 | 0 | 0 | 0 | 0 | 6 | 1 | 0 |
| Mandeville, Robert, Peoria | .255 | 78 | 239 | 37 | 61 | 72 | 6 | 1 | 1 | 23 | 4 | 5 | 2 | 1 | 27 | 1 | 42 | 13 | 0 |
| Manto, Jeffrey, Quad Cities | .197 | 74 | 233 | 34 | 46 | 88 | 5 | 2 | 11 | 34 | 3 | 1 | 5 | 5 | 40 | 0 | 74 | 3 | 1 |
| Manzon, Howard, Kenosha | .311 | 75 | 267 | 46 | 83 | 101 | 11 | 2 | 1 | 30 | 2 | 4 | 6 | 3 | 36 | 0 | 42 | 11 | 6 |
| Markert, James, Quad Cities° | .278 | 100 | 356 | 52 | 99 | 150 | 20 | 2 | 9 | 61 | 4 | 4 | 7 | 2 | 30 | 0 | 72 | 2 | 0 |
| Marquez, Edwin, Quad Cities | .191 | 35 | 110 | 14 | 21 | 31 | 2 | 1 | 2 | 10 | 0 | 1 | 0 | 2 | 19 | 0 | 25 | 0 | 2 |
| Martin, Norberto, Appleton† | .198 | 30 | 96 | 15 | 19 | 21 | 2 | 0 | 0 | 5 | 0 | 3 | 0 | 0 | 9 | 0 | 23 | 2 | 2 |

| Player and Club | Pct. | G. | AB. | R. | H. | TB. | 2B. | 3B. | HR. | RBI. | GW. | SH. | SF. | HP. | BB. | Int. BB. | SO. | SB. | CS. |
|---|---|---|---|---|---|---|---|---|---|---|---|---|---|---|---|---|---|---|---|
| Mattox, Frank, Beloit† | .282 | 126 | 476 | 92 | 134 | 159 | 16 | 3 | 1 | 34 | 6 | 6 | 1 | 2 | 63 | 3 | 58 | 59 | 17 |
| McCulla, Henry, Springfield | .317 | 112 | 382 | 61 | 121 | 184 | 21 | 3 | 12 | 70 | 7 | 1 | 2 | 5 | 57 | 1 | 77 | 2 | 1 |
| McDonald, Thomas, Clinton | .235 | 129 | 446 | 51 | 105 | 148 | 14 | 7 | 5 | 58 | 5 | 3 | 1 | 5 | 54 | 2 | 119 | 25 | 5 |
| McDougal, Julius, Peoria† | .243 | 125 | 441 | 66 | 107 | 143 | 17 | 2 | 5 | 38 | 2 | 3 | 2 | 5 | 34 | 1 | 85 | 20 | 11 |
| McGrath, Charles, Springfield | .167 | 25 | 6 | 0 | 1 | 1 | 0 | 0 | 0 | 0 | 0 | 2 | 0 | 0 | 0 | 0 | 4 | 0 | 0 |
| McGuire, William, Wausau | .246 | 56 | 191 | 24 | 47 | 65 | 9 | 0 | 3 | 15 | 1 | 1 | 4 | 4 | 19 | 1 | 22 | 1 | 3 |
| Menendez, Antonio, Appleton | .000 | 24 | 1 | 0 | 0 | 0 | 0 | 0 | 0 | 0 | 0 | 0 | 0 | 0 | 0 | 0 | 0 | 0 | 0 |
| Messier, Thomas, Clinton | .091 | 22 | 11 | 0 | 1 | 1 | 0 | 0 | 0 | 0 | 0 | 1 | 0 | 0 | 0 | 0 | 4 | 0 | 0 |
| Miley, David, Cedar Rapids* | .205 | 12 | 39 | 2 | 8 | 11 | 0 | 0 | 1 | 6 | 0 | 0 | 0 | 0 | 2 | 0 | 1 | 0 | 1 |
| Mitchell, Joseph, Beloit | .244 | 117 | 397 | 50 | 97 | 152 | 19 | 0 | 12 | 47 | 3 | 7 | 3 | 10 | 22 | 0 | 92 | 14 | 3 |
| Moncerratt, Pablo, Wausau* | .200 | 30 | 90 | 7 | 18 | 26 | 5 | 0 | 1 | 9 | 0 | 2 | 0 | 0 | 9 | 0 | 27 | 0 | 0 |
| Monda, Gregory, Cedar Rapids* | .276 | 138 | 503 | 79 | 139 | 198 | 32 | 3 | 7 | 66 | 5 | 2 | 4 | 6 | 54 | 5 | 91 | 2 | 2 |
| Monico, Mario, Beloit* | .284 | 47 | 141 | 17 | 40 | 45 | 5 | 0 | 0 | 14 | 1 | 1 | 2 | 2 | 29 | 2 | 20 | 4 | 5 |
| Montanari, David, Quad Cities* | .272 | 107 | 379 | 39 | 103 | 123 | 15 | 1 | 1 | 53 | 3 | 5 | 4 | 3 | 60 | 6 | 30 | 3 | 1 |
| Morfin, Arvid, Wausau | .103 | 9 | 29 | 0 | 3 | 3 | 0 | 0 | 0 | 0 | 0 | 0 | 0 | 0 | 3 | 0 | 9 | 0 | 0 |
| Munoz, Omer, Clinton | .207 | 47 | 121 | 9 | 25 | 29 | 4 | 0 | 0 | 11 | 1 | 4 | 0 | 0 | 7 | 0 | 7 | 3 | 2 |
| North, Jay, Springfield | .231 | 24 | 13 | 1 | 3 | 4 | 1 | 0 | 0 | 2 | 0 | 1 | 0 | 0 | 0 | 0 | 8 | 0 | 0 |
| Nunez, Dario, Quad Cities | .174 | 54 | 172 | 14 | 30 | 32 | 2 | 0 | 0 | 17 | 2 | 1 | 0 | 1 | 6 | 0 | 30 | 2 | 1 |
| Nunley, Angelo, Springfield | .265 | 97 | 344 | 66 | 91 | 106 | 7 | 4 | 0 | 31 | 4 | 4 | 1 | 5 | 48 | 0 | 73 | 46 | 11 |
| O'Connor, Michael, Peoria | .000 | 1 | 1 | 0 | 0 | 0 | 0 | 0 | 0 | 0 | 0 | 0 | 0 | 0 | 0 | 0 | 1 | 0 | 0 |
| O'Hearn, Robert, Burlington | .244 | 53 | 135 | 12 | 33 | 39 | 3 | 0 | 1 | 14 | 0 | 2 | 1 | 1 | 15 | 0 | 23 | 0 | 1 |
| O'Leary, William, Wausau | .212 | 41 | 137 | 23 | 29 | 41 | 2 | 2 | 2 | 11 | 1 | 3 | 1 | 1 | 16 | 1 | 23 | 2 | 1 |
| Oliverio, Stephen, Cedar Rapids | .067 | 20 | 15 | 1 | 1 | 1 | 0 | 0 | 0 | 0 | 0 | 1 | 0 | 0 | 2 | 0 | 6 | 0 | 0 |
| Olker, Joseph, Clinton | .571 | 16 | 7 | 3 | 4 | 4 | 0 | 0 | 0 | 2 | 0 | 1 | 0 | 0 | 1 | 0 | 2 | 0 | 1 |
| Oppenheimer, Damon, Beloit | .000 | 12 | 17 | 3 | 0 | 0 | 0 | 0 | 0 | 0 | 0 | 0 | 0 | 1 | 3 | 0 | 5 | 0 | 0 |
| Owen, Timothy, Burlington | .231 | 72 | 199 | 22 | 46 | 61 | 6 | 0 | 3 | 20 | 2 | 2 | 1 | 1 | 14 | 0 | 40 | 1 | 0 |
| Pace, George, Cedar Rapids* | .237 | 43 | 139 | 12 | 33 | 51 | 6 | 0 | 4 | 21 | 4 | 0 | 2 | 0 | 9 | 0 | 28 | 0 | 1 |
| Palma, Jay, Waterloo | .111 | 15 | 54 | 3 | 6 | 6 | 0 | 0 | 0 | 5 | 1 | 0 | 0 | 0 | 3 | 1 | 11 | 2 | 1 |
| Palmeiro, Rafael, Peoria* | .297 | 73 | 279 | 34 | 83 | 128 | 22 | 4 | 5 | 51 | 5 | 1 | 2 | 2 | 31 | 2 | 34 | 9 | 3 |
| Pappas, Erik, Quad Cities | .240 | 100 | 317 | 53 | 76 | 98 | 8 | 4 | 2 | 29 | 6 | 3 | 1 | 3 | 61 | 1 | 56 | 16 | 6 |
| Paul, Jeffrey, Waterloo* | .236 | 90 | 259 | 28 | 61 | 67 | 6 | 0 | 0 | 14 | 2 | 5 | 0 | 0 | 53 | 1 | 59 | 4 | 3 |
| Pavlas, David, Peoria | .000 | 17 | 11 | 0 | 0 | 0 | 0 | 0 | 0 | 0 | 0 | 2 | 0 | 0 | 0 | 0 | 8 | 0 | 0 |
| Pena, Jose, Clinton | .263 | 82 | 262 | 26 | 69 | 92 | 20 | 0 | 1 | 24 | 4 | 2 | 1 | 2 | 22 | 1 | 53 | 2 | 2 |
| Peraza, Luis, Appleton | .228 | 29 | 101 | 24 | 23 | 40 | 5 | 0 | 4 | 25 | 2 | 0 | 1 | 0 | 10 | 0 | 25 | 2 | 1 |
| Perez, Edgar, Wausau | .209 | 61 | 201 | 16 | 42 | 49 | 2 | 1 | 1 | 19 | 1 | 2 | 2 | 1 | 11 | 0 | 40 | 6 | 4 |
| Perez, Oriol, Wausau | .281 | 117 | 427 | 56 | 120 | 188 | 22 | 2 | 14 | 67 | 7 | 5 | 7 | 1 | 55 | 2 | 85 | 5 | 9 |
| Perezchica, Antonio, Clinton | .241 | 127 | 452 | 54 | 109 | 158 | 21 | 8 | 4 | 40 | 6 | 6 | 5 | 9 | 28 | 0 | 77 | 23 | 7 |
| Peterson, Allen, Quad Cities† | .243 | 41 | 144 | 28 | 35 | 63 | 9 | 2 | 5 | 29 | 4 | 2 | 2 | 2 | 22 | 1 | 31 | 8 | 3 |
| Phillips, Joseph, Beloit | .170 | 25 | 53 | 7 | 9 | 11 | 2 | 0 | 0 | 4 | 1 | 1 | 0 | 0 | 4 | 0 | 10 | 2 | 1 |
| Pico, Jeffrey, Peoria | .133 | 27 | 15 | 2 | 2 | 2 | 0 | 0 | 0 | 2 | 0 | 1 | 0 | 0 | 0 | 0 | 6 | 0 | 0 |
| Pleis, Scott, Springfield | 1.000 | 5 | 1 | 0 | 1 | 2 | 1 | 0 | 0 | 1 | 0 | 0 | 0 | 0 | 0 | 0 | 0 | 0 | 0 |
| Pobur, Hugh, Peoria | .000 | 28 | 0 | 0 | 0 | 0 | 0 | 0 | 0 | 0 | 0 | 0 | 0 | 0 | 0 | 0 | 0 | 0 | 0 |
| Pohle, Walter, Beloit | .274 | 129 | 434 | 65 | 119 | 157 | 16 | 2 | 6 | 52 | 6 | 6 | 2 | 7 | 45 | 0 | 58 | 26 | 9 |
| Porte, Carlos, Cedar Rapids | .232 | 87 | 276 | 43 | 64 | 85 | 14 | 2 | 1 | 28 | 0 | 1 | 0 | 0 | 25 | 1 | 32 | 6 | 3 |
| Porter, Bradley, Clinton | .159 | 28 | 82 | 9 | 13 | 18 | 2 | 0 | 1 | 8 | 1 | 2 | 0 | 1 | 16 | 0 | 40 | 1 | 0 |
| Pruitt, Darrell, Appleton | .287 | 80 | 314 | 61 | 90 | 108 | 7 | 1 | 3 | 28 | 2 | 4 | 2 | 0 | 24 | 0 | 39 | 31 | 4 |
| Quinones, Rene, Waterloo† | .264 | 25 | 91 | 14 | 24 | 40 | 4 | 0 | 4 | 12 | 0 | 1 | 0 | 1 | 16 | 0 | 19 | 7 | 2 |
| Ray, Bregg, Wausau | .194 | 76 | 170 | 16 | 33 | 41 | 5 | 0 | 1 | 9 | 1 | 3 | 1 | 1 | 20 | 0 | 32 | 3 | 5 |
| Reboulet, James, Springfield | .250 | 42 | 140 | 22 | 35 | 39 | 2 | 1 | 0 | 9 | 0 | 0 | 1 | 0 | 17 | 2 | 13 | 20 | 4 |
| Reilly, Neil, Burlington | .125 | 16 | 40 | 0 | 5 | 6 | 1 | 0 | 0 | 2 | 0 | 0 | 2 | 3 | 0 | 0 | 20 | 0 | 0 |
| Reimer, Kevin, Burlington* | .229 | 80 | 292 | 25 | 67 | 103 | 12 | 0 | 8 | 33 | 4 | 0 | 1 | 8 | 22 | 0 | 43 | 0 | 4 |
| Renfroe, Cohen, Peoria | .200 | 57 | 5 | 0 | 1 | 1 | 0 | 0 | 0 | 1 | 0 | 1 | 0 | 0 | 0 | 0 | 2 | 0 | 0 |
| Rice, Timothy, Peoria | .000 | 36 | 6 | 0 | 0 | 0 | 0 | 0 | 0 | 1 | 0 | 0 | 1 | 0 | 0 | 0 | 5 | 0 | 0 |
| Richardson, Donald, Peoria | .242 | 73 | 244 | 35 | 59 | 74 | 8 | 2 | 1 | 15 | 3 | 1 | 1 | 3 | 25 | 0 | 30 | 11 | 4 |
| Rigos, John, Springfield | .224 | 90 | 330 | 44 | 74 | 108 | 12 | 2 | 6 | 38 | 3 | 1 | 7 | 5 | 35 | 0 | 62 | 15 | 7 |
| Riley, Darren, Cedar Rapids* | .230 | 131 | 508 | 86 | 117 | 180 | 17 | 2 | 14 | 49 | 5 | 2 | 6 | 2 | 61 | 1 | 121 | 34 | 11 |
| Riley, Thomas, Cedar Rapids | .182 | 6 | 22 | 4 | 4 | 4 | 0 | 0 | 0 | 0 | 0 | 0 | 1 | 0 | 6 | 0 | 4 | 0 | 0 |
| Robinson, Brian, Cedar Rapids | .242 | 83 | 289 | 54 | 70 | 94 | 11 | 2 | 3 | 31 | 4 | 3 | 3 | 1 | 37 | 1 | 64 | 22 | 2 |
| Robinson, Michael, Springfield | .255 | 126 | 502 | 77 | 128 | 185 | 16 | 7 | 9 | 54 | 9 | 6 | 4 | 5 | 32 | 0 | 126 | 21 | 15 |
| Rodgers, Darrell, Clinton | .600 | 6 | 5 | 0 | 3 | 4 | 1 | 0 | 0 | 3 | 0 | 1 | 0 | 0 | 0 | 0 | 0 | 0 | 0 |
| Rodriguez, Angel, Beloit | .290 | 42 | 131 | 18 | 38 | 51 | 8 | 1 | 1 | 5 | 1 | 2 | 1 | 4 | 15 | 1 | 18 | 0 | 3 |
| Rodriguez, Ulisses, Kenosha | .211 | 41 | 152 | 17 | 32 | 44 | 6 | 0 | 2 | 18 | 1 | 2 | 2 | 1 | 13 | 0 | 42 | 1 | 0 |
| Rolland, David, Burlington | .190 | 86 | 289 | 32 | 55 | 94 | 10 | 1 | 9 | 25 | 1 | 4 | 1 | 0 | 26 | 0 | 87 | 6 | 8 |
| Roman, Miguel, Waterloo | .263 | 136 | 548 | 81 | 144 | 224 | 19 | 2 | 19 | 76 | 8 | 3 | 3 | 3 | 28 | 0 | 97 | 11 | 5 |
| Romanovsky, Michael, Quad Cities* | .500 | 25 | 2 | 1 | 1 | 1 | 0 | 0 | 0 | 1 | 0 | 0 | 0 | 0 | 0 | 0 | 1 | 0 | 0 |
| Ryan, Michael, Kenosha* | .217 | 111 | 382 | 44 | 83 | 132 | 19 | 3 | 8 | 45 | 6 | 4 | 1 | 3 | 45 | 5 | 83 | 1 | 3 |
| Sabo, Scott, Madison* | .000 | 34 | 0 | 0 | 0 | 0 | 0 | 0 | 0 | 0 | 0 | 0 | 0 | 0 | 2 | 0 | 0 | 0 | 0 |
| St. Laurent, James, Burlington* | .282 | 130 | 471 | 66 | 133 | 184 | 25 | 1 | 8 | 63 | 6 | 4 | 3 | 2 | 46 | 0 | 64 | 11 | 11 |
| Samuel, Michael, Beloit | .238 | 27 | 80 | 13 | 19 | 20 | 1 | 0 | 0 | 8 | 0 | 1 | 1 | 0 | 15 | 0 | 16 | 2 | 5 |
| Santos, Fausto, Madison | .193 | 70 | 197 | 19 | 38 | 52 | 2 | 0 | 4 | 22 | 4 | 5 | 0 | 2 | 13 | 0 | 39 | 0 | 2 |
| Scaletta, Thomas, Kenosha* | .192 | 54 | 167 | 17 | 32 | 41 | 3 | 0 | 2 | 18 | 3 | 2 | 1 | 2 | 27 | 2 | 35 | 1 | 1 |
| Schwarz, Jeffrey, Peoria | .188 | 27 | 16 | 1 | 3 | 3 | 0 | 0 | 0 | 1 | 0 | 0 | 0 | 1 | 0 | 4 | 0 | 0 | 0 |
| Schwarz, Thomas, Kenosha | .249 | 121 | 454 | 76 | 113 | 167 | 23 | 2 | 9 | 71 | 10 | 7 | 3 | 4 | 58 | 3 | 71 | 2 | 2 |
| Sciacca, Christopher, Quad Cities | .276 | 24 | 76 | 12 | 21 | 27 | 2 | 2 | 0 | 12 | 0 | 0 | 2 | 0 | 1 | 0 | 20 | 0 | 1 |
| Sedar, Edward, Appleton | .444 | 13 | 9 | 3 | 4 | 5 | 1 | 0 | 0 | 1 | 0 | 0 | 0 | 3 | 0 | 0 | 2 | 1 | 0 |
| Senne, Timothy, Kenosha† | .241 | 95 | 299 | 39 | 72 | 101 | 11 | 6 | 2 | 23 | 0 | 6 | 0 | 1 | 52 | 4 | 80 | 5 | 5 |
| Siemers, Henry, Kenosha | .250 | 33 | 92 | 8 | 23 | 25 | 2 | 0 | 0 | 6 | 2 | 1 | 0 | 1 | 15 | 0 | 17 | 2 | 3 |
| Sigler, Allen, Cedar Rapids* | .232 | 108 | 345 | 46 | 80 | 132 | 10 | 3 | 12 | 52 | 8 | 1 | 1 | 2 | 3 | 40 | 0 | 101 | 6 | 4 |
| Silver, Keith, Clinton | .238 | 29 | 21 | 4 | 5 | 6 | 1 | 0 | 0 | 1 | 0 | 1 | 1 | 0 | 0 | 0 | 3 | 0 | 0 |
| Simonson, Robert, Beloit | .125 | 9 | 24 | 1 | 3 | 4 | 1 | 0 | 0 | 2 | 0 | 0 | 0 | 0 | 7 | 0 | 12 | 1 | 0 |
| Skurla, John, Clinton* | .272 | 128 | 426 | 52 | 116 | 160 | 25 | 5 | 3 | 52 | 9 | 6 | 7 | 0 | 56 | 1 | 71 | 17 | 9 |
| Smith, Daniel, Cedar Rapids* | .500 | 42 | 2 | 0 | 1 | 1 | 0 | 0 | 0 | 0 | 0 | 0 | 0 | 0 | 0 | 0 | 0 | 0 | 0 |
| Smith, Michael, Cedar Rapids | .000 | 8 | 3 | 0 | 0 | 0 | 0 | 0 | 0 | 0 | 0 | 0 | 0 | 0 | 0 | 0 | 0 | 0 | 0 |
| Smith, Richard, Quad Cities | .321 | 13 | 28 | 2 | 9 | 13 | 1 | 0 | 1 | 1 | 0 | 0 | 0 | 1 | 0 | 0 | 5 | 0 | 0 |
| Smith, Todd, Peoria | .280 | 90 | 304 | 40 | 85 | 118 | 16 | 1 | 5 | 37 | 5 | 1 | 2 | 5 | 20 | 2 | 49 | 7 | 2 |
| Smith, Tommy, Clinton† | .237 | 66 | 228 | 16 | 54 | 70 | 10 | 0 | 2 | 21 | 1 | 1 | 0 | 2 | 8 | 1 | 44 | 1 | 1 |
| Smith, William, Clinton | .246 | 45 | 122 | 11 | 30 | 38 | 3 | 1 | 1 | 12 | 3 | 0 | 1 | 0 | 12 | 0 | 24 | 4 | 4 |
| Solz, Mark, Peoria* | .228 | 84 | 237 | 30 | 54 | 84 | 13 | 1 | 5 | 26 | 3 | 1 | 3 | 3 | 29 | 1 | 86 | 1 | 3 |
| Soto, Osvaldo, Cedar Rapids | .200 | 26 | 15 | 0 | 3 | 4 | 1 | 0 | 0 | 1 | 0 | 2 | 0 | 0 | 4 | 0 | 4 | 0 | 0 |
| Spear, Frank, Peoria* | .000 | 24 | 1 | 0 | 0 | 0 | 0 | 0 | 0 | 0 | 0 | 0 | 0 | 0 | 0 | 0 | 0 | 0 | 0 |
| Spring, James, Clinton* | .248 | 127 | 447 | 58 | 111 | 168 | 22 | 4 | 9 | 47 | 8 | 0 | 1 | 3 | 56 | 4 | 85 | 14 | 14 |
| Stanley, Michael, Burlington | .310 | 13 | 42 | 8 | 13 | 18 | 2 | 0 | 1 | 6 | 0 | 0 | 0 | 0 | 6 | 0 | 5 | 0 | 1 |

| Player and Club | Pct. | G. | AB. | R. | H. | TB. | 2B. | 3B. | HR. | RBI. | GW. | SH. | SF. | HP. | BB. | Int. BB. | SO. | SB. | CS. |
|---|---|---|---|---|---|---|---|---|---|---|---|---|---|---|---|---|---|---|---|
| Steinbach, Thomas, Beloit | .192 | 55 | 151 | 9 | 29 | 41 | 6 | 0 | 2 | 15 | 1 | 0 | 1 | 1 | 9 | 0 | 55 | 4 | 5 |
| Stewart, David, Wausau° | .289 | 71 | 246 | 29 | 71 | 108 | 11 | 1 | 8 | 32 | 4 | 0 | 0 | 0 | 26 | 2 | 35 | 3 | 4 |
| Surhoff, William, Beloit° | .332 | 76 | 289 | 39 | 96 | 138 | 13 | 4 | 7 | 58 | 12 | 2 | 5 | 0 | 22 | 0 | 35 | 10 | 9 |
| Swepson, Lyle, Clinton | .179 | 73 | 212 | 28 | 38 | 62 | 12 | 0 | 4 | 23 | 4 | 2 | 2 | 3 | 22 | 3 | 85 | 5 | 2 |
| Tarnow, Greg, Appleton | .195 | 23 | 41 | 3 | 8 | 12 | 2 | 1 | 0 | 1 | 0 | 2 | 0 | 1 | 4 | 0 | 17 | 0 | 0 |
| Taylor, Michael, Appleton | .281 | 131 | 513 | 107 | 144 | 218 | 30 | 7 | 10 | 69 | 9 | 1 | 6 | 2 | 106 | 3 | 98 | 51 | 18 |
| Thomas, Thomas, Kenosha° | .284 | 130 | 482 | 97 | 137 | 168 | 18 | 5 | 1 | 51 | 5 | 2 | 8 | 5 | 102 | 6 | 55 | 39 | 14 |
| Thomas, Troy, Appleton° | .290 | 131 | 462 | 94 | 134 | 171 | 19 | 6 | 2 | 72 | 12 | 0 | 2 | 3 | 105 | 5 | 76 | 43 | 9 |
| Threadgill, George, Burlington | .233 | 114 | 343 | 52 | 80 | 107 | 12 | 3 | 3 | 37 | 3 | 5 | 4 | 3 | 46 | 0 | 69 | 12 | 7 |
| Toler, Gregory, Cedar Rapids | .253 | 86 | 289 | 29 | 73 | 98 | 16 | 0 | 3 | 35 | 7 | 0 | 4 | 1 | 17 | 0 | 53 | 5 | 1 |
| Torve, Kenton, Appleton° | .276 | 33 | 123 | 16 | 34 | 46 | 6 | 3 | 0 | 16 | 3 | 1 | 2 | 1 | 10 | 0 | 24 | 3 | 4 |
| Tullier, Michael, Peoria° | .236 | 47 | 148 | 32 | 35 | 52 | 8 | 0 | 3 | 21 | 4 | 3 | 2 | 1 | 24 | 0 | 18 | 4 | 4 |
| Turgeon, Stephen, Springfield | .265 | 39 | 132 | 18 | 35 | 51 | 5 | 1 | 3 | 18 | 3 | 0 | 2 | 1 | 22 | 1 | 35 | 7 | 2 |
| Turner, John, Peoria° | .263 | 106 | 365 | 69 | 96 | 110 | 12 | 1 | 0 | 34 | 3 | 3 | 2 | 1 | 61 | 1 | 29 | 21 | 9 |
| Uribe, Jorge, Wausau | .169 | 32 | 89 | 9 | 15 | 25 | 2 | 1 | 2 | 10 | 0 | 1 | 0 | 2 | 9 | 0 | 39 | 8 | 1 |
| Van Houten, James, Springfield | .000 | 40 | 1 | 0 | 0 | 0 | 0 | 0 | 0 | 0 | 0 | 0 | 0 | 0 | 0 | 0 | 1 | 0 | 0 |
| Vanstone, Paul, Clinton† | .280 | 57 | 182 | 21 | 51 | 62 | 5 | 3 | 0 | 19 | 2 | 3 | 1 | 2 | 24 | 0 | 38 | 5 | 7 |
| Vasquez, Angelo, Burlington° | .236 | 105 | 313 | 39 | 74 | 95 | 10 | 1 | 3 | 30 | 2 | 1 | 5 | 5 | 36 | 0 | 65 | 11 | 12 |
| Velasquez, Javier, Kenosha | .225 | 65 | 209 | 26 | 47 | 63 | 5 | 1 | 3 | 32 | 4 | 1 | 4 | 0 | 25 | 0 | 32 | 3 | 1 |
| Ventura, Jose, Beloit° | .235 | 52 | 98 | 14 | 23 | 25 | 2 | 0 | 0 | 9 | 0 | 2 | 1 | 1 | 8 | 1 | 22 | 7 | 0 |
| Venturini, Peter, Appleton | .270 | 115 | 448 | 85 | 121 | 166 | 23 | 8 | 2 | 39 | 5 | 7 | 1 | 2 | 45 | 0 | 60 | 16 | 9 |
| Villa, Michael, Clinton° | .500 | 28 | 4 | 0 | 2 | 2 | 0 | 0 | 0 | 1 | 0 | 2 | 0 | 0 | 0 | 0 | 0 | 0 | 0 |
| Villanueva, Hector, Peoria | .233 | 65 | 193 | 22 | 45 | 55 | 7 | 0 | 1 | 19 | 3 | 2 | 1 | 3 | 27 | 0 | 36 | 0 | 2 |
| Walker, Darcy, Peoria° | .278 | 124 | 413 | 64 | 115 | 185 | 21 | 2 | 15 | 68 | 9 | 1 | 4 | 6 | 55 | 4 | 75 | 2 | 4 |
| Walker, Michael, Madison | .201 | 54 | 164 | 12 | 33 | 42 | 5 | 2 | 0 | 11 | 0 | 1 | 1 | 1 | 14 | 0 | 37 | 1 | 3 |
| Walters, Darryel, Beloit | .269 | 113 | 417 | 61 | 112 | 215 | 21 | 5 | 24 | 75 | 9 | 4 | 4 | 1 | 40 | 2 | 141 | 11 | 5 |
| Ward, Timothy, Wausau° | .226 | 109 | 349 | 40 | 79 | 122 | 10 | 0 | 11 | 58 | 3 | 2 | 2 | 4 | 56 | 2 | 107 | 3 | 1 |
| Williams, Bruce, Peoria | .000 | 11 | 1 | 0 | 0 | 0 | 0 | 0 | 0 | 0 | 0 | 1 | 0 | 0 | 0 | 0 | 1 | 0 | 0 |
| Williams, David, Kenosha | .220 | 25 | 59 | 9 | 13 | 17 | 2 | 1 | 0 | 4 | 0 | 1 | 0 | 1 | 8 | 0 | 6 | 4 | 1 |
| Williams, Edward, Cedar Rapids | .261 | 119 | 406 | 71 | 106 | 185 | 13 | 3 | 20 | 83 | 4 | 0 | 5 | 15 | 62 | 4 | 101 | 5 | 4 |
| Williams, Fred, Beloit | .265 | 51 | 151 | 35 | 40 | 45 | 2 | 0 | 1 | 17 | 1 | 4 | 1 | 1 | 32 | 0 | 30 | 12 | 6 |
| Wilmet, Paul, Springfield | .000 | 41 | 3 | 0 | 0 | 0 | 0 | 0 | 0 | 0 | 0 | 0 | 0 | 0 | 0 | 0 | 1 | 0 | 0 |
| Wilson, Craig, Springfield | .262 | 133 | 504 | 64 | 132 | 180 | 16 | 4 | 8 | 52 | 6 | 4 | 6 | 1 | 47 | 0 | 67 | 33 | 14 |
| Winters, James, Appleton | .267 | 125 | 465 | 66 | 124 | 191 | 27 | 8 | 8 | 91 | 12 | 1 | 7 | 3 | 63 | 6 | 107 | 10 | 8 |
| Woodhouse, Kevin, Clinton° | .189 | 40 | 111 | 12 | 21 | 28 | 7 | 0 | 0 | 9 | 1 | 1 | 3 | 0 | 22 | 1 | 27 | 3 | 4 |
| Worden, William, Wausau | .257 | 78 | 268 | 34 | 69 | 127 | 13 | 0 | 15 | 38 | 8 | 1 | 0 | 4 | 19 | 0 | 66 | 3 | 2 |
| Wrona, Richard, Peoria† | .250 | 6 | 16 | 2 | 4 | 5 | 1 | 0 | 0 | 2 | 1 | 0 | 0 | 2 | 0 | 0 | 5 | 0 | 0 |
| Yanes, Edward, Kenosha | .195 | 129 | 416 | 63 | 81 | 134 | 18 | 1 | 11 | 58 | 5 | 4 | 5 | 8 | 63 | 0 | 98 | 2 | 7 |

The following pitchers, listed alphabetically by club, with games in parentheses, had no plate appearances, primarily through use of designated hitters:

APPLETON—Anderson, Jeffrey (38); Bartolomucci, Anthony (10); Carr, Donald (14); Correa, Edwin (18); Filippi, James (16); Jefts, Christopher (16); Lahrman, Thomas (14); Oswald, Steven (11); Phelps, James (4); Reed, Kenneth (29); Renz, Kevin (19); Ruckebeil, Mark (31); Stein, John (8); Thigpen, Robert (1); White, David (53).

BELOIT—Adkins, Terence (4); Alicea, Miguel (11); Diaz, Derek (59); Evans, Gary (1); Fitzpatrick, Danny (6); Freeland, Dean (12); Frew, Michael (8); Kanwisher, Gary (25); Kleean, Thomas (14); Ludy, John (29); Madrid, Alexander (19); Montano, Martin (42); Morris, James (1); Peterek, Jeffrey (14); Porter, Charles (3); Ratliff, Daniel (11); Sadler, Alan (13); Scarpetta, Daniel (22); Simmons, Gregory (11); Tichy, Paul (6).

BURLINGTON—Adams, Terrill (14); Akins, Sidney (27); Allison, James (14); Bridges, James (19); Daniel, Stephen (20); Dial, Bryan (23); Fay, Michael (7); Harden, Ty (32); Hernandez, Carlos (28); Hibberd, Huck (8); Johnson, Ronald (10); Jones, Ross (5); Keathley, Robin (2); Lankard, Steven (4); Larsen, Daniel (21); Olsson, Daniel (28); Pardo, Lawrence (15); Rogers, Kenneth (33); Rogers, Stuart (3); Shamblin, William (15); Whitaker, Darrell (45); Wilson, Stephen (21).

CEDAR RAPIDS—Pettibone, James (1).

CLINTON—Moriarty, Todd (20); Stangel, Christopher (17).

KENOSHA—Adams, Michael (2); Andrus, Mark (13); Cardwood, Alfredo (17); Cloninger, Michael (30); Davis, Mark (8); Dodd, John (31); Gomez, Steven (52); Iasparro, Donnie (31); Malec, Jason (12); Prickett, Scott (28); Sontag, Alan (28); Tabeling, Robert (32).

MADISON—Applegate, Russell (38); Brake, Gregory (20); Burns, Todd (20); Criswell, Brian (26); Edwards, David (22); Ferreira, Jose (23); Figueroa, Victor (6); Hansen, Darel (41); John, Thomas (1); Kibler, Russell (26); Leonette, Mark (42); McDonald, Kirk (3); Whaley, Scott (10).

PEORIA—Reid, Timothy (24).

QUAD CITIES—Banning, Douglas (11); Butler, Michael (27); Cedeno, Vinicio (8); Cook, Larry (37); Cook, Michael (2); Eggersten, Todd (26); Franco, Julio (13); Fraser, William (13); Garcia, Miguel (29); Harvey, Bryan (30); Horrell, Christopher (2); Martinez, David (18); Venturino, Philip (15).

SPRINGFIELD—Livchak, Robert (5).

WATERLOO—Beasley, Christopher (17); Belleman, Michael (10); Clark, Edward (14); Encarnacion, Luis (53); Galloway, Kenneth (30); Ghelfi, Andrew (10); Greer, Michael (29); Karpuk, Gregory (12); Link, Robert (16); Minyard, John (9); Murphy, Kent (5); Murphy, Michael (8); Piphus, Benjamin (10); Robertson, Andrew (15); Sharp, Richard (34); Smith, Daryl (1); Soma, Charles (11); Stephenson, Joe (32); Whitmyer, Stephen (27).

WAUSAU—Baldrick, Robert (39); Burden, John (6); Davis, Bret (14); Higgs, Darrell (17); Jones, Calvin (20); Malave, Benito (5); Meister, Mickey (13); Mendek, William (49); Neufelder, Donald (27); Oizumi, Steven (8); Reinholtz, Jack (22); Rousey, Stephen (26); Ruzek, Donald (6); Siegel, Robert (6); Spratke, Kenneth (27); White, Logan (51).

GRAND SLAM HOME RUNS—Amante, Bertolani, Bichette, Clements, Dietrick, Digioia, Fitzgerald, Fulgencio, V. Garcia, Grant, Grayston, Jennings, Komeiji, McCulla, T. McDonald, Pace, Rigos, B. Robinson, Roman, St. Laurent, Santos, Taylor, Venturini, Walters, Worden, 1 each.

AWARDED FIRST BASE ON CATCHER'S INTERFERENCE—Pohle 8 (Kreuter 2, Caianiello, Cosby, Cupples, Fitzgerald, Owen, Pena); B. Hill 6 (Pappas 4, G. Hill, Markert); Monda 2 (G. Hill, Pappas); Bates (Pappas); H. Davis (Owen); Gonzalez (Glendening); T. Jones (Gobbo); Pruitt (Gonzalez); T. Schwarz (Gonzalez); Tom Smith (R. Anderson).

## CLUB FIELDING

| Club | Pct. | G. | PO. | A. | E. | DP. | PB. | Club | Pct. | G. | PO. | A. | E. | DP. | PB. |
|---|---|---|---|---|---|---|---|---|---|---|---|---|---|---|---|
| Cedar Rapids | .965 | 139 | 3557 | 1386 | 181 | 111 | 10 | Springfield | .960 | 140 | 3705 | 1528 | 218 | 113 | 34 |
| Beloit | .965 | 136 | 3520 | 1350 | 179 | 105 | 25 | Clinton | .959 | 140 | 3637 | 1399 | 216 | 114 | 15 |
| Kenosha | .964 | 139 | 3681 | 1497 | 195 | 117 | 26 | Appleton | .958 | 139 | 3684 | 1483 | 227 | 122 | 14 |
| Peoria | .963 | 140 | 3658 | 1530 | 199 | 123 | 28 | Wausau | .958 | 137 | 3511 | 1495 | 220 | 125 | 24 |
| Madison | .961 | 138 | 3676 | 1560 | 210 | 115 | 16 | Quad Cities | .956 | 140 | 3623 | 1471 | 233 | 133 | 31 |
| Waterloo | .960 | 140 | 3605 | 1531 | 212 | 145 | 24 | Burlington | .953 | 138 | 3556 | 1516 | 250 | 118 | 35 |

Triple Plays—Beloit, Burlington.

## INDIVIDUAL FIELDING

*Throws Lefthanded.

### FIRST BASEMEN

| Player and Club | Pct. | G. | PO. | A. | E. | DP. | Player and Club | Pct. | G. | PO. | A. | E. | DP. |
|---|---|---|---|---|---|---|---|---|---|---|---|---|---|
| Alfredson, Quad Cities | 1.000 | 1 | 4 | 1 | 0 | 1 | Lanik, Burlington* | .974 | 45 | 351 | 25 | 10 | 31 |
| Alvis, Waterloo* | .984 | 32 | 291 | 20 | 5 | 18 | Markert, Appleton | .933 | 2 | 12 | 2 | 1 | 3 |
| Amante, Springfield | 1.000 | 8 | 71 | 6 | 0 | 6 | McCulla, Springfield | .964 | 5 | 51 | 2 | 2 | 2 |
| Anderson, Madison | .990 | 12 | 93 | 2 | 1 | 8 | Mitchell, Beloit | 1.000 | 2 | 14 | 0 | 0 | 1 |
| ARIAS, Madison | .991 | 130 | 1161 | 80 | 11 | 99 | Moncerratt, Wausau* | .966 | 30 | 238 | 15 | 9 | 20 |
| Autry, Appleton | .750 | 1 | 3 | 0 | 1 | 1 | Monda, Cedar Rapids* | .988 | 137 | 1130 | 100 | 15 | 98 |
| Bates, Burlington | .971 | 4 | 29 | 4 | 1 | 3 | Montanari, Quad Cities | .990 | 64 | 540 | 36 | 6 | 55 |
| Bichette, Quad Cities | .976 | 16 | 116 | 7 | 3 | 14 | Oppenheimer, Beloit | 1.000 | 1 | 10 | 0 | 0 | 0 |
| Boever, Cedar Rapids | 1.000 | 3 | 20 | 5 | 0 | 2 | Peraza, Appleton | .984 | 25 | 236 | 16 | 4 | 14 |
| Borg, Kenosha* | .984 | 74 | 602 | 33 | 10 | 49 | Peterson, Quad Cities | .971 | 5 | 34 | 0 | 1 | 1 |
| Brilinski, Madison* | .939 | 6 | 30 | 1 | 2 | 3 | Porter, Clinton | .972 | 24 | 166 | 9 | 5 | 14 |
| Clements, Beloit | .975 | 10 | 75 | 2 | 2 | 10 | Reimer, Burlington | .979 | 74 | 685 | 29 | 15 | 54 |
| Coin, Beloit | 1.000 | 6 | 34 | 2 | 0 | 4 | Rodriguez, Kenosha | .987 | 41 | 354 | 24 | 5 | 31 |
| Cooper, Clinton | .964 | 10 | 53 | 1 | 2 | 3 | Ryan, Kenosha* | .991 | 27 | 202 | 12 | 2 | 17 |
| Crabbe, Peoria | 1.000 | 4 | 16 | 1 | 0 | 1 | Skurla, Clinton* | .976 | 49 | 377 | 26 | 10 | 39 |
| Cullers, Burlington | 1.000 | 1 | 5 | 0 | 0 | 1 | T. Smith, Clinton | .988 | 57 | 474 | 33 | 6 | 41 |
| Demeter, Springfield | .984 | 130 | 1131 | 89 | 20 | 102 | Solz, Peoria | .983 | 63 | 517 | 47 | 10 | 48 |
| Forrester, Appleton* | .984 | 92 | 760 | 36 | 13 | 67 | Stanley, Burlington | 1.000 | 1 | 11 | 0 | 0 | 0 |
| Gobbo, Beloit | 1.000 | 1 | 3 | 0 | 0 | 0 | Stewart, Wausau | .989 | 69 | 567 | 36 | 7 | 56 |
| Grayston, Burlington | 1.000 | 2 | 3 | 0 | 0 | 0 | Swepson, Clinton | 1.000 | 7 | 54 | 0 | 0 | 5 |
| Harper, Waterloo | .990 | 58 | 547 | 32 | 6 | 59 | Tarnow, Appleton | .990 | 17 | 95 | 6 | 1 | 11 |
| Higgins, Waterloo | .991 | 54 | 422 | 30 | 4 | 49 | Thomas, Appleton | .993 | 13 | 127 | 8 | 1 | 11 |
| Hill, Burlington | .975 | 22 | 172 | 20 | 5 | 17 | Vanstone, Clinton | 1.000 | 3 | 26 | 4 | 0 | 3 |
| Jones, Quad Cities* | .985 | 62 | 483 | 37 | 8 | 44 | Velasquez, Kenosha | 1.000 | 7 | 43 | 7 | 0 | 2 |
| Kelley, Burlington | 1.000 | 1 | 4 | 0 | 0 | 0 | Walker, Peoria* | .989 | 88 | 727 | 65 | 9 | 63 |
| B. Kent, Beloit* | .986 | 121 | 1040 | 50 | 15 | 80 | Ward, Wausau | .979 | 28 | 220 | 14 | 5 | 19 |
| W. Kent, Appleton | 1.000 | 1 | 1 | 0 | 0 | 0 | Worden, Wausau | .980 | 20 | 184 | 10 | 4 | 21 |

Triple Plays—B. Kent, Reimer.

### SECOND BASEMEN

| Player and Club | Pct. | G. | PO. | A. | E. | DP. | Player and Club | Pct. | G. | PO. | A. | E. | DP. |
|---|---|---|---|---|---|---|---|---|---|---|---|---|---|
| Alfonzo, Quad Cities | .786 | 2 | 4 | 7 | 3 | 1 | Larson, Wausau | .958 | 91 | 194 | 221 | 18 | 52 |
| Alfredson, Quad Cities | 1.000 | 5 | 11 | 14 | 0 | 7 | Mandeville, Peoria | .955 | 21 | 29 | 34 | 3 | 12 |
| Bates, Burlington | .972 | 27 | 40 | 63 | 3 | 8 | Mattox, Beloit | .955 | 122 | 233 | 293 | 25 | 59 |
| Beardman, Madison | .933 | 5 | 7 | 7 | 1 | 2 | Munoz, Clinton | .978 | 19 | 18 | 26 | 1 | 5 |
| Bertolani, Appleton | .945 | 133 | 314 | 351 | 39 | 79 | Nunley, Springfield | .947 | 71 | 136 | 185 | 18 | 29 |
| Blair, Clinton | .973 | 107 | 225 | 247 | 13 | 56 | Paul, Waterloo | 1.000 | 4 | 4 | 4 | 0 | 2 |
| Bucci, Burlington | .500 | 2 | 0 | 2 | 2 | 0 | E. Perez, Wausau | .952 | 47 | 103 | 136 | 12 | 32 |
| Byrd, Appleton | .980 | 11 | 23 | 27 | 1 | 9 | Phillips, Beloit | .920 | 9 | 10 | 13 | 2 | 6 |
| Carrasco, Waterloo | .946 | 50 | 80 | 129 | 12 | 24 | Porte, Cedar Rapids | .956 | 78 | 146 | 178 | 15 | 36 |
| Casey, Kenosha | .963 | 22 | 36 | 43 | 3 | 4 | Quinones, Waterloo | .985 | 13 | 23 | 44 | 1 | 11 |
| Coachman, Quad Cities | .974 | 132 | 353 | 370 | 19 | 87 | Ray, Wausau | .952 | 10 | 6 | 14 | 1 | 1 |
| Daddario, Waterloo | .956 | 83 | 193 | 241 | 20 | 61 | Reboulet, Springfield | .960 | 36 | 70 | 99 | 7 | 15 |
| Denbo, Cedar Rapids | .956 | 42 | 79 | 94 | 8 | 18 | Scaletta, Kenosha | .911 | 9 | 15 | 26 | 4 | 5 |
| Dunlap, Cedar Rapids | .990 | 27 | 59 | 43 | 1 | 16 | Sciacca, Quad Cities | 1.000 | 2 | 1 | 3 | 0 | 1 |
| Garner, Burlington | .962 | 47 | 89 | 114 | 8 | 19 | Senne, Kenosha | .965 | 87 | 190 | 219 | 15 | 39 |
| Grayston, Burlington | .952 | 15 | 26 | 33 | 3 | 7 | Thomas, Kenosha | .954 | 15 | 29 | 33 | 3 | 5 |
| Higgins, Waterloo | 1.000 | 1 | 1 | 6 | 0 | 0 | Vanstone, Clinton | .979 | 25 | 43 | 52 | 2 | 9 |
| House, Peoria | .964 | 126 | 261 | 352 | 23 | 73 | Ventura, Beloit | 1.000 | 3 | 1 | 1 | 0 | 1 |
| Jagnow, Burlington | .961 | 29 | 66 | 82 | 6 | 22 | Walker, Madison | 1.000 | 9 | 14 | 23 | 0 | 4 |
| KANTER, Madison | .977 | 115 | 239 | 320 | 13 | 64 | D. Williams, Kenosha | .944 | 20 | 34 | 34 | 4 | 8 |
| Klein, Burlington | .955 | 33 | 70 | 98 | 8 | 18 | F. Williams, Beloit | .943 | 14 | 21 | 29 | 3 | 4 |
| Krause, Madison | .926 | 18 | 28 | 47 | 6 | 7 | Wilson, Springfield | .957 | 42 | 88 | 114 | 9 | 34 |

Triple Plays—Garner, Mattox.

### THIRD BASEMEN

| Player and Club | Pct. | G. | PO. | A. | E. | DP. | Player and Club | Pct. | G. | PO. | A. | E. | DP. |
|---|---|---|---|---|---|---|---|---|---|---|---|---|---|
| Alfonzo, Quad Cities | .750 | 6 | 3 | 9 | 4 | 0 | Paul, Waterloo | .925 | 77 | 50 | 135 | 15 | 15 |
| Alfredson, Quad Cities | 1.000 | 1 | 1 | 0 | 0 | 0 | E. Perez, Wausau | 1.000 | 2 | 0 | 4 | 0 | 0 |
| Amante, Springfield | .776 | 21 | 16 | 22 | 11 | 1 | Phillips, Beloit | 1.000 | 7 | 1 | 7 | 0 | 1 |
| Anderson, Madison | .929 | 8 | 6 | 20 | 2 | 2 | Pohle, Beloit | .909 | 22 | 16 | 34 | 5 | 5 |
| Autry, Appleton | .904 | 82 | 60 | 147 | 22 | 11 | Quinones, Waterloo | .952 | 9 | 3 | 17 | 1 | 1 |
| Beardman, Madison | .886 | 18 | 8 | 31 | 5 | 5 | Ray, Wausau | .909 | 20 | 12 | 38 | 5 | 2 |
| Byrd, Appleton | .848 | 35 | 27 | 51 | 14 | 6 | Robinson, Cedar Rapids | 1.000 | 1 | 1 | 2 | 0 | 0 |
| Carrasco, Waterloo | .878 | 19 | 12 | 24 | 5 | 1 | Rolland, Burlington | .906 | 70 | 44 | 140 | 19 | 10 |
| Coin, Beloit | .600 | 6 | 4 | 2 | 4 | 0 | Roman, Waterloo | .000 | 1 | 0 | 0 | 1 | 0 |
| Crabbe, Peoria | .913 | 120 | 84 | 211 | 28 | 17 | Santos, Springfield | .880 | 68 | 43 | 125 | 23 | 12 |
| Cullers, Burlington | .900 | 5 | 4 | 5 | 1 | 1 | Scaletta, Kenosha | .935 | 21 | 15 | 28 | 3 | 2 |
| Daddario, Waterloo | .919 | 35 | 31 | 71 | 9 | 2 | Schwarz, Kenosha | .903 | 116 | 92 | 252 | 37 | 26 |
| Denbo, Cedar Rapids | .947 | 31 | 22 | 49 | 4 | 8 | Sciacca, Quad Cities | 1.000 | 5 | 2 | 9 | 0 | 1 |
| Eichorst, Madison | .913 | 16 | 12 | 30 | 4 | 4 | Senne, Kenosha | .714 | 3 | 4 | 1 | 2 | 0 |
| Fazzini, Beloit | 1.000 | 1 | 0 | 2 | 0 | 0 | Siemers, Kenosha | .750 | 1 | 1 | 2 | 1 | 0 |
| Grant, Quad Cities | .907 | 135 | 115 | 245 | 37 | 35 | Solz, Peoria | .800 | 3 | 1 | 3 | 1 | 0 |
| Grayston, Burlington | .868 | 48 | 23 | 76 | 15 | 6 | Spring, Clinton | .896 | 120 | 83 | 245 | 38 | 24 |
| Howie, Madison | .970 | 12 | 8 | 24 | 1 | 0 | Swepson, Clinton | .714 | 9 | 4 | 16 | 8 | 2 |
| Kanter, Madison | .700 | 4 | 2 | 5 | 3 | 1 | Torve, Appleton | .925 | 30 | 20 | 54 | 6 | 5 |
| Klein, Burlington | .875 | 22 | 13 | 43 | 8 | 3 | Turgeon, Springfield | 1.000 | 2 | 3 | 2 | 0 | 0 |
| Krause, Madison | .879 | 30 | 30 | 57 | 12 | 3 | Vanstone, Clinton | 1.000 | 9 | 4 | 10 | 0 | 1 |
| Luther, Springfield | .911 | 34 | 26 | 56 | 8 | 6 | Ventura, Beloit | .853 | 20 | 6 | 23 | 5 | 2 |
| Mandeville, Peoria | .946 | 22 | 10 | 43 | 3 | 3 | Venturini, Appleton | .800 | 1 | 0 | 4 | 1 | 0 |
| Manto, Quad Cities | .667 | 1 | 2 | 0 | 1 | 0 | Walker, Madison | .571 | 2 | 1 | 3 | 3 | 0 |
| McCulla, Springfield | 1.000 | 2 | 2 | 1 | 0 | 0 | Ward, Wausau | .906 | 79 | 40 | 153 | 20 | 15 |
| Mitchell, Beloit | .918 | 88 | 64 | 148 | 19 | 15 | D. Williams, Kenosha | 1.000 | 2 | 2 | 0 | 0 | 0 |
| Munoz, Clinton | .905 | 9 | 4 | 15 | 2 | 0 | E. Williams, Cedar Rapids | .897 | 114 | 83 | 204 | 33 | 23 |
| Nunley, Springfield | .500 | 3 | 0 | 1 | 1 | 0 | F. Williams, Beloit | .857 | 10 | 8 | 16 | 4 | 0 |
| O'Leary, Wausau | .883 | 36 | 24 | 82 | 14 | 12 | WILSON, Springfield | .932 | 93 | 68 | 179 | 18 | 12 |
| Owen, Burlington | .846 | 10 | 5 | 17 | 4 | 2 | Worden, Wausau | .817 | 21 | 17 | 41 | 13 | 4 |
| Palma, Waterloo | .857 | 14 | 14 | 34 | 8 | 3 | | | | | | | |

## SHORTSTOPS

| Player and Club | Pct. | G. | PO. | A. | E. | DP. |
|---|---|---|---|---|---|---|
| Alfredson, Quad Cities | .912 | 86 | 117 | 215 | 32 | 40 |
| Aragon, Kenosha | .935 | 120 | 195 | 327 | 36 | 59 |
| Autry, Appleton | 1.000 | 3 | 2 | 5 | 0 | 1 |
| Balelo, Wausau | .953 | 68 | 76 | 209 | 14 | 36 |
| Barton, Wausau | .923 | 21 | 32 | 52 | 7 | 10 |
| Bennett, Waterloo | .905 | 32 | 48 | 76 | 13 | 13 |
| Bucci, Burlington | 1.000 | 1 | 2 | 1 | 0 | 1 |
| Carganilla, Waterloo | .915 | 110 | 155 | 318 | 44 | 80 |
| Daddario, Waterloo | .938 | 3 | 6 | 9 | 1 | 3 |
| Darretta, Burlington | .924 | 97 | 145 | 269 | 34 | 52 |
| Denbo, Cedar Rapids | .947 | 7 | 13 | 23 | 2 | 1 |
| Dunlap, Cedar Rapids | .935 | 55 | 85 | 132 | 15 | 25 |
| Fregosi, Springfield | .958 | 54 | 88 | 162 | 11 | 32 |
| Grayston, Burlington | .952 | 33 | 46 | 72 | 6 | 14 |
| Howie, Madison | .938 | 105 | 151 | 273 | 28 | 45 |
| Klein, Burlington | .936 | 20 | 36 | 67 | 7 | 12 |
| Krause, Madison | .875 | 3 | 6 | 8 | 2 | 2 |
| Luther, Springfield | .938 | 78 | 116 | 234 | 23 | 42 |
| Mandeville, Peoria | .893 | 23 | 25 | 67 | 11 | 12 |
| Martin, Appleton | .912 | 28 | 39 | 86 | 12 | 13 |
| McDougal, Peoria | .939 | 120 | 196 | 356 | 36 | 73 |
| Morfin, Wausau | .857 | 9 | 16 | 20 | 6 | 2 |
| Munoz, Clinton | .821 | 17 | 21 | 25 | 10 | 7 |
| Nunez, Quad Cities | .897 | 53 | 72 | 136 | 24 | 21 |
| Nunley, Springfield | .841 | 19 | 10 | 43 | 10 | 4 |
| Perez, Wausau | .912 | 14 | 25 | 37 | 6 | 8 |
| Perezchica, Clinton | .928 | 127 | 224 | 332 | 43 | 54 |
| Phillips, Beloit | .800 | 3 | 3 | 5 | 2 | 1 |
| POHLE, Beloit | .945 | 104 | 129 | 281 | 24 | 45 |
| Quinones, Waterloo | 1.000 | 1 | 1 | 1 | 0 | 0 |
| Ray, Wausau | .954 | 36 | 50 | 94 | 7 | 19 |
| T. Riley, Cedar Rapids | .903 | 6 | 10 | 18 | 3 | 4 |
| Robinson, Cedar Rapids | .924 | 75 | 107 | 221 | 27 | 44 |
| Rolland, Burlington | .500 | 1 | 0 | 1 | 1 | 0 |
| Samuel, Beloit | .936 | 27 | 46 | 71 | 8 | 19 |
| Scaletta, Kenosha | .949 | 21 | 35 | 59 | 5 | 9 |
| Sciacca, Quad Cities | .944 | 9 | 11 | 23 | 2 | 5 |
| Senne, Kenosha | 1.000 | 1 | 3 | 4 | 0 | 1 |
| Vanstone, Clinton | 1.000 | 6 | 8 | 7 | 0 | 1 |
| Ventura, Beloit | .794 | 15 | 8 | 19 | 7 | 3 |
| Venturini, Appleton | .937 | 110 | 174 | 315 | 33 | 66 |
| Walker, Madison | .894 | 39 | 57 | 121 | 21 | 21 |
| Williams, Beloit | 1.000 | 2 | 0 | 4 | 0 | 0 |

Triple Play—Pohle.

## OUTFIELDERS

| Player and Club | Pct. | G. | PO. | A. | E. | DP. |
|---|---|---|---|---|---|---|
| Amante, Springfield | .981 | 28 | 50 | 1 | 1 | 0 |
| J. Anderson, Wausau | .931 | 64 | 78 | 3 | 6 | 0 |
| R. Anderson, Madison | 1.000 | 6 | 5 | 0 | 0 | 0 |
| Aragon, Kenosha | 1.000 | 1 | 4 | 1 | 0 | 0 |
| Arias, Madison | .000 | 2 | 0 | 0 | 1 | 0 |
| Autry, Appleton | 1.000 | 4 | 2 | 1 | 0 | 1 |
| Bayron, Kenosha* | .846 | 12 | 11 | 0 | 2 | 0 |
| Bennett, Waterloo | 1.000 | 4 | 7 | 0 | 0 | 0 |
| Bichette, Quad Cities | .941 | 121 | 179 | 12 | 12 | 2 |
| Blair, Clinton | 1.000 | 2 | 2 | 1 | 0 | 0 |
| Boderick, Peoria | .842 | 13 | 15 | 1 | 3 | 1 |
| Boever, Cedar Rapids | .969 | 126 | 178 | 11 | 6 | 2 |
| Brito, Waterloo | .951 | 132 | 160 | 15 | 9 | 2 |
| Brown, Beloit | .947 | 17 | 18 | 0 | 1 | 0 |
| Bruno, Beloit* | .988 | 45 | 79 | 5 | 1 | 3 |
| Campbell, Quad Cities | .953 | 53 | 75 | 6 | 4 | 2 |
| Cantrell, Quad Cities | .981 | 81 | 155 | 3 | 3 | 3 |
| Clements, Beloit | .900 | 10 | 18 | 0 | 2 | 0 |
| Coin, Beloit | 1.000 | 30 | 41 | 3 | 0 | 1 |
| Cooper, Clinton | 1.000 | 46 | 81 | 2 | 0 | 0 |
| Coyle, Madison | .918 | 21 | 51 | 5 | 5 | 0 |
| Crosby, Kenosha* | .917 | 44 | 71 | 6 | 7 | 1 |
| Davis, Clinton | .974 | 92 | 188 | 3 | 5 | 0 |
| DeWolf, Beloit* | .958 | 101 | 181 | 3 | 8 | 0 |
| Dietrick, Madison | .969 | 44 | 94 | 1 | 3 | 0 |
| Digioia, Springfield | .953 | 43 | 38 | 3 | 2 | 0 |
| Eichorst, Madison | 1.000 | 12 | 24 | 4 | 0 | 0 |
| Fazzini, Madison | .950 | 41 | 54 | 3 | 3 | 1 |
| Fulgencio, Cedar Rapids | .981 | 85 | 201 | 3 | 4 | 1 |
| Gould, Madison | .984 | 88 | 183 | 2 | 3 | 1 |
| Haley, Wausau | .971 | 67 | 98 | 4 | 3 | 0 |
| Hardamon, Peoria | .968 | 40 | 87 | 4 | 3 | 1 |
| Harper, Waterloo | .989 | 41 | 84 | 5 | 1 | 1 |
| Harvey, Peoria | 1.000 | 9 | 10 | 0 | 0 | 0 |
| B. Hill, Burlington | .949 | 61 | 72 | 2 | 4 | 1 |
| R. Hill, Wausau | .963 | 54 | 98 | 5 | 4 | 0 |
| House, Peoria | 1.000 | 1 | 3 | 0 | 0 | 0 |
| Howie, Madison | 1.000 | 15 | 26 | 1 | 0 | 0 |
| Jenkins, Waterloo | .879 | 28 | 28 | 1 | 4 | 0 |
| Jennings, Quad Cities* | .948 | 91 | 187 | 12 | 11 | 1 |
| Jimenez, Quad Cities | .846 | 8 | 11 | 0 | 2 | 0 |
| Jones, Quad Cities* | 1.000 | 2 | 2 | 0 | 0 | 0 |
| Jordan, Waterloo | .955 | 95 | 168 | 3 | 8 | 1 |
| Jose, Madison | .942 | 111 | 187 | 9 | 12 | 2 |
| Kelley, Burlington | 1.000 | 10 | 7 | 0 | 0 | 0 |
| Kent, Appleton | .929 | 60 | 78 | 1 | 6 | 0 |
| J. Kramer, Madison | .986 | 82 | 199 | 6 | 3 | 0 |
| M. Kramer, Burlington* | .966 | 79 | 108 | 4 | 4 | 1 |
| Krause, Madison | .961 | 60 | 91 | 8 | 4 | 0 |
| Larson, Wausau | 1.000 | 1 | 0 | 2 | 0 | 0 |
| Leon, Springfield* | .948 | 62 | 101 | 8 | 6 | 1 |
| Lezcano, Peoria | .939 | 54 | 83 | 9 | 6 | 0 |
| MACHALEC, Wausau | .987 | 114 | 208 | 16 | 3 | 4 |
| Manto, Quad Cities | .979 | 64 | 85 | 8 | 2 | 1 |
| Manzon, Kenosha | .987 | 73 | 139 | 9 | 2 | 2 |
| McCulla, Springfield | .936 | 55 | 86 | 2 | 6 | 0 |
| McDonald, Clinton | .967 | 128 | 248 | 15 | 9 | 2 |
| Monico, Beloit* | .978 | 43 | 86 | 1 | 2 | 0 |
| Nunley, Springfield | 1.000 | 1 | 2 | 0 | 0 | 0 |
| Pace, Cedar Rapids* | .900 | 11 | 9 | 0 | 1 | 0 |
| Palmeiro, Peoria* | .992 | 70 | 113 | 7 | 1 | 1 |
| O. Perez, Wausau* | .943 | 106 | 189 | 8 | 12 | 3 |
| Peterson, Quad Cities | .963 | 14 | 25 | 1 | 1 | 0 |
| Pruitt, Appleton | .964 | 77 | 128 | 4 | 5 | 0 |
| Reilly, Burlington | 1.000 | 2 | 2 | 0 | 0 | 0 |
| Richardson, Peoria | .993 | 71 | 134 | 4 | 1 | 0 |
| Rigos, Springfield | .926 | 89 | 165 | 9 | 14 | 2 |
| D. Riley, Cedar Rapids | .961 | 123 | 208 | 13 | 9 | 0 |
| M. Robinson, Springfield | .976 | 124 | 235 | 9 | 6 | 1 |
| Rolland, Burlington | 1.000 | 13 | 21 | 0 | 0 | 0 |
| Roman, Waterloo | .972 | 135 | 299 | 8 | 9 | 3 |
| Ryan, Kenosha* | .968 | 48 | 87 | 4 | 3 | 2 |
| St. Laurent, Burlington | .968 | 129 | 231 | 8 | 8 | 0 |
| Sedar, Appleton | 1.000 | 3 | 4 | 0 | 0 | 0 |
| Siemers, Kenosha | .969 | 22 | 29 | 2 | 1 | 0 |
| Sigler, Cedar Rapids | .969 | 86 | 149 | 6 | 5 | 2 |
| Simonson, Beloit | 1.000 | 7 | 10 | 2 | 0 | 1 |
| Skurla, Clinton* | 1.000 | 73 | 127 | 9 | 0 | 0 |
| T. Smith, Peoria | .992 | 77 | 118 | 4 | 1 | 0 |
| W. Smith, Clinton | .957 | 40 | 40 | 5 | 2 | 1 |
| Steinbach, Beloit | .918 | 45 | 54 | 2 | 5 | 0 |
| Swepson, Clinton | .984 | 38 | 56 | 6 | 1 | 1 |
| Taylor, Appleton | .933 | 60 | 93 | 4 | 7 | 1 |
| Th. Thomas, Kenosha | .970 | 114 | 256 | 6 | 8 | 1 |
| Tr. Thomas, Appleton | .939 | 113 | 208 | 9 | 14 | 2 |
| Threadgill, Burlington | .927 | 109 | 158 | 7 | 13 | 0 |
| Tullier, Peoria* | .970 | 45 | 94 | 3 | 3 | 2 |
| Turgeon, Springfield | .938 | 39 | 55 | 6 | 4 | 0 |
| Turner, Peoria* | .979 | 66 | 93 | 2 | 2 | 0 |
| Uribe, Wausau | 1.000 | 26 | 51 | 2 | 0 | 1 |
| Vanstone, Clinton | 1.000 | 2 | 3 | 0 | 0 | 0 |
| Vasquez, Burlington* | .895 | 62 | 87 | 7 | 11 | 3 |
| Ventura, Beloit | 1.000 | 2 | 2 | 0 | 0 | 0 |
| Walters, Beloit | .988 | 85 | 163 | 7 | 2 | 0 |
| Williams, Beloit | .974 | 25 | 32 | 5 | 1 | 0 |
| Winters, Appleton | .980 | 118 | 282 | 10 | 6 | 4 |
| Woodhouse, Clinton* | .932 | 37 | 64 | 4 | 5 | 1 |
| Yanes, Kenosha | .967 | 129 | 226 | 11 | 8 | 4 |

Triple Play—Threadgill.

## CATCHERS

| Player and Club | Pct. | G. | PO. | A. | E. | DP. | PB. |
|---|---|---|---|---|---|---|---|
| Amante, Springfield | .952 | 3 | 18 | 2 | 1 | 1 | 2 |
| Anderson, Madison | .978 | 43 | 276 | 32 | 7 | 3 | 10 |
| BERRY, Cedar Rapids | .990 | 70 | 475 | 35 | 5 | 1 | 5 |
| Bichette, Quad Cities | 1.000 | 1 | 5 | 2 | 0 | 0 | 0 |
| Bresnahan, Wausau | .978 | 19 | 120 | 13 | 3 | 2 | 4 |
| Caianiello, Appleton | .987 | 57 | 325 | 42 | 5 | 3 | 2 |
| Cosby, Clinton | .977 | 39 | 236 | 14 | 6 | 3 | 2 |
| Cullers, Burlington | .955 | 11 | 60 | 3 | 3 | 0 | 7 |
| Cupples, Madison | .988 | 71 | 376 | 48 | 5 | 4 | 3 |
| Dorsett, Madison | .979 | 31 | 194 | 40 | 5 | 3 | 3 |
| Fitzgerald, Springfield | .977 | 97 | 673 | 56 | 17 | 1 | 23 |
| Garcia, Waterloo | .989 | 79 | 460 | 60 | 6 | 6 | 13 |
| Glendening, Peoria | .966 | 94 | 580 | 53 | 22 | 7 | 15 |
| Gobbo, Beloit | .979 | 47 | 288 | 35 | 7 | 4 | 9 |
| Gonzalez, Clinton | .965 | 62 | 409 | 61 | 17 | 2 | 10 |
| Hill, Kenosha | .986 | 110 | 730 | 112 | 12 | 17 | 19 |
| Hopkins, Waterloo | .976 | 13 | 71 | 10 | 2 | 1 | 3 |
| Johnigan, Waterloo | .982 | 25 | 152 | 15 | 3 | 1 | 3 |
| Johnson, Peoria | 1.000 | 2 | 11 | 1 | 0 | 0 | 0 |
| Komeiji, Wausau | .971 | 66 | 431 | 43 | 14 | 2 | 16 |

## CATCHERS—Continued

| Player and Club | Pct. | G. | PO. | A. | E. | DP. | PB. | Player and Club | Pct. | G. | PO. | A. | E. | DP. | PB. |
|---|---|---|---|---|---|---|---|---|---|---|---|---|---|---|---|
| Kreuter, Burlington | .980 | 55 | 349 | 34 | 8 | 3 | 7 | Pena, Clinton | .973 | 50 | 321 | 43 | 10 | 6 | 3 |
| A. Lopez, Kenosha | .987 | 11 | 71 | 7 | 1 | 1 | 2 | Peterson, Quad Cities | .923 | 2 | 12 | 0 | 1 | 0 | 0 |
| J. Lopez, Waterloo | .991 | 39 | 209 | 21 | 2 | 3 | 5 | Reilly, Burlington | .980 | 9 | 45 | 5 | 1 | 0 | 2 |
| Markert, Appleton | .983 | 92 | 607 | 82 | 12 | 3 | 12 | Rodriguez, Beloit | .975 | 18 | 109 | 10 | 3 | 0 | 1 |
| Marquez, Quad Cities | .975 | 33 | 254 | 20 | 7 | 4 | 5 | Smith, Quad Cities | .987 | 11 | 72 | 3 | 1 | 1 | 4 |
| McCulla, Springfield | .991 | 46 | 316 | 32 | 3 | 1 | 9 | Stanley, Burlington | 1.000 | 7 | 34 | 2 | 0 | 0 | 0 |
| McGuire, Wausau | .973 | 49 | 304 | 26 | 9 | 4 | 4 | Surhoff, Beloit | .994 | 61 | 475 | 44 | 3 | 2 | 9 |
| Miley, Cedar Rapids | 1.000 | 12 | 97 | 8 | 0 | 1 | 0 | Tarnow, Appleton | 1.000 | 3 | 3 | 0 | 0 | 0 | 0 |
| Mitchell, Beloit | .986 | 22 | 122 | 16 | 2 | 1 | 6 | Toler, Cedar Rapids | .972 | 66 | 408 | 50 | 13 | 4 | 5 |
| O'Hearn, Burlington | .969 | 36 | 160 | 28 | 6 | 1 | 12 | Velasquez, Kenosha | .989 | 25 | 149 | 23 | 2 | 4 | 5 |
| Oppenheimer, Beloit | 1.000 | 6 | 14 | 1 | 0 | 0 | 0 | Villanueva, Peoria | .968 | 54 | 322 | 43 | 12 | 4 | 10 |
| Owen, Burlington | .978 | 53 | 273 | 37 | 7 | 5 | 7 | Worden, Wausau | 1.000 | 9 | 40 | 3 | 0 | 0 | 0 |
| Pappas, Quad Cities | .974 | 100 | 632 | 74 | 19 | 11 | 22 | Wrona, Peoria | .941 | 6 | 31 | 1 | 2 | 1 | 3 |

## PITCHERS

| Player and Club | Pct. | G. | PO. | A. | E. | DP. | Player and Club | Pct. | G. | PO. | A. | E. | DP. |
|---|---|---|---|---|---|---|---|---|---|---|---|---|---|
| Ackerman, Clinton | .947 | 45 | 4 | 14 | 1 | 2 | Goedde, Cedar Rapids | .857 | 28 | 6 | 6 | 2 | 0 |
| M. Adams, Kenosha | 1.000 | 2 | 1 | 3 | 0 | 1 | Gomez, Kenosha | .962 | 52 | 7 | 18 | 1 | 1 |
| T. Adams, Burlington | .818 | 14 | 1 | 8 | 2 | 0 | Greer, Waterloo | .944 | 29 | 3 | 14 | 1 | 3 |
| Adkins, Beloit | 1.000 | 4 | 0 | 3 | 0 | 0 | Hamstra, Clinton | .941 | 33 | 8 | 24 | 2 | 4 |
| Akins, Burlington | .931 | 27 | 8 | 19 | 2 | 3 | Hansen, Madison | 1.000 | 41 | 2 | 12 | 0 | 1 |
| Alicea, Beloit | 1.000 | 11 | 0 | 4 | 0 | 0 | Harden, Burlington | .933 | 31 | 9 | 33 | 3 | 4 |
| Allison, Burlington | .800 | 14 | 1 | 3 | 1 | 1 | Hartley, Springfield | .893 | 33 | 9 | 16 | 3 | 1 |
| Anderson, Appleton | .944 | 38 | 1 | 16 | 1 | 2 | Harvey, Quad Cities | 1.000 | 30 | 2 | 9 | 0 | 1 |
| Andrus, Kenosha | 1.000 | 13 | 2 | 1 | 0 | 1 | Hernandez, Burlington | 1.000 | 28 | 2 | 1 | 0 | 0 |
| Applegate, Madison | .818 | 38 | 3 | 15 | 4 | 1 | Hibberd, Burlington | 1.000 | 8 | 2 | 1 | 0 | 0 |
| Autry, Appleton | 1.000 | 2 | 0 | 1 | 0 | 0 | Higgs, Wausau | 1.000 | 17 | 4 | 2 | 0 | 0 |
| Baldrick, Wausau° | .938 | 39 | 2 | 13 | 1 | 1 | Hinnrichs, Clinton | .917 | 31 | 10 | 12 | 2 | 2 |
| Banning, Quad Cities | .923 | 11 | 5 | 19 | 2 | 0 | Iasparro, Kenosha | .902 | 31 | 8 | 29 | 4 | 3 |
| Bartolomucci, Appleton° | 1.000 | 10 | 0 | 2 | 0 | 0 | Jefts, Appleton | .935 | 16 | 8 | 21 | 2 | 0 |
| Beasley, Waterloo | .956 | 17 | 7 | 36 | 2 | 3 | John, Madison° | 1.000 | 1 | 1 | 4 | 0 | 0 |
| Belinskas, Cedar Rapids | .667 | 11 | 0 | 2 | 1 | 0 | Johnson, Burlington | 1.000 | 10 | 2 | 9 | 0 | 2 |
| Bell, Peoria° | .857 | 9 | 2 | 4 | 1 | 1 | C. Jones, Wausau | .950 | 20 | 11 | 8 | 1 | 0 |
| Belleman, Waterloo | .903 | 10 | 10 | 18 | 3 | 0 | T. Jones, Quad Cities° | 1.000 | 1 | 0 | 1 | 0 | 0 |
| Boyles, Cedar Rapids | .970 | 27 | 10 | 22 | 1 | 1 | KAMPSEN, Cedar Rapids | 1.000 | 29 | 10 | 25 | 0 | 2 |
| Brake, Madison° | .935 | 19 | 5 | 24 | 2 | 4 | Kanwisher, Beloit | .970 | 25 | 6 | 26 | 1 | 0 |
| Bridges, Burlington | .929 | 19 | 3 | 10 | 1 | 0 | Karpuk, Waterloo | .917 | 12 | 6 | 5 | 1 | 1 |
| Brinkman, Wausau | .956 | 27 | 13 | 30 | 2 | 3 | Kavanaugh, Springfield | 1.000 | 9 | 2 | 1 | 0 | 0 |
| Burden, Wausau | 1.000 | 6 | 2 | 1 | 0 | 0 | Keathley, Burlington | 1.000 | 2 | 1 | 5 | 0 | 1 |
| Burns, Madison | .929 | 20 | 8 | 18 | 2 | 1 | Kibler, Madison | .967 | 26 | 20 | 38 | 2 | 0 |
| Butler, Quad Cities° | .882 | 27 | 4 | 41 | 6 | 1 | Kindred, Kenosha | 1.000 | 9 | 0 | 10 | 0 | 0 |
| Cardwood, Kenosha | 1.000 | 17 | 4 | 8 | 0 | 0 | Kinzer, Springfield | 1.000 | 11 | 2 | 3 | 0 | 1 |
| Carr, Appleton | .714 | 14 | 1 | 4 | 2 | 0 | Kleean, Springfield | .900 | 14 | 1 | 8 | 1 | 0 |
| Cedeno, Quad Cities | 1.000 | 8 | 1 | 1 | 0 | 0 | Lahrman, Appleton | 1.000 | 14 | 2 | 7 | 0 | 0 |
| Cieslak, Cedar Rapids° | .889 | 9 | 2 | 6 | 1 | 0 | Lankard, Burlington | 1.000 | 3 | 0 | 2 | 0 | 0 |
| Clark, Waterloo° | .800 | 14 | 3 | 1 | 1 | 0 | Larsen, Burlington | .833 | 19 | 4 | 11 | 3 | 0 |
| Cloninger, Kenosha | .935 | 30 | 7 | 22 | 2 | 3 | Leonette, Madison | .875 | 42 | 6 | 15 | 3 | 0 |
| Coffey, Cedar Rapids | .923 | 9 | 2 | 10 | 1 | 0 | Link, Waterloo | .929 | 16 | 3 | 10 | 1 | 0 |
| Conley, Cedar Rapids° | .958 | 33 | 1 | 22 | 1 | 2 | Livchak, Springfield° | 1.000 | 5 | 1 | 5 | 0 | 0 |
| D. Cook, Clinton | 1.000 | 13 | 2 | 12 | 0 | 0 | Ludy, Beloit | .957 | 29 | 6 | 16 | 1 | 0 |
| L. Cook, Quad Cities° | .941 | 37 | 3 | 13 | 1 | 0 | Maddux, Peoria | .930 | 27 | 16 | 37 | 4 | 1 |
| M. Cook, Quad Cities | 1.000 | 2 | 1 | 1 | 0 | 1 | Madrid, Peoria | .966 | 19 | 4 | 24 | 1 | 0 |
| Correa, Appleton | 1.000 | 18 | 6 | 20 | 0 | 1 | Malave, Wausau | 1.000 | 5 | 4 | 2 | 0 | 0 |
| Costello, Springfield | .948 | 28 | 21 | 34 | 3 | 0 | Malec, Kenosha° | 1.000 | 12 | 1 | 5 | 0 | 2 |
| Criswell, Madison° | .972 | 26 | 7 | 28 | 1 | 3 | Martinez, Quad Cities | .909 | 18 | 8 | 12 | 2 | 4 |
| Cullers, Burlington | 1.000 | 2 | 0 | 1 | 0 | 0 | McDonald, Madison | .938 | 3 | 2 | 13 | 1 | 2 |
| Dacus, Quad Cities | 1.000 | 51 | 6 | 16 | 0 | 1 | McGrath, Springfield | .892 | 25 | 9 | 24 | 4 | 1 |
| Danek, Peoria | 1.000 | 16 | 0 | 1 | 0 | 0 | Meister, Wausau | 1.000 | 13 | 0 | 2 | 0 | 0 |
| C. Daniel, Cedar Rapids° | 1.000 | 25 | 9 | 21 | 0 | 0 | Mendek, Wausau° | .944 | 49 | 4 | 13 | 1 | 2 |
| S. Daniel, Burlington | .800 | 19 | 4 | 4 | 2 | 0 | Menendez, Appleton | .944 | 24 | 7 | 27 | 2 | 1 |
| Davidson, Peoria | .879 | 25 | 9 | 20 | 4 | 2 | Messier, Clinton° | .935 | 22 | 7 | 22 | 2 | 1 |
| B. Davis, Wausau° | 1.000 | 14 | 0 | 7 | 0 | 0 | Minyard, Waterloo | .667 | 9 | 0 | 2 | 1 | 1 |
| M. Davis, Kenosha | 1.000 | 8 | 0 | 5 | 0 | 1 | Montano, Beloit° | .939 | 42 | 9 | 22 | 2 | 2 |
| Dial, Beloit | .970 | 22 | 12 | 20 | 1 | 2 | Moriarty, Clinton° | 1.000 | 20 | 4 | 5 | 0 | 0 |
| Diaz, Beloit | 1.000 | 59 | 3 | 17 | 0 | 1 | Morris, Beloit° | 1.000 | 1 | 0 | 1 | 0 | 0 |
| Dibble, Cedar Rapids | .867 | 45 | 4 | 9 | 2 | 0 | M. Murphy, Waterloo | 1.000 | 8 | 3 | 15 | 0 | 0 |
| Dodd, Kenosha° | .917 | 31 | 1 | 10 | 1 | 0 | Neufelder, Wausau° | .947 | 27 | 13 | 23 | 2 | 2 |
| Dressler, Clinton | .848 | 38 | 6 | 22 | 5 | 3 | North, Springfield | .939 | 24 | 10 | 36 | 3 | 1 |
| Dunn, Springfield | 1.000 | 55 | 5 | 8 | 0 | 1 | Oizumi, Wausau | 1.000 | 8 | 1 | 2 | 0 | 0 |
| Edwards, Madison | .857 | 22 | 4 | 8 | 2 | 0 | Oliverio, Cedar Rapids | 1.000 | 20 | 6 | 15 | 0 | 1 |
| Eggersten, Quad Cities | .839 | 26 | 16 | 36 | 10 | 4 | Olker, Clinton° | .929 | 15 | 4 | 9 | 1 | 0 |
| Embser, Springfield° | .967 | 23 | 8 | 21 | 1 | 4 | Olsson, Burlington | .944 | 28 | 6 | 11 | 1 | 0 |
| Encarnacion, Waterloo | .929 | 53 | 5 | 8 | 1 | 0 | Oswald, Appleton° | .967 | 11 | 8 | 21 | 1 | 1 |
| Erickson, Clinton° | .882 | 39 | 6 | 9 | 2 | 1 | Pardo, Burlington | .833 | 15 | 3 | 7 | 2 | 0 |
| Evans, Beloit | 1.000 | 1 | 1 | 1 | 0 | 0 | Pavlas, Peoria | 1.000 | 17 | 4 | 16 | 0 | 0 |
| Fassero, Springfield° | .933 | 29 | 7 | 21 | 2 | 2 | Peterek, Beloit | 1.000 | 14 | 0 | 9 | 0 | 1 |
| Fay, Clinton | .800 | 7 | 1 | 3 | 1 | 0 | Phelps, Appleton | 1.000 | 4 | 0 | 1 | 0 | 1 |
| Felt, Kenosha° | 1.000 | 12 | 5 | 10 | 0 | 0 | Pico, Peoria | .962 | 27 | 23 | 53 | 3 | 2 |
| Ferreira, Madison | .838 | 23 | 8 | 23 | 6 | 1 | Piphus, Waterloo | 1.000 | 10 | 1 | 5 | 0 | 1 |
| Fick, Cedar Rapids° | .938 | 31 | 5 | 10 | 1 | 0 | Pleis, Springfield | .500 | 5 | 0 | 1 | 1 | 0 |
| Figueroa, Madison | 1.000 | 6 | 1 | 2 | 0 | 2 | Pobur, Peoria | 1.000 | 28 | 3 | 4 | 0 | 0 |
| Filippi, Appleton | .962 | 16 | 5 | 20 | 1 | 0 | Porter, Beloit | 1.000 | 3 | 0 | 3 | 0 | 0 |
| Fitzpatrick, Beloit | 1.000 | 6 | 2 | 4 | 0 | 0 | Prickett, Kenosha° | .906 | 28 | 1 | 28 | 3 | 2 |
| Franco, Quad Cities | 1.000 | 13 | 2 | 3 | 0 | 0 | Ratliff, Beloit | 1.000 | 11 | 2 | 9 | 0 | 0 |
| Fraser, Quad Cities | .857 | 13 | 4 | 14 | 3 | 0 | Reed, Appleton | .967 | 29 | 6 | 23 | 1 | 0 |
| Freeland, Beloit | .882 | 12 | 6 | 9 | 2 | 0 | Reid, Peoria | 1.000 | 24 | 6 | 8 | 0 | 1 |
| Frew, Beloit | .857 | 8 | 2 | 4 | 1 | 0 | Reinholtz, Wausau° | .900 | 22 | 2 | 7 | 1 | 0 |
| Galloway, Waterloo° | .913 | 30 | 6 | 15 | 2 | 1 | Renfroe, Peoria | 1.000 | 57 | 6 | 20 | 0 | 2 |
| Garcia, Quad Cities° | .846 | 29 | 0 | 11 | 2 | 1 | Renz, Appleton | .818 | 19 | 4 | 14 | 4 | 2 |
| Gass, Springfield | 1.000 | 8 | 1 | 2 | 0 | 0 | Rice, Peoria° | .962 | 36 | 16 | 34 | 2 | 1 |
| Ghelfi, Waterloo | .964 | 10 | 5 | 22 | 1 | 1 | Robertson, Waterloo | .905 | 15 | 11 | 8 | 2 | 3 |
| Glidewell, Springfield | .889 | 7 | 4 | 4 | 1 | 0 | Rodgers, Clinton | .800 | 6 | 2 | 6 | 2 | 0 |

## PITCHERS—Continued

| Player and Club | Pct. | G. | PO. | A. | E. | DP. | Player and Club | Pct. | G. | PO. | A. | E. | DP. |
|---|---|---|---|---|---|---|---|---|---|---|---|---|---|
| K. Rogers, Burlington* | .906 | 33 | 9 | 20 | 3 | 2 | Soto, Cedar Rapids | .927 | 26 | 14 | 24 | 3 | 1 |
| S. Rogers, Burlington* | 1.000 | 3 | 0 | 1 | 0 | 0 | Spear, Peoria* | .875 | 24 | 3 | 11 | 2 | 0 |
| Romanovsky, Quad Cities* | .900 | 25 | 3 | 24 | 3 | 2 | Spratke, Wausau | .942 | 27 | 15 | 34 | 3 | 3 |
| Rousey, Wausau | .923 | 26 | 7 | 17 | 2 | 1 | Stangel, Clinton | 1.000 | 17 | 2 | 4 | 0 | 1 |
| Ruckebeil, Appleton | .917 | 31 | 7 | 4 | 1 | 1 | Stein, Appleton | .882 | 8 | 3 | 12 | 2 | 0 |
| Ruzek, Wausau | 1.000 | 6 | 6 | 9 | 0 | 2 | Stephenson, Waterloo | 1.000 | 32 | 2 | 8 | 0 | 1 |
| Sabo, Madison* | 1.000 | 34 | 3 | 20 | 0 | 3 | Swepson, Clinton | 1.000 | 3 | 0 | 1 | 0 | 0 |
| Sadler, Beloit | 1.000 | 13 | 1 | 9 | 0 | 1 | Tabeling, Kenosha | .923 | 32 | 8 | 16 | 2 | 4 |
| Scarpetta, Beloit* | .947 | 22 | 4 | 32 | 2 | 6 | Thigpen, Appleton | 1.000 | 1 | 0 | 1 | 0 | 0 |
| Schwarz, Peoria | .870 | 27 | 12 | 8 | 3 | 0 | Tichy, Beloit | .714 | 6 | 0 | 5 | 2 | 1 |
| Sedar, Appleton | .750 | 7 | 1 | 8 | 3 | 0 | Van Houten, Springfield | .947 | 40 | 6 | 12 | 1 | 0 |
| Shamblin, Burlington | .778 | 15 | 2 | 12 | 4 | 3 | Venturino, Quad Cities | .957 | 15 | 5 | 17 | 1 | 0 |
| Sharp, Waterloo | .905 | 34 | 7 | 12 | 2 | 2 | Villa, Clinton | .920 | 28 | 8 | 15 | 2 | 0 |
| Siegel, Wausau | .889 | 6 | 2 | 6 | 1 | 1 | Whaley, Madison | .917 | 10 | 4 | 7 | 1 | 0 |
| Silver, Clinton | .960 | 29 | 15 | 33 | 2 | 5 | Whitaker, Burlington | 1.000 | 45 | 7 | 23 | 0 | 1 |
| Simmons, Beloit | .857 | 11 | 1 | 5 | 1 | 0 | D. White, Appleton | .880 | 53 | 2 | 20 | 3 | 0 |
| Dan. Smith, Cedar Rapids* | .952 | 42 | 5 | 15 | 1 | 0 | L. White, Wausau | .846 | 51 | 4 | 18 | 4 | 1 |
| Dar. Smith, Waterloo | 1.000 | 1 | 1 | 0 | 0 | 0 | Whitmyer, Waterloo | .833 | 27 | 9 | 16 | 5 | 3 |
| M. Smith, Cedar Rapids | .875 | 8 | 3 | 4 | 1 | 0 | Williams, Peoria | 1.000 | 11 | 0 | 3 | 0 | 0 |
| Soma, Waterloo | 1.000 | 11 | 4 | 7 | 0 | 1 | Wilmet, Springfield | .957 | 41 | 5 | 17 | 1 | 0 |
| Sontag, Wausau | .903 | 28 | 11 | 45 | 6 | 0 | Wilson, Burlington* | .850 | 21 | 3 | 14 | 3 | 0 |

The following players do not have any recorded accepted chances at the positions indicated, therefore, are not listed in the fielding averages for those particular positions: Alfredson, of; Arias, p; Borg, of; Byrd, ss; DeWolf, p; Digioia, p; Dunlap, of; Gobbo, 3b, of; Gonzalez, p; Gould, 2b; Grayston, of; Horrell, p; Jagnow, ss; R. Jones, p; Kindred, of; Machalec, 1b; McCulla, p; Mitchell, of, p; K. Murphy, p; Peraza, 3b; Pettibone, p; Ray, of; Reimer, of; B. Robinson, of; Rogers, of; Rolland, 2b; Senne, of; R. Smith, p; Stanley, of; Tarnow, 3b, p; Toler, 3b; Torve, 2b; Villanueva, p; M. Walker, c; C. Wilson, of; Worden, of.

## CLUB PITCHING

| Club | ERA. | G. | CG. | ShO. | Sv. | IP. | H. | R. | ER. | HR. | HB. | BB. | Int. BB. | SO. | WP. | Bk. |
|---|---|---|---|---|---|---|---|---|---|---|---|---|---|---|---|---|
| Beloit | 3.22 | 136 | 23 | 16 | 31 | 1173.1 | 1108 | 536 | 420 | 63 | 35 | 448 | 13 | 980 | 73 | 6 |
| Clinton | 3.27 | 140 | 22 | 14 | 32 | 1212.1 | 1029 | 541 | 440 | 74 | 49 | 610 | 7 | 908 | 86 | 19 |
| Cedar Rapids | 3.32 | 139 | 27 | 13 | 32 | 1185.2 | 1053 | 551 | 438 | 93 | 23 | 457 | 14 | 954 | 71 | 6 |
| Peoria | 3.36 | 140 | 29 | 9 | 25 | 1219.1 | 1105 | 571 | 455 | 59 | 43 | 514 | 6 | 908 | 70 | 8 |
| Appleton | 3.42 | 139 | 25 | 10 | 27 | 1228.0 | 1122 | 614 | 467 | 70 | 33 | 485 | 13 | 908 | 83 | 6 |
| Madison | 3.61 | 138 | 26 | 11 | 26 | 1225.1 | 1204 | 597 | 492 | 61 | 39 | 449 | 10 | 814 | 61 | 15 |
| Kenosha | 3.79 | 139 | 32 | 16 | 26 | 1227.0 | 1159 | 631 | 517 | 83 | 37 | 544 | 15 | 883 | 64 | 3 |
| Quad Cities | 3.91 | 140 | 28 | 9 | 30 | 1207.1 | 1206 | 673 | 525 | 75 | 58 | 567 | 11 | 938 | 87 | 27 |
| Springfield | 3.98 | 140 | 18 | 5 | 27 | 1235.0 | 1192 | 686 | 546 | 88 | 40 | 598 | 25 | 979 | 73 | 11 |
| Wausau | 3.98 | 137 | 19 | 4 | 23 | 1170.1 | 1115 | 644 | 518 | 86 | 39 | 548 | 36 | 856 | 75 | 6 |
| Waterloo | 4.28 | 140 | 17 | 12 | 31 | 1201.2 | 1179 | 685 | 572 | 99 | 58 | 540 | 12 | 863 | 88 | 7 |
| Burlington | 4.59 | 138 | 17 | 6 | 23 | 1185.1 | 1132 | 756 | 604 | 90 | 57 | 692 | 37 | 894 | 99 | 22 |

## PITCHERS' RECORDS
### (Leading Qualifiers for Earned-Run Average Leadership — 112 or More Innings)

*Throws lefthanded.

| Pitcher—Club | W. | L. | Pct. | ERA. | G. | GS. | CG. | GF. | ShO. | Sv. | IP. | H. | R. | ER. | HR. | HB. | BB. | Int. BB. | SO. | WP. |
|---|---|---|---|---|---|---|---|---|---|---|---|---|---|---|---|---|---|---|---|---|
| Silver, Clinton | 17 | 9 | .654 | 2.24 | 29 | 29 | 9 | 0 | 4 | 0 | 205.0 | 169 | 68 | 51 | 8 | 5 | 87 | 0 | 133 | 8 |
| Scarpetta, Beloit* | 13 | 3 | .813 | 2.27 | 22 | 20 | 8 | 2 | 4 | 0 | 150.2 | 126 | 41 | 38 | 6 | 2 | 34 | 1 | 139 | 2 |
| Sontag, Kenosha | 15 | 11 | .577 | 2.33 | 28 | 28 | 15 | 0 | 6 | 0 | 220.1 | 171 | 65 | 57 | 7 | 13 | 59 | 2 | 213 | 8 |
| Correa, Appleton | 13 | 3 | .813 | 2.53 | 18 | 18 | 6 | 0 | 2 | 0 | 139.0 | 93 | 45 | 39 | 13 | 2 | 56 | 0 | 128 | 8 |
| C. Daniel, Cedar Rapids* | 13 | 8 | .619 | 2.58 | 25 | 25 | 7 | 0 | 3 | 0 | 178.0 | 138 | 62 | 51 | 12 | 2 | 50 | 0 | 142 | 8 |
| Kanwisher, Beloit | 13 | 4 | .765 | 2.66 | 25 | 24 | 2 | 0 | 0 | 0 | 165.2 | 123 | 67 | 49 | 7 | 6 | 89 | 0 | 158 | 13 |
| Menendez, Appleton | 13 | 4 | .765 | 2.74 | 24 | 24 | 2 | 0 | 0 | 0 | 148.0 | 134 | 67 | 45 | 8 | 4 | 55 | 0 | 100 | 11 |
| Boyles, Cedar Rapids | 15 | 5 | .750 | 2.85 | 27 | 27 | 4 | 0 | 1 | 0 | 164.1 | 133 | 66 | 52 | 12 | 1 | 67 | 0 | 155 | 7 |
| Madrid, Beloit | 8 | 5 | .615 | 2.85 | 19 | 18 | 7 | 0 | 1 | 0 | 135.2 | 144 | 55 | 43 | 7 | 1 | 26 | 0 | 99 | 4 |
| Oliverio, Cedar Rapids | 13 | 4 | .765 | 2.86 | 20 | 18 | 5 | 2 | 1 | 0 | 125.2 | 105 | 51 | 40 | 10 | 2 | 30 | 0 | 132 | 6 |
| Pico, Peoria | 11 | 10 | .524 | 3.06 | 27 | 27 | 8 | 0 | 1 | 0 | 179.1 | 186 | 76 | 61 | 5 | 7 | 56 | 0 | 109 | 7 |

Departmental Leaders: G—Diaz, 59; W—Silver, 17; L—Butler, 14; Pct.—Correa, Scarpetta, .813; GS—Silver, 29; CG—Sontag, 15; GF—Diaz, Encarnacion, 49; ShO—Sontag, 6; Sv.—Encarnacion, 23; IP—Sontag, 220.1; H—Butler, 190; R—Butler, 118; ER—Costello, 87; HR—Brinkman, 19; HB—Hamstra, 15; BB—Eggersten, 94; IBB—L. White, 10; SO—Sontag, 213; WP—Harden, 18.

### (All Pitchers—Listed Alphabetically)

| Pitcher—Club | W. | L. | Pct. | ERA. | G. | GS. | CG. | GF. | ShO. | Sv. | IP. | H. | R. | ER. | HR. | HB. | BB. | Int. BB. | SO. | WP. |
|---|---|---|---|---|---|---|---|---|---|---|---|---|---|---|---|---|---|---|---|---|
| Ackerman, Clinton | 4 | 2 | .667 | 2.98 | 45 | 1 | 0 | 32 | 0 | 9 | 87.2 | 80 | 37 | 29 | 8 | 6 | 34 | 3 | 42 | 3 |
| M. Adams, Kenosha | 1 | 0 | 1.000 | 1.46 | 2 | 1 | 0 | 1 | 0 | 0 | 12.1 | 9 | 4 | 2 | 0 | 0 | 3 | 1 | 9 | 0 |
| T. Adams, Burlington | 2 | 1 | .667 | 2.45 | 14 | 4 | 1 | 2 | 0 | 2 | 40.1 | 27 | 13 | 11 | 0 | 1 | 19 | 0 | 23 | 2 |
| Adkins, Beloit | 0 | 1 | .000 | 11.12 | 4 | 0 | 0 | 1 | 0 | 0 | 5.2 | 12 | 9 | 7 | 2 | 0 | 5 | 0 | 4 | 2 |
| Akins, Burlington | 4 | 8 | .333 | 4.07 | 27 | 12 | 2 | 6 | 1 | 0 | 97.1 | 88 | 60 | 44 | 9 | 3 | 48 | 7 | 70 | 7 |
| Alicea, Beloit | 1 | 3 | .250 | 5.32 | 11 | 0 | 0 | 9 | 0 | 1 | 22.0 | 35 | 21 | 13 | 1 | 1 | 7 | 1 | 15 | 2 |
| Allison, Burlington | 0 | 3 | .000 | 6.43 | 14 | 2 | 0 | 0 | 0 | 0 | 35.0 | 37 | 28 | 25 | 6 | 2 | 38 | 0 | 33 | 5 |
| Anderson, Appleton | 6 | 4 | .600 | 2.56 | 37 | 1 | 0 | 17 | 0 | 9 | 84.1 | 85 | 33 | 24 | 0 | 5 | 25 | 4 | 59 | 4 |
| Andrus, Kenosha | 0 | 0 | .000 | 6.83 | 13 | 0 | 0 | 5 | 0 | 0 | 27.2 | 35 | 23 | 21 | 1 | 3 | 29 | 0 | 25 | 4 |
| Applegate, Madison | 4 | 1 | .800 | 3.59 | 38 | 0 | 0 | 24 | 0 | 4 | 82.2 | 76 | 35 | 33 | 4 | 5 | 19 | 2 | 50 | 2 |
| Arias, Madison | 0 | 0 | .000 | 0.00 | 1 | 0 | 0 | 1 | 0 | 0 | 1.0 | 0 | 0 | 0 | 0 | 0 | 0 | 0 | 1 | 0 |
| Autry, Appleton | 0 | 0 | .000 | 12.00 | 2 | 0 | 0 | 1 | 0 | 0 | 3.0 | 3 | 4 | 4 | 0 | 0 | 4 | 0 | 2 | 0 |
| Baldrick, Wausau* | 8 | 2 | .800 | 2.24 | 39 | 3 | 0 | 13 | 0 | 1 | 104.2 | 90 | 33 | 26 | 2 | 1 | 41 | 7 | 106 | 3 |
| Banning, Quad Cities | 7 | 3 | .700 | 3.40 | 11 | 11 | 6 | 0 | 0 | 0 | 82.0 | 83 | 41 | 31 | 1 | 7 | 29 | 0 | 58 | 2 |
| Bartolomucci, Appleton* | 1 | 5 | .167 | 4.05 | 10 | 1 | 0 | 7 | 0 | 0 | 26.2 | 23 | 12 | 12 | 2 | 2 | 8 | 1 | 9 | 1 |
| Beasley, Waterloo | 6 | 7 | .462 | 3.30 | 17 | 17 | 6 | 0 | 1 | 0 | 120.0 | 110 | 55 | 44 | 6 | 2 | 47 | 2 | 87 | 7 |
| Belinskas, Cedar Rapids | 0 | 0 | .000 | 3.31 | 11 | 0 | 0 | 6 | 0 | 0 | 16.1 | 15 | 6 | 6 | 1 | 0 | 6 | 0 | 12 | 2 |
| Bell, Peoria* | 1 | 1 | .500 | 4.35 | 9 | 2 | 0 | 2 | 0 | 0 | 20.2 | 24 | 14 | 10 | 1 | 0 | 11 | 0 | 18 | 0 |
| Belleman, Waterloo | 6 | 4 | .600 | 1.65 | 10 | 10 | 2 | 0 | 1 | 0 | 71.0 | 45 | 19 | 13 | 1 | 2 | 14 | 0 | 54 | 2 |
| Boyles, Cedar Rapids | 15 | 5 | .750 | 2.85 | 27 | 27 | 4 | 0 | 1 | 0 | 164.1 | 133 | 66 | 52 | 12 | 1 | 67 | 0 | 155 | 7 |
| Brake, Madison* | 4 | 4 | .500 | 3.81 | 19 | 19 | 2 | 0 | 0 | 0 | 80.1 | 104 | 41 | 34 | 6 | 1 | 31 | 0 | 47 | 1 |
| Bridges, Burlington* | 1 | 4 | .200 | 6.58 | 19 | 3 | 0 | 4 | 0 | 0 | 39.2 | 54 | 37 | 29 | 3 | 0 | 19 | 1 | 32 | 2 |

| Pitcher—Club | W. | L. | Pct. | ERA. | G. | GS. | CG. | GF. | ShO. | Sv. | IP. | H. | R. | ER. | HR. | HB. | BB. | Int. BB. | SO. | WP. |
|---|---|---|---|---|---|---|---|---|---|---|---|---|---|---|---|---|---|---|---|---|
| Brinkman, Wausau | 7 | 11 | .389 | 3.79 | 27 | 27 | 6 | 0 | 0 | 0 | 159.0 | 160 | 93 | 67 | 19 | 6 | 50 | 1 | 94 | 9 |
| Burden, Wausau | 0 | 0 | .000 | 3.09 | 6 | 0 | 0 | 2 | 0 | 2 | 11.2 | 7 | 5 | 4 | 2 | 1 | 6 | 1 | 6 | 0 |
| Burns, Madison | 8 | 8 | .500 | 3.66 | 20 | 19 | 5 | 0 | 3 | 0 | 123.0 | 109 | 55 | 50 | 8 | 3 | 40 | 0 | 94 | 12 |
| Butler, Quad Cities° | 8 | 14 | .364 | 4.77 | 27 | 27 | 4 | 0 | 1 | 0 | 162.1 | 190 | 118 | 86 | 11 | 5 | 71 | 1 | 95 | 6 |
| Cardwood, Kenosha | 6 | 5 | .545 | 3.70 | 17 | 16 | 4 | 0 | 2 | 0 | 114.1 | 87 | 55 | 47 | 10 | 2 | 65 | 0 | 79 | 6 |
| Carr, Appleton | 0 | 0 | .000 | 4.63 | 14 | 0 | 0 | 10 | 0 | 0 | 23.1 | 16 | 15 | 12 | 1 | 2 | 27 | 0 | 23 | 2 |
| Cedeno, Quad Cities | 2 | 1 | .667 | 1.80 | 8 | 0 | 0 | 6 | 0 | 1 | 15.0 | 10 | 6 | 3 | 0 | 2 | 16 | 1 | 20 | 3 |
| Cieslak, Cedar Rapids° | 1 | 0 | 1.000 | 1.48 | 9 | 4 | 0 | 3 | 0 | 0 | 30.1 | 12 | 7 | 5 | 3 | 0 | 23 | 0 | 21 | 3 |
| Clark, Waterloo° | 1 | 0 | 1.000 | 7.45 | 14 | 0 | 0 | 6 | 0 | 0 | 29.0 | 30 | 24 | 24 | 6 | 5 | 22 | 0 | 14 | 7 |
| Cloninger, Kenosha | 6 | 9 | .400 | 5.84 | 30 | 15 | 1 | 5 | 0 | 0 | 114.0 | 130 | 85 | 74 | 12 | 6 | 56 | 1 | 47 | 10 |
| Coffey, Cedar Rapids | 3 | 5 | .375 | 5.84 | 9 | 9 | 0 | 0 | 0 | 0 | 44.2 | 49 | 33 | 29 | 4 | 1 | 14 | 1 | 29 | 9 |
| Conley, Cedar Rapids° | 2 | 3 | .400 | 3.55 | 33 | 4 | 0 | 15 | 0 | 5 | 71.0 | 70 | 35 | 28 | 2 | 1 | 20 | 0 | 66 | 2 |
| D. Cook, Clinton° | 5 | 4 | .556 | 3.36 | 13 | 13 | 1 | 0 | 0 | 0 | 83.0 | 73 | 35 | 31 | 7 | 2 | 27 | 0 | 40 | 5 |
| L. Cook, Quad Cities° | 6 | 5 | .545 | 4.30 | 37 | 3 | 0 | 22 | 0 | 2 | 88.0 | 85 | 52 | 42 | 4 | 5 | 69 | 0 | 89 | 17 |
| M. Cook, Quad Cities | 0 | 0 | .000 | 1.80 | 2 | 2 | 0 | 0 | 0 | 0 | 10.0 | 6 | 3 | 2 | 0 | 1 | 7 | 0 | 10 | 1 |
| Correa, Appleton | 13 | 3 | .813 | 2.53 | 18 | 18 | 6 | 0 | 2 | 0 | 139.0 | 93 | 45 | 39 | 13 | 2 | 56 | 0 | 128 | 8 |
| Costello, Springfield | 8 | 13 | .381 | 4.16 | 28 | 28 | 7 | 0 | 0 | 0 | 188.0 | 188 | 105 | 87 | 17 | 4 | 60 | 1 | 127 | 9 |
| Criswell, Burlington° | 8 | 11 | .421 | 3.66 | 26 | 26 | 2 | 0 | 0 | 0 | 169.2 | 143 | 93 | 69 | 13 | 5 | 86 | 0 | 108 | 8 |
| Cullers, Burlington | 0 | 0 | .000 | 12.00 | 2 | 0 | 0 | 2 | 0 | 0 | 3.0 | 4 | 4 | 4 | 1 | 1 | 3 | 0 | 0 | 0 |
| Dacus, Quad Cities | 2 | 6 | .250 | 3.41 | 51 | 0 | 0 | 44 | 0 | 22 | 71.1 | 64 | 32 | 27 | 2 | 3 | 32 | 4 | 61 | 4 |
| Danek, Peoria | 2 | 1 | .667 | 3.92 | 16 | 0 | 0 | 8 | 0 | 1 | 20.2 | 23 | 13 | 9 | 2 | 0 | 9 | 0 | 13 | 5 |
| C. Daniel, Cedar Rapids° | 13 | 8 | .619 | 2.58 | 25 | 25 | 7 | 0 | 3 | 0 | 178.0 | 138 | 62 | 51 | 12 | 2 | 50 | 0 | 142 | 8 |
| S. Daniel, Burlington | 0 | 3 | .000 | 6.51 | 19 | 3 | 0 | 4 | 0 | 0 | 37.1 | 39 | 32 | 27 | 3 | 2 | 29 | 2 | 22 | 4 |
| Davidson, Peoria | 10 | 6 | .625 | 3.35 | 25 | 25 | 3 | 0 | 1 | 0 | 166.1 | 153 | 88 | 62 | 10 | 5 | 76 | 0 | 152 | 11 |
| B. Davis, Wausau° | 3 | 6 | .333 | 5.14 | 14 | 10 | 1 | 2 | 0 | 0 | 56.0 | 63 | 37 | 32 | 4 | 1 | 42 | 3 | 47 | 6 |
| M. Davis, Kenosha° | 0 | 2 | .000 | 5.61 | 8 | 4 | 0 | 3 | 0 | 1 | 25.2 | 27 | 17 | 16 | 2 | 0 | 17 | 0 | 20 | 2 |
| DeWolf, Beloit° | 0 | 1 | .000 | 4.50 | 1 | 1 | 1 | 0 | 0 | 0 | 8.0 | 8 | 4 | 4 | 1 | 0 | 2 | 0 | 3 | 1 |
| Dial, Burlington | 7 | 11 | .389 | 3.50 | 22 | 22 | 4 | 0 | 0 | 0 | 133.2 | 114 | 68 | 52 | 11 | 6 | 63 | 1 | 93 | 4 |
| Diaz, Beloit | 9 | 6 | .600 | 1.87 | 59 | 0 | 0 | 49 | 0 | 18 | 86.2 | 58 | 19 | 18 | 5 | 2 | 28 | 3 | 112 | 6 |
| Dibble, Cedar Rapids | 5 | 5 | .500 | 3.84 | 45 | 1 | 0 | 30 | 0 | 12 | 65.2 | 67 | 37 | 28 | 3 | 1 | 28 | 2 | 73 | 6 |
| Digioia, Springfield | 0 | 0 | .000 | 3.86 | 2 | 0 | 0 | 2 | 0 | 0 | 2.1 | 0 | 1 | 1 | 0 | 0 | 4 | 0 | 3 | 3 |
| Dodd, Kenosha° | 8 | 2 | .800 | 3.74 | 31 | 4 | 2 | 18 | 2 | 2 | 89.0 | 92 | 44 | 37 | 6 | 0 | 33 | 3 | 80 | 2 |
| Dressler, Clinton | 3 | 11 | .214 | 4.77 | 38 | 15 | 1 | 15 | 0 | 2 | 115.0 | 128 | 80 | 61 | 8 | 2 | 51 | 2 | 73 | 7 |
| Dunn, Springfield | 4 | 9 | .308 | 2.48 | 55 | 0 | 0 | 48 | 0 | 20 | 80.0 | 56 | 29 | 22 | 4 | 0 | 62 | 3 | 115 | 2 |
| Edwards, Madison | 1 | 4 | .200 | 5.31 | 22 | 7 | 1 | 8 | 0 | 1 | 78.0 | 93 | 55 | 46 | 3 | 4 | 37 | 0 | 48 | 3 |
| Eggersten, Quad Cities | 6 | 12 | .333 | 3.62 | 26 | 26 | 7 | 0 | 0 | 0 | 174.0 | 165 | 110 | 70 | 16 | 12 | 94 | 1 | 112 | 11 |
| Ember, Springfield° | 12 | 9 | .571 | 3.97 | 23 | 23 | 1 | 0 | 0 | 0 | 142.2 | 113 | 71 | 63 | 6 | 1 | 83 | 0 | 158 | 10 |
| Encarnacion, Waterloo | 8 | 5 | .615 | 2.64 | 53 | 0 | 0 | 49 | 0 | 24 | 92.0 | 63 | 31 | 27 | 8 | 3 | 36 | 3 | 108 | 3 |
| Erickson, Clinton° | 3 | 3 | .500 | 3.81 | 39 | 1 | 0 | 29 | 0 | 10 | 56.2 | 43 | 29 | 24 | 1 | 4 | 58 | 2 | 48 | 6 |
| Evans, Beloit | 0 | 1 | .000 | 3.60 | 1 | 1 | 0 | 0 | 0 | 0 | 5.0 | 3 | 2 | 2 | 0 | 1 | 5 | 0 | 6 | 1 |
| Fassero, Springfield° | 4 | 8 | .333 | 4.01 | 29 | 15 | 1 | 2 | 0 | 1 | 119.0 | 125 | 78 | 53 | 11 | 3 | 45 | 3 | 65 | 4 |
| Fay, Burlington | 0 | 3 | .000 | 9.42 | 7 | 3 | 0 | 2 | 0 | 0 | 14.1 | 22 | 17 | 15 | 2 | 2 | 12 | 0 | 7 | 1 |
| Felt, Kenosha | 2 | 2 | .500 | 6.11 | 12 | 4 | 0 | 4 | 0 | 1 | 35.1 | 35 | 33 | 24 | 1 | 3 | 26 | 0 | 41 | 3 |
| Ferreira, Springfield | 7 | 12 | .368 | 4.43 | 23 | 22 | 3 | 1 | 0 | 0 | 128.0 | 142 | 75 | 63 | 5 | 1 | 54 | 0 | 67 | 10 |
| Fick, Cedar Rapids° | 5 | 1 | .833 | 3.59 | 31 | 1 | 0 | 9 | 0 | 3 | 57.2 | 68 | 30 | 23 | 5 | 2 | 19 | 1 | 37 | 4 |
| Figueroa, Madison | 1 | 1 | .500 | 4.15 | 6 | 1 | 0 | 4 | 0 | 0 | 17.1 | 19 | 10 | 8 | 1 | 1 | 10 | 0 | 11 | 1 |
| Filippi, Appleton | 1 | 7 | .125 | 6.69 | 16 | 13 | 1 | 3 | 0 | 0 | 79.1 | 78 | 70 | 59 | 11 | 4 | 59 | 0 | 52 | 5 |
| Fitzpatrick, Beloit | 0 | 0 | .000 | 10.93 | 6 | 0 | 0 | 1 | 0 | 0 | 14.0 | 21 | 17 | 17 | 2 | 1 | 7 | 0 | 6 | 3 |
| Franco, Quad Cities | 0 | 0 | .000 | 3.60 | 13 | 0 | 0 | 7 | 0 | 1 | 25.0 | 27 | 11 | 10 | 1 | 1 | 7 | 0 | 8 | 0 |
| Fraser, Quad Cities | 2 | 6 | .250 | 5.40 | 13 | 13 | 1 | 0 | 0 | 0 | 81.2 | 95 | 53 | 49 | 8 | 8 | 32 | 0 | 72 | 12 |
| Freeland, Beloit | 1 | 6 | .143 | 6.47 | 12 | 12 | 1 | 0 | 0 | 0 | 64.0 | 78 | 53 | 46 | 4 | 2 | 33 | 2 | 37 | 11 |
| Frew, Beloit | 2 | 1 | .667 | 2.54 | 8 | 4 | 0 | 2 | 0 | 1 | 28.1 | 21 | 10 | 8 | 0 | 1 | 17 | 0 | 27 | 4 |
| Galloway, Waterloo° | 4 | 2 | .667 | 3.93 | 30 | 7 | 0 | 7 | 0 | 1 | 75.2 | 81 | 44 | 33 | 4 | 3 | 39 | 1 | 53 | 8 |
| Garcia, Quad Cities° | 3 | 2 | .600 | 2.89 | 29 | 1 | 0 | 10 | 0 | 0 | 65.1 | 60 | 25 | 21 | 6 | 4 | 21 | 2 | 50 | 4 |
| Gass, Springfield | 1 | 1 | .500 | 2.70 | 8 | 0 | 0 | 4 | 0 | 0 | 16.2 | 12 | 15 | 5 | 1 | 2 | 4 | 0 | 10 | 0 |
| Ghelfi, Waterloo | 4 | 5 | .444 | 3.03 | 10 | 10 | 3 | 0 | 1 | 0 | 74.1 | 69 | 26 | 25 | 5 | 3 | 16 | 1 | 31 | 0 |
| Glidewell, Springfield | 0 | 2 | .000 | 2.97 | 7 | 7 | 0 | 0 | 0 | 0 | 30.1 | 36 | 19 | 10 | 0 | 1 | 22 | 0 | 20 | 4 |
| Goedde, Cedar Rapids | 2 | 4 | .333 | 4.80 | 28 | 2 | 0 | 11 | 0 | 0 | 54.1 | 46 | 38 | 29 | 7 | 2 | 47 | 2 | 33 | 5 |
| Gomez, Kenosha | 8 | 6 | .571 | 1.96 | 52 | 0 | 0 | 48 | 0 | 18 | 87.1 | 76 | 25 | 19 | 0 | 1 | 18 | 4 | 57 | 0 |
| Gonzalez, Clinton | 0 | 0 | .000 | 0.00 | 1 | 0 | 0 | 1 | 0 | 0 | 2.1 | 1 | 0 | 0 | 0 | 0 | 2 | 0 | 2 | 0 |
| Greer, Waterloo | 7 | 8 | .467 | 3.69 | 29 | 8 | 0 | 4 | 0 | 0 | 95.0 | 83 | 47 | 39 | 4 | 12 | 42 | 2 | 75 | 6 |
| Hamstra, Clinton | 6 | 13 | .316 | 3.88 | 33 | 21 | 2 | 4 | 1 | 0 | 141.2 | 125 | 81 | 61 | 12 | 15 | 74 | 0 | 93 | 11 |
| Hansen, Madison | 4 | 7 | .364 | 2.62 | 41 | 0 | 0 | 29 | 0 | 8 | 79.0 | 73 | 33 | 23 | 1 | 2 | 32 | 5 | 63 | 10 |
| Harden, Burlington | 5 | 10 | .333 | 5.08 | 31 | 21 | 1 | 2 | 0 | 0 | 118.2 | 127 | 81 | 67 | 9 | 4 | 79 | 1 | 63 | 18 |
| Hartley, Springfield | 2 | 7 | .222 | 5.12 | 33 | 12 | 0 | 10 | 0 | 0 | 114.1 | 119 | 77 | 65 | 9 | 8 | 62 | 2 | 100 | 9 |
| Harvey, Quad Cities | 5 | 6 | .455 | 3.53 | 30 | 7 | 0 | 17 | 0 | 4 | 81.2 | 66 | 37 | 32 | 5 | 2 | 37 | 0 | 111 | 4 |
| Hernandez, Burlington | 3 | 1 | .750 | 4.82 | 28 | 0 | 0 | 24 | 0 | 6 | 28.0 | 28 | 21 | 15 | 2 | 6 | 18 | 2 | 28 | 1 |
| Hibberd, Burlington | 0 | 0 | .000 | 12.75 | 8 | 0 | 0 | 2 | 0 | 0 | 12.0 | 23 | 27 | 17 | 4 | 2 | 17 | 0 | 9 | 6 |
| Higgs, Wausau | 1 | 1 | .500 | 1.93 | 17 | 0 | 0 | 12 | 0 | 2 | 23.1 | 19 | 5 | 5 | 0 | 0 | 8 | 0 | 19 | 1 |
| Hinnrichs, Clinton | 8 | 7 | .533 | 3.26 | 31 | 8 | 3 | 10 | 0 | 3 | 94.0 | 87 | 38 | 34 | 8 | 1 | 35 | 0 | 56 | 6 |
| Horrell, Quad Cities | 0 | 1 | .000 | 27.00 | 2 | 0 | 0 | 0 | 0 | 0 | 2.2 | 8 | 8 | 8 | 1 | 0 | 6 | 1 | 3 | 0 |
| Iasparro, Kenosha | 9 | 7 | .563 | 3.18 | 31 | 14 | 4 | 12 | 0 | 2 | 136.0 | 123 | 60 | 48 | 12 | 8 | 53 | 0 | 96 | 7 |
| Jefts, Appleton | 6 | 6 | .500 | 4.01 | 16 | 13 | 1 | 3 | 0 | 0 | 83.0 | 105 | 60 | 37 | 3 | 3 | 27 | 0 | 61 | 11 |
| John, Madison | 0 | 0 | .000 | 3.00 | 1 | 1 | 0 | 0 | 0 | 0 | 6.0 | 4 | 2 | 2 | 0 | 0 | 3 | 0 | 3 | 0 |
| Johnson, Burlington | 2 | 2 | .500 | 3.94 | 10 | 3 | 0 | 3 | 0 | 0 | 32.0 | 34 | 21 | 14 | 0 | 0 | 15 | 1 | 21 | 5 |
| C. Jones, Wausau | 4 | 11 | .267 | 3.91 | 20 | 19 | 1 | 0 | 0 | 0 | 106.0 | 96 | 59 | 46 | 10 | 5 | 65 | 1 | 71 | 9 |
| R. Jones, Burlington | 0 | 1 | .000 | 13.09 | 5 | 3 | 0 | 1 | 0 | 0 | 11.0 | 28 | 23 | 16 | 2 | 0 | 13 | 1 | 8 | 1 |
| T. Jones, Quad Cities° | 0 | 0 | .000 | 0.00 | 1 | 0 | 0 | 1 | 0 | 0 | 2.0 | 1 | 0 | 0 | 0 | 0 | 2 | 0 | 0 | 0 |
| Kampsen, Cedar Rapids | 3 | 5 | .375 | 4.10 | 29 | 13 | 1 | 4 | 0 | 0 | 105.1 | 104 | 57 | 48 | 13 | 1 | 41 | 0 | 54 | 5 |
| Kanwisher, Beloit | 13 | 4 | .765 | 2.66 | 25 | 24 | 2 | 0 | 0 | 0 | 165.2 | 123 | 67 | 49 | 7 | 6 | 89 | 0 | 158 | 13 |
| Karpuk, Waterloo | 2 | 6 | .250 | 7.83 | 12 | 11 | 1 | 0 | 0 | 0 | 56.1 | 70 | 53 | 49 | 10 | 5 | 20 | 0 | 28 | 2 |
| Kavanaugh, Springfield | 0 | 0 | .000 | 1.32 | 9 | 0 | 0 | 5 | 0 | 0 | 13.2 | 13 | 7 | 2 | 0 | 0 | 11 | 1 | 5 | 1 |
| Keathley, Burlington | 1 | 1 | .500 | 1.69 | 2 | 2 | 0 | 0 | 0 | 0 | 10.2 | 7 | 4 | 2 | 0 | 1 | 6 | 0 | 4 | 0 |
| Kibler, Madison | 9 | 10 | .474 | 3.44 | 26 | 26 | 7 | 0 | 2 | 0 | 188.1 | 180 | 88 | 72 | 8 | 10 | 51 | 2 | 131 | 7 |
| Kindred, Kenosha | 0 | 5 | .000 | 5.88 | 9 | 9 | 1 | 0 | 0 | 0 | 49.0 | 59 | 36 | 32 | 5 | 0 | 26 | 0 | 38 | 2 |
| Kinzer, Springfield | 5 | 4 | .556 | 3.70 | 11 | 9 | 1 | 0 | 1 | 0 | 58.1 | 56 | 26 | 24 | 8 | 2 | 21 | 0 | 36 | 3 |
| Kleean, Beloit° | 3 | 1 | .750 | 2.92 | 14 | 3 | 0 | 2 | 0 | 0 | 52.1 | 44 | 22 | 17 | 4 | 4 | 15 | 0 | 40 | 2 |
| Lahrman, Appleton | 3 | 0 | 1.000 | 2.35 | 14 | 1 | 0 | 7 | 0 | 0 | 30.2 | 24 | 11 | 8 | 0 | 0 | 12 | 0 | 24 | 1 |
| Lankard, Burlington | 2 | 1 | .667 | 0.56 | 3 | 2 | 1 | 1 | 0 | 0 | 16.0 | 8 | 1 | 1 | 0 | 1 | 4 | 0 | 8 | 0 |
| Larsen, Burlington | 2 | 5 | .286 | 4.69 | 19 | 6 | 0 | 5 | 0 | 0 | 55.2 | 47 | 35 | 29 | 3 | 4 | 38 | 1 | 47 | 8 |
| Leonette, Madison | 4 | 3 | .571 | 2.11 | 42 | 0 | 0 | 31 | 0 | 10 | 72.2 | 61 | 21 | 17 | 1 | 0 | 19 | 1 | 51 | 2 |
| Link, Waterloo | 6 | 4 | .600 | 3.70 | 16 | 9 | 3 | 2 | 2 | 0 | 73.0 | 68 | 35 | 30 | 3 | 1 | 19 | 0 | 53 | 2 |

| Pitcher—Club | W. | L. | Pct. | ERA. | G. | GS. | CG. | GF. | ShO. | Sv. | IP. | H. | R. | ER. | HR. | HB. | BB. | Int. BB. | SO. | WP. |
|---|---|---|---|---|---|---|---|---|---|---|---|---|---|---|---|---|---|---|---|---|
| Livchak, Springfield° | 0 | 0 | .000 | 9.75 | 5 | 0 | 0 | 1 | 0 | 0 | 12.0 | 11 | 14 | 13 | 0 | 0 | 19 | 2 | 16 | 2 |
| Ludy, Beloit | 3 | 8 | .273 | 3.28 | 29 | 7 | 0 | 15 | 0 | 1 | 82.1 | 95 | 46 | 30 | 3 | 4 | 20 | 2 | 46 | 5 |
| Maddux, Peoria | 13 | 9 | .591 | 3.19 | 27 | 27 | 6 | 0 | 0 | 0 | 186.0 | 176 | 86 | 66 | 9 | 6 | 52 | 0 | 125 | 5 |
| Madrid, Beloit | 8 | 5 | .615 | 2.85 | 19 | 18 | 7 | 0 | 1 | 0 | 135.2 | 144 | 55 | 43 | 7 | 1 | 26 | 0 | 99 | 4 |
| Malave, Wausau | 0 | 1 | .000 | 3.38 | 5 | 1 | 0 | 0 | 0 | 0 | 13.1 | 10 | 7 | 5 | 2 | 2 | 6 | 0 | 7 | 1 |
| Malec, Kenosha° | 2 | 0 | 1.000 | 2.41 | 12 | 1 | 0 | 5 | 0 | 0 | 33.2 | 24 | 11 | 9 | 2 | 0 | 21 | 1 | 19 | 1 |
| Martinez, Quad Cities | 5 | 7 | .417 | 5.02 | 18 | 18 | 2 | 0 | 0 | 0 | 100.1 | 101 | 67 | 56 | 6 | 2 | 61 | 0 | 75 | 15 |
| McCulla, Springfield | 0 | 0 | .000 | 54.00 | 1 | 0 | 0 | 0 | 0 | 0 | 1.2 | 6 | 10 | 10 | 2 | 0 | 4 | 0 | 1 | 0 |
| McDonald, Madison | 0 | 2 | .000 | 3.91 | 3 | 3 | 1 | 0 | 0 | 0 | 23.0 | 23 | 10 | 10 | 1 | 1 | 6 | 0 | 10 | 1 |
| McGrath, Springfield | 6 | 7 | .462 | 3.44 | 25 | 21 | 3 | 2 | 0 | 0 | 144.0 | 151 | 70 | 55 | 7 | 7 | 56 | 0 | 83 | 12 |
| Meister, Wausau | 1 | 1 | .500 | 5.87 | 13 | 0 | 0 | 3 | 0 | 0 | 23.0 | 14 | 17 | 15 | 3 | 0 | 12 | 1 | 22 | 0 |
| Mendek, Wausau° | 3 | 7 | .300 | 2.45 | 49 | 0 | 0 | 39 | 0 | 13 | 69.2 | 50 | 22 | 19 | 5 | 2 | 37 | 2 | 92 | 3 |
| Menendez, Appleton | 13 | 4 | .765 | 2.74 | 24 | 24 | 2 | 0 | 0 | 0 | 148.0 | 134 | 67 | 45 | 8 | 4 | 55 | 0 | 100 | 11 |
| Messier, Clinton° | 7 | 8 | .467 | 3.32 | 22 | 22 | 2 | 0 | 0 | 0 | 127.1 | 97 | 55 | 47 | 5 | 3 | 80 | 0 | 136 | 17 |
| Minyard, Waterloo | 0 | 1 | .000 | 5.40 | 9 | 0 | 0 | 1 | 0 | 0 | 13.1 | 12 | 10 | 8 | 1 | 1 | 13 | 0 | 10 | 2 |
| Mitchell, Beloit | 0 | 0 | .000 | 0.00 | 1 | 0 | 0 | 1 | 0 | 0 | 0.1 | 0 | 0 | 0 | 0 | 0 | 0 | 0 | 1 | 0 |
| Montano, Beloit° | 8 | 7 | .533 | 2.74 | 42 | 5 | 1 | 23 | 0 | 5 | 98.2 | 102 | 47 | 30 | 6 | 5 | 38 | 3 | 66 | 7 |
| Moriarty, Clinton° | 1 | 0 | 1.000 | 2.95 | 20 | 0 | 0 | 6 | 0 | 1 | 39.2 | 23 | 13 | 13 | 3 | 0 | 19 | 0 | 35 | 3 |
| Morris, Beloit° | 0 | 0 | .000 | 0.00 | 1 | 0 | 0 | 1 | 0 | 1 | 3.0 | 0 | 0 | 0 | 0 | 0 | 0 | 0 | 4 | 0 |
| K. Murphy, Waterloo° | 1 | 1 | .500 | 1.04 | 5 | 0 | 0 | 5 | 0 | 0 | 8.2 | 6 | 1 | 1 | 0 | 0 | 5 | 0 | 13 | 1 |
| M. Murphy, Waterloo | 2 | 2 | .500 | 3.66 | 8 | 8 | 1 | 0 | 0 | 0 | 51.2 | 60 | 24 | 21 | 1 | 3 | 16 | 0 | 40 | 8 |
| Neufelder, Wausau° | 10 | 8 | .556 | 3.26 | 27 | 21 | 4 | 1 | 0 | 0 | 132.1 | 115 | 59 | 48 | 4 | 1 | 64 | 0 | 77 | 9 |
| North, Springfield | 11 | 4 | .733 | 3.47 | 24 | 23 | 6 | 1 | 0 | 1 | 158.0 | 148 | 79 | 61 | 12 | 2 | 58 | 0 | 96 | 7 |
| Oizumi, Wausau | 1 | 2 | .333 | 4.29 | 8 | 0 | 0 | 3 | 0 | 0 | 21.0 | 19 | 10 | 10 | 2 | 0 | 9 | 0 | 11 | 3 |
| Oliverio, Cedar Rapids | 13 | 4 | .765 | 2.86 | 20 | 18 | 5 | 2 | 1 | 0 | 125.2 | 105 | 51 | 40 | 10 | 2 | 30 | 0 | 132 | 6 |
| Olker, Clinton° | 8 | 2 | .800 | 2.96 | 15 | 15 | 1 | 0 | 1 | 0 | 82.0 | 61 | 31 | 27 | 8 | 3 | 43 | 0 | 87 | 4 |
| Olsson, Burlington | 5 | 5 | .500 | 2.18 | 28 | 4 | 1 | 18 | 0 | 3 | 66.0 | 52 | 25 | 16 | 2 | 3 | 29 | 2 | 66 | 4 |
| Oswald, Appleton° | 8 | 2 | .800 | 1.78 | 11 | 11 | 1 | 0 | 0 | 0 | 81.0 | 65 | 25 | 16 | 3 | 2 | 14 | 0 | 49 | 4 |
| Pardo, Burlington | 0 | 5 | .000 | 9.61 | 15 | 12 | 0 | 1 | 0 | 0 | 39.1 | 43 | 46 | 42 | 1 | 6 | 60 | 1 | 25 | 8 |
| Pavlas, Peoria | 8 | 3 | .727 | 2.62 | 17 | 15 | 3 | 2 | 1 | 1 | 110.0 | 90 | 40 | 32 | 7 | 3 | 32 | 0 | 86 | 6 |
| Peterek, Beloit | 6 | 2 | .750 | 2.88 | 14 | 11 | 1 | 2 | 1 | 2 | 75.0 | 68 | 31 | 24 | 4 | 1 | 24 | 0 | 64 | 2 |
| Pettibone, Cedar Rapids | 0 | 0 | .000 | 10.80 | 1 | 0 | 0 | 0 | 0 | 0 | 1.2 | 1 | 2 | 2 | 0 | 0 | 3 | 0 | 1 | 1 |
| Phelps, Appleton | 0 | 0 | .000 | 7.36 | 4 | 0 | 0 | 1 | 0 | 0 | 7.1 | 9 | 7 | 6 | 0 | 0 | 4 | 0 | 6 | 0 |
| Pico, Peoria | 11 | 10 | .524 | 3.06 | 27 | 27 | 8 | 0 | 1 | 0 | 179.1 | 186 | 76 | 61 | 5 | 7 | 56 | 0 | 109 | 7 |
| Piphus, Waterloo | 4 | 2 | .667 | 4.01 | 10 | 10 | 0 | 0 | 0 | 0 | 51.2 | 53 | 30 | 23 | 4 | 4 | 27 | 0 | 21 | 3 |
| Pleis, Springfield | 0 | 0 | .000 | 4.32 | 5 | 0 | 0 | 2 | 0 | 0 | 8.1 | 8 | 5 | 4 | 2 | 1 | 11 | 1 | 9 | 0 |
| Pobur, Peoria | 3 | 3 | .500 | 5.16 | 28 | 0 | 0 | 14 | 0 | 4 | 45.1 | 53 | 29 | 26 | 3 | 2 | 30 | 0 | 32 | 5 |
| Porter, Beloit | 1 | 0 | 1.000 | 3.29 | 3 | 3 | 0 | 0 | 0 | 0 | 13.2 | 15 | 5 | 5 | 0 | 0 | 5 | 0 | 12 | 0 |
| Prickett, Kenosha° | 11 | 8 | .579 | 4.62 | 28 | 27 | 3 | 0 | 0 | 0 | 146.0 | 166 | 104 | 75 | 8 | 0 | 84 | 2 | 77 | 9 |
| Ratliff, Beloit | 1 | 1 | .500 | 4.20 | 11 | 3 | 0 | 3 | 0 | 1 | 30.0 | 39 | 17 | 14 | 1 | 1 | 10 | 0 | 27 | 1 |
| Reed, Appleton | 12 | 4 | .750 | 3.48 | 29 | 18 | 5 | 5 | 1 | 0 | 132.0 | 112 | 62 | 51 | 5 | 4 | 59 | 1 | 87 | 16 |
| Reid, Peoria | 3 | 4 | .429 | 3.91 | 24 | 5 | 0 | 14 | 0 | 4 | 48.1 | 44 | 29 | 21 | 3 | 0 | 39 | 2 | 28 | 6 |
| Reinholtz, Wausau° | 0 | 2 | .000 | 4.98 | 22 | 1 | 0 | 13 | 0 | 1 | 43.1 | 54 | 33 | 24 | 7 | 1 | 19 | 2 | 46 | 4 |
| Renfroe, Peoria | 10 | 6 | .625 | 3.20 | 57 | 0 | 0 | 37 | 0 | 8 | 95.2 | 79 | 36 | 34 | 2 | 5 | 39 | 2 | 56 | 1 |
| Renz, Appleton | 6 | 8 | .429 | 4.03 | 19 | 18 | 3 | 0 | 1 | 0 | 114.0 | 120 | 71 | 51 | 7 | 1 | 49 | 0 | 104 | 6 |
| Rice, Peoria° | 4 | 9 | .308 | 3.30 | 36 | 14 | 3 | 15 | 1 | 3 | 125.1 | 116 | 58 | 46 | 9 | 3 | 33 | 0 | 71 | 8 |
| Robertson, Waterloo | 0 | 7 | .000 | 6.47 | 15 | 10 | 0 | 2 | 0 | 0 | 64.0 | 79 | 57 | 46 | 8 | 2 | 39 | 0 | 27 | 11 |
| Rodgers, Clinton | 2 | 2 | .500 | 1.98 | 6 | 6 | 1 | 0 | 1 | 0 | 41.0 | 28 | 10 | 9 | 0 | 1 | 23 | 0 | 46 | 3 |
| K. Rogers, Burlington° | 2 | 5 | .286 | 2.84 | 33 | 4 | 2 | 12 | 1 | 4 | 95.0 | 67 | 34 | 30 | 3 | 6 | 62 | 9 | 96 | 5 |
| S. Rogers, Burlington | 0 | 0 | .000 | 13.50 | 3 | 0 | 0 | 1 | 0 | 0 | 4.0 | 4 | 6 | 6 | 1 | 0 | 6 | 1 | 2 | 2 |
| Romanovsky, Quad Cities° | 12 | 8 | .600 | 3.76 | 25 | 21 | 6 | 2 | 2 | 0 | 158.0 | 169 | 81 | 66 | 9 | 6 | 49 | 1 | 114 | 5 |
| Rousey, Wausau | 4 | 12 | .250 | 6.66 | 26 | 19 | 2 | 2 | 0 | 0 | 105.1 | 131 | 95 | 78 | 12 | 5 | 52 | 5 | 47 | 14 |
| Ruckebeil, Appleton | 2 | 2 | .500 | 4.95 | 31 | 6 | 1 | 13 | 0 | 2 | 80.0 | 89 | 57 | 44 | 7 | 2 | 30 | 0 | 53 | 10 |
| Ruzek, Wausau | 1 | 1 | .500 | 3.00 | 6 | 4 | 1 | 0 | 0 | 0 | 30.0 | 22 | 10 | 10 | 3 | 0 | 6 | 0 | 19 | 1 |
| Sabo, Madison° | 9 | 8 | .529 | 3.85 | 34 | 16 | 3 | 8 | 1 | 3 | 117.0 | 127 | 58 | 50 | 8 | 4 | 42 | 0 | 76 | 2 |
| Sadler, Beloit | 5 | 2 | .714 | 2.68 | 13 | 12 | 0 | 0 | 0 | 0 | 57.0 | 49 | 23 | 17 | 4 | 0 | 27 | 0 | 52 | 2 |
| Scarpetta, Beloit° | 13 | 3 | .813 | 2.27 | 22 | 20 | 8 | 2 | 4 | 0 | 150.2 | 126 | 41 | 38 | 6 | 2 | 34 | 1 | 139 | 2 |
| Schwarz, Peoria | 7 | 9 | .438 | 3.20 | 27 | 19 | 6 | 3 | 2 | 0 | 143.1 | 99 | 60 | 51 | 4 | 9 | 79 | 2 | 140 | 9 |
| Sedar, Appleton | 1 | 3 | .250 | 4.20 | 7 | 7 | 2 | 0 | 0 | 0 | 40.2 | 44 | 23 | 19 | 2 | 0 | 12 | 1 | 24 | 3 |
| Shamblin, Burlington | 6 | 6 | .500 | 3.60 | 15 | 15 | 5 | 0 | 1 | 0 | 85.0 | 80 | 45 | 34 | 6 | 4 | 41 | 1 | 49 | 6 |
| Sharp, Waterloo | 4 | 7 | .364 | 7.37 | 34 | 12 | 0 | 15 | 0 | 1 | 94.0 | 134 | 92 | 77 | 17 | 7 | 47 | 0 | 52 | 9 |
| Siegel, Wausau | 0 | 4 | .000 | 8.23 | 6 | 5 | 0 | 0 | 0 | 0 | 27.1 | 38 | 27 | 25 | 2 | 2 | 20 | 0 | 18 | 1 |
| Silver, Clinton | 17 | 9 | .654 | 2.24 | 29 | 29 | 9 | 0 | 4 | 0 | 205.0 | 169 | 68 | 51 | 8 | 5 | 87 | 0 | 133 | 8 |
| Simmons, Beloit | 4 | 4 | .500 | 3.96 | 11 | 8 | 1 | 0 | 1 | 0 | 52.1 | 39 | 29 | 23 | 6 | 0 | 37 | 1 | 52 | 3 |
| Dan. Smith, Cedar Rapids° | 3 | 7 | .300 | 2.78 | 42 | 1 | 0 | 32 | 0 | 12 | 68.0 | 63 | 27 | 21 | 4 | 6 | 34 | 3 | 61 | 1 |
| Dar. Smith, Waterloo | 0 | 0 | .000 | 1.93 | 9 | 0 | 0 | 4 | 0 | 0 | 4.2 | 4 | 1 | 1 | 1 | 0 | 2 | 0 | 5 | 0 |
| M. Smith, Cedar Rapids | 5 | 1 | .833 | 3.25 | 8 | 8 | 4 | 0 | 3 | 0 | 44.1 | 38 | 20 | 16 | 2 | 3 | 22 | 1 | 28 | 4 |
| R. Smith, Quad Cities | 0 | 0 | .000 | 9.00 | 1 | 0 | 0 | 1 | 0 | 0 | 1.0 | 2 | 1 | 1 | 0 | 0 | 2 | 0 | 1 | 1 |
| Soma, Waterloo | 3 | 3 | .500 | 2.28 | 11 | 9 | 1 | 1 | 1 | 0 | 55.1 | 44 | 23 | 14 | 3 | 2 | 19 | 0 | 37 | 7 |
| Sontag, Kenosha | 15 | 11 | .577 | 2.33 | 28 | 28 | 15 | 0 | 6 | 0 | 220.1 | 171 | 65 | 57 | 7 | 13 | 59 | 2 | 213 | 8 |
| Soto, Cedar Rapids | 8 | 13 | .381 | 3.41 | 26 | 26 | 6 | 0 | 2 | 0 | 158.1 | 144 | 80 | 60 | 15 | 1 | 53 | 4 | 110 | 8 |
| Spear, Peoria° | 2 | 4 | .333 | 3.23 | 24 | 2 | 0 | 12 | 0 | 3 | 47.1 | 41 | 22 | 17 | 2 | 0 | 18 | 0 | 45 | 4 |
| Spratke, Wausau | 7 | 10 | .412 | 3.54 | 27 | 27 | 4 | 0 | 1 | 0 | 157.2 | 148 | 81 | 62 | 8 | 5 | 67 | 3 | 96 | 8 |
| Stangel, Clinton | 0 | 3 | .000 | 6.16 | 17 | 0 | 0 | 6 | 0 | 0 | 30.2 | 37 | 24 | 21 | 2 | 3 | 18 | 0 | 29 | 0 |
| Stein, Appleton | 3 | 2 | .600 | 3.92 | 8 | 8 | 3 | 0 | 1 | 0 | 59.2 | 47 | 29 | 26 | 2 | 5 | 21 | 0 | 40 | 0 |
| Stephenson, Waterloo | 3 | 3 | .500 | 4.45 | 32 | 0 | 0 | 27 | 0 | 5 | 54.2 | 58 | 29 | 27 | 5 | 0 | 15 | 3 | 54 | 1 |
| Swepson, Clinton | 0 | 0 | .000 | 4.15 | 3 | 0 | 0 | 2 | 0 | 0 | 4.1 | 3 | 2 | 2 | 0 | 0 | 5 | 0 | 2 | 2 |
| Tabeling, Kenosha | 11 | 3 | .786 | 3.83 | 32 | 16 | 1 | 7 | 1 | 2 | 136.1 | 135 | 69 | 58 | 17 | 1 | 54 | 1 | 82 | 10 |
| Tarnow, Appleton | 0 | 0 | .000 | 0.00 | 1 | 0 | 0 | 1 | 0 | 0 | 2.0 | 0 | 0 | 0 | 0 | 0 | 1 | 0 | 4 | 0 |
| Thigpen, Appleton | 1 | 0 | 1.000 | 0.00 | 1 | 0 | 0 | 0 | 0 | 0 | 2.2 | 1 | 0 | 0 | 0 | 0 | 1 | 0 | 1 | 0 |
| Tichy, Beloit | 1 | 1 | .500 | 5.87 | 6 | 4 | 1 | 2 | 0 | 1 | 23.0 | 28 | 18 | 15 | 0 | 3 | 19 | 0 | 10 | 2 |
| Van Houten, Springfield | 6 | 2 | .750 | 5.40 | 40 | 2 | 0 | 17 | 0 | 1 | 68.1 | 80 | 47 | 41 | 6 | 4 | 36 | 2 | 59 | 5 |
| Venturino, Quad Cities | 8 | 3 | .727 | 2.27 | 15 | 11 | 2 | 2 | 1 | 0 | 87.1 | 74 | 27 | 22 | 5 | 0 | 32 | 0 | 59 | 2 |
| Villa, Clinton | 7 | 5 | .583 | 2.65 | 28 | 9 | 2 | 13 | 0 | 7 | 102.0 | 74 | 38 | 30 | 4 | 4 | 54 | 0 | 86 | 11 |
| Villanueva, Peoria | 0 | 0 | .000 | 0.00 | 1 | 0 | 0 | 1 | 0 | 0 | 1.0 | 0 | 0 | 0 | 0 | 0 | 1 | 0 | 1 | 0 |
| Whaley, Madison | 6 | 2 | .750 | 2.28 | 10 | 7 | 2 | 1 | 2 | 0 | 59.1 | 50 | 21 | 15 | 2 | 2 | 18 | 0 | 54 | 2 |
| D. White, Appleton | 9 | 4 | .692 | 1.38 | 53 | 0 | 0 | 46 | 0 | 17 | 91.1 | 74 | 23 | 14 | 1 | 2 | 22 | 5 | 83 | 1 |
| L. White, Wausau | 2 | 6 | .250 | 4.38 | 51 | 0 | 0 | 27 | 0 | 4 | 86.1 | 79 | 51 | 42 | 1 | 7 | 44 | 10 | 78 | 3 |
| Whitmyer, Waterloo | 6 | 6 | .500 | 5.37 | 27 | 19 | 0 | 4 | 0 | 0 | 117.1 | 110 | 84 | 70 | 12 | 3 | 92 | 0 | 101 | 9 |
| Williams, Peoria | 1 | 0 | 1.000 | 6.00 | 11 | 4 | 0 | 3 | 0 | 1 | 30.0 | 21 | 20 | 20 | 2 | 3 | 39 | 0 | 32 | 3 |
| Wilmet, Springfield | 7 | 8 | .467 | 3.49 | 41 | 0 | 0 | 27 | 0 | 4 | 77.1 | 70 | 33 | 30 | 3 | 5 | 32 | 6 | 79 | 2 |
| Wilson, Burlington° | 3 | 5 | .375 | 4.58 | 21 | 10 | 0 | 4 | 0 | 0 | 72.2 | 71 | 44 | 37 | 11 | 2 | 27 | 1 | 76 | 1 |

BALKS—Ackerman, Eggersten, 5 each; D. Cook, 4; Butler, Criswell, S. Daniel, Fassero, Kibler, Olker, Pardo, Rousey, Venturino, Wilson, 3 each; Akins, Banning, Bridges, Cedeno, Clark, Costello, Dacus, Dial, Dressler, Ferreira, Fraser, Harvey, Hernandez, C. Jones, Larsen, Livchak, Ludy, Maddux, Messier, Montano, Piphus, Romanovsky, Sabo, Sedar, Sharp, Sontag, 2 each; T. Adams, Applegate, Beasley, Boyles, Brinkman, Coffey, Conley, L. Cook, C. Daniel, Dunn, Edwards, Erickson, Fay, Fick, Figueroa, Garcia, Hansen, Horrell, Lahrman, Madrid, Martinez, McDonald, Menendez, North, Oliverio, Pavlas, Pleis, Pobur, Prickett, Reed, Reid, Rice, K. Rogers, Ruckebeil, Sadler, Silver, Spear, Stangel, Williams, Wilmet, 1 each.

COMBINATION SHUTOUTS—Oswald-White, Reed-Anderson, Filippi-Reed, Menendez-White, Reed-White, Appleton; Kanwisher-Ratliff 2, Kleean-Diaz, Scarpetta-Frew-Montano, Kanwisher-Montano, Kanwisher-Diaz, Simmons-Peterek, Sadler-Diaz, Peterek-Ratliff, Beloit; Dial-Hernandez, Lankard-Harden, Burlington; Boyles-D. Smith, Boyles-Dibble-D. Smith, Oliverio-D. Smith, Cedar Rapids; Cook-Villa, Cook-Dressler, Hamstra-Villa, Hinnrichs-Dressler-Erickson, Villa-Erickson, Cook-Ackerman, Messier-Hinnrichs, Clinton; Sontag-Iasparro, Malec-Gomez, Iasparro-Gomez, Sontag-Dodd, Tabeling-Gomez, Kenosha; Criswell-Hansen, Ferreira-Leonette, Brake-Leonette, Madison; Williams-Renfroe, Spear-Renfroe-Rice, Schwarz-Renfroe-Spear, Peoria; Romanovsky-L. Cook, Eggersten-Dacus, Eggersten-Harvey, Martinez-Garcia-Dacus, Venturino-Dacus, Quad Cities; North-Dunn, Costello-Dunn, Ember-Dunn, Ember-Van Houten, Kinzer-Dunn, Springfield; Beasley-Stephenson, Whitmyer-Encarnacion, Belleman-Sharp, Belleman-Encarnacion, Belleman-K. Murphy, Galloway-Greer, Waterloo; Jones-Higgs, Baldrick-Mendek, Brinkman-Jones-Baldrick, Wausau.

NO-HIT GAMES—Soto, Cedar Rapids, defeated Clinton, 2-0 (second game), June 12; Link, Waterloo, defeated Clinton, 10-0 (second game), July 25.

# NY-Pennsylvania League

## CLASS A

### CHAMPIONSHIP WINNERS IN PREVIOUS YEARS

| | | |
|---|---|---|
| 1939—Olean* .631 | 1956—Wellsville* .617 | 1971—Oneonta .662 |
| 1940—Olean* .625 | 1957—Wellsville .632 | 1972—Niagara Falls .686 |
| 1941—Jamestown .618 | Erie (2nd)† .598 | 1973—Auburn .667 |
| Bradford (2nd)† .549 | 1958—Wellsville .556 | 1974—Oneonta .768 |
| 1942—Jamestown* .672 | Geneva (2nd)† .548 | 1975—Newark .688 |
| 1943—Lockport .591 | 1959—Wellsville† .635 | Newark .714 |
| Wellsville (3rd)† .532 | 1960—Erie .643 | 1976—Elmira .727 |
| 1944—Lockport .608 | Wellsville (2nd)† .535 | Elmira .703 |
| Jamestown (2nd)† .565 | 1961—Geneva .616 | 1977—Oneonta y .671 |
| 1945—Batavia* .677 | Olean (4th)† .512 | Batavia .600 |
| 1946—Jamestown‡ .672 | 1962—Jamestown .580 | 1978—Oneonta .729 |
| Batavia‡ .672 | Auburn (3rd)† .521 | Geneva z .718 |
| 1947—Jamestown* .690 | 1963—Auburn .585 | 1979—Geneva .725 |
| 1948—Lockport* .603 | Batavia (3rd)† .485 | Oneonta z .618 |
| 1949—Bradford* .635 | 1964—Auburn§ .622 | 1980—Oneonta y .662 |
| 1950—Hornell .653 | 1965—Binghamton .677 | Geneva .649 |
| Olean (2nd)† .568 | Binghamton .607 | 1981—Oneonta y .658 |
| 1951—Olean .622 | 1966—Auburn x .620 | Jamestown .649 |
| Hornell (3rd)† .568 | Binghamton .646 | 1982—Oneonta .566 |
| 1952—Hamilton .659 | 1967—Auburn .667 | Niagara Falls y .553 |
| Jamestown (2nd)† .643 | 1968—Auburn .645 | 1983—Utica y .649 |
| 1953—Jamestown* .704 | Oneonta (2nd)* .558 | Newark .649 |
| 1954—Corning* .621 | 1969—Oneonta .662 | 1984—Newark .622 |
| 1955—Hamilton* .656 | 1970—Auburn .623 | Little Falls y .587 |

*Won championship and four-club playoff. †Won four-club playoff. ‡Jamestown and Batavia declared co-champions; Batavia defeated Jamestown in final of four-club playoff. §Won championship and two-club playoff. xWon split-season playoff. yLeague divided into Eastern and Western Divisions; won playoff. zLeague divided into Wrigley and Yawkey Divisions; won playoff. (NOTE—Known as Pennsylvania-Ontario-New York League from 1939 through 1956.)

### STANDING OF CLUBS AT CLOSE OF SEASON, SEPTEMBER 2

#### NORTHERN DIVISION

| Club | W. | L. | T. | Pct. | G.B. |
|---|---|---|---|---|---|
| Oneonta (Yankees) | 55 | 23 | 0 | .705 | ....... |
| Utica (Independent) | 35 | 41 | 0 | .461 | 19 |
| Little Falls (Mets) | 34 | 41 | 0 | .453 | 19½ |
| Watertown (Pirates) | 22 | 54 | 0 | .289 | 32 |

#### CENTRAL DIVISION

| Club | W. | L. | T. | Pct. | G.B. |
|---|---|---|---|---|---|
| Auburn (Astros) | 47 | 31 | 0 | .603 | ....... |
| Geneva (Cubs) | 45 | 33 | 0 | .577 | 2 |
| Newark (Orioles) | 41 | 36 | 0 | .532 | 5½ |
| Elmira (Red Sox) | 28 | 49 | 0 | .364 | 18½ |

#### SOUTHERN DIVISION

| Club | W. | L. | T. | Pct. | G.B. |
|---|---|---|---|---|---|
| Jamestown (Expos) | 45 | 33 | 0 | .577 | ....... |
| Erie (Cardinals) | 44 | 34 | 0 | .564 | 1 |
| Niagara Falls (White Sox) | 34 | 43 | 0 | .442 | 10½ |
| Batavia (Indians) | 33 | 45 | 0 | .423 | 12 |

### COMPOSITE STANDING OF CLUBS AT CLOSE OF SEASON, SEPTEMBER 2

| Club | Ont. | Aub. | Jam. | Gen. | Eri. | New. | Uti. | L.F. | N.F. | Bat. | Elm. | Wat. | W. | L. | T. | Pct. | G.B. |
|---|---|---|---|---|---|---|---|---|---|---|---|---|---|---|---|---|---|
| Oneonta (Yankees) | .... | 2 | 2 | 1 | 2 | 2 | 13 | 12 | 4 | 2 | 3 | 12 | 55 | 23 | 0 | .705 | ....... |
| Auburn (Astros) | 2 | .... | 1 | 5 | 3 | 11 | 3 | 1 | 3 | 3 | 12 | 3 | 47 | 31 | 0 | .603 | 8 |
| Jamestown (Expos) | 2 | 3 | .... | 2 | 8 | 2 | 2 | 3 | 8 | 8 | 4 | 3 | 45 | 33 | 0 | .577 | 10 |
| Geneva (Cubs) | 3 | 9 | 2 | .... | 1 | 6 | 2 | 3 | 2 | 2 | 12 | 3 | 45 | 33 | 0 | .577 | 10 |
| Erie (Cardinals) | 2 | 1 | 8 | 3 | .... | 1 | 2 | 3 | 8 | 11 | 1 | 4 | 44 | 34 | 0 | .564 | 11 |
| Newark (Orioles) | 2 | 5 | 2 | 10 | 3 | .... | 3 | 2 | 3 | 3 | 7 | 1 | 41 | 36 | 0 | .532 | 13½ |
| Utica (Independent) | 3 | 1 | 2 | 2 | 2 | 1 | .... | 6 | 2 | 4 | 3 | 9 | 35 | 41 | 0 | .461 | 19 |
| Little Falls (Mets) | 4 | 3 | 1 | 1 | 1 | 2 | 6 | .... | 3 | 2 | 1 | 10 | 34 | 41 | 0 | .453 | 19½ |
| Niagara Falls (White Sox) | 0 | 1 | 6 | 2 | 8 | 1 | 2 | 1 | .... | 8 | 2 | 3 | 34 | 43 | 0 | .442 | 20½ |
| Batavia (Indians) | 2 | 1 | 8 | 2 | 3 | 1 | 0 | 2 | 8 | .... | 2 | 4 | 33 | 45 | 0 | .423 | 22 |
| Elmira (Red Sox) | 1 | 4 | 0 | 4 | 3 | 6 | 1 | 3 | 2 | 2 | .... | 2 | 28 | 49 | 0 | .364 | 26½ |
| Watertown (Pirates) | 2 | 1 | 1 | 1 | 0 | 3 | 7 | 5 | 0 | 0 | 2 | .... | 22 | 54 | 0 | .289 | 32 |

Major league affiliations in parentheses.

Playoffs—Oneonta defeated Geneva and Auburn defeated Jamestown in one game semifinal. Oneonta defeated Auburn, two games to none, to win league championship.

Regular-Season Attendance—Auburn, 23,966; Batavia, 35,581; Elmira, 66,636; Erie, 48,347; Geneva, 31,298; Jamestown, 52,576; Little Falls, 27,950; Newark, 22,888; Niagara Falls, 31,149; Oneonta, 42,372; Utica, 56,390; Watertown, 51,840. Total—490,793. Playoffs —2,552 (4 games).

Managers—Auburn, Bob Hartsfield; Batavia, Eddie Bane; Elmira, Dick Berardino; Erie, Fred Koenig; Geneva, Tony Franklin; Jamestown, Ed Creech; Little Falls, Dan Radison; Newark, Art Mazmanian; Niagara Falls, Luis Lagunas, Oneonta, Buck Showalter; Utica, Ken Brett; Watertown, Woody Hunt.

All-Star Team—1B—Rich Johnson, Auburn; 2B—Jose Mota, Niagara Falls; 3B—Scott Shaw, Oneonta; SS—Scott Gray, Auburn; OF— Doug Dascenzo, Geneva; Dennis Carter, Erie; Louis Medina, Batavia; Andre Tolliver, Niagara Falls; C—Jorge Alcazar, Niagara Falls; Geoff Davis, Jamestown; RHP's—Dody Rather, Oneonta; Mike Christopher, Oneonta; LHPs—Blaise Ilsley, Auburn; Jeff Ballard, Newark; DH—Don Lovell, Batavia; Manager of the Year—Buck Showalter, Oneonta.

(Compiled by Howe News Bureau, Boston, Mass.)

## CLUB BATTING

| Club | Pct. | G. | AB. | R. | OR. | H. | TB. | 2B. | 3B. | HR. | RBI. | GW. | SH. | SF. | HP. | BB. | Int. BB. | SO. | SB. | CS. | LOB. |
|---|---|---|---|---|---|---|---|---|---|---|---|---|---|---|---|---|---|---|---|---|---|
| Oneonta | .256 | 78 | 2540 | 401 | 205 | 649 | 895 | 98 | 29 | 30 | 339 | 50 | 29 | 20 | 16 | 417 | 11 | 589 | 110 | 30 | 664 |
| Jamestown | .254 | 78 | 2531 | 385 | 327 | 642 | 933 | 111 | 21 | 46 | 316 | 33 | 18 | 17 | 31 | 337 | 17 | 548 | 97 | 44 | 564 |
| Auburn | .250 | 78 | 2573 | 380 | 317 | 643 | 927 | 103 | 20 | 47 | 331 | 39 | 17 | 28 | 36 | 324 | 16 | 489 | 79 | 21 | 594 |
| Niagara Falls | .242 | 77 | 2494 | 325 | 376 | 604 | 874 | 100 | 22 | 42 | 281 | 29 | 21 | 19 | 17 | 281 | 14 | 587 | 70 | 38 | 533 |
| Geneva | .240 | 78 | 2526 | 388 | 343 | 605 | 832 | 98 | 12 | 35 | 323 | 42 | 40 | 18 | 23 | 410 | 27 | 509 | 114 | 45 | 596 |
| Batavia | .236 | 78 | 2540 | 359 | 385 | 599 | 887 | 115 | 7 | 53 | 296 | 26 | 17 | 14 | 21 | 318 | 4 | 572 | 73 | 31 | 544 |
| Erie | .233 | 78 | 2485 | 387 | 359 | 580 | 869 | 93 | 14 | 56 | 323 | 34 | 44 | 23 | 26 | 410 | 10 | 542 | 140 | 52 | 600 |
| Newark | .228 | 77 | 2495 | 357 | 331 | 570 | 804 | 94 | 16 | 36 | 301 | 34 | 36 | 14 | 26 | 375 | 26 | 505 | 108 | 45 | 562 |
| Little Falls | .224 | 75 | 2366 | 291 | 312 | 531 | 762 | 82 | 22 | 35 | 239 | 27 | 22 | 20 | 11 | 288 | 11 | 536 | 111 | 51 | 466 |
| Elmira | .224 | 77 | 2474 | 276 | 389 | 553 | 771 | 95 | 15 | 31 | 237 | 24 | 29 | 12 | 33 | 337 | 10 | 534 | 54 | 20 | 610 |
| Watertown | .215 | 76 | 2437 | 261 | 417 | 523 | 722 | 72 | 23 | 27 | 208 | 17 | 26 | 12 | 20 | 255 | 7 | 688 | 108 | 43 | 508 |
| Utica | .214 | 76 | 2468 | 275 | 324 | 528 | 683 | 77 | 18 | 14 | 228 | 27 | 38 | 11 | 25 | 291 | 11 | 656 | 140 | 57 | 519 |

## INDIVIDUAL BATTING
(Leading Qualifiers for Batting Championship—211 or More Plate Appearances)

*Bats lefthanded.    †Switch-hitter.

| Player and Club | Pct. | G. | AB. | R. | H. | TB. | 2B. | 3B. | HR. | RBI. | GW. | SH. | SF. | HP. | BB. | Int. BB. | SO. | SB. | CS. |
|---|---|---|---|---|---|---|---|---|---|---|---|---|---|---|---|---|---|---|---|
| Flower, George, Jamestown | .336 | 66 | 235 | 34 | 79 | 122 | 13 | 0 | 10 | 45 | 4 | 0 | 1 | 3 | 30 | 2 | 40 | 9 | 5 |
| Dascenzo, Douglas, Geneva† | .333 | 70 | 252 | 59 | 84 | 110 | 15 | 1 | 3 | 23 | 2 | 1 | 4 | 2 | 61 | 4 | 20 | 33 | 9 |
| Johnson, Richard, Auburn | .313 | 70 | 214 | 43 | 67 | 117 | 10 | 2 | 12 | 48 | 5 | 0 | 4 | 3 | 39 | 5 | 43 | 3 | 0 |
| Lotzar, Gregory, Elmira* | .310 | 56 | 187 | 40 | 58 | 83 | 6 | 5 | 3 | 21 | 2 | 5 | 1 | 2 | 34 | 1 | 23 | 14 | 2 |
| Donatelli, Andrew, Utica | .306 | 74 | 284 | 39 | 87 | 97 | 8 | 1 | 0 | 20 | 3 | 1 | 0 | 1 | 49 | 0 | 32 | 28 | 14 |
| Mota, Jose, Niagara Falls† | .303 | 65 | 254 | 35 | 77 | 90 | 9 | 2 | 0 | 27 | 1 | 5 | 2 | 2 | 28 | 3 | 29 | 8 | 5 |
| Shaw, Scott, Oneonta | .293 | 72 | 276 | 40 | 81 | 113 | 8 | 6 | 4 | 37 | 9 | 3 | 0 | 4 | 23 | 0 | 54 | 5 | 4 |
| Drew, Cameron, Auburn* | .291 | 72 | 278 | 48 | 81 | 114 | 10 | 4 | 5 | 45 | 5 | 0 | 0 | 5 | 34 | 1 | 53 | 10 | 5 |
| Smith, Dwight, Geneva* | .289 | 73 | 232 | 44 | 67 | 94 | 11 | 2 | 4 | 32 | 4 | 0 | 1 | 1 | 31 | 3 | 33 | 30 | 10 |
| Maas, Jason, Oneonta* | .286 | 67 | 234 | 37 | 67 | 81 | 7 | 2 | 1 | 23 | 4 | 4 | 1 | 0 | 51 | 2 | 42 | 16 | 3 |

Departmental Leaders: G—Den. Carter, Fishel, Gilkey, 77; AB—Gilkey, 294; R—Dascenzo, 59; H—Donatelli, 87; TB—Den. Carter, 152; 2B—Den. Carter, Rogalski, 20; 3B—B. Anderson, Shaw, 6; HR—Den. Carter 16; RBI—Den. Carter, 77; GWRBI—Den. Carter, 10; SH—T. Nichols, 9; SF—Den. Carter, 8; HP—Roberts, Speakman, 7; BB—B. Anderson, 67; IBB—Bellino, 8; SO—Den. Carter, 93; SB—Warmbier, 42; CS—Donatelli, 14.

(All Players—Listed Alphabetically)

| Player and Club | Pct. | G. | AB. | R. | H. | TB. | 2B. | 3B. | HR. | RBI. | GW. | SH. | SF. | HP. | BB. | Int. BB. | SO. | SB. | CS. |
|---|---|---|---|---|---|---|---|---|---|---|---|---|---|---|---|---|---|---|---|
| Adams, Gerald, Newark | .000 | 12 | 1 | 0 | 0 | 0 | 0 | 0 | 0 | 0 | 0 | 0 | 0 | 0 | 0 | 0 | 0 | 0 | 0 |
| Adams, Kevin, Auburn | .125 | 11 | 16 | 3 | 2 | 2 | 0 | 0 | 0 | 0 | 0 | 1 | 0 | 0 | 5 | 0 | 6 | 1 | 0 |
| Alcazar, Jorge, Niagara Falls | .237 | 58 | 190 | 33 | 45 | 87 | 11 | 2 | 9 | 35 | 4 | 4 | 1 | 1 | 18 | 0 | 53 | 2 | 3 |
| Alvis, David, Batavia* | .268 | 16 | 56 | 6 | 15 | 20 | 2 | 0 | 1 | 6 | 0 | 0 | 1 | 4 | 0 | 3 | 1 | 0 | |
| Anders, Scott, Geneva | .222 | 43 | 126 | 14 | 28 | 33 | 5 | 0 | 0 | 6 | 0 | 4 | 0 | 1 | 11 | 4 | 30 | 1 | 0 |
| Anderson, Brady, Elmira* | .256 | 71 | 215 | 36 | 55 | 89 | 7 | 6 | 5 | 21 | 3 | 1 | 0 | 2 | 67 | 0 | 32 | 13 | 9 |
| Armstrong, Kevin, Little Falls | .000 | 15 | 6 | 0 | 0 | 0 | 0 | 0 | 0 | 0 | 0 | 0 | 1 | 0 | 1 | 0 | 4 | 0 | 0 |
| Arnsberg, Timothy, Auburn | .429 | 7 | 7 | 1 | 3 | 3 | 0 | 0 | 0 | 0 | 0 | 0 | 0 | 0 | 0 | 0 | 1 | 0 | 0 |
| Ayers, Scott, Jamestown | .182 | 14 | 11 | 0 | 2 | 3 | 1 | 0 | 0 | 3 | 1 | 3 | 0 | 0 | 2 | 0 | 1 | 0 | 0 |
| Bafia, Robert, Geneva | .252 | 65 | 234 | 32 | 59 | 92 | 12 | 0 | 7 | 38 | 5 | 2 | 2 | 2 | 28 | 2 | 64 | 2 | 3 |
| Barker, Timothy, Jamestown | .343 | 43 | 166 | 32 | 57 | 71 | 6 | 4 | 0 | 19 | 3 | 0 | 1 | 0 | 26 | 1 | 19 | 35 | 9 |
| Bautista, Bienvenido, Newark | .133 | 20 | 30 | 7 | 4 | 5 | 1 | 0 | 0 | 0 | 0 | 0 | 0 | 0 | 4 | 0 | 16 | 2 | 1 |
| Bellino, Frank, Newark* | .236 | 72 | 246 | 24 | 58 | 86 | 8 | 4 | 4 | 32 | 3 | 1 | 0 | 0 | 37 | 8 | 28 | 6 | 5 |
| Beltre, Esteban, Utica | .199 | 72 | 241 | 19 | 48 | 58 | 6 | 2 | 0 | 22 | 1 | 8 | 1 | 3 | 18 | 0 | 58 | 8 | 7 |
| Bennett, Keith, Batavia | .208 | 7 | 24 | 7 | 5 | 8 | 3 | 0 | 0 | 0 | 0 | 1 | 0 | 0 | 2 | 0 | 5 | 2 | 0 |
| Bernaldo, Richard, Oneonta | .000 | 1 | 1 | 0 | 0 | 0 | 0 | 0 | 0 | 0 | 0 | 0 | 0 | 0 | 0 | 0 | 0 | 0 | 0 |
| Berry, Scott, Watertown | .083 | 11 | 24 | 2 | 2 | 3 | 1 | 0 | 0 | 0 | 0 | 0 | 0 | 0 | 2 | 0 | 5 | 0 | 0 |
| Bigden, Maurice, Jamestown | .205 | 29 | 78 | 14 | 16 | 19 | 0 | 0 | 1 | 7 | 1 | 2 | 0 | 0 | 13 | 0 | 23 | 3 | 1 |
| Bochesa, Gregory, Elmira | .320 | 7 | 25 | 5 | 8 | 12 | 4 | 0 | 0 | 1 | 1 | 0 | 0 | 0 | 4 | 1 | 5 | 0 | 0 |
| Boyd, Steven, Erie† | .200 | 14 | 35 | 6 | 7 | 9 | 0 | 1 | 0 | 3 | 1 | 0 | 0 | 0 | 2 | 0 | 8 | 1 | 1 |
| Brady, Lawrence, Watertown | .125 | 45 | 64 | 9 | 8 | 9 | 1 | 0 | 0 | 2 | 1 | 1 | 0 | 2 | 14 | 0 | 25 | 7 | 2 |
| Bridges, James, Watertown* | .250 | 13 | 4 | 0 | 1 | 1 | 0 | 0 | 0 | 0 | 0 | 0 | 0 | 0 | 0 | 0 | 1 | 0 | 0 |
| Brown, Michael, Auburn | .217 | 31 | 60 | 10 | 13 | 17 | 2 | 1 | 0 | 8 | 0 | 0 | 0 | 4 | 8 | 0 | 9 | 4 | 1 |
| Brown, Robert, Utica* | .200 | 53 | 145 | 15 | 29 | 43 | 5 | 0 | 3 | 17 | 2 | 2 | 0 | 0 | 35 | 3 | 52 | 5 | 1 |
| Brueggemann, Steven, Little Falls | .500 | 14 | 4 | 0 | 2 | 2 | 0 | 0 | 0 | 0 | 0 | 0 | 1 | 0 | 1 | 0 | 0 | 0 | 0 |
| Brunswick, Mark, Little Falls | .165 | 51 | 121 | 7 | 20 | 26 | 4 | 1 | 0 | 8 | 0 | 2 | 1 | 1 | 13 | 0 | 29 | 0 | 0 |
| Burke, Kevin, Newark* | .302 | 18 | 53 | 8 | 16 | 21 | 5 | 0 | 0 | 6 | 0 | 0 | 0 | 0 | 9 | 1 | 11 | 0 | 0 |
| Cabrera, Victor, Batavia | .000 | 11 | 16 | 0 | 0 | 0 | 0 | 0 | 0 | 0 | 1 | 0 | 0 | 0 | 2 | 0 | 5 | 0 | 0 |
| Calvert, Arthur, Oneonta | .312 | 22 | 77 | 12 | 24 | 35 | 2 | 0 | 3 | 14 | 2 | 0 | 1 | 1 | 7 | 0 | 22 | 1 | 1 |
| Candelino, Anthony, Jamestown | .205 | 33 | 88 | 16 | 18 | 24 | 1 | 1 | 1 | 4 | 0 | 1 | 0 | 0 | 19 | 0 | 21 | 1 | 3 |
| Carter, Dell, Elmira† | .207 | 51 | 111 | 12 | 23 | 33 | 4 | 0 | 2 | 11 | 1 | 3 | 1 | 4 | 17 | 0 | 37 | 6 | 2 |
| Carter, Dennis, Erie | .284 | 77 | 282 | 45 | 80 | 152 | 20 | 2 | 16 | 77 | 10 | 0 | 8 | 2 | 47 | 1 | 93 | 10 | 3 |
| Castro, Ruben, Geneva | .217 | 25 | 60 | 7 | 13 | 20 | 2 | 1 | 1 | 9 | 0 | 0 | 1 | 0 | 9 | 0 | 24 | 0 | 0 |
| Cento, Anthony, Niagara Falls | .138 | 12 | 29 | 3 | 4 | 9 | 0 | 0 | 0 | 1 | 0 | 0 | 0 | 0 | 0 | 0 | 6 | 0 | 0 |
| Cepeda, Octavio, Watertown | .000 | 18 | 1 | 0 | 0 | 0 | 0 | 0 | 0 | 0 | 0 | 0 | 0 | 0 | 0 | 0 | 1 | 0 | 0 |
| Cepero, Edwin, Erie | .133 | 4 | 15 | 2 | 2 | 2 | 0 | 0 | 0 | 1 | 0 | 1 | 0 | 0 | 1 | 0 | 4 | 0 | 0 |
| Channing, Kyle, Watertown | .313 | 15 | 16 | 3 | 5 | 11 | 0 | 2 | 0 | 3 | 0 | 2 | 0 | 0 | 1 | 0 | 7 | 0 | 0 |
| Cijntje, Sherwin, Newark | .248 | 56 | 145 | 29 | 36 | 41 | 1 | 2 | 0 | 9 | 0 | 4 | 1 | 2 | 20 | 1 | 27 | 14 | 5 |
| Clark, Daniel, Watertown | .207 | 66 | 217 | 30 | 45 | 57 | 3 | 3 | 1 | 10 | 1 | 2 | 1 | 1 | 25 | 0 | 50 | 17 | 2 |
| Clark, Randall, Watertown | .252 | 46 | 155 | 14 | 39 | 53 | 3 | 1 | 3 | 22 | 1 | 0 | 3 | 1 | 8 | 0 | 37 | 3 | 1 |
| Clark, Rodney, Utica* | .153 | 42 | 124 | 7 | 19 | 27 | 6 | 1 | 0 | 6 | 0 | 3 | 1 | 1 | 10 | 1 | 38 | 0 | 1 |
| Coker, Reginald, Batavia† | .167 | 4 | 6 | 1 | 1 | 1 | 0 | 0 | 0 | 0 | 0 | 0 | 0 | 0 | 2 | 0 | 3 | 1 | 0 |
| Colescott, Robert, Little Falls | .156 | 31 | 77 | 9 | 12 | 18 | 3 | 0 | 1 | 3 | 0 | 1 | 0 | 0 | 9 | 0 | 30 | 1 | 0 |
| Collins, Allen, Jamestown | .000 | 18 | 2 | 0 | 0 | 0 | 0 | 0 | 0 | 0 | 0 | 0 | 0 | 0 | 0 | 0 | 1 | 0 | 0 |
| Colombino, Carlo, Auburn | .261 | 58 | 188 | 19 | 49 | 60 | 6 | 1 | 1 | 17 | 3 | 2 | 2 | 2 | 8 | 1 | 20 | 3 | 3 |
| Contreras, Joaquin, Little Falls† | .257 | 48 | 175 | 26 | 45 | 74 | 7 | 5 | 4 | 24 | 1 | 2 | 1 | 1 | 22 | 1 | 30 | 17 | 1 |
| Cooley, Jeffrey, Little Falls | .071 | 6 | 14 | 1 | 1 | 1 | 0 | 0 | 0 | 0 | 0 | 0 | 0 | 0 | 3 | 0 | 8 | 0 | 0 |
| Cowan, John, Newark* | .244 | 27 | 45 | 4 | 11 | 13 | 0 | 1 | 0 | 4 | 0 | 0 | 0 | 0 | 9 | 0 | 14 | 1 | 1 |
| Cox, James, Elmira* | .000 | 15 | 1 | 0 | 0 | 0 | 0 | 0 | 0 | 0 | 0 | 0 | 0 | 0 | 0 | 0 | 0 | 0 | 0 |
| Crone, Raymond, Newark* | .286 | 8 | 14 | 2 | 4 | 4 | 0 | 0 | 0 | 0 | 0 | 0 | 0 | 0 | 0 | 0 | 3 | 0 | 1 |
| Cronkright, Daniel, Niagara Falls* | .247 | 73 | 259 | 38 | 64 | 86 | 12 | 2 | 2 | 22 | 1 | 2 | 4 | 3 | 46 | 3 | 47 | 6 | 4 |
| Cunningham, William, Jamestown* | .250 | 15 | 12 | 0 | 3 | 3 | 0 | 0 | 0 | 0 | 0 | 1 | 0 | 0 | 3 | 0 | 2 | 1 | 0 |
| Dallaire, Jean, Jamestown | .173 | 43 | 98 | 10 | 17 | 19 | 2 | 0 | 0 | 5 | 0 | 1 | 2 | 2 | 9 | 1 | 10 | 2 | 0 |
| Danek, William, Geneva | .250 | 15 | 16 | 1 | 4 | 5 | 1 | 0 | 0 | 0 | 0 | 5 | 0 | 1 | 0 | 5 | 0 | 0 | |
| Daniels, Ronnell, Watertown* | .256 | 29 | 90 | 12 | 23 | 29 | 3 | 0 | 1 | 7 | 1 | 0 | 0 | 2 | 0 | 19 | 1 | 0 | |

| Player and Club | Pct. | G. | AB. | R. | H. | TB. | 2B. | 3B. | HR. | RBI. | GW. | SH. | SF. | HP. | BB. | Int. BB. | SO. | SB. | CS. |
|---|---|---|---|---|---|---|---|---|---|---|---|---|---|---|---|---|---|---|---|
| Dascenzo, Douglas, Geneva† | .333 | 70 | 252 | 59 | 84 | 110 | 15 | 1 | 3 | 23 | 2 | 1 | 4 | 2 | 61 | 4 | 20 | 33 | 9 |
| Davins, James, Watertown | .000 | 16 | 1 | 0 | 0 | 0 | 0 | 0 | 0 | 0 | 0 | 0 | 0 | 0 | 0 | 0 | 0 | 0 | 0 |
| Davis, Geffrey, Jamestown | .270 | 54 | 185 | 28 | 50 | 73 | 8 | 3 | 3 | 18 | 0 | 1 | 1 | 6 | 15 | 0 | 49 | 8 | 2 |
| Dean, Roger, Utica | .255 | 69 | 243 | 32 | 62 | 83 | 10 | 1 | 3 | 29 | 4 | 1 | 2 | 1 | 30 | 0 | 68 | 18 | 1 |
| DeBoever, William, Jamestown* | .000 | 23 | 1 | 0 | 0 | 0 | 0 | 0 | 0 | 0 | 0 | 0 | 0 | 0 | 0 | 0 | 1 | 0 | 0 |
| DeCordova, David, Erie* | .000 | 16 | 4 | 1 | 0 | 0 | 0 | 0 | 0 | 0 | 0 | 2 | 0 | 0 | 0 | 0 | 2 | 0 | 0 |
| Dedos, Felix, Geneva | .250 | 16 | 4 | 1 | 1 | 1 | 0 | 0 | 0 | 1 | 0 | 0 | 0 | 0 | 0 | 0 | 1 | 0 | 0 |
| DeLaCruz, Laito, Auburn | .254 | 24 | 67 | 10 | 17 | 18 | 1 | 0 | 0 | 6 | 0 | 0 | 1 | 0 | 6 | 0 | 15 | 4 | 0 |
| DeLuca, Kurt, Little Falls | .270 | 46 | 159 | 32 | 43 | 74 | 5 | 4 | 6 | 19 | 4 | 1 | 2 | 0 | 28 | 0 | 24 | 15 | 3 |
| Denczi, Edward, Watertown | .000 | 2 | 6 | 0 | 0 | 0 | 0 | 0 | 0 | 0 | 0 | 0 | 0 | 1 | 0 | 0 | 4 | 0 | 0 |
| Dineen, Anthony, Auburn | .200 | 17 | 5 | 0 | 1 | 1 | 0 | 0 | 0 | 0 | 0 | 0 | 0 | 0 | 0 | 0 | 4 | 0 | 0 |
| Dishman, Curtis, Auburn* | .269 | 65 | 234 | 36 | 63 | 102 | 7 | 4 | 8 | 37 | 4 | 0 | 2 | 2 | 20 | 1 | 39 | 4 | 3 |
| Dixon, William, Jamestown | .000 | 23 | 3 | 0 | 0 | 0 | 0 | 0 | 0 | 0 | 0 | 0 | 0 | 0 | 0 | 0 | 2 | 0 | 0 |
| Dominico, Ronald, Little Falls* | .250 | 23 | 4 | 0 | 1 | 1 | 0 | 0 | 0 | 1 | 0 | 2 | 0 | 0 | 1 | 0 | 0 | 0 | 0 |
| Donatelli, Andrew, Utica | .306 | 74 | 284 | 39 | 87 | 97 | 8 | 1 | 0 | 20 | 3 | 1 | 0 | 1 | 49 | 0 | 32 | 28 | 14 |
| Drew, Cameron, Auburn* | .291 | 72 | 278 | 48 | 81 | 114 | 10 | 4 | 5 | 45 | 5 | 0 | 0 | 5 | 34 | 1 | 53 | 10 | 5 |
| Dromerhouser, Robert, Newark | .154 | 20 | 26 | 3 | 4 | 5 | 1 | 0 | 0 | 3 | 0 | 0 | 0 | 0 | 6 | 0 | 13 | 0 | 0 |
| Dunster, Donald, Auburn | .000 | 15 | 6 | 0 | 0 | 0 | 0 | 0 | 0 | 0 | 0 | 0 | 0 | 0 | 0 | 0 | 0 | 0 | 0 |
| Edwards, Jeff, Auburn | .167 | 41 | 126 | 11 | 21 | 31 | 2 | 1 | 2 | 12 | 2 | 0 | 2 | 2 | 10 | 0 | 38 | 1 | 0 |
| Espinoza, Andres, Little Falls* | .276 | 51 | 145 | 17 | 40 | 55 | 6 | 0 | 3 | 15 | 0 | 0 | 1 | 0 | 12 | 2 | 31 | 2 | 1 |
| Ezold, Todd, Oneonta | .216 | 31 | 88 | 8 | 19 | 24 | 5 | 0 | 0 | 12 | 3 | 1 | 0 | 1 | 9 | 0 | 28 | 1 | 2 |
| Fairchild, Glenn, Batavia† | .185 | 66 | 184 | 33 | 34 | 40 | 6 | 0 | 0 | 15 | 1 | 7 | 0 | 3 | 27 | 0 | 61 | 12 | 2 |
| Fascher, Stanley, Auburn | .250 | 21 | 8 | 0 | 2 | 2 | 0 | 0 | 0 | 1 | 0 | 0 | 0 | 0 | 1 | 0 | 2 | 1 | 0 |
| Fishel, John, Auburn | .261 | 77 | 268 | 53 | 70 | 116 | 15 | 2 | 9 | 42 | 5 | 3 | 3 | 4 | 50 | 2 | 39 | 8 | 0 |
| Fletcher, Joseph, Jamestown | .000 | 16 | 1 | 0 | 0 | 0 | 0 | 0 | 0 | 0 | 0 | 0 | 0 | 0 | 0 | 0 | 0 | 0 | 0 |
| Flower, George, Jamestown | .336 | 66 | 235 | 34 | 79 | 122 | 13 | 0 | 10 | 45 | 4 | 0 | 1 | 3 | 30 | 2 | 40 | 9 | 5 |
| Forbes, John, Newark | .200 | 44 | 65 | 6 | 13 | 16 | 3 | 0 | 0 | 4 | 0 | 0 | 0 | 0 | 9 | 1 | 24 | 0 | 0 |
| Fortner, Dennis, Geneva* | .250 | 41 | 92 | 20 | 23 | 24 | 1 | 0 | 0 | 14 | 1 | 2 | 0 | 0 | 26 | 1 | 21 | 4 | 1 |
| Fox, James, Erie | .206 | 69 | 228 | 32 | 47 | 64 | 8 | 0 | 3 | 21 | 1 | 6 | 3 | 2 | 37 | 0 | 31 | 3 | 2 |
| Fox, Kenneth, Jamestown | .000 | 9 | 4 | 0 | 0 | 0 | 0 | 0 | 0 | 0 | 0 | 0 | 0 | 0 | 0 | 0 | 2 | 1 | 0 |
| Franzen, Jules, Batavia* | .250 | 1 | 4 | 1 | 1 | 1 | 0 | 0 | 0 | 0 | 0 | 0 | 0 | 0 | 0 | 0 | 1 | 0 | 0 |
| Freed, Michael, Erie | .250 | 14 | 8 | 1 | 2 | 3 | 1 | 0 | 0 | 1 | 0 | 0 | 0 | 0 | 0 | 0 | 2 | 0 | 0 |
| Fuentes, Roberto, Elmira | .221 | 57 | 172 | 13 | 38 | 46 | 6 | 1 | 0 | 15 | 4 | 6 | 0 | 2 | 14 | 0 | 31 | 2 | 0 |
| Gaeta, Christopher, Newark | .000 | 5 | 8 | 2 | 0 | 0 | 0 | 0 | 0 | 0 | 0 | 0 | 0 | 0 | 1 | 0 | 3 | 0 | 0 |
| Galbato, Chan, Jamestown* | .333 | 12 | 3 | 1 | 1 | 1 | 0 | 0 | 0 | 0 | 0 | 0 | 0 | 0 | 0 | 0 | 0 | 0 | 0 |
| Gambino, Raymond, Watertown* | .103 | 13 | 29 | 2 | 3 | 3 | 0 | 0 | 0 | 0 | 0 | 1 | 0 | 0 | 2 | 0 | 7 | 1 | 0 |
| Garcia, Cornelio, Niagara Falls* | .273 | 70 | 231 | 29 | 63 | 90 | 11 | 2 | 4 | 38 | 6 | 1 | 2 | 0 | 36 | 5 | 80 | 18 | 4 |
| Garcia, Raymond, Utica* | .163 | 18 | 49 | 8 | 8 | 10 | 2 | 0 | 0 | 4 | 0 | 0 | 1 | 1 | 12 | 0 | 10 | 1 | 0 |
| Gardner, Mark, Jamestown | .000 | 3 | 1 | 0 | 0 | 0 | 0 | 0 | 0 | 0 | 0 | 0 | 0 | 0 | 0 | 0 | 0 | 0 | 0 |
| Gelatt, David, Little Falls | .237 | 74 | 245 | 46 | 58 | 75 | 7 | 2 | 2 | 21 | 3 | 3 | 2 | 4 | 42 | 2 | 41 | 19 | 8 |
| Gelmine, Steven, Auburn* | .333 | 23 | 3 | 1 | 1 | 1 | 0 | 0 | 0 | 0 | 0 | 1 | 0 | 0 | 0 | 0 | 1 | 0 | 0 |
| Gilkey, Otis, Erie | .204 | 77 | 294 | 57 | 60 | 92 | 9 | 1 | 7 | 27 | 2 | 4 | 2 | 3 | 55 | 1 | 57 | 34 | 10 |
| Gilles, Thomas, Oneonta | .220 | 40 | 118 | 16 | 26 | 39 | 6 | 2 | 1 | 19 | 3 | 4 | 2 | 1 | 14 | 0 | 28 | 2 | 1 |
| Givens, Brian, Little Falls | .200 | 11 | 10 | 1 | 2 | 2 | 0 | 0 | 0 | 0 | 0 | 0 | 0 | 0 | 0 | 0 | 4 | 0 | 0 |
| Glidewell, John, Jamestown | .000 | 4 | 1 | 0 | 0 | 0 | 0 | 0 | 0 | 0 | 0 | 0 | 0 | 0 | 0 | 0 | 1 | 0 | 0 |
| Gonzalez, Clifford, Little Falls* | .201 | 52 | 144 | 14 | 29 | 36 | 1 | 3 | 0 | 11 | 1 | 2 | 0 | 0 | 18 | 0 | 29 | 8 | 5 |
| Gooden, Maury, Little Falls* | .250 | 32 | 44 | 14 | 11 | 15 | 4 | 0 | 0 | 6 | 0 | 0 | 0 | 0 | 14 | 0 | 8 | 12 | 5 |
| Gouldrup, Gary, Elmira* | .193 | 58 | 166 | 11 | 32 | 40 | 6 | 1 | 0 | 10 | 1 | 0 | 1 | 0 | 13 | 0 | 32 | 1 | 0 |
| Graff, Stephen, Watertown | .221 | 49 | 140 | 16 | 31 | 48 | 5 | 0 | 4 | 23 | 2 | 0 | 2 | 4 | 14 | 0 | 54 | 1 | 3 |
| Graves, Kevin, Auburn* | .167 | 24 | 24 | 7 | 4 | 4 | 0 | 0 | 0 | 2 | 0 | 0 | 0 | 0 | 6 | 0 | 9 | 7 | 0 |
| Gray, Scott, Auburn | .205 | 75 | 254 | 33 | 52 | 68 | 11 | 1 | 1 | 21 | 6 | 2 | 4 | 0 | 58 | 1 | 49 | 7 | 4 |
| Green, Robert, Oneonta | .260 | 39 | 150 | 24 | 39 | 63 | 9 | 3 | 3 | 26 | 4 | 0 | 0 | 0 | 23 | 0 | 47 | 3 | 2 |
| Grimes, Lee, Geneva | .245 | 76 | 273 | 40 | 67 | 93 | 6 | 1 | 6 | 44 | 4 | 4 | 0 | 1 | 44 | 1 | 31 | 9 | 2 |
| Guerrero, Jonas, Auburn | .200 | 20 | 40 | 3 | 8 | 9 | 1 | 0 | 0 | 1 | 0 | 0 | 0 | 1 | 2 | 0 | 19 | 3 | 0 |
| Gutierrez, Roberto, Newark | .111 | 6 | 9 | 1 | 1 | 1 | 0 | 0 | 0 | 0 | 0 | 0 | 0 | 0 | 4 | 0 | 1 | 1 | 0 |
| Hackett, John, Erie* | .000 | 8 | 2 | 0 | 0 | 0 | 0 | 0 | 0 | 0 | 0 | 0 | 0 | 0 | 0 | 0 | 1 | 0 | 0 |
| Halasz, Michael, Newark | .244 | 21 | 45 | 5 | 11 | 12 | 1 | 0 | 0 | 4 | 0 | 0 | 0 | 0 | 13 | 0 | 14 | 2 | 0 |
| Hall, Andrew, Watertown | .121 | 15 | 33 | 2 | 4 | 5 | 1 | 0 | 0 | 1 | 0 | 3 | 1 | 3 | 6 | 0 | 14 | 0 | 0 |
| Hansen, Todd, Watertown | .000 | 11 | 5 | 2 | 0 | 0 | 0 | 0 | 0 | 0 | 0 | 1 | 0 | 0 | 1 | 0 | 2 | 0 | 0 |
| Hardamon, Derrick, Geneva | .236 | 42 | 123 | 24 | 29 | 36 | 3 | 2 | 0 | 8 | 3 | 1 | 0 | 2 | 19 | 1 | 29 | 22 | 5 |
| Hartley, Thomas, Niagara Falls | .213 | 62 | 197 | 26 | 42 | 51 | 7 | 1 | 0 | 11 | 4 | 0 | 1 | 0 | 27 | 0 | 51 | 11 | 2 |
| Harwick, Clinton, Geneva | .258 | 35 | 89 | 8 | 23 | 31 | 6 | 1 | 0 | 14 | 1 | 1 | 1 | 1 | 15 | 0 | 24 | 0 | 1 |
| Heakins, Craig, Watertown | .050 | 42 | 100 | 4 | 5 | 8 | 1 | 1 | 0 | 1 | 0 | 0 | 0 | 1 | 18 | 0 | 47 | 0 | 0 |
| Hedfelt, Francisco, Utica | .103 | 14 | 39 | 2 | 4 | 4 | 0 | 0 | 0 | 0 | 0 | 3 | 0 | 1 | 5 | 0 | 17 | 0 | 0 |
| Helton, Kevin, Watertown | .000 | 18 | 2 | 0 | 0 | 0 | 0 | 0 | 0 | 0 | 0 | 0 | 0 | 0 | 0 | 0 | 1 | 0 | 0 |
| Hibbs, Albert, Utica | .185 | 42 | 119 | 11 | 22 | 36 | 0 | 1 | 4 | 13 | 0 | 0 | 1 | 2 | 20 | 1 | 56 | 1 | 0 |
| Higgins, Theodore, Oneonta* | 1.000 | 1 | 1 | 1 | 1 | 4 | 0 | 0 | 1 | 1 | 0 | 0 | 0 | 0 | 0 | 0 | 0 | 0 | 0 |
| Hillman, Thomas, Batavia | .113 | 27 | 62 | 14 | 7 | 10 | 1 | 1 | 0 | 7 | 0 | 1 | 0 | 0 | 15 | 0 | 12 | 3 | 0 |
| Hilton, Howard, Erie | .200 | 24 | 5 | 1 | 1 | 1 | 0 | 0 | 0 | 0 | 0 | 0 | 0 | 0 | 0 | 0 | 2 | 0 | 0 |
| Hirsch, Jeffrey, Geneva† | .000 | 22 | 1 | 0 | 0 | 0 | 0 | 0 | 0 | 0 | 0 | 0 | 0 | 0 | 0 | 0 | 1 | 0 | 0 |
| Houston, Melvin, Jamestown† | .245 | 55 | 212 | 22 | 52 | 70 | 11 | 2 | 1 | 20 | 0 | 1 | 1 | 9 | 0 | 27 | 3 | 5 |
| Howard, Brian, Watertown | .224 | 18 | 76 | 6 | 17 | 26 | 4 | 1 | 1 | 6 | 0 | 1 | 1 | 0 | 2 | 0 | 19 | 4 | 4 |
| Howes, Jeff, Little Falls | .000 | 3 | 1 | 0 | 0 | 0 | 0 | 0 | 0 | 0 | 0 | 0 | 0 | 0 | 0 | 0 | 0 | 0 | 0 |
| Hunter, James, Jamestown | .100 | 14 | 10 | 0 | 1 | 1 | 0 | 0 | 0 | 0 | 0 | 0 | 0 | 0 | 2 | 0 | 2 | 0 | 0 |
| Hurst, Rock, Batavia | .244 | 37 | 119 | 16 | 29 | 42 | 8 | 1 | 1 | 10 | 1 | 0 | 1 | 1 | 7 | 0 | 33 | 4 | 0 |
| Hutson, Lee, Jamestown | .235 | 56 | 162 | 38 | 38 | 63 | 13 | 3 | 2 | 24 | 7 | 0 | 2 | 6 | 31 | 0 | 32 | 7 | 2 |
| Iavarone, Gregory, Oneonta | .315 | 28 | 54 | 9 | 17 | 24 | 1 | 0 | 2 | 9 | 1 | 4 | 0 | 0 | 18 | 0 | 17 | 1 | 1 |
| Iglesias, Luis, Erie | .286 | 4 | 14 | 3 | 4 | 7 | 0 | 0 | 1 | 1 | 0 | 0 | 0 | 2 | 1 | 0 | 4 | 1 | 0 |
| Ilsley, Blaise, Auburn* | .400 | 13 | 10 | 1 | 4 | 4 | 0 | 0 | 0 | 2 | 0 | 0 | 0 | 0 | 0 | 0 | 2 | 0 | 0 |
| James, Calvin, Auburn* | .263 | 10 | 38 | 9 | 10 | 13 | 3 | 0 | 0 | 4 | 0 | 0 | 0 | 1 | 5 | 0 | 5 | 4 | 0 |
| Jaster, Scott, Little Falls | .236 | 61 | 225 | 24 | 53 | 88 | 12 | 1 | 7 | 26 | 3 | 0 | 2 | 1 | 21 | 1 | 73 | 7 | 3 |
| Jenkins, David, Batavia | .213 | 29 | 75 | 7 | 16 | 18 | 2 | 0 | 0 | 6 | 0 | 0 | 1 | 0 | 2 | 0 | 21 | 4 | 2 |
| Jester, Timothy, Auburn* | .274 | 59 | 208 | 29 | 57 | 78 | 7 | 1 | 4 | 22 | 5 | 7 | 1 | 1 | 17 | 1 | 24 | 5 | 2 |
| Jimenez, Raul, Erie | .222 | 10 | 27 | 4 | 6 | 6 | 0 | 0 | 0 | 1 | 0 | 1 | 0 | 0 | 6 | 0 | 6 | 0 | 2 |
| Johnigan, Stephen, Batavia | .000 | 1 | 3 | 0 | 0 | 0 | 0 | 0 | 0 | 0 | 0 | 0 | 0 | 0 | 0 | 0 | 0 | 0 | 0 |
| Johnson, Everton, Little Falls | .252 | 45 | 127 | 27 | 32 | 55 | 4 | 2 | 5 | 13 | 0 | 0 | 0 | 0 | 23 | 0 | 21 | 6 | 4 |
| Johnson, Randall, Jamestown | .000 | 8 | 2 | 1 | 0 | 0 | 0 | 0 | 0 | 0 | 0 | 0 | 0 | 0 | 1 | 0 | 1 | 0 | 0 |
| Johnson, Richard, Auburn | .313 | 70 | 214 | 43 | 67 | 117 | 10 | 2 | 12 | 48 | 5 | 0 | 4 | 3 | 39 | 5 | 43 | 3 | 0 |
| Johnson, Terence, Little Falls* | .136 | 11 | 22 | 1 | 3 | 5 | 0 | 1 | 0 | 1 | 0 | 0 | 0 | 0 | 0 | 0 | 7 | 0 | 0 |
| Jordan, Ian, Watertown | .196 | 41 | 97 | 4 | 19 | 22 | 3 | 0 | 0 | 3 | 0 | 0 | 0 | 0 | 5 | 0 | 31 | 1 | 2 |
| Jordan, Scott, Batavia | .206 | 20 | 68 | 8 | 14 | 26 | 3 | 0 | 3 | 9 | 2 | 1 | 0 | 0 | 12 | 0 | 13 | 5 | 2 |
| Kelly, Leonard, Jamestown | .750 | 11 | 4 | 0 | 3 | 5 | 0 | 1 | 0 | 1 | 0 | 0 | 0 | 0 | 0 | 0 | 1 | 0 | 0 |
| Khoury, Scott, Newark* | .257 | 57 | 210 | 30 | 54 | 106 | 6 | 2 | 14 | 42 | 6 | 1 | 1 | 0 | 23 | 3 | 36 | 6 | 2 |

| Player and Club | Pct. | G. | AB. | R. | H. | TB. | 2B. | 3B. | HR. | RBI. | GW. | SH. | SF. | HP. | BB. | Int. BB. | SO. | SB. | CS. |
|---|---|---|---|---|---|---|---|---|---|---|---|---|---|---|---|---|---|---|---|
| Knowles, Rob, Erie° | .219 | 59 | 201 | 23 | 44 | 74 | 9 | 3 | 5 | 28 | 2 | 3 | 1 | 1 | 23 | 1 | 61 | 7 | 3 |
| Koopman, Robert, Watertown° | .000 | 14 | 9 | 1 | 0 | 0 | 0 | 0 | 0 | 0 | 0 | 0 | 0 | 0 | 3 | 0 | 7 | 0 | 0 |
| LaMarr, Jeffrey, Jamestown | .250 | 15 | 32 | 7 | 8 | 12 | 1 | 0 | 1 | 6 | 0 | 2 | 0 | 0 | 8 | 0 | 12 | 0 | 0 |
| Lambert, Robert, Oneonta | .000 | 1 | 0 | 1 | 0 | 0 | 0 | 0 | 0 | 0 | 0 | 0 | 0 | 0 | 2 | 0 | 0 | 2 | 0 |
| Lara, Crucito, Erie† | .230 | 54 | 161 | 25 | 37 | 43 | 3 | 0 | 1 | 14 | 2 | 2 | 2 | 1 | 22 | 2 | 37 | 4 | 3 |
| Laseke, Eric, Elmira | .207 | 59 | 193 | 17 | 40 | 45 | 5 | 0 | 0 | 11 | 1 | 3 | 1 | 0 | 19 | 1 | 29 | 5 | 1 |
| Lashua, Ricky, Oneonta† | .000 | 4 | 4 | 0 | 0 | 0 | 0 | 0 | 0 | 0 | 0 | 0 | 0 | 0 | 1 | 0 | 1 | 0 | 0 |
| Lee, Harvey, Oneonta | .249 | 52 | 169 | 35 | 42 | 60 | 7 | 1 | 3 | 22 | 6 | 3 | 2 | 1 | 25 | 0 | 41 | 16 | 4 |
| Leslie, William, Batavia | .000 | 10 | 22 | 1 | 0 | 0 | 0 | 0 | 0 | 0 | 0 | 0 | 0 | 0 | 3 | 0 | 12 | 0 | 0 |
| Lester, James, Jamestown | .285 | 54 | 158 | 27 | 45 | 56 | 7 | 2 | 0 | 14 | 3 | 1 | 1 | 4 | 26 | 0 | 29 | 2 | 5 |
| Livchak, Robert, Erie° | .200 | 27 | 35 | 1 | 7 | 8 | 1 | 0 | 0 | 0 | 0 | 1 | 0 | 0 | 4 | 0 | 12 | 0 | 1 |
| Lochow, Scott, Geneva | .217 | 22 | 60 | 6 | 13 | 16 | 3 | 0 | 0 | 7 | 1 | 1 | 0 | 1 | 3 | 0 | 15 | 0 | 0 |
| Lombardozzi, Christopher, Oneonta°.. | .246 | 66 | 207 | 33 | 51 | 70 | 9 | 2 | 2 | 25 | 3 | 5 | 0 | 1 | 57 | 1 | 55 | 11 | 3 |
| Lotzar, Gregory, Elmira° | .310 | 56 | 187 | 40 | 58 | 83 | 6 | 5 | 3 | 21 | 2 | 5 | 1 | 2 | 34 | 1 | 23 | 14 | 2 |
| Lovell, Donald, Batavia° | .282 | 74 | 277 | 38 | 78 | 129 | 19 | 4 | 8 | 51 | 5 | 0 | 3 | 3 | 29 | 1 | 26 | 8 | 6 |
| Maas, Jason, Oneonta° | .286 | 67 | 234 | 37 | 67 | 81 | 7 | 2 | 1 | 23 | 4 | 4 | 1 | 0 | 51 | 2 | 42 | 16 | 3 |
| Mainini, Matthew, Oneonta° | .260 | 70 | 196 | 30 | 51 | 69 | 7 | 1 | 3 | 23 | 4 | 0 | 5 | 0 | 52 | 2 | 46 | 4 | 4 |
| Malizia, Ricky, Newark | .200 | 33 | 50 | 13 | 10 | 15 | 3 | 1 | 0 | 5 | 1 | 3 | 0 | 0 | 15 | 0 | 15 | 4 | 2 |
| Mancini, Peter, Newark | .316 | 10 | 19 | 3 | 6 | 6 | 0 | 0 | 0 | 3 | 0 | 1 | 0 | 2 | 2 | 0 | 3 | 0 | 0 |
| Marston, Tod, Oneonta | .202 | 36 | 109 | 16 | 22 | 34 | 2 | 2 | 2 | 15 | 1 | 2 | 0 | 0 | 15 | 0 | 28 | 3 | 1 |
| Marte, Roberto, Erie | .250 | 15 | 20 | 0 | 5 | 7 | 2 | 0 | 0 | 5 | 1 | 0 | 0 | 1 | 3 | 0 | 10 | 0 | 0 |
| Martin, Norberto, Niagara Falls† | .253 | 60 | 217 | 22 | 55 | 67 | 9 | 0 | 1 | 13 | 0 | 5 | 0 | 1 | 7 | 0 | 41 | 6 | 4 |
| Martineau, Paul, Jamestown° | .253 | 68 | 229 | 30 | 58 | 92 | 14 | 1 | 6 | 31 | 2 | 0 | 2 | 1 | 26 | 7 | 55 | 1 | 1 |
| Martinez, William, Newark | .106 | 18 | 47 | 7 | 5 | 6 | 1 | 0 | 0 | 6 | 0 | 0 | 0 | 1 | 9 | 0 | 16 | 1 | 1 |
| Mauch, Thomas, Erie° | .200 | 23 | 10 | 1 | 2 | 3 | 1 | 0 | 0 | 3 | 0 | 0 | 0 | 0 | 0 | 0 | 2 | 0 | 0 |
| McCandlish, Robert, Geneva | .000 | 17 | 1 | 0 | 0 | 0 | 0 | 0 | 0 | 0 | 0 | 0 | 0 | 0 | 0 | 0 | 1 | 0 | 0 |
| McFarlane, Hermanus, Newark | .250 | 6 | 4 | 0 | 1 | 1 | 0 | 0 | 0 | 0 | 0 | 0 | 0 | 0 | 0 | 0 | 2 | 0 | 0 |
| McMillan, Timothy, Watertown | .245 | 44 | 159 | 19 | 39 | 70 | 5 | 4 | 6 | 21 | 3 | 0 | 2 | 0 | 7 | 0 | 53 | 4 | 4 |
| McNeely, Michael, Erie | .286 | 14 | 7 | 2 | 2 | 3 | 1 | 0 | 0 | 1 | 0 | 0 | 0 | 0 | 0 | 0 | 0 | 0 | 0 |
| McWilliams, Juan, Watertown | .111 | 8 | 18 | 1 | 2 | 3 | 1 | 0 | 0 | 3 | 0 | 0 | 0 | 0 | 1 | 0 | 7 | 0 | 0 |
| Medina, Luis, Batavia | .266 | 76 | 290 | 43 | 77 | 129 | 16 | 0 | 12 | 43 | 7 | 0 | 0 | 3 | 32 | 1 | 72 | 7 | 3 |
| Mejia, Simon, Geneva† | .183 | 30 | 82 | 8 | 15 | 19 | 2 | 1 | 0 | 6 | 0 | 1 | 1 | 1 | 11 | 2 | 22 | 3 | 5 |
| Melton, Lawrence, Watertown | .111 | 15 | 9 | 1 | 1 | 1 | 0 | 0 | 0 | 1 | 0 | 1 | 1 | 0 | 2 | 0 | 4 | 0 | 0 |
| Menendez, William, Geneva° | .000 | 8 | 1 | 0 | 0 | 0 | 0 | 0 | 0 | 0 | 0 | 0 | 0 | 0 | 0 | 0 | 1 | 0 | 0 |
| Meucci, Thomas, Newark | .083 | 14 | 24 | 2 | 2 | 2 | 0 | 0 | 0 | 0 | 0 | 0 | 0 | 0 | 3 | 0 | 8 | 1 | 0 |
| Meyer, Gordon, Oneonta | .182 | 6 | 11 | 2 | 2 | 3 | 1 | 0 | 0 | 0 | 0 | 0 | 0 | 1 | 0 | 0 | 3 | 0 | 0 |
| Monell, Johnny, Little Falls† | .213 | 67 | 211 | 17 | 45 | 64 | 9 | 2 | 2 | 25 | 4 | 1 | 4 | 0 | 20 | 3 | 25 | 7 | 7 |
| Moore, Michael, Niagara Falls | .245 | 55 | 184 | 22 | 45 | 60 | 7 | 4 | 0 | 15 | 4 | 2 | 0 | 2 | 13 | 0 | 26 | 3 | 3 |
| Mota, Jose, Niagara Falls† | .303 | 65 | 254 | 35 | 77 | 90 | 9 | 2 | 0 | 27 | 1 | 5 | 2 | 2 | 28 | 3 | 29 | 8 | 5 |
| Murphy, Gary, Auburn | .100 | 18 | 10 | 0 | 1 | 1 | 0 | 0 | 0 | 1 | 0 | 0 | 0 | 0 | 0 | 0 | 2 | 0 | 0 |
| Murphy, Joseph, Geneva° | .145 | 69 | 207 | 31 | 30 | 42 | 3 | 0 | 3 | 31 | 7 | 1 | 2 | 3 | 54 | 1 | 68 | 2 | 0 |
| Narcisse, Ronald, Little Falls | .178 | 37 | 73 | 8 | 13 | 16 | 3 | 0 | 0 | 9 | 1 | 0 | 0 | 0 | 11 | 0 | 37 | 1 | 4 |
| Natera, Luis, Little Falls | .175 | 61 | 160 | 7 | 28 | 33 | 5 | 0 | 0 | 3 | 0 | 3 | 1 | 0 | 16 | 0 | 43 | 1 | 3 |
| Nemeth, Carey, Erie | .232 | 64 | 198 | 34 | 46 | 80 | 8 | 1 | 8 | 25 | 1 | 5 | 1 | 3 | 47 | 0 | 63 | 14 | 5 |
| Nichols, Scott, Erie | .200 | 7 | 20 | 3 | 4 | 6 | 0 | 1 | 0 | 2 | 0 | 1 | 0 | 0 | 0 | 0 | 4 | 0 | 0 |
| Nichols, Ty, Newark† | .199 | 68 | 196 | 18 | 39 | 50 | 5 | 0 | 2 | 22 | 2 | 9 | 2 | 1 | 31 | 4 | 48 | 2 | 3 |
| Noble, Ramon, Utica | .195 | 61 | 190 | 21 | 37 | 46 | 1 | 4 | 0 | 12 | 1 | 2 | 0 | 2 | 22 | 0 | 64 | 14 | 3 |
| O'Connor, James, Erie | .182 | 3 | 11 | 3 | 2 | 5 | 0 | 0 | 1 | 3 | 0 | 0 | 0 | 0 | 2 | 0 | 5 | 0 | 0 |
| Oberholtzer, Mark, Watertown | .000 | 15 | 1 | 0 | 0 | 0 | 0 | 0 | 0 | 0 | 0 | 0 | 0 | 0 | 0 | 0 | 1 | 0 | 0 |
| Odle, Page, Watertown | .281 | 72 | 228 | 40 | 64 | 109 | 13 | 4 | 8 | 35 | 4 | 0 | 0 | 3 | 49 | 0 | 45 | 19 | 9 |
| Ojea, Alexander, Erie | .230 | 68 | 213 | 36 | 49 | 61 | 7 | 1 | 1 | 21 | 1 | 7 | 2 | 2 | 39 | 0 | 37 | 9 | 8 |
| Oller, Jeffrey, Jamestown° | .244 | 65 | 213 | 26 | 52 | 79 | 8 | 2 | 5 | 30 | 3 | 1 | 3 | 0 | 34 | 4 | 65 | 3 | 4 |
| Orsag, James, Elmira° | .226 | 66 | 212 | 26 | 48 | 68 | 14 | 0 | 2 | 22 | 3 | 1 | 1 | 2 | 37 | 4 | 49 | 3 | 1 |
| Oyster, Jeffrey, Erie | .000 | 14 | 0 | 1 | 0 | 0 | 0 | 0 | 0 | 0 | 0 | 0 | 0 | 0 | 2 | 0 | 0 | 0 | 0 |
| Page, Kelvin, Little Falls | .000 | 23 | 0 | 0 | 0 | 0 | 0 | 0 | 0 | 0 | 0 | 0 | 0 | 0 | 1 | 0 | 0 | 0 | 0 |
| Paul, Grady, Newark | .000 | 7 | 11 | 1 | 0 | 0 | 0 | 0 | 0 | 1 | 0 | 0 | 0 | 0 | 1 | 0 | 7 | 1 | 1 |
| Peraza, Luis, Niagara Falls | .241 | 72 | 274 | 35 | 66 | 121 | 15 | 2 | 12 | 47 | 7 | 0 | 3 | 0 | 19 | 1 | 65 | 3 | 1 |
| Perez, Alfredo, Auburn | .143 | 18 | 21 | 4 | 3 | 3 | 0 | 0 | 0 | 3 | 0 | 0 | 1 | 1 | 3 | 0 | 8 | 0 | 0 |
| Perez, Freddy, Utica | .193 | 39 | 109 | 13 | 21 | 28 | 5 | 1 | 0 | 7 | 1 | 0 | 1 | 1 | 9 | 0 | 36 | 8 | 6 |
| Perez, Julio, Watertown | .259 | 47 | 170 | 24 | 44 | 54 | 6 | 2 | 0 | 16 | 2 | 2 | 1 | 0 | 13 | 1 | 18 | 14 | 4 |
| Picota, Lenin, Erie | .500 | 16 | 2 | 0 | 1 | 1 | 0 | 0 | 0 | 1 | 0 | 0 | 0 | 0 | 0 | 0 | 1 | 0 | 0 |
| Plante, William, Elmira | .182 | 44 | 137 | 13 | 25 | 38 | 4 | 0 | 3 | 17 | 2 | 0 | 2 | 3 | 19 | 0 | 50 | 2 | 0 |
| Pliecones, Johnnie, Oneonta | .221 | 46 | 145 | 17 | 32 | 36 | 2 | 1 | 0 | 16 | 0 | 2 | 3 | 1 | 11 | 0 | 17 | 5 | 0 |
| Power, John, Batavia° | .103 | 11 | 29 | 2 | 3 | 7 | 1 | 0 | 1 | 4 | 0 | 0 | 0 | 0 | 4 | 0 | 6 | 0 | 0 |
| Pratt, Todd, Elmira | .134 | 39 | 119 | 7 | 16 | 19 | 1 | 1 | 0 | 5 | 1 | 3 | 1 | 1 | 10 | 0 | 27 | 0 | 1 |
| Puzey, James, Erie° | .247 | 66 | 215 | 24 | 53 | 78 | 7 | 0 | 6 | 28 | 4 | 2 | 2 | 3 | 34 | 4 | 20 | 2 | 7 |
| Quintana, Carlos, Elmira | .277 | 65 | 220 | 27 | 61 | 81 | 8 | 0 | 4 | 35 | 2 | 0 | 2 | 3 | 29 | 0 | 31 | 3 | 0 |
| Rauth, Christopher, Little Falls | .083 | 15 | 12 | 1 | 1 | 1 | 0 | 0 | 0 | 0 | 0 | 1 | 0 | 0 | 2 | 0 | 5 | 0 | 0 |
| Ray, Randy, Jamestown | .268 | 46 | 157 | 29 | 42 | 63 | 9 | 0 | 4 | 22 | 3 | 2 | 1 | 3 | 15 | 0 | 33 | 5 | 1 |
| Repoz, Craig, Little Falls | .249 | 71 | 249 | 27 | 62 | 87 | 11 | 1 | 4 | 40 | 7 | 0 | 3 | 4 | 11 | 1 | 47 | 12 | 4 |
| Reynolds, Anthony, Batavia° | .214 | 6 | 14 | 1 | 3 | 5 | 2 | 0 | 0 | 4 | 0 | 0 | 0 | 0 | 3 | 0 | 5 | 0 | 0 |
| Richardson, Jeffrey, Little Falls | .222 | 11 | 9 | 1 | 2 | 2 | 0 | 0 | 0 | 2 | 0 | 1 | 0 | 0 | 1 | 0 | 2 | 0 | 0 |
| Ricker, Troy, Utica | .157 | 34 | 89 | 9 | 14 | 18 | 1 | 0 | 1 | 9 | 0 | 2 | 0 | 0 | 14 | 0 | 37 | 7 | 4 |
| Rinehart, Robert, Little Falls° | .218 | 36 | 78 | 6 | 17 | 17 | 0 | 0 | 0 | 3 | 1 | 0 | 0 | 9 | 1 | 24 | 3 | 2 |
| Roberts, Norman, Newark | .255 | 63 | 208 | 44 | 53 | 81 | 8 | 1 | 6 | 27 | 5 | 4 | 3 | 7 | 31 | 4 | 27 | 12 | 9 |
| Robertson, Bryant, Little Falls° | .282 | 20 | 39 | 5 | 11 | 15 | 1 | 0 | 1 | 8 | 2 | 0 | 1 | 0 | 9 | 0 | 9 | 0 | 1 |
| Robinson, Emmett, Watertown | .259 | 65 | 193 | 16 | 50 | 65 | 7 | 4 | 0 | 15 | 0 | 1 | 0 | 0 | 16 | 0 | 47 | 18 | 3 |
| Robles, Gabaliel, Geneva | .143 | 18 | 7 | 0 | 1 | 1 | 0 | 0 | 0 | 3 | 1 | 4 | 0 | 0 | 0 | 0 | 1 | 0 | 0 |
| Rodriguez, Alejandro, Erie | .000 | 15 | 0 | 0 | 0 | 0 | 0 | 0 | 0 | 0 | 0 | 0 | 0 | 0 | 0 | 0 | 0 | 0 | 0 |
| Rodriguez, Ignacio, Jamestown | .229 | 64 | 192 | 23 | 44 | 67 | 3 | 1 | 6 | 26 | 2 | 0 | 0 | 1 | 27 | 2 | 48 | 6 | 2 |
| Rodriguez, Nelson, Oneonta° | .258 | 61 | 198 | 16 | 51 | 60 | 9 | 0 | 0 | 16 | 0 | 1 | 0 | 0 | 14 | 1 | 52 | 4 | 1 |
| Roebuck, Ron, Auburn† | .000 | 21 | 2 | 0 | 0 | 0 | 0 | 0 | 0 | 0 | 0 | 0 | 0 | 0 | 0 | 0 | 1 | 0 | 0 |
| Rogalski, Wayne, Auburn | .270 | 72 | 252 | 35 | 68 | 107 | 20 | 2 | 5 | 42 | 3 | 0 | 4 | 5 | 32 | 1 | 52 | 10 | 3 |
| Rogers, Marte, Elmira | .195 | 51 | 123 | 10 | 24 | 33 | 6 | 0 | 1 | 4 | 1 | 3 | 0 | 2 | 4 | 0 | 38 | 0 | 1 |
| Rosario, Victor, Elmira | .203 | 59 | 177 | 11 | 36 | 49 | 8 | 1 | 1 | 14 | 0 | 1 | 1 | 1 | 19 | 0 | 47 | 1 | 2 |
| Rossy, Elam, Newark | .215 | 73 | 246 | 38 | 53 | 80 | 14 | 2 | 3 | 25 | 5 | 3 | 1 | 1 | 32 | 1 | 22 | 17 | 7 |
| Roth, Kris, Geneva | .125 | 16 | 16 | 3 | 2 | 2 | 0 | 0 | 0 | 0 | 0 | 1 | 0 | 1 | 2 | 0 | 5 | 0 | 0 |
| Rountree, Michael, Erie° | .215 | 46 | 121 | 17 | 26 | 33 | 4 | 0 | 1 | 8 | 1 | 0 | 0 | 1 | 26 | 0 | 51 | 5 | 3 |
| Santana, Ernesto, Watertown | .000 | 19 | 2 | 0 | 0 | 0 | 0 | 0 | 0 | 0 | 0 | 0 | 0 | 0 | 0 | 0 | 2 | 0 | 0 |
| Santana, Jose, Erie | .114 | 17 | 44 | 1 | 5 | 6 | 1 | 0 | 0 | 1 | 0 | 1 | 0 | 0 | 2 | 0 | 13 | 3 | 0 |
| Santo, Robert, Newark° | .276 | 51 | 163 | 19 | 45 | 63 | 10 | 1 | 2 | 27 | 4 | 0 | 1 | 3 | 15 | 1 | 36 | 0 | 0 |
| Santos, Donaciano, Batavia | .225 | 14 | 40 | 6 | 9 | 13 | 1 | 0 | 1 | 4 | 0 | 0 | 0 | 1 | 2 | 0 | 13 | 0 | 1 |

| Player and Club | Pct. | G. | AB. | R. | H. | TB. | 2B. | 3B. | HR. | RBI. | GW. | SH. | SF. | HP. | BB. | Int. BB. | SO. | SB. | CS. |
|---|---|---|---|---|---|---|---|---|---|---|---|---|---|---|---|---|---|---|---|
| Satzinger, Jeffrey, Watertown | .400 | 18 | 5 | 1 | 2 | 2 | 0 | 0 | 0 | 0 | 0 | 0 | 0 | 0 | 0 | 0 | 0 | 0 | 0 |
| Schulte, Joseph, Auburn | 1.000 | 27 | 1 | 0 | 1 | 1 | 0 | 0 | 0 | 0 | 0 | 0 | 0 | 0 | 0 | 0 | 0 | 0 | 0 |
| Scott, Charles, Batavia | .200 | 18 | 5 | 1 | 1 | 1 | 0 | 0 | 0 | 0 | 0 | 0 | 0 | 0 | 1 | 0 | 3 | 0 | 0 |
| Sehlhorst, Daniel, Niagara Falls | .000 | 1 | 2 | 0 | 0 | 0 | 0 | 0 | 0 | 0 | 0 | 0 | 0 | 0 | 0 | 0 | 2 | 0 | 0 |
| Sepanek, Robert, Oneonta° | .275 | 63 | 211 | 34 | 58 | 96 | 13 | 5 | 5 | 43 | 6 | 0 | 3 | 0 | 23 | 2 | 37 | 5 | 0 |
| Shaw, Scott, Oneonta | .293 | 72 | 276 | 40 | 81 | 113 | 8 | 6 | 4 | 37 | 9 | 3 | 0 | 4 | 23 | 0 | 54 | 5 | 4 |
| Sheaffer, Jeffrey, Utica° | .207 | 67 | 217 | 30 | 45 | 56 | 7 | 2 | 0 | 19 | 4 | 6 | 2 | 2 | 34 | 2 | 49 | 26 | 7 |
| Sheldon, David, Niagara Falls | .186 | 47 | 145 | 17 | 27 | 45 | 3 | 0 | 5 | 16 | 1 | 0 | 3 | 1 | 17 | 0 | 41 | 1 | 0 |
| Shepis, Robert, Auburn° | .171 | 36 | 76 | 9 | 13 | 17 | 2 | 1 | 0 | 7 | 1 | 0 | 1 | 4 | 12 | 3 | 16 | 3 | 0 |
| Shockman, Mark, Newark° | .204 | 20 | 54 | 8 | 11 | 22 | 6 | 1 | 1 | 8 | 0 | 0 | 0 | 0 | 4 | 0 | 16 | 0 | 1 |
| Shouse, John, Watertown | .194 | 32 | 67 | 4 | 13 | 18 | 3 | 1 | 0 | 6 | 0 | 2 | 1 | 1 | 4 | 0 | 21 | 0 | 1 |
| Skinner, Matthew, Newark | .176 | 41 | 74 | 10 | 13 | 15 | 2 | 0 | 0 | 6 | 0 | 1 | 2 | 1 | 7 | 1 | 27 | 6 | 0 |
| Small, Jeffrey, Geneva | .220 | 75 | 259 | 32 | 57 | 97 | 13 | 3 | 7 | 39 | 7 | 2 | 0 | 2 | 35 | 1 | 46 | 2 | 2 |
| Smith, Dwight, Geneva° | .289 | 73 | 232 | 44 | 67 | 94 | 11 | 2 | 4 | 32 | 4 | 0 | 1 | 1 | 31 | 3 | 33 | 30 | 10 |
| Smith, Kevin, Auburn | .000 | 15 | 8 | 0 | 0 | 0 | 0 | 0 | 0 | 0 | 0 | 0 | 1 | 0 | 0 | 0 | 7 | 0 | 0 |
| Smith, Timothy, Newark | .281 | 17 | 57 | 12 | 16 | 23 | 1 | 0 | 2 | 15 | 2 | 0 | 1 | 0 | 12 | 1 | 9 | 0 | 0 |
| Speakman, Timothy, Elmira | .219 | 36 | 114 | 9 | 25 | 37 | 6 | 0 | 2 | 13 | 1 | 1 | 0 | 7 | 4 | 0 | 37 | 1 | 0 |
| St. Claire, Steven, Utica | .180 | 47 | 139 | 20 | 25 | 37 | 7 | 1 | 1 | 18 | 2 | 2 | 0 | 3 | 8 | 0 | 44 | 8 | 2 |
| Stanicek, Peter, Newark | .251 | 69 | 255 | 39 | 64 | 84 | 12 | 1 | 2 | 25 | 3 | 6 | 1 | 6 | 51 | 0 | 44 | 30 | 4 |
| Stanko, Edward, Oneonta° | .162 | 27 | 37 | 11 | 6 | 7 | 1 | 0 | 0 | 3 | 0 | 0 | 0 | 0 | 13 | 1 | 14 | 0 | 1 |
| Startoni, Troy, Batavia | .281 | 46 | 146 | 20 | 41 | 56 | 9 | 0 | 2 | 12 | 0 | 0 | 0 | 0 | 15 | 0 | 34 | 1 | 2 |
| Stauffacher, Stuart, Jamestown | .000 | 20 | 2 | 0 | 0 | 0 | 0 | 0 | 0 | 0 | 0 | 0 | 0 | 0 | 0 | 0 | 0 | 0 | 0 |
| Stephens, Carl, Erie | .290 | 9 | 31 | 3 | 9 | 15 | 1 | 1 | 1 | 5 | 1 | 0 | 0 | 0 | 7 | 0 | 6 | 0 | 0 |
| Stevanus, Michael, Watertown† | .192 | 64 | 167 | 22 | 32 | 38 | 2 | 2 | 0 | 20 | 0 | 3 | 0 | 3 | 30 | 1 | 65 | 9 | 4 |
| Stewart, Anthony, Watertown | .143 | 19 | 56 | 1 | 8 | 9 | 1 | 0 | 0 | 5 | 0 | 2 | 0 | 1 | 0 | 0 | 18 | 2 | 0 |
| Strickland, Robert, Geneva | .219 | 25 | 32 | 3 | 7 | 11 | 1 | 0 | 1 | 5 | 0 | 0 | 0 | 0 | 3 | 0 | 9 | 1 | 0 |
| Sullivan, Daniel, Elmira† | .167 | 2 | 6 | 1 | 1 | 1 | 0 | 0 | 0 | 0 | 0 | 0 | 0 | 0 | 1 | 0 | 3 | 0 | 0 |
| Sundgren, Scott, Jamestown | .000 | 17 | 0 | 0 | 0 | 0 | 0 | 0 | 0 | 0 | 0 | 0 | 1 | 0 | 0 | 0 | 0 | 0 | 0 |
| Swain, Robert, Batavia | .206 | 65 | 228 | 25 | 47 | 56 | 6 | 0 | 1 | 17 | 2 | 2 | 2 | 1 | 30 | 0 | 30 | 5 | 1 |
| Swanzy, Lawrence, Jamestown | .199 | 51 | 151 | 25 | 30 | 38 | 8 | 0 | 0 | 12 | 1 | 1 | 2 | 4 | 22 | 0 | 40 | 10 | 3 |
| Tackett, Jeffrey, Newark | .209 | 62 | 187 | 21 | 39 | 45 | 6 | 0 | 0 | 22 | 2 | 3 | 1 | 2 | 22 | 0 | 33 | 2 | 2 |
| Takach, David, Little Falls° | .000 | 15 | 2 | 0 | 0 | 0 | 0 | 0 | 0 | 0 | 1 | 0 | 0 | 0 | 0 | 0 | 1 | 0 | 0 |
| Tavarez, Alfonso, Utica | .223 | 74 | 264 | 25 | 59 | 74 | 11 | 2 | 0 | 24 | 5 | 6 | 1 | 2 | 7 | 0 | 37 | 4 | 5 |
| Thigpen, Robert, Niagara Falls | .200 | 29 | 5 | 2 | 1 | 1 | 0 | 0 | 0 | 0 | 0 | 0 | 0 | 0 | 2 | 0 | 0 | 0 | 0 |
| Toale, John, Elmira° | .230 | 72 | 248 | 32 | 57 | 90 | 9 | 0 | 8 | 35 | 1 | 2 | 1 | 4 | 36 | 3 | 45 | 2 | 0 |
| Todd, Charles, Batavia | .302 | 31 | 96 | 13 | 29 | 41 | 9 | 0 | 1 | 14 | 0 | 1 | 1 | 1 | 12 | 0 | 24 | 2 | 1 |
| Toliver, Andre, Niagara Falls | .282 | 51 | 174 | 22 | 49 | 73 | 7 | 4 | 3 | 24 | 1 | 2 | 0 | 6 | 20 | 0 | 39 | 2 | 6 |
| Tuozzo, John, Little Falls | .000 | 21 | 3 | 0 | 0 | 0 | 0 | 0 | 0 | 0 | 0 | 0 | 0 | 0 | 0 | 0 | 2 | 0 | 0 |
| Turner, Shane, Oneonta° | .246 | 64 | 228 | 35 | 56 | 69 | 7 | 3 | 0 | 26 | 2 | 1 | 2 | 3 | 35 | 2 | 44 | 12 | 0 |
| Turney, David, Erie | .234 | 52 | 154 | 24 | 36 | 49 | 11 | 1 | 0 | 22 | 2 | 5 | 1 | 2 | 29 | 1 | 29 | 10 | 1 |
| Urzendowski, Michael, Geneva | .250 | 32 | 80 | 9 | 20 | 23 | 3 | 0 | 0 | 6 | 2 | 1 | 0 | 3 | 12 | 0 | 23 | 1 | 2 |
| Valverde, Miguel, Watertown | .227 | 6 | 22 | 4 | 5 | 5 | 0 | 0 | 0 | 1 | 0 | 1 | 0 | 0 | 3 | 0 | 6 | 2 | 1 |
| Van Heyningen, Patrick, Newark° | .333 | 2 | 3 | 1 | 1 | 1 | 0 | 0 | 0 | 0 | 0 | 0 | 0 | 0 | 0 | 0 | 2 | 0 | 0 |
| Velarde, Randy, Niagara Falls | .220 | 67 | 218 | 28 | 48 | 64 | 7 | 3 | 1 | 16 | 0 | 0 | 1 | | 35 | 2 | 72 | 8 | 3 |
| Viltz, Corey, Oneonta° | .246 | 61 | 224 | 39 | 55 | 68 | 11 | 1 | 0 | 25 | 2 | 0 | 1 | 2 | 38 | 1 | 65 | 23 | 3 |
| Von Ahnen, John, Niagara Falls | .157 | 35 | 115 | 13 | 18 | 35 | 2 | 0 | 5 | 16 | 0 | 3 | 0 | | 7 | 0 | 35 | 2 | 3 |
| Wachs, Thomas, Little Falls° | .000 | 19 | 4 | 0 | 0 | 0 | 0 | 0 | 0 | 0 | 0 | 1 | 0 | 0 | 0 | 0 | 2 | 0 | 0 |
| Walker, Larry, Utica° | .223 | 62 | 215 | 24 | 48 | 66 | 8 | 2 | 2 | 26 | 4 | 2 | 1 | 5 | 18 | 4 | 57 | 12 | 6 |
| Wallace, Timothy, Geneva | .226 | 76 | 270 | 42 | 61 | 81 | 11 | 0 | 3 | 37 | 4 | 6 | 6 | 1 | 44 | 5 | 31 | 4 | 5 |
| Walters, Daniel, Auburn | .208 | 44 | 144 | 15 | 30 | 36 | 6 | 0 | 0 | 10 | 0 | 3 | 1 | | 8 | 0 | 23 | 1 | 0 |
| Warmbier, Kenneth, Erie | .280 | 72 | 246 | 54 | 69 | 94 | 3 | 2 | 6 | 32 | 5 | 4 | 1 | 3 | 45 | 0 | 30 | 42 | 6 |
| Webster, Casey, Batavia | .227 | 71 | 251 | 36 | 57 | 107 | 5 | 0 | 15 | 44 | 4 | 0 | 1 | 4 | 35 | 1 | 61 | 3 | 2 |
| Welborn, Todd, Little Falls | .000 | 6 | 3 | 0 | 0 | 0 | 0 | 0 | 0 | 0 | 0 | 0 | 0 | 0 | 0 | 0 | 0 | 0 | 0 |
| Wells, Terry, Auburn° | .400 | 13 | 5 | 0 | 2 | 2 | 0 | 0 | 0 | 0 | 0 | 0 | 0 | 0 | 0 | 0 | 2 | 0 | 0 |
| White, Loren, Jamestown | .220 | 41 | 118 | 18 | 26 | 52 | 6 | 1 | 6 | 28 | 3 | 1 | 0 | | 17 | 0 | 32 | 0 | 1 |
| Wilkes, William, Batavia° | .230 | 36 | 87 | 11 | 20 | 33 | 7 | 0 | 2 | 9 | 0 | 1 | 1 | 0 | 19 | 1 | 19 | 0 | 0 |
| Williams, Kerman, Elmira | .125 | 31 | 48 | 6 | 6 | 7 | 1 | 0 | 0 | 2 | 0 | 0 | 0 | 0 | 10 | 0 | 17 | 1 | 1 |
| Williams, Robert, Elmira | .000 | 21 | 1 | 0 | 0 | 0 | 0 | 0 | 0 | 0 | 0 | 0 | 0 | 0 | 0 | 0 | 1 | 0 | 0 |
| Williams, Roger, Geneva | .167 | 15 | 6 | 3 | 1 | 1 | 0 | 0 | 0 | 0 | 0 | 2 | 0 | 1 | 0 | 0 | 2 | 0 | 0 |
| Workman, Michael, Batavia | .270 | 56 | 196 | 34 | 53 | 63 | 8 | 1 | 0 | 16 | 2 | 3 | 1 | 0 | 27 | 0 | 22 | 8 | 4 |
| Wrigley, David, Watertown | .137 | 42 | 73 | 5 | 10 | 13 | 0 | 0 | 1 | 9 | 2 | 2 | 0 | 0 | 12 | 0 | 18 | 1 | 2 |
| Zapolski, Timothy, Batavia | .273 | 40 | 121 | 18 | 33 | 48 | 3 | 0 | 4 | 15 | 1 | 0 | 3 | 2 | 7 | 0 | 37 | 2 | 2 |
| Zarranz, Fernando, Geneva | .000 | 19 | 3 | 1 | 0 | 0 | 0 | 0 | 0 | 0 | 0 | 0 | 0 | 0 | 1 | 0 | 2 | 0 | 0 |

The following pitchers, listed alphabetically by club, with games in parentheses, had no plate appearances, primarily through use of designated hitters:

AUBURN—Vike, James (1).

BATAVIA—Belleman, Michael (3); Compres, Fidel (4); Farr, Michael (29); Gardner, Myron (6); Ghelfi, Andrew (6); Githens, John (14); Kahler, Christopher (5); Karpuk, Gregory (2); LaFever, Gregory (16); Link, Robert (3); Mercado, Manuel (5); Mora, Abraham (4); Murphy, Kent (13); Nichols, Rodney (13); Poehl, Michael (10); Robertson, Andrew (11); Snyder, Mark (6); Soma, Charles (1); Stender, Scott (1); Williamson, Gregg (13).

ELMIRA—Abbott, John (15); Bayer, Christopher (14); Carista, Michael (16); Clarkin, Michael (6); Gabriele, Daniel (11); Knight, Brock (14); Livernois, Derek (17); Magistri, Gregg (18); Manzanillo, Josia (19); McGowan, Donald (15); Sanderski, John (14); Vasquez, Luis (18); Zupka, William (20).

ERIE—Dumas, Donald (30); Kavanaugh, Timothy (15); Tarasovitch, Scott (1).

GENEVA—Horn, John (20); Villanueva, Hector (1).

JAMESTOWN—Ahearne, Michael (3); Haines, Michael (7); Jones, Shawn (16); Shannon, Robert (5).

LITTLE FALLS—Anderson, Michael (3); Dedicke, Edward (1).

NEWARK—Ballard, Jeffrey (13); Concepcion, Carlos (2); Egelston, Christopher (5); Gonzales, Henry (14); Holm, Michael (3); King, Randy (15); Koonce, Alan (15); Lackie, Jeffrey (2); Palermo, Peter (4); Rohan, Edward (2); Rone, Charles (12); Sanchez, Geraldo (12); Talamantez, Gregory (15); Thorpe, Paul (25); Vazquez, Jesse (18); Williams, Scott (4); Wilson, Wayne (16).

NIAGARA FALLS—Gilmore, William (19); Hendricks, Kenneth (15); Kershaw, Scott (14); Lahrman, Thomas (14); Lampkin, Steven (6); Nossek, Scott (21); Pawlowski, John (15); Peterson, Adam (14); Stacey, Shawn (12); Stone, George (21).

ONEONTA—Azocar, Oscar (15); Balabon, Richard (12); Carroll, Christopher (12); Christopher, Michael (15); Davidson, Robert (29); Dougherty, Patrick (13); Evers, Troy (14); Gay, Scott (2); Leiter, Alois (6); O'Connor, Garrett (2); Patterson, Kenneth (6); Rather, Dody (8); Tirado, Aristarco (22); Torres, Ricardo (3); Trudeau, Kevin (16); Yeager, Charles (1).

UTICA—Allison, James (9); Hendrix, James (23); Jones, Ross (14); LaMarche, Michel (10); Linton, David (15); Paixao, Paulino (15); Pruett, David (21); Sudo, Robert (15); Travels, Darren (15); Valdez, Sergio (15).

WATERTOWN—Martin, Timothy (7); Sampen, William (6).

GRAND SLAM HOME RUNS—Quintana, Webster, 2 each; Alcazar, Contreras, Flower, Gilkey, Hibbs, Ri. Johnson, Knowles, LaMarr, McMillan, Medina, Peraza, Plante, Ricker, Shaw, Toliver, Wrigley, 1 each.

AWARDED FIRST BASE ON CATCHER'S INTERFERENCE—D. Smith 4 (Brunswick, Dean, Speakman, Tackett); Graff (Dean); Ri. Johnson (Marston); Medina (Boyd); Ojea (Cento); F. Perez (Graff); Rogalski (Marston); Rountree (J. O'Connor); Santo (Hibbs).

## CLUB FIELDING

| Club | Pct. | G. | PO. | A. | E. | DP. | PB. | Club | Pct. | G. | PO. | A. | E. | DP. | PB. |
|---|---|---|---|---|---|---|---|---|---|---|---|---|---|---|---|
| Auburn | .968 | 78 | 2031 | 817 | 94 | 78 | 21 | Newark | .954 | 77 | 2037 | 894 | 140 | 76 | 26 |
| Oneonta | .964 | 78 | 2005 | 787 | 105 | 59 | 18 | Niagara Falls | .951 | 77 | 1962 | 838 | 145 | 62 | 10 |
| Erie | .963 | 78 | 2016 | 892 | 112 | 72 | 14 | Elmira | .950 | 77 | 1966 | 733 | 143 | 57 | 34 |
| Geneva | .958 | 78 | 2047 | 884 | 127 | 78 | 21 | Jamestown | .949 | 78 | 2001 | 813 | 151 | 68 | 22 |
| Little Falls | .958 | 75 | 1952 | 827 | 122 | 72 | 22 | Batavia | .948 | 78 | 1994 | 796 | 152 | 45 | 25 |
| Utica | .958 | 76 | 2030 | 875 | 128 | 61 | 26 | Watertown | .943 | 76 | 1928 | 767 | 164 | 49 | 39 |

## INDIVIDUAL FIELDING

☆Throws lefthanded.

### FIRST BASEMEN

| Player and Club | Pct. | G. | PO. | A. | E. | DP. | Player and Club | Pct. | G. | PO. | A. | E. | DP. |
|---|---|---|---|---|---|---|---|---|---|---|---|---|---|
| Alvis, Batavia☆ | .974 | 14 | 105 | 8 | 3 | 6 | Marte, Erie | 1.000 | 2 | 19 | 0 | 0 | 0 |
| Bafia, Geneva | .966 | 4 | 27 | 1 | 1 | 2 | Martineau, Jamestown☆ | .979 | 67 | 509 | 44 | 12 | 48 |
| Burke, Newark☆ | .974 | 11 | 69 | 6 | 2 | 8 | Martinez, Newark | .930 | 8 | 50 | 3 | 4 | 1 |
| Castro, Geneva | 1.000 | 17 | 124 | 10 | 0 | 14 | McFarlane, Newark | 1.000 | 2 | 10 | 0 | 0 | 0 |
| D. Clark, Watertown | 1.000 | 1 | 7 | 0 | 0 | 0 | Medina, Batavia☆ | 1.000 | 1 | 7 | 0 | 0 | 0 |
| Ra. Clark, Watertown☆ | .987 | 41 | 286 | 23 | 4 | 18 | Murphy, Geneva☆ | .983 | 67 | 578 | 43 | 11 | 53 |
| Ro. Clark, Utica☆ | .983 | 37 | 345 | 10 | 6 | 28 | Nemeth, Erie | 1.000 | 2 | 17 | 0 | 0 | 3 |
| Colescott, Little Falls | 1.000 | 1 | 3 | 0 | 0 | 0 | Odle, Watertown | .981 | 22 | 153 | 6 | 3 | 11 |
| Dascenzo, Geneva☆ | 1.000 | 2 | 2 | 0 | 0 | 1 | Orsag, Elmira | .972 | 23 | 195 | 17 | 6 | 14 |
| Davis, Jamestown | .984 | 8 | 58 | 4 | 1 | 7 | Peraza, Niagara Falls | .990 | 46 | 372 | 31 | 4 | 29 |
| Dean, Auburn | .905 | 5 | 37 | 1 | 4 | 2 | Perez, Auburn | 1.000 | 1 | 1 | 0 | 0 | 0 |
| DeLuca, Little Falls | .979 | 36 | 316 | 15 | 7 | 32 | Power, Batavia☆ | .941 | 5 | 44 | 4 | 3 | 1 |
| Dishman, Auburn | .995 | 43 | 356 | 28 | 2 | 38 | Puzey, Erie | .979 | 12 | 86 | 7 | 2 | 9 |
| Espinoza, Little Falls☆ | .989 | 40 | 331 | 21 | 4 | 25 | Rinehart, Little Falls☆ | 1.000 | 3 | 14 | 0 | 0 | 2 |
| Flower, Jamestown | .919 | 7 | 30 | 4 | 3 | 4 | Rodriguez, Jamestown | .950 | 5 | 18 | 1 | 1 | 2 |
| Forbes, Newark | 1.000 | 16 | 51 | 4 | 0 | 7 | Santo, Newark☆ | .983 | 51 | 385 | 17 | 7 | 37 |
| FOX, Erie | .994 | 66 | 608 | 40 | 4 | 50 | Santos, Batavia | .833 | 1 | 5 | 0 | 1 | 1 |
| Fuentes, Elmira | 1.000 | 1 | 1 | 0 | 0 | 0 | Sepanek, Oneonta☆ | .986 | 60 | 456 | 50 | 7 | 40 |
| Garcia, Niagara Falls☆ | .980 | 35 | 279 | 22 | 6 | 17 | Shockman, Newark☆ | .988 | 8 | 73 | 6 | 1 | 12 |
| Gilles, Oneonta | 1.000 | 26 | 154 | 8 | 0 | 10 | Shouse, Watertown | .750 | 1 | 3 | 0 | 1 | 1 |
| Graff, Watertown | .963 | 21 | 134 | 22 | 6 | 9 | Skinner, Newark | .984 | 11 | 52 | 9 | 1 | 6 |
| Hibbs, Utica | 1.000 | 3 | 16 | 0 | 0 | 1 | St. Claire, Utica | 1.000 | 1 | 9 | 0 | 0 | 0 |
| E. Johnson, Little Falls | 1.000 | 1 | 1 | 0 | 0 | 0 | Stanko, Oneonta☆ | 1.000 | 3 | 3 | 0 | 0 | 0 |
| R. Johnson, Auburn | .982 | 38 | 306 | 23 | 6 | 31 | Sullivan, Elmira | 1.000 | 2 | 27 | 0 | 0 | 1 |
| T. Johnson, Little Falls | 1.000 | 6 | 30 | 2 | 0 | 6 | Toale, Elmira | .966 | 54 | 381 | 21 | 14 | 29 |
| Jordan, Watertown | .943 | 7 | 29 | 4 | 2 | 3 | Todd, Batavia | .903 | 4 | 24 | 4 | 3 | 0 |
| Knowles, Erie | 1.000 | 1 | 2 | 0 | 0 | 0 | Walker, Utica | .989 | 42 | 338 | 29 | 4 | 23 |
| Leslie, Batavia | 1.000 | 1 | 8 | 0 | 0 | 2 | Wilkes, Batavia☆ | .994 | 21 | 162 | 8 | 1 | 7 |
| Lester, Jamestown | 1.000 | 1 | 3 | 0 | 0 | 0 | Zapolski, Batavia | .994 | 21 | 154 | 6 | 1 | 10 |
| Lovell, Batavia☆ | .972 | 19 | 162 | 10 | 5 | 10 | | | | | | | |

### SECOND BASEMEN

| Player and Club | Pct. | G. | PO. | A. | E. | DP. | Player and Club | Pct. | G. | PO. | A. | E. | DP. |
|---|---|---|---|---|---|---|---|---|---|---|---|---|---|
| Barker, Jamestown | .958 | 30 | 88 | 71 | 7 | 21 | McWilliams, Watertown | .857 | 1 | 2 | 4 | 1 | 1 |
| Bautista, Newark | .891 | 9 | 17 | 24 | 5 | 4 | Meyer, Oneonta | 1.000 | 4 | 4 | 9 | 0 | 2 |
| Bennett, Batavia | .903 | 6 | 8 | 20 | 3 | 3 | Mota, Niagara Falls | .951 | 65 | 154 | 156 | 16 | 33 |
| Bigden, Jamestown | .957 | 6 | 9 | 13 | 1 | 2 | Natera, Little Falls | .957 | 5 | 8 | 14 | 1 | 1 |
| Brown, Auburn | .902 | 15 | 19 | 18 | 4 | 3 | Ojea, Erie | .956 | 67 | 148 | 196 | 16 | 40 |
| Clark, Watertown | .966 | 14 | 23 | 33 | 2 | 5 | Perez, Watertown | .938 | 44 | 69 | 113 | 12 | 14 |
| Cooley, Little Falls | 1.000 | 1 | 1 | 3 | 0 | 0 | Pliecones, Oneonta | .969 | 17 | 32 | 31 | 2 | 5 |
| Crone, Newark | .846 | 4 | 5 | 6 | 2 | 2 | Robinson, Watertown | 1.000 | 1 | 2 | 4 | 0 | 1 |
| Flower, Jamestown | .977 | 11 | 25 | 17 | 1 | 4 | Rogalski, Auburn | .964 | 70 | 150 | 202 | 13 | 43 |
| Fortner, Geneva | .930 | 18 | 29 | 51 | 6 | 10 | Rossy, Newark | 1.000 | 1 | 1 | 0 | 0 | 0 |
| Fuentes, Elmira | .943 | 33 | 67 | 82 | 9 | 10 | Santana, Erie | .960 | 8 | 11 | 13 | 1 | 2 |
| Gambino, Watertown | .889 | 3 | 4 | 4 | 1 | 0 | Sheaffer, Utica | .933 | 3 | 7 | 7 | 1 | 4 |
| Gelatt, Little Falls | .973 | 73 | 141 | 215 | 10 | 46 | Stanicek, Newark | .976 | 69 | 162 | 198 | 9 | 50 |
| Halasz, Newark | 1.000 | 1 | 1 | 1 | 0 | 1 | Swain, Batavia | .974 | 60 | 96 | 163 | 7 | 19 |
| Hillman, Batavia | .895 | 8 | 14 | 20 | 4 | 4 | Swanzy, Jamestown | .895 | 26 | 50 | 52 | 12 | 12 |
| Howard, Watertown | .933 | 17 | 39 | 58 | 7 | 8 | Tavarez, Little Falls | .951 | 74 | 153 | 238 | 20 | 38 |
| Lambert, Oneonta | 1.000 | 1 | 1 | 1 | 0 | 0 | Turner, Oneonta | 1.000 | 1 | 2 | 0 | 0 | 0 |
| Laseke, Elmira | .968 | 52 | 76 | 135 | 7 | 24 | Turney, Erie | .982 | 9 | 29 | 25 | 1 | 8 |
| Lester, Jamestown | .921 | 15 | 39 | 31 | 6 | 9 | Velarde, Niagara Falls | .964 | 13 | 29 | 51 | 3 | 8 |
| Lombardozzi, Oneonta | .911 | 62 | 99 | 147 | 24 | 24 | WALLACE, Geneva | .994 | 65 | 123 | 188 | 2 | 45 |
| Maas, Oneonta | 1.000 | 1 | 0 | 1 | 0 | 0 | Zapolski, Batavia | .950 | 6 | 10 | 9 | 1 | 2 |

### THIRD BASEMEN

| Player and Club | Pct. | G. | PO. | A. | E. | DP. | Player and Club | Pct. | G. | PO. | A. | E. | DP. |
|---|---|---|---|---|---|---|---|---|---|---|---|---|---|
| Bafia, Geneva | .875 | 58 | 44 | 124 | 24 | 15 | Gilles, Oneonta | .926 | 11 | 5 | 20 | 2 | 0 |
| Bennett, Batavia | 1.000 | 1 | 1 | 0 | 0 | 1 | Gouldrup, Elmira | .787 | 32 | 20 | 28 | 13 | 3 |
| Bernaldo, Oneonta | 1.000 | 1 | 0 | 2 | 0 | 0 | Halasz, Newark | .900 | 6 | 4 | 14 | 2 | 0 |
| Brown, Auburn | 1.000 | 3 | 0 | 6 | 0 | 0 | Harwick, Geneva | .920 | 21 | 11 | 35 | 4 | 1 |
| D. Clark, Watertown | .826 | 49 | 34 | 56 | 19 | 3 | Hibbs, Utica | .905 | 8 | 3 | 16 | 2 | 2 |
| R. Clark, Watertown | .714 | 5 | 1 | 4 | 2 | 0 | Hillman, Batavia | 1.000 | 2 | 0 | 1 | 0 | 0 |
| Colescott, Little Falls | .857 | 17 | 9 | 27 | 6 | 5 | Iglesias, Erie | .778 | 4 | 2 | 5 | 2 | 0 |
| Colombino, Auburn | .906 | 56 | 33 | 93 | 13 | 11 | Leslie, Batavia | .889 | 7 | 3 | 5 | 1 | 0 |
| Cooley, Little Falls | 1.000 | 5 | 1 | 6 | 0 | 0 | Lester, Jamestown | .938 | 8 | 5 | 10 | 1 | 3 |
| Cronkright, Niagara Falls | .897 | 73 | 48 | 134 | 21 | 9 | Maas, Oneonta | .947 | 23 | 15 | 39 | 3 | 5 |
| DeLuca, Little Falls | .821 | 9 | 8 | 15 | 5 | 1 | Mancini, Newark | .600 | 2 | 1 | 2 | 2 | 1 |
| Donatelli, Utica | 1.000 | 1 | 1 | 0 | 0 | 0 | McWilliams, Watertown | 1.000 | 2 | 1 | 0 | 0 | 0 |
| Fishel, Auburn | .903 | 31 | 24 | 41 | 7 | 5 | Monell, Little Falls | .784 | 15 | 6 | 23 | 8 | 1 |
| Flower, Jamestown | .886 | 19 | 10 | 29 | 5 | 7 | Natera, Little Falls | 1.000 | 17 | 5 | 21 | 0 | 0 |
| Forbes, Newark | .889 | 6 | 4 | 4 | 1 | 2 | NEMETH, Erie | .938 | 60 | 28 | 139 | 11 | 9 |
| Fuentes, Elmira | 1.000 | 3 | 0 | 2 | 0 | 0 | Oller, Jamestown | .820 | 58 | 33 | 117 | 33 | 11 |

## THIRD BASEMEN—Continued

| Player and Club | Pct. | G. | PO. | A. | E. | DP. | Player and Club | Pct. | G. | PO. | A. | E. | DP. |
|---|---|---|---|---|---|---|---|---|---|---|---|---|---|
| Plante, Elmira | .860 | 17 | 20 | 23 | 7 | 4 | Swain, Batavia | .750 | 3 | 2 | 4 | 2 | 0 |
| Pliecones, Oneonta | 1.000 | 5 | 1 | 5 | 0 | 0 | Swanzy, Jamestown | 1.000 | 2 | 0 | 1 | 0 | 0 |
| Repoz, Little Falls | .929 | 35 | 11 | 80 | 7 | 8 | Toale, Elmira | 1.000 | 2 | 0 | 3 | 0 | 1 |
| Robinson, Watertown | .864 | 24 | 17 | 21 | 6 | 3 | Turney, Erie | .786 | 8 | 6 | 16 | 6 | 1 |
| Rodriguez, Watertown | .750 | 17 | 5 | 19 | 8 | 2 | Velarde, Niagara Falls | .909 | 4 | 4 | 6 | 1 | 1 |
| Rogers, Elmira | .893 | 44 | 35 | 40 | 9 | 1 | Walker, Utica | .925 | 19 | 16 | 33 | 4 | 3 |
| Rossy, Newark | .899 | 73 | 64 | 159 | 25 | 15 | Wallace, Geneva | 1.000 | 4 | 4 | 10 | 0 | 1 |
| Santana, Erie | .833 | 7 | 3 | 17 | 4 | 2 | Webster, Batavia | .879 | 66 | 41 | 97 | 19 | 12 |
| Shaw, Oneonta | .870 | 43 | 32 | 68 | 15 | 7 | Zapolski, Batavia | .947 | 6 | 5 | 13 | 1 | 0 |
| Sheaffer, Utica | .908 | 58 | 42 | 116 | 16 | 11 | | | | | | | |

## SHORTSTOPS

| Player and Club | Pct. | G. | PO. | A. | E. | DP. | Player and Club | Pct. | G. | PO. | A. | E. | DP. |
|---|---|---|---|---|---|---|---|---|---|---|---|---|---|
| Beltre, Utica | .923 | 72 | 106 | 206 | 26 | 33 | Natera, Little Falls | .916 | 41 | 52 | 111 | 15 | 21 |
| Bigden, Jamestown | .911 | 11 | 16 | 35 | 5 | 6 | Nichols, Newark | .934 | 68 | 114 | 183 | 21 | 46 |
| Brown, Auburn | .900 | 2 | 6 | 3 | 1 | 0 | Ojea, Erie | 1.000 | 2 | 1 | 0 | 0 | 0 |
| Clark, Watertown | .909 | 2 | 3 | 7 | 1 | 2 | Pliecones, Oneonta | .963 | 24 | 23 | 55 | 3 | 6 |
| Fairchild, Batavia | .862 | 65 | 111 | 177 | 46 | 21 | Repoz, Little Falls | .900 | 39 | 58 | 104 | 18 | 20 |
| Fuentes, Elmira | .924 | 23 | 35 | 50 | 7 | 13 | Robinson, Watertown | .850 | 19 | 21 | 30 | 9 | 6 |
| Gambino, Watertown | .625 | 6 | 1 | 4 | 3 | 0 | Rogalski, Auburn | .857 | 4 | 2 | 10 | 2 | 1 |
| Gelatt, Little Falls | .667 | 1 | 1 | 1 | 1 | 0 | Rogers, Elmira | .857 | 3 | 3 | 3 | 1 | 1 |
| Gouldrup, Elmira | .947 | 9 | 5 | 13 | 1 | 1 | Rosario, Elmira | .893 | 57 | 70 | 130 | 24 | 21 |
| Gray, Auburn | .947 | 74 | 118 | 221 | 19 | 46 | Rossy, Newark | .667 | 2 | 2 | 0 | 1 | 0 |
| Halasz, Newark | .944 | 11 | 12 | 39 | 3 | 6 | Sheaffer, Utica | .920 | 8 | 6 | 17 | 2 | 3 |
| Harwick, Geneva | .846 | 8 | 5 | 17 | 4 | 3 | Small, Geneva | .912 | 74 | 108 | 204 | 30 | 45 |
| Hillman, Batavia | .896 | 14 | 14 | 29 | 5 | 1 | Stevanus, Watertown | .912 | 62 | 86 | 151 | 23 | 26 |
| Houston, Jamestown | .927 | 37 | 39 | 100 | 11 | 15 | Swanzy, Jamestown | .890 | 20 | 24 | 57 | 10 | 10 |
| Lara, Erie | .929 | 53 | 71 | 164 | 18 | 26 | TURNER, Oneonta | .948 | 61 | 107 | 164 | 15 | 32 |
| Lester, Jamestown | .968 | 14 | 21 | 39 | 2 | 3 | Turney, Erie | .906 | 32 | 29 | 77 | 11 | 16 |
| Mancini, Newark | .857 | 8 | 9 | 15 | 4 | 0 | Velarde, Niagara Falls | .898 | 20 | 30 | 58 | 10 | 10 |
| Martin, Niagara Falls | .881 | 60 | 85 | 173 | 35 | 30 | Zapolski, Batavia | .667 | 5 | 3 | 5 | 4 | 2 |

## OUTFIELDERS

| Player and Club | Pct. | G. | PO. | A. | E. | DP. | Player and Club | Pct. | G. | PO. | A. | E. | DP. |
|---|---|---|---|---|---|---|---|---|---|---|---|---|---|
| Adams, Auburn | 1.000 | 6 | 10 | 0 | 0 | 0 | LaMarr, Jamestown | 1.000 | 1 | 1 | 0 | 0 | 0 |
| Anderson, Elmira* | .976 | 69 | 119 | 5 | 3 | 0 | Lara, Erie | 1.000 | 1 | 4 | 0 | 0 | 0 |
| Bafia, Geneva | 1.000 | 2 | 3 | 0 | 0 | 0 | Lee, Oneonta | .952 | 42 | 57 | 3 | 3 | 0 |
| Barker, Jamestown | 1.000 | 15 | 20 | 0 | 0 | 0 | Lotzar, Newark | .968 | 50 | 89 | 2 | 3 | 1 |
| Bellino, Newark | .944 | 68 | 81 | 3 | 5 | 1 | Lovell, Batavia* | .900 | 12 | 9 | 0 | 1 | 0 |
| Berry, Watertown | 1.000 | 7 | 8 | 0 | 0 | 0 | Maas, Oneonta | 1.000 | 32 | 37 | 0 | 0 | 0 |
| Brady, Watertown | .889 | 40 | 34 | 6 | 5 | 3 | Mainini, Oneonta* | .991 | 67 | 102 | 5 | 1 | 1 |
| M. Brown, Auburn | 1.000 | 3 | 3 | 0 | 0 | 0 | Malizia, Newark | 1.000 | 26 | 14 | 1 | 0 | 0 |
| R. Brown, Utica | .976 | 31 | 40 | 1 | 1 | 1 | Mancini, Newark | 1.000 | 1 | 1 | 0 | 0 | 0 |
| Calvert, Oneonta | 1.000 | 23 | 46 | 2 | 0 | 0 | Martinez, Newark | .846 | 10 | 11 | 0 | 2 | 0 |
| Candelino, Jamestown | .903 | 30 | 26 | 2 | 3 | 1 | McMillan, Watertown* | .954 | 44 | 82 | 1 | 4 | 1 |
| Del. Carter, Elmira | .978 | 46 | 84 | 4 | 2 | 2 | McWilliams, Watertown | 1.000 | 2 | 4 | 0 | 0 | 0 |
| Den. Carter, Erie | .985 | 77 | 119 | 10 | 2 | 2 | Medina, Geneva | .990 | 72 | 94 | 3 | 1 | 1 |
| Cento, Niagara Falls | 1.000 | 1 | 2 | 1 | 0 | 0 | Mejia, Geneva | .933 | 15 | 27 | 1 | 2 | 0 |
| Cepero, Erie | 1.000 | 4 | 2 | 0 | 0 | 0 | Meucci, Newark | 1.000 | 7 | 1 | 0 | 0 | 0 |
| Cijntje, Newark | .964 | 48 | 79 | 2 | 3 | 0 | Monell, Little Falls | .975 | 32 | 37 | 2 | 1 | 1 |
| Clark, Watertown | 1.000 | 1 | 2 | 1 | 0 | 0 | Moore, Niagara Falls | .952 | 51 | 75 | 5 | 4 | 0 |
| Coker, Batavia | .800 | 2 | 4 | 0 | 1 | 0 | Noble, Watertown | .976 | 56 | 81 | 1 | 2 | 1 |
| Contreras, Little Falls* | .976 | 47 | 79 | 3 | 2 | 1 | Odle, Watertown | .967 | 54 | 58 | 1 | 2 | 1 |
| Cowan, Newark* | .667 | 9 | 1 | 1 | 1 | 0 | Orsag, Elmira | .935 | 24 | 40 | 3 | 3 | 0 |
| Dallaire, Jamestown | .958 | 41 | 57 | 11 | 3 | 1 | Paul, Newark | 1.000 | 3 | 4 | 0 | 0 | 0 |
| Daniels, Watertown* | .951 | 22 | 35 | 4 | 2 | 1 | Perez, Utica | .925 | 30 | 44 | 5 | 4 | 1 |
| Dascenzo, Geneva* | .972 | 67 | 131 | 7 | 4 | 1 | Plante, Elmira | .957 | 17 | 21 | 1 | 1 | 0 |
| DeLaCruz, Auburn | .970 | 22 | 32 | 0 | 1 | 0 | Quintana, Elmira | .952 | 42 | 55 | 5 | 3 | 2 |
| Donatelli, Utica | .972 | 73 | 136 | 4 | 4 | 1 | Ray, Jamestown | 1.000 | 22 | 27 | 2 | 0 | 0 |
| Drew, Auburn | .975 | 72 | 152 | 1 | 4 | 0 | Reynolds, Batavia | 1.000 | 4 | 4 | 1 | 0 | 0 |
| Fishel, Auburn | .978 | 50 | 84 | 3 | 2 | 2 | Ricker, Utica | .909 | 19 | 29 | 1 | 3 | 0 |
| Flower, Jamestown | .978 | 33 | 40 | 5 | 1 | 0 | Rinehart, Little Falls* | 1.000 | 4 | 3 | 0 | 0 | 0 |
| Forbes, Newark | 1.000 | 2 | 2 | 0 | 0 | 0 | Roberts, Newark | .956 | 62 | 125 | 5 | 6 | 0 |
| Fortner, Geneva | 1.000 | 2 | 0 | 1 | 0 | 0 | Robertson, Little Falls | 1.000 | 9 | 9 | 0 | 0 | 0 |
| Fox, Jamestown | 1.000 | 2 | 3 | 0 | 0 | 0 | Robinson, Watertown | .943 | 26 | 49 | 1 | 3 | 1 |
| Gaeta, Newark | 1.000 | 3 | 1 | 0 | 0 | 0 | I. Rodriguez, Jamestown | .936 | 52 | 85 | 3 | 6 | 0 |
| Garcia, Utica* | 1.000 | 3 | 2 | 0 | 0 | 0 | N. Rodriguez, Watertown* | 1.000 | 6 | 12 | 0 | 0 | 0 |
| Gilkey, Erie | .957 | 77 | 164 | 13 | 8 | 1 | Rogers, Elmira | 1.000 | 2 | 1 | 0 | 0 | 0 |
| Gilles, Oneonta | .500 | 1 | 1 | 0 | 1 | 0 | Rountree, Batavia* | .956 | 43 | 65 | 0 | 3 | 0 |
| Gonzalez, Little Falls | 1.000 | 44 | 75 | 4 | 0 | 1 | Santos, Batavia | .917 | 11 | 11 | 0 | 1 | 0 |
| Gooden, Little Falls | .900 | 12 | 9 | 0 | 1 | 0 | Sheldon, Niagara Falls | .941 | 10 | 12 | 4 | 1 | 1 |
| Graves, Auburn | 1.000 | 8 | 8 | 0 | 0 | 0 | Shepis, Auburn* | 1.000 | 20 | 30 | 1 | 0 | 0 |
| Green, Oneonta | .953 | 35 | 37 | 4 | 2 | 1 | D. Smith, Geneva | .924 | 53 | 81 | 4 | 7 | 1 |
| Grimes, Geneva | .973 | 73 | 99 | 11 | 3 | 2 | T. Smith, Newark* | 1.000 | 1 | 2 | 0 | 0 | 0 |
| Guerrero, Auburn | .875 | 17 | 12 | 2 | 2 | 0 | St. Claire, Utica | .966 | 31 | 53 | 2 | 2 | 0 |
| Gutierrez, Newark* | 1.000 | 6 | 5 | 0 | 0 | 0 | Startoni, Batavia | .944 | 10 | 16 | 1 | 1 | 0 |
| Hardamon, Geneva | .958 | 39 | 63 | 6 | 3 | 1 | Stewart, Watertown | .909 | 16 | 20 | 0 | 2 | 0 |
| Hartley, Jamestown | .935 | 62 | 96 | 5 | 7 | 3 | Swanzy, Jamestown | 1.000 | 2 | 1 | 0 | 0 | 0 |
| Houston, Jamestown | .920 | 18 | 22 | 1 | 2 | 0 | Toliver, Niagara Falls | .972 | 51 | 67 | 3 | 2 | 0 |
| Hutson, Jamestown | .953 | 52 | 76 | 5 | 4 | 1 | Valverde, Jamestown | 1.000 | 6 | 9 | 0 | 0 | 0 |
| James, Auburn* | 1.000 | 10 | 17 | 2 | 0 | 1 | Van Heyningen, Newark* | .667 | 2 | 2 | 0 | 1 | 0 |
| Jaster, Little Falls | .990 | 61 | 97 | 5 | 1 | 1 | Velarde, Niagara Falls | .984 | 32 | 61 | 2 | 1 | 0 |
| Jenkins, Batavia | 1.000 | 23 | 36 | 0 | 0 | 0 | Viltz, Oneonta* | .921 | 48 | 58 | 0 | 5 | 0 |
| JESTER, Auburn* | 1.000 | 58 | 69 | 10 | 0 | 1 | Von Ahnen, Niagara Falls | .922 | 33 | 56 | 3 | 5 | 0 |
| E. Johnson, Little Falls | .897 | 37 | 32 | 3 | 4 | 1 | Warmbier, Erie | .969 | 30 | 28 | 3 | 1 | 0 |
| T. Johnson, Little Falls | .000 | 1 | 0 | 0 | 1 | 0 | Wilkes, Batavia* | 1.000 | 4 | 4 | 0 | 0 | 0 |
| I. Jordan, Watertown | .929 | 21 | 24 | 2 | 2 | 1 | Williams, Newark | .913 | 19 | 21 | 0 | 2 | 0 |
| S. Jordan, Batavia | 1.000 | 19 | 35 | 1 | 0 | 0 | Workman, Batavia | .979 | 55 | 90 | 2 | 2 | 0 |
| Khoury, Newark* | .980 | 32 | 46 | 2 | 1 | 1 | Wrigley, Watertown | .968 | 34 | 30 | 0 | 1 | 0 |
| Knowles, Erie | .945 | 49 | 66 | 3 | 4 | 1 | | | | | | | |

# OFFICIAL BASEBALL GUIDE

## CATCHERS

| Player and Club | Pct. | G. | PO. | A. | E. | DP. | PB. |
|---|---|---|---|---|---|---|---|
| Alcazar, Niagara Falls | .976 | 57 | 396 | 56 | 11 | 5 | 6 |
| Anders, Geneva | .986 | 41 | 251 | 26 | 4 | 4 | 3 |
| Bochesa, Elmira | 1.000 | 7 | 37 | 4 | 0 | 2 | 2 |
| Boyd, Erie | .976 | 13 | 72 | 9 | 2 | 0 | 1 |
| Brunswick, Little Falls | .981 | 51 | 336 | 34 | 7 | 3 | 10 |
| Cabrera, Batavia | .971 | 11 | 32 | 2 | 1 | 0 | 1 |
| Cento, Niagara Falls | .964 | 11 | 62 | 18 | 3 | 4 | 1 |
| Colescott, Little Falls | 1.000 | 12 | 60 | 3 | 0 | 1 | 3 |
| DAVIS, Jamestown | .989 | 42 | 331 | 29 | 4 | 0 | 10 |
| Dean, Utica | .981 | 60 | 380 | 44 | 8 | 4 | 20 |
| Dromerhouser, Newark | .920 | 10 | 23 | 0 | 2 | 1 | 2 |
| Edwards, Auburn | .986 | 40 | 251 | 31 | 4 | 5 | 13 |
| Ezold, Oneonta | .996 | 30 | 208 | 23 | 1 | 2 | 2 |
| Fox, Erie | 1.000 | 2 | 13 | 2 | 0 | 0 | 0 |
| Franzen, Batavia | 1.000 | 1 | 9 | 0 | 0 | 0 | 0 |
| Graff, Watertown | .965 | 24 | 125 | 11 | 5 | 0 | 5 |
| Hall, Watertown | .976 | 15 | 114 | 9 | 3 | 1 | 6 |
| Heakins, Watertown | .977 | 38 | 260 | 32 | 7 | 2 | 15 |
| Hedfelt, Utica | .991 | 14 | 103 | 10 | 1 | 2 | 3 |
| Hibbs, Utica | .935 | 9 | 37 | 6 | 3 | 1 | 3 |
| Hurst, Batavia | .988 | 32 | 230 | 23 | 3 | 2 | 5 |
| Iavarone, Oneonta | .985 | 27 | 186 | 14 | 3 | 0 | 5 |
| Jimenez, Erie | .966 | 9 | 49 | 8 | 2 | 1 | 0 |
| Johnigan, Batavia | 1.000 | 1 | 17 | 0 | 0 | 0 | 1 |
| LaMarr, Jamestown | .969 | 3 | 28 | 3 | 1 | 0 | 1 |
| Lochow, Geneva | .987 | 22 | 144 | 10 | 2 | 2 | 6 |
| Marston, Oneonta | .991 | 33 | 291 | 31 | 3 | 3 | 11 |
| Narcisse, Little Falls | .979 | 35 | 173 | 16 | 4 | 1 | 9 |
| Nichols, Erie | .969 | 4 | 27 | 4 | 1 | 0 | 1 |
| O'Connor, Erie | .971 | 3 | 31 | 3 | 1 | 0 | 1 |
| Perez, Auburn | 1.000 | 2 | 5 | 0 | 0 | 0 | 0 |
| Pratt, Elmira | .979 | 36 | 254 | 29 | 6 | 2 | 14 |
| Puzey, Erie | .987 | 47 | 271 | 35 | 4 | 2 | 8 |
| Ray, Jamestown | 1.000 | 15 | 96 | 16 | 0 | 1 | 3 |
| Sehlhorst, Niagara Falls | 1.000 | 1 | 3 | 2 | 0 | 0 | 0 |
| Sheldon, Niagara Falls | .981 | 16 | 90 | 13 | 2 | 0 | 3 |
| Shouse, Watertown | .983 | 20 | 105 | 11 | 2 | 1 | 13 |
| Skinner, Newark | .978 | 24 | 107 | 24 | 3 | 0 | 6 |
| Speakman, Elmira | .971 | 33 | 222 | 13 | 7 | 1 | 14 |
| St. Claire, Utica | 1.000 | 3 | 1 | 1 | 0 | 0 | 0 |
| Startoni, Batavia | .978 | 22 | 161 | 18 | 4 | 1 | 8 |
| Stephens, Erie | .988 | 8 | 68 | 17 | 1 | 1 | 3 |
| Tackett, Newark | .971 | 62 | 412 | 63 | 14 | 2 | 18 |
| Toale, Elmira | .980 | 6 | 41 | 7 | 1 | 1 | 4 |
| Todd, Batavia | .959 | 22 | 147 | 16 | 7 | 2 | 10 |
| Urzendowski, Geneva | .970 | 31 | 141 | 21 | 5 | 1 | 12 |
| Walters, Auburn | .985 | 44 | 294 | 33 | 5 | 1 | 8 |
| White, Jamestown | .990 | 26 | 175 | 21 | 2 | 2 | 8 |

## PITCHERS

| Player and Club | Pct. | G. | PO. | A. | E. | DP. |
|---|---|---|---|---|---|---|
| Abbott, Elmira* | 1.000 | 15 | 0 | 4 | 0 | 0 |
| Adams, Newark | 1.000 | 11 | 3 | 10 | 0 | 1 |
| Ahearne, Jamestown | .500 | 3 | 1 | 0 | 1 | 0 |
| Allison, Utica | .667 | 9 | 2 | 2 | 2 | 0 |
| Armstrong, Little Falls | .895 | 15 | 4 | 13 | 2 | 0 |
| Arnsberg, Auburn | 1.000 | 7 | 2 | 3 | 0 | 0 |
| Ayers, Jamestown | .857 | 14 | 8 | 16 | 4 | 2 |
| Azocar, Oneonta* | .800 | 14 | 3 | 1 | 1 | 0 |
| Balabon, Oneonta | .857 | 12 | 9 | 9 | 3 | 4 |
| Ballard, Newark* | 1.000 | 13 | 4 | 15 | 0 | 0 |
| Bayer, Elmira | .913 | 14 | 6 | 15 | 2 | 0 |
| Belleman, Batavia | 1.000 | 3 | 3 | 1 | 0 | 1 |
| Bridges, Watertown* | .947 | 13 | 6 | 12 | 1 | 0 |
| Brueggemann, Little Falls | .714 | 14 | 1 | 4 | 2 | 0 |
| Carista, Elmira | 1.000 | 16 | 5 | 10 | 0 | 0 |
| Carroll, Oneonta | .714 | 12 | 2 | 3 | 2 | 0 |
| Cepeda, Watertown | .750 | 18 | 3 | 3 | 2 | 0 |
| Channing, Watertown* | .900 | 15 | 4 | 23 | 3 | 1 |
| Christopher, Oneonta | .923 | 15 | 1 | 11 | 1 | 0 |
| Clarkin, Elmira | .909 | 6 | 4 | 6 | 1 | 2 |
| Collins, Jamestown | .667 | 18 | 1 | 1 | 1 | 0 |
| Compres, Batavia | 1.000 | 4 | 0 | 1 | 0 | 0 |
| Cox, Elmira* | 1.000 | 15 | 2 | 8 | 0 | 0 |
| Cunningham, Jamestown* | 1.000 | 15 | 4 | 15 | 0 | 2 |
| Danek, Geneva | .905 | 15 | 10 | 28 | 4 | 1 |
| Davidson, Oneonta | .909 | 29 | 1 | 9 | 1 | 0 |
| Davins, Watertown | 1.000 | 16 | 3 | 4 | 0 | 0 |
| DeBoever, Jamestown | .917 | 22 | 4 | 7 | 1 | 1 |
| DeCordova, Erie* | .833 | 16 | 3 | 2 | 1 | 0 |
| Dedos, Geneva | .846 | 16 | 4 | 7 | 2 | 0 |
| Dineen, Auburn | 1.000 | 17 | 5 | 8 | 0 | 2 |
| Dixon, Jamestown | 1.000 | 23 | 2 | 2 | 0 | 1 |
| Dominico, Little Falls | .667 | 23 | 4 | 6 | 5 | 0 |
| Dougherty, Oneonta | .933 | 13 | 5 | 9 | 1 | 1 |
| Dumas, Erie | 1.000 | 30 | 1 | 4 | 0 | 0 |
| Dunster, Auburn | .870 | 15 | 8 | 12 | 3 | 1 |
| Egelston, Newark* | 1.000 | 5 | 2 | 2 | 0 | 0 |
| Evers, Oneonta | .971 | 14 | 10 | 23 | 1 | 2 |
| Ezold, Oneonta | .750 | 1 | 2 | 1 | 1 | 0 |
| Farr, Batavia | .952 | 29 | 4 | 16 | 1 | 1 |
| Fascher, Auburn | .933 | 21 | 6 | 8 | 1 | 1 |
| Fletcher, Jamestown | 1.000 | 16 | 0 | 4 | 0 | 0 |
| Freed, Erie | 1.000 | 14 | 6 | 16 | 0 | 3 |
| Gabriele, Elmira | .917 | 11 | 3 | 8 | 1 | 1 |
| Galbato, Jamestown | .889 | 12 | 4 | 4 | 1 | 0 |
| My. Gardner, Batavia | 1.000 | 6 | 2 | 2 | 0 | 0 |
| Gay, Oneonta | 1.000 | 2 | 0 | 1 | 0 | 0 |
| Gelmine, Auburn* | 1.000 | 23 | 3 | 3 | 0 | 0 |
| Ghelfi, Batavia | .947 | 6 | 4 | 14 | 1 | 0 |
| Gilmore, Niagara Falls | .875 | 19 | 0 | 7 | 1 | 0 |
| Githens, Batavia | .833 | 14 | 4 | 16 | 4 | 0 |
| Givens, Little Falls* | .952 | 11 | 4 | 16 | 1 | 1 |
| Glidewell, Jamestown | 1.000 | 4 | 0 | 1 | 0 | 0 |
| Gonzales, Newark | 1.000 | 14 | 4 | 5 | 0 | 0 |
| Hackett, Erie* | 1.000 | 8 | 1 | 5 | 0 | 0 |
| Haines, Jamestown | .667 | 7 | 0 | 2 | 1 | 0 |
| Hansen, Watertown | .875 | 11 | 1 | 13 | 2 | 0 |
| Helton, Watertown | .857 | 18 | 2 | 10 | 2 | 1 |
| Hendricks, Niagara Falls | 1.000 | 14 | 1 | 5 | 0 | 0 |
| Hendrix, Utica | .846 | 23 | 0 | 11 | 2 | 0 |
| Hilton, Erie | .900 | 24 | 6 | 3 | 1 | 0 |
| Hirsch, Geneva | 1.000 | 22 | 2 | 4 | 0 | 1 |
| Holm, Newark* | 1.000 | 3 | 1 | 1 | 0 | 0 |
| Horn, Geneva* | .750 | 20 | 1 | 2 | 1 | 0 |
| Howes, Little Falls | 1.000 | 3 | 1 | 0 | 0 | 0 |
| Hunter, Jamestown | .857 | 14 | 4 | 8 | 2 | 0 |
| Ilsley, Auburn* | .950 | 13 | 7 | 12 | 1 | 2 |
| Johnson, Jamestown* | 1.000 | 8 | 0 | 9 | 0 | 0 |
| R. Jones, Utica | 1.000 | 14 | 2 | 12 | 0 | 1 |
| S. Jones, Jamestown | .833 | 16 | 1 | 4 | 1 | 1 |
| Kahler, Batavia | 1.000 | 5 | 0 | 2 | 0 | 0 |
| Karpuk, Batavia | .667 | 2 | 0 | 2 | 1 | 0 |
| Kavanaugh, Erie | 1.000 | 15 | 1 | 3 | 0 | 1 |
| Kelly, Jamestown | .857 | 11 | 1 | 5 | 1 | 0 |
| Kershaw, Niagara Falls | .727 | 14 | 2 | 6 | 3 | 0 |
| King, Newark | 1.000 | 15 | 2 | 2 | 0 | 0 |
| Knight, Elmira | 1.000 | 14 | 3 | 4 | 0 | 0 |
| Koonce, Newark | .900 | 15 | 3 | 6 | 1 | 0 |
| Koopman, Watertown* | .966 | 14 | 3 | 25 | 1 | 0 |
| Lackie, Newark* | 1.000 | 2 | 1 | 1 | 0 | 0 |
| LaFever, Batavia | .914 | 16 | 12 | 20 | 3 | 2 |
| Lahrman, Niagara Falls | 1.000 | 14 | 3 | 9 | 0 | 0 |
| LaMarche, Utica | .800 | 10 | 0 | 4 | 1 | 0 |
| Lampkin, Niagara Falls* | 1.000 | 6 | 4 | 5 | 0 | 0 |
| Leiter, Oneonta* | 1.000 | 6 | 3 | 7 | 0 | 0 |
| Link, Batavia | 1.000 | 3 | 1 | 1 | 0 | 1 |
| Linton, Utica* | .786 | 15 | 0 | 11 | 3 | 0 |
| Livchak, Erie* | .909 | 16 | 4 | 16 | 2 | 0 |
| Livernois, Elmira | .900 | 17 | 6 | 3 | 1 | 0 |
| Magistri, Elmira* | .778 | 18 | 3 | 4 | 2 | 0 |
| Manzanillo, Elmira | .800 | 19 | 3 | 5 | 2 | 1 |
| Martin, Watertown | 1.000 | 7 | 0 | 1 | 0 | 0 |
| Mauch, Erie | .917 | 20 | 5 | 17 | 2 | 1 |
| McCandlish, Geneva | .950 | 17 | 8 | 11 | 1 | 0 |
| McGowan, Elmira | .857 | 15 | 3 | 9 | 2 | 0 |
| McNeely, Erie | 1.000 | 14 | 8 | 9 | 0 | 1 |
| Melton, Watertown | .929 | 15 | 6 | 7 | 1 | 0 |
| Menendez, Geneva* | 1.000 | 8 | 0 | 1 | 0 | 0 |
| Mercado, Batavia* | .800 | 5 | 0 | 4 | 1 | 0 |
| Mora, Batavia | 1.000 | 4 | 0 | 4 | 0 | 0 |
| G. Murphy, Auburn | .846 | 18 | 3 | 8 | 2 | 2 |
| K. Murphy, Batavia* | 1.000 | 13 | 1 | 0 | 0 | 0 |
| Nichols, Batavia | 1.000 | 13 | 5 | 12 | 0 | 1 |
| Nossek, Niagara Falls* | 1.000 | 21 | 7 | 10 | 0 | 0 |
| O'Connor, Oneonta | 1.000 | 2 | 2 | 0 | 0 | 0 |
| Oberholtzer, Watertown | .778 | 15 | 1 | 6 | 2 | 0 |
| Oyster, Erie | 1.000 | 13 | 3 | 2 | 0 | 0 |
| Page, Little Falls | 1.000 | 23 | 2 | 6 | 0 | 2 |
| Paixao, Utica | .944 | 15 | 8 | 9 | 1 | 0 |
| Palermo, Newark | 1.000 | 4 | 3 | 6 | 0 | 0 |
| Patterson, Oneonta* | .875 | 6 | 1 | 6 | 1 | 0 |
| Pawlowski, Niagara Falls | .923 | 15 | 3 | 9 | 1 | 0 |
| Peterson, Niagara Falls | .762 | 14 | 7 | 9 | 5 | 0 |
| Picota, Erie | .846 | 16 | 3 | 9 | 2 | 1 |
| Poehl, Batavia | .955 | 10 | 2 | 19 | 1 | 1 |
| Pruett, Little Falls | 1.000 | 21 | 2 | 4 | 0 | 1 |
| Rather, Oneonta | .917 | 8 | 5 | 6 | 1 | 1 |
| Rauth, Little Falls | .889 | 15 | 5 | 19 | 3 | 2 |
| Richardson, Little Falls | 1.000 | 11 | 16 | 6 | 0 | 0 |
| Robertson, Batavia | 1.000 | 11 | 3 | 4 | 0 | 0 |
| Robles, Geneva | 1.000 | 18 | 7 | 9 | 0 | 2 |
| Rodriguez, Erie | .667 | 15 | 2 | 0 | 1 | 0 |
| Roebuck, Auburn* | .889 | 21 | 0 | 8 | 1 | 1 |
| Rone, Newark* | .333 | 12 | 0 | 1 | 0 | 0 |
| Roth, Geneva | .952 | 15 | 7 | 13 | 1 | 2 |
| Sampen, Watertown | 1.000 | 5 | 0 | 2 | 0 | 0 |
| Sanchez, Newark | .875 | 12 | 2 | 12 | 2 | 0 |
| Sanderski, Elmira | .938 | 14 | 0 | 15 | 1 | 1 |

## PITCHERS—Continued

| Player and Club | Pct. | G. | PO. | A. | E. | DP. | Player and Club | Pct. | G. | PO. | A. | E. | DP. |
|---|---|---|---|---|---|---|---|---|---|---|---|---|---|
| Santana, Watertown | 1.000 | 19 | 0 | 8 | 0 | 1 | Tirado, Oneonta | 1.000 | 22 | 2 | 5 | 0 | 0 |
| Satzinger, Watertown | .895 | 18 | 7 | 10 | 2 | 2 | Torres, Oneonta | 1.000 | 3 | 1 | 3 | 0 | 0 |
| Schulte, Auburn | 1.000 | 27 | 2 | 9 | 0 | 1 | TRAVELS, Utica | 1.000 | 15 | 12 | 17 | 0 | 2 |
| Scott, Batavia | .929 | 16 | 3 | 10 | 1 | 0 | Trudeau, Oneonta | .846 | 16 | 1 | 10 | 2 | 2 |
| Shannon, Jamestown | 1.000 | 5 | 0 | 3 | 0 | 0 | Tuozzo, Little Falls | 1.000 | 21 | 3 | 5 | 0 | 0 |
| Sheldon, Niagara Falls | 1.000 | 1 | 1 | 0 | 0 | 0 | Valdez, Utica | .926 | 15 | 8 | 17 | 2 | 0 |
| Smith, Auburn | .944 | 15 | 9 | 8 | 1 | 2 | Vasquez, Elmira | 1.000 | 18 | 4 | 15 | 0 | 2 |
| Snyder, Batavia | 1.000 | 6 | 3 | 5 | 0 | 0 | Vazquez, Newark* | 1.000 | 18 | 1 | 2 | 0 | 1 |
| Stacey, Niagara Falls | .889 | 12 | 7 | 9 | 2 | 1 | Vike, Auburn | 1.000 | 1 | 0 | 2 | 0 | 0 |
| Stauffacher, Jamestown* | .800 | 20 | 0 | 4 | 1 | 0 | Wachs, Little Falls* | .933 | 19 | 4 | 10 | 1 | 2 |
| Stewart, Watertown | 1.000 | 2 | 1 | 1 | 0 | 0 | Welborn, Little Falls | .700 | 6 | 1 | 6 | 3 | 1 |
| Stone, Niagara Falls | .957 | 21 | 3 | 19 | 1 | 0 | Wells, Auburn* | 1.000 | 13 | 4 | 8 | 0 | 1 |
| Strickland, Geneva | .889 | 14 | 5 | 11 | 2 | 1 | Rob. Williams, Utica | .870 | 21 | 3 | 17 | 3 | 2 |
| Sudo, Utica | .968 | 15 | 8 | 22 | 1 | 2 | Rog. Williams, Geneva | .889 | 15 | 4 | 20 | 3 | 0 |
| Sundgren, Jamestown | 1.000 | 17 | 6 | 5 | 0 | 1 | S. Williams, Newark | 1.000 | 4 | 1 | 5 | 0 | 0 |
| Takach, Little Falls* | .900 | 15 | 1 | 8 | 1 | 0 | Williamson, Batavia | .800 | 13 | 3 | 13 | 4 | 0 |
| Talamantez, Newark | .765 | 15 | 1 | 12 | 4 | 2 | Wilson, Newark | .895 | 16 | 3 | 14 | 2 | 0 |
| Tarasovitch, Erie | .000 | 1 | 0 | 0 | 1 | 0 | Zarranz, Geneva | .923 | 19 | 4 | 8 | 1 | 1 |
| Thigpen, Niagara Falls | 1.000 | 28 | 3 | 7 | 0 | 0 | Zupka, Elmira | .857 | 20 | 5 | 7 | 2 | 1 |
| Thorpe, Newark | .923 | 25 | 3 | 9 | 1 | 2 | | | | | | | |

The following players do not have any recorded accepted chances at the positions indicated; therefore, are not listed in the fielding averages for those particular positions: G. Adams, 3b; M. Anderson, p; Bautista, 3b, ss; Bigden, 3b; Brady, 3b, p; Colescott, p; Concepcion, p; Crone, of; Dedicke, of; Fortner, 3b; Ma. Gardner, p; Graves, 1b; Harwick, 2b, c; Higgins, of; Lashua, of; Marte, c; McFarlane, 1b; Robinson, p; Rohan, p; Sheldon, 3b; Skinner, of; Soma, p; Speakman, p; Stanko, of; Stender, of; Toale, of; Villanueva, c; K. Williams, p; Yeager, p.

## CLUB PITCHING

| Club | ERA. | G. | CG. | ShO. | Sv. | IP. | H. | R. | ER. | HR. | HB. | BB. | Int. BB. | SO. | WP. | Bk. |
|---|---|---|---|---|---|---|---|---|---|---|---|---|---|---|---|---|
| Oneonta | 1.87 | 78 | 20 | 13 | 13 | 667.1 | 453 | 205 | 139 | 17 | 22 | 257 | 6 | 690 | 38 | 1 |
| Utica | 3.25 | 76 | 12 | 1 | 16 | 676.2 | 606 | 324 | 244 | 24 | 21 | 276 | 13 | 494 | 44 | 10 |
| Little Falls | 3.32 | 75 | 14 | 5 | 11 | 650.2 | 574 | 312 | 240 | 40 | 19 | 333 | 18 | 559 | 34 | 2 |
| Jamestown | 3.39 | 78 | 7 | 6 | 20 | 667.0 | 583 | 327 | 251 | 29 | 19 | 372 | 9 | 615 | 50 | 6 |
| Newark | 3.41 | 77 | 18 | 13 | 14 | 679.0 | 597 | 353 | 257 | 26 | 20 | 368 | 13 | 538 | 61 | 7 |
| Auburn | 3.42 | 78 | 3 | 5 | 27 | 677.0 | 590 | 317 | 257 | 40 | 33 | 333 | 12 | 539 | 28 | 2 |
| Geneva | 3.55 | 78 | 15 | 3 | 23 | 682.1 | 616 | 343 | 269 | 47 | 30 | 350 | 12 | 520 | 53 | 4 |
| Elmira | 3.85 | 77 | 4 | 6 | 11 | 655.1 | 580 | 389 | 280 | 34 | 24 | 384 | 33 | 548 | 86 | 7 |
| Batavia | 3.90 | 78 | 11 | 5 | 13 | 664.2 | 595 | 385 | 288 | 48 | 22 | 322 | 13 | 590 | 83 | 8 |
| Niagara Falls | 4.03 | 77 | 12 | 4 | 16 | 654.0 | 589 | 376 | 293 | 49 | 29 | 353 | 8 | 534 | 60 | 6 |
| Erie | 4.06 | 78 | 12 | 6 | 10 | 672.0 | 666 | 359 | 303 | 66 | 23 | 285 | 25 | 520 | 35 | 4 |
| Watertown | 4.41 | 76 | 15 | 2 | 8 | 642.2 | 578 | 417 | 315 | 32 | 23 | 409 | 2 | 607 | 83 | 9 |

## PITCHERS' RECORDS
### (Leading Qualifiers for Earned-Run Average Leadership — 62 or More Innings)

*Throws lefthanded.

| Pitcher—Club | W. | L. | Pct. | ERA. | G. | GS. | CG. | GF. | ShO. | Sv. | IP. | H. | R. | ER. | HR. | HB. | BB. | Int. BB. | SO. | WP. |
|---|---|---|---|---|---|---|---|---|---|---|---|---|---|---|---|---|---|---|---|---|
| Evers, Oneonta | 10 | 1 | .909 | 1.18 | 14 | 12 | 4 | 1 | 1 | 0 | 99.1 | 69 | 21 | 13 | 2 | 5 | 25 | 1 | 85 | 4 |
| Ilsley, Auburn* | 9 | 1 | .900 | 1.40 | 13 | 12 | 2 | 1 | 0 | 0 | 90.0 | 55 | 18 | 14 | 1 | 3 | 32 | 0 | 116 | 0 |
| Ballard, Newark* | 10 | 2 | .833 | 1.41 | 13 | 13 | 6 | 0 | 3 | 0 | 96.0 | 78 | 20 | 15 | 2 | 0 | 20 | 1 | 91 | 1 |
| Christopher, Oneonta | 8 | 1 | .889 | 1.46 | 15 | 9 | 2 | 3 | 2 | 0 | 80.1 | 58 | 21 | 13 | 2 | 3 | 22 | 0 | 84 | 3 |
| Trudeau, Oneonta | 8 | 3 | .727 | 1.64 | 16 | 8 | 3 | 3 | 2 | 1 | 71.1 | 42 | 22 | 13 | 1 | 4 | 24 | 1 | 75 | 4 |
| Balabon, Oneonta | 5 | 2 | .714 | 1.74 | 12 | 12 | 3 | 0 | 2 | 0 | 72.1 | 50 | 16 | 14 | 1 | 1 | 39 | 0 | 68 | 6 |
| Dougherty, Oneonta | 6 | 2 | .750 | 1.96 | 13 | 11 | 2 | 0 | 1 | 0 | 73.1 | 53 | 24 | 16 | 2 | 2 | 30 | 0 | 62 | 2 |
| Mauch, Erie | 7 | 2 | .778 | 2.03 | 20 | 7 | 3 | 8 | 0 | 3 | 80.0 | 54 | 20 | 18 | 4 | 2 | 23 | 2 | 61 | 4 |
| Pawlowski, Niagara Falls | 9 | 3 | .750 | 2.13 | 15 | 15 | 4 | 0 | 2 | 0 | 97.0 | 74 | 41 | 23 | 7 | 3 | 35 | 0 | 82 | 6 |
| Sudo, Utica | 4 | 6 | .400 | 2.14 | 15 | 14 | 3 | 0 | 0 | 0 | 105.0 | 90 | 32 | 25 | 1 | 4 | 28 | 2 | 74 | 3 |

Departmental Leaders: G—Dumas, 30; W—Ballard, Evers, 10; L—Channing, 11; Pct.—Rather, 1.000; GS—14 pitchers with 15; CG—Koopman, 8; GF—Farr, 27; ShO—Ballard, Freed, 3; Sv.—Hirsch, 13; IP—Danek, 115.1; H—McNeely, 110; R—Channing, 63; ER—Channing, 46; HR—McNeely, 13; HB—Kershaw, Strickland, 8; BB—Talamantez, 77; IBB—Hilton, 8; SO—Cunningham, Ilsley, 116; WP—LaFever, Talamantez, 15.

### (All Pitchers—Listed Alphabetically)

| Pitcher—Club | W. | L. | Pct. | ERA. | G. | GS. | CG. | GF. | ShO. | Sv. | IP. | H. | R. | ER. | HR. | HB. | BB. | Int. BB. | SO. | WP. |
|---|---|---|---|---|---|---|---|---|---|---|---|---|---|---|---|---|---|---|---|---|
| Abbott, Elmira* | 2 | 1 | .667 | 2.89 | 15 | 0 | 0 | 6 | 0 | 2 | 37.1 | 29 | 18 | 12 | 3 | 3 | 26 | 1 | 41 | 7 |
| Adams, Newark | 4 | 2 | .667 | 2.14 | 11 | 7 | 2 | 3 | 0 | 2 | 54.2 | 40 | 13 | 13 | 2 | 1 | 21 | 1 | 33 | 6 |
| Ahearne, Jamestown | 0 | 0 | .000 | 0.00 | 3 | 0 | 0 | 3 | 0 | 0 | 4.0 | 2 | 0 | 0 | 0 | 0 | 0 | 0 | 3 | 1 |
| Allison, Utica | 1 | 1 | .500 | 5.59 | 9 | 1 | 0 | 4 | 0 | 0 | 19.1 | 17 | 15 | 12 | 1 | 2 | 18 | 1 | 34 | 3 |
| Anderson, Little Falls | 0 | 1 | .000 | 19.29 | 3 | 3 | 0 | 0 | 0 | 0 | 2.1 | 3 | 5 | 5 | 1 | 0 | 4 | 0 | 4 | 0 |
| Armstrong, Little Falls | 5 | 5 | .500 | 2.63 | 15 | 13 | 2 | 0 | 1 | 0 | 92.1 | 77 | 34 | 27 | 4 | 3 | 32 | 0 | 69 | 1 |
| Arnsberg, Auburn | 5 | 1 | .833 | 2.28 | 7 | 7 | 1 | 0 | 0 | 0 | 43.1 | 32 | 17 | 11 | 1 | 3 | 18 | 0 | 43 | 4 |
| Ayers, Jamestown | 9 | 1 | .900 | 2.32 | 14 | 14 | 2 | 0 | 0 | 0 | 89.1 | 66 | 28 | 23 | 4 | 3 | 26 | 0 | 89 | 2 |
| Azocar, Oneonta* | 0 | 2 | .000 | 4.86 | 14 | 2 | 0 | 6 | 0 | 0 | 16.2 | 21 | 16 | 9 | 3 | 0 | 9 | 0 | 13 | 3 |
| Balabon, Oneonta | 5 | 2 | .714 | 1.74 | 12 | 12 | 3 | 0 | 2 | 0 | 72.1 | 50 | 16 | 14 | 1 | 1 | 39 | 0 | 68 | 6 |
| Ballard, Newark* | 10 | 2 | .833 | 1.41 | 13 | 13 | 6 | 0 | 3 | 0 | 96.0 | 78 | 20 | 15 | 2 | 0 | 20 | 1 | 91 | 1 |
| Bayer, Elmira | 1 | 5 | .167 | 3.35 | 14 | 6 | 0 | 5 | 0 | 0 | 53.2 | 44 | 30 | 20 | 1 | 1 | 26 | 1 | 48 | 3 |
| Belleman, Batavia | 0 | 1 | .000 | 7.27 | 3 | 0 | 0 | 2 | 0 | 0 | 8.2 | 7 | 11 | 7 | 2 | 1 | 6 | 0 | 10 | 2 |
| Brady, Watertown | 0 | 0 | .000 | 40.50 | 1 | 0 | 0 | 0 | 0 | 0 | 0.2 | 5 | 3 | 3 | 0 | 0 | 2 | 0 | 0 | 0 |
| Bridges, Watertown* | 2 | 4 | .333 | 3.23 | 13 | 8 | 1 | 1 | 0 | 0 | 64.0 | 58 | 37 | 23 | 1 | 2 | 32 | 1 | 76 | 7 |
| Brueggemann, Little Falls | 2 | 2 | .000 | 5.25 | 14 | 7 | 0 | 3 | 0 | 0 | 48.0 | 43 | 32 | 28 | 8 | 0 | 33 | 3 | 34 | 6 |
| Carista, Elmira | 6 | 5 | .545 | 2.30 | 16 | 15 | 2 | 0 | 1 | 0 | 90.0 | 53 | 26 | 23 | 5 | 2 | 27 | 1 | 92 | 2 |
| Carroll, Oneonta | 1 | 0 | 1.000 | 0.37 | 12 | 0 | 0 | 7 | 0 | 3 | 24.1 | 13 | 4 | 1 | 0 | 0 | 10 | 0 | 21 | 3 |
| Cepeda, Watertown | 1 | 2 | .333 | 5.77 | 18 | 1 | 0 | 8 | 0 | 2 | 34.1 | 40 | 27 | 22 | 3 | 1 | 28 | 0 | 37 | 3 |
| Channing, Watertown* | 1 | 11 | .083 | 4.45 | 15 | 15 | 2 | 0 | 0 | 0 | 93.0 | 96 | 63 | 46 | 11 | 3 | 49 | 0 | 87 | 8 |
| Christopher, Oneonta | 8 | 1 | .889 | 1.46 | 15 | 9 | 2 | 3 | 2 | 0 | 80.1 | 58 | 21 | 13 | 2 | 3 | 22 | 0 | 84 | 3 |
| Clarkin, Elmira | 1 | 2 | .333 | 4.19 | 6 | 2 | 0 | 3 | 0 | 1 | 19.1 | 25 | 14 | 9 | 1 | 0 | 6 | 0 | 7 | 7 |
| Colescott, Little Falls | 0 | 0 | .000 | 0.00 | 1 | 0 | 0 | 1 | 0 | 0 | 1.0 | 0 | 0 | 0 | 0 | 0 | 0 | 0 | 0 | 0 |
| Collins, Jamestown | 2 | 1 | .667 | 4.96 | 18 | 0 | 0 | 15 | 0 | 5 | 16.1 | 12 | 12 | 9 | 1 | 3 | 16 | 1 | 14 | 2 |

| Pitcher—Club | W. | L. | Pct. | ERA. | G. | GS. | CG. | GF. | ShO. | Sv. | IP. | H. | R. | ER. | HR. | HB. | BB. | Int. BB. | SO. | WP. |
|---|---|---|---|---|---|---|---|---|---|---|---|---|---|---|---|---|---|---|---|---|
| Compres, Batavia | 0 | 1 | .000 | 13.50 | 4 | 1 | 0 | 3 | 0 | 0 | 4.0 | 5 | 6 | 6 | 0 | 0 | 6 | 0 | 4 | 0 |
| Concepcion, Newark | 0 | 0 | .000 | 45.00 | 2 | 0 | 0 | 1 | 0 | 0 | 1.0 | 1 | 5 | 5 | 0 | 0 | 7 | 0 | 0 | 0 |
| Cox, Elmira* | 1 | 3 | .250 | 5.45 | 15 | 0 | 0 | 3 | 0 | 0 | 34.2 | 45 | 28 | 21 | 1 | 2 | 19 | 4 | 21 | 3 |
| Cunningham, Jamestown* | 8 | 5 | .615 | 3.18 | 15 | 15 | 2 | 0 | 1 | 0 | 96.1 | 89 | 42 | 34 | 4 | 0 | 34 | 1 | 116 | 6 |
| Danek, Geneva | 8 | 5 | .615 | 2.42 | 15 | 15 | 5 | 0 | 1 | 0 | 115.1 | 96 | 45 | 31 | 5 | 3 | 38 | 2 | 75 | 8 |
| Davidson, Oneonta | 1 | 2 | .333 | 2.50 | 29 | 0 | 0 | 24 | 0 | 5 | 36.0 | 28 | 14 | 10 | 2 | 2 | 13 | 3 | 44 | 1 |
| Davins, Watertown | 2 | 0 | 1.000 | 3.64 | 16 | 0 | 0 | 13 | 0 | 3 | 29.2 | 15 | 14 | 12 | 1 | 0 | 22 | 0 | 39 | 8 |
| DeBoever, Jamestown | 2 | 0 | 1.000 | 3.22 | 22 | 0 | 0 | 7 | 0 | 4 | 44.2 | 48 | 23 | 16 | 2 | 0 | 27 | 1 | 35 | 4 |
| DeCordova, Erie* | 1 | 4 | .200 | 5.75 | 16 | 8 | 0 | 3 | 0 | 0 | 40.2 | 49 | 33 | 26 | 6 | 2 | 21 | 4 | 30 | 0 |
| Dedos, Geneva | 2 | 3 | .400 | 3.60 | 16 | 2 | 0 | 10 | 0 | 0 | 35.0 | 36 | 21 | 14 | 2 | 1 | 8 | 1 | 18 | 0 |
| Dineen, Auburn | 2 | 3 | .400 | 5.15 | 17 | 5 | 0 | 6 | 0 | 1 | 50.2 | 45 | 33 | 29 | 4 | 0 | 24 | 0 | 39 | 0 |
| Dixon, Jamestown | 1 | 3 | .250 | 3.30 | 23 | 1 | 0 | 10 | 0 | 4 | 43.2 | 41 | 19 | 16 | 3 | 4 | 13 | 1 | 34 | 5 |
| Dominico, Little Falls | 1 | 3 | .250 | 1.99 | 23 | 0 | 0 | 14 | 0 | 1 | 49.2 | 38 | 20 | 11 | 5 | 2 | 24 | 3 | 55 | 5 |
| Dougherty, Oneonta | 6 | 2 | .750 | 1.96 | 13 | 11 | 2 | 0 | 1 | 0 | 73.1 | 53 | 24 | 16 | 2 | 2 | 30 | 0 | 62 | 2 |
| Dumas, Erie | 5 | 2 | .714 | 4.88 | 30 | 0 | 0 | 19 | 0 | 0 | 48.0 | 43 | 28 | 26 | 8 | 0 | 26 | 3 | 42 | 7 |
| Dunster, Auburn | 5 | 5 | .500 | 3.61 | 15 | 15 | 0 | 0 | 0 | 0 | 89.2 | 101 | 48 | 36 | 5 | 5 | 24 | 1 | 51 | 5 |
| Egelston, Newark* | 0 | 0 | .000 | 1.50 | 5 | 1 | 0 | 2 | 0 | 2 | 18.0 | 8 | 4 | 3 | 0 | 0 | 2 | 0 | 14 | 0 |
| Evers, Oneonta | 10 | 1 | .909 | 1.18 | 14 | 12 | 4 | 1 | 1 | 0 | 99.1 | 69 | 21 | 13 | 2 | 5 | 25 | 1 | 85 | 4 |
| Ezold, Oneonta | 0 | 0 | .000 | 3.00 | 1 | 0 | 0 | 0 | 0 | 0 | 3.0 | 2 | 1 | 1 | 0 | 0 | 2 | 0 | 2 | 0 |
| Farr, Batavia | 6 | 4 | .600 | 1.93 | 29 | 0 | 0 | 27 | 0 | 7 | 60.2 | 43 | 18 | 13 | 3 | 0 | 41 | 6 | 66 | 8 |
| Fascher, Auburn | 1 | 1 | .500 | 4.95 | 21 | 5 | 0 | 13 | 0 | 6 | 60.0 | 62 | 35 | 33 | 7 | 3 | 20 | 1 | 44 | 3 |
| Fletcher, Jamestown | 2 | 2 | .500 | 6.45 | 16 | 0 | 0 | 6 | 0 | 0 | 22.1 | 19 | 18 | 16 | 3 | 1 | 27 | 1 | 23 | 3 |
| Freed, Erie | 7 | 2 | .778 | 2.35 | 14 | 13 | 5 | 1 | 3 | 0 | 95.2 | 74 | 34 | 25 | 5 | 2 | 18 | 1 | 69 | 2 |
| Gabriele, Elmira | 2 | 3 | .400 | 1.89 | 11 | 11 | 1 | 0 | 1 | 0 | 57.0 | 37 | 22 | 12 | 1 | 1 | 29 | 4 | 38 | 2 |
| Galbato, Jamestown | 3 | 2 | .600 | 3.71 | 12 | 2 | 0 | 4 | 0 | 0 | 26.2 | 21 | 18 | 11 | 0 | 1 | 28 | 1 | 11 | 2 |
| Ma. Gardner, Jamestown | 0 | 0 | .000 | 2.77 | 3 | 3 | 0 | 0 | 0 | 0 | 13.0 | 9 | 4 | 4 | 0 | 1 | 4 | 0 | 16 | 0 |
| My. Gardner, Batavia | 0 | 1 | .000 | 8.76 | 6 | 0 | 0 | 1 | 0 | 0 | 12.1 | 18 | 18 | 12 | 2 | 0 | 19 | 0 | 11 | 7 |
| Gay, Oneonta | 0 | 1 | .000 | 1.80 | 2 | 0 | 0 | 2 | 0 | 1 | 5.0 | 3 | 1 | 1 | 0 | 0 | 1 | 0 | 6 | 0 |
| Gelmine, Auburn* | 5 | 2 | .714 | 3.32 | 23 | 0 | 0 | 11 | 0 | 4 | 38.0 | 30 | 14 | 14 | 2 | 0 | 23 | 3 | 33 | 4 |
| Ghelfi, Batavia | 2 | 0 | 1.000 | 1.35 | 6 | 5 | 2 | 1 | 1 | 1 | 40.0 | 22 | 8 | 6 | 0 | 0 | 9 | 0 | 31 | 2 |
| Gilmore, Niagara Falls | 2 | 5 | .286 | 4.38 | 19 | 7 | 0 | 7 | 0 | 2 | 63.2 | 67 | 35 | 31 | 6 | 4 | 30 | 1 | 33 | 7 |
| Githens, Batavia | 2 | 6 | .250 | 4.04 | 14 | 8 | 2 | 1 | 0 | 0 | 64.2 | 56 | 36 | 29 | 3 | 3 | 19 | 0 | 43 | 5 |
| Givens, Little Falls | 3 | 4 | .429 | 2.93 | 11 | 11 | 3 | 0 | 1 | 0 | 73.2 | 54 | 28 | 24 | 1 | 2 | 43 | 0 | 81 | 2 |
| Glidewell, Jamestown | 0 | 1 | .000 | 5.93 | 4 | 2 | 0 | 0 | 0 | 0 | 13.2 | 11 | 11 | 9 | 2 | 0 | 10 | 0 | 9 | 1 |
| Gonzales, Newark | 2 | 3 | .400 | 3.60 | 14 | 6 | 2 | 4 | 1 | 2 | 60.0 | 54 | 28 | 24 | 2 | 1 | 29 | 1 | 40 | 7 |
| Hackett, Erie* | 3 | 2 | .600 | 3.52 | 8 | 7 | 1 | 0 | 1 | 0 | 46.0 | 48 | 18 | 18 | 4 | 0 | 12 | 2 | 39 | 1 |
| Haines, Jamestown | 0 | 0 | .000 | 1.04 | 7 | 0 | 0 | 3 | 0 | 0 | 8.2 | 6 | 2 | 1 | 0 | 0 | 6 | 0 | 5 | 1 |
| Hansen, Watertown | 2 | 6 | .250 | 6.08 | 11 | 9 | 0 | 0 | 0 | 0 | 40.0 | 43 | 39 | 27 | 3 | 3 | 41 | 0 | 13 | 10 |
| Helton, Watertown | 1 | 5 | .167 | 4.74 | 18 | 6 | 0 | 7 | 0 | 1 | 43.2 | 32 | 38 | 23 | 3 | 1 | 45 | 0 | 44 | 9 |
| Hendricks, Niagara Falls | 1 | 3 | .250 | 9.64 | 14 | 4 | 0 | 3 | 0 | 0 | 37.1 | 52 | 53 | 40 | 4 | 0 | 54 | 0 | 19 | 6 |
| Hendrix, Utica | 1 | 2 | .333 | 2.15 | 23 | 0 | 0 | 15 | 0 | 4 | 46.0 | 26 | 18 | 11 | 1 | 3 | 23 | 0 | 45 | 2 |
| Hilton, Erie | 3 | 7 | .300 | 4.27 | 24 | 5 | 0 | 13 | 0 | 7 | 65.1 | 73 | 46 | 31 | 6 | 2 | 26 | 8 | 65 | 5 |
| Hirsch, Geneva | 1 | 1 | .500 | 2.05 | 22 | 0 | 0 | 19 | 0 | 13 | 30.2 | 24 | 11 | 7 | 1 | 3 | 20 | 5 | 40 | 6 |
| Holm, Newark* | 0 | 0 | .000 | 0.00 | 3 | 0 | 0 | 1 | 0 | 0 | 2.2 | 2 | 0 | 0 | 0 | 0 | 1 | 0 | 3 | 0 |
| Horn, Geneva* | 1 | 2 | .333 | 5.84 | 20 | 0 | 0 | 11 | 0 | 5 | 24.2 | 25 | 16 | 16 | 1 | 1 | 16 | 2 | 14 | 2 |
| Howes, Little Falls | 0 | 0 | .000 | 3.72 | 3 | 0 | 0 | 2 | 0 | 1 | 9.2 | 9 | 5 | 4 | 2 | 2 | 4 | 0 | 6 | 0 |
| Hunter, Jamestown | 3 | 3 | .500 | 2.80 | 14 | 13 | 1 | 1 | 0 | 0 | 70.2 | 65 | 30 | 22 | 1 | 1 | 34 | 1 | 41 | 3 |
| Ilsley, Auburn* | 9 | 1 | .900 | 1.40 | 13 | 12 | 1 | 1 | 0 | 0 | 90.0 | 55 | 18 | 14 | 1 | 3 | 32 | 0 | 116 | 0 |
| Johnson, Jamestown* | 0 | 3 | .000 | 5.93 | 8 | 8 | 0 | 0 | 0 | 0 | 27.1 | 29 | 22 | 18 | 2 | 0 | 24 | 0 | 21 | 3 |
| R. Jones, Utica | 3 | 1 | .750 | 3.03 | 14 | 5 | 1 | 3 | 0 | 1 | 59.1 | 60 | 29 | 20 | 1 | 1 | 24 | 0 | 29 | 3 |
| S. Jones, Jamestown | 4 | 2 | .667 | 3.28 | 16 | 2 | 0 | 7 | 0 | 1 | 35.2 | 32 | 18 | 13 | 1 | 1 | 17 | 0 | 21 | 2 |
| Kahler, Batavia | 1 | 2 | .333 | 5.25 | 5 | 0 | 0 | 2 | 0 | 0 | 12.0 | 10 | 7 | 7 | 0 | 1 | 9 | 0 | 7 | 2 |
| Karpuk, Batavia | 0 | 1 | .000 | 9.95 | 2 | 0 | 0 | 0 | 0 | 0 | 6.1 | 10 | 10 | 7 | 0 | 0 | 7 | 0 | 8 | 1 |
| Kavanaugh, Erie | 0 | 0 | .000 | 3.42 | 15 | 0 | 0 | 10 | 0 | 0 | 23.2 | 19 | 10 | 9 | 3 | 3 | 17 | 0 | 26 | 1 |
| Kelly, Jamestown | 2 | 4 | .333 | 4.23 | 11 | 9 | 0 | 1 | 0 | 0 | 44.2 | 45 | 30 | 21 | 3 | 1 | 43 | 0 | 45 | 5 |
| Kershaw, Niagara Falls | 0 | 3 | .000 | 5.86 | 14 | 3 | 0 | 7 | 0 | 0 | 35.1 | 29 | 28 | 23 | 1 | 8 | 44 | 0 | 41 | 10 |
| King, Newark | 2 | 2 | .500 | 2.72 | 15 | 1 | 0 | 5 | 0 | 0 | 36.1 | 34 | 24 | 11 | 3 | 2 | 21 | 1 | 35 | 2 |
| Knight, Elmira | 1 | 3 | .250 | 8.22 | 14 | 6 | 0 | 5 | 0 | 0 | 30.2 | 47 | 38 | 28 | 2 | 1 | 23 | 1 | 12 | 4 |
| Koonce, Newark | 0 | 2 | .000 | 6.06 | 15 | 1 | 0 | 7 | 0 | 2 | 35.2 | 40 | 26 | 24 | 2 | 0 | 17 | 1 | 36 | 2 |
| Koopman, Watertown | 7 | 5 | .583 | 2.54 | 14 | 14 | 8 | 0 | 1 | 0 | 102.2 | 86 | 39 | 29 | 4 | 1 | 21 | 0 | 97 | 5 |
| Lackie, Newark* | 0 | 2 | .000 | 10.50 | 2 | 1 | 0 | 0 | 0 | 0 | 6.0 | 7 | 7 | 7 | 0 | 0 | 7 | 0 | 3 | 0 |
| LaFever, Batavia | 8 | 5 | .615 | 2.85 | 16 | 14 | 4 | 0 | 1 | 0 | 101.0 | 89 | 49 | 32 | 9 | 1 | 29 | 0 | 81 | 15 |
| Lahrman, Niagara Falls | 3 | 5 | .375 | 4.53 | 14 | 8 | 2 | 2 | 0 | 1 | 57.2 | 59 | 31 | 29 | 5 | 3 | 22 | 1 | 35 | 3 |
| LaMarche, Utica | 0 | 1 | .000 | 6.08 | 10 | 1 | 0 | 7 | 0 | 1 | 13.1 | 21 | 15 | 9 | 1 | 0 | 11 | 2 | 11 | 2 |
| Lampkin, Niagara Falls* | 0 | 1 | .000 | 4.15 | 6 | 2 | 0 | 3 | 0 | 1 | 17.1 | 19 | 11 | 8 | 5 | 1 | 6 | 0 | 12 | 0 |
| Leiter, Oneonta* | 3 | 2 | .600 | 2.37 | 6 | 6 | 2 | 0 | 0 | 0 | 38.0 | 27 | 14 | 10 | 0 | 0 | 25 | 0 | 34 | 5 |
| Link, Batavia | 0 | 1 | .000 | 15.00 | 3 | 0 | 0 | 0 | 0 | 0 | 3.0 | 3 | 5 | 5 | 0 | 0 | 7 | 0 | 2 | 2 |
| Linton, Utica | 2 | 5 | .286 | 4.82 | 15 | 13 | 1 | 0 | 0 | 0 | 71.0 | 64 | 46 | 38 | 3 | 3 | 52 | 0 | 38 | 10 |
| Livchak, Erie* | 4 | 6 | .400 | 5.14 | 16 | 15 | 1 | 1 | 0 | 0 | 75.1 | 80 | 47 | 43 | 6 | 4 | 49 | 0 | 63 | 5 |
| Livernois, Jamestown | 2 | 3 | .400 | 3.83 | 17 | 2 | 0 | 7 | 0 | 2 | 47.0 | 44 | 26 | 20 | 5 | 2 | 18 | 4 | 55 | 2 |
| Magistri, Elmira* | 2 | 0 | 1.000 | 3.08 | 18 | 0 | 0 | 8 | 0 | 1 | 38.0 | 25 | 18 | 13 | 0 | 2 | 36 | 1 | 38 | 10 |
| Manzanillo, Elmira | 2 | 4 | .333 | 3.86 | 19 | 4 | 0 | 10 | 0 | 1 | 39.2 | 36 | 19 | 17 | 1 | 2 | 36 | 4 | 43 | 12 |
| Martin, Watertown | 0 | 1 | .000 | 8.00 | 7 | 0 | 0 | 2 | 0 | 0 | 9.0 | 10 | 9 | 8 | 0 | 0 | 9 | 0 | 8 | 2 |
| Mauch, Erie | 7 | 2 | .778 | 2.03 | 20 | 7 | 3 | 8 | 0 | 3 | 80.0 | 54 | 20 | 18 | 4 | 2 | 23 | 2 | 61 | 4 |
| McCandlish, Geneva | 1 | 2 | .333 | 4.92 | 17 | 5 | 0 | 5 | 0 | 1 | 53.0 | 59 | 40 | 29 | 6 | 3 | 38 | 0 | 39 | 6 |
| McFarlane, Newark | 0 | 0 | .000 | 18.00 | 2 | 0 | 0 | 1 | 0 | 0 | 2.0 | 5 | 7 | 4 | 0 | 1 | 3 | 1 | 3 | 1 |
| McGowan, Elmira | 3 | 9 | .250 | 3.42 | 15 | 10 | 0 | 2 | 0 | 0 | 55.1 | 56 | 39 | 21 | 2 | 2 | 36 | 2 | 46 | 7 |
| McNeely, Erie | 6 | 2 | .750 | 4.68 | 14 | 14 | 0 | 0 | 0 | 0 | 84.2 | 110 | 48 | 44 | 13 | 0 | 20 | 3 | 35 | 0 |
| Melton, Watertown | 3 | 7 | .300 | 3.67 | 15 | 15 | 4 | 0 | 1 | 0 | 100.2 | 91 | 48 | 41 | 3 | 3 | 46 | 0 | 103 | 7 |
| Menendez, Geneva* | 2 | 2 | .500 | 3.38 | 8 | 0 | 0 | 5 | 0 | 2 | 16.0 | 12 | 7 | 6 | 2 | 3 | 10 | 0 | 21 | 2 |
| Mercado, Batavia* | 0 | 0 | .000 | 5.23 | 5 | 0 | 0 | 3 | 0 | 0 | 10.1 | 10 | 7 | 6 | 1 | 2 | 12 | 1 | 11 | 1 |
| Mora, Batavia | 0 | 0 | .000 | 3.75 | 4 | 1 | 0 | 3 | 0 | 0 | 12.0 | 13 | 7 | 5 | 1 | 4 | 6 | 1 | 6 | 1 |
| G. Murphy, Auburn | 4 | 5 | .444 | 4.16 | 18 | 9 | 0 | 8 | 0 | 4 | 71.1 | 72 | 43 | 33 | 3 | 4 | 48 | 1 | 41 | 6 |
| K. Murphy, Batavia* | 1 | 3 | .250 | 3.34 | 13 | 1 | 0 | 9 | 0 | 2 | 29.2 | 24 | 12 | 11 | 1 | 0 | 9 | 1 | 40 | 6 |
| Nichols, Batavia | 5 | 5 | .500 | 3.00 | 13 | 13 | 0 | 0 | 0 | 0 | 84.0 | 74 | 40 | 28 | 10 | 3 | 33 | 0 | 93 | 6 |
| Nossek, Niagara Falls* | 1 | 3 | .250 | 7.03 | 21 | 2 | 0 | 6 | 0 | 0 | 48.2 | 51 | 42 | 38 | 4 | 0 | 53 | 1 | 36 | 0 |
| O'Connor, Oneonta | 0 | 0 | .000 | 9.00 | 2 | 0 | 0 | 2 | 0 | 0 | 6.0 | 5 | 6 | 6 | 1 | 2 | 3 | 0 | 5 | 0 |
| Oberholtzer, Watertown | 0 | 3 | .000 | 6.35 | 15 | 0 | 0 | 8 | 0 | 0 | 22.2 | 19 | 24 | 16 | 1 | 2 | 24 | 0 | 18 | 6 |
| Oyster, Erie | 2 | 1 | .667 | 1.74 | 15 | 1 | 1 | 6 | 1 | 0 | 31.0 | 29 | 10 | 6 | 1 | 0 | 7 | 1 | 32 | 2 |
| Page, Little Falls | 2 | 2 | .500 | 2.08 | 23 | 1 | 0 | 15 | 0 | 3 | 34.2 | 20 | 10 | 8 | 2 | 1 | 32 | 5 | 50 | 2 |
| Paixao, Utica | 4 | 5 | .444 | 2.92 | 15 | 11 | 1 | 4 | 0 | 1 | 71.0 | 66 | 29 | 23 | 5 | 3 | 22 | 0 | 30 | 3 |
| Palermo, Newark | 2 | 0 | 1.000 | 0.67 | 4 | 3 | 1 | 1 | 1 | 0 | 27.0 | 20 | 3 | 2 | 1 | 2 | 13 | 0 | 16 | 0 |

| Pitcher—Club | W. | L. | Pct. | ERA. | G. | GS. | CG. | GF. | ShO. | Sv. | IP. | H. | R. | ER. | HR. | HB. | BB. | Int. BB. | SO. | WP. |
|---|---|---|---|---|---|---|---|---|---|---|---|---|---|---|---|---|---|---|---|---|
| Patterson, Oneonta* | 2 | 2 | .500 | 4.84 | 6 | 6 | 0 | 0 | 0 | 0 | 22.1 | 23 | 14 | 12 | 0 | 2 | 14 | 0 | 21 | 1 |
| Pawlowski, Niagara Falls | 9 | 3 | .750 | 2.13 | 15 | 15 | 4 | 0 | 2 | 0 | 97.0 | 74 | 41 | 23 | 7 | 3 | 35 | 0 | 82 | 6 |
| Peterson, Niagara Falls | 7 | 6 | .538 | 3.02 | 14 | 14 | 5 | 0 | 0 | 0 | 92.1 | 74 | 39 | 31 | 9 | 0 | 34 | 1 | 79 | 5 |
| Picota, Erie | 3 | 5 | .375 | 6.22 | 16 | 6 | 0 | 3 | 0 | 0 | 46.1 | 47 | 37 | 32 | 4 | 6 | 36 | 0 | 25 | 7 |
| Poehl, Batavia | 3 | 2 | .600 | 2.10 | 10 | 9 | 0 | 1 | 0 | 1 | 55.2 | 48 | 22 | 13 | 2 | 2 | 21 | 2 | 48 | 8 |
| Pruett, Utica | 7 | 1 | .875 | 0.68 | 21 | 0 | 0 | 18 | 0 | 7 | 40.0 | 24 | 5 | 3 | 0 | 0 | 19 | 3 | 34 | 1 |
| Rather, Oneonta | 8 | 0 | 1.000 | 0.31 | 8 | 8 | 4 | 0 | 2 | 0 | 58.0 | 22 | 5 | 2 | 1 | 0 | 16 | 0 | 88 | 4 |
| Rauth, Little Falls | 6 | 5 | .545 | 3.84 | 15 | 15 | 4 | 0 | 1 | 0 | 103.0 | 109 | 52 | 44 | 2 | 2 | 40 | 1 | 60 | 5 |
| Richardson, Little Falls | 4 | 3 | .571 | 3.61 | 11 | 10 | 3 | 1 | 2 | 0 | 62.1 | 58 | 32 | 25 | 6 | 4 | 32 | 3 | 56 | 4 |
| Robertson, Batavia | 1 | 2 | .333 | 5.93 | 11 | 3 | 0 | 6 | 0 | 1 | 27.1 | 25 | 24 | 18 | 3 | 3 | 15 | 2 | 25 | 7 |
| Robinson, Watertown | 0 | 0 | .000 | 54.00 | 1 | 0 | 0 | 0 | 0 | 0 | 0.1 | 4 | 2 | 2 | 0 | 0 | 0 | 0 | 1 | 0 |
| Robles, Geneva | 8 | 3 | .727 | 3.51 | 18 | 11 | 1 | 3 | 0 | 0 | 89.2 | 84 | 45 | 35 | 9 | 4 | 46 | 1 | 58 | 5 |
| Rodriguez, Erie | 3 | 1 | .750 | 5.67 | 15 | 2 | 1 | 2 | 0 | 0 | 33.1 | 35 | 24 | 21 | 3 | 2 | 28 | 1 | 31 | 1 |
| Roebuck, Auburn* | 3 | 2 | .600 | 3.49 | 21 | 1 | 0 | 10 | 0 | 2 | 49.0 | 35 | 23 | 19 | 1 | 2 | 41 | 3 | 51 | 1 |
| Rohan, Newark | 0 | 0 | .000 | 16.88 | 2 | 0 | 0 | 1 | 0 | 0 | 2.2 | 7 | 5 | 5 | 0 | 1 | 1 | 1 | 3 | 1 |
| Rone, Newark* | 0 | 0 | .000 | 4.26 | 12 | 0 | 0 | 4 | 0 | 0 | 12.2 | 11 | 7 | 6 | 0 | 1 | 9 | 1 | 11 | 1 |
| Roth, Geneva | 7 | 5 | .583 | 3.42 | 15 | 15 | 4 | 0 | 1 | 0 | 100.0 | 83 | 47 | 38 | 5 | 3 | 50 | 0 | 78 | 10 |
| Sampen, Watertown | 0 | 0 | .000 | 1.80 | 5 | 0 | 0 | 2 | 0 | 1 | 10.0 | 9 | 3 | 2 | 0 | 1 | 7 | 0 | 11 | 2 |
| Sanchez, Newark | 4 | 2 | .667 | 3.32 | 12 | 9 | 0 | 1 | 0 | 0 | 62.1 | 60 | 34 | 23 | 3 | 1 | 27 | 0 | 43 | 3 |
| Sanderski, Elmira | 3 | 5 | .375 | 5.77 | 14 | 12 | 1 | 1 | 1 | 0 | 48.1 | 45 | 41 | 31 | 1 | 3 | 40 | 5 | 26 | 13 |
| Santana, Watertown | 1 | 2 | .333 | 5.65 | 19 | 0 | 0 | 9 | 0 | 0 | 36.2 | 28 | 26 | 23 | 0 | 4 | 37 | 0 | 23 | 6 |
| Satzinger, Watertown | 2 | 8 | .200 | 6.58 | 18 | 8 | 0 | 9 | 0 | 1 | 53.1 | 44 | 43 | 39 | 2 | 2 | 48 | 1 | 50 | 10 |
| Schulte, Auburn | 5 | 3 | .625 | 2.27 | 27 | 0 | 0 | 23 | 0 | 9 | 39.2 | 26 | 18 | 10 | 3 | 6 | 24 | 1 | 34 | 1 |
| Scott, Batavia | 1 | 3 | .250 | 5.33 | 16 | 5 | 0 | 6 | 0 | 1 | 52.1 | 58 | 37 | 31 | 5 | 0 | 21 | 1 | 42 | 3 |
| Shannon, Jamestown | 1 | 3 | .250 | 3.70 | 5 | 3 | 1 | 1 | 0 | 0 | 24.1 | 24 | 15 | 10 | 0 | 1 | 4 | 0 | 29 | 1 |
| Sheldon, Niagara Falls | 0 | 0 | .000 | 0.00 | 1 | 0 | 0 | 1 | 0 | 0 | 1.0 | 0 | 0 | 0 | 0 | 0 | 0 | 0 | 1 | 1 |
| Smith, Auburn | 4 | 4 | .500 | 4.42 | 15 | 14 | 0 | 1 | 0 | 0 | 79.1 | 96 | 48 | 39 | 10 | 6 | 20 | 1 | 40 | 3 |
| Snyder, Batavia | 0 | 3 | .000 | 11.49 | 6 | 5 | 0 | 0 | 0 | 0 | 15.2 | 27 | 22 | 20 | 2 | 2 | 9 | 0 | 7 | 2 |
| Soma, Batavia | 0 | 0 | .000 | 0.00 | 1 | 0 | 0 | 1 | 0 | 0 | 1.0 | 0 | 0 | 0 | 0 | 0 | 0 | 0 | 3 | 0 |
| Speakman, Elmira | 0 | 0 | .000 | 0.00 | 1 | 0 | 0 | 1 | 0 | 0 | 1.0 | 0 | 0 | 0 | 0 | 0 | 0 | 0 | 0 | 0 |
| Stacey, Niagara Falls | 3 | 6 | .333 | 4.82 | 12 | 12 | 1 | 0 | 0 | 0 | 65.1 | 66 | 43 | 35 | 2 | 6 | 37 | 0 | 45 | 10 |
| Stauffacher, Jamestown* | 2 | 2 | .500 | 4.88 | 20 | 2 | 0 | 12 | 0 | 6 | 31.1 | 24 | 23 | 17 | 1 | 1 | 35 | 0 | 56 | 7 |
| Stender, Batavia* | 0 | 0 | .000 | 9.00 | 1 | 0 | 0 | 1 | 0 | 0 | 2.0 | 4 | 2 | 2 | 0 | 0 | 0 | 0 | 0 | 0 |
| Stewart, Watertown | 0 | 0 | .000 | 0.00 | 2 | 0 | 0 | 2 | 0 | 0 | 2.0 | 1 | 0 | 0 | 0 | 0 | 1 | 0 | 0 | 1 |
| Stone, Niagara Falls | 6 | 5 | .545 | 2.62 | 21 | 9 | 0 | 11 | 0 | 3 | 86.0 | 68 | 41 | 25 | 6 | 3 | 19 | 2 | 77 | 2 |
| Strickland, Geneva | 1 | 3 | .250 | 5.69 | 14 | 10 | 0 | 2 | 0 | 0 | 55.1 | 51 | 38 | 35 | 4 | 8 | 38 | 0 | 40 | 7 |
| Sudo, Utica | 4 | 6 | .400 | 2.14 | 15 | 14 | 3 | 0 | 0 | 0 | 105.0 | 90 | 32 | 25 | 1 | 4 | 28 | 2 | 74 | 3 |
| Sundgren, Jamestown | 6 | 1 | .857 | 1.82 | 17 | 4 | 1 | 4 | 0 | 0 | 54.1 | 40 | 12 | 11 | 2 | 1 | 24 | 2 | 47 | 2 |
| Takach, Little Falls* | 3 | 2 | .600 | 2.18 | 15 | 1 | 0 | 7 | 0 | 2 | 41.1 | 36 | 11 | 10 | 2 | 1 | 14 | 1 | 29 | 2 |
| Talamantez, Newark | 4 | 7 | .364 | 4.36 | 15 | 15 | 3 | 0 | 1 | 0 | 88.2 | 76 | 56 | 43 | 4 | 2 | 77 | 0 | 87 | 15 |
| Tarasovitch, Erie | 0 | 0 | .000 | 18.00 | 1 | 0 | 0 | 0 | 0 | 0 | 2.0 | 5 | 4 | 4 | 3 | 0 | 2 | 0 | 1 | 0 |
| Thigpen, Niagara Falls | 2 | 3 | .400 | 1.72 | 28 | 1 | 0 | 25 | 0 | 9 | 52.1 | 30 | 12 | 10 | 0 | 1 | 19 | 2 | 74 | 2 |
| Thorpe, Newark | 4 | 4 | .500 | 3.77 | 25 | 0 | 0 | 19 | 0 | 5 | 28.2 | 19 | 15 | 12 | 0 | 3 | 18 | 3 | 20 | 2 |
| Tirado, Oneonta | 2 | 3 | .400 | 1.99 | 22 | 1 | 0 | 10 | 0 | 3 | 45.1 | 20 | 15 | 10 | 0 | 1 | 15 | 1 | 68 | 1 |
| Torres, Oneonta | 1 | 2 | .333 | 4.50 | 3 | 3 | 0 | 0 | 0 | 0 | 16.0 | 17 | 10 | 8 | 2 | 0 | 10 | 0 | 13 | 1 |
| Travels, Utica | 4 | 7 | .364 | 3.59 | 15 | 14 | 1 | 1 | 0 | 1 | 95.1 | 90 | 42 | 38 | 3 | 2 | 16 | 1 | 48 | 2 |
| Trudeau, Oneonta | 8 | 3 | .727 | 1.64 | 16 | 8 | 3 | 3 | 2 | 1 | 71.1 | 42 | 22 | 13 | 1 | 4 | 24 | 1 | 75 | 4 |
| Tuozzo, Little Falls | 3 | 7 | .300 | 3.15 | 21 | 2 | 0 | 16 | 0 | 4 | 40.0 | 44 | 19 | 14 | 0 | 0 | 16 | 2 | 30 | 1 |
| Valdez, Utica | 6 | 5 | .545 | 3.07 | 15 | 15 | 5 | 0 | 0 | 0 | 105.2 | 98 | 53 | 36 | 6 | 1 | 36 | 1 | 86 | 8 |
| Vasquez, Elmira | 2 | 4 | .333 | 3.45 | 18 | 9 | 0 | 9 | 0 | 0 | 57.1 | 50 | 28 | 22 | 6 | 0 | 24 | 4 | 42 | 2 |
| Vazquez, Newark* | 1 | 2 | .333 | 1.69 | 18 | 1 | 0 | 10 | 0 | 1 | 26.2 | 18 | 9 | 5 | 0 | 4 | 22 | 2 | 31 | 6 |
| Vike, Auburn | 0 | 0 | .000 | 2.45 | 1 | 1 | 0 | 0 | 0 | 0 | 3.2 | 1 | 1 | 1 | 0 | 0 | 8 | 0 | 1 | 0 |
| Wachs, Little Falls* | 6 | 3 | .667 | 3.89 | 19 | 7 | 2 | 2 | 0 | 0 | 71.2 | 71 | 38 | 31 | 5 | 1 | 26 | 0 | 66 | 1 |
| Welborn, Little Falls | 1 | 4 | .200 | 6.00 | 6 | 6 | 0 | 0 | 0 | 0 | 21.0 | 12 | 26 | 14 | 2 | 1 | 33 | 0 | 19 | 5 |
| Wells, Auburn* | 4 | 4 | .500 | 2.74 | 13 | 9 | 0 | 2 | 0 | 1 | 62.1 | 35 | 19 | 19 | 3 | 1 | 51 | 1 | 46 | 1 |
| K. Williams, Elmira | 0 | 0 | .000 | 27.00 | 3 | 0 | 0 | 3 | 0 | 0 | 3.0 | 5 | 9 | 9 | 1 | 1 | 6 | 0 | 2 | 3 |
| Rob. Williams, Utica | 3 | 7 | .300 | 5.15 | 21 | 2 | 0 | 11 | 0 | 1 | 50.2 | 50 | 40 | 29 | 2 | 2 | 27 | 3 | 65 | 7 |
| Rog. Williams, Geneva | 8 | 4 | .667 | 2.86 | 15 | 15 | 4 | 0 | 0 | 0 | 110.0 | 85 | 43 | 35 | 8 | 1 | 55 | 1 | 105 | 3 |
| S. Williams, Newark | 1 | 2 | .333 | 5.79 | 4 | 4 | 0 | 0 | 0 | 0 | 18.2 | 16 | 16 | 12 | 0 | 0 | 23 | 0 | 7 | 7 |
| Williamson, Batavia | 3 | 4 | .429 | 4.35 | 13 | 11 | 0 | 0 | 0 | 0 | 62.0 | 49 | 44 | 30 | 4 | 3 | 46 | 0 | 52 | 5 |
| Wilson, Newark | 7 | 6 | .538 | 3.90 | 16 | 15 | 4 | 0 | 0 | 0 | 99.1 | 101 | 52 | 43 | 7 | 1 | 50 | 0 | 62 | 7 |
| Yeager, Oneonta* | 0 | 0 | .000 | 0.00 | 1 | 0 | 0 | 1 | 0 | 0 | 1.0 | 0 | 0 | 0 | 0 | 0 | 0 | 0 | 2 | 0 |
| Zarranz, Geneva | 6 | 3 | .667 | 4.10 | 19 | 5 | 1 | 8 | 0 | 2 | 52.2 | 61 | 30 | 24 | 4 | 0 | 31 | 0 | 32 | 4 |
| Zupka, Elmira | 0 | 2 | .000 | 4.60 | 20 | 0 | 0 | 10 | 0 | 4 | 43.0 | 39 | 33 | 22 | 4 | 2 | 32 | 1 | 37 | 9 |

BALKS—Paixao, Robles, 4 each; Sanchez, Valdez, 3 each; Bridges, Carista, Channing, Hendricks, McNeely, Scott, Stone, Vasquez, Williamson, Zupka, 2 each; Ballard, Cepeda, Cunningham, Davins, Evers, Farr, Galbato, Ma. Gardner, Ghelfi, Haines, Helton, Hilton, Howes, Johnson, King, Koopman, Linton, Livchak, Magistri, G. Murphy, Palermo, Peterson, Poehl, Santana, Schulte, Snyder, Stacey, Sundgren, Takach, Travels, R. Williams, Wilson, 1 each.

COMBINATION SHUTOUTS—Arnsberg-Murphy, Dunster-Gelmine, Wells-Dineen, Ilsley-Dineen, Dunster-Gelmine-Fascher, Auburn; Nichols-Murphy, Poehl-Ghelfi, Williamson-Pohel, Batavia; McGowan-Livernois-Manzanillo, Carista-Magistri-Manzanillo, Carista-Livernois, Elmira; Picota-Freed, Erie; Roth-Horn-Hirsch, Geneva; Stacey-Stone, Hunter-Dixon, Hunter-DeBoever-Collins, Ayers-Collins, Cunningham-Collins, Jamestown; Ballard-Adams, Williams-Koonce, Adams-Gonzales, Wilson-Gonzales-Thorpe, Ballard-Gonzales, Vazquez-King, Palermo-Thorpe, Newark; Pawlowski-Lahrman-Thigpen, Peterson-Thigpen, Niagara Falls; Dougherty-Gay, Evers-Davidson, Evers-Carroll, Oneonta; Sudo-Pruett, Utica; Melton-Davins, Watertown.

NO-HIT GAME—Rather, Oneonta, defeated Watertown, 6-0, July 24.

# Northwest League

## CLASS A

### CHAMPIONSHIP WINNERS IN PREVIOUS YEARS

| | | |
|---|---|---|
| 1901—Portland .675 | 1946—Wenatchee .622 | 1968—Tri-City .600 |
| 1902—Butte .608 | 1947—Vancouver .566 | 1969—Rogue Valley .633 |
| 1903—Butte .578 | 1948—Spokane .614 | 1970—Lewiston a .538 |
| 1904—Boise .625 | 1949—Yakima .660 | Coos Bay-No. Bend .563 |
| 1905—Vancouver .586 | Vancouver (2nd)† .615 | 1971—Tri-City a .625 |
| Everett° .667 | 1950—Yakima .613 | Bend .538 |
| 1906—Tacoma .600 | 1951—Spokane .655 | 1972—Lewiston a .675 |
| 1907—Aberdeen .625 | 1952—Victoria .631 | Walla Walla .513 |
| 1908—Vancouver .578 | 1953—Salem .635 | 1973—Walla Walla b .638 |
| 1909—Seattle .653 | Spokane° .590 | Portland .563 |
| 1910—Spokane .596 | 1954—Vancouver° .636 | 1974—Bellingham .619 |
| 1911—Vancouver .628 | Lewiston .629 | Eugene c .571 |
| 1912—Seattle .600 | 1955—Salem .646 | 1975—Portland .545 |
| 1913—Vancouver .600 | Eugene° .639 | Eugene d .684 |
| 1914—Vancouver .632 | 1956—Yakima .691 | 1976—Portland .556 |
| 1915—Seattle .564 | Yakima .619 | Walla Walla d .639 |
| 1916—Spokane .622 | 1957—Eugene .576 | 1977—Bellingham e .618 |
| 1917—Great Falls .592 | Wenatchee° .647 | Portland .667 |
| 1918—Seattle .588 | 1958—Lewiston .621 | 1978—Grays Harbor f .671 |
| 1919—Seattle .590 | Yakima° .594 | Eugene .514 |
| 1920—Victoria .600 | 1959—Salem .623 | 1979—Central Oregon d .606 |
| 1921—Yakima .710 | Yakima° .563 | Walla Walla .571 |
| Yakima .660 | 1960—Yakima .638 | 1980—Bellingham g .643 |
| 1922—Calgary† .600 | Yakima .562 | Eugene g .529 |
| 1923-36—Did not operate. | 1961—Lewiston° .621 | 1981—Medford d .600 |
| 1937—Wenatchee .603 | Yakima .600 | Bellingham .557 |
| Tacoma° .627 | 1962—Wenatchee° .574 | 1982—Medford .757 |
| 1938—Yakima .583 | Tri-City .580 | Salem d .486 |
| Bellingham (2nd)† .511 | 1963—Lewiston .594 | 1983—Medford h .735 |
| 1939—Wenatchee .601 | Yakima° .613 | Bellingham .588 |
| Tacoma (2nd)† .533 | 1964—Eugene .636 | 1984—Tri-Cities h .622 |
| 1940—Spokane .587 | Yakima° .611 | Medford .608 |
| Tacoma (4th)† .500 | 1965—Lewiston .667 | |
| 1941—Spokane .669 | Tri-City° .681 | |
| 1942—Vancouver .594 | 1966—Tri-City .679 | |
| 1943-45—Did not operate. | 1967—Medford .607 | |

°Won split-season playoff. †Won four-club playoff. §League disbanded June 18. aLeague divided into Northern and Southern divisions, declared champion under league rules. bLeague divided into Eastern and Western divisions, declared champion under league rules. cLeague divided into Eastern and Western divisions; won two-team playoff. dLeague divided into Northern and Southern divisions; won two-team playoff. eLeague divided into Affiliate and Independent divisions; won two-team playoff. fDeclared league champion after winning one-game playoff. Balance of playoff canceled due to rain and wet grounds. gDeclared co-champion after winning one game. Balance of playoff canceled due to rain and wet grounds. hLeague divided into Washington and Oregon divisions; won two-team playoff. (NOTE—Known as Pacific Northwest League 1901-02, Pacific National League 1903-04, Northwestern League 1905-18, Pacific Coast International League 1919-22 and Western International League 1937-54.)

### STANDING OF CLUBS AT CLOSE OF SEASON, SEPTEMBER 1

#### WASHINGTON DIVISION

| Club | Ev. | Bell. | Spo. | T.C. | Eug. | Bend | Sal. | Med. | W. | L. | T. | Pct. | G.B. |
|---|---|---|---|---|---|---|---|---|---|---|---|---|---|
| Everett (Giants) | ... | 10 | 9 | 8 | 3 | 3 | 3 | 4 | 40 | 34 | 0 | .541 | ........ |
| Bellingham (Mariners) | 6 | ... | 9 | 10 | 2 | 4 | 4 | 4 | 39 | 35 | 0 | .527 | 1 |
| Spokane (Padres) | 6 | 6 | ... | 9 | 1 | 5 | 3 | 3 | 33 | 41 | 0 | .446 | 7 |
| Tri-Cities (Independent) | 7 | 5 | 7 | ... | 4 | 5 | 2 | 3 | 33 | 41 | 0 | .446 | 7 |

#### OREGON DIVISION

| Club | | | | | | | | | W. | L. | T. | Pct. | G.B. |
|---|---|---|---|---|---|---|---|---|---|---|---|---|---|
| Eugene (Royals) | 4 | 5 | 6 | 3 | ... | 7 | 8 | 7 | 40 | 34 | 0 | .541 | ........ |
| Bend (Phillies) | 4 | 3 | 2 | 2 | 8 | ... | 9 | 11 | 39 | 35 | 0 | .527 | 1 |
| Salem (Angels) | 4 | 3 | 4 | 5 | 8 | 6 | ... | 9 | 39 | 35 | 0 | .527 | 1 |
| Medford (A's) | 3 | 3 | 4 | 4 | 8 | 5 | 6 | ... | 33 | 41 | 0 | .446 | 7 |

Tri-Cities represented Richland, Pasco and Kennewick, Wash.

Major league affiliations in parentheses.

Playoff—Everett defeated Eugene, one game to none.

Regular-Season Attendance—Bellingham, 18,343; Bend, 30,507; Eugene, 103,193; Everett, 53,869; Medford, 64,720; Salem, 34,450; Spokane, 70,576; Tri-Cities, 32,424. Total, 408,082. Playoff, 5,097.

Managers—Bellingham, Gary Pellant; Bend, Paul Carey; Eugene, Frank Funk; Everett, Joe Strain; Medford, Grady Fuson; Salem, Bruce Hines; Spokane, Jack Maloof; Tri-Cities, Ed Olsen.

All-Star Team: 1B—Jim McCollom, Salem; 2B—Julio Alcala, Eugene; 3B—Dave Cortez, Tri-Cities; SS—John Verducci, Everett; OF—Ron Jones, Bend; Mike Loggins, Eugene; Jerald Clark, Spokane; C—Chris Jelic, Eugene; DH—Keith Foley, Tri-Cities; RHP—Randy McCament, Everett; LHP—Dave Otto, Medford; Most Valuable Player—Jerald Clark, Spokane; Manager of the Year—Frank Funk, Eugene.

(Compiled by William J. Weiss, League Statistician, San Mateo, Calif.)

### CLUB BATTING

| Club | Pct. | G. | AB. | R. | OR. | H. | TB. | 2B. | 3B. | HR. | RBI. | GW. | SH. | SF. | HP. | BB. | Int. BB. | SO. | SB. | CS. | LOB. |
|---|---|---|---|---|---|---|---|---|---|---|---|---|---|---|---|---|---|---|---|---|---|
| Tri-Cities | .286 | 74 | 2660 | 485 | 475 | 760 | 1102 | 118 | 10 | 68 | 406 | 32 | 27 | 20 | 32 | 320 | 8 | 522 | 35 | 24 | 591 |
| Medford | .261 | 74 | 2562 | 430 | 412 | 668 | 941 | 90 | 30 | 41 | 346 | 23 | 9 | 23 | 31 | 363 | 9 | 520 | 131 | 46 | 597 |
| Bend | .257 | 74 | 2525 | 441 | 433 | 649 | 956 | 117 | 11 | 56 | 370 | 35 | 5 | 24 | 31 | 320 | 6 | 582 | 101 | 49 | 533 |

## CLUB BATTING—Continued

| Club | Pct. | G. | AB. | R. | OR. | H. | TB. | 2B. | 3B. | HR. | RBI. | GW. | SH. | SF. | HP. | BB. | Int. BB. | SO. | SB. | CS. | LOB. |
|------|------|----|-----|----|----|----|----|-----|-----|-----|------|-----|-----|-----|-----|-----|----|-----|-----|-----|-----|
| Eugene | .256 | 74 | 2509 | 387 | 411 | 643 | 893 | 110 | 19 | 34 | 317 | 33 | 16 | 26 | 23 | 345 | 11 | 550 | 138 | 41 | 592 |
| Salem | .254 | 74 | 2496 | 363 | 372 | 634 | 862 | 93 | 18 | 33 | 293 | 32 | 13 | 24 | 30 | 283 | 7 | 499 | 102 | 41 | 551 |
| Spokane | .253 | 74 | 2504 | 346 | 357 | 634 | 821 | 110 | 10 | 19 | 306 | 27 | 29 | 24 | 25 | 370 | 5 | 494 | 65 | 35 | 634 |
| Everett | .248 | 74 | 2530 | 363 | 359 | 627 | 897 | 107 | 20 | 41 | 309 | 37 | 12 | 26 | 28 | 361 | 11 | 654 | 66 | 30 | 616 |
| Bellingham | .242 | 74 | 2459 | 351 | 347 | 595 | 847 | 110 | 11 | 40 | 275 | 34 | 19 | 20 | 33 | 309 | 8 | 548 | 78 | 43 | 541 |

## INDIVIDUAL BATTING
(Leading Qualifiers for Batting Championship—200 or More Plate Appearances)

*Bats lefthanded.    †Switch-hitter.

| Player and Club | Pct. | G. | AB. | R. | H. | TB. | 2B. | 3B. | HR. | RBI. | GW. | SH. | SF. | HP. | BB. | Int. BB. | SO. | SB. | CS. |
|------|------|----|-----|----|----|----|-----|-----|-----|------|-----|-----|-----|-----|-----|----|-----|-----|-----|
| Foley, Keith, Tri-Cities | .376 | 57 | 234 | 54 | 88 | 142 | 9 | 0 | 15 | 55 | 3 | 2 | 3 | 2 | 26 | 2 | 26 | 0 | 1 |
| Lamar, Daniel, Tri-Cities | .375 | 64 | 256 | 65 | 96 | 170 | 19 | 2 | 17 | 69 | 3 | 0 | 4 | 4 | 32 | 3 | 42 | 0 | 2 |
| Cortez, David, Tri-Cities | .353 | 64 | 258 | 45 | 91 | 111 | 15 | 1 | 1 | 33 | 6 | 9 | 1 | 1 | 26 | 0 | 51 | 3 | 3 |
| Dabney, Ty, Everett* | .329 | 57 | 210 | 36 | 69 | 110 | 13 | 5 | 6 | 31 | 3 | 0 | 2 | 1 | 33 | 2 | 32 | 0 | 2 |
| Clark, Jerald, Spokane | .325 | 73 | 283 | 45 | 92 | 128 | 24 | 3 | 2 | 50 | 3 | 1 | 6 | 4 | 34 | 0 | 38 | 9 | 4 |
| Cora, Jose, Spokane† | .324 | 43 | 170 | 48 | 55 | 79 | 11 | 2 | 3 | 26 | 2 | 4 | 1 | 8 | 27 | 0 | 24 | 13 | 2 |
| McCollom, James, Salem | .318 | 73 | 267 | 48 | 85 | 136 | 18 | 0 | 11 | 47 | 5 | 0 | 2 | 10 | 31 | 3 | 39 | 7 | 2 |
| Jones, Ronald, Bend* | .315 | 73 | 286 | 54 | 90 | 135 | 13 | 1 | 10 | 60 | 10 | 0 | 4 | 4 | 34 | 2 | 28 | 9 | 7 |
| Gibree, Robert, Bellingham | .315 | 53 | 178 | 25 | 56 | 82 | 11 | 0 | 5 | 29 | 2 | 0 | 1 | 3 | 23 | 0 | 31 | 1 | 4 |
| Martig, Richard, Medford | .313 | 49 | 179 | 40 | 56 | 102 | 12 | 5 | 8 | 36 | 2 | 0 | 0 | 4 | 35 | 1 | 29 | 4 | 0 |

Departmental Leaders: G—Baham, Meyers, 74; AB—Baham, 305; R—Lamar, 65; H—Lamar, 96; TB—Lamar, 170; 2B—Clark, Lundblade, 24; 3B—Arndt, 6; HR—Lamar, 17; RBI—Lamar, 69; GWRBI—R. Jones, 10; SH—Cortez, 9; SF—Alcala, 7; HP—McCollom, 10; BB—Stevenson, 67; IBB—Ladnier, Meyers, 4; SO—Holyfield, 80; SB—Loggins, 35; CS—Jacas, 10.

(All Players—Listed Alphabetically)

| Player and Club | Pct. | G. | AB. | R. | H. | TB. | 2B. | 3B. | HR. | RBI. | GW. | SH. | SF. | HP. | BB. | Int. BB. | SO. | SB. | CS. |
|------|------|----|-----|----|----|----|-----|-----|-----|------|-----|-----|-----|-----|-----|----|-----|-----|-----|
| Alcala, Julio, Eugene | .225 | 70 | 262 | 30 | 59 | 83 | 12 | 3 | 2 | 32 | 3 | 7 | 7 | 0 | 20 | 0 | 42 | 10 | 4 |
| Alfonzo, Edgar, Salem | .273 | 56 | 209 | 29 | 57 | 83 | 10 | 2 | 4 | 25 | 4 | 2 | 2 | 2 | 17 | 0 | 28 | 0 | 3 |
| Armstrong, Eldridge, 4 Med.-26 TC .. | .240 | 30 | 104 | 20 | 25 | 37 | 4 | 1 | 2 | 10 | 1 | 0 | 0 | 4 | 12 | 0 | 28 | 0 | 0 |
| Arndt, Larry, Medford | .289 | 69 | 266 | 47 | 77 | 118 | 11 | 6 | 6 | 48 | 9 | 3 | 1 | 3 | 31 | 1 | 70 | 13 | 6 |
| Arnold, Timothy, Salem | .364 | 23 | 77 | 11 | 28 | 32 | 4 | 0 | 0 | 11 | 1 | 1 | 1 | 2 | 6 | 0 | 8 | 4 | 3 |
| Baham, Leon, Tri-Cities† | .308 | 74 | 305 | 62 | 94 | 134 | 14 | 1 | 8 | 55 | 4 | 1 | 3 | 1 | 40 | 1 | 35 | 12 | 3 |
| Baker, Gerald, Tri-Cities | .282 | 54 | 181 | 38 | 51 | 84 | 9 | 0 | 8 | 31 | 1 | 2 | 2 | 3 | 28 | 0 | 52 | 1 | 1 |
| Ban, Mark, Salem* | .181 | 53 | 166 | 18 | 30 | 35 | 5 | 0 | 0 | 12 | 0 | 0 | 0 | 2 | 16 | 0 | 27 | 4 | 0 |
| Bauer, Eric, Spokane | .250 | 8 | 8 | 0 | 2 | 3 | 1 | 0 | 0 | 1 | 0 | 0 | 0 | 0 | 0 | 0 | 2 | 0 | 0 |
| Beck, Dion, Bend* | .000 | 25 | 1 | 0 | 0 | 0 | 0 | 0 | 0 | 0 | 0 | 0 | 0 | 0 | 0 | 0 | 0 | 0 | 0 |
| Bedell, Jeffrey, Eugene† | .223 | 63 | 233 | 33 | 52 | 78 | 11 | 0 | 5 | 37 | 4 | 2 | 2 | 3 | 15 | 1 | 71 | 4 | 5 |
| Bernardo, Robert, Bellingham | .500 | 1 | 4 | 1 | 2 | 5 | 0 | 0 | 1 | 2 | 0 | 0 | 0 | 0 | 1 | 0 | 0 | 0 | 0 |
| Blackmun, Benjamin, Bend | .238 | 65 | 239 | 41 | 57 | 72 | 12 | 0 | 1 | 26 | 2 | 1 | 1 | 4 | 24 | 0 | 31 | 13 | 7 |
| Blount, William, Spokane* | .200 | 23 | 5 | 0 | 1 | 1 | 0 | 0 | 0 | 1 | 0 | 1 | 0 | 0 | 1 | 0 | 2 | 0 | 0 |
| Bonilla, George, Everett* | .000 | 13 | 4 | 1 | 0 | 0 | 0 | 0 | 0 | 0 | 0 | 0 | 0 | 0 | 1 | 0 | 2 | 0 | 0 |
| Bowden, Stephen, Bend* | .000 | 7 | 3 | 0 | 0 | 0 | 0 | 0 | 0 | 0 | 0 | 0 | 0 | 0 | 0 | 0 | 1 | 0 | 0 |
| Britt, Patrick, Medford | .252 | 40 | 135 | 20 | 34 | 46 | 7 | 1 | 1 | 15 | 0 | 0 | 3 | 1 | 14 | 0 | 25 | 1 | 0 |
| Brock, Kyle, Tri-Cities† | .304 | 28 | 115 | 21 | 35 | 41 | 6 | 0 | 0 | 26 | 4 | 0 | 1 | 0 | 12 | 0 | 20 | 0 | 0 |
| Brunelle, Rodney, Bend | .283 | 49 | 166 | 23 | 47 | 64 | 11 | 0 | 2 | 33 | 4 | 0 | 1 | 4 | 13 | 0 | 47 | 2 | 2 |
| Butcher, Matthew, Tri-Cities | .249 | 64 | 241 | 30 | 60 | 76 | 10 | 0 | 2 | 30 | 1 | 3 | 4 | 0 | 16 | 0 | 59 | 0 | 1 |
| Carey, Peter, Eugene* | .268 | 69 | 220 | 39 | 59 | 84 | 11 | 4 | 2 | 37 | 3 | 1 | 5 | 2 | 45 | 0 | 44 | 24 | 5 |
| Carter, Clarence, Tri-Cities | .000 | 4 | 12 | 1 | 0 | 0 | 0 | 0 | 0 | 0 | 0 | 0 | 0 | 1 | 2 | 0 | 4 | 0 | 0 |
| Carter, Jeffrey, Everett† | .304 | 54 | 207 | 45 | 63 | 92 | 9 | 4 | 4 | 22 | 1 | 1 | 1 | 2 | 36 | 0 | 33 | 28 | 8 |
| Carter, Marvin, Tri-Cities | .214 | 4 | 14 | 2 | 3 | 3 | 0 | 0 | 0 | 1 | 0 | 0 | 0 | 1 | 0 | 0 | 3 | 1 | 0 |
| Casey, Brian, Bellingham | .173 | 28 | 81 | 8 | 14 | 17 | 3 | 0 | 0 | 6 | 1 | 0 | 0 | 0 | 19 | 1 | 28 | 3 | 0 |
| Clark, Jerald, Spokane | .325 | 73 | 283 | 45 | 92 | 128 | 24 | 3 | 2 | 50 | 3 | 1 | 6 | 4 | 34 | 0 | 38 | 9 | 4 |
| Clem, John, Bellingham† | .260 | 65 | 219 | 38 | 57 | 82 | 8 | 1 | 5 | 30 | 6 | 0 | 2 | 4 | 40 | 3 | 52 | 8 | 3 |
| Cicione, Michael, Tri-Cities | .200 | 26 | 90 | 8 | 18 | 23 | 5 | 0 | 0 | 7 | 0 | 0 | 0 | 0 | 7 | 0 | 6 | 0 | 0 |
| Collins, Timothy, Bend | .500 | 18 | 2 | 1 | 1 | 1 | 0 | 0 | 0 | 0 | 0 | 0 | 0 | 0 | 0 | 0 | 0 | 0 | 0 |
| Cora, Jose, Spokane† | .324 | 43 | 170 | 48 | 55 | 79 | 11 | 2 | 3 | 26 | 2 | 4 | 1 | 8 | 27 | 0 | 24 | 13 | 2 |
| Cortez, David, Tri-Cities | .353 | 64 | 258 | 45 | 91 | 111 | 15 | 1 | 1 | 33 | 6 | 9 | 1 | 1 | 26 | 0 | 51 | 3 | 3 |
| Dabney, Ty, Everett* | .329 | 57 | 210 | 36 | 69 | 110 | 13 | 5 | 6 | 31 | 3 | 0 | 2 | 1 | 33 | 2 | 32 | 0 | 2 |
| Dandos, Michael, Everett | .255 | 43 | 161 | 23 | 41 | 54 | 8 | 1 | 1 | 21 | 0 | 0 | 1 | 0 | 12 | 0 | 20 | 1 | 2 |
| David, Amin, Medford | .273 | 64 | 231 | 37 | 63 | 90 | 8 | 2 | 5 | 32 | 0 | 1 | 1 | 2 | 28 | 3 | 26 | 1 | 1 |
| Davis, Rodney, Tri-Cities | .182 | 19 | 66 | 9 | 12 | 25 | 3 | 2 | 2 | 10 | 2 | 2 | 0 | 1 | 8 | 1 | 18 | 4 | 1 |
| De Leon, Rafael, Eugene | .250 | 40 | 144 | 23 | 36 | 47 | 5 | 0 | 2 | 9 | 0 | 0 | 1 | 3 | 14 | 0 | 18 | 4 | 2 |
| Dorsey, Maurice, Eugene | .184 | 13 | 38 | 6 | 7 | 13 | 0 | 0 | 2 | 4 | 0 | 0 | 0 | 4 | 0 | 0 | 12 | 1 | 0 |
| Duncan, Michael, Medford* | .274 | 66 | 241 | 50 | 66 | 115 | 14 | 1 | 11 | 50 | 5 | 0 | 6 | 3 | 53 | 3 | 47 | 7 | 2 |
| Ealy, Thomas, Everett | .203 | 25 | 74 | 11 | 15 | 17 | 2 | 0 | 0 | 6 | 0 | 0 | 2 | 0 | 11 | 1 | 20 | 0 | 4 |
| Eccleston, Thomas, Bellingham* | .262 | 59 | 191 | 32 | 50 | 73 | 10 | 2 | 3 | 20 | 2 | 0 | 0 | 3 | 26 | 1 | 44 | 8 | 7 |
| Ferraro, Carl, Spokane* | .000 | 11 | 1 | 0 | 0 | 0 | 0 | 0 | 0 | 0 | 0 | 0 | 0 | 0 | 1 | 0 | 1 | 0 | 0 |
| Flowers, Kim, Everett | .257 | 40 | 136 | 18 | 35 | 43 | 6 | 1 | 0 | 12 | 1 | 0 | 2 | 2 | 19 | 0 | 30 | 8 | 1 |
| Foley, Keith, Tri-Cities | .376 | 57 | 234 | 54 | 88 | 142 | 9 | 0 | 15 | 55 | 3 | 2 | 3 | 2 | 26 | 2 | 26 | 0 | 1 |
| Fulton, Gregory, Bellingham† | .200 | 63 | 215 | 25 | 43 | 58 | 8 | 2 | 1 | 17 | 1 | 0 | 3 | 3 | 20 | 0 | 44 | 8 | 0 |
| Geivett, William, Salem | .255 | 67 | 231 | 35 | 59 | 83 | 7 | 4 | 3 | 21 | 2 | 3 | 2 | 1 | 37 | 0 | 53 | 13 | 6 |
| Gibree, Robert, Bellingham | .315 | 53 | 178 | 25 | 56 | 82 | 11 | 0 | 5 | 29 | 2 | 0 | 1 | 3 | 23 | 0 | 31 | 1 | 4 |
| Ging, Adam, Spokane† | .199 | 51 | 171 | 19 | 34 | 43 | 6 | 0 | 1 | 15 | 2 | 1 | 2 | 0 | 37 | 0 | 35 | 3 | 3 |
| Graves, Kenley, Bend | .205 | 18 | 39 | 7 | 8 | 9 | 1 | 0 | 0 | 2 | 0 | 0 | 1 | 0 | 4 | 0 | 4 | 2 | 0 |
| Gray, Jeffrey, Spokane | .241 | 41 | 116 | 13 | 28 | 32 | 2 | 1 | 0 | 11 | 0 | 0 | 1 | 0 | 10 | 0 | 25 | 6 | 3 |
| Greaves, Barrymore, Bellingham | .214 | 36 | 117 | 16 | 25 | 29 | 2 | 1 | 0 | 4 | 0 | 4 | 0 | 0 | 10 | 0 | 18 | 6 | 1 |
| Greene, Nathaniel, Bend | .236 | 66 | 242 | 41 | 57 | 94 | 8 | 4 | 7 | 39 | 2 | 0 | 3 | 1 | 27 | 0 | 63 | 12 | 2 |
| Hall, Gregory, Spokane | .257 | 52 | 167 | 19 | 43 | 50 | 4 | 0 | 1 | 20 | 3 | 1 | 2 | 4 | 22 | 0 | 22 | 1 | 2 |
| Harris, Gregory, Spokane | .091 | 13 | 11 | 2 | 1 | 1 | 0 | 0 | 0 | 0 | 0 | 1 | 0 | 0 | 0 | 0 | 3 | 0 | 0 |
| Hayden, Richard, Bellingham | .111 | 4 | 9 | 1 | 1 | 2 | 1 | 0 | 0 | 0 | 0 | 0 | 0 | 0 | 2 | 0 | 2 | 0 | 0 |
| Hill, Nathaniel, Spokane | .189 | 37 | 95 | 12 | 18 | 24 | 6 | 0 | 0 | 8 | 0 | 0 | 2 | 1 | 10 | 0 | 42 | 2 | 3 |
| Holyfield, Vincent, Bend. | .248 | 71 | 278 | 42 | 69 | 113 | 14 | 3 | 8 | 42 | 2 | 1 | 2 | 4 | 22 | 1 | 80 | 11 | 7 |
| Hornsby, David, Everett | .227 | 32 | 110 | 9 | 25 | 33 | 2 | 0 | 2 | 11 | 1 | 0 | 0 | 1 | 14 | 2 | 38 | 0 | 1 |
| Howard, John, Tri-Cities* | .263 | 7 | 19 | 2 | 5 | 7 | 2 | 0 | 0 | 1 | 0 | 0 | 0 | 1 | 0 | 0 | 6 | 0 | 0 |
| Howarth, Paul, Eugene | .276 | 55 | 181 | 33 | 50 | 68 | 13 | 1 | 1 | 25 | 3 | 1 | 1 | 2 | 29 | 2 | 24 | 6 | 3 |
| Hurtado, Jose, Bend | .183 | 25 | 71 | 7 | 13 | 19 | 3 | 0 | 1 | 9 | 0 | 0 | 1 | 3 | 0 | 0 | 33 | 2 | 0 |
| Jacas, Andre, Medford | .300 | 56 | 217 | 57 | 65 | 84 | 9 | 5 | 0 | 16 | 2 | 0 | 3 | 8 | 44 | 1 | 27 | 27 | 10 |
| Jackson, Jimothy, Bend† | .000 | 5 | 7 | 0 | 0 | 0 | 0 | 0 | 0 | 0 | 0 | 0 | 0 | 0 | 1 | 0 | 6 | 1 | 0 |
| Jackson, Lloyd, Everett* | .205 | 43 | 161 | 18 | 33 | 55 | 5 | 1 | 5 | 23 | 3 | 0 | 2 | 1 | 7 | 1 | 65 | 3 | 0 |

| Player and Club | Pct. | G. | AB. | R. | H. | TB. | 2B. | 3B. | HR. | RBI. | GW. | SH. | SF. | HP. | BB. | Int. BB. | SO. | SB. | CS. |
|---|---|---|---|---|---|---|---|---|---|---|---|---|---|---|---|---|---|---|---|
| Jackson, Robert, Everett | .244 | 28 | 86 | 14 | 21 | 26 | 2 | 0 | 1 | 9 | 1 | 0 | 2 | 1 | 18 | 0 | 33 | 2 | 3 |
| James, Darin, Everett | .173 | 30 | 110 | 13 | 19 | 27 | 2 | 0 | 2 | 11 | 2 | 1 | 0 | 0 | 10 | 0 | 33 | 0 | 0 |
| James, Mark, Tri-Cities | .000 | 24 | 1 | 0 | 0 | 0 | 0 | 0 | 0 | 0 | 0 | 0 | 0 | 0 | 0 | 0 | 1 | 0 | 0 |
| Jelic, Christopher, Eugene | .313 | 42 | 144 | 24 | 45 | 64 | 7 | 3 | 2 | 22 | 1 | 0 | 1 | 0 | 37 | 0 | 24 | 7 | 3 |
| Jimenez, Genaro, Tri-Cities | .000 | 2 | 4 | 0 | 0 | 0 | 0 | 0 | 0 | 0 | 0 | 0 | 0 | 0 | 0 | 0 | 2 | 0 | 0 |
| Jones, Jerry (George), Everett* | .185 | 26 | 65 | 9 | 12 | 16 | 4 | 0 | 0 | 3 | 0 | 0 | 0 | 0 | 10 | 0 | 33 | 2 | 1 |
| Jones, Ronald, Bend* | .315 | 73 | 286 | 54 | 90 | 135 | 13 | 1 | 10 | 60 | 10 | 0 | 4 | 4 | 34 | 2 | 28 | 9 | 7 |
| Jordan, Joe, Everett | .213 | 33 | 108 | 10 | 23 | 32 | 7 | 1 | 0 | 12 | 2 | 0 | 2 | 3 | 17 | 1 | 24 | 0 | 0 |
| Kmak, Joseph, Everett | .310 | 40 | 129 | 21 | 40 | 55 | 10 | 1 | 1 | 14 | 1 | 0 | 2 | 3 | 20 | 0 | 23 | 0 | 1 |
| Knabenshue, Christopher, Spokane* .. | .279 | 71 | 258 | 50 | 72 | 92 | 13 | 2 | 1 | 34 | 2 | 2 | 2 | 0 | 57 | 1 | 42 | 10 | 4 |
| Kritsonis, John, Tri-Cities* | .262 | 31 | 126 | 32 | 33 | 38 | 5 | 0 | 0 | 12 | 1 | 1 | 0 | 3 | 28 | 0 | 5 | 9 | 4 |
| Kuiper, Glen, Spokane* | .319 | 18 | 47 | 5 | 15 | 17 | 2 | 0 | 0 | 1 | 0 | 0 | 0 | 0 | 8 | 0 | 9 | 0 | 1 |
| Kunz, Kurt, Eugene | .268 | 35 | 82 | 18 | 22 | 27 | 3 | 1 | 0 | 6 | 1 | 0 | 0 | 0 | 10 | 0 | 24 | 16 | 1 |
| Ladnier, Deric, Eugene† | .275 | 59 | 222 | 32 | 61 | 77 | 9 | 2 | 1 | 25 | 2 | 0 | 2 | 2 | 26 | 4 | 57 | 5 | 3 |
| Lamar, Daniel, Tri-Cities | .375 | 64 | 256 | 65 | 96 | 170 | 19 | 2 | 17 | 69 | 3 | 0 | 4 | 4 | 32 | 3 | 42 | 0 | 2 |
| Lambert, Reginald, Salem | .278 | 55 | 162 | 25 | 45 | 59 | 8 | 0 | 2 | 25 | 3 | 1 | 5 | 2 | 29 | 0 | 33 | 4 | 4 |
| Lemons, Timothy, Eugene | .239 | 12 | 46 | 7 | 11 | 21 | 4 | 0 | 2 | 11 | 2 | 0 | 0 | 0 | 7 | 0 | 7 | 0 | 0 |
| Leonard, Andrew, Eugene | .302 | 46 | 162 | 23 | 49 | 67 | 9 | 0 | 3 | 18 | 5 | 2 | 1 | 0 | 16 | 0 | 47 | 0 | 1 |
| Lewis, James, Spokane | .000 | 20 | 3 | 1 | 0 | 0 | 0 | 0 | 0 | 0 | 0 | 1 | 0 | 0 | 2 | 0 | 3 | 0 | 0 |
| Loggins, Michael, Eugene† | .311 | 73 | 289 | 52 | 90 | 122 | 13 | 2 | 5 | 31 | 4 | 2 | 2 | 6 | 52 | 2 | 40 | 35 | 6 |
| Lopez, George, Bellingham | .291 | 51 | 175 | 33 | 51 | 73 | 8 | 1 | 4 | 30 | 5 | 0 | 4 | 1 | 33 | 0 | 39 | 4 | 3 |
| Lundblade, Frederick, Bend | .281 | 68 | 260 | 56 | 73 | 142 | 24 | 0 | 15 | 55 | 4 | 0 | 2 | 2 | 44 | 0 | 56 | 4 | 3 |
| Luttrull, Bruce, Bend | .000 | 10 | 1 | 0 | 0 | 0 | 0 | 0 | 0 | 0 | 0 | 0 | 0 | 0 | 0 | 0 | 0 | 0 | 0 |
| Lynch, Joseph, Spokane | .333 | 32 | 3 | 0 | 1 | 1 | 0 | 0 | 0 | 2 | 0 | 0 | 0 | 0 | 1 | 0 | 1 | 0 | 0 |
| Marquez, Edwin, Salem | .215 | 27 | 79 | 10 | 17 | 17 | 0 | 0 | 0 | 6 | 0 | 0 | 1 | 1 | 13 | 0 | 11 | 0 | 0 |
| Marsh, Scott, Spokane* | .000 | 6 | 2 | 0 | 0 | 0 | 0 | 0 | 0 | 0 | 0 | 0 | 0 | 0 | 0 | 0 | 1 | 0 | 0 |
| Martig, Richard, Medford | .313 | 49 | 179 | 40 | 56 | 102 | 12 | 5 | 8 | 36 | 2 | 0 | 0 | 4 | 35 | 1 | 29 | 4 | 0 |
| Martinez, Luis, Medford† | .191 | 61 | 194 | 25 | 37 | 43 | 2 | 2 | 0 | 18 | 0 | 0 | 2 | 3 | 24 | 0 | 59 | 8 | 3 |
| Marx, William, Spokane | .500 | 15 | 8 | 0 | 4 | 4 | 0 | 0 | 0 | 1 | 1 | 1 | 1 | 0 | 0 | 0 | 2 | 0 | 0 |
| McCall, Roy, Bend | .224 | 42 | 134 | 19 | 30 | 46 | 4 | 0 | 4 | 23 | 4 | 0 | 2 | 1 | 23 | 2 | 53 | 3 | 1 |
| McCament, Randall, Everett | .143 | 14 | 14 | 0 | 2 | 2 | 0 | 0 | 0 | 2 | 0 | 0 | 0 | 0 | 0 | 0 | 10 | 0 | 0 |
| McCollom, James, Salem | .318 | 73 | 267 | 48 | 85 | 136 | 18 | 0 | 11 | 47 | 5 | 0 | 2 | 10 | 31 | 3 | 39 | 7 | 2 |
| McKinney, John, Bend | .000 | 13 | 2 | 0 | 0 | 0 | 0 | 0 | 0 | 0 | 0 | 1 | 0 | 0 | 0 | 0 | 1 | 0 | 0 |
| Mead, Timber, Everett | .176 | 15 | 17 | 1 | 3 | 5 | 2 | 0 | 0 | 1 | 0 | 1 | 0 | 0 | 0 | 0 | 2 | 0 | 0 |
| Meagher, Thomas, Spokane | .000 | 14 | 3 | 0 | 0 | 0 | 0 | 0 | 0 | 0 | 0 | 1 | 0 | 0 | 1 | 0 | 0 | 0 | 0 |
| Meyers, Glenn, Salem | .270 | 74 | 289 | 44 | 78 | 120 | 14 | 5 | 6 | 46 | 8 | 0 | 4 | 1 | 28 | 4 | 56 | 16 | 4 |
| Miller, Todd, Everett† | .216 | 43 | 139 | 16 | 30 | 35 | 3 | 1 | 0 | 12 | 1 | 0 | 0 | 4 | 12 | 0 | 55 | 7 | 3 |
| Minch, John, Medford | .274 | 32 | 95 | 8 | 26 | 28 | 2 | 0 | 0 | 9 | 0 | 0 | 0 | 2 | 8 | 0 | 9 | 2 | 1 |
| Monceratt, Pablo, Bellingham* | .232 | 47 | 181 | 28 | 42 | 72 | 13 | 1 | 5 | 31 | 1 | 2 | 3 | 5 | 12 | 0 | 50 | 4 | 1 |
| Montero, Armando, Salem | .278 | 31 | 72 | 8 | 20 | 28 | 5 | 0 | 1 | 8 | 1 | 0 | 2 | 2 | 8 | 0 | 18 | 0 | 0 |
| Moreno, Angel, Spokane | .063 | 23 | 48 | 3 | 3 | 3 | 0 | 0 | 0 | 2 | 1 | 2 | 0 | 1 | 4 | 0 | 12 | 1 | 0 |
| Morfin, Arvid, Bellingham | .204 | 47 | 162 | 9 | 33 | 39 | 6 | 0 | 0 | 22 | 4 | 3 | 2 | 1 | 10 | 0 | 36 | 5 | 3 |
| Morris, David, Everett | .000 | 18 | 1 | 0 | 0 | 0 | 0 | 0 | 0 | 0 | 0 | 0 | 0 | 0 | 0 | 0 | 1 | 0 | 0 |
| Morrison, Matthew, Tri-Cities* | .179 | 17 | 39 | 4 | 7 | 8 | 1 | 0 | 0 | 4 | 0 | 0 | 0 | 0 | 4 | 0 | 9 | 1 | 0 |
| Morton, Maurice, Spokane* | .252 | 44 | 131 | 23 | 33 | 35 | 2 | 0 | 0 | 11 | 0 | 3 | 1 | 0 | 26 | 1 | 31 | 13 | 3 |
| Munson, Jay, Tri-Cities† | .156 | 25 | 45 | 7 | 7 | 8 | 1 | 0 | 0 | 3 | 1 | 0 | 0 | 1 | 5 | 0 | 12 | 2 | 1 |
| Murphy, Daniel, Medford | .227 | 63 | 207 | 33 | 47 | 72 | 7 | 0 | 6 | 30 | 1 | 1 | 3 | 1 | 41 | 0 | 50 | 10 | 3 |
| Nalls, Gary, Salem | .209 | 57 | 191 | 32 | 40 | 54 | 5 | 0 | 3 | 16 | 1 | 0 | 2 | 3 | 26 | 0 | 49 | 5 | 6 |
| Nazabal, Robert, Bend | .000 | 19 | 2 | 0 | 0 | 0 | 0 | 0 | 0 | 0 | 0 | 0 | 0 | 0 | 0 | 0 | 2 | 0 | 0 |
| Nelson, Jerome, Salem | .270 | 69 | 263 | 50 | 71 | 84 | 7 | 3 | 0 | 30 | 5 | 1 | 1 | 3 | 28 | 0 | 25 | 26 | 7 |
| Nelson, Richard, Everett | .264 | 46 | 148 | 28 | 39 | 73 | 7 | 0 | 9 | 35 | 4 | 1 | 1 | 1 | 47 | 1 | 54 | 3 | 0 |
| Nieporte, James, Spokane | .265 | 60 | 223 | 22 | 59 | 77 | 13 | 1 | 1 | 42 | 8 | 1 | 2 | 0 | 21 | 0 | 39 | 3 | 2 |
| Nolte, Eric, Spokane* | .200 | 14 | 5 | 1 | 1 | 1 | 0 | 0 | 0 | 2 | 0 | 0 | 0 | 0 | 2 | 0 | 0 | 0 | 0 |
| Ohnoutka, Brian, Everett | .000 | 2 | 1 | 0 | 0 | 0 | 0 | 0 | 0 | 0 | 0 | 0 | 0 | 0 | 0 | 0 | 0 | 0 | 0 |
| O'Hoppe, Robert, Eugene | .198 | 48 | 167 | 20 | 33 | 38 | 3 | 1 | 0 | 15 | 0 | 1 | 0 | 2 | 18 | 1 | 40 | 7 | 2 |
| Olden, Bryan, Medford | .167 | 28 | 90 | 15 | 15 | 17 | 0 | 1 | 0 | 10 | 0 | 0 | 0 | 1 | 13 | 0 | 25 | 12 | 1 |
| Paris, Juan, Spokane | .216 | 31 | 97 | 13 | 21 | 25 | 1 | 0 | 1 | 5 | 0 | 1 | 0 | 0 | 3 | 0 | 17 | 3 | 4 |
| Parker, Richard, Bend | .249 | 55 | 205 | 45 | 51 | 68 | 9 | 1 | 2 | 20 | 3 | 0 | 3 | 4 | 40 | 0 | 42 | 14 | 7 |
| Parks, Jeffrey, Spokane | .000 | 10 | 0 | 0 | 0 | 0 | 0 | 0 | 0 | 0 | 0 | 0 | 0 | 0 | 1 | 0 | 0 | 0 | 0 |
| Pearson, Darren, Everett† | .000 | 15 | 1 | 0 | 0 | 0 | 0 | 0 | 0 | 0 | 0 | 0 | 0 | 0 | 0 | 0 | 0 | 0 | 0 |
| Peguero, Geremia, Medford | .283 | 67 | 258 | 27 | 73 | 87 | 9 | 1 | 1 | 32 | 1 | 1 | 1 | 0 | 10 | 0 | 51 | 7 | 6 |
| Perez, Mario, Bend | .000 | 17 | 2 | 0 | 0 | 0 | 0 | 0 | 0 | 0 | 0 | 0 | 0 | 0 | 0 | 0 | 0 | 0 | 0 |
| Petersen, Geoffrey, Eugene | .173 | 42 | 127 | 16 | 22 | 43 | 4 | 1 | 5 | 16 | 2 | 0 | 2 | 0 | 15 | 1 | 49 | 8 | 2 |
| Petty, Brian, Everett | .200 | 3 | 10 | 0 | 2 | 2 | 0 | 0 | 0 | 1 | 0 | 0 | 0 | 0 | 2 | 0 | 3 | 0 | 0 |
| Pimentel, Roberto, Bend† | .093 | 14 | 43 | 4 | 4 | 6 | 2 | 0 | 0 | 4 | 1 | 0 | 1 | 0 | 2 | 0 | 13 | 2 | 0 |
| Powell, Clyde, 32 TC-9 Bend | .227 | 41 | 110 | 15 | 25 | 27 | 2 | 0 | 0 | 5 | 0 | 0 | 0 | 1 | 17 | 0 | 20 | 1 | 5 |
| Ray, Louis, Bend | .277 | 13 | 47 | 6 | 13 | 18 | 2 | 0 | 1 | 4 | 0 | 0 | 0 | 1 | 4 | 0 | 16 | 0 | 0 |
| Reed, Donald, Medford* | .254 | 53 | 169 | 35 | 43 | 45 | 0 | 1 | 0 | 20 | 3 | 0 | 2 | 3 | 35 | 0 | 19 | 19 | 7 |
| Richardson, Derrick, Bend | .280 | 51 | 164 | 27 | 46 | 49 | 3 | 0 | 0 | 16 | 1 | 1 | 1 | 2 | 17 | 0 | 28 | 9 | 2 |
| Robertson, Douglas, Everett | .091 | 13 | 11 | 2 | 1 | 1 | 0 | 0 | 0 | 1 | 0 | 1 | 0 | 0 | 0 | 0 | 6 | 0 | 0 |
| Rodgers, Darrell, Everett ... | .500 | 7 | 2 | 1 | 1 | 1 | 0 | 0 | 0 | 0 | 0 | 0 | 0 | 0 | 0 | 0 | 0 | 0 | 0 |
| Rodriguez, Ernie, Bend* | .325 | 49 | 151 | 44 | 49 | 56 | 5 | 1 | 0 | 12 | 1 | 0 | 0 | 2 | 38 | 1 | 23 | 13 | 6 |
| Rose, Robert, Salem | .222 | 50 | 167 | 15 | 37 | 47 | 6 | 2 | 0 | 16 | 1 | 1 | 0 | 0 | 14 | 0 | 43 | 8 | 2 |
| Rossum, Floyd, Bend | .333 | 17 | 3 | 0 | 1 | 1 | 0 | 0 | 0 | 0 | 0 | 0 | 1 | 0 | 0 | 1 | 2 | 0 | 0 |
| Santora, Steve, Everett* | .227 | 53 | 172 | 28 | 39 | 68 | 7 | 2 | 6 | 29 | 6 | 1 | 5 | 1 | 41 | 1 | 62 | 3 | 0 |
| Sharts, Stephen, Bend* | .200 | 14 | 5 | 2 | 1 | 2 | 1 | 0 | 0 | 2 | 0 | 0 | 0 | 0 | 1 | 0 | 3 | 0 | 0 |
| Shockman, Mark, Tri-Cities* | .243 | 20 | 74 | 13 | 18 | 30 | 1 | 1 | 3 | 11 | 0 | 0 | 0 | 3 | 9 | 1 | 18 | 0 | 0 |
| Silva, Ryan, 26 TC-4 Bend | .275 | 30 | 91 | 11 | 25 | 41 | 4 | 0 | 4 | 18 | 3 | 0 | 1 | 1 | 13 | 0 | 28 | 0 | 0 |
| Silvera, Alby, Tri-Cities* | .240 | 40 | 150 | 24 | 36 | 51 | 3 | 0 | 4 | 20 | 2 | 3 | 1 | 4 | 18 | 0 | 26 | 0 | 3 |
| Simon, Michael, Bellingham | .245 | 47 | 159 | 23 | 39 | 58 | 13 | 0 | 2 | 12 | 0 | 2 | 0 | 3 | 22 | 0 | 29 | 7 | 6 |
| Slocum, Wayne, Eugene | .063 | 12 | 32 | 7 | 2 | 2 | 0 | 0 | 0 | 1 | 0 | 0 | 0 | 1 | 8 | 0 | 14 | 0 | 1 |
| Slominski, Richard, Bellingham | .255 | 41 | 145 | 29 | 37 | 62 | 5 | 1 | 6 | 23 | 3 | 0 | 2 | 4 | 18 | 1 | 50 | 1 | 0 |
| Smiciklas, Michael, Tri-Cities | .171 | 12 | 41 | 5 | 7 | 14 | 1 | 0 | 2 | 3 | 0 | 0 | 0 | 0 | 7 | 0 | 23 | 0 | 0 |
| Smith, William, Everett | .200 | 5 | 15 | 3 | 3 | 6 | 0 | 0 | 1 | 3 | 1 | 0 | 1 | 0 | 4 | 0 | 3 | 1 | 1 |
| Stevenson, William, Spokane* | .249 | 71 | 233 | 27 | 58 | 94 | 12 | 0 | 8 | 37 | 3 | 1 | 3 | 0 | 67 | 3 | 62 | 1 | 2 |
| Stewart, David, Bellingham* | .500 | 1 | 4 | 0 | 2 | 2 | 0 | 0 | 0 | 0 | 0 | 0 | 0 | 0 | 0 | 0 | 1 | 0 | 0 |
| Suhajda, Gregory, Bend | .311 | 18 | 61 | 10 | 19 | 35 | 2 | 1 | 4 | 10 | 1 | 0 | 0 | 0 | 9 | 0 | 18 | 2 | 2 |
| Suris, Jorge, Spokane | .215 | 42 | 135 | 21 | 29 | 39 | 4 | 0 | 5 | 0 | 4 | 0 | 0 | 1 | 17 | 0 | 21 | 0 | 1 |
| Tatum, Jimmy, Spokane | .228 | 74 | 281 | 21 | 64 | 78 | 9 | 1 | 1 | 32 | 2 | 4 | 1 | 5 | 20 | 0 | 60 | 0 | 1 |
| Tauanuu, Jack, Medford* | .114 | 20 | 44 | 4 | 5 | 5 | 0 | 0 | 0 | 1 | 0 | 0 | 0 | 0 | 2 | 0 | 13 | 2 | 1 |
| Thomas, Brian, Bellingham | .231 | 47 | 147 | 16 | 34 | 39 | 5 | 0 | 0 | 13 | 2 | 0 | 1 | 2 | 23 | 0 | 23 | 3 | 3 |
| Townsend, Howard, Everett† | .200 | 18 | 5 | 0 | 1 | 1 | 0 | 0 | 0 | 1 | 0 | 1 | 0 | 0 | 0 | 0 | 3 | 0 | 0 |

| Player and Club | Pct. | G. | AB. | R. | H. | TB. | 2B. | 3B. | HR. | RBI. | GW. | SH. | SF. | HP. | BB. | Int. BB. | SO. | SB. | CS. |
|---|---|---|---|---|---|---|---|---|---|---|---|---|---|---|---|---|---|---|---|
| Uribe, Jorge, Bellingham | .220 | 44 | 132 | 16 | 29 | 37 | 3 | 1 | 1 | 6 | 1 | 2 | 1 | 2 | 14 | 1 | 39 | 5 | 4 |
| Van Stone, Paul, Everett† | .143 | 7 | 14 | 2 | 2 | 2 | 0 | 0 | 0 | 0 | 0 | 0 | 0 | 0 | 7 | 0 | 2 | 1 | 0 |
| Veras, Camilo, Medford* | .266 | 64 | 229 | 42 | 61 | 89 | 9 | 5 | 3 | 29 | 0 | 3 | 1 | 0 | 25 | 0 | 66 | 18 | 5 |
| Verducci, John, Everett | .237 | 52 | 219 | 21 | 52 | 64 | 7 | 1 | 1 | 24 | 5 | 4 | 2 | 1 | 16 | 1 | 29 | 7 | 2 |
| Vizquel, Omar, Bellingham | .225 | 50 | 187 | 24 | 42 | 66 | 9 | 0 | 5 | 17 | 3 | 4 | 1 | 0 | 12 | 1 | 27 | 4 | 3 |
| Walker, Clifton, Bend | .000 | 15 | 2 | 0 | 0 | 0 | 0 | 0 | 0 | 0 | 0 | 0 | 0 | 0 | 0 | 0 | 1 | 0 | 0 |
| Walling, Kendall, Salem | .211 | 38 | 133 | 18 | 28 | 38 | 1 | 0 | 3 | 15 | 1 | 0 | 1 | 1 | 14 | 0 | 47 | 1 | 1 |
| Washington, Glenn, Salem | .200 | 39 | 95 | 14 | 19 | 23 | 0 | 2 | 0 | 5 | 0 | 1 | 0 | 0 | 8 | 0 | 38 | 14 | 2 |
| Watson, DeJon, Eugene* | .281 | 52 | 160 | 24 | 45 | 59 | 6 | 1 | 2 | 28 | 3 | 0 | 2 | 2 | 34 | 0 | 37 | 11 | 3 |
| Whitt, Michael, Everett | .280 | 52 | 200 | 33 | 56 | 77 | 11 | 2 | 2 | 25 | 5 | 1 | 2 | 4 | 24 | 1 | 38 | 0 | 2 |
| Williams, Scott, Tri-Cities | .000 | 11 | 1 | 0 | 0 | 0 | 0 | 0 | 0 | 0 | 0 | 0 | 0 | 0 | 0 | 0 | 1 | 0 | 0 |
| Wisdom, Allen, Bend† | .000 | 14 | 3 | 0 | 0 | 0 | 0 | 0 | 0 | 0 | 0 | 0 | 0 | 0 | 0 | 0 | 3 | 0 | 0 |
| Woods, Anthony, Bellingham† | .248 | 47 | 153 | 27 | 38 | 51 | 5 | 1 | 2 | 13 | 3 | 0 | 0 | 1 | 24 | 0 | 35 | 11 | 5 |
| Zayas, Carlos, Bend | .193 | 28 | 88 | 12 | 17 | 23 | 3 | 0 | 1 | 12 | 0 | 2 | 1 | 9 | 0 | 21 | 1 | 1 |
| Zellner, Joey, Tri-Cities† | .250 | 30 | 108 | 17 | 27 | 35 | 4 | 2 | 0 | 3 | 0 | 3 | 0 | 2 | 12 | 0 | 38 | 2 | 1 |
| Zottneck, Roger, Salem | .211 | 32 | 95 | 6 | 20 | 23 | 3 | 0 | 0 | 10 | 0 | 3 | 1 | 0 | 8 | 0 | 24 | 0 | 1 |

The following pitchers, listed alphabetically by club, with games in parentheses, had no plate appearances, primarily through use of designated hitters:

BELLINGHAM—Darby, Michael (22); Georger, Joseph (1); Givler, Douglas (27); McCorkle, David (6); McLain, Timothy (11); Oizumi, Steven (13); Parker, Clayton (10); Quince, Dana (6); Roberts, Jeffrey (16); Rohde, Brad (8); Schooler, Michael (10); Snell, David (19); West, Edwin (13); Zavaras, Clinton (12).

BEND—Faccio, Luis (7); Grimsley, Jason (6); Harris, Steve (11); McClanahan, Scott (2); Pruett, David (4); Ritchie, Wallace (2).

EUGENE—Berrios, Hector (13); Crew, Kenneth (3); Crouch, Matthew (8); Duane, Dean (17); Karcher, Kevin (17); Koller, David (2); Morgan, Eugene (16); Mulligan, William (17); Perez, Melido (17); Robinson, Henry (17); Schmidt, Gregory (8); Solberg, Eric (23); Vaccaro, Salvatore (22); Woyce, Donald (9).

EVERETT—Blakley, David (27); Gambee, Bradley (2); Van Kempen, John (16); Wilson, Trevor (17).

MEDFORD—Cullison, Gary (22); Cundari, Felice (10); Deabenderfer, Blaine (3); Gonzalez, John (18); Horrell, Christopher (18); Otto, David (11); Parrish, Scott (24); Perez, William (18); Shaver, Jeffrey (15); Tortorice, Mark (16); Whitehurst, Walter (14); Wilridge, James (19).

SALEM—Auth, Robert (21); Burcham, Timothy (14); Cannon, Scott (3); Cipres, Mark (11); Collins, Christopher (11); DiMichele, Frank (9); Finley, Charles (18); Franco, Julio (4); Johnson, David (22); Kesler, Michael (16); Marino, Mark (15); McGuire, Stephen (13); Morehouse, Richard (13); Sharpnack, Robert (9).

SPOKANE—Batista, Miguel (5); Maysey, Matthew (7); Morales, Edwin (2); Rodriguez, Ramon (13).

TRI-CITIES—Bowe, Michael (5); Brauckmiller, Kurt (1); Dye, Mark (3); Hatch, Brett (16); Koske, Kenneth (14); McQueen, Mark (8); Minutelli, Gino (20); Murphy, Patrick (17); Parker, Darren (14); Petersen, Frederick (10); Plumleigh, Charles (8); Smith, Marc (15); Thomas, Steven (2); Weatherly, John (2); Young, Bruce (23).

GRAND SLAM HOME RUNS—Baham, Foley, L. Jackson, 2 each; Clark, Gibree, Meyers, Murphy, Silvera, Stevenson, Vizquel, 1 each.

AWARDED FIRST BASE ON CATCHER'S INTERFERENCE—Hill 3 (Foley, Jordan, Kmak); Alcala (Nieporte); Lundblade (Leonard).

## CLUB FIELDING

| Club | Pct. | G. | PO. | A. | E. | DP. | PB. | Club | Pct. | G. | PO. | A. | E. | DP. | PB. |
|---|---|---|---|---|---|---|---|---|---|---|---|---|---|---|---|
| Bellingham | .9531 | 74 | 1955 | 829 | 137 | 53 | 25 | Eugene | .948 | 74 | 1949 | 788 | 150 | 57 | 21 |
| Tri-Cities | .9528 | 74 | 1970 | 878 | 141 | 69 | 42 | Salem | .944 | 74 | 1932 | 755 | 159 | 41 | 33 |
| Everett | .9527 | 74 | 1985 | 853 | 141 | 61 | 17 | Bend | .942 | 74 | 1943 | 779 | 167 | 61 | 29 |
| Spokane | .9526 | 74 | 1960 | 793 | 137 | 69 | 19 | Medford | .941 | 74 | 1956 | 816 | 175 | 63 | 27 |

## INDIVIDUAL FIELDING

*Throws lefthanded.

### FIRST BASEMEN

| Player and Club | Pct. | G. | PO. | A. | E. | DP. | Player and Club | Pct. | G. | PO. | A. | E. | DP. |
|---|---|---|---|---|---|---|---|---|---|---|---|---|---|
| Arndt, Medford | .973 | 12 | 97 | 12 | 3 | 9 | Lopez, Bellingham | .903 | 4 | 25 | 3 | 3 | 4 |
| Ban, Salem* | .857 | 4 | 24 | 0 | 4 | 1 | Lundblade, Bend | .971 | 33 | 286 | 20 | 9 | 21 |
| Bedell, Eugene | .973 | 36 | 301 | 20 | 9 | 31 | McCall, Bend | .978 | 19 | 165 | 14 | 4 | 12 |
| Britt, Medford | .900 | 1 | 8 | 1 | 1 | 0 | McCOLLOM, Salem | .987 | 72 | 571 | 50 | 8 | 37 |
| Brock, Tri-Cities | .981 | 27 | 243 | 17 | 5 | 15 | Monceratt, Bellingham* | .979 | 43 | 396 | 19 | 9 | 30 |
| Butcher, Tri-Cities | 1.000 | 1 | 10 | 0 | 0 | 0 | R. Nelson, Everett | .987 | 44 | 425 | 21 | 6 | 34 |
| Clem, Bellingham | .965 | 2 | 75 | 8 | 3 | 2 | Petersen, Eugene | .971 | 7 | 33 | 0 | 1 | 2 |
| Cicione, Tri-Cities | 1.000 | 10 | 83 | 10 | 0 | 10 | Ray, Bend | 1.000 | 5 | 42 | 4 | 0 | 5 |
| David, Medford | 1.000 | 3 | 16 | 2 | 0 | 0 | Richardson, Bend | .974 | 16 | 144 | 5 | 4 | 12 |
| Davis, Tri-Cities* | 1.000 | 2 | 13 | 1 | 0 | 3 | Shockman, Tri-Cities | .976 | 14 | 116 | 4 | 3 | 12 |
| Duncan, Medford* | .983 | 62 | 543 | 34 | 10 | 48 | Silva, Bend | 1.000 | 1 | 4 | 0 | 0 | 0 |
| Fulton, Bellingham | 1.000 | 17 | 170 | 4 | 0 | 9 | Slominski, Bellingham | 1.000 | 2 | 20 | 0 | 0 | 3 |
| Geivett, Salem | 1.000 | 2 | 16 | 2 | 0 | 0 | Smiciklas, Tri-Cities* | .983 | 11 | 106 | 10 | 2 | 11 |
| Gibree, Bellingham | 1.000 | 1 | 9 | 0 | 0 | 1 | Stevenson, Spokane | .980 | 70 | 586 | 38 | 13 | 57 |
| Greene, Bend | .800 | 2 | 16 | 0 | 4 | 4 | Stewart, Bellingham | .900 | 1 | 8 | 1 | 1 | 0 |
| Hall, Spokane | 1.000 | 5 | 48 | 4 | 0 | 5 | Walling, Salem | 1.000 | 1 | 1 | 0 | 0 | 0 |
| James, Everett | .971 | 7 | 62 | 4 | 2 | 5 | Watson, Eugene* | .983 | 26 | 223 | 11 | 4 | 14 |
| Lamar, Tri-Cities | .969 | 13 | 122 | 1 | 4 | 9 | Whitt, Everett | .977 | 28 | 206 | 7 | 5 | 16 |
| Lemons, Eugene | .983 | 11 | 112 | 5 | 2 | 7 | | | | | | | |

### SECOND BASEMEN

| Player and Club | Pct. | G. | PO. | A. | E. | DP. | Player and Club | Pct. | G. | PO. | A. | E. | DP. |
|---|---|---|---|---|---|---|---|---|---|---|---|---|---|
| ALCALA, Eugene | .969 | 70 | 177 | 204 | 12 | 44 | Moreno, Spokane | 1.000 | 1 | 2 | 2 | 0 | 1 |
| Alfonzo, Salem | .960 | 49 | 83 | 131 | 9 | 15 | Nalls, Salem | .000 | 1 | 0 | 0 | 1 | 0 |
| Arndt, Medford | .966 | 7 | 13 | 15 | 1 | 1 | O'Hoppe, Eugene | 1.000 | 7 | 12 | 9 | 0 | 2 |
| Butcher, Tri-Cities | .941 | 53 | 88 | 136 | 14 | 27 | Olden, Medford | .919 | 21 | 42 | 49 | 8 | 12 |
| J. Carter, Everett | .951 | 31 | 70 | 86 | 8 | 14 | Peguero, Medford | .944 | 8 | 12 | 22 | 2 | 6 |
| Cora, Bellingham | .960 | 43 | 92 | 123 | 9 | 30 | Petty, Everett | 1.000 | 2 | 2 | 5 | 0 | 2 |
| Cortez, Tri-Cities | .981 | 9 | 23 | 30 | 1 | 8 | Pimentel, Bend | .952 | 11 | 31 | 29 | 3 | 7 |
| Dabney, Everett | .951 | 39 | 61 | 113 | 9 | 22 | Richardson, Bend | .936 | 24 | 39 | 49 | 6 | 12 |
| Dandos, Everett | 1.000 | 2 | 3 | 2 | 0 | 0 | Rodriguez, Bend | .963 | 49 | 79 | 102 | 7 | 19 |
| Fulton, Bellingham | .957 | 9 | 22 | 23 | 2 | 6 | Rose, Salem | .933 | 8 | 10 | 18 | 2 | 1 |
| Geivett, Salem | .950 | 27 | 56 | 59 | 6 | 9 | Suris, Spokane | .953 | 21 | 34 | 47 | 4 | 16 |
| Graves, Bend | .765 | 4 | 5 | 8 | 4 | 0 | Thomas, Bellingham | .976 | 38 | 56 | 106 | 4 | 16 |
| Hill, Spokane | 1.000 | 1 | 0 | 1 | 0 | 0 | Van Stone, Everett | .933 | 4 | 3 | 11 | 1 | 1 |
| Howarth, Eugene | 1.000 | 1 | 0 | 1 | 0 | 0 | Vizquel, Bellingham | .870 | 7 | 12 | 8 | 3 | 1 |
| Kuiper, Spokane | .925 | 14 | 28 | 21 | 4 | 3 | Woods, Bellingham | .943 | 27 | 51 | 65 | 7 | 8 |
| Martinez, Medford | .904 | 43 | 81 | 117 | 21 | 30 | Zellner, Tri-Cities | .938 | 17 | 30 | 45 | 5 | 10 |

## THIRD BASEMEN

| Player and Club | Pct. | G. | PO. | A. | E. | DP. | Player and Club | Pct. | G. | PO. | A. | E. | DP. |
|---|---|---|---|---|---|---|---|---|---|---|---|---|---|
| Alfonzo, Salem | .933 | 5 | 2 | 12 | 1 | 0 | R. Jackson, Everett | .724 | 27 | 13 | 42 | 21 | 5 |
| Arndt, Medford | .899 | 35 | 30 | 59 | 10 | 4 | Kunz, Eugene | .833 | 23 | 12 | 43 | 11 | 7 |
| Blackmun, Bend | .868 | 46 | 33 | 92 | 19 | 10 | Ladnier, Eugene | .892 | 32 | 20 | 54 | 9 | 5 |
| Butcher, Tri-Cities | 1.000 | 7 | 5 | 10 | 0 | 0 | Lamar, Tri-Cities | .667 | 1 | 1 | 1 | 1 | 0 |
| Cicione, Tri-Cities | .909 | 14 | 6 | 24 | 3 | 1 | Lopez, Bellingham | .886 | 21 | 12 | 50 | 8 | 3 |
| CORTEZ, Tri-Cities | .929 | 55 | 42 | 114 | 12 | 4 | Martig, Medford | .851 | 35 | 26 | 71 | 17 | 4 |
| Dabney, Everett | 1.000 | 1 | 0 | 1 | 0 | 0 | Morfin, Bellingham | .890 | 40 | 27 | 70 | 12 | 5 |
| Dandos, Everett | .929 | 27 | 19 | 59 | 6 | 1 | Munson, Tri-Cities | 1.000 | 3 | 0 | 4 | 0 | 0 |
| David, Medford | 1.000 | 3 | 4 | 10 | 0 | 1 | Nalls, Salem | .000 | 1 | 0 | 0 | 1 | 0 |
| Flowers, Everett | .877 | 23 | 17 | 40 | 8 | 1 | O'Hoppe, Eugene | .800 | 2 | 0 | 4 | 1 | 0 |
| Fulton, Bellingham | .842 | 11 | 3 | 13 | 3 | 3 | Olden, Medford | .857 | 4 | 1 | 5 | 1 | 0 |
| Geivett, Salem | .908 | 41 | 22 | 57 | 8 | 3 | Richardson, Bend | 1.000 | 5 | 2 | 16 | 0 | 0 |
| Ging, Spokane | .889 | 9 | 6 | 10 | 2 | 1 | Tatum, Spokane | .874 | 67 | 38 | 149 | 27 | 11 |
| Greene, Bend | .837 | 18 | 9 | 27 | 7 | 0 | Thomas, Bellingham | .667 | 7 | 1 | 5 | 3 | 0 |
| Howarth, Eugene | .892 | 25 | 14 | 52 | 8 | 7 | Walling, Salem | .865 | 34 | 28 | 55 | 13 | 5 |
| Hurtado, Bend | .960 | 7 | 9 | 15 | 1 | 0 | Zellner, Tri-Cities | 1.000 | 2 | 1 | 0 | 0 | 0 |

## SHORTSTOPS

| Player and Club | Pct. | G. | PO. | A. | E. | DP. | Player and Club | Pct. | G. | PO. | A. | E. | DP. |
|---|---|---|---|---|---|---|---|---|---|---|---|---|---|
| Baham, Tri-Cities | .933 | 72 | 160 | 228 | 28 | 49 | O'Hoppe, Eugene | .873 | 41 | 41 | 110 | 22 | 14 |
| Blackmun, Bend | .905 | 16 | 17 | 50 | 7 | 8 | Olden, Medford | .917 | 4 | 4 | 7 | 1 | 2 |
| Butcher, Tri-Cities | .895 | 3 | 5 | 12 | 2 | 3 | Parker, Bend | .899 | 50 | 79 | 143 | 25 | 26 |
| C. Carter, Tri-Cities | .883 | 12 | 17 | 36 | 7 | 10 | Peguero, Medford | .868 | 59 | 79 | 196 | 42 | 30 |
| Cortez, Tri-Cities | .667 | 1 | 1 | 3 | 2 | 1 | Richardson, Bend | .913 | 9 | 10 | 32 | 4 | 5 |
| Dandos, Everett | 1.000 | 12 | 15 | 34 | 0 | 6 | Rose, Salem | .877 | 40 | 48 | 94 | 20 | 10 |
| De Leon, Eugene | .884 | 39 | 49 | 96 | 19 | 13 | Suris, Spokane | .905 | 19 | 25 | 51 | 8 | 8 |
| Fulton, Bellingham | .949 | 17 | 18 | 56 | 4 | 5 | Tatum, Spokane | .914 | 7 | 13 | 19 | 3 | 3 |
| Ging, Spokane | .917 | 41 | 56 | 98 | 14 | 19 | VERDUCCI, Everett | .943 | 51 | 81 | 184 | 16 | 29 |
| Martig, Medford | 1.000 | 2 | 3 | 4 | 0 | 0 | Vizquel, Bellingham | .938 | 45 | 73 | 167 | 16 | 23 |
| Martinez, Medford | .808 | 18 | 19 | 40 | 14 | 7 | Woods, Bellingham | .852 | 16 | 18 | 34 | 9 | 5 |
| Moreno, Spokane | .913 | 20 | 21 | 42 | 6 | 11 | Zellner, Tri-Cities | 1.000 | 1 | 2 | 3 | 0 | 0 |
| Nalls, Salem | .811 | 46 | 59 | 100 | 37 | 11 | | | | | | | |

## OUTFIELDERS

| Player and Club | Pct. | G. | PO. | A. | E. | DP. | Player and Club | Pct. | G. | PO. | A. | E. | DP. |
|---|---|---|---|---|---|---|---|---|---|---|---|---|---|
| Armstrong, Med-TC | .944 | 27 | 33 | 1 | 2 | 1 | Knabenshue, Spokane | .968 | 70 | 172 | 7 | 6 | 0 |
| Arndt, Medford | 1.000 | 4 | 1 | 0 | 0 | 0 | Kritsonis, Tri-Cities° | .962 | 31 | 74 | 2 | 3 | 0 |
| Ban, Salem° | 1.000 | 17 | 18 | 2 | 0 | 0 | Kunz, Eugene | 1.000 | 4 | 4 | 0 | 0 | 0 |
| Bernardo, Bellingham | 1.000 | 1 | 1 | 0 | 0 | 0 | Lambert, Salem | .907 | 51 | 59 | 9 | 7 | 0 |
| Brunelle, Bend | .829 | 21 | 26 | 3 | 6 | 1 | Loggins, Eugene° | .941 | 73 | 136 | 7 | 9 | 0 |
| Butcher, Tri-Cities | 1.000 | 3 | 1 | 1 | 0 | 0 | Meyers, Salem | .970 | 74 | 120 | 8 | 4 | 1 |
| Carey, Eugene° | .938 | 68 | 118 | 4 | 8 | 2 | Miller, Everett | .973 | 39 | 68 | 3 | 2 | 0 |
| C. Carter, Tri-Cities | .857 | 4 | 6 | 0 | 1 | 0 | Morrison, Tri-Cities | .900 | 17 | 9 | 0 | 1 | 0 |
| J. Carter, Everett | 1.000 | 1 | 1 | 0 | 0 | 0 | Morton, Spokane | .667 | 11 | 7 | 1 | 4 | 0 |
| M. Carter, Tri-Cities | .857 | 4 | 6 | 0 | 1 | 0 | Munson, Tri-Cities | .952 | 11 | 20 | 0 | 1 | 0 |
| Casey, Bellingham | 1.000 | 13 | 15 | 0 | 0 | 0 | Murphy, Medford | .955 | 49 | 63 | 1 | 3 | 0 |
| Clark, Spokane | .962 | 72 | 145 | 7 | 6 | 0 | Nalls, Salem | 1.000 | 3 | 2 | 0 | 0 | 0 |
| Clem, Bellingham | .987 | 56 | 70 | 5 | 1 | 0 | J. Nelson, Salem | .968 | 62 | 147 | 2 | 5 | 0 |
| David, Medford | 1.000 | 3 | 3 | 0 | 0 | 0 | Paris, Spokane | .973 | 21 | 33 | 3 | 1 | 1 |
| Davis, Tri-Cities° | 1.000 | 17 | 28 | 1 | 0 | 0 | Peterson, Eugene | .915 | 31 | 42 | 1 | 4 | 0 |
| Ealy, Everett | .949 | 23 | 29 | 5 | 2 | 0 | Powell, Tri-Cities-Bend | .929 | 33 | 37 | 2 | 3 | 0 |
| Eccleston, Bellingham° | .965 | 55 | 79 | 4 | 3 | 2 | Ray, Bend | 1.000 | 5 | 12 | 0 | 0 | 0 |
| Flowers, Everett | .917 | 12 | 8 | 3 | 1 | 0 | Reed, Medford° | .925 | 49 | 61 | 1 | 5 | 0 |
| Foley, Tri-Cities | .941 | 43 | 47 | 1 | 3 | 1 | Santora, Everett° | .947 | 52 | 82 | 8 | 5 | 1 |
| Graves, Bend | .933 | 8 | 14 | 0 | 1 | 0 | Shockman, Tri-Cities | .750 | 3 | 3 | 0 | 1 | 0 |
| Gray, Spokane | .968 | 35 | 59 | 2 | 2 | 2 | Silva, Tri-Cities | 1.000 | 7 | 4 | 0 | 0 | 0 |
| Greaves, Bellingham | .948 | 31 | 51 | 4 | 3 | 0 | Silvera, Tri-Cities | .969 | 39 | 57 | 6 | 2 | 0 |
| Greene, Bend | .920 | 37 | 63 | 6 | 6 | 1 | Simon, Bellingham | .923 | 43 | 68 | 4 | 6 | 2 |
| Hill, Spokane | .946 | 27 | 51 | 2 | 3 | 1 | Slocum, Eugene | .867 | 11 | 12 | 1 | 2 | 0 |
| HOLYFIELD, Bend | .975 | 70 | 151 | 3 | 4 | 0 | Smith, Everett | 1.000 | 4 | 9 | 1 | 0 | 0 |
| Howard, Tri-Cities | .500 | 5 | 1 | 0 | 1 | 0 | Suhajda, Bend | .826 | 16 | 18 | 1 | 4 | 1 |
| Howarth, Eugene | .966 | 30 | 53 | 3 | 2 | 0 | Tauanuu, Medford° | 1.000 | 17 | 11 | 3 | 0 | 0 |
| Jacas, Medford | .972 | 56 | 103 | 1 | 3 | 1 | Uribe, Bellingham | .938 | 43 | 54 | 7 | 4 | 0 |
| J. Jackson, Bend | 1.000 | 2 | 1 | 0 | 0 | 0 | Veras, Medford° | .940 | 64 | 128 | 12 | 9 | 4 |
| L. Jackson, Everett° | .943 | 42 | 79 | 3 | 5 | 1 | Washington, Salem | .946 | 27 | 51 | 2 | 3 | 0 |
| D. James, Everett | .970 | 21 | 32 | 0 | 1 | 0 | Watson, Eugene° | .902 | 26 | 37 | 0 | 4 | 0 |
| Jimenez, Tri-Cities | 1.000 | 2 | 2 | 0 | 0 | 0 | Whitt, Everett | .892 | 21 | 23 | 2 | 3 | 0 |
| J. Jones, Everett | .917 | 18 | 33 | 0 | 3 | 0 | Zellner, Tri-Cities | 1.000 | 8 | 15 | 2 | 0 | 0 |
| R. Jones, Bend | .893 | 69 | 88 | 4 | 11 | 0 | | | | | | | |

## CATCHERS

| Player and Club | Pct. | G. | PO. | A. | E. | DP. | PB. | Player and Club | Pct. | G. | PO. | A. | E. | DP. | PB. |
|---|---|---|---|---|---|---|---|---|---|---|---|---|---|---|---|
| Arnold, Salem | .976 | 23 | 182 | 22 | 5 | 1 | 7 | Kmak, Everett | .985 | 24 | 175 | 21 | 3 | 1 | 6 |
| Baker, Tri-Cities | .974 | 48 | 318 | 63 | 10 | 5 | 28 | Lamar, Tri-Cities | .965 | 17 | 119 | 17 | 5 | 0 | 7 |
| Britt, Medford | .982 | 37 | 297 | 33 | 6 | 1 | 14 | Leonard, Eugene | .982 | 35 | 236 | 36 | 5 | 1 | 7 |
| Casey, Bellingham | 1.000 | 2 | 1 | 0 | 0 | 0 | 2 | Lundblade, Bend | .981 | 34 | 231 | 22 | 5 | 6 | 6 |
| David, Medford | .974 | 39 | 273 | 31 | 8 | 3 | 13 | Marquez, Salem | .972 | 25 | 158 | 17 | 5 | 0 | 14 |
| Dorsey, Eugene | 1.000 | 5 | 21 | 1 | 0 | 0 | 1 | McCall, Bend | .983 | 21 | 154 | 15 | 3 | 2 | 11 |
| Foley, Tri-Cities | .950 | 13 | 94 | 19 | 6 | 1 | 7 | Minch, Medford | 1.000 | 1 | 2 | 0 | 0 | 0 | 0 |
| Gibree, Bellingham | .966 | 50 | 372 | 53 | 15 | 5 | 16 | Montero, Salem | .957 | 3 | 20 | 2 | 1 | 0 | 2 |
| Hall, Spokane | .964 | 27 | 199 | 13 | 8 | 1 | 8 | Nieporte, Eugene | .989 | 50 | 314 | 49 | 4 | 4 | 11 |
| Hayden, Bellingham | .960 | 14 | 22 | 2 | 1 | 0 | 0 | Slominski, Bellingham | .986 | 22 | 187 | 31 | 3 | 1 | 7 |
| Hornsby, Everett | .991 | 29 | 206 | 24 | 2 | 0 | 5 | Suhajda, Bend | 1.000 | 1 | 4 | 1 | 0 | 0 | 0 |
| JELIC, Eugene | .997 | 39 | 263 | 36 | 1 | 2 | 13 | Zayas, Bend | .956 | 21 | 159 | 16 | 8 | 0 | 12 |
| Jordan, Everett | .971 | 27 | 212 | 26 | 7 | 4 | 6 | Zottneck, Salem | .975 | 31 | 217 | 18 | 6 | 0 | 10 |

## PITCHERS

| Player and Club | Pct. | G. | PO. | A. | E. | DP. | Player and Club | Pct. | G. | PO. | A. | E. | DP. |
|---|---|---|---|---|---|---|---|---|---|---|---|---|---|
| Auth, Salem | 1.000 | 21 | 1 | 2 | 0 | 0 | Morgan, Eugene | .667 | 16 | 0 | 2 | 1 | 0 |
| Batista, Spokane | .667 | 5 | 0 | 2 | 1 | 0 | Morris, Everett | 1.000 | 18 | 2 | 6 | 0 | 0 |
| Bauer, Spokane* | 1.000 | 8 | 2 | 14 | 0 | 3 | Mulligan, Eugene* | 1.000 | 17 | 0 | 5 | 0 | 0 |
| Beck, Bend* | 1.000 | 25 | 5 | 10 | 0 | 0 | Munson, Tri-Cities | .500 | 10 | 0 | 1 | 1 | 0 |
| Berrios, Eugene* | .786 | 13 | 4 | 7 | 3 | 0 | Murphy, Tri-Cities | .957 | 17 | 5 | 17 | 1 | 1 |
| Blakley, Everett | 1.000 | 27 | 0 | 4 | 0 | 1 | Nazabal, Bend | .905 | 19 | 7 | 12 | 2 | 3 |
| Blount, Spokane* | 1.000 | 23 | 3 | 11 | 0 | 0 | Nolte, Spokane* | 1.000 | 14 | 3 | 9 | 0 | 0 |
| Bonilla, Everett* | .944 | 13 | 1 | 16 | 1 | 2 | Ohnoutka, Everett | .333 | 2 | 1 | 0 | 2 | 0 |
| Bowden, Bend | 1.000 | 7 | 4 | 4 | 0 | 0 | Oizumi, Bellingham | .833 | 13 | 2 | 3 | 1 | 0 |
| Bowe, Tri-Cities* | .000 | 5 | 0 | 0 | 1 | 0 | Otto, Medford* | 1.000 | 11 | 1 | 4 | 0 | 0 |
| Burcham, Salem | .913 | 14 | 4 | 17 | 2 | 2 | C. Parker, Bellingham | 1.000 | 10 | 3 | 9 | 0 | 0 |
| Cipres, Salem | .778 | 11 | 2 | 5 | 2 | 0 | D. Parker, Tri-Cities | .944 | 14 | 5 | 12 | 1 | 0 |
| C. Collins, Salem | 1.000 | 11 | 1 | 6 | 0 | 1 | Parks, Spokane | .500 | 10 | 0 | 2 | 2 | 0 |
| T. Collins, Bend | 1.000 | 18 | 4 | 4 | 0 | 0 | Parrish, Medford | 1.000 | 24 | 2 | 7 | 0 | 0 |
| Crew, Medford | 1.000 | 3 | 1 | 1 | 0 | 0 | Pearson, Everett | 1.000 | 15 | 2 | 2 | 0 | 1 |
| Crouch, Eugene | 1.000 | 8 | 1 | 6 | 0 | 0 | Ma. Perez, Bend | .778 | 17 | 1 | 6 | 2 | 1 |
| Cullison, Medford* | 1.000 | 22 | 1 | 7 | 0 | 0 | Me. Perez, Eugene | .900 | 17 | 5 | 13 | 2 | 0 |
| Cundari, Medford | .900 | 10 | 4 | 5 | 1 | 0 | W. Perez, Medford | 1.000 | 18 | 4 | 3 | 0 | 0 |
| Darby, Bellingham | .875 | 22 | 1 | 6 | 1 | 0 | Petersen, Tri-Cities* | .500 | 10 | 1 | 0 | 1 | 0 |
| Deabenderfer, Medford | 1.000 | 3 | 1 | 1 | 0 | 0 | Plumleigh, Tri-Cities | 1.000 | 8 | 2 | 1 | 0 | 0 |
| DiMichele, Salem* | .778 | 9 | 3 | 4 | 2 | 0 | Pruett, Bend | 1.000 | 4 | 0 | 1 | 0 | 0 |
| Duane, Eugene | 1.000 | 17 | 7 | 13 | 0 | 1 | Quince, Bellingham | 1.000 | 6 | 2 | 0 | 0 | 0 |
| Faccio, Bend | .000 | 7 | 0 | 0 | 2 | 0 | Ritchie, Bend* | 1.000 | 2 | 2 | 5 | 0 | 0 |
| Ferraro, Spokane* | 1.000 | 11 | 0 | 2 | 0 | 0 | Roberts, Bellingham | .810 | 16 | 4 | 13 | 4 | 2 |
| Finley, Salem* | 1.000 | 18 | 0 | 7 | 0 | 1 | Robertson, Everett | .667 | 13 | 3 | 7 | 5 | 1 |
| Givler, Bellingham | 1.000 | 27 | 3 | 10 | 0 | 0 | Robinson, Eugene | .750 | 16 | 7 | 17 | 8 | 1 |
| Gonzalez, Medford | .909 | 18 | 1 | 9 | 1 | 0 | Rodgers, Everett | 1.000 | 7 | 5 | 6 | 0 | 1 |
| G. Harris, Spokane | .882 | 13 | 8 | 7 | 2 | 1 | Rodriguez, Spokane* | .500 | 13 | 0 | 2 | 2 | 0 |
| S. Harris, Bend | 1.000 | 11 | 0 | 2 | 0 | 0 | Rohde, Bellingham | .500 | 8 | 1 | 0 | 1 | 0 |
| Hatch, Tri-Cities | .929 | 16 | 6 | 20 | 2 | 1 | Rossum, Bend | .692 | 17 | 4 | 5 | 4 | 0 |
| Horrell, Medford | .750 | 18 | 2 | 4 | 2 | 2 | Schmidt, Eugene | 1.000 | 8 | 0 | 1 | 0 | 0 |
| M. James, Tri-Cities | .850 | 24 | 3 | 14 | 3 | 2 | Schooler, Bellingham | .824 | 10 | 5 | 9 | 3 | 1 |
| Johnson, Salem | .917 | 22 | 4 | 7 | 1 | 0 | Sharpnack, Salem | 1.000 | 9 | 0 | 10 | 0 | 1 |
| Karcher, Eugene | .778 | 17 | 3 | 4 | 2 | 0 | Sharts, Bend* | .960 | 14 | 2 | 22 | 1 | 3 |
| Kesler, Salem* | 1.000 | 16 | 1 | 2 | 0 | 0 | Shaver, Medford | .871 | 15 | 10 | 17 | 4 | 0 |
| Koske, Tri-Cities | .895 | 14 | 6 | 11 | 2 | 1 | Smith, Tri-Cities* | 1.000 | 15 | 3 | 12 | 0 | 1 |
| Lewis, Spokane | .938 | 20 | 4 | 11 | 1 | 0 | Snell, Bellingham | .867 | 19 | 3 | 10 | 2 | 1 |
| Luttrull, Bend | 1.000 | 10 | 2 | 1 | 0 | 0 | Solberg, Eugene | 1.000 | 23 | 2 | 4 | 0 | 1 |
| Lynch, Spokane | .932 | 32 | 1 | 11 | 1 | 1 | Thomas, Tri-Cities | .000 | 2 | 0 | 0 | 1 | 0 |
| Marino, Salem | .667 | 15 | 1 | 5 | 3 | 0 | Tortorice, Medford* | .909 | 16 | 1 | 9 | 1 | 0 |
| Marsh, Spokane | .875 | 6 | 1 | 6 | 1 | 0 | Townsend, Everett* | 1.000 | 18 | 0 | 14 | 0 | 0 |
| Marx, Spokane | .929 | 15 | 6 | 20 | 2 | 1 | Vaccaro, Eugene* | 1.000 | 22 | 3 | 13 | 0 | 0 |
| Maysey, Spokane | 1.000 | 7 | 1 | 1 | 0 | 0 | Van Kempen, Everett | 1.000 | 16 | 0 | 5 | 0 | 0 |
| McCament, Everett | .895 | 14 | 7 | 27 | 4 | 3 | Walker, Bend | .875 | 15 | 8 | 13 | 3 | 0 |
| McCorkle, Bellingham | .889 | 6 | 2 | 6 | 1 | 1 | West, Bellingham | 1.000 | 13 | 7 | 10 | 0 | 0 |
| McGUIRE, Salem | 1.000 | 13 | 11 | 16 | 0 | 0 | Whitehurst, Medford | .957 | 14 | 4 | 18 | 1 | 0 |
| McKinney, Bend | 1.000 | 13 | 6 | 10 | 0 | 1 | Wilridge, Medford | 1.000 | 19 | 5 | 6 | 0 | 0 |
| McLain, Bellingham | 1.000 | 11 | 4 | 6 | 0 | 0 | Williams, Tri-Cities | .750 | 10 | 3 | 3 | 2 | 0 |
| McQueen, Tri-Cities | .667 | 8 | 0 | 2 | 1 | 0 | Wilson, Everett* | .833 | 17 | 7 | 8 | 3 | 2 |
| Mead, Everett | .885 | 15 | 6 | 17 | 3 | 1 | Wisdom, Bend* | .923 | 14 | 5 | 7 | 1 | 1 |
| Meagher, Spokane | 1.000 | 14 | 2 | 6 | 0 | 0 | Woyce, Eugene | .800 | 9 | 0 | 4 | 1 | 0 |
| Minutelli, Tri-Cities* | .727 | 20 | 2 | 6 | 3 | 1 | Young, Tri-Cities | 1.000 | 23 | 5 | 11 | 0 | 2 |
| Morales, Spokane | .000 | 2 | 0 | 0 | 1 | 0 | Zavaras, Bellingham | .875 | 12 | 2 | 5 | 1 | 1 |
| Morehouse, Salem | .857 | 13 | 10 | 14 | 4 | 0 | | | | | | | |

The following players do not have any recorded accepted chances at the positions indicated; therefore, are not listed in the fielding averages for those particular positions: Brauckmiller, p; Cannon, p; Clem, p; Dye, p; Franco, p; Fulton, of; Gambee, p; Georger, p; Gibree, p; Grimsley, p; J. Jackson, 2b; Koller, p; Kunz, p; McClanahan, p; Minch, 2b, of; Silva, c; Smiciklas, of; Weatherly, p.

## CLUB PITCHING

| Club | ERA. | G. | CG. | ShO. | Sv. | IP. | H. | R. | ER. | HR. | HB. | BB. | Int. BB. | SO. | WP. | Bk. |
|---|---|---|---|---|---|---|---|---|---|---|---|---|---|---|---|---|
| Bellingham | 3.63 | 74 | 8 | 4 | 18 | 651.2 | 595 | 347 | 263 | 42 | 20 | 300 | 11 | 573 | 73 | 3 |
| Everett | 3.74 | 74 | 17 | 6 | 14 | 661.2 | 648 | 359 | 275 | 44 | 34 | 284 | 5 | 592 | 52 | 3 |
| Spokane | 3.77 | 74 | 4 | 4 | 18 | 653.1 | 651 | 357 | 274 | 31 | 25 | 305 | 11 | 503 | 71 | 4 |
| Salem | 3.90 | 74 | 11 | 2 | 17 | 644.0 | 619 | 372 | 279 | 42 | 37 | 359 | 5 | 552 | 54 | 2 |
| Medford | 4.13 | 74 | 9 | 4 | 12 | 652.0 | 657 | 412 | 299 | 35 | 29 | 330 | 13 | 566 | 47 | 4 |
| Eugene | 4.35 | 74 | 6 | 5 | 19 | 649.2 | 667 | 411 | 314 | 56 | 25 | 313 | 7 | 525 | 51 | 5 |
| Bend | 4.36 | 74 | 4 | 1 | 15 | 647.2 | 632 | 433 | 314 | 33 | 24 | 406 | 11 | 531 | 61 | 7 |
| Tri-Cities | 5.30 | 74 | 1 | 1 | 9 | 656.2 | 741 | 475 | 387 | 49 | 39 | 374 | 2 | 527 | 76 | 1 |

## PITCHERS' RECORDS

(Leading Qualifiers for Earned-Run Average Leadership—59 or More Innings)

*Throws lefthanded.

| Pitcher—Club | W. | L. | Pct. | ERA. | G. | GS. | CG. | GF. | ShO. | Sv. | IP. | H. | R. | ER. | HR. | HB. | BB. | Int. BB. | SO. | WP. |
|---|---|---|---|---|---|---|---|---|---|---|---|---|---|---|---|---|---|---|---|---|
| C. Parker, Bellingham | 6 | 1 | .857 | 1.55 | 10 | 9 | 2 | 1 | 0 | 0 | 63.2 | 40 | 16 | 11 | 1 | 2 | 16 | 0 | 69 | 5 |
| Sharts, Bend* | 5 | 2 | .714 | 2.11 | 14 | 14 | 2 | 0 | 0 | 0 | 93.2 | 74 | 34 | 22 | 5 | 3 | 33 | 1 | 55 | 1 |
| Roberts, Bellingham | 4 | 1 | .800 | 2.11 | 16 | 4 | 1 | 5 | 1 | 1 | 64.0 | 41 | 23 | 15 | 3 | 1 | 35 | 1 | 64 | 7 |
| West, Bellingham | 8 | 4 | .667 | 2.44 | 13 | 13 | 3 | 0 | 1 | 0 | 81.0 | 67 | 29 | 22 | 10 | 1 | 20 | 0 | 69 | 5 |
| Shaver, Medford | 8 | 4 | .667 | 2.54 | 15 | 14 | 3 | 0 | 0 | 0 | 95.2 | 66 | 39 | 27 | 6 | 4 | 48 | 1 | 81 | 2 |
| Blount, Spokane* | 6 | 4 | .600 | 2.64 | 23 | 2 | 0 | 13 | 0 | 3 | 64.2 | 61 | 30 | 19 | 1 | 2 | 12 | 2 | 58 | 2 |
| McCament, Everett | 7 | 3 | .700 | 2.90 | 14 | 14 | 5 | 0 | 2 | 0 | 105.2 | 98 | 46 | 34 | 6 | 5 | 20 | 0 | 66 | 5 |
| Burcham, Salem | 8 | 4 | .667 | 2.96 | 14 | 14 | 4 | 0 | 1 | 0 | 94.1 | 72 | 40 | 31 | 5 | 6 | 52 | 0 | 91 | 8 |
| McGuire, Salem | 8 | 3 | .727 | 3.03 | 13 | 13 | 6 | 0 | 0 | 0 | 98.0 | 87 | 37 | 33 | 3 | 4 | 34 | 1 | 65 | 4 |
| Beck, Bend* | 4 | 3 | .571 | 3.13 | 25 | 1 | 0 | 20 | 0 | 8 | 69.0 | 67 | 28 | 24 | 3 | 3 | 24 | 1 | 81 | 4 |

Departmental Leaders: G—Lynch, 32; W—Burcham, McGuire, Shaver, West, 8; L—Minutelli, Nolte, 8; Pct.—C. Parker, .857; GS—Marx, Mead, Me. Perez, Robinson, Smith, 15; CG—McGuire, 6; GF—Lynch, 29; ShO—McCament, 2; Sv.—Lynch, 12; IP—McCament, 105.2; H—Murphy, 125; R—Murphy, 67; ER—Me. Perez, 61; HR—Bonilla, Me. Perez, 13; HB—Morehouse, Pearson, Whitehurst, 7; BB—Hatch, 62; IBB—Givler, 5; SO—Burcham, Whitehurst, 91; WP—Robertson, 12.

(All Pitchers—Listed Alphabetically)

| Pitcher—Club | W. | L. | Pct. | ERA. | G. | GS. | CG. | GF. | ShO. | Sv. | IP. | H. | R. | ER. | HR. | HB. | BB. | Int. BB. | SO. | WP. |
|---|---|---|---|---|---|---|---|---|---|---|---|---|---|---|---|---|---|---|---|---|
| Auth, Salem | 1 | 2 | .333 | 4.09 | 21 | 0 | 0 | 13 | 0 | 5 | 33.0 | 27 | 18 | 15 | 3 | 3 | 29 | 0 | 32 | 6 |
| Batista, Spokane | 0 | 0 | .000 | 9.53 | 5 | 0 | 0 | 3 | 0 | 0 | 5.2 | 5 | 8 | 6 | 1 | 3 | 9 | 0 | 3 | 2 |
| Bauer, Spokane* | 4 | 2 | .667 | 1.88 | 8 | 8 | 0 | 0 | 0 | 0 | 43.0 | 43 | 13 | 9 | 1 | 1 | 17 | 0 | 27 | 0 |
| Beck, Bend* | 4 | 3 | .571 | 3.13 | 25 | 1 | 0 | 20 | 0 | 8 | 69.0 | 67 | 28 | 24 | 3 | 3 | 24 | 1 | 81 | 0 |
| Berrios, Eugene* | 6 | 4 | .600 | 5.33 | 13 | 13 | 1 | 0 | 0 | 0 | 76.0 | 85 | 60 | 45 | 12 | 2 | 30 | 0 | 65 | 2 |
| Blakley, Everett | 2 | 4 | .333 | 2.89 | 27 | 0 | 0 | 23 | 0 | 7 | 28.0 | 28 | 9 | 9 | 0 | 3 | 8 | 0 | 37 | 1 |
| Blount, Spokane* | 6 | 4 | .600 | 2.64 | 23 | 2 | 0 | 13 | 0 | 3 | 64.2 | 61 | 30 | 19 | 1 | 2 | 12 | 2 | 58 | 2 |
| Bonilla, Everett* | 4 | 6 | .400 | 4.12 | 13 | 12 | 3 | 0 | 0 | 0 | 87.1 | 93 | 47 | 40 | 13 | 0 | 36 | 0 | 82 | 9 |
| Bowden, Bend | 1 | 4 | .200 | 5.50 | 7 | 7 | 0 | 0 | 0 | 0 | 34.1 | 48 | 34 | 21 | 2 | 1 | 17 | 1 | 29 | 3 |
| Bowe, Tri-Cities* | 0 | 0 | .000 | 13.50 | 5 | 0 | 0 | 1 | 0 | 0 | 4.0 | 6 | 7 | 6 | 0 | 0 | 8 | 0 | 1 | 2 |
| Brauckmiller, Tri-Cities | 0 | 0 | .000 | 27.00 | 1 | 0 | 0 | 0 | 0 | 0 | 1.0 | 1 | 3 | 3 | 0 | 0 | 2 | 0 | 0 | 3 |
| Burcham, Salem | 8 | 4 | .667 | 2.96 | 14 | 14 | 4 | 0 | 1 | 0 | 94.1 | 72 | 40 | 31 | 5 | 6 | 52 | 0 | 91 | 8 |
| Cannon, Salem | 0 | 1 | .000 | 4.09 | 3 | 0 | 0 | 1 | 0 | 0 | 11.0 | 12 | 8 | 5 | 0 | 0 | 7 | 0 | 7 | 0 |
| Cipres, Salem | 0 | 3 | .000 | 1.91 | 11 | 2 | 0 | 2 | 0 | 0 | 37.2 | 35 | 15 | 8 | 1 | 1 | 28 | 0 | 47 | 4 |
| Clem, Bellingham | 0 | 0 | .000 | 36.00 | 1 | 0 | 0 | 0 | 0 | 0 | 1.0 | 3 | 5 | 4 | 0 | 0 | 3 | 0 | 1 | 1 |
| C. Collins, Salem | 4 | 4 | .500 | 5.23 | 11 | 11 | 0 | 0 | 0 | 0 | 53.1 | 70 | 44 | 31 | 5 | 3 | 28 | 1 | 42 | 4 |
| T. Collins, Bend | 0 | 2 | .000 | 6.21 | 18 | 4 | 0 | 6 | 0 | 2 | 33.1 | 32 | 32 | 23 | 0 | 2 | 39 | 0 | 29 | 11 |
| Crew, Eugene | 1 | 1 | .500 | 2.25 | 3 | 3 | 0 | 0 | 0 | 0 | 16.0 | 11 | 4 | 4 | 0 | 0 | 9 | 0 | 14 | 1 |
| Crouch, Eugene | 1 | 4 | .200 | 7.62 | 8 | 5 | 0 | 2 | 0 | 0 | 26.0 | 35 | 25 | 22 | 4 | 2 | 17 | 0 | 21 | 3 |
| Cullison, Medford* | 0 | 4 | .000 | 4.55 | 22 | 3 | 0 | 10 | 0 | 2 | 55.1 | 63 | 36 | 28 | 3 | 0 | 19 | 1 | 50 | 1 |
| Cundari, Medford | 3 | 6 | .333 | 3.62 | 10 | 9 | 2 | 0 | 0 | 0 | 59.2 | 56 | 32 | 24 | 1 | 0 | 26 | 0 | 51 | 4 |
| Darby, Bellingham | 2 | 3 | .400 | 3.48 | 22 | 3 | 0 | 18 | 0 | 9 | 51.2 | 44 | 24 | 20 | 6 | 0 | 27 | 1 | 38 | 5 |
| Deabenderfer, Medford | 0 | 1 | .000 | 3.52 | 3 | 2 | 0 | 0 | 0 | 0 | 7.2 | 5 | 3 | 3 | 0 | 0 | 11 | 0 | 10 | 1 |
| DiMichele, Salem* | 1 | 5 | .167 | 5.83 | 9 | 8 | 0 | 1 | 0 | 0 | 41.2 | 50 | 33 | 27 | 2 | 1 | 19 | 0 | 40 | 2 |
| Duane, Eugene | 3 | 1 | .750 | 4.66 | 17 | 7 | 0 | 5 | 0 | 1 | 65.2 | 81 | 47 | 34 | 1 | 1 | 27 | 1 | 44 | 9 |
| Dye, Tri-Cities | 0 | 0 | .000 | 21.60 | 2 | 0 | 0 | 0 | 0 | 0 | 1.2 | 4 | 4 | 4 | 0 | 0 | 3 | 0 | 1 | 0 |
| Faccio, Bend | 0 | 0 | .000 | 7.04 | 7 | 0 | 0 | 3 | 0 | 0 | 7.2 | 5 | 12 | 6 | 0 | 4 | 18 | 0 | 5 | 4 |
| Ferraro, Spokane* | 1 | 1 | .500 | 1.42 | 11 | 0 | 0 | 8 | 0 | 1 | 12.2 | 12 | 4 | 2 | 0 | 1 | 6 | 2 | 10 | 2 |
| Finley, Salem* | 3 | 1 | .750 | 4.66 | 18 | 0 | 0 | 12 | 0 | 5 | 29.0 | 34 | 21 | 15 | 1 | 0 | 10 | 0 | 32 | 4 |
| Franco, Salem | 1 | 1 | .500 | 3.00 | 4 | 0 | 0 | 1 | 0 | 0 | 12.0 | 9 | 5 | 4 | 1 | 0 | 2 | 0 | 10 | 0 |
| Gambee, Everett | 0 | 0 | .000 | 20.25 | 2 | 0 | 0 | 0 | 0 | 0 | 2.2 | 7 | 8 | 6 | 0 | 1 | 3 | 0 | 4 | 1 |
| Georger, Bellingham | 0 | 0 | .000 | 27.00 | 1 | 0 | 0 | 1 | 0 | 0 | 0.1 | 3 | 1 | 1 | 0 | 0 | 0 | 0 | 0 | 0 |
| Gibree, Bellingham | 0 | 0 | .000 | 20.25 | 1 | 0 | 0 | 1 | 0 | 0 | 1.1 | 2 | 3 | 3 | 0 | 0 | 4 | 0 | 1 | 0 |
| Givler, Bellingham | 2 | 3 | .400 | 4.37 | 27 | 0 | 0 | 22 | 0 | 4 | 59.2 | 62 | 33 | 29 | 3 | 5 | 30 | 5 | 68 | 11 |
| Gonzalez, Medford | 4 | 1 | .800 | 5.22 | 18 | 6 | 1 | 5 | 0 | 2 | 58.2 | 62 | 41 | 34 | 2 | 2 | 42 | 0 | 38 | 4 |
| Grimsley, Bend | 0 | 1 | .000 | 13.50 | 6 | 1 | 0 | 2 | 0 | 0 | 11.1 | 12 | 21 | 17 | 0 | 1 | 25 | 0 | 10 | 3 |
| G. Harris, Spokane | 5 | 4 | .556 | 3.40 | 13 | 13 | 1 | 0 | 0 | 0 | 87.1 | 80 | 36 | 33 | 5 | 3 | 36 | 0 | 90 | 6 |
| S. Harris, Bend | 1 | 1 | .500 | 2.41 | 11 | 1 | 0 | 6 | 0 | 2 | 18.2 | 12 | 7 | 5 | 1 | 1 | 8 | 2 | 17 | 3 |
| Hatch, Tri-Cities | 5 | 5 | .500 | 3.74 | 16 | 12 | 1 | 1 | 1 | 0 | 84.1 | 66 | 47 | 35 | 2 | 3 | 62 | 0 | 63 | 10 |
| Horrell, Medford | 1 | 4 | .200 | 9.38 | 18 | 0 | 0 | 11 | 0 | 1 | 31.2 | 50 | 37 | 33 | 4 | 3 | 18 | 1 | 26 | 1 |
| James, Tri-Cities | 4 | 5 | .444 | 2.32 | 24 | 0 | 0 | 21 | 0 | 6 | 50.1 | 50 | 20 | 13 | 2 | 4 | 13 | 2 | 37 | 3 |
| Johnson, Salem | 4 | 1 | .800 | 2.95 | 22 | 0 | 0 | 17 | 0 | 4 | 42.2 | 45 | 15 | 14 | 4 | 4 | 18 | 2 | 45 | 3 |
| Karcher, Eugene | 2 | 1 | .667 | 4.55 | 17 | 7 | 1 | 4 | 0 | 0 | 55.1 | 47 | 33 | 28 | 4 | 3 | 31 | 0 | 36 | 5 |
| Kesler, Salem* | 1 | 3 | .250 | 3.31 | 16 | 4 | 0 | 7 | 0 | 1 | 32.2 | 33 | 24 | 12 | 4 | 1 | 19 | 0 | 22 | 4 |
| Koller, Eugene | 0 | 0 | .000 | 3.86 | 2 | 0 | 0 | 1 | 0 | 0 | 2.1 | 2 | 3 | 1 | 0 | 1 | 7 | 0 | 4 | 4 |
| Koske, Tri-Cities | 1 | 4 | .200 | 5.40 | 14 | 6 | 0 | 4 | 0 | 1 | 48.1 | 65 | 43 | 29 | 2 | 3 | 17 | 0 | 25 | 7 |
| Kunz, Eugene | 0 | 0 | .000 | 0.00 | 1 | 0 | 0 | 1 | 0 | 0 | 1.0 | 1 | 0 | 0 | 0 | 0 | 1 | 0 | 1 | 0 |
| Lewis, Spokane | 4 | 4 | .500 | 3.88 | 20 | 6 | 1 | 0 | 0 | 0 | 67.1 | 60 | 34 | 29 | 4 | 2 | 21 | 0 | 54 | 6 |
| Luttrull, Bend | 1 | 0 | 1.000 | 7.91 | 10 | 2 | 0 | 3 | 0 | 0 | 19.1 | 18 | 20 | 17 | 3 | 0 | 24 | 0 | 9 | 4 |
| Lynch, Spokane | 4 | 2 | .667 | 1.28 | 32 | 0 | 0 | 29 | 0 | 12 | 49.1 | 29 | 7 | 7 | 1 | 2 | 24 | 4 | 39 | 2 |
| Marino, Salem | 1 | 0 | 1.000 | 3.60 | 15 | 0 | 0 | 9 | 0 | 2 | 35.0 | 28 | 18 | 14 | 2 | 3 | 36 | 0 | 33 | 7 |
| Marsh, Spokane* | 1 | 0 | 1.000 | 3.18 | 6 | 0 | 0 | 0 | 0 | 0 | 17.0 | 13 | 10 | 6 | 0 | 0 | 12 | 0 | 11 | 5 |
| Marx, Spokane | 3 | 6 | .333 | 3.88 | 15 | 15 | 2 | 0 | 0 | 0 | 92.2 | 98 | 54 | 40 | 2 | 2 | 50 | 0 | 65 | 11 |
| Maysey, Spokane | 0 | 3 | .000 | 4.66 | 7 | 4 | 0 | 2 | 0 | 0 | 29.0 | 27 | 18 | 15 | 3 | 1 | 16 | 0 | 18 | 5 |
| McCament, Everett | 7 | 3 | .700 | 2.90 | 14 | 14 | 5 | 0 | 2 | 0 | 105.2 | 98 | 46 | 34 | 6 | 5 | 20 | 0 | 66 | 5 |
| McClanahan, Bend | 0 | 0 | .000 | 9.00 | 2 | 0 | 0 | 1 | 0 | 0 | 4.0 | 8 | 6 | 4 | 0 | 0 | 3 | 1 | 5 | 0 |
| McCorkle, Bellingham | 2 | 0 | 1.000 | 4.68 | 6 | 6 | 0 | 0 | 0 | 0 | 32.2 | 39 | 21 | 17 | 2 | 0 | 7 | 0 | 19 | 1 |
| McGuire, Spokane | 8 | 3 | .727 | 3.03 | 13 | 13 | 6 | 0 | 0 | 0 | 98.0 | 87 | 37 | 33 | 3 | 4 | 34 | 1 | 65 | 4 |
| McKinney, Bend | 2 | 2 | .500 | 6.06 | 13 | 3 | 0 | 6 | 0 | 1 | 35.2 | 45 | 26 | 24 | 4 | 1 | 21 | 1 | 20 | 3 |
| McLain, Bellingham | 1 | 3 | .250 | 4.31 | 11 | 6 | 0 | 1 | 0 | 0 | 39.2 | 52 | 30 | 19 | 2 | 2 | 24 | 0 | 23 | 3 |
| McQueen, Tri-Cities | 0 | 0 | .000 | 9.26 | 8 | 1 | 0 | 2 | 0 | 0 | 11.2 | 14 | 13 | 12 | 2 | 2 | 8 | 0 | 16 | 4 |
| Mead, Everett | 7 | 5 | .583 | 4.58 | 15 | 15 | 3 | 0 | 1 | 0 | 94.1 | 104 | 55 | 48 | 4 | 2 | 37 | 1 | 59 | 4 |
| Meagher, Spokane | 1 | 4 | .200 | 3.50 | 14 | 6 | 0 | 5 | 0 | 0 | 46.1 | 56 | 27 | 18 | 1 | 3 | 23 | 2 | 34 | 5 |
| Minutelli, Tri-Cities* | 4 | 8 | .333 | 8.05 | 20 | 10 | 0 | 7 | 0 | 0 | 57.0 | 61 | 57 | 51 | 3 | 6 | 57 | 0 | 79 | 6 |
| Morales, Tri-Cities | 1 | 0 | 1.000 | 8.10 | 2 | 2 | 0 | 0 | 0 | 0 | 10.0 | 11 | 9 | 9 | 2 | 1 | 4 | 0 | 6 | 1 |
| Morehouse, Salem | 6 | 5 | .545 | 4.15 | 13 | 13 | 1 | 0 | 0 | 0 | 80.1 | 71 | 52 | 37 | 5 | 7 | 47 | 1 | 62 | 6 |
| Morgan, Eugene | 2 | 0 | 1.000 | 1.42 | 16 | 0 | 0 | 16 | 0 | 8 | 19.0 | 10 | 3 | 3 | 0 | 0 | 4 | 0 | 25 | 1 |
| Morris, Everett | 3 | 1 | .750 | 4.99 | 18 | 0 | 0 | 10 | 0 | 2 | 30.2 | 27 | 20 | 17 | 5 | 2 | 17 | 0 | 29 | 3 |
| Mulligan, Eugene* | 4 | 0 | 1.000 | 0.55 | 17 | 0 | 0 | 13 | 0 | 5 | 33.0 | 16 | 4 | 2 | 0 | 0 | 22 | 3 | 44 | 0 |
| Munson, Tri-Cities | 1 | 0 | 1.000 | 5.13 | 10 | 0 | 0 | 8 | 0 | 0 | 26.1 | 23 | 20 | 15 | 2 | 0 | 19 | 0 | 33 | 6 |
| Murphy, Tri-Cities | 5 | 5 | .500 | 5.32 | 17 | 11 | 2 | 5 | 0 | 1 | 89.2 | 125 | 67 | 53 | 8 | 5 | 27 | 0 | 56 | 6 |
| Nazabal, Bend | 5 | 2 | .714 | 5.63 | 19 | 5 | 0 | 9 | 0 | 2 | 56.0 | 61 | 42 | 35 | 2 | 1 | 41 | 2 | 40 | 4 |
| Nolte, Spokane* | 3 | 8 | .273 | 3.99 | 14 | 14 | 0 | 0 | 0 | 0 | 76.2 | 79 | 50 | 34 | 6 | 3 | 46 | 0 | 52 | 11 |
| Ohnoutka, Everett | 0 | 1 | .000 | 3.86 | 2 | 0 | 0 | 0 | 0 | 0 | 7.0 | 9 | 12 | 3 | 2 | 1 | 6 | 0 | 7 | 2 |
| Oizumi, Bellingham | 2 | 4 | .333 | 5.11 | 13 | 4 | 0 | 4 | 0 | 1 | 37.0 | 43 | 33 | 21 | 3 | 2 | 15 | 2 | 40 | 9 |
| Otto, Medford* | 2 | 2 | .500 | 4.04 | 11 | 11 | 0 | 0 | 0 | 0 | 42.1 | 42 | 27 | 19 | 1 | 2 | 22 | 0 | 27 | 5 |
| C. Parker, Bellingham | 6 | 1 | .857 | 1.55 | 10 | 9 | 2 | 1 | 0 | 0 | 63.2 | 40 | 16 | 11 | 1 | 2 | 16 | 0 | 69 | 5 |
| D. Parker, Tri-Cities | 2 | 4 | .333 | 4.62 | 14 | 12 | 0 | 0 | 0 | 0 | 62.1 | 76 | 41 | 32 | 6 | 6 | 30 | 0 | 32 | 10 |
| Parks, Eugene | 0 | 1 | .000 | 7.45 | 10 | 2 | 0 | 5 | 0 | 0 | 19.1 | 33 | 17 | 16 | 2 | 1 | 6 | 0 | 20 | 3 |
| Parrish, Medford | 3 | 3 | .500 | 3.15 | 24 | 0 | 0 | 17 | 0 | 4 | 45.2 | 41 | 19 | 16 | 2 | 4 | 21 | 2 | 45 | 3 |
| Pearson, Tri-Cities | 1 | 3 | .250 | 8.07 | 15 | 2 | 0 | 4 | 0 | 0 | 29.0 | 33 | 32 | 26 | 4 | 7 | 24 | 0 | 30 | 3 |
| Ma. Perez, Bend | 3 | 3 | .500 | 2.83 | 17 | 3 | 0 | 4 | 0 | 0 | 47.2 | 37 | 23 | 15 | 2 | 1 | 36 | 1 | 43 | 6 |
| Me. Perez, Eugene | 6 | 7 | .462 | 5.44 | 17 | 15 | 2 | 1 | 0 | 0 | 101.0 | 116 | 65 | 61 | 13 | 1 | 35 | 2 | 88 | 4 |
| W. Perez, Medford | 0 | 1 | .000 | 2.68 | 18 | 0 | 0 | 10 | 0 | 2 | 37.0 | 30 | 16 | 11 | 4 | 1 | 23 | 3 | 34 | 3 |
| Petersen, Tri-Cities* | 0 | 0 | .000 | 4.50 | 10 | 0 | 0 | 2 | 0 | 0 | 14.0 | 10 | 8 | 7 | 0 | 0 | 16 | 0 | 9 | 1 |
| Plumleigh, Tri-Cities | 0 | 0 | .000 | 9.95 | 8 | 0 | 0 | 2 | 0 | 0 | 19.0 | 25 | 22 | 21 | 4 | 3 | 9 | 0 | 18 | 1 |
| Pruett, Bend | 0 | 0 | .000 | 1.13 | 4 | 0 | 0 | 3 | 0 | 0 | 8.0 | 7 | 4 | 1 | 0 | 4 | 1 | 0 | 9 | 2 |
| Quince, Salem | 0 | 0 | .000 | 10.29 | 6 | 1 | 0 | 2 | 0 | 0 | 7.0 | 8 | 8 | 8 | 2 | 0 | 11 | 0 | 5 | 1 |
| Ritchie, Bend* | 1 | 0 | 1.000 | 4.50 | 2 | 1 | 0 | 0 | 0 | 0 | 10.0 | 10 | 11 | 5 | 0 | 0 | 3 | 0 | 6 | 0 |
| Roberts, Bellingham | 4 | 1 | .800 | 2.11 | 16 | 4 | 1 | 5 | 1 | 1 | 64.0 | 41 | 23 | 15 | 3 | 1 | 35 | 1 | 64 | 7 |
| Robertson, Everett | 4 | 4 | .500 | 4.43 | 13 | 13 | 1 | 0 | 0 | 0 | 81.1 | 77 | 56 | 40 | 4 | 3 | 59 | 0 | 85 | 12 |

| Pitcher—Club | W. | L. | Pct. | ERA. | G. | GS. | CG. | GF. | ShO. | Sv. | IP. | H. | R. | ER. | HR. | HB. | BB. | Int. BB. | SO. | WP. |
|---|---|---|---|---|---|---|---|---|---|---|---|---|---|---|---|---|---|---|---|---|
| Robinson, Eugene | 5 | 7 | .417 | 4.83 | 16 | 15 | 2 | 0 | 1 | 0 | 91.1 | 105 | 63 | 49 | 11 | 5 | 37 | 0 | 41 | 2 |
| Rodgers, Everett | 5 | 0 | 1.000 | 0.47 | 7 | 7 | 4 | 0 | 0 | 0 | 57.2 | 28 | 11 | 3 | 1 | 1 | 19 | 0 | 86 | 4 |
| Rodriguez, Spokane* | 0 | 2 | .000 | 8.63 | 13 | 2 | 0 | 5 | 0 | 2 | 32.1 | 44 | 40 | 31 | 2 | 0 | 23 | 1 | 16 | 10 |
| Rohde, Bellingham | 0 | 1 | .000 | 4.82 | 8 | 0 | 0 | 5 | 0 | 1 | 18.2 | 20 | 20 | 10 | 0 | 1 | 14 | 0 | 9 | 7 |
| Rossum, Bend | 7 | 3 | .700 | 4.94 | 17 | 7 | 0 | 4 | 0 | 0 | 54.2 | 63 | 44 | 30 | 3 | 3 | 42 | 0 | 35 | 8 |
| Schmidt, Eugene | 1 | 1 | .500 | 3.46 | 8 | 2 | 0 | 4 | 0 | 0 | 26.0 | 36 | 21 | 10 | 1 | 2 | 13 | 0 | 13 | 2 |
| Schooler, Bellingham | 4 | 3 | .571 | 2.93 | 10 | 10 | 0 | 0 | 0 | 0 | 55.1 | 42 | 24 | 18 | 5 | 2 | 15 | 0 | 48 | 1 |
| Sharpnack, Salem | 1 | 2 | .333 | 6.85 | 9 | 9 | 0 | 0 | 0 | 0 | 43.1 | 46 | 42 | 33 | 6 | 4 | 30 | 0 | 24 | 2 |
| Sharts, Bend* | 5 | 2 | .714 | 2.11 | 14 | 14 | 2 | 0 | 0 | 0 | 93.2 | 74 | 34 | 22 | 5 | 3 | 33 | 1 | 55 | 1 |
| Shaver, Medford | 8 | 4 | .667 | 2.54 | 15 | 14 | 3 | 0 | 0 | 0 | 95.2 | 66 | 39 | 27 | 6 | 4 | 48 | 1 | 81 | 2 |
| Smith, Tri-Cities* | 7 | 4 | .636 | 5.49 | 15 | 15 | 0 | 0 | 0 | 0 | 77.0 | 94 | 52 | 47 | 4 | 4 | 42 | 0 | 66 | 7 |
| Snell, Bellingham | 4 | 5 | .444 | 3.28 | 19 | 7 | 2 | 7 | 0 | 2 | 82.1 | 80 | 40 | 30 | 3 | 3 | 32 | 1 | 58 | 6 |
| Solberg, Eugene | 4 | 3 | .571 | 4.47 | 23 | 0 | 0 | 11 | 0 | 1 | 46.1 | 43 | 32 | 23 | 6 | 5 | 27 | 1 | 53 | 4 |
| Thomas, Tri-Cities | 1 | 0 | 1.000 | 6.00 | 2 | 0 | 0 | 0 | 0 | 0 | 3.0 | 2 | 2 | 2 | 2 | 0 | 3 | 0 | 2 | 0 |
| Tortorice, Medford* | 3 | 5 | .375 | 4.94 | 16 | 9 | 1 | 2 | 0 | 0 | 78.1 | 80 | 59 | 43 | 4 | 4 | 47 | 2 | 72 | 6 |
| Townsend, Everett* | 4 | 1 | .800 | 1.98 | 18 | 2 | 1 | 5 | 0 | 1 | 50.0 | 47 | 12 | 11 | 2 | 4 | 17 | 2 | 35 | 0 |
| Vaccaro, Eugene* | 2 | 2 | .500 | 3.42 | 22 | 0 | 0 | 10 | 0 | 4 | 47.1 | 41 | 25 | 18 | 2 | 1 | 32 | 0 | 31 | 8 |
| Van Kempen, Everett | 1 | 2 | .333 | 3.31 | 16 | 0 | 0 | 7 | 0 | 1 | 32.2 | 30 | 15 | 12 | 1 | 4 | 12 | 2 | 22 | 2 |
| Walker, Bend | 6 | 5 | .545 | 3.23 | 15 | 13 | 1 | 2 | 0 | 0 | 78.0 | 60 | 37 | 28 | 3 | 1 | 35 | 0 | 77 | 0 |
| Weatherly, Tri-Cities | 0 | 0 | .000 | 5.14 | 2 | 1 | 0 | 0 | 0 | 0 | 7.0 | 9 | 4 | 4 | 4 | 0 | 5 | 0 | 0 | 0 |
| West, Bellingham | 8 | 4 | .667 | 2.44 | 13 | 13 | 3 | 0 | 1 | 0 | 81.0 | 67 | 29 | 22 | 10 | 1 | 20 | 0 | 69 | 5 |
| Whitehurst, Medford | 7 | 5 | .583 | 3.58 | 14 | 14 | 2 | 0 | 0 | 0 | 88.0 | 92 | 51 | 35 | 6 | 7 | 29 | 1 | 91 | 11 |
| Williams, Tri-Cities | 1 | 4 | .200 | 7.06 | 10 | 2 | 0 | 5 | 0 | 0 | 29.1 | 39 | 27 | 23 | 6 | 1 | 14 | 0 | 22 | 4 |
| Wilridge, Medford | 2 | 5 | .286 | 4.50 | 19 | 6 | 0 | 10 | 0 | 1 | 52.0 | 70 | 52 | 26 | 2 | 2 | 24 | 2 | 41 | 6 |
| Wilson, Everett* | 2 | 4 | .333 | 4.23 | 17 | 7 | 0 | 8 | 0 | 3 | 55.1 | 67 | 36 | 26 | 2 | 1 | 26 | 0 | 50 | 6 |
| Wisdom, Bend* | 4 | 6 | .400 | 5.02 | 14 | 12 | 1 | 1 | 0 | 0 | 66.1 | 73 | 52 | 37 | 5 | 1 | 31 | 0 | 64 | 5 |
| Woyce, Eugene | 3 | 3 | .500 | 3.12 | 9 | 7 | 0 | 1 | 0 | 0 | 43.1 | 38 | 26 | 15 | 2 | 2 | 21 | 0 | 45 | 6 |
| Young, Tri-Cities | 2 | 2 | .500 | 3.82 | 23 | 4 | 1 | 11 | 0 | 1 | 70.2 | 71 | 38 | 30 | 2 | 2 | 39 | 0 | 67 | 6 |
| Zavaras, Bellingham | 4 | 7 | .364 | 5.59 | 12 | 11 | 0 | 0 | 0 | 0 | 56.1 | 49 | 37 | 35 | 2 | 1 | 47 | 1 | 62 | 11 |

BALKS—Nolte, Me. Perez, Rossum, Whitehurst, Wilson, Wisdom, 2 each; Batista, Bauer, Berrios, C. Collins, Darby, Duane, Gonzalez, Hatch, Morehouse, Ma. Perez, Robinson, Rohde, Schooler, Sharts, Tortorice, Townsend, Walker, 1 each.

COMBINATION SHUTOUTS—Parker-Darby, Schooler-Oizumi-Givler, Bellingham; Sharts-Perez, Bend; Berrios-Karcher-Morgan, Crew-Vaccaro, Robinson-Vaccaro-Mulligan, Schmidt-Mulligan, Eugene; Mead-Pearson-Wilson, Robertson-Van Kempen-Blakley, Townsend-Blakley, Everett; Otto-Gonzalez-Cullison, Otto-Perez, Shaver-Horrell, Shaver-Perez, Medford; DiMichele-Franco, Salem; Bauer-Lewis-Ferraro, Bauer-Lynch, Harris-Lynch, Lewis-Blount, Spokane.

NO-HIT GAMES—None.

# South Atlantic League

## CLASS A

### CHAMPIONSHIP WINNERS IN PREVIOUS YEARS

| | | |
|---|---|---|
| 1948—Lincolnton* ............................ .627 | 1965—Salisbury.............................. .641 | 1975—Spartanburg.......................... .543 |
| 1949—Newton-Conover.................. .667 |     Rock Hill‡............................ .603 |     Spartanburg.......................... .614 |
|     Ruth'ford Co. (2nd)† .......... .627 | 1966—Spartanburg.......................... .682 | 1976—Asheville.............................. .544 |
| 1950—Newton-Conover.................. .627 |     Spartanburg.......................... .767 |     Greenwood‡.......................... .600 |
|     Lenoir (2nd)† .................... .626 | 1967—Spartanburg.......................... .730 | 1977—Greenwood.......................... .557 |
| 1951—Morganton.......................... .645 |     Spartanburg.......................... .567 |     Gastonia‡ .......................... .590 |
|     Shelby (2nd)† .................... .604 | 1968—Spartanburg.......................... .597 | 1978—Greenwood.......................... .614 |
| 1952—Lincolnton .......................... .649 |     Greenwood‡.......................... .597 |     Greenwood .......................... .565 |
|     Shelby (2nd)† .................... .645 | 1969—Greenwood‡.......................... .587 | 1979—Greenwood‡.......................... .565 |
| 1953-59—League inactive. |     Shelby .......................... .565 |     Spartanburg.......................... .525 |
| 1960—Lexington .......................... .707 | 1970—Greenville.......................... .576 | 1980—Greensboro .......................... .590 |
|     Salisbury (2nd)† .......... .650 |     Greenville.......................... .619 |     Charleston.......................... .561 |
| 1961—Salisbury.......................... .627 | 1971—Greenwood .......................... .631 | 1981—Greensboro‡.......................... .695 |
|     Shelby (4th)† .................... .481 |     Greenwood .......................... .759 |     Greenwood.......................... .549 |
| 1962—Statesville .......................... .563 | 1972—Spartanburg‡.......................... .788 | 1982—Greensboro‡.......................... .681 |
|     Statesville .......................... .700 |     Greenville.......................... .652 |     Florence.......................... .546 |
| 1963—Greenville† .......................... .576 | 1973—Spartanburg‡.......................... .646 | 1983—Columbia.......................... .620 |
|     Salisbury.......................... .631 |     Gastonia .......................... .619 |     Gastonia‡ .......................... .587 |
| 1964—Rock Hill .......................... .672 | 1974—Gastonia .......................... .606 | 1984—Charleston.......................... .549 |
|     Salisbury‡ .......................... .631 |     Gastonia .......................... .672 |     Asheville‡.......................... .510 |

*Won championship and four-club playoff. †Won four-club playoff. ‡Won split-season playoff. (NOTE—Known as Western Carolina League from 1948 through 1962 and known as Western Carolinas League through 1979.)

### STANDING OF CLUBS AT CLOSE OF FIRST HALF, JUNE 19

#### NORTHERN DIVISION

| Club | W. | L. | T. | Pct. | G.B. |
|---|---|---|---|---|---|
| Sumter (Braves)................................. | 37 | 29 | 0 | .561 | ...... |
| Asheville (Astros)................................. | 36 | 33 | 0 | .522 | 2½ |
| Spartanburg (Phillies)......................... | 35 | 33 | 0 | .515 | 3 |
| Greensboro (Red Sox)......................... | 33 | 35 | 0 | .485 | 5 |
| Gastonia (Independent)......................... | 24 | 43 | 0 | .358 | 13½ |

#### SOUTHERN DIVISION

| Club | W. | L. | T. | Pct. | G.B. |
|---|---|---|---|---|---|
| Columbia (Mets)................................. | 45 | 23 | 0 | .662 | ...... |
| Florence (Blue Jays)......................... | 39 | 28 | 0 | .582 | 5½ |
| Charleston (Padres)......................... | 40 | 29 | 0 | .580 | 5½ |
| Macon (Pirates)................................. | 28 | 43 | 0 | .394 | 18½ |
| Savannah (Cardinals)......................... | 23 | 44 | 0 | .343 | 21½ |

### STANDING OF CLUBS AT CLOSE OF SECOND HALF, AUGUST 31

#### NORTHERN DIVISION

| Club | W. | L. | T. | Pct. | G.B. |
|---|---|---|---|---|---|
| Greensboro (Red Sox)......................... | 41 | 28 | 0 | .594 | ...... |
| Asheville (Astros)................................. | 40 | 29 | 0 | .580 | 1 |
| Sumter (Braves)................................. | 35 | 34 | 0 | .507 | 6 |
| Spartanburg (Phillies)......................... | 31 | 37 | 0 | .456 | 9½ |
| Gastonia (Independent)......................... | 20 | 50 | 0 | .286 | 21½ |

#### SOUTHERN DIVISION

| Club | W. | L. | T. | Pct. | G.B. |
|---|---|---|---|---|---|
| Florence (Blue Jays)......................... | 43 | 27 | 0 | .614 | ...... |
| Charleston (Padres)......................... | 38 | 32 | 0 | .543 | 5 |
| Savannah (Cardinals)......................... | 34 | 34 | 1 | .500 | 8 |
| Columbia (Mets)................................. | 34 | 34 | 0 | .500 | 8 |
| Macon (Pirates)................................. | 28 | 39 | 1 | .418 | 13½ |

### COMPOSITE STANDING OF CLUBS AT CLOSE OF SEASON, AUGUST 31

| Club | Flo. | Col. | Char. | Ash. | Gbr. | Sum. | Spar. | Sav. | Mac. | Gas. | W. | L. | T. | Pct. | G.B. |
|---|---|---|---|---|---|---|---|---|---|---|---|---|---|---|---|
| Florence (Blue Jays)..................... | .... | 11 | 11 | 8 | 6 | 4 | 7 | 12 | 12 | 11 | 82 | 55 | 0 | .599 | ...... |
| Columbia (Mets)......................... | 9 | .... | 7 | 6 | 10 | 6 | 5 | 13 | 14 | 9 | 79 | 57 | 0 | .581 | 2½ |
| Charleston (Padres)..................... | 8 | 13 | .... | 4 | 9 | 9 | 7 | 9 | 12 | 7 | 78 | 61 | 0 | .561 | 5 |
| Asheville (Astros)......................... | 4 | 6 | 8 | .... | 10 | 13 | 8 | 6 | 8 | 13 | 76 | 62 | 0 | .551 | 6½ |
| Greensboro (Red Sox).................. | 6 | 2 | 3 | 8 | .... | 10 | 13 | 9 | 8 | 15 | 74 | 63 | 0 | .540 | 8 |
| Sumter (Braves)......................... | 8 | 6 | 3 | 7 | 10 | .... | 14 | 8 | 5 | 11 | 72 | 63 | 0 | .533 | 9 |
| Spartanburg (Phillies)................. | 5 | 5 | 5 | 12 | 7 | 5 | .... | 6 | 10 | 11 | 66 | 70 | 0 | .485 | 15½ |
| Savannah (Cardinals)................. | 6 | 6 | 11 | 6 | 2 | 3 | 6 | .... | 11 | 6 | 57 | 78 | 1 | .422 | 24 |
| Macon (Pirates)......................... | 8 | 5 | 8 | 4 | 4 | 7 | 1 | 9 | .... | 10 | 56 | 82 | 1 | .406 | 26½ |
| Gastonia (Independent).................. | 1 | 3 | 5 | 7 | 5 | 6 | 9 | 6 | 2 | .... | 44 | 93 | 0 | .321 | 38 |

Major league affiliations in parentheses.

Playoffs—Florence defeated Columbia, two games to none; Greensboro defeated Sumter, two games to none; Florence defeated Greensboro, three games to two to win league championship.

Regular-Season Attendance—Asheville, 73,888; Charleston, 105,647; Columbia, 101,277; Florence, 41,546; Gastonia, 53,307; Greensboro, 172,626; Macon, 39,679; Savannah, 34,287; Spartanburg, 48,742; Sumter, 36,518. Total—707,517. Total Playoff Attendance—7,584. All-Star Attendance—3,791.

Managers—Asheville, Fred Hatfield; Charleston, Jim Skalen; Columbia, Bud Harrelson (thru May 15) and Rich Miller (May 16 thru end of season); Florence, Hector Torres; Gastonia, Bob McBee; Greensboro, Doug Camilli; Macon, Mike Quade; Savannah, Gaylen Pitts; Spartanburg, Rolando Dearmas; Sumter, Buddy Bailey.

All-Star Team—1B—Carey Cheek, Macon; 2B—Jeff Gardner, Columbia; 3B—Zoilo Sanchez, Columbia, Roberto Zambrano, Greensboro; SS—Santiago Garcia, Florence; OF—Sil Campusano, Florence; Marcus Lawton, Columbia; Andrew Denson, Sumter; Shawn Dantzler, Spartanburg; C—Jaime Williams, Asheville; DH—Pat Jelks, Greensboro; RHP—Tim Englund, Florence; LHP—Mike Miller, Spartanburg; Relief Pitcher (RHP)—Mike Shelton, Spartanburg; Relief Pitcher (LHP)—Tom Funk, Asheville; Most Valuable Player—Sil Campusano, Florence; Manager of the Year—Hector Torres, Florence.

(Compiled by Howe News Bureau, Boston, Mass.)

### CLUB BATTING

| Club | Pct. | G. | AB. | R. | OR. | H. | TB. | 2B. | 3B. | HR. | RBI. | GW. | SH. | SF. | HP. | BB. | Int. BB. | SO. | SB. | CS. | LOB. |
|---|---|---|---|---|---|---|---|---|---|---|---|---|---|---|---|---|---|---|---|---|---|
| Greensboro .............. | .270 | 137 | 4569 | 813 | 710 | 1234 | 1759 | 177 | 45 | 86 | 674 | 66 | 23 | 46 | 47 | 688 | 16 | 855 | 159 | 50 | 1115 |
| Asheville .................. | .266 | 138 | 4549 | 694 | 597 | 1210 | 1745 | 202 | 21 | 97 | 595 | 70 | 71 | 43 | 37 | 592 | 20 | 816 | 114 | 42 | 1071 |

## CLUB BATTING—Continued

| Club | Pct. | G. | AB. | R. | OR. | H. | TB. | 2B. | 3B. | HR. | RBI. | GW. | SH. | SF. | HP. | BB. | Int. BB. | SO. | SB. | CS. | LOB. |
|---|---|---|---|---|---|---|---|---|---|---|---|---|---|---|---|---|---|---|---|---|---|
| Florence | .263 | 137 | 4529 | 755 | 609 | 1193 | 1780 | 209 | 12 | 118 | 661 | 69 | 20 | 52 | 43 | 558 | 81 | 019 | 138 | 57 | 984 |
| Columbia | .259 | 136 | 4521 | 781 | 671 | 1169 | 1593 | 160 | 30 | 68 | 655 | 65 | 52 | 47 | 40 | 803 | 20 | 866 | 289 | 58 | 1174 |
| Charleston | .258 | 139 | 4603 | 697 | 591 | 1186 | 1596 | 179 | 24 | 61 | 586 | 68 | 61 | 46 | 32 | 566 | 25 | 813 | 162 | 52 | 1024 |
| Sumter | .244 | 135 | 4446 | 647 | 633 | 1083 | 1528 | 179 | 28 | 70 | 549 | 65 | 36 | 36 | 67 | 597 | 15 | 899 | 162 | 61 | 1021 |
| Savannah | .235 | 136 | 4284 | 504 | 575 | 1008 | 1364 | 130 | 29 | 56 | 421 | 49 | 60 | 43 | 47 | 441 | 5 | 794 | 138 | 56 | 945 |
| Gastonia | .234 | 137 | 4396 | 555 | 827 | 1028 | 1481 | 165 | 21 | 82 | 445 | 35 | 40 | 23 | 29 | 494 | 7 | 1047 | 160 | 116 | 879 |
| Spartanburg | .231 | 136 | 4361 | 578 | 686 | 1009 | 1510 | 188 | 26 | 87 | 500 | 57 | 20 | 32 | 43 | 461 | 12 | 1079 | 148 | 44 | 871 |
| Macon | .228 | 139 | 4509 | 539 | 664 | 1028 | 1387 | 155 | 24 | 52 | 442 | 41 | 58 | 35 | 40 | 564 | 18 | 1048 | 139 | 53 | 1055 |

## INDIVIDUAL BATTING

(Leading Qualifiers for Batting Championship—389 or More Plate Appearances)

*Bats lefthanded.       †Switch-hitter.

| Player and Club | Pct. | G. | AB. | R. | H. | TB. | 2B. | 3B. | HR. | RBI. | GW. | SH. | SF. | HP. | BB. | Int. BB. | SO. | SB. | CS. |
|---|---|---|---|---|---|---|---|---|---|---|---|---|---|---|---|---|---|---|---|
| Jose, Manuel, Greensboro† | .323 | 116 | 402 | 75 | 130 | 166 | 19 | 7 | 1 | 48 | 8 | 2 | 3 | 2 | 36 | 1 | 67 | 38 | 17 |
| Byers, Randall, Charleston* | .319 | 133 | 501 | 79 | 160 | 231 | 32 | 9 | 7 | 94 | 22 | 0 | 8 | 1 | 30 | 6 | 48 | 12 | 3 |
| Murphy, John, Savannah | .317 | 132 | 464 | 85 | 147 | 198 | 17 | 2 | 10 | 51 | 5 | 11 | 3 | 7 | 56 | 1 | 56 | 35 | 11 |
| Campusano, Silvestre, Florence | .313 | 88 | 348 | 80 | 109 | 187 | 31 | 1 | 15 | 56 | 4 | 3 | 4 | 3 | 58 | 0 | 84 | 21 | 14 |
| Moritz, Christopher, Greensboro | .313 | 135 | 534 | 109 | 167 | 231 | 19 | 9 | 9 | 87 | 9 | 5 | 5 | 7 | 57 | 0 | 92 | 27 | 12 |
| Kaiser, Bart, Spartanburg* | .312 | 122 | 433 | 77 | 135 | 212 | 28 | 5 | 13 | 52 | 7 | 1 | 0 | 2 | 53 | 4 | 83 | 24 | 3 |
| Westbrook, Michael, Columbia* | .305 | 118 | 377 | 80 | 115 | 137 | 11 | 4 | 1 | 46 | 4 | 4 | 1 | 5 | 67 | 1 | 48 | 57 | 15 |
| Jelks, Patrick, Greensboro | .301 | 118 | 439 | 90 | 132 | 215 | 13 | 8 | 18 | 87 | 5 | 0 | 5 | 2 | 69 | 1 | 134 | 23 | 7 |
| Denson, Andrew, Sumter | .300 | 111 | 383 | 59 | 115 | 183 | 18 | 4 | 14 | 74 | 6 | 0 | 4 | 4 | 53 | 3 | 76 | 5 | 3 |
| Garcia, Santiago, Florence | .298 | 128 | 514 | 86 | 153 | 216 | 35 | 2 | 8 | 79 | 10 | 1 | 5 | 5 | 41 | 0 | 67 | 25 | 10 |
| Cheek, Carey, Macon | .297 | 136 | 485 | 70 | 144 | 230 | 29 | 3 | 17 | 82 | 10 | 0 | 4 | 6 | 78 | 10 | 84 | 4 | 2 |
| Mueller, Peter, Asheville* | .297 | 133 | 445 | 89 | 132 | 250 | 26 | 4 | 28 | 93 | 11 | 1 | 5 | 5 | 93 | 8 | 93 | 7 | 2 |
| Stark, Matthew, Florence | .297 | 110 | 381 | 66 | 113 | 167 | 15 | 0 | 13 | 70 | 8 | 1 | 6 | 2 | 83 | 2 | 29 | 7 | 3 |

Departmental Leaders: G—R. Alomar, 137; AB—R. Alomar, 546; R—Ashkinazy, 115; H—Moritz, 167; TB—Mueller, 250; 2B—Garcia, 35; 3B—Byers, Moritz, 9; HR—Mueller, 28; RBI—A. Cuevas, 101; GWRBI—Byers, 22; SH—Elliott, 15; SF—Pounders, 10; HP—Cron, Dantzler, 18; BB—Gardner, 142; IBB—Cheek, 10; SO—Landrum, 208; SB—Lawton, 111; CS—Adkins, 20.

(All Players—Listed Alphabetically)

| Player and Club | Pct. | G. | AB. | R. | H. | TB. | 2B. | 3B. | HR. | RBI. | GW. | SH. | SF. | HP. | BB. | Int. BB. | SO. | SB. | CS. |
|---|---|---|---|---|---|---|---|---|---|---|---|---|---|---|---|---|---|---|---|
| Adams, Ralph, Columbia | .000 | 24 | 19 | 3 | 0 | 0 | 0 | 0 | 0 | 2 | 0 | 2 | 0 | 0 | 9 | 0 | 10 | 0 | 0 |
| Adkins, Todd, Gastonia† | .260 | 116 | 366 | 43 | 95 | 106 | 6 | 1 | 1 | 29 | 4 | 4 | 2 | 0 | 28 | 0 | 71 | 17 | 20 |
| Agar, Jeffrey, Gastonia | .000 | 37 | 0 | 1 | 0 | 0 | 0 | 0 | 0 | 0 | 0 | 0 | 0 | 0 | 1 | 0 | 0 | 0 | 0 |
| Alomar, Roberto, Charleston† | .293 | 137 | 546 | 89 | 160 | 180 | 14 | 3 | 0 | 54 | 7 | 12 | 4 | 0 | 61 | 3 | 73 | 36 | 19 |
| Alomar, Santos, Charleston† | .207 | 100 | 352 | 38 | 73 | 89 | 7 | 0 | 3 | 43 | 3 | 5 | 2 | 3 | 31 | 1 | 30 | 3 | 1 |
| Andersh, Kevin, Macon | .043 | 27 | 23 | 1 | 1 | 4 | 0 | 0 | 1 | 1 | 0 | 7 | 0 | 0 | 4 | 0 | 12 | 0 | 0 |
| Archibald, Jaime, Columbia* | .143 | 10 | 28 | 2 | 4 | 8 | 1 | 0 | 1 | 5 | 1 | 0 | 2 | 0 | 2 | 0 | 11 | 0 | 0 |
| Arnold, Scott, Savannah | .250 | 24 | 12 | 2 | 3 | 3 | 0 | 0 | 0 | 0 | 0 | 4 | 0 | 0 | 3 | 0 | 4 | 0 | 0 |
| Arnsberg, Timothy, Asheville | .000 | 7 | 2 | 0 | 0 | 0 | 0 | 0 | 0 | 0 | 0 | 0 | 0 | 0 | 0 | 0 | 1 | 0 | 0 |
| Ashkinazy, Alan, Greensboro | .255 | 130 | 483 | 115 | 123 | 141 | 10 | 4 | 0 | 55 | 8 | 2 | 3 | 3 | 132 | 1 | 28 | 53 | 8 |
| Atkinson, Timothy, Savannah | .000 | 28 | 0 | 0 | 0 | 0 | 0 | 0 | 0 | 0 | 0 | 0 | 0 | 0 | 2 | 0 | 0 | 0 | 0 |
| Barba, Douglas, Columbia | .167 | 32 | 6 | 0 | 1 | 1 | 0 | 0 | 0 | 0 | 0 | 0 | 0 | 0 | 0 | 0 | 4 | 0 | 0 |
| Barnard, Steve, Macon† | .227 | 54 | 181 | 24 | 41 | 56 | 10 | 1 | 1 | 20 | 0 | 1 | 0 | 1 | 17 | 0 | 35 | 2 | 1 |
| Barrios, Gregg, Greensboro | .263 | 111 | 400 | 64 | 105 | 147 | 24 | 3 | 4 | 47 | 3 | 3 | 3 | 2 | 63 | 3 | 68 | 1 | 1 |
| Bates, Douglas, Savannah* | .000 | 13 | 2 | 0 | 0 | 0 | 0 | 0 | 0 | 0 | 0 | 0 | 0 | 0 | 1 | 0 | 1 | 0 | 0 |
| Bautista, German, Macon | .240 | 15 | 25 | 4 | 6 | 10 | 1 | 0 | 1 | 5 | 0 | 0 | 1 | 0 | 2 | 0 | 7 | 0 | 0 |
| Behrend, Michael, Savannah | .600 | 14 | 5 | 1 | 3 | 4 | 1 | 0 | 0 | 0 | 0 | 1 | 0 | 0 | 0 | 0 | 1 | 0 | 0 |
| Benkert, Robert, Macon | .171 | 13 | 35 | 2 | 6 | 7 | 1 | 0 | 0 | 3 | 0 | 0 | 0 | 0 | 3 | 0 | 9 | 0 | 0 |
| Bennett, Eric, Spartanburg | .255 | 47 | 161 | 18 | 41 | 49 | 4 | 2 | 0 | 24 | 0 | 0 | 2 | 1 | 22 | 0 | 40 | 1 | 0 |
| Berroa, Geronimo, Florence | .318 | 19 | 66 | 7 | 21 | 32 | 2 | 0 | 3 | 20 | 3 | 1 | 1 | 0 | 6 | 0 | 13 | 0 | 1 |
| Billinger, Jon, Savannah | .095 | 13 | 42 | 0 | 4 | 4 | 0 | 0 | 0 | 3 | 0 | 2 | 1 | 2 | 5 | 0 | 13 | 0 | 0 |
| Bitker, Joseph, Charleston | .222 | 13 | 18 | 3 | 4 | 4 | 0 | 0 | 0 | 3 | 0 | 2 | 0 | 1 | 2 | 0 | 2 | 0 | 0 |
| Blaine, Gary, Savannah | .211 | 80 | 204 | 20 | 43 | 68 | 9 | 2 | 4 | 24 | 2 | 1 | 4 | 17 | 0 | 61 | 0 | 1 |
| Blake, Keith, Gastonia | .140 | 35 | 86 | 4 | 12 | 16 | 1 | 0 | 1 | 3 | 0 | 2 | 0 | 0 | 9 | 0 | 36 | 3 | 1 |
| Blauser, Jeffrey, Sumter | .235 | 125 | 422 | 74 | 99 | 133 | 19 | 0 | 5 | 49 | 5 | 2 | 5 | 9 | 82 | 1 | 94 | 36 | 6 |
| Bonk, Thomas, Greensboro* | .251 | 93 | 307 | 53 | 77 | 122 | 13 | 1 | 10 | 66 | 5 | 0 | 5 | 1 | 75 | 7 | 40 | 1 | 0 |
| Brock, Norman, Asheville* | .280 | 112 | 311 | 49 | 87 | 116 | 11 | 3 | 4 | 33 | 7 | 5 | 2 | 0 | 44 | 0 | 36 | 12 | 3 |
| Brooks, Desmond, Columbia | .287 | 88 | 272 | 60 | 78 | 102 | 12 | 0 | 4 | 41 | 3 | 3 | 5 | 2 | 64 | 0 | 52 | 1 | 1 |
| Broussard, Woodrow, Spartanburg†.. | .000 | 27 | 3 | 0 | 0 | 0 | 0 | 0 | 0 | 0 | 0 | 0 | 0 | 0 | 0 | 0 | 1 | 0 | 0 |
| Brunswick, Mark, Columbia | .182 | 6 | 11 | 0 | 2 | 2 | 0 | 0 | 0 | 1 | 0 | 0 | 0 | 0 | 2 | 0 | 3 | 0 | 0 |
| Byers, Randall, Charleston* | .319 | 133 | 501 | 79 | 160 | 231 | 32 | 9 | 7 | 94 | 22 | 0 | 8 | 1 | 30 | 6 | 48 | 12 | 3 |
| Camilli, Kevin, Greensboro* | .264 | 40 | 125 | 13 | 33 | 47 | 5 | 0 | 3 | 13 | 0 | 1 | 0 | 1 | 15 | 1 | 31 | 0 | 0 |
| Campusano, Silvestre, Florence | .313 | 88 | 348 | 80 | 109 | 187 | 31 | 1 | 15 | 56 | 4 | 3 | 4 | 3 | 58 | 0 | 84 | 21 | 14 |
| Carrion, Jesus, Asheville | .230 | 46 | 113 | 13 | 26 | 31 | 2 | 0 | 1 | 8 | 3 | 0 | 2 | 1 | 8 | 0 | 31 | 1 | 1 |
| Carter, Dennis, Savannah ...† | .128 | 15 | 39 | 2 | 5 | 6 | 1 | 0 | 0 | 2 | 0 | 0 | 0 | 0 | 9 | 0 | 11 | 1 | 0 |
| Cash, Johnny, Sumter* | .231 | 20 | 13 | 3 | 3 | 4 | 1 | 0 | 0 | 3 | 0 | 2 | 0 | 0 | 4 | 0 | 2 | 0 | 0 |
| Cepeda, Octavio, Macon | .000 | 10 | 5 | 0 | 0 | 0 | 0 | 0 | 0 | 1 | 0 | 0 | 0 | 0 | 1 | 0 | 0 | 0 | 0 |
| Chambers, Travis, Spartanburg* | .000 | 12 | 3 | 0 | 0 | 0 | 0 | 0 | 0 | 0 | 0 | 1 | 0 | 0 | 1 | 0 | 0 | 0 | 0 |
| Chance, Anthony, 6 Mac-56 Gas | .242 | 62 | 231 | 34 | 56 | 79 | 8 | 0 | 5 | 19 | 5 | 2 | 0 | 0 | 18 | 0 | 57 | 17 | 7 |
| Cheek, Carey, Macon | .297 | 136 | 485 | 70 | 144 | 230 | 29 | 3 | 17 | 82 | 10 | 0 | 4 | 6 | 78 | 10 | 84 | 4 | 2 |
| Cisco, Jeffrey, Charleston† | .252 | 43 | 115 | 13 | 29 | 37 | 6 | 1 | 0 | 14 | 1 | 3 | 2 | 2 | 23 | 2 | 16 | 1 | 0 |
| Ciszkowski, Jeffrey, Columbia | .237 | 38 | 38 | 8 | 9 | 15 | 0 | 0 | 2 | 4 | 0 | 4 | 0 | 0 | 1 | 0 | 10 | 1 | 0 |
| Clark, Daniel, Macon | .168 | 54 | 202 | 20 | 34 | 39 | 1 | 2 | 0 | 7 | 0 | 3 | 3 | 0 | 16 | 0 | 29 | 13 | 3 |
| Clawson, Kenneth, Charleston | .240 | 107 | 217 | 24 | 52 | 58 | 3 | 0 | 1 | 25 | 5 | 2 | 2 | 0 | 28 | 4 | 41 | 2 | 0 |
| Clemente, Roberto, Gastonia | .186 | 37 | 97 | 8 | 18 | 21 | 1 | 1 | 0 | 8 | 1 | 1 | 0 | 0 | 10 | 0 | 28 | 6 | 2 |
| Clossen, William, Sumter | .133 | 26 | 15 | 0 | 2 | 2 | 0 | 0 | 0 | 1 | 0 | 1 | 0 | 0 | 2 | 0 | 4 | 0 | 0 |
| Coffman, Kevin, Sumter | .500 | 24 | 2 | 1 | 1 | 4 | 0 | 0 | 1 | 0 | 0 | 0 | 0 | 0 | 0 | 0 | 1 | 0 | 0 |
| Colpitt, Michael, Spartanburg | .000 | 24 | 2 | 1 | 0 | 0 | 0 | 0 | 0 | 0 | 0 | 0 | 0 | 0 | 1 | 0 | 2 | 1 | 0 |
| Constanzo, Fernando, Sumter | .190 | 56 | 126 | 7 | 24 | 30 | 2 | 2 | 0 | 9 | 1 | 1 | 0 | 1 | 5 | 0 | 29 | 0 | 0 |
| Contreras, Joaquin, Columbia† | .209 | 16 | 43 | 7 | 9 | 17 | 0 | 1 | 2 | 8 | 1 | 0 | 2 | 0 | 3 | 0 | 12 | 1 | 1 |
| Cooley, Jeffrey, Columbia | .050 | 13 | 20 | 1 | 1 | 1 | 0 | 0 | 0 | 0 | 0 | 3 | 0 | 0 | 0 | 0 | 12 | 0 | 0 |
| Cooper, David, Gastonia | .194 | 38 | 67 | 4 | 13 | 18 | 2 | 0 | 1 | 4 | 0 | 0 | 0 | 0 | 8 | 0 | 22 | 0 | 1 |
| Costello, Michael, Charleston | .093 | 29 | 43 | 3 | 4 | 4 | 0 | 0 | 0 | 5 | 1 | 5 | 2 | 0 | 3 | 0 | 13 | 0 | 0 |
| Crispin, Alberto, Spartanburg | .189 | 69 | 233 | 16 | 44 | 62 | 10 | 1 | 2 | 22 | 3 | 2 | 4 | 3 | 7 | 0 | 51 | 8 | 3 |
| Criswell, Timothy, Sumter | .259 | 77 | 224 | 27 | 58 | 70 | 5 | 2 | 1 | 25 | 4 | 0 | 3 | 5 | 15 | 0 | 26 | 10 | 3 |
| Cron, Christopher, Sumter | .240 | 119 | 425 | 53 | 102 | 143 | 20 | 0 | 7 | 59 | 10 | 0 | 1 | 18 | 51 | 2 | 98 | 5 | 2 |

| Player and Club | Pct. | G. | AB. | R. | H. | TB. | 2B. | 3B. | HR. | RBI. | GW. | SH. | SF. | HP. | BB. | Int. BB. | SO. | SB. | CS. |
|---|---|---|---|---|---|---|---|---|---|---|---|---|---|---|---|---|---|---|---|
| Crossley, David, Savannah | .077 | 23 | 13 | 1 | 1 | 1 | 0 | 0 | 0 | 1 | 0 | 2 | 0 | 0 | 0 | 0 | 3 | 0 | 0 |
| Cuevas, Angelo, Columbia* | .290 | 130 | 473 | 68 | 137 | 188 | 20 | 5 | 7 | 101 | 14 | 0 | 9 | 0 | 83 | 9 | 52 | 10 | 5 |
| Cuevas, Johnny, Sumter | .192 | 77 | 234 | 31 | 45 | 63 | 12 | 0 | 2 | 24 | 5 | 2 | 5 | 1 | 30 | 1 | 55 | 1 | 0 |
| Cunningham, Charles, Macon | .000 | 9 | 0 | 0 | 0 | 0 | 0 | 0 | 0 | 0 | 0 | 1 | 0 | 0 | 0 | 0 | 0 | 0 | 0 |
| Cunningham, Joseph, Savannah | .151 | 29 | 86 | 4 | 13 | 15 | 2 | 0 | 0 | 8 | 1 | 1 | 2 | 1 | 9 | 0 | 17 | 1 | 1 |
| Cusack, David, Gastonia | .254 | 132 | 460 | 78 | 117 | 221 | 17 | 3 | 27 | 79 | 5 | 0 | 4 | 2 | 82 | 3 | 101 | 6 | 6 |
| Czyzewski, Tracey, Charleston* | .182 | 31 | 11 | 3 | 2 | 2 | 0 | 0 | 0 | 4 | 0 | 1 | 2 | 0 | 2 | 0 | 4 | 0 | 0 |
| Dantzler, Shawn, Spartanburg | .289 | 122 | 409 | 67 | 118 | 218 | 26 | 4 | 22 | 70 | 8 | 0 | 1 | 18 | 40 | 1 | 90 | 15 | 2 |
| Davis, Mark, Savannah | .000 | 49 | 4 | 0 | 0 | 0 | 0 | 0 | 0 | 0 | 0 | 0 | 0 | 0 | 0 | 0 | 3 | 0 | 0 |
| DeFrancesco, Anthony, Greensboro | .205 | 48 | 156 | 16 | 32 | 36 | 4 | 0 | 0 | 18 | 0 | 3 | 3 | 21 | 0 | 29 | 2 | 0 |
| DeLaCruz, Hector, Florence | .227 | 21 | 44 | 5 | 10 | 12 | 2 | 0 | 0 | 4 | 1 | 1 | 0 | 0 | 2 | 0 | 14 | 1 | 0 |
| DeLuca, Kurt, Columbia | .147 | 11 | 34 | 1 | 5 | 5 | 0 | 0 | 0 | 2 | 0 | 1 | 1 | 1 | 0 | 6 | 1 | 0 |
| Denson, Andrew, Sumter | .300 | 111 | 383 | 59 | 115 | 183 | 18 | 4 | 14 | 74 | 6 | 0 | 4 | 4 | 53 | 3 | 76 | 5 | 3 |
| DePrimo, John, Greensboro | .167 | 36 | 90 | 15 | 15 | 16 | 1 | 0 | 0 | 10 | 0 | 4 | 3 | 1 | 18 | 0 | 13 | 0 | 0 |
| Diaz, Jose, Florence | .667 | 2 | 3 | 0 | 2 | 3 | 1 | 0 | 0 | 0 | 0 | 0 | 0 | 0 | 0 | 0 | 1 | 0 | 0 |
| Dillard, David, Charleston* | .233 | 45 | 103 | 17 | 24 | 37 | 5 | 1 | 2 | 15 | 2 | 0 | 2 | 0 | 25 | 1 | 31 | 1 | 2 |
| Dillenberger, David, Savannah | .000 | 44 | 1 | 0 | 0 | 0 | 0 | 0 | 0 | 0 | 0 | 0 | 0 | 0 | 0 | 0 | 0 | 0 | 0 |
| Drummond, Timothy, Macon | .207 | 27 | 29 | 1 | 6 | 6 | 0 | 0 | 0 | 2 | 1 | 1 | 0 | 0 | 5 | 0 | 14 | 1 | 0 |
| Ducey, Robert, Florence* | .251 | 134 | 529 | 78 | 133 | 198 | 22 | 2 | 13 | 86 | 7 | 3 | 7 | 1 | 49 | 2 | 103 | 12 | 4 |
| Durocher, Francois, Asheville | .000 | 26 | 1 | 0 | 0 | 0 | 0 | 0 | 0 | 0 | 0 | 0 | 0 | 0 | 0 | 0 | 1 | 0 | 0 |
| Dyrek, David, Asheville* | .194 | 34 | 103 | 18 | 20 | 31 | 3 | 1 | 2 | 12 | 0 | 2 | 0 | 0 | 25 | 2 | 15 | 3 | 0 |
| Elliott, John, Asheville | .267 | 130 | 390 | 54 | 104 | 116 | 12 | 0 | 0 | 36 | 4 | 15 | 5 | 2 | 71 | 1 | 55 | 13 | 4 |
| Escobar, Santiago, Florence | .269 | 115 | 376 | 63 | 101 | 135 | 16 | 3 | 4 | 43 | 7 | 2 | 4 | 5 | 34 | 0 | 72 | 14 | 8 |
| Evans, Evan, Macon | .217 | 46 | 129 | 22 | 28 | 38 | 5 | 1 | 1 | 10 | 3 | 1 | 1 | 1 | 9 | 0 | 40 | 7 | 2 |
| Ferreiras, Salvador, 10 Mac-52 Gas | .204 | 62 | 167 | 11 | 34 | 39 | 5 | 0 | 0 | 6 | 0 | 5 | 0 | 1 | 14 | 0 | 38 | 2 | 1 |
| Flores, Jose, Greensboro† | .155 | 28 | 58 | 7 | 9 | 10 | 1 | 0 | 0 | 3 | 0 | 2 | 0 | 1 | 4 | 0 | 14 | 2 | 0 |
| Ford, Russell, Charleston | .143 | 66 | 7 | 0 | 1 | 1 | 0 | 0 | 0 | 0 | 0 | 0 | 0 | 0 | 0 | 0 | 5 | 0 | 0 |
| Fortenberry, Jimmy, Gastonia* | .234 | 99 | 354 | 42 | 83 | 147 | 19 | 3 | 13 | 48 | 3 | 0 | 1 | 2 | 26 | 0 | 59 | 7 | 7 |
| Franchi, Kevin, Macon* | .000 | 26 | 5 | 0 | 0 | 0 | 0 | 0 | 0 | 0 | 0 | 0 | 0 | 0 | 1 | 0 | 4 | 0 | 0 |
| Frazier, Heath, Spartanburg | .180 | 105 | 323 | 44 | 58 | 72 | 8 | 3 | 0 | 24 | 6 | 1 | 4 | 4 | 38 | 0 | 99 | 20 | 5 |
| Frazier, Shawn, Sumter | .238 | 120 | 407 | 50 | 97 | 109 | 10 | 1 | 0 | 43 | 5 | 3 | 2 | 3 | 24 | 1 | 72 | 15 | 5 |
| Fredymond, Juan, Sumter | .160 | 40 | 94 | 10 | 15 | 20 | 3 | 1 | 0 | 7 | 1 | 0 | 0 | 0 | 8 | 0 | 17 | 3 | 2 |
| Friedel, Charles, Columbia | 1.000 | 10 | 1 | 1 | 1 | 1 | 0 | 0 | 0 | 0 | 0 | 0 | 0 | 0 | 0 | 0 | 0 | 0 | 0 |
| Frierson, John, Gastonia | .273 | 108 | 333 | 52 | 91 | 153 | 16 | 2 | 14 | 52 | 1 | 0 | 5 | 0 | 44 | 2 | 81 | 9 | 8 |
| Fulgencio, Jose, Gastonia | .164 | 90 | 238 | 27 | 39 | 51 | 5 | 2 | 1 | 18 | 1 | 5 | 0 | 1 | 32 | 0 | 58 | 9 | 4 |
| Funk, Thomas, Asheville* | .125 | 40 | 8 | 0 | 1 | 1 | 0 | 0 | 0 | 0 | 0 | 0 | 0 | 0 | 0 | 0 | 3 | 0 | 0 |
| Gambino, Raymond, Macon* | .202 | 41 | 124 | 13 | 25 | 26 | 1 | 0 | 0 | 10 | 1 | 4 | 0 | 2 | 19 | 0 | 14 | 2 | 1 |
| Gant, Ronald, Sumter | .256 | 102 | 305 | 46 | 78 | 121 | 14 | 4 | 7 | 37 | 3 | 1 | 0 | 2 | 33 | 2 | 59 | 19 | 10 |
| Garcia, Santiago, Florence | .298 | 128 | 514 | 86 | 153 | 216 | 35 | 2 | 8 | 79 | 10 | 1 | 5 | 5 | 41 | 0 | 67 | 25 | 10 |
| Gardner, Jeffrey, Columbia* | .294 | 123 | 401 | 80 | 118 | 129 | 9 | 1 | 0 | 50 | 6 | 10 | 1 | 5 | 142 | 1 | 40 | 31 | 5 |
| Gass, Jeffrey, Savannah | .000 | 6 | 8 | 0 | 0 | 0 | 0 | 0 | 0 | 0 | 0 | 0 | 2 | 0 | 0 | 0 | 3 | 0 | 0 |
| Gay, Steven, Columbia | .100 | 6 | 10 | 0 | 1 | 1 | 0 | 0 | 0 | 0 | 0 | 0 | 3 | 0 | 0 | 0 | 4 | 0 | 0 |
| Gideon, Brett, Macon | .067 | 15 | 15 | 0 | 1 | 1 | 0 | 0 | 0 | 1 | 0 | 0 | 0 | 0 | 2 | 0 | 6 | 0 | 0 |
| Gildehaus, Michael, Charleston* | .500 | 5 | 2 | 0 | 1 | 1 | 0 | 0 | 0 | 0 | 0 | 0 | 0 | 0 | 0 | 0 | 1 | 0 | 0 |
| Gjesdal, Brent, Charleston | .268 | 129 | 429 | 82 | 115 | 199 | 23 | 2 | 19 | 70 | 4 | 0 | 2 | 6 | 71 | 2 | 120 | 6 | 4 |
| Glavine, Thomas, Sumter* | .121 | 26 | 33 | 3 | 4 | 5 | 1 | 0 | 0 | 2 | 0 | 2 | 0 | 0 | 5 | 0 | 17 | 0 | 0 |
| Gonzalez, Roberto, Macon† | .213 | 47 | 136 | 9 | 29 | 32 | 3 | 0 | 0 | 8 | 1 | 2 | 0 | 4 | 0 | 30 | 1 | 1 |
| Gozzo, Mauro, Columbia | .300 | 49 | 10 | 0 | 3 | 4 | 1 | 0 | 0 | 0 | 0 | 0 | 0 | 0 | 0 | 0 | 4 | 0 | 0 |
| Green, Terry, Asheville | .255 | 128 | 502 | 66 | 128 | 154 | 19 | 2 | 1 | 48 | 5 | 9 | 2 | 0 | 40 | 2 | 64 | 11 | 6 |
| Greenlee, Robert, Charleston* | .000 | 35 | 15 | 1 | 0 | 0 | 0 | 0 | 0 | 0 | 0 | 0 | 0 | 0 | 1 | 0 | 4 | 0 | 0 |
| Gregg, Thomas, Macon* | .313 | 72 | 259 | 43 | 81 | 102 | 14 | 2 | 1 | 18 | 2 | 1 | 0 | 0 | 49 | 3 | 38 | 16 | 7 |
| Grosdidier, William, Sumter | .500 | 33 | 2 | 0 | 1 | 1 | 0 | 0 | 0 | 0 | 0 | 1 | 0 | 0 | 0 | 0 | 0 | 0 | 0 |
| Groves, Jeffrey, Sumter | .000 | 18 | 4 | 0 | 0 | 0 | 0 | 0 | 0 | 0 | 0 | 0 | 0 | 0 | 0 | 0 | 2 | 0 | 0 |
| Gsellman, Bob, Spartanburg | .222 | 43 | 108 | 14 | 24 | 49 | 2 | 1 | 7 | 7 | 2 | 1 | 0 | 1 | 18 | 0 | 46 | 1 | 0 |
| Guzman, Rodolfo, Sumter | .000 | 8 | 5 | 0 | 0 | 0 | 0 | 0 | 0 | 0 | 0 | 2 | 0 | 0 | 0 | 0 | 3 | 0 | 0 |
| Hall, David, Greensboro | .187 | 45 | 134 | 23 | 25 | 42 | 4 | 2 | 3 | 18 | 0 | 1 | 3 | 2 | 22 | 0 | 44 | 1 | 0 |
| Hammonds, Reginald, Macon | .318 | 51 | 201 | 35 | 64 | 79 | 5 | 2 | 2 | 20 | 3 | 1 | 1 | 1 | 19 | 1 | 36 | 12 | 1 |
| Hampton, Anthony, Asheville* | .278 | 76 | 302 | 55 | 84 | 112 | 12 | 2 | 4 | 51 | 2 | 3 | 1 | 3 | 48 | 1 | 51 | 19 | 9 |
| Helton, Kevin, Macon | 1.000 | 11 | 1 | 1 | 1 | 1 | 0 | 0 | 0 | 0 | 0 | 0 | 0 | 0 | 0 | 0 | 0 | 0 | 0 |
| Hendrix, James, Spartanburg | .000 | 16 | 1 | 0 | 0 | 0 | 0 | 0 | 0 | 0 | 0 | 0 | 0 | 0 | 0 | 0 | 0 | 0 | 0 |
| Heredia, Geysi, Asheville | .200 | 19 | 25 | 1 | 5 | 5 | 0 | 0 | 0 | 3 | 0 | 0 | 0 | 0 | 0 | 10 | 0 | 0 |
| Hill, Richard, Savannah | .207 | 29 | 82 | 8 | 17 | 21 | 2 | 1 | 0 | 6 | 1 | 1 | 0 | 3 | 4 | 0 | 12 | 0 | 0 |
| Hill, Stephen, Savannah* | .300 | 27 | 10 | 0 | 3 | 3 | 0 | 0 | 0 | 1 | 0 | 0 | 0 | 1 | 0 | 0 | 2 | 0 | 0 |
| Howard, James, Florence | .265 | 74 | 219 | 49 | 58 | 77 | 7 | 0 | 4 | 30 | 1 | 2 | 3 | 0 | 33 | 0 | 51 | 4 | 3 |
| Howey, Todd, Spartanburg | .227 | 68 | 238 | 30 | 54 | 83 | 14 | 0 | 5 | 33 | 7 | 2 | 3 | 1 | 23 | 0 | 66 | 5 | 1 |
| Hubbard, Marlon, Charleston | .250 | 47 | 12 | 1 | 3 | 4 | 1 | 0 | 0 | 1 | 0 | 2 | 0 | 0 | 2 | 0 | 4 | 0 | 0 |
| Huchingson, Christopher, Asheville | .118 | 23 | 34 | 4 | 4 | 4 | 0 | 0 | 0 | 5 | 0 | 2 | 0 | 0 | 4 | 0 | 13 | 0 | 0 |
| Hufford, Scott, Spartanburg | .209 | 113 | 349 | 51 | 73 | 124 | 16 | 4 | 9 | 44 | 1 | 1 | 1 | 4 | 48 | 0 | 110 | 9 | 3 |
| Hurtado, Jose, Spartanburg | .173 | 36 | 110 | 16 | 19 | 36 | 5 | 0 | 4 | 13 | 2 | 0 | 0 | 1 | 10 | 0 | 49 | 2 | 2 |
| Iglesias, Luis, Savannah | .206 | 21 | 63 | 11 | 13 | 16 | 3 | 0 | 0 | 3 | 1 | 0 | 1 | 2 | 8 | 0 | 14 | 0 | 0 |
| Infante, Kennedy, Savannah | .259 | 113 | 401 | 44 | 104 | 157 | 13 | 2 | 12 | 58 | 8 | 1 | 5 | 7 | 17 | 1 | 78 | 4 | 3 |
| Isner, Donald, Savannah | .169 | 56 | 166 | 13 | 28 | 43 | 4 | 1 | 3 | 15 | 1 | 4 | 2 | 3 | 24 | 0 | 46 | 3 | 1 |
| Jackson, Lavern, Greensboro | .260 | 95 | 296 | 54 | 77 | 112 | 6 | 4 | 7 | 36 | 6 | 2 | 0 | 3 | 52 | 0 | 64 | 9 | 3 |
| James, Calvin, Asheville* | .321 | 62 | 234 | 33 | 75 | 81 | 6 | 0 | 0 | 24 | 2 | 4 | 3 | 1 | 32 | 0 | 45 | 11 | 5 |
| James, Troy, Columbia | .200 | 41 | 5 | 0 | 1 | 1 | 0 | 0 | 0 | 1 | 0 | 0 | 0 | 0 | 0 | 0 | 2 | 0 | 0 |
| Jaster, Scott, Columbia | .171 | 10 | 41 | 4 | 7 | 8 | 1 | 0 | 0 | 2 | 0 | 0 | 0 | 0 | 4 | 0 | 13 | 1 | 1 |
| Jefferies, Gregg, Columbia† | .281 | 20 | 64 | 7 | 18 | 27 | 2 | 2 | 1 | 12 | 1 | 0 | 0 | 0 | 4 | 0 | 4 | 7 | 0 |
| Jelks, Patrick, Greensboro | .301 | 118 | 439 | 90 | 132 | 215 | 13 | 8 | 18 | 87 | 5 | 0 | 5 | 2 | 69 | 1 | 134 | 23 | 7 |
| Jimenez, Cesar, Sumter | .400 | 35 | 5 | 0 | 2 | 2 | 0 | 0 | 0 | 0 | 0 | 0 | 0 | 0 | 0 | 0 | 2 | 0 | 0 |
| Jimenez, Raul, Savannah | .142 | 36 | 106 | 7 | 15 | 20 | 3 | 1 | 0 | 6 | 2 | 2 | 2 | 0 | 19 | 0 | 27 | 0 | 0 |
| Johnson, Dodd, Sumter | .108 | 13 | 37 | 4 | 4 | 6 | 2 | 0 | 0 | 4 | 0 | 0 | 0 | 0 | 8 | 0 | 16 | 0 | 0 |
| Johnson, Issac, Spartanburg | .203 | 82 | 300 | 33 | 61 | 71 | 5 | 1 | 1 | 22 | 1 | 1 | 4 | 1 | 15 | 0 | 67 | 3 | 1 |
| Johnson, John, Macon | .264 | 89 | 235 | 27 | 62 | 86 | 9 | 3 | 3 | 34 | 4 | 1 | 0 | 1 | 27 | 1 | 52 | 5 | 5 |
| Johnson, Roger, Spartanburg | .165 | 24 | 79 | 3 | 13 | 16 | 3 | 0 | 0 | 5 | 1 | 0 | 0 | 0 | 9 | 0 | 19 | 0 | 0 |
| Jones, Geary, Columbia | .111 | 8 | 18 | 3 | 2 | 2 | 0 | 0 | 0 | 1 | 0 | 0 | 0 | 0 | 1 | 6 | 0 | 13 | 0 |
| Jones, Labarry, Sumter* | .210 | 52 | 138 | 21 | 29 | 35 | 0 | 3 | 0 | 8 | 2 | 2 | 1 | 1 | 13 | 0 | 17 | 8 | 3 |
| Jones, Mike, Florence | .282 | 40 | 149 | 30 | 42 | 56 | 6 | 1 | 2 | 17 | 3 | 3 | 3 | 0 | 10 | 0 | 28 | 8 | 1 |
| Jongewaard, Steven, Sumter | .219 | 100 | 292 | 40 | 64 | 81 | 11 | 0 | 2 | 28 | 3 | 5 | 1 | 5 | 49 | 0 | 69 | 5 | 1 |
| Jose, Manuel, Greensboro† | .323 | 116 | 402 | 75 | 130 | 166 | 19 | 7 | 1 | 48 | 8 | 2 | 3 | 2 | 36 | 1 | 67 | 38 | 17 |
| Kaiser, Bart, Spartanburg* | .312 | 122 | 433 | 77 | 135 | 212 | 28 | 5 | 13 | 52 | 7 | 1 | 0 | 2 | 53 | 4 | 83 | 24 | 3 |
| Karr, Jeffrey, Columbia | .182 | 9 | 33 | 6 | 6 | 7 | 1 | 0 | 0 | 2 | 0 | 0 | 0 | 0 | 8 | 0 | 13 | 0 | 0 |
| Kilner, John, Sumter* | .167 | 23 | 24 | 5 | 4 | 6 | 2 | 0 | 0 | 1 | 0 | 3 | 0 | 0 | 4 | 0 | 6 | 0 | 0 |

| Player and Club | Pct. | G. | AB. | R. | H. | TB. | 2B. | 3B. | HR. | RBI. | GW. | SH. | SF. | HP. | BB. | Int. BB. | SO. | SB. | CS. |
|---|---|---|---|---|---|---|---|---|---|---|---|---|---|---|---|---|---|---|---|
| Kiluk, Richard, Macon | .200 | 26 | 50 | 4 | 10 | 11 | 1 | 0 | 0 | 5 | 0 | 1 | 2 | 1 | 8 | 1 | 16 | 5 | 2 |
| Kinard, Charles, Savannah | .233 | 94 | 318 | 30 | 74 | 87 | 5 | 4 | 0 | 29 | 3 | 4 | 2 | 3 | 25 | 1 | 61 | 3 | 0 |
| Knox, Jeffrey, Spartanburg | .071 | 22 | 14 | 1 | 1 | 1 | 0 | 0 | 0 | 1 | 1 | 3 | 0 | 0 | 1 | 0 | 4 | 0 | 0 |
| Kolb, Jonathan, Macon | .000 | 39 | 6 | 0 | 0 | 0 | 0 | 0 | 0 | 0 | 0 | 1 | 0 | 1 | 0 | 0 | 2 | 0 | 0 |
| Kwolek, Joseph, Asheville | .290 | 90 | 276 | 41 | 80 | 111 | 19 | 0 | 4 | 30 | 5 | 2 | 5 | 2 | 49 | 2 | 47 | 2 | 4 |
| Landrum, Darryl, Florence | .205 | 130 | 453 | 71 | 93 | 161 | 11 | 0 | 19 | 52 | 3 | 1 | 3 | 14 | 44 | 1 | 208 | 25 | 6 |
| Lawrence, Theodore, Gastonia | .333 | 2 | 6 | 1 | 2 | 3 | 1 | 0 | 0 | 0 | 0 | 0 | 0 | 0 | 0 | 0 | 3 | 0 | 0 |
| Lawton, Marcus, Columbia† | .268 | 128 | 470 | 113 | 126 | 150 | 11 | 5 | 1 | 53 | 4 | 4 | 2 | 2 | 83 | 0 | 80 | 111 | 8 |
| Leiper, Timothy, Gastonia† | .283 | 31 | 106 | 16 | 30 | 41 | 4 | 2 | 1 | 14 | 2 | 2 | 1 | 0 | 9 | 0 | 17 | 4 | 3 |
| Lemke, Mark, Sumter† | .216 | 90 | 231 | 25 | 50 | 56 | 6 | 0 | 0 | 20 | 4 | 2 | 1 | 6 | 34 | 2 | 22 | 2 | 2 |
| Lemon, Ricky, Savannah° | .182 | 11 | 22 | 2 | 4 | 6 | 2 | 0 | 0 | 3 | 0 | 0 | 0 | 6 | 0 | 5 | 0 | 0 |
| Livin, Jeffrey, Asheville | .158 | 27 | 19 | 3 | 3 | 3 | 0 | 0 | 0 | 1 | 0 | 2 | 0 | 1 | 0 | 6 | 0 | 0 |
| Llewellyn, Paul, Sumter | .177 | 24 | 62 | 8 | 11 | 21 | 4 | 0 | 2 | 6 | 0 | 2 | 1 | 0 | 0 | 0 | 27 | 1 | 0 |
| Lowe, Dion, Gastonia° | .273 | 34 | 110 | 22 | 30 | 41 | 5 | 0 | 2 | 13 | 0 | 0 | 0 | 2 | 27 | 0 | 26 | 7 | 5 |
| Lynn, Charles, Columbia | .263 | 96 | 320 | 56 | 84 | 136 | 17 | 1 | 11 | 60 | 5 | 2 | 5 | 2 | 73 | 3 | 65 | 3 | 0 |
| Machado, Julio, Spartanburg | .667 | 32 | 3 | 0 | 2 | 2 | 0 | 0 | 0 | 0 | 0 | 1 | 0 | 0 | 0 | 0 | 0 | 0 | 0 |
| Mack, Jeremiah, Gastonia | .208 | 116 | 365 | 50 | 76 | 103 | 11 | 2 | 4 | 24 | 1 | 2 | 1 | 5 | 57 | 0 | 111 | 27 | 11 |
| Marquardt, Roger, Florence | .000 | 4 | 8 | 2 | 0 | 0 | 0 | 0 | 0 | 0 | 0 | 0 | 0 | 0 | 0 | 0 | 2 | 0 | 0 |
| Martin, Charles, Sumter | .000 | 43 | 3 | 0 | 0 | 0 | 0 | 0 | 0 | 0 | 0 | 0 | 0 | 0 | 0 | 0 | 2 | 0 | 0 |
| Martinez, Enrique, 50 Gas-4 Spt | .139 | 54 | 108 | 8 | 15 | 21 | 3 | 0 | 1 | 9 | 0 | 4 | 3 | 2 | 10 | 0 | 36 | 0 | 3 |
| Martinez, Miguel, Gastonia | .182 | 4 | 11 | 0 | 2 | 2 | 0 | 0 | 0 | 0 | 0 | 0 | 0 | 0 | 0 | 0 | 2 | 1 | 0 |
| Martinez, Porfirio, Gastonia† | .274 | 80 | 288 | 35 | 79 | 119 | 19 | 3 | 5 | 36 | 4 | 2 | 2 | 1 | 10 | 1 | 71 | 13 | 6 |
| Mathews, Thomas, Savannah° | .251 | 122 | 415 | 42 | 104 | 148 | 15 | 7 | 5 | 52 | 7 | 2 | 5 | 0 | 36 | 0 | 56 | 2 | 2 |
| Mauch, Thomas, Savannah° | .233 | 16 | 30 | 3 | 7 | 8 | 1 | 0 | 0 | 0 | 0 | 0 | 0 | 0 | 3 | 0 | 6 | 0 | 1 |
| McClain, Gregory, Macon | .238 | 57 | 143 | 16 | 34 | 43 | 6 | 0 | 1 | 15 | 0 | 1 | 1 | 4 | 22 | 0 | 35 | 1 | 3 |
| McCray, Rodney, Charleston | .206 | 117 | 373 | 81 | 77 | 90 | 8 | 1 | 1 | 27 | 0 | 5 | 1 | 6 | 80 | 2 | 88 | 49 | 7 |
| McKnight, Jefferson, Columbia° | .264 | 67 | 159 | 26 | 42 | 53 | 6 | 1 | 1 | 24 | 1 | 0 | 2 | 1 | 21 | 2 | 18 | 6 | 2 |
| McWilliams, Juan, Gastonia | .136 | 9 | 22 | 1 | 3 | 3 | 0 | 0 | 0 | 0 | 0 | 0 | 2 | 0 | 1 | 4 | 0 | 1 | 0 |
| Mercedes, Guillermo, Macon | .222 | 54 | 9 | 0 | 2 | 2 | 0 | 0 | 0 | 1 | 0 | 0 | 0 | 0 | 1 | 0 | 4 | 0 | 0 |
| Merklen, Edward, Macon° | .417 | 50 | 12 | 1 | 5 | 6 | 1 | 0 | 0 | 1 | 0 | 1 | 0 | 0 | 0 | 0 | 2 | 0 | 0 |
| Mikulik, Joseph, Asheville | .267 | 135 | 529 | 87 | 141 | 243 | 27 | 3 | 23 | 87 | 14 | 3 | 5 | 10 | 37 | 0 | 94 | 18 | 3 |
| Miller, John, Gastonia | .079 | 13 | 38 | 1 | 3 | 3 | 0 | 0 | 0 | 2 | 0 | 0 | 0 | 0 | 2 | 0 | 10 | 0 | 0 |
| Miller, Michael, Spartanburg° | .143 | 25 | 21 | 4 | 3 | 3 | 0 | 0 | 0 | 4 | 1 | 1 | 0 | 0 | 0 | 0 | 9 | 0 | 0 |
| Minick, Jeffrey, Columbia | .276 | 31 | 87 | 5 | 24 | 28 | 4 | 0 | 0 | 6 | 1 | 2 | 2 | 1 | 8 | 0 | 21 | 1 | 6 |
| Mitchell, Thomas, Asheville | .294 | 61 | 231 | 49 | 68 | 128 | 14 | 2 | 14 | 43 | 4 | 1 | 4 | 3 | 25 | 0 | 48 | 5 | 0 |
| Moore, Sam, Asheville | .125 | 28 | 8 | 1 | 1 | 1 | 0 | 0 | 0 | 0 | 0 | 0 | 0 | 0 | 1 | 0 | 4 | 0 | 0 |
| Moreland, Oscar, Columbia | .500 | 4 | 2 | 0 | 1 | 1 | 0 | 0 | 0 | 1 | 0 | 0 | 0 | 0 | 0 | 0 | 0 | 0 | 0 |
| Morelock, Charles, Sumter | .000 | 16 | 3 | 0 | 0 | 0 | 0 | 0 | 0 | 0 | 0 | 1 | 0 | 0 | 0 | 0 | 2 | 0 | 0 |
| Moreno, Jaime, Charleston | .175 | 23 | 63 | 4 | 11 | 13 | 2 | 0 | 0 | 7 | 0 | 0 | 1 | 0 | 4 | 0 | 7 | 1 | 0 |
| Moritz, Christopher, Greensboro | .313 | 135 | 534 | 109 | 167 | 231 | 19 | 9 | 9 | 87 | 9 | 5 | 5 | 7 | 57 | 0 | 92 | 27 | 12 |
| Morrison, Brian, Florence | .100 | 22 | 40 | 1 | 4 | 4 | 0 | 0 | 0 | 1 | 0 | 0 | 0 | 0 | 2 | 0 | 15 | 0 | 0 |
| Mueller, Peter, Asheville° | .297 | 133 | 445 | 89 | 132 | 250 | 26 | 4 | 28 | 93 | 11 | 1 | 5 | 5 | 93 | 8 | 93 | 7 | 2 |
| Murphy, John, Savannah | .317 | 132 | 464 | 85 | 147 | 198 | 17 | 2 | 10 | 51 | 5 | 11 | 3 | 7 | 56 | 1 | 56 | 35 | 11 |
| Myers, Gregory, Florence° | .223 | 134 | 489 | 52 | 109 | 147 | 19 | 2 | 5 | 62 | 8 | 2 | 7 | 2 | 39 | 0 | 54 | 0 | 0 |
| Newell, Thomas, Savannah | .136 | 30 | 22 | 4 | 3 | 3 | 0 | 0 | 0 | 0 | 0 | 0 | 0 | 0 | 1 | 0 | 6 | 0 | 0 |
| Nowakowski, Joseph, 49 Gas-9 Flo | .307 | 58 | 199 | 22 | 61 | 82 | 15 | 0 | 2 | 31 | 4 | 1 | 0 | 1 | 12 | 0 | 37 | 8 | 6 |
| Palmer, David, Asheville° | .250 | 24 | 4 | 1 | 1 | 4 | 0 | 0 | 1 | 4 | 0 | 1 | 0 | 0 | 1 | 0 | 1 | 0 | 0 |
| Parker, Christopher, Asheville | .000 | 34 | 5 | 0 | 0 | 0 | 0 | 0 | 0 | 0 | 0 | 1 | 0 | 0 | 0 | 0 | 3 | 0 | 0 |
| Parsons, Scott, Charleston | .306 | 93 | 301 | 30 | 92 | 121 | 17 | 0 | 4 | 40 | 1 | 1 | 3 | 1 | 24 | 1 | 33 | 1 | 2 |
| Pender, Shawn, Macon | .231 | 34 | 104 | 17 | 24 | 30 | 3 | 0 | 1 | 4 | 0 | 1 | 0 | 1 | 16 | 0 | 14 | 3 | 2 |
| Perez, Freddy, Spartanburg | .219 | 28 | 64 | 7 | 14 | 17 | 3 | 0 | 0 | 5 | 0 | 1 | 1 | 0 | 6 | 0 | 24 | 3 | 0 |
| Perez, Hector, Columbia° | .252 | 95 | 234 | 41 | 59 | 80 | 11 | 2 | 2 | 26 | 3 | 0 | 1 | 0 | 35 | 1 | 61 | 9 | 3 |
| Perry, Jeff, Savannah | .091 | 7 | 11 | 0 | 1 | 1 | 0 | 0 | 0 | 0 | 0 | 0 | 0 | 0 | 0 | 0 | 5 | 0 | 0 |
| Pettit, Steven, Savannah | .000 | 42 | 3 | 0 | 0 | 0 | 0 | 0 | 0 | 0 | 0 | 0 | 0 | 0 | 0 | 0 | 1 | 0 | 0 |
| Pierce, Chris, Macon | .153 | 51 | 131 | 16 | 20 | 20 | 0 | 0 | 0 | 8 | 1 | 2 | 2 | 1 | 15 | 0 | 35 | 0 | 1 |
| Plesac, Joseph, Charleston | .100 | 19 | 10 | 1 | 1 | 1 | 0 | 0 | 0 | 0 | 0 | 1 | 0 | 0 | 0 | 0 | 3 | 0 | 0 |
| Pounders, Bradley, Charleston | .265 | 126 | 449 | 74 | 119 | 189 | 16 | 0 | 18 | 86 | 9 | 1 | 10 | 3 | 64 | 1 | 100 | 2 | 0 |
| Powers, Scott, Sumter | .268 | 87 | 314 | 47 | 84 | 106 | 12 | 2 | 2 | 34 | 4 | 2 | 4 | 0 | 37 | 0 | 59 | 6 | 1 |
| Pregon, David, Savannah° | .237 | 88 | 304 | 45 | 72 | 126 | 14 | 2 | 12 | 49 | 6 | 1 | 3 | 3 | 37 | 0 | 74 | 3 | 1 |
| Prince, Thomas, Macon | .208 | 124 | 360 | 60 | 75 | 127 | 20 | 1 | 10 | 42 | 3 | 1 | 5 | 12 | 96 | 0 | 92 | 13 | 3 |
| Reboulet, James, Savannah | .235 | 40 | 136 | 27 | 32 | 34 | 2 | 0 | 0 | 8 | 1 | 1 | 1 | 0 | 28 | 0 | 19 | 29 | 5 |
| Reid, Philip, Charleston | .249 | 110 | 329 | 47 | 82 | 105 | 14 | 3 | 1 | 32 | 4 | 3 | 1 | 0 | 54 | 2 | 77 | 20 | 7 |
| Reyna, Luis, Florence° | .378 | 21 | 45 | 12 | 17 | 22 | 2 | 0 | 1 | 5 | 1 | 0 | 0 | 1 | 4 | 0 | 6 | 4 | 0 |
| Richardson, Jeffrey, Columbia | .000 | 5 | 3 | 0 | 0 | 0 | 0 | 0 | 0 | 0 | 0 | 0 | 0 | 0 | 1 | 0 | 0 | 0 | 0 |
| Ritter, Christopher, Macon | .125 | 25 | 24 | 0 | 3 | 3 | 0 | 0 | 0 | 1 | 0 | 3 | 1 | 0 | 3 | 0 | 11 | 0 | 0 |
| Rivas, Rafael, Florence† | .272 | 105 | 382 | 69 | 104 | 161 | 19 | 1 | 12 | 61 | 7 | 0 | 3 | 8 | 40 | 2 | 106 | 4 | 2 |
| Rivera, Luis, Gastonia | .000 | 4 | 6 | 1 | 0 | 0 | 0 | 0 | 0 | 0 | 0 | 0 | 0 | 0 | 4 | 0 | 4 | 0 | 0 |
| Rivera, Pablo, Charleston | .285 | 133 | 470 | 73 | 134 | 179 | 22 | 4 | 5 | 57 | 8 | 6 | 4 | 7 | 37 | 0 | 53 | 21 | 5 |
| Robertson, Michael, Savannah | .077 | 24 | 13 | 2 | 1 | 1 | 0 | 0 | 0 | 0 | 0 | 2 | 0 | 0 | 3 | 0 | 3 | 0 | 0 |
| Robertson, Randy, Charleston | .231 | 14 | 13 | 1 | 3 | 5 | 2 | 0 | 0 | 1 | 0 | 1 | 0 | 0 | 2 | 0 | 4 | 0 | 0 |
| Roca, Gilberto, Macon | .227 | 18 | 44 | 1 | 10 | 13 | 3 | 0 | 0 | 6 | 0 | 0 | 0 | 1 | 2 | 0 | 11 | 0 | 0 |
| Rodriguez, Aristides, Asheville | .184 | 21 | 38 | 3 | 7 | 8 | 1 | 0 | 0 | 5 | 0 | 2 | 2 | 1 | 0 | 0 | 9 | 0 | 0 |
| Rodriguez, Manuel, Gastonia | .212 | 26 | 66 | 11 | 14 | 15 | 1 | 0 | 0 | 0 | 0 | 0 | 1 | 9 | 1 | 21 | 2 | 0 |
| Rodriguez, Richard, Columbia° | .000 | 49 | 8 | 0 | 0 | 0 | 0 | 0 | 0 | 0 | 0 | 1 | 0 | 0 | 0 | 0 | 6 | 0 | 0 |
| Rooker, David, Macon | .421 | 19 | 19 | 4 | 8 | 18 | 0 | 2 | 2 | 8 | 1 | 0 | 0 | 0 | 2 | 0 | 3 | 0 | 1 |
| Roque, Gustavo, Macon | .159 | 105 | 302 | 18 | 48 | 54 | 4 | 1 | 0 | 23 | 1 | 7 | 4 | 2 | 26 | 0 | 75 | 9 | 4 |
| Ross, Cordell, Gastonia† | .300 | 29 | 110 | 23 | 33 | 39 | 6 | 0 | 0 | 9 | 1 | 1 | 1 | 1 | 10 | 0 | 29 | 1 | 4 |
| Russell, Ronald, Gastonia† | .208 | 84 | 240 | 26 | 50 | 59 | 7 | 1 | 0 | 16 | 1 | 5 | 1 | 2 | 29 | 0 | 48 | 7 | 10 |
| Rypien, Timothy, Florence | .250 | 11 | 36 | 4 | 9 | 10 | 1 | 0 | 0 | 8 | 1 | 0 | 1 | 0 | 2 | 0 | 9 | 0 | 0 |
| Salisbury, James, Sumter | .000 | 33 | 3 | 0 | 0 | 0 | 0 | 0 | 0 | 0 | 0 | 0 | 0 | 0 | 0 | 0 | 3 | 0 | 0 |
| Sanchez, Juan, Spartanburg | .234 | 87 | 329 | 42 | 77 | 109 | 20 | 3 | 2 | 43 | 5 | 0 | 2 | 1 | 7 | 0 | 71 | 8 | 6 |
| Sanchez, Zoilo, Columbia | .236 | 129 | 496 | 68 | 117 | 189 | 21 | 3 | 15 | 94 | 11 | 1 | 9 | 10 | 54 | 1 | 118 | 7 | 2 |
| Sarmiento, Ramon, Gastonia | .320 | 24 | 75 | 15 | 24 | 35 | 3 | 1 | 2 | 8 | 1 | 0 | 0 | 3 | 14 | 0 | 23 | 9 | 1 |
| Satzinger, Jeffrey, Macon | .000 | 10 | 7 | 0 | 0 | 0 | 0 | 0 | 0 | 0 | 0 | 0 | 0 | 0 | 0 | 0 | 2 | 0 | 0 |
| Scales, Richard, Charleston | .205 | 78 | 171 | 27 | 35 | 41 | 6 | 0 | 0 | 6 | 0 | 0 | 1 | 2 | 18 | 0 | 35 | 6 | 2 |
| Scanlan, Robert, Spartanburg | .133 | 26 | 15 | 1 | 2 | 2 | 0 | 0 | 0 | 1 | 0 | 2 | 0 | 0 | 1 | 0 | 8 | 0 | 0 |
| Schaum, Brian, Macon | .237 | 49 | 156 | 18 | 37 | 46 | 6 | 0 | 1 | 11 | 1 | 8 | 0 | 0 | 19 | 1 | 29 | 9 | 3 |
| Scott, Tary, Greensboro | .244 | 85 | 324 | 39 | 79 | 128 | 16 | 0 | 11 | 56 | 10 | 0 | 5 | 2 | 24 | 1 | 74 | 0 | 0 |
| Shelton, Michael, Spartanburg | .000 | 51 | 3 | 1 | 0 | 0 | 0 | 0 | 0 | 0 | 0 | 0 | 0 | 0 | 0 | 0 | 3 | 0 | 0 |
| Sherlock, Glenn, Asheville° | .274 | 22 | 62 | 5 | 17 | 23 | 3 | 0 | 1 | 8 | 1 | 0 | 0 | 4 | 1 | 0 | 8 | 0 | 0 |
| Siblerud, Daniel, Spartanburg | .000 | 38 | 5 | 1 | 0 | 0 | 0 | 0 | 0 | 1 | 0 | 0 | 0 | 0 | 1 | 0 | 3 | 0 | 0 |
| Siebert, Richard, Sumter | .188 | 28 | 16 | 2 | 3 | 3 | 0 | 0 | 0 | 0 | 0 | 1 | 0 | 0 | 0 | 0 | 7 | 0 | 0 |

| Player and Club | Pct. | G. | AB. | R. | H. | TB. | 2B. | 3B. | HR. | RBI. | GW. | SH. | SF. | HP. | BB. | Int. BB. | SO. | SB. | CS. |
|---|---|---|---|---|---|---|---|---|---|---|---|---|---|---|---|---|---|---|---|
| Silver, Roy, Savannah† | .288 | 118 | 410 | 53 | 118 | 152 | 15 | 2 | 5 | 44 | 2 | 2 | 7 | 5 | 36 | 1 | 49 | 14 | 5 |
| Smiley, John, Macon° | .167 | 16 | 18 | 0 | 3 | 3 | 0 | 0 | 0 | 0 | 0 | 1 | 0 | 1 | 0 | 4 | 0 | 0 |  |
| Smith, Henry, Asheville | .105 | 11 | 19 | 1 | 2 | 2 | 0 | 0 | 0 | 0 | 0 | 0 | 0 | 0 | 3 | 0 | 8 | 0 | 0 |
| Smith, Todd, Macon | .187 | 101 | 326 | 31 | 61 | 82 | 10 | 4 | 1 | 33 | 2 | 0 | 2 | 2 | 30 | 1 | 111 | 15 | 6 |
| Snowberger, Thomas, Gastonia° | .194 | 31 | 67 | 12 | 13 | 18 | 2 | 0 | 1 | 3 | 0 | 0 | 0 | 1 | 10 | 0 | 26 | 2 | 1 |
| Snyder, Doug, Asheville° | .252 | 54 | 163 | 27 | 41 | 57 | 8 | 1 | 2 | 15 | 0 | 3 | 1 | 0 | 26 | 0 | 21 | 6 | 0 |
| Soto, Miguel, Savannah | .225 | 127 | 431 | 34 | 97 | 110 | 5 | 4 | 0 | 28 | 5 | 4 | 4 | 1 | 17 | 0 | 51 | 6 | 10 |
| Stading, Gregory, Macon | .118 | 33 | 17 | 1 | 2 | 2 | 0 | 0 | 0 | 2 | 0 | 1 | 0 | 0 | 7 | 0 | 0 | 0 |  |
| Stampfl, Eric, Columbia | .200 | 23 | 15 | 3 | 3 | 4 | 1 | 0 | 0 | 1 | 0 | 3 | 0 | 0 | 1 | 0 | 6 | 0 | 0 |
| Stark, Matthew, Florence | .297 | 110 | 381 | 66 | 113 | 167 | 15 | 0 | 13 | 70 | 8 | 1 | 6 | 2 | 83 | 2 | 29 | 7 | 3 |
| Steen, Scott, Spartanburg | .231 | 86 | 264 | 26 | 61 | 90 | 12 | 1 | 5 | 35 | 3 | 0 | 3 | 3 | 43 | 0 | 84 | 2 | 2 |
| Stephens, Carl Ray, Savannah | .205 | 39 | 127 | 11 | 26 | 32 | 6 | 0 | 0 | 6 | 0 | 1 | 1 | 1 | 14 | 0 | 32 | 1 | 1 |
| Stevens, Michael, Macon | .236 | 58 | 182 | 21 | 43 | 70 | 6 | 0 | 7 | 25 | 5 | 1 | 2 | 1 | 17 | 0 | 58 | 3 | 0 |
| Stevenson, Craig, Asheville | .244 | 53 | 127 | 18 | 31 | 41 | 8 | 1 | 0 | 18 | 4 | 3 | 2 | 0 | 15 | 0 | 18 | 0 | 0 |
| Stewart, Jeffrey, Charleston | .000 | 26 | 18 | 2 | 0 | 0 | 0 | 0 | 0 | 0 | 0 | 3 | 0 | 3 | 0 | 10 | 0 | 0 |  |
| Stiles, William, Columbia | .200 | 37 | 5 | 0 | 1 | 2 | 1 | 0 | 0 | 1 | 0 | 0 | 0 | 0 | 0 | 0 | 3 | 0 | 0 |
| Stottlemyre, Melvin, Asheville | .308 | 14 | 13 | 1 | 4 | 6 | 2 | 0 | 0 | 1 | 0 | 0 | 0 | 0 | 6 | 0 | 5 | 0 | 0 |
| Suris, Jorge, Charleston | .000 | 5 | 2 | 2 | 0 | 0 | 0 | 0 | 0 | 0 | 0 | 0 | 0 | 0 | 0 | 0 | 0 | 0 | 0 |
| Swain, Steven, Asheville | .163 | 37 | 98 | 11 | 16 | 17 | 1 | 0 | 0 | 3 | 1 | 1 | 0 | 2 | 6 | 0 | 35 | 4 | 2 |
| Takach, David, Columbia° | .333 | 18 | 3 | 1 | 1 | 1 | 0 | 0 | 0 | 0 | 0 | 0 | 0 | 0 | 0 | 0 | 1 | 0 | 0 |
| Taylor, Paul, Asheville | .244 | 45 | 90 | 10 | 22 | 32 | 7 | 0 | 1 | 9 | 2 | 0 | 0 | 5 | 5 | 0 | 22 | 0 | 1 |
| Thompson, Scott, Columbia | .263 | 52 | 171 | 23 | 45 | 86 | 8 | 0 | 11 | 32 | 2 | 0 | 3 | 1 | 18 | 0 | 36 | 1 | 1 |
| Thomson, Robert, Gastonia | .187 | 39 | 123 | 7 | 23 | 31 | 5 | 0 | 1 | 10 | 0 | 1 | 0 | 1 | 8 | 0 | 24 | 0 | 2 |
| Todd, Kyle, Macon | .263 | 72 | 266 | 28 | 70 | 94 | 14 | 2 | 2 | 26 | 2 | 1 | 4 | 0 | 18 | 0 | 53 | 5 | 1 |
| Tonucci, Norman, Florence | .248 | 133 | 420 | 76 | 104 | 177 | 19 | 0 | 18 | 61 | 5 | 0 | 5 | 2 | 109 | 1 | 153 | 13 | 4 |
| Traylor, Keith, Columbia | .229 | 104 | 240 | 61 | 55 | 75 | 4 | 2 | 4 | 23 | 3 | 8 | 0 | 3 | 42 | 0 | 39 | 37 | 6 |
| Tubbs, Gregory, Sumter | .356 | 61 | 239 | 53 | 85 | 128 | 11 | 7 | 6 | 36 | 3 | 1 | 3 | 2 | 33 | 0 | 36 | 30 | 18 |
| Tunison, Mark, Spartanburg | .000 | 24 | 13 | 2 | 0 | 0 | 0 | 0 | 0 | 0 | 0 | 2 | 0 | 0 | 2 | 0 | 5 | 0 | 0 |
| Valverde, Miguel, Macon | .184 | 56 | 196 | 27 | 36 | 38 | 2 | 0 | 0 | 5 | 0 | 6 | 0 | 4 | 25 | 0 | 55 | 11 | 4 |
| Vargas, Jose, Asheville | .250 | 24 | 24 | 2 | 6 | 8 | 2 | 0 | 0 | 2 | 2 | 3 | 0 | 0 | 2 | 0 | 5 | 0 | 0 |
| Verrone, Stephen, Asheville | .111 | 32 | 9 | 1 | 1 | 1 | 0 | 0 | 0 | 0 | 0 | 0 | 0 | 0 | 1 | 0 | 4 | 0 | 0 |
| Villanueva, Juan, Columbia | .246 | 100 | 281 | 36 | 69 | 102 | 15 | 3 | 4 | 39 | 4 | 3 | 3 | 7 | 33 | 1 | 60 | 4 | 6 |
| Visor, Michael, Charleston | .121 | 31 | 33 | 2 | 4 | 5 | 1 | 0 | 0 | 2 | 1 | 6 | 0 | 0 | 1 | 0 | 11 | 1 | 0 |
| Vogel, George, Savannah | .206 | 118 | 355 | 57 | 73 | 100 | 10 | 1 | 5 | 24 | 4 | 14 | 3 | 4 | 60 | 1 | 80 | 36 | 14 |
| Wagner, Gerald, Sumter | .000 | 42 | 2 | 0 | 0 | 0 | 0 | 0 | 0 | 0 | 0 | 1 | 0 | 0 | 0 | 0 | 1 | 0 | 0 |
| Walters, Daniel, Asheville | .036 | 15 | 28 | 1 | 1 | 1 | 0 | 0 | 0 | 1 | 0 | 1 | 0 | 1 | 0 | 11 | 0 | 0 |  |
| Washington, Marc, Gastonia | .167 | 16 | 54 | 5 | 9 | 12 | 0 | 0 | 1 | 4 | 0 | 0 | 1 | 10 | 0 | 16 | 4 | 2 |  |
| Wellman, Phillip, Sumter† | .269 | 123 | 383 | 78 | 103 | 196 | 26 | 2 | 21 | 78 | 9 | 0 | 5 | 10 | 105 | 3 | 85 | 16 | 5 |
| West, David, Columbia° | .174 | 28 | 23 | 4 | 4 | 4 | 0 | 0 | 0 | 2 | 0 | 1 | 0 | 5 | 0 | 9 | 0 | 0 |  |
| Westbrook, Michael, Columbia° | .305 | 118 | 377 | 80 | 115 | 137 | 11 | 4 | 1 | 46 | 4 | 4 | 1 | 5 | 67 | 1 | 48 | 57 | 15 |
| Wheeler, Rodney, Spartanburg° | .261 | 116 | 410 | 70 | 107 | 129 | 11 | 1 | 3 | 35 | 4 | 1 | 2 | 2 | 63 | 3 | 47 | 41 | 16 |
| Whitaker, Kevin, Savannah | .000 | 5 | 1 | 0 | 0 | 0 | 0 | 0 | 0 | 0 | 0 | 0 | 0 | 0 | 0 | 0 | 1 | 0 | 0 |
| White, Calvin, Spartanburg | .000 | 10 | 2 | 0 | 0 | 0 | 0 | 0 | 0 | 0 | 0 | 0 | 0 | 0 | 0 | 0 | 0 | 0 | 0 |
| Williams, Jaime, Asheville | .304 | 98 | 336 | 50 | 102 | 158 | 19 | 2 | 11 | 58 | 3 | 1 | 4 | 2 | 44 | 3 | 50 | 2 | 2 |
| Williams, Steven, Spartanburg° | .224 | 124 | 434 | 47 | 97 | 160 | 21 | 0 | 14 | 60 | 5 | 0 | 5 | 0 | 51 | 4 | 89 | 5 | 0 |
| Wilson, Allen, Columbia | .221 | 56 | 154 | 17 | 34 | 42 | 5 | 0 | 1 | 12 | 1 | 1 | 0 | 31 | 1 | 47 | 1 | 2 |  |
| Young, Shane, Columbia° | .303 | 26 | 33 | 1 | 10 | 12 | 2 | 0 | 0 | 9 | 1 | 2 | 0 | 0 | 5 | 0 | 4 | 0 | 0 |
| Zambrano, Eduardo, Greensboro | .271 | 115 | 443 | 63 | 120 | 146 | 17 | 3 | 1 | 51 | 6 | 1 | 5 | 13 | 31 | 0 | 61 | 1 | 1 |
| Zambrano, Roberto, Greensboro | .291 | 112 | 378 | 77 | 110 | 200 | 25 | 4 | 19 | 79 | 6 | 0 | 3 | 4 | 69 | 1 | 96 | 1 | 1 |

The following pitchers, listed alphabetically by club, with games in parentheses, had no plate appearances, primarily through use of designated hitters:

ASHEVILLE—Mangham, Mark (8); Metoyer, Tony (5).

CHARLESTON—Rodriguez, Ramon (11).

COLUMBIA—Givens, Brian (3).

FLORENCE—Anthony, Dane (40); Bautista, Camilo (15); Burgos, Enrique (26); Diaz, Victor (8); Englund, Timothy (32); Ferlenda, Gregory (35); Holbrook, Robert (37); Humphries, Bobbie Joe (6); Johnson, Dane (10); Mejia, Cesar (7); Moyer, Richard (23); Mumaw, Stephen (11); Provence, Todd (28); Saitta, Patrick (27); Wasilewski, Thomas (32).

GASTONIA—Burduan, Rafael (26); Butters, David (6); Delgado, Jose (6); Duffy, Thomas (35); Edge, Michael (8); Hill, Kenneth (15); Johnson, Jason (25); McBee, Robert (1); Meads, David (33); Morrow, Benjamin (19); Nicholson, Keith (21); Ocharzak, David (24); Raubolt, Arthur (17); Schedeneck, James (30); Schultz, Scott (13); Stock, Ronald (5); Williams, Kenneth (11).

GREENSBORO—Abril, Ernest (22); Corsi, James (41); Crouch, Zachary (26); Gakeler, Daniel (23); Hetzel, Eric (15); Irvine, Daryl (8); Lockhart, Bruce (35); Manzanillo, Josia (7); Mettler, Bradley (22); Peterson, David (43); Skripko, Scott (28); Stephenson, Joseph (15); Tremblay, Wayne (20).

SAVANNAH—Farley, Brian (1); Valliant, Robert (6).

SPARTANBURG—Simpson, Gregory (13).

SUMTER—Stringfellow, Thornton (5).

GRAND SLAM HOME RUNS—Z. Sanchez, 2; Bonk, Campusano, Coffman, Denson, Hampton, Hufford, Hurtado, Jelks, Lynn, Mikulik, Palmer, Pounders, Prince, Rivas, Rooker, J. Sanchez, Stark, Tonucci, Wellman, R. Zambrano, 1 each.

AWARDED FIRST BASE ON CATCHER'S INTERFERENCE—A. Cuevas 2 (Prince, J. Williams); Pierce 2 (J. Cuevas, A. Rodriguez); Constanzo (Thomson); Ducey (Brooks); Evans (G. Jones); Schaum (Brooks); Silver (G. Jones); Westbrook (Prince); Wilson (Roca).

## CLUB FIELDING

| Club | Pct. | G. | PO. | A. | E. | DP. | PB. | Club | Pct. | G. | PO. | A. | E. | DP. | PB. |
|---|---|---|---|---|---|---|---|---|---|---|---|---|---|---|---|
| Savannah | .965 | 136 | 3383 | 1371 | 174 | 91 | 18 | Greensboro | .953 | 137 | 3460 | 1302 | 233 | 111 | 38 |
| Asheville | .963 | 138 | 3549 | 1520 | 194 | 124 | 29 | Columbia | .953 | 136 | 3553 | 1400 | 244 | 127 | 40 |
| Sumter | .962 | 135 | 3542 | 1371 | 194 | 85 | 48 | Florence | .952 | 137 | 3499 | 1475 | 250 | 122 | 29 |
| Macon | .955 | 139 | 3577 | 1507 | 239 | 103 | 35 | Gastonia | .946 | 137 | 3477 | 1451 | 279 | 117 | 83 |
| Charleston | .955 | 139 | 3611 | 1392 | 238 | 104 | 23 | Spartanburg | .946 | 136 | 3458 | 1473 | 281 | 114 | 37 |

Triple Plays—Gastonia, Savannah.

## INDIVIDUAL FIELDING

°Throws lefthanded.

### FIRST BASEMEN

| Player and Club | Pct. | G. | PO. | A. | E. | DP. | Player and Club | Pct. | G. | PO. | A. | E. | DP. |
|---|---|---|---|---|---|---|---|---|---|---|---|---|---|
| Archibald, Columbia° | .973 | 7 | 35 | 1 | 1 | 4 | Bennett, Spartanburg | .990 | 10 | 90 | 11 | 1 | 8 |
| Barnard, Macon | .947 | 3 | 16 | 2 | 1 | 2 | Bonk, Greensboro | .990 | 24 | 181 | 8 | 2 | 20 |

## FIRST BASEMEN—Continued

| Player and Club | Pct. | G. | PO. | A. | E. | DP. |
|---|---|---|---|---|---|---|
| Cheek, Macon | .980 | 134 | 1070 | 102 | 24 | 84 |
| Clawson, Charleston | .931 | 7 | 27 | 0 | 2 | 3 |
| Clemente, Gastonia | 1.000 | 11 | 92 | 3 | 0 | 5 |
| Cooper, Gastonia | 1.000 | 2 | 4 | 1 | 0 | 0 |
| Criswell, Sumter | 1.000 | 1 | 1 | 0 | 0 | 0 |
| Cron, Sumter | .976 | 114 | 930 | 68 | 25 | 61 |
| Cunningham, Savannah | .965 | 10 | 72 | 10 | 3 | 6 |
| Cusack, Gastonia | .986 | 111 | 981 | 60 | 15 | 93 |
| DeLaCruz, Florence | .974 | 5 | 34 | 3 | 1 | 2 |
| DeLuca, Columbia | 1.000 | 1 | 8 | 0 | 0 | 0 |
| Dillard, Charleston* | 1.000 | 1 | 2 | 1 | 0 | 0 |
| Ducey, Florence | .972 | 4 | 34 | 1 | 1 | 1 |
| Dyrek, Asheville* | 1.000 | 1 | 7 | 0 | 0 | 1 |
| Fortenberry, Gastonia | .947 | 6 | 35 | 1 | 2 | 2 |
| Fulgencio, Gastonia | 1.000 | 4 | 15 | 1 | 0 | 1 |
| Howard, Florence | 1.000 | 16 | 119 | 11 | 0 | 9 |
| Hufford, Spartanburg | 1.000 | 1 | 1 | 1 | 0 | 0 |
| Jelks, Greensboro | .975 | 45 | 300 | 13 | 8 | 27 |
| Johnson, Macon | 1.000 | 7 | 45 | 1 | 0 | 3 |
| Jongewaard, Sumter | .976 | 30 | 183 | 17 | 5 | 9 |
| Kaiser, Spartanburg | .972 | 65 | 565 | 27 | 17 | 55 |
| Lynn, Columbia | .979 | 76 | 584 | 27 | 13 | 56 |
| Mathews, Savannah | .987 | 60 | 488 | 37 | 7 | 32 |
| McClain, Macon | 1.000 | 3 | 8 | 0 | 0 | 0 |
| McKnight, Columbia | 1.000 | 19 | 53 | 2 | 0 | 11 |
| Miller, Gastonia | .961 | 7 | 48 | 1 | 2 | 5 |
| Moreno, Charleston | 1.000 | 4 | 25 | 2 | 0 | 1 |
| Morrison, Florence | .833 | 1 | 4 | 1 | 1 | 0 |
| MUELLER, Asheville* | .994 | 132 | 1173 | 64 | 8 | 105 |
| Nowakowski, Florence | 1.000 | 2 | 12 | 0 | 0 | 1 |
| Parsons, Charleston | .986 | 10 | 66 | 4 | 1 | 2 |
| Perez, Columbia* | .996 | 63 | 452 | 27 | 2 | 42 |
| Pounders, Charleston | .984 | 124 | 1004 | 58 | 17 | 80 |
| Pregon, Savannah | .988 | 71 | 604 | 40 | 8 | 46 |
| Reyna, Florence* | 1.000 | 13 | 90 | 0 | 0 | 6 |
| Rivas, Florence | .979 | 99 | 838 | 56 | 19 | 84 |
| Russell, Gastonia | 1.000 | 1 | 8 | 0 | 0 | 0 |
| Rypien, Florence | 1.000 | 9 | 82 | 5 | 0 | 7 |
| Scott, Greensboro | .976 | 75 | 547 | 33 | 14 | 48 |
| Taylor, Asheville | .976 | 13 | 79 | 1 | 2 | 6 |
| J. Williams, Asheville | 1.000 | 1 | 5 | 0 | 0 | 0 |
| S. Williams, Spartanburg | .990 | 65 | 573 | 34 | 6 | 46 |

Triple Plays—Fortenberry, Pregon.

## SECOND BASEMEN

| Player and Club | Pct. | G. | PO. | A. | E. | DP. |
|---|---|---|---|---|---|---|
| Alomar, Charleston | .944 | 129 | 282 | 313 | 35 | 61 |
| Ashkinazy, Greensboro | .970 | 129 | 334 | 321 | 20 | 67 |
| Clark, Macon | .935 | 50 | 99 | 118 | 15 | 19 |
| Cooley, Columbia | 1.000 | 4 | 0 | 2 | 0 | 0 |
| Crispin, Spartanburg | .892 | 19 | 31 | 35 | 8 | 8 |
| Elliott, Asheville | .956 | 126 | 228 | 312 | 25 | 66 |
| Escobar, Florence | .938 | 112 | 207 | 273 | 32 | 62 |
| Flores, Greensboro | .897 | 6 | 11 | 15 | 3 | 7 |
| Frazier, Spartanburg | .941 | 103 | 197 | 283 | 30 | 61 |
| Frierson, Gastonia | 1.000 | 1 | 0 | 2 | 0 | 0 |
| Fulgencio, Gastonia | 1.000 | 5 | 13 | 10 | 0 | 0 |
| Gambino, Macon | .939 | 34 | 75 | 78 | 10 | 16 |
| Gant, Sumter | .973 | 85 | 160 | 199 | 10 | 27 |
| GARDNER, Columbia | .971 | 122 | 284 | 349 | 19 | 86 |
| Gonzalez, Macon | .857 | 11 | 14 | 22 | 6 | 1 |
| Green, Asheville | 1.000 | 2 | 7 | 3 | 0 | 3 |
| Hall, Greensboro | .889 | 4 | 9 | 7 | 2 | 4 |
| Hill, Savannah | .885 | 22 | 47 | 38 | 11 | 7 |
| Howard, Florence | .932 | 30 | 48 | 75 | 9 | 17 |
| Iglesias, Savannah | .979 | 15 | 17 | 30 | 1 | 3 |
| Infante, Savannah | 1.000 | 1 | 2 | 1 | 0 | 0 |
| Jefferies, Columbia | 1.000 | 12 | 23 | 19 | 0 | 6 |
| Kinard, Savannah | .960 | 63 | 121 | 146 | 11 | 24 |
| Lawton, Columbia | .923 | 5 | 8 | 4 | 1 | 1 |
| Lemke, Sumter | .964 | 72 | 119 | 174 | 11 | 28 |
| Mack, Gastonia | .948 | 109 | 227 | 270 | 27 | 62 |
| McClain, Macon | 1.000 | 2 | 5 | 1 | 0 | 1 |
| McKnight, Columbia | .857 | 5 | 2 | 4 | 1 | 1 |
| McWilliams, Gastonia | .931 | 6 | 10 | 17 | 2 | 4 |
| Morrison, Florence | .000 | 2 | 0 | 0 | 1 | 0 |
| Pender, Macon | .800 | 1 | 4 | 0 | 1 | 1 |
| Powers, Sumter | .917 | 2 | 5 | 6 | 1 | 0 |
| Reboulet, Savannah | .988 | 40 | 81 | 88 | 2 | 17 |
| Reid, Charleston | .972 | 10 | 13 | 22 | 1 | 2 |
| Roque, Macon | .895 | 5 | 12 | 5 | 2 | 1 |
| Ross, Gastonia | .926 | 11 | 23 | 27 | 4 | 3 |
| Russell, Gastonia | .888 | 21 | 37 | 34 | 9 | 7 |
| Sanchez, Spartanburg | .937 | 28 | 40 | 64 | 7 | 9 |
| Scales, Charleston | .971 | 10 | 18 | 15 | 1 | 4 |
| Schaum, Macon | .945 | 44 | 87 | 103 | 11 | 18 |
| Soto, Savannah | 1.000 | 2 | 0 | 5 | 0 | 0 |
| Stevenson, Asheville | .934 | 25 | 30 | 41 | 5 | 8 |
| Suris, Charleston | 1.000 | 1 | 2 | 1 | 0 | 0 |
| Westbrook, Columbia | .917 | 2 | 1 | 10 | 1 | 0 |

Triple Play—Mack.

## THIRD BASEMEN

| Player and Club | Pct. | G. | PO. | A. | E. | DP. |
|---|---|---|---|---|---|---|
| Barnard, Macon | .883 | 37 | 21 | 70 | 12 | 3 |
| Bennett, Spartanburg | .833 | 1 | 1 | 4 | 1 | 0 |
| Blake, Gastonia | .826 | 19 | 10 | 28 | 8 | 1 |
| Byers, Charleston | .852 | 114 | 72 | 181 | 44 | 12 |
| Clawson, Charleston | .929 | 72 | 24 | 54 | 6 | 2 |
| Clemente, Gastonia | .813 | 6 | 6 | 7 | 3 | 1 |
| Cooley, Columbia | 1.000 | 2 | 2 | 3 | 0 | 0 |
| Crispin, Spartanburg | .883 | 38 | 22 | 76 | 13 | 3 |
| Cunningham, Savannah | .938 | 13 | 6 | 24 | 2 | 1 |
| DeLuca, Columbia | .632 | 8 | 3 | 9 | 7 | 2 |
| Flores, Greensboro | .813 | 8 | 7 | 6 | 3 | 1 |
| Frazier, Spartanburg | 1.000 | 1 | 0 | 4 | 0 | 1 |
| Fredymond, Sumter | .833 | 11 | 6 | 14 | 4 | 1 |
| Frierson, Gastonia | .727 | 4 | 2 | 6 | 3 | 1 |
| Fulgencio, Gastonia | .919 | 55 | 43 | 82 | 11 | 7 |
| Gonzalez, Macon | 1.000 | 4 | 2 | 4 | 0 | 0 |
| Green, Asheville | .857 | 2 | 1 | 5 | 1 | 0 |
| Hall, Greensboro | .844 | 36 | 25 | 56 | 15 | 8 |
| Howard, Florence | .818 | 10 | 0 | 9 | 2 | 1 |
| Hurtado, Spartanburg | .837 | 29 | 19 | 53 | 14 | 7 |
| Iglesias, Savannah | .857 | 4 | 0 | 6 | 1 | 0 |
| Infante, Savannah | .908 | 110 | 80 | 236 | 32 | 15 |
| Johnson, Sumter | .889 | 12 | 7 | 17 | 3 | 0 |
| Jongewaard, Sumter | .941 | 51 | 27 | 85 | 7 | 6 |
| Kinard, Savannah | .929 | 11 | 6 | 20 | 2 | 0 |
| Kwolek, Asheville | .937 | 67 | 40 | 168 | 14 | 11 |
| Leiper, Gastonia | .944 | 30 | 22 | 62 | 5 | 6 |
| McClain, Macon | .928 | 27 | 17 | 47 | 5 | 1 |
| McKnight, Columbia | .714 | 4 | 0 | 5 | 2 | 0 |
| McWilliams, Gastonia | .833 | 2 | 2 | 3 | 1 | 0 |
| Mitchell, Asheville | .909 | 61 | 48 | 142 | 19 | 10 |
| Nowakowski, Gastonia | 1.000 | 1 | 0 | 1 | 0 | 0 |
| Powers, Sumter | .924 | 71 | 68 | 126 | 16 | 8 |
| Pregon, Savannah | .750 | 4 | 2 | 7 | 3 | 0 |
| Ross, Gastonia | .877 | 14 | 9 | 41 | 7 | 4 |
| Russell, Gastonia | .778 | 12 | 3 | 11 | 4 | 1 |
| J. Sanchez, Spartanburg | 1.000 | 4 | 2 | 5 | 0 | 0 |
| Z. SANCHEZ, Columbia | .918 | 128 | 80 | 276 | 32 | 24 |
| Scales, Charleston | 1.000 | 12 | 4 | 7 | 0 | 1 |
| Soto, Savannah | .667 | 1 | 0 | 2 | 1 | 0 |
| Steen, Spartanburg | .825 | 69 | 38 | 103 | 30 | 9 |
| Stevenson, Asheville | .955 | 11 | 6 | 15 | 1 | 3 |
| Taylor, Asheville | .882 | 7 | 3 | 12 | 2 | 0 |
| Thomson, Gastonia | .815 | 24 | 16 | 37 | 12 | 3 |
| Todd, Macon | .912 | 72 | 63 | 134 | 19 | 14 |
| Tonucci, Florence | .911 | 133 | 95 | 255 | 34 | 27 |
| Villanueva, Columbia | .200 | 2 | 0 | 1 | 4 | 0 |
| Wellman, Sumter | .000 | 2 | 0 | 0 | 4 | 0 |
| Williams, Spartanburg | .857 | 3 | 1 | 5 | 1 | 2 |
| R. Zambrano, Greensboro | .859 | 100 | 66 | 160 | 37 | 13 |

## SHORTSTOPS

| Player and Club | Pct. | G. | PO. | A. | E. | DP. |
|---|---|---|---|---|---|---|
| Adkins, Gastonia | .905 | 115 | 156 | 312 | 49 | 59 |
| Alomar, Charleston | .977 | 8 | 16 | 26 | 1 | 5 |
| Blauser, Sumter | .929 | 117 | 150 | 306 | 35 | 36 |
| Clawson, Charleston | .965 | 24 | 18 | 65 | 3 | 8 |
| Cooley, Columbia | .889 | 4 | 2 | 6 | 1 | 1 |
| Crispin, Spartanburg | .959 | 11 | 13 | 34 | 2 | 6 |
| Diaz, Florence | .750 | 2 | 2 | 1 | 1 | 0 |
| Elliott, Asheville | 1.000 | 2 | 6 | 8 | 0 | 3 |
| Escobar, Florence | .600 | 1 | 0 | 3 | 2 | 0 |
| Flores, Greensboro | .783 | 9 | 6 | 12 | 5 | 4 |
| Fredymond, Sumter | .979 | 19 | 13 | 33 | 1 | 5 |
| Fulgencio, Gastonia | .884 | 29 | 30 | 69 | 13 | 9 |
| Gant, Sumter | 1.000 | 2 | 0 | 1 | 0 | 0 |
| Garcia, Florence | .904 | 128 | 165 | 390 | 59 | 69 |
| Gonzalez, Macon | .897 | 7 | 10 | 16 | 3 | 3 |
| Green, Asheville | .937 | 123 | 171 | 350 | 35 | 76 |
| Howard, Florence | .941 | 9 | 15 | 17 | 2 | 4 |
| Jefferies, Columbia | .857 | 3 | 5 | 7 | 2 | 1 |

## SHORTSTOPS—Continued

| Player and Club | Pct. | G. | PO. | A. | E. | DP. | Player and Club | Pct. | G. | PO. | A. | E. | DP. |
|---|---|---|---|---|---|---|---|---|---|---|---|---|---|
| I. Johnson, Spartanburg | .920 | 76 | 105 | 228 | 29 | 43 | Reid, Charleston | .916 | 85 | 128 | 208 | 31 | 35 |
| Kinard, Savannah | .980 | 12 | 16 | 32 | 1 | 6 | Roque, Macon | .939 | 96 | 146 | 286 | 28 | 50 |
| Kwolek, Asheville | 1.000 | 2 | 0 | 4 | 0 | 0 | Ross, Gastonia | .783 | 5 | 10 | 8 | 5 | 2 |
| Lawton, Columbia | .865 | 56 | 72 | 120 | 30 | 31 | Russell, Gastonia | .600 | 5 | 3 | 3 | 4 | 1 |
| McClain, Macon | .800 | 1 | 3 | 1 | 1 | 0 | Sanchez, Spartanburg | .923 | 57 | 80 | 194 | 23 | 31 |
| McKnight, Columbia | 1.000 | 3 | 4 | 4 | 0 | 1 | Scales, Charleston | .911 | 42 | 49 | 84 | 13 | 18 |
| Moritz, Greensboro | .926 | 134 | 200 | 399 | 48 | 63 | SOTO, Savannah | .947 | 125 | 192 | 324 | 29 | 50 |
| Pierce, Macon | .952 | 51 | 65 | 152 | 11 | 20 | Stevenson, Asheville | .894 | 16 | 12 | 30 | 5 | 6 |
| Powers, Sumter | .977 | 13 | 12 | 30 | 1 | 6 | Villanueva, Columbia | .907 | 96 | 114 | 247 | 37 | 47 |

## OUTFIELDERS

| Player and Club | Pct. | G. | PO. | A. | E. | DP. | Player and Club | Pct. | G. | PO. | A. | E. | DP. |
|---|---|---|---|---|---|---|---|---|---|---|---|---|---|
| Alomar, Charleston | 1.000 | 1 | 1 | 0 | 0 | 0 | Lemon, Savannah* | 1.000 | 5 | 19 | 0 | 0 | 0 |
| Barrios, Greensboro | .974 | 57 | 107 | 7 | 3 | 4 | Llewellyn, Sumter | 1.000 | 22 | 35 | 3 | 0 | 1 |
| Berroa, Florence | .923 | 19 | 24 | 0 | 2 | 0 | Lowe, Gastonia | 1.000 | 28 | 61 | 5 | 0 | 0 |
| Blaine, Savannah | .978 | 27 | 44 | 1 | 1 | 1 | Mack, Gastonia | 1.000 | 3 | 3 | 0 | 0 | 0 |
| Brock, Asheville* | .927 | 58 | 83 | 6 | 7 | 3 | Martinez, Gastonia | .938 | 65 | 98 | 7 | 7 | 1 |
| Campusano, Florence | .980 | 88 | 188 | 12 | 4 | 5 | Mathews, Savannah | .909 | 4 | 10 | 0 | 1 | 0 |
| Carter, Savannah | .967 | 13 | 27 | 2 | 1 | 1 | Mauch, Savannah | 1.000 | 10 | 8 | 0 | 0 | 0 |
| Chance, 6 Mac-55 Gas | .964 | 61 | 128 | 4 | 5 | 0 | McClain, Macon | .692 | 13 | 7 | 2 | 4 | 0 |
| Clemente, Gastonia | .857 | 15 | 11 | 1 | 2 | 0 | McCray, Charleston | .936 | 115 | 177 | 13 | 13 | 3 |
| Contreras, Columbia* | .966 | 15 | 26 | 2 | 1 | 0 | McKnight, Columbia | .971 | 27 | 33 | 1 | 1 | 0 |
| Cooper, Gastonia | 1.000 | 1 | 1 | 1 | 0 | 0 | Mikulik, Asheville | .991 | 131 | 207 | 7 | 2 | 2 |
| Cuevas, Columbia | .937 | 118 | 201 | 21 | 15 | 0 | Minick, Gastonia* | 1.000 | 26 | 32 | 2 | 0 | 0 |
| Cusack, Gastonia | .667 | 2 | 2 | 0 | 1 | 0 | Mitchell, Asheville | 1.000 | 4 | 3 | 0 | 0 | 0 |
| Dantzler, Spartanburg | .914 | 100 | 145 | 3 | 14 | 0 | Moreno, Charleston | 1.000 | 3 | 4 | 0 | 0 | 0 |
| DeLaCruz, Florence | .875 | 12 | 12 | 2 | 2 | 1 | Morrison, Florence | .933 | 14 | 14 | 0 | 1 | 0 |
| Denson, Sumter | .976 | 93 | 119 | 5 | 3 | 1 | Murphy, Savannah | .971 | 130 | 193 | 8 | 6 | 0 |
| Dillard, Charleston* | .875 | 17 | 13 | 1 | 2 | 1 | Nowakowski, 7 Gas-2 Flo | 1.000 | 9 | 13 | 1 | 0 | 0 |
| Ducey, Florence | .962 | 129 | 194 | 7 | 8 | 1 | Parsons, Charleston | .957 | 58 | 79 | 9 | 4 | 2 |
| Dyrek, Asheville* | 1.000 | 27 | 38 | 3 | 0 | 0 | Pender, Macon | 1.000 | 25 | 53 | 3 | 0 | 0 |
| Evans, Macon | .987 | 34 | 72 | 4 | 1 | 3 | F. Perez, Spartanburg | .884 | 21 | 33 | 5 | 5 | 0 |
| Fortenberry, Gastonia | .936 | 89 | 156 | 6 | 11 | 0 | H. Perez, Columbia* | 1.000 | 1 | 1 | 0 | 0 | 0 |
| Frazier, Sumter | .951 | 112 | 188 | 8 | 10 | 2 | Reid, Charleston | 1.000 | 3 | 5 | 1 | 0 | 0 |
| Frierson, Gastonia | .988 | 58 | 78 | 7 | 1 | 2 | Reyna, Florence* | 1.000 | 4 | 6 | 0 | 0 | 0 |
| Gjesdal, Charleston | .965 | 125 | 182 | 12 | 7 | 4 | P. Rivera, Charleston | .976 | 132 | 270 | 10 | 7 | 4 |
| Gonzalez, Macon* | 1.000 | 2 | 2 | 0 | 0 | 0 | Rodriguez, Gastonia | .935 | 22 | 28 | 1 | 2 | 0 |
| Gregg, Macon* | .992 | 72 | 117 | 4 | 1 | 0 | Rooker, Macon | 1.000 | 1 | 1 | 0 | 0 | 0 |
| Hammonds, Macon | .978 | 50 | 81 | 7 | 2 | 0 | Russell, Gastonia | .968 | 38 | 58 | 2 | 2 | 0 |
| Hampton, Asheville* | .952 | 76 | 149 | 8 | 8 | 0 | Sarmiento, Gastonia | .972 | 17 | 34 | 1 | 1 | 0 |
| Howey, Spartanburg | .952 | 57 | 95 | 4 | 5 | 0 | SILVER, Savannah | .995 | 106 | 191 | 8 | 1 | 0 |
| Hufford, Spartanburg | .954 | 90 | 181 | 7 | 9 | 0 | H. Smith, Asheville | .875 | 6 | 6 | 1 | 1 | 1 |
| Hurtado, Spartanburg | 1.000 | 1 | 1 | 0 | 0 | 0 | T. Smith, Macon | .961 | 91 | 166 | 6 | 7 | 1 |
| Jackson, Greensboro | .978 | 79 | 130 | 6 | 3 | 0 | Snowberger, Gastonia | .909 | 17 | 19 | 1 | 2 | 0 |
| James, Asheville* | .965 | 59 | 132 | 5 | 5 | 1 | Snyder, Asheville | .980 | 42 | 46 | 3 | 1 | 1 |
| Jaster, Columbia | 1.000 | 10 | 15 | 1 | 0 | 1 | Steen, Spartanburg | 1.000 | 1 | 2 | 0 | 0 | 0 |
| Jelks, Greensboro | .943 | 61 | 108 | 7 | 7 | 2 | Stevens, Macon | .892 | 43 | 64 | 2 | 8 | 0 |
| J. Johnson, Macon | .956 | 32 | 39 | 4 | 2 | 0 | Swain, Asheville | .905 | 27 | 34 | 4 | 4 | 1 |
| R. Johnson, Spartanburg | 1.000 | 1 | 1 | 0 | 0 | 0 | Thompson, Columbia | .959 | 33 | 43 | 4 | 2 | 0 |
| L. Jones, Sumter | .958 | 43 | 67 | 1 | 3 | 1 | Traylor, Columbia | .970 | 89 | 122 | 7 | 4 | 2 |
| M. Jones, Florence | .943 | 34 | 47 | 3 | 3 | 1 | Tubbs, Sumter | .961 | 58 | 93 | 6 | 4 | 3 |
| Jongewaard, Sumter | .923 | 13 | 12 | 0 | 1 | 0 | Valverde, Macon | .928 | 54 | 111 | 5 | 9 | 2 |
| Jose, Greensboro | .938 | 111 | 244 | 12 | 17 | 4 | Vogel, Savannah | .980 | 117 | 231 | 13 | 5 | 2 |
| Kaiser, Spartanburg | .945 | 48 | 82 | 4 | 5 | 0 | Washington, Gastonia | 1.000 | 15 | 27 | 1 | 0 | 0 |
| Kiluk, Macon | .909 | 17 | 18 | 2 | 2 | 0 | Wellman, Sumter | .962 | 100 | 163 | 12 | 7 | 0 |
| Kinard, Savannah | .905 | 8 | 18 | 1 | 2 | 1 | Westbrook, Columbia | .938 | 107 | 152 | 13 | 11 | 1 |
| Kwolek, Asheville | 1.000 | 7 | 6 | 1 | 0 | 0 | Wheeler, Spartanburg* | .955 | 107 | 231 | 4 | 11 | 0 |
| Landrum, Florence | .916 | 130 | 221 | 9 | 21 | 1 | E. Zambrano, Greensboro | .979 | 113 | 221 | 10 | 5 | 1 |
| Lawton, Columbia | .949 | 66 | 143 | 5 | 8 | 2 | R. Zambrano, Greensboro | 1.000 | 6 | 8 | 1 | 0 | 0 |

## CATCHERS

| Player and Club | Pct. | G. | PO. | A. | E. | DP. | PB. | Player and Club | Pct. | G. | PO. | A. | E. | DP. | PB. |
|---|---|---|---|---|---|---|---|---|---|---|---|---|---|---|---|
| Alomar, Charleston | .979 | 100 | 778 | 75 | 18 | 7 | 14 | Johnson, Spartanburg | .960 | 21 | 142 | 24 | 7 | 2 | 9 |
| Bautista, Macon | 1.000 | 7 | 11 | 0 | 0 | 0 | 2 | Jones, Florence | .927 | 7 | 46 | 5 | 4 | 0 | 2 |
| Benkert, Macon | .984 | 12 | 60 | 3 | 1 | 0 | 1 | Karr, Columbia | .978 | 9 | 81 | 9 | 2 | 3 | 2 |
| Bennett, Spartanburg | .969 | 31 | 172 | 14 | 6 | 4 | 2 | Lawrence, Gastonia | 1.000 | 1 | 4 | 3 | 0 | 0 | 1 |
| Billinger, Savannah | .989 | 13 | 85 | 7 | 1 | 0 | 0 | Marquardt, Florence | 1.000 | 4 | 17 | 1 | 0 | 0 | 0 |
| Blake, Gastonia | .963 | 12 | 49 | 3 | 2 | 1 | 4 | E. Martinez, 48 Gas-4 Spt | .974 | 52 | 227 | 40 | 7 | 3 | 23 |
| Bonk, Greensboro | .981 | 46 | 280 | 22 | 6 | 1 | 20 | M. Martinez, Gastonia | .958 | 4 | 21 | 2 | 1 | 0 | 4 |
| Brooks, Columbia | .982 | 80 | 509 | 25 | 10 | 2 | 15 | Moreno, Charleston | 1.000 | 5 | 29 | 4 | 0 | 2 | 0 |
| Brunswick, Columbia | 1.000 | 6 | 29 | 6 | 0 | 1 | 4 | MYERS, Charleston | .989 | 76 | 551 | 61 | 7 | 8 | 18 |
| Camilli, Greensboro | .978 | 22 | 123 | 8 | 3 | 1 | 3 | Nowakowski, 38 Gas-2 Flo | .955 | 40 | 197 | 38 | 11 | 2 | 20 |
| Carrion, Asheville | .971 | 31 | 181 | 18 | 6 | 0 | 7 | Prince, Macon | .980 | 117 | 810 | 101 | 19 | 10 | 27 |
| Cisco, Charleston | .980 | 40 | 277 | 23 | 6 | 3 | 9 | Rivera, Gastonia | .875 | 2 | 11 | 3 | 2 | 0 | 4 |
| Constanzo, Sumter | .971 | 51 | 312 | 28 | 10 | 1 | 12 | Roca, Macon | .963 | 11 | 73 | 5 | 3 | 0 | 4 |
| Cooper, Gastonia | 1.000 | 6 | 30 | 1 | 0 | 0 | 3 | Rodriguez, Asheville | .946 | 18 | 76 | 11 | 5 | 0 | 4 |
| Criswell, Sumter | .996 | 39 | 250 | 19 | 1 | 1 | 15 | Rypien, Florence | 1.000 | 2 | 5 | 1 | 0 | 0 | 1 |
| Cuevas, Sumter | .981 | 74 | 565 | 56 | 12 | 2 | 21 | Sherlock, Asheville | .977 | 21 | 115 | 15 | 3 | 0 | 3 |
| Dantzler, Spartanburg | .889 | 1 | 7 | 1 | 1 | 0 | 0 | Stark, Florence | .962 | 58 | 392 | 36 | 17 | 4 | 10 |
| DeFrancesco, Greensboro | .974 | 47 | 292 | 42 | 9 | 5 | 9 | Stephens, Savannah | .985 | 39 | 229 | 30 | 4 | 1 | 5 |
| DePrimo, Greensboro | .983 | 34 | 213 | 15 | 4 | 1 | 6 | Thomson, Gastonia | .949 | 13 | 69 | 6 | 4 | 0 | 3 |
| Ferreiras, 6 Mac-51 Gas | .965 | 57 | 322 | 33 | 13 | 2 | 23 | Walters, Asheville | .969 | 13 | 54 | 8 | 2 | 0 | 4 |
| Gsellman, Spartanburg | .968 | 37 | 191 | 21 | 7 | 1 | 6 | J. Williams, Asheville | .983 | 82 | 549 | 73 | 11 | 5 | 13 |
| Isner, Savannah | .982 | 55 | 284 | 38 | 6 | 1 | 12 | S. Williams, Spartanburg | .983 | 51 | 318 | 34 | 6 | 1 | 19 |
| Jimenez, Savannah | .969 | 35 | 229 | 18 | 8 | 0 | 1 | Wilson, Columbia | .974 | 53 | 353 | 27 | 10 | 1 | 17 |

## PITCHERS

| Player and Club | Pct. | G. | PO. | A. | E. | DP. |
|---|---|---|---|---|---|---|
| Abril, Greensboro | .815 | 22 | 7 | 15 | 5 | 1 |
| Adams, Columbia | .875 | 24 | 7 | 14 | 3 | 1 |
| Agar, Gastonia | 1.000 | 37 | 2 | 9 | 0 | 0 |
| Andersh, Macon° | .906 | 27 | 9 | 39 | 5 | 0 |
| Anthony, Florence | .960 | 40 | 5 | 19 | 1 | 2 |
| Arnold, Savannah | .868 | 24 | 12 | 21 | 5 | 2 |
| Arnsberg, Asheville | 1.000 | 7 | 4 | 6 | 0 | 1 |
| Atkinson, Savannah | .960 | 28 | 4 | 20 | 1 | 0 |
| Barba, Columbia | .688 | 32 | 4 | 7 | 5 | 0 |
| Bates, Savannah° | 1.000 | 13 | 2 | 7 | 0 | 1 |
| Bautista, Florence | .857 | 15 | 1 | 5 | 1 | 1 |
| Behrend, Savannah | .938 | 14 | 10 | 20 | 2 | 0 |
| Bitker, Charleston | .963 | 13 | 6 | 20 | 1 | 0 |
| Broussard, Spartanburg° | .842 | 27 | 1 | 15 | 3 | 1 |
| BURDUAN, Gastonia | 1.000 | 26 | 7 | 11 | 0 | 0 |
| Burgos, Florence° | .833 | 26 | 3 | 12 | 3 | 0 |
| Butters, Gastonia | 1.000 | 6 | 1 | 0 | 0 | 0 |
| Cash, Sumter° | .880 | 20 | 4 | 18 | 3 | 0 |
| Cepeda, Macon | 1.000 | 10 | 4 | 2 | 0 | 0 |
| Chambers, Spartanburg | 1.000 | 12 | 4 | 6 | 0 | 1 |
| Ciszkowski, Columbia | .903 | 25 | 9 | 19 | 3 | 2 |
| Clossen, Sumter | 1.000 | 26 | 3 | 11 | 0 | 0 |
| Coffman, Sumter | 1.000 | 24 | 2 | 14 | 0 | 2 |
| Colpitt, Spartanburg | 1.000 | 22 | 4 | 6 | 0 | 0 |
| Cooper, Gastonia | .900 | 11 | 2 | 7 | 1 | 0 |
| Corsi, Greensboro | 1.000 | 41 | 2 | 12 | 0 | 0 |
| Costello, Charleston | .947 | 29 | 8 | 28 | 2 | 0 |
| Criswell, Sumter | 1.000 | 2 | 1 | 0 | 0 | 0 |
| Crossley, Savannah° | .833 | 23 | 1 | 14 | 3 | 0 |
| Crouch, Greensboro° | .969 | 26 | 6 | 25 | 1 | 0 |
| Cunningham, Macon | .714 | 9 | 1 | 4 | 2 | 0 |
| Czyzewski, Charleston | .895 | 31 | 5 | 12 | 2 | 0 |
| Davis, Florence | .938 | 49 | 3 | 12 | 1 | 0 |
| Delgado, Gastonia | 1.000 | 6 | 0 | 2 | 0 | 0 |
| Diaz, Florence° | 1.000 | 8 | 1 | 1 | 0 | 0 |
| Dillenberger, Savannah | 1.000 | 44 | 4 | 15 | 0 | 2 |
| Drummond, Macon | .925 | 27 | 22 | 27 | 4 | 0 |
| Duffy, Gastonia | .789 | 35 | 1 | 14 | 4 | 1 |
| Durocher, Asheville | .909 | 26 | 5 | 5 | 1 | 0 |
| Edge, Gastonia | 1.000 | 8 | 0 | 2 | 0 | 0 |
| Englund, Florence | .981 | 32 | 9 | 42 | 1 | 2 |
| Farley, Savannah | 1.000 | 1 | 0 | 1 | 0 | 0 |
| Ferlenda, Florence | .973 | 35 | 14 | 22 | 1 | 3 |
| Ford, Charleston | .964 | 66 | 4 | 23 | 1 | 0 |
| Franchi, Macon° | 1.000 | 26 | 1 | 6 | 0 | 0 |
| Friedel, Columbia | 1.000 | 10 | 3 | 0 | 0 | 0 |
| Funk, Asheville° | 1.000 | 40 | 2 | 8 | 0 | 1 |
| Gakeler, Greensboro | .789 | 23 | 6 | 9 | 4 | 0 |
| Gass, Savannah | .909 | 6 | 8 | 2 | 1 | 0 |
| Gay, Columbia | 1.000 | 6 | 4 | 11 | 0 | 0 |
| Gideon, Macon | .800 | 15 | 4 | 8 | 3 | 1 |
| Gildehaus, Charleston | .667 | 5 | 1 | 1 | 1 | 0 |
| Givens, Columbia | 1.000 | 3 | 2 | 2 | 0 | 1 |
| Glavine, Sumter° | .975 | 26 | 11 | 28 | 1 | 5 |
| Gozzo, Columbia | .917 | 49 | 4 | 7 | 1 | 2 |
| Greenlee, Charleston° | .900 | 35 | 2 | 34 | 4 | 1 |
| Grosdidier, Sumter | 1.000 | 33 | 3 | 11 | 0 | 0 |
| Groves, Sumter | .400 | 18 | 1 | 1 | 3 | 0 |
| Guzman, Sumter | .923 | 8 | 4 | 8 | 1 | 0 |
| Helton, Macon | 1.000 | 11 | 2 | 5 | 0 | 0 |
| Hendrix, Spartanburg | 1.000 | 16 | 2 | 2 | 0 | 0 |
| Heredia, Asheville | .905 | 19 | 9 | 10 | 2 | 1 |
| Hetzel, Greensboro | .833 | 15 | 2 | 8 | 2 | 1 |
| K. Hill, Gastonia | 1.000 | 15 | 4 | 16 | 0 | 2 |
| S. Hill, Savannah° | .966 | 27 | 6 | 22 | 1 | 1 |
| Holbrook, Florence | .958 | 37 | 7 | 16 | 1 | 0 |
| Hubbard, Charleston | .850 | 47 | 4 | 13 | 3 | 0 |
| Huchingson, Asheville | .930 | 23 | 8 | 32 | 3 | 3 |
| Humphries, Florence | .833 | 6 | 1 | 4 | 1 | 0 |
| Irvine, Greensboro | .667 | 8 | 2 | 0 | 1 | 0 |
| James, Columbia | 1.000 | 41 | 3 | 4 | 0 | 0 |
| Jimenez, Sumter | .950 | 35 | 4 | 15 | 1 | 0 |
| D. Johnson, Florence | 1.000 | 10 | 1 | 7 | 0 | 0 |
| J. Johnson, Gastonia | .962 | 25 | 5 | 20 | 1 | 0 |
| Kilner, Sumter° | .875 | 23 | 6 | 15 | 3 | 0 |
| Knox, Spartanburg | .944 | 22 | 8 | 26 | 2 | 3 |
| Kolb, Macon | .885 | 39 | 3 | 20 | 3 | 2 |
| Livin, Asheville | .900 | 27 | 4 | 23 | 3 | 0 |
| Lockhart, Greensboro° | .933 | 35 | 2 | 12 | 1 | 0 |
| Machado, Spartanburg | .947 | 32 | 8 | 10 | 1 | 0 |
| Mangham, Asheville | .800 | 8 | 0 | 4 | 1 | 0 |
| Manzanillo, Greensboro | 1.000 | 7 | 0 | 4 | 0 | 1 |
| Martin, Sumter | .857 | 43 | 1 | 5 | 1 | 1 |
| McBee, Gastonia | 1.000 | 1 | 1 | 0 | 0 | 0 |
| Meads, Gastonia° | .964 | 33 | 6 | 21 | 1 | 1 |
| Mejia, Florence | 1.000 | 7 | 1 | 3 | 0 | 0 |
| Mercedes, Macon | .909 | 54 | 4 | 16 | 2 | 1 |
| Merklen, Macon° | .971 | 50 | 11 | 23 | 1 | 2 |
| Metoyer, Asheville | 1.000 | 5 | 0 | 1 | 0 | 0 |
| Mettler, Greensboro | 1.000 | 22 | 4 | 11 | 0 | 0 |
| Miller, Spartanburg° | .912 | 25 | 8 | 23 | 3 | 0 |
| Moore, Asheville | .929 | 28 | 5 | 8 | 1 | 0 |
| Moreland, Columbia | 1.000 | 4 | 1 | 0 | 0 | 0 |
| Morelock, Sumter | .778 | 16 | 2 | 5 | 2 | 0 |
| Morrow, Gastonia | .778 | 19 | 3 | 4 | 2 | 0 |
| Moyer, Florence | 1.000 | 23 | 3 | 10 | 0 | 2 |
| Mumaw, Florence° | .778 | 11 | 3 | 4 | 2 | 0 |
| Newell, Spartanburg | .903 | 28 | 6 | 22 | 3 | 2 |
| Nicholson, Gastonia | .931 | 21 | 6 | 21 | 2 | 0 |
| Ocharzak, Gastonia | .882 | 24 | 12 | 18 | 4 | 1 |
| Palmer, Asheville° | .786 | 24 | 2 | 9 | 3 | 1 |
| Parker, Asheville | .964 | 34 | 3 | 24 | 1 | 1 |
| Parsons, Charleston | .800 | 7 | 1 | 3 | 1 | 0 |
| Perry, Savannah | .800 | 7 | 2 | 10 | 3 | 0 |
| Peterson, Greensboro | 1.000 | 43 | 4 | 11 | 0 | 0 |
| Pettit, Savannah | .953 | 42 | 15 | 26 | 2 | 0 |
| Plesac, Charleston | .833 | 19 | 2 | 8 | 2 | 1 |
| Provence, Florence | .937 | 28 | 11 | 48 | 4 | 1 |
| Raubolt, Gastonia | .943 | 17 | 7 | 26 | 2 | 1 |
| Richardson, Columbia | 1.000 | 5 | 3 | 8 | 0 | 0 |
| Ritter, Macon | .938 | 25 | 13 | 17 | 2 | 0 |
| M. Robertson, Savannah | .881 | 24 | 12 | 25 | 5 | 3 |
| R. Robertson, Charleston | .875 | 14 | 4 | 10 | 2 | 1 |
| Ra. Rodriguez, Charleston° | .500 | 11 | 1 | 0 | 1 | 0 |
| Ri. Rodriguez, Columbia° | 1.000 | 49 | 5 | 13 | 0 | 1 |
| Rooker, Macon | .933 | 13 | 6 | 8 | 1 | 1 |
| Russell, Gastonia | 1.000 | 2 | 0 | 1 | 0 | 0 |
| Saitta, Florence | .935 | 27 | 6 | 23 | 2 | 1 |
| Salisbury, Sumter | .600 | 33 | 1 | 2 | 2 | 1 |
| Satzinger, Macon | .833 | 10 | 3 | 7 | 2 | 0 |
| Scanlan, Spartanburg | .833 | 26 | 9 | 16 | 5 | 2 |
| Schedeneck, Gastonia° | .842 | 30 | 2 | 14 | 3 | 0 |
| Schultz, Gastonia | 1.000 | 13 | 2 | 8 | 0 | 0 |
| Shelton, Spartanburg | .889 | 51 | 2 | 14 | 2 | 2 |
| Siblerud, Spartanburg | .909 | 38 | 3 | 7 | 1 | 0 |
| Siebert, Sumter | .931 | 28 | 9 | 18 | 2 | 0 |
| Simpson, Spartanburg° | .833 | 13 | 0 | 5 | 1 | 0 |
| Skripko, Greensboro | .911 | 28 | 10 | 31 | 4 | 2 |
| Smiley, Macon° | .870 | 16 | 4 | 16 | 3 | 1 |
| Stading, Macon | .900 | 33 | 5 | 13 | 2 | 1 |
| Stampfl, Columbia | .829 | 21 | 6 | 23 | 6 | 2 |
| Stephenson, Greensboro° | 1.000 | 15 | 0 | 1 | 0 | 1 |
| Stewart, Charleston | .912 | 26 | 3 | 28 | 3 | 3 |
| Stiles, Columbia | .917 | 37 | 4 | 7 | 1 | 0 |
| Stock, Gastonia° | .500 | 5 | 0 | 1 | 1 | 0 |
| Stottlemyre, Asheville | .941 | 14 | 4 | 12 | 1 | 0 |
| Stringfellow, Sumter° | 1.000 | 5 | 1 | 0 | 0 | 0 |
| Takach, Columbia° | 1.000 | 18 | 1 | 5 | 0 | 1 |
| Tremblay, Greensboro° | .857 | 20 | 3 | 3 | 1 | 0 |
| Tunison, Spartanburg | .972 | 24 | 3 | 32 | 1 | 1 |
| Valliant, Savannah° | 1.000 | 6 | 1 | 1 | 0 | 0 |
| Vargas, Asheville | .953 | 24 | 5 | 36 | 2 | 4 |
| Verrone, Asheville | .871 | 32 | 3 | 24 | 4 | 1 |
| Visor, Charleston | .903 | 31 | 5 | 23 | 3 | 3 |
| Wagner, Sumter° | .909 | 42 | 4 | 6 | 1 | 0 |
| Wasilewski, Florence | .879 | 32 | 7 | 22 | 4 | 0 |
| West, Columbia° | .885 | 26 | 5 | 18 | 3 | 1 |
| Whitaker, Savannah° | 1.000 | 5 | 1 | 2 | 0 | 0 |
| White, Spartanburg | 1.000 | 10 | 1 | 3 | 0 | 1 |
| Williams, Gastonia° | 1.000 | 7 | 0 | 5 | 0 | 1 |
| Young, Columbia° | .950 | 15 | 6 | 13 | 1 | 0 |

The following players do not have any recorded accepted chances at the positions indicated; therefore, are not listed in the fielding averages for those particular positions: Barnard, ss; Blake, ss; Byers, of; Clawson, p; Cusack, 3b; DeLuca, of; Gant, of; Howard, p; Iglesias, ss; Jo. Johnson, ss; Kwolek, 2b; Leiper, of; McKnight, p; Murphy, 3b; L. Rivera, of; Roque, 3b, of; Snowberger, 3b.

## CLUB PITCHING

| Club | ERA. | G. | CG. | ShO. | Sv. | IP. | H. | R. | ER. | HR. | HB. | BB. | Int. BB. | SO. | WP. | Bk. |
|---|---|---|---|---|---|---|---|---|---|---|---|---|---|---|---|---|
| Charleston | 3.40 | 139 | 28 | 15 | 27 | 1203.2 | 1080 | 591 | 455 | 60 | 34 | 622 | 20 | 1024 | 75 | 11 |
| Asheville | 3.52 | 138 | 31 | 11 | 28 | 1183.0 | 1109 | 597 | 463 | 87 | 36 | 469 | 11 | 957 | 96 | 11 |
| Florence | 3.60 | 137 | 10 | 6 | 29 | 1166.1 | 1079 | 609 | 466 | 72 | 33 | 536 | 8 | 944 | 85 | 13 |
| Savannah | 3.73 | 136 | 29 | 7 | 17 | 1127.2 | 1029 | 575 | 467 | 92 | 54 | 508 | 14 | 798 | 66 | 24 |
| Sumter | 3.83 | 135 | 16 | 14 | 36 | 1180.2 | 1057 | 633 | 502 | 76 | 37 | 570 | 8 | 1092 | 121 | 9 |
| Macon | 3.84 | 139 | 18 | 9 | 21 | 1192.1 | 1135 | 664 | 509 | 74 | 46 | 636 | 16 | 941 | 110 | 15 |
| Spartanburg | 3.93 | 136 | 17 | 10 | 33 | 1152.2 | 1154 | 686 | 503 | 55 | 42 | 511 | 4 | 823 | 112 | 10 |
| Columbia | 4.05 | 136 | 21 | 9 | 32 | 1184.1 | 1093 | 671 | 533 | 86 | 44 | 629 | 28 | 968 | 112 | 8 |
| Greensboro | 4.27 | 137 | 26 | 6 | 23 | 1153.1 | 1243 | 710 | 547 | 84 | 37 | 574 | 10 | 846 | 72 | 6 |
| Gastonia | 4.87 | 137 | 11 | 6 | 20 | 1159.0 | 1169 | 827 | 627 | 91 | 62 | 709 | 27 | 843 | 123 | 21 |

## PITCHERS' RECORDS
### (Leading Qualifiers for Earned-Run Average Leadership — 115 or More Innings)

*Throws lefthanded.

| Pitcher—Club | W. | L. | Pct. | ERA. | G. | GS. | CG. | GF. | ShO. | Sv. | IP. | H. | R. | ER. | HR. | HB. | BB. | Int. BB. | SO. | WP. |
|---|---|---|---|---|---|---|---|---|---|---|---|---|---|---|---|---|---|---|---|---|
| Glavine, Sumter* | 9 | 6 | .600 | 2.35 | 26 | 26 | 2 | 0 | 1 | 0 | 168.2 | 114 | 58 | 44 | 6 | 9 | 73 | 0 | 174 | 19 |
| Pettit, Savannah | 8 | 8 | .500 | 2.56 | 42 | 13 | 3 | 20 | 0 | 2 | 133.2 | 96 | 50 | 38 | 9 | 4 | 67 | 2 | 98 | 6 |
| Englund, Florence | 18 | 6 | .750 | 2.58 | 32 | 30 | 4 | 2 | 1 | 0 | 199.0 | 158 | 73 | 57 | 13 | 1 | 49 | 0 | 210 | 5 |
| Costello, Charleston | 16 | 8 | .667 | 2.61 | 29 | 29 | 9 | 0 | 4 | 0 | 200.0 | 161 | 77 | 58 | 5 | 6 | 86 | 0 | 193 | 11 |
| M. Miller, Spartanburg* | 15 | 7 | .682 | 2.67 | 25 | 25 | 7 | 0 | 3 | 0 | 161.2 | 142 | 64 | 48 | 4 | 3 | 50 | 0 | 96 | 4 |
| Provence, Florence | 11 | 9 | .550 | 2.84 | 28 | 26 | 2 | 1 | 1 | 0 | 145.2 | 142 | 73 | 46 | 7 | 5 | 52 | 1 | 60 | 5 |
| Ritter, Macon | 7 | 7 | .500 | 2.89 | 25 | 25 | 5 | 0 | 2 | 0 | 161.2 | 140 | 64 | 52 | 11 | 11 | 61 | 0 | 124 | 11 |
| Huchingson, Asheville | 10 | 5 | .667 | 3.13 | 23 | 23 | 5 | 0 | 2 | 0 | 132.1 | 137 | 62 | 46 | 4 | 9 | 32 | 0 | 72 | 2 |
| Vargas, Asheville | 13 | 7 | .650 | 3.19 | 24 | 24 | 7 | 0 | 2 | 0 | 161.0 | 135 | 70 | 57 | 9 | 3 | 64 | 3 | 136 | 18 |
| Ferlenda, Florence | 12 | 5 | .706 | 3.27 | 35 | 26 | 0 | 4 | 0 | 0 | 165.1 | 152 | 83 | 60 | 10 | 4 | 75 | 0 | 160 | 19 |

Departmental Leaders: G—Ford, 66; W—Englund, 18; L—Newell, 13; Pct.—Anthony, Cash, Funk, .818; GS—Englund, 30; CG—Costello, 9; GF—Ford, 60; ShO—Bitker, Costello, 4; Sv.—Ford, 24; IP—Costello, 200.0; H—Skripko, 192; R—Skripko, 113; ER—Skripko, 84; HR—Verrone, 20; HB—Raubolt, 12; BB—West, 111; IBB—Gozzo, Mercedes, 7; SO—Englund, 210; WP—Newell, 26.

### (All Pitchers—Listed Alphabetically)

| Pitcher—Club | W. | L. | Pct. | ERA. | G. | GS. | CG. | GF. | ShO. | Sv. | IP. | H. | R. | ER. | HR. | HB. | BB. | Int. BB. | SO. | WP. |
|---|---|---|---|---|---|---|---|---|---|---|---|---|---|---|---|---|---|---|---|---|
| Abril, Greensboro | 12 | 5 | .706 | 3.45 | 22 | 22 | 4 | 0 | 0 | 0 | 141.0 | 146 | 69 | 54 | 9 | 6 | 51 | 0 | 108 | 6 |
| Adams, Columbia | 9 | 6 | .600 | 4.76 | 24 | 23 | 5 | 1 | 2 | 0 | 140.0 | 135 | 89 | 74 | 14 | 2 | 72 | 2 | 89 | 8 |
| Agar, Gastonia | 4 | 5 | .444 | 2.52 | 37 | 0 | 0 | 30 | 0 | 10 | 64.1 | 29 | 25 | 18 | 3 | 3 | 45 | 2 | 69 | 4 |
| Andersh, Macon* | 7 | 12 | .368 | 3.43 | 27 | 27 | 3 | 0 | 2 | 0 | 152.1 | 141 | 82 | 58 | 8 | 6 | 85 | 0 | 120 | 16 |
| Anthony, Florence | 9 | 2 | .818 | 1.73 | 40 | 0 | 0 | 34 | 0 | 9 | 73.0 | 65 | 24 | 14 | 2 | 0 | 10 | 1 | 72 | 3 |
| Arnold, Savannah | 8 | 9 | .471 | 3.30 | 24 | 24 | 7 | 0 | 1 | 0 | 169.0 | 131 | 76 | 62 | 9 | 10 | 70 | 0 | 169 | 14 |
| Arnsberg, Asheville | 3 | 4 | .429 | 4.82 | 7 | 7 | 0 | 0 | 0 | 0 | 37.1 | 43 | 30 | 20 | 7 | 2 | 11 | 0 | 32 | 4 |
| Atkinson, Savannah | 4 | 3 | .571 | 4.20 | 28 | 1 | 0 | 10 | 0 | 3 | 60.0 | 56 | 30 | 28 | 4 | 3 | 30 | 3 | 46 | 4 |
| Barba, Columbia | 3 | 4 | .429 | 4.88 | 31 | 9 | 0 | 7 | 0 | 1 | 79.1 | 71 | 61 | 43 | 7 | 6 | 68 | 2 | 61 | 15 |
| Bates, Savannah* | 1 | 2 | .333 | 3.94 | 13 | 6 | 2 | 2 | 1 | 0 | 48.0 | 45 | 25 | 21 | 4 | 0 | 20 | 0 | 30 | 3 |
| Bautista, Florence | 1 | 1 | .500 | 4.45 | 15 | 0 | 0 | 8 | 0 | 1 | 28.1 | 32 | 17 | 14 | 1 | 2 | 8 | 1 | 8 | 2 |
| Behrend, Savannah | 7 | 4 | .636 | 3.03 | 14 | 14 | 7 | 0 | 1 | 0 | 101.0 | 94 | 39 | 34 | 6 | 7 | 24 | 0 | 39 | 3 |
| Bitker, Charleston | 9 | 3 | .750 | 2.59 | 13 | 13 | 6 | 0 | 4 | 0 | 90.1 | 74 | 35 | 26 | 3 | 2 | 31 | 0 | 85 | 3 |
| Broussard, Spartanburg* | 1 | 5 | .167 | 4.67 | 27 | 7 | 0 | 6 | 0 | 1 | 71.1 | 74 | 49 | 37 | 7 | 1 | 51 | 0 | 68 | 3 |
| Burduan, Gastonia | 5 | 11 | .313 | 5.05 | 26 | 15 | 0 | 5 | 0 | 0 | 112.1 | 106 | 78 | 63 | 10 | 4 | 71 | 2 | 73 | 5 |
| Burgos, Florence* | 3 | 1 | .750 | 6.61 | 26 | 0 | 0 | 12 | 0 | 1 | 47.2 | 55 | 39 | 35 | 2 | 1 | 44 | 2 | 32 | 7 |
| Butters, Gastonia | 0 | 1 | .000 | 9.82 | 6 | 0 | 0 | 5 | 0 | 0 | 7.1 | 12 | 15 | 8 | 0 | 0 | 14 | 0 | 7 | 4 |
| Cash, Sumter* | 9 | 2 | .818 | 2.92 | 20 | 13 | 7 | 4 | 3 | 0 | 101.2 | 87 | 39 | 33 | 12 | 0 | 20 | 0 | 63 | 8 |
| Cepeda, Macon | 0 | 0 | .000 | 8.00 | 10 | 1 | 0 | 6 | 0 | 0 | 18.0 | 14 | 18 | 16 | 1 | 0 | 26 | 0 | 13 | 3 |
| Chambers, Spartanburg | 1 | 0 | 1.000 | 2.13 | 12 | 1 | 0 | 7 | 0 | 2 | 25.1 | 23 | 13 | 6 | 0 | 1 | 13 | 0 | 15 | 2 |
| Ciszkowski, Columbia | 10 | 8 | .556 | 4.64 | 25 | 23 | 2 | 0 | 0 | 0 | 151.1 | 151 | 108 | 78 | 17 | 8 | 83 | 2 | 85 | 9 |
| Clawson, Charleston | 0 | 0 | .000 | 0.00 | 1 | 0 | 0 | 1 | 0 | 0 | 1.0 | 0 | 0 | 0 | 0 | 0 | 0 | 0 | 2 | 0 |
| Clossen, Sumter | 7 | 12 | .368 | 5.17 | 26 | 24 | 2 | 1 | 2 | 0 | 130.2 | 133 | 89 | 75 | 6 | 2 | 84 | 0 | 116 | 13 |
| Coffman, Sumter | 1 | 3 | .250 | 3.16 | 24 | 4 | 1 | 10 | 0 | 3 | 62.2 | 42 | 25 | 22 | 1 | 2 | 26 | 0 | 43 | 6 |
| Colpitt, Spartanburg | 0 | 0 | .000 | 10.37 | 22 | 1 | 0 | 12 | 0 | 0 | 37.1 | 43 | 46 | 43 | 3 | 3 | 51 | 1 | 18 | 17 |
| Cooper, Gastonia | 2 | 2 | .500 | 3.94 | 11 | 3 | 0 | 5 | 0 | 0 | 29.2 | 25 | 16 | 13 | 1 | 4 | 14 | 0 | 15 | 5 |
| Corsi, Greensboro | 5 | 8 | .385 | 4.23 | 41 | 2 | 1 | 36 | 0 | 9 | 78.2 | 94 | 49 | 37 | 1 | 4 | 23 | 3 | 84 | 4 |
| Costello, Charleston | 16 | 8 | .667 | 2.61 | 29 | 29 | 9 | 0 | 4 | 0 | 200.0 | 161 | 77 | 58 | 5 | 6 | 86 | 0 | 193 | 11 |
| Criswell, Sumter | 0 | 0 | .000 | 3.38 | 2 | 0 | 0 | 2 | 0 | 0 | 2.2 | 3 | 1 | 1 | 1 | 0 | 2 | 0 | 1 | 1 |
| Crossley, Savannah* | 5 | 11 | .313 | 5.35 | 23 | 20 | 2 | 1 | 1 | 0 | 111.0 | 105 | 83 | 66 | 13 | 8 | 64 | 0 | 94 | 9 |
| Crouch, Greensboro* | 8 | 5 | .615 | 3.78 | 26 | 22 | 4 | 2 | 1 | 0 | 131.0 | 141 | 63 | 55 | 9 | 3 | 65 | 0 | 103 | 7 |
| Cunningham, Macon | 2 | 2 | .500 | 5.40 | 9 | 0 | 0 | 6 | 0 | 0 | 8.1 | 8 | 7 | 5 | 2 | 1 | 6 | 1 | 8 | 2 |
| Czyzewski, Charleston | 5 | 6 | .455 | 6.02 | 31 | 13 | 0 | 6 | 0 | 0 | 101.2 | 114 | 72 | 68 | 10 | 0 | 80 | 1 | 86 | 16 |
| Davis, Savannah | 8 | 6 | .571 | 3.98 | 49 | 0 | 0 | 38 | 0 | 10 | 83.2 | 84 | 46 | 37 | 9 | 2 | 23 | 4 | 59 | 4 |
| Delgado, Gastonia | 0 | 0 | .000 | 10.13 | 6 | 1 | 0 | 1 | 0 | 0 | 18.2 | 22 | 23 | 21 | 4 | 2 | 15 | 2 | 9 | 6 |
| Diaz, Florence* | 0 | 0 | .000 | 1.00 | 8 | 0 | 0 | 7 | 0 | 1 | 9.0 | 3 | 2 | 1 | 0 | 0 | 12 | 0 | 8 | 1 |
| Dillenberger, Savannah | 4 | 5 | .444 | 3.31 | 44 | 1 | 0 | 28 | 0 | 2 | 65.1 | 71 | 34 | 24 | 2 | 5 | 42 | 0 | 49 | 3 |
| Drummond, Macon | 8 | 11 | .421 | 4.12 | 27 | 27 | 4 | 0 | 0 | 0 | 168.1 | 171 | 100 | 77 | 10 | 9 | 73 | 0 | 91 | 8 |
| Duffy, Gastonia | 2 | 9 | .182 | 6.67 | 35 | 9 | 0 | 16 | 0 | 0 | 81.0 | 99 | 84 | 60 | 6 | 5 | 53 | 1 | 62 | 13 |
| Durocher, Asheville | 2 | 7 | .222 | 1.90 | 26 | 0 | 0 | 25 | 0 | 9 | 42.2 | 31 | 17 | 9 | 3 | 1 | 17 | 3 | 42 | 2 |
| Edge, Gastonia | 0 | 1 | .000 | 6.59 | 8 | 0 | 0 | 6 | 0 | 0 | 13.2 | 14 | 12 | 10 | 2 | 0 | 6 | 0 | 16 | 4 |
| Englund, Florence | 18 | 6 | .750 | 2.58 | 32 | 30 | 4 | 2 | 1 | 0 | 199.0 | 158 | 73 | 57 | 13 | 1 | 49 | 0 | 210 | 5 |
| Farley, Savannah | 0 | 1 | .000 | 81.00 | 1 | 0 | 0 | 0 | 0 | 0 | 0.1 | 1 | 3 | 3 | 1 | 0 | 2 | 0 | 0 | 0 |
| Ferlenda, Florence | 12 | 5 | .706 | 3.27 | 35 | 26 | 0 | 4 | 0 | 0 | 165.1 | 152 | 83 | 60 | 10 | 4 | 75 | 0 | 160 | 19 |
| Ford, Charleston | 7 | 6 | .538 | 2.67 | 66 | 0 | 0 | 60 | 0 | 24 | 91.0 | 77 | 33 | 27 | 5 | 3 | 40 | 3 | 93 | 3 |
| Franchi, Macon* | 3 | 5 | .375 | 2.21 | 26 | 3 | 0 | 9 | 0 | 1 | 53.0 | 38 | 23 | 13 | 1 | 2 | 40 | 0 | 73 | 9 |
| Friedel, Columbia | 1 | 0 | 1.000 | 7.02 | 10 | 0 | 0 | 2 | 0 | 0 | 16.2 | 19 | 17 | 13 | 2 | 0 | 11 | 2 | 16 | 0 |
| Funk, Asheville* | 9 | 2 | .818 | 1.74 | 40 | 1 | 0 | 35 | 0 | 12 | 72.1 | 51 | 17 | 14 | 3 | 1 | 28 | 0 | 69 | 1 |
| Gakeler, Greensboro | 7 | 5 | .583 | 5.50 | 23 | 16 | 3 | 2 | 1 | 0 | 108.0 | 135 | 86 | 66 | 8 | 3 | 54 | 0 | 51 | 4 |
| Gass, Savannah | 1 | 2 | .333 | 3.44 | 6 | 6 | 0 | 0 | 0 | 0 | 36.2 | 33 | 17 | 14 | 2 | 3 | 11 | 0 | 22 | 2 |
| Gay, Columbia | 1 | 0 | 1.000 | 2.92 | 6 | 6 | 0 | 0 | 0 | 0 | 37.0 | 35 | 14 | 12 | 2 | 3 | 9 | 0 | 26 | 2 |
| Gideon, Macon | 4 | 7 | .364 | 3.28 | 15 | 14 | 1 | 1 | 1 | 0 | 82.1 | 71 | 38 | 30 | 4 | 2 | 46 | 0 | 62 | 8 |
| Gildehaus, Charleston | 0 | 1 | .000 | 5.23 | 5 | 1 | 0 | 1 | 0 | 0 | 10.1 | 15 | 8 | 6 | 2 | 1 | 4 | 0 | 4 | 0 |
| Givens, Columbia | 1 | 2 | .333 | 2.95 | 3 | 3 | 1 | 0 | 0 | 0 | 21.1 | 15 | 7 | 7 | 2 | 0 | 13 | 0 | 25 | 6 |
| Glavine, Sumter* | 9 | 6 | .600 | 2.35 | 26 | 26 | 2 | 0 | 1 | 0 | 168.2 | 114 | 58 | 44 | 6 | 9 | 73 | 0 | 174 | 19 |
| Gozzo, Columbia | 11 | 4 | .733 | 2.54 | 49 | 0 | 0 | 42 | 0 | 14 | 78.0 | 62 | 22 | 22 | 2 | 2 | 39 | 7 | 66 | 4 |
| Greenlee, Charleston* | 8 | 7 | .533 | 3.33 | 35 | 17 | 1 | 6 | 1 | 0 | 138.0 | 126 | 71 | 51 | 5 | 2 | 82 | 1 | 108 | 10 |
| Grosdidier, Sumter | 3 | 3 | .500 | 4.83 | 33 | 2 | 0 | 7 | 0 | 2 | 63.1 | 75 | 39 | 34 | 6 | 3 | 37 | 1 | 59 | 9 |
| Groves, Sumter | 2 | 2 | .500 | 2.20 | 18 | 0 | 0 | 5 | 0 | 0 | 28.2 | 23 | 12 | 7 | 1 | 2 | 16 | 0 | 27 | 3 |
| Guzman, Sumter | 4 | 0 | 1.000 | 2.51 | 8 | 8 | 1 | 0 | 1 | 0 | 46.2 | 36 | 15 | 13 | 1 | 1 | 14 | 2 | 39 | 6 |
| Helton, Macon | 0 | 0 | .000 | 6.50 | 11 | 0 | 0 | 7 | 0 | 0 | 18.0 | 22 | 14 | 13 | 1 | 0 | 18 | 0 | 14 | 6 |
| Hendrix, Spartanburg | 0 | 0 | .000 | 6.30 | 16 | 0 | 0 | 7 | 0 | 1 | 20.0 | 29 | 25 | 14 | 2 | 1 | 12 | 1 | 21 | 6 |
| Heredia, Asheville | 4 | 10 | .286 | 4.05 | 19 | 17 | 4 | 1 | 0 | 0 | 117.2 | 123 | 67 | 53 | 10 | 2 | 55 | 0 | 92 | 5 |
| Hetzel, Greensboro | 7 | 5 | .583 | 5.57 | 15 | 15 | 1 | 0 | 0 | 0 | 76.0 | 87 | 54 | 47 | 9 | 0 | 48 | 0 | 82 | 8 |
| K. Hill, Gastonia | 3 | 6 | .333 | 4.96 | 15 | 12 | 0 | 0 | 0 | 0 | 69.0 | 60 | 51 | 38 | 5 | 1 | 37 | 1 | 48 | 15 |
| S. Hill, Savannah* | 5 | 10 | .333 | 3.44 | 27 | 17 | 3 | 6 | 1 | 0 | 115.0 | 101 | 55 | 44 | 13 | 4 | 50 | 1 | 71 | 5 |
| Holbrook, Florence | 2 | 8 | .200 | 4.28 | 37 | 0 | 0 | 27 | 0 | 10 | 73.2 | 61 | 43 | 35 | 4 | 4 | 35 | 1 | 61 | 3 |
| Howard, Florence | 0 | 0 | .000 | 27.00 | 1 | 0 | 0 | 1 | 0 | 0 | 0.2 | 2 | 2 | 2 | 1 | 0 | 0 | 0 | 1 | 0 |
| Hubbard, Charleston | 6 | 2 | .750 | 1.69 | 47 | 0 | 0 | 20 | 0 | 3 | 96.0 | 75 | 27 | 18 | 3 | 2 | 39 | 6 | 84 | 3 |
| Huchingson, Asheville | 10 | 5 | .667 | 3.13 | 23 | 23 | 5 | 0 | 2 | 0 | 132.1 | 137 | 62 | 46 | 4 | 9 | 32 | 0 | 72 | 2 |
| Humphries, Florence | 2 | 1 | .667 | 3.23 | 6 | 6 | 0 | 0 | 0 | 0 | 30.2 | 34 | 14 | 11 | 1 | 0 | 17 | 0 | 25 | 2 |
| Irvine, Greensboro | 4 | 2 | .667 | 4.38 | 8 | 7 | 0 | 0 | 0 | 0 | 37.0 | 46 | 26 | 18 | 3 | 1 | 17 | 0 | 19 | 3 |

| Pitcher—Club | W. | L. | Pct. | ERA. | G. | GS. | CG. | GF. | ShO. | Sv. | IP. | H. | R. | ER. | HR. | HB. | BB. | Int. BB. | SO. | WP. |
|---|---|---|---|---|---|---|---|---|---|---|---|---|---|---|---|---|---|---|---|---|
| James, Columbia | 5 | 3 | .625 | 3.30 | 41 | 0 | 0 | 21 | 0 | 5 | 71.0 | 74 | 35 | 26 | 4 | 0 | 36 | 0 | 66 | 5 |
| Jimenez, Sumter | 8 | 4 | .667 | 3.25 | 35 | 4 | 0 | 9 | 0 | 1 | 97.0 | 101 | 51 | 35 | 9 | 4 | 34 | 1 | 71 | 7 |
| D. Johnson, Florence | 0 | 4 | .000 | 6.29 | 10 | 7 | 0 | 2 | 0 | 1 | 34.1 | 27 | 31 | 24 | 1 | 3 | 37 | 0 | 25 | 7 |
| J. Johnson, Gastonia | 2 | 8 | .200 | 4.98 | 25 | 15 | 2 | 5 | 0 | 1 | 97.2 | 109 | 73 | 54 | 8 | 5 | 51 | 2 | 70 | 7 |
| Kilner, Sumter* | 8 | 5 | .615 | 3.80 | 23 | 23 | 0 | 0 | 0 | 0 | 130.1 | 111 | 67 | 55 | 4 | 9 | 60 | 0 | 163 | 6 |
| Knox, Spartanburg | 11 | 8 | .579 | 3.82 | 22 | 22 | 2 | 0 | 2 | 0 | 129.2 | 149 | 81 | 55 | 6 | 7 | 30 | 0 | 75 | 6 |
| Kolb, Macon | 2 | 4 | .333 | 5.43 | 39 | 2 | 0 | 15 | 0 | 0 | 68.0 | 94 | 59 | 41 | 3 | 2 | 39 | 2 | 50 | 13 |
| Livin, Asheville | 15 | 7 | .682 | 3.48 | 27 | 26 | 8 | 0 | 3 | 0 | 175.2 | 188 | 83 | 68 | 17 | 5 | 43 | 1 | 139 | 15 |
| Lockhart, Greensboro* | 2 | 5 | .286 | 3.53 | 35 | 0 | 0 | 14 | 0 | 3 | 89.1 | 71 | 46 | 35 | 4 | 1 | 56 | 4 | 59 | 2 |
| Machado, Spartanburg | 4 | 5 | .444 | 4.32 | 32 | 3 | 1 | 13 | 0 | 0 | 81.1 | 75 | 50 | 39 | 5 | 4 | 38 | 1 | 71 | 4 |
| Mangham, Asheville | 0 | 1 | .000 | 2.60 | 8 | 0 | 0 | 4 | 0 | 0 | 17.1 | 16 | 12 | 5 | 0 | 0 | 11 | 1 | 6 | 4 |
| Manzanillo, Greensboro | 1 | 1 | .500 | 9.75 | 7 | 0 | 0 | 2 | 0 | 0 | 12.0 | 12 | 13 | 13 | 1 | 0 | 18 | 0 | 10 | 2 |
| Martin, Sumter | 4 | 4 | .500 | 2.67 | 43 | 1 | 0 | 34 | 0 | 13 | 54.0 | 42 | 22 | 16 | 5 | 1 | 19 | 1 | 53 | 3 |
| McBee, Gastonia | 0 | 0 | .000 | 0.00 | 1 | 0 | 0 | 1 | 0 | 0 | 2.1 | 3 | 0 | 0 | 0 | 1 | 1 | 0 | 0 | 0 |
| McKnight, Columbia | 0 | 0 | .000 | 9.00 | 3 | 0 | 0 | 3 | 0 | 0 | 4.0 | 4 | 5 | 4 | 1 | 1 | 3 | 0 | 8 | 0 |
| Meads, Gastonia* | 3 | 10 | .231 | 4.37 | 33 | 19 | 5 | 11 | 2 | 1 | 146.1 | 160 | 91 | 71 | 13 | 2 | 50 | 5 | 118 | 10 |
| Mejia, Florence | 0 | 0 | .000 | 4.82 | 7 | 1 | 0 | 1 | 0 | 0 | 18.2 | 20 | 14 | 10 | 0 | 2 | 12 | 0 | 19 | 2 |
| Mercedes, Macon | 5 | 11 | .313 | 2.90 | 54 | 0 | 0 | 32 | 0 | 7 | 96.1 | 94 | 48 | 31 | 6 | 0 | 31 | 7 | 72 | 5 |
| Merklen, Macon* | 4 | 3 | .571 | 3.15 | 50 | 1 | 0 | 27 | 0 | 5 | 94.1 | 82 | 44 | 33 | 5 | 3 | 36 | 1 | 80 | 4 |
| Metoyer, Asheville | 0 | 0 | .000 | 4.05 | 5 | 0 | 0 | 3 | 0 | 0 | 6.2 | 4 | 3 | 3 | 1 | 0 | 4 | 0 | 6 | 2 |
| Mettler, Greensboro | 8 | 7 | .533 | 3.27 | 22 | 16 | 5 | 2 | 2 | 0 | 113.0 | 110 | 53 | 41 | 9 | 5 | 41 | 1 | 71 | 5 |
| Miller, Spartanburg* | 15 | 7 | .682 | 2.67 | 25 | 25 | 7 | 0 | 3 | 0 | 161.2 | 142 | 64 | 48 | 4 | 3 | 50 | 0 | 96 | 4 |
| Moore, Asheville | 3 | 3 | .500 | 4.92 | 28 | 5 | 1 | 10 | 0 | 2 | 67.2 | 55 | 44 | 37 | 5 | 2 | 48 | 0 | 76 | 16 |
| Moreland, Columbia | 0 | 1 | .000 | 5.00 | 4 | 4 | 0 | 0 | 0 | 0 | 18.0 | 29 | 13 | 10 | 4 | 2 | 2 | 0 | 9 | 1 |
| Morelock, Sumter | 5 | 6 | .455 | 3.43 | 16 | 0 | 0 | 7 | 0 | 2 | 39.1 | 33 | 23 | 15 | 5 | 0 | 16 | 2 | 25 | 1 |
| Morrow, Gastonia | 2 | 3 | .400 | 5.13 | 19 | 0 | 0 | 13 | 0 | 3 | 33.1 | 31 | 24 | 19 | 2 | 0 | 23 | 1 | 42 | 2 |
| Moyer, Florence | 4 | 3 | .571 | 4.97 | 23 | 0 | 0 | 11 | 0 | 1 | 50.2 | 46 | 31 | 28 | 9 | 2 | 27 | 0 | 39 | 2 |
| Mumaw, Florence* | 6 | 0 | 1.000 | 1.47 | 11 | 5 | 2 | 2 | 1 | 1 | 49.0 | 33 | 10 | 8 | 1 | 1 | 19 | 0 | 49 | 7 |
| Newell, Spartanburg | 7 | 13 | .350 | 3.82 | 28 | 26 | 1 | 0 | 1 | 0 | 150.2 | 127 | 76 | 64 | 5 | 1 | 102 | 0 | 118 | 26 |
| Nicholson, Gastonia | 7 | 8 | .467 | 3.61 | 21 | 17 | 3 | 3 | 0 | 1 | 109.2 | 95 | 58 | 44 | 10 | 6 | 62 | 2 | 83 | 4 |
| Ocharzak, Gastonia | 4 | 7 | .364 | 5.81 | 24 | 18 | 0 | 2 | 0 | 0 | 113.0 | 133 | 95 | 73 | 12 | 6 | 74 | 1 | 50 | 23 |
| Palmer, Asheville* | 2 | 1 | .667 | 5.36 | 24 | 3 | 0 | 11 | 0 | 1 | 50.1 | 55 | 38 | 30 | 3 | 1 | 25 | 0 | 39 | 3 |
| Parker, Asheville | 3 | 2 | .600 | 3.59 | 34 | 3 | 2 | 13 | 1 | 1 | 85.1 | 75 | 47 | 34 | 1 | 3 | 43 | 2 | 69 | 13 |
| Parsons, Charleston | 1 | 1 | .500 | 4.98 | 7 | 3 | 0 | 3 | 0 | 0 | 21.2 | 24 | 17 | 12 | 0 | 1 | 10 | 1 | 20 | 2 |
| Perry, Savannah | 0 | 3 | .000 | 3.82 | 7 | 7 | 0 | 0 | 0 | 0 | 37.2 | 32 | 21 | 16 | 3 | 2 | 22 | 1 | 26 | 2 |
| Peterson, Greensboro | 5 | 5 | .500 | 2.83 | 43 | 0 | 0 | 38 | 0 | 11 | 89.0 | 83 | 34 | 28 | 8 | 5 | 35 | 2 | 101 | 7 |
| Pettit, Savannah | 8 | 8 | .500 | 2.56 | 42 | 13 | 3 | 20 | 0 | 2 | 133.2 | 96 | 50 | 38 | 9 | 4 | 67 | 2 | 98 | 6 |
| Plesac, Charleston | 2 | 4 | .333 | 6.52 | 19 | 6 | 0 | 1 | 0 | 0 | 49.2 | 60 | 45 | 36 | 3 | 3 | 42 | 0 | 30 | 9 |
| Provence, Florence | 11 | 9 | .550 | 2.84 | 28 | 26 | 2 | 1 | 1 | 0 | 145.2 | 142 | 73 | 46 | 7 | 5 | 52 | 1 | 60 | 5 |
| Raubolt, Gastonia | 4 | 9 | .308 | 4.47 | 17 | 17 | 1 | 0 | 0 | 0 | 104.2 | 112 | 66 | 52 | 6 | 12 | 73 | 2 | 75 | 9 |
| Richardson, Columbia | 3 | 2 | .600 | 1.77 | 5 | 5 | 2 | 0 | 0 | 0 | 35.2 | 25 | 11 | 7 | 1 | 3 | 11 | 0 | 33 | 3 |
| Ritter, Macon | 7 | 7 | .500 | 2.89 | 25 | 25 | 5 | 0 | 2 | 0 | 161.2 | 140 | 64 | 52 | 11 | 11 | 61 | 0 | 124 | 11 |
| M. Robertson, Savannah | 6 | 12 | .333 | 4.38 | 24 | 24 | 5 | 0 | 1 | 0 | 141.2 | 151 | 83 | 69 | 13 | 6 | 70 | 2 | 83 | 10 |
| R. Robertson, Charleston | 5 | 6 | .455 | 3.15 | 14 | 13 | 7 | 1 | 1 | 0 | 97.0 | 83 | 47 | 34 | 8 | 3 | 33 | 4 | 67 | 3 |
| Ra. Rodriguez, Charleston* | 0 | 0 | .000 | 4.50 | 11 | 0 | 0 | 7 | 0 | 0 | 14.0 | 16 | 12 | 7 | 1 | 1 | 10 | 0 | 6 | 2 |
| Ri. Rodriguez, Columbia* | 6 | 3 | .667 | 4.03 | 49 | 3 | 0 | 19 | 0 | 6 | 80.1 | 89 | 41 | 36 | 4 | 1 | 36 | 2 | 71 | 7 |
| Rooker, Macon | 3 | 2 | .600 | 5.02 | 13 | 4 | 0 | 2 | 0 | 0 | 43.0 | 44 | 31 | 24 | 0 | 0 | 40 | 2 | 35 | 10 |
| Russell, Gastonia | 0 | 1 | .000 | 9.95 | 2 | 1 | 0 | 1 | 0 | 0 | 6.1 | 7 | 7 | 7 | 0 | 1 | 10 | 0 | 8 | 0 |
| Saitta, Florence | 2 | 10 | .167 | 5.61 | 27 | 16 | 1 | 6 | 0 | 1 | 104.1 | 126 | 89 | 65 | 11 | 5 | 63 | 2 | 68 | 9 |
| Salisbury, Sumter | 2 | 2 | .500 | 6.47 | 33 | 4 | 0 | 12 | 0 | 5 | 57.0 | 61 | 64 | 41 | 4 | 0 | 70 | 0 | 70 | 14 |
| Satzinger, Macon | 2 | 5 | .286 | 7.29 | 10 | 10 | 1 | 0 | 1 | 0 | 42.0 | 39 | 40 | 34 | 2 | 2 | 52 | 0 | 27 | 5 |
| Scanlan, Spartanburg | 8 | 12 | .400 | 4.14 | 26 | 25 | 4 | 0 | 1 | 0 | 152.1 | 160 | 95 | 70 | 7 | 4 | 53 | 0 | 108 | 8 |
| Schedeneck, Gastonia* | 4 | 6 | .400 | 4.19 | 30 | 2 | 0 | 16 | 0 | 3 | 73.0 | 73 | 43 | 34 | 4 | 3 | 38 | 5 | 53 | 7 |
| Schultz, Gastonia | 1 | 4 | .200 | 6.02 | 13 | 6 | 0 | 1 | 0 | 0 | 49.1 | 59 | 40 | 33 | 3 | 5 | 27 | 1 | 27 | 1 |
| Shelton, Gastonia | 5 | 4 | .556 | 1.87 | 51 | 0 | 0 | 45 | 0 | 23 | 72.1 | 59 | 21 | 15 | 0 | 2 | 24 | 1 | 69 | 4 |
| Siblerud, Spartanburg | 4 | 4 | .500 | 4.06 | 38 | 2 | 0 | 16 | 0 | 5 | 71.0 | 76 | 48 | 32 | 4 | 7 | 24 | 0 | 45 | 9 |
| Siebert, Sumter | 7 | 8 | .467 | 5.02 | 28 | 26 | 3 | 1 | 0 | 0 | 147.0 | 149 | 93 | 82 | 12 | 4 | 72 | 0 | 145 | 12 |
| Simpson, Spartanburg* | 2 | 1 | .667 | 3.94 | 13 | 0 | 0 | 9 | 0 | 1 | 16.0 | 12 | 7 | 7 | 1 | 0 | 8 | 0 | 14 | 1 |
| Skripko, Greensboro | 12 | 9 | .571 | 4.18 | 28 | 27 | 8 | 1 | 2 | 0 | 180.2 | 192 | 113 | 84 | 12 | 5 | 74 | 0 | 104 | 11 |
| Smiley, Macon* | 3 | 8 | .273 | 4.67 | 16 | 16 | 1 | 0 | 1 | 0 | 88.2 | 84 | 55 | 46 | 12 | 2 | 37 | 0 | 70 | 4 |
| Stading, Macon | 6 | 5 | .545 | 3.31 | 38 | 9 | 3 | 16 | 1 | 8 | 98.0 | 93 | 41 | 36 | 8 | 6 | 46 | 3 | 102 | 6 |
| Stampfl, Columbia | 8 | 7 | .533 | 4.19 | 21 | 19 | 1 | 0 | 0 | 0 | 120.1 | 127 | 68 | 56 | 10 | 4 | 41 | 3 | 76 | 12 |
| Stephenson, Greensboro* | 1 | 1 | .500 | 6.20 | 15 | 0 | 0 | 11 | 0 | 0 | 24.2 | 38 | 33 | 17 | 3 | 0 | 15 | 0 | 8 | 4 |
| Stewart, Charleston | 3 | 11 | .421 | 3.41 | 26 | 25 | 3 | 0 | 1 | 0 | 140.0 | 115 | 74 | 53 | 6 | 3 | 101 | 1 | 155 | 9 |
| Stiles, Columbia | 3 | 2 | .600 | 4.66 | 37 | 0 | 0 | 16 | 0 | 5 | 48.1 | 48 | 29 | 25 | 3 | 1 | 32 | 5 | 33 | 9 |
| Stock, Gastonia* | 1 | 1 | .500 | 0.75 | 5 | 0 | 0 | 4 | 0 | 0 | 12.0 | 8 | 5 | 1 | 0 | 1 | 7 | 0 | 8 | 2 |
| Stottlemyre, Asheville | 5 | 4 | .556 | 2.75 | 14 | 13 | 0 | 0 | 1 | 0 | 78.2 | 65 | 33 | 24 | 4 | 2 | 38 | 0 | 70 | 4 |
| Stringfellow, Sumter* | 1 | 0 | 1.000 | 0.00 | 5 | 0 | 0 | 2 | 0 | 0 | 6.2 | 3 | 0 | 0 | 0 | 2 | 5 | 0 | 5 | 0 |
| Takach, Columbia* | 2 | 0 | 1.000 | 3.30 | 18 | 1 | 0 | 7 | 0 | 0 | 43.2 | 43 | 18 | 16 | 6 | 1 | 22 | 1 | 29 | 2 |
| Tremblay, Greensboro* | 2 | 5 | .286 | 6.53 | 20 | 10 | 0 | 3 | 0 | 0 | 73.0 | 88 | 71 | 53 | 8 | 4 | 77 | 0 | 46 | 9 |
| Tunison, Spartanburg | 7 | 11 | .389 | 3.86 | 24 | 24 | 3 | 0 | 0 | 0 | 142.1 | 153 | 90 | 61 | 9 | 8 | 40 | 0 | 92 | 16 |
| Valliant, Savannah* | 0 | 1 | .000 | 3.38 | 6 | 2 | 0 | 1 | 0 | 0 | 10.2 | 7 | 4 | 4 | 2 | 0 | 9 | 1 | 8 | 1 |
| Vargas, Asheville | 13 | 7 | .650 | 3.19 | 24 | 24 | 7 | 0 | 2 | 0 | 161.0 | 135 | 70 | 57 | 9 | 3 | 64 | 3 | 136 | 18 |
| Verrone, Asheville | 7 | 9 | .438 | 4.11 | 32 | 16 | 3 | 5 | 1 | 3 | 138.0 | 131 | 74 | 63 | 20 | 5 | 50 | 1 | 109 | 7 |
| Visor, Charleston | 11 | 6 | .647 | 3.47 | 31 | 19 | 2 | 5 | 1 | 0 | 153.0 | 140 | 73 | 59 | 8 | 7 | 64 | 3 | 91 | 4 |
| Wagner, Sumter | 2 | 6 | .250 | 5.89 | 42 | 0 | 0 | 24 | 0 | 8 | 44.1 | 44 | 35 | 29 | 3 | 0 | 25 | 1 | 38 | 13 |
| Wasilewski, Florence | 12 | 5 | .706 | 3.70 | 32 | 20 | 1 | 9 | 0 | 3 | 136.1 | 123 | 64 | 56 | 9 | 3 | 76 | 0 | 107 | 11 |
| West, Columbia* | 10 | 9 | .526 | 4.56 | 26 | 25 | 5 | 0 | 2 | 0 | 150.0 | 105 | 97 | 76 | 6 | 9 | 111 | 1 | 194 | 23 |
| Whitaker, Savannah* | 0 | 1 | .000 | 4.50 | 5 | 1 | 0 | 1 | 0 | 0 | 14.0 | 22 | 9 | 7 | 2 | 0 | 4 | 0 | 4 | 0 |
| White, Spartanburg | 1 | 0 | 1.000 | 6.33 | 10 | 0 | 0 | 3 | 0 | 0 | 21.1 | 32 | 21 | 15 | 2 | 0 | 15 | 0 | 13 | 6 |
| Williams, Gastonia* | 0 | 1 | .000 | 5.87 | 7 | 2 | 0 | 1 | 0 | 0 | 15.1 | 12 | 21 | 10 | 2 | 1 | 18 | 0 | 10 | 2 |
| Young, Columbia* | 8 | 4 | .667 | 2.82 | 15 | 15 | 4 | 0 | 1 | 0 | 89.1 | 61 | 36 | 28 | 1 | 1 | 40 | 1 | 81 | 6 |

BALKS—Burduan, Mercedes, 6 each; S. Hill, M. Robertson, Siebert, 5 each; Crossley, Stottlemyre, 4 each; Bitker, Englund, Kilner, Machado, Pettit, Saitta, Siblerud, Visor, West, 3 each; Andersh, Arnold, Bates, Duffy, Holbrook, Meads, Parsons, Peterson, Provence, Schultz, Stewart, Vargas, Williams, 2 each; Agar, Arnsberg, Atkinson, Barba, Broussard, Burgos, Cash, Cepeda, Ciszkowski, Colpitt, Costello, Davis, Delgado, Drummond, Durocher, Edge, Ferlenda, Franchi, Gozzo, Heredia, Hetzel, Irvine, Da. Johnson, Ja. Johnson, Kolb, Lockhart, Mangham, Miller, Nicholson, Ocharzak, Palmer, Perry, Ri. Rodriguez, Satzinger, Smiley, Stading, Stock, Tremblay, Tunison, Young, 1 each.

COMBINATION SHUTOUTS—Verrone-Moore, Vargas-Durocher, Asheville; Visor-Ford, Stewart-Hubbard, Visor-Hubbard-Ford, Charleston; Gay-Gozzo, Young-Rodriguez, Moreland-Adams, Young-Gozzo, Columbia; Ferlenda-Anthony, Wasilewski-Moyer-Burgos, Mumaw-Wasilewski, Florence; Ocharzak-Meads-Morrow, Schedeneck-Agar, Raubolt-Agar, Cooper-Duffy, Gastonia; Andersh-Stading, Macon; S. Hill-Davis, Savannah; Miller-Shelton 2, Newell-Hendrix, Newell-Siblerud, Spartanburg; Kilner-Groves-Salisbury, Glavine-Salisbury, Glavine-Coffman-Wagner, Martin-Salisbury-Wagner, Sumter.

NO-HIT GAMES—Clossen, Sumter, defeated Florence, 2-0 (second game), April 15; Saitta-Moyer, Florence, defeated Charleston, 4-3 (first game), June 7; West-Rodriguez-Barba, Columbia, defeated Charleston, 12-4, July 22; West, Columbia, defeated Spartanburg, 3-0, August 14.

# Appalachian League

## SUMMER CLASS A CLASSIFICATION

### CHAMPIONSHIP WINNERS IN PREVIOUS YEARS

| | | |
|---|---|---|
| 1921—Greenville .608 | 1948—Pulaski‡ .680 | 1969—Pulaski a .576 |
|     Johnson City° .627 | 1949—Bluefield‡ .721 |     Johnson City .544 |
| 1922—Bristol .557 | 1950—Bluefield .600 | 1970—Bluefield .638 |
| 1923—Knoxville .635 |     Bluefield z .745 | 1971—Bluefield a .609 |
| 1924—Knoxville° .642 | 1951—Kingsport‡ .659 |     Kingsport .559 |
|     Bristol .607 | 1952—Johnson City .595 | 1972—Bristol a .588 |
| 1925—Greenville .667 |     Welch (3rd)† .509 |     Covington .586 |
| 1926-36—Did not operate. | 1953—Welch° .705 | 1973—Kingsport .757 |
| 1937—Elizabethton .559 |     Johnson City .672 | 1974—Bristol a .754 |
|     Pennington Gap° .580 | 1954—Bluefield‡ .619 |     Bluefield .536 |
| 1938—Elizabethton .664 | 1955—Salem°° .689 | 1975—Marion .515 |
|     Greenville (3rd)† .571 | 1956—Did not operate. |     Johnson City a .603 |
| 1939—Elizabethton‡ .597 | 1957—Bluefield .701 | 1976—Johnson City a .714 |
| 1940—Johnson City§ .726 | 1958—Johnson City .662 |     Bluefield .600 |
|     Elizabethton .750 | 1959—Morristown .603 | 1977—Kingsport .623 |
| 1941—Johnson City .614 | 1960—Wytheville .614 | 1978—Elizabethton .594 |
|     Elizabethton° .661 | 1961—Middlesboro .591 | 1979—Paintsville .800 |
| 1942—Bristol .667 | 1962—Bluefield .671 | 1980—Paintsville .657 |
|     Bristol x .660 | 1963—Bluefield .652 | 1981—Paintsville .657 |
| 1943—Bristol .755 | 1964—Johnson City .662 | 1982—Bluefield a .681 |
|     Bristol y .617 | 1965—Salem .614 |     Johnson City .478 |
| 1944—Kingsport‡ .575 | 1966—Marion .623 | 1983—Paintsville .653 |
| 1945—Kingsport‡ .670 | 1967—Bluefield .627 | 1984—Elizabethton b .580 |
| 1946—New River‡ .675 | 1968—Marion .583 |     Pulaski .536 |
| 1947—Pulaski .648 | | |
|     New River (3rd)† .516 | | |

°Won split-season playoff. †Won four-team playoff. ‡Won championship and four-team playoff. §Johnson City, first-half winner, won playoff involving six clubs. xWon both halves and defeated second-place Elizabethton in playoff. yWon both halves, but Erwin won four-team playoff. zWon both halves, but Bristol won two-club playoff. °°Salem and Johnson City declared playoff co-champions when weather forced cancellation of final series. aLeague was divided into Northern, Southern divisions; declared league champion, based on highest won-lost percentage. bLeague was divided into Northern, Southern divisions; won one-game playoff for league championship.

### COMPOSITE STANDING OF CLUBS AT CLOSE OF SEASON, AUGUST 30

| Club | Bri. | J.C. | Wyt. | Blu. | Eliz. | Pul. | Kng. | W. | L. | T. | Pct. | G.B. |
|---|---|---|---|---|---|---|---|---|---|---|---|---|
| Bristol (Tigers) | .... | 7 | 5 | 8 | 9 | 8 | 7 | 44 | 25 | 0 | .638 | ........ |
| Johnson City (Cardinals) | 4 | .... | 6 | 6 | 7 | 7 | 9 | 39 | 29 | 0 | .574 | 4½ |
| Wytheville (Cubs) | 7 | 5 | .... | 6 | 8 | 6 | 7 | 39 | 31 | 0 | .557 | 5½ |
| Bluefield (Orioles) | 4 | 6 | 6 | .... | 7 | 6 | 7 | 36 | 34 | 0 | .514 | 8½ |
| Elizabethton (Twins) | 3 | 5 | 3 | 5 | .... | 8 | 7 | 31 | 40 | 0 | .437 | 14 |
| Pulaski (Braves) | 4 | 3 | 6 | 4 | 4 | .... | 7 | 28 | 40 | 0 | .412 | 15½ |
| Kingsport (Mets) | 3 | 3 | 5 | 5 | 5 | 5 | .... | 26 | 40 | 0 | .371 | 18½ |

Major league affiliations in parentheses.

Playoffs—None. Bristol declared league champion based on regular-season record.

Regular-Season Attendance—Bluefield, 24,511; Bristol, 10,218; Elizabethton, 7,172; Johnson City, 12,998; Kingsport, 20,817; Pulaski, 10,198; Wytheville, 26,696. Total—112,610.

Managers—Bluefield, Mike Verdi; Bristol, Tom Burgess; Elizabethton, Fred Waters; Johnson City, Rich Hacker; Kingsport, Tucker Ashford; Pulaski, Craig Robinson; Wytheville, Ramon Conde.

All-Star Team—1B-Mark McMorris, Wytheville; 2B-Gator Thiesen, Johnson City; 3B-Craig Worthington, Bluefield; SS-Gregg Jefferies, Kingsport; OF-Alex Cole, Johnson City; Tony Hamza, Wytheville; Jaime Archibald, Kingsport; C-Dave Liddell, Wytheville; DH-Tim Leiper, Bristol; LHP-Barry Hightower, Kingsport; RHP-Mike Adams, Elizabethton; Player of the Year-Greg Jefferies, Kingsport; Manager of the Year-Tom Burgess, Bristol.

(Compiled by Howe News Bureau, Boston, Mass.)

### CLUB BATTING

| Club | Pct. | G. | AB. | R. | OR. | H. | TB. | 2B. | 3B. | HR. | RBI. | GW. | SH. | SF. | HP. | BB. | Int. BB. | SO. | SB. | CS. | LOB. |
|---|---|---|---|---|---|---|---|---|---|---|---|---|---|---|---|---|---|---|---|---|---|
| Wytheville | .264 | 70 | 2113 | 359 | 345 | 558 | 775 | 85 | 18 | 32 | 273 | 30 | 33 | 16 | 11 | 307 | 12 | 374 | 87 | 18 | 493 |
| Johnson City | .262 | 68 | 1977 | 340 | 319 | 518 | 714 | 82 | 8 | 33 | 281 | 33 | 12 | 22 | 17 | 259 | 7 | 329 | 144 | 25 | 443 |
| Bristol | .261 | 69 | 2099 | 390 | 293 | 548 | 800 | 104 | 17 | 38 | 327 | 38 | 19 | 22 | 17 | 281 | 9 | 351 | 58 | 22 | 450 |
| Bluefield | .249 | 70 | 2057 | 353 | 345 | 513 | 753 | 101 | 14 | 37 | 287 | 32 | 23 | 28 | 13 | 252 | 2 | 389 | 40 | 23 | 425 |
| Elizabethton | .248 | 71 | 2095 | 348 | 340 | 520 | 726 | 97 | 8 | 31 | 277 | 21 | 11 | 19 | 24 | 326 | 5 | 380 | 60 | 18 | 478 |
| Pulaski | .242 | 68 | 2058 | 308 | 370 | 498 | 753 | 92 | 11 | 47 | 261 | 24 | 16 | 14 | 15 | 288 | 7 | 398 | 16 | 4 | 468 |
| Kingsport | .233 | 70 | 2025 | 301 | 387 | 472 | 683 | 79 | 12 | 36 | 254 | 24 | 14 | 13 | 23 | 291 | 5 | 504 | 111 | 27 | 444 |

### INDIVIDUAL BATTING

(Leading Qualifiers for Batting Championship—194 or More Plate Appearances)

°Bats lefthanded.    †Switch-hitter.

| Player and Club | Pct. | G. | AB. | R. | H. | TB. | 2B. | 3B. | HR. | RBI. | GW. | SH. | SF. | HP. | BB. | Int. BB. | SO. | SB. | CS. |
|---|---|---|---|---|---|---|---|---|---|---|---|---|---|---|---|---|---|---|---|
| McMorris, Mark, Wytheville° | .370 | 64 | 227 | 45 | 84 | 118 | 10 | 3 | 6 | 53 | 6 | 2 | 5 | 0 | 31 | 3 | 19 | 5 | 1 |
| Jones, Timothy, Johnson City° | .319 | 68 | 235 | 33 | 75 | 96 | 10 | 1 | 3 | 48 | 5 | 0 | 5 | 0 | 27 | 1 | 19 | 28 | 6 |
| Hamza, Antonio, Wytheville | .319 | 65 | 229 | 48 | 73 | 110 | 10 | 3 | 7 | 37 | 4 | 1 | 1 | 0 | 30 | 1 | 39 | 22 | 3 |
| Lanoux, Marty, Elizabethton° | .313 | 68 | 217 | 48 | 68 | 106 | 17 | 0 | 7 | 45 | 2 | 0 | 2 | 4 | 39 | 1 | 21 | 4 | 2 |
| Iglesias, Luis, Johnson City | .313 | 59 | 166 | 33 | 52 | 96 | 17 | 0 | 9 | 41 | 4 | 1 | 4 | 3 | 34 | 1 | 32 | 3 | 0 |
| Thiesen, Michael, Johnson City | .309 | 61 | 191 | 42 | 59 | 76 | 9 | 1 | 2 | 28 | 7 | 0 | 3 | 2 | 30 | 1 | 14 | 16 | 3 |
| Leiper, Timothy, Bristol† | .308 | 61 | 211 | 37 | 65 | 90 | 16 | 0 | 3 | 47 | 4 | 0 | 2 | 1 | 15 | 1 | 18 | 7 | 4 |

| Player and Club | Pct. | G. | AB. | R. | H. | TB. | 2B. | 3B. | HR. | RBI. | GW. | SH. | SF. | HP. | BB. | Int. BB. | SO. | SB. | CS. |
|---|---|---|---|---|---|---|---|---|---|---|---|---|---|---|---|---|---|---|---|
| Strange, Douglas, Bristol† | .305 | 65 | 226 | 43 | 69 | 105 | 16 | 1 | 6 | 45 | 6 | 4 | 3 | 3 | 22 | 1 | 30 | 6 | 0 |
| Perry, Robert, Elizabethton | .302 | 67 | 215 | 43 | 65 | 106 | 20 | 0 | 7 | 39 | 2 | 1 | 1 | 5 | 47 | 0 | 43 | 6 | 2 |
| Rowland, Donald, Bristol | .299 | 59 | 194 | 44 | 58 | 75 | 10 | 2 | 1 | 21 | 4 | 3 | 1 | 2 | 28 | 0 | 20 | 14 | 4 |
| Bailey, Brandon, Kingsport | .299 | 69 | 211 | 34 | 63 | 100 | 7 | 0 | 10 | 39 | 6 | 0 | 4 | 4 | 38 | 0 | 60 | 7 | 1 |
| Ewart, Ronald, Wytheville° | .297 | 57 | 165 | 33 | 49 | 63 | 7 | 2 | 1 | 20 | 2 | 2 | 1 | 2 | 47 | 3 | 15 | 6 | 0 |
| Anderson, Bernard, Bristol° | .294 | 62 | 218 | 47 | 64 | 93 | 13 | 2 | 4 | 31 | 3 | 1 | 2 | 0 | 31 | 0 | 27 | 6 | 2 |

Departmental Leaders: G—Bailey, 69; AB—T. Jones, 235; R—Cole, 60; H—McMorris, 84; TB—McMorris, 118; 2B—R. Perry, 20; 3B—Fox, 4; HR—Bailey, Justice, Tomberlin, 10; RBI—McMorris, 53; GWRBI—Thiesen, 7; SH—Sullivan, 8; SF—Dulin, T. Jones, Justice, McMorris, 5; HP—Alfano, R. Perry, 5; BB—Blackwell, Ewart, R. Perry, 47; IBB—Daily, 5; SO—Bailey, Stainbrook, 60; SB—Cole, 46; CS—Cole, 8.

(All Players—Listed Alphabetically)

| Player and Club | Pct. | G. | AB. | R. | H. | TB. | 2B. | 3B. | HR. | RBI. | GW. | SH. | SF. | HP. | BB. | Int. BB. | SO. | SB. | CS. |
|---|---|---|---|---|---|---|---|---|---|---|---|---|---|---|---|---|---|---|---|
| Aldrich, Monty, Pulaski° | .273 | 55 | 198 | 35 | 54 | 88 | 11 | 1 | 7 | 18 | 2 | 1 | 1 | 1 | 28 | 2 | 32 | 5 | 2 |
| Alfano, Michael, Pulaski | .227 | 51 | 150 | 21 | 34 | 44 | 5 | 1 | 1 | 15 | 0 | 1 | 1 | 5 | 20 | 0 | 34 | 0 | 0 |
| Alva, John, Pulaski | .227 | 63 | 216 | 33 | 49 | 64 | 5 | 2 | 2 | 27 | 3 | 1 | 1 | 2 | 26 | 0 | 33 | 0 | 0 |
| Anderson, Bernard, Bristol° | .294 | 62 | 218 | 47 | 64 | 93 | 13 | 2 | 4 | 31 | 3 | 1 | 2 | 0 | 31 | 0 | 27 | 6 | 2 |
| Archibald, Jaime, Kingsport° | .282 | 47 | 149 | 31 | 42 | 82 | 11 | 1 | 9 | 40 | 4 | 0 | 2 | 1 | 24 | 0 | 43 | 0 | 2 |
| Bailey, Brandon, Kingsport | .299 | 69 | 211 | 34 | 63 | 100 | 7 | 0 | 10 | 39 | 6 | 0 | 4 | 4 | 38 | 0 | 60 | 7 | 1 |
| Balthazar, Doyle, Bristol | .275 | 16 | 40 | 6 | 11 | 15 | 2 | 1 | 0 | 3 | 0 | 0 | 1 | 0 | 4 | 0 | 9 | 0 | 1 |
| Bastinck, Derek, Bristol | .263 | 37 | 99 | 21 | 26 | 41 | 4 | 1 | 3 | 12 | 2 | 1 | 1 | 2 | 18 | 0 | 22 | 0 | 0 |
| Bautista, Angel, Johnson City | .000 | 10 | 1 | 0 | 0 | 0 | 0 | 0 | 0 | 0 | 0 | 1 | 0 | 0 | 0 | 0 | 0 | 0 | 0 |
| Bautista, Bienvenido, Bluefield† | .115 | 10 | 26 | 3 | 3 | 3 | 0 | 0 | 0 | 1 | 0 | 0 | 0 | 0 | 3 | 0 | 7 | 0 | 0 |
| Beasant, Darrel, Kingsport | .156 | 21 | 45 | 5 | 7 | 12 | 2 | 0 | 1 | 7 | 1 | 0 | 0 | 0 | 6 | 0 | 11 | 1 | 1 |
| Beer, Steven, Pulaski | .000 | 20 | 4 | 0 | 0 | 0 | 0 | 0 | 0 | 0 | 0 | 1 | 0 | 0 | 0 | 0 | 2 | 0 | 0 |
| Bellini, Robert, Bluefield | .231 | 50 | 156 | 34 | 36 | 50 | 12 | 1 | 0 | 9 | 1 | 3 | 0 | 1 | 31 | 0 | 25 | 4 | 3 |
| Bernard, Rusbel, Bluefield | .159 | 24 | 44 | 3 | 7 | 8 | 1 | 0 | 0 | 6 | 0 | 1 | 0 | 0 | 4 | 0 | 8 | 1 | 0 |
| Billmeyer, Michael, Bluefield† | .321 | 27 | 81 | 17 | 26 | 53 | 1 | 1 | 8 | 32 | 2 | 0 | 4 | 2 | 18 | 0 | 17 | 0 | 0 |
| Blackwell, Larry, Elizabethton | .246 | 63 | 211 | 55 | 52 | 80 | 7 | 3 | 5 | 24 | 1 | 1 | 2 | 0 | 47 | 0 | 31 | 23 | 7 |
| Blake, Keith, Bristol | .400 | 2 | 5 | 2 | 2 | 2 | 0 | 0 | 0 | 1 | 0 | 1 | 0 | 1 | 1 | 0 | 2 | 0 | 0 |
| Boyce, Joseph, Elizabethton° | .254 | 44 | 142 | 24 | 36 | 55 | 5 | 1 | 4 | 17 | 2 | 2 | 0 | 2 | 20 | 0 | 28 | 5 | 2 |
| Boyd, Steven, Johnson City† | .157 | 21 | 51 | 1 | 8 | 9 | 1 | 0 | 0 | 1 | 0 | 1 | 0 | 0 | 4 | 0 | 2 | 1 | 1 |
| Brooks, Samuel, Kingsport | .000 | 23 | 0 | 0 | 0 | 0 | 0 | 0 | 0 | 0 | 0 | 0 | 0 | 0 | 1 | 0 | 0 | 0 | 0 |
| Buglione, Anthony, Johnson City | .257 | 64 | 206 | 32 | 53 | 84 | 13 | 0 | 6 | 37 | 5 | 0 | 2 | 2 | 29 | 2 | 46 | 0 | 0 |
| Burke, Kevin, Bluefield° | .234 | 26 | 64 | 11 | 15 | 26 | 5 | 0 | 2 | 10 | 1 | 2 | 0 | 1 | 6 | 0 | 14 | 2 | 1 |
| Butler, Leon, Pulaski | .036 | 11 | 28 | 2 | 1 | 1 | 0 | 0 | 0 | 1 | 1 | 0 | 0 | 0 | 8 | 1 | 8 | 0 | 0 |
| Buzzard, Lawrence, Elizabethton | .161 | 33 | 93 | 6 | 15 | 15 | 0 | 0 | 0 | 7 | 2 | 0 | 0 | 1 | 8 | 0 | 16 | 1 | 0 |
| Canan, Richard, Wytheville | .277 | 40 | 130 | 22 | 36 | 59 | 4 | 2 | 5 | 26 | 1 | 2 | 2 | 0 | 23 | 0 | 20 | 3 | 2 |
| Casteel, Brent, Wytheville | .226 | 45 | 137 | 17 | 31 | 45 | 6 | 1 | 2 | 18 | 3 | 4 | 0 | 0 | 7 | 0 | 22 | 6 | 0 |
| Castro, Genaro, Kingsport | .225 | 66 | 213 | 32 | 48 | 61 | 6 | 2 | 1 | 17 | 1 | 4 | 0 | 1 | 25 | 0 | 34 | 10 | 5 |
| Celis, Johnny, Kingsport† | .190 | 27 | 63 | 12 | 12 | 15 | 3 | 0 | 0 | 4 | 1 | 1 | 0 | 2 | 14 | 1 | 21 | 3 | 3 |
| Cloninger, Todd, Wytheville° | .000 | 6 | 1 | 0 | 0 | 0 | 0 | 0 | 0 | 0 | 0 | 0 | 0 | 0 | 0 | 0 | 1 | 0 | 0 |
| Colavito, Steven, Bluefield† | .111 | 36 | 54 | 5 | 6 | 6 | 0 | 0 | 0 | 4 | 0 | 1 | 0 | 0 | 6 | 0 | 28 | 0 | 1 |
| Cole, Alexander, Johnson City° | .263 | 66 | 232 | 60 | 61 | 71 | 5 | 1 | 1 | 13 | 3 | 0 | 1 | 1 | 30 | 0 | 27 | 46 | 8 |
| Cooley, Jeffrey, Kingsport | .375 | 2 | 8 | 2 | 3 | 3 | 0 | 0 | 0 | 1 | 0 | 0 | 0 | 0 | 1 | 0 | 3 | 1 | 0 |
| Crews, Marty, Kingsport | .212 | 45 | 132 | 8 | 28 | 35 | 4 | 0 | 1 | 12 | 0 | 0 | 2 | 2 | 7 | 1 | 55 | 0 | 0 |
| Crosby, Patrick, Elizabethton° | .236 | 58 | 182 | 21 | 43 | 51 | 6 | 1 | 0 | 14 | 0 | 1 | 1 | 0 | 15 | 1 | 11 | 1 | 1 |
| Daily, Richard, Bristol† | .232 | 59 | 185 | 34 | 43 | 77 | 10 | 0 | 8 | 30 | 5 | 1 | 0 | 3 | 46 | 5 | 49 | 1 | 1 |
| Damian, Leonard, Wytheville | .214 | 14 | 14 | 1 | 3 | 5 | 2 | 0 | 0 | 2 | 0 | 1 | 0 | 0 | 3 | 0 | 4 | 0 | 0 |
| Delancer, Julio, Elizabethton | .234 | 40 | 128 | 24 | 30 | 42 | 4 | 1 | 2 | 18 | 1 | 0 | 1 | 0 | 20 | 0 | 20 | 3 | 0 |
| Deloach, Bobby, Johnson City | .221 | 46 | 136 | 12 | 30 | 36 | 6 | 0 | 0 | 19 | 1 | 0 | 1 | 0 | 2 | 0 | 30 | 2 | 0 |
| Dewey, Todd, Pulaski° | .261 | 46 | 138 | 14 | 36 | 48 | 4 | 1 | 2 | 18 | 0 | 1 | 0 | 0 | 18 | 0 | 24 | 1 | 0 |
| Douglas, Arthur, Kingsport | .210 | 36 | 81 | 8 | 17 | 21 | 4 | 0 | 0 | 9 | 1 | 0 | 0 | 1 | 10 | 0 | 22 | 6 | 2 |
| Dulin, Timothy, Bluefield | .271 | 66 | 192 | 44 | 52 | 78 | 15 | 1 | 3 | 29 | 5 | 0 | 5 | 0 | 38 | 1 | 18 | 7 | 1 |
| Ewart, Ronald, Wytheville° | .297 | 57 | 165 | 33 | 49 | 63 | 7 | 2 | 1 | 20 | 2 | 2 | 1 | 2 | 47 | 3 | 15 | 6 | 0 |
| Farmer, Kennedy, Kingsport | .226 | 47 | 133 | 20 | 30 | 35 | 1 | 2 | 0 | 22 | 2 | 2 | 1 | 2 | 10 | 0 | 16 | 14 | 3 |
| Ford, David, Pulaski | .231 | 48 | 160 | 17 | 37 | 61 | 6 | 0 | 6 | 20 | 1 | 1 | 0 | 1 | 12 | 0 | 36 | 0 | 0 |
| Forrest, Christopher, Johnson City | .000 | 4 | 2 | 0 | 0 | 0 | 0 | 0 | 0 | 0 | 0 | 0 | 0 | 0 | 0 | 0 | 0 | 0 | 0 |
| Fortner, Dennis, Wytheville° | .220 | 14 | 41 | 5 | 9 | 9 | 0 | 0 | 0 | 3 | 1 | 2 | 1 | 0 | 7 | 1 | 15 | 0 | 0 |
| Fox, Blake, Bristol° | .236 | 59 | 195 | 34 | 46 | 74 | 11 | 4 | 3 | 38 | 6 | 0 | 2 | 2 | 29 | 0 | 22 | 5 | 1 |
| Fregosi, James, Johnson City | .382 | 12 | 34 | 10 | 13 | 20 | 1 | 0 | 2 | 5 | 1 | 0 | 0 | 0 | 14 | 0 | 3 | 4 | 1 |
| Garcia, Victor, Kingsport | .750 | 14 | 4 | 1 | 3 | 3 | 0 | 0 | 0 | 1 | 0 | 0 | 0 | 0 | 1 | 0 | 0 | 0 | 0 |
| Gardner, Daniel, Bristol° | .438 | 5 | 16 | 6 | 7 | 8 | 1 | 0 | 0 | 6 | 0 | 0 | 1 | 0 | 2 | 0 | 2 | 1 | 0 |
| Gardner, Jimmie, Wytheville | .000 | 10 | 3 | 0 | 0 | 0 | 0 | 0 | 0 | 0 | 0 | 0 | 0 | 0 | 0 | 0 | 2 | 0 | 0 |
| Garrison, David, Pulaski | .213 | 41 | 122 | 13 | 26 | 33 | 7 | 0 | 0 | 6 | 1 | 1 | 1 | 0 | 22 | 0 | 34 | 2 | 0 |
| Gliha, Patrick, Pulaski | .000 | 19 | 3 | 0 | 0 | 0 | 0 | 0 | 0 | 0 | 0 | 0 | 0 | 0 | 1 | 0 | 3 | 0 | 0 |
| Goodwin, Mark, Bluefield° | .256 | 58 | 164 | 24 | 42 | 59 | 8 | 0 | 3 | 23 | 2 | 0 | 3 | 0 | 9 | 0 | 23 | 1 | 0 |
| Green, John, Wytheville | .000 | 20 | 1 | 0 | 0 | 0 | 0 | 0 | 0 | 0 | 0 | 0 | 0 | 0 | 0 | 0 | 1 | 0 | 0 |
| Greene, Thomas, Pulaski | .000 | 12 | 4 | 0 | 0 | 0 | 0 | 0 | 0 | 0 | 0 | 2 | 0 | 0 | 0 | 0 | 0 | 0 | 0 |
| Greene, Jeffrey, Pulaski | .111 | 15 | 9 | 1 | 1 | 3 | 0 | 1 | 0 | 1 | 0 | 0 | 0 | 0 | 1 | 0 | 3 | 0 | 0 |
| Griffith, Kerry, Johnson City | .385 | 18 | 13 | 2 | 5 | 5 | 0 | 0 | 0 | 5 | 0 | 1 | 0 | 0 | 2 | 0 | 0 | 0 | 0 |
| Guerra, Orlando, Bluefield° | .000 | 24 | 1 | 0 | 0 | 0 | 0 | 0 | 0 | 0 | 0 | 0 | 0 | 0 | 0 | 0 | 1 | 0 | 0 |
| Hamilton, James, Pulaski° | .141 | 40 | 78 | 12 | 11 | 15 | 1 | 0 | 1 | 6 | 1 | 0 | 0 | 0 | 14 | 1 | 30 | 0 | 0 |
| Hamza, Antonio, Wytheville | .319 | 65 | 229 | 48 | 73 | 110 | 10 | 3 | 7 | 37 | 4 | 1 | 1 | 0 | 30 | 1 | 39 | 22 | 3 |
| Harwick, Clinton, Wytheville | .214 | 17 | 56 | 9 | 12 | 14 | 2 | 0 | 0 | 4 | 1 | 0 | 0 | 1 | 3 | 0 | 12 | 2 | 0 |
| Hayden, Alan, Kingsport° | .308 | 57 | 146 | 41 | 45 | 58 | 7 | 3 | 0 | 11 | 2 | 5 | 0 | 2 | 21 | 0 | 13 | 24 | 2 |
| Hayes, Christopher, Kingsport | .083 | 13 | 12 | 0 | 1 | 1 | 0 | 0 | 0 | 0 | 0 | 1 | 0 | 0 | 0 | 0 | 4 | 0 | 0 |
| Haynes, Kevin, Johnson City | .000 | 20 | 0 | 0 | 0 | 0 | 0 | 0 | 0 | 0 | 0 | 0 | 0 | 0 | 0 | 0 | 0 | 0 | 0 |
| Henry, Michael, Johnson City | .000 | 11 | 2 | 1 | 0 | 0 | 0 | 0 | 0 | 0 | 0 | 0 | 3 | 0 | 0 | 0 | 1 | 0 | 0 |
| Hightower, Barry, Kingsport | .500 | 10 | 2 | 1 | 1 | 1 | 0 | 0 | 0 | 0 | 0 | 0 | 0 | 0 | 0 | 0 | 0 | 0 | 0 |
| Holder, Richard, Kingsport | .500 | 25 | 2 | 2 | 1 | 1 | 0 | 0 | 0 | 1 | 0 | 0 | 0 | 0 | 1 | 0 | 0 | 0 | 0 |
| Howes, Jeff, Kingsport | .000 | 8 | 1 | 0 | 0 | 0 | 0 | 0 | 0 | 0 | 0 | 0 | 0 | 0 | 0 | 0 | 1 | 0 | 0 |
| Iglesias, Luis, Johnson City | .313 | 59 | 166 | 33 | 52 | 96 | 17 | 0 | 9 | 41 | 4 | 1 | 4 | 3 | 34 | 1 | 32 | 3 | 0 |
| Jackson, Mark, Johnson City | .243 | 60 | 177 | 33 | 43 | 59 | 6 | 2 | 2 | 20 | 2 | 0 | 2 | 3 | 27 | 0 | 27 | 17 | 2 |
| Jackson, Ruben, Bristol° | .265 | 19 | 49 | 14 | 13 | 16 | 3 | 0 | 0 | 5 | 0 | 0 | 0 | 0 | 7 | 0 | 8 | 1 | 3 |
| Jefferies, Gregg, Kingsport† | .343 | 47 | 166 | 27 | 57 | 88 | 18 | 2 | 3 | 29 | 2 | 0 | 1 | 1 | 14 | 2 | 16 | 21 | 1 |
| Jefferson, Mark, Wytheville° | .000 | 9 | 2 | 0 | 0 | 0 | 0 | 0 | 0 | 0 | 0 | 0 | 0 | 0 | 1 | 0 | 1 | 0 | 0 |
| Jones, Timothy, Johnson City° | .319 | 68 | 235 | 33 | 75 | 96 | 10 | 1 | 3 | 48 | 5 | 0 | 5 | 0 | 27 | 1 | 19 | 28 | 6 |
| Jones, Jeffery, Kingsport | .120 | 15 | 25 | 3 | 3 | 3 | 0 | 0 | 0 | 1 | 0 | 0 | 0 | 0 | 6 | 0 | 13 | 1 | 1 |
| Jones, Michael, Wytheville° | .196 | 46 | 107 | 17 | 21 | 28 | 4 | 0 | 1 | 9 | 2 | 0 | 1 | 0 | 24 | 2 | 39 | 1 | 0 |
| Justice, David, Pulaski° | .245 | 66 | 204 | 39 | 50 | 88 | 8 | 0 | 10 | 46 | 4 | 0 | 5 | 0 | 40 | 0 | 30 | 0 | 1 |

| Player and Club | Pct. | G. | AB. | R. | H. | TB. | 2B. | 3B. | HR. | RBI. | GW. | SH. | SF. | HP. | BB. | Int. BB. | SO. | SB. | CS. |
|---|---|---|---|---|---|---|---|---|---|---|---|---|---|---|---|---|---|---|---|
| Kallevig, Gregory, Wytheville | .067 | 14 | 15 | 2 | 1 | 1 | 0 | 0 | 0 | 0 | 0 | 0 | 0 | 0 | 0 | 0 | 3 | 0 | 0 |
| Kline, Stewart, Bluefield† | .245 | 51 | 143 | 15 | 35 | 56 | 3 | 3 | 4 | 30 | 5 | 1 | 3 | 0 | 16 | 0 | 19 | 0 | 2 |
| Knapp, Thomas, Bristol° | .238 | 43 | 130 | 15 | 31 | 43 | 3 | 3 | 1 | 21 | 1 | 1 | 2 | 0 | 10 | 0 | 15 | 7 | 1 |
| Kraemer, Joseph, Wytheville° | .200 | 22 | 5 | 0 | 1 | 1 | 0 | 0 | 0 | 0 | 0 | 0 | 0 | 0 | 1 | 0 | 2 | 0 | 0 |
| Kraiss, Stephen, Bluefield | .224 | 49 | 116 | 19 | 26 | 42 | 8 | 1 | 2 | 19 | 6 | 0 | 0 | 1 | 22 | 0 | 34 | 1 | 0 |
| Lancaster, Lester, Wytheville | .167 | 20 | 24 | 5 | 4 | 9 | 2 | 0 | 1 | 3 | 1 | 2 | 0 | 0 | 3 | 0 | 3 | 0 | 0 |
| Lanoux, Marty, Elizabethton° | .313 | 68 | 217 | 48 | 68 | 106 | 17 | 0 | 7 | 45 | 2 | 0 | 2 | 4 | 39 | 1 | 21 | 4 | 2 |
| Latmore, Robert, Bluefield | .258 | 59 | 190 | 29 | 49 | 62 | 6 | 2 | 1 | 20 | 3 | 2 | 1 | 1 | 19 | 0 | 34 | 4 | 4 |
| Lee, Anthony, Wytheville | .333 | 12 | 3 | 0 | 1 | 1 | 0 | 0 | 0 | 0 | 0 | 0 | 0 | 0 | 0 | 0 | 0 | 0 | 0 |
| Leiper, Timothy, Bristol† | .308 | 61 | 211 | 37 | 65 | 90 | 16 | 0 | 3 | 47 | 4 | 0 | 2 | 1 | 15 | 1 | 18 | 7 | 4 |
| Lemle, Robert, Kingsport | .173 | 51 | 133 | 17 | 23 | 32 | 1 | 1 | 2 | 9 | 0 | 0 | 1 | 0 | 25 | 0 | 43 | 11 | 4 |
| Lewis, John, Wytheville° | .282 | 58 | 202 | 48 | 57 | 77 | 8 | 3 | 2 | 19 | 0 | 1 | 0 | 3 | 39 | 0 | 29 | 22 | 4 |
| Liddell, David, Wytheville | .231 | 36 | 104 | 21 | 24 | 41 | 5 | 0 | 4 | 11 | 1 | 1 | 0 | 3 | 15 | 1 | 29 | 0 | 1 |
| Liebert, Allen, Bristol° | .235 | 33 | 98 | 14 | 23 | 30 | 4 | 0 | 1 | 13 | 1 | 0 | 1 | 0 | 8 | 1 | 9 | 0 | 1 |
| Lopez, Anthony, Elizabethton | .262 | 14 | 42 | 6 | 11 | 14 | 0 | 0 | 1 | 15 | 0 | 0 | 4 | 1 | 7 | 0 | 6 | 1 | 0 |
| Magrane, Joseph, Johnson City | .333 | 6 | 3 | 1 | 1 | 1 | 0 | 0 | 0 | 0 | 0 | 0 | 0 | 0 | 0 | 0 | 1 | 0 | 0 |
| Mancini, Peter, Bluefield | .235 | 18 | 51 | 5 | 12 | 14 | 2 | 0 | 0 | 2 | 0 | 0 | 1 | 4 | 0 | 0 | 5 | 1 | 1 |
| Mann, Kelly, Wytheville | .200 | 26 | 75 | 6 | 15 | 21 | 3 | 0 | 1 | 10 | 1 | 0 | 0 | 0 | 6 | 0 | 21 | 0 | 0 |
| Marina, Juan, Kingsport | .063 | 13 | 16 | 0 | 1 | 1 | 0 | 0 | 0 | 0 | 0 | 0 | 0 | 0 | 0 | 0 | 9 | 0 | 0 |
| Martel, Jay, Johnson City | .000 | 17 | 5 | 0 | 0 | 0 | 0 | 0 | 0 | 0 | 0 | 0 | 0 | 0 | 0 | 0 | 3 | 0 | 0 |
| Martinez, Julian, Johnson City | .194 | 21 | 62 | 4 | 12 | 17 | 2 | 0 | 1 | 8 | 0 | 3 | 0 | 1 | 3 | 0 | 12 | 3 | 1 |
| Masters, Frank, Bristol | .250 | 13 | 40 | 4 | 10 | 11 | 1 | 0 | 0 | 4 | 1 | 0 | 1 | 0 | 5 | 0 | 10 | 0 | 1 |
| McDonald, Bruce, Wytheville° | .000 | 15 | 1 | 0 | 0 | 0 | 0 | 0 | 0 | 0 | 0 | 0 | 0 | 0 | 0 | 0 | 0 | 0 | 0 |
| McGinnis, Shawn, Johnson City° | .067 | 28 | 30 | 2 | 2 | 2 | 0 | 0 | 0 | 1 | 0 | 0 | 0 | 0 | 6 | 1 | 7 | 0 | 1 |
| McMorris, Mark, Wytheville° | .370 | 64 | 227 | 45 | 84 | 118 | 10 | 3 | 6 | 53 | 6 | 2 | 5 | 0 | 31 | 3 | 19 | 5 | 1 |
| Mejias, Simeon, Wytheville† | .250 | 65 | 192 | 25 | 48 | 57 | 5 | 2 | 0 | 15 | 3 | 6 | 1 | 0 | 28 | 0 | 30 | 6 | 3 |
| Miller, Michael, Wytheville | .171 | 18 | 41 | 5 | 7 | 12 | 2 | 0 | 1 | 6 | 1 | 3 | 1 | 0 | 5 | 0 | 10 | 0 | 0 |
| Miller, Ted, Elizabethton | .268 | 25 | 71 | 7 | 19 | 26 | 2 | 1 | 1 | 16 | 3 | 0 | 1 | 0 | 9 | 0 | 14 | 2 | 0 |
| Mueller, William, Johnson City | .298 | 41 | 124 | 19 | 37 | 52 | 6 | 0 | 3 | 13 | 3 | 0 | 1 | 3 | 2 | 0 | 24 | 2 | 0 |
| Murphy, Miguel, Elizabethton | .266 | 51 | 169 | 18 | 45 | 58 | 7 | 0 | 2 | 23 | 3 | 1 | 0 | 1 | 11 | 0 | 29 | 5 | 1 |
| Murrell, Rodney, Kingsport° | .257 | 54 | 148 | 22 | 38 | 55 | 8 | 0 | 3 | 24 | 2 | 0 | 3 | 1 | 27 | 0 | 20 | 2 | 0 |
| Nowlin, James, Pulaski† | .250 | 15 | 8 | 1 | 2 | 2 | 0 | 0 | 0 | 0 | 0 | 0 | 0 | 0 | 0 | 0 | 2 | 0 | 0 |
| O'Connor, James, Johnson City | .231 | 6 | 13 | 1 | 3 | 4 | 1 | 0 | 0 | 0 | 0 | 0 | 0 | 0 | 1 | 0 | 1 | 0 | 0 |
| Paulino, Ernesto, Bluefield | .319 | 40 | 113 | 18 | 36 | 51 | 13 | 1 | 0 | 20 | 2 | 0 | 3 | 0 | 14 | 0 | 21 | 0 | 0 |
| Pena, Victor, Wytheville° | .000 | 7 | 1 | 0 | 0 | 0 | 0 | 0 | 0 | 0 | 0 | 0 | 0 | 0 | 0 | 0 | 1 | 0 | 0 |
| Perez, Francisco, Johnson City | .231 | 10 | 13 | 2 | 3 | 7 | 1 | 0 | 1 | 4 | 1 | 0 | 0 | 0 | 2 | 0 | 3 | 0 | 0 |
| Perry, Parnell, Wytheville | .253 | 48 | 150 | 22 | 38 | 49 | 8 | 0 | 1 | 21 | 2 | 2 | 2 | 0 | 11 | 0 | 29 | 6 | 3 |
| Perry, Robert, Elizabethton | .302 | 67 | 215 | 43 | 65 | 106 | 20 | 0 | 7 | 39 | 2 | 1 | 1 | 5 | 47 | 0 | 43 | 6 | 2 |
| Plecker, Michael, Kingsport | .070 | 19 | 43 | 1 | 3 | 6 | 0 | 0 | 1 | 4 | 0 | 0 | 0 | 0 | 5 | 0 | 20 | 1 | 0 |
| Polanco, Radhames, Kingsport | .167 | 47 | 138 | 16 | 23 | 29 | 3 | 0 | 1 | 5 | 0 | 1 | 0 | 0 | 25 | 1 | 47 | 3 | 0 |
| Poore, William, Johnson City | .000 | 13 | 1 | 0 | 0 | 0 | 0 | 0 | 0 | 0 | 0 | 0 | 0 | 0 | 0 | 0 | 0 | 0 | 0 |
| Prioleau, Thelanius, Bristol° | .224 | 55 | 152 | 24 | 34 | 50 | 5 | 1 | 3 | 20 | 3 | 4 | 3 | 1 | 19 | 0 | 31 | 3 | 1 |
| Ramon, Ernesto, Kingsport | .000 | 20 | 2 | 0 | 0 | 0 | 0 | 0 | 0 | 0 | 0 | 0 | 0 | 0 | 0 | 0 | 0 | 0 | 0 |
| Robertson, Michael, Johnson City | .259 | 55 | 135 | 32 | 35 | 52 | 4 | 2 | 3 | 27 | 0 | 0 | 2 | 1 | 36 | 1 | 35 | 14 | 1 |
| Roby, Ellis, Pulaski† | .224 | 33 | 116 | 27 | 26 | 37 | 3 | 1 | 2 | 15 | 0 | 1 | 1 | 2 | 17 | 0 | 22 | 6 | 1 |
| Rocca, Jose, Johnson City | .156 | 20 | 32 | 3 | 5 | 5 | 0 | 0 | 0 | 2 | 0 | 1 | 0 | 0 | 3 | 0 | 13 | 0 | 0 |
| Rockey, James, Pulaski | .290 | 63 | 214 | 34 | 62 | 84 | 14 | 1 | 2 | 28 | 3 | 4 | 2 | 3 | 26 | 2 | 28 | 1 | 0 |
| Rosthenhausler, Ramon, Bristol | .198 | 55 | 172 | 36 | 34 | 52 | 4 | 1 | 4 | 21 | 2 | 2 | 1 | 2 | 23 | 0 | 55 | 5 | 2 |
| Rowe, Mathew, Pulaski | .000 | 19 | 4 | 0 | 0 | 0 | 0 | 0 | 0 | 0 | 0 | 0 | 0 | 0 | 1 | 0 | 1 | 0 | 0 |
| Rowland, Donald, Bristol | .299 | 59 | 194 | 44 | 58 | 75 | 10 | 2 | 1 | 21 | 4 | 3 | 1 | 2 | 28 | 0 | 20 | 14 | 4 |
| Roy, Michael, Elizabethton | .247 | 33 | 85 | 16 | 21 | 28 | 7 | 0 | 0 | 16 | 1 | 0 | 4 | 1 | 31 | 2 | 22 | 0 | 0 |
| Sanchez, Adolfo, Bluefield | .211 | 20 | 38 | 7 | 8 | 11 | 3 | 0 | 0 | 3 | 0 | 0 | 0 | 0 | 4 | 0 | 13 | 0 | 0 |
| Sanders, David, Kingsport | .000 | 10 | 1 | 0 | 0 | 0 | 0 | 0 | 0 | 0 | 0 | 0 | 0 | 0 | 0 | 0 | 0 | 0 | 0 |
| Santo, Robert, Bluefield° | .283 | 16 | 46 | 7 | 13 | 23 | 1 | 0 | 3 | 9 | 1 | 0 | 1 | 0 | 5 | 0 | 8 | 0 | 0 |
| Scott, Jerry, Johnson City | .000 | 5 | 1 | 0 | 0 | 0 | 0 | 0 | 0 | 0 | 0 | 0 | 0 | 0 | 0 | 0 | 1 | 0 | 0 |
| Seitz, David, Pulaski° | .333 | 14 | 6 | 1 | 2 | 2 | 0 | 0 | 0 | 0 | 0 | 0 | 0 | 0 | 1 | 0 | 3 | 0 | 0 |
| Sherman, Harrison, Elizabethton | .248 | 38 | 109 | 16 | 27 | 38 | 6 | 1 | 1 | 12 | 1 | 0 | 1 | 1 | 12 | 0 | 20 | 2 | 0 |
| Sims, Kinney, Bluefield° | .200 | 46 | 65 | 13 | 13 | 15 | 0 | 1 | 0 | 4 | 1 | 2 | 0 | 1 | 7 | 0 | 27 | 3 | 2 |
| Singletary, Nathan, Johnson City† | .179 | 51 | 112 | 17 | 20 | 22 | 0 | 1 | 0 | 9 | 1 | 0 | 1 | 1 | 7 | 0 | 27 | 8 | 1 |
| Skeete, Rafael, Bluefield° | .125 | 5 | 8 | 2 | 1 | 1 | 0 | 0 | 0 | 1 | 0 | 0 | 0 | 0 | 1 | 0 | 4 | 0 | 0 |
| Slocumb, Heath, Kingsport | .222 | 11 | 9 | 2 | 2 | 2 | 0 | 0 | 0 | 0 | 0 | 0 | 0 | 0 | 0 | 0 | 1 | 0 | 0 |
| Smith, Gregory, Wytheville† | .235 | 51 | 179 | 28 | 42 | 52 | 6 | 2 | 0 | 15 | 1 | 3 | 1 | 2 | 20 | 1 | 27 | 8 | 1 |
| Smith, Jeffrey, Elizabethton° | .136 | 7 | 22 | 1 | 3 | 4 | 1 | 0 | 0 | 0 | 0 | 1 | 0 | 0 | 2 | 0 | 3 | 0 | 0 |
| Smith, Terrance, Pulaski | .188 | 19 | 48 | 3 | 9 | 15 | 4 | 1 | 0 | 4 | 0 | 1 | 0 | 0 | 4 | 0 | 15 | 0 | 0 |
| Snowberger, Thomas, Bristol° | .143 | 10 | 28 | 3 | 4 | 7 | 0 | 0 | 1 | 5 | 0 | 0 | 0 | 0 | 5 | 0 | 11 | 0 | 0 |
| St. Hill, Steve, Bluefield | .173 | 38 | 81 | 10 | 14 | 23 | 3 | 0 | 2 | 10 | 1 | 0 | 2 | 1 | 3 | 0 | 21 | 1 | 0 |
| Stainbrook, John, Elizabethton | .230 | 59 | 174 | 24 | 40 | 45 | 5 | 0 | 0 | 11 | 2 | 2 | 0 | 1 | 17 | 0 | 60 | 3 | 2 |
| Strange, Douglas, Bristol† | .305 | 65 | 226 | 43 | 69 | 105 | 16 | 1 | 6 | 45 | 6 | 4 | 3 | 3 | 22 | 1 | 30 | 6 | 0 |
| Stringfellow, Thornton, Pulaski° | .500 | 21 | 2 | 0 | 1 | 1 | 0 | 0 | 0 | 0 | 0 | 0 | 0 | 0 | 0 | 0 | 0 | 0 | 0 |
| Sullivan, James, Wytheville | .259 | 64 | 216 | 41 | 56 | 68 | 8 | 2 | 0 | 23 | 0 | 8 | 4 | 1 | 23 | 0 | 19 | 11 | 5 |
| Swenson, Lee, Elizabethton | .169 | 20 | 59 | 12 | 10 | 15 | 2 | 0 | 1 | 6 | 0 | 0 | 1 | 1 | 8 | 0 | 15 | 0 | 0 |
| Thiesen, Michael, Johnson City | .309 | 61 | 191 | 42 | 59 | 76 | 9 | 1 | 2 | 28 | 7 | 0 | 3 | 2 | 30 | 1 | 14 | 16 | 3 |
| Thomason, Gary, Elizabethton | .202 | 34 | 94 | 13 | 19 | 24 | 5 | 0 | 0 | 9 | 0 | 1 | 0 | 3 | 14 | 0 | 22 | 3 | 1 |
| Thompson, Anthony, Kingsport† | .210 | 32 | 81 | 12 | 17 | 34 | 3 | 1 | 4 | 14 | 2 | 0 | 0 | 2 | 21 | 0 | 29 | 5 | 2 |
| Thomson, Robert, Bristol | .000 | 2 | 5 | 0 | 0 | 0 | 0 | 0 | 0 | 0 | 0 | 0 | 0 | 0 | 0 | 0 | 3 | 0 | 0 |
| Tomberlin, Robert, Pulaski | .291 | 62 | 206 | 42 | 60 | 110 | 18 | 1 | 10 | 36 | 6 | 0 | 1 | 0 | 35 | 0 | 29 | 1 | 0 |
| Trapasso, Michael, Pulaski° | .000 | 13 | 1 | 0 | 0 | 0 | 0 | 0 | 0 | 0 | 0 | 0 | 0 | 0 | 0 | 0 | 1 | 0 | 0 |
| Tubbleville, Randal, Kingsport | .054 | 28 | 56 | 4 | 3 | 3 | 0 | 0 | 0 | 2 | 0 | 0 | 0 | 1 | 8 | 0 | 21 | 1 | 0 |
| Van Dehey, Daniel, Elizabethton | .195 | 29 | 82 | 14 | 16 | 19 | 3 | 0 | 0 | 5 | 1 | 1 | 1 | 3 | 19 | 1 | 19 | 1 | 0 |
| Vasquez, Steven, Pulaski | .000 | 20 | 1 | 0 | 0 | 0 | 0 | 0 | 0 | 0 | 0 | 0 | 0 | 0 | 0 | 0 | 0 | 0 | 0 |
| Waylock, Edmund, Bristol | .222 | 11 | 36 | 9 | 8 | 11 | 1 | 1 | 0 | 4 | 0 | 1 | 0 | 0 | 7 | 1 | 8 | 2 | 0 |
| Weems, Danny, Pulaski | .000 | 13 | 10 | 0 | 0 | 0 | 0 | 0 | 0 | 0 | 0 | 0 | 0 | 0 | 0 | 0 | 3 | 0 | 0 |
| Whitford, Larry, Wytheville | .222 | 13 | 9 | 0 | 2 | 3 | 1 | 0 | 0 | 1 | 0 | 0 | 0 | 0 | 4 | 0 | 1 | 0 | 0 |
| Willoughby, Mark, Kingsport | .250 | 15 | 4 | 0 | 1 | 2 | 1 | 0 | 0 | 2 | 0 | 0 | 0 | 0 | 0 | 0 | 2 | 0 | 0 |
| Wills, Adrian, Pulaski° | .289 | 41 | 128 | 13 | 37 | 57 | 6 | 1 | 4 | 20 | 2 | 0 | 1 | 1 | 12 | 1 | 25 | 0 | 0 |
| Worthington, Craig, Bluefield | .341 | 39 | 129 | 33 | 44 | 76 | 9 | 1 | 7 | 20 | 0 | 3 | 1 | 2 | 10 | 1 | 19 | 3 | 2 |
| Young, Ernest, Bluefield† | .241 | 33 | 79 | 13 | 19 | 28 | 3 | 0 | 2 | 12 | 2 | 0 | 1 | 1 | 9 | 0 | 25 | 1 | 1 |

The following pitchers, listed alphabetically by club, with games in parentheses, had no plate appearances, primarily through use of designated hitters:

BLUEFIELD—Constand, Andres (6); Dubois, Brian (10); Gast, Joseph (9); Hixson, Lester (2); Llanes, Pedro (13); Ludwig, Frederick, (10); Maro, William (11); McCall, Terrell (8); Meilleur, Jon (18); Mercedes, Juan (6); Peguero, Soto (11); Powell, Bradley (14); Stanhope, Chester (26); Wilson, Chaunan (12).

BRISTOL—Boling, John (5); Carter, Richard (10); Friesen, Robert (11); Gohmann, Kenneth (15); Jackson, Paul (14); Lee, Mark (15); Patenaude, Alain (8); Pifer, Gary (12); Schultz, Scott (14); Searcy, Stephen (4); Slavik, Joseph (12); Wetherell, Gerry (5); Williams, Kenneth (12); Wohlmacher, Richard (7); York, Michael (21).

ELIZABETHTON—Abbott, Paul (10); Adams, Michael (12); Bumgarner, Jeffrey (10); Coleman, DeWayne (16); Cook, James (20); Gasser, Steven (12); Honeycutt, Brian (11); Malec, Jason (4); O'Connor, Timothy (12); Olson, Steven (4); Redding, Michael (9); Rohlof, Scott (13); Strube, Robert (8); Wright, Kenneth (2).

JOHNSON CITY—Diaz, Felix (4); Farmer, Joseph (9); Hughes, Warren (11); Ittner, Lee (3); O'Keefe, Timothy (5); Peters, Steven (3).

KINGSPORT—Bohne, Mark (12).

PULASKI—Sheldon, Keith (10); Shotkoski, David (1).

WYTHEVILLE—Dedos, Felix (3).

GRAND SLAM HOME RUNS—Kline, Lopez, 1 each.

AWARDED FIRST BASE ON CATCHER'S INTERFERENCE—Goodwin 4 (M. Miller 2, Beasant, Buzzard); Archibald 3 (Kline, M. Miller, J. O'Connor); Bellini 2 (Lopez, Mann); Thiesen 2 (Buzzard, Swenson); Douglas (Swenson); T. Jones (Crews).

## CLUB FIELDING

| Club | Pct. | G. | PO. | A. | E. | DP. | PB. | Club | Pct. | G. | PO. | A. | E. | DP. | PB. |
|---|---|---|---|---|---|---|---|---|---|---|---|---|---|---|---|
| Bristol | .959 | 69 | 1623 | 667 | 99 | 52 | 14 | Wytheville | .942 | 70 | 1639 | 618 | 139 | 50 | 30 |
| Johnson City | .958 | 68 | 1517 | 633 | 94 | 53 | 5 | Kingsport | .940 | 70 | 1598 | 676 | 144 | 57 | 22 |
| Pulaski | .957 | 68 | 1609 | 654 | 102 | 46 | 11 | Elizabethton | .939 | 71 | 1631 | 681 | 149 | 49 | 18 |
| Bluefield | .947 | 70 | 1606 | 626 | 126 | 45 | 18 | | | | | | | | |

## INDIVIDUAL FIELDING

*Throws lefthanded.

### FIRST BASEMEN

| Player and Club | Pct. | G. | PO. | A. | E. | DP. | Player and Club | Pct. | G. | PO. | A. | E. | DP. |
|---|---|---|---|---|---|---|---|---|---|---|---|---|---|
| Archibald, Kingsport* | .976 | 11 | 78 | 3 | 2 | 6 | Iglesias, Johnson City | .976 | 12 | 73 | 7 | 2 | 8 |
| Bailey, Kingsport | .977 | 60 | 465 | 43 | 12 | 46 | Kraiss, Bluefield | .986 | 41 | 268 | 12 | 4 | 19 |
| Bastinck, Bristol | 1.000 | 1 | 2 | 0 | 0 | 0 | Leiper, Bristol | .984 | 29 | 243 | 9 | 4 | 14 |
| Billmeyer, Bluefield | 1.000 | 1 | 1 | 0 | 0 | 0 | McMORRIS, Wytheville* | .989 | 64 | 518 | 22 | 6 | 38 |
| Buglione, Johnson City | .997 | 43 | 311 | 30 | 1 | 32 | Mueller, Johnson City | 1.000 | 4 | 20 | 1 | 0 | 3 |
| Burke, Bluefield* | .983 | 17 | 104 | 9 | 2 | 6 | Perry, Elizabethton | .977 | 57 | 446 | 26 | 11 | 33 |
| Buzzard, Elizabethton | 1.000 | 1 | 2 | 0 | 0 | 0 | Robertson, Johnson City | .975 | 18 | 110 | 7 | 3 | 7 |
| Daily, Bristol | .974 | 41 | 367 | 15 | 10 | 33 | Rockey, Pulaski | 1.000 | 10 | 88 | 6 | 0 | 8 |
| Dewey, Pulaski | .988 | 11 | 77 | 6 | 1 | 5 | Roy, Elizabethton | 1.000 | 15 | 127 | 5 | 0 | 12 |
| Farmer, Kingsport | 1.000 | 1 | 11 | 0 | 0 | 0 | Sanchez, Bluefield | 1.000 | 1 | 2 | 0 | 0 | 0 |
| Ford, Pulaski | .982 | 47 | 411 | 15 | 8 | 30 | Santo, Bluefield* | .978 | 11 | 85 | 6 | 2 | 4 |
| Goodwin, Bluefield* | 1.000 | 1 | 4 | 0 | 0 | 0 | Sims, Bluefield* | 1.000 | 2 | 1 | 0 | 0 | 0 |
| Hamilton, Pulaski | 1.000 | 3 | 5 | 0 | 0 | 0 | Young, Bluefield* | .980 | 12 | 96 | 3 | 2 | 7 |
| Hamza, Wytheville | .933 | 6 | 51 | 5 | 4 | 9 | | | | | | | |

### SECOND BASEMEN

| Player and Club | Pct. | G. | PO. | A. | E. | DP. | Player and Club | Pct. | G. | PO. | A. | E. | DP. |
|---|---|---|---|---|---|---|---|---|---|---|---|---|---|
| Bautista, Bluefield | .950 | 6 | 6 | 13 | 1 | 2 | Latmore, Bluefield | 1.000 | 1 | 0 | 1 | 0 | 0 |
| Bernard, Bluefield | .750 | 3 | 0 | 3 | 1 | 0 | Leiper, Bristol | 1.000 | 1 | 1 | 1 | 0 | 0 |
| Boyce, Elizabethton | .919 | 36 | 56 | 102 | 14 | 19 | Mancini, Bluefield | .833 | 3 | 1 | 4 | 1 | 1 |
| Butler, Pulaski | 1.000 | 1 | 5 | 1 | 0 | 1 | Martinez, Johnson City | .936 | 12 | 18 | 26 | 3 | 4 |
| Castro, Kingsport | .939 | 62 | 107 | 153 | 17 | 32 | Mejias, Wytheville | .932 | 52 | 101 | 120 | 16 | 26 |
| Delancer, Elizabethton | .891 | 13 | 24 | 33 | 7 | 7 | Roby, Pulaski | .958 | 30 | 46 | 91 | 6 | 9 |
| Dulin, Bluefield | .933 | 55 | 78 | 145 | 16 | 25 | ROWLAND, Bristol | .967 | 58 | 85 | 123 | 7 | 24 |
| Fortner, Wytheville | .909 | 14 | 24 | 26 | 5 | 6 | Sanchez, Bluefield | .906 | 11 | 16 | 13 | 3 | 3 |
| Garrison, Pulaski | .926 | 40 | 79 | 96 | 14 | 19 | Singletary, Johnson City | .800 | 2 | 1 | 3 | 1 | 1 |
| Harwick, Wytheville | .952 | 7 | 7 | 13 | 1 | 4 | Strange, Bristol | .901 | 14 | 26 | 38 | 7 | 4 |
| Jefferies, Kingsport | 1.000 | 3 | 6 | 6 | 0 | 0 | Thiesen, Johnson City | .965 | 58 | 86 | 161 | 9 | 35 |
| Jones, Kingsport | .912 | 12 | 11 | 20 | 3 | 2 | Van Dehey, Elizabethton | .962 | 27 | 37 | 64 | 4 | 12 |

### THIRD BASEMEN

| Player and Club | Pct. | G. | PO. | A. | E. | DP. | Player and Club | Pct. | G. | PO. | A. | E. | DP. |
|---|---|---|---|---|---|---|---|---|---|---|---|---|---|
| Alfano, Pulaski | .893 | 11 | 4 | 21 | 3 | 1 | Kraiss, Bluefield | 1.000 | 4 | 1 | 4 | 0 | 0 |
| Bautista, Bluefield | 1.000 | 3 | 3 | 3 | 0 | 0 | LANOUX, Elizabethton | .904 | 62 | 50 | 101 | 16 | 3 |
| Bernard, Bluefield | .647 | 7 | 3 | 8 | 6 | 0 | Leiper, Bristol | .941 | 17 | 13 | 35 | 3 | 4 |
| Blake, Bristol | 1.000 | 1 | 1 | 1 | 0 | 0 | Mancini, Bluefield | .886 | 15 | 10 | 21 | 4 | 0 |
| Butler, Pulaski | .889 | 7 | 4 | 12 | 2 | 0 | Martinez, Johnson City | 1.000 | 7 | 1 | 5 | 0 | 1 |
| Canan, Wytheville | .893 | 30 | 33 | 42 | 9 | 3 | Mejias, Wytheville | .806 | 13 | 8 | 21 | 7 | 2 |
| Casteel, Wytheville | .750 | 30 | 19 | 26 | 15 | 5 | Miller, Wytheville | 1.000 | 1 | 0 | 1 | 0 | 0 |
| Cooley, Kingsport | .875 | 2 | 4 | 3 | 1 | 0 | Murrell, Kingsport | .839 | 25 | 21 | 31 | 10 | 2 |
| Delancer, Elizabethton | .821 | 11 | 9 | 14 | 5 | 1 | Polanco, Kingsport | .850 | 46 | 35 | 67 | 18 | 4 |
| Deloach, Johnson City | 1.000 | 1 | 0 | 1 | 0 | 0 | Rosthenhausler, Bristol | .942 | 36 | 28 | 69 | 6 | 4 |
| Dewey, Pulaski | .667 | 2 | 0 | 4 | 2 | 1 | Sanchez, Bluefield | 1.000 | 5 | 3 | 10 | 0 | 1 |
| Dulin, Bluefield | 1.000 | 5 | 2 | 9 | 0 | 0 | Singletary, Johnson City | 1.000 | 1 | 5 | 0 | 0 | 0 |
| Fregosi, Johnson City | .947 | 7 | 8 | 10 | 1 | 0 | Strange, Bristol | .895 | 10 | 3 | 14 | 2 | 1 |
| Iglesias, Johnson City | .882 | 43 | 37 | 60 | 13 | 9 | Tomberlin, Pulaski | .875 | 50 | 39 | 59 | 14 | 5 |
| Jackson, Johnson City | .947 | 8 | 9 | 9 | 1 | 2 | Waylock, Bristol | .957 | 8 | 5 | 17 | 1 | 1 |
| Jones, Johnson City | .778 | 5 | 4 | 3 | 2 | 0 | Worthington, Bluefield | .893 | 38 | 32 | 68 | 12 | 6 |
| Kline, Bluefield | 1.000 | 2 | 3 | 1 | 0 | 0 | | | | | | | |

### SHORTSTOPS

| Player and Club | Pct. | G. | PO. | A. | E. | DP. | Player and Club | Pct. | G. | PO. | A. | E. | DP. |
|---|---|---|---|---|---|---|---|---|---|---|---|---|---|
| ALVA, Pulaski | .942 | 63 | 78 | 183 | 16 | 29 | Jefferies, Kingsport | .903 | 44 | 72 | 124 | 21 | 27 |
| Bautista, Bluefield | .857 | 2 | 3 | 3 | 1 | 0 | Jones, Johnson City | .922 | 63 | 105 | 143 | 21 | 30 |
| Bernard, Bluefield | .821 | 12 | 11 | 12 | 5 | 4 | Latmore, Bluefield | .920 | 55 | 86 | 133 | 19 | 21 |
| Blackwell, Elizabethton | .858 | 58 | 73 | 133 | 34 | 26 | Murrell, Kingsport | .966 | 25 | 31 | 53 | 3 | 10 |
| Butler, Pulaski | .909 | 3 | 3 | 7 | 1 | 3 | Prioleau, Bristol | .921 | 52 | 71 | 139 | 18 | 19 |
| Canan, Wytheville | .861 | 11 | 17 | 14 | 5 | 5 | Roby, Pulaski | 1.000 | 1 | 2 | 4 | 0 | 0 |
| Castro, Kingsport | .778 | 5 | 2 | 5 | 2 | 0 | Rosthenhausler, Bristol | .940 | 18 | 34 | 45 | 5 | 8 |
| Delancer, Elizabethton | .922 | 18 | 23 | 24 | 4 | 3 | Smith, Wytheville | .900 | 50 | 56 | 160 | 24 | 21 |
| Dulin, Bluefield | 1.000 | 8 | 9 | 12 | 0 | 4 | Tomberlin, Pulaski | 1.000 | 2 | 2 | 2 | 0 | 1 |
| Fregosi, Johnson City | .944 | 5 | 3 | 14 | 1 | 3 | Van Dehey, Elizabethton | .800 | 1 | 4 | 4 | 2 | 1 |
| Harwick, Wytheville | .918 | 10 | 24 | 32 | 5 | 4 | | | | | | | |

## OUTFIELDERS

| Player and Club | Pct. | G. | PO. | A. | E. | DP. |
|---|---|---|---|---|---|---|
| Aldrich, Pulaski* | .980 | 45 | 92 | 4 | 2 | 0 |
| Alfano, Pulaski | .918 | 37 | 54 | 2 | 5 | 1 |
| Anderson, Bristol* | .936 | 61 | 98 | 5 | 7 | 0 |
| Archibald, Kingsport* | .902 | 33 | 33 | 4 | 4 | 1 |
| Balthazar, Bristol | 1.000 | 7 | 9 | 1 | 0 | 0 |
| Bellini, Bluefield* | .967 | 49 | 86 | 3 | 3 | 1 |
| Celis, Kingsport | .837 | 20 | 33 | 3 | 7 | 0 |
| Colavito, Bluefield | .920 | 25 | 22 | 1 | 2 | 0 |
| Cole, Johnson City* | .979 | 66 | 127 | 12 | 3 | 0 |
| Crosby, Elizabethton | .946 | 55 | 81 | 7 | 5 | 0 |
| DeLoach, Johnson City | .778 | 28 | 27 | 1 | 8 | 0 |
| Douglas, Kingsport | .946 | 27 | 32 | 3 | 2 | 0 |
| Ewart, Wytheville* | .971 | 51 | 62 | 5 | 2 | 1 |
| Farmer, Kingsport | 1.000 | 31 | 42 | 1 | 0 | 0 |
| Fox, Bristol* | .986 | 54 | 66 | 6 | 1 | 2 |
| Goodwin, Bluefield* | .892 | 25 | 29 | 4 | 4 | 0 |
| Hamilton, Pulaski | .952 | 14 | 18 | 2 | 1 | 0 |
| Hamza, Wytheville | .971 | 58 | 99 | 3 | 3 | 1 |
| Hayden, Kingsport* | .868 | 23 | 30 | 3 | 5 | 1 |
| M. Jackson, Johnson City | .986 | 53 | 64 | 7 | 1 | 1 |
| R. Jackson, Bristol | .846 | 18 | 10 | 1 | 2 | 1 |
| M. Jones, Wytheville | .857 | 9 | 12 | 0 | 2 | 0 |
| Justice, Pulaski* | .957 | 64 | 86 | 2 | 4 | 0 |
| Knapp, Bristol | .957 | 31 | 43 | 2 | 2 | 1 |
| Leiper, Bristol | 1.000 | 1 | 1 | 0 | 0 | 0 |
| Lemle, Kingsport | .961 | 49 | 95 | 3 | 4 | 0 |
| Lewis, Wytheville | .972 | 56 | 102 | 2 | 3 | 0 |
| McGinnis, Johnson City* | 1.000 | 14 | 14 | 2 | 0 | 0 |
| Murphy, Elizabethton | .921 | 43 | 54 | 4 | 5 | 0 |
| Perez, Johnson City | 1.000 | 5 | 7 | 0 | 0 | 0 |
| P. Perry, Wytheville | .949 | 41 | 55 | 1 | 3 | 1 |
| R. Perry, Elizabethton | 1.000 | 2 | 2 | 0 | 0 | 0 |
| Polanco, Kingsport | 1.000 | 1 | 2 | 0 | 0 | 0 |
| Robertson, Johnson City | .958 | 37 | 42 | 4 | 2 | 2 |
| Rockey, Pulaski | .978 | 52 | 87 | 3 | 2 | 1 |
| Sherman, Elizabethton | .938 | 33 | 42 | 3 | 3 | 0 |
| Sims, Bluefield* | .960 | 33 | 24 | 0 | 1 | 0 |
| Singletary, Johnson City | .923 | 32 | 33 | 3 | 3 | 0 |
| Skeete, Bluefield* | .750 | 4 | 3 | 0 | 1 | 0 |
| Smith, Elizabethton* | 1.000 | 5 | 8 | 0 | 0 | 0 |
| Snowberger, Bristol | 1.000 | 8 | 10 | 2 | 0 | 0 |
| St. Hill, Bluefield | 1.000 | 31 | 27 | 2 | 0 | 1 |
| Stainbrook, Elizabethton | .943 | 59 | 90 | 10 | 6 | 3 |
| Strange, Bristol | .969 | 44 | 55 | 7 | 2 | 1 |
| SULLIVAN, Bluefield* | .992 | 64 | 119 | 9 | 1 | 4 |
| Thiesen, Johnson City | 1.000 | 2 | 2 | 0 | 0 | 0 |
| Thomason, Elizabethton | .977 | 30 | 40 | 3 | 1 | 0 |
| Thompson, Kingsport | .958 | 26 | 44 | 2 | 2 | 2 |
| Tubbleville, Kingsport | .892 | 26 | 30 | 3 | 4 | 0 |
| Young, Bluefield* | .967 | 19 | 25 | 4 | 1 | 0 |

## CATCHERS

| Player and Club | Pct. | G. | PO. | A. | E. | DP. | PB. |
|---|---|---|---|---|---|---|---|
| Balthazar, Bristol | .966 | 5 | 27 | 1 | 1 | 0 | 3 |
| Bastinck, Bristol | .985 | 30 | 181 | 17 | 3 | 4 | 3 |
| Beasant, Kingsport | .977 | 21 | 78 | 7 | 2 | 0 | 7 |
| Billmeyer, Bluefield | .989 | 13 | 76 | 10 | 1 | 0 | 5 |
| Boyd, Johnson City | .966 | 19 | 99 | 14 | 4 | 1 | 1 |
| Buglione, Johnson City | .991 | 21 | 97 | 8 | 1 | 1 | 1 |
| Buzzard, Elizabethton | .959 | 32 | 184 | 28 | 9 | 0 | 6 |
| Crews, Kingsport | .970 | 43 | 196 | 30 | 7 | 6 | 13 |
| Dewey, Pulaski | .971 | 25 | 121 | 11 | 4 | 0 | 7 |
| Gardner, Bristol | .933 | 2 | 14 | 0 | 1 | 0 | 2 |
| Kline, Bluefield | .966 | 39 | 207 | 18 | 8 | 3 | 6 |
| LIDDELL, Wytheville | .978 | 36 | 204 | 18 | 5 | 1 | 10 |
| Liebert, Bristol | .979 | 25 | 127 | 15 | 3 | 4 | 3 |
| Lopez, Elizabethton | .932 | 7 | 37 | 4 | 3 | 1 | 1 |
| Mann, Wytheville | .963 | 22 | 118 | 11 | 5 | 0 | 10 |
| Masters, Bristol | 1.000 | 13 | 79 | 11 | 0 | 1 | 3 |
| M. Miller, Wytheville | .950 | 17 | 101 | 12 | 6 | 1 | 10 |
| T. Miller, Elizabethton | .965 | 16 | 78 | 5 | 3 | 1 | 2 |
| Mueller, Johnson City | .983 | 23 | 104 | 14 | 2 | 3 | 1 |
| O'Connor, Johnson City | .962 | 3 | 23 | 2 | 1 | 0 | 0 |
| Paulino, Bluefield | .954 | 24 | 131 | 14 | 7 | 1 | 7 |
| Plecker, Kingsport | .977 | 16 | 82 | 3 | 2 | 0 | 2 |
| Robertson, Johnson City | 1.000 | 2 | 8 | 1 | 0 | 0 | 0 |
| Rocca, Johnson City | .966 | 18 | 49 | 8 | 2 | 0 | 2 |
| Smith, Pulaski | .979 | 17 | 81 | 13 | 2 | 1 | 0 |
| Swenson, Elizabethton | .969 | 20 | 135 | 19 | 5 | 1 | 9 |
| Wills, Pulaski | .977 | 33 | 203 | 12 | 5 | 2 | 4 |

## PITCHERS

| Player and Club | Pct. | G. | PO. | A. | E. | DP. |
|---|---|---|---|---|---|---|
| Abbott, Elizabethton | 1.000 | 10 | 3 | 5 | 0 | 0 |
| Adams, Elizabethton | 1.000 | 12 | 6 | 12 | 0 | 1 |
| Bautista, Johnson City | .750 | 10 | 0 | 3 | 1 | 1 |
| Beer, Pulaski | 1.000 | 20 | 2 | 2 | 0 | 0 |
| Bohne, Kingsport | .625 | 12 | 1 | 4 | 3 | 0 |
| Boling, Bristol* | 1.000 | 5 | 2 | 4 | 0 | 0 |
| Brooks, Kingsport | 1.000 | 23 | 5 | 6 | 0 | 0 |
| Bumgarner, Elizabethton | .880 | 10 | 7 | 15 | 3 | 0 |
| Carter, Bristol | 1.000 | 10 | 4 | 3 | 0 | 0 |
| Cloninger, Wytheville* | 1.000 | 6 | 1 | 2 | 0 | 0 |
| Coleman, Elizabethton | .846 | 16 | 1 | 10 | 2 | 0 |
| Constand, Bluefield | 1.000 | 6 | 1 | 1 | 0 | 0 |
| Cook, Elizabethton | .667 | 20 | 0 | 2 | 1 | 0 |
| Damian, Wytheville | 1.000 | 14 | 1 | 5 | 0 | 0 |
| Dedos, Wytheville | 1.000 | 3 | 0 | 1 | 0 | 0 |
| Diaz, Johnson City | 1.000 | 4 | 0 | 4 | 0 | 0 |
| Dubois, Bluefield* | .882 | 10 | 2 | 13 | 2 | 0 |
| Farmer, Johnson City | 1.000 | 9 | 5 | 13 | 0 | 0 |
| Forrest, Johnson City | 1.000 | 4 | 1 | 2 | 0 | 0 |
| Friesen, Bristol | 1.000 | 11 | 2 | 3 | 0 | 3 |
| Garcia, Kingsport* | .900 | 14 | 4 | 5 | 1 | 0 |
| Gardner, Wytheville | .588 | 10 | 2 | 8 | 7 | 0 |
| Gasser, Elizabethton | 1.000 | 12 | 4 | 11 | 0 | 1 |
| Gast, Bluefield* | 1.000 | 9 | 0 | 2 | 0 | 0 |
| Gliha, Pulaski | .875 | 19 | 0 | 7 | 1 | 0 |
| Gohmann, Bristol | .833 | 15 | 0 | 10 | 2 | 0 |
| Green, Wytheville | .750 | 20 | 1 | 2 | 1 | 1 |
| J. Greene, Pulaski | 1.000 | 15 | 3 | 14 | 0 | 1 |
| T. Greene, Pulaski | .769 | 12 | 4 | 6 | 3 | 0 |
| Griffith, Johnson City | 1.000 | 18 | 3 | 14 | 0 | 0 |
| Guerra, Bluefield | .800 | 23 | 2 | 6 | 2 | 0 |
| Hayes, Kingsport | .893 | 13 | 11 | 14 | 3 | 0 |
| Haynes, Johnson City | .833 | 20 | 3 | 7 | 2 | 0 |
| Henry, Johnson City | 1.000 | 11 | 3 | 8 | 0 | 0 |
| Hightower, Kingsport* | .857 | 10 | 4 | 8 | 2 | 2 |
| Hixson, Bluefield | 1.000 | 2 | 2 | 0 | 0 | 0 |
| Holder, Kingsport | 1.000 | 25 | 3 | 10 | 0 | 1 |
| Honeycutt, Elizabethton | .778 | 11 | 3 | 4 | 2 | 0 |
| Howes, Kingsport | .818 | 8 | 3 | 6 | 2 | 0 |
| Hughes, Johnson City | 1.000 | 11 | 4 | 5 | 0 | 0 |
| Ittner, Johnson City | 1.000 | 3 | 0 | 1 | 0 | 0 |
| Jackson, Bristol | .857 | 14 | 0 | 6 | 1 | 0 |
| Jefferson, Wytheville* | .750 | 9 | 0 | 3 | 1 | 0 |
| Kallevig, Wytheville | .955 | 14 | 7 | 14 | 1 | 0 |
| Kraemer, Wytheville* | .889 | 22 | 1 | 7 | 1 | 0 |
| LANCASTER, Wytheville* | 1.000 | 20 | 6 | 20 | 0 | 1 |
| A. Lee, Wytheville | 1.000 | 12 | 4 | 2 | 0 | 0 |
| M. Lee, Bristol* | 1.000 | 15 | 0 | 4 | 0 | 0 |
| Llanes, Bluefield | .750 | 13 | 4 | 14 | 6 | 1 |
| Ludwig, Bluefield | .667 | 10 | 0 | 2 | 1 | 0 |
| Magrane, Johnson City* | .923 | 6 | 2 | 10 | 1 | 3 |
| Malec, Elizabethton* | 1.000 | 4 | 0 | 1 | 0 | 0 |
| Marina, Kingsport | .947 | 13 | 6 | 12 | 1 | 1 |
| Maro, Bluefield | .750 | 11 | 2 | 4 | 2 | 0 |
| Martel, Johnson City | .500 | 17 | 1 | 2 | 3 | 0 |
| McCall, Bluefield* | .000 | 8 | 0 | 0 | 1 | 0 |
| McDonald, Kingsport | 1.000 | 15 | 4 | 4 | 0 | 1 |
| Meilleur, Bluefield | .800 | 18 | 1 | 3 | 1 | 1 |
| Nowlin, Pulaski | .909 | 15 | 2 | 8 | 1 | 1 |
| O'Connor, Elizabethton | 1.000 | 12 | 1 | 3 | 0 | 1 |
| O'Keefe, Johnson City | 1.000 | 5 | 5 | 5 | 0 | 2 |
| Olson, Elizabethton* | 1.000 | 4 | 0 | 6 | 0 | 0 |
| Patenaude, Bristol | .889 | 8 | 2 | 6 | 1 | 0 |
| Peguero, Bluefield | .929 | 11 | 6 | 7 | 1 | 1 |
| Pena, Wytheville* | 1.000 | 7 | 2 | 2 | 0 | 0 |
| Peters, Johnson City* | .800 | 3 | 1 | 3 | 1 | 0 |
| Pifer, Bristol | .875 | 12 | 1 | 6 | 1 | 0 |
| Poore, Johnson City | .667 | 13 | 2 | 0 | 1 | 0 |
| Powell, Bluefield | .833 | 14 | 3 | 7 | 2 | 1 |
| Ramon, Kingsport | 1.000 | 20 | 4 | 5 | 0 | 0 |
| Redding, Elizabethton | 1.000 | 9 | 1 | 6 | 0 | 0 |
| Rohlof, Elizabethton | .800 | 13 | 0 | 12 | 3 | 0 |
| Rowe, Pulaski | 1.000 | 19 | 2 | 10 | 0 | 0 |
| Sanders, Kingsport | .857 | 10 | 0 | 6 | 1 | 1 |
| Schultz, Bristol | .833 | 14 | 2 | 8 | 2 | 1 |
| Searcy, Bristol* | 1.000 | 4 | 2 | 2 | 0 | 0 |
| Seitz, Pulaski* | .962 | 14 | 5 | 20 | 1 | 1 |
| Sheldon, Pulaski | .857 | 10 | 0 | 6 | 1 | 0 |
| Slavik, Bristol* | 1.000 | 12 | 1 | 6 | 0 | 0 |
| Slocumb, Kingsport | .889 | 11 | 10 | 14 | 3 | 3 |
| Stanhope, Bluefield | 1.000 | 26 | 5 | 6 | 0 | 1 |
| Stringfellow, Kingsport* | 1.000 | 21 | 0 | 2 | 0 | 0 |
| Strube, Elizabethton* | .875 | 8 | 3 | 4 | 1 | 1 |
| Trapasso, Pulaski* | 1.000 | 13 | 1 | 3 | 0 | 0 |
| Vasquez, Pulaski | 1.000 | 20 | 2 | 9 | 0 | 1 |
| Weems, Pulaski | .824 | 13 | 3 | 11 | 3 | 1 |
| Wetherell, Bristol | .714 | 5 | 1 | 4 | 2 | 1 |
| Whitford, Wytheville | .846 | 13 | 3 | 8 | 2 | 0 |
| Williams, Bristol* | .810 | 12 | 6 | 11 | 4 | 3 |
| Willoughby, Kingsport* | 1.000 | 15 | 3 | 12 | 0 | 0 |
| Wilson, Bluefield | 1.000 | 12 | 1 | 3 | 0 | 0 |
| Wohlmacher, Bristol | 1.000 | 7 | 0 | 7 | 0 | 0 |
| Wright, Elizabethton | 1.000 | 2 | 0 | 1 | 0 | 0 |
| York, Bristol | .933 | 21 | 1 | 13 | 1 | 2 |

The following players do not have any recorded accepted chances at the positions indicated; therefore, are not listed in the fielding averages for those particular positions: Billmeyer, of; Blackwell, of; Burke, of; Crews, p; Daily, 3b; J. Jones, of; Mercedes, p; Murphy, 3b; Paulino, 3b; Plecker, p; Roy, of; Sanchez, ss; Scott, p; Shotkoski, p; Thomason, 1b; Tubbleville, p; Van Dehey, 3b.

## CLUB PITCHING

| Club | ERA. | G. | CG. | ShO. | Sv. | IP. | H. | R. | ER. | HR. | HB. | BB. | Int. BB. | SO. | WP. | Bk. |
|------|------|----|-----|------|-----|-----|----|----|----|----|----|----|------|----|----|----|
| Bristol | 3.89 | 69 | 10 | 8 | 16 | 541.0 | 462 | 293 | 234 | 30 | 18 | 296 | 7 | 425 | 62 | 10 |
| Elizabethton | 4.25 | 71 | 20 | 2 | 11 | 543.2 | 543 | 340 | 257 | 32 | 10 | 276 | 7 | 407 | 47 | 5 |
| Wytheville | 4.65 | 70 | 22 | 2 | 8 | 546.1 | 521 | 345 | 282 | 38 | 15 | 298 | 14 | 420 | 63 | 10 |
| Johnson City | 4.68 | 68 | 20 | 9 | 7 | 505.2 | 492 | 319 | 263 | 42 | 22 | 259 | 3 | 354 | 35 | 4 |
| Bluefield | 4.71 | 70 | 10 | 2 | 11 | 535.1 | 528 | 345 | 280 | 39 | 19 | 270 | 3 | 391 | 37 | 6 |
| Kingsport | 4.87 | 70 | 11 | 3 | 13 | 532.2 | 550 | 387 | 288 | 31 | 20 | 289 | 4 | 336 | 69 | 5 |
| Pulaski | 5.40 | 68 | 7 | 3 | 10 | 536.1 | 530 | 370 | 322 | 42 | 16 | 316 | 9 | 392 | 44 | 3 |

## PITCHERS' RECORDS
(Leading Qualifiers for Earned-Run Average Leadership — 58 or More Innings)

°Throws lefthanded.

| Pitcher — Club | W. | L. | Pct. | ERA. | G. | GS. | CG. | GF. | ShO. | Sv. | IP. | H. | R. | ER. | HR. | HB. | BB. | Int. BB. | SO. | WP. |
|------|----|----|------|------|----|-----|-----|-----|------|-----|-----|----|----|----|----|----|----|------|----|----|
| Adams, Elizabethton | 7 | 3 | .700 | 2.19 | 12 | 11 | 5 | 0 | 1 | 0 | 74.0 | 61 | 32 | 18 | 3 | 2 | 44 | 0 | 64 | 5 |
| Schultz, Bristol° | 7 | 3 | .700 | 2.45 | 14 | 5 | 2 | 8 | 1 | 0 | 58.2 | 41 | 23 | 16 | 4 | 3 | 24 | 0 | 44 | 1 |
| Williams, Bristol° | 3 | 2 | .600 | 3.02 | 12 | 9 | 1 | 0 | 1 | 0 | 59.2 | 42 | 41 | 22 | 20 | 1 | 0 | 37 | 0 | 67 | 10 |
| Griffith, Johnson City | 9 | 2 | .818 | 3.15 | 18 | 7 | 5 | 8 | 2 | 3 | 68.2 | 59 | 28 | 24 | 2 | 7 | 31 | 2 | 42 | 0 |
| Damian, Wytheville | 7 | 3 | .700 | 3.59 | 14 | 12 | 5 | 3 | 1 | 1 | 77.2 | 66 | 38 | 31 | 6 | 0 | 27 | 0 | 55 | 4 |
| Lancaster, Wytheville | 7 | 4 | .636 | 3.62 | 20 | 10 | 7 | 8 | 1 | 3 | 102.0 | 98 | 49 | 41 | 6 | 1 | 24 | 5 | 81 | 4 |
| Kallevig, Wytheville | 6 | 7 | .462 | 3.81 | 14 | 14 | 5 | 0 | 0 | 0 | 82.2 | 81 | 45 | 35 | 7 | 4 | 20 | 1 | 56 | 4 |
| Gasser, Elizabethton | 4 | 7 | .364 | 3.91 | 12 | 12 | 3 | 0 | 0 | 0 | 76.0 | 72 | 38 | 33 | 6 | 3 | 36 | 2 | 77 | 5 |
| Coleman, Elizabethton | 5 | 1 | .833 | 3.92 | 16 | 5 | 1 | 8 | 1 | 2 | 59.2 | 54 | 38 | 26 | 4 | 0 | 26 | 0 | 32 | 4 |
| Martel, Johnson City | 7 | 7 | .500 | 4.02 | 17 | 10 | 3 | 4 | 1 | 0 | 71.2 | 74 | 43 | 32 | 4 | 0 | 29 | 1 | 55 | 4 |

Departmental Leaders: G—Stanhope, 26; W—Griffith, York, 9, L—Gasser, Kallevig, Martel, 7; Pct.—Griffith, York, .818; GS—J. Greene, Kallevig, Seitz, 14; CG—Lancaster, 7; GF—Stringfellow, 19; ShO—Griffith, Magrane, 2; Sv.—Stringfellow, 7; IP—Lancaster, 102.0; H—Lancaster, 98; R—Hayes, 57; ER—Henry, 49; HR—Henry, 9; HB—Henry, 9; BB—Whitford, 57; IBB—Lancaster, 5; SO—Lancaster, 81; WP—Gardner, 17.

## (All Pitchers—Listed Alphabetically)

| Pitcher — Club | W. | L. | Pct. | ERA. | G. | GS. | CG. | GF. | ShO. | Sv. | IP. | H. | R. | ER. | HR. | HB. | BB. | Int. BB. | SO. | WP. |
|------|----|----|------|------|----|-----|-----|-----|------|-----|-----|----|----|----|----|----|----|------|----|----|
| Abbott, Elizabethton | 1 | 5 | .167 | 6.94 | 10 | 10 | 1 | 0 | 0 | 0 | 35.0 | 33 | 32 | 27 | 3 | 0 | 32 | 0 | 34 | 7 |
| Adams, Elizabethton | 7 | 3 | .700 | 2.19 | 12 | 11 | 5 | 0 | 1 | 0 | 74.0 | 61 | 32 | 18 | 3 | 2 | 44 | 0 | 64 | 5 |
| Bautista, Johnson City | 0 | 3 | .000 | 7.67 | 10 | 7 | 0 | 1 | 0 | 0 | 29.1 | 33 | 29 | 25 | 3 | 1 | 24 | 0 | 20 | 3 |
| Beer, Pulaski | 3 | 0 | 1.000 | 5.70 | 20 | 2 | 0 | 7 | 0 | 2 | 36.1 | 44 | 23 | 23 | 3 | 0 | 17 | 3 | 26 | 3 |
| Bohne, Kingsport | 1 | 2 | .333 | 6.92 | 12 | 1 | 0 | 6 | 0 | 0 | 13.0 | 15 | 20 | 10 | 0 | 1 | 18 | 0 | 4 | 5 |
| Boling, Bristol° | 2 | 1 | .667 | 2.08 | 5 | 4 | 2 | 0 | 1 | 0 | 26.0 | 16 | 10 | 6 | 1 | 0 | 13 | 0 | 20 | 3 |
| Brooks, Kingsport | 2 | 3 | .400 | 4.82 | 23 | 0 | 0 | 16 | 0 | 6 | 37.1 | 30 | 21 | 20 | 4 | 4 | 20 | 0 | 19 | 1 |
| Bumgarner, Elizabethton | 5 | 5 | .500 | 3.09 | 10 | 9 | 4 | 0 | 0 | 0 | 55.1 | 56 | 33 | 19 | 1 | 0 | 31 | 1 | 36 | 3 |
| Carter, Bristol | 4 | 2 | .667 | 3.69 | 10 | 10 | 1 | 0 | 0 | 0 | 46.1 | 41 | 23 | 19 | 4 | 1 | 30 | 0 | 36 | 6 |
| Cloninger, Wytheville° | 0 | 0 | .000 | 10.13 | 6 | 0 | 0 | 1 | 0 | 0 | 10.2 | 12 | 13 | 12 | 2 | 0 | 16 | 0 | 9 | 1 |
| Coleman, Elizabethton | 5 | 1 | .833 | 3.92 | 16 | 5 | 1 | 8 | 1 | 2 | 59.2 | 54 | 38 | 26 | 4 | 0 | 26 | 0 | 32 | 4 |
| Constand, Bluefield | 0 | 1 | .000 | 7.56 | 6 | 1 | 0 | 1 | 0 | 0 | 8.1 | 12 | 7 | 7 | 1 | 1 | 9 | 0 | 1 | 1 |
| Cook, Elizabethton | 2 | 2 | .500 | 5.13 | 20 | 0 | 0 | 18 | 0 | 6 | 26.1 | 28 | 19 | 15 | 1 | 0 | 11 | 1 | 21 | 2 |
| Crews, Kingsport | 0 | 0 | .000 | 0.00 | 1 | 0 | 0 | 0 | 0 | 0 | 1.0 | 1 | 0 | 0 | 0 | 0 | 1 | 0 | 1 | 0 |
| Damian, Wytheville | 7 | 3 | .700 | 3.59 | 14 | 12 | 5 | 3 | 1 | 1 | 77.2 | 66 | 38 | 31 | 6 | 0 | 27 | 0 | 55 | 4 |
| Dedos, Wytheville | 0 | 0 | .000 | 21.21 | 3 | 1 | 0 | 1 | 0 | 0 | 4.2 | 11 | 11 | 11 | 0 | 0 | 3 | 0 | 1 | 2 |
| Diaz, Johnson City | 0 | 0 | .000 | 2.00 | 4 | 1 | 0 | 2 | 0 | 0 | 9.0 | 6 | 2 | 2 | 0 | 0 | 5 | 0 | 7 | 0 |
| Dubois, Bluefield° | 5 | 4 | .556 | 2.50 | 10 | 9 | 2 | 1 | 1 | 0 | 57.2 | 42 | 23 | 16 | 1 | 2 | 20 | 0 | 67 | 5 |
| Farmer, Johnson City | 5 | 3 | .625 | 4.01 | 9 | 9 | 3 | 0 | 0 | 0 | 49.1 | 44 | 25 | 22 | 5 | 1 | 20 | 0 | 29 | 5 |
| Forrest, Johnson City | 1 | 2 | .333 | 4.22 | 4 | 3 | 1 | 0 | 0 | 0 | 21.1 | 19 | 11 | 10 | 3 | 2 | 13 | 0 | 13 | 4 |
| Friesen, Bristol | 4 | 2 | .667 | 4.99 | 11 | 11 | 0 | 0 | 0 | 0 | 48.2 | 48 | 37 | 27 | 1 | 0 | 32 | 0 | 19 | 5 |
| Garcia, Kingsport° | 1 | 4 | .200 | 4.24 | 14 | 5 | 0 | 5 | 0 | 1 | 34.0 | 37 | 20 | 16 | 1 | 0 | 23 | 0 | 21 | 9 |
| Gardner, Wytheville | 2 | 5 | .286 | 6.94 | 10 | 9 | 0 | 1 | 0 | 0 | 35.0 | 33 | 35 | 27 | 1 | 2 | 35 | 0 | 26 | 17 |
| Gasser, Elizabethton | 4 | 7 | .364 | 3.91 | 12 | 12 | 3 | 0 | 0 | 0 | 76.0 | 72 | 38 | 33 | 6 | 3 | 36 | 2 | 77 | 5 |
| Gast, Bluefield° | 1 | 3 | .250 | 5.02 | 9 | 7 | 0 | 0 | 0 | 0 | 37.2 | 36 | 26 | 21 | 3 | 0 | 17 | 0 | 17 | 2 |
| Gliha, Pulaski | 1 | 2 | .333 | 3.89 | 19 | 1 | 0 | 7 | 0 | 0 | 41.2 | 29 | 19 | 18 | 2 | 0 | 29 | 1 | 42 | 4 |
| Gohmann, Bristol | 1 | 1 | .500 | 3.76 | 15 | 2 | 0 | 5 | 0 | 3 | 38.1 | 32 | 21 | 16 | 3 | 3 | 14 | 3 | 24 | 1 |
| Green, Wytheville | 4 | 0 | 1.000 | 7.11 | 20 | 1 | 0 | 11 | 0 | 0 | 38.0 | 44 | 34 | 30 | 3 | 2 | 23 | 0 | 25 | 7 |
| J. Greene, Pulaski | 2 | 5 | .286 | 5.16 | 15 | 14 | 2 | 0 | 1 | 0 | 75.0 | 75 | 46 | 43 | 8 | 3 | 32 | 1 | 69 | 2 |
| T. Greene, Pulaski | 2 | 5 | .286 | 7.64 | 12 | 12 | 1 | 0 | 1 | 0 | 50.2 | 49 | 45 | 43 | 7 | 2 | 27 | 0 | 32 | 4 |
| Griffith, Johnson City | 9 | 2 | .818 | 3.15 | 18 | 7 | 5 | 8 | 2 | 3 | 68.2 | 59 | 28 | 24 | 2 | 7 | 31 | 2 | 42 | 0 |
| Guerra, Bluefield | 4 | 2 | .667 | 4.21 | 23 | 1 | 0 | 13 | 0 | 2 | 36.1 | 30 | 21 | 17 | 3 | 1 | 23 | 1 | 42 | 2 |
| Hayes, Kingsport | 4 | 6 | .400 | 5.07 | 13 | 13 | 4 | 0 | 0 | 0 | 76.1 | 88 | 57 | 43 | 6 | 4 | 31 | 2 | 36 | 6 |
| Haynes, Johnson City | 1 | 2 | .333 | 3.82 | 20 | 1 | 0 | 15 | 0 | 3 | 33.0 | 38 | 27 | 14 | 1 | 0 | 18 | 0 | 20 | 3 |
| Henry, Johnson City | 5 | 3 | .625 | 7.35 | 11 | 10 | 2 | 0 | 0 | 0 | 60.0 | 56 | 55 | 49 | 9 | 9 | 42 | 0 | 31 | 8 |
| Hightower, Kingsport° | 5 | 5 | .500 | 2.45 | 10 | 9 | 5 | 1 | 1 | 0 | 55.0 | 32 | 21 | 15 | 6 | 2 | 25 | 0 | 50 | 4 |
| Hixson, Bluefield | 0 | 0 | .000 | 6.75 | 2 | 1 | 0 | 0 | 0 | 0 | 4.0 | 5 | 3 | 3 | 1 | 1 | 4 | 0 | 5 | 2 |
| Holder, Kingsport | 1 | 4 | .200 | 4.91 | 25 | 0 | 0 | 12 | 0 | 3 | 33.0 | 44 | 31 | 18 | 1 | 1 | 18 | 1 | 21 | 4 |
| Honeycutt, Elizabethton | 1 | 1 | .500 | 4.67 | 11 | 1 | 0 | 7 | 0 | 0 | 27.0 | 34 | 17 | 14 | 1 | 1 | 17 | 0 | 24 | 4 |
| Howes, Kingsport | 1 | 6 | .143 | 5.40 | 8 | 8 | 1 | 0 | 0 | 0 | 40.0 | 46 | 32 | 24 | 3 | 4 | 14 | 0 | 14 | 2 |
| Hughes, Johnson City | 2 | 2 | .500 | 5.27 | 11 | 5 | 0 | 5 | 0 | 0 | 42.2 | 50 | 30 | 25 | 2 | 1 | 12 | 0 | 27 | 3 |
| Ittner, Johnson City | 0 | 0 | .000 | 12.00 | 3 | 2 | 0 | 1 | 0 | 0 | 6.0 | 14 | 8 | 8 | 1 | 0 | 7 | 0 | 10 | 0 |
| Jackson, Bristol | 3 | 6 | .333 | 6.84 | 14 | 7 | 1 | 4 | 0 | 2 | 50.0 | 66 | 42 | 38 | 7 | 0 | 15 | 1 | 28 | 5 |
| Jefferson, Wytheville° | 1 | 0 | 1.000 | 2.60 | 9 | 0 | 0 | 6 | 0 | 0 | 17.1 | 20 | 9 | 5 | 0 | 0 | 16 | 0 | 9 | 2 |
| Kallevig, Wytheville | 6 | 7 | .462 | 3.81 | 14 | 14 | 5 | 0 | 0 | 0 | 82.2 | 81 | 45 | 35 | 7 | 4 | 20 | 1 | 56 | 4 |
| Kraemer, Wytheville° | 4 | 2 | .667 | 3.35 | 22 | 3 | 1 | 12 | 0 | 4 | 45.2 | 33 | 21 | 17 | 3 | 1 | 36 | 4 | 52 | 5 |
| Lancaster, Wytheville | 7 | 4 | .636 | 3.62 | 20 | 10 | 7 | 8 | 1 | 3 | 102.0 | 98 | 49 | 41 | 6 | 1 | 24 | 5 | 81 | 4 |
| A. Lee, Wytheville | 1 | 4 | .200 | 4.78 | 12 | 6 | 0 | 3 | 0 | 0 | 37.2 | 35 | 23 | 20 | 5 | 3 | 23 | 2 | 23 | 4 |
| M. Lee, Bristol° | 3 | 0 | 1.000 | 1.09 | 15 | 1 | 0 | 11 | 0 | 5 | 33.0 | 18 | 5 | 4 | 1 | 0 | 12 | 0 | 40 | 2 |
| Llanes, Bluefield | 6 | 6 | .500 | 5.04 | 13 | 12 | 0 | 0 | 0 | 0 | 69.2 | 77 | 52 | 39 | 6 | 3 | 41 | 0 | 27 | 3 |
| Ludwig, Bluefield | 3 | 1 | .750 | 4.70 | 10 | 5 | 1 | 2 | 0 | 0 | 30.2 | 31 | 21 | 16 | 1 | 1 | 11 | 0 | 21 | 1 |
| Magrane, Johnson City° | 2 | 1 | .667 | 0.60 | 6 | 5 | 2 | 0 | 2 | 0 | 30.0 | 15 | 4 | 2 | 0 | 1 | 11 | 0 | 31 | 0 |
| Malec, Elizabethton° | 0 | 0 | .000 | 6.14 | 4 | 0 | 0 | 1 | 0 | 0 | 7.1 | 9 | 5 | 5 | 1 | 0 | 4 | 1 | 4 | 1 |
| Marina, Kingsport | 3 | 4 | .429 | 4.94 | 13 | 10 | 0 | 1 | 0 | 0 | 62.0 | 60 | 41 | 34 | 4 | 0 | 29 | 1 | 45 | 8 |

| Pitcher—Club | W. | L. | Pct. | ERA. | G. | GS. | CG. | GF. | ShO. | Sv. | IP. | H. | R. | ER. | HR. | HB. | BB. | Int. BB. | SO. | WP. |
|---|---|---|---|---|---|---|---|---|---|---|---|---|---|---|---|---|---|---|---|---|
| Maro, Bluefield | 4 | 3 | .571 | 4.02 | 11 | 6 | 3 | 3 | 0 | 2 | 47.0 | 41 | 21 | 21 | 4 | 0 | 14 | 0 | 41 | 1 |
| Martel, Johnson City | 7 | 7 | .500 | 4.02 | 17 | 10 | 3 | 4 | 1 | 0 | 71.2 | 74 | 43 | 32 | 4 | 0 | 29 | 1 | 55 | 4 |
| McCall, Bluefield° | 0 | 2 | .000 | 15.83 | 8 | 1 | 0 | 3 | 0 | 0 | 9.2 | 11 | 17 | 17 | 1 | 0 | 17 | 1 | 10 | 4 |
| McDonald, Kingsport | 1 | 2 | .333 | 7.97 | 15 | 5 | 0 | 2 | 0 | 0 | 35.0 | 45 | 36 | 31 | 2 | 0 | 24 | 0 | 18 | 1 |
| Meilleur, Bluefield° | 3 | 2 | .600 | 2.40 | 18 | 1 | 0 | 13 | 0 | 2 | 30.0 | 20 | 13 | 8 | 2 | 2 | 13 | 0 | 21 | 2 |
| Mercedes, Bluefield | 0 | 0 | .000 | 12.38 | 6 | 0 | 0 | 2 | 0 | 0 | 8.0 | 12 | 13 | 11 | 0 | 1 | 12 | 1 | 3 | 1 |
| Nowlin, Pulaski | 3 | 5 | .375 | 7.97 | 15 | 9 | 0 | 1 | 0 | 0 | 49.2 | 55 | 50 | 44 | 7 | 0 | 42 | 0 | 25 | 4 |
| O'Connor, Elizabethton | 2 | 1 | .667 | 1.66 | 12 | 2 | 1 | 7 | 0 | 2 | 43.1 | 22 | 10 | 8 | 1 | 0 | 10 | 0 | 27 | 1 |
| O'Keefe, Johnson City | 1 | 1 | .500 | 4.67 | 5 | 2 | 1 | 2 | 0 | 0 | 27.0 | 29 | 15 | 14 | 2 | 0 | 10 | 0 | 17 | 1 |
| Olson, Elizabethton° | 0 | 1 | .000 | 7.71 | 4 | 0 | 0 | 3 | 0 | 0 | 7.0 | 12 | 8 | 6 | 0 | 0 | 1 | 0 | 6 | 2 |
| Patenaude, Bristol | 3 | 1 | .750 | 5.19 | 8 | 4 | 1 | 1 | 1 | 1 | 26.0 | 30 | 16 | 15 | 0 | 0 | 15 | 0 | 16 | 1 |
| Peguero, Bluefield | 5 | 3 | .625 | 5.37 | 11 | 11 | 1 | 0 | 0 | 0 | 60.1 | 67 | 42 | 36 | 8 | 2 | 28 | 0 | 31 | 5 |
| Pena, Wytheville° | 2 | 1 | .667 | 7.11 | 7 | 1 | 0 | 2 | 0 | 0 | 12.2 | 10 | 14 | 10 | 0 | 0 | 18 | 1 | 7 | 1 |
| Peters, Johnson City° | 3 | 0 | 1.000 | 0.47 | 3 | 3 | 2 | 0 | 1 | 0 | 19.0 | 5 | 1 | 1 | 1 | 0 | 3 | 0 | 30 | 0 |
| Pifer, Bristol | 0 | 2 | .000 | 5.97 | 12 | 3 | 0 | 5 | 0 | 1 | 28.2 | 28 | 29 | 19 | 2 | 4 | 16 | 0 | 16 | 5 |
| Plecker, Kingsport | 0 | 0 | .000 | 0.00 | 1 | 0 | 0 | 1 | 0 | 0 | 0.1 | 0 | 0 | 0 | 0 | 0 | 1 | 0 | 0 | 0 |
| Poore, Johnson City | 3 | 2 | .600 | 6.82 | 13 | 2 | 1 | 7 | 0 | 1 | 30.1 | 38 | 26 | 23 | 5 | 0 | 24 | 0 | 17 | 1 |
| Powell, Bluefield | 3 | 2 | .600 | 3.60 | 14 | 10 | 2 | 1 | 0 | 0 | 55.0 | 54 | 29 | 22 | 2 | 3 | 29 | 0 | 49 | 5 |
| Ramon, Kingsport | 3 | 0 | 1.000 | 4.45 | 20 | 0 | 0 | 11 | 0 | 2 | 32.1 | 33 | 20 | 16 | 1 | 2 | 11 | 0 | 24 | 7 |
| Redding, Elizabethton | 2 | 5 | .286 | 6.57 | 9 | 7 | 2 | 1 | 0 | 1 | 37.0 | 53 | 34 | 27 | 6 | 1 | 17 | 1 | 18 | 3 |
| Rohlof, Elizabethton | 2 | 5 | .286 | 4.35 | 13 | 10 | 3 | 2 | 0 | 0 | 62.0 | 66 | 40 | 30 | 2 | 2 | 26 | 0 | 45 | 4 |
| Rowe, Pulaski | 2 | 6 | .250 | 4.55 | 19 | 5 | 0 | 6 | 0 | 0 | 55.1 | 47 | 34 | 28 | 5 | 3 | 27 | 0 | 45 | 4 |
| Sanders, Kingsport | 0 | 1 | .000 | 7.88 | 10 | 0 | 0 | 2 | 0 | 1 | 16.0 | 22 | 17 | 14 | 2 | 0 | 8 | 0 | 12 | 3 |
| Schultz, Bristol | 7 | 3 | .700 | 2.45 | 14 | 5 | 2 | 8 | 1 | 0 | 58.2 | 41 | 23 | 16 | 4 | 3 | 24 | 0 | 44 | 1 |
| Scott, Johnson City | 0 | 1 | .000 | 12.96 | 5 | 1 | 0 | 3 | 0 | 0 | 8.1 | 12 | 15 | 12 | 4 | 0 | 10 | 0 | 5 | 3 |
| Searcy, Bristol° | 1 | 1 | .500 | 2.05 | 4 | 4 | 2 | 0 | 1 | 0 | 22.0 | 15 | 6 | 5 | 0 | 0 | 2 | 0 | 24 | 1 |
| Seitz, Pulaski° | 5 | 6 | .455 | 4.54 | 14 | 14 | 1 | 0 | 0 | 0 | 71.1 | 70 | 42 | 36 | 2 | 1 | 52 | 1 | 39 | 11 |
| Sheldon, Pulaski | 0 | 0 | .000 | 4.50 | 10 | 0 | 0 | 3 | 0 | 0 | 18.0 | 22 | 17 | 9 | 1 | 1 | 10 | 0 | 17 | 2 |
| Shotkowski, Pulaski | 1 | 0 | 1.000 | 0.00 | 1 | 0 | 0 | 0 | 0 | 0 | 1.0 | 1 | 0 | 0 | 0 | 0 | 1 | 0 | 0 | 0 |
| Slavik, Bristol° | 2 | 1 | .667 | 4.78 | 12 | 4 | 0 | 4 | 0 | 0 | 37.2 | 32 | 24 | 20 | 3 | 2 | 35 | 1 | 35 | 11 |
| Slocumb, Kingsport | 3 | 2 | .600 | 3.78 | 11 | 9 | 1 | 0 | 0 | 0 | 52.1 | 47 | 32 | 22 | 0 | 1 | 31 | 0 | 29 | 15 |
| Stanhope, Bluefield | 2 | 4 | .333 | 4.42 | 26 | 3 | 1 | 17 | 0 | 5 | 57.0 | 57 | 35 | 28 | 5 | 1 | 17 | 0 | 29 | 2 |
| Stringfellow, Bluefield° | 3 | 3 | .500 | 2.13 | 21 | 0 | 0 | 19 | 0 | 7 | 25.1 | 13 | 7 | 6 | 0 | 0 | 11 | 0 | 35 | 0 |
| Strube, Elizabethton° | 0 | 3 | .000 | 7.85 | 8 | 3 | 0 | 3 | 0 | 0 | 28.2 | 37 | 30 | 25 | 3 | 1 | 18 | 1 | 17 | 5 |
| Trapasso, Pulaski° | 1 | 3 | .250 | 4.78 | 13 | 1 | 1 | 8 | 0 | 0 | 26.1 | 25 | 16 | 14 | 2 | 3 | 16 | 1 | 14 | 3 |
| Tubbleville, Kingsport | 0 | 0 | .000 | 0.00 | 1 | 0 | 0 | 1 | 0 | 0 | 1.0 | 0 | 0 | 0 | 0 | 0 | 0 | 0 | 0 | 0 |
| Vasquez, Pulaski | 2 | 1 | .667 | 5.93 | 20 | 0 | 0 | 10 | 0 | 1 | 30.1 | 35 | 28 | 20 | 4 | 1 | 26 | 2 | 28 | 2 |
| Weems, Pulaski | 3 | 4 | .429 | 6.18 | 13 | 10 | 2 | 0 | 0 | 0 | 55.1 | 65 | 43 | 38 | 1 | 2 | 26 | 0 | 20 | 5 |
| Wetherell, Bristol | 0 | 1 | .000 | 8.36 | 5 | 5 | 0 | 0 | 0 | 0 | 14.0 | 15 | 14 | 13 | 1 | 2 | 10 | 0 | 16 | 3 |
| Whitford, Wytheville | 5 | 5 | .500 | 4.70 | 13 | 13 | 4 | 0 | 0 | 0 | 82.1 | 78 | 53 | 43 | 5 | 2 | 57 | 1 | 76 | 12 |
| Williams, Bristol° | 3 | 2 | .600 | 3.02 | 12 | 9 | 1 | 0 | 1 | 0 | 59.2 | 41 | 22 | 20 | 1 | 0 | 37 | 0 | 67 | 10 |
| Willoughby, Kingsport° | 1 | 5 | .167 | 5.11 | 15 | 8 | 0 | 2 | 0 | 0 | 44.0 | 50 | 39 | 25 | 1 | 0 | 33 | 0 | 42 | 4 |
| Wilson, Bluefield | 0 | 1 | .000 | 6.75 | 12 | 2 | 0 | 4 | 0 | 0 | 24.0 | 33 | 22 | 18 | 1 | 1 | 15 | 0 | 27 | 1 |
| Wohlmacher, Bluefield | 2 | 0 | 1.000 | 3.86 | 7 | 0 | 0 | 3 | 0 | 2 | 14.0 | 15 | 9 | 6 | 1 | 1 | 7 | 0 | 9 | 2 |
| Wright, Elizabethton | 0 | 1 | .000 | 7.20 | 2 | 1 | 0 | 1 | 0 | 0 | 5.0 | 6 | 4 | 4 | 0 | 0 | 3 | 0 | 2 | 1 |
| York, Bristol | 9 | 2 | .818 | 2.37 | 21 | 0 | 0 | 18 | 0 | 2 | 38.0 | 24 | 12 | 10 | 1 | 2 | 34 | 2 | 31 | 6 |

BALKS—Whitford, 3; Carter, Gohman, Holder, Kallevig, Kraemer, Magrane, 2 each; Abbott, Adams, Beer, Coleman, Dedos, Garcia, Gardner, Gast, Hayes, Henry, Howes, Ludwig, Malec, Martel, McCall, Meilleur, Mercedes, Nowlin, Pena, Pifer, Rowe, Searcy, Slavik, Strube, Wetherell, Williams, Wilson, York, 1 each.

COMBINATION SHUTOUTS—Dubois-Stanhope, Bluefield; Carter-Jackson, Williams-Schultz, Wetherell-Slavik-Lee, Bristol; Diaz-Griffith, Hughes-Griffith, Johnson City; Marina-Brooks, Hayes-Brooks, Kingsport; Rowe-Beer, Pulaski.

NO-HIT GAME—None.

# Gulf Coast League

## SUMMER CLASS A CLASSIFICATION

### CHAMPIONSHIP WINNERS IN PREVIOUS YEARS

| | | |
|---|---|---|
| 1964—Sarasota Braves ........... .610 | 1972—Chicago N.L. a ............... .651 | 1979—Houston ........................ .635 |
| 1965—Bradenton Astros ......... .632 | Kansas City a ...................... .651 | 1980—Kansas City-Blue ........... .635 |
| 1966—New York A.L. ............... .667 | 1973—Texas ............................ .732 | 1981—Kansas City-Gold .......... .688 |
| 1967—Kansas City ................... .614 | 1974—Chicago N.L. ................. .702 | 1982—New York-A.L. ............... .667 |
| 1968—Oakland ........................ .650 | 1975—Texas ............................ .774 | 1983—Texas ............................ .645 |
| 1969—Montreal ...................... .585 | 1976—Texas ............................ .704 | Los Angeles b ....................... .617 |
| 1970—Chicago A.L. ................. .600 | 1977—Chicago-A.L. ................. .731 | 1984—White Sox ..................... .651 |
| 1971—Kansas City ................... .755 | 1978—Texas ............................ .600 | Rangers b ............................ .571 |

(Note—Known as Sarasota Rookie League in 1964 and Florida Rookie League in 1965.) aDeclared co-champions; no playoff. bLeague divided into Northern and Southern divisions; won one-game playoff for league championship.

### STANDING OF CLUBS AT CLOSE OF SEASON, AUGUST 30

| NORTHERN DIVISION | | | | | | SOUTHERN DIVISION | | | | | |
|---|---|---|---|---|---|---|---|---|---|---|---|
| Club | W. | L. | T. | Pct. | G.B. | Club | W. | L. | T. | Pct. | G.B. |
| Rangers ........................ | 33 | 29 | 0 | .532 | ........ | Yankees ........................ | 43 | 18 | 1 | .705 | ........ |
| Dodgers ........................ | 28 | 33 | 0 | .459 | 4½ | White Sox ..................... | 40 | 22 | 2 | .645 | 3½ |
| Braves .......................... | 26 | 35 | 0 | .426 | 6½ | Royals ........................... | 38 | 24 | 0 | .613 | 5½ |
| Blue Jays ...................... | 23 | 39 | 0 | .371 | 10 | Reds .............................. | 38 | 24 | 0 | .613 | 5½ |
| Pirates .......................... | 15 | 47 | 0 | .242 | 18 | Astros ........................... | 24 | 37 | 1 | .393 | 19 |

### COMPOSITE STANDING OF CLUBS AT CLOSE OF SEASON, AUGUST 30

| Club | Yan. | W.S. | Royl | Rds. | Rng. | Dod. | Brv. | Ast. | B.J. | Pir. | W. | L. | T. | Pct. | G.B. |
|---|---|---|---|---|---|---|---|---|---|---|---|---|---|---|---|
| Yankees ............... | .... | 3 | 3 | 6 | 4 | 5 | 4 | 7 | 6 | 5 | 43 | 18 | 1 | .705 | ........ |
| White Sox ............ | 4 | .... | 2 | 1 | 7 | 6 | 4 | 4 | 6 | 6 | 40 | 22 | 2 | .645 | 3½ |
| Royals .................. | 3 | 5 | .... | 3 | 6 | 4 | 5 | 3 | 5 | 4 | 38 | 24 | 0 | .613 | 5½ |
| Reds .................... | 1 | 6 | 4 | .... | 3 | 4 | 5 | 4 | 5 | 6 | 38 | 24 | 0 | .613 | 5½ |
| Rangers ............... | 3 | 0 | 1 | 3 | .... | 5 | 6 | 5 | 4 | 6 | 33 | 29 | 0 | .532 | 10½ |
| Dodgers ............... | 2 | 1 | 3 | 3 | 2 | .... | 2 | 6 | 5 | 4 | 28 | 33 | 0 | .459 | 15 |
| Braves ................. | 2 | 3 | 2 | 2 | 1 | 4 | .... | 5 | 3 | 4 | 26 | 35 | 0 | .426 | 17 |
| Astros ................. | 0 | 2 | 4 | 3 | 2 | 0 | 2 | .... | 5 | 6 | 24 | 37 | 1 | .393 | 19 |
| Blue Jays ............. | 1 | 1 | 2 | 2 | 3 | 2 | 4 | 2 | .... | 6 | 23 | 39 | 0 | .371 | 20½ |
| Pirates ................. | 2 | 1 | 3 | 1 | 1 | 3 | 3 | 1 | 0 | .... | 15 | 47 | 0 | .242 | 28½ |

Games played at Bradenton and Sarasota, Fla.

Club names are major league affiliations.

Playoffs—League championship game between Yankees (Southern Division winner) and Rangers (Northern Division winner) was rained out. Yankees declared league champion based on overall winning percentage.

Regular Season Attendance—5,468 total paid for 20 openings (only games for which admission was charged).

Managers—Astros, Julio Linares; Blue Jays, Rockett Wheeler; Braves, Pedro Gonzalez; Dodgers, Jose Alvarez; Pirates, Woody Huyke; Rangers, Rudy Jaramillo; Reds, Sam Mejias; Royals, Joe Jones; White Sox, J.C. Martin; Yankees, Carlos Tosca.

All-Star Team—1B—Isidore Rondon, Reds; 2B—Rob Lambert, Yankees; 3B—Domingo Martinez, Blue Jays; SS—Francisco Burgos, Rangers; OF—Fred Carter, Yankees; Jovon Edwards, Dodgers; Ted Higgins, Yankees; C—Michael Dotzler, Rangers; Starting Pitcher—Dan Belinskas, Reds; Relief Pitcher—Phil Dale, Reds; Manager—Carlos Tosca, Yankees.

(Compiled by Howe News Bureau, Boston, Mass.)

### CLUB BATTING

| Club | Pct. | G. | AB. | R. | OR. | H. | TB. | 2B. | 3B. | HR. | RBI. | GW. | SH. | SF. | HP. | BB. | Int. BB. | SO. | SB. | CS. | LOB. |
|---|---|---|---|---|---|---|---|---|---|---|---|---|---|---|---|---|---|---|---|---|---|
| Yankees ............... | .275 | 62 | 2070 | 347 | 226 | 569 | 731 | 88 | 25 | 8 | 279 | 37 | 21 | 25 | 33 | 273 | 11 | 386 | 109 | 53 | 492 |
| Dodgers ............... | .254 | 61 | 2039 | 297 | 309 | 517 | 650 | 75 | 17 | 8 | 238 | 23 | 25 | 19 | 20 | 239 | 9 | 341 | 76 | 26 | 471 |
| Royals .................. | .246 | 62 | 1979 | 325 | 259 | 486 | 643 | 52 | 30 | 15 | 264 | 29 | 23 | 25 | 38 | 226 | 2 | 431 | 105 | 51 | 421 |
| Rangers ............... | .242 | 62 | 2066 | 257 | 246 | 501 | 641 | 70 | 23 | 8 | 212 | 32 | 19 | 14 | 31 | 208 | 7 | 421 | 66 | 42 | 453 |
| Blue Jays ............. | .240 | 62 | 2116 | 249 | 299 | 508 | 644 | 66 | 14 | 14 | 188 | 15 | 6 | 11 | 24 | 170 | 3 | 428 | 72 | 37 | 432 |
| Pirates ................. | .240 | 62 | 2072 | 237 | 376 | 497 | 615 | 63 | 17 | 7 | 199 | 11 | 7 | 11 | 15 | 152 | 1 | 442 | 79 | 41 | 415 |
| White Sox ............ | .238 | 64 | 2076 | 316 | 228 | 495 | 666 | 70 | 25 | 17 | 244 | 33 | 35 | 18 | 22 | 250 | 10 | 367 | 67 | 32 | 446 |
| Astros ................. | .233 | 62 | 1979 | 226 | 288 | 461 | 582 | 59 | 19 | 8 | 187 | 18 | 26 | 18 | 29 | 214 | 7 | 404 | 94 | 50 | 443 |
| Reds .................... | .233 | 62 | 2000 | 274 | 211 | 465 | 597 | 59 | 14 | 15 | 195 | 26 | 32 | 17 | 17 | 198 | 6 | 403 | 121 | 38 | 403 |
| Braves ................. | .221 | 61 | 2005 | 225 | 331 | 444 | 555 | 71 | 5 | 10 | 185 | 23 | 38 | 12 | 25 | 242 | 11 | 460 | 40 | 25 | 477 |

### INDIVIDUAL BATTING

(Leading Qualifiers for Batting Championship—170 or More Plate Appearances)

°Bats lefthanded.    †Switch-hitter.

| Player and Club | Pct. | G. | AB. | R. | H. | TB. | 2B. | 3B. | HR. | RBI. | GW. | SH. | SF. | HP. | BB. | Int. BB. | SO. | SB. | CS. |
|---|---|---|---|---|---|---|---|---|---|---|---|---|---|---|---|---|---|---|---|
| Lambert, Robert, Yankees ............... | .350 | 59 | 226 | 51 | 79 | 92 | 9 | 2 | 0 | 21 | 2 | 6 | 2 | 3 | 29 | 1 | 32 | 34 | 12 |
| Rondon, Isidro, Reds ...................... | .338 | 52 | 195 | 29 | 66 | 83 | 10 | 2 | 1 | 17 | 5 | 0 | 2 | 3 | 21 | 2 | 35 | 5 | 5 |
| Dotzler, Michael, Rangers° ............... | .317 | 62 | 208 | 38 | 66 | 90 | 14 | 5 | 0 | 28 | 2 | 0 | 3 | 1 | 30 | 3 | 26 | 4 | 6 |
| Mandel, Darren, Yankees ................. | .317 | 55 | 180 | 33 | 57 | 90 | 16 | 4 | 3 | 31 | 4 | 1 | 1 | 3 | 29 | 2 | 23 | 4 | 2 |
| Edwards, Jovon, Dodgers° ............... | .314 | 60 | 223 | 49 | 70 | 83 | 9 | 2 | 0 | 18 | 5 | 2 | 1 | 1 | 41 | 1 | 13 | 30 | 5 |
| Higgins, Theodore, Yankees° ............ | .306 | 55 | 196 | 38 | 60 | 79 | 7 | 6 | 0 | 36 | 6 | 1 | 4 | 4 | 30 | 3 | 14 | 9 | 6 |
| Caceres, Edgar, Dodgers° ................. | .301 | 53 | 176 | 37 | 53 | 59 | 6 | 0 | 0 | 22 | 2 | 2 | 0 | 2 | 18 | 1 | 11 | 5 | 2 |
| Robles, Daniel, Dodgers° ................. | .297 | 50 | 158 | 24 | 47 | 59 | 6 | 3 | 0 | 21 | 2 | 2 | 2 | 0 | 18 | 1 | 26 | 6 | 3 |
| Martinez, Domingo, Blue Jays .......... | .297 | 58 | 219 | 36 | 65 | 91 | 10 | 2 | 4 | 19 | 0 | 0 | 0 | 2 | 12 | 0 | 42 | 3 | 4 |
| Hindman, Randall, Reds ................... | .294 | 55 | 194 | 34 | 57 | 68 | 6 | 1 | 1 | 20 | 2 | 5 | 0 | 1 | 20 | 0 | 20 | 18 | 11 |
| Browne, James, Rangers° ................. | .293 | 59 | 191 | 22 | 56 | 76 | 8 | 3 | 2 | 29 | 6 | 1 | 1 | 0 | 31 | 0 | 32 | 0 | 2 |
| Guerrero, Epifano, Blue Jays° ........... | .288 | 56 | 229 | 34 | 66 | 78 | 8 | 2 | 0 | 18 | 0 | 1 | 2 | 1 | 14 | 0 | 20 | 8 | 5 |

Departmental Leaders: G—Dotzler, 62; AB—E. Guerrero, 229; R—Lambert, 51; H—Lambert, 79; TB—Lambert, 92; 2B—Mandel, 16; 3B—A. Clark, Higgins, T. Johnson, 6; HR—Alvarez, 5; RBI—Higgins, 36; GWRBI—Alvarez, 9; SH—J. Mota, 9; SF—Asbe, 6; HP—R. Bell, 11; BB—Waggoner, 49; IBB—Alvarez, 5; SO—W. Davis, 64; SB—Lambert, 34; CS—Lambert, McRae, 12.

| Player and Club | Pct. | G. | AB. | R. | H. | TB. | 2B. | 3B. | HR. | RBI. | GW. | SH. | SF. | HP. | BB. | Int. BB. | SO. | SB. | CS. |
|---|---|---|---|---|---|---|---|---|---|---|---|---|---|---|---|---|---|---|---|
| Abrell, Thomas, Braves | .000 | 12 | 4 | 0 | 0 | 0 | 0 | 0 | 0 | 0 | 0 | 3 | 0 | 0 | 0 | 0 | 4 | 0 | 0 |
| Acosta, Carlos, Reds | .248 | 48 | 153 | 34 | 38 | 49 | 5 | 0 | 2 | 13 | 4 | 2 | 1 | 2 | 5 | 0 | 26 | 12 | 1 |
| Adams, Steven, Pirates | .500 | 12 | 4 | 0 | 2 | 2 | 0 | 0 | 0 | 1 | 0 | 1 | 0 | 0 | 1 | 0 | 1 | 0 | 0 |
| Alcantara, Julio, Braves | .172 | 37 | 87 | 9 | 15 | 17 | 2 | 0 | 0 | 6 | 0 | 2 | 0 | 1 | 6 | 0 | 22 | 5 | 1 |
| Aleshire, Troy, Astros | .213 | 40 | 108 | 9 | 23 | 27 | 2 | 1 | 0 | 11 | 1 | 2 | 3 | 1 | 23 | 1 | 24 | 3 | 2 |
| Allen, Larry, White Sox* | .277 | 58 | 220 | 27 | 61 | 76 | 10 | 1 | 1 | 24 | 3 | 2 | 2 | 0 | 12 | 0 | 25 | 2 | 2 |
| Almonte, Heriberto, Astros | .220 | 20 | 59 | 8 | 13 | 17 | 4 | 0 | 0 | 5 | 0 | 3 | 0 | 2 | 1 | 0 | 13 | 0 | 2 |
| Alvarez, Jesus, White Sox* | .276 | 54 | 156 | 20 | 43 | 70 | 4 | 4 | 5 | 31 | 9 | 1 | 2 | 2 | 45 | 5 | 8 | 5 | 1 |
| Ames, Douglas, Dodgers* | .333 | 6 | 3 | 0 | 1 | 1 | 0 | 0 | 0 | 0 | 0 | 1 | 0 | 0 | 0 | 0 | 1 | 0 | 0 |
| Aquino, Diego, Astros | .240 | 7 | 25 | 3 | 6 | 8 | 2 | 0 | 0 | 4 | 0 | 1 | 0 | 0 | 1 | 0 | 3 | 1 | 0 |
| Arias, Cornelio, Dodgers† | .000 | 10 | 8 | 3 | 0 | 0 | 0 | 0 | 0 | 0 | 0 | 0 | 0 | 0 | 3 | 0 | 7 | 0 | 0 |
| Asbe, Daryl, Royals | .250 | 57 | 196 | 30 | 49 | 72 | 9 | 4 | 2 | 35 | 5 | 1 | 6 | 4 | 20 | 0 | 47 | 2 | 1 |
| Audain, Miguel, White Sox | .185 | 20 | 27 | 7 | 5 | 7 | 2 | 0 | 0 | 3 | 0 | 2 | 1 | 0 | 0 | 0 | 3 | 2 | 0 |
| Baldwin, Jeffrey, Astros* | .261 | 47 | 138 | 17 | 36 | 42 | 2 | 2 | 0 | 12 | 2 | 1 | 2 | 2 | 23 | 0 | 22 | 5 | 3 |
| Balli, Michael, White Sox | .109 | 26 | 46 | 3 | 5 | 6 | 1 | 0 | 0 | 6 | 1 | 2 | 1 | 0 | 5 | 0 | 9 | 3 | 1 |
| Banks, David, Yankees* | .228 | 43 | 145 | 15 | 33 | 42 | 7 | 1 | 0 | 21 | 4 | 0 | 0 | 0 | 24 | 2 | 24 | 2 | 1 |
| Barberich, Craig, Dodgers* | .188 | 21 | 32 | 2 | 6 | 7 | 1 | 0 | 0 | 2 | 0 | 2 | 0 | 0 | 8 | 0 | 7 | 0 | 1 |
| Barry, Kirk, Pirates | .236 | 21 | 72 | 12 | 17 | 22 | 3 | 1 | 0 | 8 | 0 | 0 | 0 | 2 | 10 | 1 | 1 | 1 |
| Basora, Edward, Dodgers | .000 | 12 | 3 | 6 | 0 | 0 | 0 | 0 | 0 | 0 | 0 | 0 | 0 | 1 | 0 | 0 | 2 | 1 | 0 |
| Bautista, Ruben, Braves† | .170 | 33 | 88 | 5 | 15 | 16 | 1 | 0 | 0 | 11 | 2 | 2 | 2 | 4 | 3 | 0 | 21 | 3 | 0 |
| Bautista, German, Pirates | .333 | 23 | 78 | 10 | 26 | 34 | 3 | 1 | 1 | 7 | 0 | 0 | 0 | 7 | 0 | 16 | 2 | 2 |
| Beaupre, Richard, Reds* | .160 | 40 | 119 | 11 | 19 | 21 | 2 | 0 | 0 | 9 | 0 | 0 | 0 | 4 | 12 | 1 | 21 | 1 | 1 |
| Beeler, Robert, Reds | .207 | 27 | 82 | 11 | 17 | 22 | 3 | 1 | 0 | 5 | 1 | 0 | 1 | 1 | 6 | 0 | 19 | 1 | 1 |
| Belinskas, Dan, Reds | .000 | 7 | 5 | 1 | 0 | 0 | 0 | 0 | 0 | 0 | 0 | 1 | 0 | 1 | 0 | 0 | 4 | 1 | 0 |
| Bell, Juan, Dodgers† | .160 | 42 | 106 | 11 | 17 | 17 | 0 | 0 | 0 | 8 | 1 | 2 | 0 | 1 | 12 | 0 | 20 | 2 | 1 |
| Bell, Robert, Royals | .223 | 61 | 206 | 33 | 46 | 68 | 4 | 3 | 4 | 35 | 3 | 0 | 3 | 11 | 29 | 0 | 62 | 17 | 5 |
| Benitez, Manuel, Dodgers | .257 | 52 | 175 | 30 | 45 | 69 | 13 | 1 | 3 | 28 | 0 | 4 | 4 | 15 | 2 | 26 | 2 | 2 |
| Bettencourt, Bobby, Yankees | .143 | 2 | 7 | 2 | 1 | 1 | 0 | 0 | 0 | 1 | 0 | 0 | 0 | 1 | 0 | 0 | 0 | 0 | 0 |
| Bledsoe, James, White Sox | .150 | 17 | 40 | 2 | 6 | 7 | 1 | 0 | 0 | 4 | 0 | 3 | 1 | 1 | 5 | 0 | 16 | 0 | 1 |
| Bond, David, Dodgers† | .000 | 16 | 2 | 0 | 0 | 0 | 0 | 0 | 0 | 0 | 0 | 0 | 0 | 0 | 0 | 0 | 1 | 0 | 0 |
| Braxton, Glen, White Sox* | .255 | 56 | 204 | 35 | 52 | 62 | 2 | 4 | 0 | 21 | 1 | 4 | 0 | 2 | 19 | 1 | 49 | 11 | 1 |
| Brown, Don, Reds | .187 | 43 | 107 | 24 | 20 | 37 | 4 | 2 | 3 | 10 | 0 | 2 | 1 | 0 | 20 | 0 | 25 | 11 | 2 |
| Brown, Kurt, White Sox | .205 | 49 | 176 | 24 | 36 | 55 | 8 | 1 | 3 | 23 | 5 | 1 | 1 | 4 | 13 | 0 | 32 | 0 | 2 |
| Browne, James, Rangers* | .293 | 59 | 191 | 22 | 56 | 76 | 8 | 3 | 2 | 29 | 6 | 1 | 1 | 0 | 31 | 0 | 32 | 0 | 2 |
| Bruno, Joseph, Reds* | .000 | 10 | 3 | 0 | 0 | 0 | 0 | 0 | 0 | 0 | 0 | 0 | 0 | 0 | 0 | 0 | 0 | 0 | 0 |
| Brusky, Brad, Reds | .000 | 12 | 9 | 0 | 0 | 0 | 0 | 0 | 0 | 0 | 0 | 0 | 0 | 0 | 0 | 0 | 5 | 0 | 0 |
| Burgos, Francisco, Rangers† | .257 | 56 | 206 | 29 | 53 | 63 | 6 | 2 | 0 | 19 | 5 | 1 | 3 | 2 | 14 | 0 | 22 | 6 | 8 |
| Burke, Robert, Braves | .000 | 12 | 2 | 0 | 0 | 0 | 0 | 0 | 0 | 0 | 0 | 1 | 0 | 0 | 0 | 0 | 1 | 0 | 0 |
| Butler, Leon, Braves | .185 | 31 | 81 | 10 | 15 | 15 | 0 | 0 | 0 | 3 | 0 | 4 | 0 | 1 | 12 | 1 | 19 | 1 | 2 |
| Caceres, Edgar, Dodgers† | .301 | 53 | 176 | 37 | 53 | 59 | 6 | 0 | 0 | 22 | 2 | 2 | 2 | 18 | 1 | 11 | 5 | 2 |
| Calvert, Arthur, Yankees | .316 | 36 | 136 | 19 | 43 | 57 | 8 | 3 | 0 | 26 | 4 | 0 | 5 | 1 | 15 | 2 | 28 | 4 | 6 |
| Canseco, Osvaldo, Yankees | .179 | 20 | 39 | 2 | 7 | 12 | 0 | 1 | 1 | 5 | 1 | 0 | 0 | 0 | 2 | 0 | 18 | 0 | 0 |
| Cantrell, Thomas, Braves | .214 | 43 | 145 | 17 | 31 | 42 | 4 | 2 | 1 | 10 | 1 | 0 | 1 | 0 | 19 | 1 | 27 | 3 | 2 |
| Cargile, Neal, Yankees | .280 | 48 | 118 | 17 | 33 | 43 | 3 | 2 | 1 | 20 | 3 | 1 | 1 | 2 | 14 | 0 | 29 | 9 | 4 |
| Caro, Bienvenido, Braves | .163 | 26 | 43 | 4 | 7 | 9 | 2 | 0 | 0 | 4 | 0 | 1 | 0 | 0 | 2 | 0 | 8 | 0 | 0 |
| Carter, Frederick, Yankees | .284 | 57 | 215 | 28 | 61 | 76 | 13 | 1 | 0 | 29 | 3 | 0 | 1 | 5 | 11 | 0 | 45 | 9 | 3 |
| Casey, Jermaine, Braves* | .214 | 52 | 159 | 21 | 34 | 43 | 6 | 0 | 1 | 15 | 4 | 0 | 1 | 0 | 32 | 1 | 36 | 3 | 2 |
| Chance, Anthony, Pirates | .333 | 10 | 33 | 7 | 11 | 14 | 1 | 1 | 0 | 2 | 0 | 0 | 0 | 4 | 0 | 4 | 2 | 0 |
| Charles, Juan, Dodgers | .273 | 13 | 11 | 2 | 3 | 6 | 1 | 1 | 0 | 0 | 0 | 0 | 0 | 0 | 0 | 0 | 5 | 0 | 1 |
| Clark, Anthony, Rangers | .235 | 35 | 115 | 11 | 27 | 39 | 0 | 6 | 0 | 12 | 4 | 0 | 0 | 0 | 11 | 0 | 27 | 4 | 1 |
| Clawson, Christopher, Braves | .270 | 46 | 148 | 26 | 40 | 49 | 6 | 0 | 1 | 20 | 3 | 4 | 0 | 4 | 29 | 0 | 30 | 8 | 4 |
| Clemente, Luis, Pirates | .235 | 7 | 17 | 0 | 4 | 4 | 0 | 0 | 0 | 2 | 0 | 0 | 0 | 2 | 0 | 6 | 0 | 1 |
| Colon, Emmanuel, Pirates | .000 | 9 | 1 | 0 | 0 | 0 | 0 | 0 | 0 | 0 | 0 | 0 | 0 | 0 | 0 | 0 | 1 | 0 | 0 |
| Converse, Michael, Reds | .000 | 12 | 6 | 0 | 0 | 0 | 0 | 0 | 0 | 0 | 0 | 0 | 0 | 0 | 0 | 0 | 3 | 0 | 0 |
| Cook, Jeffrey, Pirates | .263 | 46 | 167 | 32 | 44 | 50 | 1 | 1 | 1 | 13 | 1 | 1 | 0 | 0 | 14 | 0 | 25 | 19 | 8 |
| Corcino, Luis, Royals | .296 | 46 | 125 | 19 | 37 | 44 | 3 | 2 | 0 | 16 | 2 | 4 | 3 | 2 | 7 | 0 | 28 | 3 | 2 |
| Cox, Douglas, Dodgers* | .000 | 5 | 1 | 0 | 0 | 0 | 0 | 0 | 0 | 0 | 0 | 0 | 0 | 0 | 0 | 0 | 1 | 0 | 0 |
| Creager, David, Reds | .226 | 38 | 124 | 14 | 28 | 46 | 6 | 0 | 4 | 18 | 5 | 1 | 0 | 0 | 15 | 0 | 24 | 2 | 1 |
| Cruz, Marino, Braves | .283 | 24 | 60 | 7 | 17 | 19 | 2 | 0 | 0 | 12 | 2 | 1 | 1 | 0 | 7 | 0 | 2 | 0 | 0 |
| Cruz, Rafael, Rangers† | .269 | 43 | 130 | 10 | 35 | 48 | 6 | 2 | 1 | 15 | 2 | 4 | 1 | 1 | 12 | 0 | 32 | 4 | 6 |
| Cuadrado, Roberto, Yankees | .120 | 14 | 25 | 3 | 3 | 4 | 1 | 0 | 0 | 1 | 0 | 0 | 0 | 1 | 0 | 5 | 0 | 0 |
| Dale, Phil, Reds | .500 | 15 | 2 | 0 | 1 | 1 | 0 | 0 | 0 | 0 | 0 | 0 | 0 | 0 | 0 | 0 | 0 | 0 | 0 |
| Daniels, Ronnell, Pirates* | .750 | 2 | 8 | 2 | 6 | 6 | 0 | 0 | 0 | 1 | 0 | 0 | 0 | 0 | 0 | 0 | 0 | 0 | 0 |
| Davis, Kevin, Pirates | .294 | 5 | 17 | 2 | 5 | 6 | 1 | 0 | 0 | 0 | 0 | 0 | 0 | 0 | 0 | 4 | 0 | 0 |
| Davis, Wayne, Blue Jays | .197 | 55 | 218 | 26 | 43 | 64 | 8 | 2 | 3 | 23 | 1 | 0 | 2 | 3 | 8 | 0 | 64 | 18 | 7 |
| Day, Richard, Royals | .091 | 7 | 22 | 2 | 2 | 2 | 0 | 0 | 0 | 2 | 0 | 0 | 0 | 1 | 2 | 0 | 7 | 0 | 0 |
| DeLaCruz, Hector, Blue Jays | .337 | 20 | 83 | 9 | 28 | 35 | 3 | 2 | 0 | 13 | 2 | 1 | 1 | 4 | 0 | 7 | 5 | 1 |
| DeLeon, Pedro, Astros | .167 | 12 | 6 | 1 | 1 | 1 | 0 | 0 | 0 | 1 | 0 | 1 | 0 | 0 | 0 | 0 | 2 | 0 | 0 |
| Denkenberger, Ralph, Pirates* | .281 | 42 | 139 | 14 | 39 | 49 | 4 | 3 | 0 | 16 | 0 | 0 | 1 | 8 | 0 | 37 | 5 | 0 |
| Dennis, Gregory, Blue Jays | .000 | 1 | 4 | 0 | 0 | 0 | 0 | 0 | 0 | 0 | 0 | 0 | 0 | 0 | 0 | 0 | 0 | 0 | 0 |
| Dickerson, Brian, Pirates | .000 | 10 | 1 | 0 | 0 | 0 | 0 | 0 | 0 | 0 | 0 | 0 | 0 | 0 | 0 | 0 | 1 | 0 | 0 |
| Didder, Rayborne, Yankees | .167 | 18 | 30 | 6 | 5 | 5 | 0 | 0 | 0 | 4 | 0 | 0 | 1 | 3 | 0 | 11 | 2 | 2 |
| Dilone, Ivan, Dodgers | .000 | 25 | 2 | 0 | 0 | 0 | 0 | 0 | 0 | 0 | 0 | 0 | 0 | 0 | 0 | 0 | 1 | 0 | 0 |
| Dotzler, Michael, Rangers* | .317 | 62 | 208 | 38 | 66 | 90 | 14 | 5 | 0 | 28 | 2 | 0 | 3 | 1 | 30 | 3 | 26 | 4 | 6 |
| Driver, Frank, Reds | .333 | 9 | 3 | 0 | 1 | 1 | 0 | 0 | 0 | 0 | 0 | 1 | 0 | 0 | 1 | 0 | 1 | 0 | 0 |
| Duran, Jose, Dodgers | .250 | 32 | 56 | 5 | 14 | 18 | 4 | 0 | 0 | 6 | 1 | 0 | 0 | 2 | 6 | 0 | 9 | 0 | 0 |
| Dyer, Linton, Royals | .303 | 18 | 33 | 5 | 10 | 10 | 0 | 0 | 0 | 2 | 0 | 0 | 0 | 5 | 0 | 8 | 2 | 1 |
| Edge, Michael, Pirates | .000 | 3 | 1 | 0 | 0 | 0 | 0 | 0 | 0 | 0 | 0 | 0 | 0 | 0 | 0 | 0 | 0 | 0 | 0 |
| Edwards, Jovon, Dodgers* | .314 | 60 | 223 | 49 | 70 | 83 | 9 | 2 | 0 | 18 | 5 | 2 | 1 | 1 | 41 | 1 | 13 | 30 | 5 |
| Epps, Ricky, Reds | .208 | 42 | 125 | 14 | 26 | 35 | 3 | 3 | 0 | 9 | 1 | 1 | 0 | 1 | 9 | 0 | 37 | 10 | 2 |
| Escalera, Carlos, Royals | .220 | 40 | 141 | 18 | 31 | 41 | 4 | 0 | 2 | 15 | 1 | 0 | 2 | 4 | 4 | 0 | 31 | 4 | 2 |
| Eusebio, Raul, Astros | .000 | 1 | 1 | 0 | 0 | 0 | 0 | 0 | 0 | 0 | 0 | 0 | 0 | 0 | 0 | 0 | 0 | 0 | 0 |
| Eveline, William, White Sox* | .297 | 30 | 101 | 23 | 30 | 47 | 3 | 3 | 3 | 13 | 2 | 0 | 0 | 4 | 0 | 6 | 2 | 0 |
| Farley, Darren, Rangers† | .244 | 26 | 78 | 12 | 19 | 24 | 1 | 2 | 0 | 12 | 1 | 0 | 0 | 1 | 12 | 0 | 18 | 0 | 0 |
| Fiala, Mark, Astros | .000 | 6 | 2 | 0 | 0 | 0 | 0 | 0 | 0 | 0 | 0 | 0 | 0 | 0 | 0 | 0 | 0 | 0 | 0 |
| Ford, Ondra, Pirates* | .191 | 29 | 94 | 9 | 18 | 21 | 3 | 0 | 0 | 10 | 1 | 1 | 0 | 5 | 0 | 30 | 6 | 1 |
| Frias, Adolfo, Blue Jays† | .140 | 34 | 93 | 11 | 13 | 14 | 1 | 0 | 0 | 3 | 1 | 0 | 0 | 0 | 9 | 0 | 28 | 8 | 2 |
| Garcia, Rene, Dodgers* | .500 | 7 | 2 | 0 | 1 | 1 | 0 | 0 | 0 | 1 | 0 | 2 | 0 | 0 | 0 | 0 | 0 | 0 | 0 |

| Player and Club | Pct. | G. | AB. | R. | H. | TB. | 2B. | 3B. | HR. | RBI. | GW. | SH. | SF. | HP. | BB. | Int. BB. | SO. | SB. | CS. |
|---|---|---|---|---|---|---|---|---|---|---|---|---|---|---|---|---|---|---|---|
| Garcia, Victor, Pirates | .174 | 7 | 23 | 1 | 4 | 4 | 0 | 0 | 0 | 2 | 0 | 0 | 0 | 2 | 0 | 10 | 1 | 0 |
| Garner, Darrin, Rangers | .333 | 16 | 57 | 16 | 19 | 24 | 3 | 1 | 0 | 2 | 1 | 2 | 0 | 2 | 8 | 0 | 5 | 8 | 1 |
| Garrison, James, Dodgers | .167 | 21 | 12 | 5 | 2 | 2 | 0 | 0 | 0 | 0 | 0 | 0 | 0 | 2 | 0 | 1 | 1 | 0 |
| Gibbs, Austin, Dodgers* | .256 | 50 | 125 | 16 | 32 | 52 | 5 | 3 | 3 | 25 | 2 | 0 | 4 | 0 | 9 | 0 | 36 | 4 | 0 |
| Gibson, Brian, Yankees | .250 | 2 | 8 | 1 | 2 | 2 | 0 | 0 | 0 | 1 | 0 | 0 | 0 | 0 | 0 | 0 | 3 | 1 | 0 |
| Gilliam, Darryl, Dodgers | .319 | 38 | 119 | 13 | 38 | 42 | 4 | 0 | 0 | 11 | 0 | 2 | 1 | 2 | 14 | 0 | 13 | 5 | 6 |
| Girdner, Troy, Reds | .000 | 12 | 5 | 1 | 0 | 0 | 0 | 0 | 0 | 0 | 0 | 2 | 0 | 0 | 0 | 0 | 0 | 0 | 0 |
| Glasker, Stephen, Rangers* | .225 | 55 | 187 | 23 | 42 | 52 | 7 | 0 | 1 | 18 | 0 | 2 | 1 | 0 | 18 | 1 | 51 | 10 | 8 |
| Gonring, Douglas, Blue Jays* | .293 | 42 | 140 | 10 | 41 | 49 | 3 | 1 | 1 | 17 | 1 | 0 | 1 | 1 | 10 | 2 | 9 | 3 | 3 |
| Gonzalez, Andres, Yankees | .196 | 33 | 107 | 9 | 21 | 24 | 1 | 1 | 0 | 7 | 1 | 1 | 1 | 1 | 9 | 0 | 25 | 1 | 2 |
| Gonzalez, Carlos, Royals | .246 | 40 | 134 | 13 | 33 | 52 | 8 | 1 | 3 | 26 | 2 | 1 | 3 | 1 | 5 | 0 | 28 | 1 | 1 |
| Green, Carmelo, Reds | .160 | 10 | 25 | 1 | 4 | 5 | 1 | 0 | 0 | 2 | 0 | 0 | 0 | 3 | 0 | 5 | 0 | 0 |
| Grimes, Darin, Royals | .108 | 27 | 74 | 9 | 8 | 8 | 0 | 0 | 0 | 7 | 1 | 1 | 1 | 2 | 7 | 0 | 27 | 0 | 3 |
| Guerrero, Epifano, Blue Jays* | .288 | 56 | 229 | 34 | 66 | 78 | 8 | 2 | 0 | 18 | 0 | 1 | 2 | 1 | 14 | 0 | 20 | 8 | 5 |
| Guerrero, Sixto, Astros | .200 | 29 | 85 | 6 | 17 | 21 | 2 | 1 | 0 | 8 | 1 | 1 | 1 | 3 | 6 | 0 | 24 | 3 | 0 |
| Guthrie, Kelly, Braves | .111 | 19 | 36 | 1 | 4 | 5 | 1 | 0 | 0 | 2 | 1 | 0 | 0 | 0 | 4 | 0 | 8 | 0 | 0 |
| Guzman, Hector, Yankees | .244 | 15 | 45 | 4 | 11 | 12 | 1 | 0 | 0 | 5 | 2 | 1 | 1 | 1 | 1 | 0 | 5 | 7 | 0 |
| Guzman, Juan, Dodgers | .000 | 21 | 2 | 0 | 0 | 0 | 0 | 0 | 0 | 0 | 0 | 0 | 0 | 0 | 0 | 0 | 2 | 0 | 0 |
| Guzman, Rodolfo, Braves | .000 | 6 | 6 | 0 | 0 | 0 | 0 | 0 | 0 | 0 | 0 | 0 | 0 | 0 | 0 | 0 | 2 | 0 | 0 |
| Hackett, Roger, Braves* | .333 | 19 | 6 | 0 | 2 | 4 | 0 | 1 | 0 | 2 | 0 | 0 | 0 | 1 | 0 | 0 | 1 | 0 |
| Hall, Andrew, Pirates | .222 | 5 | 9 | 0 | 2 | 2 | 0 | 0 | 0 | 0 | 0 | 0 | 0 | 1 | 3 | 0 | 1 | 0 | 0 |
| Hansel, Damon, Pirates | .127 | 23 | 63 | 5 | 8 | 9 | 1 | 0 | 0 | 3 | 0 | 0 | 0 | 0 | 10 | 0 | 27 | 1 | 0 |
| Hart, Edwin, Dodgers* | .200 | 12 | 5 | 0 | 1 | 1 | 0 | 0 | 0 | 0 | 0 | 1 | 0 | 0 | 0 | 0 | 1 | 0 | 0 |
| Hartman, Jeffrey, Dodgers | .188 | 46 | 138 | 10 | 26 | 28 | 2 | 0 | 0 | 11 | 0 | 0 | 0 | 0 | 17 | 1 | 27 | 7 | 1 |
| Hartman, Robert, Astros | .250 | 10 | 4 | 0 | 1 | 1 | 0 | 0 | 0 | 1 | 0 | 1 | 0 | 0 | 0 | 0 | 2 | 0 | 1 |
| Hauradou, Hal, Yankees | .309 | 45 | 139 | 19 | 43 | 48 | 5 | 0 | 0 | 16 | 1 | 4 | 2 | 3 | 14 | 0 | 16 | 5 | 3 |
| Hern, John, Braves | .250 | 16 | 8 | 2 | 2 | 3 | 1 | 0 | 0 | 0 | 0 | 0 | 0 | 1 | 1 | 0 | 2 | 1 | 0 |
| Hernandez, Carlos, Dodgers | .245 | 22 | 49 | 3 | 12 | 13 | 1 | 0 | 0 | 6 | 0 | 0 | 0 | 3 | 0 | 8 | 0 | 0 |
| Hernandez, William, Yankees | .250 | 41 | 108 | 18 | 27 | 43 | 6 | 2 | 2 | 14 | 1 | 0 | 2 | 2 | 19 | 1 | 30 | 5 | 4 |
| Herrera, Rene, Reds† | .286 | 9 | 28 | 9 | 8 | 10 | 0 | 1 | 0 | 3 | 0 | 1 | 1 | 0 | 6 | 0 | 4 | 4 | 2 |
| Higgins, Theodore, Yankees* | .306 | 55 | 196 | 38 | 60 | 79 | 7 | 6 | 0 | 36 | 6 | 1 | 4 | 4 | 30 | 3 | 14 | 9 | 6 |
| Hildebrand, Thomas, White Sox | .262 | 50 | 172 | 23 | 45 | 60 | 7 | 1 | 2 | 26 | 2 | 4 | 2 | 2 | 8 | 0 | 24 | 4 | 2 |
| Hindman, Randall, Reds | .294 | 55 | 194 | 34 | 57 | 68 | 6 | 1 | 1 | 20 | 2 | 5 | 0 | 1 | 20 | 0 | 20 | 18 | 11 |
| Hithe, Victor, Astros | .229 | 56 | 175 | 19 | 40 | 50 | 8 | 1 | 0 | 15 | 1 | 0 | 1 | 3 | 38 | 2 | 48 | 11 | 9 |
| Hoffman, Hunter, Royals* | .230 | 38 | 122 | 12 | 28 | 33 | 3 | 1 | 0 | 15 | 0 | 1 | 0 | 1 | 13 | 0 | 38 | 0 | 0 |
| Hood, Dennis, Braves | .240 | 59 | 204 | 19 | 49 | 66 | 14 | 0 | 1 | 17 | 4 | 3 | 3 | 6 | 21 | 1 | 59 | 7 | 3 |
| Hornacek, Jay, Dodgers | .143 | 8 | 21 | 2 | 3 | 6 | 3 | 0 | 0 | 2 | 0 | 0 | 1 | 0 | 2 | 0 | 2 | 0 | 0 |
| Horta, Neder, Yankees | .245 | 53 | 147 | 42 | 36 | 39 | 3 | 0 | 0 | 23 | 3 | 6 | 3 | 3 | 46 | 0 | 33 | 9 | 3 |
| Horton, Darryl, Yankees | .050 | 19 | 20 | 8 | 1 | 1 | 0 | 0 | 0 | 0 | 0 | 0 | 0 | 3 | 4 | 0 | 7 | 4 | 0 |
| Hunter, Bertram, Astros | .210 | 56 | 210 | 17 | 44 | 51 | 4 | 0 | 1 | 17 | 2 | 1 | 2 | 2 | 15 | 0 | 51 | 12 | 8 |
| Isaac, Richard, White Sox | .243 | 21 | 37 | 6 | 9 | 12 | 3 | 0 | 0 | 3 | 0 | 0 | 0 | 0 | 3 | 0 | 7 | 2 | 1 |
| Jackson, Gayron, Astros† | .227 | 54 | 194 | 24 | 44 | 55 | 4 | 2 | 1 | 18 | 2 | 1 | 0 | 3 | 16 | 2 | 33 | 15 | 4 |
| Jackson, Michael, Rangers | .190 | 33 | 105 | 7 | 20 | 23 | 1 | 1 | 0 | 10 | 2 | 1 | 1 | 1 | 3 | 1 | 25 | 1 | 1 |
| Jeter, Shawn, Blue Jays* | .205 | 56 | 219 | 25 | 45 | 56 | 2 | 3 | 1 | 16 | 0 | 0 | 0 | 1 | 22 | 0 | 50 | 8 | 6 |
| Jimenez, Israel, Blue Jays | .242 | 33 | 95 | 13 | 23 | 28 | 2 | 0 | 1 | 7 | 1 | 0 | 0 | 7 | 4 | 1 | 35 | 0 | 0 |
| Johnson, Dino, Yankees | .287 | 41 | 143 | 31 | 41 | 55 | 7 | 2 | 1 | 16 | 2 | 0 | 2 | 1 | 18 | 0 | 27 | 4 | 5 |
| Johnson, Dodd, Braves | .250 | 39 | 136 | 16 | 34 | 46 | 6 | 0 | 2 | 11 | 1 | 0 | 2 | 1 | 17 | 0 | 21 | 1 | 1 |
| Johnson, Thomas, Royals* | .319 | 40 | 135 | 35 | 43 | 65 | 4 | 6 | 2 | 20 | 4 | 0 | 0 | 1 | 24 | 1 | 23 | 8 | 2 |
| Jordan, Ian, Pirates | .250 | 1 | 4 | 2 | 1 | 1 | 0 | 0 | 0 | 0 | 0 | 0 | 0 | 0 | 0 | 0 | 0 | 0 | 0 |
| Kelley, Thomas, Rangers* | .243 | 51 | 177 | 18 | 43 | 56 | 6 | 2 | 1 | 20 | 3 | 1 | 0 | 2 | 19 | 0 | 38 | 7 | 3 |
| Kelly, Jimy, Blue Jays† | .193 | 48 | 145 | 14 | 28 | 32 | 4 | 0 | 0 | 8 | 3 | 3 | 1 | 2 | 32 | 0 | 47 | 5 | 2 |
| Kiluk, Richard, Pirates | .292 | 7 | 24 | 6 | 7 | 10 | 1 | 1 | 0 | 3 | 1 | 0 | 0 | 2 | 1 | 0 | 6 | 5 | 1 |
| King, William, Astros | .190 | 9 | 21 | 3 | 4 | 5 | 1 | 0 | 0 | 2 | 0 | 0 | 0 | 1 | 4 | 0 | 6 | 0 | 0 |
| Klemp, Nicholas, Reds | .200 | 13 | 5 | 1 | 1 | 1 | 0 | 0 | 0 | 1 | 0 | 3 | 0 | 0 | 1 | 0 | 1 | 0 | 0 |
| Koller, Mark, Pirates | .000 | 13 | 3 | 0 | 0 | 0 | 0 | 0 | 0 | 0 | 0 | 0 | 0 | 0 | 1 | 0 | 3 | 0 | 0 |
| Kopetsky, Brian, Dodgers | .150 | 8 | 20 | 1 | 3 | 3 | 0 | 0 | 0 | 2 | 0 | 1 | 0 | 0 | 3 | 0 | 5 | 1 | 0 |
| Koslofski, Kevin, Royals* | .250 | 33 | 108 | 17 | 27 | 35 | 4 | 2 | 0 | 11 | 2 | 2 | 0 | 3 | 12 | 0 | 19 | 7 | 2 |
| Kupfner, Robert, Yankees | .000 | 3 | 6 | 0 | 0 | 0 | 0 | 0 | 0 | 0 | 0 | 0 | 0 | 0 | 2 | 0 | 3 | 0 | 0 |
| Lambert, Robert, Yankees | .350 | 59 | 226 | 51 | 79 | 92 | 9 | 2 | 0 | 21 | 2 | 6 | 2 | 3 | 29 | 1 | 32 | 34 | 12 |
| Lawhon, Duane, Yankees | .000 | 7 | 7 | 0 | 0 | 0 | 0 | 0 | 0 | 0 | 0 | 0 | 0 | 0 | 0 | 0 | 4 | 0 | 0 |
| Lopez, Vincent, White Sox | .224 | 51 | 170 | 30 | 38 | 50 | 8 | 2 | 0 | 12 | 3 | 3 | 1 | 6 | 22 | 1 | 31 | 7 | 3 |
| Lorenzetti, Gregory, Blue Jays | .286 | 53 | 192 | 26 | 55 | 70 | 12 | 0 | 1 | 18 | 1 | 0 | 1 | 0 | 29 | 0 | 28 | 6 | 3 |
| Magallanes, William, White Sox | .208 | 30 | 77 | 9 | 16 | 21 | 2 | 0 | 1 | 5 | 1 | 0 | 0 | 0 | 4 | 0 | 20 | 1 | 1 |
| Mandel, Darren, Yankees | .317 | 55 | 180 | 33 | 57 | 90 | 16 | 4 | 3 | 31 | 4 | 1 | 1 | 3 | 29 | 2 | 23 | 4 | 2 |
| Marak, Paul, Braves | .222 | 12 | 9 | 0 | 2 | 2 | 0 | 0 | 0 | 0 | 0 | 1 | 0 | 0 | 0 | 2 | 0 | 0 |
| Marshall, Gregory, Braves* | .275 | 35 | 80 | 11 | 22 | 26 | 4 | 0 | 0 | 10 | 2 | 2 | 0 | 0 | 12 | 2 | 22 | 2 | 3 |
| Martin, Albert, Braves* | .232 | 40 | 138 | 16 | 32 | 35 | 3 | 0 | 0 | 9 | 0 | 0 | 1 | 2 | 19 | 2 | 36 | 1 | 4 |
| Martinez, Domingo, Blue Jays | .297 | 58 | 219 | 36 | 65 | 91 | 10 | 2 | 4 | 19 | 0 | 0 | 2 | 12 | 0 | 42 | 3 | 4 |
| Martinez, Luis, Reds | .232 | 21 | 56 | 8 | 13 | 15 | 2 | 0 | 0 | 6 | 1 | 0 | 1 | 0 | 5 | 0 | 6 | 4 | 0 |
| Martinez, Ramon, Dodgers | .333 | 23 | 6 | 0 | 2 | 2 | 0 | 0 | 0 | 0 | 0 | 0 | 0 | 0 | 0 | 0 | 0 | 0 | 0 |
| Martinez, Ricardo, Yankees | .190 | 16 | 21 | 1 | 4 | 5 | 1 | 0 | 0 | 1 | 0 | 0 | 0 | 0 | 1 | 0 | 4 | 0 | 0 |
| Mathews, Edward, Braves | .000 | 17 | 3 | 0 | 0 | 0 | 0 | 0 | 0 | 0 | 0 | 0 | 0 | 0 | 1 | 0 | 1 | 0 | 0 |
| Maynard, Daniel, Rangers | .211 | 15 | 19 | 2 | 4 | 4 | 0 | 0 | 0 | 2 | 0 | 1 | 0 | 0 | 3 | 0 | 9 | 0 | 0 |
| McMillan, Timothy, Pirates | .222 | 14 | 54 | 5 | 12 | 24 | 1 | 1 | 3 | 7 | 1 | 0 | 0 | 0 | 5 | 0 | 16 | 1 | 2 |
| McNally, Robert, Yankees | .174 | 11 | 23 | 1 | 4 | 4 | 0 | 0 | 0 | 0 | 0 | 0 | 0 | 1 | 6 | 0 | 0 | 0 | 0 |
| McRae, Brian, Royals† | .267 | 60 | 217 | 40 | 58 | 74 | 6 | 5 | 0 | 23 | 5 | 4 | 2 | 2 | 28 | 0 | 34 | 27 | 12 |
| Mealy, Anthony, Pirates | .143 | 6 | 14 | 1 | 2 | 2 | 0 | 0 | 0 | 1 | 0 | 0 | 0 | 2 | 0 | 8 | 0 | 0 |
| Mendez, Lucas, Braves | .200 | 6 | 5 | 0 | 1 | 1 | 0 | 0 | 0 | 0 | 0 | 0 | 0 | 0 | 1 | 0 | 4 | 0 | 0 |
| Mendoza, Jesus, Braves | .179 | 30 | 78 | 6 | 14 | 19 | 2 | 0 | 1 | 9 | 0 | 0 | 0 | 3 | 0 | 27 | 0 | 0 |
| Merced, Luis, White Sox* | .211 | 32 | 71 | 11 | 15 | 19 | 2 | 1 | 0 | 9 | 0 | 0 | 0 | 8 | 0 | 7 | 5 | 1 |
| Merced, Luis, Pirates† | .228 | 40 | 136 | 16 | 31 | 40 | 6 | 0 | 1 | 13 | 1 | 0 | 0 | 1 | 9 | 0 | 9 | 3 | 1 |
| Metoyer, Tony, Astros | .600 | 11 | 5 | 2 | 3 | 5 | 2 | 0 | 0 | 0 | 0 | 0 | 0 | 0 | 1 | 0 | 0 | 0 | 0 |
| Michel, Domingo, Dodgers | .350 | 35 | 123 | 23 | 43 | 63 | 8 | 3 | 2 | 21 | 3 | 0 | 3 | 2 | 15 | 2 | 13 | 3 | 4 |
| Milholland, Eric, White Sox | .295 | 37 | 112 | 8 | 33 | 35 | 2 | 0 | 0 | 16 | 4 | 0 | 0 | 1 | 8 | 0 | 13 | 1 | 2 |
| Mitchell, Reginald, Reds* | .000 | 2 | 0 | 0 | 0 | 0 | 0 | 0 | 0 | 0 | 0 | 0 | 0 | 1 | 0 | 0 | 0 | 0 |
| Moreno, Douglas, Pirates | .200 | 12 | 10 | 0 | 2 | 2 | 0 | 0 | 0 | 0 | 1 | 0 | 1 | 0 | 4 | 0 | 3 | 0 | 0 |
| Mota, Bienvenido, Braves | .000 | 14 | 2 | 0 | 0 | 0 | 0 | 0 | 0 | 0 | 0 | 0 | 0 | 0 | 0 | 0 | 1 | 0 | 0 |
| Mota, Jose, Braves | .176 | 54 | 131 | 16 | 23 | 23 | 0 | 0 | 0 | 2 | 0 | 9 | 0 | 9 | 0 | 30 | 1 | 1 |
| Mullins, Christopher, Braves | .174 | 25 | 69 | 4 | 12 | 13 | 1 | 0 | 0 | 3 | 0 | 1 | 0 | 2 | 4 | 1 | 20 | 1 | 1 |
| Mullins, Ronald, Reds | .333 | 15 | 6 | 1 | 2 | 3 | 1 | 0 | 0 | 0 | 0 | 0 | 0 | 2 | 0 | 1 | 2 | 0 | 0 |
| Munoz, Pedro, Blue Jays | .262 | 40 | 145 | 14 | 38 | 47 | 3 | 0 | 2 | 17 | 1 | 1 | 1 | 4 | 9 | 0 | 20 | 4 | 1 |
| Natera, Antonio, Braves* | .000 | 12 | 5 | 0 | 0 | 0 | 0 | 0 | 0 | 0 | 0 | 0 | 0 | 0 | 0 | 0 | 2 | 0 | 0 |

| Player and Club | Pct. | G. | AB. | R. | H. | TB. | 2B. | 3B. | HR. | RBI. | GW. | SH. | SF. | HP. | BB. | Int. BB. | SO. | SB. | CS. |
|---|---|---|---|---|---|---|---|---|---|---|---|---|---|---|---|---|---|---|---|
| Nelson, Jeffrey, Dodgers | .000 | 14 | 3 | 0 | 0 | 0 | 0 | 0 | 0 | 0 | 0 | 0 | 0 | 0 | 0 | 0 | 0 | 0 | 0 |
| Newton, Marvin, Dodgers | .355 | 17 | 31 | 3 | 11 | 14 | 1 | 1 | 0 | 6 | 2 | 0 | 0 | 0 | 7 | 0 | 4 | 3 | 0 |
| Nina, Hector, Reds | .206 | 42 | 131 | 10 | 27 | 37 | 3 | 2 | 1 | 16 | 2 | 2 | 2 | 1 | 6 | 0 | 24 | 4 | 1 |
| Nowakowski, Joseph, Blue Jays | .216 | 33 | 125 | 12 | 27 | 35 | 4 | 2 | 0 | 10 | 1 | 0 | 0 | 0 | 1 | 0 | 18 | 1 | 2 |
| Nunez, Venicio, Astros | .500 | 6 | 6 | 4 | 3 | 4 | 1 | 0 | 0 | 2 | 0 | 0 | 0 | 0 | 1 | 0 | 2 | 0 | 0 |
| O'Bryan, Lloyd, Rangers | .195 | 46 | 128 | 23 | 25 | 35 | 5 | 1 | 1 | 10 | 3 | 1 | 1 | 9 | 13 | 0 | 36 | 8 | 2 |
| Parker, Brett, Dodgers | .230 | 25 | 74 | 8 | 17 | 19 | 2 | 0 | 0 | 8 | 0 | 0 | 1 | 0 | 9 | 0 | 12 | 1 | 0 |
| Peralta, Modesto, Reds | .000 | 19 | 2 | 0 | 0 | 0 | 0 | 0 | 0 | 0 | 0 | 0 | 0 | 0 | 0 | 0 | 1 | 0 | 0 |
| Perez, Manuel, Pirates° | .667 | 11 | 6 | 2 | 4 | 6 | 2 | 0 | 0 | 0 | 0 | 0 | 0 | 0 | 1 | 0 | 0 | 0 | 0 |
| Perez, Julio, Pirates | .394 | 17 | 71 | 8 | 28 | 30 | 0 | 1 | 0 | 9 | 1 | 0 | 0 | 0 | 4 | 0 | 2 | 7 | 3 |
| Pfaff, Robert, Braves | .224 | 40 | 125 | 5 | 28 | 38 | 8 | 1 | 0 | 13 | 0 | 2 | 1 | 0 | 7 | 0 | 29 | 0 | 1 |
| Pichardo, Feliciano, White Sox | .000 | 2 | 1 | 0 | 0 | 0 | 0 | 0 | 0 | 0 | 0 | 0 | 0 | 0 | 1 | 0 | 0 | 0 | 0 |
| Pierce, Chris, Pirates | .250 | 2 | 8 | 0 | 2 | 2 | 0 | 0 | 0 | 1 | 0 | 0 | 0 | 0 | 0 | 0 | 3 | 0 | 0 |
| Pinelli, Willie, Dodgers | .218 | 34 | 87 | 10 | 19 | 21 | 2 | 0 | 0 | 13 | 3 | 1 | 2 | 2 | 5 | 0 | 18 | 4 | 0 |
| Pittman, Douglas, Pirates | .217 | 21 | 69 | 6 | 15 | 18 | 3 | 0 | 0 | 7 | 0 | 0 | 1 | 2 | 3 | 0 | 13 | 0 | 1 |
| Pujols, Ramon, Rangers | .239 | 34 | 88 | 6 | 21 | 25 | 4 | 0 | 0 | 7 | 1 | 0 | 0 | 0 | 2 | 0 | 9 | 1 | 0 |
| Quintero, Enrique, Pirates | .205 | 37 | 127 | 8 | 26 | 33 | 5 | 1 | 0 | 9 | 0 | 0 | 1 | 1 | 4 | 0 | 36 | 0 | 2 |
| Rahming, Kenneth, White Sox | .230 | 26 | 87 | 14 | 20 | 26 | 4 | 1 | 0 | 17 | 1 | 0 | 3 | 0 | 3 | 0 | 27 | 3 | 4 |
| Ramirez, Jose, Pirates† | .226 | 31 | 84 | 7 | 19 | 22 | 1 | 1 | 0 | 4 | 0 | 1 | 0 | 0 | 4 | 0 | 15 | 1 | 2 |
| Randle, Randy, Astros | .244 | 41 | 127 | 25 | 31 | 42 | 3 | 4 | 0 | 3 | 1 | 0 | 1 | 1 | 21 | 0 | 17 | 14 | 5 |
| Redus, Jeffrey, Royals | .227 | 25 | 66 | 15 | 15 | 21 | 2 | 2 | 0 | 10 | 0 | 0 | 0 | 0 | 14 | 0 | 15 | 10 | 4 |
| Remigio, Jose, Pirates | .000 | 11 | 1 | 0 | 0 | 0 | 0 | 0 | 0 | 0 | 0 | 0 | 0 | 0 | 0 | 0 | 1 | 0 | 0 |
| Renteria, Edinson, Astros† | .164 | 40 | 110 | 12 | 18 | 18 | 0 | 0 | 0 | 7 | 0 | 1 | 1 | 3 | 8 | 0 | 14 | 1 | 1 |
| Reyes, Carlos, Astros | .281 | 56 | 196 | 21 | 55 | 71 | 8 | 1 | 2 | 25 | 2 | 0 | 2 | 3 | 16 | 0 | 25 | 8 | 4 |
| Reynolds, David, White Sox | .202 | 35 | 84 | 12 | 17 | 21 | 0 | 2 | 0 | 8 | 0 | 3 | 1 | 0 | 7 | 0 | 15 | 1 | 0 |
| Rivas, Juan, Yankees† | .500 | 2 | 2 | 0 | 1 | 1 | 0 | 0 | 0 | 1 | 0 | 0 | 0 | 0 | 0 | 0 | 0 | 0 | 0 |
| Robles, Daniel, Dodgers° | .297 | 50 | 158 | 24 | 47 | 59 | 6 | 3 | 0 | 21 | 2 | 2 | 2 | 2 | 18 | 1 | 26 | 6 | 3 |
| Roca, Gilberto, Pirates | .200 | 13 | 40 | 6 | 8 | 10 | 2 | 0 | 0 | 6 | 0 | 0 | 2 | 0 | 1 | 0 | 5 | 0 | 0 |
| Rodriguez, Nelson, Pirates | .444 | 3 | 9 | 1 | 4 | 7 | 1 | 1 | 0 | 1 | 1 | 0 | 0 | 0 | 0 | 0 | 0 | 0 | 0 |
| Rodriguez, Pete, Dodgers | .169 | 36 | 65 | 3 | 11 | 15 | 2 | 1 | 0 | 9 | 0 | 0 | 0 | 1 | 6 | 1 | 15 | 0 | 0 |
| Rogers, Danilo, Braves | .276 | 22 | 29 | 10 | 8 | 9 | 1 | 0 | 0 | 6 | 0 | 0 | 0 | 1 | 2 | 0 | 8 | 0 | 0 |
| Romero, Charles, Blue Jays† | .175 | 30 | 97 | 8 | 17 | 24 | 4 | 0 | 1 | 6 | 1 | 0 | 1 | 1 | 2 | 0 | 33 | 2 | 0 |
| Romo, Robert, Astros | .000 | 12 | 5 | 0 | 0 | 0 | 0 | 0 | 0 | 0 | 0 | 1 | 0 | 0 | 1 | 0 | 4 | 0 | 0 |
| Rondon, Isidro, Reds | .338 | 52 | 195 | 29 | 66 | 83 | 10 | 2 | 1 | 17 | 5 | 0 | 2 | 3 | 21 | 2 | 35 | 5 | 5 |
| Roque, Omar, Astros | .272 | 42 | 114 | 10 | 31 | 37 | 1 | 1 | 1 | 10 | 1 | 4 | 1 | 0 | 6 | 1 | 20 | 5 | 5 |
| Rosario, Melvin, Dodgers | .178 | 40 | 101 | 15 | 18 | 22 | 4 | 0 | 0 | 4 | 1 | 2 | 0 | 1 | 12 | 0 | 29 | 0 | 1 |
| Ruiz, Samuel, White Sox° | .277 | 17 | 47 | 8 | 13 | 13 | 0 | 0 | 0 | 2 | 0 | 2 | 0 | 1 | 5 | 0 | 3 | 2 | 2 |
| Russell, Ronald, Rangers | .219 | 55 | 178 | 25 | 39 | 50 | 5 | 0 | 2 | 17 | 0 | 3 | 2 | 5 | 10 | 1 | 25 | 2 | 0 |
| Russell, Scott, Rangers | .278 | 19 | 36 | 5 | 10 | 11 | 1 | 0 | 0 | 3 | 0 | 0 | 0 | 2 | 4 | 0 | 9 | 1 | 1 |
| Ruzich, Steve, White Sox | .000 | 6 | 5 | 2 | 0 | 0 | 0 | 0 | 0 | 0 | 0 | 0 | 0 | 0 | 2 | 0 | 4 | 0 | 0 |
| Sanchez, Francisco, Royals† | .298 | 21 | 57 | 18 | 17 | 17 | 0 | 0 | 0 | 7 | 1 | 1 | 0 | 4 | 8 | 1 | 13 | 5 | 4 |
| Sanchez, Pedro, Astros† | .249 | 50 | 173 | 23 | 43 | 59 | 10 | 3 | 0 | 12 | 3 | 4 | 0 | 1 | 18 | 0 | 31 | 13 | 6 |
| Sanders, Brian, Royals° | .225 | 51 | 160 | 28 | 36 | 37 | 1 | 0 | 0 | 13 | 0 | 4 | 1 | 0 | 23 | 0 | 23 | 12 | 9 |
| Santana, Leonel, Astros | .227 | 32 | 88 | 5 | 20 | 25 | 1 | 2 | 0 | 10 | 1 | 1 | 1 | 0 | 3 | 1 | 20 | 2 | 0 |
| Sassone, Michael, Astros | .000 | 6 | 1 | 0 | 0 | 0 | 0 | 0 | 0 | 0 | 0 | 1 | 0 | 0 | 0 | 0 | 0 | 0 | 0 |
| Scieneaux, Desmond, Pirates° | .194 | 32 | 103 | 11 | 20 | 25 | 5 | 0 | 0 | 11 | 0 | 0 | 1 | 0 | 13 | 0 | 26 | 2 | 0 |
| Scott, Michael, Braves | .200 | 10 | 5 | 0 | 1 | 3 | 0 | 1 | 0 | 2 | 1 | 2 | 0 | 0 | 0 | 0 | 4 | 0 | 0 |
| Scruggs, Ronald, White Sox° | .238 | 44 | 101 | 19 | 24 | 39 | 6 | 3 | 1 | 14 | 0 | 1 | 1 | 2 | 27 | 0 | 28 | 4 | 1 |
| Seay, Mark, Rangers° | .103 | 24 | 39 | 6 | 4 | 5 | 1 | 0 | 0 | 4 | 0 | 0 | 2 | 2 | 13 | 0 | 29 | 2 | 1 |
| Sheehan, John, Astros | .000 | 5 | 0 | 0 | 0 | 0 | 0 | 0 | 0 | 0 | 0 | 1 | 0 | 0 | 0 | 0 | 0 | 0 | 0 |
| Sheffield, Travis, Rangers† | .210 | 34 | 62 | 8 | 13 | 14 | 1 | 0 | 0 | 1 | 0 | 0 | 0 | 8 | 1 | 22 | 7 | 1 | — |
| Silverio, Francisco, Reds | .234 | 53 | 201 | 24 | 47 | 55 | 4 | 2 | 0 | 22 | 2 | 1 | 3 | 0 | 12 | 0 | 57 | 22 | 3 |
| Simms, Michael, Astros | .271 | 21 | 70 | 10 | 19 | 32 | 2 | 1 | 3 | 18 | 1 | 0 | 3 | 4 | 6 | 0 | 26 | 0 | 0 |
| Slocum, Wayne, Royals | .289 | 29 | 90 | 17 | 26 | 38 | 4 | 1 | 2 | 11 | 2 | 1 | 1 | 1 | 13 | 0 | 12 | 3 | 1 |
| Smith, Gerald, Royals | .111 | 17 | 18 | 5 | 2 | 2 | 0 | 0 | 0 | 3 | 0 | 1 | 0 | 0 | 5 | 0 | 3 | 1 | 1 |
| Smith, Henry, Astros | .167 | 10 | 6 | 4 | 1 | 2 | 1 | 0 | 0 | 0 | 0 | 0 | 0 | 0 | 4 | 0 | 1 | 0 | 0 |
| Stewart, Anthony, Pirates | .157 | 31 | 102 | 12 | 16 | 19 | 3 | 0 | 0 | 7 | 1 | 2 | 2 | 1 | 4 | 0 | 14 | 0 | 1 |
| Sullivan, Patrick, Blue Jays | .170 | 33 | 112 | 11 | 19 | 21 | 2 | 0 | 0 | 13 | 2 | 0 | 1 | 1 | 14 | 0 | 27 | 1 | 1 |
| Swartzlander, Keith, Pirates | .143 | 10 | 14 | 1 | 2 | 2 | 0 | 0 | 0 | 1 | 0 | 0 | 0 | 0 | 0 | 0 | 4 | 0 | 0 |
| Taylor, Stephon, Pirates | .220 | 44 | 127 | 14 | 28 | 33 | 1 | 2 | 0 | 11 | 0 | 0 | 2 | 0 | 18 | 1 | 37 | 4 | 7 |
| Thomas, Frank, Braves | .000 | 8 | 2 | 0 | 0 | 0 | 0 | 0 | 0 | 0 | 0 | 0 | 0 | 0 | 1 | 0 | 0 | 0 | 0 |
| Tinkle, David, Royals° | .176 | 12 | 34 | 3 | 6 | 8 | 0 | 1 | 0 | 3 | 0 | 2 | 1 | 0 | 4 | 0 | 8 | 0 | 1 |
| Torre, Paul, Reds | .198 | 37 | 101 | 9 | 20 | 21 | 1 | 0 | 0 | 7 | 0 | 1 | 0 | 1 | 16 | 0 | 25 | 3 | 2 |
| Torres, Roberto, Royals | .200 | 4 | 5 | 1 | 1 | 1 | 0 | 0 | 0 | 1 | 0 | 0 | 0 | 0 | 0 | 0 | 0 | 1 | 0 |
| Trillo, Luis, Dodgers | .000 | 6 | 7 | 1 | 0 | 0 | 0 | 0 | 0 | 0 | 0 | 0 | 0 | 0 | 0 | 0 | 1 | 0 | 0 |
| Troncoso, Victor, Rangers | .171 | 49 | 140 | 8 | 24 | 26 | 2 | 0 | 0 | 15 | 3 | 2 | 1 | 4 | 9 | 0 | 30 | 1 | 1 |
| Tuttle, John, Reds | .229 | 35 | 118 | 13 | 27 | 37 | 4 | 0 | 2 | 15 | 2 | 0 | 2 | 0 | 11 | 1 | 24 | 12 | 2 |
| Valenzuela, Manuel, Pirates° | .000 | 13 | 0 | 0 | 0 | 0 | 0 | 0 | 0 | 0 | 0 | 0 | 0 | 0 | 1 | 0 | 0 | 0 | 0 |
| Valverde, Miguel, Pirates | .246 | 34 | 126 | 12 | 31 | 38 | 5 | 1 | 0 | 16 | 0 | 0 | 0 | 1 | 9 | 0 | 21 | 9 | 5 |
| Vaughn, Robin, Pirates | .255 | 50 | 192 | 21 | 49 | 63 | 9 | 1 | 1 | 25 | 3 | 0 | 1 | 3 | 12 | 0 | 37 | 7 | 3 |
| Victor, Miguel, Astros | .000 | 11 | 4 | 0 | 0 | 0 | 0 | 0 | 0 | 0 | 0 | 0 | 0 | 0 | 0 | 0 | 3 | 0 | 0 |
| Vike, James, Astros | .000 | 11 | 4 | 0 | 0 | 0 | 0 | 0 | 0 | 0 | 0 | 0 | 0 | 1 | 0 | 0 | 3 | 0 | 0 |
| Waggoner, Aubrey, White Sox° | .190 | 49 | 142 | 33 | 27 | 40 | 6 | 2 | 1 | 10 | 1 | 3 | 2 | 1 | 49 | 3 | 40 | 12 | 7 |
| Wakefield, Terry, Pirates | .190 | 11 | 21 | 3 | 4 | 5 | 1 | 0 | 0 | 0 | 0 | 0 | 0 | 1 | 2 | 0 | 9 | 1 | 0 |
| Watson, DeJon, Royals° | .306 | 10 | 36 | 5 | 11 | 15 | 0 | 2 | 0 | 9 | 1 | 0 | 0 | 0 | 2 | 0 | 5 | 2 | 0 |
| Wetherby, Jeffrey, Braves° | .364 | 26 | 88 | 19 | 32 | 48 | 7 | 0 | 3 | 18 | 2 | 0 | 0 | 0 | 20 | 2 | 12 | 2 | 0 |
| Wilcox, Leon, Reds | .231 | 33 | 104 | 13 | 24 | 28 | 1 | 0 | 1 | 12 | 0 | 4 | 1 | 1 | 10 | 0 | 29 | 4 | 1 |
| Williams, Jimmy, Dodgers° | .200 | 13 | 15 | 3 | 3 | 3 | 0 | 0 | 0 | 1 | 0 | 3 | 0 | 0 | 2 | 0 | 4 | 1 | 0 |
| Wilmore, Orlando, Astros | .167 | 18 | 6 | 1 | 1 | 1 | 0 | 0 | 0 | 0 | 0 | 0 | 0 | 0 | 0 | 0 | 2 | 0 | 0 |
| Wilson, Thomas, Reds | .195 | 33 | 87 | 10 | 17 | 20 | 3 | 0 | 0 | 8 | 1 | 2 | 2 | 2 | 16 | 1 | 5 | 7 | 3 |
| Zayas, Pedro, Astros | .194 | 20 | 36 | 1 | 7 | 8 | 1 | 0 | 0 | 3 | 0 | 0 | 0 | 2 | 0 | 0 | 8 | 1 | 0 |
| Zielinski, Glenn, Reds | .500 | 16 | 4 | 2 | 2 | 2 | 0 | 0 | 0 | 1 | 0 | 1 | 0 | 0 | 0 | 0 | 0 | 0 | 0 |

The following pitchers, listed alphabetically by club, with games in parentheses, had no plate appearances, primarily through use of designated hitters:

ASTROS—Camp, Scott (13); Talbott, Shawn (22).

BLUE JAYS—Anderson, Richard (15); Brinson, Hugh (11); DeLaCruz, Jose (15); DeLaRosa, Francisco (16); DeLeon, Juan (5); Felden, Keith (18); Jones, Dennis (15); Kwiatkowski, Glen (14); Mejia, Cesar (10); Mumaw, Stephen (6); Palma, Ruben (17); Tracy, James (17).

BRAVES—Eave, Gary (6); Huff, Roger (1); Prentice, Douglas (3).

DODGERS—Arbelo, Ediberto (7); Irizarry, Pablo (12); Sepulveda, Jorge (2); Shields, Steven (3); Thomas, Carl (11).

PIRATES—Almonte, Eduardo (5); Bauer, Frank (3); Castro, Jorge (3); Dixon, Carl (14); Franchi, Kevin (2); Martin, Timothy (5); Massa, Juan (6); Olivares, Jose (9); Smallwood, Douglas (10); Winfield, Stephen (6).

RANGERS—Adams, Terrill (1); Booker, William (8); Bryan, Frank (9); Busick, Warren (10); James, Paul (15); Lankard, Steven (13); Larsen, Daniel (3); Meadows, Jimmy (3); Mielke, Gary (19); Mortimer, Robert (9); Nannierello, Joseph (14); Pardo, Lawrence (1); Patterson, Glenn (5); Reynolds, Jay (4); Rivera, Lino (16); Schofield, John (13); Soto, Edwardo (11); Thomas, Mitchell (7); Vlcek, James (8); West, Alvin (14).

REDS—Pace, George (12).

ROYALS—Boroski, Stanley (16); Buntzen, James (6); DeLosSantos, Julio (12); Ellis, Rufus (13); Franklin, Jimmy (10); Goodenough, Randy (10); McCormack, Brian (4); Payne, Carl (14); Peluso, Albert (13); Rodriguez, Jose (11); Rojas, Ricardo (13); Tanner, John (21); Van Vuren, Robert (13); Woyce, Donald (6).

WHITE SOX—Bartolomucci, Anthony (9); Brito, Modesto (6); Cortez, Argenis (3); Drees, Thomas (12); Edwards, Wayne (11); Henry, Mark (16); Lee, David (14); Pall, Donn (13); Sandoval, Jesus (18); Stein, John (6); Warren, Marty (11) Wilson, Eric (22).

YANKEES—Azocar, Oscar (5); Bauza, Carlos (4); Blum, Brent (8); Cantrell, Scott (13); Carreno, Amalio (1); Carroll, Christopher (11); Clark, David (8); Hellman, Jeffrey (7); McClear, Michael (20); Reker, Timothy (10); Rodriguez, Gabriel (13); Shane, Jon (11); Sisler, Dick (13); Starling, James (2).

GRAND SLAM HOME RUNS—Cook, R. Russell, 1 each.

AWARDED FIRST BASE ON CATCHER'S INTERFERENCE—Banks 4 (Roca 2, Beeler, Hall); Balli (Beeler); Burgos (C. Gonzalez); Fiala (Rosario); Hauradou (Hern).

## CLUB FIELDING

| Club | Pct. | G. | PO. | A. | E. | DP. | PB. | Club | Pct. | G. | PO. | A. | E. | DP. | PB. |
|------|------|----|-----|-----|-----|-----|-----|------|------|----|-----|-----|-----|-----|-----|
| White Sox | .953 | 64 | 1656 | 732 | 118 | 46 | 6 | Astros | .940 | 62 | 1584 | 658 | 143 | 44 | 25 |
| Royals | .952 | 62 | 1571 | 629 | 110 | 45 | 25 | Dodgers | .939 | 61 | 1567 | 640 | 144 | 61 | 21 |
| Yankees | .952 | 62 | 1620 | 699 | 118 | 45 | 20 | Reds | .934 | 62 | 1615 | 666 | 160 | 46 | 19 |
| Blue Jays | .948 | 62 | 1623 | 711 | 129 | 56 | 11 | Braves | .931 | 61 | 1612 | 708 | 172 | 48 | 29 |
| Rangers | .947 | 62 | 1631 | 705 | 131 | 40 | 12 | Pirates | .929 | 62 | 1553 | 603 | 164 | 38 | 23 |

Triple Play—White Sox.

## INDIVIDUAL FIELDING

*Throws lefthanded.

### FIRST BASEMEN

| Player and Club | Pct. | G. | PO. | A. | E. | DP. | Player and Club | Pct. | G. | PO. | A. | E. | DP. |
|-----------------|------|----|-----|-----|-----|-----|-----------------|------|----|-----|-----|-----|-----|
| Allen, White Sox* | .989 | 54 | 499 | 39 | 6 | 31 | Kelley, Rangers | 1.000 | 2 | 18 | 1 | 0 | 1 |
| Asbe, Royals | .987 | 56 | 437 | 34 | 6 | 34 | King, Astros | .875 | 1 | 6 | 1 | 1 | 0 |
| Baldwin, Astros* | .973 | 26 | 204 | 13 | 6 | 18 | Lorenzetti, Blue Jays | .972 | 44 | 395 | 23 | 12 | 36 |
| Banks, Yankees* | .979 | 43 | 391 | 28 | 9 | 33 | Mandel, Yankees | .955 | 8 | 60 | 3 | 3 | 2 |
| Bautista, Braves | .941 | 4 | 14 | 2 | 1 | 2 | Martin, Braves* | .943 | 30 | 234 | 13 | 15 | 15 |
| Beaupre, Reds | 1.000 | 1 | 7 | 1 | 0 | 0 | Mendoza, Braves | .965 | 30 | 212 | 10 | 8 | 18 |
| BROWNE, Rangers | .990 | 43 | 397 | 20 | 4 | 24 | Michel, Dodgers | .969 | 21 | 179 | 11 | 6 | 17 |
| Carter, Yankees | .974 | 14 | 106 | 5 | 3 | 4 | Newton, Dodgers | .967 | 5 | 28 | 1 | 1 | 4 |
| Creager, Reds | .986 | 31 | 265 | 16 | 4 | 25 | Pittman, Pirates | .500 | 1 | 0 | 1 | 1 | 0 |
| DeLaCruz, Blue Jays | 1.000 | 4 | 46 | 2 | 0 | 5 | Redus, Royals | 1.000 | 5 | 23 | 1 | 0 | 3 |
| Denkenberger, Pirates* | .979 | 32 | 273 | 12 | 6 | 14 | Rodriguez, Dodgers | 1.000 | 4 | 10 | 2 | 0 | 2 |
| Dotzler, Rangers | 1.000 | 1 | 5 | 0 | 0 | 0 | Rondon, Dodgers | .963 | 29 | 270 | 14 | 11 | 14 |
| Gibbs, Dodgers* | .970 | 41 | 235 | 27 | 8 | 25 | Santana, Astros | .983 | 23 | 159 | 16 | 3 | 9 |
| Gonring, Blue Jays | .982 | 15 | 154 | 9 | 3 | 10 | Scieneaux, Pirates* | .949 | 30 | 225 | 16 | 13 | 17 |
| Hern, Braves | 1.000 | 1 | 5 | 0 | 0 | 1 | Scruggs, White Sox* | .935 | 17 | 113 | 2 | 8 | 9 |
| Hernandez, Dodgers | .979 | 7 | 43 | 4 | 1 | 4 | Simms, Astros | .975 | 21 | 186 | 7 | 5 | 14 |
| Hornacek, Dodgers | 1.000 | 1 | 2 | 0 | 0 | 0 | Smith, Astros | 1.000 | 3 | 11 | 1 | 0 | 0 |
| Jackson, Rangers | .976 | 23 | 189 | 12 | 5 | 13 | Watson, Royals* | 1.000 | 5 | 46 | 4 | 0 | 3 |
| Johnson, Braves | .969 | 3 | 28 | 3 | 1 | 3 | Wetherby, Braves* | .978 | 9 | 83 | 7 | 2 | 5 |
| Jordan, Pirates | 1.000 | 1 | 14 | 0 | 0 | 1 | Wilcox, Reds | .957 | 2 | 21 | 1 | 1 | 3 |

### SECOND BASEMEN

| Player and Club | Pct. | G. | PO. | A. | E. | DP. | Player and Club | Pct. | G. | PO. | A. | E. | DP. |
|-----------------|------|----|-----|-----|-----|-----|-----------------|------|----|-----|-----|-----|-----|
| Aquino, Astros | 1.000 | 7 | 13 | 19 | 0 | 3 | Hindman, Reds | .954 | 54 | 120 | 130 | 12 | 21 |
| Basora, Dodgers | .000 | 1 | 0 | 0 | 1 | 0 | King, Astros | .857 | 2 | 1 | 5 | 1 | 0 |
| Bautista, Braves | .909 | 3 | 3 | 7 | 1 | 0 | Lambert, Yankees | .961 | 57 | 120 | 125 | 10 | 25 |
| Bell, Dodgers | .857 | 2 | 2 | 4 | 1 | 1 | Martinez, Blue Jays | 1.000 | 1 | 2 | 0 | 0 | 0 |
| Burgos, Rangers | .778 | 3 | 3 | 4 | 2 | 0 | McRae, Royals | .967 | 40 | 87 | 91 | 6 | 19 |
| Butler, Braves | .941 | 16 | 14 | 34 | 3 | 9 | Merced, Pirates | 1.000 | 1 | 0 | 2 | 0 | 0 |
| Caceres, Dodgers | .943 | 18 | 48 | 34 | 5 | 12 | Mota, Braves | .910 | 45 | 87 | 114 | 20 | 17 |
| Caro, Braves | .853 | 25 | 26 | 32 | 10 | 5 | Nunez, Astros | 1.000 | 1 | 1 | 0 | 0 | 0 |
| Clemente, Pirates | 1.000 | 5 | 6 | 3 | 0 | 0 | Parker, Dodgers | .800 | 4 | 6 | 2 | 2 | 1 |
| Cruz, Rangers | .962 | 35 | 59 | 93 | 6 | 15 | Perez, Pirates | .960 | 14 | 26 | 46 | 3 | 8 |
| Dennis, Blue Jays | 1.000 | 1 | 2 | 8 | 0 | 0 | Ramirez, Pirates | .889 | 9 | 16 | 16 | 4 | 5 |
| Didder, Yankees | .935 | 11 | 15 | 14 | 2 | 4 | Renteria, Astros | .942 | 37 | 63 | 84 | 9 | 20 |
| Eveline, White Sox | .953 | 15 | 29 | 32 | 3 | 7 | Rivas, Yankees | .800 | 2 | 3 | 1 | 1 | 0 |
| Frias, Blue Jays | 1.000 | 8 | 11 | 12 | 0 | 4 | Roque, Astros | 1.000 | 2 | 1 | 0 | 0 | 0 |
| Garner, Rangers | .988 | 14 | 40 | 39 | 1 | 7 | Ruiz, White Sox | .881 | 12 | 28 | 24 | 7 | 5 |
| Garrison, Dodgers | 1.000 | 3 | 3 | 2 | 0 | 0 | F. Sanchez, Royals | .886 | 17 | 30 | 40 | 9 | 10 |
| Gilliam, Dodgers | .714 | 1 | 5 | 0 | 2 | 0 | P. Sanchez, Astros | .922 | 21 | 43 | 52 | 8 | 7 |
| Grimes, Royals | .966 | 6 | 13 | 15 | 1 | 3 | Sheffield, Rangers | .824 | 6 | 10 | 4 | 3 | 2 |
| Guerrero, Blue Jays | .965 | 56 | 123 | 155 | 10 | 35 | Taylor, Pirates | .884 | 41 | 70 | 67 | 18 | 7 |
| Hartman, Dodgers | .947 | 45 | 94 | 86 | 10 | 19 | Torre, Rangers | 1.000 | 1 | 4 | 5 | 0 | 0 |
| Herrera, Reds | .920 | 8 | 21 | 25 | 4 | 5 | Troncoso, Rangers | .879 | 16 | 30 | 28 | 8 | 2 |
| HILDEBRAND, White Sox | .966 | 46 | 98 | 128 | 8 | 24 | Wilcox, Reds | 1.000 | 3 | 4 | 12 | 0 | 2 |

Triple Play—Ruiz.

### THIRD BASEMEN

| Player and Club | Pct. | G. | PO. | A. | E. | DP. | Player and Club | Pct. | G. | PO. | A. | E. | DP. |
|-----------------|------|----|-----|-----|-----|-----|-----------------|------|----|-----|-----|-----|-----|
| Almonte, Astros | .795 | 16 | 8 | 23 | 8 | 2 | R. Cruz, Rangers | 1.000 | 1 | 1 | 1 | 0 | 0 |
| Alvarez, White Sox | .955 | 41 | 29 | 77 | 5 | 6 | Day, Royals | .958 | 7 | 7 | 16 | 1 | 0 |
| Barberich, Dodgers | .875 | 7 | 1 | 6 | 1 | 1 | Farley, Dodgers | 1.000 | 1 | 0 | 1 | 0 | 0 |
| Bautista, Braves | .796 | 17 | 11 | 32 | 11 | 2 | Frias, Blue Jays | .913 | 8 | 7 | 14 | 2 | 2 |
| Beaupre, Reds | .824 | 6 | 5 | 9 | 3 | 1 | Grimes, Royals | .852 | 18 | 11 | 35 | 8 | 3 |
| Brown, Reds | 1.000 | 1 | 2 | 0 | 0 | 0 | Hauradou, Yankees | .885 | 30 | 26 | 66 | 12 | 6 |
| Butler, Braves | .000 | 1 | 0 | 0 | 1 | 0 | Hernandez, Dodgers | .944 | 8 | 5 | 12 | 1 | 1 |
| Caceres, Dodgers | .925 | 32 | 21 | 53 | 6 | 6 | Hildebrand, White Sox | .842 | 4 | 3 | 13 | 3 | 1 |
| Clemente, Pirates | 1.000 | 1 | 0 | 1 | 0 | 0 | Hoffman, Royals | .860 | 37 | 21 | 53 | 12 | 3 |

## THIRD BASEMEN—Continued

| Player and Club | Pct. | G. | PO. | A. | E. | DP. | Player and Club | Pct. | G. | PO. | A. | E. | DP. |
|---|---|---|---|---|---|---|---|---|---|---|---|---|---|
| Hornacek, Dodgers | .875 | 4 | 4 | 10 | 2 | 2 | Pinelli, Dodgers | .784 | 23 | 17 | 41 | 16 | 7 |
| Isaac, White Sox | .789 | 8 | 4 | 11 | 4 | 2 | Quintero, Pirates | .865 | 21 | 11 | 53 | 10 | 2 |
| Di. Johnson, Yankees | .849 | 33 | 23 | 56 | 14 | 7 | Reyes, Astros | .833 | 15 | 12 | 23 | 7 | 2 |
| Do. Johnson, Braves | .847 | 32 | 16 | 67 | 15 | 3 | Reynolds, White Sox | .958 | 26 | 11 | 57 | 3 | 2 |
| King, Astros | 1.000 | 2 | 4 | 3 | 0 | 0 | Rodriguez, Pirates | 1.000 | 2 | 1 | 4 | 0 | 1 |
| Kopetsky, Dodgers | .667 | 1 | 1 | 1 | 1 | 0 | Roque, Astros | .908 | 39 | 28 | 61 | 9 | 4 |
| Lorenzetti, Blue Jays | .909 | 7 | 3 | 27 | 3 | 1 | R. RUSSELL, Rangers | .864 | 46 | 29 | 66 | 15 | 4 |
| Martinez, Blue Jays | .837 | 50 | 37 | 102 | 27 | 5 | S. Russell, Rangers | 1.000 | 3 | 1 | 9 | 0 | 0 |
| Merced, Pirates | .870 | 15 | 17 | 23 | 6 | 1 | Tinkle, Royals | .875 | 5 | 4 | 10 | 2 | 1 |
| Michel, Dodgers | .800 | 2 | 0 | 8 | 2 | 1 | Torres, Royals | .500 | 4 | 1 | 1 | 2 | 0 |
| Mullins, Braves | .830 | 19 | 10 | 29 | 8 | 1 | Troncoso, Rangers | .776 | 24 | 11 | 41 | 15 | 4 |
| Nina, Reds | .844 | 39 | 31 | 61 | 17 | 6 | Vaughn, Pirates | .857 | 26 | 37 | 53 | 15 | 4 |
| Perez, Pirates | .818 | 3 | 5 | 4 | 2 | 0 | Wilcox, Reds | .782 | 25 | 16 | 45 | 17 | 3 |

## SHORTSTOPS

| Player and Club | Pct. | G. | PO. | A. | E. | DP. | Player and Club | Pct. | G. | PO. | A. | E. | DP. |
|---|---|---|---|---|---|---|---|---|---|---|---|---|---|
| Arias, Dodgers | 1.000 | 1 | 1 | 1 | 0 | 0 | Kopetsky, Dodgers | .800 | 7 | 4 | 12 | 4 | 1 |
| Audain, White Sox | .818 | 15 | 15 | 21 | 8 | 4 | Lopez, White Sox | .926 | 51 | 67 | 134 | 16 | 21 |
| Barberich, Dodgers | .833 | 10 | 9 | 11 | 4 | 3 | Martinez, Yankees | .867 | 16 | 7 | 19 | 4 | 5 |
| Beaupre, Reds | .912 | 25 | 36 | 67 | 10 | 13 | McRae, Royals | .870 | 19 | 29 | 51 | 12 | 12 |
| Bell, Dodgers | .866 | 38 | 54 | 69 | 19 | 13 | Merced, Pirates | .788 | 19 | 29 | 53 | 22 | 6 |
| Brown, Reds | .903 | 9 | 9 | 19 | 3 | 1 | Mota, Braves | .818 | 10 | 12 | 15 | 6 | 3 |
| Burgos, Rangers | .899 | 55 | 74 | 167 | 27 | 21 | Nina, Reds | 1.000 | 2 | 3 | 6 | 0 | 0 |
| Butler, Braves | .921 | 17 | 22 | 36 | 5 | 9 | Parker, Dodgers | .961 | 21 | 21 | 53 | 3 | 15 |
| Cantrell, Braves | .893 | 43 | 70 | 122 | 23 | 20 | Pierce, Pirates | .900 | 2 | 1 | 8 | 1 | 0 |
| CORCINO, Royals | .927 | 45 | 57 | 96 | 12 | 17 | Ramirez, Pirates | .851 | 21 | 26 | 37 | 11 | 4 |
| Cruz, Rangers | 1.000 | 3 | 3 | 4 | 0 | 2 | Randle, Astros | .901 | 38 | 59 | 87 | 16 | 8 |
| Frias, Blue Jays | .908 | 17 | 26 | 53 | 8 | 9 | Renteria, Astros | 1.000 | 3 | 4 | 6 | 0 | 0 |
| Garrison, Dodgers | .700 | 2 | 2 | 5 | 3 | 0 | Reynolds, White Sox | .878 | 9 | 15 | 21 | 5 | 2 |
| Grimes, Royals | .000 | 1 | 0 | 0 | 1 | 0 | P. Sanchez, Astros | .893 | 26 | 49 | 76 | 15 | 16 |
| Hartman, Dodgers | 1.000 | 1 | 2 | 0 | 0 | 0 | Tinkle, Royals | 1.000 | 4 | 2 | 10 | 0 | 1 |
| Hauradou, Yankees | .946 | 10 | 15 | 20 | 2 | 1 | Torre, Reds | .896 | 37 | 59 | 96 | 18 | 11 |
| Horta, Yankees | .920 | 52 | 68 | 150 | 19 | 19 | Troncoso, Rangers | .880 | 13 | 12 | 32 | 6 | 4 |
| Kelly, Blue Jays | .880 | 48 | 72 | 119 | 26 | 27 | Vaughn, Pirates | .851 | 23 | 35 | 51 | 15 | 9 |

Triple Play—Reynolds.

## OUTFIELDERS

| Player and Club | Pct. | G. | PO. | A. | E. | DP. | Player and Club | Pct. | G. | PO. | A. | E. | DP. |
|---|---|---|---|---|---|---|---|---|---|---|---|---|---|
| Acosta, Reds | .943 | 44 | 79 | 3 | 5 | 1 | Hunter, Astros | .953 | 55 | 99 | 3 | 5 | 0 |
| Alcantara, Braves | .956 | 36 | 42 | 1 | 2 | 0 | Jackson, Astros | .968 | 46 | 87 | 3 | 3 | 1 |
| Alvarez, White Sox | 1.000 | 2 | 0 | 1 | 0 | 0 | Jeter, Blue Jays | .956 | 54 | 104 | 4 | 5 | 1 |
| Arias, Dodgers | 1.000 | 5 | 1 | 0 | 0 | 0 | Jimenez, Blue Jays | .949 | 22 | 34 | 3 | 2 | 1 |
| Baldwin, Astros* | .909 | 13 | 18 | 2 | 2 | 0 | Johnson, Royals* | .955 | 28 | 61 | 2 | 3 | 0 |
| Balli, White Sox | .952 | 25 | 20 | 0 | 1 | 0 | Kelley, Rangers | .948 | 48 | 54 | 1 | 3 | 0 |
| Barry, Pirates | .875 | 13 | 19 | 2 | 3 | 1 | Kiluk, Pirates | 1.000 | 4 | 10 | 2 | 0 | 0 |
| Basora, Dodgers | 1.000 | 2 | 1 | 0 | 0 | 0 | Koslofski, Royals | .979 | 28 | 43 | 3 | 1 | 0 |
| Bell, Royals | .986 | 61 | 135 | 4 | 2 | 3 | Magallanes, White Sox | .967 | 29 | 28 | 1 | 1 | 0 |
| Benitez, Dodgers | .941 | 37 | 44 | 4 | 3 | 0 | Marshall, Braves* | 1.000 | 16 | 15 | 1 | 0 | 0 |
| Bledsoe, White Sox | .895 | 16 | 15 | 2 | 2 | 0 | Martin, Braves* | 1.000 | 9 | 12 | 0 | 0 | 0 |
| Braxton, White Sox* | .950 | 54 | 72 | 4 | 4 | 2 | McMillan, Pirates* | .960 | 12 | 24 | 0 | 1 | 0 |
| Brown, Reds | .958 | 27 | 44 | 2 | 2 | 0 | Mealy, Pirates | 1.000 | 4 | 3 | 0 | 0 | 0 |
| Calvert, Yankees | 1.000 | 25 | 38 | 1 | 0 | 0 | Merced, White Sox* | 1.000 | 26 | 24 | 0 | 0 | 0 |
| Canseco, Yankees | 1.000 | 1 | 1 | 1 | 0 | 0 | Munoz, Blue Jays | .980 | 32 | 46 | 2 | 1 | 0 |
| Cargile, Yankees | .953 | 41 | 59 | 2 | 3 | 0 | O'Bryan, Rangers | .930 | 43 | 51 | 2 | 4 | 0 |
| Carter, Yankees | .952 | 39 | 51 | 8 | 3 | 0 | Quintero, Pirates | 1.000 | 14 | 18 | 3 | 0 | 0 |
| CASEY, Braves | 1.000 | 42 | 58 | 3 | 0 | 1 | Rahming, White Sox | .852 | 25 | 21 | 2 | 4 | 0 |
| Chance, Pirates | 1.000 | 7 | 12 | 1 | 0 | 0 | Redus, Royals | 1.000 | 1 | 1 | 0 | 0 | 0 |
| Clark, Rangers | 1.000 | 27 | 28 | 0 | 0 | 0 | Robles, Dodgers* | .986 | 42 | 63 | 6 | 1 | 2 |
| Clawson, Braves | .975 | 44 | 75 | 4 | 2 | 1 | N. Rodriguez, Pirates | 1.000 | 1 | 2 | 0 | 0 | 0 |
| Cook, Pirates | .991 | 43 | 100 | 5 | 1 | 2 | P. Rodriguez, Dodgers | 1.000 | 5 | 4 | 0 | 0 | 0 |
| Daniels, Pirates* | .500 | 2 | 1 | 0 | 1 | 0 | Rogers, Braves | 1.000 | 7 | 4 | 0 | 0 | 0 |
| Davis, Blue Jays | .950 | 51 | 84 | 12 | 5 | 1 | Romero, Blue Jays | .957 | 22 | 39 | 5 | 2 | 3 |
| DeLaCruz, Blue Jays | .952 | 11 | 20 | 0 | 1 | 0 | Rondon, Reds | 1.000 | 3 | 3 | 0 | 0 | 0 |
| Denkenberger, Pirates* | 1.000 | 6 | 13 | 0 | 0 | 0 | R. Russell, Rangers | 1.000 | 8 | 14 | 0 | 0 | 0 |
| Edwards, Dodgers* | .976 | 56 | 114 | 9 | 3 | 2 | S. Russell, Rangers | .900 | 13 | 9 | 0 | 1 | 0 |
| Epps, Reds* | .927 | 34 | 37 | 1 | 3 | 0 | Sanders, Royals | .975 | 46 | 69 | 8 | 2 | 2 |
| Farley, Dodgers* | .943 | 20 | 31 | 2 | 2 | 0 | Scruggs, White Sox* | .929 | 12 | 12 | 1 | 1 | 0 |
| Ford, Pirates* | .970 | 19 | 32 | 0 | 1 | 0 | Seay, Rangers | .889 | 16 | 16 | 0 | 2 | 0 |
| Garcia, Pirates | 1.000 | 6 | 7 | 0 | 0 | 0 | Sheffield, Rangers | .963 | 22 | 26 | 0 | 1 | 0 |
| Gilliam, Dodgers | .953 | 31 | 39 | 2 | 2 | 0 | Silverio, Reds | .935 | 53 | 85 | 1 | 6 | 1 |
| Glasker, Rangers* | .952 | 54 | 71 | 9 | 4 | 0 | Slocum, Royals | .971 | 27 | 32 | 2 | 1 | 0 |
| Green, Reds | 1.000 | 4 | 7 | 0 | 0 | 0 | Smith, Astros | 1.000 | 1 | 1 | 0 | 0 | 0 |
| Guerrero, Astros | .945 | 25 | 49 | 3 | 3 | 0 | Stewart, Astros | .938 | 26 | 55 | 5 | 4 | 1 |
| Guzman, Yankees | .963 | 12 | 24 | 2 | 1 | 1 | Trillo, Dodgers | .750 | 4 | 3 | 0 | 1 | 0 |
| Hauradou, Yankees | 1.000 | 1 | 1 | 0 | 0 | 0 | Tuttle, Reds | .966 | 31 | 53 | 3 | 2 | 1 |
| Hernandez, Yankees | .939 | 33 | 44 | 2 | 3 | 0 | Valverde, Pirates | .934 | 32 | 70 | 1 | 5 | 0 |
| Higgins, Yankees* | .977 | 51 | 80 | 5 | 2 | 1 | Waggoner, White Sox | .970 | 48 | 62 | 3 | 2 | 0 |
| Hithe, Astros | .956 | 56 | 81 | 5 | 4 | 0 | Wakefield, Pirates | .867 | 9 | 12 | 1 | 2 | 0 |
| Hood, Braves | .949 | 57 | 103 | 8 | 6 | 2 | Watson, Royals* | 1.000 | 4 | 8 | 1 | 0 | 0 |
| Horton, Yankees | 1.000 | 6 | 5 | 0 | 0 | 0 | Wetherby, Braves* | .923 | 8 | 12 | 0 | 1 | 0 |

## CATCHERS

| Player and Club | Pct. | G. | PO. | A. | E. | DP. | PB. | Player and Club | Pct. | G. | PO. | A. | E. | DP. | PB. |
|---|---|---|---|---|---|---|---|---|---|---|---|---|---|---|---|
| Aleshire, Astros | .952 | 39 | 195 | 44 | 12 | 0 | 11 | Cuadrado, Yankees | .972 | 9 | 31 | 4 | 1 | 0 | 0 |
| Alvarez, White Sox | 1.000 | 5 | 23 | 5 | 0 | 0 | 1 | Davis, Pirates | 1.000 | 5 | 19 | 1 | 0 | 0 | 2 |
| Bautista, Pirates | .992 | 22 | 105 | 17 | 1 | 1 | 7 | Dotzler, Rangers | .988 | 51 | 348 | 60 | 5 | 2 | 9 |
| Beeler, Reds | .962 | 25 | 136 | 14 | 6 | 0 | 8 | Duran, Dodgers | .987 | 31 | 137 | 20 | 2 | 2 | 6 |
| Bettencourt, Yankees | 1.000 | 2 | 7 | 0 | 0 | 0 | 0 | Dyer, Royals | .966 | 16 | 50 | 6 | 2 | 1 | 3 |
| BROWN, White Sox | .996 | 35 | 236 | 28 | 1 | 1 | 3 | Escalera, Royals | .985 | 30 | 164 | 38 | 3 | 0 | 8 |
| Cruz, Braves | .955 | 22 | 115 | 12 | 6 | 2 | 5 | Eusebio, Astros | 1.000 | 1 | 4 | 0 | 0 | 0 | 0 |

## CATCHERS—Continued

| Player and Club | Pct. | G. | PO. | A. | E. | DP. | PB. | Player and Club | Pct. | G. | PO. | A. | E. | DP. | PB. |
|---|---|---|---|---|---|---|---|---|---|---|---|---|---|---|---|
| Gonring, Blue Jays | 1.000 | 2 | 2 | 0 | 0 | 0 | 0 | Nowakowski, Blue Jays | .972 | 33 | 205 | 36 | 7 | 1 | 6 |
| A. Gonzalez, Yankees | .987 | 28 | 185 | 35 | 3 | 0 | 10 | Pfaff, Braves | .980 | 40 | 206 | 38 | 5 | 3 | 22 |
| C. Gonzalez, Royals | .964 | 25 | 173 | 14 | 7 | 1 | 14 | Pichardo, White Sox | 1.000 | 1 | 2 | 0 | 0 | 0 | 0 |
| Hall, Pirates | .900 | 5 | 17 | 1 | 2 | 0 | 1 | Pittman, Pirates | 1.000 | 14 | 73 | 8 | 0 | 1 | 0 |
| Hansel, Pirates | .944 | 13 | 58 | 10 | 4 | 2 | 8 | Pujols, Rangers | .984 | 15 | 53 | 9 | 1 | 0 | 0 |
| Hern, Braves | .923 | 3 | 11 | 1 | 1 | 0 | 0 | Reyes, Astros | .975 | 24 | 128 | 26 | 4 | 1 | 8 |
| Lawhon, Yankees | 1.000 | 2 | 3 | 0 | 0 | 0 | 0 | Roca, Pirates | .967 | 13 | 79 | 10 | 3 | 1 | 5 |
| Mandel, Yankees | .978 | 33 | 222 | 45 | 6 | 5 | 10 | Rodriguez, Dodgers | .944 | 19 | 60 | 7 | 4 | 0 | 2 |
| Martinez, Reds | .960 | 15 | 108 | 11 | 5 | 0 | 6 | Rosario, Dodgers | .978 | 40 | 234 | 36 | 6 | 6 | 13 |
| Maynard, Rangers | .977 | 12 | 36 | 6 | 1 | 0 | 3 | Ruzich, White Sox | 1.000 | 5 | 9 | 1 | 0 | 0 | 0 |
| McNally, Braves | 1.000 | 11 | 55 | 7 | 0 | 0 | 1 | Smith, Royals | .950 | 10 | 19 | 0 | 1 | 0 | 0 |
| Mendez, Braves | 1.000 | 5 | 6 | 2 | 0 | 0 | 1 | Sullivan, Blue Jays | .983 | 31 | 188 | 39 | 4 | 3 | 5 |
| Milholland, White Sox | .977 | 28 | 184 | 28 | 5 | 2 | 2 | Wilson, Reds | .969 | 31 | 159 | 29 | 6 | 2 | 5 |
| Newton, Dodgers | 1.000 | 2 | 6 | 0 | 0 | 0 | 0 | Zayas, Astros | .957 | 16 | 35 | 9 | 2 | 0 | 6 |

## PITCHERS

| Player and Club | Pct. | G. | PO. | A. | E. | DP. | Player and Club | Pct. | G. | PO. | A. | E. | DP. |
|---|---|---|---|---|---|---|---|---|---|---|---|---|---|
| Abrell, Braves | .952 | 12 | 5 | 15 | 1 | 1 | Lawhon, Yankees | 1.000 | 5 | 1 | 1 | 0 | 0 |
| S. Adams, Pirates | .875 | 12 | 2 | 5 | 1 | 0 | Lee, White Sox | .913 | 14 | 10 | 11 | 2 | 0 |
| T. Adams, Rangers | 1.000 | 1 | 0 | 2 | 0 | 0 | Marak, Braves | .778 | 12 | 4 | 10 | 4 | 1 |
| Almonte, Pirates | 1.000 | 5 | 0 | 1 | 0 | 0 | Martin, Pirates | 1.000 | 5 | 1 | 1 | 0 | 0 |
| Ames, Dodgers* | .778 | 6 | 3 | 4 | 2 | 0 | MARTINEZ, Dodgers | 1.000 | 23 | 6 | 18 | 0 | 0 |
| Anderson, Blue Jays | .905 | 15 | 4 | 15 | 2 | 1 | Massa, Royals | .750 | 6 | 0 | 3 | 1 | 0 |
| Arbelo, Dodgers | .800 | 7 | 1 | 3 | 1 | 0 | Mathews, Braves | .800 | 17 | 1 | 11 | 3 | 0 |
| Azocar, Yankees* | .929 | 5 | 4 | 9 | 1 | 0 | McClear, Yankees | 1.000 | 20 | 1 | 12 | 0 | 0 |
| Bartolomucci, White Sox* | .750 | 9 | 0 | 3 | 1 | 0 | McCormack, Royals | 1.000 | 4 | 0 | 3 | 0 | 0 |
| Bauer, Pirates | 1.000 | 3 | 1 | 1 | 0 | 0 | Mejia, Blue Jays | .778 | 10 | 2 | 5 | 2 | 0 |
| Bauza, Yankees | 1.000 | 4 | 2 | 4 | 0 | 0 | Metoyer, Astros | 1.000 | 11 | 1 | 2 | 0 | 1 |
| Belinskas, Reds | .889 | 7 | 2 | 6 | 1 | 0 | Mielke, Rangers | 1.000 | 19 | 2 | 7 | 0 | 0 |
| Blum, Rangers* | .952 | 8 | 6 | 14 | 1 | 1 | Moreno, Pirates | 1.000 | 12 | 3 | 10 | 0 | 1 |
| Bond, Dodgers | .667 | 16 | 0 | 2 | 1 | 0 | Mortimer, Rangers* | .800 | 9 | 2 | 2 | 1 | 0 |
| Booker, Rangers | 1.000 | 8 | 4 | 4 | 0 | 0 | Mota, Braves | .929 | 14 | 4 | 9 | 1 | 0 |
| Boroski, Royals | .909 | 16 | 6 | 4 | 1 | 0 | Mullins, Reds | 1.000 | 15 | 5 | 7 | 0 | 0 |
| Brinson, Blue Jays | 1.000 | 11 | 2 | 2 | 0 | 1 | Mumaw, Blue Jays* | 1.000 | 6 | 1 | 6 | 0 | 0 |
| Brito, White Sox | .667 | 6 | 1 | 1 | 1 | 0 | Nannierello, Rangers | .875 | 14 | 1 | 6 | 1 | 0 |
| Bruno, Reds | 1.000 | 10 | 3 | 7 | 0 | 0 | Natera, Braves* | .714 | 12 | 4 | 6 | 4 | 1 |
| Brusky, Reds | .950 | 12 | 1 | 18 | 1 | 4 | Nelson, Dodgers | .909 | 14 | 1 | 9 | 1 | 0 |
| Bryan, Rangers | .909 | 9 | 2 | 8 | 1 | 0 | Olivares, Pirates* | .750 | 9 | 0 | 3 | 1 | 1 |
| Buntzen, Royals | 1.000 | 6 | 0 | 1 | 0 | 0 | Pace, Astros | 1.000 | 12 | 1 | 2 | 0 | 0 |
| Burke, Braves | .846 | 12 | 5 | 6 | 2 | 0 | Pall, White Sox | .808 | 13 | 5 | 16 | 5 | 0 |
| Busick, Rangers | .900 | 10 | 3 | 6 | 1 | 0 | Palma, Blue Jays | .842 | 17 | 1 | 15 | 3 | 1 |
| Camp, Astros* | .786 | 13 | 2 | 9 | 3 | 0 | Pardo, Rangers | 1.000 | 1 | 1 | 3 | 0 | 0 |
| Canseco, Yankees | .778 | 9 | 3 | 11 | 4 | 0 | Patterson, Rangers | .000 | 5 | 0 | 0 | 2 | 0 |
| Cantrell, Yankees | .857 | 13 | 4 | 14 | 3 | 1 | Payne, Royals | .938 | 14 | 4 | 11 | 1 | 0 |
| Carroll, Yankees | .909 | 11 | 3 | 7 | 1 | 0 | Peluso, Royals | 1.000 | 13 | 5 | 9 | 0 | 0 |
| Castro, Pirates | .000 | 2 | 0 | 0 | 1 | 0 | Peralta, Pirates | .750 | 19 | 0 | 3 | 1 | 1 |
| Charles, Dodgers | .955 | 13 | 10 | 11 | 1 | 3 | Perez, Pirates* | 1.000 | 11 | 4 | 6 | 0 | 0 |
| Clark, Yankees* | 1.000 | 8 | 2 | 5 | 0 | 0 | Prentice, Braves | .750 | 3 | 2 | 1 | 1 | 1 |
| Colon, Pirates | 1.000 | 9 | 4 | 4 | 0 | 0 | Reker, Yankees* | 1.000 | 10 | 1 | 5 | 0 | 0 |
| Converse, Reds | .696 | 12 | 8 | 8 | 7 | 0 | Remigio, Pirates | 1.000 | 11 | 0 | 1 | 0 | 0 |
| Cortez, White Sox | .500 | 3 | 0 | 1 | 1 | 0 | J. Reynolds, Rangers | 1.000 | 4 | 1 | 1 | 0 | 0 |
| Cox, Dodgers* | 1.000 | 5 | 0 | 3 | 0 | 0 | Rivera, Rangers | .833 | 16 | 0 | 5 | 1 | 0 |
| Dale, Reds | 1.000 | 15 | 1 | 5 | 0 | 0 | G. Rodriguez, Yankees | 1.000 | 13 | 3 | 9 | 0 | 1 |
| DeLaCruz, Blue Jays | .750 | 15 | 3 | 3 | 2 | 0 | J. Rodriguez, Royals | 1.000 | 11 | 6 | 6 | 0 | 0 |
| DeLaRosa, Blue Jays | 1.000 | 16 | 1 | 3 | 0 | 0 | Rojas, Royals | .923 | 13 | 5 | 7 | 1 | 0 |
| J. DeLeon, Blue Jays | 1.000 | 5 | 2 | 0 | 0 | 0 | Romo, Reds | .682 | 12 | 6 | 9 | 7 | 0 |
| P. DeLeon, Astros | .882 | 12 | 4 | 11 | 2 | 1 | Sandoval, White Sox | 1.000 | 18 | 0 | 2 | 0 | 0 |
| DeLosSantos, Royals | .667 | 12 | 1 | 7 | 4 | 0 | Schofield, Rangers | .826 | 13 | 8 | 11 | 4 | 2 |
| Dickerson, Pirates | 1.000 | 10 | 1 | 4 | 0 | 0 | Scott, Braves | 1.000 | 10 | 7 | 13 | 0 | 0 |
| Dilone, Dodgers | .643 | 25 | 0 | 9 | 5 | 3 | Shane, Yankees | .800 | 11 | 3 | 1 | 1 | 0 |
| Dixon, Pirates | 1.000 | 14 | 1 | 9 | 0 | 0 | Sheehan, Astros | 1.000 | 5 | 1 | 1 | 0 | 0 |
| Drees, White Sox* | .952 | 12 | 7 | 13 | 1 | 0 | Shields, Dodgers | .000 | 3 | 0 | 0 | 1 | 0 |
| Driver, Reds | .615 | 17 | 2 | 6 | 5 | 0 | Sisler, Yankees | .750 | 13 | 2 | 10 | 4 | 0 |
| Eave, Braves | 1.000 | 6 | 1 | 7 | 0 | 1 | Smallwood, Pirates | .933 | 10 | 1 | 13 | 1 | 2 |
| Edge, Pirates | 1.000 | 3 | 0 | 4 | 0 | 0 | Smith, Rangers | 1.000 | 3 | 0 | 1 | 0 | 0 |
| Edwards, White Sox* | .947 | 11 | 4 | 14 | 1 | 0 | Soto, Rangers | .667 | 11 | 0 | 2 | 1 | 0 |
| Ellis, Royals | .857 | 13 | 4 | 8 | 2 | 0 | Starling, White Sox | 1.000 | 2 | 0 | 2 | 0 | 0 |
| Felden, Blue Jays | 1.000 | 18 | 2 | 9 | 0 | 2 | Stein, White Sox | .917 | 6 | 3 | 8 | 1 | 0 |
| Fiala, Astros | 1.000 | 6 | 3 | 2 | 0 | 0 | Swartzlander, Pirates | 1.000 | 10 | 4 | 9 | 0 | 0 |
| Franklin, Royals | 1.000 | 10 | 1 | 3 | 0 | 0 | Talbott, Astros | 1.000 | 22 | 1 | 5 | 0 | 0 |
| Garcia, Dodgers* | .833 | 7 | 2 | 3 | 1 | 1 | Tanner, Royals | .833 | 21 | 1 | 4 | 1 | 0 |
| Girdner, Reds | .833 | 12 | 3 | 7 | 2 | 0 | C. Thomas, Dodgers* | .500 | 11 | 0 | 1 | 1 | 0 |
| Goodenough, Royals* | .737 | 10 | 3 | 11 | 5 | 2 | F. Thomas, Braves | .875 | 8 | 2 | 5 | 1 | 1 |
| J. Guzman, Dodgers | 1.000 | 21 | 1 | 7 | 0 | 0 | M. Thomas, Rangers* | 1.000 | 7 | 2 | 8 | 0 | 0 |
| R. Guzman, Braves | .900 | 6 | 2 | 7 | 1 | 0 | Tracy, Blue Jays | 1.000 | 17 | 1 | 13 | 0 | 0 |
| Hackett, Braves* | .962 | 19 | 9 | 16 | 1 | 1 | Valenzuela, Pirates* | .800 | 13 | 2 | 2 | 1 | 0 |
| Hart, Dodgers* | .944 | 12 | 4 | 13 | 1 | 0 | Van Vuren, Royals | .955 | 13 | 9 | 12 | 1 | 1 |
| Hartman, Astros | .941 | 10 | 6 | 10 | 1 | 0 | Victor, Astros | .833 | 11 | 3 | 7 | 2 | 1 |
| Hellman, Astros | .600 | 7 | 0 | 3 | 2 | 0 | Vike, Astros | .857 | 11 | 6 | 18 | 4 | 1 |
| Henry, White Sox* | .875 | 16 | 2 | 5 | 1 | 0 | Vlcek, Rangers | .800 | 8 | 3 | 5 | 2 | 0 |
| Hern, Braves | 1.000 | 10 | 5 | 2 | 0 | 0 | Warren, White Sox | .750 | 11 | 3 | 15 | 6 | 0 |
| Irizarry, Dodgers* | 1.000 | 12 | 0 | 3 | 0 | 0 | West, Rangers | .933 | 14 | 3 | 11 | 1 | 1 |
| James, Rangers | .889 | 15 | 5 | 11 | 2 | 0 | Williams, Dodgers* | .739 | 13 | 5 | 12 | 6 | 0 |
| Jones, Blue Jays* | .933 | 15 | 2 | 12 | 1 | 1 | Wilmore, Astros | .929 | 18 | 2 | 11 | 1 | 1 |
| Klemp, Reds* | .767 | 13 | 2 | 21 | 7 | 1 | Wilson, White Sox | .909 | 22 | 2 | 8 | 1 | 1 |
| Koller, Astros | .842 | 13 | 7 | 9 | 3 | 1 | Winfield, Pirates | 1.000 | 6 | 1 | 1 | 0 | 0 |
| Kwiatkowski, Blue Jays | .833 | 14 | 2 | 3 | 1 | 0 | Woyce, Royals | 1.000 | 6 | 3 | 8 | 0 | 0 |
| Lankard, Rangers | 1.000 | 13 | 6 | 4 | 0 | 0 | Zielinski, Reds | .889 | 16 | 3 | 5 | 1 | 0 |
| Larsen, Rangers | 1.000 | 3 | 0 | 1 | 0 | 0 | | | | | | | |

The following players do not have any recorded accepted chances at the positions indicated, therefore, are not listed in the fielding averages for those particular positions: Carreno, p; Castro, 1b; Corcino, 3b; M. Cruz, 3b; J. Edwards, 1b; Eveline, ss; Franchi, p; C. Gonzalez, of; Higgins, 1b; Hithe, 1b; Horta, 2b; Huff, p; Isaac, 2b; G. Jackson, 2b; Kupfner, of; Meadows, p; Mitchell, of; C. Mullins, of; Nina, 2b; Nunez, of; D. Reynolds, p; F Sanchez, 1b, ss; P. Sanchez, c; Sassone, p.

## CLUB PITCHING

| Club | ERA. | G. | CG. | ShO. | Sv. | IP. | H. | R. | ER. | HR. | HB. | BB. | Int. BB. | SO. | WP. | Bk. |
|------|------|----|-----|------|-----|-----|-----|-----|-----|-----|-----|-----|----------|-----|-----|-----|
| Reds | 2.14 | 62 | 8 | 5 | 12 | 538.1 | 406 | 211 | 128 | 9 | 32 | 232 | 12 | 402 | 44 | 8 |
| Yankees | 2.50 | 62 | 13 | 7 | 10 | 540.0 | 483 | 226 | 150 | 10 | 23 | 175 | 6 | 448 | 45 | 9 |
| Royals | 2.53 | 62 | 4 | 8 | 23 | 523.2 | 461 | 239 | 147 | 6 | 19 | 191 | 9 | 408 | 49 | 1 |
| White Sox | 2.61 | 64 | 14 | 7 | 11 | 552.0 | 484 | 228 | 160 | 12 | 29 | 152 | 10 | 474 | 30 | 10 |
| Rangers | 2.75 | 62 | 1 | 5 | 14 | 543.2 | 456 | 246 | 166 | 7 | 22 | 204 | 2 | 440 | 47 | 14 |
| Astros | 3.12 | 62 | 10 | 4 | 10 | 528.0 | 509 | 288 | 183 | 12 | 23 | 210 | 6 | 361 | 34 | 6 |
| Dodgers | 3.51 | 61 | 5 | 5 | 11 | 522.1 | 501 | 309 | 204 | 16 | 34 | 274 | 11 | 430 | 59 | 15 |
| Blue Jays | 3.54 | 62 | 1 | 5 | 10 | 541.0 | 531 | 299 | 213 | 10 | 28 | 245 | 5 | 398 | 46 | 9 |
| Braves | 3.65 | 61 | 3 | 3 | 7 | 537.1 | 561 | 331 | 218 | 11 | 16 | 221 | 6 | 381 | 58 | 4 |
| Pirates | 4.49 | 62 | 3 | 2 | 5 | 517.2 | 551 | 376 | 258 | 17 | 28 | 268 | 0 | 341 | 53 | 10 |

## PITCHERS' RECORDS
(Leading Qualifiers for Earned-Run Average Leadership — 50 or More Innings)

°Throws lefthanded.

| Pitcher—Club | W. | L. | Pct. | ERA. | G. | GS. | CG. | GF. | ShO. | Sv. | IP. | H. | R. | ER. | HR. | HB. | BB. | Int. BB. | SO. | WP. |
|--------------|----|----|------|------|----|-----|-----|-----|------|-----|-----|-----|----|-----|-----|-----|-----|----------|-----|-----|
| West, Rangers | 6 | 0 | 1.000 | 1.33 | 14 | 5 | 0 | 5 | 0 | 2 | 54.1 | 38 | 13 | 8 | 0 | 0 | 12 | 0 | 26 | 3 |
| Blum, Yankees° | 6 | 0 | 1.000 | 1.38 | 8 | 8 | 3 | 0 | 0 | 0 | 58.2 | 36 | 16 | 9 | 1 | 0 | 23 | 0 | 62 | 5 |
| Klemp, Reds° | 5 | 2 | .714 | 1.43 | 13 | 9 | 2 | 1 | 0 | 0 | 69.0 | 51 | 21 | 11 | 1 | 2 | 36 | 0 | 58 | 11 |
| Canseco, Yankees | 3 | 2 | .600 | 1.57 | 9 | 7 | 1 | 2 | 0 | 0 | 51.2 | 43 | 19 | 9 | 0 | 2 | 11 | 0 | 39 | 8 |
| Girdner, Reds | 5 | 3 | .625 | 1.63 | 12 | 9 | 1 | 0 | 0 | 0 | 71.2 | 42 | 22 | 13 | 1 | 5 | 35 | 2 | 77 | 7 |
| Converse, Reds | 3 | 3 | .500 | 1.67 | 12 | 12 | 1 | 0 | 1 | 0 | 70.0 | 47 | 30 | 13 | 1 | 7 | 25 | 1 | 40 | 5 |
| Pall, White Sox | 7 | 5 | .583 | 1.67 | 13 | 13 | 4 | 0 | 2 | 0 | 86.0 | 68 | 34 | 16 | 2 | 2 | 10 | 0 | 63 | 3 |
| Schofield, Rangers | 5 | 4 | .556 | 1.89 | 13 | 11 | 0 | 0 | 0 | 0 | 66.2 | 44 | 18 | 14 | 0 | 4 | 32 | 0 | 34 | 2 |
| Van Vuren, Royals | 6 | 1 | .857 | 2.12 | 13 | 13 | 0 | 0 | 0 | 0 | 68.0 | 56 | 32 | 16 | 0 | 4 | 31 | 2 | 47 | 9 |
| Warren, White Sox | 4 | 3 | .571 | 2.26 | 11 | 11 | 2 | 0 | 1 | 0 | 71.2 | 61 | 29 | 18 | 1 | 6 | 15 | 0 | 52 | 3 |
| Edwards, White Sox° | 7 | 3 | .700 | 2.49 | 11 | 11 | 3 | 0 | 0 | 0 | 68.2 | 52 | 26 | 19 | 0 | 3 | 18 | 0 | 61 | 2 |

Departmental Leaders: G—Dilone, 25; W—Edwards, Pall, Sisler, 7; L—Palma, 8; Pct.—Van Vuren, .857; GS—Anderson, 14; CG—Charles, Pall, 4; GF—Talbott, 19; ShO—Cantrell, Pall, 2; Sv.—Dale, Tanner, 7; IP—Pall, 86.0; H—Cantrell, 93; R—Palma, 64; ER—Palma, 46; HR—Cantrell, Charles, Dickerson, Sisler, 4; HB—Palma, 12; BB—Williams, 55; IBB—Dale, McClear, Tanner, 5; SO—Rojas, 78; WP—J. Guzman, 15.

## (All Pitchers—Listed Alphabetically)

| Pitcher—Club | W. | L. | Pct. | ERA. | G. | GS. | CG. | GF. | ShO. | Sv. | IP. | H. | R. | ER. | HR. | HB. | BB. | Int. BB. | SO. | WP. |
|--------------|----|----|------|------|----|-----|-----|-----|------|-----|-----|-----|----|-----|-----|-----|-----|----------|-----|-----|
| Abrell, Braves | 2 | 4 | .333 | 3.79 | 12 | 12 | 2 | 0 | 0 | 0 | 59.1 | 59 | 38 | 25 | 1 | 1 | 29 | 0 | 30 | 5 |
| S. Adams, Pirates | 3 | 2 | .600 | 6.00 | 12 | 2 | 0 | 2 | 0 | 0 | 33.0 | 38 | 28 | 22 | 0 | 5 | 18 | 0 | 25 | 3 |
| T. Adams, Pirates | 1 | 0 | 1.000 | 0.00 | 1 | 0 | 0 | 0 | 0 | 0 | 4.0 | 2 | 0 | 0 | 0 | 1 | 0 | 0 | 3 | 0 |
| Almonte, Pirates | 0 | 0 | .000 | 2.70 | 5 | 0 | 0 | 2 | 0 | 0 | 6.2 | 9 | 5 | 2 | 0 | 0 | 2 | 0 | 6 | 0 |
| Ames, Dodgers° | 2 | 3 | .400 | 3.13 | 6 | 5 | 0 | 0 | 0 | 0 | 31.2 | 35 | 20 | 11 | 0 | 0 | 7 | 0 | 26 | 6 |
| Anderson, Blue Jays | 4 | 5 | .444 | 2.56 | 15 | 14 | 0 | 1 | 0 | 1 | 81.0 | 82 | 34 | 23 | 2 | 0 | 21 | 0 | 48 | 4 |
| Arbelo, Dodgers | 2 | 1 | .667 | 3.24 | 7 | 0 | 0 | 4 | 0 | 0 | 8.1 | 5 | 4 | 3 | 0 | 2 | 6 | 0 | 6 | 0 |
| Azocar, Yankees° | 4 | 0 | 1.000 | 1.45 | 5 | 4 | 2 | 1 | 1 | 0 | 37.1 | 30 | 8 | 6 | 0 | 0 | 14 | 0 | 36 | 3 |
| Bartolomucci, White Sox° | 1 | 0 | 1.000 | 3.44 | 9 | 0 | 0 | 3 | 0 | 0 | 18.1 | 21 | 7 | 7 | 0 | 1 | 7 | 1 | 10 | 0 |
| Bauer, Pirates | 0 | 2 | .000 | 6.35 | 3 | 0 | 0 | 2 | 0 | 0 | 5.2 | 2 | 4 | 4 | 0 | 0 | 6 | 0 | 5 | 0 |
| Bauza, Yankees | 1 | 2 | .333 | 4.30 | 4 | 4 | 0 | 0 | 0 | 0 | 23.0 | 27 | 14 | 11 | 0 | 0 | 7 | 0 | 20 | 0 |
| Belinskas, Reds | 6 | 0 | 1.000 | 0.82 | 7 | 7 | 0 | 0 | 0 | 0 | 44.0 | 28 | 7 | 4 | 0 | 1 | 10 | 0 | 35 | 3 |
| Blum, Yankees° | 6 | 0 | 1.000 | 1.38 | 8 | 8 | 3 | 0 | 0 | 0 | 58.2 | 36 | 16 | 9 | 1 | 0 | 23 | 0 | 62 | 5 |
| Bond, Dodgers | 2 | 3 | .400 | 2.35 | 16 | 0 | 0 | 7 | 0 | 2 | 23.0 | 17 | 13 | 6 | 0 | 3 | 16 | 2 | 16 | 1 |
| Booker, Rangers | 2 | 0 | 1.000 | 1.88 | 8 | 1 | 0 | 1 | 0 | 1 | 24.0 | 16 | 9 | 5 | 2 | 2 | 11 | 0 | 14 | 2 |
| Boroski, Royals | 3 | 2 | .600 | 4.38 | 16 | 2 | 0 | 8 | 0 | 4 | 39.0 | 35 | 23 | 19 | 1 | 2 | 11 | 0 | 31 | 9 |
| Brinson, Blue Jays | 4 | 3 | .571 | 1.51 | 11 | 4 | 0 | 6 | 0 | 0 | 41.2 | 23 | 9 | 7 | 0 | 0 | 20 | 2 | 53 | 4 |
| Brito, White Sox | 0 | 3 | .000 | 6.75 | 6 | 3 | 0 | 2 | 0 | 1 | 20.0 | 25 | 16 | 15 | 0 | 1 | 17 | 0 | 23 | 3 |
| Bruno, Reds | 3 | 2 | .600 | 1.67 | 10 | 4 | 1 | 4 | 0 | 1 | 37.2 | 25 | 9 | 7 | 0 | 0 | 6 | 1 | 34 | 2 |
| Brusky, Reds | 5 | 3 | .625 | 2.95 | 12 | 9 | 2 | 1 | 1 | 0 | 61.0 | 58 | 30 | 20 | 1 | 1 | 19 | 0 | 31 | 4 |
| Bryan, Rangers | 2 | 3 | .400 | 4.32 | 9 | 5 | 0 | 0 | 0 | 0 | 33.1 | 30 | 20 | 16 | 1 | 2 | 8 | 0 | 18 | 4 |
| Buntzen, Royals | 0 | 3 | .000 | 2.08 | 6 | 0 | 0 | 4 | 0 | 0 | 8.2 | 12 | 8 | 2 | 0 | 0 | 3 | 0 | 10 | 1 |
| Burke, Braves | 1 | 3 | .250 | 5.92 | 12 | 2 | 0 | 4 | 0 | 1 | 38.0 | 39 | 30 | 25 | 0 | 1 | 26 | 0 | 29 | 8 |
| Busick, Rangers | 0 | 5 | .000 | 3.70 | 10 | 9 | 0 | 0 | 0 | 0 | 41.1 | 45 | 28 | 17 | 1 | 1 | 19 | 0 | 44 | 7 |
| Camp, Astros° | 2 | 0 | 1.000 | 0.72 | 13 | 3 | 1 | 7 | 1 | 0 | 37.1 | 31 | 4 | 3 | 0 | 1 | 13 | 0 | 26 | 1 |
| Canseco, Yankees | 3 | 2 | .600 | 1.57 | 9 | 7 | 1 | 2 | 0 | 0 | 51.2 | 43 | 19 | 9 | 0 | 2 | 11 | 0 | 39 | 8 |
| Cantrell, Yankees | 5 | 4 | .556 | 3.08 | 13 | 13 | 3 | 0 | 2 | 0 | 84.2 | 93 | 37 | 29 | 4 | 1 | 11 | 1 | 48 | 5 |
| Carreno, Yankees | 0 | 0 | .000 | 4.50 | 1 | 0 | 0 | 0 | 0 | 0 | 2.0 | 1 | 1 | 1 | 0 | 0 | 1 | 0 | 1 | 2 |
| Carroll, Yankees | 2 | 0 | 1.000 | 2.10 | 11 | 0 | 0 | 8 | 0 | 4 | 25.2 | 18 | 8 | 6 | 0 | 6 | 11 | 0 | 33 | 0 |
| Castro, Pirates | 0 | 0 | .000 | 4.50 | 2 | 0 | 0 | 1 | 0 | 0 | 2.0 | 3 | 2 | 1 | 0 | 0 | 3 | 0 | 2 | 0 |
| Charles, Dodgers | 3 | 5 | .375 | 4.06 | 13 | 11 | 4 | 1 | 0 | 0 | 75.1 | 79 | 43 | 34 | 4 | 5 | 14 | 3 | 46 | 3 |
| Clark, Yankees° | 4 | 1 | .800 | 3.31 | 8 | 6 | 0 | 1 | 0 | 0 | 35.1 | 34 | 17 | 13 | 0 | 1 | 13 | 0 | 31 | 1 |
| Colon, Pirates | 1 | 3 | .250 | 3.60 | 9 | 1 | 0 | 7 | 0 | 1 | 15.0 | 19 | 17 | 6 | 2 | 0 | 12 | 0 | 3 | 1 |
| Converse, Reds | 3 | 3 | .500 | 1.67 | 12 | 12 | 1 | 0 | 1 | 0 | 70.0 | 47 | 30 | 13 | 1 | 7 | 25 | 1 | 40 | 5 |
| Cortez, White Sox | 0 | 1 | .000 | 3.86 | 3 | 0 | 0 | 2 | 0 | 0 | 7.0 | 5 | 5 | 3 | 1 | 1 | 4 | 0 | 5 | 0 |
| Cox, Dodgers° | 2 | 0 | 1.000 | 0.73 | 5 | 2 | 0 | 0 | 0 | 0 | 12.1 | 11 | 1 | 1 | 0 | 0 | 5 | 0 | 16 | 0 |
| Dale, Reds | 2 | 2 | .500 | 0.89 | 15 | 0 | 0 | 14 | 0 | 7 | 20.1 | 18 | 3 | 2 | 0 | 0 | 9 | 5 | 12 | 0 |
| DeLaCruz, Blue Jays | 3 | 2 | .400 | 4.50 | 15 | 1 | 0 | 7 | 0 | 1 | 38.0 | 42 | 23 | 19 | 2 | 1 | 14 | 0 | 12 | 2 |
| DeLaRosa, Blue Jays | 0 | 1 | .000 | 5.52 | 16 | 0 | 0 | 13 | 0 | 1 | 31.0 | 43 | 24 | 19 | 1 | 2 | 5 | 1 | 19 | 0 |
| J. DeLeon, Blue Jays | 0 | 0 | .000 | 1.06 | 5 | 0 | 0 | 2 | 0 | 0 | 17.0 | 13 | 4 | 2 | 0 | 1 | 10 | 0 | 11 | 1 |
| P. DeLeon, Astros | 3 | 6 | .333 | 4.44 | 12 | 12 | 2 | 0 | 0 | 0 | 73.0 | 73 | 43 | 36 | 3 | 3 | 21 | 0 | 39 | 3 |
| DeLosSantos, Royals | 3 | 0 | 1.000 | 3.06 | 12 | 0 | 0 | 8 | 0 | 2 | 32.1 | 40 | 21 | 11 | 0 | 2 | 8 | 0 | 16 | 0 |
| Dickerson, Pirates | 0 | 2 | .000 | 4.81 | 10 | 4 | 0 | 1 | 0 | 0 | 33.2 | 28 | 24 | 18 | 4 | 1 | 19 | 0 | 16 | 6 |
| Dilone, Dodgers | 0 | 3 | .000 | 2.66 | 25 | 0 | 0 | 12 | 0 | 1 | 44.0 | 35 | 20 | 13 | 1 | 11 | 31 | 2 | 50 | 4 |
| Dixon, Pirates | 0 | 0 | .000 | 5.12 | 14 | 0 | 0 | 10 | 0 | 0 | 19.1 | 14 | 11 | 11 | 0 | 3 | 14 | 0 | 13 | 1 |
| Drees, White Sox° | 6 | 3 | .667 | 2.78 | 12 | 12 | 2 | 0 | 0 | 0 | 74.1 | 75 | 29 | 23 | 1 | 4 | 17 | 0 | 75 | 6 |
| Driver, Reds | 0 | 2 | .000 | 3.79 | 17 | 4 | 0 | 7 | 0 | 2 | 40.1 | 29 | 24 | 17 | 2 | 5 | 23 | 0 | 27 | 3 |
| Eave, Braves | 2 | 1 | .667 | 1.76 | 6 | 4 | 0 | 1 | 0 | 0 | 30.2 | 28 | 7 | 6 | 0 | 0 | 8 | 0 | 21 | 3 |

| Pitcher—Club | W. | L. | Pct. | ERA. | G. | GS. | CG. | GF. | ShO. | Sv. | IP. | H. | R. | ER. | HR. | HB. | BB. | Int. BB. | SO. | WP. |
|---|---|---|---|---|---|---|---|---|---|---|---|---|---|---|---|---|---|---|---|---|
| Edge, Pirates | 1 | 0 | 1.000 | 1.06 | 3 | 1 | 1 | 0 | 1 | 0 | 17.0 | 9 | 2 | 2 | 1 | 0 | 4 | 0 | 8 | 0 |
| Edwards, White Sox* | 7 | 3 | .700 | 2.49 | 11 | 11 | 3 | 0 | 0 | 0 | 68.2 | 52 | 26 | 19 | 0 | 3 | 18 | 0 | 61 | 2 |
| Ellis, Royals | 4 | 3 | .571 | 3.72 | 13 | 3 | 0 | 3 | 0 | 1 | 36.1 | 31 | 16 | 15 | 0 | 1 | 18 | 0 | 40 | 8 |
| Felden, Blue Jays | 0 | 4 | .000 | 4.04 | 18 | 2 | 1 | 11 | 0 | 3 | 49.0 | 53 | 28 | 22 | 3 | 3 | 19 | 0 | 26 | 1 |
| Fiala, Astros | 1 | 2 | .333 | 2.05 | 6 | 2 | 0 | 1 | 0 | 0 | 22.0 | 22 | 12 | 5 | 2 | 1 | 10 | 1 | 10 | 1 |
| Franchi, Pirates* | 0 | 0 | .000 | 0.00 | 2 | 0 | 0 | 0 | 0 | 0 | 4.0 | 2 | 0 | 0 | 0 | 0 | 1 | 0 | 9 | 2 |
| Franklin, Royals | 1 | 0 | 1.000 | 2.87 | 10 | 0 | 0 | 5 | 0 | 1 | 15.2 | 18 | 8 | 5 | 1 | 0 | 11 | 0 | 7 | 2 |
| Garcia, Dodgers* | 2 | 3 | .400 | 3.60 | 7 | 6 | 0 | 1 | 0 | 0 | 30.0 | 26 | 15 | 12 | 2 | 2 | 14 | 0 | 37 | 5 |
| Girdner, Reds | 5 | 3 | .625 | 1.63 | 12 | 9 | 1 | 0 | 0 | 0 | 71.2 | 42 | 22 | 13 | 1 | 5 | 35 | 2 | 77 | 7 |
| Goodenough, Royals* | 3 | 4 | .429 | 1.63 | 10 | 10 | 0 | 0 | 0 | 0 | 49.2 | 36 | 20 | 9 | 0 | 2 | 34 | 1 | 39 | 3 |
| J. Guzman, Dodgers | 5 | 1 | .833 | 3.86 | 21 | 3 | 0 | 12 | 0 | 4 | 42.0 | 39 | 26 | 18 | 2 | 1 | 25 | 3 | 43 | 15 |
| R. Guzman, Braves | 1 | 3 | .250 | 3.69 | 6 | 6 | 1 | 0 | 0 | 0 | 39.0 | 42 | 24 | 16 | 1 | 0 | 15 | 0 | 30 | 2 |
| Hackett, Braves* | 5 | 3 | .625 | 2.81 | 19 | 2 | 0 | 12 | 0 | 3 | 67.1 | 70 | 27 | 21 | 3 | 1 | 15 | 2 | 58 | 3 |
| Hart, Dodgers* | 2 | 4 | .333 | 3.71 | 12 | 8 | 0 | 0 | 0 | 0 | 51.0 | 47 | 26 | 21 | 2 | 2 | 16 | 1 | 41 | 3 |
| Hartman, Astros | 3 | 6 | .333 | 2.62 | 10 | 10 | 3 | 0 | 0 | 0 | 65.1 | 63 | 34 | 19 | 2 | 2 | 20 | 0 | 53 | 5 |
| Hellman, Yankees | 4 | 0 | 1.000 | 0.87 | 7 | 6 | 2 | 0 | 1 | 0 | 41.1 | 21 | 9 | 4 | 0 | 1 | 15 | 0 | 44 | 4 |
| Henry, White Sox* | 5 | 0 | 1.000 | 1.97 | 16 | 1 | 0 | 9 | 0 | 2 | 32.0 | 31 | 12 | 7 | 1 | 3 | 15 | 2 | 28 | 2 |
| Hern, Braves | 0 | 1 | .000 | 3.60 | 10 | 0 | 0 | 9 | 0 | 0 | 20.0 | 27 | 18 | 8 | 0 | 1 | 15 | 0 | 12 | 2 |
| Huff, Braves | 0 | 0 | .000 | 2.25 | 1 | 0 | 0 | 0 | 0 | 0 | 4.0 | 1 | 1 | 1 | 0 | 0 | 3 | 0 | 2 | 0 |
| Irizarry, Dodgers* | 0 | 0 | .000 | 4.63 | 11 | 0 | 0 | 4 | 0 | 0 | 11.2 | 7 | 11 | 6 | 0 | 3 | 13 | 0 | 6 | 1 |
| James, Rangers | 4 | 2 | .667 | 1.74 | 15 | 3 | 1 | 6 | 0 | 0 | 46.2 | 35 | 19 | 9 | 0 | 2 | 10 | 0 | 49 | 5 |
| Jones, Blue Jays* | 2 | 6 | .250 | 3.41 | 15 | 9 | 0 | 3 | 0 | 0 | 58.0 | 45 | 35 | 22 | 0 | 0 | 41 | 0 | 77 | 5 |
| Klemp, Reds* | 5 | 2 | .714 | 1.43 | 13 | 9 | 2 | 1 | 0 | 0 | 69.0 | 51 | 21 | 11 | 1 | 2 | 36 | 0 | 58 | 11 |
| Koller, Pirates | 1 | 7 | .125 | 4.81 | 13 | 13 | 1 | 0 | 0 | 0 | 67.1 | 84 | 50 | 36 | 2 | 3 | 29 | 0 | 36 | 7 |
| Kwiatkowski, Blue Jays | 1 | 5 | .167 | 4.95 | 14 | 9 | 0 | 1 | 0 | 0 | 40.0 | 54 | 37 | 22 | 0 | 4 | 34 | 0 | 33 | 9 |
| Lankard, Rangers | 0 | 0 | .000 | 1.66 | 13 | 0 | 0 | 11 | 0 | 2 | 21.2 | 19 | 6 | 4 | 0 | 0 | 4 | 1 | 14 | 0 |
| Larsen, Rangers | 0 | 0 | .000 | 9.00 | 3 | 1 | 0 | 2 | 0 | 0 | 6.0 | 8 | 7 | 6 | 0 | 0 | 1 | 0 | 9 | 3 |
| Lawhon, Yankees | 0 | 0 | .000 | 0.00 | 5 | 0 | 0 | 2 | 0 | 1 | 8.0 | 4 | 3 | 0 | 0 | 4 | 4 | 0 | 5 | 1 |
| Lee, White Sox | 3 | 1 | .750 | 3.75 | 14 | 7 | 2 | 4 | 1 | 1 | 57.2 | 60 | 29 | 24 | 1 | 2 | 13 | 2 | 44 | 1 |
| Marak, Braves | 2 | 6 | .250 | 5.57 | 12 | 12 | 0 | 0 | 0 | 0 | 63.0 | 80 | 58 | 39 | 1 | 1 | 36 | 0 | 33 | 11 |
| Martin, Pirates | 0 | 1 | .000 | 2.35 | 5 | 0 | 0 | 3 | 0 | 1 | 7.2 | 5 | 6 | 2 | 0 | 0 | 5 | 0 | 0 | 0 |
| Martinez, Dodgers | 4 | 1 | .800 | 2.59 | 23 | 6 | 0 | 6 | 0 | 1 | 59.0 | 57 | 30 | 17 | 1 | 1 | 23 | 0 | 42 | 5 |
| Massa, Pirates | 0 | 0 | .000 | 6.46 | 6 | 0 | 0 | 4 | 0 | 0 | 15.1 | 23 | 20 | 11 | 0 | 1 | 4 | 0 | 10 | 2 |
| Mathews, Braves | 5 | 3 | .625 | 2.23 | 17 | 0 | 0 | 16 | 0 | 2 | 32.1 | 33 | 14 | 8 | 0 | 2 | 10 | 3 | 31 | 7 |
| McClear, Yankees | 6 | 3 | .667 | 1.40 | 20 | 0 | 0 | 18 | 0 | 2 | 38.2 | 25 | 9 | 6 | 0 | 3 | 12 | 5 | 46 | 5 |
| McCormack, Royals | 0 | 0 | .000 | 4.91 | 4 | 0 | 0 | 2 | 0 | 0 | 3.2 | 6 | 5 | 2 | 0 | 0 | 6 | 1 | 1 | 0 |
| Meadows, Rangers | 0 | 0 | .000 | 0.00 | 3 | 0 | 0 | 2 | 0 | 0 | 3.0 | 2 | 0 | 0 | 0 | 0 | 1 | 0 | 2 | 0 |
| Mejia, Blue Jays | 3 | 1 | .750 | 2.37 | 10 | 3 | 0 | 5 | 0 | 3 | 38.0 | 31 | 12 | 10 | 2 | 2 | 7 | 0 | 26 | 0 |
| Metoyer, Astros | 3 | 1 | .750 | 0.62 | 11 | 0 | 0 | 9 | 0 | 3 | 29.0 | 15 | 10 | 2 | 0 | 0 | 7 | 0 | 32 | 1 |
| Mielke, Rangers | 2 | 2 | .500 | 0.96 | 19 | 0 | 0 | 14 | 0 | 6 | 37.2 | 25 | 8 | 4 | 0 | 0 | 14 | 1 | 49 | 2 |
| Moreno, Pirates | 2 | 5 | .286 | 3.84 | 12 | 12 | 0 | 0 | 0 | 0 | 68.0 | 70 | 46 | 29 | 2 | 3 | 34 | 0 | 58 | 7 |
| Mortimer, Rangers* | 1 | 1 | .500 | 5.74 | 9 | 3 | 0 | 0 | 0 | 0 | 26.2 | 27 | 21 | 17 | 0 | 1 | 11 | 0 | 22 | 1 |
| Mota, Braves | 1 | 0 | 1.000 | 4.73 | 14 | 0 | 0 | 11 | 0 | 0 | 32.1 | 30 | 22 | 17 | 0 | 3 | 19 | 0 | 11 | 3 |
| Mullins, Reds | 2 | 1 | .667 | 3.12 | 15 | 8 | 1 | 2 | 0 | 0 | 52.0 | 40 | 26 | 18 | 1 | 2 | 34 | 0 | 35 | 4 |
| Mumaw, Blue Jays* | 3 | 1 | .750 | 0.77 | 6 | 6 | 0 | 0 | 0 | 0 | 35.0 | 23 | 5 | 3 | 0 | 2 | 10 | 0 | 35 | 3 |
| Nannierello, Rangers | 1 | 2 | .333 | 1.46 | 14 | 0 | 0 | 8 | 0 | 1 | 24.2 | 18 | 8 | 4 | 0 | 1 | 6 | 0 | 18 | 1 |
| Natera, Rangers* | 3 | 3 | .500 | 2.93 | 12 | 6 | 0 | 3 | 0 | 0 | 46.0 | 53 | 29 | 15 | 1 | 1 | 18 | 1 | 34 | 5 |
| Nelson, Dodgers | 0 | 5 | .000 | 5.51 | 14 | 7 | 0 | 3 | 0 | 0 | 47.1 | 72 | 50 | 29 | 1 | 0 | 32 | 0 | 31 | 8 |
| Olivares, Pirates* | 0 | 0 | .000 | 6.75 | 9 | 0 | 0 | 3 | 0 | 0 | 17.1 | 22 | 20 | 13 | 0 | 1 | 12 | 0 | 11 | 5 |
| Pace, Reds* | 2 | 0 | 1.000 | 3.29 | 12 | 0 | 0 | 5 | 0 | 1 | 13.2 | 16 | 7 | 5 | 1 | 1 | 8 | 0 | 9 | 3 |
| Pall, White Sox | 7 | 5 | .583 | 1.67 | 13 | 13 | 4 | 0 | 2 | 0 | 86.0 | 68 | 34 | 16 | 2 | 2 | 10 | 0 | 63 | 3 |
| Palma, Blue Jays | 1 | 8 | .111 | 6.37 | 17 | 11 | 0 | 1 | 0 | 0 | 65.0 | 70 | 64 | 46 | 0 | 12 | 51 | 0 | 27 | 10 |
| Pardo, Rangers | 1 | 0 | 1.000 | 0.00 | 1 | 1 | 0 | 0 | 0 | 0 | 5.0 | 5 | 0 | 0 | 0 | 0 | 3 | 0 | 5 | 0 |
| Patterson, Rangers | 1 | 0 | 1.000 | 5.54 | 5 | 2 | 0 | 0 | 0 | 0 | 13.0 | 11 | 12 | 8 | 0 | 1 | 15 | 0 | 13 | 1 |
| Payne, Royals | 0 | 2 | .000 | 3.03 | 14 | 0 | 0 | 10 | 0 | 6 | 29.2 | 28 | 12 | 10 | 1 | 0 | 5 | 0 | 30 | 1 |
| Peluso, Reds | 3 | 0 | 1.000 | 1.69 | 13 | 5 | 1 | 3 | 0 | 2 | 42.2 | 26 | 12 | 8 | 0 | 0 | 20 | 0 | 25 | 6 |
| Peralta, Reds | 1 | 4 | .200 | 2.40 | 19 | 0 | 0 | 10 | 0 | 1 | 30.0 | 21 | 18 | 8 | 1 | 4 | 14 | 1 | 21 | 1 |
| Perez, Pirates* | 3 | 7 | .300 | 5.28 | 11 | 11 | 1 | 0 | 0 | 0 | 61.1 | 74 | 48 | 36 | 2 | 3 | 24 | 0 | 37 | 2 |
| Prentice, Braves | 1 | 1 | .500 | 6.55 | 3 | 2 | 0 | 1 | 0 | 0 | 11.0 | 18 | 14 | 8 | 0 | 0 | 4 | 0 | 4 | 3 |
| Reker, Yankees* | 1 | 2 | .333 | 2.73 | 10 | 4 | 1 | 3 | 0 | 0 | 29.2 | 37 | 15 | 9 | 0 | 1 | 2 | 0 | 17 | 2 |
| Remigio, Pirates | 0 | 2 | .000 | 3.09 | 11 | 0 | 0 | 9 | 0 | 1 | 11.2 | 17 | 5 | 4 | 0 | 0 | 9 | 0 | 11 | 0 |
| D. Reynolds, White Sox | 0 | 0 | .000 | 0.00 | 1 | 0 | 0 | 1 | 0 | 0 | 1.0 | 1 | 0 | 0 | 0 | 0 | 1 | 0 | 1 | 0 |
| J. Reynolds, Rangers | 1 | 0 | 1.000 | 1.86 | 4 | 1 | 0 | 2 | 0 | 1 | 9.2 | 6 | 2 | 2 | 0 | 0 | 5 | 0 | 10 | 1 |
| Rivera, Rangers | 0 | 1 | .000 | 2.86 | 16 | 0 | 0 | 8 | 0 | 0 | 34.2 | 30 | 18 | 11 | 2 | 2 | 17 | 0 | 30 | 2 |
| G. Rodriguez, Yankees | 0 | 1 | .000 | 4.03 | 13 | 1 | 0 | 5 | 0 | 2 | 22.1 | 26 | 15 | 10 | 0 | 1 | 10 | 0 | 14 | 3 |
| J. Rodriguez, Royals | 5 | 2 | .714 | 2.67 | 11 | 10 | 1 | 0 | 0 | 0 | 54.0 | 54 | 25 | 16 | 1 | 3 | 14 | 0 | 37 | 2 |
| Rojas, Royals | 5 | 4 | .556 | 2.75 | 13 | 13 | 1 | 0 | 1 | 0 | 72.0 | 69 | 33 | 22 | 1 | 3 | 16 | 0 | 78 | 4 |
| Romo, Astros | 3 | 6 | .333 | 3.56 | 12 | 12 | 1 | 0 | 1 | 0 | 68.1 | 67 | 45 | 27 | 1 | 4 | 35 | 0 | 48 | 3 |
| Sandoval, White Sox | 1 | 1 | .500 | 2.19 | 18 | 0 | 0 | 13 | 0 | 3 | 37.0 | 30 | 14 | 9 | 2 | 1 | 16 | 2 | 31 | 3 |
| Sassone, White Sox | 1 | 0 | 1.000 | 8.03 | 6 | 0 | 0 | 1 | 0 | 0 | 12.1 | 20 | 13 | 11 | 1 | 0 | 4 | 0 | 11 | 1 |
| Schofield, Rangers | 5 | 4 | .556 | 1.89 | 13 | 11 | 0 | 0 | 0 | 0 | 66.2 | 44 | 18 | 14 | 0 | 4 | 32 | 0 | 34 | 2 |
| Scott, Braves | 3 | 5 | .375 | 3.09 | 10 | 10 | 0 | 0 | 0 | 0 | 64.0 | 63 | 32 | 22 | 3 | 5 | 19 | 0 | 65 | 6 |
| Shane, Yankees | 0 | 1 | .000 | 5.40 | 11 | 0 | 0 | 7 | 0 | 1 | 16.2 | 19 | 15 | 10 | 1 | 3 | 16 | 0 | 9 | 1 |
| Sheehan, Astros | 0 | 2 | .000 | 3.52 | 5 | 4 | 0 | 1 | 0 | 0 | 15.1 | 15 | 9 | 6 | 0 | 0 | 5 | 0 | 9 | 0 |
| Shields, Dodgers | 0 | 0 | .000 | 2.45 | 3 | 0 | 0 | 1 | 0 | 0 | 3.2 | 1 | 2 | 1 | 0 | 0 | 3 | 0 | 2 | 1 |
| Sisler, Yankees | 7 | 2 | .778 | 3.63 | 13 | 9 | 1 | 1 | 0 | 0 | 62.0 | 67 | 37 | 25 | 4 | 0 | 19 | 0 | 41 | 5 |
| Smallwood, Pirates | 1 | 7 | .125 | 4.96 | 14 | 8 | 0 | 0 | 0 | 0 | 45.1 | 52 | 38 | 25 | 1 | 3 | 19 | 0 | 28 | 5 |
| Smith, Astros | 0 | 1 | .000 | 1.17 | 3 | 0 | 0 | 3 | 0 | 0 | 7.2 | 4 | 1 | 1 | 0 | 1 | 5 | 0 | 6 | 1 |
| Soto, Rangers | 2 | 5 | .286 | 5.20 | 11 | 7 | 0 | 1 | 0 | 0 | 36.1 | 47 | 31 | 21 | 0 | 2 | 10 | 0 | 30 | 3 |
| Starling, Yankees | 0 | 0 | .000 | 6.00 | 2 | 0 | 0 | 1 | 0 | 0 | 3.0 | 2 | 3 | 2 | 0 | 0 | 6 | 0 | 2 | 0 |
| Stein, White Sox | 2 | 1 | .667 | 2.75 | 6 | 6 | 1 | 0 | 0 | 0 | 39.1 | 26 | 15 | 12 | 1 | 3 | 4 | 0 | 43 | 3 |
| Swartzlander, Pirates | 2 | 4 | .333 | 3.10 | 10 | 10 | 0 | 0 | 0 | 0 | 49.1 | 35 | 27 | 17 | 0 | 4 | 34 | 0 | 38 | 9 |
| Talbott, Astros | 0 | 2 | .000 | 3.89 | 22 | 0 | 0 | 19 | 0 | 6 | 39.1 | 49 | 25 | 17 | 0 | 0 | 8 | 2 | 24 | 3 |
| Tanner, Royals | 3 | 3 | .500 | 1.80 | 21 | 0 | 0 | 15 | 0 | 7 | 35.0 | 30 | 13 | 7 | 0 | 2 | 10 | 5 | 20 | 1 |
| C. Thomas, Dodgers* | 0 | 0 | .000 | 2.20 | 11 | 0 | 0 | 5 | 0 | 1 | 16.1 | 16 | 13 | 4 | 1 | 2 | 14 | 0 | 9 | 2 |
| F. Thomas, Braves | 2 | 0 | .000 | 2.08 | 8 | 3 | 0 | 2 | 0 | 1 | 30.1 | 18 | 17 | 7 | 1 | 0 | 8 | 0 | 21 | 0 |
| M. Thomas, Rangers | 4 | 1 | .800 | 2.37 | 7 | 6 | 0 | 0 | 0 | 0 | 30.1 | 21 | 9 | 8 | 0 | 2 | 8 | 0 | 29 | 4 |
| Tracy, Blue Jays | 3 | 2 | .600 | 3.42 | 17 | 3 | 0 | 11 | 0 | 1 | 47.1 | 52 | 24 | 18 | 0 | 1 | 13 | 2 | 31 | 7 |
| Valenzuela, Pirates* | 1 | 3 | .250 | 5.46 | 13 | 0 | 0 | 9 | 0 | 2 | 29.2 | 36 | 22 | 18 | 3 | 1 | 18 | 0 | 20 | 3 |
| Van Vuren, Royals | 6 | 1 | .857 | 2.12 | 13 | 13 | 0 | 0 | 0 | 0 | 68.0 | 56 | 32 | 16 | 0 | 4 | 31 | 2 | 47 | 5 |
| Victor, Astros | 2 | 2 | .500 | 3.41 | 11 | 4 | 0 | 3 | 0 | 0 | 34.1 | 32 | 17 | 13 | 1 | 5 | 20 | 2 | 20 | 1 |
| Vike, Astros | 4 | 3 | .571 | 3.24 | 11 | 11 | 3 | 0 | 0 | 0 | 66.2 | 66 | 37 | 24 | 1 | 2 | 29 | 0 | 36 | 7 |
| Vlcek, Rangers | 0 | 3 | .000 | 4.38 | 8 | 7 | 0 | 1 | 0 | 0 | 24.2 | 27 | 17 | 12 | 1 | 1 | 17 | 0 | 21 | 6 |

| Pitcher—Club | W. | L. | Pct. | ERA. | G. | GS. | CG. | GF. | ShO. | Sv. | IP. | H. | R. | ER. | HR. | HB. | BB. | Int. BB. | SO. | WP. |
|---|---|---|---|---|---|---|---|---|---|---|---|---|---|---|---|---|---|---|---|---|
| Warren, White Sox | 4 | 3 | .571 | 2.26 | 11 | 11 | 2 | 0 | 1 | 0 | 71.2 | 61 | 29 | 18 | 1 | 6 | 15 | 0 | 52 | 3 |
| West, Rangers | 6 | 0 | 1.000 | 1.33 | 14 | 5 | 0 | 5 | 0 | 2 | 54.1 | 38 | 13 | 8 | 0 | 0 | 12 | 0 | 26 | 3 |
| Williams, Dodgers° | 4 | 4 | .500 | 3.78 | 13 | 13 | 1 | 0 | 1 | 0 | 66.2 | 54 | 35 | 28 | 1 | 2 | 55 | 0 | 59 | 5 |
| Wilmore, Astros | 2 | 6 | .250 | 3.45 | 18 | 4 | 0 | 8 | 0 | 1 | 57.1 | 52 | 38 | 22 | 1 | 4 | 33 | 1 | 47 | 7 |
| Wilson, White Sox | 4 | 1 | .800 | 1.62 | 22 | 0 | 0 | 16 | 0 | 4 | 39.0 | 29 | 12 | 7 | 2 | 2 | 16 | 3 | 38 | 4 |
| Winfield, Pirates | 0 | 0 | .000 | 1.08 | 6 | 0 | 0 | 6 | 0 | 0 | 8.1 | 9 | 1 | 1 | 0 | 0 | 1 | 0 | 5 | 0 |
| Woyce, Royals | 2 | 0 | 1.000 | 1.22 | 6 | 6 | 1 | 0 | 1 | 0 | 37.0 | 20 | 11 | 5 | 1 | 0 | 4 | 0 | 27 | 3 |
| Zielinski, Reds | 4 | 2 | .667 | 3.14 | 16 | 0 | 0 | 10 | 0 | 0 | 28.2 | 31 | 14 | 10 | 0 | 4 | 13 | 2 | 23 | 1 |

BALKS—Williams, 4; Busick, J. Guzman, Olivares, Pall, C. Thomas, 3 each; Abrell, Azocar, Bauza, Booker, Clark, DeLaRosa, Dilone, Girdner, Jones, Klemp, Lee, Mortimer, Palma, Rivera, Valenzuela, Wilmore, Wilson, 2 each; Bond, Brinson, Brusky, Canseco, Carreno, J. DeLeon, Drees, Driver, Garcia, Henry, Hern, Koller, Martin, McClear, Metoyer, Mielke, Mullins, Nannierello, Natera, Nelson, Perez, Rojas, Romo, Sandoval, Smallwood, Soto, Swartzlander, Talbott, Tracy, Victor, Vlcek, West, Zielinski, 1 each.

COMBINATION SHUTOUTS—Sheehan-Fiala-Talbott, DeLeon-Talbott, Astros; Mumaw-Mejia 2, Mumaw-Mejia-Tracy, Jones-Felden-DeLaCruz, Brinson-DeLeCruz-Tracy, Blue Jays; Eave-Mota, Scott-Hackett, Eave-Hackett, Braves; Garcia-Dilone-Martinez, Guzman-Cox-Martinez, Williams-Garcia, Cox-Martinez-Bond, Dodgers; Swartzlander-Valenzuela, Pirates; Pardo-Reynolds-Mielke, Patterson-Booker-Nannierello-Mielke, Schofield-James-Mielke, Soto-Booker, Schofield-Nannierello, Rangers; Belinskas-Peralta, Belinskas-Mullins-Peralta-Driver-Bruno, Klemp-Dale, Reds; Van Vuren-Peluso, Rojas-Tanner-Franklin, Peluso-Tanner, Rodriguez-Ellis-Peluso, Rojas-Ellis, Rodriguez-DeLosSantos-Tanner, Royals; Edwards-Lee, Edwards-Wilson, Edwards-Sandoval, White Sox; Clark-Shane, Canseco-McClear, Hellman-McClear, Yankees.

NO-HIT GAMES—Swartzlander-Valenzuela, Pirates, defeated Dodgers, 6-0, July 1; Eave-Mota, Braves, defeated White Sox, 8-0 (seven innings, second game), July 25; Converse, Reds, defeated Astros, 3-0 (seven innings, second game), August 20.

# Pioneer League

## SUMMER CLASS A CLASSIFICATION

### CHAMPIONSHIP WINNERS IN PREVIOUS YEARS

| | | | | | |
|---|---|---|---|---|---|
| 1939—Twin Falls* | .581 | 1954—Salt Lake City | .595 | 1969—Ogden | .620 |
| 1940—Salt Lake City | .608 | Great Falls (4th)* | .530 | 1970—Idaho Falls | .629 |
| Ogden (4th)* | .492 | 1955—Boise | .588 | 1971—Great Falls | .643 |
| 1941—Boise | .623 | Magic Valley (4th)* | .489 | 1972—Billings | .694 |
| Ogden (2nd)* | .598 | 1956—Boise | .561 | 1973—Billings | .629 |
| 1942—Pocatello† | .690 | 1957—Salt Lake City | .650 | 1974—Idaho Falls | .569 |
| Boise | .683 | Billings† | .582 | 1975—Great Falls | .577 |
| 1943-44-45—Did not operate. | | 1958—Great Falls | .582 | 1976—Great Falls | .577 |
| 1946—Twin Falls‡ | .585 | Boise† | .615 | 1977—Lethbridge | .629 |
| Salt Lake City† | .585 | 1959—Boise | .633 | 1978—Billings x | .735 |
| 1947—Salt Lake City | .618 | Billings (2nd)* | .523 | 1979—Helena | .623 |
| Twin Falls† | .600 | 1960—Boise† | .686 | Lethbridge y | .559 |
| 1948—Pocatello | .611 | Idaho Falls | .650 | 1980—Lethbridge y | .743 |
| Twin Falls (2nd)* | .595 | 1961—Boise | .638 | Billings | .629 |
| 1949—Twin Falls | .624 | Great Falls* | .571 | 1981—Calgary | .657 |
| Pocatello (3rd)* | .595 | 1962—Boise§ | .565 | Butte y | .557 |
| 1950—Pocatello | .635 | Billings* | .706 | 1982—Medicine Hat y | .629 |
| Billings (3rd)* | .571 | 1963—Idaho Falls | .702 | Idaho Falls | .600 |
| 1951—Salt Lake City | .618 | Magic Valley† | .643 | 1983—Billings y | .614 |
| Great Falls (3rd)* | .559 | 1964—Treasure Valley | .615 | Calgary | .600 |
| 1952—Pocatello | .595 | 1965—Treasure Valley | .530 | 1984—Billings | .691 |
| Idaho Falls (2nd)* | .573 | 1966—Ogden | .591 | Helena y | .647 |
| 1953—Ogden | .679 | 1967—Ogden | .621 | | |
| Salt Lake C. (4th)* | .527 | 1968—Ogden | .609 | | |

*Won four-club playoff. †Won split-season playoff. ‡Ended first half in tie with Salt Lake City and won one-game playoff. §Ended first half in tie with Billings and Great Falls and won playoff. xBillings (first place) defeated Idaho Falls (second place) in First Place-Second Place playoff. yLeague divided in Northern and Southern divisions; won two-club playoff.

### STANDING OF CLUBS AT CLOSE OF SEASON, AUGUST 29

#### NORTHERN DIVISION

| Club | GF. | Hel. | MH | But. | SLC | Bil. | Poc. | IF | W. | L. | T. | Pct. | G.B. |
|---|---|---|---|---|---|---|---|---|---|---|---|---|---|
| Great Falls (Dodgers) | .... | 10 | 10 | 10 | 5 | 6 | 7 | 6 | 54 | 16 | 0 | .771 | ........ |
| Helena (Brewers) | 4 | .... | 12 | 11 | 4 | 2 | 3 | 6 | 42 | 26 | 0 | .618 | 11 |
| Medicine Hat (Blue Jays) | 4 | 2 | .... | 7 | 4 | 0 | 6 | 3 | 26 | 44 | 0 | .371 | 28 |
| Butte (Co-op) | 4 | 3 | 7 | .... | 0 | 2 | 4 | 4 | 24 | 45 | 0 | .348 | 29½ |

#### SOUTHERN DIVISION

| Club | GF. | Hel. | MH | But. | SLC | Bil. | Poc. | IF | W. | L. | T. | Pct. | G.B. |
|---|---|---|---|---|---|---|---|---|---|---|---|---|---|
| Salt Lake City (Independent) | 2 | 3 | 3 | 7 | .... | 10 | 11 | 10 | 46 | 24 | 0 | .657 | ........ |
| Billings (Reds) | 1 | 4 | 7 | 5 | 4 | .... | 11 | 9 | 41 | 27 | 0 | .603 | 4 |
| Pocatello (A's) | 0 | 3 | 1 | 3 | 3 | 3 | .... | 11 | 24 | 45 | 0 | .348 | 21½ |
| Idaho Falls (Independent) | 1 | 1 | 4 | 2 | 4 | 4 | 3 | .... | 19 | 49 | 0 | .279 | 26 |

Major league affiliations in parentheses.

Playoff—Salt Lake City defeated Great Falls, three games to two, to win league championship.

Regular-Season Attendance—Billings, 97,773; Butte, 20,573; Great Falls, 85,193; Helena, 23,276; Idaho Falls, 20,647; Medicine Hat, 46,284; Pocatello, 22,397; Salt Lake City, 57,683. Total, 373,826. Playoffs, 12,262.

Managers—Billings, Jim Lett; Butte, Harold Dyer; Great Falls, Kevin Kennedy; Helena, Mike Easom; Idaho Falls, Ruben Rodriguez; Medicine Hat, Ralph Wheeler; Pocatello, Dave Hudgens; Salt Lake City, Jim Gattis.

All-Star Team: 1B—Marty Brown, Billings; 2B—Mike Watters, Great Falls; 3B—Mark Grimes, Salt Lake City; SS—Walter Weiss, Pocatello; OF—Michael Devereaux, Great Falls; Todd Brown, Helena; Brian Morrison, Medicine Hat; C—Greg David, Medicine Hat; DH—Joe Shotnick, Salt Lake City; P—Fred Farwell, Great Falls; Bill Ray, Great Falls; Ed McCarter, Salt Lake City; Manager of the Year—Kevin Kennedy, Great Falls.

(Compiled by William J. Weiss, League Statistician, San Mateo, Calif.)

### CLUB BATTING

| Club | Pct. | G. | AB. | R. | OR. | H. | TB. | 2B. | 3B. | HR. | RBI. | GW. | SH. | SF. | HP. | BB. | Int. BB. | SO. | SB. | CS. | LOB. |
|---|---|---|---|---|---|---|---|---|---|---|---|---|---|---|---|---|---|---|---|---|---|
| Helena | .309 | 68 | 2373 | 485 | 428 | 734 | 1029 | 113 | 19 | 48 | 417 | 34 | 23 | 39 | 12 | 408 | 12 | 365 | 134 | 36 | 540 |
| Great Falls | .307 | 70 | 2390 | 508 | 290 | 734 | 1022 | 118 | 43 | 28 | 423 | 49 | 25 | 39 | 20 | 348 | 12 | 502 | 109 | 53 | 549 |
| Salt Lake City | .303 | 70 | 2359 | 461 | 311 | 715 | 974 | 105 | 47 | 20 | 395 | 41 | 28 | 32 | 14 | 268 | 8 | 412 | 50 | 31 | 482 |
| Medicine Hat | .268 | 70 | 2301 | 318 | 378 | 616 | 837 | 95 | 18 | 30 | 284 | 24 | 18 | 23 | 28 | 221 | 13 | 463 | 66 | 17 | 498 |
| Billings | .266 | 68 | 2260 | 363 | 293 | 602 | 830 | 109 | 16 | 29 | 313 | 38 | 29 | 26 | 10 | 328 | 5 | 541 | 57 | 30 | 558 |
| Idaho Falls | .255 | 68 | 2199 | 330 | 514 | 560 | 774 | 99 | 17 | 31 | 296 | 18 | 10 | 20 | 21 | 277 | 3 | 526 | 57 | 18 | 473 |
| Butte | .254 | 69 | 2300 | 355 | 508 | 584 | 798 | 85 | 18 | 16 | 248 | 23 | 17 | 14 | 17 | 285 | 3 | | 58 | | 557 |
| Pocatello | .252 | 69 | 2355 | 309 | 407 | 593 | 777 | 94 | 21 | 16 | 248 | 23 | 17 | 14 | 17 | 285 | | | | | |

### INDIVIDUAL BATTING

(Leading Qualifiers for Batting Championship—189 or More Plate Appearances)

*Bats lefthanded. †Switch-hitter.

| Player and Club | Pct. | G. | AB. | R. | H. | TB. | 2B. | 3B. | HR. | RBI. | GW. | SH. | SF. | HP. | BB. | Int. BB. | SO. | SB. | CS. |
|---|---|---|---|---|---|---|---|---|---|---|---|---|---|---|---|---|---|---|---|
| Brown, Todd, Helena | .447 | 53 | 208 | 42 | 93 | 123 | 10 | 1 | 6 | 53 | 4 | 0 | 4 | 3 | 21 | 4 | 20 | 5 | 1 |
| Devereaux, Michael, Great Falls | .356 | 70 | 289 | 73 | 103 | 152 | 17 | 10 | 4 | 67 | 6 | 0 | 6 | 2 | 32 | 1 | 29 | 40 | 9 |
| Melvin, Scott, Salt Lake City | .351 | 59 | 231 | 43 | 81 | 107 | 10 | 8 | 0 | 37 | 4 | 4 | 3 | 1 | 19 | 0 | 34 | 8 | 6 |
| Escalera, Ruben, Helena* | .349 | 60 | 229 | 59 | 80 | 95 | 11 | 2 | 0 | 32 | 1 | 1 | 2 | 8 | 35 | 1 | 24 | 8 | 5 |
| Haney, Joseph, Helena* | .344 | 62 | 247 | 43 | 85 | 112 | 19 | 1 | 2 | 51 | 4 | 1 | 5 | 2 | 13 | 1 | 19 | 7 | 3 |
| Munford, Willie, Salt Lake City | .343 | 67 | 245 | 52 | 84 | 98 | 7 | 2 | 1 | 45 | 4 | 0 | 3 | 0 | 29 | 0 | 15 | 17 | 7 |

| Player and Club | Pct. | G. | AB. | R. | H. | TB. | 2B. | 3B. | HR. | RBI. | GW. | SH. | SF. | HP. | BB. | Int. BB. | SO. | SB. | CS. |
|---|---|---|---|---|---|---|---|---|---|---|---|---|---|---|---|---|---|---|---|
| Berroa, Geronimo, Medicine Hat | .343 | 54 | 201 | 39 | 69 | 113 | 22 | 2 | 6 | 45 | 6 | 0 | 1 | 3 | 18 | 0 | 40 | 7 | 2 |
| Grimes, Mark, Salt Lake City | .342 | 61 | 225 | 38 | 77 | 114 | 14 | 4 | 5 | 55 | 4 | 2 | 2 | 1 | 21 | 1 | 31 | 13 | 6 |
| Ramsey, Michael, Billings° | .342 | 59 | 184 | 37 | 63 | 85 | 12 | 2 | 2 | 40 | 5 | 4 | 6 | 2 | 44 | 2 | 22 | 1 | 2 |
| Callas, Peter, Idaho Falls° | .339 | 58 | 183 | 30 | 62 | 114 | 17 | 1 | 11 | 56 | 4 | 0 | 4 | 2 | 19 | 2 | 51 | 2 | 0 |

Departmental Leaders: G—Batiste, Devereaux, Huff, Watters, 70; AB—Devereaux, 289; R—Devereaux, 73; H—Devereaux, 103; TB—Devereaux, 152; 2B—Berroa, 22; 3B—Heist, Slotnick, 11; HR—Callas, 11; RBI—Devereaux, 67; GWRBI—Slotnick, 8; SH—Sardinha, 6; SF—Moralez, 7; HP—Escalera, 8; BB—Watters, 57; IBB—Reyna, 5; SO—Batiste, 83; SB—Devereaux, 40; CS—Baggott, 15.

(All Players—Listed Alphabetically)

| Player and Club | Pct. | G. | AB. | R. | H. | TB. | 2B. | 3B. | HR. | RBI. | GW. | SH. | SF. | HP. | BB. | Int. BB. | SO. | SB. | CS. |
|---|---|---|---|---|---|---|---|---|---|---|---|---|---|---|---|---|---|---|---|
| Acevedo, Ernesto, Butte | .203 | 28 | 64 | 7 | 13 | 13 | 0 | 0 | 0 | 5 | 1 | 0 | 1 | 0 | 2 | 0 | 8 | 0 | 0 |
| Alcantara, Roberto, Pocatello° | .212 | 47 | 146 | 22 | 31 | 36 | 5 | 0 | 0 | 10 | 3 | 1 | 0 | 1 | 18 | 0 | 54 | 1 | 1 |
| Alyea, Brant, Medicine Hat | .337 | 51 | 181 | 22 | 61 | 74 | 8 | 1 | 1 | 21 | 0 | 1 | 1 | 0 | 21 | 0 | 27 | 1 | 2 |
| Ames, Douglas, Great Falls° | .000 | 5 | 2 | 0 | 0 | 0 | 0 | 0 | 0 | 0 | 0 | 0 | 0 | 0 | 0 | 0 | 2 | 0 | 0 |
| Anthony, Andrew, Great Falls° | .390 | 38 | 123 | 36 | 48 | 62 | 10 | 2 | 0 | 16 | 2 | 3 | 0 | 0 | 31 | 0 | 18 | 11 | 1 |
| Ashley, Shon, Helena | .295 | 46 | 132 | 30 | 39 | 55 | 8 | 4 | 0 | 17 | 3 | 0 | 4 | 1 | 23 | 0 | 31 | 8 | 3 |
| Ayers, Kevin, Great Falls | .207 | 46 | 164 | 22 | 34 | 44 | 4 | 3 | 0 | 25 | 2 | 5 | 5 | 1 | 13 | 0 | 20 | 9 | 4 |
| Baab, Lawrence, Idaho Falls | .086 | 14 | 35 | 2 | 3 | 5 | 2 | 0 | 0 | 3 | 0 | 0 | 1 | 0 | 8 | 1 | 14 | 0 | 0 |
| Baggott, David, Idaho Falls† | .299 | 68 | 254 | 55 | 76 | 101 | 11 | 4 | 2 | 33 | 1 | 1 | 4 | 2 | 56 | 0 | 40 | 20 | 15 |
| Barnett, Micheal, Salt Lake City | .212 | 16 | 33 | 10 | 7 | 7 | 0 | 0 | 0 | 2 | 1 | 2 | 0 | 0 | 10 | 1 | 10 | 9 | 0 |
| Batesole, Michael, Great Falls | .262 | 54 | 195 | 29 | 51 | 71 | 20 | 0 | 0 | 33 | 4 | 2 | 4 | 4 | 15 | 0 | 26 | 2 | 4 |
| Batiste, Kevin, Medicine Hat | .248 | 70 | 274 | 45 | 68 | 85 | 6 | 4 | 1 | 20 | 2 | 0 | 1 | 7 | 14 | 0 | 83 | 13 | 8 |
| Bautista, Camilo, Medicine Hat | .000 | 20 | 1 | 0 | 0 | 0 | 0 | 0 | 0 | 0 | 0 | 0 | 0 | 0 | 0 | 0 | 1 | 0 | 0 |
| Bernardo, Robert, Butte | .235 | 24 | 98 | 15 | 23 | 34 | 5 | 0 | 2 | 16 | 1 | 0 | 1 | 1 | 7 | 0 | 24 | 2 | 0 |
| Berroa, Geronimo, Medicine Hat | .343 | 54 | 201 | 39 | 69 | 113 | 22 | 2 | 6 | 45 | 6 | 0 | 1 | 3 | 18 | 0 | 40 | 7 | 2 |
| Bluhm, William, Great Falls | .288 | 22 | 52 | 9 | 15 | 18 | 1 | 1 | 0 | 10 | 1 | 0 | 2 | 0 | 4 | 0 | 17 | 0 | 0 |
| Bolt, James, Salt Lake City | .278 | 41 | 108 | 22 | 30 | 35 | 5 | 0 | 0 | 15 | 4 | 4 | 2 | 2 | 9 | 0 | 12 | 2 | 2 |
| Bowens, Howard, Idaho Falls | .400 | 7 | 10 | 2 | 4 | 4 | 0 | 0 | 0 | 0 | 0 | 0 | 0 | 0 | 0 | 0 | 6 | 0 | 1 |
| Brito, Adan, Pocatello | .260 | 18 | 73 | 8 | 19 | 20 | 1 | 0 | 0 | 6 | 0 | 0 | 0 | 1 | 2 | 0 | 6 | 6 | 0 |
| Brown, Marty, Billings | .339 | 68 | 248 | 50 | 84 | 141 | 21 | 3 | 10 | 45 | 6 | 2 | 4 | 0 | 50 | 3 | 44 | 11 | 3 |
| Brown, Todd, Helena | .447 | 53 | 208 | 42 | 93 | 123 | 10 | 1 | 6 | 53 | 4 | 0 | 4 | 3 | 21 | 4 | 20 | 5 | 1 |
| Burke, Michael, Great Falls° | .339 | 55 | 192 | 37 | 65 | 102 | 10 | 3 | 7 | 46 | 6 | 1 | 3 | 1 | 29 | 2 | 36 | 8 | 2 |
| Caci, Robert, Helena | .251 | 53 | 191 | 34 | 48 | 59 | 5 | 0 | 2 | 24 | 1 | 4 | 2 | 1 | 17 | 1 | 31 | 3 | 2 |
| Cain, Calvin, Billings° | .309 | 58 | 194 | 21 | 60 | 84 | 9 | 0 | 5 | 41 | 6 | 2 | 3 | 0 | 23 | 2 | 22 | 2 | 1 |
| Caldwell, Roger, Butte | .231 | 50 | 143 | 27 | 33 | 47 | 4 | 2 | 2 | 15 | 0 | 1 | 0 | 5 | 16 | 0 | 25 | 5 | 0 |
| Callas, Peter, Idaho Falls° | .339 | 58 | 183 | 30 | 62 | 114 | 17 | 1 | 11 | 56 | 4 | 0 | 4 | 2 | 19 | 2 | 51 | 2 | 0 |
| Campbell, Richard, Billings | .161 | 40 | 124 | 20 | 20 | 27 | 5 | 1 | 0 | 9 | 2 | 3 | 2 | 0 | 20 | 0 | 34 | 3 | 1 |
| Canepa, Robert, Idaho Falls | .195 | 60 | 195 | 19 | 38 | 52 | 8 | 0 | 2 | 23 | 0 | 4 | 3 | 0 | 30 | 0 | 53 | 3 | 3 |
| Castillo, David, Butte | .306 | 66 | 252 | 36 | 77 | 113 | 16 | 4 | 4 | 44 | 1 | 1 | 6 | 0 | 24 | 1 | 46 | 6 | 5 |
| Champoux, Anthony, Idaho Falls | .316 | 59 | 206 | 43 | 65 | 78 | 5 | 4 | 0 | 26 | 2 | 3 | 2 | 3 | 46 | 0 | 43 | 6 | 4 |
| Chavez, Luis, Idaho Falls† | .125 | 6 | 8 | 2 | 1 | 2 | 1 | 0 | 0 | 0 | 0 | 1 | 0 | 0 | 1 | 0 | 2 | 0 | 0 |
| Claudio, Sindulfo, Pocatello° | .206 | 47 | 141 | 19 | 29 | 42 | 4 | 0 | 3 | 11 | 2 | 2 | 0 | 0 | 23 | 0 | 46 | 2 | 2 |
| Coffey, Michael, Billings | .000 | 11 | 3 | 0 | 0 | 0 | 0 | 0 | 0 | 0 | 0 | 0 | 0 | 0 | 0 | 0 | 2 | 0 | 0 |
| Cohoon, Donald, Butte† | .232 | 56 | 168 | 25 | 39 | 49 | 4 | 0 | 2 | 20 | 1 | 2 | 2 | 4 | 28 | 0 | 48 | 6 | 3 |
| Cowans, Eddie, Salt Lake City° | .260 | 24 | 77 | 14 | 20 | 23 | 1 | 1 | 0 | 7 | 0 | 3 | 0 | 1 | 7 | 0 | 14 | 8 | 1 |
| Cox, Terry, Medicine Hat° | .183 | 20 | 60 | 1 | 11 | 13 | 2 | 0 | 0 | 2 | 0 | 0 | 0 | 1 | 5 | 0 | 12 | 0 | 0 |
| Cummings, Patrick, Salt Lake City | .262 | 19 | 42 | 8 | 11 | 11 | 0 | 0 | 0 | 3 | 0 | 0 | 1 | 0 | 12 | 1 | 7 | 3 | 1 |
| Curtis, Gary, Billings | .217 | 26 | 69 | 12 | 15 | 20 | 3 | 1 | 0 | 7 | 0 | 0 | 0 | 0 | 18 | 0 | 18 | 2 | 2 |
| David, Gregory, Medicine Hat° | .234 | 51 | 154 | 21 | 36 | 59 | 7 | 2 | 4 | 22 | 0 | 0 | 3 | 0 | 17 | 2 | 35 | 0 | 0 |
| Davis, Steven, Billings° | .196 | 14 | 51 | 4 | 10 | 12 | 2 | 0 | 0 | 5 | 1 | 0 | 0 | 0 | 3 | 1 | 13 | 2 | 0 |
| Deitz, Timothy, Billings | .000 | 26 | 1 | 0 | 0 | 0 | 0 | 0 | 0 | 0 | 0 | 0 | 0 | 0 | 0 | 0 | 0 | 0 | 0 |
| Delgado, Alvaro, 3 Hel.-12 IF | .077 | 15 | 26 | 3 | 2 | 2 | 0 | 0 | 0 | 2 | 0 | 0 | 0 | 0 | 4 | 0 | 12 | 0 | 0 |
| Dennis, Gregory, Medicine Hat | .289 | 31 | 90 | 13 | 26 | 27 | 1 | 0 | 0 | 8 | 0 | 3 | 2 | 0 | 10 | 0 | 6 | 1 | 0 |
| Devereaux, Michael, Great Falls | .356 | 70 | 289 | 73 | 103 | 152 | 17 | 10 | 4 | 67 | 6 | 0 | 6 | 2 | 32 | 1 | 29 | 40 | 9 |
| Diaz, Serafin (Tony), Butte° | .227 | 51 | 154 | 25 | 35 | 58 | 8 | 3 | 3 | 23 | 2 | 1 | 3 | 2 | 17 | 1 | 27 | 2 | 2 |
| Donahue, Charles, Billings° | .305 | 60 | 220 | 47 | 67 | 87 | 9 | 1 | 3 | 29 | 4 | 0 | 2 | 3 | 40 | 2 | 33 | 9 | 2 |
| Dorsey, Craig, Butte° | .279 | 55 | 204 | 29 | 57 | 75 | 9 | 3 | 1 | 20 | 1 | 2 | 0 | 1 | 15 | 0 | 33 | 7 | 2 |
| Escalara, Ruben, Helena° | .349 | 60 | 229 | 59 | 80 | 95 | 11 | 2 | 0 | 32 | 1 | 1 | 2 | 8 | 35 | 1 | 24 | 8 | 5 |
| Faria, Skylar, Idaho Falls° | .260 | 60 | 196 | 24 | 51 | 72 | 6 | 2 | 3 | 29 | 1 | 2 | 1 | 0 | 21 | 1 | 42 | 9 | 5 |
| Farley, Darren, Great Falls† | .200 | 3 | 5 | 1 | 1 | 2 | 1 | 0 | 0 | 0 | 0 | 0 | 0 | 0 | 2 | 0 | 1 | 0 | 0 |
| Farwell, Frederick, Great Falls° | .500 | 12 | 2 | 0 | 1 | 1 | 0 | 0 | 0 | 0 | 0 | 0 | 0 | 0 | 1 | 0 | 1 | 0 | 0 |
| Fazzini, Frank, Helena | .457 | 12 | 46 | 15 | 21 | 36 | 7 | 1 | 2 | 21 | 4 | 0 | 1 | 1 | 11 | 0 | 14 | 0 | 0 |
| Fiala, Michael, Great Falls | .000 | 22 | 1 | 0 | 0 | 0 | 0 | 0 | 0 | 0 | 0 | 0 | 0 | 0 | 0 | 0 | 0 | 0 | 0 |
| Forney, Jeffrey, Billings | .220 | 56 | 177 | 29 | 39 | 50 | 8 | 0 | 1 | 19 | 3 | 3 | 2 | 0 | 35 | 0 | 40 | 7 | 4 |
| Geist, Peter, Great Falls | .286 | 50 | 168 | 27 | 48 | 59 | 4 | 2 | 1 | 14 | 3 | 3 | 0 | 2 | 20 | 2 | 39 | 3 | 1 |
| Goldman, James, Butte | .286 | 22 | 7 | 2 | 2 | 3 | 1 | 0 | 0 | 0 | 0 | 0 | 0 | 0 | 4 | 0 | 4 | 1 | 0 |
| Goodwin, Bradley, Salt Lake City° | .249 | 60 | 189 | 39 | 47 | 61 | 7 | 2 | 1 | 29 | 3 | 2 | 5 | 3 | 28 | 3 | 23 | 8 | 5 |
| Gossett, Steven, Butte | .000 | 15 | 4 | 0 | 0 | 0 | 0 | 0 | 0 | 0 | 0 | 0 | 0 | 0 | 0 | 0 | 1 | 0 | 0 |
| Gray, Richard, Idaho Falls† | .155 | 35 | 71 | 7 | 11 | 13 | 2 | 0 | 0 | 7 | 1 | 0 | 0 | 0 | 14 | 1 | 15 | 1 | 2 |
| Greene, Edward, Helena | .298 | 52 | 161 | 36 | 48 | 65 | 3 | 4 | 2 | 16 | 0 | 1 | 1 | 0 | 18 | 0 | 14 | 4 | 2 |
| Grimes, Mark, Salt Lake City | .342 | 61 | 225 | 38 | 77 | 114 | 14 | 4 | 5 | 55 | 4 | 2 | 2 | 1 | 21 | 1 | 31 | 13 | 6 |
| Groot, Scott, Idaho Falls | .239 | 66 | 218 | 35 | 52 | 71 | 11 | 1 | 2 | 25 | 1 | 0 | 2 | 2 | 31 | 0 | 67 | 4 | 2 |
| Guenther, Robert, Medicine Hat | .000 | 26 | 1 | 0 | 0 | 0 | 0 | 0 | 0 | 0 | 0 | 1 | 0 | 0 | 0 | 0 | 0 | 0 | 0 |
| Guillory, Walter, Pocatello | .247 | 44 | 158 | 18 | 39 | 46 | 4 | 0 | 1 | 15 | 1 | 1 | 0 | 0 | 17 | 0 | 40 | 3 | 1 |
| Haney, Joseph, Helena° | .344 | 62 | 247 | 43 | 85 | 112 | 19 | 1 | 2 | 51 | 4 | 1 | 5 | 2 | 13 | 1 | 19 | 7 | 3 |
| Harrison, Keith, Salt Lake City | .091 | 11 | 11 | 1 | 1 | 1 | 0 | 0 | 0 | 0 | 0 | 0 | 0 | 0 | 4 | 0 | 4 | 0 | 0 |
| Hayden, Richard, Butte | .240 | 38 | 96 | 12 | 23 | 24 | 1 | 0 | 0 | 12 | 0 | 0 | 0 | 0 | 19 | 0 | 43 | 5 | 0 |
| Heist, Charles, 17 IF-48 SLC° | .322 | 65 | 264 | 63 | 85 | 126 | 10 | 11 | 3 | 48 | 2 | 2 | 2 | 3 | 18 | 1 | 49 | 12 | 10 |
| Horsman, Vincent, Medicine Hat | .000 | 18 | 2 | 0 | 0 | 0 | 0 | 0 | 0 | 0 | 0 | 0 | 0 | 0 | 0 | 0 | 2 | 0 | 0 |
| Housley, Sterling, Medicine Hat | .227 | 32 | 75 | 7 | 17 | 19 | 0 | 0 | 0 | 4 | 0 | 1 | 2 | 1 | 10 | 1 | 25 | 1 | 1 |
| Huff, Michael, Great Falls | .316 | 70 | 247 | 70 | 78 | 96 | 6 | 0 | 4 | 35 | 3 | 2 | 1 | 4 | 56 | 0 | 44 | 28 | 6 |
| Huseby, Kenneth, Billings | .000 | 10 | 2 | 0 | 0 | 0 | 0 | 0 | 0 | 0 | 0 | 0 | 0 | 0 | 0 | 0 | 2 | 0 | 0 |
| Hyde, Scott, Pocatello | .263 | 50 | 160 | 14 | 42 | 55 | 10 | 0 | 1 | 22 | 3 | 0 | 2 | 3 | 23 | 0 | 44 | 1 | 0 |
| Iannini, Steven, Pocatello | .250 | 62 | 220 | 36 | 55 | 75 | 9 | 4 | 1 | 26 | 3 | 1 | 2 | 3 | 38 | 1 | 50 | 11 | 1 |
| Ingle, Michael, Salt Lake City† | .289 | 68 | 253 | 31 | 73 | 93 | 14 | 3 | 0 | 35 | 4 | 0 | 2 | 0 | 20 | 0 | 28 | 6 | 3 |
| Jackson, Ronald, Great Falls | .200 | 13 | 10 | 4 | 2 | 4 | 2 | 0 | 0 | 1 | 0 | 0 | 0 | 0 | 5 | 0 | 4 | 1 | 0 |
| Jaha, John, Helena | .265 | 24 | 68 | 13 | 18 | 27 | 3 | 0 | 2 | 14 | 1 | 0 | 0 | 1 | 14 | 0 | 23 | 4 | 0 |
| Johnson, Lindsey, Salt Lake City | .308 | 64 | 195 | 37 | 60 | 82 | 11 | 4 | 1 | 19 | 0 | 5 | 1 | 0 | 14 | 0 | 23 | 4 | 0 |
| Jones, Carl, Pocatello | .276 | 63 | 225 | 38 | 62 | 97 | 13 | 5 | 4 | 28 | 3 | 0 | 1 | 1 | 20 | 0 | 39 | 2 | 2 |
| Jones, Christopher, Billings | .258 | 63 | 240 | 43 | 62 | 96 | 12 | 5 | 4 | 33 | 0 | 1 | 1 | 1 | 19 | 0 | 72 | 13 | 0 |
| Karmeris, Joseph, Butte | .231 | 63 | 221 | 33 | 51 | 75 | 9 | 0 | 5 | 35 | 2 | 0 | 2 | 1 | 31 | 0 | 71 | 2 | 4 |

| Player and Club | Pct. | G. | AB. | R. | H. | TB. | 2B. | 3B. | HR. | RBI. | GW. | SH. | SF. | HP. | BB. | Int. BB. | SO. | SB. | CS. |
|---|---|---|---|---|---|---|---|---|---|---|---|---|---|---|---|---|---|---|---|
| Kennelley, Steve, Billings | .263 | 63 | 255 | 50 | 67 | 99 | 17 | 3 | 3 | 33 | 5 | 4 | 3 | 2 | 27 | 1 | 65 | 12 | 1 |
| Lambert, Kenneth, Great Falls | .283 | 32 | 99 | 16 | 28 | 36 | 3 | 1 | 1 | 17 | 2 | 3 | 0 | 0 | 13 | 0 | 10 | 1 | 1 |
| Lambert, Reese, Pocatello° | .333 | 15 | 3 | 0 | 1 | 1 | 0 | 0 | 0 | 0 | 0 | 1 | 0 | 0 | 0 | 0 | 0 | 0 | 0 |
| Larsen, James, Idaho Falls | .000 | 6 | 7 | 0 | 0 | 0 | 0 | 0 | 0 | 0 | 0 | 0 | 0 | 0 | 0 | 0 | 4 | 0 | 0 |
| Lilly, Michael, Great Falls | .000 | 15 | 2 | 0 | 0 | 0 | 0 | 0 | 0 | 0 | 0 | 0 | 0 | 0 | 0 | 0 | 0 | 0 | 0 |
| Love, John, Idaho Falls | .307 | 68 | 264 | 34 | 81 | 104 | 12 | 1 | 3 | 36 | 2 | 4 | 5 | 3 | 23 | 0 | 38 | 4 | 2 |
| Marquardt, Roger, Medicine Hat | .227 | 22 | 66 | 6 | 15 | 21 | 3 | 0 | 1 | 7 | 0 | 2 | 2 | 0 | 3 | 0 | 13 | 0 | 0 |
| Masten, William, Salt Lake City | .194 | 9 | 31 | 6 | 6 | 8 | 2 | 0 | 0 | 1 | 0 | 1 | 0 | 0 | 2 | 0 | 6 | 1 | 0 |
| McConnell, Walter, Great Falls° | .412 | 28 | 97 | 28 | 40 | 71 | 10 | 3 | 5 | 34 | 6 | 0 | 2 | 0 | 23 | 0 | 10 | 3 | 0 |
| McGee, Ronald, Butte° | .250 | 6 | 12 | 2 | 3 | 4 | 1 | 0 | 0 | 3 | 0 | 0 | 0 | 1 | 1 | 0 | 2 | 0 | 1 |
| McGinnis, Russell, Helena | .307 | 48 | 150 | 33 | 46 | 68 | 7 | 0 | 5 | 38 | 3 | 0 | 2 | 4 | 31 | 1 | 19 | 2 | 2 |
| McGrew, Charles, Helena° | .280 | 44 | 118 | 24 | 33 | 57 | 9 | 0 | 5 | 21 | 2 | 1 | 1 | 2 | 14 | 1 | 29 | 0 | 0 |
| Melvin, Scott, Salt Lake City | .351 | 59 | 231 | 43 | 81 | 107 | 10 | 8 | 0 | 37 | 4 | 4 | 3 | 1 | 19 | 0 | 34 | 8 | 6 |
| Mendenhall, Shannon, Pocatello | .172 | 42 | 151 | 19 | 26 | 29 | 1 | 1 | 0 | 9 | 2 | 4 | 0 | 0 | 24 | 1 | 49 | 5 | 3 |
| Messenger, Henry, Idaho Falls | .176 | 13 | 17 | 4 | 3 | 5 | 2 | 0 | 0 | 0 | 0 | 0 | 0 | 0 | 2 | 0 | 2 | 0 | 0 |
| Michel, Domingo, Great Falls | .333 | 15 | 57 | 7 | 19 | 26 | 0 | 2 | 1 | 10 | 3 | 1 | 1 | 0 | 5 | 1 | 8 | 3 | 1 |
| Miller, James, Butte | .266 | 59 | 218 | 37 | 58 | 66 | 6 | 1 | 0 | 21 | 2 | 2 | 2 | 3 | 20 | 0 | 42 | 4 | 5 |
| Moore, Barry, Butte† | .250 | 7 | 4 | 2 | 1 | 1 | 0 | 0 | 0 | 1 | 0 | 0 | 0 | 0 | 2 | 0 | 2 | 1 | 0 |
| Moralez, Paul, Great Falls | .237 | 39 | 118 | 19 | 28 | 44 | 6 | 2 | 2 | 22 | 2 | 0 | 7 | 0 | 8 | 1 | 20 | 0 | 0 |
| Morhardt, Darryl, Butte | .190 | 15 | 21 | 4 | 4 | 7 | 0 | 0 | 1 | 2 | 0 | 0 | 0 | 1 | 3 | 0 | 7 | 0 | 0 |
| Morrison, Brian, Medicine Hat | .238 | 61 | 210 | 27 | 50 | 81 | 7 | 3 | 6 | 36 | 6 | 0 | 2 | 0 | 22 | 1 | 75 | 4 | 5 |
| Munford, Willie, Salt Lake City | .343 | 67 | 245 | 52 | 84 | 98 | 7 | 2 | 1 | 45 | 4 | 0 | 3 | 0 | 29 | 0 | 15 | 17 | 7 |
| Naworski, Andrew, Great Falls | .000 | 17 | 0 | 0 | 0 | 0 | 0 | 0 | 0 | 0 | 0 | 1 | 0 | 0 | 0 | 0 | 0 | 0 | 0 |
| Nutt, James, Salt Lake City | .203 | 44 | 118 | 26 | 24 | 35 | 4 | 2 | 1 | 19 | 2 | 2 | 3 | 0 | 17 | 0 | 44 | 4 | 0 |
| Olden, Bryan, Pocatello | .267 | 23 | 86 | 15 | 23 | 24 | 1 | 0 | 0 | 6 | 0 | 1 | 0 | 2 | 11 | 0 | 22 | 3 | 0 |
| Olson, Warren, Helena | .285 | 49 | 158 | 32 | 45 | 74 | 7 | 2 | 6 | 28 | 2 | 1 | 2 | 3 | 13 | 0 | 39 | 0 | 1 |
| Palo, David, Medicine Hat | .000 | 7 | 0 | 1 | 0 | 0 | 0 | 0 | 0 | 0 | 0 | 0 | 0 | 0 | 0 | 0 | 0 | 0 | 0 |
| Pappas, Robert, Salt Lake City° | .111 | 14 | 18 | 5 | 2 | 2 | 0 | 0 | 0 | 2 | 0 | 0 | 1 | 1 | 4 | 0 | 8 | 1 | 0 |
| Parker, Brett, Great Falls | .000 | 1 | 1 | 0 | 0 | 0 | 0 | 0 | 0 | 0 | 0 | 0 | 0 | 0 | 0 | 0 | 0 | 0 | 0 |
| Patterson, Michael, Idaho Falls | .176 | 27 | 74 | 7 | 13 | 13 | 0 | 0 | 0 | 6 | 1 | 3 | 1 | 0 | 6 | 0 | 22 | 0 | 1 |
| Petty, Brian, Butte | .247 | 48 | 174 | 22 | 43 | 49 | 6 | 0 | 0 | 23 | 2 | 1 | 0 | 1 | 11 | 0 | 37 | 3 | 0 |
| Ramsey, Michael, Billings° | .342 | 59 | 184 | 37 | 63 | 85 | 12 | 2 | 2 | 40 | 5 | 4 | 6 | 2 | 44 | 2 | 22 | 1 | 2 |
| Ray, William, Great Falls | .250 | 14 | 8 | 0 | 2 | 2 | 0 | 0 | 0 | 3 | 0 | 0 | 1 | 0 | 0 | 0 | 2 | 0 | 0 |
| Reyes, Jose, Medicine Hat | .233 | 69 | 249 | 28 | 58 | 88 | 9 | 3 | 5 | 25 | 0 | 2 | 0 | 5 | 10 | 0 | 69 | 8 | 7 |
| Reyna, Luis, Medicine Hat° | .303 | 67 | 254 | 48 | 77 | 105 | 14 | 1 | 4 | 40 | 3 | 0 | 2 | 4 | 28 | 5 | 38 | 5 | 0 |
| Roesler, Michael, Billings | .000 | 13 | 2 | 0 | 0 | 0 | 0 | 0 | 0 | 0 | 0 | 0 | 0 | 0 | 0 | 0 | 1 | 0 | 0 |
| Rogers, Sebastian, Billings | .000 | 13 | 3 | 0 | 0 | 0 | 0 | 0 | 0 | 0 | 0 | 0 | 1 | 0 | 0 | 0 | 0 | 0 | 0 |
| Rosso, Pascual, Pocatello° | .209 | 48 | 139 | 19 | 29 | 49 | 6 | 4 | 2 | 18 | 1 | 0 | 1 | 1 | 21 | 0 | 48 | 5 | 2 |
| Rowan, Paul, Idaho Falls° | .220 | 61 | 200 | 24 | 44 | 69 | 12 | 2 | 3 | 25 | 2 | 1 | 2 | 2 | 18 | 0 | 69 | 2 | 3 |
| Russ, Kevin, Pocatello | .292 | 12 | 48 | 3 | 14 | 15 | 1 | 0 | 0 | 5 | 0 | 0 | 0 | 3 | 0 | 0 | 8 | 0 | 0 |
| St. Clair, Kerry, Medicine Hat | .200 | 23 | 30 | 0 | 6 | 7 | 1 | 0 | 0 | 1 | 0 | 0 | 0 | 0 | 6 | 0 | 13 | 0 | 0 |
| Sanchez, Pablo, Helena† | .216 | 44 | 139 | 21 | 30 | 35 | 1 | 2 | 0 | 10 | 0 | 5 | 1 | 2 | 15 | 0 | 31 | 5 | 1 |
| Sapienza, Richard, Billings | .167 | 18 | 42 | 6 | 7 | 7 | 0 | 0 | 0 | 5 | 0 | 1 | 0 | 0 | 3 | 0 | 6 | 0 | 0 |
| Sardinha, Eduardo, Helena | .329 | 44 | 143 | 27 | 47 | 59 | 7 | 1 | 1 | 21 | 1 | 6 | 3 | 0 | 14 | 0 | 25 | 5 | 1 |
| Savage, John, Great Falls | .000 | 24 | 1 | 0 | 0 | 0 | 0 | 0 | 0 | 0 | 0 | 0 | 0 | 0 | 0 | 0 | 0 | 0 | 0 |
| Scharkey, Brian, Salt Lake City° | .357 | 17 | 14 | 5 | 5 | 9 | 1 | 0 | 1 | 2 | 0 | 0 | 0 | 0 | 6 | 0 | 5 | 1 | 0 |
| Silverio, Nelson, Pocatello | .280 | 56 | 200 | 30 | 56 | 67 | 11 | 0 | 0 | 24 | 1 | 2 | 4 | 1 | 18 | 0 | 46 | 0 | 0 |
| Simonson, Robert, Helena | .265 | 51 | 166 | 39 | 44 | 76 | 6 | 1 | 8 | 27 | 1 | 1 | 3 | 5 | 16 | 1 | 50 | 9 | 1 |
| Slotnick, Joseph, Salt Lake City | .324 | 68 | 259 | 56 | 84 | 141 | 17 | 11 | 6 | 53 | 8 | 3 | 5 | 0 | 28 | 0 | 44 | 13 | 9 |
| Smith, Bryan, Great Falls | .000 | 15 | 1 | 0 | 0 | 0 | 0 | 0 | 0 | 0 | 0 | 0 | 0 | 0 | 1 | 0 | 1 | 0 | 0 |
| Smith, Daniel, Great Falls | .273 | 52 | 194 | 41 | 53 | 77 | 12 | 3 | 2 | 25 | 2 | 1 | 2 | 1 | 27 | 1 | 41 | 3 | 0 |
| Smith, Jackson, Billings | .255 | 61 | 208 | 19 | 53 | 56 | 3 | 0 | 0 | 18 | 3 | 4 | 1 | 1 | 12 | 0 | 43 | 3 | 1 |
| Smit, Michael, Billings | .000 | 7 | 1 | 0 | 0 | 0 | 0 | 0 | 0 | 0 | 0 | 0 | 0 | 0 | 0 | 0 | 0 | 0 | 0 |
| Stitch, Dennis, Butte° | .188 | 44 | 101 | 12 | 19 | 24 | 3 | 1 | 0 | 8 | 0 | 1 | 1 | 0 | 21 | 0 | 34 | 3 | 3 |
| Stocker, Robert, Pocatello | .000 | 14 | 0 | 0 | 0 | 0 | 0 | 0 | 0 | 0 | 0 | 0 | 0 | 0 | 1 | 0 | 0 | 0 | 0 |
| Stull, Walter, Great Falls | .250 | 12 | 4 | 1 | 1 | 1 | 0 | 0 | 0 | 0 | 0 | 0 | 0 | 0 | 0 | 0 | 1 | 0 | 0 |
| Sullivan, Daniel, Butte† | .331 | 47 | 157 | 34 | 52 | 87 | 7 | 2 | 8 | 28 | 3 | 0 | 1 | 2 | 33 | 1 | 28 | 2 | 1 |
| Tinkey, Robert, Helena | .301 | 42 | 123 | 25 | 37 | 55 | 6 | 0 | 4 | 21 | 3 | 1 | 1 | 3 | 23 | 0 | 19 | 3 | 0 |
| Torchia, James, Idaho Falls | .230 | 51 | 174 | 28 | 40 | 49 | 6 | 0 | 1 | 10 | 1 | 3 | 1 | 3 | 15 | 0 | 35 | 4 | 2 |
| Tucker, Robert, Great Falls | .000 | 1 | 1 | 0 | 0 | 0 | 0 | 0 | 0 | 0 | 0 | 0 | 0 | 0 | 0 | 0 | 0 | 0 | 0 |
| Tutt, Eric, Butte | .252 | 56 | 202 | 31 | 51 | 69 | 5 | 2 | 3 | 20 | 2 | 0 | 0 | 0 | 23 | 0 | 59 | 8 | 4 |
| Verdugo, Armando, Helena | .217 | 32 | 92 | 11 | 20 | 33 | 4 | 0 | 3 | 23 | 4 | 1 | 6 | 0 | 11 | 2 | 19 | 1 | 0 |
| Vincent, Michael, Billings | .154 | 12 | 39 | 5 | 6 | 10 | 1 | 0 | 1 | 5 | 0 | 0 | 0 | 0 | 9 | 0 | 11 | 0 | 0 |
| Wakamatsu, Donald, Billings | .250 | 58 | 196 | 20 | 49 | 56 | 7 | 0 | 0 | 24 | 3 | 5 | 2 | 0 | 25 | 2 | 36 | 1 | 0 |
| Walton, Bruce, Pocatello | 1.000 | 18 | 1 | 1 | 1 | 2 | 1 | 0 | 0 | 0 | 0 | 0 | 0 | 0 | 0 | 0 | 0 | 0 | 0 |
| Watford, Walter, Medicine Hat | .273 | 68 | 253 | 31 | 69 | 85 | 10 | 0 | 2 | 34 | 2 | 6 | 4 | 4 | 26 | 0 | 23 | 1 | 1 |
| Watkins, Timothy, Billings† | .000 | 17 | 1 | 0 | 0 | 0 | 0 | 0 | 0 | 0 | 0 | 0 | 0 | 0 | 0 | 0 | 1 | 0 | 0 |
| Watters, Michael, Great Falls° | .332 | 70 | 265 | 63 | 88 | 102 | 6 | 4 | 0 | 48 | 5 | 2 | 4 | 2 | 57 | 2 | 23 | 14 | 6 |
| Weiss, Walter, Pocatello† | .310 | 40 | 158 | 19 | 49 | 64 | 9 | 3 | 0 | 21 | 1 | 0 | 4 | 1 | 12 | 0 | 18 | 6 | 0 |
| Wentz, Keith, Great Falls | .273 | 58 | 216 | 26 | 59 | 78 | 7 | 3 | 2 | 25 | 1 | 0 | 1 | 1 | 14 | 0 | 29 | 5 | 3 |
| Whisler, Randy, Medicine Hat† | .265 | 58 | 200 | 29 | 53 | 60 | 5 | 1 | 0 | 19 | 1 | 3 | 3 | 4 | 31 | 3 | 40 | 9 | 5 |
| White, Kenneth, Salt Lake City | .294 | 39 | 109 | 17 | 32 | 40 | 3 | 1 | 1 | 13 | 2 | 1 | 1 | 1 | 10 | 0 | 22 | 3 | 2 |
| White, Michael, Great Falls | .315 | 27 | 92 | 25 | 29 | 52 | 6 | 1 | 5 | 17 | 2 | 0 | 1 | 3 | 10 | 2 | 15 | 8 | 0 |
| Xavier, Joseph, Pocatello° | .252 | 61 | 230 | 22 | 58 | 77 | 11 | 1 | 2 | 22 | 2 | 2 | 0 | 3 | 32 | 1 | 27 | 7 | 3 |

The following pitchers, listed alphabetically by club, with games in parentheses, had no plate appearances, primarily through use of designated hitters:

BILLINGS—Cieslak, Mark (7); Hayward, Jeffrey (14); Lopez, Robert (16); Summers, Thomas (15); Willis, Scott (17).

BUTTE—Asbell, John (18); Brevell, Ronald (23); Columbano, John (4); Dickey, Warren (3); Griffey, Louis (15); Halverstadt, Scott (11); Hein, Gustav (2); Holmes, Brian (15); Hovorka, James (19); Ipsen, Christian (2); Jones, Douglas (5); Nelson, Douglas (14); Swain, Gregory (10); Weatherly, John (3).

GREAT FALLS—Garcia, Rene (1); Hardwick, Anthony (2); Nelson, Kevin (15); Roche, Roderick (7); Wetteland, John (11); Zeinert, Bradley (1).

HELENA—Bosley, Richard (22); Coin, Michael (17); Fitzpatrick, Danny (23); Freeland, Dean (13); Gosling, Mark (13); Hajdasz, Rodney (7); Miramontes, David (4); Moraw, Carl (13); Nichols, Oliver (8); Pilkington, Eric (15); Signore, Thomas (9); Smith, Jeffrey (10); Taylor, Robert (8); Veres, Randolf (13); Watts, Dustin (4); Wilder, John (9).

IDAHO FALLS—Baumhouer, John (6); Dunn, Richard (14); Haringa, Kenneth (14); Klawonn, Stephen (7); Lingren, Richard (9); Mayes, LaCurtis (14); Reyes, Juan (12); Ronquillo, William (12); Sauer, Richard (9); Shelton, Eddie (7); Smith, Jon (10); Strickland, Lonnie (7); Townsend, Benjamin (25); Tuchalski, Bruce (7).

MEDICINE HAT—Bilawey, John (17); Diaz, Victor (15); Hickey, Daniel (1); Humphries, Bobbie Joe (7); Jones, Christopher (12); Mays, Jeffery (17); Musselman, Jeffrey (16); Rohde, John (18); Schlieper, Richard (20).

POCATELLO—Balsley, Darren (8); Caceres, Ernesto (23); Cundari, Felice (2); Groves, Frank (16); Hall, Martin (23); McDonald, Kirk (12); Nunez, Ramon (16); Suero, Fernando (8); Toribio, Guadalupe (2); Williamson, Kevin (8).

SALT LAKE CITY—Arrington, Thomas (16); Garrick, Darren (15); Kolovitz, Michael (21); Larsen, Chad (3); McCarter, Edward (15); Olson, Steven (16); Rollo, Victor (14); Smith, Jon (4); Strickland, Lonnie (4); Van Roy, Darrell (10); Webb, Roger (16); Woodard, Thane (18).

GRAND SLAM HOME RUNS—Grimes, 2; Burke, Canepa, Donahue, McGinnis, Verdugo, 1 each.

AWARDED FIRST BASE ON CATCHER'S INTERFERENCE—Huff 2 (Marquardt 2); K. Lambert 2 (Marquardt, Olson); Davis (Acevedo); Dorsey (McGrew); Goodwin (Smith); Love (Verdugo); Munford (Caldwell); Simonson (Caldwell).

## CLUB FIELDING

| Club | Pct. | G. | PO. | A. | E. | DP. | PB. | Club | Pct. | G. | PO. | A. | E. | DP. | PB. |
|---|---|---|---|---|---|---|---|---|---|---|---|---|---|---|---|
| Medicine Hat | .956 | 70 | 1754 | 743 | 116 | 52 | 28 | Billings | .953 | 68 | 1753 | 738 | 124 | 60 | 20 |
| Great Falls | .955 | 70 | 1813 | 771 | 121 | 75 | 18 | Pocatello | .943 | 69 | 1795 | 697 | 151 | 35 | 27 |
| Helena | .955 | 68 | 1754 | 776 | 119 | 69 | 36 | Butte | .939 | 69 | 1772 | 798 | 168 | 65 | 15 |
| Salt Lake City | .953 | 70 | 1792 | 763 | 127 | 79 | 17 | Idaho Falls | .938 | 68 | 1688 | 775 | 162 | 68 | 16 |

## INDIVIDUAL FIELDING

*Throws lefthanded

### FIRST BASEMEN

| Player and Club | Pct. | G. | PO. | A. | E. | DP. | Player and Club | Pct. | G. | PO. | A. | E. | DP. |
|---|---|---|---|---|---|---|---|---|---|---|---|---|---|
| Baab, Idaho Falls | .971 | 4 | 31 | 2 | 1 | 2 | McGinnis, Helena | .985 | 25 | 182 | 11 | 3 | 27 |
| Brito, Pocatello | 1.000 | 1 | 10 | 1 | 0 | 1 | Moralez, Great Falls | .985 | 25 | 179 | 16 | 3 | 16 |
| M. Brown, Billings | .985 | 68 | 590 | 49 | 10 | 57 | Morhardt, Butte | .966 | 6 | 54 | 3 | 2 | 4 |
| Burke, Great Falls* | .977 | 53 | 446 | 20 | 11 | 47 | Munford, Salt Lake City | .980 | 67 | 545 | 44 | 12 | 69 |
| Callas, Idaho Falls* | .967 | 23 | 198 | 7 | 7 | 23 | Reyna, Medicine Hat* | .982 | 67 | 563 | 33 | 11 | 37 |
| Campbell, Billings | 1.000 | 2 | 6 | 0 | 0 | 1 | Rosso, Pocatello* | .958 | 43 | 324 | 21 | 15 | 12 |
| Castillo, Butte | 1.000 | 1 | 9 | 0 | 0 | 0 | Rowan, Idaho Falls* | .983 | 46 | 381 | 16 | 7 | 30 |
| Escalera, Helena* | 1.000 | 1 | 12 | 2 | 0 | 1 | Silverio, Pocatello | .980 | 18 | 135 | 9 | 3 | 9 |
| Gray, Idaho Falls | 1.000 | 4 | 7 | 0 | 0 | 0 | Sullivan, Butte | .977 | 19 | 149 | 19 | 4 | 18 |
| HANEY, Helena | .994 | 49 | 433 | 32 | 3 | 34 | Tutt, Butte | .980 | 45 | 362 | 26 | 8 | 33 |
| Housley, Medicine Hat | 1.000 | 3 | 32 | 1 | 0 | 4 | Vincent, Billings | 1.000 | 1 | 1 | 1 | 0 | 0 |
| Hyde, Pocatello | .943 | 4 | 32 | 1 | 2 | 1 | Wentz, Pocatello | .969 | 8 | 58 | 5 | 2 | 4 |
| R. Lambert, Pocatello* | 1.000 | 1 | 2 | 0 | 0 | 0 | K. White, Salt Lake City | .962 | 6 | 49 | 1 | 2 | 5 |
| McGee, Butte* | .913 | 3 | 21 | 0 | 2 | 2 | | | | | | | |

### SECOND BASEMEN

| Player and Club | Pct. | G. | PO. | A. | E. | DP. | Player and Club | Pct. | G. | PO. | A. | E. | DP. |
|---|---|---|---|---|---|---|---|---|---|---|---|---|---|
| Ayers, Great Falls | 1.000 | 1 | 4 | 2 | 0 | 2 | Mendenhall, Pocatello | .879 | 7 | 14 | 15 | 4 | 1 |
| Baggott, Idaho Falls | .941 | 63 | 149 | 183 | 21 | 41 | Miller, Butte | .919 | 55 | 118 | 153 | 24 | 29 |
| Bolt, Salt Lake City | .867 | 11 | 21 | 18 | 6 | 8 | Moore, Butte | .917 | 2 | 4 | 7 | 1 | 2 |
| Bowens, Idaho Falls | .722 | 7 | 6 | 7 | 5 | 0 | Nutt, Salt Lake City | .813 | 5 | 7 | 6 | 3 | 2 |
| Brito, Pocatello | .667 | 1 | 1 | 1 | 1 | 0 | Olden, Pocatello | .942 | 22 | 34 | 47 | 5 | 5 |
| Chavez, Idaho Falls | 1.000 | 1 | 2 | 1 | 0 | 1 | Petty, Butte | .953 | 20 | 53 | 49 | 5 | 11 |
| Dennis, Medicine Hat | .833 | 3 | 3 | 2 | 1 | 1 | Reyes, Medicine Hat | .947 | 68 | 135 | 187 | 18 | 29 |
| Donahue, Billings | .902 | 16 | 35 | 48 | 9 | 11 | Sanchez, Helena | .934 | 42 | 95 | 144 | 17 | 32 |
| Housley, Medicine Hat | .933 | 5 | 7 | 7 | 1 | 3 | Sardinha, Helena | .947 | 23 | 43 | 65 | 6 | 11 |
| Kennelley, Billings | .943 | 52 | 99 | 133 | 14 | 37 | Tinkey, Helena | .892 | 8 | 13 | 20 | 4 | 7 |
| Love, Idaho Falls | 1.000 | 5 | 4 | 9 | 0 | 1 | Watters, Great Falls | .936 | 70 | 150 | 199 | 24 | 49 |
| MELVIN, Salt Lake City | .961 | 59 | 111 | 187 | 12 | 47 | Xavier, Pocatello | .943 | 42 | 79 | 103 | 11 | 17 |

### THIRD BASEMEN

| Player and Club | Pct. | G. | PO. | A. | E. | DP. | Player and Club | Pct. | G. | PO. | A. | E. | DP. |
|---|---|---|---|---|---|---|---|---|---|---|---|---|---|
| Ayers, Great Falls | .929 | 8 | 8 | 18 | 2 | 3 | McConnell, Great Falls | .850 | 21 | 15 | 36 | 9 | 4 |
| Batesole, Great Falls | .938 | 42 | 22 | 84 | 7 | 11 | McGinnis, Helena | .883 | 25 | 13 | 40 | 7 | 4 |
| Bernardo, Butte | .875 | 1 | 1 | 6 | 1 | 1 | Melvin, Salt Lake City | 1.000 | 1 | 0 | 1 | 0 | 0 |
| Bolt, Salt Lake City | .921 | 20 | 12 | 23 | 3 | 6 | Mendenhall, Pocatello | .914 | 23 | 14 | 39 | 5 | 2 |
| Brito, Pocatello | .892 | 14 | 8 | 25 | 4 | 2 | Miller, Butte | 1.000 | 1 | 1 | 0 | 0 | 0 |
| Campbell, Billings | .897 | 35 | 25 | 45 | 8 | 3 | Petty, Butte | .825 | 19 | 8 | 25 | 7 | 1 |
| Champoux, Idaho Falls | .750 | 4 | 4 | 5 | 3 | 1 | St. Clair, Medicine Hat | .750 | 2 | 2 | 4 | 2 | 0 |
| Cohoon, Butte | .891 | 53 | 40 | 99 | 17 | 10 | Silverio, Pocatello | 1.000 | 1 | 0 | 1 | 0 | 0 |
| Delgado, Helena-Idaho Falls | .875 | 8 | 2 | 5 | 1 | 0 | J. Smith, Billings | 1.000 | 1 | 1 | 2 | 0 | 0 |
| Diaz, Butte | .556 | 4 | 1 | 4 | 4 | 0 | Sullivan, Butte | .500 | 1 | 0 | 1 | 1 | 0 |
| Donahue, Billings | .899 | 33 | 26 | 54 | 9 | 5 | Tinkey, Helena | .875 | 33 | 17 | 53 | 10 | 7 |
| Goldman, Butte | .400 | 1 | 0 | 2 | 3 | 0 | WATFORD, Medicine Hat | .931 | 59 | 47 | 114 | 12 | 13 |
| Grimes, Salt Lake City | .863 | 55 | 34 | 92 | 20 | 8 | Wentz, Pocatello | .880 | 36 | 24 | 57 | 11 | 2 |
| Groot, Idaho Falls | .910 | 62 | 51 | 150 | 20 | 23 | Whisler, Medicine Hat | .923 | 10 | 9 | 15 | 2 | 2 |
| Housley, Medicine Hat | .500 | 1 | 0 | 1 | 1 | 0 | K. White, Salt Lake City | 1.000 | 1 | 1 | 1 | 0 | 0 |
| Jaha, Helena | .976 | 24 | 9 | 32 | 1 | 1 | | | | | | | |

### SHORTSTOPS

| Player and Club | Pct. | G. | PO. | A. | E. | DP. | Player and Club | Pct. | G. | PO. | A. | E. | DP. |
|---|---|---|---|---|---|---|---|---|---|---|---|---|---|
| Ayers, Great Falls | .925 | 24 | 28 | 70 | 8 | 14 | Ingle, Salt Lake City | .918 | 68 | 114 | 232 | 31 | 51 |
| Bolt, Salt Lake City | .947 | 6 | 5 | 13 | 1 | 3 | Love, Idaho Falls | .887 | 66 | 104 | 211 | 40 | 31 |
| Brito, Pocatello | 1.000 | 1 | 0 | 3 | 0 | 1 | Mendenhall, Pocatello | .900 | 13 | 25 | 29 | 6 | 4 |
| CACI, Helena | .937 | 53 | 75 | 148 | 15 | 35 | Parker, Great Falls | .833 | 1 | 2 | 3 | 1 | 0 |
| Castillo, Butte | .915 | 65 | 85 | 195 | 26 | 35 | Petty, Butte | 1.000 | 5 | 4 | 17 | 0 | 1 |
| Chavez, Idaho Falls | .700 | 5 | 1 | 13 | 6 | 2 | Sardinha, Helena | .837 | 22 | 24 | 53 | 15 | 14 |
| Cohoon, Butte | 1.000 | 5 | 5 | 4 | 0 | 3 | J. Smith, Billings | .931 | 58 | 78 | 206 | 21 | 31 |
| Curtis, Billings | .925 | 16 | 31 | 43 | 6 | 10 | Watford, Medicine Hat | .889 | 8 | 12 | 20 | 4 | 5 |
| Dennis, Medicine Hat | .949 | 30 | 39 | 91 | 7 | 14 | Weiss, Great Falls | .941 | 38 | 51 | 126 | 11 | 16 |
| Diaz, Butte | 1.000 | 1 | 1 | 1 | 0 | 0 | Whisler, Medicine Hat | .922 | 37 | 46 | 95 | 12 | 11 |
| Geist, Great Falls | .908 | 50 | 68 | 170 | 24 | 31 | Xavier, Pocatello | .943 | 19 | 21 | 45 | 4 | 4 |
| Goldman, Butte | 1.000 | 1 | 1 | 0 | 0 | 0 | | | | | | | |

## OUTFIELDERS

| Player and Club | Pct. | G. | PO. | A. | E. | DP. |
|---|---|---|---|---|---|---|
| Alcantara, Pocatello* | .911 | 44 | 68 | 4 | 7 | 0 |
| Alyea, Medicine Hat | .982 | 33 | 52 | 2 | 1 | 0 |
| Anthony, Great Falls | .966 | 34 | 25 | 3 | 1 | 3 |
| Ashley, Helena | .973 | 33 | 34 | 2 | 1 | 0 |
| Ayers, Great Falls | .667 | 3 | 2 | 2 | 2 | 0 |
| Baggott, Idaho Falls | 1.000 | 8 | 8 | 1 | 0 | 0 |
| Barnett, Salt Lake City | 1.000 | 12 | 16 | 1 | 0 | 0 |
| Batiste, Medicine Hat | .959 | 64 | 135 | 6 | 6 | 3 |
| Bernardo, Butte | .850 | 21 | 33 | 1 | 6 | 0 |
| Berroa, Medicine Hat | .953 | 50 | 58 | 3 | 3 | 1 |
| Bluhm, Great Falls | 1.000 | 19 | 17 | 3 | 0 | 0 |
| M. Brown, Billings | 1.000 | 2 | 2 | 1 | 0 | 0 |
| T. Brown, Helena | .938 | 31 | 42 | 3 | 3 | 2 |
| Cain, Billings* | .944 | 33 | 49 | 2 | 3 | 0 |
| Champoux, Idaho Falls | .910 | 35 | 56 | 5 | 6 | 2 |
| Claudio, Pocatello* | .921 | 44 | 80 | 2 | 7 | 0 |
| Cowans, Salt Lake City* | .917 | 11 | 9 | 2 | 1 | 0 |
| Davis, Billings | .960 | 14 | 22 | 2 | 1 | 0 |
| Delgado, Idaho Falls | .667 | 2 | 2 | 0 | 1 | 0 |
| Devereaux, Great Falls | .954 | 70 | 100 | 4 | 5 | 1 |
| Diaz, Butte | .947 | 46 | 66 | 5 | 4 | 0 |
| Dorsey, Butte* | .961 | 55 | 113 | 9 | 5 | 3 |
| Escalera, Helena* | .944 | 59 | 99 | 3 | 6 | 0 |
| Faria, Idaho Falls | .964 | 58 | 130 | 4 | 5 | 2 |
| Farley, Great Falls | 1.000 | 3 | 1 | 0 | 0 | 0 |
| Fazzini, Helena | .846 | 9 | 10 | 1 | 2 | 0 |
| Forney, Billings | .929 | 54 | 86 | 5 | 7 | 1 |
| Goldman, Butte | 1.000 | 4 | 5 | 0 | 0 | 0 |
| Goodwin, Salt Lake City* | .966 | 54 | 108 | 7 | 4 | 0 |
| Greene, Helena | .986 | 47 | 64 | 6 | 1 | 0 |
| Guillory, Pocatello | .953 | 42 | 80 | 1 | 4 | 1 |
| Haney, Helena | 1.000 | 12 | 13 | 1 | 0 | 0 |
| Hayden, Butte | .833 | 3 | 3 | 2 | 1 | 0 |
| Heist, Idaho Falls-Salt Lake | .943 | 64 | 125 | 7 | 8 | 0 |
| Huff, Great Falls | .962 | 70 | 120 | 5 | 5 | 0 |
| Jackson, Great Falls | .000 | 1 | 0 | 0 | 1 | 0 |
| Ca. Jones, Pocatello | .943 | 59 | 81 | 2 | 5 | 1 |
| Ch. Jones, Billings | .899 | 63 | 112 | 4 | 13 | 0 |
| Karmeris, Butte | .966 | 54 | 105 | 8 | 4 | 3 |
| J. Larsen, Idaho Falls | 1.000 | 3 | 1 | 1 | 0 | 0 |
| Messenger, Idaho Falls | .875 | 5 | 5 | 2 | 1 | 0 |
| Miller, Butte | 1.000 | 4 | 8 | 0 | 0 | 0 |
| Morrison, Medicine Hat | .962 | 48 | 92 | 10 | 4 | 2 |
| Nutt, Salt Lake City | .981 | 35 | 50 | 1 | 1 | 0 |
| Patterson, Idaho Falls | .965 | 23 | 51 | 4 | 2 | 3 |
| Petty, Butte | 1.000 | 6 | 13 | 3 | 0 | 1 |
| RAMSEY, Billings* | .975 | 54 | 75 | 2 | 2 | 1 |
| Rowan, Idaho Falls* | .848 | 17 | 27 | 1 | 5 | 0 |
| Russ, Pocatello* | 1.000 | 12 | 19 | 0 | 0 | 0 |
| St. Clair, Medicine Hat | .800 | 8 | 3 | 1 | 1 | 0 |
| Scharkey, Salt Lake City* | 1.000 | 5 | 7 | 0 | 0 | 0 |
| Silverio, Pocatello | .857 | 4 | 6 | 0 | 1 | 0 |
| Simonson, Helena | .978 | 40 | 44 | 1 | 1 | 0 |
| Slotnick, Salt Lake City | .966 | 50 | 78 | 6 | 3 | 0 |
| Stitch, Butte | .967 | 41 | 56 | 3 | 2 | 0 |
| Stocker, Pocatello | 1.000 | 1 | 1 | 0 | 0 | 1 |
| Torchia, Medicine Hat | .959 | 50 | 64 | 6 | 3 | 0 |
| Wentz, Pocatello | .846 | 14 | 22 | 0 | 4 | 0 |
| Whisler, Medicine Hat | .923 | 11 | 10 | 2 | 1 | 1 |
| M. White, Great Falls | 1.000 | 23 | 31 | 2 | 0 | 0 |
| K. White, Salt Lake City | .941 | 13 | 15 | 1 | 1 | 0 |

## CATCHERS

| Player and Club | Pct. | G. | PO. | A. | E. | DP. | PB. |
|---|---|---|---|---|---|---|---|
| Acevedo, Butte | .906 | 26 | 92 | 14 | 11 | 0 | 7 |
| Caldwell, Butte | .976 | 41 | 214 | 35 | 6 | 1 | 3 |
| Canepa, Idaho Falls | .965 | 58 | 271 | 58 | 12 | 3 | 12 |
| Cox, Medicine Hat | .974 | 20 | 103 | 9 | 3 | 1 | 7 |
| Cummings, Salt Lake City | .984 | 7 | 60 | 1 | 1 | 0 | 1 |
| David, Medicine Hat | .983 | 36 | 266 | 21 | 5 | 3 | 18 |
| Gray, Idaho Falls | .934 | 16 | 75 | 10 | 6 | 1 | 4 |
| Harrison, Salt Lake City | 1.000 | 5 | 24 | 1 | 0 | 0 | 1 |
| Hayden, Butte | .968 | 23 | 107 | 13 | 4 | 3 | 5 |
| Hyde, Pocatello | .964 | 41 | 293 | 27 | 12 | 1 | 17 |
| Jackson, Great Falls | 1.000 | 2 | 3 | 0 | 0 | 0 | 0 |
| Johnson, Salt Lake City | .979 | 57 | 343 | 27 | 8 | 2 | 10 |
| K. Lambert, Great Falls | 1.000 | 26 | 186 | 21 | 0 | 4 | 7 |
| Marquardt, Medicine Hat | .965 | 22 | 120 | 16 | 5 | 1 | 3 |
| McGinnis, Helena | 1.000 | 1 | 5 | 0 | 0 | 0 | 3 |
| McGrew, Helena | .975 | 9 | 38 | 1 | 1 | 0 | 1 |
| Olson, Helena | .978 | 46 | 281 | 31 | 7 | 0 | 13 |
| Pappas, Salt Lake City | 1.000 | 11 | 54 | 3 | 0 | 0 | 5 |
| Sapienza, Billings | .949 | 17 | 86 | 7 | 5 | 0 | 8 |
| Silverio, Pocatello | .975 | 33 | 286 | 21 | 8 | 2 | 10 |
| J.D. Smith, Great Falls | .983 | 49 | 377 | 28 | 7 | 3 | 11 |
| Verdugo, Helena | .975 | 29 | 164 | 30 | 5 | 4 | 19 |
| Vincent, Billings | .977 | 5 | 41 | 2 | 1 | 0 | 2 |
| WAKAMATSU, Billings | .988 | 56 | 367 | 44 | 5 | 3 | 10 |

## PITCHERS

| Player and Club | Pct. | G. | PO. | A. | E. | DP. |
|---|---|---|---|---|---|---|
| Ames, Great Falls* | 1.000 | 5 | 2 | 2 | 0 | 0 |
| Arrington, Salt Lake City | 1.000 | 16 | 6 | 17 | 0 | 3 |
| Asbell, Butte | .750 | 18 | 4 | 8 | 4 | 1 |
| Balsley, Pocatello | .750 | 8 | 1 | 5 | 2 | 1 |
| Baumhouer, Idaho Falls | .833 | 6 | 1 | 4 | 1 | 0 |
| Bautista, Medicine Hat | .786 | 20 | 2 | 9 | 3 | 0 |
| Bilawey, Medicine Hat | .800 | 17 | 2 | 6 | 2 | 0 |
| Bosley, Helena | 1.000 | 22 | 3 | 3 | 0 | 1 |
| Brevell, Butte | .917 | 23 | 8 | 14 | 2 | 0 |
| Caceres, Pocatello | .882 | 23 | 3 | 12 | 2 | 0 |
| Callas, Idaho Falls* | 1.000 | 4 | 0 | 2 | 0 | 0 |
| Cieslak, Billings* | .889 | 7 | 2 | 6 | 1 | 1 |
| Coin, Helena | 1.000 | 17 | 0 | 7 | 0 | 1 |
| Coffey, Billings | 1.000 | 11 | 2 | 9 | 0 | 0 |
| Cundari, Pocatello | 1.000 | 2 | 1 | 0 | 0 | 0 |
| Deitz, Billings | 1.000 | 26 | 2 | 5 | 0 | 0 |
| Dickey, Butte | .833 | 3 | 2 | 3 | 1 | 1 |
| Diaz, Medicine Hat* | 1.000 | 15 | 6 | 9 | 0 | 1 |
| Dunn, Idaho Falls | 1.000 | 14 | 2 | 10 | 0 | 1 |
| Farwell, Great Falls* | 1.000 | 12 | 3 | 17 | 0 | 0 |
| Fiala, Great Falls | .800 | 22 | 1 | 3 | 1 | 0 |
| Fitzpatrick, Helena | 1.000 | 23 | 4 | 8 | 0 | 0 |
| Freeland, Helena | .955 | 13 | 8 | 13 | 1 | 0 |
| Garrick, Salt Lake City | 1.000 | 15 | 7 | 12 | 0 | 0 |
| Goldman, Butte | .909 | 16 | 3 | 7 | 1 | 1 |
| Gosling, Helena | .857 | 13 | 2 | 4 | 1 | 0 |
| Gossett, Billings | .938 | 13 | 4 | 11 | 1 | 2 |
| Griffey, Butte* | 1.000 | 15 | 1 | 4 | 0 | 0 |
| Groves, Pocatello | .875 | 16 | 2 | 5 | 1 | 3 |
| Guenther, Medicine Hat | 1.000 | 26 | 2 | 6 | 0 | 0 |
| Hajdasz, Helena | .857 | 7 | 1 | 5 | 1 | 0 |
| Hall, Pocatello | .833 | 23 | 2 | 8 | 2 | 0 |
| Halverstadt, Butte | 1.000 | 11 | 2 | 0 | 0 | 0 |
| Hardwick, Great Falls* | .000 | 2 | 0 | 0 | 2 | 0 |
| Haringa, Idaho Falls* | 1.000 | 14 | 3 | 4 | 0 | 0 |
| Hayward, Billings | .875 | 14 | 3 | 11 | 2 | 0 |
| Hickey, Medicine Hat* | 1.000 | 1 | 1 | 0 | 0 | 0 |
| Holmes, Butte | .833 | 15 | 1 | 9 | 2 | 0 |
| Horsman, Medicine Hat* | .857 | 18 | 0 | 6 | 1 | 1 |
| Hovorka, Butte* | .842 | 19 | 5 | 11 | 3 | 2 |
| Humphries, Medicine Hat | .833 | 7 | 1 | 4 | 1 | 0 |
| Huseby, Billings | .500 | 10 | 2 | 1 | 3 | 1 |
| Ipsen, Butte | 1.000 | 14 | 1 | 5 | 0 | 0 |
| C. Jones, Medicine Hat | .600 | 11 | 1 | 5 | 4 | 1 |
| D. Jones, Butte | 1.000 | 5 | 0 | 1 | 0 | 0 |
| Klawonn, Idaho Falls | .800 | 7 | 2 | 2 | 1 | 0 |
| Kolovitz, Salt Lake City | .867 | 21 | 3 | 10 | 2 | 2 |
| R. Lambert, Pocatello* | .900 | 14 | 2 | 25 | 3 | 1 |
| C. Larsen, Salt Lake City* | 1.000 | 3 | 1 | 0 | 0 | 0 |
| Lilly, Great Falls | .900 | 15 | 8 | 10 | 2 | 1 |
| Lingren, Idaho Falls* | 1.000 | 9 | 1 | 5 | 0 | 0 |
| Lopez, Billings | 1.000 | 16 | 1 | 12 | 0 | 0 |
| Mayes, Idaho Falls | 1.000 | 14 | 4 | 11 | 0 | 2 |
| Mays, Medicine Hat | .857 | 17 | 2 | 10 | 2 | 0 |
| McCarter, Salt Lake City | .895 | 15 | 5 | 12 | 2 | 0 |
| McDonald, Pocatello | .793 | 12 | 5 | 18 | 6 | 1 |
| McGrew, Helena | 1.000 | 1 | 0 | 0 | 0 | 0 |
| Messenger, Idaho Falls | 1.000 | 5 | 1 | 0 | 0 | 0 |
| Miramontes, Helena | 1.000 | 4 | 1 | 0 | 0 | 0 |
| Moraw, Helena | .962 | 13 | 6 | 19 | 1 | 1 |
| Morhardt, Butte | .667 | 8 | 1 | 1 | 1 | 0 |
| MUSSELMAN, Medicine Hat* | 1.000 | 16 | 3 | 26 | 0 | 2 |
| Naworski, Great Falls | 1.000 | 17 | 3 | 3 | 0 | 2 |
| D. Nelson, Butte | .885 | 14 | 6 | 17 | 3 | 0 |
| K. Nelson, Great Falls | .600 | 15 | 1 | 2 | 2 | 0 |
| Nichols, Helena | 1.000 | 8 | 2 | 5 | 0 | 0 |
| Olson, Salt Lake City* | .750 | 16 | 1 | 5 | 2 | 0 |
| Pilkington, Helena* | .923 | 15 | 3 | 9 | 1 | 0 |
| Ray, Great Falls | .867 | 14 | 1 | 12 | 2 | 2 |
| Reyes, Idaho Falls | .818 | 12 | 2 | 7 | 2 | 1 |
| Roche, Great Falls | 1.000 | 7 | 1 | 0 | 0 | 0 |
| Roesler, Billings | 1.000 | 13 | 4 | 13 | 0 | 2 |
| Rogers, Billings* | .818 | 13 | 1 | 8 | 2 | 2 |
| Rohde, Medicine Hat* | .900 | 18 | 0 | 9 | 1 | 2 |
| Rollo, Salt Lake City | .667 | 14 | 2 | 0 | 1 | 1 |
| Ronquillo, Idaho Falls | .818 | 12 | 2 | 7 | 2 | 0 |
| St. Clair, Medicine Hat | .909 | 10 | 0 | 10 | 1 | 0 |
| Sauer, Idaho Falls* | .750 | 9 | 3 | 3 | 2 | 0 |
| Savage, Great Falls | .923 | 24 | 4 | 8 | 1 | 2 |
| Scharkey, Salt Lake City* | .750 | 11 | 2 | 1 | 1 | 0 |
| Schlieper, Medicine Hat* | .750 | 20 | 0 | 3 | 1 | 0 |
| Shelton, Idaho Falls* | 1.000 | 7 | 1 | 0 | 0 | 0 |
| Signore, Helena | .769 | 9 | 2 | 8 | 3 | 1 |
| Silverio, Pocatello | 1.000 | 2 | 0 | 1 | 0 | 0 |
| B. Smith, Great Falls* | 1.000 | 15 | 2 | 12 | 0 | 0 |
| Je. Smith, Helena | 1.000 | 10 | 3 | 0 | 0 | 0 |

PITCHERS—Continued

| Player and Club | Pct. | G. | PO. | A. | E. | DP. | Player and Club | Pct. | G. | PO. | A. | E. | DP. |
|---|---|---|---|---|---|---|---|---|---|---|---|---|---|
| Jo. Smith, Salt Lake-Ida. Falls.. | .900 | 14 | 2 | 7 | 1 | 0 | Van Roy, Salt Lake City | 1.000 | 10 | 1 | 1 | 0 | 0 |
| M. Smith, Billings | 1.000 | 7 | 0 | 5 | 0 | 0 | Veres, Helena | .909 | 13 | 7 | 13 | 2 | 1 |
| Stocker, Pocatello | .917 | 13 | 2 | 20 | 2 | 0 | Walton, Pocatello | .944 | 18 | 6 | 11 | 1 | 0 |
| Strickland, Ida. Falls-Salt Lake | 1.000 | 11 | 2 | 3 | 0 | 0 | Watkins, Billings | .933 | 17 | 2 | 12 | 1 | 0 |
| Stull, Great Falls | 1.000 | 12 | 2 | 14 | 0 | 1 | Webb, Salt Lake City | .903 | 16 | 6 | 22 | 3 | 3 |
| Suero, Pocatello* | 1.000 | 8 | 3 | 3 | 0 | 0 | Wetteland, Great Falls | .750 | 11 | 1 | 2 | 1 | 0 |
| Summers, Billings* | 1.000 | 15 | 2 | 5 | 0 | 0 | Wilder, Helena | 1.000 | 9 | 1 | 1 | 0 | 0 |
| Swain, Butte* | .667 | 10 | 1 | 3 | 2 | 0 | Williamson, Pocatello | 1.000 | 8 | 0 | 3 | 0 | 0 |
| Taylor, Helena | 1.000 | 8 | 1 | 1 | 0 | 0 | Willis, Billings | .500 | 17 | 0 | 1 | 1 | 0 |
| Townsend, Idaho Falls | 1.000 | 25 | 1 | 2 | 0 | 0 | Woodard, Salt Lake City | .909 | 18 | 1 | 9 | 1 | 0 |
| Tuchalski, Idaho Falls | 1.000 | 7 | 0 | 1 | 0 | 0 | | | | | | | |

The following players do not have any recorded accepted chances at the positions indicated; therefore, are not listed in the fielding averages for those particular positions: Caci, 2b; Castillo, of; Columbano, p; Donahue, c; Garcia, p; Gossett, 2b; Groot, of; Hein, p; Housley, of; Iannini, of; J. Larsen, p; Nunez, p; Palo, p; Petty, p; Toribio, p; Watts, p; Weatherly, p; Zeinert, p.

## CLUB PITCHING

| Club | ERA. | G. | CG. | ShO. | Sv. | IP. | H. | R. | ER. | HR. | HB. | BB. | Int. BB. | SO. | WP. | Bk. |
|---|---|---|---|---|---|---|---|---|---|---|---|---|---|---|---|---|
| Great Falls | 3.38 | 70 | 16 | 7 | 16 | 604.1 | 597 | 290 | 227 | 19 | 20 | 256 | 6 | 556 | 53 | 2 |
| Salt Lake City | 3.63 | 70 | 24 | 4 | 9 | 597.1 | 656 | 311 | 241 | 36 | 10 | 212 | 8 | 463 | 29 | 4 |
| Billings | 3.63 | 68 | 15 | 9 | 15 | 584.1 | 528 | 293 | 236 | 26 | 22 | 282 | 7 | 491 | 43 | 9 |
| Pocatello | 4.50 | 69 | 10 | 0 | 15 | 598.1 | 615 | 407 | 299 | 34 | 26 | 325 | 14 | 561 | 43 | 13 |
| Medicine Hat | 4.57 | 70 | 5 | 2 | 9 | 584.2 | 568 | 378 | 297 | 24 | 21 | 362 | 20 | 473 | 81 | 9 |
| Helena | 5.22 | 68 | 7 | 3 | 17 | 584.2 | 632 | 428 | 339 | 28 | 24 | 319 | 0 | 488 | 83 | 10 |
| Idaho Falls | 6.11 | 68 | 16 | 2 | 3 | 562.2 | 775 | 514 | 382 | 27 | 14 | 259 | 7 | 328 | 53 | 9 |
| Butte | 6.13 | 69 | 3 | 1 | 9 | 590.2 | 767 | 508 | 402 | 35 | 27 | 303 | 6 | 384 | 66 | 17 |

## PITCHERS' RECORDS
(Leading Qualifiers for Earned-Run Average Leadership — 56 or More Innings)

*Throws lefthanded.

| Pitcher—Club | W. | L. | Pct. | ERA. | G. | GS. | CG. | GF. | ShO. | Sv. | IP. | H. | R. | ER. | HR. | HB. | BB. | Int. BB. | SO. | WP. |
|---|---|---|---|---|---|---|---|---|---|---|---|---|---|---|---|---|---|---|---|---|
| Lopez, Billings | 8 | 2 | .800 | 1.32 | 16 | 8 | 6 | 7 | 4 | 1 | 75.0 | 60 | 14 | 11 | 1 | 0 | 8 | 0 | 78 | 2 |
| Roesler, Billings | 8 | 2 | .800 | 2.33 | 13 | 13 | 4 | 0 | 1 | 0 | 88.2 | 72 | 32 | 23 | 3 | 2 | 28 | 0 | 73 | 5 |
| Garrick, Salt Lake City | 7 | 1 | .875 | 2.45 | 15 | 10 | 3 | 4 | 1 | 0 | 73.1 | 80 | 26 | 20 | 6 | 3 | 19 | 0 | 46 | 2 |
| Ray, Great Falls | 8 | 2 | .800 | 2.55 | 14 | 14 | 4 | 0 | 0 | 0 | 99.0 | 89 | 43 | 28 | 5 | 3 | 23 | 0 | 80 | 4 |
| Farwell, Great Falls* | 10 | 1 | .909 | 2.57 | 12 | 12 | 4 | 0 | 3 | 0 | 84.0 | 81 | 32 | 24 | 2 | 0 | 15 | 0 | 75 | 2 |
| Stull, Great Falls | 8 | 1 | .889 | 2.64 | 12 | 12 | 3 | 0 | 1 | 0 | 81.2 | 74 | 30 | 24 | 2 | 2 | 33 | 0 | 90 | 9 |
| Stocker, Pocatello* | 2 | 6 | .250 | 2.85 | 13 | 13 | 5 | 0 | 0 | 0 | 94.2 | 87 | 41 | 30 | 5 | 5 | 29 | 4 | 88 | 2 |
| Diaz, Medicine Hat* | 3 | 5 | .375 | 3.07 | 15 | 14 | 1 | 1 | 0 | 0 | 76.1 | 62 | 39 | 26 | 2 | 3 | 35 | 0 | 57 | 2 |
| Rogers, Billings | 6 | 4 | .600 | 3.11 | 13 | 13 | 0 | 0 | 0 | 0 | 72.1 | 52 | 35 | 25 | 4 | 1 | 41 | 0 | 95 | 6 |
| Reyes, Idaho Falls | 3 | 6 | .333 | 3.15 | 12 | 8 | 3 | 4 | 0 | 0 | 60.0 | 67 | 37 | 21 | 2 | 1 | 21 | 1 | 38 | 7 |

Departmental Leaders: G—Deitz, Guenther, 26; W—Farwell, B. Smith, 10; L—Dunn, McDonald, 8; Pct.—Farwell, .909; GS—Arrington, McCarter, Musselman, Webb, 15; CG—McCarter, 8; ShO—Lopez, 4; GF—Deitz, 25; Sv.—Deitz, Savage, 8; IP—Arrington, 111.0; H—Arrington, Webb, 108; R—Hovorka, 68; ER—Hovorka, 54; HR—Signore, 8; HB—Caceres, 8; BB—Hovorka, 48; IBB—Bautista, Caceres, McCarter, Stocker, 4; SO—McCarter, 111; WP—Bilawey, 17.

(All Pitchers—Listed Alphabetically)

| Pitcher—Club | W. | L. | Pct. | ERA. | G. | GS. | CG. | GF. | ShO. | Sv. | IP. | H. | R. | ER. | HR. | HB. | BB. | Int. BB. | SO. | WP. |
|---|---|---|---|---|---|---|---|---|---|---|---|---|---|---|---|---|---|---|---|---|
| Ames, Great Falls* | 0 | 0 | .000 | 7.11 | 5 | 2 | 0 | 1 | 0 | 0 | 12.2 | 20 | 10 | 10 | 1 | 1 | 9 | 0 | 5 | 1 |
| Arrington, Salt Lake City | 9 | 4 | .692 | 3.16 | 16 | 15 | 7 | 0 | 1 | 0 | 111.0 | 108 | 45 | 39 | 4 | 0 | 39 | 2 | 98 | 5 |
| Asbell, Butte | 3 | 2 | .600 | 5.81 | 18 | 5 | 0 | 5 | 0 | 0 | 57.1 | 80 | 48 | 37 | 4 | 1 | 21 | 0 | 35 | 7 |
| Balsley, Pocatello | 1 | 3 | .250 | 5.27 | 8 | 8 | 1 | 0 | 0 | 0 | 41.0 | 59 | 35 | 24 | 1 | 1 | 20 | 0 | 41 | 4 |
| Baumhouer, Idaho Falls | 0 | 2 | .000 | 12.08 | 6 | 2 | 0 | 2 | 0 | 0 | 12.2 | 27 | 22 | 17 | 2 | 0 | 8 | 0 | 9 | 1 |
| Bautista, Medicine Hat | 2 | 4 | .333 | 4.17 | 20 | 0 | 0 | 3 | 0 | 1 | 45.1 | 49 | 30 | 21 | 5 | 0 | 20 | 4 | 32 | 8 |
| Bilawey, Medicine Hat | 1 | 4 | .200 | 5.04 | 17 | 9 | 0 | 5 | 0 | 0 | 55.1 | 57 | 37 | 31 | 1 | 1 | 40 | 2 | 23 | 17 |
| Bosley, Helena | 3 | 0 | 1.000 | 2.83 | 22 | 0 | 0 | 20 | 0 | 7 | 28.2 | 19 | 13 | 9 | 0 | 2 | 15 | 0 | 30 | 1 |
| Brevell, Butte | 6 | 4 | .600 | 1.90 | 23 | 1 | 0 | 21 | 0 | 3 | 52.0 | 43 | 16 | 11 | 2 | 1 | 23 | 3 | 50 | 7 |
| Caceres, Pocatello | 4 | 3 | .571 | 5.02 | 23 | 3 | 0 | 12 | 0 | 1 | 61.0 | 57 | 51 | 34 | 5 | 8 | 39 | 4 | 42 | 7 |
| Callas, Idaho Falls* | 0 | 0 | .000 | 12.86 | 4 | 1 | 0 | 2 | 0 | 0 | 7.0 | 14 | 10 | 10 | 0 | 1 | 5 | 0 | 9 | 2 |
| Cieslak, Billings* | 2 | 2 | .500 | 6.53 | 7 | 2 | 0 | 1 | 0 | 0 | 20.2 | 20 | 18 | 15 | 1 | 1 | 25 | 0 | 9 | 2 |
| Coffey, Billings | 3 | 5 | .375 | 6.08 | 11 | 10 | 2 | 0 | 0 | 0 | 50.1 | 61 | 39 | 34 | 3 | 3 | 27 | 2 | 30 | 7 |
| Coin, Helena | 3 | 0 | 1.000 | 3.61 | 17 | 1 | 1 | 9 | 0 | 1 | 42.1 | 39 | 22 | 17 | 0 | 2 | 18 | 0 | 23 | 3 |
| Columbano, Butte* | 0 | 0 | .000 | 21.21 | 4 | 0 | 0 | 1 | 0 | 0 | 4.2 | 11 | 12 | 11 | 0 | 2 | 5 | 0 | 3 | 1 |
| Cundari, Pocatello | 0 | 1 | .000 | 8.38 | 2 | 2 | 0 | 0 | 0 | 0 | 9.2 | 14 | 10 | 9 | 1 | 1 | 8 | 0 | 10 | 1 |
| Deitz, Billings | 5 | 1 | .833 | 1.98 | 26 | 0 | 0 | 25 | 0 | 8 | 41.0 | 25 | 10 | 9 | 0 | 2 | 22 | 0 | 47 | 3 |
| Diaz, Medicine Hat* | 3 | 5 | .375 | 3.07 | 15 | 14 | 1 | 1 | 0 | 0 | 76.1 | 62 | 39 | 26 | 2 | 3 | 35 | 0 | 57 | 2 |
| Dickey, Butte | 1 | 2 | .333 | 10.34 | 3 | 3 | 0 | 0 | 0 | 0 | 15.2 | 32 | 20 | 18 | 1 | 1 | 6 | 0 | 3 | 0 |
| Dunn, Idaho Falls | 5 | 8 | .385 | 3.35 | 14 | 13 | 7 | 1 | 1 | 0 | 91.1 | 98 | 49 | 34 | 5 | 2 | 22 | 1 | 42 | 0 |
| Farwell, Great Falls* | 10 | 1 | .909 | 2.57 | 12 | 12 | 4 | 0 | 3 | 0 | 84.0 | 81 | 32 | 24 | 2 | 0 | 15 | 0 | 75 | 2 |
| Fiala, Great Falls | 2 | 2 | .500 | 4.88 | 22 | 0 | 0 | 16 | 0 | 4 | 27.2 | 41 | 20 | 15 | 0 | 0 | 15 | 0 | 24 | 7 |
| Fitzpatrick, Helena | 5 | 2 | .714 | 4.15 | 23 | 1 | 1 | 13 | 0 | 6 | 47.2 | 40 | 30 | 22 | 1 | 2 | 29 | 0 | 63 | 10 |
| Freeland, Helena | 4 | 6 | .400 | 3.84 | 13 | 13 | 1 | 0 | 0 | 0 | 84.1 | 93 | 54 | 36 | 4 | 4 | 36 | 0 | 60 | 7 |
| Garcia, Great Falls* | 0 | 0 | .000 | 0.00 | 1 | 0 | 0 | 1 | 0 | 0 | 1.0 | 2 | 2 | 0 | 0 | 0 | 1 | 0 | 1 | 0 |
| Garrick, Salt Lake City | 7 | 1 | .875 | 2.45 | 15 | 10 | 3 | 4 | 1 | 0 | 73.1 | 80 | 26 | 20 | 6 | 3 | 19 | 0 | 46 | 2 |
| Goldman, Butte | 2 | 6 | .250 | 3.91 | 16 | 6 | 1 | 6 | 0 | 1 | 48.1 | 49 | 34 | 21 | 1 | 2 | 29 | 0 | 31 | 9 |
| Gosling, Helena | 3 | 1 | .750 | 5.67 | 13 | 0 | 0 | 3 | 0 | 1 | 33.1 | 42 | 26 | 21 | 0 | 1 | 18 | 0 | 26 | 5 |
| Gossett, Butte* | 4 | 4 | .500 | 4.70 | 13 | 9 | 1 | 1 | 0 | 0 | 67.0 | 62 | 39 | 35 | 5 | 5 | 36 | 0 | 35 | 8 |
| Griffey, Butte* | 1 | 3 | .250 | 8.04 | 15 | 3 | 0 | 1 | 0 | 0 | 31.1 | 52 | 36 | 28 | 4 | 0 | 19 | 0 | 23 | 3 |
| Groves, Pocatello | 3 | 3 | .500 | 7.16 | 16 | 3 | 0 | 6 | 0 | 2 | 32.2 | 33 | 32 | 26 | 3 | 2 | 30 | 1 | 36 | 2 |
| Guenther, Medicine Hat | 4 | 4 | .500 | 3.15 | 26 | 0 | 0 | 22 | 0 | 4 | 40.0 | 25 | 19 | 14 | 1 | 2 | 25 | 3 | 42 | 5 |
| Hajdasz, Helena | 2 | 2 | .500 | 4.81 | 7 | 7 | 1 | 0 | 0 | 0 | 33.2 | 36 | 23 | 18 | 1 | 2 | 11 | 0 | 24 | 7 |
| Hall, Pocatello | 3 | 3 | .500 | 3.07 | 23 | 1 | 0 | 18 | 0 | 7 | 44.0 | 33 | 20 | 15 | 2 | 2 | 35 | 1 | 62 | 3 |
| Halverdick, Butte | 1 | 5 | .167 | 8.90 | 11 | 5 | 1 | 5 | 1 | 1 | 29.1 | 46 | 33 | 29 | 2 | 2 | 35 | 1 | 62 | 3 |
| Hardwick, Great Falls* | 0 | 0 | .000 | 8.31 | 2 | 0 | 0 | 1 | 0 | 0 | 4.1 | 4 | 5 | 4 | 1 | 1 | 7 | 0 | 5 | 1 |
| Haringa, Idaho Falls* | 3 | 4 | .429 | 5.24 | 14 | 11 | 3 | 3 | 0 | 0 | 67.0 | 87 | 55 | 39 | 0 | 2 | 27 | 0 | 44 | 3 |
| Hayward, Billings | 3 | 2 | .600 | 3.75 | 14 | 7 | 0 | 0 | 0 | 0 | 62.1 | 55 | 33 | 26 | 2 | 3 | 33 | 1 | 44 | 3 |
| Hein, Butte | 0 | 0 | .000 | 81.00 | 2 | 1 | 0 | 0 | 0 | 0 | 0.2 | 8 | 8 | 6 | 1 | 0 | 2 | 0 | 0 | 1 |

| Pitcher—Club | W | L | Pct | ERA | G | GS | CG | GF | ShO | Sv | IP | H | R | ER | HR | HB | BB | Int. BB | SO | WP |
|---|---|---|---|---|---|---|---|---|---|---|---|---|---|---|---|---|---|---|---|---|
| Hickey, Medicine Hat* | 0 | 1 | .000 | 9.00 | 1 | 0 | 0 | 0 | 0 | 0 | 2.0 | 3 | 2 | 2 | 1 | 0 | 0 | 0 | 0 | 0 |
| Holmes, Butte | 0 | 4 | .000 | 5.76 | 15 | 7 | 0 | 3 | 0 | 1 | 54.2 | 73 | 47 | 35 | 3 | 1 | 24 | 0 | 26 | 4 |
| Horsman, Medicine Hat* | 0 | 3 | .000 | 6.25 | 18 | 1 | 0 | 2 | 0 | 1 | 40.1 | 56 | 31 | 28 | 1 | 0 | 23 | 3 | 30 | 1 |
| Hovorka, Butte* | 3 | 6 | .333 | 6.34 | 19 | 12 | 0 | 3 | 0 | 0 | 76.2 | 94 | 68 | 54 | 2 | 3 | 48 | 0 | 52 | 10 |
| Humphries, Medicine Hat | 4 | 0 | 1.000 | 3.24 | 7 | 7 | 1 | 0 | 0 | 0 | 41.2 | 43 | 21 | 15 | 1 | 2 | 14 | 1 | 36 | 3 |
| Huseby, Billings | 1 | 3 | .250 | 6.08 | 10 | 5 | 0 | 1 | 0 | 0 | 26.2 | 39 | 20 | 18 | 3 | 1 | 17 | 0 | 16 | 2 |
| Ipsen, Butte | 0 | 1 | .000 | 5.70 | 14 | 0 | 0 | 10 | 0 | 1 | 30.0 | 39 | 25 | 19 | 0 | 6 | 14 | 2 | 29 | 1 |
| C. Jones, Medicine Hat | 0 | 6 | .000 | 5.56 | 11 | 10 | 1 | 0 | 0 | 0 | 34.0 | 31 | 23 | 21 | 4 | 1 | 18 | 0 | 23 | 5 |
| D. Jones, Butte | 0 | 0 | .000 | 3.38 | 5 | 0 | 0 | 2 | 0 | 1 | 8.0 | 11 | 4 | 3 | 1 | 0 | 4 | 0 | 8 | 1 |
| Klawonn, Idaho Falls | 0 | 1 | .000 | 8.10 | 7 | 1 | 0 | 1 | 0 | 0 | 13.1 | 23 | 18 | 12 | 2 | 0 | 10 | 0 | 10 | 3 |
| Kolovitz, Salt Lake City | 5 | 3 | .625 | 4.78 | 21 | 4 | 0 | 13 | 0 | 2 | 43.1 | 49 | 29 | 23 | 3 | 0 | 20 | 2 | 25 | 3 |
| Lambert, Pocatello* | 4 | 7 | .364 | 4.67 | 14 | 13 | 0 | 1 | 0 | 1 | 79.0 | 73 | 48 | 41 | 5 | 0 | 43 | 0 | 88 | 6 |
| C. Larsen, Salt Lake City* | 1 | 0 | 1.000 | 4.91 | 3 | 0 | 0 | 1 | 0 | 0 | 3.2 | 5 | 4 | 2 | 0 | 0 | 4 | 0 | 4 | 1 |
| J. Larsen, Idaho Falls | 0 | 0 | .000 | 36.00 | 1 | 0 | 0 | 0 | 0 | 0 | 1.0 | 2 | 5 | 4 | 0 | 0 | 6 | 1 | 1 | 2 |
| Lilly, Great Falls | 6 | 2 | .750 | 3.33 | 15 | 13 | 2 | 1 | 0 | 0 | 75.2 | 80 | 38 | 28 | 3 | 4 | 36 | 0 | 67 | 8 |
| Lingren, Idaho Falls* | 1 | 1 | .500 | 6.75 | 9 | 2 | 0 | 5 | 0 | 0 | 29.1 | 44 | 26 | 22 | 1 | 3 | 10 | 0 | 10 | 4 |
| Lopez, Billings | 8 | 2 | .800 | 1.32 | 16 | 8 | 6 | 7 | 4 | 1 | 75.0 | 60 | 14 | 11 | 1 | 0 | 8 | 0 | 78 | 2 |
| Mayes, Idaho Falls | 0 | 6 | .000 | 6.23 | 14 | 8 | 2 | 3 | 0 | 0 | 56.1 | 76 | 48 | 39 | 4 | 0 | 32 | 2 | 33 | 4 |
| Mays, Idaho Falls | 2 | 5 | .286 | 6.24 | 17 | 6 | 0 | 6 | 0 | 2 | 53.1 | 58 | 48 | 37 | 4 | 4 | 41 | 2 | 40 | 9 |
| McCarter, Salt Lake City | 7 | 5 | .583 | 3.20 | 15 | 15 | 8 | 0 | 1 | 0 | 107.0 | 99 | 50 | 38 | 5 | 2 | 40 | 4 | 111 | 0 |
| McDonald, Pocatello | 1 | 8 | .111 | 3.99 | 12 | 11 | 2 | 0 | 0 | 0 | 79.0 | 90 | 56 | 35 | 3 | 4 | 39 | 0 | 55 | 3 |
| McGrew, Helena | 0 | 0 | .000 | 0.00 | 1 | 0 | 0 | 1 | 0 | 0 | 1.0 | 1 | 0 | 0 | 0 | 0 | 0 | 0 | 0 | 1 |
| Messenger, Idaho Falls | 1 | 2 | .333 | 9.88 | 5 | 0 | 0 | 2 | 0 | 0 | 13.2 | 18 | 15 | 15 | 2 | 0 | 6 | 1 | 3 | 0 |
| Miramontes, Helena | 0 | 0 | .000 | 15.19 | 4 | 1 | 0 | 0 | 0 | 0 | 5.1 | 13 | 9 | 9 | 1 | 0 | 4 | 0 | 5 | 2 |
| Moraw, Helena | 8 | 3 | .727 | 5.24 | 13 | 13 | 0 | 0 | 0 | 0 | 80.2 | 85 | 58 | 47 | 3 | 2 | 40 | 0 | 68 | 6 |
| Morhardt, Butte | 0 | 2 | .000 | 22.00 | 8 | 2 | 0 | 4 | 0 | 0 | 9.0 | 17 | 23 | 22 | 1 | 1 | 18 | 0 | 4 | 2 |
| Musselman, Medicine Hat* | 6 | 4 | .600 | 3.99 | 16 | 15 | 2 | 0 | 0 | 0 | 88.0 | 75 | 41 | 39 | 2 | 1 | 44 | 1 | 96 | 5 |
| Naworski, Great Falls | 2 | 0 | 1.000 | 5.74 | 17 | 0 | 0 | 2 | 0 | 2 | 31.1 | 35 | 21 | 20 | 2 | 4 | 25 | 0 | 21 | 7 |
| D. Nelson, Butte | 2 | 3 | .400 | 4.77 | 14 | 9 | 0 | 1 | 0 | 1 | 66.0 | 88 | 46 | 35 | 4 | 1 | 27 | 1 | 37 | 7 |
| K. Nelson, Great Falls | 2 | 2 | .500 | 5.68 | 15 | 1 | 0 | 6 | 0 | 2 | 31.2 | 34 | 21 | 20 | 0 | 1 | 26 | 2 | 24 | 5 |
| Nichols, Helena | 1 | 1 | .500 | 7.66 | 8 | 5 | 0 | 2 | 0 | 0 | 24.2 | 35 | 25 | 21 | 1 | 1 | 23 | 0 | 14 | 2 |
| Nunez, Pocatello | 1 | 3 | .250 | 5.23 | 16 | 1 | 0 | 5 | 0 | 1 | 32.2 | 25 | 24 | 19 | 1 | 2 | 27 | 0 | 43 | 6 |
| Olson, Salt Lake City* | 1 | 2 | .333 | 2.43 | 16 | 0 | 0 | 9 | 0 | 4 | 29.2 | 26 | 11 | 8 | 1 | 1 | 13 | 0 | 27 | 6 |
| Palo, Medicine Hat | 0 | 1 | .000 | 5.11 | 6 | 0 | 0 | 5 | 0 | 1 | 12.1 | 11 | 9 | 7 | 0 | 0 | 5 | 1 | 13 | 1 |
| Petty, Butte | 0 | 0 | .000 | 0.00 | 1 | 0 | 0 | 0 | 0 | 0 | 1.0 | 1 | 0 | 0 | 0 | 0 | 0 | 0 | 0 | 0 |
| Pilkington, Helena* | 2 | 2 | .500 | 4.63 | 15 | 2 | 0 | 5 | 0 | 1 | 35.0 | 31 | 21 | 18 | 2 | 1 | 33 | 0 | 42 | 7 |
| Ray, Great Falls | 8 | 2 | .800 | 2.55 | 14 | 14 | 4 | 0 | 0 | 0 | 99.0 | 89 | 43 | 28 | 5 | 3 | 23 | 0 | 80 | 4 |
| Reyes, Idaho Falls | 3 | 6 | .333 | 3.15 | 12 | 8 | 3 | 4 | 0 | 0 | 60.0 | 67 | 37 | 21 | 2 | 1 | 21 | 1 | 38 | 7 |
| Roche, Great Falls | 0 | 0 | .000 | 5.40 | 7 | 0 | 0 | 3 | 0 | 0 | 8.1 | 8 | 6 | 5 | 1 | 1 | 3 | 0 | 10 | 2 |
| Roesler, Billings | 8 | 2 | .800 | 2.33 | 13 | 13 | 4 | 0 | 1 | 0 | 88.2 | 72 | 32 | 23 | 3 | 2 | 28 | 0 | 73 | 5 |
| Rogers, Billings* | 6 | 4 | .600 | 3.11 | 13 | 13 | 0 | 0 | 0 | 0 | 72.1 | 52 | 35 | 25 | 4 | 1 | 41 | 0 | 95 | 6 |
| Rohde, Medicine Hat* | 3 | 3 | .500 | 5.59 | 18 | 2 | 0 | 7 | 0 | 1 | 38.2 | 38 | 32 | 24 | 1 | 4 | 45 | 1 | 32 | 8 |
| Rollo, Salt Lake City | 0 | 0 | .000 | 5.06 | 14 | 0 | 0 | 4 | 0 | 1 | 16.0 | 23 | 9 | 9 | 2 | 1 | 6 | 0 | 16 | 1 |
| Ronquillo, Idaho Falls | 1 | 2 | .333 | 7.65 | 12 | 3 | 0 | 5 | 0 | 0 | 40.0 | 64 | 41 | 34 | 5 | 2 | 18 | 0 | 26 | 6 |
| St. Clair, Medicine Hat | 0 | 2 | .000 | 5.82 | 10 | 6 | 0 | 2 | 0 | 0 | 34.0 | 38 | 32 | 22 | 1 | 2 | 33 | 1 | 21 | 8 |
| Sauer, Idaho Falls* | 2 | 1 | .667 | 8.72 | 9 | 4 | 0 | 1 | 0 | 0 | 21.2 | 35 | 33 | 21 | 0 | 0 | 21 | 0 | 19 | 7 |
| Savage, Great Falls | 5 | 1 | .833 | 1.01 | 24 | 0 | 0 | 20 | 0 | 8 | 44.2 | 26 | 5 | 5 | 0 | 2 | 18 | 3 | 51 | 0 |
| Scharkey, Salt Lake City* | 1 | 0 | 1.000 | 6.84 | 11 | 5 | 0 | 4 | 0 | 0 | 25.0 | 39 | 22 | 19 | 2 | 0 | 12 | 0 | 21 | 1 |
| Schlieper, Medicine Hat* | 1 | 2 | .333 | 3.86 | 20 | 0 | 0 | 12 | 0 | 1 | 23.1 | 22 | 14 | 10 | 0 | 1 | 19 | 1 | 28 | 5 |
| Shelton, Idaho Falls* | 0 | 3 | .000 | 5.02 | 7 | 1 | 0 | 1 | 0 | 0 | 14.1 | 17 | 20 | 8 | 1 | 0 | 14 | 1 | 11 | 4 |
| Signore, Helena* | 4 | 4 | .500 | 7.02 | 9 | 8 | 0 | 1 | 0 | 0 | 41.0 | 58 | 38 | 32 | 8 | 2 | 10 | 0 | 31 | 6 |
| Silverio, Pocatello | 0 | 0 | .000 | 6.75 | 2 | 0 | 0 | 2 | 0 | 0 | 4.0 | 3 | 3 | 3 | 1 | 0 | 2 | 0 | 4 | 0 |
| B. Smith, Great Falls* | 10 | 3 | .769 | 3.78 | 15 | 13 | 3 | 0 | 1 | 0 | 78.2 | 80 | 41 | 33 | 2 | 1 | 26 | 0 | 78 | 6 |
| Je. Smith, Helena | 0 | 0 | .000 | 11.68 | 10 | 0 | 0 | 4 | 0 | 0 | 12.1 | 17 | 20 | 16 | 0 | 0 | 16 | 0 | 9 | 7 |
| Jo. Smith, 4 SLC–10 IF* | 2 | 7 | .222 | 6.82 | 14 | 10 | 1 | 2 | 0 | 1 | 60.2 | 94 | 58 | 46 | 1 | 0 | 19 | 0 | 31 | 5 |
| M. Smith, Billings | 2 | 2 | .500 | 2.94 | 7 | 5 | 1 | 0 | 1 | 0 | 33.2 | 24 | 15 | 11 | 0 | 2 | 24 | 0 | 24 | 2 |
| Stocker, Pocatello | 2 | 6 | .250 | 2.85 | 13 | 13 | 5 | 0 | 0 | 0 | 94.2 | 87 | 41 | 30 | 5 | 5 | 29 | 4 | 88 | 2 |
| Strickland, 7 IF–4 SLC | 0 | 2 | .000 | 6.51 | 11 | 5 | 0 | 3 | 0 | 0 | 37.1 | 57 | 29 | 27 | 2 | 2 | 12 | 0 | 14 | 4 |
| Stull, Great Falls | 8 | 1 | .889 | 2.64 | 12 | 12 | 3 | 0 | 1 | 0 | 81.2 | 74 | 30 | 24 | 2 | 2 | 33 | 0 | 90 | 9 |
| Suero, Pocatello* | 1 | 0 | 1.000 | 6.61 | 8 | 0 | 0 | 7 | 0 | 0 | 16.1 | 23 | 16 | 12 | 1 | 0 | 10 | 0 | 9 | 4 |
| Summers, Billings* | 1 | 0 | 1.000 | 4.81 | 15 | 0 | 0 | 8 | 0 | 2 | 24.1 | 18 | 15 | 13 | 3 | 4 | 12 | 0 | 16 | 1 |
| Swain, Butte* | 1 | 2 | .333 | 6.15 | 10 | 5 | 0 | 1 | 0 | 0 | 33.2 | 50 | 33 | 23 | 2 | 1 | 15 | 0 | 24 | 1 |
| Taylor, Helena | 0 | 0 | .000 | 6.43 | 8 | 0 | 0 | 2 | 0 | 0 | 14.0 | 12 | 12 | 10 | 1 | 1 | 10 | 0 | 12 | 4 |
| Toribio, Pocatello* | 0 | 0 | .000 | Infin | 2 | 0 | 0 | 0 | 0 | 0 | 0.0 | 1 | 5 | 4 | 0 | 0 | 4 | 0 | 0 | 1 |
| Townsend, Idaho Falls | 2 | 3 | .400 | 5.36 | 25 | 0 | 0 | 17 | 0 | 2 | 45.1 | 61 | 37 | 27 | 1 | 1 | 17 | 0 | 35 | 3 |
| Tuchalski, Idaho Falls | 0 | 3 | .000 | 9.92 | 7 | 3 | 0 | 2 | 0 | 0 | 16.1 | 24 | 25 | 18 | 0 | 0 | 17 | 0 | 11 | 0 |
| Van Roy, Salt Lake City | 1 | 1 | .500 | 5.00 | 10 | 0 | 0 | 8 | 0 | 0 | 18.0 | 26 | 11 | 10 | 5 | 2 | 7 | 0 | 7 | 1 |
| Veres, Helena | 7 | 4 | .636 | 3.84 | 13 | 13 | 3 | 0 | 2 | 0 | 77.1 | 66 | 43 | 33 | 3 | 2 | 36 | 0 | 67 | 9 |
| Walton, Pocatello | 3 | 7 | .300 | 4.11 | 18 | 9 | 2 | 6 | 0 | 3 | 76.2 | 89 | 46 | 35 | 2 | 1 | 27 | 3 | 69 | 2 |
| Watkins, Billings | 1 | 3 | .250 | 4.85 | 17 | 5 | 2 | 4 | 0 | 1 | 65.0 | 71 | 44 | 35 | 4 | 3 | 26 | 3 | 41 | 8 |
| Watts, Helena | 0 | 0 | .000 | 16.50 | 4 | 0 | 0 | 1 | 0 | 1 | 6.0 | 16 | 13 | 11 | 0 | 0 | 1 | 0 | 4 | 2 |
| Weatherly, Butte | 0 | 1 | .000 | 27.00 | 3 | 1 | 0 | 0 | 0 | 0 | 5.0 | 11 | 16 | 15 | 2 | 0 | 7 | 0 | 3 | 0 |
| Webb, Salt Lake City | 9 | 4 | .692 | 3.90 | 16 | 15 | 6 | 0 | 0 | 0 | 97.0 | 108 | 65 | 42 | 7 | 1 | 32 | 0 | 63 | 0 |
| Wetteland, Great Falls | 1 | 1 | .500 | 3.92 | 11 | 2 | 0 | 3 | 0 | 0 | 20.2 | 17 | 10 | 9 | 0 | 0 | 15 | 1 | 23 | 0 |
| Wilder, Helena | 0 | 1 | .000 | 9.87 | 9 | 4 | 0 | 0 | 0 | 0 | 17.1 | 29 | 21 | 19 | 3 | 2 | 19 | 0 | 10 | 4 |
| Williamson, Pocatello | 1 | 1 | .500 | 3.90 | 8 | 5 | 0 | 2 | 0 | 0 | 27.2 | 28 | 20 | 12 | 4 | 0 | 12 | 1 | 14 | 2 |
| Willis, Billings | 1 | 1 | .500 | 5.92 | 17 | 0 | 0 | 7 | 0 | 3 | 24.1 | 31 | 18 | 16 | 0 | 2 | 19 | 1 | 18 | 2 |
| Woodard, Salt Lake City | 4 | 2 | .667 | 3.51 | 18 | 3 | 0 | 3 | 0 | 1 | 48.2 | 60 | 25 | 19 | 0 | 0 | 19 | 0 | 27 | 7 |
| Zeinert, Great Falls* | 0 | 0 | .000 | 6.00 | 1 | 0 | 0 | 0 | 0 | 0 | 3.0 | 6 | 6 | 2 | 0 | 0 | 4 | 0 | 2 | 1 |

BALKS—R. Lambert, 6; Bilawey, Cieslak, Gossett, Hovorka, McDonald, 3 each; Asbell, Brevell, Coffey, Diaz, Dunn, Freeland, Griffey, Haringa, Morhardt, Reyes, Veres, 2 each; Caceres, Fitzpatrick, Garrick, Guenther, Hajdasz, Hall, Lopez, Mayes, Moraw, Musselman, D. Nelson, Nunez, Olson, Petty, Pilkington, Ray, Roesler, Rohde, Ronquillo, St. Clair, Signore, Jo. Smith, Stocker, Strickland, Stull, Swain, Watkins, Weatherly, Webb, Wilder, Willis, 1 each.

COMBINATION SHUTOUTS—Coffey-Smith-Willis, Roesler-Deitz, Rogers-Summers, Billings; Ray-Savage, Wetteland-Fiala, Great Falls; Freeland-Bosley, Helena; Sauer-Shelton-Callas, Idaho Falls; Jones-Horsman-Guenther, Musselman-St. Clair-Rohde, Medicine Hat; Arrington-Olson-Kolovitz, Garrick-Kolovitz, Salt Lake City.

NO-HIT GAMES—None.

# 1986 A.L. EAST DIVISION SLATE . . .

| 1986 | EAST | | | | | | |
|---|---|---|---|---|---|---|---|
| | AT MILWAUKEE | AT DETROIT | AT CLEVELAND | AT TORONTO | AT BALTIMORE | AT NEW YORK | AT BOSTON |
| **MILWAUKEE...** | | June 27*, 28, **29-29** Sept. 9*, 10*, 11* | May 30*, 31 June **1** Aug. 18*, 19*, 20* | June 23*, 24*, 25 Oct. 3*, 4, **5** | June 30* July 1*, 2* Sept. 19*, 20*, **21** | April 11*, 12, **13** Aug. 4*, 5*, 6*, 7* | June 12*, 13*, 14, **15** Sept. 16*, 17*, 18* |
| **DETROIT.........** | June 20*, 21, **22** Sept. 30* Oct. 1*, 2* | | April 11, 12, **13** July 28*,29*,30*,31* | June 12*, 13*, 14, **15** Sept. 16*, 17* | June 16*,17*,18*,19* Oct. 3*, 4, **5** | June 30* July 1*, 2*, 3* Sept. 26*, 27, **28** | April 21, 22*, 23* Aug. 15*, 16, **17** |
| **CLEVELAND ...** | May 20*, 21*, 22 Sept. 4*, 5*, 6*, **7** | April 18*, 19, **20** Aug. 5*, 6*, 7* | | May 16*, 17, **18**, 19 Sept. 1, 2*, 3* | April 7, 9, 10* Aug. 8*, 9*, **10** | April 24*, 25*, 26, **27** Aug. 11*, 12*, 13* | June 2*, 3*, 4* Aug. 29*, 30, **31** |
| **TORONTO .......** | June 16*, 17*, 18 Sept. 12*, 13*,**14**,15* | June 6*, 7*, **8** Sept.22*,23*,24*,25* | May 23*, 24, **25** Aug. 26*, 27*, 28* | | April 25*, 26*, **27** Aug. 11*, 12*, 13* | June 27*, 28, **29** Sept. 29*, 30* Oct. 1 | June 30* July 1*, 2*, 3* Sept. 26*, 27, **28** |
| **BALTIMORE....** | June 9*, 10*, 11 Sept.25*,26*,27*,**28** | June 24*, 25*, 26* Sept. 12*, 13, **14** | April 21*, 22*, 23* Aug. 14*, 15*, 16, **17** | April 14, 16, 17 Aug. 1*, 2, **3**, 4 | | June 6*, 7, **8** Sept. 15*, 16*, 17* | June 20*, 21, **22** Sept. 29*, 30* Oct. 1* |
| **NEW YORK .....** | April 18*, 19, **20** July 28*, 29*, 30 | June 9*, 10*, 11* Sept. 19*, 20, 21 | April 15*, 16*, 17* Aug. 1*, 2, **3** | June 19*,20*,21,**22** Sept. 9*, 10*, 11* | June 12*, 13*, 14, **15** Sept. 22*, 23*, 24* | | June 23*, 24*, 25* Oct. 2*, 3*, 4, **5** |
| **BOSTON .........** | June 5*, 6*, 7*, **8** Sept. 23*, 24* | April 7, 9, 10 Aug. 8*, 9*, **10**, 11* | May 26, 27*, 28* Aug. 21*,22*, 23, **24** | June 9*, 10*, 11* Sept. 19*, 20, **21** | June 27*, 28, **29** Sept. 8*,9*, 10*, 11* | June 16*, 17*, 18* Sept. 12*, 13, **14** | |
| **SEATTLE.........** | May 5*, 6 July 10*,11*,12*,**13*** | May 20*, 21*, 22 Aug. 22*, 23*, **24** | June 17*, 18*, 19* Oct. 3*, 4, **5** | May 2*, 3, **4** July 7*, 8*, 9* | June 3*, 4*, 5* Sept. 5*, 6*, **7** | May 16*, 17, **18** Aug. 19*, 20, 21* | April 29*, 30* May 1* July 4*, 5, **6** |
| **OAKLAND ......** | April 29*, 30* May 1 July 4*, 5*, **6** | May 23*, 24*, **25**, 26 Aug. 25*, 26* | June 9*, 10*, 11* Sept. 12*, 13, **14** | May 5*, 6 July 10*, 11*, 12, **13*** | May 16*, 17*, **18** Aug. 19*, 20*, 21* | May 20*, 21*, 22* Aug. 22*, 23*, **24** | May 2*, 3, **4** July 7*, 8*, 9* |
| **CALIFORNIA...** | May 2*, 3, **4** July 7*, 8*, 9 | May 16*, 17, **18** Aug. 19*, 20*, 21* | June 6*, 7, **8** Sept. 9*, 10*, 11* | April 29*, 30* May 1* July 4*, 5, **6** | May 19*, 20*, 21* Aug. 22*, 23, **24** | May 23*, 24, **25**, 26 Aug. 25*, 26* | May 5*, 6 July 10*, 11*, 12, **13** |
| **TEXAS ..........** | April 14, 16*, 17 Aug. 1*, 2*, **3** | May 14*, 15* July 17*, 18*, 19*, **20** | May 12*, 13* July 10*, 11*, 12, **13** | April 21*, 22*, 23 Aug. 15*, 16, **17** | April 18*, 19*, **20** Aug. 5*, 6*, 7* | May 2*, 3, **4** July 21*, 22, 23 | May 16*, 17, **18** Sept. 1*, 2*, 3* |
| **KANSAS CITY** | June 2*, 3*, 4 Aug. 22*, 23*, **24** | April 29*, 30* July 24*, 25*, 26*, **27** | May 5*, 6*, 7* July 4*, 5, **6** | April 18*, 19, **20** Aug. 5*, 6*, 7* | May 9*, 10*, **11** July 21*, 22*, 23* | April 8, 9*, 10 Aug. 8*, 9, **10** | April 14, 16, 17 Aug. 1*, 2, **3** |
| **MINNESOTA...** | May 16*, 17, **18** Aug. 26*, 27*, 28 | May 2*, 3*, **4** July 21*, 22*, 23* | June 13*, 14, **15** Sept. 15*, 16*, 17* | June 2*, 3*, 4* Aug. 29*, 30, **31** | May 14*, 15* July 17*, 18*, 19*, **20** | April 29*, 30* May 1* July 25*, 26, **27** | May 19*, 20*, 21* Sept. 5*, 6, **7** |
| **CHICAGO.........** | April 22*, 23* Aug. 8*, 9*, **10**, 11* | April 25*, 26, **27** Aug. 12*, 13*, 14 | May 9*, 10, **11** July 21*, 22*, 23* | May 30*, 31 June **1** Aug. 18*, 19*, 20 | May 12*, 13* July 24*, 25*, 26, **27** | May 14*, 15* July 24*, 25*, 26, **27** | April 18*, 19, **20** Aug. 4*, 5*, 6* |
| **1986** | 81 HOME DATES 54 NIGHTS | 80 HOME DATES 55 NIGHTS | 81 HOME DATES 53 NIGHTS | 81 HOME DATES 45 NIGHTS | 81 HOME DATES 61 NIGHTS | 81 HOME DATES 50 NIGHTS | 81 HOME DATES 50 NIGHTS |

*NIGHT GAME
NIGHT GAME: Any game starting after 5:00 p.m.
HEAVY BLACK FIGURES DENOTE SUNDAY

# AND COMPLETE WEST SCHEDULES

| 1986 | WEST | | | | | | |
|---|---|---|---|---|---|---|---|
| | AT SEATTLE | AT OAKLAND | AT CALIFORNIA | AT TEXAS | AT KANSAS CITY | AT MINNESOTA | AT CHICAGO |
| **MILWAUKEE...** | May 12*, 13*, 14 July 25*, 26*, **27** | May 7*, 8 July 18*, 19, **20-20** | May 9*, 10, **11** July 21, 22*, 23* | April 25*, 26*, **27** Aug. 12*, 13*, 14* | May 26*, 27*, 28* Aug. 29*, 30*, **31** | May 23*, 24*, **25** Sept. 1, 2*, 3* | April 7, 9, 10 Aug. 15*, 16*, **17** |
| **DETROIT.........** | May 30*, 31* June **1** Sept. 1, 2*, 3* | June 2*, 3*, 4 Sept. 5*, 6, **7** | May 28*, 29* Aug. 28*,29*,30*,**31** | May 5*, 6*, 7* July 4*, 5*, **6*** | May 12*, 13* July 10*, 11*, 12, **13** | May 9*, 10*, **11** July 7*, 8*, 9 | April 14*, 15*, 16* Aug. 1*, 2*, **3** |
| **CLEVELAND ...** | June 23*, 24*, 25 Sept. 26*, 27*, **28** | June 30* July 1, 2 Sept. 19*, 20, **21** | June 27*, 28*, **29** Sept. 22*, 23*, 24* | April 29*, 30* July24*,25*,26*,**27*** | May 14*, 15* July 17*, 18*, 19*, **20** | June 20*, 21*, **22** Sept. 29*, 30* Oct. 1 | May 2*, 3*, **4** July 7*, 8*, 9 |
| **TORONTO .......** | May 9*, 10*, **11** July 21*, 22*, 23 | May 12*, 13*, 14 July 25*, 26, **27** | May 7*, 8* July 17*, 18*, 19, **20** | April 8*, 9*, 10* Aug. 8*, 9*, **10*** | April 11, 12, **13** July 28*, 29*, 30* | May 26, 27*, 28* Aug. 22*, 23*, **24** | May 20*, 21*, 22* Sept. 5*, 6, 7 |
| **BALTIMORE....** | May 23*,24*,**25*,**26 Aug. 26*,27* | May 28, 29 Aug. 28*,29*, 30, **31** | May 30*, 31* June 1 Sept. 1, 2*, 3* | April 11*, 12*, **13** July 28*, 29*, 30* | May 2*, 3*, **4** July 7*, 8*, 9* | May 6*, 7* July 3*, 4, 5, **6** | April 29*, 30* July 10*, 11*, 12*, **13** |
| **NEW YORK .....** | May 28*, 29* Aug.28*,29*,30*,**31*** | May 30*, 31 June **1** Sept. 1*, 2*, 3 | June 2*, 3*, 4* Sept. 5*, 6*, **7** | May 9*, 10*, **11** July 7*, 8*, 9* | April 21*, 22*, 23* Aug. 15*, 16, **17** | May 12*, 13 July 10*, 11*, 12*, **13** | May 5*, 6*, 7* July 4*, 5, 6 |
| **BOSTON .........** | May 7*, 8* July 17*, 18*, 19*, **20** | May 9*, 10, **11** July 21*, 22, 23 | May 12*, 13*, 14* July 25*, 26*, **27** | May 23*, 24*, **25** Aug. 25*, 26*, 27* | April 25*, 26*, **27** Aug. 12*, 13*, 14* | May 30*, 31* June **1** Aug. 18*, 19*, 20* | April 11*, 12*, **13** July 28*, 29*, 30* |
| **SEATTLE........** | | April 24*,25*, 26, **27** Aug. 11*, 12, 13 | April 14, 15*, 16* Aug. 7*, 8*, 9*, **10** | June 6*, 7 (Tn), **8*** Sept. 9*, 10 | June 9*, 10*, 11* Sept.11*,12*,13*,**14** | April 11*, 12, **13** July 28*, 29*, 30* | June 20*, 21, **22** Sept. 29*, 30* Oct. 1* |
| **OAKLAND ......** | April 18*, 19*, **20** Aug. 4*, 5*, 6* | | April 21*, 22*, 23* Aug. 15*, 16*, **17** | June 19*,20*,21*,**22*** Sept. 29*, 30* Oct. 1* | June23*,24*,25*,26* Sept. 26*, 27*, **28** | April 14*, 15*, 16 Aug. 1*, 2*, **3** | June 5*, 6*, 7*, **8** Sept. 9*, 10*, 11* |
| **CALIFORNIA ...** | April 8*, 9*, 10* Aug. 1, 2*, **3** | April 11*, 12, **13** July 28*, 29*, 30, 31 | | June 23*, 24*, 25* Oct. 2*, 3*, 4*, **5** | June 20*, 21*, **22** Sept. 29*, 30* Oct. 1* | April 25*, 26*, **27** Aug. 4*, 5*, 6 | June 9*, 10*, 11 Sept. 12*, 13*, **14**, 15* |
| **TEXAS ...........** | June26*,27*,28*,**29** Sept. 22*, 23*, 24* | June 13*, 14, **15** Sept. 15*, 16, 17 | June 16*, 17*, 18* Sept. 26*, 27, **28** | | May 30*, 31* June **1** Aug. 19*, 20*, 21* | June 9*, 10*, 11* Sept.11*,12*,13,**14** | June 2*, 3*, 4* Aug.28*,29*,30*,**31** |
| **KANSAS CITY** | June 30* July 1*, 2* Sept. 19*, 20*, **21** | June 16*, 17, 18 Oct. 3*, 4, **5** | June 12*, 13*, 14, **15** Sept. 16*, 17*, 18* | May19*,20*,21*,22* Sept. 5*, 6*, **7*** | | June 27*, 28*, **29** Sept.22*,23*,24*,25 | May 16*, 17, **18** Aug. 25*, 26*, 27* |
| **MINNESOTA ...** | April 21*, 22*, 23 Aug. 14*, 15*, 16*, **17** | April 8*, 9, 10 Aug. 8*, 9, **10-10** | April 17*, 18*, 19, **20** Aug. 11*, 12*, 13* | June 30* July 1*, 2* Sept. 19*, 20*, **21** | June 5*, 6*, 7*, **8** Sept. 8*, 9* | | June 23*, 24*, 25* Sept. 26*, 27*, **28** |
| **CHICAGO........** | June 12*, 13*, 14*, **15** Sept. 16*, 17*, 18* | June 27*, 28, **29** Sept. 22*, 23, 24 | June 30 July 1*, 2* Sept. 19*, 20, **21** | May 26*, 27*, 28* Aug. 22*, 23*, **24*** | May 23*, 24*, **25** Sept. 1*, 2*, 3*, 4* | June 17*, 18*, 19 Oct. 2*, 3*, 4*, **5** | |
| **1986** | 81 HOME DATES 63 NIGHTS | 79 HOME DATES 31 NIGHTS | 81 HOME DATES 58 NIGHTS | 80 HOME DATES 74 NIGHTS | 81 HOME DATES 64 NIGHTS | 81 HOME DATES 55 NIGHTS | 81 HOME DATES 59 NIGHTS |

JULY 15—ALL-STAR GAME AT HOUSTON

# 1986 N.L. EAST DIVISION SLATE . . .

| 1986 | EAST | | | | | |
|---|---|---|---|---|---|---|
| | **AT CHICAGO** | **AT MONTREAL** | **AT NEW YORK** | **AT PHILADELPHIA** | **AT PITTSBURGH** | **AT ST. LOUIS** |
| **CHICAGO........** | | April 15, 17<br>Aug. 14*, 15 (Tn), 16*, **17**<br>Sept. 15*, 16* | June 19*, 20*, 21, **22**<br>July 28*, 29*, 30*<br>Sept. 17*, 18 | June 23*, 24*, 25*<br>Aug. 1*, 2, **3**<br>Sept. 29*, 30*<br>Oct. 1* | April 11*, 12, **13**<br>June 9*, 10*, 11*<br>Sept. 12*, 13*, **14** | April 8*, 10<br>June 5*, 6*, 7, **8**<br>Sept. 26*, 27, **28** |
| **MONTREAL ....** | April 24, 25, 26, **27**<br>June 30<br>July 1, 2<br>Sept. 22, 23 | | June 23*, 24*, 25<br>Aug. 1*, 2*, **3**<br>Sept. 8*, 9*, 10* | May 5*, 6*, 7*<br>June 13*, 14*, **15**<br>Oct. 3*, 4*, **5** | June 27*, 28*, **29**<br>Aug. 4*, 5*, 6*, 7*<br>Sept. 24*, 25* | April 11*, 12*, **13**<br>June 9*, 10*, 11*<br>Sept. 12*, 13*, **14** |
| **NEW YORK .....** | June 27, 28, **29**<br>Aug. 4, 5, 6, 7<br>Sept. 24, 25 | June 16*, 17*, 18*<br>Aug. 8*, 9*, **10**<br>Sept. 30*<br>Oct. 1*, 2* | | April 11*, 12, **13**<br>Aug. 11*, 12*, 13*<br>Sept. 12*, 13*, **14** | April 8*, 10*<br>June 5*, 6*, 7*, **8**<br>Sept. 26*, 27*, **28** | April 24*, 25*, 26, **27**<br>June 30*<br>July 1*, 2*<br>Sept. 15*, 16* |
| **PHILADELPHIA** | June 16, 17, 18<br>Aug. 8, 9, **10**<br>Sept. 8, 9, 10 | April 22, 23<br>June 5*, 6*, 7*, **8**<br>Sept. 26*, 27*, **28** | April 18*, 19, **20**<br>June 9*, 10*, 11*<br>Sept. 19*, 20*, **21** | | April 24*, 25*, 26, **27**<br>June 30*<br>July 1*, 2<br>Sept. 22*, 23* | June 27*, 28*, **29**<br>Aug. 4*, 5*, 6*, 7<br>Sept. 24*, 25* |
| **PITTSBURGH..** | April 18, 19, **20**<br>Aug. 11, 12, 13<br>Sept. 19, 20, **21** | June 19*, 20*, 21*, **22**<br>July 28*, 29*, 30*<br>Sept. 17*, 18 | April 21*, 22*<br>June 13*, 14, **15-15**<br>Oct. 3*, 4, **5** | April 14*, 15*, 16*<br>Aug. 14, 15*, 16*, **17**<br>Sept. 15*, 16* | | June 23*, 24*, 25*<br>Aug. 8*, 9*, **10**<br>Sept. 30*<br>Oct. 1*, 2* |
| **ST. LOUIS ......** | April 21, 22, 23<br>June 13, 14, **15**<br>Oct. 3, 4, **5** | April 18, 19, **20**<br>Aug. 11*, 12*, 13*<br>Sept. 19*, 20*, **21** | April 14, 16, 17<br>Aug. 14*, 15*, 16, **17**<br>Sept. 22*, 23 | June 19*, 20*, 21*, **22**<br>July 28*, 29*, 30*<br>Sept. 17*, 18* | June 16*, 17*, 18*<br>Aug. 1*, 2*, **3**<br>Sept. 8*, 9*, 10* | |
| **ATLANTA.......** | May 30, 31<br>June **1**<br>Aug. 19, 20, 21 | May 14*, 15<br>July 17*, 18*, 19*, **20** | May 12*, 13*<br>July 10*, 11*, 12, **13** | May 2*, 3, **4**<br>July 7*, 8*, 9 | May 26, 27*, 28*<br>Aug. 22*, 23*, **24** | May 23*, 24*, **25**<br>Aug. 25*, 26*, 27* |
| **CINCINNATI ...** | May 26, 27, 28<br>Aug. 22, 23, **24** | May 12*, 13<br>July 10*, 11*, 12*, **13** | May 9*, 10, **11**<br>July 7*, 8*, 9 | May 14*, 15*<br>July 3*, 4*, 5*, **6** | May 23*, 24*, **25**<br>Aug. 25*, 26*, 27* | May 20*, 21*, 22<br>Aug. 29*, 30*, **31** |
| **HOUSTON.......** | May 23, 24, **25**<br>Sept. 1, 2, 3 | May 2, 3, **4**<br>July 7*, 8*, 9* | May 6*, 7*<br>July 3*, 4, 5*, **6** | April 29*, 30*<br>July 24*, 25*, 26*, **27** | May 9*, 10*, **11**<br>Aug. 18*, 19*, 20* | May 26*, 27*, 28<br>Aug. 22*, 23*, **24** |
| **LOS ANGELES** | May 6, 7, 8<br>July 25, 26, **27** | May 9, 10, **11**<br>Sept. 1*, 2*, 3* | May 27*, 28*, 29*<br>Aug. 29*, 30, **31** | June 2*, 3*, 4*<br>Sept. 5*, 6*, **7** | May 30*, 31*<br>June **1**<br>July 22*, 23*, 24* | May 13*, 14*<br>July 17*, 18*, 19, **20** |
| **SAN DIEGO.....** | May 9, 10, **11**<br>July 21, 22, 23 | May 26*, 27*, 28*<br>Aug. 29*, 30*, **31** | June 2*, 3*, 4*<br>Sept. 5*, 6, **7** | May 30*, 31<br>June **1**<br>Sept. 1*, 2*, 3* | May 13*, 14*<br>July 17*, 18*, 19, **20** | May 6*, 7*, 8<br>July 25*, 26, **27** |
| **SAN FRAN......** | May 13, 14<br>July 17, 18, 19, **20** | June 3*, 4*<br>Sept. 4*, 5*, 6*, **7** | May 30*, 31*<br>June **1**<br>Sept. 1, 2*, 3* | May 27*, 28*, 29*<br>Aug. 29*, 30*, **31** | May 6*, 7*, 8*<br>July 25*, 26*, **27** | May 9*, 10*, **11**<br>July 21*, 22*, 23* |
| **1986** | 81 HOME DATES<br>0 NIGHTS | 80 HOME DATES<br>55 NIGHTS | 80 HOME DATES<br>49 NIGHTS | 81 HOME DATES<br>62 NIGHTS | 81 HOME DATES<br>63 NIGHTS | 81 HOME DATES<br>57 NIGHTS |

*NIGHT GAME
NIGHT GAME: Any game starting after 5:00 p.m.
HEAVY BLACK FIGURES DENOTE SUNDAY

# AND COMPLETE WEST SCHEDULES

| 1986 | AT ATLANTA | AT CINCINNATI | AT HOUSTON | AT LOS ANGELES | AT SAN DIEGO | AT SAN FRANCISCO |
|---|---|---|---|---|---|---|
| **CHICAGO........** | May 20*, 21*, 22<br>Aug. 29*, 30, **31** | June 2*, 3*, 4*<br>Sept. 5*, 6*, **7** | May 16*, 17*, **18**<br>Aug. 25*, 26*, 27* | April 30*<br>May 1*<br>July 10*, 11*, 12*, **13** | April 28*, 29*<br>July 3*, 4*, 5, **6** | May 2*, 3, **4-4**<br>July 8*, 9 |
| **MONTREAL ....** | April 8*, 10*<br>July 3*, 4*, 5, **6** | April 29*, 30<br>July 24*, 25*, 26*, **27** | May 30*, 31*<br>June **1**<br>July 21*, 22*, 23 | May 20*, 21*, 22*<br>Aug. 22*, 23*, **24** | May 16*, 17*, **18**<br>Aug. 19*, 20*, 21 | May 23*, 24, **25**<br>Aug. 25, 26*, 27 |
| **NEW YORK .....** | April 29*, 30*<br>May 1*<br>July 25*, 26*, **27** | May 2*, 3, **4**<br>July 21*, 22*, 23* | May 14*, 15*<br>July 17*, 18*, 19*, **20** | May 16*, 17, **18**<br>Aug. 18*, 19*, 20* | May 23*, 24*, **25**<br>Aug. 25*, 26*, 27* | May 20*, 21, 22<br>Aug. 22*, 23, **24** |
| **PHILADELPHIA** | May 9*, 10*, **11**<br>July 21*, 22*, 23* | April 7, 9*<br>July 17*, 18*, 19, **20** | May 12*, 13*<br>July 10*, 11*, 12, **13** | May 23*, 24*, **25**<br>Aug. 25*, 26*, 27 | May 20*, 21*, 22<br>Aug. 22*, 23*, **24** | May 16*, 17, **18**<br>Aug. 19*, 20, 21 |
| **PITTSBURGH..** | June 2*, 3*, 4*<br>Sept. 5*, 6, **7** | May 16*, 17*, **18**<br>Sept. 1*, 2*, 3* | May 20*, 21*, 22<br>Aug. 29*, 30*, **31** | April 28*, 29*<br>July 3*, 4*, 5*, **6** | May 2*, 3*, **4**<br>July 7*, 8*, 9* | April 30<br>May 1<br>July 10, 11*, 12, **13** |
| **ST. LOUIS ......** | May 16*, 17, **18**<br>Sept. 1*, 2*, 3* | May 30*, 31<br>June **1**<br>Aug. 19*, 20*, 21* | June 2*, 3*, 4*<br>Sept. 5*, 6*, **7** | May 2*, 3*, **4**<br>July 7*, 8*, 9* | April 30*<br>May 1<br>July 10, 11*, 12*, **13** | April 28*, 29*<br>July 3*, 4, 5, **6** |
| **ATLANTA.......** | | May 5*, 6*, 7*, **8**<br>June 20*, 21*, **22**<br>Sept. 24*, 25 | April 11*, 12*, **13**<br>June 28*, 29*, 30*<br>Oct. 3*, 4*, **5** | April 24*, 25*, 26*, **27**<br>June 23*, 24*, 25*<br>Sept. 8*, 9* | June 5*, 6*, 7*, **8**<br>Aug. 4*, 5*, 6*<br>Sept. 10*, 11* | June 10*, 11<br>July 31*<br>Aug. 1*, 2, **3**<br>Sept. 12*, 13, **14** |
| **CINCINNATI ...** | April 15*, 16*<br>June 13*, 14, **15**, 16*<br>Sept. 30*<br>Oct. 1*, 2* | | April 24*, 25*, 26*, **27**<br>June 23*, 24*, 25*<br>Sept. 8*, 9 | June 9*, 10*, 11*<br>Aug. 1*, 2, **3**<br>Sept. 12*, 13, **14** | April 11*, 12*, **13**<br>July 28*, 29*, 30*<br>Sept. 26*, 27*, **28** | June 6*, 7, **8-8**<br>Aug. 4, 5*, 6<br>Sept. 10, 11 |
| **HOUSTON.......** | April 21*, 22*, 23*<br>Aug. 15*, 16*, **17**<br>Sept. 26*, 27, **28** | April 18*, 19, **20**<br>June 17*, 18*, 19*<br>Sept. 16*, 17*, 18 | | June 5*, 6*, 7, **8**<br>Aug. 4*, 5*, 6<br>Sept. 10*, 11* | June 9*, 10*, 11<br>Aug. 1*, 2*, **3**<br>Sept. 12*, 13*, **14** | April 15, 16<br>June 20*, 21, **22-22**<br>Sept. 30*<br>Oct. 1, 2 |
| **LOS ANGELES** | April 18*, 19, **20**<br>June 17*, 18*, 19*<br>Sept. 16*, 17*, 18* | June 30,<br>July 1*, 2*<br>Aug. 8*, 9, **10**<br>Sept. 19*, 20*, **21** | June 27*, 28*, **29**<br>Aug. 11*, 12*, 13*, **14**<br>Sept. 22*, 23* | | April 14*, 15*, 16*<br>June 13*, 14*, **15**<br>Sept. 29*, 30*<br>Oct. 1* | April 21*, 22*, 23<br>Aug. 15*, 16, **17**<br>Sept. 26*, 27, **28** |
| **SAN DIEGO.....** | June 27*, 28*, **29**<br>Aug. 11*, 12*, 13*, 14*<br>Sept. 22*, 23* | April 22*, 23<br>Aug. 15*, 16*, **17**, 18<br>Oct. 3*, 4, **5** | June 30*<br>July 1*, 2<br>Aug. 8*, 9*, **10**<br>Sept. 19*, 20*, **21** | April 7, 8*, 9*, 10*<br>June 20*, 21*, **22**<br>Sept. 24*, 25* | | April 17, 18*, 19, **20**<br>June 23, 24*, 25<br>Sept. 8*, 9* |
| **SAN FRAN......** | June 30*<br>July 1*, 2*<br>Aug. 8*, 9, **10**<br>Sept. 19*, 20, **21** | June 27*, 28*, **29**<br>Aug. 11*, 12*, 13*, 14*<br>Sept. 22*, 23* | April 8*, 9*, 10*<br>June 12*, 13*, 14*, **15**<br>Sept. 24*, 25 | April 11*, 12*, **13**<br>July 28*, 29*, 30*<br>Oct. 3*, 4, **5** | April 25*, 26*, **27**<br>June 16*, 17*, 18*, 19<br>Sept. 16*, 17* | |
| **1986** | 81 HOME DATES<br>59 NIGHTS | 81 HOME DATES<br>55 NIGHTS | 81 HOME DATES<br>62 NIGHTS | 81 HOME DATES<br>60 NIGHTS | 81 HOME DATES<br>61 NIGHTS | 78 HOME DATES<br>27 NIGHTS |

JULY 15—ALL-STAR GAME AT HOUSTON

**DON MATTINGLY**
● YANKEES ●
RBIs (145)
GAME-WINNING RBIs (21)
TOTAL BASES (370)
DOUBLES (48)

**WADE BOGGS**
● RED SOX ●
BATTING CHAMPION (.368)
HITS (240)

**DARRELL EVANS**
● TIGERS ●
HOME RUNS (40)

# 1985 A.L. LEADERS

**BERT BLYLEVEN**
● INDIANS-TWINS ●
STRIKEOUTS (206)
INNINGS (293.2)
COMPLETE GAMES (24)
SHUTOUTS (5)

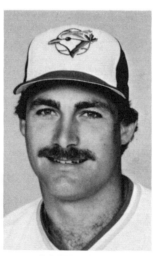

**DAVE STIEB**
● BLUE JAYS ●
ERA (2.48)

**RON GUIDRY**
● YANKEES ●
WINS (22)

**WILLIE McGEE**
● CARDINALS ●
BATTING CHAMPION (.353)
HITS (216)
TRIPLES (18)

**DALE MURPHY**
● BRAVES ●
HOME RUNS (37)
RUNS (118)
WALKS (90)

**DAVE PARKER**
● REDS ●
RBIs (125)
TOTAL BASES (350)
DOUBLES (42)

# 1985 N.L. LEADERS

**DWIGHT GOODEN**
● METS ●
WINS (24)
ERA (1.53)
STRIKEOUTS (268)
INNINGS (276.2)
COMPLETE GAMES (16)

**OREL HERSHISER**
● DODGERS ●
WINNING PCT. (.864)

**JOHN TUDOR**
● CARDINALS ●
SHUTOUTS (10)

# Index to Contents

1985 All-Star Game ....................................... 227
All-Star Teams (The Sporting News)............. 262
Baseball Writers' Awards
    (MVP, Rookie of Year, Cy Young)............. 271
Directory of Organized Ball............................. 300
Farm Systems for 1986 ............................... 332
Five-Hit Games ............................................ 245
Gold Glove Teams ....................................... 267
Hall of Fame................................................ 274
Home Runs, Grand-Slam ............................. 243
Home Runs by Parks..................................... 253
Home Runs, Three in One Game....................... 241
Low-Hit Games ........................................... 235
Major League Draft ..................................... 287
Most Valuable Player and

Cy Young voting for 1985........................ 23-24
Necrology ................................................... 288
No. 1 Men Selections ................................... 329
1-0 Games................................................... 240
Pinch-Hitting ............................................... 247
Player Deals ............................................... 279
Player Debuts.............................................. 250
Players' Association, Major League ............... 330
Presidents of Minor Leagues, 1986................. 331
Relief Pitcher Ratings ................................. 238
Review of Year ............................................. 3
Silver Slugger Teams..................................... 270
Strikeout Performances, Top......................... 237
THE SPORTING NEWS Awards ..................... 257
1985 World Series ....................................... 209

## AMERICAN LEAGUE

Attendance, 1985........................................... 287
Batting Averages, 1985.................................. 85
Batting Statistics, Miscellaneous, 1985.......... 90
Championship Series ..................................... 191
Designated Hitting, 1985.............................. 92
Directory for 1986......................................... 301
Fielding Averages, 1985 ............................... 95
Pennant Winners Each Year........................... 84
Pitchers vs. Individual Clubs........................... 108
Pitching Averages, 1985.............................. 101
Schedule, 1986 ........................................... 504
Standings, 1985 ........................................... 84
Team Reviews ............................................. 29

## NATIONAL LEAGUE

Attendance, 1985........................................... 287
Batting Averages, 1985.................................. 163
Batting Statistics, Miscellaneous, 1985.......... 170
Championship Series ..................................... 199
Directory for 1986......................................... 316
Fielding Averages, 1985 ............................... 173
Pennant Winners Each Year........................... 162
Pitchers vs. Individual Clubs........................... 185
Pitching Averages, 1985.............................. 179
Schedule, 1986 ........................................... 506
Standings, 1985 ........................................... 162
Team Reviews ............................................. 115

### 1985 Game Scores

Baltimore ................ 70     Milwaukee............... 78
Boston...................... 74     Minnesota ............... 42
California ................ 34     New York.................. 62
Chicago ................... 38     Oakland................... 46
Cleveland................. 82     Seattle..................... 50
Detroit .................... 66     Texas ...................... 54
Kansas City............. 30     Toronto................... 58

### 1985 Game Scores

Atlanta ................ 156     New York .............. 120
Chicago ................ 128     Philadelphia .......... 132
Cincinnati............. 144     Pittsburgh.............. 136
Houston ................ 148     St. Louis ............... 116
Los Angeles .......... 140     San Diego ............. 152
Montreal................ 124     San Francisco....... 160

## NATIONAL ASSOCIATION (MINOR LEAGUE) AVERAGES

American Association.......... 334     Gulf Coast............................. 487     Pacific Coast........................ 365
Appalachian.......................... 480     International ......................... 343     Pioneer ................................ 497
California ............................. 407     Mexican ............................... 352     South Atlantic ..................... 470
Carolina ............................. 416     Midwest ............................... 439     Southern.............................. 386
Eastern................................ 377     New York-Pennsylvania........ 451     Texas ................................... 397
Florida State ....................... 426     Northwest ............................ 462

# Index to Minor League Clubs, Cities

Aguascalientes, Mexico...............352
Albany, N.Y. ...............................377
Albuquerque, N.M. .......................365
Appleton, Wis...............................439
Arkansas.....................................397
Asheville, N.C. .............................470
Auburn, N.Y.................................451

Bakersfield, Calif. .........................407
Batavia, N.Y.................................451
Beaumont, Tex. ............................397
Bellingham, Wash..........................462
Beloit, Wis. .................................439
Bend, Ore. ..................................462
Bettendorf, Ia.
  (see Quad Cities)....................439
Billings, Mont...............................497
Birmingham, Ala...........................386
Bluefield, W.Va. ...........................480
Bradenton, Fla..............................487
Bristol, Va....................................480
Buffalo, N.Y. ................................334
Burlington, Ia................................439
Burlington, Vt.
  (see Vermont).........................377
Butte, Mont. ................................497

Calgary, Alberta, Can. ...................365
Campeche, Mexico.........................352
Cedar Rapids, Ia...........................439
Charleston, S.C. ...........................470
Charlotte, N.C. .............................386
Chattanooga, Tenn.........................386
Clearwater, Fla..............................426
Clinton, Ia....................................439
Columbia, S.C...............................470
Columbus, Ga...............................386
Columbus, O.................................343
Cordoba, Mexico...........................352

Davenport, Ia.
  (see Quad Cities)....................439
Daytona Beach, Fla........................426
Denver, Colo.................................334
Des Moines, Ia. (see Iowa)........334
Durham, N.C.................................416

Edmonton, Alberta, Can..............365
Elizabethton, Tenn. ...................480
Elmira, N.Y..................................451
El Paso, Tex.................................397
Erie, Pa. .....................................451
Eugene, Ore.................................462
Everett, Wash...............................462

Florence, S.C. ..............................470
Fort Lauderdale, Fla. ................426
Fort Myers, Fla.............................426
Fresno, Calif.................................407

Gastonia, N.C. .............................470
Geneva, N.Y.................................451
Glens Falls, N.Y............................377
Great Falls, Mont..........................497
Greensboro, N.C............................470
Greenville, S.C..............................386

Hagerstown, Md.........................416
Hampton, Va.
  (see Peninsula).......................416

Hawaii.........................................365
Helena, Mont................................497
Honolulu, Hawaii
  (see Hawaii) ...........................365
Huntsville, Ala..............................386

Idaho Falls, Ida............................497
Indianapolis, Ind...........................334
Iowa............................................334

Jackson, Miss...............................397
Jacksonville, Fla............................386
Jamestown, N.Y............................451
Johnson City, Tenn........................480

Kennewick, Wash.
  (see Tri-Cities) ......................462
Kenosha, Wis................................439
Kingsport, Tenn. ...........................480
Kinston, N.C.................................416
Knoxville, Tenn.............................386

Lakeland, Fla................................426
Las Vegas, Nev.............................365
Leon, Mexico................................352
Little Falls, N.Y. ...........................451
Little Rock, Ark.
  (see Arkansas)........................397
Louisville, Ky................................334
Lynchburg, Va...............................416

Macon, Ga. ..................................470
Madison, Wis................................439
Maine..........................................343
Medicine Hat, Alberta, Can.........497
Medford, Ore................................462
Memphis, Tenn.............................386
Mexico City, Reds.........................352
Mexico City, Tigers.......................352
Miami, Fla....................................426
Midland, Tex................................397
Modesto, Calif...............................407
Moline, Ill.
  (see Quad Cities)....................439
Monclova, Mexico .........................352
Monterrey, Mexico......................352

Nashua, N.H.................................377
Nashville, Tenn.............................334
Newark, N.Y.................................451
New Britain, Conn.........................377
Niagara Falls, N.Y.........................451
Norfolk, Va.
  (see Tidewater).......................343
Nuevo Laredo, Mexico...................352

Oklahoma City, Okla.....................334
Old Orchard Beach, Me.
  (see Maine)............................343
Omaha, Neb.................................334
Oneonta, N.Y................................451
Orlando, Fla.................................386
Osceola, Fla.................................426

Pasco, Wash.
  (see Tri-Cities) ......................462
Pawtucket, R.I..............................343
Peninsula, Va................................416
Peoria, Ill....................................439
Phoenix, Ariz. ..............................365

Pittsfield, Mass.............................377
Pocatello, Ida. .............................497
Portland, Ore................................365
Portsmouth, Va.
  (see Tidewater)......................343
Prince William, Va. .......................416
Puebla, Mexico.............................352
Pulaski, Tenn...............................480

Quad Cities..................................439

Reading, Pa..................................377
Redwood, Calif..............................407
Reno, Nev....................................407
Richland, Wash.
  (see Tri-Cities) ......................462
Richmond, Va................................343
Rochester, N.Y..............................343
Rock Island, Ill.
  (see Quad Cities)....................439

St. Petersburg, Fla........................426
Salem, Ore...................................462
Salem, Va.....................................416
Salinas, Calif................................407
Saltillo, Mexico ............................352
Salt Lake City, Utah......................497
San Antonio, Tex...........................397
San Jose, Calif..............................407
Sarasota, Fla.................................487
Savannah, Ga. ..............................470
Shreveport, La...............................397
Spartanburg, S.C...........................470
Spokane, Wash..............................462
Springfield, Ill...............................439
Stockton, Calif...............................407
Sumter, S.C..................................470
Syracuse, N.Y...............................343

Tabasco, Mexico............................352
Tacoma, Wash...............................365
Tampa, Fla....................................426
Tampico, Mexico ..........................352
Tidewater, Va................................343
Toledo, O.....................................343
Tri-Cities.....................................462
Tucson, Ariz.................................365
Tulsa, Okla...................................397

Union Laguna, Mexico .................352
Utica, N.Y. ..................................451

Vancouver, B.C., Can.....................365
Veracruz, Mexico...........................352
Vermont.......................................377
Vero Beach, Fla.............................426
Villahermosa, Mexico
  (see Tabasco).........................352
Visalia, Calif.................................407

Waterbury, Conn............................377
Waterloo, Ia.................................439
Watertown, N.Y.............................451
Wausau, Wis.................................439
West Palm Beach, Fla.................426
Winston-Salem, N.C. ....................416
Winter Haven, Fla..........................426
Wytheville, Va. .............................480

Yucatan, Mexico ........................352

# NOTES